Textbook Internet resources are just a click away!

STEP 1 → Go to glencoe.com

STEP 2 → Connect to resources by entering 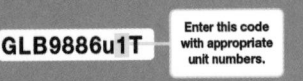 codes.

GLB9886u1T — Enter this code with appropriate unit numbers.

STEP 3 → Access your **Online Student Edition**, teaching resources, and more:

Literature and Reading Resources

- Author Search
- Literature Classics
- Big Idea Web Quests
- Interactive Timelines and Being There Online
- Literary and Text Elements eFlashcards and Games
- Interactive Reading Practice

Selection Resources

- Audio Summaries
- Selection Quizzes
- Selection Vocabulary eFlashcards and Games
- Reading-Writing Connection Activities

Vocabulary Resources

- Academic and Selection Vocabulary eFlashcards and Games
- Multi-Language Glossaries

Writing, Grammar, and Research Resources

- Interactive Writing Models
- Writing and Research Handbook
- Graphic Organizers
- Sentence-Combining Activities
- Publishing Options

Media Literacy, Speaking, Listening, and Viewing Resources

- Media Analysis Guides
- Project Ideas and Templates
- Presentation Tips and Strategies

Assessment Resources

- End-of-Unit Assessment
- ACT/SAT Vocabulary eFlashcards and Games
- Test-Taking Tips and Strategies

TEACHER EDITION

Program Consultants

Jeffrey D. Wilhelm, Ph.D.

Douglas Fisher, Ph.D.

Beverly Ann Chin, Ph.D.

Jacqueline Jones Royster, DA

Acknowledgments

Grateful acknowledgment is given authors, publishers, photographers, museums, and agents for permission to reprint the following copyrighted material. Every effort has been made to determine copyright owners. In case of any omissions, the Publisher will be pleased to make suitable acknowledgments in future editions.

Acknowledgments continued on page R98.

Cover Lee Campbell/The Bridgeman Art Library/Getty Images, MaryBeth Thielhelm/Getty Images; **T6** (t)Erich Lessing/Art Resource, NY, (b)akg-images; **T7** Scala/Art Resource, NY; **T8** THE KOBAL COLLECTION/NEW LINE CINEMA; **T9** Southampton City Art Gallery, Hampshire, UK/Bridgeman Art Library; **T10** Musee Conde, Chantilly, France, Giraudon/Bridgeman Art Library; **T12** Lambeth Palace Library, London/Bridgeman Art Library; **T15** akg-images; **T16** Private Collection/Bridgeman Art Library; **T18** Réunion des Musées Nationaux/Art Resource, NY; **T21** Neue Pinakothek/akg Images; **T23** Mary Evans Picture Library/INS. OF CIVIL ENGINEERS; **T25** Mary Evans Picture Library; **T26** Charles Plante Fine Arts/Bridgeman Art Library; **T28** Tretjakov Gallery/akg-images; **T31** Geoffrey Clements/CORBIS; **T33** Private Collection, Christie's Images/Bridgeman Art Library; **T38** Nimatallah/Art Resource, NY; **T66** David Schmidt/Masterfile.

Glencoe

The McGraw·Hill Companies

Send all inquiries to:
Glencoe/McGraw-Hill
8787 Orion Place
Columbus, OH 43240-4027

ISBN: (student edition) 978-0-07-877981-7
MHID: (student edition) 0-07-877981-2
ISBN: (teacher edition) 978-0-07-877988-6
MHID: (teacher edition) 0-07-877988-X

Printed in the United States of America.

1 2 3 4 5 6 7 8 9 10 027/043 13 12 11 10 09 08

Consultants

Senior Program Consultants

Jeffrey D. Wilhelm, PhD, a former middle and secondary school English and reading teacher, is currently Professor of Education at Boise State University. He is the author or coauthor of numerous articles and several books on the teaching of reading and literacy, including award-winning titles such as *You Gotta BE the Book* and *Reading Don't Fix No Chevys.* He also works with local schools as part of the Adolescent Literacy Project and recently helped establish the National Writing Project site at Boise State University.

Douglas Fisher, PhD, is Professor of Language and Literacy Education and Director of Professional Development at San Diego State University, where he teaches English language development and literacy. He also serves as Director of City Heights Educational Pilot, which won the Christa McAuliffe Award from the American Association of State Colleges and Universities. He has published numerous articles on reading and literacy, differentiated instruction, and curriculum design. He is coauthor of the book *Improving Adolescent Literacies: Strategies That Work* and coeditor of the book *Inclusive Urban Schools.*

Program Consultants

Beverly Ann Chin, PhD, is Professor of English, Director of the English Teaching Program, former Director of the Montana Writing Project, and former Director of Composition at the University of Montana in Missoula. She currently serves as a Member at Large of the Conference of English Leadership. Dr. Chin is a nationally recognized leader in English language arts standards, curriculum, and assessment. Formerly a high school teacher and an adult education reading teacher, Dr. Chin has taught in English language arts education at several universities and has received awards for her teaching and service.

Jacqueline Jones Royster, DA, is Professor of English and Senior Vice Provost and Executive Dean of the Colleges of Arts and Sciences at The Ohio State University. She is currently on the Writing Advisory Committee of the National Commission on Writing and serves as chair for both the Columbus Literacy Council and the Ohioana Library Association. In addition to the teaching of writing, Dr. Royster's professional interests include the rhetorical history of African American women and the social and cultural implications of literate practices. She has contributed to and helped to edit numerous books, anthologies, and journals.

T3

Advisory Board

Special Consultants

Donald R. Bear, PhD.
Professor, Department of
Curriculum and Instruction
Director, E. L. Cord Foundation
Center for Learning and Literacy
at the University of Nevada,
Reno. Author of *Words Their
Way* and *Words Their Way with
English Learners.*

Jana Echevarria, PhD.
Professor, Educational
Psychology, California State
University, Long Beach.
Author of *Making Content
Comprehensible for English
Learners: the SIOP Model.*

FOLDABLES ® **Dinah Zike, MEd,**
was a classroom teacher and
a consultant for many years
before she began to develop
Foldables™—a variety of easily
created graphic organizers. Zike
has written and developed more
than 150 supplemental books
and materials used in classrooms
worldwide. Her *Big Book of Books
and Activities* won the Teachers'
Choice Award.

The Writers' Express®
Immediate Impact. Lasting Transformation.   wex.org

Glencoe National Reading and Language Arts Advisory Council

Mary A. Avalos, PhD
Assistant Department Chair,
   Department of Teaching
   and Learning
Research Assistant Professor,
   Department of Teaching
   and Learning
University of Miami
Coral Gables, Florida

Wanda J. Blanchett, PhD
Associate Dean for Academic
   Affairs and Associate Professor
   of Exceptional Education
School of Education
University of Wisconsin–
   Milwaukee
Milwaukee, Wisconsin

William G. Brozo, PhD
Professor of Literacy
Graduate School of Education
College of Education and
   Human Development
George Mason University
Fairfax, Virginia

Nancy Drew, EdD
LaPointe Educational Consultants
Corpus Christi, Texas

Susan Florio-Ruane, EdD
Professor
College of Education
Michigan State University
East Lansing, Michigan

**Sharon Fontenot O'Neal,
PhD**
Associate Professor
Texas State University
San Marcos, Texas

Nancy Frey, PhD
Associate Professor of Literacy
   in Teacher Education
School of Teacher Education
San Diego State University
San Diego, California

**Victoria Ridgeway Gillis,
PhD**
Associate Professor
Reading Education
Clemson University
Clemson, South Carolina

Kimberly Lawless, PhD
Associate Professor
Curriculum, Instruction
   and Evaluation
College of Education
University of Illinois at Chicago
Chicago, Illinois

William Ray, MA
Lincoln-Sudbury Regional
   High School
Sudbury, Massachusetts

Janet Saito-Furukawa, MEd
English Language Arts Specialist
District 4
Los Angeles, California

Bonnie Valdes, MEd
Independent Reading Consultant
CRISS Master Trainer
Largo, Florida

Teacher Reviewers

The following teachers contributed to the review of *Glencoe Literature.*

Bridget M. Agnew
St. Michael School
Chicago, Illinois

Monica Anzaldua Araiza
Dr. Juliet V. Garcia Middle School
Brownsville, Texas

Katherine R. Baer
Howard County Public Schools
Ellicott City, Maryland

Tanya Baxter
Roald Amundsen High School
Chicago, Illinois

Danielle R. Brain
Thomas R. Proctor Senior High
    School
Utica, New York

Yolanda Conder
Owasso Mid-High School
Owasso, Oklahoma

Gwenn de Mauriac
The Wiscasset Schools
Wiscasset, Maine

Courtney Doan
Bloomington High School
Bloomington, Illinois

Susan M. Griffin
Edison Preparatory School
Tulsa, Oklahoma

Cindi Davis Harris
Helix Charter High School
La Mesa, California

Joseph F. Hutchinson
Toledo Public Schools
Toledo, Ohio

Ginger Jordan
Florien High School
Florien, Louisiana

Dianne Konkel
Cypress Lake Middle School
Fort Myers, Florida

Melanie A. LaFleur
Many High School
Many, Louisiana

Patricia Lee
Radnor Middle School
Wayne, Pennsylvania

Linda Copley Lemons
Cleveland High School
Cleveland, Tennessee

Heather S. Lewis
Waverly Middle School
Lansing, Michigan

Sandra C. Lott
Aiken Optional School
Alexandria, Louisiana

Connie M. Malacarne
O'Fallon Township High School
O'Fallon, Illinois

Lori Howton Means
Edward A. Fulton Junior High
    School
O'Fallon, Illinois

Claire C. Meitl
Howard County Public Schools
Ellicott City, Maryland

Patricia P. Mitcham
Mohawk High School (Retired)
New Castle, Pennsylvania

Lisa Morefield
South-Western Career Academy
Grove City, Ohio

Kevin M. Morrison
Hazelwood East High School
St. Louis, Missouri

Jenine M. Pokorak
School Without Walls Senior
    High School
Washington, DC

Susan Winslow Putnam
Butler High School
Matthews, North Carolina

Paul C. Putnoki
Torrington Middle School
Torrington, Connecticut

Jane Thompson Rae
Cab Calloway High School of
    the Arts
Wilmington, Delaware

Stephanie L. Robin
N. P. Moss Middle School
Lafayette, Louisiana

Ann C. Ryan
Lindenwold High School
Lindenwold, New Jersey

Pamela Schoen
Hopkins High School
Minnetonka, Minnesota

Megan Schumacher
Friends' Central School
Wynnewood, Pennsylvania

Fareeda J. Shabazz
Paul Revere Elementary School
Chicago, Illinois

Molly Steinlage
Brookpark Middle School
Grove City, Ohio

Barry Stevenson
Garnet Valley Middle School
Glen Mills, Pennsylvania

Paul Stevenson
Edison Preparatory School
Tulsa, Oklahoma

Kathy Thompson
Owasso Mid-High School
Owasso, Oklahoma

TEACHER EDITION OVERVIEW

Book Overview

In the Park, (St. James's Park), Malcolm Drummond. Southampton City Art Gallery, Hampshire, UK.

Contents

> "my hands
> Alone shall fight for me, struggle for life
> Against the monster. God must decide
> Who will be given to death's cold grip."
>
> —Beowulf

Connect to Contemporary Issues

Mood,
Make Inferences About Theme

Part 2

The Power of Faith

Historical Narrative,
Summarize

Characterization, Paraphrase

Irony, Analyze Tone

Humor, Analyze Form

Part 3   The World of Romance

*"King Arthur smote Sir Mordred under the shield
with a thrust of his spear on through the body
more than a fathom."*

—Sir Thomas Malory

UNIT TWO

The English
RENAISSANCE *1485–1650*

"To be, or not to be—that is the question.
Whether 'tis nobler in the mind to suffer
The slings and arrows of outrageous fortune,
Or to take arms against a sea of troubles,
And by opposing end them."

—William Shakespeare

PART 3   *The Sacred and the Secular*

"Who bends not his ear to any bell which upon any
occasion rings? but who can remove it from that bell
which is passing a piece of himself out of this world?"

—John Donne

UNIT THREE

From PURITANISM *to the* ENLIGHTENMENT 1640–1780

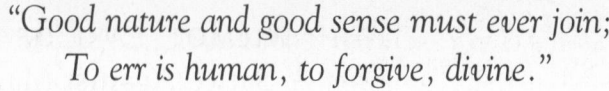

"*Good nature and good sense must ever join;*
To err is human, to forgive, divine."

—Alexander Pope

The Thinker. Auguste Rodin. Bronze, height: 49 cm.
Musee des Beaux-Arts, Lyon, France.

The Triumph of

ROMANTICISM *1750–1837*

UNIT FOUR

PART 1 *The Stirrings of Romanticism*

"*I wish to persuade women to endeavor to acquire strength, both of mind and body, and to convince them that the soft phrases, susceptibility of heart, delicacy of sentiment, and refinement of taste are almost synonymous with epithets of weakness . . .*"

—Mary Wollstonecraft

Young Woman Sewing by Lamplight, 1825. Georg Friedrich Kersting. Oil on Canvas 40.3 x 34.2 cm. Private collection.

> "My name is Ozymandias, king of kings:
> Look on my works, ye Mighty, and despair!"
>
> —Percy Bysshe Shelley

<table>
<tr><td>UNIT FIVE</td><td></td></tr>
</table>

The Victorian Age 1837–1901

Part 1   Optimism and the Belief in Progress

> "'Beware the Jabberwock, my son!
> The jaws that bite, the claws that catch!
> Beware the Jubjub bird, and shun
> The frumious Bandersnatch!"
>
> —Lewis Carroll

Part 2 𝔕𝔢𝔞𝔩𝔦𝔰𝔪 𝔞𝔫𝔡 𝔑𝔞𝔱𝔲𝔯𝔞𝔩𝔦𝔰𝔪

"*And we are here as on a darkling plain*
Swept with confused alarms of struggle and flight,
Where ignorant armies clash by night."

—Matthew Arnold

Seaside View. David Cox. Watercolor on paper. Private collection.

PART 1   **Class, Colonialism, and the Great War**

Motivation, Connect to Contemporary Issues

PART 2   Modernism

"Turning and turning in the widening gyre
The falcon cannot hear the falconer;
Things fall apart; the center cannot hold"

—William Butler Yeats

The New Planet, 1921. Konstantin Fiodorvich Juon.
Tempera on cardboard, 71 x 101 cm. Tretjakov Gallery, Moscow.

PART 3　World War II and Its Aftermath

UNIT SEVEN

An International Literature
1950–Present

Part 1

The British Isles: Making and Remaking Traditions

Speaker, Question

Vernacular, Synthesize

Part 2

Around the World: Extending and Evaluating Traditions

*"The train had cast the station like a skin.
It called out to the sky, I'm coming, I'm coming;
and again, there was no answer."*

—Nadine Gordimer

Compartment C, Car 293, 1938. Edward Hopper.
Oil on canvas. IBM Collection.

Reference Section

A View of Westminster with the Royal Barge and Other Shipping. Joseph Nicholls. Oil on canvas, 61 x 111.7 cm. Private collection.

Selections by Genre

Letter, Journal, or Diary

Speech

Women carrying water, Black figure Attic hydria from Vulci. Second half, sixth century BC.

Skills Workshops

Features

Perspectives

Award-winning nonfiction book excerpts and primary source documents

TIME

High-interest, informative magazine articles

Comparing Literature

Across Time and Place

Literary History

Independent Reading

ASSESSMENT

How to Use *Glencoe Literature*

Organization

The literature you will read is organized chronologically into seven units spanning the Anglo-Saxon period to the present.

Each unit contains the following:

A **UNIT INTRODUCTION** provides you with the background information to help make your reading experience more meaningful.

- The **TIMELINE** helps you keep track of major literary and historical events.

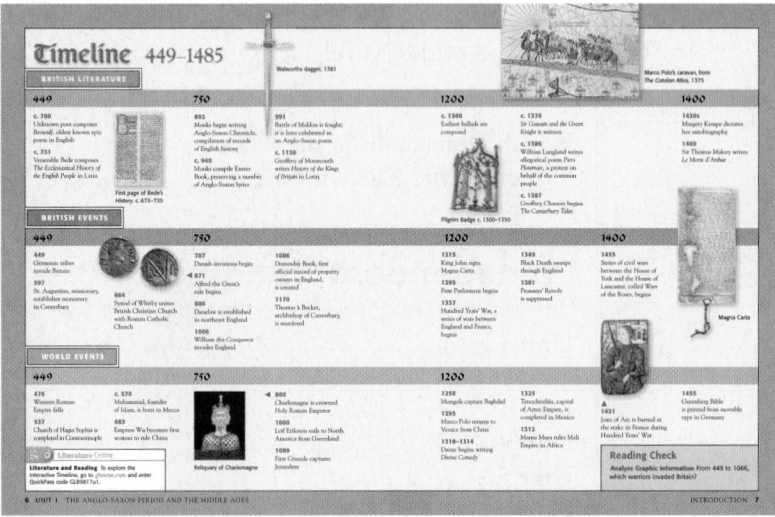

- **BY THE NUMBERS** shows you figures and key data at a glance.
- **BEING THERE** gives you a glimpse of the geography related to the period.
- **HISTORICAL, CULTURAL, AND SOCIAL FORCES** explains the influences that shape a specific literary period.
- **BIG IDEAS** target three concepts that you can trace as you read the literature.

LITERARY SELECTIONS follow each Unit Introduction. The selections are organized as follows.

Why do I need this book?

Glencoe Literature is more than just a collection of stories, poems, nonfiction articles, and other literary works. Every part is built around **Big Ideas,** concepts that you will want to think about, talk about, and maybe even argue about. Big Ideas help you become part of an important conversation. You can join in lively discussions about who we are, where we have been, and where we are going.

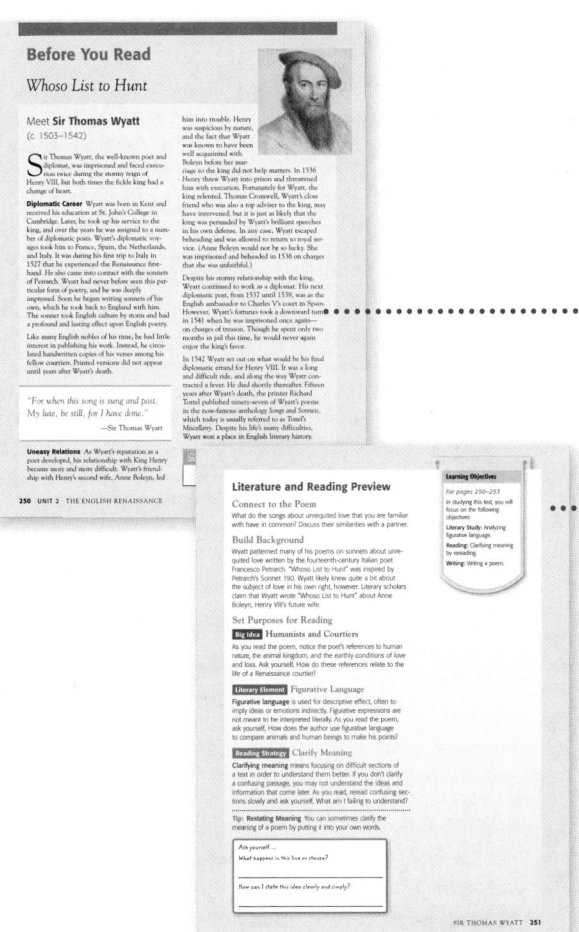

Reading and Thinking

The main literary works in your textbook are arranged in three parts.

- Start with **BEFORE YOU READ**. Learn valuable background information about the literature and preview the skills and strategies that will guide your reading.

MEET THE AUTHOR presents a detailed biography of the writer whose work you will read and analyze.

LITERATURE AND READING PREVIEW lists the basic tools you will use to read and analyze the literary work.

- Next, read the **LITERATURE SELECTION**. As you flip through the selections, you will notice that parts of the text are highlighted in different colors. At the bottom of the page are color-coded questions that relate to the highlighted text. Yellow represents a *Big Idea*, magenta represents a *Literary Element*, and blue represents a *Reading Strategy*. These questions will help you gain a better understanding of the text.

- Wrap up the literature with **AFTER YOU READ**. Explore what you have learned through a wide range of reading, thinking, vocabulary, and writing activities.

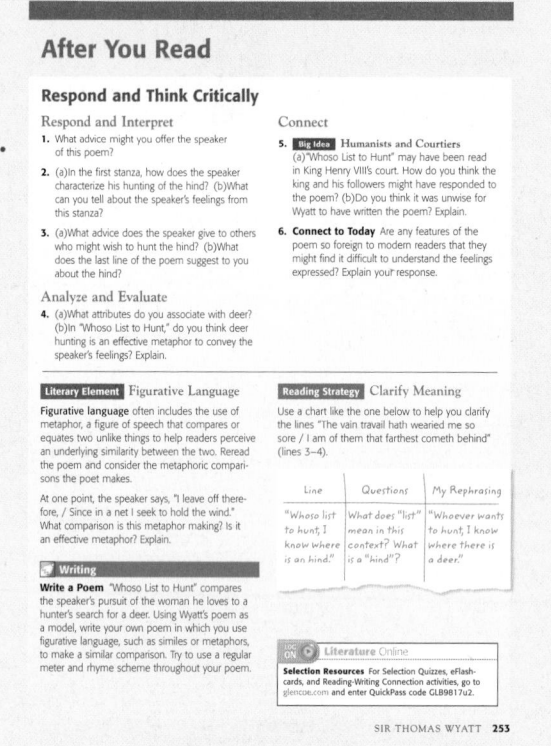

Vocabulary

VOCABULARY WORDS that may be new or difficult are chosen from most selections. They are introduced on the **BEFORE YOU READ** page. Each word is accompanied by its pronunciation, its part of speech, its definition, and the page number on which it appears. The vocabulary word is also used in a sample sentence. Vocabulary words are highlighted in the literary work.

VOCABULARY PRACTICE On the **AFTER YOU READ** pages, you will be able to practice using the vocabulary words in an exercise. This exercise will show you how to apply a vocabulary strategy to understand new or difficult words.

ACADEMIC VOCABULARY Many of the **AFTER YOU READ** pages will also introduce you to a word that is frequently used in academic work. You will be prompted to complete an activity based on that word.

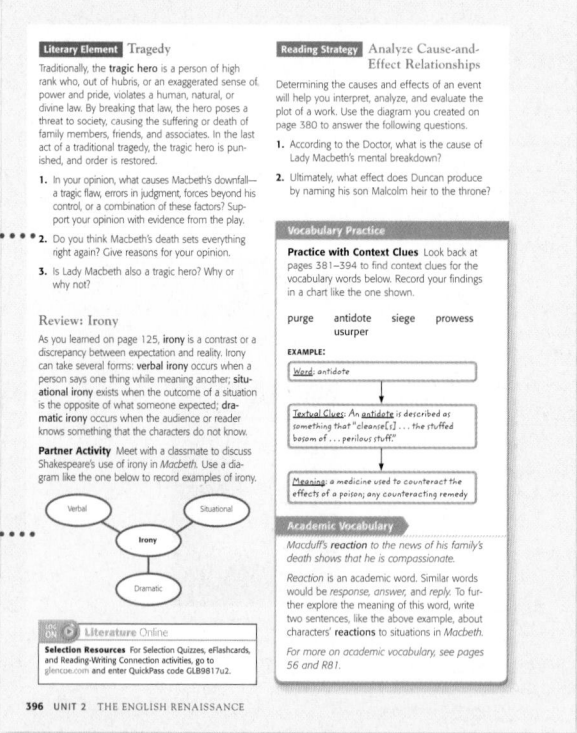

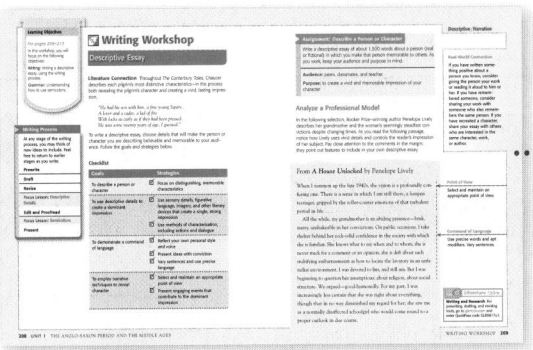

Writing Workshops

Each unit in **_Glencoe Literature_** includes a Writing Workshop. The workshop walks you through the writing process as you work on an extended piece of writing related to the unit.

- You will create writing goals and apply strategies to meet them.

- You will pick up tips and polish your critical skills as you analyze professional and workshop models.

- You will focus on mastering specific aspects of writing, including organization, grammar, and vocabulary.

- You will use a checklist to evaluate your own writing.

Assessment

At the end of each unit, you will be tested on the literature, reading, and vocabulary skills you have just learned. Designed to simulate standardized tests, this test will give you the practice you need to succeed while providing an assessment of how you have met the unit objectives.

Organizing Information

Graphic organizers—such as Foldables®, diagrams, and charts—help you keep your information and ideas organized.

FOLDABLES Study Organizer   **BOUND BOOK**

Try using this organizer to explore your personal responses to poetry, plays and nonfiction.

This chart provides an overview of the scope and sequence for *Glencoe British Literature*. For a detailed scope and sequence of skills, see the chart at the beginning of each unit in the Teacher Edition. Refer also to the Index of Skills in the Reference Section in the back of the book for a comprehensive listing of all skills and concepts taught in *British Literature*.

✔ = Introduced   ✔ = Reviewed

	UNIT ONE	UNIT TWO	UNIT THREE	UNIT FOUR	UNIT FIVE	UNIT SIX	UNIT SEVEN
Literary Periods and Movements							
Anglo-Saxon Period	✔						
Medieval Period	✔	✔					
English Renaissance		✔	✔	✔			
Puritanism to the Enlightenment (17th and 18th centuries)			✔	✔			
Romantic Period				✔	✔	✔	
Victorian Period					✔	✔	
Realism					✔		
Naturalism					✔		
Modern Period							
International (World) Literature:						✔	✔
Contemporary Period and Postmodern Period							✔
Literary Criticism							
Analyzing Literature in Context							
Political		✔			✔		✔
Historical	✔	✔	✔	✔	✔	✔	✔
Social	✔	✔	✔	✔	✔	✔	✔
Cultural	✔	✔	✔	✔	✔	✔	✔
Biographical		✔	✔	✔			
Philosophical	✔	✔	✔	✔	✔	✔	✔
Literary Genres							
Oral Tradition Forms							
Song	✔	✔			✔		✔
Myth, Folklore, and Legend	✔		✔				✔
Fiction							
Short Story						✔	✔
Novel Excerpt	✔		✔	✔	✔	✔	

	UNIT ONE	UNIT TWO	UNIT THREE	UNIT FOUR	UNIT FIVE	UNIT SIX	UNIT SEVEN
Nonfiction							
Autobiography or Memoir	✔						
Biography			✔				
Essay			✔	✔	✔	✔	✔
Magazine Article	✔	✔	✔	✔	✔	✔	✔
Speech		✔	✔			✔	✔
Informational Text	✔	✔	✔	✔	✔	✔	✔
Public Document		✔	✔			✔	✔
Political Document		✔	✔			✔	✔
Journal or Diary				✔	✔		
Letter			✔				
Poetry							
Narrative Poem	✔	✔	✔	✔			
Ballad	✔			✔			
Sonnet		✔		✔	✔	✔	
Free Verse						✔	✔
Epic	✔		✔				
Drama							
Tragedy			✔				
Comedy			✔				✔

Literary Elements

	UNIT ONE	UNIT TWO	UNIT THREE	UNIT FOUR	UNIT FIVE	UNIT SIX	UNIT SEVEN
Literary Structure							
Plot		✔	✔		✔	✔	
Setting	✔		✔	✔			✔
Characters	✔	✔	✔	✔	✔	✔	✔
Point of View	✔	✔	✔	✔	✔	✔	✔
Theme	✔	✔	✔	✔	✔	✔	✔
Voice and Tone	✔	✔	✔		✔	✔	
Author's Purpose	✔	✔	✔	✔	✔	✔	
Literary Language							
Imagery	✔	✔	✔	✔	✔	✔	✔
Symbolism			✔	✔		✔	✔
Figures of Speech		✔		✔		✔	✔

SCOPE AND SEQUENCE

✔ = Introduced ✔ = Reviewed

	UNIT ONE	UNIT TWO	UNIT THREE	UNIT FOUR	UNIT FIVE	UNIT SIX	UNIT SEVEN
Sound Devices		✔		✔			✔
Diction			✔	✔		✔	✔
Rhetorical Strategies		✔		✔		✔	
Reading Skills							
Strategies							
Analyzing	✔	✔	✔	✔	✔	✔	✔
Clarifying		✔			✔	✔	✔
Drawing Conclusions		✔	✔	✔		✔	✔
Making Inferences	✔	✔	✔			✔	✔
Making Predictions		✔				✔	
Monitoring Comprehension	✔			✔	✔		
Paraphrasing	✔	✔	✔	✔	✔		
Previewing	✔	✔	✔	✔	✔	✔	✔
Questioning		✔	✔			✔	✔
Recognizing Bias						✔	✔
Summarizing	✔	✔	✔	✔		✔	
Sythesising						✔	✔
Text Structures							
Cause and Effect	✔	✔	✔	✔	✔	✔	
Chronological Order			✔			✔	
Compare and Contrast		✔		✔	✔	✔	✔
Vocabulary Development							
Analogies	✔	✔	✔	✔	✔	✔	✔
Antonyms	✔	✔	✔	✔		✔	
Context Clues	✔	✔	✔	✔	✔	✔	✔
Denotation and Connotation		✔	✔	✔	✔	✔	✔
Multiple-Meaning Words							✔
Prefixes and Suffixes	✔	✔	✔	✔		✔	✔
Synonyms	✔	✔	✔	✔	✔	✔	✔
Word Roots	✔	✔	✔	✔		✔	✔

	UNIT ONE	UNIT TWO	UNIT THREE	UNIT FOUR	UNIT FIVE	UNIT SIX	UNIT SEVEN
Writing and Grammar							
Types of Writing							
Descriptive Essay	✔						
Research Report		✔					
Persuasive Speech		✔	✔	✔			
Reflective Essay	✔	✔	✔	✔			✔
Literary Analysis	✔	✔	✔	✔	✔	✔	
Short Story	✔			✔		✔	
Literary Critical Review				✔	✔	✔	✔
Writing Process							
Prewriting, Drafting, Revising, Editing and Proofreading, Presenting	✔	✔	✔	✔	✔	✔	✔
Traits of Strong Writing	✔	✔	✔	✔	✔	✔	✔
Grammar, Usage, and Mechanics							
Parts of Speech	✔	✔	✔	✔	✔	✔	
Capitalization and Punctuation	✔	✔	✔	✔	✔	✔	✔
Sentence Structure	✔	✔	✔	✔	✔	✔	✔
Speaking, Listening, and Viewing							
Photo Essay	✔						
Multimedia Presentation		✔					
Persuasive Speech			✔				
Reflective Presentation				✔			
Oral Response to Literature		✔			✔	✔	✔
Oral Interpretation		✔			✔	✔	
Literary Critical Review							✔
Analyzing Media Messages							✔

Teaching the Standards: Grade 12

The following abbreviated curriculum is a suggestion for addressing those objectives that students commonly encounter on standardized tests. You may use it as a guide for prioritizing instruction in preparation for the tests.

Unit 1

Selections/Lessons	Pacing/Days	Genre	Where to Find Instruction	Commonly Tested Objectives
from **Beowulf**	2–9	Epic Poem	SE, p. 24 RW, RW-APP, pp. 1–18 RW-EL, pp. 1–18, 346	**Literary Study:** Analyzing conflict. **Reading:** Identifying sequence.
from **The Pardoner's Tale**	2–8	Narrative Poem	SE, p. 125 RW, RW-APP, pp. 19–38 RW-EL, pp. 19–38, 347	**Literary Study:** Analyzing irony. **Reading:** Analyzing tone.
from **Sir Gawain and the Green Knight**	3–16	Romance	SE, p. 164 RW, RW-APP, pp. 39–76 RW-EL, pp. 39–76, 348	**Literary Study:** Analyzing archetype. **Reading:** Monitoring comprehension.

Unit 2

Selections/Lessons	Pacing/Days	Genre	Where to Find Instruction	Commonly Tested Objectives
On Monsieur's Departure AND Speech to the Troops at Tilbury	1–4	Speech	SE, p. 244 RW, RW-APP, pp. 77–84, 346 RW-EL, pp. 77–84, 349–350	**Literary Study:** Analyzing tone. **Reading:** Analyzing text structure.
The Passionate Shepherd to His Love	1–3	Poetry	SE, p. 265 RW, RW-APP, pp. 85–90, 347 RW-EL, pp. 85–90, 351–352	**Literary Study:** Analyzing point of view. **Reading:** Analyzing sound devices.
Sonnet 73 AND Sonnet 29	1–3	Sonnets	SE, p. 288 RW, RW-APP, pp. 91–96, 348 RW-EL, pp. 91–96, 353–354	**Literary Study:** Analyzing simile. **Reading:** Drawing conclusions about speaker's meaning.
from **The Tragedy of Macbeth, Act 1, Scenes 1–2**	3–7	Drama	SE, p. 306 RW, RW-APP, pp. 97–112 RW-EL, pp. 97–112, 355	**Literary Study:** Analyzing atmosphere. **Reading:** Applying background knowledge.
Eve's Apology	1–3	Poetry	SE, p. 416 RW, RW-APP, pp. 113–120 RW-EL, pp. 113–120, 356	**Literary Study:** Analyzing argument. **Reading:** Drawing conclusions about author's beliefs.

[Note: **SE**= Student Edition; **RW**= *Read and Write;* **RW-APP**= Approaching Level; **RW-EL**= English Learner]

| Meditation 17 | 1–3 | Nonfiction | SE, p. 430
RW, RW-APP, pp. 121–128
RW-EL, pp. 121–128, 357 | **Literary Study:** Analyzing metaphysical conceit.
Reading: Making inferences about theme. |

Unit 3

Selections/Lessons	Pacing/Days	Genre	Where to Find Instruction	Commonly Tested Objectives
from **The Diary of Samuel Pepys**	2–5	Diary	SE, p. 537 RW, RW-APP, pp. 129–140, 349 RW-EL, pp.129–140, 358–359	**Literary Study:** Analyzing a historical diary. **Reading:** Drawing conclusions about the author's beliefs.
A Modest Proposal	2–6	Essay	SE, p. 548 RW, RW-APP, pp. 141–154 RW-EL, pp. 141–154, 360	**Literary Study:** Analyzing satire. **Reading:** Analyzing text structure.
Letter to Her Daughter	1–4	Letter	SE, p. 585 RW, RW-APP, pp. 155–164 RW-EL, pp. 155–164, 361	**Literary Study:** Analyzing extended metaphor. **Reading:** Analyzing argument.

Unit 4

Selections/Lessons	Pacing/Days	Genre	Where to Find Instruction	Commonly Tested Objectives
Elegy Written in a Country Churchyard	2–7	Poetry	SE, p. 680 RW, RW-APP, pp. 165–180 RW-EL, pp. 165–180, 362	**Literary Study:** Analyzing an epitaph. **Reading:** Interpreting imagery.
from **A Vindication of the Rights of Woman**	2–8	Essay	SE, p. 695 RW, RW-APP, pp. 181–196, 350–351 RW-EL, pp. 181–196, 363–365	**Literary Study:** Analyzing thesis. **Reading:** Evaluating argument.
Lines Composed a Few Miles Above Tintern Abbey	1–4	Poetry	SE, p. 744 RW, RW-APP, pp. 197–206, 352 RW-EL, pp. 197–206, 366–367	**Literary Study:** Analyzing diction. **Reading:** Analyzing sensory details.
from **The Journals of Dorothy Wordsworth**	1–3	Journal	SE, p. 753 RW, RW-APP, pp. 207–212, 353 RW-EL, pp. 207–212, 368–369	**Literary Study:** Analyzing a historical journal. **Reading:** Analyzing mood.
Ode on a Grecian Urn	1–4	Poetry	SE, p. 831 RW, RW-APP, pp. 213–222 RW-EL, pp. 213–222, 370	**Literary Study:** Analyzing ode. **Reading:** Analyzing parallelism.

Unit 5

Selections/Lessons	Pacing/Days	Genre	Where to Find Instruction	Commonly Tested Objectives
TIME: What Is Love?	2–6	Science Article	SE, p. 904 RW, RW-APP, pp. 223–234, 354 RW-EL, pp. 223–234, 371–372	**Reading:** Examining connotation and denotation.
Jabberwocky	1–3	Poetry	SE, p. 913 RW, RW-APP, pp. 235–240, 355 RW-EL, pp. 235–240, 373–374	**Literary Study:** Analyzing nonsense verse. **Reading:** Analyzing style.
Dover Beach	1–4	Poetry	SE, p. 953 RW, RW-APP, pp. 241–248, 356 RW-EL, pp. 241–248, 375–376	**Literary Study:** Analyzing meter. **Reading:** Comparing and contrasting imagery.
To an Athlete Dying Young	1–3	Poetry	SE, p. 955 RW, RW-APP, pp. 249–256 RW-EL, pp. 249–256, 377	**Literary Study:** Analyzing lyric poetry. **Reading:** Connecting to personal experience.

Unit 6

Selections/Lessons	Pacing/Days	Genre	Where to Find Instruction	Commonly Tested Objectives
Sailing to Byzantium AND Second Coming	1–4	Poetry	SE, p. 1065 RW, RW-APP, pp. 257–266 RW-EL, pp. 257–266, 378	**Literary Study:** Analyzing structure. **Reading:** Analyzing figurative language: metaphor.
Preludes	1–3	Poetry	SE, p. 1073 RW, RW-APP, pp. 267–274 RW-EL, pp. 267–274, 379	**Literary Study:** Analyzing imagery. **Reading:** Analyzing style.
from **A Room of One's Own**	1–4	Essay	SE, p. 1103 RW, RW-APP, pp. 275–284 RW-EL, pp. 275–284, 380	**Literary Study:** Analyzing argument. **Reading:** Analyzing tone.
Be Ye Men of Valor	2–5	Speech	SE, p. 1112 RW, RW-APP, pp. 285–296, 357–358 RW-EL, pp. 285–296, 381–383	**Literary Study:** Analyzing rhetoric. **Reading:** Distinguishing fact and opinion.

[Note: **SE**= Student Edition; **RW**= *Read and Write;* **RW-APP**= Approaching Level; **RW-EL**= English Learner]

Unit 7

Selections/Lessons	Pacing/Days	Genre	Where to Find Instruction	Commonly Tested Objectives
A Mild Attack of Locusts	2–6	Short Story	SE, p. 1238 RW, RW-APP, pp. 297–310 RW-EL, pp. 297–310, 384	**Literary Study:** Analyzing theme. **Reading:** Analyzing conflict.
Two Sheep	1–4	Fable	SE, p. 1272 RW, RW-APP, pp. 311–320 RW-EL, pp. 311–320, 385	**Literary Study:** Analyzing anthropomorphism. **Reading:** Identifying sequence.
Comparing Literature: Shall We Choose Death? AND The Tribe with Its Eyes on the Sky AND Political Science	2–6	Radio Address AND Short Story AND Song	SE, p. 1205 RW, RW-APP, pp. 321–334 RW-EL, pp. 321–334, 386	**Literary Study:** Analyzing structure. **Reading:** Analyzing political assumptions. **Reading:** Comparing literature.

Reference Section

Selections/Lessons	Pacing/Days	Genre	Where to Find Instruction	Commonly Tested Objectives
Functional Documents	2–5	Poetry	SE, p. R22 RW, RW-APP, pp. 335–345, 359 RW-EL, pp. 335–345, 387–389	**Reading:** Analyzing expository texts.
	Total: 44–150 days			

To Teachers

Welcome to the Teacher Edition of *Glencoe Literature*. We have created this teacher edition based on the standards developed by experienced teachers and educational consultants. Teaching suggestions, additional resources, and leveled activities for differentiated instruction are all labeled and wrapped around the student text for your convenience.

Unit Scope and Sequence

Every unit of *Glencoe Literature* is organized around a carefully researched scope and sequence that includes the reading skills and strategies, literary elements, writing skills, and listening, speaking and viewing skills that students need in order to successfully progress through the program.

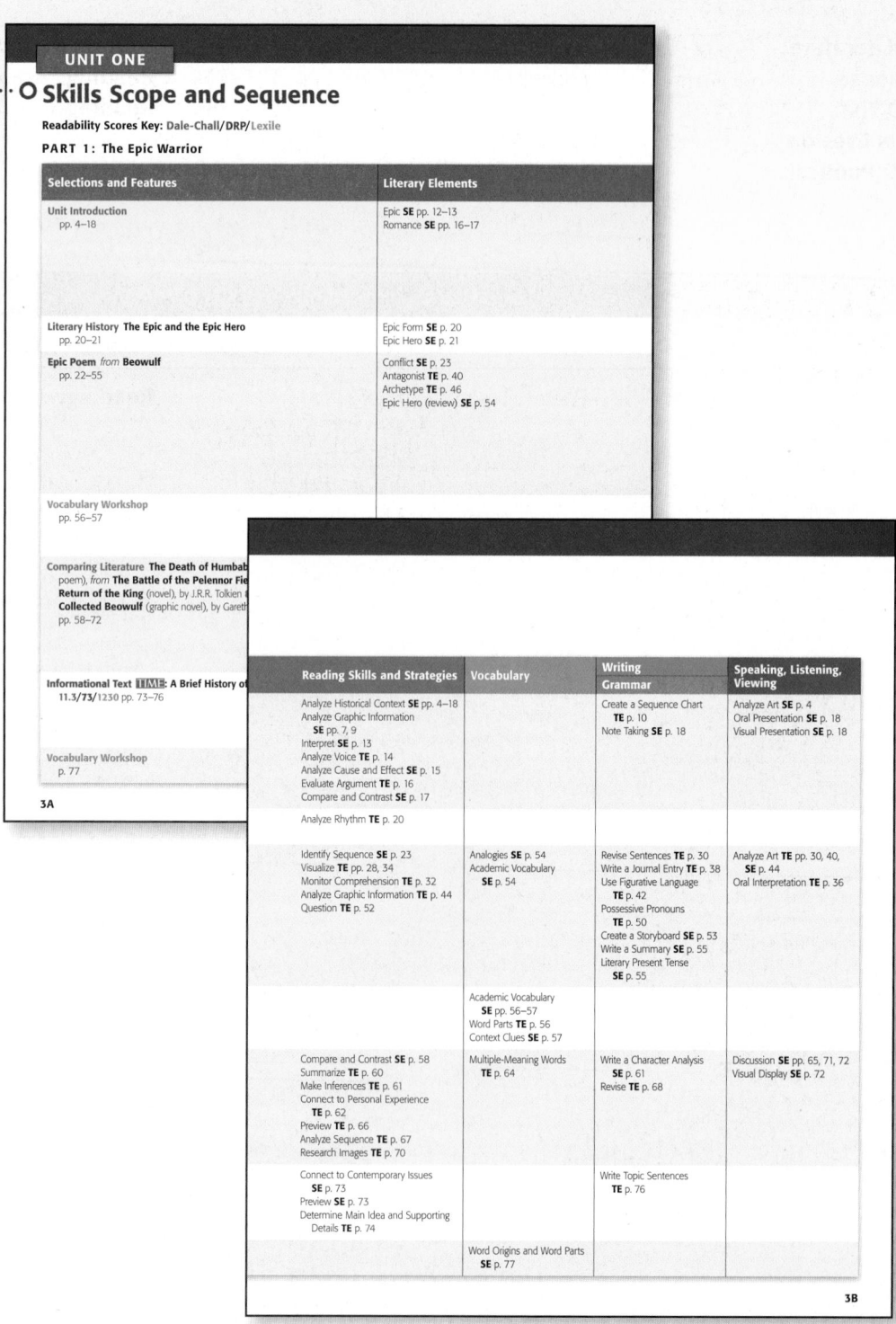

UNIT ONE

○ Skills Scope and Sequence

Readability Scores Key: Dale-Chall/**DRP**/Lexile

PART 1: The Epic Warrior

Selections and Features	Literary Elements
Unit Introduction pp. 4–18	Epic **SE** pp. 12–13 Romance **SE** pp. 16–17
Literary History **The Epic and the Epic Hero** pp. 20–21	Epic Form **SE** p. 20 Epic Hero **SE** p. 21
Epic Poem *from* Beowulf pp. 22–55	Conflict **SE** p. 23 Antagonist **TE** p. 40 Archetype **TE** p. 46 Epic Hero (review) **SE** p. 54
Vocabulary Workshop pp. 56–57	
Comparing Literature **The Death of Humbab** (poem), *from* **The Battle of the Pelennor Fie** **Return of the King** (novel), by J.R.R. Tolkien **Collected Beowulf** (graphic novel), by Gareth pp. 58–72	
Informational Text **TIME: A Brief History of** 11.3/**73**/1230 pp. 73–76	
Vocabulary Workshop p. 77	

3A

Reading Skills and Strategies	Vocabulary	Writing Grammar	Speaking, Listening, Viewing
Analyze Historical Context **SE** pp. 4–18 Analyze Graphic Information **SE** pp. 7, 9 Interpret **SE** p. 13 Analyze Voice **TE** p. 14 Analyze Cause and Effect **SE** p. 15 Evaluate Argument **TE** p. 16 Compare and Contrast **SE** p. 17 Analyze Rhythm **TE** p. 20		Create a Sequence Chart **TE** p. 10 Note Taking **SE** p. 18	Analyze Art **SE** p. 4 Oral Presentation **SE** p. 18 Visual Presentation **SE** p. 18
Identify Sequence **SE** p. 23 Visualize **TE** pp. 28, 34 Monitor Comprehension **TE** p. 32 Analyze Graphic Information **TE** p. 44 Question **TE** p. 52	Analogies **SE** p. 54 Academic Vocabulary **SE** p. 54	Revise Sentences **TE** p. 30 Write a Journal Entry **TE** p. 38 Use Figurative Language **TE** p. 42 Possessive Pronouns **TE** p. 50 Create a Storyboard **SE** p. 53 Write a Summary **SE** p. 55 Literary Present Tense **SE** p. 55	Analyze Art **TE** pp. 30, 40, **SE** p. 44 Oral Interpretation **TE** p. 36
	Academic Vocabulary **SE** pp. 56–57 Word Parts **TE** p. 56 Context Clues **TE** p. 57		
Compare and Contrast **SE** p. 58 Summarize **TE** p. 60 Make Inferences **TE** p. 61 Connect to Personal Experience **TE** p. 62 Preview **TE** p. 66 Analyze Sequence **TE** p. 67 Research Images **TE** p. 70	Multiple-Meaning Words **TE** p. 64	Write a Character Analysis **SE** p. 61 Revise **TE** p. 68	Discussion **SE** pp. 65, 71, 72 Visual Display **SE** p. 72
Connect to Contemporary Issues **SE** p. 73 Preview **SE** p. 73 Determine Main Idea and Supporting Details **TE** p. 74		Write Topic Sentences **TE** p. 76	
	Word Origins and Word Parts **SE** p. 77		

3B

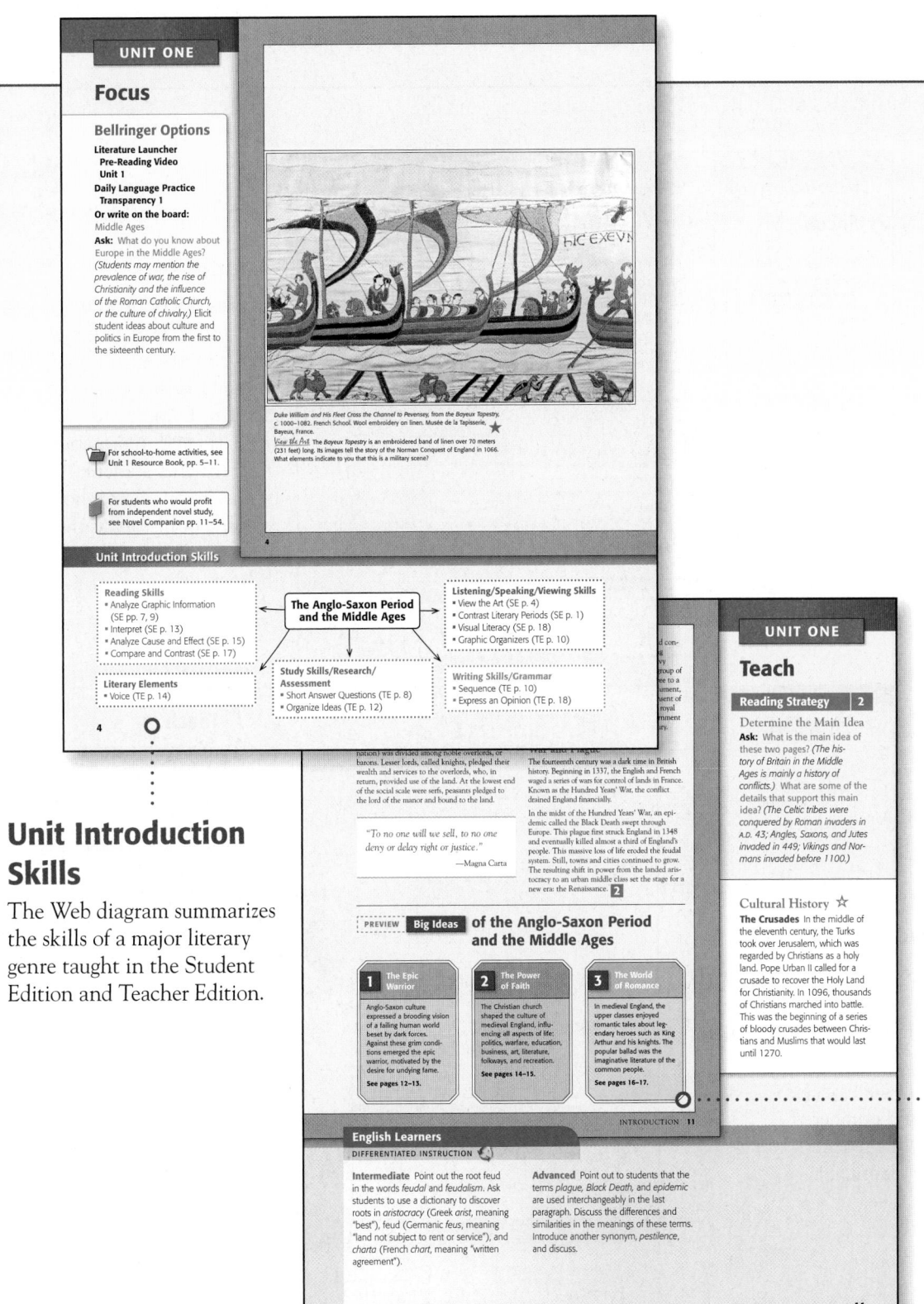

Unit Introduction Skills

The Web diagram summarizes the skills of a major literary genre taught in the Student Edition and Teacher Edition.

Big Idea

The three Big Ideas from a literary period or movement help your students focus on key concepts that they can trace through the reading selections in each unit.

Three Part Lesson Plan

The Teacher Edition of *Glencoe Literature* is organized in a three-part structure: Focus, Teach, and Assess.

Focus

Focus activities help you prepare students for the day's lessons. The **Bellringer** Activity provides a choice of transparencies and other teaching strategies that engage students and focus their attention.

Teach

In these sections, you will find leveled activities that correspond to and extend instruction in the Student Edition. Here you will also find information that enriches students' appreciation of art, photos, culture, or history as they apply to the selections being taught.

Brackets and Numbers

When students are asked to think about the text, you will see brackets that are color-coded and numbered so that the corresponding teacher information is readily identifiable.

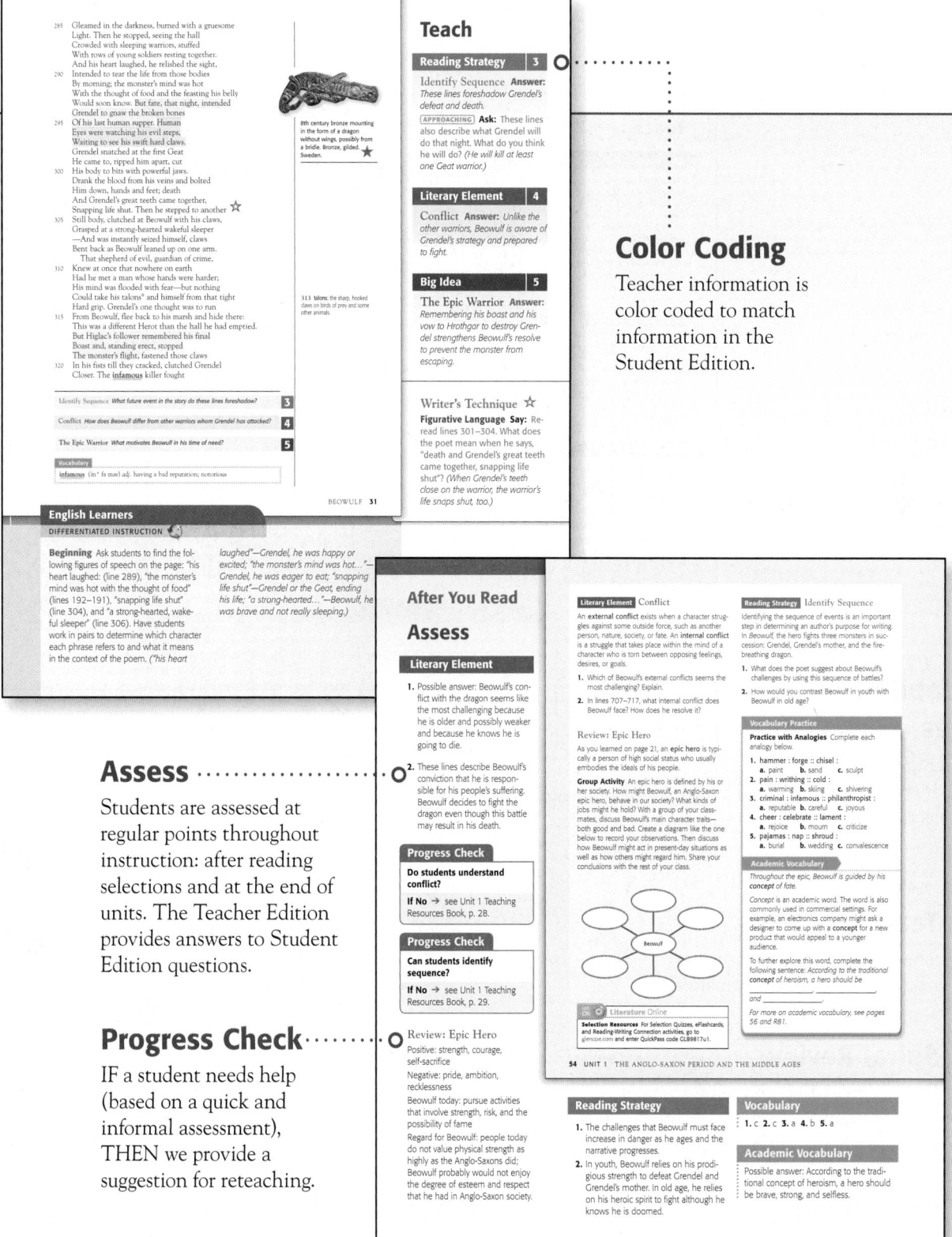

285 Gleamed in the darkness, burned with a gruesome
Light. Then he stopped, seeing the hall
Crowded with sleeping warriors, stuffed
With rows of young soldiers resting together.
And his heart laughed, he relished the sight,
290 Intended to tear the life from those bodies
By morning; the monster's mind was hot
With the thought of food and the feasting his belly
Would soon know. But fate, that night, intended
Grendel to gnaw the broken bones
295 Of his last human supper. Human
Eyes were watching his evil steps,
Waiting to see his swift hard claws.
Grendel snatched at the first Geat
He came to, ripped him apart, cut
300 His body to bits with powerful jaws,
Drank the blood from his veins and bolted
Him down, hands and feet; death
And Grendel's great teeth came together,
Snapping life shut. Then he stepped to another
305 Still body, clutched at Beowulf with his claws,
Grasped at a strong-hearted wakeful sleeper
—And was instantly seized himself, claws
Bent back as Beowulf leaned up on one arm.
That shepherd of evil, guardian of crime,
310 Knew at once that nowhere on earth
Had he met a man whose hands were harder;
His mind was flooded with fear—but nothing
Could take his talons° and himself from that tight
Hard grip. Grendel's one thought was to run
315 From Beowulf, flee back to his marsh and hide there:
This was a different Herot than the hall he had emptied.
But Higlac's follower remembered his final
Boast and, standing erect, stopped
The monster's flight, fastened those claws
320 In his fists till they cracked, clutched Grendel
Closer. The **infamous** killer fought

8th century bronze mounting in the form of a dragon without wings, possibly from a bridle. Bronze, gilded. Sweden. ★

313 **talons:** the sharp, hooked claws on birds of prey and some other animals.

Identify Sequence *What future event in the story do these lines foreshadow?* 3

Conflict *How does Beowulf differ from other warriors whom Grendel has attacked?* 4

The Epic Warrior *What motivates Beowulf in his time of need?* 5

Vocabulary
infamous (in' fə məs) adj. having a bad reputation; notorious

BEOWULF **31**

English Learners
DIFFERENTIATED INSTRUCTION

Beginning Ask students to find the following figures of speech on the page: "his heart laughed: (line 289), "the monster's mind was hot with the thought of food" (lines 192–191), "snapping life shut" (line 304), and "a strong-hearted, wakeful sleeper" (line 306). Have students work in pairs to determine which character each phrase refers to and what it means in the context of the poem. ("his heart laughed"—Grendel, he was happy or excited; "the monster's mind was hot..."—Grendel, he was eager to eat; "snapping life shut"—Grendel or the Geat, ending his life; "a strong-hearted..."—Beowulf, he was brave and not really sleeping.)

Teach

Reading Strategy 3

Identify Sequence **Answer:** *These lines foreshadow Grendel's defeat and death.*

[APPROACHING] **Ask:** These lines also describe what Grendel will do that night. What do you think he will do? *(He will kill at least one Geat warrior.)*

Literary Element 4

Conflict **Answer:** *Unlike the other warriors, Beowulf is aware of Grendel's strategy and prepared to fight.*

Big Idea 5

The Epic Warrior **Answer:** *Remembering his boast and his vow to Hrothgar to destroy Grendel strengthens Beowulf's resolve to prevent the monster from escaping.*

Writer's Technique ★
Figurative Language Say: Re-read lines 301–304. What does the poet mean when he says, "death and Grendel's great teeth came together, snapping life shut"? *(When Grendel's teeth close on the warrior, the warrior's life snaps shut, too.)*

Color Coding

Teacher information is color coded to match information in the Student Edition.

After You Read

Assess

Literary Element

1. Possible answer: Beowulf's conflict with the dragon seems like the most challenging because he is older and possibly weaker and because he knows he is going to die.

2. These lines describe Beowulf's conviction that he is responsible for his people's suffering. Beowulf decides to fight the dragon even though this battle may result in his death.

Progress Check

Do students understand conflict?

If No → see Unit 1 Teaching Resources Book, p. 28.

Progress Check

Can students identify sequence?

If No → see Unit 1 Teaching Resources Book, p. 29.

Review: Epic Hero
Positive: strength, courage, self-sacrifice
Negative: pride, ambition, recklessness
Beowulf today: pursue activities that involve strength, risk, and the possibility of fame
Regard for Beowulf: people today do not value physical strength as highly as the Anglo-Saxons did; Beowulf probably would not enjoy the degree of esteem and respect that he had in Anglo-Saxon society.

Reading Strategy

1. The challenges that Beowulf must face increase in danger as he ages and the narrative progresses.
2. In youth, Beowulf relies on his prodigious strength to defeat Grendel and Grendel's mother. In old age, he relies on his heroic spirit to fight although he knows he is doomed.

54

Literary Element Conflict

An **external conflict** exists when a character struggles against some outside force, such as another person, nature, society, or fate. An **internal conflict** is a struggle that takes place within the mind of a character who is torn between opposing feelings, desires, or goals.

1. Which of Beowulf's external conflicts seems the most challenging? Explain.
2. In lines 707–717, what internal conflict does Beowulf face? How does he resolve it?

Review: Epic Hero
As you learned on page 21, an **epic hero** is typically a person of high social status who usually embodies the ideals of his people.

Group Activity An epic hero is defined by his or her society. How might Beowulf, an Anglo-Saxon epic hero, behave in our society? What kinds of jobs might he hold? With a group of your classmates, discuss Beowulf's main character traits—both good and bad. Create a diagram like the one below to record your observations. Then discuss how Beowulf might act in present-day situations as well as how others might regard him. Share your conclusions with the rest of your class.

[diagram with "Beowulf" in center]

LIT ON Literature Online
Selection Resources For Selection Quizzes, eFlashcards, and Reading-Writing Connection activities, go to glencoe.com and enter QuickPass code GL89817u1.

54 UNIT 1 THE ANGLO-SAXON PERIOD AND THE MIDDLE AGES

Reading Strategy Identify Sequence

Identifying the sequence of events is an important step in determining an author's purpose for writing. In *Beowulf*, the hero fights three monsters in succession: Grendel, Grendel's mother, and the fire-breathing dragon.

1. What does the poet suggest about Beowulf's challenges by using this sequence of battles?
2. How would you contrast Beowulf in youth with Beowulf in old age?

Vocabulary Practice

Practice with Analogies Complete each analogy below.

1. hammer : forge :: chisel :
   a. paint   b. sand   c. sculpt
2. pain : writhing :: cold :
   a. warming   b. skiing   c. shivering
3. criminal : infamous :: philanthropist :
   a. reputable   b. careful   c. joyous
4. cheer : celebrate :: lament :
   a. rejoice   b. mourn   c. criticize
5. pajamas : nap :: shroud :
   a. burial   b. wedding   c. convalescence

Academic Vocabulary

Throughout the epic, Beowulf is guided by his *concept* of fate.

Concept is an academic word. The word is also commonly used in commercial settings. For example, an electronics company might ask a designer to come up with a **concept** for a new product that would appeal to a younger audience.

To further explore this word, complete the following sentence: According to the traditional *concept* of heroism, a hero should be

and

For more on academic vocabulary, see pages 56 and R81.

Vocabulary
1. c **2.** c **3.** a **4.** b **5.** a

Academic Vocabulary

Possible answer: According to the traditional concept of heroism, a hero should be brave, strong, and selfless.

Assess

Students are assessed at regular points throughout instruction: after reading selections and at the end of units. The Teacher Edition provides answers to Student Edition questions.

Progress Check

IF a student needs help (based on a quick and informal assessment), THEN we provide a suggestion for reteaching.

Teaching Support

Big Idea Connection

Thought-provoking statements prompt students to explore the Big Idea in context to the reading selection.

Readability Scores

Dale-Chall, DRP, and Lexiles are provided for every selection

Teaching Notes

These notes give you extra teaching hints and information.

Spiral Review

Because repetition and reinforcement are important for students' learning, we indicate when a skill is being reviewed.

Skills Support

Glencoe Literature provides addition support with the skills, such as reading, writing, literature, listening, speaking, and viewing, research, that provide the framework for all academic success.

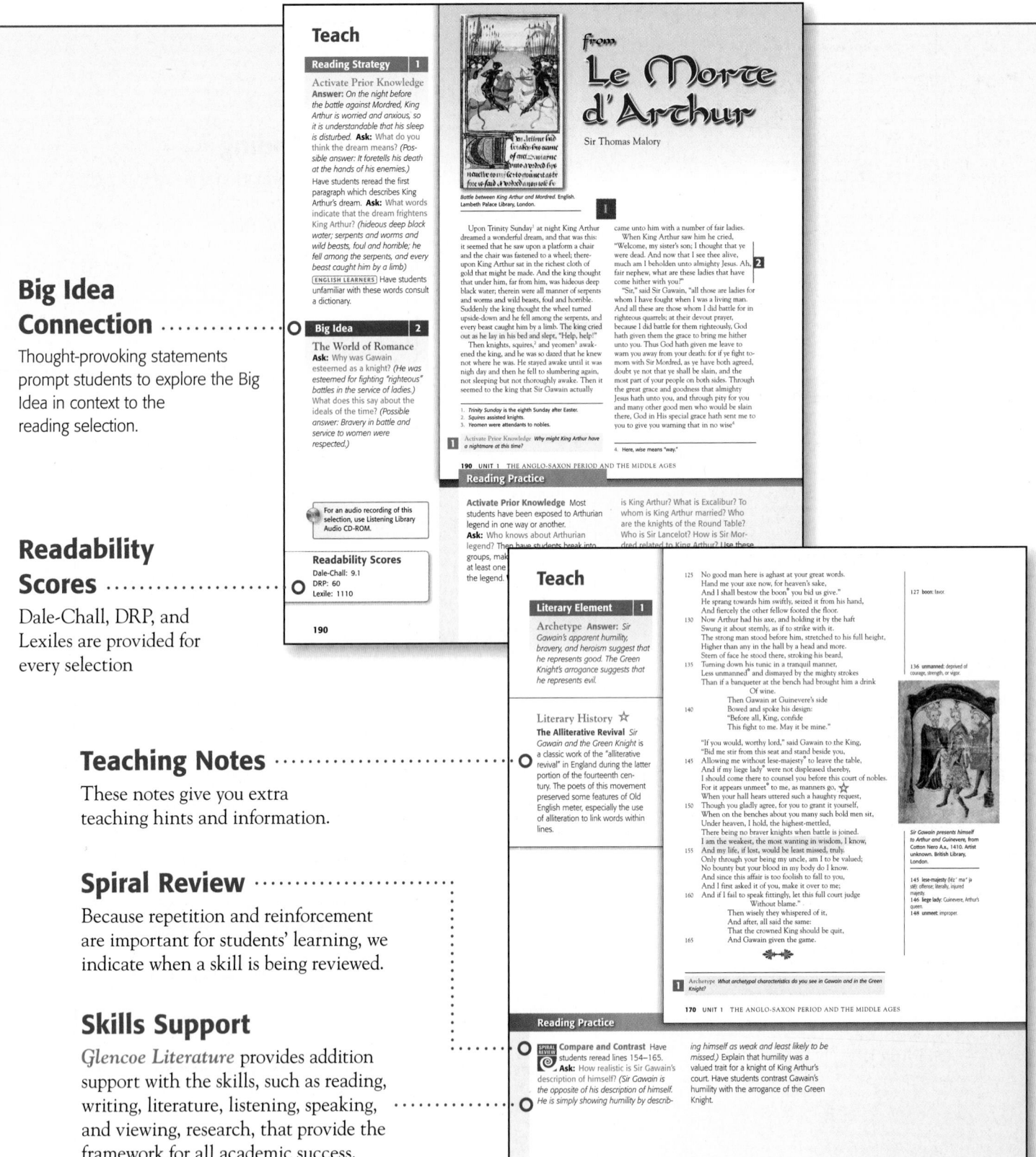

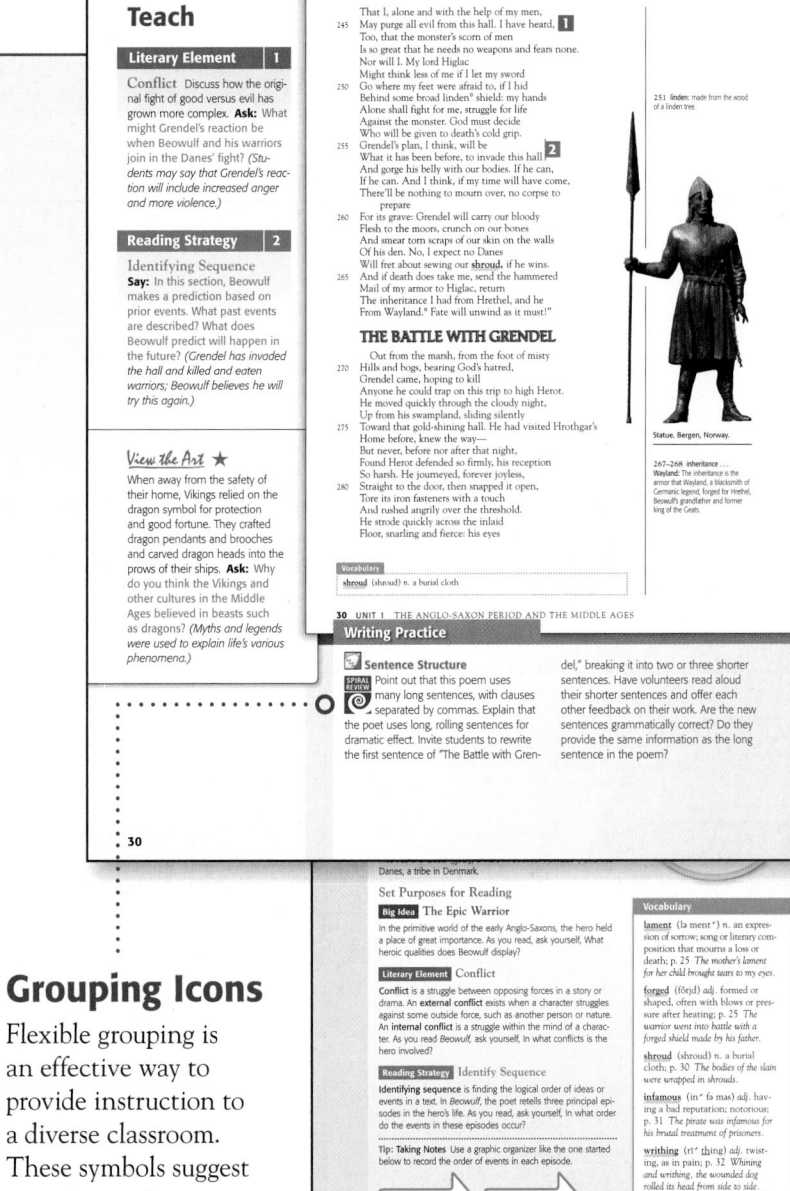

Teach

Literary Element · 1

Conflict Discuss how the original fight of good versus evil has grown more complex. **Ask:** What might Grendel's reaction be when Beowulf and his warriors join in the Danes' fight? *(Students may say that Grendel's reaction will include increased anger and more violence.)*

Reading Strategy · 2

Identifying Sequence
Say: In this section, Beowulf makes a prediction based on prior events. What past events are described? What does Beowulf predict will happen in the future? *(Grendel has invaded the hall and killed and eaten warriors; Beowulf believes he will try this again.)*

View the Art ★

When away from the safety of their home, Vikings relied on the dragon symbol for protection and good fortune. They crafted dragon pendants and brooches and carved dragon heads into the prows of their ships. **Ask:** Why do you think the Vikings and other cultures in the Middle Ages believed in beasts such as dragons? *(Myths and legends were used to explain life's various phenomena.)*

(Main sample page text)

That I, alone and with the help of my men,
245 May purge all evil from this hall. I have heard, 1
Too, that the monster's scorn of men
Is so great that he needs no weapons and fears none.
Nor will I. My lord Higlac
Might think less of me if I let my sword
250 Go where my feet were afraid to, if I hid
Behind some broad linden° shield: my hands
Alone shall fight for me, struggle for life
Against the monster. God must decide
Who will be given to death's cold grip.
255 Grendel's plan, I think, will be 2
What it has been before, to invade this hall
And gorge his belly with our bodies. If he can,
If he can. And I think, if my time will have come,
There'll be nothing to mourn over, no corpse to prepare
260 For its grave: Grendel will carry our bloody
Flesh to the moors, crunch on our bones
And smear torn scraps of our skin on the walls
Of his den. No, I expect no Danes
Will fret about sewing our **shroud**, if he wins.
265 And if death does take me, send the hammered
Mail of my armor to Higlac, return
The inheritance I had from Hrethel, and he
From Wayland.° Fate will unwind as it must!"

THE BATTLE WITH GRENDEL

Out from the marsh, from the foot of misty
270 Hills and bogs, bearing God's hatred,
Grendel came, hoping to kill
Anyone he could trap on this trip to high Herot.
He moved quickly through the cloudy night,
Up from his swampland, sliding silently
275 Toward that gold-shining hall. He had visited Hrothgar's
Home before, knew the way—
But never, before nor after that night,
Found Herot defended so firmly, his reception
So harsh. He journeyed, forever joyless,
280 Straight to the door, then snapped it open,
Tore its iron fasteners with a touch
And rushed angrily over the threshold.
He strode quickly across the inlaid
Floor, snarling and fierce: his eyes

251 **linden:** made from the wood of a linden tree.

Statue. Bergen, Norway.

267–268 **inheritance . . . Wayland:** The inheritance is the armor that Wayland, a blacksmith of Germanic legend, forged for Hrethel, Beowulf's grandfather and former king of the Geats.

Vocabulary
shroud (shroud) n. a burial cloth

30 UNIT 1 THE ANGLO-SAXON PERIOD AND THE MIDDLE AGES

Writing Practice

Sentence Structure
SPIRAL REVIEW Point out that this poem uses many long sentences, with clauses separated by commas. Explain that the poet uses long, rolling sentences for dramatic effect. Invite students to rewrite the first sentence of "The Battle with Grendel," breaking it into two or three shorter sentences. Have volunteers read aloud their shorter sentences and offer each other feedback on their work. Are the new sentences grammatically correct? Do they provide the same information as the long sentence in the poem?

30

Danes, a tribe in Denmark.

Set Purposes for Reading

Big Idea The Epic Warrior
In the primitive world of the early Anglo-Saxons, the hero held a place of great importance. As you read, ask yourself, What heroic qualities does Beowulf display?

Literary Element Conflict
Conflict is a struggle between opposing forces in a story or drama. An external conflict exists when a character struggles against some outside force, such as another person or nature. An internal conflict is a struggle within the mind of a character. As you read Beowulf, ask yourself, In what conflicts is the hero involved?

Reading Strategy Identify Sequence
Identifying sequence is finding the logical order of ideas or events in a text. In Beowulf, the poet retells three principal episodes in the hero's life. As you read, ask yourself, In what order do the events in these episodes occur?

Tip: Taking Notes Use a graphic organizer like the one started below to record the order of events in each episode.

Danes celebrate in Herot. → The warriors' rejoicing enrages Grendel.

Vocabulary
lament (la ment´) n. an expression of sorrow; song or literary composition that mourns a loss or death; p. 25 *The mother's lament for her child brought tears to my eyes.*

forged (fôrjd) adj. formed or shaped, often with blows or pressure after heating; p. 25 *The warrior went into battle with a forged shield made by his father.*

shroud (shroud) n. a burial cloth; p. 30 *The bodies of the slain were wrapped in shrouds.*

infamous (in´ fə məs) adj. having a bad reputation; notorious; p. 31 *The pirate was infamous for his brutal treatment of prisoners.*

writhing (rī´ thing) adj. twisting, as in pain; p. 32 *Whining and writhing, the wounded dog rolled its head from side to side.*

BEOWULF 23

English Learners
DIFFERENTIATED INSTRUCTION

Intermediate The word *infamous* can present difficulties to English learners and native speakers alike. **Say:** Look at the word *infamous*. What parts make up the word? Help students observe that the word consists of the prefix *in-* and *famous*. If necessary, explain that *in-* means "not." **Say:** Read the definition. Does *infamous* mean "not famous"? *(no)* Ask students to name well-known historical or fictional characters or celebrities who could be clas- sified as "famous" or "infamous." *(Answers will vary. To make certain students understand the concept, ask them to explain their reasons for labeling a given person or character as infamous.)*

23

Resource Suggestions at Point-of-Use

Helpful suggestions for using *Glencoe Literature* ancillary material support and simplify instruction.

(Sample annotation)
Before You Read

Focus

Summary
Denmark's King Hrothgar builds a huge banquet hall for his people. Their noisy celebrations infuriate a monster named Grendel, who terrorizes and attacks them, killing many. A young hero named Beowulf from nearby Geatland saves the Danes by killing Grendel and later Grendel's mother. Beowulf eventually becomes king of Geatland and dies an old man, defending his people from a dragon.

For summaries in languages other than English, see Unit 1 Teaching Resources Book, pp. 22–27.

Interactive Read and Write
Other options for teaching this selection can be found in
• Interactive Read and Write for English Learners, pp. 1–18
• Interactive Read and Write for Approaching-Level Learners, pp. 1–18
• Interactive Read and Write for On-Level Learners, pp. 1–18

Vocabulary

Diction Diction encompasses an author's choices of words, sentence length, and sentence complexity. The translator of Beowulf has chosen words that create a formal, old-fashioned feeling appropriate for an ancient epic. **Ask:** What word would you use instead of lament in common speech? *(cry, wail)*

Vocabulary Preteaching

Because vocabulary is a key component of reading success, we provide for the struggling students and English Learners in your classroom additional vocabulary preteaching activities.

Grouping Icons

Flexible grouping is an effective way to provide instruction to a diverse classroom. These symbols suggest grouping options.

Differentiated Instruction

Activities for your diverse classrooms are clearly labeled.

Informational Text

The wide range of informational text in *Glencoe Literature* broadens the students' reading to include more than just poetry, short stories, and plays.

Perspectives

Award-winning book excerpts provide students with the in-depth information they need to explore the cultural, political, historical, and literary contexts of a reading selection.

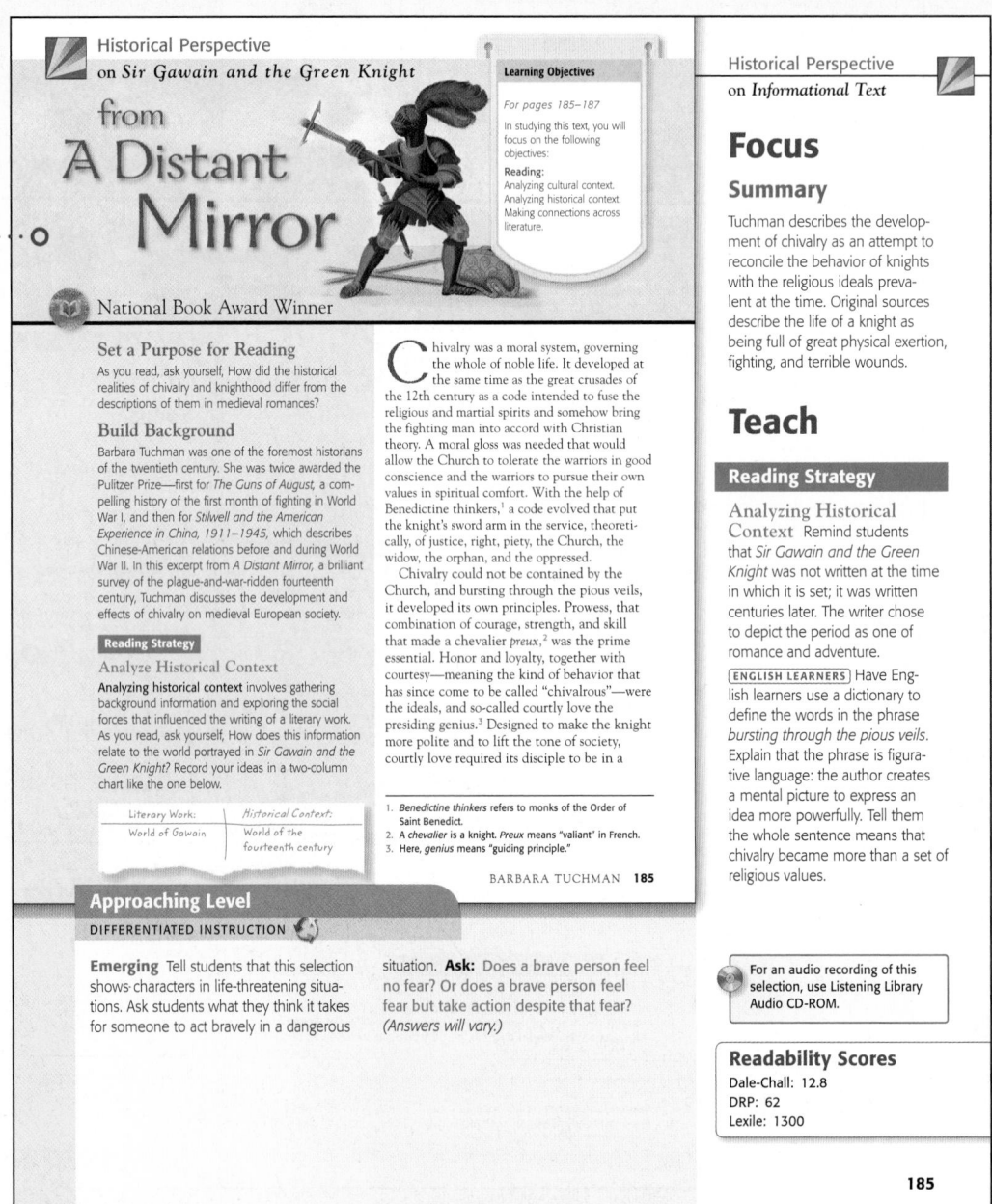

Historical Perspective
on *Sir Gawain and the Green Knight*

from
A Distant
Mirror

National Book Award Winner

Learning Objectives

For pages 185–187

In studying this text, you will focus on the following objectives:

Reading:
Analyzing cultural context.
Analyzing historical context.
Making connections across literature.

Set a Purpose for Reading
As you read, ask yourself, How did the historical realities of chivalry and knighthood differ from the descriptions of them in medieval romances?

Build Background
Barbara Tuchman was one of the foremost historians of the twentieth century. She was twice awarded the Pulitzer Prize—first for *The Guns of August*, a compelling history of the first month of fighting in World War I, and then for *Stilwell and the American Experience in China, 1911–1945*, which describes Chinese-American relations before and during World War II. In this excerpt from *A Distant Mirror*, a brilliant survey of the plague-and-war-ridden fourteenth century, Tuchman discusses the development and effects of chivalry on medieval European society.

Reading Strategy

Analyze Historical Context

Analyzing historical context involves gathering background information and exploring the social forces that influenced the writing of a literary work. As you read, ask yourself, How does this information relate to the world portrayed in *Sir Gawain and the Green Knight*? Record your ideas in a two-column chart like the one below.

Literary Work:	Historical Context:
World of Gawain	World of the fourteenth century

Chivalry was a moral system, governing the whole of noble life. It developed at the same time as the great crusades of the 12th century as a code intended to fuse the religious and martial spirits and somehow bring the fighting man into accord with Christian theory. A moral gloss was needed that would allow the Church to tolerate the warriors in good conscience and the warriors to pursue their own values in spiritual comfort. With the help of Benedictine thinkers,[1] a code evolved that put the knight's sword arm in the service, theoretically, of justice, right, piety, the Church, the widow, the orphan, and the oppressed.

Chivalry could not be contained by the Church, and bursting through the pious veils, it developed its own principles. Prowess, that combination of courage, strength, and skill that made a chevalier *preux*,[2] was the prime essential. Honor and loyalty, together with courtesy—meaning the kind of behavior that has since come to be called "chivalrous"—were the ideals, and so-called courtly love their presiding genius.[3] Designed to make the knight more polite and to lift the tone of society, courtly love required its disciple to be in a

---

1. *Benedictine thinkers* refers to monks of the Order of Saint Benedict.
2. A *chevalier* is a knight. *Preux* means "valiant" in French.
3. Here, *genius* means "guiding principle."

BARBARA TUCHMAN **185**

Approaching Level

DIFFERENTIATED INSTRUCTION

Emerging Tell students that this selection shows characters in life-threatening situations. Ask students what they think it takes for someone to act bravely in a dangerous situation. **Ask:** Does a brave person feel no fear? Or does a brave person feel fear but take action despite that fear? *(Answers will vary.)*

Historical Perspective
on *Informational Text*

Focus

Summary

Tuchman describes the development of chivalry as an attempt to reconcile the behavior of knights with the religious ideals prevalent at the time. Original sources describe the life of a knight as being full of great physical exertion, fighting, and terrible wounds.

Teach

Reading Strategy

Analyzing Historical Context Remind students that *Sir Gawain and the Green Knight* was not written at the time in which it is set; it was written centuries later. The writer chose to depict the period as one of romance and adventure.

(ENGLISH LEARNERS) Have English learners use a dictionary to define the words in the phrase *bursting through the pious veils*. Explain that the phrase is figurative language: the author creates a mental picture to express an idea more powerfully. Tell them the whole sentence means that chivalry became more than a set of religious values.

For an audio recording of this selection, use Listening Library Audio CD-ROM.

Readability Scores
Dale-Chall: 12.8
DRP: 62
Lexile: 1300

185

TIME Articles

Linked to the Big Idea, an author, or a reading selection, these articles deliver the facts on topical issues.

TIME

Focus

Summary

There are almost 100 outdoor theaters around the country running Shakespeare festivals during the summer months. Almost all are thriving because of the enthusiasm for Shakespeare.

📁 For summaries in languages other than English, see Unit 2 Teaching Resources Book, pp. 229–234.

Teach

Reading Strategy 1

Distinguish Fact from Opinion Say: Informational text contains facts about a subject. Sometimes, however, a writer inserts his or her opinions. **Ask:** Has the writer inserted opinions at the beginning of his article? If so, give examples. *(Yes; summer evening seems too balmy for indoors; "fortunately, they need not choose between pleasures.")* Have students look for examples of opinions as they read.

📁 For additional practice using the reading skill or strategy, see Unit 2 Teaching Resources Book, p. 235.

Readability Scores

Dale-Chall: 10.7
DRP: 69
Lexile: 1240

402

Learning Objectives

For pages 402–404
In studying this text, you will focus on the following objectives:

Reading:
Analyzing informational text.
Preview.
Distinguishing fact from opinion.

Set a Purpose for Reading

As you read, ask yourself, How can a playwright from the English Renaissance continue to entertain and inspire modern audiences?

Preview the Article

"Midsummer Night's Spectacle" examines the popularity of outdoor Shakespeare performances during the summer.

1. Read the title of the article. What clues does the word spectacle give you about the content of the article?

2. Read the deck, or the sentences in large type that appear below the title. **Say:** What problem or problems do you think the article will examine?

Reading Strategy

Distinguish Fact from Opinion

When you **distinguish fact from opinion,** you determine which statements can or cannot be confirmed as true.

As you read, ask yourself, Which statements can be proven as fact?

402

TIME

Midsummer Night's
SPECTACLE

Shakespeare is a reliable summer hit, especially performed outdoors.

So why is he a hard sell under a roof in winter?

By WILLIAM A. HENRY III

AS TWILIGHT SLIPS OVER THE HILLY COLLEGE TOWN OF Ashland, Oregon, the sweet summer evening seems too balmy for whiling away indoors, even to the vacationing crowds who have journeyed to attend the theater here. Fortunately, they need not choose between pleasures. Night after night, vividly costumed Shakespeare—preceded by the singing of madrigals and heralded by a flag raising and trumpet fanfare from the topmost gables of a Tudor stagehouse—unfolds here beneath a starry sky.

The scene takes place at the Oregon Shakespeare Festival (OSF), the largest regional theater in the United States and one of the oldest (it was founded in 1935). The theater is a three-stage jamboree built on a love of Shakespeare that draws almost 400,000 spectators a year. Ninety percent of those are from more than 125 miles away. With minor variations, this scene also takes place at dozens of outdoor theaters around the country, including one in an inner-city park in Louisville, Kentucky, and another on the grounds of a legendary mansion alongside the Hudson River in New York. According to Felicia Londre, former secretary of the Shakespeare Theater Association of America, the United States has about 100 outdoor Shakespeare festivals. Some, like Ashland's and New York City's Shakespeare in the Park, have grown into major institutions offering varied repertoires. Others operate just a few weeks a year. Nearly all rely on a lot of novice, non-union actors. But almost all are thriving.

1

Reading Practice

SPIRAL REVIEW Main Idea and Supporting Details Say: To find the main idea, examine how the author organizes ideas. Have students look at the second paragraph on this page. **Ask:** What is the main idea of this paragraph? *(Outdoor summertime presentations of Shakespeare's plays take place around the country.)* Where does the main idea appear? *(It appears in the fourth sentence.)* What details support the main idea? *(Examples of places where there are theaters: Ashland, Oregon; Louisville, Kentucky; on the grounds of a mansion along the Hudson River in New York City.)*

402

Guide to Readability

Throughout the teacher materials in your Teacher Edition, you will encounter DRP readability measures assigned to the reading selections in *Glencoe Literature*. You will also find readability scores based on the Lexile Framework® for Reading and the Dale-Chall Readability Formula. You can use these scores to select reading materials that are suitable for your entire class or for individual students.

Degrees of Reading Power® (DRP)

DRP values indicate the readability of prose text. The higher the value, the more difficult the text. The scale ranges from 1 to 100; commonly encountered English text tends to fall somewhere between 25 and 85. Although middle school texts have an average difficulty of 56, and high school texts have an average difficulty of 62, no single readability level is appropriate for each grade level. Rather, a typical classroom has materials with a range of readability levels available for use—some intended for less proficient readers, some for average readers, and some for stronger readers. The following chart shows the average DRP readability range for materials widely available for use at each grade. Some materials you might use, however, will certainly fall outside of the range for your particular grade.

Grade	DRP Readability Ranges
6	51–61
7	52–62
8	53–64
9	53–65
10	51–68
11	56–67
12	57–68

The Lexile® Framework

A Lexile measure assigned to a text is the specific number that describes the reading demands of the text. The typical Lexile Scale ranges from 200 to 1700 Lexiles. As with the DRP measures, there is not a direct translation from a specific Lexile measure to a specific grade level. Within any classroom, there will be a range of readers and a range of materials to be read. The levels shown on the following chart indicate the approximate range of Lexile scores for 50 percent of the materials found in a typical grade-level classroom. For example, the middle half of the instructional materials typically found in a sixth-grade classroom ranges in difficulty from about 850L to 1050L.

Grade	Text Measures (from Lexile Framework Map)
6	850L to 1050L
7	950L to 1075L
8	1000L to 1100L
9	1050L to 1150L
10	1100L to 1200L
11 and 12	1100L to 1300L

Dale-Chall Readability Formula

The Dale-Chall Formula is based on the average sentence length and the number of unfamiliar words in a passage. The idea behind this formula is that readers typically find it easier to read, process, and recall a passage if the words and sentences are familiar and grade appropriate. The Dale-Chall Formula assesses the difficulty of a passage by computing two different values from the text. The first measure is the average number of words per sentence. The second measure is the percentage of words in the passage not found on the grade appropriate Dale Word List. The following chart shows the average Dale-Chall readability scores for grades 5 thru 12.

Grade	Dale-Chall Readability Score
5-6th Grade	5.0 to 5.9
7-8th Grade	6.0 to 6.9
9-10th Grade	7.0 to 7.9
11-12th Grade	8.0 to 8.9

African American Vernacular English (AAVE)

Some of your students will be speakers of African American Vernacular English (AAVE). AAVE is a language system with well-formed rules for sounds, grammar, and meanings. Throughout the year you will help these students learn standard academic English by focusing on those places where AAVE differs from the standard and on those patterns that will have the most immediate impact on the students' reading and writing development.

These students will need help in understanding that what is appropriate in one setting is not appropriate in another, so they can shift easily and competently between varieties in different social contexts. Instruction will be more effective if it identifies nonstandard varieties of English as different, rather than inferior. All students should be taught standard English in a way that respects their home language.

Use the charts that follow to identify AAVE linguistic differences and instructional modifications that can help students as they learn to successfully and fluently speak, read, and write standard English. The modifications focus on the following:

- Providing students with clear enunciation examples during phonics and phonemic awareness lessons targeting difficult sounds. Then additional pronunciation practice is provided during small group phonics lessons.

- Using contrastive analysis during whole group and small group time in which students code switch between AAVE and standard English. The difference in each grammatical structure is highlighted and students are provided ample opportunities to practice standard English in speaking and writing. They are also taught the proper context for each usage.

- Using Discrimination Drills in which two sentences are read aloud or written on the board. One is standard English, the other reflects common AAVE structures. Students must determine which is standard English.

- Using Translation Drills in which students change an AAVE sentence into standard English.

Phonics Differences

English/Language Arts Skill	Linguistic Differences and Instructional Modifications
Digraph *th* as in bathroom	For many speakers of African American Vernacular English, the initial /th/ sound in function words such as *this* and *then* is often produced as a /d/ sound. In some words, such as *thing* and *through,* the /th/ sound is produced as a /t/ sound. At the ends of words and syllables, such as *bathroom* and *death,* the /th/ sound is replaced by the /f/ sound. This will affect students' spelling and speaking. Students will need additional articulation support prior to spelling these words.
Final Consonant *r*	Many speakers of African American Vernacular English drop the /r/ sound in words. For example, these students will say *sto'* for *store* or *do'* for *door.* Clearly pronounce these words, emphasizing the /r/ sound. Have students repeat several times, exaggerating the sound before spelling these words.
r-Blends	Many speakers of African American Vernacular English drop the /r/ in words with *r*-Blends. For example, these students will say *th'ow* for *throw.* Clearly pronounce these words in the lesson, emphasizing the sounds of the *r*-Blend. Have students repeat several times, exaggerating the sound.

Final Consonant *l* and Final *l*-Blends	Many speakers of African American Vernacular English drop the /l/ sound in words, particularly in words with *-ool* and *-oal* spelling patterns, such as *cool* and *coal*, and when the letter *l* precedes the consonants *p, t,* or *k* as in *help, belt,* and *milk.* These students will drop the *l* when spelling these words, as well. Provide additional articulation support prior to reading and spelling these words.
Final Consonant Blends	Many speakers of African American Vernacular English drop the final letter in a consonant blend *(e.g., mp, nt, nk, lo, lt, lk).* For example, they will say *des'* for *desk.* Clearly pronounce the final sound in these words and have students repeat several times, exaggerating the sound.
Plurals	When the letter *-s* is added to a word ending in a consonant blend, such as *test (tests),* many speakers of African American Vernacular English will drop the final sounds. Therefore they will say *tes'* or *tesses.* These students will need additional articulation support.
Contractions	Many speakers of African American Vernacular English drop the /t/ sound when pronouncing the common words *it's, that's,* and *what's.* These words sound more like *i's, tha's,* and *wha's.* These students will need additional articulation support in order to pronounce and spell these words.
Short Vowels *i* and *e*	When the /i/ and /e/ sounds appear before the consonants m or n in words, such as *pen/pin* and *him/hem,* many speakers of African American Vernacular English won't pronounce or hear the difference. Focus on articulation, such as mouth position for each vowel sound, during the lesson.
Inflectional Ending *-ing*	Many speakers of African American Vernacular English will pronounce words with *-ing* as /ang/. For example, they will say *thang* for *thing.* Emphasize the /i/ sound in these words to help students correctly spell and pronounce them.

Grammar, Usage, Mechanics Differences

English/Language Arts Skill	Linguistic Differences and Instructional Modifications
Subject-Verb Agreement *(he is , he goes)*	To acquire standard academic English speech and writing, speakers of African American Vernacular English need to learn to use -s with a verb and the third person and only there, as in *he is* and *he goes.* Many speakers of AAVE will leave out the -s or place it elsewhere, as in *he go* or *we goes.* Write a sentence from students' speech or writing. Then provide contrastive analysis work. Write the standard English form above that sentence. Discuss the key differences.
Subject-Verb Agreement *(do/does, have/has, was/were)*	Many speakers of African American Vernacular English have difficulties with subject-verb agreement when the verbs *do/does, have/has,* and *was/were* are used. Additional grammar instruction and practice will be needed. Write a sentence from students' speech or writing. Then provide contrastive analysis work. Write the standard English form above that sentence. Discuss the key differences.
Past Tense *(-ed)*	Many speakers of African American Vernacular English understand the use of *-ed* to form the past tense but leave it out or add sounds when pronouncing the word, as in *pick* or *pickted* for *picked.* Students will need additional work during small group time with *-ed* in order to know when and where to use it in writing.

Past Tense (simple past tense vs. past perfect tense)	Many speakers of African American Vernacular English will add *had* to the simple past tense, saying *We had picked* for *We picked.* The use of *had* indicates the past perfect tense in standard academic English. Other common nonstandard forms of irregular past-tense verbs include *He seen that* and *He had ran over there.*
The Verb "to be" (pronunciation)	In the first person present tense, many speakers of African American Vernacular English will properly use *I am* or *I'm*, but say it more like *"uhm."* Focus on pronunciation.
The Verb "to be" (writing)	To learn standard academic English, many speakers of African American Vernacular English will need to learn not to delete *is* and *are* when speaking and writing. For example, students might say *He my brother* or *She goin' over there.* Additional grammar instruction and practice will be needed. Use Discrimination and Translation Drills.
The Verb "to be" (speaking)	Many speakers of African American Vernacular English will use *was* in the singular and plural forms, as in *He was* and *They was.* Additional grammar instruction and practice will be needed.
The Verb "to be"	To learn standard academic English, many speakers of African American Vernacular English will need to learn to avoid using nonstandard forms, such as *He always be doing this,* in favor of *am, are,* and *is.* Also, additional instruction and practice will be needed to show the proper placement of the adverbs *always, never,* and *others.* For example, *He is always doing this* rather than *He always is doing this.* Write a sentence from students' speech or writing. Then provide contrastive analysis work. Write the standard English form above that sentence. Discuss the key differences.
Possessives ('s)	In standard academic English, *'s* is added to a noun to show possession. For many speakers of African American Vernacular English, the *'s* is absent. However, the *'s* is regularly added to *mine*, as in *This is mines.*
Possessive (whose)	The possessive pronoun *whose* is often not used by many speakers of African American Vernacular English. For example, students will say *I don't know who book this was.* Students will need additional instruction and practice to acquire this skill.
There is/There are	Many speakers of African American Vernacular English will need help in pronouncing *its* in standard academic English and in properly using the patterns *there is* and *there are.* In AAVE it is common to replace the word there with *it,* as in *It's a man at the door* rather than *There's a man at the door.* Use Discrimination and Translation Drills.
Plurals (nouns of measure)	Most speakers of African American Vernacular English correctly use the plural, except when it involves "nouns of measure," as in *It cost five dollars* or *She owe me five dollars*. However, the plural /s/ is often absent in writing, and students will need additional instruction and practice during small group time.
Negatives	Many speakers of African American Vernacular English will use several negatives in a sentence when only one is required, as in *Nobody never said nothing.* To master standard academic English, speakers of AAVE will need considerable practice to gain control of any, ever, and either after a negative word. Write a sentence from students' speech or writing. Then provide contrastive analysis work. Write the standard English form above that sentence. Discuss the key differences. In addition, use Discrimination and Translation Drills.

The Interaction Between English and Students' Primary Languages

By Jana Echevarria, PhD
California State University, Long Beach

Donald Bear, PhD
University of Nevada, Reno

It is important for teachers to understand why English Learners (ELs) use alternative pronunciations for some English words. Many English sounds do not exist or transfer to other languages, so English Learners may lack the auditory acuity to "hear" these English sounds and have difficulty pronouncing them. These students are not accustomed to positioning their mouth in a way the sound requires. The charts that appear on the following pages show that there is variation among languages, with some languages having more sounds in common and thus greater transfer to English than others.

For example, an English speaker may be able to pronounce the /r/ in the Spanish word pero ("but"), but not the /rr/ trill in perro ("dog"). The English speaker may also lack the auditory acuity to detect and the ability to replicate the tonal sounds of some Chinese words. Similarly, a Vietnamese speaker may have difficulty pronouncing /th/ in words such as thin or thanks.

Further, English Learners make grammatical errors due to interference from their native languages. In Spanish, the adjective follows the noun, so often English Learners say "the girl pretty" instead of "the pretty girl." While English changes the verb form with a change of subject (I walk. She walks.), some Asian languages keep the verb form constant across subjects. Adding /s/ to the third person may be difficult for some English Learners. Students may know the grammatical rule, but applying it consistently may be difficult, especially in spoken English.

When working with English Learners, you should also be aware of sociocultural factors that affect pronunciation. Students may retain an accent because it marks their social identity. Speakers of other languages may feel at a social distance from members of the dominant English-speaking culture.

English Learners improve their pronunciation in a nonthreatening atmosphere in which participation is encouraged. Opportunities to interact with native English speakers provide easy access to language models and give English Learners practice using English. However, students should not be forced to participate. Pressure to perform—or to perform in a certain way—can inhibit participation. In any classroom, teacher sensitivity to pronunciation differences contributes to a more productive learning environment.

Phonics, word recognition, and spelling are influenced by what students know about the sounds, word structure, and spelling in their primary languages. For example, beginning readers who speak Spanish and are familiar with its spelling will often spell short o with an a, a letter that in Spanish makes the short o sound. Similarly, English Learners who are unaccustomed to English consonant digraphs and blends (e.g., /ch/ and s-blends) spell /ch/ as sh because /sh/ is the sound they know that is closest to /ch/. Students learn about the way pronunciation influences their reading and spelling, beginning with large contrasts among sounds, then they study the finer discriminations. As vocabulary advances, the meaning of words leads students to the sound contrasts. For example, shoe and chew may sound alike initially, but meaning indicates otherwise. Students' reading and discussions of what they read advances their word knowledge as well as their knowledge in all language and literacy systems, including phonics, pronunciation, grammar, and vocabulary.

Phonics Transfers: Sound Transfers

This chart indicates areas where a positive transfer of sounds and symbols occurs for English Learners from their native languages into English. This symbol (✔) identifies a positive transfer. "Approximate" indicates that the sound is similar.

Consonants

Sound Transfers	Spanish	Cantonese	Vietnamese	Hmong	Korean	Khmer
/b/ as in bat	✔	approximate	approximate	approximate	approximate	✔
/k/ as in cake, kitten, peck	✔	✔	✔	✔	✔	✔
/d/ as in dog	✔	approximate	approximate	✔	approximate	✔
/f/ as in farm	✔	✔	✔	✔		
/g/ as in girl	✔	approximate	✔	approximate	approximate	
/h/ as in ham	✔	✔	✔	✔	✔	approximate
/j/ as in jet, page, ledge		approximate	approximate		approximate	
/l/ as in lion	✔	✔	✔	✔	✔	
/m/ as in mat	✔	✔	✔	✔	✔	✔
/n/ as in night	✔	✔	✔	✔	✔	✔
/p/ as in pen	✔	✔	✔	approximate	✔	✔
/kw/ as in queen	✔	approximate	✔		✔	✔
/r/ as in rope	approximate					✔
/s/ as in sink, city	✔	✔	✔	✔	✔	approximate
/t/ as in ton	✔	✔	approximate	approximate	✔	✔
/v/ as in vine	✔		✔	✔		
/w/ as in wind	✔	✔			✔	✔
/ks/ as in six	✔				✔	✔
/y/ as in yak	✔	✔		✔	✔	✔
/z/ as in zebra			✔			

Diagraphs

	Spanish	Cantonese	Vietnamese	Hmong	Korean	Khmer
/ch/ as in cheek, patch	✔	approximate		✔	✔	✔
/sh/ as in shadow			✔	✔	✔	
/hw/ as in whistle					✔	✔
/th/ as in path	approximate		approximate			
/TH/ as in that	approximate					

Diagraphs (continued)

Sound Transfers	Spanish	Cantonese	Vietnamese	Hmong	Korean	Khmer
/ng/ as in sting	✔	✔	✔	✔	✔	approximate
Short Vowels						
/a/ as in cat	approximate		approximate	✔	✔	
/e/ as in net	✔	approximate	approximate		✔	
/i/ as in kid	approximate	approximate			✔	
/o/ as in spot	approximate	approximate	approximate	approximate	approximate	✔
/u/ as in cup	approximate	approximate	✔		✔	✔
Long Vowels						
/ā/ as in lake, nail, bay	✔	approximate	approximate	approximate	✔	✔
/ē/ as in bee, meat, cranky	✔	approximate	✔	✔	✔	✔
/ī/ as in kite, tie, light, dry	✔	approximate	✔	✔	✔	✔
/ō/ as in home, road, row	✔	approximate	approximate		✔	
/ū/ as in dune, fruit, blue	✔	approximate	✔	✔	✔	✔
/yü/ as in mule, cue	✔	approximate			✔	
r-Controlled Vowels						
/är/ as in far	approximate	approximate				
/ôr/ as in corn	approximate	approximate				
/ûr/ as in stern, bird, suburb	approximate	approximate				
/âr/ as in air, bear						
/îr/ as in deer, ear						
Variant Vowels						
/oi/ as in boil, toy	✔	approximate	approximate		✔	✔
/ou/ as in loud, down	✔	approximate	✔	approximate	✔	✔
/ô/ as in law	approximate	✔	✔	approximate	approximate	✔
/ô/ as in laundry	approximate	approximate	✔	approximate	approximate	✔
/ôl/ as in salt, call	approximate	approximate			approximate	✔
/ōō/ as in moon, drew	✔	approximate	approximate	✔	✔	✔
/oo/ as in look		approximate	approximate		approximate	✔
/ə/ as in askew			approximate		✔	

Phonics Transfers: Sound Symbol Match

Consonants						
Sound Transfers	**Spanish**	**Cantonese**	**Vietnamese**	**Hmong**	**Korean**	**Khmer**
/b/ as in bat	✔		✔			
/k/ as in cake	✔		✔			
/k/ as in kitten	✔		✔	✔		
/k/ as in peck						
/d/ as in dog	✔		✔	✔		
/f/ as in farm	✔			✔		
/g/ as in girl	✔		✔			
/h/ as in ham			✔	✔		
/j/ as in jet, page, ledge						
/l/ as in lion	✔		✔	✔		
/m/ as in mat	✔		✔	✔		
/n/ as in night	✔		✔	✔		
/p/ as in pen	✔		✔	✔		
/kw/ as in queen			✔			
/r/ as in rope	approximate					
/s/ as in sink, city	✔		✔			
/t/ as in ton	✔		✔	✔		
/v/ as in vine	✔		✔	✔		
/w/ as in wind	✔					
/ks/ as in six	✔					
/y/ as in yak	✔			✔		
/z/ as in zebra						

Diagraphs

Sound Transfers	Spanish	Cantonese	Vietnamese	Hmong	Korean	Khmer
/ch/ as in cheek, patch	✔					
/sh/ as in shadow						
/hw/ as in whistle						
/th/ as in path			✔			
/TH/ as in that						
/ng/ as in sting	✔		✔			

Short Vowels

/a/ as in cat			✔	✔		
/e/ as in net	✔		✔			
/i/ as in kid						
/o/ as in spot			✔	✔		
/u/ as in cup						

Long Vowels

/ā/ as in lake						
/ā/ as in nail						
/ā/ as in bay						
/ē/ as in bee						
/ē/ as in meat						
/ē/ as in cranky						
/ī/ as in kite, tie, light, dry						
/ō/ as in home, road, row						
/ū/ as in dune			✔	✔		
/ū/ as in fruit, blue						
/yū/ as in mule, cue						

r-Controlled Vowels

Sound Transfers	Spanish	Cantonese	Vietnamese	Hmong	Korean	Khmer
/är/ as in far	✔					
/ôr/ as in corn	✔					
/ûr/ as in stern	✔					
/ûr/ as in bird, suburb						
/âr/ as in air, bear						
/îr/ as in deer, ear						

Variant Vowels

/oi/ as in boil	✔		✔			
/oi/ as in toy	✔					
/ou/ as in loud						
/ou/ as in down						
/ô/ as in law						
/ô/ as in laundry						
/ôl/ as in salt	✔					
/ôl/ as in call						
/o͞o/ as in moon, drew						
/oo/ as in look						
/ə/ as in askew						

Grammar Transfers: Grammatical Form

This chart can be used to address common mistakes that some English Learners make when they transfer grammatical forms from their native languages into English.

Nouns

Grammatical Form	Transfer Mistakes in English	Native Language	Cause of Difficulty
Plural Marker -s	**Forgets plural marker -s** *I have 3 sister.*	Cantonese, Haitian Creole, Hmong, Korean, Vietnamese, Khmer	Native language does not use a plural marker.
Countable and Uncountable Nouns	**Confuses countable and uncountable nouns** *the homeworks* or *the informations*	Haitian Creole, Spanish	Countable and uncountable nouns are different in English and native language.
Possessives	**Uses prepositions to describe possessives** *the book of my brother* as opposed to *my brother's book*	Haitian Creole, Hmong, Spanish, Vietnamese	Possession is often described using a prepositional phrase.
	Avoids using 's *dog my father* as opposed to *my father's dog*	Haitian Creole, Vietnamese, Khmer	A noun follows the object in the native language.

Articles

Grammatical Form	Transfer Mistakes in English	Native Language	Cause of Difficulty
	Consistently omits articles *He has book. They want dog not cat.*	Cantonese, Haitian Creole, Hmong, Korean, Vietnamese, Khmer	There is no article in the native language or no difference between the and a.
	Overuses articles *The English is difficult. The soccer is popular in the Europe.*	Haitian Creole, Hmong, Spanish	Some languages use articles that are omitted in English.
a/an	**Mistakes one for a/an** *She is one nurse.*	Haitian Creole, Hmong, Vietnamese	The native language either does not use articles or uses articles differently.

Pronouns

Grammatical Form	Transfer Mistakes in English	Native Language	Cause of Difficulty
Gender-Specific Pronouns	**Uses pronouns with the inappropriate gender** *He is my sister.*	Cantonese, Haitian Creole, Hmong, Korean, Spanish, Khmer	The third person pronoun in the native language is gender free, or the personal pronoun is omitted.
	Uses inappropriate gender, particularly with neutral nouns *The day is sunny. She is beautiful.*	Spanish	Nouns have feminine or masculine gender in the native language, and the gender may be carried over into English.

Pronouns

Grammatical Form	Transfer Mistakes in English	Native Language	Cause of Difficulty
Object Pronouns	**Confuses subject and object pronouns** *Her talks to me.*	Cantonese, Hmong, Khmer	The same pronoun form is used for subject and object in the native language.
	Omits object pronouns *That girl is very rude, so nobody likes.*	Korean, Vietnamese	The native language does not use direct objects.
Pronoun and Number Agreement	**Uses the wrong number for pronouns** *I saw many red birds. It was pretty.*	Cantonese, Korean	The native language does not require number agreement.
Subject Pronouns	**Omits subject pronouns** *Mom isn't home. Is at work.*	Korean, Spanish	Subject pronouns may be dropped because in the native language the verb ending gives information about the number and/or gender.
Pronouns in Clauses	**Omits pronouns in clauses** *If don't do homework, they will not learn.*	Cantonese, Vietnamese	The native language does not need a subject in the subordinate clause.
Pronouns and Nouns	**Overuses pronouns with nouns** *This school, it very good.*	Hmong, Vietnamese	This is popular in speech in some languages. The speaker mentions a topic, then makes a comment about it.
	Avoids pronouns and repeats nouns *Carla visits her sister every Sunday, and Carla makes a meal.*	Korean, Vietnamese	In the native language, the speaker repeats nouns and does not use pronouns.
Pronoun one	**Omits the pronoun one** *I saw two dogs, and I like the small.*	Spanish	Adjectives can stand alone in the native language, but English requires a *noun* or *one.*
Possessive Forms	**Confuses possessive forms** *The book is my.*	Cantonese, Hmong, Vietnamese	Cantonese and Hmong speakers tend to omit the final *n* sound, which may create confusion between my and mine.

Verbs

Grammatical Form	Transfer Mistakes in English	Native Language	Cause of Difficulty
Present Tense	**Omits -s in present tense, third person agreement** *He like pizza.*	Cantonese, Haitian Creole, Hmong, Korean, Vietnamese, Khmer	Subject-verb agreement is not used in the native language.
Irregular Verbs	**Has problems with irregular subject-verb agreement** *Tom and Sue has a new car.*	Cantonese, Hmong, Korean, Khmer	Verbs' forms do not change to show the number of the subject in the native language.
Inflectional Endings	**Omits tense markers** *I study English yesterday.*	Cantonese, Haitian Creole, Hmong, Korean, Vietnamese, Khmer	The native language does not use inflectional endings to change verb tense.
Present and Future Tenses	**Incorrectly uses the present tense for the future tense** *I go next week.*	Cantonese, Korean	The native language may use the present tense to imply the future tense.
Negative Statements	**Omits helping verbs in negative statements** *Sue no coming to school.*	Cantonese, Korean, Spanish	The native language does not use helping verbs in negative statements.
Present-Perfect Tense	**Avoids the present-perfect tense** *Marcos live here for three months.*	Haitian Creole, Vietnamese	The native language does not use the present-perfect verb form.
Past-Continuous Tense	**Uses the past-continuous tense for recurring action in the past** *When I was young, I was talking a lot.*	Korean, Spanish	In the native language, the past-continuous tense is used but in English the expression used to or the simple past tense is used.
Main Verb	**Omits the main verb** *Talk in class not good.*	Cantonese	Cantonese does not require an infinitive marker when using a verb as a noun. Speakers may confuse the infinitive for the main verb.
Main Verbs in Clauses	**Uses two or more main verbs in one clause without any connectors** *I took a book went studied at the library.*	Hmong	In Hmong, verbs can be used consecutively without conjunctions or punctuation.
Linking Verbs	**Omits the linking verb** *He hungry.*	Cantonese, Haitian Creole, Hmong, Vietnamese, Khmer	In some languages, be is implied in the adjective form. In other languages, the concept is expressed with a verb.
Helping Verb in Passive Voice	**Omits the helping verb in the passive voice** *The homework done.*	Cantonese, Vietnamese	In Cantonese and Vietnamese, the passive voice does not require a helping verb.

Verbs

Grammatical Form	Transfer Mistakes in English	Native Language	Cause of Difficulty
Passive Voice	**Avoids the passive voice** *They speak English here.* *One speaks English here.* **English is spoken here.**	Haitian Creole	The passive voice does not exist in the native language.
Transitive Verbs	**Confuses transitive and intransitive verbs** *The child broke. The child broke <u>the plate</u>.*	Cantonese, Korean, Spanish	Verbs that require a direct object differ between English and the native language.
Phrasal Verbs	**Confuses related phrasal verbs** *I ate at the apple.* *I ate up the apple.*	Korean, Spanish	Phrasal verbs are not used in the native language, and there is often confusion over their meaning.
Have **and** *be*	**Uses have instead of be** *I have thirst. He has right.*	Spanish	Spanish and English have different uses for ***have*** and ***be***.

Adjectives

Grammatical Form	Transfer Mistakes in English	Native Language	Cause of Difficulty
Word Order	**Places adjectives after nouns** *I saw a car red.*	Haitian Creole, Hmong, Spanish, Vietnamese, Khmer	Nouns often precede adjectives in the native language.
	Consistently places adjectives after nouns **This is a lesson new.**	Cantonese, Korean	Adjectives always follow nouns in the native language.
-er and -est Endings	**Avoids -er and -est endings** *I am more old than you.*	Hmong, Korean, Spanish, Khmer	The native language shows comparative and superlative forms with separate words.
-ing and ed Endings	**Confuses -ing and -ed forms** *Math is bored.*	Cantonese, Korean, Spanish, Khmer	Adjectives in the native language do not have active and passive meanings.

Adverbs

Grammatical Form	Transfer Mistakes in English	Native Language	Cause of Difficulty
Adjectives and Adverbs	**Uses an adjective where an adverb is needed** *Talk quiet.*	Haitian Creole, Hmong, Khmer	Adjectives and adverb forms are interchangeable in the native language.
Word Order	**Places adverbs before verbs** *He quickly ran.* *He ran quickly.*	Cantonese, Korean	Adverbs usually come before verbs in the native language, and this tendency is carried over into English.

Prepositions

Grammatical Form	Transfer Mistakes in English	Native Language	Cause of Difficulty
	Omits prepositions *I like come school.*	Cantonese	Cantonese does not use prepositions the way that English does.

How to Use the Grammar Transfer Charts

The grammar of many languages differs widely from English. For example, a student's primary language may use a different word order than English, may not use parts of speech in the same way, or may use different verb tenses. The Grammar Transfer Charts are designed to help you anticipate and understand possible student errors in speaking and writing standard English. With all grammar exercises, the emphasis is on oral communication, both as a speaker and listener.

1. Highlight Transferrable Skills

If the grammar skill transfers from the student's primary language to English, state that during the lesson. In many lessons an English Learner feature will indicate which skills do and do not transfer.

2. Preteach Non-Transferrable Skills

Prior to teaching a grammar lesson, check the chart to determine if the skill transfers from the student's primary language into English. If it does not, preteach the skill. Provide sentence frames and ample structured opportunities to use the skill in spoken English. Students need to talk, talk, and talk some more to master these skills.

3. Provide Additional Practice and Time

If the skill does NOT transfer from the student's primary language into English, the student will require more time and practice mastering it. Continue to review the skill using additional resources, such as the grammar lessons in the **Grammar and Language Workbook** in upcoming weeks.

4. Use Contrastive Analysis

Tell students when a skill does not transfer and include contrastive analysis work to make the student aware of how to correct their speaking and writing for standard English. For example, when a student uses an incorrect grammatical form, write the student sentence, then write the correct English form underneath. Explain the difference between the student's primary language and English. Have the student correct several other sentences using this skill.

5. Increase Writing and Speaking Opportunities

Increase the amount of structured writing and speaking opportunities for students needing work on specific grammatical forms. Sentence starters and paragraph frames, such as those found in the lessons, are ideal for both written and oral exercises.

6. Focus on Meaning

Always focus on the meanings of sentences in all exercises. As they improve and fine-tune their English speaking and writing skills, work with students on basic comprehension of spoken and written English.

To help students move to the next level of language acquisition and master English grammatical forms, recast their responses during classroom discussions or provide additional language for them to use as they respond further. Provide leveled-language sentence frames orally or in writing for students to use as they respond to questions and prompts. Below are samples.

English Learner Response Chart

Beginning (will respond by pointing or saying one word answers)	**Sample Frames** (simple, short sentences) *I see a _____.* *This is a _____.* *I like the _____.*
Early Intermediate (will respond with phrases or simple sentences)	**Sample Frames** (simple sentences with adjectives and adverbs added, and compound subjects or predicates) *I see a _____ _____.* *The _____ animal is _____.* *There are _____ and _____.*
Intermediate (will respond with simple sentences and limited academic language)	**Sample Frames** (harder sentences with simple phrases in consistent patterns; some academic language included) *The animal's prey is _____ because _____.* *The main idea is _____ because _____.* *He roamed the park so that _____.*
Early Advanced (will begin to use more sophisticated sentences and some academic language)	**Sample Frames** (complex sentences with increased academic language, beginning phrases and clauses, and multiple-meaning words) *When the violent storm hit, _____.* *As a result of the revolution, the army_____.* *Since most endangered animals are _____, they _____.*
Advanced (will have mastered some more complex sentence structures and is increasing the amount of academic language used)	Use the questions and prompts provided in the lessons for the whole group. Provide additional support learning and using academic language. These words are boldfaced throughout the lessons and sentence starters are often provided.

Classroom Resources: Print

Blackline Masters

Unit Teaching Resources

These blackline master booklets provide all the teaching materials you need to reinforce the content in each unit of *Glencoe Literature.* Worksheets include the following:

Unit Introduction
Big Idea Foldable
Big Idea School-to-Home Connection
- English
- Spanish
- Vietnamese
- Tagalog
- Cantonese
- Haitian Creole
- Hmong
Challenge Planner
Academic Vocabulary Development
Part Opener
Literary Focus
English Language Coach
Literary History
Comparing Literature Graphic Organizer
Grammar Workshop Practice
Media Workshop Practice
Selection Summaries
- English
- Spanish
- Vietnamese
- Tagalog
- Cantonese
- Haitian Creole
- Hmong
Literary Element
Reading Strategy
Selection Vocabulary Practice
Grammar Practice
Vocabulary Strategy
Selection Quick Check
- English
- Spanish
Spelling Practice
Writing Workshop Graphic Organizer
Writing Workshop Rubric
Speaking, Listening, and Viewing Activities
Speaking, Listening, and Viewing Workshop Rubric

Practice Books

Read and Write

INTERACTIVE These leveled consumable worktexts provide structured instruction and practice with selected readings from the anthology.

- On-Level provides fast-track instruction for on-level students.

- Approaching provides scaffolding for struggling or reluctant readers.

- English Learners helps students whose primary language is not English read and comprehend selection.

The Novel Companion

This worktext provides accelerated instruction for advanced students through novel study. With the tools for a detailed analysis of a novel and related reading for every unit of the anthology, students explore in more depth the Big Ideas around which the anthology is organized.

Spelling Power Workbook

Provides additional support for practice and mastery of spelling.

Writing

Glencoe Language Arts Writing Resources

This writing resource contains the following transparencies:

Writing Process Strategies Transparencies provide graphic organizers to help you guide your students through the various stages of the writing process.

Writing Practice Transparencies provide opportunities for students to practice writing in modes that are appropriate for their grade level including Narrative, Expository, and Persuasive Writing and Responding to Literary Texts.

Process of Revision Transparencies use base transparencies and corresponding overlays to show and explain actual revisions and edits. The set of revision transparencies guides students through the process of improving a sample essay. A blank Student Revision transparency is included so student volunteers can make their own revisions to improve the quality of an essay.

Writing Constructed Responses

This sourcebook with blackline masters helps students respond effectively to short essay questions.

Success in Writing: Research and Reports

These blackline masters reinforce and extend the coverage of research presented in the student edition.

Grammar and Language Workbook

This workbook provides full coverage of grammar, usage, and mechanics rules, examples, and practice exercises.

Grammar and Composition Handbook

This handbook is a handy desk reference tool providing full coverage of the writing process as well as rules and practice exercises for grammar, usage, and mechanics.

Grammar and Writing Transparencies

Help reinforce the skills taught in the grammar links and writing workshops.

Classroom Resources: Print

Assessment

Assessment Resources

This assessment tool provides three types of tests:

- Diagnostic assessment by learning objectives
- Formative tests and answer keys for selections
- Summative unit tests and answer keys

Standardized Test Prep and Practice

These materials feature exercises and activities that get students ready for standardized exams.

ACT/SAT Preparation and Practice Workbook

Fluency Practice and Assessment

English Language Development

English Language Coach

These worksheets provide extra support for English Learners.

Independent Reading

Ethnic Anthologies

The following anthologies offer students introductions to the richness and variety of literature written by African, Asian, Hispanic, and Native Americans. A Teacher's Guide for each anthology suggests answers to questions accompanying each selection to help further student discussion.

- *Glencoe African American Literature*
- *Glencoe Asian American Literature*
- *Glencoe Hispanic American Literature*
- *Glencoe Native American Literature*

InTIME Magazines

This lively collection of articles drawn from TIME helps students develop skills for reading informational text.

Transparencies

Bellringer Transparencies

include warm-up exercises to engage students and to provide a quick review of previously taught skills.

Fine Art Transparencies

enhance visual literacy and provide a strong humanities approach to literature.

Literary Elements Transparencies

help reinforce literary elements that are the focus of each lesson.

Read Aloud, Think Aloud Transparencies

model active reading

Classroom Resources: Technology

Classroom Planning, Management, and Instruction

TeacherWorks Plus CD-ROM

- Plan and manage daily lessons and activities
- Access all program resources
- Edit lesson plans and worksheets
- Track the standards taught in your classroom

Classroom Presentation Toolkit CD-ROM or DVD-ROM

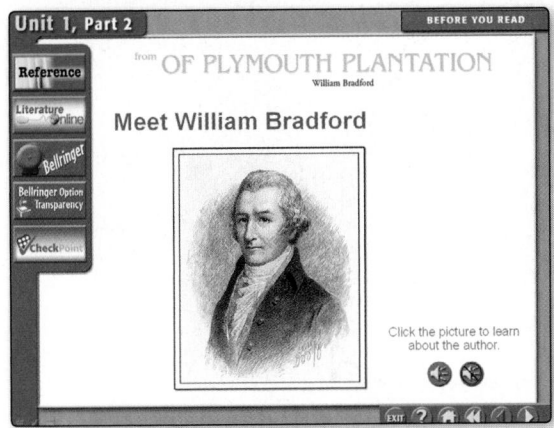

- Present customizable lessons via PowerPoint
- Launch transparencies, audio, video, and software at point-of-use during instruction

Digital Learning

Online Student Edition and StudentWorks Plus CD-ROM or DVD-ROM

- Full-text synced-audio selection read support
- Audio summaries in multiple languages
- Search, highlighting, and notes tools
- Multimedia links to video, activities, animations, and graphic graphic organizers
- Access student workbooks, Student Media Toolkit, and Student Presentation Builder
- Daily Assignments and Grade Log

Assessment and Progress Monitoring

ExamView Assessment Suite CD-ROM

- Administer ready-made diagnostic, formative, and summative assessments in English or Spanish
- Edit assessment items or create new items as needed
- Monitor student progress through a variety of reporting options
- Provides real assessment-driven remediation options

Progress Reporter Online Assessment

- Administer ready-made diagnostic, formative, and summative assessments online in English or Spanish
- Edit assessment items or create new items as needed
- Assessments administered online are scored automatically
- Essay questions are scored automatically
- Ready-made exams provide students with item rationales, explaining why each answer choice is correct or incorrect
- Automatically assigns reteaching and remediation based on student performance
- Monitor student progress by standard or by standard strand or through a variety of other reporting options

Literature Online: Assessment Resources

- End-of-Unit Assessment
- Test-taking Tips and Strategies

Literature and Reading

Literature Classics

- Choose from over 1,100 additional classic literature selections
- Search selections by author, title, date, genre, country, course/grade level, and Big Question or Big Idea
- Reinforce instruction with Genre Focus Lesson Plans and blackline masters
- Available on CD-ROM and access via glencoe.com

Classroom Resources: Technology

Listening Library CD

- Help students improve overall comprehension and reading fluency with engaging recordings of the selections in *Glencoe Literature*
- Assist English Learners with audio selection summaries in their native language
- Use the Listening Library CDs in conjunction with the Listening Library Sourcebook, a collection of standards-based strategies and activities, found on your TeacherWorks™ Plus CD-ROM

Literature Launchers: Pre-Reading Videos DVD

- Each of the engaging video segments on this DVD brings the literature to life, providing a visual context for every Unit and key selections
- Use this DVD in conjunction with the Literature Launchers Teacher Guide, found on your TeacherWorks™ Plus CD-ROM, which provides teaching strategies and video-specific blackline masters.
- English and Spanish subtitles

Literature Library Teacher Resources CD-ROM

- Access all Glencoe Literature Library Study Guides
- Develop vocabulary with Vocabulary Puzzlemaker
- Assess with ExamView Assessment Suite

BookLink K-12 CD-ROM

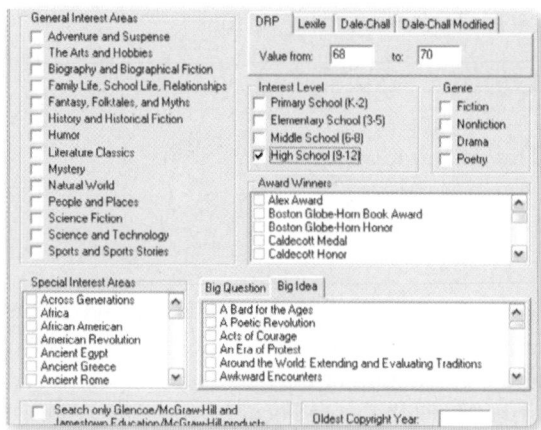

- Create customized reading lists for your students from a database of over 30,000 titles

- Search for award-winning titles and for books on state recommended reading lists
- Organize reading lists by students' reading level, author, genre, theme, or area of interest
- Find Degrees of Reading Power™ (DRP), Lexile™, and Dale-Chall scores for all selections in the Glencoe Literature program

Skill Level Up! A Skills-Based Language Arts Game CD-ROM

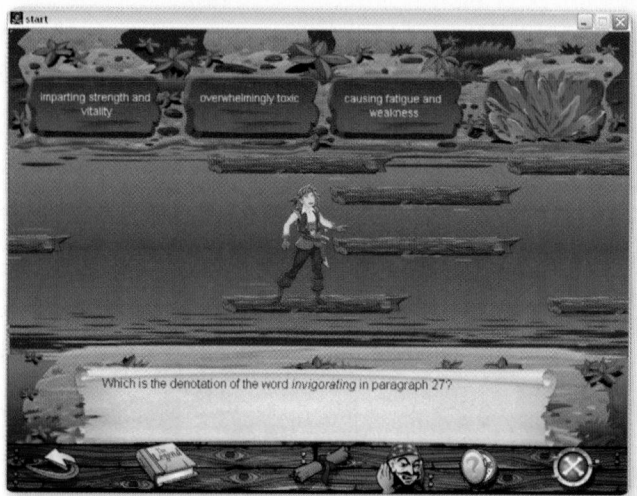

- Offers an innovative approach to Language Arts and Reading skills practice, assessment and remediation
- Skill Level Up!'s networkable game environment provides a context and purpose for learning by immersing students in an engaging adventure
- Features two access modes: the immersive story mode, which covers all the skills in the context of the adventure game play, or the skill-based assignment mode, which allows teachers to assign discrete activities according to their curriculum plan
- Adapts to each student's performance by offering remediation when necessary or enrichment activities when applicable
- Manage and track student performance using convenient assignment, tracking, and reporting functions featured in the program's management system
- Covers the following Reading Skills and Literary Elements:
  - Connecting
  - Questioning
  - Predicting
  - Point of View
  - Visualizing

- Rhyme
- Dialog
- Main Idea and Supporting Details/Paraphrasing and Summarizing
- Plot
- Conflict
- Interpreting
- Drawing Conclusions
- Setting
- Fact and Opinion
- Theme
- Author's Purpose and Perspective
- Voice, Style, Tone, Narrator
- Description, Imagery, Sensory Details
- Symbolism
- Inferring
- Figurative Language
- Analyzing Text Structure
- Meter and Rhythm
- Character and Characterization
- Sound Devices
- Genre
- Synthesizing

Literature Online: Literature, Reading, and Selection Resources (glencoe.com)

- Author and Artist Search
- Web Quest
- Selection Quizzes
- Selection Vocabulary eFlashcards
- Selection Reading-Writing Connection activities
- Reading Skills Review
- Interactive Reading Practice
- Literary Elements eFlashcards
- Fluency Practice
- Games

Vocabulary Development

Glencoe Interactive Vocabulary CD-ROM

- Generate flashcard sets from a visual glossary of selection, academic, content area, and social vocabulary terms
- Includes audio support in multiple languages for all terms
- Provides instructional modules and practice via an engaging game environment:

- signal words
- cognates/false cognates
- multiple meaning words
- synonyms and antonyms
- idioms
- analogies
- figures of speech
- context clues
- etymology
- troublesome words
- text features
- compound words
- homonyms

Vocabulary PuzzleMaker

- Create crossword puzzles, word search puzzles, and jumble puzzles in an instant
- Choose from selection and academic vocabulary (in both English and Spanish) and literary terms
- Available on CD-ROM and for download via glencoe.com

Skill Level Up! A Skills-Based Language Arts Game CD-ROM

- Using Context Clues
- Multiple Meaning Words
- Examining Words Origins
- Words with Special Meanings
- Denotation and Connotation
- Using Analogies
- Synonyms
- Antonyms
- Homonyms
- Word Parts/Structural Analysis: Base Words
- Word Parts/Structural Analysis: Prefixes
- Word Parts/Structural Analysis: Suffixes

Classroom Resources: Technology

Literature Online: Vocabulary and Spelling Resources (glencoe.com)

- Multi-Language Glossary
- Selection Vocabulary eFlashcards
- Academic Vocabulary eFlashcards
- Vocabulary Games
- Spelling Lessons
- Spelling Games

Writing

Glencoe Online Essay Grader powered by Bookette SkillWriter™ (glencoewriting.com)

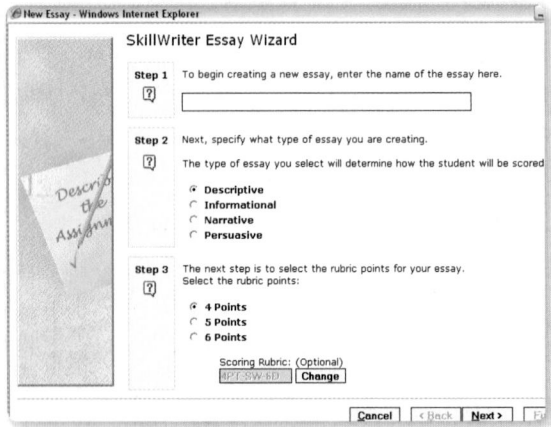

- Score student writing assignments and provide individualized feedback to each student automatically
- Assign prompts from Glencoe Literature Writing Workshops or create your own prompts!
- Manage demographic data, assign tests and run a variety of progress monitoring reports using the program's management system.

Literature Online: Writing and Research Resources (glencoe.com)

- Annotated Writing Models
- Interactive Writing Models
- Writing and Research Handbook
- Research Tips and Strategies
- Graphic Organizers
- Transition Bank
- Grammar Troubleshooter
- Sentence-Combining Practice

- Editing and Proofreading Marks
- Publishing Options

Speaking, Listening and Viewing

Skill Level Up! A Skills-Based Language Arts Game CD-ROM

- Analyzing Persuasive Techniques
- Listening Critically
- Examining Visuals in Literature and Media: Maps, Charts, Graphs
- Examining Visuals in Literature and Media: Visual Techniques

Student Presentation Builder

- Assign additional Unit-based multimedia presentation projects
- Includes a PowerPoint™ tutorial, a PowerPoint™ presentation template, and an image bank
- Available on StudentWorks Plus or via the Online Student Edition
- Teacher Guide is available on TeacherWorks Plus

Literature Online: Speaking, Listening, and Viewing Resources (glencoe.com)

- Project Ideas and Templates
- Presentation Tips and Strategies

Media Literacy

Glencoe Media Workshop DVD

- Engage students in the study and critical review of media from film footage of important events in history to analysis of commercials
- English and Spanish subtitles

Student Media Toolkit

- Provides additional interactive media analysis activities
- Includes media generator tools

Literature Online: Media Literacy Resources (glencoe.com)

- Media Analysis Guides
- Project Ideas

Library Resources

Glencoe Literature Library

Each *Glencoe Literature* Library volume consists of at least one complete extended-length reading accompanied by several related readings from a broad range of genres. A separate Study Guide for each book provides teaching notes and reproducible activity pages for students. Students may also find these activity pages at glencoe.com.

The Adventures of Huckleberry Finn by Mark Twain **DRP 54***

All Quiet on the Western Front by Erich Maria Remarque **DRP 52**

. . . And the Earth Did Not Devour Him by Tomas Rivera **DRP 52**

Animal Farm by George Orwell **DRP 60**

The Autobiography of Benjamin Franklin by Benjamin Franklin **DRP 64**

The Autobiography of Miss Jane Pittman by Ernest J. Gaines **DRP 49**

The Awakening by Kate Chopin **DRP 58**

Beowulf

Billy Budd by Herman Melville **DRP 68**

The Bridge of San Luis Rey by Thornton Wilder **DRP 55**

The Brothers Karamazov by Fyodor Dostoevsky **DRP 55**

The Canterbury Tales by Geoffrey Chaucer **DRP 59**

The Chosen by Chaim Potok **DRP 56**

A Country Doctor by Sarah Orne Jewett **DRP 59**

Cyrano de Bergerac by Edmond Rostand **DRP**

Ethan Frome by Edith Wharton **DRP 59**

Fallen Angels by Walter Dean Myers **DRP 47**

Frankenstein by Mary Shelley **DRP 64**

Great Expectations by Charles Dickens **DRP 60**

Gulliver's Travels by Jonathan Swift **DRP 67**

Hamlet by William Shakespeare

Heart of Darkness and *The Secret Sharer* by Joseph Conrad **DRP 58**

A House for Mr Biswas by V. S. Naipaul **DRP 58**

The House of the Seven Gables by Nathaniel Hawthorne **DRP 65**

The Importance of Being Earnest by Oscar Wilde **DRP**

Invisible Man by Ralph Ellison **DRP 57**

Jane Eyre by Charlotte Brontë **DRP 61**

Julius Caesar by William Shakespeare

The Jungle by Upton Sinclair **DRP 59**

The Mayor of Casterbridge by Thomas Hardy **DRP 60**

The Metamorphosis by Franz Kafka **DRP 57**

A Midsummer Night's Dream by William Shakespeare

My Ántonia by Willa Cather **DRP 57**

Narrative of the Life of Frederick Douglass by Frederick Douglass **DRP 62**

Nectar in a Sieve by Kamala Markandaya **DRP 56**

Night by Elie Wiesel **DRP 51**

One Day in the Life of Ivan Denisovich by Aleksandr Solzhenitsyn **DRP 56**

Our Town by Thornton Wilder

Picture Bride by Yoshiko Uchida **DRP 55**

Pride and Prejudice by Jane Austen **DRP 61**

A Raisin in the Sun by Lorraine Hansberry

The Red Badge of Courage by Stephen Crane **DRP 60**

The Return of the Native by Thomas Hardy **DRP 61**

The Scarlet Letter by Nathaniel Hawthorne **DRP 67**

Sense and Sensibility by Jane Austen **DRP 63**

A Separate Peace by John Knowles **DRP 59**

Silas Marner by George Eliot **DRP 55**

The Souls of Black Folk by W. E. B. Du Bois **DRP 66**

The Story of My Life by Helen Keller **DRP 59**

The Strange Case of Dr Jekyll and Mr Hyde by Robert Louis Stevenson **DRP 63**

A Tale of Two Cities by Charles Dickens **DRP 62**

The Tempest by William Shakespeare

Things Fall Apart by Chinua Achebe **DRP 56**

The Time Machine and *The War of the Worlds* by H. G. Wells **DRP 59**

To Kill a Mockingbird by Harper Lee **DRP 51**

Walden by Henry David Thoreau **DRP 62**

The Way to Rainy Mountain by N. Scott Momaday **DRP 55**

Wuthering Heights by Emily Brontë **DRP 61**

The Yearling by Marjorie Kinnan Rawlings **DRP 53**

*Degrees of Reading Power® DRP values indicate the readability of prose text. The higher the value, the more difficult the text. Though the scale ranges from 0 to 100, texts widely available for use at grades nine through twelve typically range from 53 to 68. Some materials, however, may certainly fall outside of this range.

Literary Map of London

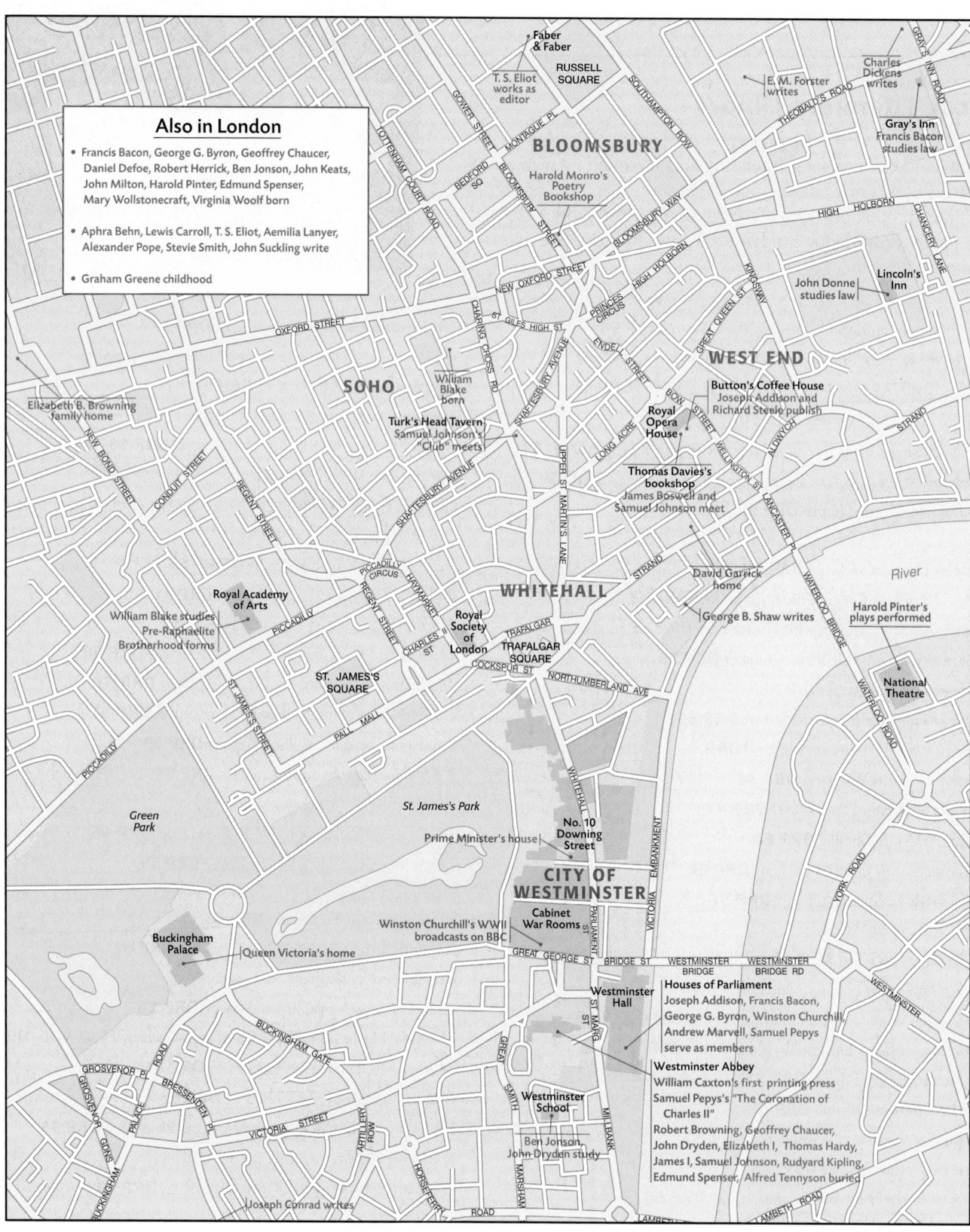

Also in London

- Francis Bacon, George G. Byron, Geoffrey Chaucer, Daniel Defoe, Robert Herrick, Ben Jonson, John Keats, John Milton, Harold Pinter, Edmund Spenser, Mary Wollstonecraft, Virginia Woolf born

- Aphra Behn, Lewis Carroll, T. S. Eliot, Aemilia Lanyer, Alexander Pope, Stevie Smith, John Suckling write

- Graham Greene childhood

Faber & Faber

T. S. Eliot works as editor

RUSSELL SQUARE

E. M. Forster writes

Charles Dickens writes

Gray's Inn Francis Bacon studies law

BLOOMSBURY

Harold Monro's Poetry Bookshop

John Donne studies law

Lincoln's Inn

WEST END

William Blake born

SOHO

Button's Coffee House Joseph Addison and Richard Steele publish

Royal Opera House

Turk's Head Tavern Samuel Johnson's "Club" meets

Thomas Davies's bookshop James Boswell and Samuel Johnson meet

Elizabeth B. Browning family home

David Garrick home

River

Harold Pinter's plays performed

Royal Academy of Arts

WHITEHALL

George B. Shaw writes

William Blake studies Pre-Raphaelite Brotherhood forms

Royal Society of London

National Theatre

PICCADILLY CIRCUS

Trafalgar

ST. JAMES'S SQUARE

TRAFALGAR SQUARE

Green Park

St. James's Park

Prime Minister's house

No. 10 Downing Street

CITY OF WESTMINSTER

Buckingham Palace

Queen Victoria's home

Winston Churchill's WWII broadcasts on BBC

Cabinet War Rooms

Westminster Hall

Houses of Parliament
Joseph Addison, Francis Bacon, George G. Byron, Winston Churchill, Andrew Marvell, Samuel Pepys serve as members

Westminster School

Ben Jonson, John Dryden study

Westminster Abbey
William Caxton's first printing press
Samuel Pepys's "The Coronation of Charles II"
Robert Browning, Geoffrey Chaucer, John Dryden, Elizabeth I, Thomas Hardy, James I, Samuel Johnson, Rudyard Kipling, Edmund Spenser, Alfred Tennyson buried

Joseph Conrad writes

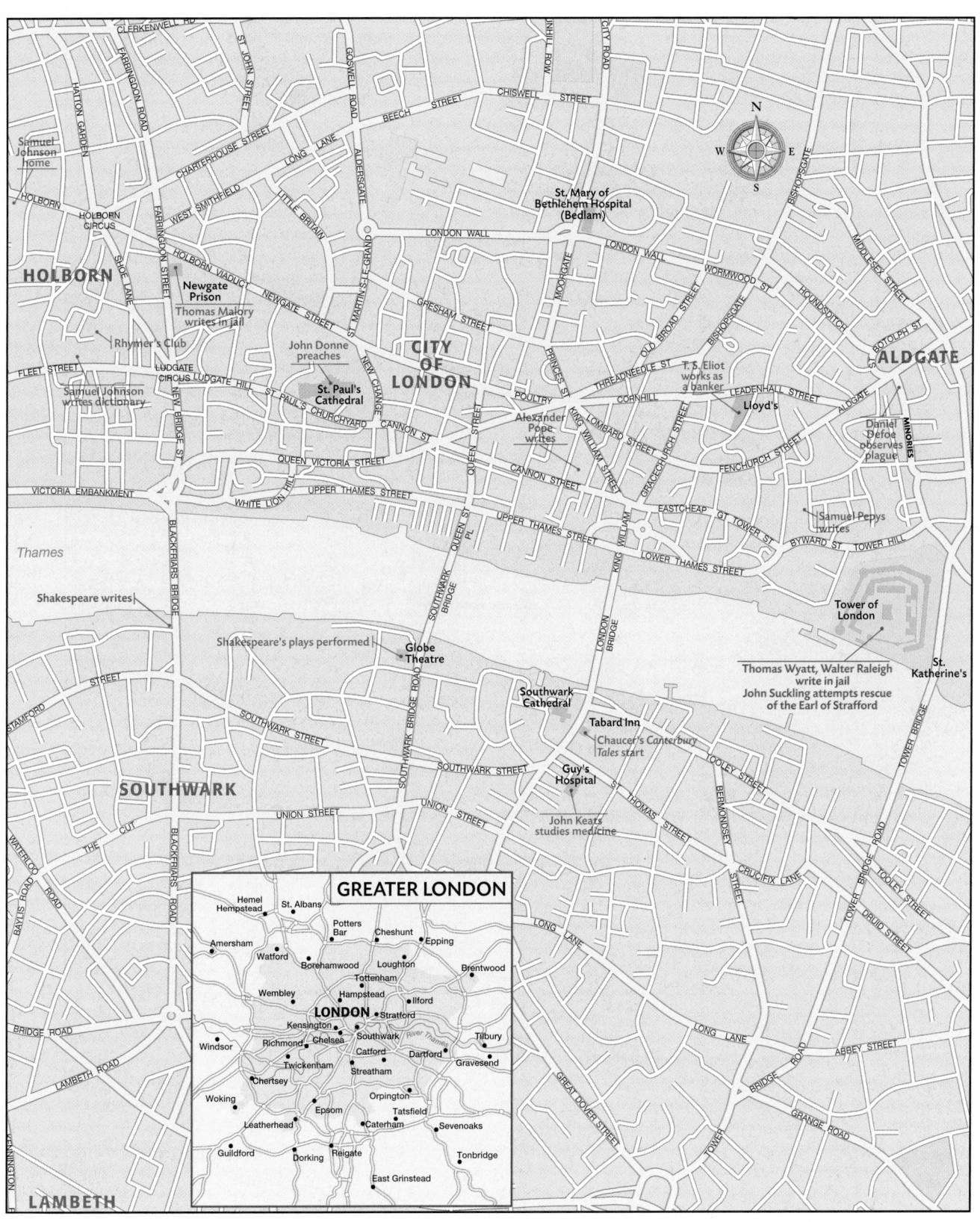

HOLBORN

Samuel Johnson home

HOLBORN CIRCUS

HOLBORN

Newgate Prison
Thomas Malory writes in jail

Rhymer's Club

Samuel Johnson writes dictionary

John Donne preaches

CITY OF LONDON

St. Paul's Cathedral

St. Mary of Bethlehem Hospital (Bedlam)

ALDGATE

T. S. Eliot works as a banker

Lloyd's

Daniel Defoe observes plague

Alexander Pope writes

Samuel Pepys writes

Thames

Shakespeare writes

Shakespeare's plays performed

Globe Theatre

Southwark Cathedral

Tabard Inn
Chaucer's Canterbury Tales start

SOUTHWARK

Guy's Hospital

John Keats studies medicine

Tower of London

Thomas Wyatt, Walter Raleigh write in jail
John Suckling attempts rescue of the Earl of Strafford

St. Katherine's

GREATER LONDON

Hemel Hempstead
St. Albans
Potters Bar
Cheshunt
Epping
Amersham
Watford
Borehamwood
Loughton
Brentwood
Tottenham
Wembley
Hampstead
Ilford
LONDON
Kensington
Stratford
Richmond
Chelsea
Southwark
Windsor
Twickenham
Catford
Dartford
Tilbury
Streatham
Gravesend
Chertsey
Orpington
Woking
Epsom
Tatsfield
Leatherhead
Caterham
Sevenoaks
Guildford
Dorking
Reigate
Tonbridge
East Grinstead

LAMBETH

Map of Great Britain

N W E S

King Duncan's palace
Forres
Inverness
Macbeth slain
Dunsinane
Aberdeen
Sir Patrick Spens drowns
George G. Byron childhood
SCOTLAND
Dundee
North Sea
James Boswell born
Wilfred Owen meets
Siegfried Sassoon (WWI)
Dumferling
Greenock
Glasgow
Edinburgh
ATLANTIC OCEAN
Ayrshire
Robert Burns's poetry
Newcastle Upon Tyne
Venerable Bede writes
Jarrow
Caedmon's hymns
Londonderry
Seamus Heaney born
Carlisle
Middlesbrough
William Wordsworth's poetry
Dorothy Wordsworth's journal
LAKE DISTRICT
William B. Yeats's childhood
NORTHERN IRELAND
Belfast
Whitby
Andrew Marvell born
Sligo
UNITED
York
W. H. Auden born
John Dryden
Winestead
Blackpool
Haworth
Kingston
Brontës born
Leeds
Irish Sea
Bolton
Manchester
IRELAND
Sheffield
Birkenhead
Liverpool
Dublin
George G. Byron home
Gawain vs. Green Knight
Newstead
Nottingham
King's Lynn (Bishop's Lynn)
Eastwood
Norwich
D. H. Lawrence born
ENGLAND
Samuel Johnson born
Lichfield
Rupert Brooke born
John Bunyan born
Fanny Burney born
Margery Kempe writes
Edmund Spenser writes
Birmingham
Cambridge
Limerick
John Dryden born
Rugby
Ipswich
Kilcolman
Shakespeare born
Aldwinkle
Elstow
Clonmel
Stratford-upon-Avon
KINGDOM
Laurence Sterne born
Jane Austen writes
Oxford
Elizabeth I palace
Lady Mary W. Montagu writes
Alexander Pope writes
Cork
Frank O'Connor born
WALES
Thomas Wyatt born
London
Alfred Tennyson writes
Swansea
Newport
Bristol
Richmond
Allington
Canterbury
Dylan Thomas's poetry
Cardiff
Bath
Twickenham
Maidstone
Matthew Arnold's "Dover Beach"
Wordsworth's Tintern Abbey
Nether Stowey
Southampton
Chaucer's Canterbury Tales
Samuel T. Coleridge writes Rime of the Ancient Mariner
Mary Shelley buried
Portsmouth
Christopher Marlowe born
Richard Lovelace home
Exeter Book written
Exeter
Dorchester
Bournemouth
King Arthur born
East Budleigh
Tintagel
Plymouth
Thomas Hardy writes
Walter Raleigh born
English Channel
FRANCE

Cambridge University

Francis Bacon	Andrew Marvell
Rupert Brooke	John Milton
George G. Byron	Samuel Pepys
Samuel T. Coleridge	Siegfried Sassoon
John Dryden	Edmund Spenser
Thomas Gray	John Suckling
Robert Herrick	Alfred Tennyson
Ted Hughes	William Wordsworth
Christopher Marlowe	Thomas Wyatt

Jonathan Swift preaches
Gerard M. Hopkins teaches
Eavan Boland, Elizabeth Bowen, James Joyce, Richard Steele, Jonathan Swift, William B. Yeats born

Oxford University

Joseph Addison	Penelope Lively
W. H. Auden	Richard Lovelace
Lewis Carroll	V. S. Naipaul
John Donne	Walter Raleigh
T. S. Eliot	Percy B. Shelley
Graham Greene	Philip Sidney
Gerard M. Hopkins	Richard Steele
A. E. Housman	Jonathan Swift
Samuel Johnson	J. R. R. Tolkien

Miles
0 25 50 75 100
0 50 100
Kilometers

Be Cyber Safe and Smart

Cyber Safety

As you explore the *Glencoe Literature* program, you will have many opportunities to go online. When you use the Internet at school or home, you enter a kind of community—the cyber world. In this online world, you need to follow safety rules and protect yourself. Here are some tips to keep in mind:

> **Words to Know**
>
> **cyber world** the world of computers and high-tech communications
> **cyber safety** actions that protect Internet users from harm
> **cyber ethics** responsible code of conduct for using the Internet
> **cyber bully** a person who uses technology to frighten, bother, or harm someone else
> **cyber citizen** a person who uses the Internet to communicate

☑ Be a responsible cyber citizen. Use the Internet to share knowledge that makes people's lives better. Respect other people's feelings and do not break any laws.

☑ Beware of cyber bullying. People can be hurt and embarrassed by comments that have been made public. You should immediately tell your teacher or counselor if you feel threatened by another student's computer postings.

☑ Do not give out personal information, such as your address and telephone number, without your parents' or guardians' permission.

☑ Tell your teacher, parent, or guardian right away if you find or read any information that makes you feel uneasy or afraid.

☑ Do not email your picture to anyone.

☑ Do not open email or text messages from strangers.

☑ Do not tell anyone your Internet password.

☑ Do not make illegal copies of computer games and programs, and software CDs.

LOG ON ▶ **Literature** Online

For more about internet safety and responsibility, go to glencoe.com

Skills Scope and Sequence

Readability Scores Key: Dale-Chall/**DRP**/Lexile

PART 1: The Epic Warrior

Selections and Features	Literary Elements
Unit Introduction pp. 4–18	Epic **SE** pp. 12–13 Romance **SE** pp. 16–17
Literary History The Epic and the Epic Hero pp. 20–21	Epic Form **SE** p. 20 Epic Hero **SE** p. 21
Epic Poem *from* **Beowulf** pp. 22–55	Conflict **SE** p. 23 Antagonist **TE** p. 40 Archetype **TE** p. 46 Epic Hero (review) **SE** p. 54
Vocabulary Workshop pp. 56–57	
Comparing Literature The Death of Humbaba *from* **Gilgamesh** (epic poem), *from* **The Battle of the Pelennor Fields,** *from* **Lord of the Rings: Return of the King** (novel), by J.R.R. Tolkien **8.5/58/900,** and *from* **The Collected Beowulf** (graphic novel), by Gareth Hinds pp. 58–72	Epic Hero **SE** p. 58 Symbol **TE** pp. 60, 63 Simile **TE** p. 65 Alliteration **TE** p. 71
Informational Text TIME**: A Brief History of Heroes,** by Tristram Hunt **11.3/73/1230** pp. 73–76	Subheadings **TE** p. 73
Vocabulary Workshop p. 77	

Reading Skills and Strategies	Vocabulary	Writing Grammar	Speaking, Listening, Viewing

Analyze Historical Context **SE** pp. 4–18
Analyze Graphic Information
   SE pp. 7, 9
Interpret **SE** p. 13
Analyze Voice **TE** p. 14
Analyze Cause and Effect **SE** p. 15
Evaluate Argument **TE** p. 16
Compare and Contrast **SE** p. 17
		Create a Sequence Chart
		   TE p. 10
		Note Taking **SE** p. 18
			Analyze Art **SE** p. 4
			Oral Presentation **SE** p. 18
			Visual Presentation **SE** p. 18

Analyze Rhythm **TE** p. 20			

Identify Sequence **SE** p. 23
Visualize **TE** pp. 28, 34
Monitor Comprehension **TE** p. 32
Analyze Graphic Information **TE** p. 44
Question **TE** p. 52
	Analogies **SE** p. 54
	Academic Vocabulary
	   SE p. 54
		Revise Sentences **TE** p. 30
		Write a Journal Entry **TE** p. 38
		Use Figurative Language
		   TE p. 42
		Possessive Pronouns
		   TE p. 50
		Create a Storyboard **SE** p. 53
		Write a Summary **SE** p. 55
		Literary Present Tense
		   SE p. 55
			Analyze Art **TE** pp. 30, 40,
			   SE p. 44
			Oral Interpretation **TE** p. 36

	Academic Vocabulary **SE** pp. 56–57 Word Parts **TE** p. 56 Context Clues **SE** p. 57		

Compare and Contrast **SE** p. 58
Summarize **TE** p. 60
Make Inferences **TE** p. 61
Connect to Personal Experience
   TE p. 62
Preview **TE** p. 66
Analyze Sequence **TE** p. 67
Research Images **TE** p. 70
	Multiple-Meaning Words
	   TE p. 64
		Write a Character Analysis
		   SE p. 61
		Revise **TE** p. 68
			Discussion **SE** pp. 65, 71, 72
			Visual Display **SE** p. 72

Connect to Contemporary Issues
   SE p. 73
Preview **SE** p. 73
Determine Main Idea and Supporting
   Details **TE** p. 74
		Write Topic Sentences
		   TE p. 76	

	Word Origins and Word Parts **SE** p. 77		

PART 1: The Epic Warrior *(continued)*

Selections and Features	Literary Elements
Poem The Seafarer pp. 78–84	Mood **SE** p. 78 Conflict (review) **SE** p. 83

PART 2: The Power of Faith

Selections and Features	Literary Elements
Nonfiction *from* **The Ecclesiastical History of the English People,** by the Venerable Bede **8.0**/**63**/1290 pp. 86–95	Historical Narrative **SE** p. 87 Internal Conflict (review) **SE** p. 94
Grammar Workshop pp. 96–97	
Literary History The Development of English pp. 98–99	English Language **SE** pp. 98–99 Dialect **TE** p. 98
Narrative Poem *from* **The Canterbury Tales,** *from* **The Prologue,** by Geoffrey Chaucer pp. 100–124	Characterization **SE** p. 101 Enjambment **TE** p. 102 Figures of Speech **TE** p. 122
Narrative Poem *from* **The Canterbury Tales,** *from* **The Pardoner's Tale,** by Geoffrey Chaucer pp. 100–124	Irony **SE** p. 125
Narrative Poem *from* **The Canterbury Tales,** *from* **The Wife of Bath's Tale,** by Geoffrey Chaucer pp. 133–151	Humor **SE** p. 133 Characterization (review) **SE** p. 150
Informational Text TIME: The Roads Now Taken, by Jeff Chu **8.8**/**66**/1170 pp. 152–154	
Autobiography *from* **The Book of Margery Kempe,** by Margery Kempe **8.5**/**60**/1200 pp. 155–161	Autobiography **SE** p. 156 Characterization (review) **SE** p. 160
Grammar Workshop p. 162	

Readability Scores Key: Dale-Chall/DRP/Lexile

PART 3: The World of Romance

Selections and Features	Literary Elements
Romance *from* **Sir Gawain and the Green Knight** pp. 164–184	Archetype **SE** p. 164 Conflict (review) **SE** p. 183
Historical Perspective *from* **A Distant Mirror,** by Barbara Tuchman **12.8/62/**1300 pp. 185–187	
Legend *from* **Le Morte d'Arthur,** by Sir Thomas Malory **9.1/60/**1110 pp. 188–198	Legend **SE** p. 189 Archetype (review) **SE** p. 197
Vocabulary Workshop p. 199	
Literary History The Ballad Tradition pp. 200–201	Ballad **SE** p. 200 Ballad Hero **SE** p. 201
Ballad Bonny Barbara Allan and **Get Up and Bar the Door** pp. 202–207	Ballad Stanza **SE** p. 202
Writing Workshop pp. 208–215	Figurative Language **TE** p. 210
Speaking, Listening, and Viewing Workshop pp. 216–217	
Independent Reading pp. 218–219	
Assessment pp. 220–225	

Reading Skills and Strategies	Vocabulary	Writing / Grammar	Speaking, Listening, Viewing
Monitor Comprehension **SE** p. 164 Make Inferences **TE** p. 166 Compare and Contrast **TE** p. 170 Summarize **TE** p. 172 Clarify **TE** p. 176	Synonyms **SE** p. 183 Academic Vocabulary **SE** p. 183	Write a Description **TE** p. 168 Write a Summary **TE** p. 174 Write a Short Story **SE** p. 184 Action Verbs **SE** p. 184	Analyze Art **SE** p. 172 Oral Interpretation **TE** p. 178 Discussion **SE** p. 182
Analyze Historical Context **SE** p. 185	Shades of Meaning **TE** p. 186		Analyze Art **TE** p. 186
Activate Prior Knowledge **SE** p. 189 Summarize **TE** p. 198	Analogies **SE** p. 198 Academic Vocabulary **SE** p. 198	Punctuate Dialogue **TE** p. 192 Write a Review **TE** p. 196	Analyze Art **TE** p. 192 Oral Report **TE** p. 194 Speech **SE** p. 198
	Context Clues **SE** p. 199		
Analyze Genre **TE** p. 200			
Respond to Characters **SE** p. 202	Word Usage **SE** p. 207	Interrogative Pronouns **TE** p. 206 Write a Story **SE** p. 207	Analyze Art **TE** p. 203 Readers Theater **TE** p. 204
		Prewrite **SE** p. 211 Draft **SE** p. 212 Dialogue **TE** p. 212 Revise **SE** p. 214 Descriptive Details **SE** p. 214 Semicolons **SE** p. 215 Write a Biographical Narrative **SE** p. 215	
		Write a Narrative **TE** p. 216	Photo Essay **SE** pp. 216–217
		Write a Riddle **TE** p. 218 Write a Review **SE** p. 219	
		Write a Descriptive Essay **SE** p. 225	

Focus

Bellringer Options

Literature Launcher
  Pre-Reading Video
  Unit 1
Daily Language Practice
  Transparency 1
Or write on the board:
Middle Ages

Ask: What do you know about Europe in the Middle Ages? *(Students may mention the prevalence of war, the rise of Christianity and the influence of the Roman Catholic Church, or the culture of chivalry.)* Elicit student ideas about culture and politics in Europe from the first to the sixteenth century.

For school-to-home activities, see Unit 1 Resource Book, pp. 5–11.

For students who would profit from independent novel study, see Novel Companion pp. 11–54.

Duke William and His Fleet Cross the Channel to Pevensey, from *the Bayeux Tapestry,* c. 1000–1082. French School. Wool embroidery on linen. Musée de la Tapisserie, Bayeux, France. ★

View the Art The *Bayeux Tapestry* is an embroidered band of linen over 70 meters (231 feet) long. Its images tell the story of the Norman Conquest of England in 1066. What elements indicate to you that this is a military scene?

4

Unit Introduction Skills

Reading Skills
- Analyze Graphic Information (SE pp. 7, 9)
- Interpret (SE p. 13)
- Analyze Cause and Effect (SE p. 15)
- Compare and Contrast (SE p. 17)

Literary Elements
- Voice (TE p. 14)

The Anglo-Saxon Period and the Middle Ages

Study Skills/Research/ Assessment
- Short Answer Questions (TE p. 8)
- Organize Ideas (TE p. 12)

Listening/Speaking/Viewing Skills
- View the Art (SE p. 4)
- Contrast Literary Periods (SE p. 1)
- Visual Literacy (SE p. 18)
- Graphic Organizers (TE p. 10)

Writing Skills/Grammar
- Sequence (TE p. 10)
- Express an Opinion (TE p. 18)

The Anglo-Saxon Period and the Middle Ages

449–1485

Looking Ahead

British literature developed in an era characterized by foreign invasions and social turbulence. Germanic tribes left northern Europe and invaded the island of Britain. The dialects spoken by these tribes, now separated by water from the European mainland, evolved into a separate language called English. Writers used that language to create works of great power and beauty—works that formed the foundation of British literature.

Keep the following questions in mind as you read:

➜ How did foreign invasions affect British history and culture?

➜ Why was the Roman Catholic Church important to medieval culture?

➜ What cultural forces does the medieval romance reflect?

Focus

Summary

This introduction gives an overview of British literature and world events from 449 to 1485. It discusses the ideal of the epic warrior, the role of the Christian church in shaping culture, and the place of romantic tales and popular ballads in medieval England. Economics and geography are also covered.

View the Art

Answer: *The ships are crowded close together, suggesting that they are traveling as a fleet. They have brought horses, and many of the men seem to be carrying shields.* The Bayeux Tapestry is an embroidered band of linen over 70 meters (231 feet) long. Its images tell the story of the Norman Conquest of England in 1066.

For diagnostic and end-of-unit assessment, see Assessment Resources, pp. 1–8, 57–84.

5

Unit Resources

Print Materials

- Unit 1 Teaching Resources, pp. 1–216
- Interactive Read and Write (On Level, Approaching, EL), pp. 1–76
- Novel Companion, pp. 7–50
- Bellringer Option Transparencies: Selection Focus 1–9; Daily Language Practice 1–18
- Literary Element Transparencies 22, 63, 49, 21, 54, 50, 16, 11, 57

- Assessment Resources, Unit Assessment, pp. 1–8
- Assessment Resources, Selection Assessment, pp. 57–84

Technology

- TeacherWorks Plus CD
- StudentWorks Plus CD
- Literature Launchers: Pre-Reading Videos DVD, Unit 1
- Literature Online
- Interactive Vocabulary CD-ROM
- Listening Library CD-ROM
- ExamView CD-ROM
- Skill Level Up! CD-ROM

Reading Strategy | 1

Analyze Graphic Information Have students examine the timeline and relate key events in British literature to British and world history.

- Explain that this unit covers ten centuries defined by wars. It begins with Anglo-Saxons invading Britain in the fifth century and ends in civil wars of the fifteenth century.
- Have students articulate a connection between British events of 449 and British literature from 892 to 991.

Language History ☆

Evolution of English The words *English* and *England* have the same root: *Engle,* meaning "the Angles" and referring to one of the three Germanic tribes—Angles, Saxons, and Jutes—who migrated in 449 to what is now England. *English* means "the language of the Angles."

Reading Practice

Understand Timelines Explain that a timeline is a chart that shows a sequence of events. Point out and name the three timelines on this chart. Then,

- review briefly that events appear in time order, from left to right, with the earliest events on the far left
- relate the three timelines by pointing out how events from 449 to 750, and so on, appear in two columns
- check comprehension

6

Timeline 449–1485 ⬛1

Walworth's dagger, 1381

BRITISH LITERATURE

449

c. 700
Unknown poet composes *Beowulf*, oldest known epic poem in English ☆

c. 731
Venerable Bede composes *The Ecclesiastical History of the English People* in Latin

First page of Bede's *History*, c. 673–735

750

892
Monks begin writing *Anglo-Saxon Chronicle*, compilation of records of English history

c. 940
Monks compile *Exeter Book*, preserving a number of Anglo-Saxon lyrics

991
Battle of Maldon is fought; it is later celebrated in an Anglo-Saxon poem

c. 1136
Geoffrey of Monmouth writes *History of the Kings of Britain* in Latin

BRITISH EVENTS

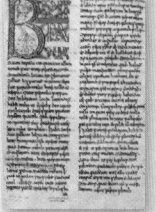

449

449
Germanic tribes invade Britain

597
St. Augustine, missionary, establishes monastery in Canterbury

664
Synod of Whitby unites British Christian Church with Roman Catholic Church

750

787
Danish invasions begin

◀ **871**
Alfred the Great's rule begins

886
Danelaw is established in northeast England

1066
William the Conqueror invades England ⬛2

1086
Domesday Book, first official record of property owners in England, is created

1170
Thomas à Becket, archbishop of Canterbury, is murdered

WORLD EVENTS

449

476
Western Roman Empire falls

537
Church of Hagia Sophia is completed in Constantinople

c. 570
Muhammad, founder of Islam, is born in Mecca

683
Empress Wu becomes first woman to rule China

750

◀ **800**
Charlemagne is crowned Holy Roman Emperor

1000
Leif Eriksson sails to North America from Greenland

1099
First Crusade captures Jerusalem

Reliquary of Charlemagne

LOG ON ▶ **Literature** Online

Literature and Reading To explore the Interactive Timeline, go to glencoe.com and enter QuickPass code GLB9817u1.

6 UNIT 1   THE ANGLO-SAXON PERIOD AND THE MIDDLE AGES

Marco Polo's caravan, from *The Catalan Atlas*, 1375

1200

c. 1300
Earliest ballads are composed

c. 1370
Sir Gawain and the Green Knight is written

1400

1420s
Margery Kempe dictates her autobiography

1469
Sir Thomas Malory writes *Le Morte d'Arthur*

c. 1386
William Langland writes allegorical poem *Piers Plowman*, a protest on behalf of the common people

c. 1387
Geoffrey Chaucer begins *The Canterbury Tales*

Pilgrim Badge c. 1300–1350

1200

1215
King John signs Magna Carta

1295
First Parliament begins

1337
Hundred Years' War, a series of wars between England and France, begins

1349
Black Death sweeps through England

1381
Peasants' Revolt is suppressed

1400

1455
Series of civil wars between the House of York and the House of Lancaster, called Wars of the Roses, begins

Magna Carta

1200

1258
Mongols capture Baghdad

1295
Marco Polo returns to Venice from China

1310–1314
Dante begins writing *Divine Comedy*

1325
Tenochtitlán, capital of Aztec Empire, is completed in Mexico

1312
Mansa Musa rules Mali Empire in Africa

1431
Joan of Arc is burned at the stake in France during Hundred Years' War

1455
Gutenberg Bible is printed from movable type in Germany

Reading Check

Analyze Graphic Information From 449 to 1066, which warriors invaded Britain?

Approaching Level

DIFFERENTIATED INSTRUCTION

Emerging Help students make meaningful "before" and "after" statements about events shown on the timelines. For example, "St. Augustine established a monastery in Canterbury long before Chaucer began the *Canterbury Tales.*" Ask students to make predictions about what they might notice in the literature they read in this unit. For example, a monastery might appear in the *Canterbury Tales*.

Teach

Reading Check

Answer: *Germanic tribes and William the Conquerer invaded Britain during those dates.*

Reading Strategy 2

Make Inferences Ask: What can you infer about British literature after 1066? *(One can infer that after William the Conquerer invaded England, he influenced British literature.)*

Political History ☆

Magna Carta The first document written to limit the power of a king was signed by King John in 1215. In January of that year, a group of barons demanded a charter to ensure liberties that seemed threatened by this capricious king. By June, the king consented to sign a document stating that his power could be limited in certain ways. This document influenced the framers of the United States Constitution.

Political History ☆

Peasants' Revolt Around 1380, King Richard II instituted a war tax and passed additional laws that laborers considered unfair. A leader arose among the laborers by the name of Wat Tyler. Tyler led a bloody revolt that forced the king to repeal the tax. Tyler gave his life for the cause. The revolt is remembered as "Wat Tyler's Rebellion."

Teach

Draw Conclusions Refer students to the text and list under the heading "Medieval Wealth."

Ask: What can you conclude about medieval lifestyles? *(They were not extravagant by our standards today.)* Point out the "Peasant's Wheel of Life."

Ask: What can you conclude about peasant life? *(There was a lot of hard work most of the year.)*

By the Numbers

MEDIEVAL WEALTH

The household goods of a wealthy thirteenth-century butcher in the English town of Colchester included the following:

- one trestle table (with boards stored in a corner except at mealtimes)
- probably some settles, or stools
- two silver spoons
- one cup
- one tablecloth and two towels
- one brass cauldron
- one brass dish
- one iron candlestick
- one washing basin and pitcher

PEASANT'S WHEEL OF LIFE

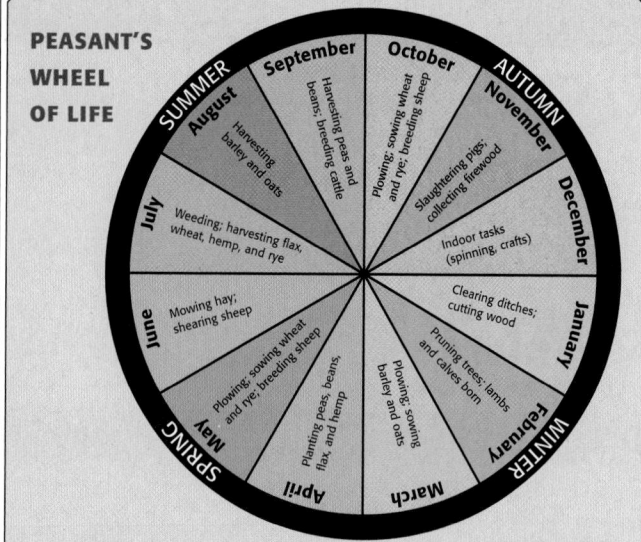

In the Middle Ages, the life of English peasants was a cycle of recurring labor. Each season brought new tasks. Harvest time in August and September was especially laborious. A good harvest of grains for making bread and brewing ale was crucial to survival in the winter months.

WERGILD

In Anglo-Saxon society, blood feuds avenged wrongdoings but claimed many lives. To avoid revenge from a slain man's kin, one could pay them *wergild,* or "man price," a sum of money that reflected the deceased's importance. In Wessex, a fixed scale was observed:

- Nobleman or member of the warrior class: 1200 shillings
- Free peasant: 200 shillings

DOMESDAY BOOK

Commissioned in 1085 by William the Conqueror, the first draft of the *Domesday Book* contained census-type records for 13,418 English estates for tax purposes. William later imposed "danegeld," a tax to pay for defense against Viking invasions.

LAND OWNERS IN ENGLAND IN THE ELEVENTH CENTURY,
according to the *Domesday Book*

- King and his family   17%
- Barons, lords, and church tenants   54%*
- Bishops and abbots   26%

* About a dozen barons controlled a quarter of the land in England.

Assessment Practice

Short-Answer Questions Discuss strategies for reading and responding to short-answer questions. Provide students with copies of these questions. Allow ten minutes.

1. What tasks occupied the daily lives of medieval peasants?

2. What threats to health marked the medieval period?

3. Who had power and wealth in the medieval period?

(Answers: 1. planting, harvesting, caring for livestock; 2. blood feuds, invasions; 3. king, barons, lords, abbots, bishops)

Being There

July: Harvest, sowing, c. 16th century. British Library, London.

June: Jousting and a game with hobby horses, c. 1520–30. From the workshop of Simon Bening. British Library, London.

The fertile soil and mild climate of Britain's southern lowlands attracted a series of invaders, who established small kingdoms that eventually merged into a single nation. Some of the displaced native peoples fled west and north to the highlands of Wales and Scotland. **2**

LOG ON ▶ **Literature** Online

Literature and Reading For more about the history and literature of this period, go to glencoe.com and enter QuickPass code GLB9817u1.

Reading Check

Analyze Graphic Information:

1. On the basis of *wergild,* how valuable was a nobleman in comparison to a free peasant?

2. In which months of the year did medieval peasants harvest crops?

3. Where were most of the towns located in medieval England?

INTRODUCTION **9**

Teach

Reading Check

Answers:

1. *Six times as valuable*
2. *In July, August, and September*
3. *In the eastern and southern parts of England*

Reading Strategy | 2

Use Maps If necessary, help students interpret the map.

Ask: Which countries are shown? *(Scotland, Ireland, Wales, England)* What convention is followed for naming bodies of water? *(Italic type is used.)*

APPROACHING If students are having difficulty, direct them to trace the borders of each country with a finger. Point out in particular the border between England and Scotland, and comment on the different shades of green used to make this border clear.

View the Art ★

Simon Bening (1483–1561) was a widely celebrated master of illumination. Illumination is the decoration of manuscripts. His clients included powerful aristocrats and royalty.

English Learners

DIFFERENTIATED INSTRUCTION

Intermediate Help students locate the bodies of water that surround Britain: to the east, the North Sea; to the west, the Irish Sea; and to the south, the English Channel.

Ask: How might these bodies of water have aided the people of medieval Britain?

If students have trouble with the question, explain that invaders had to cross the seas to attack Britain. Explain that France, to the south, and Germanic tribes from the east and north threatened British towns.

Teach

Understand Sequence of Events Have students read the text on page 10 and the top of page 11. **Ask:** What group was residing in Britain when the Romans invaded? *(the Celts)* What event ended the Anglo-Saxon era? *(the Battle of Hastings)*

Literary History ☆

Producing Books Before the advent of the printing press in the latter half of the fifteenth century, books were very difficult and expensive to produce. Their subjects had to be considered worthy of the effort. The lives of some saints were considered worthy of recording, and the first use of the English word legends referred to writings about the lives of saints.

Learning Objectives

For pages 4–18
In studying this text, you will focus on the following objectives:

Literary Study:
Analyzing literary periods.
Analyzing literary genres.

Reading:
Evaluating historical influences.
Connecting to the literature.

The Anglo-Saxon Period and the Middle Ages
449–1485

Historical and Cultural Forces

Battle Between Britons and the Invaders. From Life, Passion and Miracles of St. Edmund, King and Martyr. England, c. 1130. The Pierpont Morgan Library, New York. ☆

The Anglo-Saxons

In A.D. 43 the Romans conquered the Celtic tribes of southern Britain and introduced a standard of living more advanced than any the Celtic tribes had ever known. Early in the fifth century, however, when the Roman Empire began to fall, the Roman legions left Britain to defend Rome, and the Britons became easy prey to invaders. Angles, Saxons, and Jutes—Germanic tribes collectively referred to as Anglo-Saxons—began invading Britain's eastern shores. Gradually, their warriors drove the Britons into the mountains and took the land for their own. It was a bloody beginning for the nation that would come to be known as England.

Vikings and Normans

During the eighth and ninth centuries, Vikings from Scandinavia took to the seas in an attempt to win Britain by force. By the middle of the ninth century, much of England had fallen to the invaders. However, the tide turned in 878, when Alfred, the Saxon king of Wessex, led his warriors to victory in the Battle of Edington. During the next century, Alfred the Great's son and grandson won back all of England, and at last the country was at peace.

The peace was short-lived. When King Edward died in 1066, William, duke of Normandy, laid claim to the English throne. After the English council of elders chose Harold II as king, William

Writing Practice

Sequence Explain to students that understanding the sequence of events in writing can enhance their understanding of whatever they are reading. After students have read to the end of "War and Plague," discuss the sequence of events related in "Historical and Cultural Forces."

Ask: What political system was introduced after the Norman Conquest? *(feudalism)*

Ask students to record the sequence of events in sequence charts. Discuss with students what they included in their charts and why. Encourage them to complete sequence charts as they read the remaining Unit One introductory materials.

retaliated by attacking and defeating the Anglo-Saxons in the Battle of Hastings. He emerged as the first Norman king of England, ending the Anglo-Saxon era.

Feudal England

Following the Norman Conquest, the Anglo-Saxons became the subjects of the Norman aristocracy. The Normans introduced the continental social, economic, and political system called feudalism, under which land (the real wealth of the nation) was divided among noble overlords, or barons. Lesser lords, called knights, pledged their wealth and services to the overlords, who, in return, provided use of the land. At the lowest end of the social scale were serfs, peasants pledged to the lord of the manor and bound to the land.

> *"To no one will we sell, to no one deny or delay right or justice."*
> —Magna Carta

Feudal relationships sometimes led to heated conflicts. In the early 1200s, King John, needing money for military campaigns, imposed heavy financial burdens on his barons. In 1215 a group of the barons forced the unpopular king to agree to a "great charter," or Magna Carta. In this document, he agreed not to raise taxes without the consent of the barons. Many see in this curtailment of royal power the beginning of constitutional government in England, including the right to trial by jury.

War and Plague

The fourteenth century was a dark time in British history. Beginning in 1337, the English and French waged a series of wars for control of lands in France. Known as the Hundred Years' War, the conflict drained England financially.

In the midst of the Hundred Years' War, an epidemic called the Black Death swept through Europe. This plague first struck England in 1348 and eventually killed almost a third of England's people. This massive loss of life eroded the feudal system. Still, towns and cities continued to grow. The resulting shift in power from the landed aristocracy to an urban middle class set the stage for a new era: the Renaissance.

PREVIEW **Big Ideas** ## of the Anglo-Saxon Period and the Middle Ages

1 The Epic Warrior	**2** The Power of Faith	**3** The World of Romance
Anglo-Saxon culture expressed a brooding vision of a failing human world beset by dark forces. Against these grim conditions emerged the epic warrior, motivated by the desire for undying fame. **See pages 12–13.**	The Christian church shaped the culture of medieval England, influencing all aspects of life: politics, warfare, education, business, art, literature, folkways, and recreation. **See pages 14–15.**	In medieval England, the upper classes enjoyed romantic tales about legendary heroes such as King Arthur and his knights. The popular ballad was the imaginative literature of the common people. **See pages 16–17.**

INTRODUCTION **11**

UNIT ONE

Teach

Reading Strategy 2

Determine the Main Idea

Ask: What is the main idea of these two pages? *(The history of Britain in the Middle Ages is mainly a history of conflicts.)* What are some of the details that support this main idea? *(The Celtic tribes were conquered by Roman invaders in A.D. 43; Angles, Saxons, and Jutes invaded in 449; Vikings and Normans invaded before 1100.)*

Cultural History ☆

The Crusades In the middle of the eleventh century, the Turks took over Jerusalem, which was regarded by Christians as a holy land. Pope Urban II called for a crusade to recover the Holy Land for Christianity. In 1096, thousands of Christians marched into battle. This was the beginning of a series of bloody crusades between Christians and Muslims that would last until 1270.

English Learners

DIFFERENTIATED INSTRUCTION

Intermediate Point out the root *feud* in the words *feudal* and *feudalism*. Ask students to use a dictionary to discover roots in *aristocracy* (Greek *arist*, meaning "best"), feud (Germanic *feus*, meaning "land not subject to rent or service"), and *charta* (French *chart*, meaning "written agreement").

Advanced Point out to students that the terms *plague, Black Death,* and *epidemic* are used interchangeably in the last paragraph. Discuss the differences and similarities in the meanings of these terms. Introduce another synonym, *pestilence,* and discuss.

Teach

Reading Strategy | 1

Summarize **Ask:** How would you summarize what you have learned about Old English literature? *(Since war was a constant reality for Anglo-Saxons, the literary tradition revolved around heroic songs. Germanic and Christian influences produced work that was mythic and Christian.)*

[ENGLISH LEARNERS] Remind students that to **summarize** is to briefly restate in your own words the most important ideas from what you read. Have students write a one-sentence summary of each paragraph.

Language History ☆

Wyrd *Wyrd* is the ancestor of our modern English word *weird*. The modern meaning—"of, or relating to, or suggestive of the preternatural or supernatural"—retains some suggestion of the original meaning—"fate." Before arriving in Modern English, the word traveled through Middle English (about 1100–1500) as *werde*.

Big Idea 1
The Epic Warrior

A complex society such as that of the modern United States offers a wide range of heroic types. The Anglo-Saxons, however, recognized only a single heroic type: the warrior, who embodied the qualities valued by the tribes who settled on Britain's shores. Courage was an important virtue because through it a warrior could achieve fame and immortality. Loyalty to one's tribal lord was also important, as was wisdom in making decisions and guiding others. Physical strength was crucial to overcoming one's enemies.

A Warrior Society

For the early Anglo-Saxons, warfare was a way of life; their tribal organization, values, and beliefs—as well as their poetry—reflected that reality. Every family or tribe had a warrior chief, who in turn served a noble or royal warlord. Each warlord and his followers formed a close-knit group known as a *comitatus*. Warlords rewarded the bravest of their followers with treasure, and warriors responded by showing absolute loyalty to their leaders. The Roman historian Tacitus described the fierce loyalty of the Germanic warriors from whom the Anglo-Saxons were descended: "On the field of battle it is a disgrace to a chief to be surpassed in courage by his followers, and to the followers not to equal the courage of their chief. And to leave a battle alive after their chief has fallen means lifelong infamy and shame."

Oral Literature

The Anglo-Saxons brought their Germanic language, culture, and literary traditions to Britain. Anglo-Saxon storytellers created heroic songs describing warriors' great deeds and celebrating qualities such as strength, courage, and loyalty. Minstrels known as *scops* (shōps) performed these songs during banquets in the mead-halls of Anglo-Saxon rulers. (Mead is an alcoholic beverage

made from fermented honey.) In a mostly illiterate society, such songs served as literary entertainment. To the warriors who listened to them, the songs also provided models to emulate and a goal to pursue—namely, to win fame and be remembered after death for one's deeds.

> *"He who earns praise / Has under heaven the greatest glory."*
> —"Widsith"

Germanic and Christian Traditions

The two most important influences on Anglo-Saxon, or Old English, literature were the Germanic tradition and the Christian religion. Anglo-Saxon literary tradition was deeply rooted in the dark, heroic tales of Germanic mythology, which depict a tragic world in which even the gods ultimately perish. Since Germanic religious beliefs held no promise of an afterlife, the warrior's primary goal was to achieve fame in this life. The coming of Christianity, with its omnipotent God and promise of eternal life, did not so much replace this stark Germanic mythology as coexist with it. In works such as *Beowulf* (see page 22), the poet combines Germanic and Christian elements. **1**

Importance of *Wyrd*

Because of constant intertribal warfare and the primitive state of science and medicine, life in early Anglo-Saxon times was strife-ridden and brief. As a result, the early Anglo-Saxons believed that fate, which they called *wyrd*, controlled human destiny and that one's ultimate and inescapable fate was ☆ death. The hero's only appropriate response was to face this somber destiny with courage. Beowulf's

Study Skills Practice

Organizing Ideas
Help students complete this outline:
The Epic Warrior
I. Warrior society
  A. Tribal organization
    1. Warrior families
    2. Comitatus

  B. Values and beliefs
    1. Bravery
    2. Treasure
    3. Loyalty
II. Oral literature

last words express the Germanic view of *wyrd*: "Fate has swept our race away, / Taken warriors in their strength and led them / To the death that was waiting. And now I follow them."

Dragon ships (drakkars) of King Olaf of Norway, 1885. Rafael Monleon Y Torres. Watercolor. Museo Naval Madrid.

In 991 Viking raiders defeated an Anglo-Saxon force, killing its leader and many of his followers. In a heroic song written a few years later, a poet commemorated the Anglo-Saxons' heroic last stand.

from *The Battle of Maldon*

The strife was stern, warriors were steadfast,
Bold in battle; fighters fell
Weary with wounds. Death covered earth.
Oswold and Ealdwald all the while,
Both the brothers, marshalled their men;
Bade friend and kinsmen endure in combat
And never weaken, but wield the sword.
Byrhtwold encouraged them, brandishing buckler,
Aged companion shaking ash-spear;
Stout were the words he spoke to his men:

"Heart must be braver, courage the bolder,
Mood the stouter as our strength grows less!
Here on the ground my good lord lies
Gory with wounds. Always will he regret it
Who now from this battle thinks to turn back.
I am old in years; I will never yield,
But here at the last beside my lord,
By the leader I love I think to lie."

2

Reading Check

Interpreting Which values of the Anglo-Saxons does this passage from *The Battle of Maldon* reflect?

INTRODUCTION **13**

Teach

Reading Check

Answer: *Courage, loyalty, endurance, and the desire for fame*

Literary Element | 2

Alliteration Remind students that alliteration is the repetition of consonant sounds at the beginnings of words. **Ask:** What examples of alliteration do you find in this excerpt from The Battle of Maldon? *(Possible answers: strife, stern, steadfast; bold, battle; fighters, fell; weary, wounds; Both, brothers; marshalled, men; kinsmen, combat)*

Cultural History

Dragon Ships Be afraid! That is the message of the dragon ship to the coastal towns. She is built flat, so that she can sail in shallow water, and lightweight, so that she can achieve speeds up to 17 mph. Her mast is blood red, and she is carrying up to 60 strong-bodied oarsmen-warriors. Tall sides and shields protect her rowers.

13

Teach

Reading Strategy | 1

Connecting Ask: Do you think that a community's tallest buildings reveal its dominant values? Why?

[APPROACHING] If students are struggling, ask them to name the buildings in their city a visitor would see first. **Ask:** What kinds of activities take place in these buildings? What is the purpose of these buildings?

Invite students to explain what the message these tall buildings send about their community.

Reading Strategy | 2

Make Inferences Ask: How might the rise of Christianity have affected Britain's literary history? (*It could affect the themes, characters, settings, and plots of literature.*)

Cultural History ☆

Thomas à Becket Once friend and chancellor of King Henry II, Thomas à Becket first declined to become archbishop, explaining that in the position he would be forced into opposition to the king. Under pressure from the king, he accepted the position. Differences between the two became so violent that in 1170 knights loyal to Henry II murdered Becket in full view of the people at the evening service in Canterbury Cathedral.

Big Idea 2
The Power of Faith

1 t has been observed that a community's tallest buildings reveal its dominant values. On the basis of this standard, modern skyscrapers strikingly indicate the importance of commercial values in U.S. society. By contrast, in medieval English cities, the tallest buildings were towering stone cathedrals, which symbolized the importance of the Roman Catholic Church in the life of the people. The first English cathedral was built in Canterbury between 1070 and 1180, beginning a period of more than four hundred years of cathedral-building. These awesome and towering cathedrals were artistic masterpieces, created by the most talented architects, masons, artists, and craftspeople of the time to celebrate the glory of God.

Christianizing England

In 596 Pope Gregory I sent missionaries to convert the Anglo-Saxons to Christianity. By the year 650, most of England was Christian in name, though many people retained some pagan beliefs and traditions. Meanwhile, Celtic monks from Ireland had brought Christianity to other parts of England, establishing England's first monastery on the coastal island of Lindisfarne. With Christianity came the glimmerings of education and culture. In the eighth century, Anglo-Saxon culture reached its peak in the Northumbrian monasteries that produced elaborately decorated manuscript books, some of which, such as the *Book of Durrow* and the *Lindisfarne Gospels*, rank among the most beautiful works of art produced in the Middle Ages.

Monasteries

As Christianity spread throughout Anglo-Saxon England, some men and women chose to dedicate their lives to work and prayer. These men (known as monks) and women (known as nuns) joined religious orders, which varied greatly in their rules for communal living. Some religious orders were very strict, demanding poverty, fasting, absolute obedience, and manual labor.

English monks established libraries and schools within their monasteries, where they emphasized the importance of the written word—especially of the Bible. Working as scribes, Anglo-Saxon monks copied manuscripts by hand, thereby preserving much of the classical and Anglo-Saxon literature that survives today. The Venerable Bede and other monks also composed their own scholarly literature, which represents the first written literature in England. The earliest important work of this kind was Bede's *Ecclesiastical History of the English People* (see page 86), which offers a remarkably complete picture of early Anglo-Saxon life and times. However, like most monastic scholars of the era, Bede composed his *History* in Latin, the language of church scholarship. It was Alfred the Great, the era's most important political leader, who first encouraged the widespread use of Old English in written literature. Alfred's greatest achievement in this regard was the *Anglo-Saxon Chronicle*, an Old English history in prose and poetry.

Pilgrimages

One way to express religious devotion in the Middle Ages was to undertake a pilgrimage, or journey, to a sacred site. If English pilgrims were unable to go on a pilgrimage to Jerusalem, Rome, or the famous shrine at Santiago de Compostela in Spain, they could still visit various holy sites in their own country. One of the most important destinations for English pilgrims was Canterbury Cathedral, where in 1170 Archbishop Thomas à Becket had been slain. The pilgrims described in ☆ Chaucer's *Canterbury Tales* (see page 100) are journeying to this holy site to seek blessings from the martyred archbishop.

Reading Practice

Voice Ask: How would you describe the voice of this author? (*authoritative, positive, neutral, text bookish*) Do you think the author's tone is effective? Why? (*Yes; the purpose is to inform, not to entertain or persuade.*) Have students analyze the word choices and sentence lengths in one section. Then have students select any topic about which they feel they are authorities and mimic this author's tone in single paragraphs of their own writing. Discuss whether it is easy or difficult to maintain an authoritative voice.

Religious Drama

In a time when few people could read, the church used sermons, stained-glass windows, and popular entertainment to teach the truths and historical events of religion. English drama developed from enactments of biblical stories during church services on feast days such as Palm Sunday and Easter. Eventually, these dramatic scenes moved from the cathedral to the village green and finally to pageant wagons. The actors in such a scene were often common people, such as members of a bakers' guild, dressed up as biblical characters. In several cities in England, these plays were well attended, and as a result complete cycles developed, beginning with the creation of the world and concluding with the last judgment. These plays were known as **mystery plays** because they were performed by trade guilds (at that time *mystery* meant "trade" or "craft"). Less realistic dramas called **morality plays** were also popular. Featuring allegorical figures representing good, evil, and other abstract qualities, these plays presented moral lessons.

The following passage comes from a cycle of mystery plays performed in the city of York.

from *The Creation of Adam and Eve*

GOD: In paradise shall ye sam won;   sam won: together dwell
Of earthly thing get ye no need.
Ill and good both shall ye con;   con: know
I shall you learn your life to lead.

ADAM: Ah, Lord since we shall do no thing
But lof thee for thy great goodness,   lof: love
We shall obey to thy bidding,
3 And fulfil it both more and less.

EVE: His sign since he has on us set
Before all other thing, certain,
Him for to lof we shall not let,   let: stop
And worship him with might and main.

GOD: At heaven and earth first I began,
And six days wrought ere I would rest;
My work is ended now at man:
All likes me well, but this the best.

Stained glass window panel, Canterbury Cathedral, 12th century. Panel in the west window depicts Adam digging. Canterbury Cathedral, UK. ★

Reading Check

Analyzing Cause and Effect How did the lack of literacy in the Middle Ages indirectly lead to the emergence of drama in England?

Teach

Reading Check

Answer: *Because few people could read, the church used religious services and popular entertainment to instruct believers. Medieval drama began in the context of these services.*

Literary Element   3

Rhyme Scheme Ask: What rhyming words do you find in "from The Creation of Adam and Eve"? *(won and con, need and lead, thing and bidding, goodness and less, set and let, began and man, rest and best)* What slant rhyme do you find in the selection? *(certain and main)* What rhyme scheme do Eve's lines follow? *(abab)*

View the Art ★

The murder of Thomas à Becket made Canterbury Cathedral a popular destination for pilgrims, who brought wealth that was used to purchase the stained glass window shown on this page. This panel originally appeared in a sequence of 86 figures illustrating the genealogy of Jesus Christ. The entire sequence once began with the Creation and ended with the Virgin Mary and Christ.

Advanced Learners

DIFFERENTIATED INSTRUCTION

Word Choice Have students make lists of words in the dramatic excerpt that are not commonly used today. Ask them to look up the meanings of words they are unfamiliar with. Ask students to analyze the grammar used in the excerpt. **Ask:** How would the line "Him for to lof we shall not let" be spoken today? Have students translate the poem into Modern English. Schedule a reading and compare the different versions.

Determine the Main Idea

Ask: What is the main idea of "The World of Romance"? *(Knights and the traditions of chivalry and courtly love were central in the imaginations of medieval artists.)*

Literary History ☆

Lancelot and Guinevere

A twelfth-century Frenchman, Chrétien de Troyes, was inspired by the stories of the passion between Lancelot and Guinevere. He was one of the first to tell of their romance. Over the course of a century, scribes copied his stories and changes were introduced. Scholars believe that the element of romance in the stories is rightly attributed to Chrétien, as when Lancelot, while riding his horse, finds a comb with a few golden hairs and nearly faints with emotion upon finding that the comb belongs to Guinevere.

Big Idea 3
The World of Romance

For many people today, the knight in shining armor is emblematic of the Middle Ages. This is partly because of the enduring popularity of medieval romances. With their descriptions of brave knights, lovely maidens, mysterious castles, and splendid tournaments, romances convey a striking, albeit mostly imaginary, picture of medieval life.

The Knight

Constant warfare characterized life in the Middle Ages, with troops of heavily armed warriors, or knights, fighting one another for supremacy. These knights enjoyed great social prestige and formed the nucleus of the feudal aristocracy, which was based on the relationship between lords and vassals. In exchange for tracts of land, vassals pledged to fulfill various obligations to their lords, the foremost of which was military service.

Trained as warriors but with few other responsibilities, knights had little to do but fight. When not engaged in actual warfare, knights provided sport and entertainment for others by participating in showy tournaments, which gave them the opportunity to practice fighting and improve their skills. Even these mock battles, however, were dangerous and sometimes fatal.

Chivalry and Courtly Love

In the eleventh and twelfth centuries, under the influence of the church, an ideal of civilized behavior, called chivalry, gradually took hold among the nobility of Europe. The code of chivalry encouraged knights to be honorable, generous, brave, skillful in battle, respectful to women, and protective of widows and orphans. Although only partly successful, the code did help to civilize the conduct of knights and to elevate the status of women.

Closely allied to the code of chivalry, courtly love was an idealized picture of a relationship between a knight and a courtly lady, who was usually married to someone else. In medieval times, upper-class marriage was usually a commercial arrangement involving an exchange of property or an alliance of families. However, courtly love, as popularized in the songs and poems of the troubadours in southern France, proclaimed the transcendent value of passionate love and the all-consuming devotion of a knight toward his lady—the kind of relationship shared by Sir Lancelot and Guinevere in Arthurian legend. ☆

> *"Whither has not flying fame spread and familiarized the name of Arthur the Briton, even as far as the empire of Christendom extends?"*
>
> —Alain de Lille

The Rise of Romance

Originating in France in the 1100s, the romance became the most popular literary genre in medieval England. Many romances describe the adventures of legendary knights and celebrate chivalry and courtly love. Working in both verse and prose, English writers produced romances about the legendary King Arthur and his knights of the Round Table. The most highly regarded verse romance in English is *Sir Gawain and the Green Knight*. This seriocomic tale of a quest undertaken by King Arthur's finest knight was written in the 1300s by an unidentified poet. Around 1470, as the Middle Ages were waning, Sir Thomas Malory retold an entire cycle of Arthurian legends in *Le Morte d'Arthur* ("The Death of Arthur"), a superb work of English prose. **1**

Evaluate Logical Arguments Help students evaluate the argument contained in "The World of Romance." Remind students that inductive reasoning works from specific facts to a general statement and deductive reasoning works from a general statement to specific examples. **Ask:** What does the writer of these two pages want you to believe, and how does the writer go about persuading you?

Teach

from *Le Morte d'Arthur*
by Sir Thomas Malory

So [Arthur and Merlin] rode till they came to a lake, the which was a fair water and broad, and in the midst of the lake Arthur was ware of an arm clothed in white samite, that held a fair sword in **2** that hand. Lo! said Merlin, yonder is that sword that I spake of. With that they saw a damosel going upon the lake. What damosel is that? said Arthur. That is the Lady of the Lake, said Merlin; and within that lake is a rock, and therein is as fair a place as any on earth, and richly beseen; and this damosel will come to you anon, and then speak ye fair to her that she will give you that sword. Anon withal came the damosel unto Arthur, and saluted him, and he her again. Damosel, said Arthur, what sword is that, that yonder the arm holdeth above the water? I would it were mine, for I have no sword. Sir Arthur, king, said the damosel, that sword is mine, and if ye will give me a gift when I ask it you, ye shall have it. By my faith, said Arthur, I will give you what gift ye will ask. Well! said the damosel, go ye into yonder barge, and row yourself to the sword, and take it and the scabbard with you, and I will ask my gift when I see my time. So Sir Arthur and Merlin alit and tied their horses to two trees, and so they went into the ship, and when they came to the sword that the hand held, Sir Arthur took it up by the handles, and took it with him, and the arm and the hand went under the water.

King Arthur with a shield, from A Chronicle of England, c. 1300–1325. British Library, London.

Reading Check

Comparing and Contrasting How would you compare medieval knights with Anglo-Saxon warriors?

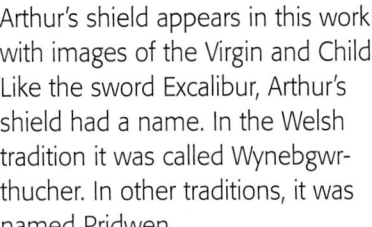

View the Art ★

Arthur's shield appears in this work with images of the Virgin and Child. Like the sword Excalibur, Arthur's shield had a name. In the Welsh tradition it was called Wynebgwr-thucher. In other traditions, it was named Pridwen.

Ask: What might the crowns beneath Arthur's feet represent? *(Possible answer: kingdoms Arthur has united under his rule)*

Literary Element | 2

Symbol Tell students that the sword in this excerpt is Excalibur, symbol of Arthur's kingship.

ENGLISH LEARNERS Ask students to think about a nation's flag. Point out that the flag is just that—a flag. Yet it also stands for another thing: for a nation. Tell students that symbols are what they are, yet at the same time, they stand for something else. Challenge students to think of common symbols.

Reading Check

Answer: *Medieval knights and Anglo-Saxon warriors had a similar primary function: to excel at warfare. In addition, both valued courage, loyalty, and heroic fame. Knights, at least in theory, adhered to the code of chivalry. That code was not part of the value system of Anglo-Saxon warriors.*

Approaching Level

DIFFERENTIATED INSTRUCTION ↻

Established Have students work in pairs to determine the meanings of unfamiliar words in the excerpt. Have students take turns reading aloud one line at a time, noting and discussing any new vocabulary. Encourage them to ask for help if needed. Then divide students into groups of four.

Have the members of each group choose the parts of the narrator, Merlin, Arthur, and Lady of the Lake. They can then read the script together.

Assess

Legacy of the Period

Refer to paragraphs 1 and 2. **Ask:** What past peoples helped to develop the English language that we read, write, and speak today? *(Germanic peoples, Norman/French peoples)*

Cultural and Literary Links

Suggest students look for ways in which Anglo-Saxon and medieval literature have influenced today's writers.

Activities

1. **Follow Up** Answers will vary.
2. **Contrast Literary Periods** Students will focus on one of the big ideas: heroism, faith, or romance
3. **Build Visual Literacy** The Catholic Encyclopedia at www.newadvent.org provides an extensive history under "Illuminated Manuscripts."
4. **Take Notes** The Foldable is an ideal way to order and store notes. To learn more about Foldables, see page R20–R21.

FOLDABLES®
Study Organizer

Have students make and label the Three-Tab Book Foldable. They can take notes about each Big Idea in one of the three sections.

Wrap-Up

Legacy of the Period

The Anglo-Saxon invasion brought the Germanic traditions that influenced British culture and society. It also introduced the Germanic language, many words of which still form the basic vocabulary of English-speakers throughout the world.

After the Norman Conquest, the French language, culture, and institutions profoundly affected society in medieval England. By establishing basic political rights, the Magna Carta became the foundation of modern law and government in Great Britain and in the United States.

The Romantic movement of the late 1800s and early 1900s found one of its primary sources of inspiration in medieval romances. One category of romance literature—the legends of King Arthur—remains popular to this day.

Cultural and Literary Links

 The Anglo-Saxon epic *Beowulf* inspired the novel *Grendel* by the modern American writer John Gardner, which tells the story from the monster's point of view.

 Geoffrey Chaucer's *Canterbury Tales* is an example of a literary form used worldwide: a collection of tales within a frame story. Other notable examples of tales in frames include the *Metamorphoses* by Ovid and *The Arabian Nights*.

 Based on earlier versions of the Arthurian legend, Sir Thomas Malory's *Le Morte d'Arthur*, in turn, inspired Alfred, Lord Tennyson's *The Idylls of the King* and T. H. White's *The Once and Future King*.

LOG ON ▶ **Literature** Online

Unit Resources For additional skills practice, go to glencoe.com and enter QuickPass code GLB9817u1.

Activities → Choose one of the following activities to explore and develop as you read this unit.

1. Follow Up Go back to Looking Ahead on page 5 and answer the questions.

2. Contrast Literary Periods Work with several other students to create a brief presentation for your class, contrasting one of this period's big ideas with a facet of modern American culture. Use examples from literature, fine art, music, movies, and other kinds of expression to support your ideas.

3. Build Visual Literacy Research one of the illuminated manuscripts produced in medieval monasteries, such as the *Book of Kells*. Then create a visual display of photocopies of some of its most remarkable pages. Include an explanation of how the manuscript was produced and descriptions of its stylistic features.

4. Take Notes Use this study organizer to keep track of the three big ideas in the unit.

FOLDABLES **THREE-TAB BOOK**
Study Organizer

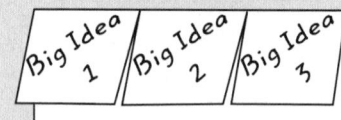

Writing Practice

Express an Opinion Ask students to imagine what their lives would be like as teens living in the Anglo-Saxon or medieval period. Have them make a two-column chart and label the left column "Anglo-Saxon Teens" and the right column "Medieval Teens."

Tell students to review the material in the Unit Opener, listing details about life in each period. Then, ask students to write two or three paragraphs explaining in which period they would prefer to live.

The Epic Warrior

Detail of the Gundestrup cauldron, c. 100 B.C. Silver. National Museum, Copenhagen, Denmark.

 View the Art The origins of the Gundestrup cauldron are unknown, but some scholars think it depicts figures from Celtic mythology. With this in mind, what can you infer about the large bearded figure in this image? Explain.

"Fate often spares the undoomed
warrior if his courage holds good."

—*Beowulf*

19

Analyze and Extend

Reading Strategy

Use Context Clues Invite a student to read the quotation aloud. **Ask:** Given the context, what do you think the word "undoomed" means? *(Possible answer: not cursed)* Is the image a good choice to accompany the quotation? Explain.

View the Art

Say: The origins of the Gundestrup cauldron are mostly unknown, but some scholars think it depicts scenes and figures from Celtic mythology. **Ask:** With this in mind, what can you infer about the large, bearded figure in this image? Explain. *(Many students will infer that the bearded figure is a king, a god, or a hero; he is much larger than all the other people and animals in the scene, and seems to have power over them—he holds each smaller man by the arm.)*

English Learners

DIFFERENTIATED INSTRUCTION

Intermediate Discuss the words *fate* and *doom*. *Fate* has a broader meaning, whereas *doom* suggests that things will turn out badly. **Ask:** Can you think of synonyms for fate? *(luck, destiny, predestination)*

Approaching Level

DIFFERENTIATED INSTRUCTION

Emerging Read the quotation aloud to students. **Ask:** What kind of behavior is required of warriors? *(standing firm against the opposition)* Have students rewrite the quotation in their own words.

For additional support for English Learners, see Unit 1 Teaching Resources Book, p. 21.

Focus

Bellringer Options

Daily Language Practice Transparency 2

Or have students discuss the following question: Can you think of examples of epics in the making? (*Students may mention the Shoah Foundation, established by filmmaker Steven Spielberg, or other local oral history projects.*)

 For an activity related to this selection, see Unit 1 Teaching Resources Book, p. 19.

 For an audio recording of this selection, use Listening Library Audio CD-ROM.

View the Art ★

Although Tyr is an obscure figure, his name is prevalent in Danish geography, indicating he was once an important diety. Initially, Tyr represented the principles of law and justice, but he went on to become a warrior god. **Ask:** What does the size of the chained animal indicate? (*Possible answers: Tyr is powerful and capable of defeating ferocious enemies.*)

Learning Objectives

For pages 20–21

In studying this text, you will focus on the following objectives:

Literary Study:
Analyzing the epic hero.
Analyzing literary genres.
Evaluating historical influences.
Connecting to the literature.

The Epic and the Epic Hero

PEOPLE ARE LIVING IN FEAR AS AN EVIL FORCE threatens to destroy the land. Then a hero appears. Brave, strong, and good, the hero defeats the evil force and saves the land and its people. You know this story well. It is one of the most widely told stories in literature, as well as one of the oldest. In times past, the deeds of the hero were told in the form of an **epic**—a long narrative poem that recounts, in formal language, the exploits of a larger-than-life hero. Ancient epic poets and their audiences viewed their epics as records of their peoples' early histories.

The earliest epics date back to a time when most people were illiterate. Recited by poets, probably with musical accompaniment, these epics were the movies of their day. Audiences were enthralled by monsters, perilous journeys, and fierce battles. Some of the early epics were eventually written down. Of most, we have only fragments, but a few complete epics have survived. Historians and anthropologists look at epics as cultural records of the societies that produced them.

> "I will proclaim to the world the deeds of Gilgamesh."
> —Gilgamesh

The epic is found in cultures around the world, thus indicating the timeless and universal human need to transmit legends from one generation to another. The earliest surviving epic is *Gilgamesh* (pages 60–61), composed by the Sumerians in one of the ancient languages of Mesopotamia (what is now Iraq). It tells of the great deeds of Gilgamesh, a legendary king who had ruled hundreds of years earlier. Centuries later, the ancient Greeks had their epics: the *Iliad* and the *Odyssey*. The Spanish had *The Song of El Cid*; the French, *The Song of Roland*; and the Anglo-Saxons, *Beowulf*. Works about modern heroes such as Superman and Luke Skywalker continue the epic tradition today.

Tyr, sky-god of the Germanic tribes, with chained animal, 6th century. Bronze. Torslunda parish, Öland, Sweden. Statens Historiska Museet, Stockholm. ★

Epic Form

More than a thousand years after *Gilgamesh*, the ancient Greek poet Homer established the standard features of the epic form in Western literature with the *Iliad* and the *Odyssey*. These features include

- poetic lines that have a regular meter and formal, elevated, or even lofty language
- main characters who have heroic or superhuman qualities
- gods or godlike beings who intervene in the events

Reading Practice

SPIRAL REVIEW **Rhythm** Tell students that a pattern of stressed and unstressed syllables establishes rhythm in poetry. Have students mark the stressed syllables with ´ and the unstressed syllables with ˘ in the following excerpt from *Gilgamesh*:

He was the slave who did the work for gods
But whom the gods would never notice.

- action on a huge scale, often involving the fates of entire peoples
- stories that begin *in medias res* (Latin for "in the middle of things") or at a critical point in the action

The classical Greek epics also established the use of certain literary devices. One of these is the **epithet,** a word or brief phrase often used to characterize a particular person, place, or thing. For example, the goddess Athena is "gray-eyed" and the sea is "wine-dark." Standardized comparisons known as **kennings** perform a similar function in the Anglo-Saxon epic *Beowulf.* For example, a king is a "ring-giver" and the sea is the "whale-road." Both epithets and kennings helped epic poets mold their ideas to their poetic forms.

The Epic Hero

The epic hero is a man—women take subordinate roles in traditional epics—of high social status whose fate affects the destiny of his people. Epic plots typically involve supernatural events, long periods of time, distant journeys, and life-and-death struggles between good and evil. Through physical strength, skill as a warrior, nobility of character, and quick wits, the epic hero almost always defeats his enemies, be they human or demonic. The hero is rarely modest, and boasting is almost a ritual in epics.

The epic hero embodies the ideals and values of his people. Odysseus, for example, displays the Greek ideal of *aretē,* or all-around excellence. He is a great warrior, a cunning leader, a clever speaker, and highly skilled at everything from sailing to plowing. Rooted in ancient Germanic tradition, the values celebrated in *Beowulf* include courage and loyalty. The end of the poem praises Beowulf for "a life / As noble as his name," a compliment that could

Grendel, 1908. From *Brave Beowulf.* British Library, London.

extend to heroes throughout history, from Gilgamesh to today's comic book and movie heroes. **1**

LOG ON ▶ **Literature** Online

Literature and Reading For more about the epic and epic heroes, go to glencoe.com and enter QuickPass code GLB9817u1.

Respond and Think Critically

1. In your opinion, what are today's epics? How do modern audiences differ from ancient ones in their responses to epics?

2. Identify three characteristics that we might expect today's epic heroes to exhibit.

3. Which characteristics of the traditional epic hero might be difficult for readers today to accept?

4. What characteristics do the epics in world literature have in common?

Teach

Big Idea   1

The Epic Warrior Say: The Anglo-Saxons descended from Germanic tribes who had a dark vision of life. Because death was deemed the fate of all humans, warriors sought fame that would preserve the memory of their deeds after death. **Ask:** How is this evident in the selection? *(Beowulf wants to slay the powerful monster, thus gaining fame and a sense of immortality.)*

Assess

1. Answers will vary. Unlike ancient audiences, modern audiences do not think of these epics as presenting real events.

2. Students may identify strength, courage, and leadership.

3. Most students will probably feel that high social status and boastfulness would be less acceptable today.

4. The epic hero is usually a person of high position, like a king, who faces monumental struggles or challenges. His actions determine the fate of his people; he embodies what is best in his culture.

Focus

from *Beowulf*

Bellringer Options

Literature Launchers:
Pre-Reading Videos DVD,
Selection Launcher

Selection Focus
Transparency 1

Daily Language Practice
Transparency 3

Or tell students that they are about to read parts of an epic poem written centuries ago. It tells about a larger-than-life fictional hero. **Ask:** If you were to imagine a hero in today's world, what heroic qualities would he or she have? What feats would your hero perform?

Meet the *Beowulf* Poet

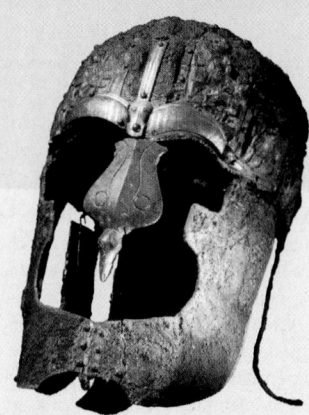

It is a curious fact that the writers of some of the world's greatest literature are unknown to us. *Beowulf* ranks high among such literature. It is the oldest of the surviving national epics produced in Western Europe after the fall of Rome. It is one of Europe's first literary works to be composed in the vernacular, or the language of the people, rather than in Latin, the language of church scholarship. Like other national epics—Spain's *The Song of El Cid* and France's *Song of Roland*, for example—*Beowulf* relates the deeds of a great national hero. That hero arose in the Anglo-Saxons' ancestral home on the European mainland, where legends about him were part of the oral tradition of the Germanic tribes.

> *"The newly Christian understanding of the world which operates in the poet's designing mind displaces him from his imaginative at-homeness in the world of his poem—a pagan Germanic society governed by a heroic code of honor."*
>
> —Seamus Heaney

Anglo-Saxon Poet Beginning in the 400s, those Germanic tribes, later known collectively as the Anglo-Saxons, invaded and settled the territory that later would become known as England. They brought their songs and legends about heroes with them, passed down from one scop (shōp), or oral poet, to another and reshaped with each performance. In the early eighth century, scholars believe, an Anglo-Saxon poet thoroughly versed in the scops' stock of legends, historical accounts, and poetic devices composed *Beowulf*. By that time, the Anglo-Saxons had converted to Christianity, and the Vikings had not yet begun their invasions in England. The *Beowulf* poet was clearly a Christian, for his poem contains references to the Bible, and was apparently well educated, displaying a familiarity with the *Aeneid*, the great Latin epic by the ancient Roman poet Virgil.

It is uncertain whether the *Beowulf* poet composed the poem orally and later transcribed it, or wrote it down in the form in which we now have it. But at some time the poem was written down, and Christian scribes made a copy of it in the late tenth century. It is their manuscript that has survived over the years, despite various misadventures. Today, the *Beowulf* manuscript is carefully preserved in the British Library in London.

In his groundbreaking essay "*Beowulf*: The Monsters and the Critics," J. R. R. Tolkien stated that the *Beowulf* poet presented a vision of the past, "pagan but noble and fraught with a deep significance—a past that itself had depth and reached back into a dark antiquity of sorrow." By vividly imagining that pagan past, the *Beowulf* poet created an inspiring tale of courage—and the first great heroic poem in the English language.

 Literature Online

Author Search For more about the *Beowulf* poet, go to glencoe.com and enter QuickPass code GLB9817u1.

Selection Skills

Literary Elements
- Conflict (SE pp. 23, 25, 28, 31, 33, 36, 39, 40, 42, 54)
- Antagonist (TE p. 40)

Reading Skills
- Identify Sequence (SE pp. 25, 28, 31, 32, 34, 37, 38, 40, 43, 45, 54)
- Active Reading (TE p. 28)

Beowulf

Vocabulary Skills
- Academic Vocab (SE p. 54)

Listening/Speaking/Viewing Skills
- Read with Expression (TE p. 36)

Writing Skills/Grammar
- Summary (SE p. 55)
- Sentence Structure (TE p. 30)
- Possessive Pronouns (TE p. 50)

Literature and Reading Preview

Connect to the Epic
Who are some heroes or role models in society today? Discuss these heroes with a partner, trying to determine what qualities they share.

Build Background
The story of Beowulf is set in the sixth century A.D., but it is not set in England. The story takes place in Scandinavia, and it involves the Geats (gēts), a tribe in southern Sweden, and the Danes, a tribe in Denmark.

Set Purposes for Reading

Big Idea The Epic Warrior

In the primitive world of the early Anglo-Saxons, the hero held a place of great importance. As you read, ask yourself, What heroic qualities does Beowulf display?

Literary Element Conflict

Conflict is a struggle between opposing forces in a story or drama. An **external conflict** exists when a character struggles against some outside force, such as another person or nature. An **internal conflict** is a struggle within the mind of a character. As you read *Beowulf,* ask yourself, In what conflicts is the hero involved?

Reading Strategy Identify Sequence

Identifying sequence is finding the logical order of ideas or events in a text. In *Beowulf,* the poet retells three principal episodes in the hero's life. As you read, ask yourself, In what order do the events in these episodes occur?

....

Tip: Taking Notes Use a graphic organizer like the one started below to record the order of events in each episode.

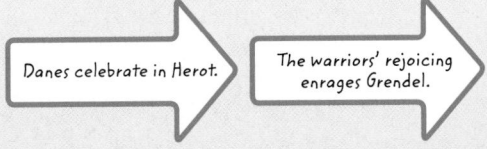

Danes celebrate in Herot. → The warriors' rejoicing enrages Grendel.

Learning Objectives

For pages 22–55
In studying this text, you will focus on the following objectives:

Literary Study: Analyzing literary genres.

Reading:
Identifying sequence.
Analyzing historical context.

Vocabulary

lament (lə ment′) *n.* an expression of sorrow; song or literary composition that mourns a loss or death; p. 25 *The mother's lament for her child brought tears to my eyes.*

forged (fôrjd) *adj.* formed or shaped, often with blows or pressure after heating; p. 25 *The warrior went into battle with a forged shield made by his father.*

shroud (shroud) *n.* a burial cloth; p. 30 *The bodies of the slain were wrapped in shrouds.*

infamous (in′ fə məs) *adj.* having a bad reputation; notorious; p. 31 *The pirate was infamous for his brutal treatment of prisoners.*

writhing (rī′ thing) *adj.* twisting, as in pain; p. 32 *Whining and writhing, the wounded dog rolled its head from side to side.*

BEOWULF 23

Focus

Summary
Denmark's King Hrothgar builds a huge banquet hall for his people. Their noisy celebrations infuriate a monster named Grendel, who terrorizes and attacks them, killing many. A young hero named Beowulf from nearby Geatland saves the Danes by killing Grendel and later Grendel's mother. Beowulf eventually becomes king of Geatland and dies an old man, defending his people from a dragon.

 For summaries in languages other than English, see Unit 1 Teaching Resources Book, pp. 22–27.

 Interactive Read and Write
Other options for teaching this selection can be found in
- Interactive Read and Write for English Learners, pp. 1–18
- Interactive Read and Write for Approaching-Level Learners, pp. 1–18
- Interactive Read and Write for On-Level Learners, pp. 1–18

Vocabulary

Diction Diction encompasses an author's choices of words, sentence length, and sentence complexity. The translator of *Beowulf* has chosen words that create a formal, old-fashioned feeling appropriate for an ancient epic. **Ask:** What word would you use instead of lament in common speech? *(cry, wail)*

English Learners

DIFFERENTIATED INSTRUCTION

Intermediate The word *infamous* can present difficulties to English learners and native speakers alike. **Say:** Look at the word *infamous*. What parts make up the word? Help students observe that the word consists of the prefix *in-* and *famous*. If necessary, explain that *in-* means "not." **Say:** Read the definition. Does *infamous* mean "not famous"? *(no)* Ask students to name well-known historical or fictional characters or celebrities who could be clas-

sified as "famous" or "infamous." *(Answers will vary. To make certain students understand the concept, ask them to explain their reasons for labeling a given person or character as infamous.)*

Teach

Big Idea | 1

The Epic Warrior **Say:**
Though this poem was created more than 1,000 years ago, Beowulf is still one of the best known heroes in English literature. Why might people still want to read about a warrior created over ten centuries ago? *(Beowulf shows timeless courage and strength in fighting deadly foes. These heroic qualities are among the most compelling human traits.)*

Literary History ☆

Scops Oral poets, or scops, relied on poetic devices to aid their memory and give their performances structure and power. One of the devices used in *Beowulf* is alliteration—the repetition of consonant sounds at the beginnings of words. Examples: *down in the darkness* (lines 1–2); *happy in his hall* (line 15); *sprawled in sleep, suspecting nothing* (lines 33–34).

 For an audio recording of this selection, use Listening Library Audio CD-ROM.

from

BEOWULF 1

Translated by Burton Raffel

GRENDEL ATTACKS THE DANES

A powerful monster, living down
In the darkness, growled in pain, impatient
As day after day the music rang
Loud in that hall,° the harp's rejoicing
5   Call and the poet's clear songs, sung
Of the ancient beginnings of us all, recalling
The Almighty making the earth, shaping
These beautiful plains marked off by oceans,
Then proudly setting the sun and moon
10   To glow across the land and light it;
The corners of the earth were made lovely with trees
And leaves, made quick with life, with each
Of the nations who now move on its face. And then
As now warriors sang of their pleasure:
15   So Hrothgar's men lived happy in his hall
Till the monster stirred, that demon, that fiend,
Grendel, who haunted the moors, the wild
Marshes, and made his home in a hell
Not hell but earth. He was spawned° in that slime,
20   Conceived by a pair of those monsters born
Of Cain,° murderous creatures banished
By God, punished forever for the crime
Of Abel's death. The Almighty drove
Those demons out, and their exile was bitter,
25   Shut away from men; they split
Into a thousand forms of evil—spirits
And fiends, goblins, monsters, giants,
A brood forever opposing the Lord's
Will, and again and again defeated.

30   Then, when darkness had dropped, Grendel
Went up to Herot, wondering what the warriors
Would do in that hall when their drinking was done.
He found them sprawled in sleep, suspecting
Nothing, their dreams undisturbed. The monster's ☆

4 hall: The Danish King Hrothgar's mead hall, Herot.

19 spawned: born. Usually, *spawned* refers to the production of young by fish, amphibians, or other water-dwelling creatures.
21 Cain: According to the Bible (Genesis 4:8), *Cain,* the eldest son of Adam and Eve, murdered his brother, Abel.

Reading Practice

SPIRAL REVIEW **Capital Letters in Poetry** Tell students that in poetry a capital letter does not always signal the beginning of a new sentence. Have a volunteer read the first section aloud. Discuss how the lines should be read, calling on multiple students to practice reading the section aloud. Remind students to pay close attention to the periods, commas, and semicolons for cues as to how to break up the lines.

35 Thoughts were as quick as his greed or his claws:
    He slipped through the door and there in the silence
    Snatched up thirty men, smashed them
    Unknowing in their beds and ran out with their bodies,
    The blood dripping behind him, back
40 To his lair,° delighted with his night's slaughter.
        At daybreak, with the sun's first light, they saw
    How well he had worked, and in that gray morning
    Broke their long feast with tears and **laments**
    For the dead. Hrothgar, their lord, sat joyless
45 In Herot, a mighty prince mourning
    The fate of his lost friends and companions,
    Knowing by its tracks that some demon had torn
    His followers apart. He wept, fearing
    The beginning might not be the end. And that night
50 Grendel came again, so set
    On murder that no crime could ever be enough,
    No savage assault quench his lust
    For evil. Then each warrior tried
    To escape him, searched for rest in different
55 Beds, as far from Herot as they could find,
    Seeing how Grendel hunted when they slept.
    Distance was safety; the only survivors
    Were those who fled him. Hate had triumphed.
        So Grendel ruled, fought with the righteous,
60 One against many, and won; so Herot
    Stood empty, and stayed deserted for years,
    Twelve winters of grief for Hrothgar, king
    Of the Danes, sorrow heaped at his door
    By hell-**forged** hands. His misery leaped
65 The seas, was told and sung in all
    Men's ears: how Grendel's hatred began,
    How the monster relished his savage war
    On the Danes, keeping the bloody feud
    Alive, seeking no peace, offering
70 No truce, accepting no settlement, no price

40 **lair:** den of a wild animal.

Viking pendants from Sweden

Conflict *What does the conflict between the Danes and Grendel symbolize?* **2**

Identify Sequence *By the time Hrothgar's grief is told and sung, what events have occurred in the poem? List them in order.* **3**

Vocabulary

lament (lə ment′) *n.* an expression of sorrow; song or literary composition that mourns a loss or death

forged (fôrjd) *adj.* formed or shaped, often with blows or pressure after heating

---

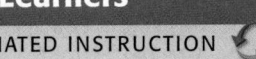

English Learners

DIFFERENTIATED INSTRUCTION

Intermediate Compound words are made up of two or more words that are sometimes joined by hyphens. Write and display these words: *hell-forged, oak-hard, round-curled, rock-steep, sea-road.* Have students supply a definition for each word and discuss the mental pictures it creates.

Approaching Level

DIFFERENTIATED INSTRUCTION

Emerging Have students use context clues to figure out the meaning of *moors* in line 17 and *plundering* in line 73. (moors: *"the wild marshes"*, *"that slime"*; plundering: *"bloody feud"*, *"crime"*) Invite students to identify other clues to each word's meaning.

Literary Element **2**

Conflict **Answer:** *The conflict between the Danes and Grendel symbolizes the struggle between good and evil*

Reading Strategy **3**

Identify Sequence
Answer: *Hrothgar has built Herot, a banquet hall where his warriors gather and listen to scops singing of the wonders of God's creation. The monster Grendel cannot bear to hear the heroes' rejoicing. He attacks Herot, slaughtering thirty warriors. He raids the hall nightly, leaving Herot deserted and Hrothgar in misery.* **Ask:** What do you think will happen next? *(Answers will vary but should be supported with evidence from the text.)*

View the Art ★
Much of what we know about life in ancient and medieval Scandinavia is based on archaeological evidence, like these amulets, which may depict the face of Odin, the chief of the Norse gods. A number of such amulets would have been strung together on a single necklace. **Ask:** Based on what is carved into these amulets, what can you infer was valued during this time period? *(The carvings show a sword and a fierce warrior, so bravery and fierceness on the battle field were likely important values.)*

Teach

Big Idea   1

The Epic Warrior Answer:
*Beowulf is committed to coura-
geous action. Upon learning of
Hrothgar's plight, Beowulf immediately sets out to rescue him.*

(ADVANCED) What effect does
Beowulf have on other people?
How does this influence your view
of him? *(They love him, and he
inspires them to do brave deeds.
This makes him seem even more
heroic.)*

Writer's Technique ☆

Kennings The author uses *kennings* throughout this poem. A
kenning is an imaginative meta-
phorical phrase used in place of a
simple noun. For example, "mankind's enemy" (line 79) and "that
shadow of death" (line 74) are
kennings that refer to Grendel.

In gold or land, and paying the living
For one crime only with another. No one
Waited for reparation° from his plundering claws:
That shadow of death hunted in the darkness,
75   Stalked Hrothgar's warriors, old
And young, lying in waiting, hidden
In mist, invisibly following them from the edge
Of the marsh, always there, unseen.
     So mankind's enemy continued his crimes, ☆
80   Killing as often as he could, coming
Alone, bloodthirsty and horrible. Though he lived
In Herot, when the night hid him, he never
Dared to touch king Hrothgar's glorious
Throne, protected by God.

THE COMING OF BEOWULF

85   So the living sorrow of Healfdane's son°
Simmered, bitter and fresh, and no wisdom
Or strength could break it: that agony hung
On king and people alike, harsh
And unending, violent and cruel, and evil.
90   In his far-off home Beowulf, Higlac's
Follower° and the strongest of the Geats—greater
And stronger than anyone anywhere in this world—
Heard how Grendel filled nights with horror
And quickly commanded a boat fitted out,
95   Proclaiming that he'd go to that famous king,
Would sail across the sea to Hrothgar,
Now when help was needed. None
Of the wise ones regretted his going, much
As he was loved by the Geats: the omens were good,
100   And they urged the adventure on. So Beowulf
Chose the mightiest men he could find,
The bravest and best of the Geats, fourteen
In all, and led them down to their boat;
He knew the sea, would point the prow°
105   Straight to that distant Danish shore.
     Then they sailed, set their ship
Out on the waves, under the cliffs.
Ready for what came they wound through the currents,
The seas beating at the sand, and were borne
110   In the lap of their shining ship, lined
With gleaming armor, going safely
In that oak-hard boat to where their hearts took them.

---

1 | The Epic Warrior *What are your first impressions of Beowulf?*

---

73 reparation: payment or action
done to make amends for a wrong
or an injury.

85 Healfdane's son: Hrothgar.

90–91 Higlac's Follower: Higlac,
king of the Geats, is Beowulf's uncle.
Higlac's follower, then, refers to
Beowulf.

104 prow: the bow, or forwardmost
part of a ship.

Reading Practice

PARTNERS **Poetic Structure** Have students locate the beginning of the
section "The Coming of Beowulf." Explain
that each section of the poem relates an
episode in the story of Beowulf. Students
can aid their comprehension of the text
by identifying the main events in a section
and summarizing the significance to the
plot. Have students work with partners
to identify important plot events in the
first section, "Grendel Attacks the Danes,"
and the second section, "The Coming of
Beowulf." Hold a brief class discussion of
students' findings.

The wind hurried them over the waves,
The ship foamed through the sea like a bird
115 Until, in the time they had known it would take,
Standing in the round-curled prow they could see
Sparkling hills, high and green,
Jutting up over the shore, and rejoicing
In those rock-steep cliffs they quietly ended
120 Their voyage. Jumping to the ground, the Geats
Pushed their boat to the sand and tied it
In place, mail shirts° and armor rattling
As they swiftly moored their ship. And then
They gave thanks to God for their easy crossing.
125   High on a wall a Danish watcher
Patrolling along the cliffs saw
The travelers crossing to the shore, their shields
Raised and shining; he came riding down,
Hrothgar's lieutenant, spurring his horse,
130 Needing to know why they'd landed, these men
In armor. Shaking his heavy spear
In their faces he spoke:
                    "Whose soldiers are you,
You who've been carried in your deep-keeled ship°
135 Across the sea-road to this country of mine?
Listen! I've stood on these cliffs longer
Than you know, keeping our coast free
Of pirates, raiders sneaking ashore
From their ships, seeking our lives and our gold.
140 None have ever come more openly—
And yet you've offered no password, no sign
From my prince, no permission from my people for your landing
Here. Nor have I ever seen,
Out of all the men on earth, one greater
145 Than has come with you; no commoner carries
Such weapons, unless his appearance, and his beauty,
Are both lies. You! Tell me your name,
And your father's; no spies go further onto Danish
Soil than you've come already. Strangers,
150 From wherever it was you sailed, tell it,
And tell it quickly, the quicker the better,
I say, for us all. Speak, say
Exactly who you are, and from where, and why."

    Their leader answered him, Beowulf unlocking
155 Words from deep in his breast:

122 **mail shirts:** a type of flexible body armor usually made of linked metal loops.

134 **deep-keeled ship:** a ship that possesses a deep bottom—the *keel* being the main piece of timber that runs the length of the bottom of the ship to support the ship's frame.

Beowulf, travelling to the Court of King Hrothgar to kill the monster Grendel, is challenged by the Danish coastguard. Beowulf is welcomed when he explains. Eveyln Paul. Illustration. Edwin Wallace Collection.

The Epic Warrior *How do the watchman's words help characterize Beowulf?* **2**

BEOWULF **27**

Teach

Big Idea   2

The Epic Warrior Answer:
To the watchman, Beowulf has the look of an overconfident intruder. The watchman says that Beowulf seems arrogant and may be a threat. **Ask:** The watchman's observations help readers to learn more about Beowulf and his men. How? *(The watchman's words offer readers descriptive details about Beowulf and his men.)*

Literary History ☆

Who Wrote This Poem? Some experts believe that *Beowulf* was written by more than one author. The only existing manuscript of this epic contains the handwriting of two different people. In addition, the poem contains both pagan and Christian elements. Other scholars believe that only one author wrote the poem. They attribute the presence of both pagan and Christian elements to the period in which the work was written. At that time, England was undergoing a cultural shift from paganism to Christianity.

English Learners
DIFFERENTIATED INSTRUCTION

Advanced Lines 154 and 155 describe Beowulf "unlocking/Words from deep in his breast." Invite students to discuss the meaning of this phrase. *(The phrase is a metaphor that compares Beowulf's heart to a locked treasure box that is opened to share Beowulf's thoughts and feelings.)*

Approaching Level
DIFFERENTIATED INSTRUCTION

Established Have volunteers practice **reading fluency** by reading aloud lines 133–153. Invite students to paraphrase the watchman's statement to Beowulf's men orally or in writing.

27

Teach

Literary Element 1

Conflict Answer: *Hrothgar can either accept Beowulf's help or continue to suffer Grendel's attacks.*

Ask: Do you think the Danes should accept Beowulf's help in fighting Grendel? Why or why not? *(Yes, the Danes have been unable to stop Grendel's reign of terror by themselves. Beowulf and his men are strong, brave, and well armed, and they may provide crucial help.)*

Reading Strategy 2

Identify Sequence Answer: *The watchman promises to escort them to Hrothgar and have his men guard their ship.*

[APPROACHING] Have students guess the meaning of *sentinel* from context *(guard)*. Invite them to imitate the upright posture of a marching guard.

Cultural History ☆

Gold Early Anglo-Saxons led simple, nomadic lives. Their only luxury was gold. This precious metal was hoarded, melted down, and taken along wherever they went. Gold was a precious commodity then, as it is today.

      "We are Geats,
Men who follow Higlac. My father
Was a famous soldier, known far and wide
As a leader of men. His name was Edgetho.
160   His life lasted many winters;
Wise men all over the earth surely
Remember him still. And we have come seeking
Your prince, Healfdane's son, protector
Of this people, only in friendship: instruct us,
165   Watchman, help us with your words! Our errand
Is a great one, our business with the glorious king
Of the Danes no secret; there's nothing dark
Or hidden in our coming. You know (if we've heard
The truth, and been told honestly) that your country
170   Is cursed with some strange, vicious creature
That hunts only at night and that no one
Has seen. It's said, watchman, that he has slaughtered
Your people, brought terror to the darkness. Perhaps
Hrothgar can hunt, here in my heart,
175   For some way to drive this devil out—
If anything will ever end the evils
Afflicting your wise and famous lord.
Here he can cool his burning sorrow.
Or else he may see his suffering go on
180   Forever, for as long as Herot towers
High on your hills."
                    The mounted officer
Answered him bluntly, the brave watchman:
      "A soldier should know the difference between words
185   And deeds, and keep that knowledge clear
In his brain. I believe your words, I trust in
Your friendship. Go forward, weapons and armor
And all, on into Denmark. I'll guide you
Myself—and my men will guard your ship,
190   Keep it safe here on our shores,
Your fresh-tarred boat, watch it well,
Until that curving prow carries
Across the sea to Geatland a chosen
Warrior who bravely does battle with the creature
195   Haunting our people, who survives that horror
Unhurt, and goes home bearing our love."
      Then they moved on. Their boat lay moored,
Tied tight to its anchor. Glittering at the top
Of their golden helmets wild boar heads gleamed,

Conflict *According to Beowulf, what are Hrothgar's options?* **1**

Identify Sequence *What happens before Beowulf and his followers leave their ship?* **2**

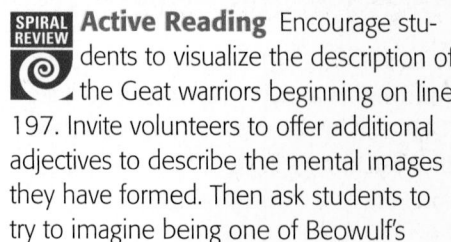

First folio of the oldest surviving Beowulf manuscript. Cotton Vitellius A.xv. By permission of the British Library, London.

Reading Practice

[SPIRAL REVIEW] **Active Reading** Encourage students to visualize the description of the Geat warriors beginning on line 197. Invite volunteers to offer additional adjectives to describe the mental images they have formed. Then ask students to try to imagine being one of Beowulf's men. **Ask:** How might you feel as you move toward battle with the deadly monster Grendel? Suggest that students try to visualize and imagine what it would be like to be a character in each part of the poem as they continue reading the selection.

200 Shining decorations, swinging as they marched,
     Erect like guards, like sentinels, as though ready
     To fight. They marched, Beowulf and his men
     And their guide, until they could see the gables
     Of Herot, covered with hammered gold ☆
205 And glowing in the sun—that most famous of all dwellings,
     Towering majestic, its glittering roofs
     Visible far across the land.
     Their guide reined in his horse, pointing
     To that hall, built by Hrothgar for the best
210 And bravest of his men; the path was plain,
     They could see their way.

          Beowulf arose, with his men
     Around him, ordering a few to remain
     With their weapons, leading the others quickly
215 Along under Herot's steep roof into Hrothgar's
     Presence. Standing on that prince's own hearth,
     Helmeted, the silvery metal of his mail shirt
     Gleaming with a smith's high art, he greeted
     The Danes' great lord:
220   "Hail, Hrothgar!
     Higlac is my cousin° and my king; the days
     Of my youth have been filled with glory. Now Grendel's
     Name has echoed in our land: sailors
     Have brought us stories of Herot, the best
225 Of all mead-halls, deserted and useless when the moon
     Hangs in skies the sun had lit,
     Light and life fleeing together.
     My people have said, the wisest, most knowing
     And best of them, that my duty was to go to the Danes'
230 Great king. They have seen my strength for themselves,
     Have watched me rise from the darkness of war,
     Dripping with my enemies' blood. I drove
     Five great giants into chains, chased
     All of that race from the earth. I swam
235 In the blackness of night, hunting monsters
     Out of the ocean, and killing them one
     By one; death was my errand and the fate
     They had earned. Now Grendel and I are called ☆
     Together, and I've come. Grant me, then,
240 Lord and protector of this noble place,
     A single request! I have come so far,
     Oh shelterer of warriors and your people's loved friend,
     That this one favor you should not refuse me—

221 **cousin:** in this case, used broadly to mean any relative.

Ship full of Viking warriors. 10th century artifact.

The Epic Warrior *What are Beowulf's credentials as a warrior?* **3**

BEOWULF **29**

Teach

Big Idea 3

The Epic Warrior Answer:
Beowulf has defeated warriors in battle, as well as giants and monsters.

Literary History ☆

Boasting and Fame The heroes of epic poetry sometimes boast of their achievements. By boasting, the hero shows that he has already won fame and intends to do so again. Fame was especially important to Anglo-Saxons. Many pagan religions offered no hope of redemption in an afterlife. Fame was the best prospect they had for a kind of immortality.

View the Art ★

This image of a Viking ship was found on the Swedish island of Gotland, in the Baltic Sea. Capable of being sailed both on the open ocean and in shallow rivers, long ships enabled the Vikings to further their trading and raiding in northern Europe.

English Learners

DIFFERENTIATED INSTRUCTION

Advanced In lines 237–238 Beowulf declares, "death was my errand and the fate/They had earned." Invite students to offer ideas about the meaning of this statement. *(Beowulf intended to kill his opponents and felt their evil actions had earned them their punishment.)*

Approaching Level

DIFFERENTIATED INSTRUCTION

PARTNERS

Emerging Distribute index cards to students and have them work in pairs to list the main events in "The Coming of Beowulf." Partners should use this list to write a summary of the plot of the poem thus far.

29

Teach

Literary Element | **1**

Conflict Discuss how the original fight of good versus evil has grown more complex. **Ask:** What might Grendel's reaction be when Beowulf and his warriors join in the Danes' fight? *(Students may say that Grendel's reaction will include increased anger and more violence.)*

Reading Strategy | **2**

Identifying Sequence
Say: In this section, Beowulf makes a prediction based on prior events. What past events are described? What does Beowulf predict will happen in the future? *(Grendel has invaded the hall and killed and eaten warriors; Beowulf believes he will try this again.)*

View the Art ★

When away from the safety of their home, Vikings relied on the dragon symbol for protection and good fortune. They crafted dragon pendants and brooches and carved dragon heads into the prows of their ships. **Ask:** Why do you think the Vikings and other cultures in the Middle Ages believed in beasts such as dragons? *(Myths and legends were used to explain life's various phenomena.)*

That I, alone and with the help of my men,
245 May purge all evil from this hall. I have heard, **1**
Too, that the monster's scorn of men
Is so great that he needs no weapons and fears none.
Nor will I. My lord Higlac
Might think less of me if I let my sword
250 Go where my feet were afraid to, if I hid
Behind some broad linden° shield: my hands
Alone shall fight for me, struggle for life
Against the monster. God must decide
Who will be given to death's cold grip.
255 Grendel's plan, I think, will be **2**
What it has been before, to invade this hall
And gorge his belly with our bodies. If he can,
If he can. And I think, if my time will have come,
There'll be nothing to mourn over, no corpse to
        prepare
260 For its grave: Grendel will carry our bloody
Flesh to the moors, crunch on our bones
And smear torn scraps of our skin on the walls
Of his den. No, I expect no Danes
Will fret about sewing our **shroud,** if he wins.
265 And if death does take me, send the hammered
Mail of my armor to Higlac, return
The inheritance I had from Hrethel, and he
From Wayland.° Fate will unwind as it must!"

THE BATTLE WITH GRENDEL

    Out from the marsh, from the foot of misty
270 Hills and bogs, bearing God's hatred,
Grendel came, hoping to kill
Anyone he could trap on this trip to high Herot.
He moved quickly through the cloudy night,
Up from his swampland, sliding silently
275 Toward that gold-shining hall. He had visited Hrothgar's
Home before, knew the way—
But never, before nor after that night,
Found Herot defended so firmly, his reception
So harsh. He journeyed, forever joyless,
280 Straight to the door, then snapped it open,
Tore its iron fasteners with a touch
And rushed angrily over the threshold.
He strode quickly across the inlaid
Floor, snarling and fierce: his eyes

> **Vocabulary**
>
> **shroud** (shroud) *n.* a burial cloth

251 **linden:** made from the wood of a linden tree.

Statue. Bergen, Norway.

267–268 **inheritance . . . Wayland:** The inheritance is the armor that Wayland, a blacksmith of Germanic legend, forged for Hrethel, Beowulf's grandfather and former king of the Geats.

Writing Practice

 Sentence Structure

SPIRAL REVIEW Point out that this poem uses many long sentences, with clauses separated by commas. Explain that the poet uses long, rolling sentences for dramatic effect. Invite students to rewrite the first sentence of "The Battle with Grendel," breaking it into two or three shorter sentences. Have volunteers read aloud their shorter sentences and offer each other feedback on their work. Are the new sentences grammatically correct? Do they provide the same information as the long sentence in the poem?

285 Gleamed in the darkness, burned with a gruesome
     Light. Then he stopped, seeing the hall
     Crowded with sleeping warriors, stuffed
     With rows of young soldiers resting together.
     And his heart laughed, he relished the sight,
290 Intended to tear the life from those bodies
     By morning; the monster's mind was hot
     With the thought of food and the feasting his belly
     Would soon know. But fate, that night, intended
     Grendel to gnaw the broken bones
295 Of his last human supper. Human
     Eyes were watching his evil steps,
     Waiting to see his swift hard claws.
     Grendel snatched at the first Geat
     He came to, ripped him apart, cut
300 His body to bits with powerful jaws.
     Drank the blood from his veins and bolted
     Him down, hands and feet; death
     And Grendel's great teeth came together,
     Snapping life shut. Then he stepped to another
305 Still body, clutched at Beowulf with his claws,
     Grasped at a strong-hearted wakeful sleeper
     —And was instantly seized himself, claws
     Bent back as Beowulf leaned up on one arm.
        That shepherd of evil, guardian of crime,
310 Knew at once that nowhere on earth
     Had he met a man whose hands were harder;
     His mind was flooded with fear—but nothing
     Could take his talons° and himself from that tight
     Hard grip. Grendel's one thought was to run
315 From Beowulf, flee back to his marsh and hide there:
     This was a different Herot than the hall he had emptied.
     But Higlac's follower remembered his final
     Boast and, standing erect, stopped
     The monster's flight, fastened those claws
320 In his fists till they cracked, clutched Grendel
     Closer. The **infamous** killer fought

8th century bronze mounting in the form of a dragon without wings, possibly from a bridle. Bronze, gilded. Sweden. ★

313 **talons:** the sharp, hooked claws on birds of prey and some other animals.

Identify Sequence	*What future event in the story do these lines foreshadow?*	**3**
Conflict	*How does Beowulf differ from other warriors whom Grendel has attacked?*	**4**
The Epic Warrior	*What motivates Beowulf in his time of need?*	**5**

Vocabulary

infamous (in′ fə məs) *adj.* having a bad reputation; notorious

BEOWULF **31**

 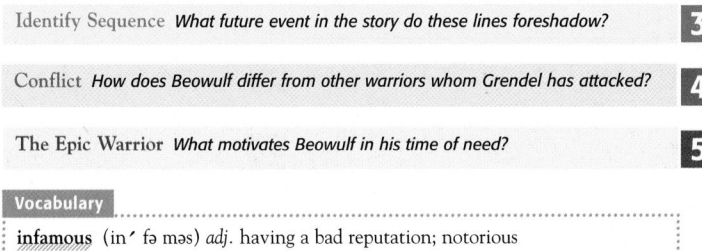

Teach

Reading Strategy   1

Identify Sequence **Answer:**
Grendel ripped apart a sleeping warrior and devoured him and then grabbed Beowulf, who was awake and ready for the attack. Beowulf seized Grendel's claw with his powerful grip and refused to let go. The intense combat that ensued battered Hrothgar's hall.

Big Idea   2

The Epic Warrior **Answer:**
Beowulf's followers show courage and loyalty to their chief. **Ask:** How do they show these traits? *(They know how deadly Grendel is, but they attack him anyway because he is engaged in battle with their leader.)*

Writer's Technique ☆

Figurative Language Have students reread lines 344–353. **Say:** The poet refers to Grendel four times in these lines without using his name. What four terms refer to Grendel? *(the Almighty's enemy; hell's captive; monster; fiend)* **Ask:** Why does the poet use these terms rather than just calling Grendel by name? *(The descriptions add variation and remind the reader of Grendel's malice.)*

For his freedom, wanting no flesh but retreat,
Desiring nothing but escape; his claws
Had been caught, he was trapped. That trip to Herot
325 Was a miserable journey for the **writhing** monster!
     The high hall rang, its roof boards swayed,
And Danes shook with terror. Down
The aisles the battle swept, angry
And wild. Herot trembled, wonderfully
330 Built to withstand the blows, the struggling
Great bodies beating at its beautiful walls;
Shaped and fastened with iron, inside
And out, artfully worked, the building
Stood firm. Its benches rattled, fell
335 To the floor, gold-covered boards grating
As Grendel and Beowulf battled across them.
Hrothgar's wise men had fashioned Herot
To stand forever; only fire,
They had planned, could shatter what such skill had put
340 Together, swallow in hot flames such splendor
Of ivory and iron and wood. Suddenly
The sounds changed, the Danes started
In new terror, cowering in their beds as the terrible
Screams of the Almighty's enemy sang
345 In the darkness, the horrible shrieks of pain
And defeat, the tears torn out of Grendel's
Taut throat, hell's captive caught in the arms
Of him who of all the men on earth
Was the strongest.

350   That mighty protector of men
Meant to hold the monster till its life
Leaped out, knowing the fiend was no use
To anyone in Denmark. All of Beowulf's ☆
Band had jumped from their beds, ancestral
355 Swords raised and ready, determined
To protect their prince if they could. Their courage
Was great but all wasted: they could hack at Grendel
From every side, trying to open

Identify Sequence *What events have occurred since Grendel entered Herot on this night?*   **1**

The Epic Warrior *What heroic traits do Beowulf's followers show?*   **2**

Vocabulary

writhing (rī′ thing) *adj.* twisting, as in pain

A helmet made of iron, bronze, and silver from the Sutton Hoo ship burial. Seventh century.

Reading Practice

SPIRAL REVIEW **Support Comprehension** Hold a brief question-and-answer session to ensure student comprehension. Have a volunteer read aloud lines 350–367. **Ask:** What happens in these lines? *(Beowulf's men attack Grendel, but their weapons are useless because Grendel has put a spell on "all men's weapons.")* Why is Beowulf successful in battling Grendel? *(Beowulf uses his bare hands, and he is extraordinarily powerful.)* Have another volunteer read the remaining lines aloud, summarizing the events.

A path for his evil soul, but their points
360 Could not hurt him, the sharpest and hardest iron
Could not scratch at his skin, for that sin-stained demon
Had bewitched all men's weapons, laid spells
That blunted every mortal man's blade.
And yet his time had come, his days
365 Were over, his death near; down
To hell he would go, swept groaning and helpless
To the waiting hands of still worse fiends.
Now he discovered—once the afflictor
Of men, tormentor of their days—what it meant
370 To feud with Almighty God: Grendel
Saw that his strength was deserting him, his claws
Bound fast, Higlac's brave follower tearing at
His hands. The monster's hatred rose higher,
But his power had gone. He twisted in pain,
375 And the bleeding sinews° deep in his shoulder
Snapped, muscle and bone split
And broke. The battle was over, Beowulf
Had been granted new glory: Grendel escaped,
But wounded as he was could flee to his den,
380 His miserable hole at the bottom of the marsh,
Only to die, to wait for the end
Of all his days. And after that bloody
Combat the Danes laughed with delight.
He who had come to them from across the sea,
385 Bold and strong-minded, had driven affliction
Off, purged Herot clean. He was happy,
Now, with that night's fierce work; the Danes
Had been served as he'd boasted he'd serve them; Beowulf,
A prince of the Geats, had killed Grendel,
390 Ended the grief, the sorrow, the suffering
Forced on Hrothgar's helpless people
By a bloodthirsty fiend. No Dane doubted
The victory, for the proof, hanging high
From the rafters where Beowulf had hung it, was the monster's
395 Arm, claw and shoulder and all.

And then, in the morning, crowds surrounded
Herot, warriors coming to that hall
From faraway lands, princes and leaders
Of men hurrying to behold the monster's
400 Great staggering tracks. They gaped with no sense
Of sorrow, felt no regret for his suffering,

375 **sinews:** bands of tissue, or tendons, that connect muscle and bone.

Norse chessmen, from a Viking hoard, Isle of Lewis, Scotland.

Conflict *Why does Beowulf hang Grendel's arm in the rafters?* **3**

Teach

Literary Element | 3

Conflict **Answer:** *Beowulf is proud. He wants to show his conquest over Grendel—the victory of good over evil—and the freedom he has brought to the Danes.*

(ENGLISH LEARNERS) Have students reread lines 374–382. **Ask:** How did Grendel lose his arm? *(Beowulf tore it off)* What happened to Grendel after that? *(He fled to the bottom of the lake and died.)*

View the Art ★

These rooks from a trove of chess pieces depict berserks—Norse warriors who worked themselves into such a frenzy before battle that they scorned the use of armor and became heedless of any wounds that they might receive. The name berserk means "bear shirt," since these warriors wore bearskins to endow themselves with the might and fierceness of the beasts.

Teach

Reading Strategy | 1

Identify Sequence **Answer:**
Warriors throng to Herot, tracing Grendel's footprints to the bloody lake where he died. Later they retell the story of the battle, extolling Beowulf's valor.

Big Idea | 2

The Epic Warrior **Answer:**
Beowulf's journey might symbolize the descent into hell. Like the epic heroes Odysseus and Aeneas, Beowulf, too, descends to the underworld.

APPROACHING **Ask:** How is Beowulf's journey to face Grendel's mother similar to a journey into the underworld? *(Beowulf has to go down to a great depth.)* To what might you compare Grendel's mother and the other monsters? *(devils, demons, or other underworld-dwellers from myths or religion)*

View the Art ★

Sutton Hoo, near Woodbridge, Suffolk, is the site of one of the most important archaeological discoveries ever made in Britain and arguably in the world. Since archaeological work at the site began in 1938, the ship burial and surrounding mounds have yielded a wealth of glittering treasures and artifacts that have given researchers new insights into Anglo-Saxon life.

Went tracing his bloody footprints, his beaten
And lonely flight, to the edge of the lake
Where he'd dragged his corpselike way, doomed
405 And already weary of his vanishing life.
The water was bloody, steaming and boiling
In horrible pounding waves, heat
Sucked from his magic veins; but the swirling
Surf had covered his death, hidden
410 Deep in murky darkness his miserable
End, as hell opened to receive him.
    Then old and young rejoiced, turned back
From that happy pilgrimage, mounted their hard-hooved
Horses, high-spirited stallions, and rode them
415 Slowly toward Herot again, retelling
Beowulf's bravery as they jogged along.
And over and over they swore that nowhere
On earth or under the spreading sky
Or between the seas, neither south nor north,
420 Was there a warrior worthier to rule over men.

THE BATTLE WITH GRENDEL'S MOTHER

The night after Grendel's defeat, his mother, a monster who lives at the bottom of a cold, dark lake, goes to Herot to avenge her son's death. She kills Hrothgar's closest friend, retrieves Grendel's arm from the rafters where Beowulf had hung it, and returns to her lake. When Beowulf hears of this, he pursues her.

He leaped into the lake, would not wait for anyone's
Answer; the heaving water covered him
Over. For hours he sank through the waves;
At last he saw the mud of the bottom.
425 And all at once the greedy she-wolf
Who'd ruled those waters for half a hundred
Years discovered him, saw that a creature
From above had come to explore the bottom
Of her wet world. She welcomed him in her claws,
430 Clutched at him savagely but could not harm him,
Tried to work her fingers through the tight
Ring-woven mail on his breast, but tore
And scratched in vain. Then she carried him, armor
And sword and all, to her home; he struggled
435 To free his weapon, and failed. The fight
Brought other monsters swimming to see

Hinged clasp from the Sutton Hoo ship burial. Seventh century. ★

Identify Sequence *Summarize what happens the morning after Beowulf's triumph.*   **1**

The Epic Warrior *What might Beowulf's journey to the she-wolf's lair symbolize?*   **2**

Reading Practice

SPIRAL REVIEW **Visualize** Read aloud or have a student read aloud lines 421–439 as listeners close their eyes and visualize what is happening. Afterward, ask students what they "saw" as they listened.

Work with students to make a web for Beowulf's fight with Grendel's mother. Ask for nouns, modifiers, and verbs that describe the battle.

Her catch, a host of sea beasts who beat at
His mail shirt, stabbing with tusks and teeth
As they followed along. Then he realized, suddenly,
440 That she'd brought him into someone's battle-hall,
And there the water's heat could not hurt him,
Nor anything in the lake attack him through
The building's high-arching roof. A brilliant
Light burned all around him, the lake
445 Itself like a fiery flame.
                                Then he saw
The mighty water witch, and swung his sword,
His ring-marked blade, straight at her head;
The iron sang its fierce song,
450 Sang Beowulf's strength. But her guest
Discovered that no sword could slice her evil
Skin, that Hrunting° could not hurt her, was useless
Now when he needed it. They wrestled, she ripped
And tore and clawed at him, bit holes in his helmet,
455 And that too failed him; for the first time in years
Of being worn to war it would earn no glory;
It was the last time anyone would wear it. But Beowulf
Longed only for fame, leaped back
Into battle. He tossed his sword aside,
460 Angry; the steel-edged blade lay where
He'd dropped it. If weapons were useless he'd use
His hands, the strength in his fingers. So fame
Comes to the men who mean to win it
And care about nothing else! He raised
465 His arms and seized her by the shoulder; anger
Doubled his strength, he threw her to the floor.
She fell, Grendel's fierce mother, and the Geats'
Proud prince was ready to leap on her. But she rose
At once and repaid him with her clutching claws,
470 Wildly tearing at him. He was weary, that best
And strongest of soldiers; his feet stumbled
And in an instant she had him down, held helpless.
Squatting with her weight on his stomach, she drew
A dagger, brown with dried blood, and prepared
475 To avenge her only son. But he was stretched
On his back, and her stabbing blade was blunted
By the woven mail shirt he wore on his chest.
The hammered links held; the point
Could not touch him. He'd have traveled to the bottom of
         the earth,
480 Edgetho's son, and died there, if that shining

The Epic Warrior *What qualities of Beowulf does this passage reveal?* **3**

452 **Hrunting:** a sword that a
Danish warrior had lent to Beowulf.

Silver Viking figurine. ★

Teach

Big Idea | 3

The Epic Warrior Answer:
This passage reveals how Beowulf's strong desire for fame motivates him in battle, inspiring his courage and tenacity. He fights on, although he may be doomed. One of Beowulf's most striking qualities is his persistence in the face of adversity.

ENGLISH LEARNERS Have students find the word *fame* in the passage (lines 458 and 462). **Ask:** *Fame normally refers to the fact of being well-known. What additional meaning does fame have in this passage? (being famous for doing something great)*

View the Art ★

This figurine from about A.D. 900 was found with other silver pendants in a hoard on the Isle of Öland, Sweden. It probably represents a Valkyrie, one of the daughters of Odin who visited battlefields to choose the warriors who would be slain. By wearing a pendant like this, a warrior hoped to ensure that he would fight bravely and be worthy of a seat in Valhalla, the feasting hall of the gods, if he died.

Approaching Level

DIFFERENTIATED INSTRUCTION

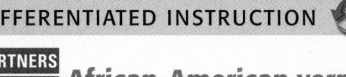

African-American vernacular English Have approaching-level students who are users of African-American vernacular English (AAVE) work to formulate 5W and How questions about Beowulf's actions while he is at the lake bottom. They may write one question of each type. Remind them to use correct syntax for questions. Have students exchange questions with a partner and write answers to their partners' questions. *(Examples: What did Beowulf use instead of his sword? He used his hands. Why did Grendel drop his sword? It could not wound the monster.)*

35

Teach

Big Idea   1

The Epic Warrior   Answer:
Beowulf surpasses ordinary war-riors in strength. His strength is comparable to that of the giants who forged the sword.

ENGLISH LEARNERS   **Ask:** What Spanish word does *ordinary* (line 488) look like? *(ordinario)* What does it mean that "no ordi-nary man" could lift this blade? *(Beowulf is stronger than other men.)*

Literary Element   2

Conflict   Answer: *Beowulf kills Grendel's mother with her own sword. Although she was attempt-ing to avenge the death of Gren-del, she herself is slain by Beowulf.*

View the Art ★

Viking women carried the keys to their houses, chests, and cabinets as a symbol of their power. Saga sources tell us that Viking brides were typically given these keys dur-ing the wedding ceremony.

Woven metal had not helped—and Holy
God, who sent him victory, gave judgment
For truth and right, Ruler of the Heavens,
Once Beowulf was back on his feet and fighting.

485   Then he saw, hanging on the wall, a heavy
Sword, hammered by giants, strong
And blessed with their magic, the best of all weapons
But so massive that no ordinary man could lift
Its carved and decorated length. He drew it
490   From its scabbard,° broke the chain on its hilt,°
And then, savage, now, angry
And desperate, lifted it high over his head
And struck with all the strength he had left,
Caught her in the neck and cut it through,
495   Broke bones and all. Her body fell
To the floor, lifeless, the sword was wet
With her blood, and Beowulf rejoiced at the sight.
    The brilliant light shone, suddenly,
As though burning in that hall, and as bright as Heaven's
500   Own candle, lit in the sky. He looked
At her home, then following along the wall
Went walking, his hands tight on the sword,
His heart still angry. He was hunting another
Dead monster, and took his weapon with him
505   For final revenge against Grendel's vicious
Attacks, his nighttime raids, over
And over, coming to Herot when Hrothgar's
Men slept, killing them in their beds,
Eating some on the spot, fifteen
510   Or more, and running to his loathsome moor
With another such sickening meal waiting
In his pouch. But Beowulf repaid him for those visits,
Found him lying dead in his corner,
Armless, exactly as that fierce fighter
515   Had sent him out from Herot, then struck off
His head with a single swift blow. The body
Jerked for the last time, then lay still.
    The wise old warriors who surrounded Hrothgar,
Like him staring into the monster's lake,
520   Saw the waves surging and blood
Spurting through. They spoke about Beowulf,

490 scabbard: a case that protects a sword's blade. **hilt:** the sword's handle, which protrudes from the scabbard.

Viking keys. ★

The Epic Warrior *What does this description imply about Beowulf's strength?*   **1**

Conflict *Irony is a discrepancy between expectation and reality. What is ironic about the way Beowulf kills Grendel's mother?*   **2**

36   UNIT 1   THE ANGLO-SAXON PERIOD AND THE MIDDLE AGES

Speaking and Listening Practice

SPIRAL REVIEW   **Read with Expression** Discuss what happens in lines 500–517. *(Beowulf exacts final revenge on Grendel by cutting off his head.)* Have students practice **reading fluency** by reading the lines aloud, varying inflection and tone of voice to convey emotion.

Use a similar procedure with lines 518–533. Before volunteers read, help students describe the emotional contrast between this passage and the previous one. *(The tone of the first passage is vengeful and aggressive; the tone of the second is mournful, passive, and reflective.)*

All the graybeards, whispered together
And said that hope was gone, that the hero
Had lost fame and his life at once, and would never
525 Return to the living, come back as triumphant
As he had left; almost all agreed that Grendel's
Mighty mother, the she-wolf, had killed him.
The sun slid over past noon, went further
Down. The Danes gave up, left
530 The lake and went home, Hrothgar with them.
The Geats stayed, sat sadly, watching,
Imagining they saw their lord but not believing
They would ever see him again.
                                    —Then the sword
535 Melted, blood-soaked, dripping down
Like water, disappearing like ice when the world's
Eternal Lord loosens invisible
Fetters and unwinds icicles and frost
As only He can, He who rules
540 Time and seasons, He who is truly
God. The monsters' hall was full of
Rich treasures, but all that Beowulf took
Was Grendel's head and the hilt of the giants'
Jeweled sword; the rest of that ring-marked
545 Blade had dissolved in Grendel's steaming
Blood, boiling even after his death.
And then the battle's only survivor
Swam up and away from those silent corpses;
The water was calm and clean, the whole
550 Huge lake peaceful once the demons who'd lived in it
Were dead.
              Then that noble protector of all seamen°
Swam to land, rejoicing in the heavy
Burdens he was bringing with him. He
555 And all his glorious band of Geats
Thanked God that their leader had come back unharmed;
They left the lake together. The Geats
Carried Beowulf's helmet, and his mail shirt.
Behind them the water slowly thickened
560 As the monsters' blood came seeping up.
They walked quickly, happily, across
Roads all of them remembered, left
The lake and the cliffs alongside it, brave men
Staggering under the weight of Grendel's skull,

Carved dragon-head post from the ship burial at Oseberg, c. A.D. 850. Viking Ship Museum, Bygdøy, Norway. ★

552 that noble protector of all seamen: Beowulf. This phrase recalls an account Beowulf tells earlier in the epic and sums up in lines 234–238, in which he boasts of having slain sea monsters and thus prevented them from attacking other seamen.

Identify Sequence *Why does the poet include this detail about the passage of time?* **3**

The Epic Warrior *What traits do Beowulf's followers show here?* **4**

English Learners

DIFFERENTIATED INSTRUCTION

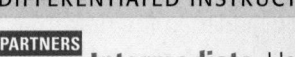 **Intermediate** Have partners take turns reading aloud lines 534–541, practicing until they are able to read smoothly at a normal speaking pace. Suggest that they start by reading from comma to comma, and then add the parts together to read the long sentence.

Approaching Level

DIFFERENTIATED INSTRUCTION

Emerging Take advantage of the selection's graphic nature by inviting students to transform the poet's words into visual art. Have small groups produce murals showing scenes from the epic. Encourage students to incorporate as many details of dress, demeanor, and action as possible.

Teach

Reading Strategy **3**

Identify Sequence Answer:
This detail emphasizes the long duration of Beowulf's absence, making his return seem highly unlikely to his followers.

Big Idea **4**

The Epic Warrior Answer:
Beowulf's followers show devotion and loyalty to their leader, who presumably has been slain.
(APPROACHING) **Ask:** What phrase does the poet use to describe the Geats after Beowulf emerges from the lake? *(his glorious band of Geats)* How does the poet feel about the Geats? *(He admires them.)*

View the Art ★

The Oseberg ship is a Viking ship that was found in a large burial mound at the Oseberg farm near Tønsberg in Vestfold County, Norway. It was excavated by the Swedish archaeologist Gabriel Gustafson and the Norwegian archaeologist Haakon Shetelig in 1904–1905. **Ask:** Why do you think the Vikings chose a dragon to decorate the ship's post? *(To invoke fear in those who saw the ship)*

Teach

Big Idea   1

The Epic Warrior Say:
Beowulf becomes king of Geatland and rules successfully for 50 years. Now he is old, and has a grave new challenge. Knowing what you know about Beowulf, how will he deal with the dragon that terrorizes his people? *(He will probably fight and defeat the dragon.)*

Reading Strategy   2

Identify Sequence Answer:
The theft of a gem-studded cup by someone who accidentally stumbles on the entrance to the stone tower precedes the dragon's attack on the Geats.

[ENGLISH LEARNERS] Point out the phrase *The beast / Had slept in a huge stone tower.* Help students identify *had slept* as the past perfect form of the verb, indicating action that took place before the time when the man stumbled on the entrance.

Literary History ☆

Triumphal Procession Many epic poems feature a triumphal procession after the hero's victory. In Greek and Roman epics, this procession featured the hero's chariot, wagonloads of treasure, and many captives. *Beowulf,* an epic from a more violent time, uses a gruesome head impaled on a spear and a band of weary warriors carrying the hero's helmet and mail shirt.

---

565   Too heavy for fewer than four of them to handle—
      Two on each side of the spear jammed through it—
      Yet proud of their ugly load and determined
      That the Danes, seated in Herot, should see it.
      Soon, fourteen Geats arrived
570   At the hall, bold and warlike, and with Beowulf,
      Their lord and leader, they walked on the mead-hall
      Green. Then the Geats' brave prince entered
      Herot, covered with glory for the daring
      Battles he had fought; he sought Hrothgar
575   To salute him and show Grendel's head.
      He carried that terrible trophy by the hair,
      Brought it straight to where the Danes sat,
      Drinking, the queen among them. It was a weird
      And wonderful sight, and the warriors stared. ☆

THE BATTLE WITH THE DRAGON

Beowulf presents Hrothgar with the jeweled hilt of the magic sword. In recognition of Beowulf's heroic services to Denmark, Hrothgar proclaims the Danes and the Geats to be allies. The following morning, Beowulf sets sail for Geatland. After he arrives in his homeland, he meets with his uncle, Higlac, the king, to recount the slayings of the monsters and to convey Hrothgar's pledge of friendship.

580   Afterwards, in the time when Higlac was dead
      And Herdred, his son, who'd ruled the Geats
      After his father, had followed him into darkness—
      Killed in battle with the Swedes, who smashed
      His shield, cut through the soldiers surrounding
585   Their king—then, when Higd's one son°
      Was gone, Beowulf ruled in Geatland,
      Took the throne he'd refused, once,°
      And held it long and well. He was old
      With years and wisdom, fifty winters
590   A king, when a dragon awoke from its darkness
      And dreams and brought terror to his people. The beast
      Had slept in a huge stone tower, with a hidden
      Path beneath; a man stumbled on
      The entrance, went in, discovered the ancient
595   Treasure, the pagan jewels and gold
      The dragon had been guarding, and dazzled and greedy
      Stole a gem-studded cup, and fled.
      But now the dragon hid nothing, neither
      The theft nor itself; it swept through the darkness,
600   And all Geatland knew its anger.

585 Higd's one son: Herdred, the son of Queen Higd and King Higlac.

587 Beowulf . . . took the throne he'd refused, once: The widowed queen, fearful that her son would be unable to defend Geatland against invaders, had offered Beowulf the throne; but he chose to support Herdred, the rightful heir.

Identify Sequence **What events precede the dragon's attack on the Geats?**   2

38   UNIT 1   THE ANGLO-SAXON PERIOD AND THE MIDDLE AGES

Writing Practice

 Diary Entry

SPIRAL REVIEW Review the events that led to the dragon's attack on Beowulf's people. Have students write a diary entry as the man who stole the gem-studded cup describing the man's feelings about what he has done. Does he feel justified in having hidden in the dragon's tower and then stolen the cup? What is his reaction to the catastrophe his country faces because of his theft? What will the man's life be like now that his theft has caused the dragon to terrorize the Geats?

But the thief had not come to steal; he stole,
And roused the dragon, not from desire
But need. He was someone's slave, had been beaten
By his masters, had run from all men's sight,
605 But with no place to hide; then he found the hidden
Path, and used it. And once inside,
Seeing the sleeping beast, staring as it
Yawned and stretched, not wanting to wake it,
Terror-struck, he turned and ran for his life,
610 Taking the jeweled cup.
                              That tower
Was heaped high with hidden treasure, stored there
Years before by the last survivor
Of a noble race, ancient riches
615 Left in the darkness as the end of a dynasty
Came. Death had taken them, one
By one, and the warrior who watched over all
That remained mourned their fate, expecting,
Soon, the same for himself, knowing
620 The gold and jewels he had guarded so long
Could not bring him pleasure much longer. He brought
The precious cups, the armor and the ancient
Swords, to a stone tower built
Near the sea, below a cliff, a sealed
625 Fortress with no windows, no doors, waves
In front of it, rocks behind. Then he spoke:
    "Take these treasures, earth, now that no one
Living can enjoy them. They were yours, in the beginning;
Allow them to return. War and terror
630 Have swept away my people, shut
Their eyes to delight and to living, closed
The door to all gladness. No one is left
To lift these swords, polish these jeweled
Cups: no one leads, no one follows. These hammered
635 Helmets, worked with gold, will tarnish
And crack; the hands that should clean and polish them
Are still forever. And these mail shirts, worn
In battle, once, while swords crashed
And blades bit into shields and men,
640 Will rust away like the warriors who owned them.
None of these treasures will travel to distant
Lands, following their lords. The harp's
Bright song, the hawk crossing through the hall

Pendant of a Viking. Statens Historiska Museum, Stockholm, Sweden.

Conflict *What does this passage suggest about Beowulf's upcoming conflict with the dragon?* **3**

Teach

Literary Element **3**

Conflict **Answer:** *This passage has an elegiac mood, stating that not only the accoutrements of war but the warriors who owned them eventually pass away. By creating this mood, the poet suggests that Beowulf's conflict with the dragon might result in his death and his people's demise.*

Approaching Level

DIFFERENTIATED INSTRUCTION

Emerging Students may need help following the transition to an earlier time that takes place in line 610. Ask them to find the words that clue the reader in to the change *(Years before)*. This passage also introduces a different perspective on the theme of war. Have students list words or phrases that demonstrate this view *(for example: War and terror / Have swept away my people; No one is left / to lift these swords)*. Have students create a T chart and help them list adjectives that describe the attitude toward battle in this passage and in the earlier parts of the poem *(earlier: heroic, glorious, brave; this passage: destructive, sad)*.

Teach

Literary Element | 1

Conflict **Answer:** *Grendel attacks out of hatred for humankind; the dragon attacks out of revenge.*

Reading Strategy | 2

Identify Sequence **Answer:** *It is ironic that in resolving a problem with his master, the slave triggers a conflict that threatens the entire kingdom.*

View the Art ★

The Spangenhelm was a popular European war helmet design of the Early Middle Ages. The name is of German origin. *Spangen* refers to the metal strips that form the framework for the helmet, and *helm* means "helmet." The front of the helmet may include a nose protector and eye protection in a shape that resembles modern eyeglass frames. Contrary to popular belief, Vikings never wore horned helmets.

On its swift wings, the stallion tramping
645 In the courtyard—all gone, creatures of every
Kind, and their masters, hurled to the grave!"
    And so he spoke, sadly, of those
Long dead, and lived from day to day,
Joyless, until, at last, death touched
650 His heart and took him too. And a stalker
In the night, a flaming dragon, found
The treasure unguarded; he whom men fear
Came flying through the darkness, wrapped in fire,
Seeking caves and stone-split ruins°
655 But finding gold. Then it stayed, buried
Itself with heathen silver and jewels
It could neither use nor ever abandon.
    So mankind's enemy, the mighty beast,
Slept in those stone walls for hundreds
660 Of years; a runaway slave roused it,
Stole a jeweled cup and bought
His master's forgiveness, begged for mercy
And was pardoned when his delighted lord took the present
He bore, turned it in his hands and stared
665 At the ancient carvings. The cup brought peace
To a slave, pleased his master, but stirred
A dragon's anger. It turned, hunting
The thief's tracks, and found them, saw
Where its visitor had come and gone. He'd survived,
670 Had come close enough to touch its scaly
Head and yet lived, as it lifted its cavernous
Jaws, through the grace of almighty God
And a pair of quiet, quick-moving feet.
The dragon followed his steps, anxious
675 To find the man who had robbed it of silver
And sleep; it circled around and around
The tower, determined to catch him, but could not,
He had run too fast, the wilderness was empty.
The beast went back to its treasure, planning
680 A bloody revenge, and found what was missing,
Saw what thieving hands had stolen.
Then it crouched on the stones, counting off
The hours till the Almighty's candle went out,
And evening came, and wild with anger

654 Seeking caves and stone-split ruins: It was believed that dragons made their dens in caves and stone burial mounds.

Helmet from a Vendel boat grave. Seventh century. ★

Conflict *How do the dragon's motives differ from those of Grendel?* **1**

Identify Sequence *What is ironic about this sequence of events?* **2**

Literary Element Practice

Antagonists Explain that an *antagonist* is a person or force that opposes the protagonist, or central character, in a work of literature. Have students identify *Beowulf's* protagonist *(Beowulf)* and the three main antagonists *(Grendel, Grendel's mother, the dragon).* Discuss qualities shared by the three antagonists and ways in which each of Beowulf's foes is unique.

You may wish to have students work together to create lists of details about each antagonist, and then use the lists to compare and contrast these villains.

685 It could fly burning across the land, killing
     And destroying with its breath. Then the sun was gone,
     And its heart was glad: glowing with rage
     It left the tower, impatient to repay
     Its enemies. The people suffered, everyone
690 Lived in terror, but when Beowulf had learned
     Of their trouble his fate was worse, and came quickly.

        Vomiting fire and smoke, the dragon
     Burned down their homes. They watched in horror
     As the flames rose up: the angry monster
695 Meant to leave nothing alive. And the signs
     Of its anger flickered and glowed in the darkness,
     Visible for miles, tokens of its hate
     And its cruelty, spread like a warning to the Geats
     Who had broken its rest. Then it hurried back
700 To its tower, to its hidden treasure, before dawn
     Could come. It had wrapped its flames around
     The Geats; now it trusted in stone
     Walls, and its strength, to protect it. But they would not.
        Then they came to Beowulf, their king, and announced
705 That his hall, his throne, the best of buildings,
     Had melted away in the dragon's burning
     Breath. Their words brought misery, Beowulf's
     Sorrow beat at his heart: he accused
     Himself of breaking God's law, of bringing
710 The Almighty's anger down on his people.
     Reproach pounded in his breast, gloomy
     And dark, and the world seemed a different place.
     But the hall was gone, the dragon's molten
     Breath had licked across it, burned it
715 To ashes, near the shore it had guarded. The Geats
     Deserved revenge; Beowulf, their leader
     And lord, began to plan it, ordered
     A battle-shield shaped of iron, knowing that
     Wood would be useless, that no linden shield
720 Could help him, protect him, in the flaming heat
     Of the beast's breath. That noble prince
     would end his days on earth, soon,
     Would leave this brief life, but would take the dragon
     With him, tear it from the heaped-up treasure
725 It had guarded so long. And he'd go to it alone,
     Scorning to lead soldiers against such
     An enemy: he saw nothing to fear, thought nothing

Viking pendant from Sweden.

The Epic Warrior *What does this passage reveal about Beowulf as a ruler of his people?* **3**

Big Idea **3**

The Epic Warrior Answer:
Beowulf is a humble and conscientious ruler. He respects the tradition that a kingdom is punished for the sins of its king, and he accepts moral responsibility for his people's suffering.

(**ENGLISH LEARNERS**) Point out the word *misery* in line 708 and explain that it is a false cognate: the Spanish word *miseria* means "poverty." Ask students to find the word in the following line that is a synonym for *misery (sorrow).*

English Learners

DIFFERENTIATED INSTRUCTION

Beginning Point out the metaphor *the Almighty's candle* went out (line 683). Help students note that the word *Almighty* is composed of *all* and *mighty* and that it is another name for God. **Ask:** What does the metaphor mean? *(the sun set)*

Advanced Learners

DIFFERENTIATED INSTRUCTION

Research Students can use the Internet to learn about symbols of evil, such as giants and dragons in Anglo-Saxon and medieval literature. Allow time for students to share the findings that interest them most. Challenge students to create a brief illustrated report of their findings.

Teach

The Epic Warrior Answer:
Hrothgar does not try to slay Grendel, the monster that is slaughtering his people. Beowulf, however, decides to fight the dragon that threatens his people. Beowulf is either braver or more powerful than Hrothgar, or (probably) both.

Literary Element   2

Conflict Answer: *Some students may say Beowulf is foolhardy to believe that he, an elderly warrior, can conquer a powerful adversary without help from other warriors. Other students may say Beowulf is noble for trying to protect his warriors from certain death.*

Of the beast's claws, or wings, or flaming
Jaws—he had fought, before, against worse
730   Odds, had survived, been victorious, in harsher
Battles, beginning in Herot, Hrothgar's
Unlucky hall.

And Beowulf uttered his final boast:
    "I've never known fear; as a youth I fought
735   In endless battles. I am old, now,
But I will fight again, seek fame still,
If the dragon hiding in his tower dares
To face me."
              Then he said farewell to his followers,
740   Each in his turn, for the last time:
    "I'd use no sword, no weapon, if this beast
Could be killed without it, crushed to death
Like Grendel, gripped in my hands and torn
Limb from limb. But his breath will be burning
745   Hot, poison will pour from his tongue.
I feel no shame, with shield and sword
And armor, against this monster: when he comes to me
I mean to stand, not run from his shooting
Flames, stand till fate decides
750   Which of us wins. My heart is firm,
My hands calm: I need no hot
Words. Wait for me close by, my friends.
We shall see, soon, who will survive
This bloody battle, stand when the fighting
755   Is done. No one else could do
What I mean to, here, no man but me
Could hope to defeat this monster. No one
Could try. And this dragon's treasure, his gold
And everything hidden in that tower, will be mine
760   Or war will sweep me to a bitter death!"
    Then Beowulf rose, still brave, still strong,
And with his shield at his side, and a mail shirt on his breast,
Strode calmly, confidently, toward the tower, under
The rocky cliffs: no coward could have walked there!
765   And then he who'd endured dozens of desperate
Battles, who'd stood boldly while swords and shields
Clashed, the best of kings, saw

The Epic Warrior *How would you contrast Beowulf's and Hrothgar's responses to attack?*   **1**

Conflict *Is Beowulf being foolhardy or noble in deciding to fight alone? Explain.*   **2**

Viking amulet in the shape of a cross with a dragon's head. 8th century, silver. National Museum of Iceland, Reykjavik.

Writing Practice

Imitating Style

SPIRAL REVIEW Have students re-read Beowulf's final boast and his farewell to his followers. Ask them to identify the tone of the boasts (*proud, courageous, bold*) and list some of the words and phrases that help set this tone (*i.e., I . . . seek fame still; if the dragon . . . dares face me; I mean to stand*). Have students think about a challenge they face in their lives and write a boast, similar in style to Beowulf's declamations, stating how they will meet the challenge. Encourage them to use figures of speech and heroic language, as does the Beowulf poet.

Huge stone arches and felt the heat
Of the dragon's breath, flooding down
770 Through the hidden entrance, too hot for anyone
To stand, a streaming current of fire
And smoke that blocked all passage. And the Geats'
Lord and leader, angry, lowered
His sword and roared out a battle cry,
775 A call so loud and clear that it reached through
The hoary rock, hung in the dragon's
Ear.° The beast rose, angry,
Knowing a man had come—and then nothing
But war could have followed. Its breath came first.
780 A steaming cloud pouring from the stone,
Then the earth itself shook. Beowulf
Swung his shield into place, held it
In front of him, facing the entrance. The dragon
Coiled and uncoiled, its heart urging it
785 Into battle. Beowulf's ancient sword
Was waiting, unsheathed, his sharp and gleaming
Blade. The beast came closer; both of them
Were ready, each set on slaughter. The Geats'
Great prince stood firm, unmoving, prepared
790 Behind his high shield, waiting in his shining
Armor. The monster came quickly toward him,
Pouring out fire and smoke, hurrying
To its fate. Flames beat at the iron
Shield, and for a time it held, protected
795 Beowulf as he'd planned; then it began to melt,
And for the first time in his life that famous prince
Fought with fate against him, with glory
Denied him. He knew it, but he raised his sword
And struck at the dragon's scaly hide.
800 The ancient blade broke, bit into
The monster's skin, drew blood, but cracked
And failed him before it went deep enough, helped him
Less than he needed. The dragon leaped
With pain, thrashed and beat at him, spouting
805 Murderous flames, spreading them everywhere.
And the Geats' ring-giver did not boast of glorious
Victories in other wars: his weapon
Had failed him, deserted him, now when he needed it
Most, that excellent sword. Edgetho's

775–777 A call . . . ear: The dragon hears the echoing sound of Beowulf's battle cry.

Vendel brooch

Identify Sequence *What effect does this sequence of events create?* **3**

The Epic Warrior *What does this passage reveal about Beowulf?* **4**

Reading Strategy 3

Identify Sequence Answer:
This sequence of events creates suspense—first a cloud of hot breath, then a shuddering of the ground as the dragon plods forward. The poet slows down the action of the narrative as Beowulf and the dragon approach each other.

Big Idea 4

The Epic Warrior Answer:
Beowulf courageously fights although he knows that he is doomed. Beowulf seems more heroic because he accepts his fate even as he fights the only losing battle of his life.

View the Art ★

This seventh-century brooch was found at Aker, Norway. At the bottom, the torso of the human figure splits to form the upward-curving necks and heads of a pair of dragons. The clasp at the top depicts two facing eagles.

Approaching Level

DIFFERENTIATED INSTRUCTION

Established Text structure helps the writer to determine what information to give and when. The structure of a text can be organized in many ways. The most common are chronological or time-order, cause-and-effect order, or in compare-contrast order. Discuss features and possible uses for each kind of organizing structure. Have students determine the text structure of *Beowulf*. (Chronological order)

Teach

Big Idea 1

The Epic Warrior Answer:
The bond of kinship entailed that a warrior must remain to fight alongside his kinsman even in the face of extreme danger and death.

Say: All but one of Beowulf's comrades run for their lives. Why does the poet call them "brave and noble followers"? *(The poet is using verbal irony. The fearsome foe has turned the men into cowards.)*

View the Art ★

Sample answer: This drawing looks more like my image of Beowulf's dragon because it looks as if it could spit white-hot flames.

Best known for his work as a critic, John Ruskin (1819–1900) is also remembered as an author, poet, and artist. He believed that great art is the expression of an epoch in which people are united by a common faith and a common purpose, accept laws, believe in leaders, and take a serious view of human destiny.

Study of a Dragon's Head after Michelangelo. John Ruskin (1819–1900). Ink on paper. Abbot Hall Art Gallery, Kendal, Cumbria, UK.

View the Art Dragons have been depicted in many ways in the visual arts. Does this drawing or the illustration on page 45 better match your own mental picture of the dragon Beowulf faces?

810   Famous son stared at death,
    Unwilling to leave this world, to exchange it
    For a dwelling in some distant place—a journey
    Into darkness that all men must make, as death
    Ends their few brief hours on earth.
815   Quickly, the dragon came at him, encouraged
    As Beowulf fell back; its breath flared,
    And he suffered, wrapped around in swirling
    Flames—a king, before, but now
    A beaten warrior. None of his comrades
820   Came to him, helped him, his brave and noble
    Followers; they ran for their lives, fled
    Deep in a wood. And only one of them
    Remained, stood there, miserable, remembering,
    As a good man must, what kinship should mean.

825   His name was Wiglaf, he was Wexstan's son
    And a good soldier; his family had been Swedish,°
    Once. Watching Beowulf, he could see
    How his king was suffering, burning. Remembering
    Everything his lord and cousin had given him,
830   Armor and gold and the great estates
    Wexstan's family enjoyed, Wiglaf's
    Mind was made up; he raised his yellow
    Shield and drew his sword—an ancient
    Weapon that had once belonged to Onela's

826 his family had been Swedish: Wiglaf, though of Swedish descent, considers himself to be a Geat. It was not unusual for a warrior from one people to serve the chief or king of another people.

The Epic Warrior *How does this passage show the bond of kinship in Anglo-Saxon culture?* **1**

Reading Practice

SPIRAL REVIEW **Graphic Organizers** This section recounts the first part of Beowulf's battle with the dragon and incorporates several changes of mood. Have students make a timeline to show the events of the battle so far (lines 761–819). Use chart paper or the board so that several students can contribute. Ask students to identify the mood that accompanies each event. Discuss the mood at the end of this section and have students predict the outcome of the battle. Ask students to name instances from movies or other stories of heroes winning a fight when it seems that all has been lost.

835　　　Nephew, and that Wexstan had won,° killing
　　　　The prince when he fled from Sweden, sought safety
　　　　With Herdred, and found death. And Wiglaf's father
　　　　Had carried the dead man's armor, and his sword,
　　　　To Onela, and the king had said nothing, only
840　　　Given him armor and sword and all,
　　　　Everything his rebel nephew had owned
　　　　And lost when he left this life. And Wexstan
　　　　Had kept those shining gifts, held them
　　　　For years, waiting for his son to use them,
845　　　Wear them as honorably and well as once
　　　　His father had done; then Wexstan died
　　　　And Wiglaf was his heir, inherited treasures
　　　　And weapons and land. He'd never worn
　　　　That armor, fought with that sword, until Beowulf
850　　　Called him to his side, led him into war.
　　　　But his soul did not melt, his sword was strong;
　　　　The dragon discovered his courage, and his weapon,
　　　　When the rush of battle brought them together.
　　　　　　And Wiglaf, his heart heavy, uttered
855　　　The kind of words his comrades deserved:
　　　　　"I remember how we sat in the mead-hall, drinking
　　　　And boasting of how brave we'd be when Beowulf
　　　　Needed us, he who gave us these swords
　　　　And armor: all of us swore to repay him,
860　　　When the time came, kindness for kindness
　　　　—With our lives, if he needed them. He allowed us to join him,
　　　　Chose us from all his great army, thinking
　　　　Our boasting words had some weight, believing
　　　　Our promises, trusting our swords. He took us
865　　　For soldiers, for men. He meant to kill
　　　　This monster himself, our mighty king,
　　　　Fight this battle alone and unaided,
　　　　As in the days when his strength and daring dazzled
　　　　Men's eyes. But those days are over and gone
870　　　And now our lord must lean on younger
　　　　Arms. And we must go to him, while angry
　　　　Flames burn at his flesh, help
　　　　Our glorious king! By almighty God,
　　　　I'd rather burn myself than see

Identify Sequence *What sequence of events led to Wiglaf's receiving his armor and sword?* **2**

The Epic Warrior *What does this passage reveal about the relationship between a chief and his followers?* **3**

833–835 **an ancient weapon . . . that Wexstan had won:** Wexstan killed the rebellious nephew of Onela, the king of Sweden, in battle. Wexstan was therefore entitled to the nephew's sword.

Page of text with a dragon illustration on vellum. 15th century. Flemish School, 43 x 31 cm. Musée Condé, Chantilly, France.

Teach

Reading Strategy　2

Identify Sequence Answer:
Wiglaf's father, Wexstan, won the armor and the sword in battle by killing King Onela's nephew. Wexstan kept the armor and the sword to give to his son when Wiglaf came of age. When Wexstan died, Wiglaf inherited the battle gear.

Big Idea　3

The Epic Warrior Answer:
A chief gave weapons, armor, and other goods to his followers in return for their loyal service in time of need.

Say: Beowulf has stated his intention to fight the dragon alone. According to Wiglaf, it is still wrong for Beowulf's warriors to run off instead of helping him. Why? *(Wiglaf believes Beowulf is too old now and "must lean on younger arms.")*

Teach

View the Art ★

Along with swords and spears, axes were important weapons in medieval Scandinavia. They could also be status symbols, like this bronze example, richly inlaid with silver wire, that was found in a nobleman's grave at Mammen, Denmark. **Ask:** Why might objects such as this be a status symbol? *(Metals were expensive and difficult to acquire.)*

---

875 Flames swirling around my lord.
   And who are we to carry home
   Our shields before we've slain his enemy
   And ours, to run back to our homes with Beowulf
   So hard-pressed here? I swear that nothing
880 He ever did deserved an end
   Like this, dying miserably and alone,
   Butchered by this savage beast: we swore
   That these swords and armor were each for us all!"
      Then he ran to his king, crying encouragement
885 As he dove through the dragon's deadly fumes:
      "Belovèd Beowulf, remember how you boasted,
   Once, that nothing in the world would ever
   Destroy your fame: fight to keep it,
   Now, be strong and brave, my noble
890 King, protecting life and fame
   Together. My sword will fight at your side!"
      The dragon heard him, the man-hating monster,
   And was angry; shining with surging flames
   It came for him, anxious to return his visit.
895 Waves of fire swept at his shield
   And the edge began to burn. His mail shirt
   Could not help him, but before his hands dropped
   The blazing wood Wiglaf jumped
   Behind Beowulf's shield; his own was burned
900 To ashes. Then the famous old hero, remembering
   Days of glory, lifted what was left
   Of Nagling, his ancient sword, and swung it
   With all his strength, smashed the gray
   Blade into the beast's head. But then Nagling
905 Broke to pieces, as iron always
   Had in Beowulf's hands. His arms
   Were too strong, the hardest blade could not help him,
   The most wonderfully worked. He carried them to war
   But fate had decreed that the Geats' great king
910 Would be no better for any weapon.
      Then the monster charged again, vomiting
   Fire, wild with pain, rushed out
   Fierce and dreadful, its fear forgotten.
   Watching for its chance it drove its tusks

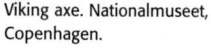

Viking axe. Nationalmuseet, Copenhagen. ★

Conflict *How might Wiglaf's actions affect the fight?* **1**

Conflict *What is ironic about Beowulf's strength?* **2**

Literary Element Practice

SPIRAL REVIEW **Archetypes** Remind students that an archetype is an idea, often symbolized by a character or characters, that appears consistently throughout the ages in literature from all parts of the world. **Ask:** How do Beowulf and Wigalf fit the hero archetype? *(They are courageous in battle and true to their word. They protect others.)* What archetype does the conflict with the dragon represent? *(the battle between good and evil)* Challenge students to name contemporary heroes and conflicts from books and film that fit the hero and good/evil conflict archetypes. **Ask:** Are these archetypes portrayed the same way as in Beowulf? *(Sample answer: No, the conflict does not take the form of a physical battle.)*

915 Into Beowulf's neck; he staggered, the blood
     Came flooding forth, fell like rain.

          And then when Beowulf needed him most
     Wiglaf showed his courage, his strength
     And skill, and the boldness he was born with. Ignoring
920 The dragon's head, he helped his lord
     By striking lower down. The sword
     Sank in; his hand was burned, but the shining
     Blade had done its work, the dragon's
     Belching flames began to flicker
925 And die away. And Beowulf drew
     His battle-sharp dagger: the blood-stained old king
     Still knew what he was doing. Quickly, he cut
     The beast in half, slit it apart.
     It fell, their courage had killed it, two noble
930 Cousins had joined in the dragon's death.
     Yet what they did all men must do
     When the time comes! But the triumph was the last
     Beowulf would ever earn, the end
     Of greatness and life together. The wound
935 In his neck began to swell and grow;
     He could feel something stirring, burning
     In his veins, a stinging venom, and knew
     The beast's fangs had left it. He fumbled
     Along the wall, found a slab
940 Of stone, and dropped down; above him he saw
     Huge stone arches and heavy posts,
     Holding up the roof of that giant hall.
     Then Wiglaf's gentle hands bathed
     The blood-stained prince, his glorious lord,
945 Weary of war, and loosened his helmet.
          Beowulf spoke, in spite of the swollen,
     Livid wound, knowing he'd unwound
     His string of days on earth, seen
     As much as God would grant him; all worldly
950 Pleasure was gone, as life would go,
     Soon:
               "I'd leave my armor to my son,
     Now, if God had given me an heir,
     A child born of my body, his life
955 Created from mine. I've worn this crown
     For fifty winters: no neighboring people
     Have tried to threaten the Geats, sent soldiers
     Against us or talked of terror. My days

Brooch, 9th century.
Goldwork.

Big Idea   3

The Epic Warrior Ask:
How is Wiglaf similar to the young Beowulf? (Like Beowulf when he was young, Wiglaf courageously fights a formidable foe to help an old king.)

(ADVANCED) Ask: Why do you think the poet included the heroic young Wigalf? (Wigalf symbolizes the idea of younger generations of heroes succeeding their elders. It is a kind of hereditary nobility, even though Wigalf is not Beowulf's son.)

View the Art ★
This ninth-century gold brooch, set with precious stones, was discovered at Eiker, in the Norwegian county of Buskerud.

Approaching Level
DIFFERENTIATED INSTRUCTION

SMALL GROUP **Established** Have students make a list of the main characters in *Beowulf* (Beowulf, King Hrothgar, Grendel, Grendel's mother, the dragon, Wiglaf).

Write and display the following questions; ask students to work in small groups to write a one-paragraph response to each: **1.** *Which character is your favorite, and why?* **2.** *Which character do you identify with, and why?* Leave time for volunteers to share their work aloud.

The Epic Warrior Answer:
Beowulf has managed to maintain peace for fifty years, has never sworn an unholy oath, and has never engaged in battle against a kinsman.

The Epic Warrior Answer:
The treasure is proof of his greatness and will bring glory and security to his people.

Have gone by as fate willed, waiting
960 For its word to be spoken, ruling as well
As I knew how, swearing no unholy oaths,
Seeking no lying wars. I can leave
This life happy; I can die, here,
Knowing the Lord of all life has never
965 Watched me wash my sword in blood
Born of my own family. Belovèd
Wiglaf, go, quickly, find
The dragon's treasure: we've taken its life,
But its gold is ours, too. Hurry,
970 Bring me ancient silver, precious
Jewels, shining armor and gems,
Before I die. Death will be softer,
Leaving life and this people I've ruled
So long, if I look at this last of all prizes."

975   Then Wexstan's son went in, as quickly
As he could, did as the dying Beowulf
Asked, entered the inner darkness
Of the tower, went with his mail shirt and his sword.
Flushed with victory he groped his way,
980 A brave young warrior, and suddenly saw
Piles of gleaming gold, precious
Gems, scattered on the floor, cups
And bracelets, rusty old helmets, beautifully
Made but rotting with no hands to rub
985 And polish them. They lay where the dragon left them;
It had flown in the darkness, once, before fighting
Its final battle. (So gold can easily
Triumph, defeat the strongest of men,
No matter how deep it is hidden!) And he saw,
990 Hanging high above, a golden
Banner, woven by the best of weavers
And beautiful. And over everything he saw
A strange light, shining everywhere,
On walls and floor and treasure. Nothing
995 Moved, no other monsters appeared;
He took what he wanted, all the treasures
That pleased his eye, heavy plates
And golden cups and the glorious banner,
Loaded his arms with all they could hold.

The Epic Warrior *Why does Beowulf believe that he has been a good king?* **1**

The Epic Warrior *Why does the treasure mean so much to Beowulf?* **2**

1 Bronze helmet, late Bronze Age (800–400 B.C.), from Veksø bog, Denmark. National Museum, Copenhagen.

Assessment Practice

SPIRAL REVIEW Reading Comprehension Test Tips For reading comprehension questions on an open-book test, you should look at the passage as you write answers to the questions. **Ask:** Why did Beowulf leave his kingdom to Wiglaf? Have students write their answers in three to five lines. *(Students' responses should mention that Wiglaf was the only warrior who fought with Beowulf against the dragon instead of fleeing. They should also mention that Beowulf had no son or other heir of his own.)*

1000 Beowulf's dagger, his iron blade,
     Had finished the fire-spitting terror
     That once protected tower and treasures
     Alike; the gray-bearded lord of the Geats
     Had ended those flying, burning raids
1005 Forever.
             Then Wiglaf went back, anxious
     To return while Beowulf was alive, to bring him
     Treasure they'd won together. He ran,
     hoping his wounded king, weak
1010 And dying, had not left the world too soon.
     Then he brought their treasure to Beowulf, and found
     His famous king bloody, gasping
     For breath. But Wiglaf sprinkled water
     Over his lord, until the words
1015 Deep in his breast broke through and were heard.
     Beholding the treasure he spoke, haltingly:
         "For this, this gold, these jewels, I thank
     Our Father in Heaven, Ruler of the Earth—
     For all of this, that His grace has given me,
1020 Allowed me to bring to my people while breath
     Still came to my lips. I sold my life
     For this treasure, and I sold it well. Take
     What I leave, Wiglaf, lead my people,
     Help them; my time is gone. Have
1025 The brave Geats build me a tomb,
     When the funeral flames° have burned me, and build it
     Here, at the water's edge, high
     On this spit of land, so sailors can see
     This tower, and remember my name, and call it
1030 Beowulf's tower, and boats in the darkness
     And mist, crossing the sea, will know it."
         Then that brave king gave the golden
     Necklace from around his throat to Wiglaf,
     Gave him his gold-covered helmet, and his rings,
1035 And his mail shirt, and ordered him to use them well:
         "You're the last of all our far-flung family.
     Fate has swept our race away,
     Taken warriors in their strength and led them
     To the death that was waiting. And now I follow them."
1040   The old man's mouth was silent, spoke
     No more, had said as much as it could;
     He would sleep in the fire, soon. His soul
     Left his flesh, flew to glory.

1026 **funeral flames:** It was the custom to cremate the bodies of the dead on a pile of flammable materials known as a funeral pyre.

The Epic Warrior *Why does Beowulf plan the tower so carefully?* **3**

Teach

Big Idea 3

The Epic Warrior Answer: *For Beowulf, immortality consists solely of fame, so he plans his monument carefully. He wants to ensure that his people will cherish his memory for as long as possible.*

Ask: Beowulf says that he has sold his life for this treasure and sold it well. What does he mean? (*A warrior's treasure is an important part of his legacy. The treasure won in this battle will help the Geats and make them remember Beowulf always.*)

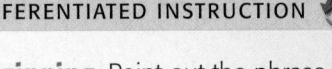

English Learners

DIFFERENTIATED INSTRUCTION

Beginning Point out the phrase *spit of land* (line 1028). **Ask:** What does the verb *spit* mean? (*expel saliva*) Does this definition makes sense in the sentence? (*no*) Model looking up *spit* in the dictionary to find the appropriate definition for the context. (*small point of land*)

Approaching Level

DIFFERENTIATED INSTRUCTION

PARTNERS **Established** Have students work in pairs using the Internet to learn more about the importance of honor, fame, and fate to the Anglo-Saxons. Have strong readers work with less proficient readers to complete this research project.

Teach

Reading Strategy | **1**

Identify Sequence Answer:
With the exception of Wiglaf, who is loyal and brave, Beowulf's followers turn out to be cowards and traitors. They violate the heroic code because of their fear.

And when the battle was over Beowulf's followers
1045 Came out of the wood, cowards and traitors,
Knowing the dragon was dead. Afraid,
While it spit its fires, to fight in their lord's
Defense, to throw their javelins and spears,
They came like shamefaced jackals, their shields
1050 In their hands, to the place where the prince lay dead,
And waited for Wiglaf to speak. He was sitting
Near Beowulf's body, wearily sprinkling
Water in the dead man's face, trying
To stir him. He could not. No one could have kept
1055 Life in their lord's body, or turned
Aside the Lord's will: world
And men and all move as He orders,
And always have, and always will.
    Then Wiglaf turned and angrily told them
1060 What men without courage must hear.
Wexstan's brave son stared at the traitors,
His heart sorrowful, and said what he had to:
    "I say what anyone who speaks the truth
Must say. Your lord gave you gifts,
1065 Swords and the armor you stand in now;
You sat on the mead-hall benches, prince
And followers, and he gave you, with open hands,
Helmets and mail shirts, hunted across
The world for the best of weapons. War
1070 Came and you ran like cowards, dropped
Your swords as soon as the danger was real.
Should Beowulf have boasted of your help, rejoiced
In your loyal strength? With God's good grace
He helped himself, swung his sword
1075 Alone, won his own revenge.
The help I gave him was nothing, but all
I was able to give; I went to him, knowing
That nothing but Beowulf's strength could save us,
And my sword was lucky, found some vital
1080 Place and bled the burning flames
Away. Too few of his warriors remembered
To come, when our lord faced death, alone.
And now the giving of swords, of golden
Rings and rich estates, is over,
1085 Ended for you and everyone who shares
Your blood: when the brave Geats hear
How you bolted and ran none of your race

Maes-how tomb near the Stones of Stenness and the Ring of Brodgar on the Orkney Mainland. Artist unknown. Engraving.

Identify Sequence *Beowulf's followers return to their leader after, not during, the battle. What can you conclude about them?* | **1** |

Grammar Practice

SPIRAL REVIEW **Possessive Pronouns** Explain that possessive pronouns show possession, or ownership. Write the following sentences on the board. Have students replace each underlined phrase with the appropriate possessive pronoun and identify whether it is first, second, or third person.

1. The monster's head lay on the ground at Beowulf's feet. *(its/third person)*
2. If I had found riches in Grendel's lair, they would have become treasures that belonged to me. *(mine/first person)*

Will have anything left but their lives. And death
Would be better for them all, and for you, than the kind
1090 Of life you can lead, branded with disgrace!"

THE FUNERAL FIRE

A huge heap of wood was ready,
Hung around with helmets, and battle
Shields, and shining mail shirts, all
As Beowulf had asked. The bearers brought
1095 Their belovèd lord, their glorious king,
And weeping laid him high on the wood.
Then the warriors began to kindle that greatest
Of funeral fires; smoke rose
Above the flames, black and thick,
1100 And while the wind blew and the fire
Roared they wept, and Beowulf's body
Crumbled and was gone. The Geats stayed,
Moaning their sorrow, lamenting their lord:
A gnarled old woman, hair wound
1105 Tight and gray on her head, groaned
A song of misery, of infinite sadness
And days of mourning, of fear and sorrow
To come, slaughter and terror and captivity.
And Heaven swallowed the billowing smoke.
1110 Then the Geats built the tower, as Beowulf
Had asked, strong and tall, so sailors
Could find it from far and wide; working
For ten long days they made his monument,
Sealed his ashes in walls as straight
1115 And high as wise and willing hands
Could raise them. And the riches he and Wiglaf
Had won from the dragon, rings, necklaces,
Ancient, hammered armor—all
The treasures they'd taken were left there, too,
1120 Silver and jewels buried in the sandy
Ground, back in the earth, again
And forever hidden and useless to men.
And then twelve of the bravest Geats
Rode their horses around the tower,
1125 Telling their sorrow, telling stories

The Epic Warrior *Why did the Anglo-Saxons regard cowardice as particularly shameful?* **2**

The Epic Warrior *What does the hero's death mean to his people?* **3**

Big Idea | 2

The Epic Warrior Answer:
The Anglo-Saxons valued the heroic code and its virtues, particularly courage and loyalty. Any violation of this code was looked upon with contempt.

Big Idea | 3

The Epic Warrior Answer:
The hero's death plunges his people into abysmal misery, compounded by a pessimistic fear of the future.

English Learners

DIFFERENTIATED INSTRUCTION

Intermediate Point out the phrase *And Heaven swallowed the billowing smoke* (line 1109). Make sure students understand what *billowing* means. **Ask:** Did Heaven actually "swallow" the smoke? What really happened? *(No, the smoke disappeared into the sky.)* Have students speculate on why the poet used Heaven in this metaphor. *(The smoke symbolizes Beowulf's soul rising to heaven.)*

Advanced Learners

DIFFERENTIATED INSTRUCTION

Funerals Have students use the Internet to research Anglo-Saxon funeral customs. Have them discuss the symbolism of Christian and pagan elements they find in their research and the poem.

Teach

The Epic Warrior Ask:
What wish of Beowulf's is accomplished when the Geats proclaim his many virtues? *(He receives his "fame" as a great warrior and king.)*

View the Art ★

The Russian-born artist Nikolai Roerich (1874–1947) was also a world traveler and a prominent student of spiritual philosophy. His painting *Visitors from Overseas* depicts a group of Varangians—medieval Scandinavians who traded, raided, and settled along the rivers of what would become Russia. **Ask:** What does the painting make you think about Varangians? *(The ships look disorganized but well-stocked; students may feel this meant that the Varangians were warriors who fought at random and did not plan out their conquests far in advance.)*

> To check students' understanding of the selection, see Unit 1 Teaching Resources Book, p. 33.

Visitors from Overseas. Nikolai Roerich. Tretyakov Gallery, Moscow, Russia.

> Of their dead king and his greatness, his glory,
> Praising him for heroic deeds, for a life
> As noble as his name. So should all men
> Raise up words for their lords, warm
> 1130 With love, when their shield and protector leaves
> His body behind, sends his soul
> On high. And so Beowulf's followers
> Rode, mourning their belovèd leader,
> Crying that no better king had ever
> 1135 Lived, no prince so mild, no man
> So open to his people, so deserving of praise. **1**

Reading Practice

 SPIRAL REVIEW Question Draw a T chart on the board or on chart paper. Ask students to re-read the events following Beowulf's death, beginning with line 1103. Have students think of questions about the text as they read and jot them down. Then call on them to ask their questions aloud as you write them on one side of the T chart. Once you have written five or six questions, have the class suggest answers and write them on the other side of the chart. *(Sample questions and answers: Why did the old woman sing of fear and sorrow to come? The Geats would be vulnerable without their great leader; Why did they bury the dragon's treasure? The items were tainted because they were the cause of Beowulf's death.)*

After You Read

Respond and Think Critically

Respond and Interpret

1. What are your impressions of Beowulf? Explain.

2. (a)Summarize what happens during the battle between Grendel and Beowulf. (b)How does learning about Grendel's fears and feelings during the battle affect your impression of the monster?

3. (a)Why does Grendel's mother try to kill Beowulf? Describe their struggle and its outcome. (b)After the struggle with Grendel's mother, why does Beowulf search for Grendel? Why does he feel the way he does?

4. (a)Why does Wiglaf come to Beowulf's aid in his fight with the dragon? (b)In what ways are Beowulf and Wiglaf similar? In what ways are they different?

Analyze and Evaluate

5. Given the fact that most of Beowulf's men abandon him during his fight with the dragon, what might this indicate about the future of the kingdom?

6. A symbol is a person, thing, or event that stands for something else, often an idea or concept. What might Beowulf symbolize? What might Grendel and the dragon represent?

Connect

7. **Big Idea** The Epic Warrior From the description of Beowulf's character, what traits do you think the Anglo-Saxons considered heroic?

8. **Connect to Today** Which character is a modern reader likely to find most appealing? Why?

Visual Literacy

Creating a Storyboard

One way to visualize the flow of events in an epic poem is to create a storyboard—a series of sketches depicting the most important events in sequence. Each sketch illustrates a single scene or action.

Group Activity With a group of classmates, list details about the setting, characters, and events in a selected passage from the poem. For example, review lines 658–693, and then add details to the third column in the chart shown. Refer to the graphic organizer you made for Reading Strategy on page 23 to be sure the order of events is correct.

Then turn your chart into a storyboard, or a series of cartoon panels, to illustrate the events. Consider how graphic storytelling increases your understanding of the poem.

Setting	Characters	Events
inside the dragon's lair	• a runaway slave • a sleeping dragon	The dragon sleeps inside stone walls.

BEOWULF **53**

Visual Literacy

Make sure students include a title with their storyboards indicating the episode from the poem that is being depicted. Display the storyboards in the classroom and allow students to view each other's work. Have students choose a storyboard created by another group and write a summary of the episode based on the storyboard. Ask students to explain in a few sentences how the storyboard helped them clarify their understanding of the episode or gain a new perspective.

After You Read

Assess

1. Students should consider Beowulf as a product of his culture's highest values.

2. (a) When Grendel claws at Beowulf, the hero jumps up, seizes Grendel by one hand, and holds on until Grendel's arm is twisted off. (b) Learning about Grendel's feelings generates more awareness of Grendel as a symbol of evil, defeated by Beowulf, God's warrior.

3. (a) Grendel's mother wants revenge for her son's death. She prepares to deliver a death-blow when Beowulf seizes her sword and kills her. (b) Beowulf wants to avenge the deaths of Hrothgar's men. He is angry about Grendel's massacre of the sleeping warriors.

4. (a) Wiglaf feels a sense of duty toward his leader. (b) Both warriors are honorable and courageous. Beowulf is old and experienced; Wiglaf is young and inexperienced.

5. It may indicate that the kingdom will never have a leader as courageous as Beowulf.

6. Students might say that Beowulf symbolizes good or humanity, and that Grendel and the dragon symbolize evil, the devil, darkness, or death.

7. The Anglo-Saxons considered fearlessness, self-sacrifice, loyalty to one's kin, and a conquering spirit to be heroic.

8. Beowulf. He demonstrates qualities—such as courage, perseverance, and self-sacrifice—that are still valued in a hero today.

 For additional assessment, see Assessment Resources, pp. 57–60.

53

After You Read

Assess

Literary Element

1. Possible answer: Beowulf's conflict with the dragon seems like the most challenging because he is older and possibly weaker and because he knows he is going to die.

2. These lines describe Beowulf's conviction that he is responsible for his people's suffering. Beowulf decides to fight the dragon even though this battle may result in his death.

Progress Check

Do students understand conflict?

If No → see Unit 1 Teaching Resources Book, p. 28.

Progress Check

Can students identify sequence?

If No → see Unit 1 Teaching Resources Book, p. 29.

Review: Epic Hero

Positive: strength, courage, self-sacrifice

Negative: pride, ambition, recklessness

Beowulf today: pursue activities that involve strength, risk, and the possibility of fame

Regard for Beowulf: people today do not value physical strength as highly as the Anglo-Saxons did; Beowulf probably would not enjoy the degree of esteem and respect that he had in Anglo-Saxon society.

Literary Element Conflict

An **external conflict** exists when a character struggles against some outside force, such as another person, nature, society, or fate. An **internal conflict** is a struggle that takes place within the mind of a character who is torn between opposing feelings, desires, or goals.

1. Which of Beowulf's external conflicts seems the most challenging? Explain.

2. In lines 707–717, what internal conflict does Beowulf face? How does he resolve it?

Review: Epic Hero

As you learned on page 21, an **epic hero** is typically a person of high social status who usually embodies the ideals of his people.

Group Activity An epic hero is defined by his or her society. How might Beowulf, an Anglo-Saxon epic hero, behave in our society? What kinds of jobs might he hold? With a group of your classmates, discuss Beowulf's main character traits—both good and bad. Create a diagram like the one below to record your observations. Then discuss how Beowulf might act in present-day situations as well as how others might regard him. Share your conclusions with the rest of your class.

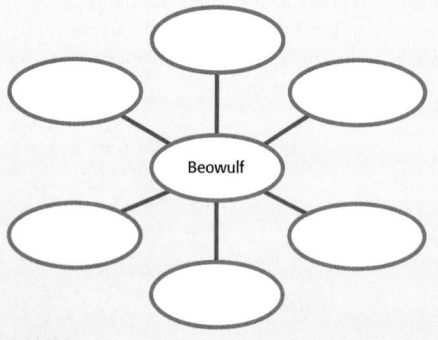

LOG ON ► **Literature** Online

Selection Resources For Selection Quizzes, eFlashcards, and Reading-Writing Connection activities, go to glencoe.com and enter QuickPass code GLB9817u1.

Reading Strategy Identify Sequence

Identifying the sequence of events is an important step in determining an author's purpose for writing. In *Beowulf,* the hero fights three monsters in succession: Grendel, Grendel's mother, and the fire-breathing dragon.

1. What does the poet suggest about Beowulf's challenges by using this sequence of battles?

2. How would you contrast Beowulf in youth with Beowulf in old age?

Vocabulary Practice

Practice with Analogies Complete each analogy below.

1. hammer : forge :: chisel :
   a. paint **b.** sand **c.** sculpt
2. pain : writhing :: cold :
   a. warming **b.** skiing **c.** shivering
3. criminal : infamous :: philanthropist :
   a. reputable **b.** careful **c.** joyous
4. cheer : celebrate :: lament :
   a. rejoice **b.** mourn **c.** criticize
5. pajamas : nap :: shroud :
   a. burial **b.** wedding **c.** convalescence

Academic Vocabulary

Throughout the epic, Beowulf is guided by his **concept** *of fate.*

Concept is an academic word. The word is also commonly used in commercial settings. For example, an electronics company might ask a designer to come up with a **concept** for a new product that would appeal to a younger audience.

To further explore this word, complete the following sentence: *According to the traditional* **concept** *of heroism, a hero should be*

_____, _____,

and _____.

For more on academic vocabulary, see pages 56 and R81.

Reading Strategy

1. The challenges that Beowulf must face increase in danger as he ages and the narrative progresses.

2. In youth, Beowulf relies on his prodigious strength to defeat Grendel and Grendel's mother. In old age, he relies on his heroic spirit to fight although he knows he is doomed.

Vocabulary

1. c **2.** c **3.** a **4.** b **5.** a

Academic Vocabulary

Possible answer: According to the traditional concept of heroism, a hero should be brave, strong, and selfless.

54

Respond Through Writing

Summary

Report Story Events When you write a summary of a story, you tell a short version of the original and report the main events in sequence. A summary does not include personal opinions. In about 100 words, write a plot summary of the episode "The Battle with Grendel's Mother" from *Beowulf*. Write your summary in the present tense.

Prewrite As you read through the text, use a flowchart like the one below to note the main characters and ideas and to trace the sequence of events. In your flowchart, enter the characters and events in the order they appear. The example shown here lists events from "The Battle with Grendel."

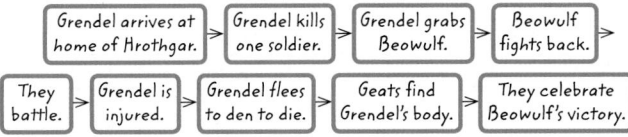

Draft Write your summary, following the order of events established in your flowchart. Include enough information to explain the characters' motivations and to clarify the logical connections between their actions. Be sure to note the relative significance of events where necessary.

> "The Battle with Grendel" begins as Grendel arrives at Hrothgar's hall. He begins by killing one Geat soldier, but the second soldier he attacks is Beowulf. Beowulf fights back, and the two begin a long and violent battle. Finally, Beowulf fatally injures Grendel at the climax of the episode. The Geat people search for Grendel's body, and when they find him dead, they celebrate Beowulf's victory.

Revise Ask a peer reader to review your summary, checking to be sure that it accurately identifies the characters and their motivations and presents all the important events in the order they occur. If your peer's comments suggest that your summary needs clarification, make the necessary changes in it.

Edit and Proofread Proofread your paper, correcting any errors in spelling, grammar, and punctuation. Use the Grammar Tip in the side column for help with the literary present tense.

Learning Objectives

In this assignment, you will focus on the following objectives:

Writing: Writing a summary.

Grammar: Understanding correct verb tense.

> ### Grammar Tip
>
> #### Literary Present Tense
>
> The **literary present tense** is used in writing about fictional events in literature, no matter when they take place. Unlike historical events, which you discuss in the past tense because they are frozen in time, fictional events come alive again whenever someone reads about them.
>
> Writing your summary in the literary present tense will help make it lively and maintain readers' interest.
>
> *After Grendel **dies,** his mother **arrives** to avenge his death.*

After You Read

Assess

 ## Respond Through Writing

Use these criteria when evaluating student summaries:

- The summary states the main points of the text in the present tense without offering personal opinions.
- Events and ideas are presented in the order they appear in the text, and characters and their motivations are accurately depicted.
- The summary is written in the literary present tense.

A student who meets all of these criteria should receive the equivalent of a 4-point response.

A student who fully meets two or partially meets three of these criteria should receive the equivalent of a 3-point response.

A student who fully meets one or partially meets two of these criteria should receive the equivalent of a 2-point response.

A student who partially meets one of these criteria should receive the equivalent of a 1-point response.

 For grammar practice, see Unit 1 Teaching Resources Book, p. 32.

To create custom assessments using software, use ExamView Assessment Suite.

Literary Present Tense

Students should keep the tense consistent. Watch out for shifts in tense: *Grendel kills a sleeping Geat soldier. But when Beowulf was attacked, he fought back.*

Focus

Write the following two headings on the board:
Discipline Specific and General Academic.

Have students brainstorm a list of words that would be considered academic vocabulary. *(Words will vary.)* Ask volunteers to write their words on the board under the correct category heading. Discuss why these words are considered academic.

Teach

Use a dictionary

When you run across an academic vocabulary word whose meaning you do not know, look it up in a dictionary. Once you know the meaning, try using the word in a sentence of your own to help you remember it.

 For additional vocabulary practice, see Glencoe Interactive Vocabulary CD-ROM.

Learning Objectives

For pages 56–57

In this workshop, you will focus on the following objectives:

Vocabulary: Understanding academic vocabulary.

For a complete list of academic vocabulary words, see pages R81–R83.

Test-Taking Tip

These key academic vocabulary words often appear on standardized tests.

- **Analyze:** to systematically examine all parts of a thing

- **Classify** or **categorize:** to put into groups, based on a common set of characteristics

- **Compare:** to show how things are alike

- **Contrast:** to show how things are different

- **Describe:** to present a sketch or an impression

- **Discuss:** to systematically write about all sides of an issue or event

- **Evaluate:** to make a judgment and support it with evidence

 Literature Online

Vocabulary For more vocabulary practice, go to glencoe.com and enter QuickPass code GLB9817u1.

Vocabulary Workshop

Academic Vocabulary

What Is Academic Vocabulary? Words that are commonly used in academic works—such as textbooks, scholarly books and articles, and tests—are called **academic vocabulary.** Learning academic vocabulary is important because these words will help you read, write, and research in many academic areas. These words will also help you succeed on standardized tests.

Different Kinds of Words Some terms are specific to certain disciplines, or areas of study. For example, the terms *sonnet, persuasive essay,* and *alliteration* pertain to literature. Others—such as *distorted, qualitative,* and *accumulation*—are used in many areas of study. The charts below show more examples of both kinds of words.

Discipline-Specific Words

Discipline	Words
Math	calculus, factorization, parabola
Science	protist, quasar, volcanism
Social studies	annal, oligarchic, vassal

General Academic Vocabulary

abstract	external
intrinsic	investigation
perspective	random
topic	underlying

Academic Words in This Book You will learn about both discipline-specific and general academic vocabulary words in this book. Words that are specific to literature and language arts will most often be introduced and explained in Literary Element and Reading Strategy features before and after you read literature selections. You will encounter more general academic vocabulary words in Academic Vocabulary features that appear after literature selections.

Multiple-Meaning Words Many academic vocabulary words, such as *vehicle,* have more than one meaning. One may be a common meaning that you are already familiar with (*vehicle* in the sense of "a means of transportation"). Another, more academic meaning may be unfamiliar to you (*vehicle* also means "a medium through which something is expressed"). The definitions are often related, however. In the case of *vehicle,* for example, both meanings are based on the underlying

---

Vocabulary Practice

Word Parts To help students understand the meaning of unfamiliar words, remind them to break down the words into their parts.

Word Part 1	Word Part 1 Meaning	Word Part 2	Word Part 2 Meaning	Word	Word Meaning
geo	Greek for earth	*centric*	Latin for center	*geocentric*	earth centered

idea of conveying something from one place to another. The chart below lists additional examples of academic words with more than one meaning.

Word	Definitions	Relationship
extract	*v.* to pull out *n.* a selection or excerpt from a written work	Both definitions involve the taking of one thing out of another.
revolution	*n.* a circular movement around an object or axis *n.* a fundamental change in government	Both definitions involve a turning around and lack of stability.
sphere	*n.* a ball-like geometric figure *n.* the area within which something acts or exists	Both definitions involve an enclosed region.

As you encounter academic vocabulary words in this book, you will master the words through various activities. You'll have a chance to practice these activities in the exercises below.

Practice Follow the instructions to complete each exercise.

1. *Even more exciting than Beowulf's battle against Grendel is his* **subsequent** *battle against the monster's mother.*

   Subsequent is an academic word. More familiar words that are similar in meaning are *later* and *following*. To study this word further, copy and fill in the graphic organizer below. Use a dictionary to help you.

   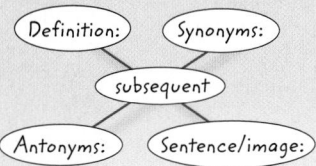

2. *Although Anglo-Saxon technology was primitive, in many ways the Anglo-Saxons' culture was quite* **complex.**

   Complex is a word that has several different meanings. Using context clues, try to figure out the meaning of *complex* in each sentence and explain the difference between the two meanings.

   a. Jennifer seemed to be able to solve the most **complex** math problems with ease.

   b. President Eisenhower warned the nation about the growing power of the military-industrial **complex.**

Assess

1. Possible answer: *subsequent*
   Definition: *occurring or coming later or after*
   Synonyms: *later, following*
   Antonyms: *before, preceding*
   Sentence/image: *Danielle met with her doctor, and then made a subsequent visit to the pharmacy to pick up her prescription.*
2. In **a.**, *complex* means "complicated" or "difficult." In **b.**, *complex* means "associated things or units forming a whole."

Test-Taking Tip

These key academic vocabulary words often appear on standardized tests.

- **Illustrate:** to provide examples or to show with a picture or another graphic

- **Infer:** to read between the lines or to use knowledge or experience to draw conclusions, make generalizations, or form predictions

- **Justify:** to prove or to support a position with specific facts and reasons

- **Predict:** to guess what will happen in the future on the basis of prior events and behaviors

- **State:** to briefly and concisely present information

- **Summarize:** to give a brief overview of the main points of an event or issue

- **Trace:** to present the steps or stages of a process or an event in sequential or chronological order

---

English Learners

DIFFERENTIATED INSTRUCTION

Beginning Students should begin to recognize that some English words have multiple meanings. Give students a list of common words that have more than one meaning, such as dog *(an animal* or *to trail)*, fan *(a cooling device* or *an admirer)*, or speaker *(an audio device* or *a person* giving a speech). Ask students to write sentences using each word's multiple meanings *(The fan made the hot weather bearable. His fan asked for an autograph.)* Encourage students to use a dictionary if needed.

Focus

Bellringer Options

**Selection Focus
Transparency 2**

**Daily Language Practice
Transparency 4**

Or have students name heroes from movies, television shows, graphic novels, and books. Write the names they give on the board. **Ask:** What qualities make these characters heroic? Make a list of the qualities students identify as heroic and discuss which are the most important.

Connect to the Reading Selections

Have volunteers who are familiar with *The Lord of the Rings* describe the various ways good and evil are represented throughout the trilogy.

Comparing Literature
Across Time and Place

Compare Literature About Heroes

Throughout history, writers from different cultures have explored the terrifying intrusion of dark forces into human life and the heroic struggles to destroy those forces. The four writers compared here—the *Beowulf* poet, the creator of *Gilgamesh*, J. R. R. Tolkien, and Gareth Hinds—portray this timeless conflict between good and evil.

COMPARE THE Big Idea **The Epic Warrior**

Epic warriors face life-threatening challenges. Their responses to these challenges define them as heroes and help characterize them as individuals. As you read, ask yourself, How do the *Beowulf* poet, the creator of *Gilgamesh*, J. R. R. Tolkien, and Gareth Hinds portray larger-than-life warriors who struggle against the forces of evil?

COMPARE Heroes' Goals

From Odysseus and Beowulf to Batman and Luke Skywalker, the superhero represents goodness and nobility. Heroes' personal goals motivate them to take risks, pursue adventures, and perform great deeds. As you read, ask yourself, How do these goals not only drive the plot of the story but suggest its **theme,** or the writer's message about life?

COMPARE Cultures

The values of a culture find expression in its art, music, and literature. As you read, ask yourself, How do the heroes in these stories embody the values cherished by their respective cultures?

 Literature Online

Author Search For information about J. R. R. Tolkien and Gareth Hinds, go to glencoe.com and enter QuickPass code GLB9817u1.

Objectives

For pages 58–72

In studying these texts, you will focus on the following objectives:

Literary Study:
Analyzing the epic hero.

Reading:
Connecting to the literature. Interpreting graphic representations of literature.

Selection Skills

Literary Elements
- Symbol (TE pp. 60, 63)
- Similes (TE p. 65)
- Alliteration (TE p. 71)

Comparing Literature

Writing Skills/Grammar
- Retell (TE p. 68)
- Topic Sentences (TE p. 76)

Reading Skills
- Summarize (TE p. 60)
- Connect (TE pp. 62, 64, 73)
- Preview (TE pp. 66, 73)
- Reread (TE p. 72)

Vocabulary Skills
- Word Origins (SE p. 77)
- Archaic Language (TE p. 64)
- Context Clues (TE p. 61)
- Multiple Word Meanings (TE p. 64)

Before You Read

The Death of Humbaba from *Gilgamesh*

Build Background

The epic *Gilgamesh* was lost for more than two thousand years. Only because of an ancient king named Assurbanipal (ä′ sər bä′ nə päl′) and an accidental discovery by a British archeologist do we know it today.

From 668 to 627 B.C., Assurbanipal reigned over the ancient empire of Assyria. During his reign, Assurbanipal sent men out to find ancient texts at such historical sites of learning as Babylon, Uruk, and Nippur. He then asked that these texts be translated into Akkadian Semitic, the language of his empire. *Gilgamesh* was one of the works found and was transcribed onto clay tablets, which were then stored in Assurbanipal's library at Nineveh.

Thousands of years later, in 1839, a British traveler named Austen Henry Layard, on his way to Ceylon (today known as Sri Lanka), stopped to investigate some mounds in Mesopotamia. What was intended as a brief delay became the work of years for Layard, as the mounds eventually proved to be the buried library of Assurbanipal. Here, among nearly twenty-five thousand broken tablets, Layard unearthed the text of *Gilgamesh.*

Who Was Gilgamesh? Gilgamesh was an actual king who lived sometime between 2800 and 2500 B.C. and reigned over the ancient Sumerian city-state of Uruk (ōō′ rook), located in what is now south-eastern Iraq. During the first several hundred years following Gilgamesh's death, people recited tales of his adventures as separate stories. Then, sometime between 2000 and 1600 B.C., storytellers began to string these tales together, forming the work that is now known as *Gilgamesh.* The following selection is taken from that epic.

Context At the point in the epic in which the tale reprinted here begins, Gilgamesh's ambition to build great walls and temples to glorify his name has driven him to the forest for building materials. There, he and his friend, Enkidu, plan to chop down a great cedar tree. However, they both believe that these precious trees are guarded by supernatural forces that will attempt to block their efforts—the greatest of these forces being Humbaba, a giant who serves the gods and protects the woods with his own physical strength and magical powers. Therefore, Gilgamesh has asked the sun-god Shamash for protection and has promised, in return, to build a great temple for him.

Seventh century B.C. cuneiform tablet.

Before You Read

Focus

Summary

Gilgamesh and his friend Enkidu begin to chop down the cedar. Immediately, Humbaba attacks them. Badly wounded, Enkidu manages to knock Humbaba down. The monster pleads for mercy. Enkidu reminds Gilgamesh that Humbaba cannot be trusted, and Gilgamesh cuts off the monster's head

English Learners

DIFFERENTIATED INSTRUCTION

Beginning Before reading, explain that the prefix *un–* means "not" and the suffix *–less* means "not having." Ask what the words "pitiless" and "unable" mean.

Intermediate Have students think of movies in which there are heroes and villains, such as *Lord of the Rings, Star Wars,* or *Superman.* Have them describe the clothing that the heroes and villains wear.

Teach

Literary Element   1

Symbol   Ask: How does the writer describe Humbaba's appearance? *(He has "a great head…like a water buffalo's," his legs are "huge and clumsy," and he is "monstrous in his contortion…") What might his appearance symbolize? (His terrible, merciless character)*

View the Art ★

Ask: Which characters in the story might be represented by the sculpture? *(The hero in the sculpture could be compared to Gilgamesh; the lion could represent Humbaba.)*

For an audio recording of this selection, use Listening Library Audio CD-ROM.

Reading Practice

SMALL GROUP SPIRAL REVIEW Summarize Have volunteers read lines 1 through 34 to the class. Have small groups summarize the beginning of the poem. When the groups are done, ask volunteers to share their groups' summary

statements. Discuss the qualities of a good summary. Ask students how they think summarizing can aid reading comprehension.

---

from Gilgamesh
The Death of Humbaba

Retold by Herbert Mason

At dawn Gilgamesh raised his ax
And struck at the great cedar.
When Humbaba heard the sound of falling trees,
He hurried down the path that they had seen
5 But only he had traveled. Gilgamesh felt weak
At the sound of Humbaba's footsteps and called to Shamash
Saying, I have followed you in the way decreed;
Why am I abandoned now? Suddenly the winds
Sprang up. They saw the great head of Humbaba
10 Like a water buffalo's bellowing down the path,
His huge and clumsy legs, his flailing arms
Thrashing at phantoms in his precious trees.
His single stroke could cut a cedar down
And leave no mark on him. His shoulders,
15 Like a porter's under building stones,
Were permanently bent by what he bore;
He was the slave who did the work for gods
But whom the gods would never notice.
Monstrous in his contortion, he aroused
20 The two almost to pity.
But pity was the thing that might have killed.
It made them pause just long enough to show
How pitiless he was to them. Gilgamesh in horror saw
Him strike the back of Enkidu and beat him to the ground
25 Until he thought his friend was crushed to death.
He stood still watching as the monster leaned to make
His final strike against his friend, unable
To move to help him, and then Enkidu slid
Along the ground like a ram making its final lunge
30 On wounded knees. Humbaba fell and seemed
To crack the ground itself in two, and Gilgamesh, **2**
As if this fall had snapped him from his daze,

Statue of a Hero Taming a Lion.
722–705 B.C. From the palace of Sargon II, King of Assur in Khorsabad. Height: 445 cm. Louvre Museum, Département des Antiquités Orientales, Paris. ★

The Demon Humbaba.
1800 B.C., Sippar.

Returned to life
And stood over Humbaba with his ax
35 Raised high above his head watching the monster plead
In strangled sobs and desperate appeals
The way the sea contorts under a violent squall.[1]
I'll serve you as I served the gods, Humbaba said;
I'll build you houses from their sacred trees.

40 Enkidu feared his friend was weakening
And called out: Gilgamesh! Don't trust him!
As if there were some hunger in himself
That Gilgamesh was feeling
That turned him momentarily to yearn
45 For someone who would serve, he paused;
And then he raised his ax up higher
And swung it in a perfect arc **3**
Into Humbaba's neck. He reached out
To touch the wounded shoulder of his friend,

50 And late that night he reached again
To see if he was yet asleep, but there was only
Quiet breathing. The stars against the midnight sky
Were sparkling like mica[2] in a riverbed. **4**
In the slight breeze
55 The head of Humbaba was swinging from a tree.

---

1. A *squall* is a sudden, violent storm.
2. *Mica* is a mineral that sparkles in the light.

Quickwrite

In what ways is Gilgamesh a heroic character? What qualities make him seem to be an ordinary human being? Write a brief essay exploring his character.

GILGAMESH **61**

Comparing Literature

Teach

The Big Idea 2

The Epic Warrior Ask: What words or phrases describe Humbaba's strength? *(single stroke could cut a cedar down; beat him to the ground; crack the ground itself in two)* **Ask:** Why does a hero need such a strong opponent? *(to show how strong the hero is; to show that no else could conquer the enemy)*

Reading Strategy 3

Make Inferences Ask: What do you think would have happened if Gilgamesh had spared Humbaba's life? *(It is likely that Humbaba would have continued his attack on the two heroes.)* What evidence in the text supports your inference? *(Enkidu tells Gilgamesh not to trust Humbaba.)*

Vocabulary 4

Context Clues Ask: Which words and phrases suggest the meaning of mica? *(Stars; sparkling; in a riverbed)*

English Learners

DIFFERENTIATED INSTRUCTION

Intermediate Remind students that in English, quotation marks usually enclose a direct quotation. Explain that this translation does not follow that convention.

Write on the board:

And called out: Gilgamesh! Don't trust him!

Have students rewrite the quotation, using quotation marks and proper punctuation. *(And called out, "Gilgamesh! Don't trust him!")* Then have students find other lines in the poem where quotation marks might be used.

Before You Read

Focus

Summary

Théoden and his knights engage and defeat the main force of the Haradrim. As the Haradrim flee, the Lord of the Nazgûl swoops down on his foul flying steed. Dernhelm, who stands between Théoden and his attacker, reveals herself to be Éowyn, a woman, and kills the flying steed. Wounded, Éowyn waits for the killing blow. From behind, Merry cuts the Nazgûl Lord's knee, making him fall, and Éowyn kills him.

Teach

Literary History ☆

Children's Literature Tolkien was not the first writer to turn children's stories into literature. *The Adventures of Winnie the Pooh* began as stories A. A. Milne told his son, Christopher Robin Milne. L. Frank Baum entertained the neighborhood children by telling them tales of the land of Oz. Only later did he write them down.

Reading Practice

SPIRAL REVIEW **Connect** Tell students that this selection describes characters in life-threatening situations.
Ask: What do you think it takes for someone to act bravely when in danger? Is a brave person always unafraid? Or does a brave person feel fear but act despite that fear? Encourage students to relate events in their own lives to events in the narrative. Remind them that although they are reading fantasy, many feelings and emotions expressed by the characters are common responses to dramatic situations.

Before You Read
from *The Battle of the Pelennor Fields*
from *The Lord of the Rings: The Return of the King*

Build Background

While grading papers in 1928, J. R. R. Tolkien (1892–1973) came across a page left blank by a student. On this blank page, Tolkien scribbled, "In a hole in the ground there lived a hobbit." From that sentence evolved his vastly popular children's fantasy *The Hobbit*. This novel in turn helped Tolkien crystallize his musings about an imaginary realm—Middle Earth, later the setting for the most influential body of fantasy writing in the twentieth century.

Born in South Africa, John Ronald Reuel Tolkien moved with his family to England at the age of four after his father's death. A devout Roman Catholic, like his mother, Tolkien served in World War I and afterward became a professor of English language and literature at Oxford University. His academic achievements included an edition of *Sir Gawain and the Green Knight* and an acclaimed lecture, "*Beowulf*: The Monsters and the Critics," that greatly influenced subsequent studies of that epic.

An Imaginary World In his spare time, Tolkien developed an intricate fictional world, complete with its own languages, history, geography, and characters—including dwarves and elves. He created some of his early fantasy writing to entertain his four children. Included in these writings is *The Hobbit*, which was published in 1937. As an extension of this popular work, Tolkien continued developing the story of Middle Earth into *The Lord of the Rings,* published seventeen years later. Because of its length, this work was originally divided into three volumes: *The Fellowship of the Ring, The Two Towers,* and *The Return of the King.* Into this modern fantasy epic, Tolkien wove elements drawn from the heroic traditions of the Germanic and Celtic peoples.

In the United States, *The Lord of the Rings* became a cult classic on college campuses when it was published in paperback in 1965. In the late 1990s, New Zealand–born film director Peter Jackson began adapting Tolkien's work in the form of a trilogy for the screen. Jackson's film version of *The Lord of the Rings: The Return of the King* won eleven Oscars, including Best Picture, in 2004.

Context At the point in *The Lord of the Rings* in which this episode occurs, the conflict between the forces of good and evil is nearing its climax. The Dark Lord, Sauron, has sent his vast armies to besiege the city of Minas Tirith. The leader of Sauron's forces is the Lord of the Nazgûl, a spectral figure astride a huge, foul, dragonlike steed. Among those defending the city are the Rohirrim, the mounted warriors of the Mark of Rohan, led by their aged king, Théoden. Unknown to Théoden, his beloved niece, Éowyn, disguised as the warrior Dernhelm, has accompanied his troops. With her is Merry, a hobbit.

LOG ON **Literature** Online

Author Search For more about J. R. R. Tolkien, go to glencoe.com and enter QuickPass code GLB9817u1.

from The Battle of the Pelennor Fields

J. R. R. Tolkien

Théoden King of the Mark had reached the road from the Gate to the River, and he turned towards the City that was now less than a mile distant. He slackened his speed a little, seeking new foes, and his knights came about him, and Dernhelm was with them. Ahead nearer the walls Elfhelm's[1] men were among the siege-engines, hewing, slaying, driving their foes into the fire-pits. Well nigh all the northern half of the Pelennor[2] was overrun, and there camps were blazing, orcs[3] were flying towards the River like herds before the hunters; and the Rohirrim went hither and thither at their will. But they had not yet overthrown the siege, nor won the Gate. Many foes stood before it, and on the further half of the plain were other hosts still unfought. Southward beyond the road lay the main force of the Haradrim,[4] and there their horsemen were gathered about the standard[5] of their chieftain. And he looked out, and in the growing light he saw the banner of the king, and that it was far ahead of the battle with few men about it. Then he was filled with a red wrath and shouted aloud, and displaying his standard, black serpent upon scarlet, he came against the white horse and the green with great press of men; and the drawing of the scimitars of the Southrons was like a glitter of stars.

1

Then Théoden was aware of him, and would not wait for his onset, but crying to Snowmane[6] he charged headlong to greet him. Great was the clash of their meeting. But the white fury of the Northmen burned the hotter, and more skilled was their knighthood with long spears and bitter. Fewer were they but they clove through the Southrons like a fire-bolt in a forest. Right through the press drove Théoden Thengel's son, and his spear was shivered as he threw down their chieftain. Out swept his sword, and he spurred to the standard, hewed[7]

2

---

1. *Elfhelm* is one of the Rohirrim.
2. The *Pelennor* is the region immediately around Minas Tirith.
3. *Orcs* are troll-like beings who form one of the principal groups serving the Dark Lord.
4. The *Haradrim* are the men of Harad, a region to the south, who serve Sauron. They are also known as *Southrons*.

---

5. A *standard* is a banner or emblem.
6. *Snowmane* is Théoden's horse.
7. *Hewed* means "cut."

J. R. R. TOLKIEN **63**

Comparing Literature

Teach

Literary Element   1

Symbol Tell students that Tolkien uses each king's standard to symbolize the king and his forces. **Ask:** In the description of the start of the attack what does "the white horse and the green" mean? *(Théoden's standard shows a white horse on a green field.)*

The Big Idea   2

The Epic Warrior   **Ask:** What verbs does Tolkien use to describe Theoden's heroic actions as he confronts the chieftain of the Southrons? *(aware; not wait; charged; drove; threw; spurred; hewed)*

Readability Scores

Dale-Chall: 8.5
DRP: 58
Lexile: 900

Approaching Level

DIFFERENTIATED INSTRUCTION

 SMALL GROUP

Emerging Some students may have trouble following the action because of the proper nouns in the selection. Have students draw a chart with three columns labeled "Good Guys," "Bad Guys," and "Places." Students should scan the selection before reading it. As they scan, they should fill in the chart with the proper nouns they encounter. Suggest they work in groups and use context clues and the footnotes to decide where to place each entry.

Established Ask students to find context clues that help define the word "standard." *(banner of the king; displaying his standard; black serpent upon scarlet)* **Ask:** What other word could you use to mean "standard"? *(flag)*

Comparing Literature

Teach

Vocabulary   1

Multiple Word Meanings

Ask: What does it mean to have a mantle in your home? *(It means that there is a shelf over a fireplace.)* If the Lord of the Nazgûl is "black-mantled," what is a mantle? *(It is a cloak or robe.)* What words help you figure out what mantle means? *("A crown of steel he bore, but between rim and robe . . .")*

Reading Strategy   2

Connect Ask: Is the Lord of the Nazgûl human? What does his face look like? *(No; his face is invisible, except for glowing eyes.)*

ADVANCED Ask: How is this tradition of nonhuman villains carried through in 21st-century entertainment? *(In many video games, the object is to destroy aliens, zombies, monsters, or some other nonhuman creatures.)*

Writer's Technique ☆

Flashback Here, Tolkien reveals the history of the demonic steed. A narrative passage set in an earlier time that interrupts the chronological order of the rest of a story is called a flashback.

staff and bearer; and the black serpent foundered.[8] Then all that was left unslain of their cavalry turned and fled far away.

But lo! suddenly in the midst of the glory of the king his golden shield was dimmed. The new morning was blotted from the sky. Dark fell about him. Horses reared and screamed. Men cast from the saddle lay groveling on the ground. "To me! To me!" cried Théoden. "Up, Eorlingas![9] Fear no darkness!" But Snowmane wild with terror stood up on high, fighting with the air, and then with a great scream he crashed upon his side: a black dart had pierced him. The king fell beneath him.

The great shadow descended like a falling cloud. And behold! it was a winged creature: if bird, then greater than all other birds, and it was naked, and neither quill nor feather did it bear, and its vast pinions[10] were as webs of hide between horned fingers; and it stank. A creature of an older world maybe it was, whose kind, lingering in forgotten mountains cold beneath the Moon, outstayed their day, and in hideous eyrie[11] bred this last untimely brood, apt to evil. And the Dark Lord took it, and nursed it with fell[12] meats, until it grew beyond the measure of all other things that fly; and he gave it to his servant to be his steed. Down, down it came, and then, folding its fingered webs, it gave a croaking cry, and settled upon the body of Snowmane, digging in its claws, stooping its long naked neck.

1 Upon it sat a shape, black-mantled, huge and threatening. A crown of steel he bore, but between rim and robe naught was there to see, **2** save only a deadly gleam of eyes: the Lord of the Nazgûl. To the air he had returned, summoning his steed ere the darkness failed, and now he was come again, bringing ruin, turning hope to despair, and victory to death. A great black mace[13] he wielded.

---

8. *Foundered* means "fell."
9. The *Eorlingas* are the men of Rohan, whose ancestor was Eorl.
10. *Pinions* means "wings."
11. *Eyrie* means "nest."
12. *Fell* means "deadly."
13. A *mace* is a war-club.

But Théoden was not utterly forsaken. The knights of his house lay slain about him, or else mastered by the madness of their steeds were borne far away. Yet one stood there still: Dernhelm the young, faithful beyond fear; and he wept, for he had loved his lord as a father. Right through the charge Merry had been borne unharmed behind him, until the Shadow came; and then Windfola[14] had thrown them in his terror, and now ran wild upon the plain. Merry crawled on all fours like a dazed beast, and such a horror was on him that he was blind and sick.

"King's man! King's man!" his heart cried within him. "You must stay by him. As a father you shall be to me, you said." But his will made no answer, and his body shook. He dared not open his eyes or look up.

Then out of the blackness in his mind he thought that he heard Dernhelm speaking; yet now the voice seemed strange, recalling some other voice that he had known.

"Begone, foul dwimmerlaik, lord of carrion![15] Leave the dead in peace!"

A cold voice answered: "Come not between the Nazgûl and his prey! Or he will not slay thee in thy turn. He will bear thee away to the houses of lamentation, beyond all darkness, where thy flesh shall be devoured, and thy shriveled mind be left naked to the Lidless Eye."

A sword rang as it was drawn. "Do what you will; but I will hinder it, if I may."

"Hinder me? Thou fool. No living man may hinder me!"

Then Merry heard of all sounds in that hour the strangest. It seemed that Dernhelm laughed, and the clear voice was like the ring of steel. "But no living man am I! You look upon a woman. Éowyn I am, Éomund's daughter. You stand between me and my lord and kin. Begone, if you be not deathless! For living or dark undead, I will smite you, if you touch him."

The winged creature screamed at her, but the Ringwraith made no answer, and was silent, as if in sudden doubt. Very amazement for a moment conquered Merry's fear. He opened his eyes and the blackness was lifted from them.

---

14. *Windfola* is Dernhelm's horse.
15. *Carrion* refers to the flesh of dead people and animals.

Vocabulary Practice

 SPIRAL REVIEW Heightened/Archaic Language Tell students that Tolkien wrote *The Lord of the Rings* in a heightened, poetic style. Many of the words he uses are not common now and were not common in England during the 1930s and 1940s. Have students go through the selection and identify unusual words that are not defined in the footnotes or words used in an unusual way. Examples on this page include *behold, mantled, lamentation, untimely,* and *begone.* Have students suggest definitions for each word, using a dictionary, if necessary.

There some paces from him sat the great beast, and all seemed dark about it, and above it loomed the Nazgûl Lord like a shadow of despair. A little to the left facing them stood she whom he had called Dernhelm. But the helm of her secrecy had fallen from her, and her bright hair, released from its bonds, gleamed with pale gold upon her shoulders. Her eyes grey as the sea were hard and fell, and yet tears were on her cheek. A sword was in her hand, and she raised her shield against the horror of her enemy's eyes.

Éowyn it was, and Dernhelm also. For into Merry's mind flashed the memory of the face that he saw at the riding from Dunharrow: the face of one that goes seeking death, having no hope. Pity filled his heart and great wonder, and suddenly the slow-kindled courage of his race awoke. He clenched his hand. She should not die, so fair, so desperate! At least she should not die alone, unaided.

The face of their enemy was not turned towards him, but still he hardly dared to move, dreading lest the deadly eyes should fall on him. Slowly, slowly he began to crawl aside; but the Black Captain, in doubt and malice intent upon the woman before him, heeded him no more than a worm in the mud.

Suddenly the great beast beat its hideous wings, and the wind of them was foul. Again it leaped into the air, and then swiftly fell down upon Éowyn, shrieking, striking with beak and claw.

Still she did not blench:[16] maiden of the Rohirrim, child of kings, slender but as a steel-blade, fair but terrible. A swift stroke she dealt, skilled and deadly. The outstretched neck she clove asunder,[17] and the hewn head fell like a stone. Backward she sprang as the huge shape crashed to ruin, vast wings outspread, crumpled on the earth; and with its fall the shadow passed away. A light fell about her, and her hair shone in the sunrise.

Out of the wreck rose the Black Rider, tall and threatening, towering above her. With a cry of hatred that stung the very ears like venom he let fall his mace. Her shield was shivered in many pieces, and her arm was broken; she stumbled to her knees. He bent over her like a cloud, and his eyes glittered; he raised his mace to kill.

But suddenly he too stumbled forward with a cry of bitter pain, and his stroke went wide, driving into the ground. Merry's sword had stabbed him from behind, shearing through the black mantle, and passing up beneath the hauberk[18] had pierced the sinew behind his mighty knee.

"Éowyn! Éowyn!" cried Merry. Then tottering, struggling up, with her last strength she drove her sword between crown and mantle, as the great shoulders bowed before her. The sword broke sparkling into many shards. The crown rolled away with a clang. Éowyn fell forward upon her fallen foe. But lo! the mantle and hauberk were empty. Shapeless they lay now on the ground, torn and tumbled; and a cry went up into the shuddering air, and faded to a shrill wailing, passing with the wind, a voice bodiless and thin that died, and was swallowed up, and was never heard again in that age of this world.

💬 Discussion Starter

What background knowledge of *The Lord of the Rings* did you bring to your reading of this selection? How would you account for the enduring popularity of Tolkien's epic?

---

16. *Blench* means "turn white, as with fear."
17. *Asunder* means "in half."

18. A *hauberk* is a long coat of chain armor.

J. R. R. TOLKIEN **65**

English Learners

DIFFERENTIATED INSTRUCTION

Intermediate Remind students that in English, the verb usually follows the subject. Point out examples such as "The winged creature screamed." Have students look for examples of inverted order in which the verb precedes the subject. Ask students to rewrite each sentence so that the verb follows the subject.

Teach

Literary Element   3

Similes Remind students that a simile is a figure of speech that uses the words *like* or *as* to compare two seemingly unlike things. **Ask:** What similes can you find on this page? (*"like a shadow of despair," "grey as the sea," "slender but as a steel blade," "like a stone," "like venom," "like a cloud"*)

(ENGLISH LEARNERS) Check to make sure that English Learners understand that *to compare* is to show how two things are similar. As an example, point out that "slender but as a steel blade" compares Éowyn to the blade of a sword, showing that she is slender but strong.

Assess

Discussion Starter

Students' discussions should address their responses to both the film adaptation (if they have seen it) and the selection from the novel. Challenge students to identify the particular strengths and methods of characterization found in each version. Tolkien's work remains popular for many reasons: it tells a story of heroism filled with exciting adventures and memorable characters.

Focus

Summary

This selection depicts scenes from *Beowulf*. The Danish watcher leads the Geats to Herot. There, Beowulf asks Hrothgar for permission to fight Grendel, using only his bare hands. He tells Hrothgar what to do with his possessions should he lose.

Teach

Literary History ☆

Comic Books Comic books have traditionally been aimed at children and teens, but comic books for older readers have become more common. Japanese comic books, called *manga*, were developed after World War II. The term *graphic novel* came into widespread use in the United States in the 1970s and connotes comic books aimed at adults.

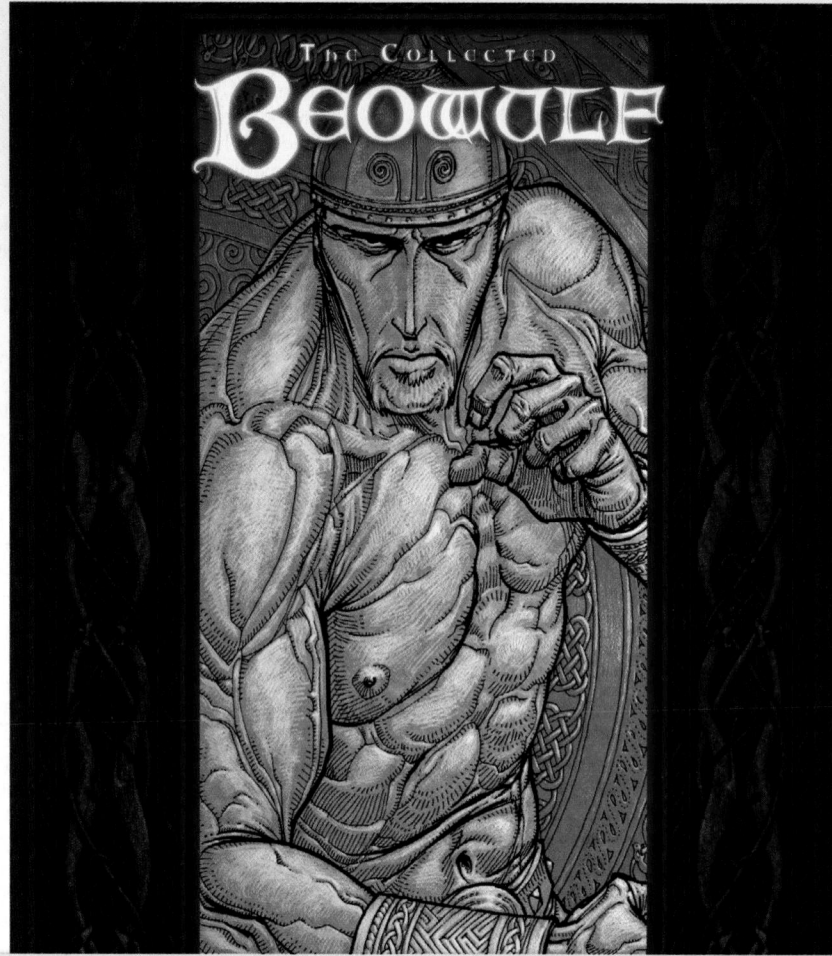

Build Background

☆ In a recent interview, Gareth Hinds explained his choice of *Beowulf* as a subject for a graphic novel by saying that he "wanted to do a superhero book, without the modern superhero conventions." For the text of his graphic novel, Hinds used a 1910 translation of *Beowulf* by Francis Gummere, which he felt provides a sense, "to the greatest extent possible in modern English, that you were actually reading the Old English poem." The excerpt you are about to read shows Beowulf's arrival in Denmark.

66 UNIT 1 THE ANGLO-SAXON PERIOD AND THE MIDDLE AGES

Reading Practice

SPIRAL REVIEW **Preview** Have students look through the selection, focusing on the pictures and not the words (which should be easy, given the typeface). Discuss which section of *Beowulf* they think is being depicted. Then discuss whether a work as long as *Beowulf* can be faithfully adapted into a graphic novel. **Ask:** Would parts of the story have to be left out? Do you think this process is similar to the process of turning a novel into a movie? If something is left out, is the story still as valuable as the original?

GARETH HINDS **67**

Comparing Literature

Teach

Big Idea | 1

The Epic Warrior Ask: Is Beowulf shown on this page? If so, where? *(Yes; he is the man standing at the front of the boat in the last panel.)* What does Hinds do to let us know he is a hero? *(Beowulf is pictured from below, which makes him appear big. His posture conveys certitude. The other men on the boat all look alike; only Beowulf stands out.)*

Reading Strategy | 2

Establish Sequence Ask: In what direction do we read a line of English text? *(from left to right)* In what direction do we read a page of English text? *(from top to bottom)* Tell students that an American graphic novel is usually read from left to right and top to bottom. (*Manga* pages, like the Japanese language, are often read from top to bottom first.) Ask a volunteer to name the order in which these panels should be read. *(top panel, middle panel, bottom left panel, bottom right panel)*

English Learners

DIFFERENTIATED INSTRUCTION

Intermediate English learners may come from countries with strong comic and graphic traditions. China, Korea, India, and many Latin American countries have large comic book publishing industries. Ask students to describe what comic books in their home country are like and how they compare with the selection from *Beowulf*.

Comparing Literature

Cultural History ☆

Vikings Here Hrothgar is depicted wearing a horned Viking helmet. Today's popular impression of a Viking probably consists of two elements: a ship with a dragon carved on the front and a horned helmet. The truth is that Vikings rarely, if ever, wore helmets with horns on them. The use of horned helmets stretches back through many ancient civilizations. They have been found in sites associated with pre-Viking Scandinavia and elsewhere in Europe. These helmets did not have horns from a cow or another animal, as shown here. Some of these helmets had stylized metal horns, snakes, and dragons, but these helmets were purely ceremonial and were worn only by priests. The pre-Viking era may be appropriate for *Beowulf*. However, Hrothgar was not a priest, and there is no religious ceremony taking place here, so it is unlikely anyone would be wearing a horned helmet.

Writing Practice

 **Retell**

SPIRAL REVIEW Discuss the contents of this page with students. Ask them to describe what happens and what mood is conveyed. Discuss Hinds's use of light and shadow, as well as viewing angle. **Ask:** Which character is this page really about? *(Beowulf)* Is he shown on the page? *(no)* Have students rewrite this page in text-only format. Tell them to try to capture the mood and feeling of the page, and not just the event that it depicts.

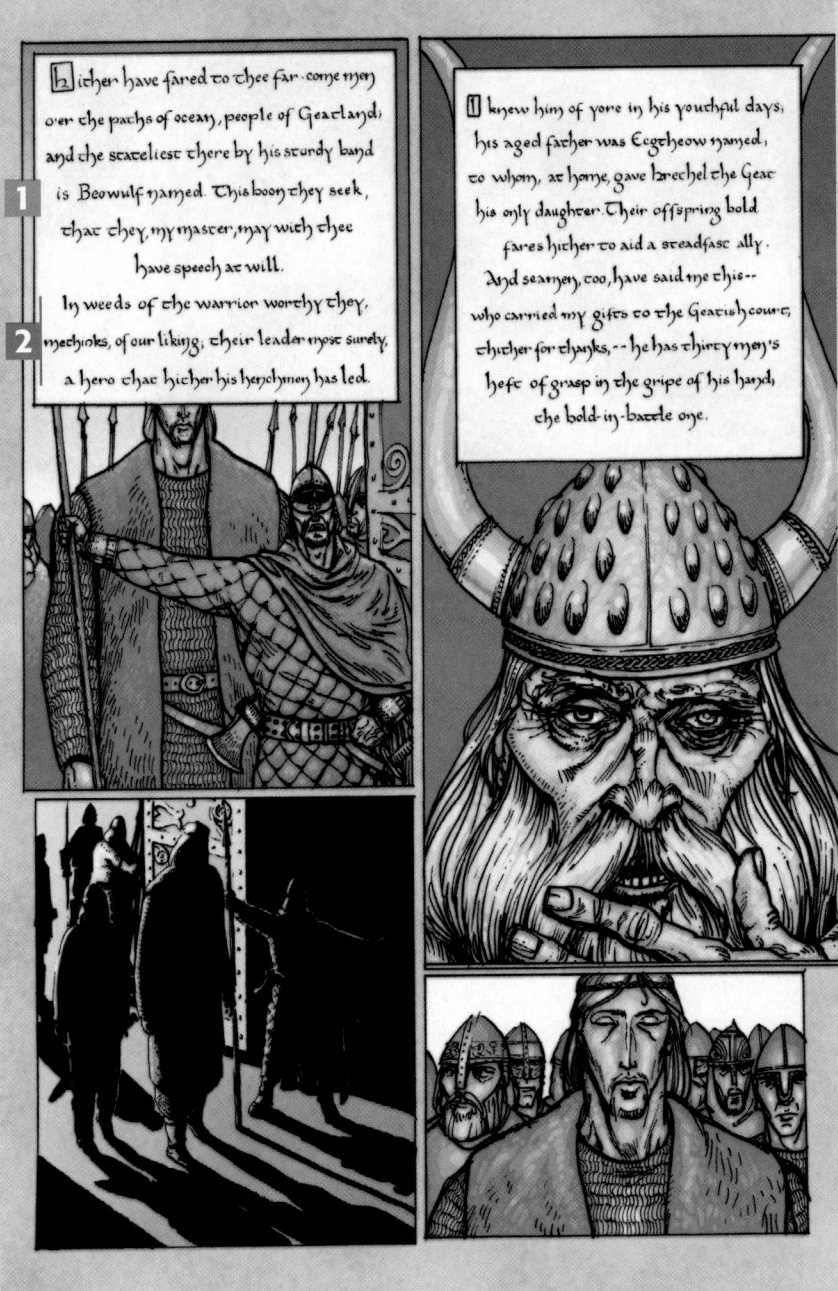

Hither have fared to thee far-come men
o'er the paths of ocean, people of Geatland;
and the stateliest there by his sturdy band
is Beowulf named. This boon they seek,
that they, my master, may with thee
have speech at will.
In weeds of the warrior worthy they,
methinks, of our liking, their leader most surely,
a hero that hither his henchmen has led.

I knew him of yore in his youthful days;
his aged father was Ecgtheow named,
to whom, at home, gave Hrethel the Geat
his only daughter. Their offspring bold
fares hither to aid a steadfast ally.
And seamen, too, have said me this,—
who carried my gifts to the Geatish court,
thither for thanks,—he has thirty men's
heft of grasp in the gripe of his hand,
the bold-in-battle one.

GARETH HINDS **69**

Comparing Literature

Teach

Vocabulary 1

Make a Vocabulary File If necessary, tell students that boon means "favor." **Ask:** How would you rephrase this sentence in your own words? *(Students may suggest something such as, "They ask if you will honor and speak with them.")* Students will continue to encounter words they don't understand. To aid their studying, have students keep a list of each word and its meaning.

Reading Strategy 2

Invert Word Order Point out to students that many of the sentences in this translation have an unusual word order. Write this sentence on the board: "In weeds of the warrior worthy they, methinks, of our liking." Below it, write: In weeds of the warrior, methinks they are worthy of our liking. **Ask:** How would you rewrite the rest of the sentence to change the word order: "their leader, most surely, a hero that hither his henchmen has lead"? *(most surely their leader, a hero who has led his henchmen hither [here])*

Approaching Level

DIFFERENTIATED INSTRUCTION

Emerging Some students may find it difficult to read this text smoothly the first time through. This is not related to ability or fluency, but rather to pattern recognition skills. Some of the letters—most noticeably *h*, *m*, and *n*—are shaped very differ- ently from those that students are used to seeing. You may want to suggest that students copy the text into their notebooks in their own handwriting before reading the selection.

Comparing Literature

Teach

Literary Element   1

Create Words Point out the word *Grendel-deeds*. **Ask:** What does this word mean? *(deeds performed by Grendel)* Is it a real word? *(no)* Are there any other improvised words on this page? *(Shining-Danes; friend-of-the-folk)*

[ADVANCED] Challenge students to take a paragraph from a modern text and replace one or more groups of words with new words such as those mentioned here.

Vocabulary   2

Decode Alternative Spellings Point out the word used to describe Hrothgar here. If no one knows, say the word aloud. *(sovran)* **Ask:** What other word does it sound like? *(sovereign)* Explain that *sovran* is an alternative spelling of *sovereign*, which means "leader" or "ruler."

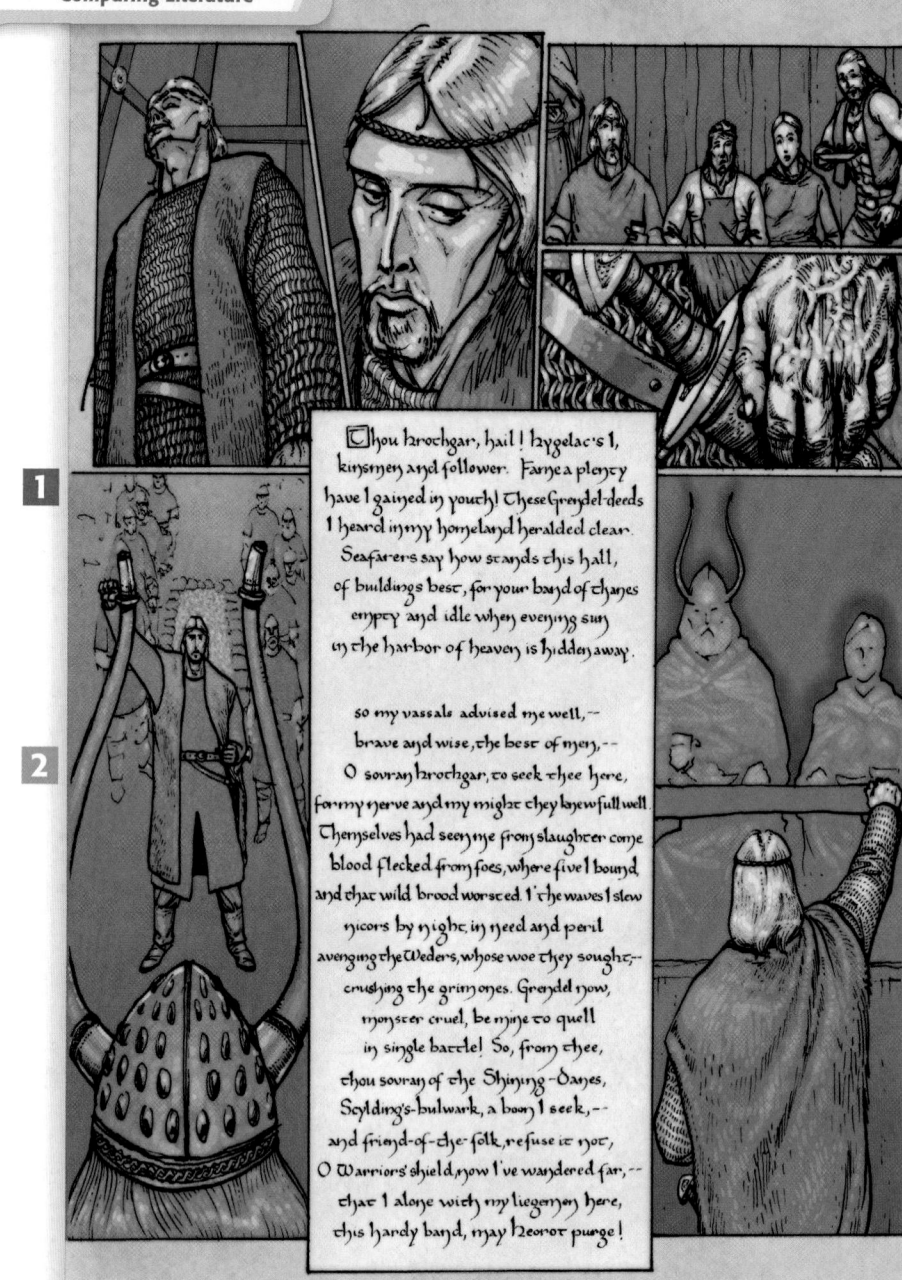

1
2

Thou hrothgar, hail! hygelac's l,
kinsmen and follower. Fame a plenty
have l gained in youth! These Grendel-deeds
l heard in my homeland heralded clear.
Seafarers say how stands this hall,
of buildings best, for your band of thanes
empty and idle when evening sun
in the harbor of heaven is hidden away.

so my vassals advised me well,—
brave and wise, the best of men,—
O sovran hrothgar, to seek thee here,
for my nerve and my might they knew full well
Themselves had seen me from slaughter come
blood flecked from foes, where five l bound
and that wild brood worsted. I' the waves l slew
nicors by night, in need and peril
avenging the Weders, whose woe they sought,—
crushing the grim ones. Grendel now,
monster cruel, be mine to quell
in single battle! So, from thee,
thou sovran of the Shining-Danes,
Scylding's-bulwark, a boon l seek,—
and friend-of-the-folk, refuse it not,
O Warriors' shield, now l've wandered far,—
that l alone with my liegemen here,
this hardy band, may heorot purge!

Research Practice

SPIRAL REVIEW **Confirm Information** Discuss with students what pieces of information are presented in these illustrations, such as the type of clothing and armor people are wearing, the size and scale of Herot, and the design of Beowulf's sword, belt, and battle axe. Challenge students to research Scandinavian artifacts from A.D. 600–1100 to determine the accuracy of these illustrations.

Comparing Literature

Teach

Discussion Starter

Students may discuss the perspective Hinds shows in depicting Beowulf traveling across the sea to Geatland and the sequence of panels in the selection. Encourage students to discuss how Hinds's graphic novel adaptation of *Beowulf* impacts their understanding of the epic.

Literary Element | 3

Alliteration Tell students that the original, Old English version of *Beowulf* is noted for its alliteration.
Ask: What examples of alliteration can you find in the top text box? Have students read their suggested passages aloud. (*"More I hear, that the <u>m</u>onster dire, in his wanton <u>m</u>ood"; "scorn <u>b</u>and or <u>b</u>uckler to <u>b</u>ear in the fight"; "I <u>f</u>ront the <u>f</u>iend and <u>f</u>ight for life, <u>f</u>oe against <u>f</u>oe. Then <u>f</u>aith be his . . ."*)

💬 **Discussion Starter**

Comic books use various conventions, such as panels, to organize narrative. Discuss how Hinds uses this graphic convention to effectively present part of the story of Beowulf.

English Learners

DIFFERENTIATED INSTRUCTION

Intermediate The section of text includes many archaic words, in part to allow alliteration. You may want to write this list of definitions of the board: dire—causing horror; recks—cares about; brand—sword; buckler—a small, round shield; gripe—grasp, or the power to grab and hold; front—confront; doom—judgment.

Have students work in small groups to list other archaic words used in the selection. Have them use a dictionary to find the meanings of these words.

Assess

Compare the Big Idea

Critique student discussions on these criteria. Do students

- identify the challenges and compare the qualities displayed by the epic warriors?
- support their views about which warrior is most heroic?
- Describe what characteristics the warriors have in common?

Compare Heroes' Goals

1. Beowulf is motivated to help his people by destroying Grendel; Gilgamesh is motivated to save his wounded friend's life; Éowyn is motivated to protect her dead king's body from desecration; in the graphic novel, Beowulf wants to rid Herot of Grendel.

2. Beowulf also wants to gain fame. Gilgamesh must resist Humbaba's plea. Éowyn wants to show her courage and loyalty as a warrior and a descendant of mighty kings. In the graphic novel, Beowulf wants to extend his fame, be fair in his fight with Grendel, and submit himself to the will of God.

Compare Cultures

Students' displays should provide visuals and information about one of the cultures represented in this feature

 To create custom assessments using software, use ExamView Assessment Suite.

Wrap-Up: Comparing Literature

Across Time and Place

- from *Beowulf*
- *The Death of Humbaba,* from *Gilgamesh*
- *The Battle of the Pellenor Fields,* from *The Lord of the Rings: The Return of the King* by J. R. R. Tolkien
- from *The Collected Beowulf* by Gareth Hinds

COMPARE THE Big Idea The Epic Warrior

Partner Activity These four selections present similar views of the epic warrior. With a partner, discuss the particular challenges faced by each epic warrior as you answer the following questions.

1. What are the specific challenges faced by Beowulf, Gilgamesh, and Éowyn in the selections?

2. Which warrior strikes you as the most heroic in his or her response to the challenges?

3. What heroic characteristics do the epic warriors in these selections have in common?

COMPARE Heroes' Goals

Group Discussion With a small group of classmates, compare the personal goals of Beowulf (in the epic and the graphic novel), Gilgamesh, and Éowyn. Discuss the following questions:

1. Why does each hero put himself or herself at risk?

2. What other motives surface during the course of each hero's struggle?

COMPARE Cultures

Visual Display Create a visual display, such as a chart or a collage, to accompany one of these selections. In your display, present images that depict the culture in the selection you chose. Use the Internet and library materials as research sources.

 Literature Online

Selection Resources For Selection Quizzes, eFlashcards, and Reading-Writing Connection activities, go to glencoe.com and enter QuickPass code GLB9817u1.

Reading Practice

SPIRAL REVIEW **Reread** Tell students that rereading a selection such as the excerpt from *The Lord of the Rings* can help them clarify events in the plot, identify rhetorical devices, and appreciate the author's diction. Write the following headings on the board and have students copy them onto a sheet of paper.

Action

Rhetorical Devices

Unusual Words

Have them add items to each column as they reread.

Learning Objectives

For pages 73–76

In studying this text, you will focus on the following objectives:

Reading:
Analyzing and evaluating informational text. Connecting to contemporary issues.

Set a Purpose for Reading

As you read, ask yourself, How has the concept of heroism evolved over time?

Preview the Article

Tristram Hunt describes how the concept of heroism has changed through the centuries.

1. Skim the article by glancing quickly over it. What pattern of organization do you think the writer uses?

2. Notice the first question following the title. Consider how you might answer it yourself.

Reading Strategy Connect to Contemporary Issues

In **connecting an informational text to contemporary issues**, you relate it to your understanding of current events and concerns. As you read, ask yourself, How is my understanding affected by this work?

Use a chart to list the connections you make between ideas in this article and issues in today's world.

Ideas	Issues

A Brief History of
HEROES

What does it mean to be a hero? Definitions of heroism have changed through the ages, but are there certain qualities that all heroes have in common?

By TRISTRAM HUNT

MOST OF US HAVE OUR OWN DEFINITION OF heroism—we think we know a hero when we see one. History and literature are filled with both epic and ordinary heroes, but pinning down the attributes of a hero is a challenge. Your hero may not look much like mine. So it's worth asking: Are there certain unchallengeable characteristics that have defined heroism across the ages? Do today's heroes share personality traits with heroes of the past? Or are heroes shaped mostly by circumstance? Although most would agree that there are some timeless, universal qualities known as heroic, throughout history the idea of the hero has fluctuated and evolved to suit the culture of the times.

1 ### The Renaissance Hero

The modern concept of the hero would not have been possible without the Renaissance, a period in European history that saw a revived interest in the classical art, literature, and learning of ancient Greece and Rome. Previously, the Middle Ages had not looked favorably upon man's achievements. Living under the shadow of human sin, the Roman Catholic scholars of medieval Europe stressed the afterlife. Greatness came from God, not man, so the true heroes of Christendom were the martyrs, missionaries, and priests preparing for salvation.

The Renaissance challenged this bleak vision. Part of the challenge came from 14th-century Italy's rediscovery of classical literature. The writings of the

A BRIEF HISTORY OF HEROES **73**

Focus

Summary

This article discusses the concept of heroism and how it has developed across the ages to reflect cultural values.

Teach

Text Element **1**

Subheadings This article has six subheadings. **Ask**: How do the subheadings help you understand the material? *(The subheadings reveal how the article is organized, in this case by progression through the centuries, and suggest what the content of each section will be.)*

For activities related to this selection, see Unit 1 Teaching Resources Book, pp. 36–44.

For an audio recording of this selection, use Listening Library Audio CD-ROM.

Readability Scores

Dale-Chall: 11.3
DRP: 73
Lexile: 1230

Approaching Level

DIFFERENTIATED INSTRUCTION

Emerging Approaching level students may have difficulty in determining the main idea of the selection *(that some heroic traits are timeless, while others are connected to a period in history)* among the questions in the first paragraph. Have students brainstorm a list of traits that come to mind when they hear the word "hero." Have them label which are universal and which are connected to a particular time period.

(Students may list "brave", "intelligent", "good" as universal; they may list "fighter", "rich", handsome" as dated.)

TIME

Teach

Big Idea   1

The Epic Warrior The characteristics of heroes change with time, reflecting the values of a particular culture. **Ask:** How would you summarize the changes that took place within the Renaissance? *(Students may talk about going from serving society to serving oneself.)*

Reading Strategy   2

Timeline Make a timeline that covers the years 1300 to 2000 and label the different historical periods correctly on the timeline. Then list the heroic qualities valued by each period. Having a visual layout is a good way to remember the sequence of historical periods.

Literary History ☆

Lord Byron A famous Romantic poet and satirist, Lord Byron was notorious for his many love affairs. His first literary success came in 1812, when he published *Childe Harold's Pilgrimage,* after his own tour of Spain, Albania, Greece, and the Aegean.

Roman historian Tacitus, the biographies of the Greek philosopher Plutarch, but above all, the letters and speeches of the Roman orator Cicero opened the classical world anew. What they all emphasized was man's capacity for greatness.

 In the 14th century, it was the Italian poet Francesco Petrarca, known as Petrarch, who ushered in the new humanism, a philosophy that focused on human values and capabilities. What excited Petrarch was the classical tradition of education. The aim of education, according to Cicero, was not to teach a narrow range of technical skills, like those needed to practice a trade, but rather to cultivate the single, noble virtue of manliness. During the Renaissance, this classical idea of *virtus* (moral excellence and goodness) went on to inspire many advice books outlining what was needed to become a well-rounded man. A manly man was proficient in warfare, scholarship, government, literature, and even the art of love. In the city-states of 15th-century Italy arose a new belief in human potential. The modern hero was born, and the ideal of the Renaissance man remains a heroic value today.

From this Renaissance culture—this new stress on the capabilities and virtue of man—came a series of histories in the late 14th century that recounted the inspirational lives of great men. Petrarch's *De Viris Illustribus* (On Famous Men) ignored saints and martyrs, concentrating instead on the achievements of generals and statesmen. For Petrarch, heroism demanded the purposeful display of virtus: from Romulus, the

founder of Rome, to the war leader Scipio, Petrarch celebrated heroes who conquered fortune, beat the odds and rose to the top.

There was, however, one dissenting voice: that of the Florentine diplomat Niccolò Machiavelli. He ridiculed Cicero's lofty sentiments about *virtus*. In his book, *The Prince* (1513), Machiavelli turned these Renaissance ideas on their head. Where Petrarch had stressed the virtues of justice, mercy, and honesty in great men, Machiavelli offered the more ruthless concepts of realpolitik, which focuses on the advancement of individual interests—be they the interests of a person or nation. Machiavelli's heroes were those who thought it was better to be feared than loved; who practiced cruelty rather than charity; who didn't base their conduct on firm principles or values, but on the winds of fortune. Machiavelli's hero was not the valiant General Scipio, but the scheming, manipulative prince Cesare Borgia. This notion of antiheroism represented a shocking reversal of thinking and secured Machiavelli his everlasting notoriety (and it finds its echo today in some scheming statesmen and princes of industry).

The Hero of Romanticism

Yet Petrarch's more benevolent vision of classical heroism continued to dominate European culture for centuries to come. Only in the 18th century did the well-rounded Renaissance man finally fall out of fashion. The philosophers of Europe's Enlightenment period had little time for the vanity of personal greatness. As part of a movement that considered reason the highest virtue, these thinkers instead

advocated the heroism of humanity. A scientific approach to social problems and a belief in universal human progress were to be honored, not the petty achievements of politicians and conquerors, or "celebrated villains," as the French writer Voltaire called them.

Inevitably, the impersonal equality of the Enlightenment produced a reaction: Romanticism. Beginning in the late 1790s with the writings of Johann von Schiller, August von Schlegel, and Novalis, the early German Romantics criticized the elevation of logic and reason above feeling. Instead, through art, literature, music, and love they celebrated the inner emotions and creative development of the human spirit. The Romantics believed in man's natural goodness and the call of individuals to develop their personality to the full. If the Renaissance tradition had emphasized military glory and outward achievement, the German Romantics emphasized the uniqueness of each meaningful experience. The heroes of the day were not warriors but poets, dreamers, philosophers, and rebels. Britain's Lord Byron (1788–1824) ☆ managed to embody it all: author, lover, and revolutionary. Through the work of writers such as William Wordsworth, Samuel Taylor Coleridge, and Robert Southey, British culture became steeped in Romanticism, which stressed individual imagination and rebellion against social conventions and injustice. In France, Victor Hugo, author of *Les Misérables* and *The Hunchback of Notre-Dame*, championed the human spirit in the face of all adversity. And Italy awaited its own Romantic hero in the form of revolutionary

Reading Practice

SPIRAL REVIEW **Main Idea and Supporting Details Say:** To find the main idea in an informational text, examine how the author organizes ideas. Have students look at the first paragraph on page 73. **Ask:** What is the main idea of this article? *(Although some qualities of heroes are timeless,* *the concept of the hero has varied as the culture changes.)* Where does the main idea of this article appear? *(In the last sentence of the first paragraph)* What details in the next paragraph support the main idea? *(With the passage of time, the idea of the hero changed.)*

Giuseppe Garibaldi, who fought to unify Italy.

The Victorian Hero

But it was the Victorian author Thomas Carlyle who turned the countercultural Romantic hero into the Great Man of history. A painfully tortured genius, Carlyle found in the humanism of the Romantics a refuge from his own brutal, mechanical age. For Carlyle, the Britain of the Industrial Revolution was a petty, soulless society run by technocrats lacking any conception of greatness.

In 1840, he delivered a series of lectures, titled *On Heroes, Hero-Worship, and the Heroic in History*, lamenting this cultural poverty and championing the role of great men in history. From the prophet Muhammad to William Shakespeare to Martin Luther to Napoleon Bonaparte, Carlyle argued, "Universal History, the history of what man has accomplished in this world, is at bottom the History of the Great Men who have worked here." For Carlyle, heroic conduct was not a skill that could be taught, as Renaissance thinkers had hoped. It was something individuals were gifted with. Moreover, heroes were not people to be emulated, but rather demigods to be acknowledged as possessing greater power. It was a potentially dangerous idea, but one that struck a chord in Victorian Britain and led to such national saviors of the 20th century as Winston Churchill and General de Gaulle.

The Quiet Hero of the 19th Century

Yet even as Carlyle praised his Great Men, there emerged an alternative: the earnest heroism of middle-class virtue. Where the Renaissance hero achieved greatness in battle and the Romantic hero turned his back on society, the 19th-century hero quietly did his duty. As the British lecturer Samuel Smiles put it in his global best seller, *Self-Help*, "Many are the lives of men unwritten, which have nevertheless as powerfully influenced civilization and progress as the more fortunate Great whose names are recorded in biography." Heroism had become democratized, and the earnest, unpublicized work of those who provided people with their basic needs was now considered heroic.

As the democratic 20th century dawned, there was an ever-stronger emphasis on those whom history forgot. For the traditional marks of heroism had passed over the worthy lives of millions. Some seemed even to believe that every human being was intrinsically heroic. The late-19th-century Russian anarchist Alexander Herzen suggested that it was "quite enough to be simply a human being, to have something to tell." British writer, Virginia Woolf remarked: "Since so much is known that used to be unknown, the question now inevitably asks itself, whether the lives of great men only should be recorded. Is not anyone who has lived a life, and left a record of that life, worthy of biography—the failures as well as the successes, the humble as well as the illustrious? And what is greatness? And what smallness?" It was up to modern biographers to set up new standards of merit and "new heroes for our admiration."

The 20th-Century Hero [2]

As the 20th century progressed, many felt the need to reject heroism altogether. Carlyle's Great Man had morphed into German philosopher Friedrich Nietzsche's Super-Man with devastating global consequences. The warmongering of European statesmen led British novelist E.M. Forster to condemn hero-worship as "a dangerous vice." For Forster, one of democracy's merits was that "it does not . . . produce that unmanageable type of citizen known as the Great Man," but "produces instead different kinds of small men—a much finer achievement." [3]

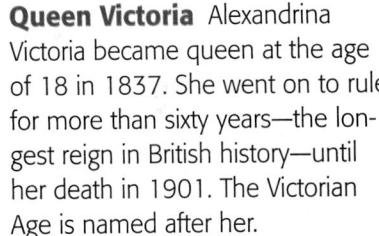

GREAT MEN
Would Machiavelli (top) have recognized Shakespeare as a hero?

Corbis

TIME

Teach

Reading Strategy [3]

Take Notes Say: Why is it helpful to take notes as you read? *(It helps to be able to summarize an article and prepare for test-taking.)*

[APPROACHING] Encourage approaching level students to stop at the end of each paragraph and write down the main idea of the paragraph.

Cultural History ☆

Queen Victoria Alexandrina Victoria became queen at the age of 18 in 1837. She went on to rule for more than sixty years—the longest reign in British history—until her death in 1901. The Victorian Age is named after her.

Advanced Learners

DIFFERENTIATED INSTRUCTION

Research Ask students to research one of the writers mentioned using print and online resources. Students should note important bibliographic information about the author, major literary works, and any additional life events that may have contributed to his or her writings. Have students present an oral report to the class, including details about the writer's attitude toward heroes.

TIME

Assess

1. Answers will vary.

2. (a) People with a love of God—martyrs, saints, and priests (b) The Renaissance emphasized potential for greatness in this life rather than in an afterlife.

3. (a) Mastery of such fields as scholarship, warfare, government, and letters (b) He believed it was better to be cruel and feared than charitable and loved, basing actions on expediency rather than principle.

4. (a) The ability to reason (b) Emotion and the development of the human spirit

5. Carlyle: Heroism is limited to only a few individuals, or "Great Men," who are gifted and god-like. Woolf: All humans are heroic and fitting subjects of biographies.

6. Answers will vary.

7. Answers will vary but should be supported with examples from the text and timeline.

8. Answers will vary. Students should note that an author's idea of heroism reflects "the ethos of the times."

 For additional assessment, see Assessment Resources, p. 61.

Informational Text

Small heroes seemed absolutely necessary in the face of Adolf Hitler. The thinkers of the mid-20th century fled from the idea of connecting militarism with greatness. Even during wartime, the British novelist George Orwell felt able to write in 1944, "The English people have no love of military glory and not much admiration for great men." Orwell did not assign to heroism semidivine greatness or classical *virtus*; instead he admired "a moral quality which must be vaguely described as decency."

The Multicultural Media Age Hero

Heroism today is even more complex. The lack of privacy that mass media demands means that personal failings can, in the public imagination, often overshadow great acts. Today, John F. Kennedy is as much remembered for his love life as for the achievements of his

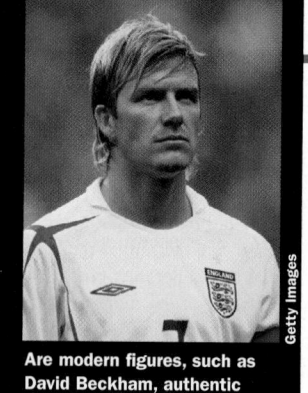

Are modern figures, such as David Beckham, authentic heroes or just celebrities of the media age?

presidency. The cult of celebrity often threatens to undermine true heroism. On the other hand, some celebrities, like the British actress Emma Thompson and U2's Bono, have used their fame to further the public good.

Perhaps most problematic—and most encouraging—is that few modern Western states are uniform societies that can instinctively rally around "national heroes." An educated, multicultural citizenry rarely shares a common idea of heroism—which is why everyday people like Fadéla Amara, a French woman of Algerian descent fighting for women's rights, and Hasan Saltik, a half-Turkish, half-Kurdish man who's been persecuted for trying to preserve Kurdish music, can be singled out as heroes. At the same time, when Hicham El Guerrouj, Morocco's star runner wins an Olympic medal after years of struggle, how many among us can fully resist sharing the national pride?

The tension between multiculturalism and national pride is precisely why it's important to focus on the qualities which all heroes share. Perhaps that's why when people today think about heroes, many choose an encompassing definition of heroism based on merit and humanity; one that seeks to recognize the often forgotten achievements of ordinary people; and one that values overcoming adversity and celebrates selfless acts to help others.

Respond and Think Critically

Respond and Interpret

1. Which ideas in this article did you find most interesting? Why?

2. (a) Which people were regarded as heroes during the Middle Ages? (b) What shift occurred that affected people's view of heroes during the Renaissance?

3. (a) What accomplishments distinguished the Renaissance man? (b) How did Machiavelli challenge the Renaissance ideal of a hero?

4. (a) Which faculty did people during the Enlightenment value the most? (b) What faculty did the Romantics emphasize instead?

Analyze and Evaluate

5. How does Thomas Carlyle's view of heroism differ from Virginia Woolf's?

6. How well do you think the writer supports the thesis, or main idea, of this article? Explain.

7. Review the chart you made for the Reading Strategy on page 73. Which of the ideas presented in this article most enhances your understanding of contemporary issues? Explain.

Connect

8. How does this article affect your understanding of the epic warriors featured in Unit One: Beowulf, Gilgamesh, and Éowyn? Support your answer with evidence from this article and the selections.

76 UNIT 1 THE ANGLO-SAXON PERIOD AND THE MIDDLE AGES

Writing Practice

 Topic Sentences

SPIRAL REVIEW In this article, some topic sentences only introduce what is to follow, while others act as transitional sentences, leading in new directions or advancing the points of the previous paragraph. Have students work in groups to look at the subheads and break down the article into historical sections. Each group should choose one section. Have each student write down one summative topic sentence and one transitional topic sentence. Have them share their findings with the group.

Vocabulary Workshop

Old English Word Parts

Literature Connection Some of the words in the modern English translation of *Beowulf* are derived from Old English words.

> *"Then, when darkness had dropped, Grendel*
> *Went up to Herot, wondering what the warriors*
> *Would do in that hall when their drinking was done."*
> —*Beowulf*

In the quotation above, the word *darkness* comes from the Old English word *deorc* (dark), *wondering* comes from *wundor* (to wonder), *drinking* comes from *drincan* (to drink), and *do* and *done* both come from the word *dōn* (to act).

Old English Word Parts

Knowing Old English word parts can make analyzing unfamiliar language much easier. Below is a chart listing some of these word parts and their meanings.

Prefix or Suffix	Meaning	Example Words
a-	in a condition	asleep
be-	completely, thoroughly	befuddle
for-	completely, detrimentally	forsake
un-	opposite of	unfold
-ful	full of	plentiful
-ly	in the manner of	quickly
-ness	state or condition	likeness
-ship	quality, state, or condition	kinship
-some	having the quality of	burdensome

Practice Read the following passages from *Beowulf*. Using the chart above, determine which word or words contain an Old English suffix or prefix. Explain how each word is derived from Old English.

1. "Of Cain, murderous creatures banished / By God, punished forever for the crime / Of Abel's death." (lines 21–23)
2. "That agony hung / On king and people alike, harsh / And unending, violent and cruel, and evil." (lines 87–89)
3. "In the lap of their shining ship, lined / With gleaming armor, going safely." (lines 110–111)

Learning Objectives

In this workshop, you will focus on the following objectives:

Vocabulary:
Understanding word origins.
Understanding word parts.

Vocabulary Terms

Old English was the language of Anglo-Saxon England. Some Old English word parts survive in today's English.

Test-Taking Tip

You can identify unfamiliar words more easily in a test-taking situation by memorizing a few common word parts, such as the ones listed in the chart.

  Literature Online

Vocabulary For more vocabulary practice, go to glencoe.com and enter QuickPass code GLB9817u1.

Focus

Point out to students that many words are formed by combining prefixes, roots, and suffixes.

Teach

Anglo-Saxon Language
Say: Old English developed when Germanic tribes (Angles, Saxons, and Jutes) invaded Britain after the Roman Empire in the West collapsed in the fifth century. Old English was the language of England until the Norman Conquest in 1066, when French became the language of the aristocracy.

Assess

1. forever, *for-*
2. alike, *a-*; unending, *un-*
3. safely, *-ly*

> For additional vocabulary practice, see Glencoe Interactive Vocabulary CD-ROM.

English Learners

DIFFERENTIATED INSTRUCTION

Intermediate An adverb modifies a verb, an adjective, or another adverb. Adverbs answer questions such as *how, when, where,* and *to what degree*. Write the following sentences on the board and have groups of students identify the questions the adverbs answer:

1. The seamstress <u>quickly</u> sewed the wedding clothes. *(how)*
2. The soldiers arrived <u>yesterday</u>. *(when)*
3. The train headed <u>west</u>. *(where)*
4. The temperature is <u>dangerously</u> cold. *(to what degree)*

Focus

Bellringer Options

Selection Focus
  Transparency 3
Daily Language Practice
  Transparency 5

Summary

The speaker vividly describes the pain, loneliness, and almost mystical attraction of life at sea. He then reflects on the transitory nature of life and urges the reader to become worthy of God's judgment.

Vocabulary

Intensity Nouns and verbs can have varying intensity. Choosing the correct word requires an understanding of intensity. **Ask:** What is a less intense word for *rancor*? *(grudge)* Berate? *(admonish)*

 For additional vocabulary practice, see Unit 1 Resource Book, pp. 53–54.

The Seafarer

Connect to the Poem

How do you deal with circumstances that are both unavoidable and unpleasant? Write a journal entry in which you describe such a situation and the way you dealt with it.

Build Background

Created by an unknown writer, "The Seafarer" is representative of the somewhat grim Anglo-Saxon worldview. The Anglo-Saxons believed that a person's *wyrd,* or fate, was unavoidable—that all roads led inescapably to death. In "The Seafarer," this view is united with Christian notions of heaven and God.

Set Purposes for Reading

Big Idea **The Epic Warrior**

As you read, ask yourself, How does the speaker combine descriptions of the failed human world with the "hope of Heaven"?

Literary Element **Mood**

Mood is the emotional quality of a work of literature. A number of elements may contribute to creating mood, such as a writer's choice of language, subject matter, setting, and tone, as well as sound devices such as rhyme, rhythm, and meter. As you read, ask yourself, How does the poet create a somber, mournful mood?

Reading Strategy **Make Inferences About Theme**

To **make inferences about theme** is to make a reasonable guess about the main idea of a literary work and express it as a general statement about life. In many works, the theme is implied, not stated explicitly. As you read, ask yourself, What idea about life is the poet conveying?

Tip: Taking Notes Use a chart like the one below to record the inferences you draw from the details presented in the poem.

Detail	Inference About Theme
Line 86 Those powers have vanished.	The human world is impermanent.

Learning Objectives

For pages 78–84

In studying this text, you will focus on the following objectives:

Literary Study: Analyzing mood.

Reading: Making inferences about theme.

Writing: Applying imagery in a paragraph or poem.

Vocabulary

admonish (ad mon´ ish) *v.* to warn; reprimand; p. 80 *The teacher was forced to admonish his class for their lack of effort.*

rancor (rang´ kər) *n.* bitter malice or resentment; p. 81 *The rancor Herman felt was visible in the scowl on his face.*

flourish (flur´ ish) *v.* to exist at the peak of development or achievement; thrive; p. 81 *With enough water and sun, the plants should flourish.*

blanch (blanch) *v.* to turn white or become pale; p. 82 *The chemicals that the painter used caused her skin to blanch.*

Selection Skills

Literary Elements
- Mood (SE pp. 79, 81–82)
- Conflict (SE p. 83)

Reading Skills
- Make Inferences (SE pp. 81–82)
- Monitor Comprehension (TE p. 80)

The Seafarer

Vocabulary Skills
- Academic Vocabulary (SE p. 84)
- Intensity (TE p. 78)

Writing Skills/Grammar
- Write with Style (SE p. 84)

Study Skills/Research/ Assessment
- Long Responses (TE p. 82)

The Seafarer

Translated by Burton Raffel

Three ceramic tiles depicting a ship sailing at sunset. William De Morgan. The De Morgan Centre, London.

This tale is true, and mine. It tells
How the sea took me, swept me back
And forth in sorrow and fear and pain,
Showed me suffering in a hundred ships, **1**
5 In a thousand ports, and in me. It tells
Of smashing surf when I sweated in the cold
Of an anxious watch,° perched in the bow°
As it dashed under cliffs. My feet were cast
In icy bands, bound with frost,
10 With frozen chains, and hardship groaned
Around my heart. Hunger tore
At my sea-weary soul. No man sheltered
On the quiet fairness of earth can feel
How wretched I was, drifting through winter
15 On an ice-cold sea, whirled in sorrow,
Alone in a world blown clear of love,
Hung with icicles. The hailstorms flew.
The only sound was the roaring sea,
The freezing waves. The song of the swan
20 Might serve for pleasure, the cry of the sea-fowl,
The death-noise of birds instead of laughter,
The mewing of gulls instead of mead.
Storms beat on the rocky cliffs and were echoed
By icy-feathered terns° and the eagle's screams;

7 watch: a period of time during a day on a ship in which a crew member is on duty. **bow:** the front section of the ship.

24 terns: seabirds that resemble small gulls and have forked tails.

Mood *How do these images contribute to the poem's mood?* **2**

Teach

Reading Strategy 1

Make Inferences Ask:
Why does the speaker begin the poem by saying that the tale is true and about him? *(Truth has a greater emotional impact than fiction.)*

Literary Element 2

Mood Answer: *They add a feeling of starkness and loneliness to the poem's dark, somber mood.*

 For additional literary element practice, see Unit 1 Resource Book, p. 51.

Cultural History ☆

Origins "The Seafarer" is one of a handful of elegies preserved in the Exeter Book, a rare collection of Old English poetry that was compiled and copied by monks during the 900s. The book is named after Exeter Cathedral, where it has been housed since about 1050. "The Seafarer" has its origins in 450–1000, a time when very few people knew how to read or write.

 For summaries in languages other than English, see Unit 1 Resource Book, pp. 45–50.

 For an audio recording of this selection, use Listening Library Audio CD-ROM.

English Learners

DIFFERENTIATED INSTRUCTION

Intermediate Tell students that compound words, such as *upstairs*, are made up of two smaller words. Note the two words that make up *seafarer*, and explain that *farer* is another word for *traveler*. **Ask:** What other word can you use to describe a seafarer? *(sailor)*

Teach

Literary Element | 1

Mood **Answer:** *These images create a dark, somber mood.*

[ENGLISH LEARNERS] Ask English learners to work with partners to review the first 24 lines of "The Seafarer" and make a list of words and phrases that help to create the poem's dark mood.

Literary History ☆

Musical Tradition "The Seafarer" was probably first sung by a poet playing a harp. The oral, musical nature of Anglo-Saxon poetry is reflected in its alliteration and its pattern of four stressed syllables in each line.

25   No kinsman could offer comfort there, ☆
      To a soul left drowning in desolation.
             And who could believe, knowing but
      The passion of cities, swelled proud with wine
      And no taste of misfortune, how often, how wearily,
30   I put myself back on the paths of the sea.
      Night would blacken; it would snow from the north;
      Frost bound the earth and hail would fall,
      The coldest seeds. And how my heart
      Would begin to beat, knowing once more
35   The salt waves tossing and the towering sea!
      The time for journeys would come and my soul
      Called me eagerly out, sent me over
      The horizon, seeking foreigners' homes.
             But there isn't a man on earth so proud,
40   So born to greatness, so bold with his youth,
      Grown so brave, or so graced by God,
      That he feels no fear as the sails unfurl,
      Wondering what Fate has willed and will do.
      No harps ring in his heart, no rewards,
45   No passion for women, no worldly pleasures,
      Nothing, only the ocean's heave;
      But longing wraps itself around him.
      Orchards blossom, the towns bloom,
      Fields grow lovely as the world springs fresh,
50   And all these **admonish** that willing mind
      Leaping to journeys, always set
      In thoughts traveling on a quickening tide.
      So summer's sentinel,° the cuckoo, sings
      In his murmuring voice, and our hearts mourn
55   As he urges. Who could understand,
      In ignorant ease, what we others suffer
      As the paths of exile stretch endlessly on?
             And yet my heart wanders away,
      My soul roams with the sea, the whales'
60   Home, wandering to the widest corners
      Of the world, returning ravenous with desire,
      Flying solitary, screaming, exciting me
      To the open ocean, breaking oaths
      On the curve of a wave.
                Thus the joys of God

Mood *What mood do the images in these lines create?*   **1**

Vocabulary

admonish (ad mon´ ish) *v.* to warn; reprimand

53 **sentinel:** one who keeps guard.

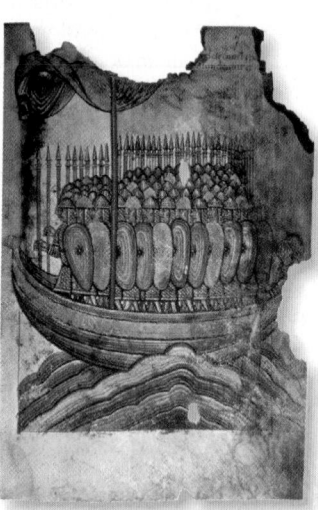

Norman soldiers crossing the English channel, from "La Vie de Saint Aubin d'Angers," 11th century. French School. Vellum. Bibliothèque Nationale, Paris.

Reading Practice

[SPIRAL REVIEW] **Monitor Comprehension** Explain that the seafarer seems to have contradictory feelings about his life at sea. **Ask:** What are these conflicting feelings? What lines from the poem reveal each of the seafarer's feelings? *(Students should note lines that show the seafarer's pain and loneliness. They should also notes lines such as "And yet my heart wanders away, / My soul roams with the sea" that show the seafarer's powerful connection to the sea.)*

Vikingesnekke' Norwegian warriors in a half-decked warship. 9th–10th centuries. Anker Lund in Billeder til Norgeshistorien.

65   Are fervent° with life, where life itself
Fades quickly into the earth. The wealth
Of the world neither reaches to Heaven nor remains.
No man has ever faced the dawn
Certain which of Fate's three threats
70   Would fall: illness, or age, or an enemy's
Sword, snatching the life from his soul.
The praise the living pour on the dead
Flowers from reputation: plant
An earthly life of profit reaped
75   Even from hatred and **rancor,** of bravery
Flung in the devil's face, and death
Can only bring you earthly praise
And a song to celebrate a place
With the angels, life eternally blessed
80   In the hosts of Heaven.
                   The days are gone
When the kingdoms of earth **flourished** in glory;
Now there are no rulers, no emperors,
No givers of gold, as once there were,

65 **fervent:** Here, *fervent* means "glowing" or "burning."

Make Inferences About Theme *How do these lines help you make inferences about the poem's theme?* **2**

The Epic Warrior *What do lines 80–83 suggest about the era in which "The Seafarer" was composed?* **3**

Vocabulary

rancor (rang´ ker) *n.* bitter malice or resentment
flourish (flur´ ish) *v.* to exist at the peak of development or achievement; thrive

Reading Strategy **2**

Make Inferences About Theme **Answer:** *These lines express the idea that God is the sole source of salvation in a world where life is fleeting.*

(APPROACHING) Help struggling students see that these lines say that life "fades quickly," or does not last. **Ask:** What does not fade quickly? What remains "fervent with life"? *(the joys of God)*

Big Idea **3**

The Epic Warrior **Answer:** *They suggest that the era was a time of cultural decline.*

English Learners

DIFFERENTIATED INSTRUCTION

Advanced Tell English learners that *snatching* (line 71) means "grabbing or seizing something very suddenly." **Ask:** What is being snatched away from humans? What three different ways might it be snatched away? *(Life is being snatched away by sickness, old age, or an enemy.)*

Approaching Level

DIFFERENTIATED INSTRUCTION

Emerging Students may not notice, at first, the subtle shifts in subject as they read the poem. Help them see the shift that begins in lines 64–67. Have them make a list of words and phrases that indicate the shift in subject in these and later lines. Point out words and phrases, such as "life itself/ Fades quickly into the earth."

Teach

Make Inferences About Theme Answer: *You can infer that because fate and God are more powerful than humanity, it is vain to struggle against the will of either one.*

(ENGLISH LEARNERS) Tell English learners that *stronger* and *mightier* are synonyms, or words with almost the same meaning. **Ask:** What other words do you know that have a similar meaning? *(tougher, more powerful)* **Ask:** How do these words help convey the meaning of the lines? *(They emphasize God's power over man.)*

 To check students' understanding of the selection, see Unit 1 Resource Book, pp. 55–56.

When wonderful things were worked among them
85 And they lived in lordly magnificence.
Those powers have vanished, those pleasures are dead.
The weakest survives and the world continues,
Kept spinning by toil. All glory is tarnished,
The world's honor ages and shrinks,
90 Bent like the men who mold it. Their faces
Blanch as time advances, their beards
Wither and they mourn the memory of friends.
The sons of princes, sown in the dust.
The soul stripped of its flesh knows nothing
95 Of sweetness or sour, feels no pain,
Bends neither its hand nor its brain. A brother
Opens his palms and pours down gold
On his kinsman's grave, strewing his coffin
With treasures intended for Heaven, but nothing
100 Golden shakes the wrath of God
For a soul overflowing with sin, and nothing
Hidden on earth rises to Heaven.
       We all fear God. He turns the earth,
He set it swinging firmly in space,
105 Gave life to the world and light to the sky.
Death leaps at the fools who forget their God.
He who lives humbly has angels from Heaven
To carry him courage and strength and belief.
A man must conquer pride, not kill it,
110 Be firm with his fellows, chaste for himself,
Treat all the world as the world deserves,
With love or with hate but never with harm,
Though an enemy seek to scorch him in hell,
Or set the flames of a funeral pyre°
115 Under his lord. Fate is stronger
And God mightier than any man's mind.
Our thoughts should turn to where our home is,
Consider the ways of coming there,
Then strive for sure permission for us
120 To rise to that eternal joy,
That life born in the love of God
And the hope of Heaven. Praise the Holy
Grace of Him who honored us,
Eternal, unchanging creator of earth. Amen.

Make Inferences About Theme *What can you infer about the theme from these lines?* 1

Vocabulary

blanch (blanch) *v.* to turn white or become pale

The Coming of the Norsemen in 1000 AD, 20th century. Mabelle Linnea Holmes. Tapestry. Jamestown-Yorktown Educational Trust, VA.

114 **funeral pyre:** a heap of flammable material on which a dead body is burned.

Assessment Practice

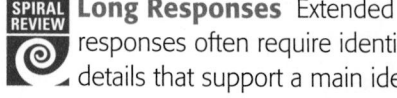 **Long Responses** Extended responses often require identifying details that support a main idea.

Ask: What factors contribute to the Seafarer's feelings of loneliness? *(Students' responses might include references to the seafarer's suffering in isolation, his frozen chains, and sea-weary soul. Students might also cite the disillusionment that the seafarer feels because of the mutability of his world.)*

After You Read

Respond and Think Critically

Respond and Interpret

1. Which images in the poem did you find the most memorable? Explain.

2. (a)What hardships of life at sea does the speaker describe at the beginning of the poem (lines 1–26)? (b)What mood do these lines create?

3. (a)What pleasures of life on the land does the speaker mention? (b)In your opinion, does the speaker long for a comfortable life on land or does he willingly go to sea? Explain.

4. (a)What does the speaker say is different about life in his time as compared with life in the past? (b)What does the speaker's attitude about the past suggest about his feelings for the time in which he lives?

Analyze and Evaluate

5. (a)How does the sea function literally and figuratively in the poem? (b)In what ways is the sea an effective symbol?

6. (a)What change do you notice in the focus and tone midway through the poem? (b)Which half of the poem do you prefer? Explain.

7. How does the poem's imagery help to convey the speaker's conflicted emotions?

Connect

8. **Big Idea** The Epic Warrior In what ways does this poem capture the brooding worldview of the Anglo-Saxons?

9. Connect to Today What kinds of experiences in today's world might affect a person in the way that seafaring has affected the poem's speaker?

Literary Element Mood

While there are many contributing factors to a literary work's **mood,** imagery is one of the most significant elements. Frequent use of dark, strange, or repellent images can help create a bleak mood. Lighthearted images help create a pleasant mood. However, authors sometimes use images as a counterpoint to the prevailing mood of a piece. By including images that conflict with the mood, authors can create more complicated or ironic works.

1. What is the principal mood of "The Seafarer"?

2. Identify several images from the poem that contribute to this mood.

3. Are there any images that conflict with the principal mood of the piece? List any that you find.

Review: Conflict

As you learned on page 23, **conflict** is a struggle between two opposing forces in a story or drama. There are two main types of conflict that can occur in a work of literature. **External conflict** exists when a character struggles against an outside force, such as a human enemy or nature. **Internal conflict** is a struggle that takes place within the mind of a character. In "The Seafarer," the speaker experiences both types of conflict.

Partner Activity Meet with another classmate to discuss the speaker's conflicts, the causes of these conflicts, and the ways they affect the poem's mood. Be sure to cite textual evidence during your discussion to support your claims.

After You Read

Assess

1. Answers will vary.

2. (a) The cold, danger, loneliness, and storms of the sea (b) One of suffering and danger.

3. (a) Springtime, birdsongs, and worldly pleasures (b) The speaker feels drawn to the sea and discontented unless he is aboard ship.

4. (a) In the past, the kingdoms of the earth flourished. Now, all that remains is hard work, tarnished glory, and images of death. (b) He understands the impermanence of earthly objects and ideas.

5. (a) The sea is a literal place of privation and danger. Figuratively, it is a symbol for the speaker's vast despair and loneliness. (b) Students' answers will vary.

6. (a) The poem becomes explicitly religious starting at line 64. (b) Students' answers will vary.

7. Students may say that the violent, brooding imagery of the sea reflects the speaker's internal conflict.

8. The worldview of the Anglo-Saxons is reflected in the speaker's sense of powerlessness. Fate directs his life, so he must accept the dangers he faces at sea.

9. Answers will vary but should pertain to a daunting experience or perilous journey.

Literary Element

1. The mood is dark and somber.

2. Some examples include "Alone in a world blown clear of love,/Hung with icicles," and "The death-noise of birds instead of laughter."

3. Yes, the descriptions of the land add a counterpoint to the poem. Some examples include "the cuckoo, sings / In his murmuring voice," and "Fields grow lovely as the world springs fresh."

Review: Conflict

Students should cite evidence to support their analysis of conflicts.

After You Read

Assess

Reading Strategy

1. The poem's theme could be described as "work as well as you can, be steadfast during change, and trust God to bring you home."

2. Students' answers will vary. Students might cite lines 103–115, which describe the speaker's pronouncements on life, or lines 64–66: "Thus the joys of God/ Are fervent with life, where life itself/Fades quickly into the earth."

Progress Check

Can students make inferences about the theme?

If No → See Unit 1 Resource Book, p. 52

Vocabulary

Answers will vary but may include:

1. disobeying a request, being mean to another child

2. a person in a theater talks during the movie

3. an environment rich in consideration and support

4. receiving an expensive bill, hearing a rude remark

Academic Vocabulary

Answers will vary but may include: study, pace yourself during the exam, get a good night's sleep before the test.

Reading Strategy Make Inferences About Theme

The theme of a literary work can have multiple interrelated parts. The theme of "The Seafarer," for example, has several aspects. The conflict within the speaker and the speaker's feelings about fate and eternity contribute different elements to the poem's broader theme.

1. What is the theme of "The Seafarer"?

2. In support of your response to question 1, list three important details from the poem and the inferences you drew from them.

Vocabulary Practice

Practice with Word Usage Respond to these statements to help you explore the meanings of vocabulary words from the selection.

1. List some behaviors for which a parent might **admonish** a child.

2. Give an example from a movie in which one person's actions incited another person's **rancor**.

3. Describe the type of living situation in which you **flourish**.

4. List some situations that might cause a person to **blanch**.

Academic Vocabulary

The poem suggests that heavenly judgment is **ensured** for all earthly things.

Ensure is an academic word. Other words that are similar in meaning are *secure*, *confirm*, and *guarantee*.

To further explore this word, answer the following question: What actions would you take if you wanted to **ensure** your success on a difficult exam?

For more on academic vocabulary, see pages 56 and R81.

 Write with Style

Apply Imagery

Assignment Writers use imagery to create vivid descriptions conveying a multitude of moods. Reread "The Seafarer," paying attention to the images that make the scene so desolate and threatening. Then use concrete sensory images to create a compelling mood in a descriptive paragraph or short poem of your own.

Get Ideas Write in your journal about a place you have visited recently. What mood does this place evoke? Take inventory of the most significant details about the place, as well as the senses to which the details appeal. Then choose a form—either a descriptive paragraph or a poem—that best fits your subject and its mood.

Give It Structure Organize your images in spatial order (from top to bottom, left to right, or front to back), in temporal order (as people experience them), or in order of power or importance.

Look at Language Be alert for vague terms you can replace with concrete, sensory words. Also watch for repetitive or unnecessary words that can be deleted. Vary the lengths of sentences to make your writing interesting.

EXAMPLE:

buzzing like a swarm of bees
The crowd was ~~really excited~~. As the ~~banging~~
~~and~~ ear-shattering thudding of the bass drums
announced the arrival of the band, a giant's
bouquet of brightly colored balloons floated into
the street.

LOG ON ▶ **Literature** Online

Selection Resources For Selection Quizzes, eFlashcards, and Reading-Writing Connection activities, go to glencoe.com and enter QuickPass code GLB9817u1.

 Write with Style

Use these criteria in evaluating student writing:

- It includes concrete sensory images, expressed with precise word choice.
- The details are organized in a logical way.
- The images work together to create a strong, identifiable mood.

To create custom assessments using software, use ExamView Assessment Suite.

Part 2

The Power of Faith

Lydgate and the Canterbury Pilgrims Leaving Canterbury (detail), from *The Troy Book and the Siege of Thebes*, c. 1412–1422. Vellum. British Library, London.

 View the Art This painting is from a manuscript of a long poem by John Lydgate, a fourteenth-century poet who admired Chaucer's *Canterbury Tales*. What does the picture tell you about medieval people who took pilgrimages? ⭐

> "And specially, from every shire's end
> Of England, down to Canterbury they wend
> To seek the holy blissful martyr, quick
> To give his help to them when they were sick."

—Geoffrey Chaucer, *The Canterbury Tales* **1**

85

Analyze and Extend

Reading Strategy 1

Draw Conclusions Direct students to read the quotation from Chaucer. **Ask:** According to the quotation, why do people travel to Canterbury? *(They go there to pray and give thanks to a saint.)*

View the Art ⭐

Answer: *Some students may say that the pilgrims were quite diverse, judging by the differences in clothing and weaponry. Students may also note that they traveled in groups and that they seemed to befriend one another.*

This image of pilgrims leaving Canterbury originally illustrated a long poem by John Lydgate, a monk and poet from the 14th century. Imitating Chaucer, Lydgate used a pilgrimage to Canterbury as the central plot of his poem.

English Learners
DIFFERENTIATED INSTRUCTION

Intermediate English language learners are likely to struggle with words such as *specially, shire,* and *wend.* Advise them to maintain a personal glossary of unfamiliar words as they read the Chaucer selections. Check comprehension frequently by asking students to paraphrase what they have read.

Approaching Level
DIFFERENTIATED INSTRUCTION

Emerging Read aloud the quotation from Chaucer. **Ask:** What did the martyr once do for the pilgrims? *(The martyr helped them when they were sick.)* Have students rewrite the quotation in their own words.

Before You Read

Focus

Bellringer Options

Selection Focus Transparency 4

Daily Language Practice Transparency 6

Or display images of medieval monasteries and monks working on manuscripts. **Ask:** Why do you suppose a person would choose to live as a monk? *(Possible responses: devotion; basic survival; education)*

As they read, have students consider the contributions Bede made to medieval culture.

Before You Read

from *The Ecclesiastical History of the English People*

Meet the **Venerable Bede**
(c. 632–735)

A bout the same time that a scop may have been singing in a hushed mead-hall about the heroic deeds of Beowulf, a monk named Bede was studying and writing in the equally quiet library of a monastery. Whereas the gifted scop remained forever nameless, this monk's name became known throughout the world.

"It has ever been a delight to learn or teach or write."

—Bede

A Life of Religious Study When Bede was a boy of seven, he went to study and live in a monastery at Wearmouth, England. About two years later, Bede moved to a monastery at Jarrow, just a short distance away. There he remained for the rest of his life, devoting himself to religion and scholarly pursuits.

A man of great learning, Bede had far-ranging interests that included religion, poetry, grammar, music, art, mathematics, and science. His passion for calculating time and dates led him to use a method of dating still in use today. This method starts from the birth of Jesus in the year A.D. 1 (A.D. stands for Latin *Anno Domini*, "in the year of our Lord"). Bede's use of this form of dating in his histories helped to popularize it.

Bede wrote in Latin, the language of religion and learning, rather than in Old English, the language of the people. With almost forty works bearing his name, Bede is the first important writer of prose in England and is considered the father of English history. Bede's masterpiece, *The Ecclesiastical History of the English People*, documents the influence of the church on the development of English civilization.

Writing History Fortunately for us, Bede was a talented storyteller. His histories are far more than mere chronicles of events; they present meticulously researched stories of conquests, saints, missionaries, and monasteries. To write his great works, Bede did research in the library of the monastery, sent letters all over Europe, and spoke with artists and scholars from afar who visited the monastery. Bede reveals in his histories how people actually lived, providing most of what we know about life in Britain between the years 46 and 731.

Except for visits to York and Lindisfarne, Bede never left Jarrow. Nevertheless, his reputation spread widely. About a century after his death, he was given the title "Venerable" to honor his wisdom and piety. In 1899 he was declared a saint of the Catholic Church. Historian Kemp Malone writes of Bede's legacy, "Bede makes every effort to be accurate. He admits wonders only after he has investigated them and found them well authenticated. His standards of verification are not ours, of course. If today a victim of snakebite were to drink down some scrapings of Irish books and get well, we should not conclude that the scrapings had worked the cure."

LOG ON **Literature** Online

Author Search For more about the Venerable Bede, go to glencoe.com and enter QuickPass code GLB9817u1.

Selection Skills

Literary Elements
- Historical Narrative (SE pp. 87, 89, 90, 95)
- Internal Conflict (SE p. 94)

Study Skills/Research/ Assessment
- Internet (TE p. 90)
- Short Responses (TE p. 92, 94)

from **The Ecclesiastical History of the English People**

Reading Skills
- Summarize (SE pp. 87, 89, 90, 92, 93)
- Skim (TE p. 88)

Vocabulary Skills
- Word Origins (SE pp. 87, 94)

Literature and Reading Preview

Connect to the Chronicle

Have you ever had to face a major change in your life? Freewrite for a few minutes about a change you faced and your reaction to it.

Build Background

The first excerpt from Bede's *History* describes events in the early 600s. Edwin, who has recently conquered his enemies to become king of Northumbria in northern England, is discussing Christianity with Paulinus, his wife's religious counselor. The second excerpt describes events in the late 600s in Whitby, England. It tells of the miraculous talent of Caedmon, the first poet to compose religious poetry in Old English.

Set Purposes for Reading

Big Idea The Power of Faith

As you read, ask yourself, What role did faith play in the lives of people living in Anglo-Saxon England?

Literary Element Historical Narrative

A **historical narrative** is a factual account of events that occurred in the past. As you read the two excerpts from *The Ecclesiastical History of the English People*, ask yourself, What features make this a historical narrative?

Reading Strategy Summarize

A **summary** is a brief restatement, in one's own words, of the main ideas and events in a literary work. Summarizing what you have read is an excellent tool for understanding and remembering a passage. As you read each passage, ask yourself, What main ideas and events are being presented?

Tip: Taking Notes Stop periodically to summarize and record important ideas and events. Use a chart to organize your notes.

Main Event or Idea	Summary
Paulinus visits the king.	

Learning Objectives

For pages 86–95

In studying this text, you will focus on the following objectives:

Literary Study:
Analyzing a historical narrative.
Analyzing internal conflict.

Reading: Summarizing.

Vocabulary Practice

expound (iks pound′) *v.* to set forth in detail; explain; p. 89 *I didn't understand the theory, so I asked the teacher to expound its meaning.*

diligently (dil′ ə jənt lē) *adv.* persistently; p. 90 *After diligently submitting many applications, I finally found a job.*

aspire (əs pīr′) *v.* to strive for; p. 91 *I practice the guitar often because I aspire to become a famous musician.*

frivolous (friv′ ə ləs) *adj.* not serious; silly; p. 91 *His frivolous manner made him seem incapable of taking on anything responsibly.*

BEDE **87**

Before You Read

Focus

Summary

In the first excerpt from the *Ecclesiastical History,* Bede describes King Edwin's wrestling with the question of converting to Christianity. After Paulinus describes God's many blessings to the king, Edwin and his council convert. They proceed to destroy the shrines of the gods they once worshiped.

In the second excerpt, a man named Caedmon has been blessed with a gift for composing religious songs. He spends the rest of his life praising God in song and encouraging others in their faith.

Vocabulary

Have partners look up the etymology of each vocabulary word in a dictionary. **Ask:** What do these words have in common? *(They are based on Latin.)* Then have students compare the meanings of the Latin roots with the English definitions of the words.

 For additional vocabulary practice, see Unit 1 Teaching Resources Book, p. 67.

English Learners

DIFFERENTIATED INSTRUCTION

Intermediate Remind students that a historical narrative is often presented chronologically, that is, in the order of events as they happened. Guide students in making a list of words or phrases that give clues to the sequence of events: *one day, when, in the morning, the next day, suddenly, after,* etc.

Have partners use words from the list to create sentences.

Teach

Big Idea   **1**

The Power of Faith   Say:

Keep the following question in mind as you read: How were people persuaded to convert to the Christian faith? *(The Christian God is depicted as powerful, generous, having knowledge of that which happens before and after life; as possessing the Truth; as bestower of grace; as personally related to his followers; and able to soothe the agony of death.)*

View the Art ★

Answer: *Students may note that the scribe is very simply dressed, has an expression of concentration, and is very serious about his work.*

This painting reflects some of the preoccupations of early Christian art, in which the outside world was of little importance, and the inner world of one's soul and salvation was foremost. This page from an illuminated manuscript showing a scribe lost in his spiritual work, emphasizes how a monk led a life of isolation from the outside world.

Readability Scores

Dale-Chall: 8.0
DRP: 63
Lexile: 1290

A Scribe Writing, 12th century. Latin (Durham). Illumination from Bede's *Life and Miracles of St. Cuthbert.* British Library, London.

View the Art In the Middle Ages, members of religious orders worked to preserve written knowledge in a time when most people could not read or write. What do you notice about the scribe depicted here? ★

Reading Practice

SPIRAL REVIEW **Skim** Have students preview the text by reading the title, caption, subheads, and first lines of each paragraph. Skimming can help students orient themselves to the material, so they will know what to expect when they begin a close reading. This allows them to absorb the details more effectively than a cold reading. **Ask:** What do you expect the selection to be about?

Lead the class in a discussion of students' ideas.

from

THE ECCLESIASTICAL HISTORY OF THE ENGLISH PEOPLE

The Venerable Bede
Translated by Bertram Colgrave

The Anglo-Saxons Embrace Christianity 1

King Edwin hesitated to accept the word of God which Paulinus preached but, as we have said, used to sit alone for hours at a time, earnestly debating within himself what he ought to do and what religion he should follow. One day Paulinus came to him and, placing his right hand on the king's head, asked him if he recognized this sign.

The king began to tremble and would have thrown himself at the bishop's feet but Paulinus raised him up and said in a voice that seemed familiar, "First you have escaped with God's help from the hands of the foes you feared; secondly you have acquired by His gift the kingdom you desired; now, in the third place, remember your own promise; do not delay in fulfilling it but receive the faith and keep the commandments of Him who rescued you from your earthly foes

and raised you to the honor of an earthly kingdom. If from henceforth you are willing to follow His will which is made known to you through me, He will also rescue you from the everlasting torments of the wicked and make you a partaker with Him of His eternal kingdom in heaven."

When the king had heard his words, he answered that he was both willing and bound to accept the faith which Paulinus taught. He said, however, that he would confer about this with his loyal chief men and his counsellors so that, if they agreed with him, they might all be consecrated together in the waters of life. Paulinus agreed, and the king did as he had said. A meeting of his council was held, and each one was asked in turn what he thought of this doctrine[1] hitherto unknown to them and this new worship of God which was being proclaimed.

Coifi, the chief of the priests, answered at once, "Notice carefully, King, this doctrine which is now being **expounded** to us. I frankly admit that, for my part, I have found that the

---

1. A *doctrine* is a body of principles taught or advocated, as in a religion.

Vocabulary

expound (iks pound´) *v.* to set forth in detail; explain

Summarize *Summarize the argument that Paulinus makes in the following speech.* 2

Teach

Reading Strategy | 2

Summarize **Answer:** *Paulinus says that God has rescued the king from his enemies and given him a kingdom, reminds Edwin of his promise to convert to Christianity, and says that God will rescue Edwin from hell.*

Political History

Edwin's Promise This promise occurred in A.D. 626, after Edwin survived an assassination attempt and had a daughter born on the same day. Edwin promised to devote his daughter to God if the assassin was destroyed.

English Learners

DIFFERENTIATED INSTRUCTION

Intermediate Ask: In what tense is the selection written? *(past)* What are some of the past tense verbs on the page? *(hesitated; came; asked; began; seemed; rescued)* What are some examples of other verb forms on this page? *(to accept—infinitive; will rescue—future tense)*

Approaching Level

DIFFERENTIATED INSTRUCTION

Established Ask students to read the speech by Coifi that begins in the second column on this page. **Ask:** Which part of the speech gives evidence of Coifi's dissatisfaction? *(the last line)* What other emotions can you find evidence for? *(Students' answers will vary.)*

Teach

View the Art ★
Decorated with gold or silver, illuminated manuscripts are the most common item to survive from the Middle Ages. Had it not been for the monastic scribes who copied these manuscripts, the entire content of western literature from Greece and Rome could have perished.

Illuminated manuscript page. Kungl. Bernadotte-Biblioteket, The Royal Collection, Sweden. ★

religion which we have hitherto held has no virtue nor profit in it. None of your followers has devoted himself more earnestly than I have to the worship of our gods, but nevertheless there are many who receive greater benefits and greater honor from you than I do and are more successful in all their undertakings. If the gods had any power, they would have helped me more readily, seeing that I have always served them with greater zeal.[2] So it follows that if, on examination, these new doctrines which have now been explained to us are found to be better and more effectual, let us accept them at once without any delay."

Another of the king's chief men agreed with this advice and with these wise words and then added, "This is how the present life of man on earth, King, appears to me in comparison with that time which is unknown to us. You are sitting feasting with your eldermen and thanes[3] in winter time; the fire is burning on the hearth in the middle of the hall and all inside is warm,

---

2. *Zeal* means "enthusiastic devotion."
3. *Eldermen* are advisers; *thanes* are nobles.

while outside the wintry storms of rain and snow are raging; and a sparrow flies swiftly through the hall. It enters in at one door and quickly flies out through the other. For the few moments it is inside, the storm and wintry tempest cannot touch it, but after the briefest moment of calm, it flits from your sight, out of the wintry storm and into it again. So this life of man appears but for a moment; what follows or indeed what went before, we know not at all. If this new doctrine brings us more certain information, it seems right that we should accept it." Other elders and counsellors of the king continued in the same manner, being divinely prompted to do so.

Coifi added that he would like to listen still more carefully to what Paulinus himself had to say about God. The king ordered Paulinus to speak, and when he had said his say, Coifi exclaimed, "For a long time now I have realized that our religion is worthless; for the more **diligently** I sought the truth in our cult, the less I found it. Now I confess openly that the truth shines out clearly in this teaching which can bestow on us the gift of life, salvation, and eternal happiness. Therefore, I advise your Majesty that we should promptly abandon and commit to the flames the temples and the altars which we have held sacred without reaping any benefit." Why need I say more? The king publicly accepted the gospel which Paulinus preached, renounced idolatry, and confessed his faith in Christ. When he asked the high priest of their religion which of them should be the first to profane[4] the altars and the shrines of the idols, together with their precincts, Coifi answered, "I will; for through the wisdom the

---

4. *Profane* means "to treat with disrespect; to desecrate."

The Power of Faith *What point do you think Bede is making about the afterlife by relating this parable of the sparrow?* **1**

Historical Narrative *How might a modern historian present this scene differently?* **2**

Vocabulary

diligently (dĭl′ ə jənt lē) *adv.* persistently

Research Practice

true God has given me no one can more suitably destroy those things which I once foolishly worshipped, and so set an example to all." And at once, casting aside his vain superstitions, he asked the king to provide him with arms and a stallion; and mounting it, he set out to destroy the idols. Now a high priest of their religion was not allowed to carry arms or to ride except on a mare. So, girded with a sword, he took a spear in his hand, and mounting the king's stallion, he set off to where the idols were. The common people who saw him thought he was mad. But as soon as he approached the shrine, without any hesitation he profaned it by casting the spear which he held into it; and greatly rejoicing in the knowledge of the worship of the true God, he ordered his companions to destroy and set fire to the shrine and all the enclosures. The place where the idols once stood is still shown, not far from York, to the east, over the river Derwent. Today it is called Goodmanham, the place where the high priest, through the inspiration of the true God, profaned and destroyed the altars which he himself had consecrated.[5]

Caedmon[6]
Translated by Leo Sherley-Price

In this monastery of Whitby there lived a brother[7] whom God's grace made remarkable. So skilful was he in composing religious and devotional songs, that he could quickly turn whatever passages of Scripture were explained to him into delightful and moving poetry in his own English tongue. These verses of his stirred the hearts of many folk to despise the world and **aspire** to

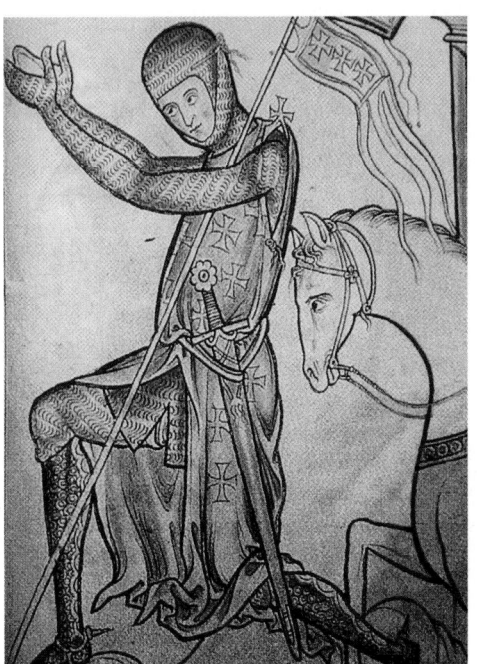

Kneeling crusader with his horse behind him (page from Westminster Psalter), 13th Century. Illuminated manuscript. The British Library, London. ★

heavenly things. Others after him tried to compose religious poems in English, but none could compare with him, for he received this gift of poetry as a gift from God and did not acquire it through any human teacher. For this reason he could never compose any **frivolous** or profane[8] verses, but only such as had a religious theme fell fittingly from his devout lips. And although he followed a secular[9] occupation until well advanced in years, he had never learned anything about poetry: indeed, whenever all those present at a feast took it in turns to sing and entertain the company, he would get up from

---

5. *Consecrated* means "set apart as sacred."
6. *Caedmon* (kad´ mən)
7. A *brother* is a member of a religious community who is not a priest or a monk.

3 **The Power of Faith** *What historical fact about religion do Coifi's actions illustrate?*

aspire (əs pīr´) *v.* to strive for

---

8. Here, *profane* means "worldly."
9. *Secular* means "not religious."

frivolous (friv´ ə ləs) *adj.* not serious; silly

Teach

Big Idea **3**

The Power of Faith
Answer: *Coifi's destruction of the shrine illustrates that some religious zealots have caused violence and bloodshed in the name of their faiths.*

Have advanced learners identify words that Coifi and Bede use to justify or explain Coifi's actions. *(For instance, "set an example to all;" "worship of the true God")*

View the Art ★

At a time when maintaining the status of knighthood was becoming expensive, a call to war in a land said to be rich in precious metals and gems fueled visions of ransoms and booty. In the First Crusade, Pope Urban II not only paid 4,000 knights to fight but promised to protect their lands and give them tax exemption while on campaign. The mark of this special status was a cross on the knight's clothes.

Approaching Level

DIFFERENTIATED INSTRUCTION

AAVE Approaching-level students who use African American Vernacular English (AAVE) may have difficulty recognizing the simple past tense. To clarify, have students compose sentences using the verb forms in the table below.

Present Tense	Present Tense
He asks	He asked
It takes	It took
She sees	She saw

Emerging Refer students to the first paragraph of the excerpt about Caedmon. **Ask:** What was Caedmon like before receiving the gift of poetry? *(nonreligious and shy)* Why do you think Bede included this information? *(to emphasize Caedmon's transformation)*

Teach

Reading Strategy 1

Summarize Answer: *Students' responses should reflect Caedmon's focus on the glory of God and God's role as creator.*

ENGLISH LEARNERS Make sure English Learners know that the "general sense" of Caedmon's song is in quotation marks. Point out that Caedmon is asked to "Sing about the Creation of all things."

Big Idea 2

The Power of Faith
Answer: *Bede is emphasizing the rewards of Christianity. By being a good Christian, Caedmon has won eternal happiness in heaven.*

Cultural History ☆

Benedictine Monks, such as Caedmon, were governed by the *Rule of Saint Benedict*. This *Rule* was a book of instructions regarding how community life in the monastery was to be carried out. Monks were not permitted to own anything, and they were required to participate in religious services at specific times each day. Their daily life was divided into periods of prayer, manual labor, and study.

table and go home directly he saw the harp approaching him.

On one such occasion he had left the house in which the entertainment was being held and went out to the stable, where it was his duty to look after the beasts that night. He lay down there at the appointed time and fell asleep, and in a dream he saw a man standing beside him who called him by name. "Caedmon," he said, "sing me a song." "I don't know how to sing," he replied. "It is because I cannot sing that I left the feast and came here." The man who addressed him then said: "But you shall sing to me." "What should I sing about?" he replied. "Sing about the Creation of all things," the other answered. And Caedmon immediately began to sing verses in praise of God the Creator that he had never heard before, and their theme ran thus: "Let us praise the Maker of the kingdom of heaven, the power and purpose of our Creator, and the acts of the Father of glory. Let us sing how the eternal God, the Author of all marvels, first created the heavens for the sons of men as a roof to cover them, and how their almighty Protector gave them the earth for their dwelling place." This is the general sense, but not the actual words that Caedmon sang in his dream; for however excellent the verses, it is impossible to translate them from one language into another[10] without losing much of their beauty and dignity. When Caedmon awoke, he remembered everything that he had sung in his dream, and soon added more verses in the same style to the glory of God.

Early in the morning he went to his superior the reeve,[11] and told him about this gift that he had received. The reeve took him before the abbess,[12] who ordered him to give an account of his dream and repeat the verses in the presence of many learned men, so that they might decide their quality and origin. All of them agreed that Caedmon's gift had been given him by our Lord, and when they had explained to him a passage of scriptural history or doctrine, they asked him to render[13] it into verse if he could. He promised to do this, and returned next morning with excellent verses as they had ordered him. The abbess was delighted that God had given such grace to the man, and advised him to abandon secular life and adopt the monastic state. And when she had admitted him into the Community as a brother, she ordered him to ☆ be instructed in the events of sacred history.[14] So Caedmon stored up in his memory all that he learned, and after meditating on it, turned it into such melodious verse that his delightful renderings turned his instructors into his audience. He sang of the creation of the world, the origin of the human race, and the whole story of Genesis. He sang of Israel's departure from Egypt, their entry into the land of promise, and many other events of scriptural history. He sang of the Lord's Incarnation, Passion, Resurrection, and Ascension into heaven, the coming of the Holy Spirit, and the teaching of the Apostles. He also made many poems on the terrors of the Last Judgement, the horrible pains of Hell, and the joys of the kingdom of heaven. In addition to these, he composed several others on the blessings and judgements of God, by which he sought to turn his hearers from delight in wickedness, and to inspire them to love and do good. For Caedmon was a deeply religious man, who humbly submitted to regular discipline, and firmly resisted all who tried to do evil, thus winning a happy death. ∿

---

10. In Bede's *History*, Caedmon's poem was translated from Old English into Latin.
11. A *reeve* is the manager of a manor or farm.
12. An *abbess* is the female head of a convent or monastery.

13. *Render* means "to express in another form."
14. The abbess is delighted with Caedmon's gift and advises him to join the monastery and learn the narratives of the Bible.

1 **Summarize** *Put the "general sense" of Caedmon's song into your own words.*

The Power of Faith *What does Bede mean by "a happy death"?* **2**

Assessment Practice

SPIRAL REVIEW **Short Responses Say:** Short-response questions usually do not have one correct answer. Instead, an answer is generally judged by its insightfulness and how well it is supported with textual evidence. Have students write three to five lines to answer the following question.

Ask: Does Bede use persuasion in his writing? **Explain.** *(Students may cite examples of logic, emotion, entreaty, or salesmanship, such as the promise of a "happy death.")*

After You Read

Respond and Think Critically

Respond and Interpret

1. After reading the selections, what questions would you like to ask Bede? Why?

2. (a)What arguments convince Edwin to convert to Christianity? (b)What does Edwin's reaction to the arguments reveal about his personality?

3. (a)Summarize the **analogy**, or comparison, made by one of the king's chief men. (b)What do the sparrow and the storm symbolize?

4. (a)Why does Coifi volunteer to be the first person to profane the shrine? (b)Why might the "common people" be impressed by Coifi's actions?

5. (a)What is Caedmon's life like before his dream? (b)How does it change after the dream?

Analyze and Evaluate

6. (a)Which of Paulinus's arguments for conversion did you find the most convincing? Explain. (b)Which of the arguments by Edwin's advisers did you find the most convincing? Explain.

7. (a)Analyze the poem that came to Caedmon in his dream. To what is heaven compared? (b)Why is Caedmon's dream considered to be a miracle?

Connect

8. **Big Idea** **The Power of Faith** How do the events in the two excerpts from the *Ecclesiastical History* portray the power of faith in England during the Anglo-Saxon period?

9. **Connect to Today** (a)Why was a humble poet such as Caedmon so revered in his time? (b)Do you think that a poet could be regarded as equally important today? Explain.

Primary Visual Artifact

Bede Manuscript

Before the introduction of printing in the fifteenth century, all copies of books had to be written by hand. Some, like the manuscript of Bede's *Ecclesiastical History* shown here, featured colored decorations or illustrations; others, like the *Beowulf* manuscript (page 28), were rather plain.

Group Activity With a group of classmates, discuss the following questions.

1. Why might much of the work of producing books during the Middle Ages have been carried out by monks?

2. Why might monks have chosen to decorate some books elaborately and to omit decorations in others?

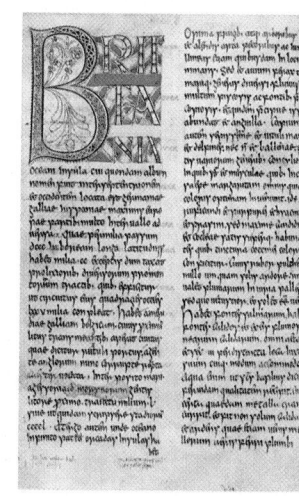

Primary Visual Artifact

1. Students may suggest that monks could read and write well, or that they had time to devote to the task of copying books.

2. Students may say that books the monks thought were more important or sacred received elaborate decorations.

Progress Check

Can students summarize?

If No → See Unit 1 Teaching Resources Book, p. 66.

After You Read

Assess

1. Students may ask about people, events, or aspects of daily life.

2. (a) The Christian God has protected Edwin and given him a kingdom; if he converts, he will go to heaven. (b) Edwin is practical and he honors his promise.

3. (a) Life is brief, and all that comes before and after is uncertain and frightening. (b) Sparrow: transitory nature of human life; storm: the void

4. (a) Coifi had consecrated the shrine himself. (b) They may worship at those shrines.

5. (a) Caedmon holds a secular job. He cannot compose or recite poetry. (b) He recites religious verse and enters a monastery.

6. Students' answers will vary.

7. (a) A kingdom with God as its king (b) Before the dream he knew nothing about poetry and was afraid to sing; he did not acquire his gift "through any human teacher."

8. The important decisions made by both kings and commoners are based on religious faith.

9. (a) Few people could read then. (b) Answers will vary.

After You Read

Literary Element

1. Answers will vary.
2. Bede was biased because he practiced Christianity. He does not explain the belief system that Christianity replaced, nor does he show anyone seriously objecting to Christianity.

Review: Internal Conflict

Internal conflict includes situations in which a character has to decide between two courses of action, has mixed feelings about something, or struggles within him- or herself in some other way.

Reading Strategy

1. Paulinus convinces Edwin to convert, with the agreement of his counselors; Coifi desecrates their former shrines.
2. Caedmon is able to compose and sing religious songs after a dream in which he is told by God to compose verses about "the Creation of all things."

Vocabulary Practice

Answers will vary but may include:
aspire
Definition: *to pursue something of high value*
Etymology: *from Latin aspirare, meaning "to breathe upon"*
Sample Sentence: *She aspired to become the mayor.*

Academic Vocabulary

Answers will vary but may include *trust, honesty,* or *respect.*

Literary Element Historical Narrative

A **historical narrative** tells the story of real people and events during a particular time and place. For this reason, a historical narrative contains many details about the period that it describes. These details are intended to present an objective rendering of reality.

1. In your opinion, do the excerpts from Bede's *Ecclesiastical History* fit the above definition of a historical narrative? Explain.
2. Although historians try to be objective, they are nevertheless influenced by the time in which they live. What biases, prejudices, or other "blind spots" might have colored Bede's work?

Review: Internal Conflict

As you learned on page 23, an **internal conflict** is a struggle that takes place within the mind of a character.

Partner Activity Work with a classmate to fill in a chart similar to the one shown below, identifying the internal conflicts faced by Edwin and Caedmon in Bede's account.

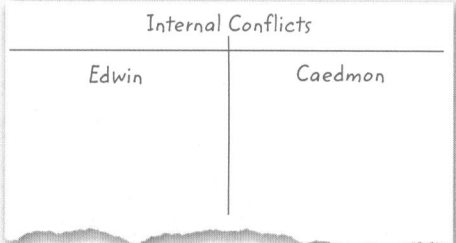

Internal Conflicts	
Edwin	Caedmon

Reading Strategy Summarize

The best summaries can easily be understood by people who have not read the works that are summarized.

1. What are the main ideas or events in the first excerpt, "The Anglo-Saxons Embrace Christianity"?
2. What are the main ideas and events in the second excerpt, "Caedmon"?

Vocabulary Practice

Practice with Word Origins Studying the etymology, or origin and history, of a word can help you better understand and explore its meaning. Create a word map, like the one below, for each of the vocabulary words in the selection. Use a dictionary for help.

aspire   diligently   expound   frivolous

Definition: *having an abundance of wealth*   Etymology: *from Latin affluens, meaning "rich"*

affluent

Sample Sentence: *Because he made very little money, Jason was forced to borrow from his more affluent relatives.*

Academic Vocabulary

The Ecclesiastical History of the English People *describes the* **foundations** *of English Christianity.*

Foundation is an academic word. In an everyday setting, *foundation* can refer to the base on which a house or other building rests.

To further explore the meaning of this word, complete the following sentence: *In my opinion, _____ is the* **foundation** *of a good friendship.*

For more on academic vocabulary, see pages 56 and R81.

 **Literature** Online

Selection Resources For Selection Quizzes, eFlashcards, and Reading-Writing Connection activities, go to glencoe.com and enter QuickPass code GLB9817u1.

Assessment Practice

SPIRAL REVIEW **Short-Answer Questions** Explain to students that short answer questions often ask you to infer a character's beliefs and assumptions. Your answer should include evidence from the text that supports your conclusions.

Have students use a graphic organizer like the one below to make inferences about characters in the text.

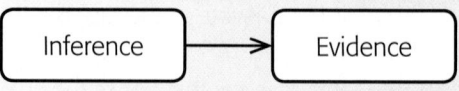

| Inference | → | Evidence |

Respond Through Writing

Reflective Essay

Compare Events The first excerpt from Bede's *History* describes how an internal conflict caused King Edwin to abandon his worship of idols and become a Christian. In a reflective essay, compare Edwin's experience to an experience that led you to change a long-held opinion. Clearly describe your original viewpoint, the event that caused your internal conflict, and the way your outlook changed.

Prewrite Review your journals, talk with family members and friends, and brainstorm to identify a situation in which you experienced an internal conflict. Then freewrite to generate details about your original belief, the events that forced you to change it, and your current belief.

Draft Make a chart or Venn diagram to clarify which aspects of your experience you will compare with King Edwin's experience.

Me	King Edwin
Believed that I'd get into first-choice college, but was rejected	Believed in idols

Be sure to explain why this event was significant for you, as King Edwin's was for him. You may want to employ rhetorical devices such as repetition or parallelism to help highlight the similarities and differences between your circumstances and Edwin's. Take a broad view of the situations, focusing both on concrete events and the more abstract ideas they involve.

Revise Reread your essay to make sure you have accurately reported Edwin's experience and your own and have compared the experiences in specific ways. Use statements such as this to make the comparison clear:

Like/Unlike Edwin's conclusion that _____,
my conclusion was that _____.

Use the Writing Workshop checklist on page 852 to check other elements of your draft.

Edit and Proofread Proofread your paper, correcting any errors in spelling, grammar, and punctuation. Use the Grammar Tip in the side column to help you with verb tenses.

Learning Objectives

In this assignment, you will focus on the following objectives:

Writing: Writing a reflective essay.

Reading: Connecting to personal experience.

Grammar: Using correct verb tenses.

> ### Grammar Tip
>
> **Verb Tenses**
>
> When comparing your own experience with King Edwin's, use the literary present tense to describe his experience, just as you would for other events in a work of literature. However, use the past tense to report what happened to you.
>
> *Unlike King Edwin, who **seems** to embrace Christianity once and for all, I **had** to remind myself repeatedly of the lesson I had learned.*
>
> Make sure you use these tenses correctly and consistently throughout your essay.

After You Read

Respond Through Writing

Use these criteria in evaluating student reflective essays:

- The essay accurately reports King Edwin's internal conflict and logically and vividly describes the student's personal experience.
- The two internal conflicts are compared on the basis of clear, specific criteria.
- King Edwin's experience is reported in the literary present, and the student's, in the past tense.

A student who meets all of these criteria should receive the equivalent of a 4-point response.

A student who fully meets two or partially meets three of these criteria should receive the equivalent of a 3-point response.

A student who fully meets one or partially meets two of these criteria should receive the equivalent of a 2-point response.

A student who partially meets one of these criteria should receive the equivalent of a 1-point response.

English Learners

DIFFERENTIATED INSTRUCTION

Beginning Recall with students that King Edwin believed in multiple gods for many years before he converted to Christianity. Ask them to write a paragraph about a time when they, like Edwin, changed their opinion about something. Remind them that a paragraph needs a main idea and details that support that main idea.

Focus

Combine Sentences

Write on the board: Yesterday I ate oranges. They were full of vitamins. They tasted good.

Have students combine these three short sentences into one or two sentences. *(Sentences will vary.)* Ask volunteers to share their sentences with the class.

Teach

Long or Short Sentences?

Long sentences generally result in a slower pace, while short sentences move the reader along more quickly.

 For additional grammar practice, see Unit 1 Teaching Resources Book, p. 72.

Learning Objectives

For pages 96–97
In this workshop, you will focus on the following objectives:

Grammar:
Understanding how to use coordinating conjunctions. Understanding how to use main and subordinate clauses.

Drafting Tip

Vary the length and structure of your sentences. Work for a rhythmic, interesting balance of long and short sentences, remembering that brevity often has dramatic force. By using different kinds of sentence openers—and by sometimes tucking information in the middle of a sentence—you can create stylistic interest.

Revising Tip

Read your draft aloud, stopping now and then to experiment with clusters of sentences. Whisper them to yourself in various combinations to find out which version sounds most effective. This process is faster than rewriting and helps you decide on a "best sentence" to write down.

Grammar Workshop

Sentence Combining

Literature Connection Writing always involves choices.

"One day Paulinus came to him and, placing his right hand on the king's head, asked him if he recognized this sign."

—The Venerable Bede, from *The Ecclesiastical History of the English People*

Consider that the sentence above might have been written "One day Paulinus came to him. He placed his right hand on the king's head. He asked the king if he recognized this sign." Instead, Bede's translator chose to combine these ideas into one sentence. Making short sentences into longer ones can help you develop your own writing style.

Strategies for Sentence Combining

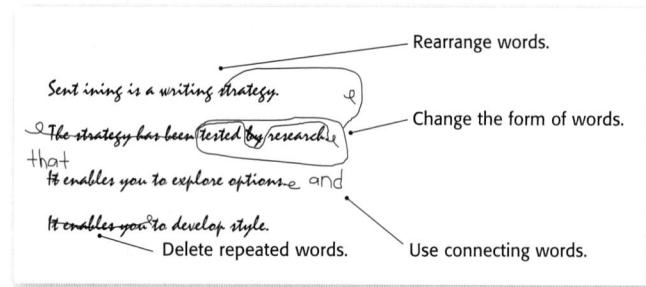

Edited Version: *Sentence combining is a research-tested writing strategy that enables you to explore options and to develop style.*

Here are some specific ways in which you can combine sentences:

Use a **prepositional phrase,** a group of words that begins with a preposition and ends with a noun or a pronoun.

Separate: *Caedmon's talent for poetry was a gift. God gave it to him.*

Combined with prepositional phrase: *Caedmon's talent for poetry was a gift <u>from God</u>.*

Use an **appositive,** a noun or pronoun placed next to another noun or pronoun to give additional information about it. An **appositive phrase** is an appositive plus words that modify it.

Separate: *The Venerable Bede lived in the eighth century. He was an English monk.*

Combined with appositive phrase: *The Venerable Bede, <u>an English monk</u>, lived in the eighth century.*

Grammar Practice

Comma Usage To help students understand how to use commas when combining sentences, focus on the following points:

- Commas may be placed before a coordinating conjunction, especially in a long sentence.

- Commas are often used before and after an appositive phrase. For example: My brother, *a musician,* just bought a new guitar.

- Commas may be placed after an introductory clause or introductory phrase.

Use a **participial phrase**. A **participle** is a verb form, often ending in *-ing* or *-ed,* that functions as an adjective. A participial phrase—a participle and other words that add to it—also functions as an adjective.

Separate: *Edwin was inspired by Paulinus. He became a Christian.*

Combined with participial phrase: *Inspired by Paulinus, Edwin became a Christian.*

Use a **coordinating conjunction** to join words or groups of words with equal grammatical weight in a sentence. Coordinating conjunctions are words such as *and, but, or, so, nor, for,* and *yet.*

Separate: *Life is a bird that escapes from the storm. It flits into the hall. It stays for only a moment.*

Combined with coordinating conjunctions: *Life is a bird that escapes from the storm <u>and</u> flits into the hall <u>but stays for only a moment</u>.*

Use a **subordinating conjunction** to join two clauses, in a way that makes one dependent upon the other. Subordinating conjunctions are words such as *after, although, as, because, if, since,* and *when.*

Separate: *Caedmon was a poet. He did not write in Latin. He had no formal education.*

Combined with subordinating conjunctions: *<u>Although</u> Caedmon was a poet, he did not write in Latin <u>because</u> he had no formal education.*

Use an **adjective clause**, a group of words with a subject and a predicate that modifies a noun or a pronoun. Adjective clauses often begin with *who, whom, whose, that,* or *which.*

Separate: *People heard Caedmon's verses. They were deeply moved.*

Combined with adjective clause: *People <u>who heard Caedmon's verses</u> were deeply moved.*

Revise Combine each group of sentences into a single sentence

1. Caedmon was a simple man. He had a gift for poetry. He had a deep faith in God.
2. Edwin heard what Paulinus had to say. He consulted with his counselors. They persuaded him to embrace Christianity.
3. Coifi destroyed the shrine and its idols. Coifi was Edwin's chief priest. He was convinced that his old religion was false.

Tip

Remember that there are many ways of combining sentences. When deciding which solution works best, ask yourself the following questions:

- Is this solution free of excess words?
- Does this solution emphasize the important idea of the sentence?
- Does this solution flow naturally when I read it aloud?
- Is this solution a complete sentence, with a subject and predicate, and not just a long fragment?

 **Literature** Online

Grammar For more grammar practice, go to glencoe.com and enter QuickPass code GLB9817u1.

Grammar Workshop

Teach

While there are many ways to combine sentences, some combinations may be clearer or have a more interesting rhythm. One way to decide between two different combinations is to read them aloud. Your ear may tell you which one works best.

Assess

Possible answers:

1. Caedmon was a simple man with a gift for poetry and a deep faith in God.
2. After hearing what Paulinus had to say, Edwin consulted with his counselors, who persuaded him to embrace Christianity.
3. Convinced that his old religion was false, Edwin's chief priest, Coifi, destroyed the shrine and its idols.

Approaching Level

DIFFERENTIATED INSTRUCTION

Emerging Students may find it difficult to understand the various strategies for sentence combining without a firm grasp of parts of speech. Help them review parts of speech by focusing on each example sentence. Guide students in identifying the nouns, verbs, prepositions, conjunctions, adverbs, and adjectives in each sentence.

Focus

Bellringer Options

Daily Language Practice Transparency 7

Or say: Many words from other languages were adopted into English as it developed. Can you name words that come from other languages that are now part of English? *(Possible answers: garage [French]; data [Latin]; rodeo [Spanish]; umbrella [Italian]; algebra [Arabic])*

Teach

Literary Element | 1

Dialect Remind students that a dialect is a way of speaking that is characteristic of a particular region or group of people. **Ask:** What kinds of dialects are spoken in the United States? *(Students may mention Southern and New England dialects.)*

Vocabulary Practice

 SPIRAL REVIEW French Words Say: Many French words are found in English today. **On the board, write:** amateur, ballet, beau, boulevard, brochure, bureau, café, envoy, glacier, invalid, limousine, morale, plateau, and restaurant. Have students use a dictionary to research the etymology of each word and how it became a part of the English language. Then, have students pick at least four of the words and use

each in a sentence that use context clues to indicate the meaning of the word. *(Sentences will vary.)*

Learning Objectives

For pages 98–99

In studying this text, you will focus on the following objective:

Reading: Analyzing historical context.

The Development of English

THE ENGLISH LANGUAGE BEGAN AS *Englisc*, the speech of a scattered population of Anglo-Saxon peoples on an island off the European coast. Today, English is a global language spoken by perhaps a billion people around the world. This is largely due to the political power and cultural influence of the British Empire and the United States. However, it is also the result of the simplicity that English grammar has acquired during its long history. Before reaching its modern form, English passed through two major stages, Old English and Middle English.

> *"One cannot but be impressed by the amazing hospitality of the English language."*
>
> —Robert Burchfield

Old English: 450–1150

1 The Anglo-Saxons spoke various Germanic dialects, a mixture of which are the basis of Old English, the form of the English language used from the mid-400s to the early 1100s. To present-day readers of English, Old English looks like a foreign language, as these lines from the Old English epic poem *Beowulf* show:

*Ða com of more   under mist-hleoþum
Grendel gongan,   Godes yrre bær*

(Then out of the marsh, under mist-covered cliffs,
  Grendel stalked, bearing God's wrath)

Old English has had a significant effect on Modern English. Although less than one percent of the words—4,500 out of 500,000—in the *Oxford English Dictionary* are from Old English, these words form our most basic (*man, wife, work, Friday, house*) and functional (*to, for, but, and*) vocabulary. One computer analysis revealed that all of the hundred most commonly used English words are of Anglo-Saxon origin.

Interior of Scriptorium, School of Segovia. Spanish School. Oil on panel. Museo Lazaro Galdiano, Madrid, Spain.

By the 600s, Christian scribes had further developed English by replacing the ancient Germanic characters known as runes with the Old English alphabet of twenty-four letters. The scribes who transcribed *Beowulf* around the year 1000 used this alphabet.

98 UNIT 1   THE ANGLO-SAXON PERIOD AND THE MIDDLE AGES

Middle English: 1150–1500

Between 450 and 1200, Latin, Danish, Old Norse, and Norman French fed the growing English language. After the Norman Conquest in 1066, England's new aristocracy spoke French. Well-educated people needed to know three languages, however: French for dealing with the nobility or the courts; Latin for the church, business, and scholarship; and English for communication with the majority of the common people. French had a strong influence on English. Many French words were introduced into the language that was becoming Middle English, and many Old English words were dropped. In fact, French increased the English vocabulary by a

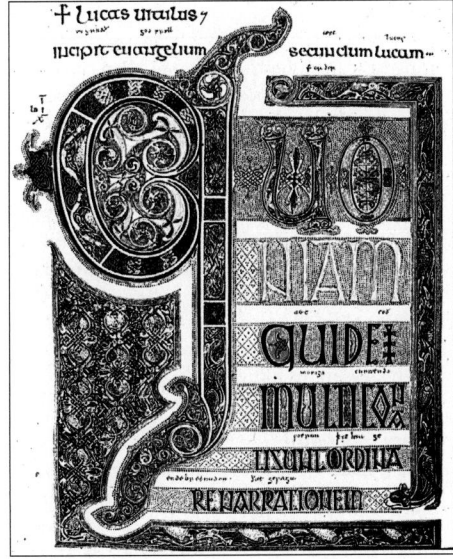

Illuminated page from St. Luke's Gospel taken from Lindisfarne Gospels, c. 695.

staggering 10,000 words, 7,500 of which are still in use. Today, almost half of Modern English's vocabulary comes from Latin and French. French influence also led to the gradual simplification of English grammar and spelling. Middle English slowly developed into a language somewhat similar to the English used today.

Linguistic diversity, however, remained so great during this period that people in one part of England could often not understand people who lived in another part. Over time, the dialect spoken in London—the language in which Geoffrey Chaucer wrote—eventually became the standard. Compare these opening lines of his *Canterbury Tales* with the passage from *Beowulf* quoted earlier:

Whan that Aprille with his shoures soote
The droghte of March hath perced to the roote,
And bathed every veyne in swich licour
Of which vertu engendred is the flour;
Whan Zephirus eek with his sweete breeth
Inspired hath in every holt and heeth
The tendre croppes, and the yonge sonne
Hath in the Ram his halve cours yronne,
And smale foweles maken melodye,
That slepen al the nyght with open ye
(So priketh hem nature in hir corages);
Thanne longen folk to goon on pilgrimages,
And palmeres for to seken straunge strondes,
To ferne halwes, kowthe in sondry londes;
And specially from every shires ende
Of Engelond to Caunterbury they wende,
The hooly blisful martir for to seke,
That hem hath holpen whan that they were seeke.

LOG ON ▶ **Literature** Online

Literature and Reading For more about the development of English, go to glencoe.com and enter QuickPass code GLB9817u1.

Respond and Think Critically

1. What most surprises you about the development of the English language? Explain.

2. Why do you think Old English remained an important influence on the development of English even after the Norman Conquest?

3. Why do you think the form of Middle English used in the London region became the standard form?

4. In what ways is the language of *The Canterbury Tales* more accessible to a modern reader than the language of *Beowulf*?

LITERARY HISTORY **99**

Advanced Learners

DIFFERENTIATED INSTRUCTION

French Influence Tell students that one result of French influence was the gradual simplification of English grammar and spelling in Middle English.

- The Norman scribes introduced *gh* and changed *cw* to w*qu*.

- Prepositions began to replace Old English word endings.

- A fixed word order of subject-verb-object began to dominate prose sentences.

- Classification of nouns by gender (masculine, feminine, or neuter) disappeared.

Have students find examples of Middle English writings and write a paragraph summary of what the text states.

Teach

Big Idea	2

The Power of Faith Explain to students that many of the Latin words that entered Old English were church-related terms brought to England by Christian missionaries. Have students use dictionaries to find common words that derive from Latin.

Assess

1. Answers will vary. Students might note the following: Many languages have contributed to the English language; English has an early connection to German, as seen in *Beowulf;* although French was the language of the Norman conquerors, it did not become the vernacular; Latin has contributed heavily to English vocabulary.

2. Students may suggest that it was because the common people continued to use Old English.

3. Students may conclude that it was because London dominated the rest of England politically, economically, and culturally.

4. The vocabulary and word order are recognizable; the nouns have some, but fewer inflections.

 For an audio recording of this selection, use Listening Library Audio CD-ROM.

 For an activity related to this selection, see Unit 1 Teaching Resources Book, p. 73.

99

Before You Read

Focus

Bellringer Options

Literature Launchers:
  Pre-Reading Videos DVD,
  Selection Launcher

Selection Focus
  Transparencies 5 and 6

Daily Language Practice
  Transparency 8

Or display a reproduction of a portrait. Point out that a portrait shows physical characteristics of a person and sometimes reveals personality qualities as well. **Ask:** How else can you determine the qualities of someone's personality and character?

Have students analyze, as they read, the narrator's descriptions of the pilgrims gathered at the inn.

Before You Read

from *The Canterbury Tales*

Initial with a portrait of Chaucer holding a book. English illumination, c. 1400.

Meet **Geoffrey Chaucer**

(c. 1342–1400)

Geoffrey Chaucer has often been called the father of English poetry. In the Prologue to *The Canterbury Tales*, Chaucer presents a portrait gallery virtually unparalleled in English literature. Its catalog of the virtues, vices, and idiosyncrasies of a cross section of medieval English society still resonates for modern readers.

A Man of the World Chaucer understood how a variety of people spoke and acted. This knowledge proved invaluable to his writing. Chaucer's father was a prosperous middle-class wine merchant, and the young Chaucer was likely exposed to the colorful banter of the characters who frequented the London docks. Chaucer became a page in the royal household while still a teenager. Despite the lowly duties of the job, such as running errands, the position offered Chaucer exposure to a world of fine manners and high-born people. In 1359 he went to France to fight in the Hundred Years' War. Taken prisoner, he was ransomed in the following year with money contributed by King Edward himself.

> "Although Chaucer's invented personages are now six hundred years old, they are flesh and blood today; they are, in fact, the people whom we have known all our lives."
>
> —Louis Untermeyer

Public Servant While in his twenties, Chaucer was made a court official, an appointment that was the start of many years of public service.

During his career, he traveled abroad on diplomatic missions to France, Spain, and Italy and became familiar with the literature and culture of these countries. Thereafter he held a variety of governmental posts.

Despite his busy professional duties, Chaucer managed to write a large body of work. His early poetry, such as the *Book of the Duchess*, was influenced by the French medieval tradition. Later he wrote the *Parliament of Fowls* and the masterly *Troilus and Cressida*. Chaucer's most mature writing, crafted while he was in his forties, includes the *Legend of Good Women* and *The Canterbury Tales*.

Literary Innovator *The Canterbury Tales* is considered Chaucer's masterpiece for several reasons. First, it marks the beginning of a new tradition—the use of Middle English, rather than French or Latin, as a vehicle for major literary works in England. Second, because *The Canterbury Tales* focuses on an assortment of people who are thrown together on a journey, it gives a lifelike and engaging picture of the various strata of English society during the 1300s. Finally, it is an outstanding literary achievement. Chaucer created approximately 17,000 lines of vivid poetry that still entertains readers six centuries later.

 Literature Online

Author Search For more about Geoffrey Chaucer, go to glencoe.com and enter QuickPass code GLB9817u1.

Selection Skills

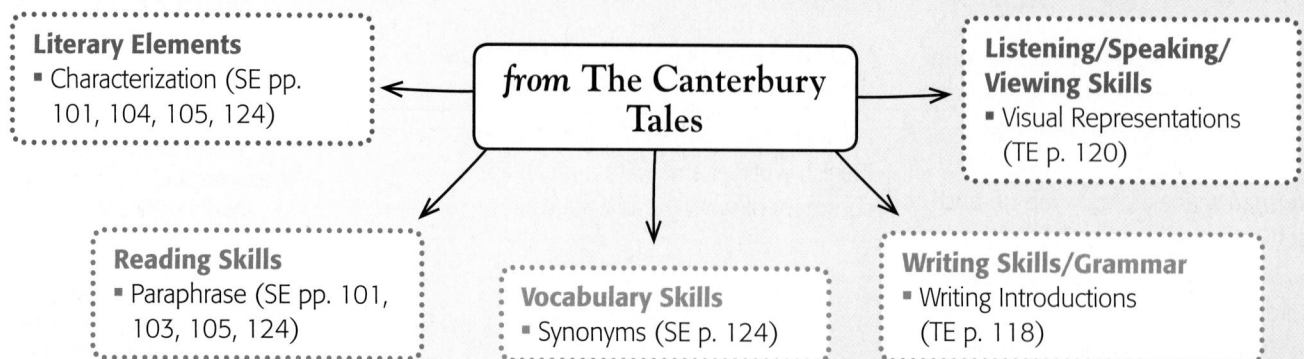

Literary Elements
- Characterization (SE pp. 101, 104, 105, 124)

***from* The Canterbury Tales**

Listening/Speaking/ Viewing Skills
- Visual Representations (TE p. 120)

Reading Skills
- Paraphrase (SE pp. 101, 103, 105, 124)

Vocabulary Skills
- Synonyms (SE p. 124)

Writing Skills/Grammar
- Writing Introductions (TE p. 118)

Literature and Reading Preview

Connect to the Poem

Have you ever tried to imagine what other people's lives are like? Write a journal entry about someone you have observed, explaining what conclusions you drew from his or her appearance and manner.

Build Background

In *The Canterbury Tales,* Chaucer uses a **frame story**—a plot structure that involves the telling of one or more stories within another story. The pilgrims' contest and journey, narrated in the Prologue and elsewhere, is the frame story. The various tales told by the pilgrims on their journey are set within this frame.

The version of *The Canterbury Tales* that you will read is a modern English translation. To sample Chaucer's Middle English, read the famous opening lines of the Prologue in the Literary History feature on page 99.

Set Purposes for Reading

Big Idea The Power of Faith

As you read the Prologue, ask yourself, In what ways do the pilgrims interpret and act upon the requirements of their religious faith?

Literary Element Characterization

Characterization involves all the methods a writer uses to reveal the values and personalities of his or her characters. A writer may make explicit statements about a character or may reveal a character indirectly through well-chosen words, thoughts, and actions. As you read, ask yourself, How does Chaucer reveal the characteristics of each pilgrim?

Reading Strategy Paraphrase

When you **paraphrase,** you put a text you have read into your own words to check your understanding of its content. A paraphrase differs from a summary in that a summary is always shorter than the original, while a paraphrase may be approximately the same length as the original. As you read, ask yourself, How could I restate this material in my own words?

....

Tip: Finding Subjects and Verbs You may find it helpful, especially when paraphrasing long, complex sentences or passages, to search for the simple subject and simple predicate in each sentence.

Learning Objectives

For pages 100–124

In studying this text, you will focus on the following objectives:

Literary Study: Analyzing characterization.

Reading: Paraphrasing.

Writing: Writing a character sketch.

Vocabulary

solicitous (sə lis′ ə təs) *adj.* full of concern; p. 106 *The shopkeeper was solicitous toward Helen because of her accident on store property.*

estimable (es′ tə mə bəl) *adj.* deserving of esteem; admirable; p. 110 *The estimable volunteers raised five thousand dollars.*

discreet (dis krēt′) *adj.* showing careful judgment in speech and action; prudent; p. 111 *The talk-show guest was discreet and did not criticize his fellow actors.*

disdainful (dis dān′ fəl) *adj.* feeling or showing contempt; scornful; p. 115 *Although he had come from an impoverished background, Robert was disdainful toward the homeless.*

prevarication (pri var′ ə kā′ shən) *n.* an act of evading the truth; lie; p. 120 *You had better tell the truth; your prevarication will only get you into more trouble.*

Before You Read

Focus

Summary

The narrator describes a group of pilgrims assembled at an inn near London prior to their journey to Canterbury. The host proposes that each pilgrim tell two tales on the journey. Whoever tells the best tale will win a dinner paid for by the group. The host joins the pilgrims and becomes their judge. The travelers draw lots to decide the order of the tales, and the cut falls to the knight.

 For summaries in language other than English, see Unit 1 Teaching Resources Book, pp. 75–80.

Vocabulary

Word Origins Tell students that looking up a related word may help them find the origin of a word (for example, *esteem* for *estimable*). Have students consult a dictionary for etymologies.

 For additional vocabulary practice, see Unit 1 Teaching Resources Book, p. 83.

 For additional context, see Glencoe Interactive Vocabulary CD-ROM.

English Learners

DIFFERENTIATED INSTRUCTION

Intermediate Incorrect pronunciation can prevent English language learners from identifying rhyming words in couplets. To help students hear the rhyming sounds, have them take turns reading aloud eight to ten lines from the poem. Help them pronounce the rhyming words correctly.

Advanced Students may concentrate solely on word definitions, losing sight of the mood of what they are reading. Have students read lines 475 through 486 and identify the humor Chaucer uses in describing the wife of Bath.

Teach

Reading Strategy   1

Paraphrase **Answer:** *The narrator describes spring and people's awakened desire to go on pilgrimages.*

Big Idea   2

The Power of Faith

Say: Keep these questions in mind as you read: What do the occupations of many of the pilgrims have in common? *(Possible response: Many of them are involved with the church.)* Which of the pilgrims seem the most pious? *(Possible responses: Parson; Plowman)* Which seem corrupt in some way? *(Possible answers: Pardoner; Skipper; Friar)*

APPROACHING For students having difficulty, point out the place where each character is described. Students may want to mark these places with sticky notes.

View the Art ★

The word *illuminated* originally referred to the use of gold to decorate letters in hand-copied books. Today, however, the word generally refers to the illustrations in these kinds of books, such as the one shown here.

First page of the *Canterbury Tales.* Illuminated manuscript, early 15th century. ★

from
The Canterbury Tales

Geoffrey Chaucer
Translated by Nevill Coghill

from The Prologue

When in April the sweet showers fall
And pierce the drought of March to the root, and all
The veins are bathed in liquor of such power
As brings about the engendering of the flower,
5 When also Zephyrus° with his sweet breath
Exhales an air in every grove and heath
Upon the tender shoots, and the young sun
His half-course in the sign of the *Ram*° has run,
And the small fowl are making melody
10 That sleep away the night with open eye
(So nature pricks them and their heart engages)
Then people long to go on pilgrimages
And palmers° long to seek the stranger strands
Of far-off saints, hallowed° in sundry° lands,
15 And specially, from every shire's end
Of England, down to Canterbury they wend
To seek the holy blissful martyr,° quick
To give his help to them when they were sick.
    It happened in that season that one day
20 In Southwark,° at *The Tabard,*° as I lay
Ready to go on pilgrimage and start
For Canterbury, most devout at heart,
At night there came into that hostelry°

5 Zephyrus (zef′ ə rəs): the Greek mythological god of the west wind, which brings mild weather.

8 Ram: the constellation Aries and the first sign of the zodiac. Evidence suggests that the pilgrimage began on April 11, 1387.

13 palmers: pilgrims who wore palm leaves as a sign that they had visited the Holy Land.
14 hallowed: regarded as sacred or holy. **sundry:** various.
17 martyr: Thomas à Becket, archbishop of Canterbury, who was murdered in 1170.

20 Southwark (suth′ ərk): a town just across the river Thames from London (today, part of Greater London). **The Tabard** (tab′ ərd): an inn in Southwark.
23 hostelry (hos′ təl rē): inn.

Paraphrase *Paraphrase the opening lines (1–12), which introduce the subject of the poem.*   1

Writing Practice

End-Stopped vs. Enjambed Lines

SPIRAL REVIEW Explain to students that when a line ends with a comma or a period, the line is end-stopped. As you read, pause at the end of such a line. When a line is enjambed, the sentence continues to the next line with less of a pause. Ask students to find examples of both types of line and to practice reading them aloud.

Some nine and twenty in a company
25 Of sundry folk happening then to fall
In fellowship, and they were pilgrims all
That towards Canterbury meant to ride.
The rooms and stables of the inn were wide;
They made us easy, all was of the best.
30 And, briefly, when the sun had gone to rest,
I'd spoken to them all upon the trip
And was soon one with them in fellowship,
Pledged to rise early and to take the way
To Canterbury, as you heard me say.
35   But none the less, while I have time and space,
Before my story takes a further pace,
It seems a reasonable thing to say
What their condition was, the full array°
Of each of them, as it appeared to me,
40 According to profession and degree,
And what apparel they were riding in;
And at a Knight I therefore will begin.
There was a *Knight*, a most distinguished man,
Who from the day on which he first began
45 To ride abroad had followed chivalry, ☆
Truth, honor, generousness and courtesy.
He had done nobly in his sovereign's° war
And ridden into battle, no man more,
As well in Christian as in heathen places,
50 And ever honored for his noble graces.
    When we took Alexandria,° he was there.
He often sat at table in the chair
Of honor, above all nations, when in Prussia.
In Lithuania he had ridden, and Russia,
55 No Christian man so often, of his rank.
When, in Granada, Algeciras sank
Under assault, he had been there, and in
North Africa, raiding Benamarin;
In Anatolia he had been as well
60 And fought when Ayas and Attalia fell,
For all along the Mediterranean coast
He had embarked with many a noble host.°
In fifteen mortal battles he had been
And jousted° for our faith at Tramissen
65 Thrice in the lists,° and always killed his man.
This same distinguished knight had led the van
Once with the Bey of Balat,° doing work

38 the full array: all of the outfit or trappings.

47 sovereign's: ruler's; king's or queen's.

51 Alexandria: This and the places named in the following lines were sites of wide-ranging military campaigns and crusades by medieval Christians against Muslims and other non-Christians.

62 host: army.

64 jousted: fought in formal combat as part of a knightly tournament.
65 lists: the fenced areas where jousts were held.
67 Bey of Balat: a Turkish governor.

Paraphrase *What does the narrator intend to do?* **3**

GEOFFREY CHAUCER **103**

Teach

Reading Strategy | 3

Paraphrase **Answer:** *The narrator plans to describe the people who will undertake the pilgrimage.*

Language History ☆

Chivalry Tell students that *chivalry* comes from the French word *cheval*, which means "horse." *Cheval* is derived from the Latin word *caballus*. A *caballarius* was a horseman; a *chevalier* was a knight.

English Learners

DIFFERENTIATED INSTRUCTION 🔄

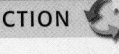
Intermediate Have students work in small groups to summarize the main actions of each stanza and then make a prediction about the thoughts, beliefs, and motivations of each character. Have them organize their predictions in a graphic organizer, supporting their assumptions with textual evidence.

Prediction	Evidence

Teach

Literary Element | 1

Characterization Answer:
The speaker praises the Knight's military success and admires his bravery and sense of honor. The Knight displays the qualities of chivalry to perfection: truthfulness, generosity, courtesy, wisdom, modesty, gentleness, and noble grace.

Literary Element | 2

Characterization Answer:
Whereas the Knight is modest and soberly dressed, his son the Squire is flamboyantly and ostentatiously attired. In contrast to the Knight, the Squire is frivolous and fond of sensual pleasure.

The Pilgrimage to Canterbury, 1806–1807. Thomas Stothard. Oil on wood, 31.8 x 95.2 cm. Tate Gallery, London.

For him against another heathen Turk;
He was of sovereign value in all eyes.
70   And though so much distinguished, he was wise
And in his bearing modest as a maid.
He never yet a boorish° thing had said
In all his life to any, come what might;
He was a true, a perfect gentle-knight.
75   Speaking of his equipment, he possessed
Fine horses, but he was not gaily dressed.
He wore a fustian° tunic stained and dark
With smudges where his armor had left mark;
Just home from service, he had joined our ranks
80   To do his pilgrimage and render thanks.
He had his son with him, a fine young Squire,
A lover and cadet, a lad of fire
With locks as curly as if they had been pressed.
He was some twenty years of age, I guessed.
85   In stature he was of a moderate length,
With wonderful agility and strength.
He'd seen some service with the cavalry
In Flanders and Artois and Picardy°
And had done valiantly in little space
90   Of time, in hope to win his lady's grace.
He was embroidered like a meadow bright
And full of freshest flowers, red and white.

72 boorish: crude; ill-mannered.

77 fustian: a coarse, heavy fabric of cotton and linen.

88 Flanders . . . Picardy: historic regions of Belgium, Holland, and northern France.

Characterization *What qualities does the speaker admire in the Knight?* **1**

Characterization *How does the Squire's character differ from that of the Knight?* **2**

Reading Practice

SPIRAL REVIEW **Inferences about Characters**
In reading this work, students must often pause to look up words or read annotations. As a result, they may lose track of which character is being described. Have students make a chart with a column for each character. In these columns, students can list details about each character's appearance, age, personality, words, and actions. This may help students make inferences and draw conclusions about the characters.

View the Art Which of the characters in the painting match the descriptions of the pilgrims given in the poem? ★
What mood is suggested by the pilgrims' expressions and stances?

Singing he was, or fluting all the day;
He was as fresh as is the month of May.
95   Short was his gown, the sleeves were long and wide;
He knew the way to sit a horse and ride.
He could make songs and poems and recite,
Knew how to joust and dance, to draw and write.
He loved so hotly that till dawn grew pale
100 He slept as little as a nightingale.
Courteous he was, lowly and serviceable,
And carved to serve his father at the table.
    There was a *Yeoman*° with him at his side,
No other servant; so he chose to ride.
105 This Yeoman wore a coat and hood of green,
And peacock-feathered arrows, bright and keen
And neatly sheathed, hung at his belt the while
—For he could dress his gear in yeoman style,
His arrows never drooped their feathers low—
110 And in his hand he bore a mighty bow.
His head was like a nut, his face was brown.
He knew the whole of woodcraft up and down.
A saucy brace° was on his arm to ward

3

It from the bow-string, and a shield and sword
115 Hung at one side, and at the other slipped
A jaunty dirk,° spear-sharp and well-equipped.
A medal of St. Christopher° he wore
Of shining silver on his breast, and bore
A hunting-horn, well slung and burnished clean,
120 That dangled from a baldrick° of bright green.
He was a proper forester, I guess.
    There also was a *Nun*, a Prioress,°

103 **Yeoman** (yō´ mən): a nobleman's attendant.

113 **brace**: a leather guard worn on an archer's forearm.

116 **dirk**: a small dagger.
117 **St. Christopher**: the patron saint of travelers. **4**

120 **baldrick**: a shoulder belt.
122 **Prioress**: the nun ranking next below the head nun in an abbey.

GEOFFREY CHAUCER **105**

Teach

Reading Strategy | 3

Paraphrase Have students paraphrase the details that the narrator provides about the Yeoman in this passage. **Ask:** What did you learn about the Yeoman in this passage? *(The Yeoman is wearing a green coat and hood and carries several weapons. He may be a forester.)*

(APPROACHING) If students are having difficulty, ask them to read aloud sentences that contain details about the Yeoman.

Literary Element | 4

Characterization Have students read the side note about St. Christopher. **Ask:** Why is this saint a perfect match for the Yeoman character? *(St. Christopher is the patron saint of foresters and travelers, and at this time the Yeoman is both.)*

View the Art ★

Answer: *Students' answers will vary.*

Skilled in several arts, Thomas Stothard (1775–1834) designed works both small and large, including delicate jewelry and national monuments.

English Learners

DIFFERENTIATED INSTRUCTION

Beginning Ask students to find the word *pilgrim* in a dictionary and to note that this word has several related definitions. **Ask:** Which definition best fits the meaning of "pilgrim" as it is used in the poem? *(A traveler or someone who wanders.)*

Teach

Big Idea   1

The Power of Faith

Answer: *Students may say that she seems too worldly and vain to be a devoted nun in a medieval abbey. There is also an air of insincerity about the Prioress in that she "counterfeits" her courtly grace.*

Literary Element   2

Characterization   Answer:

Some students will admire the Prioress's kindness toward animals. Others may say that the speaker's words here are intended to be ironic. Christian charity is generally extended to people, yet no mention is made of the Prioress's extending herself to alleviate the plight of the poor.

ENGLISH LEARNERS English learners may miss the subtle irony implicit in this description. To clarify it, make sure that they understand the meaning of "straining to counterfeit" and "seem dignified."

Her way of smiling very simple and coy.
Her greatest oath was only "By St. Loy!"°
125 And she was known as Madam Eglantyne.
And well she sang a service,° with a fine
Intoning through her nose, as was most seemly,
And she spoke daintily in French, extremely,
After the school of Stratford-atte-Bowe;°
130 French in the Paris style she did not know.
At meat her manners were well taught withal;
No morsel from her lips did she let fall,
Nor dipped her fingers in the sauce too deep;
But she could carry a morsel up and keep
135 The smallest drop from falling on her breast.
For courtliness she had a special zest,
And she would wipe her upper lip so clean
That not a trace of grease was to be seen
Upon the cup when she had drunk; to eat,
140 She reached a hand sedately for the meat.
She certainly was very entertaining,
Pleasant and friendly in her ways, and straining
To counterfeit a courtly kind of grace,
A stately bearing fitting to her place,
145 And to seem dignified in all her dealings.
As for her sympathies and tender feelings,
She was so charitably **solicitous**
She used to weep if she but saw a mouse
Caught in a trap, if it were dead or bleeding.
150 And she had little dogs she would be feeding
With roasted flesh, or milk, or fine white bread.
And bitterly she wept if one were dead
Or someone took a stick and made it smart;
She was all sentiment and tender heart.
155 Her veil was gathered in a seemly way,
Her nose was elegant, her eyes glass-gray;
Her mouth was very small, but soft and red,
Her forehead, certainly, was fair of spread,
Almost a span° across the brows, I own;
160 She was indeed by no means undergrown.

124 St. Loy: St. Eligius, patron saint of goldsmiths and jewelers, known for his good looks and sumptuous attire.
126 service: daily prayers.

129 Stratford-atte-Bowe: a nunnery near London where provincial, rather than courtly, French was taught.

159 span: nine inches. A broad forehead was considered a sign of beauty in Chaucer's day.

The Power of Faith *Does the Prioress conform to your conception of a high-ranking official of the church? Explain.*   **1**

Characterization *What is your opinion of the Prioress's "charity" toward animals? Explain.*   **2**

Vocabulary

solicitous (sə lisʹ ə təs) *adj.* full of concern

Writing Practice

 Point of View

SPIRAL REVIEW The Prioress is the picture of refinement, but she strains to "counterfeit a courtly kind of grace" (line 143). Encourage students to think of people they know or have seen who struggle to maintain an image. **Ask:** Do you think the Prioress is conscious of her "counterfeiting"?

Have students make a word web with the word "Prioress" at the center. Then have them write a short narrative, told from the Prioress's point of view, that reflects some of the ideas in the web.

Bird's eye view of Canterbury. Georg Braun and Franz Hogenberg. Copper engraving. Civitates Orbis Terrarum, Cologne, Germany.

View the Art During the Renaissance, mapmaking was a hobby of many statesmen. What elements of this map strike you as different from modern maps? What does the map tell you about medieval cities like Canterbury? ★

Her cloak, I noticed, had a graceful charm.
She wore a coral trinket on her arm,
A set of beads, the gaudies° tricked in green,
Whence hung a golden brooch of brightest sheen
165 On which there first was graven a crowned A,
And lower, *Amor vincit omnia.*°
    Another Nun, the secretary at her cell,
Was riding with her, and *three Priests* as well.
    A *Monk* there was, one of the finest sort
170 Who rode the country; hunting was his sport.
A manly man, to be an Abbot° able;
Many a dainty horse he had in stable.
His bridle, when he rode, a man might hear
Jingling in a whistling wind as clear,
175 Aye, and as loud as does the chapel bell
Where my lord Monk was Prior of the cell.°
The Rule of good St. Benet or St. Maur°
As old and strict he tended to ignore;
He let go by the things of yesterday
180 And took the modern world's more spacious way.
He did not rate that text at a plucked hen
Which says that hunters are not holy men
And that a monk uncloistered° is a mere
Fish out of water, flapping on the pier,
185 That is to say a monk out of his cloister.
That was a text he held not worth an oyster;
And I agreed and said his views were sound;
Was he to study till his head went round
Poring over books in cloisters? Must he toil
190 As Austin° bade and till the very soil?
Was he to leave the world upon the shelf?
Let Austin have his labor to himself.
    This Monk was therefore a good man to horse;
Greyhounds he had, as swift as birds, to course.°

3

163 gaudies: large beads used in counting prayers.

166 Amor vincit omnia (ä´ môr win´ kit ôm´ nē ə): Latin for "Love conquers all."

171 Abbot: the head of a monastery.

176 Prior of the cell: the head of a subordinate monastery.
177 St. Benet or St. Maur: French versions of the names of St. Benedict, who established the rules of European monasticism, and St. Maurus, one of his followers. Monastic life is governed by strict rules requiring poverty, chastity, and obedience.
183 uncloistered: not cloistered, or retired or secluded from the world, as most monks were.

190 Austin: an English version of the name of St. Augustine (A.D. 354–430), a church father who instructed monks to avoid idleness by performing manual labor.
194 to course: for hunting.

GEOFFREY CHAUCER **107**

Teach

Paraphrase **Answer:** *Students' paraphrases should mention the Monk's worldliness and his flippant dismissal of the austere rules of his monastic order.*

Literary Element　2

Characterization Have students reread the physical description of the Monk, beginning on page 107. **Ask:** What do the details in this description reveal about the Monk? (*He seems prosperous and fun loving, with an affinity for opulence and worldly goods. He does not seem religious.*)

Make sure that English learners understand lines 225–236—that is, that the Friar considers a "gift" of money a "sure sign" of a person's repentance that warrants absolution.

Big Idea　3

The Power of Faith
Answer: *Answers will vary but may include that the Friar accepts money and gifts for hearing confessions and granting people absolution of their sins.*

195　Hunting a hare or riding at a fence
　　　Was all his fun, he spared for no expense.
　　　I saw his sleeves were garnished at the hand
　　　With fine grey fur, the finest in the land,
　　　And on his hood, to fasten it at his chin
200　He had a wrought-gold cunningly fashioned pin;
　　　Into a lover's knot it seemed to pass.
　　　His head was bald and shone like looking-glass;
　　　So did his face, as if it had been greased.
　　　He was a fat and personable priest;
205　His prominent eyeballs never seemed to settle.
　　　They glittered like the flames beneath a kettle;
　　　Supple his boots, his horse in fine condition.
　　　He was a prelate° fit for exhibition,
　　　He was not pale like a tormented soul.
210　He liked a fat swan best, and roasted whole.
　　　His palfrey° was as brown as is a berry.　**2**
　　　　　There was a *Friar*, a wanton° one and merry,
　　　A Limiter,° a very festive fellow.
　　　In all Four Orders° there was none so mellow,
215　So glib with gallant phrase and well-turned speech.
　　　He'd fixed up many a marriage, giving each
　　　Of his young women what he could afford her.
　　　He was a noble pillar to his Order.
　　　Highly beloved and intimate was he
220　With County folk° within his boundary,
　　　And city dames of honor and possessions;
　　　For he was qualified to hear confessions,
　　　Or so he said, with more than priestly scope;
　　　He had a special license from the Pope.
225　Sweetly he heard his penitents at shrift°
　　　With pleasant absolution,° for a gift.
　　　He was an easy man in penance-giving
　　　Where he could hope to make a decent living;
　　　It's a sure sign whenever gifts are given
230　To a poor Order that a man's well shriven,°
　　　And should he give enough he knew in verity
　　　The penitent repented in sincerity.
　　　For many a fellow is so hard of heart
　　　He cannot weep, for all his inward smart.
235　Therefore instead of weeping and of prayer
　　　One should give silver for a poor Friar's care.

Paraphrase　*Paraphrase the Monk's philosophy of life.*　**1**

The Power of Faith　*How does the Friar represent the corruption in the medieval church?*　**3**

208 prelate: a high-ranking clergyman.

211 palfrey: a horse that is saddled and ready for riding.
212 wanton: lively, but here also meaning "morally lax."
213 Limiter: a friar licensed to beg in a certain district.
214 Four Orders: the four religious orders in which friars lived by begging: Dominicans, Franciscans, Carmelites, and Augustinians.

220 County folk: wealthy and socially prominent rural landowners.

225 shrift: confession.
226 absolution: formal forgiveness.

230 well shriven: completely forgiven, through confession, of his sins.

Reading Practice

SPIRAL REVIEW　Rereading Remind students that rereading a passage will help them to recognize an author's tone and purpose for writing and to appreciate the writer's rhetorical or literary devices. Write the following headings on the board:

Tone, Author's Purpose, and *Rhetorical and Literary Devices.* Have students copy them onto a piece of paper to guide their note taking as they reread.

He kept his tippet° stuffed with pins for curls,
And pocket-knives, to give to pretty girls.
And certainly his voice was gay and sturdy,
240 For he sang well and played the hurdy-gurdy.°
At sing-songs he was champion of the hour.
His neck was whiter than a lily-flower
But strong enough to butt a bruiser down.
He knew the taverns well in every town
245 And every innkeeper and barmaid too
Better than lepers, beggars and that crew,
For in so eminent a man as he
It was not fitting with the dignity
Of his position, dealing with a scum
250 Of wretched lepers; nothing good can come
Of commerce with such slum-and-gutter dwellers,
But only with the rich and victual-sellers.
But anywhere a profit might accrue
Courteous he was and lowly of service too.
255 Natural gifts like his were hard to match.
He was the finest beggar of his batch,
And, for his begging-district, paid a rent;
His brethren did no poaching where he went.
For though a widow mightn't have a shoe,
260 So pleasant was his holy how-d'ye-do
He got his farthing° from her just the same
Before he left, and so his income came
To more than he laid out. And how he romped,
Just like a puppy! He was ever prompt
265 To arbitrate disputes on settling days°
(For a small fee) in many helpful ways,
Not then appearing as your cloistered scholar
With threadbare habit hardly worth a dollar,
But much more like a Doctor or a Pope.
270 Of double-worsted was the semi-cope°
Upon his shoulders, and the swelling fold
About him, like a bell about its mold
When it is casting, rounded out his dress.
He lisped a little out of wantonness
275 To make his English sweet upon his tongue.
When he had played his harp, or having sung,
His eyes would twinkle in his head as bright
As any star upon a frosty night.
This worthy's name was Hubert, it appeared.
280   There was a *Merchant* with a forking beard

The Power of Faith *How does the Friar misuse his position and power within the church?* **4**

The Monk, c.15th century. Facsimile of Ellesmere Chaucer illuminated manuscript. The Victoria and Albert Museum, London. ★

---

237 **tippet:** hood.
240 **hurdy-gurdy:** a stringed instrument played by turning a hand crank.

261 **farthing:** an old British coin.

265 **settling days:** days on which disputes could be settled out of court.

270 **semi-cope:** a short robe. A robe made of double worsted, a fine woolen fabric, would be a luxury unsuitable for a friar.

Teach

Big Idea **4**

The Power of Faith
Answer: *The Friar considers it beneath his dignity to associate with the poor, yet he is eager to please the rich, because he receives material favors from them.*

View the Art ★

Monks of this time were thought to be strict and steadfast in their adherence to the rules of their orders. The Monk in this story, however, is motivated by greed and the indulgences of the modern world. **Ask:** Does the Monk in this facsimile reflect the character in the story? *(Answers will vary but should be supported by the text.)*

English Learners

DIFFERENTIATED INSTRUCTION 🖐

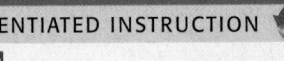 **Intermediate** Figurative language can make comprehension challenging for English learners. They may have trouble understanding similes such as "And how he romped, just like a puppy" (lines 263–264). Have English learners work with strong English-speaking partners to identify other similes and to write an explanation or interpretation for each.

Teach

Literary Element   1

Characterization Answer:
He uses his wits to present himself as a person of wealth and eminence, but he is secretly in debt.

[APPROACHING] Remind students that a hypocrite is a person who creates a false impression about him- or herself or one whose outward appearance is different from his or her true nature. Have students differentiate between the Merchant's image and his true self.

Literary Element   2

Characterization Answer:
Unlike the Friar, the Cleric is poor, honest, and unworldly. He prefers reading philosophy to wearing fine clothes and frequenting taverns. He is a virtuous man of learning, in contrast to the Friar, who is a corrupt hedonist.

Language History ☆

Discreet The word *discreet* descends from the Latin verb *discernere*, "to separate or distinguish." A discreet person, like the Sergeant at the Law, knows how to distinguish between what should be done or said and what should not.

And motley° dress; high on his horse he sat,
Upon his head a Flemish° beaver hat
And on his feet daintily buckled boots.
He told of his opinions and pursuits
285 In solemn tones, he harped on his increase
Of capital; there should be sea-police
(He thought) upon the Harwich-Holland ranges;°
He was expert at dabbling in exchanges.
This **estimable** Merchant so had set
290 His wits to work, none knew he was in debt,
He was so stately in administration,
In loans and bargains and negotiation.
He was an excellent fellow all the same;
To tell the truth I do not know his name.
295   An *Oxford Cleric*, still a student though,
One who had taken logic long ago,
Was there; his horse was thinner than a rake,
And he was not too fat, I undertake,
But had a hollow look, a sober stare;
300 The thread upon his overcoat was bare.
He had found no preferment° in the church
And he was too unworldly to make search
For secular employment. By his bed
He preferred having twenty books in red
305 And black, of Aristotle's° philosophy,
Than costly clothes, fiddle or psaltery.°
Though a philosopher, as I have told,
He had not found the stone for making gold.°
Whatever money from his friends he took
310 He spent on learning or another book
And prayed for them most earnestly, returning
Thanks to them thus for paying for his learning.
His only care was study, and indeed
He never spoke a word more than was need,
315 Formal at that, respectful in the extreme,
Short, to the point, and lofty in his theme.
A tone of moral virtue filled his speech
And gladly would he learn, and gladly teach.

---

281 **motley:** many-colored or varied.
282 **Flemish:** from Flanders, a region of northwestern Europe.

287 **Harwich-Holland ranges:** North Sea shipping lanes between Harwich (har´ ij), an English port, and Holland.

301 **preferment:** position; sponsorship.

305 **Aristotle's:** referring to the Greek philosopher (384–322 B.C.).
306 **psaltery** (sôl´ tər ē): a stringed musical instrument played by plucking.
308 **stone . . . gold:** Medieval alchemists believed that there existed a "philosopher's stone" capable of turning ordinary metals into gold.

Characterization *How is the Merchant characterized as a hypocrite?* **1**

Characterization *How does the character of the Cleric contrast with that of the Friar?* **2**

Vocabulary

estimable (es´ tə mə bəl) *adj.* deserving of esteem; admirable

110 UNIT 1   THE ANGLO-SAXON PERIOD AND THE MIDDLE AGES

Assessment Practice

SPIRAL REVIEW   **Short Responses** Explain that short-response questions often do not have single correct answers. Instead, an answer may be judged by its insightfulness and the quality of textual evidence included in it. **Ask:** Is the Cleric a good example of the "professional student" stereotype? Have students write answers in 3 to 5 lines.

(Possible responses: examples from the text such as "preferred having twenty books," " unworldly," and "only care was study.")

A *Sergeant at the Law*° who paid his calls,
320　Wary and wise, for clients at St. Paul's°
There also was, of noted excellence.
Discreet he was, a man to reverence,° ☆
Or so he seemed, his sayings were so wise.
He often had been Justice of Assize°
325　By letters patent,° and in full commission.
His fame and learning and his high position
Had won him many a robe and many a fee.
There was no such conveyancer° as he;
All was fee-simple° to his strong digestion,
330　Not one conveyance could be called in question.
Though there was nowhere one so busy as he,
He was less busy than he seemed to be.
He knew of every judgment, case and crime
Ever recorded since King William's time.°
335　He could dictate defenses or draft deeds;
No one could pinch a comma from his screeds°
And he knew every statute off by rote.
He wore a homely parti-colored coat,
Girt with a silken belt of pin-stripe stuff;
340　Of his appearance I have said enough.
　　　There was a *Franklin*° with him, it appeared;
White as a daisy-petal was his beard.
A sanguine° man, high-colored and benign,°
He loved a morning sop° of cake in wine.
345　He lived for pleasure and had always done,
For he was Epicurus'° very son,
In whose opinion sensual delight
Was the one true felicity in sight.
As noted as St. Julian° was for bounty ▐3▌
350　He made his household free to all the County.
His bread, his ale were finest of the fine
And no one had a better stock of wine.
His house was never short of bake-meat pies,
Of fish and flesh, and these in such supplies
355　It positively snowed with meat and drink
And all the dainties that a man could think.
According to the seasons of the year
Changes of dish were ordered to appear.

▐4▌　Paraphrase　*What motivates the Franklin? Paraphrase lines 345–348.*

Vocabulary

discreet (dis krēt´) *adj.* showing careful judgment in speech and action; prudent

319　**Sergeant at the Law:** a lawyer appointed by the king to serve as a judge.
320　**St. Paul's:** the cathedral of London, outside which lawyers often met clients when the courts were closed.
322　**reverence:** respect deeply.
324　**Assize:** a traveling law court.
325　**letters patent:** royal documents commissioning assize judges.
328　**conveyancer:** The Sergeant specializes in land sales and leases as well as property disputes.
329　**fee-simple:** property owned outright.

334　**King William's time:** the reign of William the Conqueror, king of England from 1066 to 1087.
336　**screeds:** long, tiresome writings.

341　**Franklin:** a wealthy landowner.

343　**sanguine:** cheerful; optimistic. **benign:** of a kind or gentle disposition.
344　**sop:** piece.

346　**Epicurus':** referring to the Greek philosopher (341?–270 B.C.) who taught that the goal of life was real and enduring pleasure, in the sense of peace of mind—a view of pleasure commonly mischaracterized as mere gratification of physical appetites.
349　**St. Julian:** patron saint of hospitality.

The Man of Law, 15th century. (detail from *The Canterbury Tales*), English School. Huntington Library and Art Gallery, San Marino, CA. ⭐

Teach

Reading Strategy　▐3▌

Characterization Have students review this passage. **Ask:** What details has the author provided in the text that make Franklin seem like a "good" pilgrim? *(Students may mention that despite his wealth and love of pleasure, the Franklin seems to have come by his riches honestly and shows hospitality to everyone.)*

ENGLISH LEARNERS Have English learners reread the description of the Franklin and write down any words or expressions they don't understand. They should use a dictionary to clarify the meaning of any unknown words.

Reading Strategy　▐4▌

Paraphrase Answer: *Students' paraphrases should include the information that the Franklin lives for pleasure, with gratification of the senses as his most important goal.*

View the Art ⭐

This detail of the Man of the Law is from the Ellesmere manuscript of *The Canterbury Tales,* which was probably created around 1400. The manuscript is lavishly decorated with floral borders, illuminated initial letters, and the famous portraits of the 23 pilgrims. These miniature portraits serve as visual cues that signal when each pilgrim is telling his or her tale.

Teach

Reading Strategy   1

Paraphrase Ask: What does the speaker say about the Cook? Have students answer by paraphrasing lines 389–397. *(The Cook has many skills, such as boiling, roasting, and baking. He also has an ulcer on his knee.)*

ADVANCED **Ask:** How does the speaker feel about the Cook's having an ulcer on his knee? Why? *(The speaker expresses concern either for the cook, who is suffering or because it is worrisome to have someone with an open sore preparing food.)*

He kept fat partridges in coops, beyond,
360 Many a bream and pike° were in his pond.
Woe to the cook unless the sauce was hot
And sharp, or if he wasn't on the spot!
And in his hall a table stood arrayed
And ready all day long, with places laid.
365 As Justice at the Sessions none stood higher;°
He often had been Member for the Shire.°
A dagger and a little purse of silk
Hung at his girdle, white as morning milk.
As Sheriff° he checked audit, every entry.
370 He was a model among landed gentry.
    A *Haberdasher,*° a *Dyer,* a *Carpenter,*
A *Weaver* and a *Carpet-maker* were
Among our ranks, all in the livery
Of one impressive guild-fraternity.°
375 They were so trim and fresh their gear would pass
For new. Their knives were not tricked out with brass
But wrought with purest silver, which avouches
A like display on girdles and on pouches.
Each seemed a worthy burgess,° fit to grace
380 A guild-hall with a seat upon the dais.
Their wisdom would have justified a plan
To make each one of them an alderman;°
They had the capital and revenue,
Besides their wives declared it was their due.
385 And if they did not think so, then they ought;
To be called "*Madam*" is a glorious thought,
And so is going to church and being seen
Having your mantle° carried, like a queen.
    They had a *Cook* with them who stood alone
390 For boiling chicken with a marrow-bone,
Sharp flavoring-powder and a spice for savor.
He could distinguish London ale by flavor,
And he could roast and seethe and broil and fry,
Make good thick soup and bake a tasty pie.
395 But what a pity—so it seemed to me,
That he should have an ulcer° on his knee.
As for blancmange,° he made it with the best.
    There was a *Skipper* hailing from far west;
He came from Dartmouth, so I understood.
400 He rode a farmer's horse as best he could,
In a woolen gown that reached his knee.
A dagger on a lanyard falling free
Hung from his neck under his arm and down.
The summer heat had tanned his color brown,
405 And certainly he was an excellent fellow.

360 **bream and pike:** kinds of fishes.

365 **Justice . . . higher:** When a justice of the peace heard a case, he was the presiding judge.
366 **Member for the Shire:** representative of his county in Parliament.
369 **Sheriff:** royal tax collector.

371 **Haberdasher:** one who sells men's clothing.

373–374 **livery . . . guild-fraternity:** The five tradesmen all belong to the same fraternal trade organization and wear its livery, or identifying uniform.

The Physician, (detail from *The Canterbury Tales*). Private collection.

379 **burgess:** a citizen or freeman of a British borough; townsman.
382 **alderman:** a high-ranking member of a town council.
388 **mantle:** cloak; cape.
396 **ulcer:** open sore.
397 **blancmange** (blə mänj´): a white pudding made of milk, rice, and seasonings.

Reading Practice

Read Aloud Have student volunteers read sections of the text aloud, taking care to pause slightly at marks of punctuation. Have other students listen to the "music" of the poem: the meter, the rhyme scheme, the variation in sentence length. Invite students to suggest ways the story would be different if it were in prose form.

As students read pages 112–113, have them list 5–10 words they do not understand. Have them look up the meanings and etymologies of these words and write their definitions on sticky notes. As they reread the pages, have them stick the definitions near the words to aid in understanding the text.

Many a draught of vintage, red and yellow,
He'd drawn at Bordeaux,° while the trader snored.
The nicer rules of conscience he ignored.
If, when he fought, the enemy vessel sank,
410 He sent his prisoners home; they walked the plank.
As for his skill in reckoning his tides,
Currents and many another risk besides,
Moons, harbors, pilots, he had such dispatch
That none from Hull to Carthage° was his match.
415 Hardy he was, prudent in undertaking;
His beard in many a tempest had its shaking,
And he knew all the havens as they were
From Gottland to the Cape of Finisterre,
And every creek in Brittany and Spain;
420 The barge he owned was called *The Maudelayne*.
    A *Doctor* too emerged as we proceeded;
No one alive could talk as well as he did
On points of medicine and of surgery,
For, being grounded in astronomy,°
425 He watched his patient closely for the hours
When, by his horoscope, he knew the powers
Of favorable planets, then ascendent,
Worked on the images for his dependent.
The cause of every malady you'd got
430 He knew, and whether dry, cold, moist or hot;°
He knew their seat, their humor and condition.
He was a perfect practicing physician.
These causes being known for what they were,
He gave the man his medicine then and there.
435 All his apothecaries° in a tribe
Were ready with the drugs he would prescribe
And each made money from the other's guile;°
They had been friendly for a goodish while.
He was well-versed in Aesculapius° too
440 And what Hippocrates and Rufus knew
And Dioscorides, now dead and gone,
Galen and Rhazes, Hali, Serapion,
Averroes, Avicenna, Constantine,
Scotch Bernard, John of Gaddesden, Gilbertine.
445 In his own diet he observed some measure;
There were no superfluities for pleasure,
Only digestives, nutritives and such.
He did not read the Bible very much.
In blood-red garments, slashed with bluish gray

Characterization *Given this information, how is line 405 ironic?* **2**

406–407 vintage . . . Bordeaux:
Bordeaux (bôr dō´), France, was
famous for its red and white (here,
"yellow") wine.

414 Hull to Carthage: These and
the place names in lines 418–419
indicate how widely the Skipper has
traveled.

424 astronomy: in Chaucer's day,
astrology. The planets' positions
supposedly determined the best
time to treat a patient.

430 dry, cold, moist or hot: In
Chaucer's day people believed that
the body was composed of four
"humors": black bile (said to be cold
and dry), phlegm (cold and moist),
blood (hot and moist), and yellow
bile (hot and dry). Excess of any
humor could lead to illness.
435 apothecaries: druggists.

437 guile: cunning; deceit; slyness.

439 Aesculapius (es´ kyə lā´ pē
əs): This and the names that
immediately follow identify medical
experts from ancient times to
Chaucer's day.

Teach

Literary Element   2

Characterization **Answer:**
*The Skipper's actions belie the
speaker's characterization by
ignoring "the nicer rules of conscience" when he executes his
prisoners by making them walk
the plank.*

Cultural History ☆

Medieval Health Care Doctors
in Chaucer's time believed that
humors, or bodily fluids, ruled
one's health. It was thought that a
person's health and temperament
were governed by the proportion of blood, phlegm, choler, and
melancholy in the body. Illness was
sometimes treated by prescribing a
change in diet to bring the humors
back into balance.

English Learners

DIFFERENTIATED INSTRUCTION

PARTNERS **Beginning** Have English learners
work together in pairs to write
simple sentences that describe the
illustrations of Chaucer's characters. For
each character, read the corresponding
description from the poem. Guide students
in identifying one or two details from the
text that are reflected in the illustrations.

Teach

Literary Element   1

Characterization Answer:
Here again, the speaker is being ironic. The Doctor can hardly be "perfect" when he enters into lucrative drug deals with his apothecaries and profits greatly from extorting wealthy victims of the plague.

Big Idea   2

The Power of Faith
Answer: *The religious journey known as a pilgrimage was a key feature of Christianity in medieval England. The Wife of Bath exemplifies this link with her many pilgrimages.*

Literary Element   3

Characterization Answer:
She is an expert on love because "she'd had five husbands, all at the church door."

[ENGLISH LEARNERS] Make sure English learners understand that *company* can mean a business, but it can also mean "companionship" and "people you spend time with." **Ask:** What is the "other company" referred to in line 471? *(other male friends)*

Cultural History ☆

Clothing Dyes The Wife of Bath's hose "of the finest scarlet red" were not just impressive for their color but for their cost. Scarlet was an expensive dye in her time because it was made from the dried bodies of red beetles or other red insects.

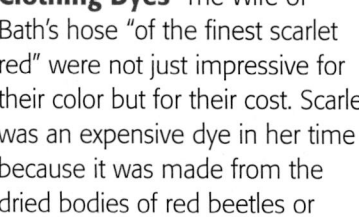

---

450 And lined with taffeta, he rode his way;
    Yet he was rather close as to expenses
    And kept the gold he won in pestilences.°
    Gold stimulates the heart, or so we're told.
    He therefore had a special love of gold.
455   A worthy *woman* from beside *Bath*° city
    Was with us, somewhat deaf, which was a pity.
    In making cloth she showed so great a bent
    She bettered those of Ypres and of Ghent.°
    In all the parish not a dame dared stir
460 Towards the altar steps in front of her,
    And if indeed they did, so wrath was she
    As to be quite put out of charity.
    Her kerchiefs were of finely woven ground;°
    I dared have sworn they weighed a good ten pound,
465 The ones she wore on Sunday, on her head.
    Her hose were of the finest scarlet red ☆
    And gartered tight; her shoes were soft and new.
    Bold was her face, handsome, and red in hue.
    A worthy woman all her life, what's more
470 She'd had five husbands, all at the church door,
    Apart from other company in youth;
    No need just now to speak of that, forsooth.
    And she had thrice been to Jerusalem,°
    Seen many strange rivers and passed over them;
475 She'd been to Rome and also to Boulogne,
    St. James of Compostella and Cologne,
    And she was skilled in wandering by the way.
    She had gap-teeth, set widely, truth to say.
    Easily on an ambling horse she sat
480 Well wimpled° up, and on her head a hat
    As broad as is a buckler° or a shield;
    She had a flowing mantle that concealed
    Large hips, her heels spurred sharply under that.
    In company she liked to laugh and chat
485 And knew the remedies for love's mischances,
    An art in which she knew the oldest dances.
      A holy-minded man of good renown

452 **pestilences:** plagues.

455 **Bath:** a city in southwestern England.

458 **Ypres** (ē ′ prə) . . . **Ghent:** Flemish cities known for weaving and wool making.

463 **ground:** a composite fabric.

473 **Jerusalem:** This and the place names immediately following were famous pilgrimage sites during the Middle Ages.
480 **wimpled:** A wimple is a cloth that covers the head and neck.
481 **buckler:** a small round shield.

The Parson, detail from *The Canterbury Tales.* c.1342–1400. English School. Vellum. Huntington Library and Art Gallery, San Marino, CA.

Characterization *What information about the Doctor in lines 435–454 contradicts the characterization in line 432?* **1**

The Power of Faith *How were religion and traveling linked in the Middle Ages?* **2**

Characterization *What qualifies the Wife of Bath as an expert on love?* **3**

114   UNIT 1   THE ANGLO-SAXON PERIOD AND THE MIDDLE AGES

Writing Practice

⚡ Analyze Imagery

SPIRAL REVIEW   Remind students that effective writers use adjectives to paint a vivid picture in the reader's mind. An adjective or an adjective phrase can make the text more meaningful. Have students list the adjectives used to describe the Wife of Bath, and then write a paragraph explaining how these adjectives affect how they imagine her.

There was, and poor, the *Parson* to a town,
Yet he was rich in holy thought and work.
490   He also was a learned man, a clerk,
Who truly knew Christ's gospel and would preach it
Devoutly to parishioners, and teach it.
Benign and wonderfully diligent,
And patient when adversity was sent
495   (For so he proved in much adversity)
He hated cursing to extort a fee,
Nay rather he preferred beyond a doubt
Giving to poor parishioners round about
Both from church offerings and his property;
500   He could in little find sufficiency.°
Wide was his parish, with houses far asunder,
Yet he neglected not in rain or thunder,
In sickness or in grief, to pay a call
On the remotest, whether great or small,
505   Upon his feet, and in his hand a stave.
This noble example to his sheep he gave
That first he wrought, and afterwards he taught;
And it was from the Gospel he had caught
Those words, and he would add this figure too,
510   That if gold rust, what then will iron do?
For if a priest be foul in whom we trust
No wonder that a common man should rust;
The true example that a priest should give
Is one of cleanness, how the sheep should live. ☆
515   He did not set his benefice to hire°
And leave his sheep encumbered in the mire
Or run to London to earn easy bread
By singing masses for the wealthy dead,
Or find some Brotherhood and get enrolled.
520   He stayed at home and watched over his fold
So that no wolf should make the sheep miscarry.
He was a shepherd and no mercenary.
Holy and virtuous he was, but then
Never contemptuous of sinful men,
525   Never **disdainful,** never too proud or fine,
But was discreet in teaching and benign.
His business was to show a fair behavior

500 **He . . . sufficiency:** He required little to satisfy his own needs.

515 **set . . . hire:** pay someone else to perform clerical duties.

Characterization *How does this proverb contrast the Parson's character with that of other clerics, such as the Monk and the Friar?*   **4**

Vocabulary

disdainful (dĭs dān′ fəl) *adj.* feeling or showing contempt; scornful

Teach

Literary Element   4

Characterization   Answer:
The Parson believes that he should set a good example for those to whom he preaches good behavior.

Writer's Technique ☆

Allusion Tell students that writers sometimes use allusions or references to well-known people, places, events, written works, or artworks. In line 514, Chaucer alludes to the Bible's frequent use of sheep and shepherds as metaphors for believers and their leaders. **Ask:** In what other lines does this allusion appear? *(lines 520–522)*

Approaching Level

DIFFERENTIATED INSTRUCTION

Emerging Point out to students that Chaucer describes the Parson by explaining what he is and does as well as what he is not or will not do: "Holy and virtuous he was, but then / Never contemptuous of sinful men." As students read the description of the Parson, have them use a two-column chart to keep track of what he *is,* and what he is *not.*

The Power of Faith

Answer: *The qualities mentioned by the speaker—including honesty, generosity, and hard work—make the Plowman an ideal Christian.*

View the Art ★

This image of the Friar is an illumination from a medieval manuscript. Tell students that an average day's journey on horseback was 30 to 40 miles. **Ask:** What would it have been like to travel in this fashion? *(Possible answer: It would have been tiring and dirty and would have taken great stamina.)*

And draw men thus to Heaven and their Savior,
Unless indeed a man were obstinate;
530　And such, whether of high or low estate,
He put to sharp rebuke, to say the least.
I think there never was a better priest.
He sought no pomp or glory in his dealings,
No scrupulosity° had spiced his feelings.
535　Christ and His Twelve Apostles and their lore
He taught, but followed it himself before.
　　There was a *Plowman* with him there, his brother;
Many a load of dung one time or other
He must have carted through the morning dew.
540　He was an honest worker, good and true,
Living in peace and perfect charity,
And, as the gospel bade him, so did he,
Loving God best with all his heart and mind
And then his neighbor as himself, repined
545　At no misfortune, slacked for no content,
For steadily about his work he went
To thrash his corn, to dig or to manure
Or make a ditch; and he would help the poor
For love of Christ and never take a penny
550　If he could help it, and, as prompt as any,
He paid his tithes° in full when they were due
On what he owned, and on his earnings too.
He wore a tabard smock° and rode a mare.
　　There was a *Reeve,*° also a *Miller,* there,
555　A College *Manciple* from the Inns of Court,°
A papal *Pardoner* and, in close consort,°
A Church-Court *Summoner,*° riding at a trot,
And finally myself—that was the lot.
　　The *Miller* was a chap of sixteen stone,°
560　A great stout fellow big in brawn and bone.
He did well out of them, for he could go
And win the ram at any wrestling show.
Broad, knotty and short-shouldered, he would boast
He could heave any door off hinge and post,
565　Or take a run and break it with his head.
His beard, like any sow or fox, was red
And broad as well, as though it were a spade;
And, at its very tip, his nose displayed
A wart on which there stood a tuft of hair
570　Red as the bristles in an old sow's ear.

The Friar, detail from *The Canterbury Tales.* 15th century. English School. Huntington Library and Art Gallery, San Marino, CA. ★

534 scrupulosity: here, overly careful attention to social niceties.

551 tithes (tīthz): offerings made to the church, consisting of one-tenth of a person's income.
553 tabard smock: a loose jacket of heavy fabric.
554 Reeve: the manager of a landowner's estate.
555 Manciple . . . Court: an administrator in charge of providing food for the lawyers who lived and trained at London's Inns of Court.
556 Pardoner: a church employee licensed by the pope to dispense papal pardons, which released people from punishment for sins, and to collect money for church charities. consort: accompaniment.
557 Summoner: a layman charged with summoning sinners before a church court.
559 sixteen stone: 224 pounds. A stone is a British unit of weight equal to 14 pounds.

The Power of Faith *How does the Plowman demonstrate the ideals of the Christian religion?* 　**1**

Speaking and Listening Practice

SMALL GROUP

Dramatic Reading
Have students work in groups of 4 to 5 and read aloud the description of the Miller, the Manciple, or the Reeve. Each student should read 4 lines (2 couplets), taking care to pronounce words correctly. Have groups rehearse their readings and present them to the class.

His nostrils were as black as they were wide.
He had a sword and buckler at his side,
His mighty mouth was like a furnace door.
A wrangler and buffoon, he had a store
575 Of tavern stories, filthy in the main.
His was a master-hand at stealing grain.
He felt it with his thumb and thus he knew
Its quality and took three times his due—
A thumb of gold, by God, to gauge an oat!
580 He wore a hood of blue and a white coat.
He liked to play his bagpipes up and down **3**
And that was how he brought us out of town.
     The *Manciple* came from the Inner Temple;°
All caterers might follow his example
585 In buying victuals; he was never rash
Whether he bought on credit or paid cash.
He used to watch the market most precisely
And got in first, and so he did quite nicely.
Now isn't it a marvel of God's grace
590 That an illiterate fellow can outpace
The wisdom of a heap of learned men?
His masters—he had more than thirty then—
All versed in the abstrusest° legal knowledge,
Could have produced a dozen from their College
595 Fit to be stewards in land and rents and game
To any Peer° in England you could name,
And show him how to live on what he had
Debt-free (unless of course the Peer were mad)
Or be as frugal as he might desire,
600 And make them fit to help about the Shire
In any legal case there was to try;
And yet this Manciple could wipe their eye.°
    The *Reeve* was old and choleric° and thin;
His beard was shaven closely to the skin,
605 His shorn hair came abruptly to a stop
Above his ears, and he was docked on top
Just like a priest in front; his legs were lean,
Like sticks they were, no calf was to be seen.
He kept his bins and garners° very trim;
610 No auditor could gain a point on him.
And he could judge by watching drought and rain
The yield he might expect from seed and grain.
His master's sheep, his animals and hens,

583 Inner Temple: one of the four Inns of Court.

593 abstrusest: hardest to understand.

596 stewards . . . any Peer: estate managers for any nobleman.

602 wipe their eye: get the better of or outdo them.
603 choleric: easily irritated or angered.

609 garners: buildings for storing grain.

Characterization *From the characterization of the Miller, what sort of tale would you expect him to tell when his time comes?* **2**

Literary Element | **2**

Characterization Answer:
Students might predict that the Miller will tell a tale full of bawdy humor.

Literary Element | **3**

Characterization Have students think about what they already know about the Miller.
Ask: Why would bagpipes be a fitting instrument for him? *(Bagpipes attract attention, they take a good deal of effort to play, and they can make quite a lot of noise. The Miller likes to show off in both his actions and his words.)*
[APPROACHING] For students having difficulty, have them reread lines 570–575 to discover the kinds of stories the Miller knows.

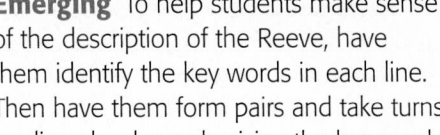

Approaching Level

DIFFERENTIATED INSTRUCTION

Emerging To help students make sense of the description of the Reeve, have them identify the key words in each line. Then have them form pairs and take turns reading aloud, emphasizing the key words. Have partners keep track of any questions they have about the meaning of words or phrases and share them with the class.

Teach

Reading Strategy | 1

Paraphrase Answer: *Students' paraphrases should include how the Reeve looks, what kind of work he does, how he does it, and how he positions himself in the pilgrim cavalcade.*

ENGLISH LEARNERS Remind English learners that they can use details in the text to help them guess what kind of man the Reeve is. **Ask:** What is the Reeve good at? *(making money, bargaining, making business deals)*

Literary Element | 2

Characterization Ask: What trait in the Reeve's character might make him choose to ride at the back of the group of pilgrims? *(Students may suggest that he is not very sociable or that he wants to keep an eye on the others in the group because he is suspicious by nature.)*

Cultural History ☆

Safety of Cures In search of a cure for his carbuncles, the Summoner is willing to try medicines that today would be unlikely to meet federal safety guidelines: quicksilver, or mercury; lead; brimstone, or sulfur; boracic, or boric acid; and possibly other salves with "the power to bite."

Pigs, horses, dairies, stores and cattle-pens
615 Were wholly trusted to his government.
He had been under contract to present
The accounts, right from his master's earliest years.
No one had ever caught him in arrears.
No bailiff, serf or herdsman dared to kick,
620 He knew their dodges, knew their every trick;
Feared like the plague he was, by those beneath.
He had a lovely dwelling on a heath,
Shadowed in green by trees above the sward.°
A better hand at bargains than his lord,
625 He had grown rich and had a store of treasure
Well tucked away, yet out it came to pleasure
His lord with subtle loans or gifts of goods,
To earn his thanks and even coats and hoods.
When young he'd learnt a useful trade and still
630 He was a carpenter of first-rate skill.
The stallion-cob he rode at a slow trot
Was dapple-gray and bore the name of Scot.
He wore an overcoat of bluish shade
And rather long; he had a rusty blade
635 Slung at his side. He came, as I heard tell,
From Norfolk, near a place called Baldeswell.
His coat was tucked under his belt and splayed.
He rode the hindmost of our cavalcade.   **2**
    There was a *Summoner* with us at that Inn,
640 His face on fire, like a cherubin,°
For he had carbuncles.° His eyes were narrow,
He was as hot and lecherous as a sparrow.
Black scabby brows he had, and a thin beard.
Children were afraid when he appeared.
645 No quicksilver, lead ointment, tartar creams, ☆
No brimstone, no boracic,° so it seems,
Could make a salve that had the power to bite,
Clean up or cure his whelks° of knobby white
Or purge the pimples sitting on his cheeks.
650 Garlic he loved, and onions too, and leeks,
And drinking strong red wine till all was hazy.
Then he would shout and jabber as if crazy,
And wouldn't speak a word except in Latin
When he was drunk, such tags° as he was pat in;
655 He only had a few, say two or three,
That he had mugged up° out of some decree;

623 **sward:** grassland; lawn.

640 **cherubin:** one of the angels who, in medieval art, usually had flame-colored faces.
641 **carbuncles:** large pimples and patches of red skin, often seen as a sign of lechery or drunkenness in Chaucer's time.

645–646 **quicksilver . . . boracic:** medieval skin medicines.

648 **whelks:** pustules.

654 **tags:** brief quotations.

656 **mugged up:** memorized.

Paraphrase *Paraphrase Chaucer's description of the Reeve in lines 603–638.*   **1**

Writing Practice

Writing Introductions

SPIRAL REVIEW Point out that Chaucer begins to introduce the Pardoner at line 665. Tell students to read through line 710, taking notes about the information Chaucer provides. Have students write short paragraphs that serve as oral introductions of the Pardoner to his fellow travelers. Explain that students do not need to mention all of the details that Chaucer includes. They may also wish to make up additional information they think the others would want to know (such as his name and hometown) Have students compare their introductions.

No wonder, for he heard them every day.
And, as you know, a man can teach a jay°
To call out "Walter" better than the Pope.
660 But had you tried to test his wits and grope
For more, you'd have found nothing in the bag.
Then "*Questio quid juris*"° was his tag.
He was a noble varlet° and a kind one,
You'd meet none better if you went to find one.

665   He and a gentle *Pardoner* rode together,
A bird from Charing Cross° of the same feather,
Just back from visiting the Court of Rome.
He loudly sang "*Come hither, love, come home!*"
The Summoner sang deep seconds to this song,
670 No trumpet ever sounded half so strong.
This Pardoner had hair as yellow as wax,
Hanging down smoothly like a hank of flax.
In driblets fell his locks behind his head
Down to his shoulders which they overspread; **4**
675 Thinly they fell, like rat-tails, one by one.
He wore no hood upon his head, for fun;
The hood inside his wallet° had been stowed,
He aimed at riding in the latest mode;
But for a little cap his head was bare
680 And he had bulging eye-balls, like a hare.
He'd sewed a holy relic° on his cap;
His wallet lay before him on his lap,
Brimful of pardons come from Rome, all hot.
He had the same small voice a goat has got.
685 His chin no beard had harbored, nor would harbor,
Smoother than ever chin was left by barber.
I judge he was a gelding, or a mare.
As to his trade, from Berwick down to Ware
There was no pardoner of equal grace,
690 For in his trunk he had a pillow-case
Which he asserted was Our Lady's veil.
He said he had a gobbet° of the sail
St. Peter had the time when he made bold
To walk the waves, till Jesu Christ took hold.°
695 He had a cross of metal set with stones
And, in a glass, a rubble of pigs' bones.
And with these relics, any time he found
Some poor up-country parson to astound,
In one short day, in money down, he drew

Paraphrase *What does the speaker say about the Summoner's knowledge and intelligence? Paraphrase lines 660–662.* **3**

658 jay: a bird that can be taught to mimic human speech but cannot understand what it says.

662 *Questio quid juris*: Latin for "The question is, What point of the law applies?"
663 varlet: rascal.

666 Charing Cross: a district of London.

677 wallet: pack; knapsack.

681 relic: an object cherished for its association with a saint or holy person.

692 gobbet: large piece.
693–694 St. Peter . . . hold: In the Christian Bible (Matthew 14:29–31), Jesus extended a helping hand to Peter when Peter became afraid while walking on water.

Teach

Reading Strategy **3**

Paraphrase Answer: *Students' paraphrases should note that the Summoner is educated enough to spout two or three Latin phrases in conversation but in actuality is a man of meager knowledge and intelligence.*

(ENGLISH LEARNERS) Have English Learners clarify the meaning of "pat" (line 654) using a dictionary. Ask students to find evidence in lines 653–658 for the assertion that the Summoner can speak some Latin but does not really understand it.

Literary Element **4**

Characterization Have students reread lines 671–676.
Ask: How does this description characterize the Pardoner? *(Students might suggest that his long yellow hair makes him seem unkempt. Since it hangs in "locks . . . like rat-tails," it gives the impression of uncleanliness.)*

English Learners

DIFFERENTIATED INSTRUCTION

Intermediate The relative pronouns *that, which, who, whom,* and *whose* refer to nouns. In line 691, the relative clause "Which he asserted was Our Lady's veil," cannot stand on its own. It is a subordinate clause. *Which* refers to *pillow-case* in line 690. Have students look through the selection for other lines containing relative pronouns. Then ask them to rewrite the lines in their own words. Monitor students' work to ensure grammaticality.

The Power of Faith

Answer: *The Pardoner takes advantage of the religious faith of his victims by selling fake relics for a considerable profit. He manages to treat both clergymen and laypeople this way.*

(ADVANCED) Have advanced students discuss the factors that allowed the Pardoner to take advantage of others. **Ask:** Why was the Pardoner able to become so corrupt? *(Students may suggest that the religious institutions of the time emphasized the authority of clergy.)*

Paraphrase Answer: *Students' paraphrases should note that the speaker asks his audience to forgive him for his candor in describing the crude speech and manners of some of the pilgrims.*

Writer's Technique ☆

Point of View Draw attention to line 711 and point out the pronoun *I*. Explain that by changing from the third person to the first person, Chaucer is referring to himself as the narrator of the tale. He explains to readers why he is presenting the tales just as he heard them.

To create custom assessments using software, use ExamView Assessment Suite.

---

700 More than the parson in a month or two,
And by his flatteries and **prevarication**
Made monkeys of the priest and congregation.
But still to do him justice first and last
In church he was a noble ecclesiast.°
705 How well he read a lesson or told a story!
But best of all he sang an Offertory,°
For well he knew that when that song was sung
He'd have to preach and tune his honey-tongue
And (well he could) win silver from the crowd.
710 That's why he sang so merrily and loud.
      Now I have told you shortly, in a clause,
The rank, the array, the number and the cause
Of our assembly in this company
In Southwark, at that high-class hostelry
715 Known as *The Tabard*, close beside *The Bell*.°
And now the time has come for me to tell
How we behaved that evening; I'll begin
After we had alighted at the Inn,
Then I'll report our journey, stage by stage,
720 All the remainder of our pilgrimage.
But first I beg of you, in courtesy,
Not to condemn me as unmannerly
If I speak plainly and with no concealings
And give account of all their words and dealings,
725 Using their very phrases as they fell.
For certainly, as you all know so well,
He who repeats a tale after a man
Is bound to say, as nearly as he can,
Each single word, if he remembers it,
730 However rudely spoken or unfit,
Or else the tale he tells will be untrue,
The things pretended and the phrases new.
He may not flinch although it were his brother,
He may as well say one word as another.
735 And Christ Himself spoke broad° in Holy Writ,
Yet there is no scurrility° in it,
And Plato° says, for those with power to read,

Pilgrims. Illustration from *The Troy Book and the Siege of Thebes.*

704 ecclesiast (i klē′ zē əst′): clergyman.
706 Offertory: a song accompanying the collection of the offering in church.
715 The Bell: another inn.

735 broad: bluntly; plainly.
736 scurrility: coarseness; indecency.
737 Plato: a Greek philosopher (427?–347? B.C.).

The Power of Faith *How does the Pardoner abuse his holy office and take advantage of the religious faith of his victims?* **1**

Paraphrase *Paraphrase the speaker's disclaimer in lines 721–723.* **2**

Vocabulary

prevarication (pri var′ ə ka′ shən) *n.* an act of evading the truth; lie

120 UNIT 1   THE ANGLO-SAXON PERIOD AND THE MIDDLE AGES

Viewing Practice

Visual Representations Have students view the various illustrations throughout the selection. Explain that many of these illustrations appeared in the first printings of The Canterbury Tales. Have students describe the appearance of the Pilgrims in each illustration, including the Physician (p. 112) and the Parson (p. 114). Ask students whether or not they feel the illustrations match what they know so far about each Pilgrim. (Some students may feel that the images accurately reflect each Pilgrim. Other students may feel that they do not, citing the example of the Physician, who would not have been likely to mix medicines while riding on horseback.) You may want to have students do additional research at the library or online to see what life would have been like for Chaucer's Pilgrims.

"The word should be as cousin to the deed."
Further I beg you to forgive it me
740   If I neglect the order and degree
And what is due to rank in what I've planned.
I'm short of wit as you will understand.
    Our *Host* gave us great welcome; everyone
Was given a place and supper was begun.
745   He served the finest victuals° you could think,
The wine was strong and we were glad to drink.
A very striking man our Host withal,
And fit to be a marshal in a hall.°
His eyes were bright, his girth a little wide;
750   There is no finer burgess in Cheapside.°
Bold in his speech, yet wise and full of tact,
There was no manly attribute he lacked,
What's more he was a merry-hearted man.
After our meal he jokingly began
755   To talk of sport, and, among other things
After we'd settled up our reckonings,
He said as follows: "Truly, gentlemen,
You're very welcome and I can't think when
—Upon my word I'm telling you no lie—
760   I've seen a gathering here that looked so spry,
No, not this year, as in this tavern now.
I'd think you up some fun if I knew how.
And, as it happens, a thought has just occurred
To please you, costing nothing, on my word.
765   You're off to Canterbury—well, God speed!
Blessed St. Thomas° answer to your need!
And I don't doubt, before the journey's done
You mean to while the time in tales and fun.
Indeed, there's little pleasure for your bones
770   Riding along and all as dumb° as stones.
So let me then propose for your enjoyment,
Just as I said, a suitable employment.
And if my notion suits and you agree
And promise to submit yourselves to me
775   Playing your parts exactly as I say
Tomorrow as you ride along the way,
Then by my father's soul (and he is dead)
If you don't like it you can have my head!
Hold up your hands, and not another word."

745 **victuals** (vit′ əlz): food.

748 **marshal in a hall:** a manager in charge of making the arrangements for a banquet.
750 **Cheapside:** in Chaucer's day, London's main business district.

766 **St. Thomas:** here, St. Thomas à Becket.

770 **dumb:** silent.

Characterization *How does the speaker characterize himself in this passage? How is his self-portrait here consistent with the way he has portrayed himself throughout "The Prologue"?*   **3**

Teach

Literary Element   3

Characterization Answer:
Chaucer, through the speaker, is being disingenuous in order to produce a humorous effect. Throughout "The Prologue," the speaker feigns naiveté when he praises certain pilgrims who are guilty of immorality and corruption. This technique adds a layer of ironic humor to "The Prologue" that ranges from grim to ridiculous.

English Learners

DIFFERENTIATED INSTRUCTION

Intermediate Have English learners pair with English speakers to identify the sequence of events from line 771–850. Students may want to use a chart, numbered list, or timeline to keep track of events in order similar to the one shown. Ask pairs to share their work with the class.

Teach

Reading Strategy   1

Paraphrase Answer: *The Host suggests that each pilgrim tell two stories on the way to Canterbury and two on the way back. The teller of the best story will receive a supper paid for by the others. The Host will join the pilgrimage and be the judge.*

(ENGLISH LEARNERS) If English learners have difficulty understanding the question, explain that a *notion* is an idea. **Ask:** What is the Host's idea?

Literary Element   2

Characterization Answer:
The Host is a hospitable man of wit, good humor, and charm. He entices the pilgrims with his proposal to provide entertainment and guidance on their journey. His flair for planning and organization wins the confidence of the pilgrims. Finally, he ingratiates himself with flattery and a modest, diffident manner.

(APPROACHING) If students have trouble deciding which traits have gained the pilgrim's trust, have them make a list of all the Host's character traits. Discuss which traits would help gain the trust of strangers.

Writer's Technique ☆

Introductions Writers often do not want to tell readers what comes next in their stories. They want events to unfold on their own. In lines 785–805, Chaucer has the Host explain what will happen next. **Ask:** Why might Chaucer have included this introduction? *(Perhaps he wanted readers to understand why the pilgrims were telling their tales. Chaucer gives nothing away about the stories themselves.)*

780   Well, our opinion was not long deferred,
It seemed not worth a serious debate;
We all agreed to it at any rate
And bade him issue what commands he would.
"My lords," he said, "now listen for your good,
785   And please don't treat my notion with disdain. ☆
This is the point. I'll make it short and plain.
Each one of you shall help to make things slip
By telling two stories on the outward trip
To Canterbury, that's what I intend,
790   And, on the homeward way to journey's end
Another two, tales from the days of old;
And then the man whose story is best told,
That is to say who gives the fullest measure
Of good morality and general pleasure,
795   He shall be given a supper, paid by all,
Here in this tavern, in this very hall,
When we come back again from Canterbury.
And in the hope to keep you bright and merry
I'll go along with you myself and ride
800   All at my own expense and serve as guide.
I'll be the judge, and those who won't obey
Shall pay for what we spend upon the way.
Now if you all agree to what you've heard
Tell me at once without another word,
805   And I will make arrangements early for it."
    Of course we all agreed, in fact we swore it
Delightedly, and made entreaty° too
That he should act as he proposed to do,
Become our Governor in short, and be
810   Judge of our tales and general referee,
And set the supper at a certain price.
We promised to be ruled by his advice
Come high, come low; unanimously thus
We set him up in judgment over us.
815   More wine was fetched, the business being done;
We drank it off and up went everyone
To bed without a moment of delay.
    Early next morning at the spring of day
Up rose our Host and roused us like a cock,
820   Gathering us together in a flock,

807 entreaty: an enthusiastic request.

Thomas Becket is consecrated Archbishop of Canterbury. 14th century illuminated manuscript. From the Queen Mary Psalter.

Paraphrase *What "notion" does the Host propose in lines 785–805?*   **1**

Characterization *What character traits of the Host have gained him the trust of the pilgrims?*   **2**

Literary Practice

SMALL GROUP
Figures of Speech Point out the simile "Up rose our Host and roused us like a cock." **Ask:** What is the Host being compared to? *(the Host is compared to a rooster crowing at the break of day)* Show students that there is a comparison inherent in the line "Gathering us together in a flock," in which the people are gathered like a flock of birds or sheep.

Have small groups of students work together to identify other similes and metaphors used throughout the Prologue. Groups may also choose to illustrate one of the figures of speech.

And off we rode at slightly faster pace
Than walking to St. Thomas' watering-place;°
And there our Host drew up, began to ease
His horse, and said, "Now, listen if you please,
825 My lords! Remember what you promised me.
If evensong and matins will agree°
Let's see who shall be first to tell a tale.
And as I hope to drink good wine and ale
I'll be your judge. The rebel who disobeys,
830 However much the journey costs, he pays.
Now draw for cut and then we can depart;
The man who draws the shortest cut shall start.
My Lord the Knight," he said, "step up to me
And draw your cut, for that is my decree.
835 And come you near, my Lady Prioress,
And you, Sir Cleric, drop your shamefastness,
No studying now! A hand from every man!"
Immediately the draw for lots began
And to tell shortly how the matter went,
840 Whether by chance or fate or accident,
The truth is this, the cut fell to the Knight,
Which everybody greeted with delight.
And tell his tale he must, as reason was
Because of our agreement and because
845 He too had sworn. What more is there to say?
For when this good man saw how matters lay,
Being by wisdom and obedience driven
To keep a promise he had freely given,
He said, "Since it's for me to start the game,
850 Why, welcome be the cut in God's good name!
Now let us ride, and listen to what I say."
And at the word we started on our way
And in a cheerful style he then began
At once to tell his tale, and thus it ran.

Paraphrase *How does the Host decide who will tell the first tale?*
Paraphrase lines 838–841. **3**

822 St. Thomas' watering-place:
a brook two miles from London.

826 If evensong . . . agree: a
reference to evening and morning
prayer services, here meaning "If
what you said last night is what you
mean this morning."

Teach

Reading Strategy   3

Paraphrase Answer: *The
pilgrims draw lots to determine
who will tell the first tale. The luck
of the draw goes to the Knight.*

(ENGLISH LEARNERS) Make sure that
English Learners understand the
meanings of *draw* and *lots* as they
are used in this section. Have them
use a dictionary if necessary.

> To check students' understanding
> of the selection, see Unit 1 Teach-
> ing Resources Book, p. 86

Progress Check

**Can students identify
characterization?**

If No → See Unit 1 Teaching
Resources Book, p. 81.

Approaching Level

DIFFERENTIATED INSTRUCTION

Emerging Predicting the events of a story
helps students identify their expectation
before they begin reading. Tell students
that they are going to read two of the tales
told by the travelers: "The Pardoner's Tale"
and "The Wife of Bath's Tale." Have each
student write paragraphs predicting what
kind of tale the Pardoner and the Wife of
Bath will tell. Later, students can compare
their predictions with the actual stories.

After You Read

Assess

1. Students' answers will vary.
2. (a) London to Canterbury to visit the shrine of Thomas à Becket (b) Spring is the traditional time of year for pilgrimage, rebirth, and renewal.
3. (a) He was at the Tabard Inn, ready to go on a pilgrimage and "most devout at heart." (b) He seems to remain aloof.
4. (a) *Trades or Professions:* Merchant, Sergeant at the Law, Cook, Skipper, Doctor, Wife of Bath, Manciple, Host; *Church:* Prioress, Nun, Priest, Monk, Friar, Cleric, Parson, Summoner, Pardoner; *Feudal System:* Knight, Squire, Yeoman, Franklin, Plowman, Miller, Reeve (b) They present a broad cross section of mid-range English society. The nobility and the poor are absent.
5. Students' answers will vary.
6. Characters are defined by how well they follow Christian tenets.
7. (a) They read, listen to recorded music, chat, or observe the scenery. (b) People created their own entertainment.

 For additional selection assessment, see Assessment Resources, pp. 67–68.

After You Read

Respond and Think Critically

Respond and Interpret

1. (a)Which characters remind you in some way of people you know? Explain. (b)Do any of the characters seem unrealistic to you? Explain.
2. (a)Where are the pilgrims traveling and for what reason? (b)How is the time of year in which they are traveling meaningful?
3. (a)What information does the speaker give about himself? (b)Does the speaker seem to fit in with the band of pilgrims? Explain.

Analyze and Evaluate

4. (a)Categorize the twenty-nine pilgrims according to their roles in fourteenth-century English society. Use the headings "Trades and Professions," "Church," and "Feudal System." (b)How well do these people represent the whole of medieval society? Are any groups of people missing?
5. (a)Which character appeals to you the most? Why? (b)Which character appeals to you the least? Why?

Connect

6. **Big Idea** The Power of Faith How does the Christian faith of the Middle Ages inform the the Prologue to *The Canterbury Tales?*
7. **Connect to Today** (a)How do people today amuse themselves on trips? (b)How do these activities compare with the amusements of Chaucer's time?

Literary Element Characterization

In **direct characterization**, the writer makes explicit statements about a character. In **indirect characterization**, the writer reveals a character through the character's words, thoughts, actions, and appearance, as well as through what other characters say or think about the character.

Find one example of direct characterization and one example of indirect characterization in the Prologue.

Writing

Write a Character Sketch In the Prologue to *The Canterbury Tales,* Chaucer characterizes the pilgrims both directly and indirectly. Choose a person that you see frequently, and combine direct and indirect characterization to create a description of the person, capturing his or her essential qualities.

 Literature Online

Selection Resources For Selection Quizzes, eFlashcards, and Reading-Writing Connection activities, go to glencoe.com and enter QuickPass code GLB9817u1.

Reading Strategy Paraphrase

When you paraphrase a passage, you restate it in your own words. Paraphrase Chaucer's description of the Manciple in lines 583–602.

Vocabulary Practice

Practice with Synonyms A synonym is a word that has the same, or nearly the same, meaning as another word. With a partner, match each boldfaced vocabulary word below with a synonym. You will not use all the answer choices..

1. discreet
2. disdainful
3. estimable
4. prevarication
5. solicitous

a. aloof
b. careful
c. falsehood
d. scornful
e. helpful
f. ambitious
g. admirable

Literary Element

Students' answers will vary.

 **Writing**

Tell students to be guided by Chaucer's direct observations as well as by how the strengths and weaknesses of the characters are revealed.

Reading Strategy

Answers will vary but should mention that the Manciple, although he is illiterate, is a shrewd man who knows much more than his masters.

Vocabulary

1. b 2. d 3. g 4. c 5. e

 To create custom assessments using software, use Exam View Assessment Suite.

from *The Pardoner's Tale*

Connect to the Poem

Is there any goal or reward that would tempt you to betray one of your friends? Discuss this question with a group of classmates. Compare the circumstances in which different students might be tempted.

Build Background

In the Middle Ages, pardoners were licensed by the pope to grant indulgences, gifts of divine mercy to repentant sinners. By Chaucer's time, corrupt pardoners were selling indulgences for personal gain rather than granting them to penitents in return for voluntary donations to the church. "The Pardoner's Tale" is an **exemplum**—a brief story used to teach a lesson.

Set Purposes for Reading

Big Idea The Power of Faith

As you read, ask yourself, How are the sins of greed and betrayal leading to moral chaos and self-destruction?

Literary Element Irony

Irony is a contrast or discrepancy between expectation and reality. **Situational irony** exists when an occurrence is the opposite of a character's expectations. **Dramatic irony** occurs when readers or audiences have information unknown to the characters. **Verbal irony** occurs when a character says one thing while meaning another. As you read "The Pardoner's Tale," ask yourself, Is irony present here? Which type of irony?

Reading Strategy Analyze Tone

Tone expresses an author's attitude toward his or her subject. It is conveyed through such elements as word choice, sentence structure, and figures of speech. As you read, ask yourself, What attitude does Chaucer have toward these events?

....

Tip: Analyzing Objectivity How emotionally involved a speaker is can contribute to a work's tone. As you read, use a continuum similar to the one below to record the speaker's involvement in different passages.

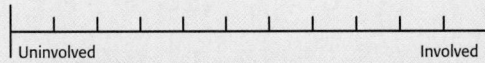

| Uninvolved | Involved |

GEOFFREY CHAUCER **125**

Learning Objectives

For pages 125–132

In studying this text, you will focus on the following objectives:

Literary Study: Analyzing irony.

Reading: Analyzing tone.

Writing: Writing a movie scene.

Vocabulary

adversary (ad′ vər ser′ ē) *n.* an opponent; enemy; p. 126 *Louise and Frank were worthy adversaries at playing Scrabble because each had an extensive vocabulary.*

prudent (prōōd′ ənt) *adj.* cautious; careful; p. 129 *Be prudent in divulging your Social Security number because it can be misused by an unscrupulous person.*

gratify (grat′ ə fī′) *v.* to satisfy; indulge; p. 130 *Grandfather likes to gratify his sweet tooth with chocolate ice cream.*

deftly (deft′ lē) *adv.* skillfully; nimbly; p. 131 *Working in the bakery window, the pizza chef deftly spun the dough into a large circle.*

Focus

Summary

Three men pledge to find and kill Death. An old man points them to a tree, where they find gold. One man goes to town for bread and wine. The other two plot to kill him and keep his gold. After they kill him, they drink the wine, which the dead man had poisoned. All three find Death.

Interactive Read and Write

Other options for teaching this selection can be found in

- Interactive Read and Write for English Learners, pp. 19–38
- Interactive Read and Write for Approaching-Level Learners, pp. 19–38
- Interactive Read and Write for On-Level Learners, pp. 19–38

| Vocabulary | 1 |

Word Origins Have students look up the origin of each vocabulary word. Remind students that sometimes you have to look up a related word (for example, *adverse* for *adversary*) to find its etymology.

Selection Skills

Literary Elements
- Irony (SE pp. 125, 127, 128, 129, 132)

from The Pardoner's Tale

Writing Skills/Grammar
- Write a Movie Scene (SE p. 132)

Reading Skills
- Analyze Tone (SE pp. 125, 126, 127, 132)

Vocabulary Skills
- Word Origins (TE p. 125)

Teach

Big Idea 1

The Power of Faith Say:

Keep these questions in mind as you read: Why do the rioters focus on the gold rather than on the plague? *(Students may say that the men see the gold as something that could bring them pleasure, whereas they can do nothing about the plague.)* How are the deaths the men create different from Death? *(They control the deaths they inflict.)*

Reading Strategy 2

Analyze Tone Answer:

His tone is objective and emotionally detached. The large number of plague victims has probably dulled the shock he feels from another death.

Cultural History ☆

The Seven Deadly Sins As an exemplum, this story focuses on the disastrous effects of two of the "seven deadly sins": *gluttony* and *greed (or covetousness)*. The other five are envy, anger, sloth, lust, and pride. This list was compiled by Pope Gregory I.

For an audio recording of this selection, use Listening Library Audio CD-ROM

For additional reading strategy practice, see Unit 1 Teaching Resources Book, p. 95.

126

---

from The Pardoner's Tale

It's of three rioters° I have to tell **1**
Who, long before the morning service bell,°
Were sitting in a tavern for a drink.
And as they sat, they heard the hand-bell clink
5   Before a coffin going to the grave;°
One of them called the little tavern-knave°
And said "Go and find out at once—look spry!—
Whose corpse is in that coffin passing by;
And see you get the name correctly too."
10   "Sir," said the boy, "no need, I promise you;
Two hours before you came here I was told.
He was a friend of yours in days of old,
And suddenly, last night, the man was slain,
Upon his bench, face up, dead drunk again.
15   There came a privy° thief, they call him Death,
Who kills us all round here, and in a breath
He speared him through the heart, he never stirred.
And then Death went his way without a word.
He's killed a thousand in the present plague,°
20   And, sir, it doesn't do to be too vague
If you should meet him; you had best be wary.
Be on your guard with such an **adversary**,
Be primed to meet him everywhere you go,
That's what my mother said. It's all I know."
25   The publican° joined in with, "By St. Mary,
What the child says is right; you'd best be wary,
This very year he killed, in a large village
A mile away, man, woman, serf at tillage,°
Page in the household, children—all there were.
30   Yes, I imagine that he lives round there.
It's well to be prepared in these alarms,
He might do you dishonor." "Huh, God's arms!"
The rioter said, "Is he so fierce to meet?
I'll search for him, by Jesus, street by street.
35   God's blessed bones! I'll register a vow!

Analyze Tone *How would you describe the tone of the tavern-knave's report?* **2**

Vocabulary

adversary (ad′ vər ser′ ē) n. an opponent; enemy

---

1 rioters: people given to unrestrained revelry and debauchery.
2 long before . . . bell: long before 9 A.M.
4–5 hand-bell . . . grave: During this time, a bell was rung next to the coffin in a funeral procession.
6 tavern-knave: serving boy.

15 privy: secretive.

19 killed . . . plague: In 1348 and 1349 at least a third of the population of England perished from the plague called the Black Death.

25 publican: a tavernkeeper or innkeeper.

28 tillage: plowing.

Research Practice

SPIRAL REVIEW **Historical Context** Tell students that the Black Death was a phantom enemy in medieval times, mostly because people were ignorant of its causes. The horrific nature of the disease, the swift certainty of its outcome, and the huge toll it took on populations only increased people's fears. It wasn't until hundreds of years later that the bacterium responsible for the plague was discovered. Have students use the library or Internet resources to compile notes on the cause of the plagues and the ways it was spread.

Here, chaps! The three of us together now,
Hold up your hands, like me, and we'll be brothers
In this affair, and each defend the others,
And we will kill this traitor Death, I say!
40 Away with him as he has made away
With all our friends. God's dignity! Tonight!"
    They made their bargain, swore with appetite,
These three, to live and die for one another
As brother-born might swear to his born brother.
45 And up they started in their drunken rage
And made towards this village which the page
And publican had spoken of before.
Many and grisly were the oaths they swore,
Tearing Christ's blessed body to a shred;°
50 "If we can only catch him, Death is dead!"
    When they had gone not fully half a mile,
Just as they were about to cross a stile,°
They came upon a very poor old man
Who humbly greeted them and thus began,
55 "God look to you, my lords, and give you quiet!"
To which the proudest of these men of riot
Gave back the answer, "What, old fool? Give place!
Why are you all wrapped up except your face?
Why live so long? Isn't it time to die?"
60   The old, old fellow looked him in the eye
And said, "Because I never yet have found,
Though I have walked to India, searching round
Village and city on my pilgrimage,
One who would change his youth to have my age.
65 And so my age is mine and must be still
Upon me, for such time as God may will.
    "Not even Death, alas, will take my life;
So, like a wretched prisoner at strife
Within himself, I walk alone and wait
70 About the earth, which is my mother's gate,°
Knock-knocking with my staff from night to noon
And crying, 'Mother, open to me soon!
Look at me, mother, won't you let me in?
See how I wither, flesh and blood and skin!
75 Alas! When will these bones be laid to rest?
Mother, I would exchange—for that were best—
The wardrobe in my chamber, standing there

49 **Tearing . . . shred:** Their swearing included such expressions as "God's arms" (line 32) and "God's blessed bones" (line 35).
52 **stile:** a stairway used to climb over a wall or fence.

70 **mother's gate:** the entrance to the grave.

The Pardoner (detail). Illumination from Geoffrey Chaucer's *The Canterbury Tales.* The Huntington Art Collection, San Marino, CA.

Irony *What is ironic about the rioters' resolution?* **3**

Analyze Tone *In what tone does the rioter answer the "poor old man"?* **4**

Literary Element 3

Irony **Answer:** *Death is personified throughout the tale, and the rioters ironically confuse the abstract and the concrete by speaking of Death as if it were a living person. "Killing Death" is an oxymoron.*

(ENGLISH LEARNERS) Have English Learners focus on finding irony in line 50: "If we can only catch him, Death is dead!"

Reading Strategy 4

Analyze Tone **Answer:** *He uses a cruel, demeaning tone. Some students may say that by presuming to decide when the old man should die, the rioter is "playing God."*

Cultural History ☆

Relics In the Middle Ages, it was common for people to revere (and swear by) relics—the remains of saints, usually bones. According to St. Thomas Aquinas, showing reverence for the remains of a holy person is one way to honor that person.

Approaching Level

DIFFERENTIATED INSTRUCTION

Emerging Approaching level students may benefit from connecting the Pardoner's Tale with stories in contemporary society. Point out to students that the killing of a comrade for the sake of greed is similar to stories that are often found in modern newspapers. Ask students to find an article in a newspaper or magazine that reminds them of "The Pardoner's Tale" in some way. Have students take notes in their journals, summarizing the article and identifying comparisons between it and the Pardoner's story. Invite students to share their comparisons with the class and to add any comments or opinions of their own.

Teach

Literary Element | 1

Irony Answer: *In discovering the treasure, the rioters no longer seek Death.*

APPROACHING If students are having difficulty, ask them to identify what the rioters were planning to do before they found the treasure, and how finding it changes their plans.

View the Art ★

Answer: *Chaucer is probably the figure on the right. He is facing the others and leaning in toward them as if telling them a story.*

So long, for yours! Aye, for a shirt of hair°
To wrap me in!' She has refused her grace,
80   Whence comes the pallor of my withered face.
    "But it dishonored you when you began
To speak so roughly, sir, to an old man,
Unless he had injured you in word or deed.
It says in holy writ, as you may read,
85   'Thou shalt rise up before the hoary° head
And honor it.' And therefore be it said
'Do no more harm to an old man than you,
Being now young, would have another do
When you are old'—if you should live till then.
90   And so may God be with you, gentlemen,
For I must go whither I have to go."
    "By God," the gambler said, "you shan't do so,
You don't get off so easy, by St. John!
I heard you mention, just a moment gone,
95   A certain traitor Death who singles out
And kills the fine young fellows hereabout.
And you're his spy, by God! You wait a bit.
Say where he is or you shall pay for it,
By God and by the Holy Sacrament!
100   I say you've joined together by consent
To kill us younger folk, you thieving swine!"
    "Well, sirs," he said, "if it be your design
To find out Death, turn up this crooked way
Towards that grove, I left him there today
105   Under a tree, and there you'll find him waiting.
He isn't one to hide for all your prating.
You see that oak? He won't be far to find.
And God protect you that redeemed mankind,
Aye, and amend° you!" Thus that ancient man.
110   At once the three young rioters began
To run, and reached the tree, and there they found
A pile of golden florins on the ground,
New-coined, eight bushels of them as they thought.
No longer was it Death those fellows sought,
115   For they were all so thrilled to see the sight,
The florins were so beautiful and bright,
That down they sat beside the precious pile.
The wickedest spoke first after a while.
"Brothers," he said, "you listen to what I say.
120   I'm pretty sharp although I joke away.
It's clear that Fortune° has bestowed this treasure

78 shirt of hair: usually a rough shirt worn as self-punishment; here, a shroud

85 hoary: white with age.

Chaucer, the Knight and the Squire from "The Pardoner's Prologue" of *The Canterbury Tales.* Harry Mileham (1873–1957). Private collection.

View the Art Of the figures shown here, which do you think represents Chaucer? What about this character's body language leads you to your conclusion? ★

109 amend: improve.

121 Fortune: fate.

Irony *What is ironic about the rioters' discovery?* **1**

Vocabulary Practice

SPIRAL REVIEW **Context Clues** Remind students that writers often give context clues to the meanings of unfamiliar words. Write these examples on the board and ask volunteers for the meanings of the underlined words. Have students demonstrate their understanding by using each word in a sentence of their own.

- To let us live in <u>jollity</u> and pleasure
- Shall run to town as quickly as he can/ To <u>fetch</u> us bread and wine
- And on he ran, he had no thought to <u>tarry</u>

To let us live in jollity and pleasure.
Light come, light go! We'll spend it as we ought.
God's precious dignity! Who would have thought
125   This morning was to be our lucky day?
        "If one could only get the gold away,
Back to my house, or else to yours, perhaps—
For as you know, the gold is ours, chaps—
We'd all be at the top of fortune, hey?
130   But certainly it can't be done by day.
People would call us robbers—a strong gang,
So our own property would make us hang.
No, we must bring this treasure back by night
Some **prudent** way, and keep it out of sight.
135   And so as a solution I propose
We draw for lots and see the way it goes;
The one who draws the longest, lucky man,
Shall run to town as quickly as he can
To fetch us bread and wine—but keep things dark°—
140   While two remain in hiding here to mark
Our heap of treasure. If there's no delay,
When night comes down we'll carry it away,
All three of us, wherever we have planned."
        He gathered lots and hid them in his hand
145   Bidding them draw for where the luck should fall.
It fell upon the youngest of them all,
And off he ran at once towards the town.
        As soon as he had gone the first sat down
And thus began a parley° with the other:
150   "You know that you can trust me as a brother;
Now let me tell you where your profit lies;
You know our friend has gone to get supplies
And here's a lot of gold that is to be   **2**
Divided equally amongst us three.
155   Nevertheless, if I could shape things thus
So that we shared it out—the two of us—
Wouldn't you take it as a friendly act?" ☆
        "But how?" the other said. "He knows the fact
That all the gold was left with me and you;
160   What can we tell him? What are we to do?"
        "Is it a bargain," said the first, "or no?
For I can tell you in a word or so

139 **keep things dark:** act in secret; don't give us away.

149 **parley** (pär′ lē): a discussion, as with an enemy.

Irony *What ironic thread runs through the dialogue among the three rioters?* **3**

Vocabulary

prudent (prood′ ənt) *adj.* cautious; careful

Reading Strategy **2**

Predicting Have students reread lines 148–157. **Ask:** What prediction might you make about the proposal the first rioter will make? *(He will somehow suggest tricking or doing away with the youngest one.)*

Literary Element **3**

Irony Answer: *The three rioters pledge trust and friendship to each other while harboring treachery and betrayal in their hearts.*

Writer's Technique ☆

Plot Point out that the storyteller does not allow the action to lag. Instead, the tension begins to build as soon as the youngest departs, leaving the other two alone.

Approaching Level

DIFFERENTIATED INSTRUCTION

AAVE Approaching level students who use African American vernacular English (AAVE) may have trouble recognizing the past tense of some verbs. Remind students that the suffix -ed indicates the past tense. Have students find examples on the page.

Teach

Big Idea   **1**

The Power of Faith

Answer: *The Pardoner attests that God allows the Devil to put evil thoughts into the minds of humans and to tempt them into sin and damnation.*

What's to be done to bring the thing about."
"Trust me," the other said, "you needn't doubt
165   My word. I won't betray you, I'll be true."
     "Well," said his friend, "you see that we are two,
And two are twice as powerful as one.
Now look; when he comes back, get up in fun
To have a wrestle; then, as you attack,
170   I'll up and put my dagger through his back
While you and he are struggling, as in game;
Then draw your dagger too and do the same.
Then all this money will be ours to spend,
Divided equally of course, dear friend.
175   Then we can **gratify** our lusts and fill
The day with dicing at our own sweet will."
Thus these two miscreants° agreed to slay
The third and youngest, as you heard me say.
     The youngest, as he ran towards the town,
180   Kept turning over, rolling up and down
Within his heart the beauty of those bright
New florins, saying, "Lord, to think I might
Have all that treasure to myself alone!
Could there be anyone beneath the throne
185   Of God so happy as I then should be?"
     And so the Fiend, our common enemy,
Was given power to put it in his thought
That there was always poison to be bought,
And that with poison he could kill his friends.
190   To men in such a state the Devil sends
Thoughts of this kind, and has a full permission
To lure them on to sorrow and perdition;°
For this young man was utterly content
To kill them both and never to repent.
195   And on he ran, he had no thought to tarry,
Came to the town, found an apothecary
And said, "Sell me some poison if you will,
I have a lot of rats I want to kill
And there's a polecat too about my yard
200   That takes my chickens and it hits me hard;

Florin, a coin of the thirteenth century

---

177 miscreants (mis′ krē ənts): evildoers, villains.

192 perdition: damnation.

The Power of Faith *What point about the Devil is the Pardoner expressing here?*   **1**

Vocabulary

gratify (grat′ ə fī′) *v.* to satisfy; indulge

Reading Practice

Summarize Remind students that a plot is the sequence of events in a narrative work. Review the components of plot: exposition (including characters, setting, and conflict), action, climax, and resolution. Afterward have students summarize the plot of "The Pardoner's Tale." Students can work in pairs to create graphic organizers that show the stages of the plot.

But I'll get even, as is only right,
With vermin that destroy a man by night."
　　The chemist answered, "I've a preparation
Which you shall have, and by my soul's salvation
205　If any living creature eat or drink
A mouthful, ere he has the time to think,
Though he took less than makes a grain of wheat,
You'll see him fall down dying at your feet;
Yes, die he must, and in so short a while
210　You'd hardly have the time to walk a mile,
The poison is so strong, you understand."
　　This cursed fellow grabbed into his hand
The box of poison and away he ran
Into a neighboring street, and found a man
215　Who lent him three large bottles. He withdrew
And **deftly** poured the poison into two.
He kept the third one clean, as well he might,
For his own drink, meaning to work all night
Stacking the gold and carrying it away.
220　And when this rioter, this devil's clay,
Had filled his bottles up with wine, all three,
Back to rejoin his comrades sauntered he.
　　Why make a sermon of it? Why waste breath?
Exactly in the way they'd planned his death
225　They fell on him and slew him, two to one.
Then said the first of them when this was done,
"Now for a drink. Sit down and let's be merry,
For later on there'll be the corpse to bury."
And, as it happened, reaching for a sup,
230　He took a bottle of poison up
And drank; and his companion, nothing loth,°
Drank from it also, and they perished both.
　　There is, in Avicenna's long relation°
Concerning poison and its operation,
235　Trust me, no ghastlier section to transcend
What these two wretches suffered at their end.
Thus these two murderers received their due,
So did the treacherous young poisoner too.

Apothecary's pestle and mortar, early 18th century. Brass and copper. Private collection.

231 nothing loth: very willingly.

233 Avicenna's (av′ ə sen′ əz) **long relation:** a medieval book on medicine by the Arab physician Avicenna (980–1037), which contains a chapter on poisons.

Analyze Tone *How would you describe the Pardoner's tone in relating the deaths of the last two rioters?*

Vocabulary

deftly (deft′ lē) *adv.* skillfully; nimbly

Teach

Reading Strategy 2

Analyze Tone **Answer:** *Although he is relating a grisly death, his tone is cool and objective—for example, he cites a scholarly treatise on poisons.*

Literary Element 3

Irony After students finish reading the tale, have them return to the old man's speech in lines 102–109. **Ask:** How does the old man's comment prove to be true? *(The old man knows—and once readers are familiar with the story, they too know—that the Death awaiting the rioters beneath the oak tree is their own.)*

To check students' understanding of the selection, see Unit 1 Teaching Resources Book, p. 99.

Progress Check

Can students identify irony?

If No → See Unit 1 Teaching Resources Book, p. 94.

English Learners

DIFFERENTIATED INSTRUCTION

Beginning Have English Learners read the exchange between the young man and the chemist. Then direct their attention to the illustration of the mortar and pestle. Have them describe orally what a chemist or apothecary's job was. **Ask:** Why would a chemist use a mortar and pestle? *(to grind or mix herbs)*

After You Read

Assess

1. Students' answers will vary. Make sure that they support their opinions with reasons and examples from the text.
2. (a) They show no respect for other people. (b) As a "wretched prisoner" waiting to die
3. (a) A large pile of gold coins (b) Between love of money and the death of the soul
4. (a) Students' answers will vary but should include money. (b) Given the characterization of the Pardoner in "The Prologue," it is ironic that the Pardoner tells a tale warning against his own vice.
5. In rejecting Christian morality, the rioters bring about their own deaths.
6. Answers will vary.

Vocabulary

Students should provide specific examples from the selection that provided context clues to define the vocabulary words.

 For additional assessment, see Assessment Resources, pp. 69–70.

 To create custom assessments using software, use ExamView Assessment Suite.

After You Read

Respond and Think Critically

Respond and Interpret

1. (a)Were you surprised by the way the tale ends? Why or why not? (b)Would any other ending have been as satisfactory? Explain.
2. (a)How does the rioters' treatment of the tavern-knave and the old man characterize the rioters? (b)How does the old man characterize himself?
3. (a)When the rioters go in search of Death, what do they find under the oak tree? (b)What symbolic association about greed might Chaucer be making here?

Analyze and Evaluate

4. (a)What do you think is the moral of this exemplum? (b)Do you find it ironic that the Pardoner has told a moralistic tale? Explain.

Connect

5. **Big Idea** **The Power of Faith** In what way does this tale illustrate the power of faith in medieval society?
6. **Connect to Today** If this tale were set in modern times, what sort of characters might be used in place of the medieval rioters?

Literary Element Irony

"The Pardoner's Tale" contains examples of verbal irony, situational irony, and dramatic irony.

1. One rioter says, "We'll be brothers in this affair, and each defend the others." How is this an example of verbal irony?
2. When the rioters find the treasure, the "wickedest" says that Fortune gave it to them so that they could live "in jollity and pleasure." How is this an example of situational irony?
3. What example of dramatic irony occurs near the end of the tale?

 Writing

Write a Movie Scene Choose a section of "The Pardoner's Tale" to rewrite as a brief movie scene. Try to reproduce the overall tone of that section of Chaucer's tale—is the section mostly humorous? mostly suspenseful? mostly ironic? As a challenging alternative, rewrite a selected passage as a modern crime drama, using the same basic characters and events.

LOG ON ▶ **Literature** Online

Selection Resources For Selection Quizzes, eFlashcards, and Reading-Writing Connection activities, go to glencoe.com and enter QuickPass code GLB9817u1.

Reading Strategy Analyze Tone

A work's tone may include the moral outlook that the writer conveys through the voice of the narrator.

Partner Activity With a partner, discuss the moral tone of "The Pardoner's Tale." Do you think the tone is appropriate? Explain.

Vocabulary Practice

Practice with Context Clues Look back at "The Pardoner's Tale" to find context clues for the vocabulary words below. Record your findings in a chart like the one shown here.

adversary   prudent   gratify   deftly

EXAMPLE:

Word: miscreant

↓

Textual Clues: Two of the rioters are referred to as miscreants just after they plot to kill the third, so miscreant probably indicates that the two rioters are evil or criminals.

↓

Meaning: evildoer; villain

Literary Element

1. The rioters' actions are completely unbrotherly.
2. The rioters will die because of their greed before they can enjoy their wealth.
3. The two rioters celebrate their murder of the youngest rioter by drinking the poisoned wine that the youngest rioter concocted for them.

Reading Strategy

Students' answers will vary. Some may say that the detached tone enhances the chilling effect of the tale.

 **Writing**

Scenes will vary.

from *The Wife of Bath's Tale*

Connect to the Poem

What are the benefits of submitting oneself to the superior arguments of another? Discuss this question with a partner, considerng situations in which an insistence on getting one's own way might be ill-advised.

Build Background

That the Wife has had five husbands would not have seemed remarkable to Chaucer's contemporaries; in the Middle Ages, a woman with property was very eligible. What they might have found remarkable is her success in governing her husbands.

Set Purposes for Reading

Big Idea **The Power of Faith**

The Wife's tale is set in the shadowy margin between the pagan and Christian worlds. As you read, ask yourself, Which events belong to each of these worlds?

Literary Element **Humor**

The quality of a literary work that makes characters and their situations seem funny, amusing, or ludicrous is called humor. Types of humor range widely, from puns and word play to broad satire, sarcasm, parody, and subtle wit. As you read, ask yourself, What forms of humor are present in this tale?

Reading Strategy **Analyze Form**

"The Wife of Bath's Tale," like many other tales from Chaucer's era, is told in the form of a narrative poem. **Narrative poetry** is verse that is specifically meant to tell a story. To analyze a work of narrative poetry, you can look at the ways in which an author combines structure, word choice, and literary elements (such as character, narrator, and conflict) to express a theme or idea.

....

Tip: Analyzing Structure "The Wife of Bath's Tale" consists of the Wife's introduction, followed by a tale in which events are told in chronological order. Use a timeline like the one below to help you keep track of what happens in each part.

"Knight attacks the maiden."   "Wife tells the tale to the pilgrims."

Learning Objectives

For pages 133–151

In studying this text, you will focus on the following objectives:

Literary Study:
Analyzing humor.
Analyzing characterization.

Reading:
Analyzing form.
Understanding historical context.

Vocabulary

reprove (ri prōōv′) *v.* to scold or correct, usually gently or out of kindness; p. 135 *Felicia's mother reproved her for not sharing her toys.*

concede (kən sēd′) *v.* to admit as true; acknowledge; p. 137 *Reuben had to concede that Charles's fund-raising scheme was best.*

disperse (dis purs′) *v.* to scatter about; distribute widely; p. 141 *After the family reunion, all the relatives dispersed to their homes around the country.*

arrogance (ar′ ə gəns) *n.* over-bearing pride or self-importance; p. 144 *In his arrogance, the ruler built a monument to himself.*

suffice (sə fīs′) *v.* to be enough; p. 148 *You said you hoped for rain; will this downpour suffice?*

GEOFFREY CHAUCER **133**

Before You Read

Focus

Summary

A knight can escape execution by finding out what women most desire. After a year of searching, he meets an old woman. She gives him the answer in exchange for granting her a wish. After he reluctantly marries her, she turns into a lovely young woman.

 For summaries in langauges other than English, see Unit 1 Teaching Resources Book, pp. 101–106.

Vocabulary

Have students use a dictionary to identify the etymology of each vocabulary word. Then have them write sentences that describe the way each word has developed.

 For additional vocabulary practice, see Unit 1 Teaching Resources Book, p. 109.

 For additional context, see Glencoe Interactive Vocabulary CD-ROM.

Selection Skills

Literary Elements
- Humor (SE pp. 133, 134, 138, 142, 143)
- Mood (TE p. 139)

***from* The Wife of Bath's Tale**

Writing Skills/Grammar
- Expository Essay (SE p. 151)
- Verbs (TE p. 136)
- Persuasion (TE p. 138)
- Gerunds (TE p. 140)

Reading Skills
- Evaluate Argument (SE pp. 133, 140, 141, 146, 147)
- Analyze Tone (TE pp. 140, 147)

Vocabulary Skills
- Word Origins (TE p. 136)

Teach

Literary Element   1

Humor **Answer:** *Their exchange is an amusing quibble between two people who like to talk. The Pardoner claims to be intimidated by the Wife's citation of St. Paul that grants a wife power over her husband's body. The Pardoner jokes that he has cancelled his marriage plans.*

For an audio recording of this selection, use Listening Library Audio CD-ROM.

The Wife of Bath (detail). Illumination from Geoffrey Chaucer's *The Canterbury Tales.* The Huntington Art Collection, San Marino, CA.

from The Wife of Bath's Tale

The Wife of Bath prefaces her tale by saying that she has a right to speak of the woes of marriage since she has had considerable experience in the matter. Apparently, the object of marriage for her is to have mastery over her husband, "who shall be both my debtor and my slave." To support this view, she cites part of a statement by St. Paul that grants a wife power over her husband's body. This prompts the Pardoner to interrupt.

> The Pardoner started up, and thereupon
> 'Madam,' he said, 'by God and by St John,
> That's noble preaching no one could surpass!
> I was about to take a wife; alas!
> 5 Am I to buy it on my flesh so dear?
> There'll be no marrying for me this year!'
> 'You wait,' she said, 'my story's not begun.
> You'll taste another brew before I've done;
> You'll find it doesn't taste as good as ale;
> 10 And when I've finished telling you my tale
> Of tribulation in the married life
> In which I've been an expert as a wife,
> That is to say, myself have been the whip.
> So please yourself whether you want to sip
> 15 At that same cask of marriage I shall broach.
> Be cautious before making the approach,
> For I'll give instances, and more than ten.

Humor *What is humorous in this exchange between the Wife and the Pardoner?* 1

Vocabulary Practice

SPIRAL REVIEW **Compound Words** Review with students that a compound word is made up of two or more words. Readers can increase their understanding of unfamiliar words by examining the meaning of the separate parts. Examples on pages 135–136 include *countryside,* *outhouses,* and *daylight.*

Give students practice by asking them to define these compound words: *housewife, sportsman, nighttime, seaside, sunshine, schoolhouse, butterfly.*

And those who won't be warned by other men,
By other men shall suffer their correction,
20 So Ptolemy° has said, in this connection.
You read his *Almagest*; you'll find it there.
    'Madam, I put it to you as a prayer,'
The Pardoner said, 'go on as you began!
Tell us your tale, spare not for any man.
25 Instruct us younger men in your technique.'
    'Gladly,' she said, 'if you will let me speak,
But still I hope the company won't **reprove** me
Though I should speak as fantasy may move me,
And please don't be offended at my views;
30 They're really only offered to amuse.

The Wife proceeds to tell a series of vivid private anecdotes of her five
marriages, supposedly as exempla of her beliefs about relationships.
She boasts of how she controlled her first three husbands by always
making them feel at fault. Her last two husbands proved less coopera-
tive. The fourth cheated on her, and the most she could do to retaliate
was to pretend to be interested in other men. The fifth would beat
her, and yet she loved him most, because "he was disdainful in his
love." A scholar, he would try to educate her to be submissive by
forcing her to listen to authoritative readings on wicked women. This
finally provoked her to start a brawl. In the end, she made him burn
the texts and surrender his mastery to her, and from then on, she
says, she was kind and true to him and he to her. In the tale that fol-
lows, it is the wife who subjects the husband to a course of education.

2

    When good King Arthur ruled in ancient days
    (A king that every Briton loves to praise)
    This was a land brim-full of fairy folk.
    The Elf-Queen and her courtiers joined and broke
35 Their elfin dance on many a green mead,°
    Or so was the opinion once, I read,
    Hundreds of years ago, in days of yore.
    But no one now sees fairies any more.
    For now the saintly charity and prayer
40 Of holy friars seem to have purged the air;
    They search the countryside through field and stream
    As thick as motes° that speckle a sun-beam,

The Power of Faith *How has Christianity supplanted paganism in King* **3**
Arthur's day?

---

20 Ptolemy (täl′ ə mē): Claudius Ptolemaeus was a second-century Greek astronomer whose *Almagest* served as the definitive textbook for medieval astronomers. The proverb in the preceding lines was added by someone else to a particular edition of the *Almagest*.

35 mead: meadow.

42 motes: particles of dust.

GEOFFREY CHAUCER **135**

Teach

Literary Element **2**

Foreshadow Tell students to take note of the Wife of Bath's own marital history and keep it in mind as they read her tale. **Ask:** How might her life foreshadow the tale she tells? *(In her fifth marriage, she gains mastery over her husband and the marriage thrives.)*

Big Idea **3**

The Power of Faith
Answer: *The fairies have been purged by the prayers and blessings of the friars who wander the town and countryside.*

Cultural History ☆

Early Marriage In medieval times, girls and boys were considered adults in their mid-teens. High-born girls were often contracted in marriage in their infancy or early childhood. Marriages themselves generally took place at age 14 or so.

English Learners

DIFFERENTIATED INSTRUCTION

Intermediate To facilitate reading for students learning English, suggest that they break up the reading into smaller parts of several lines each. Instruct students to practice saying the lines until they know them well enough to enjoy their rhythm.

Approaching Level

DIFFERENTIATED INSTRUCTION

Emerging Draw attention to the typeface at the beginning of the selection and have students compare it with the type used in the poem itself. Explain that the words at the beginning are not part of the actual poem but a summary of what has happened before. Have students note the summary on page 126 as well.

Teach

Word Origins The Latin word *statuere* means "to set up" or "to decree." *Statute,* which denotes a decree or law that stands on the books, comes from the past participle of this Latin word. Have students use dictionaries to find another word that derives from *statuere. (Possible answer:* statue)

View the Art  ★

Answer: *Most students will say that the painting's mood is cheerful and calm and that it is very similar to the mood in Chaucer's description. Some may say that Chaucer's description is more fantastical than the painted image.*

This painting portrays Bath, a small town outside of London.

The City Weir, Bath, Looking Towards Walcot, 18th century. Thomas Ross. Oil on canvas, 91.5 x 121.5 cm. Victoria Art Gallery, Bath and North East Somerset Council, England.

View the Art Painters use color, light, and shape to create overall moods, or feelings, in their works. How would you describe the mood this image evokes? How does it compare to the mood evoked by Chaucer's description of the countryside? ★

> Blessing the halls, the chambers, kitchens, bowers,
> Cities and boroughs, castles, courts and towers,
> 45   Thorpes,° barns and stables, outhouses and dairies,
> And that's the reason why there are no fairies.
> Wherever there was wont to walk° an elf
> To-day there walks the holy friar himself
> As evening falls or when the daylight springs,
> 50   Saying his mattins and his holy things,
> Walking his limit round from town to town.
> Women can now go safely up and down
> By every bush or under every tree;
> There is no other incubus° but he,
> 55   So there is really no one else to hurt you
> And he will do no more than take your virtue.
>   Now it so happened, I began to say,
> Long, long ago in good King Arthur's day,
> There was a knight who was a lusty liver.
> 60   One day as he came riding from the river
> He saw a maiden walking all forlorn
> Ahead of him, alone as she was born.
> And of that maiden, spite of all she said,
> By very force he took her maidenhead. ☆
> 65   This act of violence made such a stir,
> So much petitioning to the king for her,
> That he condemned the knight to lose his head

45 Thorpes: villages.

47 was wont to walk: habitually walked.

54 incubus: an evil spirit that attacks women in their sleep.

136   UNIT 1   THE ANGLO-SAXON PERIOD AND THE MIDDLE AGES

Vocabulary Practice

SPIRAL REVIEW **Verbs** Point out to students that a varied and specific use of verbs helps make writing more effective. Have students look at these examples in Chaucer's poem: *expressed* (line 77), *concede* (line 84), *seek* (line 85). Write the following verbs on the board:

said   walked   held

Ask students to brainstorm more specific verbs for each of these words. List them on the board, then review the words with the class. Have students suggest how each word could affect a reader's perception of a text.

By course of law. He was as good as dead
(It seems that then the statutes took that view) **1**
70 But that the queen, and other ladies too,
Implored° the king to exercise his grace
So ceaselessly, he gave the queen the case
And granted her his life, and she could choose
Whether to show him mercy or refuse.
75   The queen returned him thanks with all her might,
And then she sent a summons to the knight
At her convenience, and expressed her will:
'You stand, for such is the position still,
In no way certain of your life,' said she,
80 'Yet you shall live if you can answer me:
What is the thing that women most desire?
Beware the axe and say as I require.
     'If you can't answer on the moment, though,
I will **concede** you this: you are to go
85 A twelvemonth and a day to seek and learn
Sufficient answer, then you shall return.
I shall take gages° from you to extort
Surrender of your body to the court.'
     Sad was the knight and sorrowfully sighed,
90 But there! All other choices were denied,
And in the end he chose to go away
And to return after a year and day
Armed with such answer as there might be sent
To him by God. He took his leave and went. **2**
95   He knocked at every house, searched every place,
Yes, anywhere that offered hope of grace.
What could it be that women wanted most?
But all the same he never touched a coast,
Country or town in which there seemed to be
100 Any two people willing to agree.
     Some said that women wanted wealth and treasure,
'Honour,' said some, some 'Jollity and pleasure,'
Some 'Gorgeous clothes' and others 'Fun in bed,'
'To be oft widowed and remarried,' said
105 Others again, and some that what most mattered
Was that we should be cosseted° and flattered.
That's very near the truth, it seems to me;

The Power of Faith *How does the knight expect ultimately to free himself through faith?* **3**

Vocabulary

concede (kən sēd´) *v.* to admit as true; acknowledge

71 **implored:** pleaded with.

87 **gages:** valuable items pledged in support of a promise, such as money posted for bail.

Manuscript Illumination of a Knight from the Codex Capodilista, 15th century.

106 **cosseted:** pampered.

Teach

Literary Element **2**

Characterization Ask: Why can't the knight answer the queen's question? *(His behavior so far shows no understanding of what women might want. He violated the maiden he came upon as if it were his right.)*

Big Idea **3**

**The Power of Faith
Answer:** *He has faith that God will send him the answer when he needs it.*

Cultural History ☆

Uncourtly Love Despite the legend of courtly love, wandering knights were not always concerned with loyalty and chivalry. Often, they deceived ladies with false oaths and pledges.

Approaching Level

DIFFERENTIATED INSTRUCTION

Emerging Remind students that alliteration is the repetition of initial consonant sounds in a series of words. Chaucer uses alliteration to produce a musical quality to his verse. Draw attention to examples such as *wont to walk* (line 47), *lusty liver* (line 59), and *riding from the river* (line 60). Encourage students to find additional examples on neighboring pages. Then, have students practice **reading fluency** by reading these examples aloud, to the class or to each other.

Teach

Literary Element 1

Humor **Answer:** *The Wife is ridiculing one of the suggested answers to the question of what women most desire—a reputation for dependability, discretion, and the ability to keep secrets. According to the Wife, women are incapable of keeping secrets.*

[APPROACHING] Students may find line 125 difficult. To clarify, have students suggest other words that might complete the sentence "But that's not worth _____."

View the Art ★

A knight's relationship with his "courtly lady" was very similar to his relationship with his liege lord. He was supposed to give her the same obedience and loyalty. **Ask:** What aspects of this painting show that the woman is in control of the love relationship? *(Possible answers: His bent knees; her placement as raised and seated above him; his submissive expression and her confident one.)*

Knight Visiting His Lady, 1475 (detail). Artist unknown. Manuscript illumination. ★

A man can win us best with flattery.
To dance attendance on us, make a fuss,
110 Ensnares° us all, the best and worst of us.
    Some say the things we most desire are these:
Freedom to do exactly as we please,
With no one to reprove our faults and lies,
Rather to have one call us good and wise.
115 Truly there's not a woman in ten score°
Who has a fault, and someone rubs the sore,
But she will kick if what he says is true;
You try it out and you will find so too.
However vicious we may be within
120 We like to be thought wise and void of sin.
Others assert we women find it sweet
When we are thought dependable, discreet
And secret, firm of purpose and controlled,
Never betraying things that we are told.
125 But that's not worth the handle of a rake;
Women conceal a thing? For Heaven's sake!
Remember Midas? Will you hear the tale?
    Among some other little things, now stale,
Ovid° relates that under his long hair
130 The unhappy Midas grew a splendid pair
Of ass's ears; as subtly as he might,

110 **ensnares:** captures or traps.

115 **ten score:** two hundred.

129 **Ovid:** a Roman poet (43 B.C.?–A.D. 17) best known for the *Metamorphoses*, a collection of mythological tales in verse.

Humor *What is the Wife making fun of here?* **1**

138 UNIT 1 THE ANGLO-SAXON PERIOD AND THE MIDDLE AGES

Writing Practice

 **Persuasion**

[SPIRAL REVIEW] The knight is originally sentenced by the king to lose his head for his act of violence. The queen persuades the king to give her the case, and she then imposes a very different punishment. Encourage students to think about the justice of the task the queen sets for the knight. **Ask:** Could the queen's approach rehabilitate the knight?

Have students write persuasive essays in which they defend or argue against the queen's handling of the case. Remind them to include logical reasons, evidence, and examples to support their positions.

Illustration of
a Knight and
Horse in Armor.
Friedrich Martin
von Reibisch.
Stapleton
Collection. ★

View the Art ★

The covering of the horse in this
illustration is called a bard. Bards
came in a number of different
styles, colors, and shapes. The
open type was mostly decorative
and covered little of the horse. The
type shown is the "full blanket,"
which most knights used. It often
carried the knight's crest and colors.

He kept his foul deformity from sight;
Save for his wife, there was not one that knew.
He loved her best, and trusted in her too.
135   He begged her not to tell a living creature
That he possessed so horrible a feature.
And she—she swore, were all the world to win,
She would not do such villainy and sin
As saddle her husband with so foul a name;
140   Besides to speak would be to share the shame.
Nevertheless she thought she would have died
Keeping this secret bottled up inside;
It seemed to swell her heart and she, no doubt,
Thought it was on the point of bursting out.
145   Fearing to speak of it to woman or man,
Down to reedy marsh she quickly ran
And reached the sedge.° Her heart was all on fire
And, as a bittern° bumbles in the mire,
She whispered to the water, near the ground,
150   'Betray me not, O water, with thy sound!

147 sedge: any of a family of
marsh plants.
148 bittern: heron.

GEOFFREY CHAUCER   **139**

English Learners

DIFFERENTIATED INSTRUCTION

Intermediate English learners may have
trouble with figurative language in the tale.
Draw students' attention to the expression
bottled up inside in line 143. Have a volunteer explain the meaning of the phrase.
(Emotion not expressed). Encourage students to take the time to understand the
meaning of such expressions.

Teach

Reading Strategy 1

Evaluate Argument
Answer: *No, an anecdote may bolster an argument, but it cannot be sufficient to prove the argument. Logic, reasons, and evidence are required to prove an argument.*

Literary Element 2

Mood Have students read lines 162–166. **Ask:** What is the mood of these lines? *(It is one of defeat, sadness, dejection.)*

Big Idea 3

The Power of Faith
Answer: *The knight's vision of the dancing women suggests a coven of witches.*

Literary History ☆

Plot Structure In return for the answer he needs, the knight promises to do whatever the old woman wants. The book *Dr. Faustus* is based on a medieval legend of a man who promises his soul to the Devil in return for life. In the fairy tale *Rumpelstiltskin*, the miller's daughter promises her firstborn to Rumpelstiltskin if he will spin straw into gold for her.

To thee alone I tell it: it appears
My husband has a pair of ass's ears!
Ah! My heart's well again, the secret's out!
I could no longer keep it, not a doubt.'
155 And so you see, although we may hold fast°
A little while, it must come out at last,
We can't keep secrets; as for Midas, well,
Read Ovid for his story°; he will tell.
    This knight that I am telling you about
160 Perceived at last he never would find out
What it could be that women loved the best.
Faint was the soul within his sorrowful breast,
As home he went, he dared no longer stay;
His year was up and now it was the day.
165   As he rode home in a dejected mood
Suddenly, at the margin of a wood,
He saw a dance upon the leafy floor
Of four and twenty ladies, nay, and more.
Eagerly he approached, in hope to learn
170 Some words of wisdom ere he should return;
But lo! Before he came to where they were,
Dancers and dance all vanished into air!
There wasn't a living creature to be seen
Save one old woman crouched upon the green.
175 A fouler-looking creature I suppose
Could scarcely be imagined. She arose
And said, 'Sir knight, there's no way on from here.
Tell me what you are looking for, my dear,
For peradventure° that were best for you;
180 We old, old women know a thing or two.'
    'Dear Mother,' said the knight, 'alack the day!
I am as good as dead if I can't say
What thing it is that women most desire;
If you could tell me I would pay your hire.'
185 'Give me your hand,' she said, 'and swear to do
Whatever I shall next require of you ☆
—If so to do should lie within your might—
And you shall know the answer before night.'
'Upon my honour,' he answered, 'I agree.'
190 'Then,' said the crone,° 'I dare to guarantee
Your life is safe; I shall make good my claim.

155 hold fast: restrain firmly.

158 Read . . . story: In the *Metamorphoses,* the marsh weeds whisper Midas's secret whenever the wind blows.

179 peradventure: perhaps.

190 crone: a withered old woman.

Evaluate Argument *Is Ovid's tale convincing proof of the Wife's argument that women cannot keep secrets? Explain.*

The Power of Faith *How does the knight's encounter at the edge of the wood evoke the pagan world?*

Grammar Practice

SPIRAL REVIEW | PARTNERS

Gerunds Have students read line 246. Tell them the word *pleading* is called a gerund. Explain that a gerund is a verb form ending in *-ing* that is used as a noun. Point out that a gerund can be used as a subject, an object, a predicate nominative, or an appositive. A gerund phrase includes a gerund and any complements and modifiers of it. Confirm that *pleading* is used as a subject.

Have students write sentences about the knight, using gerunds in each of the four ways mentioned here. Have pairs of students exchange sentences and review each other's work.

Upon my life the queen will say the same.
Show me the very proudest of them all
In costly coverchief or jewelled caul°
195 That dare say no to what I have to teach.
Let us go forward without further speech.'
And then she crooned her gospel in his ear
And told him to be glad and not to fear.
    They came to court. This knight, in full array,
200 Stood forth and said, 'O Queen, I've kept my day
And kept my word and have my answer ready.'
    There sat the noble matrons and the heady
Young girls, and widows too, that have the grace
Of wisdom, all assembled in that place,
205 And there the queen herself was throned to hear
And judge his answer. Then the knight drew near
And silence was commanded through the hall.
    The queen gave order he should tell them all
What thing it was that women wanted most.
210 He stood not silent like a beast or post,
But gave his answer with the ringing word
Of a man's voice and the assembly heard:
    'My liege and lady, in general,' said he,
'A woman wants the self-same sovereignty°   **4**
215 Over her husband as over her lover,
And master him; he must not be above her.
That is your greatest wish, whether you kill
Or spare me; please yourself. I wait your will.'
    In all the court not one that shook her head
220 Or contradicted what the knight had said;
Maid, wife and widow cried, 'He's saved his life!'
    And on the word up started the old wife,
The one the knight saw sitting on the green,
And cried, 'Your mercy, sovereign lady queen!
225 Before the court **disperses**, do me right!
'Twas I who taught this answer to the knight,
For which he swore, and pledged his honour to it,
That the first thing I asked of him he'd do it,
So far as it should lie within his might.
230 Before this court I ask you then, sir knight,
To keep your word and take me for your wife;

Evaluate Argument *What criterion do the women use to evaluate the*   **5**
knight's answer?

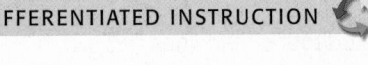

Vocabulary

disperse (dĭs pûrs´) *v.* to scatter about; distribute widely

194 **caul**: a net cap worn over the hair.

214 **sovereignty**: power to rule another person or group of people.

GEOFFREY CHAUCER **141**

Reading Strategy   **4**

Analyze Tone Have students review lines 210–216. **Ask:** What is the tone of the knight when he knows the answer to the queen's question? *(He is more confident than before.)*

(ENGLISH LEARNERS) Have English Learners point out words that create tone in the knight's reply, such as "not silent," and "ringing word."

Reading Strategy   **5**

Evaluate Argument
Answer: *They seem to know intuitively that his answer is correct.*

Approaching Level

DIFFERENTIATED INSTRUCTION

Emerging Point out words in the poem—such as *ere* (line 170), *lo* (line 171), and *peradventure* (line 179)—that were once common in English but sound strange today. Have students practice reading lines containing such words to improve their fluency.

Emerging Have students note how the characters address one another. The old woman addresses the knight as "Sir knight," and he addresses her as "Dear Mother." **Ask:** How does the knight address the queen? *("O Queen" and later "My liege and lady")*

Teach

Humor **Answer:** *Students'*
answers will vary. Some may
find poetic justice in the fact that
the knight, who violated a young
maiden, is now forced to marry an
ugly old crone. Others may find it
amusing that the knight's "reward"
for answering the question correctly
is his subjugation to such a woman.

View the Art ★

Note that this painting illustrates a
dance of the fifteenth century.
Say: To perform this dance,
couples often lined up and
performed simple movements.
However, since their clothing
was very restrictive, the dances
stressed footwork. How does
this dance differ from the way
you dance? *(Answers will vary.)*

Writer's Technique ☆

Point of View Draw attention
to lines 249–252 and point out
the use of the pronouns *I* and *me.*
Explain that the author is showing
that the Wife of Bath is switching
from third-person narration to first-
person narration.

Month of May: May Dance and Game of
Small Papers, c. 1459. Artist unknown.
From the Hours of the Duchess of
Burgundy. Musée Condé, Chantilly, France.

For well you know that I have saved your life.
If this be false, deny it on your sword!'
   'Alas!' he said, 'Old lady, by the Lord
235 I know indeed that such was my behest,°
But for God's love think of a new request,
Take all my goods, but leave my body free.'
'A curse on us,' she said, 'If I agree!
I may be foul, I may be poor and old,
240 Yet will not choose to be, for all the gold
That's bedded in the earth or lies above,
Less than your wife, nay, than your very love!'
   'My love?' said he. 'By heaven, my damnation!
Alas that any of my race and station
245 Should ever make so foul a misalliance!'°
Yet in the end his pleading and defiance
All went for nothing, he was forced to wed.
He takes his ancient wife and goes to bed.
   Now peradventure some may well suspect ☆

235 behest: command.

245 misalliance: a marriage
between people unsuitable for each
other.

Humor *Do you see any humor in the knight's predicament? Explain.*   **1**

142   UNIT 1   THE ANGLO-SAXON PERIOD AND THE MIDDLE AGES

Grammar Practice

SPIRAL REVIEW **Conditional Sentences** Have
students look at lines 285–288.
Explain that line 287 begins a
conditional sentence. **Say:** A conditional
sentence presents two events linked
by a cause-effect relationship. In other
words, if A happens, then B will follow.
A conditional sentence is often introduced by the word *if,* but the words
when, whenever, or *should* can also
introduce conditional sentences.

Have students reread lines 282–284.
Ask: What is the cause-effect relationship in this conditional sentence? *(If the*
knight shows courtesy [cause], then the
wife can set things right [effect].)

Pilgrims Going to Canterbury, 13th century. Artist unknown. Stained glass. Canterbury Cathedral, Kent, UK.

View the Art The stained-glass windows in Canterbury Cathedral are the only surviving examples of English stained glass from their era. What does this portrayal of Canterbury pilgrims have in common with other images of pilgrims you have seen in this unit?

250   A lack of care in me since I neglect
       To tell of the rejoicing and display
       Made at the feast upon their wedding-day.
       I have but a short answer to let fall;
       I say there was no joy or feast at all,
255   Nothing but heaviness of heart and sorrow.
       He married her in private on the morrow
       And all day long stayed hidden like an owl,
       It was such torture that his wife looked foul.
         Great was the anguish churning in his head
260   When he and she were piloted to bed;
       He wallowed back and forth in desperate style.
       His ancient wife lay smiling all the while;
       At last she said, 'Bless us! Is this, my dear,
       How knights and wives get on together here?
265   Are these the laws of good King Arthur's house?
       Are knights of his all so contemptuous?
       I am your own beloved and your wife,
       And I am she, indeed, that saved your life;
       And certainly I never did you wrong.
270   Then why, this first of nights, so sad a song?
       You're carrying on as if you were half-witted.
       Say, for God's love, what sin have I committed?
       I'll put things right if you will tell me how.'
         'Put right?' he cried. 'That never can be now!
275   Nothing can ever be put right again!
       You're old, and so abominably plain,
       So poor to start with, so low-bred to follow;
       It's little wonder if I twist and wallow!
       God, that my heart would burst within my breast!'

Humor *How is the old woman making fun of the knight? Why does she appear to be unoffended by his aversion to her age and appearance?* **2**

GEOFFREY CHAUCER   **143**

Teach

| Literary Element | 2 |

Humor Answer: *She is making fun of the knight's lack of chivalry, honor, and gratitude. Some students may say that she is amused rather than offended because she harbors a secret that the knight knows nothing about.*

ADVANCED **Ask:** Why does she pretend not to understand the knight's distress? *(Students may suggest that she is tormenting him.)*

View the Art

This is a photograph of one of the stained-glass windows in Canterbury Cathedral. The pilgrim trade provided most of the funding needed to build what is one of the most important stained-glass collections in the world. Although this scene depicts pilgrims making their way to Canterbury, most of the scenes in the cathedral have a biblical emphasis.

Approaching Level

DIFFERENTIATED INSTRUCTION

Established One way to understand a character is to understand his or her goals. Discuss the goals of the knight and his wife. **Ask:** What does each one want? *(The knight wants to get out of the marriage; his wife wants to be beloved by him.)* Encourage students to think about how each character might achieve his or her goal. **Ask:** Which character seems optimistic? *(the wife)* Does she have a plan? *(Students will most likely say yes. Encourage them to explain why they think so.)*

Remind students of who is telling the tale and how her experience and point of view might affect her narration.

Teach

Evaluate Argument

Answer: *The old woman corrects the knight's false notion of gentility. She argues that gentility does not stem from one's ancestry, but from one's gentle and virtuous nature. Most students will find her argument persuasive because she cites reasons, examples, and various learned authorities to support her contention.*

280 'Is that,' said she, 'the cause of your unrest?'
     'Yes, certainly,' he said, 'and can you wonder?'
     'I could set right what you suppose a blunder,
     That's if I cared to, in a day or two,
     If I were shown more courtesy by you.
285 Just now,' she said, 'you spoke of gentle birth,
     Such as descends from ancient wealth and worth.
     If that's the claim you make for gentlemen
     Such **arrogance** is hardly worth a hen.
     Whoever loves to work for virtuous ends,
290 Public and private, and who most intends
     To do what deeds of gentleness he can,
     Take him to be the greatest gentleman.
     Christ wills we take our gentleness from Him,
     Not from a wealth of ancestry long dim,
295 Though they bequeath their whole establishment
     By which we claim to be of high descent.
     Our fathers cannot make us a bequest
     Of all those virtues that became them best
     And earned for them the name of gentlemen,
300 But bade us follow them as best we can.
        'Thus the wise poet of the Florentines,
     Dante° by name, has written in these lines,
     For such is the opinion Dante launches;
     "Seldom arises by these slender branches°
305 Prowess of men, for it is God, no less,
     Wills us to claim of Him our gentleness."
     For of our parents nothing can we claim
     Save temporal° things, and these may hurt and maim.
        'But everyone knows this as well as I;
310 For if gentility° were implanted by
     The natural course of lineage down the line,
     Public or private, could it cease to shine
     In doing the fair work of gentle deed?
     No vice or villainy could then bear seed.
315   'Take fire and carry it to the darkest house
     Between this kingdom and the Caucasus,°
     And shut the doors on it and leave it there,
     It will burn on, and it will burn as fair
     As if ten thousand men were there to see,
320 For fire will keep its nature and degree,

302 Dante Alighieri (dän′ tā
ä′ lə gyar′ ē): an Italian poet
(1265–1321), author of the *Divine
Comedy.*
304 slender branches: branches
of the family tree.

308 temporal: worldly.

310 gentility: courteous behavior
befitting a person of noble birth.

316 Caucasus: the Caucasus
Mountains in southeastern Europe.

Evaluate Argument *Summarize and evaluate the old woman's argument against the knight's accusation that she is not a gentlewoman.*   **1**

Vocabulary

arrogance (ar′ ə gəns) n. overbearing pride or self-importance

---

Reading Practice

SPIRAL REVIEW **Summarize** Remind students that a summary is a brief telling of the main idea and supporting details of a selection. Ask students to choose sections of the tale they have already read and write short summaries of them. Provide these tips:

- Identify the main ideas.
- Determine the supporting details.
- Relate the main ideas and the essential details in a logical sequence.
- Use your own words; paraphrase.
- Where possible, answer the five "W questions" in your summary.

Chaucer at the Court of Edward III, 1856–1868.
Ford Madox Brown. Oil on canvas, 123.2 x 99.1
cm. Tate Gallery, London.

View the Art This painting was done more
than four centuries after Chaucer's death by
an artist who hoped to find a new way of
portraying historical and religious subjects.
In what ways does it differ from medieval
illustrations? What qualities does it share
with them? ★

I can assure you, sir, until it dies.
  'But gentleness, as you will recognize,
Is not annexed° in nature to possessions.
Men fail in living up to their professions;
325 But fire never ceases to be fire.
God knows you'll often find, if you enquire,
Some lording full of villainy and shame.
If you would be esteemed for the mere name
Of having been by birth a gentleman
330 And stemming from some virtuous, noble clan,
And do not live yourself by gentle deed
Or take your father's noble code and creed,
You are no gentleman, though duke or earl.
Vice and bad manners are what make a churl.°
335 'Gentility is only the renown
For bounty that your fathers handed down,
Quite foreign to your person, not your own;
Gentility must come from God alone.
That we are gentle comes to us by grace
340 And by no means is it bequeathed with place.
  'Reflect how noble (says Valerius°)

323 **annexed:** attached as a quality
or consequence.

334 **churl:** a discourteous, ill-bred
person.

341 **Valerius:** Valerius Maximus, a
Roman author (c. 20 B.C.–A.D. 50)
whose work was widely popular as a
source for writers.

The Power of Faith How does the old woman use the power of faith
to support her argument?

Teach

Big Idea	**2**

The Power of Faith
Answer: *She contends that
gentility is a gift from God, not a
privilege handed down by one's
ancestors.*

View the Art ★

Possible answer: *Brown's painting is more detailed and realistic
than illustrations in medieval
manuscripts. It also uses perspective differently and focuses on the
author rather than the pilgrims.
Like the manuscript illustrations,
however, Brown's painting makes
use of a few vibrant colors—
especially red.*

Ford Madox Brown (1821–1893)
was an English painter who concentrated on painting moral and
historical subjects. This painting
depicts Chaucer speaking at the
court of one of the most successful kings of medieval times,
Edward III.)

English Learners

DIFFERENTIATED INSTRUCTION

Beginning Read aloud line 315:
"Take fire and carry it to the darkest
house." **Ask:** What is the subject of the
verbs here? *(You is understood as the
subject.)* Explain that this kind of sentence
is called an imperative; it usually gives a
command. Have students identify other
imperative sentences in the tale.

Advanced Learners

DIFFERENTIATED INSTRUCTION

Research Students can use the Internet
to learn more about Seneca and the other
people the wife mentions. Allow time for
students to share their findings. Challenge
students to use the results of their research
to create multimedia presentations.

The Power of Faith

Answer: *Since God himself, in the person of Jesus, chose to live in poverty, it cannot be a shameful condition. On the contrary, virtuous Christians should emulate the example of Jesus (as the Plowman in "The Prologue" does).*

Evaluate Argument

Answer: *Appeal to authority is not sufficient to prove an argument. Strictly speaking, it is a logical fallacy. However, if the authorities cited are eminent experts, their testimonies can enhance an argument that is solidly based on logic, reasons, and evidence.*

(ENGLISH LEARNERS) Remind English Learners that Dante, Valerius, Boethius, Seneca, and Juvenal are very respected by the old woman's audience. **Ask:** How do people feel when famous or respected people support an opinion? *(They may be more likely to agree.)*

Was Tullius surnamed Hostilius,
Who rose from poverty to nobleness.
And read Boethius,° Seneca° no less,
345   Thus they express themselves and are agreed:
"Gentle is he that does a gentle deed."
And therefore, my dear husband, I conclude
That even if my ancestors were rude,
Yet God on high—and so I hope He will—
350   Can grant me grace to live in virtue still,
A gentlewoman only when beginning
To live in virtue and to shrink from sinning.
   'As for my poverty which you reprove,
Almighty God Himself in whom we move,
355   Believe and have our being, chose a life
Of poverty, and every man or wife
Nay, every child can see our Heavenly King
Would never stoop to choose a shameful thing.
No shame in poverty if the heart is gay,
360   As Seneca and all the learned say.
He who accepts his poverty unhurt
I'd say is rich although he lacked a shirt.
But truly poor are they who whine and fret
And covet what they cannot hope to get.
365   And he that, having nothing, covets not,
Is rich, though you may think he is a sot.°
   'True poverty can find a song to sing.
Juvenal° says a pleasant little thing:
"The poor can dance and sing in the relief
370   Of having nothing that will tempt a thief."
Though it be hateful, poverty is good,
A great incentive to a livelihood,
And a great help to our capacity
For wisdom, if accepted patiently.
375   Poverty is, though wanting in estate,
A kind of wealth that none calumniate.°
Poverty often, when the heart is lowly,
Brings one to God and teaches what is holy,
Gives knowledge of oneself and even lends
380   A glass° by which to see one's truest friends.

344 Boethius (bō ē´ thē əs): a Roman philosopher and statesman (c. 480–c. 524) best known for his *Consolation of Philosophy,* written while he was imprisoned for treason. **Seneca:** a Roman playwright and philosopher (4 B.C.?–A.D. 65).

366 sot: habitual drunkard.

368 Juvenal: a Roman poet and satirist (A.D. 60?–127?).

376 calumniate: utter false and vicious statements about.

380 glass: mirror.

The Power of Faith *How does the old woman's first argument against the knight's accusation of poverty illustrate her religious faith?*   **1**

Evaluate Argument *The old woman has cited Dante, Valerius, Boethius, Seneca, and now Juvenal. How well do these citations support her argument?*   **2**

Grammar Practice

(SPIRAL REVIEW) **Simple and Compound Sentences** Review that a simple sentence has only one main clause. Simple sentences can, however, contain compound subjects and compound predicates. A compound sentence has two or more main clauses. The main clauses are usually joined by a comma followed by a coordinating conjunction, such as *and, but, or nor, yet, or for*. Have students write a simple sentence, a simple sentence with a compound subject, a simple sentence with a compound predicate, and three compound sentences with different coordinating conjunctions.

Month of April, Wedding Procession. Grimani Breviary. Biblioteca Marciana, Venice, Italy.

View the Art In Chaucer's day, marriages were often arranged by the couples' families. Grooms tended to be much older than their brides. What do you notice about the wedding procession in this painting? Do you think it matches Chaucer's description of the knight's wedding day? Explain.

And since it's no offence, let me be plain;
Do not rebuke my poverty again.
    'Lastly you taxed me, sir, with being old.
    Yet even if you never had been told
385 By ancient books, you gentlemen engage,
    Yourselves in honour to respect old age.
    To call an old man "father" shows good breeding,
    And this could be supported from my reading.
        'You say I'm old and fouler than a fen.°
390 You need not fear to be a cuckold,° then.
    Filth and old age, I'm sure you will agree,
    Are powerful wardens over chastity.
    Nevertheless, well knowing your delights,
    I shall fulfil your worldly appetites.
395   'You have two choices; which one will you try?
    To have me old and ugly till I die,
    But still a loyal, true, and humble wife
    That never will displease you all her life,
    Or would you rather I were young and pretty
400 And chance your arm what happens in a city
    Where friends will visit you because of me,

389 fen: lowland wholly or partly covered with water.
390 cuckold: a man whose wife is unfaithful to him.

Evaluate Argument *Summarize the six reasons the old woman uses to support her argument that poverty is beneficial.* **3**

Evaluate Argument *Summarize and evaluate the old woman's argument that the knight should not scorn her for being old and ugly.* **4**

GEOFFREY CHAUCER **147**

Teach

Reading Strategy | 3

Evaluate Argument
Answer: *(1) Poverty makes one fearless of thieves. (2) It is an incentive to work. (3) It teaches wisdom. (4) It teaches holiness. (5) It brings self-knowledge. (6) It enables one to identify one's truest friends.*

Reading Strategy | 4

Evaluate Argument
Answer: *The old woman argues that the husband of an old and ugly wife need never fear that his wife will be unfaithful. Most students will deny the validity of this argument, since an old, ugly wife is repellent to her husband as well as to potential rivals.*

View the Art
Answer: *Most students will notice the bride's averted eyes and the difference between modern and medieval wedding clothes. Students may say that the couple's somber expressions reflect Chaucer's description but the youth and beauty of the bride do not.*

During the Middle Ages, a husband was usually much older than his wife, as is the case in this painting.

Approaching Level

DIFFERENTIATED INSTRUCTION

Emerging To help visual learners reflect on what they have read, have them draw sketches of the scene in which the knight capitulates and tells his wife to make the decision. Instruct them to use lines 404– 411 as a guide to their depiction of the knight and lines 412–413 as a guide to their depiction of the wife. Have partners trade sketches and react to each other's interpretations of the scene.

Teach

Literary Element 1

Humor **Answer:** *Most students will find humor in the irony of the knight's response. Forced to choose between two undesirable alternatives and subdued by the old woman's arguments, he sensibly surrenders his powers of choice to his wife, thus giving her the very thing she has said that women desire most—mastery over their husbands and lovers.*

Literary Element 2

Humor **Answer:** *Most students will see her prayer as a humorous parody of a conventional prayer in its worldly lust and plea for revenge.*

Reading Strategy 3

Analyze Tone **Ask:** What is the tone of the Wife of Bath's final words? *(Students may say that it is triumphant or defiant.)*

(APPROACHING) If students have difficulty understanding the wife's tone, have them paraphrase the content of her final words.

To check students' understanding of the selection, see Unit 1 Teaching Resources Book, p. 112

Progress Check

Can students analyze humor?

If No → See Unit 1 Teaching Resources Book, p. 107.

Yes, and in other places too, maybe.
Which would you have? The choice is all your own.'
   The knight thought long, and with a piteous groan
405   At last he said, with all the care in life,
'My lady and my love, my dearest wife,
I leave the matter to your wise decision.
You make the choice yourself, for the provision
Of what may be agreeable and rich
410 In honour to us both, I don't care which;
Whatever pleases you **suffices** me.'
   'And have I won the mastery?' said she,
'Since I'm to choose and rule as I think fit?'
'Certainly, wife,' he answered her, 'that's it.'
415 'Kiss me,' she cried. 'No quarrels! On my oath
And word of honour, you shall find me both,
That is, both fair and faithful as a wife;
May I go howling mad and take my life
Unless I prove to be as good and true
420 As ever wife was since the world was new!
And if to-morrow when the sun's above
I seem less fair than any lady-love,
Than any queen or empress east or west,
Do with my life and death as you think best.
425 Cast up the curtain, husband. Look at me!'
   And when indeed the knight had looked to see,
Lo, she was young and lovely, rich in charms.
In ecstasy he caught her in his arms,
His heart went bathing in a bath of blisses
430 And melted in a hundred thousand kisses,
And she responded in the fullest measure
With all that could delight or give him pleasure.
   So they lived ever after to the end
In perfect bliss; and may Christ Jesus send
435 Us husbands meek and young and fresh in bed,
And grace to overbid them when we wed.
And—Jesu hear my prayer!—cut short the lives
Of those who won't be governed by their wives;
And all old, angry niggards° of their pence,°
440 God send them soon a very pestilence! **3**

439 niggards: misers. pence: pennies.

Humor *Do you find any humor in the knight's response to the choice offered him by the old woman? Explain.* **1**

Humor *Do you find any humor in the Wife's prayer? Explain.* **2**

Vocabulary

suffice (sə fīs´) *v.* to be enough

Reading Practice

SPIRAL REVIEW **Compare and Contrast**
Comparing and contrasting two characters is one way to understand them better. Have students choose two characters from *The Wife of Bath's Tale* (including the wife of Bath herself) and describe the ways they are similar and different. Students may find it helpful to note their observations as well as evidence from the text in a two-column chart.

After You Read

Respond and Think Critically

Respond and Interpret

1. Do you think the knight gets what he deserves? Explain.

2. (a)What question does the knight have to answer in order to save his life? (b)How do you think the knight feels when he provides the queen with the correct answer? Explain.

3. (a)What bargain does the old woman make with the knight? (b)What is the ironic connection between the answer to the queen's question and the requirement that the old woman demands of the knight?

4. (a)Summarize the ending of "The Wife of Bath's Tale." (b)What lesson does the ending teach?

Analyze and Evaluate

5. (a)How does the old woman get the knight to change his attitude toward marrying her? (b)Do you find her method convincing? Explain.

6. (a)Through her arguments, what is the old woman ultimately demanding that the knight acknowledge? (b)How does the knight's acknowledgment transform both the knight and the old woman?

7. Do you think Chaucer's portrayal of the Wife indicates that he was ahead of his time in his view of women? Why or why not?

Connect

8. **Big Idea** The Power of Faith To what extent does "The Wife of Bath's Tale" illustrate the power of Christian faith?

9. **Connect to Today** In your opinion, is the lesson that the Wife teaches relevant to today's world? Explain.

Daily Life & Culture

The Medieval Pilgrimage

A pilgrimage is a journey made to a holy place, or shrine, to venerate it, ask for supernatural aid, or to fulfill a religious obligation. In medieval England the most popular pilgrimage was the one made each year to Canterbury Cathedral. The cathedral achieved renown as the place where Archbishop Thomas à Becket was murdered by agents of King Henry II in 1170 during a struggle for power between church and state.

The journey from London to Canterbury was expensive because the pilgrims had to stay at inns along the way. Also, they had to endure the hardships of life on horseback over unpaved roads for several days on their way to Canterbury and back.

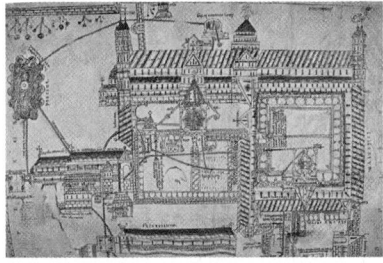

1. Of Chaucer's twenty-nine pilgrims, which ones strike you as making this pilgrimage for spiritual reasons?

2. Do any of the pilgrims seem to be making the journey for other reasons? Explain.

Twelfth-century plan of Canterbury Cathedral

GEOFFREY CHAUCER **149**

Daily Life & Culture

1. Students may say the Knight, Cleric, Parson, and Plowman.

2. The Squire and the Monk are seeking recreation. The Friar and the Pardoner are motivated by the opportunity to make money by hearing confessions or selling pardons and indulgences.

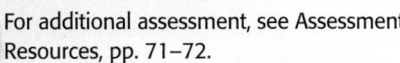

For additional assessment, see Assessment Resources, pp. 71–72.

After You Read

Assess

1. Answers will vary.

2. (a) "What is the thing that women most desire?" (b) Relieved and elated

3. (a) The old woman will tell the knight the answer to the queen's question if the knight promises to do whatever the old woman requires of him. (b) The answer is that women most desire mastery over their husbands, which is what the old woman achieves.

4. (a) The old woman becomes a beautiful woman. (b) Students may respond that the tale teaches the answer to the queen's question.

5. (a) She refutes his objections to her lack of gentility, her poverty, and her age and ugliness, and reminds him that she saved his life. (b) Most students will agree that it is.

6. (a) Her intelligence, humanity, and inner worth (b) He is transformed into a modest gentleman and she is transformed into a beautiful young woman.

7. Answers will vary but should include that his portrayal of the Wife is humorous, not disparaging.

8. Some students may say that the tale has little to do with Christianity because the knight escapes punishment for a grave sin. Others may say that the transformation of the old woman rewards the Christian virtues of trust and fidelity.

9. Students may say that the tale has a strong feminist message that resonates with the modern principle of the intellectual equality between the sexes. In this sense, Chaucer's thinking was ahead of its time.

After You Read

Assess

Literary Element

1. She implies that the Pardoner will not let her get a word in; yet, she talks more than any of the other pilgrims.

2. The Wife makes fun of friars by giving a long list of the places that friars bless.

3. The Wife has spent the previous sixteen lines extolling the holiness and benevolence of friars, only to tell us in the concluding couplet that these holy friars are sexual predators.

Review: Characterization

Possible answer:

On his quest: The knight is diligent. "He knocked at every house, searched every place, . . ."

After he is freed: The knight is desperate. "Think of a new request, Take all my goods, but leave my body free, . . ."

After he is married: The knight is dejected. "Nothing can ever be put right again!"

At the end: The knight is ecstatic. "His heart went bathing in a bath of blisses, . . ."

Reading Strategy

1. Yes. It presents events in chronological order; the elements of the tale support the theme—a woman most desires sovereignty over her husband.

2. Answers will vary.

3. Answers will vary but may include: It is effective in that the knight comes to respect and honor women.

Literary Element Humor

Among the types of humor that Chaucer uses in "The Wife of Bath's Tale" are exaggeration, understatement, and incongruity. Incongruity involves the juxtaposition of two or more jarring or unexpected pieces of information.

1. How is the Wife's reply to the Pardoner in line 26 of "The Wife of Bath's Tale" an example of understatement?

2. How is the Wife's account of the way in which friars have banished fairies (lines 38–46) an example of exaggeration?

3. How is the Wife's comment on friars in lines 55–56 an example of incongruity?

Review: Characterization

As you learned on page 101, **characterization** consists of the various methods a writer uses to develop the personality of a character.

Partner Activity Meet with another classmate to discuss the character of the knight in "The Wife of Bath's Tale." Use a graphic organizer similar to the one below to describe his character at several points during the tale. Write your description under the heading in the first column and cite the knight's words or actions that support your descriptions in the second column. When you finish filling in your chart, summarize how the knight changes throughout the tale.

Character Description	Words or Actions
At the beginning: The knight is immoral and violent.	"By very force he took her maidenhead."
On his quest:	
After he is freed:	
After he is married:	
At the end:	

 Literature Online

Selection Resources For Selection Quizzes, eFlashcards, and Reading-Writing Connection activities, go to glencoe.com and enter QuickPass code GLB9817u1.

Reading Strategy Analyze Form

In "The Wife of Bath's Tale," Chaucer uses poetry as a means to present a narrative.

1. Look back at the timeline you completed. Does this tale seem to follow a traditional narrative structure? Explain how it does or does not.

2. What poetic elements, such as rhythm and sound devices, appear in the tale? In what ways do they help emphasize Chaucer's message?

3. In your opinion, is telling the story of the knight and the old woman an effective way for the Wife to express her attitude about relationships? Why or why not?

Vocabulary Practice

Practice with Analogies Complete each analogy below. Use a dictionary if you need help.

1. reprove : fault :: applaud :
   a. honor   **b.** good deed   **c.** smile

2. concede : deny :: trust :
   a. honor   **b.** payment   **c.** doubt

3. disperse : scatter :: spoil :
   a. ruin   **b.** robbery   **c.** improve

4. arrogance : attitude :: wave :
   a. greet   **b.** enjoyment   **c.** gesture

5. suffice : lack :: raise :
   a. lower   **b.** crops   **c.** bonus

Academic Vocabulary

The knight's deference to his wife's judgment results in his **acquisition** *of a beautiful young bride and a happy marriage.*

Acquisition is an academic word. The word is also used in the art world. For example, a painting newly purchased by a museum might be called a recent **acquisition.**

To further explore this word, complete the following sentence: *In my opinion, successful* **acquisition** *of knowledge requires _____.*

For more on academic vocabulary, see pages 56 and R81.

Vocabulary

1. b 2. c 3. a 4. c 5. a

Academic Vocabulary

Possible answers: *persistence; open-mindedness*

For grammar practice, see Unit 1 Teaching Resources Book, p. 111.

 To create custom assessments using software, use ExamView Assessment Suite.

Progress Check

Can students identify sequence?

If No → See Unit 1 Teaching Resources Book, p. 108.

Respond Through Writing

Expository Essay

Analyze Style In addition to conveying a message about life and relationships, "The Wife of Bath's Tale" is also a humorous and entertaining story. Analyze the way in which Chaucer uses his unique style and humor to bring out the nuances and complexities of the tale's message, or theme. Support your ideas with examples from the text.

Understand the Task Style consists of all of the expressive techniques found in a particular work. Elements of style include word choice, sentence length and structure, figurative language, and imagery.

Prewrite Plan carefully before you begin to write. You may wish to skim through the selection and record instances of humor in a graphic organizer like the one shown below.

Instance of Humor	Effect
"There'll be no marrying for me this year!"	Clarifies the Pardoner's feelings about marriage

Once you have completed your graphic organizer, use the collected information to establish a controlling idea and general structure for your essay. What will your overall point be? How will you organize your information?

Draft Identify the significant ideas in the Wife's tale. Then consider the role humor plays in conveying each idea and in the tale overall. What types of humor does Chaucer rely upon most, and how does his use of language create a humorous tone? Also, consider that "The Wife of Bath's Tale" is an *exemplum*, or a story in which the theme is a sort of moral lesson. What effect does the use of humor have on your understanding of the theme? In what ways does it make the tale more complex?

Revise Exchange essays with a classmate and evaluate your partner's work. Are the claims or viewpoints well supported with logical assertions? Provide comments for your partner, and revise your own paper according to the comments you receive.

Edit and Proofread Proofread your paper, correcting any errors in grammar, spelling, and punctuation. Use the Grammar Tip in the side column to help you with degrees of comparison.

Learning Objectives

In this assignment. you will focus on the following objectives:

Writing: Writing an expository essay.

Literary Study: Analyzing style.

> **Grammar Tip**
>
> **Degrees of Comparison**
>
> The comparative form of an adjective or adverb is used to compare two things. It is often formed by adding the suffix *-er* or the word *more* to the modifier.
>
> *December is a* **stormier** *month than May.*
>
> *He walks* **more quickly** *than she does.*
>
> The superlative form is used to compare more than two things. It is often formed by adding the suffix *-est* or the word *most* to the modifier.
>
> *February can be the* **stormiest** *month of all.*
>
> *Of the three of them, he walks* **most quickly**.

After You Read

Assess

Respond Through Writing

Use these criteria in evaluating student expository essays:

- The essay correctly identifies the theme and analyzes Chaucer's style and use of humor in conveying that theme.
- Statements are supported with quotations from the text.
- The essay includes correct comparative and superlative forms of words that can be used as either adjectives or adverbs.
- A student who meets all of these criteria should receive the equivalent of a 4-point response.
- A student who fully meets two or partially meets three of these criteria should receive the equivalent of a 3-point response.
- A student who fully meets one or partially meets two of these criteria should receive the equivalent of a 2-point response.
- A student who partially meets one of these criteria should receive the equivalent of a 1-point response.

Approaching Level
UNIVERSAL ACCESS

Emerging To help students see the humor in the tale, direct their attention to the closing lines (434–440). **Ask:** What type of husbands does the Wife of Bath ask for in her prayer? (*husbands who young, passionate, and humble*) What type of husbands does The Wife of Bath ask Jesu to punish? (*those who won't obey their wives and those who are stingy with their money*) What type of punishment does she want inflicted upon them? (*a pestilence*)

Advanced Learners
UNIVERSAL ACCESS

Ask: Do you consider the Wife of Bath to be a feminist? Explain. (*Some students may say she doesn't want equality with men, but superiority. Others may feel she needs to carry her struggle to the extreme in a male-dominated society.*)

Focus

Summary

In the past, most pilgrimages were of a religious nature, but today they are just as likely to be secular. Muslim pilgrims continue to make their way to Mecca, but others become "pilgrims" by hiking, cycling, or climbing mountains. They seek to test their physical limits, while also nourishing their spirits.

Teach

Reading Strategy | 1

Connect to Personal Experience There are different ways to connect with a text. The most obvious is to empathize through a similar experience. Sometimes a reader may not connect with any of the specific events or experiences in a text. In these cases it helps to seek out a more general connection. Students should ask themselves, have I ever felt this way? What else have I read that is like this text? Do I know someone like this?

> For an audio recording of this selection, use Listening Library Audio CD-ROM.

> For activities related to this selection, see Unit 1 Teaching Resources Book, pp. 114–122.

Readability Scores

Dale-Chall: 8.8
DRP: 66
Lexile: 1170

Set a Purpose for Reading

As you read, ask yourself, How has the traditional pilgrimage evolved?

Preview the Article

In "The Roads Now Taken," the writer examines the rise of the secular pilgrimage.

Skim the first two paragraphs of the article. What main point do you think the writer might try to prove?

Reading Strategy Connect to Personal Experience

Connecting to personal experience means relating what you read to events in your own life. As you read, ask yourself, What parallels do these events have in my life? Create a chart like the one below.

Event	Every year, thousands of people in Germany go on communal hikes.
My Experience	Every year, my family goes camping in the woods together.
Shared Significance	These events allow participants to explore a common bond.

152 UNIT 1

Vocabulary Practice

SPIRAL REVIEW **Adjectives** Remind students that an adjective is a word that modifies a noun or pronoun by limiting its meaning. **Say:** Reread the first paragraph of the article and find at least five adjective-noun word pairs in it. Have students list the adjective-noun pairs in a graphic organizer like this:

Adjective	Noun
Benedictine	monks
monkish	contemplation
grand	seat
English	Christianity
saintly	intercession

The Roads Now Taken

It's a secular age, but Europeans still go on quests, treks, and pilgrimages to test their limits and nourish their souls.

By JEFF CHU

THE BENEDICTINE MONKS WERE FED UP. BY 1420, TRAFFIC was so bad inside England's Canterbury Cathedral that the Benedictines were constantly being diverted from their duties and contemplations by hordes of pilgrims. Ever since the martyrdom of Archbishop Thomas Becket 250 years earlier, people had been flocking here—to the grand seat of English Christianity and the scene of Becket's murder. They came to ask for Becket's saintly help in personal problems and to plead for healing and good health. This was all good and holy of the pilgrims, but who could hear themselves pray with all these visitors tramping around?

So the monks built a tunnel under the stairs at the center of the church, a sort of express lane to the spot where Becket was killed. Over the years, thousands of faithful shuffled through the cool, stone corridor, but gradually, what with King Henry VIII's break with Roman Catholicism, the Reformation, and later, creeping secularization, the pilgrims' numbers shrank to the point that the passageway became more useful as a broom closet. In 2004, however, officials at Canterbury reopened the tunnel. This time the passageway wasn't for Benedictines and pilgrims. It was for tourists, their digital cameras in hand, visiting one of the most famous cathedrals in England.

Where have all the pilgrims gone? They serve as a barometer for the values of an age. Their habits tell us about the spiritual state of a people. What temples do they worship in? To whom do they pay their tithes and offerings? Where do they seek their soul food? The fashionable answer is to say that faith in Europe is nearly extinct. Some theologians call the

Xurxo Lobato

THE HARD WAY On Spain's Camino de Santiago, pilgrims battle blisters, fatigue, and the elements over hundreds of miles of ancient trail. ★

TIME

Teach

Big Idea   **2**

The Power of Faith Point out that there are many kinds of pilgrimages: a trip to a holy site; a return to one's origins; a test of endurance; a spiritual quest. In some ways, each of us is on a pilgrimage, traveling from one event in life to the next.

View the Art ★

Saint James (Sant' Iago) is the patron saint of Spain. The pilgrims' road to the site of his tomb in Santiago de Compostela is almost 500 miles long, running east to west across northern Spain. The true pilgrim makes the trip on foot, bicycle, or horseback.

Continent "post-Christian." But the truth is that neither faith nor pilgrimage is dead in Europe.

Spiritual Experiences

TIME decided to hitch a ride with modern-day pilgrims to find out what moves people today—how travel helps test physical limits and nourish the spirit. Yes, there are still religious roamers out there: the constantly faithful Muslims, whose visits to Mecca have given us a word for a center of shared interest that draws people from all over; the Christians who walk the great pilgrim's way of El Camino de Santiago in Spain.

But in a secular age, the spiritual impulse is more likely to show itself in a cycling or mountain-climbing adventure, or the quiet contemplation of an English garden. Mass worship may take place in a football stadium. Many of today's most secular pilgrimages have a ritualistic quality that makes them part of the ancient tradition. It is what the Very Rev. Robert Willis, dean of Canterbury, calls the search for "blessing and enrichment. In pilgrimage, body, mind, and spirit come together in an individual quest," he says. "Jesus was always walking, walking, walking—all the way to Calvary."

Our quest need not be so momentous: "Any journey that adds a mini-jigsaw piece to the puzzle of you can be a mini-pilgrimage."

Part of the joy of pilgrimage is a spirit of community that comes from identifying with something bigger than oneself. The pilgrim who sets out solo shares a bond with others who journey on the same path: the aches, the pains, and the triumphs. "The experience is very much about helping other pilgrims," says Abbot Christopher Dillon of Ireland's Glenstal Abbey, who walked the rugged Camino last year and hosts occasional pilgrims at his monastery in County

Approaching Level

DIFFERENTIATED INSTRUCTION

Established Approaching Level students may benefit from focusing on the reasons why the Plymouth Pilgrims came to America. **Ask:** What motivated pilgrims to travel to Plymouth Rock? *(religious and political freedom)*, Why have "pilgrims" from other nations traveled to America in more recent times? *(Political freedom, economic opportunity, escaping from hardships, etc.)*

TIME

Assess

1. Answers will vary.

2. (a) King Henry broke with Catholicism, the Reformation spread, European society has secularized. (b) Religious pilgrimages have dwindled, and more people are taking secular pilgrimages.

3. (a) "Any journey that adds a mini-jigsaw piece to the puzzle of you can be a mini-pilgrimage." (b) Answers will vary.

4. Communal hikes in Germany; trips to European battlefields

5. **Religious pilgrimage:** organized religion; ritual that may be thousands of years old; **Secular pilgrimage:** may have to do with faith or spirituality; way of paying homage to a person one admires. Pilgrimages—either secular or religious—are driven by ritual, love, and a shared sense of purpose.

6. The human need for community, faith, and love is still as powerful today as it was in 1420. Evidence: "Part of the joy of pilgrimage is a spirit of community that comes from identifying with something bigger than oneself."

7. Answers will vary.

8. The pilgrimages in the article are about personal and spiritual fulfillment. The Wife of Bath hoped to change or contemplate something about herself.

For additional assessment, see Assessment Resources, pp. 73–74.

Informational Text

Limerick. "There is great companionship on the road." That's the whole point of the Volksmarches, the communal hikes in Germany that attract thousands every year. The preservation of generational bonds is at the heart of the pilgrimages made to the battlefields of Europe, where families go to honor ancestors they never knew but will never forget.

A Journey into the Soul
And yet each pilgrim is utterly alone, because a pilgrimage is a trip not just to a physical place but also into a person's soul. So one can travel to Stratford-upon-Avon to celebrate Shakespeare's writings, be surrounded by thousands of other Shakespeare lovers, and yet be absolutely alone with one's own epiphanies about the Bard's works.

The traditional may argue that only a religious person is a true pilgrim, but as Phil Cousineau, the author of *The Art of Pilgrimage*, says, "The phenomenon of pilgrimage tends to hold up a mirror to what is sacred for the times." The world has

PILGRIMS' PROGRESS Muslims pray en route to Mecca (top); tourists pose at Canterbury.

changed, and so has pilgrimage. There will also always be those who label it foolishness, whether you embark with a belief in an unseen God's promise of salvation or in the power of a pair of devilish stilettos, as the amazingly committed shoppers at the Prada outlet in Montevarchi, Italy, do. A modern miracle—say, a game-winning goal that curled magnetically into the net at a world championship soccer match—works as much magic for some as the reenactment of medieval ones does for others. Faith is not rational. You can't argue a doubter into belief or force anyone onto the pilgrim's path.

In Chaucer's *Canterbury Tales*, the Prioress wears a brooch inscribed *Amor vincit omnia* (Love conquers all). This is true, not least, of pilgrimage. The love that drives it springs from faith, from mockery-proof loyalty, from unwavering belief in the power of a religion, or a great idea, or even a beautiful game. The pilgrim is no ordinary traveler. His map is in the heart.

Respond and Think Critically

Respond and Interpret

1. How have your ideas about pilgrimages changed after reading the article?

2. (a) Why did the number of Canterbury pilgrims dwindle? (b) Why is this relevant to the article?

3. (a) How does the Very Rev. Robert Willis define a "mini-pilgrimage"? (b) Why do you think people go on these mini-pilgrimages?

4. According to the article, what are some examples of secular pilgrimages that people go on?

Analyze and Evaluate

5. How do religious and secular pilgrimages differ? How are they alike?

6. How do you think the writer feels about the shift from religious to secular pilgrimages? Cite specific examples from the text to support your opinion.

Connect

7. Have you ever been on a religious or secular pilgrimage? If so, how did that experience affect you?

8. Think about the pilgrimage of the Wife of Bath. What does her journey have in common with the pilgrimages discussed in this article?

154 UNIT 1 THE ANGLO-SAXON PERIOD AND THE MIDDLE AGES

Reading Practice

SPIRAL REVIEW Clarify Say: The author uses the terms "spiritual" *(relating to God and religion)* and "secular" *(relating to the world and nature)* to describe different types of pilgrimages and different places for pilgrimages. **Ask:** What is one example given by the author of a spiritual pilgrimage and one of a secular pilgrimage? *(Students may respond: Mecca or El Camino de Santiago for spiritual; cycling or mountain-climbing for secular.)*

Before You Read

from *The Book of Margery Kempe*

Meet **Margery Kempe**
(c. 1373–1440)

The Exorcism of the Demon. Master of Saint Severin. Museo Horne, Florence, Italy.

Daughter of a mayor, wife of a tax collector, and mother of fourteen children, Margery Kempe might seem a conventional woman of the 1400s; however, she was anything but typical. She was a mystic, a pilgrim, and the author of the first English-language autobiography.

Born into a prosperous family in Norfolk, England, Kempe had both money and status. She married John Kempe at twenty and soon after, during a serious illness, had an intense religious experience that, she believed, restored her health.

In the following years, Kempe dedicated her energy to her children and two business ventures—a brewery and a mill. When both businesses failed, she decided to change her life. At the age of forty, Kempe devoted her life entirely to Christ. She took a vow of chastity and received permission from an archbishop to wear white clothes and receive weekly communion.

> *"This is a short account of someone who had high status and worldly reputation but was later drawn to our Lord by severe poverty, sickness, humiliation . . . "*
>
> —Margery Kempe, from *The Book of Margery Kempe*

Spiritual Pilgrim After a visit to Canterbury, Kempe began her life as a pilgrim. She traveled first to Jerusalem and then to Rome. Her spells of excessive sobbing, however, annoyed both priests and fellow travelers. After her return to England, she set out on a pilgrimage to Spain and then journeyed to Germany and Northern Europe. Later, she visited sacred sites in England.

Despite Kempe's devotion and her claims to mysticism, or the direct experience of the reality of God, she made some church officials uneasy. She was arrested and tried for the heresy of Lollardy but was acquitted. The Lollards were supporters of John Wycliffe, a priest and Oxford scholar who was highly critical of the church and some of its practices. The church, in turn, attempted to suppress followers of Wycliffe.

Staunch in Her Faith Given to spells of "boisterous crying," mystical visions, and spontaneous preaching against all "merriment," Kempe had few friends, but her faith in God and in her calling remained unshaken. Nothing is known of the last years of her life. Medical experts have commented on her excessive weeping and shouting. Feminists have pondered her situation as a medieval woman in a male-dominated society. Theologians have studied the descriptions of her visions and marveled at her devotion. Though she related many details about her life in her autobiography, she remains an enigma to the modern world.

LOG ON **Literature** Online

Author Search For more about Margery Kempe, go to glencoe.com and enter QuickPass code GLB9817u1.

Before You Read

Focus

Selection Skills

Literary Elements
- Autobiography (SE p. 156, 160)

from **The Book of Margery Kempe**

Reading Skills
- Analyze Cause-and-Effect Relationships (SE p. 156, 161)

Vocabulary Skills
- Word Origins (TE p. 156)
- Academic Vocabulary (SE p. 161)

Writing Skills/Grammar
- Apply Tone (SE p. 161)

Before You Read

Focus

Summary

Margery Kempe writes about a mental illness she developed after the birth of her first child. It led to a religious experience that she says restored her health and changed her life.

For summaries in languages other than English, see Unit 1 Teaching Resources Book, pp. 123–128.

For summaries in languages other than English, see Unit 1 Teaching Resources Book, pp. 123–128.

Vocabulary   1

Have students use a dictionary to trace the etymology of each vocabulary word. Discuss the meanings of the original Latin terms. **Ask:** Are the Latin words synonyms for the English words? Why or why not? *(Answers will vary; many words will be synonyms.)*

For additional vocabulary practice, see Unit 1 Teaching Resources Book, p. 131.

For additional vocabulary practice, see Unit 1 Teaching Resources Book, p. 131.

For additional context, see Glencoe Interactive Vocabulary CD-ROM.

For additional context, see Glencoe Interactive Vocabulary CD-ROM.

Before You Read

Literature and Reading Preview

Connect to the Autobiography

Why do people write autobiographies? List at least five reasons that seem plausible to you.

Build Background

Although Margery Kempe wanted to record the events of her life so that others might learn from them, she, like most women of her time, was illiterate. Therefore, Kempe dictated her autobiography to a scribe, possibly her eldest son. The autobiography was then revised by a priest. *The Book of Margery Kempe,* lost for centuries, was rediscovered in 1934.

Set Purposes for Reading

Big Idea The Power of Faith

As you read, ask yourself, What does this selection reveal about the importance of the church in medieval life?

Literary Element Autobiography

An **autobiography** is a person's account of his or her own life. Told from the first-person point of view, an autobiography can offer revealing insights into a person's view of herself or himself. As you read, ask yourself, What do the details in this autobiography reveal about Margery Kempe's personality?

Reading Strategy Analyze Cause-and-Effect Relationships

When you **analyze cause-and-effect relationships,** you look for the causes, or reasons, why something happened and relate them to the effects, or results. Writers often signal cause-and-effect relationships with words such as *therefore, because, subsequently,* and *consequently.* Identifying these relationships will help you better understand the connections between events. As you read, ask yourself, How is each event related to preceding and following events?

Tip: Using a Cause-and-Effect Organizer Use a chart to record cause-and-effect relationships.

Cause	Effect

Learning Objectives

For pages 155–161

In studying this text, you will focus on the following objectives:

Literary Study: Analyzing autobiography. Analyzing characterization.

Reading: Analyzing cause-and-effect relationships.

Writing: Applying tone in an autobiographical sketch.

Vocabulary

divulge (di vulj′) *v.* to make known; disclose; p. 158 *Though many people knew the secret, no one divulged it.*

slander (slan′ dər) *v.* to utter false or malicious statements about; p. 158 *By spreading rumors and telling lies, he slandered his former friend.*

instigation (in′stə gā′ shən) *n.* an act of urging on; p. 158 *At the instigation of the leader, the crowd shouted.*

restrain (ri strān′) *v.* to hold back; restrict; p. 159 *The owner used a leash to restrain his dog.*

composure (kəm pō′ zhər) *n.* a calm or tranquil state of mind; p. 159 *After avoiding the collision, we could not regain our composure.*

Reading Practice

Build Background Explain that at the time Margery Kempe lived, people did not understand the scientific causes of disease. Many Christians believed that illness occurred when a demon entered a person's body. Some religious leaders treated the sick by trying to expel the demons. People who had diseases prayed and performed other religious tasks in the hope that they would get well. **Ask:** For diseases that had no medical cure, do you think a religious approach was helpful? Why or why not? *(Some students may say no, because the disease could never be cured. Others may feel religion provided hope for the sick.)*

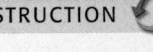 *Saint Bernard exorcising an evil spirit,* panel from the Altar of Saint Bernard, 1500. Jörg Breu the Elder. Tempera on wood.

from The Book of

Margery Kempe

Margery Kempe

MARGERY KEMPE **157**

View the Art ★

In the Roman Catholic tradition, many mental illnesses were attributed to demonic possession. In order to free a person of possession, a priest or religious person performed an exorcism. **Ask:** How does this painting show the possession of the woman? *(Answers may include her crazed eyes, open mouth, unstable figure, and unruly garments.)* What is the relationship between Saint Bernard and the possessed woman? *(Saint Bernard is determined and stable, while he performs an exorcism on a possessed woman who is being restrained and is out of control.)*

 For an audio recording of this selection, use Listening Library Audio CD-ROM.

Readability Scores
Dale-Chall: 8.5
DRP: 60
Lexile: 1200

English Learners

DIFFERENTIATED INSTRUCTION

Beginning/Early Intermediate Ask students to describe the people in the painting. **Ask:** What are the people wearing? What are they doing? Write the words students use on the board. Have them work with a partner to write three sentences that describe one of the figures. Then, explain that the woman in the painting may have an illness similar to Margery Kempe's. Kempe had difficulty controlling her words and actions. In the painting, a religious leader is trying to cure the woman. Kempe also relies on her faith for help.

Teach

Literary Element | 1

Autobiography Ask: From what point of view is the story told? *(first person)* How does the point of view help to identify the kind of literature you are reading? *(Autobiographies are told from a first-person point of view.)*

APPROACHING For approaching level students, ask which pronoun or group of pronouns the author uses most: *I, you,* or *he/she/they.* *(I)* Explain that authors of auto-biographies tend to use "I" most often because they are writing about themselves.

Reading Strategy | 2

Analyze Cause-and Effect Relationships Answer: *According to her, the Devil has kept telling her that as long as she is in good health, there is no need for her to confess.*

Literary Element | 3

Autobiography Answer: *She wants to explain the causes of her subsequent behavior.*

When I was twenty, or a little older, I was married to a well-respected burgess,[1] and, things being what they are, I quickly found myself pregnant. During the pregnancy and up to the time the child was born I suffered from severe attacks of illness; and then, what with the labor of giving birth on top of my previous illness, I despaired of my life and thought that I would not survive.

At that point I sent for my priest, because I had something on my conscience which I had never before **divulged** in my life. For I was con-stantly hindered by my enemy, the devil, who was always telling me that so long as I was in good health I had no need to make confession; I should just do penance[2] by myself, in private, and God, in his all-sufficient mercy, would for-give me for everything.

And therefore I often did harsh penances, restricting myself to bread and water; I also did other godly deeds, praying devoutly but never revealing my guilty secret in the course of confession.

But when I was ever sick or out of spirits, the devil whispered to me that I would be damned because I had not been absolved of[3] that special sin. Therefore, not expecting to survive the birth of my child, I sent for my priest, as I've already told you, fully intending to be absolved for everything I had done in my life.

But when I was on the point of revealing my long-concealed secret, my confessor[4] was a lit-tle too hasty with me; he began to tell me off in no uncertain terms, before I had even cov-ered all I meant to say; and after that, try as he might, he couldn't get me to say a word.

Eventually, what with my fear of damnation on one hand and the priest's sharp tongue on the other, I became insane, and for half a year, eight weeks and a few days I was prodigiously[5] plagued and tormented by spirits.

During that time I saw (or I believed I saw) devils opening their mouths as if to swallow me, and revealing waves of fire that were burn-ing inside their bodies. Sometimes they grabbed at me, sometimes they threatened me; they tugged and pulled me, night and day for a whole eight months. They also bayed[6] at me fearsomely, and told me to forsake the church and its faith and deny my God, his mother, and all the saints in heaven.

They told me to deny my good works and all my good qualities, and turn my back on my father, my mother, and all my friends. And that's what I did: I **slandered** my husband, my friends, and my own self. I said many wicked and cruel things; I was empty of any virtue or goodness; I was bent on every wickedness; I said and did whatever the spirits tempted me to say and do. At their **instigation** I would have

---

1. A *burgess* is a citizen of an English borough, or town.
2. *Penance* is a religious act, such as praying, done to show sorrow or repentance for sin.
3. *Absolved of* means "pardoned for."

4. The *confessor* was the priest to whom Kempe confessed.
5. *Prodigiously* means "exceedingly."
6. *Bayed* means "shouted" or "roared."

2 Analyze Cause-and-Effect Relationships *Why does Kempe put off confessing her sin?*

Vocabulary

divulge (di vulj´) *v.* to make known; disclose

Autobiography *Read ahead to the end of the next paragraph. Why does Kempe include this detail about the devils here?* **3**

Vocabulary

slander (slan´ dər) *v.* to utter false or malicious statements about

instigation (in´ stə ga´ shən) *n.* an act of urging on

Reading Practice

 SMALL GROUP

Evaluate Information Remind students that autobiographies tell stories about the authors' lives. Sometimes an autobiography contains the whole truth, sometimes the truth is embellished, and sometimes the truth is incomplete or biased. Students must use their own background knowledge to evaluate the information in autobiogra-phies. Have students work in small groups to discuss whether this excerpt from *The Book of Margery Kempe* gives an accurate account of Kempe's experiences.

The birth of Louis, son of Isabella, future Louis VIII the Good, in 1187. From "Histoire des nobles princes de Hainaut", late 15th century. Jacques de Guise. Bibliothèque Municipale, Boulogne-sur-Mer, France.

destroyed myself many times over and been damned to hell; and as if to show determination I bit my own hand so savagely that the mark has been visible ever since.

What's more, I used my nails (for I had no other instrument) to scratch myself viciously, ripping the skin on my chest near my heart. And if I'd had my own way I would have done even more to myself, but I was bound and **restrained** by force day and night. I suffered from these and other temptations for such a long while that people thought I'd never recover or even survive, but then something happened: as I lay by myself, without my attendants, our merciful Lord Jesus Christ—ever to be trusted! his name be praised!—never forsaking his servant in a time of need, appeared to me—his creature who had forsaken him—in human

form, the most pleasing, most beautiful, loveliest sight that human eyes could ever behold. Dressed in a mantle[7] of purple silk, he sat by the bed, looking at me with so much holiness in his face that I felt myself inwardly fortified. And he spoke to me in the following way:

"Daughter, why have you abandoned me, when I never thought to abandon you?"

And instantly, as he spoke these words, I swear that I saw the air open up as brightly as any shaft of lightning. And he rose up into the air, not very fast or quickly but with grace and ease, so that I could clearly see him in the air until it closed again.

And at once my **composure** and mental faculties came back to me, just as they had been before, and I begged my husband, as soon as he came, for the keys of the cellar so that I could get myself food and drink as I had done in the past. My maids and attendants advised him not to hand over any keys; they said I would only give away any such stores[8] as we had, for they thought that I was beside myself.

Nevertheless, my husband, who was always kind and sympathetic to me, ordered them to give me the keys; and I got myself food and drink, insofar as my physical health would allow me to do so. And I recognized my friends, the members of my household, and all the others who came to see the act of mercy which our Lord Jesus Christ had performed on me. Blessed may he be, who is always close to us in our troubles. When people think he is far away, he is right beside them, full of grace.

Afterwards, I returned to all my other household duties, doing everything in a quite level-headed and sober way but not really knowing the call of our Lord.

5

---

7. A *mantle* is a long sleeveless garment worn over other clothes.

8. Here, *stores* refers to food stored for future use.

The Power of Faith *To what does Kempe credit the restoration of her mental faculties?*

4

Vocabulary

restrain (ri strān´) v. to hold back; restrict

Vocabulary

composure (kəm pō´ zhər) n. a calm or tranquil state of mind

MARGERY KEMPE **159**

Teach

Big Idea   4

The Power of Faith
Answer: *She thinks that seeing a vision of Jesus Christ and hearing his words cured her.*

Reading Strategy   5

Respond **Ask:** How do you feel about Margery Kempe after reading this excerpt from her autobiography? *(Students may express both positive and negative reactions toward Kempe.)* Encourage students to give reasons for their reactions.

ENGLISH LEARNERS Ask English learners to describe an action Margery Kempe takes and their response to it. Have them explain why they feel the way they do.

View the Art ★

Explain that medieval childbirth was both a joyous and risky event. Have students examine this painting and note the differences between modern and medieval childbirth. *(Possible answers: There are only women in the room; the father is not present; a nurse holds the baby.)* Also, note that the baby is wrapped in linen because it was believed that this would make his or her limbs grow straight.

 To check students' understanding of the selection, see Unit 1 Teaching Resources Book, p. 134.

Approaching Level

DIFFERENTIATED INSTRUCTION

Emerging Students may have difficulty understanding the connections Margery Kempe makes between her religious beliefs and her illness. Tell students to create a two-column, two-row chart with the column headings "Cause" and "Effect." Under "Effect," have students write the phrase "becoming sick" in the top row and "getting well" in the bottom row. As they read, students should list the events Kempe believes cause and cure her illness in the correct rows.

After You Read

Assess

1. Encourage questions showing sympathy for her, such as "What could others do to help you?"

2. The priest reacted harshly to her less serious sins.

3. (a) It makes her frightened, tormented, and self-destructive. (b) She becomes violent.

4. (a) Christ appears at her bedside and assures her that he will never abandon her. (b) She regains her sanity, an apparent miracle.

5. Students might mention the description of Kempe using her nails to rip the skin on her chest or imagining devils with waves of fire burning inside their bodies.

6. Answers will vary.

7. Agree, because Kempe did something so wrong that she became insane.

8. She survives a moral crisis by acknowledging her sins and trusting in Jesus.

9. Answers will vary.

Literary Element

1. Possible responses: Priests, the church, and confession played important roles in the lives of ordinary people. People with mental illness were cared for at home.

2. Religion, honesty, and kindness

Progress Check

Can students identify autobiography?

If No → See Unit 1 Teaching Resources Book, p. 129.

After You Read

Respond and Think Critically

Respond and Interpret

1. What questions would you like to ask Margery Kempe?

2. Why does Kempe refuse to tell her secret to the priest?

3. (a)How does Kempe's illness affect her personality? (b)Why is she "restrained by force"?

4. (a)Describe the vision that changes the course of Kempe's illness. (b)Why is that vision a turning point in her life? Explain.

Analyze and Evaluate

5. Which **images** in the selection did you find the most powerful? Why?

6. In your opinion, would the selection be more interesting if Kempe had revealed her secret to readers? Explain why or why not.

7. The poet William Wordsworth once wrote, "From the body of one guilty deed, / A thousand ghostly fears, and haunting thoughts, proceed!" Would Kempe agree with this statement? Support your answer with evidence from the selection.

Connect

8. **Big Idea** The Power of Faith Which of the church's teachings about confession and Jesus profoundly affect Kempe's life? Explain.

9. **Connect to the Author** From what you learned about Kempe's life on page 155, how do you think her later experiences might have influenced her perspective on the events she describes in this excerpt?

Literary Element Autobiography

Autobiographies not only provide details about the author's personality but usually impart information about the society in which the author lived.

1. What did you learn about medieval life in an English town from reading this selection?

2. From the details Kempe chose to include in this excerpt, what values do you think were most important to her?

Review: Characterization

As you learned on page 101, **characterization** comprises all the techniques that writers use to reveal the personalities of characters. The writer of an autobiography uses the same techniques to convey his or her own personality traits.

Partner Activity Discuss Margery Kempe's personality with a classmate, citing details from this excerpt to support your inferences about her. Then make a chart like the one below. For each characteristic you identify, list a passage in which Kempe reveals that trait.

Characteristic	Evidence

LOG ON ▶ **Literature** Online

Selection Resources For Selection Quizzes, eFlashcards, and Reading-Writing Connection activities, go to glencoe.com and enter QuickPass code GLB9817u1.

Review: Characterization

Possible answers:

Characteristic	Evidence
Religious	"I also did other godly deeds, praying devoutly," "Blessed may he be, who is always close to us in our troubles"
Feels guilty/sinful	"I had something on my conscience," "I often did harsh penances," "my fear of damnation"
Prone to exaggeration	"I became insane," "I was bent on every wickedness"
Extreme in her actions	"I used my nails to scratch myself viciously"

Reading Strategy | Analyze Cause-and-Effect Relationships

To understand this selection, you must consider the reasons why Margery Kempe and the people in her life act as they do. Review the cause-and-effect chart you filled in as you read the selection.

1. What causes Kempe to inflict pain on herself?

2. After her recovery, why do her attendants advise her husband not to give her the keys to the cellar?

3. Why does her husband disregard this advice?

Vocabulary Practice

Practice with Antonyms An antonym is a word that has a meaning opposite to that of another word. With a partner, brainstorm three antonyms for each boldfaced vocabulary word below. Then discuss your choices with your classmates. Be prepared to explain why you chose your words.

> divulge   slander   instigation
> restrain   composure

EXAMPLE:
loyal

<u>Antonyms:</u> unreliable, disloyal, treacherous

<u>Explanation:</u> Someone who is treacherous would betray you, but someone who is <u>loyal</u> would not.

Academic Vocabulary

*In her autobiography, Kempe describes how she was tormented by religious guilt and **eventually** went mad.*

Eventually is an academic word. Other words that are similar in meaning are *finally, ultimately,* and *later.*

To further explore the meaning of this word, use *eventually* in a sentence of your own, in which you describe a time you came to an important realization.

For more on academic vocabulary, see pages 56 and R81.

Write with Style

 Apply Tone

Assignment Margery Kempe describes her spiritual suffering in a serious, self-critical tone. Write a brief autobiographical sketch about one of your experiences with illness, using either a tone similar to Kempe's or one that expresses another attitude, such as sarcasm, humor, disdain, or indifference.

Get Ideas What attitude will you take toward your illness? Once you have settled on an attitude, or tone, begin thinking about specific details that will help you convey that tone. Make notes or an informal outline to help guide your writing.

EXAMPLE:
My bout of mumps: a mouth of bumps

A. Humorous tone—humiliating, looking way worse than I felt
B. Swelling up like a chipmunk in math class
C. Getting it on the other side the next day
D. Not well enough to go out, but not sick enough to avoid doing schoolwork

Give It Structure Using the outline or notes you developed, fill in the details of your experience. Decide whether you will organize your details chronologically or in some other way, such as order of importance. Use concrete sensory details and precise word choice to show, rather than tell, the reader what you experienced. As you write, be sure your work maintains a consistent tone.

Look at Language Read your sketch aloud—it should sound like your own voice. Then reread it as if someone else had written it, to make sure it holds your interest. Use the active rather than the passive voice, and select strong, precise verbs.

MARGERY KEMPE **161**

After You Read

Reading Strategy

1. She felt controlled by demons and tried to get rid of them through self-inflicted punishments.

2. They think that in her deranged state, she will simply give away the food stored there.

3. Her husband is sympathetic and demonstrates it by giving her the keys.

Vocabulary

Answers will vary.

 Write with Style

Use these criteria in evaluating student writing:

- It identifies and describes a personal experience with illness.
- The details are specific, organized logically, and contribute to a consistent tone.
- A consistent personal voice comes through.

> For additional assessment, see Assessment Resources, pp. 75–76.

 To create custom assessments using software, use Exam View Assessment Suite.

Focus

Ask: Are there volunteers who will read the problem samples aloud?

Point out that reading a text aloud often makes correct and incorrect verb tenses more obvious.

Teach

Future Tense Tell students that the future tense of a verb is usually formed by combining *will* or *going to* with the verb. Have students use the future tense in a sentence.

Assess

Possible rewrites:

1. Margery Kempe traveled on several religious pilgrimages.
2. Like Kempe, the Venerable Bede recorded English history.
3. Chaucer, Kempe, and Bede influenced society.
4. Kempe stayed in bed most of the time when she was ill.

For additional grammar practice, see Unit 1 Teaching Resources Book, p. 136.

Verb Tenses

Verb tenses are the different forms verbs take to indicate when actions occur.

Tip

To identify the correct verb tense in a test-taking situation, think about how different verb forms would sound in the sentence. Often, an irregular verb will sound incorrect if you form the past tense by adding *-ed.*

Language Handbook

For more about verb tenses, see Language Handbook, p. R46.

 Literature Online

Grammar For more grammar practice, go to glencoe.com and enter QuickPass code GLB9817u1.

Grammar Workshop

Verb Tense

Literature Connection The **tenses** of a verb are different forms that help show time.

> *"And at once my composure and mental faculties came back to me, just as they had been before . . . "*
>
> —Margery Kempe, from *The Book of Margery Kempe*

Margery Kempe uses the past-tense form *came* to describe events at a particular past time. Then she uses the past-perfect form *had been* to describe an earlier situation. In your writing and speaking, using the correct verb tenses informs your audience of when specific events occurred and helps the audience keep track of a sequence of events.

Here are some ways to recognize and solve problems with verb tense.

Problem 1 A verb ending is incorrect or missing.

Margery Kempe confess to her priest before giving birth.
Mental illness tormenting Kempe for more than eight months.

Solution Add *-ed* to a regular verb to form its past tense or past participle.

Margery Kempe confessed to her priest before giving birth.
Mental illness tormented Kempe for more than eight months.

Problem 2 The past tense and the past participle forms are confused.

She had wrote her autobiography in order to describe her faith.

Solution Irregular verbs may have different past-tense and past-participle forms. For example, the past tense of *write* is *wrote*; the past participle of *write* is *written.*

She had written her autobiography in order to describe her faith.

Revise Rewrite the following sentences, correcting any errors in verb form.

1. Margery Kempe travel on several religious pilgrimages.
2. Like Kempe, the Venerable Bede recording English history.
3. Chaucer, Kempe, and Bede had influence society.
4. Kempe stay in bed most of the time when she was ill.

Approaching Level

DIFFERENTIATED INSTRUCTION

Emerging Regular verbs can be changed from present to past tense by adding *-ed.* The past tenses of irregular verbs are formed in other ways. Ask students to supply the past tense of each of the following words. Allow them to use a dictionary if necessary.

Present	Past
think	*(thought)*
buy	*(bought)*
seek	*(sought)*
swim	*(swam)*
run	*(ran)*
write	*(wrote)*

Part 3

The World of Romance

Roman de Tristan: Tournament, c. 15th century.

 This painting shows a *mêlée*—a mock battle in which teams of mounted knights demonstrated their skill and strength. What details indicate that the painting does not depict actual warfare? Explain.

"On a great festival such as this [King Arthur] would eat no meat till he had heard some strange tale of adventure, of the deeds of princes, or feats of arms, some great wonder which he might listen to and believe."

—*Sir Gawain and the Green Knight*

163

UNIT ONE
PART 3

Analyze and Extend

Reading Strategy | 1

Evaluate Text Invite a student to read the quotation aloud. **Ask:** Why does "King Arthur" appear in brackets? *(It is not part of the original text but was inserted to clarify the text for the purposes of the excerpt. [The original text has the word he.])*

View the Art ★

Possible answer: *The women calmly watching the combat from a viewing stand suggests that this is a sport rather than an actual battle.*

For additional support for English Learners, see Unit 1 Teaching Resources Book, p. 138.

English Learners
UNIVERSAL ACCESS

Advanced Ask: Which words in this quotation are prepositions? *(on; of; to)* What synonym can you find for the idiom "such as"? *(for example)*

Intermediate Read the quotation aloud to students. **Ask:** When looking at the art, what do you imagine is meant by "great festival"? *(competitions for knights)* Have students rewrite the quotation in their own words.

Focus

Bellringer Options

Selection Focus Transparency 8

Daily Language Practice Transparency 12

Or write on the board: honor, good name, reputation. Display an image of a hero facing a challenger, such as a knight facing a dragon. **Ask:** How do you define personal honor? What qualities and actions make a person honorable? Have students discuss characters from their favorite films who have undergone tests of honor.

from *Sir Gawain and the Green Knight*

Connect to the Story

How do you define *honor*? Freewrite for a few minutes about actions that you think show a person to be honorable.

Build Background

The author of *Sir Gawain and the Green Knight* is unknown to us; but because of the dialect in which the poem is written, scholars have concluded that it was composed in northwest England about 1370. The poet's sophisticated technique and his knowledge of French and Latin point to an educated man who was familiar with the ways of the aristocracy.

Set Purposes for Reading

Big Idea The World of Romance

Sir Gawain and the Green Knight is set in an imaginary medieval world of mysterious castles and perilous quests. As you read, ask yourself, What challenges does Sir Gawain face in his test of honor?

Literary Element Archetype

An **archetype** is a character type, a setting, an image, or a story pattern that appears in the literature of many cultures. As you read, ask yourself, What features of this poem are archetypes?

Reading Strategy Monitor Comprehension

When you read, stop periodically to check your **comprehension**, or understanding, of the story. Ask yourself, How might I summarize key ideas, characters, and events?

Tip: Taking Notes As you read, jot down notes on important characters and events. Use a chart similar to the one below.

Character or Event	Significance
Sir Gawain accepts a challenge from the Green Knight.	Gawain is risking his life and his honor for the king.

Learning Objectives

For pages 164–184

In studying this text, you will focus on the following objectives:

Literary Study: Analyzing archetypes. Analyzing conflict.

Reading: Monitoring comprehension by reviewing and summarizing.

Vocabulary Preview

copiously (kō′ pē əs le) *adv.* plentifully; p. 167 *The seashells were scattered copiously around the beach after they had been washed in at high tide.*

intrepid (in trep′ id) *adj.* fearless; courageous; p. 169 *The intrepid woman dashed back into the burning house to save the family dog.*

dauntless (dônt′ lis) *adj.* daring; not easily discouraged; p. 178 *Dauntless despite the loss of his supplies, the explorer pressed forward.*

blithe (blīth) *adj.* carefree; light-hearted; p. 179 *I wish we could be children again, when we were naively blithe.*

Selection Skills

Literary Elements
- Archetype (SE pp. 164, 168–180, 183)
- Conflict (SE p. 183)

Sir Gawain and the Green Knight

Listening/Speaking/ Viewing Skills
- Analyze Art (SE pp. 172, 174, 176)

Reading Skills
- Monitor Comprehension (SE pp. 164, 169–179, 183)

Vocabulary Skills
- Synonyms (SE p. 183)
- Academic Vocabulary (SE p. 183)

Writing Skills/Grammar
- Short Story (SE p. 184)
- Action Verbs (SE p. 184)

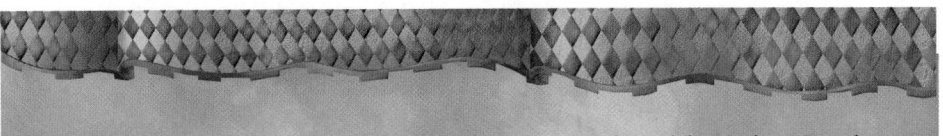

Translated by John Gardner

Splendid that knight errant° stood in a splay of green, **1**
And green, too, was the mane of his mighty destrier;°
Fair fanning tresses enveloped the fighting man's shoulders,
And over his breast hung a beard as big as a bush;
5 The beard and the huge mane burgeoning° forth from his head
Were clipped off clean in a straight line over his elbows,
And the upper half of each arm was hidden underneath
As if covered by a king's chaperon,° closed round the neck.
The mane of the marvelous horse was much the same,
10 Well crisped° and combed and carefully pranked with knots,°
Threads of gold interwoven with the glorious green,
Now a thread of hair, now another thread of gold;
The tail of the horse and the forelock were tricked the
    same way,
And both were bound up with a band of brilliant green
15 Adorned with glittering jewels the length of the dock,°
Then caught up tight with a thong° in a criss-cross knot
Where many a bell tinkled brightly, all burnished° gold.
So monstrous a mount, so mighty a man in the saddle
Was never once encountered on all this earth
20   till then;
        His eyes, like lightning, flashed,
        And it seemed to many a man,
        That any man who clashed
        With him would not long stand.

1 **knight errant:** a knight who wanders the land, searching for adventure.
2 **destrier** (des´ trē ər): war horse.
5 **burgeoning** (bər´ jə ning): sprouting; growing.

8 **chaperon** (sha´ pə rōn): hood.

10 **crisped:** curled. **pranked with knots:** decorated with bows.

15 **dock:** the fleshy part of a horse's tail.
16 **thong:** a narrow strip of leather used for binding.
17 **burnished:** polished or rubbed smooth.

English Learners

DIFFERENTIATED INSTRUCTION

Intermediate Tell English Learners that much of the conflict in Gawain surrounds the idea of chivalry. Ask students to use a dictionary to look up the meaning of *chivalry*. Then discuss how chivalry will be explored as Sir Gawain is tested by the Green Knight and a beautiful queen.

Before You Read

Focus

Summary

Sir Gawain, a knight in King Arthur's court, accepts a challenge from the terrifying Green Knight, who possesses supernatural powers. Gawain passes a test of honor by risking his life to meet the challenge and resisting the temptations of a beautiful lady.

For summaries in languages other than English, see Unit 1 Teaching Resources Book, pp. 139–144.

Interactive Read and Write
Other options for teaching this selection can be found at:
- Interactive Read and Write for EL Students, pp. 39–76
- Interactive Read and Write for Approaching-Level Learners, pp. 39–76
- Interactive Read and Write for On-Level Learners, pp. 39–76

Vocabulary **1**

Have students identify one difference in word choice between the translations by John Gardner and by Brian Stone. They should choose words that are almost synonyms, but have slightly different meanings. **Ask:** How are the words you chose similar? How are they different?

For additional vocabulary practice, see Unit 1 Teaching Resources Book, p. 147.

For additional context, see Glencoe Visual Vocabulary CD-ROM.

Teach

Monitor Comprehension
Make sure students understand the importance of the color green throughout the description of the rider (The Green Knight). **Ask:** How is the rider described? *(The rider is green, with long hair and a substantial beard.)* **Ask:** What might the color green predict about the rider's future behavior? *(The rider's behavior may be unusual just as his color is.)*

View the Art ★

Though the legend of King Arthur originated in medieval Britain, stories involving Arthur and his knights inspired stories and artwork—like this Italian fresco—throughout Europe. Observe the dress and behavior of Arthur and his court: do they fit the general image you have of knights? If not, what might be the reason for the difference? *(Most students will say that the knights do not fit their usual ideas of knights; most of them are unarmed, and they do not wear armor of any kind. Reasons for the difference might include the setting, which is in peacetime, or the culture; Italian knights at the time may have dressed differently from British knights.)*

 For an audio recording of this selection, use Listening Library Audio CD-ROM.

from
Sir Gawain and the Green Knight

Translated by Brian Stone

King Arthur and his knights sit at the Round Table, 14th century fresco. Runkelstein Castle, South Tyrol, Italy. ★

> Yes, garbed all in green was the gallant rider,
>   And the hair of his head was the same hue as his horse,   **1**
> And floated finely like a fan round his shoulders;
> And a great bushy beard on his breast flowing down,
> 5 With the heavy hair hanging from his head,
> Was shorn below the shoulder, sheared right round,
> So that half his arms were under the encircling hair,

Reading Practice

SPIRAL REVIEW **Make Inferences** Have students reread the description of the Green Knight on page 167. **Ask:** Are the knight's intentions peaceful, or is he looking for combat? Which details give clues that he is or is not looking for a fight? *(It would appear that he is looking for a fight: He carried a huge and monstrous axe, he was "dreading no danger," and he was grim.)*

Covered as by a king's cape, that closes at the neck.
The mane of that mighty horse, much like the beard,
10 Well crisped and combed, was **copiously** plaited
With twists of twining gold, twinkling in the green,
First a green gossamer, a golden one next.
His flowing tail and forelock followed suit,
And both were bound with bands of bright green,
15 Ornamented to the end with exquisite stones,
While a thong running through them threaded on high
Many bright golden bells, burnished and ringing.
Such a horse, such a horseman, in the whole wide world
Was never seen or observed by those assembled before,
20   Not one. ☆
                 Lightning like he seemed
                 And swift to strike and stun.
                 His dreadful blows, men deemed,
                 Once dealt, meant death was done.

25 Yet hauberk° and helmet had he none,
Nor plastron° nor plate-armor proper to combat,
Nor shield for shoving, nor sharp spear for lunging;
But he held a holly cluster° in one hand, holly
That is greenest when groves are gaunt and bare,
30 And an axe in his other hand, huge and monstrous,
A hideous helmet-smasher for anyone to tell of;
The head of that axe was an ell-rod° long.
Of green hammered gold and steel was the socket,
And the blade was burnished bright, with a broad edge,
35 Acutely honed° for cutting, as keenest razors are.
The grim man gripped it by its great strong handle,
Which was wound with iron all the way to the end,
And graven° in green with graceful designs.
A cord curved round it, was caught at the head,
40 Then hitched to the haft° at intervals in loops,
With costly tassels attached thereto in plenty
On bosses° of bright green embroidered richly.
In he rode, and up the hall, this man,
Driving towards the high dais,° dreading no danger. **3**
45 He gave no one a greeting, but glared over all.
His opening utterance was, "Who and where
Is the governor of this gathering? Gladly would I

25 **hauberk** (hô′bərk′): a long shirt of chain mail worn as armor.
26 **plastron:** a metal breastplate worn under a hauberk.
28 **holly cluster:** Holly represents good luck and shows that the knight comes in peace.

32 **ell-rod:** almost four feet.

35 **honed:** sharpened.

38 **graven:** carved.

40 **haft:** handle.

42 **bosses:** raised decorations.

44 **dais** (dā′ əs): a raised platform.

The World of Romance *How can you tell from the description in lines 1–20 that the "gallant rider" is a knight?* **2**

Vocabulary

copiously (kō′ pē əs lē) *adv.* plentifully

Teach

Big Idea | 2

The World of Romance
Answer: *Although the rider wears green, he nonetheless has long hair, wears a cape and armor, and rides a horse, as any other knight would.*

Reading Strategy | 3

Monitor Comprehension
Ask: What emotions would the appearance of the Green Knight and his horse be likely to inspire in the knights of King Arthur's court? *(Their appearance would inspire both fear and wonder.)*

Writer's Technique ☆
Poetry In each stanza of this poem, the poet follows a series of long lines with five short lines. Tell students to think about what kind of information is presented in the short lines. Ask them why the poet presents that information in short lines rather than the long ones.

Teach

Literary Element | 1

Rhyme Ask: What is the rhyme scheme found in the groups of short lines on this page? *(Words at the end of the first, third, and fifth lines rhyme, and words at the end of the second and fourth lines rhyme. The rhyme scheme is* ababa.*)*

Literary Element | 2

Archetype Answer: *Green in this selection represents spring and renewal of life.*

ENGLISH LEARNERS **Ask:** What qualities do you associate with the color green? *(life, nature, envy, mold)* Tell English Learners that the color green can symbolize many things. The meaning of the color of the Green Knight has been discussed for centuries, but scholars do not necessarily agree on what the green color means.

Literary Element | 3

Alliteration Explain that alliteration is a literary device in which a writer repeats an initial consonant sound to emphasize certain words or to create a musical effect. Help students locate the repetition of the *g* sound in line 71 (*Greet, gruesome, guest*).

Behold him with my eyes and have speech with him."

He frowned;
50   Took note of every knight
As he ramped and rode around;
Then stopped to study who might
Be the noble most renowned.

The assembled folk stared, long scanning the fellow,
55   For all men marveled what it might mean
That a horseman and his horse should have such a color
As to grow green as grass, and greener yet, it seemed,
More gaudily glowing than green enamel on gold.
Those standing studied him and sidled towards him
60   With all the world's wonder as to what he would do.
For astonishing sights they had seen, but such a one never;
Therefore a phantom from Fairyland the folk there deemed him.
So even the doughty° were daunted° and dared not reply,
All sitting stock-still, astounded by his voice.
65   Throughout the high hall was a hush like death;
Suddenly as if all had slipped into sleep, their voices were
At rest;
Hushed not wholly for fear,
But some at honor's behest;°
70   But let him whom all revere
Greet that gruesome guest. **3**

For Arthur sensed an exploit before the high dais,
And accorded him courteous greeting, no craven° he,
Saying to him, "Sir knight, you are certainly welcome.
75   I am head of this house:° Arthur is my name.
Please deign to dismount and dwell with us
Till you impart your purpose, at a proper time."
"May he that sits in heaven help me," said the knight,
"But my intention was not to tarry in this turreted hall.
80   But as your reputation, royal sir, is raised up so high,
And your castle and cavaliers° are accounted the best,
The mightiest of mail-clad men in mounted fighting,
The most warlike, the worthiest the world has bred,
Most valiant to vie with in virile contests,
85   And as chivalry is shown here, so I am assured,
At this time, I tell you, that has attracted me here.
By this branch that I bear, you may be certain
That I proceed in peace, no peril seeking;
For had I fared forth in fighting gear,

King Arthur and the knights of the Round Table.

---

63 doughty (dou′ tē): courageous, valiant. **daunted:** fearful.

69 behest: command.

73 craven: coward.

75 this house: Arthur's court at Camelot.

81 cavaliers: knights.

---

2 Archetype *What might the Green Knight's color represent?*

Writing Practice

📝 **Use Alliteration and Figurative Language** Review alliteration by having students read various examples in this poem. Alliteration may also be combined with figurative language (as in "As to grow green as grass,") to create vivid images that have a musical quality when read aloud. Have students write descriptive sentences containing figurative language and alliteration. Then have them read their sentences aloud in small groups.

90 My hauberk and helmet, both at home now,
My shield and sharp spear, all shining bright,
And other weapons to wield, I would have brought;
However, as I wish for no war here, I wear soft clothes.
But if you are as bold as brave men affirm,
95 You will gladly grant me the good sport I demand
        By right."
        Then Arthur answer gave:
        "If you, most noble knight,
        Unarmored combat crave,
100   We'll fail you not in fight."

"No, it is not combat I crave, for come to that,
On this bench only beardless boys are sitting.
If I were hasped° in armor on a high steed,
No man among you could match me, your might being meagre.
105 So I crave in this court a Christmas game,
For it is Yuletide and New Year, and young men abound here.
If any in this household is so hardy in spirit,
Of such mettlesome° mind and so madly rash
As to strike a strong blow in return for another,
110 I shall offer to him this fine axe freely;
This axe, which is heavy enough, to handle as he please.
And I shall bide the first blow, as bare as I sit here.
If some **intrepid** man is tempted to try what I suggest,
Let him leap towards me and lay hold of this weapon,
115 Acquiring clear possession of it, no claim from me ensuing.
Then shall I stand up to his stroke, quite still on this floor—
So long as I shall have leave to launch a return blow
        Unchecked.
        Yet he shall have a year
120   And a day's reprieve,° I direct.
        Now hasten and let me hear
        Who answers, to what effect."

"By heaven," then said Arthur, "what you ask is foolish,
But as you firmly seek folly, find it you shall.

Gawain. From *Le Roman de Lancelot du Lac,* 14th century. The Pierpont Morgan Library, New York. ★

---

103 **hasped:** fastened.

108 **mettlesome:** spirited; plucky.

120 **reprieve:** a postponement or temporary relief from danger.

Monitor Comprehension *What impression do you have of the Green Knight so far?* [4]

Monitor Comprehension *What "game" is the Green Knight proposing?* [6]

Vocabulary

intrepid (in trep′ id) *adj.* fearless; courageous

SIR GAWAIN AND THE GREEN KNIGHT **169**

Teach

Literary Element   1

Archetype Answer: *Sir Gawain's apparent humility, bravery, and heroism suggest that he represents good. The Green Knight's arrogance suggests that he represents evil.*

Literary History ☆

The Alliterative Revival *Sir Gawain and the Green Knight* is a classic work of the "alliterative revival" in England during the latter portion of the fourteenth century. The poets of this movement preserved some features of Old English meter, especially the use of alliteration to link words within lines.

---

125 No good man here is aghast at your great words.
     Hand me your axe now, for heaven's sake,
     And I shall bestow the boon° you bid us give."
     He sprang towards him swiftly, seized it from his hand,
     And fiercely the other fellow footed the floor.
130 Now Arthur had his axe, and holding it by the haft
     Swung it about sternly, as if to strike with it.
     The strong man stood before him, stretched to his full height,
     Higher than any in the hall by a head and more.
     Stern of face he stood there, stroking his beard,
135 Turning down his tunic in a tranquil manner,
     Less unmanned° and dismayed by the mighty strokes
     Than if a banqueter at the bench had brought him a drink
             Of wine.
             Then Gawain at Guinevere's side
140   Bowed and spoke his design:
             "Before all, King, confide
             This fight to me. May it be mine."

     "If you would, worthy lord," said Gawain to the King,
     "Bid me stir from this seat and stand beside you,
145 Allowing me without lese-majesty° to leave the table,
     And if my liege lady° were not displeased thereby,
     I should come there to counsel you before this court of nobles.
     For it appears unmeet° to me, as manners go, ☆
     When your hall hears uttered such a haughty request,
150 Though you gladly agree, for you to grant it yourself,
     When on the benches about you many such bold men sit,
     Under heaven, I hold, the highest-mettled,
     There being no braver knights when battle is joined.
     I am the weakest, the most wanting in wisdom, I know,
155 And my life, if lost, would be least missed, truly.
     Only through your being my uncle, am I to be valued;
     No bounty but your blood in my body do I know.
     And since this affair is too foolish to fall to you,
     And I first asked it of you, make it over to me;
160 And if I fail to speak fittingly, let this full court judge
             Without blame."
             Then wisely they whispered of it,
             And after, all said the same:
             That the crowned King should be quit,
165   And Gawain given the game.

127 boon: favor.

136 unmanned: deprived of courage, strength, or vigor.

Sir Gawain presents himself to Arthur and Guinevere, from Cotton Nero A.x., 1410. Artist unknown. British Library, London.

145 lese-majesty (lēz´ ma´ jə stē): offense; literally, injured majesty.
146 liege lady: Guinevere, Arthur's queen.
148 unmeet: improper.

 **Archetype** *What archetypal characteristics do you see in Gawain and in the Green Knight?*

Reading Practice

SPIRAL REVIEW **Compare and Contrast** Have students reread lines 154–165. **Ask:** How realistic is Sir Gawain's description of himself? *(Sir Gawain is the opposite of his description of himself. He is simply showing humility by describing himself as weak and least likely to be missed.)* Explain that humility was a valued trait for a knight of King Arthur's court. Have students contrast Gawain's humility with the arrogance of the Green Knight.

"By God," said the Green Knight, "Sir Gawain, I rejoice
That I shall have from your hand what I have asked for here.
And you have gladly gone over, in good discourse,°
The covenant° I requested of the King in full,

170 Except that you shall assent, swearing in truth,
To seek me yourself, in such place as you think
To find me under the firmament, and fetch your payment
For what you deal me today before this dignified gathering."
"How shall I hunt for you? How find your home?"

175 Said Gawain, "By God that made me, I go in ignorance;
Nor, knight, do I know your name or your court.
But instruct me truly thereof, and tell me your name,
And I shall wear out my wits to find my way there;
Here is my oath on it, in absolute honor!"

180 "That is enough this New Year, no more is needed,"
Said the gallant in green to Gawain the courteous,
"To tell you the truth, when I have taken the blow
After you have duly dealt it, I shall directly inform you
About my house and my home and my own name.

185 Then you may keep your covenant, and call on me,
And if I waft you no words, then well may you prosper,
Stay long in your own land and look for no further
          Trial.
          Now grip your weapon grim;

190   Let us see your fighting style."
          "Gladly," said Gawain to him,
          Stroking the steel the while.

On the ground the Green Knight graciously stood,
With head slightly slanting to expose the flesh.

195 His long and lovely locks he laid over his crown,
Baring the naked neck for the business now due.
Gawain gripped his axe and gathered it on high,
Advanced the left foot before him on the ground,
And slashed swiftly down on the exposed part,

200 So that the sharp blade sheared through, shattering the bones,
Sank deep in the sleek flesh, split it in two,
And the scintillating° steel struck the ground.
The fair head fell from the neck, struck the floor,
And people spurned it° as it rolled around.

205 Blood spurted from the body, bright against the green.

168 **discourse:** speech.
169 **covenant:** binding agreement.

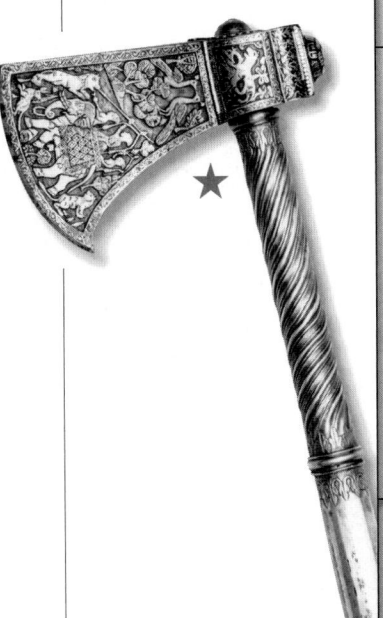

202 **scintillating:** sparkling; brilliant.

204 **spurned it:** fended it off with their feet.

The World of Romance *What does this oath reveal about the values of this time?* **2**

View the Art ★

Tell students that axes were common weapons in medieval battle. Point out the decorations on the head of this axe and note that axes were much longer than what is shown here. Discuss with students characteristics of this axe and the violent description of Gawain slashing the Green Knight.

Advanced Learners

DIFFERENTIATED INSTRUCTION

Career Like King Arthur, leaders in today's world are protected by those who serve them. The president of the United States, for example, is protected by Secret Service agents who vow to risk their own lives to protect that of the president. By providing this invaluable and dangerous service, Secret Service agents exhibit a sense of loyalty to the president and a sense of duty to their country. Have students research the 1981 assassination attempt on President Reagan to discover more about the role of a Secret Service agent.

Teach

The World of Romance

Answer: *Medieval romance contains elements of magic and fantasy.*

(APPROACHING) A supernatural act is one in which the laws of science are broken. **Ask:** What might you have expected to happen to the Green Knight when he was beheaded? *(He might have fallen to the floor and died.)*

View the Art ★

Only one manuscript of *Sir Gawain and the Green Knight* has survived from medieval times. This illustration is from the banquet scene in that manuscript.

Answer: *Answers will vary, but most students will say that the illustration accurately depicts the details given in lines 212–222.*

The Headless Green Knight in Arthur's Hall, from Cotton Nero A.x., 1410. Artist unknown. British Library, London.

View the Art This illustration is from the only surviving medieval manuscript of *Sir Gawain and the Green Knight*. How does the artist's depiction of the Green Knight compare with your impressions of him? ★

Yet the fellow did not fall, nor falter one whit,
But stoutly sprang forward on legs still sturdy,
Roughly reached out among the ranks of nobles,
Seized his splendid head and straightway lifted it.
210   Then he strode to his steed, snatched the bridle,
Stepped into the stirrup and swung aloft,
Holding his head in his hand by the hair.
He settled himself in the saddle as steadily
As if nothing had happened to him, though he had
215   No head.
       He twisted his trunk about,
       That gruesome body that bled;
       He caused much dread and doubt
       By the time his say was said.

220   For he held the head in his hand upright,

---

1   **The World of Romance** *What does this supernatural event suggest about the elements of medieval romance?*

Reading Practice

SPIRAL REVIEW   **SMALL GROUP**   **Summarize** Have small groups pause at the end of line 242 to summarize what has occurred so far in the story. Tell students to break the poem into chunks in which they can find main ideas and details to support them. Ask students in each group to prepare one overall summary of the text so far. Encourage them to take notes as they discover more main ideas and details. They can then incorporate their notes in their overall summaries. Have volunteers present their groups' summaries.

Pointed the face at the fairest in fame° on the dais;
And it lifted its eyelids and looked glaringly,
And menacingly said with its mouth as you may now hear:
"Be prepared to perform what you promised, Gawain;
225   Seek faithfully till you find me, my fine fellow,
According to your oath in this hall in these knights' hearing.
Go to the Green Chapel without gainsaying° to get
Such a stroke as you have struck. Strictly you deserve
That due redemption on the day of New Year.
230   As the Knight of the Green Chapel I am known to many; **2**
Therefore if you ask for me, I shall be found.
So come, or else be called coward accordingly!"
Then he savagely swerved, sawing at the reins,
Rushed out at the hall door, his head in his hand,
235   And the flint-struck fire flew up from the hooves.
What place he departed to no person there knew,
Nor could any account be given of the country he had come
    from.
              What then?
         At the Green Knight Gawain and King
240   Grinned and laughed again;
         But plainly approved the thing
         As a marvel in the world of men.

As the end of the next year approaches, Sir Gawain sets out on his horse Gringolet to seek the Green Knight. After fruitless searching and many adventures, he arrives at a castle whose lord, Bercilak, can direct him to the Green Chapel nearby. Gawain is invited to stay until his appointment. The lord proposes a game: he will give Gawain the winnings of his hunt each day in return for whatever Gawain has won while staying in his castle. For two days, while the lord is hunting, the lady of the castle attempts to seduce Gawain, but Gawain nobly rejects her advances. He accepts only a kiss each day which he exchanges with the lord in return for his hunting spoils. On the third day, Gawain continues to resist the lady, but she presses him to accept one small gift by which to remember her.

    She proffered him a rich ring wrought in red gold,
    With a sparkling stone set conspicuously in it,
245   Which beamed as brilliantly as the bright sun;
    You may well believe its worth was wonderfully great.
    But the courteous man declined it and quickly said,
    "Before God, gracious lady, no giving just now!
    Not having anything to offer, I shall accept nothing."
250   She offered it him urgently and he refused again,

221 **fairest in fame:** Guinevere.

227 **gainsaying:** contradicting; opposing.

Monitor Comprehension *How do you think Sir Gawain feels now about his oath to the Green Knight?* **3**

SIR GAWAIN AND THE GREEN KNIGHT **173**

Teach

Reading Strategy	2

Monitor Comprehension
Ask: What will happen to Sir Gawain if he does not find the Green Knight in a year? (*Gawain will be considered a coward.*)

Reading Strategy	3

Monitor Comprehension
Answer: *Students will most likely say that Sir Gawain feels some apprehension about the promise.*

Approaching Level
DIFFERENTIATED INSTRUCTION

Emerging The many unfamiliar words in this selection may be overwhelming for some students. Suggest that they read the definitions on each page before reading the text. Then encourage them to read at a pace that keeps them from stopping at every unknown word. In that way they can concentrate on following the plot and getting a general sense of the text. Have students work in pairs to read a part of the selection and then recount it in their own words to a partner.

173

Teach

Monitor Comprehension
Have students summarize the scene between Sir Gawain and the lady of the castle. **Ask:** Why won't Gawain accept the lady's gifts? *(She is a married woman, and he is resisting her advances.)*

Predict **Ask:** Will Gawain accept the green sash from the lady? *Why or why not? How might his actions affect the outcome of the story? Tell students to jot down their answers and review their prediction as they read.*

View the Art ★

This illustration comes from a collection of love songs. **Ask:** What about the image strikes you as romantic or suggestive of courtly love? Explain. *(Possible answers: the knight's bowed head, the idea of giving a token before a dangerous tournament, the body positions and eye contact of the two lovers.)*

Knight receiving tokens from his lady love whilst preparing for tournament, from facsimile of the Manesse Codex, 1305–40. German manuscript. University Library, Heidelberg, Germany.

View the Art This illustration comes from a collection of love songs. What about the image strikes you as romantic or suggestive of courtly love?

Fast affirming his refusal on his faith as a knight.
Put out by this repulse, she presently said,
"If you reject my ring as too rich in value,
Doubtless you would be less deeply indebted to me
255 If I gave you my girdle,° a less gainful gift."
She swiftly slipped off the cincture° of her gown
Which went round her waist under the wonderful mantle,
A girdle of green silk with a golden hem,
Embroidered only at the edges, with hand-stitched ornament.
260 And she pleaded with the prince in a pleasant manner
To take it notwithstanding° its trifling worth;
But he told her that he could touch no treasure at all, **1**
Not gold nor any gift, till God gave him grace
To pursue to success the search he was bound on. **2**
265 "And therefore I beg you not to be displeased:
Press no more your purpose, for I promise it never
      Can be.
      I owe you a hundredfold
      For grace you have granted me;
270   And ever through hot and cold
      I shall stay your devotee."

"Do you say 'no' to this silk?" then said the beauty,
"Because it is simple in itself? And so it seems.
Lo! It is little indeed, and so less worth your esteem.
275 But one who was aware of the worth twined in it
Would appraise its properties as more precious perhaps,
For the man that binds his body with this belt of green,
As long as he laps it closely about him,

255 girdle: a belt or sash.
256 cincture: belt; sash.

261 notwithstanding: in spite of.

174 UNIT 1 THE ANGLO-SAXON PERIOD AND THE MIDDLE AGES

Reading Practice

SPIRAL REVIEW **Summary Charts** Ask students to write a three-sentence summary of the content on p. 174. Summaries should include who the characters are, what they did, and why they did it. Have students make a chart like the one below in order to organize their thoughts.

Who	What	Why

No hero under heaven can hack him to pieces,
280 For he cannot be killed by any cunning on earth."
Then the prince pondered, and it appeared to him
A precious gem to protect him in the peril appointed him
When he gained the Green Chapel to be given checkmate:° **3**
It would be a splendid stratagem° to escape being slain.
285 Then he allowed her to solicit° him and let her speak.
She pressed the belt upon him with potent words
And having got his agreement, she gave it him gladly,
Beseeching him for her sake to conceal it always,
And hide it from her husband with all diligence.
290 That never should another know of it, the noble swore
              Outright.
          Then often his thanks gave he
          With all his heart and might,
          And thrice by then had she
295   Kissed the constant knight.

**The time comes for Gawain to keep his appointment with the Green
Knight. He dresses carefully, wrapping the green sash around his waist,
and sets off with a guide, who leaves him as they near the Green Chapel.**

      Then he gave the spur to Gringolet and galloped down the path,
      Thrust through a thicket there by a bank,
      And rode down the rough slope right into the ravine.
      Then he searched about, but it seemed savage and wild,
300   And no sign did he see of any sort of building;
      But on both sides banks, beetling° and steep,
      And great crooked crags, cruelly jagged;
      The bristling barbs of rock seemed to brush the sky.
      Then he held in his horse, halted there,
305   Scanned on every side in search of the chapel.
      He saw no such thing anywhere, which seemed remarkable,
      Save, hard by in the open, a hillock of sorts,
      A smooth-surfaced barrow° on a slope beside a stream
      Which flowed forth fast there in its course,
310   Foaming and frothing as if feverishly boiling.
      The knight, urging his horse, pressed onwards to the mound,
      Dismounted manfully and made fast to a lime-tree
      The reins, hooking them round a rough branch;
      Then he went to the barrow, which he walked round, inspecting,
315   Wondering what in the world it might be.
      It had a hole in each end and on either side,
      And was overgrown with grass in great patches.
      All hollow it was within, only an old cavern

283 checkmate: inescapable
defeat.
284 stratagem: a clever, often
underhanded scheme.
285 solicit: persuade.

301 beetling: overhanging.

308 barrow: a mound of earth,
often over a grave.

Archetype *Why might the lady be considered a literary archetype?* **4**

Teach

Reading Strategy 3

Monitor Comprehension
Ask: Why does Sir Gawain
finally decide to accept the sash?
*(He decides it might protect him
when he encounters the Green
Knight.)*

Literary Element 4

Archetype **Answer:** *The
woman as a forbidden love interest and one for whom the hero
fights to win love or appreciation
is a recurring theme throughout
literature.*

Cultural History

The word *chivalry* comes from the
French word for a knight. At first,
chivalry referred to the training of
knights for battle, but eventually
came to mean the courtly behavior of a knight off the battlefield.
Knights were expected to champion the weak, to act devoutly and
piously, and to uphold the truth.
Chivalry also became associated
with courtly love, in which a knight
showed skill in poetry and music
and pledged to defend and protect
a noblewoman.

Approaching Level
DIFFERENTIATED INSTRUCTION

AAVE While engrossed in the poem,
approaching-level students who are users
of African-American Vernacular English may
not be paying attention to verb tense. Have
them make a list of verbs on p. 175 and
indicate the tense of each verb. Point out
that the text in the narration is in the past
tense while the dialogue is in the present
tense.

Teach

Archetype **Answer:** *This comparison represents the archetype of good versus evil; Sir Gawain feels that he is the hero fighting the evil Green Knight.*

View the Art ★

Fresco painting involves the application of paint to a still-wet plaster surface.

Answer: *Students may note that the fresco consists of softer lines and colors, more realistic detail, and more movement than the illustration. Some students may point out that the illustration tells a story, while the fresco does not.*

Knight on horseback, from series of frescoes of tournaments, 14th century. Museo Civico, San Gimignano, Italy.

<u>View the Art</u> Fresco painting, which involves the application of paint to a still-wet plaster surface, was very popular in Italy during the fourteenth and fifteenth centuries. How is this fresco different in appearance and style from the illustration on page 172?

> Or the crevice of an ancient crag: he could not explain it
> 320   Aright.
>   "O God, is the Chapel Green
>   This mound?" said the noble knight.
>   "At such might Satan be seen
>   Saying matins° at midnight."
>
> 325   "Now certainly the place is deserted," said Gawain,
>   "It is a hideous oratory,° all overgrown,
>   And well graced for the gallant garbed in green
>   To deal out his devotions in the Devil's fashion.
>   Now I feel in my five wits, it is the Fiend himself
> 330   That has tricked me into this tryst, to destroy me here.
>   This is a chapel of mischance—checkmate to it!
>   It is the most evil holy place I ever entered."
>   With his high helmet on his head, and holding his lance,
>   He roamed up to the roof of that rough dwelling.
> 335   Then from that height he heard, from a hard rock

324 matins (mat´ inz): a liturgical prayer traditionally beginning at midnight.

326 oratory: a place of prayer.

---

1 Archetype *Why do you think the poet has Sir Gawain compare the Green Knight to the devil?*

Reading Practice

SPIRAL REVIEW 🌀 **Clarify** Students may be confused when the same character is referred to with different names. In line 323, Gawain mentions that *Satan* might be in the Green Chapel. Then he later refers to "the Fiend." These are both references to the same character. **Ask:** *Who is the Fiend?* (Satan, but also the Green Knight)

On the bank beyond the brook, a barbarous noise.
What! It clattered amid the cliffs fit to cleave° them apart,
As if a great scythe° were being ground on a grindstone there.
What! It whirred and it whetted like water in a mill.
340   What! It made a rushing, ringing din, rueful° to hear.
"By God!" then said Gawain, "that is going on,
I suppose, as a salute to myself, to greet me
                    Hard by.
              God's will be warranted:
345   'Alas!' is a craven cry.
              No din shall make me dread
              Although today I die."

Then the courteous knight called out clamorously,
"Who holds sway here and has an assignation° with me?
350   For the good knight Gawain is on the ground here.
If anyone there wants anything, wend your way hither fast,
And further your needs either now, or not at all."
"Bide there!" said one on the bank above his head,
"And you shall swiftly receive what I once swore to give you."
355   Yet for a time he continued his tumult° of scraping,
Turning away as he whetted,° before he would descend.
Then he thrust himself round a thick crag through a hole,
Whirling round a wedge of rock with a frightful weapon,
A Danish axe duly honed for dealing the blow,
360   With a broad biting edge, bow-bent along the handle,
Ground on a grindstone, a great four-foot blade—
No less, by that love-lace gleaming so brightly!
And the gallant in green was garbed as at first,
His looks and limbs the same, his locks and beard;
365   Save that steadily on his feet he strode on the ground,
Setting the handle to the stony earth and stalking beside it.
He would not wade through the water when he came to it,
But vaulted over on his axe, then with huge strides
Advanced violently and fiercely along the field's width
370   On the snow.
              Sir Gawain went to greet
              The knight, not bowing low.
              The man said, "Sir so sweet,
              You honor the trysts you owe."

375   "Gawain," said the green knight, "may God guard you!
You are welcome to my dwelling, I warrant you,
And you have timed your travel here as a true man ought.
You know plainly the pact we pledged between us:

Monitor Comprehension *What is happening here, and what is its effect on
the story?*

SIR GAWAIN AND THE GREEN KNIGHT   **177**

---

337 cleave: split.
338 scythe (sīth): a tool used for
mowing or reaping, consisting of a
long curved blade and a long bent
handle.
340 rueful: mournful.

349 assignation: an appointment
for a meeting.

355 tumult (tōo′ məlt): a noisy
commotion; disturbance.
356 whetted: sharpened.

Teach

Reading Strategy   2

Monitor Comprehension
Answer: *The noise is the sharp-
ening of the axe that the Green
Knight will use to cut off Sir
Gawain's head. Students should
recognize that this element builds
suspense in the story.*

Literary Element   3

Onomatopoeia A word that
imitates or suggests the sound it
describes is called *onomatopoeia*.
For example, the word *buzz* is an
onomatopoeic word. **Ask:** What
other onomatopoeic words can
you think of? (*moo, oink, crack,
hiss*)

[ENGLISH LEARNERS] **Ask:** What
functions do these words serve in
the story? (*They build tension.*)

Teach

Vocabulary | 1

Tools for Word Meaning

In line 400, Gawain is described as "the daring dauntless man." Have students use context clues to ascertain the meaning of *dauntless*. Write the word on the board and divide it into the base word *daunt* and the suffix *-less*, meaning "without." Have students check the meaning of *dauntless* and *daunt* in a dictionary. Ask them to suggest synonyms for *dauntless*. *(fearless, courageous)*

Reading Strategy | 2

Monitor Comprehension
Ask: How does Sir Gawain behave differently than the Green Knight did when accepting the blow? *(Sir Gawain flinches.)* Why does the Green Knight refuse to complete the strike? *(He does not strike the blow because Gawain flinched. The Green Knight considers Gawain a coward.)*

Big Idea | 3

The World of Romance
Answer: *Cowardice is the opposite of the ideal qualities of a knight: nobility and bravery. If Sir Gawain were a coward, he would be undeserving of knighthood.*

This time a twelvemonth ago you took your portion,
380 And now at this New Year I should nimbly requite° you.
And we are on our own here in this valley
With no seconds° to sunder° us, spar° as we will.
Take your helmet off your head, and have your payment here.
And offer no more argument or action than I did
385 When you whipped off my head with one stroke."
"No," said Gawain, "by God who gave me a soul,
The grievous gash to come I grudge you not at all;
Strike but the one stroke and I shall stand still
And offer you no hindrance; you may act freely,
390   I swear."
     Head bent, Sir Gawain bowed,
     And showed the bright flesh bare.
     He behaved as if uncowed,°
     Being loth° to display his care.

395 Then the gallant in green quickly got ready,
Heaved his horrid weapon on high to hit Gawain,
With all the brute force in his body bearing it aloft,
Swinging savagely enough to strike him dead.
Had it driven down as direly as he aimed,
400 The daring **dauntless** man would have died from the blow. [1]
But Gawain glanced up at the grim axe beside him
As it came shooting through the shivering air to shatter him, [2]
And his shoulders shrank slightly from the sharp edge.
The other suddenly stayed the descending axe,
405 And then reproved the prince with many proud words:
"You are not Gawain," said the gallant, "whose greatness is such
That by hill or hollow no army ever frightened him;
For now you flinch for fear before you feel harm.
I never did know that knight to be a coward.
410 I neither flinched nor fled when you let fly your blow,
Nor offered any quibble in the house of King Arthur.
My head flew to my feet, but flee I did not.
Yet you quail° cravenly though unscathed so far.
So I am bound to be called the better man
415   Therefore."
     Said Gawain, "Not again
     Shall I flinch as I did before;
     But if my head pitch to the plain,
     It's off for evermore.

380 requite: repay.

382 second: an official attendant of a contestant in a duel. **sunder:** separate. **spar:** fight.

393 uncowed: not frightened by threats.
394 loth: reluctant.

413 quail: flinch.

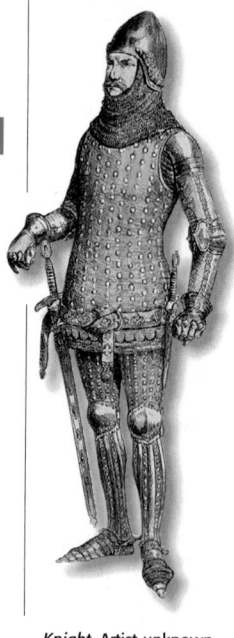

Knight. Artist unknown. Antique hand-colored print.

---

3   **The World of Romance** *Why does the Green Knight call Sir Gawain a coward?*

Vocabulary

dauntless (dônt′ lis) *adj.* daring; not easily discouraged

178   UNIT 1   THE ANGLO-SAXON PERIOD AND THE MIDDLE AGES

Speaking and Listening Practice

SMALL GROUP

Oral Reading Have groups of three students present oral readings of the conversation between Gawain and the Green Knight. Two students should read the parts of the characters, and the third should act as the narrator. Ask students to evaluate how the experience increased their understanding of the story.

420   "But be brisk, man, by your faith, and bring me to the point;
     Deal me my destiny and do it out of hand,
     For I shall stand your stroke, not starting at all
     Till your axe has hit me. Here is my oath on it."
     "Have at you then!" said the other, heaving up his axe,

425   Behaving as angrily as if he were mad.
     He menaced him mightily, but made no contact,
     Smartly withholding his hand without hurting him.
     Gawain waited unswerving, with not a wavering limb,
     But stood still as a stone or the stump of a tree

430   Gripping the rocky ground with a hundred grappling roots.
     Then again the green knight began to gird:°
     "So now you have a whole heart I must hit you.
     May the high knighthood which Arthur conferred
     Preserve you and save your neck, if so it avail you!"

435   Then said Gawain, storming with sudden rage,
     "Thrash on, you thrustful fellow, you threaten too much.
     It seems your spirit is struck with self-dread."
     "Forsooth,"° the other said, "You speak so fiercely
     I will no longer lengthen matters by delaying your business,

440   I vow."
         He stood astride to smite,°
         Lips pouting, puckered brow.
         No wonder he lacked delight
         Who expected no help now.

445   Up went the axe at once and hurtled down straight
     At the naked neck with its knife-like edge.
     Though it swung down savagely, slight was the wound,
     A mere snick on the side, so that the skin was broken.
     Through the fair fat to the flesh fell the blade,

450   And over his shoulders the shimmering blood shot to the ground.
     When Sir Gawain saw his gore glinting on the snow,
     He leapt feet close together a spear's length away,
     Hurriedly heaved his helmet on to his head,
     And shrugging his shoulders, shot his shield to the front,

455   Swung out his bright sword and said fiercely,
     (For never had the knight since being nursed by his mother
     Been so buoyantly happy, so **blithe** in this world)
     "Cease your blows, sir, strike me no more.
     I have sustained a stroke here unresistingly,

431 gird: get ready.

438 Forsooth: in truth.

441 smite: strike.

Monitor Comprehension   *What has happened on the Green Knight's third strike?*   **4**

Vocabulary

blithe (blīth) *adj.* carefree; lighthearted

SIR GAWAIN AND THE GREEN KNIGHT   **179**

 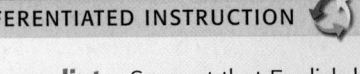
Teach

Reading Strategy   4

Monitor Comprehension
Answer: *He has nicked Sir Gawain's neck, causing a slight wound but no serious injury.*

(APPROACHING) **Ask:** In which line do you find out that Sir Gawain isn't seriously injured? Which words describe Sir Gawain's wound? *(Line 447, "slight was the wound")*

Writer's Technique ☆
Repetition The writer shows the Green Knight attempting to behead Gawain three times. Not only does the repetition of the beheading attempts add to the tension in the scene, but it also introduces the number three. In literature, three often refers to the Christian trinity. The wound that Sir Gawain acquires is thought to be a comparison to the wounds of Christ on the cross. Sir Gawain is wounded to illustrate that he broke his promise under duress; however, Christ was loyal.

Teach

Archetype Answer: *She serves as the test that challenges a knight's character.*

View the Art ★

The Imperial crown of the Holy Roman Empire is thought to be created between 955 and 962 for Emperor Otto I. **Ask:** How would you describe the imperial crown of the Holy Roman Empire? *(It is covered in gold and jewels.)*

Ask: Why do you think the crown was decorated in this fashion? *(to convey that its wearer had wealth and power)*

---

460 And if you offer any more I shall earnestly reply.
    Resisting, rest assured, with the most rancorous
               Despite.°
           The single stroke is wrought
           To which we pledged our plight°
465   In high King Arthur's court:
           Enough now, therefore, knight!"

    The bold man stood back and bent over his axe,
    Putting the haft to earth, and leaning on the head.
    He gazed at Sir Gawain on the ground before him,
470 Considering the spirited and stout way he stood,
    Audacious° in arms; his heart warmed to him.
    Then he gave utterance gladly in his great voice,
    With resounding speech saying to the knight,
    "Bold man, do not be so bloodily resolute.°
475 No one here has offered you evil discourteously,
    Contrary to the covenant made at the King's court.
    I promised a stroke, which you received: consider yourself paid.
    I cancel all other obligations of whatever kind.
    If I had been more active, perhaps I could
480 Have made you suffer by striking a savager stroke.
    First in foolery I made a feint° at striking,
    Not rending° you with a riving cut—and right I was,
    On account of the first night's covenant we accorded;
    For you truthfully kept your trust in troth with me,
485 Giving me your gains, as a good man should.
    The further feinted blow was for the following day,
    When you kissed my comely wife, and the kisses came to me:
    For those two things, harmlessly I thrust twice at you
               Feinted blows.
490   Truth for truth's the word;
         No need for dread, God knows.
         From your failure at the third
         The tap you took arose.

    "For that braided belt you wear belongs to me.
495 I am well aware that my own wife gave it you.
    Your conduct and your kissings are completely known to me,
    And the wooing by my wife—my work set it on.
    I instructed her to try you, and you truly seem
    To be the most perfect paladin° ever to pace the earth.
500 As the pearl to the white pea in precious worth,

Imperial crown of the Holy Roman Empire. ★

461–462 **rancorous Despite:** bitter ill will or malice.
464 **plight:** promise.
471 **Audacious:** daring; bold.
474 **resolute:** determined.

481 **feint** (fānt): here, a deceptive action designed to draw attention away from one's real purpose.
482 **rending:** tearing apart.

499 **paladin:** a model of chivalry.

---

1   **Archetype** *At this point in the story, how has the lady developed into an archetype?*

180   UNIT 1   THE ANGLO-SAXON PERIOD AND THE MIDDLE AGES

Assessment Practice

Short Responses Explain that a short-response question may not have just one correct answer. Instead, an answer is generally judged by its insightfulness and the quality of textual evidence included.

Ask: How was the lady of the castle Gawain's fierce foe? Have students write their answers, using words from the text as evidence to support their ideas. Pair students as needed to write their responses.

So in good faith is Gawain to other gay knights.
But here your faith failed you, you flagged° somewhat, sir,
Yet it was not for a well-wrought thing, nor for wooing either,
But for love of your life, which is less blameworthy."

502 **flagged:** grew weak.

2

505 The other strong man stood considering this a while,
So filled with fury that his flesh trembled,
And the blood from his breast burst forth in his face
As he shrank for shame at what the chevalier° spoke of.
The first words the fair knight could frame were:

508 **chevalier:** knight.

510 "Curses on both cowardice and covetousness!
Their vice and villainy are virtue's undoing."
Then he took the knot, with a twist twitched it loose,
And fiercely flung the fair girdle to the knight.
"Lo! There is the false thing, foul fortune befall it!

515 I was craven about our encounter, and cowardice taught me
To accord with covetousness and corrupt my nature
And the liberality and loyalty belonging to chivalry.
Now I am faulty and false and found fearful always.
In the train of treachery and untruth go woe

520   And shame.
        I acknowledge, knight, how ill
        I behaved, and take the blame.
        Award what penance you will:
        Henceforth I'll shun ill-fame."

525 Then the other lord laughed and politely said,
"In my view you have made amends for your misdemeanor;
You have confessed your faults fully with fair acknowledgment,
And plainly done penance at the point of my axe.
You are absolved° of your sin and as stainless now

4

529 **absolved:** forgiven.

530 As if you had never fallen in fault since first you were born.
As for the gold-hemmed girdle, I give it you, sir,
Seeing it is as green as my gown. Sir Gawain, you may
Think about this trial when you throng in company
With paragons° of princes, for it is a perfect token,°

534 **paragons:** models of perfection. **token:** a keepsake or souvenir.

535 At knightly gatherings, of the great adventure at the Green
    Chapel.
You shall come back to my castle this cold New Year,
And we shall revel° away the rest of this rich feast;
            Let us go."
        Thus urging him, the lord

537 **revel:** make merry.

540   Said, "You and my wife, I know
        We shall bring to clear accord,
        Though she was your fierce foe."

The World of Romance *How does Sir Gawain exhibit both heroism and humbleness?*

3

Teach

Reading Strategy   **2**

Critical Thinking **Ask:**
How did Sir Gawain's behavior in his test of honor show his weaknesses of character?
(He accepted the green sash because he feared for his life. He succumbed to the lady by kissing her three times.)

Big Idea   **3**

The World of Romance
Answer: *Sir Gawain is a hero because he is so chivalrous, brave, and gallant, yet he is humble in accepting responsibility for his own wrongdoing.*

Reading Strategy   **4**

Critical Thinking **Ask:** Why do you think the author did not portray Sir Gawain as a "perfect" person? *(His struggle to overcome his faults is more meaningful and instructive to the reader.)*

 To check students' understanding of the selection, see Unit 1 Teaching Resources Book, p. 150.

English Learners

DIFFERENTIATED INSTRUCTION

Beginning Tell students that the phrases *made amends* and *done penance* both have a similar meaning; however, the word *penance* is often used in a religious context. **Ask:** What other words on this page are used in a religious context? *(faith, sin)*

After You Read

Assess

1. Answers will vary.

2. (a) He challenges them to exchange blows. (b) By not killing Sir Gawain, the Green Knight proves that he is not evil.

3. (a) He says that he is the weakest of the knights and the least likely to be missed. (b) The king may be permitting Sir Gawain to display his loyalty and bravery.

4. (a) He rejects the ring because he says that he has nothing to offer for it. He accepts the sash because he can't resist the protection it offers. (b) She represents a challenge to Sir Gawain's chivalry.

5. (a) The Green Knight stops before the first blow because Sir Gawain flinches. He stops before the second blow to make sure that Sir Gawain has not flinched. On the third stroke, he inflicts a minor gash. He says the third stroke is to punish Sir Gawain for accepting the sash. (b) Some may say that the real test is the lady's offer of the girdle. He fails this test and gives in to his fear of being killed.

6. (a) The two translations tell the same story but use different descriptive words and alliteration. (b) Answers will vary.

7. (a) Sir Gawain may seem one-dimensional, as he is playing the part of the gallant knight. Later, as he almost succumbs to the lady's advances, he becomes a more fully developed character. (b) Answers will vary.

8. Answers will vary.

9. Answers will vary.

After You Read

Respond and Think Critically

Respond and Interpret

1. Were you surprised by the Green Knight's actions at the end of the story? Why or why not?

2. (a)In your own words, state the challenge that the Green Knight offers the members of the Round Table. (b)Do you think the Green Knight is meant to be viewed as evil? Use evidence from the text to support your opinion.

3. (a)Why does Sir Gawain consider himself the knight best qualified to accept the Green Knight's challenge? (b)Why do you think King Arthur allows Sir Gawain to take up the challenge?

4. (a)Why does Sir Gawain refuse the lady's gift of a gold ring but accept her green silk girdle? (b) In the final line of the selection, the Green Knight claims that his wife was Sir Gawain's "fierce foe." In what ways might the lady be considered Sir Gawain's foe?

5. (a)During the incident at the Green Chapel, what reasons does the Green Knight give for the three blows of the axe? (b)What was Sir Gawain's real test? Did he pass? Explain.

Analyze and Evaluate

6. (a)Compare the two translations of the opening stanza of the poem, on pages 165–167. How are they similar and different? (b)Which of the translations do you prefer? Why?

7. (a)How realistic is the character of Sir Gawain? (b)Explain why the author may have developed his character the way he did.

Connect

8. **Big Idea** The World of Romance Do you think Sir Gawain is a hero by the standards of knightly behavior in his time? Why or why not?

9. **Connect to Today** Would you consider Sir Gawain a hero by today's standards? Why or why not?

Primary Visual Artifact

A Knight's Armor

Early knights wore simple knee-length suits of chain mail, a netting made of interlocking metal rings. During the 1300s and 1400s, armor improved. New types of furnaces allowed metalsmiths to create lightweight yet strong steel plates.

Group Activity What were the advantages and disadvantages of armor as it changed over time? Discuss this question with your classmates. Refer to the image and captions on the right and cite evidence from the selection to support your answers.

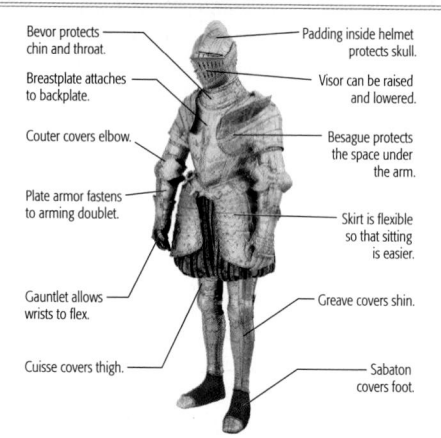

Bevor protects chin and throat.

Breastplate attaches to backplate.

Couter covers elbow.

Plate armor fastens to arming doublet.

Gauntlet allows wrists to flex.

Cuisse covers thigh.

Padding inside helmet protects skull.

Visor can be raised and lowered.

Besague protects the space under the arm.

Skirt is flexible so that sitting is easier.

Greave covers shin.

Sabaton covers foot.

Group Activity

Early armor was heavy and did not offer protection from arrows. Later armor was ineffective against more modern weapons.

 For additional assessment, see Assessment Resources, pp. 77–78.

 To create custom assessments online, go to Progress Reporter Online Assessment.

 To create custom assessments using software, use ExamView Assessment Suite.

Literary Element | Archetype

An **archetype** represents a pattern that has recurred in literature throughout time. Because the audience is already familiar with what archetypes represent, they often evoke a strong response from the reader.

1. What archetypes are present in *Sir Gawain and the Green Knight*?

2. In what ways are archetypes used to further the plot of the poem?

Review: Conflict

As you learned on page 23, **conflict** is the central struggle between two opposing forces in a story or drama. An **external conflict** exists when a character struggles against some outside force. Many stories, such as *Sir Gawain and the Green Knight*, feature conflict between the **protagonist**, or central character, and the **antagonist**, a person or force that opposes the protagonist. An antagonist may try to prevent the protagonist from doing something or may simply have beliefs that contradict those of the protagonist.

Partner Activity Meet with another classmate to discuss the conflicts in *Sir Gawain and the Green Knight*. With your partner, create a web diagram like the one below. Fill in the diagram, listing each antagonist and conflict Sir Gawain must face throughout the story.

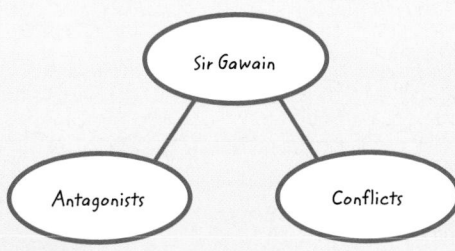

Literature Online

Selection Resources For Selection Quizzes, eFlash-cards, and Reading-Writing Connection activities, go to glencoe.com and enter QuickPass code GLB9817u1.

Reading Strategy | Monitor Comprehension

You may need to reread challenging material to gain a better understanding of it. You should be able to summarize important ideas after your first reading so that you can pay closer attention to supporting details in your second reading.

Summarize the conflicts in *Sir Gawain and the Green Knight* and the way each is resolved.

Vocabulary Practice

Practice with Synonyms Synonyms are words with nearly the same meaning. With a partner, brainstorm three synonyms for each boldfaced vocabulary word. Be prepared to explain why you chose your words.

copiously   intrepid   dauntless   blithe

EXAMPLE:
veneration

Synonyms: admiration, adoration, worship

Explanation: Both veneration and admiration mean "respect," but veneration has stronger positive connotations.

Academic Vocabulary

*During Sir Gawain's visit to his castle, the Green Knight was able to **achieve** his goal of testing Gawain's knightly virtue.*

Achieve is an academic word. The word is also used in everyday life. For example, a runner who beats an Olympic record has **achieved** a significant goal. To study this word further, copy and fill in the graphic organizer below.

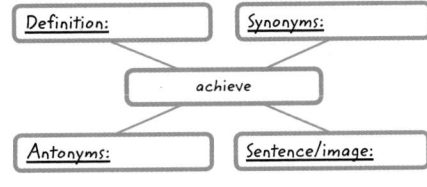

For more on academic vocabulary, see pages 56 and R81.

SIR GAWAIN AND THE GREEN KNIGHT   **183**

After You Read

Assess

Literary Element

1. Some archetypes present are the quest, the battle between good and evil, and the heroic character.

2. Because readers think of Sir Gawain as representing good, or the "hero," the readers want him to succeed at the end of the story.

Review: Conflict

After students make their diagrams identifying Gawain's external conflicts, you may wish to have them identify the internal conflicts that Gawain faces.

Reading Strategy

Students should understand that each conflict Sir Gawain faces is a part of the Green Knight's challenge and, once the challenge is revealed to Sir Gawain, all of the conflicts are resolved.

Progress Check

Can students identify archetype?

If No → See Unit 1 Teaching Resources Book, p. 145.

Progress Check

Can students monitor comprehension?

If No → See Unit 1 Teaching Resources Book, p. 146.

Vocabulary

Possible answers:

copiously
Synonyms: *richly, abundantly, plentifully*

intrepid
Synonyms: *fearless, dauntless, courageous*

dauntless
Synonyms: *bold, brave, unwavering*

blithe
Synonyms: *lighthearted, pleasant, cheerful*

Academic Vocabulary

achieve
Definition: *succeed in doing or accomplishing*
Synonyms: *accomplish, attain*
Antonyms: *fail, loss*
Sentence/image: *If Darryl works hard, he'll achieve his goal.*

After You Read

Assess

Respond Through Writing

Use these criteria in evaluating student short stories:

- The story recasts the main character and conflict of *Sir Gawain and the Green Knight* in modern times.
- It establishes a realistic setting and believable characters, provides a clear conflict that comes to a climax, and offers a satisfying resolution.
- Strong action verbs reveal the characters, create interest, and move the plot forward.

A student who meets all of these criteria should receive the equivalent of a 4-point response.

A student who fully meets two or partially meets three of these criteria should receive the equivalent of a 3-point response.

A student who fully meets one or partially meets two of these criteria should receive the equivalent of a 2-point response.

A student who partially meets one of these criteria should receive the equivalent of a 1-point response.

Respond Through Writing

Short Story

Apply Characterization The story of Sir Gawain and the Green Knight presents an ideal archetype of medieval British heroes and culture. Write a short story of 1,500 words or more, in which you adapt the character of Sir Gawain and the legend's main conflict to modern times. Incorporate interior monologue to develop and deepen your characterization.

Prewrite Review the excerpt from *Sir Gawain and the Green Knight*, noting the important elements of the conflict and of Gawain's character. Then write in your journal an idea for a modern situation and setting for your short story.

Draft Keeping in mind the elements of conflict and characterization that you will recreate, use a story map to flesh out your setting, characters, and sequence of events. Locate your events in specific places, choosing concrete sensory details that bring those places to life.

> **Settings:** Soccer field (fresh-cut grass, strong winds, bright sun), school hallways (crowded, noisy, hot)
>
> **Characters:** Gawain (high school soccer forward, honorable, brave, modest); Greene (goalie for a rival school, vicious, taunting)
>
> **Problem/conflict:** Greene challenges Gawain to a kickoff to see who is the better soccer player.
>
> **Main events:** Gawain wins the kickoff, agrees to another one in one year. A "friend" of Greene's tries to get Gawain to cheat but he refuses. He does accept a good-luck jersey.
>
> **Climax:** The second kickoff between Gawain and Greene (use internal monologue showing Gawain's thoughts)
>
> **Resolution:** Greene reveals that he was the "friend," and knows Gawain took the good-luck jersey. Gawain apologizes, and the two agree to be friends and equals.

Revise Use the criteria listed in the Writing Workshop checklist on page 1160 to evaluate your draft. Look for places where you can add concrete sensory details to make characters and settings convincing and realistic. Use changes in pace to reflect changes in setting or mood.

Edit and Proofread Proofread your paper, correcting any errors in spelling, grammar, and punctuation. Use the Grammar Tip in the side column to help you with action verbs.

Grammar Tip

Action Verbs

Action verbs are verbs that describe what people do. Use strong, specific action verbs in your short story to move the plot forward and reveal your characters' unique feelings and personalities.

*Gawain ~~hit~~ **slammed** his fist into the boy's locker. "Leave me alone," he ~~said~~ **snarled**. "I'm no cheater!"*

Writing Practice

Point of View Explain that writing this short story involves choosing the most convincing point of view. Have students write the first paragraph of their short stories in their choice of the first, second or third person. Then ask them to write the same paragraph in the other two points of view. **Ask:** Which point of view was most convincing in terms of characterization?

 For grammar practice, see Unit 1 Teaching Resources Book, p. 149.

from
A Distant Mirror

National Book Award Winner

Learning Objectives

For pages 185–187

In studying this text, you will focus on the following objectives:

Reading:
Analyzing cultural context.
Analyzing historical context.
Making connections across literature.

Set a Purpose for Reading

As you read, ask yourself, How did the historical realities of chivalry and knighthood differ from the descriptions of them in medieval romances?

Build Background

Barbara Tuchman was one of the foremost historians of the twentieth century. She was twice awarded the Pulitzer Prize—first for *The Guns of August,* a compelling history of the first month of fighting in World War I, and then for *Stilwell and the American Experience in China, 1911–1945,* which describes Chinese-American relations before and during World War II. In this excerpt from *A Distant Mirror,* a brilliant survey of the plague-and-war-ridden fourteenth century, Tuchman discusses the development and effects of chivalry on medieval European society.

Reading Strategy

Analyze Historical Context

Analyzing historical context involves gathering background information and exploring the social forces that influenced the writing of a literary work. As you read, ask yourself, How does this information relate to the world portrayed in *Sir Gawain and the Green Knight*? Record your ideas in a two-column chart like the one below.

Literary Work:	Historical Context:
World of Gawain	World of the fourteenth century

Chivalry was a moral system, governing the whole of noble life. It developed at the same time as the great crusades of the 12th century as a code intended to fuse the religious and martial spirits and somehow bring the fighting man into accord with Christian theory. A moral gloss was needed that would allow the Church to tolerate the warriors in good conscience and the warriors to pursue their own values in spiritual comfort. With the help of Benedictine thinkers,[1] a code evolved that put the knight's sword arm in the service, theoretically, of justice, right, piety, the Church, the widow, the orphan, and the oppressed.

Chivalry could not be contained by the Church, and bursting through the pious veils, it developed its own principles. Prowess, that combination of courage, strength, and skill that made a chevalier *preux,*[2] was the prime essential. Honor and loyalty, together with courtesy—meaning the kind of behavior that has since come to be called "chivalrous"—were the ideals, and so-called courtly love the presiding genius.[3] Designed to make the knight more polite and to lift the tone of society, courtly love required its disciple to be in a

---

1. *Benedictine thinkers* refers to monks of the Order of Saint Benedict.
2. A *chevalier* is a knight. *Preux* means "valiant" in French.
3. Here, *genius* means "guiding principle."

Approaching Level

DIFFERENTIATED INSTRUCTION

Emerging Tell students that this selection shows characters in life-threatening situations. Ask students what they think it takes for someone to act bravely in a dangerous situation. **Ask:** Does a brave person feel no fear? Or does a brave person feel fear but take action despite that fear? *(Answers will vary.)*

Focus
Summary

Tuchman describes the development of chivalry as an attempt to reconcile the behavior of knights with the religious ideals prevalent at the time. Original sources describe the life of a knight as being full of great physical exertion, fighting, and terrible wounds.

Teach

Reading Strategy

Analyzing Historical Context Remind students that *Sir Gawain and the Green Knight* was not written at the time in which it is set; it was written centuries later. The writer chose to depict the period as one of romance and adventure.

[ENGLISH LEARNERS] Have English learners use a dictionary to define the words in the phrase *bursting through the pious veils.* Explain that the phrase is figurative language: the author creates a mental picture to express an idea more powerfully. Tell them the whole sentence means that chivalry became more than a set of religious values.

 For an audio recording of this selection, use Listening Library Audio CD-ROM.

Readability Scores

Dale-Chall: 12.8
DRP: 62
Lexile: 1300

Teach

Big Idea   1

The World of Romance

Say: Using examples from the selection, explain whether the knights Tuchman describes lived by the romantic ideals of honor and loyalty. *(Possible answer: No, because some fought for selfish reasons.)*

Reading Strategy   2

Draw Conclusions **Ask:**

What do you think a knight's life was like? Was it romantic and exciting? *(A knight's life was very difficult, with constant exertion, bad food, and the possibility of wounds or death.)*

View the Art ★

This painting depicts a typical scene of battle on horseback.
Ask: What aspects of this illustration do you find in Tuchman's descriptions of knighthood and battle? *(Possible answers: the heavy armor, the collision of opponents, the length of lances and other weapons, the confusion.)*

Informational Text

Scene from the *Battle of Crecy*, 1346. From *Les Chroniques de France*. British Library, London. ★

1 chronically amorous[4] condition, on the theory that he would thus be rendered[5] more courteous, gay, and gallant, and society in consequence more joyous.

Prowess was not mere talk, for the function of physical violence required real stamina. To fight on horseback or foot wearing 55 pounds of plate armor, to crash in collision with an opponent at full gallop while holding horizontal an eighteen-foot lance half the length of an average telephone pole, to give and receive blows with sword or battle-ax that could cleave[6] a skull or slice off a limb at a stroke, to spend half of life in the saddle through all weathers and for days at a time, was not a weakling's work. Hardship and fear were part of it. "Knights who are at the wars . . . are 2 forever swallowing their fear," wrote the companion and biographer of Don Pero Niño,

the "Unconquered Knight" of the late 14th century. "They expose themselves to every peril; they give up their bodies to the adventure of life in death. Moldy bread or biscuit, meat cooked or uncooked; today enough to eat and tomorrow nothing, little or no wine, water from a pond or a butt,[7] bad quarters, the shelter of a tent or branches, a bad bed, poor sleep with their armor still on their backs, burdened with iron, the enemy an arrow-shot off. 'Ware! Who goes there? To arms! To arms!' With the first drowsiness, an alarm; at dawn, the trumpet. 'To horse! To horse! Muster! Muster!' As lookouts, as sentinels,[8] keeping watch by day and by night, fighting without cover, as foragers,[9] as scouts, guard after guard, duty after duty. 'Here they come! Here! They are so many—No, not as many as that—This way—that—Come this side—Press them there—News! News! They come back hurt, they have prisoners—no, they bring none back. Let us go! Let us go! Give no ground! On!' Such is their calling."

Horrid wounds were part of the calling. In one combat Don Pero Niño was struck by an arrow that "knit together his gorget[10] and his neck," but he fought on against the enemy on the bridge. "Several lance stumps were still in his shield and it was that which hindered him most." A bolt[11] from a crossbow "pierced his nostrils most painfully whereat he was dazed, but his daze lasted but a little time." He pressed forward, receiving many sword blows on head and shoulders which "sometimes hit the bolt embedded in his nose making him

---

4. *Amorous* means "being in love."
5. Here, *rendered* means "made."
6. *Cleave* means "to cut" or "to slash."

7. Here, *butt* means "barrel."
8. *Sentinels* are guards.
9. *Foragers* are scavengers.
10. A *gorget* is a piece of armor worn around the neck.
11. Here, *bolt* refers to a type of small arrow.

186   UNIT 1   THE ANGLO-SAXON PERIOD AND THE MIDDLE AGES

Vocabulary Practice

SPIRAL REVIEW **Shades of Meaning** Remind students that an adjective tells something about a person, place, or thing. **Ask:** What adjectives can you find in the last paragraph on page 187? *(long, interminable,* and *workless)* Which two have similar meanings? *(long* and

interminable) What is the difference between the two meanings? *(Long means "extended," whereas* interminable *means "without end." Long is simply a statement of fact. Winter nights are long. Interminable is pejorative and implies that people want the verse to end.)*

suffer great pain." When weariness on both sides brought the battle to an end, Pero Niño's shield "was tattered and all in pieces; his sword blade was toothed like a saw and dyed with blood . . . his armor was broken in several places by lance-heads of which some had entered the flesh and drawn blood, although the coat was of great strength." Prowess was not easily bought.

In the performance of his function, the knight must be prepared, as John of Salisbury[12] wrote, "to shed your blood for your brethren"— he meant brethren in the universal sense— "and, if needs must, to lay down your life." Many were thus prepared, though perhaps more from sheer love of battle than concern for a cause. Blind King John of Bohemia[13] met death in that way. He loved fighting for its own sake, not caring whether the conflict was important.

As an ally of Philip VI,[14] at the head of 500 knights, the sightless King fought the English through Picardy,[15] always rash and in the avant-garde. At Crécy he asked his knights to lead him deeper into the battle so that he might strike further blows with his sword. Twelve of them tied their horses' reins together and, with the King at their head, advanced into the thick of the fight, "so far as never to return." His body was found next day among his knights, all slain with their horses still tied together.

Fighting filled the noble's need of something to do, a way to exert himself. It was his substitute for work. His leisure time was spent chiefly in hunting, otherwise in games of chess, backgammon, and dice, in songs, dances, pageants, and other entertainments. Long winter evenings were occupied listening to the recital of interminable[16] verse epics. The sword offered the workless noble an activity with a purpose, one that could bring him honor, status, and, if he was lucky, gain.

---

12. *John of Salisbury* (1115–1180) was a writer, historian, secretary to two archbishops of Canterbury, and bishop of Chartres.
13. *King John of Bohemia* (1296–1346) was a popular heroic figure who ruled from 1311 until his death at the Battle of Crécy in France.

---

14. *Philip VI* (1293–1350) was king of France from 1328 until his death.
15. *Picardy* is a region of northern France.
16. *Interminable* means "never-ending."

Respond and Think Critically

Respond and Interpret

1. How have your ideas about knights and chivalry changed as a result of reading this excerpt?

2. How does this excerpt define chivalry?

3. (a)According to Tuchman, why did chivalry develop? (b)Why do you think chivalry eventually took on a life of its own and burst "through [its] pious veils"?

4. (a)Why did Blind King John fight so many battles? (b)What does this suggest to you about chivalry?

Analyze and Evaluate

5. (a)What assertions does Tuchman make about the life of a knight? (b)How does she support these assertions?

6. Overall, do you think the author has a positive or a negative view of chivalry? Cite specific examples to support your opinion.

7. (a)Compare and contrast this passage's depiction of chivalry and knighthood with the depiction of them in *Sir Gawain and the Green Knight.* (b)Which depiction seems more accurate?

Connect

8. The portrayal of chivalry and knighthood in medieval tales is often not accurate. Despite this, do you think that these myths and legends are important? Explain.

BARBARA TUCHMAN **187**

For activities related to this selection, see Unit 1 Teaching Resources Book, pp. 152–160.

For additional selection assessment, see Assessment Resources, pp. 79–80.

Assess

1. Students may feel that the realities of medieval culture are not romantic.

2. As a code or system that provided a moral framework for noble life

3. (a) Chivalry developed as a result of the Crusades. (b) Students may argue that knighthood was inherently incompatible with the values of the church.

4. (a) Tuchman claims that "He loved fighting for its own sake." (b) Tuchman notes the original goal of placing the knight in the service of "justice, right, piety, the Church, the widow, the orphan and the oppressed."

5. (a) Tuchman asserts that the life of a knight was one of extreme physical violence that required an enormous amount of stamina. It was mostly a matter of brute physicality, not courtly love or spirituality. (b) She quotes extensively from primary sources.

6. Tuchman has a negative view of chivalry. Students should point to her descriptions of King John's motives or to the passage's final paragraph, in which she describes the leisurely lifestyle of knights.

7. (a) Tuchman does not romantically depict chivalry and knighthood. The motivations of the knights she describes are not the same as those of Gawain or the Round Table. However, the graphic depictions of violence in each are similar. (b) Tuchman's history is probably more accurate.

8. Students' answers will vary.

Before You Read

Focus

Bellringer Options

Selection Focus
Transparency 9

Daily Language Practice
Transparency 13

Or display pictures or paintings of knights in their regalia. **Ask:** What do you know about knighthood? What do you know about the legend of King Arthur and the Knights of the Round Table? Tell students to keep these ideas in mind as they prepare to read the following selection.

Before You Read

Le Morte d'Arthur

How Morgan le Fay Gave a Shield to Sir Tristram, 1893–1894. Aubrey Vincent Beardsley. Illustration.

Meet **Sir Thomas Malory**
(c. 1405–1471)

"Syr Thomas Maleore, knyght" reads the name of the author on the first printing of *Le Morte d'Arthur* in 1485. That simple listing tells everything that is definitely known about the author, for there was more than one Thomas Malory. Most evidence suggests, however, that the writer was the hot-blooded Thomas Malory who represented Warwickshire in Parliament in 1445 and spent much of his later life in jail.

Knighthood and Prison Malory lived in troubled times. Though his family held land and was well respected, he found himself supporting the wrong side—the Lancasters—during the Wars of the Roses, a bloody, drawn-out conflict to determine which family would rule England. That conflict pitted the House of Lancaster, whose symbol was a red rose, against the House of York, whose symbol was a white rose. A long list of crimes was attributed to Malory, from extortion and attempted murder to cattle rustling. In one notorious incident, he escaped from prison by swimming across a moat and then attacked a nearby abbey that he believed was holding possessions stolen from him. Malory's behavior outraged King Edward IV, who specifically excluded him from four general pardons for criminals, issued between 1468 and 1470.

> *"It is as if the book were the production of no one mind, nor even of a score of successive minds, nor even of any one place or time, but were a rolling body of British-Norman legend."*
>
> —David Masson

Le Morte d'Arthur Malory was in jail when he composed the great English prose work that related the heroic adventures of King Arthur and his knights of the Round Table. The narrative is a reworking of English, French, and Latin tales. Malory translated and organized the diverse body of Arthurian romance that had developed in England and France since Anglo-Saxon times. In the process, he created the first prose masterpiece in English.

Malory died in jail and was buried in the Chapel of St. Francis at Grey Friars. After his death, his manuscript was published by William Caxton, the man who introduced the printing press to England. Caxton gave the work its famous title, *Le Morte d'Arthur,* which is French for "The Death of Arthur." Caxton's title highlighted the story's tragic end.

Never before had a work of English prose matched the elegance and force of English verse. Through the centuries, *Le Morte d'Arthur* has influenced the imaginations of many writers. As American novelist and satirist Mark Twain said, "From time to time I dipped into old Sir Thomas Malory's enchanting book, and fed at its rich feast of prodigies and adventures, breathed in the fragrance of its obsolete names, and dreamed again."

 Literature Online

Author Search For more about Sir Thomas Malory, go to glencoe.com and enter QuickPass code GLB9817u1.

Selection Skills

Literary Elements
- Legend (SE pp. 189, 193, 196, 197)
- Archetype (SE p. 197)

Reading Skills
- Activate Prior Knowledge (SE pp. 189, 190, 194, 198)

Le Morte d'Arthur

Vocabulary Skills
- Analogies (SE pp. 189, 198)

Listening/Speaking/ Viewing Skills
- Analyze Art (SE pp. 191, 192, 195)
- Speech (SE p. 198)

Writing Skills/Grammar
- Punctuate Dialogue (TE p. 192)
- Review (TE p. 196)

Study Skills/Research/ Assessment
- Castle Life (TE p. 194)

Literature and Reading Preview

Connect to the Story

Do you think dreams can foretell the future? With a group of classmates, discuss the possibility of foreseeing the future.

Build Background

In Malory's *Le Morte d'Arthur,* King Arthur creates the brotherhood of the Round Table—an assembly of knights including Sir Lancelot and Sir Gawain, Arthur's nephew—who pledge loyalty to Arthur and to the code of chivalry. As the selection begins, Arthur prepares for battle against his illegitimate son, Mordred, who has raised an army against him.

Set Purposes for Reading

Big Idea **The World of Romance**

In his writing, Malory sought to recapture the Arthurian romantic ideals. As you read, ask yourself, What ideals do King Arthur and his knights represent?

Literary Element **Legend**

A **legend** is a tale that is based on history and handed down from one generation to the next. Usually, a legend celebrates the heroic qualities of a national or cultural leader. As you read, ask yourself, What characteristic qualities of a legend does this story possess?

Reading Strategy **Activate Prior Knowledge**

Reading is an interactive process. When you recall information and personal experiences that are uniquely your own while you are reading, you draw on your personal background. By thus **activating prior knowledge**, and combining it with the words on a page, you create meaning in a selection. As you read, ask yourself, How does what I already know about King Arthur help me understand the story?

Tip: Taking Notes Use a chart to connect your prior knowledge to specific events in the story.

Prior Knowledge	Events in the Story
Sir Lancelot was King Arthur's bravest knight.	Gawain warns Arthur to wait for Lancelot to defeat Mordred.

Learning Objectives

For pages 188–198

In studying this text, you will focus on the following objectives:

Literary Study: Analyzing a legend. Analyzing archetypes.

Reading: Activating prior knowledge.

Speaking and Listening: Delivering a speech.

Vocabulary

doleful (dōl′ fəl) *adj.* sad; p. 192 *The wind in the trees made a doleful sound.*

peril (per′ əl) *n.* risk of injury, loss, or destruction; p. 193 *Police officers face great perils in chasing hit-and-run drivers.*

jeopardy (jep′ ər dē) *n.* danger; p. 195 *The fire in the warehouse put nearby buildings in jeopardy.*

brandish (bran′ dish) *v.* to shake or swing threateningly, as a weapon; p. 195 *Pretending he was a knight, the boy brandished a plastic sword.*

Tip: Analogies To complete an analogy, determine the relationship between the ideas represented by the first pair of words. Then apply that relationship to the second pair.

Before You Read

Focus

Summary

King Arthur has a disturbing dream in which Gawain warns him to postpone fighting Mordred. Arthur makes a treaty with Mordred, and the two meet. Both sides misinterpret the actions of a knight who draws a sword, and a terrible battle ensues. Arthur kills Mordred, but not before Mordred wounds Arthur. Bedivere puts Arthur aboard a barge that will take him to Avalon so that he can heal.

 For summaries in languages other than English, see Unit 1 Teaching Resources Book, pp. 161–166.

Vocabulary

Analogies Have small groups of students use 3- x 5-inch note cards to make a word analogy game. For each word, students should write an analogy based on a synonym relationship, an antonym relationship, and one other relationship of their choosing. Each group then uses its cards to quiz other groups.

 For additional vocabulary practice, see Unit 1 Teaching Resources Book, p. 169.

 For additional context, see Glencoe Interactive Vocabulary CD-ROM.

English Learners

DIFFERENTIATED INSTRUCTION

Intermediate Students may benefit from considering the genre of legend and heroism in legends. **Ask:** What does it mean for a character, or a real person, to be a legend? Invite students to generate a list of characters in novels, poems, and short stories as well as real people in various fields of skill and knowledge that they consider legendary.

Ask: What does it mean when we say that a hero is "larger than life"? What character traits does the hero of a legend have? Elicit and write on the board the traits students mention. Tell students to think about these traits as they read about Arthur and his knights.

Teach

Reading Strategy | 1

Activate Prior Knowledge
Answer: *On the night before the battle against Mordred, King Arthur is worried and anxious, so it is understandable that his sleep is disturbed.* **Ask:** What do you think the dream means? *(Possible answer: It foretells his death at the hands of his enemies.)*
Have students reread the first paragraph which describes King Arthur's dream. **Ask:** What words indicate that the dream frightens King Arthur? *(hideous deep black water; serpents and worms and wild beasts, foul and horrible; he fell among the serpents, and every beast caught him by a limb)*
ENGLISH LEARNERS Have students unfamiliar with these words consult a dictionary.

Big Idea | 2

The World of Romance

Ask: Why was Gawain esteemed as a knight? *(He was esteemed for fighting "righteous" battles in the service of ladies.)* What does this say about the ideals of the time? *(Possible answer: Bravery in battle and service to women were respected.)*

 For an audio recording of this selection, use Listening Library Audio CD-ROM.

Readability Scores

Dale-Chall: 9.1
DRP: 60
Lexile: 1110

Battle between King Arthur and Mordred. English. Lambeth Palace Library, London.

from
Le Morte d'Arthur

Sir Thomas Malory

I

Upon Trinity Sunday[1] at night King Arthur dreamed a wonderful dream, and that was this: it seemed that he saw upon a platform a chair and the chair was fastened to a wheel; thereupon King Arthur sat in the richest cloth of gold that might be made. And the king thought that under him, far from him, was hideous deep black water; therein were all manner of serpents and worms and wild beasts, foul and horrible. Suddenly the king thought the wheel turned upside-down and he fell among the serpents, and every beast caught him by a limb. The king cried out as he lay in his bed and slept, "Help, help!"

Then knights, squires,[2] and yeomen[3] awakened the king, and he was so dazed that he knew not where he was. He stayed awake until it was nigh day and then he fell to slumbering again, not sleeping but not thoroughly awake. Then it seemed to the king that Sir Gawain actually came unto him with a number of fair ladies.

When King Arthur saw him he cried, "Welcome, my sister's son; I thought that ye were dead. And now that I see thee alive, much am I beholden unto almighty Jesus. Ah, fair nephew, what are these ladies that have come hither with you?"

"Sir," said Sir Gawain, "all those are ladies for whom I have fought when I was a living man. And all these are those whom I did battle for in righteous quarrels; at their devout prayer, because I did battle for them righteously, God hath given them the grace to bring me hither unto you. Thus God hath given me leave to warn you away from your death: for if ye fight to-morn with Sir Mordred, as ye have both agreed, doubt ye not that ye shall be slain, and the most part of your people on both sides. Through the great grace and goodness that almighty Jesus hath unto you, and through pity for you and many other good men who would be slain there, God in His special grace hath sent me to you to give you warning that in no wise[4]

---

1. *Trinity Sunday* is the eighth Sunday after Easter.
2. *Squires* assisted knights.
3. *Yeomen* were attendants to nobles.

Activate Prior Knowledge **Why might King Arthur have a nightmare at this time?**

4. Here, *wise* means "way."

Reading Practice

Activate Prior Knowledge Most students have been exposed to Arthurian legend in one way or another.
Ask: Who knows about Arthurian legend? Then have students break into groups, making sure that each group has at least one student who is familiar with the legend. **Write on the board:** Who is King Arthur? What is Excalibur? To whom is King Arthur married? Who are the knights of the Round Table? Who is Sir Lancelot? How is Sir Mordred related to King Arthur? Use these questions to facilitate students' discussion about their prior knowledge.

Teach

St. Bedivere returns Excalibur to the lake at the death of King Arthur, early 14th century. Illuminated manuscript.

 View the Art This illumination depicts the return of Arthur's sword to the Lady of the Lake, from whom it had originally come. What is the mood of the image? What details contribute to the mood? ★

should ye do battle to-morn; but ye should make a treaty for a month. And make this offer generously to-morn so as to assure the delay, for within a month Sir Lancelot shall come with all his noble knights and rescue you worshipfully and slay Sir Mordred and all who ever will hold with him."

Then Sir Gawain and all the ladies vanished; at once the king called upon his knights, squires, and yeoman and charged them quickly to fetch his noble lords and wise bishops unto him. When they had come the king told them of his vision and what Sir Gawain had said to him: that if he fought on the morn, he would be slain. Then the king commanded and charged Sir Lucan le Butler, his brother Sir Bedivere, and two bishops to make a treaty in any way for a month with Sir Mordred: "And

spare not; offer him lands and goods, as much as ye think best."

They departed and came to Sir Mordred, where he had a grim host[5] of a hundred thousand men. There they entreated Sir Mordred a long time, and at the last it was agreed for Sir Mordred to have Cornwall and Kent during King Arthur's days and all England after the king's days.

Then they agreed that King Arthur and Sir Mordred should meet between their two hosts, and that each of them should bring fourteen

---

5. Here, *host* means "army."

SIR THOMAS MALORY **191**

Teach

View the Art ★

The Holy Grail as we picture it today appears first in the work of Robert de Boron, a French poet of the late twelfth and early thirteenth centuries. According to Boron, the Grail was the cup used at the Last Supper and also the cup in which Joseph of Arimathea caught drops of Jesus' blood as he hung on the cross. Then, Boron wrote, Joseph went on to create the Grail—or Round—Table in memory of the Last Supper. **Ask: How does this painting depict religious imagery?** *(Students may point out that the top half of the picture appears similar to a painting of the Last Supper, or that the building near the bottom looks like a church.)*

King Arthur and His Knights Around the Table. Manuscript on vellum. Bibliothèque Nationale, Paris. ★

persons with him. They came back with this word to King Arthur.

Then he said, "I am glad that this is done." So he went into the field.

When King Arthur prepared to depart for the meeting in the field he warned all his host that if they should see any sword drawn, "see that ye come on fiercely and slay that traitor Sir Mordred, for I in no wise trust him."

In like wise Sir Mordred warned his host: "If ye see any sword drawn, see that ye come on fiercely and then slay all who stand before you, for in no way will I trust in this treaty; I know well that my father wishes to be avenged upon me."

So they met for their appointment and were thoroughly agreed and accorded;[6] wine was fetched and they drank together. Just then an adder came out of a little heath-bush and stung a knight on the foot. When the knight felt the sting, he looked down and saw the adder; at once he drew his sword to slay the adder, and thought to cause no harm. But when the hosts on both sides saw that sword drawn, they blew trumpets and horns and shouted grimly, and the two hosts rushed toward each other.

Then King Arthur mounted his horse and said, "Alas, this unhappy day!" So he rode to join his party, and Sir Mordred did in like wise. And never since was there seen a more **doleful** battle in any Christian land, for there was great rushing and riding, thrusting and striking, and many a grim word was spoken by each side, and

Vocabulary

doleful (dōl′ fəl) *adj.* sad

---

6. *Accorded* means "reconciled."

Grammar Practice

Punctuate Dialogue Point out that much of the story is told through dialogue, or characters' speech. As a class, review the rules for punctuating dialogue: Characters' words go inside quotation marks. Commas go inside quotation marks. Semicolons and colons go outside quotation marks. Question marks and exclamation points appear within quotation marks when they are part of characters' speeches.

Have students write a brief dialogue between Arthur and Bedivere, paying particular attention to the punctuation of the quotations.

many a deadly stroke was dealt. But King Arthur rode steadily throughout the army of Sir Mordred many times and did full nobly, as a noble king should; never at any time did he weaken. And Sir Mordred did his duty that day and put him-self in great **peril**. Thus they fought all the long day, and no knight ever stinted[7] till he was laid to the cold earth. So they fought on till it was near night, and by that time there were a hundred thousand who lay dead upon the ground. Then King Arthur was madly wroth[8] out of measure, when he saw that so many of his people were slain. When the king looked about him he was aware that of all his host and of all his good knights no more were left alive but two: one was Sir Lucan le Butler, and the other his brother Sir Bedivere; and they were both sorely wounded.

"Jesus, mercy!" said the king. "Where are all my noble knights? Alas, that ever I should see this doleful day! For now I have come to my end. But would to God that I knew where that traitor Sir Mordred, who hath caused all this mischief, is."

Then King Arthur looked about and saw where Sir Mordred stood leaning upon his sword among a great heap of dead men. "Now give me my spear," said King Arthur to Sir Lucan, "for yonder I have spied the traitor who hath wrought all this woe."

"Sir, let him be," said Sir Lucan, "for he brings ill fortune. And if ye can pass through this unlucky day, ye shall be right well revenged upon him. Good lord, remember your night's dream and what the spirit of Sir Gawain

---

7. Here, *stinted* means "ceased" or "stopped."
8. *Wroth* means "angered."

1 The World of Romance *What does this detail suggest about King Arthur?*

2 Legend *What seems exaggerated in this description?*

told you last night. God in His great goodness hath preserved you so far. Therefore for God's sake, my lord, leave off now; for, blessed be God, ye have won the field: here we three are alive, but with Sir Mordred no one is alive. Therefore if ye leave off now, this wicked day of destiny is over."

"Now betide[9] me death, betide me life," said the king, "now that I see him yonder alone, he shall never escape my hands! For I shall never have him at better avail."[10]

"God speed you well!" said Sir Bedivere.

Then the king got his spear in both his hands and ran toward Sir Mordred, crying, "Traitor, now has thy death-day come!"

When Sir Mordred heard King Arthur he ran toward him with his sword drawn in his hand. Then King Arthur smote[11] Sir Mordred under the shield with a thrust of his spear on through the body more than a fathom. When Sir Mordred felt that he had his death-wound, he thrust himself with all his might up to the handguard of King Arthur's spear; and right so, holding his sword in both his hands, he smote his father King Arthur upon the side of the head so that the sword pierced the helmet and the brain-pan. Therewith Sir Mordred fell stark dead to the earth; and the noble King Arthur fell to the earth and there he swooned often, and Sir Lucan and Sir Bedivere lifted him up each time. So they led him, weak between them, to a little chapel not far from the sea, and when the king was there he seemed reasonably comfortable.

Then they heard people cry out in the field.

"Now go thou, Sir Lucan," said the king, "and let me know what that noise in the field betokens."[12]

So Sir Lucan departed slowly, for he was grievously wounded in many places; as he went he saw and noticed by the moonlight how plunderers and robbers had come into the field to plunder and to rob many a full noble knight

---

9. *Betide* means "come to."
10. Here, *avail* means "advantage."
11. *Smote* means "struck."
12. *Betokens* means "signifies."

SIR THOMAS MALORY **193**

| **Big Idea** | **1** |

The World of Romance
Answer: *This detail reveals King Arthur's fighting prowess, courage, and devotion to duty.*

Ask: How does this reflect the ideals of the time period? *(Much importance was placed on these characteristics. Those that held the highest social positions were expected to have these qualities.)*

| **Literary Element** | **2** |

Legend **Answer:** *The number of the slain is probably exaggerated to suggest the epic scale of the battle.*

| **Big Idea** | **3** |

The World of Romance
[APPROACHING] **Ask:** What does the text indicate about the religious beliefs of the time? *(King Arthur and his knights beseech God and Jesus. They adhere to Christian beliefs.)*

If students are struggling, point out the characters' reliance on guidance from God. For example, Lucan reminds Arthur that God sent Gawain in a dream to warn Arthur not to fight.

Approaching Level

DIFFERENTIATED INSTRUCTION

Emerging Introduce students to story mapping. Tell them to write the title of the work at the top of a blank piece of paper. Then, have them write *Characters* and list all of the main characters they have encountered. After students have read each section of the story, have them stop and write a brief summary of it. You might help students complete a summary for the first section: "King Arthur has a dream that warns him not to fight Mordred. He makes a treaty with Mordred to wait for Lancelot's arrival." Have students create similar summaries for the remaining sections.

Teach

Activate Prior Knowledge

Answer: *Students might recall that the sword Excalibur has magical properties, that it was given to Arthur by the Lady of the Lake, or that by pulling it from a stone Arthur became the King of England.* **Ask:** What does Arthur expect Bedivere to see when he throws the sword into the water? *(He expects something magical to happen.)*

Literary History ☆

Arthurian Legend T. H. White, a British novelist, wrote a best-selling interpretation of the Arthurian legend called *The Once and Future King*. It was published in 1958. This novel was a compilation of four different books, or parts. The first three were published individually. The last was published with the compilation as a whole. White was a well-known scholar of Arthurian legend.

Research Practice

Castle Life Ask students to do research on what daily life in a medieval castle was like. Students can present their findings in "A Day in the Life of . . . " narratives. Some students might write about knights, some about ladies of the court, and some, perhaps, about knaves or jesters. Remind students that their reports should describe their subjects' dress, food, responsibilities, luxuries, and hardships. Also, the reports should explain how their subjects celebrated festivals or other significant occasions.

---

of brooches and beads, of many a good ring, and of many a rich jewel. And whoever was not fully dead, the robbers slew them for their armor and their riches. When Sir Lucan understood this work, he came back to the king as quickly as he could and told him all that he had heard and seen.

"Therefore, by my counsel," said Sir Lucan, "it is best that we bring you to some town."

III

"I would it could be so," said the king, "but I cannot stand, my head aches so. Ah, Sir Lancelot, this day have I sorely missed thee! And alas, that ever I was against thee! For now I have my death, whereof Sir Gawain warned me in my dream."

Then Sir Lucan took up the king on one side and Sir Bedivere did so on the other side, and in the lifting the king swooned. Also with the lifting, Sir Lucan fell into a swoon and part of his guts fell out of his body, and therewith the noble knight's heart burst. When the king awoke he beheld Sir Lucan, how he lay foaming at the mouth, and how part of his guts lay at his feet.

"Alas," said the king, "this is to me a full heavy sight to see this noble duke die so for my sake; for he wished to help me, he who had more need of help than I. Alas, he would not complain, his heart was so set upon helping me. Now Jesus have mercy upon his soul!"

Then Sir Bedivere wept for the death of his brother.

"Leave this mourning and weeping," said the king, "for all this will not avail me. For wit thou well,[13] if I might live myself the death of

> **Then King Arthur smote Sir Mordred under the shield with a thrust of his spear on through the body more than a fathom.**

Sir Lucan would grieve me evermore, but my time passeth on fast. Therefore take thou here Excalibur, my good sword, and go with it to yonder water's side; when thou comest there, I charge thee to throw my sword into that water and come again and tell me what thou saw there."

"My lord," said Sir Bedivere, "your command shall be done, and quickly I shall bring you word back."

So Sir Bedivere departed. And along the way he beheld that noble sword, that the pommel and the haft were all of precious stones. Then he said to himself, "If I throw this rich sword into the water, thereof shall never come good, but only harm and loss." Then Sir Bedivere hid Excalibur under a tree, and as soon as he might he came again unto the king and said that he had been at the water and had thrown the sword into the water.

"What saw thou there?" said the king.

"Sir," he said, "I saw nothing but waves and winds."

"That is untruly said by thee," said the king. "Therefore go thou quickly again and do my command. As thou art dear to me, spare not but throw it in."

Then Sir Bedivere returned again and took the sword in his hand, and again he thought it a sin and a shame to throw away that noble sword. So once more he hid the sword and returned again and told the king that he had been at the water and done his command.

"What saw thou there?" said the king.

"Sir," he said, "I saw nothing but waves and winds."

"Ah, traitor untrue," said King Arthur, "now hast thou betrayed me twice! Who would have

---

13. The expression *wit thou well* means "heed what I say."

The Death of Arthur. John Mulcaster Carrick.

 View the Art How does this painting compare with how you imagine this scene? ★

Teach

Big Idea   **2**

The World of Romance
Answer: *By lying to his king, Bedivere betrays his knightly honor.* **Ask:** What does Bedivere risk by not listening to Arthur? *(He risks Arthur's life because it is taking so long to get him help.)*
(APPROACHING) Check to make sure that students understand the two conflicting urges Bedivere faces: his duty to his king, and his desire to save the beautiful sword. **Ask:** In this legend, which is more important—Bedivere's duty to help Arthur or his desire to save this important sword?

thought that thou who hast been to me so lief[14] and dear and thou who art called a noble knight would betray me for the richness of this sword? But now go again quickly; thy long tarrying[15] putteth me in great **jeopardy** of my life, for I have taken cold. And unless thou do now as I bid thee, if ever I may see thee again I shall slay thee with my own hands; for thou would for my rich sword see me dead."

Then Sir Bedivere departed and went to the sword and quickly took it up and went to the water's side, and there he bound the girdle[16]

14. *Lief* means "beloved."
15. *Tarrying* means "delaying."
16. *The girdle* is the sash around the sword's handle.

2   **The World of Romance** *In addition to betraying King Arthur, what does Bedivere betray by lying to his king?*

Vocabulary

jeopardy (jep′ ər dē) *n.* danger

about the hilt;[17] then he threw the sword as far into the water as he might. And there came an arm and a hand above the water which caught it and shook and **brandished** it thrice and then vanished with the sword into the water. So Sir Bedivere came back to the king and told him what he saw.

"Alas," said the king, "help me hence, for I fear that I have tarried over-long."

Then Sir Bedivere took the king upon his back and so went with him to the water's side. When they reached there they saw a little barge which waited fast by the bank with many fair ladies in it. Among them all was a queen, and they all had black hoods; they all wept and shrieked when they saw King Arthur.

17. The *hilt* is the handle, also called the haft, of the sword.

Vocabulary

brandish (bran′ dish) *v.* to shake or swing threateningly, as a weapon

SIR THOMAS MALORY **195**

View the Art ★

Answer: *Students may say that the painting effectively captures the ethereal atmosphere of the scene in Malory's work.*

An artist of the Pre-Raphaelite School, John Mulcaster Carrick (1833–1896) is known for rendering his subjects in meticulous detail. His *Death of Arthur* reflects the Pre-Raphaelites' preoccupation with myth, legend, and ancient history.

Teach

Big Idea   1

The World of Romance
Answer: *Sir Bedivere's decision to remain with the hermit reflects his loyalty to King Arthur and the strength of his religious beliefs.*

Ask: Do you think that chivalric ideals are still appreciated today? *(Students may say that less emphasis is placed on them in our capitalistic society, in which every person fends for himself or herself.)*

Literary Element   2

Legend   Answer: *By suggesting that King Arthur might return, the writer makes him into a symbol of the indomitability of the English warrior.* **Say:** Name three elements that make Arthur a legendary figure. *(Students may cite his bravery, his skill in battle, and the possibility of his immortality)*

To check students' understanding of the selection, see Unit 1 Teaching Resources Book, p. 172.

Progress Check

Can students identify elements of legend?

If No → See Unit 1 Teaching Resources Book, p. 167.

Writing Practice

 Review When students have finished reading the selection, have them write reviews of the story. Give students sample reviews, possibly from the local paper or the *New York Times Book Review*. Tell students to include a brief description of the plot but to focus mainly on whether they recommend the story and why or why not. Remind students to support their opinions with examples from the text. Invite volunteers to share their reviews with the class.

"Now put me into that barge," said the king. Sir Bedivere did so gently, and three queens received him there with great mourning and put him down; in one of their laps King Arthur laid his head. Then that queen said, "Ah, dear brother, why have ye tarried so long from me? Alas, this wound on your head hath caught over-much cold."

So they rowed from the land and Sir Bedivere beheld all those ladies go from him. Then Sir Bedivere cried, "Ah, my lord Arthur, what shall become of me, now that ye go from me and leave me here alone among my enemies?"

"Comfort thyself," said the king, "and do as well as thou may, for in me is no more trust to trust in. I must go into the Vale of Avalon[18] to heal me of my grievous wound. And if thou hear nevermore of me, pray for my soul!"

But ever the queens and ladies wept and shrieked, so that it was a pity to hear. As soon as Sir Bedivere had lost sight of the barge, he wept and wailed and then took to the forest and walked all night. And in the morning he was aware of a chapel and a hermitage[19] between two ancient woods.

Then Sir Bedivere was glad, and thither he went. When he came into the chapel he saw where a hermit lay grovelling on all fours fast[20] by a tomb that was newly made. When the hermit saw Sir Bedivere he knew him at once, for he was the Bishop of Canterbury whom Sir Mordred recently put to flight.

"Sir," said Sir Bedivere, "what man is interred[21] there whom you pray so earnestly for?"

"Fair son," said the hermit, "I know not truly but by deeming.[22] But this night at midnight a number of ladies came here and brought hither a dead corpse and prayed me to bury him. And

---

18. *Avalon* is a legendary island paradise.
19. A *hermitage* is the home of a hermit, a person who lives in solitude for religious reasons.
20. Here, *fast* means "near."
21. *Interred* means "buried."
22. *Deeming* is guessing.

---

here they offered a hundred tapers[23] and they gave me a thousand besants."[24]

"Alas," said Sir Bedivere, "that was my lord King Arthur who here lieth buried in this chapel." Then Sir Bedivere swooned and when he awoke he prayed the hermit that he might remain with him always, there to live with fasting and prayers. "For hence I will never go," said Sir Bedivere, "of my own will. But all the days of my life I will be here to pray for my lord Arthur."

"Ye are welcome to me here," said the hermit, "for I know you better than ye think I do. Ye are Sir Bedivere the Bold, and the full noble duke Sir Lucan le Butler was your brother."

Then Sir Bedivere told the hermit all, as ye have heard before, and he remained with the hermit who was earlier the Bishop of Canterbury. There he put on poor clothes and served the hermit full humbly in fasting and in prayers.

Thus, concerning Arthur I find no more written in books which are authorized. Nor did I ever hear or read more with true certainty concerning his death. . . .

Yet some men say in many parts of England that King Arthur is not dead, but was taken by the will of our Lord Jesus into another place. And men say that he shall come again and shall win the Holy Cross. Yet I will not say that it shall be so; rather, I would say that here in this world he changed his form of life. But many men say that there is written upon his tomb this line:

HERE LIES ARTHUR, THE ONCE AND FUTURE KING.

ॐ

---

23. *Tapers* are candles.
24. *Besants* are gold coins.

The World of Romance *What chivalric ideals does Bedivere's decision reflect?*   1

Legend *Why does the writer conclude the story with this statement?*   2

After You Read

Respond and Think Critically

Respond and Interpret

1. What are your impressions of King Arthur and the decisions that he makes? Explain.

2. (a)Summarize the content of Arthur's dreams. (b)What might the overturned chair symbolize? What might the serpents represent?

3. (a)What accident triggers the battle between the two armies? (b)What part does Arthur and Mordred's mutual distrust play in triggering the battle?

4. (a)What does Arthur ask Sir Bedivere to do with his sword, Excalibur? (b)What do Bedivere's actions regarding Excalibur reveal about his character?

Analyze and Evaluate

5. (a)What motivates Arthur to fight Mordred to the death? (b)In your opinion, is Arthur's decision wise? Why or why not?

6. (a)How would you describe the **mood** of this selection? Does it change as the story progresses? Explain. (b)What details does Malory use to achieve this mood?

7. Evaluate Malory's use of **dialogue**. How does it help develop the characters? How does it help move the narrative along?

Connect

8. **Big Idea** The World of Romance In the literature of medieval Europe, King Arthur came to represent the ideal of chivalry. In what ways does he embody this ideal?

9. **Connect to the Author** Malory's personal behavior seems to have been less than chivalrous. Why might he have chosen to write tales that exalt the ideal of chivalry?

Literary Element Legend

A **legend** is different from a myth in that a legend has fewer supernatural elements and more historical truth than a myth does. Because legends are stories of the people, they are often expressions of the spirit, values, or character of the culture that creates them.

1. Find examples in the selection that contribute to the perception of King Arthur as a legendary hero. Explain your choices.

2. In your opinion, why has the legend of King Arthur endured?

Review: Archetype

As you learned on page 164, an **archetype** is a character type, a setting, an image, or a story pattern that occurs frequently in literature across many cultures.

Partner Activity Meet with another classmate to identify and discuss archetypal elements in this selection. Working with your partner, list these archetypes and the emotional responses they evoke in a chart like the one below.

Archetypes	Emotional Responses

Literary Element

1. Arthur does not weaken in the battle. He defeats the evil Mordred. His magic sword is returned to the water. Preternatural women escort him in a barge.

2. The legend is an adventure story, full of human emotion and high drama.

After You Read

Assess

1. Answers will vary.

2. (a) Arthur sits in a chair attached to a wheel and turned upside down. He falls into black water filled with serpents. Then he has a vision of Sir Gawain warning him not to fight Mordred. (b) The overturned chair may symbolize the end of Arthur's reign. The serpents may represent terrible events.

3. (a) A soldier draws his sword to kill an adder that has stung him. (b) Arthur and Mordred had told their men to attack if they should see a sword drawn.

4. (a) Arthur asks Bedivere to throw Excalibur into the water. (b) Bedivere's reluctance suggests his practical nature and love of material things.

5. (a) He wants to avenge his knights. (b) Some may see his decision as unwise, especially given the warning in his dream.

6. (a) The mood early on is foreboding. At the end it is sad yet hopeful. (b) A foreboding mood is created by the black water filled with serpents. Details that create a sad but hopeful mood include the dead knights, the heroic death of Sir Lucan, and the epitaph on Arthur's tomb.

7. It reveals the chivalry of King Arthur and his knights and events soon to take place.

8. Arthur's actions show strength, loyalty, generosity, honor, and courtesy.

9. Answers will vary.

Review: Archetype

Archetypes include the epic confrontation between good and evil, the snake as an agent of evil, a magic sword, and the hero's victory over death.

After You Read

Assess

Reading Strategy

1. Ask students to share any knowledge they might have of Arthur's court.
2. Students' answers will vary. Some students may say that this portrayal is more violent than others with which they are familiar.

Vocabulary

1. c 2. c 3. b 4. a

Academic Vocabulary

Possible answer: To join a team in the park district, you may have to submit an application, attend tryouts, and purchase a uniform. If you fail to do any of these, you may not be eligible to play.

Speaking and Listening

Use these criteria in evaluating student speeches.

- Information is presented in a logical order.
- The speaker effectively makes eye contact and incorporates body language, pacing, and tone of voice.
- The speaker accurately assesses the speech and identifies ways to improve.

Reading Strategy Activate Prior Knowledge

To read effectively, you must **activate your prior knowledge** of people, places, history, languages, and literature. For example, while reading *Le Morte d'Arthur,* you might recall other portrayals of King Arthur and his knights. Drawing upon this prior knowledge can help you identify the qualities that distinguish Malory's story.

1. What prior knowledge about King Arthur did you bring to your reading of this story?

2. What makes Malory's portrayal of King Arthur different from other portrayals of him?

Vocabulary Practice

Practice with Analogies Choose the pair of words that best completes each analogy.

1. safety : jeopardy ::
   a. peace : harmony   c. joy : sorrow
   b. affection : regard

2. whimper : doleful ::
   a. crash : accidental   c. laugh : amused
   b. shriek : distant

3. danger : peril ::
   a. fear : cowardice   c. luck : diligence
   b. weakness : frailty

4. sword : brandish ::
   a. pencil : write   c. marathon : sprint
   b. student : teach

Academic Vocabulary

King Arthur commands Sir Bedivere to follow a specific **procedure** *to return the sword.*

Procedure is an academic word. In the justice system, it is essential to follow proper legal **procedure** when handling a case.

To further explore this word, answer the following question: What is another enterprise in which it is important to follow the correct **procedure,** and why is it important?

For more on academic vocabulary, see pages 56 and R81.

Speaking and Listening

Speech

Assignment King Arthur has figured prominently in legends for centuries and is still seen today as a heroic figure. After reviewing the excerpt from *Le Morte d'Arthur* and noting the qualities and actions that make Arthur heroic, deliver a brief speech describing a living person who shares these heroic qualities. Focus on both the person's actions and his or her effect on the world.

Prepare List the ideas you want to convey about the person, providing vivid facts and examples to support your statements. You can choose to organize your ideas chronologically or in order of importance, but be sure your argument has a logical structure. Include analogies or syllogisms where appropriate to clarify the relationships among ideas and strengthen your message.

Deliver As you present your speech, frequently make eye contact with people in various parts of the audience. Use your voice and body to enhance the impact of your words:

- Walk around in front of the audience or change your posture.
- Gesture with your hands, shoulders, or torso.
- Use facial expressions to express surprise, anger, and other emotions that support your points.
- Alter your tone of voice and pacing to keep your audience interested.

Evaluate Consult the checklist on page 655 to review the elements of a successful speech. Then write a critique of your performance, indicating which skills you have mastered and which ones you will need to work on.

 Literature Online

Selection Resources For Selection Quizzes, eFlashcards, and Reading-Writing Connection activities, go to glencoe.com and enter QuickPass code GLB9817u1.

198 UNIT 1   THE ANGLO-SAXON PERIOD AND THE MIDDLE AGES

Reading Practice

Summarize Ask students to demonstrate their knowledge of the main characters by creating a graphic organizer of character relationships. **Ask:** How will you show which knights are loyal to the king and which are treacherous?

Challenge students to think of ways to include Gawain (who is dead) and Lancelot (who is far from the battle) in their graphic organizers. Students may compare their graphic organizers and discuss other Arthurian characters they know of who do not appear in the selection.

Vocabulary Workshop

Context Clues

Literature Connection Sometimes an unfamiliar word's **context**, or the words that surround that word, can provide clues to the word's meaning.

> *"Welcome, my sister's son; I thought that ye were dead. And now that I see thee alive, much am I beholden unto almighty Jesus."*

> —Sir Thomas Malory, from *Le Morte d'Arthur*

For example, in the line above, you can infer the meaning of *beholden* from its context. Because Arthur is happy that his nephew is alive, you can infer that Arthur feels indebted or grateful to Jesus for saving Gawain.

Types of Context Clues

- The context can provide an **example** that clarifies a word.
  The boy took the teacher's remark literally. *When she said, "We'll take the bull by the horns," he looked around for a bull.*

- There may be a **contrast** between the word and a familiar one.
  It is difficult to use literal *language to talk about being in love; people tend to use figurative language and imagery.*

- A **restatement** expresses a word in a more familiar way.
  In poetry, a literal *style seems out of place; however, in an essay, a matter-of-fact style is appropriate.*

- The context may include a **synonym** of the word.
  Nancy was so literal *that she thought every comment I made was exact.*

Practice Use context clues to determine the meaning of each underlined word. Identify which type of context clue you used.

1. Sir Gawain was sent to Arthur to quickly warn him of the <u>portending</u> danger of the next day's battle.
   a. impending   **b.** bold   **c.** horrifying   **d.** pleasant

2. *Sir Gawain and the Green Knight* and *Le Morte d'Arthur* are <u>indigenous</u> English writings because they were written in England.
   a. rich   **b.** native   **c.** rare   **d.** fictitious

3. In *Le Morte d'Arthur,* Malory shaped a loose group of Arthurian legends into a single, <u>homogeneous</u> narrative.
   a. unexpected   **b.** complicated   **c.** multiple   **d.** unified

Vocabulary Terms

Context clues are the words and phrases surrounding an unfamiliar word that can provide hints about the word's meaning.

Test-Taking Tip

To use context clues in a test-taking situation, underline words and phrases surrounding the unfamiliar word. Use these words as context clues to define the unfamiliar word.

 Literature Online

Vocabulary For more vocabulary practice, go to glencoe.com and enter QuickPass code GLB9817u1.

VOCABULARY WORKSHOP **199**

English Learners

DIFFERENTIATED INSTRUCTION

Intermediate Write the following two sentences on the board. Help students figure out the meanings of the underlined words by using context clues.

1. There they <u>entreated</u> and begged Sir Mordred a long time. *(begged or pleaded with)*

2. Therewith Sir Mordred fell <u>stark</u> dead to the earth. *(utterly)*

Vocabulary Workshop

Context Clues

Focus

Write on the board: Having the proper decorum during class means arriving on time and paying attention. Underline decorum in the sentence. Ask students to use context clues in the sentence to define decorum. Have them jot down their definitions *(manners or conduct)*. Ask volunteers to share their definitions. Discuss which parts of the sentence alerted them to the word's meaning *(arriving on time and paying attention)*.

Teach

Context Clues Say: Knowing a word's part of speech or how a word functions in a sentence can help you determine the word's meaning. **Give students the following examples:** If the word in question is the subject of the sentence, it is probably a noun. If the word in question ends in *-ly,* it is probably an adverb.

Assess

Exercise

1. a; example

2. b; restatement

3. d; contrast

 For additional vocabulary practice, see Glencoe Interactive Vocabulary CD-ROM.

199

Focus

Bellringer Options

Daily Language Practice Transparency 14

Or have students discuss this question: What do today's journalists have in common with balladeers from the Middle Ages? *(Both report actual events with similar subject matter: murder, revenge, personal tragedies, honorable goals, and misfortunes of love.)*

Teach

Literary Element | 1

Tropes Tell students that a trope is a commonly used theme or literary device. Ask them to name some tropes found in contemporary popular music.

Cultural History ☆

Jesse James The outlaw and legendary figure was born in Missouri in 1847. During the Civil War, he joined a guerrilla band, fighting for the South. Because of this, he was declared an outlaw in 1866. James then carried out a campaign of banditry for the next 16 years, gaining notoriety as a train robber. He was shot to death in 1882.

Learning Objectives

For pages 200–201

Literary Study:
Analyzing literary genres.
Analyzing literary periods.
Evaluating historical influences.

The Ballad Tradition

> "O I fear ye are poisoned, Lord
>   Randall, my son!
> O I fear ye are poisoned, my
>   handsome young man!"
> "O yes, I am poisoned; Mother,
>   make my bed soon,
> For I'm sick at the heart, and I fain
>   would lie doon."
>
> —from "Lord Randall"

SIX CENTURIES AGO, MOST PEOPLE IN THE British Isles were unable to read or write. For entertainment, they relied upon traveling minstrels and local storytellers. These musicians and poets created **folk ballads,** or rhymed verse that is recited or sung, out of local stories and tall tales. During the Middle Ages, balladeers often resembled today's journalists; many ballads recounted actual events. Similar to American blues songs, folk ballads contain common tropes and characteristics. Typical ballads deal with topics such as these:

- murderous acts and the desire for revenge
- tragic accidents and sudden disasters
- heroic deeds and quests for honor
- jealous sweethearts and unrequited love

The Ballad's Influence

Most of the English and Scottish ballads we know today date from after the fifteenth century. The authors of these ballads are unknown. In fact, a given ballad may exist in any number of versions, because of the memories and personal tastes of the many different people who passed it on from generation to generation. Ballads were first collected and published in the late eighteenth and early nineteenth centuries, most notably by Thomas Percy in *Reliques of Ancient English Poetry* (1765) and Sir Walter Scott in *Minstrelsy of the Scottish Border* (1802–1803). Samuel Coleridge, John Keats, and other Romantic poets were inspired by such collections of folk and medieval literature. These authors began to write **literary ballads**—ballads purposely written, by known authors, in imitation of folk ballads.

Robin Hood, Will Scarlet and Little John, 17th century. Ballad in woodcut form.

Literary Element Practice

Genre The folk ballad and the literary ballad are distinct genres. **Ask:** What are some differences between these genres? Make a list of characteristics, like the following, on the board:

Folk Ballad
1. Unknown author
2. Passed on orally for generations

Literary Ballad
1. Known author
2. Written down and published

Robin Hood—Ballad Hero

One of the most enduringly popular and widespread ballad themes is that of the noble outlaw. Robin Hood, the legendary bandit of Sherwood Forest who robbed from the rich and gave to the poor, became the hero of a cycle of ballads. The earliest of the surviving Robin Hood ballads date from the fifteenth and sixteenth centuries. In the same tradition, ballads have immortalized the American outlaw Jesse James as a modern Robin Hood.

Characteristics of the Folk Ballad

English and Scottish ballads share many characteristics:

- *Dramatization of a single incident.* The story begins abruptly, often in the middle of the action. Little attention is paid to characterization, background exposition, or description.

- *Little reflection or expression of sentiment.* Ballads focus on telling a story rather than what people thought or felt about the events.

- *Dialogue that furthers the story.* The tales are often mainly told through the speech of the characters rather than by a narrator.

- *A strong, simple beat and an uncomplicated rhyme scheme or pattern.*

- *Use of a refrain repeated regularly throughout the ballad, often at the end of stanzas, to emphasize ideas and add to the musical quality of the verse.* Ballads often employ incremental repetition, in which a line is repeated with small but significant changes as the poem approaches its climax.

- *Use of a burden, or a complete lyrical stanza that is repeated after a narrative stanza.* Some ballads use a burden rather than a refrain. A burden is

Robin Hood, Holding a Bow and Arrow,
c. 1650. Woodcut.

like a modern chorus. It allowed listeners to join in and gave singers time to remember verses.

- *The tendency to suggest rather than directly state.* Although sparsely told, ballads often contain sharp psychological portraits and much folk wisdom.

- *Stories that are often based on actual events.* These incidents—shipwrecks, murders, accidental deaths—might make headlines today. **2**

The best of the folk ballads are among the most haunting narrative poems in British literature. They are still popular today, particularly among Irish folk singers. In the twentieth century, musical artists such as Bob Dylan and B. B. King employed variations of this storied lyrical form.

 Literature Online

Literature and Reading For more about the ballad tradition, go to glencoe.com and enter QuickPass code GLB9817u1.

Respond and Think Critically

1. Given the content of most ballads, what conclusions might you draw about the people who created them and the people who enjoyed them?

2. Why do you think musicians and poets continue to write and perform ballads?

3. (a)Who was the audience for most of the early folk ballads? (b)Why do you think Robin Hood became the hero of many of these ballads?

Literary History

Teach

| Big Idea | 2 |

The World of Romance

Many ballads were based on true incidents, but others were based on imaginary people and events. **Ask:** Why might balladeers have invented imaginary people and events? *(Students may mention the need for a hero or something reflecting the romantic nature of the times, such as chivalry and courtly love.)*

Assess

1. Those who created and enjoyed ballads cherished tradition, had strong family ties, and admired courage and audacity.

2. The subject matter of most ballads is timeless, and many ballads record actual events.

3. (a) The common people were the audience. (b) The common people would have seen Robin Hood as an ally.

 For activities related to this feature, see Unit 1 Teaching Resources Book, pp. 174–175.

 For an audio recording of this feature, use Listening Library Audio CD-ROM.

English Learners

DIFFERENTIATED INSTRUCTION

Intermediate Be aware that students may react to the topics of some ballads—revenge, the quest for honor, or a lover's betrayal, for example—in ways that reflect their diverse cultural upbringings. **Ask:** In your culture, are there topics that would not be used as subject matter of ballads because they are considered in poor taste or for some other reason? *(Answers may include unrequited love or betrayal, out of deference to the feelings of the persons involved.)*

Before You Read

Focus

Bellringer Options

Daily Language Practice Transparency 15

Or have students vote on their favorite popular song. Discuss why the song is popular. Answers may center on the song's message, beats, melody, or style.

Vocabulary

Connotation Point out that words that have similar meanings can differ in their tone or emotional associations. **Ask:** In a scientific paper, would you be more likely to say *inhabit* or *dwell*? (*inhabit*) Which of the following words is more formal: *foremost* or *top*? (*foremost*)

Before You Read

Ballads

Connect to the Poems

What are some of your favorite popular songs? Write a journal entry about what makes certain songs appealing.

Build Background

Both of the ballads you are about to read are Scottish. "Bonny Barbara Allan" tells a familiar, tragic story of disappointment in love. "Get Up and Bar the Door" is a comic ballad about married life—a favorite target of medieval humor.

Set Purposes for Reading

Big Idea The World of Romance

As you read the ballads, ask yourself, How do the ballads romanticize the stories they tell?

Literary Element Ballad Stanza

The **ballad stanza** is a quatrain, or four-line stanza. The first and third lines have four stressed syllables; the second and fourth lines have three. Only the second and fourth lines rhyme. As you read, ask yourself, How does each stanza exemplify or diverge from the ballad stanza form?

Reading Strategy Respond to Characters

Responding to characters involves thinking about how characters make you feel. As you read, ask yourself, how am I reacting to the characters' actions and dialogue?

Tip: Making a Response-Evidence Chart Use a chart to list the evidence that prompts your responses.

> Character: Barbara Allan
> Response: She is selfish and capricious.
> Evidence:
> She refuses to pity a man who she thinks slighted her.

Learning Objectives

For pages 202–207

In studying these texts, you will focus on the following objectives:

Literary Study: Analyzing ballads.

Reading: Responding to characters.

Writing: Writing a story.

Vocabulary

dwell (dwel) *v.* to live as a resident; p. 203 *Before moving to London, Sayed dwelled in a small town.*

foremost (fôr′ mōst′) *adj.* ahead of all others or in the first position; p. 206 *As the foremost authority in his field, he was the obvious choice for department chair.*

Selection Skills

Literary Elements
- Ballad Stanza (SE pp. 202–203, 206, 207)

Bonny Barbara Allan/ Get Up and Bar the Door

Listening/Speaking/ Viewing Skills
- Readers Theater (TE p. 204)

Reading Skills
- Respond to Characters (SE pp. 202, 204, 206, 207)

Vocabulary Skills
- Word Usage (SE p. 207)

Writing Skills/Grammar
- Write a Story (SE p. 207)
- Interrogative Pronouns (TE p. 206)

At Harvest Time, 1880. Jules Bastien-Lepage. Oil on canvas, 81.3 x 105.4 cm. Sotheby's, New York.

Bonny Barbara Allan

It was in and about the Martinmas[1] time,
    When the green leaves were a falling,
That Sir John Graeme, in the West Country,
    Fell in love with Barbara Allan.

5 He sent his men down through the town,
    To the place where she was **dwelling:**
"O haste and come to my master dear,
    Gin[2] ye be Barbara Allan."

    O hooly,[3] hooly rose she up,
10   To the place where he was lying,

---

1. *Martinmas* (St. Martin's Day) is celebrated on November 11.
2. *Gin* means "if."
3. *Hooly* means "slowly."

Ballad Stanza *Does this quatrain follow the typical rhyme scheme of the ballad stanza? How might singing or reciting the ballad contribute to the rhyme in a way that simply seeing it on the page might not?*

Vocabulary

dwell (dwel) *v.* to live as a resident

BALLADS **203**

English Learners

DIFFERENTIATED INSTRUCTION

Intermediate Tell students that ballads provide an excellent opportunity to practice **reading fluency** because they were written to be read aloud or sung. Have students work in pairs to practice reading the ballad aloud. Students should read silently first, noting any words or phrases they find difficult. They can then consult the footnotes or a dictionary for clarification. Once they have established the correct pronunciation, they should attempt to read the poem aloud with their partner. On the second read, students should be expressive with their voices to indicate changes of speaker in the poem.

Focus

Summary

"Bonny Barbara Allan" tells of a young man and a woman who die for love. The comic ballad "Get Up and Bar the Door" tells of a husband and wife who agree that the first to speak will have to bar the door.

 For summaries in languages other than English, see Unit 1 Teaching Resources Book, pp. 176–181.

Teach

Literary Element

Ballad Stanza **Answer:**
Students may disagree on whether the rhyme scheme is abcb.

Point out that in a ballad, near rhyme often takes the place of exact rhyme. Also, the rhyme is more apparent when recited or sung, particularly with a Scottish accent.

View the Art ★

Jules Bastien-Lepage (1848–1884) was a French Naturalist painter. He frequently painted scenes of rural and peasant life.
Ask: What does Bastien-Lepage's painting share with the first stanza of "Bonny Barbara Allan"? (*Possible answers include an autumn setting and a nostalgic, wishful tone.*)

 For an audio recording of this selection, use Listening Library Audio CD-ROM.

Teach

Reading Strategy   1

Respond to Characters

Answer: *Students might sympathize with him now that Graeme admits his error and tries to redeem himself on his deathbed. Some students might suggest that he is ridiculous for letting her rejection ruin him.* **Ask:** What is Graeme's dying wish? *(That his friends be kind to Barbara Allan.)*

 For additional practice using the reading skill or strategy, see Unit 1 Teaching Resources Book, p. 183.

Big Idea   2

The World of Romance

Answer: *Despite having been wronged by Graeme, Barbara Allan recognizes that he truly loved her. He has shown his devotion by dying for her; she will show her devotion by dying for him. This tragic ending reflects the chivalry, loyalty, and romantic love typical of the literature of the time.*

And when she drew the curtain by,
"Young man, I think you're dying."

"O it's I'm sick, and very, very sick,
And 'tis a' for Barbara Allan:"
15 "O the better for me ye's[4] never be,
Though your heart's blood were a spilling.

"O dinna ye mind,[5] young man," said she,
"When ye was in the tavern a drinking,
That ye made the healths gae[6] round and round,
20   And slighted Barbara Allan?"

He turned his face unto the wall,
And death was with him dealing:
"Adieu, adieu, my dear friends all,
And be kind to Barbara Allan."

25 And slowly, slowly raise she up,
And slowly, slowly left him,
And sighing said, she coud not stay,
Since death of life had reft[7] him.

She had not gane[8] a mile but twa[9]
30   When she heard the dead-bell[10] ringing,
And every jow[11] that the dead-bell geid,[12]
It cry'd, "Woe to Barbara Allan!"

"O mother, mother, make my bed!
O make it saft and narrow!
35 Since my love died for me today,
I'll die for him tomorrow."

---

4. *Ye's* means "you shall."
5. *Dinna ye mind* means "don't you remember."
6. *Healths gae* means "toasts go."
7. *Reft* means "deprived."
8. *Gane* means "gone."
9. *Twa* means "two."
10. A *dead-bell* is a church bell rung when someone dies.
11. *Jow* means "stroke."
12. *Geid* means "gave."

1 Respond to Characters *Knowing that Graeme slighted Barbara Allan publicly, how might you respond to his character after these last words?*

2 The World of Romance *How does Barbara Allan's final action reflect the attitudes toward romantic love that were popular during medieval times?*

Speaking Practice

Readers Theater Have students work together to put on a Readers' Theater performance of the ballad. Students will need a narrator, Barbara Allan, John Graeme, and friends of Graeme. You might have students work in groups and take turns presenting their renditions of the ballad. Suggest that students copy the ballad and include stage directions or notations to follow as they perform their pieces for the class.

Cottage and Pond, Moonlight, c. 1780. Thomas Gainsborough. Oil on glass, 28 x 33.6 cm. Victoria and Albert Museum, London.

Get Up and Bar the Door

It fell about the Martinmas time,
　　And a gay time it was then,
When our goodwife got puddings¹ to make,
　　And she's boiled them in the pan.

5　The wind sae cauld blew south and north
　　And blew into the floor;
Quoth our goodman to our goodwife,
　　"Gae out and bar the door."

"My hand is in my hussyfskap,²
10　Goodman, as ye may see;
An it should nae³ be barred this hundred year,
　　It s' no be barred for me."

They made a paction⁴ tween them twa,
　　They made it firm and sure,
15　That the first word whaeer⁵ should speak
　　Should rise and bar the door.
　　Should rise and bar the door.

Then by there came two gentlemen,
　　At twelve o'clock at night,
And they could neither see house nor hall,
20　　Nor coal nor candle-light.

---

1. *Puddings* are sausages.
2. *Hussyfskap* means "household chores."
3. *An it should nae* means "if it should not."
4. A *paction* is an agreement.
5. *Whaeer* means "whoever."

BALLADS　**205**

Teach

Ballad Stanza Answer: *The quatrain maintains the traditional pattern of four stressed and three unstressed syllables, although the third line diverges slightly.*

 To check students' understanding of the selection, see Unit 1 Teaching Resources Book, p. 185.

| Big Idea | 2 |

The World of Romance

Answer: *This ballad is a comic portrayal of married life. Instead of behaving heroically by defending his home and his wife against intruders, the husband keeps quiet so as not to lose the wager and have to bar the door.*

(ENGLISH LEARNERS) Have English learners put lines 37–40 into their own words. **Ask:** What reasons does the husband give for being angry? *(The strangers threaten to kiss his wife and burn him with hot water.)*

| Reading Strategy | 3 |

Respond to Characters

Answer: *Students may consider her response humorous and justified. Her stubbornness and independence help her win in the end. Others may consider her stubbornness extreme.*

"Now whether is this a rich man's house,
    Or whether is it a poor?"
But neer a word wad ane o' them speak,
    For barring of the door.

25 And first they[6] ate the white puddings,
    And then they ate the black;
Tho muckle[7] thought the goodwife to hersel,
    Yet neer a word she spake.

Then said the one unto the other,
30   "Here, man, tak ye my knife;
Do ye tak aff the auld man's beard,
    And I'll kiss the goodwife."

"But there's nae water in the house,
    And what shall we do then?"
35 "What ails ye at the pudding-broo[8]
    That boils into the pan?"

O up then started our goodman,
    An angry man was he:
"Will ye kiss my wife before my een
40   And scad[9] me wi' pudding-bree?"[10]

Then up and started our goodwife,
    Gied three skips on the floor:
"Goodman, you've spoken the **foremost** word,
    Get up and bar the door!"

---

6. *They* refers to the two gentlemen.
7. *Muckle* means "much."
8. *What ails ye at the pudding-broo* means "What's wrong with using the pudding broth?"
9. *Scad* means "scald."
10. *Bree* means "broth."

| **1** | Ballad Stanza *How does this quatrain maintain or diverge from the traditional ballad stanza form?* |

| **2** | The World of Romance *How are the ideals of heroism, chivalry, and romantic love portrayed in this ballad?* |

| **3** | Respond to Characters *What is your response to the wife's comment?* |

Vocabulary

foremost (fôr′ mōst′) *adj.* ahead of all others or in the first position

Grammar Practice

Interrogative Pronouns Write on the board: "What ails ye at the pudding-broo that boils into the pan?" Explain that "What" is used here as an interrogative pronoun, a pronoun that asks a question. Ask students to identify other interrogative pronouns. *(who, whom, whose, which)* Have students write questions that begin with each of the interrogative pronouns. Students should structure their questions as if they were writing a quiz. When students finish writing their questions, have them trade papers and answer the questions posed by their partners.

After You Read

Respond and Think Critically

Respond and Interpret

1. (a)What does Barbara Allan ask her mother to do for her? (b)What does her request suggest about her true feelings for John Graeme?

2. (a)In "Get Up and Bar the Door," what excuse does the wife give to her husband for not barring the door herself? (b)Is this her real reason? Explain.

Analyze and Evaluate

3. How might "Bonny Barbara Allan" have been more or less effective if the writer had included the characters' thoughts and emotions?

4. What techniques does the writer use to create a humorous tone in "Get Up and Bar the Door"? Support your answer with details from the poem.

Connect

5. **Big Idea** **The World of Romance** How is marriage in "Get Up and Bar the Door" shown to be at odds with the ideals of the medieval period?

6. **Connect to Today** Identify a modern film or TV show that features a character similar to Barbara Allan. What do she and Barbara have in common?

Literary Element Ballad Stanza

Repetition of lines, phrases, and words is common in ballads. Such repetition is often used to emphasize a particular tone or theme.

1. In "Bonny Barbara Allan," how does the repetition of "slowly, slowly" in the seventh stanza contribute to the emotional effect of the ballad?

2. (a)How is the expression "bar the door" expressed throughout "Get Up and Bar the Door"? (b)What effect does this imprecise repetition have on the poem?

Reading Strategy Responding to Characters

A **dynamic character** grows and changes, whereas a **static character** remains basically unchanged, even though things happen to him or her.

1. Are Barbara Allan and Sir John Graeme dynamic characters or static ones? How can you tell?

2. Are the husband and wife in "Get Up and Bar the Door" dynamic characters or static ones? How do you know?

 **Writing**

Write a Story These ballads focus on pairs of very stubborn characters. Choose a secondary character from one of the ballads—such as Barbara Allan's mother or one of the intruders—and write a short story describing the events of the ballad from that character's perspective. For help in writing a story, see page 1154.

Vocabulary Practice

Practice with Word Usage Respond to these statements to help you explore the meanings of the vocabulary words in the selection.

1. Describe a place where you have always wanted to **dwell**.

2. Name a goal that is of **foremost** importance to you.

LOG ON ▶ **Literature** Online

Selection Resources For Selection Quizzes, eFlashcards, and Reading-Writing Connection activities, go to glencoe.com and enter QuickPass code GLB9817u1.

BALLADS **207**

Vocabulary

1–2. Answers will vary. Students should demonstrate an understanding of the definitions of *dwell* and *foremost*.

 For additional selection assessment, see Assessment Resources, pp. 83–84.

Reading Strategy

1. Both are static characters. Not enough information is given about them to show growth or change in character.

2. Both are static characters. Neither grows or changes.

After You Read

Assess

1. (a) To prepare a deathbed (b) She may love Graeme. She may feel responsible for his death.

2. (a) She says she is too busy. (b) Answers will vary.

3. Many students may think the ballad provides enough details as it is.

4. The story's plot hinges on a ridiculous wager. The characters' stubbornness is humorous.

5. The realistic rather than idealistic portrayal of marriage is not in accord with the medieval ideals of chivalry.

6. Answers will vary.

Literary Element

1. The repetition in the first and third lines emphasizes the contrast between his bitter "laugh" and his realization in the second and fourth stanzas.

2. (a) Slightly different versions are repeated. (b) The audience expects the repetition, which makes the last line humorous.

Progress Check

Can students identify ballad stanzas?

If No → See Unit 1 Teaching Resources Book, p. 182.

 Writing

Evaluate students' stories based on whether they are told from a single character's perspective and whether the details—what the character thinks and does—are true to that perspective.

Focus

Bellringer

Discuss various characters in fiction and history, such as Ebenezer Scrooge, Captain Ahab, Amelia Earhart, and Abraham Lincoln. **Ask:** How would you describe these individuals? What makes each one memorable? *Have students list a few traits for each one, including their physical attributes, personalities, and accomplishments.*

Summary

In this workshop, students will write and present descriptive essays. They will follow the stages of the writing process, including prewriting, drafting, revising, and editing. In addition, two mini-lessons, on elaborating with descriptive details and using semicolons, are provided.

 For Writing Workshop graphic organizer and rubric, see Unit 1 Teaching Resources, pp. 187-189.

Workshop Resources

Print Materials

- Unit 1 Teaching Resources pp. 187–189
- Writing Kit
- Success in Writing: Research and Reports
- Grammar and Language Transparency 13
- Writing Workshop Transparencies 6–10
- Daily Language Practice Transparencies 21, 44, 135, 150

Technology

- Literature Online: Writing Resources and Grammar Resources, www.glencoe.com
- Online Essay Grader, www.glencoe.com
- Student Presentation Builder on Student-Works Plus CD-ROM
- Media Workshop DVD
- Online Student Edition

208

Learning Objectives

For pages 208–215

In this workshop, you will focus on the following objectives:

Writing: Writing a descriptive essay, using the writing process.

Grammar: Understanding how to use semicolons.

Writing Process

At any stage of the writing process, you may think of new ideas to include. Feel free to return to earlier stages as you write.

Prewrite

Draft

Revise

Focus Lesson: Descriptive Details

Edit and Proofread

Focus Lesson: Semicolons

Present

Writing Workshop

Descriptive Essay

Literature Connection Throughout *The Canterbury Tales,* Chaucer describes each pilgrim's most distinctive characteristics—in the process both revealing the pilgrim's character and creating a vivid, lasting impression.

> *"He had his son with him, a fine young Squire,*
> *A lover and a cadet, a lad of fire*
> *With locks as curly as if they had been pressed.*
> *He was some twenty years of age, I guessed."*

To write a descriptive essay, choose details that will make the person or character you are describing believable and memorable to your audience. Follow the goals and strategies below.

Checklist

Goals	Strategies
To describe a person or character	☑ Focus on distinguishing, memorable characteristics
To use descriptive details to create a dominant impression	☑ Use sensory details, figurative language, imagery, and other literary devices that create a single, strong impression
	☑ Use methods of characterization, including actions and dialogue
To demonstrate a command of language	☑ Reflect your own personal style and voice
	☑ Present ideas with conviction
	☑ Vary sentences and use precise language
To employ narrative techniques to reveal character	☑ Select and maintain an appropriate point of view
	☑ Present engaging events that contribute to the dominant impression

Assignment: Describe a Person or Character

Write a descriptive essay of about 1,500 words about a person (real or fictional) in which you make that person memorable to others. As you work, keep your audience and purpose in mind.

Audience: peers, classmates, and teacher

Purpose: to create a vivid and memorable impression of your character

Analyze a Professional Model

In the following selection, Booker Prize–winning author Penelope Lively describes her grandmother and the woman's seemingly steadfast convictions despite changing times. As you read the following passage, notice how Lively uses vivid details and controls the reader's impression of her subject. Pay close attention to the comments in the margin; they point out features to include in your own descriptive essay.

From *A House Unlocked* by Penelope Lively

When I summon up the late 1940s, the vision is a profoundly confusing one. There is a sense in which I am still there, a lumpen teenager, gripped by the roller-coaster emotions of that turbulent period in life. . . .

All the while, my grandmother is an abiding presence—brisk, merry, unshakeable in her convictions. On public occasions, I take shelter behind her rock-solid confidence in the society with which she is familiar. She knows what to say when and to whom, she is never stuck for a comment or an opinion, she is deft about such stultifying embarrassments as how to locate the lavatory in an unfamiliar environment. I was devoted to her, and still am. But I was beginning to question her assumptions: about religion, about social structure. We argued—good-humoredly. For my part, I was increasingly less certain that she was right about everything, though that in no way diminished my regard for her; she saw me as a normally disaffected schoolgirl who would come round to a proper outlook in due course.

Real-World Connection

If you have written something positive about a person you know, consider giving the person your work or reading it aloud to him or her. If you have remembered someone, consider sharing your work with someone who also remembers the same person. If you have recreated a character, share your essay with others who are interested in the same character, work, or author.

Point of View

Select and maintain an appropriate point of view.

Command of Language

Use precise words and apt modifiers. Vary sentences.

 Literature Online

Writing and Research For prewriting, drafting, and revising tools, go to glencoe.com and enter QuickPass code GLB9817u1.

WRITING WORKSHOP **209**

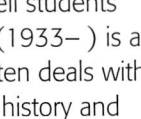
Teach

Big Idea

The Power of Faith In *The Canterbury Tales,* Chaucer describes pilgrims who journeyed to Canterbury Cathedral more than a thousand years ago to seek blessings from the martyred Archbishop Thomas à Becket. **Say:** Describe some of today's pilgrims, religious and nonreligious. **Ask:** What do they look like? Where do they journey? How are they similar to Chaucer's pilgrims? How are they different?

Literary History ☆

Penelope Lively Tell students that Penelope Lively (1933–) is a writer whose work often deals with the relation between history and personal memory. Lively's novel *Moon Tiger* won the Booker Prize in 1987. She first gained acclaim as a children's writer.

English Learners
DIFFERENTIATED INSTRUCTION

Intermediate English learners who are hesitant when using descriptive adjectives may benefit from consulting a thesaurus or a dictionary of synonyms to find vivid, interesting words. Write the word *happy* on the board. Have students find more vivid synonyms in a thesaurus.

Advanced Learners
DIFFERENTIATED INSTRUCTION

Descriptive Language Have students reread the second paragraph of the Lively passage to find several adjectives. Then have them rewrite the paragraph, replacing those words with weaker ones. Ask students to compare the versions to determine why the original is more effective.

 **Writing Workshop**

**Descriptive Essay**

Teach

Writing Skills

Descriptive Details Tell students that in order to make a character memorable, one needs to create his or her portrait with details that are colorful and vivid. Plain or neutral language will make a plain or neutral character. **Say:** When you know that you are using a weak word but just cannot think of a stronger synonym, highlight the word in parentheses or brackets and return to it later for another try.

Cultural History ☆

Corsets Corsets came into vogue in the sixteenth century and were used by men and women alike so that they could wear the small-waisted fashions of the day. In the nineteenth century, some doctors claimed the corset to be a medical necessity even though corsets deformed the internal organs.

Descriptive Details
Use vivid details and sensory images to describe the character.

Methods of Characterization
Use precise details about appearance and actions to help create your dominant impression.

Events
Present engaging events.

Methods of Characterization/ Dominant Impression
Use dialogue and other methods of characterization to create a lasting impression of the character.

In my head, my grandmother is always aged around seventy. Her grey hair is set in neat rolls and confined within an invisible net. She wears a tweed skirt, a blouse and cardigan in winter, linen dresses in summer. Lisle stockings, always. A large hessian apron is tied round her waist for gardening, its pockets bristling with secateurs, raffia, pruning knife. When I hugged her I could feel the carapace of her corset, never discarded, even in the hottest weather. For the evening, she changed into a long red velveteen housecoat, worn with a rope of ivory beads. Her presence seemed to animate the house. When she was out, the whole place went very still; when she was at home, her brisk step rang on the stairs and along the passages, you heard her humming and singing, you heard her laughter. She could share a joke, and had a sense of the ridiculous. But there was an implacable code of conduct, and minefields on all sides. Good manners were considered paramount—the decent consideration of each towards all. Excessive behavior or bad language brought instant disapproval: once, a young woman visitor, inflamed by sherry, tossed a cushion across the Golsoncott drawing-room to a friend, and was never invited to the house again. My grandmother became tight-lipped at any sexual inference. On another occasion, when she was in her eighties, we had to leave a concert in the interval because a couple in the row in front had been kissing. Sheltered from the tabloid press, and listening only to BBC Home Service and Third Programme, she was immune to much of the changing climate of the fifties, let alone the sixties. But occasionally the licence of the times filtered through to her; her condemnation was absolute and unrelenting. Skimpy clothing on women was a particular affront. The miniskirt made public outings an ordeal. But then, bizarrely, she rounded on the ankle-length skirts and coats of the seventies: "Ridiculous! Why go back to all that clutter!"

Reading–Writing Connection Think about the writing techniques that you just encountered and try them out in the descriptive essay you write.

Writing Practice

Figurative Language and Clichés
Point out to students that figurative language can enhance a description by means of comparisons. However, many similes and metaphors have become clichés. Encourage students to think of fresh, concrete comparisons to substitute for clichéd ones.

Have students rewrite the comparisons below with fresh similes and metaphors.
1. My cousin is as smart as a whip and as sly as a fox.
2. Mr. Berson is a giant among men.
3. Raul appears to be as strong as an ox, but he's really just a lamb.

Prewrite

Gather Ideas As you ponder subjects to write about, think of people who have had a significant effect on you. Alternatively, create a fictional character that will leave your audience with a lasting impression.

Choose a Subject Use the following criteria to help you choose a memorable character to describe.

▶ **Choose a familiar subject.** It is easier to write vividly about a subject you know or remember well. Think about someone who has influenced you directly. If you are making up a character, fully imagine the physical traits and behaviors that will make the character believable.

▶ **Choose a meaningful subject.** Choose a character who is meaningful to you personally. Consider what specifically makes that character memorable to you and how to leave your audience with a similar impression.

▶ **Choose a complex subject or a new approach.** To hold your readers' interest, choose a subject who is unusual or multifaceted. Try to choose a character that is not obviously important (or one that is important for unexpected reasons). For example, an eccentric neighbor from your childhood may have made a strong impression on you.

Organize Details Visualize the character you have chosen, concentrating on his or her most striking characteristics. To organize your description, arrange the important details in a graphic organizer.

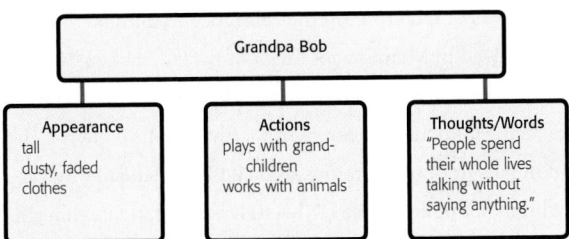

Make an Impression Before you begin drafting, clarify the overall impression you want to create for your audience. What makes the character special to you? The overall impression you want to create will help you decide which details to include and which to omit.

Talk About Your Ideas To help develop a natural writing voice and a conversational tone, describe your character aloud to a partner. Check to ensure that your partner's impression of your character matches the one you want to convey, and note which details you should add or delete.

Characters and Traits

Character	Character Traits
Grandpa Bob	is a good listener, loves animals, loves the outdoors, is timid
Lisbeth, my neighbor	is friendly, funny, a good gardener, a great storyteller
Marco	is a great best friend, loyal, funny; loves soccer

Avoid Plagiarism

Resist the temptation to submit someone else's work as your own by chunking the assignment into manageable steps that you can complete one by one. Begin work on the first day you receive the assignment, and work steadily to avoid a crisis.

WRITING WORKSHOP **211**

Teach

Writing Process

Prewrite Have students think of people in their lives—past and present—who have made an impact on them in some way. These will serve as possible subjects. **Say:** What makes the individuals memorable or special to you? Have students visualize the characters they select to write about and list their qualities in a graphic organizer as shown. Remind them that the traits do not all have to be good, bad, exciting, or unusual. To help students brainstorm, have them consider what they find most admirable, quirky, striking, or irritating about their subjects.

Writing Skills

Peer Response Have each student describe his or her subject aloud to a partner. Encourage the partners to listen closely and to offer ideas for better means (a stronger adjective, a revealing anecdote) to describe the characters.

English Learners
DIFFERENTIATED INSTRUCTION

Beginning Encourage students with limited English speaking ability to describe their characters to you. Help them find better words and techniques, wherever needed, to make their characters come alive on the page.

Approaching Level
DIFFERENTIATED INSTRUCTION

Established Students with well-developed visual abilities often learn best by visualizing a subject. Have students close their eyes and visualize the persons they've chosen to write about. Then have them try to transfer their images to written words.

 **Writing Workshop**

Teach

Writing Skills

Descriptive Details Answer:
Sensory details in this passage include visual details such as "bronzed, weathered face" and "clothes always seem fairly dusty." The passage also includes olfactory details such as "the smell of hay and damp soil." The details begin to create the impression of a man whom people avoid.

Writing Skills

Methods of Characterization

Answer: *Methods of characterization used by this author include a physical description of Grandpa Bob's appearance, as well as details about his behavior ("likes to keep his coat on") and emotions ("he gets along better with animals than most people").*

Writing Skills

Events Answer: *It shows his love for animals and his persistence in the face of opposition.*

Writing Skills

Dialogue Answer: *His words give insight into his outlook on the world.*

Writing Frames

As you read the workshop model, think about the writer's use of the following frames:

- _____ looks as if s/he belongs _____.

- In his/her way, _____ is _____.

- Despite _____, s/he is _____.

Consider using frames like these in your own descriptive essay.

Descriptive Details

How do sensory details and images begin to create an impression of Grandpa Bob?

Methods of Characterization

Which methods of characterization does the writer use here?

Events

How does this event engage the reader?

Dialogue

How does including dialogue help create the character? How does it contribute to the dominant impression?

Draft

Bring Your Character to Life Using your plan as a guide, begin drafting your descriptive essay. Refer often to the notes you made earlier but feel free to add new ideas that come to you as you write. Occasionally, check to be sure that the details you include contribute to the overall impression you want to give your readers.

Analyze a Workshop Model

Here is a final draft of a descriptive essay. Read it and answer the questions in the margin. Use the answers to guide you as you write.

Gruff Grandpa Bob

Standing about six feet tall in cowboy boots, wearing a faded bandana below his bronzed, weathered face, my grandpa Bob looks as if he belongs outdoors. His clothes always seem faintly dusty, even right after they have been washed, and his hair is bleached and wild from decades in the sun and wind. He never sits down unless he's eating—sometimes not even then. As my grandpa himself would admit, he gets along better with animals than most people. Most people tend to keep their distance from him.

He has lived in Montana for much of his life, making house calls as the local veterinarian. I've seen him at work, stomping into a stranger's house or barn with hardly a "hello," often rushing ahead in pursuit of the suffering animal. One offended woman kicked him out of her house for his rudeness. Grandpa, though, wouldn't abandon her sick dog. He paced for half an hour on the woman's porch; finally, she let him in. "What's more important," he said frankly, "making small talk with someone or healing her poor dog?" When they see him on the street, people approach him to thank him—sometimes years later—for coming out after midnight to set a horse's leg or to perform emergency surgery on a dog. He reddens and looks down at the sidewalk with his hands thrust deep in the pockets of his faded jeans. "All right, then," he

Writing Practice

 **Effective Dialogue** Encourage students to use dialogue to develop their characters. What characters say can reveal their emotional states, personalities, backgrounds, and levels of education.

Give students these guidelines:

- Make sure the dialogue has a purpose.

- Keep each character's dialogue consistent with his or her personality, background, education, and time period.
- Make dialogue sound like natural speech by including pauses, interruptions, and even repetition where these might naturally occur.

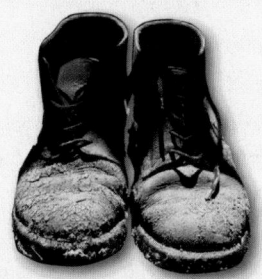

says, nodding shyly. "All right." Then he makes a dash for his truck.

My grandparents have been married for forty-five years, although I've rarely caught them having a typical conversation together. My grandma does most of the talking, but Grandpa never seems to grow tired of her company. Even though he inevitably grumbles under his breath every time Grandma tells him to take off his muddy boots when he comes inside (and she does tell him, every time), you can tell by the way he looks at her and listens to her that he respects her completely. If she's happy, he'll shoot her a wink when he thinks no one's looking; and if she's upset, he'll reach across the table and softly enclose her tiny, shaking hand between his own callused palms.

In his quiet way, Grandpa is a supportive father. He gives my dad and his brothers a hand—whether it's as someone to listen to their troubles or just someone to help paint the garage. Despite his gruff reputation, he's also a great grandpa. He plays games with us, such as soccer, horseshoes and chess; takes us with him to treat dogs, cats, and horses; and always keeps our secrets, no matter what.

Now that he's in his seventies, he's traded in his walking stick for a cane. Most of the townspeople are used to him by now, but the new ones are often a little shocked when they first meet him. "People spend their whole lives talking without saying anything," he once told me. "They might accomplish something worthwhile if they just listened to someone else for a minute." I couldn't agree more.

Command of Language

Which choices show the writer's style? What do you hear in the writer's voice? How does the writer vary sentences and use precise language?

Point of View

What point of view has the writer maintained? How is the choice related to purpose and audience?

Dominant Impression

How does the conclusion help give the audience a lasting impression of Grandpa?

Writing Workshop

Descriptive Essay

Teach

Writing Skills

Command of Language
Answer: *The language seems conversational and down-to-earth, and the use of parentheses ("and she does tell him, every time") makes the language informal. An example of parallel structure: "If she's happy, he'll shoot her a wink… and if she's upset, he'll reach across…" An example of vivid word choice: "callused palms."*

Writing Skills

Point of View/Dominant Impression Answer: *The point of view is third person. It lends an air of objectivity. The impression of Grandpa Rob is that a gruff exterior hides a caring, compassionate man. The last two paragraphs drive home that there is more to him than what the townspeople initially see.*

Cultural History ☆

Horseshoes Horseshoes, or horseshoe pitching, is played with either two or four players in the United States and Canada. The player whose horseshoe is thrown closest to a stake wins a point.

English Learners

DIFFERENTIATED INSTRUCTION

Intermediate English learners may have difficulty finding English words that accurately convey their general ideas, let alone descriptive details. Listing descriptive words and phrases in their native languages before writing may facilitate the writing process. Have these students consult a bilingual dictionary or thesaurus for a list of English equivalent for their words and phrases. Students can then refer to the list to aid them when writing their descriptive essays.

213

Descriptive Essay

Teach

Writing Process

Revise Tell students that they need to grab readers' attention in their opening sentences. Explain that anecdotes, details, and dialogue can bring a subject "to life" for readers.

Writing Skills

Peer Review Remind students who are evaluating others' work to make constructive suggestions. Peer reviewers should keep the following questions in mind as they read the drafts:

- What effect does the description have on me? Is this the effect the writer intended?
- Is there anything in the description I find awkward or confusing?
- What do I like best about the description?

Traits of Strong Writing

Include these traits of strong writing to express your ideas effectively.

Ideas message or theme and the details that develop it

Organization arrangement of main ideas and supporting details

Voice writer's unique way of using tone and style

Word Choice vocabulary a writer uses to convey meaning

Sentence Fluency rhythm and flow of sentences

Conventions correct spelling, grammar, usage, and mechanics

For more information on using the Traits of Strong Writing, see pages R28–R30.

Word Choice

This academic vocabulary word appears in the student model:

abandon (ə ban′ dən) *v.* 1. to withdraw one's support or help from; 2. to give up the control or ownership of forever; *Grandpa, though, wouldn't abandon her sick dog.*

Using academic vocabulary may help strengthen your writing. Try to use one or two academic vocabulary words in your descriptive essay. See the complete list on pages R81–R83.

Revise

Peer Review Once you complete your draft, exchange papers with a partner. Have your partner note any areas that could use more vivid details, better pacing, or more relevant examples. Then have your partner tell his or her impression of your subject. If the impression is not what you intended, discuss ways to clarify your description. Use the checklist below to evaluate and strengthen each other's essays.

Checklist

- ☑ Do you create a dominant impression?
- ☑ Do you select and maintain an appropriate point of view?
- ☑ Do you use methods of characterization such as appearance, words, and actions?
- ☑ Do you present events that reveal character? Do you include sensory details, figurative language, imagery, or other literary devices?
- ☑ Do you reflect a personal style and voice?

▶ Focus Lesson

Elaborate with Descriptive Details

After you delete unimportant details from your essay, focus on elaborating with details that will make your character seem real to your audience. Enhance descriptions with sensory details, and include actions, gestures, and dialogue that reveal personality and emotion.

Draft:

> He gets embarrassed and doesn't say much.

Revision:

> He reddens and <u>looks down at the sidewalk with his hands thrust deep in the pockets</u>[1] of his faded jeans. <u>"All right, then," he says, nodding shyly. "All right."</u>[2] Then he <u>makes a dash for his truck.</u>[3]

1: Describe gestures that reveal emotion.

2: Use dialogue to reveal attitudes and personality.

3: Describe actions that show the character's thoughts.

214 UNIT 1 THE ANGLO-SAXON PERIOD AND THE MIDDLE AGES

Assessment Practice

Writer's Portfolio Writer's portfolios are places where students can store their writing. They are similar to artists' portfolios—collections of drafts and polished work. At the end of the semester, students can include those compositions that they feel best represent their writing abilities and progress.

Tell students that one of the major values of writing portfolios is the opportunity they provide for students to assess themselves.

Edit and Proofread

Get It Right When you have completed the final draft of your essay, proofread it for errors in grammar, usage, mechanics, and spelling. Refer to the Language Handbook, pages R47–R59, as a guide.

Focus Lesson

Use Semicolons as Separators

One use of a semicolon (;) is to separate main clauses joined by a coordinating conjunction if there are commas in the clauses. Another is to separate items in a series if the items contain commas.

Problem: Main clauses run together

If she's happy, he'll shoot her a wink when he thinks no one's looking, and if she's upset, he'll reach across the table and softly enclose her tiny, shaking hand between his own callused palms.

Solution: Separate the two main clauses with a semicolon.

If she's happy, he'll shoot her a wink when he thinks no one's looking; and if she's upset, he'll reach across the table and softly enclose her tiny, shaking hand between his own callused palms.

Problem: Items in a series run together

He plays games with us, such as soccer, horseshoes, and chess, takes us with him to treat dogs, cats, and horses, and always keeps our secrets, no matter what.

Solution: Separate items with a semicolon.

He plays games with us, such as soccer, horseshoes, and chess; takes us with him to treat dogs, cats, and horses; and always keeps our secrets, no matter what.

Present

Finishing Touches Before handing in your revised descriptive essay, be sure that it is typed or neatly handwritten and that you turn in the correct, revised version. Check to see that you have followed your teacher's general guidelines, including length, spacing, font size, and margin requirements.

Peer Review Tips

A classmate may ask you to read his or her descriptive essay. Take your time and jot down notes as you read so you can give constructive feedback. Use the following questions to get started:

- Can you identify the dominant impression of the person or character?
- What narrative techniques contribute to that impression?

Word-Processing Tip

Never rely exclusively on a spelling or grammar check. A program can identify possible errors, but—especially in matters of grammar and punctuation—may be wrong nearly as often as it is right. You must be the final judge of correctness.

 Writer's Portfolio
Place a clean copy of your descriptive essay in your portfolio to review later.

 LOG ON ▶ **Literature** Online

Writing and Research For editing and publishing tools, go to glencoe.com and enter QuickPass code GLB9817u1.

WRITING WORKSHOP **215**

Teach

Writing Process

Edit and Proofread Encourage students to use the Proofreading Checklist on the inside back cover of the textbook. Before they share their work, encourage students to read their essays aloud to themselves, listening not only for errors in grammar but also for the cadence or rhythm of their words. Suggest that students try this technique both as a way of checking for errors or weak spots and as a way of rehearsing for public recitations of the essays.

Writing Process

Present The ways of presenting student writing are numerous: shared reading, bulletin board postings, individual books, class/school/city newspapers, student anthologies, or literary contests. Having a wider audience often will lead students to take more care and pride in their writing.

Writer's Technique ☆

Sentence Variety Sentence variety is one way to make writing more interesting for readers. Using semicolons, commas, conjunctions, and dependent clauses, students can combine some shorter sentences and avoid repetitive sentence formats (example: I went to the store. I bought a pear. I ate it on the way home. *When I went to the store, I bought a pear and ate it on the way home.*).

Approaching Level

DIFFERENTIATED INSTRUCTION

🖥 **Emerging** Approaching-level readers may have trouble understanding that an effective description shows rather than tells readers what the subject is like. As an example, read aloud the following sentence:

She dresses in casual clothes.

Ask students for ways to revise the sentence to make it more lively. *(Possible response: Jeans, canvas shoes, and T-shirts are more her style.)*

Have approaching-level students work with other students to revise their descriptions so that they show rather than tell.

Focus

Summary

In this workshop, students will learn techniques for planning, rehearsing, and delivering a presentation of a photo essay.

Teach

Speaking Skills

Stage Fright Share the following strategies for students who may be nervous about speaking in class:

- Rehearse the presentation often.
- Use note cards.
- Pretend that you are just chatting with a group of friends.
- Make eye contact with the friendliest faces in the classroom.

 For help with creating presentations, see Student Presentation Builder on StudentWorks Plus.

 For Speaking, Listening, and Viewing rubric, see Unit 1 Teaching Resources, pp. 192–193.

216

Learning Objectives

For pages 216–217
In this workshop, you will focus on the following objective:

Speaking and Listening: Presenting a photo-essay.

Find the Right Image
Photo essays often include other kinds of images besides photographs. You can also use drawings, illustrations, or visuals such as posters or collages. You might also use digital images, or digitize your own images, for a slide presentation.

Speaking, Listening, and Viewing Workshop

Photo Essay

Literature Connection In the Prologue to *The Canterbury Tales,* Chaucer describes his characters in great detail.

"He had his son with him, a fine young Squire, a lover and cadet, a lad of fire with locks as curly as if they had been pressed."
—Geoffrey Chaucer, *The Canterbury Tales*

Artists have since used Chaucer's description to create images of what the characters may have looked like, as the pictures on this page show.

You can also use images to describe or represent a person. In a photo essay, an artist combines photographs and other images to represent a person or time in history. The images should combine to create a single controlling impression—perhaps showing the audience why the person represented is noteworthy.

The Squire, detail from *The Canterbury Tales,* 15th c. English School. Vellum. Huntington Library and Art Gallery, San Marino, CA.

> **Assignment** Plan and deliver a photo essay about someone you admire.

The Prioress, detail from *The Canterbury Tales,* 15th c. English School. Vellum. Huntington Library and Art Gallery, San Marino, CA.

The Manciple, detail from *The Canterbury Tales,* 15th c. English School. Vellum. Huntington Library and Art Gallery, San Marino, CA.

The Canon's Yeoman, detail from *The Canterbury Tales,* 15th c. English School. Vellum. Huntington Library and Art Gallery, San Marino, CA.

216 UNIT 1 THE ANGLO-SAXON PERIOD AND THE MIDDLE AGES

Writing Practice

Narrative Remind students that a narrative form will help make their presentation more engaging. Encourage students to

- include a compelling introduction when they are presenting

- use the body of their narrative to weave the images together into a story about the individual's life-changing events and complexities

- write a conclusion that summarizes the most significant aspects of the individual

Plan Your Presentation

Follow these steps to plan your photo essay.

- **Select your subject.** Choose someone interesting or influential in your own life, or in society or history, or use the subject of your descriptive essay.
- **Determine or review your main idea or controlling impression,** and select images that support it.
- **Decide how you will showcase your work.** Will you use an easel, posters, a slide projector, or a computer presentation?
- **Consider the size of the audience** as you determine how large to make your images and where you will display or project them.
- **Evaluate when to use different types of effects.** For example, decide whether to enlarge or crop images. Consider presenting some images as a **montage,** that is, as a single visual display made up of several different images.
- **Order your images** in a logical sequence.
- **Add identifying labels** where you think they might assist your audience in focusing on your controlling impression.
- **Create credit lines for all images,** using standardized citation styles like those for the images on page 216. Place the citations at the bottom of each slide, poster, or picture. Use a readable type, but make it smaller than the type you use for labels.
- **Create a narrative that accompanies and explains the images.** Incorporate transitional words and phrases that show relationships.

Techniques for Delivering a Photo Essay

Verbal Techniques	Nonverbal Techniques
☑ **Volume** Speak loudly and slowly enough so that your audience can understand the background information you provide.	☑ **Eye Contact** Make frequent eye contact with the audience; however, you should also look at the photographs or art to draw attention to important details.
☑ **Pace** Allow the audience enough time to view and react before moving on to the next image.	☑ **Gestures** Use gestures to emphasize ideas in your essay when appropriate.
☑ **Tone** Define any terms your audience may be unfamiliar with; describe any places your audience may not have visited.	☑ **Display** Show your images prominently enough so that your entire audience can see them clearly.

Speaking Frames

Consider using the following frames to explain and link your images:

- This photo/image shows _____.
- Just as in the previous image, here _____.
- Unlike the picture of _____, this illustration/photo/image reflects _____.

Rehearse

You do not need to memorize your presentation. However, you should practice several times to familiarize yourself with what you intend to say and to coordinate your narrative with your images.

Presentation Tips

Use the following checklist to evaluate the presentation of your photo essay.

- Did you choose and display images that the entire audience could see?
- Did you explain and link the images to create and support a single controlling impression of your subject?
- Did you use nonverbal techniques such as gestures and eye contact to connect effectively with your audience?

Literature Online

Speaking, Listening, and Viewing For project ideas, templates, and presentation tips, go to glencoe.com and enter QuickPass code GLB9817u1.

Teach

Viewing Skills

Models Have students go to washingtonpost.com to look at some examples of photo essays. Point out the variety of perspectives, images, and elements in the photographs, and emphasize how, presented together, the photographs tell a complete story of an event, a concept, or a person.

Listening Skills

Peer Assessment Ask students to respond to one another's presentations, using the following criteria:

- Did the speaker engage the audience?
- Was his or her rehearsal evident and delivery smooth?
- Did he or she use effective pacing, volume, and eye contact?
- Were the images prominently displayed?

English Learners

DIFFERENTIATED INSTRUCTION

Beginning English learners need strategies to follow a speaker's presentation. Explain that transitions are words and phrases that introduce new information and signal how that information relates to the rest of the text. Have students brainstorm to develop a list of transitions for future reference. Here are a few examples:

Cause/effect: because, due to, as a result, consequently, therefore

Change in time/location: afterward, suddenly, beyond, in front of

Contrast: but, on the other hand

Degree of importance: above all, least important, primarily

Focus

Summary

The purpose of Independent Reading is to encourage students to read other works from the time period that they have learned about in this unit.

Teach

Literary History ☆

Riddle Me This Encourage students to find more translations of Old English riddles in the library or on the Internet. Have them share what they find with the rest of the class. **Ask:** What do these riddles have in common? How are they different? What purposes do you think the authors had for writing the riddles? Guide students in understanding that the riddles are alike in that they pose questions and the answers often are personified. The riddles differ in length and in the sophistication of their language. Point out that the purpose of the riddles is to entertain, much as riddles and puzzles still do today.

Anglo-Saxon and Medieval Periods

BEFORE THE ADVENT OF CHRISTIANITY IN BRITAIN, THERE WERE NO BOOKS. The first books were produced in monasteries where Anglo-Saxon monks copied religious texts written in Latin onto vellum, a fine parchment made from the skin of a calf. Printing did not come to England until 1476, when William Caxton set up a wooden printing press in a shop near Westminster Abbey. Even with this advance, few people of the time could read. They could listen, however, and traveling minstrels and members of the clergy created a great body of oral literature in order to teach and entertain. Much of this literature was eventually written down.

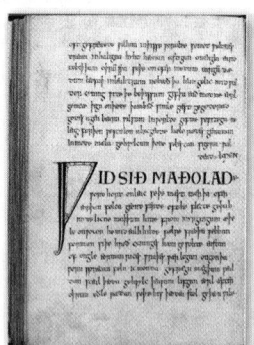

Anglo-Saxon Riddles

We know about Old English riddles today because of their inclusion in the *Exeter Book,* which Leofric, the first bishop of Exeter, willed to the library of Exeter Cathedral before his death in 1072. The book contains thirty-one poems and ninety-five riddles. Try to guess the answer to the following riddle. (A lay is a short poem meant to be sung.)

> *A moth ate words; a marvelous event*
> *I thought it when I heard about that wonder,*
> *A worm had swallowed some man's lay, a thief*
> *In darkness had consumed the mighty saying*
> *With its foundation firm. The thief was not*
> *One whit the wiser when he ate those words.*

Anglo-Saxon riddles can be quite clever, as evidenced by the answer to the one above—a bookworm.

Heroic Poems

Old English poetry often is about brave deeds, allegiance to a military leader, and accounts of victories or, sometimes, defeats. "The Battle of Maldon" is one such poem, inspired by a battle between invading Danes and English defenders in 991. The beginning and ending of the poem no longer exist, but enough remains for readers to visualize what happened during that battle in southeastern England. The English army, led by Byrtnoth, lost the battle. Byrtnoth was killed, and his most faithful men fought on until they, too, were killed. Some soldiers fled the battle, however, and are condemned by the unknown poet.

Writing Practice

Riddles After students have read translations of Old English riddles, have them practice writing their own. Students may choose to rewrite Old English riddles in contemporary style or to make up completely new riddles to entertain the class.

Explain to students that they can use personification when writing the riddles—for example, "I turn up at night, though I have not been fetched. I am gone in the day without being stolen." (a star) Have students try to solve one another's riddles.

Beowulf

This powerful Anglo-Saxon epic follows Beowulf, the greatest of the Geat warriors through various adventures including his battle with Grendel, Grendel's mother, and his final encounter with a dragon before his death.

The Canterbury Tales

In *The Canterbury Tales*, a group of men and women meet at an inn to begin a pilgrimage to the shrine of Thomas à Becket in Canterbury. The inn's host suggests that they while away their time on the long journey by telling stories. Chaucer presents an array of colorful characters who vary widely in social standing, occupation, morality, and wit. The pilgrims come to life through the narrator's vivid descriptions and through the tales they tell.

CRITICS' CORNER

" . . . Sheffelde, a mercer, cam in-to an hows and axed for mete; and specyally he axyed after eggys; and the good wyf answerde, that she coude speke no frenshe. And the merchaunt was angry, for he also coude speke no frenshe, but wolde haue hadde 'egges' and she vunderstode hym not. And theene at laste another sayd that he wolde haue 'eyren' then the good wyf sayd that she vunderstod hym wel. Loo, what sholde a man in thyse dayes now wryte, 'egges' or 'eyren'?"

—William Caxton

When William Caxton began printing in 1476, many forms of English existed. In the anecdote above, Caxton expresses his frustration over the various words being used for eggs.

 Write a Review

Read another tale from *The Canterbury Tales* and write a review of it for your classmates. Be sure to explain why other students might enjoy the tale, and offer suggestions on how they might overcome difficulties in reading it. Present your review to the class.

INDEPENDENT READING **219**

Students' reviews should be geared toward classmates. They should include reading strategies.

Cultural History

Caxton's Press Explain to students that William Caxton began his career by translating a French work, *The Recuyell of the History of Troy.* His translation became very popular, and many important people wanted copies. Because the work of copying the book by hand was wearisome, Caxton set up a printing press like one he had seen in Cologne. His books were the first to be printed in England.

Glencoe Literature Library

Glencoe Literature Library offers an extensive collection of hardcover books that help you encourage your students to read independently. Choose from among the more than 120 full-length literary works—novels, novellas, plays, and nonfiction. Each book includes related readings from a broad range of genres. Go to www.glencoe.com for more information.

 For access to all study guides for the Glencoe Literature Library, see the Literature Library Teacher Resources CD-ROM.

 To create customized reading lists from a database of more than 30,000 titles, use BookLink K-12 CD-ROM.

Established Literature from the Anglo-Saxon period and the Middle Ages will be especially difficult for approaching-level readers. To help these students understand what they read, have them pause to reread passages that are confusing. Explain that rereading is the quickest and most basic way to clarify a passage's meaning. If, after rereading the passage, students still find sentences that they do not understand, have them try to rewrite these sentences in their own words. Remind them that they can use a dictionary and a thesaurus to replace unfamiliar words with words that they already know.

Focus

Bellringer

Say: No matter how hard you study as a student, if you don't know how to go about taking a test, whether multiple choice or essay, you won't score the highest possible mark.

Have students brainstorm to develop a list of key test-taking strategies that have helped them on past tests.

Teach

Assessment Explain to students that the Assessment section will reinforce their general test-taking strategies as well as to test them on the skills and vocabulary covered in the unit. Students will first read a nonfiction selection and answer comprehension, context-clue, and inference questions. After that, they will answer ten sentence-completion questions and seven paragraph-improvement questions and write a short descriptive essay.

 To create custom assessments online, go to Progress Reporter Online Assessment.

 To create custom assessments using software, see ExamView Assessment Suite.

Assessment

English–Language Arts

Reading: Nonfiction

Carefully read the following passage. Use context clues to help you define any words with which you are unfamiliar. Pay close attention to cause-and-effect relationships, the conflicts described, and the tone. Then, on a separate sheet of paper, answer the questions that follow.

*from **The Ecclesiastical History of the English People*** by the Venerable Bede

line

From that time, the south part of Britain, destitute of armed soldiers, of martial stores, and of all its active youth, which had been led away by the rashness of the tyrants, never to return . . . suffered many years under two very savage foreign nations, the Scots from the west, and the Picts from the north. We call these foreign nations, not on account of their being seated out of Britain, but because
5 they were remote from that part of it which was possessed by the Britons . . .

On account of the irruption of these nations, the Britons sent messengers to Rome with letters in mournful manner . . . An armed legion was immediately sent them, which, arriving in the island, and engaging the enemy, slew a great multitude of them, drove the rest out of the territories of their allies, and having delivered them from their cruel oppressors, advised them to build a wall between the two
10 seas across the island, that it might secure them, and keep off the enemy; and thus they returned home with great triumph . . .

But the former enemies, when they perceived that the Roman soldiers were gone, immediately coming by sea, broke into the borders, trampled and overran all places, and like men mowing ripe corn, bore down all before them. Hereupon messengers are again sent to Rome, imploring aid . . . A
15 legion is accordingly sent again, and, arriving unexpectedly in autumn, made great slaughter of the enemy . . . Then the Romans declared to the Britons, that they could not for the future undertake such troublesome expeditions for their sake, advising them rather to handle their weapons like men, and undertake themselves the charge of engaging their enemies, who would not prove too powerful for them, unless they were deterred by cowardice; and, thinking that it might be some help to the
20 allies, whom they were forced to abandon, they built a strong stone wall from sea to sea . . . This famous wall, which is still to be seen, was built at the public and private expense, the Britons also lending their assistance. It is eight feet in breadth, and twelve in height, in a straight line from east to west, as is still visible to beholders . . .

After their departure, the Scots and Picts, understanding that they had declared they would come
25 no more, speedily returned, and growing more confident than they had been before, occupied all the northern and farthest part of the island, as far as the wall . . . At last, the Britons, forsaking their cities and wall, took to flight and were dispersed. The enemy pursued, and the slaughter was greater than

---

Reading Practice

Daily Practice Tell students that reading a little every day not only helps build their vocabulary but also sharpens their critical-thinking skills and prepares them for the type of reading passages in the SAT. One of the best ways to improve writing is to read the works of great writers, such as John Steinbeck and Toni Morrison, and nonfiction from periodicals, such as the *New York Times* and *Scientific American,* which they can find online or in a library.

on any former occasion; for the wretched natives were torn in pieces by their enemies, as lambs are torn by wild beasts. Thus, being expelled their dwellings and possessions, they saved themselves from
30 starvation, by robbing and plundering one another, adding to the calamities occasioned by foreigners . . . till the whole country was left destitute of food, except such as could be procured in the chase.

1. According to Bede, what caused the lack of an active youth in Britain?
   (A) The youth had gone to sea.
   (B) The youth had been killed in battles with the Scots and Picts.
   (C) The people were destitute.
   (D) The people were afraid to fight.
   (E) Tyrants took them away.

2. For what reason does Bede claim that the Scots and Picts were "foreign nations"?
   (A) They lived in a remote part of the island.
   (B) They were invaders.
   (C) They were from outside Britain.
   (D) They were not Christian.
   (E) They were Nordic raiders.

3. Which of the following was an immediate effect of the first invasion of Britain described in the passage?
   (A) The Picts and Scots were slaughtered.
   (B) The Britons sent messengers to Rome.
   (C) The Romans abandoned the Britons.
   (D) The Romans were forced to flee.
   (E) A defensive wall was built to defend the Britons.

4. According to the context, what does the word *slew*, in line 8, mean?
   (A) chased
   (B) killed
   (C) overran
   (D) frightened
   (E) removed

5. According to Bede, what caused the Scots and Picts to return?
   (A) The defensive wall was never built.
   (B) The Britons were unable to defend themselves.
   (C) There were too few resources in their own countries.
   (D) They realized that the Romans had departed.
   (E) They wished to join the Romans.

6. According to the context, what does the word *imploring*, in line 14, mean?
   (A) refusing
   (B) expecting
   (C) issuing
   (D) begging
   (E) remembering

7. According to the context, what does the word *deterred*, in line 19, mean?
   (A) frightened
   (B) ashamed
   (C) restrained
   (D) amused
   (E) reassured

8. Why did the Scots and Picts become "more confident than they had been before"?
   (A) They had overcome Roman defenses.
   (B) They knew that the Romans would not return.
   (C) They had captured the northernmost part of the island.
   (D) The Britons had abandoned their cities.
   (E) The Britons had demonstrated their inability to fight.

Assessment

Assess

1. **E** is the correct answer. Bede explicitly states that all of Britain's active youth "had been led away by the rashness of the tyrants." `DOK 1`

2. **A** is the correct answer. Bede states that the Picts and Scots were foreign because they lived in "remote" parts of the island. `DOK 1`

3. **B** is the correct answer. Bede states that "the Britons sent messengers to Rome" before the other events occurred. `DOK 1`

4. **B** is the correct answer. *Killed* is a synonym of *slew*. `DOK 1`

5. **D** is the correct answer. Nowhere do the claims that the wall was never built, that the invaders had insufficient resources in their countries, or that they wished to join the Romans appear. `DOK 1`

6. **D** is the correct answer. *Begging* is a synonym of *imploring*. `DOK 1`

7. **C** is the correct answer. *Restrained* is a synonym of *deterred*. `DOK 1`

8. **B** is the correct answer. Bede explicitly states that the cause of the invaders' confidence was the permanent departure of the Romans. `DOK 1`

Approaching Level

DIFFERENTIATED INSTRUCTION

Emerging Explain that when students encounter unfamiliar words in their reading, they might use context clues to figure out a word's meaning. Write on board: To end the argument, Steve <u>acquiesced</u> to his sister's demand. Have students focus on the context, or the words around acqui-esced, namely "end the argument" and "his sister's demand." Based on the context of the sentence, what word might be a synonym for *acquiesced*? (accepted).

Assessment

Assess

9. **C** is the correct answer. Bede compares the Britons to lambs and the Scots and Picts to wild beasts. **DOK 1**

10. **B** is the correct answer. Bede states, "They saved themselves from starvation, by robbing and plundering one another." **DOK 1**

11. **E** is the correct answer. Wars, illnesses, and deaths are all types of calamities, but they do not fully define the word in this context, so **A, C,** and **D** are incorrect. *Friendships* makes no sense in this context, so **B** is also incorrect. **DOK 1**

12. **D** is the correct answer. The Romans are less central than the Britons, so **A** is incorrect. The Picts and Scots are the antagonists, and Bede is not a character in this passage, so **B, C,** and **E** are incorrect. **DOK 2**

13. **A** is the correct answer. The conflict is between the Britons and the Scots and Picts. **DOK 2**

14. **C** is the correct answer. The passage is a historical narrative with a reportorial and authoritative tone. **DOK 4**

15. **A** is the correct answer. Clearly, Bede's main purpose was to inform. **DOK 4**

---

9. To what does Bede compare the Scots and Picts?
   - **(A)** Britons
   - **(B)** Romans
   - **(C)** wild beasts
   - **(D)** lambs
   - **(E)** the natives

10. According to Bede, how did some Britons save themselves?
   - **(A)** They joined the Scots and Picts.
   - **(B)** They robbed other Britons.
   - **(C)** They fled to Rome.
   - **(D)** They defeated the invaders.
   - **(E)** They built a defensive wall.

11. From the context, what do you conclude that the word *calamities*, in line 30, means?
   - **(A)** wars
   - **(B)** friendships
   - **(C)** illnesses
   - **(D)** deaths
   - **(E)** disasters

12. Which group or individual is the main protagonist in this passage?
   - **(A)** the Romans
   - **(B)** the Picts
   - **(C)** the Scots
   - **(D)** the Britons
   - **(E)** Bede

13. Which of the following best describes the main external conflict represented in this passage?
   - **(A)** man against man
   - **(B)** man against nature
   - **(C)** man against society
   - **(D)** man against fate
   - **(E)** man against the divine

14. What is the overall tone of this passage?
   - **(A)** angry
   - **(B)** ironic
   - **(C)** authoritative
   - **(D)** skeptical
   - **(E)** sarcastic

15. From this selection, what do you conclude the author's main purpose was?
   - **(A)** to inform
   - **(B)** to persuade
   - **(C)** to instruct
   - **(D)** to entertain
   - **(E)** to tell a story

LOG ON **Literature** Online
Assessment For additional test practice, go to glencoe.com and enter QuickPass code GLB9817u1.

Reading Practice

Find the Main Idea Explain that a main idea is the subject of a passage, which can be stated or implied. Sometimes the main idea is stated in the first paragraph. If it is not stated but implied, one needs to read the entire passage carefully. Students can use the *STAR* method:

Stop—Slow down and relax.

Think—Think it through. How are all the sentences related?

Act—Skim the text and ask, What is the writer trying to say? Choose an answer.

Review—When you have completed the section, quickly review your work.

Vocabulary Skills: Sentence Completion

For each item in the Vocabulary Skills section, choose the word or words that best complete the sentence.

1. Who can say which of the three monsters was Beowulf's greatest _____?
   (A) arrogance
   (B) adversary
   (C) instigation
   (D) rancor
   (E) slander

2. The _____ Viking raiders were known throughout Europe for their unmerciful violence.
   (A) solicitous
   (B) discreet
   (C) infamous
   (D) forged
   (E) writhing

3. During England's Anglo-Saxon period, seafaring was filled with _____ and misery.
   (A) writhing
   (B) instigation
   (C) prevarication
   (D) shroud
   (E) peril

4. Medieval knights were expected to be gallant and to _____ to attain the chivalrous ideal.
   (A) blanch
   (B) aspire
   (C) slander
   (D) dwell
   (E) divulge

5. Anglo-Saxon poetry is filled with _____ imagery that conveys themes of loss and misery.
   (A) doleful
   (B) estimable
   (C) blithe
   (D) intrepid
   (E) frivolous

6. The clergy and the nobility were required at various times to _____ the power of overreaching monarchs.
   (A) disperse
   (B) brandish
   (C) gratify
   (D) restrain
   (E) flourish

7. The two _____ causes of death during the 1300s were war and the bubonic plague.
   (A) dauntless
   (B) diligent
   (C) disdainful
   (D) discreet
   (E) foremost

8. Intense _____ culminated in the brutal Hundred Years' War.
   (A) rancor
   (B) jeopardy
   (C) lament
   (D) composure
   (E) arrogance

9. The power of the church _____ during the Medieval period as at no other time.
   (A) expounded
   (B) admonished
   (C) flourished
   (D) divulged
   (E) slandered

10. Those who _____ in Europe's monasteries dedicated their lives to work and prayer.
    (A) dispersed
    (B) dwelled
    (C) blanched
    (D) sufficed
    (E) brandished

Approaching Level

DIFFERENTIATED INSTRUCTION

Established Explain that comparing and contrasting the possible choices will help students determine a correct answer. Suggest that when they are struggling with a sentence-completion exercise, they should try out each choice and think about whether the word makes sense in the sentence.

Assess

1. **B** is the correct answer. No other option makes sense in this context. (DOK 1)

2. **C** is the correct answer. No other option makes sense in this context. (DOK 1)

3. **E** is the correct answer. **A, B,** and **C** make little sense in this context. **D** makes no sense grammatically. (DOK 1)

4. **B** is the correct answer. No other option makes sense in this context. (DOK 1)

5. **A** is the correct answer. **B** makes no sense in this context. The phrase *loss* and *misery* makes *blithe, intrepid,* and *frivolous* inappropriate, so **C, D,** and **E** are all incorrect. (DOK 1)

6. **D** is the correct answer. **E** makes no sense in context. *Perceive, brandish,* and *deceive* all seem possible; but the word *unwieldy* implies the need for restraint, not perception, the brandishing of power, or deception, so **A, B,** and **C** are all incorrect. (DOK 1)

7. **E** is the correct answer. No other option makes sense in this context. (DOK 1)

8. **A** is the correct answer. **C** makes no sense grammatically. **B, D,** and **E** make no sense in this context. (DOK 1)

9. **C** is the correct answer. No other option makes sense in this context. (DOK 1)

10. **B** is the correct answer. No other option makes sense in this context. (DOK 1)

Assess

1. D is the correct answer. This sentence contains an incorrectly formed contraction. No other option corrects this problem without changing the content or introducing further errors. 〔DOK 1〕

2. B is the correct answer. This sentence contains an incorrect verb tense. No other option corrects this problem without changing the content or introducing further errors. 〔DOK 1〕

3. E is the correct answer. This sentence contains an incorrect verb tense. No other option corrects this problem without changing the content or introducing further errors. 〔DOK 1〕

Grammar and Writing: Paragraph Improvement

Read carefully through the opening paragraphs from the first draft of a student's descriptive essay. Pay close attention to the writer's use of verb tense, commas, and pronouns. Then, on a separate sheet of paper, answer the questions below.

(1) My father is one of the most amazing men I have ever met. (2) Hes a big guy. (3) At over six feet tall, with big suntanned hands that look like baseball mitts, and dark green eyes, dad cuts an impressive figure. (4) He was a fisherman, a painter, and (perhaps most important of all) the person who saved my little brother's life.

(5) When I was fifteen, my father, my brother John, and I are all on an extended fishing trip in the boundary waters, near the Canadian border. (6) Its a wonderful part of the world, lush and clean. (7) We had planned to be gone for a little over two weeks, camping, fishing, canoeing, and trying with little luck to stay dry. (8) "What's the weather going to be like this time of year?" (9) I asked, as we loaded up the van. (10) "Cold, and probably rainy," Dad replied he wasn't lying.

(11) For the first five days there was a constant drizzle, the temperature never climbed above 50 degrees. (12) Then, on the sixth day, rain started lashing down and thunder could be heard at a distance. (13) The wind picked up. (14) The temperature dropped considerably. (15) As the weather rolls in, we huddled in our canoe, trying to catch that night's dinner. (16) None of us had expected this, it arrived so suddenly.

1. Which of the following is the best revision of sentence 2?
   (A) He was a big guy.
   (B) My father and I are big guys.
   (C) We are big guys.
   (D) He's a big guy.
   (E) He's that big of a guy.

2. Which of the following is the best revision of sentence 4?
   (A) He was a fisherman, a painter; and (perhaps most important of all) the person who saved my little brother's life.
   (B) He is a fisherman, a painter, and (perhaps most important of all) the person who saved my little brother's life.
   (C) He was a fisherman, and a painter.
   (D) He was a fisherman, and a painter, and (perhaps most important of all) the person who saved my little brother's life.
   (E) We were fishermen, painters, and people who saved my little brother's life.

3. Which of the following is the best revision of sentence 5?
   (A) When I was fifteen, my father, my brother John, and me are all on an extended fishing trip in the boundary waters, near the Canadian border.
   (B) When I was fifteen, my father, my brother John, and I are all on an extended fishing trip.
   (C) When I was fifteen, my father, my brother John, and me are all on an extended fishing trip.
   (D) My father, my brother John, and I are all on a fishing trip, near the Canadian border.
   (E) When I was fifteen, my father, my brother John, and I were all on an extended fishing trip in the boundary waters, near the Canadian border.

Reading Practice

Reread Tell students that paragraph-improvement exercises are like puzzles. They will have to read the passage more than once to figure out the most logical sequence of sentences. To help students become more comfortable with these exercises, provide practice models that they can work on during their free time. You might take a passage from a book that the class is reading and rearrange the sentences.

4. Which of the following is the best revision of sentence 6?
   - **(A)** It's a wonderful part of the world, lush and clean.
   - **(B)** Its a wonderful part of the world; lush and clean.
   - **(C)** It was a wonderful part of the world, lush and clean.
   - **(D)** Its a wonderful part of the world.
   - **(E)** A wonderful part of the world, its lush and clean.

5. Which of following is the best revision of sentence 10?
   - **(A)** "Probably rainy," Dad wasn't lying.
   - **(B)** "Cold, and probably rainy."
   - **(C)** "Cold, and probably rainy," Dad replied. He wasn't lying.
   - **(D)** Cold, and probably rainy, Dad replied and he wasn't lying.
   - **(E)** My dad replied, and he wasn't lying.

6. Which of the following errors appears in sentence 11?
   - **(A)** run-on sentence
   - **(B)** misplaced modifier
   - **(C)** fragment
   - **(D)** incorrect verb tense
   - **(E)** incorrect parallelism

7. To improve sentence fluency, which of the following sentences in the third paragraph might be enhanced by combining them with a semicolon?
   - **(A)** 11 and 12
   - **(B)** 12 and 13
   - **(C)** 13 and 14
   - **(D)** 14 and 15
   - **(E)** 15 and 16

8. Which of the following is the best revision of sentence 15?
   - **(A)** As the weather rolls in, we huddled in our canoe.
   - **(B)** The weather rolled in, we huddled in our canoe.
   - **(C)** The weather rolls in. We huddled in our canoe. We tried to catch that night's dinner.
   - **(D)** We huddled in our canoe, trying to catch that night's dinner.
   - **(E)** As the weather rolled in, we huddled in our canoe, trying to catch that night's dinner.

9. Which of the following is the best revision of sentence 16?
   - **(A)** None of us expected this, suddenly.
   - **(B)** None of us had expected this, it had arrived so suddenly.
   - **(C)** None of us had expected this, it was arriving so suddenly.
   - **(D)** None of us had expected this; it arrived so suddenly.
   - **(E)** None of us had expected this.

10. While writing the concluding paragraphs of this draft, what should the writer include?
   - **(A)** a description of how the father saved John's life
   - **(B)** a description of the types of fish that can be caught in the boundary waters
   - **(C)** a description of John's appearance
   - **(D)** a statement on the importance of family relationships
   - **(E)** further description of the father's appearance

Essay

Write a descriptive essay in which you explore the character of a person who has had an important influence on your life. How did you first come to know this person? In what ways has he or she influenced you? As you write, keep in mind that your essay will be checked for **ideas, organization, voice, word choice, sentence fluency, conventions,** and **presentation.**

Assess

4. **A** is the correct answer. This sentence incorrectly contains a possessive pronoun. The possessive *its* is being confused with the contraction *it's*. **DOK 1**

5. **C** is the correct answer. This is a run-on sentence. No other option corrects this problem without changing the content or introducing further errors. **DOK 1**

6. **A** is the correct answer. This sentence contains two main clauses separated only by a comma. It is a run-on. **DOK 2**

7. **C** is the correct answer. Sentences 13 and 14 are short and choppy. Combining them with a semicolon would improve sentence fluency. **DOK 4**

8. **E** is the correct answer. This sentence contains and incorrect verb tense. No other option corrects this problem without changing the content or introducing further errors. **DOK 1**

9. **D** is the correct answer. This sentence contains and incorrect verb tense. No other option corrects this problem without changing the content or introducing further errors. **DOK 1**

10. **A** is the correct answer. As is clear from the opening paragraph, what must be included is a description of how John's life was saved. **DOK 4**

Essay

Check to be sure that each student's essay focuses on a person's character and influence and that it is well organized and free of grammatical errors. **DOK 3**

AAVE Remind approaching-level students who are users of African American vernacular English (AAVE) that possessives and contractions can be easily confused. **Write on the board:** The dog lost ___ bone. **Say:** One way to know which form to use is to read the sentence with the contraction spelled out. (in this case, as *The dog lost it is bone.* Since that does not sound right, you know that the contraction is not the correct form to use. Use this technique so that you will always remember whether to use a contraction or the possessive form of a word.

Skills Scope and Sequence

Readability Scores Key: Dale-Chall/DRP/Lexile

PART 1: Humanists and Courtiers

Selections and Features	Literary Elements
Unit Introduction pp. 226–240	Formal Essay **TE** p. 235 Thesis **TE** p. 237 Simile **TE** p. 239
Literary History The Development of the Sonnet pp. 242–243	Sonnet **TE** p. 242
Poem and Speech On Monsieur's Departure and **Speech to the Troops at Tilbury,** by Elizabeth I 9.3/59/1430 pp. 244–249	Tone **SE** p. 245 Internal Conflict (review) **SE** p. 248
Poem Whoso List to Hunt, by Sir Thomas Wyatt pp. 250–253	Figurative Language **SE** p. 251 Rhyme Scheme **TE** p. 252
Vocabulary Workshop p. 254	
Sonnets Sonnet 30 and **Sonnet 75,** by Edmund Spenser pp. 255–260	Rhyme Scheme **SE** p. 256 Tone (review) **SE** p. 259
Sonnet Sonnet 31, by Sir Philip Sidney pp. 261–264	Apostrophe **SE** p. 262
Poem The Passionate Shepherd to His Love, by Christopher Marlowe pp. 265–268	Point of View **SE** p. 266
Poem The Nymph's Reply to the Shepherd, by Sir Walter Raleigh pp. 269–272	Author's Purpose **SE** p. 270
Essay Of Studies, by Sir Francis Bacon 10.2/65/700 pp. 273–279	Parallelism **SE** p. 274 Author's Purpose **SE** p. 278
Grammar Workshop p. 280	

Reading Skills and Strategies	Vocabulary	Writing Grammar	Speaking, Listening, Viewing
Use the Timeline **TE** p. 228 Make Inferences **TE** p. 229 Construct Graphic Organizers **TE** p. 230 Use Maps **TE** p. 231 Identify Main Idea and Details **TE** p. 232			View the Art **SE** p. 226 Organize Ideas **TE** p. 236
Analyze Text Structure **SE** p. 245 Compare and Contrast **TE** p. 246	Synonyms **SE** p. 249 Academic Vocabulary **SE** p. 249	Write a Persuasive Speech or Essay **SE** p. 249	
Clarify Meaning **SE** p. 251		Write a Poem **SE** p. 253	
	Dictionary Use **SE** p. 254 Word Choice **TE** p. 254		
Connect to Personal Experience **SE** p. 256	Word Origins **SE** p. 260 Academic Vocabulary **SE** p. 260	Write a Sonnet **TE** p. 258	Conduct an Interview **SE** p. 260
Examine Denotation and Connotation **SE** p. 262	Analogies **SE** p. 264	Write a Letter **SE** p. 264	
Analyze Sound Devices **SE** p. 266 Predict **TE** p. 266	Academic Vocabulary **SE** p. 268	Write a Poem **SE** p. 268	
Compare and Contrast Speakers **SE** p. 270 Build Background **SE** p. 270	Academic Vocabulary **SE** p. 272	Write a List **SE** p. 272	
Determine Main Idea and Supporting Details **SE** p. 274	Word Parts **SE** p. 278 Academic Vocabulary **SE** p. 278	Write an Expository Essay **SE** p. 279 Semicolons **SE** p. 279	Create a Concept Map **SE** p. 277
		Subject-Verb Agreement **SE** p. 280 Predicate Nominative **TE** p. 280	

Readability Scores Key: Dale-Chall/DRP/Lexile

PART 2: A Bard for the Ages

Selections and Features	Literary Elements
Sonnets Sonnet 116 and **Sonnet 130,** by William Shakespeare pp. 282–287	Simile and Metaphor **SE** p. 284
Sonnets Sonnet 73 and **Sonnet 29,** by William Shakespeare pp. 288–290	Simile **SE** p. 288
Songs Fear No More the Heat o' the Sun and **Blow, Blow, Thou Winter Wind,** by William Shakespeare pp. 291–294	Theme **SE** p. 291
Soliloquies To be or not to be *from* **Hamlet,** and **All the world's a stage** *from* **As You Like It,** and **Our revels now are ended** *from* **The Tempest,** by William Shakespeare pp. 295–303	Voice **SE** p. 295 Extended Metaphor **TE** p. 298 Figurative Language (review) **SE** p. 302
Literary History Shakespeare's Theater pp. 304–305	Blank Verse **TE** p. 305
Play Macbeth, Act 1, by William Shakespeare pp. 306–326	Atmosphere **SE** p. 306 Drama **TE** p. 308
Play Macbeth, Act 2, by William Shakespeare pp. 327–341	Motif **SE** p. 327 Verse and Meter **TE** p. 330
Play Macbeth, Act 3, by William Shakespeare pp. 342–359	Foil **SE** p. 342 Dynamic Characters **TE** p. 346
Play Macbeth, Act 4, by William Shakespeare pp. 360–379	Plot **SE** p. 360 Imagery **TE** p. 362 Meter and Rhyme Scheme **TE** p. 364 Dramatic Irony **TE** p. 370
Play Macbeth, Act 5, by William Shakespeare pp. 380–397	Tragedy **SE** p. 380 Dialogue **SE** p. 382 Irony (review) **SE** p. 396

Reading Skills and Strategies	Vocabulary	Writing / Grammar	Speaking, Listening, Viewing
Analyze Figures of Speech **SE** p. 284 Analyze Text **TE** p. 286	Synonyms **TE** p. 284 Synonyms **SE** p. 287	Write a Poem **SE** p. 287	
Draw Conclusions About Speaker's Meaning **SE** p. 288	Academic Vocabulary **SE** p. 290	Write an Essay **SE** p. 290	
Respond to Tone **SE** p. 291 Analyze Tone **TE** p. 292	Word Origins **SE** p. 294	Write a Movie Scene **SE** p. 294	
Draw Conclusions About Theme **SE** p. 295	Context Clues **TE** p. 300, **SE** p. 302 Academic Vocabulary **SE** p. 302	Write a Reflective Essay **SE** p. 303	Compare Speeches **SE** p. 296 Use a Text Diagram **SE** p. 301
Preview **TE** p. 304			
Apply Background Knowledge **SE** p. 306 Predict **TE** p. 312 Make Inferences **TE** p. 322	Word Parts **TE** p. 318, **SE** p. 326	Sentence Structure **TE** p. 310 Write a Description **TE** p. 314 Write a Narrative **TE** p. 320 Write a Brochure **SE** p. 326	Readers' Theater **TE** p. 316 View the Art **TE** p. 321
Evaluate Credibility **SE** p. 327 Make Inferences **TE** p. 332 Analyze Tragedy **TE** p. 340	Prefixes **TE** p. 338 Word Origins **SE** p. 341	Subordinate Conjunctions **TE** p. 328 Write a Scene **TE** p. 334 Write a Summary **SE** p. 341	Read Aloud **TE** p. 336
Evaluate Style **SE** p. 342 Paraphrase **TE** p. 344 Visualize **TE** p. 350	Antonyms **SE** p. 359	Write an Essay **TE** p. 348 Write a Paragraph **TE** p. 352 Write a Research Report **TE** p. 356 Write a Letter **SE** p. 359	
Make and Verify Predictions **SE** p. 360 Analyze Literary Periods **TE** p. 366 Make Inferences **TE** p. 376	Word Usage **SE** p. 379	Write a Letter **TE** p. 368 Write a Campaign Speech **TE** p. 372 Write an Essay **TE** p. 378 Write a Dramatic Monologue **SE** p. 379	Read Aloud **TE** p. 362 Read Speeches Aloud **TE** p. 374
Analyze Cause-and-Effect Relationships **SE** p. 380 Question **TE** p. 386 Analyze Character Transformation **TE** p. 388	Context Clues **SE** p. 396 Academic Vocabulary **SE** p. 396	Write a Speech **TE** p. 384 Write a Narrative **TE** p. 390 Conjunctions **TE** p. 392 Write an Expository Essay **SE** p. 397 Colons **SE** p. 397	

Readability Scores Key: Dale-Chall/DRP/Lexile

PART 2: A Bard for the Ages *(continued)*

Selections and Features	Literary Elements
Visual Perspective **Throne of Blood** *from* **Shakespeare on Screen,** by Daniel Rosenthal **10.0**/**69**/1350 pp. 398–401	
Informational Text **TIME**: **Midsummer Night's Spectacle,** by William A. Henry III **10.7**/**69**/1240 pp. 402–404	

PART 3: The Sacred and the Secular

Selections and Features	Literary Elements
Sacred Texts *from* **Genesis** 6.9/57/970 and **Psalm 23** pp. 406–415	Style **SE** p. 407 Parallelism (review) **SE** p. 414
Poem **Eve's Apology,** by Aemilia Lanyer pp. 416–419	Argument **SE** p. 417
Literary History **The Metaphysical Poets** pp. 420–421	Figurative Language **TE** p. 420
Poems **Song** and **A Valediction: Forbidding Mourning** and **Death Be Not Proud,** by John Donne pp. 422–429	Meter **SE** p. 423 Metaphysical Conceit **TE** p. 424 Theme (review) **TE** p. 428
Prose Meditation **Meditation 17,** by John Donne **7.6**/**60**/1140 pp. 430–435	Metaphysical Conceit **SE** p. 430 Motif (review) **SE** p. 434
Vocabulary Workshop p. 436	
Poem **On My First Son,** by Ben Jonson pp. 437–440	Elegy **SE** p. 438
Poem **Song: To Celia,** by Ben Jonson pp. 441–443	Lyric Poetry **SE** p. 441 Rhyme Scheme (review) **SE** p. 442
Literary History **The Cavalier Poets** pp. 444–445	Conceit **SE** p. 444
Comparing Literature **To the Virgins, to Make Much of Time** (poem), by Robert Herrick, **Carpe Diem** (poem), by Horace, **To Helene** (poem), by Pierre de Ronsard, and *from* **The Rubáiyát** (poem), by Omar Khayyám pp. 446–455	Universal Theme **SE** p. 446 Carpe Diem **SE** p. 448

Reading Skills and Strategies	Vocabulary	Writing / Grammar	Speaking, Listening, Viewing
Compare and Contrast Genres **SE** p. 398	Word Origins **TE** p. 400	Appositives **TE** p. 398	
Distinguish Fact from Opinion **SE** p. 402 Main Idea and Supporting Details **TE** p. 402		Write a Summary **SE** p. 404	
Analyze Text Structure **SE** p. 407	Synonyms **SE** p. 415	Write a Definition **TE** p. 412	Illustrations **TE** p. 410 Oral Interpretation **SE** p. 415
Draw Conclusions About Author's Beliefs **SE** p. 417 Evaluate **TE** p. 418	Context Clues **SE** p. 419	Write an Editorial **SE** p. 419	
	Words in Context **TE** p. 420		
Analyze Figures of Speech **SE** p. 423	Word Usage **SE** p. 429 Academic Vocabulary **SE** p. 429	Compound Subjects and Predicates **TE** p. 424 Paraphrase the Poem **TE** p. 426	Oral Report **SE** p. 429
Make Inferences About Theme **SE** p. 430 Summarize **TE** p. 432	Analogies **SE** p. 434 Academic Vocabulary **SE** p. 434	Write a Summary **SE** p. 435 Introductory Clauses **SE** p. 435	
	Analogies **SE** p. 436		
Question **SE** p. 438 Preview **TE** p. 438	Academic Vocabulary **SE** p. 440	Write a Dialogue **SE** p. 440	
Make Inferences **SE** p. 441	Academic Vocabulary **SE** p. 443		Literature Groups **SE** p. 443
	Multiple Meanings **TE** p. 444		
Compare and Contrast **SE** p. 446 Analyze Sound Devices **SE** p. 448 Evaluate **TE** p. 448 Preview **TE** p. 448 Main Idea and Supporting Details **TE** p. 454	Academic Vocabulary **SE** p. 450	Write a Poem **SE** p. 450 Write a Comparison **TE** p. 452	

Readability Scores Key: Dale-Chall/DRP/Lexile

PART 3: The Sacred and the Secular *(continued)*

Selections and Features	Literary Elements
Poem Why So Pale and Wan, Fond Lover?, by Sir John Suckling pp. 456–459	Form **SE** p. 457
Poem To Lucasta, Going to the Wars, by Richard Lovelace pp. 460–463	Paradox **SE** p. 461
Poem To His Coy Mistress, by Andrew Marvell pp. 464–469	Hyperbole **SE** p. 465 Carpe Diem (review) **SE** p. 468
Writing Workshop pp. 470–479	
Speaking, Listening, and Viewing Workshop pp. 480–483	
Independent Reading pp. 484–485	
Assessment pp. 486–491	

Reading Skills and Strategies	Vocabulary	Writing Grammar	Speaking, Listening, Viewing
Apply Background Knowledge **SE** p. 457 Summarize and Evaluate **SE** p. 458	Synonyms **SE** p. 459	Write a Journal Entry **SE** p. 459	
Paraphrase **SE** p. 461	Context Clues **SE** p. 463	Write a Letter **SE** p. 463	
Preview **SE** p. 465 Analyze Humor **TE** p. 466	Analogies **SE** p. 469 Academic Vocabulary **SE** p. 469	Write an Essay **SE** p. 469	
		Write a Historical Investigation Report **SE** p. 470 Prewrite **SE** p. 471 Draft **SE** p. 473 Revise **SE** p. 478	
		Make an Outline **TE** p. 482	Multimedia Presentation **SE** p. 480 Make a Storyboard **TE** p. 480
Identify Tone **TE** p. 484			
		Write an Essay **SE** p. 491	

Focus

Bellringer Options

Literature Launcher
  Pre-Reading Video: Unit 2

Daily Language Practice
  Transparency 16

Or write on the board:
Renaissance

Ask: What do you know about the meaning of this word? Elicit students' ideas about the etymology and definition of the word as well as details about the culture of the period. *(Students may define Renaissance as "rebirth." They may mention fifteenth through seventeenth century Europe. They may know that the Renaissance started in Italy and spread throughout Europe.)*

 For students who would profit from independent novel study, see Novel Companion pp. 51–118.

 For school-to-home activities, see Unit 2 Teaching Resources Book, pp. 5–11.

The Family of Henry VIII: An Allegory of the Tudor Succession, c. 1570–1575. Lucas de Heere. Oil on panel. National Museum and Gallery of Wales, Cardiff.

View the Art Queen Elizabeth I (shown in the right foreground) commissioned this allegorical painting after taking over the throne from Mary I, shown on the left. What do the figures accompanying each woman suggest about Elizabeth's reasons for having the painting done? ★

226

Unit Introduction Skills

Reading Skills
- Analyze Graphic Information (SE pp. 223–231)
- Interpret (SE pp. 235–239)

The English Renaissance

Listening/Speaking/Viewing Skills
- Group Debate (SE p. 240)
- Create Visual Displays (SE p. 240)

Literary Elements
- Soliloquy (TE p. 237)

Writing Skills/Grammar
- Write a Journal (SE p. 240)

The English RENAISSANCE

1485–1650

Looking Ahead

Near the end of the 1400s, a cultural movement known as the Renaissance, which had begun in Italy a century earlier, reached England. Although the next one hundred fifty years in England were marked by bitter conflicts at home and military threats from abroad, they also produced some of the greatest works of English literature, notably William Shakespeare's plays and the King James Bible.

Keep the following questions in mind as you read:

➤➤ What were the characteristics of Renaissance humanism?

➤➤ How is humanism reflected in Shakespeare's works?

➤➤ How did the metaphysical and Cavalier poets respond to the religious conflicts of their time?

227

Focus

Summary

This introduction gives an overview of British literature and events and world events from 1485 to 1650. It covers the transition in literature to a focus on secular subjects, the role of William Shakespeare in the English Renaissance, and the sharp contrast between the sacred and the secular during this period. Economics and geography are also discussed.

View the Art ★

Lucas de Heere (1534–1584) was a Flemish painter who fled religious persecution to settle in England. This work was commissioned by Queen Elizabeth, who appears in the foreground of the painting.

Answer: *Students may infer that Mary brings war, while Elizabeth brings peace and prosperity.*

Unit Resources

Print Materials

- Unit 2 Teaching Resources, pp. 1–374.
- Standards Practice Reader (On Level, Approaching, EL), pp. 83–128.
- Novel Companion, pp. 51–118
- Bellringer Option Transparencies: Selection Focus 10–22; Daily Language Practice 16–28
- Literary Element Transparencies 105, 106, 61, 98, 18

- Assessment Resources, Unit Assessment, pp. 9–16
- Assessment Resources, Selection Assessment, pp. 85–140

Technology

- TeacherWorks Plus CD
- StudentWorks Plus CD
- Literature Launchers: Pre-Reading Videos DVD, Unit 2
- Literature Online
- Interactive Vocabulary CD-ROM
- Listening Library CD-ROM
- ExamView CD-ROM
- Skill Level Up! CD-ROM

UNIT TWO

Teach

Use the Timeline Help students read the timeline and relate key events in British literature to British and world history.

- Explain that the Renaissance began in Italy in the fourteenth century and arrived in England around 1475.
- The English Renaissance was defined by a humanistic revival in art, literature, and learning.
- Tell students that Sir Francis Bacon is called the father of inductive reasoning, which became very important to scientific study.

Say: Identify on the timeline two scientific events that occurred after the publication of Bacon's essays. *(Students will likely choose Harvey's discovery of blood circulation in 1616 and Galileo's telescope in 1609.)*

Political History ☆

Henry VIII The monarch Henry VIII served as King of England from 1509 to 1547. He may be most remembered for breaking ties with the Catholic Church. Pope Clement VII would not permit Henry to divorce his wife, Catherine of Aragon. Henry VIII blamed her for not producing a son to inherit the crown. Thomas Cromwell, Henry's advisor, led a revolution which led to the formation of the Church of England and permitted Henry to marry his second wife, Anne Boleyn.

228

Timeline
1485–1650

Dr. Faustus, seventeenth c. engraving.

BRITISH LITERATURE

1475

1476
William Caxton establishes first printing press in England

1516
Sir Thomas More writes *Utopia* ▶

1549
Book of Common Prayer is published

1550

1557
Tottel's Miscellany, an early collection of English songs and sonnets, is published

1564
William Shakespeare is born

1576
First professional playhouse opens in London

c. 1582
Sir Philip Sidney writes *Astrophel and Stella*

1590
Sir Edmund Spenser publishes first part of *The Faerie Queene*

1597
Sir Francis Bacon's first **1**
essays are published

1599
Globe Theatre, home of Shakespeare's company, is founded

BRITISH EVENTS

1475

1485
Wars of the Roses end; Henry VII begins reign (until 1509)

1509
Henry VIII begins reign (until 1547)

1534 ☆
Henry VIII breaks with Roman Catholic Church ▶

1547
Edward VI begins reign (until 1553)

1550

1553
Mary I begins reign (until 1558)

1558
Elizabeth I begins reign (until 1603)

1580
Sir Francis Drake circumnavigates globe

1588
English navy defeats Spanish Armada

Queen Elizabeth I medal c. 1588

WORLD EVENTS

1475

1492
Columbus reaches New World

1498
Vasco Da Gama reaches India

1550

1520
Suleiman the Magnificent becomes ruler of Ottoman Empire

1543
Copernicus publishes heliocentric theory ▶

1556
Akbar becomes ruler of Mughal Empire

1580
Michel de Montaigne publishes *Essais* (*Essays*)

LOG ON ▶ **Literature** Online

Literature and Reading To explore the Interactive Timeline, go to glencoe.com and enter QuickPass code GLB9817u2.

Reading Practice

Timeline Explain that a timeline is a chart that shows a sequence of events. Point out and name the three timelines on these pages.

- Review briefly that events appear in time order, from left to right.
- Point out how events from 1475 to 1650 appear in a double-wide column.
- Check comprehension.

Ask: How many years elapsed between Vasco Da Gama's reaching India and the East India Company's being chartered? *(102 years)*

1600

1604
☆ Christopher Marlowe's *Doctor Faustus* is published

1609
Shakespeare's sonnets are published

1610–1611
John Donne writes *Holy Sonnets*

▲
1611
King James Bible is published

1616
William Shakespeare dies

1623
First Folio, Shakespeare's collected works, is published

1640

1642
Theaters are closed by order of Puritans

1648
Robert Herrick publishes *Hesperides*

Map of Virginia, c. 1590

1600

1600
East India Company is chartered

1603
Elizabeth I dies; James I begins reign (until 1625)

1605
Gunpowder Plot is uncovered

2 **1607**
Jamestown colony is established ▶

1616
William Harvey discovers circulation of the blood

1625
Charles I begins reign (until 1649)

1642
Civil war erupts

1649
Charles I is beheaded; Oliver Cromwell becomes Lord Protector

1600

1603
Edo (Tokyo) becomes new capital of Tokugawa Japan

1605
Miguel de Cervantes writes *Don Quixote*, Part I

1606
Dutch painter Rembrandt is born

▲
1609
Galileo constructs his first telescope

1619
First enslaved Africans arrive in America

1624
Japan prohibits European contact

1640

1644
Ming Dynasty ends in China ▶

Hizen ware, c. seventeenth century

Reading Check

Analyze Graphic Information Who ruled England longer, Queen Elizabeth I or King James I?

INTRODUCTION **229**

UNIT TWO

Teach

Reading Check

Answer: *Queen Elizabeth I ruled England longer than King James I.*

| **Reading Strategy** | **2** |

Make Inferences Ask: What are some general topic categories that would cover several events on the timelines? *(Students may say religion, exploration, and science.)*

ENGLISH LEARNERS Help English Learners understand the significance of these timeline elements by briefly reviewing the historic background. Involve other students in the process.. **Say:** Can someone explain the importance of the Jamestown Colony? *(Answers should focus on the settlement being the first colony of Europeans in America.)*

Literary History ☆

Faust The play *Doctor Faustus* by Christopher Marlowe was based on a translation of a German Faust text. Faust is a character with artistic and intellectual gifts who trades his soul to the devil for greater power over matter. He is unconcerned about his soul because he does not believe in eternal life. It seems Marlowe did, however, as the play ends with Faust's being carried away by demons.

Approaching Level

DIFFERENTIATED INSTRUCTION

Established Have students choose an event from the timelines. Each student should use online or offline sources to learn more about the event and to prepare a brief oral presentation. During the presentations students should address the following questions: When and where did the event occur? Who was involved in the event? What caused the event? Why is the event significant? Have students find and show a visual related to the event during the presentation.

229

Teach

Interpret Graphic Aids

Refer students to the two graphs under the heading "Spanish and English Losses."

Ask: What can you conclude about the conflict on the basis of the two graphs? *(The English had more ships and fewer personnel engaged in battle. The Spanish suffered much greater losses in the conflict.)*

Political History ☆

Earning Power Today in the United States, about 10 percent of the population controls 69.8 percent of the nation's wealth, while about 50 percent of the population shares just 2.8 percent of the nation's wealth.

By the Numbers

The Spanish Armada

In 1588, during the reign of Elizabeth I, England became one of the great sea powers of the world. In that year, Philip II of Spain sent the Spanish Armada, a huge fleet of warships, to fight England's small navy. Philip sought to overthrow England's Protestant monarch and restore the supremacy of the Roman Catholic Church in England. The English navy won an impressive victory, aided by the inhospitable climate of the English seas. The defeated survivors of the "invincible Armada" returned to Spain, and England's mastery over the seas was unchallenged thereafter.

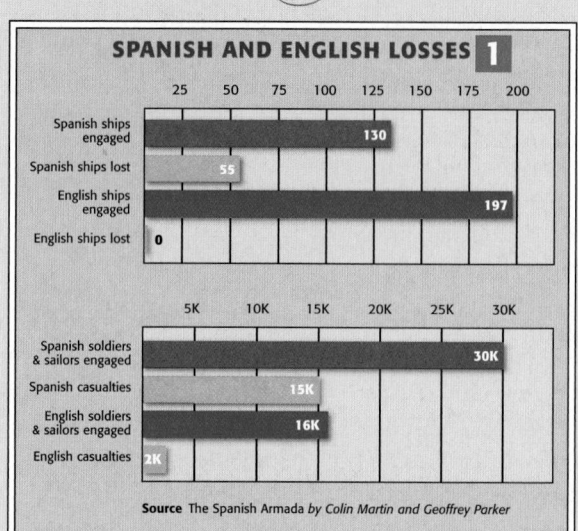

SPANISH AND ENGLISH LOSSES

	25	50	75	100	125	150	175	200
Spanish ships engaged					130			
Spanish ships lost		55						
English ships engaged								197
English ships lost	0							

	5K	10K	15K	20K	25K	30K
Spanish soldiers & sailors engaged						30K
Spanish casualties			15K			
English soldiers & sailors engaged				16K		
English casualties	2K					

Source *The Spanish Armada* by Colin Martin and Geoffrey Parker

HOLIDAYS

A 1552 act prohibited work on Sundays and listed 23 feast day holidays, with 11 more days off at Easter, Whitsun (the seventh Sunday after Easter), and Christmas.

EXECUTIONS

In Tudor England, executions for treason were not uncommon. According to a recent study, Henry VIII executed 308 people for treason between 1532 and 1540. Mary I, Henry's Catholic daughter, executed 132 for that crime during her five-year reign. Later, Elizabeth I, Henry's Protestant daughter, executed 183 traitors during her long reign.

LONDON'S POPULATION

During this period, plague swept through London in 1498, 1535, 1543, 1563, 1589, 1593 (over 10,000 deaths), 1603 (over 25,000 deaths), 1625 (over 26,000 deaths), and 1636. Nevertheless, the population of the city grew steadily. In 1500 approximately 50,000 people lived in London; a century later, approximately four times as many inhabitants lived there.

THEATER PRICES

The Globe and other outdoor playhouses held approximately 3,000 spectators. The "groundlings," who stood in the large central courtyard, paid a penny to enter— roughly equivalent to the price of a movie ticket today; those who wished to sit in the covered galleries paid from two to twelve pennies.

EARNING POWER ☆

During Shakespeare's time, approximately 2 percent of the population controlled most of the nation's land and wealth. The incomes for some members of this upper class reached nearly $94,000 a year. Yeomen—free, land-owning farmers—earned from $94 to $188 a year. A teacher earned about $28.80 a year; a laborer, a shilling, or about 9 cents, a day.

Reading Practice

SPIRAL REVIEW **Construct Graphic Organizers** Refer students to the text under the heading "Executions." **Ask:** What kind of graphic organizer might provide a good summary of this information? *(Students might propose a three-column chart with headings "Monarch," "Years of Reign," and "Number Executed for Treason")* Have students create graphic representations of the information under the headings "Executions," "London's Population," and "Earning Power."

Being There

A *Musicians at Wadley House,* detail from *The Life and Death of Sir Henry Unton,* c. 1596. English school. Oil on panel. National Portrait Gallery, London.

B *The Southeast Prospect of Hampton Court, Herefordshire,* c. 1699. Leonard Knyff. Oil on canvas, 58½ x 84½ in. Yale Center for British Art, Paul Mellon Collection, New Haven, CT.

C *A Fete at Bermondsey,* c. 1570. Joris Hoefnagel. Hatfield House, Hertfordshire, England.

By the early 1600s, England, Scotland, and Wales were politically united under King James I. London, the hub of the nation's economy, was now one of the great capitals of Europe with a population exceeding 100,000. Tudor and Stuart monarchs lived in gorgeous palaces in or near London. Many writers spent their entire lives working in London or its suburbs.

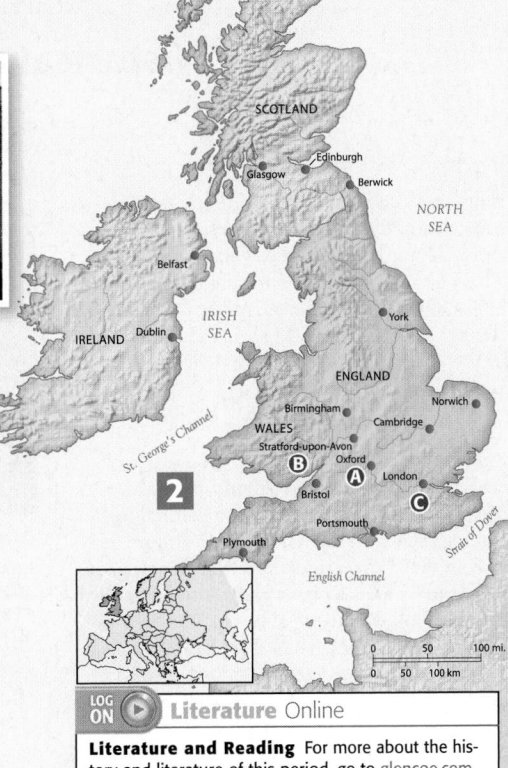

LOG ON ▶ **Literature** Online

Literature and Reading For more about the history and literature of this period, go to glencoe.com and enter QuickPass code GLB9817u2.

Reading Check

Analyze Graphic Information:

1. In 1588, what percentage of the ships in the Spanish Armada were lost?

2. At the Globe Theatre, how many times more was the highest price of admission than the lowest one?

3. About how many miles from London is Shakespeare's birthplace, Stratford-upon-Avon?

Advanced Learners

DIFFERENTIATED INSTRUCTION

Research Ask students to select one of the Renaissance Britain cities on the map during the 1400s and 1500s. Have them research the city and answer the following questions: What was the city's population at this time? What did the city's population do for a living? Did the city's location provide any special benefits for the city (i. e. water supply, transportation, defense, etc.)? How did the city contribute to the arts and sciences of the time? What ordinary day like? Why was the city significant to Renaissance Britain? Have each student present his or her research to the class.

Teach

Reading Check

Answers:

1. *Approximately 42 percent*
2. *12 times*
3. *Approximately 80 miles (130 kilometers)*

Reading Strategy | 2

Use Maps If necessary, help students interpret the map. **Ask:** Which place is closest to London: Wadley House, Hampton Court, or Bermondsey? *(Bermondsey is closest to London.)*

View the Art ★

A. It is believed that the painting of scenes from Sir Henry Unton's life was created at the request of a family member after his death.

B. During most of the English Renaissance, Hampton Court was the seat of the noble Coningsby family.

C. Hoefnagel's piece shows a lavish wedding banquet.

Ask: What can you learn about Renaissance lifestyles from the art? *(Lifestyles of the wealthy could be quite extravagant.)*

Teach

Reading Strategy   1

Ask Questions Have students read the first two sections of text on page 232. **Ask:** What questions do you have about what you have read so far? *(Some students may not understand the references to "Tudor," and "House of York" or know the significance of the Wars of the Roses.)* Where could you find answers to your questions? *(Students may mention dictionaries, encyclopedias, and on-line resources.)*

View the Art ★

The battle between the English forces and the Spanish Armada in 1588 was the first naval battle in history that relied on heavy artillery. The English ships had an advantage because they were better armed than the Spanish ships. This, along with the violent weather that inflicted heavy damage on the Armada, resulted in the Armada's eventual defeat.

Learning Objectives

For pages 226–240
In studying this text, you will focus on the following objectives:

Reading:
Analyzing a literary period.
Evaluating historical influences.
Connecting to the literature.

The English Renaissance

1485–1650

Historical and Cultural Forces

Tudor England

Henry VII's defeat of Richard III and marriage to a member of the House of York ended the thirty-year civil war known as the Wars of the Roses. Although religious and political conflicts divided England under the Tudor monarchs—Henry VII, Henry VIII, Edward VI, Mary I, and Elizabeth I—by the late 1500s, a burst of creative energy had brought a golden age to England.

The Renaissance

As England became an economic and naval power, it was also influenced by a cultural movement known as the Renaissance. Beginning in Italy in the fourteenth century, the Renaissance ("rebirth" in French) later swept into France, Holland, and the other nations of Western Europe, including England. This period marked the transition between the Middle Ages and the modern world and was characterized by a renewed interest in science, art, and all learning that had flourished in ancient Greece and Rome.

During the Middle Ages, many pre-Christian literary masterpieces gathered dust in monastery libraries, largely unnoticed. In the early Renaissance, however, scholars such as the Italian poet Francesco Petrarch (pē´ trärk) rediscovered these classical works. Dazzled by what he found,

Sea Battle Between the Spanish Armada and English Naval Forces, 1600. Hendrik Cornelisz Vroom. Oil on canvas, 91 x 153 cm. Landesmuseum Ferdinandeum, Innsbruck, Austria. ★

Petrarch was angry at earlier generations who had "permitted . . . the writings that their ancestors had produced by toil and application, to perish through insufferable neglect."

Humanism

An era of intellectual inquiry and artistic activity, the Renaissance produced a new movement called humanism. In general, humanists relished new ideas and shared a lively interest in the affairs of this world, not the afterlife. Political and scientific

Reading Practice

SPIRAL REVIEW **Identify Main Idea and Details** Work with students to analyze the paragraphs under the heading "The Renaissance." **Ask:** What is the main idea of the first paragraph? *(The Renaissance involved a departure from the values of the Middle Ages.)* How do the details in the sec-ond paragraph support the main idea? *(The Middle Ages were less notable for education and literature than the Renaissance was.)*

questions intrigued them, as did philosophical and religious ones. People painted, sculpted, and composed music as never before. The act of reading classical works emphasized the ability of the individual to think independently, without guidance from higher authorities.

The French writer Michel de Montaigne (mon tän´) exemplified the new humanistic ideal. In 1571 he retired from public life to devote himself to reading and reflection on subjects that piqued his curiosity. Modeling his skeptical, independent quest for truth on that of the ancient Greek philosopher Socrates, Montaigne took as his motto the question "Que sais-je?" ("What do I know?"). To explore that question, he wrote brief prose discussions, which he called **essais**, or "attempts."

The Protestant Refomation

During the early 1500s, a religious revolution that had begun in central Europe was spreading across the continent. It was called the Protestant Reformation and was a protest against the powerful Roman Catholic Church that significantly influenced the social, political, and economic structure of sixteenth-century Europe. In 1517 the German monk Martin Luther helped spur on this movement by protesting against the sale of indulgences and certain other perceived abuses ☆ of the Roman Catholic Church. His protests helped trigger a widespread rejection of the pope's authority in Europe.

By 1530 Henry VIII had reasons to align himself and England with the Protestants. He wanted his marriage to Catherine of Aragon annulled because she had not given him a male heir. When the pope in Rome refused, Henry VIII broke with the Roman Catholic Church, proclaiming himself the sole head of the Church of England, or the Anglican Church. This split led to bitter and long-lasting conflicts among religious factions in England that lasted until the end of the 1600s. When Henry VIII's Catholic daughter, Mary I, became queen, she executed Protestants; later, Henry VIII's Protestant daughter, Elizabeth I, executed Catholics. In an attempted invasion in 1588 launched by Philip II, the Catholic monarch of Spain, Elizabeth I's navy defeated the Spanish Armada. England thus remained Protestant under Elizabeth I and her cousin, James I.

PREVIEW **Big Ideas** of the English Renaissance

1 Humanists and Courtiers	**2** A Bard for the Ages	**3** The Sacred and the Secular
To the humanists, human endeavor had dignity and worth in its own right. Influenced by that idea, English writers began to shift their focus from otherworldly concerns and concentrate on secular subjects, such as love, politics, science, and philosophy. **See pages 234–235.**	William Shakespeare, a singular genius, wrote poems and plays that represent the full flowering of the English Renaissance. His works focus on individuals: heroes and villains who grapple with painful dilemmas. **See pages 236–237.**	The English Renaissance was an age of extreme contrasts. It produced literature that includes devotional meditations as well as witty reflections on time, transience, and erotic love. The contrast between the sacred and the secular was sharply drawn. **See pages 238–239.**

INTRODUCTION **233**

Teach

Reading Strategy 2

Support Generalizations

Ask: What generalization does the author make? *(The Renaissance was "a golden age" in England.)* How does the author support this generalization? *(The author cites examples that demonstrate England's political, economic, and military power.)*

ENGLISH LEARNERS Make sure English learners understand the term "generalization." Explain the word's root is "general," which means not specific or not limited to a certain group. Generalizations, therefore, are ideas or statements which could be applied to larger groups.

Language History ☆

Indulgences Pope Leo X empowered agents to travel throughout England selling letters that granted pardons for sins. The profits were used for church business, such as the construction of cathedrals.

Compare and Contrast
Guide students in creating a Venn diagram to show what they have learned about similarities and differences between the Middle Ages and the Renaissance in England.

Cultural History ☆

Sir Walter Raleigh Raleigh (c. 1552–1618) was a favorite courtier of Queen Elizabeth I, and as such he received land, knighthood, and leadership of the Queen's Guard. A friend to Edmund Spenser, and a subject of satire to Shakespeare, Raleigh was a prominent personality of his time. His fame could not help him, however, when he angered the queen by secretly marrying her maid, and he spent some time in the Tower of London as punishment. Raleigh funded an expedition to the New World around 1585, but failed to colonize Roanoke Island. He was executed in 1618 after a second stint in the Tower for suspicion of opposing James I.

Big Idea 1

Humanists and Courtiers

Unlike scholars in the Middle Ages, the humanists of the Renaissance focused on this world. Many of their studies—including grammar, rhetoric, and logic—reflect this shift in emphasis. For example, medieval scholars believed the form of words revealed part of the essential meaningfulness of God's creation. Renaissance scholars, on the other hand, were curious about how human languages were related to one another. **1**

Humanism in England
Living up to its name, humanism depended more on personal contact than on systematic instruction at schools and universities. The friendships formed by humanists—in private study with one another, in the royal courts where they served as political advisers, and in their personal correspondence—inspired many significant works in this period. Reading humanist works often seems like overhearing a conversation between friends.

> *"Nature herself prescribes a life of joy (that is, pleasure)."*
>
> —Thomas More, *Utopia*

Sir Thomas More, lord chancellor of England, and Desiderius Erasmus of Holland shared one of the most remarkable of these friendships. Whenever he visited London, Erasmus lived in More's home. There, he wrote his best-known work, *The Praise of Folly*, which he dedicated to his English friend. Erasmus considered More, with his cultivated intellect, sparkling wit, deep learning, and broad culture, to be the ideal humanist, calling him *omnium horarum homo*, which is usually translated "a man for all seasons." More's most celebrated

work, his satire *Utopia* (1516), presents his vision of an ideal society, freed from convention and ruled by reason. More coined the title of this work from Greek words that mean "no place."

Elizabeth I and Her Court
Queen Elizabeth I, Henry VIII's second daughter, came to the throne in 1558. Famous for her wit and eloquence, she knew Greek, Latin, and several modern languages and loved music, dancing, and the theater. Her long reign of forty-five years was marked by religious conflicts, political intrigue, and threats of war. She turned England into a great sea power capable of defeating the feared Spanish Armada. With a nimble intelligence and strong personality, she also supported a flourishing period of cultural achievement. Elizabeth's court served as a forum for daring displays of wit that the queen greatly admired—and in which she skillfully participated. Her favorites, privileged members of the court, exemplified the qualities she most admired. Sir Walter Raleigh, ☆ for example, combined many occupations: soldier and sailor, explorer of Virginia and Guiana, poet and scientist, possible spy. He began to write his *History of the World* while imprisoned in the Tower of London by Elizabeth's successor, her cousin James I.

The Court of James I
When Elizabeth I died in 1603, the throne passed peacefully to her cousin James, king of Scotland and a member of the Stuart family that would rule England through most of the 1600s. Thus James VI of Scotland became James I of England; all of Britain (England, Scotland, and Wales) was at last ruled by one monarch. Elizabeth I had been worldly and practical; James I, however, was theological and disputatious. He commissioned the translation of the Bible into English, still known as the King James Bible, a masterpiece of English

Writing Practice

⚡ Organize Ideas

SPIRAL REVIEW Point out that each paragraph in the body of an essay should have a topic sentence. Remind students that structuring their paragraphs in this way will make writing easier.

Read aloud the topic sentence of the first paragraph. "Unlike scholars in the Middle Ages, the humanists of the Renaissance focused on this world." **Ask:** How does the author support the topic sentence?

(The author uses an example of how scholars in each period thought about language.)

Ask students to analyze other paragraphs in the text.

Edward Herbert, 1st Baron Herbert of Cherbury, c. 1610–14. Isaac Oliver. Vellum mounted on card, 9¹/₁₀ x 7¹/₁₀ in. Powis Castle, Wales.

prose. He wrote on a variety of subjects, including witchcraft and government, and argued for the divine right of kings. Like Elizabeth I, James I enjoyed theatrical performances. In fact, he admired one troupe of players so much that he gave it his patronage, commissioning it to give special performances at court. Formerly known as the Lord Chamberlain's Men, the King's Men included William Shakespeare, whose tragedy *Macbeth* was first performed before the king in 1605.

In the early 1580s, Sir Philip Sidney wrote a defense of literature in response to Puritan attacks claiming that all art was immoral.

from **A Defence of Poesie** by Sir Philip Sidney

Now therin of all sciences (I speak still of human, and according to the humane conceits) is our poet the monarch. For he doth not only show the way, but giveth so sweet a prospect into the way, as will entice any man to enter into it. Nay, he doth, as if your journey should lie through a fair vineyard, at the very first give you a cluster of grapes, that, full of that taste, you may long to pass further. He beginneth not with obscure definitions, which must blur the margent with interpretations, and load the memory with doubtfulness; but he cometh to you with words set in delightful proportion, . . . and with a tale forsooth he cometh unto you, with a tale which holdeth children from play, and old men from the chimney corner. And, pretending no more, doth intend the winning of the mind from wickedness to virtue: even as the child is often brought to take most wholesome things by hiding them in such other as have a pleasant taste. . . . So is it in men (most of which are childish in the best things, till they be cradled in their graves): glad they will be to hear the tales of Hercules, Achilles, Cyrus, and Aeneas; and, hearing them, must needs hear the right description of wisdom, valor, and justice.

Reading Check

Interpret According to Sidney, how does poetry fulfill a moral purpose?

English Learners

DIFFERENTIATED INSTRUCTION

Intermediate Suggest that students begin a personal glossary of new terms and words found in Renaissance literature. Words like *doth*, *margent*, and *forsooth* may be unfamiliar to English learners.

Approaching Level

DIFFERENTIATED INSTRUCTION

Established Have students develop **reading fluency** by taking turns reading aloud parts of *A Defence of Poesie*. Encourage them to match Sidney's intended tone.

Teach

Reading Check

Answer: *Sidney believes that poetry fulfills a moral purpose by combining moral instruction with delight.*

Literary Element | 2

Formal Essay If necessary, remind students that a formal essayist writes as an impersonal, objective authority with the purpose of instructing or persuading an audience. The author uses a serious tone and develops a thesis in a highly organized way.

Ask: What details tell you that the tone of Sidney's essay is serious? *(Sidney discusses the importance of poetry to virtue and how the poet can guide people of all ages along a virtuous path.)*

View the Art ★

Isaac Oliver (c. 1560–1617) traveled from France to England, probably as a refugee from religious wars. In England, he learned to paint miniatures like the one shown.

Ask: How does the artist's depiction of a man enjoying nature reflect Renaissance humanist values? *(The Renaissance promoted taking pleasure and interest in the world around you more than in the afterlife.)*

Teach

Reading Strategy | 1

Thesis **Ask:** What is the thesis sentence of "A Bard for the Ages"? ("William Shakespeare . . . is said to be the world's favorite author.")

[APPROACHING] Remind students that these statements normally appear at the beginning of a piece. The thesis tells the reader the main idea of the passage.

Literary History ☆

Sonnets Shakespearian sonnets, also called Elizabethan sonnets or English sonnets, have fourteen lines divided into three quatrains and a final couplet. The rhyming couplet often presents a conclusion to the issues brought up in the preceding quatrains. Each line is written in iambic pentameter. The rhyme scheme is *abab cdcd efef gg*.

Reading Practice

 Organize Ideas Have students create a web showing the main idea and details.

Say: Write the main idea in the center circle. Add details in the surrounding circles.

Big Idea 2
A Bard for the Ages

William Shakespeare, poet and playwright, is said to be the world's favorite author. No other playwright's works have been produced so often and read so widely in so many different countries. On the one hand, little is known about Shakespeare as a person. He left behind no letters or manuscripts to provide clues about his personality or the inner workings of his mind. On the other hand, Shakespeare imbued the characters in his plays with such rich humanity that they live on the page and on the stage, still inspiring readers and theater audiences more than four hundred years after their creation.

> *"Soul of the age! / The applause! delight! the wonder of our stage!"*
>
> —Ben Jonson

Shakespeare's Theaters

No one knows when Shakespeare first arrived in London, but his name first appears in London theatrical records as an actor and a playwright. His career in the theater proved profitable for him. Around 1610, he had earned enough money to leave London and retire to an estate in the small country town of Stratford-upon-Avon, where he had grown up. His fortune, however, did not come directly from his plays. An astute businessman, Shakespeare was a shareholder, or part owner, in one of London's most popular acting companies, the Lord Chamberlain's Men. In 1599 the company built the Globe Theatre, the most famous of Elizabethan theaters.

Located on the disreputable south bank of the river Thames, the Globe was designed to provide inexpensive entertainment for approximately three thousand spectators. Built roughly in the shape of an O, this playhouse was open to the air. Galleries of seats and areas for standing ringed three-quarters of the platform stage.

Shakespeare was also a shareholder in the Blackfriars Theatre, a more intimate and expensive playhouse. Closer to the center of London and attracting a wealthier audience, the Blackfriars was roofed and provided candlelight for evening performances.

Shakespeare's Learning

Alluding to Shakespeare's lack of higher learning, Ben Jonson wrote that Shakespeare had "small Latin and less Greek." In fact, while there is no indication that Shakespeare knew any Greek at all, Latin works by the poet Ovid and the playwrights Plautus and Seneca, which he read at the local grammar school in Stratford-upon-Avon, deeply influenced him. Shakespeare imaginatively incorporated much of what he read into his plays.

Shakespeare's Humanism

Shakespeare's ability to absorb and transform different kinds of material—from political issues of the day to events from Roman and English history—reflects a humanistic ideal. His characters, seeking to fulfill their potential, are constantly probing and striving, demonstrating their wit at court, displaying their courage on the battlefield, falling in love and writing poetry, or devising plots to bring about their deepest desires, whether loving or vengeful. No other writer has seen more deeply into the many manifestations of human nature. In an uncanny way, Shakespeare understands why people behave the way they do. Young and old, women and men, good and evil, beggars and kings—all live in his plays.

William Shakespeare is a timeless author.

- widely read around the world
- complex, realistic characters in his plays
- understands human nature

David Garrick as Richard III, 1745. William Hogarth. Oil on canvas, 75 x 98⅕ in. Walker Art Gallery, National Museums, Liverpool.

The power of Shakespeare's imagination informs his understanding of even his villains' complexities. In the following passage from Richard III, *the title character vows to become a villain because of his physical repugnance and the unhappiness it has brought him.*

from *Richard III*, Act 1, scene 1 by William Shakespeare

Now is the winter of our discontent
Made glorious summer by this sun of York;
And all the clouds that loured upon our house
In the deep bosom of the ocean buried.
Now are our brows bound with victorious wreaths;
Our bruiséd arms hung up for monuments;
Our stern alarums changed to merry meetings;
Our dreadful marches to delightful measures.
Grim-visaged war hath smoothed his wrinkléd front;
And now, instead of mounting barbéd steeds
To fright the souls of fearful adversaries,
He capers nimbly in a lady's chamber
To the lascivious pleasing of a lute.
But I, that am not shaped for sportive tricks,
Nor made to court an amorous looking-glass;
I, that am rudely stamped, and want love's majesty
To strut before a wanton ambling nymph;

I, that am curtailed of this fair proportion,
Cheated of feature by dissembling Nature,
Deformed, unfinished, sent before my time
Into this breathing world, scarce half made up,
And that so lamely and unfashionable
That dogs bark at me as I halt by them;
Why I, in this weak piping time of peace,
Have no delight to pass away the time,
Unless to spy my shadow in the sun
And descant on mine own deformity:
And therefore, since I cannot prove a lover,
To entertain these fair well-spoken days,
I am determinéd to prove a villain
And hate the idle pleasures of these days.

Reading Check

Interpret How does Richard's speech reflect Shakespeare's humanism?

Approaching Level

DIFFERENTIATED INSTRUCTION

Emerging Have students draw a picture of what Richard III might look like to himself—not to others—based on his description. Schedule time to share and discuss students' drawings.

Advanced Learners

DIFFERENTIATED INSTRUCTION

Translate Have students translate the excerpt into their own words. Schedule a reading, and discuss the different versions.

Teach

Reading Check

Answer: *Shakespeare examines the psychology behind Richard's decision to become a villain and presents his physical deformity as debilitating and humiliating.*

Literary Element | 2

Soliloquy Let students know that the excerpt from *Richard III* is a soliloquy—a passage in which a character alone on a stage reveals his or her private thoughts and feelings as if thinking aloud.
Say: Find three lines or phrases in Richard's soliloquy that show how he feels about his appearance. *("am not shaped for sportive tricks"; "am rudely stamped"; "cheated of feature by dissembling nature")*

View the Art ★

William Hogarth (1697–1764) apprenticed as a silver engraver before he decided he wasn't making enough money doing that or painting portraits. An innovative man, he decided to create an art form that he called "the modern moral subject." These works were so popular, and copied so frequently, that Hogarth lobbied for the Copyright Act of 1735.

Main Idea **Ask:** What is the main idea of "The Sacred and the Secular"? *(Renaissance thinkers sought to redefine themselves in relation to church and state.)*

APPROACHING Help students find the main idea of the passage. **Say:** While you read, ask yourself what is this author trying to tell me? What does the author want me to remember? This answer is the main idea.

Literary History ☆

The Bible In 500 B.C., the 39 books which make up the Hebrew Bible were completed. These were written in Hebrew. In 200 B.C., a translation of the Hebrew Bible into Greek was completed, including 14 books of Apocrypha. Greek was also the first language of the New Testament's 27 books, written in the first several centuries A.D. It wasn't until A.D. 382 that all 80 books appeared together in Latin. Even though many translations followed, by A.D. 600 Latin had become the only language allowed for scripture in Western Europe.

Big Idea 3
The Sacred and the Secular 1

Should limits be imposed on the quest for knowledge? That question was as relevant in the Renaissance as it is today. With its emphasis on investigation rather than revelation, humanism inevitably roused the concern of religious authorities. Not all humanists, however, saw a contradiction between religious faith and free inquiry. After all, had not God endowed human beings with intelligence?

Humanism and Religion

Sir Thomas More's humanism, for example, was grounded in the Roman Catholic religion. He never allowed public affairs, however important, to distract him from private prayer and charities dear to his heart. He ran his home as a school for his daughters, whom he educated in Christian and classical subjects. It was a matter of conscience—his opposition to Henry VIII's intended divorce—that led to his execution for treason, ordered by the very king whom he had served so well. As he was about to be beheaded, More defined his relationship to both the sacred and secular realms: "The King's good servant, but God's first."

> *"As thou readest therefore think that every syllable pertaineth to thine own self, and suck out the pith of the scripture, and arm thyself against all assaults."*
>
> —William Tyndale

The Bible in English ☆

Many Renaissance writers who did not associate with humanists such as More nonetheless were eager to wrest the control of learning from religious authorities. An important way to do so was to bring the Christian sacred writings down from the pulpit and into people's homes. The new printing presses made translations of the Bible into modern languages relatively affordable. By 1522 Martin Luther had translated the New Testament into German. In the 1520s and 1530s, William Tyndale, one of the leaders of the Protestant Reformation in England, followed Luther's example by translating the Bible into English. He sought to bring the words of scripture into the hearts and minds of individual readers.

These "assaults" were real. The penalties for translating the Bible without official approval from either the pope or—after Henry VIII took control of the Church of England—the government were often deadly. Tyndale was burned at the stake for heresy in 1536. Ironically, the scholars who later worked on the official translation of the Bible, the King James Version (see page 406), borrowed heavily from Tyndale's work.

Metaphysical and Cavalier Poets

Growing up as a Catholic in Protestant England, the poet John Donne learned early about the dangers of religious conflict. In his youth, however, Donne wrote witty poems about romantic love. Many of his contemporaries also delighted in writing about subjects far removed from the entangled and divisive religious issues of the day. Donne was the most notable of a group of writers later referred to as the metaphysical poets (see page 420). Poets such as Donne and Andrew Marvell shared a strong sense of the contradictions inherent in life, such as that between the beauty of the sensual world and the ravages of time.

Writing Practice

 Word Choice

SPIRAL REVIEW Read aloud to students the first sentence under the heading: "The Bible in English." **Ask:** What do you think about the author's choice of the verb to wrest? Encourage discussion about other choices the author might have made. **Ask:** What are some synonyms of "wrest"? *(take; extort; squeeze; wrench; wring)* Why might the author have chosen this word?

Vanitas, Self Portrait of the Artist, Still Life, c. 17th century. David Bailly. Stedelijk Museum de Lakenhal, Leiden, The Netherlands.

In 1625 King James I was succeeded by his son, Charles I, whose court was more pleasure-loving than his father's had been. His courtiers were called cavaliers, after the Italian word for *knight*. They still aspired to the grace and elegance of Renaissance gallantry, but they cared little for its high seriousness and Christian chivalry.

The Cavalier poets (see page 444), such as Robert Herrick, Sir John Suckling, and Richard Lovelace, wrote lyrical poems of great polish, sophistication, wit, and raciness. They celebrated earthly pleasures, especially quick-blooming love, and lamented its inevitable fading.

Batter my heart, three-personed God by John Donne

Batter my heart, three-personed God; for, you
As yet but knock, breathe, shine, and seek to mend;
That I may rise, and stand, o'erthrow me, and bend
Your force to break, blow, burn and make me new.
2 I, like an usurped town, to another due,
Labor to admit you, but oh, to no end,
Reason your viceroy in me, me should defend,
But is captived, and proves weak or untrue,

Yet dearly I love you, and would be loved fain,
But am betrothed unto your enemy:
Divorce me, untie, or break that knot again,
Take me to you, imprison me, for I
Except you enthral me, never shall be free,
Nor ever chaste, except you ravish me.

Reading Check

Interpret How does the word choice in this sonnet reflect both the sacred and the secular?

INTRODUCTION **239**

Approaching Level

DIFFERENTIATED INSTRUCTION

PARTNERS **Emerging** Have students work in pairs to determine the meanings of unfamiliar words in the poem. Have them take turns reading aloud one line at a time, noting and discussing any new vocabulary. Encourage them to ask for help if needed.

UNIT TWO

Teach

Reading Check

Answer: *In addressing God, Donne uses language that relates to romantic love (for example, "enthral," "chaste," "ravish") and politics (for example, "usurped town," "viceroy," "enemy").*

Literary Element | 2

Simile If necessary, remind students that a simile is a figure of speech in which the word *like* or *as* is used to compare two seemingly unlike things. Discuss the comparison Donne makes in the line "I, like an usurped town, to another due." **Ask:** What does Donne refer to with the word "another"? *(the secular world, life, concerns)*

View the Art ★

David Bailly (1584–1657) was a Dutch painter. In this self-portrait, the primary figure on the left is the artist as a young man, while the portrait in his hands shows the artist at 67, the age at which he made the portrait. **Ask:** What other symbols show the passage of time? *(skull, pocket watch, wilted flowers, snuffed candle)*

239

Assess

Connect to Today

1. Follow Up Students' initial responses should reflect the information in this introduction. As they complete the lessons in the unit, have them revisit their responses and use what they have learned to refine the responses and add additional supporting details.

2. Contrast Literary Periods Encourage students to discuss their opinions about specialization, teamwork, and introspection.

3. Build Visual Literacy Have students form groups based on media interests, such as painting or video.

4. Note Taking After students finish each selection, have them keep a record of their responses in the Foldable.

FOLDABLES®
Study Organizer

Have students make and label the Bound Book Foldable to take notes on the poetry, play, and nonfiction in the unit.

Wrap-Up

Legacy of the Period

The value that humanism placed on human experience has permanently altered the way people judge the world. Moreover, humanism's emphasis on intellectual questioning and direct observation gave birth to modern scientific methods. As Sir Francis Bacon wrote, "Knowledge is power."

The literature of the English Renaissance—particularly the plays of William Shakespeare—is one of the pinnacles of world culture. The reign of Elizabeth I also witnessed the beginning of England's three-hundred-year transformation from a small island nation into a global empire ruling one quarter of the world. The growth of the British Empire, in turn, spread the influence of English culture to most corners of the world.

The cultural products of the Protestant Reformation including the *Book of Common Prayer* and the King James Bible, have enriched the spiritual lives and the language of countless English speakers throughout the world.

Cultural and Literary Links

 Shakespeare's plays and poems continue to enthrall audiences—on stage and on film, in adaptations into operas and hip-hop musicals, in historically faithful productions with male actors playing female parts, and in iconoclastic productions set in inner-city slums and high-rise penthouses. Biographies and novels about Shakespeare appear frequently, attesting to his undiminished appeal.

 The King James Bible has profoundly influenced the development of the English language, introducing many phrases into the language that are still in use. These phrases include "fall flat on his face," "a man after my own heart," "to pour one's heart out," and "the land of the living."

LOG ON **Literature** Online

Unit Resources For additional skills practice, go to glencoe.com and enter QuickPass code GLB9817u2.

Activities

➤ Choose one of the following activities to explore and develop as you read this unit.

1. Follow Up Go back to Looking Ahead on page 227 and answer the questions.

2. Contrast Literary Periods The Renaissance ideal was a person skilled in many fields, from writing sonnets to fighting in battles. Does this ideal still have value in the modern world? Work with a group of classmates to stage a debate on whether modern concepts of specialization and teamwork have rendered the Renaissance ideal obsolete.

3. Build Visual Literacy From paintings of her own day to films and TV programs today, Elizabeth I has been one of the most widely depicted monarchs of all time. With a group of classmates, create a gallery of images of Elizabeth that show various facets of her personality and public role.

4. Take Notes Use the bound-book organizer to explore your personal responses to the selections in this unit.

FOLDABLES®
Study Organizer

BOUND BOOK

Reader-Response Journal

Assessment Practice

SPIRAL REVIEW **Note Taking** Explain to students note taking is an important skill because it can help you remember information about the subject. When you take notes, review them before your next class so the details will be fresh in your mind. Mark the most important points with an asterisk or a highlighter so you can find them quickly in the future. Ask students to practice taking notes during your lecture and/or their reading. Review their notes and make suggestions for improving their note taking techniques.

PART 1

Humanists and Courtiers

Queen Elizabeth I Being Carried in Procession, c. 1601. Robert Peake. Oil on canvas, 51.97 x 75 in. Private collection.

View the Art Robert Peake was one of the most talented painters of royalty in the late sixteenth century. From this image, what can you infer about royal life in Elizabeth I's time?

"I have taken all knowledge to be my province." **1**

—Sir Francis Bacon

241

UNIT TWO

PART 1

Analyzing and Extending

Reading Strategy | 1

Interpret Meaning Invite a student to read the quotation aloud. **Ask:** What do you think is meant by "province"? (*Province refers to the range of one's proper duties, functions, scope or jurisdiction.*)

View the Art

Robert Peake (c. 1551–c. 1619) was one of the finest late-sixteenth-century painters. Born in London, he was apprenticed to a goldsmith in Cheapside. He was a court employee in the "Office of the Revels" for most of his adult life. In this position, he was principal Picture Maker to Henry, Prince of Wales, and Sergeant Painter to King James I.

Ask: What can you learn about royal life in Elizabeth I's time? (*Possible response: Queen Elizabeth I was a powerful person at the time.*)

For additional support for English Learners, see Unit 2 Teaching Resources Book, p. 19.

English Learners

DIFFERENTIATED INSTRUCTION

Intermediate *Province* can refer to an area of land. It can also refer to an area of interest or expertise. **Ask:** How can you tell which meaning of *province* is intended by Sir Francis Bacon? (*The province is said to be "all knowledge," so "area of land" does not apply.*)

Approaching Level

DIFFERENTIATED INSTRUCTION

Established Read the quotation aloud to students. **Ask:** Is Bacon a humanist? Explain. (*Bacon is not limited by the authority of the church with regard to what he will think or what knowledge he will pursue. Therefore, he is a humanist.*)

Focus

Bellringer Options

Daily Language Practice
Transparency 17

Or have students discuss the following question: Why have so many poets decided to use the sonnet structure when writing poems? As they read, students should consider the different types of sonnets brought to life by different poets.

Teach

Big Idea | 1

Secular Topics The sonnet was developed when poets began to focus on secular subjects.
Ask: What are some of the secular subjects of the poetry? *(Students' answers may include questions of love and mortality and personal experiences.)*

Literary Element | 2

Sonnet Remind students that, generally, a series of sonnets focused on a particular theme. Petrarch wrote hundreds of poems about a woman named Laura. English poets Sir Philip Sidney and Edmund Spenser both wrote sonnet sequences examining love.

For an audio recording of this selection, use Listening Library Audio CD-ROM.

242

Learning Objectives

For pages 242–243
In studying this text, you will focus on the following objectives:

Literary Study:
Analyzing literary genres. Identifying characteristics of a sonnet.

Reading: Monitoring comprehension.

The Development of the Sonnet

2 During the 1300s, Italian poet Francesco Petrarch (1304–1374) popularized the sonnet. By the end of the sixteenth century, poets throughout much of Europe were writing sonnets. Many of the most recognizable poems in history were written in sonnet form. Romantic poet William Wordsworth wrote that the sonnet was the key with which "Shakespeare unlocked his heart."

Henry Percy, 9th Earl of Northumberland. Nicholas Hilliard, (1547–1619). Rijksmuseum, Amsterdam.

THE WORD *SONNET* COMES FROM THE ITALIAN *sonetto*, meaning "a little sound or song." For more than seven hundred years, poets have used these highly structured fourteen-line poems to explore such issues as the fleeting nature of love and profound questions of mortality. **1**

Meter and Rhyme Patterns

Traditional sonnets have fourteen lines, each of which is written in **iambic pentameter.** That is, each line has five metric units, or feet, and each foot consists of an unstressed syllable (marked ˘) followed by a stressed syllable (marked ´). The rhythm of a line of iambic pentameter is shown in this example from Spenser's Sonnet 30:

> My love is like to ice, and I to fire

Sonnets also have set rhyme schemes, determined by the final sounds in the lines. To identify the rhyme scheme of a poem, begin with the first line and assign letters, in alphabetical order, to the sounds at the end of the lines. Lines that end with the same sound should be assigned the same letter. In Sidney's Sonnet 39, for example, the rhyme scheme for the first four lines would be *abab*.

Come sleep! O sleep, the certain knot of peace,	a
The baiting place of wit, the balm of woe,	b
The poor man's wealth, the prisoner's release,	a
The indifferent judge between the high and low	b

Sonnet Forms

There are three major sonnet forms: the **Italian,** or **Petrarchan;** the **English,** or **Shakespearean;** and the **Spenserian.**

The Italian Sonnet The Italian sonnet is often called the Petrarchan sonnet after Francesco Petrarch, the poet who made it famous. Many of Petrarch's sonnets are about unrequited love, a common topic for sonnets that follow this form.

Literary Element Practice

SPIRAL REVIEW **Sonnet** Have students reread the text and define each of the following terms:

rhyme scheme	*(the pattern of rhyming of end lines—e.g., abab cdcd)*
octave	*(the first 8 lines in a Petrarchan sonnet)*
sestet	*(the last 6 lines in a Petrarchan sonnet)*
couplet	*(a group of 2 lines ending a Shakespearean or Spenserian sonnet)*
quatrain	*(a group of 4 lines containing its own rhyme scheme)*

Portrait of Frances Howard, Countess of Essex and Somerset, c. sixteenth–seventeenth century. Isaac Oliver. Victoria and Albert Museum, London.

SONNET XII
by Francesco Petrarch
translated by Marion Shore

Octave: *Problem or situation is described.*

If my life find strength enough to fight
the grievous battle of each passing day,
that I may meet your gaze, years from today,
lady, when your eyes have lost their light,
　　and when your golden curls have turned to white,
and vanished are your wreaths and green array,
and when your youthful hue has fled away,
whose beauty makes me tremble in its sight,

Sestet: *Problem or situation is resolved.*

　　perhaps then Love will overcome my fears } *Turn*
enough that I may let my secret rise
and tell you what I've suffered all these years;
and if no flame be kindled in your eyes,
at least I may be granted for my tears
the comfort of a few belated sighs.

In an Italian sonnet, the first eight lines (called an **octave**) present a problem or situation. The last six lines (called a **sestet**) provide an answer or resolution to the problem. The switch from problem to resolution is called the turn. The octave of a typical Italian sonnet has the rhyme scheme *abbaabba*, and the sestet follows either *cdecde* or *cdcdcd*, as shown above.

The English Sonnet The English sonnet is also called the Shakespearean sonnet because Shakespeare was the master of this sonnet form. English sonnets are divided into three **quatrains** (groups of four lines, with each containing its own rhyme scheme) and one **couplet** (a group of two lines). The rhyme scheme is usually *abab cdcd efef gg*. The English form allows for a more detailed

development of the question or problem in the first three quatrains, but it demands a quick summary and solution in the couplet.

The Spenserian Sonnet Edmund Spenser crafted his own version of the sonnet. Like the Shakespearean sonnet, the Spenserian version has three quatrains and a couplet, but it follows the rhyme scheme *abab bcbc cdcd ee*. This interlocking rhyme scheme pushes the sonnet toward the final couplet, in which the writer typically makes a key point or comment.

 Literature Online

Literature and Reading For more about sonnets, go to glencoe.com and enter QuickPass code GLB9817u2.

Respond and Think Critically

1. Read Sonnet XII above. What is the "puzzle" of the poem, or the issue that the speaker is exploring? How is the situation resolved in the sestet?

2. Why do you think some modern poets still write in the highly structured sonnet form as well as in free verse?

3. What is the major difference between the Italian sonnet and the English sonnet?

LITERARY HISTORY **243**

English Learners
DIFFERENTIATED INSTRUCTION

Intermediate Invite students to discuss how romantic love is viewed in their cultures. Keep in mind that not all cultures allow dating before marriage. Find out if any of the students are from cultures where marriages are still arranged, and ask them to comment on this topic.

As part of the discussion, bring up the notion of unrequited love, explaining that the word *unrequited* refers to love that

is not returned. Then invite students to compare the sonnet to similar poems in their own languages, especially poems about love.

Literary History

Teach

View the Art ★

Isaac Oliver (1565?–1617) is best known for painting miniatures.

Ask: How is a sonnet like a miniature portrait? *(Both create their effects in a small space.)*

Assess

1. Students can discuss the meaning of the sonnet in small groups. Students may say that the speaker is in love with a woman but is afraid of her rejection.

2. Many poets enjoy the challenge of writing in a highly structured form.

3. The Italian sonnet contains an octave that presents a problem followed by a sestet that resolves the problem. An English sonnet contains three quatrains that present a problem followed by a couplet that resolves the problem. The main difference is that the English form allows for a more detailed development of the problem in the three quatrains but requires a brief resolution in the couplet, while the Italian form allows for greater balance between problem and resolution in the octave and sestet.

 For an activity related to this section, see Unit 2 Teaching Resources Book, pp. 20–21.

 For additional assessment, see Assessment Resources.

Bellringer Options

Literature Launchers:
  Pre-Reading Videos DVD,
  Selection Launcher
Selection Focus
  Transparency 10
Daily Language Practice
  Transparency 18

Or say: Think of a time when you felt you had to hide your feelings about someone else.

Invite students to discuss why they or others might feel a need to conceal feelings about another person. **Say:** As you read this poem, try to figure out what feelings the speaker is hiding.

Meet **Elizabeth I**
(1533–1603)

Queen Elizabeth I had a turbulent youth. When she was only two, her father, King Henry VIII, had her mother, Anne Boleyn, beheaded. Elizabeth had four stepmothers over the next ten years. Thanks to Catherine Parr, Henry's sixth wife, Elizabeth received a rigorous education. When Elizabeth was fourteen, her father died. Her ten-year-old half brother, Edward, ascended the throne but died six years later, and Elizabeth's half sister, Mary, came to power. Mary, a devout Catholic, sought to purge Protestantism from the nation. Her executions of Protestants as rebels or heretics earned her the nickname Bloody Mary. Elizabeth, a Protestant, was compelled to observe Catholicism or risk execution. Upon Mary's death in 1558, Elizabeth took the throne. She was only twenty-five at the time, but her study of languages, history, and philosophy had prepared her to be a great ruler.

Religious Tensions Elizabeth's first major act as queen was to issue a proclamation called the Act of Supremacy, which re-established the Church of England as the nation's official religion. With this decree, Elizabeth began to guide the nation toward a more moderate stance that would enable both Protestants and Catholics to practice their religions peacefully. This position was unpopular with the extremists of both groups, who would rather have punished, or even killed, those who did not share their convictions.

Elizabeth's Catholic cousin, Mary Queen of Scots, was one of these extremists. Mary's opinions were important because she was next in line for the English throne. If Elizabeth died without producing an heir, Mary would become the next queen of England; but Mary did not seem to be willing to wait for Elizabeth to die of natural causes to acquire this position. Shortly after she settled in

England in 1568, Mary was linked to two attempts on the queen's life. In 1570, Pope Pius V, unhappy with Elizabeth's religious policies, tried to aid Mary by excommunicating Elizabeth and declaring that English Catholics did not have to obey their queen's dictates.

"Though God hath raised me high, yet this I count the glory of my crown: that I have reigned with your loves."

—Elizabeth I, from *"The Golden Speech"*

Political Savvy Over the next fifteen years, Protestants pressured Elizabeth to execute the Queen of Scots, make a politically favorable marriage, and produce a Protestant heir. Instead, Elizabeth simply kept Mary prisoner until a third assassination attempt in 1587 prompted her to order Mary's execution. As for making a favorable marriage, Elizabeth turned that possibility into a brilliant political maneuver. By hinting at a possible marriage to King Philip II of Spain, Elizabeth stalled him from attacking England until she had prepared her nation to resist a Spanish invasion.

During the course of her forty-five-year reign, Elizabeth demonstrated a shrewdness for politics, enhanced the country's wealth and power, and saw England emerge as a major naval power. She even managed to write a few poems.

 Literature Online

Author Search For more about Elizabeth I, go to glencoe.com and enter QuickPass code GLB9817u2.

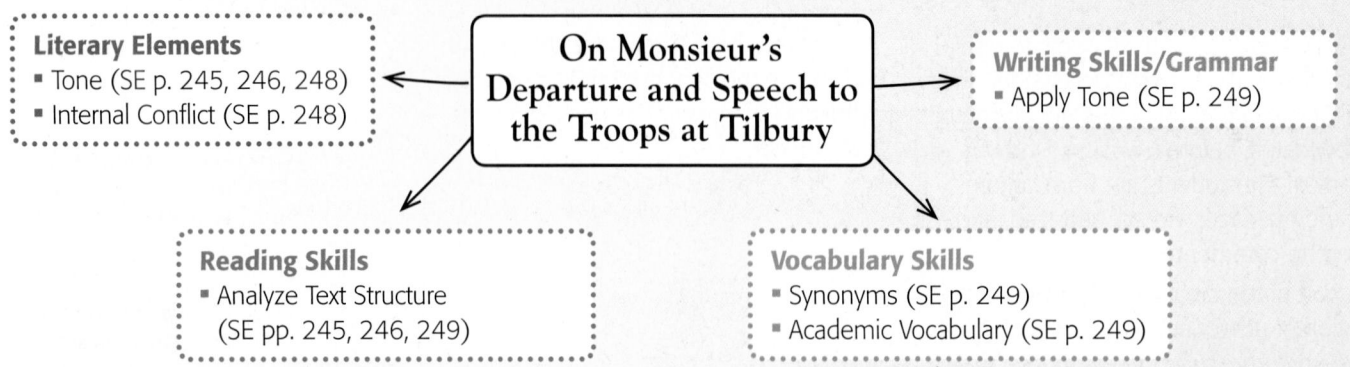

Literary Elements
- Tone (SE p. 245, 246, 248)
- Internal Conflict (SE p. 248)

On Monsieur's Departure and Speech to the Troops at Tilbury

Writing Skills/Grammar
- Apply Tone (SE p. 249)

Reading Skills
- Analyze Text Structure (SE pp. 245, 246, 249)

Vocabulary Skills
- Synonyms (SE p. 249)
- Academic Vocabulary (SE p. 249)

Literature and Reading Preview

Connect to the Texts

Have you ever had to balance feelings of love and duty? Write a journal entry about one such instance, explaining how you decided which was more important.

Build Background

Among Elizabeth's foreign suitors was the duke of Alençon, a young Frenchman. He was most likely the "Monsieur" of the poem you are about to read.

Elizabeth delivered the speech to the troops at Tilbury to the land forces assembled to prevent the invasion of the Spanish Armada, a fleet of warships sent by Philip II. The Armada was defeated at sea and never reached England.

Set Purposes for Reading

Big Idea Humanists and Courtiers

As you read, notice how Elizabeth focuses on secular subjects, such as love and politics, rather than on religious concerns. Ask yourself, How do these works reflect the Renaissance spirit?

Literary Element Tone

Tone is an expression of an author's attitude toward the subject matter or audience. A writer can convey tone through word choice, punctuation, sentence structure, and figures of speech. Works' tones can be described with words like *formal, playful, objective,* and *humorous.* As you read, ask yourself, What are the tones of the poem and the speech?

Reading Strategy Analyze Text Structure

Analyzing text structure means studying the way an author organizes material and presents ideas. In "On Monsieur's Departure," Elizabeth explores her feelings through a series of contrasting images. As you read the poem, ask yourself, How does its structure reinforce the expression of feelings?

....

Tip: Analyzing Contrasting Images Record examples of the speaker's state of mind in a chart like this one. When you have finished, evaluate the effect of the contrasts.

Image	Contrasting Image
grieving	not showing emotion

ELIZABETH I **245**

Learning Objectives

For pages 244–249

In studying these texts, you will focus on the following objectives:

Literary Study: Analyzing tone.

Reading: Analyzing text structure.

Writing: Applying tone in a persuasive speech or essay.

Vocabulary

mute (mūt) *adj.* unable to speak; silent; p. 246 *Izzy was struck mute by the beauty of the scene.*

suppressed (sə prest′) *adj.* subdued; held back; p. 246 *Andy's suppressed emotions bubbled out.*

treachery (trech′ ər ē) *n.* willful betrayal of trust; treason; p. 247 *The soldier's treachery caused great losses in the war.*

concord (kon′ kôrd) *n.* an agreement of interests or feelings; p. 247 *The concord between the nations helped them achieve their goals.*

valor (val′ ər) *n.* courage and boldness, as in battle; p. 247 *Dana's valor earned him a medal.*

Before You Read

Focus

Summary

"On Monsieur's Departure" is a poem about hiding deep love. The speaker uses starkly contrasting images to express her private consternation and staunch outward resolve.

"Speech to the Troops at Tilbury" is a rallying cry from Queen Elizabeth to her troops, meant to spur them to victory over the Spanish Armada that threatened to attack England.

 For summaries in languages other than English, see Unit 2 Teaching Resources Book, pp. 23–28.

 Interactive Read and Write

Other options for teaching this selection can be found in:

- Interactive Read and Write for EL students, pp. 77–84.
- Interactive Read and Write for Approaching-Level students, pp. 77–84.
- Interactive Read and Write for On-Level students, pp. 77–84.

Vocabulary

Word Origins Have students find the etymologies of the vocabulary words in a dictionary. Divide the class into pairs in which students take turns giving the meaning of a Latin or an Old French root and asking for the English word.

 For additional vocabulary practice, see Unit 2 Teaching Resources Book, pp. 31–32.

English Learners

DIFFERENTIATED INSTRUCTION

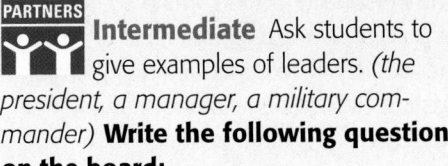 **PARTNERS**

Intermediate Ask students to give examples of leaders. *(the president, a manager, a military commander)* **Write the following questions on the board:**

Does a good leader show his or her feelings? Why? Why not?

How can a leader get others to do their best?

Have students discuss those questions with a partner. Then ask each pair to give a brief summary of the conversation.

Humanists and Courtiers

Say: Elizabeth's role as a monarch influenced the degree to which she felt free to express emotion. **Ask:** What sort of public behavior do people expect of a king or queen? *(Monarchs are generally expected to be dignified, calm, and serious.)*

Reading Strategy 2

Analyze Text Structure

Answer: *They express the confusion and inner turmoil of the speaker and make it easier for the reader to understand her dilemma.*

[ENGLISH LEARNERS] Explain to English learners that the speaker compares her sadness to her shadow, which is always with her.

Literary Element 3

Tone **Answer:** *The author's attitude is one of love, along with anguish that the love cannot be enjoyed.*

View the Art ★

This formal portrait by an unknown artist is one of the foremost images of Elizabeth I. The portrait's style is more lifelike than many later images of Elizabeth. **Ask:** On the basis of the portrait, how would you describe the queen's personality? *(confident; commanding)*

On Monsieur's Departure

Elizabeth I 1

I grieve and dare not show my discontent,
I love and yet am forced to seem to hate,
I do, yet dare not say I ever meant,
I seem stark **mute** but inwardly do prate.[1]
5   I am and not, I freeze and yet am burned,
    Since from myself another self I turned.

My care[2] is like my shadow in the sun,
Follows me flying, flies when I pursue it,
Stands and lies by me, doth what I have done.
10 His too familiar care doth make me rue it.[3]
    No means I find to rid him from my breast,
    Till by the end of things it be **suppressed**.

Some gentler passion slide into my mind,
For I am soft and made of melting snow;
15 Or be more cruel, love, and so be kind.
Let me float or sink, be high or low.
    Or let me live with some more sweet content,
    Or die and so forget what love ere meant.

---

1. *Prate* means "chatter."
2. Here, *care* means "sorrow."
3. *His . . . it* can be restated as "His superficial sorrow makes me regret my own sorrow."

Analyze Text Structure *How do the contrasting elements in these lines lend intensity to the poem?* 2

Tone *How would you describe the author's attitude toward her subject?* 3

Vocabulary

mute (mūt) *adj.* unable to speak; silent
suppressed (sə prest′) *adj.* subdued; held back

Reading Practice

SPIRAL REVIEW **Compare and Contrast**
Work with students to find contrasting pairs of elements in the first stanza *(love/hate, do/dare not say I ever, seem stark mute/do prate, am/not, freeze/burned, myself/another self)*. Discuss each opposition. Then discuss how one personality could contain so much opposition. Encourage students to work independently to continue finding contrasting elements in stanzas 2 and 3. Ask students to explain how pairs of elements in stanzas 2 and 3 contrast.

Speech to the Troops at Tilbury

Elizabeth I

My loving people,

    We have been persuaded by some that are careful of[1] our safety, to take heed how we commit our selves to armed multitudes, for fear of **treachery**; but I assure you I do not desire to live to distrust my faithful and loving people. Let tyrants fear, I have always so behaved myself that, under God, I have placed my chiefest strength and safeguard in the loyal hearts and good-will of my subjects; and therefore I am come amongst you, as you see, at this time, not for my recreation and disport, but being resolved, in the midst and heat of the battle, to live or die amongst you all; to lay down for my God, and for my kingdom, and my people, my honor and my blood, even in the dust. I know I have the body but of a weak and feeble woman; but I have the heart and stomach[2] of a king, and of a king of England too,[3] and think foul scorn that Parma[4] or Spain, or any prince of Europe, should dare to invade the borders of my realm; to which rather than any dishonor shall grow by me, I myself will take up arms, I myself will be your general, judge, and rewarder of every one of your virtues in the field. I know already, for your forwardness you have deserved rewards and crowns;[5] and We do assure you in the word of a prince, they shall be duly paid you. In the mean time, my lieutenant general[6] shall be in my stead, than whom never prince commanded a more noble or worthy subject; not doubting but by your obedience to my general, by your **concord** in the camp, and your **valor** in the field, we shall shortly have a famous victory over those enemies of my God, of my kingdom, and of my people.

---

1. *Careful of* means "anxious about."
2. Here, *stomach* means "courage."
3. This statement alludes to the concept of the king's (or queen's) two bodies, the one natural and mortal, the other political and immortal.
4. The dukedom of Parma, in northern Italy, was an ally of Spain in the effort to invade England.
5. A *crown* was an English monetary unit.
6. Elizabeth's *lieutenant general* was Robert Dudley, Earl of Leicester. In addition to leading her armies, he was Elizabeth's favorite courtier. He was once rumored to be her lover and potential husband.

Humanists and Courtiers *What evidence in this passage points to a shift from otherworldly concerns to a concentration on secular subjects?* **4**

Vocabulary

treachery (trech′ ər ē) *n.* willful betrayal of trust; treason

concord (kon′ kôrd) *n.* an agreement of interests or feelings

valor (val′ ər) *n.* courage and boldness, as in battle

ELIZABETH I **247**

Teach

Big Idea   4

Humanists and Courtiers
Answer: *Elizabeth focuses here on her own strength and determination to defend England. God is mentioned, but the queen assumes control and responsibility herself.*

Political History ☆

Spanish Armada In 1588, Spain sent a huge fleet of warships to invade England. Spain had far more fire-power than the English, but England's smaller, faster vessels held their own against Spain's heavy ships. The weather helped England, too, when a terrible storm scattered the Spanish vessels. Good planning and bad weather helped England to defeat Spain.

Readability Scores

Dale-Chall: 9.3
DRP: 59
Lexile: 1430

To check students' understanding of the selection, see Unit 2 Teaching Resources Book, p. 34

Advanced Learners

DIFFERENTIATED INSTRUCTION

Research Students can research more about England's battle against the Spanish Armada. A useful source is http://www.historylearningsite.co.uk/spanish_armada.htm. The site explains Spain's motives for attacking and details how and why its master plan failed.

English Learners

DIFFERENTIATED INSTRUCTION

Advanced Have volunteers read aloud the speech's salutation and first two sentences. Help students understand that Elizabeth is saying she has been warned that her people may betray her, but she knows she can trust them because she is a fair ruler who lives and who will die among them.

After You Read

Assess

1. Some students may sympathize because she is torn between love and duty.

2. (a) Her shadow (b) Her regret that her sorrow was greater than his at parting.

3. (a) They have told her someone might assassinate her. (b) To show she does not distrust her people (c) To show that she is afraid of nothing and is committed to defending her people

4. Students may choose the melting snow, as it shows the speaker's vulnerability.

5. (a) Take up arms herself and be "general, judge, and rewarder of every one of your virtues in the field." (b) That a woman is too weak to lead. (c) Yes, she will do everything a man can do, even lead the armies.

6. In the poem, Elizabeth I is concerned with her feelings of love and how they conflict with duty. In the speech she mentions God, but the emphasis is on her resolve to defend England.

7. It shows how her feelings might conflict with duty.

Progress Check

Can students identify tone?

If No → See Unit 2 Teaching Resources Book p. 29

248

After You Read

Respond and Think Critically

Respond and Interpret

1. Can you sympathize with the feelings of the speaker in "On Monsieur's Departure"? Why or why not?

2. (a)In the second stanza of the poem, to what does the speaker compare her feelings? (b)What does the second stanza reveal about her feelings for Monsieur?

3. (a)According to the opening lines of the speech to the troops at Tilbury, what warning have some of Elizabeth's advisers given her? (b)According to Elizabeth, why does she ignore their advice? (c)What effect do you think Elizabeth hopes to have on her audience by opening her speech in this way?

Analyze and Evaluate

4. In your opinion, what image in the poem is most effective in conveying the speaker's feelings? Explain your answer.

5. (a)In her speech, what does Elizabeth say she will do rather than see her country dishonored? (b)Against what criticism of her ability as a ruler is she defending herself? (c)Do you think this is an adequate defense? Explain your answer.

Connect

6. **Big Idea** Humanists and Courtiers In what ways do these works demonstrate the idea that the English were beginning to focus more on secular subjects than on religious subjects?

7. **Connect to the Author** How does knowing the identity of the poem's author deepen your understanding of the conflict that the poem describes?

Literary Element Tone

Just as a queen's attitude can set the tone of her court, a writer's attitude toward subject matter or audience can set the tone of a literary work.

In the speech to the troops at Tilbury, what evidence can you find that Elizabeth I's attitude toward her audience is one of deep respect?

Review: Internal Conflict

As you learned on page 23, an **internal conflict** is a struggle that takes place within the mind of a character. Much of "On Monsieur's Departure" deals with a conflict in the mind of the speaker.

Group Activity Get together with a small group of classmates and discuss the following questions.

1. According to the first stanza of the poem, what feelings has the speaker been forced to hide?

2. What reasons might she have for hiding her feelings?

Literary Element

She opens by calling her audience "loving people," says she is resolved "to live or die" among them, and says they deserve rewards for battling invaders.

Review: Internal Conflict

1. Love and grief
2. Political reasons—her subjects may not approve.

Reading Strategy Analyze Text Structure

Elizabeth I uses comparison and contrast to make her points in both the poem and the speech.

Partner Activity With a partner, list three examples of the use of comparison and contrast in the poem and the speech. Then discuss how this structure adds to the emotional impact of the poem.

Vocabulary Practice

Practice with Synonyms A synonym is a word that has the same, or nearly the same, meaning as another word. With a partner, match each boldfaced vocabulary word below with its synonym. You will not use all the answer choices. Use a thesaurus or dictionary to check your answers.

1. mute
2. suppressed
3. treachery
4. concord
5. valor

a. deceit
b. humanism
c. silent
d. harmony
e. restrained
f. courage
g. cowardice

Academic Vocabulary

*In her speech to the troops at Tilbury, Elizabeth proposes a **strategy** to defeat Spain.*

Strategy is an academic word. Elizabeth's **strategy** for defeating Spain included having her troops follow their general, get along with each other, and act with courage.

To further explore the meaning of this word, answer the following question: Do you have any **strategies** for success? Explain.

For more on academic vocabulary, see pages 56 and R81.

Write with Style

 Apply Tone

Assignment The great respect and trust that Elizabeth had for her troops came through powerfully when she addressed them at Tilbury. Write a persuasive speech or essay, adapting Elizabeth's tone to a subject you feel strongly about.

Get Ideas Alone or with several classmates, brainstorm a list of topics. Then choose a topic, making sure that it is an issue with two distinct sides. Make a pro-and-con chart showing the arguments on each side of the issue and the details that support them.

Give It Structure Consider the audience you're addressing and how best to persuade them. Look over your pro-and-con chart and find the details that most strongly support your point. Make these details the focus of your speech or essay. Address possible counterarguments with relevant facts, statistics, or expert opinions.

EXAMPLE:
Support Our School's Cleanup Project

Arguments:
* *Creates a pleasant, healthful environment*
* *Clears land for the new running track*
* *Shows our responsibility and earns respect*

Counterarguments and rebuttals:
* *Too busy to pitch in (but school is about developing citizenship as well as grades)*

Look at Language Like Elizabeth I, you will want to convey a tone of authority in your writing. Express your ideas in strong, clear language to emphasize the importance of your position. Replace words or phrases that are vague with terms that express your ideas in precise and interesting ways.

 Literature Online

Selection Resources For Selection Quizzes, eFlashcards, and Reading-Writing Connection activities, go to glencoe.com and enter QuickPass code GLB9817u2.

ELIZABETH I **249**

After You Read
Assess

 Write with Style

Use these criteria in evaluating student writing:

* The writing clearly identifies the topic.
* The arguments are clear and supported with logic and relevant details.
* Precise language creates a tone of authority.

> For grammar practice, see Unit 2 Teaching Resources Book, p. 33.

Reading Strategy

Examples include "I grieve and dare not show my discontent" (line 1), "I love and yet am forced to seem to hate" (line 2), and "Let me float or sink, be high or low" (line 16). Students may feel this structure reflects the speaker's conflicting feelings.

Progress Check

Can students analyze text structure?

If No → See Unit 2 Teaching Resources Book p. 30

 To create custom assessments using software use ExamView Assessment Suite.

Vocabulary

1. c **2.** e **3.** a **4.** d **5.** f

Academic Vocabulary

Students may respond that they schedule their time outside school, work at part-time jobs, or make responsible choices.

Before You Read

Focus

Bellringer Options

Daily Language Practice Transparency 19

Or explain that unrequited love is love that is not returned. Point out that there are countless accounts of unrequited love in movies, television shows, songs, and books. Invite students to discuss examples of unrequited love from books, movies, or television shows. **Ask:** What happens in the plot of the book (movie, show)? What does the person who loves unrequitedly feel, say, or act like?

Before You Read

Whoso List to Hunt

Meet **Sir Thomas Wyatt**

(c. 1503–1542)

Sir Thomas Wyatt, the well-known poet and diplomat, was imprisoned and faced execution twice during the stormy reign of Henry VIII, but both times the fickle king had a change of heart.

Diplomatic Career Wyatt was born in Kent and received his education at St. John's College in Cambridge. Later, he took up his service to the king, and over the years he was assigned to a number of diplomatic posts. Wyatt's diplomatic voyages took him to France, Spain, the Netherlands, and Italy. It was during his first trip to Italy in 1527 that he experienced the Renaissance firsthand. He also came into contact with the sonnets of Petrarch. Wyatt had never before seen this particular form of poetry, and he was deeply impressed. Soon he began writing sonnets of his own, which he took back to England with him. The sonnet took English culture by storm and had a profound and lasting effect upon English poetry.

Like many English nobles of his time, he had little interest in publishing his work. Instead, he circulated handwritten copies of his verses among his fellow courtiers. Printed versions did not appear until years after Wyatt's death.

> *"For when this song is sung and past, My lute, be still, for I have done."*
>
> —Sir Thomas Wyatt

Uneasy Relations As Wyatt's reputation as a poet developed, his relationship with King Henry became more and more difficult. Wyatt's friendship with Henry's second wife, Anne Boleyn, led him into trouble. Henry was suspicious by nature, and the fact that Wyatt was known to have been well acquainted with Boleyn before her marriage to the king did not help matters. In 1536 Henry threw Wyatt into prison and threatened him with execution. Fortunately for Wyatt, the king relented. Thomas Cromwell, Wyatt's close friend who was also a top adviser to the king, may have intervened; but it is just as likely that the king was persuaded by Wyatt's brilliant speeches in his own defense. In any case, Wyatt escaped beheading and was allowed to return to royal service. (Anne Boleyn would not be so lucky. She was imprisoned and beheaded in 1536 on charges that she was unfaithful.)

Despite his stormy relationship with the king, Wyatt continued to work as a diplomat. His next diplomatic post, from 1537 until 1539, was as the English ambassador to Charles V's court in Spain. However, Wyatt's fortunes took a downward turn in 1541 when he was imprisoned once again—on charges of treason. Though he spent only two months in jail this time, he would never again enjoy the king's favor.

In 1542 Wyatt set out on what would be his final diplomatic errand for Henry VIII. It was a long and difficult ride, and along the way Wyatt contracted a fever. He died shortly thereafter. Fifteen years after Wyatt's death, the printer Richard Tottel published ninety-seven of Wyatt's poems in the now-famous anthology *Songs and Sonnets*, which today is usually referred to as *Tottel's Miscellany*. Despite his life's many difficulties, Wyatt won a place in English literary history.

LOG ON ▶ **Literature** Online

Author Search For more about Sir Thomas Wyatt, go to glencoe.com and enter QuickPass code GLB9817u2.

Selection Skills

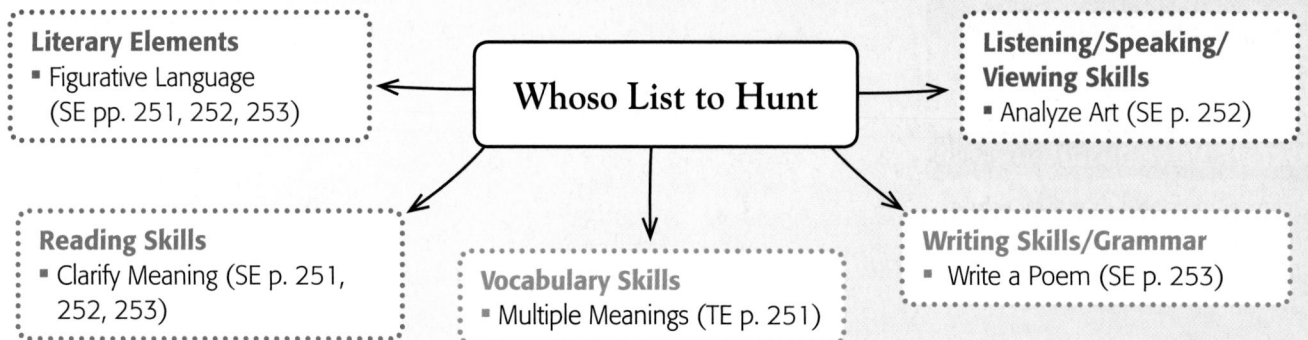

Literary Elements
- Figurative Language (SE pp. 251, 252, 253)

Whoso List to Hunt

Listening/Speaking/ Viewing Skills
- Analyze Art (SE p. 252)

Reading Skills
- Clarify Meaning (SE p. 251, 252, 253)

Vocabulary Skills
- Multiple Meanings (TE p. 251)

Writing Skills/Grammar
- Write a Poem (SE p. 253)

Literature and Reading Preview

Connect to the Poem

What do the songs about unrequited love that you are familiar with have in common? Discuss their similarities with a partner.

Build Background

Wyatt patterned many of his poems on sonnets about unrequited love written by the fourteenth-century Italian poet Francesco Petrarch. "Whoso List to Hunt" was inspired by Petrarch's Sonnet 190. Wyatt likely knew quite a bit about the subject of love in his own right, however. Literary scholars claim that Wyatt wrote "Whoso List to Hunt" about Anne Boleyn, Henry VIII's future wife.

Set Purposes for Reading

Big Idea Humanists and Courtiers

As you read the poem, notice the poet's references to human nature, the animal kingdom, and the earthly conditions of love and loss. Ask yourself, How do these references relate to the life of a Renaissance courtier?

Literary Element Figurative Language

Figurative language is used for descriptive effect, often to imply ideas or emotions indirectly. Figurative expressions are not meant to be interpreted literally. As you read the poem, ask yourself, How does the author use figurative language to compare animals and human beings to make his points?

Reading Strategy Clarify Meaning

Clarifying meaning means focusing on difficult sections of a text in order to understand them better. If you don't clarify a confusing passage, you may not understand the ideas and information that come later. As you read, reread confusing sections slowly and ask yourself, What am I failing to understand?

···

Tip: Restating Meaning You can sometimes clarify the meaning of a poem by putting it into your own words.

> *Ask yourself...*
> *What happens in this line or stanza?*
> _____
> _____
> *How can I state this idea clearly and simply?*
> _____

Learning Objectives

For pages 250–253

In studying this text, you will focus on the following objectives:

Literary Study: Analyzing figurative language.

Reading: Clarifying meaning by rereading.

Writing: Writing a poem.

Before You Read

Focus

Summary

"Whoso List to Hunt" is about a woman the speaker courted unsuccessfully in the past. The poem expresses vividly the keen pain of love that is not returned.

 For summaries in languages other than English, see Unit 2 Teaching Resources Book, pp. 36–41.

Vocabulary

Multiple Meanings Write the following words on the board: *vain, sore, draw, fair*. Have students find at least two definitions of each word in a dictionary. Write the definitions on the board. As students read the poems, have them choose the definition for each word that matches the context.

 For additional context, see Glencoe Interactive Vocabulary CD-ROM.

English Learners

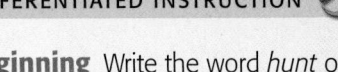
DIFFERENTIATED INSTRUCTION

Beginning Write the word *hunt* on the board and define it as "to chase an animal for sport or food." Tell students that the speaker of the poem "Whoso List to Hunt" knows where to find a good animal. He has been hunting it himself but is tired of chasing it. He thinks about the animal all the time and he must make a decision about whether to continue hunting it. **Ask:** Why would someone continue to hunt an animal even when he is tired? *(He wants the animal very much.)*

Teach

Reading Strategy | 1

Clarify Meaning
Answer: *He is saying that if anyone wants to hunt, he knows where there is a deer; however, he will hunt no longer.*

Literary Element | 2

Figurative Language
Answer: *The deer may represent Anne Boleyn, and Caesar may represent Henry VIII.*

[ENGLISH LEARNERS] Remind English learners that Wyatt may have loved Anne Boleyn, who married Henry VIII. **Ask:** Why might Wyatt compare Anne Boleyn to a deer owned by Caesar? *(Both Boleyn and the deer are under the power of powerful men.)*

View the Art ★

Anne Boleyn was the second of King Henry VIII's six wives. She secretly married him in 1533 while he was still married to Catherine of Aragon. Anne gave birth to a daughter who would later become Queen Elizabeth I. In 1536, Anne was accused of adultery and beheaded.

Whoso List to HUNT

Sir Thomas Wyatt

Anne Boleyn, c. 1530. Artist unknown. Oil on panel, 54.3 x 41.6 in. National Portrait Gallery, London. ★

View the Art Anne Boleyn was the second wife of Henry VIII, who would eventually have her beheaded. What lines of the poem does this image reflect? Explain.

Whoso list[1] to hunt, I know where is an hind,[2]
But as for me, alas, I may no more.
The vain travail[3] hath wearied me so sore
I am of them that farthest cometh behind.
5 Yet may I, by no means, my wearied mind
Draw from the deer, but as she fleeth afore,
Fainting[4] I follow. I leave off therefore,
Since in a net I seek to hold the wind.

Whoso list her hunt, I put him out of doubt,[5]
10 As well as I, may spend his time in vain.
And graven[6] with diamonds in letters plain
There is written, her fair neck round about,
"*Noli me tangere,* for Caesar's I am,[7]
And wild for to hold, though I seem tame."

---

1. *List* here is a verb meaning "desires."
2. A *hind* is a female deer.
3. *Travail* means "hard work."
4. Here, *fainting* means "growing weak."
5. *I put him out of doubt* means "I assure him."
6. *Graven* means "carved."
7. There is a story that the Roman dictator Julius Caesar kept tame deer on whose collars were inscribed the words *Noli me tangere,* Latin for "Touch me not."

1 Clarify Meaning *Restate these lines in your own words. What is the speaker trying to say?*

2 Figurative Language *Given what you know about Wyatt's life, who might the tame deer and Caesar represent?*

Literary Element Practice

SPIRAL REVIEW **Rhyme Schemes** Point out that this poem, like many, contains rhyming words at the ends of lines. Explain that the pattern of rhyme in a poem is called a rhyme scheme. Use the first four lines to show how to denote a rhyme scheme. (The first rhyming sound is *a*, the second is *b*, and so on; the first four lines follow the pattern *abba*.) Invite students to help you write the rhyme scheme for the rest of the octave. *(abba)* Then have students work independently to write the rhyme scheme for the sestet. *(cddcee)*

After You Read

Respond and Think Critically

Respond and Interpret

1. What advice might you offer the speaker of this poem?

2. (a)In the first stanza, how does the speaker characterize his hunting of the hind? (b)What can you tell about the speaker's feelings from this stanza?

3. (a)What advice does the speaker give to others who might wish to hunt the hind? (b)What does the last line of the poem suggest to you about the hind?

Analyze and Evaluate

4. (a)What attributes do you associate with deer? (b)In "Whoso List to Hunt," do you think deer hunting is an effective metaphor to convey the speaker's feelings? Explain.

Connect

5. **Big Idea** Humanists and Courtiers
(a)"Whoso List to Hunt" may have been read in King Henry VIII's court. How do you think the king and his followers might have responded to the poem? (b)Do you think it was unwise for Wyatt to have written the poem? Explain.

6. **Connect to Today** Are any features of the poem so foreign to modern readers that they might find it difficult to understand the feelings expressed? Explain your response.

Literary Element Figurative Language

Figurative language often includes the use of metaphor, a figure of speech that compares or equates two unlike things to help readers perceive an underlying similarity between the two. Reread the poem and consider the metaphoric comparisons the poet makes.

At one point, the speaker says, "I leave off therefore, / Since in a net I seek to hold the wind." What comparison is this metaphor making? Is it an effective metaphor? Explain.

Reading Strategy Clarify Meaning

Use a chart like the one below to help you clarify the lines "The vain travail hath wearied me so sore / I am of them that farthest cometh behind" (lines 3–4).

Line	Questions	My Rephrasing
"Whoso list to hunt, I know where is an hind."	What does "list" mean in this context? What is a "hind"?	"Whoever wants to hunt, I know where there is a deer."

Writing

Write a Poem "Whoso List to Hunt" compares the speaker's pursuit of the woman he loves to a hunter's search for a deer. Using Wyatt's poem as a model, write your own poem in which you use figurative language, such as similes or metaphors, to make a similar comparison. Try to use a regular meter and rhyme scheme throughout your poem.

Literature Online

Selection Resources For Selection Quizzes, eFlashcards, and Reading-Writing Connection activities, go to glencoe.com and enter QuickPass code GLB9817u2.

SIR THOMAS WYATT **253**

After You Read

Assess

1. They might advise speaker to find someone else.

2. (a) As hard and tiring work (b) He is sad and discouraged.

3. (a) Not to waste their time (b) The hind belongs to someone else.

4. (a) Students may say that deer are fast, beautiful, and gentle. (b) Some students may say the metaphor is effective because the speaker had been pursuing the woman and has found her to be elusive. Others may object to comparing women to animals.

5. (a) The king might have inferred that the poem was about his wife and reacted with jealousy. (b) Students may say Wyatt was reckless.

6. The vocabulary and the Latin motto could be obstacles to understanding the feelings expressed in the poem.

Progress Check

Can students identify figurative language?

If No → See Unit 2 Teaching Resources Book, p. 42.

Progress Check

Can students clarify meaning?

If No → See Unit 2 Teaching Resources Book, p. 43.

Literary Element

1. The metaphor compares the possibility of winning his beloved's favor to catching the wind with a net. Students may appreciate this witty metaphor.

Reading Strategy

Check students' charts to be sure that the tones listed are plausibly related to the passages that students cite.

Writing

Students' poems will vary but should include similes or metaphors to make comparisons and feature a rhyme scheme.

253

Focus

Write on the board: betwixt, methinks, verily. Ask students to look up definitions for these words. Have them write sentences using the words. Ask volunteers to share their sentences. *(Sentences will vary).*

Teach

Use Etymologies Many dictionaries include word histories, known as etymologies, which can help identify definitions of archaic words.

Assess

1. They both derive from Old English.

2. fled

3. adverb, preposition, or conjunction; Wyatt uses *afore* as an adverb.

4. Possible answer: "runs away in front of me"

 For additional vocabulary practice, see Glencoe Interactive Vocabulary CD-ROM.

Vocabulary Practice

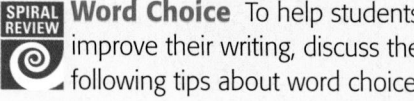 **Word Choice** To help students improve their writing, discuss the following tips about word choice:

1. Do not use unfamiliar words. If you are unsure of a word's definition, consult a dictionary before including it in your writing.

2. Do not overuse the same word. When you are writing, you may initially use the same words repeatedly. During your revisions, watch for repeated words and replace them with appropriate synonyms.

3. Think about your reader. The words you choose should be easy for your reader to understand. Readers are more impressed with clarity than with big words. Have students revise their writing based on these tips.

254

Learning Objectives

In this workshop, you will focus on the following objective:

Vocabulary: Understanding the use of a dictionary.

Tip

Homographs are words that are spelled alike but have different etymologies and meanings (for example, *sole* meaning "only" and *sole* meaning "a flat fish"). Homographs have separate entries in a dictionary, each marked with a small raised number immediately before or after the entry word.

Technology

You can obtain CD-ROM versions of many major dictionaries. In addition, you can access numerous dictionaries, such as *WWWebster's Dictionary*, on the Internet. When using an online dictionary, you simply enter a search word to find its entry. Often, you can hear the word spoken.

 **Literature** Online

Vocabulary For more vocabulary practice, go to glencoe.com and enter QuickPass Code GLB9817u2.

Vocabulary Workshop

Dictionary Use

Literature Connection Sir Thomas Wyatt wrote these lines nearly 500 years ago:

> *"Yet may I, by no means, my wearied mind*
> *Draw from the deer, but as she fleeth afore,*
> *Fainting I follow."*
> —Sir Thomas Wyatt, from "Whoso List to Hunt"

It is no wonder that some of the words are unfamiliar to modern readers. What does *fleeth afore* mean? And will a dictionary even tell you?

Looking for a Word Dictionaries identify words no longer used in modern English—like *afore* in the passage above—with the label "Archaic." But what about words that simply aren't there, like *fleeth*? The solution is to look for an entry close in spelling to the word you want, then apply your knowledge of the language and the context in which the word is used. Because the word just before *fleeth* in Wyatt's poem is *she*, you are probably looking for a verb to explain what "she" is doing. The closest verb to *fleeth* is *flee*. You may already know that in Wyatt's day people added -th rather than -s to make the third-person singular form of a verb.

A Word's Entry A main entry in a dictionary tells you far more than a word's definition. Here is what one dictionary says about *afore* and *flee*.

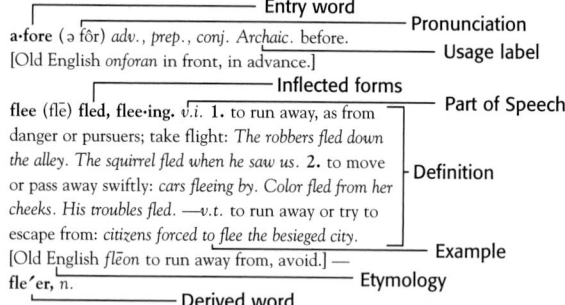

a·fore (ə fôr) *adv., prep., conj. Archaic.* before. [Old English *onforan* in front, in advance.]

flee (flē) **fled, flee·ing.** *v.i.* **1.** to run away, as from danger or pursuers; take flight: *The robbers fled down the alley. The squirrel fled when he saw us.* **2.** to move or pass away swiftly: *cars fleeing by. Color fled from her cheeks. His troubles fled.* —*v.t.* to run away or try to escape from: *citizens forced to flee the besieged city.* [Old English *flēon* to run away from, avoid.] — **fle´er,** n.

Labels: Entry word, Pronunciation, Usage label, Inflected forms, Part of Speech, Definition, Example, Etymology, Derived word

Practice Use the dictionary entries in this lesson to answer the following questions.

1. What do the etymologies of *afore* and *flee* have in common?

2. What is the past tense of *flee*?

3. What parts of speech can *afore* be used as? How does Wyatt use it in his poem?

4. How would you translate *fleeth afore* into modern English?

Before You Read

Sonnet 30 and Sonnet 75

Meet **Edmund Spenser**
(c. 1552–1599)

In his day, Edmund Spenser was considered one of the greatest poets of England and the first major English writer since Chaucer. He rose from humble beginnings to become a respected literary figure who received a life pension from Queen Elizabeth I after he personally presented his work to her.

> *"Sleep after toil, port after stormy seas, Ease after war, death after life does greatly please."*
>
> —Edmund Spenser

Student and Diplomat Spenser was the son of a cloth maker. He attended the Merchant Taylors' School in London as a "poor boy" before going to Cambridge University as a scholarship student, where he received his bachelor of arts and master of arts degrees. Shortly after leaving Cambridge, Spenser published *The Shepheardes Calender*, a collection of twelve short pastoral poems, one for each month of the year. The pastoral is a traditional English verse form that idealizes the rural pleasures of shepherds and innocent country people living in harmony with nature.

In 1580 Spenser was hired as secretary to Arthur Lord Grey, the harsh Lord Deputy of Ireland, who attempted to crush the frequent Irish rebellions against English rule. In war-ravaged Ireland, Spenser made his fortune by acquiring the lands of defeated Irish rebels. He eventually settled at Kilcolman Castle near the city of Cork.

Major Poet and Courtier In Ireland, Spenser began his most famous work, the great Elizabethan epic, *The Faerie Queene*. The poem, divided into books, is more than a thousand pages long. It depicts heroism in an enchanted world of dragons, monsters, and other marvels. Spenser planned for his epic to have twelve books, but he completed only six. Each book has as its hero a knight who performs noble deeds for a glorious fairy queen, based on Queen Elizabeth.

Spenser became friendly with Sir Walter Raleigh, a favorite courtier of Queen Elizabeth's. Raleigh took Spenser to London, introduced him at court, and helped him publish the first three books of *The Faerie Queen* in 1590. The work was a resounding success, and three more books followed in 1596.

Unrest at Home Returning to Ireland in 1591, Spenser faced another rebellion. As a supporter of English rule, he was a natural target of the rebels, who set fire to Kilcolman Castle. Spenser and his family escaped, but many of his papers were destroyed, possibly including additional books of *The Faerie Queene*. He returned to London but died soon afterward and was buried near Chaucer in the Poets' Corner in Westminster Abbey. At the funeral, admiring fellow poets are said to have honored Spenser by dropping verse tributes into his open grave.

 Literature Online

Author Search For more about Edmund Spenser, go to glencoe.com and enter QuickPass code GLB9817u2.

Before You Read

Focus

Bellringer Options

Selection Focus Transparency 11

Daily Language Practice Transparency 20

Or say: Think about depictions of romantic love you have seen in paintings, literature, music, television shows, and movies. How are people in love depicted? What do they say and do? How do they appear? How are they described? What feelings do they express, and how?

Approaching Level

DIFFERENTIATED INSTRUCTION

Established Have students preview the poems by looking at the painting included for each one. Ask students to compare and contrast the paintings by describing what each painting depicts and what emotions each person in the paintings probably feels. Then invite students to write one prediction about each sonnet's content. Have them revisit their predictions after reading to see if they were correct.

Before You Read

Focus

Summary

The speaker of Sonnet 30 is a man who passionately loves a woman indifferent to his affections. He describes how her indifference and his ardor accentuate each other.

The speaker of Sonnet 75 is a man driven to sing of his beloved's glorious virtues. He writes a poem in order to immortalize her.

Vocabulary

Affixes Write the words *congealing*, *vainly*, and *immortal* on the board. Have students use the definitions of the vocabulary words and their own understanding of affixes to write a definition for each of the three words.

For additional vocabulary practice, see Unit 2 Teaching Resources Book, p. 54.

For additional context, see Glencoe Interactive Vocabulary CD-ROM.

Literature and Reading Preview

Connect to the Poems

Does the desire to immortalize one's beloved in a work of art motivate poets and artists today? Discuss this question with a group of classmates, citing any examples you can think of.

Build Background

After the death of his first wife, Spenser began courting an Anglo-Irish woman named Elizabeth Boyle. His series of eighty-nine sonnets called *Amoretti* ("little love songs") was probably about his courtship of Elizabeth, whom he married in 1594.

Set Purposes for Reading

Big Idea Humanists and Courtiers

As you read, ask yourself, How do the two sonnets illustrate the humanist ideals of courtly love and the power of art?

Literary Element Rhyme Scheme

A **rhyme scheme** is the pattern of end rhymes in a poem. To identify the rhyme scheme, assign a letter, in alphabetical order, to each new end rhyme. The rhyme scheme for these opening lines of Spenser's Sonnet 54 is *abab*:

Of this world's theatre in which we **stay**,	a
My love, like the spectator, idly **sits**,	b
Beholding me, that all the pageants **play**,	a
Disguising diversely my troubled **wits**.	b

As you read, ask yourself, What pattern can be seen in the end rhymes in these poems?

Reading Strategy Connect to Personal Experience

Connecting to personal experience means applying the ideas, feelings, or events in a work of literature to aspects of your life. As you read, ask yourself, What similarities are there between the situations depicted in the poems and experiences I have had in my own life?

....

Tip: Taking Notes Use a chart like the one below to record connections between the poems and your own experiences.

Expression of Love	My Experience

Vocabulary

congeal (kən jēl′) *v.* to harden; thicken; p. 257 *After several hours in the refrigerator, the gravy congealed.*

vain (vān) *adj.* conceited; excessively pleased with oneself; p. 258 *Although the actor was handsome, he was not vain.*

mortal (môrt′ əl) *adj.* destined to die; p. 258 *All human beings are mortal.*

Selection Skills

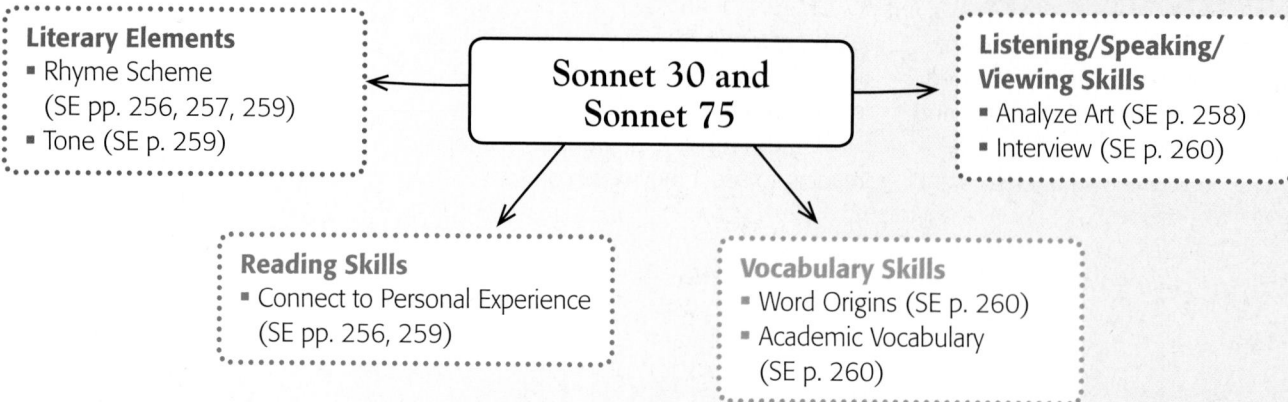

Literary Elements
- Rhyme Scheme (SE pp. 256, 257, 259)
- Tone (SE p. 259)

Sonnet 30 and Sonnet 75

Listening/Speaking/Viewing Skills
- Analyze Art (SE p. 258)
- Interview (SE p. 260)

Reading Skills
- Connect to Personal Experience (SE pp. 256, 259)

Vocabulary Skills
- Word Origins (SE p. 260)
- Academic Vocabulary (SE p. 260)

256

Sonnet 30

Edmund Spenser ☆

Unrequited Love. Colored print. O'Shea Gallery, London.

My love is like to ice, and I to fire;
How comes it then that this her cold so great
Is not dissolv'd through my so hot desire,
But harder grows the more I her entreat?[1]
5   Or how comes it that my exceeding heat
Is not delayed[2] by her heart frozen cold,
But that I burn much more in boiling sweat,
And feel my flames augmented manifold?[3]
What more miraculous thing may be told,
10 That fire, which all things melts, should harden ice,
And ice, which is **congealed** with senseless cold,
Should kindle fire by wonderful device?
Such is the power of love in gentle mind,
That it can alter all the course of kind.[4]

---

1. *Entreat* means "beg."
2. In this context, *delayed* means "lessened."
3. *Augmented manifold* means "increased greatly."
4. *Kind* means "nature."

> **Rhyme Scheme** *How does the concluding rhyming couplet summarize the contradictions in the poem?*

> **Vocabulary**
> **congeal** (kən jēl´) *v.* to harden; thicken

EDMUND SPENSER **257**

Teach

TLiterary Element   1

Rhyme Scheme Answer:
The poem draws an elaborate analogy between heat, representing the passion of the lover, and cold, representing the indifference of the beloved. The speaker wonders why his "hot desire" does not melt his beloved's "frozen cold." Alternatively, he wonders why his beloved's "ice" kindles rather than cools his fiery desire. In the final couplet, he concludes that love can change the laws of nature.

Reading Strategy   2

Connect to Personal Experience Ask: Have you ever had the experience of being drawn to someone (a potential friend, boyfriend, or girlfriend) who was indifferent to you? Was your experience like that of the speaker in this poem? Can you relate to the feelings he expresses? Explain.

Cultural History ☆

The Individual Before the Renaissance, a person was typically viewed as a part of the community, but in the sixteenth century, there was increasing interest in the idea of a person as a unique individual. This individualism is reflected in Elizabethan poetry, of which Spenser is one of the most well-known writers.

For an audio recording of this selection, use Listening Library Audio CD-ROM.

Teach

Big Idea   1

Humanists and Courtiers

Answer: *A favorite human-ist theme of the Elizabethan poets was that the poet had the power to immortalize the beloved through his or her verse.*

Explain that the power to immortalize was traditionally ascribed to God; in this poem, though, a mortal human has the power to immortalize someone through art.

(APPROACHING) Ask students having difficulty to identify the method by which the poet plans to "eternalize" his love and avoid death.

View the Art ★

Ingres (1780–1867) is considered to be the last important champion of the French classical tradition. He was a perfectionist who often revisited his works.

To check students' understanding of the selection, see Unit 2 Teaching Resources Book, p. 56.

Sonnet 75

Edmund Spenser

One day I wrote her name upon the strand,[1]
But came the waves and washèd it away:
Again I wrote it with a second hand,
But came the tide, and made my pains his prey.
5   "**Vain** man," said she, "that dost in vain assay,[2]
A **mortal** thing so to immortalize,
For I myself shall like to this decay,
And eke[3] my name be wipèd out likewise."
"Not so," quod[4] I, "let baser things devise[5]
10 To die in dust, but you shall live by fame:
My verse your virtues rare shall eternize,[6]
And in the heavens write your glorious name,
Where whenas death shall all the world subdue,
Our love shall live, and later life renew."

---

1. *Strand* means "beach."
2. *Assay* means "try."
3. *Eke* means "also."
4. *Quod* means "said."
5. *Devise* means "plan."
6. *Eternize* means "make eternal."

Humanists and Courtiers *What humanist theme of the Elizabethan period does this line express?*   **1**

Vocabulary

vain (vān) *adj.* conceited; excessively pleased with oneself
mortal (môrt´ əl) *adj.* destined to die

258   UNIT 2   THE ENGLISH RENAISSANCE

Paolo and Francesca. Jean Auguste Dominique Ingres. Oil on wood. Musée Condé, Chantilly, France.

View the Art Paolo Malatesta and Francesca de Rimini were real-life doomed lovers who inspired a memorable passage in Dante Alighieri's *Inferno*. In what ways is this image similar to the one on page 257? ★

Writing Practice

Rhyme Scheme Invite students to help you write the rhyme scheme for this poem (*abab bcbc cdcd ee*). Ask students to write a list of three words that match each end sound in the rhyme scheme for this poem. (Words should end in /and/, /a–/, /ı-z/, /a–m/, /––oo/.)

Have students try writing a sonnet that matches the rhyme scheme *abbaabba cdecde*. Suggest that they choose end sounds and brainstorm words before writing, so that they choose sounds for which there are enough words to write a poem.

After You Read

Respond and Think Critically

Respond and Interpret

1. In your opinion, which sonnet is more idealistic? Explain.

2. (a)In Sonnet 30, to what does the speaker compare his and his beloved's feelings? (b)What do these comparisons indicate about the feelings of the two people?

3. (a)Paraphrase the question the speaker asks in lines 5–8 of Sonnet 30. (b)What does this question indicate about the speaker's love?

4. (a)What **paradox**, or apparent contradiction, does the speaker point out in lines 9–12 of Sonnet 30? (b)Is the paradox resolved? Explain.

5. (a)How does the speaker's beloved respond to the speaker's actions in Sonnet 75? (b)What do you think she means by what she says?

Analyze and Evaluate

6. Assuming that these two sonnets are about the same speaker and the same woman, has their relationship changed between Sonnet 30 and Sonnet 75? Explain.

7. (a)Which sonnet employs a narrative structure? Which sonnet employs a comparison-contrast structure? (b)In your opinion, which sonnet is more effective as a love poem? Explain.

Connect

8. **Big Idea** **Humanists and Courtiers** How does Spenser reconcile humanism and religion at the end of Sonnet 75?

9. **Connect to Today** (a)What does the end of Sonnet 75 suggest about the power of poetry? (b)Is this view of poetry's power one that can be seriously held today? Why or why not?

Literary Element Rhyme Scheme

A poem's **rhyme scheme** is its pattern of end rhymes in each stanza.

1. Identify the rhyme scheme of Sonnet 30 and Sonnet 75.

2. (a)Where does the couplet, or pair of successive rhyming lines, appear in each sonnet? (b)What does Spenser accomplish in these rhyming couplets?

Reading Strategy Connect to Personal Experience

Spenser's sonnets are in the courtly love tradition, which involved the lover's idealization of the beloved and desire to immortalize her in verse.

1. How do the conventions or rituals of modern love differ from those of sixteenth-century love?

2. Do you think the desire to achieve lasting fame motivates writers and artists today? Explain.

Review: Tone

As you learned on page 245, **tone** is an expression of a writer's attitude toward his or her subject matter or audience. Tone is conveyed through such elements as word choice, sentence structure, and figures of speech. A variety of attitudes can be expressed by writers, including sympathy, objectivity, and amusement.

Partner Activity Create a chart like the one below for each poem. Then work with a partner to fill in your charts with words that convey particular tones you identify in the poems.

Word Choice	Tone
"made my pains his prey"	disappointed

After You Read

Assess

1. Answers will vary.

2. (a) fire and ice (b) They suggest his passion for her and her indifference.

3. (a) Sample answer: "Why does my passion grow as she turns colder?" (b) The speaker's love grows despite being unrequited.

4. (a) Fire hardens ice, and ice kindles fire. (b) No—his love makes her less responsive; her aloofness makes him more ardent.

5. (a) She says that trying to immortalize her is vanity. (b) She will die, and so will her memory.

6. Students may say that the words "our love" in Sonnet 75 imply that the woman has warmed to the speaker.

7. (a) Sonnet 75—narrative; Sonnet 30—comparison/contrast (b) Answers will vary.

8. The speaker says that his beloved and their love will be doubly immortalized—first in verse and later in heaven.

9. (a) It can transcend earthly decay. (b) Students may say that modern song lyrics may be seen as a type of verse that can immortalize the subject.

Reading Strategy

1. Students' answers will vary.

2. Students' answers will vary. They should provide support.

Progress Check

Can students analyze rhyme scheme?

If No → See Unit 2 Teaching Resources Book, p. 52.

Literary Element

1. Both use *abab bcbc cdcd ee*.

2. (a) At the end (b) He makes a key point that provides resolution.

Review: Tone

Focusing on the imagery in a poem can help students understand its tone. Students may want to use their charts to explore the emotions conveyed by particular images in addition to words and phrases.

After You Read
Assess

Vocabulary Practice

Possible answer:

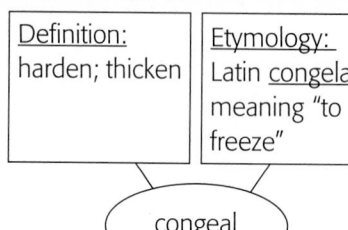

Definition: harden; thicken

Etymology: Latin <u>congelare</u>, meaning "to freeze"

congeal

Sample Sentence: After I blew out the candle, the wax began to <u>congeal</u>.

Other answers:

vain

Definition: *conceited; excessively pleased with oneself.*

Etymology: Latin <u>vanus</u>, meaning "empty"

Sample Sentence: *The vain critic treated the waiter poorly.*

mortal

Definition: *destined to die*

Etymology: Latin <u>mors</u>, meaning "death"

Sample Sentence: *Even the healthiest people are mortal.*

Academic Vocabulary

An essay consists of an introduction, thesis, body, and conclusion.

Vocabulary Practice

Practice with Word Origins Studying the etymology, or origin and history, of a word can help you better understand its meaning. Create a word map, like the one below, for each of these vocabulary words from the selection. Use a dictionary for help.

congeal   vain   mortal

EXAMPLE:

<u>Definition</u>: overcome; vanquish

<u>Etymology</u>: from Latin <u>domare</u>, meaning "to tame"

daunt

<u>Sample Sentence</u>: When the child saw how long the slide was, he was <u>daunted</u> and did not climb the ladder.

Academic Vocabulary

*The **structure** of Spenser's sonnets is different from that of English or Italian sonnets.*

Structure is an academic word. The **structure** of a sonnet includes its rhyme scheme and meter.

To further explore this word, answer the following question: What is the basic **structure** of an essay?

For more on academic vocabulary, see pages 56 and R81.

 Literature Online

Selection Resources For Selection Quizzes, eFlashcards, and Reading-Writing Connection activities, go to glencoe.com and enter QuickPass code GLB9817u2.

Speaking and Listening

Interview

Assignment Imagine that you are a parent of the woman addressed in Spenser's sonnets. Interview your daughter about her suitor, asking questions whose answers can be found in or inferred from the poems.

Prepare Create a list of relevant questions phrased in mature, sensitive, respectful language. The questions should reflect your understanding of the poems and of parents' attitudes toward their children. Leave space under each question to record the response.

Interview At a time when you won't be interrupted, conduct your interview, having a classmate play the part of your daughter. Take notes on her answers, and encourage her to add any other relevant information. Follow these tips:

- Listen respectfully without interrupting.
- Look at the interviewee frequently while she's speaking, but don't stare.
- Adjust your tone of voice and body language to make her comfortable.
- Ask questions to clarify information.
- Review all of the responses with the interviewee, make any necessary changes, and thank her for her cooperation.
- If possible, tape-record your interview so that you can refer to it later on.

Report Summarize what you learned about the suitor in a written statement. Present the information in the order of its importance—to either you or your interviewee. Be sure to note when something is your own interpretation, instead of a response from the interview itself.

Evaluate Evaluate your interview and summary for clarity, accuracy, and completeness.

Speaking and Listening

Use these criteria in evaluating student interviews:

- Interview questions are open-ended and phrased with sensitivity and respect.
- The interviewer uses good listening techniques and gathers useful information.
- The interview summary is well-organized and accurate.

For additional selection assessment, see Assessment Resources, pp. 89–90.

Before You Read

Sonnet 31

Meet **Sir Philip Sidney**
(1554–1586)

Sir Philip Sidney was truly a Renaissance man—someone who can do a variety of things exceptionally well—like so many of the great figures of the Renaissance. Sidney was a brilliant courtier whose refined, aristocratic behavior made him for a time a particular favorite of Queen Elizabeth's. He also was a statesman, a brave soldier, a noted patron of the arts, and a gifted writer of both poetry and prose.

Educated by private tutors until he was ten, Sidney then entered Shrewsbury School, where he met his lifelong friend Fulke Greville, who later became his biographer. Sidney studied at Oxford from 1568 to 1571 but left before receiving a degree because of an outbreak of the plague. He completed his education by traveling abroad, visiting cities such as Paris, Frankfurt, Venice, and Vienna.

Literary Renown Sidney's diverse talents are reflected in his writings. He has been called the "father of English literary criticism" for his extended essay *The Defence of Poesie*, an eloquent argument against Puritan charges that poetry is immoral. His romance the *Arcadia* is one of the finest imaginative prose works of Elizabethan times. Sidney is best known, however, for his sonnet sequence *Astrophel and Stella*, first published in 1591. In this work, which includes 108 sonnets and eleven songs, Sidney examines love from many different perspectives.

Like most members of the upper class, Sidney wrote for himself and his friends; only a few of his works were published during his lifetime. He spent his time traveling, encouraging other writers (including Edmund Spenser), and volunteering for causes in which he believed.

> *"They are never alone that are accompanied with noble thoughts."*
>
> —Sir Philip Sidney

Tragic Death In 1585 Sidney was appointed governor of Flushing, an important English fortress in the Netherlands. There, at age thirty-one, while fighting alongside Dutch Protestants in their battle against Spanish Catholics in the Netherlands, he was seriously wounded by a musket shot that shattered his thighbone. Even in this debilitated state, Sidney was the picture of gentility. Just as he was about to take a drink, he saw a soldier nearby who was dying and offered his drink to the man, saying, "Thy necessity is greater than mine." Sidney succumbed to infection and died twenty-six days after being wounded. His death caused much grief in England. Queen Elizabeth and her subjects mourned the passing of this poet, the embodiment of Renaissance nobility.

 Literature Online

Author Search For more about Sir Philip Sidney, go to glencoe.com and enter QuickPass code GLB9817u2.

SIR PHILIP SIDNEY   **261**

Before You Read

Focus

Bellringer Options

Daily Language Practice Transparency 21

Or ask: What words, images, and feelings do you associate with the word *love*? Work with students to make a concept web about love. **Say:** As you read this poem, pay attention to the words, images, and feelings that this poet associates with love.

Approaching Level

DIFFERENTIATED INSTRUCTION

Established The title of this selection tells the reader that Sidney's poem is a sonnet. **Say:** There are two major types of sonnets in English. Petrarchan sonnets feature an *abbaabba* rhyme scheme in the first eight lines. Shakespearean sonnets have an *abab cdcd* rhyme scheme in the first eight lines.

Ask students to look at the rhyme scheme before they read the poem and determine whether the poem is a Petrarchan or a Shakespearian sonnet. *(Petrarchan)*

Before You Read

Focus

Summary

In this sonnet, the speaker beseeches the moon to tell him whether romantic love is as disappointing and painful on the Moon as the speaker clearly finds it to be on Earth.

 For summaries in languages other than English, see Unit 2 Teaching Resources Book, pp. 58–63.

Vocabulary

Analogy Write on the board: assist : helpful :: scorn : proud.
Say: Use analogies to draw connections between things of different types. Someone who assists is helpful, while someone who scorns is proud. Have students create an analogy for each of the vocabulary words.

 For additional vocabulary practice, see Unit 2 Teaching Resources Book, p. 66.

 For additional context, see Glencoe Interactive Vocabulary CD-ROM.

Selection Skills

Literature and Reading Preview

Connect to the Poem

Why do people sometimes associate moonlight and the moon with love and romance? Freewrite for a few minutes to explore your ideas about this question.

Build Background

This sonnet is from *Astrophel and Stella,* which is a **sonnet sequence**, or a series of sonnets interrelated by content or theme. In Sidney's sonnets, the speaker is called Astrophel. The real Stella was Penelope Devereux, to whom Sidney was briefly engaged, though the engagement was broken off when Devereux's family required her to marry the wealthy Lord Rich.

Set Purposes for Reading

Big Idea Humanists and Courtiers

This sonnet focuses on romantic passion rather than religious concerns. As you read, ask yourself, How does the poem reflect humanist interests?

Literary Element Apostrophe

Apostrophe is a figure of speech in which a writer addresses an absent person, an inanimate object, or an idea. Often, the word *O* is used in apostrophe, as in lines 1 and 9 of Sidney's poem. As you read, ask yourself, What effect does the poet's use of apostrophe have?

Reading Strategy Examine Denotation and Connotation

The **denotation** of a word is its direct meaning or dictionary definition. A word's **connotations** are the ideas and emotions associated with it. Connotations may be positive, negative, or neutral. For example, if you want to compliment a friend on her ability to save money, you would be wise to call her *thrifty* rather than *cheap*. As you read, ask yourself, How does Sidney draw on words' connotations to convey the speaker's feelings?

Tip: Taking Notes Use word webs to record words from Sidney's poem, along with their connotations.

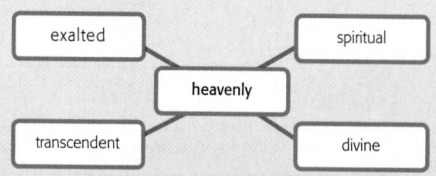

Learning Objectives

For pages 261–264

In studying this text, you will focus on the following objectives:

Literary Study: Analyze apostrophe.

Reading: Examining denotation and connotation.

Writing: Writing a letter.

Vocabulary

wan (won) *adj.* pale; p. 263 *Her wan complexion and watery eyes revealed that she was ill.*

languished (lang′ gwisht) *adj.* dispirited; lacking vitality; p. 263 *After a long stay in the hospital, he felt droopy and languished.*

deem (dēm) *v.* to regard as; consider; p. 263 *Marla's essay was deemed worthy of publication.*

scorn (skôrn) *v.* to reject as contemptible or unworthy; p. 263 *Heather and Jillian scorn those who do not belong to their social circle.*

Tip: Analogies To complete an analogy, decide on the relationship between the ideas represented by the first pair of words. Then apply that relationship to the second pair.

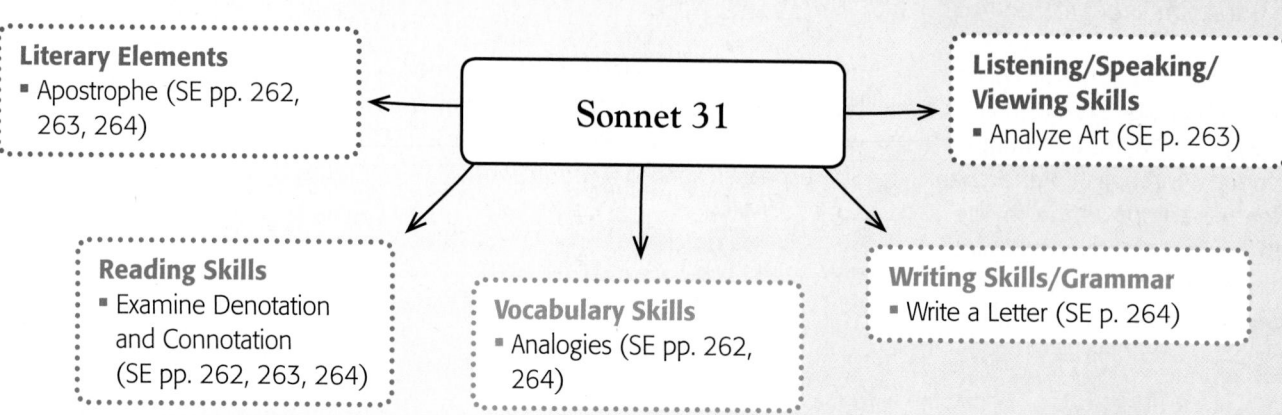

Literary Elements
- Apostrophe (SE pp. 262, 263, 264)

Sonnet 31

Listening/Speaking/Viewing Skills
- Analyze Art (SE p. 263)

Reading Skills
- Examine Denotation and Connotation (SE pp. 262, 263, 264)

Vocabulary Skills
- Analogies (SE pp. 262, 264)

Writing Skills/Grammar
- Write a Letter (SE p. 264)

Sonnet 31

from *Astrophel and Stella*

Sir Philip Sidney

Astronomical Observation: Venus. Donato Creti. Pinacoteca, Vatican Museums.

<u>View the Art</u> This painting was one in a series meant to persuade Pope Clement XI to finance the construction of an observatory. What does the sense of scale in the image—the relative sizes of objects—suggest about the artist's view of human importance? Why might this have been a wise view for him to have?

With how sad steps, O Moon, thou climb'st the skies!
How silently, and with how **wan** a face!
What, may it be that even in heavenly place
That busy archer his sharp arrows tries?[1]
5   Sure, if that long-with-love-acquainted eyes
Can judge of love, thou feel'st a lover's case,
I read it in thy looks; thy **languished** grace,
To me, that feel the like, thy state descries.[2]
Then, even of fellowship, O Moon, tell me,
10 Is constant love **deemed** there but want of wit?[3]
Are beauties there as proud as here they be?
Do they above love to be loved, and yet
Those lovers **scorn** whom that love doth possess?
Do they call virtue there ungratefulness?

---

1. The *busy archer* is Cupid, the Roman god of love.
2. *Descries* is another word for "reveals."
3. Here, *wit* refers to intelligence.

> **Apostrophe** *What does the speaker imagine that he and the moon have in common?* **1**

> **Examine Denotation and Connotation** *What does the word* fellowship *suggest about the speaker's attitude toward the moon?* **2**

Vocabulary

wan (won) *adj.* pale
languish (lang′ gwish) *adj.* dispirited; lacking vitality
deem (dēm) *v.* to regard as; consider
scorn (skôrn) *v.* to reject as contemptible or unworthy

SIR PHILIP SIDNEY **263**

After You Read

Assess

1. Students might advise the speaker to keep busy with other interests and to try to get over the heartache of unrequited love.

2. (a) A face and emotions (b) The speaker wants to share his sadness.

3. (a) In the heavens, is enduring love a sign of stupidity? Are beautiful women there as proud as they are on earth? Do women love being loved but scorn those who love them? (b) His beloved is fickle, haughty, and contemptuous.

4. It imitates the moon's slow climb through the sky and the slow movements of a sad person.

5. It focuses on the experience of love and loss, a secular concern.

6. Students may say that the poem does not accurately portray Sidney's relationship with Penelope, since their engagement was broken off because of her parents' wishes rather than her coldness.

Literary Element

1. It reveals a feeling of helplessness.

2. Students might share the idea that the moon, or the "man in the moon," has a melancholy face.

Progress Check

Can students identify apostrophe?

If No → See Unit 2 Teaching Resources Book, p. 64.

After You Read

Respond and Think Critically

Respond and Interpret

1. What advice would you give to the speaker of this sonnet? Explain.

2. (a) What human qualities does the speaker attribute to the moon? (b) What does this use of **personification** reveal about the speaker's emotional state?

3. (a) Paraphrase the questions that the speaker asks in lines 10–14. (b) What do these questions imply about the object of the speaker's love?

Analyze and Evaluate

4. When a line of poetry consists of one-syllable words, readers are forced to read it slowly. How does the slow pace support the meaning of lines 1–2?

Connect

5. **Big Idea** Humanists and Courtiers In what ways does this sonnet reflect humanist concerns?

6. **Connect to the Author** Does your knowledge that Sidney was unable to marry Penelope Devereux affect your reading of this poem? Explain your answer.

Literary Element Apostrophe

In poetry, **apostrophe** and **personification** are figures of speech that often go hand in hand. For example, in this sonnet, Sidney both addresses the moon and gives it human qualities. Poets often use apostrophe to achieve a sense of emotional immediacy.

1. How does the apostrophe help reveal the speaker's emotional state?

2. In what ways are your thoughts and feelings about the moon similar to or different from the speaker's?

Reading Strategy Examine Denotation and Connotation

Paying attention to words' **connotations** can provide you with clues about the author's attitude toward his or her subject.

Select three words from Sonnet 31 and explain how their connotations enhance your understanding of the speaker.

Writing

Write a Letter In Sonnet 31, Sir Philip Sidney addresses the moon as if it were able to reply to him. Use the techniques of apostrophe and personification to write a letter to an inanimate object, asking questions you wish it would answer. Your letter should be informal, with a polite tone.

LOG ON ▶ **Literature** Online

Selection Resources For Selection Quizzes, eFlashcards, and Reading-Writing Connection activities, go to glencoe.com and enter QuickPass code GLB9817u2.

264 UNIT 2   THE ENGLISH RENAISSANCE

Vocabulary Practice

Practice with Analogies Choose the word that best completes each analogy below.

1. silent : loud :: languished :
   a. energetic   **b.** lethargic
2. scare : frighten :: deem :
   a. earn   **b.** evaluate
3. praise : scold :: scorn :
   a. display   **b.** accept
4. loyal : faithful :: wan :
   a. pastel   **b.** sickly

Reading Strategy

Answers will vary.

Vocabulary

1. a **2.** b **3.** b **4.** b

Writing

Letters will vary, but they should demonstrate an understanding of apostrophe and personification.

 For additional assessment, see Assessment Resources, pp. 91–92.

Before You Read

The Passionate Shepherd to His Love

Meet **Christopher Marlowe**

(1564–1593)

The nineteenth-century poet Alfred, Lord Tennyson, wrote, "If Shakespeare is the dazzling sun of this mighty period, Marlowe is certainly the morning star." Born two months before William Shakespeare, Christopher Marlowe, with his innovative verse and shocking tragedies, led the way for Shakespeare and other Elizabethan writers. Though his literary career spanned only six years, Marlowe is considered by many critics to be the father of English drama. With the premiere of *Tamburlaine the Great*, blank verse, which Ben Jonson called Marlowe's "mighty line," became the staple of Elizabethan writing.

> *"Nature that fram'd us of four elements,*
> *Warring within our breasts for regiment,*
> *Doth teach us all to have aspiring minds."*
>
> —Christopher Marlowe, *Tamburlaine*

From Humble Beginnings Born in 1564, Marlowe was the son of a shoemaker. At age seventeen, he received a scholarship to attend Cambridge. While there, Marlowe was recruited by Sir Francis Walsingham to serve as a secret agent for Queen Elizabeth—a path that led to trouble.

Marlowe was nearly denied his master of arts because the university found his lengthy absences suspicious and potentially heretical. However, a letter from the Privy Council righted the situation: "It was not Her Majesty's pleasure that anyone employed, as he [Marlowe] had been, in matters touching the benefit of his country, should be defamed by those that are ignorant in th' affairs he went about." Some believe his "affairs" helped uncover the most dangerous conspiracy to assassinate the queen.

Poetry and Drama
While at Cambridge, Marlowe translated Ovid's *Amores* into English by using blank verse and rhyming pentameter couplets. He also wrote *Tamburlaine*, the play that launched him into the London spotlight in 1587. Marlowe's plays, including *The Tragicall History of Dr. Faustus*, *Edward II*, *The Massacre at Paris*, and *The Jew of Malta*, provide a social commentary and reveal his feelings about Queen Elizabeth's rule, as well as his deep awareness of corruption through power, the darkness of individual suffering, the danger of greed, and the need for social responsibility.

A Dramatic Ending While in London, Marlowe met the dramatist Thomas Kyd, an acquaintance that would later prove fatal. In 1593 Kyd was arrested by officers of the court. Papers denying the divinity of Jesus Christ and referring to the Roman Catholic Church had been found in Kyd's room. Under torture and duress, Kyd professed his innocence and claimed the papers belonged to Marlowe and had been merely "shuffled" into his. Marlowe was arrested on May 20, 1593, on the charges of atheism and blasphemy.

Ten days later, Marlowe was stabbed in the eye and died at the lodging house of Dame Eleanor Bull in Deptford. Marlowe had spent the afternoon with three other men, all of whom were associated with Sir Francis Walsingham, head of the queen's secret service. The circumstances of his death have been debated for centuries. Some believe the murder was the result of a dispute over a bill, but many believe Marlowe was assassinated.

LOG ON ▶ **Literature** Online

Author Search For more about Christopher Marlowe, go to glencoe.com and enter QuickPass code GLB9817u2.

CHRISTOPHER MARLOWE **265**

Before You Read

Focus

Bellringer Options

Selection Focus Transparency 12

Daily Language Practice Transparency 22

Or ask: Are you more drawn to urban or rural life? Why? How familiar are you with life in urban (rural) places? What are some common ways that urban (rural) life is idealized by people from rural (urban) places? What are some drawbacks that these ideals don't consider? Lead a discussion with students, based on these questions.

Selection Skills

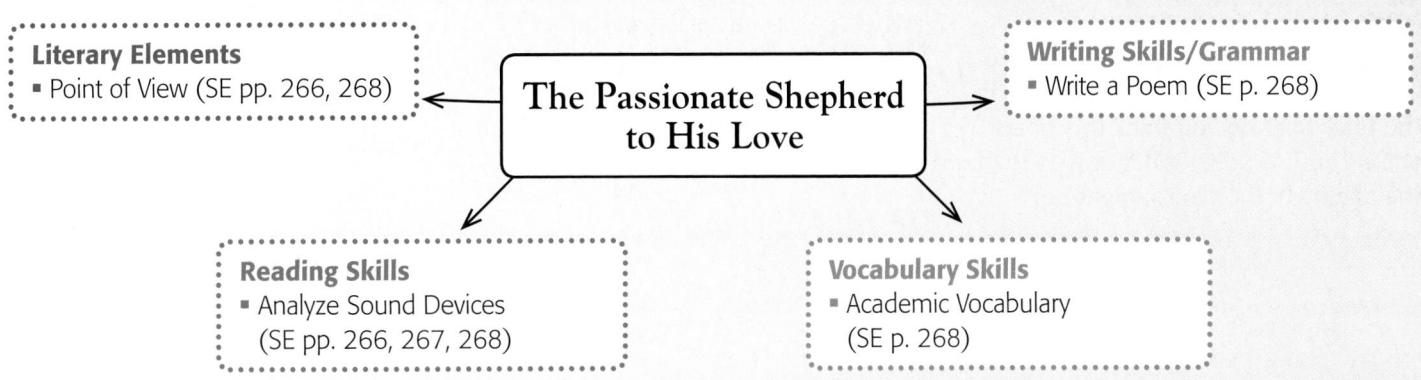

Literary Elements
- Point of View (SE pp. 266, 268)

Writing Skills/Grammar
- Write a Poem (SE p. 268)

The Passionate Shepherd to His Love

Reading Skills
- Analyze Sound Devices (SE pp. 266, 267, 268)

Vocabulary Skills
- Academic Vocabulary (SE p. 268)

Before You Read

Focus

Summary

"The Passionate Shepherd to His Love" is a pastoral poem—one that idealizes simple lives lived in rural settings, in harmony with nature. The speaker asks his beloved to join him in a life of rural bliss. In typical pastoral tradition, the speaker delights in the beauty and innocence of rural life.

For summaries in languages other than English, see Unit 2 Teaching Resources Book, pp. 70–75.

Interactive Read and Write

Other options for teaching this selection can be found in

- Interactive Read and Write for EL Students pp. 85–90
- Interactive Read and Write for Approaching-Level Students, pp. 85–90
- Interactive Read and Write for On-Level Students, pp. 85–90

Literature and Reading Preview

Connect to the Poem

How might a setting of rustic simplicity lend itself to a depiction of love? List some characteristics of such a setting that make it an appropriate backdrop for lovers.

Build Background

Written in the pastoral tradition, "The Passionate Shepherd to His Love" was not meant to be realistic, but an idealized celebration of the "natural life." Considered one of the greatest pastoral poems ever written, it inspired several responses from other poets, including John Donne and Sir Walter Raleigh.

Set Purposes for Reading

Big Idea Humanists and Courtiers

As you read, ask yourself, How does the exaggerated style and setting of "The Passionate Shepherd to His Love" reflect the shift in focus from otherworldly concerns to secular subjects like love, politics, and science?

Literary Element Point of View

The standpoint from which a poem is told is called **point of view.** A first-person speaker uses *I* and *me*. A third-person speaker is an observer, not a participant in the action. In this poem, Marlowe uses a first-person point of view. The speaker is a humble shepherd, not a sophisticated city dweller like Marlowe. As you read, ask yourself, How does Marlowe exploit this point of view in speaking about the joys of love?

Reading Strategy Analyze Sound Devices

Sound devices are techniques used to enhance a poem's sense of rhythm, to emphasize particular sounds, or to add to the musical quality of poetry. One sound device is **alliteration**, or the repetition of consonant sounds at the beginnings of words. As you read this poem, ask yourself, How is alliteration used to reinforce meaning or tone and create a musical effect?

Tip: Taking Notes Use a chart to record Marlowe's uses of alliteration and their effects.

Alliteration	Effects

Shepherd Piping to a Shepherdess, 1747–1750. Francois Boucher. 94 x 142 cm. Wallace Collection, London.

Reading Practice

SPIRAL REVIEW **Predict** Ask students to think about the title of the poem and to look at the illustration. **Ask:** From the title, what do you think this poem will be about? *(love)* What do you think the setting of the poem might be?

Why? *(a pastoral setting, because the title includes the word "shepherd")* Now have students read the first line of each stanza. **Ask:** Were your guesses about the subject and setting correct?

The Passionate Shepherd to His Love

Christopher Marlowe

Come live with me, and be my love,
And we will all the pleasures prove[1]
That valleys, groves, hills, and fields,
Woods or steepy mountain yields.

5 And we will sit upon the rocks,
Seeing the shepherds feed their flocks,
By shallow rivers to whose falls
Melodious birds sing madrigals.[2]

And I will make thee beds of roses,
10 And a thousand fragrant posies,
A cap of flowers, and a kirtle[3]
Embroidered all with leaves of myrtle.

A gown made of the finest wool,
Which from our pretty lambs we pull,
15 Fair lined slippers for the cold,
With buckles of the purest gold.

A belt of straw and ivy buds,
With coral clasps and amber studs.
And if these pleasures may thee move,
20 Come live with me and be my love.

The shepherd swains[4] shall dance and sing
For thy delight each May morning;
If these delights thy mind may move,
Then live with me and be my love.

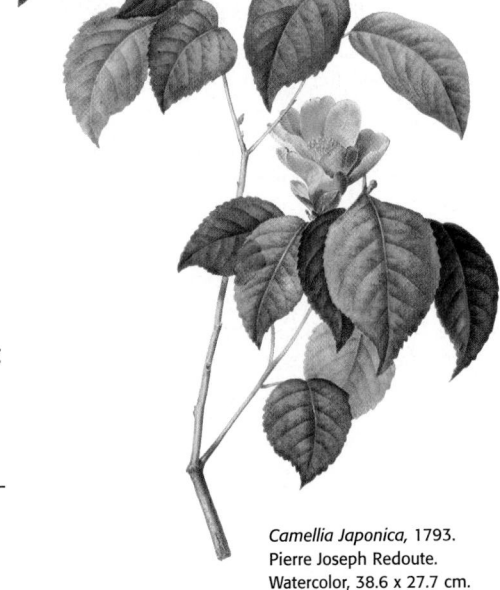

Camellia Japonica, 1793.
Pierre Joseph Redoute.
Watercolor, 38.6 x 27.7 cm.
Fitzwilliam Museum,
University of Cambridge.

---

1. Marlowe uses *prove* here to mean "experience."
2. *Madrigals* are harmonious songs.
3. A *kirtle* is a dress.
4. *Swains* means "youths."

Analyze Sound Devices *How does the alliteration in this line contribute to the effect of the poem?*

CHRISTOPHER MARLOWE **267**

Teach

Literary Element   1

Point of View   Ask: How would you describe this speaker's view of rural life? (*He idealizes rural life; he portrays it as innocent and romantic.*)

Reading Strategy   2

Analyze Sound Devices

Answer: *The line has many soft, flowing sounds; the alliteration of* melodious *and* madrigals *contributes to the gentle flow of the verse.*

(APPROACHING) Have students group together all the words in this stanza that begin with the same consonant sounds. (*w:* we will; *s:* sit, seeing, sing; *sh:* shepherds, shallow; *r:* rocks, rivers; *f:* feed, flocks, falls; *m:* melodious, madrigals)

For additional practice using the reading skill or strategy, see Unit 2 Teaching Resources Book, p. 77.

Big Idea   3

Humanists and Courtiers

Ask: How do the subject of this poem and the concerns of the speaker express a humanist stance? (*A relationship between two individuals is the poem's subject. This speaker's concerns are human love and daily life. He does not mention—and does not seem concerned about— God or an afterlife. All of this shows the poem's humanist stance.*)

After You Read

Assess

1. Students should be able to articulate their views about love and discuss whether the poem reflects those views.

2. (a) Beds of roses, a woolen gown, lined slippers, and dancing youths (b) They show his desire to please.

3. (a) Carefree and leisurely (b) This description does not reflect the hard work required of a shepherd.

4. (a) It creates a simple, musical quality, similar to children's poems. They contribute to the speaker's idyllic, innocent tone. (b) He may be trying to emphasize the beauty and ease of rural life.

5. They suggest the dissatisfaction of urban people who yearn for the innocence of a simpler time and place.

6. Students may say that a modern woman would realize that the day-to-day life of a shepherd is tedious and dirty, not idyllic.

Writing

Students' poems will vary, but each should employ a similiar rhyme scheme and a modern point of view.

Progress Check

Can students analyze point of view?

If No → See Unit 2 Teaching Resources Book, p. 76.

For additional assessment, see Assessment Resources, pp. 93–94.

268

After You Read

Respond and Think Critically

Respond and Interpret

1. Has your view of love changed after reading this poem? Why or why not?

2. (a)How does the nymph characterize all the treasures the shepherd offers? (b)What does the nymph's response to the shepherd reveal about her view of life?

Analyze and Evaluate

3. (a)Would the meaning of this poem be different if you had not already read "The Passionate Shepherd to His Love"? Explain. (b)How does reading these two poems together increase the impact of the poems?

4. How does Raleigh use imagery to express the nymph's views of life and the shepherd's promises?

Connect

5. **Big Idea** **Humanists and Courtiers** At this time, writers were focusing on the concerns of love, politics, science, and philosophy. (a)What do you think the theme of Raleigh's poem is? (b)How does the theme reflect Raleigh's views on these worldly subjects? Explain.

6. **Connect to Today** Can you think of any modern movies, TV shows, or literary works that are direct responses to previous works? How do they relate to the previous works?

Literary Element **Author's Purpose**

An **author's purpose** can be to persuade, to describe, to inform, to explain, or to entertain.

1. Why might Raleigh have written a response to Marlowe's "The Passionate Shepherd to His Love"?

2. Why did Raleigh use the same meter and references that Marlowe used?

Reading Strategy **Compare and Contrast Speakers**

The nymph in Raleigh's poem responds to each of the shepherd's pleas, and her responses establish the tone of the poem.

1. How does the nymph's tone compare to the shepherd's tone?

2. What words or phrases help you determine the nymph's tone?

 Writing

Write a List Reread "The Nymph's Reply to the Shepherd" and make a list of the reasons the nymph gives for refusing the shepherd's offer. Which reasons do you agree with? Which seem less persuasive? Reorganize your list to show the nymph's reasons in order, from most important to least important.

LOG ON ▶ **Literature** Online

Selection Resources For Selection Quizzes, eFlashcards, and Reading-Writing Connection activities, go to glencoe.com and enter QuickPass code GLB9817u2.

Academic Vocabulary

In Raleigh's poem, the girl from Marlowe's poem **amends** the shepherd's statements about love.

Amend is an academic word. More familiar words that are similar in meaning are *change*, *improve*, and *correct*.

To further explore the meaning of this word, answer the following question: How does the nymph **amend** what the shepherd has said?

For more on academic vocabulary, see pages 56 and R81.

Literary Element

1. Students might respond that Marlowe chose a male's point of view because he could easily relate to it.

2. The responding poets could have easily written from the beloved's point of view, or they could have used an urban man rather than a shepherd.

Reading Strategy

Students may say that the repeated use of the *l* sound adds a lulling, musical mood.

Academic Vocabulary

Students might describe a situation in which a person behaved selfishly under a guise of selflessness.

Before You Read

The Nymph's Reply to the Shepherd

Meet **Sir Walter Raleigh**
(1552–1618)

Sir Walter Raleigh was a soldier, explorer, colonizer, courtier, poet, scientist, and historian—perhaps the best example of a Renaissance man to emerge from the Elizabethan Age. He was described as "the most romantic figure of the most romantic age in the annals of English history" by biographer Hugh de Selincourt. Like Christopher Marlowe, Raleigh was brilliant and ambitious. He is credited as the father of both the British Empire and modern historical writing. He also introduced the potato to Ireland and tobacco to England. Even so, Raleigh experienced several spectacular failures. In his lifetime, he went from a war hero, favorite of the queen, and most loved man in England to a heretic accused of high treason and a prisoner of the court for more than a decade.

> *"We should begin by such a parting light*
> *To write the story of all ages past,*
> *And end the same before th' approaching night."*
>
> —Sir Walter Raleigh, *Ocean to Cynthia*

Quest for Excellence Raleigh began his career as a soldier and persuaded Elizabeth and her council to sponsor a voyage that established the first English colony—named Virginia after Queen Elizabeth, the Virgin Queen—in the hope of furthering England's position in the New World. However, his attempt to found a colony at Roanoke Island failed, as did most of his later overseas enterprises, such as his quest to find gold in Guiana.

Literary Man A patron of poets, Raleigh was also a poet himself. Fellow poet Edmund Spenser,

whom Raleigh brought to Elizabeth's court from Ireland, claimed Raleigh's verse was "the sommers Nightingale." Critics, however, disagree about Raleigh's stature as a poet. Some argue that he "ranks even better amongst the minor poets of his time" and is indeed "extraordinary by any standards," while others label him "sometimes a Poet, not often."

The authenticity of some poems credited to Raleigh has been debated, but much of his best work simply disappeared or was left unsigned. Like many court poets, he resisted the "stigma of print." However, his remaining poems, his many papers, and his only book, *The History of the World*, mark Raleigh as a gifted writer who deserves his place in English literature.

Imprisonment When Raleigh secretly married one of the queen's ladies-in-waiting, Elizabeth turned on him and sent him to the Tower of London. He was briefly released, but after James I came to power in 1603, Raleigh was falsely accused of treason and sentenced to death. He remained in the Tower for the rest of his life, and it was there that he wrote his long, incomplete book *The History of the World*. He was to dedicate it to the Prince of Wales, his most powerful supporter, who is said to have declared, "None but my father would keep such a bird in a cage." The prince died in 1612 before he could help Raleigh, who was finally beheaded in 1618. As he examined his executioner's ax, Raleigh remarked, "This is a sharp medicine, but it is a cure for all diseases." His final words, as the executioner hesitated, were "Strike, man!"

Literature Online

Author Search For more about Sir Walter Raleigh, go to glencoe.com and enter QuickPass code GLB9817u2.

SIR WALTER RALEIGH **269**

Before You Read

Focus

Bellringer Options

Daily Language Practice Transparency 23

Or ask: When it comes to love, are you a romantic or a realist? Do you like to dream about how perfect things could be with your beloved? Or, do you try to see all good and bad aspects of people and relationships? What are the advantages and disadvantages of being a romantic? A pragmatist? Lead a discussion with students, based on these questions.

Selection Skills

Literary Elements
- Author's Purpose (SE pp. 270, 271, 272)

The Nymph's Reply to the Shepherd

Listening/Speaking/Viewing Skills
- Analyze Art (SE p. 271)

Reading Skills
- Compare and Contrast Speakers (SE pp. 270, 271, 272)

Writing Skills/Grammar
- Write a List (SE p. 272)

Vocabulary Skills
- Academic Vocabulary (SE p. 272)

Before You Read

Focus

Summary

"The Nymph's Reply to the Shepherd" contains pastoral imagery like that in "The Passionate Shepherd to His Love." The speaker of this poem, however, has a much different stance toward the material. This poem is a point-by-point rebuttal of the romantic portrayal of rustic life in Marlowe's poem. Rather than being swept away by romantic notions, the speaker points out the difficulties inherent to rustic life.

 For summaries in languages other than English, see Unit 2 Teaching Resources Book, pp. 80–85.

Literature and Reading Preview

Connect to the Poem

What is your view of love? Are you romantic? Are you realistic? Or are you a little bit of both? Write a journal entry in which you analyze your view.

Build Background

This poem is a response to Christopher Marlowe's pastoral "The Passionate Shepherd to His Love" (page 267). Raleigh's nymph rejects each worldly pleasure the shepherd offers. The themes of the poem—the swiftness of time's passage, the corruption of society through greed and power, the inevitability of death, and the lies of lovers—appeared in many of Raleigh's works.

Set Purposes for Reading

Big Idea Humanists and Courtiers

Like Marlowe and other sixteenth-century writers, Raleigh explored love, politics, science, and philosophy in his writing and in his life. As you read this poem, ask yourself, How does Raleigh address some of these issues?

Literary Element Author's Purpose

An **author's intent** when writing a literary work is called the author's purpose. Authors typically write to persuade, to inform, to explain, to entertain, or to describe. As you read, ask yourself, What was Raleigh's purpose in responding to Marlowe's poem?

Reading Strategy Compare and Contrast Speakers

The **speaker** of a poem is similar to the narrator in a work of prose. The speaker's words communicate a particular tone toward the subject of the work. The nymph—the shepherd's love—is the speaker in Raleigh's poem, and she responds to the pleas of Marlowe's shepherd. As you read, ask yourself, How is the nymph's point of view similar to or different from that of the shepherd in Marlowe's poem?

Tip: Comparing and Contrasting Read both poems stanza by stanza, and use a chart to compare and contrast the speakers' points of view.

Stanza	Nymph	Shepherd
1.		
2.		

Learning Objectives

For pages 269–272

In studying this text, you will focus on the following objectives:

Literary Study: Analyzing author's purpose.

Reading: Comparing and contrasting speakers.

Writing: Writing a list.

Reading Practice

SPIRAL REVIEW Build Background Tell students that "The Nymph's Reply to the Shepherd" was written in response to "The Passionate Shepherd to His Love." **Ask:** What do you think the nymph's reply will be? *(Some students may say that the nymph will live with the shepherd; others will have different ideas.)* **Say:** Now read the first stanza of the poem. What words make you think the nymph might be skeptical of the shepherd's promises? *("If all the world and love were young, / And truth in every shepherd's tongue")*

The Nymph's Reply to the Shepherd

Sir Walter Raleigh

Shepherd and Shepherdess. Abraham Bloemaert. Oil on canvas. Collection of the Earl of Pembroke, Wilton House, Wilts, UK.

View the Art Peasants, shepherds, and shepherdesses were recurring figures in Bloemaert's work. Does the pair in this image more closely resemble the subjects of Marlowe's poem or of Raleigh's? ★

If all the world and love were young,
And truth in every shepherd's tongue,
These pretty pleasures might me move,
To live with thee and be thy love.

5 Time drives the flocks from field to fold,[1]
When rivers rage, and rocks grow cold,
And Philomel[2] becometh dumb,
The rest complains of cares to come.

The flowers do fade, and wanton[3] fields
10 To wayward winter reckoning yields;
A honey tongue, a heart of gall,[4]
Is fancy's spring but sorrow's fall.

Thy gowns, thy shoes, thy beds of roses,
Thy cap, thy kirtle, and thy posies,
15 Soon break, soon wither, soon forgotten;
In folly ripe, in reason rotten.

Thy belt of straw and ivy buds,
Thy coral clasps and amber studs,
All these in me no means can move
20 To come to thee and be thy love.

But could youth last, and love still breed,
Had joys no date[5] nor age no need,
Then these delights my mind might move
To live with thee and be thy love.

---

1. The flocks are driven to a *fold,* or sheep enclosure.
2. *Philomel* refers to the nightingale. In Greek mythology, Philomela was turned into a nightingale by the gods.
3. *Wanton* means "ample" or "luxuriant."
4. Here, *gall* is bitterness.
5. Raleigh uses *date* to mean "end."

Author's Purpose *How do these lines help to establish Raleigh's purpose?* **1**

Compare and Contrast Speakers *Compare lines 13–15 with lines 9–16 in "The Passionate Shepherd to His Love." How do the speakers' tones differ?* **2**

After You Read

Assess

1. Students should be able to articulate any changes in their views of love.

2. (a) They lack permanence. (b) The nymph is practical—pleasures are fleeting.

3. (a) Students may say that they might not have understood the meaning or tone. (b) Marlowe idealizes rural life. Raleigh points out the gap between pastoral ideals and reality.

4. Examples include cooling rocks and withering flowers.

5. (a) Lovers lie, and worldly delights cannot stop time. (b) It shows that earthly pleasures cannot provide lasting happiness.

6. Answers will vary. Many of the responses they cite may be parodies of previous works.

Literary Element

1. He may have wanted to give his perspective on the pastoral tradition.

2. Raleigh wanted to create an obvious and direct reply, so he matched Marlowe stanza for stanza and used the same meter. Also, Marlowe's poem was extremely popular, so people would immediately recognize to whom the nymph was replying.

Progress Check

Can students analyze author's purpose?

If No → See Unit 2 Teaching Resources Book, p. 86.

 For additional assessment, see Assessment Resources, pp. 97–98.

Reading Strategy

1. The nymph's tone is realistic; the shepherd's is idealistic and fanciful.

2. *cold, folly, rotten*

Writing

Items on students' lists will vary, but they should be arranged in order of importance.

After You Read

Respond and Think Critically

Respond and Interpret

1. Does this poem reflect your idea of love? Why or why not?

2. (a)What things does the shepherd promise to give his beloved? (b)What do these promises tell you about the shepherd and his love for the woman?

3. (a)Describe the kind of life the couple would have according to the shepherd. (b)Is this a realistic possibility? Explain.

Analyze and Evaluate

4. Marlowe uses rhymes at the ends of each pair of lines. (a)What effect does this use of rhyme have on the tone of the poem? (b)What might Marlowe be trying to emphasize with his rhymes?

Connect

5. **Big Idea** **Humanists and Courtiers**
Marlowe's work, like that of many of his contemporaries, reflects ideas about love, politics, and philosophy. While the main subjects of this poem are love and the simple life, the poem also suggests other ideas. How might the ideas of this poem reflect the politics and society of the time?

6. **Connect to Today** Do you think a modern woman would find the shepherd's words persuasive? Why or why not?

Literary Element Point of View

Marlowe wrote his poem from the point of view of the shepherd, who is attempting to persuade his love to live with him. This poem inspired many responses from other poets.

1. Why might Marlowe have chosen to write from the point of view of the shepherd?

2. What point of view might other poets have used when writing their responses?

Writing

Write a Poem Suppose the speaker of Marlowe's poem were a modern person, writing a poem to his beloved. What might his profession be? What kind of setting and lifestyle might he promise her? Write a poem from the point of view of a modern "shepherd." Try to employ rhyme schemes and rhythms like those used in the original poem.

LOG ON ▶ **Literature** Online

Selection Resources For Selection Quizzes, eFlashcards, and Reading-Writing Connection activities, go to glencoe.com and enter QuickPass code GLB9817u2.

Reading Strategy Analyze Sound Devices

Marlowe uses **alliteration** to reinforce the poem's meaning and tone. Review the chart you made.

Marlowe uses the alliteration of *live* and *love* in the poem's first line and in the last lines of the fifth and sixth stanzas. What does this repeated alliteration contribute to the poem's mood?

Academic Vocabulary ▶

The shepherd does not explicitly reveal his motivation for promising his love fine things.

Motivation is an academic word that appears in everyday usage. In a criminal procedure, prosecutors attempt to establish an accused person's **motivation** for committing a crime.

To further explore the meaning of this word, describe a situation you once observed in which a person's **motivations** were different from what they appeared to be.

For more on academic vocabulary, see pages 56 and R81.

272 UNIT 2   THE ENGLISH RENAISSANCE

Academic Vocabulary

Possible answers: Life's pleasures cannot last forever because everything must grow old and die; the things he promises are not practical; she's not motivated by material delights, but she might consider his offer if they could simply live and be happy forever.

Before You Read

Of Studies

Meet **Sir Francis Bacon**

(1561–1626)

The poet and playwright Ben Jonson called Sir Francis Bacon "one of the greatest men, and most worthy of admiration, that had been in many ages." Not everyone shared this high opinion. The physician William Harvey, for example, said that Bacon had "the eye of a viper."

Political Rise and Fall Bacon was born in London, the son of a civil servant in Queen Elizabeth's court. After attending Trinity College, Cambridge, and training as a lawyer, Bacon held a series of government posts and was knighted in 1603. As a supporter of King James I, Bacon rose to the position of Lord Chancellor of England, the highest honor in the British legal profession. However, his career soured in 1621, when he was convicted of taking bribes to support his extravagant lifestyle. After resigning in disgrace, Bacon devoted himself to scholarly pursuits.

> "I have taken all knowledge to be my province."
>
> —Sir Francis Bacon

Scientist and Philosopher A true Renaissance man, Bacon contributed to many diverse fields: philosophy, biology, physics, chemistry, and architecture. He also wrote a digest of British laws, a history of Great Britain, and biographies of Tudor monarchs. In his writings *Advancement of Learning* and *De Dignitate et Augmentis Scientiarum*, he presented a thorough systematization of the whole range of human knowledge. Scientists today owe their reliance on the inductive method of reasoning to Bacon, who promoted the idea that generalizations should be based on facts. That idea, while obvious today, was revolutionary during Bacon's lifetime, when scholars still preferred deductive reasoning—moving from generalizations to specifics rather than vice versa.

In addition, Bacon introduced the concept of hypotheses to scientists, arguing that scientists needed to make initial assumptions before beginning their experiments. He also pioneered the idea of a scientific research establishment that would work collaboratively in a methodical fashion to give material benefits to humankind. This innovative idea eventually led to the founding of Britain's Royal Society, an organization dedicated to the advancement of scientific endeavors.

Bacon even died in the service of science. At the age of sixty-five, while riding in his carriage, he impulsively decided to test the powers of refrigeration. He exited the carriage to collect snow, which he stuffed into a dead hen. Unfortunately, he caught a chill in the process and died of bronchitis a few days later.

Acclaimed Stylist Of all Bacon's writings, the most popular remains his *Essays and Counsels*, which he first published in 1597. This work was a landmark in English prose composition. Bacon packed his essays with pithy insights and shrewd observations about human nature that apply as well to modern times as to his own. This characteristic has earned him literary immortality: he remains one of the most quotable authors in the English language.

 Literature Online

Author Search For more about Sir Francis Bacon, go to glencoe.com and enter QuickPass code GLB9817u2.

SIR FRANCIS BACON **273**

Before You Read

Focus

Bellringer Options

Selection Focus
  Transparency 13

Daily Language Practice
  Transparency 24

Or write and display this excerpt from the essay: *Some books are to be tasted, others to be swallowed, and some few to be chewed and digested.* Invite volunteers to recount their experiences with books they merely "tasted," or read part of. Ask about books they have "swallowed," or read eagerly. Then have them tell about books they have "chewed and digested," or read carefully and were nourished by.

For summaries in languages other than English, see Unit 2 Teaching Resources Book, pp. 90–95.

Selection Skills

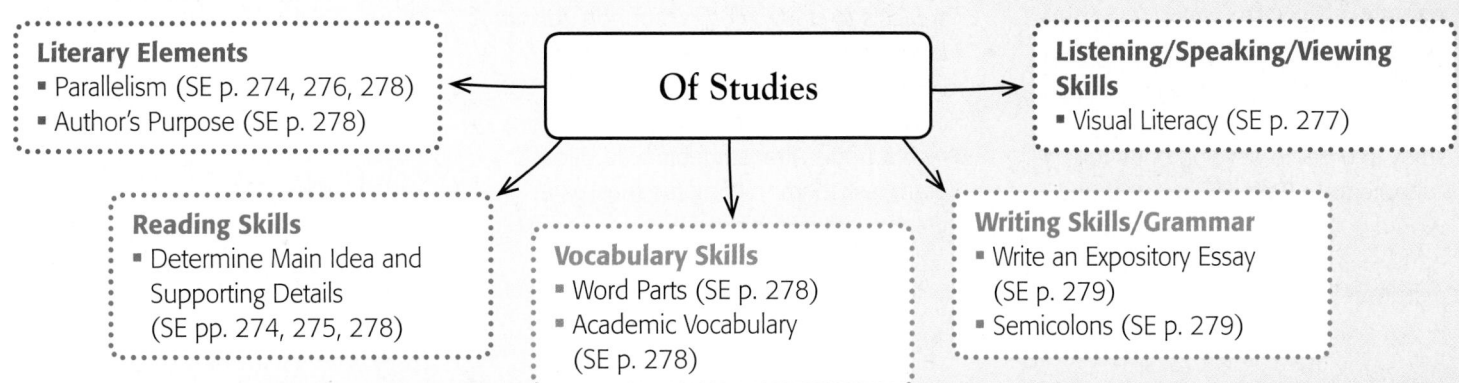

Literary Elements
- Parallelism (SE p. 274, 276, 278)
- Author's Purpose (SE p. 278)

Of Studies

Listening/Speaking/Viewing Skills
- Visual Literacy (SE p. 277)

Reading Skills
- Determine Main Idea and Supporting Details (SE pp. 274, 275, 278)

Vocabulary Skills
- Word Parts (SE p. 278)
- Academic Vocabulary (SE p. 278)

Writing Skills/Grammar
- Write an Expository Essay (SE p. 279)
- Semicolons (SE p. 279)

Before You Read

Focus

Summary

"Of Studies" is a persuasive essay that outlines the varied benefits of reading different kinds of books. Bacon states that study gives personal pleasure, hones one's skills in conversation, and imparts wisdom and knowledge that cannot be gained in other ways. He counsels that just as certain physical activities benefit the body, well-rounded studies improve the mind.

Vocabulary

Word Parts Write on the board: *executive function, discourse analysis, impedance.*
Ask: From the unit vocabulary, which of these words do you think means "electrical resistance"? *(impedance)* Which is a system that controls mental processes? *(executive function)*

 For additional vocabulary practice, see Unit 2 Teaching Resources Book, p. 98.

Literature and Reading Preview

Connect to the Essay

How and why do you study? What benefits do reading and studying offer? Discuss these questions with a partner. Consider whether it is possible to read or study too much.

Build Background

The **essay,** a brief prose composition exploring a single subject, was a development of the Renaissance. The French writer Michel de Montaigne (mon tān´) published a collection of writings that he called *Essais* ("attempts"). Bacon borrowed the title and thus became the "father" of the English essay.

Set Purposes for Reading

Big Idea Humanists and Courtiers

As you read, ask yourself, How does this essay reflect the Renaissance focus on secular concerns?

Literary Element Parallelism

The use of words, phrases, or sentences that have similar grammatical structures is called **parallelism.** Consider the following example: *Sir Francis Bacon was **a distinguished scientist** and **an elegant stylist.*** The boldfaced phrases are parallel, each consisting of an indefinite article followed by an adjective and a noun. As you read, ask yourself, What examples of parallelism can I see in Bacon's essay?

Reading Strategy Determine Main Idea and Supporting Details

Determining an author's main idea is finding the most important thought in a paragraph or a work. An essay typically states or implies a **thesis,** or main idea, which is developed through the use of **supporting details,** such as examples, reasons, or facts. As you read, ask yourself, What is the main idea of this passage, and what details support it?

Tip: Using an Idea Web Use a web to record details and the main idea they support.

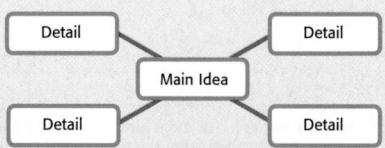

Learning Objectives

For pages 273–279
In studying this text, you will focus on the following objectives:

Literary Study:
Analyzing parallelism.
Analyzing author's purpose.

Reading: Determining main idea and supporting details.

Vocabulary

discourse (dis´ kôrs´) *n.* verbal communication in speech or writing; p. 275 *His discourse left the audience bored and somewhat confused.*

execute (ek´ sə kūt´) *v.* to carry out; put into effect; p. 275 *To execute her orders, the housekeeper polished the silverware with extreme care.*

sloth (slôth) *n.* laziness; p. 275 *His sloth prevented him from completing the required courses.*

impediment (im ped´ ə mənt) *n.* an obstruction; obstacle; p. 276 *Her limited income was an impediment to a lavish lifestyle.*

Literary Element Practice

SPIRAL REVIEW **Author's Purpose** Point out that Bacon wrote his essay "On Studies" in order to give advice about what and how one should study in order to develop one's fullest potential. **Ask:** What questions would you expect an author to address if he or she were advising a student? *(Possible answers: useful subjects to study; methods of note taking; ideas about the purpose of studying.)* Have each student write a paragraph advising a student who is about to begin high school. After students read Bacon's essay, ask them to compare their paragraphs with Bacon's essay.

OF STUDIES

Sir Francis Bacon

Teach

Big Idea | 1

Humanists and Courtiers
Answer: *Learning helps practical people conduct their affairs more effectively because it enables them to understand the total picture as well as the details.*

Ask: How does Bacon's advice exemplify the humanist philosophy? *(Bacon aims to optimize rationality and learning. He counsels that people can increase their virtues through effort; he makes no mention of God-given virtues.)*

ENGLISH LEARNERS Ask: Which part of Bacon's sentence contains a conclusion, and which part contains his reasons for the conclusion? *(Conclusion: Studies perfect nature and are perfected by experience; reasons: for natural abilities are like natural plants . . .)*

Reading Strategy | 2

Determine Main Idea and Supporting Details
Answer: *The author suggests that talents and abilities are vital and natural and require discipline and training. Just as plants must be pruned, talents must be cultivated.*

Studies serve for delight, for ornament, and for ability. Their chief use for delight is in privateness and retiring; for ornament, is in **discourse**; and for ability, is in the judgment and disposition of business. For expert men can **execute**, and perhaps judge of particulars, one by one; but the general counsels, and the plots and marshaling of affairs, come best from those that are learned. To spend too much time in studies is **sloth**; to use them too much for ornament, is affectation;[1] to make judgment wholly by their rules, is the humor[2] of a scholar. They perfect nature, and are perfected by experience: for natural abilities are like natural plants, that need proyning[3] by study; and studies themselves do give forth directions too much at large, except they be bounded in by experience. Crafty men contemn[4] studies, simple men admire them, and wise men use them; for they teach not their own use; but that is a wisdom without them and above them, won by observation. Read not to contradict and confute;[5] nor to believe and take for granted; nor to find talk and discourse; but to weigh and consider. Some books are to be tasted, others to be swallowed, and some few to be chewed and digested; that is, some books are to be read only in parts; others to be read, but not curiously;[6] and some few to be read wholly, and with diligence and

---

1. *Affectation* is artificial behavior meant to be impressive.
2. Here, *humor* means "whim."

---

3. *Proyning* means "pruning."
4. *Contemn* means "to view with scorn or contempt."
5. *Confute* means "prove wrong."
6. *Curiously* means "carefully."

---

1 Humanists and Courtiers *What advantage does learning provide for practical people?*

Vocabulary

discourse (dis′ kôrs′) *n.* verbal communication in speech or writing
execute (ek′ sə kūt′) *v.* to carry out; put into effect
sloth (slôth) *n.* laziness

Determine Main Idea and Supporting Details
What does the author suggest about talents and abilities by using this simile? **2**

SIR FRANCIS BACON **275**

For additional practice using the reading skill or strategy, see Unit 2 Teaching Resources Book, p. 97.

For an audio recording of this selection, use Listening Library Audio CD-ROM.

Readability Scores
Dale-Chall: 10.2
DRP: 65
Lexile: 700

English Learners

DIFFERENTIATED INSTRUCTION

Intermediate Bacon uses many words likely to be unfamiliar to English learners. He also uses familiar words in unfamiliar ways. Before students read the essay, review the meanings of vocabulary words. Ask volunteers to use the words in oral sentences.

Advanced Learners

DIFFERENTIATED INSTRUCTION

Persuasive Essay Explain that this is a persuasive essay—it attempts to sway readers toward a set of beliefs and course of action. Ask what Bacon is trying to persuade readers to believe and do. Have students identify claims that support Bacon's argument. Have them evaluate each claim.

Teach

Literary Element | 1

Parallelism Answer: *The nouns* reading, conference, *and* writing *are parallel. So are the phrases* a full man, a ready man, *and* an exact man. *Each phrase contains an indefinite article, an adjective, and a noun.*

[ADVANCED] **Ask:** How does this use of parallelism improve Bacon's essay? *(It gives structure and coherence to his argument.)*

View the Art ★

Edwaert Collier (1640–1709) was a Dutch painter who spent many years in London. This still life depicts items typically found on a desk of the time. Included is a speech by Queen Anne, a geography book, an inkwell, a sand shaker for blotting, sealing wax, and a seal. The Latin quotation "Vita brevis ars longa" is a translation by Horace of an aphorism by Hippocrates. It means "Life is short; art endures."

> To check students' understanding of the selection, see Unit 2 Teaching Resources Book, p. 101.

Still Life with Inkstand and Books, 1702. Edwaert Collier. Oil on canvas. Private collection. ★

attention. Some books also may be read by deputy, and extracts made of them by others; but that would be only in the less important arguments, and the meaner sort of books, else distilled books[7] are like common distilled waters,[8] flashy[9] things. Reading maketh a full man; conference[10] a ready man; and writing an exact man. And therefore, if a man write little, he had need have a great memory; if he confer little, he had need have a present wit;[11] and if he read little, he had need have much cunning, to seem to know that he doth not. Histories make men wise; poets witty; the mathematics subtile; natural philosophy deep; moral grave; logic and rhetoric[12] able to contend. *Abeunt studia in mores.*[13]

Nay, there is no stond[14] or **impediment** in the wit but may be wrought out by fit studies; like as diseases of the body may have appropriate exercises. Bowling is good for the stone and reins;[15] shooting for the lungs and breast; gentle walking for the stomach; riding for the head; and the like. So if a man's wit be wandering, let him study the mathematics; for in demonstrations, if his wit be called away never so little, he must begin again. If his wit be not apt to distinguish or find differences, let him study the Schoolmen;[16] for they are *cymini sectores.*[17] If he be not apt to beat over[18] matters, and to call up one thing to prove and illustrate another, let him study the lawyers' cases. So every defect of the mind may have a special receipt.[19] ∾

---

7. *Distilled books* are books that have been abridged, or condensed.
8. *Distilled waters* are homemade remedies.
9. *Flashy* means "tasteless."
10. A *conference* is a conversation.
11. A *present wit* is a quick, alert mind.
12. *Rhetoric* is the skill of speaking or writing effectively or persuasively.
13. *Abeunt studia in mores* is Latin for "Studies affect people's behavior."

14. *Stond* means "obstruction."
15. *Stone and reins* are kidney stones and other kidney disorders.
16. *Schoolmen* refers to medieval philosophers.
17. *Cymini sectores* is Latin for "hairsplitters" (literally, "seed splitters").
18. *Beat over* means "reason through."
19. Here, *receipt* means "remedy."

Vocabulary

impediment (im pedʹ ə mənt) *n.* an obstruction; obstacle

1 **Parallelism** *What are the parallel structures in this sentence?*

Reading Practice

 Independent Reading Point out that Bacon's essay provides guidance for how students can approach learning in school and also their own enrichment and enjoyment in the outside world. Discuss where people gain knowledge outside of academic settings. Have volunteers recount their own experiences with outside learning related to personal interests. **Ask:** If Bacon were alive today, what might he think of the Internet? Why? *(He would probably be enthusiastic about it, because it provides ready access to learning about a myriad of topics.)*

After You Read

Respond and Think Critically

Respond and Interpret

1. Did Bacon change your opinion of studies? Why or why not?

2. (a)According to Bacon, what are the three main benefits of study, and what danger can result from each benefit? (b)Why do people need more than knowledge to make wise decisions?

3. (a)Summarize the benefits Bacon mentions for studying history, poetry, mathematics, philosophy, logic, and rhetoric. (b)What do these benefits have in common?

Analyze and Evaluate

4. Bacon believes that spending "too much time in studies is sloth." What might be his reasons for

that belief? Explain why you agree or disagree with him.

5. (a)How valid is Bacon's statement that some books should be tasted, some swallowed, and some chewed and digested? Explain your response. (b)In your opinion, should this essay be tasted, swallowed, or chewed and digested? Support your evaluation.

Connect

6. **Big Idea** Humanists and Courtiers
Why might this essay have appealed to young people during the Renaissance?

7. Connect to Today Are Bacon's ideas relevant to learning today? Why or why not?

Visual Literacy

Creating a Concept Map

Though brief, "Of Studies" is complex and dense in meaning. By creating a concept map—a visual representation that enables you to process information quickly—you can organize Bacon's ideas.

Group Activity With a small group, complete the concept map below by filling in the empty boxes. Then discuss your findings.

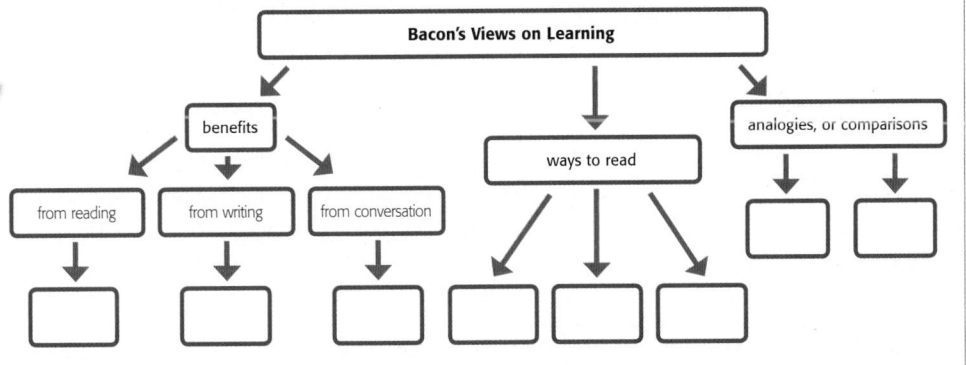

Visual Literacy

Benefits: fullness; readiness; exactness. *ways to read:* in parts; not carefully; with diligence. *analogies:* reading books as eating; studying as treating diseases with exercise

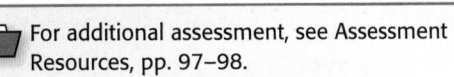
For additional assessment, see Assessment Resources, pp. 97–98.

After You Read

Assess

1. Some students may say they now view studies as more important to future endeavors.

2. (a) The three main benefits are delight, ornament, and ability; the dangers are sloth, affectation, and simplified judgments. (b) People must evaluate what they learn from books in light of what they learn through observation and experience.

3. (a) History helps readers avoid mistakes. Poetry helps them learn to use language. Mathematics makes them perceptive. Philosophy helps them be profound and serious. Logic and rhetoric help with debate. (b) All of these benefits promote worldly success.

4. Bacon realizes that studying is primarily an inactive pursuit (physically) and recognizes that a person needs practical experience to complement the knowledge gained from books.

5. (a) Some books are intended mainly to entertain, others give only general overviews of topics, and scholarly books provide detailed information. (b) Students may say that this essay should be chewed and digested; its ideas merit careful reading and reflection.

6. The essay focuses on secular, not spiritual, concerns. It provides practical instructions for studying.

7. Students may say that Bacon's ideas remain relevant because they accurately reflect unchanging aspects of human nature. Studies still affect people's behavior.

After You Read

Assess

Literary Element

1. Sample answer: "Crafty men contemn studies, simple men admire them, and wise men use them."

2. Parallelism shows how ideas are related by expressing them in the same grammatical structure.

Progress Check

Can students analyze parallelism?

If No ➔ See Unit 2 Teaching Resources Book, p. 96.

Review: Author's Purpose

Sample answers:

Bacon's Purpose: to both inform and persuade

Form: persuasive essay

Content: "Nay, there is no stond or impediment in the wit but may be wrought out by fit studies . . ."

Tone: The essay has a refreshing conciseness of expression and a serious though occasionally humorous, insistent tone.

Reading Strategy

1. Students may say they like Bacon's analogy comparing physical and mental exercise because it is simple and sensible.

2. Studies are a tool meant to be used in the affairs of living. They should not be pursued for their own sake.

Literary Element Parallelism

Parallelism affects a piece of writing in many ways. It helps words flow together; it calls attention to important ideas; it balances different ideas in a composition; and it sets up a cadence, or rhythm. In "Of Studies," for example, Bacon writes:

"Studies serve **for delight, for ornament, and for ability.**"

In this example, each boldfaced phrase consists of the preposition *for* followed by a noun.

1. Find three more examples of parallelism in "Of Studies."

2. Explain how Bacon's use of parallelism helps emphasize his ideas.

Review: Author's Purpose

As you learned on page 270, an **author's purpose** is his or her intent in writing a literary work. An author typically writes to accomplish one or more of the following purposes: to persuade, to instruct, to inform or explain, to entertain, to describe, or to tell a story.

Partner Activity With another classmate, discuss Bacon's purposes for writing this essay. To present your evidence, create a web like the one below. Fill it in with an example for each item listed.

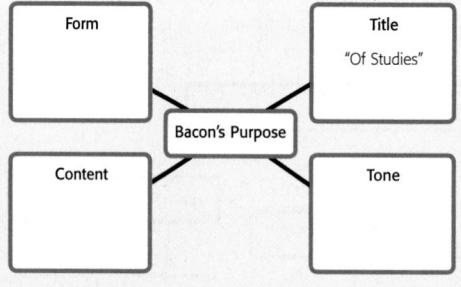

 Literature Online

Selection Resources For Selection Quizzes, eFlashcards, and Reading-Writing Connection activities, go to glencoe.com and enter QuickPass code GLB9817u2.

Reading Strategy Determine Main Idea and Supporting Details

In order to figure out a text's main idea, note passages that express important points. Then try to sum up the thesis, or main idea. Refer to the web you created as you answer the following questions.

1. Choose one idea from Bacon's essay that you find interesting. Explain why it appeals to you.

2. What idea seems to be at the heart of Bacon's views about studies?

Vocabulary Practice

Practice with Word Parts For each word in the left-hand column, identify the word containing the same root in the right-hand column. Write the words and underline the parts they have in common. Use a dictionary to find the meaning of the word you identified, and explain how it is related to that of the vocabulary word.

1. discourse   executor

2. execute   coursing

3. impediment   pedal

EXAMPLE: <u>divide</u>, in<u>divid</u>uality

<u>Divide</u> means "separate." <u>Individuality</u> is what makes someone distinct, or separate, from others.

Academic Vocabulary

*Bacon developed ideas that are still part of the modern scientific **paradigm**.*

Paradigm is an academic word. It is often used in the sciences. For example, because Albert Einstein's theory of relativity introduced a radically new way of thinking about the universe, it is said to have caused a "**paradigm** shift."

To further explore the meaning of this word, answer the following question: How did Renaissance humanism challenge the medieval Christian **paradigm**?

For more on academic vocabulary, see pages 56 and R81.

Vocabulary

1. **discourse,** <u>coursing</u>; *coursing* means "running"; *discourse* is the course, or process, of communication.

2. **execute,** <u>executor</u>; an *executor* is one who *executes*, or carries out, a plan.

3. **impediment,** <u>pedal</u>; an *impediment* is something that prevents movement; a *pedal* is an aid to movement.

Academic Vocabulary

Possible answer: Renaissance humanism challenged the medieval Christian paradigm by diverting attention from divine concerns to earthly ones.

Respond Through Writing

Expository Essay

Analyze Rhetorical Devices In "Of Studies," Sir Francis Bacon argues convincingly about the broad advantages of learning. Analyze how Bacon's use of rhetorical devices—such as repetition, analogy, and parallelism—helps him develop and strengthen his argument.

Prewrite Reread Bacon's essay, taking notes on the rhetorical devices he uses. List each example of repetition, analogy, and parallelism that you find, being sure to quote his statements accurately. Decide how you will present and organize the information in your analysis.

Draft Using the examples of rhetorical devices you identified during prewriting, create a chart indicating how each example contributes to Bacon's significant ideas and overall message.

Analogy	Function
"... natural abilities are like natural plants, that need proyning by study ..."	Supports idea that people's minds must be nurtured to grow
Parallelism	
"Crafty men contemn studies, simple men admire them, and wise men use them ..."	Clearly categorizes and contrasts people on the basis of their attitudes toward studies

Incorporate the information you've gathered into your essay, using statements like the following to present your evidence:

The author uses _____ to represent _____.

Revise Exchange papers with a classmate, checking that your partner has correctly identified rhetorical devices and used accurately quoted examples from the text to support statements about their effects in Bacon's arguments. After reviewing your peer reader's comments, consult the Writing Workshop checklist on page 972 and make appropriate changes in your own draft.

Edit and Proofread Proofread your paper, correcting any errors in spelling, grammar, and punctuation. Use the Grammar Tip in the side column to help you with semicolons.

Learning Objectives

In this assignment, you will focus on the following activities:

Literary Study: Analyzing rhetorical devices.

Writing: Writing an expository essay.

Grammar: Understanding how to use semicolons.

> **Grammar Tip**
>
> **Semicolons**
>
> Use **semicolons** (;) to separate these elements in sentences:
>
> - clauses not joined by a conjunction
> - clauses joined by a conjunctive adverb
> - phrases in a series when they include commas
>
> Semicolons are especially useful in writing about literature that uses complex rhetorical devices.
>
> *In his statement "Crafty men contemn studies, simple men admire them, and wise men use them. . . ." Bacon employs parallelism to compare types of people; however, I think this he oversimplifies it.*

After You Read

Respond Through Writing

Use these criteria in evaluating students' expository essays:

- The essay correctly identifies Bacon's rhetorical devices.
- It accurately analyzes the contribution of those devices to Bacon's argument.
- The analysis is supported with logical explanations and quotations from the text.
- A student who meets all of these criteria should receive the equivalent of a 4-point response.
- A student who fully meets two or partially meets all of these criteria should receive the equivalent of a 3-point response.
- A student who fully meets one or partially meets two of these criteria should receive the equivalent of a 2-point response.
- A student who partially meets one of these criteria should receive the equivalent of a 1-point response.

 For grammar practice, see Unit 2 Teaching Resources Book, p. 100.

SIR FRANCIS BACON **279**

 To create custom assessments using software, use ExamView Assessment Suite.

Grammar Workshop

Subject-Verb Agreement

Focus

Write this sentence on the board: There have been no change since the last time we asked.

Discuss why this sentence is confusing. *(The plural verb have does not match the singular noun change.)* Remind students to be careful about using proper subject-verb agreement when writing sentences.

Teach

Subject-Verb Agreement

Call upon individual students to read the problem samples aloud. Hearing the samples can make correct and incorrect subject verb-agreement obvious in some cases.

Revise

1. change verb to *have*
2. change verb to *has*
3. no errors

Subjects and Verbs

A **subject** tells who or what a sentence is about. A **verb** tells the action that a subject takes.

Tip

Avoid using forms of the verb *to be* when possible. Instead, write in the active voice.

Language Handbook

For more about subjects and verbs, see Language Handbook, pp. R45–R46.

Phrases and Clauses as Subjects

If the subject of a verb is a single phrase or clause, the verb should be singular. Don't be misled by plural words within the phrase or clause: *How she managed to write such interesting essays* **was** *a mystery to me.*

LOG ON ▶ **Literature** Online

Grammar For more grammar practice, go to glencoe.com and enter QuickPass code GLB9817u2.

Grammar Workshop

Subject-Verb Agreement

Literature Connection In every sentence and clause, the subject and verb must agree; that is, if the **subject**—who or what is doing something—is singular, the **verb** that describes the action must also be singular. If the subject is plural, the verb must be plural.

"Crafty men contemn studies, simple men admire them, and wise men use them."

—Sir Francis Bacon, from "Of Studies"

In the sentence above, *men* is the subject of each clause, so the verbs *contemn, admire,* and *use* must be in plural form. You can avoid many subject-verb agreement errors in your own writing by following the guidelines below.

Common Agreement Problems

Problem 1 **A compound subject is joined by *or* or *nor*.**

> *Neither "Of Studies" nor Bacon's other works* <u>*teaches*</u> *us that learning is the same for every person.*

Solution **Make the verb agree with the part of the compound subject that is closer to it.**

> *Neither "Of Studies" nor Bacon's other works* <u>*teach*</u> *us that learning is the same for every person.*

Problem 2 **An indefinite pronoun is the subject.**

> *Everyone* <u>*have encountered*</u> *a hobby to "chew up and digest."*

Solution **Determine whether the indefinite pronoun is singular or plural and make the verb agree with it.**

> *Everyone* <u>*has encountered*</u> *a hobby to "chew up and digest."*

Revise Correct any errors in subject-verb agreement. If there are none, write *no errors*.

1. Neither Bacon nor other writers has put the full value of learning into words.
2. Everyone have interests and subjects to pursue.
3. Histories or philosophy is important to study.

Grammar Practice

Predicate Nominative Tell students that a noun or pronoun that follows a linking verb and gives more information about the subject is a predicate nominative. Write the following sentence on the board: *Many governments are* <u>*democracies*</u>.

Ask: Which sentence in the exercise has a linking verb? *(sentence 3)* What is the linking verb in each sentence? *(is; are)*

PART 2

A Bard for the Ages

Portrait of William Shakespeare, 1623 (detail). Martin Droeshout. Engraving.

 View the Art Engravings like this one use thin, cross-hatched lines to create shape and shadow. What is your impression of Shakespeare from this detail of his portrait?

*"O! for a Muse of fire, that would ascend
The brightest heaven of invention."*

—William Shakespeare, *Henry V*

281

English Learners

DIFFERENTIATED INSTRUCTION

Beginning English language learners may not know the words *bard, ages,* and *ascend.* Advise them to maintain a personal glossary of the new words they learn to refer to as they read Shakespeare's writing. Ask students to paraphrase the title and the quotation.

Approaching Level

DIFFERENTIATED INSTRUCTION

Emerging Read aloud the quotation from Shakespeare. **Ask:** What can you infer about Shakespeare's beliefs and his creative process? *(He believed the creative process was aided by unseen forces.)*

Analyzing and Extending

Reading Strategy 1

Context Clues Direct students to read the part title and to look at the portrait of Shakespeare. **Ask:** If you did not know the meaning of *bard*, what clues on the page could help you determine its meaning? *(Students may say that if you know who William Shakespeare is, you might guess that a bard is a poet or playwright.)*

View the Art

Martin Droeshout (c. 1601–1650) lived in London, England, and, like his father before him, was employed as an engraver. He is best known for this portrait of Shakespeare, which appeared in the first edition of Shakespeare's collected plays. The portrait was highly praised by Ben Jonson, a contemporary of Shakespeare's, who said the image looked very much like the man. **Ask:** How does the art relate to the quotation? *(It is a portrait of the writer.)*

Shakespeare's Poetry

Bellringer Options

Selection Focus
Transparency 14

Daily Language Practice
Transparencies 25, 27

Or say: Shakespeare is responsible for many common sayings in the English language, such as "neither rhyme nor reason" and "method in the madness." Have students jot down what they know about Shakespeare and his work. Encourage them to share their prior knowledge with the rest of the class.

Meet **William Shakespeare**
(1564–1616)

William Shakespeare is the most celebrated English poet and dramatist of all time. Nearly four centuries after his death, his works continue to delight readers and audiences around the world. In fact, Shakespeare's writings are more widely read and more often quoted than any other works ever written, except the Bible. Yet, while Shakespeare's literature endures, we know very little about the man himself. The meager information we do have about Shakespeare's life has been pieced together from anecdotes, gossip, clues found in his poems and plays, legal documents, entries in the public record, and the memorials and reminiscences by his fellow writers.

Early Life Shakespeare was born in the small town of Stratford-upon-Avon. His father, John Shakespeare, was a prosperous glove maker, butcher, and tradesman who also filled several local government positions, including high bailiff (the equivalent of mayor). His mother, Mary Arden, was the daughter of a wealthy landowner. William Shakespeare was the third of at least eight children born to this well-to-do couple. He was their first son and their first child to survive past childhood. As a young boy, Shakespeare likely attended the local grammar school, studying Latin and classical literature.

When Shakespeare was about thirteen, however, his father started to lose his social standing and to have serious financial problems. Shakespeare was forced to leave school in order to work to help support his family. Just what type of work he did remains unknown, but he may have apprenticed as a butcher. Shakespeare may also have served for a time as a schoolmaster in the country, where he would have acquired the familiarity with outdoor sports, such as hunting, hawking, and falconry, that manifests itself throughout his literary works.

At the age of eighteen, Shakespeare married a twenty-six-year-old local woman named Anne Hathaway and began a family of his own. The couple had a daughter, Susanna, and twins, Hamnet and Judith. Sadly, Hamnet died at the age of eleven.

The London Theater Scene Shakespeare moved to London to pursue a career in the theater, but, according to poet William Davenant, he arrived without friends or money. His first "theater job" actually consisted of tending the horses of theater patrons—the equivalent of parking cars at a theater today. Nevertheless, his wit attracted the attention of the actors, who apparently thought him clever enough to improve a few of their plays (revising plays to add scenes or to bring them up to date was a common practice at the time), and the actors eventually recommended him for a job. If Davenant's tale is true, this is how Shakespeare got his chance to write for the stage—and to act in small parts as well.

Dramatic Success The production of *Henry VI* in 1592 appears to have been Shakespeare's first theatrical success. Later, he wrote and published two long narrative poems, which became immediate favorites: *Venus and Adonis* and *The Rape of Lucrece*. He dedicated these works to a newfound patron and friend, the young Earl of Southampton.

Selection Skills

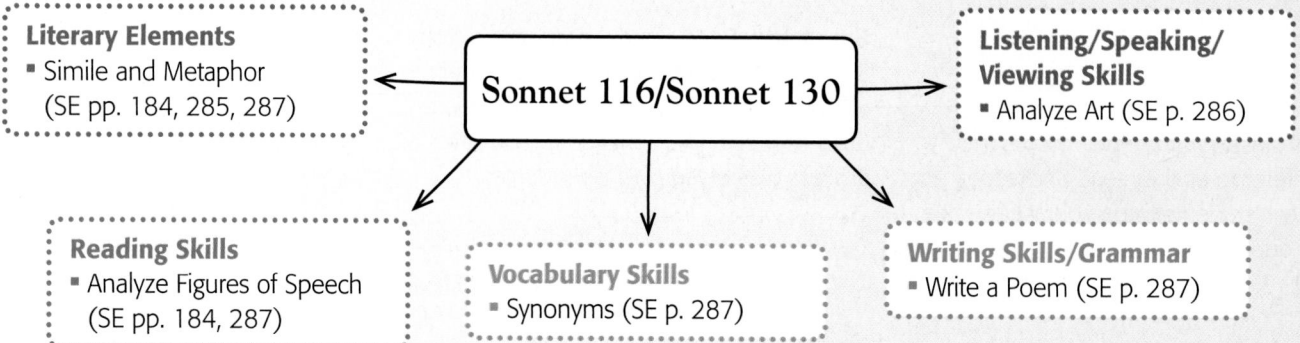

Literary Elements
- Simile and Metaphor
(SE pp. 184, 285, 287)

Sonnet 116/Sonnet 130

Listening/Speaking/Viewing Skills
- Analyze Art (SE p. 286)

Reading Skills
- Analyze Figures of Speech
(SE pp. 184, 287)

Vocabulary Skills
- Synonyms (SE p. 287)

Writing Skills/Grammar
- Write a Poem (SE p. 287)

The Room in Which Shakespeare Was Born, 1853. Henry Wallis. Oil on board, 29.2 x 41.9 cm. Tate Gallery, London.

The earl, upon reaching maturity and thereby gaining access to his fortune, expressed his thanks for these dedications by giving Shakespeare a large sum of money, which enabled him to become partial owner of a theatrical company, the Lord Chamberlain's Men. As part owner, Shakespeare became the main playwright for the troupe.

The playhouse in which they had been performing, called simply the "Theatre," was torn down and rebuilt in a larger, more splendid form south of the Thames River. This new playhouse, opened in 1599, was called the Globe, which is the name still associated with Shakespearean theater today.

Building a Career and an Estate By the time the Globe opened, Shakespeare had earned enough money to enable him to purchase several properties and a large estate for his family in Stratford, although he continued to live primarily in London. By 1599 the thirty-five-year-old playwright was producing two plays a year and drawing tremendous audiences as well as critical acclaim. A literary handbook of the time calls Shakespeare "most excellent" in both comedy and tragedy and "the most passionate among us to bewail and bemoan the perplexities of love."

> "*He was not of an age, but for all time!*"
>
> —Ben Jonson

The Pinnacle of Genius Shakespeare's greatest creative period had just begun in 1599. Between 1601 and 1607, he wrote the tragic masterpieces *Hamlet, Othello, Macbeth,* and *King Lear.* He also wrote comedies that were darker and more complex than his previous works. As well as performing in the Globe, the Lord Chamberlain's Men performed several times at the courts of Elizabeth I and James I. In fact, James's patronage enabled the troupe to call itself the King's Men. Besides their performances at court, the King's Men also performed after 1609 in an indoor, heated, and candle-lit playhouse called the Blackfriars Theatre. Their performances in this aristocratic venue proved much more profitable than those in the Globe.

Shakespeare's finest plays, though much admired by his contemporaries, achieved less literary status than his narrative and lyrical poems in his lifetime. During Shakespeare's career, his reputation as a great writer was based mainly on his nondramatic poems and on his sonnets. Shakespeare published his sonnets in 1609, although he had actually written and circulated the bulk of them in handwritten form in the 1590s.

In 1610, for reasons not known to us today, Shakespeare moved back to Stratford, where he lived comfortably as a semi-retired gentleman, writing fewer plays than before. Among these was a supreme romance, *The Tempest,* in which the main character's farewell speech (see page 300) is generally regarded as Shakespeare's farewell to writing and perhaps to life. He died in Stratford on his fifty-second birthday.

 Literature Online

Author Search For more about William Shakespeare, go to glencoe.com and enter QuickPass code GLB9817u2.

Literary History

Did Shakespeare Write the Plays? There have always been people who have doubted that William Shakespeare could have been the genius who wrote the plays that are credited to him. They reason that Shakespeare was not raised in London, had little education, and knew nothing about court life, law, medicine, or many other subjects about which the author of the plays seems to have known. One theory proposes that the plays were actually written by a nobleman, such as Sir Walter Raleigh or the Earl of Southampton, but credited to Shakespeare, the actor and stage manager, because it was unseemly for the nobility to be associated with the theater.

English Learners

DIFFERENTIATED INSTRUCTION

Intermediate In the sonnets on the following pages, students will encounter difficult vocabulary words. For example, in Sonnet 116, the imagery in lines 5–7 has to do with sailing and ships at sea. Make sure students understand *tempest, bark,* and the sailors' use of stars to guide their ships. Then, have students paraphrase lines 5–7, asking questions if necessary.

Advanced Tell students to make a two-column chart with the headings *New Words* and *Definitions.* Ask them to list any unfamiliar words from the sonnets in the first column. Have students use a dictionary to find the definitions and record them in the second column.

Before You Read

Focus

Summary

Both of these sonnets deal with aspects of love. In Sonnet 116, the speaker focuses on the constancy that results from "the marriage of true minds." The speaker of Sonnet 130 finds that figurative language fails to capture the beauty of his beloved.

 For summaries in languages other than English, see Unit 2 Teaching Resourcees Book, pp. 106–111.

Vocabulary

Have students use a dictionary to research the etymologies of the vocabulary words. **Say:** Often, a word's meaning changes over time. What possible connections can you make between the vocabulary words and the meanings of their Latin or Middle English roots? *(Students' responses will vary.)*

 For additional vocabulary practice, see Unit 2 Teaching Resources Book, pp. 114–115.

 For additional context, see Glencoe Interactive Vocabulary CD-ROM.

 For an audio recording of this selection, use Listening Library Audio CD-ROM.

284

Literature and Reading Preview

Connect to the Poems

What is the essence of true love? Discuss this question with a small group of classmates. Consider what various authors and songwriters have had to say about the subject of love.

Build Background

Long before Shakespeare's time, writing a sonnet was one way for a poet to demonstrate mastery of the technical aspects of poetry. It was also a way for the poet to demonstrate his or her creative ingenuity. Sonnets often relied heavily on literary conventions such as eternal love shared between two people, often in an idealized setting. A poet might demonstrate ingenuity either by composing clever variations on these conventions or by parodying them. A **parody** is a humorous imitation of a literary work that aims to point out its shortcomings.

Set Purposes for Reading

Big Idea A Bard for the Ages

Shakespeare was a deep thinker and a learned man as well as a great poet. As you read, ask yourself, How does Shakespeare use the sonnet form to express his ideas about love?

Literary Element Simile and Metaphor

Simile and **metaphor** are figures of speech that make comparisons between two seemingly unlike things or ideas in order to suggest an underlying similarity between them. In a simile, the words *like* or *as* are used to express the comparison explicitly. The comparison in a metaphor is implicit. As you read, ask yourself, What purposes do these devices serve in the sonnets?

Reading Strategy Analyze Figures of Speech

A **figure of speech** is a specific kind of figurative language, such as metaphor, simile, personification, or symbol. Figures of speech are not to be taken literally; they express a truth beyond the literal level. As you read, ask yourself, How do figures of speech contribute to the meaning of each poem as a whole?

Tip: Taking Notes Use a chart to record the figures of speech in Sonnets 116 and 130.

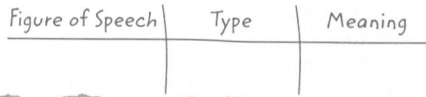

Figure of Speech	Type	Meaning

284 UNIT 2   THE ENGLISH RENAISSANCE

Learning Objectives

For pages 282–290

In studying these texts, you will focus on the following objectives:

Literary Study: Analyzing simile and metaphor.

Reading:
Analyzing figures of speech. Drawing conclusions about speaker's meaning.

Writing:
Writing a poem.
Writing an essay.

Vocabulary

alteration (ôl′ tə rā′ shən) *n.* change; modification; p. 285 *Although I was gone for only a short time, I noticed a subtle alteration in the mood of the party.*

tempest (tem′ pist) *n.* a violent storm; a violent outburst or disturbance; p. 285 *The tempest left many people homeless.*

doom (doo-m) *n.* that which cannot be escaped; death, ruin, or destruction; p. 285 *The residents fearfully awaited the hurricane and its doom.*

tread (tred) *v.* to walk or step; p. 286 *Please do not tread on the flower beds.*

Vocabulary Practice

SPIRAL REVIEW **Synonyms** Direct students' attention to the vocabulary for the lesson. Have students review the words and their meanings. Then have them identify synonyms of each word. *(Possible responses: alteration—change, adjustment; tempest—storm, outburst; doom—ill fate, destiny; tread—walk)* Invite students to write sentences containing the vocabulary words. When they finish, have them replace each of the vocabulary words with a synonym. Lead a class discussion about the differences in connotation produced by the changes.

Promenading Noblemen. Central section from the Garden of Love at the court of Philippe III the Good, Duke of Burgundy (1396–1467), in the gardens of Hesdin Castle in 1432, fifteenth century. Anonymous. Chateaux de Versailles et de Trianon, France.

SONNET 116

William Shakespeare

Let me not to the marriage of true minds
Admit impediments;[1] love is not love
Which alters when it **alteration** finds,
Or bends with the remover to remove.[2]
5   Oh no, it is an ever-fixèd mark[3]
That looks on **tempests** and is never shaken;
It is the star to every wand'ring bark,[4]
Whose worth's unknown, although his height be taken.
Love's not Time's fool, though rosy lips and cheeks
10 Within his bending sickle's compass[5] come,
Love alters not with his brief hours and weeks,
But bears it out even to the edge of **doom**.[6]   **2**
        If this be error and upon me proved,
        I never writ, nor no man ever loved.

Simile and Metaphor *Explain the metaphor in this line. What is being compared?*   **1**

Vocabulary

alteration (ôl′tə rā′shən) *n.* change; modification
tempest (tem′pist) *n.* a violent storm; a violent outburst or disturbance
doom (do͞om) *n.* that which cannot be escaped; death, ruin, or destruction

1. *Impediments* means "obstacles." The speaker is referring to the traditional Christian marriage service in which the clergy member says, "If any of you know cause or just impediment why these persons should not be joined together . . ."
2. *Bends . . . to remove* means the person changes when his or her sweetheart is inconstant.
3. *Mark* refers to a landmark that sailors can see from the water and that is used as a navigational guide.
4. A *bark* is a boat.
5. Here, *compass* means "range."
6. *The edge of doom* refers to the end of the world.

WILLIAM SHAKESPEARE   **285**

Teach

A Bard for the Ages

Answer: *Through the speaker, Shakespeare is stating that a person should be judged on intrinsic qualities, not on false ideals expressed through preposterous comparisons.*

APPROACHING Check to make sure approaching level students understand that the speaker is comparing his lover to women who are dishonestly described as perfect.

View the Art ★

Answer: *Students may say that the woman in the painting seems more attractive than the woman described in the poem.)*

A Girl at a Window Holding a Bunch of Grapes. Attributed to Hieronymus van der Mij. Oil on panel, 43.5 x 34 cm. Sotheby's, London.

View the Art Dutch artists of van der Mij's time were known for keen attention to detail and symbolism. Does the woman in this image fit your impression of the woman in Shakespeare's sonnet? ★

SONNET 130
William Shakespeare

My mistress' eyes are nothing like the sun;
Coral is far more red than her lips' red;
If snow be white, why then her breasts are dun;[1]
If hairs be wires, black wires grow on her head.
5   I have seen roses damask'd,[2] red and white,
But no such roses see I in her cheeks,
And in some perfumes is there more delight
Than in the breath that from my mistress reeks.[3]
I love to hear her speak, yet well I know
10   That music hath a far more pleasing sound;
I grant I never saw a goddess go,[4]
My mistress when she walks **treads** on the ground.
    And yet, by heaven, I think my love as rare
    As any she belied with false compare.[5]

1. *Dun* is dull gray.
2. Something that is *damask'd* is multicolored.
3. Here, *reeks* simply means "is exhaled."
4. Here, *go* means "walk."
5. *As any . . . compare* means "As any woman misrepresented with false comparisons."

A Bard for the Ages *What philosophical insight is Shakespeare expressing in this couplet?*   **1**

Vocabulary

tread (tred) *v.* to walk or step

Reading Practice

SPIRAL REVIEW **Analyze Text** To analyze a text, students must identify the component parts and use them to construct meaning. Have students break the poem into sentences. Point out that the poem consists of three quatrains and one couplet. Then have students explain in their own words what each sentence means. Then ask them to identify what the poet is saying by combining the separate elements of the poem. If students are confused by the irony of the poem, help them understand that the poet is making a comment on the way people romanticize lovers. Allow students time to discuss their analyses in class.

After You Read

Respond and Think Critically

Respond and Interpret

1. (a)In your own words, summarize the two main points the speaker makes about the nature of love in Sonnet 116. (b)What is the speaker implying about failed relationships?

2. (a)How does the speaker in Sonnet 130 describe the woman he loves? (b)Does his description tell you his real opinion of her? Support your answer with lines from the poem.

Analyze and Evaluate

3. (a)What is the speaker's main point in lines 1–12 of Sonnet 116? (b)In your opinion, is the couplet a convincing conclusion to the poem?

4. (a)What sort of poetry does Sonnet 130 mock or criticize? (b)What message about love is implied in this criticism?

Connect

5. **Big Idea** **A Bard for the Ages** What can you infer about Shakespeare's philosophy of life from Sonnets 116 and 130?

6. **Connect to Today** What conventions of love songs do songwriters parody today, as Shakespeare parodied some conventions of sonnets in Sonnet 130?

Literary Element Simile and Metaphor

Sonnet 116 makes its points through a series of implicit comparisons, or **metaphors.** Sonnet 130 parodies a series of explicit comparisons, or **similes.** The word *like* appears in the first simile of Sonnet 130 and is implied in all of the similes that follow.

1. Explain the metaphor in lines 5–6 of Sonnet 116.

2. (a)List the "negative similes," or what the speaker says his beloved is *not,* in Sonnet 130. (b)Identify the sonnet's only metaphor.

Writing

Write a Poem With a partner, write a reply to Sonnet 130 from the mistress's point of view. Include metaphors, similes, and figures of speech that help convey her opinions of Sonnet 130's speaker. Partners should write alternating lines until the sonnet is complete (with fourteen lines). For help with writing a sonnet, see page 242.

>  **Literature** Online
>
> **Selection Resources** For Selection Quizzes, eFlash-cards, and Reading-Writing Connection activities, go to glencoe.com and enter QuickPass code GLB9817u2.

Reading Strategy Analyze Figures of Speech

In Sonnet 116, Shakespeare uses symbol and personification. A **symbol** is something that exists on a literal level and signifies something beyond itself. **Personification** attributes human qualities to something inhuman.

1. What examples of personification appear in lines 9–10 of Sonnet 116?

2. What might the sickle in Sonnet 116 symbolize?

Vocabulary Practice

Practice with Synonyms A synonym is a word that has the same, or nearly the same, meaning as another word. With a partner, match each boldfaced vocabulary word below with its synonym. You will not use all of the answer choices.

1. alteration	a. modification
2. doom	b. beauty
3. tempest	c. destruction
4. tread	d. step
	e. storm
	f. confrontation

WILLIAM SHAKESPEARE **287**

Before You Read

Focus

Summary

In Sonnet 73, the speaker characterizes himself as old and near death but rejoices in the strength of his beloved's love for him. The speaker of Sonnet 29, whenever he envies others' qualities, remembers that he is loved and therefore rich indeed.

 For summaries in languages other than English, see Unit 2 Teaching Resources Book, pp. 118–123.

Teach

Reading Strategy | 1

Draw Conclusions About Speaker's Meaning Answer: *He describes himself as old and possibly ill. He compares himself to the winter season, which is a common symbol of old age and death.*

(ENGLISH LEARNERS) For English learners, define *thou, mayst, behold,* and *boughs.* **Ask:** What season does the speaker describe? *(winter)* Have students restate lines 1–3 in their own words. *(You can see winter in me.)*

Literary Element Simile

A **simile** is a figure of speech that uses *like* or *as* to compare two seemingly unlike things. Not every statement with *like* or *as* is a simile—the comparison must be between things that are basically different and must create greater understanding about what is being compared. For example, "My love is like a rose" is a simile; "My backpack is like your tote bag" is not a simile. As you read, ask yourself, How do these similes help me understand the poems?

Reading Strategy Draw Conclusions About Speaker's Meaning

A **conclusion** is a general statement based on a number of specific examples. To be valid, a conclusion must make good sense and should not go beyond the evidence. As you read, ask yourself, What can I conclude from these statements?

···

Tip: Making Adjustments Be prepared to adjust your original conclusion to reflect the information you learn as you read.

SONNET 73

William Shakespeare

That time of year thou mayst in me behold
When yellow leaves, or none, or few, do hang
Upon those boughs which shake against the cold,
Bare ruin'd choirs,[1] where late the sweet birds sang.
5 In me thou seest the twilight of such day
As after sunset fadeth in the west,
Which by and by[2] black night doth take away,
Death's second self, that seals up all in rest.
In me thou seest the glowing of such fire
10 That on the ashes of his youth doth lie,
As the death-bed whereon it must expire,
Consum'd with that which it was nourish'd by.[3]
　This thou perceiv'st, which makes thy love more strong,
　To love that well, which thou must leave ere long.

1. *Choirs* is a reference to the place in a church where the choir sings. Here, it is used as a metaphor for bare tree branches.
2. *By and by* means "presently" or "soon."
3. *Consum'd . . . by* is an image that suggests that the fire was choked by the ashes of the wood that previously fueled its flame. The speaker means he has been consumed by life.

---

1 Draw Conclusions About Speaker's Meaning *What conclusion about himself does the speaker state in lines 1–4? Explain.*

288 UNIT 2　THE ENGLISH RENAISSANCE

Selection Skills

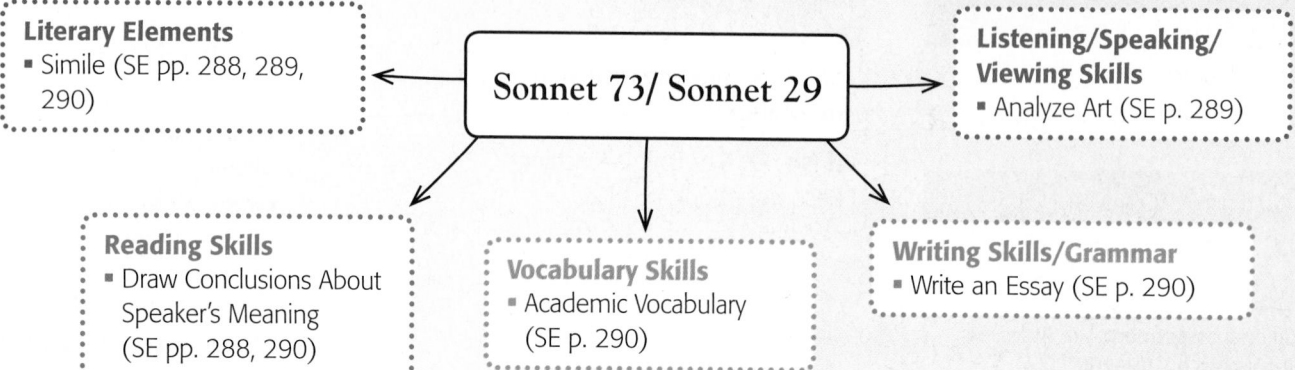

Literary Elements
- Simile (SE pp. 288, 289, 290)

Sonnet 73/ Sonnet 29

Listening/Speaking/ Viewing Skills
- Analyze Art (SE p. 289)

Reading Skills
- Draw Conclusions About Speaker's Meaning (SE pp. 288, 290)

Vocabulary Skills
- Academic Vocabulary (SE p. 290)

Writing Skills/Grammar
- Write an Essay (SE p. 290)

Double Portrait, c. 1502. Giorgione (Giorgio da Castelfranco). Oil on canvas, 77 x 66.5 cm. Palazzo Venezia, Rome.

View the Art The artist Giorgione was known for detailed portraits of Venetian citizens. What does this double portrait seem to be expressing about its subject?

SONNET 29

William Shakespeare

W hen in disgrace with Fortune and men's eyes
I all alone beweep my outcast state,
And trouble deaf heaven with my bootless cries,[1]
And look upon myself and curse my fate,
5   Wishing me like to one more rich in hope,
Featur'd like him, like him with friends possess'd,[2]
Desiring this man's art, and that man's scope,[3]
With what I most enjoy contented least;
Yet in these thoughts myself almost despising,
10 Haply[4] I think on thee, and then my state,[5]
Like to the lark at break of day arising
From sullen earth, sings hymns at heaven's gate,
     For thy sweet love rememb'red such wealth brings
     That then I scorn to change my state with kings.

---

1. *Bootless cries* are vain or futile cries.
2. The speaker compares himself to three different men in lines 5–7.
3. Here, *scope* means "mental power."
4. *Haply* means "by chance."
5. *State,* here and in line 14, refers to the speaker's condition or position in life.

2

Simile *Are lines 5–6 an example of a simile? Explain.*

WILLIAM SHAKESPEARE **289**

Teach

Literary Element   2

Simile **Answer:** *No, the speaker compares himself to other, more fortunate men, not to anything basically unlike himself.*
Ask: Which lines do include a simile? *(lines 10–12)*

Reading Strategy   3

Draw Conclusions About Speaker's Meaning **Ask:** What happens in the last five lines of the poem? *(The mood and the speaker's view of the world change because he thinks about his lover.)* What can you conclude about the speaker's relationship with his lover? *(It brings him great joy.)*

View the Art ★

Giorgione, a prominent Venetian painter, is known for his detailed portraits. Although his career lasted only about 15 years, his painting techniques inspired Titian, among others.

English Learners

DIFFERENTIATED INSTRUCTION

Intermediate Explain to students that love is an emotion that speaks across time and culture. Then have English learners share examples of love poetry and love stories from their own cultures. To spark discussion, ask students whether the ideal of love in their cultures matches the ideal of love Shakespeare portrays in his poetry. Invite students to identify the romantic notions of beauty and salvation that Shakespeare draws on in these sonnets. Then allow them to compare the poems and stories they mentioned with the sonnets.

After You Read

Assess

1. (a) A bare tree, a day at sunset, a dying fire. (b) Old age and dying.
2. (a) His ill fate and bad luck. (b) Possible answers: anguished; bitter; angry.
3. (a) Possible answer: sorrowful. (b) Possible answer: the metaphors of the bare tree, twilight, and dying fire.
4. (a) He thinks of his beloved. (b) Answers will vary.
5. Loving relationships are essential to life.
6. They all express a positive attitude toward love.

Literary Element

1. (a) The speaker's "state" is likened to a lark singing at daybreak. (b) The speaker is suddenly filled with joy.
2. Possible answer: I'm like the autumn of the year.

⚡ Writing

Be sure that students support their analyses with quotations from the poems.

Progress Check

Can students identify similes?

If No → See Unit 2 Teaching Resources Book, p. 124.

Progress Check

Can student draw conclusions about meaning?

If No → See Unit 2 Teaching Resources Book, p. 125.

After You Read

Respond and Think Critically

Respond and Interpret

1. (a) To what three things does the speaker compare himself in Sonnet 73? (b) What do you think these three things symbolize, or represent?
2. (a) What does the speaker complain about in the first part of Sonnet 29? (b) Based on the early lines of the poem, what kind of person would you say the speaker is?

Analyze and Evaluate

3. (a) How would you describe the tone of Sonnet 73? (b) What details create that tone?

4. (a) What reasons does the speaker in Sonnet 29 give for his change in mood? (b) Do you find the transition in the speaker's mood convincing? Explain.

Connect

5. **Big Idea** A Bard for the Ages Based on these two sonnets, how would you describe the value Shakespeare puts on human relationships?
6. **Connect to the Author** Recall that these two sonnets form parts of a larger sequence. How might they have been related to Sonnets 116 and 130 in Shakespeare's mind?

Literary Element Simile

A **simile** is a comparison between two basically unlike things by means of the word *like* or *as*. The comparison is meant to create greater understanding of what is being compared.

1. (a) What is the simile in lines 9–12 of Sonnet 29? (b) What understanding of the speaker and his "state" do you gain from this comparison?
2. Write a simile that expresses the speaker's attitude toward himself in lines 1–4 of Sonnet 73.

📝 Writing

Write an Essay Sonnets 73 and 29 address the idea that love is more valuable than youth, fame, or wealth. Write a brief essay describing the things that make you feel most fortunate and the reasons you chose those things. For help with writing an essay, see page 846.

LOG ON ▶ **Literature** Online

Selection Resources For Selection Quizzes, eFlash-cards, and Reading-Writing Connection activites, go to glencoe.com and enter QuickPass code GLB9817u2.

Reading Strategy Draw Conclusions About Speaker's Meaning

A **conclusion** is a general statement based on a number of specific examples.

1. What conclusion does the speaker come to in the couplet of Sonnet 73?
2. What conclusion can you draw about the speaker's emotions in lines 1–8 of Sonnet 29?

Academic Vocabulary ▶

In Sonnet 29, the speaker comes to the **conclusion** that he values the love of the person he is addressing more than material wealth.

Conclusion is an academic word. From what you know about Shakespeare's life and works, you might arrive at the **conclusion** that he led an extraordinary life.

Using context clues, try to figure out the meaning of conclusion in the following sentence: *There was not enough evidence to reasonably draw the **conclusion** that he had stolen the car.*

For more on academic vocabulary, see pages 56 and R81.

Reading Strategy

1. His failing condition makes his beloved love him more.
2. He is feeling dejected.

Academic Vocabulary

Students may respond that a *conclusion* is a judgment made about something after considering everything known about it.

Before You Read

Shakespeare's Songs

Connect to the Songs

How might emotions be expressed more powerfully through song than through speech? List some songs that convey feelings in ways that prose paraphrases could not.

Build Background

Shakespeare used songs in his plays to heighten the drama, making what is merry merrier or what is sad sadder. In Shakespeare's plays, the songs are often meditations on the action sung by minor characters. Unfortunately, most of the original music that was written to accompany these songs has been lost—if it was ever written down in the first place. However, we do know a great deal about what Elizabethan music sounded like, and using that information, many composers since Shakespeare have set his lyrics to music.

Set Purposes for Reading

Big Idea A Bard for the Ages

As you read, ask yourself, How might people of the time have responded to dirges in a tragedy or a romantic comedy?

Literary Element Theme

Theme is the central idea about life in a story, song, poem, or play. Some works have a stated theme, which is expressed explicitly. Other works have an implied theme, which is revealed gradually through events, dialogue, or description. As you read a song, ask yourself, What theme is the character conveying?

Reading Strategy Respond to Tone

An author's attitude toward his or her subject matter or the audience is called **tone**. Tone is conveyed through word choice, punctuation, sentence structure, and figures of speech. Literary characters may also express tone. As you read, ask yourself, What does the speaker's tone tell me about the work's theme?

Tip: Noting Tone of Voice Tone in literature is akin to tone of voice in conversation. To help discover a literary tone, think of how the speaker's voice would sound if the words were spoken aloud.

Learning Objectives

For pages 291–294

In studying these texts, you will focus on the following objectives:

Literary Study: Analyzing theme.

Reading: Responding to tone.

Writing: Writing a movie scene.

Vocabulary

tyrant (tī′ rənt) *n.* a cruel, oppressive ruler; a ruler with unlimited power; p. 292 *Years of spoiling turned her brother into a tyrant.*

censure (sen′ shər) *n.* strong disapproval; condemnation as wrong; p. 292 *The council called for the official censure of the mayor, due to her offensive remark.*

keen (kēn) *adj.* having a sharp edge or point; p. 293 *Tom kept a keen edge on his hunting knife.*

folly (fol′ ē) *n.* foolishness; an irrational and useless undertaking; p. 293 *Having the picnic during a thunderstorm was sheer folly.*

WILLIAM SHAKESPEARE **291**

Before You Read

Focus

Summary

The first song, "Fear No More the Heat o' the Sun," expresses the idea that everyone must die, regardless of his or her station in life. In "Blow, Blow, Thou Winter Wind," the speaker compares the winter to man's inhumanity and unkindness.

 For summaries in languages other than English, see Unit 2 Teaching Resources Book, pp. 128–133.

Vocabulary

Sound and Sense Write the following pairs of words on the board: *keen* and *pointed, folly* and *stupidity, censure* and *scolding, tyrant* and *despot.* **Ask:** *How do you respond to these synonyms? Does despot sound more or less offensive than tyrant? Does censure or scolding seem more intense? Does keen or pointed sound sharper? (Students' emotional responses to the words will vary.)*

Selection Skills

Literary Elements
- Theme (SE pp. 291, 292, 294)

⟵

> **Fear No More the Heat o' the Sun/ Blow, Blow, Thou Bitter Wind**

⟶

Vocabulary Skills
- Word Origins (SE p. 294)

Reading Skills
- Respond to Tone (SE pp. 291, 293, 294)

Writing Skills/Grammar
- Write a Movie Scene (SE p. 294)

Teach

Theme **Answer:** *The topic of death.* **Say:** Express the theme in your own words. *(Possible response: Death can be viewed as a liberation from the troubles of life.)*

(APPROACHING) **Ask:** What do you think the phrase *come to dust* may mean? If necessary, explain that the phrase means "die." **Ask:** Which words in the poem seem negative or unpleasant? *(Students should mention words such as* furious, rages, frown, *and* all-dreaded.*)*

Ask: Does the speaker associate death with suffering or relief? *(relief)*

 For an audio recording of this selection, use Listening Library Audio CD-ROM.

In the play Cymbeline, *Imogen, the daughter of King Cymbeline, is falsely accused of adultery. To clear herself, she wears a man's disguise. Falling ill, she takes a drug that puts her into a deathlike coma. The characters Guiderius and Arviragus (actually Imogen's brothers, also in disguise) express their sorrow for this "most rare boy" and sing this funeral dirge.*

Fear No More the Heat o' the Sun

William Shakespeare

Fear no more the heat o' the sun,
Nor the furious winter's rages,
Thou thy worldly task hast done,
Home art gone, and ta'en thy wages.
5 Golden lads and girls all must,
As[1] chimney-sweepers, come to dust.

Fear no more the frown o' the great,
Thou art past the **tyrant's** stroke;
Care no more to clothe and eat,
10 To thee the reed is as the oak.
The scepter, learning, physic,[2] must
All follow this and come to dust.

Fear no more the lightning-flash
Nor the all-dreaded thunder-stone.[3]
15 Fear not slander, **censure** rash.
Thou hast finish'd joy and moan.
All lovers young, all lovers must
Consign[4] to thee and come to dust.

No exorciser harm thee.
20 Nor no witchcraft charm thee.
Ghost unlaid forbear[5] thee.
Nothing ill come near thee.
Quiet consummation[6] have,
And renownèd be thy grave.

1. The speaker uses *as* to mean "like."
2. *Scepter, learning,* and *physic* refer to kings, scholars, and doctors.
3. The sound of thunder was thought to be caused by falling stones. Hence they were called *thunder-stones.*
4. *Consign* means "submit."
5. *Forbear* means "leave alone."
6. *Consummation* means "fulfillment."

---

1 Theme *What topic will the theme of this poem comment upon?*

Vocabulary

tyrant (tī′rənt) *n.* a cruel, oppressive ruler; a ruler with unlimited power
censure (sen′shər) *n.* strong disapproval; condemnation as wrong

292 UNIT 2 THE ENGLISH RENAISSANCE

Reading Practice

Analyze Tone Divide students into pairs and have them take turns reading the poem aloud while their partner reads along silently. Then have students identify the poem's tone. *(Possible responses: consoling; sad but hopeful)* Ask students to identify the elements of the poem that express this tone. Students might begin by discussing how the repetition of "Fear no more" affects the tone. Invite partners to share the highlights of their conversations with the rest of the class.

In As You Like It, *the former Duke Senior, whose title has been usurped by his younger brother, has been living in exile in the Forest of Arden, where he enjoys the simple delights of nature—as opposed to the treachery of life at court. With him are Lord Amiens and other former attendants. This song occurs when the former duke requests Amiens to "Give us some music."*

Blow, Blow, Thou Winter Wind

William Shakespeare

Blow, blow, thou winter wind,
Thou art not so unkind
   As man's ingratitude;
Thy tooth is not so **keen**,
5 Because thou art not seen,
   Although thy breath be rude.
Heigh-ho! sing, heigh-ho! unto the green holly,
Most friendship is feigning,[1] most loving mere folly.
  Then, heigh-ho, the holly!
10   This life is most jolly.

Freeze, freeze, thou bitter sky,
That dost not bite so nigh[2]
   As benefits forgot;
Though thou the waters warp,[3]
15 Thy sting is not so sharp
   As friend remembered not.
Heigh-ho! sing, heigh-ho! unto the green holly,
Most friendship is feigning, most loving mere **folly**.
  Then, heigh-ho, the holly!
20   This life is most jolly.

---

1. *Feigning* means "pretending."
2. *Nigh* means "near."
3. *Warp* means "make rough by freezing."

Respond to Tone *Do these two lines express the same tone? Explain.* **2**

Vocabulary

keen (kēn) *adj.* having a sharp edge or point
folly (fol′ē) *n.* foolishness; an irrational and useless undertaking

Winter, c. 1820. William Blake. Tempera on pine, 90.2 x 29.7 cm. Tate Gallery, London.

WILLIAM SHAKESPEARE **293**

After You Read

Assess

1. (a) They all die. (b) Kings, scholars, and doctors.

2. (a) "Man's ingratitude" (b) Being forgotten by one's friends

3. (a) A peaceful death and a respected grave (b) Possible answer: The song is meant to console the living.

4. (a) Love is characterized as folly and friendship as false. (b) Many of the words seem to encourage jollity, but the song expresses bitterness over a lost friendship.

5. The Elizabethans knew that death was always close at hand. They may have felt relief in knowing that life's struggles would be over when death came.

6. False friendships and the inevitability of death are modern themes.

Literary Element

1. (a) All life comes to an end; death need not be feared. (b) It is universal.

2. (a) It is explicitly stated. (b) Most friendship is false; most love is folly.

⚡ Writing

Students' scenes will vary but should include descriptions of the setting, the actions of the singer, and the reactions of the characters to the song.

After You Read

Respond and Think Critically

Respond and Interpret

1. (a) In "Fear No More . . ." what happens to all the "golden lads and girls," "the scepter, learning, physic," and the "lovers"? (b) What do "the scepter, learning, physic" in line 11 represent?

2. (a) According to "Blow, Blow, Thou Winter Wind," what is more unkind than the winter wind? (b) What has a sharper sting than ice water?

Analyze and Evaluate

3. (a) In the last stanza of "Fear No More . . .," what does the speaker wish for the person being addressed? (b) Do you think this song is meant to be consoling? Explain.

4. (a) According to the **refrain**, how does "Blow, Blow, Thou Winter Wind" characterize love and friendship? (b) How do the words of this song contrast with its purpose?

Connect

5. **Big Idea** A Bard for the Ages In what way does "Fear No More the Heat o' the Sun" express a particularly Elizabethan attitude toward death?

6. **Connect to Today** Are the attitudes expressed in these songs at all relevant today? Explain your response.

Literary Element Theme

A **theme** is a central idea about life in a literary work. Some works have a stated theme, while in other works the theme is implied. In addition, some themes are universal, meaning they can be found in literature all over the world.

1. (a) What is the theme of "Fear No More the Heat o' the Sun"? (b) Is this theme universal? Explain.

2. (a) Is the theme of "Blow, Blow, Thou Winter Wind" stated or implied? (b) What is the theme?

💻 Writing

Write a Movie Scene Reread the background information about "Blow, Blow, Thou Winter Wind" on page 293. Write a brief movie scene in which this song is performed, using what you know about its original context. Decide on an appropriate setting and on appropriate tone of voice and gestures for the actors.

> **LOG ON** ▶ **Literature** Online
>
> **Selection Resources** For selection Quizzes, eFlashcards, and Reading-Writing Connection activities, go to glencoe.com and enter QuickPass code GLB9817u2.

Reading Strategy Respond to Tone

Tone is an author's or character's attitude toward his or her subject matter or audience.

How would you describe the tones of each of these songs? Which words help create the tones?

Vocabulary Practice

Practice with Word Origins Studying the origin and history of a word can help you better understand and explore its meaning. Create a word map, like the one below, for each of these vocabulary words. Use a dictionary for help.

tyrant   censure   keen   folly

EXAMPLE:

Definition: failure to show or express thanks		Etymology: from Latin gratis, meaning "thankful"
	ingratitude	
	Sample Sentence: After all her hard work on the project, the ingratitude of her co-workers made her angry.	

Reading Strategy

Possible answers: "Fear No More the Heat o' the Sun"—sad but hopeful, consoling; "Blow, Blow, Thou Bitter Wind"—bitter but jocular, resigned.

Vocabulary

Sample setences will vary.

tyrant—*definition:* a cruel, oppressive ruler; *etymology:* from Greek *tyrannos,* meaning "absolute ruler"

censure—*definition:* strong disapproval; *etymology:* from Latin *censura,* meaning "judgment"

keen—*definition:* having a sharp edge or point; *etymology:* from Old English *cene,* meaning "brave"

folly—*definition:* foolishness; *etymology:* from Old French *fol,* meaning "fool."

Shakespeare's Soliloquies

Connect to the Texts

What prompts a person to wonder about the meaning of life? In a journal entry, recall a situation that caused you to consider what your life means.

Build Background

Soliloquies were a common feature in Elizabethan theater. In a **soliloquy**, a character, alone onstage, reveals his or her private thoughts and feelings. In *Hamlet*, the ghost of Hamlet's father has urged Hamlet to avenge his murder. Hamlet hesitates, unsure that he has seen a true ghost, and uncertain of how to go about killing the murderer. Hamlet then ponders the idea of being dead, and free from care.

Set Purposes for Reading

Big Idea A Bard for the Ages

As you read, ask yourself, How might the themes of these speeches be important in Elizabethan drama?

Literary Element Voice

The distinctive use of language that conveys the author's or speaker's personality to the reader or viewer is called **voice**. Voice is determined by elements of style such as word choice and tone. As you read each speech, ask yourself, How would I describe the distinctive voice of the speaker?

Reading Strategy Draw Conclusions About Theme

A **conclusion** is a general statement drawn from specific examples. **Theme** is the overall message about life in a work of literature. To draw a conclusion about theme, consider what has happened, how the characters feel about it, and how you—the reader or audience member—are supposed to react.

···

Tip: Taking Notes As you read the following speeches and soliloquies, jot down your conclusions in a chart.

Selection	Conclusions

Learning Objectives

For pages 295–303

In studying these texts, you will focus on the following objectives:

Literary Study:
Analyzing voice.
Analyzing figurative language.

Reading: Drawing conclusions about theme.

Vocabulary

calamity (kə lam′ə tē) *n.* disaster; extreme misfortune; p. 297 *It was a calamity when the levees broke and the river flooded the city.*

awry (ə rī′) *adv.* wrong; in a faulty way; p. 297 *All our careful vacation plans went awry when the airport was closed.*

oblivion (ə bliv′ ē ən) *n.* a state of forgetting; p. 299 *Jesse was in a state of oblivion after her surgery.*

pageant (paj′ ənt) *n.* an elaborately staged drama or spectacular exhibition; p. 300 *Our community staged a grand historical pageant.*

infirmity (in fur′ mə tē) *n.* weakness; state of being feeble or unable; p. 300 *Russell didn't let his infirmity ruin his life.*

WILLIAM SHAKESPEARE **295**

Focus

Summary

The first soliloquy comes from *Hamlet*. The title character reflects on the question of whether to live or die and the consequences of a choice. The second soliloquy comes from *As You Like It*. The character Jaques compares life to a play and identifies the circularity of the stages of life. In the last soliloquy, from *The Tempest*, Prospero describes the ending of a play.

 For summaries in languages other than English, see Unit 2 Teaching Resources Book, pp. 140–145.

Vocabulary

Tone Remind students that a writer's tone is his or her attitude toward a subject—cheerful, for example, or pessimistic, ironic, sorrowful, or angry. **Say:** Use each vocabulary word in a sentence that demonstrates its distinct tone. Invite students to read their sentences aloud so that others may identify the tone of each.

Selection Skills

Literary Elements
- Voice (SE pp. 295, 299, 302)
  Figurative Language
  (SE p. 302)

To be or not to be/
All the world's a stage/
Our revels now are ended

Listening/Speaking/Viewing Skills
- Visual Literacy (SE p. 301)

Reading Skills
- Draw Conclusions About Theme (SE pp. 295, 297, 302)

Vocabulary Skills
- Tone (TE p. 295)
- Context Clues (SE pp. 299, 300, 302)
- Academic Vocabulary (SE p. 302)

Writing Skills/Grammar
- Coordinating Conjunctions (SE p. 303)
- Write a Reflective Essay (SE p. 303)

Teach

 For additional vocabulary practice, see Unit 2 Teaching Resources Book, p. 149.

 For additional context, see Glencoe Interactive Vocabulary CD-ROM.

View the Art ★

This image is a woodcut by Edward Gordon Craig from a German edition of Hamlet published in 1928.

Ask: How does this image of Hamlet compare with how you imagine him? *(Responses will vary.)*

 For an audio recording of this selection, use Listening Library Audio CD-ROM.

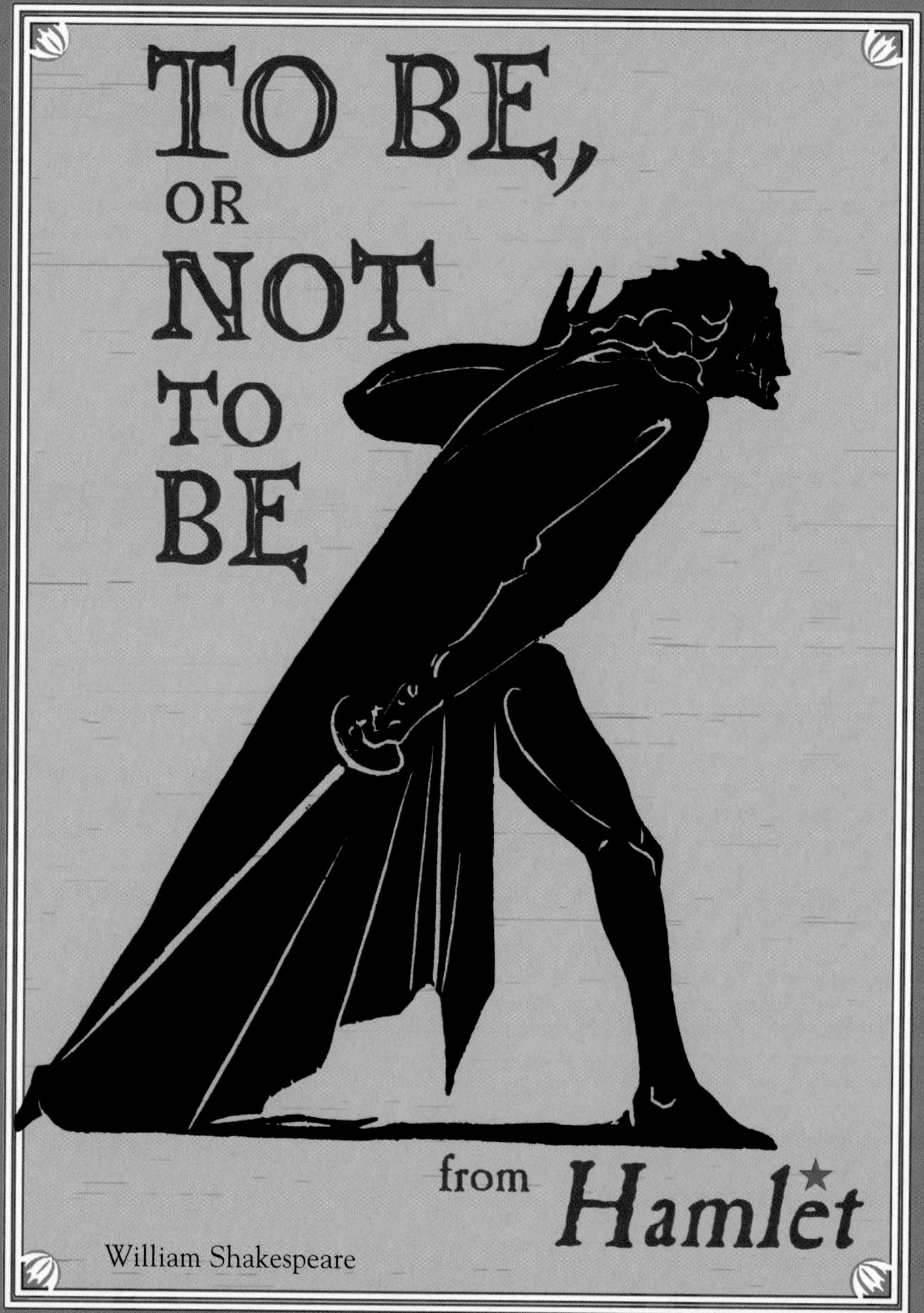

TO BE,
OR
NOT
TO
BE

from *Hamlet*

William Shakespeare

Listening and Viewing Practice

Compare Speeches Find copies of several film versions of *Hamlet*. Locate the "To be or not to be" speech in each of the movies and cue the tapes or DVDs. Play each version of the speech for students. Then lead a class discussion about the different representations of the character of Hamlet as presented in this speech. Have students evaluate each actor's performance, analyzing the voice that comes across. Invite students to suggest improvements that could be made in the performances.

Hamlet.

To be, or not to be—that is the question.
Whether 'tis nobler in the mind to suffer
The slings and arrows of outrageous fortune,
Or to take arms against a sea of troubles,
5 And by opposing end them. To die, to sleep—
No more, and by a sleep to say we end
The heartache and the thousand natural shocks
That flesh is heir to. 'Tis a consummation
Devoutly to be wished. To die, to sleep,
10 To sleep—perchance to dream. Aye, there's the rub,[1]
For in that sleep of death what dreams may come
When we have shuffled off this mortal coil[2]
Must give us pause. There's the respect
That makes **calamity** of so long life.
15 For who would bear the whips and scorns of time,
The oppressor's wrong, the proud man's contumely,[3]
The pangs of despised love, the law's delay,
The insolence of office, and the spurns
That patient merit of the unworthy takes,[4]
20 When he himself might his quietus make
With a bare bodkin?[5] Who would fardels[6] bear,
To grunt and sweat under a weary life,
But that the dread of something after death,
The undiscovered country from whose bourn[7]
25 No traveler returns, puzzles the will,
And makes us rather bear those ills we have
Than fly to others that we know not of?
Thus conscience does make cowards of us all,
And thus the native hue[8] of resolution
30 Is sicklied o'er with the pale cast of thought,
And enterprises of great pitch[9] and moment
With this regard their currents turn **awry**
And lose the name of action. . . .

1. Here, *rub* refers to an obstacle.
2. *Coil* means "turmoil."
3. *Contumely* refers to abuse.
4. The phrase *of the unworthy takes* means "receives from unworthy persons."
5. A *bare bodkin* is a dagger out of its sheath.
6. *Fardels* are "burdens."
7. Here, *bourn* means "boundary."
8. *Native hue* means "natural color."
9. Here, *pitch* means "height."

Draw Conclusions About Theme *What conclusion can you draw from lines 21–28 about Hamlet's fear of death?* **1**

Vocabulary

calamity (kə lam′ə tē) *n.* disaster; extreme misfortune
awry (ə rī′) *adv.* wrong; in a faulty way

Teach

Reading Strategy | 1

Draw Conclusions About Theme **Answer:** *Hamlet fears death because beyond it is something unknown from which there is no return.* **Ask:** According to the text, what results from this common human fear and belief? *(It makes "cowards of us all." In other words, people fear to end their own lives. They prefer their known torture to the unknown.)*

(ENGLISH LEARNERS) Have English learners find the definitions of unfamiliar terms in a dictionary. Then help students paraphrase the ideas in lines 21–28.

Literary Element | 2

Voice **Ask:** What is the tone of this soliloquy? *(Possible responses: contemplative; dark; pessimistic)* From his voice, how would you describe the speaker? *(Possible response: troubled and morose but intelligent and realistic.)*

(APPROACHING) Have approaching-level students identify words with negative associations. **Ask:** What emotions is the speaker expressing here? *(Possible responses: sadness; depression)*

Advanced Learners

DIFFERENTIATED INSTRUCTION

Understanding Context This soliloquy is located in Act 3, scene 1, of a five-act play. Challenge students to build a context for the soliloquy by reading *Hamlet* up to this point. Then have them write one-page essays, discussing what leads Hamlet to these thoughts and expressing their opinions about Hamlet's situation. **Ask:**

Do you believe that Hamlet is right? Do you think that he is insane? Remind students to provide specific text examples to support their opinions. After they finish reading and writing, have students share their findings with the rest of the class.

Cultural History ☆

The Many Faces of Hamlet
Many movies have been made of *Hamlet*, one of Shakespeare's most popular dramas. Distinguished actors, such as Laurence Olivier and Mel Gibson, have played the title character in well-known versions. A recent movie version, starring Ethan Hawke, is set in the present day.

Teach

View the Art ★

This painting from 1670 depicts French and Italian comedians performing in the style of *commedia dell'arte* (comedy of art), an Italian form of comic theater that was popular throughout Europe from the sixteenth to the eighteenth centuries. *Commedia dell'arte* actors were known for their use of improvisation, masks, and stock plots and scenarios. This type of theater was practiced in England in the Punch-and-Judy puppet shows that featured Punch, a *commedia dell'arte* character (*Pulcinella* in Italian) who was cruel and rebellious. **Ask:** How does the painting relate to the soliloquy? *(Possible response: The actors in the painting represent many different parts, just as Jaques says man plays many roles in life.)*

All the world's a stage

from *As You Like It*

William Shakespeare

Literary Element Practice

Extended Metaphor Explain to students that the soliloquy on page 299 is an extended metaphor. Remind students that a metaphor is a comparison in which one thing is discussed as if it were another.

Tell students that an extended metaphor is one that runs throughout a passage or an entire work. As they read the soliloquy, have them note the main metaphor and its parts. *(Main metaphor: The world is a stage. Parts: People are actors; different ages are like a play's acts.)*

In As You Like It, *the former Duke, whose title has been usurped by his younger brother, has been living in exile in the Forest of Arden. With him are Jaques, a melancholy lord, and other former attendants. The former Duke has just commented that the "wide and universal theater" of the world presents scenes sadder than theirs. Jaques picks up on the word* theater *in this meditation on life.*

Jaques.

All the world's a stage
And all the men and women merely players:
They have their exits and their entrances;
And one man in his time plays many parts,

5   His acts being seven ages. At first the infant,
Mewling[1] and puking in the nurse's arms.
And then the whining school-boy, with his satchel
And shining morning face, creeping like snail
Unwillingly to school. And then the lover,

10   Sighing like furnace, with a woeful ballad
Made to his mistress' eyebrow. Then a soldier,
Full of strange oaths, and bearded like the pard,[2]
Jealous in honor,[3] sudden[4] and quick in quarrel,
Seeking the bubble reputation

15   Even in the cannon's mouth. And then the justice,
In fair round belly with good capon lin'd,
With eyes severe, and beard of formal cut,
Full of wise saws[5] and modern instances;
And so he plays his part. The sixth age shifts

20   Into the lean and slipper'd pantaloon,[6]
With spectacles on nose and pouch on side,
His youthful hose, well sav'd, a world too wide
For his shrunk shank;[7] and his big manly voice,
Turning again toward childish treble, pipes

25   And whistles in his sound. Last scene of all,
That ends this strange eventful history,
Is second childishness and mere **oblivion**,
Sans[8] teeth, sans eyes, sans taste, sans everything.

1. *Mewling* is a catlike cry.
2. The phrase *bearded like the pard* means the soldier had a moustache like a leopard's.
3. *Jealous in honor* means "being easily angered in matters of honor."
4. Here, *sudden* means "rash" or "impetuous."
5. Here, *saws* mean "sayings."
6. A *pantaloon* is a stock character in Italian comedy, usually portrayed as a ridiculous, helpless old man.
7. Here, *shank* means "calf."
8. *Sans* is French for "without."

Voice *How would you describe Jaques's voice in these lines?*

Vocabulary

oblivion (ə bliv´ē ən) *n.* a state of forgetting

French and Italian comedians, 1670. Anonymous. Canvas. Comédie Française, Paris.

WILLIAM SHAKESPEARE   **299**

Teach

Literary Element   **1**

Voice **Answer:** *His voice is objective and removed; he speaks of "one man" rather than himself or any particular person.* **Ask:** How would you describe his voice overall? *(Possible responses: pessimistic; sad; hopeless)*

Reading Strategy   **2**

Draw Conclusions About Theme **Ask:** What can you conclude about the speaker's view of life from the description at the end? *(Possible response: Life is cyclical. We all end where we began. The choice of words (e.g., "oblivion" and "sans everything") suggests an essentially pessimistic view of hopelessness.)* What idea do the last four lines emphasize? *(Possible response: We are born with nothing and we die with nothing.)*

ENGLISH LEARNERS Help English learners connect to the text by having them describe what happens to people when they become old. Have students find vocabulary in the text that relates to aging.

Approaching Level

DIFFERENTIATED INSTRUCTION

Emerging Point out that Jaques compares life to a play in acts. He describes the progressing stages of life. Have students draw a timeline featuring seven cross marks with *Infant* on the far left and six more stages of life inserted in order on the timeline.

English Learners

DIFFERENTIATED INSTRUCTION

Intermediate List the soliloquy's seven ages—infant, school-boy, lover, soldier, justice, pantaloon, old age—on the board. Read aloud Shakespeare's description, as students follow along. Have students demonstrate the aspects of the age through gestures and facial expressions.

Teach

A Bard for the Ages

Answer: *The speech is all about impermanence: All life is a dream, with death (sleep) at the end.*

Ask: How do the ideas expressed in this speech relate to life today? *(Possible response: The ideas presented are universal concerns that poets and dramatists address today.)*

Literary Element | **2**

Voice **Ask:** On the basis of lines 11–16, how would you describe Prospero's voice? *(Possible response: He is self-effacing. He calls people from thinking of the universal to living in the moment.)*

[APPROACHING] **Say:** Prospero describes himself as weak, troubled, and infirm. What sort of personality do you think he has? *(Possible responses: modest, falsely humble.)*

In The Tempest, *Prospero, Duke of Milan, and his daughter, Miranda, end up shipwrecked on an island after escaping an attempt on their lives by Prospero's brother. Years later, Prospero, who is also a powerful magician, has caused the wreck of another ship, one bearing Ferdinand, Prince of Naples. Hoping that Miranda and Ferdinand will fall in love, Prospero has just staged an elaborate show in which island spirits, portraying Roman goddesses, bless their union.*

Our revels now are ended

from *The Tempest*

William Shakespeare

Prospero.
    Our revels[1] now are ended. These our actors,
    As I foretold you, were all spirits and
    Are melted into air, into thin air;
    And, like the baseless fabric of this vision,[2]
5   The cloud-capped towers, the gorgeous palaces,
    The solemn temples, the great globe[3] itself,
    Yea, all which it inherit,[4] shall dissolve,
    And, like this insubstantial **pageant** faded,
    Leave not a rack[5] behind. We are such stuff
10   As dreams are made on,[6] and our little life
    Is rounded[7] with a sleep. Sir, I am vexed.
    Bear with my weakness. My old brain is troubled.
    Be not disturbed with my **infirmity**.
    If you be pleased, retire into my cell
15   And there repose. A turn or two I'll walk
    To still my beating[8] mind.

2

1. *Revels* refers to entertainment, specifically the pageant the spirits recently presented in the play.
2. This phrase refers to the flimsy theater edifice or background.
3. *Great globe* refers to the Globe Theatre in London, where Shakespeare worked and performed.
4. *Which it inherit* means "those who will occupy it."
5. A *rack* is a small part of a cloud.
6. Here, *on* means "of."
7. Here, *rounded* means "surrounded," (that is, before birth and after death).
8. Here, *beating* means "disrupted" or "agitated."

1 | **A Bard for the Ages** *How does Prospero's speech reflect the Elizabethan concern with impermanence and death?*

Vocabulary

pageant (paj′ənt) *n.* an elaborately staged drama or spectacular exhibition

infirmity (in fur′mə tē) *n.* weakness; state of being feeble or unable

Vocabulary Practice

[SPIRAL REVIEW] **Context Clues** Remind students that context clues can help them determine the meanings of unfamiliar words. Have students skim the speech and record any unfamiliar words and their line numbers. Work through the selection line by line, identifying the unfamiliar words and helping students use context clues to determine their meanings. Tell students to record these meanings and double-check them with a dictionary. If you wish, have students use the words in original sentences in order to cement their understanding.

After You Read

Respond and Think Critically

Respond and Interpret

1. Which character—Hamlet, Jaques, or Prospero—comes closest to your own views on life and death? Explain.

2. (a)In "To be, or not to be," what do you think Hamlet means by "the slings and arrows of outrageous fortune" in line 3? Give some examples mentioned in the text. (b)What does Hamlet mean by the "undiscovered country" in line 24?

3. (a)What are the "many parts" everyone must play, according to Jaques in "All the world's a stage"? (b)What does he mean by "second childishness"?

4. (a)In "Our revels now are ended," how does Prospero explain the disappearance of the actors? (b)What does he say corresponds in real life with the vision he has just shown?

Analyze and Evaluate

5. Hamlet is wondering if he should murder his uncle, the king. How does the possibility of death affect his decision in lines 29–33?

6. (a)In "All the world's a stage," does Jaques seem to respect the people who play "many parts"? Explain. (b)What does he mean by "strange, eventful history"? Is he being sarcastic? Explain.

Connect

7. **Big Idea** **A Bard for the Ages** What ideas about life and death do these three speeches and soliloquies have in common? Explain.

8. **Connect to Today** Do you think most people today would agree with Hamlet about fearing death? Explain.

Visual Literacy

Use a Text Diagram

Putting aspects of a literary selection into visual form can enrich your understanding of them. Construct a diagram to order the "seven ages"

Seven Ages of Mankind	
Age	Characteristics
1.	
2.	
3.	
4.	
5.	
6.	
7.	

in Jaques's "All the world's a stage." First copy this graphic organizer below on a separate piece of paper. Then complete it, using words and phrases from Jaques's speech.

Group Activity Discuss the following questions with classmates. Support your answers with the diagram you created and evidence from the text.

1. Why do you think Jaques outlines seven ages? In your estimation, how old are the people represented in each?

2. Are some of the stages Jaques describes different in today's culture? Create a storyboard with illustrations to present each stage today.

After You Read

Assess

1. Students' answers will vary.

2. (a) He is referring to unfortunate things that happen in life, such as "the oppressor's wrong, the proud man's contumely, the pangs of despised love." (b) the afterlife

3. (a) stages of life or maturity (b) Senility or the helplessness of extreme old age.

4. (a) They weren't real people, but spirits who have "melted into air." (b) the fact that the world and all who live in it will disappear

5. The thought of death prevents him from committing murder.

6. (a) Possible answer: No, he has something scornful to say about each age. (b) The "strange, eventful history" is one's life. He is being sarcastic, because the life he has just described is neither "strange" nor "eventful."

7. Each speech suggests that there is something unreal, or dreamlike, about life. To Jaques, life is a series of parts to play, as on a stage. To Hamlet, the "dreams" that may come after death are more fearful than the realities that dreams evade. To Prospero, all the world is insubstantial and will dissolve like the visions he has conjured up.

8. Students' answers will vary.

Visual Literacy

1. Answers will vary, but students should provide estimates for the ages of the seven stages described: Infant, schoolboy, soldier, lover, justice, lean-and-slippered pantaloon (elderly), and oblivion.

2. Answers will vary.

After You Read

Assess

Literary Element

1. He is speaking very personally, trying to decide whether he should live or die, act or do nothing.
2. In contrast to Hamlet's immediacy, Jaques's voice is removed, impersonal, and a bit scornful of the life he describes.

Review: Figurative Language

1. It is a metaphor.
2. Students may answer that the metaphor provides insight into both. If the world is a stage, all desires and actions need not be taken very seriously. The idea that the stage is a world is exemplified by the worldly desires and actions that are demonstrated on it.

Progress Check

Can students analyze voice?

If No → See Unit 2 Teaching Resources Book, p. 146.

Literary Element Voice

Voice is the distinctive use of language that conveys a speaker's personality to the reader or viewer. Voice is determined by elements of style such as word choice and tone.

1. Describe Hamlet's voice in "To be, or not to be." Is he speaking personally and with a sense of immediacy, or objectively and with a sense of detachment?
2. Compare Hamlet's voice to that of Jaques in "All the world's a stage."

Review: Figurative Language

As you learned on page 251, **figurative language** is language used for descriptive effect or to convey ideas and emotions. Figurative expressions are not literally true but express some truth beyond the literal level. Three common types of figurative language are simile, metaphor, and personification. A **simile** is a comparison that uses words such as *like* or *as,* whereas a **metaphor** directly states a comparison without using these words. **Personification** is a figure of speech in which a nonhuman thing is given human characteristics.

Partner Activity Meet with a classmate to discuss the following questions.

1. What kind of figurative language is the phrase "all the world's a stage"?
2. Does the phrase "all the world's a stage" provide insight into the world, the stage, or both? Explain.

Prospero. Henry Fuseli.
York Art Gallery, UK.

Reading Strategy Draw Conclusions About Theme

A **conclusion** is a general statement drawn from specific examples. A conclusion about theme should take into account what has happened, and how the characters and audience respond to it.

1. Hamlet asks the question, "To be, or not to be?" Does he come to a conclusion? Explain.
2. Use the examples given in "All the world's a stage" to come to a conclusion about Jaques's philosophy: *All the world's a stage, and all the men and women merely players; therefore* _____ .

Vocabulary Practice

Practice with Context Clues Identify the context clues in the following sentences that help you determine the meaning of each boldfaced vocabulary word.

1. Our championship game was a **calamity**— we lost by twenty points.
2. The plan for our day went **awry** when I locked the keys in the car.
3. The woman was in **oblivion** and forgot that she had an appointment that day.
4. I was a turkey in the Thanksgiving **pageant**.
5. Mary's **infirmity** kept her from running.

Academic Vocabulary

*Hamlet quickly **abandons** the idea of suicide.*

Abandon is an academic word that is also used in many everyday settings. For example, animal shelters take care of **abandoned** pets.

Use context clues to figure out the meaning of the word *abandon* in the following sentence: *After years of poor reviews, the painter decided to **abandon** her artistic efforts.*

For more on academic vocabulary, see pages 56 and R81.

Reading Strategy

1. He really comes to no conclusion, except that he is too cowardly to act.
2. Students might summarize Jaques's thought as follows: It matters little, in the end, what one does or does not do.

Vocabulary

1. The context suggests that a *calamity* is a drastic turn of events.
2. The context conveys that things go *awry* when a plan is interrupted.
3. The context suggests that *oblivion* is a state in which one recalls nothing
4. The context suggests an event requiring a costume, so *pageant* must mean "exhibition," "play," or "show."

5. The sentence implies that Mary's condition prevents her from running, so *infirmity* must mean "weakness."

Academic Vocabulary

The painter abandons her art to "pursue a new career," so *abandon* must mean "leave behind."

Respond Through Writing

Reflective Essay

Explore Theme The soliloquy from "As You Like It" expresses a powerful and poetic reflection on the various stages of life. Using the theme of this speech as a basis, write a reflective essay on a rite of passage you have experienced in your own "strange eventful history."

Understanding the Task A **theme** is the central message of a work of literature—one that can often be expressed as a general statement about life. It may be stated directly, or it may be conveyed indirectly through description, dialogue, and events.

Prewrite State the theme of Jaques's speech in "As You Like It" in your own words. Then brainstorm or freewrite to identify a rite of passage in your life that illustrates the theme. Create a graphic organizer, such as a word web, to help you explore the details of that experience and the ways in which it exemplifies Shakespeare's theme.

Draft Compile the information you have gathered to vividly describe your rite of passage. You may want to present your experience chronologically, or point by point, comparing it to similar ideas in the soliloquy. Use quotations or paraphrases of the text to support any comparisons you make. Then explain the ways in which your own rite of passage connects to the larger idea of aging or "coming of age."

In stating your reflections, use structures like the following:

I'd always/never felt _____, until _____.

Revise Before rereading your draft, review the soliloquy. Have you correctly interpreted it and identified its theme? Have you made clear why your own experience was significant and how it relates to Shakespeare's theme? If necessary, rework your essay to reflect a clear understanding of the message and its connection to your experience.

EXAMPLE:
The theme of the soliloquy "All the world's a stage" is that this life is just preparation for the next stage, or a better life to come a short drama in which we each have a minor part. I'd always felt that way, too, until my eyes were dramatically opened.

Edit and Proofread Proofread your paper, correcting any errors in spelling, grammar, and punctuation. Use the Grammar Tip in the side column to help you with coordinating conjunctions.

Learning Objectives

In this assignment, you will focus on the following objectives:

Writing: Writing a reflective essay.

Literary Study: Exploring theme.

Grammar: Understanding how to use coordinating conjunctions.

> **Grammar Tip**
>
> **Coordinating Conjunctions**
>
> Combining sentences can help you vary your writing.
>
> Join related short sentences with **coordinating conjunctions** such as *and, but, or, nor, for, yet,* and *so.*
>
> *I heard that Granddad had died. I felt his hand on my shoulder at graduation.*
>
> **Combined:**
>
> *I heard that Granddad had died,* **yet** *I felt his hand on my shoulder at graduation.*

LOG ON ▶ **Literature** Online

Selection Resources For Selection Quizzes, eFlashcards, and Reading-Writing Connection activities, go to glencoe.com and enter QuickPass code GLB9817u2.

After You Read

Assess
Respond Through Writing

Use these criteria in evaluating student reflective essays:

- The theme of the Shakespeare excerpt is correctly identified.
- Descriptive details of a personal rite of passage are presented chronologically and are related to the literary theme.
- Coordinating conjunctions are correctly used to join sentences and to reveal the relationship between them.
- A student who meets all of these criteria should receive the equivalent of a 4-point response.
- A student who fully meets two or partially meets three of these criteria should receive the equivalent of a 3-point response.
- A student who fully meets one or partially meets two of these criteria should receive the equivalent of a 2-point response.
- A student who partially meets one of these criteria should receive the equivalent of a 1-point response.

Approaching Level

DIFFERENTIATED INSTRUCTION

AAVE Approaching-level speakers of African American vernacular English (AAVE) may use *was* with plural subjects. Write *was* and *were* on the board. Add the following sentences: *The moment ___ one of the most frightening of my life.*

They ___ ready for a great performance. To practice **reading fluency,** have students read each sentence aloud, inserting first *was* and then *were* in the blank. After each reading, **ask:** Is the subject singular or plural? *(singular, plural)* Explain that because the subject is singular in the first sentence, the verb *was* is needed, and because the subject is plural in the second sentence, the verb *were* is needed. Then have students check the use of *was* and *were* in their essay drafts.

Focus

Shakespeare's Theater

I N 1558, THE FIRST YEAR OF ELIZABETH I'S REIGN, THERE WERE NO playhouses in England. Actors, or "players," performed wherever they could find an audience—often in the open courtyards of London inns. Much to the distress of the mostly Puritan city council, who believed that "playacting" was a violation of the biblical commandment against idolatry, these performances attracted large and often rowdy crowds. In 1574 the Common Council of London issued an order banishing players from London. To get around the order, actor James Burbage and his company of players leased land in nearby Shoreditch, where they built the first public playhouse in England. Completed in 1576, the "Theater" was an immediate success. Several other theaters soon followed.

Bellringer Options

**Daily Language Practice
    Transparency 26**
**Selection Focus
    Transparency 15**
**Or have students discuss this
question:** How have citizens
contributed to the revival of the
theater in the past and today?
As students read, they should
consider and compare theater of
the past to theater today.

Learning Objectives

For pages 304–305
In studying this text, you will
focus on the following
objectives:

Literary Study: Analyzing
blank verse.

Reading:
Analyze literary periods.
Evaluate historical influences.

> *"The cause of plagues is sinne, if
> you look to it well: and the cause of
> sinne are playes: therefore the cause
> of plagues are playes."*
>
> —Thomas White, *Sermon*, 1576

The Globe

To theater-lovers today, one early English playhouse stands out from all the rest—the Globe, home to many of Shakespeare's plays. Built in 1599, the first Globe was, quite literally, a rebirth of the Theater. When Burbage had trouble renewing his lease, he had the Theater disassembled. The timber was carted over the Thames River to Bankside and was used to build the Globe. Although no trace of the original Globe remains today, surviving maps, construction contracts, and plays of the time have helped scholars piece together a fairly clear picture of what it looked like in its day.

This Wooden O

 In Henry V, the first play to be performed at the Globe, Shakespeare referred to the theater as "this wooden O." From that description and others, scholars believe that the Globe was a circular

The Globe Theatre. Medieval woodcut. London.

structure, formed by three-tiered, thatch-roofed galleries that served as seating. These galleries overlooked an open courtyard, into which jutted a raised platform stage. At the back of the main stage was a small curtained inner stage used for indoor scenes. Above the main stage stood a two-tiered gallery. The first tier was used to stage balcony and bedroom scenes; the second, to house musicians.

Teach

Literary History ☆

Henry V The first play presented at the Globe Theatre, *Henry V* takes place in the 1400s and is based on the life of the king who led the English army to invade and conquer France.

304 UNIT 2   THE ENGLISH RENAISSANCE

Reading Practice

Preview Have students read each heading and make predictions about what the material under the heading will include. Discuss the meanings of any unfamiliar terms in the headings. Students may need extra assistance in understanding why religious groups such as the Puritans considered theater immoral.

Lords and Groundlings

Plays were usually performed in the afternoon before a diverse audience of about two thousand people. Members of the nobility and the rising middle class generally sat in the galleries. Less well-to-do spectators, called "groundlings," could stand and watch from the courtyard for only a penny. Their close proximity to the stage made for an intimate theatrical experience, but it also made for a noisy one. Accounts of the time suggest that the groundlings did not hesitate to shout comments to the actors onstage and that vendors selling snacks circulated throughout the audience during performances.

Theatrical Conventions

Certain theatrical conventions that seemed natural to Elizabethans might strike today's audiences as strange. For example, most of Shakespeare's  characters speak in **blank verse**—unrhymed lines of iambic pentameter. In this verse form, each line is divided into five units, or feet, with stress falling on every second syllable. Because the rhythm of blank verse mimics the natural rhythm of spoken English, it is especially appropriate for dialogue.

Because acting was considered to be too indelicate for women, female roles were played by boys—apprentices to the company of players. Costumes were usually colorful and elaborate versions of regular Elizabethan dress, whether worn for *Macbeth*, set in the eleventh century, or for *Julius Caesar*, set in 44 B.C. Scenery was almost nonexistent. A single tree might stand for a forest, or a chair for a throne room. Shakespeare made up for the lack of scenery by giving characters descriptive passages to help the audience visualize the scenes.

The Elizabethan stage had no front curtain, so the beginning of a play was announced by the blaring of trumpets, and the start of a new scene was signaled by the entrance of the appropriate characters. Given the lack of scenery changes and intermissions, Elizabethan productions probably moved quickly. Scholars estimate that a typical performance of a Shakespearean play lasted only two hours, as opposed to the three or more hours that it usually takes to perform his plays today.

The Globe's Comeback

The original Globe Theatre was destroyed in 1613 when the explosion of a cannon intended to mark the entrance of the king during a performance of *Henry VIII* accidentally set the thatched roof on fire. Within an hour, the entire theater burned to the ground. Rebuilt the following year, the Globe stood until 1644, when it was torn down to clear the land for new housing.

Thanks to the late U.S. actor Sam Wanamaker, the Globe made a comeback in 1997. Wanamaker founded the new Globe, a working replica of the original. It stands on the south bank of the Thames River in London and opened, like the original, with a production of *Henry V*. After more than three centuries, Shakespeare's "wooden O" has come full circle.

LOG ON ▶ **Literature** Online

Literature and Reading For more about Shakespeare's theater, go to glencoe.com and enter QuickPass code GLB9817u2.

Respond and Think Critically

1. Why do you think Elizabethan audiences found drama so appealing?

2. Why might the Puritans have thought that playacting violated the biblical commandment against idolatry?

3. Why do you think Elizabethan plays were performed during the afternoon in an open courtyard?

Teach

Literary Element   **1**

Blank Verse Explain that blank verse has been used in English not only in dramas but also in long narrative poems, such as John Milton's *Paradise Lost* and William Wordsworth's *Prelude*. Guide students to discuss the differences between blank verse and rhyming verse with a regular meter.

Assess

1. Students may say that the theater was the prime source of entertainment for a large section of Elizabethan society.

2. The Puritans may have thought that the actors and playwrights in the Elizabethan age were being similarly idolized.

3. Possible answer: To avoid a need for artificial lighting.

Approaching Level

DIFFERENTIATED INSTRUCTION

Established Ask students to think of public performances they have attended. Have them make a list of the similarities and differences between those experiences and "the Globe experience" discussed here. Emphasize the crowded conditions, the noise, and the stage conventions.

Discuss some differences between Elizabethan theaters and modern movie theaters: Modern audiences are more likely to sit quietly and usually buy their snacks in the theater lobby; movie settings are more realistic than those on a Shakespearean stage; dialogue in modern movies is in prose, not blank verse.

Before You Read

Focus

Summary

Macbeth and Banquo crush a rebellion against King Duncan. Afterward they encounter three witches who prophesy that Macbeth will be king and that Banquo will sire kings. When Duncan visits Macbeth's castle, Lady Macbeth decides the time and place are right for assassination. Ambition and his wife's goading overcome Macbeth's misgivings.

 For summaries in languages other than English, see Unit 2 Teaching Resources Book, pp. 155–160.

Vocabulary

Language of the Times

Ask: Which of the vocabulary words might you actually use in your writing? *(prophetic, repentance)* Which ones strike you as outdated? *(direful, plenteous, peerless)* Have students say or write a sentence using each of the outdated words, then repeat the sentence using contemporary language.

Before You Read

Macbeth, Act 1

Connect to the Play

Why do some people seek power at all costs? Freewrite for a few minutes about this question.

Build Background

For the basic story of this play, Shakespeare turned to one of the most popular books of the time, Raphael Holinshed's *Chronicles of England, Scotland, and Ireland* (1587). Always fascinated by psychological truth, Shakespeare altered his source material to gain dramatic power. In Shakespeare's hands, the historical Macbeth becomes a **tragic hero**—a character, usually of high status, who suffers a downfall as a result of a fatal character flaw, errors in judgment, or forces beyond human control.

Set Purposes for Reading

Big Idea A Bard for the Ages

Shakespeare explored human nature in its many manifestations. As you read, ask yourself, How do the characters' motivations contribute to their universal appeal?

Literary Element Atmosphere

Atmosphere is the general mood, or emotional quality, of a literary work. Playwrights create atmosphere primarily through details, such as those of setting, that are conveyed through the dialogue. As you read, ask yourself, What mood is being created, and what details help to convey it?

Reading Strategy Apply Background Knowledge

Background knowledge refers to what you already know about the historical, social, and cultural forces that help shape a literary work. Background information about Shakespeare and his times is found in the unit introduction on pages 236–237, the feature on Shakespeare's theater on pages 304–305, the biography of Shakespeare on pages 282–283, and the Build Background section on this page. Also use the side notes, which provide help with unfamiliar words and complicated sentence structures, to add to your background knowledge while reading particular passages. As you read, ask yourself, How is what I already know helping me to understand what I am reading?

Learning Objectives

For pages 306–326

In studying this text, you will focus on the following objectives:

Literary Study: Analyzing atmosphere.

Reading: Applying background knowledge.

Writing: Writing a brochure.

Vocabulary

direful (dīr′ fəl) *adj.* terrible; dreadful; p. 310 *She claimed that the house was haunted because of direful events in its past.*

prophetic (prə fet′ ik) *adj.* having the quality of foretelling future events; p. 314 *With prophetic skill, he predicted the final score of the baseball game.*

repentance (ri pent′ əns) *n.* a feeling of sorrow for wrongdoing; remorse; p. 317 *Justin expressed repentance for breaking the toy.*

plenteous (plen′ tē əs) *adj.* abundant; fruitful; p. 318 *The potluck dinner featured plenteous main courses but only two desserts.*

peerless (pēr′ lis) *adj.* unrivaled; without equal; p. 319 *Grandpa is peerless when it comes to reciting Shakespearean passages.*

Selection Skills

Literary Elements
- Atmosphere (SE pp. 306–326)
- Drama (TE p. 308)

Reading Skills
- Apply Background Knowledge (SE pp. 306–326)

Macbeth, Act I

Vocabulary Skills
- Word Parts (SE p. 326; TE p. 318)

Listening/Speaking/Viewing Skills
- Analyze Art (SE pp. 312, 321; TE p. 307)

Writing Skills/Grammar
- Write a Brochure (SE p. 326)
- Sentence Structure (TE p. 310)

306

The Tragedy of
Macbeth

William Shakespeare

Macbeth and the Three Witches. John Wootton. Oil on canvas. Private collection.

Teach

View the Art

John Wootton (1686–1765) is often associated with the prominent writers and poets of his day, such as Alexander Pope, Edmund Gray, and Jonathan Swift. This painting depicts an event in Act I, scene 3, of *Macbeth*. The focus of the painting is on the dark, moody landscape. **Ask:** Based on the images in the painting, what do you think will happen when Macbeth meets the three witches? *(Responses will vary.)*

 For an audio recording of this selection, use Listening Library Audio CD-ROM.

Interactive Read and Write

Other options for teaching this selection can be found in

- Interactive Read and Write for EL Students, pp. 97–112
- Interactive Read and Write for Approaching-Level Students pp. 97–112
- Interactive Read and Write for On-Level Students, pp. 97–112

English Learners

DIFFERENTIATED INSTRUCTION

Intermediate Point out to students that all the words in the vocabulary list are formed with suffixes. Ask students to identify the suffixes and root words, or provide the root words and ask students to just identify the suffixes. Note the spelling changes in the root words when the suffixes are added. **Ask:** Based on the definition of each vocabulary word, what does each root word mean?

(direful: *terrible,* prophetic: *person who foretells the future,* repentance: *feel remorse,* plenteous: *abundance,* peerless: person of equal status)* Which word's meaning is not changed by the suffix? *(direful)*

Teach

Apply Background Knowledge **Ask:** When have you encountered a "Cast of Characters" list before? *(Possible response: when reading other plays or looking at a playbill)* What information does this list include? *(It identifies all the characters in the play and gives a brief description of each.)* How can this be a valuable tool for reading the play? *(Possible response: It provides a reference if one is confused about who a character is or how he or she relates to the other characters.)*

For additional practice using the reading skill or strategy, see Unit 2 Teaching Resources Book, p. 162.

Cultural History

Richard Burbage Scholars think that the first performance of *Macbeth* occurred in 1606. There is no official record of the opening-night cast, but many believe that Richard Burbage played Macbeth. Burbage was the most famous actor at the time of *Macbeth's* first performance and a good friend of Shakespeare. Other famous Shakespearean roles Burbage played include Richard III, Romeo, Hamlet, Othello, and King Lear.

---

1 CAST OF CHARACTERS

DUNCAN: King of Scotland

MALCOLM: Duncan's older son and heir to the throne

DONALBAIN: Duncan's younger son

☆ **MACBETH:** Thane of Glamis, a Scottish noble and general in King Duncan's army

LADY MACBETH: Macbeth's wife

BANQUO: a thane of Scotland and general in King Duncan's army

FLEANCE: Banquo's son

MACDUFF: Thane of Fife, a Scottish noble

LADY MACDUFF: Macduff's wife

SON OF MACDUFF AND LADY MACDUFF

LENNOX
ROSS
MENTEITH } thanes and nobles of Scotland
ANGUS
CAITHNESS

SIWARD: Earl of Northumberland and general of the English forces

YOUNG SIWARD: Siward's son

SEYTON: an officer attending Macbeth

THREE WITCHES

HECATE: leader of the witches

PORTER

OLD MAN

THREE MURDERERS

ENGLISH DOCTOR

SCOTTISH DOCTOR

CAPTAIN: an officer serving Duncan

GENTLEWOMAN: an attendant to Lady Macbeth

APPARITIONS

LORDS, GENTLEMEN, OFFICERS, SOLDIERS, MESSENGERS, ATTENDANTS, SERVANTS

SETTING: *Scotland and England during the eleventh century.*

Literary Element Practice

SPIRAL REVIEW **Drama** **Ask:** How does drama differ from fiction or nonfiction? *(It tells a story solely through dialogue and action. It does not include narration and is meant to be performed, not read.)* Identify the different parts of the text for students. Point out that the speakers' names appear in boldface small capitals. The dialogue appears in regular type. The stage directions are italicized. Have students identify examples of each of these elements and explain their purpose before they begin reading Act 1.

ACT 1

SCENE 1. Scotland. An open place.

[*In the midst of a great storm of thunder and lightning,* THREE WITCHES *appear in a deserted, outdoor place.*]

> FIRST WITCH. When shall we three meet again?
> In thunder, lightning, or in rain?
>
> SECOND WITCH. When the hurlyburly's° done,
> When the battle's lost and won.
>
> 5 THIRD WITCH. That will be ere° the set of sun.
>
> FIRST WITCH. Where the place?
>
> SECOND WITCH.   Upon the heath.°
>
> THIRD WITCH. There to meet with Macbeth.
>
> FIRST WITCH. I come, Graymalkin.°
>
> SECOND WITCH. Paddock° calls.
>
> THIRD WITCH.   Anon!°
>
> 10 ALL. Fair is foul, and foul is fair.°
> Hover through the fog and filthy air.

[*The* WITCHES *exit.*]

SCENE 2. A military camp near Forres, a town about a hundred miles north of Edinburgh in Scotland.

[*From offstage come the sounds of men fighting, weapons clashing, and trumpets blaring.* DUNCAN, *King of Scotland, enters with his two teenage sons.* MALCOLM, *the older, who is heir to the throne, and* DONALBAIN, *the younger. With them are a Scottish nobleman,* LENNOX, *and other attendants. They meet a* CAPTAIN *bleeding from wounds received in battle between the king's army and the forces of his two rivals, Macdonwald and the Thane of Cawdor.*]

> KING. What bloody man is that? He can report,
> As seemeth by his plight, of the revolt
> The newest state.
>
> MALCOLM.   This is the sergeant
> Who like a good and hardy soldier fought
> 5 'Gainst my captivity.° Hail, brave friend!
> Say to the king the knowledge of the broil°
> As thou didst leave it.

---

3 **hurlyburly:** commotion.

5 **ere:** before.

6 **heath:** uncultivated land covered by small shrubs.

8 **Graymalkin:** gray cat (the name of a familiar, or spirit in animal form, that serves a witch).
9 **Paddock:** toad (another familiar). **Anon:** right away!
10 In Shakespeare's time, many people believed that witches reversed normal values and practices, considering ugliness beautiful and vice versa.

1–3 The wounded officer **(sergeant)** has returned to King Duncan's military camp near Forres. Duncan hopes he can report on the progress of the rebellion.

5 **'Gainst my captivity:** to keep me from being captured.
6 **broil:** battle.

Apply Background Knowledge *Why might the witches want to meet Macbeth?*

Atmosphere *What do these lines suggest about the world of this play?*

Teach

Reading Strategy 2

Apply Background Knowledge Answer: *The witches might want to meet Macbeth to involve him in evil.*
Ask: How does this scene set the mood for the action to come? (*It establishes a creepy mood that is filled with foreboding.*)

Literary Element 3

Atmosphere Answer: *The witches reverse the values of fair and foul, or good and bad. Evil may be perceived as good in this dark and murky atmosphere.*
Ask: How do the beginning lines of scene 2 reinforce the dark and foreboding atmosphere? (*The king asks about a bloody man, indicating violence of some sort.*)

English Learners

DIFFERENTIATED INSTRUCTION

Intermediate Have students use a dictionary to look up the various meanings of *foul* and *fair*. **Ask:** What do *foul* and *fair* mean when you are talking about the weather? (*bad weather and nice weather*) What do the words mean when you are talking about justice or how people treat each other? (*wrong or against the rules and kind or equal*)

Advanced Learners

DIFFERENTIATED INSTRUCTION

Build Background In addition to reading about the real-life Macbeth and Duncan, Shakespeare also read about King Duff, who was murdered by a trusted young couple. Scholars believe Shakespeare was drawn to the story of King Duff because of similar events happening in his own time—specifically, the Gunpowder Plot of 1605. *Macbeth* likely premiered in London in 1606. Tell students to research the

political and social climate of the time and write a brief report on one specific aspect of it. Allow time for students to share their reports with the class.

Teach

Literary Element | 1

Atmosphere Ask: What kind of atmosphere do lines 25–28 create? *(They create a foreboding and scary atmosphere.)*

Writer's Technique ☆

Figurative Language

Shakespeare uses figurative language to paint a vivid picture of the battle. Here he uses a simile comparing it to two tired swimmers hanging on to each other, each nearly causing the other to drown. In line 12, he uses an implied metaphor with the word *swarm*. It brings to mind the image of a swarm of bees overtaking a man.

CAPTAIN.   Doubtful it stood,
      As two spent swimmers, that do cling together
      And choke their art.° The merciless Macdonwald—
10   Worthy to be a rebel for to that
      The multiplying villainies of nature
      Do swarm upon him°—from the Western Isles° ☆
      Of kerns and gallowglasses° is supplied;
      And Fortune, on his damnèd quarrel smiling,
15   Showed like a rebel's whore:° but all's too weak:
      For brave Macbeth—well he deserves that name—
      Disdaining Fortune, with his brandished steel,
      Which smoked with bloody execution,
      Like valor's minion° carved out his passage
20   Till he faced the slave;
      Which nev'r shook hands, nor bade farewell to him,
      Till he unseamed him from the nave to th' chops,°
      And fixed his head upon our battlements.

KING.   O valiant cousin!° Worthy gentleman!

25 **CAPTAIN.**   As whence the sun 'gins his reflection°
      Shipwracking storms and **direful** thunders break,
      So from that spring whence comfort seemed to come
      Discomfort swells.° Mark, King of Scotland, mark:
      No sooner justice had, with valor armed,
30   Compelled these skipping kerns to trust their heels
      But the Norweyan lord,° surveying vantage,°
      With furbished arms and new supplies of men,
      Began a fresh assault.

KING.   Dismayed not this
      Our captains, Macbeth and Banquo?

CAPTAIN.   Yes;
35   As sparrows eagles,° or the hare the lion.
      If I say sooth,° I must report they were
      As cannons overcharged with double cracks;°
      So they doubly redoubled strokes upon the foe.
      Except° they meant to bathe in reeking wounds,
40   Or memorize another Golgotha,°
      I cannot tell—
      But I am faint; my gashes cry for help.

KING.   So well thy words become thee as thy wounds;
      They smack of honor both. Go get him surgeons.

[As the CAPTAIN exits with the help of attendants, noblemen ROSS and ANGUS enter.]

Vocabulary

direful (dīr′fəl) *adj.* terrible; dreadful

8–9 As . . . art: like two tired swimmers who hinder their skill by clinging to each other.

10–12 Worthy . . . him: well suited to be a rebel, since he is infested with evil qualities.
12 Western Isles: the Hebrides, off Scotland's west coast.
13 kerns and gallowglasses: lightly armed Irish foot soldiers and horsemen armed with axes.
14–15 Fortune . . . whore: Fortune, approving Macdonwald's cause, appeared to favor the rebel.
19 minion: favorite.

21–22 Which . . . chops: Macbeth didn't part from Macdonwald until he had cut him open from his navel to his jaw.
24 cousin: kinsman (Macbeth and Duncan were both grandsons of King Malcolm).
25 sun 'gins his reflection: sun rises.

25–28 As . . . swells: The Captain says that Macdonwald's defeat was only a break in the storm.

31 Norweyan lord: Sweno, King of Norway. **surveying vantage:** seeing an opportunity for attack.

35 As sparrows eagles: as much as sparrows frighten eagles.
36 sooth: truth.
37 cracks: explosive charges.

39 Except: unless.
40 memorize . . . Golgotha: make the field as notorious for slaughter as Golgotha, where Christ was crucified.

Grammar Practice

SPIRAL REVIEW Sentence Structure Write on the board: subject, verb, object. Help students determine the basic parts of sentences in order to extract meaning from Shakespeare's poetic language. Read the sentence in lines 29–33 aloud. Ask students to identify the subject of the sentence *(lord)*, the verb *(began)*, and the verb's object *(assault).* Lead students to see that the rest of the sentence consists of modifying words and phrases and a subordinate clause. If students find it difficult to understand a sentence, have them repeat this exercise to identify basic meaning.

45   Who comes here?

MALCOLM.   The worthy Thane° of Ross.

LENNOX. What a haste looks through his eyes! So should he
        look
        That seems to° speak things strange.

ROSS.   God save the king!

KING. Whence cam'st thou, worthy Thane?

ROSS.   From Fife, great
        King;
        Where the Norweyan banners flout the sky
50   And fan our people cold.°
        Norway° himself, with terrible° numbers,
        Assisted by that most disloyal traitor
        The Thane of Cawdor, began a dismal° conflict;
        Till that Bellona's bridegroom, lapped in proof,°
55   Confronted him with self-comparisons,°
        Point against point rebellious, arm 'gainst arm,
        Curbing his lavish° spirit: and, to conclude,
        The victory fell on us.

KING.   Great happiness!

ROSS.   That now
        Sweno, the Norways' king, craves composition;°
60   Nor would we deign him burial of his men
        Till he disbursèd, at Saint Colme's Inch,°
        Ten thousand dollars° to our general use.

KING. No more that Thane of Cawdor shall deceive
        Our bosom interest:° go pronounce his present° death,
65   And with his former title greet Macbeth.

ROSS. I'll see it done.

KING. What he hath lost, noble Macbeth hath won.

        [They exit.]

SCENE 3. A heath.

[It is thundering as the THREE WITCHES wait on a desolate heath for MACBETH
and BANQUO. The two generals are on their way to KING DUNCAN's palace at
Forres.]

FIRST WITCH. Where hast thou been, sister?

Atmosphere *Which phrases in this passage increase the sense of fore-boding?* **2**

Apply Background Knowledge *What do you predict will happen to the former Thane of Cawdor?* **3**

MACBETH, ACT 1, SCENE 3 **311**

Side glosses

45 Thane: a Scottish title of nobility.

47 seems to: seems about to.

50 fan . . . cold: filled the Scots with cold fear.
51 Norway: the King of Norway.
terrible: terrifying.
53 dismal: ominous.
54 Bellona's . . . proof: Ross refers to Macbeth as the husband of Bellona—Roman goddess of war—clad in tested armor (**proof**).
55 Confronted . . . self-comparisons: faced him with equal courage and skill.
57 lavish: insolent.

59 craves composition: begs for terms of peace.

61 Saint Colme's Inch: Inchcolm, an island in the Firth of Forth.
62 dollars: currency that first came into use in the early sixteenth century, about five hundred years after Macbeth's time.
64 Our . . . interest: my dearest concerns. **present:** immediate.

311

Teach

View the Art ★

Answer: *Students' answers will vary. Some may think the witches in the painting are a good representation. Others may say they imagined the witches as being more grotesque.*

Alexandre Gabriel Decamps (1803–1860) was a French painter and printmaker who spent several years working in the fields as a young man. The peasant art he encountered during this time inspired him to begin drawing. After about five years of formal study under other artists, Decamps became a professional artist.

The Witches in Macbeth, c. 1841–1842. Alexandre Gabriel Decamps. The Wallace Collection, London.

View the Art Decamps was inspired by the peasant life he observed around him as a young man. How does this depiction of the witches compare with your impression of them thus far?

SECOND WITCH. Killing swine.°

THIRD WITCH. Sister, where thou?

FIRST WITCH. A sailor's wife had chestnuts in her lap,
5   And mounched, and mounched, and mounched.
         "Give me," quoth I.
      "Aroint thee,° witch!" the rump-fed ronyon° cries.
      Her husband's to Aleppo gone, master o' th' Tiger:
      But in a sieve I'll thither sail,
10   And, like a rat without a tail,
      I'll do, I'll do, and I'll do.°

SECOND WITCH. I'll give thee a wind.

FIRST WITCH. Th' art kind.

THIRD WITCH. And I another.

15 FIRST WITCH. I myself have all the other;
      And the very ports they blow,
      All the quarters that they know
      I' th' shipman's card.°
      I'll drain him dry as hay:
20   Sleep shall neither night nor day
      Hang upon his penthouse lid;°
      He shall live a man forbid:°
      Weary sev'nights° nine times nine
      Shall he dwindle, peak,° and pine:
25   Though his bark cannot be lost,°

312 UNIT 2   THE ENGLISH RENAISSANCE

2 Killing swine: It was commonly believed that witches killed domestic animals.

7 Aroint thee: Go away! **rump-fed ronyon:** fat-rumped, scabby creature.

8–11 The First Witch says she will take revenge by doing mischief against the woman's husband, who is captain of the Tiger, a ship heading toward the Middle Eastern city of Aleppo. Witches could supposedly use a leaky sieve for a boat and assume the shape of any animal, although the tail would be missing.

12–18 I'll . . . shipman's card: Witches were thought to control winds. The First Witch plans to use this power to block the Tiger from entering a port.

18 shipman's card: a compass or navigational chart.

21 penthouse lid: eyelid.
22 forbid: cursed.
23 sev'nights: weeks.
24 peak: grow peaked or emaciated.
25 Though . . . lost: Although I cannot sink his ship.

Reading Practice

SMALL GROUP SPIRAL REVIEW Predict An effective way to involve students in their reading is to have them make predictions about events and then check their predictions as they read. Have students read through the end of page 313. Then have them work in groups to fill in a predictions chart like the one shown. Have groups reconvene at the end of each scene to compile information for their group chart. Invite groups to share their charts at the end of Act 1.

Clues	Predictions	Verifications
Witches call Macbeth Thane of Cawdor. The former Thane of Cawdor has been executed.	*I predict Macbeth will be named Thane of Cawdor.*	

Yet it shall be tempest-tossed.
Look what I have.

SECOND WITCH. Show me, show me.

FIRST WITCH. Here I have a pilot's thumb,
30   Wracked as homeward he did come.

[*The sound of a drum is heard offstage.*]

THIRD WITCH. A drum, a drum!
Macbeth doth come.

ALL. The weird° sisters, hand in hand,
Posters of° the sea and land,
35   Thus do go about, about:
Thrice to thine, and thrice to mine,
And thrice again, to make up nine.
Peace! The charm's wound up.

[*MACBETH and BANQUO enter.*]

MACBETH. So foul and fair a day I have not seen.°

40   **BANQUO.** How far is 't called° to Forres? What are these
So withered, and so wild in their attire,
That look not like th' inhabitants o' th' earth,
And yet are on 't? Live you, or are you aught
That man may question? You seem to understand me,
45   By each at once her choppy° finger laying
Upon her skinny lips. You should be women,
And yet your beards forbid me to interpret
That you are so.

MACBETH.   Speak, if you can: what are you?

FIRST WITCH. All hail, Macbeth! Hail to thee, Thane of
Glamis!

50   **SECOND WITCH.** All hail, Macbeth! Hail to thee, Thane of
Cawdor!

THIRD WITCH. All hail, Macbeth, that shalt be King hereafter!

[*MACBETH is startled by the WITCHES' greeting; BANQUO notices and
addresses him.*]

BANQUO. Good sir, why do you start,° and seem to fear
Things that do sound so fair? [*To the WITCHES.*] I' th' name
of truth,
Are ye fantastical,° or that indeed

---

33 **weird:** connected with or determining fate.
34 **Posters of:** swift travelers over.

39 **So . . . seen:** Macbeth refers to the foulness of the weather and the fairness of his victory, which echoes the witches' chant in Act 1, scene 1, line 10.
40 **is 't called:** is it said to be.

45 **choppy:** chapped.

52 **start:** act startled.

54 **fantastical:** imaginary.

Atmosphere *What happens to mortals who displease the witches?*

Atmosphere *What effect does Shakespeare create by having Macbeth's first words in the play echo the witches' chant in scene 1?*

Teach

Literary Element   1

Atmosphere Answer: *Mortals who displease the witches incur dreadful punishments, such as prolonged sleeplessness and dismemberment.*

Literary Element   2

Atmosphere Answer: *Macbeth associated with moral ambiguity—with a confusion of "fair" and "foul."*

(**ENGLISH LEARNERS**) Remind English learners of the different possible interpretations of *foul* and *fair.* **Ask:** What does Macbeth mean when he says *foul* and *fair?* Which definitions is he using? *(He is talking about the weather.)*

English Learners

DIFFERENTIATED INSTRUCTION

Beginning On this spread, students encounter a number of shortened forms of words. Point them out to students (lines 8, 13, 18, 23, 40, 42, 43). Model how to figure out the words represented by the shortened forms. **Say:** There are two unusual shortened words in the phrase "master o' th' Tiger" on line 8. The "o'" could mean *on* or *of.* "Master *of* th' Tiger" makes sense as a phrase, while "master *on* th' Tiger" does not. Encourage students to use similar reasoning to decode the other shortened forms. Have them read the phrases aloud using the entire words in place of the shortened forms.

Approaching Level

DIFFERENTIATED INSTRUCTION

Emerging Have students choose a scene or character from the play to illustrate. Allow students to use the medium of their choice in the illustration. Tell students to be sure to use descriptions from the text to guide their work. Allow students to present their illustrations to the class.

313

Teach

Apply Background Knowledge **Answer:** *Banquo interprets the apparition of the witches as a hallucination.*

Ask: How does this questioning of the witches' existence affect the atmosphere of the play? *(Possible response: It adds to the feeling of dread and uncertainty produced thus far.)*

ADVANCED Ask advanced level students to research information about the miasma theory of disease, which was prevalent in Elizabethan times. Have students discuss how beliefs such as this inform Banquo's "rational" theory about the witches' appearance.

Writer's Technique ☆

Ambiguity Ambiguity is the use of a word or expression that can be interpreted in more than one way. In line 56, Banquo uses the expression *present grace* in speaking of the witches' addresses to Macbeth. This literally refers to the honor Macbeth currently receives as Thane of Glamis. However, *present grace* can also be a reference to the Christian state of grace that indicates a person is free from sin or is honored by God for his purity. To this point, Macbeth has lived virtuously. Encourage students to look for other examples of ambiguity in Shakespeare's word choice.

---

55   Which outwardly ye show? My noble partner
You greet with present grace° and great prediction ☆
Of noble having° and of royal hope,
That he seems rapt withal:° to me you speak not.
If you can look into the seeds of time,
60   And say which grain will grow and which will not,
Speak then to me, who neither beg nor fear
Your favors nor your hate.°

FIRST WITCH.   Hail!

SECOND WITCH.   Hail!

65   **THIRD WITCH.**   Hail!

FIRST WITCH.   Lesser than Macbeth, and greater.

SECOND WITCH.   Not so happy,° yet much happier.

THIRD WITCH.   Thou shalt get° kings, though thou be none.
So all hail, Macbeth and Banquo!

70   **FIRST WITCH.**   Banquo and Macbeth, all hail!

MACBETH.   Stay, you imperfect° speakers, tell me more:
By Sinel's° death I know I am Thane of Glamis;
But how of Cawdor? The Thane of Cawdor lives,
A prosperous gentleman; and to be King
75   Stands not within the prospect of belief,
No more than to be Cawdor. Say from whence
You owe° this strange intelligence?° Or why
Upon this blasted° heath you stop our way
With such **prophetic** greeting? Speak, I charge you.

[*The witches vanish.*]

80   **BANQUO.**   The earth hath bubbles as the water has,
And these are of them. Whither are they vanished?

MACBETH.   Into the air, and what seemed corporal° melted°
As breath into the wind. Would° they had stayed!

BANQUO.   Were such things here as we do speak about?
85   Or have we eaten on the insane root°
That takes the reason prisoner?

MACBETH.   Your children shall be kings.

BANQUO.   You shall be King.

---

1   Apply Background Knowledge *How does Banquo interpret the apparition of the witches?*

Vocabulary

prophetic (prə fet´ik) *adj.* having the quality of foretelling future events

56 present grace: current honor (the title Thane of Glamis).
57 noble having: possession of further titles.
58 rapt withal: carried away with it.

61–62 beg . . . hate: beg your favors nor fear your hatred.

67 happy: fortunate.

68 get: beget, father.

71 imperfect: incomplete.
72 Sinel: Macbeth's father.

77 owe: own, possess.
intelligence: information.
78 blasted: blighted.

82 corporal: flesh and blood.
melted: vanished.
83 Would: I wish.

85 insane root: A number of plants, such as henbane and hemlock, were believed to cause insanity.

Writing Practice

 Word Choice

SPIRAL REVIEW Tell students that precise word choice can help establish an atmosphere. Direct their attention to lines 55–58 on this page. Point out the words *noble, present, great, royal,* and *rapt.* **Ask:** What effect does the repetition of noble have? *(It places emphasis on Macbeth's status within society.)* Have each student choose a character from the play and write a one-paragraph description of him or her. Tell students to review their paragraphs and replace vague words with precise nouns, adjectives, and verbs.

MACBETH.   And Thane of Cawdor too. Went it not so?

BANQUO.   To th' selfsame tune and words. Who's here?

[ROSS and ANGUS enter.]

90 ROSS.   The King hath happily received, Macbeth,
The news of thy success; and when he reads°
Thy personal venture in the rebels' fight,
His wonders and his praises do contend
Which should be thine or his.° Silenced with that,
95 In viewing o'er the rest o' th' selfsame day,
He finds thee in the stout Norweyan ranks,
Nothing afeard of what thyself didst make,
Strange images of death.° As thick as tale
Came post with post,° and every one did bear
100 Thy praises in his kingdom's great defense,
And poured them down before him.

ANGUS.   We are sent
To give thee, from our royal master, thanks;
Only to herald° thee into his sight,
Not pay thee.

105 ROSS.   And for an earnest° of a greater honor,
He bade me, from him, call thee Thane of Cawdor;
In which addition,° hail, most worthy Thane!
For it is thine.

BANQUO.   [Aside.] What, can the devil speak true?

MACBETH.   The Thane of Cawdor lives: why do you dress me
110 In borrowed robes?

ANGUS.   Who° was the thane lives yet,
But under heavy judgment bears that life
Which he deserves to lose. Whether he was combined°
With those of Norway, or did line° the rebel
With hidden help and vantage, or that with both
115 He labored in his country's wrack,° I know not;
But treasons capital,° confessed and proved,
Have overthrown him.

MACBETH.   [Aside.]   Glamis, and Thane of Cawdor:
The greatest is behind.° [Addressing ROSS and ANGUS.]
Thanks for your pains.
[Aside to BANQUO.] Do you not hope your children shall be
kings,
120 When those that gave the Thane of Cawdor to me
Promised no less to them?

BANQUO.   [Aside to MACBETH.] That, trusted home,°
Might yet enkindle you unto° the crown,

---

91 reads: considers.

93–94 His . . . his: His astonishment, which leaves him speechless, conflicts with his desire to praise Macbeth.

97–98 Nothing . . . death: Not at all afraid of dying as he killed.
98–99 As thick . . . post: As fast as could be counted came messenger after messenger.

103 herald: conduct.

105 earnest: a small payment made as a pledge.

107 addition: title.

2

110 Who: he who.

112 combined: in conspiracy.
113 line: support, strengthen.

115 wrack: ruin.
116 capital: punishable by death.

119 behind: still to come.

122 home: fully.
123 enkindle you unto: enflame your hopes for.

MACBETH, ACT 1, SCENE 3   **315**

Apply Background Knowledge **Ask:** What information from the text prepared you for this event? *(The king has ordered the execution of the previous Thane of Cawdor and selected Macbeth to take his place. Also, the witches portended that Macbeth would be named the new thane.)* How do you think Macbeth will react to this event? Why? *(He will likely be happy to receive the honor. It might, however, make him believe that the witches were right, inspiring his greed to make the second prediction—that he will be king—come true.)*

Approaching Level

DIFFERENTIATED INSTRUCTION

Emerging Tell students that in older poems and plays, writers often use poetic contractions to maintain the rhythm of the text. Point students to line 89. Draw their attention to *th'.* **Ask:** What letter does the apostrophe replace in this word? *(e)* Then have them identify the missing letters in *o'er* and *o'* in line 95. *(v and f)* Explain that Shakespeare often uses the contrac-tion *'tis,* which is short for *it is.* Suggest that students make a list of such contractions and their full spellings to help them better understand the play.

Teach

A Bard for the Ages

Answer: *Banquo's warning shows how rational and perceptive he is in contrast to Macbeth.* **Ask:** How does this contrast of character reflect a universal idea? *(Flawed heroes with more sympathetic friends are seen in fiction throughout the ages.)*

Atmosphere **Answer:**
Macbeth's confusion of good and ill echoes the witches' confusion of fair and foul. **Ask:** How does this affect the atmosphere of the play? *(Possible response: It makes us further doubt Macbeth's character, thus reinforcing the sense of impending doom.)*

ENGLISH LEARNERS For English learners, **ask:** What does *ill* mean? *(Students will likely answer that it means "unhealthy.")* Have students look up the word in a dictionary to find other meanings. **Ask:** In these lines, is *ill* a synonym for *foul*? *(yes)*

Language History ☆

"Cousin" The word *cousin* is used with different meanings in the play. When Banquo calls Ross and Angus cousins, he means persons of the same race or nation. Kings, such as Duncan, often used the term when referring to other monarchs or nobles. Historically, Duncan and Macbeth were first cousins; their mothers were sisters.

Besides the Thane of Cawdor. But 'tis strange:
And oftentimes, to win us to our harm,
125   The instruments of darkness tell us truths,
Win us with honest trifles, to betray 's
In deepest consequence.°
Cousins, a word, I pray you.

[BANQUO *speaks privately to the two noblemen while* MACBETH *expresses his thoughts in an aside.*]

MACBETH.   Two truths are told,
As happy prologues to the swelling act
130   Of the imperial theme.°—I thank you, gentlemen—

[MACBETH *interrupts himself to speak to* ROSS *and* BANQUO; *he then continues his aside.*]

This supernatural soliciting°
Cannot be ill, cannot be good. If ill,
Why hath it given me earnest of success,
Commencing in a truth? I am Thane of Cawdor:
135   If good, why do I yield to that suggestion
Whose horrid image doth unfix my hair
And make my seated heart knock at my ribs,
Against the use of nature?° Present fears
Are less than horrible imaginings.°
140   My thought, whose murder yet is but fantastical,
Shakes so my single state of man that function
Is smothered in surmise, and nothing is
But what is not.°

BANQUO.   [*Speaking to* ROSS *about* MACBETH.] Look,
how our partner's rapt.

MACBETH.   [*Aside.*] If chance will have me King, why, chance
may crown me,
145   Without my stir.°

BANQUO.   New honors come upon him,
Like our strange garments, cleave not to their mold
But with the aid of use.°

MACBETH.   [*Aside.*]   Come what come may,
Time and the hour runs through the roughest day.

BANQUO.   Worthy Macbeth, we stay upon your leisure.°

150   MACBETH.   Give me your favor. My dull brain was wrought
With things forgotten.° Kind gentlemen, your pains

---

1 A Bard for the Ages *What does Shakespeare reveal about Banquo's character in these lines?*

2 Atmosphere *How do Macbeth's words echo the witches' lines?*

123–127 But . . . consequence: Banquo says that demonic forces often win our confidence by making trivial predictions that come true.

128–130 Two . . . theme: Macbeth uses theatrical terms to describe his career, which will reach a climax when he becomes king.

131 supernatural soliciting: the witches' tempting or suggesting.

135–138 If . . . nature: Macbeth says that the thought of murdering Duncan causes his hair to stand on end and his firmly-placed **(seated)** heart to pound—symptoms of fear contrary to his nature.
138–139 Present . . . imaginings: Fears of something that presently exists are less powerful than fears of imaginary horrors.
140–143 My . . . not: Macbeth says that the imaginary murder in his thoughts has caused such inner turmoil that he can no longer act. The only thing that seems real to him is this unreal murder.
145 stir: taking action.
146–147 Like . . . use: like new clothes that do not fit comfortably until worn for a while.
149 stay . . . leisure: we are waiting for you at your convenience.
150–151 Give . . . forgotten: Macbeth asks for their pardon. He excuses his inattentiveness by saying that he was trying to remember something.

Listening and Speaking Practice

SMALL GROUP   **SPIRAL REVIEW**

Readers' Theater Post these guidelines for a Readers' Theater presentation:

- Use emphasis and pauses to build suspense
- Vary reading speed
- Vary voice, pitch, and tone
- Use facial expressions and gestures

Go through the guidelines with the class. Then divide students into small groups and have each group practice and deliver oral readings of scenes from Act 1.

Are registered where every day I turn
The leaf to read them. Let us toward the King.
[*Aside to* BANQUO.] Think upon what hath chanced, and at
   more time,°
155 The interim having weighed it,° let us speak
Our free hearts° each to other.

    BANQUO.   Very gladly.

    MACBETH. Till then, enough. Come, friends.

[*They all exit together.*]

SCENE 4. The palace at Forres.

[*At* KING DUNCAN's *palace at Forres, the king and his two sons,* MALCOLM *and* DONALBAIN, *enter to a fanfare of trumpets. They are accompanied by* LENNOX *and other attendants.*]

    KING. Is execution done on Cawdor? Are not
Those in commission° yet returned?

    MALCOLM.   My liege,
They are not yet come back. But I have spoke
With one that saw him die, who did report
5 That very frankly he confessed his treasons,
Implored your Highness' pardon and set forth
A deep **repentance**: nothing in his life
Became him like the leaving it. He died
As one that had been studied° in his death,
10 To throw away the dearest thing he owed°
As 'twere a careless° trifle.

    KING.   There's no art
To find the mind's construction in the face:°
He was a gentleman on whom I built
An absolute trust.

[MACBETH, BANQUO, ROSS, *and* ANGUS *enter. The* KING *addresses* MACBETH.]

          O worthiest cousin!
15 The sin of my ingratitude even now
Was heavy on me: thou art so far before,°
That swiftest wing of recompense is slow
To overtake thee. Would thou hadst less deserved,

A Bard for the Ages *How does Malcolm's description of Cawdor's death reveal Shakespeare's humanism?*   **3**

---

154 at more time: when we have more leisure time.
155 The interim . . . it: having considered it in the meantime.
156 Our free hearts: our minds freely.

2 Those in commission: those charged with carrying out the execution.

9 studied: rehearsed.
10 owed: owned.
11 careless: worthless.

11–12 There's . . . face: There's no way to read a person's thoughts by looking at his or her face.

16 before: ahead.

Teach

Big Idea   **3**

A Bard for the Ages
Answer: *Even though Cawdor was a traitor, he is shown as repentant and somewhat worthy of respect. Instead of portraying cold stereotypes, Shakespeare creates unique, multifaceted characters.*

Tell students that "Nothing in his life / became him like the leaving of it" (lines 7–8) is one of the play's many famous quotes.
Ask: What does it mean when we say that a piece of clothing "becomes" a person? *(It suits the person, looks good on him or her.)* Help students relate this usage of *becomes* to the quote. Ask students to paraphrase the lines *(The way he died was more worthy than the way he lived.)*

(APPROACHING) For approaching level students, **say:** Think of another story or a movie that includes a person repenting for betrayal. Explain how its treatment of the person compares with Malcolm's description. *(Responses will vary.)*

English Learners

DIFFERENTIATED INSTRUCTION

Advanced Direct students' attention to the stage directions that begin Scene 4 on this page. **Ask:** Where is the action now taking place? *(the palace at Forres)* What else do you learn from the stage directions? *(the participants in the scene and their relationships to one another)*

Teach

Reading Strategy　1

Apply Background Knowledge Answer: *Because kingship was not hereditary, Macbeth might think that he, the worthiest thane, the one who saved his country, should be named heir*

Ask: How do you think Macbeth will react to the king's declaration? *(Possible response: This declaration will shake Macbeth's faith in his destiny, thus spurring him into making plans for murder.)*

Literary Element　2

Atmosphere Answer: *This image contrasts light and darkness. Light symbolizes truth, while darkness symbolizes the evil plans resulting from Macbeth's envy and greed. This descriptive contrast reflects the ambiguity of the play and the sense of foreboding.*

Ask: What information does this aside give to the audience but not to other characters? *(It enlightens the audience about Macbeth's plans to kill the king in order to gain the throne.)*

[ADVANCED] Have advanced level students go online to conduct some brief research on common Elizabethan beliefs about astrology. Ask them to speculate about additional layers of meaning an Elizabethan audience might hear in Macbeth's asking the stars to look away from his planned actions.

20　　That the proportion both of thanks and payment
　　　Might have been mine!° Only I have left to say,
　　　More is thy due than more than all can pay.°

　　MACBETH.　The service and the loyalty I owe,
　　　In doing it, pays itself. Your Highness' part
25　　Is to receive our duties: and our duties
　　　Are to your throne and state children and servants;
　　　Which do but what they should, by doing every thing
　　　Safe toward your love and honor.°

　　KING.　　　　　　　　　　　　Welcome hither.
　　　I have begun to plant thee, and will labor
　　　To make thee full of growing. Noble Banquo,
30　　That hast no less deserved, nor must be known
　　　No less to have done so,° let me enfold° thee
　　　And hold thee to my heart.

　　BANQUO.　　　　　　　　　There if I grow,
　　　The harvest is your own.

　　KING.　　　　　　　　　My **plenteous** joys,
　　　Wanton° in fullness, seek to hide themselves
35　　In drops of sorrow. Sons, kinsmen, thanes,
　　　And you whose places are the nearest,° know,
　　　We will establish our estate upon
　　　Our eldest, Malcolm, whom we name hereafter
　　　The Prince of Cumberland: which honor must
40　　Not unaccompanied invest him only,
　　　But signs of nobleness, like stars, shall shine
　　　On all deservers.° From hence to Inverness,°
　　　And bind us further to you.°

　　MACBETH.　The rest is labor, which is not used for you.°
45　　I'll be myself the harbinger,° and make joyful
　　　The hearing of my wife with your approach;
　　　So, humbly take my leave.

　　KING.　　　　　　　　　My worthy Cawdor!

　　MACBETH.　[*Aside.*] The Prince of Cumberland! That is a step
　　　On which I must fall down, or else o'erleap,
50　　For in my way it lies.° Stars, hide your fires;
　　　Let not light see my black and deep desires:

1　Apply Background Knowledge　*Read the side note about kingship and heredity. Why might Macbeth think that he should be named Duncan's heir?*

2　Atmosphere　*How does this image reinforce the mood of the play?*

Vocabulary

plenteous　(plen′tē əs)　*adj.* abundant; fruitful

318　UNIT 2　THE ENGLISH RENAISSANCE

18–20 Would . . . mine: I wish you deserved less, so that I could repay you amply.
21 than more . . . pay: than it would be possible to pay.

23–27 Your . . . honor: Macbeth compares the relationship between kings and their subjects to that between parents and children or masters and servants. By doing everything possible to protect Duncan, his subjects are merely fulfilling their obligations.
30–31 That hast . . . so: who is no less worthy and whose deeds must be acknowledged.
31 enfold: embrace.

34 Wanton: unrestrained.

36 whose . . . nearest: who are by birth closest to the throne.

37–42 We . . . deservers: The King (using the royal "we") announces that his eldest son, Malcolm, will succeed him to the throne. He gives Malcolm a new title and says that other deserving subjects will also receive honors. In Scotland at this time, the crown was not hereditary.
42 Inverness: the location of Macbeth's castle.
43 bind us further to you: make me even more indebted to Macbeth for his hospitality.
44 The rest . . . you: Any leisure not devoted to you is labor.
45 harbinger: an officer who precedes royalty to arrange reception for a visit.
48–50 The . . . lies: Macbeth realizes that he will not become king by "chance" (see Act 1, scene 3, line 144).

Vocabulary Practice

[SPIRAL REVIEW] **Word Parts** Tell students that one way to determine words' meanings is to analyze word parts. Direct students' attention to the vocabulary words *plenteous* and *peerless*. Ask students to identify the base word of each. (plenty; peer) Then have students identify the suffixes and their meanings. (-ous—*full of,* *possessing; -less—without, lacking*) Finally, help students connect the meanings of the suffixes and the bases to arrive at the given definitions. Have students practice using this technique on other unfamiliar words they encounter in the text.

The eye wink at the hand;° yet let that be
Which the eye fears, when it is done, to see. ☆

[*MACBETH exits.*]

KING. True, worthy Banquo; he is full so valiant,°
55 And in his commendations° I am fed;
It is a banquet to me. Let's after him,
Whose care is gone before to bid us welcome.
It is a **peerless** kinsman.

[*They all exit to a flourish of trumpets.*]

SCENE 5. The castle at Inverness.

[*In* MACBETH's *castle at Inverness,* LADY MACBETH *appears alone, reading a letter from her husband.*]

LADY MACBETH. [*Reads.*] "They met me in the day of success;
and I have learned by the perfect'st report° they have more
in them than mortal knowledge. When I burned in desire
to question them further, they made themselves air, into
5 which they vanished. Whiles I stood rapt in the wonder of
it, came missives° from the King, who all-hailed me 'Thane
of Cawdor'; by which title, before, these weird sisters
saluted me, and referred me to the coming on of time, with
'Hail, King that shalt be!' This have I thought good to
10 deliver° thee, my dearest partner of greatness, that thou
mightst not lose the dues of rejoicing,° by being ignorant of
what greatness is promised thee. Lay it to thy heart, and
farewell."
Glamis thou art, and Cawdor, and shalt be
15 What thou art promised. Yet do I fear thy nature;
It is too full o' th' milk of human kindness°
To catch the nearest way.° Thou wouldst be great,
Art not without ambition, but without
The illness° should attend it. What thou wouldst highly,°
20 That wouldst thou holily;° wouldst not play false,
And yet wouldst wrongly win. Thou'dst have, great Glamis,
That which cries "Thus thou must do" if thou have it;
And that which rather thou dost fear to do
Than wishest should be undone.° Hie thee hither,
25 That I may pour my spirits in thine ear,

A Bard for the Ages *What does Shakespeare reveal about Macbeth's relationship with his wife in the phrase "my dearest partner of greatness"?* **3**

Vocabulary

peerless (pēr'lis) *adj.* unrivaled; without equal

52 **The eye . . . hand:** Let my eyes be blind to my hand's deed.

54 **he . . . valiant:** Macbeth is as valiant as you say he is.
55 **his commendations:** commendations of him.

2 **perfect'st report:** best intelligence.

6 **missives:** messengers.

10 **deliver:** communicate to.
11 **lose . . . rejoicing:** be deprived of your rightful joy.

16 **milk . . . kindness:** natural feelings of compassion or loyalty.
17 **catch . . . way:** take the quickest means to the throne (that is, killing Duncan).
19 **illness:** wickedness, ruthlessness. **wouldst highly:** would greatly like.
20 **wouldst thou holily:** you would like to have virtuously.

21–24 **Thou'dst . . . undone:** What you want requires you to do certain things, and you fear taking such action rather than wishing the action were not taken.

Advanced Learners

DIFFERENTIATED INSTRUCTION

Character Analysis Have each student choose a major character from the play: Macbeth, Lady Macbeth, Banquo, King Duncan, or the witches. Prompt students to write a one-page character analysis. In their analyses, students should include a description of the character, as well as an analysis of the character's role within the plot of the play. Tell students to support their ideas with citations from the text. Invite volunteers to share their character analyses with the rest of the class.

Teach

Big Idea **3**

A Bard for the Ages
Answer: *Macbeth regards his wife as a confidant, to whom he entrusts his heartfelt yearnings. A shared ambition unites this husband and wife.*

Ask: What does Lady Macbeth's response reveal about her character? *(She is a powerful woman who is more concerned with social climbing than with compassion or loyalty.)*

ENGLISH LEARNERS Explain to English learners that *thou* is a singular form of *you* that is no longer used. It is comparable to the Spanish *tú*, although it lacks the informal/formal distinction of *tú* and *usted*. Other forms of *thou* also appear in this passage, and the verbs are conjugated in the archaic second person singular. Have students take turns reading short sections of the passage aloud, then restating the sentences using *you* and contemporary forms of the verbs.

Writer's Technique ☆

Point out to students that *Macbeth* is written in blank verse—non-rhyming lines of iambic pentameter, the meter that most closely resembles natural speech in English. Shakespeare occasionally interrupts the flow of the meter to end a speech in a rhymed couplet, as in lines 52–53. Have students read lines 48–53 aloud. **Ask:** What effect does the rhyming couplet have at the end of this speech? *(It draws the reader or audience's attention to what is said in the couplet. It sums up the speech.)*

Teach

Literary Element	**1**

Atmosphere

Answer: *The raven is a black bird, symbolic of evil. It suits the ominous mood established by the witches in the opening scene.*

Ask: What do you think the bird's hoarseness, or inability to make sound, foreshadows? *(Possible response: The hoarseness might foreshadow the omen's inability to "speak" to King Duncan or give him a warning.)*

Literary Element	**2**

Atmosphere

Answer: *Images such as "thick night," "the dunnest smoke of hell," "keen knife," "wound," and "blanket of the dark" reinforce the ominous mood.*

Say: Explain how these images work to reinforce the mood. *(They evoke darkness and hell, which signify evil. Also, they predict an injury to the king, which is the main conflict that leads to suspense in the story.)*

APPROACHING Direct approaching-level students' attention to Lady Macbeth's plea to the spirits to "unsex me here" (line 40). Explain that she is asking for these spirits to erase her womanly character.

Ask: What qualities do you think Elizabethans expected women to have? *(kindness, compassion)* Why does Lady Macbeth want to be rid of these qualities? *(She wants to do evil.)*

And chastise° with the valor of my tongue
All that impedes thee from the golden round°
Which fate and metaphysical° aid doth seem
To have thee crowned withal.

[*A* MESSENGER *enters.*]

                What is your tidings?

30   MESSENGER. The King comes here tonight.

LADY MACBETH.   Thou'rt mad to
   say it!
Is not thy master with him, who, were 't so,
Would have informed for preparation?°

MESSENGER. So please you, it is true. Our thane is coming.
One of my fellows had the speed of him,°
35   Who, almost dead for breath, had scarcely more
Than would make up his message.

LADY MACBETH.   Give him tending;
He brings great news. [*The* MESSENGER *exits.*]
                The raven° himself is hoarse
That croaks the fatal entrance of Duncan
Under my battlements. Come, you spirits
40   That tend on mortal° thoughts, unsex me here,
And fill me, from the crown° to the toe, top-full
Of direst cruelty! Make thick my blood,
Stop up th' access and passage to remorse,°
That no compunctious visitings of nature°
45   Shake my fell purpose,° nor keep peace between
Th' effect and it!° Come to my woman's breasts,
And take my milk for gall,° you murd'ring ministers,°
Wherever in your sightless° substances
You wait on nature's mischief!° Come, thick night,
50   And pall thee in the dunnest smoke° of hell,
That my keen knife see not the wound it makes,
Nor heaven peep through the blanket of the dark,
To cry "Hold, hold!"

[MACBETH *enters.*]

             Great Glamis! Worthy Cawdor!
Greater than both, by the all-hail hereafter!
55   Thy letters have transported me beyond
This ignorant present,° and I feel now

26 **chastise:** reprimand.
27 **golden round:** crown.
28 **metaphysical:** supernatural.

32 **informed for preparation:** sent word to prepare for the guest.

34 **had . . . him:** sped ahead of him.

38 **raven:** traditionally a bird of ill omen.

40 **mortal:** murderous.
41 **crown:** top of the head.

43 **remorse:** compassion.
44 **compunctious . . . nature:** natural feelings of pity.
45 **fell purpose:** cruel intentions.
45–46 **nor . . . it:** nor prevent my intentions from being carried out.
47 **take . . . gall:** exchange my milk for bile (traditionally associated with envy and hatred). **ministers:** agents.
48 **sightless:** invisible.
49 **wait . . . mischief:** serve evil.
50 **pall . . . smoke:** cover yourself in the darkest smoke.

56 **this ignorant present:** this present unaware of the future.

---

1 Atmosphere *How does the image of the hoarse raven contribute to the atmosphere?*

2 Atmosphere *Which images in these lines reinforce the ominous mood?*

320 UNIT 2 THE ENGLISH RENAISSANCE

Writing Practice

SPIRAL REVIEW **Sensory Details** Audiences who see *Macbeth* can watch and listen as the play is brought to life through expression, gestures, and scene design. Readers, however, need to visualize these sensory details. Have students choose a soliloquy or dialogue from Act I and write a short narrative about it in the third person. Encourage them to include as much sensory detail as possible with sentences such as, "Her crimson cloak swirled around her ankles as she paced frantically. Hoarsely she continued, 'Make thick my blood…'" Students can begin by creating a graphic organizer in the form of a 5-column chart in which they can list details of the five senses that they imagine.

Ellen Terry as Lady Macbeth, 1880s. John Singer Sargent. Oil on canvas, 221.0 x 114.3 cm. Tate Gallery, London.

View the Art Ellen Terry was a popular Shakespearean actress during the Victorian era. What does this painting suggest about Lady Macbeth's desires?

Teach

View the Art ★

Answer: *Lady Macbeth appears to yearn for the crown she holds high above her head. It indicates that she desires to have her husband reign as king so that she might have the power of queen.*

The American painter John Singer Sargent (1856–1925) spent most of his life in Europe. As a young man, Sargent studied art in France and Italy before settling in England. He is best recognized for his glamorous portraits of socially prominent people.

The celebrated Shakespearean actress Ellen Alicia Terry (1847–1928) was born into a family of English performers. Many of her friends attributed her success to her enchanting personality, as well as to her extraordinary artistic talents.

Approaching Level

DIFFERENTIATED INSTRUCTION

Established Have students select soliloquies from the text to act out for the class. Explain to students that the word *soliloquy* literally means "talking alone." Therefore, this type of speech is not part of a normal conversation but is an outward expression of a character's private thoughts. After students choose their soliloquies, allow them time to memorize their lines. Suggest that students practice their delivery at home in front of family members or a mirror. Allow time for students to deliver their dramatic soliloquies to the class.

Teach

Atmosphere **Answer:**
Banquo's speech shows that appearances can be deceiving. Macbeth's castle, which seems to be blessed and safe, really houses a murderous couple.

Ask: How does his description contradict the true atmosphere of the plot? *(The true atmosphere is foreboding and reeks of evildoing, whereas Banquo's description is one of religious blessedness.)*

[ENGLISH LEARNERS] For English learners, **ask:** What does *ironic* mean? *(Make sure students understand that* ironic *means "contrary to fact.") Ask students to make up their own examples of ironic speech (i.e., saying "Well, that was fun!" after taking an especially grueling test).*

Cultural History ☆
Martlets Martlets are small European swallows, birds that often nest in churches to breed. This also happens in the United States. Each spring a great number of swallows return from a migration to the mission of San Juan Capistrano in southern California.

The future in the instant.°

MACBETH.   My dearest love,
Duncan comes here tonight.

LADY MACBETH.   And when goes hence?

MACBETH. Tomorrow, as he purposes.

LADY MACBETH.   O, never
60   Shall sun that morrow see!
Your face, my Thane, is as a book where men
May read strange matters. To beguile the time,
Look like the time;° bear welcome in your eye,
Your hand, your tongue: look like th' innocent flower,
65   But be the serpent under 't. He that's coming
Must be provided for: and you shall put
This night's great business into my dispatch;°
Which shall to all our nights and days to come
Give solely sovereign sway° and masterdom.

70 MACBETH. We will speak further.

LADY MACBETH.   Only look up clear.°
To alter favor ever is to fear.°
Leave all the rest to me.

[*They exit.*]

SCENE 6. Outside the castle at Inverness.

[*Outside* MACBETH'*s castle oboes sound to announce the arrival of royalty.* KING DUNCAN *and his sons enter with a group of Scottish noblemen, including* BANQUO, LENNOX, MACDUFF, ROSS, *and* ANGUS. *It is nighttime, and they are attended by servants with torches.*]

KING. This castle hath a pleasant seat;° the air
Nimbly and sweetly recommends itself
Unto our gentle senses.

BANQUO.   This guest of summer,
The temple-haunting martlet, does approve ☆
5   By his loved mansionry that the heaven's breath
Smells wooingly here.° No jutty, frieze,
Buttress, nor coign of vantage, but this bird
Hath made his pendent bed and procreant cradle.°
Where they most breed and haunt, I have observed
10   The air is delicate.

[LADY MACBETH *enters to welcome her guests.*]

KING.   See, see, our honored hostess!

57 instant: present.

62–63 To beguile . . . time: To deceive the occasion, put on an appearance appropriate to the occasion.

67 dispatch: management.

69 solely sovereign sway: absolute power.

70 look up clear: appear undisturbed.
71 To alter . . . fear: Changing one's usual appearance always arouses suspicion.

1 seat: location.

3–6 This . . . here: The house martin, a bird that often nests in churches, proves by building its nest here that the place is heavenly.
6–8 No jutty . . . cradle: There is no projecting part of a building, decorative band on a wall, supporting structure, or convenient corner where this bird has not made its suspended bed and nest for offspring.

1 Atmosphere *What is ironic about Banquo's comments about Macbeth's castle?*

Reading Practice

SPIRAL REVIEW **Make Inferences** Tell students that the language and figures of speech that Shakespeare uses can give them insight into the playwright's own beliefs and assumptions. Have students brainstorm some of the recurring images and motifs, such as references to heaven and hell, the presence of the supernatural, and the association of Macbeth and Lady Macbeth's ambitions with dark images, and write these on the board or on chart paper. Ask students to draw inferences about Shakespeare's beliefs and assumptions based on these motifs (i.e., *He was religious and/or assumed his audience was religious; he believed in the supernatural; he thought that ambition could be dangerous.*)

The love that follows us sometime is our trouble,
Which still we thank as love. Herein I teach you
How you shall bid God 'ield us for your pains
And thank us for your trouble.°

LADY MACBETH.   All our service
15 In every point twice done, and then done double,
Were poor and single business° to contend
Against those honors deep and broad wherewith
Your Majesty loads our house: for those of old,
And the late dignities heaped up to them,
20 We rest your hermits.°

KING.   Where's the Thane of Cawdor?
We coursed him at the heels,° and had a purpose
To be his purveyor:° but he rides well,
And his great love, sharp as his spur, hath holp° him
To his home before us. Fair and noble hostess,
25 We are your guest tonight.

LADY MACBETH.   Your servants ever
Have theirs, themselves, and what is theirs, in compt,
To make their audit at your Highness' pleasure,
Still to return your own.°

KING.   Give me your hand.
Conduct me to mine host: we love him highly,
30 And shall continue our graces towards him.
By your leave, hostess.

[LADY MACBETH *and the* KING *go into the castle.*]

SCENE 7. The castle at Inverness.

[*In a torch-lit room in* MACBETH's *castle, music is heard. A steward, followed by other servants carrying dishes of food, crosses the stage. As they exit,* MACBETH *enters.*]

MACBETH. If it were done° when 'tis done, then 'twere well
It were done quickly. If th' assassination
Could trammel up the consequence, and catch,
With his surcease success; that but this blow
5 Might be the be-all and the end-all—here,
But here, upon this bank and shoal of time,
We'd jump the life to come.° But in these cases
We still have judgment here; that we but teach
Bloody instructions, which, being taught, return
10 To plague th' inventor:° this even-handed justice
Commends° th' ingredients of our poisoned chalice°
To our own lips. He's here in double trust:
First, as I am his kinsman and his subject,
Strong both against the deed; then, as his host,

11–14 **The . . . trouble:** The King says that he sometimes finds love inconvenient, but he still is grateful for it. He jokingly suggests that this will teach Lady Macbeth to be thankful for the trouble she is taking as his hostess.
16 **single business:** trivial service.

20 **We . . . hermits:** We will devote ourselves to praying for you.

21 **coursed . . . heels:** pursued him closely.
22 **purveyor:** an officer who travels ahead of a king or nobleman to make advance preparations.
23 **holp:** helped.

25–28 **Your . . . own:** Your servants forever hold their dependents, themselves, and their possessions in trust for you, and are always ready to open their accounts to you and return what is yours.

1 **were done:** were over and done with.

2–7 **If . . . come:** Macbeth says that if he could achieve his goals merely by killing Duncan, without any consequences here on earth, he would risk whatever consequences awaited him in the next world.
8–10 **We still . . . inventor:** We are always punished in this life, in that our bloody deeds provide an example for others to act against us.
11 **Commends:** offers. **chalice:** cup.

MACBETH, ACT 1, SCENE 7 **323**

Teach

| **Reading Strategy** | **2** |

Apply Background Knowledge Point out the phrase "Fair and noble hostess" in line 24. **Ask:** What does *fair* mean in this phrase (or context)? *(attractive, pleasant)* Have students list the meanings of *fair* that they have encountered in Act I *(just* or *equal, attractive* or *pleasant)*. **Ask:** What do the two meanings have in common? *(They are both positive qualities.)*

(ENGLISH LEARNERS) If necessary, have students look up the meanings of *fair* in the dictionary.

Approaching Level

DIFFERENTIATED INSTRUCTION

Established Explain to students that reading stage directions thoroughly can help them better understand the action and setting of the play. Point out that Macbeth's major speech on this page is an aside, in which he speaks directly to the audience and the other characters cannot hear him. Have students identify the stage directions that indicate this. (*Macbeth enters after the servants exit so he is alone.*) Have students write a paragraph describing the scene design for the opening of Scene 7.

Teach

Apply Background Knowledge Answer: *A subject should honor and revere a king. Rules of hospitality demand that hosts treat guests courteously.*

Ask: In line 12, what does Macbeth mean by "double trust"? *(The king trusts him as a loyal subject and a gracious host.)*

---

15   Who should against his murderer shut the door,
      Not bear the knife myself. Besides, this Duncan
      Hath borne his faculties° so meek, hath been
      So clear° in his great office, that his virtues
      Will plead like angels trumpet-tongued against
20   The deep damnation of his taking-off;°
      And pity, like a naked newborn babe,
      Striding the blast,° or heaven's cherubin° horsed
      Upon the sightless couriers° of the air,
      Shall blow the horrid deed in every eye,
25   That tears shall drown the wind. I have no spur
      To prick the sides of my intent, but only
      Vaulting ambition, which o'erleaps itself
      And falls on th' other°—

[LADY MACBETH enters.]

                              How now! What news?

LADY MACBETH.   He has almost supped. Why have
      you left the chamber?

30   MACBETH.   Hath he asked for me?

LADY MACBETH.   Know you not he has?

MACBETH.   We will proceed no further in this business:
      He hath honored me of late, and I have bought°
      Golden opinions from all sorts of people,
      Which would be worn now in their newest gloss,
35   Not cast aside so soon.

LADY MACBETH.   Was the hope drunk
      Wherein you dressed yourself? Hath it slept since?
      And wakes it now, to look so green and pale°
      At what it did so freely? From this time
      Such I account thy love. Art thou afeard
40   To be the same in thine own act and valor
      As thou art in desire? Wouldst thou have that
      Which thou esteem'st the ornament of life,°
      And live a coward in thine own esteem,
      Letting "I dare not" wait upon "I would,"
45   Like the poor cat i' th' adage?°

MACBETH.   Prithee, peace!
      I dare do all that may become a man;
      Who dares do more is none.

LADY MACBETH.   What beast was 't then
      That made you break° this enterprise to me?

---

1 Apply Background Knowledge *What do subjects owe their king? What do hosts owe their guests?*

324   UNIT 2   THE ENGLISH RENAISSANCE

---

17 **borne his faculties:** used his powers.
18 **clear:** blameless.

20 **taking-off:** murder.

22 **striding the blast:** bestriding the trumpet's blow. **cherubin:** angels.
23 **sightless couriers:** invisible messengers (the wind).

25–28 **I . . . other:** Macbeth says that his only motivation is ambition, which he compares to a rider that makes a horse fall after leaping too high over an obstacle.

32 **bought:** acquired.

37 **green and pale:** sickly.

42 **ornament of life:** the crown.

45 **Like . . . adage:** Lady Macbeth refers to an old saying about a cat that wanted to eat fish but wouldn't get its paws wet to catch them.

48 **break:** reveal.

Research Practice

SPIRAL REVIEW **Annotated Bibliography** Tell students that when they reach college they may be required to submit annotated bibliographies—lists of books about certain topics—with research reports. Each source has an annotation, or description of what it is about. Have students search the library or Internet for outside sources about *Macbeth*. Each student should choose one source. Then have students use MLA style, or a style of your choice, to cite the work. Finally, have them provide a brief description of the article or Internet site.

When you durst do it, then you were a man;
50 And to be more than what you were, you would
Be so much more the man. Nor time nor place
Did then adhere, and yet you would make both.
They have made themselves, and that their fitness now
Does unmake you.° I have given suck, and know
55 How tender 'tis to love the babe that milks me:
I would, while it was smiling in my face,
Have plucked my nipple from his boneless gums,
And dashed the brains out, had I so sworn as you
Have done to this.

MACBETH.   If we should fail?

LADY MACBETH.   We fail?
60 But screw your courage to the sticking-place,°
And we'll not fail. When Duncan is asleep—
Whereto the rather° shall his day's hard journey
Soundly invite him—his two chamberlains
Will I with wine and wassail° so convince,°
65 That memory, the warder of the brain,
Shall be a fume, and the receipt of reason
A limbeck only:° when in swinish sleep
Their drenchèd natures lies as in a death,
What cannot you and I perform upon
70 Th' unguarded Duncan, what not put upon
His spongy° officers, who shall bear the guilt
Of our great quell?°

MACBETH.   Bring forth men-children only;
For thy undaunted mettle° should compose
Nothing but males. Will it not be received,
75 When we have marked with blood those sleepy two
Of his own chamber, and used their very daggers,
That they have done 't?

LADY MACBETH.   Who dares receive it other,°
As° we shall make our griefs and clamor roar
Upon his death?

MACBETH.   I am settled,° and bend up
80 Each corporal agent° to this terrible feat.
Away, and mock the time° with fairest show:
False face must hide what the false heart doth know.

[They exit.]

Atmosphere *How does this image contribute to the atmosphere?* **2**

A Bard for the Ages *How does Shakespeare show a change in Macbeth's character at this point in the play?* **3**

51–54 **Nor time . . . you:** You were willing when neither time nor place was suitable, and now that everything has fallen into place, the convenience has unnerved you.
60 **But . . . sticking-place:** only summon up all your courage. **sticking place:** a notch on a crossbow that holds the string when it has been tightened for firing.

62 **Whereto the rather:** to which all the sooner.

64 **wassail:** "carousing" or "spiced ale." **convince:** overcome.t

65–67 **memory . . . only:** Memory, the guardian of the brain, shall become only a vapor, and the brain only the part of a still through which vapors pass.

71 **spongy:** soaked with alcohol.

72 **quell:** murder.

73 **undaunted mettle:** brave spirit.

77 **receive it other:** take it otherwise.
78 **As:** since.

79 **settled:** resolved.

79–80 **bend . . . agent:** exert every power in my body.
81 **mock the time:** deceive the present occasion.

Teach

Literary Element | 2

Atmosphere Answer: *It not only darkens the atmosphere but suggests that the enterprise that Macbeth and Lady Macbeth are about to undertake is horrible and unnatural.*

Ask: Do you think this image is effective at creating an atmosphere of dread? Explain. *(Possible response: The visual image of a mother dashing out the brains of a nursing babe is extremely violent and effective at instilling dread in the audience.)*

Big Idea | 3

A Bard for the Ages
Answer: *Macbeth, the courageous hero who saved his country, has adopted his wife's modus operandi, looking like "th' innocent flower" but being "the serpent under 't."*

Ask: Where has a reference to the "inside," namely the inner motivations, not matching the "outside," or the face, been made? *(King Duncan refers to this when he speaks about the treason of the former Thane of Cawdor.)*

To check students' understanding of the selection, see Unit 2 Teaching Resources Book, p. 166.

Progress Check

Can students interpret atmosphere?

If No → See Unit 2 Teaching Resources Book, p. 161.

Approaching Level

DIFFERENTIATED INSTRUCTION

Emerging Ask: Is Macbeth an essentially good character who has turned evil? Or is he evil all along? Ask students to raise their hands to indicate which they think is true. Divide the students into two teams on the basis of their responses. Then, hold a debate on the topic of the elasticity of Macbeth's character. Allow groups time to confer and build their arguments for their opinions. Allow the first group to present their argument, then have the second present a rebuttal. Finally, have the first group respond. Then give the second group a turn to present their argument, and follow this procedure a second time.

After You Read

Assess

1. Students' answers will vary.
2. (a) Macbeth will be Thane of Cawdor and king; Banquo's descendants will be kings. (b) Macbeth seems disturbed; Banquo distrusts the predictions.
3. (a) Macbeth thinks of murdering the king, but the idea horrifies him. (b) He is ambitious but has a conscience.
4. He understands that murdering his king is evil. He realizes he is overly ambitious.
5. (a) Lady Macbeth tells him he is a coward who does not love her. She explains it will be easy to murder Duncan. (b) It appeals to both reason and emotion.
6. (a) Possible answer: the dark impulses in Macbeth. (b) They crystallize his secret desires and compel him to act.
7. by depicting him as a brave hero, caring and sensitive.
8. Possible answer: a denizen of the streets or a sinister neighbor.

Literary Element

1. Dark and violent
2. Students should center on enhancing the sinister feeling.

 For additional assessment, see Assessment Resources, pp. 107–108.

Reading Strategy

Students should cite useful information from Act 1.

 Writing

Write a Brochure Students' brochures should:

- Reflect details in discussions of how setting affects atmosphere
- Evoke the play's atmosphere

326

After You Read

Respond and Think Critically

Respond and Interpret

1. What is your impression of Macbeth and Lady Macbeth?
2. (a)What predictions do the witches make about Macbeth's future? About Banquo's? (b)How does Macbeth's reaction differ from Banquo's?
3. (a)What conflict arises in Macbeth after the first prediction proves true? (b)What does this inner conflict reveal about his character?

Analyze and Evaluate

4. A **soliloquy** is a dramatic device in which a character, alone on the stage, reveals his or her private thoughts and feelings as if thinking aloud. What does Macbeth's soliloquy in scene 7 reveal about him?

5. (a)Summarize the arguments that Lady Macbeth uses to convince her husband to murder Duncan. (b)Do these arguments appeal to Macbeth's reason, his emotions, or both? Explain your answer.
6. (a)Review the scenes in which the witches appear. What might the witches symbolize, or stand for? (b)What is their effect on Macbeth?

Connect

7. **Big Idea** **A Bard for the Ages** How does Shakespeare make Macbeth a character with whom the audience can sympathize?
8. **Connect to Today** In a movie set in modern times, what kind of characters might perform the same function as the witches in *Macbeth*? Why?

Literary Element **Atmosphere**

The witches in *Macbeth* help to establish the **atmosphere,** or emotional quality, of the work.

1. Describe the atmosphere created by the witches' dialogue in scenes 1 and 3.
2. If you were producing scene 1 of *Macbeth* today, how would you establish the atmosphere?

Writing

Write a Brochure The events of Act 1 take place in several striking settings. With a partner, discuss how each setting affects the atmosphere, or mood, of the scene. Then create a travel brochure for eleventh-century Scotland, based on the details you have discussed. Your brochure should evoke the atmosphere established in the play.

Reading Strategy **Apply Background Knowledge**

Applying what you know to what you are reading helps you make connections that increase your understanding of a drama. Which background information was most useful to you in reading Act 1?

Vocabulary Practice

Practice with Word Parts Use a printed or online dictionary to find the meanings of the base word and the suffix that make up each vocabulary word. Then use the word correctly in a sentence.

direful   prophetic   repentance   plenteous   peerless

EXAMPLE:
rehearsal

<u>Base Word</u>
rehearse, "to practice a performance"
+
<u>Suffix</u>
-al, "the action of"

Vocabulary

Sentences will vary. Sample responses:

direful
root: "dread"
suffix: "full of"

prophetic
root: "an interpreter of the gods"
suffix: "pertaining to"

repentence
root: "suffer punishment"
prefix: "again"
suffix: "process of"

plenteous
root: "abundant supply"
suffix: "resembling"

peerless
root: "a person who is equal"
suffix: "without"

Before You Read

Macbeth, Act 2

Build Background

To Shakespeare's audience, *Macbeth*—a play depicting the horrors of regicide—would have hit close to home. The dating of the play places it in the aftermath of one of the most disturbing events in English history, the Gunpowder Plot of 1605. The Gunpowder Plot involved a conspiracy by Catholic extremists to blow up King James I and his Protestant government at the opening of Parliament on November 5. On the night of November 4, one conspirator, Guy Fawkes, was arrested with thirty-six barrels of gunpowder beneath the House of Lords.

These events are reflected in the allusions to equivocation, or deceptive testimony, in the porter's speech in scene 3 of this act. The famous Jesuit, Father Garnet, who was tried and executed for his role in the Gunpowder Plot, had made a speech defending equivocation as a legitimate means to avoid self-incrimination.

Literary Element **Motif**

A **motif** (mō tēf′) is a significant phrase, description, or image that is repeated throughout a literary work and related to its theme. For example, in Act 1 of *Macbeth,* two important motifs are the supernatural, associated with the witches, and the shedding of blood, associated with the wounded captain. As you read Act 2, ask yourself, Where do these motifs recur, and what new motifs does Shakespeare introduce and develop?

Reading Strategy **Evaluate Credibility**

Evaluating credibility involves making a judgment about whether a character is knowledgeable and truthful. As you read, ask yourself, Are the characters' statements in this act convincing?

Tip: Using a Checklist Use a checklist like the one below to evaluate the characters' credibility.

☑	Under what circumstances is the statement made?
☑	Does the character have anything to gain, lose, or hide?
☑	Can the statement be corroborated by events or by other characters?
☑	Does the statement make logical sense?

MACBETH, ACT 2 **327**

Learning Objectives

For pages 327–341

In studying this text, you will focus on the following objectives:

Literary Study: Analyzing motif.

Reading: Evaluating credibility.

Writing: Writing a summary.

Vocabulary

stealthy (stel′ thē) *adj.* secret; sly; p. 329 *The stealthy figure crept down the alley.*

surfeited (sur′ fit əd) *adj.* overfed; overcome by excess drinking, eating, etc.; p. 330 *I felt surfeited after devouring the entire pizza.*

provoke (prə vōk′) *v.* to call forth; to stir to action or feeling; p. 334 *He provoked the teacher with his chronic lateness.*

scruple (skrōō′ pəl) *n.* a moral or ethical principle that restrains action; p. 337 *Her scruples prevented her from resorting to lies.*

predominance (pri dom′ ə nəns) *n.* the state of being most important, common, or noticeable; p. 339 *The predominance of children in the theater made for a noisy movie-going experience.*

Before You Read

Teach

Summary

Lady Macbeth drugs Duncan's guards. Macbeth then murders the king. Lady Macbeth smears blood on the guards to make them look guilty. Macduff discovers the king's body. Out of fear Duncan's sons flee the country. The nobles interpret this as guilt and choose Macbeth as the successor. Macduff refuses to go to the coronation.

 For summaries in languages other than English, see Unit 2 Teaching Resources Book, pp. 168–173.

Vocabulary

Word webs Model a word web on the board for one of the vocabulary words. Write the word in the center. Other boxes in the web should be labeled *definition, synonyms, antonyms, sentence.* Have students contribute ideas for the web boxes. For the *sentence* box, have students contribute an original sentence using the word.

Selection Skills

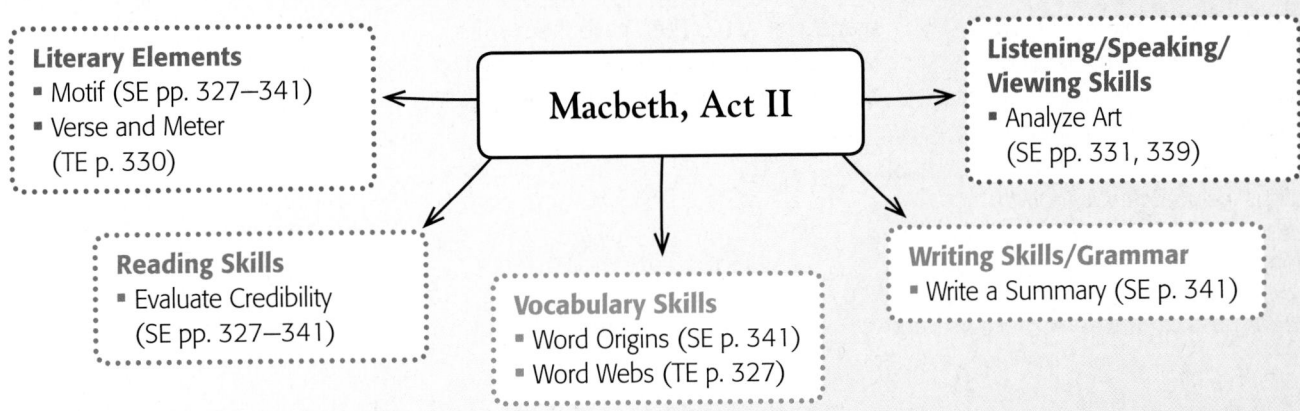

Literary Elements
- Motif (SE pp. 327–341)
- Verse and Meter (TE p. 330)

Reading Skills
- Evaluate Credibility (SE pp. 327–341)

Macbeth, Act II

Vocabulary Skills
- Word Origins (SE p. 341)
- Word Webs (TE p. 327)

Listening/Speaking/Viewing Skills
- Analyze Art (SE pp. 331, 339)

Writing Skills/Grammar
- Write a Summary (SE p. 341)

Teach

Literary Element   1

Motif   **Answer:** *Motifs include light and darkness, sleep and wakefulness.*

Reading Strategy   2

Evaluate Credibility
Answer: *Macbeth is not telling the truth. Macbeth's next lines reveal that he is eager to discuss the witches' prophecies. Banquo, who has seen the effect of the witches on Macbeth, probably does not believe him.*

[ENGLISH LEARNERS] Ask English learners to imagine what Macbeth sounds like as he tells this lie. Have them read the speech aloud several times, practicing the intonations Macbeth might use as he pretends he does not care about the witches' prophecy.

For additional practice using the reading skill or strategy, see Unit 2 Teaching Resources Book, p. 175.

For an audio recording of this selection, use Listening Library Audio CD-ROM.

ACT 2

SCENE 1. The castle at Inverness.

[*It is late at night as* BANQUO *and his son,* FLEANCE, *both guests of* MACBETH'S, *enter the courtyard of the castle.* FLEANCE *carries a torch to light the way.*]

BANQUO.   How goes the night, boy?

FLEANCE.   The moon is down; I have not heard the clock.

BANQUO.   And she goes down at twelve.

FLEANCE.   I take't, 'tis later, sir.

BANQUO.   Hold, take my sword. There's husbandry° in heaven.
5   Their candles° are all out. Take thee that° too.
A heavy summons° lies like lead upon me,
And yet I would not sleep. Merciful powers,
Restrain in me the cursèd thoughts that nature
Gives way to in respose!

[MACBETH *and a servant carrying a torch enter.*]

                               Give me my sword!
10   Who's there?

MACBETH.   A friend.

BANQUO.   What, sir, not yet at rest? The King's a-bed:
He hath been in unusual pleasure, and
Sent forth great largess to your offices:°
15   This diamond he greets your wife withal,
By the name of most kind hostess; and shut up°
In measureless content.

MACBETH.   Being unprepared,
Our will became the servant to defect,
Which else should free have wrought.°

BANQUO.   All's well.
20   I dreamed last night of the three weird sisters:
To you they have showed some truth.

MACBETH.   I think not of them.
Yet, when we can entreat an hour to serve,°
We would spend it in some words upon that business,
If you would grant the time.

BANQUO.   At your kind'st leisure.

4 husbandry: thrift.
5 candles: stars. that: perhaps his shield, cloak, or dagger.
6 summons: weariness calling him to sleep.

14 largess . . . offices: gifts to your servants' quarters.

16 shut up: concluded (his remarks).

17–19 Being . . . wrought: Our lack of preparation hindered us from entertaining as lavishly as we would have liked.

22 entreat . . . serve: arrange a suitable hour.

---

1   Motif   *Which motifs can you identify in this passage?*

2   Evaluate Credibility   *Is Macbeth telling the truth? Do you think Banquo believes him? Explain.*

Grammar Practice

SPIRAL REVIEW   **Subordinate Conjunctions**
Remind students that a subordinate conjunction joins two clauses so that one is grammatically dependent of the other. Common subordinate conjunctions include *after, although, as, because, if, since, that, unless, until, where, whereas, while,* and *which.* Have students find subordinate conjunctions in scene 1 of Act 2. Then have them write five sentences about the scene, using five different subordinate conjunctions.

25 MACBETH. If you shall cleave to my consent, when 'tis,°
    It shall make honor for you.

BANQUO.   So I lose none°
    In seeking to augment it, but still keep
    My bosom franchised and allegiance clear,°
    I shall be counseled.°

MACBETH.   Good repose the while!

30 BANQUO. Thanks, sir. The like to you!

[BANQUO and FLEANCE exit.]

MACBETH. [To the servant.] Go bid thy mistress, when my
    drink° is ready,
    She strike upon the bell. Get thee to bed.

[The servant exits. MACBETH, alone, imagines that he sees a bloody
dagger.]

    Is this a dagger which I see before me,
    The handle toward my hand? Come, let me clutch thee.
35 I have thee not, and yet I see thee still.
    Art thou not, fatal vision, sensible
    To feeling° as to sight, or art thou but
    A dagger of the mind, a false creation,
    Proceeding from the heat-oppressèd° brain?
40 I see thee yet, in form as palpable
    As this which now I draw.
    Thou marshal'st me° the way that I was going;
    And such an instrument I was to use.
    Mine eyes are made the fools o' th' other senses,
45 Or else worth all the rest.° I see thee still;
    And on thy blade and dudgeon° gouts° of blood,
    Which was not so before. There's no such thing.
    It is the bloody business which informs°
    Thus to mine eyes. Now o'er the one half-world
50 Nature seems dead, and wicked dreams abuse°
    The curtained° sleep; witchcraft celebrates
    Pale Hecate's offerings;° and withered murder,
    Alarumed by his sentinel, the wolf,
    Whose howl's his watch, thus with his **stealthy** pace,

---

25 cleave . . . 'tis: support my position when the time comes.

26 So . . . none: as long as I lose no honor.

28 My . . . clear: my heart free from guilt and my loyalty unstained.
29 I . . . counseled: I am ready to listen to you.

31 drink: posset (a hot, spiced bedtime drink).

36–37 sensible . . . feeling: capable of being perceived by touch.

39 heat-oppressèd: fevered.

42 marshal'st me: leads me.

44–45 Mine . . . rest: Either my eyes alone are deceived, or they correctly perceive what the other senses have missed.
46 dudgeon: handle. gouts: drops.
48 informs: takes shape.

50 abuse: deceive.

51 curtained: enclosed with bed curtains.
52 Hecate's offerings: rituals dedicated to Hecate, goddess of witchcraft (described as pale because she is associated with the moon).

Evaluate Credibility *Is this dagger real or a figment of Macbeth's imagination? Explain.* **3**

Motif *What might this image foreshadow?* **4**

Vocabulary

stealthy (stel´thē) *adj.* secret; sly

MACBETH, ACT 2, SCENE 1 **329**

Teach

Reading Strategy 3

Evaluate Credibility
Answer: *The dagger is a figment of Macbeth's imagination. His seeing it shows the intense emotional and moral strain he is under.*

Literary Element 4

Motif **Answer:** *The sword with "gouts of blood" suggests the shedding of someone's blood. This image foreshadows violence and murder.*

(APPROACHING) Tell approaching-level students that Macbeth's soliloquy, which begins on line 33, highlights the two principal motifs from Act I: blood and the supernatural. Write these two motifs on the board and ask students to contribute words or phrases from the speech that refer to them. *(dagger, fatal vision, blood, wicked dreams, etc.)* Have students find clues within the speech that might suggest a new motif: madness.

English Learners

DIFFERENTIATED INSTRUCTION

Intermediate Remind students that Shakespeare uses idioms that have survived or changed only slightly. Point out the phrase "The like to you!" (line 30). Guide students in understanding this expression, pointing out that "The like to you" has become "The same to you."

Approaching Level

DIFFERENTIATED INSTRUCTION

Established Have students read scene 1 aloud to practice **reading fluency** and to compare and contrast Macbeth's dialogue with his soliloquy. Encourage them to analyze Macbeth's character by comparing the diction in his conversation with that in his soliloquy. Remind them to focus on words with clear connotations. **Ask:** What differences do you notice in the way you read the dialogue and the way you read

Macbeth's soliloquy? *(Answers will vary. Students should note that the dialogue is more conversational and the soliloquy is more dramatic.)*

Big Idea | 1

A Bard for the Ages
Answer: *Shakespeare uses a ringing bell to show Macbeth's losing the struggle with his conscience. Macbeth then emphasizes his decision to murder Duncan with a rhymed couplet.*

Reading Strategy | 2

Evaluate Credibility
Answer: *Lady Macbeth's previous statements implied that nothing would stop her from murdering Duncan. This statement reveals that Lady Macbeth is not as steel-hearted as she pretends to be.*

(APPROACHING) To ensure that approaching-level students understand Lady Macbeth's statement, ask students to restate the last sentence of the speech in contemporary language *(If he had not resembled my father as he slept, I would have done it.)*

Vocabulary | 3

Word Origins Point out that the *sur-* in surfeited is an Old French prefix that comes from the Latin word *super*, meaning "over; above; beyond." **Ask:** What other words contain this prefix? *(surpass "to go beyond" and surmount "to overcome")*

(ENGLISH LEARNERS) Tell students that the Spanish equivalent to *sur-* is *sobre-*, derived from the same Latin source. Write *sobrepasar* on the board and ask students to use their knowledge of cognates to guess the English translation *(surpass)*. *Surfeit* does not translate to a Spanish *sobre-* word, but remind students that *sobrar* means "to exceed."

330

55　With Tarquin's ravishing strides, towards his design
　　Moves like a ghost.° Thou sure and firm-set earth,
　　Hear not my steps, which way they walk, for fear
　　Thy very stones prate of° my whereabout,
　　And take the present horror from the time,
60　Which now suits with it.° Whiles I threat,° he lives:
　　Words to the heat of deeds too cold breath gives.°

　　[A bell rings.]

　　　I go, and it is done: the bell invites me.°
　　　Hear it not, Duncan, for it is a knell
　　　That summons thee to heaven, or to hell.

[MACBETH *exits*.]

SCENE 2. The castle at Inverness.

[*Later the same night* LADY MACBETH *enters the empty courtyard of the castle*.]

　　LADY MACBETH. That which hath made them drunk hath
　　　　made me bold;
　　　What hath quenched them hath given me fire. Hark!
　　　　Peace!
　　　It was the owl that shrieked,° the fatal bellman,°
　　　Which gives the stern'st good night. He° is about it.
5　　The doors are open, and the **surfeited** grooms° ❸
　　　Do mock their charge° with snores. I have drugged their
　　　　possets,
　　　That death and nature do contend about them,
　　　Whether they live or die.°

　　MACBETH. [*Calling from within*.] Who's there? What, ho?

　　LADY MACBETH. Alack, I am afraid they have awaked
10　　And 'tis not done! Th' attempt and not the deed
　　　Confounds° us. Hark! I laid their daggers ready;
　　　He° could not miss 'em. Had he° not resembled
　　　My father as he slept, I had done 't.°

52–56 withered . . . ghost: Murder, alerted by the wolf's howl of the night's progress, moves toward his victim as silently as a ghost. (Tarquin was a Roman tyrant infamous for his rape of Lucrece.)
58 prate of: chatter about.
58–60 Thy . . . it: Macbeth doesn't want his footsteps to interrupt the dead silence, which he finds appropriate for the crime he is about to commit.
60 threat: threaten.
61 Words . . . gives: Talking cools off one's urge to take action.
62 the . . . me: The bell is Lady Macbeth's signal for Macbeth to go to Duncan's room.

3 the owl that shrieked: considered an omen of death. **bellman:** a watchman who rang a bell to sound the hours at night, announce a death, or signal that a prisoner would soon be executed.
4 He: Macbeth.
5 grooms: servants.
6 mock their charge: make a mockery of their duty.
6–8 I . . . die: Lady Macbeth says that she has so strongly drugged their bedtime drinks that they are in a deathlike sleep.
11 Confounds: ruins.
12 He: Macbeth. **he:** Duncan.
13 I had done 't: I would have killed him.

---

1 **A Bard for the Ages** *How does Shakespeare show a change in Macbeth by the end of this soliloquy?*

2 **Evaluate Credibility** *How would you compare this statement with Lady Macbeth's previous statements about killing the king in Act I?*

Vocabulary

surfeited (sur′fit əd) *adj.* overfed; overcome by excess drinking, eating, etc.

Literary Element Practice

SPIRAL REVIEW **Verse and Meter** Remind students that a line of iambic pentameter has five feet, each consisting of an unstressed syllable followed by a stressed one. Explain that this verse attempts to mimic speech while maintaining the regularity of poetic meter. To reinforce its crafted naturalness, have students do this activity:

- Read lines 9–11 aloud, emphasizing the stressed syllables. (A <u>lack</u>, I <u>am</u> a <u>fraid</u> they <u>have</u> a <u>waked</u> …)
- Reread the lines, this time speaking naturally. Note that they sound natural *and* poetic.

Lady Macbeth Seizing the Daggers, 1812. Henry Fuseli. Tate Gallery, London.

View the Art Fuseli's dramatic style influenced many painters of the Romantic era. What does this image suggest about the relationship between Macbeth and Lady Macbeth? ★

[MACBETH *enters, his hands covered with blood.*]

                         My husband!

    MACBETH. I have done the deed. Didst thou not hear a noise?

15   LADY MACBETH. I heard the owl scream and the crickets cry.°
      Did not you speak?

    MACBETH.   When?

    LADY MACBETH.   Now.

    MACBETH.   As I descended?

    LADY MACBETH. Ay.

    MACBETH. Hark!
      Who lies i' th' second chamber?

    LADY MACBETH.   Donalbain.

20   MACBETH. [*Looking at his hands.*] This is a sorry° sight.

15 crickets cry: another omen of death.

20 sorry: miserable.

MACBETH, ACT 2, SCENE 2 **331**

English Learners

DIFFERENTIATED INSTRUCTION

Advanced Explain that *descended* (line 18) contains the Latin prefix *de-,* "down," and the root *scend,* "climb." **Say:** Other words that contain *de-* include *demote* and *decline.* Words containing *scend* include *ascend* and *transcend.* **Ask:** What other words do you know contain the prefix *de-*? (*Students may say degrade, derail, debunk, etc.*) What other words do you know include the root *scend*? (*Students may say descendant, condescend, etc.*) Have students use each of these words in a sentence.

Teach

Motif **Answer:** *Macbeth has murdered Duncan while the king was innocently asleep. In doing this, Macbeth has "killed" sleep and innocence.*

Ask: How might "murdering sleep" affect Macbeth? *(It may ruin his ability to find relief from his troubles in sleep. In line 42, Macbeth believes the voice cursed him to "sleep no more.")* What concepts does sleep symbolize in this scene? *(life, death, innocence)*

(ADVANCED) Ask advanced level students to compare other literary selections they have read in which sleep is featured as a symbol. Encourage them to draw conclusions about sleep as a motif in literature across genres and periods.

LADY MACBETH. A foolish thought, to say a sorry sight.

MACBETH. There's one did laugh in 's sleep, and one cried
    "Murder!"
    That they did wake each other. I stood and heard them.
    But they did say their prayers, and addressed them
25   Again to sleep.°

LADY MACBETH. There are two° lodged together.

MACBETH. One cried "God bless us!" and "Amen" the other,
    As° they had seen me with these hangman's hands:°
    List'ning their fear, I could not say "Amen,"
    When they did say "God bless us!"

LADY MACBETH.   Consider it not so deeply.

30   MACBETH. But wherefore° could not I pronounce "Amen"?
    I had most need of blessing, and "Amen"
    Stuck in my throat.

LADY MACBETH.   These deeds must not be thought
    After these ways; so,° it will make us mad.

MACBETH. Methought I heard a voice cry "Sleep no more!
35   Macbeth does murder sleep"—the innocent sleep,
    Sleep that knits up the raveled sleave° of care,
    The death of each day's life, sore labor's bath,
    Balm° of hurt minds, great nature's second course,°
    Chief nourisher in life's feast—

LADY MACBETH.   What do you mean?

40   MACBETH. Still it cried "Sleep no more!" to all the house:
    "Glamis hath murdered sleep, and therefore Cawdor
    Shall sleep no more: Macbeth shall sleep no more."

LADY MACBETH. Who was it that thus cried? Why, worthy
    Thane,
    You do unbend° your noble strength, to think
45   So brainsickly of things. Go get some water,
    And wash this filthy witness° from your hand.
    Why did you bring these daggers from the place?
    They must lie there: go carry them, and smear
    The sleepy grooms with blood.

MACBETH.   I'll go no more.
50   I am afraid to think what I have done;
    Look on 't again I dare not.

LADY MACBETH.   Infirm of purpose!°
    Give me the daggers. The sleeping and the dead

---

1 Motif *In what way has Macbeth murdered sleep?*

24–25 addressed . . . sleep: fell back asleep. **two:** Malcolm and Donalbain, King Duncan's sons.

27 As: as if. **hangman's hands:** bloodstained hands. (After an execution, the executioner would cut the victim's body into pieces.)

30 wherefore: why.

33 so: if we do so.

36 raveled sleave: tangled threads.

38 Balm: healing ointment. **second course:** main (and most nourishing) course of a meal.

44 unbend: relax, weaken.

46 witness: evidence.

51 Infirm of purpose: Feebly determined.

Reading Practice

SPIRAL REVIEW **Make Inferences** Explain to students that Shakespeare uses dialogue to create characterization. To understand the Macbeths, students must make inferences based on the two characters' words and behavior following the murder of Duncan. Ask students to use evidence in lines 49–73 on this spread to make inferences about Macbeth and Lady Macbeth. *(Macbeth is unraveling under the moral and emotional strain of the murder. Lady Macbeth feels no pangs of conscience, and she seems driven and shrewish.)*

Are but as pictures.° 'Tis the eye of childhood
That fears a painted devil. If he do bleed,
55 I'll gild° the faces of the grooms withal,
For it must seem their guilt.

[*As* LADY MACBETH *exits, knocking is heard offstage.*]

MACBETH.   Whence is that knocking?
How is 't with me, when every noise appalls me?
What hands are here? Ha! They pluck out mine eyes!
Will all great Neptune's ocean wash this blood
60 Clean from my hand? No; this my hand will rather
The multitudinous seas incarnadine,°
Making the green one red.

[LADY MACBETH *returns.*]

LADY MACBETH.   My hands are of your color, but I shame
To wear a heart so white. [*Knocking within.*] I hear a
knocking
65 At the south entry. Retire we to our chamber.
A little water clears us of this deed:
How easy is it then! Your constancy
Hath left you unattended.° [*Knock.*] Hark! more knocking.
Get on your nightgown, lest occasion call us
70 And show us to be watchers.° Be not lost
So poorly in your thoughts.

MACBETH.   To know my deed, 'twere best not know myself.°
[*Knock.*]
Wake Duncan with thy knocking! I would thou couldst!

[*They exit.*]

SCENE 3. The castle at Inverness.

[*The setting is the same as above, except that now it is early morning and a
drunken* PORTER, *or doorkeeper, enters and crosses the courtyard to open the
castle gate.*]

PORTER.   Here's a knocking indeed! If a man were porter of
hell gate, he should have old° turning the key. [*Knocking
is heard offstage.*] Knock, knock, knock! Who's there, i'
th' name of Beelzebub?° Here's a farmer, that hanged
5   himself on th' expectation of plenty.° Come in time! Have
napkins enow° about you; here you'll sweat for 't.

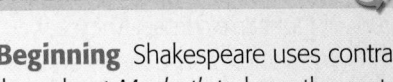

Motif *With which words spoken by Macbeth does the phrase "a little
water" contrast?* **2**

Evaluate Credibility *The porter pretends that he is guarding the
entrance to hell. What is ironic about the porter's fiction?* **3**

---

53 **but as pictures:** merely like
pictures (because they do not
move).
55 **gild:** smear, paint.

61 **The . . . incarnadine:** turn the
vast seas blood red.

67–68 **Your . . . unattended:** Your
firmness of purpose has deserted
you.
70 **show . . . watchers:** reveal that
we have been awake all night.

72 **To know . . . myself:** If I am
aware of my crime, it would be best
for me to remain in this daze.

1–16 **Here's . . . further:** As the
Porter goes to open the castle gate,
he imagines himself admitting lost
souls through the gates of hell.
2 **old:** plenty of.
4 **Beelzebub:** a devil.
4–5 **a farmer . . . plenty:** a farmer
who hoarded grain in anticipation of
higher prices, then hanged himself
when crops turned out to be
plentiful.
6 **napkins enow:** handkerchiefs
enough (to wipe up your sweat
in hell).

MACBETH, ACT 2, SCENE 3   **333**

Teach

333

Teach

Literary Element · 1

Motif Say: Compare the way the idea of sleep is treated here with images associated with sleep in Scene 2. *(Here sleep is a comical consequence of drunkenness and given crass associations. In Scene 2, sleep symbolizes innocence and purity, as well as death.)*

APPROACHING For approaching-level students, **ask:** What overall impression does the porter give of the state of the castle when he talks about drink and sleep? *(He makes it sound like people have been up late drinking and the place is in disarray.)*

Language History ☆

Puns on *Lie* Shakespeare makes a pun involving an outdated meaning of the word *lye*, which at the time was slang for "urine." Explain that a pun is a play on words, a joke based on different meanings of the same word or of words that sound alike. This exchange between the Porter and Macduff includes a multilayered pun on meanings of the word *lie*: (1) to rest, (2) to be laid out, as in wrestling, (3) to tell an untruth, (4) to cause to urinate.

[*Knock.*] Knock, knock! Who's there, in th' other devil's name? Faith, here's an equivocator,° that could swear in both the scales against either scale; who committed
10 treason enough for God's sake, yet could not equivocate to heaven. O, come in, equivocator. [*Knock.*] Knock, knock, knock! Who's there? Faith, here's an English tailor come hither for stealing out of a French hose:° come in, tailor. Here you may roast your goose.° [*Knock.*] Knock,
15 knock; never at quiet! What are you? But this place is too cold for hell. I'll devil-porter it no further. I had thought to have let in some of all professions that go the primrose way to th' everlasting bonfire.° [*Knock.*] Anon, anon! [*The PORTER opens the gate.*] I pray you, remember the porter.°

[*MACDUFF and LENNOX enter through the gate.*]

20 MACDUFF. Was it so late, friend, ere you went to bed,
        That you do lie so late?

   PORTER. Faith, sir, we were carousing till the second cock:° and drink, sir, is a great provoker of three things.

   MACDUFF. What three things does drink especially **provoke**?

25 PORTER. Marry, sir, nose-painting, sleep, and urine. Lechery, sir, it provokes and unprovokes: it provokes the desire, but it takes away the performance. Therefore much drink may be said to be an equivocator with lechery: it makes him and it mars him; it sets him on and it takes him off; it persuades
30 him and disheartens him, makes him stand to and not stand to; in conclusion, equivocates him in a sleep, and, giving him the lie, leaves him. ☆

   MACDUFF. I believe drink gave thee the lie° last night.

   PORTER. That it did, sir, i' the very throat° on me: but I
35 requited° him for his lie, and, I think, being too strong for him, though he took up my legs sometime, yet I made a shift to cast him.°

   MACDUFF. Is thy master stirring?

[*MACBETH enters in his dressing gown.*]

        Our knocking has awaked him; here he comes.

40 LENNOX. Good morrow, noble sir.

   MACBETH.   Good morrow, both.

   MACDUFF. Is the king stirring, worthy Thane?

   MACBETH.   Not yet.

Vocabulary

provoke (prə vōk′) *v.* to call forth; to stir to action or feeling

---

8 equivocator: one who gives deceptive testimony by using words that have more than one meaning.

13 stealing . . . hose: stealing cloth from a supply provided for a customer's French breeches.
14 roast your goose: heat your pressing iron.

17–18 primrose . . . bonfire: flowery path to hell.
19 I . . . porter: The Porter asks for a tip.

22 second cock: three o'clock in the morning.

33 gave . . . lie: laid you out (as in wrestling).
34 i' the very throat: an expression used to call someone a liar.
35 requited: repaid.

37 cast him: "throw him off" or "vomit him up."

Writing Practice

SPIRAL REVIEW **Scene** Dramatists use language and imagery to create mood. Through the Porter's black humor, along with Lennox and Macduff's talk of unnatural events, Shakespeare creates a dark, hallucinatory mood. Have students review the language and imagery in lines 1–59, which set the mood for the discovery of Duncan's corpse. Then ask them to write a short scene between two characters who make an eerie or shocking discovery. Suggest that students set the mood by having the characters recount a strange experience or dream. Encourage them to be creative and to select language and imagery that convey mood.

MACDUFF. He did command me to call timely° on him:
I have almost slipped the hour.°

MACBETH.   I'll bring you to him.

MACDUFF. I know this is a joyful trouble to you;
45   But yet 'tis one.

MACBETH. The labor we delight in physics pain.° **2**
This is the door.

MACDUFF.   I'll make so bold to call,
For 'tis my limited service.°

[MACDUFF goes to wake KING DUNCAN.]

LENNOX. Goes the king hence today?

MACBETH.   He does: he did
appoint so.°

50 LENNOX. The night has been unruly. Where we lay,
Our chimneys were blown down, and, as they say,
Lamentings heard i' the air, strange screams of death,
And prophesying with accents terrible
Of dire combustion° and confused events
55   New hatched to th' woeful time: the obscure bird°
Clamored the livelong night. Some say, the earth
Was feverous and did shake.°

MACBETH.   'Twas a rough night.

LENNOX. My young remembrance cannot parallel
A fellow to it.

[MACDUFF returns, appearing very shaken.]

60 MACDUFF. O horror, horror, horror! Tongue nor heart
Cannot conceive nor name thee.

MACBETH AND LENNOX.   What's the matter?

MACDUFF. Confusion° now hath made his masterpiece. ☆
Most sacrilegious murder hath broke ope
The Lord's anointed temple,° and stole thence
65   The life o' th' building.

MACBETH.   What is 't you say? The life?

LENNOX. Mean you his Majesty?

MACDUFF. Approach the chamber, and destroy your sight
With a new Gorgon:° do not bid me speak;
See, and then speak yourselves. Awake, awake!

Motif *Which motifs in lines 51–57 reinforce the atmosphere created in earlier scenes?* **3**

Side glossary

42 **timely:** early.

43 **slipped the hour:** let the hour slip by.

45 **The . . . pain:** The labor we enjoy cures any discomfort associated with it.

48 **limited service:** assigned duty.

49 **appoint so:** plan to do so.

54 **combustion:** confusion.

55 **obscure bird:** bird of darkness (the owl).

56–57 **the earth . . . shake:** Earthquakes were commonly associated with political unrest.

62 **Confusion:** destruction.

64 **The . . . temple:** the King's body.

68 **Gorgon:** a mythological monster whose gaze turned an onlooker to stone.

Teach

Reading Strategy | 2

Evaluate Credibility Have students analyze Macbeth's response to Macduff about "labor we delight in."

Ask: Do you think Macbeth's stated enjoyment of this task is credible? (*Most students will probably conclude that Macbeth is lying in order to conceal his part in Duncan's murder.*)

Literary Element | 3

Motif Answer: *Violent disturbances in nature, death screams, strange prophecies, and ominous birds reinforce atmosphere.*

(ADVANCED) Have advanced students discuss Shakespeare's use of omens and ghosts in his tragedies (i.e., King Hamlet's ghost in *Hamlet*; the omens in Julius Caesar, Act I, Scene 3). Based on his repeated use of these elements, ask them to make inferences about Elizabethan beliefs about humans, nature, and the supernatural.

Writer's Technique ☆

Figurative Language
Shakespeare uses figurative language to create memorable images. Such vivid description runs throughout his work. Using personification, he calls the destruction of Duncan's bloody corpse a "masterpiece" in line 62. He follows with a metaphor about the king's body.

Ask: To what does Shakespeare compare the king's body? (*a temple*) Why might he have chosen this image? (*to suggest that the murder was sacrilege*)

English Learners

DIFFERENTIATED INSTRUCTION

Advanced Have students use the Internet to better fathom Shakespeare's reference to a Gorgon. Suggest that they begin by finding pictures of Caravaggio's *Head of Medusa*. After researching this mythological creature, they should present their findings to the rest of the class.

Advanced Learners

DIFFERENTIATED INSTRUCTION

Research Shakespeare included references to the Gunpowder Plot of 1605 in *Macbeth*. Advanced students might enjoy learning more about this infamous affair. They can then examine how topical references that the audience would have recognized are woven into the play.

Teach

Cultural History ☆

Sleep and Death Throughout the play, Shakespeare returns to motifs of sleep and death, and lines 72–79 link these two states with an unsettling effect. Many cultures have been interested in the connection between sleep and death. Ancient Egyptians believed that the afterlife was a shadow of life much like sleep. In ancient Greece, people believed that Hypnos, god of sleep, resembled Thanatos, god of death. Miguel de Cervantes, Shakespeare's Spanish contemporary, wrote in *Don Quixote* (1605–1616) that "sleep … resembles death; there is very little difference between a man in his first sleep, and a man in his last sleep."

[*MACBETH and LENNOX rush off. MACDUFF comes forward, still upset and shouting.*]

70   Ring the alarum bell. Murder and Treason!
       Banquo and Donalbain! Malcolm! Awake!
       Shake off this downy sleep, death's counterfeit, ☆
       And look on death itself! Up, up, and see
       The great doom's image!° Malcolm! Banquo!
75   As from your graves rise up, and walk like sprites,°
       To countenance° this horror. Ring the bell.

[*A bell begins to ring offstage as LADY MACBETH enters.*]

LADY MACBETH.   What's the business,
       That such a hideous trumpet calls to parley
       The sleepers of the house? Speak, speak!

MACDUFF.   O gentle lady,
80   'Tis not for you to hear what I can speak:
       The repetition, in a woman's ear,
       Would murder as it fell.

[*BANQUO enters.*]

                     O Banquo, Banquo!
       Our royal master's murdered.

LADY MACBETH.   Woe, alas!
       What, in our house?

BANQUO.   Too cruel anywhere.
85   Dear Duff, I prithee, contradict thyself,
       And say it is not so.

[*MACBETH and LENNOX return with ROSS.*]

MACBETH.   Had I but° died an hour before this chance,°
       I had lived a blessèd time; for from this instant
       There's nothing serious in mortality:°
90   All is but toys.° Renown and grace is dead,°
       The wine of life is drawn, and the mere lees°
       Is left this vault° to brag of.

[*MALCOLM and DONALBAIN, still in their nightclothes, enter.*]

DONALBAIN.   What is amiss?

MACBETH.   You are, and do not know 't.
       The spring, the head, the fountain of your blood
95   Is stopped; the very source of it is stopped.

MACDUFF.   Your royal father's murdered.

MALCOLM.   O, by whom?

LENNOX.   Those of his chamber, as it seemed, had done 't:
       Their hands and faces were all badged° with blood;

74 great doom's image: an image of doomsday.
75 sprites: ghosts.
76 countenance: look upon.

87 but: only. **chance:** event.

89 serious in mortality: important in life.
90 toys: trifles. **Renown . . . dead:** Fame and fortune are dead.
91 lees: dregs.
92 vault: "wine vault" or "the earth vaulted by heaven."

98 badged: marked.

Listening and Speaking Practice

SMALL GROUP   SPIRAL REVIEW

Read Aloud It is important to remind students regularly that the text of *Macbeth* was meant to be spoken. Reading parts of the play aloud can bring the characters to life and give students new perspectives on the words they have read silently.

Have pairs or small groups choose a scene or a portion of a scene they would like to read aloud. Tell each group to create a T-chart. In the left column they copy the lines of dialogue. In the right column they make notes about the characters' feelings and the mood of the speech as conveyed by the figures of speech and other stylistic devices. Have students use these notes to help them practice reading their scene aloud with the emotions and intonations they feel are appropriate.

So were their daggers, which unwiped we found
100 Upon their pillows. They stared, and were distracted.°
No man's life was to be trusted with them.

MACBETH. O, yet I do repent me of my fury,
That I did kill them.

MACDUFF.   Wherefore did you so?°

MACBETH. Who can be wise, amazed,° temp'rate and furious,
105 Loyal and neutral, in a moment? No man.
The expedition° of my violent love
Outrun the pauser,° reason. Here lay Duncan,
His silver skin laced with his golden blood,
And his gashed stabs looked like a breach in nature
110 For ruin's wasteful entrance:° there, the murderers,
Steeped in the colors of their trade, their daggers
Unmannerly breeched with gore.° Who could refrain,
That had a heart to love, and in that heart
Courage to make 's° love known?

LADY MACBETH.   Help me hence, ho!

[LADY MACBETH faints.]

115 MACDUFF. Look to the lady.

MALCOLM. [Aside to DONALBAIN.] Why do we hold our
tongues,
That most may claim this argument for ours?°

DONALBAIN. [Aside to MALCOLM.] What should be spoken
here,
Where our fate, hid in an auger-hole,
May rush, and seize us?° Let's away:
120 Our tears are not yet brewed.

MALCOLM. [Aside to DONALBAIN.] Nor our strong sorrow
Upon the foot of motion.°

BANQUO.   Look to the lady.

[LADY MACBETH, faint, is carried out.]

And when we have our naked frailties hid,°
That suffer in exposure, let us meet
And question° this most bloody piece of work,
125 To know it further. Fears and **scruples** shake us.

Evaluate Credibility *Why does Lady Macbeth faint?*   **1**

Vocabulary

scruple (skrōō′pəl) *n.* a moral or ethical principle that restrains
action

---

100 **distracted:** insane.

103 **Wherefore . . . so:** Why did
you do so?
104 **amazed:** bewildered.

106 **expedition:** haste.
107 **pauser:** delayer.

109–110 **And . . . entrance:**
Macbeth compares Duncan's
wounds to a gap in a defensive wall
that allows destructive forces to
enter.
112 **breeched with gore:** covered
with blood.
114 **'s:** his.

116 **That . . . ours:** who are most
concerned with this matter.

117–119 **What . . . us:** Donalbain
advises against speaking up in the
castle, where deadly fate may
ambush them from any tiny hole.

120–121 **Nor . . . motion:** Nor
has our great sorrow begun to
express itself.

122 **when . . . hid:** "when we have
replaced our nightclothes with
proper clothing" or "when we have
covered our naked grief."
124 **question:** examine.

MACBETH, ACT 2, SCENE 3 **337**

Teach

Reading Strategy   1

Evaluate Credibility
Answer: *Most students will say
that she feigns fainting to divert
attention from Macbeth, who is
explaining at length why he killed
the guards. Others may say that
the strain of the night and the
pressure of the moment have
taken their toll on her.* **Ask:** Why
do you think Shakespeare
doesn't tell us that Lady Macbeth
is pretending to faint? *(Shakespeare probably wanted to leave
this decision to directors, actors,
and ultimately the audience.)*

(ENGLISH LEARNERS) Read to
English learners Lady Macbeth's
line 114 aloud, emphasizing the
h sounds in "Help me hence, Ho!"
English learners reading silently
may not "hear" the exhalation
caused by the English sound of *h.*
Have students repeat the line after
you, pronouncing the *h* sounds.
Ask what effect the alliteration of *h*
gives to Lady Macbeth's voice.
*(It makes her sound breathless
and faint.)*

English Learners

DIFFERENTIATED INSTRUCTION

Advanced Remind students that both
Shakespearean and modern English contain
words that have multiple meanings. Have
students create a chart of the definitions of
these multiple-meaning words: *reason* (line
107), *seize* (line 119), *tears* (line 120).

Have students continue to track any
double meanings of words in the rest of
scene 3. Then ask what effects the double
meanings create. *(In some cases, they create poetic echoes. In others, irony results.)*

Teach

Big Idea   1

A Bard for the Ages

Answer: *Banquo, who does not believe the guards are guilty, gives himself to God. In his faith and alliance with good, he serves as a foil, or contrasting character, illustrating the defects in Macbeth's character.*

Literary Element   2

Motif   **Answer:** *This event, perhaps a solar eclipse, hints that Macbeth has upset the natural order. The "dark night"—Macbeth—has extinguished the "traveling lamp," or sun—Duncan.*

Writer's Technique ☆

Theme Malcolm refers to the show of "unfelt sorrow" that comes easily to the "false man." Donalbain notes that in Scotland, there are "daggers in men's smiles." Students should see that these words underscore one of Shakespeare's frequent themes: People's moral facades can be dangerously deceptive.

> In the great hand of God I stand, and thence
> Against the undivulged pretense I fight
> Of treasonous malice.°
>
> MACDUFF.   And so do I.
>
> ALL.   So all.
>
> MACBETH.   Let's briefly put on manly readiness,°
> 130   And meet i' th' hall together.
>
> ALL.   Well contented.
>
> [*Everyone exits except* MALCOLM *and* DONALBAIN.]
>
> MALCOLM.   What will you do? Let's not consort° with them.
> To show an unfelt sorrow is an office° ☆
> Which the false man does easy. I'll to England.
>
> DONALBAIN.   To Ireland, I; our separated fortune
> 135   Shall keep us both the safer. Where we are
> There's daggers in men's smiles; the near in blood, ☆
> The nearer bloody.°
>
> MALCOLM.   This murderous shaft that's shot
> Hath not yet lighted,° and our safest way
> Is to avoid the aim. Therefore to horse;
> 140   And let us not be dainty of leave-taking,
> But shift away.° There's warrant in that theft
> Which steals itself when there's no mercy left.°
>
> [*They exit.*]

SCENE 4. The castle at Inverness.

[*The nobleman* ROSS *and an* OLD MAN *enter the courtyard.*]

> OLD MAN.   Threescore and ten° I can remember well:
> Within the volume of which time I have seen
> Hours dreadful and things strange, but this sore° night
> Hath trifled former knowings.
>
> ROSS.   Ha, good father,
> 5   Thou seest the heavens, as troubled with man's act,
> Threatens his bloody stage.° By th' clock 'tis day,
> And yet dark night strangles the traveling lamp:°

Side notes:

126–128 **In the . . . malice:** Placing myself in God's hands, I will fight against the undisclosed purpose of this treason.

129 **put . . . readiness:** prepare ourselves for taking action.

131 **consort:** associate.
132 **office:** task.

136–137 **the near . . . bloody:** The more closely one is related (to Duncan), the more likely one is to be murdered.
138 **lighted:** reached its target.
140–141 **let . . . away:** Let us not be polite about taking leave, but instead slip off unnoticed.

141–142 **There's . . . left:** stealing away is justified in these merciless times.

1 **Threescore and ten:** seventy years.

3 **sore:** dreadful.

6 **his bloody stage:** the earth.
7 **traveling lamp:** the sun.

---

1   A Bard for the Ages *How does Shakespeare use this speech to show the difference in character between Banquo and Macbeth?*

2   Motif *What does this unnatural event suggest?*

Vocabulary Practice

SPIRAL REVIEW   **Prefixes** Remind students that the prefix *pre-* means "before" but its definition is not limited to "an earlier time." In some words, *pre-* means "before in order, position, or rank." Have students determine in which of the following words *pre-* has this meaning: *prefix, predict, preside, presuppose.* Have students consult a dictionary to find the meanings of *prefect,* *precedence, preeminent, preside,* and *prerogative.*

Have them write a sentence that illustrates the meaning of each word. Suggest that, where possible, students express thoughts that are related to some aspect of *Macbeth*.

Conway Castle. John Varley (1778–1842). Watercolor, 27.7 x 42.1 cm. Agnew & Sons, London.

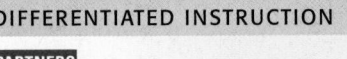 **View the Art** Conway Castle is built to appear as though it "grew" from an outcropping of rock in Wales. Does the scene depicted in this painting more closely resemble your impression of Duncan's palace or Macbeth's castle? Explain. ★

Is 't night's **predominance**, or the day's shame,
That darkness does the face of earth entomb,
10   When living light should kiss it?

OLD MAN.   'Tis unnatural,
Even like the deed that's done. On Tuesday last
A falcon, tow'ring in her pride of place,°
Was by a mousing owl hawked at° and killed.

ROSS.   And Duncan's horses—a thing most strange and
            certain—
15   Beauteous and swift, the minions of their race,°
Turned wild in nature, broke their stalls, flung out,
Contending 'gainst obedience, as they would make
War with mankind.

OLD MAN.   'Tis said they eat° each other.

ROSS.   They did so, to th' amazement of mine eyes,

12 tow'ring . . . place: circling at the height of its ascent.
13 Was by . . . at: was attacked by an owl, which normally preys on mice.

15 minions of their race: best of their breed.

18 eat: ate.

> **Vocabulary**
>
> **predominance** (pri dom´ə nəns) *n.* the state of being most important, common, or noticeable

Approaching Level

DIFFERENTIATED INSTRUCTION

PARTNERS **Emerging** Students may better comprehend the dialogue between characters by reading it aloud. Ask pairs to read aloud the exchange between Ross and the Old Man from line 1 at the beginning of scene 4 through line 19 on this spread.

English Learners

DIFFERENTIATED INSTRUCTION

PARTNERS **Intermediate** Have pairs of students read through scene 4 and jot down all the action verbs they can find, such as *remembered, trifled, entomb,* and *kiss.* Suggest that they remove any outdated endings, such as the *-st* in *seest.* Complete the activity by having students use any unfamiliar action verbs from their lists in original sentences.

Teach

Literary Element | 3

Motif Compare the mood of the action of the owl as described in this scene with the owl described in scene 3, lines 55–56. (*In the earlier scene, the owl is mournful, but here it kills another bird. The increased violence intensifies the mood of tension and fear.*)

(APPROACHING) Direct approaching-level students' attention to line 19. Ask students what connotations the word *amazement* usually carries for them. (*a positive connotation, expressing wonder*). **Ask:** What is Ross expressing? (*shock and horror*)

Literary Element | 4

Motif **Ask:** What other strange events do the old man and Ross recount? (*A falcon was attacked and killed by an owl, and the king's best horses fled their stalls and ate one another.*)

(APPROACHING) Make sure approaching-level students understand the association of darkness with Duncan's murder. Direct students' attention to lines 8–10. **Ask:** What does *entomb* mean? (*to bury in a tomb or grave*) Who else is to be entombed? (*Duncan*)

View the Art ★

Answer: *Accept all reasonable responses.*

English watercolorist John Varley turned his eye mostly to landscapes, especially of the Welsh highlands. Built by the English king Edward I between 1283 and 1289, Conway Castle was part of Edward's "iron ring" of Welsh castles. It stemmed from the outcrop of rock on which it was built.

339

Teach

Reading Strategy · 1

Evaluate Credibility
Answer: *Macduff doubts Macbeth's credibility and suspects him of murder. He feels Macbeth does not deserve his imminent coronation.*

Literary Element · 2

Motif **Answer:** *This image reflects the unnatural change of leadership: Macbeth, "our new [robes]," has replaced Duncan, the "old robes."*

Ask: How would you describe the tone of Macduff's words? *(There is a tone of distrust or uncertainty in them.)*

[ENGLISH LEARNERS] Ask English learners if they recognize a cognate for the word *adieu. (adiós)* Tell them that *adieu* is rarely used in contemporary English. Point out also that the word serves as a clue that the two men are parting ways.

Progress Check

Can students analyze motif?

If No → See Unit 2 Teaching Resources Book, p. 174.

 To check students' understanding of the selection, see Unit 2 Teaching Resources Book, p. 179.

20   That looked upon 't.
[MACDUFF *enters.*]

                                    Here comes the good Macduff.
    How goes the world, sir, now?

MACDUFF.   Why, see you not?

ROSS. Is 't known who did this more than bloody deed?

MACDUFF. Those that Macbeth hath slain.

ROSS.   Alas, the day!
    What good could they pretend?°

MACDUFF.   They were suborned:°
25   Malcolm and Donalbain, the king's two sons,
    Are stol'n away and fled, which puts upon them
    Suspicion of the deed.

ROSS.   'Gainst nature still.°
    Thriftless° ambition, that will ravin up°
    Thine own life's means! Then 'tis most like
30   The sovereignty will fall upon Macbeth.

MACDUFF. He is already named, and gone to Scone
    To be invested.°

ROSS.   Where is Duncan's body?

MACDUFF. Carried to Colmekill,°
    The sacred storehouse of his predecessors
35   And guardian of their bones.

ROSS.   Will you to Scone?

MACDUFF. No, cousin, I'll to Fife.°

ROSS.   Well, I will thither.

MACDUFF. Well, may you see things well done there. Adieu,
    Lest our old robes sit easier than our new!°

ROSS. Farewell, father.

40 OLD MAN. God's benison° go with you, and with those
    That would make good of bad, and friends of foes!

[*They exit.*]

24 What . . . pretend: What did they intend to gain by it? **suborned:** secretly hired to commit evil.

27 'Gainst nature still: even more unnatural.
28 Thriftless: wasteful. ravin up: swallow greedily.

31–32 already . . . invested: already chosen and has gone to Scone, the traditional Scottish coronation site, to be crowned.
33 Colmekill: Iona, a small island off Scotland's coast where kings were buried.
36 Fife: Macduff is Thane of Fife.
38 Lest . . . new: in case the old rule suits us better than the new.
40 benison: blessing.

Gentleman's Doublet and Hose, 1548. German School. Textile. Staatliche Kunstsammlungen Dresden, Germany.

1 Evaluate Credibility *Why does Macduff refuse to attend Macbeth's coronation?*

2 Motif *How does the image of ill-fitting robes sum up the action so far?*

340 UNIT 2   THE ENGLISH RENAISSANCE

Reading Practice

SPIRAL REVIEW **Analyze Tragedy** Ask students to list characteristics of a tragedy *(i.e. a hero with a tragic flaw, a somber mood, dark and sad events, an unhappy ending).* Write students' ideas on the board. Then ask students to skim Act II for examples of each of the elements on the list. You may ask them to predict whether or not the play will have a happy ending.

After You Read

Respond and Think Critically

Respond and Interpret

1. (a)What does the "dagger soliloquy" in scene 1 reveal about Macbeth's state of mind? (b)Why might Shakespeare have chosen to have Macbeth reveal his feelings in a soliloquy?

2. (a)How does Lady Macbeth get blood on her hands? (b)What does her reaction to the blood reveal about her character?

Analyze and Evaluate

3. In your opinion, who is more responsible for Duncan's murder—Macbeth or Lady Macbeth?

4. (a)Why do you think Shakespeare chose to have Duncan's murder occur offstage? (b) How might showing the murder have changed the audience's feelings about Macbeth?

Connect

5. **Big Idea** **A Bard for the Ages** How does Shakespeare demonstrate his deep understanding of human nature in this act? Consider Macbeth's conflict over murdering Duncan.

6. **Connect to Today** Macbeth's motive for killing Duncan is "vaulting ambition." Cite some modern instances of such ambition (not necessarily leading to murder).

Literary Element Motif

By developing **motifs**, playwrights can make sure that key elements resonate with the audience.

1. How does Shakespeare develop the motif of the supernatural in Act 2?

2. Explain how the motif of blood dominates this act.

Reading Strategy Evaluate Credibility

When you **evaluate credibility**, you express a judgment about whether a character's assertions are convincing on the basis of evidence in the text.

In scene 3, lines 102–114, Macbeth explains his motives for killing Duncan's attendants. Is Macbeth's explanation convincing? Explain.

 Writing

Write a Summary Write a summary of Act 2 of *Macbeth,* being careful to include the events of the plot that occur offstage. Remember that a summary should be shorter than the original text because its purpose is to convey the main points of the text. For help with writing a summary, see page 55.

Vocabulary Practice

Practice with Word Origins Studying the origin and history of a word can help you better understand and explore its meaning. Create a word map, like the one below, for each vocabulary word from Act 2. Use a dictionary for help.

stealthy   surfeited   provoke
scruple   predominance

EXAMPLE:

> Definition: a literary work with a disastrous conclusion

> Etymology: from Latin tragoedia, meaning "a dramatic scene"

> tragedy

> Sample Sentence: Macbeth, like most tragedies, deals with the downfall of the central character.

 Literature Online

Selection Resources For Selection Quizzes, eFlash-cards, and Reading-Writing Connection activities, go to glencoe.com and enter QuickPass code GLB9817u2.

MACBETH, ACT 2   **341**

Vocabulary

Sample sentences will vary. Students' webs should model the example:

> Definition: secret; sly

> Etymology: Old Norse *stuld-r* means "theft"

> stealthy

> Sample Sentence: The <u>stealthy</u> cat burglar escaped before the police arrived.

 For additional assessment, see Assessment Resources, pp. 109–110.

 To create custom assessments online, go to Progress Reporter Online Assessment.

 To create custom assessments using software, use ExamView Assessment Suite.

After You Read

Assess

1. (a) Macbeth is extremely anxious. (b) Macbeth doesn't want others to know these thoughts.

2. (a) She smears the grooms with Duncan's blood. (b) She is ruthless.

3. Students' answers will vary.

4. (a) To control the audience's reaction to Macbeth, who despite his crime remains sympathetic (b) The audience would hate him.

5. Shakespeare shows the human conscience vacillating between right and wrong.

6. Students' answers will vary. Some may suggest politicians or businessmen.

Literary Element

1. In the unnatural acts that Ross and the old man recount

2. Macbeth imagines a dagger with blood on its handle; Lady Macbeth smears Duncan's blood on the sleeping grooms; Macbeth doubts that he will ever be able to cleanse his hands of Duncan's blood.

Reading Strategy

No. Macbeth argues that any loyal man would have acted the same, but Lennox did not react that way.

Writing

Students' summaries should briefly convey the main points of Act 2, including any events that take place off stage.

> For grammar practice, see Unit 2 Teaching Resources Book, p. 178.

341

Focus

Summary

Macbeth hires assassins to murder Banquo. Fleance, Banquo's son, escapes. At dinner, Macbeth sees Banquo's ghost take the king's seat. Unnerved, Macbeth acts strangely. Lady Macbeth tells the guests that his behavior is due to a lifelong illness. The weird sisters and Hecate plan Macbeth's undoing.

 For summaries in languages other than English, see Unit 2 Teaching Resources Book, pp. 181–186.

Vocabulary

Classical Word Derivations

The word *jovial* is derived from Jove, another name for the ancient Roman god Jupiter. On the board, create a three-column table with the headings *Word, Meaning,* and *Character*. In the *Word* column **write** the words: *herculean, odyssey, volcano, martial,* and *titanic*. Fill in the word meanings and related characters as a class. Students may use a dictionary to look up meanings if necessary.

Macbeth, Act 3

Build Background

Macbeth first appeared in the First Folio of 1623, a collection of Shakespeare's plays compiled by John Heminge and Henry Condell, two of his Globe colleagues, after the playwright's death.

During the 1500s and 1600s, belief in the existence of witchcraft was widespread. King James I even wrote a book on the subject, titled *Demonologie,* in which he argued that witchcraft and other forms of sorcery were a threat to society. According to some scholars, the prominence of witchcraft and the supernatural in the plot of *Macbeth* is evidence that Shakespeare was using this play to secure the king's approval.

Literary Element   Foil

A **foil** is a minor character whose attitudes, beliefs, and behavior differ significantly from those of a main character. Through these differences, the foil helps highlight specific attributes—both good and bad—of the main character. One example of a foil in literature is the character of Enkidu, who is Gilgamesh's foil in the epic of *Gilgamesh* (see page 59). As you read, ask yourself, Which character or characters function as Macbeth's foil?

Reading Strategy   Evaluate Style

Style consists of the expressive qualities that make an author's work original and distinctive. An author's style includes his or her word choice, sentence structures, and use of figurative language or imagery. As you read, ask yourself, How effective are the elements of style in conveying the author's purpose and message?

Tip: Using a Chart Use a chart like the one below to record the effects that stylistic elements have in Act 3.

Element of Style	Effect
word choice	Terms like "bloody cousins" (scene 1, line 29) and cruel parricide (scene 1, line 31) illustrate the horror of Duncan's murder.

Learning Objectives

For pages 342–359

In studying this text, you will focus on the following objectives:

Literary Study: Analyzing foil.

Reading: Evaluating style.

Writing: Writing a letter.

Vocabulary

indissoluble (in′ di sol′ yə bəl) *adj.* incapable of being broken; permanent; p. 343 *The team members play as an indissoluble unit.*

incense (in sens′) *v.* to make enraged; fill with anger; p. 346 *The mistreatment of animals incensed her.*

jovial (jō′ vē al) *adj.* full of good humor; genial and playful; p. 348 *Always good-natured and jovial with his nephews, he enjoys telling them jokes.*

appall (ə pôl′) *v.* to fill with horror and shock; p. 353 *The images of poverty and starvation in that documentary appall sensitive viewers.*

amends (ə mendz′) *n.* something done or given to make up for injury, loss, etc.; p. 356 *Luke offered to replant the flowers to make amends for trampling them.*

Selection Skills

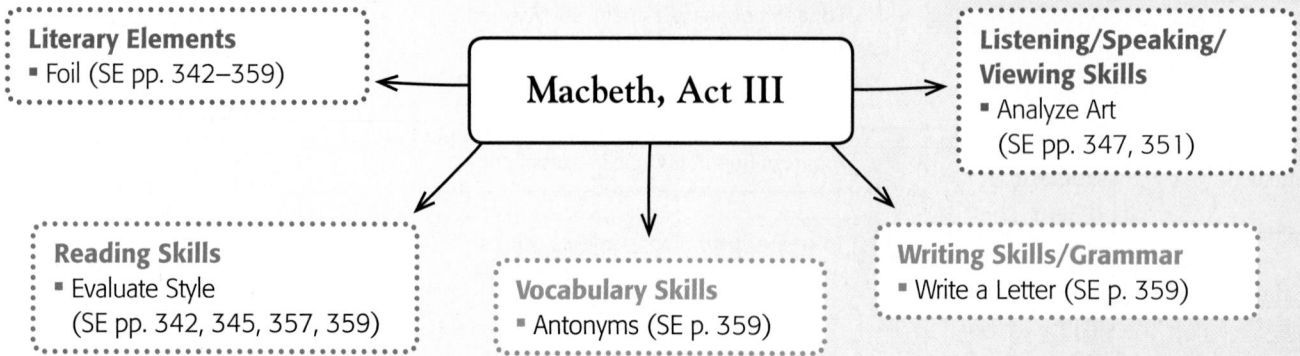

Literary Elements
- Foil (SE pp. 342–359)

Macbeth, Act III

Listening/Speaking/ Viewing Skills
- Analyze Art (SE pp. 347, 351)

Reading Skills
- Evaluate Style (SE pp. 342, 345, 357, 359)

Vocabulary Skills
- Antonyms (SE p. 359)

Writing Skills/Grammar
- Write a Letter (SE p. 359)

ACT 3

SCENE 1. The palace at Forres.

[BANQUO *is alone in a room in the royal palace at Forres.*]

BANQUO. Thou° hast it now: King, Cawdor, Glamis, all,
  As the weird women promised, and I fear
  Thou play'dst most foully for 't. Yet it was said
  It should not stand in thy posterity,°
5 But that myself should be the root and father
  Of many kings. If there come truth from them—
  As upon thee, Macbeth, their speeches shine—
  Why, by the verities on thee made good,°
  May they not be my oracles as well
10 And set me up in hope? But hush, no more!

[*A trumpet sounds as* MACBETH, *the new king, and* LADY MACBETH *enter. They are accompanied by* LENNOX, ROSS, *other* LORDS, LADIES, *and* ATTENDANTS.]

MACBETH. Here's our chief guest.

LADY MACBETH.   If he had been forgotten,°
  It had been as° a gap in our great feast,
  And all-thing° unbecoming.

MACBETH. Tonight we hold a solemn supper,° sir,
15 And I'll request your presence.

BANQUO.   Let your Highness
  Command upon me, to the which my duties
  Are with a most **indissoluble** tie
  For ever knit.°

MACBETH. Ride you this afternoon?

BANQUO.   Ay, my good lord.

20 MACBETH. We should have else desired your good advice
  (Which still hath been both grave and prosperous)°
  In this day's council; but we'll take tomorrow.°
  Is 't far you ride?

BANQUO. As far, my lord, as will fill up the time
25 'Twixt this and supper. Go not my horse the better,
  I must become a borrower of the night
  For a dark hour or twain.°

MACBETH.   Fail not our feast.

1 Thou: Macbeth.

4 stand in thy posterity: continue with your descendants.

8 by . . . good: judging by the truths regarding you that have been confirmed.

11 forgotten: absent, neglected.
12 It . . . as: it would have been like.
13 all-thing: wholly.
14 solemn supper: formal banquet.

18 knit: bound.

21 still . . . prosperous: always has been sober and profitable.
22 but . . . tomorrow: Macbeth (now using the royal "we") says that he can wait until tomorrow.

25–27 Go . . . twain: Unless my horse runs faster than I expect, I must ride an hour or two after sunset.

Vocabulary

indissoluble (in′ di sol′yə bəl) *adj.* incapable of being broken; permanent

MACBETH, ACT 3, SCENE 1 **343**

Teach

Reading Strategy   1

Evaluate Style Ask: What does Banquo reason in his soliloquy that opens scene 1? *Banquo reasons that since the witches' prophecies concerning Macbeth have come true, their prophecy concerning his children may also be fulfilled.* Why does Shakespeare use a soliloquy instead of dialogue to convey Banquo's thoughts? *(Banquo no longer trusts Macbeth so he cannot discuss his feelings with anyone.)*

(ENGLISH LEARNERS) Remind English learners that some words have multiple meanings. **Ask:** What does the word *weird* mean? *(strange, out of the ordinary)* Explain that *weird* in line 2 has a different meaning in Banquo's speech. Have students look up the word in a dictionary and tell you which meaning applies here. *(relating to witchcraft or the supernatural)*

> For an audio recording of this selection, use Listening Library Audio CD-ROM.

Approaching Level

DIFFERENTIATED INSTRUCTION

Emerging The complex syntax and abstract language in *Macbeth* can pose special challenges for struggling readers. You may need to use audiotapes and filmed versions to assist some students. Have students listen to audiotapes or watch video versions of sections of the play. Then have them read those sections in the textbook. To ensure that they are successfully relating the media to the text, have them summarize the sections orally.

Teach

Literary Element | 1

Foil Answer: *Banquo has already demonstrated his sense of honor; he is also brave and prudent. Moreover, the witches' prophecies may well come true, placing Banquo's descendants, not Macbeth's, on the Scottish throne.*

[APPROACHING] Help approaching-level students reinforce the idea of Banquo as Macbeth's foil by doing a point-by-point comparison between the two characters. List Macbeth's qualities and actions on one side of the board and Banquo's contrasting qualities and actions on the other.

> For additional literary element practice, see Unit 2 Teaching Resources Book, p. 187.

Cultural History ☆

Director's Vision Directors often make decisions that contradict Shakespeare's stage directions. In Orson Welles's 1948 film, Macbeth delivers this "soliloquy" to Lady Macbeth, emphasizing the words *barren* and *fruitless* to suggest that Macbeth blames his wife for their lack of children. Encourage students to discuss whether directors should take these kinds of liberties with the text.

BANQUO. My lord, I will not.

MACBETH. We hear our bloody cousins° are bestowed
30 In England and in Ireland, not confessing
     Their cruel parricide,° filling their hearers
     With strange invention.° But of that tomorrow,
     When therewithal we shall have cause of state
     Craving us jointly.° Hie° you to horse. Adieu,
35 Till you return at night. Goes Fleance with you?

BANQUO. Ay, my good lord: our time does call upon 's.°

MACBETH. I wish your horses swift and sure of foot,
     And so I do commend° you to their backs.
     Farewell. [BANQUO *exits.*]
40 Let every man be master of his time
     Till seven at night. To make society
     The sweeter welcome, we will keep ourself
     Till suppertime alone. While° then, God be with you!

[*Everyone exits except* MACBETH *and a* SERVANT.]

     Sirrah,° a word with you: attend those men
45 Our pleasure?°

ATTENDANT. They are, my lord, without the palace gate.

MACBETH. Bring them before us.

[*The* SERVANT *exits, leaving* MACBETH *alone.*]

     To be thus is nothing, but to be safely thus°—
     Our fears in Banquo stick deep,
50 And in his royalty of nature° reigns that
     Which would be feared. 'Tis much he dares;
     And, to° that dauntless temper° of his mind,
     He hath a wisdom that doth guide his valor
     To act in safety. There is none but he
55 Whose being I do fear: and under him
     My genius is rebuked,° as it is said
     Mark Antony's was by Caesar. He chid° the sisters,
     When first they put the name of King upon me,
     And bade them speak to him; then prophetlike
60 They hailed him father to a line of kings.
     Upon my head they placed a fruitless° crown
     And put a barren scepter in my gripe,° ☆
     Thence to be wrenched with an unlineal hand,°
     No son of mine succeeding. If 't be so,
65 For Banquo's issue have I filed° my mind;
     For them the gracious Duncan have I murdered;

29 cousins: Malcolm and Donalbain.

31 parricide: murder of a parent or close relative.
32 invention: lies.

33–34 therewithal . . . jointly: In addition to that, we will have matters of state requiring the attention of both of us.
34 Hie: hurry.
36 our . . . upon 's: We should depart soon.
38 commend: entrust.

43 While: until.

44 Sirrah: a term of address to a social inferior.
44–45 attend . . . pleasure: Are those men waiting to serve me?

48 To . . . thus: To be king is nothing unless one's rule is secure.

50 royalty of nature: regal nature.

52 to: in addition to. **dauntless temper:** fearless disposition.

56 genius is rebuked: inner spirit is repressed.
57 chid: scolded.

61 fruitless: barren, childless.
62 gripe: grip.
63 with an unlineal hand: by someone not related to me.

65 filed: defiled.

---

1 Foil *Why does Macbeth perceive Banquo as a threat?*

Reading Practice

 SPIRAL REVIEW **Paraphrase** Remind students that restating key passages in their own words is a powerful tool for understanding complex texts. Emphasize that a paraphrase does not have to follow the sentence structure of the original text; rearranging the order of words or ideas can often be helpful in making sense of a passage.

Ask: How might you paraphrase lines 49–51? (*I am really worried about Banquo. I fear him because he has a noble manner that threatens me.*)

Put rancors° in the vessel of my peace
Only for them, and mine eternal jewel°
Given to the common enemy of man,°
70 To make them kings, the seeds of Banquo kings!
Rather than so, come, fate, into the list,°
And champion me to th' utterance!° Who's there?

[*The* SERVANT *returns with two* MURDERERS, *and* MACBETH *addresses*
the SERVANT.]

Now go to the door, and stay there till we call.

[*The* SERVANT *exits.*]

Was it not yesterday we spoke together?

75 FIRST MURDERER. It was, so please your Highness.

MACBETH.   Well then, now
Have you considered of my speeches? Know
That it was he° in the times past, which held you
So under fortune,° which you thought had been
Our innocent self: this I made good to you
80 In our last conference; passed in probation° with you,
How you were born in hand,° how crossed; the
    instruments,°
Who wrought with them, and all things else that might
To half a soul° and to a notion° crazed
Say "Thus did Banquo."

FIRST MURDERER.   You made it known to us.

85 MACBETH. I did so; and went further, which is now
Our point of second meeting. Do you find
Your patience so predominant in your nature,
That you can let this go? Are you so gospeled,°
To pray for this good man and for his issue,°
90 Whose heavy hand hath bowed you to the grave
And beggared yours° for ever?

FIRST MURDERER.   We are men, my liege.

MACBETH. Ay, in the catalogue ye go for° men;
As hounds and greyhounds, mongrels, spaniels, curs,
Shoughs,° water-rugs° and demi-wolves,° are clept°
95 All by the name of dogs: the valued file°
Distinguishes the swift, the slow, the subtle,
The housekeeper, the hunter, every one
According to the gift which bounteous nature
Hath in him closed,° whereby he does receive
100 Particular addition, from the bill

Evaluate Style *What does the choice of analogy, along with Macbeth's*
word choice, convey about his attitude toward the men he is addressing? **2**

67 **rancors:** bitterness.
68 **eternal jewel:** soul.
69 **common . . . man:** devil.

71 **list:** field of combat.
72 **champion . . . utterance:** fight me
to the death.

77 **he:** Banquo.
78 **under fortune:** in poverty.

80 **passed in probation:** went through
the proof.
81 **born in hand:** deceived.
instruments: means.

83 **half a soul:** a half-wit. **notion:** mind.

88 **gospeled:** schooled in the Gospels
(which urge us to love our enemies).
89 **issue:** children.

91 **beggared yours:** impoverished your
descendants.

92 **go for:** are counted as.

94 **Shoughs:** shaggy-haired dogs.
water-rugs: rough-haired water dogs.
demi-wolves: crossbreeds between wolf
and dog. **clept:** called.
95 **valued file:** list of traits.

99 **closed:** enclosed.

Teach

Reading Strategy 2

Evaluate Style **Answer:**
By comparing the men to dogs,
Macbeth shows how little he
values them.

(ENGLISH LEARNERS) Call English
learners' attention to line 94, in
which Macbeth lists three types of
dogs. Ask students to reread the
side note for this line. **Ask:** Given
what you know from the side
note, do you think Macbeth is
using complimentary types of
dogs? *(no)* Explain that these
terms have negative connotations.
Ask: How do these unflattering
terms for dogs support the idea
that Macbeth is insulting the
men? *(Macbeth compares the*
men to these lowly types of dogs.)

English Learners

DIFFERENTIATED INSTRUCTION

Intermediate Have students create a
Venn diagram to analyze the relationship
between Macbeth and Banquo. Encourage
them to include descriptive phrases in the
appropriate sections. Suggest that they add
new information as they read. Then have
small groups discuss the diagrams to clarify
their ideas of each character.

Approaching Level

DIFFERENTIATED INSTRUCTION

Emerging Help students recognize
unfamiliar contractions such as *'tis* ("it is,"
line 51), *'t* ("it," line 64) and *th'* ("the," line
72). Encourage students to practice ***read-***
ing fluency by reading aloud sentences
with contractions to hear how these forms
maintain iambic pentameter.

Teach

Evaluate Style Ask: What exaggerations (or hyperboles) does Shakespeare use in the conversation between Macbeth and the murderers, what is the effect of these exaggerations? *(Macbeth says he is ill as long as Banquo lives; the murderers say they have suffered so much they are willing to do anything now. The exaggerations show how strongly the characters feel about their frustrations.)*

(ENGLISH LEARNERS) Ask English learners to sum up the murderers' speeches in one sentence. *(Life has been so hard on me that I'll risk anything for revenge, a solution, or just to die.)* **Ask:** Why are the murderers motivated to help Macbeth? *(They don't care what happens to them and Macbeth has convinced them that Banquo has harmed them.)*

Vocabulary | 2

Context Clues Ask: What emotion is evoked by the phrase "the vile blows and buffets of the world" in line 109? *(Possible responses: anger; sorrow)* How does this help you understand the meaning of incensed? *(The context suggests events that have enraged the speaker.)*

That writes them all alike:° and so of men.
Now if you have a station in the file,°
Not i' th' worst rank of manhood, say 't,
And I will put that business in your bosoms
105 Whose execution takes your enemy off,
Grapples you to the heart and love of us,
Who wear our health but sickly in his life,
Which in his death were perfect.°

SECOND MURDERER.   I am one, my liege,
Whom the vile blows and buffets of the world **2** | **1**
110 Hath so **incensed** that I am reckless what
I do to spite the world.

FIRST MURDERER.   And I another
So weary with disasters, tugged with fortune,
That I would set° my life on any chance,
To mend it or be rid on 't.°

MACBETH.   Both of you
115 Know Banquo was your enemy.

BOTH MURDERERS.   True, my lord.

MACBETH.   So is he mine, and in such bloody distance
That every minute of his being thrusts
Against my near'st of life:° and though I could
With barefaced power sweep him from my sight
120 And bid my will avouch it,° yet I must not,
For certain friends that are both his and mine,
Whose loves I may not drop, but wail his fall°
Who I myself struck down: and thence it is
That I to your assistance do make love,°
125 Masking the business from the common eye
For sundry weighty reasons.

SECOND MURDERER.   We shall, my lord,
Perform what you command us.

FIRST MURDERER.   Though our lives—

MACBETH.   Your spirits shine through you. Within this hour at
       most
I will advise you where to plant yourselves,
130 Acquaint you with the perfect spy o' th' time,
The moment on 't;° for 't must be done tonight,
And something° from the palace; always thought°
That I require a clearness:° and with him—
To leave no rubs° nor botches in the work—

Vocabulary

incense (in sens′) *v.* to make enraged; fill with anger

100–101 Particular . . . alike: a special designation that distinguishes him from the general category of dog.
102 station in the file: standing in the ranks.

106–108 Grapples . . . perfect: Macbeth says that their murder of Banquo will place them firmly in his affection. He is ill while Banquo lives but will be healthy again once he is dead.

113 set: risk.
114 on 't: of it.

116–118 and . . . life: Macbeth compares Banquo to a fencer standing dangerously close to him. Banquo's very existence is like a sword thrust against Macbeth's heart.
120 bid . . . it: offer my desire for Banquo's death as justification for killing him.
122 but wail his fall: but instead cry over his death.
124 to your . . . love: court your assistance.

130–131 perfect . . . on 't: precise instructions regarding exactly when to act.
132 something: at some distance.
always thought: it being understood at all times.
133 clearness: freedom from suspicion.
134 rubs: flaws.

Literary Element Practice

SPIRAL REVIEW Dynamic Characters Remind students that a dynamic character changes significantly during a work. Encourage students to notice how Macbeth has changed by comparing his actions in this scene with those in the scene leading up to Duncan's murder (Act 2, scene 1). Have students identify both similarities and differences in his character to emphasize that while dynamic characters change, some core personality traits stay the same.

Macbeth Instructing the Murderers Employed to Kill Banquo. George Cattermole. Watercolor on paper. Victoria & Albert Museum, London.

View the Art Cattermole is commonly associated with images from *Macbeth*. How do you interpret the figures to the right of Macbeth in this image? ★

135　　Fleance his son, that keeps him company,
　　　　Whose absence is no less material to me°
　　　　Than is his father's, must embrace the fate
　　　　Of that dark hour. Resolve yourselves apart:°
　　　　I'll come to you anon.

　　BOTH MURDERERS.　　　We are resolved, my lord.

140　**MACBETH.** I'll call upon you straight.° [*The* MURDERERS *exit.*]
　　　　Abide within.
　　　　It is concluded: Banquo, thy soul's flight,
　　　　If it find heaven, must find it out tonight. [MACBETH
　　　　exits.]

SCENE 2. The palace at Forres.

[LADY MACBETH *and a* SERVANT *enter another room in the palace.*]

　　LADY MACBETH. Is Banquo gone from court?

　　SERVANT. Ay, madam, but returns again tonight.

　　LADY MACBETH. Say to the King, I would attend his leisure
　　　　For a few words.

　　SERVANT.　　　Madam, I will. [*The* SERVANT *exits to*
　　　　summon MACBETH.]

　　LADY MACBETH.　　　　Nought's had, all's spent,
5　　　Where our desire is got without content:°
　　　　'Tis safer to be that which we destroy
　　　　Than by destruction dwell in doubtful° joy.

[MACBETH *enters.*]

　　　　How now, my lord! Why do you keep alone,
　　　　Of sorriest fancies your companions making,

136 Whose . . . me: whose death is no less important to me.

138 Resolve . . . apart: Make up your minds in private.

140 straight: immediately.

4–5 Nought's . . . content: We possess nothing and squander everything when we are not satisfied after getting what we wished for.
7 doubtful: apprehensive, suspicious.

3

Reading Strategy　3

Evaluate Style **Ask:** What purpose do Lady Macbeth's rhyming couplets have in lines 4–7? (*They sum up her situation and Macbeth's at this point in the play and give her justification for what's to come.*)

(APPROACHING) To check approaching-level students' understanding of what Lady Macbeth is referring to, **ask:** Is Macbeth secure now that Duncan is dead? (*no*) Why not? (*Banquo is a threat because of the witches' prophecy.*) How does this explain Lady Macbeth's assertion that they have nothing? (*If Macbeth is not secure on the throne, then all could be easily lost.*)

View the Art ★

Answer: *Students might guess that the figures to the right represent the three witches, watching over Macbeth as he sinks further and further into his fate.*

George Cattermole (1800–1868) depicted many scenes from *Macbeth*. This painting reflects his attention to detail and his ability to interpret characters' moods and personalities.

Ask: What details in the painting show Macbeth's continued moral decay? Explain. (*Macbeth is slouching. He stares into space instead of looking directly at the murderers. These details imply that Macbeth is becoming a weak leader.*)

English Learners

DIFFERENTIATED INSTRUCTION

Intermediate Point out that some scenes in Shakespeare end with a rhyming couplet that summarizes the scene. Have students read lines 141–142 of Act 3, scene 1, carefully. **Ask:** What is the main idea of these lines? (*The deal between Macbeth and the two murderers is set. They will kill Banquo tonight.*)

A Bard for the Ages

Answer: *The scorpion was considered a symbol of treachery and fear. This ghastly image suggests a mind tormented by horrible thoughts.*

ADVANCED Challenge advanced level students to explore the scorpion image more deeply. **Ask:** Do you think Macbeth views himself as the scorpion? Explain. *(possible answer: Yes. He has shown signs of anguish and guilt, so he may be accusing himself of betrayal.)*

Literary History ☆

Sleep in Shakespeare In an essay about *Macbeth*, the critic Mark Van Doren suggests that "sleep in Shakespeare is ever the privilege of the good and the reward of the innocent." Here, Macbeth and Lady Macbeth are deprived of peaceful sleep because they are neither good nor innocent, whereas Duncan "sleeps well" in death.

---

10 Using those thoughts which should indeed have died
   With them they think on? Things without all remedy
   Should be without regard:° what's done is done.

  MACBETH. We have scorched° the snake, not killed it:
   She'll close° and be herself, whilst our poor malice°
15 Remains in danger of her former tooth.°
   But let the frame of things disjoint, both the worlds suffer,°
   Ere we will eat our meal in fear, and sleep
   In the affliction of these terrible dreams
   That shake us nightly: better be with the dead,
20 Whom we, to gain our peace, have sent to peace,
   Than on the torture of the mind to lie
   In restless ecstasy.° Duncan is in his grave;
   After life's fitful fever he sleeps well. ☆
   Treason has done his worst: nor steel, nor poison,
25 Malice domestic,° foreign levy,° nothing,
   Can touch him further.

  LADY MACBETH.   Come on.
   Gentle my lord, sleek o'er your rugged looks;
   Be bright and **jovial** among your guests tonight.

  MACBETH. So shall I, love; and so, I pray, be you:
30 Let your remembrance apply to Banquo;
   Present him eminence, both with eye and tongue:°
   Unsafe the while, that we must lave
   Our honors in these flattering streams°
   And make our faces vizards° to our hearts,
35 Disguising what they are.

  LADY MACBETH.   You must leave this.

  MACBETH. O, full of scorpions is my mind, dear wife!
   Thou know'st that Banquo, and his Fleance, lives.

  LADY MACBETH. But in them nature's copy's not eterne.°

  MACBETH. There's comfort yet; they are assailable.
40 Then be thou jocund.° Ere the bat hath flown
   His cloistered flight, ere to black Hecate's summons
   The shard-borne beetle with his drowsy hums
   Hath rung night's yawning peal,° there shall be done
   A deed of dreadful note.

11–12 Things . . . regard: You shouldn't dwell upon matters beyond remedy.
13 scorched: wounded.
14 close: heal. **poor malice:** feeble power to harm.
15 in . . . tooth: in as much danger from her tooth as before she was wounded.
16 But . . . suffer: but let the universe fall apart, and let both heaven and earth perish.

22 ecstasy: frenzy.

25 Malice domestic: civil war. **foreign levy:** troops sent from abroad.

31 Present . . . tongue: Pay respect to him with both looks and speech.
32–33 Unsafe . . . streams: We are vulnerable at the moment, so we must wash our reputations in these streams of flattery.
34 vizards: masks.

38 in . . . eterne: They do not have eternal life.

40 jocund: merry.

40–43 Ere . . . peal: before sunset (when the bat begins its flight and the winged beetle's droning announces nightfall).

---

1   **A Bard for the Ages** *What does Shakespeare convey about Macbeth's state of mind with this image?*

Vocabulary

jovial (jō′vē əl) *adj.* full of good humor; genial and playful

---

Writing Practice

SPIRAL REVIEW **Analytical Essay** Have students write a brief essay analyzing one of the main characters in the play. Ask them to evaluate the character's strengths and weaknesses. Tell students that because the characters are morally complex, they will need to define the terms *strength* and *weakness* in their essay introductions. For example, Macbeth's willingness to act on his desire could be taken as a strength because it gets him what he wants or as a weakness because it indicates his willingness to be morally unscrupulous.

LADY MACBETH. What's to be done?

45 MACBETH. Be innocent of the knowledge, dearest chuck,°
Till thou applaud the deed. Come, seeling° night,
Scarf up° the tender eye of pitiful day,
And with thy bloody and invisible hand
Cancel and tear to pieces that great bond°
50 Which keeps me pale! Light thickens, and the crow
Makes wing to th' rooky° wood.
Good things of day begin to droop and drowse,
While night's black agents to their preys do rouse.
Thou marvel'st at my words: but hold thee still;
55 Things bad begun make strong themselves by ill:
So, prithee, go with me. [*They exit together.*]

SCENE 3. Outside the palace at Forres.

[*Some distance from the palace, the two assassins wait to attack* BANQUO *and* FLEANCE. *They are joined by a mysterious* THIRD MURDERER.]

FIRST MURDERER. But who did bid thee join with us?

THIRD MURDERER. Macbeth.°

SECOND MURDERER. He needs not our mistrust; since he
delivers°
Our offices° and what we have to do
To the direction just.°

FIRST MURDERER. Then stand with us.
5 The west yet glimmers with some streaks of day.
Now spurs the lated° traveler apace°
To gain the timely inn,° and near approaches
The subject of our watch.

THIRD MURDERER. Hark! I hear horses.

BANQUO. [*Calls from offstage.*] Give us a light there, ho!

SECOND MURDERER. Then 'tis he. The rest
10 That are within the note of expectation°
Already are i' th' court.

FIRST MURDERER. His horses go about.°

THIRD MURDERER. Almost a mile: but he does usually—
So all men do—from hence to th' palace gate
Make it their walk.

A Bard for the Ages *How does Shakespeare signal a change in Macbeth's relationship with his wife in these lines?* **2**

A Bard for the Ages *Why do you think Shakespeare hides the identity of this mysterious third murderer?* **3**

Side notes:

45 **chuck:** a term of endearment.
46 **seeling:** eye-closing.
47 **Scarf up:** blindfold.

49 **that great bond:** Banquo's and Fleance's lease on life.

51 **rooky:** black and full of rooks (birds similar to crows).

1 **Macbeth:** This third murderer is probably a spy sent by Macbeth to make sure the other murderers carry out his orders.
2 **delivers:** reports.
3 **offices:** duties.
4 **To . . . just:** in exact accordance with our instructions.

6 **lated:** belated. **apace:** at a swift pace.
7 **gain . . . inn:** reach a welcome inn.

10 **within . . . expectation:** included on the list of expected guests.
11 **go about:** take a roundabout route (rather than heading directly to the palace).

Teach

Foil **Answer:** *Banquo's dying words confirm his noble nature: his final concern is not for himself but for the safety of his son.*

ENGLISH LEARNERS Remind English learners that some words have multiple meanings and that the context will often help them deduce the correct meaning. **Ask:** Is Banquo begging his son to fly like a bird? *(no)* What is he telling Fleance to do? *(run away)* Tell students that this meaning of *fly* is not used in contemporary English; instead, the word *flee* is used.

Writer's Technique ☆

Plot At the end of scene 3, Macbeth has "won the battle, but lost the war." He has won a tactical, or short-term, victory but has faltered strategically, costing him in the long run. Banquo's death removes an immediate concern. However, Fleance's escape means that the witches' prophecy concerning Banquo's descendants can still come true.

[*BANQUO and FLEANCE, carrying a torch, enter on foot.*]

SECOND MURDERER.   A light, a light!

THIRD MURDERER.   'Tis he.

FIRST MURDERER.   Stand to 't.

15   BANQUO.   It will be rain tonight.

FIRST MURDERER.   Let it come down.

[*They attack* BANQUO.]

BANQUO.   O, treachery! Fly, good Fleance, fly, fly, fly!

☆ [FLEANCE *escapes.*]

      Thou mayst revenge. O slave! [BANQUO *dies.*]

THIRD MURDERER.   Who did strike out the light?

FIRST MURDERER.   Was 't not the way?°   **18 Was . . . way:** Was it not the right course of action?

THIRD MURDERER.   There's but one down; the son is fled.

20   SECOND MURDERER.   We have lost best half of our affair.

FIRST MURDERER.   Well, let's away and say how much is done. ☆

[*The* MURDERERS *exit.*]

SCENE 4. The palace at Forres.

[*A banquet has been prepared in a hall of the royal palace.* MACBETH *and* LADY MACBETH *enter with* ROSS, LENNOX, *and other* LORDS *and their* ATTENDANTS.]

MACBETH.   You know your own degrees; sit down:°
     At first and last, the hearty welcome.

1 You . . . down: At state banquets, guests were seated according to their ranks (**degrees**).

LORDS.   Thanks to your Majesty.

MACBETH.   Ourself will mingle with society
5   And play the humble host.
     Our hostess keeps her state,° but in best time
     We will require° her welcome.

6 keeps her state: remains in the chair designated for the queen.
7 require: request.

LADY MACBETH.   Pronounce it for me, sir, to all our friends,
     For my heart speaks they are welcome.

[*The first* MURDERER *enters and stands near the door.*]

10   MACBETH.   See, they encounter thee with their hearts' thanks.
     Both sides are even:° here I'll sit i' th' midst:
     Be large in mirth; anon we'll drink a measure°
     The table round. [*He goes to the* MURDERER *at the door.*]
      There's blood upon thy face.

11 Both sides are even: There are equal numbers on both sides of the table.
12 measure: toast.

---

1   **Foil** *How do Banquo's dying words leave a lasting impression of his character in the mind of the audience?*

Reading Practice

SPIRAL REVIEW **Visualize** Encourage students to visualize scenes that involve many characters. Suggest that students follow these steps:

- Jot down words and phrases that indicate positions of people and objects in the scene
- Pay close attention to stage directions and consider how they change characters' positions and relationships

- Try to imagine how all of the characters react to what is happening, not just the characters who are speaking

Some students might decide to create a paper stage design and use cardboard squares to represent characters.

The Banquet Scene from Macbeth, 1840s. Daniel Maclise. Oil on canvas. The Garrick Club, London.

View the Art Maclise was one of the most influential English painters of his time. How does the painting reflect the chaos caused by Macbeth's mad ramblings?

MURDERER. 'Tis Banquo's then.

15   MACBETH. 'Tis better thee without than he within.°
        Is he dispatched?

MURDERER. My lord, his throat is cut; that I did for him.

MACBETH. Thou art the best o' th' cutthroats.
        Yet he's good that did the like for Fleance;
20   If thou didst it, thou art the nonpareil.°

MURDERER. Most royal sir, Fleance is 'scaped.

MACBETH. [*Aside.*] Then comes my fit° again: I had else been
            perfect,
        Whole as the marble, founded as the rock,
        As broad and general as the casing air:°
25   But now I am cabined, cribbed, confined, bound in
        To saucy° doubts and fears. [*To the* MURDERER.]—But
            Banquo's safe?

MURDERER. Ay, my good lord: safe in a ditch he bides,°
        With twenty trenchèd° gashes on his head,
        The least a death to nature.°

MACBETH.   Thanks for that.

2

15 'Tis ... within: It is better on your face than in his body.

20 **nonpareil:** one without equal.

22 **fit:** violent disorder.

24 **As broad . . . air:** as free and unrestrained as the surrounding air.

26 **saucy:** insolent.

27 **bides:** remains.
28 **trenchèd:** cut.
29 **a death to nature:** enough to kill a man.

MACBETH, ACT 3, SCENE 4 **351**

Foil **Answer:** *Macbeth realizes that he cannot control the future. A time may come when Fleance will stalk him, seeking revenge for his father's murder.*

Foil **Answer:** *The ghost takes the royal seat to symbolize that Banquo's descendants will inherit Macbeth's throne.*

Literary History ☆

Ghosts on Stage Shakespeare varied his depictions of ghosts in his plays. In *Hamlet*, the ghost of Hamlet's murdered father is visible to his son as well as other characters. The ghost of Julius Caesar appears to Brutus when he is alone. In *Richard III*, the title character is visited by the ghosts of those he has killed. Some writers create ghosts that are visible to only one character as a basis for farce or comedy, as in Noel Coward's *Blithe Spirit*, in which the ghost of a deceased wife haunts a man after he has remarried.

30   [*Aside.*] There the grown serpent lies; the worm that's fled
    Hath nature that in time will venom breed,
    No teeth for th' present. [*To the* MURDERER.]—Get thee gone.
      Tomorrow
    We'll hear ourselves° again. [*The* MURDERER *exits.*]

LADY MACBETH.   My royal lord,
    You do not give the cheer.° The feast is sold
35   That is not often vouched, while 'tis a-making,
    'Tis given with welcome.° To feed were best at home;
    From thence,° the sauce to meat is ceremony;°
    Meeting were bare without it.

[*The* GHOST OF BANQUO *enters and sits in* MACBETH's *place.*] ☆

MACBETH.   Sweet remembrancer!
    Now good digestion wait on° appetite,
40   And health on both!

LENNOX.   May 't please your Highness sit.

MACBETH. Here had we now our country's honor roofed,°
    Were the graced person of our Banquo present—
    Who may I rather challenge for unkindness
    Than pity for mischance!°

ROSS.   His absence, sir,
45   Lays blame upon his promise. Please 't your Highness
    To grace us with your royal company?

[MACBETH *looks at his chair and sees the* GHOST.]

MACBETH. The table's full.

LENNOX.   Here is a place reserved, sir.

MACBETH. Where?

LENNOX. [*Indicating the place where* MACBETH *sees the* GHOST.]
    Here, my good lord. What is 't that moves your Highness?

50   MACBETH. Which of you have done this?°

LORDS.   What, my good lord?

MACBETH. Thou canst not say I did it. Never shake
    Thy gory locks at me.

ROSS. Gentlemen, rise, his Highness is not well.

LADY MACBETH. Sit, worthy friends. My lord is often thus,
55   And hath been from his youth. Pray you, keep seat.

---

1 Foil *Why does the thought of Banquo's son make Macbeth uneasy?*

2 Foil *Why does the ghost of Banquo sit in Macbeth's place?*

33 hear ourselves: discuss the matter.

34 give the cheer: provide your guests with hospitality.

34–36 The feast . . . welcome: A feast where the guests are not made to feel welcome is no better than a meal sold at an inn.
37 From thence: away from home. **ceremony:** courtesy.

39 wait on: serve.

41 Here . . . roofed: we would now have all of Scotland's noblemen under one roof.

43–44 Who . . . mischance: Macbeth says that he hopes Banquo's absence is caused by discourtesy rather than an accident.

50 done this: killed Banquo.

Writing Practice

Setting Details Shakespeare uses setting to reinforce theme through careful selection of details concerning time of day, weather, and images. Have students identify examples of this craft in Act 3.

Students can practice selecting their own details of setting by responding to the following writing prompt:

- Write a descriptive paragraph in which Macbeth is content with the honors granted to him by King Duncan. He is greeting his friend and fellow hero, Banquo, who has just arrived for a feast. Select details that enhance the atmosphere of your scene.

The fit is momentary; upon a thought°
He will again be well. If much you note him,
You shall offend him and extend his passion.°
Feed, and regard him not. [*To* MACBETH.]—Are you a man?

60   MACBETH.   Ay, and a bold one, that dare look on that
Which might **appall** the devil.

LADY MACBETH.   O proper stuff!°
This is the very painting of your fear.
This is the air-drawn dagger which, you said,
Led you to Duncan. O, these flaws° and starts,
65   Impostors to true fear, would well become
A woman's story at a winter's fire,
Authorized by her grandam.° Shame itself!
Why do you make such faces? When all's done,
You look but on a stool.

MACBETH.   Prithee, see there!
70   Behold! Look! Lo! [*To the* GHOST.] How say you?
Why, what care I? If thou canst nod, speak too.
If charnel houses° and our graves must send
Those that we bury back, our monuments
Shall be the maws of kites.° [*The* GHOST *vanishes.*]

LADY MACBETH.   What, quite unmanned in folly?

75   MACBETH.   If I stand here, I saw him.

LADY MACBETH.   Fie, for shame!

MACBETH.   Blood hath been shed ere now, i' th' olden time,
Ere humane statute purged the gentle weal;°
Ay, and since too, murders have been performed
Too terrible for the ear. The times has been
80   That, when the brains were out, the man would die,
And there an end; but now they rise again,
With twenty mortal murders on their crowns,°
And push us from our stools. This is more strange
Than such a murder is.

LADY MACBETH.   My worthy lord,
85   Your noble friends do lack you.

MACBETH.   I do forget.
Do not muse at me, my most worthy friends;

A Bard for the Ages *What does Shakespeare suggest about the power of evil in this passage?* **4**

Vocabulary

appall (ə pôl′) *v.* to fill with horror and shock

---

56 **upon a thought:** in a moment.

58 **extend his passion:** prolong his suffering.

61 **proper stuff:** nonsense.

64 **flaws:** emotional outbursts.

67 **Authorized . . . grandam:** passed down from her grandmother.

72 **charnel houses:** buildings where bones dug up from old graves were stored.
73–74 **our . . . kites:** our tombs will be the stomachs of birds of prey.

77 **Ere . . . weal:** before human laws cleansed the community of violence.

82 **mortal . . . crowns:** deadly wounds on their heads.

3

Teach

Reading Strategy **3**

Analyze Argument
Ask: How does Lady Macbeth try to persuade her husband to control his actions? (*She accuses him of giving in to his fears and calls him womanly.*) Why is Macbeth not persuaded by her argument? (*He is terrified by the ghost.*)

(**ENGLISH LEARNERS**) Have English learners read line 62 aloud. **Ask:** Is Lady Macbeth talking about an actual painting or is she using a figure of speech? (*figure of speech*) What does Lady Macbeth mean by "this is the very painting of your fear"? (*You are imagining a vision of the thing you fear.*)

Big Idea **4**

A Bard for the Ages
Answer: *The violation of the natural, moral order disrupts the supernatural order. As a result of Macbeth's crime, even the dead do not follow the normal course of nature.*

Approaching Level
DIFFERENTIATED INSTRUCTION

Emerging During scene 4, Lady Macbeth has two distinct tones: one for talking with her guests and one for her husband. Have student teams practice reading this scene aloud, using tone of voice for dramatic effect. For example, a student playing Lady Macbeth might whisper roughly when addressing Macbeth.

English Learners
DIFFERENTIATED INSTRUCTION

Intermediate Discuss Lady Macbeth's urgent need to explain her husband's strange behavior. Lady Macbeth knows that she must convince these powerful men that Macbeth is merely sick. Any sign of mental weakness could quickly become the motivation for a coup.

Teach

Foil **Answer:** *Macbeth's speech calls for Banquo's appearance, and the ghost ironically appears at his request.*

View the Art ★

The Princess's Theatre was a theater in London's West End that burned down in 1829 but was rebuilt in 1840–1841. The theater was demolished in 1931, and the site has been occupied by various retail stores since then.

The Banquet (Act 3, scene 4), *Macbeth* production at the Princess's Theatre, 1901. Victoria & Albert Museum, London. ★

I have a strange infirmity, which is nothing
To those that know me. Come, love and health to all!
Then I'll sit down. Give me some wine, fill full.

[The GHOST *reappears, but* MACBETH *does not notice him at once.]*

90   I drink to th' general joy o' th' whole table,
    And to our dear friend Banquo, whom we miss;
    Would he were here! To all and him we thirst,°
    And all to all.

  LORDS.   Our duties, and the pledge.

  MACBETH. *[To the* GHOST.] Avaunt!° and quit my sight! Let
    the earth hide thee!
95   Thy bones are marrowless, thy blood is cold;
    Thou hast no speculation° in those eyes
    Which thou dost glare with.

  LADY MACBETH.   Think of this, good peers,
    But as a thing of custom;° 'tis no other.
    Only it spoils the pleasure of the time.

100 MACBETH. What man dare, I dare.
    Approach thou like the rugged Russian bear,
    The armed rhinoceros, or th' Hyrcan° tiger;
    Take any shape but that,° and my firm nerves
    Shall never tremble. Or be alive again,
105   And dare me to the desert° with thy sword.
    If trembling I inhabit then, protest me
    The baby of a girl.° Hence, horrible shadow!
    Unreal mock'ry, hence! *[The* GHOST *vanishes again.]*
          Why, so: being gone,

92 thirst: wish to drink.

94 Avaunt: Begone!

96 speculation: vision.

98 thing of custom: a customary occurrence.

102 Hyrcan: from Hyrcania, an ancient province near the Caspian Sea.
103 that: Banquo's shape.
105 the desert: an uninhabited place.

106–107 If . . . girl: If I tremble, then call me a baby girl.

1 Foil *What is ironic about Macbeth's speech?*

Vocabulary Practice

Shakespeare's Coinages Shakespeare was an innovative writer who created, or coined, many words that are part of contemporary English. For example, the use of the word *unreal* in line 108 on this page is the first known use of this word. Other terms coined in *Macbeth* include *assassination* (Act 1, scene 7, line 2) and *drugged* (Act 2, scene 2, line 6). Have students use available technology to compile a list of additional words coined by Shakespeare. Students might also research the etymology of words coined by Shakespeare and make a generalization about their linguistic sources.

I am a man again. Pray you, sit still.

110 **LADY MACBETH.** You have displaced the mirth, broke the good
meeting,
With most admired disorder.°

MACBETH. Can such things be,
And overcome° us like a summer's cloud,
Without our special wonder? You make me strange
115 Even to the disposition that I owe,°
When now I think you can behold such sights,
And keep the natural ruby of your cheeks,
When mine is blanched with fear.

ROSS. What sights, my lord?

LADY MACBETH. I pray you, speak not: he grows worse and
worse;
Question enrages him: at once, good night.
120 Stand not upon the order of your going,°
But go at once.

LENNOX. Good night; and better health
Attend his Majesty!

LADY MACBETH. A kind good night to all!

[*Everyone exits except MACBETH and LADY MACBETH.*]

MACBETH. It will have blood, they say: blood will have blood.
Stones have been known to move and trees to speak;
125 Augures and understood relations have
By maggot-pies and choughs and rooks brought forth
The secret'st man of blood.° What is the night?

LADY MACBETH. Almost at odds with morning,° which is
which.

MACBETH. How say'st thou, that Macduff denies his person
130 At our great bidding?

LADY MACBETH. Did you send to him, sir?

MACBETH. I hear it by the way, but I will send:
There's not a one of them but in his house
I keep a servant fee'd.° I will tomorrow,
And betimes° I will, to the weird sisters:
135 More shall they speak, for now I am bent° to know
By the worst means the worst. For mine own good

Foil *Why does Macbeth begin to suspect Macduff?* **3**

A Bard for the Ages *How does Shakespeare suggest that Macbeth's character is beginning to crumble in these lines?* **4**

111 admired disorder: amazing lack of self-control.

112 overcome: pass over.

113–114 You . . . owe: You make me feel like a stranger to my own nature.

120 Stand . . . going: Do not wait to leave in order of your rank.

125–127 Augures . . . blood: Macbeth says that the cries of magpies (**maggot-pies**) and birds of the crow family (**choughs**) have provided omens and revealed hidden relationships that exposed even the most concealed murderers.
128 Almost . . . morning: almost midnight.

133 fee'd: paid to inform me.
134 betimes: early.
135 bent: determined.

Teach

Big Idea 2

A Bard for the Ages
Say: "Blood will have blood" has become a well-known saying. How do you think this phrase might be used outside the context of this play? (*The phrase can reflect any situation in which revenge is sought. One violent, or "bloody" act often leads to another in retaliation.*)

[ENGLISH LEARNERS] Explain to English learners the meaning of "blood for blood" and ask them to think of idioms in their home languages that mean the same thing (i.e. *ojo por ojo* "an eye for an eye" in Spanish). Have students discuss the way the concept of revenge, or blood debt, exists across cultures.

Literary Element 3

Foil **Answer:** *Macbeth mistrusts all his subjects, particularly Macduff for failing to attend the coronation and the royal banquet. Macduff is someone whom Macbeth cannot control.*

Big Idea 4

A Bard for the Ages
Answer: *Macbeth has become superstitious and overtly insecure in his power. He decides to seek out the agents of evil who previously sought him out and, in doing so, shows that he is losing control.*

[APPROACHING] For approaching-level students, **ask:** Who are the "weird sisters" (line 134)? (*the three witches*) What does he think they can give him? (*more information*)

English Learners
DIFFERENTIATED INSTRUCTION

Intermediate Help students avoid spending time trying to memorize archaic terms. As students compile lists of vocabulary, encourage them to talk with native English speakers to help determine which new words are common today and which words are archaic.

Approaching Level
DIFFERENTIATED INSTRUCTION

Established Explain to approaching-level students that Shakespeare's language is often outdated. For example, Lady Macbeth says "Question enrages him," meaning "Asking him questions makes him angry." **Say:** Adopt a flexible attitude as you read, interpreting these subtle differences.

Foil **Ask:** Will Hecate function as a foil for Macbeth? *(Possibly but it is unlikely since others like Banquo and MacDuff serve as better foils.)* Is it possible that Hecate serves as a foil for the three witches? *(Yes)* Which traits do these characters share and which are different? *(All the characters perform witchcraft; however, the three witches have only prophesied Macbeth's destiny, while Hecate wants to have an active role in the outcome of his destiny.)*

Literary History ☆

Hecate In Greek mythology, Hecate was a moon goddess frequently found in the company of Hades, the god of the underworld. She could cast spells to bring spirits of the dead back to earth. She took special delight in tormenting people.

All causes shall give way.° I am in blood
Stepped in so far that, should I wade no more,
Returning were as tedious as go o'er.°
140   Strange things I have in head that will to hand,°
Which must be acted ere they may be scanned.°

LADY MACBETH. You lack the season of all natures,° sleep.

MACBETH. Come, we'll to sleep. My strange and self-abuse°
Is the initiate fear that wants hard use.°
145   We are yet but young in deed.

    [*They exit.*]

SCENE 5. A heath.

[*There is thunder and lightning on a heath as the* THREE WITCHES *enter and meet* HECATE, *the goddess of witchcraft.*] **1**

    FIRST WITCH. Why, how now, Hecate! you look angerly.

    HECATE. Have I not reason, beldams° as you are,
       Saucy and overbold? How did you dare
       To trade and traffic with Macbeth
5   In riddles and affairs of death;
       And I, the mistress of your charms,
       The close contriver° of all harms,
       Was never called to bear my part,
       Or show the glory of our art?
10   And, which is worse, all you have done
       Hath been but for a wayward son,
       Spiteful and wrathful; who, as others do,
       Loves for his own ends, not for you.
       But make **amends** now: get you gone,
15   And at the pit of Acheron°
       Meet me i' th' morning: thither he
       Will come to know his destiny.
       Your vessels and your spells provide,
       Your charms and everything beside.
20   I am for th' air; this night I'll spend
       Unto a dismal° and a fatal end:
       Great business must be wrought ere noon.
       Upon the corner of the moon
       There hangs a vap'rous drop profound;°
25   I'll catch it ere it come to ground:
       And that distilled by magic sleights°
       Shall raise such artificial sprites°

> **Vocabulary**
>
> **amends** (ə mendz′) *n.* something done or given to make up for injury, loss, etc.

136–137 For mine . . . way: My own welfare takes precedence over all other interests.
139 go o'er: reaching the other shore.
140 will to hand: demand to be carried out.
141 scanned: examined.
142 season of all natures: preservative of all living things.
143 strange and self-abuse: remarkable self-delusion.
144 the initiate . . . use: the fear of a beginner who needs to be hardened by experience.

2 beldams: hags.

7 close contriver: secret plotter.

15 Acheron: a river in the underworld in Greek mythology.

21 dismal: disastrous.

24 profound: with important qualities.

26 sleights: devices.
27 artificial sprites: spirits created by magic arts.

Analyze Literary Periods The introduction of Hecate at this point has puzzled many scholars. Some believe that scene 5 was added by the playwright Thomas Middleton. **Ask:** Why do you think another writer might have added material to Shakespeare's play? *(The producer might have requested more scenes for a play that was considered short. Additional supernatural characters might have been added because these characters were popular.)* Students should research and report on the methods scholars use to determine the authenticity of texts such as Shakespeare's. Alternatively, students may research and report on Thomas Middleton as a playwright and his possible involvement in adding the character of Hecate into scene 5 of *Macbeth*.

As by the strength of their illusion
Shall draw him on to his confusion.°
30 He shall spurn fate, scorn death, and bear
His hopes 'bove wisdom, grace, and fear:
And you all know security°
Is mortals' chiefest enemy.

[*Music and a song are heard offstage.* HECATE *is called away.*]

Hark! I am called; my little spirit,° see,
35 Sits in a foggy cloud and stays for me.

[HECATE *exits*.]

FIRST WITCH. Come, let's make haste; she'll soon be back
again.

[*The* WITCHES *exit quickly.*]

SCENE 6. The palace at Forres.

[LENNOX *and another* LORD *enter a room in the palace.*]

LENNOX. My former speeches have but hit° your thoughts,
Which can interpret farther.° Only I say
Things have been strangely borne.° The gracious Duncan
Was pitied of Macbeth: marry,° he was dead.°
5 And the right-valiant Banquo walked too late;
Whom, you may say, if 't please you, Fleance killed,
For Fleance fled. Men must not walk too late.
Who cannot want the thought,° how monstrous
It was for Malcolm and for Donalbain
10 To kill their gracious father? Damnèd fact!°
How it did grieve Macbeth! Did he not straight,
In pious rage, the two delinquents tear,
That were the slaves of drink and thralls° of sleep?
Was not that nobly done? Ay, and wisely too;
15 For 'twould have angered any heart alive
To hear the men deny 't. So that I say
He has borne all things well:° and I do think
That, had he Duncan's sons under his key—
As, an 't° please heaven, he shall not—they should find
20 What 'twere to kill a father. So should Fleance.
But, peace! for from broad words,° and 'cause he failed
His presence at the tyrant's feast, I hear,
Macduff lives in disgrace. Sir, can you tell

---

29 **confusion:** ruin.

32 **security:** overconfidence.

34 **little spirit:** Hecate's helper.

1 **but hit:** only agreed with.

2 **interpret farther:** draw further conclusions.
3 **borne:** managed.
3–4 **The . . . dead:** Here, Lennox begins to mock Macbeth's explanations of the recent deaths.
4 **marry:** by the Virgin Mary (a mild oath similar to *indeed*).
8 **Who . . . thought:** who cannot help thinking.

10 **fact:** deed, crime.

13 **thralls:** slaves.

17 **borne . . . well:** managed everything cunningly.

19 **an 't:** if it.

21 **from broad words:** as a result of unrestrained speech.

A Bard for the Ages *Why does Shakespeare include these lines?* **2**

Evaluate Style *What effect does the verbal irony in Lennox's speech have?* **3**

Teach

Big Idea   2

A Bard for the Ages
Answer: *These lines suggest that overconfident people, such as Macbeth, will make fatal mistakes.*

Reading Strategy   3

Evaluate Style Answer: *By stating the opposite of what he means, Lennox not only protects himself from eavesdropping spies but subverts Macbeth's evil in a cunning way.*

(APPROACHING) Explain to approaching-level students that in addition to providing a note of irony and shining a spotlight on Macbeth's hypocrisy, Lennox's speech provides a neat summary of the play's main events and the characters involved in them. **Ask:** Who was killed first? *(Duncan)* Who is accused of killing Duncan? *(his sons Malcolm and Donalbain).* Continue asking factual questions about the speech's content, as a memory aid to students.

English Learners

DIFFERENTIATED INSTRUCTION

Beginning Have students summarize the action in Act III in numbered steps, using verbs in the past tense. First, model the activity for students by narrating the first few steps in the action of Act II. Show an example by writing on the board: *1. Macbeth decided he must have Banquo killed.* After they have written their summaries, have students write a summary in a full paragraph, introducing their sentences with sequence words such as *first, then, next, after that,* etc. Have volunteers read their summaries; encourage students to pay attention to the forms and pronunciation of the verbs.

Teach

Literary Element ⟨1⟩

Foil Answer: *King Edward I is pious and graceful, while Macbeth is neither.*

⟨ENGLISH LEARNERS⟩ For English learners, point out the word *malevolence* in line 28. Ask students who are unfamiliar with this word, to look the meaning up in a standard dictionary. *(The quality or state of being harmful or evil)* Some Spanish-speaking students may recognize the prefix *mal-* as a cognate to *malo,* which means "bad" in Spanish.

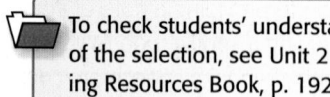 To check students' understanding of the selection, see Unit 2 Teaching Resources Book, p. 192.

Where he bestows himself?

LORD.   The son of Duncan,
25   From whom this tyrant holds the due of birth,°
     Lives in the English court, and is received
     Of the most pious Edward° with such grace
     That the malevolence of fortune nothing
     Takes from his high respect.° Thither Macduff
30   Is gone to pray the holy King, upon his aid
     To wake Northumberland° and warlike Siward;°
     That by the help of these, with Him above
     To ratify the work, we may again
     Give to our tables meat, sleep to our nights,
35   Free from our feasts and banquets bloody knives,°
     Do faithful homage and receive free honors:°
     All which we pine for now. And this report
     Hath so exasperate the King° that he
     Prepares for some attempt of war.

LENNOX.   Sent he to Macduff?

40   LORD. He did: and with an absolute "Sir, not I,"
     The cloudy messenger turns me his back,
     And hums, as who should say "You'll rue the time
     That clogs me with this answer."°

LENNOX.   And that well might
     Advise him to a caution, t' hold what distance
45   His wisdom can provide.° Some holy angel
     Fly to the court of England and unfold°
     His message ere he come, that a swift blessing
     May soon return to this our suffering country
     Under a hand accursed!

LORD.   I'll send my prayers with him.

     [*They exit.*]

---

25 holds . . . birth: withholds his birthright (the throne).

27 Edward: Edward the Confessor, King of England from 1042–1066.

28–29 That . . . respect: that Malcolm's misfortune has not diminished the great respect he is shown.

29–31 Thither . . . Siward: The Lord says that Macduff has gone to ask Edward to arouse Siward, Earl of **Northumberland** (a northern English county), to fight on Malcolm's behalf.

35 Free . . . knives: free our feasts and banquets from bloody knives.

36 free honors: the honors of free men (not enslaved to a tyrant).

38 exasperate the King: angered Macbeth.

40–43 with an . . . answer: When Macduff refused to obey the order to appear before Macbeth, the gloomy messenger turned and made a noise expressing his indignation and suggesting that Macduff will regret burdening him with such a response.

44–45 Advise . . . provide: warn him to be cautious and keep a safe distance from Macbeth.

46 unfold: reveal.

⟨**1**⟩ Foil *How does Edward I contrast with Macbeth?*

Reading Practice

⟨SPIRAL REVIEW⟩ **Side Notes** Direct students' attention to the Lord's speech (lines 24–39 of Scene 6). Have each student silently read over the speech. **Ask:** What is the purpose of this speech? *(To inform the audience that Macduff plans to go to war with Macbeth)* **Ask:** Which side note provides the best support for this interpretation? *(The side note for lines 29-31.)* Then, assign a volunteer the previous speech, made by Lennox. **Ask:** What is the purpose of this speech? *(To hold Macbeth responsible for all of the recent murders)* **Ask:** Which side note provides the best support for this interpretation? *(The side note for lines 3-4.)*

After You Read

Respond and Think Critically

Respond and Interpret

1. Did any of the events in Act 3 surprise you? Explain why or why not.

2. (a)Describe the murder plot that Macbeth devises against Banquo. (b)How is it different from the murder plot against Duncan? What do these differences suggest to you about Macbeth's character?

3. (a)Which intended victim of Macbeth's plot manages to escape? (b)What conflicts might this character cause for Macbeth in the future?

Analyze and Evaluate

4. What signs are there in this act that Macbeth's conscience is troubling him?

5. (a)What does Lennox's sarcastic tone in scene 6, lines 1–24, suggest about Macbeth's future as king? (b)Does his tone seem realistic here?

6. How has the relationship between Macbeth and Lady Macbeth changed in this act?

Connect

7. **Big Idea** **A Bard for the Ages** Many critics believe that another author may have written scene 5 after Shakespeare's death. In your opinion, does the scene enhance the play? Explain why or why not.

8. **Connect to Today** If the host of a banquet today were to behave as Macbeth did, how might the guests react?

Literary Element Foil

A **foil** character serves two main purposes: to highlight flaws in the main character's personality and to suggest what the main character might have been like if these flaws had not been present.

1. In what significant ways is Banquo similar to and different from Macbeth?

2. What flaws in Macbeth's character do these differences help reveal?

Writing

Write a Letter As Act 3 progresses, Macbeth finds himself ever deeper in trouble. Suppose you are a friend of his whom he has asked for advice. What should you tell him to do? Write a letter to Macbeth, suggesting ways for him solve his problems. If possible, refer to events in the play to support your ideas.

Reading Strategy Evaluate Style

The central action of Act 3 involves Macbeth's inward and outward responses to the murder of Banquo. Does Shakespeare's choice of words, imagery, and figurative language effectively express Macbeth's guilt and desperation? Explain why or why not, using examples from the text to support your conclusion.

Vocabulary Practice

Practice with Antonyms An antonym is a word that has a meaning opposite to that of another word. With a partner, match each bold-faced vocabulary word below with its antonym. Use a thesaurus or dictionary to check your answers. You will not use all the answer choices.

1. indissoluble
2. incensed
3. jovial
4. appall
5. amends

a. melancholy
b. temporary
c. damages
d. annoyance
e. soothe
f. placated
g. ironclad

MACBETH, ACT 3 **359**

After You Read

Assess

1. Students' answers will vary.

2. (a) Hired assassins will ambush Banquo and his son. (b) Macbeth corrupts two desperate men to do his killing for him. This signals Macbeth's moral deterioration.

3. (a) Fleance (b) His escape means that the prophecy concerning Banquo's descendants can still come true.

4. He makes plans to visit the witches and implies that he will commit more murders

5. (a) His days as king could be limited. (b) Students' answers will vary.

6. Lady Macbeth is no longer the aggressive one.

7. Students' answers will vary.

8. They might be frightened and might head for the exit.

Vocabulary

1. b 2. f 3. a 4. e 5. c

Writing

Students' letters should advise Macbeth on how to solve his problem and cite references to the text to support their ideas.

 For grammar practice, see Unit 2 Teaching Resources Book, p. 191.

 For additional assessment, see Assessment Resources, pp. 111–112.

Progress Check

Can students evaluate style?

If No → See Unit 2 Teaching Resources Book, p. 188.

Literary Element

1. Both are bold and ambitious, but Banquo is prudent and honorable.

2. Macbeth allows blind ambition to overcome his better judgment.

Reading Strategy

Students should support their argument with examples. They may mention sleep and dreams (scene 2 lines 13–26), scorpions (scene 2 line 37), and blood and decay (scene 4, lines 69–74).

Before You Read

Focus

Summary

Hecate and the witches warn Macbeth to beware of Macduff. Macbeth sends hirelings to murder Macduff's family. In England, Macduff meets with Malcolm and asks him to claim the throne. Malcolm tests Macduff, but once assured of Macduff's honesty, he reveals his true nature. They learn of the murders of Macduff's family and pledge to unseat Macbeth.

 For summaries in languages other than English, see Unit 2 Teaching Resources Book, pp. 194–199.

Vocabulary

Register Tell students that *register* refers to the types of words a person uses in different situations. Remind them of the distinction between the formal and informal registers and ask whether the vocabulary words would most likely be used in formal or informal speech. Have students rewrite the sample sentences in the informal register.

Before You Read

Macbeth, Act 4

Build Background

This act begins with the famous "cauldron scene," in which the witches prepare a ghastly brew. According to the critic D. J. Palmer, "This scene is the climactic point of the play's use of spectacle: the cauldron itself is an image traditionally associated with hell, and each of the three Apparitions in turn rises and descends from within it...." Shakespeare's audience would have thought of witches as grotesque hags possessed by evil spirits.

Literary Element Plot

A **plot** is the sequence of events in a narrative work. A plot may begin with **exposition,** or the introduction of the characters, setting, and conflict. The **rising action** adds complications to the conflicts, leading to the **climax,** or emotional high point. The climax gives way rapidly to its logical result in the **falling action,** and finally to the **resolution** (sometimes called the **dénouement**) in which the final outcome is revealed. As you read, ask yourself, At what stage is the plot now?

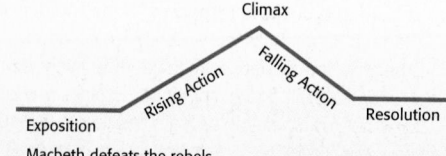

Climax

Rising Action · Falling Action

Exposition — Macbeth defeats the rebels.

Resolution

Reading Strategy Make and Verify Predictions

Predicting is making an educated guess about what will happen in a selection. When you predict, you use your prior knowledge and the clues you gather from the selection to create an expectation for what you will read. As you read, ask yourself, What do I think is going to happen in the play?

Tip: Predicting Use a chart to list clues from the play and the predictions you make. Adjust your predictions if they don't fit what you learn.

Clues	Predictions
An apparition warns Macbeth about Macduff.	Macbeth vows to kill Macduff.

360 UNIT 2   THE ENGLISH RENAISSANCE

Learning Objectives

For pages 360–379

In studying this text, you will focus on the following objectives:

Literary Study: Analyzing plot.

Reading: Making and verifying predictions.

Writing: Writing a dramatic monologue.

Vocabulary

pernicious (pər nish′ əs) *adj.* destructive; deadly; p. 366 *Parents feared that pernicious fumes from the toxic dump were harmful.*

exploit (eks′ ploit) *n.* a bold deed; p. 367 *The exploits of heroes can reveal the true meaning of courage.*

redress (ri dres′) *v.* to set right; remedy; p. 371 *I tried to redress his complaint by replacing the lost book.*

avarice (av′ ər is) *n.* greed; p. 373 *King Midas's avarice for gold brought about his downfall.*

pertain (pər tān′) *v.* to be connected to or have relevance to; p. 377 *I'll only answer questions that pertain to this assignment.*

Selection Skills

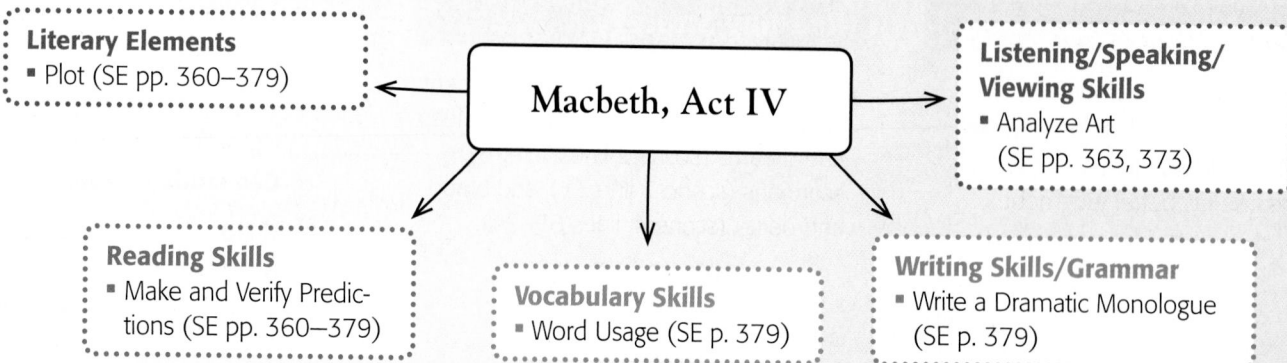

Literary Elements
- Plot (SE pp. 360–379)

Macbeth, Act IV

Listening/Speaking/ Viewing Skills
- Analyze Art (SE pp. 363, 373)

Reading Skills
- Make and Verify Predictions (SE pp. 360–379)

Vocabulary Skills
- Word Usage (SE p. 379)

Writing Skills/Grammar
- Write a Dramatic Monologue (SE p. 379)

360

ACT 4

SCENE 1. A deserted place.

[It is thundering as the THREE WITCHES enter and stand around a large caldron, or pot, in their deserted meeting place.]

    FIRST WITCH. Thrice the brinded cat hath mewed.

    SECOND WITCH. Thrice and once the hedge-pig whined.°

    THIRD WITCH. Harpier° cries. 'Tis time, 'tis time.

    FIRST WITCH. Round about the caldron go:

5   In the poisoned entrails throw.

[The WITCHES circle the caldron, and as each mentions an item, she throws it into the pot.]

      Toad, that under cold stone
      Days and nights has thirty-one
      Swelt'red venom sleeping got,°
      Boil thou first i' th' charmèd pot.

10   ALL. Double, double, toil and trouble;
      Fire burn and caldron bubble.

    SECOND WITCH. Fillet of a fenny snake,°
      In the caldron boil and bake;
      Eye of newt and toe of frog,

15   Wool of bat and tongue of dog,
      Adder's fork° and blindworm's° sting,
      Lizard's leg and howlet's° wing,
      For a charm of pow'rful trouble,
      Like a hell-broth boil and bubble.

20   ALL. Double, double, toil and trouble;
      Fire burn and caldron bubble.

    THIRD WITCH. Scale of dragon, tooth of wolf,
      Witch's mummy, maw and gulf°
      Of the ravined° salt-sea shark,

25   Root of hemlock digged i' th' dark,
      Liver of blaspheming Jew,
      Gall of goat, and slips of yew
      Slivered in the moon's eclipse,
      Nose of Turk and Tartar's lips,

30   Finger of birth-strangled babe
      Ditch-delivered by a drab,°
      Make the gruel thick and slab:°
      Add thereto a tiger's chaudron,°
      For th' ingredients of our caldron.

1–2 Thrice . . . whined: The witches respond to the calls of their familiars, which include a striped (**brinded**) cat and a hedgehog (**hedge-pig**).
3 Harpier: one of the familiar spirits attending the witches. *Harpier* is derived from *harpy*, a birdlike monster of classical mythology.

6–8 that under . . . got: which has sweated venom for thirty-one days while sleeping under a cold stone.

12 Fillet . . . snake: a slice of a snake found in marshland.

16 Adder's fork: snake's forked tongue. **blindworm:** a limbless lizard once thought to be poisonous.
17 howlet: small owl.

23 maw and gulf: stomach and gullet.
24 ravined: glutted with prey.

31 Ditch-delivered by a drab: given birth to in a ditch by a prostitute.
32 slab: sticky.
33 chaudron: entrails.

Plot *Why do you think Shakespeare shows the witches performing their satanic rites at this stage of the rising action?*

Teach

Literary Element   1

Plot **Answer:** *By showing the witches at work, Shakespeare suggests that the powers of darkness are influencing events more and more.*

ENGLISH LEARNERS English learners may find this long list of archaic terms daunting. Explain that it is not always necessary to understand each word or even each sentence in order to get the gist of the action. **Ask:** According to the stage direction after line 5, what are the witches doing? *(adding items to the pot)* What are all of the items for? *(ingredients for the potion)* So, what is the main thing you need to know about this section of the scene? *(the witches are making an evil potion)*

 For an audio recording of this selection, use Listening Library Audio CD-ROM.

English Learners

DIFFERENTIATED INSTRUCTION

Advanced Students need not look up every unfamiliar word in Shakespeare. Help them practice identifying which are essential to understanding. Ask partners to read this page and identify repeated images. Have them tell which words they will look up and which they feel they can skip.

Advanced Learners

DIFFERENTIATED INSTRUCTION

Rhymes Encourage students to read aloud sections of Act 4, scene 1, to help them recognize that the witches speak in rhyming couplets. **Ask:** What words are exact rhymes? *(trouble, bubble; snake, bake; shark, dark; etc.)* Near rhymes? *(stone, thirty-one; wolf, gulf)* Interested students can research Elizabethan pronunciation to learn about words that once rhymed but no longer do.

Teach

Imagery Shakespeare uses vivid imagery to create an atmosphere and support theme. **Ask:** What images does Macbeth use in his speech that begins on line 50? *(He describes violent storms and nature in rebellion.)* What do these images suggest about Macbeth? *(He has embraced the unnatural, turbulent world of the witches, which is associated with darkness and evil.)*

(APPROACHING) Have approaching-level students focus on the metaphor in line 52 ("Though you untie the winds"). **Ask:** What does untie mean in this metaphor? *(free, set loose)* According to Macbeth, who can set the winds loose? *(the witches)* What is he saying about the witches' power? *(They can control nature.)*

Reading Strategy   2

Make and Verify Predictions Answer: *Macbeth will ask the witches what the future holds for him.*

---

35   **ALL.** Double, double, toil and trouble;
     Fire burn and caldron bubble.

   SECOND WITCH. Cool it with a baboon's blood,
     Then the charm is firm and good.

[HECATE, *goddess of witches, enters and addresses the other* THREE WITCHES.]

   HECATE. O, well done! I commend your pains;
40   And everyone shall share i' th' gains:
     And now about the caldron sing,
     Like elves and fairies in a ring,
     Enchanting all that you put in.

[*Music and a song are heard offstage.* HECATE *exits.*]

   SECOND WITCH. By the pricking of my thumbs,°
45   Something wicked this way comes:
       Open, locks,
       Whoever knocks!

[MACBETH *enters.*]

   MACBETH. How now, you secret, black, and midnight hags!
     What is 't you do?

   ALL.   A deed without a name.

50   **MACBETH.** I conjure you, by that which you profess,°
     Howe'er you come to know it, answer me:
     Though you untie the winds and let them fight
     Against the churches; though the yesty° waves
     Confound° and swallow navigation up;
55   Though bladed corn° be lodged° and trees blown down;
     Though castles topple on their warders' heads;
     Though palaces and pyramids do slope°
     Their heads to their foundations; though the treasure
     Of nature's germens° tumble all together,
60   Even till destruction sicken, answer me
     To what I ask you.

   FIRST WITCH.   Speak.

   SECOND WITCH.   Demand.

   THIRD WITCH.   We'll answer.

   FIRST WITCH. Say, if th' hadst rather hear it from our mouths,
     Or from our masters?

   MACBETH.   Call 'em, let me see 'em.

44 By . . . thumbs: I can tell by the tingling in my thumbs.

50 by . . . profess: by the art you claim to have skill in.

53 yesty: foamy.
54 Confound: destroy.

55 bladed corn: unripe grain. **lodged:** beaten down by wind.

57 slope: bend.

59 nature's germens: the seeds of all life.

---

2 Make and Verify Predictions **What do you predict Macbeth will ask the witches?**

Reading Practice

 SMALL GROUP   SPIRAL REVIEW   **Read Aloud** This is an intensely atmospheric scene when it is performed onstage. Divide students into groups of five and have each student take one of the roles on this page. Have students practice reading the roles aloud with dramatic intonations. Remind students that Shakespeare likely intended for the witches to seem frightening and disturbed.

Once groups have had a chance to practice, you may ask them to perform for the class. Then discuss how hearing the scene altered their appreciation of it. Ask what was the effect of listening to the rhyming lines as opposed to reading them *(They lend a sing-song quality and make the words sound like a spell.)*

Teach

View the Art ★

Answer: *Accept all reasonable responses. Some students will suggest that the costumes do not match their vision of Macbeth and the witches. Others may point out that the witches' cauldron is missing.*

George Romney (1734–1802) was most successful as a portrait artist. He preferred, however, to illustrate historical events and to interpret literary works in paintings like the one shown here. His paintings reflect his talented drawing skills. His figures move with strong, natural gestures that capture spontaneous movements and emotions.

Macbeth and the Witches, 1780. George Romney. Folger Shakespeare Library, Washington, DC.

View the Art Romney's work is characterized by the natural-looking movements of his figures. How does this painting compare with your vision of the scene? ★

Advanced Learners

DIFFERENTIATED INSTRUCTION

Adaptations Shakespeare's literary influence has been far-reaching. Many of his thematic elements and plots have been used in modern entertainment. Have students find songs, novels, and other works that are clearly derived from specific elements in Shakespeare. Have students present their analysis to the class, explaining how a modern work relates to Shakespeare. Allow students to bring in visuals, props, or other media to enhance their presentations.

Teach

Plot **Ask:** How does each
of the three apparitions relate
to specific elements that have
occurred in the plot so far? *(The
first apparition, a helmeted head,
reflects Macduff, who was present
the night that Macbeth murdered
Duncan. The second apparition,
a bloody child, reflects Macbeth's
constant worries about what child
will inherit the throne. The third
apparition, a crowned child, reinforces this concern.)*

ENGLISH LEARNERS Point out
to English learners the multiple-
meaning word *issue* in line 87. Ask
students to tell you the meaning
or meanings that they already
know for the word. *(Students will
most likely say "problem or question".)* Have students read the side
note and tell you what meaning
Shakespeare intended. *(likeness,
appearance)* Then have students
look up *issue* in the dictionary
to find the other meaning of the
word that is relevant in this context
(offspring).

FIRST WITCH. Pour in sow's blood, that hath eaten
65   Her nine farrow;° grease that's sweaten°
     From the murderer's gibbet° throw
     Into the flame.

ALL.   Come, high or low,
     Thyself and office° deftly show!

*[Thunder is heard as the FIRST APPARITION, the armored head of a
warrior, appears.]*

MACBETH. Tell me, thou unknown power—

FIRST WITCH.   He knows thy thought:
70   Hear his speech, but say thou nought.

FIRST APPARITION.° Macbeth! Macbeth! Macbeth! Beware
     Macduff!
     Beware the Thane of Fife. Dismiss me: enough.

[The FIRST APPARITION disappears.]

MACBETH. Whate'er thou art, for thy good caution thanks:
     Thou has harped° my fear aright. But one word more—

75 **FIRST WITCH.** He will not be commanded. Here's another,
     More potent than the first.

[More thunder as the SECOND APPARITION, a Bloody Child, appears.]

SECOND APPARITION.° Macbeth! Macbeth! Macbeth!

MACBETH. Had I three ears, I'd hear thee.

SECOND APPARITION. Be bloody, bold, and resolute! Laugh to
     scorn
80   The pow'r of man, for none of woman born
     Shall harm Macbeth.

[The SECOND APPARITION disappears.]

MACBETH. Then live, Macduff: what need I fear of thee?
     But yet I'll make assurance double sure,
     And take a bond of fate.° Thou shalt not live;
85   That I may tell pale-hearted fear it lies,
     And sleep in spite of thunder.

*[Thunder sounds as the THIRD APPARITION, a Crowned Child with a tree
in his hand, appears.]*

           What is this,
     That rises like the issue of a king,°
     And wears upon his baby-brow the round
     And top of sovereignty?°

ALL.   Listen, but speak not to 't.

Side notes:

65 **nine farrow:** litter of nine piglets. **sweaten:** sweated.
66 **gibbet:** gallows.

68 **office:** your function.

71 **First Apparition:** The first of three ghosts whose appearance foretells Macbeth's downfall, this helmeted head probably symbolizes his confrontation with Macduff.

74 **harped:** guessed.

77 **Second Apparition:** This ghost probably represents Macduff at birth.

84 **take . . . fate:** get a guarantee from fate (by killing Macduff).

87 **rises . . . king:** rises in the likeness of a king's child.

88–89 **round . . . sovereignty:** crown.

Literary Element Practice

SPIRAL REVIEW **Meter and Rhyme Scheme** The
characters in this scene speak in different meters and rhyme schemes.
Encourage students to scan a variety of
lines from this scene. Help them see that
the witches and Hecate speak in rhymed
tetrameter (four-stress) couplets, the
apparitions speak in rhymed pentameter
(five-stress) couplets, and Macbeth and
Lennox speak in blank verse—unrhymed
lines of iambic pentameter.

Macbeth and the Witches, 1834–1835. Joseph Anton Koch. Landesmuseum Ferdinandeum, Innsbruck, Austria.

Reading Strategy   2

Make and Verify Predictions Answer:
Macbeth will probably ask the apparitions if Banquo's child will become king of Scotland.

View the Art ★

Joseph Anton Koch (1768–1839) was one of the most important landscape artists of his time. While he believed in many Neoclassical ideas, his work does reflect some Romantic characteristics, such as an interest in the natural world. **Ask:** Does this image correspond with your vision of Macbeth meeting the witches? Explain. *(Answers will vary. Students may note that the trees appear to be blowing, the waves are intense, and the clouds are swirling in the sky. All of which reflect upon the witches' implied ability to control nature.)*

---

90   THIRD APPARITION.°   Be lion-mettled, proud, and take no care
      Who chafes, who frets, or where conspirers are:
      Macbeth shall never vanquished be until
      Great Birnam Wood to high Dunsinane Hill
      Shall come against him.°

[*The* THIRD APPARITION *disappears.*]

   MACBETH.   That will never be.
95   Who can impress° the forest, bid the tree
      Unfix his earth-bound root? Sweet bodements,° good!
      Rebellious dead, rise never, till the Wood
      Of Birnam rise, and our high-placed Macbeth
      Shall live the lease of nature, pay his breath
100   To time and mortal custom.° Yet my heart
      Throbs to know one thing. Tell me, if your art
      Can tell so much: shall Banquo's issue ever
      Reign in this kingdom?

   ALL.   Seek to know no more.

   MACBETH.   I will be satisfied. Deny me this,
105   And an eternal curse fall on you! Let me know
      Why sinks that caldron? And what noise is this?

[*Oboes are heard.*]

   FIRST WITCH.   Show!

90 Third Apparition: This ghost likely represents Malcolm, Duncan's son and designated heir to the throne.

92–94 Macbeth . . . him: Macbeth shall never be conquered until the forest of Great Birnam marches to his castle on Dunsinane Hill.

95 impress: force into service.

96 bodements: prophecies.

99–100 live . . . custom: live out his natural life and die a normal death.

Make and Verify Predictions *What do you think Macbeth will do after hearing the apparitions' prophecies?*

English Learners

DIFFERENTIATED INSTRUCTION

Intermediate Remind students that, in English, words are sometimes left out or "understood." For example, when Macbeth says to the witches "I will be satisfied," he is saying that he will continue to seek more knowledge until he is satisfied.

Approaching Level

DIFFERENTIATED INSTRUCTION

Established Keeping track of the plots and subplots in a Shakespearean drama can challenge struggling readers. Encourage students to use a story map to keep track of key events. Have them fill in the details as they read. Students can compare maps with one another to make sure they have included each essential element.

Teach

Reading Strategy   1

Make and Verify Predictions **Answer:** *King James I of England, who claimed Banquo as one of his ancestors, is living proof that the prophecy has been fulfilled.*

[APPROACHING] Read lines 112–114 with approaching-level students and help them point out the words and phrases that indicate a family resemblance between the kings in the procession and Banquo. **Ask:** Why is it important that the kings look like each other and like Banquo? *(The family resemblance helps prove that they are descended from him.)*

SECOND WITCH. Show!

THIRD WITCH. Show!

110 ALL. Show his eyes, and grieve his heart;
  Come like shadows, so depart!

[A pantomime passes across the stage. In the show are the apparitions of eight kings, representing the eight Stuart kings of Scotland. The eighth king, representing James I of England, has a mirror in his hand. BANQUO'S GHOST appears at the end of the procession.]

MACBETH. Thou art too like the spirit of Banquo. Down!
  Thy crown does sear mine eyelids. And thy hair,
  Thou other gold-bound brow, is like the first.
115 A third is like the former. Filthy hags!
  Why do you show me this? A fourth! Start, eyes!
  What, will the line stretch out to th' crack of doom?
  Another yet! A seventh! I'll see no more.
  And yet the eighth° appears, who bears a glass
120 Which shows me many more; and some I see
  That twofold balls and treble scepters carry:
  Horrible sight! Now I see 'tis true;
  For the blood-boltered° Banquo smiles upon me,
  And points at them for his.°

[The APPARITIONS in the pantomime vanish.]

                    What, is this so?

125 FIRST WITCH. Ay, sir, all this is so. But why
  Stands Macbeth thus amazedly?
  Come, sisters, cheer we up his sprites,
  And show the best of our delights:
  I'll charm the air to give a sound,
130 While you perform your antic round,°
  That this great king may kindly say
  Our duties did his welcome pay.

[Music plays as the WITCHES dance and vanish.]

MACBETH. Where are they? Gone? Let this **pernicious** hour
  Stand aye accursed° in the calendar!
135 Come in, without there!°

[LENNOX enters.]

---

1 Make and Verify Predictions *How do you know that the prophecy about Banquo's descendants has come true?*

Vocabulary

pernicious (pər nish′ əs) *adj.* destructive; deadly

119–121 The **eighth** king is James VI of Scotland, who in 1603 became James I of England. He holds a magic mirror that shows future generations of Scottish rulers, some of them bearing coronation symbols of the Scottish and British thrones (**twofold balls** and **treble scepters**). James was descended from Banquo.
123 **blood-boltered:** having hair matted with blood.
124 **his:** his descendants.

130 **antic round:** fantastic circle dance.
134 **Stand aye accursed:** remain forever cursed.
135 **without there:** you who stands outside.

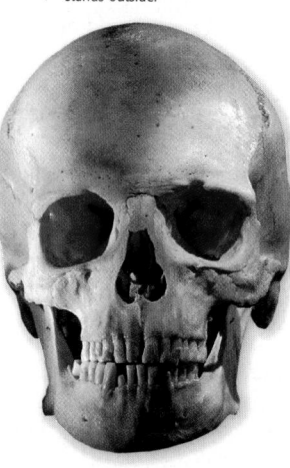

Reading Practice

SPIRAL REVIEW **Analyze Literary Periods**
Remind students that Shakespeare wrote *Macbeth* while James I was on the throne and that James I traced his ancestry directly to Banquo. Ask students to consider what choices Shakespeare might have made to honor or flatter the king, who would certainly have been in the audience. *(Shakespeare's play depicts Banquo as an honorable man who was wrongly murdered; Shakespeare's presentation of the eight Stuart kings presented an opportunity to show James's ancestors in a favorable light.)*

LENNOX.   What's your Grace's will?

MACBETH. Saw you the weird sisters?

LENNOX.   No, my lord.

MACBETH. Came they not by you?

LENNOX.   No indeed, my lord.

MACBETH. Infected be the air whereon they ride,
    And damned all those that trust them! I did hear
140   The galloping of horse. Who was 't came by?

LENNOX. 'Tis two or three, my lord, that bring you word
    Macduff is fled to England.

MACBETH.   Fled to England?

LENNOX. Ay, my good lord.

MACBETH. [Aside.] Time, thou anticipat'st° my dread **exploits.**
145   The flighty purpose never is o'ertook
    Unless the deed go with it.° From this moment
    The very firstlings of my heart shall be
    The firstlings of my hand.° And even now,
    To crown my thoughts with acts, be it thought and done:°
150   The castle of Macduff I will surprise;°
    Seize upon Fife; give to th' edge o' th' sword
    His wife, his babes, and all unfortunate souls
    That trace him in his line.° No boasting like a fool;
    This deed I'll do before this purpose cool:
155   But no more sights!—Where are these gentlemen?
    Come, bring me where they are.

[MACBETH exits with LENNOX.]

SCENE 2. MACDUFF's castle at Fife.

[In Fife, on the southeast coast of Scotland, LADY MACDUFF, her son, and
ROSS enter a room in MACDUFF's castle. LADY MACDUFF is upset and angry
with her husband for leaving Scotland.]

LADY MACDUFF. What had he done, to make him fly the land?°

ROSS. You must have patience, madam.

---

144 **anticipat'st:** prevent by acting
in advance.

145–146 **The flighty . . . it:** Our
intentions are so fleeting that they
escape unless accompanied by
immediate action.

146–148 **From . . . hand:** From
now on, the first impulses of my
heart will be matched by the actions
of my hand.

149 **be it . . . done:** Let it be done
immediately.

150 **surprise:** capture.

153 **trace . . . line:** follow in his
lineage.

1 **fly the land:** flee the country.

Plot *How does Macduff's escape frustrate Macbeth's plans?* **2**

Make and Verify Predictions *Do you think that Macduff's family will
be able to save their lives? Explain.* **3**

Vocabulary

exploit (eks′ploit) *n.* a bold deed

Literary Element **2**

Plot **Answer:** *Macbeth cannot
kill Macduff, who has removed
himself from harm's way. Macduff
might now join with others to
unseat Macbeth.*

Ask: What other character has
escaped Macbeth's murder-
ous plans earlier in the play?
*(Banquo's son Fleance escaped
in Act 3.)* Why was this event
important to the plot? *(Because
Fleance is alive, he can still
become king, fulfilling the prophecy that Banquo's descendants will
rule.)*

Reading Strategy **3**

Make and Verify
Predictions **Answer:** *Without
Macduff to protect them, they are
extremely vulnerable. Macbeth will
probably succeed in killing them.*

ENGLISH LEARNERS For English
learners, **ask:** What does this
speech tell you about Macbeth
as a character? *(Possible answer:
He has lost the mercy and guilt he
felt earlier. He has become more
crazy and violent.)*

English Learners

DIFFERENTIATED INSTRUCTION

Intermediate Review the importance
of understanding suffixes by discussing
Macbeth's curse to the witches: "Infected
be the air whereon they ride. And damned
all those that trust them!" Discuss the use
of the suffix *-ed*, which is used to form the
past tense of weak verbs. Point to the
past tense of *see* in Macbeth's line "Saw
you the weird sisters?" Explain to students
that strong verbs like *see* do not use a
suffix like *-ed* to form the past tense. Ask
students to note other examples of familiar
affixes on this page.

Approaching Level

DIFFERENTIATED INSTRUCTION

Emerging Students may better understand an exchange between two characters
by reading it aloud with a partner. Ask pairs
to read aloud the scene between Lenox
and Macbeth on this page.

Teach

Literary Element | **1**

Plot **Answer:** *Macduff fled without telling his wife for fear that she would be implicated and harmed.*

Big Idea | **2**

A Bard for the Ages

Answer: *In spite of the witty replies of Macduff's son, the mood is rather sad and melancholy.*

(ADVANCED) Have advanced students research the role of the noblewoman in medieval times and what was expected of her when her husband was absent from the castle.

Cultural History ☆

View of Childhood By modern standards, Lady Macduff's conversation with her son seems abrupt and almost cruel. She pretends that her husband is dead and speaks with her son as she would with an adult. This reflects the treatment of children in Elizabethan times—they were given adult responsibilities at an early age and were expected to behave maturely.

LADY MACDUFF.   He had none:
    His flight was madness. When our actions do not,
    Our fears do make us traitors.°

    ROSS.   You know not
5   Whether it was his wisdom or his fear.

    LADY MACDUFF. Wisdom! To leave his wife, to leave his babes,
    His mansion and his titles,° in a place
    From whence himself does fly? He loves us not;
    He wants the natural touch:° for the poor wren,
10 The most diminutive of birds, will fight,
    Her young ones in her nest, against the owl.
    All is the fear and nothing is the love;
    As little is the wisdom, where the flight
    So runs against all reason.

    ROSS.   My dearest coz,°
15 I pray you, school° yourself. But, for your husband,
    He is noble, wise, judicious, and best knows
    The fits o' th' season.° I dare not speak much further:
    But cruel are the times, when we are traitors
    And do not know ourselves;° when we hold rumor
20 From what we fear, yet know not what we fear,°
    But float upon a wild and violent sea
    Each way and move. I take my leave of you.
    Shall not be long but I'll be here again.
    Things at the worst will cease, or else climb upward
25 To what they were before. [*He addresses* MACDUFF's *son.*]
        My pretty cousin,
    Blessing upon you!

    LADY MACDUFF. Fathered he is, and yet he's fatherless.

    ROSS. I am so much a fool, should I stay longer,
    It would be my disgrace and your discomfort.°
30 I take my leave at once.

    [ROSS *exits.*]

    LADY MACDUFF.   Sirrah, your father's dead: ☆
    And what will you do now? How will you live?

    SON. As birds do, mother.

    LADY MACDUFF.   What, with worms and flies?

    SON. With what I get, I mean; and so do they.

3–4 **When . . . traitors:** Even when we are innocent of treason, our fears make us behave like traitors.

7 **titles:** possessions.

9 **wants . . . touch:** lacks natural feelings.

14 **coz:** cousin, kinswoman.
15 **school:** control.

17 **fits o' th' season:** violent disorders of the time.

18–19 **we are . . . ourselves:** We are considered traitors but do not know of any treason we have committed.
19–20 **when . . . fear:** when we believe rumors merely because we are afraid.

29 **It . . . discomfort:** I would disgrace myself and embarrass you by weeping.

---

1 Plot *Why has Macduff fled Scotland without telling his wife?*

2 A Bard for the Ages *What mood does Shakespeare create here through the dialogue between Lady Macduff and her son?*

Writing Practice

SPIRAL REVIEW **Write a Letter** Dramatists advance the plot through dialogue and action. Occasionally they will use a dramatic device such as a letter to provide the audience with relevant information. Have students review the letter Lady Macbeth is reading in Act 1, scene 5 (page 319), to illustrate the point. Then ask students to write a letter from Macduff that Lady Macduff might be reading as Ross arrives. Suggest that they consider including where Macduff has gone, whom he plans to see, and what the purpose of his trip is. Challenge them to add an explanation for leaving his family behind.

LADY MACDUFF. Poor bird! thou'dst never fear the net nor lime,°

35   The pitfall° nor the gin.°

SON. Why should I, mother? Poor birds they are not set for.° My father is not dead, for all your saying.

LADY MACDUFF. Yes, he is dead: how wilt thou do for a father?

SON. Nay, how will you do for a husband?

40 LADY MACDUFF. Why, I can buy me twenty at any market.

SON. Then you'll buy 'em to sell° again.

LADY MACDUFF. Thou speak'st with all thy wit, and yet, i' faith,
    With wit enough for thee.°

SON. Was my father a traitor, mother?

45 LADY MACDUFF. Ay, that he was.

SON. What is a traitor?

LADY MACDUFF. Why, one that swears and lies.°

SON. And be all traitors that do so?

LADY MACDUFF. Every one that does so is a traitor, and must be hanged.

50 SON. And must they all be hanged that swear and lie?

LADY MACDUFF. Every one.

SON. Who must hang them?

LADY MACDUFF. Why, the honest men.

SON. Then the liars and swearers are fools; for there are liars
55   and swearers enow° to beat the honest men and hang up them.

LADY MACDUFF. Now, God help thee, poor monkey! But how wilt thou do for a father?

SON. If he were dead, you'd weep for him. If you would not,° it were a good sign that I should quickly have a new father.

60 LADY MACDUFF. Poor prattler, how thou talk'st! **3**

[A MESSENGER enters.]

MESSENGER. Bless you, fair dame! I am not to you known, Though in your state of honor I am perfect.°
I doubt° some danger does approach you nearly:°
If you will take a homely° man's advice,
65   Be not found here; hence, with your little ones.
To fright you thus, methinks I am too savage;

---

34 lime: birdlime, a sticky substance smeared on branches to catch birds.
35 pitfall: trap. **gin:** snare.
36 Poor . . . for: People do not set traps for birds of little value.

41 sell: betray.

43 wit . . . thee: considerable understanding for a child.

47 swears and lies: takes an oath and breaks it.

55 enow: enough.

58 would not: did not care to weep.

62 in . . . perfect: I am fully aware of your noble rank.
63 doubt: fear. **nearly:** closely.
64 homely: humble.

Teach

Reading Strategy   3

Make and Verify Predictions Ask students to recall what occurred after the porter's comic speeches at the beginning of Act 2, scene 3. *(the discovery of Duncan's murder)* **Ask:** What might follow this witty exchange between Lady Macduff and her son? *(Possible responses: We might find out that Macduff is really dead; Lady Macduff and her son might be murdered.)*

ENGLISH LEARNERS Direct English learners' attention to the son's question in line 48. Explain that Shakespeare sometimes used inverted word order and left out words. Ask student who *all* refers to *(all people)*. Ask what *so* refers to *(swearing and lying)*. Ask where *that do so* would normally appear if the sentence were phrased in contemporary English *(after* all*)*. Last, ask students to restate the question in common, contemporary English. *(And are all the people who swear and lie traitors?)*

Approaching Level

DIFFERENTIATED INSTRUCTION

Emerging It may be helpful for approaching-level students to break down dialogue by paraphrasing each line. Have students read through the conversation between Lady Macduff and her son. Then ask them to go back and reread the conversation, paraphrasing each line.

For example, the son says "If he were dead, you'd weep for him. If you would not, it were a good sign that I should quickly have a new father." Students should explain that the son is saying if his father were truly dead, then his mother would be in mourning, and if she were not sad, then that would mean she had met a prospective husband to father her son. After they have completed paraphrasing each line in the conversation, have students volunteer to summarize the entire conversation to the class.

Teach

Make and Verify Predictions

Answer: *Macduff likely will return to Scotland, seeking revenge against Macbeth.*

Cultural History ☆

Violence on Stage In ancient Greek tragedies, violence usually occurred offstage. Characters would often describe the violent murders and graphic deaths in long, detailed monologues. However, in Elizabethan theater, violence and bloodshed were depicted onstage for enthusiastic, even rowdy audiences. In a sense, the Elizabethan stage was a forerunner of modern representations of violence on television and in films.

To do worse to you were fell cruelty,
Which is too nigh your person.° Heaven preserve you!
I dare abide° no longer.

[*The* MESSENGER *exits quickly.*]

LADY MACDUFF.   Whither should I fly?
70   I have done no harm. But I remember now
I am in this earthly world, where to do harm
Is often laudable, to do good sometime
Accounted dangerous folly. Why then, alas,
Do I put up that womanly defense,
75   To say I have done no harm?—What are these faces?

[*The* MURDERERS *hired by* MACBETH *enter.*]

MURDERER. Where is your husband?

LADY MACDUFF. I hope, in no place so unsanctified
Where such as thou mayst find him.

MURDERER.   He's a traitor.

SON. Thou li'st, thou shag-eared° villain!

MURDERER.   What, you egg!°

[*The* MURDERER *stabs the child.*] ☆
80   Young fry of treachery!°

SON.   He has killed me, mother:
Run away, I pray you!

[*The* BOY *dies as* LADY MACDUFF *runs off crying,* "Murder!" *The* MURDERERS *pursue her.*]

SCENE 3. The palace of the King of England.

[MACDUFF *has come to England in an attempt to ally himself with* MALCOLM, KING DUNCAN'*s older son and rightful heir to the Scottish crown.* MACDUFF *and* MALCOLM *enter and meet in front of the palace of Edward the Confessor, the devoutly religious king of England.*]

MALCOLM. Let us seek out some desolate shade, and there
Weep our sad bosoms empty.

MACDUFF.   Let us rather
Hold fast the mortal sword,° and like good men

---

1 Make and Verify Predictions *What do you think Macduff will do when he learns that his son has been murdered?*

66–68 To . . . person: The messenger says that even frightening her like this is too savage. Any action taken against her would be fierce (**fell**) cruelty, and such cruelty is all too near.
69 abide: stay.

78–79 shag-eared: hairy-eared. **egg:** a term of reproach for an impertinent boy.

80 Young . . . treachery: traitor's offspring.

3 Hold . . . sword: keep a firm grip on the deadly sword.

Literary Element Practice

SPIRAL REVIEW **Dramatic Irony** Remind students that dramatic irony arises when the audience has information unknown to the characters. Ask students to identify how Shakespeare uses dramatic irony to evoke pathos, or intense sympathy, for Macduff at the beginning of scene 3. *(Macduff speaks of the suffering of the Scots without knowing that his own family has now been affected. Malcolm says* that Macbeth's evil "hath not touched" Macduff, not knowing what the audience knows.) Have students look for other additional ironic statements in this scene.

Bestride our down-fall'n birthdom.° Each new morn
5 New widows howl, new orphans cry, new sorrows
Strike heaven on the face, that it resounds
As if it felt with Scotland and yelled out
Like syllable of dolor.°

MALCOLM.   What I believe, I'll wail;
What know, believe; and what I can **redress**,
10 As I shall find the time to friend,° I will.
What you have spoke, it may be so perchance.°
This tyrant, whose sole° name blisters our tongues,
Was once thought honest:° you have loved him well;
He hath not touched you yet. I am young; but something
15 You may deserve of him through me;° and wisdom°
To offer up a weak, poor, innocent lamb
T' appease an angry god.

MACDUFF.   I am not treacherous.

MALCOLM.   But Macbeth is.
A good and virtuous nature may recoil
20 In an imperial charge.° But I shall crave your pardon;
That which you are, my thoughts cannot transpose:°
Angels are bright still, though the brightest° fell:
Though all things foul would wear the brows of grace,
Yet grace must still look so.°

MACDUFF.   I have lost my hopes.

MALCOLM.   Perchance even there where I did find my
25   doubts.°
Why in that rawness left you wife and child,
Those precious motives, those strong knots of love,
Without leave-taking?° I pray you,
Let not my jealousies be your dishonors,
30 But mine own safeties.° You may be rightly just°
Whatever I shall think.

MACDUFF.   Bleed, bleed, poor country:
Great tyranny, lay thou thy basis sure,
For goodness dare not check thee:° wear thou thy wrongs;°
The title is affeered.° Fare thee well, lord:
35 I would not be the villain that thou think'st
For the whole space that's in the tyrant's grasp

Plot *Dramatic irony occurs when the audience knows something that
the characters do not. What is ironic about Macduff's statement?*   **2**

---

4 **Bestride . . . birthdom:**
protectively stand over our ruined
native land.

8 **Like . . . dolor:** a similar cry of
sorrow.

10 **to friend:** to be favorable to me.

11 **may be so perchance:** may
perhaps be true.
12 **sole:** mere.
13 **honest:** honorable.

14–15 **something . . . me:** You
may be rewarded by betraying me
to Macbeth.
15 **and wisdom:** it would be wise.

19–20 **A good . . . charge:** A
good man may fall away from his
virtuous nature when pressured by a
royal command.
21 **transpose:** change.
22 **the brightest:** Lucifer, the angel
cast down from heaven for rebelling
against God.
23–24 **Though . . . so:** Even if
everything evil put on the
appearance of virtue, virtue would
still appear like itself.
25 **doubts:** suspicions.

25–28 **Perchance . . . leave-
taking:** Malcolm says that he
became suspicious of Macduff
because Macduff left his family
behind in a vulnerable state
(**rawness**), which might suggest that
he really is allied with Macbeth.
29–30 **Let . . . safeties:** Do not
take my suspicions as attacks on
your honor but rather as precautions
for my safety.
30 **rightly just:** completely
honorable.
32–33 **lay . . . thee:** You can
establish yourself safely, for virtue is
afraid to stop you.
33 **wear . . . wrongs:** Display your
ill-gotten gains.
34 **afeered:** legally confirmed.

Teach

Literary Element | **2**

Plot **Answer:** *Macduff's
reference to "new widows" and
"new orphans" is ironic because
the audience knows that Macduff's
wife and child are slain.*

Writer's Technique ☆

Variety of Tone Shakespeare
often creates interest by varying
the tone from scene to scene. The
seriocomic scene between Lady
Macduff and her son abruptly shifts
tone and ends in brutal violence.
The following scene between
Malcolm and Macduff allows the
audience to recover from this
shock. As the men earnestly determine what to do next, the tone
becomes serious and heroic.

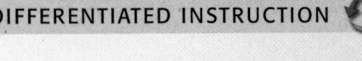

English Learners

DIFFERENTIATED INSTRUCTION

Beginning Students might try this reading plan for scene 3:

▪ Read one speech, or set of lines spoken
by one character, at a time.

▪ Use simple sentences to explain the
general idea of what the character says.

Advanced Learners

DIFFERENTIATED INSTRUCTION

Historical Research Advanced students
may wish to conduct additional research on
the historical Duncan, Macbeth, and Macduff.
Have them report their findings to the class
and lead a discussion on how Shakespeare
adapted each historical figure.

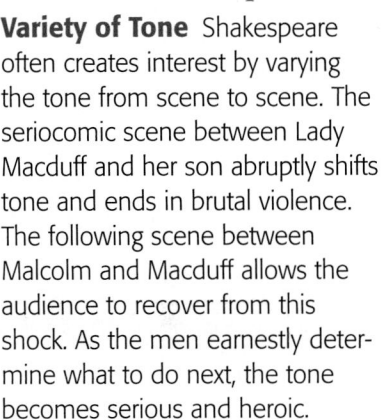

Teach

Big Idea   1

A Bard for the Ages

Answer: *Malcolm is cautious to the extent that he is willing to portray himself as a villain in order to test Macduff's honesty.*

(APPROACHING) For approaching-level students, read Malcolm's list of Macbeth's evils in lines 57–60. **Ask:** Can anyone possibly be worse than that? *(not likely)* **Say:** But then Malcolm goes on to say that he is worse than Macbeth. Does he really mean it? *(no)* What device is Shakespeare using through Malcolm? *(exaggeration)*

Big Idea   2

A Bard for the Ages

Ask: What generalization about human nature does Macduff make in these lines? *(That lust for power has led to the fall of many kings and kingdoms)* Do you think Shakespeare risked offending King James I with observations like this? *(Many students will agree that the risk of offense was slight because it presents a general statement and is applied to Macbeth, not King James.)*

Cultural History ☆

The Seven Deadly Sins

Shakespeare's audience would have been familiar with the Christian tradition of the seven deadly sins, which most endanger salvation: lust, avarice, pride, gluttony, envy, anger, and sloth. Malcolm's list of Macbeth's vices (and the virtues that he lacks) closely parallels these sins.

And the rich East to boot.

MALCOLM.   Be not offended:
I speak not as in absolute fear of you.
I think our country sinks beneath the yoke;
40   It weeps, it bleeds, and each new day a gash
Is added to her wounds. I think withal°
There would be hands uplifted in my right;°
And here from gracious England° have I offer
Of goodly thousands: but, for all this,
45   When I shall tread upon the tyrant's head,
Or wear it on my sword, yet my poor country
Shall have more vices than it had before,
More suffer, and more sundry ways° than ever,
By him that shall succeed.

MACDUFF.   What° should he be?

50   MALCOLM.   It is myself I mean, in whom I know
All the particulars of vice so grafted°
That, when they shall be opened,° black Macbeth
Will seem as pure as snow, and the poor state
Esteem him as a lamb, being compared
55   With my confineless harms.°

MACDUFF.   Not in the legions
Of horrid hell can come a devil more damned
In evils to top Macbeth.

MALCOLM.   I grant him bloody,
Luxurious,° avaricious, false, deceitful,
Sudden,° malicious, smacking of every sin ☆
60   That has a name: but there's no bottom, none,
In my voluptuousness: your wives, your daughters,
Your matrons and your maids, could not fill up
The cistern of my lust, and my desire
All continent° impediments would o'erbear,°
65   That did oppose my will. Better Macbeth
Than such an one to reign.

MACDUFF.   Boundless intemperance°
In nature° is a tyranny; it hath been
Th' untimely emptying of the happy throne,
And fall of many kings. But fear not yet
70   To take upon you what is yours: you may
Convey your pleasures in a spacious plenty,°
And yet seem cold,° the time you may so hoodwink.°

41 withal: in addition.
42 right: cause.
43 gracious England: the gracious King of England.

48 More . . . ways: shall suffer more and in more varied ways.
49 What: who.

51 grafted: implanted.
52 opened: exposed, in bloom.

55 confineless harms: boundless evils.

58 Luxurious: lecherous.
59 Sudden: violent.

64 continent: restraining. **would o'erbear:** would be overwhelmed.

66 Boundless intemperance: unrestrained lust.
67 nature: human nature.

71 Convey . . . plenty: secretly indulge your pleasures in great abundance.
72 cold: lacking in sexual desire.
the time . . . hoodwink: In this way you may blindfold the age.

---

1   **A Bard for the Ages** *What does Shakespeare reveal about Malcolm's character in lines 58–66?*

Writing Practice

SPIRAL REVIEW   **Write a Campaign Speech** In this scene, the characters discuss who should rule Scotland. Invite students to consider the characters in the play and decide who they believe would make the best ruler. Have them create Pro and Con lists for their chosen candidate, noting the qualities that would make the person a good ruler and those that could be drawbacks. Have students include examples from the play that illustrate these characteristics. Then have students write a campaign speech to be spoken either by the character or by his or her representative. The speech should point out the candidate's strengths and explain why voters should overlook any drawbacks.

Caregg Cennen Castle. John Samuel Raven (1829–1877). Oil on canvas, 42½ x 62¾ in. Private collection.

View the Art John Samuel Raven was well-known for his ability to evoke mood in landscapes. How would you describe the mood of this painting? How does it compare to the mood of this act?

> We have willing dames enough. There cannot be
> That vulture in you, to devour so many
> 75 As will to greatness dedicate themselves,
> Finding it so inclined.
>
> MALCOLM.   With this there grows
> In my most ill-composed affection° such
> A stanchless **avarice** that, were I King,
> I should cut off the nobles for their lands,
> 80 Desire his° jewels and this other's house:
> And my more-having would be as a sauce
> To make me hunger more, that I should forge
> Quarrels unjust against the good and loyal,
> Destroying them for wealth.
>
> MACDUFF.   This avarice
> 85 Sticks deeper, grows with more pernicious root
> Than summer-seeming° lust, and it hath been
> The sword° of our slain kings. Yet do not fear.
> Scotland hath foisons° to fill up your will

77 **affection:** character.

80 **his:** one man's.

86 **summer-seeming:** youthful, transitory.
87 **sword:** cause of overthrow.
88 **foisons:** abundant supplies.

Vocabulary

avarice (av′ər is) *n.* greed

MACBETH, ACT 4, SCENE 3 **373**

View the Art ★

Answer: *The mood of this painting is dark, brooding, and ominous. The painting accurately reflects the mood established in this act through plot, setting, imagery, and dialogue.*

A self-taught artist, John Samuel Raven painted a variety of scenes throughout the British Isles. This painting exemplifies his ability to capture the mood evoked by details of a natural setting.

Approaching Level

DIFFERENTIATED INSTRUCTION

AAVE Students who use African American Vernacular English (AAVE) tend to struggle with singular and plural subject-verb agreement, especially with irregular verbs, such as *has/have, was/were,* and *does/do.* **Write** the following sentence pairs on the board and ask students to read each sentence aloud and identify the correct use of each irregular verb:

We have willing dames enough. *(correct)*
We has willing dames enough.

A stanchless avarice that, was I King...
A stanchless avarice that, were I King... *(correct)*

You do not fear. *(correct)*
You does not fear.

Note that *yet* is replaced with *you* in the last sentence pair to clarify the subject. For extra practice, replace plural subjects with singular subjects and vice versa. Have students identify the correct use of the irregular verb.

373

Teach

Literary Element | **1**

Plot Answer: *Macduff emphasizes Malcolm's parents' religious purity because he believes they represent the noble and virtuous side of the current battle against evil as embodied by Macbeth. He shows his allegiance to Duncan's memory and not to the vile persona that Malcolm is presenting.*

Literary Element | **2**

Plot Answer: *Macduff has passed Malcolm's test, and Malcolm is now willing to ally himself with Macduff and his friends against Macbeth.*

[ADVANCED] Have advanced students discuss how Macduff's initial willingness to put up with Malcom's claim that Scotland has enough women and treasure to satisfy him, changes or expands their understanding of Macduff's character. Ask them to speculate on what Macduff's initial acquiescence might indicate about the times he lived in.

Of your mere own.° All these are portable,
90   With other graces weighed.°

MALCOLM. But I have none: the king-becoming graces,
As justice, verity, temp'rance, stableness,
Bounty, perseverance, mercy, lowliness,
Devotion, patience, courage, fortitude,
95   I have no relish° of them, but abound
In the division of each several crime,°
Acting it many ways. Nay, had I pow'r, I should
Pour the sweet milk of concord into hell,
Uproar the universal peace, confound°
100   All unity on earth.

MACDUFF.   O Scotland, Scotland!

MALCOLM. If such a one be fit to govern, speak:
I am as I have spoken.

MACDUFF.   Fit to govern!
No, not to live. O nation miserable!
With an untitled° tyrant bloody-sceptered,
105   When shalt thou see thy wholesome days again,
Since that the truest issue° of thy throne
By his own interdiction° stands accursed,
And does blaspheme his breed?° Thy royal father
Was a most sainted king: the queen that bore thee,
110   Oft'ner upon her knees than on her feet,
Died every day she lived.° Fare thee well!
These evils thou repeat'st upon thyself
Hath banished me from Scotland. O my breast,
Thy hope ends here!

MALCOLM.   Macduff, this noble passion,
115   Child of integrity, hath from my soul
Wiped the black scruples, reconciled my thoughts
To thy good truth and honor. Devilish Macbeth
By many of these trains° hath sought to win me
Into his power; and modest wisdom° plucks me
120   From over-credulous haste: but God above
Deal between thee and me! For even now
I put myself to thy direction, and
Unspeak mine own detraction;° here abjure
The taints and blames I laid upon myself,
125   For° strangers to my nature. I am yet

89 **Of . . . own:** merely from your royal property.
89–90 **All . . . weighed:** All of these flaws are bearable when balanced against other virtuous qualities.

95 **relish:** trace.

96 **division . . . crime:** different forms of each particular crime.

99 **confound:** destroy.

104 **untitled:** having no right to the throne.
106 **issue:** offspring.
107 **interdiction:** declaration against himself.
108 **blaspheme . . . breed:** slander his ancestry.

109–111 **the queen . . . lived:** Macduff says that Malcolm's mother lived every day as if preparing for heaven, spending more time on her knees in prayer than on her feet.

118 **trains:** lures, traps.
119 **modest wisdom:** prudence.

123 **mine own detraction:** my slander of myself.

125 **For:** as.

1 | Plot *Why does Macduff describe Malcolm's parents this way?*

2 | Plot *How does the dialogue between Macduff and Malcolm advance the plot?*

Listening and Speaking Practice

SPIRAL REVIEW **Read Speeches Aloud** Students can use speaking and listening skills to help in understanding complex texts. Have each student select a speech, such as Malcolm's revealing that he was testing Macduff (lines 114–137) and read it aloud. Provide these reading reminders:

- Read slowly and clearly.
- Use the punctuation to tell you when to pause or stop.

- Think about the meaning of the lines as you read them aloud. Your understanding will be communicated to your listeners.

Listeners can use these strategies:

- Focus attention on understanding the general meaning of the speech, not specific details.
- Jot down unfamiliar words or unclear phrases as you listen.

- After the presentation, ask questions to clarify ideas.

Unknown to woman, never was forsworn,°
Scarcely have coveted what was mine own,
At no time broke my faith, would not betray
The devil to his fellow, and delight
130   No less in truth than life. My first false speaking
Was this upon myself. What I am truly,
Is thine and my poor country's to command:
Whither indeed, before thy here-approach,°
Old Siward,° with ten thousand warlike men,
135   Already at a point,° was setting forth.
Now we'll together, and the chance of goodness
Be like our warranted quarrel!° Why are you silent?

MACDUFF. Such welcome and unwelcome things at once
    'Tis hard to reconcile.

[An ENGLISH DOCTOR enters.]

140 MALCOLM. Well, more anon. Comes the King forth,
    I pray you?

DOCTOR. Ay, sir. There are a crew of wretched souls
    That stay his cure:° their malady convinces
    The great assay of art;° but at his touch, ☆
    Such sanctity hath heaven given his hand,
145   They presently amend.°

MALCOLM.   I thank you, doctor.

[The DOCTOR exits.]

MACDUFF. What's the disease he means?

MALCOLM.   'Tis called the evil:°
    A most miraculous work in this good King,
    Which often since my here-remain° in England
    I have seen him do. How he solicits heaven,
150   Himself best knows: but strangely visited people,
    All swoll'n and ulcerous, pitiful to the eye,
    The mere° despair of surgery, he cures,
    Hanging a golden stamp° about their necks,
    Put on with holy prayers: and 'tis spoken,
155   To the succeeding royalty he leaves
    The healing benediction.° With this strange virtue°
    He hath a heavenly gift of prophecy,
    And sundry blessings hang about his throne
    That speak him full of grace.

[ROSS enters.]

A Bard for the Ages *What does this ability suggest about how subjects should regard their king?* **3**

Side notes:

126 **was forsworn:** broke my oath.

133 **here-approach:** arrival.
134 **Old Siward:** the Earl of Northumberland (general of the English forces).
135 **at a point:** in readiness.
136–137 **we'll . . . quarrel:** We will go forth together, and may our chance of success be equal to the justness of our cause.

142 **stay his cure:** wait to be healed by him (Edward the Confessor was reputed to have special healing powers).
142–143 **convinces . . . art:** defeats the greatest efforts of medical science.
145 **presently amend:** recover immediately.

146 **the evil:** scrofula, a skin disease known as "the King's evil" because the King's touch would supposedly cure it.
148 **here-remain:** stay here.

152 **mere:** utter.
153 **stamp:** coin.

155–156 **To . . . benediction:** He will pass on the power of healing to his descendants.
156 **With . . . virtue:** in addition to this remarkable power.

Teach

Big Idea   3

A Bard for the Ages
Answer: *Subjects should regard their king as God's representative on Earth.*

Writer's Technique ☆

Theme Shakespeare's plays contain intricate webs of connected images. Speeches that appear to be digressions often connect to key themes. For example, the doctor's entrance and Malcolm's description of Edward's healing powers appear to be unrelated to the topics being discussed. However, by analogy, Scotland is ill with a disease caused by Macbeth. It must be healed by the "touch" or efforts of a noble king, Malcolm.

English Learners

DIFFERENTIATED INSTRUCTION

Advanced Direct English learners attention to line 146, where Malcolm reveals the name of the disease that citizens are waiting to be cured of. Tell students to read the footnote that explains why the disease is called the evil. **Ask:** Why is the name of the disease ironic? *(Because Macbeth, who is considered evil, as the king would be the one to cure the evil disease with his touch)* Explain to them that the concept of disease is being used as a metaphor here. **Say:** Scotland is considered diseased. This does not mean that all of the citizens have a disease rather it implies that the figurative disease that has been causing harm to the country is Macbeth.

Teach

Plot **Ask:** What key decision does Malcolm announce beginning with line 188? *(Malcolm is returning to Scotland with the backing of England's king.)*

Ask: What does this development mean for Macbeth? *(He will have to fight for the throne of Scotland.)*

ENGLISH LEARNERS Tell English learners that "peace" has similar connotations in English and Spanish and that the term *rest in peace* can be translated to "descansar en paz." In light of this understanding, ask students what Ross really means when he says in line 179 that Macduff's family members were at peace when he left them.

Writer's Technique ☆

Ambiguity Shakespeare is using ambiguity here to heighten the dramatic tension. At first Ross cannot bear to tell Macduff the news. He tries to soften the blow by using "well" and "at peace" in the sense of being in heaven, not being physically healthy. Because the audience knows that Lady Macduff and her son have been killed, the audience recognizes this ambiguity as dramatic irony.

MACDUFF.   See, who comes here?

160 MALCOLM. My countryman; but yet I know him not.

MACDUFF. My ever gentle° cousin, welcome hither.

MALCOLM. I know him now: good God, betimes remove
      The means that makes us strangers!

ROSS.   Sir, amen.

MACDUFF. Stands Scotland where it did?

ROSS.   Alas, poor country!

165 Almost afraid to know itself! It cannot
      Be called our mother but our grave, where nothing
      But who knows nothing is once seen to smile;°
      Where sighs and groans, and shrieks that rend the air,
      Are made, not marked; where violent sorrow seems

170 A modern ecstasy.° The dead man's knell
      Is there scarce asked for who,° and good men's lives
      Expire before the flowers in their caps,
      Dying or ere they sicken.

MACDUFF.   O, relation
      Too nice,° and yet too true!

MALCOLM.   What's the newest grief?

175 ROSS. That of an hour's age doth hiss the speaker;°
      Each minute teems° a new one.

MACDUFF.   How does my wife?

ROSS. Why, well.

MACDUFF.   And all my children?

ROSS.   Well too.

MACDUFF. The tyrant has not battered at their peace?

ROSS. No; they were well at peace when I did leave 'em.

180 MACDUFF. Be not a niggard° of your speech: how goes 't?

ROSS. When I came hither to transport the tidings,
      Which I have heavily borne, there ran a rumor
      Of many worthy fellows that were out;°
      Which was to my belief witnessed the rather,

185 For that I saw the tyrant's power afoot.°
      Now is the time of help. Your eye° in Scotland
      Would create soldiers, make our women fight,
      To doff° their dire distresses.

MALCOLM.   Be 't their comfort
      We are coming thither. Gracious England hath

190 Lent us good Siward and ten thousand men;
      An older and a better soldier none

161 gentle: noble.

166–167 where . . . smile: where no one ever smiles except for those who are oblivious to everything.

170 modern ecstasy: common emotion.
170–171 The dead . . . who: People rarely ask for whom the funeral bells toll (because they ring so often).

174 nice: exact, precisely detailed.

175 That . . . speaker: If one describes a tragedy that occurred an hour ago, listeners hiss because the news is so old.
176 teems: brings forth.

180 niggard: miser.

183 out: in open rebellion.

184–185 Which . . . afoot: which I am ready to believe because I saw Macbeth's forces on the march.
186 Your eye: the sight of you.
188 doff: put off.

Reading Practice

SPIRAL REVIEW **Make Inferences** Actors playing roles in Shakespeare's plays must make inferences about characters' actions and emotions, but no two actors will draw exactly the same inferences. Have students imagine that they are playing Macduff in scene 3. Ask them to make inferences about why he asks Ross so many questions about the status of his country and family and have them support their inferences with details from the scene. *(Students might suggest that Macduff is ignorant of his family's state and asks questions out of concern.)*

That Christendom gives out. **1**

ROSS.   Would I could answer
This comfort with the like! But I have words
That would be howled out in the desert air,

195   Where hearing should not latch° them.

MACDUFF.   What concern they?
The general cause or is it a fee-grief°
Due to some single breast?

ROSS.   No mind that's honest
But in it shares some woe, though the main part
Pertains to you alone.

MACDUFF.   If it be mine,

200   Keep it not from me, quickly let me have it.

ROSS.   Let not your ears despise my tongue for ever,
Which shall possess them with the heaviest sound
That ever yet they heard.

MACDUFF.   Humh! I guess at it.

ROSS.   Your castle is surprised; your wife and babes

205   Savagely slaughtered. To relate the manner,
Were, on the quarry° of these murdered deer,
To add the death of you.

MALCOLM.   Merciful heaven!
What, man! Ne'er pull your hat upon your brows;°
Give sorrow words. The grief that does not speak

210   Whispers the o'er-fraught heart,° and bids it break.

MACDUFF.   My children too?

ROSS.   Wife, children, servants, all
That could be found.

MACDUFF.   And I must be from thence!
My wife killed too?   **3**

ROSS.   I have said.

MALCOLM.   Be comforted.
Let's make us med'cines of our great revenge,

215   To cure this deadly grief.

MACDUFF.   He° has no children. All my pretty ones?
Did you say all? O hell-kite!° All?

Make and Verify Predictions *What do you predict Ross is going to reveal?*   **2**

Vocabulary

pertains (pər tāns′) *v.* to be connected to or have relevance to

---

195 **latch:** catch.

196 **fee-grief:** personal grief.

206 **quarry:** heap of game slain in a hunt.

208 **pull . . . brows:** a conventional gesture of grieving.

210 **Whispers . . . heart:** whispers to the overburdened heart.

216 **He:** may refer to Malcolm (who does not understand the depth of Macduff's grief because he has no children) or to Macbeth (who could not have performed such a deed if he had children).
217 **hell-kite:** infernal bird of prey.

MACBETH, ACT 4, SCENE 3   **377**

Teach

Reading Strategy   2

Make and Verify Predictions Answer: *Ross is going to reveal that Macbeth has slaughtered Macduff's family.*

Big Idea   3

A Bard for the Ages Ask: What psychological reality does Shakespeare present about how people receive bad news? *(Macduff cannot immediately absorb the tragic information; when people are in similar situations, they often ask questions that have already been answered, as though they refuse to accept what they have heard.)*

APPROACHING Help approaching-level students understand Ross's statement in lines 205–208 ("To relate the manner . . .) **Ask:** What do these lines mean? *(Ross is telling Macduff that his family was murdered in order to heavily hurt Macduff.)*

Approaching Level

DIFFERENTIATED INSTRUCTION

Established Help approaching-level students understand what Ross is saying in lines 204–207. Explain that Ross uses a metaphor here to describe the murder of Macduff's family. **Ask:** What does he compare the murders to? *(hunting)* What does he compare the victims to? *(murdered deer)*

Say: Ross explains why the murderers came after Macduff's family in line 207

"To add the death of you." **Ask:** What might Ross mean by this? *(Students may say that the murderers were really after Macduff or that the murderers knew that they would be able to kill Macduff's family and hoped to kill Macduff as well.)*

377

Teach

Literary Element | 1

Plot **Answer:** *Macduff feels guilty because he left his family behind in order to keep them safe; however, he blames himself because his family was murdered in order to hurt him.*

APPROACHING For approaching-level students, **ask:** Do you think Macduff's family would have been spared if he had not left them? Explain. *(Answers will vary. Some students may say yes, because the murderers would have only been after Macduff. Others may say no, because his family may have been murdered if they got in the way of Macduff's assassination.)*

Reading Strategy | 2

Make and Verify Predictions **Answer:** *Answers will vary. Some students may say that Macbeth cannot escape punishment because he is fated to lose the throne to Banquo's descendants and now Macduff and Malcolm seek revenge.)*

 To check students' understanding of the selection, see Unit 2 Teaching Resources Book, p. 205.

Progress Check

Can students make and verify predictions?

If No → See Unit 2 Teaching Resources Book, p. 201.

378

What, all my pretty chickens and their dam°
At one fell swoop?

220   MALCOLM. Dispute it° like a man.

MACDUFF.   I shall do so;
But I must also feel it as a man.
I cannot but remember° such things were,
That were most precious to me. Did heaven look on,
And would not take their part? Sinful Macduff,
225   They were all struck for thee! Naught° that I am,
Not for their own demerits but for mine
Fell slaughter on their souls. Heaven rest them now!

MALCOLM. Be this the whetstone of your sword. Let grief
Convert to anger; blunt not the heart, enrage it.

230   MACDUFF. O, I could play the woman with mine eyes,
And braggart with my tongue! But, gentle heavens,
Cut short all intermission;° front to front°
Bring thou this fiend of Scotland and myself;
Within my sword's length set him. If he 'scape,
235   Heaven forgive him too!

MALCOLM.   This time goes manly.
Come, go we to the King. Our power is ready;
Our lack is nothing but our leave.° Macbeth
Is ripe for shaking, and the pow'rs above
Put on their instruments.° Receive what cheer you may.
240   The night is long that never finds the day.

[They all exit.]

218 dam: mother.

220 Dispute it: resist your grief.

222 but remember: help but remember that.

225 Naught: wicked man.

232 intermission: delay. front to front: face to face.

237 Our lack . . . leave: All we have left to do is take leave of the king.
239 Put . . . instruments: arm themselves.

---

1 Plot *Why does Macduff blame himself for the murder of his family?*

2 Make and Verify Predictions *Do you think it is possible for Macbeth to escape punishment for his crimes? Explain.*

Writing Practice

SPIRAL REVIEW **Fate Versus Free Will** In Act IV, Shakespeare sets up the catalysts for the action to follow in the final act. Ask students whether they believe that fate is the cause of the events that are being set in motion or whether the characters themselves are responsible for what happens. Suggest that students organize their thoughts by creating cause-and-effect organizers for the actions of Macbeth and Macduff *(i.e., Macbeth wanted the witches to tell him what would happen → The witches prophesied that a line of kings would descend from Banquo → etc.)* Have students write an essay using examples from the text to support their position.

After You Read

Respond and Think Critically

Respond and Interpret

1. (a)What information does Macbeth gather from the witches? (b)How does this information spur Macbeth to commit more murders?

2. (a)Describe the characters of Lady Macduff and her son. (b)Why do you think Lady Macduff calls her husband a traitor and tells her son, ". . . your father's dead"?

Analyze and Evaluate

3. (a)How might the fate of Lady Macduff and her son affect an audience's opinion of Macbeth? (b)Do you think the murder of Macduff's son should take place offstage? Explain.

4. (a)In your opinion, to what extent are the witches responsible for Macbeth's moral decay? (b)How much of the responsibility falls on Macbeth himself? Explain.

Connect

5. **Big Idea** **A Bard for the Ages** As Malcolm points out, King Edward was believed to have "healing hands." Why might Shakespeare have focused upon Edward as a healer?

6. **Connect to Today** In scene 3, Malcolm tests Macduff's loyalty. How might you test the loyalty of an associate?

| **Literary Element** | Plot |

Several incidents make up the **plot** of a drama, which consists of a beginning, a middle, and an end.

1. How would you contrast Macbeth's meeting with the witches in this act with their first meeting on the heath?

2. Macduff is the thane who first discovers Duncan's murdered body. What events in the rising action transform him into a figure of nemesis, or retribution?

| **Writing** |

Write a Dramatic Monologue Banquo's ghost never speaks. What might he say in response to Macbeth's outbursts at dinner? Would his tone be angry? sad? Write a dramatic monologue for Banquo's ghost to deliver to Macbeth. Consider the ways in which Banquo is a foil to Macbeth.

> **LOG ON** ▶ **Literature** Online
>
> **Selection Resources** For Selection Quizzes, eFlashcards, and Reading-Writing Connection activities, go to glencoe.com and enter QuickPass code GLB9817u2.

| **Reading Strategy** | Make and Verify Predictions |

Part of **predicting** is reading on to find out if your predictions are correct. Review the chart you made as you read, and answer the following questions.

1. Which of your predictions were accurate? Explain.

2. What do you predict will happen to Macbeth in Act 5? Why do you think so?

Vocabulary Practice

Practice with Word Usage Respond to these statements to help you explore the meanings of vocabulary words from Act 4.

1. Give an example of **pernicious** behavior from a book or movie.

2. Name an **exploit** you would like to attempt in the future.

3. Describe a time when you had to **redress** a situation.

4. Give an example of **avarice** from the contemporary world.

5. Write a question that **pertains** to a theme in *Macbeth*.

MACBETH, ACT 4 **379**

 Writing

Students' monologues should be written from Banquo's ghost's point of view, respond to Macbeth's erratic behavior, and reflect how Banquo is a foil to Macbeth.

Reading Strategy

1. Answers will vary.
2. Accept all reasonable responses.

Vocabulary

Possible answers:

1. Macbeth has his friend Banquo killed to expand his own power.

2. I would like to go rock climbing.

3. I broke the window, so I paid for it.

4. Some people insist on using more limited resources than necessary.

5. When might ambition transform into a destructive quality?

After You Read

Assess

1. (a) Beware Macduff. None "of woman born" will harm Macbeth. He is safe until Birnam Wood marches on Dunsinane castle. (b) Macbeth thinks he is safe from harm.

2. (a) Both seem honorable and affectionate. (b) Lady Macduff uses the terms figuratively. Macduff has betrayed them by leaving.

3. (a) The audience might decide that Macbeth is totally depraved. (b) Students' answers will vary.

4. (a) Students may say the witches' prophesies stir Macbeth's ambition. (b) Students may note that Macbeth has free will and chose to murder Duncan, Banquo, and Macduff's family.

5. Some students may suggest English patriotism or a compliment to King James I, who then occupied the English throne.

6. You could criticize an idea that you actually favor, in order to see whether your associate accepts or defends your criticism.

Literary Element

1. In their first meeting, the witches seek out Macbeth. In their second meeting, he seeks them out, demanding that they reveal his future.

2. Macduff leaves his family and goes to England to gain Malcolm's support in unseating Macbeth.

Progress Check

Can students follow the plot?

If No → See Unit 2 Teaching Resources Book, p. 200.

Before You Read

Focus

Summary

At Dunsinane castle, Lady Macbeth commits suicide. Macbeth, preoccupied with military preparations, learns of her death. For camouflage, Malcolm's troops to carry branches as they march from Birnam Forest. Seeing that the woods appear to be moving, Macbeth decides to attack. Macduff seeks out and slays Macbeth. Malcolm's forces win, and he makes plans for his coronation.

 For summaries in languages other than English, see Unit 2 Teaching Resources Book, pp. 207–212.

Vocabulary

Analogies Ask students to think of at least three analogies for each vocabulary word. *(i.e., three historical usurpers, three situations requiring an antidote)*

[ENGLISH LEARNERS] Tell English learners to identify the three cognates in the vocabulary list and tell you the Spanish equivalents. *(purga, antídoto, and usurpador)*

Before You Read

Macbeth, Act 5

Build Background

This act opens with a famous sleepwalking scene, a particular favorite of most actresses portraying Lady Macbeth. Somnambulism (som nam′ byə li′ zəm) is an abnormal condition of sleep in which actions such as walking are performed. Since sleepwalkers are not completely aware of their surroundings, they can easily injure themselves by falling down or bumping into things. In adults, sleepwalking is considered symptomatic of a troubled personality. Shakespeare obviously knew about this condition and relished its theatrical possibilities. His depiction of Lady Macbeth's symptoms is medically accurate. These symptoms indicate that Lady Macbeth, formerly so commanding and calculating, now is haunted by guilt. As the Doctor observes, "Infected minds / To their deaf pillows will discharge their secrets."

Literary Element | Tragedy

A **tragedy** is a literary work in which the main character, or hero, suffers a downfall as a result of a tragic flaw—a character weakness, an error in judgment, or forces beyond human control, such as fate. The **tragic hero** is usually a high-ranking character who ultimately gains some kind of insight into himself or herself even though he or she experiences defeat, and oftentimes death. *Macbeth* is considered to be one of Shakespeare's finest tragedies. As you read, ask yourself, What qualities of a tragedy does *Macbeth* reflect?

Reading Strategy | Analyze Cause-and-Effect Relationships

A **cause** is an action or event that makes something happen; an **effect** is the result of that action or event. You analyze cause-and-effect relationships whenever you try to answer the question *why*. As you read, ask yourself, What are the causes of these actions and events?

Tip: Noting Causes and Effects Use a diagram to help you identify cause-and-effect relationships.

Macbeth fears the witches' prophecy. → Macbeth orders the murderers to kill Fleance.

Vocabulary

purge (purj) *n.* the process of getting rid of impurities or undesirable elements; p. 385 *The mayor initiated a purge of dishonest workers.*

antidote (an′ ti dōt′) *n.* a medicine used to counteract the effects of a poison; any counteracting remedy; p. 386 *Keeping busy is the antidote to boredom.*

siege (sēj) *n.* a blockade; the surrounding of a fortified place by an opposing army; p. 388 *The siege of Troy lasted for ten years.*

prowess (prou′ is) *n.* superior ability; skill; p. 393 *Pelé is known for his prowess on the soccer field.*

usurper (ū surp′ ər) *n.* one who seizes the power, position, or rights of another by force; p. 393 *The usurper forced the elected president out of office.*

Selection Skills

Literary Elements
- Tragedy (SE pp. 380, 384–386, 389, 390, 392, 393, 396)

Macbeth, Act V

Listening/Speaking/Viewing Skills
- Analyze Art (SE p. 383)

Reading Skills
- Analyze Cause-and-Effect Relationships (SE pp. 380, 381, 387, 389, 396)

Vocabulary Skills
- Context Clues (SE p. 396; TE p. 388)
- Academic Vocabulary (SE p. 396)

Writing Skills/Grammar
- Write an Expository Essay (SE p. 397)

380

ACT 5

SCENE 1. MACBETH's castle at Dunsinane.

[It is late at night in MACBETH's *castle at Dunsinane. A* GENTLEWOMAN *who serves* LADY MACBETH *enters with a* SCOTTISH PHYSICIAN.*]*

    DOCTOR. I have two nights watched° with you, but can perceive no truth in your report. When was it she last walked?°

5   GENTLEWOMAN. Since his Majesty went into the field,° I have seen her rise from her bed, throw her nightgown upon her, unlock her closet,° take forth paper, fold it, write upon 't, read it, afterwards seal it, and again return to bed; yet all this while in a most fast sleep.

10   DOCTOR. A great perturbation in nature,° to receive at once the benefit of sleep and do the effects of watching!° In this slumb'ry agitation, besides her walking and other actual performances, what, at any time, have you heard her say?

    GENTLEWOMAN. That, sir, which I will not report after her.

15   DOCTOR. You may to me, and 'tis most meet° you should.

    GENTLEWOMAN. Neither to you nor anyone, having no witness to confirm my speech.

[LADY MACBETH enters, carrying a candlestick.]

    Lo you, here she comes! This is her very guise,° and, upon my life, fast asleep! Observe her; stand close.°

20   DOCTOR. How came she by that light?

    GENTLEWOMAN. Why, it stood by her. She has light by her continually. 'Tis her command.

[LADY MACBETH moves across the stage, unaware that others are watching her.]

    DOCTOR. You see, her eyes are open.

    GENTLEWOMAN. Ay, but their sense° are shut.

25   DOCTOR. What is it she does now? Look, how she rubs her hands.

    GENTLEWOMAN. It is an accustomed action with her, to seem thus washing her hands: I have known her continue in

---

1 watched: stayed awake.

3 walked: sleepwalked.

4 into the field: joined the army on the battlefield.

6 closet: private cabinet.

9 perturbation in nature: disruption of natural functions.
10 effects of watching: actions one does while awake.

15 meet: proper.

18 guise: custom.
19 close: hidden.

24 sense: power of perception.

Analyze Cause-and-Effect Relationships *Why has Macbeth gone into the field?* **1**

Analyze Cause-and-Effect Relationships *Why do you think Lady Macbeth goes through the motions of washing her hands while fast asleep?* **2**

MACBETH, ACT 5, SCENE 1 **381**

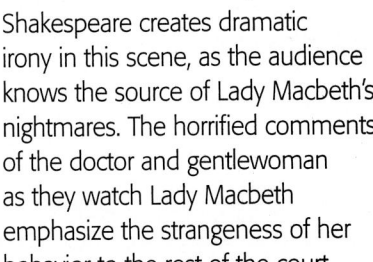

Teach

A Bard for the Ages

Answer: *After Duncan's murder, Macbeth lamented that all the world's oceans could not wash the blood from his hands; Lady Macbeth answered that a little water would clear them of the deed. Now, the smell of blood lingers on her hands, stronger than the scent of all perfumes.*

ADVANCED Ask advanced students to compare Lady Macbeth and Macbeth. In this scene, we see the change in Lady Macbeth's feelings.

Ask: Has Macbeth also undergone a change? If so, how is it similar to or different from Lady Macbeth's alteration? *(Answers will vary.)*

Writer's Technique ☆

Prose This scene is in prose rather than iambic pentameter. The doctor and gentlewoman's use of prose reflects their lower social status or limited verbal skills. However, Lady Macbeth has previously spoken in iambic pentameter. Her use of prose in this scene emphasizes her fallen mental state.

---

this a quarter of an hour.

30   LADY MACBETH.   Yet here's a spot. ☆

DOCTOR.   Hark! she speaks. I will set down what comes from her, to satisfy° my remembrance the more strongly.

LADY MACBETH.   [*She sets down the candlestick and rubs her hands as if she were washing them.*] Out, damned spot!
35   Out, I say! One: two: why, then 'tis time to do 't.° Hell is murky. Fie, my lord, fie! A soldier, and afeard? What need we fear who knows it, when none can call our pow'r to accompt?° Yet who would have thought the old man to have had so much blood in him?

DOCTOR.   Do you mark that?

40   LADY MACBETH.   The Thane of Fife had a wife. Where is she now? What, will these hands ne'er be clean? No more o' that, my lord, no more o' that! You mar all with this starting.°

DOCTOR.   Go to,° go to! You have known what you should not.

45   GENTLEWOMAN.   She has spoke what she should not, I am sure of that. Heaven knows what she has known.

LADY MACBETH.   Here's the smell of the blood still. All the perfumes of Arabia will not sweeten this little hand. Oh, oh, oh!

50   DOCTOR.   What a sigh is there! The heart is sorely charged.°

GENTLEWOMAN.   I would not have such a heart in my bosom for the dignity° of the whole body.

DOCTOR.   Well, well, well—

GENTLEWOMAN.   Pray God it be, sir.

55   DOCTOR.   This disease is beyond my practice. Yet I have known those which have walked in their sleep who have died holily in their beds.

LADY MACBETH.   Wash your hands; put on your nightgown; look not so pale! I tell you yet again, Banquo's buried.
60   He cannot come out on 's° grave.

DOCTOR.   Even so?

LADY MACBETH.   To bed, to bed! There's knocking at the gate. Come, come, come, come, give me your hand! What's done cannot be undone. To bed, to bed, to bed!

[*LADY MACBETH exits.*]

---

1   **A Bard for the Ages** *How does Shakespeare use this image to reveal Lady Macbeth's change in character?*

32 **satisfy:** support.

34 **One . . . do 't:** Lady Macbeth, counting out the chimes of a clock, imagines it is the night when Duncan was murdered.

36–37 **call . . . accompt:** force anyone as powerful as us to answer for our crimes.

42 **starting:** sudden fits.

43 **Go to:** an exclamation expressing disapproval (addressed to Lady Macbeth).

50 **charged:** burdened.

52 **dignity:** worth.

60 **on 's:** of his.

Literary Element Practice

SPIRAL REVIEW **Dialogue** To fully understand dialogue—conversation between literary characters—a reader must identify to whom each character is speaking. After the doctor and gentlewoman share their comments, Lady Macbeth enters, but she does not interact with these characters. She speaks to herself or to her own visions.

Encourage students to "fill in the blanks" in Lady Macbeth's dialogue, explaining what sights she sees that prompt each exclamation.

View the Art ★

Answer: *Lady Macbeth appears dazed. Her wide-open eyes suggest that she is horror-stricken. Her head, turned away from the outstretched arm, implies that she is trying to avoid looking at her hand and to keep it as far away as possible. Her emotional state is fragile.*

A number of Fuseli's paintings are based on scenes from Shakespeare's works. This captivating painting highlights his fascination with dream interpretation.

Lady Macbeth Sleepwalking, 1784. Henry Fuseli. Oil on canvas, 87 x 63 in. Louvre Museum, Paris.

 View the Art Many of Fuseli's images portray figures in a state of strain, or making unnaturally exaggerated gestures. What does Lady Macbeth's expression tell you about her emotional state?

383

English Learners

DIFFERENTIATED INSTRUCTION

Intermediate Say: An interjection is a word or phrase that expresses emotion. On page 382, point out Lady Macbeth's "Fie, my lord, fie!" **Say:** *fie* is an old-fashioned word used to express disgust. Also on page 382, point out the doctor's "Go to, go to!" as expressing disapproval. Have students list some contemporary interjections.

Approaching Level

DIFFERENTIATED INSTRUCTION

Emerging Suggest that students create a scene map for Act IV by folding a sheet of paper into eighths and labeling the sections "Scene 1" through "Scene 8." After reading each scene, students can write a brief summary, including details such as setting, main characters, and key events.

Reading Strategy 1

Analyze Cause-and-Effect Relationships Ask: What does the Doctor believe to be the cause of Lady Macbeth's strange behavior? *(He believes she is haunted by "unnatural deeds.")* Do you believe that his analysis of the situation is correct? *(Most students will agree that Lady Macbeth has lost her reason because of the stress caused by her role in Duncan's murder.)*

Literary Element 2

Tragedy Answer: *Angus's comment reveals that Macbeth's "secret murders" have come back to haunt him.*

ENGLISH LEARNERS After English learners have read the sidenote for line 18, ask them what *minutely* means in this line. Then have them look the word up in the dictionary and tell you the meanings they find. If their dictionary includes "every minute" as a definition for *minutely*, make sure students see it is labeled as archaic.

65 **DOCTOR.** Will she go now to bed?

GENTLEWOMAN. Directly.

DOCTOR. Foul whisp'rings are abroad. Unnatural deeds
  Do breed unnatural troubles. Infected minds
  To their deaf pillows will discharge their secrets.
70   More needs she the divine° than the physician.
  God, God forgive us all! Look after her;
  Remove from her the means of all annoyance,°
  And still° keep eyes upon her. So good night.
  My mind she has mated° and amazed my sight:
75   I think, but dare not speak.

GENTLEWOMAN.   Good night, good doctor.

[*They exit.*]

70 divine: priest.

72 annoyance: injury.
73 still: always.
74 mated: bewildered.

SCENE 2. In the countryside, near Dunsinane.

[*Soldiers enter with the Scottish noblemen* MENTEITH, CAITHNESS, ANGUS, *and* LENNOX. *The soldiers are carrying drums and flags. They are all on the way to join forces with an approaching English army to rebel against* MACBETH.]

MENTEITH. The English pow'r° is near, led on by Malcolm,
  His uncle Siward and the good Macduff.
  Revenges burn in them; for their dear causes
  Would to the bleeding and the grim alarm
5   Excite the mortified man.°

ANGUS.   Near Birnam Wood
  Shall we well° meet them; that way are they coming.

CAITHNESS. Who knows if Donalbain be with his brother?

LENNOX. For certain, sir, he is not. I have a file°
  Of all the gentry: there is Siward's son,
10   And many unrough° youths that even now
  Protest their first of manhood.°

MENTEITH.   What does the tyrant?

CAITHNESS. Great Dunsinane he strongly fortifies.
  Some say he's mad; others, that lesser hate him,
  Do call it valiant fury: but, for certain,
15   He cannot buckle his distempered cause
  Within the belt of rule.°

ANGUS.   Now does he feel
  His secret murders sticking on his hands;
  Now minutely revolts upbraid his faith-breach.°

1 pow'r: army.

3–5 their dear . . . man: Their grave cause would arouse a dead man to bloodshed and grim warfare.
6 well: no doubt.

8 file: list.

10 unrough: beardless.
11 Protest . . . manhood: proclaim the beginning of their manhood.

15–16 He . . . rule: Like a man who cannot buckle his belt because he is bloated with disease, Macbeth cannot impose order on his diseased cause.

18 minutely . . . faith-breach: Revolts occurring every minute upbraid his disloyalty.

2 Tragedy *What does Angus's comment reveal about Macbeth?*

Writing Practice

SPIRAL REVIEW **Iambic Pentameter** Point out the doctor's speech, beginning on line 67, and remind students that the doctor and gentlewoman speak in prose to signify their lower social status. Of course, today a doctor is regarded with a higher social status. Tell students to imagine they are a modern-day psychologist observing Lady Macbeth's sleepwalking behavior and commenting on it. Have them write a short speech for the psychologist in iambic pentameter. The speech should be at least six lines long and can be in contemporary English.

²⁰ Those he commands move only in command,
Nothing in love. Now does he feel his title
Hang loose about him, like a giant's robe
Upon a dwarfish thief.

MENTEITH.   Who then shall blame
His pestered° senses to recoil and start,
When all that is within him does condemn
²⁵ Itself for being there?

CAITHNESS.   Well, march we on,
To give obedience where 'tis truly owed.
Meet we the med'cine of the sickly weal,°
And with him pour we, in our country's **purge**,
Each drop of us.°

LENNOX.   Or so much as it needs
³⁰ To dew the sovereign flower and drown the weeds.°
Make we our march towards Birnam.

[*They march off.*]

SCENE 3. The castle at Dunsinane.

[MACBETH, *the* DOCTOR, *and attendants enter a room in Dunsinane Castle.*]

MACBETH. Bring me no more reports; let them fly all!°
Till Birnam Wood remove to Dunsinane
I cannot taint° with fear. What's the boy Malcolm?
Was he not born of woman? The spirits that know
⁵ All mortal consequences° have pronounced me thus:
"Fear not, Macbeth; no man that's born of woman
Shall e'er have power upon thee." Then fly, false thanes,
And mingle with the English epicures.°
The mind I sway by° and the heart I bear
¹⁰ Shall never sag with doubt nor shake with fear.

[*A* SERVANT *enters.*]

The devil damn thee black, thou cream-faced loon!°
Where got'st thou that goose look?

SERVANT. There is ten thousand—

MACBETH.   Geese, villain?

SERVANT.   Soldiers, sir.

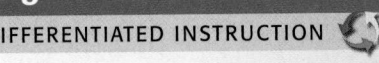 **Tragedy** *Which of Macbeth's qualities does this passage reveal?* **3**

Vocabulary

purge (purj) *n.* the process of getting rid of impurities or undesirable elements

---

23 pestered: troubled.

27 med'cine . . . weal: physician of our ailing commonwealth (Malcolm).
28–29 pour . . . us: Let us shed all our blood to restore Scotland's health.
30 To . . . weeds: to water the royal flower (Malcolm) and drown the evil (Macbeth).

1 let . . . all: Let all of the thanes desert me.

3 taint: become infected.

5 All mortal consequences: everything that will happen to human beings.

8 epicures: gluttons (The Scots, who typically ate plain food, often disapproved of English eating habits.)
9 I sway by: that directs me.

11 loon: stupid fellow.

Teach

Literary Element **3**

Tragedy **Answer:** *This passage reveals Macbeth's determination to master his fear.*

Cultural History ☆

Misinterpreted Prophecies
Like many leaders in literature and history, Macbeth interprets the witches' prophecy to suit his goals. For example, when a king of Lydia asked the oracle of Delphi whether he should fight Persia, the oracle responded that he would destroy a mighty empire. Only after his brutal defeat did the king realize that the empire destroyed was his own.

English Learners

DIFFERENTIATED INSTRUCTION

Beginning Review Shakespeare's use of contractions—for example, *pow'r* (power) in scene 2, line 1; and *med'cine* (medicine) in scene 2, line 27. Point out that each of these reduces the number of syllables in a word to maintain the meter. Students should internalize the contractions as they read silently and aloud.

Approaching Level

DIFFERENTIATED INSTRUCTION

Emerging Point out that the "tyrant" referred to in scene 2, line 11, is Macbeth. This identification is essential to understanding that the noblemen are talking about Macbeth in the rest of the scene. The pronouns *he, his,* and *him* refer to Macbeth in lines 12–25.

Teach

Literary Element 1

Tragedy **Answer:** *Though facing insurmountable opposition, Macbeth is determined not to surrender. He vows to keep fighting to the end, even if Malcolm's forces are hacking his body to pieces.*

(ADVANCED) Have advanced students list other qualities of a tragic hero, such as honor, loyalty, keeping one's word, and a tragic flaw. Ask them which characters possess these other qualities. Have students discuss whether other characters in the play can also be considered tragic heroes.

Cultural History ☆

Psychology The scientific study of psychology was developed in the later 19th century by pioneers such as Wilhelm Wundt, Hermann Ebbinghaus, Ivan Pavlov, and Sigmund Freud. However, writers and observers in all eras have drawn sharp and insightful conclusions based on observation and experience. Macbeth understands that his wife's mental disorder is caused by guilt; however, Shakespeare depicts his desire for an instant cure as obviously naïve.

MACBETH. Go prick thy face and over-red thy fear,°
15   Thou lily-livered boy. What soldiers, patch?°
  Death of thy soul! Those linen° cheeks of thine
  Are counselors to fear.° What soldiers, whey-face?

SERVANT. The English force, so please you.

MACBETH. Take thy face hence.

[*The* SERVANT *exits.*]

                    Seyton!°—I am sick at heart,
20   When I behold—Seyton, I say!—This push°
  Will cheer me ever, or disseat° me now.
  I have lived long enough. My way of life
  Is fall'n into the sear,° the yellow leaf,
  And that which should accompany old age,
25   As° honor, love, obedience, troops of friends,
  I must not look to have; but, in their stead,
  Curses not loud but deep, mouth-honor,° breath,
  Which the poor heart would fain° deny, and dare not.
  Seyton!

[SEYTON *enters.*]

30 **SEYTON.** What's your gracious pleasure?

MACBETH.   What news more?

SEYTON. All is confirmed, my lord, which was reported.

MACBETH. I'll fight, till from my bones my flesh be hacked.
  Give me my armor.

SEYTON.   'Tis not needed yet.

MACBETH. I'll put it on.
35   Send out moe° horses, skirr° the country round.
  Hang those that talk of fear. Give me mine armor.
  How does your patient, doctor?

DOCTOR.   Not so sick, my lord,
  As she is troubled with thick-coming fancies
  That keep her from her rest.

MACBETH.   Cure her of that. ☆
40   Canst thou not minister to a mind diseased,
  Pluck from the memory a rooted sorrow,
  Raze out° the written troubles of the brain,
  And with some sweet oblivious **antidote**

14 over-red thy fear: cover your white-faced fear with redness.
15 patch: fool.
16 linen: pale as linen.
17 Are . . . fear: advise others to be afraid.

19 Seyton: Macbeth's trusted officer.
20 push: effort.
21 disseat: dethrone.

23 the sear: a withered state.

25 As: such as.

27 mouth-honor: lip service.
28 fain: gladly.

35 moe: more. **skirr:** scour.

42 Raze out: erase.

---

1 Tragedy *How do these lines reinforce Macbeth's stature as a hero?*

Vocabulary

antidote (an′ti dōt′) *n.* a medicine used to counteract the effects of a poison; any counteracting remedy

Reading Practice

PARTNERS **SPIRAL REVIEW** **Question** Tell students that asking questions as they read is a good way to understand the plot. "How" questions and questions in any of the 5W categories can all be useful. Reassure students that in a complex text such as Macbeth, simple factual questions such as "Who is Siward again?" are appropriate and helpful. Have students read this scene and keep a list of questions they think of. Then have them exchange questions with a partner and ask students to answer each other's questions.

Cleanse the stuffed bosom of that perilous stuff
45 Which weighs upon the heart?

DOCTOR.   Therein the patient
Must minister to himself.

MACBETH.   Throw physic° to the dogs, I'll none of it.
Come, put mine armor on. Give me my staff.
Seyton, send out—Doctor, the thanes fly from me—
50 Come, sir, dispatch.° If thou couldst, doctor, cast
The water of my land,° find her disease
And purge it to a sound and pristine health,
I would applaud thee to the very echo,
That should applaud again—Pull 't off,° I say—
55 What rhubarb, senna,° or what purgative drug,
Would scour these English hence? Hear'st thou of them?

DOCTOR.   Ay, my good lord; your royal preparation
Makes us hear something.

MACBETH.   Bring it° after me.
I will not be afraid of death and bane°
60 Till Birnam Forest come to Dunsinane.

DOCTOR.   [Aside.] Were I from Dunsinane away and clear,
Profit again should hardly draw me here.

[They exit.]

SCENE 4. In the countryside, near Birnam Wood.

[A group of soldiers and noblemen enter marching. Among them are a drummer, flagbearer, MALCOLM, MACDUFF, MENTEITH, CAITHNESS, ANGUS, and SIWARD, the general sent by the King of England, and his son, YOUNG SIWARD.]

MALCOLM.   Cousins, I hope the days are near at hand
That chambers will be safe.°

MENTEITH.   We doubt it nothing.°

SIWARD.   What wood is this before us?

MENTEITH.   The Wood of Birnam.

MALCOLM.   Let every soldier hew him down a bough
5 And bear 't before him. Thereby shall we shadow°
The numbers of our host,° and make discovery°
Err in report of us.

Analyze Cause-and-Effect Relationships   *Why does Macbeth not fear the forces aligned against him?*   **2**

Analyze Cause-and-Effect Relationships   *How will this action reveal the flaw in Macbeth's interpretation of the witches' prophecy?*   **3**

---

47 **physic:** medicine.

50 **dispatch:** be quick (addressed to an attendant).
50–51 **cast . . . land:** diagnose the ailment of my country.

54 **Pull 't off:** remove this piece of armor (which was put on incorrectly).
55 **senna:** a purgative drug.

58 **it:** the rest of his armor.
59 **bane:** destruction.

2 **That . . . safe:** when we may be safe in our bedchambers. **nothing:** not at all.

5 **shadow:** conceal.
6 **host:** army. **discovery:** Macbeth's scouts.

Teach

Reading Strategy   2

Analyze Cause-and-Effect Relationships Answer: *Macbeth believes he is secure because it is impossible for the Birnam Forest to march towards Dunsinane.* **Ask:** What effect do you predict will occur as a result of Macbeth's sense of invulnerability? *(It will lead to his downfall because no man is as untouchable as he believes himself to be.)*

Reading Strategy   3

Analyze Cause-and-Effect Relationships Answer: *This action will transform Birnam Wood into a moving grove, showing that the advance of Birnam Wood on Dunsinane is really possible.*

Ask: Does Malcolm ask his soldiers to carry branches from Birnam Wood because he wants to make the witches' prophecy come true? *(No, he is unaware of the prophecy. He adopts this strategy because he wants to hide the size of his army.)*

ENGLISH LEARNERS Have English learners look up *hew* (line 4), *bough* (line 4), *bear* (line 5), and *Err* (line 7) in a dictionary. Help them choose the correct meaning of *bear*. Then ask students to restate Malcolm's instructions in simple language to ensure that they understand them.

English Learners

DIFFERENTIATED INSTRUCTION

Beginning Remind students that synonyms are words with similar meanings. Model how synonyms can be used to define words by providing these definitions: *wood* (line 3)—"forest"; *bough* (line 4)—"branch"; *host* (line 6)—"army." Ask students to define three more nouns with synonyms.

Approaching Level

DIFFERENTIATED INSTRUCTION

Emerging Some students may have difficulty identifying characters' emotions on the basis of dialogue. Encourage students to read short scenes aloud. Then discuss how each character probably feels during the scene.

Teach

Context Clues Model the use of context clues to find the meaning of the word *siege.* Read lines 2–3 aloud. **Say:** I know that *scorn* means "contempt." The castle's strength is mockingly contemptuous of something; it is probably either an enemy or an attack. I can use the vocabulary note to see that it is an attack on a fortified place.

SOLDIERS.   It shall be done.

SIWARD.   We learn no other but° the confident tyrant
     Keeps still in Dunsinane, and will endure
10   Our setting down before 't.°

MALCOLM.   'Tis his main hope,
     For where there is advantage to be given
     Both more and less° have given him the revolt,
     And none serve with him but constrainèd things°
     Whose hearts are absent too.

MACDUFF.   Let our just censures
15   Attend the true event,° and put we on
     Industrious soldiership.

SIWARD.   The time approaches,
     That will with due decision make us know
     What we shall say we have and what we owe.°
     Thoughts speculative their unsure hopes relate,
20   But certain issue strokes must arbitrate:°
     Towards which advance the war.°

[*They march off.*]

SCENE 5. The castle at Dunsinane.

[*Inside Dunsinane Castle,* MACBETH, SEYTON, *and other soldiers, including a drummer and flagbearer, prepare for battle.*]

MACBETH.   Hang out our banners on the outward walls.
     The cry is still "They come!" Our castle's strength
     Will laugh a **siege** to scorn. Here let them lie **1**
     Till famine and the ague° eat them up.
5   Were they not forced with those that should be ours,°
     We might have met them dareful,° beard to beard,
     And beat them backward home.

[*A cry is heard within the castle.*]

                   What is that noise?

SEYTON.   It is the cry of women, my good lord.

[*SEYTON exits.*]

MACBETH.   I have almost forgot the taste of fears:
10   The time has been, my senses would have cooled
     To hear a night-shriek, and my fell of hair°
     Would at a dismal treatise° rouse and stir

Vocabulary

siege (sēj) *n.* a blockade; the surrounding of a fortified place by an opposing army

---

Side notes

8 **no other but:** only that.

9–10 **will . . . 't:** will not try to prevent us from laying siege to it.

12 **more and less:** noblemen and commoners.
13 **constrainèd things:** people who have no choice.

14–15 **Let . . . event:** Let us reserve our judgment of this matter until the battle is over.

17–18 **with due . . . owe:** distinguish our claims from what we really own.
19–20 **Thoughts . . . arbitrate:** Speculation may express unsure hopes, but certain outcomes must be decided in battle.
21 **war:** army.

4 **ague:** fever.
5 **forced . . . ours:** reinforced with deserters or rebels.
6 **met them dareful:** confronted them defiantly.

11 **my . . . hair:** the hair on my scalp.
12 **dismal treatise:** dreadful story.

Reading Practice

SPIRAL REVIEW **Analyze Character Transformation** Students can use Macbeth's response to hearing about his wife's death in lines 17–28 on this spread as crucial evidence showing how he has changed during the play. Encourage them to compare this "tomorrow" monologue with Macbeth's hypocritical speech in Act 2, scene 3 (page 336), when he reacts publicly to the news of Duncan's murder. Students should recognize that the earlier speech shows Macbeth in firm control, whereas this one shows him darkly pessimistic. Have students summarize the events that have led to his transformation.

As life were in 't. I have supped full with horrors.
Direness,° familiar to my slaughterous thoughts,
15 Cannot once start me.

[SEYTON *returns*.]

Wherefore was that cry?

SEYTON. The Queen, my lord, is dead.

MACBETH. She should have died hereafter;°
There would have been a time for such a word.°
Tomorrow, and tomorrow, and tomorrow
20 Creeps in this petty pace from day to day,
To the last syllable of recorded time;
And all our yesterdays have lighted fools
The way° to dusty death. Out, out, brief candle!
Life's but a walking shadow,° a poor player
25 That struts and frets his hour upon the stage
And then is heard no more. It is a tale
Told by an idiot, full of sound and fury
Signifying nothing.

[A MESSENGER *enters*.]

Thou com'st to use thy tongue; thy story quickly!

30 MESSENGER. Gracious my lord,
I should report that which I say I saw,
But know not how to do 't.

MACBETH.   Well, say, sir.

MESSENGER. As I did stand my watch upon the hill,
I looked toward Birnam, and anon, methought,
35 The wood began to move.

MACBETH.   Liar and slave!

MESSENGER. Let me endure your wrath, if 't be not so.
Within this three mile may you see it coming;
I say a moving grove.

MACBETH.   If thou speak'st false,
Upon the next tree shalt thou hang alive,
40 Till famine cling° thee. If thy speech be sooth,°
I care not if thou dost for me as much.
I pull in resolution,° and begin
To doubt th' equivocation of the fiend

Analyze Cause-and-Effect Relationships *How have Macbeth's crimes affect his conscience?*   **2**

Tragedy *What does this comparison suggest about Macbeth's view of life?*   **3**

14 **Direness:** horror.

17 **She . . . hereafter:** She should have died at a later time (not when I'm preoccupied with urgent matters).
18 **word:** message that the queen is dead.

22–23 **lighted . . . way:** illuminated the path that fools take.
24 **shadow:** insubstantial image, actor.

40 **cling:** wither. **sooth:** the truth.

42 **pull in resolution:** restrain my confidence.

Teach

Reading Strategy   2

Analyze Cause-and-Effect Relationships **Answer:** *Macbeth's crimes have numbed his conscience, rendering him insensitive to appalling events.*

Literary Element   3

Tragedy **Answer:** *This comparison suggests Macbeth's utter despair and his conviction that life is meaningless.*

(ENGLISH LEARNERS) Make sure English learners understand the two comparisons. If they do not understand what a player is, encourage them to use the word *stage* as a context clue. Have them complete the sentence *Life is like . . .* once for each comparison (*Life is like an actor; life is like a story.*)

Approaching Level

DIFFERENTIATED INSTRUCTION

Emerging Students can develop ***reading fluency*** and internalize sentence structure through reciting speeches. Suggest that students memorize Macbeth's famous "tomorrow" monologue (scene 5, lines 17–28). Allow students to share oral readings or taped presentations with the rest of the class.

Advanced Learners

DIFFERENTIATED INSTRUCTION

Quotations Note that excerpts from Macbeth's "tomorrow" monologue are frequently quoted. Have advanced students use library or Internet research tools to find and read at least two such quotations. Have them explain the contexts in which the quotation is applied.

Teach

Reading Strategy | 1

Analyze Cause-and-Effect Relationships **Ask:** How and why did Macbeth change his battle strategy? *(He was planning to sit out the siege. However, seeing Birnam Wood move, he knows that the prophecy has come true and Dunsinane is no longer a safe refuge. Thus, he decides to attack and, if nothing else, go down fighting.)*

(APPROACHING) For approaching-level students **ask:** Who first said "Fear not, till Birnam Wood / Do come to Dunsinane"? *(the witches)* Why did Macbeth feel safe after hearing this prophecy? *(because a forest can't move)* What didn't he realize? *(that the witches were not speaking literally)*

Literary Element | 2

Tragedy **Answer:** *He accepts, rather than denies, the fulfillment of the prophecy. Still, he plans to die fighting rather than passively accept his doom.*

Literary Element | 3

Tragedy **Answer:** *By comparing himself to a tethered bear, Macbeth suggests that he is ferocious, a mighty creature surrounded by petty foes.*

(ENGLISH LEARNERS) Remind English learners that *fly* has multiple meanings. **Ask:** What does Macbeth mean by *fly*? *(run away)* Have students look up *stake* in the dictionary to help them more accurately visualize bear-baiting.

390

---

45   That lies like truth:° "Fear not, till Birnam Wood
     Do come to Dunsinane!" And now a wood
     Comes toward Dunsinane. Arm, arm, and out!
     If this which he avouches° does appear,
     There is nor flying hence nor° tarrying here.
     I 'gin to be aweary of the sun,
50   And wish th' estate° o' th' world were now undone.
     Ring the alarum bell! Blow wind, come wrack!°
     At least we'll die with harness° on our back.

[*They all exit.*]

SCENE 6. In the countryside, near the castle at Dunsinane.

[MALCOLM, SIWARD, MACDUFF, *and their soldiers, hidden by the tree boughs they are carrying, advance toward Dunsinane Castle.*]

     MALCOLM.   Now near enough. Your leavy° screens throw
            down,
            And show like those you are. You, worthy uncle,°
            Shall, with my cousin, your right noble son,
            Lead our first battle.° Worthy Macduff and we
5   Shall take upon 's what else remains to do,
            According to our order.
     SIWARD.   Fare you well.
            Do we but find the tyrant's power° tonight,
            Let us be beaten, if we cannot fight.
     MACDUFF.   Make all our trumpets speak; give them all breath,
10   Those clamorous harbingers° of blood and death.

[*Blaring trumpets and the sound of battle are heard as they exit.*]

SCENE 7. In the countryside, near the castle at Dunsinane.

[*On another part of the battlefield outside the castle,* MACBETH *enters.*]

     MACBETH.   They have tied me to a stake; I cannot fly,
            But bearlike, I must fight the course.° What's he
            That was not born of woman? Such a one
            Am I to fear, or none.

[YOUNG SIWARD *enters and challenges* MACBETH.]

5   YOUNG SIWARD.   What is thy name?
     MACBETH.   Thou'lt be afraid to hear it.
     YOUNG SIWARD.   No; though thou call'st thyself a hotter name
            Than any is in hell.

2   Tragedy *What does this speech reveal about Macbeth's character?*

3   Tragedy *What does Macbeth suggest about himself in this passage?*

390   UNIT 2   THE ENGLISH RENAISSANCE

43–44 doubt . . . truth: mistrust the deceptive language of the devil, who tells apparent truths in order to deceive.

47 he avouches: the Messenger assures us is true.

48 nor . . . nor: neither . . . nor.

50 estate: established order.

51 wrack: ruin.

52 harness: armor.

1 leavy: leafy.

2 uncle: Siward.

4 battle: battalion.

7 power: forces.

10 harbingers: forerunners announcing someone's approach.

2 bearlike . . . course: Like a bear tied to a stake, I must fight off this round of attack. (Macbeth's metaphor refers to bear-baiting, a popular entertainment in which bears were tied to stakes and surrounded by vicious dogs.)

Writing Practice

SPIRAL REVIEW **Descriptive Narratives** Have students rewrite the dialogue between young Siward and Macbeth as a short third-person narrative. Have students begin by visualizing Macbeth. **Ask:** What does he look like? Does his appearance reflect the changes in his character? Have students jot notes about the physical appearance of both Macbeth and young Siward in this scene. Then have them write the narrative, incorporating as many details as possible about the men's appearance and gestures.

MACBETH.   My name's Macbeth.

YOUNG SIWARD.   The devil himself could not pronounce a title
　　More hateful to mine ear.

MACBETH.   No, nor more fearful.

10 YOUNG SIWARD.   Thou liest, abhorrèd tyrant; with my sword
　　I'll prove the lie thou speak'st.

[*They fight, and* YOUNG SIWARD *is slain.*]

MACBETH.   Thou wast born of woman.
　　But swords I smile at, weapons laugh to scorn,
　　Brandished by man that's of a woman born.

[MACBETH *exits as the sounds of battle mount.* MACDUFF *enters.*]

MACDUFF.   That way the noise is. Tyrant, show thy face!
15　　If thou be'st slain and with no stroke of mine,
　　My wife and children's ghosts will haunt me still.°
　　I cannot strike at wretched kerns,° whose arms
　　Are hired to bear their staves.° Either thou, Macbeth,
　　Or else my sword, with an unbattered edge,
20　　I sheathe again undeeded.° There thou shouldst be;
　　By this great clatter, one of greatest note
　　Seems bruited.° Let me find him, Fortune!
　　And more I beg not.

[*More battle sounds are heard as* MACDUFF *exits.* MALCOLM *and* OLD
SIWARD *enter.*]

SIWARD.   This way, my lord. The castle's gently rend'red:°
25　　The tyrant's people on both sides do fight;
　　The noble thanes do bravely in the war;
　　The day almost itself professes yours,
　　And little is to do.

MALCOLM.   We have met with foes
　　That strike beside us.°

SIWARD.   Enter, sir, the castle.

[*They exit as the sounds of battle continue.*]

SCENE 8. Near the castle at Dunsinane.

[MACBETH *enters in another part of the battlefield, still ready to fight to the
end despite overwhelming opposition.*]

MACBETH.   Why should I play the Roman fool, and die
　　On mine own sword?° Whiles I see lives,° the gashes
　　Do better upon them.

A Bard for the Ages *How does Shakespeare set apart Macduff's
motives from those of Macbeth's other opponents?* **4**

16 still: always.

17 kerns: hired Irish soldiers.

18 bear their staves: carry their spears.

20 undeeded: unused.

21–22 By this . . . bruited: The noise seems to announce the presence of someone of the highest rank.

24 gently rend'red: surrendered without resistance.

29 strike beside us: fight on our side.

1–2 play . . . sword: commit suicide like a Roman was supposed to do when faced with defeat. **lives:** other living beings.

Teach

Big Idea   4

A Bard for the Ages
Answer: *Macduff has a personal vendetta against Macbeth—namely, to avenge his murdered wife and children.*

Cultural History

Stage Fighting Shakespeare's audience was familiar with swordplay and expected to see realistic duels onstage. Therefore, fencing was part of an actor's training, and sword fights were carefully choreographed. Actors sometimes used trick daggers with blades that collapsed into hollow handles. They also wore bladders (painted to look like skin and filled with sheep's blood) that would burst when punctured, giving the impression of wounds.

391

Teach

Tragedy Answer: *Evidence suggests that Macbeth does feel remorse for his actions: His conscience will not allow him to kill the man whose wife and children he slaughtered.*

[APPROACHING] Remind approaching-level students of Macbeth's crime against Macduff. **Ask:** Whose blood does Macbeth mean when he says "blood of thine"? *(He is talking about Macduff's wife and children, whom he had killed.)*

Tragedy Answer: *Answers will vary. Possible answer: Even as Macbeth nears his end, he is a man of heroic courage. This quality might have made him great.*

[ADVANCED] Have advanced students debate the question "Macbeth: Hero or Villain?" Have them use evidence from the text to support their arguments.

[*MACDUFF enters.*]

MACDUFF.   Turn, hell-hound, turn!

MACBETH. Of all men else I have avoided thee.
5   But get thee back! My soul is too much charged°
       With blood of thine already.

MACDUFF.   I have no words:
       My voice is in my sword, thou bloodier villain
       Than terms can give thee out!°

[*They fight.*]

MACBETH.   Thou losest labor:
       As easy mayst thou the intrenchant air
10   With thy keen sword impress as make me bleed:°
       Let fall thy blade on vulnerable crests;
       I bear a charmèd life, which must not yield
       To one of woman born.

MACDUFF.   Despair° thy charm,
       And let the angel° whom thou still hast served
15   Tell thee, Macduff was from his mother's womb
       Untimely ripped.°

MACBETH. Accursèd be that tongue that tells me so,
       For it hath cowed my better part of man!°
       And be these juggling fiends no more believed,
20   That palter° with us in a double sense;
       That keep the word of promise to our ear,
       And break it to our hope. I'll not fight with thee.

MACDUFF. Then yield thee, coward,
       And live to be the show and gaze o' th' time:°
25   We'll have thee, as our rarer monsters are,
       Painted upon a pole,° and underwrit,
       "Here may you see the tyrant."

MACBETH.   I will not yield,
       To kiss the ground before young Malcolm's feet,
       And to be baited° with the rabble's curse.
30   Though Birnam Wood be come to Dunsinane,
       And thou opposed,° being of no woman born,
       Yet I will try the last.° Before my body
       I throw my warlike shield. Lay on, Macduff;
       And damned be him that first cries "Hold, enough!"

---

1 Tragedy *Does Macbeth feel remorse for having murdered Macduff's family? Explain.*

2 Tragedy *What is your final impression of Macbeth?*

5 **charged:** burdened.

8 **Than . . . out:** than words can describe.

9–10 **As easy . . . bleed:** You can as easily mark the invulnerable air with your sword as make me bleed.

13 **Despair:** lose hope in.
14 **angel:** fallen angel, demon.

15–16 Macduff tells Macbeth that he was prematurely removed from his mother's womb (presumably because she died) and therefore is not "of woman born."
18 **cowed . . . man:** intimidated my courage.
20 **palter:** use trickery.

24 **show . . . time:** spectacle of the age.

25–26 **We'll . . . pole:** Macduff says that Macbeth will be treated like a sideshow freak, with his picture displayed on a pole to attract spectators.

29 **baited:** taunted.

31 **opposed:** opposing me.
32 **try the last:** try my fate to the end.

Grammar Practice

Conjunctions Review conjunctions with students, explaining that they are words used to link sentences, phrases, and other words. Have students look for examples of the conjunctions *and, though, yet,* and *but* on pages 392–393. For each conjunction, students should explain its meaning and tell what words or ideas the conjunction links. (For example, in lines 4–5, Macbeth says of all men else I have avoided thee, <u>but</u> get thee back!)

[*They exit, fighting. More trumpet blasts and battle cries are heard. They reenter fighting, and* MACBETH *is slain.* MACDUFF *removes* MACBETH's *body. After he leaves,* MALCOLM, OLD SIWARD, ROSS, *various thanes and soldiers, including a drummer and flagbearer, enter.*]

35   MALCOLM. I would the friends we miss were safe arrived.

    SIWARD. Some must go off;° and yet, by these I see,
      So great a day as this is cheaply bought.

    MALCOLM. Macduff is missing, and your noble son.

    ROSS. Your son, my lord, has paid a soldier's debt:
40   He only lived but till he was a man;
      The which no sooner had his **prowess** confirmed
      In the unshrinking station where he fought,
      But like a man he died.°

    SIWARD.   Then he is dead?

    ROSS. Ay, and brought off the field. Your cause of sorrow
45   Must not be measured by his worth, for then
      It hath no end.

    SIWARD.   Had he his hurts before?°

    ROSS. Ay, on the front.

    SIWARD.   Why then, God's soldier be he!
      Had I as many sons as I have hairs,
      I would not wish them to a fairer death: ☆
50   And so his knell is knolled.

    MALCOLM.   He's worth more sorrow,
      And that I'll spend for him.

    SIWARD.   He's worth no more:
      They say he parted well and paid his score:
      And so God be with him! Here comes newer comfort.

[MACDUFF *enters with* MACBETH's *head.*]

    MACDUFF. Hail, King! for so thou art: behold, where stands
55   Th' **usurper's** cursèd head. The time is free.° **4**
      I see thee compassed with thy kingdom's pearl,°
      That speak my salutation in their minds,
      Whose voices I desire aloud with mine:
      Hail, King of Scotland!

    ALL.   Hail, King of Scotland!

Tragedy *What is the resolution of this tragedy?* **3**

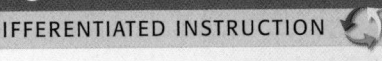

prowess (prou′is) *n.* superior ability; skill
usurper (ū surp′ər) *n.* one who seizes the power, position, or rights of another by force

---

Side notes:

36 **go off:** die.

41–43 **The which . . . died:** He died just as he had confirmed his manhood through his steadfast fighting.

46 **hurts before:** wounds on the front of his body (received while facing the enemy).

55 **The time is free:** Our age is liberated from tyranny.
56 **compassed . . . pearl:** surrounded by the noblest in the kingdom.

Teach

Literary Element **3**

Tragedy **Answer:** *Malcolm, Duncan's heir, will become king of Scotland.*

Vocabulary **4**

Forms of Words **Ask:** What verb form is related to the noun *usurper?* (usurp) What suffix is added to this verb to form the noun meaning "one who usurps"? (-er)

 For additional context, see Glencoe Visual Vocabulary CD-ROM.

Cultural History ☆
Death Before Dishonor
Some ancient peoples believed that death was preferable to life after a defeat in battle. Sparta was a Greek city-state in which every male child was trained for war. The Spartan mother presented her son with his shield as he left for battle, telling him "With this or on this." She meant for him to carry the shield home as a hero or be carried back on it dead.

English Learners
DIFFERENTIATED INSTRUCTION

Intermediate Have students use the phonetic representation of *prowess* (line 41) to recognize that the first vowel in the word is that in *cow,* not that in *low.* Challenge them to think of other words in which *ow* has this sound.

Approaching Level
DIFFERENTIATED INSTRUCTION

Emerging Ask approaching-level students to summarize the key events that occur after Macbeth's death. *(Old Siward discovers his son has been killed; Macduff enters with Macbeth's head; Malcolm prepares to take the throne.)*

Teach

Literary Element | 1

Tragedy **Ask:** Does Malcolm's description of Macbeth suggest that Macbeth is a tragic hero? *(No, Malcolm describes Macbeth as a "butcher" and does not acknowledge Macbeth's strengths, such as courage, that might have made him a great man.)*

ENGLISH LEARNERS If English learners are not familiar with the word *butcher,* have them look it up in a dictionary. **Ask:** What does a butcher do? *(kills animals and sells their meat)* Why does Malcolm compare Macbeth to a butcher? *(because Macbeth killed people with no more feeling than a butcher shows toward the animals)*

To check students' understanding of the selection, see Unit 2 Teaching Resources Book, p. 218.

Group of musicians preceding the celebratory procession, fourteenth–fifteenth century (detail). Artist unknown. Fresco. Castello di Manta Asti, Italy.

[There is a trumpet flourish.]

60   MALCOLM. We shall not spend a large expense of time
      Before we reckon with your several loves,°
      And make us even with you. My thanes and kinsmen,
      Henceforth be earls, the first that ever Scotland
      In such an honor named. What's more to do,
65   Which would be planted newly with the time°—
      As calling home our exiled friends abroad
      That fled the snares of watchful tyranny,
      Producing forth the cruel ministers°
      Of this dead butcher and his fiendlike queen, **1**
70   Who, as 'tis thought, by self and violent hands
      Took off her life—this, and what needful else
      That calls upon us, by the grace of Grace°
      We will perform in measure, time, and place:°
      So thanks to all at once and to each one,
75   Whom we invite to see us crowned at Scone.

[They all exit to a flourish of trumpets.]

61 reckon . . . loves: count up the acts of friendship that each of you has performed and reward your loyalty.

64–65 What's . . . time: what remains to be done at the beginning of this new era.

68 Producing . . . ministers: bringing to justice the cruel agents.

72 Grace: God.

73 in . . . place: with restraint and in the appropriate time and place.

Study Skills Practice

PARTNERS | **SPIRAL REVIEW** **Review a Text** Share these strategies for reviewing *Macbeth* prior to taking a comprehension test:

- Review and complete your notes. Fill in remaining boxes in any charts you have been keeping during reading.
- Try to summarize the key events of the play to a partner. Ask your partner to identify which elements you left out.

- Make a list of the literary elements you explored. Write a definition of each element and then compare your definition with the entry in the Literary Terms Handbook (pp. R1–R19).

After You Read

Respond and Think Critically

Respond and Interpret

1. Was the ending of *Macbeth* what you thought it would be? Explain why or why not.

2. (a)What does the sleepwalking scene reveal about Lady Macbeth's state of mind? (b)What might Lady Macbeth's hand movements mean?

Analyze and Evaluate

3. (a)What metaphors does Macbeth use in his soliloquy after he is told that Lady Macbeth is dead? (b)What do these metaphors reveal about Macbeth's state of mind?

4. Do Macbeth and Lady Macbeth exchange personalities as the play progresses? Use evidence from the play to support your opinion.

5. (a)Describe how the Apparitions' prophecies are fulfilled in Act 5. (b)What dramatic function do these prophecies serve in Acts 4 and 5?

Connect

6. **Big Idea** **A Bard for the Ages** Poet and playwright Ben Jonson, a contemporary of Shakespeare's, wrote that Shakespeare was "not of an age, but for all time." In your opinion, what does *Macbeth* have to offer today's audiences? Explain.

7. **Connect to the Author** James I, king of England when *Macbeth* was written, was also the king of Scotland and a descendant of Malcolm. How might this have influenced Shakespeare's decision to write the play?

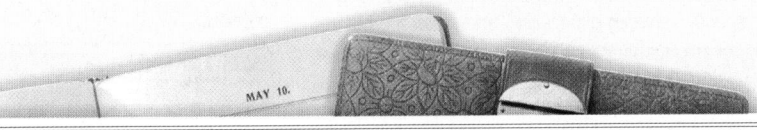

Daily Life & Culture

Eleventh-Century Scotland

During the Middle Ages, the period in which *Macbeth* is set, society in Scotland was organized under the feudal system. The king awarded land grants, or fiefs, to important nobles in return for their pledge of a specified number of armed soldiers in times of war. Fiefdoms, or manors, consisted of a castle, a church, a village, and farmland.

Most medieval houses consisted of one or two rooms with thatched roofs and dirt floors. They were dark, damp, and cold places. In the center of one room, a fire blazing in an open hearth provided warmth. Windows, which were small openings without glass, had wooden shutters that were put up at night or in foul weather.

Life in a castle revolved around a great hall, a large one-room structure with a high ceiling. At the end of the hall opposite the main entrance was a raised platform, or dais, where the nobles reclined. In early times the nobles slept in the hall behind the dais, with curtains or screens separating their sleeping quarters. Kitchens were separate rooms or separate buildings, and bathrooms—if they were indoors—contained chamber pots or latrines that opened directly into a moat or river or onto the ground outside.

Partner Activity With a classmate, answer the following questions.

1. What was life like in a Scottish manor?

2. What distinguished the upper classes from the lower classes in medieval Scotland?

After You Read

Assess

1. Students' answers will vary.

2. (a) Lady Macbeth is so tortured by guilt that her mind dwells constantly on the crimes. (b) Her scrubbing movements suggest that she is trying to cleanse the stains of blood from her hands.

3. (a) Life is a brief candle, an insubstantial shadow, a bad actor, and an exercise in futility. (b) They show his deep disillusionment.

4. Some students may point to the shift in power in their relationship. Others may point to Macbeth's apparent madness upon seeing Banquo's ghost and Lady Macbeth's sleepwalking later in the play.

5. (a) Birnam Wood comes to Dunsinane when Malcolm's soldiers carry tree branches. Macduff reveals that he is not "of woman born" and slays Macbeth. (b) They intensify the tragic flaw in Macbeth's character—his hubris.

6. Students' answers will vary.

7. Shakespeare's choice of subject made good sense from a political point of view. The play indirectly underscores the legitimacy of James I's place in the succession, since it ends with the defeat of the usurper Macbeth and the crowning of Malcolm, Duncan's rightful heir and King James's ancestor.

Daily Life & Culture

1. Manors consisted of a castle, church, village, and farmland. The manors were granted to nobles in return for soldiers.

2. The lower class lived in dark, damp one- or two-room houses. The upper class lived in lavish castles with several rooms.

After You Read
Assess

Literary Element

1. Answers will vary. Some students may say Macbeth's tragic flaw caused his downfall.

2. Possible responses: yes, because social order is restored. Or no, because Macbeth's acts can never be undone.

3. Possible responses: yes, excessive ambition is her tragic flaw. Or no, her downfall was the result of guilt not her tragic flaw.

Progress Check

Can students analyze elements of a tragedy?

If No → See Unit 2 Teaching Resources Book, p. 213.

Review: Irony

Possible responses:

Verbal: In Act III Lennox remarks that Macbeth "has borne all things well," and means the opposite.

Situational: Lady Macbeth, who has scolded Macbeth for feeling guilty, is driven to madness by her own tormented conscience.

Dramatic: In Act I, the audience knows that Lady Macbeth contemplates Duncan's murder even as she welcomes him to her castle.

Reading Strategy

1. "unnatural deeds"
2. After unseating Macbeth, Malcolm becomes king of Scotland.

Progress Check

Can students analyze cause-and-effect relationships?

If No → See Unit 2 Teaching Resources Book, p. 214.

396

Literary Element Tragedy

Traditionally, the **tragic hero** is a person of high rank who, out of hubris, or an exaggerated sense of power and pride, violates a human, natural, or divine law. By breaking that law, the hero poses a threat to society, causing the suffering or death of family members, friends, and associates. In the last act of a traditional tragedy, the tragic hero is punished, and order is restored.

1. In your opinion, what causes Macbeth's downfall—a tragic flaw, errors in judgment, forces beyond his control, or a combination of these factors? Support your opinion with evidence from the play.

2. Do you think Macbeth's death sets everything right again? Give reasons for your opinion.

3. Is Lady Macbeth also a tragic hero? Why or why not?

Review: Irony

As you learned on page 125, **irony** is a contrast or a discrepancy between expectation and reality. Irony can take several forms: **verbal irony** occurs when a person says one thing while meaning another; **situational irony** exists when the outcome of a situation is the opposite of what someone expected; **dramatic irony** occurs when the audience or reader knows something that the characters do not know.

Partner Activity Meet with a classmate to discuss Shakespeare's use of irony in *Macbeth*. Use a diagram like the one below to record examples of irony.

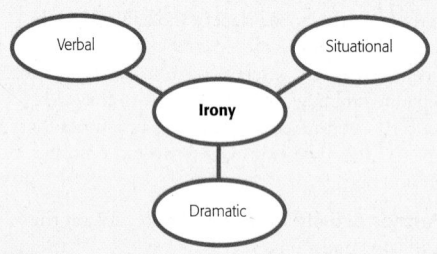

LOG ON ▶ **Literature** Online

Selection Resources For Selection Quizzes, eFlashcards, and Reading-Writing Connection activities, go to glencoe.com and enter QuickPass code GLB9817u2.

Reading Strategy Analyze Cause-and-Effect Relationships

Determining the causes and effects of an event will help you interpret, analyze, and evaluate the plot of a work. Use the diagram you created on page 380 to answer the following questions.

1. According to the Doctor, what is the cause of Lady Macbeth's mental breakdown?

2. Ultimately, what effect does Duncan produce by naming his son Malcolm heir to the throne?

Vocabulary Practice

Practice with Context Clues Look back at pages 381–394 to find context clues for the vocabulary words below. Record your findings in a chart like the one shown.

purge   antidote   siege   prowess
usurper

EXAMPLE:

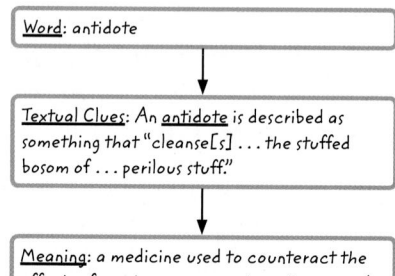

Academic Vocabulary

*Macduff's **reaction** to the news of his family's death shows that he is compassionate.*

Reaction is an academic word. Similar words would be *response, answer,* and *reply*. To further explore the meaning of this word, write two sentences, like the above example, about characters' **reactions** to situations in *Macbeth*.

For more on academic vocabulary, see pages 56 and R81.

Vocabulary

Example of chart:

Word: *siege*

Textual Clues: outward walls, strength, forced, dareful, beat them backward home

Meaning: a fortified place by an opposing army intending to invade; a blockade

Academic Vocabulary

Students' sentences should reflect an understanding of the word *reactions*.

Respond Through Writing

Expository Essay

Cause and Effect Perhaps Shakespeare's darkest work, *The Tragedy of Macbeth* traces the steady downfall of a powerful king. Identify the causes that lead to Macbeth's defeat and evaluate them to determine the one that contributes most definitively to his tragic end.

Prewrite With one or two classmates, adapt the cause-and-effect diagram below to include the entire chain of events that results in Macbeth's loss of the throne and death. Then evaluate each event and discuss which cause you think to be the most important one. State your controlling idea and support it with details from *Macbeth*. If necessary, alter your plan based on others' responses during the discussion.

Cause	Effect
Macbeth decides against killing the king	Lady Macbeth is angry
Macbeth fears losing her affection	Macbeth changes his mind.

Draft Clearly present your evaluation of the causes and effects of events in the play. Gather quotations and details from the play to support your choice of the most significant cause. Establish solid connections between events, inferring characters' motivations from both stated and implied information. Anticipate evaluations that differ from your own, and explain why yours is more accurate and complete.

Sentence structures like the following can help you in stating and supporting your descriptions of causes and effects:

As a result of _____, Macbeth _____.

Revise Ask a peer reader to respond to your draft, considering whether you've accurately identified and connected causes and effects and supported your evaluation of the most significant event with details from the text.

Edit and Proofread Proofread your paper, correcting any errors in spelling, grammar, and punctuation. Use the Grammar Tip in the side column to help you with colons.

Learning Objectives

In this assignment, you will focus on the following objectives:

Writing: Writing an expository essay.

Reading: Analyzing cause and effect.

 ### Grammar Tip

Colons

Colons (:) can be useful in incorporating supporting details—both quotations and examples—into your essay.

Use a colon to introduce a long quotation, to introduce a series after a statement that ends in *as follows* or *the following*, to separate two main clauses when the second explains the first, and to separate the title and subtitle of a work.

Macbeth reveals his dependence on his wife in his letter to her: "This have I thought good to deliver thee, my dearest partner of greatness. . . ."

Macbeth's fate is sealed by his weakness: nothing can reverse the course of events once it is set in motion.

After You Read

Assess

 ## Respond Through Writing

Students' expository essays should evaluate the causes that lead to Macbeth's defeat, include a thesis that clearly states one of the causes as the main contributor to Macbeth's tragic downfall, support ideas with examples from the text, and represent control of grammar and English usage.

A student who meets all of these criteria should receive the equivalent of a 4-point response.

A student who fully meets two or partially meets three of these criteria should receive the equivalent of a 3-point response.

A student who fully meets one or partially meets two of these criteria should receive the equivalent of a 2-point response.

A student who partially meets one of these criteria should receive the equivalent of a 1-point response.

For grammar practice, see Unit 2 Teaching Resources Book, p. 217.

 For additional assessment, see Assessment Resources, pp. 115–116.

 To create custom assessments online, go to Progress Reporter Online Assessment.

 To create custom assessments using software, use ExamView Assessment Suite.

Focus

Summary

This passage from *Shakespeare on Screen* discusses Akira Kurosawa's *Throne of Blood,* an adaptation of *Macbeth* set in fifteenth-century Japan.

For summaries in languages other than English, see Unit 2 Teaching Resources Book. p. 220–225.

Teach

Reading Strategy | 1

Compare and Contrast Genres

Before students begin reading the selection, have them recall the situations and details in *Macbeth* that they found most memorable. This will help them select features of the play to list in their charts.

APPROACHING Approaching-level students should be told that to "compare" is to find things in common, while to "contrast" is to find differences. They should always start with things in common/comparisons (such as, the film and the play are both about cruel kings) and from that draw differences/contrasts (such as, the film is set in Japan, the play in Scotland).

Readability Scores

Dale-Chall: 10.0
DRP: 69
Lexile: 1350

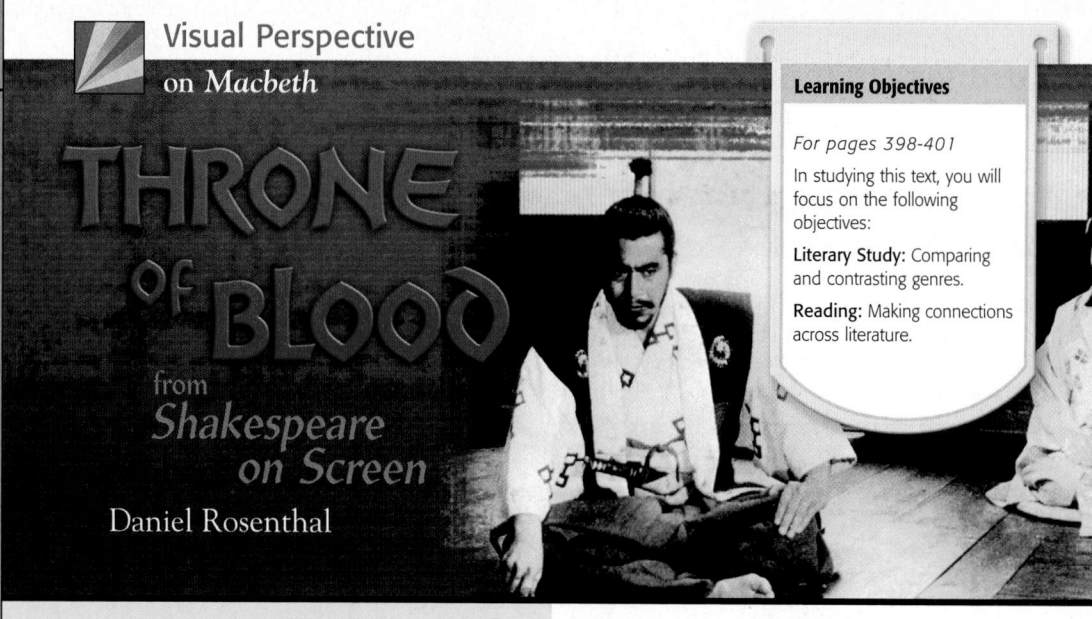

Visual Perspective
on *Macbeth*

THRONE OF BLOOD

from
Shakespeare on Screen

Daniel Rosenthal

Set a Purpose for Reading

As you read, ask yourself, What elements of *Macbeth* does Kurosawa retain in his film *Throne of Blood?*

Build Background

Shakespeare's *Macbeth* has inspired a wide range of artists from various cultures. Composers such as Dmitri Shostakovich and Giuseppe Verdi have written operas based on the play. *Macbeth* has also been interpreted in the styles of Japanese Kabuki and Chinese Beijing opera. One of the best-known treatments of *Macbeth* is the 1957 Japanese film *Throne of Blood,* created by one of Japan's greatest directors, Akira Kurosawa. In the following section from his book *Shakespeare on Screen,* Daniel Rosenthal describes Kurosawa's adaptation of Shakespeare's famous tragedy.

Reading Strategy

Compare and Contrast Genres

As you read the text and examine the photographs, ask yourself, How does the film *Throne of Blood* **compare** with and **contrast** with *Macbeth?* Note their similarities and differences in a two-column chart.

Macbeth	Throne of Blood
Set in 11th-century Scotland	Set in 15th-century Japan

398 UNIT 2   THE ENGLISH RENAISSANCE

The ambitious general Washizu (Toshiro Mifune) and his ruthless wife Asaji (Isuzu Yamada) ponder their next move.

Washizu, the Macbeth figure in *Throne of Blood* has all of his Shakespearean counterpart's courage, but none of his eloquence[1]. This wild-eyed samurai[2] (Toshiro Mifune at his fiercest) rarely says more than a dozen words at a time, and his language is as plain as the floorboards of his castle. There is no poetry in *Throne of Blood*'s sparse dialogue, and little subtlety in its characterization, but its pace, atmosphere and imagery have a power that is absolutely Shakespearean.

The Bard's evocation of 11th-century Scotland and Kurosawa's depiction of late 15th-century Japan are both marked by bestial omens and foul weather. In *Throne of Blood* a horse's wild behavior presages[3] its master's murder; galloping warriors are buffeted by howling wind and driving rain, or shrouded in fog or mist. The music of Shakespeare's verse is

---

1. *Eloquence* means "powerful speech."
2. A *samurai* is a noble warrior of medieval and early modern Japan.
3. *Presages* means "foreshadows."

Grammar Practice

SPIRAL REVIEW **Appositives** Remind students that an appositive is a noun or phrase that identifies or describes a noun in a sentence. It usually follows the noun it identifies and is set off with commas if it is not essential to the meaning of the sentence.

Write the following sentences on the board and have students identify the appositive element in each:

1. Washizu, the Macbeth figure in *Throne of Blood*, has all of his Shakespearean counterpart's courage.

2. Tsuzuki installs Washizu and his wife, Asaji, in North Mansion.

replaced by the woodwind and percussion of Masaru Sato's distinctively Japanese score.

Washizu's story is told in flashback, beginning with a shot of the monument that marks the site of Cobweb Castle, as a male chorus sings of its destruction. Next, we see the impregnable[4] castle in its former glory, as Tsuzuki (the Duncan figure) learns of heroic exploits by Washizu and his best friend, Miki (Minoru Chiaki as a jovial, trusting Banquo), against Inui (the King of Norway) and the treacherous Fujimaki (the thane of Cawdor).

2 Meanwhile, in a marvelously dynamic and eerie sequence, Washizu and Miki become lost in the maze-like Cobweb Forest, and meet an aged "evil spirit" (Chieko Naniwa). Her white make-up resembles the ghost-masks of Noh theater[5] (the ancient Japanese form that

4. *Impregnable* means "unconquerable."
5. *Noh theater* is a highly stylized form of Japanese drama that developed in the fourteenth and fifteenth centuries. Noh plays are performed by actors wearing symbolic masks.

Kurosawa adored), and she prophecies in the husky, expressionless tones of Noh actors: Washizu, commander of Fort One, will rule North Mansion and then Cobweb Castle. Miki will take over Fort One, and his son will eventually rule the castle.

Tsuzuki installs Washizu and his wife, Asaji, in North Mansion, and Kurosawa immediately uses Noh to associate Asaji (the mesmerizing Isuzu Yamada) so closely with the forest spirit that the suspicion arises they are in league **2** together. Yamada's long, oval face is like a Noh mask, she walks heel to toe, like Noh actors, and adopts an expressionless voice to suit Asaji's pitiless ambition. She convinces the unambitious Washizu that Tsuzuki and Miki are plotting his death and that he must strike while Tsuzuki is their guest.

Here, Kurosawa devises a night-time sequence of such stealth that it perfectly distills the dreadful tension of Duncan's murder in *Macbeth*. For seven minutes, in the build-up to and bloody aftermath of the crime, no words are spoken—

 View the Photograph After having his comrade Miki killed, Washizu imagines he sees his ghost at a banquet. How does this image compare to your impression of the banquet scene in Macbeth?

DANIEL ROSENTHAL **399**

Visual Perspective

on *Macbeth*

Teach

Reading Strategy   2

Imagery **Ask:** Besides describing the elements borrowed from Noh, what other descriptions does Rosenthal give? (*"dynamic and eerie sequence"; "the maze-like Cobweb Forest"; "unambitious Washizu"; "a night-time sequence of such stealth that it perfectly distills the dreadful tension of Duncan's murder"*) Help students see that these descriptions work together to create an image of creepiness, tension, and foreboding.

View the Photograph ★

Kurosawa is one of the best-known Japanese filmmakers in the world.

Answer: *Answers will vary; most students will say that the atmosphere in this image seems less ominous and less chaotic than in* Macbeth. *They may also note the different cultures' ideas of a banquet.*

Advanced Learners

DIFFERENTIATED INSTRUCTION

Adaptation Ask students to imagine that they are going to make a film adaptation of *Macbeth*. The film will be set in your community in the present day. **Ask:** What changes will you need to make in the play to fit it into your world and culture?

Have students discuss, in a group, how they would adapt the play to a modern setting. Be sure they understand that the overall plot of the play and the basic motivations of the characters should remain unaltered in their adaptation.

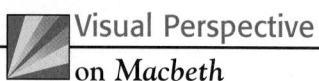

Visual Perspective
on *Macbeth*

Teach

| Vocabulary | 1 |

Prefixes Point out that there are three words on this page—*invariably, invisible,* and *invincibility*—that contain the prefix *in-,* meaning "not." Variable means "able to change," so *invariably* means "characterized as being not able to change." *Invisible* means "not visible." The Latin word *vincere* means "to conquer" or "to defeat," which explains the definition of *invincibility* in the footnote.

[ENGLISH LEARNERS] English learners can increase their word skills by knowing that –ible and –able at the end of a word is called a suffix, and both suffixes mean "able." To get the meaning of a word like "indefensible" the student would follow the formula prefix-suffix-root; thus "not able to be defended." **Ask:** What are the meanings of the following: indefinable *(not able to be defined),* inexpressible *(not able to be expressed),* inexcusable *(not able to be excused)?*

Cinema

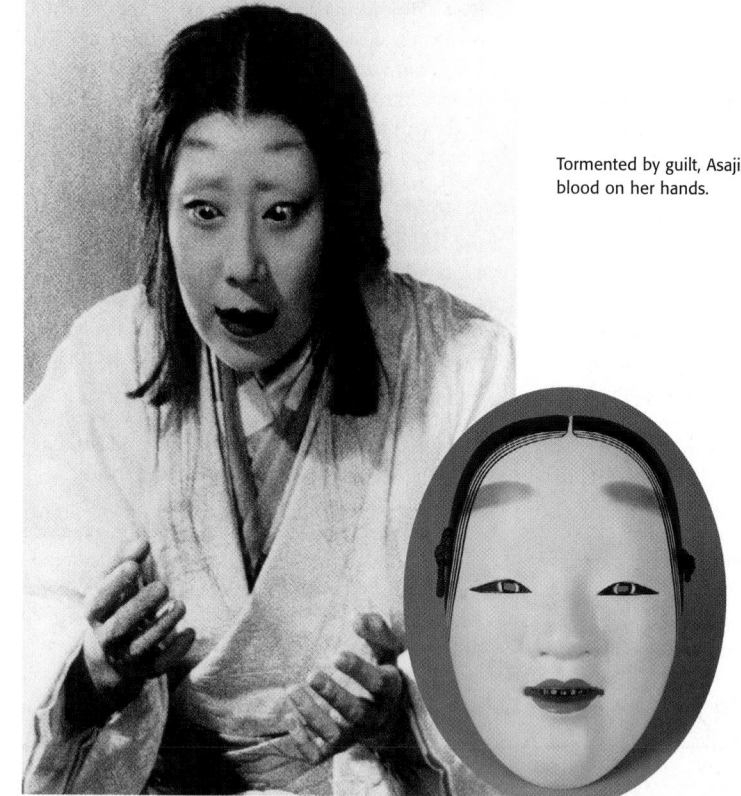

Tormented by guilt, Asaji sees blood on her hands. ★

Noh Mask of a Young Woman. Japanese, nineteenth century. Leeds Museum and Art Galleries, Great Britain.

2 nor are they necessary: the horror of the deed is writ large on Mifune and Yamada's faces.

The "guilty" flight of Kunimaru, Tsuzuki's son, and Noriyasu (Macduff) makes Washizu lord of the castle, and from now on the script begins to work devastating variations on *Macbeth.* With no children of his own, Washizu has agreed to let Miki's son, Yoshiteru, inherit the castle, but then Asaji suddenly announces that she is pregnant: Washizu *will* have an heir, so Miki and Yoshiteru must die.

Kurosawa now pulls off a unique feat: improving on Shakespeare by *not* showing a murder that is invariably depicted on stage. **1** Miki's horse refuses to be saddled, but he ignores this omen and sets off for Washizu's feast. The horse gallops, riderless, back into Fort One, showing that Miki is dead; his dazed

ghost's appearance during the feast provides confirmation.

A final reckoning

Months pass, Asaji has a stillborn child, and the realization that Yoshiteru (who escaped his father's assassin) will still inherit prompts a self-mocking shout from Washizu: "Fool! Fool!"—the closest Mifune gets to a soliloquy. **1**

With Asaji madly washing Tsuzuki's invisible blood from her hands, and his enemies preparing to attack, Washizu rides back to the spirit, who guarantees him invincibility[6] "until Cobweb Forest comes to Cobweb Castle."

---

6. *Invincibility* is the characteristic of being impossible to defeat.

400 UNIT 2 THE ENGLISH RENAISSANCE

View the Art ★

Ask: From your knowledge of *Macbeth,* which scene do you think is being shown here? *(The "mad scene"—the scene in which Lady Macbeth/Asaji tries to wash the nonexistent blood off of her hands.)*

 To check students' understanding of the selection, see Unit 2 Teaching Resources Book p. 227.

400

Vocabulary Practice

SPIRAL REVIEW **Word Origins** Draw students' attention to the name "Cobweb Castle." **Ask:** Who can tell me what cobweb means? *(It is another word for a spiderweb.)* Explain that in Middle English, the word for *spider* was *coppe* and the word for *web* was *web.* Therefore, in Middle English, the word for a spiderweb was *coppeweb,* which became *cobweb* in Modern English.

In the violent climax of *Throne of Blood*, Washizu is killed by his own men.

He reassures his soldiers with this promise, but when they see an army of pines approaching through the mist, we get the last, greatest twist on *Macbeth*: Washizu is killed by his own men. Dozens of arrows whistle into his armor, until one last arrow transfixes his neck and he collapses. Beyond the gates, Noriyasu's men prepare to raze the castle and the screen fades back to its opening image of the monument.

Astonishingly, on its first release, Kurosawa's film was dismissed by *The New York Times* for an "odd amalgamation[7] of cultural contrasts [that] hits the occidental[8] funnybone." However, by 1965, Britain's *Sight and Sound* magazine was making a bold and not unreasonable claim for *Throne of Blood* as the only work that "completely succeeded in transforming a play of Shakespeare's into a film."

---

7. **Amalgamation** means "blending."
8. **Occidental** means "relating to Europe and the Western Hemisphere."

Respond and Think Critically

Respond and Interpret

1. Write a brief summary of the main ideas in this excerpt before you answer the following questions. For help with writing a summary, see page 435.

2. (a) List the various ways in which Kurosawa's film departs from Shakespeare's play. (b) Examine the image above of the dying Washizu. Why do you think Kurosawa changed this aspect of the play?

3. (a) What is Asaji's makeup modeled on? (b) Review the image of Asaji staring at her hands on page 400. How would you describe her face?

Analyze and Evaluate

4. In his film, Kurosawa uses a flashback; he begins the film with Cobweb Castle in ruins and then presents the events that brought about the castle's decline. What effect do you think this flashback has on the action of the film?

5. What aspects of *Macbeth* do you think Kurosawa's film is most successful in capturing? Explain.

Connect

6. Why do you think artists from other cultures have been so eager to interpret and adapt Shakespeare's *Macbeth*?

7. *Throne of Blood* is an example of one film adaptation of *Macbeth*. (a) If you were writing your own version of the play for the screen, what other settings might you use? (b) What aspects of the plot would you change?

DANIEL ROSENTHAL **401**

401

Focus

Summary

There are almost 100 outdoor theaters around the country running Shakespeare festivals during the summer months. Almost all are thriving because of the enthusiasm for Shakespeare.

 For summaries in languages other than English, see Unit 2 Teaching Resources Book, pp. 229–234.

Teach

Reading Strategy   1

Distinguish Fact from Opinion Say: Informational text contains facts about a subject. Sometimes, however, a writer inserts his or her opinions. **Ask:** Has the writer inserted opinions at the beginning of his article? If so, give examples. *(Yes; summer evening seems too balmy for indoors; "fortunately, they need not choose between pleasures.")* Have students look for examples of opinions as they read.

 For additional practice using the reading skill or strategy, see Unit 2 Teaching Resources Book, p. 235.

Readability Scores

Dale-Chall: 10.7
DRP: 69
Lexile: 1240

Learning Objectives

For pages 402–404

In studying this text, you will focus on the following objectives:

Reading:
Analyzing informational text.
Preview.
Distinguishing fact from opinion.

Set a Purpose for Reading

As you read, ask yourself, How can a playwright from the English Renaissance continue to entertain and inspire modern audiences?

Preview the Article

"Midsummer Night's Spectacle" examines the popularity of outdoor Shakespeare performances during the summer.

1. Read the title of the article. What clues does the word *spectacle* give you about the content of the article?

2. Read the deck, or the sentences in large type that appear below the title. What problem or problems do you think the article will examine?

Reading Strategy

Distinguish Fact from Opinion

When you **distinguish fact from opinion,** you determine which statements can or cannot be confirmed as true.

As you read, ask yourself, Which statements can be proven as fact?

Midsummer Night's SPECTACLE

Shakespeare is a reliable summer hit, especially performed outdoors.

So why is he a hard sell under a roof in winter?

By WILLIAM A. HENRY III

AS TWILIGHT SLIPS OVER THE HILLY COLLEGE TOWN OF Ashland, Oregon, the sweet summer evening seems too balmy for whiling away indoors, even to the vacationing crowds who have journeyed to attend the theater here. Fortunately, they need not choose between pleasures. Night after night, vividly costumed Shakespeare—preceded by the singing of madrigals and heralded by a flag raising and trumpet fanfare from the topmost gables of a Tudor stagehouse—unfolds here beneath a starry sky. 1

The scene takes place at the Oregon Shakespeare Festival (OSF), the largest regional theater in the United States and one of the oldest (it was founded in 1935). The theater is a three-stage jamboree built on a love of Shakespeare that draws almost 400,000 spectators a year. Ninety percent of those are from more than 125 miles away. With minor variations, this scene also takes place at dozens of outdoor theaters around the country, including one in an inner-city park in Louisville, Kentucky, and another on the grounds of a legendary mansion alongside the Hudson River in New York. According to Felicia Londre, former secretary of the Shakespeare Theater Association of America, the United States has about 100 outdoor Shakespeare festivals. Some, like Ashland's and New York City's Shakespeare in the Park, have grown into major institutions offering varied repertoires. Others operate just a few weeks a year. Nearly all rely on a lot of novice, non-union actors. But almost all are thriving.

Reading Practice

SPIRAL REVIEW **Main Idea and Supporting Details Say:** To find the main idea, examine how the author organizes ideas. Have students look at the second paragraph on this page. **Ask:** What is the main idea of this paragraph? *(Outdoor summertime presentations of Shakespeare's plays take place around the country.)* Where does the main idea appear? *(It appears in the fourth sentence.)* What details support the main idea? *(Examples of places where there are theaters: Ashland, Oregon; Louisville, Kentucky; on the grounds of a mansion along the Hudson River in New York City.)*

David Cooper/TIME

A Passion for the Bard

Americans seemingly cannot get enough of Shakespeare in open air during the summer—though they are conspicuously less eager to see the Bard's work indoors at other times of the year. For many theatergoers, the experience of Shakespeare outdoors takes on an almost sacred character. When Richard Devin, the artistic director of the Colorado Shakespeare Festival, moved a summer's staging of Shakespeare's *The Winter's Tale* to a new indoor space and installed an adaptation of Richard Brinsley Sheridan's *The Rivals* outdoors, he quickly realized he had goofed. Not only did *The Rivals* prove an unusually tough sell, but subscribers wrote in fury. "They told me they would never come to Shakespeare indoors or accept another writer outdoors," Devin says. "They spoke of Shakespeare's universality and of what it meant to see these plays under the stars with their children. They felt we were stealing an irreplaceable opportunity from them."

Other theater executives have noted a similar audience passion for Shakespeare. Even his less-popular "problem" plays, which many people consider both difficult to produce and to watch, have more box-office appeal than masterpieces by almost anyone else. Says Bill Patton, OSF's former executive director, who oversaw its growth for many years: "Some of Shakespeare's popularity may be that it's certified as good for you, so audiences can congratulate themselves on their intellectuality, even though this was popular entertainment for its time and still is. Also the plays are taught in school, so people feel familiar with them."

Swordplay Sells

Actors and directors tend to be ambivalent about staging the Bard outdoors. Only a dozen or so of his 37 plays consistently succeed outdoors both artistically and at the box office, and those mainly when staged in broad strokes. By common consent, the lighter comedies and the more swashbuckling histories fare best because they depend less on language that is easily lost in the night air and more on pageantry and action. Intimate texts and subtle, groundbreaking performances tend not to work in the wide and windy spaces.

Soliloquies cannot compete with swordplay. Jerry Turner, who spent almost 20 years as OSF's artistic director, refused to schedule *Othello* outdoors because he felt its intimate story and rich language were ill-suited to that setting. But after OSF erected a stadium-like "acoustic shell" that surrounded the stage with tiers of balconies while leaving it open to the sky, Turner finally consented to try *Othello* outdoors. The flat and tedious result bore out his original judgment—although critics said much of the blame went to the bland performances of the three principal actors.

Some artistic directors claim to find great value in working outdoors. Says Jack O'Brien of San Diego's Old Globe Theater: "The shows are usually at their fairest and least phony outside. It's hard to stand next to a tree and speak archly. Even when we are doing Shakespeare indoors, I have often taken the cast outside during tech week and had a complete run-through just to get in touch with that honesty." O'Brien thinks of Shakespeare's earlier plays, almost all work outdoors, while his later ones mostly don't: "You can see in his poetry the adaptation from an open theater to a more enclosed one—the way, for example, he speaks of light or time of day."

The former head of the New York Shakespeare Festival, JoAnne Akalaitis, speaks enthusiastically about the "magic" of Shakespeare in Central Park: "Shakespeare in the park is part of the essence of being a cultural person in New York City. It is relaxed, warm, open, and democratic. The upsides are the wind and clouds, the informality, coupled with the power that comes with that much massed humanity." She adds dryly,

---

English Learners

DIFFERENTIATED INSTRUCTION

Intermediate The article refers to "the Bard." **Ask:** What does bard mean? *(A composer of epic or heroic verse)* Who is "the Bard" in this article? *(Shakespeare is recognized as the Bard in England and America.)* **Say:** In Scotland, Robert Burns is called the Bard. Other cultures may have a national poet who is considered their "Bard." Ask students to tell who holds that position of esteem in their native cultures. Ask them to share some of the poets' works with the rest of the class if they are available in English translation.

TIME

Teach

Big Idea 2

A Bard for the Ages

Shakespeare's writing reflects his ability to capture the true human nature of his characters, their desires and foibles. **Ask:** What, do you think, is the connection between Shakespeare's characters and his popularity as the world's favorite author? *(Audiences today can identify with the characters, who experience universal situations: moral dilemmas, loss of faith, and achievement of goals.)*

Literary History

Sheridan's Comedies Richard Brinsley Sheridan was born in Dublin in 1751 and attended Harrow School in England, where he developed an interest in the theater. Sheridan began writing plays, and in 1775 the Covent Garden Theatre produced his comedy *The Rivals.* A revised version was a success. He became a co-owner of the Drury Lane Theatre, where he produced his most popular comedy, *The School for Scandal.*

 To check students' understanding of the selection, see Unit 2 Teaching Resources Book, p. 236.

Assess

1. Students' summaries should include the main ideas from the article, including the widespread outdoor performances of and enthusiasm for Shakespeare's plays.

2. (a) "Audiences can congratulate themselves on their intellectuality" and "the plays are taught in school, so people feel familiar with them." (b) Being familiar with Shakespeare's work, audiences may already have ideas about and preferences for how the plays should be performed.

3. (a) Students may feel that a theater director is more aware of both technical and sales issues, whereas a theater patron is only aware of what he or she sees on the stage. (b) There would be less technical expertise, and the article might seem to be based more on opinions if it had less factual evidence.

4. (a) Possible answers: "Soliloquies cannot compete with swordplay"; "The flat and tedious result bore out his original judgment" (page 403). (b) The author is biased in that he consistently represents Shakespeare and theater in a positive way.

5. Students may point out that many of Shakespeare's plays were originally performed outdoors and are more authentic in an outdoor venue. Also, an audience may find theater more accessible in an outdoor setting.

David Blue/TIME

Michael Daniel/TIME

ALL'S WELL THAT ENDS WELL IN COLORADO: The experience takes on an almost sacred character.

COMEDY OF ERRORS: Making merry in New York's Central Park

"The downside is the body miking." Or at least, it was. For years, the Central Park sound system was notoriously tinny, and actors could not seem to avoid hitting their mikes when they scuffled, so every few minutes the audience heard what sounded like thunder. Today, however, the introduction of a more sophisticated sound system has largely solved that problem.

Another downside is the sheer size of the stage and audience, which can sometimes tempt film stars, fearful of understatement, into almost operatic acting. But whatever the shortcomings of these productions, audiences seem to want Shakespeare outdoors more than ever. New troupes spring up each year as producers discover what OSF's founder,

Angus Bowmer, learned in 1935. He staged boxing matches as a way to help pay for his outdoor Shakespeare shows. The boxing lost money. From the start, the Shakespeare turned a profit.

Respond and Think Critically

Respond and Interpret

1. Write a brief summary of the main ideas of this article before you answer the following questions. For help with writing a summary, see page 435.

2. (a) Why do Shakespeare's plays appeal to audiences, according to former OSF director Bill Patton? (b) How does this explain why audiences might feel protective of Shakespeare's work?

Analyze and Evaluate

3. (a) Why do you think the writer chose to quote theater and artistic directors instead of theater patrons? (b) How might "Midsummer Night's

Spectacle" be different if these quotes were removed, or if only theater patrons were quoted?

4. (a) Give one example of an instance in which the writer presents an opinion as fact. (b) In what way is the writer biased, or partial to one particular view or opinion?

Connect

5. In your opinion, are Shakespeare's plays best performed outdoors? Explain. Think about how the plays were originally performed in Shakespeare's time and what has changed since then.

404 UNIT 2   THE ENGLISH RENAISSANCE

 For additional assessment, see Assessment Resources, pp. 119–120.

 To create custom assessments sing software, use ExamView Assessment Suite.

PART 3

The Sacred and the Secular

Allegory of Fleeting Time, c. 1634. Antonio Pereda. Kunsthistorisches Museum, Vienna, Austria.

> "I write of groves, of twilights, and I sing
> The court of Mab, and of the Fairy King. **1**
> I write of hell; I sing (and ever shall)
> Of heaven, and hope to have it after all."

—Robert Herrick, "The Argument of His Book"

405

For additional support for English Learners, see Unit 2 Teaching Resources Book, p. 238.

English Learners

DIFFERENTIATED INSTRUCTION

Beginning Have students use descriptive language to write short sentences about the painting. Then ask for volunteers to share their sentences. **Ask:** Based on the words you have chosen, what kind of tone does the image create? *(Answers will vary.)*

Approaching Level

DIFFERENTIATED INSTRUCTION

Emerging Read the quotation aloud to students. **Ask:** Would you describe this quotation as sacred or secular? Explain. *(Students might say that it is both sacred and secular, as the author glorifies nature and art and aspires to heaven.)*

Analyze and Extend

Literary Element   1

Allusion If necessary, remind students that an allusion is a reference to a well-known person, place, event, written work, or work of art. Discovering the meaning of an allusion can often be essential to the understanding of a work. **Ask:** Have you heard of Mab before? *(Mab is a fairy queen of uncertain origin who appears in the work of Shakespeare, Jonson, and others.)*

View the Art

Antonio Pereda (c. 1611–1678) was a Spanish painter famous for his still-life pictures. His most famous work is titled *Life Is a Dream*. **Say:** Compare this painting with the work of David Bailly on page 239. **Ask:** What symbols do you see in both works? *(Possible answers: portraits; books; skulls; beads; hourglasses; coins; candlesticks)*

405

Before You Read

Focus

Bellringer Options

**Selection Focus
Transparency 16**

**Daily Language Practice
Transparency 28**

Or ask for a show of hands to determine how many students have read one of the Harry Potter novels (or another book currently popular among teens). **Say:** If this were the 1600s in England, the book you would most likely have read would be the Bible. When the first English version of the Bible appeared in 1611, it quickly became the best seller of its time. The King James Bible remained the most widely read book in English for centuries.

Before You Read
from the King James Version of the Bible

The Creation of Heaven and Earth (detail from the Chaos), 1200. Mosaic. Monreale Cathedral, Sicily.

The Bible is a collection of writings belonging to the sacred literature of Judaism and Christianity. Although most people think of the Bible as a single book, it is actually a collection of books. In fact, the word *Bible* comes from Greek *ta biblia*, meaning "the little books." The Hebrew Bible, also called the Tanakh, contains the sacred writings of the Jewish people and chronicles their history. The Christian Bible was originally written in Greek. It contains most of the same texts as the Hebrew Bible, as well as twenty-seven additional books, called the New Testament. The many books of the Bible were written at different times and contain various types of writing—including history, law, stories, songs, proverbs, sermons, prophecies, and letters.

> *"I perceived how that it was impossible to establish the lay people in any truth except the Scripture were plainly laid before their eyes in their mother tongue."*
>
> —William Tyndale

From Latin to English Before the Protestant Reformation began in the early 1500s, the Christian Bible was ordinarily read in Latin. As a result, few people had direct knowledge of the Bible. One of the most important goals of Protestant leaders, such as Martin Luther, was to translate the Bible into the languages that common people could read. In 1525 the English Protestant William Tyndale completed his translation of the New Testament, the first English version of the Bible to be printed. Tyndale's work on the Hebrew Bible ended abruptly, however, when authorities banned his translation and executed him for heresy.

Other English translations appeared soon after, notably the Great Bible of Miles Coverdale; the Geneva Bible, translated by a group of English Protestants living in Switzerland; and the Rheims-Douay Bible, translated by English Roman Catholics living in France. By 1603, when James I became king of England, at least seven English translations of the Bible were in use. In 1604 a conference of churchmen proposed that the English Bible be revised. King James agreed and gathered a group of forty-seven scholars to create a new English Bible. The group was instructed to correct the Bishops' Bible—a version of Coverdale's Great Bible—by comparing it with the original Hebrew and Greek texts. These scholars turned to Tyndale's masterful prose in preparing their new version. The result of their efforts, first printed in 1611, was the King James—or Authorized—Version of the Holy Bible.

The Legacy of the King James Bible For centuries, the King James Bible was not only the most widely read English Bible, but the most widely read English book. Thus it exerted an enormous stabilizing influence on the English language, which had been changing steadily since the Norman Conquest in 1066. The language and style of the King James Version of the Bible have had a profound influence on English language and literature up to the present day.

Selection Skills

Literary Elements
- Style (SE pp. 406–414)
- Parallelism (SE p. 414)

from **The King James Version of the Bible**

Listening/Speaking/Viewing Skills
- Analyze Art (SE p. 410; TE p. 408)
- Oral Interpretation (SE p. 415)
- Illustrations (TE p. 410)

Reading Skills
- Analyze Text Structure (SE pp. 406–415)

Vocabulary Skills
- Synonyms (SE p. 415)

Writing Skills/Grammar
- Characterization (TE p. 412)

Literature and Reading Preview

Connect to the Texts

Why might it be important for lay Christians—Christians who are not clergy—to understand the Bible? List several reasons.

Build Background

The first book in the Bible is Genesis, which begins with God's creation of the world. The book's title is derived from the Greek word *gignesthai*, meaning "to be born."

The Bible is written chiefly in prose, but some portions contain poetry. In fact, the book of Psalms consists of poems intended to be sung. Many of the psalms are traditionally attributed to King David, who ruled Israel from about 1000 to 962 B.C.

Set Purposes for Reading

Big Idea The Sacred and the Secular

As you read, ask yourself, What effects might this translation have had on laypeople, who could now read the Bible on their own?

Literary Element Style

Style is the way language is used to convey an idea or concept. It involves word choice and the length and arrangement of sentences, as well as the use of figurative language and imagery. As you read, ask yourself, How did the translators use repetition and other devices to create a distinctive style?

Reading Strategy Analyze Text Structure

Analyzing text structure—the organization of ideas within a work—can help you to understand the logic and message of a text. Some basic types of text structures include chronological order (order of time), cause-and-effect order, comparison-contrast order, and spatial order. As you read, ask yourself, How are the important ideas in the text organized?

Tip: Taking Notes Use a chart like the one below to record clues to the text's structure.

Genesis	
Clue Words or Phrases	Type of Connection

Learning Objectives

For pages 406–415

In studying these texts, you will focus on the following objectives:

Literary Study:
Analyzing style.
Identifying parallelism.

Reading: Analyzing text structure.

Speaking and Listening: Performing an oral interpretation.

Vocabulary

abundantly (ə bun′ dənt lē) *adv.* plentifully; p. 409 *The storeroom was packed with provisions, ensuring that we would be abundantly provided for during the long winter.*

replenish (ri plen′ ish) *v.* to refill or make complete again; add a new supply to; p. 409 *Seeing the nearly empty candy bowl, the hostess replenished it, filling the bowl to the rim.*

beguile (bi gīl′) *v.* to mislead by trickery; deceive; p. 412 *The sly suitor beguiled the naive heiress with flattery.*

enmity (en′ mə tē) *n.* ill will; hostility; p. 412 *The cruel girl's bullying earned her the enmity of all her classmates.*

Before You Read

Focus

Summary

The excerpt from Genesis tells the Judeo-Christian tale of how the earth was made by God. It recounts the story of Adam, Eve, the serpent, and the apple—telling how God drove humans from the Garden of Eden for disobeying him.

In Psalm 23, the speaker describes the power of faith to provide all that a mortal needs: green pastures, still waters, righteousness, comfort, food and drink, goodness, mercy, and a chance to live forever in heaven.

 For summaries in languages other than English, see unit 2 Teaching Resources Book, pp. 240-245.

Vocabulary

Vocabulary Have students write two sentences. In one sentence, they should use *abundantly* and *replenish* in a way that shows the relationship between the words. In the second sentence, they should use *beguile* and *enmity* to show a relationship between the words.

 For additional vocabulary practice, see Unit 2 Teaching Resources Book, p. 248.

English Learners

DIFFERENTIATED INSTRUCTION

Advanced Tell students that they will be reading from Genesis, which describes the formation of the universe. Have students work with a partner to describe what elements they would create first if they were building the universe. **Ask:** What techniques might you use to tell this story? What images and symbols might you use to tell this story? *(Answers will vary.)*

Teach

from Genesis

from the King James *version of the* Bible

Elohim Creating Adam, 1805. William Blake. Watercolor on paper, 431 x 536 cm. Tate Gallery, London.

Chapter 1

In the beginning God created the heaven and the earth. And the earth was without form and void; and darkness was upon the face of the deep. And the spirit of God moved upon the face of the waters. And God said, "Let there be light": and there was light. And God saw the light, that it was good: and God divided the light from the darkness. And God called the light Day, and the darkness he called Night. And the evening and the morning were the first day.

---

1 Analyze Text Structure *What does this phrase tell you about how the story is structured?*

2 Analyze Text Structure *What is created on the first day of the world's existence?*

408 UNIT 2   THE ENGLISH RENAISSANCE

408

And God said, "Let there be a firmament[1] in the midst of the waters, and let it divide the waters from the waters." And God made the firmament, and divided the waters which were under the firmament from the waters which were above the firmament: and it was so. And God called the firmament Heaven. And the evening and the morning were the second day.

And God said, "Let the waters under the heaven be gathered together unto one place, and let the dry land appear": and it was so. And God called the dry land Earth; and the gathering together of the waters called he Seas: and God saw that it was good. And God said, "Let the earth bring forth grass, the herb[2] yielding seed, and the fruit tree yielding fruit after his kind,[3] whose seed is in itself, upon the earth": and it was so. And the earth brought forth grass, and herb yielding seed after his kind, and the tree yielding fruit, whose seed was in itself, after his kind: and God saw that it was good. And the evening and the morning were the third day.

And God said, "Let there be lights in the firmament of the heaven to divide the day from the night; and let them be for signs, and for seasons, and for days, and years: and let them be for lights in the firmament of the heaven to give light upon the earth": and it was so. And God made two great lights; the greater light to rule the day, and the lesser light to rule the night: he made the stars also. And God set them in the firmament of the heaven to give light upon the earth, and to rule over the day and over the night, and to divide the light from the darkness: and God saw that it was

good. And the evening and the morning were the fourth day.

And God said, "Let the waters bring forth **abundantly** the moving creature that hath life, and fowl that may fly above the earth in the open firmament of heaven." And God created great whales, and every living creature that moveth, which the waters brought forth abundantly, after their kind, and every winged fowl after his kind: and God saw that it was good. And God blessed them, saying, "Be fruitful, and multiply, and fill the waters in the seas, and let fowl multiply in the earth." And the evening and the morning were the fifth day.

And God said, "Let the earth bring forth the living creature after his kind, cattle, and creeping thing, and beast of the earth after his kind": and it was so. And God made the beast of the earth after his kind, and cattle after their kind, and every thing that creepeth upon the earth after his kind: and God saw that it was good.

And God said, "Let us make man in our image, after our likeness: and let them have dominion[4] over the fish of the sea, and over the fowl of the air, and over the cattle, and over all the earth, and over every creeping thing that creepeth upon the earth." So God created man in his own image, in the image of God created he him; male and female created he them. And God blessed them, and God said unto them, "Be fruitful, and multiply, and **replenish** the earth, and subdue it: and have dominion over the fish of the sea, and over the fowl of the air, and over every living thing that moveth upon the earth."

---

4. *Dominion* means "authority" or "power to rule."

Analyze Text Structure What does this sentence tell you about how this text is organized? **4**

Analyze Text Structure On the sixth day, what is the order of creation? **5**

Vocabulary

replenish (ri plen′ ish) *v.* to refill or make complete again; add a new supply to

---

1. The *firmament* is the atmosphere surrounding the earth.
2. Here, *herb* refers to vegetation.
3. *After his kind* means "like itself."

3 *Style* These sentences are repeated with slight variations throughout the first chapter of Genesis. How do these repetitions help you to understand what is happening in the text?

Vocabulary

abundantly (ə bun′ dənt lē) *adv.* plentifully

Literary Element | 3

Style Answer: *These repetitions frame the events of the text, making the tale easy to follow. Readers begin to expect a pattern: God creates something, God sees that it is good, and then the day ends.*

(ENGLISH LEARNERS) Tell students that there is a pattern in the text. **Say:** There is a pattern in which God creates something, sees that it is good, and the day ends. So when God creates gray whales, if the pattern continues, God will see that the whales are good, and then the day will end.

Reading Strategy | 4

Analyze Text Structure
Answer: *The sentence tells the reader that chapter 1 of Genesis is organized sequentially.*

Reading Strategy | 5

Analyze Text Structure
Answer: *All the animals that live on the earth are created first. (Birds of the air and creatures of the sea have already been created on the fifth day.) Then men and women are created and given dominion over all living things on the planet.*

English Learners

DIFFERENTIATED INSTRUCTION

Intermediate Have each student choose the second or third paragraph on this page to read aloud to a small group. Students should read quietly to themselves before taking turns reading aloud. They should read their paragraph at least twice, aiming for a smooth delivery at a normal speaking pace.

Approaching Level

DIFFERENTIATED INSTRUCTION

Emerging Have students use context clues in the third paragraph on this page to figure out what the speaker means by "the greater light . . . and the lesser light." *(the sun and the moon)* Have volunteers explain how they used context to glean the meanings of these phrases.

Teach

Literary Element | 1

Style **Ask:** How does the style of this artwork complement or contrast with the style of the prose in Genesis? *(The style of the prose in Genesis is solemn and formal with use of repetition as God creates the elements of the Earth. The artwork is also solemn though slightly chaotic with the use of repetition with several kinds of birds as well as other animals.)*

View the Art ★

The Grabow Altar is the most famous work by Master Bertram of Minden (c. 1345–1415). It consists of 24 panels that portray scenes from both the Old and New Testaments of the Bible. Master Bertram's softer style of painting is considered a precursor of the Flemish school and similar to French painters of the time. **Ask:** What biblical event does this painting depict? *(It illustrates the creation of animals.)* Is this depiction similar to how you visualized that event while reading about it in the selection? *(Students' responses will vary.)*

1 *Creation of the Animals,* Grabow Altarpiece, left inner wing, exterior, 1410. Master Bertram of Minden. Tempera on wood, 80 x 51cm. Hamburg Kunsthalle Collection, Germany.

View the Art The Grabow Altarpiece is composed of 24 narrow panels like this one, each illustrating a different Biblical scene. In what ways has the artist taken advantage of the panel's shape and size to create a visually interesting image? ★

410 UNIT 2   THE ENGLISH RENAISSANCE

Viewing Practice

SPIRAL REVIEW **Illustrations** Lead a discussion about the relationship between text and images, using this selection from Genesis and the illustration as examples. **Ask:** Why do publishers often include artwork or photographs with the stories, articles, and other literary works they publish? *(Images can enhance and illustrate text, providing a clearer, richer reading experience.)* How does the art here and on page 406 illustrate or enhance the writing? *(Both paintings depict important passages in the selection. Their tones complement the text—both are solemn and have an air of mystery.)*

410

And God said, "Behold, I have given you every herb bearing seed, which is upon the face of all the earth, and every tree, in which is the fruit of a tree yielding seed; to you it shall be for meat.[5] And to every beast of the earth, and to every fowl of the air, and to every thing that creepeth upon the earth, wherein there is life, I have given every green herb for meat": and it was so.

And God saw every thing that he had made, and behold, it was very good. And the evening and the morning were the sixth day.

Chapter 2

Thus the heavens and the earth were finished, and all the host[6] of them. And on the seventh day God ended his work which he had made; and he rested on the seventh day from all his work which he had made. And God blessed the seventh day, and sanctified it: because that in it he had rested from all his work which God created and made.

These are the generations of the heavens and of the earth when they were created, in the day that the Lord God made the earth and the heavens, and every plant of the field before it was in the earth, and every herb of the field before it grew: for the Lord God had not caused it to rain upon the earth, and there was not a man to till the ground. But there went up a mist from the earth, and watered the whole face of the ground. And the Lord God formed man of the dust of the ground, and breathed into his nostrils the breath of life; and man became a living soul.

And the Lord God planted a garden eastward in Eden; and there he put the man whom he had formed. And out of the ground made the Lord God to grow every tree that is pleas-

ant to the sight, and good for food; the tree of life also in the midst of the garden, and the tree of knowledge of good and evil. . . .

And the Lord God took the man, and put him into the garden of Eden to dress it and to keep it. And the Lord God commanded the man, saying, "Of every tree of the garden thou mayest freely eat: but of the tree of knowledge of good and evil, thou shalt not eat of it: for in the day that thou eatest thereof thou shalt surely die."

And the Lord God said, "It is not good that the man should be alone; I will make him a help meet for him."[7] And out of the ground the Lord God formed every beast of the field, and every fowl of the air; and brought them unto Adam to see what he would call them: and whatsoever Adam called every living creature, that was the name thereof. And Adam gave names to all cattle, and to the fowl of the air, and to every beast of the field; but for Adam there was not found a help meet for him.

And the Lord God caused a deep sleep to fall upon Adam, and he slept: and he took one of his ribs, and closed up the flesh instead thereof; and the rib, which the Lord God had taken from man, made he a woman, and brought her unto the man.

And Adam said, "This is now bone of my bones, and flesh of my flesh: she shall be called Woman, because she was taken out of Man."

Therefore shall a man leave his father and ☆ his mother, and shall cleave unto[8] his wife: and they shall be one flesh. And they were both naked, the man and his wife, and were not ashamed.

Chapter 3

Now the serpent was more subtle than any beast of the field which the Lord God had made. And he said unto the woman, "Yea, hath God said, 'Ye shall not eat of every tree of the garden'?"

---

5. *Meat* refers to food in general.
6. *Host* refers to the great number of living things on the earth.

2 The Sacred and the Secular *What religious and secular traditions are linked to this passage?*

3 Analyze Text Structure *At this point in the narrative, why does the text go back and explain how people were created?*

---

7. *Help meet for him* means, in this case, "wife."
8. *Cleave unto* means "cling to" or "be faithful to."

Big Idea **2**

The Sacred and the Secular **Answer:** *The Sabbath resulted from this passage, as well as the secular concept of a workweek and weekend.*

Reading Strategy **3**

Analyze Text Structure Answer: *The first explanation occurs in the context of the creation of the whole universe. The explanation here gives more detail. It expands upon the concepts expressed in chapter 1 and refocuses the narrative on the creation of humanity.*

Language History ☆

Woman In *Microcosmus*, written in 1619, Samuel Purchas gives this hypothesis about the origin of the word *woman*: "A woman is a house builded for generation and gestation, when our language calls her woman, womb-man." The generally accepted etymology of *woman*, however, is that it comes from Old English *wifman*, meaning "female human being."

Approaching Level

DIFFERENTIATED INSTRUCTION

 Emerging To support students' understanding of sequence of events and to give students practice with the selection's language and concepts, have them work with partners to create timelines of what happens each day of the creation. Draw a blank timeline on the chalkboard for students to copy. Suggest that they reread the account of each day, jotting down notes about what God did or created, before creating their timelines.

Teach

Reading Strategy | 1

Analyze Text Structure

Answer: *This curse applies to both the present and the future.*

(APPROACHING) In the passage, God gives three separate curses. **Ask:** What is the curse for the serpent? *(to crawl on its belly and be hated by humans)* **Ask:** What is the curse for Eve? *(to suffer in life and in childbirth)* **Ask:** What is the curse for Adam? *(to struggle throughout life until death)*

Literary Element | 2

Style **Answer:** *The repetition of dust emphasizes the mortality of human beings and the cycle of life.*

Literary History ☆

The Pentateuch The first five books of the Bible are Genesis, Exodus, Leviticus, Numbers, and Deuteronomy. These are called the Five Books of Moses. The stories in these books were transmitted as oral narrations until they were written down sometime between 1000 and 400 B.C.

And the woman said unto the serpent, "We may eat of the fruit of the trees of the garden: but of the fruit of the tree which is in the midst of the garden, God hath said, 'Ye shall not eat of it, neither shall ye touch it, lest ye die.'"

And the serpent said unto the woman, "Ye shall not surely die: for God doth know that in the day ye eat thereof, then your eyes shall be opened, and ye shall be as gods, knowing good and evil."

And when the woman saw that the tree was good for food, and that it was pleasant to the eyes, and a tree to be desired to make one wise, she took of the fruit thereof, and did eat, and gave also unto her husband with her; and he did eat. And the eyes of them both were opened, and they knew that they were naked; and they sewed fig leaves together, and made themselves aprons.

And they heard the voice of the Lord God walking in the garden in the cool of the day: and Adam and his wife hid themselves from the presence of the Lord God amongst the trees of the garden.

And the Lord God called unto Adam, and said unto him, "Where art thou?"

And he said, "I heard thy voice in the garden, and I was afraid, because I was naked; and I hid myself."

And he said, "Who told thee that thou wast naked? Hast thou eaten of the tree, whereof I commanded thee that thou shouldest not eat?"

And the man said, "The woman whom thou gavest to be with me, she gave me of the tree, and I did eat."

And the Lord God said unto the woman, "What is this that thou hast done?"

And the woman said, "The serpent **beguiled** me, and I did eat."

And the Lord God said unto the serpent, "Because thou hast done this, thou art cursed above all cattle, and above every beast of the field; upon thy belly shalt thou go, and dust shalt thou eat all the days of thy life: and I will put **enmity** between thee and the woman, and between thy seed and her seed; it shall bruise thy head, and thou shalt bruise his heel."

Unto the woman he said, "I will greatly multiply thy sorrow and thy conception;[9] in sorrow thou shalt bring forth children; and thy desire shall be to thy husband, and he shall rule over thee."

And unto Adam he said, "Because thou hast hearkened unto the voice of thy wife, and hast eaten of the tree, of which I commanded thee, saying, 'Thou shalt not eat of it': cursed is the ground for thy sake; in sorrow shalt thou eat of it all the days of thy life; thorns also and thistles shall it bring forth to thee; and thou shalt eat the herb of the field; in the sweat of thy face shalt thou eat bread, till thou return unto the ground; for out of it wast thou taken: for dust thou art, and unto dust shalt thou return."

And Adam called his wife's name Eve; because she was the mother of all living. Unto Adam also and to his wife did the Lord God make coats of skins, and clothed them.

And the Lord God said, "Behold, the man is become as one of us, to know good and evil: and now, lest he put forth his hand, and take also of the tree of life, and eat, and live forever": therefore the Lord God sent him forth from the garden of Eden, to till the ground from whence he was taken. So he drove out the man; and he placed at the east of the garden of Eden cherubim,[10] and a flaming sword which turned every way, to keep the way of[11] the tree of life. ☙

---

9. *Conception,* as used here, refers to childbirth.
10. *Cherubim* are a class of angels.
11. *Keep the way of* means "guard."

Analyzing Text Structure *Does this curse apply to the present or the future?* **1**

Style *What is the effect of the repetition of the word dust?* **2**

Vocabulary

beguile (bi gīl′) *v.* to mislead by trickery; deceive

Vocabulary

enmity (en′ mə tē) *n.* ill will; hostility

Writing Practice

Characterization

SPIRAL REVIEW Ask a volunteer to read aloud the first sentence of chapter 3. Have students create a word web around the word *subtle.*

not obvious — sly — devious

Then have students write a definition for *subtle,* based on the context. **Ask:** How is the serpent characterized in this passage? *(as a sly and devious animal)*

Psalm 23

from the King James
version of the Bible

Agnus Dei, Lamb of God, fresco from crypt of Anagni Cathedral, thirteenth century. Anagni Cathedral, Italy.

The Lord is my shepherd; I shall not want.[1]

2 He maketh me to lie down in green pastures: he leadeth me beside the still waters.

3 He restoreth my soul: he leadeth me in the paths of righteousness for his name's sake.

4 Yea, though I walk through the valley of the shadow of death, I will fear no evil: for thou art with me; thy rod and thy staff they comfort me.

5 Thou preparest a table before me in the presence of mine enemies: thou anointest my head with oil; my cup runneth over.

6 Surely goodness and mercy shall follow me all the days of my life; and I will dwell in the house of the Lord for ever.

---

1. *Want* means "be in need of anything."

Analyze Text Structure *What does this comparison add to the earlier comparison of the Lord to a shepherd?*   **3**

The Sacred and the Secular *Why does this psalm end with a reference to the future?* **4**

KING JAMES VERSION OF THE BIBLE **413**

Teach

Reading Strategy | 3

Analyze Text Structure
Answer: *The earlier comparison suggests that God is a gentle shepherd who carefully tends his flock. This second comparison adds another dimension. The role of a host is to protect and comfort his guests.*

(ADVANCED) The speaker characterizes the Lord in several different ways including as a shepherd and host. **Ask:** What third comparison made about the Lord? *(The Lord as a priest who anoints the speaker's head with oil)* **Ask:** What is the speaker's purpose in using three comparisons? *(The speaker shows the multiple roles of the Lord.)*

Big Idea | 4

The Sacred and the Secular
Answer: *This reference supports the psalm's comforting message, suggesting God's eternal presence. It also implies the idea of an afterlife—the speaker believes that he or she will "dwell in the house of the Lord for ever."*

 To check students' understanding of the selection, see Unit 2 Teaching Resources Book, pp. 251.

Progress Check

Can students identify style?

If No → See Unit 2 Teaching Resources Book, p. 246.

After You Read

Assess

1. Students' answers will vary.
2. (a) 1: heaven, earth, light; 2: division between heaven and earth; 3: dry land, seas, and plants; 4: sun and moon; 5: animals that swim and fly; 6: animals that walk on earth, Adam and Eve (b) Humans are God's crowning achievement.
3. (a) The serpent persuades them to quench their thirst for knowledge. (b) Their "eyes were opened" by disobeying God's command.
4. (a) Adam: having to till the soil and return to dust; Eve: pains of childbirth; serpent: crawling on his belly and being the woman's enemy (b) A worry-free existence in Eden
5. (a) Mortal life on the earth (b) Because the Lord offers protection and comfort
6. That he or she will receive God's mercy throughout life and will be in heaven after death
7. (a) Immortality (b) Possible answers: wisdom; imperfection; fallibility
8. (a) A shepherd and a host (b) That God is a source of guidance, sustenance, and protection
9. (a) The Lord will care for those who trust and follow him. (b) A funeral or another occasion that involves mourning
10. They stress the importance of a life partner and the loyalty that married people owe to each other.

After You Read

Respond and Think Critically

Respond and Interpret

1. Which excerpt did you enjoy more? Explain.
2. (a)In your own words, describe the things God creates each day in Genesis. (b)Why are man and woman created last?
3. (a)According to Genesis, why do Adam and Eve disobey God and eat from the "tree of knowledge of good and evil"? (b)What causes Adam and Eve to be ashamed of their nakedness and afraid of God?
4. (a)What different punishments does God impose on Adam, Eve, and the serpent? (b)As a result of their actions, what do Adam and Eve lose?
5. (a)In Psalm 23, what is "the valley of the shadow of death"? (b)Why does the speaker "fear no evil"?
6. In the last verse of Psalm 23, what does the speaker conclude?

Literary Element **Style**

One component of **style** is word choice. Compare the following three translations of a passage from Psalm 23.

- "You spread a table for me in full view of my enemies; / You anoint my head with oil; / my drink is abundant." (Tanakh, Jewish Publication Society)

- "Thou spreadest a table for me in the sight of my enemies; / thou hast richly bathed my head with oil, / and my cup runs over." (New English Bible)

- "Thou preparest a table before me in the presence of mine enemies; thou anointest my head with oil; my cup runneth over." (King James Bible)

1. Study the following phrases from the three passages: "in full view of," "in the sight of," and "in the presence of." Do you think the difference in wording reflects an important distinction in meaning? Explain.

Analyze and Evaluate

7. (a)In Genesis, what does "the tree of life" symbolize, or stand for? (b)What does "the tree of knowledge of good and evil" symbolize?
8. (a)To what does the speaker compare the Lord in Psalm 23? (b)What do these metaphors suggest about the relationship between the speaker of the psalm and God?

Connect

9. **Big Idea** The Sacred and the Secular (a)What message does Psalm 23 contain that is particularly comforting? (b)During what occasions might it be appropriate for someone to read this psalm?
10. **Connect to Today** The last four paragraphs from chapter 2 of Genesis are often read in modern Christian wedding ceremonies. Why might they be suitable for a wedding?

---

2. Compare "my drink is abundant" with "my cup runneth over." What connotations does each phrase suggest?

Review: Parallelism

As you learned on page 274, **parallelism** is the use of a series of words, phrases, or sentences that have similar grammatical structures. For example, the following phrases are parallel: "Let the waters under the heaven be gathered" and "Let the dry land appear." Parallelism shows the relationship between ideas and helps emphasize thoughts.

Partner Activity With a partner, answer these questions.

1. Identify an example of parallelism in Genesis and explain what it adds to the telling of the story.
2. Find two examples of parallelism in Psalm 23 and explain how they contribute to the impact of the psalm.

Literary Element

1. Students' answers will vary but should be supported with reasons.
2. The first phrase suggests that the speaker is well provided for; the second suggests that the speaker is overwhelmed by the Lord's generosity.

 For grammar practice, see Unit 2 Teaching Resources Book, p. 250.

Review: Parallelism

1. Students' answers will vary. Possible answer: the phrases "And God said," "And God saw," and "And God called." The parallelism organizes the text and keeps the focus on God.
2. "He maketh me," "he leadeth me"; "Thou preparest a table," "Thou anointest my head"—the expressions with identical structure add to the musicality and rhythm of the psalm.

Reading Strategy | Analyze Text Structure

There are four basic types of text structures:

- **Chronological order:** text structured around the order of events, from beginning to end.

- **Cause-and-effect order:** text structured around causal relationships.

- **Comparison-contrast order:** text structured in a way that shows similarities and differences between ideas or events.

- **Spatial order:** text structured around the physical arrangement of things or events.

Several organizational methods may be at work in the same text. For example, a text might proceed mainly in chronological order but demonstrate cause-and-effect relationships at the same time. Use the notes that you took while reading to help you answer the following questions.

1. How is the excerpt from Genesis structured? Explain.

2. How is Psalm 23 structured? Explain.

Vocabulary Practice

Practice with Synonyms Synonyms are words with the same, or nearly the same, meaning. With a partner, brainstorm three synonyms for each vocabulary word below, keeping in mind the shades of meaning each word has. Then discuss your choices with your classmates. Be prepared to explain the choices.

abundantly   replenish   beguile   enmity

EXAMPLE: *jubilant*
<u>Synonyms</u>: glad, joyous, elated
<u>Explanation</u>: Both <u>jubilant</u> and <u>glad</u> mean "happy," but <u>jubilant</u> has slightly stronger connotations.

 **Literature** Online

Selection Resources For Selection Quizzes, eFlashcards, and Reading-Writing Connection activities, go to glencoe.com and enter QuickPass code GLB9817u2.

Speaking and Listening

Oral Interpretation

Assignment Although people often speak of the Bible as if it were a single, authoritative document, several translations exist. Choose a translation other than the King James Version and do an oral interpretation of a passage from Genesis or Psalms.

Prepare Read your selection carefully, and summarize or paraphrase the content to be sure you understand its meaning. You may want to commit the passage to memory. Then read it again, noting places to use body language or vary your tone of voice to enhance understanding. Finally, practice your delivery, using correct pronunciation and fluid, appropriate gestures.

EXAMPLE:

The Lord takes care of us as his sheep;

<soothing tone; arms gathered in to body>

I will not be without any good thing.

<arm lifted; louder voice>

He makes a resting-place for me in the green fields;

<slower pace>

he is my guide by the quiet waters.

<eyes following as hand extends; softer voice>

Perform Make frequent eye contact with your listeners, whether you are speaking from an annotated text or from memory. Relax, take your time, and think about the meaning of the words as you deliver them. Your voice and entire body should help listeners understand the passage. When you have finished, briefly explain the passage's meaning and tell why you chose to present it in the way you did.

Evaluate Evaluate the effectiveness of your oral interpretation, paying attention to ways in which you could improve your performance next time.

After You Read

Assess

Reading Strategy

1. The first chapter of Genesis is in chronological, cause-and-effect, and spatial order. The first chapter proceeds chronologically. The second chapter proceeds spatially. The third chapter proceeds largely from cause to effect. Adam and Eve disobey God, so he expels them from Eden.

2. Psalm 23 is structured spatially. There are images and metaphors that are not in chronological or cause-and-effect order. The poem moves symbolically from life to death.

Vocabulary

Sample answer:

abundantly

<u>Synonyms</u>: bountifully, copiously, plentifully

<u>Explanation</u>: Both *abundantly* and *copiously* imply a large amount, although *copiously* can sometimes have negative connotations.

Speaking and Listening

Use these criteria in evaluating student oral interpretations:

- It presents a selection from an appropriate version and section of the Bible.
- Body language and vocal pitch and pacing underscore the meaning of the passage.
- The self-evaluation is fair and accurate and identifies areas for improvement.

Focus

Bellringer Options

Literature Launchers: Pre-Reading Videos DVD, Selection Launcher

Selection Focus Transparency 17

Daily Language Practice Transparency 29

Or ask: Have you ever found it hard to decide—or explain—who should be blamed for a mistake or an act of misbehavior?

Tell students to think, as they read, about the reasons the speaker uses in assigning blame for the fall of Adam and Eve.

Interactive Read and Write

Other options for teaching this selection can be found in

- Interactive Read and Write for EL Students pp. 113–120.
- Interactive Read and Write for Approaching-Level Students pp. 113–120.
- Interactive Read and Write for On-Level Students pp. 113–120.

Before You Read

Eve's Apology

Meet **Aemilia Lanyer**
(1569–1645)

The Annunciation, c. 1430–1432 (detail). Fra Angelico. Oil on panel. Prado, Madrid, Spain.

In 1611, the same year that the King James Bible and three of Shakespeare's plays were published, forty-two-year-old Aemilia Lanyer (lən yēr´) published her landmark book of poetry, *Salve Deus Rex Judaeorum*. It was one of the first books of poetry ever published by an Englishwoman and the first such book dedicated exclusively to women patrons.

Source of the Book The book was remarkable for another reason as well. In it, according to scholar Susanne Woods, Lanyer is "attacking the vanity and blindness of men and justifying women's right to be free of masculine subjugation" at a time when few women dared to do so. Lanyer excused her boldness with the claim that her title, which means "Hail, God, King of the Jews," came to her in a dream. She said that this was "a significant token, that I was appointed to performe this Worke."

"Do not the thing that goes against thy heart."

—Aemilia Lanyer,
from *Salve Deus Rex Judaeorum*

Ironically, Lanyer may have owed some credit for her accomplishments to her father, Baptista Bassano, a musician at the English royal court. Although her father died when she was only seven, he left her with money and connections to people at the royal court who exposed her to ideas and rhetorical techniques that developed her mind and her art. She had a relationship with Lord Hunsdon, a member of Queen Elizabeth's court

and a patron of Shakespeare's theater company. When Lanyer's relationship with Hunsdon ended, she married Alfonso Lanyer, a court musician. An educated woman, Lanyer may have known Shakespeare himself, as well as Ben Jonson and Edmund Spenser. In fact, there is some evidence that Lanyer is the so-called Dark Lady whom Shakespeare addresses in many of his sonnets.

A Woman's Vision Lanyer was a friend of the countess of Cumberland, a patron of the arts and Lanyer's patron as well. The countess was one of the many women to whom Lanyer dedicated her book. Part of Lanyer's book contains what is known as a country-house poem, "The Description of Cooke-ham," about the home of the countess of Cumberland and her daughter. According to Woods, the poem "presents a woman's vision of an ideal life in harmony with nature in which neither men nor class distinctions mar conversation and song under a lovely oak tree with a wonderful view of the countryside."

LOG ON ▶ **Literature** Online

Author Search For more about Aemilia Lanyer, go to glencoe.com and enter QuickPass code GLB9817u2.

Selection Skills

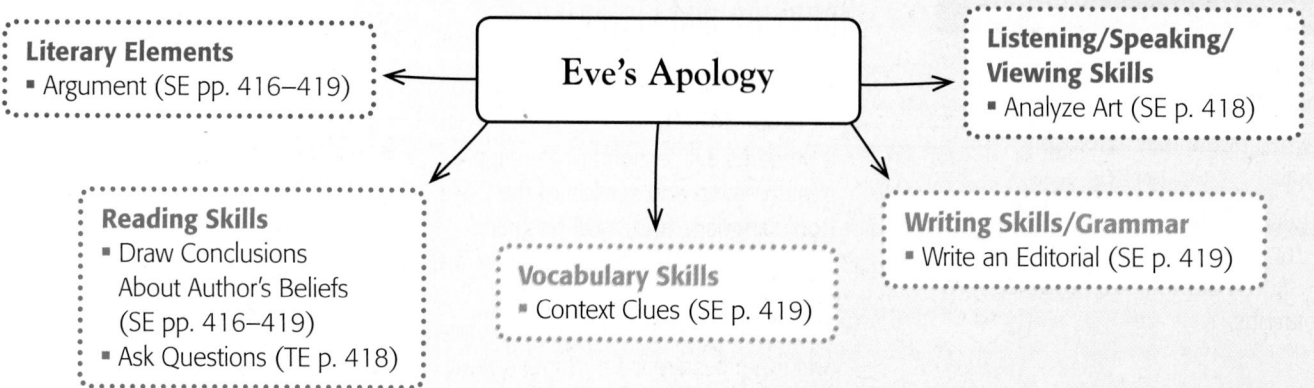

Literary Elements
- Argument (SE pp. 416–419)

Eve's Apology

Listening/Speaking/Viewing Skills
- Analyze Art (SE p. 418)

Reading Skills
- Draw Conclusions About Author's Beliefs (SE pp. 416–419)
- Ask Questions (TE p. 418)

Vocabulary Skills
- Context Clues (SE p. 419)

Writing Skills/Grammar
- Write an Editorial (SE p. 419)

Literature and Reading Preview

Connect to the Poem

Do you think Eve should be blamed for God's decision to banish the first couple from Eden? Reread chapters 2 and 3 of Genesis (page 411) and write a journal entry, giving your thoughts on this question.

Build Background

The word *apology* in the title of Lanyer's poem does not mean that Eve is sorry for her actions or is accepting the blame for them. As it is used here, *apology* refers to a defense or justification of Eve's actions.

Set Purposes for Reading

Big Idea The Sacred and the Secular

Some humanists believed that faith could be combined with the spirit of inquiry. As you read, ask yourself, Was Lanyer this kind of humanist?

Literary Element Argument

Argument is persuasive writing in which logic or reason is used to try to influence the reader's ideas or actions. In an argument, a writer states an opinion and supports that opinion with facts and reasoning. Arguments may also appeal to the reader's emotions. As you read, ask yourself, Which arguments are based on reason and which on emotion?

Reading Strategy Draw Conclusions About Author's Beliefs

A **conclusion** is a general statement about the information you have on a subject. You should back up your conclusions with supporting details. As you read, ask yourself, Which details provide clues to what Aemilia Lanyer believes?

....

Tip: Summarizing When you draw conclusions about parts of a poem, summarize the meaning of each stanza in a sentence or two. Use a chart like the one below.

Stanza	Summary
1.	
2.	
3.	
4.	

Learning Objectives

For pages 416–419

In studying this text, you will focus on the following objectives:

Literary Study: Analyzing argument.

Reading: Drawing conclusions about author's beliefs.

Writing: Writing an article.

Vocabulary

endure (en door′) *v.* to bear; tolerate; put up with; p. 418 *It was hard to endure the pain in my knee when I fell.*

discretion (dis kresh′ ən) *n.* good judgment; p. 418 *When I asked her whether I should reveal the secret, she left it to my discretion.*

Before You Read

Focus

Summary

In this excerpt, the speaker discusses Adam and Eve's tasting of the forbidden fruit of "the tree of knowledge of good and evil," arguing that Adam deserves more blame than Eve for the act.

 For summaries in languages other than English, see Unit 2 Teaching Resources Book, pp. 253–258.

Vocabulary

Say: Often a writer will choose a word with an explicit as well as an implicit meaning. **Ask:** What is the implicit meaning of *endure*? (*The word* endure *suggests that the speaker has suffered greatly and without justification.*) **Ask:** What might the implicit meaning of *discretion* be? (*The word* discretion *suggests that the speaker feels a need to be secretive.*)

 For additional vocabulary practice, see Unit 2 Teaching Resources Book, p. 261.

English Learners

DIFFERENTIATED INSTRUCTION

Intermediate Point out that the main idea in this excerpt is related to the blame Adam and Eve share for eating the forbidden fruit. Then ask students to create a graphic organizer to identify lines in the excerpt that lay blame for their actions on Adam or Eve.

(Answers will vary.)

Blame

Adam	Eve
_____	_____
_____	_____
_____	_____

Ask students to describe in writing—before they read the selection—how much blame Adam and Eve might have.

Evaluate Encourage students to evaluate the poem's view of human nature. **Ask:** Do you agree or disagree that men are boastful of the knowledge supposedly given them by Eve? *(Accept all reasonable responses.)*

Argument **Answer:** *Students may question whether Eve erred for the sake of knowledge. Some may note that the fruit was appealing to both Adam and Eve and may therefore conclude that the argument is persuasive.*

[APPROACHING] **Ask:** In what lines does Lanyer suggest that most of the blame is Adam's? *(lines 1, 2, 4, 7,19, 24)*

 For additional practice using the reading skill or strategy, see Unit 2 Teaching Resources Book, p. 260.

 To check students' understanding of the selection, see Unit 2 Teaching Resources Book, pp. 262.

View the Art ★

Christian Pierre has designed many book covers, and she has taught at La Villa School of the Arts in Jacksonville, Florida.

Eve's Apology

from **Salve Deus Rex Judaeorum**

Aemilia Lanyer

The Temptress, 1995. Christian Pierre. Acrylic on masonite, 48 x 32 in. Private collection.

View the Art. Christian Pierre uses bold color and "speedy execution" (that is, quick brushstrokes) to create vivid, spontaneous-seeming images. How does her portrayal of Eve compare with Lanyer's? ★

But surely Adam cannot be excused;
Her fault, though great, yet he was most to blame.
What weakness offered, strength might have refused;
Being lord of all, the greater was his shame;
5   Although the serpent's craft had her abused,
God's holy word ought all his actions frame;[1]
    For he was lord and king of all the earth
    Before poor Eve had either life or breath,

Who being framed[2] by God's eternal hand
10 The perfectest man that ever breathed on earth,
And from God's mouth received that strait[3] command,
The breach[4] whereof he knew was present death;
Yea, having power to rule both sea and land,
Yet with one apple won to lose that breath
15   Which God had breathèd in his beauteous face,
    Bringing us all in danger and disgrace;

And then to lay the fault on patience's back,
That we (poor women) must **endure** it all;
We know right well he did **discretion** lack,
20 Being not persuaded thereunto at all.
If Eve did err, it was for knowledge sake;
The fruit being fair persuaded him to fall.
    No subtle serpent's falsehood did betray him;
    If he would eat it, who had power to stay[5] him?

25 Not Eve, whose fault was only too much love,
Which made her give this present to her dear,
That what she tasted he likewise might prove,[6]
Whereby his knowledge might become more clear;
He never sought her weakness to reprove[7]
30 With those sharp words which he of God did hear;
    Yet men will boast of knowledge, which he took **1**
    From Eve's fair hand, as from a learnèd book.

---

1. *Frame* means "determine."
2. Here, *framed* means "formed."
3. *Strait* means "strict."
4. A *breach* is a violation.
5. *Stay* means "prevent."
6. *Prove* means "discover by experience."
7. *Reprove* means "condemn."

2 Argument *Explain why this is or is not a persuasive argument.*

Vocabulary

endure (en door´) *v.* to bear; tolerate; put up with
discretion (dis kresh´ ən) *n.* good judgment

Reading Practice

 SPIRAL REVIEW SMALL GROUP **Ask Questions** After students have read the poem, have each write down two questions about it and its meaning. Then have each write one thing he or she knows for certain about the poem. Divide the class into groups of four or five; within each group, students should share their questions and certainties. Encourage them to attempt to answer one another's questions. As a follow-up, have the entire class discuss any unanswered questions.

After You Read

Respond and Think Critically

Respond and Interpret

1. In the first stanza, who does the speaker say is most to blame for Adam and Eve's sin? Why?

2. (a)According to the second stanza, what did Adam know would result from disobeying God's command? (b)What else results from his actions?

3. (a)In the third stanza, what reasons does the speaker give for Eve's error and Adam's fall? (b)What do the reasons imply about Eve and Adam?

Analyze and Evaluate

4. (a)In the fourth stanza, what reasons does the speaker give to argue that Eve's actions were more excusable than Adam's? (b)How effec-

tively do you think these reasons support the argument? Explain.

5. What is your reaction to lines 31–32 about the source of men's knowledge?

6. Do you think this apology would be more or less effective if the speaker were Eve herself? Explain.

Connect

7. **Big Idea** The Sacred and the Secular How do you think the attitudes about women during Lanyer's time might have affected her opinions and writing?

8. **Connect to Today** In your opinion, are two people who commit the same act always equally responsible for their actions? Explain.

Literary Element Argument

Writers rely on different persuasive techniques in order to convince the reader to think in a certain way. Lanyer uses **emotional appeals**, or words and phrases that arouse strong emotions in the reader.

1. Restate the main points of the argument in "Eve's Apology." Do you think it is an effective argument? Why or why not?

2. List two or three passages in which the speaker appeals to the reader's emotions. Do these appeals enhance her argument? Explain.

 Writing

Write an Editorial Write an editorial, like those appearing in newspapers or magazines, in which you agree or disagree with the argument presented in "Eve's Apology." Before you begin, identify each of Lanyer's specific points and the support she gives for her viewpoint. Write your article in a journalistic tone, using persuasive prose whenever appropriate. For help in crafting an argument, see the Writing Workshop on page 646.

Reading Strategy Draw Conclusions About Author's Beliefs

When you draw a conclusion, you make a general statement about something you have read or found. What conclusion can you draw about Lanyer's beliefs, based on this poem?

Vocabulary Practice

Practice with Context Clues Identify the context clues in the following sentences that help you determine the meaning of each bold-faced vocabulary word.

1. I got up and walked out, unable to **endure** another minute of that terrible movie.

2. Because we vote with secret ballots, revealing your choice is up to your **discretion**.

LOG ON **Literature** Online

Selection Resources For Selection Quizzes, eFlashcards, and Reading-Writing Connection activities, go to glencoe.com and enter QuickPass code GLB9817u2.

AEMILIA LANYER **419**

After You Read

Assess

1. Adam, because he has been lord of all.

2. (a) Adam knew he would die. (b) All humans die as a result of Adam's sin.

3. (a) Eve fell to deceit and a thirst for knowledge; Adam, to the appeal of a tempting fruit. (b) That Eve was more idealistic, Adam more greedy.

4. (a) Eve wanted to give Adam the gift of knowledge; Adam's actions were motivated by greed. (b) Answers will vary.

5. Answers will vary.

6. Possible answer: It would be less effective, because Eve's arguments might be seen as self-serving.

7. Answers will vary.

8. Possible answer: A difference in motivation might result in a difference in responsibility.

Literary Element

1. Adam is more at fault because he was created to be stronger than Eve. Eve acted out of love and a desire for knowledge. Student opinions will vary.

2. "That we (poor women) must endure it all"; "Not Eve, whose fault was only too much love." Students should give valid reasons to support their opinions.

Writing

Editorials will vary, but they should agree or disagree with the poem's argument and have a journalistic tone.

Reading Strategy

Clearly, Lanyer's beliefs about gender equality are evident in this unorthodox interpretation of the story of Adam and Eve.

Vocabulary

1. The context suggests that *endure* means "tolerate something unpleasant."

2. The context suggests that *discretion* means "caution or prudent judgment."

Focus

Bellringer Options

Daily Language Practice Transparency 30

Or have students read the displayed quotation from Samuel Johnson. **Ask:** Do you think Johnson admired the work of the metaphysical poets? How can you tell?

Teach

Literary Element | 1

Figurative Language Remind students that figurative language is not meant to be interpreted literally and is often used for descriptive effect to imply ideas indirectly. Figurative language is especially prominent in poetry.

View the Art ★

Vanitas is an art term that refers to works with the message that life and time are both limited and that, as a result, life should be lived to the fullest. Northern European artists often depicted this theme in still lifes.

 For an activity related to this selection, see Unit 2 Teaching Resources Book, p. 264.

Learning Objectives

For pages 420–421

In studying this text, you will focus on the following objectives:

Literary Study:
Analyzing literary periods.
Analyzing literary genres.

The metaphysical poets derived inspiration
from the rich legacy of Elizabethan verse, their

The eighteenth-century Neoclassicist writer Samuel Johnson (see page 623), who was highly critical of the "unnatural" images and rhythms of John Donne's verse, gave it the name "metaphysical poetry," a term that has since been used by Donne's admirers as well as by his detractors. Johnson used the term to describe poetry that dealt with philosophical, abstract, and highly theoretical topics.

The Metaphysical Style

Although the metaphysical poets derived inspiration from the rich legacy of Elizabethan verse, their poetry was in part a reaction against the stylized conventions of the sixteenth-century sonnet sequence. Instead of using regular meters and "poetic" images drawn from nature, poets such as Donne often used irregular rhythms and unusual, **1** often startling, figurative language. Donne's tone is less formal and his word choice is simpler than those of most Elizabethan poets, but his verse makes far greater demands on the reader's intellect.

The Metaphysical Poets

THE TERM *METAPHYSICAL POETS* IS GENERALLY APPLIED TO A distinctive group of seventeenth-century English poets, including John Donne, George Herbert, Richard Crashaw, and Andrew Marvell. Their poetry was marked by highly complex extended metaphors, avoidance of smooth or regular meter, and a fondness for unconventional imagery often drawn from philosophy, theology, science, or the arts.

> *"The metaphysical poets were men of learning, and to show their learning was their whole endeavor. . . . Their thoughts are often new, but seldom natural."*
>
> —Samuel Johnson

Vanitas. French School. Louvre, Paris. ★

The Characteristics of Metaphysical Poetry

Like the Elizabethan poets, the metaphysical poets wrote about love and the physical attraction between men and women, but they were also attracted to darker or more somber subjects, such as death, the brevity of human life, and the **2** individual's relationship with God. A philosophical approach to everyday subjects and experience expressed in a witty, conversational style is a hallmark of metaphysical poetry. The similarities and differences between the Elizabethan and metaphysical styles may be summarized as follows.

Vocabulary Practice

 Words in Context Help students build their vocabulary with definitions of words in context. Have students work alone or with partners to define and write original sentences for the following words from the feature:

conventions
hallmarks

melodious
unravel
legacy
arresting
minted

Remind students that their definitions should fit the context of the article.

- **Use of Argument** Like much Elizabethan verse, metaphysical poetry often takes the form of an argument, but the argument in a metaphysical poem appeals to the intellect as well as to emotions.

- **Use of Conceits** Elizabethan poets were fond of **conceits,** or elaborate extended metaphors. Often these conceits compared the beauty of a woman to the beauty of a natural object, such as a star. The metaphysical poets took the use of conceits a significant step further, creating arresting comparisons between very dissimilar objects or ideas that demand thought and imagination to unravel.

- **Use of Language** Elizabethan poets usually wrote in a "high style," using melodious words, elegant phrasing, and poetic inversions of typical speech patterns. By contrast, the metaphysical poets often wrote in a "plain style" that more closely resembled speech. The first line below exemplifies the high style; the second exemplifies the plain style.

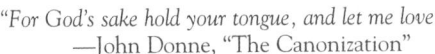

"With how sad steps, O Moon, thou climb'st the skies!"
—Sir Philip Sidney, Sonnet 31

"For God's sake hold your tongue, and let me love"
—John Donne, "The Canonization"

- **Use of Unconventional Forms** Most Elizabethan poets were content with traditional forms; the metaphysical poets often were not. In many of their poems, lines do not scan regularly, rhyme schemes cannot be predicted, and vocabulary and syntax are not elevated. The result, however, is a directness of language that often captivates the reader.

★ *Portrait of a Lady,* c. seventeenth century. English School. Private collection.

The Legacy of the Metaphysical Poets

Because of changes in literary taste, metaphysical poetry was undervalued throughout the eighteenth and nineteenth centuries. In the early twentieth century, however, poets such as William Butler Yeats, T. S. Eliot, and W. H. Auden praised the metaphysical poets for their ability to appeal to the mind as well as to the heart. When Modernist poets were overturning the values and conventions of Romanticism, the metaphysical poets were at last praised and recognized for their substantial contributions to English literature.

LOG ON ▶ **Literature** Online

Literary History For more about the metaphysical poets, go to glencoe.com and enter QuickPass code GLB9817u2.

Respond and Think Critically

1. In your opinion, should poetry primarily appeal to intellect or to emotions? Explain.

2. Why might Samuel Johnson have considered metaphysical poetry to be "unnatural"?

3. In what ways did the metaphysical poets anticipate Modernist poetry?

Advanced Learners

DIFFERENTIATED INSTRUCTION

Freewrite Say: Take five minutes to write several phrases or sentences about a subject that is important to you. Read over what you have written. Encourage students to identify whether their approach was emotional or intellectual and to explain how they made their determinations.

Teach

Reading Strategy | 2

Word Parts Write *meta + physical* on the board. Explain that *metaphysical* literally means "after or following the physical" and that it has to do with a branch of philosophy that seeks to know what truly can be called "real."

Big Idea | 3

The Sacred and the Secular

Ask: How do the differences, in topics and style, between the Elizabethan and metaphysical poets reflect different ideas about religion and its relevance to everyday life? *(The metaphysical poets addressed religious topics more directly; their plain-spoken style suggests a sense that these topics were closely related to ordinary life.)*

View the Art ★

Explain to students that "English School" refers to painters who produced works typical of the English artworks of this period.

Assess

1. Students' answers will vary.

2. Johnson was a Neoclassicist who believed that art should faithfully imitate nature and focus on human values.

3. Like Modernist poets, metaphysical poets ignored established conventions of poetry and created subtle, complex poems that appealed to intellect as well as emotion.

Bellringer Options

Selection Focus
Transparency 18
Daily Language Practice
Transparency 31

Or point out that many poems have been written with specific occasions or kinds of occasions in mind. **Ask:** Do you think some kinds of occasions are more suitable than others as subjects for poems? What kinds of occasions might be particularly good subjects?

Before You Read

Donne's Works

Meet **John Donne**
(1572–1631)

I n life and in art, John Donne traveled a unique path. Gifted with a nimble mind and astonishing talent, he created intimate portraits of human relationships and the physical world, but his foremost passion was for God. He believed that human suffering was transient, that the afterlife was real, and that people had a duty to confront their own mortality with courage. The poems and sermons in which Donne expressed his views are considered to be some of the most glorious works of English literature.

Ambitious Youth Donne was born into an affluent Roman Catholic family at a time when anti-Catholic sentiment ran high. When he was four, his father died. At twelve, Donne began studies at Oxford, continuing later at Cambridge, but as a result of his Catholicism, he received degrees from neither school. Donne would not make the oath to the Protestant Queen Elizabeth that was a requirement for graduation.

After traveling in Spain and Italy, the young Donne studied law in London. Perhaps to prove his patriotism and help pave the way for a government career, Donne then joined the Earl of Essex on two daring military expeditions against Spain. On his return to England in 1597, Donne secured the position of secretary to government minister Sir Thomas Egerton. By this time, Donne had abandoned Catholicism and joined the Church of England.

As Egerton's secretary, Donne met many important people with whom he made himself popular. His career flourished until 1601. That year, he met, fell in love with, and eloped with Egerton's seventeen-year-old niece, Anne More. Anne's father, furious, responded by having Donne fired from his post and thrown into jail. Though his

time there was brief, Donne lost all hope of a government career, his wife lost her dowry, and, suddenly without funds, the couple was forced to live on the charity of Anne's cousin.

Poet and Minister To occupy his time after being fired, Donne studied and wrote essays on theology and poems about love and religion. He supported his growing family with odd jobs, writing, and the charity of friends. His allies, moved by the power of his religious poems, urged him to enter the Anglican ministry. At forty-three he did just that, and he soon became a chaplain to King James I.

Two years later, Donne's wife died in childbirth. Grief-stricken, he poured himself into preaching with passionate intensity. The force and eloquence of these sermons helped lead to his appointment, at the age of forty-nine, to the deanship of the prestigious St. Paul's Cathedral in London.

> *"Donne's verses are like the peace of God: they pass all understanding."*
>
> —King James I

In February of 1631, Donne, who was already ill with the cancer that would kill him, gave his final sermon at court. Many believe that he intended it to be his own funeral sermon. By the time Donne died, he was considered the greatest preacher in England.

 Literature Online

Author Search For more about John Donne, go to glencoe.com and enter QuickPass code GLB9817u2.

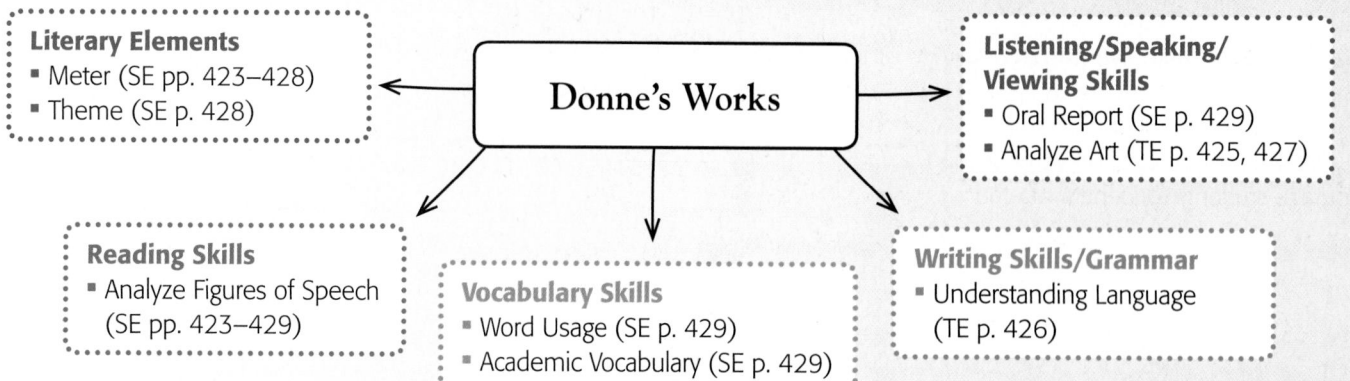

Literary Elements
- Meter (SE pp. 423–428)
- Theme (SE p. 428)

Donne's Works

Listening/Speaking/Viewing Skills
- Oral Report (SE p. 429)
- Analyze Art (TE p. 425, 427)

Reading Skills
- Analyze Figures of Speech (SE pp. 423–429)

Vocabulary Skills
- Word Usage (SE p. 429)
- Academic Vocabulary (SE p. 429)

Writing Skills/Grammar
- Understanding Language (TE p. 426)

Literature and Reading Preview

Connect to the Poems

How do you deal with loss in your life? Freewrite for a few minutes about your way of handling separation from someone important to you.

Build Background

Donne probably wrote "Song" and "A Valediction: Forbidding Mourning" to comfort Anne More just before he left on a diplomatic mission to France. He wrote "Death Be Not Proud" soon after Anne's death.

Set Purposes for Reading

Big Idea The Sacred and the Secular

As you read, ask yourself, How do Donne's religious beliefs affect his description of earthly events?

Literary Element Meter

Meter is a regular pattern of stressed and unstressed syllables in a line of poetry. The basic unit of meter is the **foot,** consisting of one or two stressed syllables (marked ´) and/or one or two unstressed syllables (marked ˘). As you read each poem, ask yourself, What rhythm is produced by the arrangement of stressed and unstressed syllables?

Reading Strategy Analyze Figures of Speech

Figurative language is language that is not meant to be interpreted literally. A **figure of speech** is a specific form of figurative language, such as metaphor, personification, or simile. A **metaphor** makes a comparison between two unlike things to help readers perceive one thing more vividly (as in *The stars are torches*). **Personification** gives human qualities to objects, animals, or ideas (as in *The trees are patient*). A **simile** compares two unlike things by means of the word *like* or *as* (as in *The moon is like a purse*). As you read, ask yourself, What effects do the figures of speech have?

Tip: Taking Notes Record figures of speech in a chart.

Figure of Speech	What the figure of speech communicates

Learning Objectives

For pages 422–429

In studying these texts, you will focus on the following objectives:

Literary Study: Analyzing meter.

Reading: Analyzing figures of speech.

Speaking and Listening: Delivering an oral report.

Vocabulary

jest (jest) *n.* an utterance or act offered humorously or mockingly; p. 424 *When I said that I would not clean the house, Mom knew my remark was in jest.*

refined (ri fīnd´) *adj.* freed from imperfections; improved; p. 426 *Refined sugar has been processed to remove unwanted particles.*

English Learners

DIFFERENTIATED INSTRUCTION

Beginning Say: Similes and metaphors are both ways of making comparisons. Similes use the words *like* or *as* to form comparisons. Metaphors don't have these connecting words. For example, the simile "A ship is like a floating city" could be changed into the metaphor "A ship is a floating city." Have students practice changing these similes into metaphors: 1) My love is like a red convertible. *(My love is a red convertible.)* 2) The company's managers are like a gang of thieves. *(The company's managers are a gang of thieves.)* 3) Marisa is as pretty as a picture. *(Marisa is a pretty picture.)*

Before You Read

Focus

Summary

In these three poems, Donne expresses feelings arising from specific occasions. "Song" is about the pain lovers feel when separated from each other. "A Valediction: Forbidding Mourning" is about acceptance of the death of a loved one. The speaker of "Death Be Not Proud" sees dying not as an end but as the beginning of the afterlife.

For summaries in languages other than English, see Unit 2 Teaching Resources Book, pp. 266–271.

Vocabulary

Related Words Students can use their knowledge of related words to guide their usage of new vocabulary. **Ask:** Which of these words is related to jest: *suggest* or *jester? (jester)* What is a jester? *(clown)* Which of these words is related to refined: refinery or finery? *(refinery)* What is a refinery? *(facility for purifying materials)*

Teach

Literary Element — 1

Metaphysical Conceit

Explain that a metaphysical conceit is an extended simile or metaphor comparing two things that are very unlike each other. Although the comparison may seem rather far fetched, it sometimes serves as a poem's main unifying element.

Ask: What metaphysical conceit can be found in lines 9–16 of "Song"? *(The speaker compares his journey to that of the sun.)*

Reading Strategy — 2

Analyze Figures of Speech

Answer: *The speaker is attempting to persuade his lover not to grieve over his leaving. By comparing her sighs to his soul, he intends to make her stop sighing.*

ENGLISH LEARNERS **Ask:** How would you put lines 25-26 into modern-day English? *(When you sigh, you don't sigh wind, but you sigh my soul away.)*

SONG

John Donne

A Market Scene with Fruit and Vegetable Sellers. Frederick van Valkenborch (1570–1623). Oil on canvas. Private collection.

Sweetest love, I do not go,
  For weariness of thee,
Nor in hope the world can show
  A fitter love for me,
5   But since that I
Must die at last, 'tis best,
To use[1] myself in **jest**
    Thus by feigned[2] deaths to die.

Yesternight the sun went hence,
10 And yet is here today,
He hath no desire nor sense,
  Nor half so short a way:
    Then fear not me,
But believe that I shall make
15 Speedier journeys, since I take
  More wings and spurs than he.

O how feeble is man's power,
  That if good fortune fall,
Cannot add another hour,
20   Nor a lost hour recall!

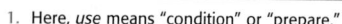

    But come bad chance,
And we join to it our strength,
And we teach it art and length,
    Itself o'er us to advance.

25 When thou sigh'st, thou sigh'st not wind,
  But sigh'st my soul away,
When thou weep'st, unkindly kind,
  My life's blood doth decay.
    It cannot be
30 That thou lov'st me as thou say'st,
If in thine my life thou waste,
  That art the best of me.

Let not thy divining heart
  Forethink me any ill,
35 Destiny may take thy part,
  And may thy fears fulfill,
    But think that we
Are but turned aside to sleep;
They who one another keep
40 Alive, ne'er parted be.

---

1. Here, *use* means "condition" or "prepare."
2. *Feigned* means "imagined" or "pretended."

> **Vocabulary**
>
> **jest** (jest) *n.* an utterance or act offered humorously or mockingly

Analyze Figures of Speech *Why does the speaker compare the sighs of his beloved to his soul?* — 2

424 UNIT 2 THE ENGLISH RENAISSANCE

Grammar Practice

SPIRAL REVIEW **Compound Subjects and Predicates** Remind students that a compound subject is made up of two or more simple subjects that are joined by a conjunction and have the same verb; a compound predicate is made up of two or more predicates joined by a conjunction and have the same subject.

Write on the board: Donne and his wife were very much in love. Help students identify Donne and his wife as the compound subject. Then have them identify the compound predicate in the last two lines of "A Valediction," on p. 424. *("makes my circle just, and makes me end where I begun")*

A VALEDICTION:
FORBIDDING MOURNING

John Donne

Ptolemy of Alexandria, c. A.D. 130 Illustration from the *Margarita Philosophica*, 1535. Science Museum, London.

*A*s virtuous men pass mildly away,
   And whisper to their souls to go,
Whilst some of their sad friends do say,
   "The breath goes now," and some say, "No";

5 So let us melt[1] and make no noise,
     No tear-floods nor sigh-tempests move;
   'Twere profanation[2] of our joys
     To tell the laity[3] our love.

   Moving of the earth[4] brings harms and fears,
10   Men reckon what it did and meant;
   But trepidation of the spheres,[5]
     Though greater far, is innocent.[6]

   Dull sublunary lovers' love,
     Whose soul[7] is sense,[8] cannot admit
15 Absence, because it doth remove
     Those things which elemented[9] it.

---

1. *Melt* means "part."
2. *Profanation* means "desecration" or "debasement."
3. *Laity* usually refers to people who are not members of the clergy, but here it may be intended to mean "outsiders" (that is, everyone but the speaker and the speaker's beloved).
4. *Moving of the earth* is a reference to earthquakes.
5. *Trepidation of the spheres* refers to a shuddering motion attributed to the eighth sphere in Ptolemy's model of the universe.
6. Here, *innocent* means "harmless."
7. Here, *soul* refers to essence.
8. *Sense* means "physical perceptions."
9. *Elemented* means "composed."

Meter *What pattern of stressed and unstressed syllables do you hear in these two lines?* **3**

Meter **Answer:** *In each line, there are four stressed syllables, each preceded by an unstressed syllable. (That is, the lines are iambic tetrameter.)*

(APPROACHING) Have students read the lines aloud, speaking the stressed syllables loudly and the unstressed syllables softly.

View the Art ★

Ptolemy (c. A.D. 100–170) was an astronomer, mathematician and geographer. He created the Ptolemaic system, a mathematical model of the universe that holds that the Earth is both the center of the universe and stationary. This was a dominant theory until the sixteenth and seventeenth centuries, when it was replaced by the Copernican system. **Ask:** How does the man in the painting appear similar to the speaker of the poem? *(He appears wistful and contemplative.)*

English Learners

DIFFERENTIATED INSTRUCTION

Advanced Explain that Donne's ordination into the Church of England produced a change in his poetry. Before then, his language had been vividly sensual. Afterward, it merged the sensual with the religious: his love poems use religious images, while his religious poems abound with sensual imagery. Have students identify how the poet uses imagery in the poem.

Approaching Level

DIFFERENTIATED INSTRUCTION

PARTNERS **Emerging** Students with short attention spans may lose interest in poems and fail to fully comprehend their meanings. Have students paraphrase, either orally or in writing, each stanza before reading the next. Have student pairs read or recite their paraphrases to each other, then discuss them.

Teach

Literary Element 1

Meter Have student volunteers read these stanzas aloud, and ask the others to listen for syllables that receive greater or lesser emphasis. **Ask:** Is the meter exactly the same in each line? *(no)* Explain that this variation makes the poem seem more conversational.

Reading Strategy 2

Analyze Figures of Speech
Answer: *Just as the legs of a compass can move apart while still remaining joined, people in love can endure physical separation but remain together in spirit.*

>
> For additional practice using the reading skill or strategy, see Unit 2 Teaching Resources Book, p. 273.

But we, by a love so much **refined**
  That ourselves know not what it is,
Inter-assurèd[10] of the mind;
20   Care less, eyes, lips, and hands to miss.

Our two souls, therefore, which are one,
  Though I must go, endure not yet
A breach,[11] but an expansion,
  Like gold to airy thinness beat.[12]

25 If they be two, they are two so
  As stiff twin compasses[13] are two:
Thy soul, the fixed foot, makes no show
  To move, but doth if the other do.

And though it in the center sit,
30   Yet when the other far doth roam,
It leans and hearkens after it,
  And grows erect as that comes home.

Such wilt thou be to me, who must,
  Like the other foot, obliquely[14] run:
35 Thy firmness[15] makes my circle[16] just,
  And makes me end where I begun.

---

10. *Inter-assurèd* means "mutually assured."
11. A *breach* is a break.
12. *Like . . . beat* refers to gold leaf, which is made by beating gold into extremely thin sheets. Baser metals would break up under the beating.
13. *Twin compasses* are the two legs of a geometrical compass.
14. *Obliquely* means "off at an angle."
15. *Firmness* implies faithfulness or perfection.
16. The *circle,* which has neither a beginning nor an end, is a symbol of perfection.

Analyze Figures of Speech *Why does the poet compare people in love to the legs of a compass in this stanza?* 2

Vocabulary

refined (ri fīnd´) *adj.* freed from imperfections; improved

Writing Practice

Understanding Language
Discuss with students how all languages change over time; elicit examples from the first languages of English language learners. Point out that poets often use contracted forms, altered syllables, or altered stresses to fit meters. Write these examples on the board: *'tis, hath, o'er, thou, sigh'st.* Invite volunteers to give their equivalents in modern English. *(it is, has, over, you, sigh)* Then have students work in small groups to paraphrase the poem and rewrite it in their own words.

DEATH
BE NOT PROUD

John Donne

Death, be not proud, though some have called thee
Mighty and dreadful, for thou art not so;
For those whom thou think'st thou dost overthrow
Die not, poor Death, nor yet canst thou kill me.
5   From rest and sleep, which but thy pictures[1] be,
Much pleasure, then from thee much more must flow,
And soonest our best men with thee do go,
Rest of their bones, and soul's delivery.[2]
Thou art slave to fate, chance, kings, and desperate men,
10 And dost with poison, war, and sickness dwell,
And poppy[3] or charms can make us sleep as well
And better than thy stroke; why swell'st thou then?[4]
One short sleep past, we wake eternally,
And death shall be no more; Death, thou shalt die.

---

1. Rest and sleep are called *thy pictures* because they resemble death.
2. *Soul's delivery* likely means "soul's salvation."
3. *Poppy* is opium, a narcotic drug that can produce sleep.
4. *Why swell'st thou then?* can be restated as "Why do you swell with pride?"

The Sacred and the Secular *What consolation do these lines suggest?* **3**

JOHN DONNE   **427**

Advanced Learners

DIFFERENTIATED INSTRUCTION

Identifying Personifications Divide the class into groups, and have each group choose a thing (e.g., America), an idea (e.g., liberty), or an intangible quality (e.g., faith, honor) to personify. Students should list the attributes of the "person" they create, then write a few lines of formal address to it. The identity of the "person" should be kept hidden so that other students can guess it. These addresses need not rhyme but should, like the poem, give clues to the personifications. Let groups take turns delivering their addresses, and award points to those whose personifications are most easily guessed.

Teach

Big Idea   **3**

The Sacred and the Secular
Answer: *The lines suggest that death, rather than meaning destruction, means peaceful rest and the salvation of one's soul.*

View the Art ★

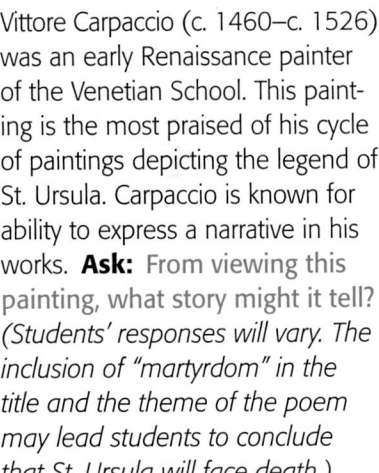

Vittore Carpaccio (c. 1460–c. 1526) was an early Renaissance painter of the Venetian School. This painting is the most praised of his cycle of paintings depicting the legend of St. Ursula. Carpaccio is known for ability to express a narrative in his works. **Ask:** From viewing this painting, what story might it tell? *(Students' responses will vary. The inclusion of "martyrdom" in the title and the theme of the poem may lead students to conclude that St. Ursula will face death.)*

 To check students' understanding of the selection, see Unit 2 Teaching Resources Book, p. 275–276.

427

After You Read

Assess

1. Students' responses will vary, but all should evidence a close reading of the poem.

2. (a) He says his reason for leaving is not that he is tired of her. (b) He means his departure is like an imagined death.

3. (a) Like the sun, he is leaving and will return. Unlike the sun, he doesn't have far to go. (b) He intends to reassure his beloved.

4. (a) He compares it to a gentle death. (b) He considers their love something sacred.

5. (a) Their love cannot withstand their absence, and so it no longer exists. (b) A higher, more spiritual and "refined" type of love

5. (a) He belittles Death, saying it has no power to kill him. (b) To rest and sleep (c) He has no fear of death.

6. (a) Death in itself has no power; it results from other causes. (b) When the speaker has passed into eternity

7. (a) He says people have little power over good luck, but they can add to bad luck by negative expectations and reactions. (b) Student responses will vary. Encourage students to support their views with textual evidence.

Progress Check

Can students identify meter?

If No → See Unit 2 Teaching Resources Book, p. 272.

After You Read

Respond and Think Critically

Respond and Interpret

1. What ideas from the poems did you find most powerful or surprising? Explain.

2. (a)In "Song," how does the speaker try to reassure his beloved in the first stanza? (b)What does the speaker mean by "[t]hus by feigned deaths to die"?

3. (a)In "Song," how is the speaker similar to and different from the sun? (b)Why might the speaker make this comparison?

4. (a)In the first two stanzas of "A Valediction: Forbidding Mourning," to what does the speaker compare his separation from his lover? (b)What do the words "profanation" and "laity" imply about his feelings?

5. (a)In "Death Be Not Proud," what does the speaker tell Death in the first four lines? (b)To what does the speaker compare Death in line five? (c)What can you infer about the speaker's attitude toward Death, on the basis of the first eight lines?

6. (a)How is Death "slave to fate, chance, kings, and desperate men"? (b)According to lines 13–14, when will Death die?

Analyze and Evaluate

7. (a)In "Song," what is the speaker saying about the power people have over good and bad luck? (b)Do you agree with his views on the subject? Explain.

8. (a)Why should the parting of two people in love not be a cause for mourning, according to "A Valediction: Forbidding Mourning"?

9. Tone is the attitude of the author toward the subject of a literary work. (a)How would you describe the tone of "Death Be Not Proud"? (b)What standard ideas about death are contradicted by the poem? Support your answer.

Connect

10. **Big Idea** The Sacred and the Secular These poems explore life, death, and love. According to the poems, what is fleeting? What is eternal? Explain what the poems suggest about Donne's views of the sacred and the secular.

11. **Connect to Today** Do you think a modern woman would find the speaker's argument in "A Valediction" persuasive? Explain.

Literary Element Meter

Meter is the pattern of stressed and unstressed syllables that gives a line of poetry a predictable rhythm. Within a poem, a poet may choose to vary the meter to create certain effects. For instance, if the reader has come to expect a line to be written in a certain rhythm, the introduction of a new rhythm may help to heighten the poem's drama.

- On a sheet of paper, copy out "Song" or "A Valediction: Forbidding Mourning." Then mark the stressed and unstressed syllables. Note how many syllables occur in each line of the poem. (a)How regular is the meter of the poem you chose? (b)Why might the poet have chosen such a meter? Explain.

Review: Theme

As you learned on page 291, the **theme** of a work is its central insight about life or human nature.

Partner Activity Meet with a classmate and discuss the themes of these three poems. For each poem, state the theme in one or two sentences. Then list evidence that supports your description of the theme. When you are done, compare and contrast the themes of the three poems.

Literature Online

Selection Resources For Selection Quizzes, eFlashcards, and Reading-Writing Connection activities, go to glencoe.com and enter QuickPass code GLB9817u2.

---

8. It can be an occasion for them to experience the true, spiritual nature of their relationship.

9. (a) The tone is defiant and confident. The speaker rejects death in favor of the afterlife. (b) Students may mention the ideas that death is fearsome and that it is final.

10. Earthly ("sublunary") life is fleeting, but spiritual life is eternal. As shown in his sensual/religious imagery, Donne does not separate these two realms.

11. Answers will vary. Some may think that a modern woman would not find much comfort in the speaker's intensely spiritual view of human relationships.

Reading Strategy Analyze Figures of Speech

In these poems, **figures of speech,** such as metaphors and similes, are used by Donne to create a variety of effects. They help to create tone, to vividly portray feelings, and to suggest fresh ideas. To convey meaning, Donne also uses **personification**—a figure of speech in which human qualities are given to objects, animals, or concepts.

1. (a) Explain one metaphor in "Song." What does the metaphor compare? (b) What meaning does the metaphor contribute to the poem?

2. (a) Explain the simile in lines 21–24 of "A Valediction: Forbidding Mourning." (b) What is the simile comparing? What is the deeper meaning of the simile?

3. What does the poem "Death Be Not Proud" achieve by personifying death? Explain.

Vocabulary Practice

Practice with Word Usage Respond to these statements to help you explore the meanings of vocabulary words from the selection.

1. Describe a **jest** that you found humorous.

2. Describe a project you worked on for which you created a very **refined** final product.

Academic Vocabulary

Apostrophe, rhyme, and meter all make **contributions** *to the greatness of Donne's verse.*

Contribution is an academic word that also appears in everyday usage. For example, a gift of money to a charity is often called a **contribution.**

To further explore the meaning of this word, complete the following sentence: *Someday, I hope to make a* **contribution** *to society by* _____.

For more on academic vocabulary, see pages 56 and R81.

Speaking and Listening

Oral Report

Assignment John Donne wrote "Death Be Not Proud" as a way of coming to terms with the death of his wife. All of us must eventually face and accept the death of people we love. Prepare an oral report on the stages of grief and methods of working through its powerful emotions.

Prepare Reread the poem and draw conclusions about attitudes toward death and dying in his time. Then search the Internet and the library for scientific studies and other materials about how death is seen in modern times. One classic source is Elizabeth Kübler-Ross's *On Death and Dying.* As you gather material, include supporting examples and evidence for your statements, being sure to quote and cite sources accurately.

Report Approach your presentation calmly and confidently. Use eye contact and appropriate gestures and facial expressions, and vary the tone, volume, and pace of your voice. Create flip charts or other visual aids to illustrate or summarize your points.

EXAMPLE:

> Five Stages of Grief
> - denial
> - anger
> - bargaining
> - depression
> - acceptance

Evaluate Write a paragraph evaluating your oral report. Use the chart on page 855 for help in your assessment. Consider how well you fulfilled each of the objectives and whether there are areas in which you could improve.

JOHN DONNE **429**

Reading Strategy

1. (a + b) Answers will vary.
2. (a) The simile suggests that the love between two people is extremely powerful and can withstand adversity. (b) The simile compares the love and connection between two people to gold that does not break apart although stretched thin.
3. Students may say that by giving death human characteristics the poem diminishes death's stature and makes it seem a thing to be scorned rather than feared.

Vocabulary

1. Students might retell a joke a friend told or recount an anecdote from a movie or book.
2. Students might mention an essay they revised extensively.

Academic Vocabulary

Possible answer: Someday, I hope to make a contribution to society by becoming a nurse.

Speaking and Listening

Use these criteria in evaluating student oral reports:

- Statement about the stages and ways of dealing with death, supported with evidence
- Clear delivery, with appropriate visual aids
- Self-evaluation, includes suggestions for improvement

Literary Element

(a) Students who choose "Song" may note a more regular meter than those who choose "A Valediction." (b) Students' answers will vary but should be supported with references to the poems.

Review: Theme

Students should restate the theme in their own words. Answers will vary but should be supported with text evidence.

Focus

Summary

Donne wrote this selection after having suffered a life-threatening illness. His theme is that all men and women are connected in sympathy because all are subject to illness, infirmity, and death.

Vocabulary

Analogies **Write on the board:** covetousness: generous :: vanity: humble.
Say: An analogy is a way of comparing similar features of different items. For instance, a generous person does not show covetousness. A humble person does not show vanity. Have students write their own analogies for each vocabulary word.

 For summaries in languages other than English, see Teaching Resources Guide, pp. 277–282.

Before You Read

Meditation 17

Connect to the Meditation

How can society function as a support system for those in need? Discuss this question with a partner, considering the ways in which people are connected in a society.

Build Background

At the age of fifty-one, Donne became seriously ill. After his recovery, he wrote a series of prose meditations—short sermons expressing his private reflections on this experience. This meditation refers to the ancient custom of ringing the bells of a village church to signal that someone was about to die.

Set Purposes for Reading

Big Idea **The Sacred and the Secular**

Even though "Meditation 17" is a sermon, it contains secular imagery and metaphors. As you read, ask yourself, Why did Donne choose these particular figures of speech?

Literary Element **Metaphysical Conceit**

A **metaphysical conceit** is an intellectual comparison that can develop a wide range of ideas and emotions. As you read, ask yourself, How does Donne use metaphysical conceits to advance an argument about mortality and salvation?

Reading Strategy **Make Inferences About Theme**

A **theme** of a work is a message about life or human nature. Often, readers can discover a theme by making inferences based on details in the work. As you read, ask yourself, What overall message is Donne trying to convey?

Tip: Taking Notes Record inferences about theme in a chart.

Details	Inference About Theme
"all mankind is of one author and is one volume"	Everyone belongs to God and is a part of the same whole.

Learning Objectives

For pages 430–434

In studying this text, you will focus on the following objectives:

Literary Study: Understanding metaphysical conceit.

Reading: Making inferences about theme.

Vocabulary

congregation (kong′ grə gā′ shən) *n.* a group of people who gather for religious worship; p. 431 *The minister greeted his congregation before beginning the sermon.*

covetousness (kuv′ it əs nəs) *n.* great desire for something belonging to another; p. 432 *Greta wanted her sister's purse; she was guilty of covetousness.*

contemplation (kon′ təm plā′ shən) *n.* careful thought or consideration; meditation; p. 432 *Tom sat under the oak tree, deep in contemplation.*

Selection Skills

Literary Elements
- Metaphysical Conceit (SE pp. 430–434)
- Motif (SE p. 434)

Meditation 17

Writing Skills/Grammar
- Summary (SE p. 435)
- Introductory Clauses (SE p. 435)

Reading Skills
- Make Inferences About Theme (SE pp. 430–434)
- Summarize (TE p. 432)

Vocabulary Skills
- Analogies (SE p. 434; TE p. 430)
- Academic Vocabulary (SE p. 434)

Dance of Death, sixteenth century. Print. Private collection.

Meditation 17

John Donne

Nunc lento sonitu dicunt, Morieris.
Now this bell, tolling softly for another, says to me, Thou must die.

Perchance he for whom this bell tolls may be so ill as that he knows not it tolls for him; and perchance I may think myself so much better than I am, as that they who are about me and see my state may have caused it to toll for me, and I know not that.

The church is catholic,[1] universal, so are all her actions; all that she does belongs to all. When she baptizes a child, that action concerns me; for that child is thereby connected to that head[2] which is my head too, and ingrafted into that body[3] whereof I am a member. And when she buries a man, that action concerns me: all mankind is of one author and is one volume; when one man dies, one chapter is not torn out of the book, but translated into a better language; and every chapter must be so translated. God employs several translators; some pieces are translated by age, some by sickness, some by war, some by justice; but God's hand is in every translation, and his hand shall bind up all our scattered leaves[4] again for that library where every book shall lie open to one another.

As therefore the bell that rings to a sermon calls not upon the preacher only, but upon the **congregation** to come, so this bell calls us all; but how much more me, who am brought so near the door by this sickness. There was a

---

4. *Leaves*, in this context, are pages.

> Metaphysical Conceit **What two things is Donne comparing here?** **1**

> Make Inferences About Theme **What does Donne mean when he says the death bell "calls us all"?** **2**

Vocabulary

congregation (kong′ grə gā′shən) *n.* a group of people who gather for religious worship

---

1. When Donne says the church is *catholic,* he means that it embraces all humankind.
2. *Head* refers to Jesus Christ, the head of the church.
3. *Body* refers to the church.

JOHN DONNE **431**

Teach

Big Idea 1

The Sacred and the Secular

Answer: *For Donne, earthly troubles are to be treasured, since they mature and ripen us and make us turn to God.*

(APPROACHING) **Ask:** What experiences might explain Donne's positive attitude toward suffering? (*His illness; his work as a minister.*)

Literary Element 2

Metaphysical Conceit

Answer: *The "gold" of a dying person's affliction can remind the living of their own danger and lead them to seek God's aid.*

Interactive Read and Write

Other options for teaching this selection can be found in

- Interactive Read and Write for EL Students pp. 121–128.
- Interactive Read and Write for Approaching-Level Students pp. 121–128.
- Interactive Read and Write for On-Level Students pp. 121–128.

contention as far as a suit[5] (in which piety[6] and dignity, religion and estimation,[7] were mingled) which of the religious orders should ring to prayers first in the morning; and it was determined that they should ring first that rose earliest. If we understand aright the dignity of this bell that tolls for our evening prayer, we would be glad to make it ours by rising early, in that application, that it might be ours as well as his whose indeed it is.

The bell doth toll for him that thinks it doth; and though it intermit[8] again, yet from that minute that that occasion wrought upon him, he is united to God.

Who casts not up his eye to the sun when it rises? but who takes off his eye from a comet when that breaks out? Who bends not his ear to any bell which upon any occasion rings? but who can remove it from that bell which is passing a piece of himself out of this world?

No man is an island, entire of itself; every man is a piece of the continent, a part of the main.[9] If a clod be washed away by the sea, Europe is the less, as well as if a promontory[10] were, as well as if a manor of thy friend's or of thine own were. Any man's death diminishes me, because I am involved in mankind, and therefore never send to know for whom the bell tolls; it tolls for thee.

Neither can we call this a begging of misery or a borrowing of misery, as though we were not miserable enough of ourselves but must fetch in

> *"No man is an island, entire of itself; every man is a piece of the continent, a part of the main."*

more from the next house, in taking upon us the misery of our neighbors. Truly it were an excusable **covetousness** if we did; for affliction[11] is a treasure, and scarce any man hath enough of it. No man hath affliction enough that is not matured and ripened by it, and made fit for God by that affliction. If a man carry treasure in bullion,[12] or in a wedge of gold, and have none coined into current moneys, his treasure will not defray him[13] as he travels. Tribulation[14] is treasure in the nature of it, but it is not current money in the use of it, except we get nearer and nearer our home, heaven, by it. Another man may be sick too, and sick to death, and this affliction may lie in his bowels as gold in a mine and be of no use to him; but this bell that tells me of his affliction digs out and applies that gold to me, if by this consideration of another's danger I take mine own into **contemplation** and so secure myself by making my recourse[15] to my God, who is our only security. ❧

---

5. A *contention as far as a suit* is a dispute or controversy that resulted in a lawsuit.
6. *Piety* means "religious devotion."
7. Here, *estimation* refers to self-esteem.
8. *Intermit* means "pause."
9. Here, *main* means "mainland."
10. A *promontory* is a ridge of land extending out into a body of water.

11. *Affliction* means "pain" or "suffering."
12. *Bullion* is precious metal in the form of bars or ingots.
13. *Defray him* means "pay his costs."
14. *Tribulation* is misery or suffering.
15. *Recourse* is an appeal for help or protection.

The Sacred and the Secular *What is Donne's attitude toward earthly troubles?* **1**

Metaphysical Conceit *According to Donne, what good is the "gold" of a dying person's affliction?* **2**

Vocabulary

covetousness (kuv′ it əs nəs) *n.* great desire for something belonging to another

contemplation (kon′ təm pla′ shən) *n.* careful thought or consideration; meditation

Reading Practice

SPIRAL REVIEW **Summarize** Tell students that this is one of the most influential sermons in all of British literature. Point out that the structure is much like that of a persuasive essay. Have students write a summary of the main points of Donne's argument. Also ask them to think about what makes Donne's meditation so powerful. (*Students may include the following points: the church embraces all humankind; all people must face death; all people are connected; affliction can help to build character; there is security only in God.*)

After You Read

Respond and Think Critically

Respond and Interpret

1. Which passages triggered the strongest reactions in you as you read this sermon? Why?

2. (a)Paraphrase Donne's words in the first paragraph. (b)In your opinion, what is Donne's message in this paragraph?

3. (a)According to Donne, in what ways is humanity like a "piece of the continent"? (b)What do you think is the main point Donne makes in the sixth paragraph? State this point in your own words.

4. (a)What act would be "an excusable covetousness"? Why? (b)Explain in your own words why Donne says "affliction is a treasure."

Analyze and Evaluate

5. (a)In the last paragraph, what does Donne think he will gain from "consideration of another's danger"? (b)What do you think Donne would

have liked his parishioners to do when they heard a bell toll? Support your answer with details from the selection.

6. Donne's statement that "No man is an island, entire of itself" is very famous. (a)What does Donne mean by this statement? (b)How do other statements by Donne lead to the conclusion that "no man is an island"? Explain.

Connect

7. **Big Idea** The Sacred and the Secular (a)What images from the secular world does Donne use to advance his argument about the sacred? (b)Why do you think Donne uses these secular images? Explain.

8. **Connect to the Author** In what specific ways might this sermon reflect Donne's experience of serious illness?

You're the Critic: Different Viewpoints

How Deep Is Donne?

The views of T. S. Eliot and C. S. Lewis, two of the twentieth century's most celebrated writers and critics, about the emotional depth of Donne's poetry sharply differed.

Group Activity Read the two quotations, and discuss the following questions with classmates. Cite evidence from Donne's works for support.

1. (a)What is the reasoning behind Lewis's claim that Donne's poetry is "too simple"? (b)For what reason does Eliot claim that Donne has "interest for the present age"?

2. To what is Lewis referring when he says that Donne's work contains "puzzles"? Explain.

> *"One of the characteristics of Donne which wins him, I fancy, his interest for the present age, is his fidelity to emotion as he finds it; his recognition of the complexity of feeling and its rapid alterations."*
>
> —T. S. Eliot

> *"Paradoxical as it may seem, Donne's poetry is too simple to satisfy. . . . There are puzzles in his work, but we can solve them all if we are clever enough; there is none of the depth and ambiguity of real experience in him."*
>
> —C. S. Lewis

JOHN DONNE **433**

You're the Critic

1. (a) Lewis feels that Donne's metaphors are too literal and explainable, rather than evocative and complex. (b) Eliot praises Donne's responsiveness to feelings and their complexity—things we are acutely aware of in the modern world.

2. The puzzles are Donne's unusual metaphors—which, for Lewis, can be understood intellectually without being true to the depths and ambiguities of actual experience.

> To check students' understanding of the selection, see Unit 2 Teaching Resources Book, p. 287.

After You Read

Assess

1. Students' answers will vary.

2. (a) A man hearing the bell toll for his own death may not know he is close to death. (b) Possible answer: We can never know the time of our death.

3. (a) Each time a clod washes away (i.e., a person dies), the mainland (humankind) is diminished. (b) Humans are all connected and what affects one affects all.

4. (a) It would be excusable to covet the suffering of others, because suffering is something valuable. (b) Affliction builds character and brings the sufferer closer to God.

5. (a) By considering another's danger, Donne is reminded that his own life is fleeting and he must be mindful of his own death. (b) He would have liked his parishioners to reflect on the death the bell signaled and on their own deaths. Donne says not to wonder for whom the bell tolls but to take it as a personal summons, and he gives many examples of how humans are interconnected in life and death.

6. (a) All people share the same fate and are therefore interconnected. (b) Students' answers will vary.

7. (a) Books, libraries, gold, and treasure (b) These images make abstractions tangible and their mysteries understandable by analogy.

8. He may have experienced such physical suffering that he felt compelled to adopt the attitude that "affliction is a treasure" simply in order to endure his day-to-day existence.

After You Read

Assess

Literary Element

1. (a) Donne compares human-kind to a book, individuals to chapters, and death to translation. (b) It provides a picture of humans reaching a state of grace after death.
2. Affliction is like gold bullion. It cannot be used to better life immediately, but it provides spiritual reserves for the future.
3. Answers will vary. Encourage students to discuss and provide textual support for their views.

Review: Motif

Have each group of students compare their list of motifs with other groups' lists. Then lead the whole class in a discussion of the most important motifs in Meditation 17 and their emotional effects.

Progress Check

Can students identify metaphysical conceit?

If No ➜ See Unit 2 Teaching Resources Book, p. 283

Progress Check

Can students make inferences about theme?

If No ➜ See Unit 2 Teaching Resources Book, p. 284

Literary Element Metaphysical Conceit

A **conceit** is an elaborate metaphor or simile that makes a comparison between two significantly different things. The comparison may seem far-fetched at first but, when examined, gains clarity and persuasion. The conceit not only brings together two entirely different images or ideas but then develops the comparison in details, so as to highlight the similarities. A **metaphysical conceit** creates an abstract or intellectual comparison rather than one based on nature.

1. (a) What conceit does Donne develop extensively in the second paragraph of "Meditation 17?" (b) How does this conceit help explain Donne's ideas about death and faith?
2. Summarize the main points of the conceit Donne develops in the last paragraph of "Meditation 17."
3. Which conceit in this sermon do you feel was the most evocative or powerful? Support your answer.

Review: Motif

As you learned on page 327, a **motif** is a significant phrase, description, or image that is repeated throughout a literary work and that provides an insight into the work's theme.

Group Activity With a group of classmates, try to identify all of the motifs that appear in this sermon. Create a list of them on the board. Then discuss why Donne chose to repeat the words, phrases, and images that he did. How do these repeated ideas and images affect the broader argument of his sermon? How do they affect the sermon's emotional power?

Reading Strategy Make Inferences About Theme

The **theme** of a work is its overall message about life or human nature. Donne develops his theme by using a number of conceits. These conceits help the reader to see different ways of arriving at the same idea.

1. What is the theme of this meditation?
2. Understanding Donne's conceits can be like unraveling a puzzle. Why could it be argued that the labor of understanding Donne's conceits helps to reinforce his theme? Explain.

Vocabulary Practice

Practice with Analogies Choose the vocabulary word that best completes each analogy.

1. worshipper : congregation :: student :
   a. chorus **b.** audience **c.** class
2. contemplation : thoughts :: behavior :
   a. actions **b.** answers **c.** ideas
3. covetousness : greed :: rivalry :
   a. pride **b.** competition **c.** hate

Academic Vocabulary

In "Meditation 17", John Donne seeks to **aid** his congregation by telling them about the transience of earthly life.

Aid is an academic word. More familiar words that are similar in meaning are *help, assist,* and *serve.*

To further explore the meaning of this word, answer the following question: What actions could you take to **aid** your community?

For more on academic vocabulary, see pages 56 and R81.

 Literature Online

Selection Resources For Selection Quizzes, eFlashcards, and Reading-Writing Connection activities, go to glencoe.com and enter QuickPass code GLB9817u2.

Reading Strategy

1. Affliction and death bring humans closer to God and to one another.
2. Students may say that the mental labor of understanding the conceits helps the reader to focus more intently on issues of morality and faith.

Vocabulary

1. c **2.** a **3.** b

Academic Vocabulary

Students might answer that they could volunteer at various organizations, work hard in school, be an informed voter, and so on.

Respond Through Writing

Summary

Report Main Ideas When you write a summary of a nonfiction work, you restate the main ideas or events in fewer words. A summary does not include personal opinions. In about 100 words, summarize "Meditation 17" by John Donne.

Understanding the Task When you **restate** written or spoken material, you retell it in your own words and do not copy exact words from the original text.

Prewrite Create a flowchart in which you trace Donne's sequence of ideas from the beginning of "Meditation 17" to the end. Be sure to include each important step in his argument.

Draft Following the sequence of ideas shown in your graphic, summarize the essay by stating each idea in a single sentence, indicating how it is related to the ideas that precede and follow it. Stick closely to Donne's meaning, even though you are putting it into your own words. The sample below shows how one writer summarized a similar essay—Sir Francis Bacon's "Of Studies."

EXAMPLE:

> Studying serves three main purposes: to give personal pleasure, to improve one's conversational skills, and to supply knowledge that can't be obtained in a different way. There are also three ways to study a book: in parts, as a whole (but not seriously), or with serious intent and focus. Different types of studying improve different parts of a person's intelligence, just as different sports exercise different parts of the body.

Revise Reread "Meditation 17" and then look over your summary. Make sure you have not copied material directly from Donne's work but have included his major ideas in the order he presented them. Check to see that you have not left out any major ideas in favor of less-important ones. Delete any irrelevant ideas or sentences you find.

Edit and Proofread Proofread your paper, correcting any errors in spelling, grammar, and punctuation. Use the Grammar Tip in the side column to help you with introductory clauses.

Learning Objectives

In this assignment, you will focus on the following objectives:

Writing: Writing a summary.

Grammar: Understanding how to use introductory clauses.

Grammar Tip

Introductory Clauses

Using **introductory clauses**—beginning your sentences with a variety of subordinate clauses that include both a subject and a predicate—can add interest to your summary.

When revising, use different types of introductory clauses to vary your writing. You can often combine related sentences by turning one into an introductory clause.

Some people are healthy and others are sick. They refuse to believe that their time is limited.

REVISED:

Whether they are healthy or sick, *people refuse to believe that their time is limited.*

After You Read

Assess

Respond Through Writing

Use these criteria in evaluating student summaries:

- It covers all the important ideas presented in "Meditation 17."
- It includes about 100 words that are the writer's own and not copied from the original.

Introductory clauses are used to vary sentence structure and maintain readers' interest.

- A student who meets all of these criteria should receive the equivalent of a 4-point response.
- A student who fully meets two or partially meets three of these criteria should receive the equivalent of a 3-point response.
- A student who fully meets one or partially meets two of these criteria should receive the equivalent of a 2-point response.
- A student who partially meets one of these criteria should receive the equivalent of a 1-point response.

 For grammar practice, see Unit 2 Teaching Resources Book, p. 286.

 To create custom assessments using software, use ExamView Assessment Suite.

English Learners

DIFFERENTIATED INSTRUCTION

Intermediate To assist English learners in proofreading their summaries of "Meditation 17," have them work with partners. Pairs can trade and read each others' papers, correcting errors in spelling, grammar, or punctuation as they read. Make sure a good dictionary is available so that students can look up troublesome words. When they finish, have partners return the papers and review them together. Encourage students to ask and answer questions about the corrections on their papers in order to enhance their understanding.

Vocabulary Workshop

Analogies

Focus

Point out that analogies can be based on relationships other than the ones listed on this page, including cause/effect, object/characteristic, and activity/goal.

Have students brainstorm different analogies that they have come across while reading.

Teach

Importance of Analogies
Remind students: Analogies play a significant role in problem solving, decision making, perception, memory, creativity, emotion, explanation, and communication.

Assess

1. a **2.** b

For additional vocabulary practice, see Glencoe Interactive Vocabulary CD-ROM.

Vocabulary Terms

An **analogy** is a type of comparison based on the relationships between pairs of things or ideas.

Tip

To complete an analogy in a test-taking situation, think about the relationship between the first pair of words. Then try to find a similar relationship in the answer choices.

LOG ON ▶ Literature Online

Vocabulary For more vocabulary practice, go to glencoe.com and enter QuickPass code GLB9817u2.

Vocabulary Workshop

Analogies

Literature Connection When John Donne compared the bond between human beings to the relationship between an island and the mainland, he created one of the most famous analogies in all of literature.

> *"No man is an island, entire of itself; every man is a piece of the continent, a part of the main."*
>
> —John Donne, from "Meditation 17"

An **analogy** is a comparison based on a similarity between things that are otherwise dissimilar. To complete an analogy on a test, you must select from a list the pair of words that represents the same relationship as is in the first pair.

Strategy A good strategy for completing analogies is to make up a sentence in which a clear relationship exists between the ideas represented in the first pair of words:

stanza : poem ::

a. flag : anthem   **c.** mural : painting

b. room : building   **d.** program : recital

To determine the relationship represented by the first pair of words, you might use them in a sentence like this one: "A stanza is a division of a poem." Only pair **b** could also work in the sentence you created: "A room is a division of a building."

Analogies can be based on a variety of relationships.

Relationship	Example
Association or usage	A *farmer* is associated with or uses a *plow*.
Part/whole	A *needle* is a part of a *compass*.
Example/class	*Asia* is a *continent*.
Synonym or antonym	*Affliction* is a synonym for *suffering*.

Practice Complete the following analogies.

1. congregation : sermon ::
   a. audience : play
   b. horse : polo
   c. fans : spectators

2. pressure : force ::
   a. weight : gravity
   b. velocity : speed
   c. suction : grip

Assessment Practice

SPIRAL REVIEW **Process of Elimination** When solving analogy problems, students may find it helpful to eliminate incorrect answers first. Write the following problem on the board:

clasp : bracelet ::
a. hook : coat
b. diamond : ring
c. buckle : belt
d. wrist : watch
e. cuff : trousers

Say: To eliminate choices from the list of paired words, pinpoint the relationship in each pair as precisely as possible. Remember that a word can refer to more than one object or idea.

Before You Read

On My First Son and Song: To Celia

Meet **Ben Jonson**
(1572–1637)

Picture a fiery-tempered man with a "mountain belly," a "rocky face," and a thumb that had been branded to show he'd once killed a man. Seat him in a tavern called the Mermaid, discussing the art of poetry with a group of young writers who so idolized him that they called themselves the "Sons of Ben." Add to this the fact that, in the prime of his career, this man was more respected for his work than his contemporary William Shakespeare was for his, and you might just begin to appreciate Ben Jonson.

Soldier, Scholar, Playwright Jonson was born in or near London in 1572. As a boy, Jonson was educated at the Westminster School of London, but, unable to afford a university education, he went on to become a mostly self-taught scholar. His first job was as apprentice to a bricklayer; then he went into the army. It wasn't until his early twenties that he joined a theater company and began acting and writing.

> "Talking and eloquence are not the same: to speak, and to speak well, are two things. A fool may talk, but a wise man speaks."
>
> —Ben Jonson

Jonson's first major literary success was a play entitled *Every Man in His Humor*. It was produced when he was only twenty-six and featured Shakespeare in a leading role. Both critics and audiences loved it.

Almost overnight, however, Jonson nearly lost everything. He killed a fellow actor in a duel and wound up sentenced to death. He managed to escape hanging only through "benefit of clergy"— that is, by proving that he could read Latin and was thus entitled to a trial in the more lenient church court. That court overturned the civil court's death sentence, but Jonson received a brand on his thumb as a convicted felon.

Poet Laureate Jonson was a proud man, and many people found him arrogant and argumentative. He also could be both warm-hearted and fearless.

Throughout his lifetime, Jonson's outspoken nature got him into trouble with the law, his critics, and many of his friends and colleagues. However, his literary career flourished. By 1616, his plays and other works were so popular that King James I gave the forty-four-year-old Jonson a lifetime pension—making him England's first poet laureate.

Yet this honor would turn out to be one of Jonson's last great career successes. Shortly after becoming poet laureate, he decided to spend a year away from London's literary scene. When he returned, he found himself unable to reclaim his former prominence in literary circles. Apparently, what Jonson liked to write had gone out of style.

Jonson suffered a stroke in 1628. After his death in 1637, he was buried at Westminster Abbey under a tombstone that reads "O rare Ben Jonson."

 Literature Online

Author Search For more about Ben Jonson, go to glencoe.com and enter QuickPass code GLB9817u2.

Before You Read

Focus

Bellringer Options

Selection Focus
Transparency 19

Daily Language Practice
Transparency 32

Or read aloud the displayed quotation on the student page.

Ask: What distinction is Jonson drawing between speaking and talking?

Lead students in a brief discussion about the value of eloquence.

 For summaries in languages other than English, see Unit 2 Teaching Resources Book, pp. 289–294.

Selection Skills

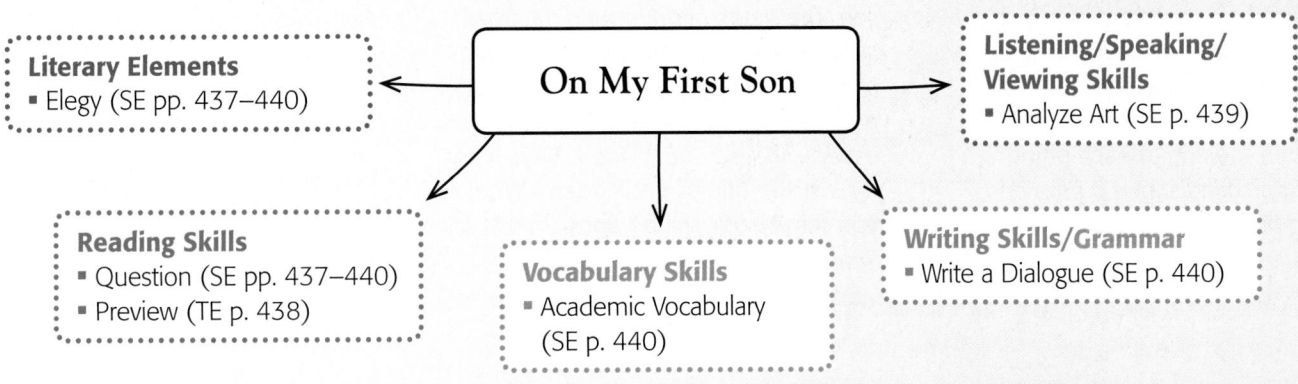

Literary Elements
- Elegy (SE pp. 437–440)

On My First Son

Listening/Speaking/Viewing Skills
- Analyze Art (SE p. 439)

Reading Skills
- Question (SE pp. 437–440)
- Preview (TE p. 438)

Vocabulary Skills
- Academic Vocabulary (SE p. 440)

Writing Skills/Grammar
- Write a Dialogue (SE p. 440)

Focus

Summary

In "On My First Son" the poet mourns the death of a young son. He calls his son his "best piece of poetry."

View the Art ★

(Answer: accept all reasonable responses.)

Henri François Riesener (1734–1806), a French painter of German descent, specialized in portraits and also worked as a miniaturist. His nephew was one of the most famous of all French painters, Eugène Delacroix. **Ask:** What does this painting express about the relationship between a father and his son? *(Students' responses will vary.)*

Literature and Reading Preview

Connect to the Poems

Have you, or has someone you know, ever lost a beloved family member or friend? Write a journal entry in which you discuss the emotions a person facing such a loss is likely to feel.

Build Background

In his elegy "On My First Son," Jonson mourns the passing of his son Benjamin, who died of the plague in 1603, on his seventh birthday. A century after "Song: To Celia" was published, it was set to music by the British composer Thomas Arne. It became wildly popular and is often performed even today.

Set Purposes for Reading

Big Idea The Sacred and the Secular

During the English Renaissance, much poetic literature consisted of devotional meditations as well as witty reflections on time, transience, and love. As you read Jonson's poems, ask yourself, In what different ways are these themes expressed?

Literary Element Elegy

An **elegy** is a poem mourning a death or other great loss. The subject is often the transience of life. As you read "On My First Son," ask yourself, What statements does the poet make about sorrow, grief, and the fleeting nature of human existence?

Reading Strategy Question

Questioning involves regularly asking yourself whether you have understood what you've read. As you answer your questions, you're making sure that you're getting the gist of a text. As you read "On My First Son," ask yourself, Am I understanding what this is about?

....

Tip: Asking Questions Record your questions and answers in a chart like the one below.

Question	Answer
1. Why does the speaker begin with the word "farewell"?	
2. Why does the speaker feel as if he is paying a debt?	

Learning Objectives

For pages 437–443

In studying these texts, you will focus on the following objectives:

Literary Study: Analyzing elegy.

Reading: Questioning.

Writing: Writing a dialogue.

Speaking and Listening: Participating in a literature group.

Reading Practice

SPIRAL REVIEW **Preview** Have students preview the poems by looking at the painting included for each one. **Ask:** What conclusions can you draw from looking at each painting? *(The first painting shows a man and a young boy, probably a father and son. The man's hand around the boy's shoulder may suggest a warm relationship. The second painting depicts a man and his beloved. The relationship looks especially close and loving.)* **Say:** Now look at the title of each poem. What do you think each will be about? ("On My First Son" will probably be about a man's relationship with his son. "Song: To Celia" will probably be a poem from a man to the woman he loves.)*

Barbet and His Son. Henri François Riesener. Oil on canvas. Musée des Beaux-Arts, Rouen, France.

View the Art Riesener was a portraitist who worked chiefly in France. How would you describe the father's expression in this picture? How does it relate to the sentiment expressed by Jonson?

On My First Son

Ben Jonson

Farewell, thou child of my right hand,[1] and joy;
  My sin was too much hope of thee, loved boy.
Seven years thou wert lent to me, and I thee pay,[2]
  Exacted by thy fate, on the just[3] day.
5   O, could I lose all father now![4] For why
  Will man lament the state he should envy?
To have so soon 'scaped world's and flesh's rage,
  And, if no other misery, yet age?
Rest in soft peace, and, asked, say here doth lie
10   Ben Jonson his[5] best piece of poetry;
For whose sake, henceforth, all his vows be such,
  As what he loves may never like too much.

1

---

1. *Child of my right hand* is the literal translation of the Hebrew name Benjamin, which was the name of Jonson's son.
2. *I thee pay* means "I pay thee back"—that is, "I return you."
3. Here, *just* may mean "exact," or it may mean "complete in amount." In Jonson's day, loans were often made for periods of seven years, and Jonson's son had completed exactly seven years of life on the day he died.
4. *Lose all father now* means "give up all thoughts of being a father."
5. *Ben Jonson his* means "Ben Jonson's."

Elegy *Why might the speaker envy his dead son?*   **2**

BEN JONSON   **439**

439

After You Read

Assess

1. (a) His sin was having too much love for his son; the price he pays is losing his son to God. (b) He seems to have a fatalistic attitude.

2. (a) Seven (b) It allows him to believe that the child died before experiencing any of life's great pain.

3. Because he is denied the joys of being with his son.

4. (a) He will never love so that he will not experience this kind of grief again. (b) Answers will vary.

5. Students might mention the way Jonson expresses both his grief over his son's death and his belief in fate and that his son is in a better place.

6. Answers will vary. Have the students suggest a song and explain why it is an elegy.

Literary Element

1. Answers may include "farewell," "why will man lament the state," "'scaped world's and flesh's rage," and "misery."

2. The sad tone is created by the subject matter, the choice of words, and the rhythm.

Writing

Dialogues should show an understanding of each poet's opinion of love and loss.

Academic Vocabulary

Students might respond that they like to talk to family members and friends, attend religious services, write in a journal, or create art.

After You Read

Respond and Think Critically

Respond and Interpret

1. (a) What does Jonson say was his sin and the price he pays for it? (b) Given these statements, how do you think Jonson is handling his son's death?

2. (a) How old was Jonson's son when he died? (b) How does the boy's youth add some relief to the sorrow Jonson expresses?

Analyze and Evaluate

3. Why might Jonson still lament his son's death despite the fact that he also envies his son?

4. (a) What will Jonson do from now on for the sake of his dead son? Why? (b) In your opinion, what is the difference between loving and liking?

Connect

5. **Big Idea** The Sacred and the Secular How does Jonson address both the sacred and the secular in his response to his son's death?

6. **Connect to Today** Think of a modern song or poem that might be considered an elegy. What characteristics does it share with Jonson's poem?

Literary Element Elegy

In ancient times, an **elegy** was a poem with a particular meter. Today, however, the term refers to a serious, formal poem of lament or sorrow. Most elegies mourn deaths or other great losses, but some reflect on common truths or life's smaller tragedies.

1. List some of the words and phrases from "On My First Son" that express the qualities of an elegy.

2. How would you describe the tone of the poem? What elements create the tone?

Writing

Write a Dialogue At the end of his elegy "On My First Son," Jonson, having lost his beloved child, swears never to love anything too much again. Many years later, the poet Alfred, Lord Tennyson, wrote, "'Tis better to have loved and lost / Than never to have loved at all." Write a brief dialogue between Jonson and Tennyson, in which each defends his position on love and loss.

LOG ON ▶ **Literature** Online

Selection Resources For Selection Quizzes, eFlashcards, and Reading-Writing Connection activities, go to glencoe.com and enter QuickPass code GLB9817u2.

Reading Strategy Question

To increase your understanding of a literary work, you should read it more than once. Continue to ask questions each time you read. After you read "On My First Son," try to answer the following questions. If you can't answer all the questions, read the poem at least once more and try again.

1. What is the work about? Who is it about?

2. What parts of this poem do you find confusing?

3. If you could talk to the poet, what would you ask him?

Academic Vocabulary

In "On My First Son," Jonson finds solace for his grief in **communication** through poetry.

Communication is an academic word. Jonson uses poetry as a medium for the **communication** of his feelings.

To further explore the meaning of this word, answer the following question: What kind of **communication** do you use to express your strong feelings?

For more on academic vocabulary, see pages 56 and R81.

Reading Strategy

1. The poem is about the poet's reaction to the death of his young son. While the poem's subject is the young boy, the poem is mostly about the speaker, the child's grieving father.

2. Students' answers should reflect any language, tone, or theme issues they found difficult to understand.

3. Students' questions should reflect elements or events that led to the writing of the poem about which they would like to know more.

Progress Check

Can students question?

If No → See Unit 2 Teaching Resources Book, p. 296.

Before You Read

Before You Read

Focus

Summary

In this song, Jonson writes of the painful but universal theme of unrequited love. The speaker is desperately in love with a woman he holds in highest regard; unfortunately, she does not return his feelings.

Literary Element **Lyric Poetry**

A **lyric poem** expresses a speaker's personal thoughts and feelings. Lyric poems are usually short and highly musical. The form is thought to have originated in ancient Greece, where the words were sung to the music of a lyre, a stringed instrument similar to a harp. Over time, people began to speak lyrics as opposed to singing them. As you read "Song: To Celia," ask yourself, What rhythm is created by its brief lines?

Reading Strategy **Make Inferences**

Authors don't always directly state what they want you to understand. By providing clues and interesting details, they imply certain information. When readers combine those clues with their own knowledge, they are **making inferences.** In "Song: To Celia," Jonson does not directly state his theme. As you read, ask yourself, What verbal clues allow me to make an inference about Jonson's views on love and attraction?

Song: To Celia Ben Jonson

Drink to me only with thine eyes,
  And I will pledge with mine;
Or leave a kiss but in the cup,
  And I'll not look for wine.
5 The thirst that from the soul doth rise
  Doth ask a drink divine;
But might I of Jove's nectar[1] sup,
  I would not change[2] for thine.
I sent thee late[3] a rosy wreath,
10 Not so much honoring thee,
As giving it a hope that there
  It could not withered be.
But thou thereon did'st only breathe,
  And sent'st it back to me;
15 Since when it grows, and smells, I swear,
  Not of itself, but thee.

---

1. *Jove's nectar* refers to ambrosia, the drink of the gods in Greek mythology, which supposedly kept them immortal.
2. *Change* means "exchange."
3. *Late* means "recently."

1 **Make Inferences** *What is the speaker saying about Celia's reaction to his gift?*

Two Lovers, c. 1525. Paris Bordone. Pinacoteca di Brera, Milan, Italy.

BEN JONSON **441**

Teach

| **Reading Strategy** | **1** |

Making Inferences
Answer: *That Celia didn't even hesitate before sending his gift back to him*

 For summaries in languages other than English, see Unit 2 Teaching Resources Book, pp. 299–304.

 For additional practice using the reading skill or strategy, see Unit 2 Teaching Resources Book, p. 306.

 To check students' understanding of the selection, see Unit 2 Teaching Resources Book, p. 307.

Selection Skills

Literary Elements
- Lyric Poetry (SE pp. 441–442)
- Rhyme Scheme (SE p. 442)

Song: To Celia

Listening/Speaking/ Viewing Skills
- Literature Groups (SE p. 443)

Reading Skills
- Make Inferences (SE pp. 441–443)

Vocabulary Skills
- Academic Vocabulary (SE p. 443)

After You Read

Assess

1. Students' answers will vary.
2. (a) The nectar of the gods (b) The speaker values Celia's kiss above all else.
3. (a) He sends Celia the wreath so that the roses will thrive. (b) He considers Celia to have life-sustaining power.
4. (a) Students may say that the speaker is desperately in love or that he is simply infatuated with her. (b) Celia does not seem to return his feelings, as she immediately sends back his gift of flowers.
5. (a) Many students may feel that they would trust his love to last because he is so passionate. (b) Students may cite details such as his language and his comparison of Celia to the gods.
6. (a) Students should see that the speaker is passionate—and perhaps a little foolish. (b) Possible answer: There are plenty of other women you can pursue.
7. Students' answers will vary.
8. The song deals with the timeless topic of romantic love.

After You Read

Respond and Think Critically

Respond and Interpret

1. Which Jonson poem appeals to you more—"Song: To Celia" or "On My First Son"? Why?
2. (a) What would the speaker sacrifice for a kiss? (b) How valuable is Celia's kiss? Explain.
3. (a) What reason does the speaker give for sending the wreath? (b) What is he implying about Celia?

Analyze and Evaluate

4. (a) How would you describe the speaker's feelings for Celia? (b) Do you think Celia returns his feelings? Explain.

5. (a) If you were Celia, would you trust the speaker's love to last? (b) What details make you think as you do?
6. (a) What can you infer about the speaker's personality? (b) What advice would you give to him?

Connect

7. **Big Idea** The Sacred and the Secular What sacred elements do you find in Jonson's expression of his love for Celia?
8. **Connect to Today** Why do you think this song is still popular after many years?

Literary Element Lyric Poetry

Because of its musicality, lyric poetry is often memorable. **Meter,** or the arrangement of stressed and unstressed syllables in a line of verse, is often an important element in the creation of lyric poetry's musical effects. Before answering the questions, review the terms used to describe meter on page 423.

1. How many stressed syllables are there in the third line of "Song: To Celia?" How many are there in the fourth?
2. Try to describe the meter in these two lines, using the correct terms.

Review: Rhyme Scheme

As you learned on page 256, a **rhyme scheme** is a pattern of end rhymes in a stanza or a poem. A rhyme scheme is described by a series of letters of the alphabet, with a different letter assigned to each end-of-line sound. The first five lines of "Song: To Celia," for example, have an *abcba* rhyme scheme. On a separate sheet of paper, list the remaining letters in the poem's rhyme scheme.

Drink to me only with thine eyes (a)
   And I will pledge with mine; (b)
Or leave a kiss but in the cup, (c)
   And I'll not look for wine. (b)
The thirst that from the soul doth rise (a)
   Doth ask a drink divine; ( )
But might I of Jove's nectar sup, ( )
   I would not change for thine. ( )
I sent thee late a rosy wreath, (d)
   Not so much honoring thee, (e)
As giving it a hope that there (f)
   It could not withered be. ( )
But thou thereon did'st only breathe, ( )
   And sent'st it back to me; ( )
Since when it grows, and smells, I swear, ( )
   Not of itself, but thee. ( )

What is the poem's complete rhyme scheme?

Literary Element

1. There are four stressed syllables in the third line. There are three in the fourth.
2. The meter in line 3 is iambic tetrameter, and in line 4 it is iambic trimeter.

Review: Rhyme Scheme
abcbabcbdefedefe

Reading Strategy   Make Inferences

Use the text and a chart like the one below to help you make inferences about the speaker's intent in "Song: To Celia."

Quotation	Question	Answer
"Drink to me only with thine eyes"	What does he actually want her to do?	He wants her to notice and pay attention to him.

1. **Quotation:** "The thirst that from the soul doth rise / Doth ask a drink divine;"

   Question:

   Answer:

2. **Quotation:** "But might I of Jove's nectar sup, / I would not change for thine."

   Question:

   Answer:

Academic Vocabulary

*In "Song: To Celia," the speaker makes his feelings for Celia **apparent** to the reader.*

Apparent is an academic word. More familiar words that are similar in meaning to *apparent* are *obvious, clear,* and *evident.*

To further explore the meaning of this word, describe a situation you have heard about or experienced in which an **apparent** truth turned out to be false.

For more on academic vocabulary, see pages 56 and R81.

Speaking and Listening

Literature Groups

Assignment With a group of classmates, discuss the theme of Jonson's lyric poem "Song: To Celia" and the differences between lyric poetry and narrative poetry. Decide what themes are best suited to each type of poetry and explain why each is suited to that type.

Prepare Before beginning, review the rules for participating in a group discussion on page 975. Agree on the purpose of your discussion. Will you just share ideas, or do you want to reach a single viewpoint? If your goal is consensus, define what that means. Do you need unanimity, or will a simple majority be sufficient?

Discuss Use good listening strategies to create a supportive atmosphere for sharing ideas. Don't just exchange opinions, though—support your statements with examples and logical explanations.

Designate one member of the group to record the group's ideas in a Venn diagram like the one shown here.

THEMES IN POETRY

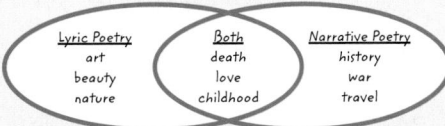

Lyric Poetry	Both	Narrative Poetry
art beauty nature	death love childhood	history war travel

Report Present the results of your discussion to the class. Be sure to speak clearly, using a classroom-appropriate volume and tone of voice. Use gestures and body language for emphasis.

Evaluate Write a brief paragraph in which you evaluate how well your group achieved its goal and communicated its results to the class.

BEN JONSON   **443**

After You Read

Assess

Reading Strategy

Possible answers:

1. *Question:* What does he want from her?
   Answer: a kiss and her love
2. *Question:* Why might he compare her to the gods?
   Answer: He is so in love with her that he sees her as more than human.

Academic Vocabulary

Students should describe a time when appearances differed from reality.

Speaking and Listening

Use these criteria in evaluating student literature groups:

- The group discussion addresses both the specific theme of Jonson's poem and general themes suitable for lyric and narrative poetry.
- Statements are well supported, and the group exhibits good speaking and listening skills.
- The group summarizes the results of its discussion for the class, incorporating appropriate presentation techniques.
- The group assesses its performance on the basis of relevant criteria.

Focus

Bellringer Options

Daily Language Practice
Transparency 33

Or have students discuss the following question: Who would you consider "cavalier" in present day?

As students read, they should note the traits attributed to the Cavalier poets.

Teach

Literary Element | 1

Conceit Remind students that a conceit is an elaborate metaphor or simile that makes an intellectual comparison rather than one based on nature.

(APPROACHING) **Ask:** If you were to write a conceit, which two objects might you choose?

Ask: How are these objects seemingly different? In what way might they be alike?

For an audio recording of this selection, use Listening Library Audio CD-ROM.

For activities related to this selection, see Unit 2 Teaching Resources Book, pp. 309–310.

Learning Objectives

For pages 444–445

In studying this text, you will focus on the following objectives:

Literary Study:
Analyzing literary periods.
Analyzing literary genres.

The Cavalier Poets

THE METAPHYSICAL POETS CAME MOSTLY FROM the middle class; but their contemporaries, the Cavalier poets, were often aristocrats. Some came from such distinguished families that they were welcomed at the court of King Charles I; others served the king as soldiers. Like his predecessors Elizabeth and James, Charles surrounded himself with well-educated, able, versatile young men who were witty writers and conversationalists. Some were literary followers of Ben Jonson, the brilliant poet and dramatist who had been a rival and friend of Shakespeare. The most gifted of the "Sons of Ben" were Sir John Suckling, Robert Herrick, and Richard Lovelace.

> *"Dum loquimur, fugerit invida Aetas; carpe diem, quam minimum credula postero."*
>
> *"As we speak, envious time runs away; seize the day, put very little faith in tomorrow."*
>
> —Horace, *Odes*, 1.11

Long before the French word *cavalier* came to describe these poets, it simply denoted a horseman, especially a mounted warrior, such as a knight. During Charles I's reign, however, *cavalier* became a political term. Supporters of the monarchy were called Cavaliers or Royalists. Their opponents, who supported the Puritan-dominated Parliament, were called Roundheads (because of their closely cropped hair). The personal style of the Cavaliers, which featured long, flowing hair and elaborate dress, contrasted sharply with that of the austerely garbed Roundheads.

Features of Cavalier Poetry

As writers affiliated with the court, the Cavalier poets generally intended to entertain their audience rather than instruct it. Their poetry displays a number of typical features.

Conversational Style Influenced by the works of John Donne and Ben Jonson, the Cavaliers cultivated a conversational style based on natural speech patterns. "I sing of brooks, of blossoms, birds, and bowers; / Of April, May, of June, and July flowers" begins one of Herrick's poems.

A Cavalier, c. 1629—1667. Edward Bower. Oil on canvas. Dunster Castle, Somerset, England.

444 UNIT 2 THE ENGLISH RENAISSANCE

Vocabulary Practice

Multiple Meanings Point out that the word *cavalier* has another meaning that is not related to politics. It can mean "arrogant" or "scornful," as in this sentence: *His cavalier attitude made working with him very difficult.*

Use the information above as a springboard to discuss other words with multiple

meanings. Shown below are a few such words from the feature. Have students write two sentences for each word—one sentence for each of the two different meanings.

term	cultivated	tone
court	patterns	simple

1 **Elaborate Conceits** Some of the Cavalier poets shared Donne's fondness for elaborate conceits. The majority of the Cavaliers' poems, however, were less obscure and more accessible than those of the metaphysical poets.

Meditative Tone Most of the Cavaliers' poems seem controlled; at times the poets even seem self-mocking—as in Suckling's lines "I must confess, when I did part from you, / I could not force an artificial dew [tears] / Upon my cheeks . . . "

Classicism Most of the "Sons of Ben" shared Jonson's admiration for the poetry of the ancient Greeks and Romans. Cavalier poetry is rich in classical allusions, such as the names of Greek and Roman gods—clearly, readers were expected to be familiar with classical works. Furthermore, the forms of the poems are often based on classical models, such as the odes of Horace, the satires of Juvenal, and the eclogues (short pastoral poems written as dialogues between shepherds) of Virgil.

Regular Poetic Form The Cavaliers' use of regular rhythmic patterns, carefully structured stanzas, and simple language also reflects the classical influence. The Cavalier poets welcomed the tidy order of regular meter and rhyme schemes. Widely used by Marvell and others, **heroic couplets** are pairs of rhymed iambic pentameter lines. Lovelace favored the four- or eight-line stanza with either an *abab* or an *aabb* rhyme scheme. Such regularity, of course, allowed the poems to be set to music.

Carpe Diem The classical influence can also be seen in the Cavaliers' choices of subject. Love was a popular theme, and some Cavaliers wrote about idealized love and addressed their poems to women to whom they gave such classical names as Julia, Althea, and Lucasta. Others, reflecting on the uncertainty and brevity of life, wrote poems that

expressed a precept known as *carpe diem* (Latin for "seize the day"). This expression, drawn from famous lines of the Roman poet Horace, urges readers to make the most of every moment—a sensible strategy, given the uncertainty of life during the English Civil War. Herrick wrote, "Gather ye rosebuds, while ye may, / Old time is still a-flying"; other poets wrote variations on this theme.

The Cavalier poets did not shrink from writing sarcastic commentaries on the pursuit of coy beauties. The seemingly amazed speaker in a Suckling poem exclaims, "Out upon it! I have loved / Three whole days together; / And am like to love three more, / If it prove fair weather."

Political and Poetical Fortunes

As King Charles's fortunes changed, so did those of the Cavalier poets. In 1649, after civil wars between Royalists and Parliamentarians had thrown the country into chaos, a parliamentary court sentenced Charles to death. When the Puritan leader Oliver Cromwell was declared head of the newly formed Commonwealth, the Cavalier poets fell into disgrace. Some fled London; others were arrested and imprisoned. Suckling is thought to have committed suicide; Lovelace died in poverty and obscurity. Only Herrick lived to see the restoration of the monarchy in 1660, when Charles II, son of the executed King Charles I, was crowned. **2**

Literature Online

Literature and Reading For more about the Cavalier poets, go to glencoe.com and enter QuickPass code GLB9817u2.

Respond and Think Critically

1. What characteristics of Cavalier poetry do you expect to enjoy the most? Why?

2. Why might the *carpe diem* philosophy have appealed to the Cavalier poets as a theme?

3. Do you think that a witty poem can make a serious comment about human nature? Explain.

Teach

Big Idea **2**

The Sacred and the Secular As they finish reading, students should note the fate of the Cavalier poets.

Ask: What major political and social commentary did the Cavalier poets offer? (*Students may note that the Cavalier poets wrote about love, hypocrisy, and carpe diem.*)

Assess

1. Students' answers will vary.

2. The "seize the day" philosophy has special appeal in uncertain times, such as the English Civil War.

3. Encourage students to cite examples of the use of humor to attract and maintain the attention of readers or viewers.

English Learners

DIFFERENTIATED INSTRUCTION

Intermediate Because of their diverse backgrounds, some students may be especially sensitive to the fate of artists who find themselves on the losing side of a power struggle—the status of the Cavalier poets after the Commonwealth came to power. Encourage students with such an understanding to draw parallels to the Cavaliers. Ask the students to share their thoughts with the rest of the class.

Focus

Bellringer Options

Selection Focus Transparency 20

Daily Language Practice Transparency 34

Or ask: Do you think an issue that was important in ancient Rome, medieval Persia, Renaissance France, and Restoration England could still be important to us today?

Compare Literature About Carpe Diem

Have students share their responses to the opening question.

Compare Literature About *Carpe Diem*

Have you ever been too preoccupied with the past or the future to enjoy the present? The four writers compared here—Robert Herrick, Horace, Pierre de Ronsard, and Omar Khayyám—urge readers to "seize the day" and warn against missing opportunities that may never come again.

COMPARE THE Big Idea **The Sacred and the Secular**

These four selections span sixteen centuries, yet they all express secular ideas about human mortality, such as the brevity of life and the uncertainty of the future. As you read, ask yourself, By ignoring the possibility of an afterlife, how do these poets seek to enhance human existence?

COMPARE Universal Theme

The dual sense of the sweetness and brevity of human life is one of the earliest themes in literature. *Carpe diem,* a recurring literary motif that originated in Horace's odes, emphasizes an awareness of the transience of life and the permanent oblivion of death. As you read, ask yourself, How does acceptance of these realities free people to make the most of life and to seek pleasure and happiness in the present?

COMPARE Cultures

Herrick in the worldly court of Restoration England, Horace amid the political turmoil of ancient Rome, Ronsard among the refined aristocrats of Renaissance France, and Omar immersed in the scientifically advanced society of twelfth-century Persia—all these writers reflected, within these diverse cultures, a shared disillusionment with their cultures' traditional philosophies. As you read, ask yourself, How does this humanistic spirit promote intellectual inquiry and the pursuit of earthly happiness?

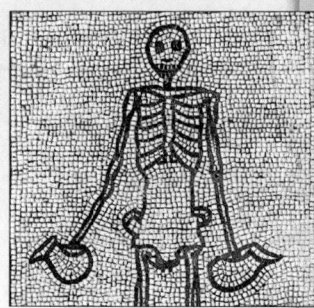

Memento mori, a skeleton (detail). Mosaic. Museo Archeologico Nazionale, Naples, Italy.

LOG ON ▶ **Literature** Online

Author Search For more about Robert Herrick, Horace, Pierre de Ronsard, and Omar Khayyám, go to glencoe.com and enter QuickPass code GLB9817u2.

446 UNIT 2 THE ENGLISH RENAISSANCE

Skills Practice

Literary Elements
- Carpe Diem (SE pp. 446–455)

Comparing Literature

Listening/Speaking/Viewing Skills
- Analyze Art (SE p. 449; TE p. 451)
- Discussion Starter (SE p. 452)
- Oral Interpretation (SE p. 455)

Reading Skills
- Analyze Sound Devices (SE pp. 446–455)

Vocabulary Skills
- Academic Vocabulary (SE p. 450)

Writing Skills/Grammar
- Write a Poem (SE p. 450)
- Quickwrite (SE pp. 451, 454)

Before You Read

To the Virgins, to Make Much of Time

Meet **Robert Herrick**
(1591–1674)

Although Robert Herrick has become one of the most celebrated Cavalier poets of the seventeenth century, literary success escaped him during his lifetime. Born the son of a goldsmith in London, Herrick spent six years as an apprentice to his uncle. Eventually, however, he abandoned the goldsmith trade to enroll at Saint John's College, Cambridge, at the age of twenty-two. After graduation, Herrick was drawn to London's literary circles. Ben Jonson, the city's literary giant, served as his mentor, father figure, and subject of several poems. Economic pressure eventually forced Herrick to abandon his leisurely literary life and accept a position as a vicar, or assistant priest, in Devonshire, a rural hamlet far from the excitement of London.

> *"It takes great wit and interest and energy to be happy. . . . It is the greatest feat man has to accomplish."*
>
> —Robert Herrick

Country Life As he gradually adapted to the country lifestyle, Herrick found poetic inspiration in his daily life and household. Many of his best-known poems are about rural life and festivals. He also composed 158 poems addressed to imaginary mistresses with exotic names, such as Anthea and Electra. But despite the relative peace and solitude of life in the country, Herrick was affected by political strife. Herrick was an Anglican priest and a supporter of King Charles I, the subject of some of his poems. When civil war broke out and the Puritans came to power, royalists like Herrick were expelled from their positions. After losing his post as vicar, Herrick returned to London at the age of fifty-seven, having composed more than 1,400 poems.

Literary Labors and Disappointment Herrick had hoped to publish his poems and reestablish a literary reputation in London, but he was disappointed to discover that the London of his youth had irreversibly changed—Ben Jonson had died, and Herrick's literary circle had dispersed. Nonetheless, Herrick became one of the first poets to collect and publish nearly all of his poetry in one carefully organized volume. This massive collection contained two parts: the first, entitled *Noble Numbers*, contained religious poems, and the second, entitled *Hesperides*—referring to mythical nymphs who guarded an apple tree that bore golden fruit—contained his secular poems. Unfortunately for Herrick, critics largely ignored his poetry until the nineteenth century. After the Restoration ended Puritan rule, Herrick returned to his post at Devonshire at the age of seventy-one, where he remained until his death. He never composed poems again.

Herrick is now recognized as one of the foremost followers of Ben Jonson, but he also established a solid reputation as a poet in his own right. His poems are unique in their ability to explore serious philosophical questions of life and death in short, playful lyrics.

ROBERT HERRICK **447**

Before You Read

Focus

Literary History ☆

In the 19th century and throughout history, many artists relied on patronage to make a living. A wealthy patron would give the artist money for sustenance and supplies in exchange for art. This meant the artist had to create art the patron liked. Herrick's job as a vicar freed him from this constraint. The job gave him money to live on and didn't demand much of his time so he was free to write poetry of his own choosing. At the time, only a very few poets—most of them rural clergymen or country doctors—enjoyed this kind of creative freedom.

English Learners

DIFFERENTIATED INSTRUCTION

Beginning Tell students that Herrick's writing was shaped by both his profession as a vicar and his lifestyle in the country.
Ask: What were Herrick's hopes for his writing? *(to publish his poems and be well-regarded)*

Intermediate Ask students to read the text and stop at the end of each of the three paragraphs to summarize to the partner what they understand and any questions they have.

Comparing Literature

Before You Read

Focus

Summary

Addressing young women, Herrick tells them that time is fleeting, that youth is the best part of life, and that they should get married before they are too old to enjoy it.

 For summaries in languages other than English, see Unit 2 Teaching Resources Book, pp. 312–317.

Reading Strategy | 1

Evaluate Have several student volunteers summarize the third stanza in their own words. Then discuss whether students agree with the ideas it expresses.

Literature and Reading Preview

Connect to the Poem

Have you ever regretted a missed opportunity? Freewrite for a few minutes about one such experience.

Build Background

The *carpe diem* attitude of Cavalier poets such as Herrick was a response to the upheavals of the seventeenth century, when Parliament and the monarchy battled for supremacy and disputes between Anglicans and Puritans intensified the conflict.

Set Purposes for Reading

Big Idea The Sacred and the Secular

Although Herrick was an Anglican priest, much of his poetry expresses a secular point of view. As you read, ask yourself, What are the secular values that the speaker espouses?

Literary Element Carpe Diem

Carpe diem is a Latin phrase meaning "Seize the day"—in other words, "make the most of each moment." In many poems treating this theme, the speaker emphasizes the brevity of life—often with the purpose of persuading a young woman to yield to love before her beauty fades. As you read the poem, ask yourself, What are the images and figures of speech that convey the *carpe diem* motif?

Reading Strategy Analyze Sound Devices

The **sound devices** in a poem may serve to give it a musical quality, to enhance its tone or mood, or to reinforce its rhythm. When you analyze sound devices, you consider how each individual device helps convey the poem's meaning or message. As you read this poem, ask yourself, How does Herrick's use of rhyme, alliteration, and assonance contribute to this message?

Tip: Taking Notes Use a chart to record examples of sound devices and the effects they have in the poem and upon you.

Sound Device	Examples	Effects
Rhyme Alliteration Assonance	a-flying/dying	links the idea of time passing to death

Reading Practice

SPIRAL REVIEW **Preview** Before students read "To the Virgins, to Make Much of Time," ask them to look at the structure of the poem on the page, which will help them develop a schematic map of the poem before reading it. **Ask:** How is the poem structured? *(four stanzas of four lines each)* **Ask:** Is there a rhyme scheme? *(lines 1 and 3 and 2 and 4 of each stanza rhyme)*

Flora, detail from the Primavera, c. 1478. Sandro Botticelli. Tempera on panel. Galleria degli Uffizi, Florence, Italy.

View the Art In poetry and literature, flowers often appear as a symbol of youthful pleasure or beauty—wonderful to behold but short-lived. This image is a small section of a painting called *Primavera,* meaning "springtime." What symbolic role might you infer the figure of Flora plays in the painting?

To the Virgins, to Make Much of Time

Robert Herrick

Gather ye rosebuds, while ye may,
  Old time is still a-flying:
And this same flower that smiles today
  Tomorrow will be dying.

5 The glorious lamp of heaven, the sun,
  The higher he's a-getting,
The sooner will his race be run,
  And nearer he's to setting.

The age is best which is the first,
10 When youth and blood are warmer;
But being spent, the worse, and worst
  Times still succeed the former. **1**

Then be not coy, but use your time,
  And, while ye may, go marry:
15 For having lost but once your prime
  You may forever tarry.[1]

---

1. *Tarry* means "linger" or "wait."

Carpe Diem *How does the figurative language in this stanza convey the* carpe diem *motif?* **2**

The Sacred and the Secular *How does this statement illustrate a secular belief of the Cavalier poets?* **3**

ROBERT HERRICK **449**

For additional literary element practice, see Unit 2 Teaching Resources Book, p. 318.

Comparing Literature

Teach

Literary Element   2

Carpe Diem **Answer:** *The rosebuds constitute a symbol for earthly pleasure. The wilting flower represents the brevity of life.*

ENGLISH LEARNERS **Say:** Think of a rosebud as it blooms, as petals fade, and the rose dies. The speaker uses the rose to show how time passes quickly.

Big Idea   3

The Sacred and the Secular
Answer: *The statement implies that youthful pleasure and passion are more valuable than the serene satisfactions that may accompany middle and old age.*

View the Art

Answer: *Flora likely represents youth, beauty, or the swift passage of the seasons.*

To check students' understanding of the selection, see Unit 2 Teaching Resources Book, p. 320.

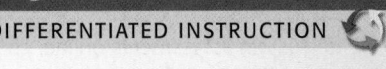
English Learners

DIFFERENTIATED INSTRUCTION

Intermediate Point out to students that there are a number of variations of words in the poem (e.g., *ye* for *you, a-flying* for *flying, a-getting* for *getting*). Ask students to identify the words that they don't hear often in contemporary English. Then ask them to rewrite the poem, using language that makes sense to them.

Approaching Level

DIFFERENTIATED INSTRUCTION

Emerging Herrick uses the metaphor of a rose and the metaphor of the sun to illustrate the same concept. **Ask:** What concept is Herrick describing in the metaphor of the rose and the sun? *(the passage of time)*

After You Read

Assess

1. Students' answers will vary.

2. (a) Young women should marry because the opportunity may be lost later. (b) Answers will vary.

3. (a) The speaker depicts youth as the prime of life and the successive periods as increasingly unpleasant. (b) Answers will vary.

4. The time allowed for the coexistence of both sacred and secular perspectives.

5. Students may say that women today might decide, not to "go marry," but to travel and get an education before taking on the responsibilities of marriage and children.

Literary Element

1. The speaker suggests that one should enjoy life and take advantage of present opportunities.

2. The duration of human life can be compared to a single day; therefore, one should "seize the day."

Writing

Students' poems will vary but should use Herrick's rhyme scheme and run eight lines long.

Academic Vocabulary

Students may respond that including an explicit message makes the tone more urgent and creates the sense that the author is speaking directly to the reader.

After You Read

Respond and Think Critically

Respond and Interpret

1. What do you think of the speaker's suggestions in this poem? Explain.

2. (a) What conclusion does the speaker reach in the last stanza? (b) How could you restate the last two lines?

Analyze and Evaluate

3. (a) What is the speaker's attitude toward youth and aging in the third stanza? (b) Do you agree with his assessment?

Connect

4. **Big Idea** The Sacred and the Secular What does the fact that Herrick, an Anglican priest, wrote poetry extolling the sensual pleasures of marriage tell us about the age and the society in which he lived?

5. **Connect to Today** How might this poem have a different significance for women today than it did in the seventeenth century?

Literary Element Carpe Diem

Carpe diem contains a form of the Latin word *carpere,* meaning "to pluck, grab, or harvest."

1. What evidence of the *carpe diem* theme do you find in the poem?

2. How might you summarize the speaker's attitude toward life and death?

Writing

Write a Poem Think back to your first year of high school. Were there any activities or opportunities you missed out on? Write a *carpe diem* poem entitled "To the Freshmen, to Make Much of High School." Urge your audience to seize opportunities while they can. Your poem should be at least eight lines long and use the same rhyme scheme as Herrick's.

Reading Strategy Analyze Sound Devices

Sound devices such as alliteration, assonance, and rhyme can have both an individual and a combined effect within a poem. Refer to your reading chart to answer the following questions.

1. Which sound devices help to create a sense of the pleasures of youth? Cite examples from the poem to support your answer.

2. What pattern do the rhyming pairs of words establish? Explain how this reinforces the message of the poem.

Academic Vocabulary

Herrick makes the message of his poem **explicit** *by stating it in the title.*

Explicit is an academic word. The title and the first line of the poem are **explicit** statements of Herrick's message.

To further explore the meaning of this word, answer the following question: How might the inclusion of an **explicit** message, rather than an implicit one, change the tone of a literary work?

For more on academic vocabulary, see pages 56 and R81.

LOG ON ▶ **Literature** Online

Selection Resources For Selection Quizzes, eFlashcards, and Reading-Writing Connection activities, go to glencoe.com and enter QuickPass code GLB2946u2.

Reading Strategy

1. Sample answer: Assonance and rhyme are used in lines 9–12, which indicate that the first age is best "when youth and blood are warmer."

2. The pairs of words that Herrick chooses establish an *abab* pattern, which reinforces the message of the poem that time is short and youth should be enjoyed because it is fleeting.

 To create custom assessments online, go to Progress Reporter Online Assessment.

Progress Check

Can students analyze sound devices?

If No → See Unit 2 Teaching Resources Book p. 319.

Build Background

Horace's **odes**—elaborate lyrics often addressed to a person, event, or force of nature—are rich in the *carpe diem* spirit. Denying the existence of an afterlife, he famously said, "Seize the day, put very little faith in tomorrow." Influenced by the Greek philosophers Epicurus and Aristotle, Horace believed in the "golden mean," a lifestyle driven by the pursuit of pleasure and the avoidance of the pain that results from excessive self-indulgence.

Carpe Diem

Horace
translated by Thomas Hawkins

Strive not, Leuconoe[1], to know what end
The gods above to me or thee will send:
Nor with astrologers consult at all,
That thou mayst better know what can befall;
5   Whether thou liv'st more winters; or thy last
Be this, which Tyrrhen[2] waves 'gainst rocks do cast.
Be wise! Drink free, and in so short a space
Do not protracted hopes of life embrace:
Whilst we are talking, envious time doth slide;
10 This day's thine own; the next may be denied.

1. *Leuconoe* (lyō̄ kō′ nō ē) is a friend of the poet.
2. *Tyrrhen* (tir′ en) is a reference to the Tyrrhenian Sea, a part of the Mediterranean southwest of Italy.

Skull, symbol of death, surrounded by symbolic objects. Mosaic from Pompeii. Museo Archeologico Nazionale, Naples, Italy.

> **Quickwrite**
>
> In these lines, the speaker advises the reader to ignore the future because it is uncertain. Do you agree with this advice? How does it apply to your goals in life? Write a paragraph expressing your views.

HORACE   **451**

Focus

Summary

Addressing his friend Leuconoe, Horace tells him that a person has no idea whether he will live for many years or die tomorrow. He tells his friend to enjoy today since he may not be here tomorrow.

View the Art ★

Many of Pompeii's beautiful mosaics survived the town's destruction by a volcanic eruption in 79 A.D. Historians have identified the drapery-like object that appears at the left in this one to be a purple robe, as worn by the nobility, while the corresponding item on the right is rags. **Ask:** What interpretation of the image might this suggest? *(Both rich and poor are equal in death.)*

Teach

Big Idea   **1**

The Sacred and the Secular Ask: Does Horace make a religious argument or a secular one? *(While he does mention the gods, Horace's argument is that we cannot know what fate has in store for us. This is a secular argument.)*

Quickwrite

Students' paragraphs should explain the logic behind the advice—that life is too uncertain for long-range plans. Evaluate students' paragraphs on their use of reasons and examples to support their opinions.

Comparing Literature

Focus

Summary

Ronsard tells Hélène that when she is old, she will regret the fact that she did not return his affections. He then tells her it is not too late; she can still avoid that terrible fate if she chooses to.

Teach

Discussion Starter

The poem is both an encouragement and a warning. The speaker begins the poem by presenting a vivid prediction of the regrets the woman will feel if she does not reciprocate the speaker's love. The last two lines indicate that the woman is still young and can "gather up the roses" before it is too late.

Literary Element | 1

Analyze Sound Devices

Ronsard uses **alliteration** to emphasize phrases and add a musical quality to the poem. The line, "Moved closer to the coals," repeats sounds in *closer* and *coal*.

(APPROACHING) **Ask:** How does Ronsard use rhyming in the first and second stanzas? *(He rhymes the first and fourth lines and the second and third lines.)* **Ask:** How does the rhyme scheme change in the last stanza? *(He rhymes the first and second lines, the third and sixth lines, the fourth and sixth lines.)*

Build Background

Revered during the Renaissance, Pierre de Ronsard earned a reputation as the "Prince of French Poets." Influenced by Horace and Virgil, he wrote odes that combined experimental forms with complex rhymes and classical allusions. He also excelled in the composition of Petrarchan sonnets.

The following poem is from Ronsard's collection *Sonnets pour Hélène* (1578), which reflects the profound melancholy that dominated Ronsard as he approached his death in 1585. This poem influenced the twentieth-century Irish poet William Butler Yeats, who wrote an adaptation of it called "When You Are Old" (see page 1062).

Saint Magdalen Reading, sixteenth century. Master of the Female Half-Figures. Oil on wood, 54 x 42 cm. Louvre, Paris.

To Hélène

Pierre de Ronsard
translated by Robert Hollander

When you are very old, in evening candlelight,
Moved closer to the coals and carding out your wool,[1] **1**
You'll sing my songs and marvel that you were such a fool:
"O Ronsard did praise me when I was young and bright."

5   Then you'll have no handmaid to help you pass the night,
Spinning while your gossip leads her into lull,
Until you say my name and her rousèd eyes grow full
In wonder of your glory in what Ronsard did write.

When I am in the earth, poor ghost without his bones,
10 A sleeper in the shade of myrtle trees and stones,
Then you, beside the hearth, old and crouched and gray,
Will yearn for all that's lost, repenting your disdain.
Live it well, I pray you, today won't come again:
Gather up the roses before they fall away.

---

1. *Carding out your wool* refers to the act of combing strands of wool to untangle them before spinning them into thread.

💬 Discussion Starter

Is this poem an encouragement to a young woman to "seize the day," or is it a lament for an old woman who has missed her opportunity for love? Discuss this question in a small group.

Writing Practice

Compare Characters

SPIRAL REVIEW Ask students to make a graphic organizer to track the characteristics of Ronsard and Hélène as the speaker describes each in the poem. Then ask them to compare and contrast Ronsard and Hélène, using evidence from the graphic organizer.

Characteristics

Ronsard	Hélène
———	———
———	———
———	———

Build Background

Manuscripts of the *Rubáiyát* (roo′ bī ät′) were not found until two hundred years after Omar Khayyám's death in 1123. Seventy-five of the 158 quatrains have come down to us in a translation made in 1859 by the Englishman Edward FitzGerald. His translation is considered to be a free, rather than a literal, translation.

Rubáiyát is the plural of *ruba'i*, or "quatrain," which is the essential unit of Persian verse. Each ruba'i has an *aaba* rhyme scheme and expresses a complete thought: the first two lines pose a situation or problem, the third line creates suspense, and the fourth line offers a resolution. The *Rubáiyát* is complex and meditative, and Omar offers a secular rather than a religious solution to the problem of existing in an uncertain world.

Comparing Literature

Focus
Summary

Omar Khayyám urges his "beloved" to enjoy life. He argues that life is short, time goes by quickly, and the only thing that is certain is that we will die. After death there will be none of life's pleasures, so we should enjoy them now.

from the Rubáiyát

Omar Khayyám
translated by Edward FitzGerald

2
Dreaming when dawn's left hand was in the sky
I heard a voice within the tavern cry,
   "Awake, my little ones, and fill the cup
Before life's liquor in its cup be dry."

20
Ah! my belovéd, fill the cup that clears
Today of past regrets and future fears—
   Tomorrow?—Why, tomorrow I may be
Myself with yesterday's sev'n thousand years.

23
Ah, make the most of what we yet may spend,
Before we too into the dust descend;
   Dust into dust, and under dust, to lie,
Sans wine, sans song, sans singer and—sans end!

OMAR KHAYYÁM **453**

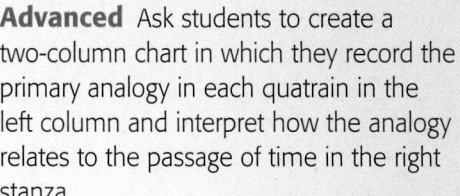

English Learners

DIFFERENTIATED INSTRUCTION

Advanced Ask students to create a two-column chart in which they record the primary analogy in each quatrain in the left column and interpret how the analogy relates to the passage of time in the right stanza.

Approaching Level

DIFFERENTIATED INSTRUCTION

Emerging Tell students that there are a number of comparisons that the speaker makes in the quatrains between the passage of time and everyday objects and sights. **Ask:** What is the passage of time compared to in the first quatrain? the second quatrain? the third quatrain? *(dawn, a cup, and dust)*

Comparing Literature

Teach

Quickwrite

Student paragraphs should explain how the sensory image of drinking and tasting reinforces the idea of taking advantage of the here and now. The cup is a symbol for human life, which is empty unless it is filled with "life's liquor," a symbol for sensual experience, "the secret well of life" that can rid the drinker of "past regrets and future fears."

Bird and Scene of Lovers With an Attendant. Persia. Seattle Art Museum, WA.

26

Oh, come with old Khayyám, and leave the wise
To talk; one thing is certain, that life flies;
  One thing is certain, and the rest is lies;
The flower that once has blown for ever dies.

34

Then to this earthen bowl did I adjourn
My lip the secret well of life to learn:
  And lip to lip it murmur'd—"While you live,
Drink!—for once dead you never shall return."

37

One moment in annihilation's waste,
One moment, of the well of life to taste—
  The stars are setting, and the caravan
Starts for the dawn of nothing—Oh, make haste!

38

Ah, fill the cup:—what boots it to repeat
How time is slipping underneath our feet:
  Unborn tomorrow and dead yesterday,
Why fret about them if today be sweet!

39

How long, how long, in infinite pursuit
Of this and that endeavor and dispute?
  Better be merry with the fruitful grape
Than sadden after none, or bitter, fruit.

> **Quickwrite**
>
> Throughout the quatrains excerpted here, Omar repeats the image of filling and drinking from a cup. How does this image symbolize his message? Using evidence from the text, write your response in a paragraph.

Reading Practice

SPIRAL REVIEW **Main Idea and Supporting Details** Tell students that poems often do not use standard paragraph structure with a topic sentence and supporting details. However, point out that the meaning of a poem can often be conveyed in a sentence or two. Have stu-dents reread the quatrains and consider if one of the lines might state the main idea. **Ask:** Is the main idea repeated in the poem? *(Yes, lines 7–8 and 14 convey the same main idea of sadness that time is passing.)*

Wrap-Up: Comparing Literature
Across Time and Place

- *To the Virgins, to Make Much of Time* by Robert Herrick
- *Carpe Diem* by Horace
- *To Hélène* by Pierre de Ronsard
- from the *Rubáiyát* by Omar Khayyám

COMPARE THE **Big Idea** The Sacred and the Secular

Group Activity Herrick, Horace, Ronsard, and Omar express secular world-views, rejecting a sacred worldview either implicitly or explicitly. With a small group of classmates, discuss the following questions.

1. Accoring to these four writers, what is the nature of life and death?

2. In each poem, the speaker offers advice to a hypothetical listener. What advice does each speaker give, and to whom is he speaking?

3. How do these four writers characterize time in their poems?

COMPARE Universal Theme

Writing The works by Herrick, Horace, Ronsard, and Omar insist that one should make every moment count. The literature of many periods explores the attempt to defeat the ravages of time by living as if each moment were one's last. How might the writing of literature be an attempt to defeat the ravages of time? In a brief essay, compare the poets' messages and the ways in which they confront the fleeting nature of life through verse.

Lady in a White Cap, c. fifteenth century. Hans Holbein the Younger.

COMPARE Cultures

Speaking and Listening Despite writing in different cultures and time periods, Herrick, Horace, Ronsard, and Omar developed similar responses to the process of aging and the inevitable mortality of human beings. Research the ways in which historical and cultural context might have affected each of the poets' themes, and make an oral presentation of your findings to the class.

Selection Resources For Selection Quizzes, eFlashcards, and Reading-Writing Connection activities, go to glencoe.com and enter QuickPass code GLB9817u2.

COMPARING LITERATURE **455**

English Learners

DIFFERENTIATED INSTRUCTION

Beginning Ask: What themes are present in all of the four selections? *(Possible answer: making every moment count)*

Intermediate In order to compare how each author explores the universal theme, ask students to make a two-column chart. In the left column, students should record the author of the selection. In the right column, students should write quotes that illustrate the theme in metaphors.

Assess

Compare the Big Idea: The Sacred and the Secular

1. Life is a brief interval between birth and death. Death is oblivion.

2. Herrick's speaker advises young virgins to enjoy youthful love before they grow old. Horace's speaker advises his friend Leuconoe to live for the present and not to worry about the future. Ronsard's speaker warns the woman he loves to reciprocate his love before it is too late. Omar's speaker addresses his "beloved" and advises her to savor life's sensual pleasures before the annihilation of death.

3. Time is characterized as an enemy that can be conquered only by living in the moment and enjoying life's sensual pleasures to the fullest extent.

Compare Universal Theme

Students' essays should

- discuss similarities in the themes of the four poems
- explain how writing literature is a way of immortalizing one's name and art
- show how the message of each poem offers an approach to life that can alleviate despair over transience, uncertainty, and death

Compare Cultures

Students may note the religious or political upheaval that existed during the lives of Herrick, Horace, and Ronsard. They may also note Omar Khayyám's scientific and philosophical background.

Bellringer Options

Daily Language Practice
Transparency 35

Or write the word *wit* on the board. **Ask:** What do we mean when we say someone is "a wit" or "witty"? *(that the person is clever or funny)*

Explain that the Cavalier poets, including Suckling, were famous for their wit. Tell students to look for witty passages as they read these poems.

Before You Read
Why So Pale and Wan, Fond Lover?

Meet **Sir John Suckling**
(1609–1642)

Imagine inheriting an immense fortune at the age of eighteen. What kind of life would you lead? When John Suckling came into his inheritance, he promptly left college to live as a gambler, big spender, and playboy, taking a grand tour of continental Europe and seeking glory as a gentleman soldier there.

Early Years Suckling was born on February 10, 1609, in Middlesex. In 1613, when Suckling was only four years old, his mother died. In 1623 Suckling enrolled in Trinity College in Cambridge. Three years later, while Suckling was still a student, his father died, leaving Suckling with the fortune that allowed him to pursue his life of extravagance. Shortly afterward, Suckling was admitted to Gray's Inn, one of four legal societies that, by tradition, govern the right of barristers to practice law in England's courts. For a while, Suckling pursued a military career, joining the army of Swedish king Gustavus Adolphus during the Thirty Years' War.

A Sparkling Wit Upon returning to England, Suckling became "famous at court for his accomplishments and ready, sparkling wit," according to his friend Sir William Davenant. In fact, he became so well liked that King Charles I knighted him when he was merely twenty-one. Regarded by many critics as the most famous member of the Cavalier poets, Suckling used his "sparkling wit" to write popular dramas, long ballads, and prose works, but he is best known today for his short, sprightly songs and verses. Suckling's attitude toward these songs and verses—casual diversions rather than things to be taken seriously—is reflected in the poems themselves. Their tone has been described as witty, light, mocking, lacking depth, and flippant. Yet, according to English critic Robin Skelton, they illustrate an admirable

> "I hold that perfect joy makes all our parts
> As joyful as our hearts."
>
> —Sir John Suckling, from
> "If You Refuse Me Once and Think Again"

quality common to Cavalier poetry: the ability "to celebrate the minor pleasures and sadnesses of life."

Politics, Intrigue, and Death In 1639 Suckling led a troop in the king's thwarted expedition against Scotland. Suckling outfitted his soldiers in brightly colored uniforms with plumed hats and provided them with horses at his own expense. As it turned out, however, the troop's poor performance and gaudy costumes became the subject of much ridicule. Two years later, Suckling made a mistake that neither his wit nor his money could correct. He joined a conspiracy to rescue the Earl of Strafford, one of the king's chief deputies, whom Parliament had imprisoned in the Tower of London. The rescue mission failed, and Suckling fled to Paris. There, early in 1642, at the age of thirty-three, he died under mysterious circumstances. According to one theory, he was murdered by a servant; according to another, he poisoned himself.

LOG ON **Literature** Online

Author Search For more about Sir John Suckling, go to glencoe.com and enter QuickPass code GLB9817u2.

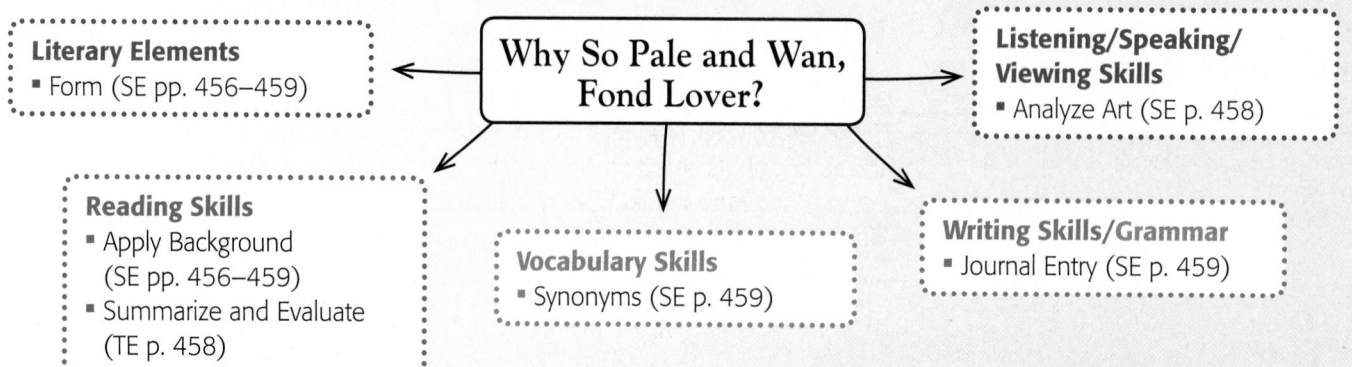

Literary Elements
- Form (SE pp. 456–459)

Why So Pale and Wan, Fond Lover?

Listening/Speaking/Viewing Skills
- Analyze Art (SE p. 458)

Reading Skills
- Apply Background (SE pp. 456–459)
- Summarize and Evaluate (TE p. 458)

Vocabulary Skills
- Synonyms (SE p. 459)

Writing Skills/Grammar
- Journal Entry (SE p. 459)

Literature and Reading Preview

Connect to the Poem

What types of remarks do you consider witty? Puns? Jokes? Sarcasm? Discuss this question with a small group of classmates. Consider the purpose of wit, and what qualities make a person or a comment witty.

Build Background

In Suckling's day, most marriages were based on financial considerations and were arranged by a couple's parents—often when the couples were just children. As a result, many young women, already engaged, may have felt it necessary to publicly ignore lovesick suitors' pleas for attention.

Set Purposes for Reading

Big Idea The Sacred and the Secular

As you read, ask yourself, How does this poem express the poet's witty reflections on amorous behavior?

Literary Element Form

A literary work's **form** is its structure. The form of a poem is determined by the number of stanzas (groups of lines that form units), the number and length of lines in each stanza, the rhythmic patterns, and the rhyme scheme (or lack of it). As you read, ask yourself, How are these elements employed to convey or reinforce meaning in the poem?

Reading Strategy Apply Background Knowledge

The ideas expressed in Suckling's poem were shaped in part by the attitudes and customs of the world in which he lived. As you read, ask yourself, How might those attitudes and customs have influenced Suckling?

....

Tip: Taking Notes Reread the preceding page and the Build Background above, noting attitudes and customs of Suckling's time. Jot down some of these in a chart, then add ideas in the poem that seem to be influenced by the attitudes and customs.

Attitudes and Customs	Illustrated in Poem
1. Cavalier poems are casual diversions—not to be taken seriously.	1. "Young sinner" suggests that the speaker is mocking the person addressed.

Learning Objectives

For pages 456–459

In studying this text, you will focus on the following objectives:

Literary Study: Analyzing form.

Reading: Applying background knowledge.

Writing: Writing a journal entry.

Vocabulary

dull (dul) *adj.* slow in thinking or responding; p. 458 *John's head cold made him feel rather dull at school.*

prevail (pri vāl´) *v.* to be in general use; succeed; p. 458 *Supporters of the tax increase trusted that the practical reasons for it would prevail.*

SIR JOHN SUCKLING **457**

Before You Read

Focus

Summary

In "Why So Pale and Wan, Fond Lover?" the speaker chides a young man for his traumatized infatuation with a woman who does not return his love.

 For summaries in languages other than English, see Unit 2 Teaching Resources Book, pp. 322–327.

Vocabulary

Synonyms Tell students that knowing synonyms for less familiar words can help them grasp the meaning of new texts. Divide the class in half, and challenge each group to suggest as many synonyms as they can for *dull* and *prevail*. Students may begin with the definitions in their books and then use dictionaries as they try to produce thorough lists.

 For additional vocabulary practice, see Unit 2 Teaching Resources Book, p. 330.

English Learners

DIFFERENTIATED INSTRUCTION

Intermediate Explain that Suckling places words in unexpected order. Point out lines 3 and 4 as an example. **Ask:** Why might Suckling have written this question in such an odd way? *(to create a certain sound or rhyme, to sound witty)*

Ask: How would you usually write this question? *(Will looking ill prevail when looking well can't move her?)* Then, ask students to identify two other places where Suckling's word order is unexpected (lines 8–9, lines 13–14). Have them try to write these lines in more usual word order.

Teach

Apply Background Knowledge **Answer:** *He is flippantly chiding the young lover for revealing how deeply he cares about his lady. This exemplifies the Cavaliers' (real or pretended) disdain for genuine expression of love.*

 For additional practice using the reading skill or strategy, see Unit 2 Teaching Resources Book, p. 329.

View the Art ★

Answer: *The man in the image also seems pale, silent, distressed, and distracted by something other than the artist in front of him.*

Sir Joshua Reynolds (1723–1792) is considered the leading British portrait painter of the 1700s. He is known for his use of strong lighting and rich colors. He often had his subjects strike poses characteristic of classical art. **Ask:** How do the colors in this poem represent the mood of the poem's speaker? *(The colors are dark and dreary, like the speaker's mood.)*

Why So Pale and Wan, Fond Lover?

Sir John Suckling

Portrait of Francis Russell, the Marquess of Tavistock, 1767. Sir Joshua Reynolds. Oil on canvas.

View the Art The pose shown in this painting has been popular with artists for many centuries as a way of demonstrating seriousness or thought. How does the man in the image compare to the "fond lover" in the poem? Explain. ★

Why so pale and wan,[1] fond[2] lover?
    Prithee,[3] why so pale?
Will, when looking well can't move her,
    Looking ill **prevail**?
5   Prithee, why so pale?

Why so **dull** and mute, young sinner?
    Prithee, why so mute?
Will, when speaking well can't win her,
    Saying nothing do 't?
10   Prithee, why so mute?

Quit, quit, for shame, this will not move:
    This cannot take her.
If of herself she will not love,
    Nothing can make her:
15   The devil take her!

---

1. *Wan* means "sickly" or "pale."
2. *Fond,* in Suckling's time, meant "foolish."
3. At the time Suckling wrote this poem, *prithee* meant "please."

1 Apply Background Knowledge *How do Suckling's observations in this poem illustrate the Cavaliers' attitudes?*

Vocabulary

prevail (pri vāl′) *v.* to be in general use; succeed
dull (dul) *adj.* slow in thinking or responding

Reading Practice

SMALL GROUP
Summarize and Evaluate
Divide the class into small groups. Assign the poem's first stanza to half of the groups and the second stanza to the second group. Ask each group to prepare answers to these questions:

- In the speaker's opinion, what is the young man in love doing wrong?
- Do you agree with the speaker that the young man is behaving foolishly?
- What advice would you give the young man as he tries to earn the love of the young woman?

Have groups compare the advice they would give and decide on the best strategy for the young lover.

After You Read

Respond and Think Critically

Respond and Interpret

1. Did you enjoy Suckling's wit in this poem? Why or why not?

2. (a)Paraphrase the speaker's questions in lines 3–4 and lines 8–9. (b)What point might the speaker be trying to make by asking these questions?

3. (a)In addition to "pale and wan," how else does the speaker describe the suitor in line 1? (b)Why might the speaker in this poem view the suitor in this way?

Analyze and Evaluate

4. (a)One definition of *passion* is "very strong love." What do you think the speaker's attitude is toward passion? (b)What do you think the suitor's attitude is toward passion? (c)Do you agree with the speaker, the suitor, or neither? Why?

Connect

5. **Big Idea** The Sacred and the Secular What types of wit does Suckling use in this poem?

6. **Connect to the Author** What characteristics of the poem might reflect the young age at which Suckling wrote it?

Literary Element Form

In this poem, Suckling employs specific rhythmic patterns, rhymes and near rhymes, and the grouping of stanzas to help convey his observations.

Partner Activity Meet with a classmate to study the poem. Then answer these questions:

1. How does the sequence of stanzas in the poem help convey meaning?

2. (a)Identify the rhyme scheme of the poem. Find two examples of slant rhyme (words that nearly rhyme but do not exactly rhyme). (b)Why might Suckling have created these slant rhymes?

 Writing

Write a Journal Entry "Why So Pale and Wan, Fond Lover" deals with a young person's behaving absurdly to win his beloved's heart. In a journal entry, write an account of an incident in which someone did an incredibly romantic—or incredibly foolish—thing to win someone's love. In the end, was it worthwhile or simply embarrassing for the person to have acted that way? Would you have done the same thing?

Reading Strategy Apply Background Knowledge

Suckling's poems reflect the attitudes and customs of the world in which he lived.

In what ways does this poem express the attitudes of the Cavalier poets toward the writing of poetry and the subject matter of poetry?

Vocabulary Practice

Practice with Synonyms Synonyms are words with the same, or nearly the same, meaning. With a partner, match each boldfaced vocabulary word below with a synonym. You will not use all the answer choices. Use a thesaurus or dictionary to check your answers.

1. prevail
2. dull

a. win
b. prevent
c. sluggish
d. wry

 Literature Online

Selection Resources For Selection Quizzes, eFlashcards, and Reading-Writing Connection activities, go to glencoe.com and enter QuickPass code GLB9817u2.

SIR JOHN SUCKLING **459**

Reading Strategy

Students should cite examples of direct, colloquial language that expresses witty observations about everyday situations, notably the pleasures and pains of amorous love.

Vocabulary

1. a 2. c

Writing

Journal entries should describe a romantic or foolish event intended to win someone's love; the worthiness of the action should be evaluated.

After You Read

Assess

1. Students' answers will vary.

2. (a) Will lovesick appearance and silence attract your beloved when healthy appearance and eloquence can't? (b) That it is pointless to pine for someone so unresponsive

3. (a) As "fond" (foolish) (b) He thinks that the suitor is throwing his heart away on this woman.

4. (a) He might consider passion foolish or even irrational. (b) He might consider passion inescapable. (c) Students' answers will vary.

5. Teasing, sarcasm, exaggeration, and irony

6. The tone is flippant. He is advising a friend, who he describes as a "young sinner."

Literary Element

1. The first and second stanzas set a pattern, and the third and fourth break it. This signals a shift in tone.

2. (a) The rhyme scheme is *ababb* in all three stanzas. Examples of slant rhyme are "lover" and "move her" in the first stanza and "move" and "love" in the third stanza. (b) To hint that the lover and the loved one are not in harmony

To check students' understanding of the selection, see Unit 2 Teaching Resources Book, p. 331.

Progress Check

Can students analyze form?

If No → See Unit 2 Teaching Resources Book, p. 328.

459

Before You Read

Focus

Bellringer Options

Selection Focus
   Transparency 21
Daily Language Practice
   Transparency 36

Or tell students to think about what it might be like to be a soldier going off to war. **Ask:** What feelings and thoughts might a person in that situation have? Lead the class in a brief discussion of their ideas.

Before You Read

To Lucasta, Going to the Wars

Meet **Richard Lovelace**
(1618–c. 1657)

Richard Lovelace seemed destined to lead a charmed life. As a handsome, wealthy young aristocrat studying at Oxford University, he caught the notice of King Charles I and Queen Henrietta Maria. He so impressed them that they arranged for him to receive an honorary degree and join their court. There, his literary talent, love of the fine arts, and superb horsemanship made him a favorite. Unfortunately, his affiliation with the king also led to his downfall.

A Renaissance Gentleman Richard Lovelace was probably born in the Netherlands, where his father was stationed with the king's military. Sadly, he died in action when Lovelace was a young boy. Lovelace eventually returned to England and attended school at Charterhouse and Oxford. While studying at Oxford, Lovelace wrote *The Scholar,* a comedy that was performed at the school in 1636. At court, Lovelace epitomized the ideal of the Renaissance gentleman: he was a lover, soldier, wit, musician, and poet. From 1639 to 1640, he participated in the king's military campaign in Scotland. In 1642, at the age of twenty-four, Lovelace led a march petitioning Parliament to grant the king broader powers. Parliamentary leaders responded by briefly imprisoning him.

Punishment and Poverty In 1646 Lovelace offered his services to King Louis XIV of France and was wounded during a battle at Dunkirk. When King Charles I was arrested in 1648, Lovelace was arrested again—this time to prevent him from leading a revolt to rescue the king. During this second imprisonment, he wrote "To Lucasta, Going to the Wars." After King Charles I was beheaded in 1649, Lovelace was released from prison, but by then he had exhausted his fortune. During the height of his popularity and influence

at court, Lovelace had worn clothes made from fabrics of gold and silver. According to biographer Anthony à Wood, Lovelace, after leaving prison for the second time, was reduced to wearing ragged clothes, living in run-down lodgings, and accepting charity. He spent his last years in ill health—a victim of tuberculosis—and is believed to have died in the squalor of Gunpowder Alley, London, at age thirty-nine.

> *"Thus richer than untempted Kings are we,*
> *That asking nothing, nothing need:*
> *Though Lord of all what Seas embrace; yet he*
> *That wants himself, is poor indeed."*
>
> —Richard Lovelace
> from "The Grasshopper"

Enduring Fame Literary historians are divided in their opinion of Lovelace's body of poetry. One scholar has even suggested that it would have been better if most of Lovelace's poems "had remained in manuscript and perished with his two plays." Most critics agree, however, that "To Lucasta, Going to the Wars" is worthy of the enduring fame it has achieved.

Literature Online

Author Search For more about Richard Lovelace, go to glencoe.com and enter QuickPass code GLB9817u2.

460 UNIT 2 THE ENGLISH RENAISSANCE

Selection Skills

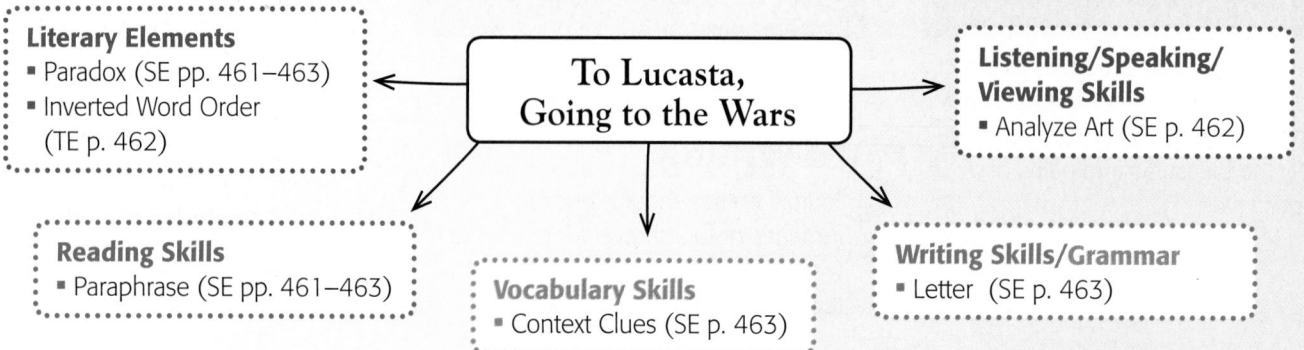

Literary Elements
- Paradox (SE pp. 461–463)
- Inverted Word Order (TE p. 462)

Reading Skills
- Paraphrase (SE pp. 461–463)

To Lucasta, Going to the Wars

Vocabulary Skills
- Context Clues (SE p. 463)

Listening/Speaking/ Viewing Skills
- Analyze Art (SE p. 462)

Writing Skills/Grammar
- Letter (SE p. 463)

Literature and Reading Preview

Connect to the Poem

What might cause you to sacrifice your freedom or love? Write a journal entry in which you record your ideas about this question.

Build Background

Lovelace wrote "To Lucasta, Going to the Wars" in 1648, during his second imprisonment. It was published in *Lucasta*, one of two collections that contain the bulk of Lovelace's literary legacy. The Lucasta who lends her name to these two volumes is said to have been Lucy Sacherevell. After hearing that Lovelace had died of wounds at Dunkirk, she married someone else. Parliamentary leaders of the time held up the publication of *Lucasta* to silence Lovelace, whom they considered to be a political enemy.

Set Purposes for Reading

Big Idea The Sacred and the Secular

As you read, ask yourself, How does this poem express the poet's secular notions of love and honor?

Literary Element Paradox

A **paradox** is a statement that appears to be contradictory but is actually true, either in fact or in a figurative sense. As you read, ask yourself, Which statements or ideas are paradoxes?

Reading Strategy Paraphrase

When you **paraphrase,** you put something you have read or heard into your own words. Paraphrasing is a useful strategy for breaking down difficult text and making it easier to understand. As you read, ask yourself, How would I express these ideas?

Tip: Taking Notes Try paraphrasing each stanza of the poem. Write down your paraphrases in a chart like the one shown here.

"To Lucasta, Going to the Wars"
Stanza 1:
Stanza 2:
Stanza 3:

Learning Objectives

For pages 460–463

In studying this text, you will focus on the following objectives:

Literary Study: Analyzing paradox.

Reading: Paraphrasing.

Writing: Writing a letter.

Vocabulary

chaste (chāst) *adj.* pure; virtuous; modest; p. 462 *Felicity's chaste behavior made it difficult for her parents to believe that she would deceive them.*

inconstancy (in kon′ stən sē) *n.* changeable nature; disloyalty; p. 462 *Nora's inconstancy in the past caused the board to doubt her.*

Before You Read

Focus

Summary

This poem deals with the separation of lovers. In "To Lucasta, Going to the Wars," the speaker is leaving his beloved for "war and arms."

 For summaries in languages other than English, see Unit 2 Teaching Resources Book, pp. 333–338.

Vocabulary

Context Clues Have students prepare to use context clues to guess the meaning of *chaste* by pointing out these words in the context: *nunnery* and *quiet*. Ask students to describe the lives of women in a nunnery. Then, have them predict what *chaste breast* might mean in this context. *(pure heart, modest soul)*

 For additional vocabulary practice, see Unit 2 Teaching Resources Book, p. 341.

English Learners

DIFFERENTIATED INSTRUCTION

Beginning/Early Intermediate Write these words from the selection on the board: *arms, foe, sword, horse, shield.* Explain that in this poem, these words have to do with war. Have students work with a partner to look up each word in a dictionary. Remind them that sometimes, as in the case of *arms*, they will need to read past the first definition to find a meaning that makes sense in the context of war.

Partners should explain what the speaker is imagining as he uses each word in saying goodbye to the woman he loves. Provide this example: *Arms* means the weapons a soldier uses. The speaker is imagining the weapons he will carry to protect himself and attack the enemy on the battlefield.

Teach

Big Idea 1

The Sacred and the Secular
Answer: *The speaker embodies the Renaissance attitudes toward courtly love and honorable behavior. He declares that his honor depends upon the faithful execution of his duties. As a gentleman he must go to war, and this takes precedence over his love for Lucasta.*

For additional practice using the reading skill or strategy, see Unit 2 Teaching Resources Book, p. 340

View the Art ★

Possible answer: *Although Brown, as the painting and poem suggest, was clearly brave for going to war, the truth of his injuries stands in contrast to the glory and honor portrayed by the artist and the poet.*

To check students' understanding of the selection, see Unit 2 Teaching Resources Book, p. 343.

To Lucasta, Going to the Wars

Richard Lovelace

Tell me not, sweet, I am unkind,
  That from the nunnery
Of thy **chaste** breast and quiet mind
  To war and arms I fly.

5 True, a new mistress now I chase,
  The first foe in the field;
And with a stronger faith embrace
  A sword, a horse, a shield.

Yet this **inconstancy** is such
10 As you too shall adore;
I could not love thee, dear, so much,
  Loved I not honor more.

1 The Sacred and the Secular *What qualities of a Renaissance gentleman and Cavalier poet does the speaker exhibit in these lines?*

Vocabulary

chaste (chāst) *adj.* pure; virtuous; modest
inconstancy (in kon′ stən sē) *n.* changeable nature; disloyalty

Thomas Brown at the Battle of Dettingen, 27th June, 1743. English school. Oil on canvas. Private collection.

View the Art The Thomas Brown depicted in this painting lost his nose, two fingers, and half an eyebrow during the battle. In what ways does this historical detail stand in contrast to the tone of both the image and the poem?

Literary Elements Practice

SPIRAL REVIEW **Inverted Word Order** On the board, write the final line of "To Lucasta, Going to the Wars": "Loved I not honor more."

Ask: In this clause, does the subject or the verb come first? *(verb)* What is the actual meaning of the clause? *(if I did not love honor more)* How is the order unusual? *(The verb comes before the subject.)* Explain that this is an example of **inverted word order.** It is used poetically to make the line read better but does not change the meaning of the clause. Have a volunteer find and reword the inversion in line 5. *(I now chase a new mistress)*

After You Read

Respond and Think Critically

Respond and Interpret

1. Which lines from the poem did you find most memorable? Why?

2. (a)Who is the "new mistress" whom the speaker is chasing? (b)Why might the poet have chosen to compare this new love to his love for Lucasta?

3. (a)What three things does the speaker "with a stronger faith embrace"? (b)What does his loyalty to these things suggest about his values?

Analyze and Evaluate

4. (a)What reasons does the speaker give for going to war? (b)Do you think these are valid reasons?

Connect

5. **Big Idea** The Sacred and the Secular What courtly attitudes are important to the speaker of the poem?

6. **Connect to Today** Do you think such courtly attitudes are still important today? Why or why not?

Literary Element Paradox

Although a **paradox** seems illogical or counterintuitive, it in fact conveys an important truth. The modern expression "Less is more" is an example of such a paradox.

Find and explain the two central paradoxes in "To Lucasta, Going to the Wars."

Writing

Write a Letter Write a letter from Lucasta to the speaker, in which she responds positively or negatively to his decision to go to war. In your letter, introduce at least one paradox into Lucasta's own position—for example, that in letting him go away she is really showing him her devotion.

Reading Strategy Paraphrase

Look back at the **paraphrases** you created in your chart as you read. What literary elements are missing from your paraphrases? In what ways do these elements contribute to your appreciation of the poem?

Vocabulary Practice

Practice with Context Clues Identify the context clues in the following sentences that help you determine the meaning of each boldfaced vocabulary word.

1. The **chaste,** or pure, behavior she usually showed changed when her parents weren't watching her.

2. His lover's **inconstancy** caused the poet to swing between emotional extremes, rejoicing one moment and lamenting the next.

LOG ON ▶ **Literature** Online

Selection Resources For Selection Quizzes, eFlashcards, and Reading-Writing Connection activities, go to glencoe.com and enter QuickPass code GLB9817u2.

After You Read

Assess

1. Students' answers will vary.

2. (a) War (b) He embraces both "mistresses" with similar passion and conviction.

3. (a) A sword, a horse, and a shield (b) He is totally committed to his cause.

4. (a) Honor and a sense of patriotic duty (b) Students' answers will vary.

5. A sense of duty, a responsibility to defend the crown, and an enthusiasm for righteous warfare

6. Students may say that such courtly attitudes, though rare today, may still be important to people who make great personal sacrifices for the public good, such as firefighters or those who serve in the military.

Literary Element

The paradox in lines 9–10 indicates that Lucasta will come to value her lover's unfaithfulness. The paradox in lines 11–12 contends that his love of honor increases his love for her.

Writing

Each letter should respond to the speaker's decision to go to war and include at least one paradox that supports and explains the letter writer's intent.

Progress Check

Can students identify paradox?

If No → See Unit 2 Teaching Resources Book, p. 339.

Reading Strategy

Students' paraphrases will probably lack the literary devices that Lovelace employs—patterns of rhythm, rhyme, parallelism, repetition, descriptive imagery, and figurative language.

 To create custom assessments online, go to Progress Reporter Online Assessment.

Vocabulary

1. The context provides a synonym, *pure*, for the word *chaste.*

2. Since his lover's inconstancy causes drastic changes in the poet's mood, it can be inferred that *inconstancy* means "changeable behavior."

Before You Read

Focus

Bellringer Options

Selection Focus
Transparency 22
Daily Language Practice
Transparency 37

Or have students write on the board things that they might say to someone who was taking too long to reach a decision (for example, "Get a move on!" or "Shake a leg!"). Explain that the poem they will be reading is about a man whose lover can't make up her mind about him.

Before You Read

To His Coy Mistress

Meet **Andrew Marvell**
(1621–1678)

Andrew Marvell's legacy has been, like that of many other poets from his era, mixed. Initially considered one of the great political satirists of his day, he is now mostly remembered for his love lyrics. During his life, Marvell brilliantly adapted his thought and art—moving with the political, religious, and artistic currents of the day. In so doing, Marvell was able to remain active and alive, producing what is now considered some of the best-loved poetry of his century.

> "The world in all doth but two nations bear—
> The good, the bad; and these mixed everywhere."
>
> —Andrew Marvell

Young Scholar Marvell was born in 1621 and educated at the University of Cambridge. He received his degree in 1639, though, as a result of his father's death two years later, his academic career came to an early end. In all likelihood, Marvell spent the next five years overseas working as a tutor.

Marvell began making favorable connections at the age of twenty-nine when he became tutor to the daughter of Sir Thomas Fairfax, Lord-General of Oliver Cromwell's Parliamentary army. At first, Marvell was opposed to the Cromwell government, but became very supportive, eventually writing such laudatory poems as "An Horatian Ode upon Cromwell's Return from Ireland" and "On the Death of O. C." By age thirty-four, Marvell was tutoring William Dutton, a boy for whom Cromwell himself was guardian. Four years later, he advanced his career further by becoming assistant to the Latin secretary for the Puritan Commonwealth: famed poet and essayist John Milton.

Parliamentarian and Poet In 1659 Marvell was elected to Parliament, in which he served for the remainder of his life. That next year, King Charles II was restored to the throne. Many supporters of the Puritan cause were imprisoned or killed. Astonishingly, Marvell managed to stay well positioned. This is doubly miraculous considering that Marvell was also writing scathing attacks on the monarchy, parodies of the king's speeches, and strongly opinionated political pamphlets and religious tracts.

The reprisals against supporters of the Commonwealth were indeed harsh. Cromwell's body was exhumed from its resting place at Westminster Abbey and put on display, various leaders were captured and executed, and prominent literary figures, including Milton, were forced into hiding. While the historical record is unclear, it is possible that Marvell intervened, saving the poet's life, thus allowing Milton to write his masterpiece, *Paradise Lost.*

When Marvell died in 1678, none of his poems had yet been printed. Even after their initial publication, Marvell was, for some time, still generally remembered as a political satirist. It wasn't until the nineteenth and twentieth centuries that Marvell's lyrics became widely read and appreciated.

 Literature Online

Author Search For more about Andrew Marvell, go to glencoe.com and enter QuickPass code GLB9817u2.

Selection Skills

Literary Elements
- Hyperbole (SE pp. 464–468)
- Carpe Diem (SE p. 468)

To His Coy Mistress

Listening/Speaking/Viewing Skills
- Analyze Art (TE p. 466)

Reading Skills
- Preview (SE pp. 464–469)

Vocabulary Skills
- Analogies (SE p. 469; TE p. 465)
- Academic Vocabulary (SE p. 469)

Writing Skills/Grammar
- Apply Hyperbole (SE p. 469)

Literature and Reading Preview

Connect to the Poem

In what ways can people's knowledge that they will eventually die give them a useful perspective on their daily life? Freewrite for a few minutes to generate ideas about this topic.

Build Background

"To His Coy Mistress" first appeared in print after Marvell's death, in a volume entitled *Miscellaneous Poems.* Mary Palmer, Marvell's housekeeper, arranged for the book's publication and referred to Marvell as her husband in its preface. Palmer claimed to be his wife by virtue of a secret marriage. Her claim was hotly disputed, however, giving rise to a lengthy lawsuit. Many people believe that she had the book published simply to give the appearance of being a devoted wife.

Set Purposes for Reading

Big Idea The Sacred and the Secular

As you read, ask yourself, How does the speaker use philosophical and religious notions to advance his secular argument?

Literary Element Hyperbole

Hyperbole is a figure of speech in which exaggeration is used to express strong emotion, make a point, or evoke humor. For example, when students say that "the lecture went on forever," they are using exaggeration to make their point and to generate a humorous effect. As you read, ask yourself, What examples of hyperbole do I see in this poem?

Reading Strategy Preview

To **preview** means to look over a selection before you read. Previewing lets you begin to see what you already know and what you'll need to know. Before you read, ask yourself, What do the title and illustration tell me about the poem's subject?

···

Tip: Taking Notes After scanning the title, the illustration, and the opening of the poem, write down predictions about the poem's content and theme. After you finish reading, verify or modify your predictions. Use a chart like this.

Predictions	Verify or Modify
The poem's title suggests that it will be addressed to a young woman.	This prediction was correct.

ANDREW MARVELL **465**

Vocabulary

hue (hū) *n.* a color, shade, or tint; p. 467 *The sky was full of many magnificent hues.*

strife (strīf) *n.* unrest or violent conflict; p. 467 *The city was engulfed in uncontrollable strife.*

Before You Read

Focus

Summary

To woo his beloved, the speaker of "To His Coy Mistress" praises her extravagantly and urges her not to waste time in giving in to him. The speaker shows both passion and wit in trying to coax his beloved.

For summaries in languages other than English, see Unit 2 Teaching Resources Book, pp. 345–350.

Vocabulary

Analogies Have groups of students use a dictionary and thesaurus to compile lists of synonyms for *hue* and synonyms and antonyms for *strife*. Then, have the groups create an analogy for each word. Each group should then present and explain their analogies.

For additional vocabulary practice, see Unit 2 Teaching Resources Book, p. 353.

English Learners

DIFFERENTIATED INSTRUCTION

Intermediate Ask English learners to list words that people in love might use to praise each other. Tell students that the speaker in this poem extremely admires the woman he loves. Then, have students use a dictionary to check the meanings of some of the words the speaker uses:

praise, gaze, adore, amorous, pleasures

Ask students to look for these words as they read the poem. Have them think about how the speaker uses the words to try to achieve his goal: the affections of the woman he loves.

Teach

Preview **Answer:** *They suggest that the poem will contain an argument or admonishment. They also convey what may be a major theme of the poem—that in a world where time is limited, we must take our pleasures as they come or risk losing them forever.*

 For additional practice using the reading skill or strategy, see Unit 2 Teaching Resources Book, p. 352.

View the Art ★

Fragonard was known for indulgent images that hint at pleasure and even scandal. **Ask:** Does this image reflect the mental picture you have of the poem's speaker and his "coy mistress"? Explain. *(Answers will vary; accept all reasonable responses.)*

Reading Practice

SPIRAL REVIEW **Humor** Remind students that writers sometimes use humor to make a serious point. **Ask:** Besides describing an amusing attempt at seduction, what other point might Marvell be making about life? *(Life is fleeting, and we should make the most of it.)* Would he be less effective if he simply stated this fact explicitly? *(He might come off as preachy or boringly puritanical.)* Point out that some of literature's most enduring writers (Mark Twain, Jane Austen) have used humor in similar ways.

The Stolen Kiss. Jean-Honore Fragonard. Oil on canvas. Hermitage Museum, St. Petersburg, Russia. ★

To His Coy Mistress

Andrew Marvell

    Had we but world enough, and time,
This coyness,[1] lady, were no crime.
We would sit down, and think which way
To walk, and pass our long love's day.
5 Thou by the Indian Ganges'[2] side
Shouldst rubies find; I by the tide
Of Humber[3] would complain.[4] I would
Love you ten years before the flood,[5]
And you should, if you please, refuse
10 Till the conversion of the Jews.[6]

1. *Coyness* may be modesty or flirtatious, playful evasiveness.
2. The *Ganges* is a great river in northern India.
3. The *Humber* is a muddy river in Marvell's hometown of Hull.
4. Here, *complain* means to write love complaints, or songs lamenting the cruelty of love.
5. By *flood,* the speaker means the flooding of the world associated with Noah in the biblical book of Genesis.
6. In Marvell's time, Christians believed that Jews would convert to Christianity just before the world's end.

1 Preview *What do these first two lines suggest to you about the content of this poem?*

My vegetable love[7] should grow
Vaster than empires, and more slow;
An hundred years should go to praise
Thine eyes, and on thy forehead gaze;

15 Two hundred to adore each breast,
But thirty thousand to the rest;
An age at least to every part,
And the last age should show your heart.
For, lady, you deserve this state,[8]

20 Nor would I love at lower rate.
   But at my back I always hear
Time's wingèd chariot hurrying near;
And yonder all before us lie
Deserts of vast eternity.

25 Thy beauty shall no more be found,
Nor, in thy marble vault, shall sound
My echoing song; then worms shall try
That long-preserved virginity,
And your quaint honor turn to dust,

30 And into ashes all my lust.
The grave's a fine and private place,
But none, I think, do there embrace.
   Now, therefore, while the youthful **hue**
Sits on thy skin like morning dew,

35 And while thy willing soul transpires
At every pore with instant fires,
Now let us sport us while we may,
And now, like amorous birds of prey,
Rather at once our time devour

40 Than languish in his slow-chapped[9] power.
Let us roll all our strength and all
Our sweetness up into one ball,
And tear our pleasures with rough **strife**
Thorough[10] the iron gates of life:

45 Thus, though we cannot make our sun
Stand still, yet we will make him run.

Hyperbole *How is this hyperbole effective?* **2**

The Sacred and the Secular *How do these lines emphasize the speaker's concern with this life as opposed to an afterlife?* **3**

Vocabulary

hue (hū) *n.* a color, shade, or tint
strife (strīf) *n.* unrest or violent conflict

---

7. *Vegetable love* is love that grows slowly and passively, like a plant.

8. Here, *state* means "dignity."

9. *Slow-chapped* means "slow-jawed," suggesting the image of time slowly chewing.

10. *Thorough* means "through."

ANDREW MARVELL **467**

Teach

Literary Element   2

Hyperbole **Answer:** *The extravagance of the speaker's argument, exaggerating everything to the point of ridiculousness, keeps the tone superficial and his appeal light-hearted. The case he makes is too extreme to be taken seriously, yet it involves issues all mortals must consider—namely, aging and death.*

Big Idea   3

The Sacred and the Secular
Answer: *The speaker refers almost exclusively to things of this world. He is preoccupied with the passage of time and on the physical attributes of his lady rather than spiritual matters.*

APPROACHING If students have difficulty, ask them to make a list of the speaker's many references to time. Remind them that the sacred is more concerned with eternal, timeless things. This speaker, in contrast, thinks more about time and its passing.

 To check students' understanding of the selection, see Unit 2 Teaching Resources Book, p. 354.

English Learners

DIFFERENTIATED INSTRUCTION

Advanced Write the following on the board: *vaster than empires, time's winged chariot, deserts of vast eternity*. After students read the poem, ask them to use context clues to explain the phrases. Students can look up the definitions of the words and speculate on their meanings.

Approaching Level

DIFFERENTIATED INSTRUCTION

Emerging In "To His Coy Mistress," Marvell employs phrases that may elude some students. Suggest students close their eyes and try to picture what each figurative expression describes.

After You Read

Assess

1. Students' answers will vary.
2. (a) Coyness (b) She is wasting time they could be spending together.
3. (a) Write love songs, allow his love to grow slowly, and praise his beloved's attributes for ages (b) They show that he would woo her slowly if he could.
4. (a) A winged chariot (b) That death is catching up to him
5. (a) First, he claims he would spend ages admiring his love. Then, he argues that time is running out. Lastly, he proposes that they should enjoy life while still young. (b) Answers will vary.
6. (a) A series of rhymed couplets (b) Possible answer: They support the playful tone of the poem.
7. (a) While still young, they should attack time rather than be its victims. In the first part of the poem, time is all powerful. (b) It ends the poem on an optimistic note.
8. The speaker claims, contrary to Christian belief, that beyond death there is nothing but "deserts of vast eternity." Thus, he focuses on earthly joys rather than on preparation for an afterlife.
9. Lines 5 through 18 are a parody of the hyperbole that sometimes appears in traditional love poems.

468

After You Read

Respond and Think Critically

Respond and Interpret

1. (a)What are your reactions to the speaker in this poem? (b)What might you like to say to him?
2. (a)According to the speaker, what is his sweetheart's crime? (b)Why do you think he regards this as a crime?
3. (a)What are some of the things the speaker claims he would do if he had unlimited time? (b)How do these claims help the speaker's argument?
4. (a)What image of time does the speaker present in lines 21–22? (b)What do you think he means to suggest with this image?

Analyze and Evaluate

5. (a)Summarize the main parts of the speaker's argument. (b)In your opinion, is this a convincing argument? Why or why not?

6. (a)What is the poem's rhyme scheme? (b)What effect do the rhymes have on the poem?
7. (a)Restate the speaker's recommendations in the poem's final paragraph, lines 33–46. How is this portion of the poem different from the rest of the poem? (b)Why is this an effective way to end the poem?

Connect

8. **Big Idea** The Sacred and the Secular What details can you identify in this poem that undercut the common religious beliefs of the time?
9. **Connect to the Author** During his lifetime, Marvell was known primarily as a writer of satire. Where in the poem does he seem to be making fun of traditional love poems?

Literary Element Hyperbole

Humor is an integral part of **hyperbole**. When hyperbole appears in literature, it is often used expressly for this purpose. Like hyperbole, which exaggerates facts or circumstances, **understatement** can be employed in a similar way. Understatement is language that makes something seem less important than it really is. Like hyperbole, it can add humor or direct the reader's attention to something the author wants to emphasize.

1. What understatement appears in lines 31–32? In what ways is this example an effective use of the device?
2. Why might hyperbole and understatement be effective techniques to use together?

Review: Carpe Diem

As you learned on page 448, *carpe diem* is a Latin phrase meaning "Seize the day"—in other words, "Make the most out of every moment." In *carpe diem* poems, the speaker emphasizes the shortness of life.

Partner Activity In "To His Coy Mistress," Marvell makes use of *carpe diem* motif. Throughout the poem, the speaker makes many references to the passing of time and urges his mistress to seize the day. Working with a partner, identify three images that further the speaker's message, and explain how they support the *carpe diem* motif.

Literary Element

1. He says that physical love does not take place in a grave. This reinforces his argument that the lovers should seize the day.
2. Together, they create delightful surprises as the reader's expectations are amusingly thwarted.

Review: Carpe Diem

Check that students' examples are indeed used in the poem to support the motif of *carpe diem*.

Reading Strategy Previewing

Previewing is the first step in encountering a text for the first time. It allows you, as a reader, to make predictions about the text and to set a purpose for your reading. While previewing, you are often able to determine the genre, the subject, and perhaps even the theme of a work. Review the chart you made while you were previewing the poem, and then answer the following questions.

1. In general, were your predictions about "To His Coy Mistress" correct? Explain.

2. Why might previewing be less than effective as a way to predict the theme of a literary work?

Vocabulary Practice

Practice with Analogies Choose the word that best completes each analogy. To complete an analogy, decide on the relationship represented by the first pair of words, then apply that relationship to the second set of words.

1. hue : color :: noise :
   a. feeling   **b.** hearing   **c.** sound

2. war : strife :: connection :
   a. disorder   **b.** bond   **c.** disruption

Academic Vocabulary

In "To His Coy Mistress," the speaker encourages his sweetheart not to waste time, because life is **brief.**

Brief is an academic word. On a quiz, you might be asked to write a **brief** summary of a literary work in order to prove that you had read it.

A four-square organizer helps you visualize a word and its meaning. Fill out a diagram like the one below for the word brief.

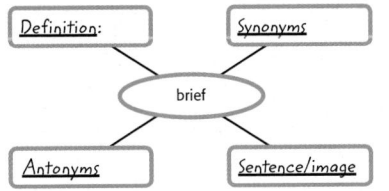

For more on academic vocabulary, see pages 56 and R81.

Write with Style

Apply Hyperbole

Assignment Though Marvell wrote "To His Coy Mistress" over three centuries ago, its message is timeless and universal. Identify a theme of the poem and provide examples of hyperbole that Marvell uses to support the theme.

Get Ideas Reread "To His Coy Mistress," stating the themes of the poem in your own words. Then identify examples of hyperbole in the poem.

EXAMPLE:

Themes

- Life is short.
- We have to make the most of the time we have.
- Love is what life is all about.

Hyperbole

- "I would / Love you ten years before the flood"
- "My vegetable love should grow / Vaster than empires, and more slow"
- "An hundred years should go to praise / Thine eyes"
- "An age at least to every part"

Finally, examine the instances of hyperbole you've identified and determine which theme they support.

Give It Structure Clearly state the theme you've chosen to focus on. Present the examples of hyperbole in a logical order—as they appear in the poem, for example, or from least to most important. Be sure to indicate how each supports the theme.

Look at Language Be sure you quote lines from the poem exactly as they appear. In your explanations, choose words that convey your ideas precisely.

LOG ON **Literature** Online

Selection Resources For Selection Quizzes, eFlashcards, and Reading-Writing Connection activities, go to glencoe.com and enter QuickPass code GLB9817u2.

ANDREW MARVELL   **469**

Reading Strategy

1. Students' answers will vary.
2. Possible answer: Early in a work, a writer may set up expectations, only to undermine them later in the work through complications or irony.

Vocabulary

1. c   **2.** b

Academic Vocabulary

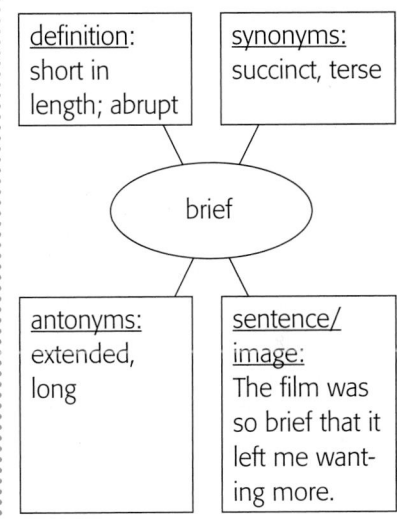

Write with Style

Use these criteria in evaluating student writing:

- It identifies a theme of the poem.
- It correctly quotes examples of hyperbole and explains how they support the theme.
- The ideas are presented in a logical order.

 For additional assessment, see Assessment Resources, pp. 139–140.

To create custom assessments online, go to Progress Reporter Online Assessment.

 To create custom assessments using software, use ExamView Assessment Suite.

Progress Check

Can students identify hyperbole?

If No → See Unit 2 Teaching Resources Book, p. 351.

Research Report

Focus

Bellringer

Ask students which historical periods intrigue them most and why. **Ask:** How can a literary text tell us something about the period in which it was written?

Have students list some works that were written in their favorite time periods. (For this, you may want to have a world history timeline available.)

Summary

In this workshop, students will write a literary research paper in which they investigate the relationship between a literary text and its historical context. In addition, focus lessons on using transitions between paragraphs and on using quotations correctly are provided.

 For Writing Workshop graphic organizer and rubric, see Unit 2 Teaching Resources, pp. 357–359.

Workshop Resources

Print Materials

- Unit 2 Teaching Resources Book pp. 357–359
- Writing Kit
- Success in Writing: Research and Reports
- Grammar and Language Transparencies 47, 87
- Writing Workshop Transparencies 11–15
- Daily Language Practice Transparencies 13, 37, 44, 94, 141, 148

470

Learning Objectives

For pages 470–479

In this workshop, you will focus on the following objectives:

Writing: Writing a research report.

Grammar: Understanding how to use quotation marks.

Writing Workshop

Research Report

Literature Connection Queen Elizabeth I's speech at Tilbury, a primary source from the English Renaissance, gives modern readers a sense of the personal and historical context of the attack of the Spanish Armada in 1588.

> *"We have been persuaded by some that are careful of our safety, to take heed how we commit our selves to armed multitudes, for fear of treachery; but I assure you I do not desire to live to distrust my faithful and loving people."*

In a **research report**, you investigate a variety of sources in order to draw and support your own conclusions about an appropriately narrow topic. Use the goals and strategies below to write a successful research report.

Checklist

Goals	Strategies
To state an original, well-researched thesis	☑ Use multiple sources to draw a central conclusion about your topic
To analyze and synthesize supporting evidence	☑ Quote, paraphrase, and summarize information from a variety of sources
	☑ Consider and comment on the relative value of sources
	☑ Combine ideas from different sources to lead to fresh insights
To organize your ideas logically	☑ Write well-structured body paragraphs to support ideas presented in your introduction and to lead smoothly to your conclusion
To use sources correctly and honestly	☑ Quote correctly and attribute all sources
	☑ Use standardized citations
	☑ Avoid copyright infringement

Writing Process

At any stage of a writing process, you may think of new ideas. Feel free to return to earlier stages as you write.

Prewrite

Draft

Revise

Focus Lesson: Transitions Between Paragraphs

Edit and Proofread

Focus Lesson: Quotations

Present

Technology

- Literature Online: Writing Resources and Grammar Resources, www.glencoe.com
- Online Essay Grader, www.glencoe.com
- Student Presentation Builder on StudentWorks Plus CD-ROM
- Media Workshop DVD
- Online Student Edition

Assignment: Write a Research Report

Write a research report of at least 1,500 words. As you work, keep your audience and purpose in mind.

Audience: other students and people familiar with your chosen literary text

Purpose: to investigate a connection between a literary text and its historical context

Prewrite

Explore Ideas As you read through Unit Two, did you wonder how Queen Elizabeth's speech at Tilbury affected the battle or what a performance of *Macbeth* would have been like in Shakespeare's time? For your own report, you might consider literary texts that interest you and explore the relationship between a text and the history, culture, and author that shaped it.

▶ **Ask Questions** Think of questions you want to answer and use your curiosity to guide your research. **1**

▶ **Narrow Your Topic** Once you have a general topic that interests you, narrow the topic to fit the scope of the assignment. Too broad a topic will be overwhelming and difficult to focus, whereas too narrow a topic may not provide enough varied, reliable sources. Revise the question guiding your research until its scope fits that of the assignment.

Gather Research Now try to answer your research questions. Search through a combination of sources, such as online databases, general reference books, periodicals, the Internet, historical records, and documents. Ask a librarian for additional ideas.

▶ **Develop a General Overview** Familiarize yourself with background information from reference books and the Internet to develop a general understanding of your topic.

▶ **Consult a Variety of Sources with Diverse Perspectives** Include information from several sources and different viewpoints. Primary sources are original documents—such as letters, newspaper articles, historical records, and interviews—from the time period. Secondary sources are written by people who did not personally experience or influence the time or event. Include relevant information on your topic from a variety of perspectives.

▶ **Use Reliable Sources** As you conduct your research, evaluate the reliability and validity of your sources to make sure that they are not outdated, biased, or inaccurate.

Real-World Connection

You might apply your research skills to planning a trip to a college campus or to learning about job opportunities at a company.

Journalists' Questions

Create a cluster diagram like the one below to explore different ways to approach a research idea. Fill in the center with an idea and write a relevant question beginning with each word surrounding the center. Then choose the most intriguing question as a starting point for further development of a topic.

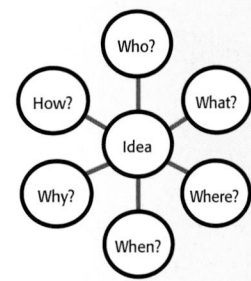

LOG ON ▶ Literature Online

Writing and Research For prewriting, drafting, and revising tools, go to glencoe.com and enter the QuickPass code GLB9817u2.

English Learners

DIFFERENTIATED INSTRUCTION

Intermediate Tell students that literary research is their response to the questions that they ask while experiencing the world an author has created. These questions may concern such elements as character, style, setting, theme, and literary movement.

▪ Their original text—the literary work they have studied firsthand—is called the **primary source**.

▪ Those works that present information as well as the opinions and ideas of other scholars are called **secondary sources**.

Writing Workshop

Research Report

Teach

Big Idea | 1

Humanists and Courtiers
Remind students that the Renaissance era, and in particular the humanist movement, was one of great intellectual inquiry and artistic activity. **Ask:** How does the literary research paper exemplify the spirit of this age? *(Like the Renaissance, the essence of a literary research paper is intellectual inquiry. And just as scholars and artists rediscovered and shed light on the literary works of their ancestors, we will make discoveries through our research and writing in this class.)*

Writing Process

Prewrite To help them focus on their topic, encourage students to brainstorm for ideas by using a cluster or web diagram. Ask them to record their generating topic or idea in the center of a blank page and then spontaneously to add related ideas around it. Allowing their instincts to guide them, students will find that what they really want to write about will begin to take shape.

Writing Workshop

Teach

Writing Skills

Thesis Statement Remind students that a thesis is a declarative sentence that

- focuses on one well-defined idea,
- makes an arguable assertion (is capable of being supported), and
- prepares readers for the body of the paper and foreshadows the conclusion.

Writing Skills

Organization Explain that when making multiple points in an essay, students should be sure to place those points in the same order in the paper as they are in in the thesis. They should think of the thesis as a map to the essay's organization. If the map does not match the layout of the essay, readers may become lost in the writing.

Take Notes As you look through sources, jot down important ideas, facts, and quotations. Whether you record your notes on note cards, in a notebook, or on separate computer files, keep your information organized. Record full publishing information for each source (see pages R31–R32) and assign it a number or the author's last name. Then use this number or name to label any notes taken from the source. This identification technique will save you time and will help you compile your works-cited list later.

> BIBLIOGRAPHY NOTE CARD
>
> Wells, Stanley   2
> Shakespeare: A Life in Drama
> New York: W. W. Norton & Company, 1995
> Wilmette Public Library
> 822.33 WE

Avoid Plagiarism

Plagiarism infringes on the author's copyright, which is his or her exclusive right to reproduce the work, or any part of it, as well as to make derivative works from it. Copyright infringement is a punishable offense.

▶ **Quote** Record direct quotations word for word, including punctuation. Use direct quotations sparingly—for emphasis or to make a point.

▶ **Paraphrase** Restate someone else's idea in your own words. If you substitute a few of your own words in a direct quotation and call it a paraphrase, you have commited plagiarism because most of the words are still the source's words, not yours.

▶ **Summarize** Condense information to its key points.

> SUMMARY NOTE CARD
>
> Shakespeare: A Life in Drama   2
> Shakespeare focused on writing dialogue
> rather than on stage directions.
> (summary) page 28

Write a Thesis and Make an Outline Write a thesis statement to sum up the main idea based on your research. The thesis will guide your report. (Keep in mind, though, that you will probably revise your thesis as you gain new insights while writing.) Finally, use your notes to help you make an outline, including only the information that is relevant to your thesis. Choose an effective way to order the main ideas in your outline and keep related ideas together.

Writing Practice

Test the Thesis Caution students not to commit themselves too soon to a thesis. They should use their original ideas as a first step that may lead to even better theses.

When they finally narrow down their working theses, they should consider the following questions:

1. Is the thesis broad enough to require a variety of resources?
2. Is it narrow enough to research in depth?
3. Is it original enough to interest both me and my readers?
4. Will it lead to new insights?

Draft

Tie It All Together To begin drafting, follow your outline, revising the order of ideas as necessary. Remember that writing a research paper is more than just reporting facts and quotations. Make distinctions between the relative worth and meaning of the facts and ideas you find, and draw your own conclusions for the reader. Show how each of your main points relates to your thesis, and explain important relationships.

Analyze a Workshop Model

Here is a final draft of a research report. Read the paper and pay close attention to the comments in the margin. They point out features to include in your own paper. Then answer the questions in the margin and use the answers to guide you as you write your own draft.

Shakespeare: Man of the Theater

Readers of Shakespeare's plays, such as <u>Macbeth</u>, will better appreciate his scripts if they consider the historical background of the Elizabethan theater and Shakespeare's versatile role as a man *of* the theater. As Stanley Wells points out, Shakespeare "was a man of the theatre in at least three different senses: as a business man, as an actor, and as a playwright" (23). <u>Macbeth</u> serves as a model to illustrate Shakespeare's broad range of theatrical talents—directing, producing, staging, performing, and writing.

At the height of his career, Shakespeare was writing plays with a single stage in mind: the Globe Theatre. Although he began his career writing for many playhouses, he wrote his most famous plays, including <u>Macbeth</u>, for the Globe. Shakespeare, one of the Globe's co-owners, helped build the theater in 1599 (Gurr 18).

The Globe was a round outdoor venue enclosed in wood. Although the stage was built so that the actors were in shadow rather than under direct sunlight (Gurr 22), there was no way to adjust the lighting onstage to suggest nighttime or a stormy setting. In addition, Shakespeare's plays had no intermissions or breaks when an act or scene changed (Gurr 38). Because of the lack of scenery, intervals, and controlled lighting, Shakespeare had

Exposition

Writing Frames

As you read the workshop model, think about the writer's use of the following frames:

- For example, note the distinctions between _____.

- Based on _____, one can conclude that _____.

- As _____ notes in <title of work>, _____.

Consider using frames like these in your own research report.

Thesis Statement

State your thesis—the main idea that you will develop in your research paper—in your introduction. How does a thesis statement help guide readers?

Organization

Present factual details and other evidence in your body paragraphs. How does this paragraph provide important background information as well as supporting details?

Teach

Writing Process

Draft Have students try freewriting their first draft. Explain that freewriting is a discovery process during which a writer freely explores a topic and lets his or her creativity be the guide. In the first draft, tell students not to stop to check spelling, punctuation, or grammar; doing so will disrupt the flow of discovery and creative energy.

(**ENGLISH LEARNERS**) During freewriting, English learners may write some of their thoughts in their primary language instead of in English. Allow them to do so if it helps them express their ideas on paper. The language can be revised in the next draft.

Writing Skills

Thesis Statement **Answer:** *It indicates the basic idea that will be elaborated on and supported throughout the paper.*

Writing Skills

Supporting Evidence **Answer:** *These details show how careful Shakespeare was to ensure that his work would be presented exactly as he had intended when he wrote it.*

English Learners

DIFFERENTIATED INSTRUCTION

Beginning When it is time for students to review and polish their sentences, encourage them to work with partners, reading their papers aloud and checking word choice and word placement. Through this process, they should be able to hear what works and what does not. Remind them also of the importance of conciseness.

Approaching Level

DIFFERENTIATED INSTRUCTION

Emerging Ask students to look at the workshop model and to phrase its thesis statement as a question. (*Do we better appreciate Shakespeare's plays if we consider the Elizabethan theater and his various roles in it?*) Then have students write their own thesis statements as questions.

Research Report

Teach

Writing Skills

Organization Answer: *The thesis posits that Shakespeare's plays directly reflect his involvement in the Elizabethan theater. After discussing how the poetry of the plays supports that idea, the writer shows in this paragraph how Shakespeare's stage directions also support the idea.*

Writing Skills

Analysis and Evaluation
Answer: *The documented facts in this selection are followed by citations. The conclusions reached or assumptions cannot be documented.*

Organization

Write well-structured paragraphs that relate to the thesis. How does this paragraph build on the thesis introduced in the first paragraph?

---

to rely mainly on dialogue to indicate setting and passage of time. He compensated by writing descriptive poetry to "paint the set" (Papp and Kirkland 138). For example, in Macbeth, Act 3, scene 2, Macbeth describes the approaching night to Lady Macbeth:

> Come, seeling night,
> Scarf up the tender eye of pitiful day,
> And with thy bloody and invisible hand
> Cancel and tear to pieces that great bond
> Which keeps me pale! Light thickens, and the crow
> Makes wing to th' rooky wood.
> Good things of day begin to droop and drowse,
> While night's black agents to their preys do rouse.

These lines help the audience envision the setting changing from dawn to dusk while revealing Macbeth's increasing remorse for Duncan's murder.

Shakespeare's stage directions, though sparse, also helped minimize the limitations of the Elizabethan stage. In addition to suggesting entrances and exits, the stage directions often include predictable sounds to summon particular characters. In Macbeth, for example, thunder always introduces the witches and apparitions, a trumpet flourish summons royalty and authority figures, and the drum signals the march of soldiers. The bell is a more sinister signal that also becomes a clue for the audience. After the bell rings in Act 2, scene 1, Macbeth says, "I go, and it is done; the bell invites me. / Hear it not, Duncan, for it is a knell, / That summons thee to heaven, or to hell." The summons of the bell is echoed later in the act, after Macduff finds Duncan's corpse and cries, "Ring the alarum bell! Murder and Treason! . . . Ring the bell" (II.iii). Ironically, once the bell rings, Lady Macbeth wakes and cries, "What's the business, / That such a hideous trumpet calls to parley / The sleepers of the house?" (II.iii).

With the exception of some key stage directions, what most contemporary audiences notice is Shakespeare's *lack* of specific direction in the existing plays. Because of Shakespeare's active

---

Writing Practice

Quotations Stress the value of using quotations from primary and secondary sources to illustrate statements and to give additional support for a main argument. Remind students, however, not to overuse them: Quotations should not constitute more than 20 percent of a paper. Explain that it is not enough just to provide a quotation; students also need to explain how the quotation illustrates the point they are trying to make. Suggest that students work in pairs to review their use of quotations.

involvement in the production of his plays, such directions were not needed at the time the plays were written. Shakespeare would have had an intimate knowledge of his company and which types of roles his talented actors could best perform. From evidence in early manuscripts, it appears that he wrote certain characters with specific actors from his company in mind (Wells 28). When his company, the Chamberlain's Men, began performing at the Globe, "Shakespeare was at the height of his powers, and his confidence in his colleagues was, by any standard, unusual" (Thompson 184).

In addition, Shakespeare as playwright was likely to be the director of his plays, guiding the actors toward his vision of the performance (Papp and Kirkland 149; Wells 29). Based on the number of plays performed and the lack of rehearsal time, one can conclude that Shakespeare's main focus was on dialogue, rather than on "prescribing the gestures, facial expressions, and actions that should accompany the words," even when such cues established meaning (Wells 28). This focus on dialogue to the exclusion of stage directions results in an openness to interpretation for modern readers, actors, and directors (Wells 28). For Shakespeare, though, who knew his actors and knew he himself would be involved in rehearsal, the method was simply more practical. Unlike modern performers, Shakespeare's did not need detailed stage directions. Shakespeare could expect an accurate performance because of his personal collaboration with the actors.

Like his stage directions, or lack of them, Shakespeare's dialogue was also influenced by the practicalities of the stage. First, to succeed, a play had to draw an audience. As Alfred Harbage notes in Shakespeare's Audience, "Unlike some other audiences existing in and near his time, Shakespeare's audience was literally popular, ascending through each gradation from potboy to prince. It was the one to which he had been conditioned early and for which he never ceased to write" (159). In addition, unlike modern audiences, Elizabethan audiences reacted more to the auditory than to the visual. Many of those who attended the Globe were illiterate,

Exposition

Analysis and Evaluation

Evaluate ideas from a variety of sources, making distinctions between offhand judgments and documented facts.

Standardized Citations

A standard citation in MLA style consists of the author's last name and page number; when more than one source is used to state a fact or idea, use a semicolon to separate them. Find the citation on the next page that has no page number. Why is it missing?

Teach

Writing Skills

Tone and Style Answer: *The writer's formal tone and style of the inclusion of citations reflects the purpose of informing and providing facts for an audience who may be unknowledgeable about how Shakespeare focused on dialogue rather than stage directions.*

Literary History ☆

Macbeth *Macbeth*, one of Shakespeare's most well-known tragedies, was written between 1606 and 1607 and was published in 1623 as part of Shakespeare's First Folio. The play was loosely based on the story of a real Macbeth, a Scottish king who took the throne in A.D. 1040 after killing King Duncan I on the battlefield. Six years after taking the throne, Macbeth was nearly dethroned by the Earl of Northumbria and was finally killed in a battle in 1057 by Malcolm, who later became king of Scotland.

English Learners

DIFFERENTIATED INSTRUCTION

Intermediate Once students have written a working outline, discuss the method of deduction for organizing it.

Explain that deduction

- is a process of development that moves from the general to the specific
- is the most commonly used form of organization for literary research.

Explain also that a thesis statement is the generalization that leads to the specific

support provided by primary and secondary sources. The thesis is stated early in the paper. The body of the paper then proceeds to provide the facts, examples, and analogies that flow logically from that thesis.

Writing Workshop

Teach

Writing Skills

Secondary Source **Answer:** *A primary source might well be long and unwieldy, so several quotations could be needed to make a single point. Using the secondary source allows the writer to make the point more succinctly.*

Writing Skills

Rhetorical Choices **Answer:** *Natural language makes the report easy to follow. Sentence variety helps to make the writing interesting. Repetition helps to emphasize key points.*

Literary History ☆

Shakespeare's Plays As was normal in the period, Shakespeare based many of his plays on the work of other playwrights and recycled older stories and historical material. For example, *Hamlet* (c. 1601) is probably a reworking of an older, lost play (the so-called *Ur-Hamlet*), and *King Lear* is an adaptation of an older play, *King Leir*.

Secondary Source

Use a variety of primary and secondary sources. Why might a secondary source be more effective than a primary source in illustrating this point?

Synthesis

Synthesize ideas to create fresh insights.

and a play's dialogue, like a church's sermon or a storytelling, became a type of learning (Gurr 26; "All About Shakespeare"). For Elizabethan audiences, "the central feature of the plays was speech" (Gurr 26). The nuances of dialogue would not be lost on an Elizabethan audience, and Shakespeare could use particular diction and rhythms to reveal character (Sutherland 119).

For example, note the distinctions between the characters' language in Macbeth. Because most of the characters in Macbeth are royalty or of the nobility, they speak in blank verse (Nostbakken 15). On the other hand, the drunken Porter, a servant, speaks in prose. The witches speak in verse that often rhymes, emphasizing a chantlike quality. Although blank verse sounds more eloquent than prose, using blank verse was also a practical maneuver; its consistent rhythm made the lines easier for the actors to memorize (Papp and Kirkland 169). Any change from verse to prose or vice versa was a signal to the audience. For example, Lady Macbeth speaks prose instead of her usual blank verse in Act 5, scene 1:

> To bed, to bed! There's knocking at the gate. Come, come, come, come, give me your hand! What's done cannot be undone. To bed, to bed, to bed!

Here Lady Macbeth is sleepwalking. Her repetitive, uncontrolled prose reveals her changed state and exposes how the murder has affected her character (Nostbakken 15).

Despite Shakespeare's attention to dialogue, as a "man of the theater" his focus was on a play's successful performance, not on its polished written form. Lines were revised during the rehearsal process, and whole parts may have been added or deleted during rehearsal as needed (Wells 29; Nostbakken 13–14). In addition, because of a dearth of copyright laws during the time and the prevailing attitude that stage plays were not serious literature, printing plays was not a priority for most playwrights (Papp and Kirkland 139). To people involved in theater during Elizabethan times, a stage play was a "passing event," not a "literary text" (Papp and Kirkland 140). About half of Shakespeare's plays were

☆

Research Practice

Navigate the Internet **Say:** Your thesis and your working outline are the primary compasses that will help you navigate the variety of sources available. These include library as well as Internet sources.

Explain that there are several Web pages devoted to individual authors. Have

students try entering an author's name on any of the popular search engines. Remind students to research with caution: The Internet is to be used as a resource tool only. Students must still do their own writing.

printed before his death, although "there is nothing to suggest that he did anything either to prepare the plays for reading or to see them through the press" (Wells 30). The written plays served as guides, but the true accomplishment was the performance.

To understand Shakespeare's <u>Macbeth</u> today, one must keep in mind the particular theater for which Shakespeare was writing. By understanding the Elizabethan stage, the needs of its audience, and Shakespeare's personal involvement in the production of his plays, modern readers, audiences, and directors gain insight into Shakespeare's artistry. The stage informed every aspect of his plays; to read Shakespeare's plays as part of the Elizabethan world enriches the theatergoer's experience.

Exposition

Conclusion

Summarize your main points and add related insight in your conclusion. What does or does not make this conclusion effective?

Works Cited

"All About Shakespeare." http://www.pbs.org/standarddeviantstv/ transcript_shakespeare.html.

Gurr, Andrew, with John Orrell. <u>Rebuilding Shakespeare's Globe.</u> New York: Routledge, 1989.

Harbage, Alfred. <u>Shakespeare's Audience.</u> New York and London: Columbia UP, 1969.

Nostbakken, Faith. <u>Understanding Macbeth: A Student Casebook to Issues, Sources, and Historical Documents.</u> Westport: Greenwood, 1997.

Papp, Joseph, and Elizabeth Kirkland. <u>Shakespeare Alive!</u> New York: Bantam, 1988.

Shakespeare, William. <u>Macbeth.</u> <u>Glencoe Literature: The Reader's Choice.</u> New York: Glencoe, 2009.

Sutherland, James. "How the Characters Talk." <u>Shakespeare's World.</u> Ed. James Sutherland and Joel Hurstfield. New York: St. Martin's, 1964.

Thompson, Peter. "English Renaissance and Restoration Theatre." <u>The Oxford Illustrated History of Theatre.</u> Ed. John Russell Brown. Oxford: Oxford UP, 1995.

Wells, Stanley. <u>Shakespeare: A Life in Drama.</u> New York: Norton, 1995.

Reliable Sources

Use a variety of reliable sources. What indicates that this source is probably reliable?

Variety of Sources

Use a variety of sources, such as books, encyclopedias, the Internet, newspapers, letters, and historical records. When might a writer use an encyclopedia?

Writing Workshop

Research Report

Teach

Writing Skills

Conclusion Answer: *The writer has returned to the thesis, synthesized the information presented in the body, and arrived at a deep understanding of the material.*

Writing Skills

Reliable Sources Answer: *PBS is a widely known and reputable public television network, often acclaimed for its in-depth coverage.*

Writing Skills

Variety of Sources Answer: *A writer might use an encyclopedia when he or she needs simple background material or a general perspective on the chosen subject matter before moving to more specific and key details.*

Cultural History ☆

Sound Effects The Elizabethan theater used a variety of sound effects. In addition to the trumpet blast that summoned the audiences to the theater, music played an important role in setting the mood of the plays. The actors also used devices to create the sounds of thunder, running horses, falling rain, and cannon blasts.

English Learners

DIFFERENTIATED INSTRUCTION

Advanced Tell students that by combining sentences they can show how ideas are related.

Ask them to compare these expressions:

- The British already controlled India. They made Burma a province of that country.

- Because the British already controlled India, they made Burma a province of that country.

Have students discuss the subtle change resulting from subordinating one of these ideas. Urge them to experiment with various combinations as they revise their drafts.

Research Report

Teach

Writing Skills

Peer Review Encourage a "cooling off" period to help students forget what they *meant* to say and see more clearly what they actually *did* say. As students exchange drafts, urge honest but constructive criticism.

ENGLISH LEARNERS Pair a stronger writer with a writer who needs more assistance. Stronger writers' work can provide a model for English learners when they are writing their own reports.

Writing Process

Revise Have students review the checklist of questions in the rubric. This time have them imagine how members of their intended audience would relate each question to the drafted paper. Then have students revise their papers accordingly.

Traits of Strong Writing

Include these traits of strong writing to express your ideas effectively.

Ideas

Organization

Voice

Word Choice

Sentence Fluency

Conventions

Presentation

For more information on using the Traits of Strong Writing, see pages R28–R30.

Word Choice

This academic vocabulary word appears in the student model:

minimize (mi´ nə mīz) *v.* to reduce or keep to a minimum; *Shakespeare's stage directions, though sparse, also helped minimize the limitations of the Elizabethan stage.* Using academic vocabulary may help strengthen your writing. Try to use one or two academic vocabulary words in your research report. See the complete list on pages R81–R83.

 **Literature** Online

Writing and Research For editing and publishing tools, go to glencoe.com and enter QuickPass code GLB9817u2.

Revise

Peer Review Exchange drafts with a partner to help you identify strengths and weaknesses in your research papers. Both you and your partner should note any passages that seem unclear, irrelevant, or out of place. Return the papers and discuss ways to improve them. Refer to the traits of strong writing as you revise. Use the checklist below to help you evaluate and strengthen each other's writing.

Checklist

☑ Do you begin with a strong, clear thesis statement to guide your paper?

☑ Do you support main points with well-documented details, facts, and examples from a variety of sources?

☑ Do you quote, paraphrase, and summarize information correctly from a variety of sources?

☑ Do you include a clear introduction, body, and conclusion?

☑ Do you synthesize information and comment on the relative value of sources?

☑ Do you use sources honestly and cite them correctly?

▶ Focus Lesson

Use Transitions Between Paragraphs

Transitions show the relationship between ideas. Guide your readers by carefully choosing transitional words and phrases to show the relationships between paragraphs and to improve the overall flow of your paper. You can also repeat key words and phrases from an earlier paragraph to create a link to a subsequent paragraph.

Draft:

Unlike modern performers, Shakespeare's did not need detailed stage directions. Shakespeare could expect an accurate performance because of his personal collaboration with the actors.

Shakespeare's dialogue was influenced by the practicalities of the stage.

Writing Practice

 **Revision** *Revision* means "looking again." Have students find peer readers to read their papers with them (the writers) present. Have students guide their readers' responses by asking specific questions, such as:

- Is the order of my paragraphs logical?
- Have I supported all of my opinions effectively?
- Are there any mistakes in punctuation or grammar?

Have the writers press their readers on these or any other concerns, but remind them that the writers are in charge.

478

Revision:

Unlike modern performers, Shakespeare's did not need detailed stage directions. Shakespeare could expect an accurate performance because of his personal collaboration with the actors. <u>Like his stage directions,</u>[1] or lack of them, Shakespeare's dialogue was <u>also</u>[2] influenced by the practicalities of the stage.

<u>1: Repeat phrases to increase coherence and create unity.</u>

<u>2: Use transitional words to clarify relationships.</u>

Edit and Proofread

Get It Right Proofread for errors in grammar, usage, mechanics, and spelling. Use the Language Handbook, pages R47–R59, as a guide.

> **Focus Lesson**

Use Quotations Correctly

Copy quotations exactly, and enclose them in quotation marks.

Problem: The direct quotation is not accurately quoted.

"As Stanley Wells points out, Shakespeare was a man of the theatre in at least three different senses: as a business man, as an actor, and as a playwright" (23).

Solution: Place quotation marks around the direct quotation only.

As Stanley Wells points out, Shakespeare "was a man of the theatre in at least three different senses: as a business man, as an actor, and as a playwright" (23).

Present

Appearance Matters Check to see that you have followed your teacher's general guidelines, including length, spacing, font size, and margin requirements.

Exposition

Peer Review Tips

A classmate may ask you to read his or her research report. Take your time and jot down notes as you read so you can give constructive feedback. Use the following questions to get started:

- Can you identify the thesis in the introduction and the main ideas that support it in the body paragraphs?

- Where do you find a comment on the relative worth of sources or a distinction between sources?

- Do all sources appear to be correctly cited?

Word-Processing Tip

Your formal bibliography should appear on a separate page; the centered title for this page should be "Works Cited." Set your margins so that each entry begins at the left margin and all turn lines indent five spaces. Double-space the list, and do not add extra lines of space between entries.

Writer's Portfolio

Place a clean copy of your research report in your portfolio to review later.

Teach and Assess

Writing Process

Edit and Proofread Encourage students to read their papers aloud. Hearing their own words puts the words in a new light. Have students listen to the flow of ideas and of the language. The students should decide whether the voice sounds honest and whether the tone is appropriate to the purpose of the paper and to the audience.

Writing Process

Edit and Proofread Encourage students to avoid the passive voice except when the subject is unknown or when the emphasis is intended to be on the verb rather than the subject. **Write on the board:** The killer was discovered by the police; he was hiding under the bed. Ask students to make the sentence active. (*The police found the killer hiding under the bed.*)

English Learners

DIFFERENTIATED INSTRUCTION

Intermediate Emphasize that using effective transitions will make sentences and paragraphs flow smoothly from one idea to the next. Ask students for examples of transitional elements (*although, despite, while, first of all, yet,* etc.). Now, going back to the workshop model on page 471, have students work with partners to find effective transitions in the text. (*with the exception of; because of; in addition; first*)

Focus

Summary

In this workshop, students will learn techniques for planning and presenting a multimedia exhibit.

Teach

Viewing Skills

Multimedia Ask students how they would define *multimedia*. Write some of their answers on the board. Explain that *multimedia* generally refers to the intermixing of different media—such as text, sound, still images, graphics, photography, and film or video—to create a presentation that communicates information.

 For Speaking, Listening, and Viewing rubric, see Unit 2 Teaching Resources, pp. 362–363.

 For help with creating presentations, see Student Presentation Builder on StudentWorks Plus.

Learning Objectives

For pages 480–483

In this workshop, you will focus on the following objective:

Speaking and Listening: Delivering a multimedia presentation.

Workshop Model

In this workshop, note the examples used from a multimedia presentation titled "Shakespeare: Versatile Man of the Stage." You might try out some of the techniques shown in the multimedia presentation that you create.

Real-World Connection

Computer slide and other multimedia presentations are used throughout the business and academic world to inform and persuade audiences large and small.

Speaking, Listening, and Viewing Workshop

Multimedia Presentation

Literature Connection When Shakespeare staged his masterpieces, he transformed written works into powerful performances. Though the Globe Theatre lacked elaborate scenery, artificial lighting, and a large stage, Shakespeare showed great ingenuity. In this workshop, your task is to transform a written work—your research report—into an engaging, informative multimedia presentation.

> **Assignment**
>
> Plan and deliver a multimedia presentation of your historical investigation report. As you develop your presentation, keep your audience and purpose in mind.
>
> Audience: classmates and teacher
> Purpose: to inform and describe; to engage

Plan Your Presentation

Multimedia is the merging of text, sound, and images (art, photos, video clips, animation, and print) into a single presentation. Forms of multimedia include narrated slide or transparency presentations, Web sites, and Web casts.

Before you decide what type of multimedia presentation you will create, find out what equipment is available at your school. For example, can you use an overhead projector, a digital camera, a video camera, a screen, or audio equipment? For a computer-based presentation, check out the kinds of hardware, including the amount of memory, that are available to you.

Consider trying out computer software too. For example, what photo, graphics, animation, or multimedia authorship programs are available for your use? Think about how much time you will need to become skillful at using any new equipment, hardware, or software.

If your software options are limited, remember that a librarian or media specialist can also point out available databases or free programs for downloadable audio and video clips. If your equipment options are limited, remember that overhead projectors are almost always available. The chart on the next page shows some options for your presentation.

Writing Practice

Storyboard Once students complete their research, have them make storyboards to organize their information. (A storyboard is a pictorial view of a presentation.) Students can create their storyboards on a computer (using a slide-show program, for example), or they can use adhesive-backed notes on large sheets of paper. On each slide or card they should include appropriate text, graphics/images, and relevant links to other slides or cards.

Ways to Create a Multimedia Presentation		
	Equipment	Application
Low-tech	Camera, slide/overhead projector, tape recorder	• Use 35-mm slides or overhead transparencies for the visuals
	Computer with speakers, monitor, and microphone	• Use presentation software to create a slide show combining text, graphics, images, and sound
High-tech	Computer with speakers, monitor, microphone, plus digital camera, video camera, and scanner	• Use a hypertext program to combine text, graphics, images, and sounds to create "cards" containing hyperlinks that make different sequences possible

Choose Your Media

After you have decided on a type of presentation, reread your historical investigation report and look for ways to add sound and images. You might also review your outline and highlight or annotate key ideas and details, as this sample shows.

Color code:  = image ■ = sound

Introduction   *Drawing—Shakespeare*

Music—wind instrument ensemble from Elizabethan era

Thesis: *Macbeth* illustrates Shakespeare's talents as a "man of the theater."

I. Had to overcome limitations of Globe (lack of scenery, control of lighting)

  Image: Globe Theater

  A. Wrote descriptive poetry

  Dramatic reading—Macbeth's "Come, seeling night, . . ."

  B. Incorporated sound effects

  Sound library clips—thunder, trumpets, drums, bells

  C. Apparently wrote with specific actors in mind

  Image: actor playing Macbeth

II. Showed virtuosity as both a director and a playwright

  A. Did not require detailed stage directions; could focus on dialogue instead

  B. Knew his audience and made the dialogue appeal to them

  Drawing —Globe stage and groundlings in Shakespeare's time

  C. Used levels of language (blank verse for nobility, prose for servants, rhymes/chants for witches)

  Video—parts of Macbeth that demonstrate levels of language

  D. Adapted plays during rehearsals

III. Conclusion

  Music—wind instrument ensemble from Elizabethan era

Select Appropriate Media

As you selected sources for your historical investigation report, you evaluated their reliability and validity. Apply similar criteria to the media you choose. For example, consider the author or sponsoring institution of any site or source you use. Ask yourself why the work was created and how much it was edited before publication or release.

Edit the Media

Choose media that explain, support, or enhance the presentation of your thesis. Use narration to help your audience understand what the sounds and images communicate.

 Literature Online

Speaking, Listening, and Viewing For project ideas, templates, and presentation tips, go to glencoe.com and enter QuickPass code GLB9817u2.

Teach

Viewing Skills

Use Models Have students visit some Web sites that feature sound, text, and video or animation. The most commonly seen are Flash-based Web sites that usually contain some sort of animation and, more and more often, sound and video.

Other types of multimedia can be found in slide presentations or on Web sites with movies embedded in them.

Listening Skills

Peer Assessment Ask students to respond to each presentation, according to the following criteria:

- Did the speaker engage the audience?
- Did he or she use effective pacing, volume, and eye contact?
- Was the topic effectively supported by the different media used?
- Did the presentation make a strong impact?

English Learners

DIFFERENTIATED INSTRUCTION

Beginning To practice **reading fluency,** allow students with limited English-speaking abilities to practice their presentations for you before or after class. Help them pronounce difficult or unfamiliar words. Then ask them to express the meaning of the passage in their own words.

Advanced Learners

DIFFERENTIATED INSTRUCTION

Research In doing their research, students can use a comprehensive search engine online, plugging in keywords such as *design, effective, multimedia, slide-show, power presentation,* and *hyperstudio.*

Teach

Viewing Skills

Assessing Images Remind students that the Internet gives them access to many images relevant to their topic. Students should choose images that convey accurate information about their topic.

Ask: Suppose your topic is Elizabeth I. What do you want the images you choose to communicate about this queen? *(Possible answers: her ability to command, her proud demeanor, etc.)* What kinds of images would—and which kinds would not—convey this idea clearly? *(Possible answers: Commissioned portraits of her in grand regalia would communicate the idea; political drawings by her detractors might not.)*

Develop Your Presentation

Follow these steps as you pull together the media you have found.

- **Evaluate and select appropriate images and sounds.** Use only balanced, reliable information. Edit media elections for conciseness.

- **Focus on your audience and purpose.** Because your purpose is to inform, you might incorporate some of the historical records that you used in your research report. Show how you drew ideas from a wide range of sources with different facts and perspectives. To help your audience see how your sources varied, you might display their title pages, along with examples. Re-create these pages by scanning them or by photocopying and enlarging them.

- **Call attention to your thesis.** Your main proposition, claim, or thesis helps unify your presentation. Display this key idea clearly to help give your audience the "big picture."

Organize Your Presentation

Create a storyboard—a series of frames—that shows text, images, or sounds for each slide, card, and transparency you will use. Add ideas for narration. Begin with a title slide that identifies your presentation and its creator. End with a Works Cited list that documents all your research sources—print, visual, and sound.

> **Avoid Plagiarism**
> Correctly credit each image, video clip, and sound, along with all your print sources, in a Works Cited slide at the end of your presentation. (See pages R35–R37 for standardized citation styles.)

• title 1 • picture of Globe Theater <u>Elizabethan music</u>	• thesis 2 <u>bring music down</u> • read thesis and 1st main idea	• drawing: 3 Globe stage • narration: no control over light; lack of scenery	• photo of 4 2 source title pages • explain how sources vary
• Shakespeare's 5 sound effects • cues for actors <u>trumpets, drums, thunder, bells</u>	• Shakespeare's 6 verse • video clip (actor as Macbeth) • narration: viewpoints on verse	• levels of 7 language <u>recordings of dialogue</u> • explanation/ commentary	• thesis (restated) 8 • Works Cited <u>Elizabethan music</u>

Writing Practice

Main Ideas When students research images, music, graphics, and other resources for a multimedia presentation, they may be overwhelmed by choices. **Ask:** What questions will guide you as you choose media? *(What main idea do I want to communicate? What details support the main idea?)*

Tell students that an outline, which they know is useful for organizing reports, can also keep them on track as they search for media. Direct students to complete a simple outline of their main ideas and supporting ideas. Students should "fill in" the outline with media choices as they research.

Outline: Queen Elizabeth I
I. Queen Elizabeth I's power
  A. as ruler
  B. as patron of the arts
  C. as model for nobility
II. Queen Elizabeth I's pride
  A.

Shakespeare: Versatile Man of the Stage
by Tyrone Johnson

Performing Macbeth
The rise and fall of a tragic hero

Note these two examples of slides based on ideas mapped out in the model storyboard.

Rehearse/Deliver Your Presentation

Delivering a multimedia presentation requires skillful timing. After you practice the entire presentation on your own, rehearse it in front of a few classmates or family members. Ask them for feedback on the organization of your ideas and the clarity of the sounds and images. As you deliver or watch a presentation keep these techniques in mind.

Techniques for a Multimedia Presentation

Presentation Techniques	Listening and Viewing Techniques
☑ **Pace** Allow the audience enough time to view and hear each segment of your presentation. Remember that the images, sounds, and research ideas are unfamiliar to your audience.	☑ **Body Language/Posture** Show respect for the presenter by sitting upright, and keeping your head up.
☑ **Volume** Present spoken words, sounds, and music loudly enough so that your entire audience can hear them.	☑ **Movement and Facial Expressions** Provide cues that you are listening and understanding, such as an occasional nod. Maintain a facial expression that shows interest.
☑ **Eye Contact** Look at your images as you direct your audience's attention to them. Make as much eye contact with your audience as possible.	☑ **Focus** Look directly either at the presenter or at the images.

Evaluation Checklist

☑ Are the thesis and main ideas clear?

☑ Do the text, images, and sounds clearly support the thesis and main ideas?

☑ Do any of the text elements, sounds, or images need editing?

☑ Does the presentation flow smoothly from beginning to end?

Teach

Speaking Skills

Fluency When students deliver their presentations, they should be prepared to pronounce correctly the names of people, places, characters, works of literature and art, and historical periods. Ask them to consult a dictionary or listen to the words pronounced online ahead of time and to practice until they can pronounce the words correctly with ease.

 For help with creating presentations, see Student Presentation Builder on StudentWorks Plus.

English Learners

DIFFERENTIATED INSTRUCTION

Intermediate Show students images of people speaking to groups. **Ask:** How would you describe the speaker's posture? Focus? Facial expressions? Have students model the posture, expressions, and gestures of practiced speakers.

Approaching Level

DIFFERENTIATED INSTRUCTION

African American Vernacular English (AAVE) Explain that when people speak to an audience, careful pronunciation helps the audience understand what is said. Have students work in pairs to mark in their speeches these words:

- words ending in *–ing*
- words with vowel + /r/
- words ending in /1/ or *–le*

Guide students in practicing clear pronunciation of these problem words.

Focus

Summary

The purpose of Literature of the Time is to encourage students to read more literature from the time period that they have learned about in this unit.

Teach

Cultural History ☆

Poetry for the Learned? Read aloud a poem from Tottel's *Miscellany*. **Ask:** What do you think this poem is about? How would you put it in your own words? Do you think that Tottel was right to be concerned about "stateliness of style"? Point out that Tottel's collection, which became very popular, helped popularize the sonnet. Lead students to perceive that its form and content were suited to the writing style of the Renaissance; people of the period could interpret the sonnet's elaborate metaphors more readily than readers today. Discuss whether contemporary poetry is aimed primarily at the well educated.

Reading Practice

Identify Tone As they read Renaissance poetry and prose independently, have students think about the writers' intentions and motivations in creating the works. Ask them also to consider the tone of each work. Does it convey humor? Anguish? Sarcasm? Romance? Tell students to think of a word that describes the tone of each work and to make that word the center of a word web. Students should expand the web by adding words or phrases from the work that help communicate the tone.

Independent Reading

DURING THE ENGLISH RENAISSANCE, LYRIC POETRY AND DRAMA FLOURISHED, REACHING unsurpassable heights. Yet, throughout the sixteenth century, aristocratic poets such as Sir Thomas Wyatt and Sir Philip Sidney rarely published their own poems. Rather, these poets circulated their poetry among friends. Eventually, however, printers gathered these poems and published collections, or anthologies, called "miscellanies." In 1557 Richard Tottel published his *Miscellany*, and for the first time the general public had widespread access to written poetry. People also read works by Richard Hakluyt (hak′ lo͞ot), an English clergyman and geographer who collected prose accounts of travel adventures. His most important work was *The Principal Navigations, Voyages, and Discoveries of the English Nation*, an anthology published in 1589. Another major work of the English Renaissance was the *Book of Common Prayer*, which was first published in 1549 and came into prominence as a result of the English Reformation.

Tottel's Miscellany

compiled by Richard Tottel

Tottel's book is usually considered the first printed collection of English poetry. It contains sonnets by Sir Thomas Wyatt; Henry Howard, Earl of Surrey; and several others. The book, originally entitled *The Book of Songs and Sonnets*, is more commonly known as *Tottel's Miscellany*. Tottel was aware that his collection might have its share of naysayers. In a message to readers, he tried to forestall criticism by writing, "If perhaps some mislike the stateliness of style removed from the rude skill of common ears: I ask help of the learned to defend their learned friends, the authors of this work." Despite his concerns, Tottel's book was successful.

Book of Common Prayer

Thomas Cranmer and others

By the end of King Edward VI's short-lived reign in 1553, Protestant churchgoers were familiar with the *Book of Common Prayer*. This book was based on the Latin liturgy and compiled in large part by Thomas Cranmer, the archbishop of Canterbury. It was written in English, which allowed people to read the prayers for themselves. In 1549 the Act of Uniformity specified that only the *Book of Common Prayer* could be used in church services. This heightened the already heated tension between Protestants and Catholics created by King Henry VIII's split from the Catholic Church. A major revision was published in 1552, and the book has been revised from time to time ever since.

Hamlet

William Shakespeare

Probably Shakespeare's best-known work, *Hamlet* is a brilliant study of revenge, madness, and appearance versus reality.

A Midsummer Night's Dream

William Shakespeare

A Midsummer Night's Dream follows young lovers into a magical forest, where a mischievous elf causes comedy and chaos.

The Tragedy of Julius Caesar

William Shakespeare

Julius Caesar relates the story of Julius Caesar's murder and the intrigues and ambitions of his supporters and enemies.

CRITICS' CORNER

"Hakluyt's Voyages is the prose epic of the English people. As Shakespeare's characters are giants, so too are Hakluyt's. As Shakespeare's language is vigorous and colorful, so too is the language of the Voyages. As Shakespeare's plays reflect the mind and spirit of his age, so too does Hakluyt's monumental work. The collection is Elizabethan in its vitality and scope, with all the greatness attributable to that age; at the same time it is more—in its panorama of the revealed birth of an empire and the opening of the globe, the Voyages has no equivalent in the English language."

—Irwin R. Blacker, Introduction to Hakluyt's *Voyages*

The Principal Navigations, Voyages, and Discoveries of the English Nation ☆

compiled by Richard Hakluyt

Richard Hakluyt, a clergyman, collected accounts from adventurous sailors, explorers, and merchants who traveled all over the world. His book includes accounts from such famous globe-trotters as Sir Francis Drake, Sir Martin Frobisher, and Sir Walter Raleigh. Hakluyt wrote that his purpose was to save the texts "which long have lain miserably scattered in musty corners, and . . . hidden in misty darkness, and were very like for the greatest part to have been buried in perpetual oblivion." His book helped to document England's growing mastery of the sea while informing readers about valuable markets and astonishing lands.

LITERATURE OF THE TIME **485**

Teach

Cultural History ☆

Discover Discoveries Explain to students that although Hakluyt's book is not widely read today, his anthology of travel and adventure stories influenced other Renaissance writers, including Shakespeare. Point out that Hakluyt's work is of lasting interest because he gathered many firsthand accounts from explorers and adventurers who made British colonies on foreign lands possible. Discuss with students what purpose Hakluyt might have had in editing a collection of stories about British voyages and discoveries.

Glencoe Literature Library

Glencoe Literature Library offers an extensive collection of hardcover books that help you encourage your students to read independently. Choose from among the more than 120 full-length literary works—novels, novellas, plays, and nonfiction. Each book includes related readings from a broad range of genres. Go to www.glencoe.com for more information.

 For access to all study guides for the Glencoe Literature Library, see the Literature Library Teacher Resources CD-ROM.

 To create customized reading lists from a database of more than 30,000 titles, use BookLink K–12 CD-ROM.

Approaching Level

DIFFERENTIATED INSTRUCTION

Established Explain to students that as they read Renaissance poetry and prose independently, they will encounter many unfamiliar words and phrases. Encourage them to use context clues, both within the sentence and in surrounding sentences, to help them figure out the meaning of each word or phrase. Have them write down their best guesses about the meaning of the words and phrases. Then ask them to consult a dictionary to learn whether their guesses were correct.

485

Focus

Bellringer Options

Say: No matter how hard you study, if you don't know how to go about taking a test—essay, multiple-choice, or any other kind—you won't score the highest possible mark.

Have students brainstorm to compile a list of key test-taking strategies that have helped them on past tests.

Teach

Assessment Explain to students that Test Preparation and Practice is intended to reinforce their general test-taking strategies, as well as to test the skills and vocabulary covered in the unit. They will first be asked to read a nonfiction selection and answer comprehension, context-clue, and inference questions. Then, they will be asked to answer ten sentence-completion exercises and seven paragraph-improvement questions and to write a short analytical essay.

Assessment

English–Language Arts

Reading: Nonfiction

Carefully read the following passage. Use context clues to help define any words with which you are unfamiliar. Pay close attention to the use of figurative language, argument, and tone. Then, on a separate sheet of paper, answer the questions that follow.

from "Of Cunning" by Sir Francis Bacon

line

We take cunning for a sinister or crooked wisdom. And certainly there is a great difference between a cunning man and a wise man; not only in point of honesty, but in point of ability. . . .

5 . . . I knew a counsellor and secretary, that never came to Queen Elizabeth of England with bills to sign, but he would always first put her into some discourse of estate, that she might the less mind the bills. . . .

10 In things that are tender and unpleasing, it is good to break the ice by some whose words are of less weight, and to reserve the more weighty voice to come in as by chance, so that he may be asked the question upon the other's speech. . . .

15 I knew one that, when he wrote a letter, he would put that which was most material in the postscript, as if it had been a by-matter.

I knew another that, when he came to have speech, he would pass over that that he intended

20 most; and go forth, and come back again, and speak of it as of a thing that he had almost forgot. . . .

It is a point of cunning, to let fall those words in a man's own name, which he would have another man learn and use, and thereupon take

25 advantage. I knew two that were competitors for the secretary's place in Queen Elizabeth's time, and yet kept good quarter between themselves; and would confer one with another upon the business; and the one of them said, That to be a secretary in

30 the *declination of a monarchy* was a ticklish thing, and that he did not affect it: the other straight caught

Vocabulary Practice

VOCABULARY: Build Vocabulary Tell students that building their vocabulary will help them maximize their scores on the SAT and other crucial tests. Often they may figure out a word's meaning from the context; in some cases, though, context might not be enough. When they come across a word whose meaning they don't know, they should write it down and look up the definition. They can then create a set of flashcards for such words. On each card, they should include a sample sentence that contains the word.

up those words and discoursed with divers of his friends, that he had no reason to desire to be secretary in the *declination of a monarchy.* The

35 first man took hold of it, and found means it was told the Queen; who, hearing of a *declination of a monarchy,* took it so ill as she would never after hear of the other's suit. . . .

Some have in readiness so many tales and

40 stories, as there is nothing they would insinuate, but they can wrap it into a tale; which serveth both to keep themselves more in guard, and to make others carry it with more pleasure.

It is a good point of cunning for a man to

45 shape the answer he would have in his own words and propositions; for it makes the other party stick the less.

It is strange how long some men will lie in wait to speak somewhat they desire to say; and how

50 far about they will fetch; and how many other matters they will beat over, to come near it. It is a thing of great patience, but yet of much use. . . .

But these small wares and petty points of cunning are infinite; and it were a good deed to

55 make a list of them; for that nothing doth more hurt in a state than that cunning men pass for wise.

But certainly some there are that know the resorts and falls of business, that cannot sink into the main of it; like a house that hath convenient

60 stairs and entries, but never a fair room. . . . Some build rather upon the abusing of others, and (as we now say) *putting tricks upon them,* than upon soundness of their own proceedings.

---

1. In the opening paragraph, what is the principal distinction that Bacon makes between cunning people and wise people?
   A. The cunning are evil; the wise are not.
   B. The cunning are different from the wise in ability and honesty.
   C. The wise will always rise to the top ranks of their professions.
   D. The wise are less honest and have less ability than the cunning.

2. From the context, what do you conclude that the word *tender* means in line 10?
   F. young
   G. loving
   H. gentle
   J. sensitive

1. **B** is the correct answer. Bacon explicitly states that "there is a great difference between a cunning man and a wise man; not only in point of honesty, but in point of ability." `DOK 2`

2. **J** is the correct answer. "Young," "loving," and "gentle" make no sense in context with *unpleasing,* so **F**, **G**, and **H** are all incorrect. `DOK 1`

Approaching Level

DIFFERENTIATED INSTRUCTION

Established Remind the class that all states are now required by law to test outgoing high school students. While the law does not require that these tests be "high-stakes," or required for graduation, many are. You may wish to discuss with your class the specific features of your state's exit exam. If possible, provide them with a sample copy of the exam and review its particulars with them. Provide one-on-one instruction for students who need extra help with any part of the exam.

Assessment

Assess

3. C is the correct answer. There is nothing in the passage to support **A**, **B**, or **D**. (DOK 4)

4. F is the correct answer. From the context, it is clear that the intended meaning is "important." (DOK 1)

5. B is the correct answer. See Bacon's explicit statement in lines 41–43. (DOK 2)

6. J is the correct answer. No other option makes sense. (DOK 1)

7. D is the correct answer. Bacon states that "it were a good deed to make a list of them." (DOK 1)

8. G is the correct answer. Bacon states "that nothing doth more hurt in a state than that cunning men pass for wise." (DOK 2)

9. A is the correct answer. Bacon uses the word *like* in comparing two essentially unlike things. (DOK 4)

10. H is the correct answer. The tone is not angry, ironic, or skeptical, so **F**, **G**, and **J** are incorrect. (DOK 4)

11. D is the correct answer. Bacon details many types of cunning, but his main idea is not that they exist, so option **A** is incorrect. Bacon explicitly disagrees with statements **B** and **C**, so they are incorrect. (DOK 2)

12. G is the correct answer. There is nothing in the passage to support **F**, **H**, or **J**. (DOK 4)

3. Why might the letter writer put the "most material" information in a postscript?
   A. to cause the reader to ignore it
   B. to make it more likely to be read
   C. to downplay the importance of the information
   D. to increase the importance of the information

4. From the context, what do you conclude that the word *material* means in line 16?
   F. important
   G. matter
   H. textile
   J. assured

5. According to Bacon, why is it useful to present information in the form of a story?
   A. to make the information seem less important
   B. to guard the speaker and make the information more pleasant to hear
   C. to confuse the listener through the distortion and manipulation of facts
   D. to bore the listener with unimportant information

6. Why might it be "of much use" to "wait to speak"?
   F. to upset the listener
   G. to prevent the listener from speaking
   H. to allow the speaker to pass as wise
   J. to wait for the appropriate moment

7. What reason does Bacon give for listing the "small wares" of cunning?
   A. to create a definitive list
   B. to make the tools of the cunning available to everyone
   C. to hurt the state
   D. to pass on this information because doing so is a good deed

LOG ON ▶ Literature Online

Assessment For additional test practice, go to glencoe.com and enter QuickPass code GLB9817u2.

8. According to Bacon, what is the most hurtful thing to a state?
   F. that the wise pass for the cunning
   G. that the cunning pass for the wise
   H. that the petty points of cunning become infinite
   J. that the state itself becomes cunning

9. What literary device is most evident in the sentence beginning in line 57?
   A. simile
   B. metaphor
   C. motif
   D. apostrophe

10. What is the overall tone of this passage?
    F. angry
    G. ironic
    H. knowing
    J. skeptical

11. What is the main idea of this passage?
    A. There are many different kinds of cunning.
    B. The wise and the cunning are essentially the same kind of people.
    C. The wise are less adept than the cunning.
    D. The cunning are different from the wise in ability and honesty.

12. On the basis of this passage, with which of the following statements would Bacon be most likely to agree?
    F. There is no such thing as wisdom.
    G. The cunning have many tools.
    H. The cunning always outwit the wise.
    J. The cunning are not intelligent.

▶ To create custom assessments online, go to Progress Reporter Online Assessment.

Vocabulary Skills: Sentence Completion

For each question in the Vocabulary Skills section, choose the word or words that best complete the sentence.

1. Although many were executed for _____ in Tudor England, their actual crime was holding religious beliefs different from those of the monarch.
   A. spite
   B. calamity
   C. treachery
   D. impediment

2. The humanists believed that limited skill in language, especially in rhetoric, was almost an _____.
   F. infirmity
   G. enmity
   H. tread
   J. discretion

3. Many Renaissance thinkers believed that learning and quiet contemplation would _____ in the effort to completely remake society.
   A. execute
   B. prevail
   C. appall
   D. provoke

4. There is nearly _____ recognition of Shakespeare's literary _____ among scholars.
   F. consistent . . . virtues
   G. vain . . . tempest
   H. continual . . . strif
   J. bitter . . . balm

5. Many in Tudor England, including King James I, believed that supernatural forces could trick or _____ the unsuspecting into performing evil acts.
   A. scorn
   B. beguile
   C. replenish
   D. prevail

6. The barely _____ tension between Protestants and Catholics in England burst into violence during the Reformation.
   F. wan
   G. suppressed
   H. vain
   J. mute

7. Before the beginning of the Renaissance, the classics of ancient Greece and Rome had _____ in near obscurity.
   A. subdued
   B. scorned
   C. executed
   D. languished

8. Though barely able to _____ the grief he felt after his wife's death, Donne transformed his sorrow into powerful sermons and verse.
   F. deem
   G. censure
   H. endure
   J. congeal

9. Little _____ existed between writers who envied one another's talents and position.
   A. concord
   B. valor
   C. inconstancy
   D. alteration

10. Some poets of the period, including Donne, attempted to strike a balance between the impermanent, _____ world and the divine.
    F. meek
    G. mute
    H. wan
    J. mortal

To create custom assessments using software, go to ExamView Assessment Suite.

Assessment

Assess

1. **C** is the correct answer. No other word makes sense in this context. (**DOK 1**)

2. **F** is the correct answer. No other word makes sense in this context. (**DOK 1**)

3. **B** is the correct answer. No other word makes sense in this context. (**DOK 1**)

4. **F** is the correct answer. Neither *vain recognition* nor *bitter recognition* would make sense in this context, so **G** and **J** are incorrect. The concept of literary strife makes no sense in any context, so **H** is incorrect. (**DOK 2**)

5. **B** is the correct answer. The word *trick* makes sense in conjunction with no word other than *beguile*. (**DOK 1**)

6. **G** is the correct answer. No other word makes sense in this context. (**DOK 1**)

7. **D** is the correct answer. No other word makes sense in this context. (**DOK 1**)

8. **H** is the correct answer. No other word makes sense in this context. (**DOK 1**)

9. **A** is the correct answer. The word *envied* suggests neither little valor nor little inconstancy, so **B** and **C** are both incorrect. *Alteration* makes no sense in this context, so **D** is also incorrect. (**DOK 1**)

10. **J** is the correct answer. The word *impermanent* makes sense in conjunction with no word other than *mortal*. (**DOK 1**)

Teach

Multiple-Choice Questions

Emphasize the following tips for best results in answering multiple-choice questions:

- Read the entire question and try to answer it before looking at the options.
- Even if you think you know the answer, be sure to read through all of the options.
- If you are uncertain, begin by eliminating answers that are wrong, thus increasing your chances of being right.

Grammar and Writing: Paragraph Improvement

In the following excerpt from a student draft of a research report, some phrases are underlined. The number beneath each underlined phrase corresponds to a numbered question on the next page, which prompts you to replace the underlined phrase. If you think the original should not be changed, choose "NO CHANGE."

Throughout the passage, boxed numbers also appear. These numbers refer to questions about specific paragraphs or to the essay as a whole. When these questions are about a paragraph's sentence order, each sentence in the paragraph is numbered.

Both the boxed numbers and the numbers beneath underlined phrases refer to question numbers, *not* to the sequence of sentences or paragraphs.

Read the passage through once before you begin to answer the questions. As you read, pay close attention to the writer's use of **verb tense, quotation marks,** and **transitions.** Write your answers on a separate sheet of paper.

> Over the past four hundred years, literary critics have had mixed responses to the works of the Metaphysical poets. Some have found their use of conceits, or extended comparisons, labored or unnecessarily complex. Others, including poet T. S. Eliot, has been
> ‾‾
> 1
> deeply affected by these poems' intellectual and emotional capacity. Often, those most critical of these works argue that they create unnatural, or forced, relationships between unlike things.
> 2 The best poets of this group did not create unnatural conceits, just that which was unexpected.
> This movement—which included John Donne, Andrew Marvell, and George Herbert,
> ‾‾‾
> 3
> among others—were not simply generating complex and irregular poems to confuse readers. They were openly rejecting the formality found in the previous generation's work. Complicated
> ‾‾‾‾‾‾‾‾‾‾‾
> 4
> conceits, irregular meter and rhyme, and unexpected intellectual maneuvers were not generally found in the works of 16th-century poets. These were revolutionary changes that did not sit well with some later critics. "[T]heir amplifications had no limits, wrote Samuel Johnson." He
> ‾‾‾‾‾‾‾‾‾‾‾‾‾‾‾‾‾‾‾‾‾‾‾‾‾‾‾‾‾‾‾‾‾‾‾‾‾‾
> 5
> goes on to state that "they left not only reason but fancy behind them; and produced combinations of confused magnificence, that not only could not be credited, but could not be imagined."
> 6 [1] Eliot, in particular, would argue with the claim that these writers created a
> ‾‾‾‾‾‾‾‾‾‾‾‾‾‾‾‾‾‾‾‾‾‾
> 7
> "confused magnificence." [2] Many would disagree with Johnson's assessment. [3] Eliot
> ‾‾‾‾‾‾‾‾‾‾‾‾‾‾
> 8
> believed that these writers created a finely tuned poetry, he saw in them great clarity. 9
> 10

Transitional Words and Phrases

Explain that transitional words and phrases are the tiny stitches that provide coherence and flow within a text. Often added to sentences as overt signs of transition, they can be effective in providing clues to relationships between ideas in a work. Ask students to suggest examples of transitional words and phrases. (*Possible answers:* however; then; next; therefore; first; moreover; on the other hand)

1. **A.** NO CHANGE
   B. Others, including poet T. S. Eliot, have been deeply affected by these poems' capacity.
   C. Others, including poet T. S. Eliot, was deeply affected by these poems' capacity.
   D. Poet T. S. Eliot has been deeply affected by these poems' capacity.

2. Which of the following transitions would work best at the start of this sentence?
   F. First
   G. For instance
   H. Therefore
   J. Yet

3. **A.** NO CHANGE
   B. This movement, among others, were not simply generating complex and irregular poems to confuse readers.
   C. This movement—which included John Donne, Andrew Marvell, and George Herbert, among others—was not simply generating complex and irregular poems to confuse readers.
   D. This movement was not simply generating complex and irregular poems to confuse readers.

4. **F.** NO CHANGE
   G. Complicated conceits were not generally found in the works of 16th-century poets.
   H. Complicated conceits and irregular meter were not generally found in the works of 16th-century poets.
   J. Complicated conceits, irregular meter and rhyme, and unexpected intellectual maneuvers was not generally found.

5. **A.** NO CHANGE
   B. [T]heir amplifications had no limits, wrote Samuel Johnson.

Essay

Write a short essay in which you examine the use of imagery, or other literary devices, in a poem from this unit. As you write, keep in mind that your essay will be checked for **ideas, organization, voice, word choice, sentence fluency, conventions,** and **presentation.**

   C. "[T]heir amplifications had no limits, Samuel Johnson wrote."
   D. "[T]heir amplifications had no limits," wrote Samuel Johnson.

6. Which of the following sentence sequences would make this paragraph logical?
   F. 1, 3, 2
   G. 2, 1, 3
   H. 3, 2, 1
   J. 2, 3, 1

7. **A.** NO CHANGE
   B. Eliot would argue with the claim that these writers created a "confused magnificence."
   C. Eliot, in particular, would argue with the claim that these writers created a confused magnificence.
   D. Eliot in particular would argue.

8. **F.** NO CHANGE
   G. Eliot believed that these writers created a finely tuned poetry; he saw in them great clarity.
   H. Eliot believed these writers created clarity.
   J. He believed that these writers created a finely tuned poetry.

9. Which of the following would be most appropriate at this point in paragraph 3?
   A. another quotation from Johnson
   B. a quotation from Eliot that demonstrates his position
   C. a quotation from Donne
   D. a restatement of the thesis

10. Which of the following must the writer include while completing this essay?
   F. footnotes
   G. quotations from Donne, Marvell, and Herbert
   H. examples of Metaphysical conceits
   J. examples of sixteenth-century poetry

Assess

1. **B** is the correct answer. The subject and verb do not agree in this sentence. No other option corrects this error without altering the sense of the sentence or introducing further errors. **DOK 1**

2. **J** is the correct answer. This sentence contrasts with the preceding sentence, so *yet* is the best choice. **DOK 2**

3. **C** is the correct answer. The subject and verb do not agree in this sentence. No other option corrects this error without changing the content or introducing further errors. **DOK 1**

4. **F** is the correct answer. This sentence contains no error. **DOK 1**

5. **D** is the correct answer. The quotation marks in this sentence are misplaced. No other option corrects this error without changing the content or introducing further errors. **DOK 1**

6. **G** is the correct answer. This is the only sequence that makes sense in the paragraph. **DOK 2**

7. **A** is the correct answer. This sentence contains no error. **DOK 1**

8. **G** is the correct answer. This sentence contains two main clauses separated only by a comma. No other option corrects this error without changing the content or introducing further errors. **DOK 1**

9. **B** is the correct answer. The most appropriate element to include would be support for the claim that Eliot saw in these writers "great clarity." **DOK 4**

Essay

Check to be sure that each student's essay focuses on the use of literary devices in a poem and that it is well organized and free of grammatical errors. **DOK 3**

10. **H** is the correct answer. Although the writer may choose to include footnotes, quotations, or examples of sixteenth-century poetry, he or she must include examples of the conceits under discussion. **DOK 4**

491

Skills Scope and Sequences

Readability Scores Key: Dale-Chall/DRP/Lexile

PART 1: The Civil War, the Commonwealth, and the Restoration

Selections and Features	Literary Elements
Unit Introduction pp. 492–506	Satire **TE** p. 495 Argument **TE** p. 501
Poems How Soon Hath Time and **When I Consider How My Light Is Spent,** by John Milton pp. 508–511	Personification **SE** p. 509
Epic *from* **Paradise Lost,** by John Milton pp. 512–523	Allusion **SE** p. 512 Alliteration **TE** p. 519 Conflict (review) **SE** p. 522
Fiction *from* **The Pilgrim's Progress,** by John Bunyan 8.5/61/1380 pp. 524–531	Allegory **SE** p. 525 Style **TE** p. 528 Characterization (review) **SE** p. 530
Vocabulary Workshop p. 532	
Poem On Her Loving Two Equally, by Aphra Behn pp. 533–536	Inversion **SE** p. 534
Diary *from* **The Diary of Samuel Pepys,** by Samuel Pepys 7.5/56/1220 pp. 537–546	Diary **SE** p. 538 Tone (review) **SE** p. 545

Reading Skills and Strategies	Vocabulary	Writing Grammar	Speaking, Listening, Viewing

Use the Timeline **TE** p. 494
Analyze Structure **TE** p. 494
Analyze Graphic Information
  SE pp. 495, 497
Confirm Predictions **TE** p. 499
Organize Ideas **TE** p. 500
Analyze Causes and Effects **TE** p. 500,
  SE p. 501
Compare and Contrast **SE** p. 503
Analyze Transitions **TE** p. 504
Interpret **SE** p. 505
Reread **TE** p. 505			

Identify Problem and Solution
  SE p. 509
	Academic Vocabulary
	  SE p. 511
		Write a Memo **SE** p. 511	

Visualize **SE** p. 512
Use Graphic Aids **TE** p. 514
Draw Conclusions **TE** p. 517
	Prefixes **TE** p. 518
	Antonyms **SE** p. 522
	Academic Vocabulary
	  SE p. 522
		Write an Expository Essay **SE**
		  p. 523
		Apostrophes **SE** p. 523
			Oral Presentation **TE** p. 520

Summarize **SE** p. 525
Understand Main Idea **TE** p. 526
	Identify the Latin Root *Dict*
	  TE p. 528
	Word Parts **SE** p. 531
	Academic Vocabulary
	  SE p. 531
		Apply Symbolism **SE** p. 531	

	Use a Thesaurus **SE** p. 532		
Question **SE** p. 534	Use a Thesaurus **TE** p. 534 Word Usage **SE** p. 536	Write a Letter **SE** p. 536	

Draw Conclusions About Author's
  Beliefs **SE** p. 538
Identify Author's Purpose **TE** p. 538
Infer **TE** p. 541
Visualize **TE** p. 544
	Etymology **TE** p. 540
	Analogies **SE** p. 546
	Academic Vocabulary
	  SE p. 546
		Appositives and Appositive
		  Phrases **TE** p. 542
		Write a Research Report
		  SE p. 546	

PART 2: The English Enlightenment and Neoclassicism

Selections and Features	Literary Elements
Essay A Modest Proposal, by Jonathan Swift 10.6/66/1750 pp. 548–558	Satire **SE** p. 549 Persona **TE** p. 556 Author's Purpose (review) **SE** p. 557
Novel *from* **Gulliver's Travels,** by Jonathan Swift 9.1/59/1510 pp. 559–570	Parody **SE** p. 559 Irony (review) **SE** p. 569
Epigrams Epigrams, by Alexander Pope pp. 571–575	Heroic Couplet **SE** p. 572
Mock-Epic *from* **The Rape of the Lock,** by Alexander Pope pp. 576–583	Mock-Epic **SE** p. 576 Scansion **TE** p. 580 Allusion (review) **SE** p. 582
Letter Letter to Her Daughter, by Lady Mary Wortley Montagu 7.6/64/1290 pp. 584–590	Extended Metaphor **SE** p. 585
Vocabulary Workshop p. 591	
Literary History The Essay pp. 592–593	Essay **SE** pp. 592–593 Genre **TE** p. 592
Essays *from* **The Spectator,** by Joseph Addison and Sir Richard Steele 10.4/65/1340 pp. 594–600	Style **SE** p. 595
Comparing Literature *from* **A Journal of the Plague Year** (historical fiction) 14.5/61/1460, by Daniel Defoe, *from* **History of the Peloponnesian War** (history) 8.9/66/1290, by Thucydides, and *from* **The Plague** (novel) 8.6/65/1300, by Albert Camus pp. 601–617	Historical Fiction **SE** p. 603 Irony **TE** p. 612 Mood **TE** p. 614

Readability Scores Key: Dale-Chall/**DRP**/Lexile

PART 2: The English Enlightenment and Neoclassicism *(continued)*

Selections and Features	Literary Elements
Informational Text TIME: Death by Mosquito, by Christine Gorman 13.3/**71**/1260 pp. 618–622	
Nonfiction *from* **A Dictionary of the English Language,** by Samuel Johnson 16.9/**74**/1340 pp. 623–630	Voice **SE** p. 624 Tone (review) **SE** p. 629
Grammar Workshop p. 631	
Biography *from* **The Life of Samuel Johnson,** by James Boswell 8.5/**64**/1440 pp. 632–641	Biography **SE** p. 633 Style (review) **SE** p. 640
Historical Perspective *from* **Samuel Johnson,** by W. Jackson Bate 5.8/**66**/1380 pp. 642–645	
Writing Workshop pp. 646–653	
Speaking, Listening, and Viewing Workshop pp. 654–655	
Independent Reading pp. 656–657	
Assessment pp. 658–663	

Focus

Literature Launchers
 Pre-Reading Videos
DVD: Unit 3
Daily Language Practice
 Transparency 38

Or **write** on the board: Puritan

Ask: What does this term mean to you? *(Possible responses: religious discipline and disregard for luxury.)* **Write** on the board: Enlightenment **Ask:** What do you know about this period? *(Possible responses: the eighteenth century, philosophy, or humanitarian reforms.)*

For school-to-home activities, see Unit 3 Teaching Resources Book, pp. 5-11.

For students who would profit from independent novel study, see Novel Companion pp. 129-172.

Dr. Johnson at Cave's the Publisher, 1854. Henry Wallis. Oil on canvas, 19½ x 23½ in. Private collection.

View the Art Samuel Johnson is widely considered to be one of the foremost British intellectuals of the eighteenth century. What impression of him does this painting convey? What details contribute to that impression? ★

492

Unit Introduction Skills

Reading Skills
- Analyze Graphic Information (SE pp. 495, 497)
- Analyze Cause and Effect (SE p. 501)
- Compare and Contrast (SE p. 503)
- Interpret (SE p. 505)

From Puritanism to the Enlightenment

Listening/Speaking/Viewing Skills
- Analyze Art (SE p. 492; TE pp. 497, 498, 501, 503, 505)
- Contrast Literary Periods (SE p. 506)

Writing Skills/Grammar
- Compare/Contrast (TE p. 496)
- Summarize and Draw Conclusions (TE p. 506)

Literary Elements
- Satire (TE pp. 495, 503)
- Argument (TE p. 501)

492

From PURITANISM to the ENLIGHTENMENT

1640–1780

Looking Ahead

In the 1640s, religious and political conflict between King Charles I and the largely Puritan supporters of Parliament led to civil war, the execution of the king, and a decade of stern Puritan rule. Following the return of the monarchy in 1660, Parliament kept much of its power, but Restoration culture reveled in a witty, worldly reaction against Puritan severity. During the same period, a scientific revolution was blossoming into the Enlightenment, an intellectual movement whose participants reexamined all aspects of life in the light of reason.

Keep the following questions in mind as you read:

>> What were the essential features of Puritanism?

>> What factors contributed to the outbreak of the English civil war?

>> What were the goals of the English Enlightenment?

493

Focus

Summary

This introduction gives an overview of British literature and events, as well as world events, from 1640 to 1780. It discusses the reaction of the Puritans against the excesses and the tyranny of the monarchy, the Restoration, and the English Enlightenment and Neoclassicism.

View the Art ★

Henry Wallis (1830–1916) was an English painter, writer, and collector. He specialized in portraits of literary figures, such as the great English writer Samuel Johnson.

Answer: *Johnson's posture and expression convey seriousness and concentration; he is hard at work and does not notice either the girl or the food she's brought him; the girl's expression suggests that she is intimidated by him or trying not to disturb him.*

For diagnostic and end-of-unit assessment, see Assessment Resources, pp. 17–24, 317–318.

Unit Resources

Print Materials

- Unit 3 Teaching Resources, pp. 1–245
- Interactive Read and Write (On Level, Approaching, EL), pp. 129–164
- Novel Companion, pp. 129–172
- Bellringer Option Transparencies: Selection Focus 25, 26, 27, 28, 29, 30, 31, 32; Daily Language Practice 38–51

- Literary Element Transparencies 1, 3, 16, 49, 53, 62, 76, 77, 90, 98, 107
- Assessment Resources, Unit Assessment, pp. 317–318
- Assessment Resources, Selection Assessment, pp. 141–172

Technology

- TeacherWorks Plus CD
- StudentWorks Plus CD
- Literature Launchers: Pre-Reading Videos DVD, Unit 3
- Literature Online
- Interactive Vocabulary CD-ROM
- Listening Library CD-ROM
- ExamView CD-ROM
- Skill Level Up! CD-ROM

UNIT THREE

Teach

Reading Strategy | 1

Use the Timeline Help students read the timeline and relate key events in British literary history to British and world history.

- Explain that around 1640 Cromwell ruled England with strict Puritan discipline.
- When Charles II was restored to the throne in 1660, a period called the Restoration began.
- The Enlightenment brought a new age of reason.

Ask: What evidence of "the Age of Reason" can you identify in the timeline? *(Students may mention the theory of gravitation, the development of the microscope, or the publication of the* Dictionary of the English Language.*)*

Political History ☆

The Glorious Revolution The Glorious Revolution occurred when King James II, a Catholic, was deposed, and William III and Mary II acceded to the throne. Mary was James's Protestant daughter and consort to the Dutch prince William of Orange.

494

Timeline 1640–1780 | 1

Satan Smitten by Michael in Milton's *Paradise Lost.*

BRITISH LITERATURE

1640

1644
John Milton publishes *Areopagitica*

1660
Samuel Pepys begins his diary

1663
Drury Lane Theatre opens

1667
John Milton publishes *Paradise Lost*

1668
John Dryden becomes poet laureate

1678
John Bunyan publishes *Pilgrim's Progress* ▶

1680

1709
The Tatler begins publication

1711
The Spectator begins publication

1714
Alexander Pope publishes *The Rape of the Lock*

1719
Daniel Defoe publishes *Robinson Crusoe*

BRITISH EVENTS

1640

1647
George Fox founds Quakers

1660
Charles II restored to throne

1662
Royal Society founded

1665
Plague ravages London

1666
Great Fire of London occurs

Sir Isaac Newton's telescope

1680

1685
Charles II dies; James II becomes king

1687
Newton publishes theory of gravitation

1688 ☆
Glorious Revolution occurs

1707
England and Scotland unite as Great Britain ▶

1710
Sir Christopher Wren completes St. Paul's Cathedral

1714
Ruling House of Hanover founded by George I

WORLD EVENTS

1640

1644
Haiku master Matsuo Bashō born

1650
Taj Mahal completed in India

1657
Fire destroys much of Japanese capital, Edo (Tokyo)

1661
Louis XIV begins Palace of Versailles in France

1680

1680
Molière's theater company becomes the Comédie Française

1682
LaSalle claims Louisiana for France

1683
Ottoman Turks besiege Vienna

c. 1697
Ashanti Empire formed in Africa ▼

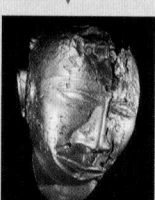

LOG ON ▶ **Literature** Online

Literature and Reading To explore the Interactive Timeline, go to glencoe.com and enter QuickPass code GLB9817u3.

494 UNIT 3 FROM PURITANISM TO THE ENLIGHTENMENT

Reading Practice

SPIRAL REVIEW **Analyze Structure** Tell students that these timelines show three sequences of events. Point out the three timelines on this chart:

- Point out to students that events appear in time order, from left to right.
- Point out how events appear in a double-wide column across the three timelines.
- Check comprehension.

Ask: In what years are political events noted for Britain? *(1660, 1685, 1688, 1707, 1714, 1746, 1757)*

Robert Lovelace Preparing to Abduct
Clarissa Harlow, c. 18th century.
Francis Hayman. Oil on canvas,
25 x 30 in. Southampton City Art
Gallery, Hampshire, UK.

1720

1720
Alexander Pope completes
translation of the *Iliad*

1726
Jonathan Swift publishes
Gulliver's Travels

1728
Alexander Pope publishes
The Dunciad

1729
Jonathan Swift publishes
A Modest Proposal

1734
Alexander Pope publishes
An Essay on Man

1747–1748
Samuel Richardson
publishes *Clarissa*

1755
Samuel Johnson publishes
*A Dictionary of the
English Language*

1760

1763
Boswell meets Johnson

1768
Encyclopaedia Britannica
begins publication

1776
Edward Gibbon publishes
first volume of *The Decline
and Fall of the Roman Empire*

1720

1721
Smallpox inoculation
introduced by Lady Mary
Wortley Montagu

1732
Covent Garden Theatre
opens

1735
William Hogarth
completes his engraving of
A Rake's Progress

1742
George Frideric Handel's
Messiah first performed

1746
Defeat at Culloden Moor
ends Jacobite Rebellion ▶

1752
Britain adopts Gregorian
calendar

1757
Victory at Plassey begins
British rule of India

1760

1768
Royal Academy of Arts
founded

1720

1722
Safavid Empire ends in Persia

1727
Coffee first planted in Brazil

1749
German composer Johann
Sebastian Bach completes
The Art of the Fugue

1752
Ben Franklin invents the
lightning rod

1755
Earthquake destroys
Lisbon in Portugal

1756
Seven Years' War begins
in Europe

1759
French writer Voltaire
publishes *Candide*

1760

1762
Catherine II becomes
ruler of Russia ▶

1775
American Revolution begins

Reading Check

Analyze Graphic Information During this period,
what three cities suffered major disasters?

Approaching Level

DIFFERENTIATED INSTRUCTION

Emerging Help approaching-level students follow the organization of the timeline. Point out the dates inside the banners
and the dates in the columns beneath.
Note that the dates in the banners are forty
years apart. Tell students that the events
are organized vertically in chronological
order beneath the dates in the banners.

Teach

Literary Element

Satire This unit contains more
than one satirical selection. Ask
students to speculate on why
satire seems like a natural type of
expression for the Enlightenment.
*(The quest for knowledge might
lead people to question assumptions.)* Have them list examples of
contemporary satires.

Literary History ☆

A Modest Proposal In this
satirical work, Jonathan Swift
(1667–1745) suggests that the
problem of poverty in Ireland could
be solved by eating Irish children.
Swift claims to have learned from
an American that a healthy child
of one year is "a most delicious,
nourishing and wholesome food,
whether stewed, roasted, baked, or
boiled." After all, Swift pointed out,
wouldn't this be a better solution
than taxing absentee landlords,
buying Irish goods, or being more
compassionate to the poor?

Assess

Reading Check

Answer: *London, Edo, and
Lisbon*

Teach

Use Multiple Sources Direct students' attention to the graph entitled "London's Population, 1600–1800" and the timelines on the previous pages. **Ask:** What generalization can you make about the year 1665? *(Despite being ravaged by plague in 1665, London's population increased steadily throughout the 1660s.)*

Cultural History ☆

St. Paul's Cathedral The first St. Paul's Cathedral was built in A.D. 604. That cathedral was ransacked by Vikings, and a more elaborate version was erected in 962. From 1087 to 1310, work was under way on a cathedral in the grand Norman style. This third version, the one destroyed in the Great Fire, took more than 220 years to complete. After the fire, Christopher Wren submitted designs for a new cathedral. It is his design that stands in London today.

BY THE NUMBERS

The Great Fire of London

On September 2, 1666, fire broke out in a London bakery. During the next four days it spread, destroying much of the city. Fortunately, the flames spread slowly, which enabled Londoners to escape. As a result, few people were killed; contemporary records indicate only five deaths from the fire. Damage to buildings and property, however, was considerable; 100,000 Londoners were homeless.

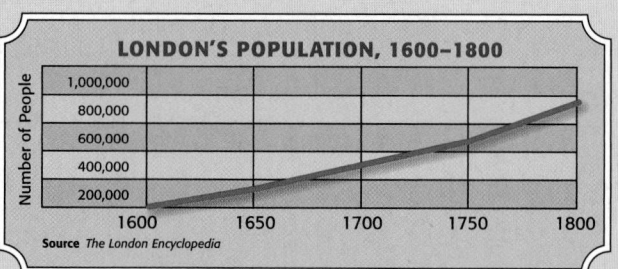

LONDON'S POPULATION, 1600–1800

Source *The London Encyclopedia*

1

BUILDINGS DESTROYED:

- 13,200 houses
- 4 river bridges
- 3 city gates
- St. Paul's Cathedral ☆
- 87 parish churches
- 6 chapels
- 52 company (guild or trade association) halls
- Royal Exchange
- Custom House
- Newgate and several other prisons

COST OF REBUILDING:

- Houses: nearly 4 million pounds
- Other public buildings: 2 million pounds
- St. Paul's Cathedral: 2 million pounds

PUNISHMENT FOR SWEARING

Under the Puritan Commonwealth, swearing in public was an offense punishable by the payment of a fine, which varied according to the social rank of the offender. A duke paid 30 shillings; a baron paid 20 shillings; a squire paid 10 shillings; and a commoner paid 3 shillings and fourpence.

TEA AND COFFEE

Drinking tea became popular in England during the Restoration. At that time, it was a very costly drink: a pound of tea cost 10 pounds. By 1700 the price was reduced to one pound, but this was still a big expense for ordinary British families, whose annual income ranged between 15 and 50 pounds a year. The first coffeehouse opened in London in 1652. By 1700 the number had grown to somewhere between 500 and 2,000.

TRAVEL RATES

In the late 1600s, stagecoaches could travel at a maximum speed of 3 to 4 miles per hour. By 1719 express coaches could travel a distance of 60 miles a day. In 1765 a coach pulled by 6 horses made the trip from London to the port of Dover, a distance of 84 miles, in one day.

THE SLAVE TRADE

In 1672 a group of merchants from London formed the Royal African Company to engage in the West African slave trade. The company transported an average of 5000 Africans a year between 1680 and 1686 to the sugar plantations of the West Indies. Daniel Defoe estimated that British ships were transporting 40,000 to 50,000 Africans a year, who were then sold for an average price of 25 pounds per person.

Writing Practice

📝 Compare and Contrast

SPIRAL REVIEW 🌀 Have students write a brief essay comparing and contrasting life in seventeenth-century England with contemporary life in the United States. Tell them to use the information from this page, although they do not need to cover every single point. Encourage students to consider broader themes such as the attitudes of the nation (which they may infer from the facts given), as well as day-to-day details.

Being There

A *In a London Coffee House*, c. 1700. Engraving.

B *Family Party*, c. eighteenth century. William Hogarth. Private collection.

C *Earl and Countess of Ossory and their Children at Ampthill Park*, 1777. Benjamin Killingbeck. Private collection, Ackermann and Johnson Ltd, London.

In 1707 the Act of Union established the state of Great Britain, composed of England and Scotland. Wales had been a part of England since the mid-1500s. In 1666 the Great Fire of London destroyed much of the city. Once London was rebuilt, however, it continued to grow throughout the 1700s, becoming Europe's largest city by 1750. **2**

LOG ON ▶ **Literature** Online

Literature and Reading For more about the history and literature of this period, go to glencoe.com and enter QuickPass code GLB9817u3.

Reading Check

Analyze Graphic Information:

1. How many times greater was London's population in 1800 than it had been in 1600?

2. Use Daniel Defoe's figures to calculate the total value of the slaves transported each year by British ships.

3. Why would a port city like Portsmouth be especially vulnerable to the spread of plague?

English Learners

DIFFERENTIATED INSTRUCTION

Intermediate Ask students to point out the graphic elements on the spread: *heads, captions, map, labels, timeline.* Have them briefly summarize the purpose of each element and then explain how each element supports the purpose of the spread.

Teach

Reading Strategy | 2

Use Maps Ask students to read the text and examine the map. **Ask:** How would you account for the fact that England expanded first to include Wales and only later united with Scotland? *(Possible answer: Scotland was more mountainous and harder to conquer than Wales.)*

View the Art ★

A. The first London coffee-house was established in Cornhill in 1652.

B. William Hogarth (1697–1764) began his career as an apprentice to a silver engraver.

C. During the sixteenth century, Ampthill Park was royal property. Henry VIII hunted there.

Assess

Reading Check

Answers:

1. *Nearly five times greater*

2. *1,000,000 to 1,250,000 pounds*

3. *As an English Channel seaport, it would be one of the first places reached by an outbreak of plague spreading from the continent of Europe.*

Teach

Make Predictions Have students read the first three paragraphs, under the headings "The Divine Right of Kings" and "Growing Conflict." **Ask:** What do you predict you will read about next? Discuss students' predictions.

(ADVANCED) Have advanced students research the differences of opinion between the king and Parliament on economic matters. Ask them to determine what the two parties disagreed about and who they think was right.

View the Art ★

The London *Times* obituary of Charles West Cope (1811–1890), published on August 27, 1890, remembered a well-known "painter of historical and domestic scenes." *The Pilgrim Fathers* is remembered as one of his noteworthy works.

Learning Objectives

For pages 492–506
In studying this text, you will focus on the following objectives:

Literary Study: Analyzing a literary period.

Reading: Evaluating historical influences.
Connecting to the literature.

From PURITANISM to the ENLIGHTENMENT

1640–1780

Historical, Social, and Cultural Forces

The Divine Right of Kings

When James I succeeded to the English throne, he firmly upheld the principle of the divine right of kings, the belief that the regent derives power directly from God. James was not interested in reforming the Church of England, but rather in making his subjects conform to its practices. Catholics were forbidden to celebrate Mass, and Puritans could not gather for religious meetings. Many religious dissidents left England. Catholics tended to emigrate to the European continent, particularly France and Italy. The Puritans first found a home in Holland, and later voyaged to North America, where they established the Plymouth Colony in 1620 in present-day Massachusetts.

The Pilgrim Fathers: Departure of a Puritan Family for New England, 1856. Charles West Cope. Oil on canvas, 87²/10 x 113²/10 in. National Gallery of Victoria, Melbourne, Australia.

Growing Conflict

When James's son Charles I came to the throne in 1625, people who hoped for a more tolerant ruler were disappointed. The new king had taken to heart his father's example of ruling by divine right. Because of his belief that he would be committing a grave sin in surrendering part of his authority, Charles disregarded Parliament's opinions on economic spending. By 1629, with Parliament and the king unable to agree on religious and economic matters, Charles dissolved Parliament and did not call it back for eleven years.

During the "eleven years' tyranny," grievances on both sides mounted. By the time Charles recalled Parliament in 1640, it was too late for any permanent compromise. Parliament called for a new constitution that included their demands to control all church and military matters and appoint ministers and judges. The king moved his court from London to the northern city of York. The ideological battle lines were drawn; by August 1642, war had begun. **1**

Civil War

The English civil war was fought between Royalist Cavaliers loyal to the king and the Puritan Roundheads (so called because their hair was cut short, unlike the long-haired courtiers). Over time, Parliament proved victorious, due largely ★ to the New Model Army of Oliver Cromwell, a

Reading Practice

SPIRAL REVIEW **Note Taking** One way to take notes on this text would be to create a three column chart with heads as follows: Historical Forces, Social Forces, and Cultural Forces. Ask students to identify at least one example for each heading. *(Historical: the reign of James I; Social:*

prejudice and intolerance toward Catholics and Puritans; Cultural: Anglican ritual)

Historical: The reign of James I	Social: Prejudice and intolerance toward Catholics and Puritans	Cultural: Anglican ritual

military genius and Puritan extremist. In April 1646, Charles surrendered himself to the Scots, who turned him over to Parliament in exchange for a large ransom.

By this time, the Parliamentary forces wanted to do away with the monarchy. The court that tried Charles accused him of being a "Tyrant, Traitor and Murderer; and a public enemy to the good people of this nation." The trial was controversial; many people who had fought against Charles were reluctant to resort to execution. Nonetheless, the death sentence was passed, and the king was publicly beheaded. A week after his death, Parliament abolished the monarchy.

The Commonwealth and The Restoration

Cromwell became the Lord Protector of the country. Until his death in 1658, Cromwell imposed strict Puritanical rules on public behavior and religious worship. He closed theaters, banned dancing and music, and caused all religious icons to be destroyed as "graven images."

In 1660 the English Parliament that had ordered the execution of Charles I invited his son Charles II to return from exile and reclaim the throne.

With the restoration of the monarchy, theaters were reopened, public festivals were celebrated, and new fashions in clothes, food, and ideas flooded in from the European continent. Intellectual life began to flourish once more and set the stage for the burgeoning Enlightenment that took hold in England during the following century.

The Enlightenment and Neoclassicism

The Enlightenment was a European philosophical and literary movement that in England is often called "The Age of Reason." It is characterized by a profound faith in the power of human reason and a devotion to clarity of thought. Other hallmarks of the age were a skeptical attitude toward traditional religion, best represented by the Scottish philosopher David Hume, and a surge of scientific discovery.

A related literary movement was Neoclassicism, which reached its pinnacle in the poetry, prose, and criticism of Samuel Johnson. Its major tenet was the conviction that the classical authors of ancient Greece and Rome had perfected the rules and norms that should govern the writing of literature for all time. **2**

PREVIEW **Big Ideas** **Puritanism to the Enlightenment**

1 Puritanism and the Civil War	**2** The Restoration	**3** The English Enlightenment & Neoclassicism
In the early 1640s, conflicts between the Anglican supporters of the monarchy and the Puritan supporters of Parliament brought about the English civil war. Many English writers of the period took sides in the struggle. **See pages 500–501.**	After ten years of stern Puritan rule, the newly restored British monarchy under King Charles II was greeted with enthusiasm. British literary culture of the Restoration was marked by a witty, cynical tone and an emphasis on worldly values. **See pages 502–503.**	The late 1600s saw the rise of the Enlightenment, an intellectual movement that accepted reason as the supreme authority. In the eighteenth century, Neoclassicists sought to revive the literary principles of ancient Greece and Rome. **See pages 504–505.**

Teach

Reading Strategy **2**

Confirm Predictions Have students reflect on their predictions after they finish reading the essay. **Ask:** Were your predictions correct? Explain to students that predictions do not have to be correct to be valuable. Their value is in engaging the reader with the text. Making predictions makes reading more interesting.

Political History

Parliament Parliament began as a group of noble advisers to the king. With the signing of the Magna Carta by King John in 1215, a 400-year power struggle began between Parliament and the monarch. The struggle was resolved in 1689 with passage of the Bill of Rights, which stated that laws could be made or repealed only by Parliament. The king could not act alone.

English Learners

DIFFERENTIATED INSTRUCTION

Intermediate Discuss the prefixes *en-, neo-, re-* and the suffixes *-ation, -ism, -ment,* using the examples *restoration, enlightenment,* and *neoclassicism.* Ask students to identify the root words and determine the correct meanings of the prefixes and suffixes. Explain that a grasp of common prefixes and suffixes is a powerful tool in reading comprehension.

Teach

Reading Strategy | 1

Analyze Causes and Effects

Have students create a chart showing the causes and effects discussed in the text on page 500. *(Possible answers: Cause: belief that authority came from God; effect: ferocity of conviction. Cause: Puritan religious intolerance of Catholics; effect: disagreement over policy toward Spain.)*

[APPROACHING] Leading questions can help approaching-level students locate causes and effects. **Ask:** Why did the Puritans feel so strongly about their cause? *(They wanted to purify the church of England.)* Why did James have problems with Parliament? *(religious differences)*

Cultural History ☆

Relics A relic is an object of religious veneration. It is usually a piece of the body or a personal item belonging to a saint. The following relics of Charles I were preserved in Ashburnham Church: the bloody shirt in which he was executed, the watch he wore the day of his execution, his "white silk knit drawers," and the sheet thrown over his body after his execution.

Big Idea 1
Puritanism and the Civil War

The Royalists and the Puritans, who would battle each other in the English civil war, both believed that all authority came from God. But they violently disagreed about how God's authority showed itself in the world, and this fierce dispute led to war.

What Was Puritanism?

Puritanism was a radical form of Calvinistic Protestantism whose adherents acknowledged only the "pure" word of God as revealed in their interpretations of the Bible. Puritans also shared the central goal of purifying the Church of England by eradicating the doctrines and rites that were retained from Catholicism.

The best thinkers among the Puritans embraced a liberal stance in politics that balanced their religious intolerance. John Milton, a democrat and pamphleteer for the anti-Royalist forces, spoke for "the true warfaring Christian" in his famous essay *Areopagitica:* "I cannot praise a fugitive and cloistered virtue, unexercised and unbreathed, that never sallies out and sees her adversary, but slinks out of the race, where that immortal garland is to be run for, not without dust and heat." Puritans such as Milton valued civil liberties and were zealous in defending their beliefs.

Religious Conflict

At least since the time of Elizabeth I, Puritans and other nonconformists (a blanket term for any Protestants who did not conform to the rites of the official Church of England) had been a thorn in the side of the monarch. James I had difficulties with Parliament, especially over government funding and foreign relations. James encouraged closer ties with Catholic Spain, even when Spain was at war with Protestant Holland. The House of Commons, with a large Puritan contingent, preferred to wage a Puritan crusade. James arrested some of his Parliamentary opponents; the Commons made a protest asserting their liberties. Ultimately, the English civil war began over questions of authority—who had it and how it should be divided.

The Civil War

At the beginning of the war, the Royalist forces won some impressive victories, particularly because of the strength of their cavalry. Under the leadership of Oliver Cromwell, however, the Parliamentary army turned the tide. At the Battle of Naseby in June 1645, a miscalculation by the king and his cavalry commander, coupled with brilliant maneuvers by Cromwell, turned the battle into a Puritan victory.

Three and a half years later, in January 1649, Parliament tried the king for treason and condemned him to death. With the fall of the axe, the Puritans demonstrated that the former subjects wielded the sovereignty now. The moan from the assembled crowd, however, suggested that many were deeply divided and fearful.

Puritan Rule

Cromwell was a complex leader who left a legacy to be both admired and deplored. He preached and practiced religious toleration—except for Catholics. Throughout England, baptismal fonts, statues of saints, ceiling and altar decorations—the Catholic devotional art of centuries—were smashed. Under Cromwell's government, the economy prospered, but there was little pleasure or entertainment in a country where public music was banned and theaters were closed. What had begun as a noble experiment in liberty ended in a military dictatorship.

After Cromwell's death in 1658, his son Richard briefly attempted to rule as Lord Protector, but he

Reading Practice

[SPIRAL REVIEW] Organize Ideas

Point out that each paragraph in the body of an essay should have a topic sentence that clearly relates to the thesis statement. **Ask:** What is the thesis statement of "Puritanism and the Civil War"? *("But they violently disagreed about how God's authority showed itself in the world, and this fierce dispute led to war.")* Ask students to identify topic sentences in the paragraphs that follow and to discuss how they support the thesis.

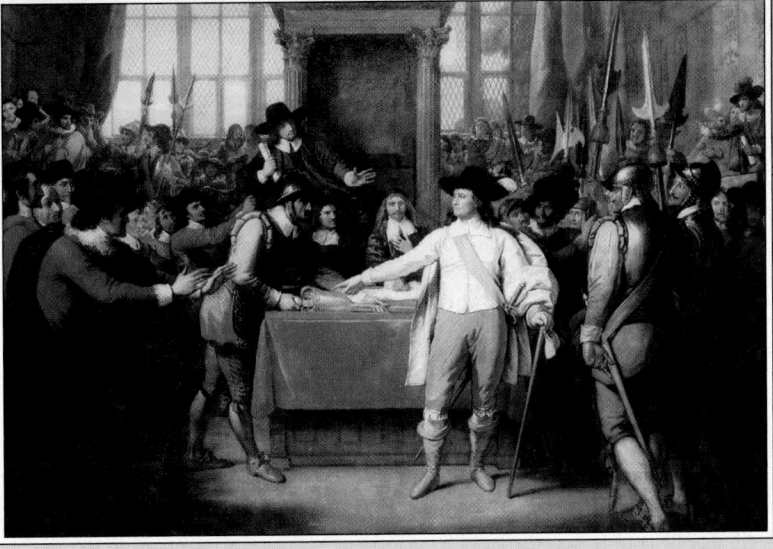
Cromwell Dissolving the Long Parliament, Benjamin West. Oil on canvas. Montclair Art Museum, NJ. ★

was ousted by the military, which disbanded Parliament and ruled incompetently. When order was restored by some of the king's old enemies, there seemed only one solution. In May 1660, Charles II returned triumphant, riding through London to the palace of Whitehall, the scene of his father's execution twelve years before.

1

In 1644, *responding to a recent government order imposing censorship, John Milton published his essay* Areopagitica, *a defense of freedom of the press.*

from **Areopagitica** by John Milton

I deny not, but that it is of greatest concernment in the Church and Commonwealth, to have a vigilant eye how books demean themselves as well as men; and thereafter to confine, imprison, and do sharpest justice on them as malefactors. For books are not absolutely dead things, but do contain a potency of life in them to be as active as that soul was whose progeny they are; nay, they do preserve as in a vial the purest efficacy and extraction of that living intellect that bred them. I know they are as lively, and as vigorously productive, as those fabulous dragon's teeth, and being sown up and down, may chance to spring up armed men. And yet, on the other hand, **2** unless wariness be used, as good almost kill a man as kill a good book: who kills a man kills a reasonable creature, God's image; but he who destroys a good book, kills reason itself, kills the image of God, as it were in the eye. Many a man lives a burden to the earth; but a good book is the precious life-blood of a master spirit, embalmed and treasured up on purpose to a life beyond life. 'Tis true, no age can restore a life, whereof perhaps there is no great loss; and revolutions of ages do not oft recover the loss of a rejected truth, for the want of which whole nations fare the worse.

2

Reading Check

Analyze Cause and Effect What made Cromwell an unpopular ruler?

Teach

Literary Element   2

Argument Ask: How would you summarize Milton's argument? *(The loss of a book is greater than the loss of a life, for the book lives on as a distillation of human intellect.)* Which part of the argument is Milton's recognition of the opposing argument? *(The allusion to the dragon's teeth)*

View the Art ★

Benjamin West (c. 1738–1820) was born in the United States, studied Neoclassical painting in Italy, and earned a living as a portrait painter in London from age 25 until he was given patronage by King George III.

Assess
Reading Check

Answer: *Cromwell was dictatorial; he forbade various forms of entertainment and persecuted non-Puritans.*

English Learners

DIFFERENTIATED INSTRUCTION

Beginning Make sure students understand that Milton is comparing the value of a good book with the value of a human life. Clarify the allusion to the dragon of Greek mythology whose teeth were planted in the soil and grew an army of men.

Approaching Level

DIFFERENTIATED INSTRUCTION

SMALL GROUP

Emerging Ask students to work in small groups to rewrite the excerpt in clear modern sentences. Make sure each group has access to a dictionary and a thesaurus. Invite students to read their rewrites aloud, and discuss the various versions.

Reading Strategy | 1

Make Predictions Have students read the opening paragraph on this page. **Ask:** What do you expect to be included in the era's "good times"? *(public entertainment and intellectual freedom)* Have students complete the reading. **Ask:** Did anything you read about surprise you? *(women on stage, bawdy literature)*

Cultural History ☆

The Tower of London Begun during the reign of William the Conqueror (1066–1087) the Tower of London was a fortification to control the "vast and fierce populace." It was used as a base for royal power in London and as a retreat during times of civil unrest. As rulers have come and gone, the tower has been used as a prison, menagerie, execution site, mint, armory, jewel house, and tourist attraction.

Reading Practice

SPIRAL REVIEW **Develop a Graphic Organizer** Guide students in creating a problem/solution chart to help them understand and enjoy "The Restoration". **Say:** Write the title as the header. As you read, add details about problems that were faced and solutions that were presented in the period called the Restoration.

Problem	Solution

Big Idea 2
The Restoration

1 We all know the sense of relief we feel when an arduous task is done or a difficult experience is finally over. After twenty years of turmoil, England was ready for a return to good times.

The Restoration Court

As he traveled through England to reclaim his throne, Charles II was greeted by many spontaneous outpourings of joy from the people. Writers and artists who looked forward to the renewal of royal patronage for their work were quick to praise his return.

Charles was a far cry from both his father and Oliver Cromwell. Known as the merry monarch, the good-natured Charles enjoyed pleasures of all kinds, from courtly entertainments to his royal mistresses. Trying to break the cycle of retribution which had plagued England for so long, Charles forgave many of his father's old enemies. His mercy did not extend, however, to most of the judges at his father's trial and signers of the order of execution. Cromwell's body, which had been buried in the Tower of London, was dug up, ☆ beheaded, and reburied in a common pit.

Public Pleasures

Charles II's taste for pleasure was shared by many of his subjects, whose lives had been dreary under Puritan rule. Holidays such as Christmas were celebrated once more, horse races—and betting—started up again, and music and evening masquerade parties filled public pleasure gardens such as Vauxhall. Charles also reopened the theaters. Audiences had an insatiable appetite for comedies about the fashionable manners of the age. Bawdy, witty, and amoral, these Restoration dramas by such playwrights as William Congreve, William Wycherley, and George Farquhar reflect a cynical frivolity in matters of love and money.

One of the most popular playwrights of the day was Aphra Behn, the first woman in England to make her living as a professional writer. Behn was often accused of lewdness, but there is no doubt that her vivacious comedies reflected the pleasure-loving attitude and carpe diem spirit of the Restoration.

The new licentiousness of public behavior was not universally shared. Puritans and others spoke out against the irreverence of the age. But dissenting too loudly could lead to jail, as it did in the case of John Bunyan, who spent more than twelve years imprisoned for his defiant Puritanism.

Plague and Fire

Perhaps the Puritans viewed the twin disasters of plague and fire as a punishment from God for what they perceived to be the immorality and corruption of the age. But the outbreak of the bubonic plague in 1665 disproportionately affected the poor. The College of Physicians ordered houses in which plague appeared to be nailed shut, leaving all the inhabitants to their fate. Wealthy people could engineer their escape and pay to leave London. So many victims died that bodies were buried in communal pits rather than in individual plots. The official number of the dead was more than 68,000; with the addition of people not usually included on official lists, such as Quakers and Jews, the actual number was probably more than 100,000.

Unlike the plague, the Great Fire of London equally affected both the rich and the poor. The fire raged for four days and continued to smolder for almost two months. An area about one and one-half miles long by a half mile wide was completely destroyed, including most of old London within its medieval walls. The king, who had shown great personal courage and intelligence in

John Rose Presenting the First English-Grown Pineapple to Charles II, 1675. Hendrick Danckerts. Victoria and Albert Museum, London. ★

fighting the fire, took a vigorous interest in rebuilding the city—in fire-resistant stone—on an elegant and systematic scale. He placed his plan in the hands of Sir Christopher Wren, an astronomer by training, who proved to be the greatest civic architect England has ever produced.

One of the most brilliant and notorious members of the Restoration was John Wilmot, Earl of Rochester.

from *A Satire Against Mankind* by John Wilmot

Were I (who to my cost already am
One of those strange, prodigious creatures, man)
A spirit free to choose, for my own share,
What case of flesh and blood I pleased to wear,
I'd be a dog, a monkey, or a bear,
Or anything but that vain animal
Who is so proud of being rational.
  The senses are too gross, and he'll contrive
A sixth to contradict the other five,
And before certain instinct will prefer
Reason, which fifty times for one does err;
Reason, an *ignis fatuus* in the mind,
Which, leaving light of nature, sense, behind,
Pathless and dangerous wandering ways it takes
Through error's fenny bogs and thorny brakes;
Whilst the misguided follower climbs with pain
Mountains of whimseys, heaped in his own brain;

Stumbling from thought to thought falls headlong down
Into doubt's boundless sea, where, like to drown,
Books bear him up a while, and make him try
To swim with bladders of philosophy;
In hopes still to o'ertake the escaping light,—
The vapor dances in his dazzling sight
Till, spent, it leaves him to eternal night.
Then old age and experience, hand in hand,
Lead him to death and make him understand,
After a search so painful and so long,
That all his life he has been in the wrong.
Huddled in dirt the reasoning engine lies,
Who was so proud, so witty, and so wise.

2

Reading Check

Compare and Contrast How did the attitude toward the arts during the Restoration differ from that during the Puritan Commonwealth?

INTRODUCTION **503**

Reading Strategy | 1

Compare and Contrast

Draw a Venn diagram on the board to compare Enlightenment approaches to science and literature (science in one circle; literature in the other; both in the intersection of the two circles).

Ask: What was similar about Enlightenment approaches to science and literature? *(Both were governed by the laws of nature.)*

Literary History ☆

Aristotle's *Poetics* The following excerpt from Aristotle's work discusses tragedy: "Tragedy is an imitation not only of a complete action, but of events inspiring fear or pity. Such an effect is best produced when the events come on us by surprise; and the effect is heightened when, at the same time, they follow as cause and effect. The tragic wonder will then be greater than if they happened of themselves or by accident; for even coincidences are most striking when they have an air of design."

Big Idea 3

English Enlightenment and Neoclassicism

Can humans understand the complexities of the natural world without the aid of divine revelation? Many eighteenth-century intellectuals were Deists, who believed that God manifests himself, not through the Bible or supernatural forces, but through the grandeur of his creation. Therefore, the way to know God is to use reason and observation to study the laws that govern the physical universe. This Enlightenment way of thinking led to a creative outburst of scientific inquiry and intellectual freedom that was unprecedented in the Western world.

A Scientific Revolution

Soon after his restoration to the throne, Charles II granted a charter to a group of "natural philosophers," or scientists, who were inspired by Francis Bacon's inductive approach to knowledge. The group became known as the Royal Society of London for the Promotion of Natural Knowledge. Early members included the astronomer and architect Christopher Wren, the chemist Robert Boyle, the astronomer Edmund Halley, and above all Isaac Newton, who made revolutionary advances in physics, mathematics, optics, and astronomy. Because of Newton, the mechanical workings of the universe were no longer considered mysterious, but instead could be understood by humans.

The Rule of Reason

In their study of nature, the members of the Royal Society emphasized the importance of experiment and observation. Nature was their sole authority. The Royal Society's Latin motto, *nullius in verba,* means "on the word of no one." Communicating their learning to others in a clear and accurate manner was a vital part of their methodology. They started the first scientific journal, *Philosophical Transactions,* which is still published today, to disseminate the discoveries of their members. Their plain style has influenced English prose—particularly in science, philosophy, and journalism—to this day.

The Rule of the Ancients

Just as the members of the Royal Society were concerned with extracting universal laws of nature from the diverse data of the real world, so too philosophers and poets set themselves the task of identifying universal laws of human nature. They believed that nature was rational and orderly, and that these underlying patterns were harmonious and beautiful. Poetry, no less than physics, was governed by natural, not man-made, laws. Therefore, the purpose of art was to imitate nature.

> *"Those RULES of old discovered, not devised / Are Nature still, but Nature methodized."*
>
> —Alexander Pope, Essay on Criticism

By "rules of old," Pope was referring to the literary norms established by classical Greek and Roman authors that eighteenth-century writers began to apply in their own work. Neoclassical writers turned to ancient texts, such as Aristotle's *Poetics,* ☆ because they believed those texts explained the natural laws that govern, for example, why audiences laugh at comic characters or feel pity and terror for the downfall of a tragic hero.

The satirist Jonathan Swift gave literary life to the conflict between the ancients and the moderns in his satire *The Battle of the Books,* which contains the story of a spider and a bee in a library. The modern spider spins "dirt and poison" out of its own entrails; the ancient bee goes to the most fragrant flowers of nature to find the "sweetness and

---

Reading Practice

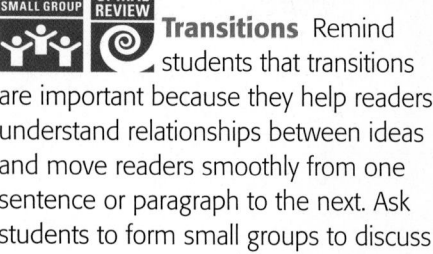

Transitions Remind students that transitions are important because they help readers understand relationships between ideas and move readers smoothly from one sentence or paragraph to the next. Ask students to form small groups to discuss the five paragraph transitions in "English Enlightenment and Neoclassicism." Ask them to assign a grade to each transition and provide a rationale for the grade. Then meet as a class, compare the grades from each group, and discuss.

Covent Garden Market, 1737. Balthazar Nebot. Tate Gallery, London.

Reading Strategy | 2

Reread Remind students that it is generally expected that a passage of verse will need to be read several times to be understood. Ask students to read the passage to themselves three times. Then pair them and have partners read to each other and work together to interpret meaning. After another silent reading, discuss the meaning of the excerpt as a class.

light" out of which it makes its honey. The poem ends with a ferocious battle between ancients, such as Homer and Aristotle, and moderns, such as Dryden and Milton. Pope, Swift, and other writers believed that satire could spur improvements in moral and social behavior. Satire, by pointing out our faults and vices, can induce us to live a more balanced, moderate, and harmonious life.

Alexander Pope's admiration for ancient Greek and Roman culture inspired one of his greatest achievements, the translation of the epics of Homer. In the following passage from Pope's Neoclassical translation of the Odyssey, the goddess Pallas Athena aids Odysseus in the destruction of his enemies by displaying her shield, the aegis, which inspires terror in all who see it.

from the **Odyssey, Book 22,** translated by Alexander Pope

Now *Pallas* shines confess'd; aloft she spreads
The arm of vengeance o'er their guilty heads;
The dreadful *Aegis* blazes in their eye;
Amaz'd they see, they tremble, and they fly:
Confus'd, distracted, thro' the rooms they fling,
Like oxen madden'd by the breeze's sting,
When sultry days, and long, succeed the gentle spring.
Not half so keen, fierce vulturs of the chace
Stoop from the mountains on the feather'd race,
When the wide field extended snares beset,

With conscious dread they shun the quiv'ring net:
No help, no flight; but wounded ev'ry way,
Headlong they drop: the fowlers seize their prey.
On all sides thus they double wound on wound,
In prostrate heaps the wretches beat the ground,
Unmanly shrieks precede each dying groan,
And a red deluge floats the reeking stone. **2**

Reading Check

Interpret Why did Neoclassical writers believe that art should imitate nature?

View the Art ★

Balthazar Nebot (active c. 1730–1765) has largely evaded the public record. It is believed he was born in Spain and married in London around 1730. He is best known for work he completed in the decade after his marriage, which included market scenes like the one shown here.

English Learners

DIFFERENTIATED INSTRUCTION

Intermediate Ask students to identify and explain the metaphors present in the passage from the *Odyssey*. If necessary, prompt them with questions such as, "Who is compared to oxen? Why does the poet use this image? What is the 'red deluge'?" Encourage students to use the dictionary to identify difficult words such as *deluge*.

Assess

Legacy of the Period

Refer students to the last sentence of the first paragraph. **Ask:** What ideas are currently fought about in print? (*Possible answers: cloning; investing in space travel*)

Cultural and Literary Links

Ask students to think, as they read, about how Enlightenment and Neoclassical authors have influenced modern world views.

Connect to Today

1. **Follow Up** (a) radical Calvinists, acknowledged only "pure" word of God (b) conflicts between Anglicans and Puritans (c) reason over religion

2. **Contrast Literary Periods** Have students consider issues such as national security and the right to privacy.

3. **Build Visual Literacy** You may wish to have students work in small groups.

4. **Take Notes** Encourage students to record questions as they read the selections in this unit in the Foldables Study Organizer. Students can then revisit and find answers to these questions after they have finished reading each selection.

FOLDABLES®
Study Organizer

Have students make and label the Layered-Look Book. They can ask questions about each Big Idea on each page.

WRAP-UP

Legacy of the Period

During this time, the British press and freedom of thought and expression became increasingly less restricted. British intellectual life was more and more marked by the desire to share information, explore new ideas, and to fight about them in print rather than on the battlefield.

The thinkers of the English Enlightenment helped to shape the ideals of the American Revolution and the U.S. government. John Locke's theory of natural rights is a key element in the Declaration of Independence. Arguments against the authoritarian rule of the king by intellectuals such as Milton, Locke, and Thomas Hobbes influenced the writers of *The Federalist Papers*, a series of articles supporting ratification of the U.S. Constitution.

The ideas of the scientific revolution and the Enlightenment laid the foundation for a modern worldview based on rationalism and secularism. The widespread use of the scientific method—the systematic procedures for collecting and analyzing evidence—was crucial to the development of modern science. The intellectuals of the Enlightenment advocated the rights of the individual, paving the way for the rise of democracy in the 1800s and 1900s.

Cultural and Literary Links

» English Puritanism was a basic element in the development of American colonial literature. Pilgrim leader William Bradford advocated the use of a plain style that became an enduring influence on American literature.

» John Milton's Satan in *Paradise Lost* is an archetypal rebel who influenced such characters as the monster in Mary Shelley's *Frankenstein* and Captain Ahab in Herman Melville's *Moby-Dick*.

» Jonathan Swift's *Gulliver's Travels* has added several words to the English language, such as *Lilliputian* (tiny) and *Yahoo* (crude person).

 **LOG ON** **Literature** Online

Unit Resources For additional skills practice, go to glencoe.com and enter QuickPass code GLB9817u3.

Activities

Choose one of the following activities to explore and develop as you read this unit.

1. Follow Up Go back to Looking Ahead on page 493 and answer the questions.

2. Contrast Literary Periods Milton's argument for freedom of the press was grounded in his religious convictions about the freedom of the individual conscience. What reasons do journalists give today when they argue against censorship? Working with other students, research contemporary issues involving freedom of the press, and hold a panel discussion dealing with the issues they raise.

3. Build Visual Literacy Make a chart contrasting the strengths and weaknesses of the Puritan Commonwealth and the Restoration monarchy. Illustrate the chart with seventeenth-century British artworks.

4. Take Notes Use this study organizer to jot down questions you have about the readings in this unit.

 FOLDABLES
Study Organizer

LAYERED LOOK BOOK

Reader's Questions
Who?
What?
Where?
When?
Why?

Writing Practice

 Summarize and Draw Conclusions

SMALL GROUP Divide students into heterogeneous groups. Ask them to create an outline summarizing the key points of the philosophies of the Puritans and of the Englightenment. Then have the groups discuss which aspects of each school of thought influence the way we think today. Ask the groups to write their conclusions in a paragraph.

Part 1

THE CIVIL WAR, THE COMMONWEALTH, AND THE RESTORATION

After van Dyck: Triple Portrait of King Charles I, c. 17th century. Henry Stone. Victoria and Albert Museum, London.

 View the Art As the title suggests, this portrait was painted in the style of Sir Anthony van Dyck, an artist Charles greatly admired. What does the artwork seem to suggest about the king? How is your impression affected by the quotation below?

"None can love freedom but good men;
the rest love not freedom but license, which never
hath more scope than under tyrants." **1**

—John Milton, *The Tenure of Kings and Magistrates*

507

Analyzing and Extending

Reading Strategy | 1

Interpret Meaning Encourage students to use a dictionary to clarify the definition of any words in the quote which are unclear. **Ask:** Why would license have greater scope under a tyrant? *(Oppression provides the necessary conditions for disregarding accepted rules or standards.)*

View the Art ★

Henry Stone (c. 1616–1653) is usually remembered for his copies of works by Italian artists. In this case, Stone has copied the famous Flemish portraitist van Dyck.

Possible Answers: *Students may say that the portrait makes the king look dignified, proper, powerful, or confident. Some students may say that their opinion of him becomes more negative after reading Milton's quote about tyrants; others may say that they view him more favorably, as one of the "good men" Milton writes about.*

 For additional support for English Learners, see Unit 3 Teaching Resources Book, p. 19.

Milton's Poetry

Bellringer Options

Selection Focus
  Transparency 23
Daily Language Practice
  Transparency 39

Or **write** this question on the board: What would you like to accomplish by the time you are 30? List some of students' responses, then repeat the question for ages 40, 50, and so on. Tell students to keep these goals in mind as they read the poems in this lesson.

Meet **John Milton**
(1608–1674)

John Milton recognized his potential as a writer at an early age. In fact, he had so much confidence in his literary talents that by the age of twenty-one he had declared it his intention to become a "great poet." The intensity of his work and the large scale of his subject matter helped him live up to this intention. He once expressed that his goal was to "justify the ways of God to men."

Early Success Milton was born in London on December 9, 1608. His early education took place at St. Paul's School, and his earliest attempts at poetry were rhymed retellings of Psalms 114 and 136. In April 1625, he became a student of Christ's College in Cambridge, where he gained the respect of his classmates, as well as the high esteem of his teachers. After graduating, Milton spent six years at his father's country home, reading extensively and writing several highly regarded works, including *Lycidas*, a poem about the death of a classmate, which is considered one of the finest elegies in the English language. When he was about thirty, Milton traveled to Italy where the artists, scholars, philosophers, and scientists whose works he had been studying hailed him as a brilliant young poet, further fueling his ambitions.

Political Pursuits However, political conflicts at home caused him to cut his trip short. Back in England, Milton gave up all his other pursuits to write pamphlets in defense of religious and civil freedoms. He believed that the people delegated power to the king, and had a right to overthrow a king who abused that power. During this time, Milton also suffered several tragedies, including the deaths of his first and second wives, the deaths of all but three of his children, and, at the age of forty-four, the loss of his eyesight.

> "Yet some there be that by due steps aspire
> To lay their just hands on that golden key
> That opes the palace of Eternity."
>
> —John Milton, from *Il Penseroso*

The Epic Poems Not until 1660 was Milton free to devote himself to writing the epic poems he had planned so many years earlier. Unfortunately, the events leading to this "free time" were less than ideal. When the Puritan government was dissolved and King Charles II ascended the throne, Milton was arrested as a traitor. Influential friends saved him from execution, but he was forced to retire and pay heavy fines. Blind, penniless, and bitterly disappointed by the collapse of the Commonwealth, Milton returned to his first love, poetry.

In the years before his death, and with the help of paid assistants, family members, and friends, he published *Paradise Lost*, his great epic masterpiece about Adam and Eve's fall from grace. He later published *Paradise Regained*, a shorter epic that tells of Christ's temptation in the wilderness.

 Literature Online

Author Search For more about John Milton, go to glencoe.com and enter QuickPass code GLB9817u3.

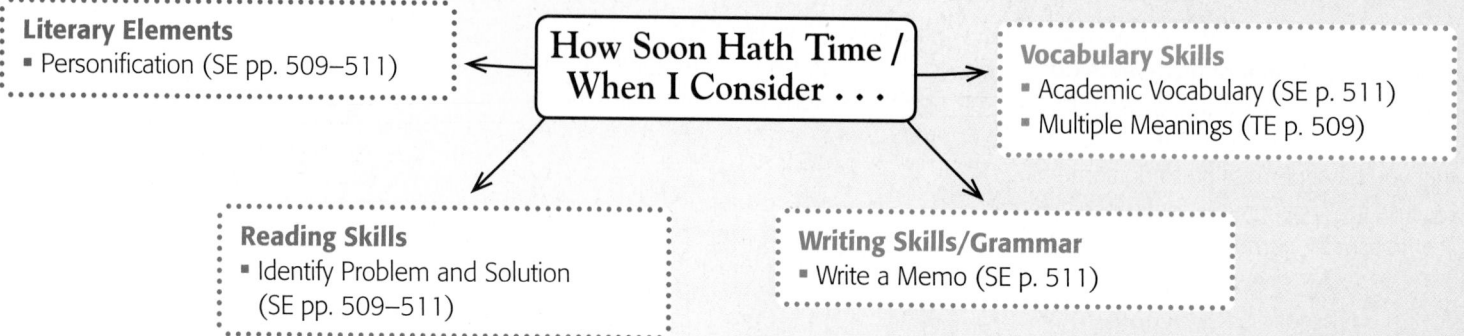

Literary Elements
- Personification (SE pp. 509–511)

**How Soon Hath Time /
When I Consider . . .**

Vocabulary Skills
- Academic Vocabulary (SE p. 511)
- Multiple Meanings (TE p. 509)

Reading Skills
- Identify Problem and Solution
  (SE pp. 509–511)

Writing Skills/Grammar
- Write a Memo (SE p. 511)

Literature and Reading Preview

Connect to the Poems

How well do you follow through on the goals you set for yourself or the goals others suggest to you? Write a journal entry in which you reflect on this topic.

Build Background

The two sonnets you are about to read are autobiographical, and Milton employed the Italian, or Petrarchan, sonnet form in both (see page 242). In "How Soon Hath Time," Milton expresses his thoughts and feelings on his twenty-third birthday. In "When I Consider How My Light Is Spent," composed twenty years later, he writes about his concerns after having just gone blind.

Set Purposes for Reading

Big Idea Puritanism and the Civil War

As you read these poems, ask yourself, What in them might help explain Milton's religious devotion and his identification with the Puritan cause?

Literary Element Personification

Personification is a figure of speech in which an animal, object, force of nature, or idea is given human characteristics. By presenting something such as the wind, the passing of time, or the virtue of patience as a person, a writer is able to intensify certain ideas. As you read, ask yourself, Where is Milton making use of personification?

Reading Strategy Identify Problem and Solution

The Italian sonnet form is conducive to presenting a **problem** and a **solution**. Review the information about this type of sonnet on pages 242–243. As you read, ask yourself, What problem and solution are presented in each poem?

Tip: Using Details to Summarize Look for details in the poems that point to the problem, as well as details that lead to the solution. Then, in your own words, summarize the problem and the solution. Use a chart like the one shown here to help you organize your thoughts.

Learning Objectives

For pages 508–511

In studying these texts, you will focus on the following objectives:

Literary Study: Analyzing a literary period.

Reading:
Evaluating historical influences.
Connecting to the literature.

"How Soon Hath Time"	"When I Consider . . ."
Details Related to Problem	Details Related to Problem
1. twenty-third birthday	1. light is spent
2.	2.
3.	3.
Summary of Problem:	Summary of Problem:
Details Related to Solution	Details Related to Solution
1.	1.
2.	2.
3.	3.
Summary of Solution:	Summary of Solution:

JOHN MILTON **509**

Before You Read

Focus

Summary

In "How Soon Hath Time," Milton speaks of the speed with which the first 23 years of life have gone and the lack of blossoming or achievement he feels. As he grows older, rather than dwell on his concern, he submits himself to God.

In "When I Consider How My Light Is Spent," Milton worries that his loss of eyesight may keep him from serving God. Patience tells him that God doesn't need his good works; those "also serve who only stand and wait."

 For summaries in languages other than English, see Unit 3 Teaching Resources Book, pp. 20–25.

Vocabulary

Multiple Meanings Say: Milton often uses words that have more than one meaning. He expects readers to notice the various meanings of his words. **Write** the words *measure* and *account* on the board. Have students give two possible meanings for each word. (*measure: amount, meter; account: narrative, worth*)

 For additional context, see Glencoe Visual Vocabulary CD-ROM.

English Learners

DIFFERENTIATED INSTRUCTION

Intermediate Say: Like many poets of his time period, Milton often uses old-fashioned, or archaic, language. For example, he uses verb forms with the ending *–th* or *–eth*. **Write** the word *showeth* on the board and circle the verb *show*. **Say:** To find the verb in these forms, remove the *–th* or *–eth*. Have students circle archaic verb forms in Milton's poems and translate them into contemporary English.

Teach

Reading Strategy   1

Identify Problem and Solution Answer: *The speaker observes that time is passing quickly. This bothers him because he feels that he should have accomplished more by this time in his life.*

For additional practice using the reading skill or strategy, see Unit 3 Teaching Resources Book, p. 27.

Literary Element   2

Personification Answer: *Patience is personified. Students may say that the personification of patience intensifies the speaker's internal conflict and the resolution that he finds.*

ENGLISH LEARNERS Remind English learners that proper names are capitalized. **Say:** By capitalizing "Patience," Milton transforms the word into a proper name, which personifies a noun that would normally be lowercase.

Cultural History

Cambridge University Milton wrote "How Soon Hath Time" shortly after graduating from Cambridge University. Founded in 1209, Cambridge is considered one of England's finest universities. Like Oxford University, Cambridge is divided into smaller colleges. Milton attended Christ's College, as did Charles Darwin and the comedian Sacha Baron Cohen.

How Soon Hath Time

John Milton

How soon hath Time, the subtle thief of youth,
Stolen on his wing my three and twentieth year!
My hasting days fly on with full career,[1]
But my late spring no bud or blossom showeth.
5 Perhaps my semblance[2] might deceive the truth,
That I to manhood am arrived so near,
And inward ripeness doth much less appear,
That some more timely-happy spirits endueth.[3]
Yet be it less or more, or soon or slow,
10 It shall be still[4] in strictest measure even[5]
To that same lot,[6] however mean[7] or high,
Toward which Time leads me, and the will of Heaven;
All is, if I have grace to use it so,
As ever in my great Taskmaster's eye.

1. *Career* means "speed."
2. *Semblance* means "outward appearance."
3. *Endueth* means "endow."
4. *Still* means "always."
5. *Even* means "equal" or "adequate."
6. *Lot* means "fate."
7. *Mean* in this context means "low in status or quality."

When I Consider How My Light Is Spent

John Milton

When I consider how my light is spent
Ere half my days in this dark world and wide,
And that one talent[1] which is death to hide,
Lodged with me useless, though my soul more bent
5 To serve therewith my Maker, and present
My true account, lest He returning chide.
"Doth God exact day-labor, light denied?"
I fondly[2] ask. But Patience, to prevent
That murmur, soon replies, "God doth not need
10 Either man's work or His own gifts. Who best
Bear His mild yoke, they serve Him best. His state
Is kingly. Thousands at His bidding speed
And post o'er land and ocean without rest;
They also serve who only stand and wait."

1. By using the word *talent*, Milton alludes to the biblical parable of the talents, in which a servant is scolded for hiding his master's *talent*, or money, in the earth instead of putting it to good use while the master was away (Matthew 25:14–30).
2. *Fondly* means "foolishly."

Identify Problem and Solution *What thought is expressed in this line? How does this thought relate to the problem presented in the poem?* **1**

Personification *What quality is personified in lines 7–14 of this poem?* **2**

Reading Practice

SPIRAL REVIEW **Problem and Solution** In both sonnets, the speaker begins in conflict and ends in a degree of resolution. Review with students the form of the Italian sonnet as described on page 242. Point out the octaves and sestets of the sonnets on this page. Have students identify the problem presented in each octave and summarize it in their own words. Have students predict what the solution will be. Then have students read and summarize the sestets and compare the summaries with their predictions. Have students evaluate the differences between their predictions and the actual resolutions.

After You Read

Respond and Think Critically

Respond and Interpret

1. (a)In "How Soon Hath Time," to what season does the speaker compare his twenty-third year? (b)What might the lack of "buds" and "blossoms" symbolize?

2. (a)What thoughts are expressed in lines 4–8 of "How Soon Hath Time"? (b)What thoughts are expressed in lines 9–14?

3. (a)In "When I Consider . . . ," what is the speaker thinking about in line 1? (b)In your own words, explain why he is worried about his situation.

Analyze and Evaluate

4. In both poems, what is the standard by which the speaker seems to judge his life?

Connect

5. **Big Idea** Puritanism and the Civil War
What is the main aspect of faith that the speaker is struggling with in "When I Consider . . ."?

6. **Connect to the Author** Considering Milton's ambition to become a great poet, do you think the disappointment he expresses in "How Soon Hath Time" is justified? Why or why not?

Literary Element Personification

You may encounter the use of **personification** in everyday contexts: *"The swirling wind taunted the field-goal kicker."* In these examples, nonhuman entities are given human characteristics.

1. What is implied about time in line 8 of "How Soon Hath Time"? What is said about time in lines 11 and 12?

2. How is patience personified in "When I Consider . . ."?

Writing

Write a Memo Milton's sonnets address the problem of having only a limited amount of time to accomplish a goal. Write a memo to your future self, describing a goal you hope to accomplish by midlife. For help with writing a memo, see page R25.

Literature Online

Selection Resources For Selection Quizzes, eFlashcards, and Reading-Writing Connection activities, go to glencoe.com and enter QuickPass code GLB9817u3.

Reading Strategy Identify Problem and Solution

Each of these poems presents a **problem** (something that concerns the speaker) and offers a **solution** (a response to his concern).

1. (a)In your own words, state the problem and the solution in each poem. (b)What details helped you identify each problem and solution?

2. How does the form and structure of each poem help reveal both the problem and the solution?

Academic Vocabulary

*As a young poet, Milton expressed concerns that usually applied only to older **adults.***

Adults is a word used in many areas of study. For example, a biologist might refer to full-grown worms as **adults**. To further explore this word, answer the following question: At what point do you think a person truly becomes an **adult**, and why?

For more on academic vocabulary, see pages 56 and R81.

JOHN MILTON **511**

Reading Strategy

1. (a) In "How Soon Hath Time" the speaker worries about his lack of accomplishments at the age of 23. His solution is to trust in God to guide him. In "When I Consider . . ." the speaker wonders how he can serve God now that he is blind. He resolves to patiently maintain his faith in God. (b) Answers will vary.

2. Both poems follow the form of the Italian sonnet. In each, the octave states the problem and the sestet offers the solution.

 To check students' understanding of the selection, see Unit 3 Teaching Resources Book, p. 28.

After You Read

Assess

1. (a) Spring (b) Lack of accomplishments

2. (a) In lines 4–8, he observes that he has made no significant accomplishments at this point in his life. (b) In lines 9–14, he observes that God will continue to direct his endeavors.

3. (a) The loss of his eyesight (b) He wonders how he can serve God if he cannot see.

4. Service to God

5. The struggle to maintain faith in the face of misfortune

6. Answers will vary.

Literary Element

1. (a) Time has been kinder to some of the speaker's peers. Time, along with the "will of Heaven," will continue to direct the speaker's fate.

2. As a disembodied adviser

Progress Check

Can students identify personification?

If No → See Unit 3 Teaching Resources Book, p. 26.

Writing

Students' essays should clearly identify future goals and reasonable ways to achieve them.

Academic Vocabulary

Students might list various mental or emotional signs of adulthood, such as independence and responsibility.

Before You Read

Focus

Summary

In this passage from the beginning of *Paradise Lost,* Milton first calls on the Holy Spirit to assist him in telling the story of the fall of mankind. The poem then tells of the casting out from heaven of Satan and the other rebellious angels, after which Satan vows to do everything in his power to thwart the will of God.

 For summaries in languages other than English, see Unit 3 Teaching Resources Book, pp. 30–35.

Vocabulary

Antonyms Say: Antonyms are words that are opposite in meaning. Have students find antonyms for the vocabulary words using a thesaurus. Then have them write a brief story using the vocabulary words and their antonyms.

 For additional vocabulary practice, see Unit 3 Teaching Resources Book, p. 38.

Before You Read

Paradise Lost

Connect to the Poem

What mental images of Satan and hell have books and movies given you? Make a list of some of the features of those images.

Build Background

Milton spent his entire adult life planning to write something of the magnitude of his 10,565-line poem *Paradise Lost.* This epic relates the story of Adam and Eve as told in the biblical book of Genesis. In this story, Satan tempts Adam and Eve to commit the "original sin." By eating the forbidden fruit from the tree of knowledge, Adam and Eve disobey God, fall from God's grace, and are banished from the Garden of Eden. As background to the story, Milton describes hell at the time Satan and the other rebellious angels were first driven from heaven.

Set Purposes for Reading

Big Idea Puritanism and the Civil War

As you read, ask yourself, In what ways does this poem reflect Milton's Puritan beliefs?

Literary Element Allusion

An **allusion** is a reference to a well-known person, place, event, written work, or work of art. Discovering the meaning of an allusion can often be essential to understanding part or all of a work of literature. As you read, ask yourself, What ideas do the allusions convey? Check a dictionary or an encyclopedia for the meanings of those that are not explained.

Reading Strategy Visualize

Visualizing is picturing a writer's ideas or descriptions in your mind's eye. Visualizing is a good way to understand and remember information in a text. As you read, ask yourself, What images does the poetry evoke for me?

Tip: Picturing Descriptions Carefully read how Milton describes people, places, and things in this excerpt. Jot down especially vivid descriptions. Next to each one, in your own words, describe the picture it evokes.

Vocabulary

transgress (trans gres′) *v.* to break or violate a law; to go beyond a limit; p. 514 *Taking the car would transgress his own ethics.*

deluge (del′ ūj) *n.* something that overwhelms as if by a flood; p. 515 *The radio host's comments provoked a deluge of angry letters.*

discern (di surn′) *v.* to perceive; to detect; p. 515 *In the snow, we could barely discern the road ahead.*

myriad (mir′ ē əd) *n.* a great or countless number; p. 516 *She had a myriad of excuses for being late.*

subterranean (sub tə rā′ ne ən) *adj.* below the earth's surface; underground; p. 520 *Moles are largely subterranean creatures.*

Selection Skills

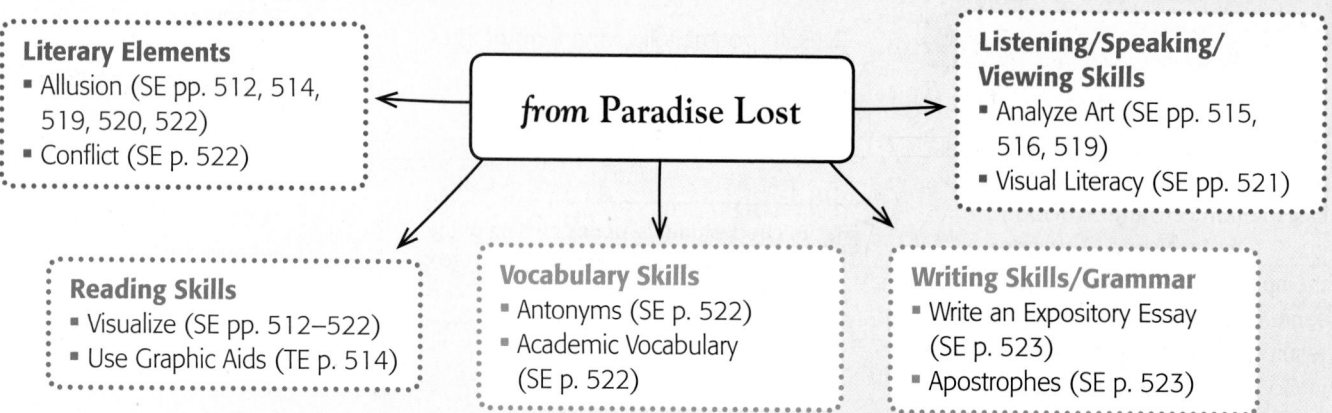

Literary Elements
- Allusion (SE pp. 512, 514, 519, 520, 522)
- Conflict (SE p. 522)

Reading Skills
- Visualize (SE pp. 512–522)
- Use Graphic Aids (TE p. 514)

from **Paradise Lost**

Vocabulary Skills
- Antonyms (SE p. 522)
- Academic Vocabulary (SE p. 522)

Writing Skills/Grammar
- Write an Expository Essay (SE p. 523)
- Apostrophes (SE p. 523)

Listening/Speaking/Viewing Skills
- Analyze Art (SE pp. 515, 516, 519)
- Visual Literacy (SE pp. 521)

512

from Paradise Lost

John Milton

from Book I

Of man's first disobedience and the fruit
Of that forbidden tree whose mortal taste
Brought death into the world and all our woe,
With loss of Eden, till one greater Man°
5 Restore us and regain the blissful seat,
Sing, Heavenly Muse,° that on the secret top
Of Oreb or of Sinai° didst inspire
That shepherd° who first taught the chosen seed°
In the beginning how the Heavens and Earth
10 Rose out of Chaos;° or if Sion hill°
Delight thee more and Siloa's brook° that flowed
Fast° by the oracle of God, I thence
Invoke thy aid to my adventurous song,
That with no middle flight intends to soar
15 Above the Aonian mount° while it pursues
Things unattempted yet in prose or rhyme.
And chiefly thou, O Spirit, that dost prefer
Before all temples the upright heart and pure,
Instruct me, for thou knowest; thou from the first
20 Wast present and with mighty wings outspread
Dovelike sat'st brooding on the vast abyss

4 greater Man: Christ

6 Heavenly Muse: In Greek mythology, the Muses were nine goddesses who presided over the arts and sciences and were believed to be sources of inspiration. Milton calls on the Holy Spirit to help him compose his epic.
7 Oreb (ôr′ ĕb) . . . **Sinai** (sī′nī): two names for the peak in Egypt where Moses was said to have received the word of God
8 shepherd: Moses. **the chosen seed:** the Jewish people
10 Chaos: infinite space; formless matter. **Sion hill:** hill in Jerusalem on which the palace of David and the Temple were built, usually spelled Zion today
11 Siloa's brook: a stream near Jerusalem
12 Fast: near
15 Aonian mount: Mount Helicon, home of the Muses

Visualize *Read the side note on Oreb and Sinai. How do you picture "the secret top"? The Old Testament account describes God descending "in fire" with smoke ascending. How does this information help you picture Milton's description?*   **1**

Puritanism and the Civil War *What help does Milton ask of God? Why does he seek this help?*   **2**

JOHN MILTON **513**

Teach

Reading Strategy   1

Visualize Answer: *God and Moses were hidden from view in some way. The Old Testament account suggests that the top of the mountain was shrouded in smoke and that Moses did not see God but only heard his voice.*

 For additional practice using the reading skill or strategy, see Unit 3 Teaching Resources Book, p. 37.

Big Idea   2

Puritanism and the Civil War Answer: *Milton asks God to help him write his epic. He recognizes that his task is an ambitious one, requiring God's guidance in order to adequately "justify the ways of God to men."*

 For an audio recording of this selection, use Listening Library Audio CD-ROM.

English Learners

DIFFERENTIATED INSTRUCTION

PARTNERS Intermediate Help English learners recognize word families. Pair students with strong English speakers to write sentences containing these word forms:

mortal—mortality, mortuary

restore—restoration

adventurous—adventuresome, adventure

Advanced To help English learners access meaning, suggest that they break up the poem into smaller parts as they read. Then have students paraphrase the main idea or central action of each part.

513

Teach

Allusion Answer: *The Serpent is Satan. Milton is alluding to the story of the Fall, in which Satan presents himself to Eve in the form of a serpent.*

Puritanism and the Civil War Answer: *Milton believed that power rested in the people and that any person—in particular, a ruler—who set himself above the will of the people was contemptible.*

Visualize Answer: *"Hurled headlong" and "hideous ruin and combustion" evoke a picture of a body plunging downward into flames. "To bottomless perdition" evokes a state of unending suffering. "In adamantine chains and penal fire" suggests a body bound by heavy metal restraints and punished with flames.*

ENGLISH LEARNERS Have English learners identify the five adjective/noun pairs in lines 45–49 and use a dictionary to put each into more familiar language. *(Possible answers: ethereal sky: heavenly sky; hideous ruin: terrible destruction; bottomless perdition: deepest hell; adamantine chains: strong chains; penal fire: punishing fire)*

And mad'st it pregnant: what in me is dark
Illumine; what is low raise and support;
That, to the height of this great argument,
25   I may assert° Eternal Providence
And justify the ways of God to men.
    Say first, for Heaven hides nothing from thy view,
Nor the deep tract of Hell, say first what cause
Moved our grand° parents in that happy state,
30   Favored of Heaven so highly, to fall off
From their Creator and **transgress** his will
For one restraint,° lords of the world besides.
Who first seduced them to that foul revolt?
The infernal Serpent; he it was whose guile,°
35   Stirred up with envy and revenge, deceived
The mother of mankind what time° his pride
Had cast him out from Heaven with all his host
Of rebel angels, by whose aid, aspiring
To set himself in glory above his peers,
40   He trusted to have equaled the Most High,
If he opposed, and with ambitious aim
Against the throne and monarchy of God,
Raised impious war in Heaven and battle proud
With vain attempt. Him the Almighty Power
45   Hurled headlong flaming from the ethereal° sky,
With hideous ruin and combustion, down
To bottomless perdition,° there to dwell
In adamantine° chains and penal fire,
Who durst defy the Omnipotent to arms.
50   Nine times the space that measures day and night
To mortal men, he with his horrid crew
Lay vanquished, rolling in the fiery gulf,
Confounded,° though immortal. But his doom
Reserved him to more wrath, for now the thought
55   Both of lost happiness and lasting pain
Torments him. Round he throws his baleful° eyes

25 assert: defend

29 grand: first (Adam and Eve)

32 one restraint: that they should not eat the fruit of the tree of knowledge of good and evil
34 guile: deceit

36 what time: when

45 ethereal: heavenly, celestial

47 perdition: damnation
48 adamantine: unyielding

53 Confounded: damned

56 baleful: evil

Allusion *Who is the Serpent? Why does Milton refer to him in this way?*

Puritanism and the Civil War *Recall Milton's belief that power belonged to all the people, who delegate it to a king. Why might Milton have been particularly disdainful of someone who aspires "to set himself in glory above his peers"?*

Visualize *What elements in this description of Satan's descent to hell in lines 44–48 evoke especially vivid pictures in your mind?* **3**

Vocabulary

transgress (trans gres´) *v.* to break or violate a law; to go beyond a limit

Reading Practice

SPIRAL REVIEW **SMALL GROUP** **Use Graphic Aids** Some students find the selection easier to understand if they narrow their focus to the events being described, instead of trying to comprehend every detail. Have pairs of students create two-column charts as shown.

As students read, have them add information beneath each heading.

What Satan Does	How Satan Feels

Judgement of Adam and Eve, 1807. William Blake. Pen and watercolor on paper, 25 x 20.2 cm. The Huntington Library, Art Collections and Botanical Gardens, San Marino, CA.

View the Art As well as a painter, William Blake was an important poet—one who valued emotion and expression over reason. Does the overall mood of this image reflect that of Milton's poetry? Why or why not?

That witnessed huge affliction and dismay
Mixed with obdurate° pride and steadfast hate.
At once, as far as angels' ken,° he views
60   The dismal situation waste and wild:
A dungeon horrible, on all sides round
As one great furnace flamed; yet from those flames
No light, but rather darkness visible
Served only to discover sights of woe,
65   Regions of sorrow, doleful shades, where peace
And rest can never dwell, hope never comes
That comes to all; but torture without end
Still urges and a fiery **deluge,** fed
With ever-burning sulfur unconsumed.
70   Such place Eternal Justice had prepared
For those rebellious, here their prison ordained
In utter darkness, and their portion set
As far removed from God and light of Heaven
As from the center thrice to the utmost pole.°
75   O how unlike the place from whence they fell!
There the companions of his fall, o'erwhelmed
With floods and whirlwinds of tempestuous fire,
He soon **discerns,** and weltering° by his side,
One next himself in power and next in crime,
80   Long after known in Palestine, and named

58 obdurate: stubborn or unyielding
59 ken: sight

4

74 center . . . pole: three times the distance from Earth's center to the outermost point of the universe

78 weltering: tossing, writhing

Vocabulary

deluge (del´ ūj) *n.* something that overwhelms as if by a flood
discern (di surn´) *v.* to perceive; to detect

JOHN MILTON **515**

Teach

Reading Strategy 1

Visualize Answer: *Students' descriptions will vary but should include the image of Beelzlebub casting a "transcendent brightness" more dazzling than that of other angels.*

Big Idea 2

Puritanism and the Civil War **Answer:** *Satan tells Beelzebub that, though they have lost this battle, their will has not been conquered. They can still seek revenge. Satan considers it "low indeed" to admit defeat and submit to God. Satan's pride, his refusal to acknowledge the authority of a higher power, and his sense of superiority over his peers echo Milton's contempt for those same characteristics in Charles I.*

(**ADVANCED**) For advanced students, **ask:** William Blake wrote that Milton was "of the Devil's party without realizing it." What did he mean by this? *(Milton made Satan a sympathetic figure.)* Ask advanced students to write a paragraph agreeing or disagreeing with Blake based on these lines.

View the Art ★

Answer: *Students' answers will vary. Most will note the great contrast between the glorious figure depicted in the painting and the figure suffering in "dungeon horrible" that Milton portrays.*

Beelzebub.° To whom the archenemy,
And thence in Heaven called Satan, with bold words
Breaking the horrid silence, thus began:
    "If thou beest he—but O, how fallen! how changed
85 From him who in the happy realms of light,
Clothed with transcendent brightness, didst outshine
Myriads, though bright—if he whom mutual league,
United thoughts and counsels, equal hope
And hazard in the glorious enterprise,
90 Joined with me once, now misery hath joined
In equal ruin: into what pit thou seest
From what height fallen! so much the stronger proved
He with his thunder; and till then who knew
The force of those dire arms? Yet not for those,
95 Nor what the potent Victor in his rage
Can else inflict, do I repent or change,
Though changed in outward luster, that fixed mind
And high disdain from sense of injured merit,
That with the Mightiest raised me to contend,
100 And to the fierce contention brought along
Innumerable force of spirits armed
That durst dislike his reign and, me preferring,
His utmost power with adverse power opposed
In dubious battle on the plains of Heaven,
105 And shook his throne. What though the field be lost?
All is not lost; the unconquerable will,
And study of revenge, immortal hate,
And courage never to submit or yield:
And what is else not to be overcome?
110 That glory never shall his wrath or might
Extort from me. To bow and sue for grace
With suppliant knee and deify his power,
Who from the terror of this arm so late
Doubted° his empire, that were low indeed;
115 That were an ignominy° and shame beneath
This downfall; since by fate the strength of gods
And this empyreal° substance cannot fail;

81 Beelzebub: Though the name is often used to mean Satan himself, Milton uses it for another fallen angel, Satan's second in command.

Satan in his Original Glory, 1805. William Blake. Watercolor on paper, 42.9 x 33.9 cm. Tate Gallery, London.

View the Art Blake once wrote that chiaroscuro (a painting style featuring sharply contrasting light and dark areas) was an "infernal machine." How would you describe the use of light and color in this painting? ★

114 Doubted: feared for

115 ignominy: disgrace or dishonor

117 empyreal: heavenly; therefore, nonmaterial and indestructible

---

Visualize *Based on Satan's description, how do you picture Beelzebub before his banishment from heaven?* **1**

Puritanism and the Civil War *What does Satan consider to be "low indeed," "ignominy and shame"? How might Milton's attitude toward Satan here connect to his feelings about tyrannical monarchs?* **2**

Vocabulary

myriad (mir′ ē əd) *n.* a great or countless number

Writing Practice

SPIRAL REVIEW **Spatial Order** Explain that writers can organize descriptive details in spatial order to present details in the order in which the eye would see them (for example, left to right, top to bottom, far to near). After students have read the first two pages of this selection, have them analyze the spatial order Milton uses.

Have students choose a location, such as the school cafeteria, and write a descriptive paragraph that uses spatial order to organize details. Suggest that students think of themselves as a movie camera, "panning" to show the scene. Encourage students to use signal words such as *beneath, next to,* and *above.*

Since, through experience of this great event,
In arms not worse, in foresight much advanced,
120   We may with more successful hope resolve
To wage by force or guile eternal war,
Irreconcilable to our grand Foe,
Who now triumphs, and in the excess of joy
Sole reigning holds the tyranny of Heaven." ☆

125   So spake the apostate° Angel, though in pain,
Vaunting° aloud, but racked with deep despair;
And him thus answered soon his bold compeer:°
"O Prince, O Chief of many thronèd Powers,
That led the embattled Seraphim° to war
130   Under thy conduct and, in dreadful deeds
Fearless, endangered Heaven's perpetual King
And put to proof his high supremacy,
Whether upheld by strength or chance or fate,
Too well I see and rue the dire event,
135   That with sad overthrow and foul defeat
Hath lost us Heaven, and all this mighty host
In horrible destruction laid thus low,
As far as gods and heavenly essences
Can perish: for the mind and spirit remains
140   Invincible, and vigor° soon returns,
Though all our glory extinct, and happy state
Here swallowed up in endless misery.
But what if he our Conqueror (whom I now
Of force believe almighty, since no less
145   Than such could have o'erpowered such force as ours)
Have left us this our spirit and strength entire,
Strongly to suffer and support our pains,
That we may so suffice his vengeful ire
Or do him mightier service as his thralls°
150   By right of war, whate'er his business be,
Here in the heart of Hell to work in fire
Or do his errands in the gloomy deep?
What can it then avail, though yet we feel
Strength undiminished, or eternal being
155   To undergo eternal punishment?"
Whereto with speedy words the Archfiend replied:
"Fallen Cherub,° to be weak is miserable,
Doing or suffering; but of this be sure,
To do aught good never will be our task,
160   But ever to do ill our sole delight,

125 **apostate:** renegade
126 **Vaunting:** boasting
127 **compeer:** companion; peer

129 **Seraphim:** the highest-ranking angels

140 **vigor:** strength, power

3

149 **thralls:** slaves

157 **Cherub:** angel

Puritanism and the Civil War *In this passage, Milton clearly defines the nature of the battle between Satan and God. What is that battle?*   **4**

Reading Strategy **3**

Draw Conclusions

Say: Beelzebub uses positive words to address Satan and words that suggest strength to speak of God. **Ask:** Why do you think Beelzebub speaks benignly about both sides? *(He doesn't want to fight any longer.)*

(ENGLISH LEARNERS) Have English learners work in pairs to compose a two to three sentence summary of Beelzebub's speech.

Big Idea **4**

Puritanism and the Civil War **Answer:** *Satan declares that his goal will be to counter God's good works with his evil works. His battle is nothing less than the ultimate contest of good versus evil.*

Writer's Technique ☆

Diction Milton could have Satan describe God as "our powerful Foe," but he chooses "our grand Foe" instead. Similarly, Satan could speak of "the stewardship of Heaven"; instead he speaks of "the tyranny of Heaven." Ask students how Milton's diction suggests Satan's contempt for God.

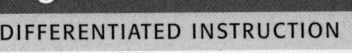

English Learners

DIFFERENTIATED INSTRUCTION

Intermediate Remind English learners that a subordinate clause has a subject and a verb but cannot stand alone as a sentence. Many subordinate clauses begin with a relative pronoun, such as *that, which, who, whom,* or *whose.* Have them look in the selection for lines with relative pronouns.

Advanced Learners

DIFFERENTIATED INSTRUCTION

Research Draw advanced students' attention to the side note about Seraphim. **Say:** Angels are present in Christianity, Judaism, and Islam. Other religions have teachings about similar spiritual beings. Ask students to research this subject through library resources and the Internet.

Teach

Visualize **Answer:** *Students might picture an army of angels robed in white equipped with tools of war ascending to heaven, with red thunderbolts gradually diminishing.*

Reading Strategy 2

Visualize **Answer:** *He spots a dreary plain away from the fiery ocean. Milton describes the place as forlorn, wild, desolate, and devoid of light—adjectives that also describe Satan and his purpose.*

(APPROACHING) **Ask:** Milton says that the only light on the plain is cast by the "pale and dreadful" flames. What does this light look like? *(It is shadowy and weak, like light from a fire at night.)*

Cultural History ☆

The Seven Deadly Sins

In traditional Christian doctrine, the seven sins of pride, envy, avarice, wrath, sloth, lust, and gluttony were believed to cause other sins. These seven sins were also deemed to be mortal, or deadly, to the Christian soul. St. Thomas Aquinas considered the sin of pride to be the chief deadly sin. Milton uses Satan's excessive pride to make him appear more damnable than those he leads.

518

As being the contrary to his high will
Whom we resist. If then his providence
Out of our evil seek to bring forth good,
Our labor must be to pervert that end
165   And out of good still° to find means of evil,
Which ofttimes may succeed so as perhaps
Shall grieve him, if I fail not,° and disturb
His inmost counsels from their destined aim.
But see! The angry Victor hath recalled
170   His ministers of vengeance and pursuit
Back to the gates of Heaven: the sulfurous hail
Shot after us in storm, o'erblown hath laid
The fiery surge that from the precipice
Of Heaven received us falling; and the thunder,
175   Winged with red lightning and impetuous rage,
Perhaps hath spent his shafts and ceases now
To bellow through the vast and boundless deep.
Let us not slip° the occasion, whether scorn
Or satiate° fury yield it from our Foe.
180   Seest thou yon dreary plain, forlorn and wild,
The seat of desolation, void of light,
Save what the glimmering of these livid flames
Casts pale and dreadful? Thither let us tend
From off the tossing of these fiery waves,
185   There rest, if any rest can harbor there,
And reassembling our afflicted powers,°
Consult how we may henceforth most offend
Our Enemy, our own loss how repair,
How overcome this dire calamity,
190   What reinforcement we may gain from hope, ☆
If not what resolution from despair."
   Thus Satan, talking to his nearest mate,
With head uplift above the wave and eyes
That sparkling blazed, his other parts besides
195   Prone on the flood, extended long and large,
Lay floating many a rood,° in bulk as huge
As whom the fables name of monstrous size,
Titanian, or Earthborn, that warred on Jove,
Briareos or Typhon, whom the den
200   By ancient Tarsus° held, or that sea beast

---

165 still: always

167 if I fail not: if I am not mistaken

178 slip: lose
179 satiate: satisfied

186 afflicted powers: stricken forces; overthrown armies

196 rood: unit of measure equaling about a quarter of an acre
197–200 fables . . . Tarsus: In Greek mythology, Zeus (the Roman Jove) successfully battled the Titans with the help of the earthborn giant Briareos; Typhon of Tarsus was a monstrous serpent who attacked Zeus.

Visualize *Picture the scene that Satan describes as the forces of God retreat to heaven. What does it look like?* 1

Visualize *Describe where Satan decides to go to escape the "fiery waves." Why might Milton have chosen this location as an appropriate place for Satan's purpose?* 2

518 UNIT 3   FROM PURITANISM TO THE ENLIGHTENMENT

Vocabulary Practice

(SPIRAL REVIEW) **Prefixes** Three common Latin prefixes are *re-*, *de-*, and *pre-*. The prefix *re-* means "again", the prefix *de-* can mean "separation, privation", and *pre-* means "before". Have students look up the definition of each of the following words and explain how the prefix affects the meaning:

1. received
2. reassembling
3. repair
4. desolation
5. despair
6. precipice

The Fallen Angels
Entering Pandemonium,
1851. John Martin.
Oil on canvas,
622 x 765 mm. Tate
Gallery, London.
View the Art Artists
use both color and
texture to create
moods. How well does
this painting reflect
Milton's description of
hell in lines 180–184?
Explain.

Leviathan,° which God of all his works
Created hugest that swim the ocean stream:
Him, haply slumbering on the Norway foam,
The pilot of some small night-foundered skiff,°
205 Deeming some island, oft, as seamen tell,
With fixèd anchor in his scaly rind,
Moors by his side under the lee while night
Invests the sea and wishèd morn delays.
So stretched out huge in length the Archfiend lay,
210 Chained on the burning lake, nor ever thence
Had risen or heaved his head, but that the will
And high permission of all-ruling Heaven
Left him at large to his own dark designs, **3**
That with reiterated crimes he might
215 Heap on himself damnation while he sought
Evil to others, and enraged might see
How all his malice served but to bring forth
Infinite goodness, grace, and mercy, shown
On man by him seduced, but on himself
220 Treble confusion, wrath, and vengeance poured.
  Forthwith upright he rears from off the pool
His mighty stature; on each hand the flames,
Driven backward, slope their pointing spires and, rolled
In billows, leave in the midst a horrid vale.
225 Then with expanded wings he steers his flight
Aloft, incumbent° on the dusky air
That felt unusual weight, till on dry land
He lights—if it were land that ever burned

201 **Leviathan:** a biblical sea monster

204 **skiff:** boat

226 **incumbent:** lying or resting

Allusion *To what does Milton compare Satan?* **4**

Visualize *Picture the scene Milton describes in lines 221—224. Where might you see a creature like this in contemporary literature, media, or art?* **5**

Teach

Literary Element | 3

Alliteration Remind students that alliteration is a device in which initial consonant sounds of words are repeated. Have students find two examples in line 213. *("Left him at large"; "dark designs")*

Literary Element | 4

Allusion Answer: *To a monstrous sea serpent that the pilot of a small boat moors next to, mistaking it for an island*

ENGLISH LEARNERS For English learners, **ask:** What words begin Milton's comparison of Satan to a sea serpent? *("as huge / As")* What words signal the end of the comparison? *("So stretched out")*

Reading Strategy | 5

Visualize Answer: *Students may relate this description of Satan to scenes in horror movies or stories.*

View the Art ★

Answer: *Most students will say that the image relates very closely to Milton's description, citing the colors and shadows, as well as particular details such as the lake of fire.*

Teach

Literary Element   1

Allusion   Answer: *With its explosions, rivers of fire, smoke, and violence, a volcano resembles the hell described by Milton.*

 To check students' understanding of the selection, see Unit 3 Teaching Resources Book, p. 41.

With solid, as the lake with liquid, fire,
230 And such appeared in hue as when the force
Of **subterranean** wind transports a hill
Torn from Pelorus,° or the shattered side
Of thundering Etna, whose combustible°
And fueled entrails, thence conceiving fire
235 Sublimed° with mineral fury, aid the winds
And leave a singèd bottom all involved°
With stench and smoke. Such resting found the sole
Of unblest feet. Him followed his next mate,
Both glorying to have scaped the Stygian° flood
240 As gods and by their own recovered strength,
Not by the sufferance of supernal° power.
   "Is this the region, this the soil, the clime,"
Said then the lost Archangel, "this the seat
That we must change for Heaven, this mournful gloom
245 For that celestial light? Be it so, since he
Who now is sovereign can dispose and bid
What shall be right: farthest from him is best;
Whom reason hath equaled, force hath made supreme
Above his equals. Farewell, happy fields,
250 Where joy forever dwells! Hail, horrors! Hail,
Infernal world! and thou, profoundest Hell,
Receive thy new possessor—one who brings
A mind not to be changed by place or time.
The mind is its own place, and in itself
255 Can make a Heaven of Hell, a Hell of Heaven.
What matter where, if I be still the same,
And what I should be, all but less than He
Whom thunder hath made greater? Here at least
We shall be free; the Almighty hath not built
260 Here for his envy, will not drive us hence:
Here we may reign secure, and in my choice
To reign is worth ambition, though in Hell:
Better to reign in Hell than serve in Heaven."

232 **Pelorus:** a cape in Sicily
233 **combustible:** capable of igniting and burning

235 **Sublimed:** vaporized
236 **involved:** enveloped

239 **Stygian:** hellish. *Stygian* is the adjective form of *Styx*, the name of the river that, in Greek mythology, flows through the Underworld.
241 **supernal:** heavenly

Allusion *Mount Etna is an active volcano in Sicily. Why is it an appropriate allusion here?*

Vocabulary

subterranean (sub′ tə ra′ nē ən) *adj.* below the surface of the earth; underground

520 UNIT 3   FROM PURITANISM TO THE ENLIGHTENMENT

Listening and Speaking Practice

  Oral Presentation Have students work in small groups to prepare oral presentations of lines 178–263. Post and discuss these guidelines beforehand:

- Vary the speed at which you read.
- Vary voice quality and tone.
- Use facial expressions and gestures to underscore the meaning of the text.

- Use stresses and dramatic pauses to hold listeners' attention and help characterize the speakers.

Have students practice several times before giving their presentations.

520

After You Read

Respond and Think Critically

Respond and Interpret

1. What was your reaction to Milton's descriptions of Satan and hell?

2. (a)According to the introduction (lines 1–26), what is the purpose of the poem? (b)Why might Milton have included a direct statement of purpose at the beginning of the poem?

3. (a)Why have Satan and his followers been cast out of heaven? (b)How does the fall of Adam and Eve parallel the fall of Satan and his followers? How does it differ?

4. (a)What reason does Satan give for choosing to "reign in Hell" rather than "serve in Heaven"? (b)Do you think Satan really believes this, or is he merely trying to "save face"? Support your answer with evidence from the text.

Analyze and Evaluate

5. (a)According to Milton, what is Satan's role in the fall of Adam and Eve? (b)Does this view of Satan's role change your impression of the story of Adam and Eve? Explain your answer.

6. (a)Satan suffers a fall from grace through his own actions. What is his "fatal flaw"? (b)How does Satan compare with other evil characters you've encountered in books or movies?

Connect

7. **Big Idea** Puritanism and the Civil War In what ways is the content of this poem influenced both by Milton's desire to serve God and by his support of Parliament's battle against Charles I?

8. **Connect to Today** Some Christians today do not believe hell to be an actual locality. Do you think Milton did? Why or why not?

Visual Literacy

Depicting the Underworld

Because Milton drew from the Bible in writing his epic poem, the art that depicts *Paradise Lost* is deeply symbolic, with stark representations of good and evil—including the role of Satan in the battle between heaven and hell. In his engraving *Satan's Flight Through Chaos*, which is based on *Paradise Lost*, Doré shows Satan's tense and tormented posture as he clings to a crag.

Group Activity Discuss these questions with your classmates.

1. How does this engraving contribute to your visualization of the scenes in *Paradise Lost*?

2. Look back at Blake's watercolor, *Satan in his Original Glory*, on page 516. How does that image of Satan contrast with Doré's?

Satan's Flight Through Chaos, 1866. Gustave Dore. Engraving.

After You Read

Assess

1. Students' reactions will vary.

2. (a) To "justify the ways of God to men" (b) The statement provides a clear objective for the reader. Also, Milton follows the traditional epic form.

3. (a) They have rebelled against God. (b) Both falls result from disobeying God. They differ in that Adam and Eve have a chance for redemption, but Satan is condemned for eternity.

4. (a) He prefers ruling his own kingdom to being God's servant. (b) Some students will suggest that Satan's pride and ambition allow him to believe that he is better off ruling in hell. Others may argue that he is deceiving himself by attempting to rationalize his defeat as a victory.

5. (a) Satan engineers Adam and Eve's fall as a way of getting revenge for his defeat by God. (b) This view might cause some students to regard Adam and Eve as having been unwittingly tricked by Satan's evil rather than having been willfully disobedient to God. Other students might suggest that because Satan is presented as fallible, Adam and Eve might have been able to resist Satan's temptation.

6. (a) Pride (b) Students' answers will vary.

7. Milton's stated purpose "to justify the ways of God to men" reveals his desire to serve God in his poetry. Milton's belief in Parliament and his disdain for Charles I are echoed in Milton's description of the battle between the forces of God and the rebellious angels in heaven.

8. Answers will vary. Students should support their opinions with text evidence.

Visual Literacy

1. Answers will vary. Challenge students to discuss whether the illustration spurs them to rethink their reading of the selection.

2. Students should contrast the elegant wings and youthful face in Blake's watercolor with the tense posture and batlike wings in Doré's work.

After You Read

Assess

Literary Element

1. Students should demonstrate how each example helps to illuminate or explain the actions or ideas being presented.

2. Encourage students to cite their favorite allusions and to explain why the allusions are effective.

Review: Conflict

1. The conflict is the external battle of good versus evil between God and Satan.

2. (a) Milton first shows God's forces driving Satan out of heaven and down to hell. He then describes Satan's suffering and his plan to seek revenge. (b) The conflict reaches a climax when Satan declares his intention to continue his battle against God.

3. Satan's decision to crown himself the ruler of hell.

Progress Check

Can students identify allusion?

If No → See Unit 3 Teaching Resources Book, p. 36.

Reading Strategy

1. (a) The rebellious angels are lying vanquished in the fires of hell. (b) Satan's "lost happiness and lasting pain" torment him. His face might be contorted in a grimace of pain and anguish.

2. The inclusion of "doleful shades" shows that hell offers only "sights of woe," scenes of despair and desolation, and forlorn spirits. This description makes hell appear dark and lonely.

Literary Element Allusion

An author often makes an **allusion** in order to point out a similarity between his or her work and the work of another author. In line 6 of *Paradise Lost* ("Sing, Heavenly Muse . . . "), Milton makes an allusion when he calls on the "Heavenly Muse" for inspiration. Ancient Greek poetry often began with a prayer to the Muses. To readers of Milton's time, most of whom were familiar with classical poetry, this allusion places *Paradise Lost* in the classical tradition of calling upon a higher power for guidance while writing. Review the excerpt from *Paradise Lost* to remind yourself of the allusions in it. Then answer the following questions:

1. How do the numerous references to Greek mythology enrich the themes expressed in *Paradise Lost*? Give specific examples from the poem to support your opinion.

2. What other allusions did you find in the poem? Explain their significance in the context in which they are mentioned.

Review: Conflict

As you learned on page 23, **conflict** is a struggle between two opposing forces in a story, drama, or narrative poem. An **external conflict** exists when a character struggles against some outside force, such as another person, nature, society, or fate. An **internal conflict** is a struggle that takes place within the mind of a character who is torn between opposing feelings, desires, or goals. A narrative's principal conflict builds until the story reaches a climax, which is the point of greatest emotional intensity.

Partner Activity With a partner, answer these questions:

1. Identify the conflict in this excerpt from *Paradise Lost*. Is this conflict external or internal? Explain why.

2. (a)How does Milton develop this conflict? (b)At what point does the conflict reach its climax?

3. Within the confines of this excerpt, what is the outcome of the conflict?

 Literature Online

Selection Resources For Selection Quizzes, eFlashcards, and Reading-Writing Connection activities, go to glencoe.com and enter QuickPass code GLB9817u3.

Reading Strategy Visualize

Vivid description helps the reader not only to picture the setting but also to understand more clearly the actions and ideas presented. Part of the greatness of *Paradise Lost* is its ability to evoke powerful pictures in the reader's mind. Review lines 50–69 ("Nine times the space . . . sulfur unconsumed.") to answer the following questions:

1. (a) Describe the position and movement of the rebellious angels. (b)Describe Satan. What torments him?

2. The word *doleful* means "dreary" or "dismal." The word *shade* has numerous meanings, including "not in the sunshine" and "ghost" or "spirit." Does this affect your picture of hell?

Vocabulary Practice

Practice with Antonyms With a partner, match each boldfaced vocabulary word below with its antonym—a word with an opposite meaning. You will not use all the answer choices. Use a thesaurus or dictionary to check your answers.

1. transgress   a. few
2. deluge   b. perceive
3. discern   c. ignore
4. myriad   d. terrestrial
5. subterranean   e. trickle
   f. obey

Academic Vocabulary

*Satan's **initial** response to finding himself in hell is despair.*

Initial is an academic word that is also used in everyday situations. For example, the **initial** step toward painting a wall is applying primer. Use context clues to figure out the meaning of the word in the sentence about *Paradise Lost* above. Check your guess in a dictionary.

For more on academic vocabulary, see pages 56 and R81.

Vocabulary Practice

1. f 2. e 3. c 4. a 5. d

Academic Vocabulary

The context indicates that Satan had one response at first, but that his response changed. This suggests that *initial* means "first" or "occurring at the beginning."

522

Respond Through Writing

Expository Essay

Analyze Imagery In *Paradise Lost*, Milton vividly re-creates the world depicted in Genesis and portrays the epic struggle played out within it. Write a response to literature in which you discuss how the imagery in Milton's masterpiece helps you visualize and appreciate the complexity of its settings and characters.

Prewrite As you review the excerpt from *Paradise Lost*, create a chart for the images Milton uses to describe his characters and settings. In one column, quote the text; in another, indicate whom or what is described; in the final column, note your reactions to the image. Use this chart to help you determine a controlling idea or thesis for your paper.

Draft Use the reactions to Milton's images you listed in your chart to explain how each image helps you understand what Milton is describing and picture it clearly in your mind. Also look for patterns in Milton's imagery. Are there words or images that repeat, or that seem to be associated with particular characters? What effect does this have on the poem?

> *The sensory images of blazing heat and unyielding metal shackles make us feel the physical and emotional pain of Satan's ejection from Heaven, which is key to Milton's portrayal of the character.*

In discussing the imagery in the poem, you can use sentence structures like the following:

The imagery of _____ creates a mood of _____.

Revise Exchange papers with a classmate and examine your partner's essay, looking for correct identification of imagery and logical explanations supported by details from the poem. Use the comments you receive as a guide to revising your own essay.

Edit and Proofread Proofread your paper, correcting any errors in spelling, grammar, and punctuation. Use the Grammar Tip in the side column to help you with apostrophes.

▶ Grammar Tip

Apostrophes

Apostrophes are used to show possession. Use *'s* with singular nouns (even ones ending in *s*—for example, *the bass's fins*) and plural subjects that don't end in *s* (for example, *men's*). Use *'* with plural nouns that end in *s*.

The words "stench and smoke" depict **Satan's** *fury and stir* **readers'** *imaginations.*

JOHN MILTON **523**

After You Read

Assess

Respond Through Writing

Use these criteria in evaluating students' expository essays:

- It identifies and accurately cites Milton's imagery.
- The contribution of the imagery to Milton's message is clearly explained.
- Apostrophes are used correctly to show possession and indicate quotations within quotations.

A student who meets all of these criteria should receive the equivalent of a 3-point response.

A student who fully meets two or partially meets two of these criteria should receive the equivalent of a 2-point response.

A student who fully meets one or partially meets two of these criteria should receive the equivalent of a 1-point response.

 For grammar practice, see Unit 3 Teaching Resources Book, p. 40.

 For additional assessment, see Assessment Resources, pp. 143–144.

 To create custom assessments using software, use ExamView Assessment Suite.

English Learners

DIFFERENTIATED INSTRUCTION

Intermediate To assist English learners in prewriting for their expository essays about *Paradise Lost*, have them add a column to the prewriting chart in which they can restate quotes from the text in their own words.

Make sure a standard dictionary is available so that students can look up troublesome words. By restating quoted text, students will enhance their understanding of the excerpt and help develop the thesis for their essays.

Bellringer Options

**Daily Language Practice
Transparency 40**

Or **draw** a web on the board and **write** *Vanity* in the center circle. Ask students to suggest ways that people are vain or display vanity. **Say:** As you read this selection, look for the author's idea of vanity.

Meet **John Bunyan**

(1628–1688)

Few English authors sprang from humbler beginnings than John Bunyan. Born in the quiet little village of Elstow, Bunyan was the son of a poverty-stricken tinker—a mender of pots and pans. He received only a basic education, leaving school at an early age to learn his father's trade and to contribute to the family income. Yet Bunyan went on to write more than fifteen books, among them the most widely read prose work of the seventeenth century, *The Pilgrim's Progress*. This achievement was just one of many in a remarkable life. In fact, according to nineteenth-century historian Thomas Babbington Macauley, "[D]uring the latter half of the seventeenth century, there were only two minds which possessed the imaginative faculty in a very eminent degree. One of those minds produced [John Milton's] *Paradise Lost*, the other *The Pilgrim's Progress*."

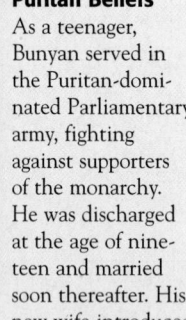

Puritan Beliefs As a teenager, Bunyan served in the Puritan-dominated Parliamentary army, fighting against supporters of the monarchy. He was discharged at the age of nineteen and married soon thereafter. His new wife introduced him to a series of religious texts including *The Plain Man's Pathway to Heaven* and *The Practice of Piety*. Moved by these books of Puritan religious philosophy, Bunyan joined a nonconformist (Puritan) church and began studying the Bible. While still in his twenties, he became one of England's best-known nonconformist preachers.

This brought him into direct conflict with another religious group, the Quakers. His first writings, *Some Gospel Truths Opened* and *A Vindication*, were created to oppose Quaker beliefs.

> "[W]ords easy to be understood do often hit the mark, when high and learned ones do only pierce the air."
>
> —John Bunyan

Setbacks and Achievements After the Puritan government was dissolved, Bunyan fell upon hard times. At age thirty-two he was arrested for preaching without a license. Refusing to renounce his faith, Bunyan spent twelve years in a Bedford prison, during which time he wrote nine books, including his autobiography and several books of spiritual instruction. He also began work on *The Pilgrim's Progress*.

Bunyan was pardoned and released from prison at age forty-four. He returned to preaching and was appointed the pastor of the same church he had been affiliated with before his imprisonment. However, sentiments against nonconformist religious groups continued to run high, and after only four years, Bunyan was again arrested and imprisoned for his beliefs. While serving his second sentence, Bunyan completed *The Pilgrim's Progress*, a work that would come to be considered a masterpiece of the plain English prose style. In 1678 the first part of this book was published, and in 1684 the work was published in its entirety.

 Literature Online

Author Search For more about John Bunyan, go to glencoe.com and enter QuickPass code GLB9817u3.

Selection Skills

Literary Elements
- Allegory (SE pp. 525, 526, 529, 530)
- Characterization (SE p. 530)

from **The Pilgrim's Progress**

Listening/Speaking/Viewing Skills
- Analyze Art (TE p. 528)

Reading Skills
- Summarize (SE pp. 525, 527, 528, 531)

Vocabulary Skills
- Word Parts (SE pp. 525, 531)
- Academic Vocabulary (SE p. 531)

Writing Skills/Grammar
- Apply Symbolism (SE p. 531)

Literature and Reading Preview

Connect to the Selection

What are some ways in which people display vanity? List several ways in which people show that they are vain.

Build Background

From the late sixteenth to the early eighteenth century, the word *Puritanism* referred to the belief that all existing churches had been corrupted, and needed to be purified. Their argument was that purification was only possible through strict belief in and interpretation of the Bible.

Set Purposes for Reading

Big Idea Puritanism and the Civil War

As you read, ask yourself, How does Bunyan employ the Puritan themes of good versus evil and destruction versus salvation?

Literary Element Allegory

An **allegory** is a narrative or dramatic work in which almost all the characters, settings, and events represent abstract ideas. The overall purpose of an allegory is to teach a moral lesson. Characters and settings are often given names that clarify the abstract qualities they represent. *The Pilgrim's Progress* focuses on a character named Christian and the obstacles he must overcome during his pilgrimage to the Celestial City. During his journey, Christian meets Faithful, who decides to join him. As you read, ask yourself, What names indicate that the people and things they are applied to have allegorical meanings?

Reading Strategy Summarize

A **summary** is a brief restatement, in one's own words, of the main ideas and events in a literary work. As you read, ask yourself, Which passages convey main ideas, and which provide supporting details?

Tip: Restating Information Summarizing small sections at a time can help you better understand a difficult selection. Use a chart to restate important information from the story.

Paragraph	Summary
Paragraph 1 (pg. 526) Then I saw in my dream that . . .	The narrator dreams that Christian and Faithful encounter a town called Vanity.

JOHN BUNYAN **525**

Learning Objectives

For pages 524–531

In studying this text, you will focus on the following objectives:

Literary Study: Analyzing allegory.

Reading: Summarizing.

Writing: Applying symbolism in an allegory.

Vocabulary

diverse (di vurs′) *adj.* markedly different; p. 527 *People of all ages and ethnicities made up the diverse crowd at the concert.*

indictment (in dīt′ mənt) *n.* a formal accusation; p. 528 *The documentary film offered a searing indictment of the effects of cigarette smoking.*

reconciled (rek′ ən sīld) *adj.* brought to acceptance of; p. 529 *The elderly couple could not be reconciled to the loss of their farm.*

Tip: Word Parts When you come across unfamiliar words, you can often break them down into parts—prefixes, roots, and suffixes—for clues to their meaning. For example, the word *insatiable*, which means "not able to be satisfied," is composed of the prefix *in-* ("not"), the root *sati* ("fill or satisfy"), and the suffix *-able* ("capable of being").

Before You Read

Focus

Summary

Christian and Faithful stop at the fair in the town of Vanity. They attract attention by their unworldly attire and speech. The two are blamed for causing a disturbance, and it is decreed that they should die. Faithful is beaten and burned at the stake, but a chariot takes Faithful's soul to the celestial gate. Christian is sent to prison. After a time, God allows him to escape, and the pilgrim continues his journey.

 For summaries in languages other than English, see Unit 3 Teaching Resources Book, pp. 43–48.

Vocabulary

Word Parts Divide the class into three groups, giving each group a dictionary. Tell students that each vocabulary word has a prefix, a suffix, or both. Set a timer and see which group can complete this activity first: 1. Identify the prefixes and suffixes. 2. Tell the meaning of each affix. 3. Look up the word and learn its meaning.

 For additional vocabulary practice, see Unit 3 Teaching Resources Book, p. 51.

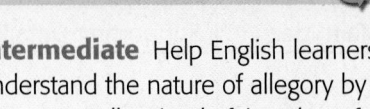

English Learners

DIFFERENTIATED INSTRUCTION

Intermediate Help English learners understand the nature of allegory by asking them to retell a simple fairy tale or folktale (for example, a version of "Little Red Riding Hood") from their first language. Point out that the tale has two meanings: the story itself and the life lesson that story teaches.

Ask students to assign allegorical meanings to the characters in a tale. For instance, Little Red Riding Hood represents children or other innocents, and the wolf represents the dangers of the world. Explain that many such tales are short, simple allegories. *The Pilgrim's Progress* functions in the same way, but the story, as well as its real-world lessons, is more complex.

Teach

Reading Strategy   1

Summarize **Answer:**
The fair was established by the demons Beelzebub, Apollyon, and Legion. They chose Vanity because it lay in the pilgrims' path.

For additional practice using the reading skill or strategy, see Unit 3 Teaching Resources Book, p. 50.

Literary Element   2

Allegory **Answer:** *The countries, titles, kingdoms, and other merchandise listed represent the worldly things that tempt people.*

Literary Element   3

Allegory **Answer:** *Heaven or the afterlife*

Literary History

World's Fair The fictional Vanity Fair in Bunyan's work represents the world at large, but the first world's fair was held in London in 1851 to celebrate progress and to promote trade among nations. The term *world's fair* was coined by William Makepeace Thackeray in a poem about the event. Coincidentally, Thackeray had already achieved fame with his novel *Vanity Fair.*

Readability Scores

Dale-Chall: 8.5
DRP: 61
Lexile: 1380

---

from The Pilgrim's Progress

John Bunyan

Vanity Fair

Then I saw in my dream that, when they[1] were got out of the wilderness, they presently saw a town before them, and the name of that town is Vanity; and at the town there is a fair kept, called Vanity Fair. It is kept all the year long. It beareth the name of Vanity Fair because the town where it is kept is lighter than vanity and also because all that is there sold, or that cometh thither, is vanity. As is the saying of the wise, "All that cometh is vanity."

This fair is no new-erected business, but a thing of ancient standing. I will show you the original of it.

Almost five thousand years ago there were pilgrims walking to the Celestial City, as these two honest persons are; and Beelzebub, Apollyon, and Legion,[2] with their companions, perceiving by the path that the pilgrims made that their way to the city lay through this town of Vanity, they contrived here to set up a fair, a fair wherein should be sold all sorts of vanity, and that it should last all the year long. Therefore, at this fair are all such merchandise sold as houses, lands, trades, places, honors, preferments,[3] titles, countries, kingdoms, lusts, pleasures, and delights of all sorts, as harlots, wives, husbands, children, masters, servants, lives, blood, bodies, souls, silver, gold, pearls, precious stones, and what not.

And, moreover, at this fair there is at all times to be seen jugglings, cheats, games, plays, fools, apes, knaves, and rogues, and that of every kind.

Here are to be seen, too, and that for nothing, thefts, murders, adulteries, false swearers, and that of a blood-red color.

And as in other fairs of less moment, there are the several rows and streets under their proper names, where such and such wares are vended; so here likewise you have the proper places, rows, streets (namely, countries and kingdoms), where the wares of this fair are soonest to be found. Here is the Britain Row, the French Row, the Italian Row, the Spanish Row, the German Row, where several sorts of vanities are to be sold. But as in other fairs some one commodity is as the chief of all the fair, so the ware of Rome[4] and her merchandise is greatly promoted in this fair; only our English nation, with some others, have taken a dislike thereat.

Now, as I said, the way to the Celestial City lies just through this town where this lusty[5] fair is kept; and he that would go to the city, and yet not go through this town, must needs "go out of the world." The Prince of princes[6] himself, when here, went through this town to his own country,

---

1. *They* refers to Christian and Faithful.
2. *Beelzebub, Apollyon,* and *Legion* are devils.
3. Appointments to government or church positions were called *preferments.*

1   Summarize *Who originally established the fair and why did they decide to locate it in the town of Vanity?*

2   Allegory *What does the merchandise sold at the fair represent?*

4. *Rome* refers to the Roman Catholic Church.
5. Here, *lusty* means "merry."
6. *The Prince of princes* is a reference to Christ, who was tempted in the wilderness, as described in the Bible (Matthew 4:1–11).

Allegory *What does the Celestial City symbolize?*   **3**

Reading Practice

SPIRAL REVIEW **Understand Main Idea** As students read this work, they will often have to pause to look up words or read annotations. As a result, they may lose track of the main idea of a section. Filling in a chart like the one shown here will help students understand a passage.

Main Idea	Supporting Details

and that upon a fair day, too; yea, and, as I think, it was Beelzebub, the chief lord of this fair, that invited him to buy of his vanities; yea, would have made him lord of the fair would he but have done him reverence as he went through the town. Yea, because he was such a person of honor, Beelzebub had him from street to street and showed him all the kingdoms of the world in a little time that he might, if possible, allure the Blessed One to cheapen[7] and buy some of his vanities; but he had no mind to the merchandise and, therefore, left the town without laying out so much as one farthing upon these vanities. This fair, therefore, is an ancient thing of long standing, and a very great fair.

Now these pilgrims, as I said, must needs go through this fair. Well, so they did; but, behold, even as they entered into the fair, all the people in the fair were moved, and the town itself, as it were, in a hubbub about them, and that for several reasons.

First, the pilgrims were clothed with such kind of raiment[8] as was **diverse** from the raiment of any that traded in that fair. The people, therefore, of the fair made a great gazing upon them: some said they were fools; some they were bedlams;[9] and some they were outlandish[10] men.

Secondly, and as they wondered at their apparel, so they did likewise at their speech; for few could understand what they said. They naturally spoke the language of Canaan,[11] but they that kept the fair were the men of this world; so that, from one end of the fair to the other, they seemed barbarians each to the other.

---

7. Bunyan uses *cheapen* to mean "inquire the price of."
8. Clothing is also called *raiment*.
9. People who were considered insane were called *bedlams*. *Bedlam* is a shortened form of St. Mary's of Bethlehem, an asylum in London.
10. Here, *outlandish* means "foreign."
11. Hebrew is the language of Canaan, the Promised Land.

---

 4 Puritanism and the Civil War *How does the townspeople's reaction to the pilgrims reflect the Puritan experience during Bunyan's lifetime?*

Vocabulary

diverse (di vurs′) *adj.* markedly different

Thirdly, but that which did not a little amuse the merchandisers was that these pilgrims set very light by their wares; they cared not so much as to look upon them; and if they called upon them to buy, they would put their fingers in their ears and cry, "Turn away mine eyes from beholding vanity," and look upwards, signifying that their trade and traffic was in heaven.

One chanced mockingly, beholding the carriage of the men, to say unto them, "What will ye buy?" But they, looking gravely upon him, answered, "We buy the truth." At that there was an occasion taken to despise the men the more; some mocking, some taunting, some speaking reproachfully, and some calling upon others to smite them. At last things came to a hubbub and great stir in the fair, insomuch that all order was confounded. Now was word presently brought to the great one of the fair, who quickly came down and deputed some of his most trusty friends to take these men into examination, about whom the fair was almost overturned. So the men were brought to examination; and they that sat upon[12] them asked them whence they came, whither they went, and what they did there in such an unusual garb? The men told them that they were pilgrims and strangers in the world and that they were going to their own country, which was the heavenly Jerusalem, and that they had given no occasion to the men of the town, nor yet to the merchandisers, thus to abuse them and to let[13] them in their journey, except it was for that, when one asked them what they would buy, they said they would buy the truth. But they that were appointed to examine them did not believe them to be any other than bedlams and mad or else such as came to put all things into a confusion in the fair. Therefore, they took them and beat them and besmeared them with dirt and then put them into the cage, that they might be made a spectacle to all the men of the fair.

---

12. Here, *sat upon* means "tried."
13. *Let* means "hinder."

Summarize *What causes this disturbance?* **5**

Big Idea **4**

Puritanism and the Civil War Answer: *The Puritans were often harassed and persecuted for their beliefs.*

[APPROACHING] If approaching-level students have difficulty connecting the plot to events of Bunyan's time, prompt them to use what they have learned about pilgrims. **Ask:** What conditions in Europe drove the pilgrims to risk their lives in the New World? *(Among others, persecution for their religious beliefs and practices)*

Reading Strategy **5**

Summarize Answer: *The pilgrims refuse to buy from the vendors and look and behave differently from the people of Vanity.*

Approaching Level

DIFFERENTIATED INSTRUCTION

 Emerging Divide approaching-level students who need work in developing **reading fluency** into groups. Have students practice reading a section from this page. Work with the groups to devise a rating system for reading with fluency. Then call on members from each group to read the section aloud. As group members read, the listeners can use the rating system to score each reader. Challenge students to continue practicing so that their fluency scores improve.

Teach

Literary Element | 1

Style John Bunyan tended to write lengthy sentences, using *and* to connect several ideas in a sentence. **Ask:** What effect does cramming several events into one sentence have? *(confusion; a rush of things happening)*

Reading Strategy | 2

Summarize Answer: *Christian and Faithful's exemplary behavior causes a divisive reaction among those at the fair. In their rage and perhaps guilt, one group insists that the two be put to death.*

View the Art ★

William Hogarth (1697–1764) was probably the greatest satirical artist of the eighteenth century, though he also painted portraits and historical subjects. Among his satirical works are several series of sequential paintings and engravings that are thought by some to be ancestors of modern comic-strip and comic-book art.

O, The Roast Beef of Olde England, 1748. William Hogarth. Oil on canvas, 78.7 cm. x 94.6 cm. Tate Gallery, London. ★

There, therefore, they lay for some time and were made the objects of any man's sport or malice or revenge, the great one of the fair laughing still at all that befell them. But the men being patient and not rendering railing[14] for railing, but contrariwise, blessing, and giving good words for bad and kindness for injuries done, some men in the fair that were more observing and less prejudiced than the rest began to check and blame the baser sort for their continual abuses done by them to the men; they,[15] therefore, in angry manner, let fly at them again, counting them as bad as the men in the cage and telling them that they seemed confederates and should be made partakers of their misfortunes. The other replied that, for aught they could see, the men were quiet and sober and intended nobody any harm and that there were many that traded in their fair that were more worthy to be put into the cage, yea, and pillory, too, than were

Visual Vocabulary
A *pillory* (pil´ ə rē) is an instrument for public punishment consisting of a wooden board with holes in which to lock the offender's head and hands.

14. *Railing* is bitter speech or strong criticism.
15. *They* refers to the baser ones.

the men they had abused. Thus, after diverse words had passed on both sides, the men behaving themselves all the while very wisely and soberly before them, they fell to some blows among themselves and did harm one to another. Then were these two poor men brought before their examiners again and there charged as being guilty of the late hubbub that had been in the fair. So they beat them pitifully and hanged irons upon them and led them in chains up and down the fair for an example and a terror to others, lest any should speak in their behalf or join themselves unto them. But Christian and Faithful behaved themselves yet more wisely and received the ignominy and shame that was cast upon them with so much meekness and patience that it won to their side, though but few in comparison of the rest, several of the men in the fair. This put the other party yet into greater rage, insomuch that they concluded[16] the death of these two men. Wherefore they threatened that neither cage nor irons should serve their turn, but that they should die for the abuse they had done and for deluding the men of the fair.

Then were they remanded to the cage again until further order should be taken with them. So they put them in and made their feet fast in the stocks. . . .[17]

Then a convenient time being appointed, they brought them forth to their trial in order to their condemnation. When the time was come, they were brought before their enemies and arraigned. The judge's name was Lord Hate-good. Their **indictment** was one and the same in substance, though somewhat varying in form; the contents whereof were this:

"That they were enemies to and disturbers of their trade; that they had made commotions

16. *Concluded* means "decided on."
17. The *stocks* were an instrument for public punishment consisting of a heavy wooden frame with holes in which to lock the offender's legs.

Summarize *Why have Christian and Faithful been condemned to die?* | 2

Vocabulary

indictment (in dīt´ mənt) n. a formal accusation

Vocabulary Practice

SPIRAL REVIEW **Identify The Latin Root *Dict*** In "Vanity Fair," Christian and Faithful receive an **indictment** and a guilty **verdict**. At the heart of these two words is the same Latin root: *dict,* meaning "stated." **Say:** Knowing the meaning of this common root can help you figure out the definitions of words that contain it. For example, an *indictment* is a statement of accusation made by a grand jury, and a *verdict* is the finding stated by the jury in a trial.

Have students write a brief definition of each of the following words:

1. edict
2. prediction
3. dictionary
4. diction

528

and divisions in the town and had won a party to their own most dangerous opinions, in contempt of the law of their prince." . . .

Then went the jury out, whose names were Mr. Blind-man, Mr. No-good, Mr. Malice, Mr. Love-lust, Mr. Live-loose, Mr. Heady, Mr. High-mind, Mr. Enmity, Mr. Liar, Mr. Cruelty, Mr. Hate-light, and Mr. Implacable—who every one gave in his private verdict against [Faithful] among themselves and afterward unanimously concluded to bring him in guilty before the judge. And first, among themselves, Mr. Blind-man, the foreman, said, "I see clearly that this man is a heretic." Then said Mr. No-good, "Away with such a fellow from the earth." "Ay," said Mr. Malice, "for I hate the very looks of him." Then said Mr. Love-lust, "I could never endure him." "Nor I," said Mr.

3 Live-loose, "for he would always be condemning my way." "Hang him, hang him," said Mr. Heady. "A sorry scrub,"[18] said Mr. High-mind. "My heart riseth against him," said Mr. Enmity. "He is a rogue," said Mr. Liar. "Hanging is too good for him," said Mr. Cruelty. "Let's dispatch him out of the way," said Mr. Hate-light. Then said Mr. Implacable, "Might I have all the world given me, I could not be **reconciled** to him; therefore, let us forthwith bring him in

---

18. An insignificant person was called a *scrub.*

Vocabulary

reconciled (rek′ ən sīld) *adj.* brought to acceptance of

guilty of death." And so they did; therefore, he was presently condemned to be had from the place where he was to the place from whence he came and there to be put to the most cruel death that could be invented.

They, therefore, brought him out, to do with him according to their law; and first they scourged[19] him, then they buffeted[20] him, then they lanced his flesh with knives; after that they stoned him with stones, then pricked him with their swords; and last of all they burned him to ashes at the stake. Thus came Faithful to his end.

Now I saw that there stood behind the multitude a chariot and a couple of horses,[21] waiting for Faithful, who, so soon as his adversaries had dispatched him, was taken up into it and straightway was carried up through the clouds with sound of trumpet, the nearest way to the celestial gate.

But as for Christian, he had some respite and was remanded back to prison. So he there remained for a space; but He that overrules all things, having the power of their rage in his own hand, so wrought it about[22] that Christian for that time escaped them and went his way.

---

19. *Scourged* means "whipped."
20. *Buffeted* means "punched."
21. The image of the *chariot and a couple of horses* is an allusion to the biblical story of Elijah, who ascended to heaven in a chariot of fire.
22. *Wrought it about* means "arranged it."

Allegory *What fate awaits Faithful and why?* **4**

Teach

Literary Element | 3

Allegory To help students understand the character of "Live-Loose's" name, **ask:** What may happen if an animal gets loose from its pen or leash? *(It may run away, get lost, or harm a pet, a person, or property.)* Help students recognize Bunyan's assumption that rules keep people from wrong behavior. Someone who lives outside the rules is bound to cause trouble.

Literary Element | 4

Allegory Answer: *Heaven and salvation await Faithful because he has lived a pure life and resisted the temptation of Vanity's fair.*

To check students' understanding of the selection, see Unit 3 Teaching Resources Book, p. 53.

JOHN BUNYAN **529**

English Learners

DIFFERENTIATED INSTRUCTION

PARTNERS **Advanced** Explain to students that word meanings change over time. To illustrate, **write** these words from *The Pilgrim's Progress* on the board: *mad, sport, railing, check, sober, stocks.* Help students use context clues to figure out how each word is being used in the text, and then discuss how each word is used most commonly today. Ask pairs of students to find other words in the selection that look familiar but are used in unfamiliar ways. *(Possible answers: counting, late, fast)* Have students analyze the words and keep lists in their journals.

After You Read

Assess

1. Students' answers will vary.

2. (a) They say they only want to buy truth. (b) They are devoutly religious and capable of resisting worldly temptation.

3. (a) The pilgrims dress differently, speak the language of Canaan, and show no interest in material goods. (b) He seems to think that Christians stand apart from the mass of humanity.

4. (a) They behave meekly and quietly. (b) Because some of the citizens begin to support Christian and Faithful (c) Christian and Faithful are blamed for the fighting.

5. (a) Vanity might symbolize greed and temptation. (b) Bunyan was trying to show the frivolousness and danger of human vanity and greed.

6. (a) Material wealth and worldly amusements are worthless compared to the glory of entering heaven. (b) Some students may say that in the allegory the theme is presented more dramatically and memorably than it would be presented in an essay.

7. They scorn the fair, showing that they have no interest in worldly matters and put their faith only in God.

8. Some may suggest shopping malls, amusement parks, carnivals, or summer fairs.

Review: Characterization

Check that students have correctly categorized the examples of characterization in their diagram.

After You Read

Respond and Think Critically

Respond and Interpret

1. If you could talk to John Bunyan, what questions would you ask him?

2. (a) What are Christian and Faithful willing to buy at the fair? (b) What does this suggest about their values?

3. (a) How do the townspeople of Vanity know that the pilgrims are foreigners? (b) What does their response to the pilgrims indicate about Bunyan's view of Christians in the world?

4. (a) Throughout the humiliation and violence to which they are subjected, how do Faithful and Christian behave? (b) What causes the citizens of Vanity to begin fighting among themselves? (c) Who is blamed for the fighting?

Analyze and Evaluate

5. (a) What might the town of Vanity symbolize, or represent? (b) How does this reflect Bunyan's Puritan beliefs?

6. (a) Sum up the theme, or central message, of the allegory. (b) What might be lost if Bunyan had expressed this theme in an essay instead?

Connect

7. **Big Idea** **Puritanism and the Civil War** How might Christian and Faithful reflect Bunyan's spiritual beliefs?

8. **Connect to Today** Today's fairs are very different from the fairs of Bunyan's time. What setting might Bunyan choose if he were writing today?

Literary Element Allegory

An **allegory** is a story with two meanings—a literal meaning and a symbolic meaning. The underlying symbolic meaning has moral, social, religious, or political significance. Characters in an allegory are often personifications of abstract concepts such as charity, greed, or envy. Think about the names Bunyan uses for his characters. Specifically, reread the list of jurors' names and pronouncements on page 529 and then answer the following questions.

1. (a) How are the names of the jurors fitting? (b) What do the names of the judge and jury members suggest about the nature of Christian and Faithful's trial?

2. What do Christian and Faithful represent?

3. Create a few names that could be used in a modern allegory. These names can be humorous, but should describe either a stereotype or a distinct personality.

Review: Characterization

As you learned on page 101, **characterization** refers to the methods a writer uses to reveal the personality of a character. In **direct characterization**, the narrator explicitly tells the reader about a character's personality. In **indirect characterization**, the character's personality is implied by his or her actions, speech, thoughts, physical appearance, and the way other characters react to him or her.

Partner Activity With a partner, discuss what you know about Faithful and Christian in "Vanity Fair." On a sheet of paper, create a diagram like the one below. Then find a strong example of each method of characterization used to portray the two pilgrims.

Literary Element

1. (a) The juror's names reflect their negative or sinful personalities. (b) Their names suggest that the trial will not be a fair one and that its outcome is predetermined.

2. Both pilgrims embody the traits of the ideal Christian: they are meek, humble, patient, and faithful.

3. Students' responses will vary.

Progress Check

Can students identify allegory?

If No → See Unit 3 Teaching Resources Book, p. 49.

Reading Strategy — Summarize

Summarizing helps you to recap the action of a story and to identify main ideas. Review the chart you made for the Reading Strategy on page 525 to answer the following questions.

1. What conflict do Faithful and Christian encounter?

2. Is this conflict avoidable? Explain.

Vocabulary Practice

Practice with Word Parts For each vocabulary word in the left-hand column, identify the word containing the same root in the right-hand column. Write the words and underline the parts they have in common. Use a printed or online dictionary to look up the meaning of the word you identified, and explain how it is related to the meaning of the vocabulary word.

1. diverse   conciliate

2. indictment   reversal

3. reconciled   dictionary

EXAMPLE

*structure, de*struction
Destruction is the opposite of *construction,*
or "building up." A structure is something
that has been built.

Academic Vocabulary

The people at Vanity Fair act against the pilgrims' **principles** *by committing such sins as lust, malice, and cruelty.*

Principles is a word that can have several different meanings. Using context clues, try to figure out the meaning of *principles* in each sentence and explain the difference between the two meanings.

1. My parents taught me sound moral **principles.**

2. To solve an equation, it is necessary to understand the basic **principles** of algebra.

For more on academic vocabulary, see pages 56 and R81.

Write with Style

 Apply Symbolism

Assignment John Bunyan shared his Puritan views of life in his allegorical work *The Pilgrim's Progress.* Adapt the allegory in the section "Vanity Fair" to a scenario from the modern world, using modern symbols for vices and virtues.

Get Ideas With a few classmates, brainstorm a list of stories you've seen recently—in the newspaper, on television or on the Internet—that illustrate human vices and virtues. If you have a hard time coming up with real stories, you might think about fictional stories you've read recently.

In the left column of a two-column chart, list the vices and virtues that figure in your story. On the right, indicate a person, animal, or other object that might symbolize each vice and virtue.

Give It Structure Decide on the purpose, audience, and form of your writing. Then make a flow-chart indicating the sequence of events, along with the characters and setting for each.

EXAMPLE

Event 1: Ms. Spoiled breaks a law in her hometown, Luxury City, and is caught by Mr. Justice.

Event 2: Mr. Justice wants to exile her to the town of Punish, but gives her a second chance.

Event 3: Ms. Spoiled breaks the law again.

Event 4: Mr. Justice finally sends Ms. Spoiled to the town of Punish, as she deserves.

Look at Language Carefully choose the names you use for characters and objects, making sure they convey exactly the characteristics you have in mind. To keep readers interested, vary the pace of your writing by mixing sentence types and structures.

Literature Online

Selection Resources For Selection Quizzes, eFlashcards, and Reading-Writing Connection activities, go to glencoe.com and enter QuickPass code GLB9817u3.

JOHN BUNYAN **531**

Reading Strategy

1. They encounter at Vanity the angry and hateful vendors who want either to sell the pilgrims goods or to harm them.

2. The conflict is unavoidable. If the pilgrims want to reach the Celestial City, they must go through Vanity. The fair was created by Beelzebub and other devils for this very reason.

Progress Check

Can students summarize?

If No → See Unit 3 Teaching Resources Book, p. 50.

 ## Write with Style

Use these criteria in evaluating student writing:

- The allegory has a focused message.
- The events are presented in a logical order.

The symbols are direct, easily understood, and clearly support the message

For grammar practice, see Unit 3 Teaching Resources Book, p. 52.

Academic Vocabulary

1. The context implies that principles means "morals" or "values."

2. The context implies that principles means "rules" or "laws."

Vocabulary Practice

1. d**i**verse, re**v**ersal
   Things that are diverse are different, or "turned apart." A reversal is a turning back.

2. in**dict**ment, **dict**ionary
   An indictment is a formal "saying," or statement, of a legal charge. A dictionary records the meanings of words, which are things said.

3. re**concil**ed, **concil**iate
   The meanings of *reconciled* and *conciliate* share the idea of becoming friendly or in harmony with.

 For additional assessment, see Assessment Resources, pp. 145–146.

Focus

Origin of Thesaurus Ask: What is the origin of the word *thesaurus*? *(It comes from a Latin word meaning "treasure" or "collection.")* **Say:** When you look up the word *thesaurus* in a thesaurus, some of the words listed are *dictionary, wordbook, lexicon, vocabulary,* and *glossary.*

Teach

Antonyms Remind students that antonyms are words with opposite meanings. Have them look in a thesaurus to find an antonym of each underlined word in the exercise sentences. Ask students to share their answers with the class.

Assess

Possible synonym choices:

1. **pious:** religious, devout; sanctimonious, self-righteous

2. **kind:** merciful, generous; category, variety; character, temper

3. **broke free:** got out, escaped; **trip:** journey, excursion; blunder, mistake; dance, skip; trap, hoodwink

4. **large:** gigantic, enormous, substantial

 For additional vocabulary practice, see Glencoe Interactive Vocabulary CD-ROM.

Thesaurus and Synonyms

A **thesaurus** is a reference source used to find words with similar meanings, or **synonyms.**

Test-Taking Tip

To decide whether two words are synonyms, first identify the part of speech of each word. Synonyms are always the same part of speech.

LOG ON ► **Literature** Online

Vocabulary For more vocabulary practice, go to glencoe.com and enter QuickPass code GLB9817u3.

Vocabulary Workshop

Thesaurus Use

Literature Connection In this passage, the narrator describes Vanity Fair as a place with "pleasures, and delights of all sorts."

> *"Therefore, at this fair are all such merchandise sold as houses, lands, trades, places, honors, preferments, titles, countries, kingdoms, lusts, pleasures, and delights of all sorts."*
>
> —John Bunyan, from *The Pilgrim's Progress*

Pleasures and *delights* are **synonyms,** or words with similar meanings. Some synonyms are interchangeable, while others have subtly different associations, or connotations. For example, the word *pleasures* refers to general gratification, but *delights* suggests extraordinary enjoyment.

Most dictionaries explain the differences between some synonyms, but for many words you must consult a **thesaurus,** a specialized dictionary of synonyms and **antonyms,** or words with opposite meanings. Thesauruses (*or thesauri*) are available in many formats—CD-ROM, Internet, word-processing software, and print—and can be organized traditionally by concept or in dictionary style.

Traditional Style

Probably the best-known traditional thesaurus is *Roget's Thesaurus.* To find a synonym for the adjective *loud,* for example, you would look it up in the alphabetical index. This list includes several entries, including *loud-sounding* and *gaudy,* with page references. On those pages, you would find synonyms related to the concepts of *loudness* and *vulgarity.*

Dictionary Style

This type of thesaurus presents words in alphabetical order. Each word is followed by several synonyms, listed by parts of speech. The entry also refers the reader to other related words, such as *audible* and *noisy,* in the case of *loud.*

Practice Using a thesaurus, find at least two synonyms for each underlined word. Then, working in small groups, discuss the connotations of each synonym.

1. Vanity Fair failed to tempt the <u>pious</u> pilgrims.
2. Christian and Faithful are both rewarded for their <u>kind</u> acts.
3. Christian <u>broke free</u> from the prison and continued his <u>trip</u>.
4. Religion played a <u>large</u> role in eighteenth-century British literature.

Listening and Speaking Practice

Find Synonyms for Political Terms A thesaurus is a good tool for increasing students' reading comprehension. Ask students to choose an article related to the democratic process from the local, national or world section of a newspaper. Have students look up isynonyms of each word that is unclear to them in a thesaurus. *(Possible words: caucus, primary, bipartisan, delegate, filibuster, etc.)* Then ask students to present to the class the effect of the media using one word over the other.

Before You Read

On Her Loving Two Equally

Meet **Aphra Behn**
(c. 1640–1689)

Poet, novelist, playwright, and sometime spy—Aphra Behn (äˊ frä bān) was England's first professional female writer. Extraordinarily prolific, Behn wrote about the social and political topics of her time. She was a versatile and talented literary craftsperson.

> *"All women together ought to let flowers fall upon the tomb of Aphra Behn, for it was she who earned them the right to speak their minds."*
>
> —Virginia Woolf

Much of Behn's early life is a mystery. Accounts vary as to when she was born, who her parents were, and even what her real name was. She was probably born in 1640 in Kent. At twenty-three, she likely traveled to Surinam (Dutch Guiana), an English sugar colony in the West Indies, although why and with whom is unclear. She returned to England the next year and married a London merchant named Behn. However, he died just a year or two after their marriage—probably from the bubonic plague.

The King's Spy Ironically, the first documented facts of Behn's life concern her work as a spy for King Charles II. Shortly after being widowed, Behn, in need of an income, arrived in Holland as an official spy to see what she could learn of Dutch military plans. At the time, England was engaged in trade wars with the Dutch. Although she obtained valuable information about a planned Dutch invasion, the king's agents did not pay her fully for it, and she was forced to borrow money to return to England. As a result, she spent part of 1668 in a London debtors' prison.

This prison experience spurred Behn to do something that no other woman had yet tried—earn a living from writing. In 1670 she wrote a romantic melodrama called *The Forc'd Marriage*—and it was a success. Encouraged, Behn continued writing plays, producing fifteen more in the next twelve years and becoming a minor celebrity in the process. *The Rover, Part I*, her most successful play, is set in Naples during the carnival season.

Early English Novelist In 1682 Behn was arrested for writing a play containing a satirical attack on the Duke of Monmouth, an illegitimate son of Charles II, and angering the king. Behn decided to take a break from writing for the stage and turned to writing poetry and fiction. Drawing upon her acquaintance with an enslaved African prince in Surinam, she wrote one of the first novels by an English author, *Oroonoko; or the History of the Royal Slave*. It was published a year before she died at the age of forty-eight.

Behn's literary contributions were undervalued during her lifetime primarily because of her gender. Although she wrote for money, she also sought recognition and acclaim. "I value fame as much as if I had been born a *Hero*," she wrote, "and if you rob me of that, I can retire from the ungrateful World, and scorn its fickle Favours."

 Literature Online

Author Search For more about Aphra Behn, go to glencoe.com and enter QuickPass code GLB9817u3.

Before You Read

Focus

Bellringer Options

Selection Focus
  Transparency 24
Daily Language Practice
  Transparency 41

Or **write** the word *choices* on the board. **Ask:** Have you ever been torn between two equally attractive choices? For example, have you ever had two invitations for the same day or two romantic interests at the same time?

After a short discussion, tell students to look for a similar situation in the poem they will read.

Selection Skills

Literary Elements
- Inversion (SE pp. 534–536)

On Her Loving Two Equally

Listening/Speaking/Viewing Skills
- Analyze Art (TE p. 535)

Reading Skills
- Question (SE pp. 534, 536)

Vocabulary Skills
- Word Usage (SE pp. 534, 536)

Writing Skills/Grammar
- Write a Letter (SE p. 536)

Before You Read

Focus

Summary

In this poem the speaker expresses ambivalence about which of two suitors, Alexis and Damon, she prefers.

 For summaries in languages other than English, see Unit 3 Teaching Resources Book, pp. 55–60.

Literature and Reading Preview

Connect to the Poem

Have you ever had to choose between two people you cared about? How did you make your choice? Freewrite for a few minutes about your experiences in such a situation.

Build Background

Charles II's reign saw the rise of a new kind of comedy, called the comedy of manners. In these plays, the heroes and heroines were shameless characters who waltzed in and out of one another's arms, exchanging witty remarks. In real life, however, respected women of the time could not behave nearly as freely as those stage characters did. For example, Behn was often labeled immoral merely for writing comedies that depicted amorous situations. Yet, throughout her career, Behn refused to modify her works. In 1684 she wrote "On Her Loving Two Equally" after more than a dozen years of defending her plays against charges of immorality.

Set Purposes for Reading

Big Idea The Restoration

The literary culture of the Restoration was marked by a witty, cynical tone and an emphasis on worldly values. As you read, ask yourself, How does this poem reflect that culture?

Literary Element Inversion

Inversion is the reversal of the typical word order in a prose sentence or a line of poetry. For example, in the sentence "Thee I love," the direct object *thee* precedes rather than follows the subject and the verb. As you read, ask yourself, Which expressions are instances of inversion?

Reading Strategy Question

Questioning is the process of asking questions as you read about things you do not understand. When you ask questions, you are reading strategically. As you read, ask yourself, What questions do these lines raise?

Tip: Taking Notes Have a running conversation with yourself while you read. Use a chart to record your questions and answers.

Questions	Answers
Who are the speaker's two suitors?	Damon and Alexis.

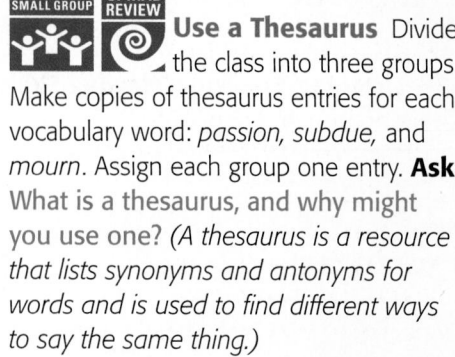
534

Two Strings to her Bow, 1887. John Pettie. Oil on canvas, 84 x 120.8 cm. Art Gallery and Museum, Kelvingrove, Glasgow, Scotland. ★

On Her Loving Two Equally

Aphra Behn

How strong does my **passion** flow,
Divided equally twixt[1] two?
Damon had ne'er[2] **subdued** my heart
Had not Alexis took his part;
5 Nor could Alexis powerful prove,
Without my Damon's aid, to gain my love.

When my Alexis present is,
Then I for Damon sigh and **mourn**;
But when Alexis I do miss,
10 Damon gains nothing but my scorn.
But if it chance they both are by,[3]
For both alike I languish, sigh, and die.

Cure then, thou mighty wingéd god,[4]
This restless fever in my blood;
15 One golden-pointed dart take back:
But which, O Cupid, wilt thou take?
If Damon's, all my hopes are crossed;
Or that of my Alexis, I am lost. **1**

1. *Twixt* means "between."
2. *Ne'er* means "never."
3. The word *by* means "near."
4. The *wingéd god* is Cupid, Roman god of love. Cupid shoots darts of gold or lead into the hearts of lovers. A golden-pointed dart would supposedly generate true love, while a leaden dart would generate false love.

Inversion *How would you write this clause in normal word order?* **2**

Vocabulary

passion (pash′ən) *n.* powerful emotion; love
subdue (səb do͞o′) *v.* to conquer
mourn (môrn) *v.* to show or feel sadness; grieve

APHRA BEHN **535**

Teach

Reading Strategy 1

Question **Ask:** Which of the two suitors, if either, does the speaker in the poem prefer? *(The speaker has not expressed a preference—despite the arguments she gives.)*

APPROACHING If students have difficulty, have them make a two-column chart listing the speaker's praise for each suitor.

Literary Element 2

Inversion **Answer:** *When my Alexis is present*

View the Art ★

John Pettie (1839–1893) was born in Scotland where he received his artistic training. He moved to London in 1862 and by 1874 he had been elected to the prestigious Royal Academy.

To check students' understanding of the selection, see Unit 3 Teaching Resources Book, p. 64.

English Learners

DIFFERENTIATED INSTRUCTION

Intermediate Remind students that the most common word order in English is subject–verb–object/complement. **Write** this example on the board:

Damon loves the lady.

Label the subject, verb, and object. Tell students that when a writer changes the normal word order, sentences can sound confusing. Rewriting a sentence in normal word order helps readers understand it.

Write lines 7, 8, 9, and 11 from the poem on the board. Label the subject, verb, and complement in line 7: When my Alexis (subject) present (complement) is (verb). Then model how to rewrite this line in normal word order: When my Alexis (subject) is (verb) present (complement).

Ask: Why is the rewritten sentence easier to understand? *(it is in the expected word order)*

Label the subject, verb, and object/complement in the other lines from the poem. Guide students as they practice writing the lines in normal word order.

After You Read

Assess

Respond and Think Critically

1. Students' answers will vary.

2. (a) The contrast between the two suitors makes both more appealing than either would be on his own. (b) Each of the rival suitors enhances the other's value.

3. (a) She languishes and sighs for both of them. (b) She enjoys being the center of attention.

4. To keep both of her admirers enamored of her

5. (a) The speaker's tone is light and playfully exaggerated. (b) The word choice supports the tone. Examples include phrases such as "sigh and mourn," "restless fever in my blood," and "all my hopes are crossed."

6. The purpose of the poem is to entertain and the emphasis is on worldly pursuits.

7. Answers will vary. Students may say that a modern woman might have many of the same feelings.

⚡ Writing

Letters should reflect the viewpoint of Damon and should include reasoned attempts at persuasion.

Vocabulary Practice

1. Students should describe an instance in which a person's emotions caused the person to act against his or her better judgment.

2. Students might list games, activities, and incentives that would capture the students' attention and calm them down.

3. Students might mention attending funerals, wearing black, and so forth.

536

After You Read

Respond and Think Critically

Respond and Interpret

1. If you were a close friend of the speaker in the poem, what advice would you give her? Why?

2. (a)According to the first stanza, why does the speaker find it hard to make up her mind? (b)What is ironic about the way her two rival suitors affect her?

3. (a)What does the speaker do when she is near both men? (b)What do the words she uses to describe her state at such times suggest about her personality and how she views her situation? Explain.

Analyze and Evaluate

4. What do you think the speaker really wants from Cupid? Explain.

5. (a)What is the speaker's tone, or attitude toward her subject? (b)How well does her word choice support that tone? Explain.

Connect

6. **Big Idea** The Restoration In what ways is this poem a product of the Restoration? Consider the poem's subject matter and purpose.

7. **Connect to Today** How might a modern woman deal with a situation like the speaker's?

Literary Element Inversion

Poets use **inversion**, or the placing of parts of speech out of their normal positions, to emphasize certain words or phrases or to maintain the rhyme scheme or the meter. For example, a poet might place a verb before its subject, as in "there go I"; an adjective after its noun, as in "the ocean wide"; or a main verb after a direct object, as in "so sweetly did me kiss."

1. Identify two inversions in Behn's poem. For each, tell what Behn inverts, or reverses.

2. Choose one inversion and tell why, in your opinion, Behn reverses the words or phrases.

⚡ Writing

Write a Letter Suppose that you are Damon, and you have just discovered the speaker's feelings for Alexis. Write a letter to the speaker in which you try to persuade her to choose you over your rival. Use persuasive techniques to strengthen your argument.

LOG ON ▶ **Literature** Online

Selection Resources For Selection Quizzes, eFlashcards, and Reading-Writing Connection activities, go to glencoe.com and enter QuickPass code GLB9817u3.

Reading Strategy Question

Questioning is a strategy that helps you create meaning while reading and reflecting on a poem. By asking questions, you deepen your understanding of a poem and the poet's intentions.

1. When was the strategy of questioning most helpful to you in reading this poem?

2. How would you evaluate the speaker of this poem? Is she really torn between her two suitors, or does she perhaps enjoy having more than one admirer? Explain.

Vocabulary Practice

Practice with Word Usage Respond to these statements to help you explore the meanings of vocabulary words in the selection.

1. Give an example from a book or movie in which **passion** made a person do something foolish.

2. List some things a teacher might do to **subdue** a rowdy kindergarten class.

3. List some conventional ways that people **mourn** for the dead.

Literary Element

1. In the phrase "Alexis powerful prove," the words *powerful* and *prove* are inverted. In the phrase "for Damon sigh and mourn," *for Damon* would follow *sigh* and *mourn* in normal word order.

2. In the case of "Alexis powerful prove," the inversion creates a slant rhyme with the word *love* in the following line.

Reading Strategy

1. Students' answers will vary.

2. The playful tone suggests that the speaker enjoys having two suitors.

Progress Check

Can students question?

If No → See Unit 3 Teaching Resources Book, p. 62.

Before You Read

from *The Diary of Samuel Pepys*

Meet **Samuel Pepys**
(1633–1703)

In his day, Samuel Pepys (pēps) was primarily recognized for his contributions to the British navy. Today he is more appreciated for his colorful and informative diary. Unnoticed for more than one hundred years after Pepys's death, the diary provides vivid accounts of some of the most stirring events of the seventeenth century, as well as an intimate portrait of Pepys himself.

> *"The instinct to live for the moment lyrically and at the same time prudently is seen nowhere better than in the Diary of Samuel Pepys."*
>
> —George Sherburn

A Distinguished Career Pepys was the fifth son of a London tailor. He attended Cambridge University on a scholarship, eventually earning a master's degree. Pepys worked as personal secretary to his influential cousin Admiral Edward Montagu, but admitted that his role as a public servant was due to "chance without merit." In 1660 Montagu brought Pepys along on a journey to Holland to bring back the exiled king Charles II and restore him to the English throne. Pepys was later appointed to a position as a clerk in the navy office, and through successive promotions he became secretary to the admiralty, the navy's top-ranking official. During his tenure, he instituted countless changes and doubled the navy's fighting strength—increasing the number of battleships from thirty to fifty-nine and the firepower from 1,730 guns to 4,492—thus transforming a poorly organized navy into a major military powerhouse.

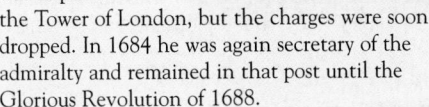

In 1679 Pepys won election to Parliament, but suffered a setback when he was falsely accused of passing secrets to the French. He was imprisoned in the Tower of London, but the charges were soon dropped. In 1684 he was again secretary of the admiralty and remained in that post until the Glorious Revolution of 1688.

Literary Legacy As a New Year's resolution, Pepys began his diary on January 1, 1660. While he probably never intended that the diary be published, he took great care with it. Much of the diary is transcribed from rough notes and carefully bound in six volumes. He wrote with extreme honesty and passion, whether he was recording his observations while witnessing important historical events or merely reflecting upon his personal interests—in music, theater, wine, clothes, and books—as well as his jealousies, weaknesses, desires, career advancements, and accumulation of wealth. His eye for detail and his vivid accounts afford a realistic glimpse into the events of the Restoration.

Pepys's diary is historically important and a literary success because he crafted his narrative with the care of a novelist, possibly with an audience in mind. According to biographer Richard Ollard: "The *Diary* is a great work, as literature, as history, as a psychological document and as a key to what has been known as the English character in an age of national cultures perhaps soon to become extinct. It is thus almost impossible to exaggerate its value and importance."

 Literature Online

Author Search For more about Samuel Pepys, go to glencoe.com and enter QuickPass code GLB9817u3.

SAMUEL PEPYS **537**

Before You Read

Focus

Summary

On April 23, 1661, Samuel Pepys witnesses the coronation of King Charles II. The pomp and ceremony impress Pepys, as does the banquet that follows.

On September 2, 1666, Pepys is awakened by the report of a great fire in London. He begins to fear that the flames will reach his house, so he spends the night carting his valuables to the home of Sir W. Rider.

 For summaries in languages other than English, see Unit 3 Teaching Resources Book, pp. 66–71.

Vocabulary

Synonym Contest Divide the class into teams. For each of the vocabulary words have students brainstorm a list of as many synonyms as possible. Allow students to use dictionaries but not a thesaurus. Have each team share their lists. Declare the team with the largest number of synonyms for all four words the winner.

 For additional vocabulary practice, see Unit 3 Teaching Resources Book, p. 74.

Literature and Reading Preview

Connect to the Diary

What recent events would you record in a diary? Write a journal entry noting the important events from one day in your life.

Build Background

During the nearly ten years Pepys kept his diary, he recorded vivid eyewitness accounts of such events as the restoration of King Charles II. He safeguarded his privacy by writing his entries in a combination of shorthand and secret code.

On September 2, 1666, a fire broke out in the residence of the king's baker. Violent winds quickly spread the flames. The Great Fire of London raged for four days, devastating four-fifths of the central city. Thirteen thousand homes were destroyed.

Set Purposes for Reading

Big Idea The Restoration

As you read, ask yourself, How do Pepys's entries reflect the new sense of freedom and the enjoyment of life that many writers of the Restoration felt?

Literary Element Diary

A **diary** is an individual's private, day-to-day account of personal thoughts, feelings, and experiences written for his or her own use rather than for publication. As you read, ask yourself, How does Pepys's account of particular types of people, events, and details convey his unique voice?

Reading Strategy Draw Conclusions About Author's Beliefs

Through close examination of an author's choice of details, tone, word choice, and use of figurative language, a reader can **draw conclusions**—or make general statements—about the author's beliefs. As you read, ask yourself, What evidence in the text helps me to draw accurate conclusions about his beliefs?

Tip: Taking Notes As you read, use a chart similar to the one below to record your conclusions about Pepys's beliefs.

Clues in Text	Conclusions
"And a great pleasure it was to see the Abbey . . ."	Pepys was a royalist.

Learning Objectives

For pages 537–546

In studying this text, you will focus on the following objectives:

Literary Study: Interpreting a historical diary.

Reading: Drawing conclusions about author's beliefs.

Research: Conducting Internet research.

Vocabulary

cavalcade (kav′əl kād′) *n.* a ceremonial procession; p. 540 *The men and women in the cavalcade wore elaborate robes.*

loath (lōth) *adj.* reluctant; unwilling; p. 542 *We were loath to leave the theater before the final encore.*

quench (kwench) *v.* to put out; to extinguish; p. 542 *The strong winds made it extremely difficult to quench the flames.*

malicious (mə lish′ əs) *adj.* deliberately harmful; p. 544 *John attacked his brother with malicious intent.*

Tip: To make sure that you have answered an analogy exercise correctly, check that the relationship between the second pair of words matches that between the first pair.

Reading Practice

SPIRAL REVIEW **Author's Purpose** Explain that authors have different reasons for writing, such as to inform or to persuade. Understanding an author's motivation can better prepare the reader for the text. **Ask:** What motivated this author to write down these events? Does his motivation for writing influence your interpretation of the text? As they read, tell students to look for clues that indicate the author's motivation for writing.

from
The Diary of Samuel Pepys

Samuel Pepys

The Coronation of Charles II

APRIL 23, 1661. Coronation Day. About four I rose and got to the Abbey,[1] where I followed Sir J. Denham, the surveyor, with some company that he was leading in. And with much ado, by the favor of Mr. Cooper, his man, did get up into a great scaffold[2] across the north end of the Abbey, where with a great deal of patience I sat from past four till eleven before the King came in. And a great pleasure it was to see the Abbey raised in the middle, all covered with red, and a throne (that is a chair) and footstool on the top of it; and all the officers of all kinds, so much as the very fiddlers, in red vests.

At last comes in the dean and prebends[3] of Westminster, with the bishops (many of them in cloth-of-gold copes[4]), and after them the nobility, all in their Parliament robes, which was a most magnificent sight. Then the Duke,[5] and the King with a scepter (carried by my Lord Sandwich) and sword and mond[6] before him, and the crown, too. The King in his robes, bare-headed, which was very fine. And after all had placed themselves, there was a sermon and the service; and then in the choir at the high altar, the King passed through all the ceremonies of the coronation, which to my great grief I and most in the Abbey could not see. The crown being put upon his head, a great shout begun, and he came forth to the throne, and there passed more ceremonies: as taking the oath and having things read to him by the bishop; and his lords (who put on their caps as soon as the King put on his crown) and bishops come and kneeled before him. And three times the King

---

1. The *Abbey* is Westminster Abbey, the London church that is the traditional site of coronations.
2. A *scaffold* is a raised platform.
3. The *dean* and *prebends* (preʹbəndz) are high church officials.
4. *Copes* are long capes worn by church officials during processions and other religious ceremonies.
5. The *Duke* is the Duke of York—the king's brother and later King James II.
6. A *mond* is a ball of gold or other precious material with a cross on top, representing the globe of Earth. It is meant to be a symbol of royal power.

Draw Conclusions About Author's Beliefs *What conclusions can you draw about Pepys's political sympathies based on his descriptions of the coronation?* **1**

SAMUEL PEPYS **539**

Advanced Learners

DIFFERENTIATED INSTRUCTION

Point of View Remind students that all writers approach their subject from a particular point of view which is shaped by their experiences and world view. **Say:** In this selection, Pepys's view of the events might be quite different than someone from a lower or higher class. When we are analyzing writing, we have to keep the author's point of view of mind. Have students write a diary entry about one of the topics in Pepys's diary but from the perspective of a different person, such as a visitor to London, a peasant, or the king.

Teach

Reading Strategy 1

Draw Conclusions About Author's Beliefs **Answer:**
Pepys's glowing description and his disappointment in not being able to see the king reveal his Royalist sympathies.

Cultural History ☆

Royal Celebration The coronation of Charles II gave Londoners an excuse to decorate their houses and wear their best clothes. The day before the coronation, Pepys put on a new velvet coat and went to see a royal procession from the Tower of London to Whitehall. Pepys notes in his diary that the route was "all graveled; and the houses, hung with carpets before them, made brave show, and the ladies out of the windows."

Interactive Read and Write
Other options for teaching this selection can be found in
- Interactive Read and Write for EL Students pp. 129–140
- Interactive Read and Write for Approaching-Level Students, pp. 129–140
- Interactive Read and Write for On-Level Students, pp. 129–140

Readability Scores
Dale-Chall: 7.5
DRP: 56
Lexile: 1220

Teach

Literary Element 1

Diary Answer: *Pepys repeats the words "very fine." Some students may say that the repetition enhances Pepys's style by establishing an informal, conversational tone. Others may say that the repetition detracts from Pepys's style because it is little more than a cliché.*

View the Art  ★

Answer: *The scepter's being carried, red vests and gold capes, the large and solemn group of people*

Dirck Stoop (1618–1686) painted and engraved portraits (including one of Charles II), battle scenes, still lifes, and hunting scenes. **Ask:** How does the artist show the pomp of the royal cavalcade? *(He depicts a long, impressive cavalcade with people dressed in finery, many on horses; the king stands out on a white horse.)*

Charles II's entry into London on the day before his Coronation in 1661. Dirck Stoop (1618–1686). Oil on canvas, 64 x 199 cm. Museum of London.

View the Art Dirck Stoop was known for his paintings of upper-class and royal life. What details in Pepys's account are reflected in the style or details of this painting? Explain. ★

at Arms[7] went to the three open places on the scaffold and proclaimed that if anyone could show any reason why Charles Stuart should not be King of England, that now he should come and speak. And a general pardon also was read by the Lord Chancellor, and medals flung up and down by my Lord Cornwallis, of silver, but I could not come by any. But so great a noise that I could make but little of the music; and indeed, it was lost to everybody . . . .

I went out a little while before the King had done all his ceremonies and went round the Abbey to Westminster Hall,[8] all the way within rails, and ten thousand people, with the ground covered with blue cloth; and scaffolds all the way. Into the hall I got, where it was very fine with hangings and scaffolds one upon another full of brave[9] ladies; and my wife in

one little one on the right hand. Here I stayed walking up and down, and at last, upon one of the side stalls, I stood and saw the King come in with all the persons (but the soldiers) that were yesterday in the **cavalcade;** and a most pleasant sight it was to see them in their several robes. And the King came in with his crown on, and his scepter in his hand, under a canopy borne up by six silver staves,[10] carried by barons of the Cinque Ports,[11] and little bells at every end.

And after a long time, he got up to the farther end, and all set themselves down at their several tables; and that was also a brave sight; and the King's first course carried up by the Knights of the Bath. And many fine ceremonies there was of the herald's leading up people before him and bowing; and my Lord of Albemarle's going to the kitchen and eat a bit of the first dish that was to go to the King's

---

7. The *King at Arms* is the chief herald, an officer whose duties include making royal proclamations and arranging public processions and ceremonies.
8. *Westminster Hall* is the court of justice.
9. As it is used here, *brave* means "finely dressed."

1 **Diary** *What words of approval used on page 539 does Pepys repeat here? In your opinion, does this repetition enhance or detract from Pepys's style?*

---

10. *Staves* is the plural of *staff.*
11. *Cinque* (singk) *Ports* are the five seaports along the English Channel that jointly provided England's naval defense.

Vocabulary

cavalcade (kav′əl kad′) *n.* a ceremonial procession

Vocabulary Practice

SPIRAL REVIEW Etymology Remind students that etymology is the study of a word's history and origins. **Say:** Understanding where a word came from can help us learn its definition and use it correctly in our writing. On the board, **write:** *chancellor, king, herald, ceremony,* and *brave.* Ask students to use a dictionary to trace the etymology of each word. Have them share their results with the class. **Ask:** Did any of the meanings change from their original use to how we use them today? *(Possible answers:* Chancellor *originally meant "doorkeeper";* king*—"kin";* herald*—"army leader";* ceremony*—no change in meaning;* brave*—"wild.")*

table. But, above all, was these three Lords, Northumberland and Suffolk and the Duke of Ormond, coming before the courses on horseback and staying so all dinnertime, and at last to bring up [Dymock] the King's champion,[12] all in armor on horseback, with his spear and target carried before him. And a herald proclaims, "That if any dare deny Charles Stuart to be lawful King of England, here was a champion that would fight with him"; and

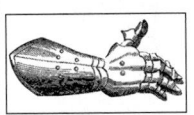

Visual Vocabulary
A *gauntlet* is a protective glove, usually made of leather or metal, worn with medieval armor. Throwing down a gauntlet symbolized a challenge.

with these words, the champion flings down his gauntlet, and all this he do three times in his going up towards the King's table. At last when he is come, the King drinks to him and then sends him the cup, which is of gold, and he drinks it off and then rides back again with the cup in his hand. I went from table to table to see the bishops and all others at their dinner and was infinitely pleased with it. And at the Lords' table, I met with William Howe, and he spoke to my Lord[13] for me, and he did give me four rabbits and a pullet, and so I got it, and Mr. Creed and I got Mr. Michell to give us some bread, and so we at a stall eat it, as everybody else did what they could get. I took a great deal of pleasure to go up and down and look upon the ladies and to hear the music of all sorts, but above all, the twenty-four violins.

---

12. At coronations, the *King's champion* ceremoniously defended the new king's title to the crown. This office had been held by the *Dymock* family since Richard II was crowned in 1377.
13. *My Lord* is Edward Montagu, the Earl of Sandwich, who was Pepys's cousin and lifelong patron.

3 The Restoration *What element of public life has been restored along with the monarchy?*

The London Fire

SEPTEMBER 2, 1666. Lord's Day.[14] Some of our maids sitting up late last night to get things ready against our feast today, Jane called us up about three in the morning to tell us of a great fire they saw in the city. So I rose and slipped on my nightgown and went to her window and thought it to be on the back side of Mark Lane at the farthest; but, being unused to such fires as followed, I thought it far enough off and so went to bed again and to sleep. About seven rose again to dress myself and there looked out at the window and saw the fire not so much as it was and further off. So to my closet[15] to set things to rights after yesterday's cleaning.

By and by Jane comes and tells me that she hears that above three hundred houses have been burned down tonight by the fire we saw and that it is now burning down all Fish Street, by London Bridge.[16] So I made myself ready presently and walked to the Tower[17] and there got up upon one of the high places, Sir J. Robinson's little son going up with me; and there I did see the houses at the end of the bridge all on fire and an infinite great fire on this and the other side the end of the bridge, which, among other people, did trouble me for poor little Michell and our Sarah[18] on the bridge. So down, with my heart full of trouble, to the lieutenant of the Tower, who tells me that it begun this morning in the King's baker's house in Pudding Lane and that it hath burned St. Magnus's Church and most part of Fish Street already. So I down to the waterside and there got a boat and through bridge and there

---

14. *Lord's Day* is Sunday.
15. A *closet* was a private room used especially for study or prayer.
16. *London Bridge* was the only bridge over the Thames River at that time. It was lined with shops and houses.
17. The *Tower* of London actually consists of a group of buildings on the Thames River constructed as a fortress and later used as a royal residence and prison.
18. *Sarah* was a maid whom Mrs. Pepys fired on December 5, 1662. Pepys still cared about her well-being.

Teach

Literary Element | **2**

Diary Have students reread the description of the banquet ceremony. **Ask:** What impressions does Pepys create with this description? (*Students may suggest that it and other details about armored knights remind them of King Arthur and underscore the "kingly" nature of the occasion.*)

Big Idea | **3**

The Restoration Answer: *The Puritans frowned on public pleasures and entertainment, including the performance of music in church. Pepys is delighting in the festive coronation music being played in Westminster Abbey.*

English Learners

DIFFERENTIATED INSTRUCTION

Intermediate Help English language learners realize that Pepys's world had some similarities to their own. Have students create a two-column chart like the one shown here.

My Thoughts	Pepys's Thoughts

Students should list sensory details or feelings they might expect to have while watching an awards show or coverage of a natural disaster. As students read the selection, have them jot down details that Pepys mentions. Then have students compare the lists and compare reactions to the event.

Teach

Infer In describing the Great Fire, Pepys tells how some people stay home "till the very fire touched them." **Ask:** Why would people act this way? *(Many were poor and had no place to go. In the confusion, it is also possible that people did not know where to go.)*

Reading Strategy 2

Drawing Conclusions About Author's Beliefs

Answer: *Throughout his description of the fire in this paragraph, Pepys shows his personal involvement with and compassion for the victims, especially the poor people.*

Literary Element 3

Diary Answer: *Most students will say that Pepys is showing off his exalted position as an adviser to the king.*

View the Art ★

Answer: *Most students will note that, unlike Pepys's depiction, the painting does not show any people or any individual circumstances. The severity and devastation of the fire, however, are much like Pepys describes.*

Point out to students that paintings and written accounts are the only sources of information about events in 1666.

The Great Fire of London, 1666. After Waggoner. Oil on canvas, 46.9 x 72.4 cm. Guildhall Art Gallery, Corporation of London.

View the Art The Great Fire has been the subject of many paintings, but Pepys's account is considered one of the best written descriptions of it. How does this visual representation compare with Pepys's written account?

saw a lamentable fire. Poor Michell's house, as far as the Old Swan,[19] already burned that way, and the fire running further, that in a very little time it got as far as the Steel Yard, while I was there. Everybody endeavoring to remove their goods and flinging into the river or bringing them into lighters[20] that lay off; poor people staying in their houses as long as till the very fire touched them and then running into boats or clambering from one pair of stairs by the waterside to another. And among other things, the poor pigeons, I perceive, were **loath** to leave their houses, but hovered about the windows and balconies till they were, some of them burned, their wings, and fell down. Having stayed, and in an hour's time seen the fire rage every way, and nobody, to my sight, endeavoring to **quench** it, but to remove their goods, and leave all to the fire, and having seen it get as far

as the Steel Yard, and the wind mighty high and driving it into the City; and everything, after so long a drought, proving combustible, even the very stones of churches, and among other things the poor steeple by which pretty Mrs. —— lives, and whereof my old schoolfellow Elborough is parson, taken fire in the very top and there burned till it fell down. I to Whitehall[21] (with a gentleman with me who desired to go off from the Tower, to see the fire, in my boat); to Whitehall, and there up to the King's closet in the Chapel, where people come about me, and I did give them an account dismayed them all, and word was carried in to the King. So I was called for and did tell the King and Duke of York what I saw, and that unless his Majesty did command houses to

---

19. Betty *Michell* was a former love interest of Pepys who lost her house in the fire. The *Old Swan* was a tavern near London Bridge.
20. *Lighters* are large, open barges.

Vocabulary

loath (lōth) *adj.* reluctant; unwilling
quench (kwench) *v.* to put out; to extinguish

---

21. *Whitehall* was the king's residence in Westminster, London, as well as the location of several government offices.

Drawing Conclusions About Author's Beliefs *Pepys uses the word* poor *three times in this paragraph. What conclusions can you draw about Pepys's social consciousness?* 2

Diary *Why do you think Pepys includes this detail about his conversation with the king in his diary?* 3

542 UNIT 3 FROM PURITANISM TO THE ENLIGHTENMENT

Vocabulary Practice

SPIRAL REVIEW **Appositives and Appositive Phrases Write** on the board: and his wife, Barbary Sheldon. Explain that Barbary Sheldon is an **appositive**—a noun or pronoun that is placed next to another noun or pronoun to identify or give additional information about it; an appositive phrase is an appositive plus words that modify it. Appositives and appositive phrases that are not essential to the meaning of a sentence are set off with commas. Have students write four sentences about Pepys's diary that contain appositives and appositive phrases.

be pulled down, nothing could stop the fire. They seemed much troubled, and the King commanded me to go to my Lord Mayor from him and command him to spare no houses, but to pull down before the fire every way. The Duke of York bid me tell him that if he would have any more soldiers, he shall; and so did my Lord Arlington afterwards, as a great secret. Here meeting with Captain Cocke, I in his coach, which he lent me, and Creed with me to Paul's,[22] and there walked along Watling Street, as well as I could, every creature coming away laden with goods to save, and here and there sick people carried away in beds. Extraordinary good goods carried in carts and on backs. At last met my Lord Mayor in Canning Street, like a man spent, with a handkerchief about his neck. To the King's message he cried, like a fainting woman, "Lord! What can I do? I am spent: people will not obey me. I have been pulling down houses, but the fire overtakes us faster than we can do it." That he needed no more soldiers and that, for himself, he must go and refresh himself, having been up all night.

So he left me, and I him, and walked home, seeing people all almost distracted, and no manner of means used to quench the fire. The houses, too, so very thick thereabouts and full of matter for burning, as pitch and tar, in Thames Street; and warehouses of oil and wines and brandy and other things. Here I saw Mr. Isaake Houblon, the handsome man, prettily dressed and dirty, at his door at Dowgate, receiving some of his brothers' things, whose houses were on fire, and, as he says, have been removed twice already; and he doubts (as it soon proved) that they must be in a little time removed from his house also, which was a sad consideration. And to see the churches all filling with goods by people who themselves should have been quietly there at this time.

By this time it was about twelve o'clock; and so home and there find my guests, which was Mr. Wood and his wife, Barbary Sheldon, and also Mr. Moone: she mighty fine, and her husband, for aught I see, a likely man. But Mr. Moone's design and mine, which was to look over my closet and please him with the sight thereof, which he hath long desired, was wholly disappointed; for we were in great trouble and disturbance at this fire, not knowing what to think of it. However, we had an extraordinary good dinner, and as merry as at this time we could be. While at dinner, Mrs. Batelier come to enquire after Mr. Woolfe and Stanes (who, it seems, are related to them), whose houses in Fish Street are all burned, and they in a sad condition. She would not stay in the fright. Soon as dined, I and Moone away and walked through the City, the streets full of nothing but people and horses and carts laden with goods, ready to run over one another, and removing goods from one burned house to another. They now removing out of Canning Street (which received goods in the morning) into Lombard Street and further; and among others I now saw my little goldsmith, Stokes, receiving some friend's goods, whose house itself was burned the day after. We parted at Paul's; he home, and I to Paul's Wharf, where I had appointed a boat to attend me, and took in Mr. Carcasse and his brother, whom I met in the street, and carried them below and above bridge to and again to see the fire, which was now got further, both below and above, and no likelihood of stopping it. Met with the King and Duke of York in their barge, and with them to Queenhithe, and there called Sir Richard Browne to them. Their order was only to pull down houses apace,[23] and so below bridge at the waterside; but little was or could be done, the fire coming upon them so fast. Good hopes there was of stopping it at the Three Cranes above, and at Buttolph's Wharf below bridge, if care be used; but the wind carries it into the City, so as we know not by the waterside what it do there. River full of lighters and boats taking in goods, and good goods swimming in the water, and only I observed that hardly one lighter or boat in three that had the goods of a

---

22. *Paul's* is St. Paul's Cathedral, which was destroyed in the fire and later rebuilt.

23. *Apace* means "swiftly."

SAMUEL PEPYS **543**

Teach

Cultural History ☆

London Fires Cities like London were subject to frequent and terrible fires during this time. In 1666, most buildings in London were made of highly flammable wood and pitch construction. Hay and feed piles for animals and riverside warehouses filled with hemp, oil, tallow, timber, and coal added to the combustible conditions. Strong winds easily carried sparks from one part of the city to another. After the fire, Charles II appointed commissioners to redesign the city, and 9,000 houses and public buildings of brick were completed along wider streets by 1671. Nevertheless, London suffered another serious fire in 1676.

Approaching Level

DIFFERENTIATED INSTRUCTION

Established Ask approaching-level students to write a brief paragraph about something happening in the classroom at that moment. **Say:** Reread your paragraph and think about how to change the sentences to past tense. Have students circle the verbs they would need to change. **Write** those verbs on the board. Guide students through changing the present tense verbs to the past tense forms. **Write** the past tense forms on the board. Then have students revise their paragraphs.

Teach

Visual Vocabulary
A *pair of virginals* is actually a single musical instrument: a small, rectangular, legless sixteenth-century harpsichord that is placed on a table or held in the lap to play.

house in but there was a pair of virginals in it.

Having seen as much as I could now, I away to Whitehall by appointment and there walked to St. James's Park and there met my wife and Creed and Wood and his wife and walked to my boat; and there upon the water again, and to the fire up and down, it still increasing, and the wind great. So near the fire as we could for smoke; and all over the Thames, with one's face in the wind, you were almost burned with a shower of fire-drops. This is very true; so as houses were burned by these drops and flakes of fire, three or four, nay, five or six houses, one from another. When we could endure no more upon the water, we to a little alehouse on the Bankside, over against the Three Cranes, and there stayed till it was dark almost and saw the fire grow; and as it grew darker, appeared more and more and in corners and upon steeples and between churches and houses as far as we could see up the hill of the City in a most horrid **malicious** bloody flame, not like the fine flame of an ordinary fire. Barbary and her husband away before us. We stayed till, it being darkish, we saw the fire as only one entire arch of fire from this to the other side the bridge and in a bow up the hill for an arch of above a mile long: it made me weep to see it. The churches, houses, and all on fire and flaming at once; and a horrid noise the flames made and the cracking of houses at their ruin.

So home with a sad heart, and there find everybody discoursing and lamenting the fire;

---

1 | **Diary** *How has the tone of this diary entry changed as the fire continued to spread?*

Vocabulary

malicious (mə lish′əs) *adj.* deliberately harmful

and poor Tom Hater come with some few of his goods saved out of his house, which is burned upon Fish Street Hill. I invited him to lie at my house and did receive his goods, but was deceived in his lying there, the news coming every moment of the growth of the fire; so as we were forced to begin to pack up our own goods and prepare for their removal and did by moonshine (it being brave dry and moonshine and warm weather) carry much of my goods into the garden, and Mr. Hater and I did remove my money and iron chests into my cellar, as thinking that the safest place. And got my bags of gold into my office, ready to carry away, and my chief papers of accounts also there, and my tallies[24] into a box by themselves. So great was our fear, as Sir W. Batten hath carts come out of the country to fetch away his goods this night. We did put Mr. Hater, poor man, to bed a little; but he got but very little rest, so much noise being in my house, taking down of goods.

3RD.[25] About four o'clock in the morning, my Lady Batten sent me a cart to carry away all my money and plate[26] and best things to Sir W. Rider's at Bednall Green. Which I did, riding myself in my nightgown in the cart; and, Lord! to see how the streets and the highways are crowded with people running and riding and getting of carts at any rate to fetch away things. I find Sir W. Rider tired with being called up all night, and receiving things from several friends. His house full of goods, and much of Sir W. Batten's and Sir W. Pen's. I am eased at my heart to have my treasure so well secured. Then home, with much ado to find a way, nor any sleep all this night to me nor my poor wife. ❧

2

---

24. *Tallies* were sticks marked with notches representing amounts of money. The tallies served as records of money paid or owed.
25. The abbreviation *3rd* refers to the date, September 3.
26. *Plate* refers to tableware or decorative objects made of a precious metal, such as silver or gold.

Draw Conclusions About Author's Beliefs *Pepys itemizes the belongings that he chose to save from the fire. What does this list of items tell you about Pepys?* **3**

544

After You Read

Respond and Think Critically

Respond and Interpret

1. What were your reactions to the events Pepys describes?

2. (a)Where does Pepys go to see the coronation of Charles II? (b)What is Pepys's attitude toward the king's restoration?

3. (a)When Pepys first views the fire burning in the distance, what does he do? Why? (b)How does his later attitude toward the fire compare with his initial reaction?

Analyze and Evaluate

4. (a)Explain the mood of Pepys's account of the night of September 2 and early the next morning. (b)What techniques does he use to create this mood?

Literary Element Diary

Pepys's diary entries offer valuable insight and impressions of historic events, such as the Great Fire and candid pictures of everyday life. In his description of the coronation of Charles II, Pepys includes both personal and historical details.

1. Identify a detail Pepys observes during the Great Fire of London that you would probably not find in a history book.

2. If Pepys had known his diary might be read or even published, how might it have been different? Explain.

Review: Tone

As you learned on page 245, **tone** refers to the author's attitude toward his or her subject matter or audience. Tone is conveyed through elements such as word choice, punctuation, sentence structure, and figures of speech. A writer's tone may convey a variety of attitudes, such as sympathy, irony, sadness, or despair.

5. (a)What does Pepys do at twelve o'clock on the night of the fire? (b)What is your opinion of his behavior?

Connect

6. **Big Idea** **The Restoration** After the repressive years of Puritan rule, the Restoration gave writers a renewed sense of freedom. How does Pepys's account of the king's coronation illustrate the exhilarating atmosphere that characterized the Restoration?

7. **Connect to the Author** If Pepys had not been well educated and well connected socially, how might the kinds of events recorded in his diary have been different?

Partner Activity With a partner, discuss the similarities and differences in Pepys's tone—first in his account of the coronation, and then in his account of the fire. Create a chart similar to the one below to compare and contrast words, phrases, and devices that Pepys uses to convey his tone.

Textual Evidence	Description of Tone
Coronation: "And a great pleasure it was to see the Abbey raised in the middle, all covered with red . . ."	festive, jubilant
Great Fire of London: "So down, with my heart full of trouble, to the lieutenant of the Tower . . ."	ominous, sad

---

After You Read

Assess

1. Students' answers will vary.

2. (a) Westminster Abbey (b) Pepys is jubilant.

3. (a) He returns to bed. (b) Initially unaware of the fire's threat, he later experiences a "heart full of trouble" at the London Bridge.

4. (a) In the beginning, the mood is objective, but as Pepys is drawn into the scene, the mood becomes somber. (b) He uses vivid details and images to describe the scene, such as "a shower of firedrops," and vivid adjectives, such as "lamentable" and "malicious."

5. (a) Pepys returns home and has a good dinner and a "merry" time with his guests. (b) Students' answers will vary.

6. His description of the lavish ceremonies and rituals surrounding the coronation reflects the general feeling that freer, more relaxed, and more pleasurable times lay ahead with the return of the monarchy.

7. Students may say that the diary events would focus more on home and work life.

 For additional assessment, see Assessment Resources, pp. 149–150.

Literary Element

1. Pepys's observation and sympathy for the endangered pigeons probably would not be mentioned in a traditional history book.

2. Knowing that people would read his diary might have caused Pepys to be more guarded about giving his opinion, or it might have made him try to be more of a historian.

Review: Tone

Students' interpretations of the tones of specific passages should be reasonable.

Progress Check

Can students identify traits of diary writing?

If No → See Unit 3 Teaching Resources Book, p. 72.

545

After You Read

Assess

Reading Strategy

1. On the basis of his descriptions of the ceremony, the reader can conclude that he is pleased to have Charles II restored to the throne.

2. Worldly goods seem important to Pepys. He repeatedly describes what belongings people were attempting to rescue from their homes. He also makes a point of mentioning that he removed his money and chests of gold to a safe place.

Research and Report

Use these criteria in evaluating student Internet use:

- A search is done for articles about the places or events referred to in Pepys's "The London Fire."
- Information is culled from reputable Internet sources, which are cited accurately.
- A report of the research findings is presented logically, using visual aids as support.

Reading Strategy Draw Conclusions About Author's Beliefs

In his description of the coronation and the Great Fire, Pepys interjects comments that give the reader insight into his personal beliefs.

1. What conclusion can you draw about Pepys's attitude toward King Charles II and the coronation ceremony?

2. Based on his description of people's actions during the fire, what conclusion can you draw about Pepys's attitude toward material wealth?

Vocabulary Practice

Practice with Analogies Choose the word that best completes each analogy below.

1. laundry : wash :: fire :
   a. quench   b. climb   c. shout

2. parade : holiday :: cavalcade :
   a. battle   b. ceremony   c. rodeo

3. courteous : polite :: malicious :
   a. tactful   b. flattering   c. spiteful

4. sarcastic : sincere :: loath :
   a. eager   b. indifferent   c. scornful

Academic Vocabulary

*Pepys's diary must be understood within the historical **context** of the Restoration.*

Context is a word that can have several different meanings. The text surrounding a specific word or phrase is often called its **context**. To further explore this word, explain an instance in which a misunderstanding resulted from someone's comments being taken out of **context**.

For more on academic vocabulary, see pages 56 and R81.

Research and Report

 Internet Connection

Assignment Use the Internet to investigate one of the places or events mentioned in "The London Fire" section of Pepys's diary. Give an oral presentation reporting your findings.

Get Ideas Review Pepys's description of the Great Fire of London and make a list of topics to pursue. Choose one topic, and compile specific questions to structure your Internet search. Enter the questions directly into a search engine or search by keywords.

Research Gather only relevant and reliable information. Use the following criteria to evaluate Web sites:

- **Authority**—Is the site sponsored by a reputable organization? Does the author have legitimate credentials? Can he or she be contacted to verify information?
- **Objectivity**—Does the author cite facts or merely offer unsupported opinions? Does he or she have a personal, political, or philosophical agenda?
- **Accuracy**—Is the material free from grammatical and factual errors? Can the information be confirmed by another source?
- **Timeliness**—When was the site last updated? Can you be sure the information is current?

Be sure to include accurate citations for any Web sites you decide to use as sources. Record the answers to your questions in a two-column chart—questions on the left and answers on the right. Then organize the material logically—in chronological order, for example, or in order of importance—to present in your report.

Report Synthesize your information into a coherent picture, being sure to address any inconsistencies in the information you found. Then share your information with the class, including relevant images as visual aids. If possible, present your report as a computer slide show or PowerPoint presentation.

Vocabulary Practice

1. a
2. b
3. c
4. a

Academic Vocabulary

Students should explain how the different context changed the meaning of the comments.

Part 2

THE ENGLISH ENLIGHTENMENT AND NEOCLASSICISM

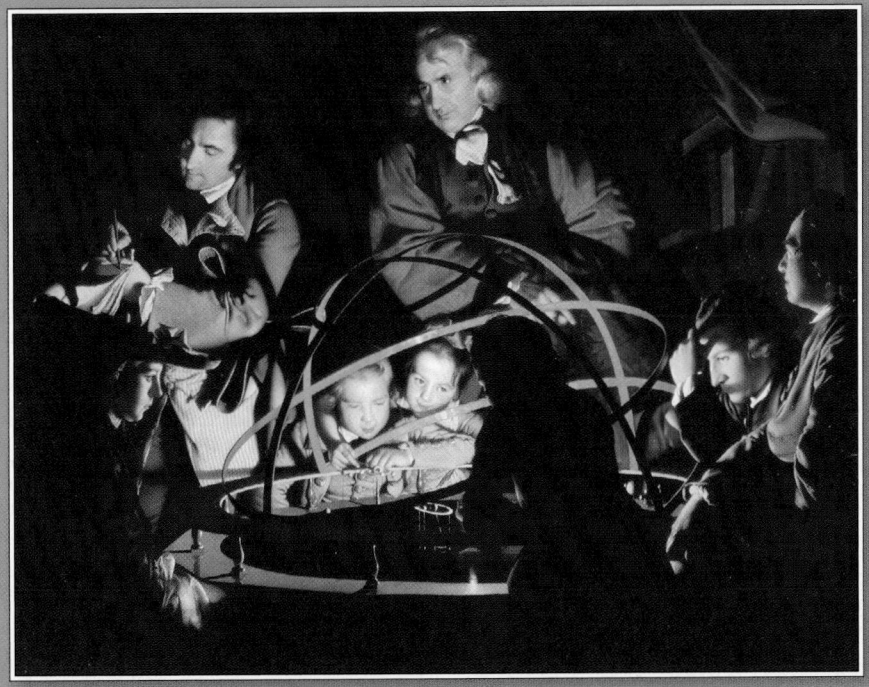

The Orrery, c. 1766. Joseph Wright of Derby. Oil on canvas. Derby Museum and Art Gallery, UK.

 View the Art An orrery is a mechanical model of the solar system, often with a lamp representing the sun. What does this painting suggest about the role of science in eighteenth-century Britain? Explain.

"Why, Sir, you find no man, at all intellectual, who is willing to leave London. No, Sir, when a man is tired of London, he is tired of life; for there is in London all that life can afford." **1**

—Samuel Johnson

547

Analyze and Extend

Reading Strategy   **1**

Interpret Meaning Direct students to read the quote from Johnson. **Ask:** What does this quote imply about life? *(That it is lived—for some—for its intellectual value.)*

View the Art

Joseph Wright (1734–1797) was born in Derby, a small town in England during the Industrial Revolution. His work combines art, science and philosophy in the style of his group of friends who met as the "Lunar Society" every Monday closest to the full moon. Together, these friends demonstrated experiments and kept abreast of advances in science. The full title of the work shown is *A Philosopher Giving that Lecture on the Orrery in which a Lamp is put in place of the Sun.* **Answer:** *The image suggests that science was considered very important and was accessible to all different ages and types of people.*

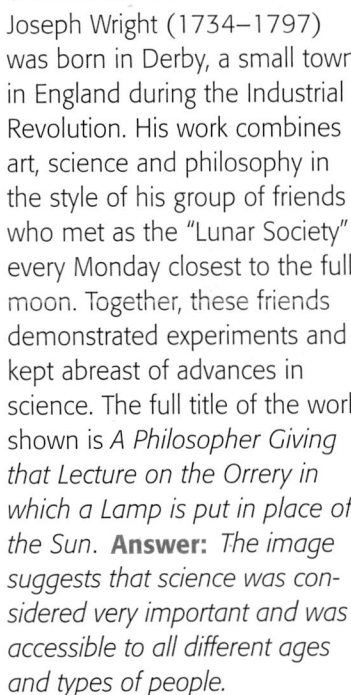
For additional support for English Learners, see Unit 3 Teaching Resources Book, p. 80.

Before You Read

Bellringer Options

Literature Launchers:
Pre-Reading Videos DVD,
Selection Launcher

Selection Focus
  Transparency 26

Daily Language Practice
  Transparency 44

Or ask students to give examples of satire on TV. *(Possible answers: Saturday Night Live; The Daily Show; The Simpsons)* **Ask:** What makes these programs satirical? *(They use irony, humor, and other techniques to point out societal problems and criticize the people who cause them.)*

Swift's Works

Meet **Jonathan Swift**
(1667–1745)

Jonathan Swift is generally thought to be the greatest prose writer of the eighteenth century and one of the world's finest satirists. He was a writer whom many considered a misanthrope (one who hates humankind) because his writings were deeply critical of humanity. It was, however, his deep love for humanity that caused him to criticize it, and his dream was to cure the ills of his age through humor.

Swift was born in Dublin, Ireland, of English parents. He had a difficult childhood. Before Swift was born, his father died, leaving the family so poor that his mother was forced to send her infant son to live with an uncle. At the age of six, he was sent to Kilkenny School, which was then the best school in Ireland. However, depression kept Swift from doing well in school, and later he barely graduated from Dublin's Trinity College.

Early Writing Swift's education as a writer began at the age of 22, when Sir William Temple, a retired diplomat living near London, hired him to be his secretary. Temple was also a noted author, and Swift learned a great deal about writing from him. Temple helped Swift obtain an M.A. degree from the University of Oxford. Through Temple, Swift also gained the notice of King William III, who suggested that he pursue a career in the Church of England. Swift became an Anglican priest and, while in his late twenties, served in Ireland. However, Swift was unhappy with his post and returned to Temple's employment.

It was in Temple's house that Swift first composed odes in the style of the ancient Greek poet Pindar. Then, realizing that he had a gift for humorous prose, he composed two of his acclaimed satires: *A Tale of a Tub*, which ridiculed the extravagances of religion, literature, and academia; and *The*

"Satire is a sort of glass, wherein beholders do generally discover everybody's face but their own."

—Jonathan Swift

Battle of the Books, which presented a mock debate between ancient and modern authors.

In 1699 Swift returned to Ireland to serve as pastor in a Protestant parish. His works had caught the eye of other authors, and he was invited to write essays for *The Tatler*, a popular English periodical. These essays and a series of political pamphlets enhanced his fame and showed that he was well informed about current events.

Master Satirist In 1713 Swift became dean of St. Patrick's Cathedral in Dublin, a post that he continued to hold for more than thirty years until his death. While living in Ireland, he wrote his satirical masterpiece, *Gulliver's Travels*.

Swift died at the age of 78. The generosity of spirit, deep learning, and humane humor that pervade his works are his rich legacy to the literary tradition.

 Literature Online

Author Search For more about Jonathan Swift, go to glencoe.com and enter QuickPass code GLB9817u3.

Selection Skills

Literary Elements
- Satire (SE pp. 549, 551, 552, 553, 554, 555, 557)
- Author's Purpose (SE p. 557)

A Modest Proposal

Listening/Speaking/Viewing Skills
- Analyze Art (SE pp. 552, 555)
- Speech (SE p. 558)

Reading Skills
- Analyze Text Structure (SE pp. 549, 551, 554, 555, 556, 558)

Vocabulary Skills
- Synonyms (SE p. 558)
- Academic Vocabulary (SE p. 558)

Writing Skills/Grammar
- Write Satire (TE p. 550)

Literature and Reading Review

Connect to the Selections

How might you persuade others to help with problems in your community? With a group of classmates, discuss your ideas.

Build Background

In *A Modest Proposal*, first published in 1729, Swift draws attention to economic conditions in Ireland. In the early 1700s, Ireland was ruled by England. Ireland could buy some products only from England and at high prices. English landlords, who owned much of Ireland's best land, charged exorbitant rents.

The narrator of *Gulliver's Travels* is Lemuel Gulliver, a doctor on a merchant ship who washes up on the shores of several fictional countries. Upon returning to England, he is painfully aware of his country's flaws.

Set Purposes for Reading

Big Idea The English Enlightenment and Neoclassicism

As you read, ask yourself, How does *A Modest Proposal* reflect reason, one of the core values of the Enlightenment?

Literary Element Satire

A Modest Proposal is a **satire**—a literary work that uses irony, humor, and other techniques to point out problems and criticize the people who are causing them. As you read, ask yourself, What is being satirized? What satirical techniques does Swift use?

Reading Strategy Analyze Text Structure

When you **analyze text structure**, you identify the pattern of organization a writer uses to present his or her ideas. As you read, ask yourself, Why did Swift choose a problem-and-solution pattern of organization for this essay?

Tip: Taking Notes Use a graphic organizer to record information about the text structure as you read.

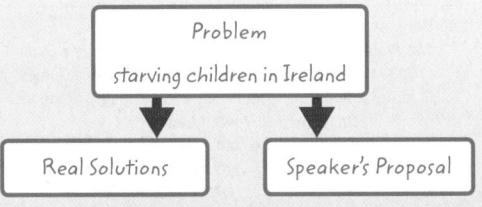

Learning Objectives

For pages 548–569

In studying this text, you will focus on the following objectives:

Literary Study: Analyzing satire.
Analyzing parody.

Reading: Analyzing text structure.
Making inferences about theme.

Writing: Delivering a speech.

Vocabulary

sustenance (sus′ tə nəns) *n.* food or items that support life; p. 550 *The volunteers gave the hurricane victims sustenance to restore their strength.*

deference (def′ ər əns) *n.* courteous respect; p. 553 *His deep admiration and deference for the teacher showed.*

digress (dī′ gres) *v.* to stray from the main subject; p. 554 *Please stay on the topic and do not digress to other subjects.*

conjecture (kən jek′ chər) *v.* to infer from inconclusive evidence; to guess; p. 559 *The fire chief conjectured that a frayed wire may have caused the blaze.*

magnitude (mag′ nə tood′) *n.* greatness of size or extent; p. 565 *A seismograph is used to measure and record the magnitude of earthquakes.*

Before You Read

Focus
Summary

An Englishman, dismayed at the pitiable sight of poor Irish mothers and children, offers a "practical" plan for alleviating the problem. He proposes that the children be bred like farm animals, slaughtered, and eaten. The speaker supports his main idea with analyses of the social and economic benefits. He then dismisses alternative plans for progressive taxes, economic prudence, and social reform.

Vocabulary

Related Forms Remind students that knowing one form of a word will enable them to recognize related forms when they encounter them. **Ask:** *Sustain* is the verb form of which noun? *(sustenance)* Ask similar questions using *defer, digression,* and *conjecture.* Students will note that *conjecture* is the same in the noun and verb forms. Have students write one example sentence for each of the related forms (*sustain, defer, digression,* and *conjecture*).

English Learners

DIFFERENTIATED INSTRUCTION

Intermediate Point out the affix *-ance/-ence* in *sustenance* and *deference.* Explain that this affix turns a verb into a noun. Ask what Spanish affix is similar *(-ancia).* Give the example *tolerate/tolerance* and ask Students to supply the Spanish translation. *(tolerar/tolerancia)*

A Modest Proposal

Jonathan Swift

Waifs and Strays, 1882. Joseph Clark. Oil on canvas, 102 x 84 cm. Sotheby's, London. ★

FOR PREVENTING THE CHILDREN OF POOR PEOPLE FROM BEING A *BURTHEN*[1] TO THEIR PARENTS OR THE COUNTRY, AND FOR MAKING THEM BENEFICIAL TO THE PUBLIC.

It is a melancholy object to those who walk through this great town,[2] or travel in the country, when they see the *streets*, the *roads*, and *cabin doors* crowded with *beggars* of the female sex, followed by three, four, or six children, *all in rags*, and importuning every passenger for an alms.[3] These *mothers*, instead of being able to work for their honest livelihood, are forced to employ all their time in strolling to beg **sustenance** for their *helpless infants* who, as they grow up, either turn *thieves* for want[4] of work or leave their *dear Native Country to fight for the Pretender*[5] in Spain or sell themselves to the Barbadoes.[6]

I think it is agreed by all parties that this prodigious number of children, in the arms or on the backs or at the *heels* of their *mothers*, and frequently of their fathers, is, *in the present deplorable state of the kingdom*, a very great additional grievance; and, therefore, whoever could find out a fair, cheap, and easy method of making these

---

1. A *burthen* is a burden.
2. The *town* referred to here is Dublin, Ireland.
3. *Importuning . . . alms* means "asking every passerby for a handout."

Vocabulary

sustenance (sus′ tə nəns) n. food or items that support life

4. Here, *want* means "lack."
5. *The Pretender* was a name given to James Edward Stuart (1688–1766), the son of England's deposed king, James II. James Edward had the loyalty and sympathy of the Irish people because he was Roman Catholic.
6. *Sell . . . Barbadoes* is a reference to the many Irish people who hoped to escape poverty by traveling to the West Indies. They obtained passage by agreeing to work as indentured servants.

550 UNIT 3 FROM PURITANISM TO THE ENLIGHTENMENT

Writing Practice

SMALL GROUP

Satire In *A Modest Proposal*, Swift satirizes the pitiable conditions of poor and abandoned children in Ireland in the early eighteenth century. Have students break into small groups and create their own "modest proposals." Have them address problems in today's society (fast food, cell-phone abusers, corrupt CEOs, politicians) and follow Swift's model: Lay out the problem, propose a solution, and back it up with supporting reasons. Encourage students to capture the biting spirit of Swift's satire in their own writing.

children sound and useful members of the commonwealth would deserve so well of the public as to have his statue set up for a preserver of the nation.

But my intention is very far from being confined to provide only for the children of *professed beggars*; it is of a much greater extent and shall take in the whole number of infants at a certain age who are born of parents in effect as little able to support them as those who demand our charity in the streets.

As to my own part, having turned my thoughts for many years upon this important subject, and maturely weighed the several *schemes of other projectors*, I have always found them grossly mistaken in their computation. It is true a child *just dropped from its dam*[7] may be supported by her milk for a solar year with little other nourishment, at most not above the value of two shillings, which the mother may certainly get, or the value in *scraps*, by her lawful occupation of *begging*. And it is exactly at one year old that I propose to provide for them in such a manner as, instead of being a charge upon their *parents* or the *parish*, or *wanting food and raiment*[8] for the rest of their lives, they shall, on the contrary, contribute to the feeding and partly to the clothing of many thousands.

There is likewise another great advantage in my scheme, that it will prevent those *voluntary abortions*, and that horrid practice of *women murdering their bastard children*, alas! too frequent among us, sacrificing the *poor innocent babes*, I doubt, more to avoid the expense than the shame, which would move tears and pity in the most savage and inhuman breast.

The number of souls in this kingdom being usually reckoned one million and a half, of these

---

7. A *dam* is a mother. The word is normally used only to refer to animals.
8. *Raiment* is clothing.

 1 **Analyze Text Structure** *What does this passage tell you about conditions in Ireland?*

2 **The English Enlightenment and Neoclassicism** *What characteristics does the speaker display in this paragraph?*

3 **Analyze Text Structure** *What details in this paragraph suggest that poverty is an urgent problem?*

I calculate there may be about two hundred thousand couples whose wives are breeders, from which number I subtract thirty thousand couples who are able to maintain their own children, although I apprehend there cannot be so many under *the present distresses of the kingdom*, but this being granted, there will remain a hundred and seventy thousand breeders. I again subtract fifty thousand for those women who miscarry or whose children die by accident or disease within the year. There only remain a hundred and twenty thousand children of poor parents annually born. The question, therefore, is how this number shall be reared and provided for, which, as I have already said, under the present situation of affairs is utterly impossible by all the methods hitherto proposed, for we can *neither employ them in handicraft* or *agriculture*; we neither build houses (I mean in the country) nor cultivate land. They can very seldom pick up a livelihood *by stealing* till they arrive at six years old, except where they are of towardly parts,[9] although I confess they learn the rudiments much earlier, during which time they can, however, be properly looked upon only as *probationers*,[10] as I have been informed by a principal gentleman in the County of Cavan, who protested to me that he never knew above one or two instances under the age of six, even in a part of the kingdom *so renowned for the quickest proficiency in that art*.

I am assured by our merchants that a boy or a girl, before twelve years old, is no saleable commodity, and even when they come to this age, they will not yield above three pounds, or three pounds and half-a-crown at most, on the Exchange, which cannot turn to account[11] either to the parents or the kingdom, the charge of nutriment and rags having been at least four times that value.

I shall now therefore humbly propose my own thoughts, which I hope will not be liable to the least objection.

I have been assured by a very knowing American of my acquaintance in London that a

---

9. *Towardly parts* means "promising talent."
10. *Probationers* are apprentices.
11. *Turn to account* means "be profitable."

Satire *What does the term breeders suggest?* **4**

JONATHAN SWIFT **551**

Teach

Teach

Satire **Answer:** *The speaker implies that his American acquaintance is an experienced cannibal.*

Big Idea 2

The English Enlightenment and Neoclassicism Answer: *He suggests that 20,000 children be held in reserve as breeders and 100,000 children be brought to market. He advises mothers to fatten their infants and specifies the portions provided by a cooked infant.*

(ENGLISH LEARNERS) Make sure students understand Swift's analogy between children and animals used for food. **Ask:** What animals are mentioned by name? *(sheep, cattle, swine)* What kind of animals are these? *(animals we raise for food)* Lead students to note that Swift refers to people as males and females, not men and women. Note that the Spanish equivalents (*macho* and *hembra* for "male" and "female") carry a similar connotation.

View the Art ★

Answer: *Students may say that the people in the painting look destitute like the people Swift describes.*

Sir Luke Fildes (1843–1927) based this painting on a scene that he witnessed while returning home from a dinner party. He was so moved that he vowed to publicize their plight. The Victorian establishment viewed such publicity as unpatriotic.

Applicants for Admission to a Casual Ward, 1874. Sir Luke Fildes. Oil on canvas, 54 x 96 cm. Royal Holloway and Bedford New College, Surrey, England.

View the Art A casual ward, or workhouse, provided the poor and the elderly with scanty food and shelter in exchange for hours of sometimes toilsome labor. What do the people in the painting have in common with the people described in *A Modest Proposal*? ★

young healthy child, well nursed, is at a year old a most delicious, nourishing, and wholesome food, whether *stewed, roasted, baked,* or *boiled,* and I make no doubt that it will equally serve in a *fricassee,* or a *ragout.*[12]

I do, therefore, humbly offer it to *public consideration* that, of the hundred and twenty thousand children already computed, twenty thousand may be reserved for breed, whereof only one-fourth part to be males, which is more than we allow to *sheep, black cattle,* or *swine;* and my reason is that these children are seldom the fruits of marriage, *a circumstance not much regarded by our savages;* therefore *one male* will be sufficient to serve *four females.* That the remaining hundred thousand may at a year old be offered in sale to the *persons of quality* and *fortune* through the kingdom, always advising the mother to let them suck

plentifully of the last month, so as to render them plump and fat for a good table. A child will make two dishes at an entertainment for friends, and when the family dines alone, the fore or hind quarter will make a reasonable dish and, seasoned with a little pepper or salt, will be very good boiled on the fourth day, especially in *winter.*

I have reckoned upon a medium, that a child just born will weigh twelve pounds and, in a solar year, if tolerably nursed, increaseth to twenty-eight pounds.

I grant this food will be somewhat dear,[13] and therefore very *proper for landlords,* who, as they have already devoured most of the parents, seem to have the best title to the children.

Infants' flesh will be in season throughout the year, but more plentiful in *March,* and a little before and after, for we are told by a grave

---

12. *Fricassee* and *ragout* are types of meat stews.

1 Satire *What does the speaker imply about his American acquaintance?*

---

13. Here, *dear* means "expensive."

The English Enlightenment and Neoclassicism 2
Despite the speaker's proposal, what details in this paragraph suggest that he is logical?

Vocabulary Practice

  Multiple-Meaning Words A number of words on these pages have more than one meaning (i.e., *dishes, medium, dear, title, grave, net, dressed*). Have students work in heterogeneous pairs or small groups to create a four-column chart with the heads: *Word, Meaning 1, Meaning 2,* and *Sentences.* Under *Word,* they should list at least four multiple-meaning words

from this spread. Under *Meaning,* they should define each word as it is used on the page and one other meaning. Under *Sentences,* have them write a sentence for both meanings of each word.

author,[14] an eminent French physician, that *fish being a prolific diet*, there are more children born in *Roman Catholic countries* about nine months after *Lent* than at any other season; therefore, reckoning a year after *Lent*, the markets will be more glutted than usual because the number of *Popish*[15] infants is at least three to one in this kingdom, and therefore it will have one other collateral advantage by lessening the number of *Papists*[16] among us.

I have already computed the charge of nursing a beggar's child (in which list I reckon all *cottagers*, *labourers*, and four-fifths of the *farmers*) to be about two shillings *per annum*, rags included, and I believe no gentleman would repine[17] to give ten shillings for the *carcass of a good fat child*, which, as I have said, will make four dishes of excellent nutritive meat when he hath only some particular friend or his own family to dine with him. Thus the Squire will learn to be a good landlord and grow popular among his tenants; the mother will have eight shillings net profit and be fit for work till she produces another child.

Those who are more thrifty (*as I must confess the times require*) may flay[18] the carcass, the skin of which, artificially[19] dressed, will make admirable *gloves for ladies* and *summer boots for fine gentlemen*.

As to our City of Dublin, shambles[20] may be appointed for this purpose in the most convenient parts of it, and butchers, we may be assured, will not be wanting, although I rather recommend buying the children alive and dressing them hot from the knife, as we do *roasting pigs*.

A very worthy person, *a true lover of his country*, and whose virtues I highly esteem, was lately pleased, in discoursing on this matter, to offer a refinement upon my scheme. He said that many gentlemen of this kingdom, having of late

destroyed their deer, he conceived that the want of venison might be well supplied by the bodies of young lads and maidens not exceeding fourteen years of age, nor under twelve, so great a number of both sexes in every country being now ready to starve for want of work and service,[21] and these to be disposed of by their parents, if alive, or otherwise by their nearest relations. But with due **deference** to so excellent a friend and so deserving a patriot, I cannot be altogether in his sentiments; for as to the males, my American acquaintance assured me from frequent experience that their flesh was generally tough and lean, like that of our schoolboys, by continual exercise, and their taste disagreeable, and to fatten them would not answer the charge. Then as to the females, it would, I think, with humble submission, *be a loss to the public* because they soon would become breeders themselves. And besides, it is not improbable that some scrupulous people might be apt to censure such a practice (although indeed very unjustly) as a little bordering upon cruelty, which, I confess, hath always been with me the strongest objection against any project, however so well intended.

But in order to justify my friend, he confessed that this expedient[22] was put into his head by the famous *Psalmanazar*,[23] a native of the island Formosa, who came from thence to London above twenty years ago and in conversation told my friend that in his country when any young person happened to be put to death, the executioner sold the carcass to *persons of quality* as a prime dainty, and that in his time, the body of a plump girl of fifteen, who was crucified for an attempt to poison the emperor, was sold to his Imperial *Majesty's Prime Minister of State* and

---

21. *Service* is work as a servant.
22. *Expedient* means "a means to an end."
23. George *Psalmanazar* was a French impostor who pretended to be from Formosa (now Taiwan) and wrote about incidences of cannibalism there.

Satire *What is ironic about the speaker's statement that he is against cruel plans?* **4**

Vocabulary

deference (def′ ər əns) *n.* courteous respect

---

14. The *grave author* is François Rabelais, a French satirist.
15. *Popish* means "Roman Catholic."
16. *Papists* are Roman Catholics.
17. *Repine* means "complain."
18. To *flay* is to strip off the skin.
19. Here, *artificially* means "skillfully."
20. *Shambles* were slaughterhouses.

3 **Satire** *What examples of irony do you see in this paragraph?*

Teach

Literary Element | 3

Satire Answer: *One who would buy a child for food is a "gentleman." Adopting the speaker's idea would improve the popularity of landlords.*

(**ENGLISH LEARNERS**) Point out the false cognate *popular*. Ask students what the word means to them in Spanish. Make certain students understand that the English *popular* means "well-liked." In Spanish, *popular* means "of the people," which is contrary to attitude Swift imputes to landlords.

Literary Element | 4

Satire Answer: *It is ironic that the speaker says this after proposing such a cruel plan of his own.*

Language History ☆

Satire This word probably comes from the Latin *satura*, meaning "mixed" (literally, "dish of mixed fruits"). The Roman poet Horace (first century B.C.) is credited as being one of the first satirists. His poetry tended to be composed of short verses that included deliberate attacks on situations and people.

English Learners

DIFFERENTIATED INSTRUCTION

Intermediate You may want students to acquire background information on several relevant topics, such as English rule over Ireland, laws that denied civil rights to Catholics, and Irish support for James Stuart, who claimed he was the rightful heir after King James II was dethroned.

Have students look for references to these issues in the selection. Then have them use the Internet and other resources to learn about these aspects of life in Ireland during the 1700s. Encourage them to report their findings to the class.

Teach

Literary Element | 1

Satire **Answer:** *The conditions referred to (cold, famine, and filth) are treated as advantageous. There is no reason to be concerned that Irish adults will be an unbearable economic burden. Poor housing, starvation, and terrible sanitation are killing them.*

Reading Strategy | 2

Analyze Text Structure
Answer: *The English landlords are the cause of Ireland's misery. They have forced their tenants to sell their corn and cattle to pay the rent.*

(ADVANCED) Have students think about Swift's solutions to the problem of Irish poverty from the point of view of the poor tenants. What practical use could the landlords serve that would alleviate the difficulties of Irish society? Have students list their arguments in favor of their solution.

Visual Vocabulary
A *groat* was an old British coin worth four pennies.

other great *Mandarins*[24] of the Court, *in joints from the gibbet,*[25] at four hundred crowns. Neither, indeed, can I deny that if the same use were made of several plump young girls in this town, who, without one single groat to their fortunes, cannot stir abroad without a chair and appear at the *playhouse* and *assemblies* in foreign fineries, which they never will pay for, the kingdom would not be the worse.

Some persons of a desponding spirit are in great concern about that vast number of poor people who are aged, diseased, or maimed, and I have been desired to employ my thoughts what course may be taken to ease the nation of so grievous an encumbrance. But I am not in the least pain upon that matter because it is very well known that they are every day *dying* and *rotting* by *cold* and *famine* and *filth* and *vermin* as fast as can be reasonably expected. And as to the younger labourers, they are now in almost as hopeful a condition. They cannot get work and consequently pine away for want of nourishment to a degree that if at any time they are accidentally hired to common labour, they have not strength to perform it; and thus the country and themselves are happily delivered from the evils to come.

I have too long **digressed** and therefore shall return to my subject. I think the advantages by the proposal which I have made are obvious and many, as well as of the highest importance.

For *first*, as I have already observed, it would greatly lessen the *number of Papists*, with whom we are yearly overrun, being the principal breeders of the nation as well as our most dangerous enemies and who stay at home on purpose with a design to *deliver the kingdom to the Pretender*, hoping to take their advantage by the absence of *so many good Protestants*, who have chosen rather to leave their country than stay at home and pay tithes against their conscience to an *Episcopal curate.*[26]

Secondly, the poorer tenants will have something valuable of their own, which by law may be made liable to distress[27] and help to pay their landlord's rent, their corn and cattle being already seized and *money a thing unknown.*

Thirdly, whereas the maintenance of a hundred thousand children, from two years old and upwards, cannot be computed at less than ten shillings a piece *per annum*, the nation's stock will be thereby increased fifty thousand pounds *per annum*, besides the profit of a new dish introduced to the tables of all *gentlemen of fortune* in the kingdom who have any refinement in taste; and the money will circulate among ourselves, the goods being entirely of our own growth and manufacture.

Fourthly, the constant breeders, besides the gain of eight shillings *sterling per annum* by the sale of their children, will be rid of the charge of maintaining them after the first year.

Fifthly, this food would likewise bring great *custom to taverns*, where the vintners[28] will certainly be so prudent as to procure the best receipts[29] for dressing it to perfection and consequently have their houses frequented by all the *fine gentlemen*, who justly value themselves upon their knowledge in good eating; and a skillful cook, who understands how to oblige his guests, will contrive to make it as expensive as they please.

Sixthly, this would be a great inducement to marriage, which all wise nations have either

---

24. *Mandarins* are powerful people.
25. *Joints from the gibbet* are pieces of meat from the gallows.

1 **Satire** *How does the language contribute to the irony in this paragraph?*

Vocabulary
digress (dī gres′) *v.* to stray from the main subject

26. *Protestants . . . curate* Swift is attacking Protestants who have left Ireland and thus avoided paying tithes to the Anglican Church. A *tithe* is one-tenth of a person's annual income.
27. *Distress* is seizure of property for payment of debt.
28. *Vintners* are wine merchants.
29. Here, *receipts* are recipes.

Analyze Text Structure *Whom does the speaker identify as the cause of Ireland's misery?* **2**

Grammar Practice

SPIRAL REVIEW **Commas in Series** Point out that commas are used to separate three or more words, phrases, or clauses in a series. No commas are necessary when all the items are connected by conjunctions. Have students rewrite the following sentences correctly, adding commas where they are needed:

1. Swift believed that merchants should be honest(,) industrious(,) and skillful.
2. The speaker claims that his proposal is of no expense(,) of little trouble(,) and within English power.

encouraged by rewards or enforced by laws and penalties. It would increase the care and tenderness of mothers toward their children when they were sure of a settlement for life to the poor babes, provided in some sort by the public to their annual profit instead of expense. We should see an honest emulation[30] among the married women, *which of them could bring the fattest child to the market.* Men would become as *fond* of their wives, during the time of their pregnancy, as they are now of their *mares* in foal, their *cows* in calf, or *sows* when they are ready to farrow,[31] nor offer to beat or kick them (as it is too *frequent* a practice) for fear of a miscarriage.

Many other advantages might be enumerated: for instance, the addition of some thousand carcasses in our exportation of barrelled beef; the propagation of *swine's flesh* and improvement in the art of making good *bacon,* so much wanted among us by the great destruction of *pigs,* too frequent at our tables, which are no way comparable in taste or magnificence to a well-grown, fat yearling child, which, roasted whole, will make a considerable figure at a *Lord Mayor's feast* or any other public entertainment. But this and many others I omit, being studious of brevity.

Supposing that one thousand families in this city would be constant customers for infants' flesh, besides others who might have it at *merry-meetings,* particularly *weddings* and *christenings,* I compute that Dublin would take off annually about twenty thousand carcasses, and the rest of the kingdom (where probably they will be sold somewhat cheaper) the remaining eighty thousand.

I can think of no one objection that will possibly be raised against this proposal, unless it should be urged that the number of people will be thereby much lessened in the kingdom. This I

---

30. Here, *emulation* means "competition."
31. *Farrow* means "produce piglets."

3 Analyze Text Structure *How does Swift suggest that the speaker's plan is ridiculous?*

4 Satire *Why does the speaker identify "weddings" and "christenings" as particularly appropriate occasions for eating children?*

Irish Emigrants. John Joseph Barker. Oil on canvas, 255 x 185.2 cm. Victoria Art Gallery, Bath and North East Somerset Council, UK.

View the Art Laws enacted in 1695 stripped Irish Catholics of rights to money and property, causing many to leave—and some to be forcibly shipped out—of the country. What does this artwork suggest about the emigrants? What details support your conclusions? ★

freely own, and it was indeed one principal design in offering it to the world. I desire the reader will observe that I calculate my remedy *for this one individual Kingdom of IRELAND and for no other that ever was, is, or, I think, ever can be upon earth.* Therefore, let no man talk to me of other expedients: *of taxing our absentees[32] at five shillings a pound; of using neither clothes, nor household furniture, except what is of our own growth and manufacture; of utterly rejecting the materials and instruments that promote foreign luxury; of curing the expensiveness of pride, vanity, idleness, and gaming in our women; of introducing a vein of parsimony,[33] prudence, and temperance; of learning to love our*

---

32. In this context, *absentees* are English people who own land in Ireland but refuse to live on it.
33. *Parsimony* (pär′ sə mō′ nē) is thriftiness.

JONATHAN SWIFT **555**

Teach

Reading Strategy | 1

Analyze Text Structure
Answer: *Swift really favors these other expedients, which are practical solutions to the problem of poverty in Ireland.*

(APPROACHING) Have students read each point in the list separately, paraphrase it, and explain why the measure makes sense as a way to alleviate Ireland's poverty.

Reading Strategy | 2

Analyze Text Structure
Answer: *The speaker alludes to England.*

Literary Element | 3

Persona *Persona* is the Latin word for a mask. Satirists often use this device to support the irony of their work. The "I" who is speaking does not represent the author's views but rather serves as a mask behind which the satirist can present the views he or she wishes to ridicule. Have students discuss Swift's use of this device.

Country, wherein we differ even from LAPLANDERS and the inhabitants of TOPINAMBOO;[34] of quitting our animosities and factions; . . . of being a little cautious not to sell our country and consciences for nothing; of teaching landlords to have at least one degree of mercy toward their tenants; lastly, of putting a spirit of honesty, industry, and skill into our shopkeepers, who, if a resolution could now be taken to buy only our native goods, would immediately unite to cheat and exact upon us in the price, the measure, and the goodness, nor could ever yet be brought to make one fair proposal of just dealing, though often and earnestly invited to it.

Therefore, I repeat, let no man talk to me of these and the like expedients till he hath at least some glimpse of hope that there will ever be some hearty and sincere attempt to put them in practice.

But as to myself, having been wearied out for many years with offering vain, idle, visionary thoughts, and at length utterly despairing of success, I fortunately fell upon this proposal, which, as it is wholly new, so it hath something solid and real, of no expense and little trouble, full in our own power, and whereby we can incur no danger in *disobliging England.* For this kind of commodity will not bear exportation, the flesh being of too tender a consistence to admit a long continuance in salt, *although perhaps I could name a country which would be glad to eat up our whole nation without it.*

After all, I am not so violently bent upon my own opinion as to reject any offer proposed by wise men, which shall be found equally innocent,

> "I have not the least personal interest in endeavouring to promote this necessary work, having no other motive than the *public good of my country*"

cheap, easy, and effectual. But before something of that kind shall be advanced in contradiction to my scheme, and offering a better, I desire the author, or authors, will be pleased maturely to consider two points. *First,* as things now stand, how they will be able to find food and raiment for a hundred thousand useless mouths and backs. And *secondly,* there being a round million of creatures in human figure throughout this kingdom, whose whole subsistence[35] put into a common stock would leave them in debt two millions of pounds *sterling;* adding those who are beggars by profession to the bulk of farmers, cottagers, and labourers with their wives and children, who are beggars in effect; I desire those *politicians* who dislike my overture and may perhaps be so bold to attempt an answer, that they will first ask the parents of these mortals whether they would not at this day think it a great happiness to have been sold for food at a year old in the manner I prescribe and thereby have avoided such a perpetual scene of misfortunes as they have since gone through by the *oppression of landlords,* the impossibility of paying rent without money or trade, the want of common sustenance, with neither house nor clothes to cover them from the inclemencies of the weather, and the most inevitable prospect of entailing[36] the like or greater miseries upon their breed for ever.

I profess in the sincerity of my heart that I **3** have not the least personal interest in endeavouring to promote this necessary work, having no other motive than the *public good of my country, by advancing our trade, providing for infants, relieving the poor, and giving some pleasure to the rich.* I have no children by which I can propose to get a single penny, the youngest being nine years old and my wife past childbearing. ∞

---

34. *Topinamboo* was an area in Brazil.

1 Analyze Text Structure *Why does the speaker include these "other expedients"?*

2 Analyze Text Structure *To which country does the speaker allude?*

---

35. *Whole subsistence* is all their possessions.
36. *Entailing* means "passing on to the next generation."

Reading Practice

(SPIRAL REVIEW) Fact and Opinion Swift makes his assertions as if they are all purely factual; in fact, he skillfully blends fact and opinion. Have students read through *A Modest Proposal* and make a list of the statements of fact and statements of opinion that they find, stated in their own words (*i.e., fact: the population of Ireland, facts about the poverty of the people, landlords leaving the country to avoid tithing; opinion:* that women would be happy to sell their children, that a child would be tasty to eat). Ask students how this blending of fact and opinion supports Swift's purpose. (*It supports his pose as a disinterested, almost scientific cobserver and creates an ironic mood.*)

After You Read

Respond and Think Critically

Respond and Interpret

1. What were your reactions to the suggestions in *A Modest Proposal*? Explain your answer.

2. (a)What problem does the speaker describe in the opening paragraphs of *A Modest Proposal*? (b)Does the speaker mainly analyze the causes of Ireland's problem or the effects? Why is it to the speaker's advantage not to analyze both?

3. (a)What solution to the problem does the speaker propose? (b)In your opinion, does Swift expect readers to take the speaker's solution seriously? Explain.

4. (a)What objection to the proposal does the speaker think readers might raise? How does he answer that objection? (b)In your opinion, does the speaker understand the real reasons that readers might object to his proposal? Explain.

Analyze and Evaluate

5. (a)List six advantages the speaker claims for his proposal. (b)How well does the speaker support these advantages?

6. (a)Summarize at least two other solutions that the speaker lists and rejects. (b)What is ironic about the speaker's rejection of these solutions?

Connect

7. **Big Idea** The English Enlightenment and Neoclassicism In writing *A Modest Proposal*, Swift adopted a **persona**, a mask or voice through which an author speaks. What Enlightenment characteristics do you see in Swift's persona?

8. **Connect to Today** Think about a modern satire (print, film, or TV) with which you are familiar. Did its author make use of the same devices Swift employed? Explain.

Literary Element Satire

Satire aims to expose the vices, follies, or flaws of a person or group of people by making them seem ridiculous. Satirists' main weapon is humor, which they create through devices such as **exaggeration** and its opposite, **understatement**. In *A Modest Proposal*, for example, Swift exaggerates the economists' indifference toward the Irish and understates the impact of his proposal by his use of the word modest. By creating a narrator who supports a position opposite to his own, Swift also employs **irony**, another common satiric device.

1. Why might satire be an effective instrument for social change?

2. What other examples of exaggeration and understatement can you find in *A Modest Proposal*? Whom or what do these statements ridicule?

3. What is ironic about the conclusion of *A Modest Proposal*?

Review: Author's Purpose

As you learned on page 270, an **author's purpose** is an author's intent in writing a literary work. An author typically writes to accomplish one or more of the following purposes: to persuade, to instruct, to inform or explain, to entertain, to describe, or to tell a story.

Partner Activity Meet with a partner to discuss Swift's purpose in writing *A Modest Proposal*. First, in a few words, describe the tone of the work. Then, quote a specific statement from the work to illustrate your description. Conclude your analysis by briefly explaining how the tone of the pamphlet helps it to fulfill its purpose.

1. What was Swift's purpose in writing this essay?

2. How does the tone of the pamphlet help fulfill that purpose?

JONATHAN SWIFT **557**

After You Read

Assess

1. Students' answers will vary.

2. (a) Ireland is overrun by poor mothers who cannot provide for their children. (b) The effects, since analyzing the causes would force him to expose English guilt.

3. (a) That children be bred like farm animals, slaughtered, and eaten (b) The speaker is serious, but Swift is not.

4. (a) Some people may object that the proposal would reduce the population. The speaker argues that the proposal is limited strictly to Ireland. (b) His inability to perceive the reasons his proposal is objectionable is at the core of the satire.

5. (a) Reducing the number of Catholics, giving the poor a valuable commodity, stimulating the economy, freeing the poor of the cost of child rearing, profiting taverns, and encouraging marriage (b) If one accepts his premise, these advantages seem reasonable consequences.

6. (a) Possible answers: taxing absentee landowners; buying domestic products; practicing thrift (b) These alternative solutions are morally sound and economically practical.

7. Evaluations should reflect an understanding of the relationship between understatement and satire.

8. Answers will vary.

Progress Check

Can students identify satire?

If No → See Unit 3 Teaching Resources Book, p. 87.

Literary Element

1. By exposing vices and follies to ridicule, satire suggests that these flaws are correctable.

2. Exaggeration: Irish children steal by age six. Understatement: making gloves from human skin as an example of thrift. The statements ridicule the Irish and English.

3. The speaker will be unaffected by his plan; he has no children.

Review: Author's Purpose

1. To focus public attention on the shameful conditions in Ireland

2. The ironic tone suggests that the speaker's proposal is barbaric, but is less inhumane than the English exploitation of Ireland.

After You Read

Assess

Reading Strategy

1. They suggest personal sacrifice for the common good of Ireland.

2. This method of organization enabled Swift to describe conditions in Ireland, to have the speaker argue for a proposal that Swift wants readers to find reprehensible, and to present other expedients that Swift really favors.

Progress Check

Can students analyze text structure?

If No ➔ See Unit 3 Teaching Resources Book, p. 88.

Vocabulary

Sample answers:

sustenance

Synonyms: livelihood, nourishment, necessities

Sample explanation: *Sustenance* and *nourishment* both refer to items necessary to sustain life.

deference

Synonyms: respect, esteem, honor

Sample explanation: You would feel both deference and respect for a person who you admired greatly.

digress

Synonyms: deviate, ramble, drift

Sample explanation: Someone who was digressing would stray from his or her point, as would someone who was rambling.

Reading Strategy Analyze Text Structure

Review the graphic organizer you created as you read, and then answer the questions below.

1. What do the speaker's alternate solutions have in common?

2. Why do you think Swift used problem and solution as the method of organization in this essay?

Vocabulary Practice

Practice with Synonyms With a partner, brainstorm three synonyms for each boldfaced vocabulary word below, keeping in mind the different shades of meaning each word has. Then discuss your choices with your classmates.

| sustenance | deference | digress |

EXAMPLE:

timid

Synonyms: shy, reticent, cautious
Explanation: Like a timid person, a cautious person might be afraid to try new things. However, the word timid has slightly more negative connotations.

Academic Vocabulary

Swift's A Modest Proposal satirizes characteristics of the Enlightenment **period** *in England.*

Period is a word that has many different meanings. For example, in a school setting, *periods* can refer to the intervals of time that divide the school day into different classes. Using context clues, try to figure out the meaning of *period* in each sentence. Explain the difference between the two meanings.

1. The 1960s were a turbulent **period** in American history.

2. He was sloppy with punctuation, often forgetting to put **periods** at the ends of his sentences.

For more on academic vocabulary, see pages 56 and R81.

Speaking and Listening

 Speech

Assignment Swift satirized a serious social problem by using irony, hyperbole, and understatement to stress the importance of dealing with it. Write and deliver a short speech using these techniques to propose a satirical solution to a current issue like homelessness or health care.

Prepare Decide on the social problem you want to address, the thesis you want to present, and the specific targets of your satire. You might want to use a word web to brainstorm rhetorical devices that will help you achieve your purpose. For example, rhetorical questions can appeal to your audience's ethics or emotions:

Why would people do _____ when _____ is so much easier?

Figurative language can also be effective in developing a satirical take on an idea.

EXAMPLE
Government-issued portable shells let you carry your home with you, like a tortoise—and have you ever seen a homeless tortoise?

Deliver Present your speech with confidence, making frequent eye contact with your audience. Using a straightforward, serious tone of voice and understated gestures can add to the effectiveness of your satirical elements.

Evaluate Write a brief critique of the effectiveness of your arguments, humor, and performance.

LOG ON ▶ **Literature** Online

Selection Resources For Selection Quizzes, eFlashcards, and Reading-Writing Connection activities, go to glencoe.com and enter QuickPass code GLB9817u3.

558 UNIT 3 FROM PURITANISM TO THE ENLIGHTENMENT

Academic Vocabulary

1. The context indicates that *period* refers to a significant era.

2. The context indicates that a *period* is a punctuation mark at the end of a sentence.

Speaking and Listening

Students' speeches should include specific and clear theses regarding Swift's strategies. There should also be supporting evidence and examples, discussion of the author's use of italics, and conclusions that restate the theses.

Before You Read

from
Gulliver's Travels

Jonathan Swift

from A Voyage to Lilliput

I lay down on the grass, which was very short and soft, where I slept sounder than ever I remember to have done in my life, and as I reckoned, above nine hours; for when I awaked, it was just daylight. I attempted to rise, but was not able to stir: for as I happened to lie on my back, I found my arms and legs were strongly fastened on each side to the ground; and my hair, which was long and thick, tied down in the same manner. I likewise felt several slender ligatures across my body, from my armpits to my thighs. I could only look upwards; the sun began to grow hot, and the light offended my eyes. I heard a confused noise about me, but in the posture I lay, could see nothing except the sky.

In a little time I felt something alive moving on my left leg, which advancing gently forward over my breast, came almost up to my chin; when bending my eyes downwards as much as I could, I perceived it to be a human creature not six inches high, with a bow and arrow in his hands, and a quiver at his back. In the meantime, I felt at least forty more of the same kind (as I **conjectured**) following the first. I was in the utmost astonishment and roared so loud

> **Vocabulary**
>
> **conjecture** (kən jek′ chur) *v.* to infer from inconclusive evidence; to guess

JONATHAN SWIFT **559**

Before You Read

Focus

Summary

In *Gulliver's Travels,* Jonathan Swift parodies the travel genre through the purported firsthand account of the exotic travels of Lemuel Gulliver—ship's surgeon and captain. At the same time, Swift satirizes human nature and English behavior. The selection includes excerpts from *A Voyage to Lilliput* and *A Voyage to Brobdingnag.* In the first, Gulliver is shipwrecked on the island of Lilliput, whose six-inch-tall inhabitants he describes as preposterous and self-important. Their absurd disputes have led to suffering, persecution, and war. In the second excerpt, Gulliver visits Brobdingnag, whose enormous inhabitants are at first amused, then outraged, and finally horrified by his descriptions of English customs.

> For summaries in languages other than English, see Unit 3 Teaching Resources Book, pp. 93–98.

Teach

Big Idea 1

The English Enlightenment and Neoclassicism Answer: *The Europeans are similar to the Lilliputians in reacting violently toward perceived threats.*

ADVANCED Ask students whether they think the comparison will be flattering of unflattering to the Europeans. Have students support their opinion with evidence from the text *(i.e., the leader is por-trayed as pompous in dress and speech, the people's tiny stature makes them amusing.)*

Reading Strategy 2

Make Inferences About Theme Answer: *The "person of quality" is self-important and likes to command attention.*

Readability Scores

Dale-Chall: 9.1
DRP: 59
Lexile: 1510

---

that they all ran back in a fright; and some of them, as I was afterwards told, were hurt with the falls they got by leaping from my sides upon the ground. However, they soon returned; and one of them, who ventured so far as to get a full sight of my face, lifting up his hands and eyes by way of admiration, cried out in a shrill but distinct voice, *Hekinah Degul.* The others repeated the same words several times, but I then knew not what they meant. I lay all this while, as the reader may believe, in great uneasiness. At length, struggling to get loose, I had the fortune to break the strings and wrench out the pegs that fastened my left arm to the ground; for by lifting it up to my face, I discovered the methods they had taken to bind me; and at the same time, with a violent pull, which gave me excessive pain, I a little loosened the strings that tied down my hair on the left side; so that I was just able to turn my head about two inches. But the creatures ran off a second time before I could seize them; whereupon there was a great shout in a very shrill accent; and after it ceased, I heard one of them cry aloud, *Tolgo Phonac*; when in an instant I felt above a hun-dred arrows discharged on my left hand, which pricked me like so many needles; and besides, they shot another flight into the air, as we do bombs in Europe. . . .

I had reason to believe I might be a match for the greatest armies they could bring against me if they were all of the same size with him that I saw. But fortune disposed otherwise of me. When the people observed I was quiet, they discharged no more arrows; but by the noise increasing, I knew their numbers were greater; and about four yards from me, over

> "In an instant I felt above a hundred arrows discharged on my left hand, which pricked me like so many needles"

against my right ear, I heard a knocking for above an hour, like people at work; when turn-ing my head that way, as well as the pegs and strings would permit me, I saw a stage erected about a foot and a half from the ground, capa-ble of holding four of the inhabitants, with two or three ladders to mount it: from whence one of them, who seemed to be a person of quality,[1] made me a long speech, whereof I understood not one syllable. . . .

He appeared to be of a middle age and taller than any of the other three who attended him, whereof one was a page,[2] who held up his train[3] and seemed to be somewhat longer than my middle finger. The other two stood one on each side to support him. He acted every part of an orator; and I could observe many periods of threatenings and others of promises, pity, and kindness.

I answered in a few words, but in the most submissive manner, lifting up my left hand and both my eyes to the sun, as calling him for a witness; and being almost famished with hun-ger, having not eaten a morsel for some hours before I left the ship, I found the demands of nature so strong upon me that I could not for-bear showing my impatience (perhaps against the strict rules of decency) by putting my finger frequently on my mouth to signify that I wanted food. The *Hurgo* (for so they call a great lord, as I afterwards learned) understood me very well. He descended from the stage and commanded that several ladders should be

---

1. Here, a *person of quality* is a nobleman.
2. A *page* is a court servant.
3. Here, a *train* is a long extension at the back of a robe that trails behind the wearer.

Make Inferences About Theme *What does the fact that a stage was erected suggest about the "person of quality"?* **2**

The English Enlightenment and Neoclassicism *What does Swift suggest about the Europeans?* **1**

Reading Practice

SPIRAL REVIEW **Visualize** Remind students to take the time to form mental pictures of what they are reading. Let them know that this will help them to under-stand the events in *Gulliver's Travels*. Invite students to create quick sketches as they read the text. For example, on this page, students might benefit from drawing a quick sketch of the stage erected by the Lil-liputians. Some students may wish to cre-ate captions and labels for their sketches. Those who are inclined may go so far as to create a *Gulliver's Travels* comic book.

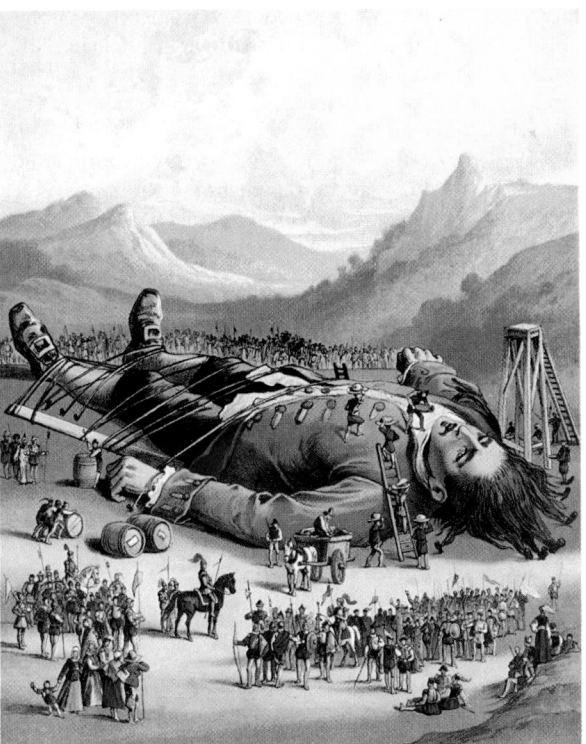

Gulliver is tied down by the people of Lilliput, 1726. From *The Coloured Picture Book for the Nursery.*

applied to my sides, on which above a hundred of the inhabitants mounted and walked towards my mouth, laden with baskets full of meat, which had been provided and sent thither by the King's orders upon the first intelligence he received of me. I observed there was the flesh of several animals but could not distinguish them by the taste. There were shoulders, legs, and loins shaped like those of mutton, and very well dressed, but smaller than the wings of a lark. I ate them by two or three at a mouthful and took three loaves at a time, about the bigness of musket bullets. They supplied me as fast as they could, showing a thousand marks of wonder and astonishment at my bulk and appetite. . . .

Because the reader may perhaps be curious to have some idea of the style and manner of expression peculiar to that people, as well as to know the articles upon which I recovered my liberty, I have made a translation of the whole instrument, word for word, as near as I was able, which I here offer to the public.

GOLBASTO MOMAREN EVLAME GURDILO SHEFIN MULLY ULLY GUE, most mighty Emperor of Lilliput, delight and terror of the universe, whose dominions extend five thousand *blustrugs* (about twelve miles in circumference) to the extremities of the globe; monarch of all monarchs, taller than the sons of men; whose feet press down to the center, and whose head strikes against the sun; at whose nod the princes of the earth shake their knees; pleasant as the spring, comfortable as the summer, fruitful as autumn, dreadful as winter. His most sublime Majesty proposeth to the Man-Mountain, lately arrived at our celestial dominions, the following articles, which by a solemn oath he shall be obliged to perform.

First, the Man-Mountain shall not depart from our dominions without our license under our great seal.

Secondly, he shall not presume to come into our metropolis without our express order, at which time the inhabitants shall have two hours warning to keep within their doors.

Thirdly, the said Man-Mountain shall confine his walks to our principal high roads and not offer to walk or lie down in a meadow or field of corn.

Fourthly, as he walks the said roads, he shall take the utmost care not to trample upon the bodies of any of our loving subjects, their horses, or carriages; nor take any of our said subjects into his hands without their own consent.

Parody *What is absurd about the emperor's claims?* **3**

JONATHAN SWIFT **561**

Teach

Literary Element 3

Parody **Answer:** *The emperor's claims are an example of the use of* **hyperbole** *for comic effect. In reality, the emperor stands only six inches tall.*

APPROACHING Ask students to identify the words that describe the imaginary extent of the emperor's reach *(universe, globe, earth, head strikes the sun)*. Then have them find the actual measurements Swift mentions *(emperor's height = six inches; emperor's dominions = twelve miles in circumference)*.

View the Art ★

A unique example of a Victorian scrap book, *The Coloured Picture Book for the Nursery* comprises thirty pages of over 250 Victorian pictures neatly pasted onto linen pages between the stories. While it is a book "for the nursery," there are also Ogden's cigarette cards of public figures of the time, as well as numerous Victorian advertising materials such as "Johnston's Corn Flour Incidents in English History series" and newspaper clippings about the Boer War. The book was first published around 1880 by Nelson and Company in London.

Ask: How does this painting reflect what Swift describes? *(The artist captures many of the details Swift mentions, such as the large numbers of soldiers, ladders, and the stream of Lilliputians bringing food to Gulliver.)*

Teach

Literary Element   1

Parody Answer: *The document is a parody of bureaucratic ideas and language.*

Big Idea   2

The English Enlightenment and Neoclassicism Answer: *Swift implies that the differences between these parties are merely trivial and superficial. Fundamentally, the parties are alike.*

Fifthly, if an express require extraordinary dispatch, the Man-Mountain shall be obliged to carry in his pocket the messenger and horse, a six days' journey once in every moon, and return the said messenger back (if so required) safe to our Imperial Presence.

Sixthly, he shall be our ally against our enemies in the island of Blefuscu and do his utmost to destroy their fleet, which is now preparing to invade us.

Seventhly, that the said Man-Mountain shall, at his times of leisure, be aiding and assisting to our workmen, in helping to raise certain great stones, towards covering the wall of the principal park and other of our royal buildings.

Eighthly, that the said Man-Mountain shall, in two moons' time, deliver in an exact survey of the circumference of our dominions, by a computation of his own paces round the coast.

Lastly, that upon his solemn oath to observe all the above articles, the said Man-Mountain shall have a daily allowance of meat and drink, sufficient for the support of 1,728 of our subjects, with free access to our Royal Person and other marks of our favor. Given at our Palace at Belfaborac the twelfth day of the ninety-first moon of our reign.

I swore and subscribed to these articles with great cheerfulness and content, although some of them were not so honorable as I could have wished. . . .

One morning, about a fortnight[4] after I had obtained my liberty, Reldresal, Principal Secretary (as they style him) of Private Affairs, came to my house attended only by one servant. He ordered his coach to wait at a distance and desired I would give him an hour's audience, which I readily consented to on account of his quality and personal merits, as well as of the many good offices he had done me during my solicitations at court. I offered to lie down

that he might the more conveniently reach my ear, but he chose rather to let me hold him in my hand during our conversation. He began with compliments on my liberty, said he might pretend to some merit in it, but, however, added that if it had not been for the present situation of things at court, perhaps I might not have obtained it so soon. "For," said he, "as flourishing a condition as we appear to be in to foreigners, we labor under two mighty evils: a violent faction at home and the danger of an invasion by a most potent enemy from abroad. As to the first, you are to understand that for about seventy moons past there have been two struggling parties in this empire, under the names of Tramecksan and Slamecksan, from the high and low heels on their shoes, by which they distinguish themselves. It is alleged, indeed, that the high heels are most agreeable to our ancient constitution: but however this be, his Majesty hath determined to make use of only low heels in the administration of the government and all offices in the gift of the Crown, as you cannot but observe; and particularly, that his Majesty's Imperial heels are lower at least by a *drurr* than any of his court (*drurr* is a measure about the fourteenth part of an inch). The animosities[5] between these two parties run so high that they will neither eat nor drink nor talk with each other. We compute the Tramecksan, or High-Heels, to exceed us in number; but the power is wholly on our side. We apprehend[6] his Imperial Highness, the Heir to the Crown, to have some tendency toward the High-Heels; at least we can plainly discover one of his heels higher than the other, which gives him a hobble in his gait. Now, in the midst of these intestine[7] disquiets, we are threatened with an invasion from the island of Blefuscu, which is the other great empire of the universe, almost as large

---

4. A *fortnight* is two weeks.

---

5. *Animosities* means "feelings of hostility or hatred."
6. *Apprehend* means "to perceive."
7. *Intestine*, here, means "internal."

---

1   Parody *What might Swift be parodying with this lengthy document?*

The English Enlightenment and Neoclassicism *What does Swift imply about political parties in England, namely the Tories and the Whigs?*   **2**

Grammar Practice

SPIRAL REVIEW   **Main and Subordinate Clauses**
A clause is a group of words that has a subject and a predicate and is used as part of a sentence. A **main clause** (also called an independent clause) can stand alone as a sentence. Every sentence must contain at least one main clause. A **subordinate clause** (also called a dependent clause) cannot stand alone as a sentence. **Ask:** What examples of subordinate clauses can you find on this page? *(Possible answer: "about a fortnight after I had obtained my liberty…")* Discuss sentence variety in Swift's writing.

and powerful as this of his Majesty. For as to what we have heard you affirm, that there are other kingdoms and states in the world inhabited by human creatures as large as yourself, our philosophers are in much doubt and would rather conjecture that you dropped from the moon or one of the stars because it is certain that an hundred mortals of your bulk would, in a short time, destroy all the fruits and cattle of his Majesty's dominions. Besides, our histories of six thousand moons make no mention of any other regions than the two great empires of Lilliput and Blefuscu, which two mighty powers have, as I was going to tell you, been engaged in a most obstinate war for six and thirty moons past. It began upon the following occasion. It is allowed on all hands that the primitive way of breaking eggs before we eat them was upon the larger end. But his present Majesty's grandfather, while he was a boy, going to eat an egg and breaking it according to the ancient practice, happened to cut one of his fingers. Whereupon the Emperor his father published an edict,[8] commanding all his subjects, upon great penalties, to break the smaller end of their eggs. The people so highly resented this law that, our histories tell us, there have been six rebellions raised on that account; wherein one Emperor lost his life, and another his crown. These civil commotions were constantly fomented[9] by the monarchs of Blefuscu; and when they were quelled,[10] the exiles always fled for refuge to that empire. It is computed that eleven thousand persons have, at several times, suffered death rather than submit to break their eggs at the smaller end. Many hundred large volumes have been published upon this controversy: but the books of the Big-Endians have been long forbidden, and the whole party rendered incapable by law of

Gulliver capturing the fleet of the Blefuscudians, enemies of his Lilliputian hosts, 1911. A. E. Jackson. Chromolithograph from an edition of Jonathan Swift's Gulliver's Travels (London & New York, 1911). Private collection.

holding employments. During the course of these troubles, the emperors of Blefuscu did frequently expostulate by their ambassadors, accusing us of making a schism[11] in religion by offending against a fundamental doctrine of our great prophet Lustrog, in the fifty-fourth chapter of the Brundrecal (which is their Alcoran).[12] This, however, is thought to be a mere strain upon the text, for the words are these: *that all true believers shall break their eggs at the convenient end;* and which is the convenient end seems, in my humble opinion, to be left to every man's conscience, or at least in the power of the chief magistrate to determine. Now the

---

8. An *edict* is an official command.
9. *Fomented* means "incited."
10. *Quelled* means "subdued."

3 Make Inferences About Theme *What generalization is Swift making about people when he has the Lilliputian philosophers doubt Gulliver's claims?*

---

11. A *schism* is a division.
12. The *Alcoran* is the Koran, Islam's sacred text.

JONATHAN SWIFT **563**

Teach

Big Idea 1

The English Enlightenment and Neoclassicism Answer:

Even when recounting the most horrible casualties of war, the secretary maintains a matter-of-fact tone. Swift's portrayal of Reldresal satirizes government officials for their easy acceptance of senseless war and much bloodshed.

ENGLISH LEARNERS Explain to students that in English the passive voice is often used to give writing an air of detachment, an unemotional tone. Ask students to find examples of passive construction in the Secretary's speech (*It is allowed; It is computed; have been published; This, however, is thought*)

Reading Strategy 2

Make Inferences About Theme Answer: *To the Brobdingnagians, Gulliver is the size of a Lilliputian and thus as insignificant as an "insect." Hoping to impress the king, Gulliver has described England in exaggerated terms that provoke laughter. Swift satirizes the absurdity of English self-importance and arrogance.*

Research Practice

SPIRAL REVIEW SMALL GROUP Eighteenth-Century Britain Tell students that their enjoyment of *Gulliver's Travels* will be enhanced by learning more about the politics and culture of eighteenth-century Britain. Have students work in small groups. Each group will research and present a different aspect of Britain's politics or culture. One group might research the conflicts Britain was engaged in during the late seventeenth and early eighteenth centuries. Another group might research George Psalmanazar, a con man.

Big-Endian exiles have found so much credit in the Emperor of Blefuscu's court, and so much private assistance and encouragement from their party here at home, that a bloody war has been carried on between the two empires for six and thirty moons with various success, during which time we have lost forty capital ships and a much greater number of smaller vessels, together with thirty thousand of our best seamen and soldiers; and the damage received by the enemy is reckoned to be somewhat greater than ours. However, they have now equipped a numerous fleet and are just preparing to make a descent upon us, and his Imperial Majesty, placing great confidence in your valor and strength, has commanded me to lay this account of his affairs before you."

I desired the Secretary to present my humble duty to the Emperor and to let him know that I thought it would not become me, who was a foreigner, to interfere with parties; but I was ready, with the hazard of my life, to defend his person and state against all invaders.

After leaving Lilliput, Gulliver goes on a second voyage, which ends with his being marooned in Brobdingnag. Everything in this imaginary country is twelve times larger than normal. As a result, Gulliver learns firsthand what it is like to feel small.

from
A Voyage to Brobdingnag

It is the custom that every Wednesday (which, as I have before observed, was their Sabbath) the King and Queen, with the royal issue of both sexes, dine together in the apartment of his Majesty, to whom I was now become a favorite; and at these times my little chair and table were placed at his left hand, before one of the saltcellars. This prince took a pleasure in conversing with me, inquiring into the manners, religion, laws, government, and learning of Europe; wherein I gave him the best account I was able. His apprehension was so clear, and his judgment so exact, that he made very wise reflections and observations upon all I said. But, I confess, that after I had been a little too copious[13] in talking of my own beloved country, of our trade, and wars by sea and land, of our schisms in religion, and parties in the state; the prejudices of his education prevailed so far that he could not forbear taking me up in his right hand and, stroking me gently with the other, after a hearty fit of laughing, asked me whether I were a Whig or a Tory.[14] Then turning to his first minister, who waited behind him with a white staff, near as tall as the mainmast of the *Royal Sovereign*, he observed how contemptible a thing was human grandeur, which could be mimicked by such diminutive insects as I. "And yet," said he, "I dare engage, those creatures have their titles and distinctions of honor, they contrive little nests and burrows that they call houses and cities; they make a figure in dress and equipage; they love, they fight, they dispute, they cheat, they betray." And thus he continued on, while my color came and went several times with indignation to hear our noble country, the mistress of arts and arms, the scourge of France, the arbitress of Europe, the seat of virtue, piety, honor, and truth, the pride and envy of the world, so contemptuously treated.

But as I was not in a condition to resent injuries, so, upon mature thoughts, I began to doubt whether I were injured or no. For after having

Visual Vocabulary
The *Royal Sovereign* was one of the largest British warships of Swift's day.

---

13. Here, *copious* means "wordy."
14. A *Whig* and a *Tory* were members of the two main political parties in Britain.

---

1 The English Enlightenment and Neoclassicism *How does Swift's portrayal of Reldresal satirize government officials? Consider Reldresal's tone in this passage.*

Make Inferences About Theme *What is ironic about this passage?* **2**

Gulliver walking about on the table at the inn as Glumdalcitch, his "little" Brobdingnagian nurse, commanded him, 1911. A. E. Jackson. Chromolithograph from an edition of Jonathan Swift's Gulliver's Travels *(London & New York, 1911).*

View the Art Swift pokes fun at the foibles of his own society through his depictions of Lilliput and Brobdingnag. Judging by their facial expressions, how do you think the Brobdingnagians feel about Gulliver? ★

most courtly manner of strutting and bowing and prating,[15] to say the truth, I should have been strongly tempted to laugh as much at them as this King and his grandees[16] did at me. . . .

He was perfectly astonished with the historical account I gave him of our affairs during the last century, protesting it was only a heap of conspiracies, rebellions, murders, massacres, revolutions, banishments, the very worst effects that avarice,[17] faction, hypocrisy, perfidiousness,[18] cruelty, rage, madness, hatred, envy, lust, malice, and ambition could produce.

been accustomed several months to the sight and converse of this people and observed every object upon which I cast my eyes to be of proportionable **magnitude**, the horror I had first conceived from their bulk and aspect was so far worn off that if I had then beheld a company of English lords and ladies in their finery and birthday clothes, acting their several parts in the

---

15. *Prating* means "chattering" or "babbling."
16. *Grandees* are important people.
17. *Avarice* is greed.
18. *Perfidiousness* is treachery.

Parody *What advantage does Swift derive by using Gulliver as his persona in this parody?* `3`

JONATHAN SWIFT **565**

Parody **Answer:** *Swift can use the persona of Gulliver to comment scathingly but with impunity on his country's history.*

View the Art ★

Possible answer: The Brobgingnagians regard Gulliver with amusement and interest.

English Learners

UNIVERSAL ACCESS

Beginning Adverbs are words that modify verbs, adjectives, or other adverbs. **Ask:** What adverbs can you identify on these pages, and what words do they modify?

(Examples include: strongly *modifies* tempted, perfectly *modifies* astonished, never *modifies* forget, clearly *modifies* proved)

Big Idea   1

The English Enlightenment and Neoclassicism Answer:
The king makes a logical induction, drawing a conclusion about the English on the basis of the evidence provided by Gulliver.

His Majesty in another audience was at the pains to recapitulate the sum of all I had spoken; compared the questions he made with the answers I had given; then taking me into his hands, and stroking me gently, delivered himself in these words, which I shall never forget, nor the manner he spoke them in. My little friend Grildrig, you have made a most admirable panegyric[19] upon your country. You have clearly proved that ignorance, idleness, and vice are the proper ingredients for qualifying a legislator; that laws are best explained, interpreted, and applied by those whose interest and abilities lie in perverting, confounding, and eluding them. I observe among you some lines of an institution, which in its original might have been tolerable; but these half erased, and the rest wholly blurred and blotted by corruptions. It doth not appear from all you have said how any one perfection is required towards the procurement of any one station among you; much less that men are ennobled on account of their virtue, that priests are advanced for their piety or learning, soldiers for their conduct or valor, judges for their integrity, senators for the love of their country, or counselors for their wisdom. As for yourself (continued the King), who have spent the greatest part of your life in traveling, I am well disposed to hope you may hitherto have escaped many vices of your country. But, by what I have gathered from your own relation, and the answers I have with much pains wrung and extorted from you,

> *"The king was struck with horror at the description I had given of those terrible engines and the proposal I had made."*

I cannot but conclude the bulk of your natives to be the most pernicious[20] race of little odious vermin that nature ever suffered to crawl upon the surface of the earth.

Nothing but an extreme love of truth could have hindered me from concealing this part of my story. It was in vain to discover my resentments, which were always turned into ridicule; and I was forced to rest with patience while my noble and most beloved country was so injuriously treated. I am heartily sorry as any of my readers can possibly be that such an occasion was given; but this prince happened to be so curious and inquisitive upon every particular that it could not consist either with gratitude or good manners to refuse giving him what satisfaction I was able. Yet thus much I may be allowed to say in my own vindication, that I artfully eluded many of his questions and gave to every point a more favorable turn by many degrees than the strictness of truth would allow. For I have always born that laudable partiality to my own country, which Dionysius Halicarnassensis[21] with so much justice recommends to a historian. I would hide the frailties and deformities of my political mother and place her virtues and beauties in the most advantageous light. This was my sincere endeavor in those many discourses I had with that mighty monarch, although it unfortunately failed of success. . . .

But great allowances should be given to a King who lives wholly secluded from the rest

---

19. A *panegyric* (pa′ nə jir′ ik) is a speech of praise.

1 The English Enlightenment and Neoclassicism *In what way is the king a man of reason?*

20. *Pernicious* means "destructive" or "malicious."
21. *Dionysius Halicarnassensis* was a Greek writer who lived in Rome and tried to persuade the conquered Greeks to submit to the Romans. Swift is being ironic.

Writing Practice

Narrative

 Remind students that narrative writing tells a story. Driven by a conflict or problem, a narrative unfolds event by event and leads to a resolution. The story is told by a narrator who is inside (first-person) or outside (third-person) the story. A narrative can take the form of a novel, an essay, a poem, or a short story. Invite students to write short first-person narratives in which they travel to an imaginary place inhabited by unknown people. Have them write about their interactions and how they come to understand and evaluate the other culture.

of the world and must therefore be altogether unacquainted with the manners and customs that most prevail in other nations, the want of which knowledge will ever produce many prejudices and a certain narrowness of thinking, from which we and the politer countries of Europe are wholly exempted. And it would be hard indeed if so remote a prince's notions of virtue and vice were to be offered as a standard for all mankind.

To confirm what I have now said and further to show the miserable effects of a confined education, I shall here insert a passage which will hardly obtain belief. In hopes to ingratiate myself further into his Majesty's favor, I told him of an invention discovered between three and four hundred years ago to make a certain powder, into a heap of which the smallest spark of fire falling, would kindle the whole in a moment, although it were as big as a mountain, and make it all fly up in the air together, with a noise and agitation greater than thunder. That a proper quantity of this powder rammed into a hollow tube of brass or iron, according to its bigness, would drive a ball of iron or lead with such violence and speed as nothing was able to sustain its force. That the largest balls thus discharged would not only destroy whole ranks of an army at once but batter the strongest walls to the ground, sink down ships with a thousand men in each to the bottom of the sea; and when linked together by a chain, would cut through masts and rigging, divide hundreds of bodies in the middle, and lay all waste before them. That we often put this powder into large hollow balls of iron and discharged them by an engine into some city we were besieg-ing, which would rip up the pavements, tear the houses to pieces, burst and throw splinters on every side, dashing out the brains of all who came near. That I knew the ingredients very well, which were cheap and common; I understood the manner of compounding them and could direct his workmen how to make those tubes of a size proportionable to all other things in his Majesty's kingdom, and the largest need not be above two hundred feet long; twenty or thirty of which tubes, charged with the proper quantity of powder and balls, would batter down the walls of the strongest town in his dominions in a few hours or destroy the whole metropolis if ever it should pretend to dispute his absolute commands. This I humbly offered to his Majesty as a small tribute of acknowledgment in return of so many marks that I had received of his royal favor and protection.

The King was struck with horror at the description I had given of those terrible engines and the proposal I had made. He was amazed how so impotent and groveling an insect as I (these were his expressions) could entertain such inhuman ideas and in so familiar a manner as to appear wholly unmoved at all the scenes of blood and desolation, which I had painted as the common effects of those destructive machines, whereof, he said, some evil genius, enemy to mankind, must have been the first contriver. As for himself, he protested that although few things delighted him so much as new discoveries in art or in nature, yet he would rather lose half his kingdom than be privy to such a secret, which he commanded me, as I valued my life, never to mention any more. ❧

---

2 Make Inferences About Theme *What is ironic about Gulliver making allowances for the king?*

Make Inferences About Theme *How does Swift expect the reader to react to Gulliver's description of gunpowder?* **3**

Teach

Reading Strategy 2

Make Inferences About Theme **Answer:** *It is ironic that Gulliver accuses the clear-sighted and rational king of "many prejudices" and "narrowness of thinking."*

Reading Strategy 3

Make Inferences About Theme **Answer:** *Swift expects the reader to react negatively, as the king does in the next paragraph.*

(APPROACHING) **Ask:** What happens when a spark of fire touches the powder? *(It explodes).* What kind of powder explodes like that when kindled? *(gunpowder)* What are the "hollow tube of brass or iron" and the "ball or iron or lead"? *(a gun and bullets)*

Cultural History ☆

When Swift was writing *Gulliver's Travels,* the seeds had already been sown for the Industrial Revolution. Thomas Savery patented a crude steam engine in 1698. By 1712, the design had been improved by Thomas Newcomen.

English Learners

UNIVERSAL ACCESS

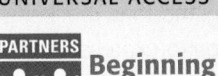 **Beginning** Organize students to work in pairs and read aloud chunks of text. Then have students make a list of any words or phrases they encounter that are unfamiliar. Stduents should use a dictionary and the selection footnotes to clarify their understanding, and then paraphrase the chunk before moving on to the next section.

After You Read

Assess

1. Students will probably identify more closely with the people of Brobdingnag.

2. (a) All subjects must break eggs at the smaller end. Many believed this decree broke with religious teachings; they rebelled and endured punishment or death rather than obey. (b)Human conflicts frequently erupt over trivial differences.

3. (a) He thinks the English are the most contemptible creatures imaginable. (b) Gulliver is small-minded in his praise of England.

4. The king's opposition to the technology suggests that the Brobdingnagians are civilized and have great respect for life.

5. Swift shared the views of the Brobdingnagians. Explanations should reflect an understanding of satire.

6. Students might say that satire is more effective because it elicits mocking laughter, which most people and institutions want to avoid.

7. Some students may feel that Swift's attacks were too personal. Others may feel that his attacks were general and satirical, and therefore similar to those of Pope.

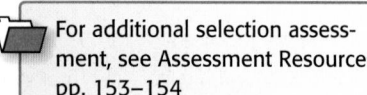
For additional selection assessment, see Assessment Resources, pp. 153–154

After You Read

Respond and Think Critically

Respond and Interpret

1. Which country do you prefer, Lilliput or Brobdingnag? Why?

2. (a)Summarize the emperor's command about eggs and the controversy it causes. (b)What point about human behavior does Swift make in his description of the egg controversy?

3. (a)What does the king of Brobdingnag think of the English? (b)Gulliver is physically smaller than the king of Brobdingnag and his people. In what other sense is Gulliver shown to be "small"?

Analyze and Evaluate

4. What does the king's reaction to technology Gulliver describes suggest about Brobdingnagians?

5. Do you believe that Swift shared the views of the Lilliputians, of the Brobdingnagians, or of Gulliver? Explain.

Connect

6. **Big Idea** The English Enlightenment and Neoclassicism Satire is a literary form that flourished during the Enlightenment. In your opinion, is Swift's use of satire more or less effective than simple, direct criticism? Why?

7. **Connect to the Author** Swift praised Alexander Pope for not making satire a personal attack: "He lash'd the Vice, but spar'd the Name." Do you think Swift succeeded in living up to that ideal in this excerpt? Explain.

You're the Critic

Was Swift a Misanthrope?

Swift has been accused of hating people in general because of his savage satires. But was he really a misanthrope? Read these excerpts of literary criticism. A. L. Rowse published a biography of Swift in 1975. William Makepeace Thackeray, who lived in the nineteenth century, had strong opinions about Swift.

"What Swift detested was the nonsensical belief that men as a whole were rational—their behavior showed that this was not true. At the utmost, they were capable of reason; then why don't they act on it more? . . . The evidences of men's refusal to use what reason they have got were all round him, especially in Ireland, and Swift was right to highlight the evidences of their idiocy . . . how otherwise can, or will, the fools learn?"

—A. L. Rowse

"If you had been his inferior in [talent or ability] . . . , his equal in mere social station, he would have bullied, scorned, and insulted you; if, undeterred by his great reputation, you had met him like a man, he would have quailed before you, and not had the pluck to reply, and gone home, and years after written a foul epigram about you."

—William Makepeace Thackeray

Group Activity Discuss these questions with classmates. Refer to the criticisms and cite Swift's work or his biography on page 548.

1. (a)What is the difference of opinion between Thackeray and Rowse? (b)Which one seems to best understand Swift? Explain.

2. In your opinion, was Swift a misanthrope or was he a realist about humans? Explain.

You're the Critic

1. (a) Thackeray believes Swift delivers cheap shots at the subjects that he satirizes, while Rowse believes that Swift's aim was to teach humanity about the errors caused by irrational thought. (b) Students will probably respond that Rowse's criticism seems closer to the truth, and that Thackeray's criticism seems to express an ad hominem attack.

2. Answers will vary. Some students may propose that he was both. Have students cite evidence from Swift's work to support their viewpoints.

Literary Element | Parody

A parodist imitates some defining feature of a work, such as its style or subject matter, exaggerating it for comic effect. *Gulliver's Travels*, Swift's **parody** of travel books, even included maps of Gulliver's imaginary voyages and a picture and biography of Lemuel Gulliver, a doctor on a merchant ship.

1. What features of government documents does Swift parody in the Lilliputians' eight commandments to Gulliver?

2. (a)In your opinion, does Swift romanticize the Lilliputians and Brobdingnagians? (b)Why might Swift have chosen to portray them as he does?

Review: Irony

As you learned on page 125, **irony** is a contrast or discrepancy between expectation and reality. **Verbal irony** exists when a person says one thing while meaning another; **situational irony** exists when the outcome of a situation is the opposite of what someone expected.

Partner Activity Meet with another classmate to discuss Swift's use of irony in *Gulliver's Travels*. Working with your partner, create a web diagram like the one below and fill it in with an example of each kind of irony.

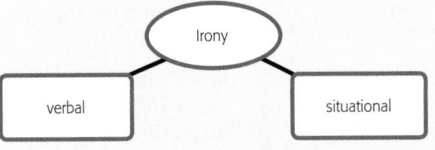

LOG ON ▶ **Literature** Online

Selection Resources For Selection Quizzes, eFlashcards, and Reading-Writing Connection activities, go to glencoe.com and enter QuickPass code GLB9817u3.

Reading Strategy | Make Inferences About Theme

It is important to distinguish the topics of a work from its **theme** or themes. *Gulliver's Travels* includes many topics, such as human folly, corruption, politics, and several others. A **theme** is the message a writer shares about one of the work's topics. For example, "It is absurd for humans to take pride in gunpowder" is one of Swift's themes, or messages.

1. How would you state another important theme of *Gulliver's Travels*?

2. To support your theme, list three important details from these excerpts and the inferences about the theme that you drew from them.

Vocabulary Practice

Practice with Synonyms With a partner, match each boldfaced vocabulary word below with a synonym. You will not use all the answer choices. Use a thesaurus or dictionary to check your answers.

1. conjecture   **a.** verify

2. magnitude   **b.** level

               c. guess

               d. size

Academic Vocabulary

Because they are so small, the Lilliputians **perceive** *Gulliver as a giant.*

Perceive is an academic word. Political candidates, in addition to taking a stand on various issues, usually need to be **perceived** by the public as trustworthy and likable in order to secure votes. To further explore this word, answer the following question: What person— either a public figure or someone you know— did you initially **perceive** in a way different from the way you do now? Explain your answer.

For more on academic vocabulary, see pages 56 and R81.

JONATHAN SWIFT   **569**

Literary Element

1. Swift parodies legalistic style.

2. (a) Students may say that Swift romanticized the Brobdingnagians. (b) Swift's portrayals reflect his political views.

Review: Irony

Answers will vary. Possible verbal irony: Swift endorses the king of Brobdingnag's moral standards although Gulliver deprecates them. Possible situational irony: Gulliver expects to impress the king of Brobdingnag with his account of the uses of gunpowder but actually appalls him.

Progress Check

Can students identify parody?

If No → See Unit 3 Teaching Resources Book, p. 99.

Reading Strategy

1. Possible response: Europeans should be horrified at the weapons produced by their technology.

2. Students' details and inferences will vary depending on their themes.

Progress Check

Can students make inferences about theme?

If No → See Unit 3 Teaching Resources Book, p. 100.

Vocabulary Practice

1. c

2. d

Academic Vocabulary

Answers will vary.

After You Read

Assess

Respond Through Writing

Use these criteria when evaluating students' writing:

- Did the thesis state a universal theme found in *Gulliver's Travels* in their own words?

- Is evidence from the selection used to good effect?

- Does the conclusion restate the writer's position, echo the main points, and add a related insight?

- Does the essay seem polished with regard to spelling, grammar, and punctuation?

A student who meets all of these criteria should receive the equivalent of a 4-point response.

A student who fully meets two or partially meets three of these criteria should receive the equivalent of a 3-point response.

A student who fully meets one or partially meets two of these criteria should receive the equivalent of a 2-point response.

A student who partially meets one of these criteria should receive the equivalent of a 1-point response.

For grammar practice, see Unit 3 Teaching Resources Book, p. 102.

Respond Through Writing

Reflective Essay

Respond to Theme Of the numerous messages about people and governments that Swift conveys in *Gulliver's Travels*, choose the theme that seems most universal. Then write a reflective essay describing how that theme applies to one or more incidents in your life.

Prewrite With several classmates, brainstorm a list of themes in *Gulliver's Travels*. Then create a list that ranks the themes on the basis of how universal you think each is. Finally, choose one of the most universal themes and write in your journal about incidents in your life that illustrate that theme. Write down as many details as you can remember; this will help you plan your paper and make specific connections to Swift's theme.

Draft A good way to begin your draft is to state the theme you have chosen in your own words. Then describe your personal incident chronologically, including sensory details and rhetorical devices where needed. Compare it with relevant events in Swift's work. Show clearly the significance of your experience, emphasizing how it illustrates the message found in *Gulliver's Travels*.

> One of Swift's most universal themes—and one I have experienced firsthand in my own life—is that people often mistrust and fear those who don't look or think the way they do.
>
> I am an albino and, as long as I can remember, have been stared at and treated differently from other children.

Use statements like the following to support your interpretation of an implied theme.

The author implies _____ by saying _____.

Revise It is helpful to get comments from a peer reader on your reflective essay, since you may be too close to the material to see it objectively. Use the comments and the Writing Workshop checklist on page 852 to improve your draft.

Edit and Proofread Proofread your paper, correcting any errors in spelling, grammar, and punctuation. Use the Grammar Tip in the side column to help you with parentheses and brackets.

570 UNIT 3   FROM PURITANISM TO THE ENLIGHTENMENT

Learning Objectives

In this assignment, you will focus on the following objectives:

Writing: Writing a reflective essay.

Grammar: Understanding how to use parentheses and brackets.

Grammar Tip

Parentheses and Brackets

Use **parentheses** to add examples or other explanatory information to your essay. Do not use a comma before the first parenthesis. When the material within parentheses is a complete sentence, begin it with a capital letter and end it with a period.

Use **brackets** to set off supplementary information within parentheses or to correct or comment on quoted material.

My affliction sets me dramatically apart from my friends, since I had to restrict my exposure to the sun. (You can imagine how much fun outdoor activities [going to the beach, for example] were for me.)

 To create custom assessments using software, use ExamView Assessment Suite.

To create custom assessments online, go to Progress Reporter Online Assessment.

Before You Read

Pope's Works

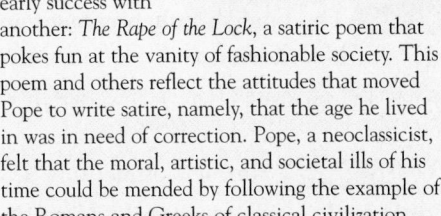

Meet Alexander Pope

(1688–1744)

Although Alexander Pope became the first English writer to earn his living solely by writing literature, the odds were against him from birth. He was chronically ill from a young age and received little formal education. In addition, he was Roman Catholic when England was ruled by Protestants. Yet, Pope overcame his obstacles to become one of England's most respected satiric poets and quotable authors.

> "Nor fame I slight, nor her favors call;
> She comes unlook'd for, if she comes
>   at all."
>
> —Alexander Pope

Overcoming Odds Though a literary giant, Pope was well under five feet tall. Tuberculosis of the spine stunted his growth in childhood, leaving him disabled and an object of ridicule for the rest of his life. As a Roman Catholic, Pope was barred from attending England's universities or holding a government office—the source of income for many writers of the time. He read widely on his own, however, perfecting his language skills by translating foreign works into English. Encouraged by his father, Pope developed an early talent for poetry. While still a teenager, he wrote a series of nature poems, his "Pastorals," which were solicited for publication by the time he was eighteen.

At 23, Pope wrote *An Essay on Criticism*. The work earned him powerful enemies, as many critics were outraged that a young writer would dare attack the literary establishment in print. However, the simple language and learned observations of the poem impressed many influential writers including Joseph Addison, Richard Steele, and Jonathan Swift. The next year, Pope followed this early success with another: *The Rape of the Lock*, a satiric poem that pokes fun at the vanity of fashionable society. This poem and others reflect the attitudes that moved Pope to write satire, namely, that the age he lived in was in need of correction. Pope, a neoclassicist, felt that the moral, artistic, and societal ills of his time could be mended by following the example of the Romans and Greeks of classical civilization.

Wit and Warfare Pope himself noted, "The life of a wit is a warfare on earth." He endured criticism from other writers his entire life, many of whom attacked not only his writing, but his religious beliefs and physical handicaps as well. In his thirties, Pope returned to Greek poetry, translating the *Iliad* and the *Odyssey*. After announcing his intention to translate the *Iliad*, he was met with great resistance. Among others, Addison—who had turned against Pope for political reasons—attempted to thwart the success of the translation. The attempts failed, however. In fact, the translations sold so well that Pope was able to lease an estate outside of London called Twickenham (twi′ kə nəm). While there, he continued writing, all the while defending himself against his enemies.

Pope's friends remained loyal throughout his life. His later works, such as *An Essay on Man*, display a thoughtfulness that even his enemies later came to respect.

 Literature Online

Author Search For more about Alexander Pope, go to glencoe.com and enter QuickPass code GLB9817u3.

English Learners

DIFFERENTIATED INSTRUCTION

Beginning **Write on the board:**

_____ rhymes with _____.

Explain that Pope's Epigrams are written in rhyming couplets—pairs of lines whose end words ends rhyme. Have students preview the text by looking at the rhyming pairs and using them to complete the sentence on the board.

Before You Read

Focus

Bellringer Options

Selection Focus
  Transparency 27
Daily Language Practice
  Transparency 45

Or write: Literary giant.
Ask: When you read that Pope was a literary giant, what does it make you expect of him? *(insight, style, wisdom)*

As they read, have students note attributes and contributions from Pope that seem to make him a literary giant. Ask them to pay particular attention to examples of his work that they personally like.

Before You Read

Focus

Summary

A collection of quotations from *An Essay on Criticism, Moral Essays* and *An Essay on Man,* under the title "Epigrams," begins the selection. (Reinforce for students that *epigram* is synonymous with *saying,* perhaps giving a simple example, such as "I think, therefore I am.")

> For summaries in languages other than English, see Unit 3 Teaching Resources Book, pp. 105–110.

Vocabulary

Dictionary Have students use a dictionary to look up each vocabulary word. Have them use a chart to list the etymology, alternate definitions, synonyms, and antonyms of each word.

> For additional vocabulary practice, see Unit 3 Teaching Resources Book, p. 113.

Literature and Reading Preview

Connect to the Essay

What expressions or sayings have you learned from older generations? Make a list of several sayings, explaining each.

Build Background

Pope was influenced by the style of classical poetry. As a Neoclassicist, he valued order and balance over emotion. The precedents set by ancient Greek and Roman authors guided Neoclassicists. One feature of ancient poetry adopted was the **epigram**—a brief, witty saying that sums up a moral point.

Set Purposes for Reading

Big Idea The English Enlightenment and Neoclassicism

As you read, ask yourself, How do these lines show that reason dominated Pope's beliefs and opinions?

Literary Element Heroic Couplet

A heroic couplet is a rhymed pair of lines in iambic pentameter that work together to express an idea or point. The following passage from *An Essay on Man* forms a heroic couplet:

> And, spite of pride, in erring reason's spite,
> One truth is clear, Whatever is, is right.

As you read, ask yourself, How do the characteristics of the heroic couplet help Pope express his ideas?

Reading Strategy Paraphrase

When you **paraphrase**, you restate something in your own words. As you read, ask yourself, How would I express these ideas?

Tip: Using a Paraphrase Chart Use a chart to record complex epigrams and to paraphrase their meaning.

Epigram	Paraphrase
p. 574; "Be thou the first true merit to befriend; His praise is lost, who stays till all commend."	One should compliment what is done well without waiting until others do so first.

Learning Objectives

For pages 571–575

In studying this text, you will focus on the following objectives:

Literary Study: Analyzing heroic couplet.

Reading: Paraphrasing.

Writing: Writing a journal entry.

Vocabulary

commend (kə mend´) *v.* to praise; express approval of; p. 574 *The association held a banquet to commend the accomplishments of its members.*

discord (dis´ kôrd) *n.* a lack of agreement or harmony; p. 574 *The blaring music, harsh lighting, and general discord of the restaurant made the customers uncomfortable.*

Tip: Context Clues You can often find clues to the meaning of an unfamiliar word by looking at words and phrases that surround the word. Context clues may be examples, definitions, synonyms, or other kinds of clues.

Selection Skills

Literary Elements
- Heroic Couplet (SE pp. 572, 573, 575)

Reading Skills
- Paraphrase (SE pp. 572, 574, 575)

Pope's Works

Vocabulary Skills
- Context Clues (SE pp. 572, 575)

Listening/Speaking/Viewing Skills
- Analyze Art (SE p. 573)

Writing Skills/Grammar
- Write a Journal Entry (SE p. 575)

572

Epigrams

Alexander Pope

from An Essay on Criticism

'Tis with our judgments as our watches, none
Go just alike, yet each believes his own.

One science only will one genius fit;
So vast is art, so narrow human wit.

A little learning is a dangerous thing;
Drink deep, or taste not the Pierian spring:[1]
There shallow drafts intoxicate the brain,
And drinking largely sobers us again.

In wit, as Nature, what affects our hearts
Is not the exactness of peculiar parts;
'Tis not a lip or eye we beauty call,
But the joint force and full result of all.

True wit is Nature to advantage dressed;
What oft was thought, but ne'er so well
 expressed.

Words are like leaves; and where they most
 abound,
Much fruit of sense beneath is rarely found.

---

1. The *Pierian spring* is a reference to a sacred spring in Greek mythology. It can also mean "a source of inspiration."

1 The English Enlightenment and Neoclassicism *What does this epigram mean, and how is it connected with the ideas of the Enlightenment?*

2 Heroic Couplet *What characteristics of these lines make them a heroic couplet?*

The Ship of Fools. Hieronymus Bosch. Louvre, Paris.

View the Art Hieronymus Bosch created complicated images full of religious and moral symbolism. What does this painting suggest about the people it depicts? Explain. ★

ALEXANDER POPE **573**

Teach

Big Idea **1**

The English Enlightenment and Neoclassicism Answer: *Shallow learning is deceptive; patient, deep learning inspires us. These ideas reflect a focus on reason.*

Literary Element **2**

Heroic Couplet Answer: *The paired lines are written in iambic pentameter, they rhyme, and they work together to express a point.*

View the Art ★

(Possible answer: The "fools" seem to be people preoccupied with food, drink, and music, or frivolous pleasures, ignorant of their surroundings or situation.)

Bosch's *Ship of Fools* was once believed to have been a depiction of medieval Europe's solution to the mental health problem: towns and villages would round up their mentally ill, load them all into a large cart, and force them into the streets where they had to beg for a living. Later, however, it was shown that Bosch actually intended the painting as a poetic religious reference.

573

Teach

Reading Strategy | 1

Paraphrase **Answer:** *Nature can never be fully understood because human reason is prone to err. However, what we observe is "right" or has a purpose, even if we do not understand it.*

Ask: Which epigram do you find difficult to understand? Discuss the meanings of some of the challenging epigrams.

[APPROACHING] If students have difficulty, have them use a dictionary to clarify the meanings of unknown words, and then paraphrase the epigram one line at a time.

 For additional practice using the reading skill or strategy, see Unit 3 Teaching Resources Book, p. 112.

 To check students' understanding of the selection, see Unit 3 Teaching Resources Book, p. 114.

Progress Check

Can students identify heroic couplets?

If No → See Unit 3 Teaching Resources Book, p. 111.

In words, as fashions, the same rule will hold;
Alike fantastic, if too new or old:
Be not the first by whom the new are tried,
Nor yet the last to lay the old aside.

True ease in writing comes from art, not chance,
As those move easiest who have learned to dance.
'Tis not enough no harshness gives offense,
The sound must seem an echo to the sense.

Avoid extremes; and shun the fault of such,
Who still are pleased too little or too much.

Regard not then if wit be old or new,
But blame the false, and value still the true.

We think our fathers fools, so wise we grow;
Our wiser sons, no doubt, will think us so.

Be thou the first true merit to befriend;
His praise is lost, who stays till all **commend**.

Good nature and good sense must ever join;
To err is human, to forgive, divine.

Vocabulary

commend (kə mend´) v. to praise; express approval of

For fools rush in where angels fear to tread.

from Moral Essays

'Tis education forms the common mind,
Just as the twig is bent, the tree's inclined.

from An Essay on Man

Hope springs eternal in the human breast:
Man never is, but always to be blest.

All Nature is but art, unknown to thee;
All chance, direction, which thou canst not see;
All **discord**, harmony not understood;
All partial evil, universal good:
And, spite of pride, in erring reason's spite,
One truth is clear, Whatever is, is right.

Vice is a monster of so frightful mien,
As, to be hated, needs but to be seen;
Yet seen too oft, familiar with her face,
We first endure, then pity, then embrace.

A wit's a feather, and a chief's a rod;
An honest man's the noblest work of God.

Paraphrase *How would you paraphrase this epigram from* An Essay on Man? | **1**

Vocabulary

discord (dis´ kôrd) n. a lack of agreement or harmony

574 UNIT 3 FROM PURITANISM TO THE ENLIGHTENMENT

Grammar Practice

SPIRAL REVIEW **Participles** Remind students that a participle is a verb form that can function as an adjective, as shown in the following sentence:

Pope's *encouraging* epigrams counsel moderation in all things.

The present participle is made up of the base form of the verb plus *–ing*. Ask students to write four sentences about the thoughts expressed in Pope's epigrams, using a participle in each of the four sentences. Remind students of the difference between participles and gerunds, which function as nouns. Have students exchange sentences with a partner and perform a peer review.

After You Read

Respond and Think Critically

Respond and Interpret

1. Which of Pope's sayings did you find particularly true or fitting? Explain.

2. (a)According to the epigrams, which qualities does Pope consider most important? (b)How can you tell that these are important to him?

3. (a)How would you describe Pope's attitude toward learning as conveyed in the epigrams? (b)Cite two examples that support your view.

Analyze and Evaluate

4. **Parallelism** is the use of phrases that have similar grammatical structures. How does parallelism in the epigrams reinforce Pope's ideas?

Connect

5. **Big Idea** The English Enlightenment and Neoclassicism Write your own epigram (as a heroic couplet) based on the attitudes of the English Enlightenment and Neoclassicism.

6. **Connect to Today** In *An Essay on Man*, Pope remarks that humans are "the glory, jest, and riddle of the world." What modern events show humans as "the glory," "jest," or "riddle" of the world?

Literary Element Heroic Couplet

Pope and other poets of his time often wrote heroic couplets as **closed couplets**, with each containing a complete thought, and a semicolon, colon, or period at its end. Many lines have a **caesura (si zyur′ ə)** or pause, near the middle, indicated by a comma.

1. Which lines in the epigrams do not form closed heroic couplets?

2. How do caesuras help emphasize meaning in the epigrams?

🚀 **Writing**

Write a Journal Entry Are epigrams an effective way of giving advice? In a journal entry, write about an instance in which you or someone you know might have benefited from the ideas in one of Pope's epigrams. Quote the epigram and explain it in your own words. Then explain the situation in which the epigram would have been helpful.

LOG ON ▶ **Literature** Online

Selection Resources For Selection Quizzes, eFlashcards, and Reading-Writing Connection activities, go to glencoe.com and enter QuickPass code GLB9817u3.

Reading Strategy Paraphrase

To maintain the rhyme scheme (*aa, bb*), meter (iambic pentameter), and form (couplet) of a heroic couplet, the word order is often presented in an irregular way. This can make it difficult to identify the main idea. To **paraphrase** the theme of a heroic couplet, first "translate" the couplet, rearranging the word order as necessary.

1. In the third epigram from *An Essay on Man*, what does "her face" refer to?

2. What do we "endure," "pity," and "embrace"?

3. What is the message or theme of the epigram?

Vocabulary Practice

Practice with Context Clues Identify the context clues in the following sentences that help you determine the meaning of each boldfaced vocabulary word.

1. Because our class did well on the annual test, the principal wants to **commend** us.

2. Even though the school band produced nothing but **discord** at the start of the year, they were in perfect harmony for the holiday concert.

After You Read

Assess

1. Answers will vary. Students should support their answers with text evidence.

2. (a) Pope valued wisdom, good judgment, and wit. (b) These qualities are mentioned frequently.

3. (a) Pope believes learning is vital to life. (b) "Drink deep, or taste not the Pierian spring" and "'Tis education forms the common mind."

4. Ideas are repeated to solidify them in the mind of the reader.

5. Students' epigrams should consist of a pair of rhymed lines in iambic pentameter that express an idea or a point having to do with the ideas of the Enlightenment or Neoclassicism.

6. Students should cite examples that show the human spirit at its best, its most foolish, and its most mysterious.

🚀 **Writing**

Students' journal entries should rephrase an idea in one of Pope's epigrams and then rephrase it in easy-to-understand language.

Literary Element

1. "'Tis with our judgments as our watches, none / Go just alike, yet each believes his own." Also, "For fools rush in where angels fear to tread" is not a couplet.

2. They reinforce breaks between thoughts, as with "A being darkly wise, and rudely great" and "Sole judge of truth, in endless error hurled."

Reading Strategy

1. It refers to vice.

2. The vices of ourselves and other people.

3. It is important to not be around too much vice or we will become more accepting of vice in our own lives.

Vocabulary

1. If the class "did well," the principal would want to praise or congratulate them, so *commend* means "praise."

2. The sentence suggests that *discord* is the opposite of *harmony*, indicating that the word's definition is "lack of harmony."

Before You Read

Focus

Summary

In Canto III of *The Rape of the Lock,* Belinda and the Baron are enjoying cards and coffee. The Baron, beside himself with adoration of Belinda, snips a lock of her hair.

 For summaries in languages other than English, see Unit 3 Teaching Resources Book, pp. 116–121.

Vocabulary

Dictionary Have students use a dictionary to research the Latin or Greek root of each vocabulary word. Then have students compare the meaning of each root word with the word's definition.

 For additional vocabulary practice, see Unit 3 Teaching Resources Book, p. 124.

Before You Read

from *The Rape of the Lock*

Connect to the Poem

What makes a story really funny? Freewrite for a few minutes about the techniques authors use to create humor.

Build Background

The Rape of the Lock was based on an actual event. A baron named Lord Petre had cut a lock of hair from beautiful Arabella Fermor's head and refused to give it back. A great scandal ensued. Pope created a masterpiece of satire from the event.

Set Purposes for Reading

Big Idea The English Enlightenment and Neoclassicism

Part of Neoclassicism involved admiration for Greek and Roman civilization. As you read, ask yourself, How does Pope use references to classical mythology to comment on his subject?

Literary Element Mock-Epic

A **mock-epic** is an imitation epic—a long narrative poem that describes subjects in a way that mimics the elaborate form of classical epics such as Homer's *Iliad*. As you read, ask yourself, How does Pope use mock-epic to poke fun at society?

Reading Strategy Interpret Imagery

To interpret is to use your own understanding of the world to decide what something means. When you **interpret imagery,** you decide what the "word pictures" and sensory details of a selection mean. As you read, ask yourself, How does my prior knowledge help me determine the meaning of Pope's images?

Imagery:		Prior Knowledge:		Interpretation:
• "glitt'ring forfex" • "Steel could . . . strike to dust th' imperial powers of Troy . . ."	**+**	Pope uses epic conventions to describe trivial events; he is a master of satire.	**+**	Pope describes a battle weapon as if it were a sword that inspired fear. It is actually a pair of scissors.

576 UNIT 3 FROM PURITANISM TO THE ENLIGHTENMENT

Learning Objectives

For pages 576–583

In studying this text, you will focus on the following objectives:

Literary Study: Analyzing mock epic.

Reading: Interpreting imagery.

Writing: Applying allusion to a poem or description.

Vocabulary

stratagem (strat′ ə jəm) *n.* a deception; a military tactic designed to surprise an enemy; p. 578 *The soldiers decided that an ambush was the only stratagem likely to defeat their powerful enemy.*

confound (kən found′) *v.* to confuse; to defeat or overthrow; p. 580 *Lars had little physical strength, but he was always able to confound his opponent in a chess match.*

Selection Skills

Literary Elements
- Mock-Epic (SE pp. 576, 577, 578, 580, 581, 582)
- Allusion (SE p. 582)

Reading Skills
- Interpret Imagery (SE pp. 576, 577, 579, 581, 583)

from **The Rape of the Lock**

Listening/Speaking/Viewing Skills
- Analyze Art (SE p. 579)

Vocabulary Skills
- Analogies (SE p. 583)
- Academic Vocabulary (SE p. 583)

Writing Skills/Grammar
- Apply Allusion (SE p. 583)

from The Rape of the Lock

Alexander Pope

from Canto III

Close by those meads,° for ever crown'd with flowers,
Where Thames with pride surveys his rising towers,
There stands a structure of majestic frame,°
Which from the neighb'ring Hampton takes its name.
5 Here Britain's statesmen oft the fall foredoom
Of foreign tyrants, and of nymphs at home;
Here thou, great Anna!° whom three realms obey,
Dost sometimes counsel take—and sometimes tea. ☆
    Hither the heroes and the nymphs resort,
10 To taste a while the pleasures of a court;
In various talk th' instructive hours they pass'd,
Who gave the ball, or paid the visit last;
One speaks the glory of the British Queen,
And one describes a charming Indian screen;
15 A third interprets motions, looks, and eyes;
At every word a reputation dies.
Snuff, or the fan, supply each pause of chat,
With singing, laughing, ogling, *and all that.*
    Meanwhile, declining from the noon of day,
20 The sun obliquely shoots his burning ray;
The hungry judges soon the sentence sign,
And wretches hang that jurymen may dine. . . .
Belinda now, whom thirst of fame invites,
Burns to encounter two adventurous knights,
25 At ombre° singly to decide their doom;
And swells her breast with conquests yet to come. . . .
The nymph exulting fills with shouts the sky;
The walls, the woods, and long canals reply.
    O thoughtless mortals! ever blind to fate,
30 Too soon dejected, and too soon elate.

The Battle of the Beaux and the Belles, drawing for the eighth illustration from *"Rape of the Lock"*, 1896. Aubrey Beardsley. 25.7 x 17.6 cm. Pen and ink on paper. The Barber Institute of Fine Arts, University of Birmingham.

1 **meads:** meadows—often wet, grassy lands.
3 **structure . . . frame:** Pope is referring to Hampton Court, the royal palace.
7 **Anna:** Queen Anne, who ruled Great Britain and Ireland and claimed to rule France; thus, "whom three realms obey."

25 **Ombre:** a card game.

1 Mock-Epic *What makes Pope's description of Queen Anne humorous and satirical?*

2 Interpret Imagery *What is happening in this image? What does the image suggest about this society?*

ALEXANDER POPE **577**

Teach

Big Idea   1

The English Enlightenment and Neoclassicism **Answer:**
The warning addresses the "rash youth" to recall Scylla's fate after cutting Nisus's hair—an allusion to classical mythology.

Literary Element   2

Mock-Epic **Answer:** *Clarissa gives the Baron a pair of scissors. Pope uses the epic convention of describing the pair of scissors as though it were a mighty double-edged sword.*

Literary History ☆

Sylph The character of Ariel in the poem is a sylph, an elemental being of the air. Pope's satirical sylphs are composed of the condensed humors of deceased peevish women.

Sudden, these honors shall be snatch'd away,
And cursed for ever this victorious day.
 For lo! the board with cups and spoons is crown'd,
The berries crackle, and the mill turns round:
35 On shining altars of Japan they raise
The silver lamp; the fiery spirits blaze:
From silver spouts the grateful liquors glide,
While China's earth receives the smoking tide: °
At once they gratify their scent and taste,
40 And frequent cups prolong the rich repast.
Straight hover round the fair her airy band;
Some, as she sipp'd, the fuming liquor fann'd,
Some o'er her lap their careful plumes display'd,
Trembling, and conscious of the rich brocade.
45 Coffee (which makes the politician wise,
And see through all things with his half-shut eyes)
Sent up in vapors to the baron's brain
New **stratagems,** the radiant lock to gain.
Ah cease, rash youth! desist ere 'tis too late,
50 Fear the just gods, and think of Scylla's fate!°
Changed to a bird, and sent to flit in air,
She dearly pays for Nisus' injured hair!
 But when to mischief mortals bend their will,
How soon they find fit instruments of ill!
55 Just then, Clarissa° drew with tempting grace
A two-edged weapon from her shining case:
So ladies, in romance, assist their knight,
Present the spear, and arm him for the fight.
He takes the gift with reverence and extends
60 The little engine° on his fingers' ends;
This just behind Belinda's neck he spread,
As o'er the fragrant steams she bends her head.
Swift to the lock a thousand sprites repair,
A thousand wings, by turns, blow back the hair;
65 And thrice they twitch'd the diamond in her ear;
Thrice she look'd back, and thrice the foe drew near.
Just in that instant, anxious Ariel sought ☆
The close recesses of the virgin's thought:
As on the nosegay in her breast reclin'd,
70 He watch'd th' ideas rising in her mind,

33–38 the board . . . tide: The *board* refers to the tray on which coffee will be served. Lines 33–38 describe the preparation and serving of coffee. The *berries* (beans) crackle when they are roasted and then are ground in the mill. The *altars of Japan* are lacquered tables. *The smoking tide* is coffee, and it is poured into *China's earth,* or Chinese porcelain cups.

50 Scylla's (si′ lə) **fate:** refers to the classical myth about Scylla, who plucked out one of her father Nisus's hairs, on which the safety of the kingdom depended. As punishment, she was turned into a bird.

55 Clarissa: a female character in the poem who disapproves of Belinda's vanity.

60 engine: device.

---

1   **The English Enlightenment and Neoclassicism** *How does this warning reflect the inspiration of classical mythology?*

2   **Mock-Epic** *What is actually happening here? Which conventions of epic poetry does Pope employ in this passage?*

Vocabulary

stratagem (strat′ ə jəm) *n.* a deception; a military tactic designed to surprise an enemy

Reading Practice

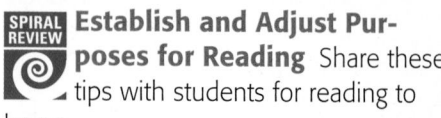

SPIRAL REVIEW   **Establish and Adjust Purposes for Reading** Share these tips with students for reading to learn:

- Read slowly and carefully.
- Reread difficult passages.
- Take careful notes or construct a graphic.

Ask students to identify a challenging section of *Canto III* and apply these strategies. Discuss whether and how students found them to be effective. Next, ask students to reread at a faster pace for their enjoyment.

Madame de Pompadour. Francois Boucher. Oil on canvas. Louvre, Paris.

 View the Art Madame de Pompadour played a significant role in the court of the French King Louis XV. What details in this portrait are reminiscent of Pope's description of Belinda?

> Sudden he view'd, in spite of all her art,
> An earthly lover lurking at her heart.
> Amazed, confused, he found his power expired,
> Resign'd to fate, and with a sigh retired.
> 75 The peer now spreads the glitt'ring forfex° wide,
> T' inclose the lock; now joins it, to divide.
> Ev'n then, before the fatal engine closed,
> A wretched sylph too fondly interposed;
> Fate urged the shears, and cut the sylph in twain,
> 80 (But airy substance soon unites again)
> The meeting points the sacred hair dissever
> From the fair head, forever, and forever!
>   Then flash'd the living lightning from her eyes,
> And screams of horror rend th' affrighted skies.
> 85 Not louder shrieks to pitying Heaven are cast,
> When husbands or when lap-dogs breathe their last;
> Or when rich China vessels, fall'n from high,
> In glitt'ring dust and painted fragments lie!
>   "Let wreaths of triumph° now my temples twine,
> 90 (The victor cried) the glorious prize is mine!

75 **forfex:** scissors.

89 **wreaths of triumph:** the wreaths that ancient Greek victors wore on their heads.

3 Interpret Imagery *What action is being described in this passage? How does the paradoxical language contribute to the effect of the image?*

ALEXANDER POPE **579**

Teach

Reading Strategy | 3

Interpret Imagery
Answer: *The Baron is about to cut a lock of Belinda's hair with the scissors. The paradoxical language ("joins it, to divide") emphasizes and exaggerates the action and the result of the loss (the close of the scissors and the "divide" created at the separation of Belinda and her lock of hair).*

Writer's Technique ☆

Repetition Remind students that writers use repetition of sounds, words, phrases and lines to emphasize an important point, expand upon an idea, help create rhythm, and increase the feeling of unity in a work. **Ask:** Do you think Pope's use of repetition in lines 90 to 100 is effective? Explain.

 View the Art ★

Answer: The woman in the portrait shares Belinda's gold hair, flowers—"nosegay in her breast"—and expensive dress—"rich brocade."

Approaching Level

DIFFERENTIATED INSTRUCTION

Benchmark Remind students that figurative language is often used in poetry for descriptive effect and is not meant to be interpreted literally. Draw students' attention to line 116 and the phrase "lightning in her eyes." **Ask:** What is Pope communicating here? (*Belinda's rage*) Ask students to identify other examples of figurative language in the selection.

Say: "Lightning in her eyes" has become an overused metaphor. What metaphor might you use to describe Belinda's rage in a fresh way? (*Answers will vary.*)

579

Teach

Mock-Epic
Answer: *Pope describes the "battle scene" after Belinda's lock is cut; the battle scene is an epic convention. The clapping fans, rustling silks, and cracking whalebones are all parts of the ladies' elaborate clothing but are made to seem like battle actions.*

ENGLISH LEARNERS Have English Learners point out words normally associated with battles, for example, combat, attack, heroes, weapons, mortal wound.

Literary History ☆

The first version of *The Rape of the Lock* was written over a period of about fourteen days (a fortnight) in 1711. This version had 2 cantos of 334 lines. In 1714, a new version of 5 cantos and 794 lines was published with 6 copper-plate engravings. The result was so popular that two more printings were done in 1714, and subsequent printings were done in 1715, 1718, and 1723.

While fish in streams, or birds delight in air,
Or in a coach and six° the British fair,
As long as *Atalantis*° shall be read,
Or the small pillow grace a lady's bed,
95 While visits° shall be paid on solemn days,
When numerous wax-lights in bright order blaze,
While nymphs take treats, or assignations give,
So long my honor, name, and praise shall live!"
What Time would spare, from steel receives its date
100 And monuments, like men, submit to fate!
Steel could the labor of the gods destroy,
And strike to dust th' imperial powers of Troy;°
Steel could the works of mortal pride **confound,**
And hew triumphal arches to the ground.
105 What wonder then, fair nymph! thy hairs should feel
The conquering force of unresisted steel?

In Canto IV, Umbriel, a "melancholy sprite," travels to the underworld to gather a vial of "soft sobs, melting griefs, and flowing tears" and a bag of "sighs, sobs, and passions." When Umbriel returns, he empties the vial and bag over Belinda and her friend. Belinda then tells the Baron that he shouldn't have taken the lock. The Baron, however, ignores her lament.

from Canto V

"To arms, to arms!" the fierce virago° cries,
And swift as lightning to the combat flies.
All side in parties, and begin th' attack:
110 Fans clap, silks rustle, and tough whalebones crack;
Heroes' and heroines' shouts confusedly rise,
And bass and treble voices strike the skies.
No common weapons in their hands are found,
Like Gods they fight, nor dread a mortal wound. . . .
115   See fierce Belinda on the baron flies,
With more than usual lightning in her eyes:
Nor fear'd the chief th' unequal fight to try,
Who sought no more than on his foe to die.
But his bold lord with manly strength endued,
120 She with one finger and a thumb subdued:
Just where the breath of life his nostrils drew,
A charge of snuff the wily virgin threw;

> **1** | **Mock-Epic** *How does Pope make use of the conventions of epic poetry in this passage? What is the effect?*

> **Vocabulary**
> **confound** (kən found´) *v.* to confuse; to defeat or overthrow

92 **coach and six:** a prestigious carriage with six horses.
93 *Atalantis:* a popular gossipy romance in which real society people were thinly disguised as fictional characters.
95 **visits:** the regular evening visits that were a serious ritual for the society lady. The society lady would be accompanied by servants carrying **wax-lights.**

101-102 **steel . . . Troy:** According to legend, the swords of the ancient Greeks conquered Troy.

107 **virago:** a "female warrior," in this case, Belinda.

Literary Element Practice

SPIRAL REVIEW **Scansion** Remind students that scansion is the analysis of the meter of a line of verse. Ask students to copy lines 100 through 106. Have them scan the lines.

And mon/uments,/ like men,/ submit/ to fate/

Steel could/ the la/bor of/ the gods/ destroy,/

And strike/to dust/th' imper/ial powers/ of Troy;/

Every first syllable receives an unstressed denotation. Every second syllable receives a stressed denotation. Stress and unstress for "powers."

The gnomes direct, to every atom just,
The pungent grains of titillating dust.
125　Sudden, with starting tears each eye o'erflows,
And the high dome re-echoes to his nose.
　　　"Now meet thy fate," incensed Belinda cried,
And drew a deadly bodkin° from her side. . . .
　　　"Boast not my fall, (he cried) insulting foe!
130　Thou by some other shalt be laid as low.
Nor think, to die dejects my lofty mind:
All that I dread is leaving you behind!
Rather than so, ah let me still survive,
And burn in Cupid's flames—but burn alive."
135　　　"Restore the lock!" she cries; and all around
"Restore the lock!" the vaulted roofs rebound.
Not fierce Othello° in so loud a strain
Roar'd for the handkerchief that caused his pain.
But see how oft ambitious aims are cross'd,
140　And chiefs contend till all the prize is lost!
The lock, obtain'd with guilt, and kept with pain,
In every place is sought, but sought in vain:
With such a prize no mortal must be blest,
So Heaven decrees! with Heaven who can contest?
145　　　Some thought it mounted to the lunar sphere,
Since all things lost on earth are treasured there.
There heroes' wits are kept in pond'rous vases,
And beaux' in snuff-boxes and tweezer-cases.
There broken vows, and death-bed alms are found,
150　And lovers' hearts with ends of riband° bound. . . .
　　　But trust the Muse—she saw it upward rise,
Though mark'd by none but quick, poetic eyes. . . .
A sudden star it shot through liquid air,
And drew behind a radiant trail of hair. . . .
155　　　Then cease, bright nymph! to mourn thy ravish'd hair,
Which adds new glory to the shining sphere!
Not all the tresses that fair head can boast
Shall draw such envy as the lock you lost.
For, after all the murders of your eye,
160　When, after millions slain, yourself shall die;
When those fair suns shall set, as set they must,
And all those tresses shall be laid in dust;
This lock, the Muse shall consecrate to fame,
And 'midst the stars inscribe Belinda's name.

128 **bodkin:** a dagger. Here, it refers to a hairpin that is shaped like a dagger.

137 **Othello:** This allusion to Shakespeare's play *Othello* (Act III, scene 4) refers to Othello's demanding to see the handkerchief he had given his wife, believing her to have given it to another man and thus having been unfaithful.

150 **riband** (ri bənd'): decorative ribbon.

2　Mock-Epic *What does the juxtaposition of these two lines about what is kept in the "lunar sphere" reveal about the characters at Hampton Court?*

3　Interpret Imagery *After Belinda's lock of hair is lost, what happens to it?*

ALEXANDER POPE **581**

Literary Element　**2**

Mock-Epic Answer: *Pope juxtaposes "heroes' wits," which are so large that they are kept in "pond'rous vases," with the wits of court dandies (beaus) that fit in much smaller containers— "snuff-boxes" and "tweezer-cases," noting that all things lost on earth will end up in the "lunar sphere." The effect reveals the ridiculousness of the characters at Hampton Court.*

(**ENGLISH LEARNERS**) Make sure English Learners understand the word *wits* and that "pond'rous vases" are large compared to tiny "snuff-boxes" and "tweezer-cases."

Reading Strategy　**3**

Interpret Imagery Answer: *The lock is lost to the "lunar sphere," or heavens. In reality, it is possible the Baron simply does not return it. The celestial, heavenly imagery suggests that the lost lock has become immortalized like a tragic hero.*

 To check students' understanding of the selection, see Unit 3 Teaching Resources Book, p. 126.

English Learners

DIFFERENTIATED INSTRUCTION

Intermediate Remind students that Pope's humor stems from his use of elevated language and style to describe everyday or trivial events. Challenge students to rewrite a portion of Pope's work. Have them replace Pope's elevated, ornate language with simpler vocabulary. Ask students to share their work with the class.

After You Read

Assess

1. Students may find that satire is more effective than direct description of the characters' personality traits.

2. (a) Society is preoccupied with superficialities. The characters engage in idle gossip, even if it is destructive. (b) Pope's tone is amused but scornful.

3. (a) Coffee service is described. (b) The language suggests distant places (Japan, China), sacred rituals ("crown'd," "shining altars," "fiery spirits") and intense action ("crackle," "turns round," "blaze") and implies the coffee service is a sacred and cosmopolitan ritual.

4. (a) The Baron cuts her lock of hair with a pair of scissors. (b) Her reaction reveals Belinda's vanity.

5. (a) The Baron is jubilant over the "victory" and thinks he should be congratulated. (b) By showing the Baron's reaction in his own words, the poet can show how arrogant he really is without comment from the narrator.

6. The allusion puts the Baron's plan to cut Belinda's hair in perspective. Unlike Scylla's act, which cost a kingdom, the Baron's act is just silly.

7. The juxtaposition of the serious with the trivial reveals the distortion of values in high society.

8. He satirizes the ideals by using a mock-epic, while epics were popular during the Greek and Roman time periods.

9. (a) Students may cite political cartoons, op-ed articles, or comments that friends or family members have made. (b) Satire can show how ridiculous certain practices, attitudes, or personalities appear to others.

582

After You Read

Respond and Think Critically

Respond and Interpret

1. How effective was Pope's use of satire in revealing the personalities of his characters?

2. (a) Reread lines 9–16. How would you interpret the society that Pope describes? (b) What is Pope's **tone**, or attitude toward his subject, in these lines?

3. (a) Reread lines 33–38. What is being described? (b) What does the descriptive language suggest about how the characters perceive the event?

4. (a) How is the lock "raped"? (b) What does Belinda's reaction reveal about her?

Analyze and Evaluate

5. (a) What is the Baron's reaction after the lock is cut? (b) What is the effect of revealing the Baron's reaction in his own words?

6. Read the side note about Scylla in line 50. What does this allusion imply about the Baron's plan?

7. What is the effect of juxtaposing the death of husbands and lap dogs in the comparison to Belinda's grief in lines 85–86?

Connect

8. **Big Idea** The English Enlightenment and Neoclassicism How does Pope's interest in Greek and Roman history affect his attitude toward high society in *The Rape of the Lock*?

9. **Connect to Today** (a) What examples of satire have you encountered in your own life? (b) How can satire be more painful than a direct insult?

Literary Element Mock-Epic

A **mock-epic** mimics the elevated style and form of epic poetry to describe trivial events in a humorous way. Literary epics are highly conventional poems, and the mock-epic, likewise, includes these epic conventions: the hero is of national or cosmic significance; the setting is broad, often worldwide or even cosmic; the action involves superhuman battle feats; the gods or other supernatural beings take interest in these battles; and the poem is narrated in a grand, ceremonial style that includes allusions and epic similes.

1. What type of diction, or word choice, does Pope use throughout *The Rape of the Lock*? Give examples from the selection that illustrate his style.

2. How does the setting and action of Pope's poem reflect or mimic the conventions of epic poetry?

3. Who is the hero of the poem? How can you tell?

Review: Allusion

As you learned on page 512, an **allusion** is a reference to a well-known character, place, or situation from history, art, or another work of literature. Epic (and mock-epic) poetry is typically full of allusions that contribute to a grand style. Several of Pope's allusions relate to figures from Greek myth. A **myth** is a story by an unknown author that deals with gods, heroes, and supernatural events.

Partner Activity Meet with a group of classmates and identify the allusions in *The Rape of the Lock*. Then record the allusions you find, give their meanings, and try to interpret their significance in Pope's poem. Use a chart like the one below.

Allusion	Meaning	Significance in Poem
"Scylla's fate" (line 50)	Scylla plucked out one of her father's, Nisus, hairs. As punishment, she was turned into a bird.	The speaker warns the Baron not to cut the lock, reminding him of the destruction a similar act caused Scylla.

Literary Element

1. Pope uses elevated, exaggerated diction in his descriptions.

2. The setting is actually a parlor or sitting room, although it is described as though it were worldwide and cosmic. The real action occurs when the Baron snips Belinda's lock and she tries to get it back. The action is described, however, as if it were an epic battle scene.

3. Belinda is the hero, because her name has become immortalized with the lock, despite her own mortality.

Review: Allusion

Allusions include the references to heroes and nymphs, *Atlantis*, "wreaths of triumph," the swords of the ancient Greeks that conquered Troy, Cupid, Othello, and the Muse, among others.

Reading Strategy | Interpret Imagery

Much of Pope's vivid imagery is figurative rather than literal. **Figurative language** is not literally true but expresses some truth beyond the literal level. In the poem, note how Pope uses elaborate, figurative language to describe mundane people and situations. Also, notice how such descriptions satirize the subjects being described.

1. (a)Reread lines 33–38. How is the coffee service described? (b)What type of figurative language is used in the lines? (c)How do these images affect your understanding of the characters in the poem?

2. Reread the final twelve lines of the poem. Which images are presented figuratively?

Vocabulary Practice

Practice with Analogies For each analogy, decide what the relationship is between the first pair of words. Then match that relationship in the second pair.

1. stratagem : enemy :: vaccine :
   a. doctor   c. medicine
   b. disease   d. patient

2. reply : respond :: confound :
   a. enemy   c. advocate
   b. quandary   d. confuse

Academic Vocabulary

The elevated style and trivial events in The Rape of the Lock **indicate** *that the poem is satirical.*

Indicate is an academic word. More familiar words that are similar in meaning are *show*, *demonstrate*, and *suggest*.

To further explore this word, complete the following sentence: *If a person _____, it would* **indicate** *that he or she was untrustworthy.*

For more on academic vocabulary, see pages 56 and R81.

Write with Style

 Apply Allusion

Assignment Many writers, like Alexander Pope, have used allusions to famous characters in literature, events in history, and ancient myths to create a lofty style. Create a poem or description that alludes to famous elements of literature or culture.

Get Ideas Make a three-column chart like the one below. Brainstorm characters and events that fit into each category.

History	Literature	Myths
invention of the airplane	Hamlet	Sisyphus
	Job	Zeus
fall of Rome		Athena
Vietnam War		

Look for a common thread in the items you've identified, or choose a single entry from your chart as your reference. Then use your journal to write about a setting, character, or event in which to incorporate your allusion.

EXAMPLE

The myth of Sisyphus, the invention of the airplane, and the Book of Job all involve facing or overcoming adversity. I could use these stories to help describe a situation where I faced adversity.

Give It Structure Using your notes as a foundation, create an informal outline, or just let your ideas flow and go back and organize them logically. You may want to focus on one allusion at a time or organize them chronologically.

Look at Language Be sure your allusions clearly support the message of your poem or description. Also consider your audience's knowledge—use allusions with which they will be familiar.

LOG ON ▶ **Literature** Online

Selection Resources For Selection Quizzes, eFlashcards, and Reading-Writing Connection activities, go to glencoe.com and enter QuickPass code GLB9817u3.

ALEXANDER POPE **583**

After You Read

Assess

Reading Strategy

1. (a) The coffee service is described in elaborate, exaggerated, vivid language. (b) Pope uses metaphors to describe the scene. (c) The images suggest the characters' illusions of self-importance.

2. Some figurative images are: "a sudden star it shot through liquid air," "drew behind a radiant trail of hair," "all those tresses shall be laid in dust," and "'midst the stars inscribe Belinda's name."

Progress Check

Can students interpret imagery?

If No → See Unit 3 Teaching Resources Book, p. 123.

Vocabulary practice

1. a
2. d

Academic Vocabulary

Possible answer: If a person consistently breaks promises, it indicates that he or she is untrustworthy.

 ## Write with Style

Students' writing should utilize a person or time period in history to depict a mock-epic situation.

 For grammar practice, see Unit 3 Teaching Resources Book, p. 125.

 To create custom assessments online, go to Progress Reporter Online Assessment.

 To create custom assessments using software, use ExamView Assessment Suite.

Before You Read

Focus

Bellringer Options

Literature Launchers:
Pre-Reading Videos DVD,
Selection Launcher

Selection Focus
   Transparency 28

Daily Language Practice
   Transparency 46

Or present these questions to students and have them respond in writing in their notebooks or journals. **Say:** Think about a time when an adult gave you advice on how to do something or solve a problem. What was the advice about? How did you react?

Interactive Read and Write

Other options for teaching this selection can be found in

- Interactive Read and Write for EL Students pp. 155–164

- Interactive Read and Write for Approaching-Level Students, pp. 155–164

- Interactive Read and Write for On-Level Students, pp. 155–164

Before You Read

Letter to Her Daughter

Meet **Lady Mary Wortley Montagu**

(1689–1762)

Lady Mary Wortley Montagu went after what she wanted in life—even when that meant defying social customs. For example, although the custom of the time was for women to receive less education than men, the young Lady Montagu sneaked a Latin dictionary and grammar book from her family's library and secretly taught herself the language. She defied convention again at twenty-three, when she chose not to marry the man her father had selected for her and eloped instead with the man she loved, Edward Wortley Montagu, a member of Parliament.

"What fire, what ease, what knowledge of Europe and Asia."

—Edward Gibbon

Life in Turkey When her husband was appointed ambassador to Turkey at Constantinople (now Istanbul) in 1716, Lady Montagu embraced the culture, learning Turkish, visiting mosques, and even getting to know harem women. She noticed the effectiveness of the Turkish practice of immunizing children against smallpox, a disease that had marred her beauty when she was a young woman. She then had both her son and daughter immunized. When her husband was recalled to England in 1718, she pushed English doctors to adopt this immunization practice—and succeeded, overcoming the considerable prejudice against women offering advice to doctors. She recorded her observations about life in Turkey in *Turkish Embassy Letters.*

Lady Montagu was acquainted with several distinguished writers of her day. For a time, she was particularly friendly with Alexander Pope (both lived in Twickenham, west of London), who was evidently infatuated with her. He even commissioned an artist to paint her portrait in Turkish costume. For reasons unclear, they had a falling out, which occasioned much bitterness on both sides. While living in Twickenham, Lady Montagu wrote essays and composed a series of letters dealing with feminism.

Living Abroad By this time, Lady Montagu's relationship with her husband had become formal and impersonal. After twenty-five years of marriage, during which she had raised a son and daughter, Lady Montagu separated from her husband and left England. She lived abroad in Italy and France for more than twenty years. On a visit to the continent, the Reverend Joseph Spence met her for the first time in Rome and wrote this assessment of her character: "She is one of the most shining characters in the world, but shines like a comet; she is all irregularity, and always wandering; the most wise, most imprudent; loveliest, most disagreeable; best-natured, cruelest woman in the world."

Lady Montagu is best known for her witty and informative correspondence. Her letters to her daughter are full of vivid details and practical advice. Lady Montagu died of cancer at the age of seventy-three, shortly after returning to England.

 Literature Online

Author Search For more about Lady Mary Wortley Montagu, go to glencoe.com and enter QuickPass code GLB9817u3.

Selection Skills

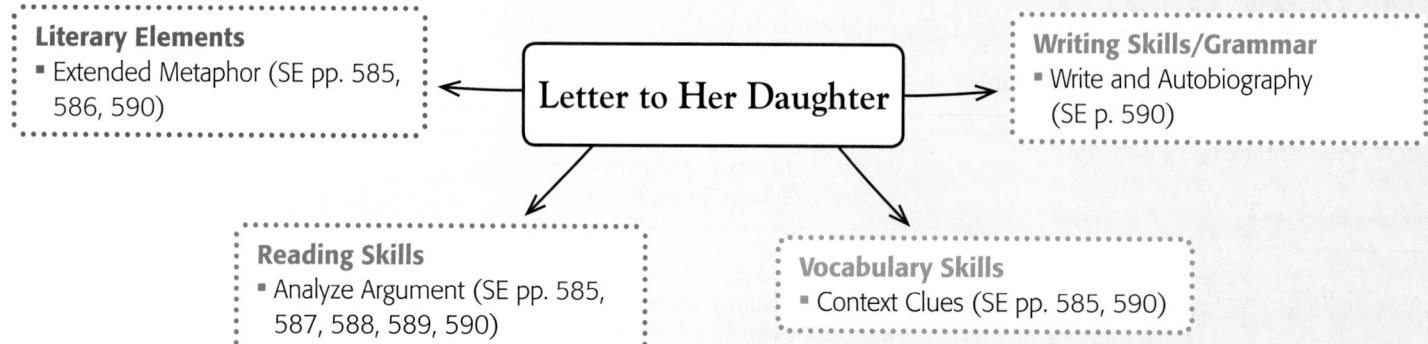

Literary Elements
- Extended Metaphor (SE pp. 585, 586, 590)

Letter to Her Daughter

Writing Skills/Grammar
- Write and Autobiography (SE p. 590)

Reading Skills
- Analyze Argument (SE pp. 585, 587, 588, 589, 590)

Vocabulary Skills
- Context Clues (SE pp. 585, 590)

Literature and Reading Preview

Connect to the Letter

How do letters differ from other forms of communication? Discuss this question with a partner. Consider why a letter might be an especially suitable way to offer advice.

Build Background

During the eighteenth century, writing letters was the primary form of long-distance communication. Lady Montagu's colorful correspondence chronicled everything from her adventures in Turkey to her exploits in Europe. Lady Montagu had been separated from her family for seventeen years when in 1753 she wrote the following letter to her daughter from Italy.

Set Purposes for Reading

Big Idea The English Enlightenment and Neoclassicism

The Enlightenment valued reason as the supreme authority in matters of opinion, belief, and conduct. As you read, ask yourself, What role does reason play in this letter?

Literary Element Extended Metaphor

Metaphors are figures of speech in which two unlike things are compared to show similarities between them. In an **extended metaphor,** two things are compared throughout a paragraph or selection. As you read, ask yourself, How is extended metaphor used by Montagu?

Reading Strategy Analyze Argument

Argument is a type of persuasive writing in which logic or reason is used to try to influence the reader's ideas or actions. As you read, ask yourself, What are Montagu's opinions? What evidence does she use to support them?

Tip: Taking Notes Use a chart like the one below to record Montagu's opinions and reasons.

Opinions	Support
"Your children should be endowed with an uncommon share of good sense."	My family and my husband's have produced several intelligent people.

Learning Objectives

For pages 584–590

In studying this text, you will focus on the following objectives:

Literary Study: Analyzing extended metaphor.

Reading: Analyzing argument.

Writing: Writing an autobiography.

Vocabulary

edifice (ed′ ə fis) *n.* a building, especially a large one; p. 586 *The new apartment complex is an edifice that towers over the neighborhood.*

diversion (di vur′ zhən) *n.* an amusement; an entertainment; p. 587 *We tried to think of diversions to occupy the noisy preschoolers.*

inveterate (in vet′ ə rit) *adj.* firmly established; deep-rooted; p. 588 *Her inveterate love for gossip made her the town busybody.*

elate (i lāt′) *v.* to make happy; p. 589 *Winning the lottery elated that struggling family.*

Tip: Context Clues To figure out the meaning of an unfamiliar word, look for clues in the context, or the surrounding words. For example, consider the phrase "edifices raised that the raisers can never inhabit." The words *raised* and *inhabit* help you figure out the meaning of *edifice* ("a building").

LADY MARY WORTLEY MONTAGU **585**

Before You Read

Focus

Summary

Lady Montagu gives advice about the education of her eldest granddaughter. Lady Montagu warns her daughter to educate the young girl for the life she is most likely to lead—that of an unmarried woman. Montagu envisions such a life as more desirable than most marriages, influenced perhaps by her own unhappy marriage. Montagu outlines the kind of education that would provide contentment for a single woman of her social class.

 For summaries in languages other than English, see Unit 3 Teaching Resources Book, pp. 128–133.

Vocabulary

Create Analogies Explain that verbal analogy expresses a relationship between two pairs of words. The relationship may involve synonyms, antonyms, cause and effect, grammatical function, or something else. **Say:** Identify the relationship of the two pairs of words in this verbal analogy: *Feigned is to false as genuine is to authentic. (Both pairs of words are synonyms.)*

 For additional vocabulary practice, see Unit 3 Teaching Resources Book, p. 137.

English Learners

DIFFERENTIATED INSTRUCTION

Intermediate Explain to students that this selection is a letter, a form of nonfiction. Direct them to create a chart and take notes about Lady Montagu as they read. Ask them to use these headings for their charts:

Her description of people and events

Her actions

How others respond

After completing the reading, have students orally summarize what they have learned.

Vocabulary · 1

Clarify Meaning Have students suggest names of well-known buildings that might be described as edifices.

Literary Element · 2

Extended Metaphor
Answer: *Both parents and builders often draw up beautiful plans for their respective creations but overlook practical considerations.*

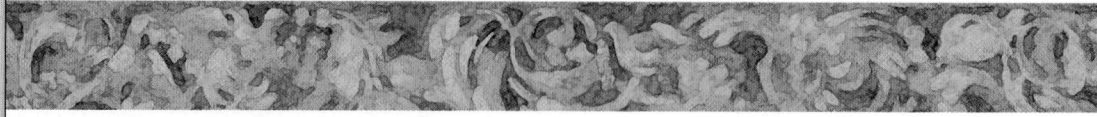

Letter to Her Daughter

Lady Mary Wortley Montagu

January 28, 1753

Dear Child,

You have given me a great deal of satisfaction by your account of your eldest daughter. I am particularly pleased to hear she is a good arithmetician; it is the best proof of understanding. The knowledge of numbers is one of the chief distinctions between us and brutes. If there is anything in blood, you may reasonably expect your children should be endowed with an uncommon share of good sense. Mr. Wortley's family and mine have both produced some of the greatest men that have been born in England. I mean Admiral Sandwich and my great-grandfather who was distinguished by the name of Wise William. I have heard Lord Bute's father mentioned as an extraordinary genius (though he had not many opportunities of showing it), and his uncle the present Duke of Argyle has one of the best heads I ever knew.

I will therefore speak to you as supposing Lady Mary not only capable but desirous of learning. In that case, by all means let her be indulged in it. You will tell me I did not make it a part of your education. Your prospect was very different from hers, as you had no defect either in mind or person to hinder, and much in your circumstances to attract, the highest offers. It seemed your business to learn how to live in the world, as it is hers to know how to be easy out of it. It is the common error of builders and parents to follow some plan they think beautiful (and perhaps is so) without considering that nothing is beautiful that is misplaced. Hence we see so many **edifices** raised that the raisers can never inhabit, being too large for their fortunes. Vistas are laid open over barren heaths, and apartments contrived for a coolness very agreeable in Italy but killing in the north of Britain. Thus

2 Extended Metaphor *How are parents similar to builders?*

Vocabulary

edifice (ed′ ə fis) n. a building, especially a large one

Reading Practice

SPIRAL REVIEW **Evaluate Arguments** Lady Montagu writes with such certainty on some points that some students may find it difficult to distinguish fact from opinion. As students read the selection, have them work in groups to make an outline of Lady Montagu's argument. Once students have finished the outline, instruct them to identify which points are best supported, which are weakest, which are facts, and which are opinions. Once students have finished, have them discuss ways in which Lady Montagu might have strengthened her argument.

every woman endeavors to breed her daughter a fine lady, qualifying her for a station in which she will never appear, and at the same time incapacitating her for that retirement to which she is destined. Learning (if she has a real taste for it) will not only make her contented but happy in it. No entertainment is so cheap as reading, nor any pleasure so lasting. She will not want new fashions nor regret the loss of expensive **diversions** or variety of company [3] if she can be amused with an author in her closet. To render this amusement extensive, she should be permitted to learn the languages. I have heard it lamented[1] that boys lose so many years in mere learning of words. This is no objection to a girl, whose time is not so precious. She cannot advance herself in any profession and has, therefore, more hours to spare; and as you say her memory is good, she will be very agreeably employed this way.

> *True knowledge consists in knowing things, not words.*

There are two cautions to be given on this subject: first, not to think herself learned when she can read Latin or even Greek. Languages are more properly to be called vehicles of learning than learning itself, as may be observed in many schoolmasters, who though perhaps critics in grammar are the most ignorant fellows upon earth. True knowledge consists in knowing things, not words. I would wish her no further a linguist than to enable her to read books in their originals, that are often corrupted and always injured by translations. Two hours' application every morning will bring this about much sooner than you can imagine, and she will have leisure enough besides to run over the English poetry, which is a more important part of a woman's education than it is generally supposed. Many a young damsel has been ruined by a fine copy of verses, which she would have laughed at if she had known it had been stolen from Mr. Waller.[2] I remember when I was a girl, I saved one of my companions from destruction, who communicated to me an epistle[3] she was quite charmed with. As she had a natural good taste, she observed the lines were not so smooth as Prior's or Pope's,[4] but had more thought and spirit than any of theirs. She was wonderfully delighted with such a demonstration of her lover's sense and passion, and not a little pleased with her own charms, that had force enough to inspire such elegancies. In the midst of this triumph,

---

1. *Lamented* means "regretted."
2. *Mr. Waller* was an English poet.
3. An *epistle* is a letter.
4. *Prior* (Matthew Prior) and *Pope* (Alexander Pope) were both English poets.

Analyze Argument Why does Montagu include this detail about schoolmasters? [4]

Vocabulary

diversion (di vur′ zhən) *n.* an amusement; an entertainment

Teach

Reading Strategy   1

Analyze Argument Answer:
The point of this anecdote is that a young woman must be well-read in English poetry in order to protect herself from dishonest suitors.

Reading Strategy   2

Analyze Argument Answer:
This reference to Newton supports Montagu's argument for education. (Newton was Montagu's contemporary.) She says that even though few people can make Newton's mathematical calculations, people with cultivated intellects can understand his results.

I showed her they were taken from Randolph's *Poems,* and the unfortunate transcriber was dismissed with the scorn he deserved. To say truth, the poor plagiary[5] was very unlucky to fall into my hands; that author, being no longer in fashion, would have escaped anyone of less universal reading than myself. You should encourage your daughter to talk over with you what she reads, and as you are very capable of distinguishing, take care she does not mistake pert folly for wit and humor, or rhyme for poetry, which are the common errors of young people, and have a train of ill consequences.

The second caution to be given her (and which is most absolutely necessary) is to conceal whatever learning she attains, with as much solicitude as she would hide crookedness or lameness. The parade of it can only serve to draw on her the envy, and consequently the most **inveterate** hatred of all he and she fools, which will certainly be at least three parts in four of all her acquaintance. The use of knowledge in our sex (beside the amusement of solitude) is to moderate the passions and learn to be contented with a small expense, which are the certain effects of a studious life and, it may be, preferable even to that fame which men have engrossed to themselves and will not suffer us to share. You will tell me I have not observed this rule myself, but you are mistaken; it is only inevitable accident that has given me any reputation that way. I have always carefully avoided it and ever thought it a misfortune.

The explanation of this paragraph would occasion a long digression, which I will not trouble you with, it being my present design only to say what I think useful for the instruction of my granddaughter, which I have much at heart. If she has the same inclination (I should say passion) for learning that I was born with, history, geography, and philosophy will furnish her with materials to pass away cheerfully a longer life than is allotted to mortals. I believe there are few heads capable of making Sir Isaac Newton's calculations, but the result of them is not difficult to be understood by a moderate capacity. Do not fear this should make her affect the character of Lady——— or Lady——— or Mrs.———————. Those women are ridiculous, not because they have learning but because they have it not. One thinks herself a complete historian after reading Echard's *Roman History,*[6] another a profound philosopher having got by heart some of Pope's unintelligible essays, and a third an able divine[7] on the strength of Whitefield's sermons.[8] Thus you hear them screaming politics

---

5. A *plagiary* is one who plagiarizes, or copies another's work and passes it off as one's own.
6. *Roman History* is a work by the English historian Lawrence Echard.
7. A *divine* is a theologian, or student of religion.
8. *Whitefield's sermons* refers to the writings of George Whitefield, a well-known English preacher of the time.

1   Analyze Argument *What is the point of this anecdote?*

2   Analyze Argument *What does this reference to Newton add to the author's argument?*

Vocabulary

inveterate (in vet′ ə rit) *adj.* firmly established; deep-rooted

Writing Practice

SPIRAL REVIEW **Persuasive Techniques** Discuss Montagu's use of persuasive techniques to convince her daughter about the granddaughter's need to conceal her knowledge. Ask students which arguments they find convincing and which they do not. Then have students write a brief essay that relates the situation described in this letter to modern life.

How have relations between the sexes changed since Montagu's day? Are there still situations in which people of both sexes purposely conceal their knowledge? What are they?

and controversy. It is a saying of Thucydides:[9] Ignorance is bold, and knowledge reserved. Indeed, it is impossible to be far advanced in it without being more humbled by a conviction of human ignorance than **elated** by learning. **4**

At the same time I recommend books, I neither exclude work nor drawing. I think it as scandalous for a woman not to know how to use a needle as for a man not to know how to use a sword. I was once extreme fond of my pencil, and it was a great mortification[10] to me when my father turned off my master,[11] having made a considerable progress for the short time I learned. My overeagerness in the pursuit of it had brought a weakness on my eyes that made it necessary to leave it off, and all the advantage I got was the improvement of my hand. I see by hers that practice will make her a ready writer. She may attain it by serving you for a secretary when your health or affairs make it troublesome to you to write yourself, and custom will make it an agreeable amusement to her. She cannot have too many for that station in life which will probably be her fate. The ultimate end of your education was to make you a good wife (and I have the comfort to hear that you are one); hers ought to be to make her happy in a virgin state. I will not say it is happier, but it is undoubtedly safer than any marriage. In a lottery where there is (at the lowest computation) ten thousand blanks to a prize, it is the most prudent choice not to venture.

I have always been so thoroughly persuaded of this truth that notwithstanding the flattering views I had for you (as I never intended you a sacrifice to my vanity) I thought I owed you the justice to lay before you all the hazards attending matrimony. You may recollect I did so in the strongest manner. Perhaps you may have more success in the instructing your daughter. She has so much company at home she will not need seeking it abroad, and will more readily take the notions you think fit to give her. As you were alone in my family, it would have been thought a great cruelty to suffer you no companions of your own age, especially having so many near relations, and I do not wonder their opinions influenced yours. I was not sorry to see you not determined on a single life, knowing it was not your father's intention, and contented myself with endeavoring to make your home so easy that you might not be in haste to leave it.

I am afraid you will think this a very long and insignificant letter. I hope the kindness of the design will excuse it, being willing to give you every proof in my power that I am your most affectionate mother,

M. Wortley

---

9. *Thucydides* was an ancient Greek historian.
10. *Mortification* means "humiliation."
11. *Turned off my master* means "dismissed my tutor."

3 The English Enlightenment and Neoclassicism *What does this reference to Thucydides suggest about the Neoclassical period?*

5 Analyze Argument *Why does Lady Montagu want her granddaughter to be made aware of the drawbacks of marriage?*

LADY MARY WORTLEY MONTAGU **589**

English Learners

DIFFERENTIATED INSTRUCTION

Intermediate Tell students that when Lady Montagu advises that a woman should know how to use a needle, she means more than simple sewing. Upper-class women of the time were expected to know how to embroider and to create decorations for the home using these skills. These women were also encouraged to draw and to play a musical instrument or sing, skills that would be attractive to potential husbands.

At this time, some children of aristocratic families were still educated at home by tutors (private teachers). However, many boys were sent to private boarding schools.

Teach

Big Idea **3**

The English Enlightenment and Neoclassicism Answer: *This reference to Thucydides, an ancient Greek historian, suggests that period's renewed interest in classical authors.*

Vocabulary **4**

Context Clues Say: Find the sentence containing the word elated. What antonym or word with an opposite meaning appears in the sentence? (*humbled*)

Reading Strategy **5**

Analyze Argument Answer: *Lady Montagu believes that her granddaughter should prepare herself to live as a single woman instead of as a wife.*

> To check students' understanding of the selection, see Unit 3 Teaching Resources Book, p. 139.

Progress Check

Can students identify extended metaphor?

If No → See Unit 3 Teaching Resources Book, p. 134.

After You Read

Assess

1. Answers will vary.
2. (a) Montagu is pleased. (b) She believes knowledge of arithmetic is indicative of cognitive ability.
3. (a) "Vehicles of learning" (b) Learning a language is a means to the acquisition of knowledge.
4. (a) Instruction in drawing and sewing (b) Women's education was often limited to those domestic skills.
5. She might have advised that her grandson be similarly educated, with instruction in swordsmanship instead of needlework, but with an emphasis on a university education.
6. Montagu would probably have agreed with Pope. Montagu advocates substantial, not little, learning, especially for an unmarried woman.
7. Montagu's letter values reason and self-improvement over marriage and child-rearing.
8. Answers will vary.

After You Read

Respond and Think Critically

Respond and Interpret

1. What ideas in the letter surprised you? Why?
2. (a) What is Montagu's reaction to the news that her granddaughter is good at arithmetic? (b) What reason does she give for feeling this way?
3. (a) What term does Montagu use to describe Latin and Greek? (b) What might she mean by this?
4. (a) Besides being taught to read, what else does Montagu believe her granddaughter's education should include? (b) What does this tell you about women's education during this period?

Analyze and Evaluate

5. If Montagu were advising on the education of a grandson, in what ways might her advice differ?

6. In your opinion, would Montagu have agreed with Alexander Pope's aphorism "A little learning is a dangerous thing"? Why or why not?

Connect

7. **Big Idea** The English Enlightenment and Neoclassicism The English Enlightenment was a movement that championed reason, science, and self-improvement. How does Montagu's letter reflect the values of that movement?
8. **Connect to Today** Would you like to lead a life like the one Montagu recommends for her granddaughter? Explain.

Literary Element Extended Metaphor

In the second paragraph, Montagu presents an **extended metaphor** in which she points out the error commonly committed by both builders and parents. She presents consequences of this error in terms of building, leaving readers to infer comparable parenting mistakes each one symbolizes.

1. Identify three results of poor planning by builders that Montagu describes.
2. Explain how one of these building problems might relate to parenting.

✍ Writing

Write an Autobiography Imagine that Montagu's daughter took the advice in the letter. Write a short autobiography in the role of Montagu's granddaughter, describing your early years, education, and family relationships.

LOG ON ▶ **Literature** Online

Selection Resources For Selection Quizzes, eFlashcards, and Reading-Writing Connection activities, go to glencoe.com and enter QuickPass code GLB9817u3.

Reading Strategy Analyze Argument

In this letter, Montagu gives advice about her granddaughter's education and voices her opinions about marriage and the life of a single woman.

1. How does Montagu support her opinion that her granddaughter should remain single?
2. How does she justify having prepared her own daughter for marriage?

Vocabulary Practice

Practice with Context Clues Identify context clues that help you determine the meaning of each boldfaced vocabulary word.

1. She lived in an impressive Victorian **edifice** located on a large plot of land.
2. After giving up hope, we were **elated** to find her diamond ring lying in the birdbath.
3. A bird called a magpie, an **inveterate** and practiced thief, had flown off with her ring.
4. The act of thievery was a **diversion** for the bird, but a cause of anxiety for the lady.

Literary Element

1. Examples: buildings too large to inhabit, vistas overlooking desolate lands, and buildings not suited to the climate.
2. Vistas that overlook wastelands are like training girls to be ladies when they may never lead glamorous lives.

Reading Strategy

1. Her granddaughter already has many companions.
2. Her own daughter was alone and did not have any companions her own age.

Vocabulary

1. "lived in"; "impressive"
2. "giving up hope" constrasts *elated*
3. *inveterate* is equivalent to "practiced"
4. "anxiety" contrasts with *diversion*

 Writing

Students should write based on information in the selection.

Vocabulary Workshop

Denotation and Connotation

Literature Connection In her letter to her daughter, Montagu uses words that have similar denotations, or dictionary definitions, but subtly different connotations, or emotional associations.

> "Learning (if she has a real taste for it) will not only make her contented but happy in it."

> —Lady Mary Wortley Montagu, from "Letter to Her Daughter"

Both *happy* and *contented* have positive connotations, but *happy* suggests a more active and highly charged emotional state than does *contented*. In using both words, Montagu expresses her awareness of the distinction.

To compare the connotations of words with similar denotations, try creating a semantic chart like the one below. Here's how:

- Write the words you're comparing in the left-hand column of the chart.
- Find the denotations and connotations of each word in a dictionary or a thesaurus.
- Write the denotations and connotations in the columns at the top of the chart.
- If a word conveys the denotation or connotation recorded at the top of the chart, put a check mark in the corresponding box. If it doesn't, put a zero there. If you're not sure, write a question mark in the space.

	Positive feeling	Fulfillment	Mental approval	Intense emotion	Overwhelming emotion
Contented	✓	✓	✓	0	0
Happy					
Satisfied					
Joyful					
Exuberant					

Practice Follow the instructions to complete each exercise.

1. Complete this semantic chart on a separate sheet of paper. Share your finished chart with your classmates and discuss which words best convey Montagu's feelings about her granddaughter's education.

2. Find three or four similar words used to describe a character in another selection in Unit 3, Part 2. Create a semantic chart for these words. Share and compare charts with your classmates.

Denotation and Connotation

The **denotation** of a word is its literal meaning; its **connotations** are the emotional associations it evokes.

Tip

If you are asked the denotation of a word, think about how you would define the word for someone else. To identify its connotations, think about the images and ideas the word brings to mind.

 Literature Online

Vocabulary For more vocabulary practice, go to glencoe.com and enter QuickPass code GLB9817u3.

English Learners

DIFFERENTIATED INSTRUCTION

 Intermediate Have English learners work in pairs to fill in their semantic charts. Afterwards, have them create sentences that use each word.

Students may want to use a frame such as "I feel _____ when _____" to complete their sentences.

> For additional vocabulary practice, see Glencoe Interactive Vocabulary CD-ROM.

Vocabulary Workshop

Denotation and Connotation

Focus

Point out to students how their choice of words can make an obvious difference in the feelings conveyed. **Ask:** Which word evokes more feeling: won or triumphed? crushed or defeated? *(triumphed/crushed)*

Teach

Positive and Negative Connotations

Say: A word may convey a positive, neutral, or negative feeling.

Write the following words on the board:

glaring   shining   dazzling
conclude   quit
glutted   brimming

Ask: What kind of feeling does each word create? *(Answers will vary.)*

Assess

1. Possible responses:
- *Happy*—positive feeling, fulfillment, mental approval, intense emotion
- *Satisfied*—positive feeling, fulfillment, mental approval
- *Joyful*—positive feeling, intense emotion
- *Exuberant*—positive feeling, overwhelming emotion

Possible answer: *contented, happy,* and *satisfied*

2. Answers will vary, but semantic charts should show that students understand the impact of connotations in conveying precise meaning.

591

Focus

Bellringer Options

Daily Language Practice Transparency 47

Or have students discuss this question: Why was the development of the essay revolutionary as a literary genre? *(As they read, students should consider how essays have brought discussions of human experiences to the masses.)*

Teach

Literary Element | 1

Genre **Remind students:**

A genre is a category or type of literature. Fiction, nonfiction, poetry, and drama are examples of genres.

 For activities related to this selection, see Unit 3 Teaching Resources Book, pp. 141–142.

 For an audio recording of this selection, use Listening Library Audio CD-ROM.

Learning Objectives

For pages 592–593

In studying this text, you will focus on the following objectives:

Literary Study: Analyzing literary genres.

Reading: Evaluating historical influences.

The Essay

AN ESSAY IS A WORK OF PROSE NONFICTION that discusses, formally or informally, any topic. Because of the wide scope and variety of the essay, modern author E. B. White believed the essay to **1** be a misunderstood literary genre, a "second-class citizen" in the world of letters. Yet, the essay in all its forms has remained immensely popular throughout the nearly six centuries since its humble origins.

> *"The essay is a literary device for saying almost everything about almost anything."*
>
> —Aldous Huxley

Michel de Montaigne

Another distinguished contemporary essayist, Joseph Epstein, calls the birth of the personal essay a "happy accident of literature." In 1580 a forty-seven-year-old French lawyer, courtier, country gentleman, and writer named Michel de Montaigne (män tän´) published a volume of short prose works that exhibited his wide interests and learning. Although his early life had been dedicated to public affairs, most of the writings in this collection were short and personal, with unpretentious titles, such as "Of Idleness," "Of Smells and Odors," and "Of Books." To distinguish them from the more methodical, scholarly writings, known as *treatises*, which were common at the time, Montaigne called his works *essais*, a French word for "attempts." By coining this term for his literary musings, Montaigne is generally considered to be the father of the modern essay.

Sir Francis Bacon

In the 1590s, English philosopher and writer

Francis Bacon, only seventeen years younger than Montaigne and clearly familiar with his work, used the term *essay* in the titles of several of his own commentaries on various subjects, such as truth, adversity, and the married versus the single life. Bacon also wrote about both personal and universal topics, but he chose a more formal and objective style than Montaigne's. Bacon wrote essays closer to treatises, which are systematic examinations of scholarly subjects in such areas as philosophy, religion, and science. His essays usually begin with a thesis that is followed by supporting arguments. To support his thesis, Bacon offered extensive **2** quotations from ancient writers, as well as short observations of his own. These concise statements (or aphorisms), which express an observation about human experience, are a hallmark of Bacon's style.

From these beginnings, the essay evolved into two distinct forms: the formal and the informal. Soon other writers were using the term *essay* for compositions in which they expressed their viewpoints on specific topics.

The Formal Essay

A **formal essay** is a prose composition in which an author writes as an impersonal, objective authority on a particular subject, with the purpose of instructing or persuading his or her readers. Using the third-person point of view instead of the first-person, the author strikes a serious tone and develops a main idea, or **thesis**, in a logical, highly organized way. Two eighteenth-century writers, Daniel Defoe and Samuel Johnson, were famous practitioners of the formal essay.

Reading Practice

SPIRAL REVIEW **Reread** Tell students that rereading an article will help them identify the main idea, supporting details, and the author's purpose for writing. Have students list the main idea for each paragraph plus any supporting details. If students have access to a word-processing program on a computer, have them indent each set of supporting details under their corresponding main idea.

Charles Lamb and William Hazlitt continued the formal essay tradition into the nineteenth century, as did Samuel Taylor Coleridge, Thomas De Quincey, Matthew Arnold, and John Stuart Mill. In the twentieth century, the formal essay was a mainstay in such fields as history, literature, and the natural and social sciences. In newspapers today, most editorials and many opinion pieces are formal essays.

The Informal Essay

By contrast, the **informal** or **personal essay** has a lighter tone, is less structured, and typically includes personal details and humor conveyed in a conversational style. Although writers may compose informal essays to instruct or persuade, they often write primarily to entertain their readers. For example, in the eighteenth century, Joseph Addison and Richard Steele wrote and published many instructive yet humorously satirical essays in *The Tatler* and *The Spectator* on such topics as marriage, education, and the folly and extravagance of the times. Nineteenth- and twentieth-century writers, including Robert Louis Stevenson, Max Beerbohm, G. K. Chesterton, Virginia Woolf, and George Orwell, contributed brilliantly to the personal essay form. Their essays address subjects ranging from the important to the trivial, in both cases providing fresh insights on life.

The formal essay has changed little since Bacon. The informal essay, however, has changed greatly. Novelist and essayist Cynthia Ozick thinks that one reason for this change might be the essayist's adaptations of fictional techniques, "including revelations, moments of suspense, moments of climax, moments of crescendo," as well as dialogue and detail. Another reason for the essay's renewed popularity may be the number and variety of forums for the personal essay in both print and electronic media—most recently in a multitude of blogs on the Internet.

Young Ladies' Finishing School. Thomas Rowlandson. Museum of London.

View the Art A finishing school is a school for girls that emphasizes proper social behavior. What is this illustration satirizing?

 Literature Online

Literature and Reading For more about the essay, go to glencoe.com and enter QuickPass code GLB9817u3.

Respond and Think Critically

1. (a) Why is Michel de Montaigne considered to be the father of the modern essay? (b) How do Sir Francis Bacon's essays differ from those of Montaigne?

2. How would you categorize the many essays that you have written for school during the last several years? Are they primarily formal or informal?

3. (a) Name some of the techniques that modern essayists have adapted from fiction. (b) How do these techniques affect your appreciation of essays?

LITERARY HISTORY **593**

Advanced Learners

DIFFERENTIATED INSTRUCTION

The Formal Essay Have students select an inanimate object in the classroom and write a formal essay about it. Tell students that the essay should be impersonal, objective, and persuasive about the object's value. Ask students to exchange their essays and critique each other's papers.

Teach

The Big Idea　2

The English Enlightenment and Neoclassicism Explain to students that neoclassicism dominated English literature from the Restoration in 1660 until the end of the eighteenth century. Neoclassic literature expressed ideals of order, logic, restraint, and accuracy and imitated the art and themes of Greek or Roman originals.

View the Art

Answer: *This illustration is satirizing the effectiveness of training in proper social etiquette. Left to their own devices and unwatched by their teachers, the girls show anything but ladylike deportment.*

Assess

1. (a) He coined the term "essay." (b) The informal essay is often associated with Montaigne; the formal essay is associated with Bacon.

2. Answers will vary. Students may note that primarily they write formal essays.

3. (a) The techniques include "revelations, moments of suspense, moments of climax, moments of crescendo," dialogue and detail. (b) Answers will vary.

Joseph Addison

Sir Richard Steele

Bellringer Options

Selection Focus
  Transparency 29
Daily Language Practice
  Transparency 48
Or ask: If you had the chance to write a newspaper column about modern life, what topics would you choose to write about? Have students discuss this topic with a partner.

Say: As you read, think about what topics interested readers of Addison and Steele's time. What do these topics show about society at that time?

Meet **Joseph Addison**
(1672–1719)

and **Sir Richard Steele**
(1672–1729)

Joseph Addison and Sir Richard Steele were about as opposite as they could be. Addison was serious, reserved, and sensible. Steele was brash, outgoing, and always in debt. Nevertheless, the two formed one of the most successful literary partnerships of all time.

Childhood Friends Addison and Steele, both born in the same year, began a friendship as boys at London's Charterhouse School and continued their friendship at Oxford University. They stayed in contact after impetuous Steele left school without a degree to make a career in the army, while scholarly Addison remained behind to earn a master's degree.

> *"[Bring] philosophy out of the closets and libraries, schools and colleges, to dwell in the clubs and assemblies, at tea-tables and in coffee-houses."*
>
> —The Spectator (March 1711)

Literary Collaboration Their literary collaboration did not begin until the two were in their thirties. By that time, Steele had become disillusioned with the army, achieved some acclaim as a playwright, and served as the primary writer for the London *Gazette*. Addison, meanwhile, had also made a reputation for himself in the literary world and launched a promising diplomatic career. Their partnership began in 1709, when Steele decided to

publish an essay-based periodical he called *The Tatler* and invited his friend Addison to contribute. Steele's purpose was to "expose the false arts of life, to pull off the disguises of cunning, vanity, and affectation, and recommend a general simplicity in our dress, our discourse, and our behavior." *The Tatler* was a hybrid newspaper, literary review, and magazine of philosophical essays. As editor, Steele assumed the sardonic persona of Isaac Bickerstaff, a fictional character created by Jonathan Swift in order to perpetrate a literary hoax.

The Spectator Addison and Steele's collaboration continued in 1711, when Steele discontinued *The Tatler* for political reasons, and they launched a new, nonpolitical, essay-based periodical they called *The Spectator*. The authors succeeded so superbly in their mission "to enliven morality with wit, and to temper wit with morality" that this periodical immediately became a popular favorite. Despite the success of the magazine, the two parted ways in 1712 and later quarreled as a result of a political disagreement.

Although the pair's accomplishments included knighthood for Steele and a position as secretary of state for Addison, the men are best remembered for their essays and brief literary collaboration.

 **Literature** Online

Author Search For more about Joseph Addison and Sir Richard Steele, go to glencoe.com and enter QuickPass code GLB9817u3.

Selection Skills

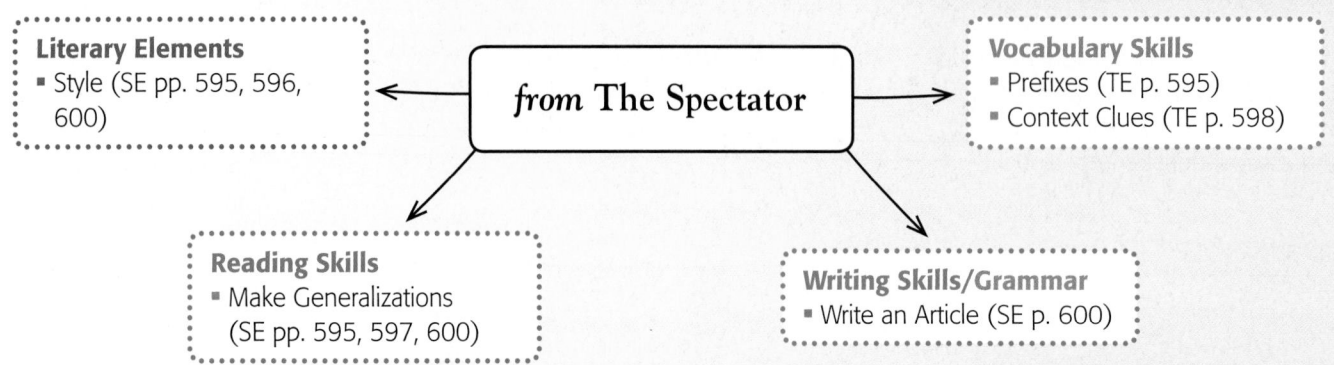

Literary Elements
- Style (SE pp. 595, 596, 600)

from The Spectator

Vocabulary Skills
- Prefixes (TE p. 595)
- Context Clues (TE p. 598)

Reading Skills
- Make Generalizations (SE pp. 595, 597, 600)

Writing Skills/Grammar
- Write an Article (SE p. 600)

Literature and Reading Preview

Connect to the Essays

If you had the chance to write a newspaper column about modern life, what topics would you write about? List several topics that you think are indicative of the qualities of society today.

Build Background

In Addison and Steele's time, Londoners gathered in coffee-shops to gossip and discuss reactions to controversial topics. Many heated conversations were inspired by pieces from *The Spectator*. As a result, the essays of Addison and Steele had an influence on the manners and culture of the time.

Addison and Steele are credited with having invented the **periodical essay**, an informal essay that appears in a periodical publication, such as a magazine or newspaper.

Set Purposes for Reading

Big Idea The English Enlightenment and Neoclassicism

As you read, ask yourself, How did the Enlightenment emphasis on reason motivate writers to satirize irrational behavior?

Literary Element Style

Style is a writer's characteristic way of writing. An author creates a unique style through expressive qualities that distinguish his or her work, including word choice and figures of speech. As you read, ask yourself, What features of the essays create a distinctive style?

Reading Strategy Make Generalizations

When you draw conclusions about a text based on specific examples or ideas, you are **making generalizations**. A generalization is an observation that may relate universal themes and ideas to a text. As you read, ask yourself, What is the author suggesting about the characters or about life in general?

....

Tip: Taking Notes Make generalizations by drawing conclusions from specific examples, ideas, or anecdotes in the text.

Text Reference	Generalization

JOSEPH ADDISON AND SIR RICHARD STEELE **595**

Learning Objectives

For pages 594–600

In studying this text, you will focus on the following objectives:

Literary Study: Analyzing style.

Reading: Making generalizations.

Writing: Writing an article.

Vocabulary

complaisance (kəm plā′ səns) *n.* a willingness to please, be gracious, or be courteous; p. 598 *The complaisance of the hotel manager made our stay comfortable and enjoyable.*

negligence (neg′ li jəns) *n.* an air of careless ease or casualness; p. 598 *His negligence in doing his job caused his dismissal.*

irrational (i rash′ ən əl) *adj.* lacking reason; ill-advised; p. 599 *The defense lawyer proved that the prosecutor's argument was irrational.*

Before You Read

Focus

Summary

These two periodical essays illustrate the collaboration of Addison and Steele. The two invented a fictitious "Spectator's Club" that had seven members. The featured member of the club was the gentleman Sir Roger de Coverley, whom Steele describes in the first essay in the selection. Steele lampoons the country gentleman in his humorous description. In the second essay, Addison makes fun of the manners, fashions, and pretensions of both city and country people in his time.

 For summaries in languages other than English, see Unit 3 Teaching Resources Book, pp. 143–148.

Vocabulary

Prefixes Tell students that the prefix in- before a word means "not" as in insincere, and indefinite. However, before words beginning with l, m, and r, the prefix changes. So, "not legal" is "illegal," "not movable" is "immovable," and "not rational" is "irrational." **Say:** Name three other words which use the prefixes *il-, im-* or *ir-* to mean "not." *(illegible, immeasurable, irregular)*

 For additional vocabulary practice, see Unit 3 Teaching Resources Book, p. 151.

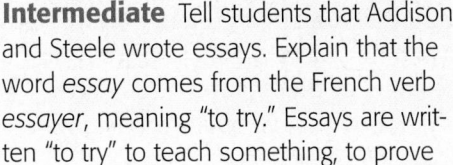

Sir Roger de Coverley and Addison with "The Saracen's Head", a scene from "The Spectator", 1867. William Powell Frith. Oil on canvas, 38.1 x 45.7 cm. Guildhall Art Gallery, Corporation of London, UK.

from The Spectator

Sir Richard Steele ☆

Sir Roger de Coverley

Friday, March 2, 1711

The first of our society is a gentleman of Worcestershire, of ancient descent, a baronet, his name Sir Roger de Coverley. His great-grandfather was inventor of that famous country-dance[1] which is called after him. All who know that shire[2] are very well acquainted with the parts and merits of Sir Roger. He is a gentleman that is very singular in his behavior, but his singularities[3] proceed from his good sense and are contradictions to the manners of the world only as he thinks the world is in the wrong. However, this humor creates him no enemies, for he does nothing with sourness or obstinacy; and his being unconfined to modes and forms makes him but the readier and more capable to please and oblige all who know him. When he is in town, he lives in Soho Square.[4] It is said he keeps hisself a bachelor by reason he was crossed in love by a perverse,[5] beautiful widow of the next county to him. Before this disappointment, Sir Roger was what you call a fine gentleman, had often supped with my Lord Rochester and Sir George Etherege,[6] fought a duel upon his first coming to town, and kicked Bully Dawson[7] in a public coffeehouse for calling him "youngster." But being ill used by the

---

1. *That famous country-dance* is a dance called the Roger of Coverley, dating from 1685.
2. A *shire* is a county.
3. *Singularities* are unique or peculiar features.
4. *Soho Square* is a fashionable district in the center of London.
5. Here, *perverse* means "willfully determined; contrary."
6. *Lord Rochester* and *Sir George Etherege* are John Wilmot, Earl of Rochester, a notorious Restoration poet, and Sir George Etherege, a playwright.
7. *Bully Dawson* was a notorious swindler.

1 The English Enlightenment and Neoclassicism *What Enlightenment value is attributed to Sir Roger in this passage?*

2 Style *What aspect of Steele's style indicates that he is satirizing the conventional notions of an English gentleman?*

Reading Practice

SPIRAL REVIEW 🌀 **Make Inferences About Character** The author presents clues to Roger de Coverley's character that may be difficult for modern readers to understand. **Ask:** What can you infer about the stereotypical behavior of a "fine gentleman" of the time? *(A fine gentleman dines with writers and defends his honor by fighting duels and beating up scoundrels.)*

Ask: What is the author revealing about Sir Roger's attitudes toward class when he points out that he "calls the servants by their names"? *(Sir Roger is gracious and not above chatting with those who rank beneath him socially.)*

above-mentioned widow, he was very serious for a year and a half; and though, his temper being naturally jovial, he at last got over it, he grew careless of himself and never dressed afterwards. He continues to wear a coat and doublet of the same cut that were in fashion at the time of his repulse,[8] which, in his merry humors, he tells us, has been in and out[9] twelve times since he first wore it. . . . He is now in his fifty-sixth year, cheerful, gay, and hearty; keeps a good house both in town and country; a great lover of mankind; but there is such a mirthful cast in his behavior that he is rather beloved than esteemed. His tenants grow rich, his servants look satisfied, all the young women profess love to him, and the young men are glad of his company; when he comes into a house, he calls the servants by their names and talks all the way upstairs to a visit. I must not omit that Sir Roger is a justice of the quorum;[10] that he fills the chair at a quarter-session[11] with great abilities; and three months ago gained universal applause by explaining a passage in the Game Act.[12]

---

8. *Repulse* means "rejection," referring to his rejection by the widow.
9. When Steele writes *in and out,* he means "in and out of fashion."
10. *A justice of the quorum* is a justice of the peace.
11. In a county court, a meeting held four times a year is called a *quarter-session.*
12. The *Game Act* was a law governing hunting.

Make Generalizations *What generalization can you make about Sir Roger from this statement?* **3**

 Coffee-House in Salisbury Market-Place.

Customers in the coffee house in Salisbury market-place. Thomas Rowlandson. Reproduced in *The Graphic,* Christmas number. 1891.

View the Art In Addison and Steele's day, coffeehouses were centers of intellectual and social activity. What mood does this artwork convey? What details help to create that mood?

SIR RICHARD STEELE **597**

Teach

Vocabulary 1

Context Clues Have students locate context clues that describe what "negligent" behavior of the time was like. *(an unconstrained carriage and a certain openness of behavior, free and easy manner)*

Reading Strategy 2

Make Generalizations

Answer: *Addison points out an ironic reversal between city and country manners. Formerly, "good breeding," or the observance of elaborate social conventions, was a characteristic of people living in courts and cities, while country people acted "bluntly and naturally." These social rituals, however, became too troublesome for city dwellers and were rejected in favor of "an agreeable negligence." Country people, in an effort to emulate the refined manners of the city, aped the social conventions of urban life only to find that good breeding was now out of fashion in the cities.*

Literary Element 3

Style Answer: *By using personal pronouns to inject his opinions and relate anecdotes about himself, Addison is demonstrating one of the defining characteristics of the informal journalistic essay.*

Country Manners Joseph Addison

Tuesday, July 17, 1711

The first and most obvious reflections which arise in a man who changes the city for the country are upon the different manners of the people whom he meets with in those two different scenes of life. By manners, I do not mean morals, but behavior and good breeding, as they show themselves in the town and in the country. And here, in the first place, I must observe a very great revolution that has happened in this article of good breeding. Several obliging deferences, condescensions, and submissions, with many outward forms and ceremonies that accompany them, were first of all brought up among the politer part of mankind, who lived in courts and cities and distinguished themselves from the rustic part of the species (who on all occasions acted bluntly and naturally) by such a mutual **complaisance** and intercourse of civilities. These forms of conversation by degrees multiplied and grew troublesome; the modish[1] world found too great a constraint in them and have, therefore, thrown most of them aside. Conversation, like the Romish religion,[2] was so encumbered with show and ceremony that it stood in need of a reformation to retrench its superfluities and restore it to its natural good sense and beauty. At present, therefore, an unconstrained carriage and a certain openness of behavior are the height of good breeding. The fashionable world is grown free and easy; our manners sit more loose upon us; nothing is so modish as an agreeable **negligence.** In a word, good breeding shows itself most where to an ordinary eye it appears the least.

---

1. *Modish* means "stylish" or "fashionable."
2. The *Romish religion* is Roman Catholicism.

Vocabulary

complaisance (kəm plā′ səns) *n.* a willingness to please, be gracious, or be courteous

negligence (neg′ li jəns) *n.* an air of careless ease or casualness

If after this we look on the people of mode in the country, we find in them the manners of the last age. They have no sooner fetched themselves up to the fashion of the polite world but the town has dropped them and are nearer to the first state of nature than to those refinements which formerly reigned in the court and still prevail in the country. One may now know a man that never conversed in the world by his excess of good breeding. A polite country squire[3] shall make you as many bows in half an hour as would serve a courtier[4] for a week. There is infinitely more to do about place and precedence in a meeting of justices' wives than in an assembly of duchesses.

This rural politeness is very troublesome to a man of my temper, who generally takes the chair that is next me and walks first or last, in the front or in the rear, as chance directs. I have known my friend Sir Roger's dinner almost cold before the company could adjust the ceremonial and be prevailed upon to sit down; and have heartily pitied my old friend when I have seen him forced to pick and cull[5] his guests, as they sat at the several parts of his table, that he might drink their healths according to their respective ranks and qualities. Honest Will Wimble, who I should have thought had been altogether uninfected with ceremony, gives me abundance of trouble in this particular. Though he has been fishing all the morning, he will not help himself at dinner till I am served. When we are going out of the hall, he runs behind me; and last night, as we

---

3. A *squire* is a gentleman and landowner.
4. A *courtier* is an attendant at a royal court.
5. *Cull* means "choose."

Make Generalizations *Based on Addison's analysis, what generalizations can you make about the difference between city manners and country manners?* 2

Style *What effect does Addison's use of personal pronouns, such as* my *and* me, *have on this essay?* 3

Writing Practice

Identify Author's Purpose

SPIRAL REVIEW Remind students that Addison and Steele's essays commented on life in the 18th century. Have students state the essay's main point. *(Country people are behind the times compared to city people)* Ask students to identify the three points of good breeding to which Addison refers in his essay. *(behavior, conversation, dress)* Under each of these points, have students write a paragraph to describing action from the text that is considered behind the times.

Visual Vocabulary
A *stile* is a set of steps for passing over a fence.

were walking in the fields, stopped short at a stile till I came up to it and, upon my making signs to him to get over, told me, with a serious smile, that sure I believed they had no manners in the country.

There has happened another revolution in the point of good breeding, which relates to the conversation among men of mode and which I cannot but look upon as very extraordinary. It was certainly one of the first distinctions of a well-bred man to express everything that had the most remote appearance of being obscene in modest terms and distant phrases; whilst the clown, who had no such delicacy of conception and expression, clothed his ideas in those plain homely terms that are the most obvious and natural. This kind of good manners was perhaps carried to an excess, so as to make conversation too stiff, formal, and precise; for which reason (as hypocrisy in one age is generally succeeded by atheism in another) conversation is in a great measure relapsed into the first extreme; so that at present several of our men of the town, and particularly those who have been polished in France, make use of the most coarse, uncivilized words in our language and utter themselves often in such a manner as a clown would blush to hear.

This infamous piece of good breeding, which reigns among the coxcombs[6] of the town, has not yet made its way into the country; and as it is impossible for such an **irrational** way of

6. *Coxcombs* are vain, foolish people.

Vocabulary
irrational (i rash′ ən əl) *adj.* lacking reason; ill-advised

Lloyd's Coffee House, London, 1798. William Holland. Intaglio print.

conversation to last long among a people that make any profession of religion or show of modesty, if the country gentlemen get into it, they will certainly be left in the lurch. Their good breeding will come too late to them, and they will be thought a parcel of lewd clowns, while they fancy themselves talking together like men of wit and pleasure.

As the two points of good breeding which I have hitherto insisted upon regard behavior and conversation, there is a third which turns upon dress. In this too the country are very much behindhand. The rural beaus are not yet got out of the fashion that took place at the time of the Revolution[7] but ride about the country in red coats and laced hats, while the women in many parts are still trying to outvie one another in the height of their headdresses.

But a friend of mine who is now upon the western circuit, having promised to give me an account of the several modes and fashions that prevail in the different parts of the nation through which he passes, I shall defer the enlarging upon this last topic till I have received a letter from him, which I expect every post.

7. *Revolution* refers to the Glorious Revolution of 1688, in which William III and Mary II took the throne of England from King James II without any bloodshed.

Make Generalizations *What is Addison both explaining and predicting in this sentence?* **4**

Teach

| **Reading Strategy** | **4** |

Make Generalizations
Answer: *Addison is explaining a current trend among fashionable city dwellers, which is to speak using coarse, uncivilized language. Addison's prediction is that country gentlemen will follow this trend too late; as a result, they will be perceived by fashionable people from the city as being lewd and foolish.*

ADVANCED Discuss the humor of this reversal by focusing on three elements of Addison's style: heightened language, parenthetical expressions (*"as hypocrisy in one age is generally succeeded by atheism in another"*), and allusions (*the French*).

To check students' understanding of the selection, see Unit 3 Teaching Resources Book, p. 153.

Approaching Level

DIFFERENTIATED INSTRUCTION

Established Because of the language, students may have difficulty understanding the main idea of the essay; namely, that problems arise when country people try to act as they think cultured city people do. Have students reread paragraph three and make two columns—one listing the good manners at dinner (*arranging seating,* *drinking to the health of all there*) and the other listing problems with these actions (*meal gets cold, people are hungry*).

After You Read

Assess

1. Students' answers may vary.
2. (a) Sir Roger was "crossed in love." (b) He no longer cares about his appearance and remains a bachelor.
3. (a) In the city, good manners are considered to be too much trouble. In the country, people imitate good manners because they are perceived as fashionable. (b) Addison is troubled by its artificiality and insincerity.
4. Steele has written a satire on the shallowness of the conventions of the English gentleman, and he portrays Sir Roger as a caricature.
5. (a) It ridicules the manners of city dwellers and country folk. (b) City dwellers are lazy and crude, while country folk are pretentious and vain.
6. Students' answers should be supported by examples.
7. Students should specify examples of humor from the essay.

Literary Element

1. Addison and Steele use humor and satire, anecdote, vivid diction, and a conversational tone.
2. Addison is making a humorous appeal to his readers, most of whom would have scorned ostentatious ceremonies.

Progress Check

Can students analyze style?

If No → See Unit 3 Teaching Resources Book, p. 149.

After You Read

Respond and Think Critically

Respond and Interpret

1. What are your impressions of Sir Roger de Coverley and the country folk?
2. (a)What disappointment did Sir Roger suffer? (b)How has it affected him?
3. (a)How does Addison describe polite behavior in the country versus in the city? (b) Why is he troubled by the "rural politeness" he sees?

Analyze and Evaluate

4. In what ways is the description of Sir Roger meant to be a **caricature**, or exaggeration, of certain individual qualities for ridiculous effect?

Literary Element Style

Although Addison and Steele's eighteenth-century English may occasionally seem long-winded to modern readers, it was an elegant and familiar **style** that was popular in its day.

1. What elements of style do the authors use to create a sense of informality in their essays?
2. In "Country Manners," what is the effect of Addison's analogy between "Romish religion" and polite converstation?

Writing

Write an Article Think about aspects of modern life, such as fashion, types of music, or lifestyles. Choose one as a topic for a contribution to a present-day version of *The Spectator*. Adopt the style used by Addison and Steele. You may wish to submit your article to your school paper.

LOG ON ▶ **Literature** Online

Selection Resources For Selection Quizzes, eFlashcards, and Reading-Writing Connection activities, go to glencoe.com and enter QuickPass code GLB9817u3.

5. (a)How is "Country Manners" a satire? (b)What do Addison's observations suggest about his opinion of city dwellers and country folk?

Connect

6. **Big Idea** The English Enlightenment and Neoclassicism The Enlightenment was an age of satire when human follies were ridiculed. Is satire a popular literary form today? Explain.
7. **Connect to the Authors** In what ways do these essays succeed in fulfilling Addison and Steele's mission "to enliven morality with wit"?

Reading Strategy Make Generalizations

When you make generalizations about essays, such as excerpts from *The Spectator*, you must support the generalizations with evidence from the text.

Partner Activity With a partner, discuss your reading of "Sir Roger de Coverley." What generalization can you make about Steele's attitude toward class distinctions in eighteenth-century society?

Vocabulary Practice

Practice with Antonyms Antonyms are words with opposite meanings. Work with a partner to match each boldfaced vocabulary word below with an antonym. You will not use all the answer choices. Use a thesaurus or dictionary to check your answers.

1. complaisance
2. negligence
3. irrational

a. logical
b. rashness
c. rudeness
d. diligence
e. stoicism

Writing

Students' articles should focus on specific interest and imitate the style of Addison and Steele.

> To create custom assessments using software, use ExamView Assessment Suite.

Reading Strategy

Steele disapproved of the pretensions of the upper class and would have probably favored a more democratic society.

Vocabulary

1. c 2. d 3. a

600

Comparing Literature

Across Time and Place

Compare Literature About Epidemics

Pandemics, or epidemics that affect multiple countries, have changed the course of civilization. Although modern vaccines have saved innumerable lives from diseases such as smallpox and bubonic plague, new threats such as the avian (bird) flu are raising alarms across the world. Could a catastrophe on the scale of the influenza epidemic of 1918–1919, which killed twenty-five million people, happen again?

from *A Journal of the Plague Year*

from *History of the Peloponnesian War*

from *The Plague*

COMPARE THE [Big Idea] **The English Enlightenment and Neoclassicism**

In the 1700s, the works of such writers as Defoe often showed how the past repeats itself, sometimes unexpectedly. As you read, ask yourself, How do the works by Defoe, Thucydides, and Camus show the importance of learning from history and the attempt to find order in chaos?

COMPARE Style

Style expresses both a writer's personality and a certain way of seeing the world. As you read, ask yourself, How does the style of these selections contribute to the writers' messages?

COMPARE Cultures

The tragedies that strike various cultures often serve as warnings for future generations and as lessons to remind people of the precarious nature of life. As you read, ask yourself, What lessons about life can be learned by the warnings in the following three selections?

 Literature Online

Author Search For more about Daniel Defoe, Thucydides, and Albert Camus, go to glencoe.com and enter QuickPass code GLB9817u3.

COMPARING LITERATURE **601**

Focus

Bellringer Options

Daily Language Practice Transparency 49

Or have students gather data on the infection and mortality rates of AIDS in the United States and Africa over the past ten years. Discuss how the disease has affected societies in both places.

Connect to the Reading Selections

The paragraph at the top of the page ends with a question. Solicit responses to the question from students. **Ask:** How different is today's world from the world of 1918? How would these differences affect the possibility of a pandemic?

Selection Skills

Literary Elements
- Historical Fiction (SE pp. 603, 606, 607, 608)
- Style (SE p. 617)

Reading Skills
- Connect to Contemporary Issues (SE pp. 603–605, 607, 608)
- Infer (TE p. 604)

Vocabulary
- Word Parts (SE pp. 603, 608)
- Analogies (TE p. 603)

Comparing Literature

Listening/Speaking/Viewing Skills
- Analyze Art (SE p. 604)
- Report on Culture (SE p. 617)

Writing Skills/Grammar
- Movie Scene (SE p. 608)
- Transitive and Intransitive Verbs (TE p. 612)

Learning Objectives

For pages 601–617

In studying these texts, you will focus on the following objectives:

Literary Study: Analyzing historical fiction.

Reading: Comparing historical context. Connecting to contemporary issues.

Writing: Writing a movie scene.

Before You Read

Focus

Summary

Defoe's narrator describes a huge pit dug in the local churchyard and a nighttime visit to the churchyard to watch scores of dead bodies being dumped into the pit. There he sees a man walking around seemingly in a daze. It turns out that the man's wife and children had all been among the dead dumped into the pit. The man faints, and the gravediggers take him to his friends so they can help him.

 For summaries in languages other than English, see Unit 3 Teaching Resources Book, pp. 155–161.

Before You Read

from *A Journal of the Plague Year*

Meet **Daniel Defoe**
(1660–1731)

Spy, satirist, journalist, merchant, and writer, Daniel Defoe bounced back and forth between bankruptcy and prosperity, prison and political favor, throughout his life. Even in his dimmest moments, he was known to keep his sense of humor. Once, as a punishment for publishing a controversial pamphlet, he was sentenced to the pillory, a wooden device used for public punishment that locked the prisoner's head and hands. For the occasion, Defoe composed and distributed a poem, "Hymn to the Pillory"—a mock-Pindaric ode that inspired audience members to decorate the pillory with flowers.

> "The best of men cannot suspend their fate:
> The good die early, and the bad die late."
>
> —Daniel Defoe

Early Schemes As the son of a Protestant Dissenter (someone who defied the Church of England), Defoe attended the Reverend Charles Morton's academy for Dissenters at Newington Green, where he developed his clear writing style. Trade and commerce fascinated Defoe, leading him to abandon his plans for the ministry to become a merchant instead. Unfortunately, Defoe's various enterprises all failed. At age twenty-five, he joined a rebellion against the Roman Catholic King James II in which six hundred rebels died, but Defoe escaped. Three years later, the king fled to France, and Defoe became the leading pamphleteer and political informant for rotestant King William III. Despite his royal connections, however, Defoe's troubles continued. He wrote a satire, *The Shortest Way with the Dissenters*, which was intended to ridicule the suppression of dissent. However, both Anglicans and Dissenters missed the point. Defoe was later jailed, but he was soon released by the Earl of Oxford, Robert Harley, for whom Defoe became a spy.

Literary Breakthrough Defoe's breakthrough work wasn't published until he was sixty—the first part of *The Life and Adventures of Robinson Crusoe*. Defoe presented this fictional work as a memoir; it is loosely based on the real-life adventures of Alexander Selkirk, a Scottish sailor who was marooned on one of the Juan Fernández Islands, off the coast of Chile, and lived there alone from October 1704 to February 1709.

Defoe again applied his journalistic method to fiction when, in 1721, reports reached London of a plague outbreak in continental Europe. His work *A Journal of the Plague Year* was presented as a first-hand account of the Great Plague of the Middle Ages. Literary critic Maximillian E. Novak points out that "Defoe never forgot that history was something that happened to masses of people, not just to Kings and Queens."

Reading Practice

SPIRAL REVIEW **Preview** Tell students that they can often identify the structure of a piece of writing by skimming a page. **Ask:** What subheadings might help you identify the structure? *(the* headings *Early Schemes* and *Literary Breakthrough)* **Ask:** What might you predict the organizational structure of this piece to be? *(chronological order)*

Literature and Reading Preview

Connect to the Story

How might you respond to witnessing a major disaster, such as a hurricane? With a partner, discuss how such an experience might affect you, both at the time and throughout your life.

Build Background

The bubonic plague first appeared in Europe in 1347. By 1351 it had killed twenty-five million people. It became known as the Black Death. Scientists now know that the plague is caused by a bacterium called *Yersinia pestis*, which is spread by fleas. Vaccines and antibiotics now combat any further outbreaks.

Set Purposes for Reading

Big Idea The English Enlightenment and Neoclassicism

As you read, ask yourself, How does Defoe's portrayal of a past outbreak of the plague fit into the concerns associated with the English Enlightenment and Neoclassicism?

Literary Element Historical Fiction

Historical fiction sets characters against the backdrop of a period other than the author's own. This type of fiction often blends actual historical people with fictitious ones and realistic details with symbolic ones. As you read, ask yourself, How is the fictional narrative grounded in history?

Reading Strategy Connect to Contemporary Issues

Connecting details from literature with those from current events can help you further understand what you read. As you read, ask yourself, How does the emergence of viruses today, such as Ebola and avian (bird) flu, relate to Defoe's narrative about the plague?

·······

Tip: Making Connections Identify things from your experience or things you've read that link to the Defoe excerpt.

Detail in selection	Detail from my experience	Connection

Vocabulary

confining (kən′ fīn ing) *adj.* restricting; limiting; p. 605 *The confining nature of the assignment frustrated Juan.*

oppressed (ə prest′) *adj.* burdened; weighed down; p. 606 *Jim felt oppressed with sadness after his cousin's funeral.*

defy (di fī′) *v.* to resist; refuse to cooperate with; p. 606 *Mrs. Johnson warned Betty not to defy her authority in the classroom.*

prodigious (prə dij′ əs) *adj.* great in size, number, or degree; enormous; p. 607 *The prodigious accomplishments of the Elizabethan theater were a testament to the importance that Queen Elizabeth I placed on drama.*

·······

Tip: Word Parts Breaking down unfamiliar words into prefixes, roots, and suffixes can help you understand the words. For example, the word *credible*, meaning "believable," consists of the root *cred* ("believe") and the suffix *-ible* ("able to be").

DANIEL DEFOE **603**

Before You Read

Focus

Vocabulary

Have students work in pairs to write four sentences in which the vocabulary words are used correctly in analogies. Then ask pairs to trade with other pairs to read and check their analogies for correct use of vocabulary and analogy.

 For additional vocabulary practice, see Unit 3 Teaching Resources Book, p. 164.

 For additional context, see Glencoe Interactive Vocabulary CD-ROM.

Approaching Level

DIFFERENTIATED INSTRUCTION

Established Ask: What are semicolons used for? *(to connect two or more independent clauses)* Tell students that writers in Defoe's time often used a large number of semicolons. A whole paragraph might consist of one sentence made up of several independent clauses joined by semicolons. Tell students they might find it easier to read the selection if they think of the semicolons as periods—which is what they would be if Defoe were writing today.

Comparing Literature

Teach

Reading Strategy   1

Connect to Contemporary Issues Answer: *Students may discuss the media's coverage of disasters, such as hurricanes, and public health concerns, such as the potential outbreak of a virus.*

View the Art ★

Possible answers: *The flying horse might represent the swiftness of infection, the scythe might represent death, and the army behind the horseman might represent the spread of disease.*

 For an audio recording of this selection, use Listening Library Audio CD-ROM.

Readability Scores

Dale-Chall: 14.5
DRP: 61
Lexile: 1460

---

from
A Journal of the Plague Year

☆ Daniel Defoe

Death on a Pale Horse, 1867. Gustave Doré. Illustration.

View the Art This image is an illustration of "Plague," one of the four horsemen of the Apocalypse mentioned in the book of Revelation in the Christian Bible. What qualities of a plague might the details in this picture represent? ★

1 went all the first part of the time freely about the streets, though not so freely as to run myself into apparent danger, except when they dug the great pit in the churchyard of our parish[1] of Aldgate. A terrible pit it was, and I could not resist my curiosity to go and see it. As near as I may judge, it was about forty feet in length, and about fifteen or sixteen feet broad, and at the time I first looked at it, about nine feet deep; but it was said they dug it near twenty feet deep afterwards in one part of it, till they could go no deeper for the water; for they had, it seems, dug several large pits before this. For though the plague was long a-coming to our parish, yet, when it did come, there was no parish in or about London where it raged with such violence as in the two parishes of Aldgate and Whitechapel.

I say they had dug several pits in another ground, when the distemper[2] began to spread in our parish, and especially when the dead

---

1. In England, a *parish* is a subdivision of a county.

1 Connecting to Contemporary Issues *How is this tendency shown in contemporary society?*

2. *Distemper* is a disease—in this case, the plague.

Reading Practice

SPIRAL REVIEW **Infer** Remind students that until the late 1800s, no one knew that germs cause disease. **Ask:** If the magistrates did not know that germs from infected bodies could spread the disease to healthy people, why would they insist that all bodies had to be buried at least six feet underground? *(People would realize that those who came into contact with sick or dead people often became sick themselves, while those who did not often remained healthy. People could tell that the disease spread without knowing how it spread.)*

carts began to go about, which was not, in our parish, till the beginning of August. Into these pits they had put perhaps fifty or sixty bodies each; then they made larger holes, wherein they buried all that the cart brought in a week, which, by the middle to the end of August, came to from two hundred to four hundred a week; and they could not well dig them larger, because of the order of the magistrates[3] **confining** them to leave no bodies within six feet of the surface; and the water coming on at about seventeen or eighteen feet, they could not well, I say, put more in one pit. But now, at the beginning of September, the plague raging in a dreadful manner, and the number of burials in our parish increasing to more than was ever buried in any parish about London of no larger extent, they ordered this dreadful gulf to be dug, for such it was, rather than a pit.

They had supposed this pit would have supplied them for a month or more when they dug it, and some blamed the churchwardens for suffering[4] such a frightful thing, telling them they were making preparations to bury the whole parish, and the like; but time made it appear the churchwardens knew the condition of the parish better than they did, for, the pit being finished the fourth of September, I think, they began to bury in it the sixth, and by the twentieth, which was just two weeks, they had thrown into it 1,114 bodies when they were obliged to fill it up, the bodies being then come to lie within six feet of the surface. I doubt not but there may be some ancient persons alive in the parish who can justify[5] the fact of this

---

3. *Magistrates* are officers empowered to administer laws.
4. As used here, *suffering* means "permitting."
5. *Justify* means "verify."

2 The English Enlightenment and Neoclassicism *How does the narrator's comment in this sentence link to the intellectual movements of Defoe's time?*

Vocabulary

confining (kən fīn´ ing) *adj.* restricting; limiting

and are able to show even in what place of the churchyard the pit lay better than I can. The mark of it also was many years to be seen in the churchyard on the surface, lying in length parallel with the passage which goes by the west wall of the churchyard out of Houndsditch, and turns east again into Whitechapel, coming out near the Three Nuns' Inn.

It was about the tenth of September that my curiosity led, or rather drove, me to go and see this pit again, when there had been near four hundred people buried in it; and I was not content to see it in the daytime, as I had done before, for then there would have been nothing to have been seen but the loose earth; for all the bodies that were thrown in were immediately covered with earth by those they called the buriers, which at other times were called bearers; but I resolved to go in the night and see some of them thrown in.

There was a strict order to prevent people coming to those pits, and that was only to prevent infection. But after some time that order was more necessary, for people that were infected and near their end, and delirious also, would run to those pits, wrapped in blankets or rugs, and throw themselves in, and, as they said, bury themselves. I cannot say that the officers suffered any willingly to lie there; but I have heard that in a great pit in Finsbury, in the parish of Cripplegate, it lying open then to the fields, for it was not then walled about, [people] came and threw themselves in, and expired there, before they threw any earth upon them; and that when they came to bury others and found them there, they were quite dead, though not cold.

This may serve a little to describe the dreadful condition of that day, though it is impossible to say anything that is able to give a true idea

---

Connect to Contemporary Issues *What public health concerns today warrant restricted access to certain places or even quarantining?* **3**

Advanced Learners

DIFFERENTIATED INSTRUCTION

Words of Numbers In order to make his account seem more like nonfiction, Defoe includes several statistical details. Have students look through the selection for numbers—expressed as numerals or in words—such as the size of the pit, the number of bodies, the number of days

that had passed, and so on. Have students determine what calculations the leaders of Aldgate or Whitechapel might have had to consider as the plague approached. Have them express these calculations as word problems.

Teach

Big Idea | **2**

The English Enlightenment and Neoclassicism Answer: *Thinkers and writers of Defoe's time were deeply interested in finding order and reason in life. By offering a way to verify facts, Defoe encourages readers to seek proof of the truth independently, much as a scientist would.*

Reading Strategy | **3**

Connect to Contemporary Issues Answer: *Students may discuss SARS, the Ebola virus, avian (bird) flu, or other public health concerns.*

Literary History ☆

Style The Canadian writer Robertson Davies (1913–1995) once said, "I used to tell young reporters that if they wanted to learn to write magnificent newspaper English, they should learn to write like Daniel Defoe." Students may wish to obtain copies of other writings from the same period, such as *Pamela (Pamela: Or Virtue Rewarded)* by Samuel Richardson (1741) or *Tom Jones (The History of Tom Jones, a Foundling)* by Henry Fielding (1749). They can read a page or two and compare the flowery language, long sentences, and frequent digressions with Defoe's straightforward writing in *A Journal of the Plague Year.*

Teach

Big Idea 1

The English Enlightenment and Neoclassicism

Answer: *The sexton tells the narrator that he should have a better reason than curiosity to venture to the burial pit. The belief that people should govern their lives by reason, not emotion, is central to the English Enlightenment.*

[ENGLISH LEARNERS] *Tell students that they may have heard the expression, "Curiosity killed the cat."* **Ask:** *What does this expression mean? How does it elate to the beliefs of English Enlightenment and Neoclassicism? (It suggests that curiosity can be dangerous. In the English Enlightenment and Neoclassicism periods, curiosity was seen as inferior to reason.)*

Literary Element 2

Historical Fiction The
dialogue adds color to the portrayal. Students may respond that a factual account of the plague, such as one detailing the number of people who died, would be interesting, but Defoe adds drama to his narration by fictionalizing it.

For additional literary element practice, see Unit 3 Teaching Resources Book, p. 162.

---

of it to those who did not see it, other than this, that it was indeed very, very, very dreadful, and such as no tongue can express.

I got admittance into the churchyard by being acquainted with the sexton[6] who attended; who, though he did not refuse me at all, yet earnestly persuaded me not to go, telling me very seriously, for he was a good, religious, and sensible man, that it was indeed their business and duty to venture, and to run all hazards,[7] and that in it they might hope to be preserved; but that I had no apparent call to it but my own curiosity, which, he said, he believed I would not pretend was sufficient to justify my running that hazard. I told him I had been pressed in my mind to go, and that perhaps it might be an instructing sight, that might not be without its uses. "Nay," says the good man, "if you will venture upon that score,[8] name of God go in; for, depend upon it, it will be a sermon to you, it may be, the best that ever you heard in your life. 'Tis a speaking sight," says he, "and has a voice with it, and a loud one, to call us all to repentance"; and with that he opened the door and said, "Go, if you will."

His discourse had shocked my resolution a little, and I stood wavering for a good while, but just at that interval I saw two links

Visual Vocabulary
Links are torches.

6. The *sexton* was responsible for maintaining church property and for digging graves for churchyard burials.
7. *Hazards* are risks.
8. *Upon that score* means "for that reason."

1 The English Enlightenment and Neoclassicism *How does the sexton's advice relate to the importance that Neoclassical writers placed on reason?*

2 Historical Fiction *How does the dialogue between the speaker and the sexton heighten Defoe's portrayal of the plague?*

---

come over from the end of the Minories,[9] and heard the bellman,[10] and then appeared a dead cart, as they called it, coming over the streets; so I could no longer resist my desire of seeing it, and went in. There was nobody, as I could perceive at first, in the churchyard, or going into it, but the buriers and the fellow that drove the cart, or rather led the horse and cart; but when they came up to the pit they saw a man go to and again,[11] muffled up in a brown cloak, and making motions with his hands under his cloak, as if he was in great agony, and the buriers immediately gathered about him, supposing he was one of those poor delirious or desperate creatures that used to pretend, as I have said, to bury themselves. He said nothing as he walked about, but two or three times groaned very deeply and loud, and sighed as he would break his heart.

When the buriers came up to him they soon found he was neither a person infected and desperate, as I have observed above, or a person distempered[12] in mind, but one **oppressed** with a dreadful weight of grief indeed, having his wife and several of his children all in the cart that was just come in with him, and he followed in an agony and excess of sorrow. He mourned heartily, as it was easy to see, but with a kind of masculine grief that could not give itself vent by tears; and calmly **defying** the buriers to let him alone, said he would only see the bodies thrown in and go away, so they left importuning[13] him. But no sooner was the cart turned round and the bodies shot into the

9. The *Minories* is a street in London.
10. The *bellman* was the town crier, who rang a bell to attract attention. Part of his job was to announce deaths.
11. *To and again* means "to and fro."
12. Here, *distempered* means "deranged."
13. *Left importuning* means "stopped troubling."

Vocabulary

oppressed (ə prest′) *adj.* burdened; weighed down
defy (di fī′) *v.* to resist; refuse to cooperate with

Reading Practice

Determine Author's Message Read this sentence aloud: "'Tis a speaking sight," says he, "and has a voice with it, and a loud one, to call us all to repentance." **Ask:** What does this sentence mean? *(The sight has a message—that everyone should repent.)* What is there about this sentence that tells the reader Defoe is doing more than just recounting events? *(The message is "us all," people of all classes and all eras, including the reader.)*

Flight of the Townspeople into the Country to Escape from the Plague, a.d. 1630. Hand-colored woodcut from *A Looking-glass for Town and Country;* broadside in the collection of the Society of Antiquaries.

View the Art People who were able to often fled into the countryside to escape a plague. What might the skeleton and the cart represent? What does this scene have in common with Defoe's account?

pit promiscuously,[14] which was a surprise to him, for he at least expected they would have been decently laid in, though indeed he was afterwards convinced that was impracticable;[15] I say, no sooner did he see the sight but he cried out aloud, unable to contain himself. I could not hear what he said, but he went backward two or three steps and fell down in a swoon. The buriers ran to him and took him up, and in a little while he came to himself, and they led him away to the Pie Tavern over against the end of Houndsditch, where, it seems, the man was known, and where they took care of him. He looked into the pit again as he went away, but the buriers had covered the bodies so immediately with throwing in earth, that though there was light enough, for there were lanterns, and candles in them, placed all night round the sides of the pit, upon heaps of earth,

seven or eight, or perhaps more, yet nothing could be seen.

This was a mournful scene indeed, and affected me almost as much as the rest; but the other was awful and full of terror. The cart had in it sixteen or seventeen bodies; some were wrapped up in linen sheets, some in rags, some little other than naked, or so loose that what covering they had fell from them in the shooting out of the cart, and they fell quite naked among the rest; but the matter was not much to them, or the indecency much to any one else, seeing they were all dead, and were to be huddled together into the common grave of mankind, as we may call it, for here was no difference made, but poor and rich went together; there was no other way of burials, neither was it possible there should, for coffins were not to be had for the **prodigious** numbers that fell in such a calamity as this.

---

14. Here, *promiscuously* means "casually" or "indiscriminately."
15. *Impracticable* means "not feasible."

3 Historical Fiction *How do the details and the characterization of the cloaked man in the preceding two paragraphs contribute to the story?*

Connect to Contemporary Issues *What contemporary disasters have caused similar shortages?* **4**

Vocabulary

prodigious (prə dij′əs) *adj.* great in size, number, or degree; enormous

DANIEL DEFOE **607**

Comparing Literature

Teach

Literary Element | 3

Historical Fiction **Answer:** *The details are both realistic and symbolic, two key aspects of historical fiction. By introducing the cloaked man, Defoe shows the reader the human tragedy of the plague. The man represents all those whose lives were changed by the plague.*

Reading Strategy | 4

Connect to Contemporary Issues **Answer:** *Natural disasters, such as hurricanes or earthquakes, or acts of war or genocide.*

View the Art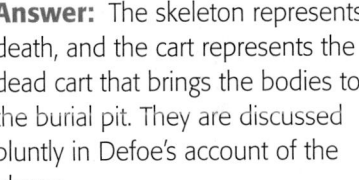

Answer: The skeleton represents death, and the cart represents the dead cart that brings the bodies to the burial pit. They are discussed bluntly in Defoe's account of the plague.

To check students' understanding of the selection, see Unit 3 Teaching Resources Book, p. 167.

English Learners

DIFFERENTIATED INSTRUCTION

Advanced Students may be confused by the vocabulary word *impracticable*. Tell them that *impracticable* means "not possible under the current circumstances," whereas *impractical* can be thought of as a synonym for "not a good idea."

Share the following example:

It would have been **impracticable** to build a modern sports car in the 1890s. There were no high-performance parts nor any way to make them.

It would have been **impractical** to have a sports car in the 1890s, because there were very few paved roads to drive it on.

After You Read

Assess

1. Answers will vary.

2. They were feeling hopeless desperation.

3. (a) Corpses are "shot into the pit" rather than laid at rest with formality. (b) All people eventually go to their graves.

4. (a) The statistics underscore that the plague took place. (b) Students may mention the dimensions of the pits and the number of bodies buried.

5. (a) Detached and journalistic (b) Students may suggest that if they were reporting, their accounts would convey more emotion.

6. The narrator may come closer to understanding God and finding repentance.

7. People might gain greater respect for life, death, and the worth of the individual.

Literary Element

1. Dimensions of burial pits, the number buried, and the order to keep people away from the pits.

2. Defoe may have wanted to include details that he was unable to document.

Reading Strategy

Students may discuss how tragedy, grief, and the threat of illness play roles in contemporary society.

Progress Check

Can students connect to contemporary issues?

If No → See Unit 3 Teaching Resources Book, p. 163.

After You Read

Respond and Think Critically

Respond and Interpret

1. Which of the narrator's observations moved you the most? Explain why it affected you.

2. What do the actions of the plague-infected people tell you about their state of mind?

3. (a)Describe the type of burial that is given to plague victims in the churchyard. (b)What does this say about the nature of death?

Analyze and Evaluate

4. (a)How do statistics and facts add to the account? (b)Which details were most powerful?

5. (a)Describe the tone of this selection. (b)Do you find it appropriate for the subject? Explain.

Connect

6. **Big Idea** The English Enlightenment and Neoclassicism How does Defoe portray religion in the time of the plague?

7. **Connect to Today** How might survivors of a plague today be affected by the experience?

Literary Element Historical Fiction

Writers of **historical fiction** sometimes present history through the eyes of a real figure from the past. Some believe Defoe used a real diary from the time of the plague for reference and that the narrator is modeled after Defoe's uncle, Henry Foe.

1. What details from *A Journal of the Plague Year* could you investigate to check Defoe's accuracy?

2. Why might Defoe have chosen to write his account as fiction, rather than nonfiction?

Writing

Write a Movie Scene This selection vividly recounts many dramatic events. With a partner, write a movie scene based on the excerpt. Be sure to include dialogue mentioned in the story. Since the story is a work of historical fiction, you may wish to research clothing, buildings, and other details from the period and include them in your scene.

LOG ON **Literature** Online

Selection Resources For Selection Quizzes, eFlashcards, and Reading-Writing Connection activities, go to glencoe.com and enter QuickPass code GLB9817u3.

Reading Strategy Connect to Contemporary Issues

Defoe's portrayal of the plague resonates in today's world—for example, disasters still create large death tolls in poor areas.

Partner Activity With a partner, discuss the connections to current issues you made while reading.

Vocabulary Practice

Practice with Word Parts Pair each vocabulary word with the word containing the same root in the right-hand column. Underline the parts they have in common. Use a dictionary to help explain how the words are related.

1. confining   prodigy

2. oppressed   finish

3. defy   fiancée

4. prodigious   pressure

EXAMPLE:

pro*vis*ion, *vis*ible
*Vis*ible means "able to be seen." A pro*vis*ion is something done as a result of looking ahead.

Writing

Scenes should incorporate dialogue from the selection and provide visual cues. Top scores should be given to those scenes that show evidence of outside research.

Vocabulary

1. con*fin*ing, *fin*ish. *Finish* means "end." To confine a thing is to seal it off or stop it.

2. opp*ress*ed, p*ress*ure. Pressure is force exerted against something. To oppress people is to weigh them down unfairly.

3. *defy*, *fian*cée. To defy someone is to refuse to cooperate with them, while a fiancée is a woman who is engaged to a man.

4. *prodig*ious, *prodig*y. One meaning of the word *prodigy* is "something abnormal or monstrous." *Prodigious* means "enormous" or "extraordinary."

Build Background

The Peloponnesian War between the great city-states Athens and Sparta was fought between 431 B.C. and 404 B.C. Nearly every other city-state in Greece was allied in some way in the war. Sparta eventually emerged victorious from the twenty-seven-year war, ending the zenith of classical Greek culture that was reached in Athens. In this passage, Thucydides describes the medical symptoms of the plague that ravaged Athens and also reports on the devastating effects the plague had on Athenian morale, spirit, and behavior.

Considered the greatest Greek historian, Thucydides was an Athenian general who recorded the battles during the Peloponnesian War. Thucydides was born sometime between 460 B.C. and 454 B.C. and probably saw first-hand the great plague that struck Athens around 430 B.C.

from *History of the* *Peloponnesian War*

Thucydides
translated by Rex Warner

At the beginning of the following summer the Peloponnesians and their allies, with two-thirds of their total forces as before, invaded Attica, again under the command of the Spartan King Archidamus, the son of Zeuxidamus. Taking up their positions, they set about the devastation of the country.

They had not been many days in Attica before the plague first broke out among the Athenians. Previously attacks of the plague had been reported from many other places in the neighborhood of Lemnos and elsewhere, but there was no record of the disease being so virulent anywhere else or causing so many deaths as it did in Athens. At the beginning the doctors were quite incapable of treating the disease because of their ignorance of the right methods. In fact mortality among the doctors was the highest of all, since they came more frequently in contact with the sick. Nor was any other human art or science of any help at all. Equally useless were prayers made in the temples, consultation of oracles, and so forth; indeed, in the end people were so overcome by their sufferings that they paid no further attention to such things.

The plague originated, so they say, in Ethiopia in upper Egypt, and spread from there into Egypt itself and Libya and much of the territory of the King of Persia. In the city of

THUCYDIDES **609**

Comparing Literature

Focus

Summary

Thucydides explains the origins of the plague and then describes the symptoms as it spreads from one organ to another. Those who survived often lost the use of their extremities or sometimes suffered amnesia. Thucydides makes the point that the disease killed both the healthy and the weak, those who were cared for and those who were ignored, those who prayed and those who didn't, those who were rich and those who were poor.

Comparing Literature

Teach

Political History ☆

The Peloponnesus is the large peninsula that makes up the southern part of Greece. Sparta is on this peninsula. Attica is the region of Greece that includes Athens. Upper Egypt is the southern, inland part of the country, up the Nile River, which flows from south to north. Because it is in the south, it lies below Lower Egypt on a standard map. Libya lies to the west of Egypt, and Persia is located in present-day Iran. Piraeus is a port city just south of Athens.

Readability Scores

Dale-Chall: 8.9
DRP: 66
Lexile: 1290

☆ Athens it appeared suddenly, and the first cases were among the population of Piraeus, so that it was supposed by them that the Peloponnesians had poisoned the reservoirs. Later, however, it appeared also in the upper city, and by this time the deaths were greatly increasing in number. As to the question of how it could first have come about or what causes can be found adequate to explain its powerful effect on nature, I must leave that to be considered by other writers, with or without medical experience. I myself shall merely describe what it was like, and set down the symptoms, knowledge of which will enable it to be recognized, if it should ever break out again. I had the disease myself and saw others suffering from it.

That year, as is generally admitted, was particularly free from all other kinds of illness, though those who did have any illness previously all caught the plague in the end. In other cases, however, there seemed to be no reason for the attacks. People in perfect health suddenly began to have burning feelings in the head; their eyes became red and inflamed; inside their mouths there was bleeding from the throat and tongue, and the breath became unnatural and unpleasant. The next symptoms were sneezing and hoarseness of voice, and before long the pain settled on the chest and was accompanied by coughing. Next the stomach was affected with stomach-aches and with vomitings of every kind of bile that has been given a name by the medical profession, all this being accompanied by great pain and difficulty. In most cases there were attacks of ineffectual retching,[1] producing violent spasms; this sometimes ended with this stage of the disease, but sometimes continued long afterwards. Externally the body was not very hot to the touch, nor was there any pallor:[2] the skin was rather reddish and livid, breaking out into small pustules and ulcers. But inside there was a feeling of burning, so that people could not bear the touch even of the lightest linen clothing, but wanted to be completely naked, and indeed most of all would have liked to plunge into cold water. Many of the sick who were uncared for actually did so, plunging into the water-tanks in an effort to relieve a thirst which was unquenchable; for it was just the same with them whether they drank much or little. Then all the time they were afflicted with insomnia and the desperate feeling of not being able to keep still.

> "*W*ords indeed fail one when one tries to give a general picture of this disease; and as for the sufferings of individuals, they seemed almost beyond the capacity of human nature to endure."

In the period when the disease was at its height, the body, so far from wasting away, showed surprising powers of resistance to all the agony, so that there was still some strength left on the seventh or eighth day, which was the time when, in most cases, death came from the internal fever. But if people survived this critical period, then the disease descended to the bowels, producing violent ulceration and uncontrollable diarrhea, so that most of them died later as a result of the weakness caused by this. For the disease, first settling in the head, went on to affect every part of the

---

1. *Retching* means "vomiting."
2. *Pallor* means "paleness."

Research Practice

Find Sources Tell students to imagine they want to find out what disease struck Athens around 430 B.C. All they have is the list of symptoms Thucydides describes. Help students brainstorm ideas about what sources they might use to match the symptoms with the correct disease.

Funeral Stele of a Young Woman, ca. 460 BCE. Classical Greek. Marble, h. 52.30 in. Antikensammlung, Staatliche Museen zu Berlin, Germany.

were many dead bodies lying about unburied, the birds and animals that eat human flesh either did not come near them or, if they did taste the flesh, died of it afterwards. Evidence for this may be found in the fact that there was a complete disappearance of all birds of prey: they were not to be seen either round the bodies or anywhere else. But dogs, being domestic animals, provided the best opportunity of observing this effect of the plague.

These, then, were the general features of the disease, though I have omitted all kinds of peculiarities which occurred in various individual cases. Meanwhile, during all this time there was no serious outbreak of any of the usual kinds of illness; if any such cases did occur, they ended in the plague. Some died in neglect, some in spite of every possible care being taken of them. As for a recognized method of treatment, it would be true to say that no such thing existed: what did good in some cases did harm in others. Those with naturally strong constitutions were no better able than the weak to resist the disease, which carried away all alike, even those who were treated and dieted with the greatest care. The most terrible thing of all was the despair into which people fell when they realized that they had caught the plague; for they would immediately adopt an attitude of utter hopelessness, and, by giving in in this way, would lose their powers of resistance. Terrible, too, was the sight of people dying like sheep through having caught the disease as a result of nursing others. This indeed caused more deaths than anything else. For when people were afraid to visit the sick, then they died with no one to look after them; indeed, there were many houses in which all the inhabitants perished through lack of any attention. When, on the other hand, they did visit the sick, they lost their own lives, and this was particularly true of those who made it a point of honor to act properly. Such people felt ashamed to think of their own safety and went into their friends' houses at times when even the members of the

body in turn, and even when people escaped its worst effects it still left its traces on them by fastening upon the extremities of the body. It affected the genitals, the fingers, and the toes, and many of those who recovered lost the use of these members; some, too, went blind. There were some also who, when they first began to get better, suffered from a total loss of memory, not knowing who they were themselves and being unable to recognize their friends.

Words indeed fail one when one tries to give a general picture of this disease; and as for the sufferings of individuals, they seemed almost beyond the capacity of human nature to endure. Here in particular is a point where this plague showed itself to be something quite different from ordinary diseases: though there

THUCYDIDES **611**

Comparing Literature

Teach

Reading Strategy   **1**

Draw Conclusions

Ask: Why do you think animals that ate the corpses died? *(They got the disease, and it killed them.)* How do you think that happened? *(Whatever germ or virus caused the disease was still in the corpses. The animals consumed the germ when they ate, and it attacked them.)* Why do you think there were no birds of prey near the bodies? *(Something about the corpses—perhaps the smell—made them unappetizing to the birds or let the birds know they were dangerous.)*

English Learners

DIFFERENTIATED INSTRUCTION

Advanced Many languages have a way to refer to a person in general. In English, we use the impersonal pronoun "one." However, many English learners may have never encountered this construction. **Write this sentence on the board:** Words fail when one tries to give a general picture of this disease. Explain to students that this is correct English, but it is considered very formal. Today it is used most often in academic and scientific writing. **Write this sentence on the board:** If one votes, one can make a difference. **Ask:** What would be the more common way to say this? *(If you vote, you can make a difference.)*

Comparing Literature

Teach

Literary Element   1

Irony Explain to students that an ironic situation is one in which an event or series of events leads to something other than the expected result—often to the opposite of the expected result. Writers sometimes create ironic situations in order to increase the drama in their stories. Here, Thucydides describes an ironic situation that occurred in real life. Moral people who thought honor demanded they visit the sick caught the disease and died. Less honorable people, who did nothing to help the sick, may have been spared from the disease and survived. We like to think that good deeds will be rewarded. But in this ironic situation, the people who perform the good deeds end up dying. And it is the good deed itself that causes their death.

(ADVANCED) **Ask:** What is the overall effect on the reader of Thucydides' use of situational irony? *(The reader wonders if good deeds are worthy dying for.)*

Quickwrite

Students should discuss the lawlessness that Thucydides describes in his report on the Athenian people's response to the plague. Challenge students to support their perspectives with evidence from the text and from contemporary society, such as looting or rioting that has followed protests, court decisions, or sporting events.

612

---

household were so overwhelmed by the weight of their calamities that they had actually given up the usual practice of making laments for the dead. Yet still the ones who felt most pity for the sick and the dying were those who had had the plague themselves and had recovered from it. They knew what it was like and at the same time felt themselves to be safe, for no one caught the disease twice, or, if he did, the second attack was never fatal. Such people were congratulated on all sides, and they themselves were so elated at the time of their recovery that they fondly imagined that they could never die of any other disease in the future.

A factor which made matters much worse than they were already was the removal of people from the country into the city, and this particularly affected the incomers. There were no houses for them, and, living as they did during the hot season in badly ventilated huts, they died like flies. The bodies of the dying were heaped one on top of the other, and half-dead creatures could be seen staggering about in the streets or flocking around the fountains in their desire for water. The temples in which they took up their quarters were full of the dead bodies of people who had died inside them. For the catastrophe was so overwhelming that men, not knowing what would happen next to them, became indifferent to every rule of religion or of law. All the funeral ceremonies which used to be observed were now disorganized, and they buried the dead as best they could. Many people, lacking the necessary means of burial because so many deaths had already occurred in their households, adopted the most shameless methods. They would

arrive first at a funeral pyre that had been made by others, put their own dead upon it and set it alight; or, finding another pyre burning, they would throw the corpse that they were carrying on top of the other one and go away.

In other respects also Athens owed to the plague the beginnings of a state of unprecedented lawlessness. Seeing how quick and abrupt were the changes of fortune which came to the rich who suddenly died and to those who had previously been penniless but now inherited their wealth, people now began openly to venture on acts of self-indulgence which before then they used to keep dark. Thus they resolved to spend their money quickly and to spend it on pleasure, since money and life alike seemed equally ephemeral. As for what is called honor, no one showed himself willing to abide by its laws, so doubtful was it whether one would survive to enjoy the name for it. It was generally agreed that what was both honorable and valuable was the pleasure of the moment and everything that might conceivably contribute to that pleasure. No fear of god or law of man had a restraining influence. As for the gods, it seemed to be the same thing whether one worshipped them or not, when one saw the good and the bad dying indiscriminately. As for offences against human law, no one expected to live long enough to be brought to trial and punished: instead everyone felt that already a far heavier sentence had been passed on him and was hanging over him, and that before the time for its execution arrived it was only natural to get some pleasure out of life. ◆

Quickwrite

Thucydides describes the despair felt by Athenians who endured the plague. How should humans respond in times such as the one detailed in Thucydides's historical account? Write a paragraph explaining your views.

Writing Practice

Transitive and Intransitive Verbs Direct students' attention to the first sentence in the first complete paragraph on this page. Point out that the noun *removal* means "the act of removing." Write "people removing from the country" on the board. Below it, write "people removing their gloves."

Explain that a transitive verb involves an action being performed on an object and an intransitive verb does not involve such an action. **Ask**: In which phrase is *removing* a transitive verb? *(people removing their gloves)* In which phrase is *removing* an intransitive verb? *(people removing from the country)*

Build Background

The Plague is set in the Algerian port of Oran in the early 1940s. At the time Albert Camus wrote it, he himself was apart from his wife, who was in the city of Oran. Camus was in a mountain village in France, seeking treatment for tuberculosis. While he was there, German troops tightened their control of the region, and Camus was not allowed to return home. "Caught like rats!" he wrote in his journal.

The plot of the novel begins when Dr. Bernard Rieux steps on a dead rat. Soon scores of rats are crawling out into the open, ready to die. The citizens' annoyance turns to alarm when they realize that the cause of the dying rats is an outbreak of the bubonic plague. The city declares a state of emergency and seals itself off from nearly all contact, and Rieux works tirelessly to combat the epidemic. The novel has a mysterious point of view. Only in the last chapter does the narrator reveal that he is Dr. Rieux.

Allegory of the Plague. A Biccherna book cover, 1437. Kunstgewerbemuseum, Staatliche Museen zu Berlin, Germany.

View the Art In an allegory, characters, objects, and events symbolize ideas and concepts. What might the elements of this painting symbolize?

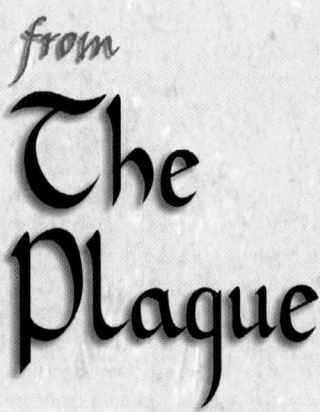

from
The Plague

Albert Camus
translated by Stuart Gilbert

The truth is that nothing is less sensational than pestilence,[1] and by reason of their very duration great misfortunes are monotonous. In the memories of those who lived through them, the grim days of plague do not stand out like vivid flames, ravenous and inextinguishable, beaconing a troubled sky, but rather like the slow, deliberate progress of some monstrous thing crushing out all upon its path.

No, the real plague had nothing in common with the grandiose imaginings that had haunted Rieux's mind at its outbreak. It was, above all, a shrewd, unflagging adversary; a skilled organizer, doing his work thoroughly and well. That, it may be said in passing, is why, so as not to play false to the facts, and,

1. *Pestilence* refers to the bubonic plague.

ALBERT CAMUS **613**

Comparing Literature

Focus

Summary

Camus discusses the psychological toll suffered by those who did not get the plague. He describes a monotonous existence in which each day seems like every other. People are no longer able to recall mental images of the faces of the loved ones from whom they have separated, and they have given up hope of ever seeing them again. People also begin to lose track of their own individuality.

Political History ☆

France took control of Algeria in 1848, and it remained a French territory until 1962. During World War II, Nazi Germany occupied the northern part of France. The southern part was unoccupied but was run by a Nazi-controlled government with its capital in the town of Vichy. The Vichy government controlled Algeria until the Allies liberated it and made it their headquarters in North Africa.

View the Art ★

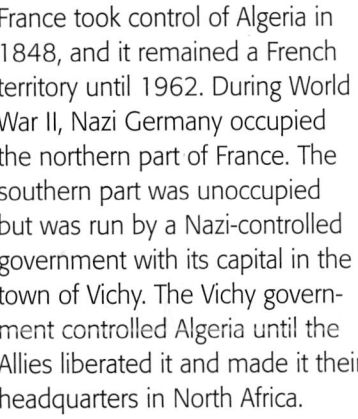

Possible answer: *The horse and horsemen represent the plague, the scythe represents death, and the roomful of people represent the unaware victims.*

Comparing Literature

Teach

Literary Element   1

Mood As students read the selection, have them note the mood that Camus creates in describing life in Oran. Suggest they take notes of what words and images Camus uses to create this mood.

Have students use a chart like the one below to track the words Camus uses.

Noun	Adjective
days	**grim**

Readability Scores

Dale-Chall: 8.6
DRP: 65
Lexile: 1300

still more, so as not to play false to himself, the narrator has aimed at objectivity. He has made hardly any changes for the sake of artistic effect, except those elementary adjustments needed to present his narrative in a more or less coherent form. And in deference to this scruple he is constrained to admit that, though the chief source of distress, the deepest as well as the most widespread, was separation—and it is his duty to say more about it as it existed in the later stages of the plague—it cannot be denied that even this distress was coming to lose something of its poignancy.

Was it that our fellow citizens, even those who had felt the parting from their loved ones most keenly, were getting used to doing without them? To assume this would fall somewhat short of the truth. It would be more correct to say that they were wasting away emotionally as well as physically. At the beginning of the plague they had a vivid recollection of the absent ones and bitterly felt their loss. But though they could clearly recall the face, the smile and voice of the beloved, and this or that occasion when (as they now saw in retrospect) they had been supremely happy, they had trouble in picturing what he or she might be doing at the moment when they conjured up these memories, in a setting so hopelessly remote. In short, at these moments memory played its part, but their imagination failed them. During the second phase of the plague their memory failed them, too. Not that they had forgotten the face itself, but—what came to the same thing—it had lost fleshly substance and they no longer saw it in memory's mirror.

Thus, while during the first weeks they were apt to complain that only shadows remained to them of what their love had been and meant, they now came to learn that even shadows can waste away, losing the faint hues of life that memory may give. And by the end of their long sundering they had also lost the power of imagining the intimacy that once was theirs or understanding what it can be to live with someone whose life is wrapped up in yours.

In this respect they had adapted themselves to the very condition of the plague, all the more potent for its mediocrity. None of us was capable any longer of an exalted emotion; all had trite, monotonous feelings. "It's high time it stopped," people would say, because in time of calamity the obvious thing is to desire its end, and in fact they wanted it to end. But when making such remarks, we felt none of the passionate yearning or fierce resentment of the early phase; we merely voiced one of the few clear ideas that lingered in the twilight of our minds. The furious revolt of the first weeks had given place to a vast despondency, not to be taken for resignation, though it was none the less a sort of passive and provisional acquiescence.[2]

Our fellow citizens had fallen into line, adapted themselves, as people say, to the situation, because there was no way of doing otherwise. Naturally they retained the attitudes of sadness and suffering, but they had ceased to feel their sting. Indeed, to some, Dr. Rieux among them, this precisely was the most disheartening thing: that the habit of despair is worse than despair itself. Hitherto those who **1** were parted had not been utterly unhappy; there was always a gleam of hope in the night of their distress; but that gleam had now died out. You could see them at street corners, in cafés or friends' houses, listless, indifferent, and looking so bored that, because of them, the whole town seemed like a railway waiting-room. Those who had jobs went about them at the exact tempo of the plague, with dreary perseverance. Everyone was modest. For the first time exiles from those they loved had no reluctance to talk freely about them, using the same words as everybody else, and regarding their deprivation from the same angle as that from which they viewed the latest statistics of the epidemic. This change was striking, since until now they had jealously withheld their personal

---

2. *Acquiescence* means "giving up."

Reading Practice

Paraphrase Suggest that when students find themselves at a particularly difficult section, they take a moment to rewrite it in their own words. Use as an example this paraphrase of the beginning of the third paragraph.

"Were our neighbors, even those mourning loved ones, getting used to people dying? Not exactly—it was more that they were becoming emotionally dead. When the plague started, they remembered the victims and missed them terribly."

grief from the common stock of suffering; now they accepted its inclusion. Without memories, without hope, they lived for the moment only. Indeed, the here and now had come to mean everything to them. For there is no denying that the plague had gradually killed off in all of us the faculty not of love only but even of friendship. Naturally enough, since love asks something of the future, and nothing was left us but a series of present moments.

However, this account of our predicament gives only the broad lines. Thus, while it is true that all who were parted came ultimately to this state, we must add that all did not attain it simultaneously; moreover, once this utter apathy had fallen on them, there were still flashes of lucidity, broken lights of memory that rekindled in the exiles a younger, keener sensibility. This happened when, for instance, they fell to making plans implying that the plague had ended. Or when, quite unexpectedly, by some kindly chance, they felt a twinge of jealousy, none the less acute for its objectlessness. Others, again, had sudden accesses of energy and shook off their languor on certain days of the week—for obvious reasons, on Sundays and Saturday afternoons, because these had been devoted to certain ritual pleasures in the days when the loved ones were still accessible. Sometimes the mood of melancholy that descended on them with the nightfall acted as a sort of warning, not always fulfilled, however, that old memories were floating up to the surface. That evening hour which for believers is the time to look into their consciences is hardest of all hours on the prisoner or exile who has nothing to look into but the void. For a moment it held

them in suspense; then they sank back into their lethargy, the prison door had closed on them once again.

Obviously all this meant giving up what was most personal in their lives. Whereas in the early days of the plague they had been struck by the host of small details that, while meaning absolutely nothing to others, meant so much to them personally, and thus had realized, perhaps for the first time, the uniqueness of each man's life; now, on the other hand, they took an interest only in what interested everyone else, they had only general ideas, and even their tenderest affections now seemed abstract, items of the common stock. So completely were they dominated by the plague that sometimes the one thing they aspired to was the long sleep it brought, and they caught themselves thinking: "A good thing if I get plague and have done with it!" But really they were asleep already; this whole period was for them no more than a long night's slumber. The town was peopled with sleepwalkers, whose trance was broken only on the rare occasions when at night their wounds, to all appearance closed, suddenly reopened. Then, waking with a start, they would run their fingers over the wounds with a sort of absentminded curiosity, twisting their lips, and in a flash their grief blazed up again, and abruptly there rose before them the mournful visage of their love. In the morning they harked back to normal conditions—in other words, the plague.

What impression, it may be asked, did these exiles of the plague make on the observer? The answer is simple; they made none. Or, to

> "The town was peopled with sleepwalkers, whose trance was broken only on the rare occasions when at night their wounds, to all appearance closed, suddenly reopened."

ALBERT CAMUS **615**

Comparing Literature

Teach

Reading Strategy 2

Compare and Contrast
Ask: How does Camus contrast the mental state of the survivors in the early and late stages of the plague? *(In the early stages, the survivors took an interest in small details; in the late stages, they lose all interest in the particular and have only general ideas.)*

(ENGLISH LEARNERS) Have English learners write two sentences using appropriate connectors (e.g., *first, then*) describing how the survivors' attitudes and beliefs changed during the plague.

English Learners

DIFFERENTIATED INSTRUCTION

Intermediate Read aloud the following sentence from the top of the second column on page 615: "[T]hen they sank back into their lethargy, the prison door had closed on them once again." **Ask:** Are the people really inside a prison? *(No)*

Then read this sentence aloud: "[T]he one thing they aspired to was the long sleep [the plague] brought." **Ask:** Do the really people want to go to sleep? *(No)* Discuss the actual meaning of the sentences.

Comparing Literature

Teach

Vocabulary · 1

Foreign Words Point out that when the right word for a situation does not exist in English, writers sometimes use a foreign word. When this happens, the foreign word is usually printed in italics. Ask if any students know the origin of the word *sang-froid. (French)* Then ask if any students can translate either of its two parts. (sang: *"blood,*: froid: *"cold."*) **Ask:** What English word does that remind you of? *(cold-blooded)* What does *cold-blooded* mean in English? *(without compassion or remorse)* Is it usually used positively or negatively? *(negatively)* Point out to students that *cold-blooded* is usually used with the word *murder* or *killer.* It is not good to be cold-blooded. On the other hand, *sang-froid* means "coolness." It can be good to have *sang-froid.*

Quickwrite

Students' responses should explore how the haunting, poetic imagery of a deserted town and aimless, sleepwalking people contributes to the selection. Encourage students to explore how the story develops Camus's response to the forced separation and lack of freedom imposed on the French by the occupying Nazi forces.

---

put it differently, they looked like everybody else, nondescript. They shared in the torpor of the town and in its puerile[3] agitations. They lost every trace of a critical spirit, while gaining an air of *sang-froid.*[4] You could see, for instance, even the most intelligent among them making a show like all the rest of studying the newspapers or listening to the radio, in the hope apparently of finding some reason to believe the plague would shortly end. They seemed to derive fantastic hopes or equally exaggerated fears from reading the lines that some journalist has scribbled at random, yawning with boredom at his desk. Meanwhile they drank their beer, nursed their sick, idled, or doped themselves with work, filed documents in offices, or played the phonograph at home without betraying any difference from the rest of us. In other words, they had ceased to choose for themselves; plague had leveled out discrimination. This could be seen by the way nobody troubled about the quality of the clothes or food he bought. Everything was taken as it came.

And, finally, it is worth noting that those who were parted ceased to enjoy the curious privilege that had been theirs at the outset. They had lost love's egoism and the benefit they derived from it. Now, at least, the position was clear: this calamity was everybody's business. What with the gunshots echoing at the gates, the punctual thuds of rubber stamps marking the rhythm of lives and deaths, the files and fires, the panics and formalities, all alike were pledged to an ugly but recorded death, and, amidst noxious fumes and the muted clang of ambulances, all of us ate the same sour bread of exile, unconsciously waiting for the same reunion, the same miracle of peace regained. No doubt our love persisted, but in practice it served nothing; it was an inert mass within us, sterile as crime or a life

sentence. It had declined on a patience that led nowhere, a dogged expectation. Viewed from this angle, the attitude of some of our fellow citizens resembled that of the long queues one saw outside the food-shops. There was the same resignation, the same long-sufferance, inexhaustible and without illusions. The only difference was that the mental state of the food-seekers would need to be raised to a vastly higher power to make it comparable with the gnawing pain of separation, since this latter came from a hunger fierce to the point of insatiability.

In any case, if the reader would have a correct idea of the mood of these exiles, we must conjure up once more those dreary evenings sifting down through a haze of dust and golden light upon the treeless streets filled with teeming crowds of men and women. For, characteristically, the sound that rose toward the terraces still bathed in the last glow of daylight, now that the noises of vehicles and motors—the sole voice of cities in ordinary times—had ceased, was but one vast rumor of low voices and incessant footfalls, the drumming of innumerable soles timed to the eerie whistling of the plague in the sultry air above, the sound of a huge concourse of people marking time, a never ending, stifling drone that, gradually swelling, filled the town from end to end, and evening after evening gave its truest, mournfulest expression to the blind endurance that had ousted love from all our hearts. ❧

Quickwrite

Camus once wrote, "A novel is never anything but a philosophy expressed in images." *The Plague,* in part, is an allegorical novel about the fascist occupation of Europe.

How do you interpret the imagery in this selection? What questions does it raise about the purpose of human suffering and the meaning of life? Write a brief essay on this topic, citing evidence from the text to support your points.

---

3. *Puerile* means "childish."
4. *Sang-froid* means "composure in tense situations."

Writing Practice

Sentence Structure Work with students to deconstruct one or more of the long sentences by removing all the clauses and extraneous modifiers. For example, the last sentence of the selection would become something like this: "For the sound that rose toward the terraces was but one vast rumor of low voices and incessant footfalls, the drumming of innumerable soles, the sound of a huge concourse of people marking time, a never-ending, stifling drone that filled the town and gave its truest expression to the endurance that had ousted love from our hearts."

Wrap-Up: Comparing Literature

Across Time and Place

- from *A Journal of the Plague Year* by Daniel Defoe
- from *History of the Peloponnesian War* by Thucydides
- from *The Plague* by Albert Camus

COMPARE THE Big Idea **The English Enlightenment and Neoclassicism**

Writing Reason and a vigorous intellectual quest to find the answers for the cause of things highlight the age of the English Enlightenment and Neoclassicism. In a brief essay, describe how Defoe, Thucydides, and Camus explore both the seeming randomness of epidemics and the causes and effects they identify in the coming of the disease.

COMPARE Style

Group Activity How do the styles of Defoe, Thucydides, and Camus compare and contrast? Meet with a group to discuss the style of each writer and the purpose each style serves, and then answer the following questions.

1. What descriptive terms would you use to compare and contrast the tone of these three selections?

2. How would you describe the contrasting imagery used by these three writers?

3. What terms would you use to describe the overall style of each of these writers?

COMPARE Cultures

Speaking and Listening Defoe, Thucydides, and Camus write about different cultures, yet they present evidence about the similar physical and psychological toll exacted by disease. With a group, research the cultures explored in each selection (seventeenth-century England, ancient Greece, and 1940s-era Algeria). Present a report to the class about how the precarious nature of life is reflected in the culture of one of the selections.

Literature Online

Selection Resources For Selection Quizzes, eFlashcards, and Reading-Writing Connection activities, go to glencoe.com and enter QuickPass code GLB9817u3.

COMPARING LITERATURE **617**

English Learners

DIFFERENTIATED INSTRUCTION

Beginning Ask students if one selection had more words they didn't know than the other selections. Discuss which words gave students the most trouble. Suggest they list the words they did not know and their definitions in their notebooks.

Assess

Compare the Big Idea

Students' responses should explore the interest in God and salvation expressed by Defoe's narrator; the exacting scientific and political explanations presented by Preston; the clear report offered by Thucydides; and the themes of evil and meaninglessness in life expressed by Camus's narrator. Encourage students to discuss the reasons each writer seems to give for how the plague takes hold.

Compare Style

Students should contrast Defoe's elegant style, serious tone, and stark imagery; Preston's reportorial, energetic style, conversational tone, and detailed, sometimes gross imagery; Thucydides' austere style, detached tone, and clear imagery; and Camus's complex and experimental style, detached tone, and poetic imagery.

Compare Cultures

Students should connect cultural forces and events to the selections. Examples include how the real plague connects with Defoe's story; how the anthrax attacks of 2001 impact Preston's account and argument; how Thucydides' account of the Peloponnesian War and the outbreak of the plague has become the authoritative report of those events; and how the Nazi occupation of France in World War II is a subject in Camus's novel.

Focus

Summary

Malaria has recently made a comeback as a disease rivaling deadly plagues. Effective treatment exists, but high costs for medicine and the worry over using DDT hamper efforts to lower the death rate. Malaria doesn't affect just the physical health of people; nations with high malarial incidence have a lower economic growth rate, which has an effect on the global economy.

For activities related to this selection, see Unit 3 Teaching Resources Book, pp. 169–177.

Teach

Reading Strategy | 1

Analyze Cause-and-Effect Relationships Identifying cause-and-effect situations can help students find the main idea and supporting arguments. **Ask:** What do you think the main idea is? *(Students may answer: It is possible to lower the death rate from malaria.)* What are some of the supporting arguments? *(There is medicine available that works quickly. Insecticide-treated nets protect people from being bitten.)*

For an audio recording of this selection, use Listening Library Audio CD-ROM.

Set a Purpose for Reading

Read to learn about malaria and its impact on Africa and the world.

Preview the Article

"Death By Mosquito" examines the malaria outbreak in Africa and the need for an international response.

1. From the title, how serious a disease do you think malaria is?

2. Read the deck—the sentence in large type that appears under the headline. What must you know to answer the question?

Reading Strategy Analyze Cause-and-Effect Relationships

An **effect,** or consequence, is a direct result of a **cause,** or action. You explore cause-and-effect relationships when answering "Why?" about events in a text.

As you read, make a list of cause-and-effect situations presented in "Death By Mosquito." Create a chart to organize your thoughts.

Cause	Effect
Malaria came to the United States via a plane flight or ocean vessel.	Seven people in Florida were hospitalized with a disease.

Grammar Practice

Adverbs Say: Reread the first paragraph in the article. Make a list of all of the adverbs you can find. Remember that adverbs can modify verbs, other adverbs, and adjectives. Then write how you can tell the word is an adverb. (***most***—how many; ***ever***—when; ***well***—how much; ***nearly-as***—how; ***particularly***—how much)

Read the paragraph aloud. **Ask:** What happens when the adverbs are removed from the sentence? *(less information, less interesting)*

Death By Mosquito

Malaria is killing millions. But it can be cured. Why isn't that happening?

By CHRISTINE GORMAN

AS CURRENT TRENDS MAKE CLEAR, AIDS IS SURPASSING the Black Death as the most devastating plague ever to afflict the human race. But all the well-deserved attention paid to AIDS over the past few years has overshadowed the rapid comeback of a second, nearly-as-deadly plague—malaria. Statistics suggest that malaria sickened 300 million people in 2003 and killed 3 million—most of them under age 5. What makes the malaria deaths particularly tragic is that malaria can be cured. **1**

Countries in sub-Saharan Africa have suffered the brunt of this assault, but nations in temperate zones, including the United States, are not immune. A malaria outbreak in Florida that hospitalized seven people in 2003 was the first widespread transmission of the disease on U.S. soil in nearly 20 years. The cause was almost certainly a parasite that hopped a ride in a human, or a mosquito on an international flight or ship, since none of the patients had recently traveled overseas.

There is reason for hope, however. Doctors have made remarkable progress over the past few years in the treatment of drug-resistant malaria by combining several compounds—the most powerful of which comes from an ancient Chinese herbal remedy that cures 90% of patients in three days. Meanwhile, community groups, nonprofit

THE CULPRIT The female mosquito needs blood to produce eggs. It transmits malaria parasites when it bites again.

TIME

Teach

Readability Scores
Dale-Chall: 13.3
DRP: 71
Lexile: 1260

THE GROWING THREAT

While the malaria problem has been dormant in the U.S., the number of cases per year in Africa has grown fourfold since the 1980s. The death rate among African children has nearly doubled since then.

Malaria mortality per 100,000
- Sub-Saharan Africa
- Worldwide

Malaria distribution, 2003
- Areas where malaria is widespread
- Areas with some malaria
- No malaria

200 —
150 —
100 —
50 —
0 —

1900 1930 1950 1970 1990 2002

Source: World Health Organization

DEATH BY MOSQUITO **619**

English Learners

DIFFERENTIATED INSTRUCTION

Intermediate Ask students from other countries if environmental hazards exist there. *(Students may mention air or water pollution.)* **Ask:** What, if anything, is the government doing about the hazardous condition? *(Answers will vary.)* What factors make a solution to the problem difficult? *(Students may say a particular solution will create other problems.)*

How are these problems different from problems we face in the United States? *(Answers will vary.)*

TIME

Teach

| Big Idea | 1 |

The Spread of Malaria

Malaria is a disease caused by parasites (organisms that live in and feed off another body) that are attracted to and carried by the anopheles mosquito. After students read the article, **Ask:** How is the disease spread among human beings? *(An infected mosquito carries parasites, which enter the bloodstream when an infected insect bites a human. The parasites multiply within the host's body and are transmitted when a mosquito bites an infected person.)*

Cultural History ☆

Mosquito-Borne Diseases

Each year, according to the World Health Organization, some 200 million people are infected with mosquito-borne illnesses other than malaria: dengue, yellow fever, and various forms of encephalitis, including the West Nile virus.

---

organizations, and governments are redoubling efforts to control the mosquitoes that cause the disease through insecticide-treated nets and the indoor spraying of antimosquito pesticides. Certainly the need for action has never been clearer.

☆ Researchers believe the average number of cases of malaria per year in Africa has quadrupled since the 1980s. A study in the journal Lancet reported that the death rate due to malaria has at least doubled among children in eastern and southern Africa. And some rural areas have seen a heartbreaking 11-fold jump in deaths. Says malaria expert Dr. Christa Hook, "In many ways, it's a kind of silent Holocaust."

Recognition of malaria's toll on the global economy is also growing. Economist Jeffrey Sachs of Columbia University estimates that countries hit hardest by the most severe form of malaria have annual economic growth rates 1.3 percentage points lower than those in which malaria is not a serious problem. In other words, fighting malaria is good for business—as many companies with overseas operations have long understood.

Understanding the Disease

To better understand why malaria has become such a threat and what can be done to stop the disease, it helps to know a little biology. Malaria is caused by four closely related parasites, some of which have a particular fondness for anopheles mosquitoes. The parasites enter the bloodstream when an infected mosquito bites a human. Then they multiply inside the host's liver and red

SLOWING THE SPREAD

The tools for fighting malaria are already at hand. It's just a matter of getting them out to those who need it.

TREATED NETS Sprayed with insecticide, they act as traps; mosquitoes are attracted by CO2 and killed on contact.

SWEET WORMWOOD A drug made from this Chinese herb cures 90% of patients within three days, but it is in short supply.

DDT When the poison is sprayed on or inside a hut, it kills mosquitoes without doing a lot of harm to the environment.

blood cells. (That's why pregnant women, who make lots of blood to nourish their growing fetus, are especially vulnerable.) Eventually the red blood cells burst with a new generation of parasites, causing fever, shivering, pain, and sometimes death. The cycle of transmission is complete when another mosquito bites an infected person and picks up more parasites. **1**

You might expect that one bout of malaria would lead to lifelong protection against the disease. But for complicated reasons, that is not the case. The illness tends to be less severe in adults who are continually exposed to the parasites. But when young children become infected, they are much more likely to suffer severe anemia and convulsions that may lead to permanent brain damage and death.

For decades, the best treatment for malaria was a relatively cheap and effective medication called chloroquine, which was discovered in Germany in 1934. But by the 1970s, the drug had been used so widely to treat all kinds of fevers, not just those caused by malaria, that the malaria parasites became resistant. So doctors had to turn to a second medication, called sulfadoxine-pyrimethamine, or SP, for short. Within five years, however, the parasites started to develop resistance to SP as well. Today resistance to both drugs is on the rise in parts of Africa, where drug-resistant malaria parasites are the leading cause of death.

At the same time, efforts to control anopheles mosquitoes have been more or less abandoned.

620 UNIT 3 FROM PURITANISM TO THE ENLIGHTENMENT

Reading Practice

Subheadings Say: Look at the sub-headings in the article. **Ask:** Do they help you understand the organization of the article? *(Answers will vary.)* Tell students to look at their answers to Reading Strategy: Analyzing Cause-and-Effect Relationships on page 618. **Ask:** How do the subheadings correspond with the main idea and the supporting

arguments? *(Students' answers will vary dependent upon their answers in the Reading Strategy.)*

TIME

Malaria struck 300 million in one year, killing as many as 3 million.

Part of the problem was the realization that malaria could never be completely wiped out from tropical regions the way it had been in the U.S. and other countries in temperate zones. There was also a growing backlash against DDT, a pesticide that is highly effective at attacking mosquitoes but whose widespread use in agriculture killed many fish, beneficial insects, and birds. Although only small amounts of DDT are needed to control malaria—usually in indoor-spraying campaigns—its toxic reputation made cash-strapped governments in Africa, which often must rely heavily on international donors, hesitant to use it.

There Is a Silver Lining

So much for how things got so bad. The silver lining to all this heartache is that the outlines of a workable solution have at long last emerged. No one is promising an end to all deaths from malaria. But doctors estimate that hundreds of millions of people could avoid the illness and the death rate could be cut in half. The catch: Although astonishingly inexpensive (at least by the industrial world's standards), an effective response is still beyond the financial resources of the poorest nations of the world, particularly those in

Africa. There simply can be no progress without help from the developed world.

To be successful, any antimalaria campaign must do two things: treat the illness and prevent the transmission of parasites. Several studies in Africa have proved that combination therapy (using several types of drugs at once), in which at least one of the medications comes from a plant called sweet wormwood, easily destroys drug-resistant malarial parasites in the bloodstream. Using combination therapy, often in the same pill, greatly decreases the risk that the parasites will become resistant. As an added bonus, artemisinin, the active ingredient in sweet wormwood, acts very quickly, further decreasing the chances of drug resistance.

The full three-day course of treatment with artemisinin-based combination therapy costs from $1 to $10 a person. Unfortunately, that's at least 10 times the price of current, though ineffective, treatment programs. Most poor African governments simply cannot afford to foot the entire bill for combination therapy and the training required to give it. And the same holds true for the majority of their private citizens, many of whom already spend a third of their income on malaria treatment.

Although nearly every developed country and most major international aid groups have said they are ready to help pay for artemisinin-based treatment in Africa, that support has not always been forthcoming. Some health experts believe a report about the many benefits of artemisinin-containing drugs from the U.S. Institute of Medicine will, over time, dissolve any reluctance.

Stop Mosquitoes Before They Bite

And what about prevention? Many African countries are working to distribute low-cost insecticide-soaked mosquito nets. These serve as traps for mosquitoes, which are attracted by the carbon dioxide that sleepers exhale and are then killed by the insecticide. The nets are portable, so they can be taken along by their owners. In villages where at least 80% of pregnant women and children under age 5 sleep beneath insecticide-sprayed mosquito nets, the rate of illness for all residents has dropped dramatically. Unfortunately, only 1% or 2% of people in malarial zones sleep under mosquito nets. Also, most nets need to be retreated every six months, and they are less effective in areas where anopheles mosquitoes bite all day long

DEATH BY MOSQUITO **621**

Statistics Many essays use statistical information as part of supporting arguments. **Ask:** How do the statistics in "Death by Mosquito" help you in reading the essay? *(Students may answer the statistics give specific information.)* **Ask:** How can you "sharpen" the statistic on page 621, or make it more meaningful? *(If 1% to 2% of people in malarial zones sleep under mosquito nets, how many people in total do so? Is the information necessary to answer that question available in the article? No.)*

Literary History ☆

Silent Spring Rachel Carson was a nature writer who became concerned about the effect DDT spraying was having on the environment. Her book *Silent Spring*, published in 1962, eventually brought about the banning of DDT. It also brought a new public awareness that nature was vulnerable to human intervention.

Approaching Level

DIFFERENTIATED INSTRUCTION

Emerging Help students to review the information about malaria on pages 620–621. **Ask:** What causes malaria? *(parasites)* How do they usually enter the human body? *(from infected mosquitoes.)* Where do the parasites breed inside the body? *(in the liver and in red blood cells)* What causes people to become ill when new parasite are born? *(Red blood cells burst.)*

Assess

1. Students will likely be surprised and angry about the lack of adequate response to the outbreak.

2. (a) approximately 300 million people (b) Malaria is curable.

3. (a) The number of malaria cases has quadrupled. (b) Countries with malaria outbreaks have lower economic growth rates.

4. (a) A bite from a mosquito infected with a kind of parasite, which enters the bloodstream and multiplies inside the host's liver and red blood cells (b) Medicines, such as chloroquine, are effective for a while, and then the parasites build up a resistance to the drugs.

5. (a) Treat the illness and prevent the transmission of parasites (b) Preventing the transmission of parasites will stop the effect of the parasites, which is causing malaria.

6. (a) The chemical kills birds and beneficial insects. (b) The author is for the use of DDT because she includes only evidence of its positive effects.

7. Answers will vary. Some students may think that the environmental risks are a small price to pay for the possible elimination of such a deadly disease. Others may feel that other, less harmful treatment options should be explored.

instead of just at night.

Another effective method of reducing transmission is to spray DDT inside huts and other buildings. Intriguingly, DDT is often better at repelling mosquitoes than killing them. This requires much less pesticide than was once sprayed on crops and swamps. An international antipesticide treaty that took effect in May 2004 makes an exception for the use of DDT in malarial areas. But some health experts are worried that the complicated process to get permission to use DDT will limit the pesticide's effectiveness.

Recent experience in South Africa shows just how well DDT can work. In 1996, the South African government, under pressure from environmental groups, decided to stop its use of DDT in residential spraying. Instead the government would use pesticides that contained safer types of chemicals. Unfortunately, it turned out that many anopheles mosquitoes in South Africa were resistant to those chemicals. The number of cases of malaria, which had been hovering between 8,000 and 13,000 a year, grew steadily worse, and by the year 2000 it had reached 64,000 cases, with 423 deaths. When the government reintroduced DDT spraying, the number of cases fell almost immediately.

Even environmentalists had to admit that DDT was necessary. "I wasn't very happy about it," says Gerhard Verdoorn, chairman of South Africa's Endangered Wildlife Trust, a conservation group which had earlier lobbied the South African government to drop the pesticide and now helps train DDT sprayers. "We can't just look after animals and not care if people die."

That's the kind of attitude that will make a difference in the battle against malaria. The know-how to control the disease already exists. What is not so clear is whether there is the necessary commitment—financial and political—to make it happen.

Respond and Think Critically

Respond and Interpret

1. Write a brief summary of the main events in this article before you answer the following questions. For help with writing a summary, see page 435.

2. (a) Approximately how many people become ill with malaria each year? (b) Why is this particularly tragic?

3. (a) By how much has the number of malaria cases grown in Africa since the 1980s? (b) What are the economic implications of a malaria outbreak?

4. (a) What causes someone to contract malaria? (b) How have the medicines used to treat the disease both failed and succeeded?

Analyze and Evaluate

5. (a) What does the writer claim are two things an anti-malaria campaign must do? (b) In what way do these things represent cause-and-effect situations?

6. (a) What effect does the chemical DDT have on wildlife? (b) Based on evidence from the text, do you think the writer is for or against the use of DDT in the fight against malaria? Explain.

Connect

7. Do you think the benefits of DDT outweigh the risks? Explain.

8. How do you think the spread and response to an epidemic like malaria is different now than it would have been in eighteenth-century England?

8. The disease can spread more easily now since international travel is common and accessible. In the eighteenth century, people were more likely to associate plagues with religion. Now, many people believe that diseases need to be treated with medicine.

Before You Read

from *A Dictionary of the English Language*

Meet **Samuel Johnson**

(1709–1784)

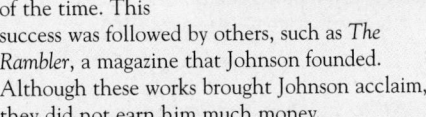

Samuel Johnson once said in his typically blunt but humorous way, "No man but a blockhead ever wrote except for money." Money was, in fact, a problem for Johnson throughout most of his life. Although he was one of the greatest writers of his time, he often had to struggle to make ends meet.

A Difficult Childhood Born in Lichfield in 1709, Samuel Johnson was the son of a bookseller. In his infancy, he contracted a disease that left him deaf in one ear, nearly blind in one eye, and badly scarred. Despite these health problems, Johnson was an exceptional student. According to his mother, he could memorize almost instantly whatever he read. In his late teens, Johnson attended Oxford University, but he could not afford to complete his education there. From the time he left school until his father died in 1731, little is known about Johnson except that he most likely suffered from mental depression.

> *"Dictionaries are like watches; the worst is better than none, and the best cannot be expected to go quite true."*
>
> —Samuel Johnson

Literary Success and Financial Strain After Oxford, Johnson unsuccessfully tried his hand at a number of jobs. At the age of twenty-six, he settled down and married a widow about twenty years his senior. He opened a school but had difficulty keeping students. Within two years, he closed the school and moved to London. Soon, Johnson began to earn his living by writing. He contributed essays to the *Gentlemen's Magazine* and attracted critical attention with his poem "London," which condemned certain political leaders and vices of the time. This success was followed by others, such as *The Rambler*, a magazine that Johnson founded. Although these works brought Johnson acclaim, they did not earn him much money.

Further Success—and Compensation Johnson's fortunes began to change when he reached his thirties. It was then that a bookseller commissioned him to write an English language dictionary. Johnson and six assistants worked for more than eight years to gather and produce the almost 40,000 entries that *A Dictionary of the English Language* contains. The sheer scope of the task—it had taken a French academy forty years to complete a comparable French dictionary—clinched Johnson's reputation as a scholar.

When Johnson was in his fifties, he was at last freed from his financial difficulties when King George III granted him a pension for life. In his later years, Johnson continued to work, editing an edition of *Lives of the English Poets*, a series of biographical and critical essays. Johnson died in 1784 at the age of seventy-five and was buried in Westminster Abbey.

Literature Online

Author Search For more about Samuel Johnson, go to glencoe.com and enter QuickPass code GLB9817u3.

SAMUEL JOHNSON **623**

Before You Read

Focus

Bellringer Options

Selection Focus
   Transparency 31
Daily Language Practice
   Transparency 50

Or share this excerpt from "London" with students: "Prepare for Death, if here at Night you roam,/And sign your Will before you sup from Home./Some fiery Fop, with new Commission vain,/Who sleeps on Brambles till he kills his Man;/Some frolick Drunkard, reeling from a Feast,/Provokes a Broil, and stabs you for a Jest."

Ask: What can you learn about Samuel Johnson from his poem? (*He is intelligent, gifted, and melancholy.*)

 For summaries in languages other than English, see Unit 3 Teaching Resources Book, pp. 178–183.

Selection Skills

Literary Elements
- Voice (SE pp. 624, 626, 629) (TE p. 626)
- Tone (SE p. 629) (TE p. 629)

A Dictionary of the English Language/Letter to Lord Chesterfield

Writing Skills/Grammar
- Apply Diction (SE p. 630) (TE p. 630)

Reading Skills
- Distinguish Fact and Opinion (SE pp. 624, 625, 628, 630) (TE p. 625)
- Use a Dictionary (TE p. 626)

Vocabulary Skills
- Analogies (TE p. 624)
- Word Parts (TE p. 624)
- Antonyms (TE p. 630)
- Update Meaning (TE p. 628)

623

Before You Read

Focus

Summary

The selection contains two selections by Johnson, from *A Dictionary of the English Language* and "Letter to Lord Chesterfield." Johnson's preface to his dictionary is very personal by today's standards, and students will notice this also in Johnson's definitions. Johnson's *Letter to Lord Chesterfield* is a rebuke to an opportunist who declined to support Johnson's dictionary project until the glory was won.

Vocabulary

Analogies Say: Choose the vocabulary word from the list that best explains what each of the following pairs has in common: a music collection and a museum *(aggregated)*; a detective and a worried parent *(vigilance)*; a lifelong memory and a mountain *(immutably)*; a naturally gifted athlete and a hunch *(intuitive)*.

 For additional vocabulary practice, see Unit 3 Teaching Resources Book, p. 186.

 For additional context, see Glencoe Interactive Vocabulary CD-ROM.

Literature and Reading Preview

Connect to the Texts

What slang phrases were once popular among your peers but now are no longer used? With a group of classmates, discuss why the phrases have gone out of fashion.

Build Background

Johnson's *A Dictionary of the English Language* was published in 1755 in London. Johnson appealed to wealthy patrons for financial backing, but while many expressed interest, few offered any funds. Johnson was forced to use much of his own income from the *Dictionary*—he received one sum when the book was published, and no payments afterward—to pay the small staff who copied his work by hand, pasted revisions, and produced the pages. Among the 42,773 definitions in the final first edition was Johnson's particularly wry definition of the word "patron": "Commonly a wretch, who supports with insolence and is paid with flattery" (see page 628).

Set Purposes for Reading

Big Idea The English Enlightenment and Neoclassicism

As you read, ask yourself, How does Johnson use reason to guide his opinions?

Literary Element Voice

Voice is the distinctive use of language that conveys to the reader the personality of a writer or narrator. Voice is determined by elements of style, such as word choice and tone. As you read, ask yourself, What are the distinctive characteristics of Johnson's voice?

Reading Strategy Distinguish Fact and Opinion

Facts are statements that can be verified or proven true. **Opinions** express beliefs, ideas, and feelings, and as such, they cannot be verified. A good reader uses prior knowledge and logic to recognize whether the author is presenting information as verifiable truth. As you read, ask yourself, How does Johnson get his opinions across—even in the traditionally factual text of a dictionary?

Tip: Compiling Emotional Language You can often spot an author's opinion by his or her use of emotional words. As you read, keep track of emotional language.

Learning Objectives

For pages 623–630

In studying this text, you will focus on the following objectives:

Literary Study: Analyzing voice.

Reading: Distinguishing fact and opinion.

Writing: Applying diction in a brief example.

Vocabulary

vigilance (vij′ ə ləns) *n.* careful watchfulness; p. 626 *Keeping up to date with clothing fashions requires a certain amount of vigilance.*

intuitive (in tōō′ ə tiv) *adj.* known or perceived without deliberate thought; p. 626 *The young man had an intuitive gift for playing the piano.*

immutably (i mū′ tə blē) *adv.* unchangeably; permanently; p. 626 *Although Perkins had retired as governor years earlier, his name was immutably linked to that office.*

aggregated (ag′ rə gā′ təd) *adj.* collected; gathered into a whole; p. 626 *The neighborhood's crime statistics were aggregated in a report and sent to the mayor's office.*

Vocabulary Practice

Word Parts Begin with the words *longevity, immortal,* and *philology.*
Ask: What word parts do you recognize? What do the prefixes and suffixes mean? (*Suffix: -ity, state or quality/Root: long; Prefix: im-, not/Root: mortal; Suffix: -ology, discourse, expression/ Prefix: phil, love of*) **Ask:** How does

knowing the definitions of prefixes and suffixes help you understand new vocabulary? Give an example. (*Recognizing the word long and knowing the suffix -ity, one can guess the meaning refers to a long-lasting state.*)

from

A Dictionary of the English Language

Trompe L'Oeil with Writing Materials. Evert Collier. Oil on canvas, 181/2 x 251/2 in. Victoria and Albert Museum, London.

Samuel Johnson

from The Preface

In hope of giving longevity to that which its own nature forbids to be immortal, I have devoted this book, the labor of years, to the honor of my country, that we may no longer yield the palm of philology[1] without a contest to the nations of the continent. The chief glory of every people arises from its authors. Whether I shall add anything by my own writings to the reputation of English literature must be left to time. Much of my life has been lost under the pressures of disease; much has been trifled away; and much has always been spent in provision for the day that was passing over me; but I shall not think my employment useless or ignoble if, by my assistance, foreign nations and distant ages gain access to the propagators[2] of knowledge and understand the teachers of truth, if my labors afford light to the repositories[3] of science and add celebrity to Bacon, to Hooker, to Milton, and to Boyle.[4]

When I am animated by this wish, I look with pleasure on my book, however defective, and deliver it to the world with the spirit of a man that has endeavored well. That it will immediately become popular I have not promised to myself. A few wild blunders and risible[5] absurdities, from which no work of such multi-

---

1. A *palm* leaf is a symbol for excellence or victory; *philology* is the study of language.

2. As used here, *propagators* are people who spread knowledge.
3. *Repositories* are storehouses.
4. Francis *Bacon,* Richard *Hooker,* John *Milton,* and Robert *Boyle* are writers and scholars whom Johnson quotes throughout his dictionary.
5. *Risible* means "laughable" or "comical."

1 Distinguish Fact and Opinion **Is this statement a fact or an opinion? Do you agree with it? Why or why not?**

The English Enlightenment and Neoclassicism
What statement is Johnson making about the place of language, ideas, and education in world culture? **2**

SAMUEL JOHNSON **625**

Teach

Reading Strategy **1**

Distinguish Fact and Opinion Answer: *It is an opinion. Some students may agree with this statement completely. Others may argue that ordinary citizens are what make a country truly great.*

ENGLISH LEARNERS Check to make sure English learners understand that here *glory* means "something that brings great honor or praise." **Ask:** What kinds of things might bring glory to a country? *(Possible responses: winning a war; scientific discoveries)*

 For additional practice using the reading skill or strategy, see Unit 3 Teaching Resources Book, p. 185.

Big Idea **2**

The English Enlightenment and Neoclassicism **Answer:** *Johnson is saying that language and ideas are of primary importance in furthering understanding.*

 For an audio recording of this selection, use Listening Library Audio CD-ROM.

Readability Scores

Dale-Chall: 16.9
DRP: 74
Lexile: 1340

Teach

Literary Element 1

Voice Answer: *Some students may say that Johnson seems detached or scholarly, recognizing imperfections while insisting on the value of his work. Others may say that he sounds apologetic or humble. They may also note the graceful parallel structure.*

(ENGLISH LEARNERS) Have English learners consult a dictionary to find several definitions of *perform*. **Ask:** What do you think *performed* means in this sentence? *(carried out; done)* What does Johnson think of his dictionary? *(Possible response: He thinks it is good but not perfect.)*

Literary Element 2

Voice Answer: *Answers will vary. Students may cite "frigid tranquility" as an example of Johnson's diction; they may note the irony with which Johnson closes his preface.*

(APPROACHING) For approaching-level students, write the words *dismiss, frigid, tranquility,* and *censure* on the board. Have students consult a dictionary to define the words. **Ask:** Which words seem negative? *(dismiss, frigid, censure)* Which seem positive? *(tranquility)* How would you describe the statement's tone? *(Possible responses: uncaring; sarcastic)*

Language History ☆

Word Origin The origin of *vigilance* is a Latin verb *(vigilare)* that means "to keep watch" or "to stay awake." Johnson uses *vigilance* in contrast to *inadvertency*

---

plicity was ever free, may for a time furnish folly with laughter and harden ignorance in contempt; but useful diligence will at last prevail, and there never can be wanting some who distinguish desert; who will consider that no dictionary of a living tongue ever can be perfect, since while it is hastening to publication, some words are budding, and some falling away; that a whole life cannot be spent upon syntax and etymology,[6] and that even a whole life would not be sufficient; that he, whose design includes whatever language can express, must often speak of what he does not understand; that a writer will sometimes be hurried by eagerness to the end and sometimes faint with weariness under a task which Scaliger[7] compares to the labors of the anvil and the mine; that what is obvious is not always known, and what is known is not always present; that sudden fits of inadvertency[8] will surprise **vigilance**, slight avocations[9] will seduce attention, and casual eclipses will darken learning; and that the writer shall often in vain trace his memory at the moment of need for that which yesterday he knew with **intuitive** readiness and which will come uncalled into his thoughts tomorrow.

In this work, when it shall be found that much is omitted, let it not be forgotten that much likewise is performed; and though no book was ever spared out of tenderness to the author, and the world is little solicitous to know whence proceeded the faults of that which it condemns; yet it may gratify curiosity to inform it that the *English Dictionary* was written with little assistance of the learned and without any patronage of the great; not in the soft obscurities of retirement or under the shelter of academic bowers,[10] but amidst inconvenience and distraction, in sickness and in sorrow. It may repress the triumph of malignant[11] criticism to observe that if our language is not here fully displayed, I have only failed in an attempt which no human powers have hitherto completed. If the lexicons[12] of ancient tongues, now **immutably** fixed and comprised in a few volumes, are yet, after the toil of successive ages, inadequate and delusive; if the **aggregated** knowledge and cooperating diligence of the Italian academicians did not secure them from the censure of Beni;[13] if the embodied critics of France, when fifty years had been spent upon their work, were obliged to change its economy[14] and give their second edition another form, I may surely be contented without the praise of perfection, which, if I could obtain, in this gloom of solitude, what would it avail me? I have protracted my work till most of those whom I wished to please have sunk into the grave, and success and miscarriage are empty sounds: I therefore dismiss it with frigid tranquility, having little to fear or hope from censure or from praise. ∾

---

6. *Syntax* is sentence structure, and *etymology* is word history.
7. *Scaliger* refers to J. J. Scaliger (1540–1609), a scholar who suggested that criminals be sentenced to writing dictionaries.
8. *Inadvertency* means "heedlessness" or "negligence."
9. *Avocations* are hobbies or other diversions.
10. By *bowers*, Johnson means "idealized settings."
11. In this case, *malignant* means "having an evil or negative influence."
12. *Lexicons* are dictionaries.
13. Paola *Beni* severely criticized the Italian Academy's dictionary.
14. Here, *economy* means "organization."

1 **Voice** *What does this statement tell you about the author's personality?*

Vocabulary

vigilance (vij′ə ləns) *n.* careful watchfulness
intuitive (in tōō′ə tiv) *adj.* known or perceived without deliberate thought

2 **Voice** *What qualities of Johnson's voice does this statement convey?*

Vocabulary

immutably (i mū′tə blē) *adv.* unchangeably; permanently
aggregated (ag′rə gā′təd) *adj.* collected; gathered into a whole

---

626 UNIT 3 FROM PURITANISM TO THE ENLIGHTENMENT

Reading Practice

Use a Dictionary Refer students to the entry for *imagination*. **Ask:** What does the stress mark indicate? *(the syllable that receives the greatest emphasis or stress)* How did Johnson indicate the end of an entry? *(with a period)* Refer students to the entry for *kind*. **Ask:** What conventions did Johnson follow for quotations? *(He indented quotations and gave their source.)* Invite students to perform a careful comparison of Johnson's style and the style used in a modern dictionary. Have them create a visual, such as a poster, comparing two entries.

from
A Dictionary of the English Language

⭐ **ANTHO′ LOGY.** *n.* 1. A collection of flowers. 2. A collection of poems.

CLUB. *n.* An assembly of good fellows, meeting under certain conditions.
> What right has any man to meet in factious *clubs* to vilify the government?
> > Dryden, *Medal, Dedication.*

IMA′ GINATION. *n.* 1. Fancy; the power of forming ideal pictures; the power of representing things absent to one's self or others. 2. Conception; image in the mind; idea. 3. Contrivance; scheme.

KIND. *adj.* Benevolent; filled with general good-will.
> By the *kind* gods, 'tis most ignobly done
> To pluck me by the beard.
> > Shakespeare, *King Lear.*

LEXICO′ GRAPHER. *n.* A writer of dictionaries; a harmless drudge that busies himself in tracing the original and detailing the signification of words.

MAN. *n.* 1. Human being.
> The king is but a *man* as I am; the violet smells to him as it doth to me; the element shows to him as it doth to me, all his senses have but human conditions.
> > Shakespeare.

2. Not a woman. 3. Not a boy. 4. A word of familiarity bordering on contempt. 5. Not a beast.

MO′ PPET. *n.* A puppet made of rags.

Dr. Samuel Johnson's house in London, designed by Johnson.

Teach

Language History ☆

Compare the recent definition of *anthology* with that given by Johnson in 1755. The first definition given by Johnson is not in use today but is suggested by the etymology of the word. **Ask:** Do you think the definition of *anthology* will be different 250 years from today? Explain. *(Students may say that the word will stabilize, or they may say that he word meaning will keep changing.)*

English Learners

DIFFERENTIATED INSTRUCTION

Beginning Ask: What are some of the adjectives on this page? *(sudden, slight, casual, intuitive)* Point out that these adjectives appear before nouns. **Ask:** What are the nouns that these adjectives modify? *(fits, avocations, eclipses, readiness)* Encourage students to identify more adjective-noun pairs.

Teach

Reading Strategy   1

Distinguish Fact and Opinion Answer: *In this definition Johnson reveals his bias against Scotland and its people.* **Ask:** Can you identify other examples of opinion among the excerpts from Johnson's dictionary? *(Possible answer: "In England [pension] is generally understood to mean pay given to a state hireling for treason to his country.")* [ENGLISH LEARNERS] Direct English learners' attention to the entry for *lexicographer*. Have students consult a dictionary to define any unfamiliar words. **Ask:** What facts are included in the entry? *(writes dictionaries, finds the origins of words, explains what words mean)* What opinions are included? *(is harmless, works very hard)*

Big Idea   2

The English Enlightenment and Neoclassicism Answer: *The length and complexity of the definition implies that Johnson views the human mind and the ability to reason as very significant.*

Literary History ☆

Although Johnson's *Dictionary* was not the first English dictionary, his method of defining words set one precedent: He was the first English lexicographer to use quotations to illustrate the use of the words he defined.

📁 To check students' understanding of the selection, see Unit 3 Teaching Resources Book, p. 189.

628

NA′TURE. *n.* 1. An imaginary being supposed to preside over the material and animal world. 2. The constitution of an animated body.

> We're not ourselves,
> When *nature*, being oppressed, commands
> the mind
☆ To suffer with the body.
> Shakespeare, *King Lear.*

3. Disposition of mind; temper. 4. The regular course of things. 5. Natural affection, or reverence; native sensations. 6. Sort; species. 7. Physics; the science which teaches the quality of things.

OATS. *n.* A grain, which in England is generally given to horses, but in Scotland supports the people.

PA′STERN. *n.* The knee of a horse.
> I will not change my horse with any that
> treads on four *pasterns*.[1]
> Shakespeare, *Henry V.*

PA′TRON. *n.* One who countenances, supports, or protects. Commonly a wretch who supports with insolence and is paid with flattery.

PE′NSION. *n.* An allowance made to anyone without an equivalent. In England it is generally understood to mean pay given to a state hireling for treason to his country.

PE′PPERMINT. *n.* Mint eminently hot.

---

1. A *pastern* is actually part of a horse's foot. When an acquaintance asked Johnson why he had defined it as a knee, he answered, "Ignorance, Madam, pure ignorance."

1 Distinguish Fact and Opinion **What opinion is hidden within this "factual" definition?**

SLO′THFUL. *adj.* Idle; lazy; sluggish; inactive; indolent; dull of motion.
> The desire of the *slothful* killeth him; for his
> hands refuse to labor.
> Proverbs, 21:25.

SMOKE. *n.* The visible effluvium, or sooty exhalation, from anything burning.

SNEEZE. *n.* Emission of wind audibly by the nose.

WIT. *n.* 1. The powers of the mind; the mental faculties; the intellects. This is the original signification. 2. Imagination; quickness of fancy. 3. Sentiments produced by quickness of fancy. 4. A man of fancy. 5. A man of genius. 6. Sense; judgment. 7. In the plural, sound mind; intellect not crazed. 8. Contrivance; stratagem; power of expedients.

X. A letter which, though found in Saxon words, begins no word in the English language.

YAWN. *v.* 1. To gape; to oscitate; to have the mouth opened involuntarily by fumes, as in sleepiness.

YOUTH. *n.* The part of life succeeding to childhood and adolescence; the time from fourteen to twenty-eight.

The English Enlightenment and Neoclassicism *This definition is nearly twice as long as any of the others in this listing. What does this suggest about Johnson's view of the human mind and reason?* **2**

Vocabulary Practice

Update Meaning Point out to students instances of outdated language and ideas. For example, point out in the definition of **yawn** that today one would not say a yawn was caused by "fumes." Have students work in pairs to select one word or definition from the list that is outdated. Ask the pairs to rewrite the entry to reflect current beliefs and usage.

Respond and Think Critically

Respond and Interpret

1. What is your impression of Johnson after reading excerpts from his works?

2. (a)In the first paragraph of the preface to *A Dictionary of the English Language*, what purpose does Johnson say he hopes the dictionary will fulfill? (b)How might the definitions in the dictionary help fulfill this purpose?

3. (a)Which of the definitions from Johnson's dictionary are sarcastic? (b)Why might Johnson have decided to include these definitions?

Analyze and Evaluate

4. (a)What is the overall tone of the preface to *A Dictionary of the English Language*? (b)What does this suggest about Johnson?

5. Which style of definition do you prefer: the straightforward or the sarcastic? Why?

Connect

6. **Big Idea** The English Enlightenment and Neoclassicism What characteristics of Johnson's works suggest the influence of the English Enlightenment? How might Johnson's style contradict the principles of reason?

7. **Connect to Today** Contemporary dictionaries are compiled by large groups of writers and editors. What might be some of the benefits of a dictionary written by such a group? What might be some of the drawbacks?

Literary Element Voice

The **voice** of a literary work is the distinctive use of language that conveys to the reader the personality of a writer or narrator. Voice is determined by elements of style such as word choice and tone. Johnson's voice is marked by long, elegant sentences; precise diction; and an expertly controlled sarcastic wit.

1. In the preface to the *Dictionary*, find an example of a long, elegant sentence that Johnson uses to witty or sarcastic effect.

2. Which word choices in the dictionary entries do you find particularly effective? Why?

Review: Tone

As you learned on page 245, **tone** is an author's attitude toward his or her subject matter. Tone is conveyed through elements such as word choice, punctuation, sentence structure, and figures of speech. The tone of Samuel Johnson's preface to his *Dictionary* is outwardly modest and deferential but contains hints of disappointment and defiance.

Partner Activity With a partner, use a chart like this one to "translate" Johnson's overt tone into his intended meanings.

| Text: I may surely be contented without the praise of perfection, which, if I could obtain, in this gloom of solitude, what would it avail me? | Meaning: Johnson has reached the point in his labor where criticism means nothing to him, as he expects no praise. |

---

1. Students may view Johnson as a real person, with opinions and doubts.

2. (a) His purpose is to glorify England. (b) By using quotations from great English writers

3. (a) *Lexicographer, oats, patron,* and *pension.* (b) To show his wit

4. (a) Proud, defensive, self-righteous. (b) He anticipated opposition.

5. The sarcasm is witty, but straightforward definitions are helpful.

6. Johnson's works apply the principles of logic and reason. Johnson often masked his opinions under the guise of reason.

7. The benefits include a shorter creation time. The drawbacks include an impersonal voice.

Progress Check

Can students analyze voice?

If No → See Unit 3 Teaching Resources Book, p. 184.

Literary Element

1. Make sure that students choose a sentence that is lengthy, witty, or barbed.

2. Students may choose words such as *overpowered, enchantment, contending, exhausted,* and *uncourtly.*

Review: Tone

Possible answers for student charts:

Meaning 1. Johnson means that having never had a patron, he did not expect encouragement or assistance.

Meaning 2. Johnson means that Chesterfield's praise now is too little, too late.

After You Read

Assess

Reading Strategy

1. (a) Johnson's dictionary includes his opinions as if they were facts—most dictionaries include only factual information. (b) The form is fitting because Johnson can present opinion and satire in concise, witty definitions.

2. (a) Harmless drudge
   (b) Wretch, insolence, flattery

Writing

Students' definitions should mimic Johnson's diction, appeal to a specific audience, and address both denotations and connotations of words.

 For grammar practice, see Unit 3 Teaching Resources Book, p. 188.

 For additional selection assessment, see Assessment Resources, pp. 167–168.

When you **distinguish fact from opinion**, you determine whether information can be verified and proved true.

1. (a) With regard to fact and opinion, how does Johnson's dictionary differ from most standard dictionaries today? (b) Why might the dictionary form be especially fitting for Johnson's style of expression?

2. Use your notes to pick out the emotional words in the following passages:

   (a) "a harmless drudge that busies himself in tracing the original and detailing the signification of words." (from "Lexicographer") (b) "Commonly a wretch who supports with insolence and is paid with flattery." (from "Patron")

Vocabulary Practice

Practice with Antonyms With a partner, brainstorm three antonyms for each boldfaced vocabulary word below. Then discuss your choices with your classmates. Be prepared to explain why you chose your words.

vigilance   intuitive   immutably
aggregated

EXAMPLE:
ambitious

<u>Antonyms</u>: unmotivated, lazy, satisfied

<u>Sample explanation</u>: An ambitious person energetically pursues his or her goals, unlike a person who is lazy.

Literature Online

Selection Resources For Selection Quizzes, eFlashcards, and Reading-Writing Connection activities, go to glencoe.com and enter QuickPass code GLB9817u3.

Write with Style

 Apply Diction

Assignment Johnson used unique and entertaining diction to write about the English language. Think of a topic that interests you and list several words related to the topic. Use diction that mimics Johnson's to write definitions of these words.

Get Ideas Make a word web to generate terms related to your topic.

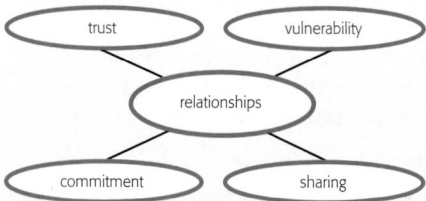

Then review the format and diction of Johnson's dictionary entries and decide how you will adapt them to your own project.

EXAMPLE:
VULNERABILITY. n. A condition best described as painting a target on one's stomach, and handing a friend the bow and arrow.

Give It Structure Before you begin defining your words, think about the audience for whom you are writing. Consider what terms and ideas they are familiar with, and give necessary background information. Decide what impression you would like your definitions to make. Will they be witty? easily remembered? catchy? Tailor your diction and word choice to support the overall impression and tone you choose.

Look at Language Pay attention to the denotations and connotations of the words you define and the words you use in your definitions. Include figurative language to add interest and convey complicated ideas in a precise way. Vary the structure of your sentences to keep your writing fresh.

Vocabulary

Possible answers:

vigilance

<u>Antonyms</u>: inattentiveness, carelessness, negligence

<u>Sample explanation</u>: A person who exhibited *vigilance* would be very careful, unlike a person who exhibited *carelessness*.

intuitive

<u>Antonyms</u>: learned, deliberate, conscious

<u>Sample explanation</u>: *Intuitive* knowledge comes naturally, unlike *learned* knowledge, which is acquired through effort.

immutably

<u>Antonyms</u>: temporarily, inconstantly, irregularly

<u>Sample explanation</u>: Something that exists *immutably* will never be gone, but something that exists *temporarily* will soon be gone.

aggregated

<u>Antonyms</u>: scattered, dispersed, dissipated

<u>Sample explanation</u>: A substance that is *aggregated* is gathered into a whole, but a substance that is *scattered* is split into many parts.

Grammar Workshop

Pronoun-Antecedent Agreement

Literature Connection In this quotation, Samuel Johnson uses the pronoun *it* in place of the noun *book*.

> "…I look with pleasure on my book, however defective, and deliver it to the world…"
>
> —Samuel Johnson, from *A Dictionary of the English Language*

When you speak or write, make sure that every **pronoun** you use has a clear **antecedent**, or noun to which the pronoun refers. Avoid these common problems in pronoun-antecedent agreement.

Problems

1. **A weak or vague pronoun antecedent**

   The *Dictionary* was well received, <u>which</u> was Johnson's reward.

2. **A pronoun that refers to more than one antecedent.**

   Francis Bacon and John Milton appear in the *Dictionary*, and <u>he</u> felt that, at least, made the book worthwhile.

Solutions

1. **Substitute a noun for the pronoun.**

   The *Dictionary*'s warm <u>reception</u> was Johnson's reward.

2. **Clarify the antecedent of the pronoun.**

   Francis Bacon and John Milton appear in the *Dictionary*, and <u>Johnson</u> felt that, at least, made the book worthwhile.

Revise Rewrite the following sentences to correct pronoun-antecedent errors. Add any necessary information.

1. Johnson wrote in a preface that he did not care if it was popular.
2. The absence of some words should not reflect badly on him.
3. The writing was filled with complex sentences, which made it seem formal.
4. Johnson's *Dictionary* was revolutionary, which received mixed reactions.
5. Several of the definitions included Johnson's own opinions, but did readers recognize it?

GRAMMAR WORKSHOP **631**

Learning Objectives

In this workshop, you will focus on the following objectives:

Grammar:
Understanding how to correct pronoun-antecedent agreement.
Understanding how to correct capitalization.

Correcting Pronoun-Antecedent Agreement

A **pronoun** substitutes for a noun and should always refer to a particular noun, or **antecedent.** Remember that pronouns should agree in number and gender with the antecedents to which they refer.

Tip

To check for pronoun-antecedent agreement when writing for a test, read the sentence to yourself. Sentences that need correction often sound strange or confusing.

Language Handbook

For more about pronouns and antecedents, see Language Handbook, p. R49.

Grammar For more grammar practice, go to glencoe.com and enter QuickPass code GLB9817u3.

Grammar Workshop

Pronoun-Antecedent Agreement

Focus

Write on the board: After we learned more details about the fire, it was depressing. Discuss why this sentence is confusing. *(Possible response: The antecedent of it is vague.)*

Teach

Pronoun Agreement
Pronouns must agree with their antecedents in person, number, and gender.

Assess

Possible responses:

1. Johnson wrote in a preface that he did not care if the book was popular.
2. The absence of some words should not reflect badly on Johnson.
3. The writing was filled with complex sentences, which made the style seem formal.
4. Johnson's *Dictionary*, which received mixed reactions, revealed a totally new approach.
5. Several of the definitions included Johnson's own opinion, but did readers recognize this fact?

 For additional grammar practice, see Unit 3 Teaching Resources Book, p. 191.

Approaching Level

DIFFERENTIATED INSTRUCTION

Established Students probably will write many friendly letters in their lifetimes. They may also want to write formal letters of complaint. These two types of letters have different styles and tones.

Lead a class discussion about the differences in these two types of letters. Have students draft two letters: a short, friendly letter that describes an unpleasant event and a formal letter to the person who caused the situation. In each, be sure to avoid unclear pronoun references. Then have students exchange letters and review each other's work.

Selection Focus
Transparency 32

Daily Language Practice
Transparency 51

Or write on the board: *Friendship.*
Ask: What are some qualities of a friend or an acquaintance that you admire? As they read, have students consider the friendship of Boswell and Johnson.

Before You Read

from *The Life of Samuel Johnson*

Meet **James Boswell**

(1740–1795)

For years, the biographer and diarist James Boswell's accomplishments were overshadowed by those of Samuel Johnson, the literary giant about whom he wrote. Before the twentieth century, Boswell was often regarded as little more than an adequate reporter. The discovery of Boswell's journals in the 1920s and 1930s, however, revealed his rare insight and his important role in the development of the modern biography.

Early Life Boswell was born in 1740 in Edinburgh, Scotland, the son of well-to-do parents. As a child he disliked the school he attended, so his father provided him with private tutors. Boswell received an excellent education in the arts and law, but he did not want to become a lawyer like his father. Instead, he was drawn to the theater and the arts. In 1760, at the age of twenty, he ran away to London, but his father soon brought him back home. Father and son struck a bargain: James could return to London as soon as he passed his law exams, so at the age of twenty-two he passed his exams and happily set out.

A Literary Friendship Boswell loved the life of the city. He made a point of introducing himself to London's intellectual elite and quickly became a part of it. His wealthy background and personal charm afforded him access to the upper crust of London society. He met such notable figures of the time as painter Joshua Reynolds, writer Oliver Goldsmith, and political reformer John Wilkes. In a London bookshop, he also met the famous man of letters Samuel Johnson, and one of the great friendships of English literary history began. At the time they met, Boswell was only twenty-two. Johnson was fifty-three.

Travels Abroad Shortly after meeting Johnson, Boswell toured Europe, spending time in Corsica, a Mediterranean island. His account of his tour across Corsica, published when he was twenty-eight, was both a popular and a critical success.

At twenty-nine, Boswell married and moved back to Scotland to practice law. Though he could see Johnson only occasionally, the two wrote to each other and, when Boswell was in his early thirties, they toured the Scottish Highlands and the Hebrides Islands, off the western coast of Scotland, together. Boswell later published his journal from the tour. However, he is best known for *The Life of Samuel Johnson*. His sharp memory and eye for detail allow readers a vivid look into the life of not just Samuel Johnson, but also of Boswell himself.

> "We cannot tell the precise moment when friendship is formed. As in filling a vessel drop by drop, there is at last a drop which makes it run over; so in a series of kindnesses there is at last one which makes the heart run over."
>
> —James Boswell

While he was proud of his literary efforts, Boswell nevertheless regarded himself as a personal failure. He died in 1795, at the age of fifty-four, never to realize the impact his work would have on English literature.

 Literature Online

Author Search For more about James Boswell, go to glencoe.com and enter QuickPass code GLB9817u3.

Selection Skills

Literary Elements
- Biography (SE pp. 633-635, 637–638, 640)

The Life of Samuel Johnson

Listening/Speaking/Viewing Skills
- View the Art (SE pp. 636, 639)

Reading Skills
- Evaluate Credibility (SE pp. 633–634, 636–637, 641)
- Summarize (TE p. 634)
- Visualize (TE p. 636)

Vocabulary Skills
- Etymology (TE p. 633)
- Practice with Denotation and Connotation (SE p. 641)

Writing Skills/Grammar
- Diction (TE p. 638)

Literature and Reading Preview

Connect to the Biography

Is there anyone in the public eye whom you admire? Write a journal entry in which you explain why you admire the person.

Build Background

Throughout his friendship with Johnson, Boswell kept detailed journals in which he recorded his conversations with his illustrious friend. Boswell later used these journals, as well as information he gathered by interviewing Johnson's friends and acquaintances, to write the story of Johnson's life. For years it was believed that Boswell's journals had been destroyed shortly after his death, but they were recovered in the 1920s at Malahide Castle in Ireland. Upon examination of the journals, scholars learned that most of Johnson's conversations, the true spice of Boswell's biography, had been copied almost directly from Boswell's initial recording of them in his journals.

Set Purposes for Reading

Big Idea The English Enlightenment and Neoclassicism

As you read, ask yourself, How does Boswell bring into prominence Samuel Johnson's intellectual rigor, strongly held opinions, and force of personality?

Literary Element Biography

A **biography** is a nonfiction account of a person's life and personality, written by someone other than the subject. Using such resources as interviews, diaries, journals, and letters, the biographer describes major events in the subject's life and provides insight into the subject's character. As you read, ask yourself, How is the biographer himself a character in the story of Johnson's life?

Reading Strategy Evaluate Credibility

To analyze what you read, you must sometimes **evaluate the credibility** of the author or source. In a biography such as Boswell's *The Life of Samuel Johnson*, you must read carefully to separate facts from opinions and detect **bias**, or an inclination toward an opinion or position. As you read, ask yourself, Does the author seem reliable? How can I tell?

....

Tip: Taking Notes Take notes on examples of bias within the text.

Learning Objectives

For pages 632–641

In studying this text, you will focus on the following objectives:

Literary Study: Analyzing biography.

Reading: Evaluating credibility.

Writing: Writing an essay.

Vocabulary

veneration (ven´ ə rā´ shən) *n.* deep respect or reverence; p. 634 *The visiting dignitary was met with veneration and cheering crowds.*

zealous (zel´ əs) *adj.* filled with intense, enthusiastic devotion; p. 637 *The principal is zealous about the need for art in the school.*

impetuous (im pech´ oo əs) *adj.* characterized by rushing headlong into things; impulsive; p. 637 *Guillermo has an impetuous nature that allows him to talk to complete strangers.*

precept (prē´ sept) *n.* a rule intended as a guide for conduct or action; p. 638 *Regular attendance and punctuality are two of our club's precepts.*

ingenuity (in´ jə noo´ ə tē´) *n.* cleverness; inventiveness; p. 639 *Jackson's brilliant model for the science fair was just one example of his ingenuity.*

JAMES BOSWELL **633**

Established Have students use the following steps to preview the selection:

1. Read the title, headings, and pulled quotations.

2. Look at the images and read the captions.

3. Skim the first and last paragraphs of the selection.

4. Write at least four specific questions about the selection.

Ask students to share their questions with the class, adding at least two of the questions they hear to their own lists. Students should write answers to the questions as they read.

Before You Read

Focus

Summary

At their first meeting James Boswell was at first put off by Samuel Johnson's rough demeanor. This was a disappointment to Boswell, as he greatly admired the man who compiled the *Dictionary of the English Language*. By the time they parted, however, Boswell sought reassurance from their host that Johnson liked him. Apparently Johnson did like Boswell. Their friendship is a lasting element of English literary history.

For summaries in languages other than English, see Unit 3 Teaching Resources Book, pp. 192–197.

Vocabulary

Have students use a dictionary to research the etymologies of the vocabulary words. **Ask:** Which words are closely related to the meanings of their Latin or Greek roots? *(veneration, zealous, impetuous)* Which words are more distantly related? *(precept, ingenuity)*

For additional vocabulary practice, see Unit 3 Teaching Resources Book, p. 200.

For additional context, see Glencoe Interactive Vocabulary CD-ROM.

Teach

Reading Strategy 1

Evaluate Credibility

Answer: *Boswell reveals his sense of awe for Johnson.*

Ask: Why do you think Boswell described his veneration as mysterious? (*Students may say that his vision of Johnson in London had dreamlike qualities.*)

[ENGLISH LEARNERS] Remind students that cognates are words with similar spellings and meanings in two languages. Write the word *reverence* on the board. **Ask:** Do you know a similar word in Spanish? (*reveréncia*) What does the word mean? (*respect*) Point out that other words with similar spellings in Spanish and English may be cognates.

Literary Element 2

Biography Answer: *Postponement of the first meeting seems to have heightened Boswell's anticipation.*

 For an audio recording of this selection, use Listening Library Audio CD-ROM

Readability Scores

Dale-Chall: 8.5
DRP: 64
Lexile: 1440

from The Life of Samuel Johnson

James Boswell

Boswell Meets Johnson 1763

This is to me a memorable year; for in it I had the happiness to obtain the acquaintance of that extraordinary man whose memoirs I am now writing, an acquaintance which I shall ever esteem as one of the most fortunate circumstances in my life.

Though then but two-and-twenty, I had for several years read his works with delight and instruction and had the highest reverence for their author, which had grown up in my fancy into a kind of mysterious **veneration,** by figuring to myself a state of solemn elevated abstraction in which I supposed him to live in the immense metropolis of London. . . .

Mr. Thomas Davies the actor, who then kept a bookseller's shop in Russel Street, Covent Garden, told me that Johnson was very much

his friend and came frequently to his house, where he more than once invited me to meet him, but by some unlucky accident or other, he was prevented from coming to us. . . .

At last, on Monday the sixteenth of May, when I was sitting in Mr. Davies's back parlor, after having drunk tea with him and Mrs. Davies, Johnson unexpectedly came into the shop; and Mr. Davies having perceived him through the glass door in the room in which we were sitting, advancing towards us—he announced his awful[1] approach to me, somewhat in the manner of an actor in the part of Horatio, when he addresses Hamlet on the appearance of his father's ghost,[2] "Look, my Lord, it comes." I found that I had a very perfect idea of Johnson's figure, from the portrait of him

---

1 Evaluate Credibility *What does the biographer reveal in this paragraph about himself and his view of Johnson?*

Vocabulary

veneration (ven′ ə ra′ shən) *n.* deep respect or reverence

1. Here, *awful* means "awe-inspiring."
2. In William Shakespeare's *Hamlet,* Act 1, scene 4, Horatio announces to his friend Hamlet the appearance of Hamlet's father's ghost.

Biography *What effect does the long-delayed first meeting with Johnson have on Boswell?* **2**

634 UNIT 3   FROM PURITANISM TO THE ENLIGHTENMENT

Reading Practice

Summarize Remind students that a summary is a short restatement of the main ideas and important details of a selection. Summarizing is a helpful tool for understanding key elements in a passage. **Ask:** How would you summarize what you have read so far? (*James Boswell met Samuel Johnson at Thomas Davies's bookshop on May 16th, 1763. In Boswell's biography* The Life of Samuel Johnson, *he relays his first impression of Johnson's appearance. Boswell poignantly portrays his own vulnerability in their initial interactions but expresses a deep admiration for Johnson.*)

painted by Sir Joshua Reynolds soon after he had published his *Dictionary*, in the attitude of sitting in his easy chair in deep meditation, which was the first picture his friend did for him, which Sir Joshua very kindly presented to me, and from which an engraving has been made for this work. Mr. Davies mentioned my name and respectfully introduced me to him. I was much agitated; and recollecting his prejudice against the Scotch, of which I had heard much, I said to Davies, "Don't tell where I come from." "From Scotland," cried Davies roguishly. "Mr. Johnson," said I, "I do indeed come from Scotland, but I cannot help it." I am willing to flatter myself that I meant this as light pleasantry to sooth and conciliate him, and not as a humiliating abasement[3] at the expense of my country. But however that might be, this speech was somewhat unlucky; for with that quickness of wit for which he was so remarkable, he seized the expression "come from Scotland," which I used in the sense of being of that country; and, as if I had said that I had come away from it, or left, retorted, "That, Sir, I find, is what a very great many of your countrymen cannot help." This stroke stunned me a good deal; and when we had sat down, I felt myself not a little embarrassed and apprehensive of what might come next. He then addressed himself to Davies: "What do you think of Garrick?[4] He has refused me an order[5] for the play for Miss Williams[6] because he knows the house will be full and that an order would be worth three shillings." Eager to take any opening to get into conversation with him, I ventured to say, "Oh, Sir, I cannot think Mr. Garrick would grudge such a trifle to you." "Sir," said he, with a stern look, "I have known David Garrick

longer than you have done, and I know no right you have to talk to me on the subject." Perhaps I deserved this check; for it was rather presumptuous in me, an entire stranger, to express any doubt of the justice of his animadversion[7] upon his old acquaintance and pupil. I now felt myself much mortified and began to think that the hope which I had long indulged of obtaining his acquaintance was blasted. And, in truth, had not my ardor been uncommonly strong, and my resolution uncommonly persevering, so rough a reception might have deterred me forever from making any further attempts. Fortunately, however, I remained upon the field not wholly discomfited[8] and was soon rewarded by hearing some of his conversation, of which I preserved the following short minute,[9] without marking the questions and observations by which it was produced.

"People," he remarked, "may be taken in once, who imagine that an author is greater in private life than other men. Uncommon parts require uncommon opportunities for their exertion.

"In barbarous society, superiority of parts is of real consequence. Great strength or great wisdom is of much value to an individual. But in more polished times there are people to do everything for money; and then there are a number of other superiorities, such as those of birth and fortune and rank that dissipate[10] men's attention and leave no extraordinary share of respect for personal and intellectual superiority. This is wisely ordered by Providence[11] to preserve some equality among mankind.

---

7. An *animadversion* (a´ nə mad´ vər´ zhən) is an unfavorable remark or criticism.
8. When Boswell says he was not *wholly discomfited*, he means he was not completely frustrated or thwarted.
9. In this instance, a *minute* is a record or a summary.
10. *Dissipate* means "waste."
11. *Providence* is divine guidance.

Biography *What is Boswell saying about his reporting of this conversation?* **4**

The English Enlightenment and Neoclassicism *How do Johnson's comments in this paragraph reflect Enlightenment ideas?* **5**

JAMES BOSWELL **635**

---

3. An *abasement* is a humbling.
4. David *Garrick* (1717–1779) was considered the greatest Shakespearean actor of his time.
5. In this context, an *order* is a free ticket.
6. Garrick gave a benefit performance for his impoverished friend, the poet Anna *Williams* (1706–1783), who was also a friend of Johnson's.

3 Biography *Why does Johnson's remark "stun" Boswell?*

Literary Element **3**

Biography Answer: *Boswell was trying to be witty, but Johnson retorted with a far wittier remark that was somewhat insulting to Boswell.*

APPROACHING Explain that when Boswell says he "cannot help" coming from Scotland, he means that it is not his fault. However, Johnson uses *come from* in a different sense, implying that the Scottish should stay in their own country. **Ask:** Why do you think that Boswell includes Johnson's statement in the biography? *(Possible response: to show Johnson's sarcasm.)*

Literary Element **4**

Biography Answer: *He is saying that he has extracted from the conversation those comments that were put in by Johnson.*

Big Idea **5**

The English Enlightenment and Neoclassicism Answer: *Johnson uses logic and reasoning to understand the world; he reasons from observed facts to develop an explanation; he has respect for order. All these processes and positions are Enlightenment ideas.*

Approaching Level

DIFFERENTIATED INSTRUCTION

Emerging Ask: Why is the word *Meets* capitalized at the beginning of page 634? *(It is part of the subheading.)* What other uses of capitalization do you notice on this page? *(title of a book,* *beginning of a sentence, personal pronoun, title of a person, person's name, place name, week day name, month name)*

Teach

Reading Strategy   1

Evaluate Credibility

Answer: *He is saying that, although Johnson was highly opinionated, he was willing to change his mind and able to recognize changes in other people.* **Ask:** Why do you think Boswell included a flash forward here? *(Possible answer: He was fond of Johnson and wanted to show him in a positive light.)*

(ENGLISH LEARNERS) Explain to students that Johnson uses *outrun* and *run away from* figuratively. **Ask:** According to Johnson, how does Derrick's character, or personality, change? *(It gets better.)*

View the Art ★

Answer: *Students may say that while Johnson looks bored and disinterested Boswell gazes admiringly at Johnson; they do not consider each other with the same level of respect.*

Samuel Johnson with James Boswell at home in Boer Court. Hand-colored engraving. *View the Art* Johnson hosted a variety of people in his home to stave off the loneliness and insomnia he suffered without company. What can you infer about Johnson and Boswell's relationship from this engraving? ★

"Sir, this book [*The Elements of Criticism*,[12] which he had taken up] is a pretty essay and deserves to be held in some estimation, though much of it is chimerical."[13]

Speaking of one who with more than ordinary boldness attacked public measures and the royal family, he said, "I think he is safe from the law, but he is an abusive scoundrel; and instead of applying to my Lord Chief Justice to punish him, I would send half a dozen footmen[14] and have him well ducked.[15]

"The notion of liberty amuses the people of England and helps to keep off the *taedium vitae*.[16] When a butcher tells you that his heart bleeds for his country, he has, in fact, no uneasy feeling.

"Sheridan[17] will not succeed at Bath with his oratory. Ridicule has gone down before him, and I doubt,[18] Derrick is his enemy.

"Derrick may do very well as long as he can outrun his character, but the moment his character gets up with him, it is all over."

---

12. *The Elements of Criticism* was written by Scottish jurist and philosopher Henry Home, Lord Kames (1696–1782).
13. *Chimerical* (ki mer´ i kəl) means "whimsical" or "fanciful."
14. *Footmen* were servants.
15. Ducking in water was a type of punishment.
16. *Taedium vitae* (tī´ dē əm ve´ tī) is Latin for "weariness of life."
17. *Sheridan* is Thomas Sheridan (1719–1788), an Irish-born actor.
18. In this context, *doubt* means "fear" or "suspect."

636 UNIT 3   FROM PURITANISM TO THE ENLIGHTENMENT

It is, however, but just to record, that some years afterwards, when I reminded him of this sarcasm, he said, "Well, but Derrick has now got a character that he need not run away from."

I was highly pleased with the extraordinary vigor of his conversation and regretted that I was drawn away from it by an engagement at another place. I had, for a part of the evening, been left alone with him and had ventured to make an observation now and then, which he received very civilly; so that I was satisfied that though there was a roughness in his manner, there was no ill nature in his disposition. Davies followed me to the door, and when I complained to him a little of the hard blows which the great man had given me, he kindly took upon him to console me by saying, "Don't be uneasy. I can see he likes you very well."

Johnson's Character

The character of Samuel Johnson has, I trust, been so developed in the course of this work that they who have honored it with a perusal[19] may be considered as well acquainted with

---

19. A *perusal* is a careful reading.

Evaluate Credibility *What is Boswell implying about Johnson's opinions of others?*   **1**

Reading Practice

Visualize Boswell is trying to give the reader a clear mental image of Samuel Johnson. Without consideration of the portraits students have seen of Johnson, let them take as their inspiration Boswell's written description to create a visual representation of Johnson in any medium from abstract collage, to a graphic organizer ordering his traits, to a portrait. Encourage students to make their visual representations suggest not merely Johnson's physical appearance but also the personality, values, and abilities that Boswell describes. Encourage students to present and explain their work.

him. As, however, it may be expected that I should collect into one view the capital and distinguishing features of this extraordinary man, I shall endeavor to acquit myself of that part of my biographical undertaking, however difficult it may be to do that which many of my readers will do better for themselves.

His figure was large and well formed, and his countenance[20] of the cast of an ancient statue; yet his appearance was rendered strange and somewhat uncouth by convulsive cramps, by the scars of that distemper[21] which it was once imagined the royal touch[22] could cure, and by a slovenly[23] mode of dress. He had the use only of one eye; yet so much does mind govern and even supply the deficiency of organs, that his visual perceptions, as far as they extended, were uncommonly quick and accurate. So morbid was his temperament that he never knew the natural joy of a free and vigorous use of his limbs: when he walked, it was like the struggling gait of one in fetters;[24] when he rode, he had no command

or direction of his horse but was carried as if in a balloon. That with his constitution and habits of life he should have lived seventy-five years is a proof that an inherent *vivida vis*[25] is a powerful preservative of the human frame.

Man is, in general, made up of contradictory qualities; and these will ever shew[26] themselves in strange succession, where a consistency in appearance at least, if not reality, has not been attained by long habits of philosophical discipline. In proportion to the native vigor of the mind, the contradictory qualities will be the more prominent and more difficult to be

adjusted; and, therefore, we are not to wonder that Johnson exhibited an eminent example of this remark which I have made upon human nature. At different times, he seemed a different man, in some respects; not, however, in any great or essential article, upon which he had fully employed his mind, and settled certain principles of duty, but only in his manners and in the display of argument and fancy in his talk. He was prone to superstition, but not to credulity.[27] Though his imagination might incline him to a belief of the marvelous and the mysterious, his vigorous reason examined the evidence with jealousy. He was a sincere and **zealous** Christian, of high Church-of-England and monarchical principles, which he would not tamely suffer to be questioned; and had, perhaps, at an early period, narrowed his mind somewhat too much, both as to religion and politics. His being impressed with the danger of extreme latitude in either, though he was of a very independent spirit, occasioned his appearing somewhat unfavorable to the prevalence of that noble freedom of sentiment which is the best possession of man. Nor can it be denied that he had many prejudices, which, however, frequently suggested many of his pointed sayings that rather shew a playfulness of fancy than any settled malignity. He was steady and inflexible in maintaining the obligations of religion and morality, both from a regard for the order of society and from a veneration for the Great Source[28] of all order; correct, nay, stern in his taste; hard to please and easily offended; **impetuous** and irritable in his temper,

---

20. Boswell refers to Johnson's *countenance*, or facial features.
21. The disease that Boswell refers to as *distemper* was scrofula, tuberculosis of the lymphatic glands.
22. Because of a popular but mistaken belief that scrofula could be cured by the *royal touch*, Johnson was taken to London at the age of two to be touched by Queen Anne.
23. *Slovenly* means "untidy" or "sloppy."
24. *Fetters* are chains or shackles on the ankles or feet.
25. *Vivida vis* (vē′ vē dä wēs) means "life force."
26. *Shew* means "show."

 2 Biography *As a biographer, what does Boswell expect from his readers?*

27. *Credulity* means "a willingness to believe without sufficient evidence; gullibility."
28. The *Great Source* refers to God as the provider.

Evaluate Credibility *Do you think Boswell can or cannot be trusted to give an accurate description of the "differences" in Johnson's personality? Explain.* **3**

Vocabulary

zealous (zel′ əs) *adj.* filled with intense, enthusiastic devotion

impetuous (im pech′ ōō əs) *adj.* characterized by rushing headlong into things; impulsive

---

Teach

Literary Element   2

Biography Answer: *He expects that many readers will draw inferences about Johnson's character based on incidents and conversations that the biography describes.*

Reading Strategy   3

Evaluate Credibility

Answer: *Students may suggest that Boswell can be trusted because he might have witnessed several private moments during which these differences surfaced. On the other hand, Boswell clearly admires Johnson, so some students may not trust Boswell to be objective.*

Writer's Technique ☆

Figurative Language is not meant to be interpreted literally and is used for descriptive effect, often to imply ideas. Boswell employs two similes to describe how Johnson moved. **Ask:** Do you think Boswell's description is effective? Explain.

English Learners

DIFFERENTIATED INSTRUCTION

Intermediate Invite students to list words and phrases that describe Samuel Johnson. Have them sort the descriptions under the headings "intelligent" and "rude." They can include adjectives, phrases, and examples. (*intelligent: vigor of conversation; rude: sarcasm*)

Approaching Level

DIFFERENTIATED INSTRUCTION

Established Invite students to form pairs and read aloud from the selection. Suggest that they read the parts of Samuel Johnson in character and take turns portraying him.

Teach

Literary Element | 1

Biography Answer: *The tone seems forgiving and even a bit apologetic. Students will have varying opinions about the accuracy of Boswell's explanation of Johnson's impatience.*

(APPROACHING) Ask students to find words that describe Johnson's physical and mental health. **Ask:** Boswell admits that Johnson had a bad temper at times. How does he explain Johnson's poor manners? *(Johnson was rude sometimes because he was sick.)*

Big Idea | 2

The English Enlightenment and Neoclassicism

Answer: *According to Boswell, Johnson had more than knowledge or an accumulation of facts; he was a powerful thinker. Reason was one of the important values of the Enlightenment.*

Writer's Technique ☆

Allusion Boswell quotes Bible verse, as in this example I Corinthians 15:19, to describe Johnson. **Ask:** Why might the Bible be a good source for allusions to describe Johnson? *(Boswell may be underscoring Johnson's personal piety. By speaking of his friend in biblical terms, he makes Johnson seem greater [in the degree of his difficulties as well as his strengths] than the average person.)*

but of a most humane and benevolent heart, which shewed itself not only in a most liberal charity, as far as his circumstances would allow, but in a thousand instances of active benevolence. He was afflicted with a bodily disease, which made him often restless and fretful, and with a constitutional melancholy, the clouds of which darkened the brightness of his fancy and gave a gloomy cast to his whole course of thinking. We, therefore, ought not to wonder at his sallies[29] of impatience and passion at any time, especially when provoked by obtrusive[30] ignorance or presuming petulance,[31] and allowance must be made for his uttering hasty and satirical sallies even against his best friends. And, surely, when it is considered, that, "amidst sickness and sorrow," he exerted his faculties in so many works for the benefit of mankind, and particularly that he achieved the great and admirable *Dictionary* of our language, we must be astonished at his resolution. The solemn text "of him to whom much is given, much will be required" seems to have been ever present to his mind, in a rigorous sense, and to have made him dissatisfied with his labors and acts of goodness, however comparatively great, so that the unavoidable consciousness of his superiority was, in that respect, a cause of disquiet. He suffered so much from this, and from the gloom which perpetually haunted him and made solitude frightful, that it may be said of him, "If in this life only he had hope, he was of all men most miserable."[32] He

> "In him were united a most logical head with a most fertile imagination, which gave him an extraordinary advantage in arguing. . . ."

loved praise when it was brought to him but was too proud to seek for it. He was somewhat susceptible of[33] flattery. As he was general and unconfined in his studies, he cannot be considered as master of any one particular science; but he had accumulated a vast and various collection of learning and knowledge, which was so arranged in his mind as to be ever in readiness to be brought forth. But his superiority over other learned men consisted chiefly in what may be called the art of thinking, the art of using his mind, a certain continual power of seizing the useful substance of all that he knew and exhibiting it in a clear and forcible manner; so that knowledge, which we often see to be no better than lumber[34] in men of dull understanding, was, in him, true, evident, and actual wisdom. His moral **precepts** are practical, for they are drawn from an intimate acquaintance with human nature. His maxims[35] carry conviction, for they are founded on the basis of common sense and a very attentive and minute survey of real life. His mind was so full of imagery that he might have been perpetually a poet; yet it is remarkable, that, however rich his prose is in this respect, his poetical pieces, in general, have not much of that splendor, but are rather distinguished by strong sentiment and acute observation conveyed in harmonious and energetic verse, particularly in heroic couplets.[36]

---

29. *Sallies* are outbursts.
30. *Obtrusive* means "pushy in a rude or bold manner."
31. *Petulance* is bad temper.
32. "*If . . . miserable.*" is based on I Corinthians 15:19: "If in this life only we have hope in Christ, we are of all men most miserable."

33. *Susceptible of* means "easily affected by."
34. Here, *lumber* means "useless material."
35. *Maxims* are sayings that express moral principles or rules of conduct.
36. *Heroic couplets* consist of paired rhyming lines written in iambic pentameter.

1 **Biography** *How would you describe Boswell's tone here? In your opinion, is Boswell just trying to make his friend look good, or is his comment accurate?*

The English Enlightenment and Neoclassicism *In what way might Boswell's version of Samuel Johnson be said to epitomize the age of the Enlightenment?* **2**

Vocabulary

precept (prē′ sept) *n.* a rule intended as a guide for conduct or action

Writing Practice

Diction Remind students that diction is the author's word choice and that good writers choose their words carefully. Draw students' attention to the phrase "a slow, deliberate utterance" in the first column. **Ask:** What other words could Boswell have used here? *(carefully chosen words, purposeful speech, halting vocalization.)* **Say:** Analyze the effect of Boswell's diction in this example and others. Have students write a paragraph or two giving their analysis of Boswell's diction.

Oliver Goldsmith, Irish playwright, poet and dramatist, with James Boswell, diarist, and Dr. Samuel Johnson, poet, critic and lexicographer.

Though usually grave, and even awful, in his deportment, he possessed uncommon and peculiar powers of wit and humor; he frequently indulged himself in colloquial pleasantry; and the heartiest merriment was often enjoyed in his company, with this great advantage, that as it was entirely free from any poisonous tincture[37] of vice or impiety,[38] it was salutary[39] to those who shared in it. He had accustomed himself to such accuracy in his common conversation that he at all times expressed his thoughts with great force and an elegant choice of language, the effect of which was aided by his having a loud voice and a slow, deliberate utterance. In him were united a most logical head with a most fertile imagination, which gave him an extraordinary advantage in arguing: for he could reason close or wide, as he saw best for the moment. Exulting in his intellectual strength and dexterity, he could, when he pleased, be the greatest sophist[40] that ever contended in the lists of decla-

mation,[41] and from a spirit of contradiction and a delight in shewing his powers, he would often maintain the wrong side with equal warmth and **ingenuity,** so that when there was an audience, his real opinions could seldom be gathered from his talk; though when he was in company with a single friend, he would discuss a subject with genuine fairness. But he was too conscientious to make error permanent and pernicious[42] by deliberately writing it, and in all his numerous works, he earnestly inculcated[43] what appeared to him to be the truth, his piety being constant and the ruling principle of all his conduct.

Such was Samuel Johnson, a man whose talents, acquirements, and virtues were so extraordinary that the more his character is considered, the more he will be regarded by the present age, and by posterity, with admiration and reverence.

41. Here, a *declamation* is a speech.
42. *Pernicious* means "destructive."
43. *Inculcated* means "encouraged by persistent teaching or indoctrination."

Vocabulary

ingenuity (in′ jə noo′ ə tē) *n.* cleverness; inventiveness

37. *Tincture* means "trace" or "tinge."
38. *Impiety* means "lack of reverence."
39. *Salutary* means "conducive to health or well-being."
40. A *sophist* is one who is skilled in using deceptive arguments.

JAMES BOSWELL **639**

View the Art ★

Boswell wrote the following in his biography of Johnson:

"I had learnt that his place of frequent resort was the Mitre tavern in Fleet-street, where he loved to sit up late, and I begged I might be allowed to pass an evening with him there soon, which he promised I should."

The illustration shows Boswell and Johnson with Oliver Goldsmith at the Mitre.

To check students' understanding of the selection, see Unit 3 Teaching Resources Book, pp. 203.

Progress Check

Can students identify biography?

If No → See Unit 3 Teaching Resources Book, p. 198.

Advanced Learners

DIFFERENTIATED INSTRUCTION

Literary Biography Ask: What writers do you admire? Encourage students to write several paragraphs about a writer who interests them. Remind them to look for books, magazine articles, interviews, Web sites, and video footage about their subjects. Suggest that students emulate Boswell in describing the writer they choose.

After You Read

Assess

1. Students may have found Johnson gruff at first but Boswell's description soon softens Johnson's image.

2. (a) Boswell was introduced to Johnson by Mr. Davies at his bookstore. (b) Boswell wanted to make a good impression on Johnson.

3. (a) Johnson joked that many Scottish people could not help leaving Scotland. (b) Students may find Johnson's remark witty.

4. (a) Johnson's narrow views on religion and politics. (b) He emphasizes Johnson's intellectual abilities, wit, and humanity but also seeks to be balanced in his judgment.

5. (a) The quotations show Johnson to be quick-witted and opinionated. (b) Boswell was an attentive friend.

6. It might have focused entirely on Johnson's negative traits.

7. Boswell, in his defense of and admiration for Johnson, exemplifies the Enlightenment's faith in reason and clarity of thought by presenting both positive and negative information.

8. (a) The friendship allowed Boswell to get close to his subject. (b) That closeness might have made Boswell reluctant to reveal less flattering information.

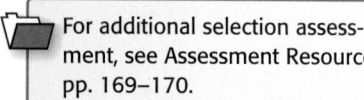
For additional selection assessment, see Assessment Resources, pp. 169–170.

After You Read

Respond and Think Critically

Respond and Interpret

1. What was your impression of Johnson during his first meeting with Boswell? Did your impression of him change as you read more about him? Explain why or why not.

2. (a)How did Boswell meet Johnson? (b)Why might Boswell have felt so nervous during that first meeting?

3. (a)Name an aspect of Johnson's personality that Boswell finds objectionable. (b)How does Boswell's overall description excuse this trait?

Analyze and Evaluate

4. (a)What parts of Boswell's description of Johnson's physical appearance are objective, or factual—and which are subjective, or personal opinion? (b)Why might Boswell have included both types of descriptions?

5. (a)What do the quotations that Boswell provides reveal about Johnson's personality? (b)What do they reveal about Boswell himself?

6. How might the portrayal of Johnson have differed had it been written by a stranger instead of a friend?

Connect

7. **Big Idea** The English Enlightenment and Neoclassicism In what ways does Boswell's biography exemplify the guiding principles of the Enlightenment?

8. **Connect to the Author** (a)How might Johnson's friendship have been helpful to Boswell as a biographer? (b)What difficulties might the friendship have posed?

Literary Element Biography

Before *The Life of Samuel Johnson*, **biographies** generally focused on describing an individual's major life events and accomplishments. Boswell's work was instrumental in developing the modern approach to biography, with its emphasis on analyzing the forces that shape personality.

1. (a)At what points in the selection does Boswell examine the forces that helped shape Johnson's opinions and behavior? (b)What are these forces?

2. In your opinion, does Boswell provide convincing reasons for Johnson's behavior? Support your opinion with evidence from the selection.

Review: Style

As you learned on page 407, **style** is the combination of expressive qualities that distinguish an author's work, including word choice and the length and arrangement of sentences, as well as the use of figurative language and imagery.

Read this passage from the preface to *A Dictionary of the English Language* by Samuel Johnson.

"In this work, when it shall be found that much is omitted, let it not be forgotten that much likewise is performed; and though no book was ever spared out of tenderness to the author, and the world is little solicitous to know whence proceeded the faults of that which it condemns; yet it may gratify curiosity to inform it that the *English Dictionary* was written with little assistance of the learned and without any patronage of the great . . ."

Use a Venn diagram to show how Boswell's and Johnson's writing styles are alike and different.

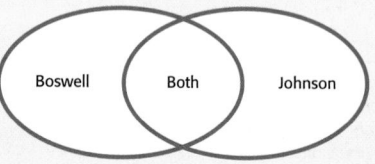

Literary Element

1. (a) In the second excerpt, Boswell refers to the belief that people may have contradictory characteristics. (b) Johnson's physical disabilities and his tendency toward prejudice and melancholy

2. Students may think that Boswell was not convincing. Some may think that he was too intent on relating causes

and effects. Students should support their answers.

Review: Style

Students may note that Boswell's sentences are shorter and his tone is more objective. Both authors use sophisticated vocabulary and figurative language. Johnson uses copious semicolons.

Reading Strategy — Evaluate Credibility

In James Boswell's account of Samuel Johnson's life, he makes every attempt to be fair. But his comments are often based upon his own subjective perspective. For each of the following phrases from the selection, decide whether the statement is objective (fact) or subjective (opinion).

1. "his appearance was rendered strange and somewhat uncouth"

2. "He had the use only of one eye"

3. "I had, for a part of the evening, been left alone with him"

Vocabulary Practice

Practice with Denotation and Connotation A word's denotation is its dictionary meaning; its **connotations** are its emotional overtones. Each of the vocabulary words is listed with a word that has a similar denotation. Choose which word has less-positive connotations.

1. veneration   idolatry

2. zealous   rabid

3. impetuous   passionate

4. petulance   irritation

5. ingenuity   genius

Academic Vocabulary

*In this excerpt, Boswell gives his **assessment** of the character of Samuel Johnson.*

Assessment is an academic word that appears in everyday usage. For example, the process by which a teacher judges a student's academic performance is called assessment.

To further explore the meaning of this word, answer this question: What is your **assessment** of Boswell's language in this excerpt?

For more on academic vocabulary, see pages 56 and R81.

Speaking and Listening

 Interview

Assignment What might Johnson have thought about his new young friend? Use the Internet, as well as the biographical information on page 632, to research Boswell's life and his friendship with Johnson. Then conduct an interview in which you ask Johnson about the pair's first meeting.

Prepare Create a list of relevant questions phrased in mature, sensitive, respectful language. The questions should reflect your understanding of Johnson's character, and any inferences you have made about Boswell himself. Leave space under each question to record the response.

Interview At a time when you won't be interrupted, conduct your interview, having a classmate play the part of Johnson. Take notes on his or her answers, and encourage your partner to add any other relevant information. Follow these tips:

- Listen respectfully without interrupting.
- Look at the interviewee frequently while "he" is speaking, but don't stare.
- Adjust your tone of voice and body language to make the interviewee comfortable.
- Ask questions to clarify information.
- Review all of the responses with the interviewee, make any necessary changes, and thank him.
- If possible, tape-record your interview so that you can refer to it later on.

Report Summarize what you learned about Boswell and Johnson's friendship in a written statement. Present the information in the order of its importance. Be sure to note when something is your own interpretation rather than a response from the interview itself.

Evaluate Evaluate your interview and summary for clarity, accuracy, and completeness.

Literature Online

Selection Resources For Selection Quizzes, eFlashcards, and Reading-Writing Connection activities, go to glencoe.com and enter QuickPass code GLB9817u3.

Reading Strategy

1. opinion
2. fact
3. fact

Progress Check

Can students evaluate credibility?

If No → See Unit 3 Teaching Resources Book, p. 199.

Speaking and Listening

Students' interviews should

- include questions that reflect Johnson's character
- include questions that are relevant and mature
- include a summary of Boswell and Johnson's friendship

Vocabulary Practice

1. Positive: veneration; negative: idolatry
2. Positive: zealous; negative: rabid
3. Positive: passionate; negative: impetuous
4. Negative: irritation; more negative: petulance
5. Positive: ingenuity; more positive: genius

Academic Vocabulary

Possible answer: Boswell's descriptive language is effective and vivid. For example, he writes that Johnson's face has "the cast of an ancient statue."

 To create custom assessments online, go to Progress Reporter Online Assessment.

 To create custom assessments using software, use ExamView Assessment Suite.

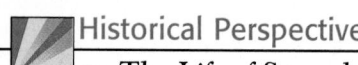
Focus

Summary

Bate provides a psychological profile of Boswell, including personality traits that made him an extraordinary biographer. Boswell rejected his father's morals and politics and looked to men of his father's generation—including Johnson—for role models. His talents included his ability to understand others, his ease in talking to them, his remarkable recall of conversations, and his determination to record them.

Teach

Reading Strategy	1

Connect Remind students that connecting what they read to what they have read will help them construct meaning. Have students recall details about Boswell's first meeting with Dr. Johnson.

For activities related to this selection, see Unit 3 Teaching Resources Book, pp. 205–213.

For an audio recording of this selection, use Listening Library Audio CD-ROM.

Readability Scores

Dale-Chall: 5.8
DRP: 66
Lexile: 1380

Historical Perspective
on *The Life of Samuel Johnson*

from

Samuel Johnson

W. Jackson Bate

Pulitzer Prize Winner

Learning Objectives

For pages 642–645
In studying this text, you will focus on the following objectives:

Literary Study: Making connections across literature.

Reading: Analyzing historical context. Determining main idea and supporting details.

Set a Purpose for Reading

Read to learn more about Boswell's life and his famed biography of Johnson.

Build Background

Walter Jackson Bate was awarded two Pulitzer Prizes during his distinguished career. He won the second prize in 1978 for his vividly written life of Samuel Johnson. The following excerpt from that work describes James Boswell's family background and his relationship with Samuel Johnson.

Reading Strategy Determine Main Idea and Supporting Details

Determining the main idea means finding the most important thought in a paragraph or a selection which is developed through the use of **supporting details**, such as examples, reasons, facts, or descriptions. As you read, ask yourself, What are the main idea and the supporting details in each passage?

Main Idea	Supporting Details

On Monday, May 16, when he[1] dropped into the small bookshop kept by his friend Tom Davies, there occurred one of the famous meetings in literary history, which began an acquaintance that was ultimately to result in one of the masterpieces of world literature—James Boswell's *Life of Johnson* (1791). The admiring young Scot was the son of Alexander Boswell, Laird of Auchinleck, a man about Johnson's age, who had studied law at Leyden and was now a judge on the Scottish bench. Though Boswell's name, because of his great work, was to become a household word not long after his death, he himself was drastically underrated until our own generation. He has proved, at the very least, to be a far more complicated person than was ever imagined. The most celebrated literary discovery of this century was the vast journal—or series of journals—he kept through most of his life, chronicling with complete frankness his own personal experiences and, more important, recording conversations and interviews with noted people he met. When published, the writings—*The Private Papers of James Boswell from Malahide Castle*

---

1. *He* refers to James Boswell.

Reading Practice

Expository Texts Tell students to use the following strategies when reading this and other expository texts.

- **Varying Reading Rate:** Slow down when encountering difficult concepts, new vocabulary, or passages with much information.

- **Monitoring Comprehension:** Question yourself as you read, and then reread, review, or read on to clarify what is unclear.

- **Tracking Information:** List key ideas as you read.

(1928–34)—filled eighteen volumes, and they were later to be supplemented by other material. The conversations in the *Life of Johnson,* together with those in Boswell's earlier *Journal of a Tour to the Hebrides with Samuel Johnson* (1785), are carved from this enormous collection of diaries.

We should remind ourselves (it is often forgotten) how extremely young Boswell was when he met Johnson—he was only twenty-two; Johnson was fifty-three—just as we should remind ourselves that he had many interests, and spent most of his adult life as an able and busy lawyer in Edinburgh, visiting London only on vacations. In some ways, he was even younger than twenty-two at this time, and was generally to remain younger than his years. The identity for which the young Boswell was searching—and continued to search—was one that could define itself against the example of his father, Lord Auchinleck, who was firm and moralistic, a Whig[2] and a Presbyterian, and who proudly spoke broad Scots. In reaction, the son was all the father was not: romantically imaginative, promiscuous, impulsively idealistic and open-natured, pliable,[3] and with an impressionable genius for mimicry.

In his search for identity, a shadow in the background was always there to make him uneasy if he allowed himself to think of it. There was a strain of mental instability in his family; and Boswell's own younger brother John, after the age of nineteen, was to suffer from marked insanity for most of his remaining life. The stability for which Boswell was always to crave was something that his gregarious[4] nature could acquire only through others. And his profoundest enjoyment, if not at the start, certainly as the years passed, was the company, example, and if possible the approval, of older men whom he admired—men of acknowledged standing who were also interesting in themselves, knew the world, and, like Johnson, symbolized the

---

2. The *Whig* party was the dominant political faction in England at the time.
3. *Pliable* means "changeable."
4. *Gregarious* means "outgoing" or "social."

---

moral rectitude he wanted desperately to impose on his own wayward nature.

Hence his injunctions to himself in his journal to identify with admired models, and acquire a stronger mind and character ("be Johnson"). At first the ideals suggest conventional notions of sophistication and elegance. After arriving in London, for example, he writes, "I felt strong dispositions to *be a Mr. Addison.*"[5] Months later—he has by now met and talked a good deal with Johnson—the rather frightened youth is to set off for Harwich to get the boat to Holland, where he is to study law. And the models now, basically so different from each other (the father from whom he is in part fleeing, Lord Chesterfield,[6] and Johnson), show what he really wants most to acquire—inner strength, reserve, calmness, and courage: "[Be] like Father, grave . . . composed. . . . Go abroad with a manly resolution. . . . Never despair. . . . Study [to be] like Lord Chesterfield, *manly.* . . . *Resemble Johnson . . . your mind will strengthen*" (August 1763); or, later in the year, "*Be* like the Duke of Sully." As he approaches and enters his thirties, there are moments of satisfaction (when he says "you," he is addressing himself—a common practice in his diaries, and typical of his attempt at detachment):

> "You felt yourself . . . *like a Johnson* in comparison of former days" (1766). "Was *powerful* like Johnson, and very much satisfied with myself" (1767). "I was in such a frame as to *think myself an Edmund Burke*"[7] (1774). "Fancied myself like Burke, and drank moderately . . ." (1775).

One of the touching entries is near the end, toward the close of his life. Much of his despair—he is now fifty—is that he felt he had no more inner strength to meet difficulties now, when he needed it badly, than he had as a youth—that

---

5. Joseph *Addison* (1672–1719) was a famed essayist.
6. *Lord Chesterfield* (1694–1773) was a statesman and the patron of many writers.
7. *Edmund Burke* (1729–1797) was a conservative British political thinker and statesman.

W. JACKSON BATE **643**

Teach

Reading Strategy | 2

Make Inferences Direct students' attention to the sentence beginning, "In some ways, he was even younger than twenty-two…" **Ask:** What do you think Bate means by that? (*He means that Boswell was naive and immature. He hadn't yet formed his identity.*)

Big Idea | 3

The English Enlightenment and Neoclassicism Ask: Did Boswell's rebellion against his father reflect the Enlightenment ideal of reason? Why or why not? Have students support their answers with evidence from the selection. (*Possible response: No. Boswell's rejection of his father's conservative views made him impulsive and quick to change his opinions.*)

English Learners

DIFFERENTIATED INSTRUCTION

Intermediate Read aloud the sentence that begins, "The most celebrated…." **Say:** Let me make sure that I understand this sentence before I go on. I know that a celebration marks something good, so the first part of the sentence means that Boswell's journals were valuable. Looking up *chronicling,* I find that it means "to record," and *frankness* means "openness" or "honesty," so the second part of the sentence means that he recorded honestly what happened to him. In the third part, Bate says that Boswell's talks with important people were the best part of the journals. Therefore, the sentence means this: Boswell's journals were valuable because he recorded what happened to him honestly and wrote about his talks with important people. Notice how I stopped at different points to make sure I understood what I have read. To practice **reading fluency,** have students read aloud part of another sentence. Ask them to explain the meaning in their own words.

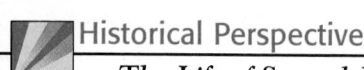
Teach

Evaluate the Credibility of Sources Say: Bate describes Boswell's advantages as a biographer. In what ways do they contribute to Boswell's credibility as a source? How might they compromise his credibility?

(Possible response: His ability to get people to talk openly and his good memory contribute to his credibility, while his empathy and admiration compromise it.)

APPROACHING Ask students to reread the sentence that begins "The talents include...." Then, have them list Boswell's strengths in their own words.

View the Art ★

Thomas Rowlandson was a popular caricature artist in the 1700s. He found comedy in all walks of life. His work is admired both for its wit and for its artistic quality.

James Boswell: Caricature, Boswell's tour of the Hebrides. May 1786. ★

he seemed to have gone through life "without any addition to my character from my having had the friendship of Dr. Johnson and many eminent men."

Many readers assume that he was constantly in Johnson's presence. But during the twenty-one years he knew Johnson, the total number of days he spent in Johnson's company amounted to 325, plus another 101 during their trip to Scotland and the Hebrides[8] in 1773.

Even so, by 1772—ten years after he met Johnson—he had accumulated what he justly called "a vast treasure of his conversation at different times," and decided that he would someday try to write a life of Johnson using these materials. It was to be a new kind of biography—a "life in Scenes," as though it were a kind of drama. And when the "life in Scenes" did appear, nothing comparable to it had existed. Nor has anything comparable been written since, because that special union of talents, opportunities, and subject

matter has never been duplicated. If there were writers who had Boswell's opportunities of knowing their subject as well, they have not had his unusual combination of talents. If they had his talents, they have lacked his opportunities. The talents include his gift for empathy and dramatic imitation, his ability to draw people out and get them to talk freely, his astonishing memory for conversations, his zest and gusto, his generous capacity for admiration, and his sheer industry as a reporter—qualities that are by no means often found together. Bringing these qualities into focus and sustaining his industry was his prevailing sense of what he called "the *waste* of good if it be not preserved," of the rapid erosion and loss of human experience through life's enemy, time, and the need to rescue it as far as possible through the recorded word. But the final indispensable element in Boswell's great work is Johnson himself. Fascinating as they are, the interviews with others—David Hume, Voltaire, Rousseau, the elder Pitt[9]—rarely approach in range of topics and personal interest any section of equal length dealing with Johnson.

The picture of Johnson, which for better or worse remains permanently imprinted because of this classic work, is inevitably, given the circumstances, somewhat specialized. Most important, it

---

8. The *Hebrides* are islands off the western coast of Scotland.

9. *David Hume* (1711–1776) was a Scottish philosopher. *Voltaire* (1694–1778) and Jean-Jacques *Rousseau* (1712–1778) were famed French writers and philosophers. William *Pitt* (1708–1778) was a powerful British statesman and orator.

Compare and Contrast Have students compare Bate's biography of Boswell with Boswell's biography of Johnson. In particular, encourage students to comment on each author's access to his subject, attitude toward him, and voice. Ask students which biography they prefer and why. *(Students should contrast Boswell's direct access to Johnson and autobiographical* *remarks with Bate's scholarly research and comparatively detached tone. Students may also note both authors' warm feelings toward their subjects.)*

is a picture of Johnson in his later years. The first half of Johnson's life occupies little more than a tenth of the work. Less than a quarter takes him up to fifty-three, when his life was more than two-thirds over; and a full half of the book is devoted to Johnson's last eight years, from sixty-seven to seventy-five. There are also personal sides of Johnson even after fifty-three of which Boswell could never know, but of which others—above all, Mrs. Thrale[10]—knew or suspected a great deal, though they did not always care to proclaim their knowledge. Moreover, it is a very masculine world in which Boswell presents him—the world of The Club and the taverns. In addition, he saw Johnson through the spectacles of his own romantic Toryism,[11] with the result that Johnson has been—and perhaps will unfortunately always be—viewed as an "arch-conservative." Even his minor dramatic touches have proved permanent: for example, his exaggerated insertion of "Sir" before so many of Johnson's remarks, as if to give them a kind of

thunderous and formal authority; or his decision to change his references to him from "Mr. Johnson" to "Dr. Johnson," with the result that Johnson alone, of all great writers who have ever received a doctor's degree, is forever known to most people as "Dr. Johnson." (Ironically Johnson himself—according to Hawkins[12]—rather disliked being called Dr. Johnson. At least, as even Boswell once admitted, he hardly ever assumed it in formal notes or on cards—"but called himself *Mr.* Johnson"; and when Boswell once noticed a letter addressed to him with the title "Esquire," and said he thought it a title inferior to "Doctor," Johnson "checked me, and seemed pleased with it.") Yet whatever its limitations, large or small, the work remains unique among all writings by one human being about another—unique in the way Boswell himself foresaw when he decided as a mature man to undertake it: that is, in the drama, fidelity, and range of interests in the conversation of one of the most fascinating individuals in history. ∾

---

10. Hester *Thrale* (1741–1821) and her husband Henry Thrale were Johnson's friends and traveling companions.
11. The principles of the English Tory party, which opposed those of the Whigs, are known as *Toryism*.

---

12. Sir John *Hawkins* (1719–1789) was a close friend and biographer of Johnson.

Respond and Think Critically

Respond and Interpret

1. Write a brief summary of the main events in this excerpt before you answer the following questions. For help writing a summary, see page 435.

2. After having read this excerpt, does Boswell's biography of Johnson seem more or less reliable? Explain.

3. (a)According to Bate, how was Boswell different from his father? (b)In his diary, what did Boswell repeatedly urge himself to do? (c)What does this suggest about Boswell's character?

Analyze and Evaluate

4. (a)According to Bate, what change did Boswell often make to Johnson's remarks? (b)How have

these types of changes affected people's perceptions of Johnson?

5. (a)What is the main idea of this excerpt? (b)Do you think Bate adequately developed and supported the main idea with details? Why or why not?

Connect

6. **Big Idea** The English Enlightenment and Neoclassicism In what ways do Boswell's life and work embody the principles of the Enlightenment? In what ways do they deviate from these principles?

6. Boswell's use of observation and reportage embodies many Enlightenment principles. His desire to create a record of experience to prevent it from being lost is a Neoclassicist impulse. Boswell's manipulation of information and his emotional instability do not embody Enlightenment principles.

 For additional selection assessment, see Assessment Resources, pp. 171–172.

Assess

1. Answers will vary.

2. Some might argue that Bate's description of Boswell suggests that he was too close to his subject to present an unbiased description. Others might argue that Boswell's "gift for empathy and dramatic imitation" and "his astonishing memory for conversation" make him a very reliable biographer.

3. (a) Boswell was "romantically imaginative, promiscuous, impulsively idealistic and open-natured, pliable, and with an impressionable genius for mimicry." (b) Boswell repeatedly orders himself to "be" like other, more notable men. (c) Boswell was aware of his faults and often sought out role models, or father figures, to help him overcome his weaknesses.

4. (a) Boswell added the word "Sir" at the beginning of many of Johnson's remarks. (b) People view Johnson as a conservative figure of formality and authority.

5. (a) Despite his personal flaws and romantic notions, Boswell created a brilliant and unique biography. (b) Answers will vary, but most will argue that the main idea is well developed and adequately supported.

Writing Workshop

Persuasive Essay

Focus

Bellringer

Bring in an editorial from your local newspaper and read it aloud to the students. **Ask:** What is the writer's topic? What is his or her position? Now have students list some of the controversial issues they feel strongly about—inside or outside school—and have them write down arguments on both sides of each issue.

Summary

In this workshop, students will write and present persuasive essays. They will follow the stages of the writing process, including prewriting, drafting, revising, editing, and presenting. In addition, focus lessons on appropriate tone and parallelism are provided.

 For Writing Workshop graphic organizer and rubric, see Unit 3 Teaching Resources, pp. 214–216.

Workshop Resources

Print Materials

- Unit 3 Teaching Resources Book pp. 214–216
- Writing Kit
- Success in Writing: Research and Reports

- Literary Element Transparency 106
- Writing Workshop Transparencies 18–20

Learning Objectives

For pages 646–653

In this workshop, you will focus on the following objective:

Writing: Writing a persuasive essay using the writing process.

Writing Workshop

Persuasive Essay

Literature Connection In *A Modest Proposal*, Jonathan Swift uses satire to take a stand on the issue of Irish poverty and, specifically, England's attitudes toward it.

> *"I repeat, let no man talk to me of these and the like expedients till he hath at least some glimpse of hope that there will ever be some hearty and sincere attempt to put them in practice."*

Through his satire, Swift attempts to persuade his English audience of the danger of their attitudes by illustrating the horrible result if these attitudes were carried to an extreme, but logical, outcome. In a persuasive essay, the writer takes a position on an issue and attempts to persuade the audience through reasoned arguments. To write a successful essay, you will need to learn the goals of persuasive writing and the strategies for achieving those goals.

Checklist

Goals	Strategies
To present and support a clearly stated opinion, position, or claim to a target audience	☑ Select a point of view that suits and furthers your purpose
	☑ Support ideas with precise, relevant, detailed evidence and examples
	☑ Select a tone that is consistent with your audience, purpose, and occasion
	☑ Organize ideas logically and for greatest rhetorical effect
To use language persuasively	☑ Use rhetorical devices
	☑ Use persuasive techniques such as appeals, repetition, testimonials, and word choice
To anticipate and address audience concerns	☑ Acknowledge and refute opposing arguments

Writing Process

At any stage of a writing process you may think of new ideas. Feel free to return to earlier stages as you write.

Prewrite

Draft

Revise

Focus Lesson: Appropriate Tone

Edit and Proofread

Focus Lesson: Parallelism

Present

 **Literature** Online

Writing and Research For prewriting, drafting, and revising tools, go to glencoe.com and enter QuickPass code GLB9817u3.

646 UNIT 3 FROM PURITANISM TO THE ENLIGHTENMENT

Technology

- Literature Online: Writing Resources and Grammar Resources, www.glencoe.com
- Online Essay Grader, www.glencoe.com
- Student Presentation Builder on Student-Works Plus CD-ROM
- Media Workshop DVD
- Online Student Edition

> **Persuasion**

Assignment Write a Persuasive Essay

Write a persuasive essay of about 1,500 words to defend your position on a controversial issue you care about. As you work, keep your audience and purpose in mind.

Audience: peers, school faculty, or community members

Purpose: to persuade others to think about and act on your issue in a certain way

Real-World Connection

If your essay focuses on an issue in the community, you may want to send it to the editor of a local newspaper. If it focuses on a school-related issue, you may wish to present it aloud at a student council meeting.

Analyze a Professional Model

In the following speech given at the outbreak of World War II, future prime minister Winston Churchill attempts to persuade the British people that war has become necessary. As you read, note Churchill's firm position on this controversial issue and his support of that position. Pay close attention to the comments in the margin. They point out features to include in your own persuasive essay.

War Speech, September 3, 1939 by Winston Churchill ☆

In this solemn hour it is a consolation to recall and to dwell upon our repeated efforts for peace. All have been ill-starred, but all have been faithful and sincere. This is of the highest moral value—and not only moral value, but practical value—at the present time, because the wholehearted concurrence of scores of millions of men and women, whose cooperation is indispensable and whose comradeship and brotherhood are indispensable, is the only foundation upon which the trial and tribulation of modern war can be endured and surmounted. This moral conviction alone affords that ever-fresh resilience which renews the strength and energy of people in long, doubtful and dark days. Outside, the storms of war may blow and the lands may be lashed with the fury of its gales, but in our own hearts this Sunday morning there is peace. Our hands may be active, but our consciences are at rest.

We must not underrate the gravity of the task which lies before us or the temerity of the ordeal, to which we shall not be found

Tone/Thesis/Claim

Present your position in a clear, potent thesis statement. Select a tone that matches the purpose and ocassion.

Emotional Appeal

Stir the audience's emotions by personalizing your issue and expressing it with fresh, vivid language.

Teach

Big Idea

English Enlightenment and Neoclassicism Remind students that the writers in the Age of Enlightenment, like Swift and Pope, believed that satire could spur improvements in moral and social behavior. **Ask:** How does the persuasive essay reflect this spirit? *(By their very nature, persuasive essays express the authors' attempts to "enlighten" the reader about an existing problem or condition, often calling for change, elimination, or at least awareness—much as Swift and his contemporaries tried to do.)*

Political History

Winston Churchill Best known as prime minister of the United Kingdom during the Second World War, Churchill (1874–1965) was at various times a soldier, a journalist, an author, and a politician. He is generally regarded as one of the most important leaders in British and world history. He won the 1953 Nobel Prize in Literature.

Writing Workshop

Persuasive Essay

Teach

Writing Skills

Ethical Appeal Explain that students, after presenting factual information, should make an ethical appeal. One way is to lay out a worst-case scenario, describing what may happen if no action is taken. **Say:** The conclusion of a persuasive essay must convince the audience to act. You must use strong language to convey your message boldly. Your closing should leave the audience with a clear understanding of the essay's intent.

Language History ☆

Slang The term *Nazi* derives from *Nationalsozialistiche Deutsche Arbeiterpartei* (National Socialist German Workers' Party). English speakers before Adolf Hitler's rise to power in 1930, spoke simply of the National Socialist party, but people who had left Germany earlier came to use the slang term *Nazi.* After the war, these Germans brought the term back with them.

Logical Appeal

Cite reasons that guide your audience through the logic of your position.

Supporting Evidence

Use precise, relevant, and detailed examples to illustrate a point.

Ethical Appeal

Appeal to the audience's sense of right and wrong to gain support for your position.

Counterarguments

Refute opposing arguments to strengthen your own position.

Rhetorical Devices

Use rhetorical devices such as repetition and parallelism to add force to your argument.

---

unequal. We must expect many disappointments, and many unpleasant surprises, but we may be sure that the task which we have freely accepted is one not beyond the compass and the strength of the British Empire and the French Republic. The Prime Minister said it was a sad day, and that is indeed true, but at the present time there is another note which may be present, and that is a feeling of thankfulness that, if these great trials were to come upon our Island, there is a generation of Britons here now ready to prove itself not unworthy of the days of yore and not unworthy of those great men, the fathers of our land, who laid the foundations of our laws and shaped the greatness of our country.

This is not a question of fighting for Danzig or fighting for Poland. We are fighting to save the whole world from the pestilence of Nazi tyranny and in defense of all that is most sacred to ☆ man. This is no war of domination or imperial aggrandizement or material gain; no war to shut any country out of its sunlight and means of progress. It is a war, viewed in its inherent quality, to establish, on impregnable rocks, the rights of the individual, and it is a war to establish and revive the stature of man. Perhaps it might seem a paradox that a war undertaken in the name of liberty and right should require, as a necessary part of its processes, the surrender for the time being of so many of the dearly valued liberties and rights. In these last few days the House of Commons has been voting dozens of Bills which hand over to the executive our most dearly valued traditional liberties. We are sure that these liberties will be in hands which will not abuse them, which will use them for no class or party interests, which will cherish and guard them, and we look forward to the day, surely and confidently we look forward to the day, when our liberties and rights will be restored to us, and when we shall be able to share them with the peoples to whom such blessings are unknown.

Reading-Writing Connection Think about the writing techniques that you just encountered and try them out in the persuasive essay you write.

Writing Practice

Persuasion Explain that readers should carefully consider the support offered by authors and speakers as an aid to evaluating the persuasiveness of arguments. Suggest that students use an idea support map to help them organize an author's reasoning and argument.

England should enter the war.

→↑

Nazi tyranny threatens the world.

→↑

→↑

→↑

Have students complete the idea support map. Ask them to evaluate the persuasiveness of the arguments. Is Churchill persuasive? Why or why not?

Prewrite

Explore Issues Think of an issue that is important to you, that is controversial, and that can be debated logically. For example, is there a school policy that you think should be updated or changed?

Clarify Your Position and Create a Call for Action Once you have chosen an issue, write a thesis statement in which you identify your issue and present your concise position. Then consider your purpose. Do you want to change opinions or offer a new perspective? Do you want to persuade your audience to act in a certain way? Develop a call for action, or a statement expressing what your audience should do.

Address Your Audience Pay particular attention to your target audience. If your audience is likely to agree with your position, you may use your argument as a means to underscore your shared position and to effect action. If your audience is likely to disagree, tailor your background information, evidence, and tone to anticipate potential objections. If your audience is unfamiliar with your issue or position, provide adequate background that explains why your issue deserves attention.

Organize Your Argument Organize your argument in a logical, coherent way. For example, to make an immediate impact on your readers, start with your most important supporting evidence. Alternately, you can build up to your strongest point, leaving it fresh in readers' minds.

Use Persuasive Techniques Try out these persuasive techniques:

Repetition: Drive your point home through intentional repetition, or repeat words with especially positive or negative connotations.

Word Choice: Select vivid, fresh words that suit your purpose, such as words that shout or sing—or words that stick, stab, jab, or prod.

Testimonials: Incorporate the supporting opinions of authorities to bolster your position or evidence.

The following techniques should be used sparingly and with care:

Irony: Use irony, or say one thing when you mean the opposite, to capture your audience's attention or elicit an emotional response.

Hyperbole: Overstate your case or deliberately exaggerate.

Bandwagon: Suggest that everyone else understands the logic or urgency of what you suggest or will be flocking to follow your advice.

Glittering Generalities: Make broad statements that overlook exceptions and all contradictory evidence, ideas, or opinions.

Persuasion

Types of Appeals

▶ **Logical Appeal** reaches an audience through reason.

▶ **Emotional Appeal** stirs an audience's feelings by personalizing the issue.

▶ **Ethical Appeal** focuses on an audience's sense of right and wrong.

Avoid Plagiarism

You may find support for your ideas on the Internet. If you do, do not cut and paste it into your essay or print it out. Instead, take careful notes at the prewriting stage. If you use the ideas or support in your essay, cite your sources.

Persuasive Essay

Teach

Writing Process

Prewrite Have students consider using a cluster diagram when they brainstorm about points for their argument. They can position their thesis in the center circle and then surround it with those points that spontaneously occur to them. Students can divide the diagram by putting the "pros" of the issue on one side and the "cons" on the other. Finally, they can rank each point in order of importance.

Writing Skills

Audience Tell students to keep in mind that their purpose is to persuade others by appealing to convictions that their audiences hold, not to express personal preferences. Remind students that different audiences may have different perspectives and that what is most convincing to one may be less persuasive to another.

English Learners
DIFFERENTIATED INSTRUCTION

Beginning Display magazine and newspaper advertisements. For each ad, ask students to identify the topic and position, the audience, and the techniques used in the appeal. Encourage students to think of a persuasive essay as a kind of advertisement, using logic, factual detail, and emotional appeals.

Approaching Level
DIFFERENTIATED INSTRUCTION

Emerging Tell students that an effective way to present supporting reasons is in order of importance. In one system of arrangement, the most important reason is stated first, followed by the second most important, and so on in descending rank. Have students arrange their supporting reasons in this order.

Teach

Writing Skills

Persuasive Techniques

Answer: *The writer raises awareness by opening with supporting evidence (background statistics) and an ethical appeal (the relative value of safety to sports advancement).*

Writing Skills

Thesis/Claim **Answer:** *The thesis addresses safety, which is an issue that is always difficult to argue against—from either position—especially where several people are concerned.*

Writing Skills

Logical Appeal **Answer:**

The writer implies a simple, inarguable truth: though a natural large-scale disaster is rare, one should always be prepared for the worst-case scenario.

Writing Frames

As you read the workshop model, think about the writer's use of the following frames:

- _____ may seem _____ at first; however, in the long run, . . .

- _____ would offer/ would help

- One of the first steps is _____.

Consider using frames like these in your own persuasive essay.

Persuasive Techniques

What persuasive techniques does the writer use to raise awareness of the issue?

Thesis/Claim

How might this thesis and call to action be persuasive both to people who agree with the writer and to those who may not at first?

Logical Appeal

Why does this reason make sense?

Draft

Go with the Flow As you develop your argument, you may think of new or better reasons and supporting evidence to include. Feel free to adjust your original outline as necessary. Reread your draft periodically, checking to see that you maintain a reasonable tone and that you firmly support your reasons with logical evidence.

Analyze a Workshop Model

Here is a final draft of a persuasive essay. Read the essay and answer the questions in the margin. Use the answers to these questions to guide you as you write.

State of Emergency: It Could Happen to Us

Lately, disasters have become a regular occurrence: wildfires blazing on the West Coast, hurricanes flooding the Gulf Coast, and even tornadoes ravaging our own state. Disturbingly, Linden High School has not updated its emergency management and response plan in more than twenty years. More disturbingly, school officials currently do not intend to review the plan, even though they admit it is outdated. Officials have cited expense as the main reason, yet Linden High intends to approve a request from the Athletic Department to build a new football field this summer. Before updating costly athletic facilities, Linden School should consider the broader needs of its students and the best use of its limited funds. Updating Linden's emergency response plan would provide for the safety of *all* Linden students and faculty, make recovery from possible emergencies faster and less expensive in the future, and encourage students to take an active role in emergency management and prevention.

The fact that Linden High has managed to avoid a major disaster so far does not mean that the school is now, or will be, prepared to face one in the future. Although it is true that large-scale natural

---

Writing Skills

Begin with the End Some students may consider writing their conclusions first. By knowing the statements they want to reinforce in their conclusions, students may be better able to draft the supporting points.

Now have students write decisive, definitive conclusions for their essays. **Ask:** Which points do you really want to emphasize? Encourage students to imagine a trial lawyer delivering a moving, resounding summation to the jury.

disasters are statistically rare in communities like ours, choosing to inform Linden's staff and students of potential emergency situations can only be helpful. This is not to say that we will or should become paranoid, as some critics have suggested. Instead, we should pay attention to emergency situations and response efforts in our community and elsewhere to learn the best ways to deal with crises.

The cost of updating Linden's emergency response plan may seem expensive at first; however, in the long run it would save money, recovery time, and possibly lives. One of the first steps in updating the response plan would involve locating and addressing current hazards. For example, John Gupta, principal of nearby Colgate High School, hired a building inspector as part of an emergency-plan update. The inspector installed fire-resistant walls in the electrical closet. Although the procedure was costly, the expense proved to be justified when a fire broke out in the room a year later. As Gupta noted, "the new walls kept the fire contained. A $2,000 renovation saved the whole school from going up in flames." The renovation probably saved hundreds of thousands of dollars and countless lives. In fact, the *Linden Times* noted that similar updates prevented almost $800,000 in property damage in Linden last year alone. Besides, although some preventive measures are expensive, many are not. "Planning in advance, keeping extra supplies, and creating routine procedures such as practice drills cost little but are extremely effective," noted Linden fire chief John Rodriguez. A preventive approach improves the overall ability to respond to emergencies. Likewise, a preventive approach decreases the overall need to respond.

Instead of putting off emergency-response planning, Linden High needs to take responsibility for the safety of its students and staff before an emergency occurs. By updating our current plan, we could save lives and money; we would encourage students to take an active role in public safety; and we would decrease the number of emergency situations overall. Why not learn from our nation's recent disasters and avoid repeating past mistakes?

Persuasion

Counterarguments
How does the writer show an understanding of both sides of the issue?

Supporting Evidence
What makes this example relevant and precise?

Persuasive Technique
What kinds of appeals do you find in this paragraph? How is the writer both attributing sources and incorporating testimonials?

Organization
How does the writer organize the essay for greatest rhetorical effect?

Rhetorical Devices
How are parallel structure and repetition effectively used in the conclusion?

Approaching Level

DIFFERENTIATED INSTRUCTION

Emerging Students may find longer paragraphs or passages difficult to comprehend. Have students pause after reading each long section to ask theselves, What was the main idea of that section of text? If they cannot recall the main idea, they should reread the text with that question in mind.

For practice in **reading fluency,** have students take turns reading a sentence at a time. Guide them as they clarify each sentence.

Teach

Writing Skills

Counterarguments Answer: *The writer appeals to logic and anticipates the criticism that he or she is being paranoid. He or she counters by calling for basic awareness and preparedness when it comes to emergency situations.*

Writing Skills

Supporting Evidence Answer: *The example demonstrates how a simple and inexpensive preventive measure can save untold lives and dollars.*

Writing Skills

Persuasive Technique Answer: *The writer appeals to logic and ethics and offers supporting evidence and repetition to reinforce the argument. The quotations serve as sources and testimonials.*

Writing Skills

Organization Answer: *The writer sums up the examples, in two succinct sentences, to point up the logic of the appeal.*

Writing Skills

Rhetorical Devices Answer: *The parallel structure and repetition in the conclusion emphasize the writer's main reasons memorably and clearly.*

Teach

Writing Process

Revising Encourage students to read their essays more than once. Tell them to focus on one of the following three aspects during each reading: (1) content, (2) organization, and (3) style and voice. Suggest that reading the essay aloud will help them find any flaws, as well as hone their own unique writing style.

Writing Skills

Peer Review Have each student "test" his or her persuasive essay with a classmate. Instruct the listener to assume the role of someone who can be persuaded. After listening to the classmate's essay, the listener should provide feedback about which points strongly supported the argument.

Traits of Strong Writing

Include these traits of strong writing to express your ideas effectively.

Ideas
Organization
Voice
Word Choice
Sentence Fluency
Conventions
Presentation

For more information on using the Traits of Strong Writing, see pages R28–R30 of the Writing Handbook.

Word Choice

This academic vocabulary word appears in the student model:

overall (ō′ vər ol) *adj.* 1. all together, including all; *adv.* as a whole; with everything taken into account. *A preventive approach improves the overall ability to respond to emergencies.*

LOG ON ▶ **Literature** Online

Writing and Research For editing and publishing tools, go to glencoe.com and enter QuickPass code GLB9817u3.

Revise

Use the checklist below to help you evaluate and strengthen your essay.

Checklist

- ☑ Do you present a clearly stated opinion, claim, or thesis?
- ☑ Do you support ideas with detailed, precise, and relevant evidence?
- ☑ Do you organize your reasons logically and for greatest audience effect?
- ☑ Do you anticipate and address audience concerns and counterarguments?
- ☑ Do you select a point of view and tone that match your audience, purpose, and occasion?
- ☑ Do you use rhetorical devices, such as parallelism, to strengthen your argument?
- ☑ Do you use persuasive techniques, such as appeals and repetition, to strengthen your argument?

▶ **Focus Lesson**

Appropriate Tone

Revise to ensure an appropriate tone. For many persuasive purposes, you will want to sound clear, reasonable, and convincing.

Draft:

Some guys can't stop complaining that talking about emergencies will make everyone paranoid, but they don't know what's happening in the real world. Let's keep our minds on emergency situations and response efforts in our community and elsewhere.

Revision:

This is not to say that we will or should become paranoid, as some critics have suggested.[1] Instead, we should pay attention to emergency situations and response efforts in our community and elsewhere[2] to learn the best ways to deal with crises.

1: Use a formal tone, avoiding contractions, slang, and colloquial language.

2: Use a reasonable, respectful tone to address opposing arguments.

Writing Skills

Revising Explain that writers often repeat the same types of errors in their work. For example, a writer may overuse commas, misspell the same words repeatedly, or misplace modifiers again and again. Encourage students to create a chart of their common writing errors based on those marked on returned papers. The chart can serve as a list of errors to check for before submitting a final draft.

Type of Error	Example of Error	Corrected Error
Comma Splice	The black dog wagged its tail, the white dog barked loudly.	The black dog wagged its tail, but the white dog barked loudly.

Edit and Proofread

Get It Right When you have completed the final draft of your essay, proofread it for errors in grammar, usage, mechanics, and spelling. Refer to the Language Handbook, pages R47–R59, as a guide.

Focus Lesson

Parallelism

Parallelism is the use of the same grammatical form to express ideas similar in content and function. To create parallel structure, balance each element in a series of words, phrases, or sentences. For example, balance nouns with nouns and participial phrases with participial phrases. Writers often use parallelism, in single sentences or a series of sentences, as a rhetorical device to add sophistication to an argument or to emphasize a point.

Original: Phrases similar in content and function are expressed using different grammatical forms.

Lately, disasters have become a regular occurrence: _wildfires on the West Coast_, _hurricanes flooding the Gulf Coast_, and even _fatal tornadoes_.

Improved: Make phrases parallel by balancing grammatical forms.

Lately, disasters have become a regular occurrence: _wildfires blazing on the West Coast_, _hurricanes flooding the Gulf Coast_, and even _tornadoes ravaging our own state_.

Present

The Power of Presentation Your presentation could have a persuasive effect on your grade. Be sure to submit a clean, final copy that follows your teacher's guidelines.

Peer Review Tips

A classmate may ask you to read his or her persuasive essay. Take your time and jot down notes as you read so you can give constructive feedback. Use the following questions to get started:

• Does the writer present convincing, well-developed, and well-supported reasons for the claim or thesis?

• Does the writer persuade through the effective use of appeals, rhetorical devices, and other persuasive techniques?

Word-Processing Tip

The typeface you select can also affect your audience; for example, bold, powerful fonts are often used effectively to deliver persuasive messages in advertising. For a formal essay, however, select a conservative, readable font and black type. Create emphasis through careful word choice rather than through italics or other format choices.

Writer's Portfolio

Place a copy of your persuasive essay in your portfolio to review later.

Teach

Writing Process

Editing and Proofreading
Have students use the Proofreading Checklist on the inside back cover of the textbook.

Before students proofread, have them brainstorm to compile lists of common grammar, mechanics, and usage problems that they encountered in previous writing assignments and exercises. Have students refer to the lists as they check their essays.

Finally, although a computer's spell-check function is handy and helpful, it does not catch everything. If they are unsure about a word, urge students to consult a dictionary.

Writing Process

Presenting Students who are submitting their works to college admissions boards, employers, or contest judges should be certain that they have formatted the documents to satisfy any required standards.

English Learners

DIFFERENTIATED INSTRUCTION

Advanced Remind English learners that a suffix can change the function of a word in a sentence. For example, the word *parallel* is usually used as an adjective; the suffix *–ism*, however, makes the word a noun. Ask students to identify and discuss other examples of words changed by suffixes. (*grammatical, sophistication, and rhetorical*)

Focus

Summary

In this workshop, students will learn techniques for planning, rehearsing, and delivering a persuasive speech.

Teach

Speaking Skills

Tips from Toastmasters International Tell students that Toastmasters International offers these effective-speaking tips:

- Imagine speaking in a loud, clear, assured voice. Visualize yourself as successful, and you will be.
- Focus attention on your message and your audience. This will help your nervousness to abate.
- Realize that audiences want you to succeed: to be interesting, stimulating, and informative.

 For Speaking, Listening, and Viewing rubric, see Unit 3 Teaching Resources, pp. 219–220.

 For help with creating presentations, see Student Presentation Builder in StudentWorks Plus.

Learning Objectives

For pages 654–655

In this workshop, you will focus on the following objective:

Speaking and Listening: Delivering a persuasive speech.

Using Visual Media

Consider using graphics to emphasize important points in your speech. A chart or graph can make facts and statistics easier to understand. A photograph can add emotional impact to your message.

Speaking Frames

Consider using the following frames in your persuasive speech:

• My own view is that _____ because _____.

• While it is true that _____, it does not necessarily mean that _____.

Presentation Tips

Use the following checklist to evaluate your speech.

• Did you capture and hold your audience's attention throughout the speech?

• Did you use appeals and rhetorical devices effectively to help persuade your audience?

Speaking, Listening, and Viewing Workshop

Persuasive Speech

Literature Connection Jonathan Swift used his satirical essay *A Modest Proposal* to convince and persuade others of his beliefs. Sometimes, such as in informal or everyday situations, a written essay may not be the best way to persuade others to agree with you. Instead, you may want to speak to your audience directly. Like a persuasive essay, a persuasive speech should be built on structured, logical arguments and should use solid evidence to support those arguments.

> **Assignment** Deliver your persuasive essay as a persuasive speech.

Plan Your Presentation

There are four basic types of persuasive speeches. A persuasive speech can propose the following:

Fact The speaker makes a claim as if it were a fact, although it is not necessarily. *A teen curfew will lower crime rates throughout the city.*

Problem The speaker claims something is a serious problem deserving immediate attention. *Teenagers with nothing to do may take part in vandalism and other crimes.*

Policy The speaker asserts that one course of action is better than another. *We should introduce a curfew for teenagers, because parental supervision alone is not enough.*

Value The speaker argues the merits of one opinion by providing another opinion. Unlike fact, problem, and policy propositions, a value proposition appeals to emotion rather than reason. *Since older teenagers are more responsible, the curfew should only apply to younger teens.*

Review your persuasive essay to determine which type of persuasive speech you will present.

Speaking and Listening Practice

Use Note Cards Explain that when delivering a speech, you are *speaking* to an audience, not reading to them. Encourage students to reread their speech aloud several times in front of a mirror until they have almost memorized it. Students should write down their key points on note cards so that the written speech is no longer needed. The note cards will serve as cues to keep them on track while delivering the speech.

 For help with creating presentations, see Student Presentation Builder on StudentWorks Plus.

Rehearse

Practice giving your speech alone, perhaps in front of a mirror, and in front of family members or friends. Ask them for feedback on your performance. Then revise your speech on the basis of your audience's reactions and suggestions. Rehearse using these verbal and nonverbal presentation techniques.

Techniques for Delivering a Persuasive Speech

Verbal Techniques	Nonverbal Techniques
☑ **Delivery** Speak from the heart; don't read your speech.	☑ **Eye Contact** Maintain eye contact with your audience. Refer to your notes only when necessary.
☑ **Pace** Speak at a moderate speed, but use your voice to emphasize main points.	☑ **Posture** Stand tall with your head straight, but be natural.
☑ **Clarity** Speak clearly and distinctly. Pronounce all words carefully.	☑ **Gestures** Use gestures and facial expressions to convey meaning and reinforce your ideas.

Listen and Demonstrate Understanding

Use these strategies to listen politely and effectively:

- Face the speaker and sit upright.
- Respond appropriately, though subtly, to shifts in the speech. Meet attempts at humor with laughter or a smile; show engagement through facial expressions or slight movements, such as leaning forward.
- Take notes by writing, or take mental notes by silently reviewing key points or consciously committing them to memory.

Use these strategies to evaluate and analyze the speech and its delivery:

- Consider the degree to which you agreed or disagreed with the claim before hearing the speech, and the degree to which you might consider, or accept, the claim now.
- Evaluate the logic, depth, and persuasiveness of the support by identifying the most effective reasons and what made them effective.
- Identify memorable words, appeals, and other persuasive techniques.
- Determine how verbal and nonverbal techniques, such as pace and gestures, added to or detracted from your appreciation of the speech or your willingness to be persuaded.

Identify Logical Fallacies

Attack *ad hominem*: an attack on the person who holds the opinion rather than on the opinion.

Overgeneralization: the act of drawing a big conclusion from a small amount of evidence.

False causality or *non sequitur*: stating a conclusion that does not logically follow from the facts or explanation that preceded it.

 LOG ON ▶ **Literature** Online

Speaking, Listening, and Viewing For project ideas, templates, and presentation tips, go to glencoe.com and enter QuickPass code GLB9817u3.

Teach

Speaking Skills

Use Visual Aids Have students practice using visual aids until they are comfortable integrating them into their speech. Remind students to use only one or two visuals to clarify key points.

Listening Skills

Peer Assessment Ask students to use the following criteria in evaluating one another's speeches:

- Does the speech persuade listeners to take action?
- Does the speaker use effective pacing, volume, and eye contact?
- In the conclusion, does the speaker restate his or her position and summarize his or her main points?

APPROACHING For students having difficulty, consider recording the speeches on tape or video. Watch the speeches as a class. Model a correct evaluation of one or two of the speeches before asking students to do the peer evaluations on their own.

English Learners

DIFFERENTIATED INSTRUCTION

Beginning Allow students with limited English speaking abilities to practice their presentations privately, before or after class. Help them pronounce difficult or unfamiliar words.

Approaching Level

DIFFERENTIATED INSTRUCTION

Established Encourage students to record themselves as they practice their speeches. Have them listen carefully to the playback, paying attention to their speaking style. Urge students to repeat this exercise until they hear that they are speaking clearly and distinctly.

Focus

Summary

The purpose of Independent Reading is to encourage students to read novels from the time period that they have learned about in this unit.

Teach

Literary History ☆

The Reading Public Explain to students that by the middle of the eighteenth century narrative fiction was popular with the British public. These narratives often centered on ordinary people, such as chambermaids or apprentices. **Ask:** Why would eighteenth-century authors write novels about ordinary people? What audience were they trying to reach? Guide students to understand that whereas some earlier authors had expected their work to reach only educated readers, writers of the eighteenth-century were interested in reaching a wider audience.

Reading Practice

Explore Satire Tell students that many eighteenth-century novels, especially those by Fielding and Swift, are satirical. Note that satire usually includes exaggeration and comedy and is often used to spur change. Ask students to discern whether the novels that they are reading are satirical. Have them list reasons for thinking that the novels are or are not satirical. If a novel is satire, have students discuss what is being satirized.

Independent Reading

DURING THE RESTORATION AND THE EIGHTEENTH CENTURY, THE NOVEL WAS considered a new and shocking literary genre. The novel began to take shape in the eighteenth century; in the nineteenth and twentieth centuries, the novel evolved into one of the crowning glories of English literature.

Daniel Defoe is often credited with writing the first English novel, *Robinson Crusoe* (1719). In Defoe's novel, the shipwrecked Crusoe survives on a Caribbean island for twenty-eight years with a few supplies and a prisoner he calls Friday. All but ignored by the upper classes because Defoe himself was only a middle-class merchant, *Robinson Crusoe* was welcomed by shopkeepers, apprentices, servants, and the country at large. Since Defoe's time, the popularity of novels has never diminished. ☆

Pamela, or Virtue Rewarded

Samuel Richardson

In *Pamela*, Richardson is the "editor" of a collection of letters and journals penned by fifteen-year-old Pamela Andrews, a maidservant in a wealthy household, and five acquaintances. These entries take the reader through Pamela's relationship with Mr. B., the son of Pamela's late employer. Mr. B. is in hot pursuit of Pamela, but she repeatedly rejects his advances because of her desire to remain chaste. Despite Mr. B.'s unorthodox method of wooing, including imprisoning her, Pamela finally falls in love with him and the two are married. During the latter part of the novel, Pamela attempts to explain her decision to her fellow letter writers.

The History of Tom Jones, a Foundling

Henry Fielding

Considered by many to be Fielding's greatest novel, *Tom Jones* seems like a precursor to the modern-day soap opera. The reader follows Tom from childhood to adulthood and witnesses the growth of his love for his childhood sweetheart, Sophia, a character likely based on Fielding's wife. As one might expect, the course of true love does not run smoothly, and the characters must overcome many obstacles. Before the two are united, they travel all over the country, giving the reader a picture of England in the mid-1700s. Fielding wrote that his purpose in writing *Tom Jones* was "to recommend goodness and innocence" and that he had "endeavored to laugh mankind out of their favorite follies and vices."

Gulliver's Travels

Jonathan Swift

Gulliver's Travels describes the journeys of Dr. Lemuel Gulliver, ship's surgeon, world traveler, and reporter. Gulliver visits strange lands that are inhabited by various bizarre creatures, from six-inch-high Lilliputians to the giant Brobdingnagians and the savage and brutal Yahoos. By contrasting these creatures with humans, Swift highlights human weakness and societal ills.

 Write a Review

Read one of the books listed on these pages and write a review of it for your classmates. Be sure to explain why others might enjoy the book, or offer suggestions about ways of overcoming difficulties in reading it. Present your review to the class.

CRITICS' CORNER

"The great aim of Sterne was to give as true a picture as possible of real human beings as they are in themselves, not as they imagine themselves to be, nor as others judge them to be by their actions and outward behavior alone. This meant the shifting of emphasis from the external to the internal event, from the patterned plot artificially conceived and imposed on the characters, to the free evocation of the fluid, ever-changing process of being."

—A. A. Mendilow in "The Revolt of Sterne," from *Time and the Novel*, 1952.

The Life and Opinions of ☆ Tristram Shandy, Gentleman

Laurence Sterne

Tristram Shandy has been described as strange, tedious, silly, and downright nasty. Yet it has also been called a forerunner of the stream-of-consciousness novel and psychological fiction, and was enormously popular with the public. Sterne depicts the life of Shandy (whose name means "half crazy") in a nine-volume book that defies all conventions: events occur out of order, stories are unfinished, and some pages are even left blank.

Approaching Level

DIFFERENTIATED INSTRUCTION

Emerging To help students better visualize the novels they are reading, have them pay special attention to the novels' settings. Remind them that the setting is the time and place of a story and that the setting can be important to the plot. Have them consider whether the authors use realistic settings or fantastical ones. Encourage each student to draw pictures of one important setting in his or her novel. Have students do historical research about the period to help them understand the authors' (and characters') environment and social world.

Independent Reading

Teach

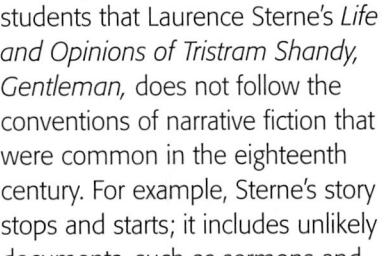 Write a Review

Students should direct reviews to their classmates and offer reading strategies.

Cultural History ☆

Shandy Started It Explain to students that Laurence Sterne's *Life and Opinions of Tristram Shandy, Gentleman,* does not follow the conventions of narrative fiction that were common in the eighteenth century. For example, Sterne's story stops and starts; it includes unlikely documents, such as sermons and legal papers; and the story line is not fully resolved.

Glencoe Literature Library

Glencoe Literature Library offers an extensive collection of hardcover books that help you encourage your students to read independently. Choose from among the more than 120 full-length literary works—novels, novellas, plays, and nonfiction. Each book includes related readings from a broad range of genres. Go to www.glencoe.com for more information.

 For access to all study guides for the Glencoe Literature Library, see the Literature Library Teacher Resources CD-ROM.

 To create customized reading lists from a database of more than 30,000 titles, use BookLink K–12 CD-ROM.

Have students suggest strategies to help reduce stress before a test. *(Possible responses: being well prepared, regularly reviewing material during the week before a test, maintaining a positive attitude, exercising regularly, taking deep breaths before the test, getting a good night's sleep)*

Teach

Assessment Explain to students that Test Preparation and Practice is intended to reinforce general test-taking strategies as well as to test the skills and vocabulary covered in the unit. They will read a passage and answer comprehension and inference questions about it. Then they will be asked to answer ten sentence-completion questions and ten paragraph-improvement questions and to write a short persuasive essay.

 To create custom assessments online, go to Progress Reporter Online Assessment.

 To create custom assessments using software, see ExamView Assessment Suite.

Assessment

English–Language Arts

Reading: Fiction

Carefully read the following passage. Use context clues to help you define any words with which you are unfamiliar. Pay close attention to the use of figurative language and tone. Then, on a separate sheet of paper, answer the questions that follow.

from **The Battle of the Books** by Jonathan Swift

line

[U]pon the highest corner of a large window there dwelt a certain spider, swollen up to the first magnitude by the destruction of infinite numbers of flies, whose spoils lay scattered before the gates of his palace, like human bones before the cave of some giant. . . . In this mansion he had for some time dwelt in peace and plenty, without danger to
5 his person by swallows from above, or to his palace by brooms from below: when it was the pleasure of fortune to conduct thither a wandering bee, to whose curiosity a broken pane in the glass had discovered itself, and in he went; where . . . he at last happened to alight upon one of the outward walls of the spider's citadel; which, yielding to the unequal weight, sunk down to the very foundation. Thrice he endeavored to force his passage, and
10 thrice the center shook. The spider within, feeling the terrible convulsion, supposed at first that nature was approaching to her final dissolution; or else, that Beelzebub, with all his legions, was come to revenge the death of many thousands of his subjects whom his enemy had slain and devoured. However, he at length valiantly resolved to issue forth and meet his fate. Meanwhile the bee had acquitted himself of his toils, and, posted
15 securely at some distance, was employed in cleansing his wings, and disengaging them from the ragged remnants of the cobweb. By this time the spider was adventured out, when, beholding the chasms, the ruins, and dilapidations of his fortress, he was very near his wits' end; he stormed and swore like a madman, and swelled till he was ready to burst. . . . "A plague split you," said he . . . "is it you, with a vengeance, that have made
20 this litter here? . . . " "Good words, friend," said the bee having now pruned himself, and being disposed to droll. . . . "Sirrah," replied the spider, "if it were not for breaking an old custom in our family, never to stir abroad against an enemy, I should come and teach you better manners." "I pray have patience," said the bee, "or you'll spend your substance, and, for aught I see, you may stand in need of it all, toward the repair of your house."
25 "Rogue, rogue," replied the spider, "yet methinks you should have more respect to a person whom all the world allows to be so much your betters. " . . . At this the spider, having swelled himself into the size and posture of a disputant, began his argument in the true spirit of controversy. . . .

Reading Practice

Hyperbole Ask students for examples of hyperbole. After their responses, explain that hyperbole is a figure of speech in which exaggeration is featured. Everyone uses expressions such as the following: *I nearly died laughing . . . He was hopping mad . . . We tried a thousand times.*

Obviously, such statements are not literally true, but people use them to express strong emotion, make a point, or evoke humor.

> "Not to disparage myself," said he, "by the comparison with such a rascal, what art
> 30 thou but a vagabond without house or home, without stock or inheritance? born to no
> possession of your own, but a pair of wings and a drone-pipe. Your livelihood is a
> universal plunder upon nature. . . . "
>
> "I am glad," answered the bee, "to hear you grant at least that I am come honestly by
> my wings and my voice; for then, it seems, I am obliged to Heaven alone for my flights
> 35 and my music. . . . I visit indeed all the flowers and blossoms of the field and garden; but
> whatever I collect thence enriches myself, without the least injury to their beauty, their
> smell, or their taste. . . . [O]ne insect furnishes you with a share of poison to destroy
> another . . . producing nothing at all but flybane and a cobweb."

1. Which of the following literary elements is Jonathan Swift using in the phrase *the destruction of infinite numbers of flies*, in line 2?
   (A) allusion
   (B) metaphor
   (C) simile
   (D) hyperbole
   (E) motif

2. Which of the following literary elements is Swift using in the phrase *like human bones before the cave of some giant*, in line 3?
   (A) conceit
   (B) hyperbole
   (C) simile
   (D) metaphor
   (E) aside

3. At first what does the spider assume is happening as the bee attempts to free itself?
   (A) The world is ending.
   (B) A sparrow has come to eat him.
   (C) A broom is sweeping away his web.
   (D) A fly has landed in his web.
   (E) A bee has landed in his web.

4. Which of the following literary elements is Swift using in the phrase *Beelzebub, with all his legions, was come to revenge the death of many thousands of his subjects*, in lines 11–12?
   (A) allusion
   (B) metaphor
   (C) simile
   (D) hyperbole
   (E) motif

5. From the context, what do you conclude that the word *acquitted*, in line 14, means?
   (A) exonerated
   (B) explained
   (C) freed
   (D) imprisoned
   (E) prosecuted

6. Which of the following literary elements is Swift using in the phrase *he stormed and swore like a madman*, in line 18?
   (A) allusion
   (B) metaphor
   (C) simile
   (D) hyperbole
   (E) motif

Assessment

Assess

1. **D** is the correct answer. Swift's use of the adjective *infinite* in reference to the number of flies is obviously exaggeration, or hyperbole. (DOK 2)

2. **C** is the correct answer. Swift uses the word *like* in a comparison of two essentially unlike things. (DOK 2)

3. **A** is the correct answer. Swift explicitly states that the spider "supposed at first that nature was approaching to her final dissolution." (DOK 1)

4. **A** is the correct answer. Swift is alluding here to a character from a written work other than *The Battle of the Books*. (DOK 2)

5. **C** is the correct answer. Option **A** is a synonym of *acquitted* but makes no sense in this context. Option **D** is an antonym of *acquitted*, so it cannot be correct. Options **B** and **E** are not synonyms of *acquitted*, so neither makes sense at all. (DOK 1)

6. **C** is the correct answer. Swift uses the word *like* in a comparison of two essentially unlike things, which means that he is using a simile. (DOK 2)

Approaching Level

DIFFERENTIATED INSTRUCTION

Emerging Frequently the anxiety of students who are anxious about taking a test is negative or self-defeating. Encourage students to try writing down any negative thoughts and then countering them with positive statements. They should repeat positive statements to help reprogram the mind to believe in successes instead of failures.

Assessment

Assess

7. D is the correct answer. "Ready to burst" is clearly an exaggeration. **DOK2**

8. E is the correct answer. The spider states, in lines 21–23, "if it were not for breaking an old custom in our family … I should come and teach you better manners." **DOK1**

9. B is the correct answer. From the context it is clear that the intended meaning of the word is "resources." **DOK1**

10. B is the correct answer. The spider states in line 29 that it does not wish "to disparage [itself] … by the comparison with such a rascal." **DOK1**

11. E is the correct answer. The bee states that heaven gave it its flight and music, but this is not the bee's response to the assertion, so **A** is incorrect. The bee may assume that the spider is more wicked but never states this, so **B** is incorrect. The bee never states that its ability to fly and hum attest to its superiority, so **C** is incorrect. The bee claims that the spider creates "flybane and a cobweb," so **D** is incorrect. **DOK2**

12. A is the correct answer. From the context, it is clear that no other option conveys the intended meaning of the word. **DOK1**

13. E is the correct answer. The passage relies on the use of personification throughout. Both the bee and the spider are personified. **DOK2**

7. Which of the following literary elements is Swift using in the phrase *swelled till he was ready to burst*, in lines 18–19?
   (A) allusion
   (B) metaphor
   (C) simile
   (D) hyperbole
   (E) motif

8. Why does the spider claim to be unable to attack the bee?
   (A) The spider is afraid of the bee.
   (B) The spider has been wounded.
   (C) The spider must rebuild his web.
   (D) There is no time for the spider to attack.
   (E) A family tradition prevents the spider.

9. From the context, what do you conclude that the word *substance*, in line 23, means?
   (A) basis
   (B) matter
   (C) theme
   (D) thought
   (E) understanding

10. What does the spider fear that he will do by comparing himself to the bee?
    (A) cause controversy
    (B) disparage himself
    (C) lose his inheritance
    (D) become a vagabond
    (E) become a disputant

11. How does the bee counter the assertion that he is *a universal plunder upon nature*, in lines 31–32?
    (A) The bee says that heaven gave it its flights and music.
    (B) The bee says that the spider is more wicked.
    (C) The bee says that it can fly and sing, and the spider cannot.
    (D) The bee says that the spider cannot create anything.
    (E) The bee says that it does not destroy what it collects.

12. From the context, what do you conclude that the word *furnishes*, in line 37, means?
    (A) supplies
    (B) removes
    (C) confiscates
    (D) undermines
    (E) collects

13. Which of the following is the most prominent literary element in this passage?
    (A) repetition
    (B) symbol
    (C) allegory
    (D) apostrophe
    (E) personification

14. According to your reading of this passage, what do you conclude that the overall tone of this piece is?
    (A) angry
    (B) humorous
    (C) skeptical
    (D) sinister
    (E) knowing

15. From your reading of this selection, what do you think the author's main purpose is?
    (A) to persuade
    (B) to instruct
    (C) to inform
    (D) to entertain
    (E) to describe

LOG ON ▶ **Literature** Online

Assessment For additional test practice, go to glencoe.com and enter QuickPass code GLB9817u3.

14. B is the correct answer. The tone of this passage is clearly not angry or sinister, so options **A** and **D** are both incorrect. Although there may be some skepticism and a somewhat knowing quality, neither accurately expresses the overall tone of this passage, so options **C** and **E** are also incorrect. **DOK4**

15. D is the correct answer. Swift's primary purpose is to entertain. **DOK4**

Vocabulary Skills: Sentence Completion

For each item in the Vocabulary Skills section, choose the word or words that best complete the sentence.

1. The violent _____ of the English Civil War ended with the execution of King Charles I.
   - (A) indictment
   - (B) discord
   - (C) precept
   - (D) ingenuity
   - (E) principle

2. The harsh ten years after the end of the English Civil War were marked by _____ Puritan rule.
   - (A) diverse
   - (B) jovial
   - (C) zealous
   - (D) aggregated
   - (E) loath

3. The Puritans' _____ censorship ended with the restoration of the king to the throne.
   - (A) oppressed
   - (B) diverse
   - (C) aggregated
   - (D) impetuous
   - (E) confining

4. The Enlightenment sprang, in part, from a newfound _____ of the power of reason by writers and philosophers.
   - (A) stratagem
   - (B) cavalcade
   - (C) veneration
   - (D) indictment
   - (E) negligence

5. The leaders of the Puritan Commonwealth attempted to _____ Royalist sentiment, but in the end they failed.
   - (A) subdue
   - (B) elate
   - (C) impose
   - (D) mourn
   - (E) commend

6. Slowly it became clear that the Puritan Commonwealth was not a benevolent power, but instead _____ and oppressive.
   - (A) reconciled
   - (B) subterranean
   - (C) impetuous
   - (D) intuitive
   - (E) malicious

7. Enlightenment thinkers rejected _____ and unsound ideas while embracing the ancient works of Western civilization.
   - (A) immutable
   - (B) jovial
   - (C) diverse
   - (D) irrational
   - (E) aggregated

8. The Restoration led to a reversal of the ban on theater, music, and other popular_____.
   - (A) diversions
   - (B) edifices
   - (C) vigilance
   - (D) stratagems
   - (E) negligence

9. Enlightenment thinkers showed their respect for reason and the natural sciences in a _____ of ways.
   - (A) deluge
   - (B) cavalcade
   - (C) conjecture
   - (D) myriad
   - (E) discord

10. Many artists, hoping for royal patronage, were _____ by the restoration of the king.
    - (A) elated
    - (B) confounded
    - (C) mourned
    - (D) quenched
    - (E) commended

ASSESSMENT **661**

Assessment

Assess

1. **B** is the correct answer. No other word makes sense in this context. (DOK 1)
2. **C** is the correct answer. The adjective *harsh* does not suggest "diverse," "jovial," or "aggregated," so options **A**, **B**, and **D** are all incorrect. *Loath* makes no sense in this context. (DOK 1)
3. **E** is the correct answer. No other word makes sense in relation to the word *censorship*. (DOK 1)
4. **C** is the correct answer. No other word makes sense in this context. (DOK 1)
5. **A** is the correct answer. No other word makes sense in this context. (DOK 1)
6. **E** is the correct answer. The sentence suggests that the correct answer must be an antonym of *benevolent*. (DOK 1)
7. **D** is the correct answer. No other word, in relation to the adjective *unsound*, makes sense. (DOK 1)
8. **A** is the correct answer. The correct answer must be a class that contains both *theater* and *music*. (DOK 1)
9. **D** is the correct answer. No other word makes sense in this context. (DOK 1)
10. **A** is the correct answer. No other word makes sense in this context. (DOK 1)

Approaching Level

DIFFERENTIATED INSTRUCTION

Established When doing the sentence-completion part of a test, students should consider these three simple steps:

1. Look ahead: Read the sentence and predict an answer.

2. Make your choice: Decide which answer choice fits best in the blank or blanks.

3. Read back the sentence: Verify your answer by positioning the word in the sentence.

Assessment

Assess

1. **D** is the correct answer. The original sentence contains incorrect parallel structure. No other option corrects this error without changing the content or introducing further errors. (DOK 1)

2. **B** is the correct answer. The nonessential parenthetical element *while genuinely felt* must be enclosed by commas, parentheses, or dashes. No other option corrects this error without changing the content. (DOK 1)

Grammar and Writing: Paragraph Improvement

Read carefully through the opening paragraphs from the first draft of a student's persuasive essay. Pay close attention to the writer's use of **parallelism, pronouns,** and **commas.** Then, on a separate sheet of paper, answer the questions below.

---

(1) Many in our community claim that their property taxes are too high. (2) They claim that the government takes too much, and they have claimed that they are voiceless in the way those taxes are spent. (3) These complaints while genuinely felt should not be acted upon by city or county officials.

(4) The property taxes in Hansen County are some of the lowest in the state. (5) All of the surrounding counties including Green Rain, Regal, South Regal, and Smith. outrank Hansen in property taxes by several percentage points. (6) Furthermore, Hansen County has the lowest rate of taxation in the state, and this rate is unmatched in all adjacent states.

(7) Many argue that our property taxes are used to fund unnecessary expenditures, such as pay increases for county employees and unwarranted road improvements. (8) The facts, however, tell a different story. (9) Twenty-seven percent of the property taxes collected approximately ten times the amount spent on road construction goes directly toward the purchase of essentials for the functioning of the public schools. (10) These essentials include heating, and air conditioning, textbooks, school lunches, busing, and computers. (11) Without these funds students will be underserved and undereducated; they will be left without a proper training in technology; current texts will not be available; some will go hungry during the day, while others will be unable to attend school at all. (12) These taxes are absolutely necessary to the future of these students.

---

1. Which is the best revision of sentence 2?
   - **(A)** They claim that the government takes too much. And they have claimed that they are voiceless in the way those taxes are spent.
   - **(B)** They claim that the government takes too much, and they have claimed that they are voiceless.
   - **(C)** They have claimed that they are voiceless in the way those taxes are spent.
   - **(D)** They claim that the government takes too much, and they claim that they are voiceless in the way those taxes are spent.
   - **(E)** They claim that the government takes too much; they are voiceless in the way they spend those taxes.

2. Which is the best revision of sentence 3?
   - **(A)** These complaints should not be acted upon by city or county officials.
   - **(B)** These complaints, while genuinely felt, should not be acted upon by city or county officials.
   - **(C)** Genuinely felt complaints should not be acted upon by city or county officials.
   - **(D)** City or county officials should not act upon genuinely felt complaints.
   - **(E)** City or county officials have acted upon these genuinely felt complaints.

Writing Practice

Parallelism Explain that parallelism is the use of a series of words, phrases, or clauses that have similar grammatical structures.

On the board or a transparency, write these (or similar) examples, and have students identify the parallel elements.

Words: He tried to find a car that was <u>fast, flashy,</u> and <u>affordable</u>.

Phrases: <u>Playing the piano</u> or <u>singing a song</u> is joyous.

Clauses: <u>Perch is less expensive</u>, but <u>salmon is more nutritious</u>.

3. Which is the best revision of sentence 5?
   - (A) All of the surrounding counties—including Green Rain, Regal, South Regal, and Smith—outrank Hansen in property taxes by several percentage points.
   - (B) The surrounding counties outrank Hansen in property taxes by several percentage points.
   - (C) All of the surrounding counties outranks Hansen in property taxes by several points.
   - (D) All of the surrounding counties, including Green Rain, and Regal, and South Regal, and Smith, outrank Hansen in property taxes by several percentage points.
   - (E) Delete this sentence.

4. Sentences 7 and 8 are an example of which persuasive technique?
   - (A) call to action
   - (B) supporting evidence
   - (C) counterargument
   - (D) ethical appeal
   - (E) emotional appeal

5. Which is the best revision of sentence 9?
   - (A) Twenty-seven percent of the property taxes collected—approximately ten times the amount spent on road construction—goes directly toward the purchase of essentials for the functioning of the public schools.
   - (B) Twenty-seven percent of property taxes go to purchase essentials for public schools.
   - (C) Twenty-seven percent of the property taxes collected is spent on road construction.

   - (D) Taxes are used for essentials for public schools.
   - (E) Approximately ten times the amount spent on road construction goes directly toward the purchase of essentials for public schools.

6. Which is the best revision of sentence 10?
   - (A) These essentials include heating and air conditioning, textbooks and school lunches, busing and computers.
   - (B) These essentials include heating and air conditioning, textbooks, school lunches, busing, and computers.
   - (C) Some of these essentials include heating, and air conditioning, textbooks, school lunches, busing, and computers.
   - (D) Essentials include heat, air conditioning, textbooks, lunches, busing, and computers.
   - (E) Delete this sentence.

7. Which error appears in sentence 11?
   - (A) incorrect use of semicolons
   - (B) fragment
   - (C) lack of pronoun-antecedent agreement
   - (D) lack of subject-verb agreement
   - (E) incorrect parallelism

8. What should the author conclude this essay with?
   - (A) counterargument
   - (B) strongest argument
   - (C) response to counterargument
   - (D) supporting evidence
   - (E) background

Essay

What do you think was the most important long-term effect of the Enlightenment? Write a short persuasive essay stating your opinion supported by evidence from this unit and any background knowledge you have. As you write, keep in mind that your essay will be checked for **ideas, organization, voice, word choice, sentence fluency, conventions,** and **presentation.**

Essay

Students may draw on the unit introduction for evidence. Be sure that they suggest and justify a plausible long-term effect of the Enlightenment. [DOK 3]

3. **A** is the correct answer. The original sentence incorrectly uses the period. No other option corrects this error without changing the content or introducing further errors. [DOK 1]

4. **C** is the correct answer. By introducing and then refuting an opposing position, the writer is using counterargument. [DOK 2]

5. **A** is the correct answer. Commas, parentheses, or dashes must enclose the parenthetical element *approximately ten times the amount spent on road construction*. No other option corrects this error without changing the content. [DOK 1]

6. **B** is the correct answer. This sentence has faulty parallelism in the series. No other option corrects this error without changing the content or introducing further errors. [DOK 1]

7. **E** is the correct answer. The last comma should have been a semicolon according to the series items preceding. [DOK 2]

8. **B** is the correct answer. For impact, climactic order would callo for saving the strongest argument for the closing. [DOK 2]

Skills Scope and Sequence

Readability Scores Key: Dale-Chall/DRP/Lexile

PART 1: The Stirrings of Romanticism

Selections and Features	Literary Elements
Unit Introduction pp. 664–678	Romanticism **SE** pp. 664–678
Poem Elegy Written in a Country Churchyard, by Thomas Gray pp. 680–688	Epitaph **SE** p. 681 Elegy (review) **SE** p. 687
Poems To a Mouse and **Auld Lang Syne,** by Robert Burns pp. 689–694	Dialect **SE** p. 690
Essay *from* **A Vindication of the Rights of Woman,** by Mary Wollstonecraft **11.4/69/**1740 pp. 695–704	Thesis **SE** p. 696
Vocabulary Workshop p. 705	
Informational Text TIME: **Raising Their Voices,** by Jeff Chu **9.5/66/**1140 pp. 706–712	
Grammar Workshop p. 713	
Poems A Poison Tree, The Lamb, and **The Tyger,** by William Blake pp. 714–719	Symbol **SE** p. 715
Poems London, and **The Chimney Sweeper** *from* **Songs of Innocence,** and **The Chimney Sweeper** *from* **Songs of Experience**, by William Blake pp. 720–725	Stanza **SE** p. 720 Meter (review) **SE** p. 724
Novel *from* **Pride and Prejudice,** by Jane Austen **6.8/53/**910 pp. 726–736	Dialogue **SE** p. 727 Foil **TE** p. 732 Point of View (review) **SE** p. 735

Reading Skills and Strategies	Vocabulary	Writing Grammar	Speaking, Listening, Viewing
Analyze Historical Context **SE** pp. 664–678 Analyze Graphic Information **SE** pp. 667, 669 Monitor Comprehension **TE** p. 668 Identify Cause-and-Effect Relationships **TE** p. 670	Context Clues **TE** p. 676	Write a Research Report **TE** p. 666 Write a Reflective Essay **TE** p. 678	Collage **TE** p. 672 Debate **SE** p. 678 Presentation **SE** p. 678
Interpret Imagery **SE** p. 681 Monitor Comprehension **TE** p. 682	Word Usage **TE** p. 686 Analogies **SE** p. 688 Academic Vocabulary **SE** p. 688	Subject-Verb Agreement **TE** p. 684 Write an Epitaph **SE** p. 688	Analyze Art **SE** p. 682
Monitor Comprehension **SE** p. 690 Paraphrase **TE** p. 692	Word Usage **SE** p. 694	Write a Poem **SE** p. 694	Oral Interpretation **TE** p. 690
Evaluate Argument **SE** p. 696 Activate Prior Knowledge **TE** p. 696 Skim **TE** p. 700	Denotation and Connotation **SE** p. 703 Academic Vocabulary **SE** p. 703	Intervening Expressions **TE** p. 698 Write a Persuasive Essay **SE** p. 704 Italics or Underscore **SE** p. 704	Analyze Art **SE** p. 698 Discussion **SE** p. 702
	Word Origins and Word Parts **SE** p. 705		
Identify Problem and Solution **SE** p. 706 Preview **SE** p. 706 Summarize **TE** p. 708		Adjectives **TE** p. 706 Write a Summary **SE** p. 712	
		Dangling Modifiers **SE** p. 713	
Visualize **SE** p. 715	Multiple-Meaning Words **TE** p. 718 Academic Vocabulary **SE** p. 719	Write a Poem **SE** p. 719	Analyze Art **SE** p. 716
Analyze Historical Context **SE** p. 720 Analyze Theme **TE** p. 722	Academic Vocabulary **SE** p. 724	Write an Expository Essay **SE** p. 725 Quotations **SE** p. 725	Analyze Art **SE** p. 721 Discussion **SE** p. 723
Analyze Characterization **SE** p. 727 Make Predictions **TE** p. 734	Multiple-Meaning Words **TE** p. 728 Word Origins **SE** p. 736 Academic Vocabulary **SE** p. 736	Write a Character Analysis **TE** p. 730 Write Dialogue **SE** p. 736	Analyze Art **SE** p. 728

Readability Scores Key: Dale-Chall/DRP/Lexile

PART 3: The Quest for Truth and Beauty *(continued)*

Selections and Features	Literary Elements
Poem Ozymandias, by Percy Bysshe Shelley pp. 808–812	Irony **SE** p. 809 Hyperbole and Understatement **TE** p. 810 Imagery (review) **SE** p. 811
Poems Ode to the West Wind and **To a Skylark,** by Percy Bysshe Shelley pp. 813–823	Diction **SE** p. 813 Romantic Poetry **TE** p. 816 Rhyme Scheme (review) **SE** p. 822
Poems La Belle Dame sans Merci and **When I Have Fears,** by John Keats pp. 824–829	Form **SE** p. 825
Poem Ode on a Grecian Urn, by John Keats pp. 830–834	Ode **SE** p. 830 Rhetorical Devices (review) **SE** p. 833
Comparing Literature To Autumn (poem), by John Keats, and **Haiku for Four Seasons** (haiku), by Matsuo Bashō, and **Untying the Knot** *from* **Pilgrim at Tinker Creek** (nonfiction), by Annie Dillard **8.5/60/1170** pp. 835–845	Imagery **SE** p. 836
Writing Workshop pp. 846–853	
Speaking, Listening, and Viewing Workshop pp. 854–855	
Independent Reading pp. 856–857	
Assessment pp. 858–863	

Reading Skills and Strategies	Vocabulary	Writing Grammar	Speaking, Listening, Viewing
Draw Conclusions About Meaning **SE** p. 809	Academic Vocabulary **SE** p. 812	Write a Research Report **SE** p. 812	Analyze Art **SE** p. 810
Recognize Author's Purpose **SE** p. 813 Identify Main Idea and Supporting Details **TE** p. 814 Monitor Comprehension **TE** p. 818	Synonyms **SE** p. 822 Academic Vocabulary **SE** p. 822	Pronouns **TE** p. 820 Write a Review **SE** p. 823	Analyze Art **SE** p. 817 Discussion **SE** p. 821
Apply Background Knowledge **SE** p. 825	Context Clues **SE** p. 829	Write a Journal Entry **TE** p. 828 Write an Internal Monologue **SE** p. 829	Analyze Art **SE** p. 826 Performance **TE** p. 826
Analyze Parallelism **SE** p. 830 Analyze Theme **TE** p. 834	Word Origins **SE** p. 834 Academic Vocabulary **SE** p. 834	Write a Research Report **SE** p. 834	Oral Report **TE** p. 832
Compare and Contrast **SE** p. 835 Analyze Sound Devices **SE** p. 836 Preview **TE** pp. 836, 842 Analyze Literary Influences **TE** p. 840	Word Usage **SE** p. 839	Write a Poem **SE** p. 839 Write a Comparison-Contrast Essay **SE** p. 845	Analyze Art **SE** p. 837 Oral Interpretation **TE** p. 838 Discussion **SE** p. 845 Oral Presentation **SE** p. 845
		Prewrite **SE** p. 849 Draft **SE** p. 850 Revise **SE** p. 852 Sentence Structure **SE** p. 852 Word Choice **TE** p. 852 Write a Reflective Essay **SE** p. 853 Active and Passive Voice **SE** p. 853	
		Revise **SE** p. 855	Reflective Presentation **SE** pp. 854–855
Make Judgments **TE** p. 856		Keep a Reader Response Journal **SE** p. 857	
		Write a Reflective Essay **SE** p. 863	

Focus

Bellringer Options

Literature Launchers: Pre-Reading Videos DVD: Unit 4

Daily Language Practice Transparency 52

Or write the unit title on the board: The Triumph of Romanticism **Say:** Think about the words *triumph* and *Romanticism*. **Ask:** What words are synonyms of *triumph*? (*conquest, victory, win*) Draw a word web on the board, with *Romanticism* at the center. **Ask:** What kinds of values do you think are part of Romanticism? (*Students may mention enjoyment of the world, emotions, imagination.*) What values do you think Romanticism would triumph over? (*Students may mention science, rational thought being more important than emotions.*)

 For school-to-home activities, see Unit 4 Teaching Resources Book, pp. 5–11.

The Hay Wain, 1821. John Constable. National Gallery, London, UK.

View the Art John Constable's paintings of the English countryside were so popular that the area where he worked became known as "Constable country." What can you tell about his attitude toward country life from this painting? ★

664

Unit Introduction Skills

Reading Skills
- Analyze Graphic Information (SE pp. 667, 669)
- Compare and Contrast (SE p. 673)
- Analyze Cause and Effect (SE pp. 675, 677)

The Triumph of Romanticism

Listening/Speaking/Viewing Skills
- Analyze Art (SE p. 664)
- Using Visuals to Enhance Meaning (TE p. 672)

Study Skills/Research/Assessment
- Resources and References (TE p. 666)

Writing Skills/Grammar
- Personal Reflections (TE p. 678)

The Triumph of
ROMANTICISM
1750-1837

Looking Ahead

Toward the end of the 1700s, industrial and political revolution overturned traditional ways of life in Europe. Bold, new ideas were beginning to challenge the belief in reason associated with the Enlightenment. In time, many of these ideas would form part of Romanticism, a broad movement in art and thought that valued feeling and imagination over reason. British Romantic writers found inspiration in nature, folk culture, the medieval past, and their own passions.

Keep the following questions in mind as you read:

◆ What were the essential features of Romanticism?

◆ How did Romantic writers respond to nature?

◆ What conception of the imagination did Romanticism express?

665

Focus

Summary

This introduction gives an overview of British literature and events and world events from 1750 to 1837. It discusses the reaction of Romantic thinkers against the reason-based thinking of the Enlightenment. The difference in their beliefs is notable in regards to nature, which the Enlightenment thinker saw as mechanistic and the Romantic thinker considered intrinsically good and not to be tamed by science. The economics and geography of the period are also presented.

Teach

View the Art ★

Answer: *Most students will say Constable regarded English country life as incredibly peaceful, lush, and even prosperous. His portrayal is very idealized.*

John Constable (1776–1837) representation of light informed the painters of the French Impressionist period. **Ask:** What does the painting suggest about the values of Romanticism? *(nature; simple life; life of common people)*

Unit Resources

Print Materials

- Unit 4 Teaching Resources, pp. 1–279
- Interactive Read and Write (On Level, Approaching, EL), pp. 165–222
- Novel Companion, pp. 163–230
- Bellringer Option Transparencies: Selection Focus 33–42; Daily Language Practice 52–69
- Literary Element Transparencies 12, 25, 26, 36, 97, 100

- Assessment Resources, Unit Assessment, pp. 25–32
- Assessment Resources, Selection Assessment, pp. 173–212

Technology

- TeacherWorks Plus CD
- StudentWorks Plus CD
- Literature Launchers: Pre-Reading Videos DVD, Unit 4
- Literature Online
- Interactive Vocabulary CD-ROM
- Listening Library CD-ROM
- ExamView CD-ROM
- Skill Level Up! CD-ROM

Teach

Reading Strategy | 1

Use the Timeline Help students read the timeline and relate key events in British literary history to British and world history.

- Explain that James Watt's invention of the steam engine in 1769 ushered in the Industrial Revolution.
- Have students identify events that reflect the revolutionary ideology of the time.

Ask: How do the publications listed reflect revolutionary ideas? *(Students may see connections between revolution and Mary Wollstonecraft's writing.)*

Cultural History ☆

The Elgin Marbles The Greek Parthenon was constructed around 450 B.C. The sculptures decorating it show Greek gods and heroes asserting civilization over barbarism. Around 1800, the seventh Lord Elgin took advantage of the Turkish occupation of Athens to "purchase" these sculptures to sell to Britain. It became a controversial issue and remains so today.

TIMELINE
1750–1837

BRITISH LITERATURE

1750

1751
Thomas Gray's "Elegy Written in a Country Churchyard" is published anonymously

1765
Bishop Percy publishes *Reliques of Ancient English Poetry*

1765
First gothic novel, Horace Walpole's *The Castle of Otranto*, is published

1786
Robert Burns publishes *Poems, Chiefly in the Scottish Dialect*

1786
William Beckford publishes *Vathek*

1790

1792
Mary Wollstonecraft publishes *A Vindication of the Rights of Woman*

1794
Ann Radcliffe publishes *The Mysteries of Udolpho*

1794
William Blake publishes *Songs of Innocence and Experience*

1798
William Wordsworth and Samuel Taylor Coleridge publish *Lyrical Ballads*

1799
William Wordsworth begins *The Prelude*

BRITISH EVENTS

1750

1753
Britain and its colonies celebrate January 1 as New Year's Day for the first time

1769
James Watt invents modern high-pressure steam engine

1771
Sir Richard Arkwright builds first water-powered cotton mill

1776 ▲
American colonists declare their independence from Britain; Adam Smith publishes *The Wealth of Nations*

1781
British surrender at Yorktown ends American Revolution ▶

1788
British establish first colony in Australia

1790

1795
Mungo Park explores Niger River in Africa

1798
Thomas Malthus publishes *An Essay on the Principle of Population*

1802
British purchase Elgin Marbles ☆

1805
British defeat Napoleon's naval forces at Trafalgar

1807
Britain outlaws slave trade

WORLD EVENTS

1750

1752
First U.S. hospital opens in Philadelphia

1752
Benjamin Franklin proves that lightning is electricity

1754
French and Indian War begins in North America

1789
French Revolution begins with storming of the Bastille prison

1790

1793
U.S. inventor Eli Whitney invents cotton gin ▶

1793
French king Louis XVI executed by revolutionaries

1794 ▶
Toussaint L'Ouverture leads Haitian revolts against France and Spain

1804
Napoleon Bonaparte proclaimed emperor of France

LOG ON ▶ **Literature** Online

Literature and Reading To explore the Interactive Timeline, go to glencoe.com and enter QuickPass code GLB9817u4.

Research Practice

Resources and References

SPIRAL REVIEW Have students identify events on the timeline that they would like to learn more about. Discuss appropriate resources for the information they would like to find and how to credit their source. Share this example for an online encyclopedia entry with students:

"Mary." <u>Encyclopædia Britannica</u>. 2006. Encyclopædia Britannica Premium Service. 8 Feb. 2006 <http://www.britannica.com/eb/article-9051212>. Have students write short research papers about the events they have chosen. Guide them in proper documentation of their work.

Frigate *Macedonian* captured by frigate *United States*, 1812.

1810

1813
Jane Austen publishes *Pride and Prejudice*

1814
First historical novel, Sir Walter Scott's *Waverley*, is published

1815
Jane Austen publishes *Emma*

1817
Samuel Taylor Coleridge's *Biographia Literaria* is published

1818
John Keats publishes *Endymion* ▼

1818 ☆
George Gordon, Lord Byron, publishes *Childe Harold's Pilgrimage*

1818
First science fiction novel, Mary Shelley's *Frankenstein*, is published

1820
Percy Bysshe Shelley publishes *Prometheus Unbound*

1824
George Gordon, Lord Byron publishes *Don Juan* ▼

1810

1811
Prince of Wales becomes regent

1811
Luddites destroy machinery

1812
War between United States and Great Britain begins

1814
George Stephenson designs first steam locomotive ▼

1819
Peterloo Massacre takes place

1824
England purchases Singapore and Malaya

1830
First public railway line opens in Britain

1810

1810
Father Hidalgo leads Mexican revolt against Spain

1812
Grimm brothers publish *Children's and Household Tales*

1815
Napoleon defeated at Waterloo, ending Napoleonic Wars

1814–1815
Congress of Vienna meets

1817
In Africa, Shaka becomes chief of Zulus

1819 ▶
Simón Bolívar leads Venezuelan revolt against Spain

1821
Greece revolts against Turkey and declares its independence

1830
France occupies Algeria

Reading Check

Analyze Graphic Information What new types of fiction first appeared during the Romantic Period?

Approaching Level

DIFFERENTIATED INSTRUCTION

Emerging Ask: How many years after James Watt designed the modern high-pressure steam engine did George Stephenson design the first steam locomotive? *(45 years)* Invite volunteers to ask and answer questions based on the timeline.

UNIT FOUR

Teach

Reading Check

Answer: *Gothic fiction, historical fiction, and science fiction.*

Reading Strategy | 2

Classify Ask students to classify the items in World Events and British Events categories under headings such as *Science* and *Politics*. Have them identify any themes or trends they perceive in the events they have grouped.

Literary History ☆

Lord Byron *Childe Harold's Pilgrimage* is an autobiographical work published after Byron traveled extensively, including a visit to Athens. Share this excerpt with students: "Dull is the eye that will not weep to see / Thy walls defaced, thy mouldering shrines removed / By British hands, which it had best behoved / To guard those relics ne'er to be restored." **Say:** This reflects Lord Byron's feelings about the Elgin Marbles situation. **Ask:** Do you think Byron approved or disapproved of the sculptures being moved to England? *(He is clearly angry and upset that they were moved.)*

Teach

Reading Strategy | 1

Make Inferences Say: Recall that Eli Whitney's cotton gin was invented in 1793. **Ask:** What connection can you infer about the Industrial Revolution and the rate of British cotton consumption? *(Students may say that mechanization made the process of growing and harvesting cotton more efficient and improvements in transportation allowed Britain to import more raw cotton.)*

APPROACHING Help students reason step by step. **Ask:** How did the cotton gin affect cotton production? *(It increased.)* How would improved transportation during this time affect the amount of goods transported? *(More could be transported.)*

Cultural History ☆

Omnibus By 1829 London's growth had created severe traffic problems. Thus, Londoners were delighted when George Shillibeer introduced the first omnibus, a horse-drawn carriage service. One carriage could transport many people at once, reducing congestion in the streets. By 1835 approximately half a million people were using omnibuses to travel in and out of the city each day.

BY THE NUMBERS

The Cost of Gentility

In the late 1700s, a well-bred person was said to be genteel. Gentility, which made a family socially acceptable, was closely related to economic status and lifestyle. The following list presents what a family could afford at various income levels.

100 pounds per year
- One ill-paid servant

300 pounds per year
- Two servants

400 pounds per year
- Three servants (including a cook)

500 pounds per year
- Gentility on a tight budget

700–1,000 pounds per year
- A carriage

More than 4,000 pounds per year
- A second house in London for the social season

TRAVEL EXPENSES

A genteel young Englishman's education included the Grand Tour, a European trip that could last three to four years. Money went much further on the Continent than in England. In the late 1700s a tourist could live better on 100 pounds a year in Italy than on 500 pounds a year in England.

MILITARY EXPANSION

Between 1793 and 1815, England spent 1,650,000,000 pounds on warfare. By the time of the Battle of Waterloo (1815), the British army had grown to about 250,000 men, more than six times its size at the time of the French Revolution (1789). The British navy had grown from 16,000 men to more than 140,000.

POPULATION BOOM ☆

Between 1760 and 1815, England's population grew five times as fast as during the preceding fifty years. One reason was falling mortality rates from epidemic diseases such as plague.

POLICING LONDON

In 1829 Parliament passed the Metropolitan Police Act, and Sir Robert Peel set up a constabulary for London. London's first police were required to be younger than 35, at least 5 feet 5 inches tall, and able to read and write. They were required to walk a beat of twenty miles a day, seven days a week.

GROWTH OF RAILROADS

The first public railway line opened in 1830 and extended 32 miles between the British cities of Liverpool and Manchester. The locomotive sped along at 16 miles per hour. Within 20 years, locomotives were able to reach 50 miles per hour, an incredible speed at the time.

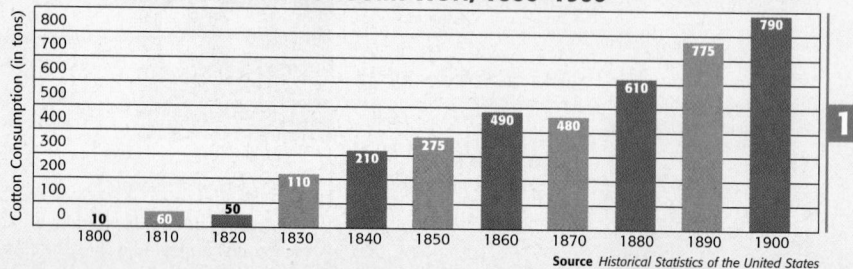

BRITISH COTTON CONSUMPTION, 1800–1900

Cotton Consumption (in tons)

Year	Consumption
1800	10
1810	60
1820	50
1830	110
1840	210
1850	275
1860	490
1870	480
1880	610
1890	775
1900	790

Source *Historical Statistics of the United States*

Reading Practice

SPIRAL REVIEW **Construct a K-W-L Chart** Invite students to translate the information on this page into a K-W-L chart so they will have a place to record any questions raised by this data. Have students enter information from the page in the "What We **K**now" column. Then, tell them to write questions in the "What We **W**ant to Know" column. After students read the information on pages 670–677, allow time for them to enter information in the "What We **L**earned" column. Encourage students to share unanswered questions as part of a class discussion. Allow students to research unanswered questions as extra-credit projects.

BEING THERE

A *Hungerford Stairs,* c.1810. George Shepherd. Guildhall Library, Corporation of London.

B *London's Royal Exchange,* 1809. Thomas Rowlandson.

C *Flatford Mill,* 1817. John Constable. Tate Gallery, London.

2 In the late 1700s, manufacturing began to assume a larger role in the British economy. As a result, industrial towns began to spread over England's landscape. To escape what they saw as a growing blight of factories and slums, many Romantic writers fled to remote areas such as the Lake District.

SCOTLAND
Edinburgh
Glasgow
NORTH SEA
Newcastle
Belfast
LAKE DISTRICT
UNITED KINGDOM
IRISH SEA
Leeds · Hull
Galway · Dublin · Liverpool · Manchester
IRELAND · Sheffield
Cork
Birmingham · ENGLAND
St. George's Channel
WALES
Swansea
Bristol · London **A** **B**
Portsmouth
Plymouth
Strait of Dover
English Channel

LOG ON ▶ **Literature** Online

Literature and Reading For more about the history and literature of this period, go to glencoe.com and enter QuickPass code GLB9817u4.

Reading Check

Analyze Graphic Information:

1. About how many times larger was the British navy in 1815 than it had been in 1789?

2. At top speed, how long would it have taken the first train to travel from Liverpool to Manchester in 1830?

3. In what part of England is the Lake District located?

English Learners

DIFFERENTIATED INSTRUCTION

Intermediate Point out the slang terms *Bobbies* and *Peelers* under the heading "Policing London." Explain that *Bob* and *Bobby* are nicknames for *Robert,* so *Bobbies* derives from *Robert.* Mention that English police officers are still commonly called *Bobbies.* Explain that *jargon* describes the words that are used in a particular profession, sport, or other area of specialization. Have students find another police jargon word in the paragraph *(beat)* and look it up in the dictionary.

Teach
Reading Check

Answers:

1. *Almost nine times larger*
2. *Two hours*
3. *Northwestern England*

Reading Strategy | 2

Make Generalizations Point out that the map on this page shows some of the industrial towns that spread across England in the late 1700s. **Ask:** How did the Industrial Revolution affect English towns? *(New industrial towns spread over the landscape. Some Romantic writers chose rural locations, such as the Lake District, for their homes.)*

View the Art ★

A. Hungerford Stairs, along the Thames River, was a point of embarkation for emigrants.

B. Thomas Rowlandson became chiefly known as a caricaturist of London daily life in the late 1700s.

C. John Constable's painting of the landscape near his home earned the area the nickname "Constable Country."

Teach

Reading Strategy | 1

Make Generalizations Have students read only the red headings on these two pages.

Ask: What generalization can you make just from reading the headings on these pages? *(Students may say that the Romantic era was a time of revolutionary ideas, great social upheaval, and war.)*

[APPROACHING] **Ask:** Which word appears most frequently in the heads? *(revolution)* Does the word mean the same thing in all the heads? *(no)* What meanings does it have? *(a radical change; a war to overthrow a ruling power)* What idea do the meanings have in common? *(violent, sudden, or intense change)*

View the Art ★

The Hero of Trafalgar shows Viscount Horatio Nelson and the gun crew firing from the quarterdeck of HMS Victory in one decisive battle of the Napoleonic Wars. Nelson was shot in the battle and died of his wounds but is to this day regarded as one of the greatest officers in the history of the Royal Navy. Byron referred to him as "Britannia's God of War."

Learning Objectives

For pages 664–678
In studying these texts, you will focus on the following objectives:

Literary Study:
Analyzing a literary period. Connecting to the literature.

Reading: Evaluating historical influences.

The Triumph of
ROMANTICISM
1750–1837

Historical, Social, and Cultural Forces

The Industrial Revolution

Beginning in Britain in the late 1700s, the Industrial Revolution brought a shift from economies based on farming and handmade goods to economies based on manufacturing by machines in industrial factories. Coal and steam replaced wind and water as new sources of energy and power. Cities and towns grew as people moved from the country to work in factories. This process produced wealth for a few factory owners but widespread misery for their workers, who struggled with long hours, bad working conditions, poverty, slums, and disease.

The Hero of Trafalgar, 1898. Orford Smith. Color lithograph.

The American and French Revolutions

The late 1700s was a period of growing political unrest that culminated in a series of revolutions. In 1776 Britain's American colonists declared their independence, resulting in a long war before the United States of America won its freedom in 1781. The French Revolution began in 1789 as a democratic protest against royal despotism and an idealistic assertion of human equality. Yet, once in power, the revolutionary government in France resorted to brutality, leading to the execution of thousands during the Reign of Terror.

Latin American Revolutions

In the early 1790s, the ideals of the American and French Revolutions began to spread throughout Latin America. In France's colony of Saint Domingue (present-day Haiti), enslaved Africans took up arms under the leadership of Toussaint L'Ouverture, winning independence in 1804. Beginning in 1810, a widespread series of revolts took place against Spanish rule in Latin America. By 1824, Argentina, Chile, Mexico, Peru, Uruguay, Paraguay, Colombia, Venezuela, and Bolivia had become independent.

★ The Napoleonic Wars

In 1793 revolutionary France declared war on Britain. From that point until 1815, with no more

Reading Practice

  Identify Causes and Effects Have small groups of students create a cause-and-effect organizer like the one below for one of the movements in this essay.

Then have pairs or groups present their organizers to the class, explaining how one thing lead to another.

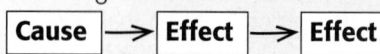

than a brief respite, Britain and France were engaged in the Napoleonic Wars. Napoleon Bonaparte first championed the French Revolution and then seized power himself, becoming emperor of France in 1804. The British naval commander Horatio Nelson became a national hero when he shattered Napoleon's fleet at the battle of Trafalgar in 1805. Britain continued to fight Napoleon on land and sea until his defeat at the climactic Battle of Waterloo in 1815.

Romanticism

Romanticism sprang from a reaction against Enlightenment values. While the Enlightenment praised reason and its limits, the Romantics were fascinated by extreme physical sensations and mental states—even terror and madness. Romantic works are filled not with moderation and social cohesion but with exotic extremes, whimsy, nightmares, innocent children, lone wanderers, and quests. The skeptical intellectual is the representative figure of the Enlightenment; for the Romantics, it is the sublimely inspired poet.

Unlike Enlightenment thinkers, the Romantics did not view feelings as untrustworthy or distracting. On the contrary, they valued expressions of feelings as authentic. Someone who was capable of feeling deeply demonstrated a natural human sympathy both to nature and to the feelings of others.

> *"It is the addition of strangeness to beauty that constitutes the romantic character in art."*
>
>  —Walter Pater

Romantic poets were particularly suspicious of the Enlightenment view that nature obeyed mechanical laws and could be mastered. In Romanticism, nature is always active, vital, and spontaneous. True enlightenment came not from bookish studies, but from nature, which for the Romantics included scenery, wilderness, and an interest in the natural state of people. The simplicity of common people—the songs they sang and the stories they told—inspired poets, as did children. Imagining what primitive people might have been like in a state of nature gave rise to the Romantic ideal of the "noble savage," a human being of instinctive goodness. Above all, Romantic writers placed their trust in instinct and the imagination.

PREVIEW **Big Ideas** of The Triumph of Romanticism

1 The Stirrings of Romanticism	**2** Nature and the Imagination	**3** The Quest for Truth and Beauty
The later 1700s saw dissident voices challenge the rule of rationalism that underpinned the Enlightenment. New literary movements, which would soon develop into Romanticism, emphasized feelings and imagination over reason. **See pages 672–673.**	As the Industrial Revolution began to transform Britain into a nation of cities and factories, Romantics sought inspiration in the beauty of the natural world, the lives of ordinary workers, the innocence of childhood, and the supernatural. **See pages 674–675.**	A second generation of English Romantics inherited many of the enthusiasms and values of their predecessors. During their tragically brief lives, Lord Byron, Percy Shelley, and John Keats each pursued the ideals of truth and beauty. **See pages 676–677.**

INTRODUCTION **671**

Teach

Main Idea Guide students in identifying the main idea of the section titled "The 'State of Nature.'" **Ask:** What is the most important thing the author is saying about Romanticism? *(Jean-Jacques Rousseau's conception of human nature as essentially good, curious, and content inspired Romantic writers.)* Encourage students to find the main ideas of the sections "Sensibility and the Emotions" and "The Imagination."

Literary History ☆

Noble Savage The term *noble savage* first appeared in John Dryden's *The Conquest of Granada,* published in 1672. However, the concept of the noble savage can be traced all the way back to the ancient Greek and Roman authors Homer, Ovid, Pliny, Horace, and Virgil. Rousseau glorified the ideal of the noble savage in *Emile* (1762) and *Reveries* (1782). In modern literature, Aldous Huxley's John the Savage in *Brave New World* is an example of the noble savage.

Big Idea 1
The Stirrings of Romanticism

The bold attempts of Enlightenment thinkers to find reason and order in the world—indeed, in the whole universe—inspired an equally bold reaction against those qualities. The reaction became Romanticism.

> *"Man was born free, and everywhere he is in chains."*
>
> —Jean-Jacques Rousseau, The Social Contract

The "State of Nature"

Interested in getting at the root causes of things, including human nature, several Enlightenment thinkers speculated about what humans in a "state of nature" might be like. One of the most influential of these thinkers was Jean-Jacques Rousseau, a Swiss who spent much of his adult life in France. He believed that humans were born naturally good, curious, and content with satisfying just their basic needs. According to Rousseau, society corrupts us so that we instead desire status, idleness, and luxuries. Can we ever regain the primitive innocence and happiness of the "noble savage"? Rousseau thought not, but he did believe in educating children in a more natural way. His ideal education would be more "natural" in two ways, both by allowing the child to be outside in nature and by attending to the unfolding of each child's inner nature as he or she develops. He believed such education would produce upstanding citizens who would be confident in their own abilities and opinions. Rousseau became an important catalyst for the new generation of Romantic writers.

Sensibility and the Emotions

Young writers increasingly wanted to reduce the Enlightenment's emphasis on reason. One solution was to replace it with a kind of sympathetic feeling called "sensibility." Whereas in the seventeenth century the physician William Harvey discovered that the heart was responsible for the circulation of the blood, the Romantics were far more interested in the way the heart represents the origin of emotion than in its mechanics. This cult of sensibility first emphasized the physical reactions we have when our hearts are moved—blushing, turning pale, and fainting. They read these visible movements of the blood as signs of inner moral sympathy and virtue.

The Imagination

Another warm, Romantic antidote to the cool reason of the Enlightenment was the imagination, which blends sensory impressions with fantasy. Enlightenment thinkers had tended to dismiss the imagination, either because they wanted to analyze pure experience in their scientific experiments or because they were interested in purely logical arguments in their philosophical searches for fundamental truths. Romantic writers valued precisely that quality of the imagination that Enlightenment writers had despised: its ability to fuse sights and sounds from wildly different kinds of experience in ways that defy sense. In fact the Romantics embraced the irrational ecstasies and horrors of the imagination. The poet William Blake (see page 714), for example, believed that imagination, rather than science, held the secrets of the universe. As he asserted, "Vision or Imagination is a Representation of what Eternally Exists, Really and Unchangeably."

Viewing Practice

SPIRAL REVIEW **Use Visuals to Enhance Meaning** Tell students that they are going to research and select visuals for this page. Ask students to focus their searches on Britain in the early 1800s. Students can determine and explain their own purposes in choosing their visuals, but you might suggest that they look for images depicting historical events, notable people, authors, cultural details such as clothing styles, and Blake's artwork. Display students' images as a "Romantic Collage" bulletin board and use it as a review at the end of the unit.

The Ancient of Days. Frontispiece, plate 1, from *Europe, a Prophecy*, 1794. William Blake. The Pierpont Morgan Library, New York.

The Pre-Romantics

The early years of this era saw several writers who straddled both Enlightenment values and the emerging ideals of Romanticism. Thomas Gray used Neoclassical techniques in his poetry, such as elevated language and classical forms, while embracing a love of nature and a belief in the common man—important ideals of later Romantic poets. Despite his acceptance in high society, Robert Burns wrote of the lives of common people in Scottish dialect characteristic of peasants and farmers. Perhaps the most famous pre-Romantic writer of all, William Blake was not content with the prevailing Neoclassical values of his day and focused on supernatural elements and imaginative experimentation thereby forging a style all his own.

A proverb is a short statement that expresses a truth. Blake wrote the following proverbs as a counterpart to the book of Proverbs in the Bible.

from *Proverbs of Hell* from *The Marriage of Heaven and Hell*
by William Blake

No bird soars too high, if he soars with his own wings.
A dead body revenges not injuries.
The most sublime act is to set another before you.
If the fool would persist in his folly he would become wise.
Folly is the cloke of knavery.
Shame is Pride's cloke.
Prisons are built with stones of Law, Brothels with bricks of Religion.
The pride of the peacock is the glory of God.
The lust of the goat is the bounty of God.
The wrath of the lion is the wisdom of God.
The nakedness of woman is the work of God.
Excess of sorrow laughs. Excess of joy weeps.
The roaring of lions, the howling of wolves, the raging of the stormy sea, and the destructive sword, are portions of eternity too great for the eye of man.

2

Reading Check

Compare and Contrast How do Blake's ideas oppose Enlightment values?

INTRODUCTION **673**

Teach
Reading Check

Answer: *Blake urged excessive behavior, celebrated chaotic and violent elements in nature, and attacked accepted social values.*

Literary Element | 2

Tone Remind students that tone reflects a writer's attitude toward his or her subject. Have students practice reading aloud Proverbs of Hell to a partner. Then, together, they should determine the tone of each line before reading the passage again to express the tone and mood in their reading.

ENGLISH LEARNERS Tell students that they need to know what the proverbs mean to read them with expression. Let students work in groups, with each student choosing two or three proverbs to read. Have the groups perform their readings and discuss the tone.

View the Art ★

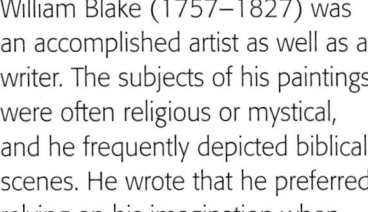

William Blake (1757–1827) was an accomplished artist as well as a writer. The subjects of his paintings were often religious or mystical, and he frequently depicted biblical scenes. He wrote that he preferred relying on his imagination when creating his art.

Rereading Before students read the section titled "What Is Nature?" have students reread the section on page 672 titled "The 'State of Nature.'" **Ask:** What have you learned about the Romantic view of nature so far? *(Romantic thinkers distrusted Enlightenment reductionism and mechanization of nature and sought beauty in wild, untamed wilderness.)*

Cultural History ☆

London In the nineteenth century, London was not a healthy place. Fumes from factories and stoves created a thick fog that often covered the city. Sometimes people walking the streets became lost, fell into the Thames River, and drowned.

Big Idea 2

Nature and the Imagination

Perhaps the most profound disagreement between Enlightenment and Romantic writers was their differing reactions to nature. What is it for? Is it good or bad? What should we do with it?

What Is Nature?

To Enlightenment thinkers, disorderly nature seemed meant for humans to tame. Nature could be made more productive in farms run on rational principles. Nature could be made more rational by being analyzed and studied in laboratories. Nature could be made more beautiful in orderly gardens with straight paths and clear views.

The answers to these questions seemed more complicated to writers a few generations later when the face of nature was literally changing. Cities and towns were sprawling into the countryside, railroads began to crisscross the landscape, smoke-belching factories were springing up. Had human intervention really made nature more rational or more beautiful? And what did these changes say about the humans who had caused them?

> *Heaven lies about us in our infancy!"*
> —William Wordsworth

Romantics preferred their nature wild and untamed. Their landscape gardens, for example, kept a space for wilderness, with winding paths through tangled woods leading to sudden, startling views. Instead of the arranged prettiness of an ornamental garden, they preferred the sublime experience of the Swiss Alps, where the overwhelming scale of nature inspires awe rather than mere appreciation. In his poem "The Tables Turned," William Wordsworth (see page 738)

recommended that we shut our books and lift our eyes to the natural world around us: "Enough of science and of art; / Close up those barren leaves; / Come forth, and bring with you a heart / That watches and receives."

The Child and the Common Man

Who led the most natural life? One answer for the Romantics was children, because they had not yet been educated by school or society. Long before the Enlightenment, thinkers had viewed children as deficient adults precisely because they had not yet been transformed by education. The Romantics, however, saw in children innocence and imagination rather than ignorance. Another group whose lives and culture had not been distorted by civilized values was the common people. Writers of the period became interested in imagining the experiences and impressions of ordinary folk.

In 1798, two young poets, William Wordsworth and Samuel Taylor Coleridge (see page 757), decided to publish a book of poetry, called *Lyrical Ballads*, that experimented with these new ideas. Their poems for the most part are written in the simple verse form of folk ballads or hymns. They use informal vocabulary, not ornate language. Their subjects, too, are drawn from the lives of uneducated people: a little girl whose brothers and sisters have died, an old Indian woman, a mentally deficient boy, an old sailor, a father going for a walk with his young son.

Dreams and Nightmares

Many Romantic writers shared a critical attitude toward the methods and promised benefits of science. Wordsworth, for instance, was concerned about our motivations in studying nature: "Our meddling intellect / Mis-shapes the beauteous forms of things; / —We murder to dissect." This Romantic indictment of how science deforms nature took life in the gothic novel *Frankenstein*

Reading Practice

SPIRAL REVIEW **Construct a Graphic Organizer** Guide students in creating an idea web for each heading on this page. An example for "What Is Nature?" is shown.

Romantics disagreed with Enlightenment urge to tame nature.

What Is Nature?

Romantics believed nature should be wild and untamed.

Nature can teach us who we are more effectively than a book can.

Romantics preferred majestic Alps instead of ordered gardens.

Cloud Study, Horizon of Trees. John Constable. Royal Academy of Arts, London.

by Mary Shelley (see page 791). As a result of views like these, many Romantics were fascinated by subjects that science could not explain. Coleridge contributed a long poem to *Lyrical Ballads* that includes nightmarish scenes set among the icebergs of the Antarctic. He later claimed

that his famous poem "Kubla Khan" appeared to him in a drug-induced dream vision. By focusing on the irrational and unnatural, Romantic writers hoped to embrace the full scope of human experience, including the pains and pleasures of the heart and the dark recesses of the mind.

from the preface to *Lyrical Ballads* by William Wordsworth

The principal object, then, which I proposed to myself in these poems was to choose incidents and situations from common life, and to relate or describe them, throughout, as far as was possible, in a selection of language really used by men; . . . Low and rustic life was generally chosen, because in that condition, the essential passions of the heart find a better soil in which they can attain their maturity, are less under restraint, and speak a plainer and more emphatic language; because in that condition of life our elementary feelings co-exist in a state of greater simplicity, and,

consequently, may be more accurately contemplated, and more forcibly communicated; because the manners of rural life germinate from those elementary feelings; and, from the necessary character of rural occupations, are more easily comprehended; and are more durable; and lastly, because in that condition the passions of men are incorporated with the beautiful and permanent forms of nature.

Reading Check

Analyze Cause and Effect How did Wordsworth and Coleridge's interest in common life influence their poetry?

Advanced Learners

DIFFERENTIATED INSTRUCTION

The Romantic Ideal The Romantics rejected the authoritarianism, materialistic values, and industrialization they saw emerging in the early years of the nineteenth century. They valued individual rights, imagination, extreme emotions, and nature. Have students research, read about, and take notes on modern artists

who have championed these values, such as Kurt Cobain, Janis Joplin, Jack Kerouac, and Louise Gluck. Invite students to share their information with the class.

Teach

Reading Check

Answer: *They used simple verse forms and ordinary language; they chose common people and everyday activities as their subjects.*

Literary Element	2

Style Remind students that *style* refers to the expressive qualities that distinguish an author's work, including word choice and sentence structure. **Ask:** How many sentences are here? Why might Wordsworth have made such liberal use of semicolons? *(two; so that closely related ideas would flow together)* Would you describe Wordsworth's diction in this preface as low and rustic? Explain. *(Students may say that Wordsworth's diction in the Preface is formal and academic and that he is referring to the poems with the terms low and rustic.)*

View the Art ★

Ask: How does the scene in this painting express the Romantic idea of nature's being wild, untamed, and overwhelming? *(Students may say that the ominous-looking clouds fill most of the painting, dwarfing the houses below.)*

Teach

Preview and Make Predictions Ask students to look at the title, headings, quote, and painting on this spread before they begin reading the text. **Ask:** How do you predict a revolutionary spirit relates to the literature of the Romantics? *(Students may say the spirit of revolution inspired resistance to authoritarianism.)*

(APPROACHING) Have students look at the painting of Shelley and describe it. Ask students which themes they recognize in the art from earlier Romantic periods and predict whether these themes influenced later Romantics.

Political History ☆

Reign of Terror The period of the French Revolution between September 5, 1793, and July 27, 1794, is known as the Reign of Terror. During this time, a small subgroup of the government used extremely harsh punishments to eliminate anyone it suspected of being an enemy of the revolution. It is estimated that hundreds of thousands were arrested and thousands executed during the Terror.

or the Romantics, the deepest human experiences were often moments of intense communication between their inner selves and the world around them. They sought these experiences by falling in love, writing poetry, and fighting for causes they believed in.

The Revolutionary Spirit

In 1789 the French Revolution seemed to offer young people a chance to realize these dreams. Wordsworth and Coleridge, among many others, responded to the ideals of "Liberty, Equality, Fraternity" and were infused with enthusiasm for the revolutionary cause. As Wordsworth exulted (in lines later included in his long autobiographical narrative poem *The Prelude*), "Bliss was it in that dawn to be alive, / But to be young was very heaven!" When these ideals seemed betrayed by the bloody excesses of the Reign of Terror, both ☆ men slipped into conservative views. The next generation of Romantics, such as Percy Bysshe Shelley (see page 808), who had been inspired by Wordsworth's and Coleridge's youthful political radicalism, felt betrayed and continued to support revolt both at home and abroad.

The Spirit of Nationalism

The Romantic interest in folk culture had important political as well as literary consequences. Many English Romantics, whose education had been steeped in the classics, were particularly stirred by the struggles of the Greek people to win independence from Turkish rule. The Romantic poet George Gordon, Lord Byron (see page 800), donated money to the Greek cause, founded an artillery unit, and died en route to fight beside the Greeks.

Exotic Places and Times

For the Romantics, a great part of the attraction of foreign lands was the glamour of their cultures. Such places held the allure of the unknown and the exotic. Actual travel was not always necessary. The Romantics could feed their imaginations with the writings of travelers to the Near East and other faraway places. Literature with exotic settings—whether experienced or imagined—proved very popular with Romantic writers and audiences. Other remote and beautiful spots appealed to them as well. The highlands of Scotland and the Swiss and Italian Alps, for example, with their rough peaks and raging torrents, provided the settings for Mary Shelley's *Frankenstein*.

The past, too, offered exotic surprises. Many Romantic writers bypassed the familiar, sunlit eras of Greece and Rome for darker, more mysterious periods. In particular, the medieval "Dark Ages" appealed to them. The Romantics were inspired by the same qualities of the Middle Ages that the Enlightenment thinkers despised—Gothic wildness, age-old ritual, and strange beliefs. Beginning in 1765 with Horace Walpole's *The Castle of Otranto*, writers used imaginary medieval settings, including weird landscapes and haunted castles, to create a new literary form, the gothic novel.

> "Much have I traveled in the realms of gold . . ."
>
> —John Keats
> "On First Looking into Chapman's Homer"

The Poetic Quest

It is not surprising that in an age so conscious of its own rebellion, Romantic poets above all reflected on their role in culture. Many poets in

Vocabulary Practice

SPIRAL REVIEW **Context Clues** Remind students to decode meaning in text using three different types of context clues: definition, inference, and contrast. Definition clues give the meaning in the text. Inference clues are implied and enable readers to infer meaning from the context. Contrast clues show what a word does not mean. Have students use context clues to figure out words they do not know on page 676 and identify the type of clue in each case. Ask them to choose a word and write three new sentences for it that include each type of context clue to its definition.

Percy Bysshe Shelley, 1845. Joseph Severn. Oil on canvas. Keats-Shelley Memorial House, Rome. ★

this period, most notably Wordsworth and Shelley, wrote manifestos declaring the supremacy of poetry. Others wrote poems that seem to be allegories of the grand poetic quest for beauty and truth that guided many Romantic poets. One of the poets who sought to capture exuberance and beauty was John Keats (see page 824). In his brief life, he traveled far in his imagination. Some of his most famous sonnets are about the ability of books to transport him to the magical realms of the imagination. Sublime thoughts demand sublime forms of expression, Romantic poets thought. They were thrilled to take on this challenge.

from *A Defense of Poetry* by Percy Bysshe Shelley

The most unfailing herald, companion, and follower of the awakening of a great people to work a beneficial change in opinion or institution, is Poetry. At such periods there is an accumulation of the power of communicating and receiving intense and impassioned conceptions respecting man and nature. The persons in whom this power resides, may often, as far as regards many portions of their nature, have little apparent correspondence with that spirit of good of which they are the ministers. But even whilst they deny and abjure, they are yet compelled to serve, the Power which is seated on the throne of their own soul. It is impossible to read the compositions of the most celebrated writers of the present day without being startled with the electric life which burns within their words. They measure the circumference and sound the depths of human nature with a comprehensive and all-penetrating spirit, and they are themselves perhaps the most sincerely astonished at its manifestations, for it is less their spirit than the spirit of the age. Poets are the hierophants [interpreters] of an unapprehended inspiration, the mirrors of the gigantic shadows which futurity casts upon the present, the words which express what they understand not; the trumpets which sing to battle, and feel not what they inspire: the influence which is moved not, but moves. Poets are the unacknowledged legislators of the World.

2

Reading Check

Analyze Cause and Effect In Shelley's view, what links poetry with revolution?

INTRODUCTION **677**

Approaching Level

DIFFERENTIATED INSTRUCTION

Emerging Remind students that an argument is persuasive writing in which logic or reason is used to try to influence the reader. Help students break down the elements of Shelley's argument. **Ask:** How does Shelley describe the poet? *(as an unknowing instrument of something larger)* What force speaks through the poet? *(the spirit of the age, the force of life, the future of humanity)* What does he mean by the last sentence? *(Poets rule the world.)* Have students discuss whether they think Shelley has proven his argument and whether they agree with him.

Teach

Reading Check

Answer: *Shelley believed that periods of revolution stimulate the imaginative power in human beings. Because poets possess this power to a high degree, their works are the truest reflection of the spirit of these times.*

Literary Element   2

Symbol Remind students that a symbol is something that exists on a literal level within a work but also represents something beyond itself on a figurative level. **Ask:** How do trumpets work as a symbol in this excerpt by Shelley? *(Trumpets here are symbols for poets; this symbol suggests poets can be heard and understood by many and can inspire many.)*

View the Art ★

Joseph Severn (1793–1879) is best known for his friendship with John Keats. He was by Keats's side at his death and is buried beside him in a cemetery in Rome. **Ask:** What symbols in the painting identify it as a Romantic work of art?

Assess

Legacy of the Period

Refer students to the second paragraph, about childhood. **Ask:** How would you describe our society's view of children today? (*Students may say that our society views children as innocent but curious about the world.*)

Cultural and Literary Links

As students read the unit, invite them to think about how Romantic authors have influenced their favorite modern authors.

Activities

1. **Follow Up** Encourage students to support their answers with specific details from the unit introduction.

2. **Contrast Literary Periods** Make sure the panels are made up of students who initially hold differing views.

3. **Build Visual Literacy** Ideally, students will use a variety of visual media for their collages.

Have students make and label the Bound Book as shown. Then have them use it to organize information they learn about each literary genre.

WRAP-UP

Legacy of the Period

Many of Romanticism's core values, such as the spiritual power of nature, the importance of the imagination, and the dignity of the artist, have become a permanent part of our civilization. Today's environmental movements and creative arts programs are part of Romanticism's legacy.

The Romantics helped change the way our civilization regards children. Previously, children were seen simply as immature adults. Romantics such as Rousseau, Blake, and Wordsworth, however, attached a central importance to what they saw as the unique experiences of childhood.

Romanticism also shaped our vision of the medieval period. Since the Renaissance, most people had viewed the Middle Ages as a time of "Gothic" barbarism, but the Romantics saw the medieval past as a glamorous era of knights and ladies, fairies and wizards, dragons and quests.

When it spread to the United States, European Romanticism helped influence American literature, inspiring writers such as Ralph Waldo Emerson, Henry David Thoreau, Edgar Allan Poe, Nathaniel Hawthorne, and Herman Melville.

Cultural and Literary Links

- Largely ignored in his own time, William Blake has had a great influence on modern writers, particularly poets, including William Butler Yeats, Theodore Roethke, and Allen Ginsberg.

- The gothic novel and the historical novel, types of fiction that remain very popular today, made their first appearance during the Romantic period.

- Often cited as the first science fiction novel, Mary Shelley's *Frankenstein* helped establish the image of the brilliant, but mad, scientist that is still a feature of popular culture. As an artificial human made from flesh (not machinery, like a robot), Frankenstein's monster is perhaps the first android in literature.

 **Literature** Online

Unit Resources For additional skills practice, go to glencoe.com and enter QuickPass code GLB9817u4.

Activities

Choose one of the following activities to explore and develop as you read this unit.

1. Follow Up Go back to the Looking Ahead section on page 665 and answer the questions.

2. Contrast Literary Periods Neoclassicists believed in traditions and reason. Romantics believed in imagination and emotion. Hold a debate on which of these philosophies is a better guide to life.

3. Build Visual Literacy Create a collage or presentation of the different ways in which Victor Frankenstein and his monster have been portrayed in popular culture.

4. Take Notes Use this organizer to explore your personal responses to the selections in this unit.

 **BOUND BOOK**

Reader-Response Journal

Writing Practice

Personal Reflections

SPIRAL REVIEW Ask students to think about whether they are more Romantic types or Enlightenment thinkers. Have them write a personal essay on aspects of Romantic and Enlightenment philosophies that they recognize in their own attitudes and beliefs. They may structure their essays by pointing out aspects of the two philosophies and comparing them to experiences or beliefs of their own. Most students will probably find a mixture of Romantic and other traits within themselves. Students should conclude their essays by stating whether their personal philosophy seems more influenced by the Romantic or Enlightenment worldview. They may conclude that the two philosophies have equal influence.

PART 1

The Stirrings of Romanticism

Autumn Leaves, 1856. Sir John Everett Millais. Manchester Art Gallery, UK.

 View the Art Millais was a founding member of an art movement known as the Pre-Raphaelite Brotherhood. The Pre-Raphaelites rebelled against the conventional painting styles of the time. Does this painting seem unconventional? Explain why or why not.

"To see a World in a Grain of Sand,
And a Heaven in a Wild Flower,
Hold Infinity in the palm of your hand,
And Eternity in an hour." **1**

—William Blake, "Auguries of Innocence"

English Learners

DIFFERENTIATED INSTRUCTION

Beginning Point out the rhyming words *flower* and *hour*. **Ask:** Can you think of other words that have the *–ower* spelling? *(Students may think of tower or shower; let them continue until they* come to words that are spelled the same but have a different pronunciation, such as *grower* or *blower*.) Remind students that one of the challenges of English is that pronunciations can change.

 For additional support for English Learners, See Unit 4 Teaching Resources Book, p. 19.

Analyze and Extend

Reading Strategy | 1 |

Make Connections Ask: How do you interpret the phrase "Eternity in an hour"? *(Students may point out that there are moments in life, such as falling in love, when all that is and all that could be seem present at once.)*

View the Art ★

Answer: *Some students may say that the subject matter and portrayal are fairly conventional. Others may note that the sharp outlines of the figures, the bright colors, and the daily-life subject matter seem unconventional compared to paintings from the English Renaissance or the Enlightenment.*

Sir John Everett Millais (1829–1896) was the youngest student ever to enter the Royal Academy. His nickname was "The Child." He was just eleven years old, and other students were envious of his talent. His early technique included painting landscapes outdoors and later adding figures in the studio.

Ask: What stirrings of Romanticism do you observe in the art? *(Students might point out the prominence of nature and the emphasis on childhood.)*

Before You Read

Elegy Written in a Country Churchyard

Meet Thomas Gray
(1716–1771)

"I shall be but a shrimp of an author," Thomas Gray noted late in his life, reflecting on the small number of works he had published. If measured only by quantity, Gray's output of poetry was indeed small. He allowed only thirteen of his poems to be published during his lifetime. Gray's reputation as an author was more secure than he imagined, however, for if he wrote little, he also wrote remarkably well. His "Elegy Written in a Country Churchyard" remains one of the best-loved poems in the English language.

> "['Elegy Written in a Country Churchyard'] abounds with images that find a mirror in every mind, and with sentiments to which every bosom returns an echo."
>
> —Samuel Johnson, "The Life of Gray"

A Good Education Gray was born in 1716 in London to a doting mother and a violent, uncaring father. His mother wanted to provide her only son (the sole survivor of twelve children) with a good education and a stable life away from his father. She sent him at the age of eight to study at Eton, a prestigious boarding school. There, Gray formed enduring friendships with Richard West, the son of a prominent lawyer, and Horace Walpole, the wealthy son of a powerful English politician.

After Eton, Gray attended Cambridge University, but interrupted his studies for two years to tour Europe with Walpole. Gray returned to Cambridge at the age of twenty-five to complete his studies and stayed on to become a resident scholar.

The Secluded Poet Gray led a quiet life, maintaining close relationships with only a handful of people. Among them was his mother, whom he often visited in the village of Stoke Poges, where she moved after his father's death. Gray came to love the natural beauty of the village and the quiet life of its people. In its peaceful surroundings he worked on two of his best poems: a sonnet on the death of his friend Richard West and "Elegy Written in a Country Churchyard," which took him nine years to complete. Gray did not plan to publish the elegy, but he had little choice in the matter. He showed it to Walpole, who shared it with friends, and an imperfect copy of the poem made its way to the editor of a popular periodical. When Gray learned that the *Magazine of Magazines* planned to print the poem without his permission, he quickly published an accurate version. Gray's "Elegy Written in a Country Churchyard" came out in February 1751 to almost immediate acclaim. Because he felt that a gentleman should not accept payment for writing poetry, he let his publisher keep all the profits.

A Perfectionist at Work At the age of forty-one, Gray was offered the position of poet laureate of England, but he turned down the honor. A perfectionist, Gray wrote very slowly and feared that as poet laureate he would have to produce works at a rate that would compromise his standards. Gray died at Cambridge at the age of fifty-five, after a long illness. He was buried in Stoke Poges next to his mother.

LOG ON ▶ **Literature** Online

Author Search For more about Thomas Gray, go to glencoe.com and enter QuickPass code GLB9817u4.

Literary Elements
- Epitaph (SE pp. 681, 686, 687)

Elegy Written in a Country Churchyard

Writing Skills/Grammar
- Apply Imagery (SE p. 688)
- Subject-Verb Agreement (TE p. 684)

Reading Skills
- Interpret Imagery (SE pp. 681, 682, 685, 688)

Vocabulary Skills
- Academic Vocabulary (SE p. 688)

Literature and Reading Preview

Connect to the Poem

How would you like to be remembered? Make a list of the achievements, favorite quotations, personality traits, activities, or talents that you would want mentioned in an elegy about you.

Build Background

Gray's "Elegy" shows the influence of two types of poetry popular in the 1700s. One type is the **elegy**, a poem that laments a death or some other great loss. The other is "landscape poetry," in which a speaker's natural surroundings evoke melancholy musings on life and death. Gray's "Elegy" belongs to a subdivision of this type—"graveyard poetry," in which the evocative scene is set in a cemetery.

Set Purposes for Reading

Big Idea The Stirrings of Romanticism

As you read, ask yourself, Which elements in the poem emphasize emotion, the imagination, and nature?

Literary Element Epitaph

Gray's poem ends with an **epitaph**—a brief statement, often inscribed on a gravestone, that commemorates a dead person. As you read the poem, ask yourself, How does the epitaph relate to the rest of the poem?

Reading Strategy Interpret Imagery

Imagery includes all the word pictures that writers create to evoke emotional responses. In creating imagery, writers use sensory details that appeal to sight, hearing, touch, taste, and smell. When you **interpret imagery**, you analyze these word pictures and determine the kinds of emotional responses the images evoke. As you read, ask yourself, What feelings do these images suggest?

....

Tip: Taking Notes Use a chart to make associations between images, the senses to which they appeal, and the feelings they suggest.

Image (line)	Appeals to Sense of...	Emotional Response

Vocabulary

pomp (pomp) *n.* splendid or dignified display; p. 683 *The pomp of the graduation ceremony emphasized its significance.*

inevitable (i nev′ ə tə bəl) *adj.* incapable of being avoided or prevented; certain; p. 683 *Realizing that defeat was inevitable, the candidate conceded the election.*

genial (jē′ nē əl) *adj.* giving warmth and comfort; pleasant or cheerful; p. 684 *The genial host enthusiastically greeted his guests.*

uncouth (un kōōth′) *adj.* crude; lacking polish, culture, or refinement; p. 685 *The uncouth couple chatted during the performance.*

kindred (kin′ drid) *adj.* like; allied; similar; p. 685 *Wanting desperately to win, the athletes shared kindred emotions.*

Before You Read

Focus

Summary

In the cemetery of a village church, the poet reflects on the people buried there and the fleeting nature of life.

Vocabulary

Analogies Analogies can be based on many types of relationships. For example, they can bring together a trait and a person or thing. Ask students to think about the four adjectives in the vocabulary box. **Ask:** What things are *inevitable*? What kind of person is *genial*, *uncouth*, or *kindred*? Have students use their answers to write analogies for each adjective. *(genial : host of a party : : uncouth : person late to a party)*

 For additional vocabulary practice, see Unit 4 Teaching Resources Book, p. 26.

THOMAS GRAY **681**

English Learners

 DIFFERENTIATED INSTRUCTION

Intermediate English learners may approach the poem with anxiety because of its length. Explain to students that each of the thirty-two four-line stanzas of the poem contains an idea, a scene, or an event. Rather than trying to comprehend the whole poem, students can work on a single stanza at a time.

Guide small groups of students in setting up a note page with thirty-two lines. On each line, have students write the main idea of each stanza in order. Tell students that when they have finished the poem, they will have created a summary that they can review.

Model the exercise by reading the first stanza aloud and then offering a simple, one-sentence summary such as *The work day has ended and night is falling.*

Teach

Reading Strategy　　1

Interpret Imagery　Answer: *The tolling of the curfew bell, the sound of the herd of cows returning to the barn, the weary plowman on his way home from working in the fields, and the solitary darkness surrounding the speaker create a mood of melancholy.*

ENGLISH LEARNERS Encourage students to picture the scene in their minds as you describe it. **Say:** A bell rings; cows walk through the meadow, mooing; a farmer stumbles home as darkness falls. Then **ask:** What feelings come to mind when you imagine these events? (*Answers will vary.*)

 For additional practice using the reading skill or strategy, see Unit 4 Teaching Resources Book, p. 27.

Writer's Technique ☆

Alliteration/Assonance Explain that alliteration (the repetition of consonant sounds at the beginning of words) and assonance (the repetition of the same or similar vowel sounds within nearby words) enhance the sounds of the words and underscore the ideas that relate to them. **Ask:** How does Gray use these sound devices in lines 5–8? (*He uses alliteration to emphasize "solemn stillness"; he uses assonance to draw attention to "beetle wheels."*)

View the Art ★

Answer: *Some students will say the image evokes calm; others might suggest melancholy.*

Stoke Poges Church, 1864. Jasper Francis Cropsey. Oil on board, 11.75 x 19 in. Johnny van Haeften Gallery, London.

View the Art The "graveyard poets" strove to evoke emotion with scenes set in churchyards. What emotions does this image evoke? ★

Elegy Written in a Country Churchyard

Thomas Gray

The curfew tolls the knell of parting day,
The lowing° herd wind slowly o'er the lea,°
The plowman homeward plods his weary way,
And leaves the world to darkness and to me.

5　Now fades the glimmering landscape on the sight,
And all the air a solemn stillness holds,
Save where the beetle wheels his droning flight,
☆ And drowsy tinklings lull the distant folds;

Save that from yonder ivy-mantled tower
10　The moping owl does to the moon complain
Of such, as wandering near her secret bower,°
Molest her ancient solitary reign.

2 **lowing:** the sound a cow makes.
lea: meadow.

11 **bower:** a shelter of leafy branches.

 Interpret Imagery *What mood does the cluster of images in the first stanza create?*

682 UNIT 4　THE TRIUMPH OF ROMANTICISM

Reading Practice

 **Focus on Questions**
One way to trace the progress of an argument is to ask and answer questions while reading. In this work, Gray has provided some of the questions. Have students look ahead to lines 41–42. Ask them to restate the question in their own words and then suggest an answer. (*Can fancy burial monuments bring a person back to life? No.*) Now have students continue to read and answer questions as they encounter them in lines 43–44 and 85–88. Have students work with a partner to ask and answer other questions that capture the poem's argument.

Beneath those rugged elms, that yew tree's shade,
Where heaves the turf in many a moldering heap,
15   Each in his narrow cell forever laid,
The rude° forefathers of the hamlet sleep.

The breezy call of incense-breathing Morn,
The swallow twittering from the straw-built shed,
The cock's shrill clarion° or the echoing horn,°
20   No more shall rouse them from their lowly bed.

2

For them no more the blazing hearth shall burn,
Or busy housewife ply her evening care;
No children run to lisp their sire's return,
Or climb his knees the envied kiss to share.

25   Oft did the harvest to their sickle yield,
Their furrow oft the stubborn glebe° has broke;
How jocund° did they drive their team afield!
How bowed the woods beneath their sturdy stroke!

Let not Ambition mock their useful toil,
30   Their homely joys, and destiny obscure;°
Nor Grandeur hear with a disdainful smile
The short and simple annals° of the poor.

The boast of heraldry,° the **pomp** of power,
And all that beauty, all that wealth e'er gave,
35   Awaits alike the **inevitable** hour.
The paths of glory lead but to the grave.

Nor you, ye proud, impute° to these the fault,
If Memory o'er their tomb no trophies° raise,
Where through the long-drawn aisle and fretted vault°
40   The pealing anthem swells the note of praise.

Can storied urn° or animated° bust
Back to its mansion call the fleeting breath?

The Stirrings of Romanticism *How does this stanza reflect the emergence of Romanticism?* **3**

Vocabulary

pomp (pomp) *n.* splendid or dignified display
inevitable (i nev′ ə tə bəl) *adj.* incapable of being avoided or prevented; certain

THOMAS GRAY   **683**

Sidenotes:

16 **rude:** uncultured; unrefined.

19 **clarion:** a crowing sound.
echoing horn: a hunter's horn.

26 **glebe:** soil.
27 **jocund** (jo′ kənd): cheerfully; lightheartedly.

30 **obscure:** undistinguished.

32 **annals:** descriptive accounts or histories.

33 **heraldry:** Here, *heraldry* means "nobility."

37 **impute:** attribute.
38 **trophies:** memorials to military heroes, usually depicting arms taken from the enemy.
39 **fretted vault:** an arched church ceiling adorned with carving in decorative patterns.
41 **storied urn:** a funeral urn depicting the life of the deceased and often inscribed with a legend.
animated: lifelike.

The Stirrings of Romanticism Answer:

Another tenet of Romanticism is the belief that all human beings are endowed with imagination and creative potential. The speaker laments the fact that the creative potential of many poor people is unappreciated, unfulfilled, and relegated to obscurity.

ENGLISH LEARNERS **Say:** Gray says that beautiful gems may exist and beautiful flowers may bloom where no one sees them. **Ask:** How are these gems and flowers like a talented but poor person living in a small village? *(Like the gems' and flowers' beauty, this person's splendid talent will not be noticed by many people.)*

Can Honor's voice provoke° the silent dust,
Or Flattery soothe the dull cold ear of Death?

45 Perhaps in this neglected spot is laid
Some heart once pregnant with celestial fire;
Hands that the rod of empire might have swayed,
Or waked to ecstasy the living lyre.

But Knowledge to their eyes her ample page
50 Rich with the spoils of time did ne'er unroll;
Chill Penury° repressed their noble rage,
And froze the genial current of the soul.

Full many a gem of purest ray serene,
The dark unfathomed° caves of ocean bear:
55 Full many a flower is born to blush unseen,
And waste its sweetness on the desert air.

Some village Hampden,° that with dauntless breast
The little tyrant of his fields withstood;
Some mute inglorious Milton° here may rest,
60 Some Cromwell° guiltless of his country's blood.

The applause of listening senates to command,
The threats of pain and ruin to despise,
To scatter plenty o'er a smiling land,
And read their history in a nation's eyes,

65 Their lot forbade: nor circumscribed° alone
Their growing virtues, but their crimes confined;
Forbade to wade through slaughter to a throne,
And shut the gates of mercy on mankind,

The struggling pangs of conscious truth to hide,
70 To quench the blushes of ingenuous° shame,
Or heap the shrine of Luxury and Pride
With incense kindled at the Muse's flame.°

43 provoke: bring to life.

51 Penury (pen' yə rē): extreme poverty.

54 unfathomed: not measured; unplumbed.

57 Hampden: a reference to John Hampden (1594–1643), an English Parliamentary leader who opposed Charles I over unfair taxation.
59 Milton: a reference to the poet John Milton (1608–1674).
60 Cromwell: a reference to Oliver Cromwell (1599–1658), an English statesman and general who was responsible for much bloodshed.

65 circumscribed: limited; restricted.

70 ingenuous: innocent; naive.

72 incense kindled at the Muse's flame: Here, *incense* means "praise," and *the Muse* stands for a poet or poetry, so this phrase means "poetic praise."

---

1   **The Stirrings of Romanticism** *What aspect of Romanticism's philosophy about the poor is evident in this stanza?*

Vocabulary

genial (jē′ nē əl) *adj.* giving warmth and comfort; pleasant or cheerful

684   UNIT 4   THE TRIUMPH OF ROMANTICISM

Grammar Practice

SPIRAL REVIEW   **Subject-Verb Agreement** Ask students to identify the subject of the sentence in lines 45–46. (*heart*) Ask if anyone thought *spot* was the subject. Point out that *spot* is the object of the preposition *in* and that the subject of a sentence never appears within a prepositional phrase. Verbs must agree with their subjects in person and number. Have students identify the subject and select the correct verb below.

1. The people in this country parish (lives/**live**) simply.
2. For all people, the hours upon earth (comes/**come**) to an inevitable end.

Far from the madding° crowd's ignoble strife, ☆
Their sober wishes never learned to stray;
75 Along the cool sequestered° vale of life
They kept the noiseless tenor° of their way.

Yet even these bones from insult to protect
Some frail memorial still erected nigh,
With **uncouth** rhymes and shapeless sculpture decked,
80 Implores the passing tribute of a sigh.

Their name, their years, spelt by the unlettered Muse,°
The place of fame and elegy supply:
And many a holy text around she strews,
That teach the rustic moralist to die.

85 For who to dumb Forgetfulness a prey,
This pleasing anxious being e'er resigned,
Left the warm precincts of the cheerful day,
Nor cast one longing lingering look behind?

On some fond breast the parting soul relies,
90 Some pious drops the closing eye requires;
Even from the tomb the voice of Nature cries,
Even in our ashes live their wonted° fires.

For thee, who mindful of the unhonored dead
Dost in these lines their artless tale relate;
95 If chance, by lonely contemplation led,
Some **kindred** spirit shall inquire thy fate,

Haply° some hoary-headed swain° may say,
"Oft have we seen him at the peep of dawn
Brushing with hasty steps the dews away
100 To meet the sun upon the upland lawn.

"There at the foot of yonder nodding beech
That wreathes its old fantastic roots so high,
His listless° length at noontide would he stretch
And pore upon the brook that babbles by.

73 madding: acting as if mad; frenzied.

75 sequestered: sheltered; secluded.
76 tenor: course; direction.

81 unlettered Muse: uneducated poet (Gray is referring to the tombstone engraver).

2

92 wonted: customary; usual.

97 Haply: perhaps.
hoary-headed swain: white-haired countryman.

103 listless: lacking in energy; sluggish.

Interpret Imagery *What two images are contrasted in this stanza?* **3**

Vocabulary

uncouth (un kōōth′) *adj.* crude; lacking polish, culture, or refinement
kindred (kin′drid) *adj.* like; allied; similar

Teach

Literary Element | 1

Personification Point out that Gray makes fortune, fame, science, melancholy, and misery seem human by capitalizing their names and suggesting they are capable of human activity. **Ask:** How does this personification affect your understanding of the speaker's ideas? *(Students may say that personification helps them visualize the concepts being discussed or makes Gray's points more forceful.)* Encourage students to look back through the poem to find other examples of personification.

Literary Element | 2

Epitaph Answer: *Gray identifies with the poor, obscure rustics mentioned earlier in the poem. He also asserts that he was born with a melancholy personality.*

[ENGLISH LEARNERS] Remind students of these facts about Gray: he lived quietly, never married, had only a few friends, and published only thirteen poems. **Ask:** In what ways does the epitaph describe Gray? *(The epitaph describes a man who was unknown but sincere in his work and who had and wanted only one dear friend.)*

Progress Check

Can students understand epitaph?

If No → See Unit 4 Teaching Resources Book, p. 26.

To check students' understanding of the selection, see Unit 4 Teaching Resources Book, p. 30.

686

105　"Hard by yon wood, now smiling as in scorn,
　　　Muttering his wayward° fancies he would rove,
　　　Now drooping, woeful wan, like one forlorn,
　　　Or crazed with care, or crossed in hopeless love.

　　　"One morn I missed him on the customed hill,
110　Along the heath° and near his favorite tree;
　　　Another came; nor yet beside the rill°
　　　Nor up the lawn nor at the wood was he;

　　　"The next with dirges° due in sad array
　　　Slow through the churchway path we saw him borne.
115　Approach and read (for thou canst read) the lay,°
　　　Graved on the stone beneath yon aged thorn."°

　　　　　　　The Epitaph

　　　Here rests his head upon the lap of Earth
　　　A youth to Fortune and to Fame unknown.
　　　Fair Science frowned not on his humble birth,
120　*And Melancholy marked him for her own.*

　　　Large was his bounty, and his soul sincere,
　　　Heaven did a recompense as largely send:
　　　He gave to Misery all he had, a tear;
　　　He gained from Heaven ('twas all he wished) a friend.

125　*No farther seek his merits to disclose,*
　　　Or draw his frailties from their dread abode
　　　(There they alike in trembling hope repose),
　　　The bosom of his Father and his God.

1

106　**wayward:** irregular; unpredictable; erratic.

110　**heath:** a stretch of land covered with heather or wild shrubs.
111　**rill:** a small stream or brook.

113　**dirges:** songs of mourning.

115　**lay:** poem.
116　**thorn:** a hawthorn, a thorny tree with white or pink flowers.

2 **Epitaph** *Some critics maintain that Gray wrote his own epitaph at the end of the poem. If so, what do these lines tell you about Gray?*

686 UNIT 4 THE TRIUMPH OF ROMANTICISM

Vocabulary Practice

SPIRAL REVIEW Changes in Language Write on the board these words from the elegy: *knell, lowing, lea, save, folds, cell, hamlet, hearth, ply, sickle, furrow, glebe,* and *jocund.* Explain that these terms are not widely used today. Words such as *cell* have acquired a very different meaning.

Call on volunteers to share dictionary definitions of these words as they were used in Gray's time. Then challenge students to write original sentences using these words with their eighteenth-century definitions.

After You Read

Respond and Think Critically

Respond and Interpret

1. (a)What emotions did you experience while reading Gray's elegy? (b)What lines or images prompted these emotions?

2. (a)In lines 17–28, what sights, sounds, and feelings does the speaker say the dead have left behind? (b)What do these **images** have in common?

3. (a)In lines 45–64, what does the speaker speculate some of the country people might have become if they had been able to fulfill their potential? (b)What kept them from fulfilling their potential?

4. (a)Summarize the speaker's feelings about the dead. (b)How does the speaker hope readers will feel about the people buried in the churchyard?

Analyze and Evaluate

5. In your opinion, what is the main **theme** of this poem? Use specific lines or phrases to support your answer.

6. (a)What does the person described in the epitaph have in common with the other people described in the elegy? (b)What evidence can you find in the poem that Gray described himself in the epitaph?

7. (a)Do you find Gray's elegy to be sad, hopeful, or both? (b)Some critics have called Gray's elegy overly sentimental. Do you agree with this criticism? Explain.

Connect

8. **Big Idea** The Stirrings of Romanticism How does "Elegy Written in a Country Churchyard" demonstrate that writers at this time were beginning to focus on emotion, imagination, and nature rather than on reason, science, and classical literature? Use details from the poem to support your answer.

9. **Connect to Today** If you were to rewrite the elegy for modern American readers, what famous people would you choose to take the place of Hampden, Milton, and Cromwell? Explain your choices.

Literary Element Epitaph

An **epitaph** may describe the merits and accomplishments of a person who has died, or it may take the form of an appeal from the dead to those who pass by the grave. A number of writers have composed their own epitaphs.

1. What form does the epitaph at the end of the poem take?

2. Assuming that Gray has written his own epitaph, how does he choose to be remembered?

Review: Elegy

As you learned on page 438, an **elegy** is a poem mourning the death of an individual or lamenting a tragic event. In the eighteenth century, the so-called graveyard school of English poets wrote elegies that were general reflections on death and immortality and combined somber imagery of human impermanence with philosophical speculation.

Group Activity Meet with a small group and discuss the following questions:

1. What characteristics make Gray's elegy an example of the graveyard-school poetry?

2. What does Gray's "Elegy" mourn? Does it just lament the loss of one individual, or does it go beyond this? Cite evidence from the poem to support your response.

THOMAS GRAY **687**

After You Read

Assess

1. (a) Sadness or consolation (b) Students' answers will vary.

2. (a) The dead no longer feel the breeze, hear the swallows, rise to the crowing cock, enjoy the fire, or interact with their families. (b) The world of the English countryside

3. (a) Political or military leaders, poets, musicians, or orators (b) They were poor and uneducated.

4. (a) The speaker expresses regret that the dead rustics had few opportunities. (b) He hopes readers will share his affection and sympathy.

5. Wasted human potential (lines 45–64), the democracy of death (lines 29–44), and the spiritual peace of the poor (lines 73–76)

6. (a) He is not famous or fortunate. (b) In lines 93–96, the speaker addresses himself and refers to the poem he is writing. In lines 98–116, the speaker imagines a speech about himself narrated by "some hoary-headed swain," who introduces the epitaph.

7. (a) Students' answers will vary. (b) Students' answers will vary.

8. Gray writes a highly emotional elegy that laments the loss of human life. Gray also uses imagination to speculate upon the lives of the people buried in the churchyard. Finally, images drawn from nature are an integral part of the poem.

9. Make sure that students justify their choices.

Literary Element

1. The epitaph primarily describes the character and personality of the dead person.

2. Gray wishes to be remembered as a melancholy youth who failed to achieve fame and fortune but was kind and blessed by Heaven with a friend.

Review: Elegy

1. The setting, the melancholy imagery, the obsession with death, and the philosophical speculations mark Gray's poem as an example of the Graveyard School.

2. Students may say that the elegy also mourns wasted human potential.

After You Read

Assess

Reading Strategy

1. In this stanza, Gray contrasts the man's "smiling as in scorn" with his "drooping, woeful wan" appearance.

2. Gray's use of contrasting imagery helps to memorialize the common people as opposed to the famous and fortunate.

Vocabulary

1. d **2.** b **3.** a **4.** c **5.** b

Academic Vocabulary

Students might respond that many minority and ethnic groups are minimized today.

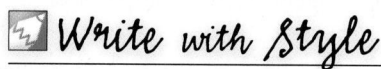 *Write with Style*

Students' epitaphs should focus on a central idea or image. They should use vivid sensory details and express a strong voice.

> For additional assessment, see Assessment Resources, pp. 173–174.

In his elegy, Gray often uses contrasting imagery. For example, the "madding crowd's ignoble strife" contrasts with the "noiseless tenor" of the village (lines 73–76).

1. Identify an example of contrasting imagery in lines 105–108.

2. How does Gray's use of contrasting images contribute to the meaning of the poem?

Vocabulary Practice

Practice with Analogies Choose the word that best completes each analogy.

1. obligatory : necessary :: certain :
   a. uncouth
   b. pomp
   c. genial
   d. inevitable

2. cold : hostile :: warm :
   a. kindred
   b. genial
   c. inevitable
   d. uncouth

3. simplicity : plainness :: magnificence :
   a. pomp
   b. genial
   c. uncouth
   d. kindred

4. rare : common :: refined :
   a. genial
   b. kindred
   c. uncouth
   d. pomp

5. restless : serene :: unlike :
   a. inevitable
   b. kindred
   c. pomp
   d. uncouth

Academic Vocabulary ▶

In "Elegy Written in a Country Churchyard" Gray writes about people whose importance society has **minimized***.*

Minimize is an academic word that can be applied to many everyday situations. For example, a campaign manager might try to **minimize** his candidate's faults.

To further explore this word, answer the following question: Are any groups of people **minimized** today in American society?

For more on academic vocabulary, see pages 56 and R81.

Write with Style

 Apply Imagery

Assignment Stark images lend power to the epitaph that ends Thomas Grey's poem "Elegy Written in a Country Churchyard." Write an epitaph of your own that commemorates a famous person, or one that you would like to appear on your own gravestone. Use vivid imagery to convey your ideas.

Get Ideas First, brainstorm or write in your journal to find a subject for your epitaph. Then make a word web or list to identify the characteristics you want to highlight. Finally, visualize and jot down images that capture those characteristics. You may also want to research famous epitaphs for inspiration.

Give It Structure Reread the last sixteen lines of Gray's poem to remind yourself of the form and purpose of an epitaph. Structure your epitaph around a central focus—for instance, something important, striking, or unusual about your subject—in order to establish an overall impression.

Look at Language Choose concrete, specific words and images to express the person's unique qualities. Even if your poem is only a few lines long, it should show variety, express your personal voice, and maintain readers' interest.

EXAMPLE:

> butterfly flown
> Here lies a ~~departed person~~.
> Who flitted through life's glorious garden.
> Taking with her a shining light.

Writing Practice

SPIRAL REVIEW **Vivid Images** After students have used a word web to identify the characteristics they want to include in their epitaph, have them use these starter sentences to generate specific, interesting details for images. They should generate more than one response to each question.

- When I think about how this person looks, what I most notice is ____.

- When I think about how this person speaks, what I most remember is ____.

- When I think of what this person has accomplished, I am most impressed by ____.

- When I think of this person, I feel ____.

Before You Read

Burns's Poetry

Meet Robert Burns
(1759–1796)

Scottish author Robert Burns was famous both for his songwriting and his poetry. Still celebrated as a Scottish national hero, he wrote simple lyrics that continue to capture the imagination of readers around the world. He had a keen ear for the speech of his native land, and in his work he employed its characteristic sound to impart a fresh vitality to English literature.

> "My heart's in the Highlands, my
>   heart is not here,
> My heart's in the Highlands a-chasing
>   the deer."
>
> —Robert Burns

Peasant-Poet Burns was born on a farm in southwestern Scotland to poor, uneducated peasants. As a boy, he worked on the farm and attended school infrequently. Whatever education Burns obtained came mainly from reading. His favorite writers were Shakespeare and Pope. Burns's mother, uneducated but imaginative, taught him the ballads, legends, and songs of the Scottish peasants. These songs inspired him to write poetry of his own.

After the death of his father, Burns quickly developed his gift for expressing emotions of love, friendship, and amusement in verse. He also attempted to keep the family farm going but failed. Soon, however, his fortunes changed for the better. At the age of twenty-seven, he published *Poems, Chiefly in the Scottish Dialect*, a work that enjoyed immediate success with simple farmers and sophisticated critics alike. Burns then temporarily gave up farming and moved to Edinburgh.

There, he played the role expected of him—that of a gifted but uncultured rustic.

Labor of Love In 1788 Burns left Edinburgh and settled on a farm in Ellisland, Dumfriesshire. When his friend James Johnson planned to compile a definitive anthology of Scottish folk songs, he asked Burns to help him, and Burns jumped at the chance. He threw himself wholeheartedly into the project and for the next three years roamed the countryside collecting, editing, and writing lyrics for many old Scottish tunes, thus preserving the rhythms and accents of his native tongue. Considering this work to be a labor of love, he declined payment, even refusing to allow his name to appear in the collection. In doing so, he created difficulties for scholars, who have found it almost impossible to determine where some of the original folk songs leave off and Burns's contributions begin.

Sadly enough, Burns's devotion to his country and to the peasant life was the cause of his early death. He had developed a heart disease from strenuous work on his father's farm as a boy, and he finally succumbed to it at the age of thirty-seven. But Burns the poet lives on in spirit when every year on New Year's Eve people join hands and sing his beautiful song "Auld Lang Syne."

 Literature Online

Author Search For more about Robert Burns, go to glencoe.com and enter QuickPass code GLB9817u4.

Before You Read

Focus

Bellringer Options

Daily Language Practice Transparency 54

Or play an association game with students. Name a holiday or other event and ask them to think of a song that they identify with it. For example, for Independence Day, students might say "The Star Spangled Banner." End the game with New Year's Eve. When students name "Auld Lang Syne," ask them to think about why this song is appropriate in marking the passage of time. Tell students they will be reading this poem and others by Robert Burns.

Selection Skills

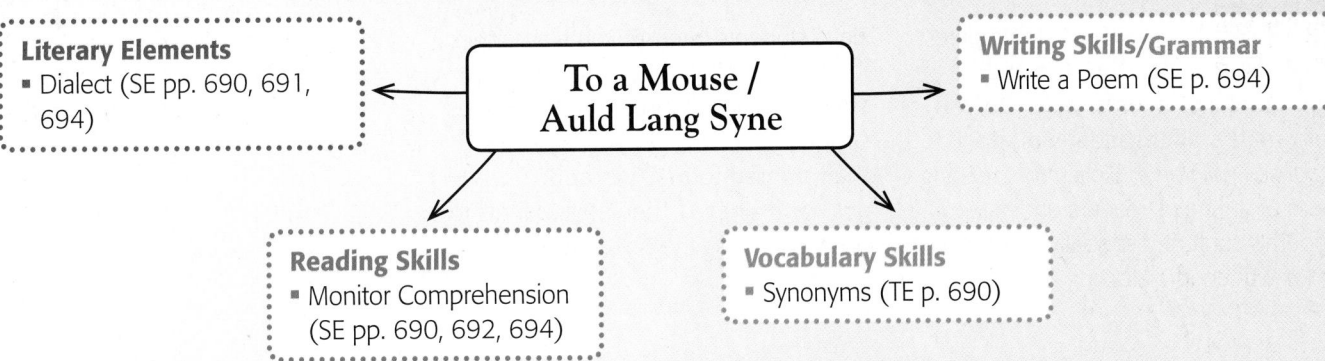

Literary Elements
- Dialect (SE pp. 690, 691, 694)

To a Mouse / Auld Lang Syne

Writing Skills/Grammar
- Write a Poem (SE p. 694)

Reading Skills
- Monitor Comprehension (SE pp. 690, 692, 694)

Vocabulary Skills
- Synonyms (TE p. 690)

Before You Read

Focus

Summary

The poems by Burns included here reflect the language and rhythms of traditional Scottish folk songs. "To a Mouse" recognizes the bond between humans and animals; "Auld Lang Syne" celebrates the past alive in memory.

 For summaries in languages other than English, see Unit 4 Teaching Resources Book, pp. 32–37.

Vocabulary

Synonyms Remind students that when they read a poem written in dialect, they will often use synonyms as they paraphrase the poem's content. Write lines 8, 23, and 38 of "To a Mouse" on the board. Ask students to practice paraphrasing these lines, substituting a synonym for each vocabulary word. Then compare students' paraphrases.

 For additional vocabulary practice, see Unit 4 Teaching Resources Book, p. 40.

Literature and Reading Preview

Connect to the Poems

How important are the people and events from your past? Discuss this question with a partner. Consider whether it is better to reflect on the past or to look toward the future.

Build Background

Robert Burns's poetry flourished during a time when the English-controlled British government was trying to subdue Scottish patriotism by depriving Scots of civil liberties. Burns's *Poems, Chiefly in the Scottish Dialect* did much to restore a sense of pride in his fellow Scots, and later his preservation of traditional Scottish songs raised Burns to the status of folk hero. His work reflects his deep connection to Scottish peasant life and nature.

Set Purposes for Reading

Big Idea The Stirrings of Romanticism

As you read, ask yourself, How do Burns's poems reflect the importance of feelings, imagination, and sensitivity to nature?

Literary Element Dialect

A **dialect** is a variety of language that is characteristic of a particular region or group of people. Burns wrote many poems in Lowland Scots, a dialect of English. In this dialect, an apostrophe often indicates missing letters: for example, the apostrophe in *tim'rous* stands for the letter *o* in the word *timorous*. As you read, ask yourself, What makes this language distinctive?

Reading Strategy Monitor Comprehension

Monitoring your comprehension means thinking about whether you are understanding what you read. Reading and understanding Burns's dialect is like breaking a code. First, read each poem silently, using the side notes for help. Then read each poem aloud, listening to its sounds and rhythms. Check your understanding by paraphrasing each stanza—restating it in your own words. As you read, ask yourself, Am I understanding the meaning of this poem?

Tip: Taking Notes Use a chart to record difficult passages and your paraphrases of them.

Passage	Paraphrase
"Should auld acquaintance be forgot"	Should we forget our old friends?

Learning Objectives

For pages 689–694

In studying these texts, you will focus on the following objectives:

Literary Study: Analyzing dialect.

Reading: Monitoring comprehension by paraphrasing.

Writing: Writing a poem.

Vocabulary

dominion (də min′ yən) *n.* control or the exercise of control; p. 691 *Gandhi spearheaded a movement to put an end to England's dominion over India.*

bleak (blēk) *adj.* cold; harsh; raw; p. 692 *The bleak wind howled through the chinks in the doors and window frames.*

foresight (fôr′ sīt′) *n.* preparation or concern for the future; p. 692 *His grandfather's foresight in saving money helped pay for Randall's education.*

Tip: Word Usage When you encounter new words, it might help you to answer a specific question about the word—for example, What was a situation in which I wish I had shown more **foresight** than I did?

Reading Practice

 Read Aloud To prepare students to read and paraphrase Burns' poems, **ask:** Do you usually read a poem silently or aloud? *(Responses will vary.)* Explain that reading a poem aloud helps readers understand the poem's content, especially when the poem is written in dialect.

Have students listen as you read aloud the first stanza of "Auld Lang Syne." Then **ask:** What words in these lines *sound* like words you know, even if their printed form *looks* odd? *(auld = old, min' = mind)* Then ask students to practice reading the poem to each other in pairs.

Students may feel shy about reading aloud at first, so encourage them to play with the language and not worry about mistakes.

To a Mouse

Robert Burns

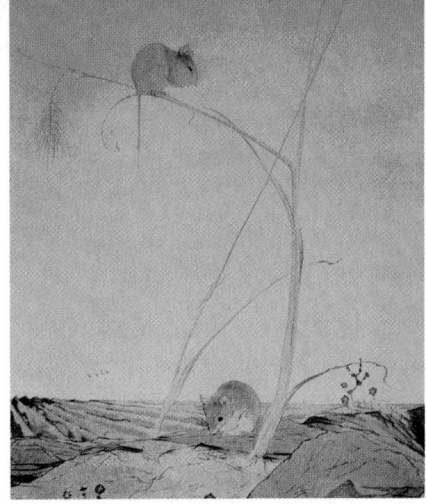

Town Mouse and Country Mouse, from *Aesop's Fables*.
Edward Julius Detmold (1883–1957). Private collection.

View the Art This illustration comes from a collection of fables—tales in which animals are often richly characterized. Do either of the mice in this image reflect Burns's description? Explain. ★

On Turning Her Up in Her Nest
with the Plow, November, 1785

Wee, sleekit,° cow'rin', tim'rous beastie,
O, what a panic's in thy breastie!
Thou need na start awa sae hasty
    Wi' bickering brattle!°
5 I wad be laith° to rin an' chase thee
    Wi' murd'ring pattle!°

I'm truly sorry man's **dominion**
Has broken Nature's social union
An' justifies that ill opinion
10   Which makes thee startle
At me, thy poor, earthborn companion
    An' fellow mortal!

I doubt na, whiles,° but thou may thieve;
What then? poor beastie, thou maun° live!

1 sleekit: sleek.

4 bickering brattle: the sudden sounds of a scamper.
5 wad be laith: would be loath, or reluctant.
6 pattle: a plowstaff (small paddle or spade with a long handle, used to clean a plow).

13 whiles: sometimes.
14 maun: must.

Dialect *How would you restate this sentence in Standard English?* **1**

Dialect *Why do you think Burns mainly uses Standard English and not Scottish dialect in this stanza?* **2**

Vocabulary

dominion (də min′yən) *n.* control or the exercise of control

ROBERT BURNS **691**

Teach

Literary Element   1

Dialect Answer: *I would be very unwilling to run after and chase you wielding a dangerous tool!*

Literary Element   2

Dialect Answer: *Burns uses Standard English to draw attention to this particular stanza, emphasizing that human interference with nature has caused animals to be suspicious of people.*

> For additional literary element practice, see Unit 4 Teaching Resources Book, p. 38.

View the Art ★

Answer: *Some students may say that the gray mouse at the bottom of the image fits the description of "wee, sleekit, cow'rin, tim'rous," because it is huddled beneath the plant and very small. Other students might say that neither mouse fits the description, because they have not been disturbed by a human.*

Edward Julius Detmold (1883–1957) and his twin brother, Maurice, began drawing plants and animals at early ages under the tutelage of their uncle. Their work shows influences of Japanese-style illustration. Among other successes, they are credited with watercolor illustrations for Rudyard Kipling's *Jungle Book*.

Teach

Reading Strategy | 1

Monitor Comprehension

Answer: *You had to work hard to make a home out of that small pile of leaves and stubble! Now, despite all your hard work, you are turned out of house and home.*

ENGLISH LEARNERS Guide English learners to rewrite these lines, making these substitutions, before they attempt the paraphrase: *stubble* for *stibble, your* for *thee, many* for *mony, you're* for *thou's, without* for *but,* and *shelter* for *hald.*

For additional practice using the reading skill or strategy, see Unit 4 Teaching Resources Book, p. 39.

---

15   A daimen-icker in a thrave°
          'S a sma' request:
        I'll get a blessin' wi' the lave°
          An' never miss 't!

        Thy wee-bit housie, too, in ruin!
20   Its silly wa's° the win's are strewin'!
        An' naething, now, to big° a new ane
          O' foggage° green!
        An' **bleak** December's winds ensuin',
          Baith snell° an' keen!

25   Thou saw the fields laid bare an' waste,
        An' weary winter comin' fast,
        An' cozie here, beneath the blast,
          Thou thought to dwell,
        Till crash! the cruel coulter° past
30   Out through thy cell.

        That wee bit heap o' leaves an' stibble°
        Has cost thee mony a weary nibble!
        Now thou's turned out, for a' thy trouble,
          But° house or hald,°
35   To thole° the winter's sleety dribble
          An' cranreuch° cauld!

        But, Mousie, thou art no thy lane°
        In proving **foresight** may be vain:
        The best laid schemes o' mice an' men
40   Gang aft a-gley°
        An' lea'e° us nought but grief an' pain
          For promised joy.

        Still thou art blest, compared wi' me!
        The present only toucheth thee:
45   But, och! I backward cast my e'e
          On prospects drear!
        An' foward, tho' I canna see,
          I guess an' fear!

---

1 Monitor Comprehension *How would you paraphrase these lines?*

Vocabulary

bleak (blēk) *adj.* cold; harsh; raw
foresight (fôr´sīt´) *n.* preparation or concern for the future

692 UNIT 4   THE TRIUMPH OF ROMANTICISM

Side notes

15 **daimen-icker in a thrave:** an occasional ear of corn in a bundle.

17 **lave:** remainder.

20 **silly wa's:** weak walls.
21 **big:** build.
22 **foggage:** moss.

24 **snell:** bitter; severe.

29 **coulter:** a plowshare (blade attached to a plow).

31 **stibble:** stubble.

34 **But:** without. **hald:** an obsolete form of *hold,* meaning "shelter."
35 **thole:** endure.
36 **cranreuch:** frost.

37 **no thy lane:** not alone.

40 **Gang aft a-gley:** go often awry; turn out badly.
41 **lea'e:** leave.

Reading Practice

SPIRAL REVIEW **Paraphrase** Burns's poetry presents an excellent opportunity to work on paraphrasing in groups since his use of dialect is challenging even to proficient English speakers. Remind students that to paraphrase means to restate something in your own words.

Assign students to small groups and have group members divide the stanzas in each poem on an equitable basis. Using the side notes as a guide for dialect, each student should paraphrase in modern English the lines for which he or she is responsible.

Auld Lang Syne

Robert Burns

Should auld acquaintance be forgot,
  And never brought to min'?
Should auld acquaintance be forgot,
  And auld lang syne?[1]

5   For auld lang syne, my dear.
    For auld lang syne,
    We'll tak a cup o' kindness yet,
    For auld lang syne.

   We twa hae run about the braes,[2]
10   And pu'd the gowans[3] fine;
   But we've wander'd mony a weary foot
    Sin' auld lang syne.

   We twa hae paidled i' the burn,[4]
    From morning sun till dine;
15 But seas between us braid hae roar'd[5]
    Sin' auld lang syne.

   And there's a hand, my trusty fiere,[6]
    And gie's a hand o' thine;
   And we'll tak a right guid-willie waught,[7]
20   For auld lang syne.

   And surely ye'll be your pint-stowp,[8]
    And surely I'll be mine;
   And we'll tak a cup o' kindness yet
    For auld lang syne.

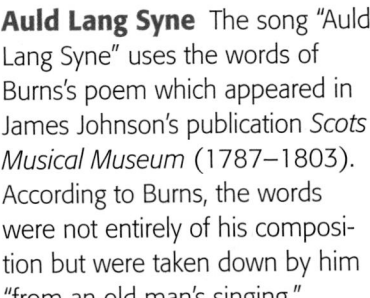

1. *Auld lang syne* means "old long ago."
2. *Braes* are hills.
3. *Pu'd the gowans* means "pulled the daisies."
4. *Hae paidled i' the burn* means "have paddled in the stream."
5. *Braid hae roar'd* means "broad have roared."
6. *Fiere* means "friend."
7. *Tak a right guid-willie waught* means "take a good drink."
8. *Ye'll be your pint-stowp* means "you'll pay for your pint."

The Stirrings of Romanticism *How does this stanza suggest the importance of human relationships and emotions?* **2**

Big Idea   2

The Stirrings of Romanticism Answer: *This stanza implies that friendships and personal relationships, which are based on emotional attachment, are worth cherishing and celebrating.*

Literary History ☆

Auld Lang Syne The song "Auld Lang Syne" uses the words of Burns's poem which appeared in James Johnson's publication *Scots Musical Museum* (1787–1803). According to Burns, the words were not entirely of his composition but were taken down by him "from an old man's singing."

Progress Check

Can students understand dialect?

If No → See Unit 4 Teaching Resources Book, p. 49.

To check students' understanding of the selection, see Unit 4 Teaching Resources Book, p. 41.

Approaching Level

DIFFERENTIATED INSTRUCTION

Emerging To help students understand this poem, describe the event and setting that prompt the speaker's words. **Say:** Two childhood friends meet in a tavern or inn. They are surprised to see each other after so many years. **Ask:** What might these old friends talk about?

(old times, what they did while children, what has happened since they last met) Then have students complete a T-chart as they read the poem to help them understand the events that the speaker mentions in each stanza.

running in the hills	weary wandering

The left side lists the childhood memories that the speaker recalls (running in the hills, etc.). The right side lists what has happened to the friends since they last met (crossing the sea, etc.).

After You Read

Assess

1. Students' responses will vary.

2. (a) The speaker accidentally destroys the mouse's nest. (b) The speaker regrets it because his action broke "nature's social union," justified the animal's fear of people, destroyed the results of its hard work, and left it unprotected as winter approaches.

3. (a) The speaker addresses a cherished person, called "my dear" and "my trusty fiere." (b) Friendship is an important value, and old times are worth recalling fondly.

4. There is a bond between humans and animals. Each must struggle to survive.

5. (a) Planning and hard work cannot guarantee success. (b) The human intellect is a disadvantage since it brings pain.

6. Burns is sympathetic to the smallest creature and use dialect as a vehicle for literature.

7. Answers will vary.

Writing

Students' poems should describe events or people from the past. The poems should use some kind of rhyme scheme, similar to Burns's poem.

Literary Element

1. Students' paraphrasing should accurately restate the main idea in each stanza.

2. Students may say that Burns sought to preserve his Scottish culture.

Reading Strategy

1. Your small house is in ruins, the weak walls crumbling.

2. Paraphrasing is a way to retell in a logical order using clear language.

Vocabulary

1. Students might mention parents, teachers, coaches, and anyone else who restricts their behavior.

2. Students should mention harsh weather conditions, like a blizzard or dry, parching heat.

3. Students should mention a time when they thought something out ahead of time.

After You Read

Respond and Think Critically

Respond and Interpret

1. Which lines from the poems did you find most memorable? Why?

2. (a)What has the speaker done to the mouse in "To a Mouse"? (b)What reasons does the speaker give for regretting what has happened?

3. (a)Whom does the speaker address in "Auld Lang Syne"? (b)What is the speaker's attitude toward friendship and old times?

Analyze and Evaluate

4. What does the second stanza in "To a Mouse" seem to suggest about the speaker's view of the relationship between nature and human beings? Explain.

5. (a)What lesson does the mouse's experience teach, according to the speaker? (b)What is **ironic**, or unexpected, about the ideas in the last stanza of the poem?

Connect

6. **Big Idea** The Stirrings of Romanticism Why do you think Burns's poems appealed so much to Scottish peasants?

7. **Connect to Today** "Auld Lang Syne" is still sung on New Year's Eve by many people. Do people still share Burns's attitudes about friendship, as well? Support your answer.

Literary Element Dialect

Dialects may differ in pronunciation, grammar, vocabulary, and spelling from standard forms of language.

1. Use Standard English to reword several stanzas from the poems. Which version of each stanza do you prefer? Why?

2. Why do you think Burns chose to write these poems in his native dialect, Lowland Scots, rather than in Standard English?

Writing

Write a Poem Using Burns's "Auld Lang Syne" as a model, write your own poem celebrating friends and events of your past. Try to incorporate the same songlike rhyme scheme that appears in Burns's poem. You may also wish to include a chorus that repeats throughout your poem, making it more of a song.

LOG ON ▶ **Literature** Online

Selection Resources For Selection Quizzes, eFlashcards, and Reading-Writing Connection activities, go to glencoe.com and enter QuickPass code GLB9817u4.

Reading Strategy Monitor Comprehension

Efficient readers **monitor their comprehension** by having mental conversations with themselves as they read. They notice when something does not make sense, and they apply strategies to aid comprehension, such as paraphrasing, that are appropriate to the work and their own learning style. Review the chart you created as you read these poems, and then answer the following questions.

1. How would you paraphrase lines 19–20 of "To a Mouse"?

2. How does paraphrasing specific lines and stanzas help you to understand them better?

Vocabulary Practice

Practice with Word Usage Respond to these statements to help you explore the meanings of vocabulary words in the poems.

1. Name some people who hold **dominion** over you.

2. Give an example of **bleak** weather.

3. Think of a time when your **foresight** served you well.

Before You Read

from A Vindication of the Rights of Woman

Meet **Mary Wollstonecraft**
(1759–1797)

When Mary Wollstonecraft wrote *A Vindication of the Rights of Woman*, she became the mother of the feminist movement and launched a struggle that would continue for more than two centuries. Through her writing, Wollstonecraft exposed injustices, challenged a society dominated by white, upper-class males, and promoted social improvement.

Awakening to Social Injustice Wollstonecraft was born in London to a violent, alcoholic father who squandered the family's fortune. Her childhood was filled with anxiety and fear, and she quickly realized the subservient role of women: her mother was abused and submissive, and her brother was well educated, while she was not. Wollstonecraft resented her family and the inequalities that existed between the sexes.

Controversial Writer With limited opportunities to support herself and her family, Wollstonecraft tried the few professions available to middle-class women—governess, lady's companion, and educator. While a governess, Wollstonecraft wrote her first novel, *Mary: A Fiction*. The novel is a cultural critique of a patriarchal and aristocratic society. It was published by Joseph Johnson, who later hired Wollstonecraft to be a reviewer for his journal *Analytical Review* and introduced her to the political theorist William Godwin, whom Wollstonecraft later married.

At the *Analytical Review*, Wollstonecraft continued to write educational tracts, believing that through education women would become an integral part of society. She published her first controversial work, *A Vindication of the Rights of Men*, anonymously in 1790, and she continued her work on education and politics with the publication of *A Vindication of the Rights of Woman* in 1792. She called for a "revolution in female manners" and for a world in which women would not be limited to menial labor or relegated to the dependent roles of wife, companion, or governess. Despite her radical determination "to loudly demand Justice for one half of the human race," the work was well received.

> *"[I]t is a farce to call any being virtuous whose virtues do not result from the exercise of its own reason. This was Rousseau's opinion respecting men: I extend it to women."*
>
> —Mary Wollstonecraft

A Troubled Life Although neither Wollstonecraft nor William Godwin believed in marriage, their bond was strong. However, their life together was cut short when Wollstonecraft died just eleven days after giving birth to her daughter Mary, who would become Mary Shelley, author of *Frankenstein*. Godwin was devastated by Wollstonecraft's death and decided to publish her unfinished novel, in which she documented "the misery and oppression, peculiar to women, that arise out of the partial laws and customs of society." Since then, her writings have been praised for their influence on the women's rights movement.

 Literature Online

Author Search For more about Mary Wollstonecraft, go to glencoe.com and enter QuickPass code GLB9817u4.

MARY WOLLSTONECRAFT **695**

Before You Read

Focus

Summary

The author states her thesis that societal neglect of women's education has made them weak. She contends that women should develop those abilities that are considered signs of noble character in men. The author then refutes those who believe the purpose of female education should be to render them pleasing. This cultivation of "artificial graces," she argues, eventually makes women servile or bitter.

 For summaries in languages other than English, see Unit 4 Teaching Resources Book, pp. 43–48.

Vocabulary

Persuasion Have students brainstorm political and social conditions about which they have strong opinions. Ask them to choose a topic and write a persuasive letter to the editor about it, using at least three of the vocabulary words. Encourage students to include specific examples.

Literature and Reading Preview

Connect to the Essay

Has the women's rights movement achieved true, full equality since Wollstonecraft's time? With a small group, discuss whether discrimination against women still exists, and in what ways.

Build Background

The English were divided on the French Revolution that broke out in 1789. The British statesman and orator Edmund Burke defended the aristocracy in *Reflections on the Revolution in France*. Wollstonecraft disagreed in *A Vindication of the Rights of Men*, citing the social and economic inequality in England. In the essay, she mentioned the rights of women—a subject she developed in *A Vindication of the Rights of Woman*.

Set Purposes for Reading

Big Idea The Stirrings of Romanticism

As you read, ask yourself, How does Wollstonecraft challenge the values of her time and call for change?

Literary Element Thesis

The **thesis** of a persuasive essay is the statement of the proposition to be proved. A thesis may be stated directly or implied and is usually expressed toward the beginning of the essay. The writer must then present convincing evidence, such as facts, reasons, and well-supported opinions. As you read, ask yourself, What thesis is Wollstonecraft trying to prove?

Reading Strategy Evaluate Argument

Argument is a type of writing in which logic and reason are used to persuade the reader. **Evaluating argument** means judging an argument and the credibility of the writer on the basis of how well he or she establishes authority and supports a thesis with convincing evidence. As you read, ask yourself, Am I convinced by this argument?

....

Tip: Taking Notes Use a chart like the one below to record the reasoning behind Wollstonecraft's argument. Determine whether her reasons are credible.

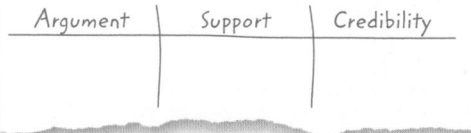

Argument	Support	Credibility

Vocabulary

indignation (in´ dig nā´ shən) n. anger aroused by something unjust or mean; p. 697 *We felt indignation at our unfair treatment.*

rational (rash´ ən əl) adj. able to reason; sensible; p. 697 *The speaker remained rational, though angry, throughout the debate.*

faculty (fak´ əl tē) n. capacity of the mind; ability; aptitude; p. 700 *Kathleen possessed the faculty to solve difficult math problems.*

congenial (kən jēn´ yəl) adj. compatible; agreeable; p. 700 *The congenial couple loved and respected each other.*

condescend (kon´ di send´) v. to lower oneself; p. 701 *She wouldn't condescend to cheat on a test.*

Reading Practice

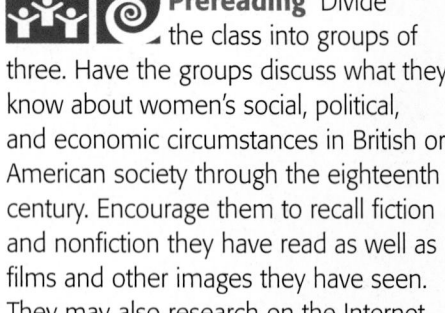 **Prereading** Divide the class into groups of three. Have the groups discuss what they know about women's social, political, and economic circumstances in British or American society through the eighteenth century. Encourage them to recall fiction and nonfiction they have read as well as films and other images they have seen. They may also research on the Internet.

Have a representative of each group report its findings to the class. *(Students should discuss women's limited educational and job opportunities, economic reliance on men, and inability to vote.)*

from
A Vindication
of the
Rights of Woman

Mary Wollstonecraft

from the Introduction

After considering the historic page and viewing the living world with anxious solicitude,[1] the most melancholy emotions of sorrowful **indignation** have depressed my spirits, and I have sighed when obliged to confess that either nature has made a great difference between man and man or that the civilization which has hitherto taken place in the world has been very partial. I have turned over various books written on the subject of education and patiently observed the conduct of parents and the management of schools, but what has been the result?—a profound conviction that the neglected education of my fellow creatures is the grand source of the misery I deplore and that women, in particular, are rendered weak and wretched by a variety of concurring causes, originating from one hasty conclusion. The conduct and manners of women, in fact, evidently prove that their minds are not in a healthy state, for like the flowers which are planted in too rich a soil, strength and usefulness are sacrificed to beauty, and the flaunting leaves, after having pleased a fastidious eye, fade, disregarded on the stalk, long before the season when they ought to have arrived at maturity. One cause of this barren blooming I attribute to a false system of education, gathered from the books written on this subject by men who, considering females rather as women than human creatures, have been more anxious to make them alluring mistresses than affectionate wives and **rational** mothers, and the understanding of the sex has been so bubbled[2] by this specious homage[3] that the civilized women of the present century, with a few exceptions, are only anxious to inspire love when they ought to cherish a nobler ambition and by their abilities and virtues exact respect. . . .

---

1. *Solicitude* is care or concern.

Evaluate Argument *How does Wollstonecraft immediately attempt to establish her credibility? Is her attempt convincing?*

Vocabulary

indignation (in´ dig nā´ shən) *n.* anger aroused by something unjust or mean

---

2. Here, *bubbled* means "fooled" or "deceived."
3. *Specious homage* means "deceptively attractive honor or respect."

Evaluate Argument *What cause-and-effect relationship does Wollstonecraft develop here? Do you find it plausible? Explain.* **2**

Thesis *Summarize Wollstonecraft's thesis in this paragraph.* **3**

Vocabulary

rational (rash´ ən əl) *adj.* able to reason; sensible

MARY WOLLSTONECRAFT **697**

Teach

View the Art ★

Answer: *She might think that they have been taught social graces, but society has allowed the better part of their intelligence to atrophy.*

The painter and graphic artist James Jacques Joseph Tissot (1836–1902) began his career in his native France. In 1871 he emigrated to England, where he lived an opulent lifestyle. Here he developed a passion for painting the costumes of elegant women. These paintings found their way into works devoted to the history of fashion. Recently, they have become recognized as masterpieces.

Interactive Read and Write

Other options for teaching this selection can be found in

- Interactive Read and Write for EL Students pp. 181–196
- Interactive Read and Write for Approaching-Level Students, pp. 181–196
- Interactive Read and Write for On-Level Students, pp. 181–196

Yet, because I am a woman, I would not lead my readers to suppose that I mean violently to agitate[4] the contested question respecting the quality or inferiority of the sex, but as the subject lies in my way, and I cannot pass it over without subjecting the main tendency of my reasoning to misconstruction, I shall stop a moment to deliver, in a few words, my opinion. In the government of the physical world, it is observable that the female in point of strength is, in general, inferior to the male. This is the law of nature, and it does not appear to be suspended or abrogated[5] in favor of woman. A degree of physical superiority cannot, therefore, be denied—and it is a noble prerogative! But not content with this natural preeminence,[6] men endeavor to sink us still lower merely to render us alluring objects for a moment, and women, intoxicated by the adoration which men, under the influence of their senses, pay them, do not seek to obtain a durable interest in their hearts or to become the friends of the fellow creatures who find amusement in their society.

I am aware of an obvious inference:[7] from every quarter have I heard exclamations against masculine women, but where are they to be found? If by this appellation[8] men mean to inveigh against their ardor[9] in hunting, shooting, and gaming, I shall most cordially join in the cry; but if it be against the imitation of manly virtues, or, more properly speaking, the attain-

The Woman of Fashion, 1883–1885. James Jacques Joseph Tissot. Oil on canvas, 148.3 x 103 cm. Private collection.

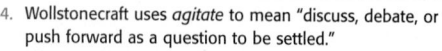 **View the Art** Tissot made a living documenting the stylish upper class of the Victorian era in images like this one. What might Wollstonecraft think of the women pictured? Why? ★

ment of those talents and virtues, the exercise of which ennobles the human character, and which raise females in the scale of animal being, when they are comprehensively termed mankind; all those who view them with a philosophic eye must, I should think, wish with me, that they may every day grow more and more masculine. . . .

My own sex, I hope, will excuse me if I treat them like rational creatures instead of flattering their fascinating graces and viewing them as if they were in a state of perpetual childhood, unable to stand alone. I earnestly wish to point out in what true dignity and human

---

4. Wollstonecraft uses *agitate* to mean "discuss, debate, or push forward as a question to be settled."
5. *Abrogated* means "abolished."
6. Here, *superiority, prerogative,* and *preeminence* are synonymous.
7. An *inference* is a conclusion based on something known or assumed.
8. An *appellation* is a name or description; here, it refers to the word *masculine* in the previous sentence.
9. *Inveigh against their ardor* means "to speak vehemently against women's enthusiasm."

Grammar Practice

PARTNERS **SPIRAL REVIEW** **Intervening Expressions** Write the following expressions on the board: *as well as, in addition to, plus,* and *together with.* Explain that the number of a subject is not affected by such expressions. These expressions do not create a compound subject. For example: Mary Wollstonecraft, as well as her daughter, Mary Shelley, is widely admired for her literary accomplishments. Have students write four sentences using each of the intervening expressions given. Then have students exchange papers with a partner to check for correct usage and subject-verb agreement.

happiness consists—I wish to persuade women to endeavor to acquire strength, both of mind and body, and to convince them that the soft phrases, susceptibility of heart, delicacy of sentiment,[10] and refinement of taste are almost synonymous with epithets[11] of weakness and that those beings who are only the objects of pity and that kind of love which has been termed its sister will soon become objects of contempt. . . .

The education of women has, of late, been more attended to than formerly; yet they are still reckoned a frivolous sex and ridiculed or pitied by the writers who endeavor by satire or instruction to improve them. It is acknowledged that they spend many of the first years of their lives in acquiring a smattering of accomplishments; meanwhile, strength of body and mind are sacrificed to libertine[12] notions of beauty, to the desire of establishing themselves—the only way women can rise in the world—by marriage. And this desire making mere animals of them, when they marry, they act as such children may be expected to act: they dress; they paint, and nickname God's creatures. Surely these weak beings are only fit for a seraglio![13] Can they be expected to govern a family with judgment or take care of the poor babes whom they bring into the world?

If then it can be fairly deduced from the present conduct of the sex, from the prevalent fondness for pleasure which takes place of ambition and those nobler passions that open and enlarge the soul, that the instruction which women have hitherto received has only tended, with the constitution of civil society, to render them insignificant objects of desire—mere propagators[14] of fools!—if it can be

proved that in aiming to accomplish them, without cultivating their understandings, they are taken out of their sphere of duties and made ridiculous and useless when the short-lived bloom of beauty is over, I presume that *rational* men will excuse me for endeavoring to persuade them to become more masculine and respectable.

Indeed, the word *masculine* is only a bugbear.[15] There is little reason to fear that women will acquire too much courage or fortitude, for their apparent inferiority with respect to bodily strength must render them, in some degree, dependent on men in the various relations of life, but why should it be increased by prejudices that give a sex to virtue and confound simple truths with sensual reveries?[16] . . .

from Chapter 2

. . . Youth is the season for love in both sexes, but in those days of thoughtless enjoyment, provision should be made for the more important years of life when reflection takes place of sensation. But Rousseau,[17] and most of the male writers who have followed his steps, have warmly inculcated[18] that the whole tendency of female education ought to be directed to one point: to render them pleasing.

Let me reason with the supporters of this opinion who have any knowledge of human nature, do they imagine that marriage can eradicate[19] the habitude of life? The woman who has only been taught to please will soon find that her charms are oblique sunbeams and that they cannot have much effect on her hus-

---

10. *Sentiment* refers to emotion or feelings.
11. *Epithets* are descriptive words.
12. *Libertine* means "morally unrestrained."
13. A *seraglio* (si ral′ yō) is a harem.
14. *Propagators* are those who produce offspring.

15. A *bugbear* is an object of needless fear.
16. *Reveries* are daydreams.
17. *Rousseau* is Jean-Jacques Rousseau (1712–1778), a French philosopher who believed humanity is essentially good but is corrupted by society.
18. *Inculcated* means "taught" or "frequently repeated."
19. *Eradicate* means "get rid of."

  Thesis *Is this deduction merely a restatement of the thesis, or is it a further conclusion based on the reasons and evidence used to support the thesis? Explain.*

Evaluate Argument *Why does Wollstonecraft refer to Rousseau? How does the reference help to develop her credibility and argument?* **3**

Literary Element 1

Thesis Answer: *This deduction is a conclusion that goes beyond the thesis. It follows that if women are trained to be alluring companions at the expense of a quality education that develops intellect, they become dehumanized ("insignificant objects of desire") and fit only to be "mere propagators of fools."*

(ENGLISH LEARNERS) Paraphrase Wollstonecraft's statement for English learners. **Say:** Wollstonecraft says that women are nothing more than pretty mothers of foolish children. Is that the author's main argument? Explain. *(No, her argument is that women suffer because of their poor education.)*

Reading Strategy 2

Evaluate Argument Answer: *The reference, which shows that she is aware of other intellectuals' thoughts and writings on the topic, gives her credibility as a knowledgeable source. It also gives her an opportunity to recognize the opposition and to refute its arguments.*

Literary Element 3

Metaphor Help students recognize how Wollstonecraft uses metaphors to enliven her writing. **Ask:** What metaphor does she use when speaking of a woman's charms? *("oblique sunbeams")*

English Learners

DIFFERENTIATED INSTRUCTION

PARTNERS **Beginning** Help students see the relationships among words with common origins. Pair students with strong English speakers to write sentences using the different forms of these words: *human:* humanity, humane *submit:* submission, submissiveness *genial:* congenial, geniality

Approaching Level

DIFFERENTIATED INSTRUCTION

Emerging Lead students in discussing the text on these pages and how different text formats support comprehension. Draw students' attention to the bottom notes, the visual, caption, and vocabulary note. Remind students to use such text support when they read.

Teach

Big Idea 1

The Stirrings of Romanticism Answer:

Wollstonecraft states that women should first be concerned with self-respect. She believes that women are the equals of men and should not rely on men to make them happy. These opinions reflect the reassessment and criticism of traditional values, such as male dominance, that characterized the Romantic movement.

ENGLISH LEARNERS Tell English learners who speak Spanish to find as many cognates as they can in the sentence that begins "But whether she be…." (*respectable, respetable; infirmity, enfermedad; neglect, negligencia; subject, sujeto*) Have them write the English word, the Spanish word, and the definition. Then, ask them to share their findings with a partner.

---

band's heart when they are seen every day, when the summer is passed and gone. Will she then have sufficient native energy to look into herself for comfort and cultivate her dormant[20] **faculties**? Or is it not more rational to expect that she will try to please other men, and in the emotions raised by the expectation of new conquests, endeavor to forget the mortification her love or pride has received? When the husband ceases to be a lover—and the time will inevitably come—her desire of pleasing will then grow languid[21] or become a spring of bitterness, and love, perhaps the most evanescent[22] of all passions, gives place to jealousy or vanity.

I now speak of women who are restrained by principle or prejudice. Such women, though they would shrink from an intrigue with real abhorrence, yet, nevertheless, wish to be convinced by the homage of gallantry that they are cruelly neglected by their husbands, or days and weeks are spent in dreaming of the happiness enjoyed by **congenial** souls till their health is undermined and their spirits broken by discontent. How then can the great art of pleasing be such a necessary study? It is only useful to a mistress; the chaste wife and serious mother should only consider her power to please as the polish of her virtues, and the affection of her husband as one of the comforts that render her talk less difficult and her life happier. But whether she be loved or neglected, her first wish should be to make herself respectable and not to rely for all her happiness on a being subject to like infirmities with herself.

---

20. *Dormant* means "in a state of rest or inactivity."
21. *Languid* means "faint" or "weak."
22. *Evanescent* means "likely to vanish."

---

1 **The Stirrings of Romanticism** *How does this statement reflect Romanticism's criticism of traditional values?*

Vocabulary

faculty (fak′ əl tē) *n.* capacity of the mind; ability; aptitude

congenial (kən jēn′ yəl) *adj.* compatible; agreeable

The worthy Dr. Gregory[23] fell into a similar error. I respect his heart but entirely disapprove of his celebrated legacy to his daughters. . . .

He actually recommends dissimulation[24] and advises an innocent girl to give the lie to her feelings and not dance with spirit, when gaiety of heart would make her feet eloquent without making her gestures immodest. In the name of truth and common sense, why should not one woman acknowledge that she can take more exercise than another or, in other words, that she has a sound constitution. And why, to damp innocent vivacity, is she darkly to be told that men will draw conclusions which she little thinks of? Let the libertine draw what inference he pleases, but I hope that no sensible mother will restrain the natural frankness of youth by instilling such indecent cautions. Out of the abundance of the heart, the mouth speaketh, and a wiser than Solomon[25] hath said that the heart should be made clean and not trivial ceremonies observed, which it is not very difficult to fulfill with scrupulous exactness when vice reigns in the heart.

Women ought to endeavor to purify their heart, but can they do so when their uncultivated understandings make them entirely dependent on their senses for employment and amusement, when no noble pursuit sets them above the little vanities of the day or enables them to curb the wild emotions that agitate a reed over which every passing breeze has power? To gain the affections of a virtuous man, is affectation necessary? Nature has given woman a weaker frame than man, but to ensure her husband's affections, must a wife, who by the exercise of her mind and body whilst she was discharging the duties of a daughter, wife, and mother, has allowed her constitution to retain its natural strength, and her nerves a healthy tone, is she, I say, to

---

23. *Dr. Gregory* is John Gregory (1724—1773), a Scottish physician who wrote the book *A Father's Legacy to His Daughters.*
24. *Dissimulation* is pretense.
25. *Solomon*, king of Israel during the tenth century B.C., was known for his wisdom.

Reading Practice

PARTNERS **SPIRAL REVIEW** **Skim** Point out that this selection is composed of two excerpts from a longer work. Explain that skimming, or glancing quickly over the excerpts and noting headings and organizational pattern, can be a helpful previewing strategy.

Have students work with partners to scan the text and draw inferences about the nature, subject, and organization of the work before they begin reading.

condescend to use art and feign a sickly delicacy in order to secure her husband's affection? Weakness may excite tenderness and gratify the arrogant pride of man, but the lordly caresses of a protector will not gratify a noble mind that pants for, and deserves to be respected. Fondness is a poor substitute for friendship! . . .

If all the faculties of woman's mind are only to be cultivated as they respect her dependence on man; if, when a husband be obtained, she have arrived at her goal, and meanly proud, rests satisfied with such a paltry crown, let her grovel contentedly, scarcely raised by her employments above the animal kingdom; but, if, struggling for the prize of her high calling, she look beyond the present scene, let her cultivate her understanding without stopping to consider what character the husband may have whom she is destined to marry. Let her only determine, without being too anxious about present happiness, to acquire the qualities that ennoble a rational being, and a rough inelegant husband may shock her taste without destroying her peace of mind. She will not model her soul to suit the frailties of her companion, but to bear with them: his character may be a trial, but not an impediment to virtue. . . .

These may be termed Utopian[26] dreams. Thanks to that Being who impressed them on my soul and gave me sufficient strength of mind to dare to exert my own reason, till, becoming dependent only on him for the support of my virtue, I view with indignation the mistaken notions that enslave my sex.

I love man as my fellow; but his scepter, real or usurped, extends not to me, unless the reason of an individual demands my homage; and even then the submission is to reason, and not to man. In fact, the conduct of an accountable being must be regulated by the operations of its own reason, or on what foundation rests the throne of God?

It appears to me necessary to dwell on these obvious truths because females have been insulated, as it were, and while they have been stripped of the virtues that should clothe humanity, they have been decked with artificial graces that enable them to exercise a short-lived tyranny. Love, in their bosoms, taking place of every nobler passion, their sole ambition is to be fair, to raise emotion instead of inspiring respect; and this ignoble desire, like the servility in absolute monarchies, destroys all strength of character. Liberty is the mother of virtue, and if women be, by their very constitution, slaves, and not allowed to breathe the sharp invigorating air of freedom, they must ever languish like exotics[27] and be reckoned beautiful flaws in nature.

---

26. *Utopian* means "impossibly ideal."

2 **Evaluate Argument** *Is this statement an effective refutation of the views of Rousseau and Dr. Gregory? Explain.*

Vocabulary

condescend (kon′ di send′) *v.* to lower oneself

27. *Languish like exotics* means "to grow weak or droop like plants out of their natural environment."

Thesis *What analogy is Wollstonecraft using here to support her thesis? In your opinion, is it a valid analogy? Explain.* **3**

Teach

Reading Strategy 2

Evaluate Argument
Answer: *Most students will agree that it is an effective refutation because Wollstonecraft has cited reasons and evidence to show that gratifying "the arrogant pride of man" will not satisfy women's needs, nor will it be conducive to harmonious relationships, which should be based on the friendship of equal partners.*

Literary Element 3

Thesis **Answer:** *Wollstonecraft is making an analogy between male dominance and absolute monarchy. Most students will agree that it is a valid analogy because both institutions victimize people through the tyrannical use of power.*

To check students' understanding of the selection, see Unit 4 Teaching Resources Book, p. 54.

Advanced Learners

DIFFERENTIATED INSTRUCTION

College In *A Vindication of the Rights of Woman,* Wollstonecraft focuses on the effects of unequal educational opportunities for women 200 years ago. Remind students that there are still places in the world where women receive an inferior education.

Ask students to read about this subject in newspapers, magazines, or journals. Have students report to the class on places where obtaining a college education is a problem for women. Students should look for the causes of this situation and the efforts to correct it.

After You Read

Assess

1. Answers will vary.

2. (a) Both cannot "stand alone." (b) Women had few rights.

3. (a) Artificial graces gain women brief control at the expense of lifelong respect. (b) Enforced obedience is not virtuous behavior.

4. (a) Forceful, authoritative, and at times sarcastic (b) Her forceful tone is compelling and persuasive.

5. Fondness implies superiority and friendship implies equality.

6. (a) Physical strength (b) Men and women are equal in intelligence, courage, and determination. This one concession strengthens her argument because acknowledging the opposition is a rhetorical advantage.

7. (a) Her writing challenges traditional male and female roles. (b) It predicts the women's rights movement.

8. Answers will vary. Most students will say that Wollstonecraft's exposure to education and educated people taught her the value of being well-informed and independent, and she sought to give that opportunity to other women.

 For additional assessment, see Assessment Resources, pp. 177–178.

702

After You Read

Respond and Think Critically

Respond and Interpret

1. Do you think you would have found Wollstonecraft's arguments convincing if you had lived during the late eighteenth century? Explain.

2. (a) What comparisons does Wollstonecraft make between women and children? (b) What do these comparisons reveal about women's status?

3. (a) Summarize the ideas Wollstonecraft presents in the last paragraph. (b) What do you think she means by "Liberty is the mother of virtue"?

Analyze and Evaluate

4. (a) How would you describe Wollstonecraft's tone? (b) Is her tone likely to persuade readers to adopt her point of view? Explain.

5. In describing the relationship between men and women, Wollstonecraft says, "Fondness is a poor substitute for friendship!" Do you agree?

6. (a) What superiority does Wollstonecraft concede to men? (b) Why does she claim that this one difference does not make one sex worthier than the other? Does her admission of this difference weaken or strengthen her argument? Explain.

Connect

7. **Big Idea** The Stirrings of Romanticism (a) How does Wollstonecraft's essay challenge the values of British society during her time period? (b) How does her essay predict change?

8. **Connect to the Author** Consider what you know of Wollstonecraft from the biography on page 695. Why might she have felt particularly strongly about the education of women, or their roles in society?

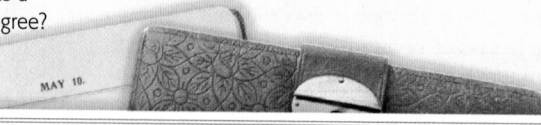

Daily Life & Culture

Women's Roles in Society

Eighteenth-century British society was divided along class and gender lines. Women were not allowed to vote, own property, or receive an equal education. With few career options—teacher, seamstress, governess, or lady's companion—marriage was the primary goal for most upper-class women. Marriage was a legal and economic contract, and for most women it was the only means of social advancement. Most aristocratic women did not attend school but were taught by their governess to be docile, fashionable, moral, and marriageable. Daily studies might include Shakespearean sonnets, singing and playing the harpsichord, and manners and morality.

Educational opportunities were determined by the station and rank a child was born into. Lower-class girls were the least educated group in England. While some attended Christian charity schools, little time was spent on lessons. The girls spun, sewed, and wove instead. When the girls were old enough, they usually worked full-time as maids and seamstresses.

Group Activity Discuss these questions with your classmates.

1. Do you think Wollstonecraft was justified in writing *A Vindication of the Rights of Woman*? Explain.

2. How do women's roles differ today? How have these differences affected modern life?

Daily Life & Culture

1. Most students will respond that she was justified in writing her essay because women suffered discrimination and were deprived of important civil rights.

2. Today, most women in the United States have the same educational opportunities as men, they have the right to vote and own property, and they can hold any job they are qualified for. However, women sometimes get paid less than men for the same job, and they are still the primary caregivers in most families. Today, most marriages are usually made for love rather than economic gain, mothers are better prepared to educate their children, and society has benefited from the contributions of women.

Literary Element | Thesis

A well-crafted **thesis** alone is not enough to persuade readers. In order to be convincing, the writer must present compelling evidence, such as facts, statistics, examples, and expert opinions, to support the thesis.

1. What is the thesis of *A Vindication of the Rights of Woman*?

2. How does Wollstonecraft support her thesis? Give specific examples from the essay.

Review: Allusion

As you learned on page 512, an **allusion** is an indirect reference to a well-known person, place, or event from history, music, art, or another literary work. Understanding allusions can be essential to interpreting a work of literature. In her essay, Wollstonecraft alludes to Sir Thomas More's book *Utopia*.

Partner Activity Work with a partner and use the Internet to research information on Thomas More's *Utopia*. Look up the meaning of the title, where the word originated, and how it is used today. Then determine why Wollstonecraft would say that her ideas "may be termed Utopian dreams."

Young Woman Sewing by Lamplight, 1825. Georg Friedrich Kersting. Oil on canvas, 40.3 x 34.2 cm. Private collection.

 Literature Online

Selection Resources For Selection Quizzes, eFlashcards, and Reading-Writing Connection activities, go to glencoe.com and enter QuickPass code GLB9817u4.

Reading Strategy | Evaluate Argument

In addition to establishing her credibility, Wollstonecraft builds her arguments logically so that the reader is led to the same conclusion she has reached. One type of reasoning she uses effectively is cause and effect.

1. (a) What makes Wollstonecraft qualified to write on the topic of women's rights? (b) How does she establish her credibility?

2. According to Wollstonecraft, what is the main cause of the "weak and wretched" state of women in late-eighteenth-century society?

Vocabulary Practice

Practice with Denotation and Connotation Each of the vocabulary words is listed with a word that has a similar denotation. Choose the word that has the stronger connotation.

1. indignation   annoyance

2. rational   wise

3. faculty   talent

4. congenial   loving

5. condescend   humiliate

Academic Vocabulary

*In Wollstonecraft's time, the structure and mores of society **prohibited** women from reaching their full potential.*

Prohibited is an academic word. According to Wollstonecraft, men in the eighteenth century **prohibited** women from being anything but mistresses, wives, and mothers.

To further explore the meaning of this word, answer the following question: Has someone ever **prohibited** you from doing something? Explain.

For more on academic vocabulary, see pages 56 and R81.

After You Read

Assess

Literary Element

1. The thesis is that, because of educational neglect, women have not been prepared for the equal status that is the basis of a healthy relationship between the sexes.

2. She supports her thesis with reasons, evidence, and logic. Make sure that students choose cogent examples from the essay.

Review: Allusion

Utopia is a place of ideal perfection, especially in laws, government, and social conditions. The word comes from the Greek, meaning "nowhere." It refers to an ideal society that never could exist. Wollstonecraft alludes to *Utopia* when referring to her dreams of equality for women. She fears that most people will never consider gender equality to be a realistic possibility, so her vision of an equal society may be deemed a fantasy.

Progress Check

Can students identify thesis?

If No → See Unit 4 Teaching Resources Book, p. 49.

Reading Strategy

1. (a) She has firsthand knowledge of what it is like to be a woman and to suffer disadvantages because of her sex. She has also done extensive reading and research on the topic. (b) She establishes her credibility by exhibiting her learning, experience, and intellectual power.

2. The lack of education available to women

Vocabulary

1. *Indignation* has the stronger connotation.

2. *Wise* has the stronger connotation.

3. *Talent* has the stronger connotation.

4. *Loving* has the stronger connotation.

5. *Humiliate* has the stronger connotation.

Academic Vocabulary

Students should describe a time when they were prevented or barred from doing something.

After You Read

Assess

⚡ Respond Through Writing

Use these criteria when evaluating students' writing:

- Does the writer paraphrase the thesis accurately?
- Does the writer summarize the introduction and Chapter 2, providing enough supporting detail?
- Does the conclusion summarize the writer's interpretation of the thesis and offer insight into the work?

A student who meets all of these criteria should receive the equivalent of a 4-point response.

A student who fully meets two or partially meets three of these criteria should receive the equivalent of a 3-point response.

A student who fully meets one or partially meets two of these criteria should receive the equivalent of a 2-point response.

A student who partially meets one of these criteria should receive the equivalent of a 1-point response.

⚡ Respond Through Writing

Persuasive Essay

Argue a Position Wollstonecraft argued powerfully for the education of women over two and a half centuries ago. Do you think that her argument is still relevant today? Explain why or why not, using persuasive techniques and evidence from the selection to support your opinion.

Understanding the Task Argument is a type of writing which uses logic, reason, and other persuasive techniques to influence readers.

Prewrite With a classmate, create an outline of the major points in Wollstonecraft's argument and the evidence she provides to support them. Discuss each point, indicating whether you think it applies to women today and explaining why or why not. You may also want to consult outside sources, such as current educational statistics, for further ideas. Summarize your position in a thesis statement that will become the basis for your persuasive essay.

Wollstonecraft: Point of education to make women "pleasing"
Now: Absolutely not—women have equal educational opportunities today and aim to compete with, rather than please, men.

Draft Organize your arguments logically, either beginning or ending with your strongest point. Include facts, statistics, quotations from experts and solid reasoning to support your claims and use persuasive techniques such as appeals to emotion or logic.

You should also try to address any counterarguments your readers might have. Statements like the following will help you strengthen your own point by rebutting a different one:

While some readers will say_____, I believe _____ because _____.

Revise Ask a peer reader to evaluate your argument, looking out for statements that are not logically explained or adequately supported. Check to see that you have acknowledged your sources wherever necessary. Lastly, evaluate your essay against the Writing Workshop checklist on page 652.

Edit and Proofread Proofread your paper, correcting any errors in spelling, grammar, and punctuation. Use the Grammar Tip in the side column to help you with using italics or underscoring.

Learning Objectives

In this assignment, you will focus on the following objectives:

Writing: Writing a persuasive essay.

Grammar: Understanding italics and underscoring.

▶ Grammar Tip

Italics or Underscore

In supporting your arguments, you will need to quote from both primary and secondary sources and cite them correctly. Use **italics** or **underscoring** to indicate the titles of books, plays, and long poems.

You can also italicize or underscore words or phrases you want to strongly emphasize, but this type of emphasis should be used sparingly.

As Wollstonecraft ironically states in <u>A Vindication of the Rights of Woman</u>, "My own sex, I hope, will excuse me if I treat them like rational creatures instead of flattering their <u>fascinating</u> graces . . . ."

Writing Practice

PARTNERS

Thesis Remind students that a thesis statement presents an author's central argument. Explain that the statement should communicate an opinion or point of view. Write the following sentences on the board:

- Obesity is increasing among children in the United States.
- The best way to reduce childhood obesity is to remove high-calorie snacks from schools.

Ask: Which sentence contains an opinion? *(the second sentence)* What sorts of details could the author include to support the thesis? *(Possible responses: doctors' opinions, statistics about snacks in schools, case studies)* What differing arguments could be made about the same topic? *(Possible responses: Children should exercise; parents should serve more nutritious meals.)* Ask students to draft a thesis statement on the topic of crime and to list three sorts of details that would support their claim. Have them exchange papers with a partner and evaluate each other's work.

Vocabulary Workshop

Greek and Latin Word Parts

Literature Connection Almost a third of the words in this sentence from *A Vindication of the Rights of Woman* are derived from Latin:

> "My own sex, I hope, will excuse me if I treat them like rational creatures instead of flattering their fascinating graces and viewing them as if they were in a state of perpetual childhood, unable to stand alone."

> —Mary Wollstonecraft, from *A Vindication of the Rights of Woman*

Examples include *rational* (from *ratio*, "reason"), *fascinating* (from *fascinum*, "witchcraft"), *viewing* (from *videre*, "to see"), and *perpetual* (from *perpetuus*, "continuous"). Many English words trace their origins to Latin or Greek, so knowing a few common word parts can help you determine the meanings of unfamiliar words.

Prefixes and suffixes are word parts that are added to **base words** (which can stand alone) or to **word roots** (bases from which words are derived but which are not complete words). Prefixes are inserted at the beginning, and suffixes at the end, of base words or word roots. For example, the word *excuse* is made up of the Latin prefix *ex-* ("from") and the root *causa* ("cause"). The following chart contains some common Greek and Latin prefixes, roots, and suffixes, and their meanings.

Prefixes	Roots	Suffixes
auto- self, same	*bio* life	*-ate* cause to be
contra- against	*dic(t)* say	*-cide* killing
dis- opposite	*gen* birth, race	*-graph* writing
im- / *in-* not	*phono* sound	*-ible* inclined to, capable of
re- back, again	*scrib* write	*-ion* state, condition

Practice Using a dictionary and the chart above, find the origin of the word parts in, and the definition of, each of the following words. Notice how the Greek or Latin word parts contribute to the English meaning.

1. phonograph
2. autobiography
3. genocide
4. contradiction
5. distensible

Vocabulary For more vocabulary practice, go to glencoe.com and enter QuickPass code GLB9817u4.

Learning Objectives

In this workshop, you will focus on the following objectives.

Vocabulary:
Understanding word origins.
Understanding word parts.

Prefixes and Suffixes

A **prefix** is a word part that is inserted at the beginning of a word root or a base word to create a new meaning; a **suffix** is added to the end. Unlike a base word, a root cannot stand alone.

Test-Taking Tip

When you find an unfamiliar word in a reading passage, break it into its word parts. Then think of words you know that contain the same word parts. Identifying familiar roots can be especially helpful.

Focus

Write on the board in 3 columns:

Prefixes
anti- (opposite; opposing)
geo- (Earth)
hyper- (excessive)
micro- (small)
neo- (new, recent)

Roots
anthrop- (human)
-chron- (time)
-dem- (people)
-path- (feeling, suffering)

Suffixes
-ism (theory of)
-ism (forms nouns)
-gram (written or drawn)
-logy (theory, study)
-meter (measure)

Say: One way new words are created is by combining prefixes, word roots, and suffixes. Ask students to make up new words using the prefixes, roots, and suffixes on the board. Ask them to give a definition of the word based on the meanings of the word parts.

Teach

Base Words Prefixes and suffixes can be added to both base words and root words. Base words can stand alone, but root words cannot. Ask students to suggest base words and then prefixes and suffixes that can be attached to create new words. (*For example, part/partly*)

 For additional vocabulary practice, see Glencoe Interactive Vocabulary CD-ROM.

Assess
Practice

1. <u>Gr. root</u> *phono*; <u>suffix</u> *-graph* (recorded sound)

2. <u>Gr. prefix</u> *auto-*; <u>root</u> *bio*; <u>suffix</u> *-graph* (story of one's own life)

3. <u>Gr. root</u> *gen*; Lat. <u>suffix</u> *-cide* (killing of an entire group)

4. <u>Lat. prefix</u> *contra-*; <u>root</u> *dict*; <u>suffix</u> *-ion* (a contrary assertion)

5. <u>Lat. prefix</u> *dis-*; root *tens*; <u>suffix</u> *-ible*; (able to be expanded)

Focus

Summary

The article examines specific issues that Arabic women face, such as women in education and government and the rise of feminism. Arabic feminists are now taking chances to raise awareness about equal rights issues.

 For summaries in languages other than English, see Unit 4 Teaching Resources Book, pp. 56–61.

Teach

Reading Strategy | 1

Identify Problem and Solution **Say:** A writer may present a problem and then provide solutions. For example, a writer may explain the problem of automobile accidents involving teenagers and then propose solutions to this problem. Have students look for examples of problem-and-solution relationships in this article as they read.

(APPROACHING) Ask approaching-level students to name two rights that American women have that Arab women have to fight for.

 For an audio recording of this selection, use Listening Library Audio CD-ROM.

Readability Scores

Dale-Chall: 9.5
DRP: 66
Lexile: 1140

706

Learning Objectives

For pages 706–712
In studying this text, you will focus on the following objectives:

Reading:
Analyzing informational text. Identifying problem and solution.

Set a Purpose for Reading

As you read, ask yourself, How are the roles of women changing in the Middle East?

Preview the Article

1. Read the **subheads,** or the headlines between paragraphs. What clues do these subheads give you about the content of the article?

2. What do you already know about feminism? How can you apply your prior knowledge to the article?

Reading Strategy Identify Problem and Solution

When you identify problems and solutions while reading, you examine issues the writer presents and evaluate how these issues might be resolved. As you read, think about the gender-inequality problems discussed in "Raising Their Voices" and ask yourself, How are Arab women attempting to solve these problems? You may want to use a chart or another graphic organizer to record your ideas.

TIME

Raising Their
VOICES

Savvy, optimistic and ambitious, a new generation of Arab women is speaking out, forging its own brand of feminism—and slowly reshaping Arab society.

By JEFF CHU

DOZENS OF MEN SCURRY AROUND A SUBURBAN CAIRO art gallery, carrying out the rapid-fire orders issued by a tall, imposing woman in black jeans and a cream cashmere sweater. "Everyone out of the way!" barks director Inas El Degheidi, scanning the set to make sure everything is in place for the next scene in *Women in Search of Freedom,* her film about the harsh lives of female migrant workers. Even in a cosmopolitan city like Cairo, most Arab men aren't used to being bossed around by a woman, but El Degheidi's confrontational style does not faze her crew; they "are used to my way by now," she says. So are audiences: The veteran Egyptian filmmaker is known for training her camera on problems that male-dominated Arab society tries to keep under wraps—marital infidelity and a legal system that's tougher on women accused of adultery than on men. "Issues need to be brought to the surface," the director says, "to create a healthy social dialogue."

Provocative? You bet. El Degheidi, 46, belongs to a rising generation of Arab women who are challenging the conservatism and sexism of the Middle East, where some 90% of the population is Muslim and females are rarely treated as equals. Across the region, these women are using their growing prominence to push for women's rights, and overcoming real obstacles in the process. In Jordan, Queen Rania is lobbying for a progressive agenda—and upsetting traditionalists. In the tiny oil-rich nation of Qatar,

---

Reading Practice

SPIRAL REVIEW **Recognize Adjectives** Point out to students that adjectives help make informational text more effective by adding vivid details and color that strengthen description. **Ask:** Which adjectives do you find in the first paragraph? (*Suburban, Cairo, art, rapid-fire, tall, imposing, black, cream, cashmere, next, harsh, female, migrant, cosmopolitan, Arab,* *confrontational, veteran, Egyptian, male-dominated, marital, legal, healthy, social*) Have a volunteer read aloud the paragraph without the adjectives. **Ask:** Do you know as much as you did before? (*No, the adjectives are necessary for description.*)

HISTORY
EL Degheidi's films are informed by the "residue" of past discrimination.

Barry Iverson

Sheika Mouza, the wife of the country's king, has become the architect of an educational expansion that's giving women new choices. And all over the Arab world, smart, ambitious, effective women in all fields—politics, business, arts, sports—are helping to claim a larger role for women in all walks of life.

Daring to Speak Out
El Degheidi is one of eight children from a conservative, middle-class family. She and her sisters "were restricted in all our comings and goings," she says.

"This discrimination must have left some residue," including a deep curiosity about relations between men and women. But probing society's fault lines can be hazardous to one's health. Some of El Degheidi's films have earned her death threats from Islamic militants. "There are people now who want to hush any loud voice with a different opinion," El Degheidi says.

Especially if the voice belongs to a woman. In January 2004, Lubna Olayan, Saudi Arabia's best-known businesswoman, spoke before an audience of men and women at an economic forum without wearing a head scarf, leading Saudi Arabia's top cleric to condemn her "shameful behavior." The topic of her speech: pursuing change while preserving core values. "To progress," Olayan said, "we have no choice but to embrace change." Throughout the Arab world, legions of young women are doing just that, studying at universities (more than half of undergraduates in Kuwait, Saudi Arabia, and Qatar are female), and preparing for a society in which it's normal for women to be called "doctor" or "entrepreneur" in

RAISING THEIR VOICES **707**

TIME

Teach

Big Idea | 2

The Stirrings of Romanticism **Ask:** What do present-day Muslim women have in common with writers from the Romantic period? *(They want to break away from the rigidity and repression of Islam as it is practiced today, just as the writers from the Romantic period found the emphasis on reason during the Enlightenment period to be narrow and restrictive.)*

View the Photograph ★

Inas El Degheidi is Egypt's most established female director-producer. Her film *Sorry for the Law* is about a legal loophole that pardons men who kill their adulterous wives while women get life in jail or a death sentence for the same crime.

English Learners

DIFFERENTIATED INSTRUCTION

Intermediate Explain to students that it is helpful to look for context clues when reading. **Say:** Context clues are the surrounding words that can help you figure out the meaning of unfamiliar words. Have students find the word *legions* in the second paragraph on page 707. **Ask:** Can you tell what the word means in its context? *(a large number)* Next, have students find the word *entrepreneur* in the same paragraph. **Ask:** Can you tell what the word means in its context? *(a person who organizes a business)* If students cannot gather the meanings from context clues, then have them look up the definitions in a standard dictionary.

TIME

Teach

Informational Text

Reading Strategy   **1**

Identify Problem and Solution Point out to students that writers use different ways to organize problems and solutions. **Say:** Try stopping after reading each subsection of the article to review the problems and solutions the writer has presented.

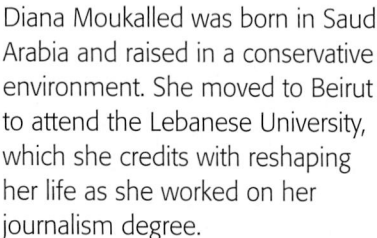

View the Photograph ★

Diana Moukalled was born in Saudi Arabia and raised in a conservative environment. She moved to Beirut to attend the Lebanese University, which she credits with reshaping her life as she worked on her journalism degree.

HEAD-ON Moukalled, who tackles topics such as Afghan refugees, says many Arabs "don't want to face problems that need to be dealt with." ★

Ayman Mroueh

addition to—and sometimes instead of—"wife" and "mother." But they don't see change as an abandonment of duty. Rather, it means choice. The right to choose, say, whether to wear a veil in public is as much a part of a woman's emancipation as the right to vote. The veil is no barrier to hijab-wearing leaders like Sheika Mouza; not wearing one is likewise no obstacle to Queen Rania.

One sign of change is the growing public role being taken by the wives of Arab leaders. (No Arab country is ruled by a woman.)

The steps may seem small, but in these conservative cultures, they are important. In 2002, when Bahrain held its first election in over 25 years, Sheika Sabeeka, the King's wife, led a campaign to encourage women to vote. When Morocco's King Mohammed VI wed Salma Bennani that year, he gave her the title "Princess." Before that, spouses of Morocco's kings had rarely been seen, let alone honored with titles. And the King has also spoken out on women's rights. Syrian President Bashar Assad's wife, Asma, travels with

her husband and promotes the cause of microfinance—small loans for entrepreneurial women who would otherwise be unable to obtain credit. Her mother-in-law made just a handful of appearances during the 30-year rule of the current President's father, Hafez. **1**

Women in Government **2**
Women are also a growing presence in the official ranks of government. In 2003, after the people of Qatar approved a constitution giving women the right to vote and run for office, the Persian Gulf state

708 UNIT 4   THE TRIUMPH OF ROMANTICISM

Reading Practice

Read Shorter Segments and Paraphrase

Suggest that students break up their reading into smaller parts of at least one paragraph in length. Then have them paraphrase the main idea or central action of each part.

Then, divide the class into three groups. Assign each group a section of the essay that has been covered so far. Have each group write a summary of the main

points in each section. Each member of the group should contribute ideas for the summary. After ten minutes, form new groups with a member of each of the four sections. Have each member share his/her summary of a section with the rest of the group.

SELF-ESTEEM Yassine urges women to be "more positive and proactive." ★

Etienne Boyer/SIPA

got its first female Cabinet member. Tunisia's Cabinet has six women; Jordan's has three. But "patriarchy is still there," says Jordan's Asma Khader, a women's-rights activist and high government official. Women hold less than 6% of the region's parliamentary seats (the global average is nearly 16%). The United Arab Emirates and Kuwait bar women from voting or running for parliament. Morocco has the highest rate of female representation—women hold 35 of the 325 seats in the Chamber of Representatives—and reserves 30 seats for women. That the half-female electorate only voted five women into at-large seats shows how hard it is to crack a male-run system. "Women in the Arab world are still operating in male-dominated societies with stale traditions," says Haifa al Kaylani. She is the founder of the Arab International Women's Forum, a networking group. Says Khader: "Women's [political] participation and equal rights are still not accepted by some extremist groups and religious interpretations."

Some governments have defied such dissenters, expanding women's legal rights. Egyptian President Hosni Mubarak, for example, has ruled that children born to Egyptian mothers would be considered Egyptian; previously, only fathers passed on citizenship. Moroccan lawmakers have approved King Mohammed VI's reforms of the country's personal-status code. Women were given the right to ask for divorce, the minimum marriage age for girls rose from 15 to 18, and polygamy was strictly limited.

Education: "The Bones of the Body"

Morocco's Nadia Yassine is a mother of four, grandmother of one, and the daughter of fundamentalist leader Sheik Abdel-Salam Yassine. As spokeswoman for his Justice and Charity Party, she is perhaps the most visible fundamentalist feminist in the Arab world.

Her hair tucked under a tight head scarf and her body cloaked in a flowing robe, Yassine, 45, hardly fits the West's image of a feminist—but neither she nor her more liberal counterparts claim to be Western-style feminists. "I adapted my feminism from Islam, not Western culture," she says. Her inspiration comes partly from Islam's history. Muhammad was "a true feminist," she says. His favorite wife, Aisha, a revered Islamic-law expert, led an army into battle. Discrimination "is a homegrown malady," Yassine says. "We can find solutions derived from our own culture, our own value system."

Perhaps the most potent solution is education. "We have to unveil the Arab woman's mind," says Egyptian activist Nawal El Saadawi. Though half of Arab women still cannot read and 4 million girls are not in school, education rates have risen rapidly across the region. In Bahrain, Jordan, Lebanon, the United Arab Emirates, and the Palestinian

> **"The lives of Arab women are still not what they should be."**
>
> —DIANA MOUKALLED, editor, Future TV international news

RAISING THEIR VOICES **709**

TIME

Teach

Reading Strategy 1

Summarize Remind students that a summary is a short restatement of the main idea and supporting details of a selection. Have students summarize the experiences of Nadia Bakhurji in Saudi Arabia.

Cultural History ☆

The wife of the king of Qatar, Sheika Mouza, has been in a position to be a role model for other Muslim women. Her husband routinely violates a traditional Islamic tenet by appearing regularly in public with her.

For activities related to this selection, see Unit 4 Teaching Resources Book, pp. 62–63.

territories, enrollment rates for girls and boys are equal among primary-school-age children. In a 2003 values survey, Saudi women ranked learning third, behind only faith and family in importance. In Qatar, where Sheika Mouza, the second of the ruler's three wives, has led a drive to build a world-class educational system, including branches of Cornell University's medical school and Texas A&M's petrochemical college, more than 70% of undergrads are women.

In Kuwait, the numbers are about the same—and girls' desire to perform is so strong that "if we left admission to grades, we would have almost 100% girls," says Fayzah al-Kharafi, a chemistry professor at Kuwait University. Al-Kharafi, 57, knows how education can break down barriers. A trailblazer in Arab higher education, she has racked up impressive firsts at K.U.—first woman to get a scientific Ph.D. there; first female science professor; and, in 1993, first woman to lead an Arab-world university when she was named president. She gave up that job in 2002 because she missed the classroom, where she says she can have a bigger role in pushing students to pursue academic excellence. "Education is the bones of the body," she says. "We cannot live without it. It gives more opportunities. Women are prepared for all jobs in society."

But once they have diplomas, can they get those jobs? In Saudi Arabia, women make up 55% of undergraduates, but only 15% of the labor force. Those who venture beyond traditional working-women's sectors like health care and education are greeted by male

skepticism. Architect Nadia Bakhurji recalls how hard it was to win funding for her Riyadh firm. Men doubted her trustworthiness, purely due to her gender. "One man said, 'Don't you have a husband? A male figure we can deal with? Between you and me, what if we don't get our money back?'" she says. "They don't have as much faith in you because you're a woman." She pressed on, thinking of her mother, who wed at 14 and never realized her dream of entering politics. "The best she could do was to concentrate on her children," Bakhurji says. "She boosted me. She told me, 'You're a star.'" Her persistence paid off in 1996, when she won the backing of billionaire investor Prince Alwaleed bin Talal bin Abdulaziz al Saud. His willingness to bet on a businesswoman shows an openness that Bakhurji, 36, hopes will soon be the norm. Her generation "will have a knock-on effect" on her son's, she says. "The next generation is going to be far more accustomed to seeing their mothers as work-oriented and high achievers." 1

Getting the Message Out

Role models matter, agrees Nawal El Moutawakel, who was the only woman on Morocco's Olympic team in 1984, when she won the 400-meter hurdles and became the first Arab woman to strike Games gold. Now an International Olympic Committee member, she notes that "it's becoming something very usual" for Arab women to have a medal-winning presence in the male-dominated sports world. El Moutawakel, 41, says her success—and that of athletes who have followed her—has opened

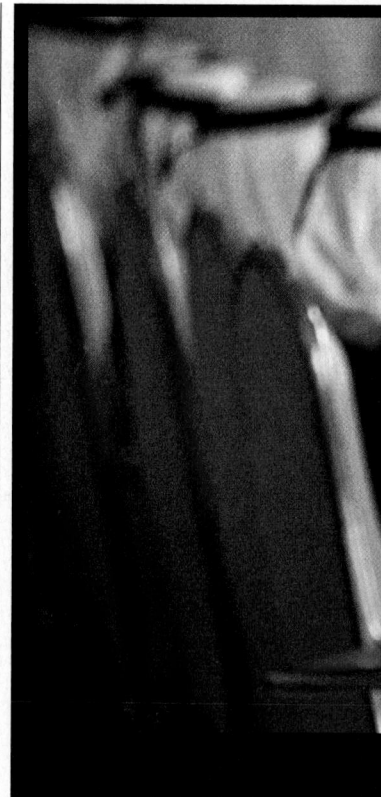

> **"We need to teach people that they can speak out, that they have a choice."**
>
> —ASSILAH AL HARTHY, executive, Oman's national oil firm

Assessment Practice

 Practice Short Response Questions

Point out that short-response questions often do not have just one correct answer. Stress that an answer to a short response question is generally judged by its insightfulness and the quality of textual evidence

included. **Write on the board:** Give two examples of how Muslim feminists are using media. Write your answers using 3 to 5 lines for each. (the films of Inas El Degheidi; Diana Moukalled is editor of Future TV's international news.)

ROYAL PREROGATIVE **Mouza** has used her power to transform education in Qatar. ★

Barry Iverson

TIME

Teach

doors and minds even for those who will never set foot on an Olympic track. She points to the Run for Fun, a 10-km race she organizes in Casablanca each May, as one symbol of the larger public space now becoming available to women. In 2003, 12,000 women— "all sizes, all ages, all dress codes, Olympic champions, members of parliament, grandmothers"—took part. "We don't exclude men; they come to help," says El Moutawakel, laughing. "But I want to push for women to understand the importance of participation."

It's not always easy to get that message to the ordinary citizen, especially when women have not had a real voice in society for so many generations. Says Assilah al-Harthy, the first female executive with Oman's national oil firm: "We need to teach people that they can speak out, that they have a choice. People may not understand the first time or the second time, but they will start asking, 'Why, where, when?'"

2 It helps if they hear others speaking out. The Arab media— more influential than ever, due in part to the growing use of satellite dishes, jokingly called the national flower in several countries—has broadened debate through the work of journalists such as Diana Moukalled. She is the editor of Lebanon-based Future TV's international news, and the Arab world's only female roving reporter. "The media has a great role to play in putting the spotlight on issues, providing a platform for women, and educating people," says Moukalled, 33, producer of about 30 hour-long documentaries. Her work is sometimes shelved; pro-Saddam Hussein sentiments in the region killed a show about Iraq's Kurds, made before the Iraq war started in 2003. "We all know there is censorship," she says. "But so many have made it on air,

RAISING THEIR VOICES   **711**

After You Read

Assess

1. Summaries will vary but should include the main ideas and most important details from the article.

2. Students may be surprised to learn about these differences.

3. (a) Marital infidelity and a legal system that is tougher on women than on men (b) They are challenging the conservatism and sexism in Arabic society.

4. (a) She has received death threats. (b) Still hostile to women who step out of their traditional roles

5. (a) Sheika Sabeeka, the wife of the king of Bahrain, led a campaign to encourage women to vote. (b) King Mohammed VI of Morocco gave his wife the title of "Princess" and has spoken out in favor of women's rights; President Hosni Mubarak of Egypt has ruled that children born to Egyptian mothers would be considered Egyptian; Saudi investor Prince Alwaleed bin Talal bin Abdulaziz al Saud decided to back business-woman Nadia Bakhurji.

6. (a) She does not want to adopt Western culture. (b) Western feminism has advanced to a greater degree and Arabic women are still struggling for basic rights.

7. (a) Women comprise 55 percent of undergraduates but only 15 percent of the work force. (b) Discrimination in hiring

8. (a) She produces documentaries that give women a platform. (b) Censorship exists, causing her documentaries to be shelved sometimes.

stirring discussions about important issues."

That women are viewing, reading, and talking is itself progress. "The lives of Arab women are still not what they should be," Moukalled says, "[but] things are moving forward." Calls for change are getting louder. In January 2004, 300 Saudi women signed a petition to Saudi Arabia's Crown Prince demanding reform, including more women in government and the relaxation of restrictions on their daily lives. Though the petition was mostly ignored by the country's rulers, the petition was a big step.

The changes may not be fast or radical by Western standards. But the women of the Arab world respond: We are not in the West. "We've always heard from the West, 'Broaden your horizons!' And we have," says Sheika Hanadi al-Thani, who heads an investment company for women in Qatar. "Now it's time for us to tell the West, 'You think outside your box.' Be patient, be more understanding of the context." "We are moving in the right direction," says al-Harthy. "But we can't go too fast. Change is not easy to take."

It's easier when many move together—a theme in El Degheidi's film. *Women in Search of Freedom* focuses on three women from different Arab lands who find themselves in a foreign country and seek strength from each other. The journey of today's Arab women is much the same. Some may be conservative, others more liberal, but as they progress, venturing into territory that's foreign to many in their society, they'll need unity to succeed. El Degheidi, for one, is sure who will succeed. "Don't be afraid to break barriers," she says to her Arab sisters. "You will be the winner in the end."

Respond and Think Critically

Respond and Interpret

1. Write a brief summary of the main ideas in this article before you answer the following questions. For help with writing a summary, see page 435.

2. How did you respond to the differences in gender equality in Arab society?

3. (a) What problems in Arab society does filmmaker Inas El Degheidi attempt to bring out into the open? (b) What is different about the new generation of Arab women?

4. (a) What response has El Degheidi's work received? (b) What does this imply about the attitude that some people in Arab societies have toward feminists and women's issues?

5. (a) What is one example of an attempt by an Arab leader's wife to effect change in society and politics? (b) Name three male Arab leaders mentioned in the article who are sympathetic to women's rights. What have they done to improve the status of women?

Analyze and Evaluate

6. (a) Why does Nadia Yassine say her feminism is "from Islam, not Western culture"? (b) How might Islamic feminism differ from Western feminism?

7. (a) What is the ratio of women undergraduates to women in the labor force in Saudi Arabia? (b) What might account for this discrepancy?

8. (a) How has the journalist Diana Moukalled used the media to call attention to the fight for women's rights? (b) How does censorship affect her work?

Connect

9. How does the role of women in late-eighteenth-century English society compare with the role of women in Arab societies today?

9. Arranged marriages, the lack of voting rights, and limited career opportunities for women in late eighteenth-century English society created obstacles similar to those faced by women in Arabic societies today.

 For additional assessment, see Assessment Resources, pp. 179–180.

Grammar Workshop

Dangling Modifiers

Literature Connection In Jeff Chu's summary of advances in the Arab women's movement, a verbal phrase adds information to his conclusion.

> *"Some may be conservative, others more liberal, but as they progress, venturing into territory that's foreign to many in their society, they'll need unity to succeed."*

> —Jeff Chu, from "Raising Their Voices"

The modifier *venturing into territory that's foreign to many in their society* adds information about progress being made. The connection between the modifier and its referent, *they,* is clear. To use a modifier that has no clear referent—a **dangling modifier**—would confuse readers.

Problem	**Dangling modifier**
	Based on this article, I can see dramatic changes in Arab society.
	Based on this article has no referent. It modifies, or is connected to, no word or phrase in the sentence. *Question:* What is based on this article? *Answer:* Nothing.
Solution 1	**Change the participle to a preposition.**
	From this article, I can see dramatic changes in Arab society.
Solution 2	**Make the phrase part of the main clause.**
	My seeing dramatic changes in Arab society is based on this article.
Solution 3	**Rewrite the sentence to make the referent clear.**
	Since reading this article, I can see dramatic changes in Arab society.

Revise Rewrite the following sentences to correct any dangling modifiers. If a sentence needs no revision, write *correct*.

1. Hanging on every word, the lecture was clearly well accepted.
2. Her hair tucked under a scarf, she hardly fits the image of a feminist.
3. What is your opinion of the issue, judging by the article?
4. Expanding women's rights, the audience showed little enthusiasm.

Learning Objectives

In this workshop, you will focus on the following objectives:

Grammar:
Understanding how to correct dangling modifiers. Understanding how to use commas with introductory phrases and clauses.

Dangling Modifiers

A **dangling modifier** is one that has no referent; it does not logically modify any word in the sentence.

Tip

To avoid dangling modifiers, think about the meaning. Make sure each phrase modifies a word close to it.

Commas with Introductory Phrases

A comma should be used to set off an introductory participial phrase from the rest of the sentence. The punctuation will help to prevent misreading.

 Literature Online

Grammar For more grammar practice, go to glencoe.com and enter QuickPass code GLB9817u4.

GRAMMAR WORKSHOP **713**

Focus

Write this sentence on the board: Running out of the room, the dishes in the cabinet rattled. Discuss why this sentence is confusing.

Remind students that the sequence of words in a sentence determines the meaning of the sentence.

Teach

Dangling Modifiers

A dangling modifier is a phrase that does not modify a specific element in a sentence or that modifies an unintended element. It is sometimes a participial phrase that contains a participle and any modifiers necessary to complete its meaning.

Assess

Possible answers:

1. Hanging on every word, the audience clearly showed that the lecture was well accepted.
2. Correct.
3. Correct.
4. The audience showed little enthusiasm for expanding women's rights.

 For additional grammar practice, see Unit 4 Teaching Resources Book, p. 65.

Approaching Level

DIFFERENTIATED INSTRUCTION

Established Misplaced and dangling modifiers often create confusion and factual errors in newspaper headlines. Have students look through a newspaper for headlines that are ambiguous.
Examples:

- Frightened Horse Injures Rancher with Shotgun

- Workers Refuse to Return to Work after Death

- High School Sweethearts Reunite after Twenty Years at Supermarket

Ask students to share their examples with the class. Ask volunteers to explain how the misplaced or dangling modifier changes the meaning of each sentence.

713

Before You Read

Focus

Bellringer Options

Selection Focus Transparency 35

Daily Language Practice Transparency 57

Or **ask:** What do we usually mean when we say someone is innocent? *(free of guilt)* What signs or symbols suggest innocence? *(Answers will vary. Some may suggest lambs or infant children.)* Point out that innocence was a major theme in the poetry of William Blake, and encourage students to keep this idea in mind as they read his works.

Before You Read

Blake's Poetry

Meet **William Blake**
(1757–1827)

Poet, artist, and mystic—William Blake was not content with the prevailing neoclassical values of his day. His interest in the supernatural and his imaginative experimentation classify him as pre-Romantic. Blake was defiantly unique, and some of his contemporaries considered him insane. As William Wordsworth said of the unworldly Blake, "There is something in the madness of this man which interests me more than the sanity of Lord Byron and Walter Scott."

> *"Poetry fettered fetters the human race. Nations are destroyed, or flourish, in proportion as their poetry, painting, and music are destroyed or flourish!"*
>
> —William Blake

Strange and Humble Beginnings Blake grew up in London, surrounded by the grit and poverty of the new industrial age. From early childhood, Blake spoke of having religious visions of angels and prophets; these visions would continue throughout his life. When, at age ten, he expressed a desire to become a painter, his parents sent him to a drawing school. At the age of fifteen, Blake was apprenticed to an engraver—an artisan who cuts or carves designs into wood blocks or metal sheets from which prints can be made.

When he was twenty-five, Blake married Catherine Boucher, an uneducated woman whom he later taught to read and trained as an engraver. She accepted his eccentric lifestyle and intense spirituality.

"I have very little of Mr. Blake's time," she once told a friend, light-heartedly. "He is always in Paradise." The couple was befriended by a group of progressive artists who admired Blake's fervent imagination and helped him publish his first book of poems when he was twenty-six. Soon after, Blake started his own print shop, taking his younger brother, Richard, as his apprentice.

A Creative Fervor The late 1780s and early 1790s found Blake at the peak of his creative powers. He discovered a new method of relief etching on copperplates, which he called "illuminated printing." Blake, with the help of Catherine, used this technique to beautifully illustrate and hand-paint nearly all of his books. Unfortunately, this method was so complex and time-consuming that relatively few copies of his work were produced; the surviving originals are ranked among the art treasures of the world. In 1794 Blake published a volume of lyric poems called *Songs of Innocence and Experience*. Blake described this work as "shewing the two contrary states of the human soul." As he grew older, Blake became more and more caught up in his mystical faith and visions of a heavenly world. His later work demonstrates his ever-deepening reflections on God, humankind, and the power of the imagination. As he famously wrote, "If the doors of perception were cleansed every thing would appear to man as it is, infinite."

LOG ON ▶ **Literature** Online

Author Search For more about William Blake, go to glencoe.com and enter QuickPass code GLB9817u4.

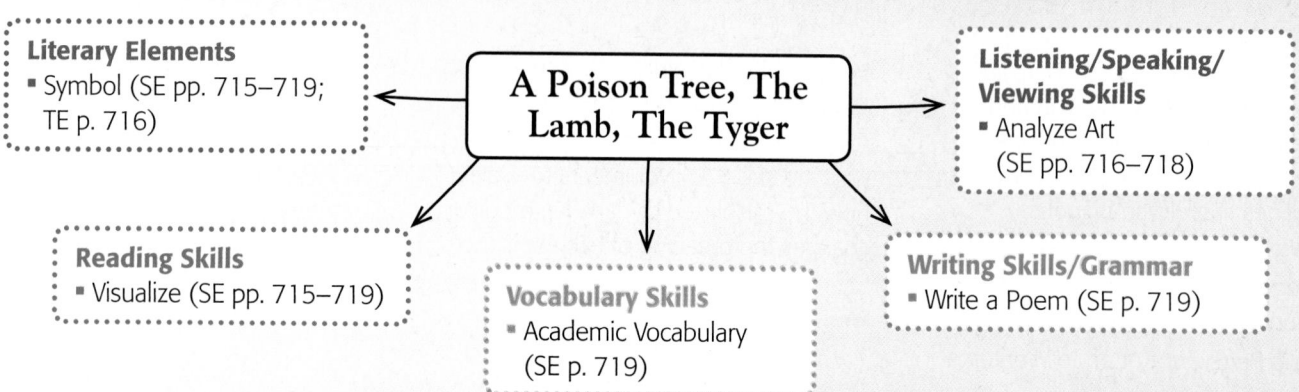

Literary Elements
- Symbol (SE pp. 715–719; TE p. 716)

A Poison Tree, The Lamb, The Tyger

Listening/Speaking/ Viewing Skills
- Analyze Art (SE pp. 716–718)

Reading Skills
- Visualize (SE pp. 715–719)

Vocabulary Skills
- Academic Vocabulary (SE p. 719)

Writing Skills/Grammar
- Write a Poem (SE p. 719)

Literature and Reading Preview

Connect to the Poems

Are there drawbacks to innocence? to knowledge? Write a journal entry about a time when you had to change your old perception of the world.

Build Background

Blake first wrote *Songs of Innocence* and then added *Songs of Experience* as a counterpoint and complement. Subsequently, both volumes were published as one book. As these titles suggest, Blake views the universe in contrasts. The poems in *Songs of Innocence* examine good, passivity, and reason; those in the companion volume explore evil, violence, and emotion.

Set Purposes for Reading

Big Idea The Stirrings of Romanticism

As you read, ask yourself, How does Blake favor imagination over deductive reasoning?

Literary Element Symbol

A **symbol** is a person, an animal, a place, an object, or an event within a text that exists on a literal level but also represents something on a figurative level. A symbol may have multiple layers of meanings or associations. The meaning of any symbol is determined by its textual surroundings. As you read, ask yourself, What else might this detail represent?

Reading Strategy Visualize

To **visualize** is to use your imagination to form pictures of settings, characters, and action. To help youself visualize, pay close attention to sensory details and descriptions, along with your responses to them. As you read these poems, ask yourself, How are my visualizations similar to or different from Blake's own engraved illustrations of his poems?

....

Tip: Comparing and Contrasting Use Venn diagrams like the one below to compare the images, colors, and sensory details of your visualizations with those in Blake's engravings.

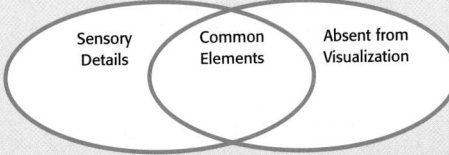
Sensory Details — Common Elements — Absent from Visualization

Learning Objectives

For pages 714–724

In studying these texts, you will focus on the following objectives:

Literary Study:
Analyzing symbol.
Analyzing stanza.

Reading:
Visualizing.
Analyzing historical context.

Writing: Writing a poem.

Child laborers at the Alioin towel mill, England.

Before You Read

Focus

Summary

William Blake was a visionary who wrote poems that ring with an intensely personal mysticism. In "A Poison Tree," the speaker nurtures his wrath against a foe, and it grows into a tree bearing evil fruit. In "The Lamb," the speaker portrays the lamb as a symbol of innocence and goodness. In "The Tyger," the speaker ponders the forces that created evil in the world.

> For summaries in languages other than English, see Unit 4 Teaching Resources Book, pp. 66–71.

Approaching Level

DIFFERENTIATED INSTRUCTION

Established Have students narrate a sequence of events in which they gained knowledge through lost innocence.
Ask: What did you know at the beginning? What did you know while you were learning? What did you know at the end once you had learned something new? *(Answers will vary.)*

Teach

Symbol **Answer:** *The reference is to a poisoned tree that symbolizes the speaker's hidden anger.*

(APPROACHING) Have approaching-level students write a paragraph identifying and describing how "A Poison Tree" explores a loss of innocence as in Genesis.

| Literary Element | 2 |

Symbol **Answer:** *The apple, the tree, and the garden allude to the Garden of Eden and the origin of Original Sin, when Adam and Eve partook of the forbidden fruit.*

View the Art ★

Possible answer: *Blake might have meant for this image to call attention to the effects of the "poison tree," since it shows the "foe outstretched."*

 For an audio recording of this selection, use Listening Library Audio CD-ROM.

A Poison Tree, Plate 49 from *Songs of Innocence and Experience*. c. 1815–1826. William Blake. Etching, ink, and watercolor. Fitzwilliam Museum, University of Cambridge.

View the Art This page comes from the *Songs of Experience* and was painted by Blake himself. Why might he have chosen this image to accompany the poem? ★

A Poison Tree

William Blake

I was angry with my friend;
I told my wrath, my wrath did end.
I was angry with my foe;
I told it not, my wrath did grow.

5 And I watered it in fears,
Night and morning with my tears;
And I sunnèd[1] it with smiles,
And with soft deceitful wiles.

And it grew both day and night,
10 Till it bore an apple bright.
And my foe beheld it shine,
And he knew that it was mine,

And into my garden stole
When the night had veiled the pole;[2]
15 In the morning glad I see
My foe outstretched beneath the tree.

---

1. The accent on the *e* shows that the word *sunnèd* is pronounced as two syllables.
2. *Pole* means "sky" or "heavens."

1 Symbol *What symbol is alluded to in this line?*

2 Symbol *How are the poison tree and the apple connected?*

Literary Element Practice

SPIRAL REVIEW **Identify Symbols** Remind students that the symbols in Blake's poems exist on both literal and figurative levels. Have students create a chart to list the poems' symbols and their meanings.

Have them list the symbols in the left column and their meaning, or meanings, in the right column. Remind students to look for textual clues in Blake's poems to determine the meanings of the symbols.

| Symbol | ⟶ | Meanings |

The Lamb

William Blake

The Shepherd, 1789. William Blake. Etching, ink, and watercolor. The Huntington Library, Art Collections, and Botanical Gardens, San Marino, CA.

View the Art Note that this image contains a different poem, also from *Songs of Innocence*. Does this image convey a similar mood to that of Blake's poem "The Lamb"? Explain why or why not. ★

Little Lamb, who made thee?
 Dost thou know who made thee?
Gave thee life and bid thee feed
By the stream and o'er the mead;[1]
5 Gave thee clothing of delight,
Softest clothing, woolly bright;
Gave thee such a tender voice,
Making all the vales rejoice!
 Little Lamb, who made thee?
10 Dost thou know who made thee?

 Little Lamb, I'll tell thee,
 Little Lamb, I'll tell thee!
He[2] is callèd by thy name,
For he calls himself a Lamb.
15 He is meek and he is mild;
He became a little child.
I a child and thou a lamb,
We are callèd by his name.
 Little Lamb, God bless thee!
20 Little Lamb, God bless thee!

---

1. Here, *mead* means "meadow."
2. *He* refers to Jesus Christ.

Visualize *How do you picture this scene? Do you see it as calm or as turbulent?* **3**

Teach

Reading Strategy 3

Visualize **Answer:** *Most students are likely to see calmness in the stream, serene landscape, and peaceably grazing sheep.*

(APPROACHING) To help approaching-level students visualize the setting of "The Lamb," have them choose adjectives to describe it.
Ask: What adjectives do you associate with "The Lamb"? *(calm, peaceful, serene, pastoral, agricultural)*

> For additional practice using the reading skill or strategy, see Unit 4 Teaching Resources Book, p. 73.

View the Art ★

Possible answers: *Most students will say the image creates much the same mood as Blake's poem, since it looks peaceful and pastoral, and is full of lambs. Some students may say that the shepherd seems to be the focus of the image, whereas the lamb itself is the focus of Blake's poem.*

The idyllic setting and simple images, combined with the words of the poem, convey Blake's vision of an idealized, pastoral England that existed before the ravages of the Industrial Revolution.

English Learners

DIFFERENTIATED INSTRUCTION

Intermediate Discuss the lamb's symbolism. **Ask** Can anyone think of an animal that is used as a symbol in American culture? Think of images that appear on public buildings, on money, or on official documents. *(The eagle is the most common animal symbol, representing the strength and nobility of the United States.)* Discuss other animals used symbolically in advertisements or by corporations. *(Examples: the lion, used by a film company; the bull, used by a financial management company)* Ask students from other cultures for parallel instances or different interpretations of animal symbolism in other parts of the world.

Teach

Reading Strategy · 1

Visualize **Answer:** *The tiger gives off a bright but sinister light in the dark forests of the night. It is both attractive and menacing.*

[ENGLISH LEARNERS] Have English learners rewrite the first and second stanzas of "The Tyger" using familiar words and traditional spellings.

Big Idea · 2

The Stirrings of Romanticism Answer: *The image of the anvil, like the hammer, chain, and furnace in stanza 4, associates the tiger with the "deadly terrors" of factories and mechanization. Blake felt that industrialization was a powerful threat both to individuals and to the pastoral English ideal.*

View the Art ★

Possible answers: *Most students will say that Blake's depiction of a tiger—"fearful symmetry," "burning bright," "sinews of thy heart"—is much darker and more fierce than the image of a tiger that accompanies it. They may also note that the forest is painted much brighter and calmer than the "forests of the night" described in the poem.*

Progress Check

Can students interpret symbol?

If No → See Unit 4 Teaching Resources Book, p. 72.

 To check students' understanding of the selection, see Unit 4 Teaching Resources Book, p. 74.

718

The Tyger, 1794–1795. William Blake. Etching, ink, and watercolor. The Huntington Library, Art Collections, and Botanical Gardens, San Marino, CA.

<u>View the Art</u> Blake painted the page for "The Tyger" himself. How does the illustration compare to Blake's description? ★

Tyger! Tyger! burning bright
In the forests of the night,
What immortal hand or eye
Could frame thy fearful symmetry?[1]

5   In what distant deeps[2] or skies
Burnt the fire of thine eyes?
On what wings dare he aspire?
What the hand dare seize the fire?

And what shoulder, and what art,
10   Could twist the sinews of thy heart?
And when thy heart began to beat,
What dread hand? and what dread feet?

What the hammer? what the chain?
In what furnace was thy brain?
15   What the anvil? what dread grasp
Dare its deadly terrors clasp?

When the stars threw down their spears
And watered heaven with their tears,
Did he smile his work to see?
20   Did he who made the Lamb make thee?

Tyger! Tyger! burning bright
In the forests of the night,
What immortal hand or eye
Dare frame thy fearful symmetry?

The Tyger

William Blake

---

1. In this context, *symmetry* means "well-proportioned form."
2. *Deeps* means "ocean" or "abyss."

Visualize *How does the description in the first four lines create a striking image?* **1**

The Stirrings of Romanticism *How do these lines reflect Blake's concerns about the industrialization of society?* **2**

Vocabulary Practice

Multiple-Meaning Words Direct attention to the word *frame,* in line 4. Ask a volunteer to look it up in a standard dictionary and read out the definitions. Focus on the fact that *frame* could mean either "to enclose," as in framing a picture, or "to build," as in framing a house. Explain that this technique of using two or more meanings of a word simultaneously is called **ambiguity**. Discuss how it enriches the possible meanings of the poem.

Have students repeat this process with the word *art* in line 9. Encourage a range of interpretations.

After You Read

Respond and Think Critically

Respond and Interpret

1. (a)Briefly summarize what happens to the speaker's anger with a friend and a foe in "A Poison Tree." (b)Why, in your opinion, does the speaker deal with his anger in this way?

2. (a)According to the speaker, what three things has the lamb been given? (c)What do these lines reveal about the speaker's attitude toward the lamb?

3. (a)In "The Tyger," what question does the speaker ask in lines 1–5 and in lines 21–24? How do these questions differ? (b)From these questions, what can you infer about the speaker's attitude toward the tiger?

Analyze and Evaluate

4. (a)At the end of "A Poison Tree," how does the speaker feel? (b)Do you think it is appropriate for the speaker to feel this way? Explain.

5. (a)How is "The Tyger" similar to "The Lamb"? How are the poems different? (b)What is gained by reading these poems together?

Connect

6. **Big Idea** **The Stirrings of Romanticism** How do these poems embody a shift toward imagination and individualism?

7. **Connect to the Author** Blake was strongly influenced by religion and spirituality. How does this influence come out in his poetry?

Literary Element Symbol

One key to understanding **symbols** is to think associatively. In Blake's poems, note how imagery and tone are used to narrow and eliminate some associations in order to specifically define the symbols.

1. (a)What ideas do you associate with a tree and an apple? (b)In "A Poison Tree," what do you think the apple and the tree symbolize?

2. (a)What ideas or characteristics do you associate with a lamb and a tiger? (b)What do you think the lamb and the tiger symbolize?

Writing

Write a Poem Using Blake's poems as a model, write a poem in which you use a symbol or symbols as a way of expressing a deeper message. Before you begin, you may wish to brainstorm about some commonly symbolic items—for example, the dawn often symbolizes birth or youth, while sunsets symbolize old age or death.

> **LOG ON** **Literature** Online
>
> **Selection Resources** For Selection Quizzes, eFlashcards, and Reading-Writing Connection activities, go to glencoe.com and enter QuickPass code GLB9817u4.

Reading Strategy Visualize

Visualizing may help you comprehend the actions or mannerisms of a character and a speaker's attitude toward what he or she is describing.

1. Which images or actions were easiest to visualize in "A Poison Tree"? Explain.

2. What images from "The Tyger" helped you understand the speaker's attitude?

> **Academic Vocabulary**
>
> *Blake's message is **implicit**: it is clear although he does not state it outright.*
>
> *Implicit* is an academic word often used in literary criticism. The meaning of "A Poison Tree" is **implicit**—the poet does not state it directly.
>
> Use context clues to figure out the meaning of the word *implicit* in the italicized sentence above. Use a dictionary to check your guess.
>
> *For more on academic vocabulary, see pages 56 and R81.*

WILLIAM BLAKE **719**

Writing

Students' poems should use a symbol in order to express a greater theme or message. You may wish to hold a brief class discussion on what makes a symbol before students begin to write.

Reading Strategy

1. Students may mention the "apple bright," the tree, or the slain foe.

2. Students may mention the stars throwing down their spears and watering heaven with their tears.

Academic Vocabulary

Implicit means "implied or indirectly stated."

After You Read

Assess

1. (a) Revealing his feelings to a friend releases his anger; hiding his feelings from a foe deepens it. (b) The speaker may trust his friend, but not his foe, to be understanding.

2. (a) Life, clothing, and a tender voice (b) The speaker is caring.

3. (a) He wonders who could have created the tiger. *Dare* replaces *could* in line 24. (b) The speaker respects the tiger's magnificence but is afraid of its savage power.

4. (a) "Glad" (b) It is normal to feel glad when an enemy disappears.

5. (a) They both ask the same basic question: Who made you? The power that made the lamb was benevolent, but the one that fashioned the tiger was sinister. (b) The contrasts help the reader better understand their meanings.

6. Each appeals to the reader's feelings, and each involves an element of mystery.

7. Answers will vary but students should note Blake's frequent references to a creator in his poetry, and the use of Biblical references.

Literary Element

1. (a) The Garden of Eden. (b) The speaker's anger

2. (a) Lambs with gentleness and tigers with violence (b) The lamb is the innocence of children; the tiger is the rapacious nature of adults.

719

Before You Read

Focus

Bellringer Options

Daily Language Practice Transparency 117

Or **ask:** How do you think the Industrial Revolution changed England during Blake's time? Explain that with the advent of the steam engine, the cotton gin, and other inventions, the factory system emerged. London became an industrial center with no laws to protect workers, women, or children.

Teach

Reading Strategy | 1

Analyze Historical Context
Answer: *The faces' "weakness" and "woe" evoke a scene of hope-lessness and death.*

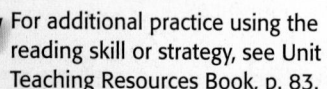
For additional practice using the reading skill or strategy, see Unit 4 Teaching Resources Book, p. 83.

Selection Skills

Before You Read

Literary Element Stanza

A **stanza** is a group of lines forming a unit in a poem. A stanza in a poem is similar to a paragraph in prose. Some of the most common types of stanzas are the couplet, or two-line stanza; the tercet, which has three lines; and the quatrain, which has four. As you read these poems, note how Blake uses the quatrain and the natural breaks at the end of stanzas to transition from one concept or thought to another.

Reading Strategy Analyze Historical Context

Analyzing historical context involves gathering background information and exploring social forces that influenced the writing of a literary work. As you read these poems, use your background knowledge of the Industrial Revolution to better understand the context in which these poems were written.

LONDON

William Blake

I wander thro' each charter'd° street,
Near where the charter'd Thames does flow,
And mark in every face I meet
Marks of weakness, marks of woe.

5 In every cry of every Man,
In every Infant's cry of fear,
In every voice, in every ban,°
The mind-forg'd manacles° I hear.

How the Chimney-sweeper's cry
10 Every black'ning Church appalls;
And the hapless° Soldier's sigh
Runs in blood down Palace walls.

But most thro' midnight streets I hear
How the youthful Harlot's° curse
15 Blasts the new born Infant's tear,
And blights with plagues the Marriage hearse.

1 charter'd: here, the meaning is "controlled."

7 ban: a legal prohibition, a public curse, or a marriage announcement.
8 manacles: shackles.

11 hapless: unfortunate; deserving pity.

14 Harlot's: prostitute's.

---

1 Analyze Historical Context *What does this suggest to you about the conditions in London at the time?*

720 UNIT 4   THE TRIUMPH OF ROMANTICISM

London, The Chimney Sweeper from *Songs of Innocence*, The Chimney Sweeper from *Songs of Experience*

Literary Elements
- Stanza (SE pp. 720–724)

Listening/Speaking/Viewing Skills
- Analyze Art (SE pp. 721, 722)

Reading Skills
- Analyze Historical Context (SE pp. 720–724)
- Analyze Theme (TE p. 722)

Vocabulary Skills
- Academic Vocabulary (SE p. 724)

Writing Skills/Grammar
- Expository Essay (SE p. 725)

720

THE CHIMNEY SWEEPER
from *Songs of Innocence*

William Blake

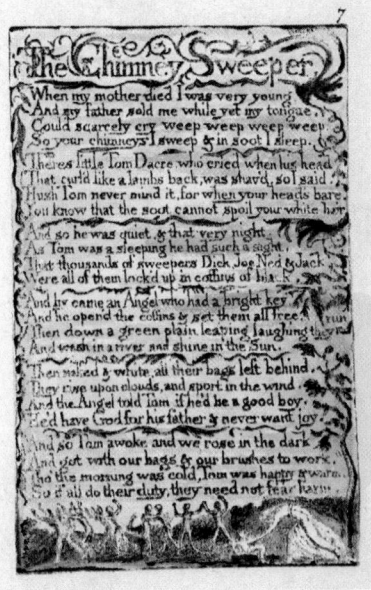

The Chimney Sweeper, plate 7 (Bentley 12) from *Songs of Innocence and of Experience* 1789–94. William Blake. Raised etching. Yale Center for British Art, Paul Mellon Collection, New Haven, CT.

View the Art Blake's *Songs of Innocence* addressed the rosy world view of an innocent child. Does this image suit the content and tone of Blake's poem? Explain why or why not. ★

When my mother died I was very young,
And my father sold me while yet my tongue
Could scarcely cry "'weep! 'weep! 'weep! 'weep!"[1]
So your chimneys I sweep, & in soot I sleep.

5   There's little Tom Dacre, who cried when his head,
That curl'd like a lamb's back, was shav'd: so I said
"Hush, Tom! never mind it, for when your head's bare
You know that the soot cannot spoil your white hair."

And so he was quiet, & that very night,
10 As Tom was a-sleeping, he had such a sight!—
That thousands of sweepers, Dick, Joe, Ned, & Jack,
Were all of them lock'd up in coffins of black.

And by came an Angel who had a bright key,
And he open'd the coffins & set them all free;
15 Then down a green plain leaping, laughing, they run,
And wash in a river, and shine in the Sun.

Then naked & white, all their bags left behind,
They rise upon clouds and sport in the wind;
And the Angel told Tom, if he'd be a good boy,
20 He'd have God for his father, & never want joy.

And so Tom awoke; and we rose in the dark,
And got with our bags & our brushes to work.
Tho' the morning was cold, Tom was happy & warm;
So if all do their duty they need not fear harm.

★ 1. "'Weep . . . 'weep" is the child's attempt to call out "Sweep!" as a chimney sweeper would.

Analyze Historical Context *Why does the speaker of the poem work as a chimney sweeper?* `2`

The Stirrings of Romanticism *What role does the imagination play in these lines?* `3`

WILLIAM BLAKE **721**

Teach

Reading Strategy `2`

Analyze Historical Context
Answer: *His father sold him while he was still very young (lines 2–3). Explain that such was the poverty in London that thousands of little boys were sold off by parents (here a widower) unable to support them.*

Say: After many years, largely in response to the writings of Blake and Dickens, Parliament passed child-protection laws that ended such practices.

Big Idea `3`

The Stirrings of Romanticism
Answer: *In their dreams, the soot-blackened little boys "wash in a river," leave their tools ("bags") behind, and ascend into heaven.*

(ENGLISH LEARNERS) Have English learners read lines 17–18 again, stopping at each comma. **Ask:** What details do you see in your imagination? *(Student responses will vary but may include the warm sun, shouts of joy, blue sky, and soft breezes.)*

View the Art ★
Possible answer: *Yes, the calligraphy and swirling art seems whimsical and childlike.*

English Learners
DIFFERENTIATED INSTRUCTION

Intermediate Have students create a two-column chart with heads "Happy Images" and "Sad Images." Ask English learners to read the poem and find words or phrases that are happy and sad and put them in the appropriate column. Words like *died, cry, coffins,* and *black* should go under "Sad Images." *Angel, bright, free* and *laughing* should go under "Happy Images." **Ask:** Which column shows what the chimney sweepers really feel? Have students write sentences that describe the sweepers' true feelings.

Teach

Reading Strategy   1

Analyze Historical Context

Answer: *He mentions the church ("God & his Priest") and the crown ("& King"). The speaker views them both as oppressive forces "who make up a heaven of our misery."*

Explain that Blake is criticizing the church's compliance with the social injustices wrought by the government, such as the unrestricted use of children as a source of unpaid, unprotected labor.

(APPROACHING) For approaching-level students, **ask:** What word choices does the speaker make in the first two lines to emphasize the misery of the chimney sweeper? *(little, crying, weep, woe)* What word choices does the speaker make in the last stanza to emphasize the hypocrisy of societal institutions? *(praise God & his Priest & King, heaven of our misery)*

View the Art ★

Answer: *This image gives a harsher depiction of life for a chimney sweeper, while the image on page 721 is more whimsical and innocent. This image matches better with experience; the other image matches better with innocence.*

To check students' understanding of the selection, see Unit 4 Teaching Resources Book, p. 84.

THE CHIMNEY SWEEPER
from *Songs of Experience*

William Blake

A little black thing among the snow,
Crying "'weep! 'weep!" in notes of woe!
"Where are thy father & mother? say?"
"They are both gone up to the church to pray.

5   "Because I was happy upon the heath,
And smil'd among the winter's snow,
They clothed me in the clothes of death,
And taught me to sing the notes of woe.

"And because I am happy & dance & sing,
10   They think they have done me no injury,
And are gone to praise God & his Priest & King,
Who make up a heaven of our misery."

---

1   Analyze Historical Context *What social institutions is the speaker commenting upon in these lines? How does the speaker view these institutions?*

The Chimney Sweeper, Plate 37 from *Songs of Innocence and of Experience,* c. 1815–26. William Blake. Etching, ink and watercolor. Fitzwilliam Museum, University of Cambridge, England.

View the Art *Songs of Experience* was meant to stand in contrast to *Songs of Innocence.* In what ways does this image contrast with the illustration on page 721? Explain. ★

Reading Practice

SPIRAL REVIEW **Analyze Theme** The *Chimney Sweeper* analyzes child labor through a child who was sold to be a chimney sweeper. Have students summarize each stanza and identify the view of the child laborer using textual evidence. (Stanza 1 acknowledges that the child has been abandoned by his parents, stanza 2 grimly emphasizes that the child's parents sent him off to be a chimney sweeper with the line "they clothed me in clothes of death", stanza 3 mentions that the parents go on with their regular routines and that heaven is seen as made up of misery.)

After You Read

Respond and Think Critically

Respond and Interpret

1. (a)What does the speaker in "London" claim to hear in "every voice, in every ban"? (b)What specific people does the speaker mention?

2. (a)At the end of "The Chimney Sweeper" from *Songs of Innocence*, why is Tom "happy"? (b)What is the message of this poem?

3. (a)In "The Chimney Sweeper" from *Songs of Experience*, how is the child clothed and what is the child taught to sing? (b)What does this imply about innocence?

Analyze and Evaluate

4. (a)In the last stanza of "London," what effect does the "youthful Harlot's curse" have on the newborn child? (b)What does this symbolize?

5. (a)In "The Chimney Sweeper" from *Songs of Innocence*, what two settings are contrasted? (b)In "The Chimney Sweeper" from *Songs of Experience*, what is the predominant setting? (c)What do the settings of both poems suggest about the relationship between youth and experience?

Connect

6. **Big Idea** The Stirrings of Romanticism What elements of Romanticism are most evident in these poems? Explain.

7. **Connect to Today** Are people in modern society as concerned with the idea of "innocence" as some were in Blake's time? Explain, using examples from recent history or culture.

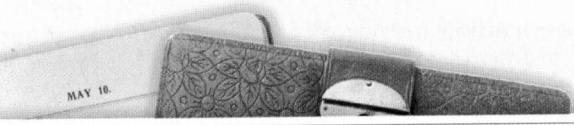

Daily Life & Culture

Chimney Sweeps and Child Labor

The Industrial Revolution in Great Britain during the middle part of the eighteenth century fundamentally altered familial and societal structures. New large-scale manufacturing techniques and tools required a large urban labor force. Tragically, children were regularly forced into dangerous, unhealthy, and cruel environments, for little or no pay. Like the chimney sweeps depicted in Blake's poems, these children were nearly always from poor families. In fact, many of them were orphans.

As a result of the alarming conditions in the factories, mines, and mills, an act was passed in 1833 that provided for the inspection of these

facilities. These inspections resulted in the Factory Act of 1847, which limited the number of hours children could work. Subsequent acts followed throughout the nineteenth century, as did greater interest in reforming societal ills. By the start of the twentieth century, child labor had all but vanished in Britain.

Group Activity Discuss these questions with a group of classmates.

1. Why might parents allow their children to be subjected to harsh factory conditions?

2. Does Blake's depiction of London seem accurate? Explain.

After You Read

Assess

1. (a) "Mind-forg'd manacles" (b) The chimney sweeper, the soldier, the prostitute, and the infant

2. (a) The angel told him that if he is "a good boy," he will go to heaven. (b) That earthly life is a living hell for children like Tom Dacre

3. (a) Clothed "in the clothes of death" and taught to sing "the notes of woe" (b) Innocence is a source of danger for children.

4. (a) Drowns out the Infant's cry (b) That innocence is withered by brutal experiences

5. (a) Urban reality and a dream world (b) The snowfilled heath (c) That youth and innocence must give way to experience

6. A preference for imagination and feeling, a concern for individual lives, the use of simple, everyday language, and the idea that modern, industrialized society has destroyed innocence

7. Answers will vary. Students should cite a recent historical or cultural development that illustrates modern society's attitude toward the idea of innocence.

Daily Life & Culture

1. Students might suggest that financial need forced the parents to subject their children to these conditions.

2. In leading this discussion, you might want to have volunteers look up encyclopedia articles on the Industrial Revolution in England, the factory system, the history of child labor, and other such topics.

After You Read

Assess

Literary Element

1. The first two stanzas introduce the setting and the fact that the speaker hears cries of woe; the last two describe the specific cries.

2. The speaker reveals that his father sold him into the trade; the speaker comforts Tom Dacre after his head is shaved; Tom dreams that the sweepers are locked in coffins; an angel releases the sweepers who clean themselves and frolic; the sweepers rise upon clouds, and Tom is promised heaven if he is good; Tom awakes and goes to work contented.

Review: Meter

In the first stanza of "London," the first three lines are written in iambic tetrameter; the fourth line is written in trochaic tetrameter with the final foot missing an unstressed syllable.

Progress Check

Can students interpret the use of a stanza?

If No → See Unit 4 Teaching Resources Book, p. 82.

Reading Strategy

1. London is filled with pain, fear, and misery.

2. Responses will vary. In "The Chimney Sweeper" from *Songs of Innocence,* the child speaker relates that Tom's head is shaved by his cruel overseer so it won't collect soot.

Literary Element Stanza

A **stanza** is a unified group of lines within a larger poem. A stanza serves a similar function to a paragraph in prose. Blake often writes in quatrains, which are one of the most commonly occurring stanzas in English lyric poetry. Think about how each quatrain forms a self-contained idea while simultaneously adding to the poem as a whole.

1. In "London," what is the connection between the first two stanzas and the last two stanzas?

2. Describe what happens in each stanza of "The Chimney Sweeper" from *Songs of Innocence.*

Review: Meter

As you learned on page 423, **meter** is the regular pattern of stressed and unstressed syllables that gives a line of poetry a predictable rhythm. The basic unit of meter is the **foot**. A foot usually contains one stressed syllable (marked ´) and one or more unstressed syllables (marked ˘).

Partner Activity Meet with another classmate and try to determine the meter in "London" and in both "Chimney Sweeper" poems. First, read each stanza aloud and try to figure out where the stresses fall. Remember that the meter of a poem is not always regular. Then, on a separate sheet of paper, rewrite the stanza, marking stressed and unstressed syllables. Finally, referring to your **scansion**, label the meter, using the appropriate terminology. For a list of terms used to describe the different types of meter, refer to the Literary Terms Handbook, page R10.

A View in Regent's Park in 1831, from *The Progress of Steam.* Henry Thomas Alken. City of Westminster Archive Centre, London.

Reading Strategy Analyze Historical Context

Writers are influenced by their environments, cultures, and experiences. Some writers, such as Blake, choose to overtly tackle the social issues and problems of their day. Often, in order to **analyze historical context,** you must bring your own knowledge of historical events to bear on a text. If you have trouble answering these questions, reread the biography on page 714 and Build Background on page 715, as well as the Unit Four introduction.

1. How does Blake characterize the urban environment of London?

2. Cite several instances from these poems that illustrate Blake's concern for the poor and destitute.

3. (a) According to the poems, how were children sometimes treated during this era? (b) Does this treatment differ from that in our own time? Explain.

Academic Vocabulary

In his poems, Blake describes the **widespread** *suffering of the lower classes.*

Widespread is an academic word. Words that are similar in meaning are *prevalent* and *common.*

To further explore the meaning of this word, answer the following question: Why were unhealthy working conditions such a **widespread** problem in Blake's time?

For more on academic vocabulary, see pages 56 and R81.

LOG ON ▶ **Literature** Online

Selection Resources For Selection Quizzes, eFlash-cards, and Reading-Writing Connection activities, go to glencoe.com and enter QuickPass code GLB9817u4.

---

3. (a) Children were sold into labor and mistreated.
   (b) Yes, child-labor laws make this type of institutionalized cruelty rare.

Academic Vocabulary

Conditions were widespread because many people were unemployed. Also, working conditions were not regulated by the government such as they are today.

Respond Through Writing

Expository Essay

Analyze Theme In his poems, William Blake depicts the harsh conditions of eighteenth-century England. Write a response to literature in which you analyze how the ambiguities and nuances of his theme are supported by stylistic devices such as diction, tone, repetition, and rhythm.

Understanding the Task Nuance refers to the subtle distinctions that distinguish and individualize a text. **Diction** is the unique choice of words that creates an author's recognizable voice. **Tone** is an author's attitude toward his or her subject. Elements such as word choice, sentence structure, figures of speech, and punctuation help create tone.

Prewrite First, reread the poems and state the themes in your own words. Then make a chart listing the stylistic elements you find. Identify each element—rhyme, rhythm, diction, or tone—and indicate how it helps support the subtleties and double meanings of Blake's theme.

Draft A good way to structure your essay is to begin by identifying the overall theme of the poems and discussing its layers of meaning, or complexities. Support your interpretation and explanations with quotations and other details from the text. Then focus on individual aspects of the theme, showing how each stylistic element helps convey that idea.

Blake's use of rhyme in these poems creates an inescapable pulse that helps readers actually feel the children's bondage and hopelessness. For example, the regular <u>abab</u> rhyme scheme in "London" mimics the repetitive rhythm of the young chimney sweepers' lives.

Use statements like the following to clarify the contribution of specific aspects of Blake's style:

The author uses _____, _____, and
_____ to represent _____.

Revise Skim Blake's poems once again, making sure you have accurately identified his style and interpreted his theme. Finally, review the Writing Workshop checklists on pages 852 and 972. Evaluate your essay on the basis of those checklists, making any necessary changes.

Edit and Proofread Proofread your paper, correcting any errors in spelling, grammar, and punctuation. Use the Grammar Tip in the side column to help you with in-text quotations.

> **Grammar Tip**
>
> **In-Text Quotations**
>
> When quoting a passage, enclose it in quotation marks, copying it exactly as it appears in the original. Use ellipses (. . .) to indicate omitted words or phrases and slashes (/) to indicate line breaks.
>
> *The lines "They clothed me in the clothes of death, / And taught me to sing the notes of woe" emphasize the sweepers' suffering.*

After You Read

Assess

Respond Through Writing

Students' expository essays should:

- analyze the ambiguities and nuances of the theme of harsh conditions in 18th-century England
- analyze Blake's stylistic devices and identify how these devices support the theme
- support interpretations and explanations with details from the text
- reflect accurate use of spelling, grammar, and punctuation

A student who meets all of these criteria should receive the equivalent of a 4-point response.

A student who fully meets two or partially meets three of these criteria should receive the equivalent of a 3-point response.

A student who fully meets one or partially meets two of these criteria should receive the equivalent of a 2-point response.

A student who partially meets one of these criteria should receive the equivalent of a 1-point response.

 For additional assessment, see Assessment Resources, pp. 183–184.

 To create custom assessments online, go to Progress Reporter Online Assessment.

 To create custom assessments using software, use ExamView Assessment Suite.

Before You Read

Focus

Before You Read

from *Pride and Prejudice*

Bellringer Options

**Daily Language Practice
Transparency 59**

Or have students discuss their favorite sitcoms and how they satirize the behavior of the characters. **Ask:** What human flaws, social customs, and attitudes do these shows mock? As they read, tell students to look for the ways in which Jane Austen uses humor to poke fun at her characters in this excerpt from her novel *Pride and Prejudice*.

Meet **Jane Austen**

(1775–1817)

A clergyman's daughter, Jane Austen never traveled beyond her middle-class circle of family and acquaintances, typical of England's villages. The lives of these small-town residents became the inspiration for Austen's most memorable works.

"3 or 4 families in a country village is the very thing to work on."

—Jane Austen, on novel writing

Family Life Jane Austen was born in 1775 to a minister, George Austen, and his wife, Cassandra. Although the Austens had a comfortable income, they were not considered rich, especially since there were seven children in the family. While not always able to provide financially for their children, Austen's parents encouraged Jane and her siblings to have a passion for learning. Her father owned a library of over five hundred books, and Austen later wrote that her family were "great novel readers, and not ashamed of being so." Austen began writing at an early age to entertain her family, reading her satirical sketches aloud.

By the time she was twenty, she had written an early version of her novel *Sense and Sensibility* and soon afterward began the manuscripts that eventually became *Pride and Prejudice* and *Northanger Abbey*. Years later, she revised and expanded these manuscripts, which were well received when they were published. During the remainder of her brief life, she wrote three more novels—*Mansfield Park*, *Emma*, and *Persuasion*.

Marriage and Manners In an age when genteel young women could not seek gainful employment, marriage meant financial security. The pressure to marry was strong, and Austen examines that pressure throughout her work with a witty and satirical eye. Although Austen never married, she is believed to have had a brief engagement in 1802 with a twenty-one-year-old suitor from her village, until she broke the engagement a day after it was formed. Little is known about these aspects of Austen's life, as her sister Cassandra was fiercely protective of her and destroyed many of Austen's private letters and correspondence once the author died.

While Austen's novels were popular with the public and many of her fellow authors, it was only after her death that she received critical acclaim. Sir Walter Scott wrote in his journal, in an entry dated March 14, 1826, "Also read again, and for the third time at least, Miss Austen's very finely written novel of *Pride and Prejudice*. That young lady had a talent for describing the involvement and feelings and characters of ordinary life which is to me the most wonderful I ever met with."

Selection Skills

Literary Elements
- Dialogue (SE pp. 727–735)
- Point of View (SE p. 735)

⟵ *from* **Pride and Prejudice** ⟶

Writing Skills/Grammar
- Apply Dialogue (SE p. 736)
- Describe Characters (TE p. 730)

Reading Skills
- Analyze Characterization (SE pp. 727–736)

Vocabulary Skills
- Word Origins (SE p. 736)
- Academic Vocabulary (SE p. 736)

Listening/Speaking/Viewing Skills
- Analyze Art (SE p. 728; TE p. 730)

Literature and Reading Preview

Connect to the Novel

How important is marriage in modern societies—your own culture and other cultures? Discuss these questions in a group.

Build Background

In eighteenth-century England, property and other finances usually belonged to the husband or father. For this reason, it was often necessary for middle-class daughters to marry into wealth. After the death of a father, a family's estate would go to another male relative instead of the wife or their daughters.

Set Purposes for Reading

Big Idea The Stirrings of Romanticism

As you read, ask yourself, Which characters show attitudes of Romanticism—such as valuing individualism and feeling over reason—and which preserve Enlightenment attitudes, valuing reason and self-control?

Literary Element Dialogue

Dialogue is conversation between characters in a literary work. Through dialogue, a writer reveals the feelings, thoughts, and intentions of characters, sets up conflicts, and moves the plot forward. As you read, ask yourself, How does the dialogue in *Pride and Prejudice* reveal the relationships between characters?

Reading Strategy Analyze Characterization

When you **analyze characterization**, you look critically at how the thoughts, actions, and motives of a character are revealed. In **direct characterization**, the author tells something outright about a character's personality. In **indirect characterization**, the author suggests traits by presenting a character's words, thoughts, actions, or appearance, as well as the reactions of other characters. As you read, ask yourself, How is Austen telling me about these characters?

Tip: Taking Notes Create a chart like the one shown below to analyze characters.

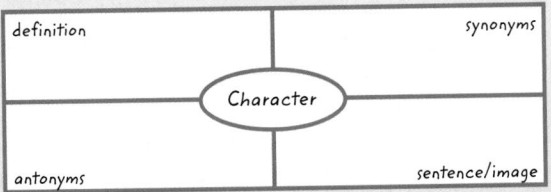

JANE AUSTEN **727**

Learning Objectives

For pages 726–736

In studying this text, you will focus on the following objectives:

Literary Study: Analyzing dialogue.

Reading: Analyzing characterization.

Writing: Applying dialogue.

Vocabulary

hypocritical (hip′ ə krit′ i kəl) *adj.* pretending to believe one thing but doing the opposite; p. 730 *It is hypocritical to urge others to recycle when you don't do the same.*

acquaintance (ə kwānt′ əns) *n.* the state of being familiar with; p. 730 *I did not know Mary well; I had only just made her acquaintance.*

emphatic (em fat′ ik) *adj.* with strong emphasis; p. 731 *My mother was emphatic about having us call home if we were going to stay out late.*

Before You Read

Focus

Summary

A wealthy, single man, Mr. Bingley moves into a small English village, causing a stir among marriage-minded mothers who view him as a potential husband for their daughters. Mrs. Bennet, with her five eligible daughters, is elated when he seems to favor her eldest, Jane. Bingley's friend, the wealthier Mr. Darcy, is introduced as arrogant and prideful and a contrast to the agreeable Mr. Bingley.

 For summaries in languages other than English, see Unit 4 Teaching Resources Book, pp. 86–91.

Vocabulary

Identify Part of Speech

Say: Changing the suffix of a word changes its part of speech. Have students use a dictionary to identify the root words of *hypocritical, acquaintance,* and *emphatic*. Then have them write one word from the same root and identify its part of speech.

 For additional vocabulary practice, see Unit 4 Teaching Resources Book, p. 94.

Approaching Level

DIFFERENTIATED INSTRUCTION

Emerging Tell students that the selection contrasts the following character types: those with Romantic attitudes of individualism and emotion and those with Enlightenment attitudes of social structure and self-control. Have students create a two-column chart to list the characters that fit each type.

One column should be labeled "Romanticism" and the other "Enlightenment." Have students identify characters that fit each type and list them in the columns as they read. Then have them explain their choices in a class discussion.

Teach

Literary Element | 1

Dialogue **Answer:** *Mr. Bennet has a sharp wit; Mrs. Bennet is not intelligent enough to notice Mr. Bennet's banter.*

[APPROACHING] If approaching-level students have difficulty understanding the structure of nineteenth century society regarding marriage, tell them about the practice of "arranging" for young people to meet. Have students read the first chapter and **ask:** What does Mrs. Bennet want Mr. Bennet to do? *(Call on Mr. Bingley to arrange a time for him to visit and meet the Bennet girls)*

  For additional literary element practice, see Unit 4 Teaching Resources Book, p. 92.

View the Art ★

Answer: *Students may infer from the women's close body language that they are friends or relative. They may also infer that the women live in a rural location and are wealthy or well-off, based on the elaborate garden and the seemingly-expensive clothing.*

Readability Scores

Dale-Chall: 6.8
DRP: 53
Lexile: 910

Promenade. Constant-Emile Troyon. Oil on canvas. Courtesy of Thomas Brod and Patrick Pilkington. Private collection.

View the Art In Austen's time, the paths through gardens were often used as social meeting-places for friends. What can you infer about the women in this painting? ★

from
Pride and Prejudice

Jane Austen

Chapter 1

It is a truth universally acknowledged that a single man in possession of a good fortune must be in want of a wife.

However little known the feelings or views of such a man may be on his first entering a neighborhood, this truth is so well fixed in the minds of the surrounding families that he is considered as the rightful property of some one or other of their daughters.

"My dear Mr. Bennet," said his lady to him one day, "have you heard that Netherfield Park is let at last?"

Mr. Bennet replied that he had not.

"But it is," returned she; "for Mrs. Long has just been here, and she told me all about it."

Mr. Bennet made no answer.

"Do not you want to know who has taken it?" cried his wife impatiently.

"*You* want to tell me, and I have no objection to hearing it."

This was invitation enough.

"Why, my dear, you must know, Mrs. Long says that Netherfield is taken by a young man of large fortune from the north of England; that he came down on Monday in a chaise and four[1] to see the place, and was so much delighted with it that he agreed with Mr. Morris immediately; that he is to take possession before Michaelmas,[2] and some of his servants are to be in the house by the end of next week."

"What is his name?"

"Bingley."

"Is he married or single?"

---

1. A *chaise and four* is an elegant coach drawn by four horses.
2. *Michaelmas* (mik′əl məs) is September 29, the feast of the archangel Michael, which is celebrated mainly in England.

Dialogue *What does this dialogue reveal about the relationship between Mr. and Mrs. Bennet?* | **1**

728 UNIT 4   THE TRIUMPH OF ROMANTICISM

Vocabulary Practice

Multiple-Meaning Words Direct students' attention to the word *mean* in the description of Mrs. Bennet on p. 729. Point out that *mean* has multiple meanings. Break students into groups and have them discuss which context clues in the passage help them understand the meaning of *mean* here. Next direct students' attention to the word *reserve* earlier in the same paragraph. Have them look up the various meanings of this word. Tell them to use context clues to decide which definition matches the word's use in this case.

"Oh! Single, my dear, to be sure! A single man of large fortune; four or five thousand a year.[3] What a fine thing for our girls!"

"How so? How can it affect them?"

"My dear Mr. Bennet," replied his wife, "how can you be so tiresome! You must know that I am thinking of his marrying one of them."

"Is that his design in settling here?"

"Design! Nonsense, how can you talk so! But it is very likely that he *may* fall in love with one of them, and therefore you must visit him as soon as he comes."

"I see no occasion for that. You and the girls may go, or you may send them by themselves, which perhaps will be still better, for as you are as handsome as any of them, Mr. Bingley might like you the best of the party."

"My dear, you flatter me. I certainly *have* had my share of beauty, but I do not pretend to be anything extraordinary now. When a woman has five grown-up daughters, she ought to give over thinking of her own beauty."

"In such cases, a woman has not often much beauty to think of."

"But, my dear, you must indeed go and see Mr. Bingley when he comes in the neighborhood."

"It is more than I engage for,[4] I assure you."

"But consider your daughters. Only think what an establishment it would be for one of them. Sir William and Lady Lucas are determined to go, merely on that account, for in general you know they visit no newcomers. Indeed you must go, for it will be impossible for *us* to visit him if you do not."

"You are overscrupulous[5] surely. I dare say Mr. Bingley will be very glad to see you; and I will send a few lines by you to assure him of my hearty consent to his marrying whichever he chooses of the girls, though I must throw in a good word for my little Lizzy."

"I desire you will do no such thing. Lizzy is not a bit better than the others; and I am sure she is not half so handsome as Jane, nor half so good-humored as Lydia. But you are always giving *her* the preference."

"They have none of them much to recommend them," replied he; "they are all silly and ignorant like other girls, but Lizzy has something more of quickness than her sisters."

"Mr. Bennet, how can you abuse your own children in such a way? You take delight in vexing me. You have no compassion on my poor nerves."

"You mistake me, my dear. I have a high respect for your nerves. They are my old friends. I have heard you mention them with consideration these twenty years at least."

"Ah! You do not know what I suffer."

"But I hope you will get over it, and live to see many young men of four thousand a year come into the neighborhood."

"It will be no use to us if twenty such should come, since you will not visit them."

"Depend upon it, my dear, that when there are twenty, I will visit them all."

Mr. Bennet was so odd a mixture of quick parts, sarcastic humor, reserve, and caprice, that the experience of three and twenty years had been insufficient to make his wife understand his character. *Her* mind was less difficult to develop. She was a woman of mean[6] understanding, little information, and uncertain temper. When she was discontented, she fancied herself nervous. The business of her life was to get her daughters married; its solace was visiting and news.

---

3. A yearly income of four or five thousand pounds was then a fairly large sum of money, probably acquired from land holdings and investments.
4. *Engage for* means "plan to undertake."
5. *Overscrupulous* means "too concerned about social niceties."
6. *Mean* means "low" or "poor."

Analyze Characterization *How does Austen characterize Lizzie as she introduces her?* **3**

The Stirrings of Romanticism *Does this description make Mr. Bennet seem like part of the Romantic age or of the Enlightenment? Explain.* **4**

JANE AUSTEN **729**

2 Analyze Characterization *How does Austen reveal Mrs. Bennet's character?*

Teach

Reading Strategy **2**

Analyze Characterization
Answer: *What Mrs. Bennet says reveals her concern with finding husbands for her daughters.*

Reading Strategy **3**

Analyze Characterization
Answer: *Austen tells what other characters think of her. Lizzy is her father's favorite because she is "quick" and her mother compares her unfavorably to her sisters.*

(ADVANCED) For advanced students, **ask:** What do the parents' opinions of their children reveal about their characters? *(Mr. Bennet values Lizzy's intelligence because of his own. Mrs. Bennet is more shallow and values beauty and easygoing temperament most.)*

Big Idea **4**

The Stirrings of Romanticism **Answer:** *His wit and sarcasm connect to Enlightenment values, but his capriciousness is closer to Romanticism's emphasis on individuality.*

(ENGLISH LEARNERS) Have English learners read the last paragraph on this page and restate in their own words the comparison of Mr. and Mrs. Bennet. *(Possible answer: Mr. Bennet is smart, sarcastic, quiet, and acts quickly. Mrs. Bennet is simple-minded, not very smart, and emotional. She can be nervous, social, and gossipy.)*

Teach

Literary Element · 1

Dialogue Answer: *The exchange introduces Elizabeth, advances the plot by mentioning the upcoming dance, and shows that Mrs. Bennet sees getting her daughters married as a cutthroat competition.*

Reading Strategy · 2

Analyze Characterization

Answer: *Austen reveals Mrs. Bennet's character both by directly stating that she scolded her daughter because of her own frustration and by reporting her energetic, scolding words.*

View the Art ★

Constant Troyon was a French painter of the Barbizon School of Art in the 1840s. Most of his paintings involved animals, such as bulls, horses, or cattle. Although he lived and painted during the Romantic Period, this painting features elements of the Enlightenment. **Ask:** What elements of the Enlightenment are shown in this painting? (*The formal dress of the men and the formal greetings, such as extending a hand or taking off one's hat, are shown.*)

Chapter 2

Mr. Bennet was among the earliest of those who waited on Mr. Bingley. He had always intended to visit him, though to the last always assuring his wife that he should not go; and till the evening after the visit was paid, she had no knowledge of it. It was then disclosed in the following manner. Observing his second daughter employed in trimming a hat, he suddenly addressed her with, "I hope Mr. Bingley will like it, Lizzy."

"We are not in a way to know *what* Mr. Bingley likes," said her mother resentfully, "since we are not to visit."

"But you forget, Mama," said Elizabeth, "that we shall meet him at the assemblies,[7] and that Mrs. Long has promised to introduce him."

"I do not believe Mrs. Long will do any such thing. She has two nieces of her own. She is a selfish, **hypocritical** woman, and I have no opinion of her."

"No more have I," said Mr. Bennet; "and I am glad to find that you do not depend on her serving you."

Mrs. Bennet deigned not to make any reply; but unable to contain herself, began scolding one of her daughters.

"Don't keep coughing so, Kitty, for heaven's sake! Have a little compassion on my nerves. You tear them to pieces."

"Kitty has no discretion in her coughs," said her father; "she times them ill."

Three Gentlemen Greeting Each Other. Richard Dighton (1795–1880). Watercolor and ink wash over pencil. Private collection. Bonhams, London. ★

"I do not cough for my own amusement," replied Kitty fretfully.

"When is your next ball to be, Lizzy?"

"Tomorrow fortnight."[8]

"Aye, so it is," cried her mother, "and Mrs. Long does not come back till the day before; so, it will be impossible for her to introduce him, for she will not know him herself."

"Then, my dear, you may have the advantage of your friend, and introduce Mr. Bingley to *her*."

"Impossible, Mr. Bennet, impossible, when I am not acquainted with him myself; how can you be so teasing?"

"I honor your circumspection. A fortnight's **acquaintance** is certainly very little. One cannot know what a man really is by the end of a fortnight. But if *we* do not venture, somebody

---

7. **Assemblies** are public dances.

1 | Dialogue **What purpose does this dialogue serve?**

2 | Analyze Characterization **Is this passage an example of direct or indirect characterization, or both? Explain.**

Vocabulary

hypocritical (hip′ ə krit′ i kəl) *adj.* pretending to believe one thing but doing the opposite

---

8. **Tomorrow fortnight** means "two weeks from tomorrow."

Vocabulary

acquaintance (ə kwānt′ əns) *n.* the state of being familiar with

Writing Practice

PARTNERS | SPIRAL REVIEW · **Describe Characters**
To help students increase their ability to recognize character traits, have them analyze the five Bennet sisters: Lizzy, Jane, Mary, Lydia, and Kitty. Tell students to base their analyses on direct evidence from the narrator's words and indirect evidence from the characters' own words and actions and from how other characters react to them. Students may work in pairs to write a few sentences describing each sister and citing evidence from the text to back up their descriptions.

else will; and after all, Mrs. Long and her nieces must stand their chance; and therefore, as she will think it an act of kindness, if you decline the office, I will take it on myself."

The girls stared at their father. Mrs. Bennet said only, "Nonsense, nonsense!"

"What can be the meaning of that **emphatic** exclamation?" cried he. "Do you consider the forms of introduction, and the stress that is laid on them, as nonsense? I cannot quite agree with you *there*. What say you, Mary, for you are a young lady of deep reflection, I know, and read great books, and make extracts."

Mary wished to say something very sensible, but knew not how.

"While Mary is adjusting her ideas," he continued, "let us return to Mr. Bingley."

"I am sick of Mr. Bingley," cried his wife.

"I am sorry to hear *that*; but why did not you tell me so before? If I had known as much this morning, I certainly would not have called on him. It is very unlucky; but as I have actually paid the visit, we cannot escape the acquaintance now."

The astonishment of the ladies was just what he wished—that of Mrs. Bennet perhaps surpassing the rest—though when the first tumult of joy was over, she began to declare that it was what she had expected all the while.

"How good it was in you, my dear Mr. Bennet! But I knew I should persuade you at last. I was sure you loved your girls too well to neglect such an acquaintance. Well, how pleased I am! And it is such a good joke, too, that you should have gone this morning, and never said a word about it till now."

"Now, Kitty, you may cough as much as you choose," said Mr. Bennet; and, as he spoke, he left the room, fatigued with the raptures of his wife.

---

3 Analyze Characterization *How does this description of Mr. Bennet's intent help you understand his character?*

Vocabulary

emphatic (em fat´ ik) *adj.* with strong emphasis

"What an excellent father you have, girls," said she, when the door was shut. "I do not know how you will ever make him amends for his kindness; or me either, for that matter. At our time of life it is not so pleasant, I can tell you, to be making new acquaintances everyday; but for your sakes, we would do anything. Lydia, my love, though you *are* the youngest, I dare say Mr. Bingley will dance with you at the next ball."

"Oh!" said Lydia stoutly, "I am not afraid; for though I *am* the youngest, I'm the tallest."

The rest of the evening was spent in conjecturing how soon he would return Mr. Bennet's visit, and determining when they should ask him to dinner.

Chapter 3

Not all that Mrs. Bennet, however, with the assistance of her five daughters, could ask on the subject was sufficient to draw from her husband any satisfactory description of Mr. Bingley. They attacked him in various ways—with barefaced questions, ingenious suppositions, and distant surmises—but he eluded the skill of them all; and they were at last obliged to accept the secondhand intelligence of their neighbor Lady Lucas. Her report was highly favorable. Sir William had been delighted with him. He was quite young, wonderfully handsome, extremely agreeable, and to crown the whole, he meant to be at the next assembly with a large party. Nothing could be more delightful! To be fond of dancing was a certain step toward falling in love; and very lively hopes of Mr. Bingley's heart were entertained.

"If I can but see one of my daughters happily settled at Netherfield," said Mrs. Bennet to her

---

The Stirrings of Romanticism *Does this description of Mr. Bingley make him seem to fit the Romantic Age or the Enlightenment? Explain.* **4**

JANE AUSTEN **731**

Teach

Reading Strategy 1

Analyze Characterization
Answer: *Mrs. Bennet's concerns may further reveal her self-absorption, wanting Mr. Bingley to stay in the neighborhood so he will fall in love with one of her daughters.*

Big Idea 2

The Stirrings of Romanticism Answer: *His unconcern for sociable behavior and conventional manners suggests that he may be a brooding man of dark moods, a character often depicted in the Romantic Age.*

husband, "and all the others equally well married, I shall have nothing to wish for."

In a few days Mr. Bingley returned Mr. Bennet's visit, and sat about ten minutes with him in his library. He had entertained hopes of being admitted to a sight of the young ladies, of whose beauty he had heard much; but he saw only the father. The ladies were somewhat more fortunate, for they had the advantage of ascertaining from an upper window that he wore a blue coat and rode a black horse.

An invitation to dinner was soon afterward dispatched, and already had Mrs. Bennet planned the courses that were to do credit to her housekeeping, when an answer arrived which deferred it all. Mr. Bingley was obliged to be in town⁹ the following day, and consequently unable to accept the honor of their invitation, etc. Mrs. Bennet was quite disconcerted. She could not imagine what business he could have in town so soon after his arrival in Hertfordshire;¹⁰ and she began to fear that he might be always flying about from one place to another, and never settled at Netherfield as he ought to be. Lady Lucas quieted her fears a little by starting the idea of his being gone to London only to get a large party for the ball, and a report soon followed that Mr. Bingley was to bring twelve ladies and seven gentlemen with him to the assembly. The girls grieved over such a number of ladies; but were comforted the day before the ball by hearing that, instead of twelve, he had brought only six with him from London, his five sisters and a cousin. And when the party entered the assembly room, it consisted of only five altogether; Mr. Bingley, his two sisters, the husband of the eldest, and another young man.

Mr. Bingley was good-looking and gentleman-like; he had a pleasant countenance, and easy, unaffected manners. His sisters were fine women, with an air of decided fashion. His brother-in-law, Mr. Hurst, merely looked the gentleman; but his friend Mr. Darcy soon drew the attention of the room by his fine, tall person, handsome features, noble mien—and the report which was in general circulation within five minutes after his entrance of his having ten thousand a year. The gentlemen pronounced him to be a fine figure of a man, the ladies declared he was much handsomer than Mr. Bingley, and he was looked at with great admiration for about half the evening, till his manners gave a disgust which turned the tide of his popularity; for he was discovered to be proud, to be above his company, and above being pleased; and not all his large estate in Derbyshire¹¹ could then save him from having a most forbidding, disagreeable countenance, and being unworthy to be compared with his friend.

Mr. Bingley had soon made himself acquainted with all the principal people in the room; he was lively and unreserved, danced every dance, was angry that the ball closed so early, and talked of giving one himself at Netherfield. Such amiable qualities must speak for themselves. What a contrast between him and his friend! Mr. Darcy danced only once with Mrs. Hurst and once with Miss Bingley, declined being introduced to any other lady, and spent the rest of the evening in walking about the room, speaking occasionally to one of his own party. His character was decided. He was the proudest, most disagreeable man in the world, and everybody hoped that he would never come there again. Among the most violent against him was Mrs. Bennet, whose dislike of his general behavior was sharpened into particular resentment by his having slighted one of her daughters.

Elizabeth Bennet had been obliged by the scarcity of gentlemen to sit down for two

---

9. *In town* means "in London" here.
10. *Hertfordshire* (härt′ fərd shər) is an English county just north of London.

1 Analyze Characterization *What does this description of Mrs. Bennet's concerns add to her characterization?*

---

11. *Derbyshire* (där′ bi shər) is a county in north-central England.

The Stirrings of Romanticism *Does Mr. Darcy seem to be part of the Romantic age or the Enlightenment? Explain.* **2**

Literary Element Practice

SPIRAL REVIEW Character Foil Point out to students the line on this page, "What a contrast between him and his friend!" in reference to the differences between Mr. Bingley and Mr. Darcy. Remind students that a character foil is a device an author uses to show traits by contrasting characters: **Ask:** Does Mr. Darcy serve as a foil for Mr. Bingley? *(Students should recognize that these characters are foils.)*

Have students write a character analysis of either Mr. Darcy or Mr. Bingley based on the qualities the character does not hold in comparison to the character's foil.

dances; and during part of that time, Mr. Darcy had been standing near enough for her to overhear a conversation between him and Mr. Bingley, who came from the dance for a few minutes to press his friend to join it.

"Come, Darcy," said he, "I must have you dance. I hate to see you standing about by yourself in this stupid manner. You had much better dance."

"I certainly shall not. You know how I detest it, unless I am particularly acquainted with my partner. At such an assembly as this, it would be insupportable. Your sisters are engaged, and there is not another woman in the room whom it would not be a punishment to me to stand up with."

"I would not be so fastidious as you are," cried Bingley, "for a kingdom! Upon my honor, I never met with so many pleasant girls in my life as I have this evening; and there are several of them you see uncommonly pretty."

"*You* are dancing with the only handsome girl in the room," said Mr. Darcy, looking at the eldest Miss Bennet.

"Oh! She is the most beautiful creature I ever beheld! But there is one of her sisters sitting down just behind you, who is very pretty, and I dare say, very agreeable. Do let me ask my partner to introduce you."

Two Women Reading in an Interior. Jean Georges Ferry. Gavin Graham Gallery, London.

"Which do you mean?" and turning round, he looked for a moment at Elizabeth, till catching her eye, he withdrew his own and coldly said, "She is tolerable; but not handsome enough to tempt *me*; and I am in no humor at present to give consequence to young ladies who are slighted by other men. You had better return to your partner and enjoy her smiles, for you are wasting your time with me."

Mr. Bingley followed his advice. Mr. Darcy walked off; and Elizabeth remained with no very cordial feelings toward him. She told the

 4 Dialogue *What does this dialogue reveal about Mr. Darcy's character?*

3

JANE AUSTEN **733**

Teach

Literary Element | 3

Dialogue **Ask:** What is revealed through the exchange between Mr. Bingley and Mr. Darcy? *(Darcy is proud; Bingley is jovial and is happy to be at the ball.)*

Literary Element | 4

Dialogue **Answer:** *He knows his own tastes and refuses to adapt to social pressures. His insistence on following his individual preference is a characteristic of Romanticism.*

(ENGLISH LEARNERS) For English learners, **ask:** How does the author show the differences between Mr. Bingley and Mr. Darcy? *(by describing and contrasting their appearance and behavior)* Have students restate the characteristics of each man in their own words.

Advanced Learners

DIFFERENTIATED INSTRUCTION

Respond to Literature Encourage students to read *Pride and Prejudice* or another of Jane Austen's novels and make an oral presentation to the class in one of the following forms:

- a critical review of the novel
- a dramatization of a scene from the novel
- drawings of scenes from the novel

- a letter to Jane Austen reflecting their response to the novel
- songs, poems, or any other creative response you find acceptable.

Teach

Reading Strategy | 1

Analyze Characterization
Answer: *Her actions show that she is self-sufficient and that she has a sense of humor. Rather than taking offense at Mr. Darcy's rudeness, she laughs at the incident.*

Literary History ☆

Reason and Emotion Jane Austen's novels show elements of Neoclassicism in their emphasis on reason and acceptance of the rigid social hierarchy of the time. In her novels, Austen often quoted her favorite writer, Samuel Johnson, whose rationality and wit epitomize the Enlightenment. Austen's novels also show elements of an emerging Romanticism: a love of natural beauty and a respect for the place of emotion in life.

> 📁 To check students' understanding of the selection, see Unit 4 Teaching Resources Book, p. 96.

---

story, however, with great spirit among her friends; for she had a lively, playful disposition, which delighted in anything ridiculous.

The evening altogether passed off pleasantly to the whole family. Mrs. Bennet had seen her eldest daughter much admired by the Netherfield party. Mr. Bingley had danced with her twice, and she had been distinguished by his sisters. Jane was as much gratified by this as her mother could be, though in a quieter way. Elizabeth felt Jane's pleasure. Mary had heard herself mentioned to Miss Bingley as the most accomplished girl in the neighborhood; and Catherine and Lydia had been fortunate enough to be never without partners, which was all that they had yet learned to care for at a ball. They returned therefore in good spirits to Longbourn, the village where they lived, and of which they were the principal inhabitants. They found Mr. Bennet still up. With a book he was regardless of time, and on the present occasion he had a good deal of curiosity as to the event of an evening which had raised such splendid expectations. He had rather hoped that all his wife's views on the stranger would be disappointed, but he soon found that he had a very different story to hear.

"Oh, my dear Mr. Bennet"—as she entered the room—"we have had a most delightful evening, a most excellent ball. I wish you had been there. Jane was so admired, nothing could be like it. Everybody said how well she looked, and Mr. Bingley thought her quite beautiful, and danced with her twice. Only think of *that*, my dear; he actually danced with her twice; and she was the only creature in the room that he asked a second time. First of all, he asked Miss Lucas. I was so vexed to see him stand up with her; but, however, he did not admire her

at all: indeed, nobody can, you know; and he seemed quite struck with Jane as she was going down the dance. So, he inquired who she was, and got introduced, and asked her for the two next. Then, the two third he danced with Miss King, and the two fourth with Maria Lucas, and the two fifth with Jane again, and the two sixth with Lizzy, and the Boulanger—"[12]

"If he had had any compassion for *me*," cried her husband impatiently, "he would not have danced half so much! For God's sake, say no more of his partners. Oh, that he had sprained his ankle in the first dance!"

"Oh! My dear," continued Mrs. Bennet, "I am quite delighted with him. He is so excessively handsome! And his sisters are charming women. I never in my life saw anything more elegant than their dresses. I dare say the lace upon Mrs. Hurst's gown—"

Here she was interrupted again. Mr. Bennet protested against any description of finery. She was therefore obliged to seek another branch of the subject, and related, with much bitterness of spirit and some exaggeration, the shocking rudeness of Mr. Darcy.

"But I can assure you," she added, "that Lizzy does not lose much by not suiting *his* fancy; for he is a most disagreeable, horrid man, not at all worth pleasing. So high and so conceited that there was no enduring him! He walked here, and he walked there, fancying himself so very great! Not handsome enough to dance with! I wish you had been there, my dear, to have given him one of your set-downs.[13] I quite detest the man." ❧

---

1 Analyze Characterization *How does this paragraph contribute to the characterization of Elizabeth?*

---

12. When a gentleman asked a lady to dance, the couple danced a two-dance set, except in the case of more complex or exhausting dances, such as the *Boulanger* (bōō län zhā'). The *two third* is the third two-dance set, the *two fourth* is the fourth, and so on.

13. *Set-downs* means "snubbing remarks" or "rebuffs."

Reading Practice

 Make Predictions After students have completed the selection, ask them to make predictions about the following:

- Which characters are likely to have a romance? Explain why you think so.
- Which character or characters are most likely to change during the course of the novel? How and why might the person or persons change?

Encourage interested students to read the entire novel and report on whether their predictions were confirmed or needed to be revised. If available, you might show a film version of *Pride and Prejudice* to the class.

After You Read

Respond and Think Critically

Respond and Interpret

1. Which character do you find most interesting? Why?

2. (a)According to the opening paragraph, what "truth" is "universally acknowledged"? (b)What is Austen implying about society here?

3. (a)Who has rented Netherfield Park? (b)Why is this important to Mrs. Bennet?

4. (a)Summarize the reasons that Bingley draws approval at the local assembly. (b)Why does Darcy first attract the attention of the room?

5. (a)What girl does Bingley show a preference for? Why? (b)What might this reveal about Bingley's character?

Analyze and Evaluate

6. (a)Identify the narrator's tone, or attitude toward the subject. (b)Toward which character(s) does she seem most sympathetic?

7. (a)Which character seems to most display the trait of pride? (b)Which most displays prejudice? Explain.

Connect

8. **Big Idea** The Stirrings of Romanticism Which character exemplifies most strongly the values of the Romantic era? Explain.

9. **Connect to Today** In what ways does the dance in this excerpt compare to modern parties? In what ways does it differ?

Literary Element Dialogue

Jane Austen was the first major British writer to make extensive use of both action and dialogue in fiction. Austen's dialogue is also realistic, in keeping with her characters' backgrounds and traits. For example, Mr. Bennet is intentionally witty, and Mrs. Bennet is not witty at all, though she often makes us laugh.

1. Identify three remarks or actions by Mr. Bennet that support the direct statements made about him at the close of Chapter 1.

2. What do we learn about Bingley's and Darcy's personalities in Chapter 3? What specific actions and lines of dialogue are revealing?

Review: Point of View

As you learned on page 266, **point of view** is the relationship of the narrator to the story. In the **third-person omniscient**, or all-knowing, point of view, the narrator is not a character in the story but someone who stands outside the story and comments on the action. A third-person omniscient narrator knows everything about the characters and events and may reveal details that the characters themselves could not reveal.

Group Activity With a group of classmates, reread this excerpt, recording specific instances where the narrator's omniscience is shown, and determining the significance of each in the story. Use a chart like the one below.

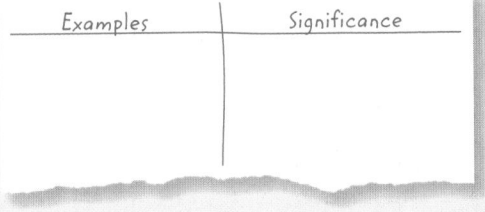

Examples	Significance

After You Read

Assess

1. Encourage discussion of what makes a character interesting.

2. (a) A single man with a good income must want a wife. (b) Austen is lightly mocking the mercenary nature of society.

3. (a) Mr. Bingley (b) She hopes he will marry one of her daughters.

4. (a) He is attractive, friendly, rich, and enjoys parties. (b) He is far richer and more handsome than Bingley.

5. (a) Jane Bennet because she is prettiest (b) Bingley seems to judge women on appearance, which might indicate his shallowness.

6. (a) Ironic (b) Mr. Bennet and Elizabeth

7. (a) Mr. Darcy (b) Mrs. Bennet shows prejudice in favor of Mr. Bingley and against Mr. Darcy and Mrs. Long.

8. Mr. Darcy, since he follows his impulses in spite of the social situation.

9. Possible answers: The dance might resemble a modern party in that people gather for music, dancing, and often hoping to meet a partner or make new acquaintances. It differs in the format (defined dances, rigid customs) and the types of people invited (both parents and their children).

Literary Element

1. Students' answers may vary but should show that Mr. Bennet is clever and enjoys mocking others.

2. Bingley is jovial and enjoys dancing and socializing. Darcy is somewhat surly and does not enjoy either dancing or socializing. The conversation that ensues when Bingley tries to convince Darcy to dance reveals their individual personalities.

Review: Point of View

Sample response:

Example: "It is a truth universally acknowledged that a single man in possession of a good fortune must be in want of a wife."

Significance: The narrator is able to reveal the opinions of the community while mocking them at the same time.

735

After You Read

Assess

Reading Strategy

1. Darcy is aloof and proud. Bingley is agreeable and sociable, if somewhat shallow. Mr. Bennet has a sharp wit and enjoys mocking others. Mrs. Bennet is foolish and overly emotional. Elizabeth Bennet is intelligent and self-confident and has a good sense of humor. Jane is beautiful.

2. Students should point out specific examples of dialogue, actions, and description.

Progress Check

Can students analyze characterization?

If No → See Unit 4 Teaching Resources Book, p. 93.

 Write with Style

Students' dialogue should develop both character and plot details. Remind students that dialogue often serves as a way to heighten tension and reveal some kind of conflict.

For grammar practice, see Unit 4 Teaching Resources Book, p. 95.

Reading Strategy Analyze Characterization

Sometimes a narrator directly reveals details about a character; other times these character traits are implied. For example, Austen explicitly states that Mrs. Bennet is "a woman of mean understanding." However, Mrs. Bennet's actions also *imply* that she is a foolish person, without explicitly stating it.

1. What do we learn about each main character's personality in this excerpt?

2. How does the author reveal these character traits directly and indirectly?

Vocabulary Practice

Practice with Word Origins Create a word map, like the one below, for each of these vocabulary words from the selection. Use a dictionary for help.

hypocritical   acquaintance   emphatic

EXAMPLE:

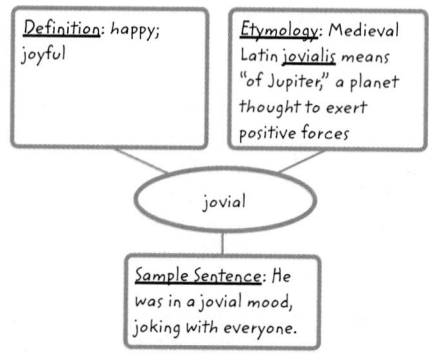

Academic Vocabulary

Mr. and Mrs. Bennet are **straightforward** *with each other because they know each other well.*

Straightforward is an academic word that appears in everyday usage. People who say what they mean are often called **straightforward**. Explore this word's meaning by completing the following sentence: *I like it when people are* **straightforward** *about*

_____ .

Write with Style

 Apply Dialogue

Assignment As you've seen in *Pride and Prejudice*, realistic dialogue can reveal much about characters, the relationships among them, and the action that takes place. Recreate the dialogue from a social event or party you recently attended. What does it reveal about the event and the people there?

Get Ideas Once you decide on the event you will describe, think about the characters you want to focus on and the main idea you want to get across. Make a chart or outline listing this information along with specific dialogue you want to include.

Event	Sura's party
People involved	
Main ideas	

Give It Structure Keep in mind that the purpose of your writing is not just to report people's conversations, but to use them to disclose the speakers' personalities and the situation they're involved in. Omit statements that don't contribute to this purpose. Avoid including too much background information—your dialogue should be what creates a sense of the overall scene.

Look at Language Use strong action verbs to report people's words and describe their attitudes and emotions. "He said" and "she said" quickly become boring for readers.

EXAMPLE:

"I wouldn't have believed it myself if I hadn't seen it with my own eyes," Elena ~~said~~ whispered.

"No way," gasped Dana.

"Yes, way," she ~~answered~~ shot back. "Evan just turned his back on Sura, galloped off, and started hitting on Lauren."

LOG ON ▶ **Literature** Online

Selection Resources For Selection Quizzes, eFlashcards, and Reading-Writing Connection activities, go to glencoe.com and enter QuickPass code GLB9817u4.

Vocabulary Practice

Sample Word Maps

hypocritical

Definition: characterized by actions contradicting personal beliefs.

Etymology: The adjective form of Middle English *ipocrite*, Latin *hypocrita*, and Greek *hypokrits* meaning "a stage actor or one who pretends to be who they are not."

Sentence: It would be *hypocritical* for Mrs. Bennet to complain about anyone judging her.

acquaintance

Definition: a person known to someone but not as a close friend

Etymology: Middle English *aquienten* meaning familiar, known and the suffix *-ance,* which forms the noun from a verb.

Sentence: The Bennet sisters and Mr. Bingley are *acquaintances.*

emphatic

Definition: strongly expressive

Etymology: Greek *emphatikós* means "indicative, forceful."

Sentence: Mr. Darcy gave an *emphatic* response, saying he detests dancing, to Mr. Bingley.

PART 2

Nature and the Imagination

The Bard, c.1817. John Martin. Oil on canvas, 50 x 39.96 in. Yale Center for British Art, Paul Mellon Collection, New Haven, CT.

 John Martin was known for his dramatic paintings of historical and biblical scenes. Here, he depicts a bard reciting his poetry to an audience. Does the image fit Wordsworth's description of poetry? Explain why or why not.

"Poetry is the spontaneous overflow of powerful feelings: it takes its origin from emotion recollected in tranquility."

—William Wordsworth, preface to *Lyrical Ballads* **1**

737

Analyzing and Extending

Reading Strategy **1**

Interpret Meaning Direct students to read the quotation from Wordsworth. **Ask:** What does this quotation reveal about the origin of poetry? *(Poetry originates when someone recalls powerful feelings in a state of calmness.)*

View the Art

Answer: *Most students will say that the details of the image—the bard's wild gestures and swirling clothing, the rushing water and dramatic cliffs and mountains—go well with Wordsworth's description of poetry as "spontaneous overflow of powerful feelings."*

John Martin's (1789–1854) inspiration for this painting was a poem by the popular poet Thomas Gray. In the poem, Gray describes King Edward I's conquest of Wales. Edward ordered all the bards to be slaughtered in an attempt to root out the cultural and national pride of the conquered people.

 For additional support for English Learners, see Unit 4 Teaching Resources Book, p. 99.

English Learners

DIFFERENTIATED INSTRUCTION

Beginning Ask: What definition can you give for *spontaneous* based on the context? *(natural, momentary, and unplanned)* **Ask:** What might *tranquility* be the opposite of in this context? *(Powerful feelings)*

Approaching Level

DIFFERENTIATED INSTRUCTION

Established Read aloud the quotation from Wordsworth. **Ask:** How would you say this in your own words? *(Quiet reflection about moments of passion leads to poetry.)*

Before You Read

Focus

Bellringer Options

Literature Launchers:

Pre-Reading Videos DVD,
Selection Launcher

Selection Focus
 Transparency 36

Daily Language Practice
 Transparency 60

Or **say:** Think about a favorite childhood place that you have not seen in a while. It might be a hideaway where you went to be alone, a friend's or a relative's home, or a neighborhood where you once lived.

Ask: Do you think your special childhood place would look the same today as it did then? Would you feel the same way about it now if you were there?

Before You Read

Wordsworth's Poetry

Meet **William Wordsworth**
(1770–1850)

William Wordsworth was a true literary pioneer. He defied the conventions of his time by insisting that poetry should express deep feelings about everyday experiences. In the process, he influenced a generation of poets and helped revolutionize English poetry.

Passion for Nature Wordsworth was born in England's Lake District, a land of breathtaking scenery. Early in life, he suffered two tragedies: the sudden death of his mother when he was eight and the death of his father about five years later. The orphaned Wordsworth children were separated. William and his brothers boarded with a couple near the school the boys attended, and their sister, Dorothy, lived with relatives. Though Wordsworth grieved over the loss of his parents, he came to love school, the people of the Lake District, and the land. The passion he developed for poetry, for simple country living, and for the natural world was to influence him for the rest of his life.

> *"Come forth into the light of things,*
> *Let Nature be your Teacher."*
>
> —William Wordsworth

Rebel in France Wordsworth furthered his education at Cambridge University, graduating at the age of twenty-one. While visiting France, he became caught up in the spirit of the French Revolution, which he viewed as a struggle for social justice. He also fell in love with a French woman named Annette Vallon. Though he wanted to stay with her, lack of money forced him to return to England. The next few years were difficult ones for Wordsworth. He felt guilty about leaving Vallon,

disillusioned by the increasing violence in France, and disappointed by the poor critical response to his volumes of poetry *An Evening Walk* and *Descriptive Sketches.* Lacking a purpose for his future, he teetered on the brink of mental collapse.

Literary Acclaim When Wordsworth was in his mid-twenties, however, his fortunes changed. He inherited money from a friend, was given a cottage in the Lake District, and was reunited with his sister, Dorothy, who was his dear friend and confidant. Soon afterward, he met Samuel Taylor Coleridge, and this meeting resulted in what is probably the most significant friendship in all of English literature. With the companionship and support of his sister and his friend, Wordsworth began to devote himself to writing poetry. He soon established his reputation as a leading young poet with a slim volume of poems entitled *Lyrical Ballads,* first published in 1798. That book, which includes Wordsworth's poem "Lines Composed a Few Miles Above Tintern Abbey" and Coleridge's *The Rime of the Ancient Mariner,* became the cornerstone of English Romanticism.

Wordsworth continued to write throughout his long life, which he spent in the Lake District with his sister and his wife, Mary. His masterpiece, *The Prelude,* a long autobiographical poem, was published after his death.

LOG ON ▶ **Literature** Online

Author Search For more about William Wordsworth, go to glencoe.com and enter QuickPass code GLB9817u4.

Selection Skills

Literary Elements
- Enjambment (SE pp. 739, 741, 743)

The World.../It Is a Beauteous.../My Heart Leaps Up/Composed Upon...

Listening/Speaking/Viewing Skills
- View the Art (SE pp. 740, 742)

Reading Skills
- Identify Genre (SE pp. 739, 742, 743)
- Text Structure (TE p. 740)
- Word Order (TE p. 742)

Vocabulary Skills
- Word Origins (SE p. 743)

Writing Skills/Grammar
- Write an Essay (SE p. 743)

Literature and Reading Preview

Connect to the Poems

What are the benefits of appreciating nature? Freewrite about an experience you've had in nature, and why it was significant.

Build Background

In 1800 Wordsworth added a preface to *Lyrical Ballads* to explain his new approach to poetry. Wordsworth's innovative ideas clashed with those of his predecessors Swift, Pope, and Johnson, the giants of Neoclassicism. Wordsworth suggested that poetry springs from the "spontaneous overflow of powerful feelings" the poet "recollect[s] in tranquility." He felt the language of poetry should be simple and natural.

Set Purposes for Reading

Big Idea **Nature and the Imagination**

As you read, ask yourself, What do these poems suggest about the relationship between humans and the natural world?

Literary Element **Enjambment**

Enjambment is the continuation of a sentence in a poem from one line to the next. Wordsworth often uses enjambment in his poetry. As you read, ask yourself, Where does the poet use this technique?

Reading Strategy Identify Genre: Romantic Poetry

In Wordsworth's view, Romantic poetry differed from Neoclassical poetry in its emphasis on spontaneity and its use of simple language. As you read, ask yourself, How does this poem fit in with what I know about Romanticism?

Tip: Taking Notes Use a web diagram to list examples of Romantic traits in Wordsworth's poems.

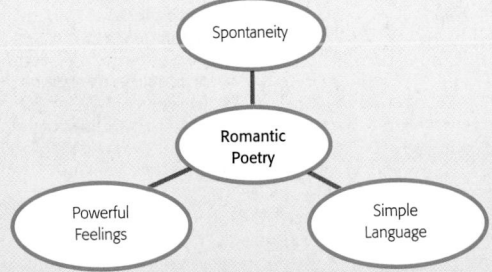

Learning Objectives

For pages 738–751
In studying these texts, you will focus on the following objectives:

Literary Study:
Analyzing enjambment.
Analyzing diction.

Reading:
Identifying genre.
Analyzing sensory details.

Writing: Writing an essay.

Vocabulary

sordid (sôr′ did) *adj.* filthy; selfish; greedy; mean; p. 740 *Putting himself before others, he used any means to achieve his sordid goals.*

piety (pī′ ə tē) *n.* devoutness; reverence; p. 741 *With heartfelt piety, he bowed his head upon entering the cathedral.*

secluded (si klo̅o̅′ did) *adj.* shut off from others; undisturbed; p. 744 *By hiding in a secluded thicket, the fox eluded the hunters.*

repose (ri pōz′) *v.* to lie at rest; rest from work or toil; p. 744 *Worn out from work, the farmer reposed for a while under a shady tree.*

WILLIAM WORDSWORTH **739**

Before You Read

Focus

Summary

"The World Is Too Much with Us" laments how caught up people get in consumerism. In "It Is a Beauteous Evening, Calm and Free," the speaker walks by the sea with a young girl and feels the presence of God. "My Heart Leaps Up" expresses the speaker's wish that his reverence for nature will stay with him always. "Composed Upon Westminster Bridge" portrays London on a silent morning.

 For summaries in languages other than English, see Unit 4 Teaching Resources Book, pp. 100-105.

Vocabulary

Word Origins Have students look up the Latin root of each vocabulary word in a dictionary. Then ask them to compare the meaning of the Latin root with the vocabulary word's definition.

 For additional context, see Glencoe Interactive Vocabulary CD-ROM.

English Learners

DIFFERENTIATED INSTRUCTION

PARTNERS **Intermediate** Have students preview the reading by looking at the title of each poem and the associated pictures. Invite students to work in pairs to describe orally what they see in the pictures. Then have them write predictions about the content of the poems. As they read, ask students to confirm and revise their predictions.

Teach

Literary Element ▮1

Enjambment Ask: What does Wordsworth achieve by using enjambment in lines 9–11? (*By beginning a new sentence with an interjection—"Great God!"—in the middle of a line, Wordsworth emphasizes the speaker's high emotion. The enjambment here also helps the poem to keep its rhyme scheme; "be" rhymes with "lea" two lines later.*)

Big Idea ▮2

Nature and the Imagination
Answer: *The speaker equates this inability with a diseased emotional life and an alienation caused by the preoccupation with money.*

View the Art ★

Answer: *Students may note the clothing and playing cards scattered around, the woman sleeping at the table, the children unattended in a corner, and the dog getting into the food. Some students will feel the painting creates a negative image of a "dissolute" life, while others might note that the room seems cheerful and full of music and think it has a positive mood.*

This slice-of-life family scene is a typical subject for Dutch painter Jan Steen. He often portrayed lively, chaotic family groupings. In fact, the Dutch have a saying based on his work: *a Jan Steen household (een huishouden van Jan Steen)* is a bustling, messy home.

The Dissolute Household, 1668. Jan Steen. Oil on canvas. Victoria and Albert Museum, London.

View the Art The word *dissolute* suggests a person or place lacking in restraint, and even in morals. What impression does this image create of a "dissolute" life? Is it a positive one, or a negative one? ★

The World Is Too Much with Us

William Wordsworth

The world is too much with us; late and soon,
Getting and spending, we lay waste our powers;
Little we see in Nature that is ours;
We have given our hearts away, a **sordid** boon!°
5   This Sea that bares her bosom to the moon;
The winds that will be howling at all hours,
And are up-gathered now like sleeping flowers;
For this, for everything, we are out of tune;
It moves us not.—Great God! I'd rather be
10   A Pagan° suckled in a creed° outworn;
So might I, standing on this pleasant lea,°
Have glimpses that would make me less forlorn;
Have sight of Proteus° rising from the sea;
Or hear old Triton° blow his wreathèd horn.

4 **boon:** gift.

10 **Pagan:** a believer in the ancient Greek or Roman gods of mythology.
creed: a statement of faith or principles.
11 **lea** (lē): meadow.
13 **Proteus** (prṓ′ tē əs): in Greek mythology, a prophet who rose from the sea and assumed different forms.
14 **Triton** (trīt′ ən): the son of the sea god Neptune, who makes the sound of the ocean by blowing through his conch-shell horn.

▮1

 **Nature and the Imagination** *Why is the inability to be moved by nature tragic to the speaker?*

Vocabulary

sordid (sôr′ did) *adj.* filthy; selfish; greedy; mean

740 UNIT 4   THE TRIUMPH OF ROMANTICISM

Reading Practice

 SMALL GROUP **SPIRAL REVIEW** **Analyze Text Structure and Paraphrase** Explain that this poem and the next ("It Is a Beauteous Evening, Calm and Free") are examples of a Petrarchan, or Italian, sonnet. In a Petrarchan sonnet, the first eight lines, or octave, describe a problem or situation. The last six lines, or sestet, suggest a resolution.

Have students work in small groups to paraphrase the problem described in the octave and the resolution in the sestet.

It Is a Beauteous Evening, Calm and Free

William Wordsworth

It is a beauteous evening, calm and free,
The holy time is quiet as a Nun
Breathless with adoration; the broad sun
Is sinking down in its tranquility;
5   The gentleness of heaven broods o'er the Sea:
Listen! the mighty Being is awake,
And doth with his eternal motion make
A sound like thunder—everlastingly.
Dear Child!° dear Girl! that walkest with me here,
10 If thou appear untouched by solemn thought,
Thy nature is not therefore less divine:
Thou liest in Abraham's bosom° all the year,
And worship'st at the Temple's inner shrine,
God being with thee when we know it not.

3

9 Dear Child: Caroline, Wordsworth's daughter with Annette Vallon.

12 Abraham's bosom: According to a Jewish tradition, souls on their way to heaven rest with Abraham, the father of the Hebrew people.

My Heart Leaps Up

William Wordsworth

My heart leaps up when I behold
    A rainbow in the sky:
So was it when my life began;
So is it now I am a man;
5   So be it when I shall grow old,
    Or let me die!
The Child is father of the Man; **4**
And I could wish my days to be
Bound each to each by natural **piety.**

Enjambment *What does Wordsworth achieve by using enjambment in lines 1 and 2?* **5**

Vocabulary

piety (pī′ ə tē) *n.* devoutness; reverence

WILLIAM WORDSWORTH **741**

Teach

Big Idea   3

Nature and the Imagination
Ask: How does the child's relationship to nature differ from the speaker's? *(Unlike the adult, the child does not reflect on nature's mysteries. Adults are rarely able to experience nature with such blessed simplicity.)*

ENGLISH LEARNERS Make sure English learners understand the phrase "untouched by solemn thought." Then have them paraphrase lines 9–11.

Reading Strategy   4

Identify Genre: Romantic Poetry **Ask:** What does line 7 in *My Heart Leaps Up* mean? How does it exemplify the philosophy of Romantic poetry? *(Line 7 means that the child is wiser than the adult he or she later becomes. Children are symbols of Romantic values: spontaneity, closeness to nature, expression of powerful feelings.)*

 For additional practice using the reading skill or strategy, see Unit 4 Teaching Resources Book, p. 107.

Literary Element   5

Enjambment **Answer:** *The use of enjambment emphasizes the object of the speaker's emotion (a rainbow), the first words in the next line, and creates a rhyme with "old" in line 5.*

Teach

A View of Westminster with the Royal Barge and Other Shipping. Joseph Nicholls. Oil on canvas, 61 x 111.7 cm. Private collection.

View the Art The city, or borough, of Westminster, contains many of the most important buildings and institutions in London, including Buckingham Palace. Is this importance reflected in Nicholls's painting?

Reading Strategy · 1

Identify Genre: Romantic Poetry **Answer:** *This poem conveys tranquility, as the speaker gazes at London in the early morning light. The mighty city is beautiful as it seems to sleep.*

APPROACHING Have approaching-level students scan the poem for words that describe the speaker's emotions.

View the Art ★

Answer: *Students should use details from the painting to support their opinions.*

This view looks west across London's Westminster Bridge to Westminster Abbey and Palace, where all but two of England's monarchs have been crowned since 1066. The Royal Barge was the monarch's main form of transportation for journeys of any length—an analogue to Air Force One, the airplane used today by presidents of the United States.

Composed Upon Westminster Bridge, September 3, 1802

William Wordsworth

Earth has not anything to show more fair:
Dull would he be of soul who could pass by
A sight so touching in its majesty:
This City now doth, like a garment, wear
5   The beauty of the morning; silent, bare,
Ships, towers, domes, theaters, and temples lie
Open unto the fields, and to the sky;
All bright and glittering in the smokeless air.
Never did sun more beautifully steep
10 In his first splendor, valley, rock, or hill;
Ne'er saw I, never felt, a calm so deep!
The river glideth at his own sweet will:
Dear God! the very houses seem asleep;
And all that mighty heart is lying still!

1 Identify Genre: Romantic Poetry *What emotion does this poem convey?*

To check students' understanding of the selection, see Unit 4 Teaching Resources Book, p. 109.

Reading Practice

SPIRAL REVIEW **Word Order** Point out that Wordsworth often uses unusual word order in his poems (e.g. "Earth has not anything to show . . ." in the first line). Reread the poem line by line with students, and have volunteers identify examples of unusual word order. Have students "unscramble" each example and paraphrase its meaning in conversational English. Discuss why the poet might have chosen to write in this way. *(Wordsworth was probably trying to help readers picture each image afresh and to emphasize certain thoughts, feelings, and images in the poem.)*

After You Read

Respond and Think Critically

Respond and Interpret

1. Which poem did you like best? Why?

2. (a)According to line 2 of "The World Is Too Much with Us," with what activities are people preoccupied? How does this change lives? (b)What does the speaker think of this change?

3. (a)In "My Heart Leaps Up," what natural phenomenon does the speaker admire? (b)What qualities are usually associated with this phenomenon?

4. (a)In "Composed Upon Westminster Bridge," when does the speaker describe London? (b)Why is that time of day significant?

Analyze and Evaluate

5. What is the **theme**, or main idea about life, in "The World Is Too Much with Us"?

6. Restate the paradox in line 7 of "My Heart Leaps Up." In what sense does that statement seem contradictory? In what sense is it true?

Connect

7. **Big Idea** **Nature and the Imagination** How does Wordsworth view the relationship between humans and the natural world? Explain.

8. **Connect to Today** Consider Wordsworth's message in "The World Is Too Much With Us." Does it apply to modern society? Explain.

Literary Element Enjambment

Poets may use enjambed lines to emphasize rhyming words or to create a conversational tone, breaking lines where people would pause in conversation.

1. What lines of "The World Is Too Much with Us" are enjambed? What rhymes are emphasized?

2. What purposes do the three examples of enjambment in the first eight lines of "It Is a Beauteous Evening, Calm and Free" serve?

Reading Strategy Identify Genre: Romantic Poetry

Review the web diagram you made as you read.

1. What elements in these poems reflect Wordsworth's idea that poetry springs from "the spontaneous overflow of powerful feelings"?

2. To what extent is the language in these poems simple and natural?

Writing

Write an Essay "Composed Upon Westminster Bridge" describes a place the poet found beautiful and impressive. Write a brief essay describing a location that inspires such feelings for you. Use elements of Romanticism, such as strong emotion and simple language, in your essay.

 **Literature** Online

Selection Resources For Selection Quizzes, eFlashcards, and Reading-Writing Connection activities, go to glencoe.com and enter QuickPass code GLB9817u4.

Vocabulary Practice

Practice with Word Origins Create a word map for each of these vocabulary words from the selection. Use a dictionary for help.

sordid   piety

EXAMPLE:

> *Definition:* facts that are recalled or retained in the mind

> *Etymology:* Latin *memoria* means "remembering"

> memories

> *Sample Sentence:* The poem's speaker relates childhood memories.

WILLIAM WORDSWORTH **743**

Literary Element

1. Lines 1, 6, 9, and 11; the rhymes *soon/boon, ours/flowers,* and *be/lea*

2. To fit the Petrarchan sonnet form

Progress Check

Can students recognize enjambment?

If No → See Unit 4 Teaching Resources Book, p. 106.

Reading Strategy

1. Word choices such as *A pagan, Listen! Dear Child! Or let me die! Dear God!*

2. Wordsworth often uses simple words of one or two syllables, as in "The world is too much with us; late and soon."

After You Read

Assess

1. Preferences will vary.

2. (a) "Getting and spending," thereby losing touch with nature (b) It is a tragic loss.

3. (a) A rainbow (b) Light, color, brightness, hope, union with heaven, and good fortune

4. (a) In the early morning (b) The city glitters in the rising sun, unobscured by smoke from chimneys and factories

5. Losing touch with nature leaves people spiritually bankrupt.

6. The statement is paradoxical because a child cannot be the father of an adult. The statement is true in that childhood experiences profoundly influence an adult's mature attitudes.

7. Nature is a divine realm and the true home of human beings.

8. Students should support their opinions using examples.

Vocabulary Practice

sordid; Definition: filthy; selfish; greedy; Etymology: Latin *sordidus* means "dirty" or "foul"; Possible sentence: His sordid means for rigging the election were discovered, and he was taken out of the running.

piety; Definition: devoutness; reverence; Etymology: Latin *pietas* means "dutifulness" ; Possible sentence: The worshippers showed piety by covering their heads in the temple.

Writing

Students' essays should use emotion, simple language and other elements of Romanticism to describe a specific location.

Focus

Summary

In "Lines Composed a Few Miles Above Tintern Abbey," the speaker looks out over a familiar and beautiful vista and meditates on his life, aging, the joys of nature, solitude, and the companionship of his beloved sister.

Teach

Reading Strategy | 1

Analyze Sensory Details
Answer: *"Waters, rolling," "mountain springs," "soft inland murmur," "steep and lofty cliffs," "wild secluded scene," and "the quiet of the sky"*

Literary History ☆

Romantic poets criticized the stiff, formal diction of 18th-century poetry. To Wordsworth, plain speech and vivid emotion were paramount. In turn, their use of simple, conversational language was attacked.

Selection Skills

Literary Elements
- Diction (SE pp. 744, 747, 749, 751)
- Mood (TE p. 746)

Reading Skills
- Analyze Sensory Details (SE pp. 744, 751)

Lines Composed a Few Miles Above Tintern Abbey

Vocabulary Skills
- Antonyms (SE p. 751)
- Academic Vocabulary (SE p. 751)

Listening/Speaking/Viewing Skills
- View the Art (SE p. 745)

Writing Skills/Grammar
- Expository Essay (SE p. 752)
- Ellipses (SE p. 752)
- Describe a Setting (TE p. 748)

744

Literary Element Diction

An author's **diction** is his or her word choice—the use of particular words to convey specific meanings. Diction is particularly important in poetry, which uses language more economically than most prose does. As you read, ask yourself, What effect does Wordsworth's diction have on the poem?

Reading Strategy Analyze Sensory Details

In creating effective images, writers use **sensory details**, or descriptions that appeal to one or more of the five senses: sight, hearing, touch, taste, and smell. Like diction and sentence structure, sensory details influence the tone and meaning of a literary work. As you read, ask yourself, How do these details contribute to this poem's meaning?

LINES COMPOSED A FEW MILES ABOVE TINTERN ABBEY

William Wordsworth

☆ Five years have past; five summers, with the length
Of five long winters! and again I hear
These waters, rolling from their mountain springs
With a soft inland murmur. Once again
5 Do I behold these steep and lofty cliffs,
That on a wild **secluded** scene impress
Thoughts of more deep seclusion; and connect
The landscape with the quiet of the sky.
The day is come when I again **repose**

Analyze Sensory Details *This poem was inspired by Wordsworth's two visits to the ruins of a medieval abbey located in an area of Wales known for its striking beauty. Which details in the first eight lines help you visualize the scene?*

1

Vocabulary

secluded (si klōō′ did) *adj.* shut off from others; undisturbed
repose (ri pōz′) *v.* to lie at rest; rest from work or toil

Interior of Tintern Abbey.
Thomas Girtin.
Watercolor on paper.
Private collection.

View the Art Tintern Abbey was constructed in 1131, as a monastery and church. To which lines in Wordsworth's poem does this image most closely correspond? Explain. ⭐

10   Here, under this dark sycamore, and view
     These plots of cottage ground, these orchard tufts,
     Which at this season, with their unripe fruits,
     Are clad in one green hue, and lose themselves
     'Mid groves and copses.¹ Once again I see
15   These hedgerows,² hardly hedgerows, little lines
     Of sportive wood run wild; these pastoral farms,
     Green to the very door; and wreaths of smoke
     Sent up, in silence, from among the trees!
     With some uncertain notice, as might seem
20   Of vagrant dwellers in the houseless woods,
     Or of some hermit's cave, where by his fire
     The hermit sits alone.

                         These beauteous forms,
     Through a long absence, have not been to me
     As is a landscape to a blind man's eye;
25   But oft, in lonely rooms, and 'mid the din
     Of towns and cities, I have owed to them
     In hours of weariness, sensations sweet,

1. *Copses* are thick, dense growths of small trees or bushes.
2. *Hedgerows* are rows of bushes, shrubs, or trees that serve as fences or boundaries.

Diction *What does the phrase "unripe fruits" suggest about the time of year?* **2**

Nature and the Imagination *What comforts the speaker while he is in the city?* **3**

WILLIAM WORDSWORTH **745**

Teach

Literary Element | 2

Diction **Answer:** *The season is late spring or early summer.*

📁 For additional literary element practice, see Unit 4 Teaching Resources Book, p. 117.

Big Idea | 3

Nature and the Imagination
Answer: *The speaker is comforted by the beauty of Tintern Abbey, which lingers in his memory and imagination.*

(APPROACHING) Have approaching-level students list the images described in lines 1–20. Point out that "These beauteous forms" refers back to these images.

View the Art ⭐

Answer: *Students should explain how the lines they have chosen correspond with the mood or details of the image.*

> **Interactive Read and Write**
> Other options for teaching this selection can be found in
> - Interactive Read and Write for EL Students pp. 197-206
> - Interactive Read and Write for Approaching-Level Students, pp. 197-206
> - Interactive Read and Write for On-Level Students, pp. 197-206

Teach

Reading Strategy | 1

Paraphrase Paraphrasing unusual figures of speech may help students make sense of the poem. **Ask:** How would you paraphrase "the fever of the world"? *(the hectic pace of daily life)* Guide students in clarifying other phrases.

Big Idea | 2

Nature and the Imagination
Answer: *The lines suggest a mystical union with nature. The speaker believes that when people open themselves to nature's influence, they can "see into the life of things" in a meditative way.*

[ENGLISH LEARNERS] Check English learners understanding of the phrase "an eye made quiet."
Ask: What do joy and harmony do to the eye? *(make it still)* What happens when our eye is quiet? *(We see into the life of things.)*

Literary Element Practice

SPIRAL REVIEW **Mood** Remind students that mood is the feeling that the poem creates in the reader. Have each student choose one word from the poem that helps set the mood, such as *tranquil* or *lightened*, and use it as the center of a word web. Have students add mood words to their webs as they read through the poem.

Felt in the blood, and felt along the heart;
And passing even into my purer mind,
30   With tranquil restoration—feelings, too,
Of unremembered pleasure: such, perhaps,
As have no slight or trivial influence
On that best portion of a good man's life,
His little, nameless, unremembered, acts
35   Of kindness and of love. Nor less, I trust,
To them I may have owed another gift,
Of aspect more sublime; that blessed mood,
In which the burthen[3] of the mystery,
In which the heavy and the weary weight
40   Of all this unintelligible[4] world,
Is lightened—that serene and blessed mood,
In which the affections gently lead us on—
Until, the breath of this corporeal[5] frame
And even the motion of our human blood
45   Almost suspended, we are laid asleep
In body, and become a living soul;
While with an eye made quiet by the power
Of harmony, and the deep power of joy,
We see into the life of things.
                                    If this
50   Be but a vain belief, yet, oh! how oft—
In darkness and amid the many shapes
Of joyless daylight; when the fretful stir
Unprofitable, and the fever of the world, **1**
Have hung upon the beatings of my heart—
55   How oft, in spirit, have I turned to thee,
O sylvan Wye![6] thou wanderer through the woods,
How often has my spirit turned to thee!

        And now, with gleams of half-extinguished thought,
With many recognitions dim and faint,
60   And somewhat of a sad perplexity,
The picture of the mind revives again;
While here I stand, not only with the sense
Of present pleasure, but with pleasing thoughts
That in this moment there is life and food

---

3. *Burthen* is a variant form of *burden.*
4. *Unintelligible* means "incapable of being understood."
5. *Corporeal* means "bodily."
6. *Sylvan* means "wooded"; the *Wye* is the river along whose banks Wordsworth walked during his visits.

2 Nature and the Imagination *What type of relationship with nature do these lines suggest?*

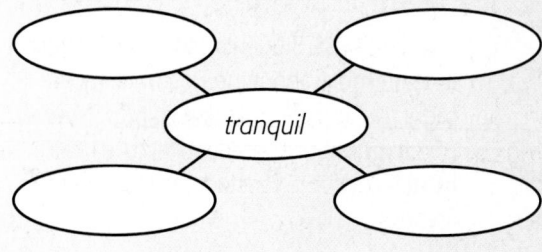

65 For future years. And so I dare to hope,
Though changed, no doubt, from what I was when first
I came among these hills; when like a roe[7]
I bounded o'er the mountains, by the sides
Of the deep rivers, and the lonely streams,
70 Wherever nature led—more like a man
Flying from something that he dreads than one
Who sought the thing he loved. For nature then
(The coarser pleasures of my boyish days,
And their glad animal movements all gone by)
75 To me was all in all—I cannot paint
What then I was. The sounding cataract[8]   **3**
Haunted me like a passion; the tall rock,
The mountain, and the deep and gloomy wood,
Their colors and their forms, were then to me
80 An appetite; a feeling and a love,
That had no need of a remoter charm,
By thought supplied, nor any interest
Unborrowed from the eye. That time is past,
And all its aching joys are now no more,
85 And all its dizzy raptures. Not for this
Faint[9] I, nor mourn nor murmur; other gifts
Have followed; for such loss, I would believe,
Abundant recompense.[10] For I have learned
To look on nature, not as in the hour
90 Of thoughtless youth; but hearing oftentimes
The still, sad music of humanity,
Nor harsh nor grating, though of ample power
To chasten and subdue. And I have felt
A presence that disturbs me with the joy
95 Of elevated thoughts; a sense sublime
Of something far more deeply interfused,
Whose dwelling is the light of setting suns,
And the round ocean and the living air,
And the blue sky, and in the mind of man;
100 A motion and a spirit, that impels
All thinking things, all objects of all thought,

---

7. A *roe* is a small Eurasian deer found in lightly forested regions.
8. A *cataract* is a waterfall.
9. Here, *faint* means "to lose heart; become depressed."
10. *Recompense* is compensation or repayment.

Diction *What do the words* roe *and* bounded *suggest about the speaker's former reaction to nature?*

Diction *How does this image contrast with the image of "the sounding cataract" in line 76?*

WILLIAM WORDSWORTH   **747**

Literary Element   3

Diction **Ask:** What do lines 75–76 mean? Why might the speaker express this thought in this way? *(This means he does not have access to the person he was when younger. He probably means to help the reader to picture what he was then, even while claiming he himself cannot.)*

ENGLISH LEARNERS If English learners have difficulty understanding the poet's unusual syntax, guide them in restructuring and clarifying the sentence without the line break: *I cannot paint ("show you," or "describe") what I was then ("in the past," "when I was young").*

Literary Element   4

Diction **Answer:** *The speaker's earlier reaction was like that of a wild, instinctive creature.*

Literary Element   5

Diction **Answer:** *This image, which reflects the speaker's mature response to nature, is meditative and quiet; the image of "the sounding cataract," which reflects the speaker's youthful response, is thunderous and energetic.*

English Learners

DIFFERENTIATED INSTRUCTION

PARTNERS **Intermediate** Help English learners with summarizing. Model careful rereading and summarizing of groups of lines. Then have students work with partners to write a one-paragraph summary of the page.

Approaching Level

DIFFERENTIATED INSTRUCTION

Emerging After approaching-level students have completed a guided reading of page 747, have them take turns reading aloud the lines of the poem to improve ***reading fluency***. Ask them to aim for smooth and evenly paced reading.

Teach

Nature and the Imagination

Answer: *Just as an anchor keeps a ship from drifting, so nature keeps the speaker from straying off course. Nature is a moral compass that points the way to truth and virtue in a confusing world.*

View the Art ★

Tintern Abbey is the beautiful, ivy-covered ruins of a medieval monastery in a remote valley in south Wales. Founded in 1131, the monastery was rebuilt and added to until about 1300. In the 1300s, the Black Death swept through Europe, causing great hardship and probably ending the heyday of this beautiful monastery. In 1536 King Henry VIII ordered the immediate closing of all monasteries in England.

Tintern Abbey, 1794. Joseph Mallord William Turner. Tate Gallery, London. ★

And rolls through all things. Therefore am I still
A lover of the meadows and the woods
And mountains; and of all that we behold
105　From this green earth; of all the mighty world
Of eye and ear—both what they half create,
And what perceive; well pleased to recognize
In nature and the language of the sense,
The anchor of my purest thoughts, the nurse,
110　The guide, the guardian of my heart, and soul
Of all my moral being.

　　　　　　　　Nor perchance,
If I were not thus taught, should I the more
Suffer my genial spirits[11] to decay;
For thou art with me here upon the banks
115　Of this fair river; thou my dearest Friend,[12]
My dear, dear Friend, and in thy voice I catch
The language of my former heart and read
My former pleasures in the shooting lights

---

11. *Suffer my genial spirits* means "allow my vital energies."
12. *My dearest Friend* refers to Wordsworth's sister, Dorothy, who accompanied him on this walking tour.

1　Nature and the Imagination *What does nature mean to the speaker?*

Writing Practice

Describe a Setting Point out that this poem, like much of Wordsworth's work, has a strong sense of place. The landscape is a canvas for the speaker's thoughts, memories, observations, and emotions. Have students create presentations about places they feel strongly about. They should write a short passage and illustrate it with one or more images—drawings, paintings, or collages. Invite students to present their work to small groups.

Of thy wild eyes. Oh! yet a little while
120 May I behold in thee what I was once,
My dear, dear Sister! and this prayer I make,
Knowing that Nature never did betray
The heart that loved her; 'tis her privilege,
Through all the years of this our life, to lead
125 From joy to joy; for she can so inform[13]
The mind that is within us, so impress
With quietness and beauty, and so feed
With lofty thoughts, that neither evil tongues,
Rash judgments, nor the sneers of selfish men,
130 Nor greetings where no kindness is, nor all
The dreary intercourse of daily life,
Shall e'er prevail against us, or disturb
Our cheerful faith, that all which we behold
Is full of blessings. Therefore let the moon
135 Shine on thee in thy solitary walk;
And let the misty mountain winds be free
To blow against thee: and, in after years,
When these wild ecstasies shall be matured
Into a sober pleasure; when thy mind
140 Shall be a mansion for all lovely forms,
Thy memory be as a dwelling place
For all sweet sounds and harmonies; oh! then,
If solitude, or fear, or pain, or grief,
Should be thy portion, with what healing thoughts
145 Of tender joy wilt thou remember me,
And these my exhortations! Nor, perchance—
If I should be where I no more can hear
Thy voice, nor catch from thy wild eyes these gleams
Of past existence—wilt thou then forget
150 That on the banks of this delightful stream
We stood together; and that I, so long
A worshipper of Nature, hither came
Unwearied in that service; rather say
With warmer love—oh! with far deeper zeal
155 Of holier love. Nor wilt thou then forget
That after many wanderings, many years
Of absence, these steep woods and lofty cliffs,
And this green pastoral landscape, were to me
More dear, both for themselves and for thy sake!

---

13. Here, *inform* means "to inspire."

Diction *What does the diction in this passage suggest about city life?* **2**

Nature and the Imagination *What does the speaker suggest about the relationship between humans and nature in lines 155–159?* **3**

WILLIAM WORDSWORTH **749**

Teach

| Literary Element | 2 |

Diction Answer: *Phrases such as "evil tongues," "rash judgments," and the "sneers of selfish men" suggest the spiritual damage that life in the city inflicts.*

APPROACHING To help approaching-level students understand the meaning of "rash judgments," "evil tongues," and "greetings where no kindness is," have them offer examples of each. For example, a rash judgment might be judging someone by their appearance.

| Big Idea | 3 |

Nature and the Imagination

Answer: *The speaker says that his sister will recognize that this beautiful scene can be appreciated not only for itself but also for its ability to connect people who share its beauty in memory. Their visit to Tintern Abbey has strengthened their familial bond.*

Approaching Level

DIFFERENTIATED INSTRUCTION

 PARTNERS

Established Assign partners and distribute three index cards to each pair. On the first card, have partners identify details that Wordsworth uses to describe the landscape near Tintern Abbey. On the second card, have them describe the emotions that the scene formerly evoked in the poet. On the third card, have them describe the emotions that the scene now evokes in him. Ask students reading above grade level to write a fourth card, stating the theme, or main message, of the poem and explaining how each section helps develop that message.

749

After You Read

Assess

1. Students' answers will vary.

2. (a) A wooded hillside above the ruins of an abbey surrounded by cottages. Sights include cliffs, the sky, orchards, groves, hedgerows, and chimney smoke. The speaker hears the soft murmuring of an inland stream. (b) He feels appreciation, wonder, and affection.

3. (a) Five (b) The memory has offered solace amid the din and confusion of city life.

4. (a) He no longer flees a world he dreads. He now has a deeper appreciation of the bond between nature and humanity. (b) He feels that his maturity and wisdom are adequate compensation for the lost ardor of youth.

5. The poem is about the natural world, human nature, and the connections between them.

6. The sentence structure, vocabulary, and conversational tone are like prose. Poetic elements include meter, alliteration, personification, and imagery.

7. The speaker also worships the divinity reflected in nature.

8. The joy Wordsworth seems to feel from being there with his sister seems to reflect their close attachment; Wordsworth says he sees his old self in her, and wishes that she will remember him fondly always.

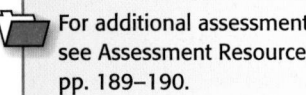 For additional assessment, see Assessment Resources, pp. 189–190.

750

After You Read

Respond and Think Critically

Respond and Interpret

1. Which lines of this poem did you find most meaningful? Which lines would you like to clarify or ask questions about?

2. (a) Describe the **setting** of the poem. What sights and sounds does the speaker mention in lines 1–22? (b) What is the speaker's attitude toward the sights and sounds around him?

3. (a) How many years have passed since the speaker's first visit to the countryside overlooking Tintern Abbey? (b) Why has the speaker so often "returned in spirit" to these powerful scenes since his first visit?

4. (a) In what ways has the speaker changed since his first visit? How does he look upon nature now? (b) How does the speaker feel about the changes he sees in himself since his first visit?

Analyze and Evaluate

5. Is this poem about nature, about human nature, or about both? Explain your opinion, citing lines from the poem to support your ideas.

6. In what ways is this poem like prose? What elements are "poetic"?

Connect

7. **Big Idea** Nature and the Imagination Compare "Lines Composed a Few Miles Above Tintern Abbey" with "It Is a Beauteous Evening, Calm and Free." Consider Wordsworth's attitude toward nature and the enjoyment of nature. What similarities do you see in these poems?

8. **Connect to the Author** Reread the biography on page 738. In what ways is Wordsworth's attachment to his sister reflected in this poem?

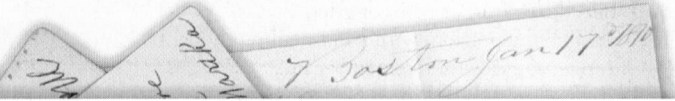

Primary Source Quotation

Evaluating a Literary Rebel

Francis Jeffrey, a literary critic, expressed these opinions about Wordsworth's poetry in articles published in the *Edinburgh Review* in 1807 and 1814. As you read, note this critic's reaction to Wordsworth's poetry and Romanticism.

"With Mr. Wordsworth and his friends, it is plain that their peculiarities of diction are things of choice, and not of accident. They write as they do, upon principle and system; and it evidently costs them much pains to keep down to the standard which they have proposed for themselves."

"If Mr. Wordsworth, instead of confining himself almost entirely to the society of . . . cottagers and little children . . . had condescended to mingle a little more with the people that were to read and judge [his book], we cannot help thinking that its texture might have been considerably improved."

Group Activity Discuss the following questions with your classmates. Cite evidence from Wordsworth's poems for support.

1. What is Jeffrey's evaluation of Wordsworth's diction?

2. What criticism does Jeffrey level at Wordsworth in the last quotation? How might Wordsworth have responded?

Primary Source Quotation

1. Wordsworth's diction is intentional, not accidental, and its quality is poor.

2. Jeffrey criticizes Wordsworth for spending his time in rural isolation, suggesting that if he associated more freely with his urban readers his poetry might improve. Wordsworth might reply that if Jeffrey spent more time in the country, he might respond better to Romantic poetry.

Literary Element Diction

Through his **diction**, or word choice, Wordsworth rebelled against the strict demands of Neo-classicism. Instead of using "poetic" language, he tried to use simple and natural language, which reflected the speech patterns of ordinary people.

1. In "Tintern Abbey," does Wordsworth fulfill his intention to write poetry "in a selection of language really spoken" by people? Explain.

2. How does the diction in this poem reflect Wordsworth's aesthetic principles and reinforce his ideas?

Review: Lyric Poetry

As you learned on page 441, **lyric poetry** expresses a speaker's personal thoughts and feelings. Lyric poems are usually short and musical, and they emphasize the experience of emotion.

Partner Activity With a partner, answer these questions:

1. Review the four poems by Wordsworth that precede "Lines Composed a Few Miles Above Tintern Abbey." In what ways are these poems examples of lyric poetry?

2. (a)In what way is "Lines Composed a Few Miles Above Tintern Abbey" a lyric poem? (b)What is the verse form of this poem?

 Literature Online

Selection Resources For Selection Quizzes, eFlashcards, and Reading-Writing Connection activities, go to glencoe.com and enter QuickPass code GLB9817u4.

Reading Strategy Analyze Sensory Details

By using **sensory details**, Wordsworth creates images, or word pictures, that evoke emotional responses in the reader. Review the examples of sensory details that you noted while reading the poems, and then answer the following questions.

1. To which senses do most of the sensory details in "Tintern Abbey" appeal? Identify images that appeal to the sense of touch.

2. Which sensory details evoke negative emotions about life in London?

3. How does the use of sensory details reinforce the theme of this poem? Cite examples to support your opinion.

Vocabulary Practice

Practice with Antonyms With a partner, match each boldfaced vocabulary word below with an antonym. You will not use all the answer choices. Use a dictionary or thesaurus to check your answers.

1. secluded
2. repose

a. crowded
b. isolated
c. toil
d. curious

Academic Vocabulary

In "Tintern Abbey," Wordsworth **highlights** the persistence of memory.

Highlight is an academic word. In the poem, Wordsworth also **highlights** the wonders of nature.

To further explore the meaning of this word, complete the following sentence: *Some other themes that Wordsworth highlights in his poetry are _____.*

For more on academic vocabulary, see pages 56 and R81.

WILLIAM WORDSWORTH **751**

After You Read

Assess

Literary Element

1. The language of this poem is very similar to the language of the people of the period.

2. Wordsworth uses simple language, which creates a conversational tone. The tone reinforces Wordsworth's message that an appreciation of nature, though deepened by mature thought, is an activity that comes mainly from the heart. His word choices reflect his belief that poetry should spring from the spontaneous overflow of powerful feelings, reveal the power of nature's beauty, and reflect the speech of common people.

Review: Lyric Poetry

1. All four are short poems that musically express the speaker's powerful feelings.

2. (a) It resembles the other four poems in its subject matter and its expression of deep emotion. (b) Blank verse, or unrhymed iambic pentameter

Reading Strategy

1. Most of the sensory details appeal to sight or hearing. Examples of details that appeal to touch include "felt in the blood," "weary weight," and "the misty mountain winds."

2. Details include "lonely rooms," "the din of towns and cities," "the sneers of selfish men," and "the dreary intercourse of daily life."

3. The sensory details support the theme that an appreciation of nature sustains people and connects them, whereas urban society is draining and alienating.

751

After You Read

Assess

📝 Respond Through Writing

Use these criteria in evaluating student essays:

- It identifies and accurately cites Wordsworth's diction.
- The contribution of the diction to Wordsworth's message is clearly explained.
- Ellipses are used to show omission of words, phrases, or whole lines in quotations.

A student who meets all of these criteria should receive the equivalent of a 3-point response.

A student who fully meets two of these criteria should receive the equivalent of a 2-point response.

A student who partially meets one of these criteria should receive the equivalent of a 1-point response.

📝 Respond Through Writing

Expository Essay

Analyze Diction The essence of poetry is precise and evocative choice of language. Wordsworth revolutionized the literary form by using the power of words to reveal the emotional depth of everyday experiences. Analyze the style of Wordsworth's poem, focusing on his use of diction to create ambiguity and nuance.

Prewrite Reread "Lines Composed a Few Miles Above Tintern Abbey," jotting down words or phrases that contribute to the poem's message and emotional effect. Then craft a controlling statement for your essay that summarizes your analysis of Wordsworth's style.

Draft Keeping your controlling statement in mind, create an informal outline of the information you will include. One effective way to clarify the nuances of Wordsworth's diction is to analyze the poem's language stanza by stanza. Note effective instances of word choice or voice, followed by the effects they have on the poem or on the reader.

Wordsworth's everyday language and concrete, sensory images help us see our familiar world with new eyes.

   I. Stanza 1—repetition in "five years . . . five summers . . . five long winters" stresses familiarity and return

   II. Stanza 2—"little, nameless, unremembered, acts / Of kindness and of love" focuses us on the small things we tend to forget: ambiguity—most easily forgotten is most important to remember

Use statements like the following to identify and interpret Wordsworth's stylistic devices:

The poet uses _____, _____, and _____ to represent _____.

Revise Consult the Writing Workshop checklist on page 972 to evaluate how well you've met the standards for an analytic essay. Make sure you've identified Wordsworth's significant ideas and elements of diction and that you have provided adequate support for your statements by citing and explaining lines from the poem.

Edit and Proofread Proofread your paper, correcting any errors in spelling, grammar, and punctuation. Use the Grammar Tip in the side column to help you with ellipses.

Learning Objectives

In this assignment, you will focus on the following objectives:

Writing: Writing an expository essay.

Grammar: Understanding ellipses.

Grammar Tip

Ellipses

When writing about literature, you often will need to quote from the text to support your points. Delete words or lines from the text that don't contribute to your point and replace them with **ellipses**—spaced dots that indicate missing information.

Use three spaced dots to indicate text omitted within a sentence.

Wordsworth contrasts the beauty of "These hedgerows . . . these pastoral farms / Green to the very door" with "the din / Of towns and cities."

Writing Practice

PARTNERS **Revise and Review** Have students revise their essays analyzing Wordsworth's use of diction. Remind them to correct spelling and grammar and to check that they have supported their statements with evidence from the text. Then have students work with a partner to review their essays. Have them exchange papers, noting any additional corrections as they read. When they finish, have partners return the papers and review them together. Encourage students to discuss the suggestions made by their partners.

Before You Read
from *The Journals of Dorothy Wordsworth*

Meet **Dorothy Wordsworth**
(1771–1855)

The depth of Dorothy Wordsworth's devotion to her brother William, the great Romantic poet, and of his devotion to her can be illustrated by a striking entry in one of Dorothy's journals that describes the events surrounding William's marriage to his childhood sweetheart, Mary Hutchinson. On the night before he was to be married, William entrusted Dorothy with the wedding ring, presumably for safekeeping. On the morning of the wedding she returned it to him. Recalling that moment in her journal, she wrote, "I gave him the wedding ring—with how deep a blessing! I took it from my forefinger where I had worn it the whole of the night before—he slipped it again onto my finger, and blessed me fervently." Modern readers might view this revelation as odd, and apparently so did the editors of the first edition of Dorothy's journals, who chose to omit it when the journals were published after her death. In fact, however, Mary was Dorothy's oldest friend. Neither woman was jealous of the other. After William married, Dorothy lived with him and his wife and helped them raise their children.

> "We walked to Rydale. It was very
> pleasant—Grasmere lake a beautiful
> image of stillness, clear as glass,
> reflecting all things. . . . The church
> and buildings, how quiet they were!"
>
> —Dorothy Wordsworth
> from *The Grasmere Journals*

Three Writers, One Soul Dorothy Wordsworth was born on Christmas Day. When she was six years old, her mother died, and Dorothy was separated from her brothers and sent to live with relatives because it was thought that an all-male household was not a fit place to raise a young girl. Many years later, Dorothy was reunited with her brother William. Dorothy and William enjoyed a deep friendship with the poet Samuel Taylor Coleridge, with whom they walked and talked daily for a number of years. The three were so close that Dorothy once described the trio as "three persons with one soul."

Observer of Nature Although Dorothy wrote some poetry, her best writing is found in her journals and letters. Her *Alfoxden Journal, 1798* and *The Grasmere Journals, 1800–1803* offer a remarkably detailed and rich view of English cottage life in the first part of the nineteenth century and provide valuable insights into her relationship with her brother and her influence on his poetry. Dorothy's journal writing (which, according to her, she pursued "because I shall give William pleasure by it") shows her to be a keen observer of nature and of the people around her. One biographer has called her "probably . . . the most distinguished of English writers who never wrote a line for the general public."

Later Years When Dorothy Wordsworth was in her mid-sixties, she fell seriously ill with arteriosclerosis. She became an invalid, and the disease apparently affected her mind. She remained in this debilitated state for more than twenty years until her death at the age of eighty-three.

Literature Online

Author Search For more about Dorothy Wordsworth, go to glencoe.com and enter QuickPass code GLB9817u4.

DOROTHY WORDSWORTH **753**

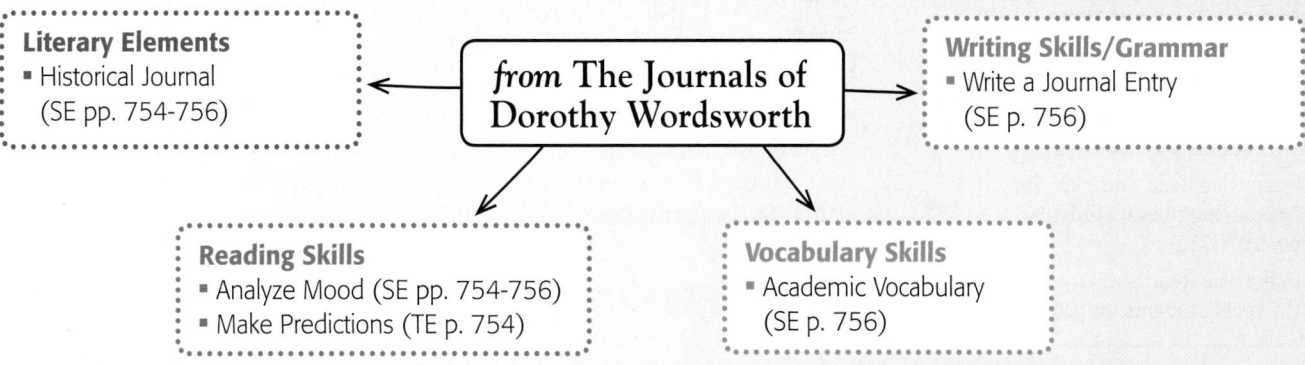

Before You Read

Focus

Summary

This entry from Dorothy Wordsworth's journal describes a walk with her brother William on a stormy spring day. She details their observations of the countryside—various plants, wind and rough waters, and a mass of daffodils along the shore.

 For summaries in languages other than English, see Unit 4 Teaching Resources Book, pp. 122–127.

Vocabulary

Synonyms Write the following words and definitions on the board: *beautiful, toss ("to be thrown around"), reel ("to sway"), change.* Have students use a thesaurus to find two synonyms for each word. **Write** their responses on the board. **Say:** Describe the mood each word creates based on its sound and associations.

Readability Scores

Dale-Chall: 6.5
DRP: 57
Lexile: 980

Interactive Read and Write

Other options for teaching this selection can be found in

- Interactive Read and Write for EL Students pp. 207–212
- Interactive Read and Write for Approaching-Level Students, pp. 207–212
- Interactive Read and Write for On-Level Students, pp. 207–212

754

Literature and Reading Preview

Connect to the Journal

Have you ever come across a scene in nature so extraordinary that you wanted to share it with someone? Create a word web using details from the scene and your reactions to them.

Build Background

In 1799 William and Dorothy Wordsworth settled in the village of Grasmere. From 1800 to 1803, Dorothy recorded descriptions of village life in and around Grasmere. William Wordsworth often turned to Dorothy's journals for inspiration as well as for details for his poems. The journal entry you are about to read inspired William to write the poem "I Wandered Lonely as a Cloud," the first stanza of which is reprinted on the next page.

Set Purposes for Reading

Big Idea Nature and the Imagination

As you read, ask yourself, How do Dorothy Wordsworth's observations reflect the Romantics' admiration for nature, and nature's effect on the imagination?

Literary Element Historical Journal

A **historical journal** is a record of events kept by a participant or witness in those events. Journals provide interesting details about daily lives and can be an important source of historical information. As you read, ask yourself, What does this journal entry reveal about Dorothy's relationship to William and her influence on his poetry?

Reading Strategy Analyze Mood

Mood is the emotional quality of a literary work. A writer's style and choice of language, as well as subject matter and setting, contribute to a work's mood. **Analyzing mood** means discovering how these components work together. As you read, ask yourself, How does Wordsworth create mood in this passage?

Tip: Taking Notes Use a chart like this one to record examples of Wordsworth's style that contribute to the mood of the journal.

Example	Style Element	Description of Mood
"Wind seized our breath"	personification	violent weather

Reading Practice

SPIRAL REVIEW **Make Predictions** Remind students that the ideals of Romanticism include imagination, individual expression, and a strong interest in nature. Have students read the first and last sentences of the selection as well as the stanza from William Wordsworth's poem. Ask them to write several sentences in which they predict the theme, style, tone, and other aspects of the selection. *(Students' predictions may incorporate Dorothy Wordsworth's references to nature and William Wordsworth's imaginative language.)*

Learning Objectives

For pages 753–756

In studying this text, you will focus on the following objectives:

Literary Study: Analyzing a historical journal.

Reading: Analyzing mood.

Writing: Writing a journal entry.

from The Journals of Dorothy Wordsworth

Dorothy Wordsworth

THURSDAY, APRIL 15.   It was a threatening misty morning—but mild. We [Dorothy and William] set off after dinner from Eusemere. Mrs. Clarkson went a short way with us but turned back. The wind was furious, and we thought we must have returned. We first rested in the large boathouse, then under a furze bush opposite Mr. Clarkson's; saw the plough going in the field. The wind seized our breath; the lake was rough. There was a boat by itself floating in the middle of the bay below Water Millock. We rested again in the Water Millock lane. The hawthorns are black and green, the birches here and there greenish, but there is yet more of purple to be seen on the twigs. We got over into a field to avoid some cows—people working, a few primroses by the roadside wood-sorrel flowers, the anemone, scentless violets, strawberries, and that starry yellow flower which Mrs. C. calls pile wort. When we were in the woods beyond Gowbarrow Park, we saw a few daffodils[1] close to the waterside. We fancied that

I wandered lonely as a cloud

That floats on high o'er vales and hills,

When all at once I saw a crowd,

A host of golden daffodils,

Beside the lake, beneath the trees,

Fluttering and dancing in the breeze.

—*William Wordsworth*

the lake had floated the seeds ashore and that the little colony had so sprung up. But as we went along there were more and yet more, and at last under the boughs of the trees, we saw that there was a long belt of them along the shore, about the breadth of a country turnpike road. I never saw daffodils so beautiful. They grew among the mossy stones about and about them; some rested their heads upon these stones as on a pillow for weariness, and the rest tossed and reeled and danced and seemed as if they verily laughed with the wind that blew upon them over the lake. They looked so gay, ever glancing, ever changing. This wind blew directly over the lake to them. There was here and there a little knot and a few stragglers a few yards higher up, but they were so few as not to disturb the simplicity and unity and life of that one busy highway. We rested again and again. The bays were stormy, and we heard the waves at different distances and in the middle of the water like the sea. ∾

---

1. The *daffodil*, also called the trumpet narcissus, has a brilliant yellow flower with a trumpet-shaped central crown.

1 Historical Journal *How might the details in this paragraph have inspired William Wordsworth to write "I Wandered Lonely as a Cloud"?*

Analyze Mood *What mood is created by this personification of the daffodils?* **2**

Nature and the Imagination *The Romantics valued the unity and simplicity of nature. What principle of Romanticism is illustrated here by Wordsworth's imaginative treatment of nature?* **3**

DOROTHY WORDSWORTH **755**

Teach

Literary Element   1

Journal **Answer:** *Dorothy Wordsworth is scrupulous in recording specific details of the setting. Her brother William turned these details into vivid images for his poem.*

Reading Strategy   2

Analyze Mood **Answer:** *The personification of the daffodils as reeling, dancing, and laughing creates a light and joyful mood.*

ENGLISH LEARNERS Ask English learners which words describe the daffodils as though they were people. *(rested their heads, weariness, danced, laughed)*

> For additional practice using the reading skill or strategy, see Unit 4 Teaching Resources Book, p. 129.

Big Idea   3

Nature and the Imagination
Answer: *Dorothy Wordsworth compares the daffodils to a group of travelers proceeding down a highway, undisturbed by the few stragglers that are not part of the group. On a symbolic level, the "highway" of daffodils represents the Romantic principle of the "simplicity and unity" of nature.*

> To check students' understanding of the selection, see Unit 4 Teaching Resources Book, p. 131.

After You Read

Assess

Respond and Think Critically

1. Responses will vary.

2. (a) They walk down to the lake, along a lane, into a field, and into the woods. (b) Encountering threatening weather, they stop at the boathouse, under a bush, in the lane, and in the woods.

3. (a) She describes the weather, the plant life, and the lake. (b) She is a keen observer and lover of nature.

4. (a) "Rested their heads," "tossed and reeled and danced," "laughed," and "glancing" (b) It helps the reader visualize the movement of the daffodils in the wind.

5. "The wind was furious," "seized our breath." Evaluations will vary.

6. Students may say that technology distances people from enjoying the natural world because they have distractions that make it easier to stay indoors.

7. She finds harmony and energy in the scene with the daffodils.

Literary Element

1. Thursday, April 15, amidst a rural, agricultural environment.

2. That she appreciated nature and simple pleasures

Progress Check

Can students analyze a journal?

If No → See Unit 4 Teaching Resources Book, p. 128.

756

After You Read

Respond and Think Critically

Respond and Interpret

1. What aspect or detail of this journal entry did you find most interesting? Explain.

2. (a) Describe the journey the Wordsworths take. (b) What weather conditions do they encounter and what stops do they make?

3. (a) What kinds of observations does the author record in this entry? (b) What do these observations suggest about her attitude toward nature?

Analyze and Evaluate

4. (a) What human qualities does the author give to the daffodils? (b) How does this use of **personification** help the reader visualize the daffodils?

5. Identify several sensory images in the journal entry and evaluate how well each one helps you imagine what the author is describing.

Connect

6. **Big Idea** **Nature and the Imagination** The Romantics often found spiritual strength in the natural world. What indications of this do you find in Dorothy Wordsworth's journal?

7. **Connect to Today** Do you think that technology has made people today less likely to appreciate the natural world in the same way Dorothy and William Wordsworth did? Explain.

Literary Element | Journal

Journals provide a glimpse into what life was like during a certain time period.

1. What does the entry reveal about the time and place in which Dorothy and William lived?

2. What does the journal entry suggest about Dorothy Wordsworth's values and outlook on life? Use details from the entry to support your ideas.

Writing

Write a Journal Entry Dorothy Wordsworth's journal entry attempts to recreate the atmosphere, or mood, of her day spent with William. Freewrite a journal entry in which you think back to a day you spent with someone important to you. Include details that help you recapture the mood of that day, in addition to specific events.

LOG ON ▶ **Literature** Online

Selection Resources For Selection Quizzes, eFlash-cards, and Reading-Writing Connection activities, go to glencoe.com and enter QuickPass code GLB9817u4.

Reading Strategy Analyze Mood

Mood, the emotional quality of a literary work, encompasses both **tone**, the attitude a writer takes toward the subject, and **atmosphere**, which refers to the physical qualities of the work's setting.

1. What mood is conveyed in the journal entry and what details help convey this mood?

2. How does the first line of William Wordsworth's poem alter the mood of Dorothy's journal entry?

Academic Vocabulary

Dorothy Wordsworth's work serves as a **complement** *to the work of her brother, William.*

Complement is an academic word. In everyday usage, someone might say that a cup of coffee was the perfect **complement** to dessert.

To further explore the meaning of this word, answer the following question: How do you and your friends serve as **complements** to one another?

For more on academic vocabulary, see pages 56 and R81.

Reading Strategy

1. The mood is happy and cheerful. Dorothy's delighted response to the sight of the daffodils and her description of them convey the happy mood.

2. William transforms the nature walk from a shared experience to a solitary one, thus interjecting a mood of Romantic melancholy.

Academic Vocabulary

My friends and I serve as complements to each other because we help make up for each other's weaknesses.

Writing

Students' journals should include specific details to recreate the mood of specific moment.

Before You Read

Kubla Khan and
The Rime of the Ancient Mariner

Meet **Samuel Taylor Coleridge**

(1772–1834)

Tales such as *Robinson Crusoe* and the *Arabian Nights* enthralled young Samuel Taylor Coleridge, and from an early age, he felt drawn to the worlds of fantasy and the exotic.

A Lonely and Friendless Youth Coleridge was born at Ottery St. Mary, Devonshire. His father was the village vicar, an unworldly but popular figure. He died when Coleridge was only nine years old. Lonely and friendless, Coleridge retreated into books and his own vivid imagination where he nurtured dreams of a better future for himself. He spent much time alone outdoors, and once, after running away after a fight and collapsing on a riverbank, spent the night there and almost froze to death. As a result, he contracted a painful case of rheumatism that plagued him for the rest of his life. At the time, opium was a standard medical treatment for such a condition, and in the course of easing his persistent attacks, Coleridge grew to depend on the drug and lamented his addiction. "Yet to my fellow men," he wrote, "I may say that I was seduced into the accursed Habit ignorantly."

While at Cambridge University, Coleridge became inspired by the democratic ideals of the French Revolution. Along with several friends, including the poet Robert Southey, he joined in a movement to establish an ideal community in the United States that would be removed from war and intolerance and would give all citizens an equal voice in the government. Coleridge, Southey, and others planned to set up their community by the Susquehanna River in Pennsylvania. However, the utopian group disintegrated, and Coleridge moved with his wife, Sarah (Southey's wife's sister), and their new baby back to England to live in a small village in Somerset.

A Turning Point When Coleridge was twenty-five, he met the poet William Wordsworth. They became good friends, and Wordsworth and his sister Dorothy moved to Somerset to be near Coleridge. The two poets spent endless hours in each other's company and soon began their famous collaboration on *Lyrical Ballads*, which was published in 1798 and included Coleridge's *The Rime of the Ancient Mariner*. For Coleridge, this period was the happiest of his life.

> *"Not the poem which we have read, but that to which we return, with the greatest pleasure, possesses the genuine power, and claims the name of essential poetry."*
>
> —Samuel Taylor Coleridge

Poet and Critic By his early thirties, Coleridge had turned most of his attention to writing prose essays and treatises on literary and religious subjects. Despite illness, depression, and drug addiction, Coleridge produced an extraordinary body of work. He became the greatest literary critic of his age, known particularly for his perceptive commentary on the plays of Shakespeare and his *Biographia Literaria*, a spiritual autobiography and a brilliant exposition of the romantic ideals of art and life.

 Literature Online

Author Search For more about Samuel Taylor Coleridge, go to glencoe.com and enter QuickPass code GLB9817u4.

SAMUEL TAYLOR COLERIDGE **757**

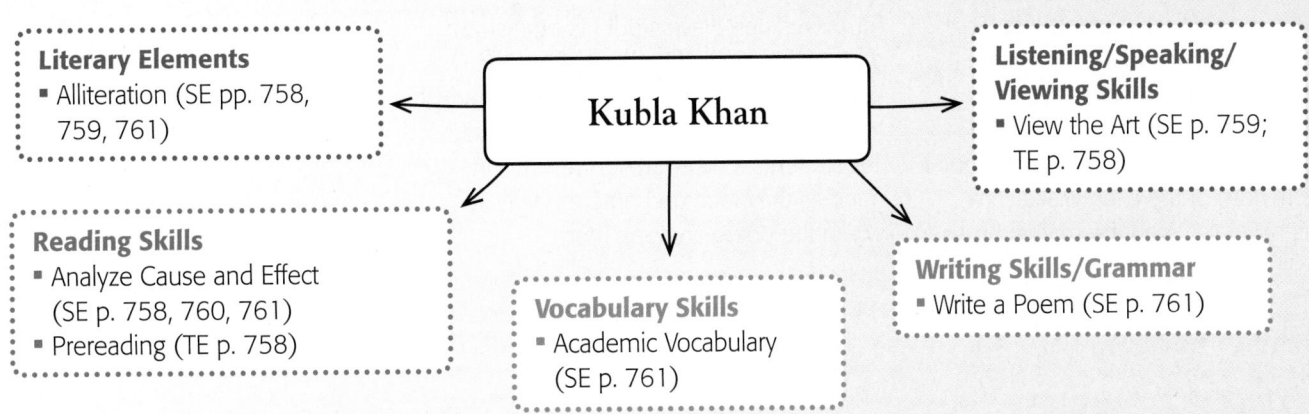
757

Before You Read

Focus

Summary

The speaker describes Kubla Khan's extravagant and mysterious pleasure dome, built in a surreal world that juxtaposes sun and ice, demons and paradise.

 For summaries in languages other than English, see Unit 4 Teaching Resources Book, pp. 133-138.

Teach

View the Art ★

Cambuluc means "residence of the Khan." This city was located on the land of modern-day Beijing. Ancient maps often combined pictorial representations of cities with geographic information. **Ask:** How does this map help you locate and envision the capital of Kubla Khan's empire? *(The landforms help you understand its location; the picture helps you imagine some of the architecture and beauty of the city.)*

Literature and Reading Preview

Connect to the Poem

Why are we excited and frightened by the unknown? With a group, discuss an experience you've had with confronting something new and unfamiliar.

Build Background

At the time when Coleridge wrote "Kubla Khan," he was reading a travel book called *Purchas His Pilgrimage*. He fell asleep after reading a passage relating how Kublai Khan, the founder of the Mongol dynasty, built a palace amid a tropical paradise. According to Coleridge, during his nap, he literally dreamed up three hundred lines of poetry. On waking, he began writing the poem but was interrupted. After returning to his work, he couldn't remember the rest, and the poem remains an unfinished fragment.

Set Purposes for Reading

Big Idea Nature and the Imagination

The Romantics were fascinated with the realm of dreams and nightmares, visions and creative madness. As you read, ask yourself, What role do dreams and visions play in "Kubla Khan"?

Literary Element Alliteration

Alliteration is a literary device in which a sound is repeated at the beginning of words or stressed syllables—for example, "meandering with a mazy motion." As you read, ask yourself, What examples of alliteration can I find?

Reading Strategy Analyze Cause-and-Effect Relationships

A **cause** is an action that makes something happen; an **effect** is the result of that action. In a complicated poem such as "Kubla Kahn," pay attention to ways in which events unfold in each stanza to determine cause-and-effect relationships. As you read, ask yourself, How do the events relate to each other?

....

Tip: Noting Causes and Effects Use a chart to record the causes and effects you discover as you read.

Cause	Effect
• Kubla Khan issued a decree.	• Walls and towers were built.

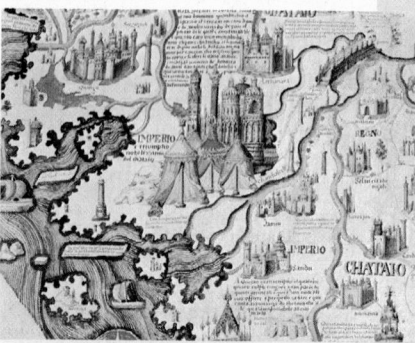

Map showing Cambuluc, the capital of Kublai Khan's Mongol Empire. British Museum, London. ★

Reading Practice

SPIRAL REVIEW **Preread** Have students look at the illustrations that accompany the poem and read the captions. Tell students to read lines 1–5 silently and then aloud, noting both the content and the rhythm of the lines. Make sure students have also read the margin notes for these lines. Have students brainstorm a list of questions they have about the poem based on what they have seen and read. **Write** the questions on the board. Tell students to keep their questions in mind as they read and note the way in which the poem answers them.

KUBLA KHAN

Samuel Taylor Coleridge

In Xanadu° did Kubla Khan
A stately pleasure dome decree:°
Where Alph,° the sacred river, ran
Through caverns measureless to man
5   Down to a sunless sea.
So twice five miles of fertile ground
With walls and towers were girdled round:
And there were gardens bright with sinuous rills,°
Where blossomed many an incense-bearing tree;
10 And here were forests ancient as the hills,
Enfolding sunny spots of greenery.

But oh! that deep romantic chasm which slanted
Down the green hill athwart a cedarn cover!°
A savage place! as holy and enchanted
15 As e'er beneath a waning moon was haunted
By woman wailing for her demon lover!
And from this chasm, with ceaseless turmoil seething,
As if this earth in fast thick pants were breathing,
A mighty fountain momently° was forced:
20 Amid whose swift half-intermitted° burst
Huge fragments vaulted like rebounding hail,
Or chaffy grain beneath the thresher's flail:
And 'mid these dancing rocks at once and ever
It flung up momently the sacred river.
25 Five miles meandering with a mazy motion
Through wood and dale the sacred river ran,

1 **Xanadu** (zaˊ nə doō): perhaps an altered form of *Xamdu* (also Shang-tu), a residence of Kublai Khan (1215—1294), a grandson of Genghis Khan who conquered China and became the first khan, or ruler, of the Mongol dynasty.
2 **decree:** order. (Kubla Khan ordered that a pleasure dome be built.)
3 **Alph:** an imaginary river, perhaps named for the Greek river Alpheus.
8 **sinuous rills:** winding streams.

13 **athwart a cedarn cover:** across a covering of cedars.

19 **momently:** from moment to moment.
20 **intermitted:** interrupted.

Alliteration *Identify five examples of alliteration in lines 1–5 of this poem.* **1**

English Learners

DIFFERENTIATED INSTRUCTION

Beginning In addition to appreciating the poet's use of alliteration, oral reading will help students focus on the imagery. Remind students to read slowly and clearly and not to emphasize the rhythm or alliteration. Students should use punctuation to guide their pauses.

Intermediate Remind students that adjectives usually precede the noun they modify: "stately pleasure dome" (line 2). However, poets sometimes reverse this order for emphasis or rhythm: "caverns measureless" (line 4). Have students identify adjectives in the poem and the nouns they modify.

Teach

Kublai Khan with Marco Polo in Peking, 1375. Bibliothèque Nationale, Paris.

Then reached the caverns measureless to man,
And sank in tumult to a lifeless ocean:
And 'mid this tumult Kubla heard from far
30   Ancestral voices prophesying war!
     The shadow of the dome of pleasure
     Floated midway on the waves;
     Where was heard the mingled measure°
     From the fountain and the caves.
35   It was a miracle of rare device,°
     A sunny pleasure dome with caves of ice!

     A damsel with a dulcimer°
     In a vision once I saw:
     It was an Abyssinian° maid,
40   And on her dulcimer she played,
     Singing of Mount Abora.°
     Could I revive within me
     Her symphony and song,
     To such a deep delight 'twould win me,
45   That with music loud and long,
     I would build that dome in air,
     That sunny dome! those caves of ice!
     And all who heard should see them there,
     And all should cry, Beware! Beware!
50   His flashing eyes, his floating hair!
     Weave a circle round him thrice,
     And close your eyes with holy dread,
     For he° on honeydew hath fed,
     And drunk the milk of Paradise.

33 measure: tune or melody; rhythmic sound.

35 device: design.

37 dulcimer (dul′ sə mər): a stringed musical instrument.

39 Abyssinian: from the country of Abyssinia (now called Ethiopia) in East Africa.
41 Mount Abora: probably a reference to Mount Amara in Ethiopia.

53 The words *his, him,* and *he* in lines 50–53 all refer to the speaker of the poem.

1 Analyze Cause-and-Effect Relationships *What causes the speaker to have this vision?*

2 Nature and the Imagination *How does this passage indicate the power of the imagination?*

 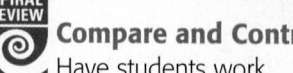

After You Read

Respond and Think Critically

Respond and Interpret

1. How did you respond to the place described?

2. (a)Describe the pleasure dome and its setting in lines 1–11. (b)How would you describe the mood of the first stanza?

3. (a)Identify images from stanza 1 that suggest the pleasure dome is beautiful and bright. (b)Identify images from stanza 2 that suggest the surroundings are dark and dangerous.

4. (a)What do the "voices" in line 30 predict? (b)How is this at odds with the description of the pleasure dome from the first stanza?

Analyze and Evaluate

5. (a)What can you infer about the speaker's character from lines 49–54? (b)Why might the speaker think that people would be filled with "holy dread" upon seeing him?

6. What does Coleridge's use of contrasting images contribute to your understanding of the poem?

Connect

7. **Big Idea** **Nature and the Imagination** What characteristics of "Kubla Khan" strike you as dreamlike? Explain.

8. **Connect to the Author** Consider what you know about Coleridge's life from the biography on page 757. Why might he have found the images in "Kubla Khan" to be so appealing?

Literary Element Alliteration

Poets often use **alliteration** to emphasize certain words, to create a musical quality, to help establish the prevailing mood of a poem, or to reinforce meaning.

1. Explain the cumulative effect of the alliterative words in lines 15–16.

2. (a)Point out all the instances of alliteration in lines 42–46. (b)Why do you think Coleridge uses this device in these lines?

 Writing

Using Coleridge's "Kubla Khan" as a model, write a poem describing your own vision of a "stately pleasure dome." Incorporate alliteration where appropriate, and employ a consistent rhyme scheme like the one in Coleridge's poem.

LOG ON ▶ **Literature** Online

Selection Resources For Selection Quizzes, eFlash-cards, and Reading-Writing Connection activities, go to glencoe.com and enter QuickPass code GLB9817u4.

Reading Strategy Analyze Cause-and-Effect Relationships

A **cause** is an event that results in an **effect**. Analyzing causes and effects in literature can help you remember and understand what is happening.

1. What are the effects of the mighty fountain that erupts from the chasm?

2. What would happen if the speaker could remember the damsel's song?

Academic Vocabulary

*"Kubla Khan" is **predominantly** a description of the great palace Xanadu.*

Predominantly is an academic word. Some more familiar words that are similar in meaning to *predominantly* are *mainly*, *principally*, and *primarily*.

To further explore the meaning of this word, answer the following question: Who figures **predominantly** in your life, and why?

For more on academic vocabulary, see pages 56 and R81.

SAMUEL TAYLOR COLERIDGE **761**

After You Read

Assess

1. Answers will vary.

2. (a) It is a compound with gardens, streams, and woods enclosed by walls (b) Mysterious and magical

3. (a) "Gardens bright with sinuous rills"; blossoming "incense-bearing" trees; "sunny spots of greenery" (b) "Savage place"; "chasm, with ceaseless turmoil seething"; "earth in fast thick pants were breathing"; "Huge fragments vaulted"; "sank in tumult to a lifeless ocean"

4. (a) The coming of war (b) It contrasts with the peace and order of the pleasure dome.

5. (a) He craves artistic fulfillment. (b) They would be in awe of his poetic powers.

6. The images suggest that the poem describes a fantasy.

7. Coleridge struggled with extremes of emotion, suffering, and addiction; the conflicting images of the poem may have appealed to his inner conflict; he may also have found the idea of an escape from worldly troubles appealing, given his illness and addiction.

8. Answers will vary.

 For additional assessment, see Assessment Resources, pp. 193–194.

Literary Element

1. "Waning," "woman," and "wailing" create a musical effect that suggests a plaintive song.

2. (a) "symphony and song," "deep delight," "loud and long" (b) To add to the poem's musicality

Reading Strategy

1. It flings up rock fragments; it forces up the sacred river; it creates a tumult containing war-prophesying voices.

2. The speaker would be able to re-create the pleasure dome.

Academic Vocabulary

Students might answer that friends, parents, classmates, teachers, or teammates figure predominantly in their lives.

Writing

Students' poems should incorporate alliteration, develop the main idea, and use a consistent rhyme scheme.

Focus

Bellringer Options

Daily Language Practice Transparency 63

Or discuss stories and storytellers with the class. **Ask:** Can you think of any examples of people telling personal stories because they feel that they *must* share their tales? What compels them to speak? *(Examples might include situations in which a witness has observed something criminal and feels compelled to tell the authorities.)* Explain that a character in this poem feels compelled to share a story.

Before You Read

The Rime of the Ancient Mariner

Connect to the Poem

Have you ever learned a valuable life lesson by experiencing hardship or encountering difficulty? Write a journal entry recounting the experience and what it taught you.

Build Background

The Rime of the Ancient Mariner is a tale of a sea voyage to distant places, with crime, death, and inhuman suffering as parts of the ghastly adventure. Coleridge's friend and fellow poet William Wordsworth suggested several memorable details, including the shooting of the albatross and the ship's navigation by dead men.

Set Purposes for Reading

Big Idea **Nature and the Imagination**

As you read, ask yourself, In what ways does the mariner interact with both the fantastic and the ordinary?

Literary Element **Narrative Poetry**

Narrative poetry is verse that tells a story. Narrative poems have characters, settings, and narrators. Many narrative poems also have literary elements such as figurative language and dialogue. A narrative poem may be written in any verse form and may be rhymed or unrhymed. As you read, ask yourself, What narrative elements can I find?

Reading Strategy **Monitor Comprehension**

When you **monitor comprehension,** you stop periodically to check your understanding of a selection. At each stopping point, you should be able to recall and summarize key events, characters, and ideas. As you read, ask yourself, Am I keeping track of what has happened so far?

Tip: Summarizing Summarizing what happens in each part of the poem will help you to understand its plot. Coleridge has helped by putting a brief summary in marginal glosses. You should incorporate Coleridge's notes into your own summary. As you read, write a summary for each of the seven parts.

Learning Objectives

For pages 762–786

In studying this text, you will focus on the following objectives:

Literary Study: Analyzing narrative poetry. Connecting literature to art.

Reading: Monitoring comprehension by summarizing.

Vocabulary

dismal (diz′ məl) *adj.* dark and gloomy; p. 766 *It was a dismal afternoon, and I was glad I could stay indoors, where it was warm and bright.*

penance (pen′ əns) *n.* an act of self-punishment to show repentance for a sin; p. 778 *In the Greek tragedy, Oedipus puts out his own eyes as penance for having killed his father.*

impart (im pärt′) *v.* to give; donate; p. 781 *Uncle Simon loves to impart little bits of wisdom to all of us at family dinners.*

Selection Skills

Literary Elements
- Narrative Poetry (SE pp. 762–785)
- Ballad Stanza (SE p. 785)
- Rhyme Scheme (TE p. 766)
- Personification (TE p. 770)
- Character (TE p. 784)

Writing Skills/Grammar
- Connect to Art (SE p. 786)
- Hypertext Links (TE p. 780)

The Rime of the Ancient Mariner

Vocabulary Skills
- Context Clues (SE p. 786)
- Academic Vocabulary (SE p. 786)
- Connotations (TE p. 782)

Reading Skills
- Monitor Comprehension (SE pp. 762–786)
- Use Text Structure (TE p. 764)
- Contrast (TE p. 776)

Listening/Speaking/Viewing Skills
- View the Art (SE pp. 765, 773, 781; TE pp. 770, 778)
- Perform a Dialogue (TE p. 778)

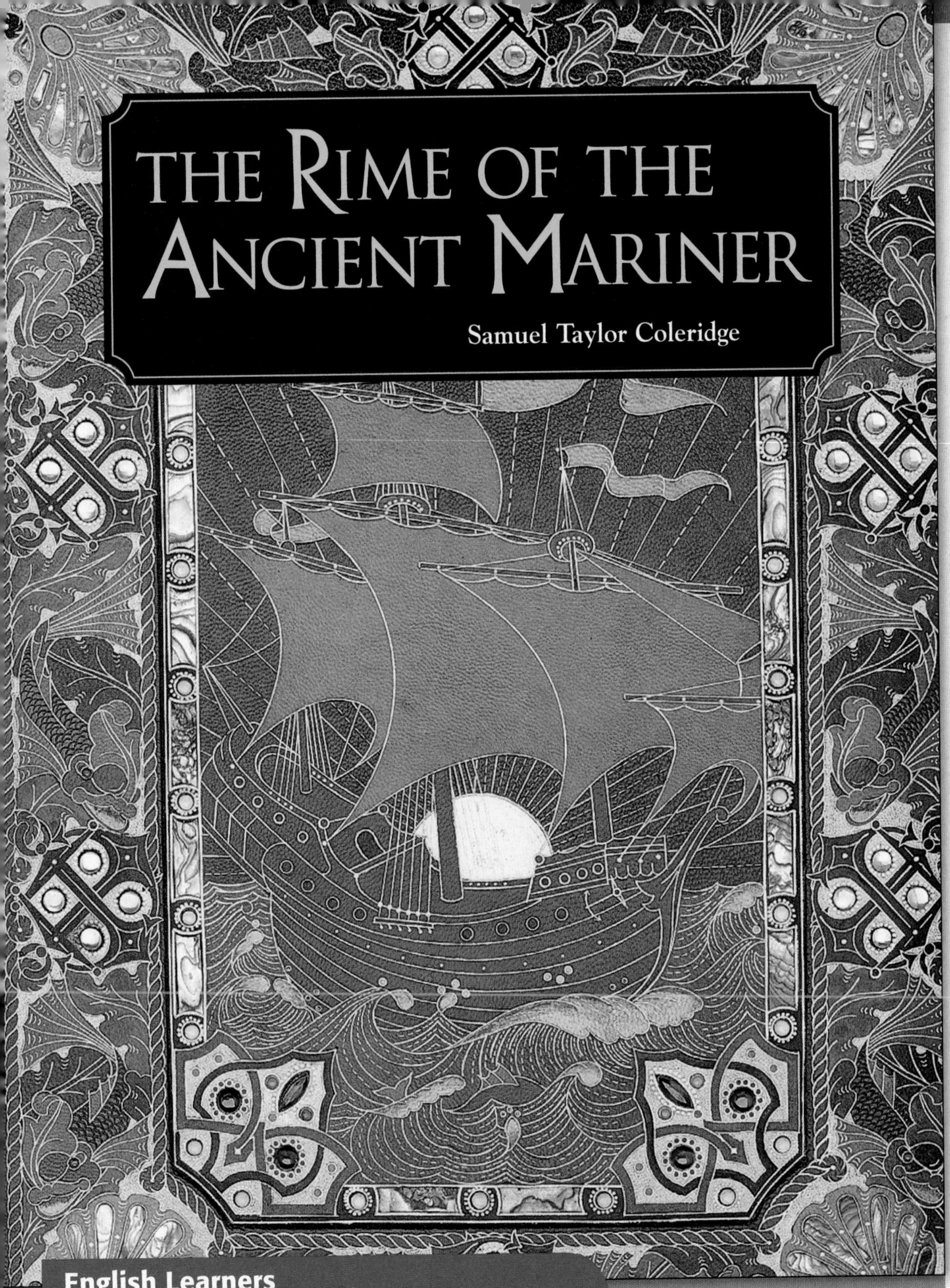
THE RIME OF THE ANCIENT MARINER
Samuel Taylor Coleridge

English Learners

DIFFERENTIATED INSTRUCTION

PARTNERS

Intermediate Allow students to connect to the poem through an oral activity. Explain that in this poem, a character learns something important about life after experiencing great suffering. Ask students to think of a difficult experience they have had and what they learned from it. Tell students to tell a partner about the experience and what was learned. The partner should ask questions to help clarify his or her understanding of the story.

Before You Read

Focus

Summary

The Ancient Mariner stops a Wedding Guest and tells him a tale of his supernatural and spiritual journey of redemption. The Mariner describes his killing of an albatross and the terrifying ordeals that followed, including the deaths of the other crew members, mystical visitations, and emotional and physical anguish. The Mariner is released from his torments only after accepting the fact that all of nature is beautiful and worthy of love. The Wedding Guest, initially a reluctant listener, awakens the next day "a sadder and wiser man."

For summaries in languages other than English, see Unit 4 Teaching Resources Book, pp. 143-148.

Vocabulary

Make a Vivid Impression

Tell students that using varied and colorful words in their writing allows them to make a strong and vivid impression on the reader. Ask them to choose a duller synonym for each vocabulary word (*i.e.*, dark *for* dismal; punishment *for* penance; give *for* impart). Have students write a new example sentence for each vocabulary word and then rewrite it using the duller synonym. Ask students to compare the two sentences in terms of the impression they make on the reader.

Teach

Narrative Poetry Answer:
The Mariner addresses the Wedding Guest outside the bridegroom's home as the wedding feast is about to begin.

ENGLISH LEARNERS Point out *kin* and *din*. Ask English learners to use context clues to guess the meanings of the words. Have them confirm their guesses by looking the words up in a dictionary. Point out also that *wherefore* does not mean "where." If students are not able to guess that it means "why," have them look it up in the dictionary.

Nature and the Imagination
Answer: *The Mariner's "glittering eye" exerts magical power over the Guest, who must stay and listen in spite of his desire to attend the wedding feast.*

Writer's Technique ☆
Coleridge's Marginal Notes
The Rime of the Ancient Mariner was first published in 1798. Coleridge added his "gloss," the marginal notes that summarize the plot, when the poem was reprinted in *Sibylline Leaves* in 1817. In addition to providing helpful guidance, these notes also mirror the appearance of the marginal notes printed in early Bibles, providing another link to writing from earlier eras.

764

ARGUMENT

How a Ship, having passed the Equator, was driven by storms to the cold Country towards the South Pole; and how from thence she made her course to the tropical Latitude of the Great Pacific Ocean; and of the strange things that befell; and in what manner the Ancient Mariner came back to his own Country.

PART I

It is an ancient Mariner,
And he stoppeth one of three.
"By thy long gray beard and glittering eye,
Now wherefore stopp'st thou me?

5   "The Bridegroom's doors are opened wide,
And I am next of kin;
The guests are met, the feast is set:
May'st hear the merry din."

He holds him with his skinny hand,
10   "There was a ship," quoth he.
"Hold off! unhand me, graybeard loon!"
Eftsoons[1] his hand dropped he.

He holds him with his glittering eye—
The Wedding Guest stood still,
15   And listens like a three years' child:
The Mariner hath his will.

The Wedding Guest sat on a stone:
He cannot choose but hear;
And thus spake on that ancient man,
20   The bright-eyed Mariner.

---

1. *Eftsoons* means "at once."

 1   Narrative Poetry *To whom does the Mariner address his tale? What is the setting of their meeting?*

2   Nature and the Imagination *What elements of the supernatural are at work in this stanza?*

764   UNIT 4   THE TRIUMPH OF ROMANTICISM

An ancient Mariner meeteth three Gallants bidden to a wedding feast and detaineth one.

The Wedding Guest is spellbound by the eye of the old seafaring man and constrained to hear his tale.

Reading Practice

SPIRAL REVIEW **Use Text Structure** Suggest that students identify these text features in Coleridge's poem:

- an initial argument that summarizes the plot of the narrative poem
- mostly four-line stanzas in which the second and fourth lines rhyme
- division into seven parts
- marginal notes that summarize events

Suggest that students preview each part of the poem by first reading Coleridge's marginal notes, which summarize the events. These notes will provide considerable support for all students as they read.

Mariner recounts story to wedding guest, 1875. Gustave Doré. Engraving.

View the Art Doré was one of the most successful illustrators of his time, in part because of the expressive nature of his work. How does the body language of the Mariner and the Wedding Guest reflect their emotions? Explain.

"The ship was cheered, the harbor cleared,
Merrily did we drop
Below the kirk,[2] below the hill,
Below the lighthouse top.

25 "The Sun came up upon the left,
Out of the sea came he!
And he shone bright, and on the right
Went down into the sea.

"Higher and higher every day,
30 Till over the mast at noon[3]—".
The Wedding Guest here beat his breast,
For he heard the loud bassoon.

The bride hath paced into the hall,
Red as a rose is she;
35 Nodding their heads before her goes
The merry minstrelsy.[4]

The Wedding Guest he beat his breast,
Yet he cannot choose but hear;
And thus spake on that ancient man,
40 The bright-eyed Mariner.

3

The Mariner tells how the ship sailed southward with a good wind and fair weather, till it reached the Line. [The line is the equator.]

The Wedding Guest heareth the bridal music; but the Mariner continueth his tale.

---

2. *Kirk* is Scottish for *church*.
3. In this line, Coleridge is saying the sun's position indicates that the ship has reached the equator.
4. A *minstrelsy* is a group of musicians.

SAMUEL TAYLOR COLERIDGE **765**

Teach

Literary Element | **3**

Narrative Poetry **Ask:** How does this stanza emphasize the story-within-a-story structure of this narrative poem? *(The Wedding Guest interrupts the Ancient Mariner's tale because he hears music and wants to join the wedding party. The Wedding Guest's story opens and closes the poem, thus framing the story; within that narrative, the Mariner tells his tale.)*

View the Art

Answer: *The Mariner stares forcefully and uses his hand to keep his listener seated. The Wedding Guest sits somewhat passively, compelled to listen. However, he does not look directly at the Mariner, suggesting that the stranger's tale has not yet captivated him.*

Paul Gustave Doré (1832–1883) was one of the most renowned and prolific French illustrators of the nineteenth century. Copies of his original illustrations of *The Rime of the Ancient Mariner* accompany the text. Several of the illustrations reflect his interest in religious works.

For an audio recording of this selection, use Listening Library Audio CD-ROM.

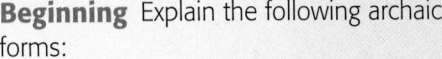

Teach

Big Idea 1

Nature and the Imagination
Answer: *The Storm Blast is a personification of a natural force; the speaker imagines this force as striking and chasing the ship. Thus, the speaker imbues this force with consciousness, imposing his own creative energies on the natural world.*

Big Idea 2

Nature and the Imagination
Answer: *These images prompt readers to experience the ice as a living, conscious menace.*

Cultural History ☆

The Albatross Sailors considered these large, white seabirds as good omens, perhaps because of their habit of following ships. A single albatross might trail a ship for days or even weeks. Other names for albatrosses include Gooney birds and mollymawks. **Ask:** Why might sailors have developed superstitions about different animals? *(Life at sea was often dangerous, so sailors might have developed superstitions to help them cope with stressful conditions.)*

"And now the Storm Blast came, and he
Was tyrannous and strong:
He struck with his o'ertaking wings,
And chased us south along.

45 "With sloping masts and dipping prow,[5]
As who pursued with yell and blow
Still treads the shadow of his foe,
And forward bends his head,
The ship drove fast, loud roared the blast,
50 And southward aye[6] we fled.

"And now there came both mist and snow,
And it grew wondrous cold:
And ice, mast-high, came floating by,
As green as emerald.

55 "And through the drifts the snowy clifts[7]
Did send a **dismal** sheen:
Nor shapes of men nor beasts we ken[8]—
The ice was all between.

"The ice was here, the ice was there,
60 The ice was all around:
It cracked and growled, and roared and howled,
Like noises in a swound![9]

"At length did cross an Albatross, ☆
Thorough the fog it came;
65 As if it had been a Christian soul,
We hailed it in God's name.

---

5. A *mast* is a vertical pole that supports a ship's sails, and the *prow* is the forward part of a ship's hull.
6. *Aye* means "always."
7. *Clifts* means "crevices."
8. *Ken* means "saw; identified."
9. A *swound* is a swoon or fainting fit.

1 Nature and the Imagination *How does the use of personification here reflect the Romantic idea that the imagination is a force within the individual that reacts to the natural world?*

2 Nature and the Imagination *What is the effect of this personification?*

Vocabulary

dismal (diz′ məl) *adj.* dark and gloomy

The ship driven by a storm toward the South Pole.

The land of ice, and of fearful sounds, where no living thing was to be seen.

Till a great sea bird, called the Albatross, came through the snow-fog, and was received with great joy and hospitality.

Literary Element Practice

SPIRAL REVIEW ⟳ **Rhyme Scheme** Ask students to identify the rhyme scheme that recurs in the four-line stanzas of the poem *(abcb)*. Students might scan ahead to see that some of the poem's stanzas contain more lines and thus vary this scheme. Encourage students to classify the rhymes they find:

- True rhymes repeat the same stressed vowel sounds and any succeeding sounds: *came* and *name*.
- Slant rhymes are approximate rhymes that repeat only a vowel or a consonant sound: *thus* and *Albatross*.
- Internal rhyme occurs within a line of poetry: *day* and *play* in line 89.

"It ate the food it ne'er had eat,
And round and round it flew.
The ice did split with a thunder-fit;
70 The helmsman steered us through!

"And a good south wind sprung up behind;
The Albatross did follow,
And every day, for food or play,
Came to the mariners' hollo!

75 "In mist or cloud, on mast or shroud,[10]
It perched for vespers[11] nine;
Whiles all the night, through fog-smoke white,
Glimmered the white Moonshine."

"God save thee, ancient Mariner!
80 From the fiends that plague thee thus!—
Why look'st thou so?"[12]—"With my crossbow
I shot the Albatross."

PART II

"The Sun now rose upon the right:[13]
Out of the sea came he,
85 Still hid in mist, and on the left
Went down into the sea.

"And the good south wind still blew behind,
But no sweet bird did follow,
Nor any day for food or play
90 Came to the mariners' hollo!

"And I had done a hellish thing,
And it would work 'em woe:
For all averred,[14] I had killed the bird
That made the breeze to blow.

---

10. A *shroud* is a rope that supports the mast of a ship.
11. Here, *vespers* means "evenings."
12. The words *"God . . . so?"* are spoken by the Wedding Guest.
13. This line indicates that the ship is heading north.
14. *Averred* means "asserted; affirmed."

Monitor Comprehension *What happens in this last stanza? Why does the Guest interrupt the Mariner?*

Narrative Poetry *Does the Mariner offer any motivation for what he has done? Explain.* **4**

And lo! the Albatross proveth a bird of good omen, and followeth the ship as it returned northward through fog and floating ice.

The ancient Mariner inhospitably killeth the pious bird of good omen.

His shipmates cry out against the ancient Mariner for killing the bird of good luck.

SAMUEL TAYLOR COLERIDGE **767**

Teach

Reading Strategy **3**

Monitor Comprehension
Answer: *The Mariner reveals that he killed an albatross befriended by the crew. The Guest interrupts the Mariner to ask why he looks haunted.*

(APPROACHING) Have approaching-level students read the Wedding Guest's interruption aloud with appropriate expression. Ask them to visualize and orally describe what the Wedding Guest must see in the ancient Mariner's face.

 For additional practice using the reading skill or strategy, see Unit 4 Teaching Resources Book, p. 150.

Literary Element **4**

Narrative Poetry **Answer:**
The Mariner offers no explanation for his action.

(ENGLISH LEARNERS) Point out the word *hellish* in line 91. Have English learners discuss the meaning and connotations of the word, which are similar in both languages *(relating to hell, evil, deserving of damnation).*

English Learners

DIFFERENTIATED INSTRUCTION

Intermediate Point out that Coleridge often uses masculine or feminine pronouns to refer to inanimate objects. For example, he uses the pronouns *he* and *his* to refer to the Storm Blast in lines 41–44. Suggest that students pause when they read a pronoun to identify the noun it replaces.

Approaching Level

DIFFERENTIATED INSTRUCTION

Emerging Remind students not to emphasize the rhythm as they read the poem because doing so can impede comprehension. Give students the following tips:

- use punctuation to guide comprehension
- rhythm and rhyme should not dominate the reading

Teach

Cultural History ☆

The Doldrums The Mariner's description of the becalmed ship suggests an area near the Equator in parts of the Atlantic and Pacific Oceans known as the Doldrums. Weather in the Doldrums is characterized by calm and light shifting winds. When a ship is becalmed, its crew depletes its precious stores of food and water without making progress toward its destination. Fresh water was especially important on an ocean voyage because the salinity of ocean water made it undrinkable and caused sickness.

95 'Ah, wretch!' said they, 'the bird to slay,
  That made the breeze to blow!'

  "Nor dim nor red, like God's own head,
  The glorious Sun uprist:¹⁵
  Then all averred, I had killed the bird
100 That brought the fog and mist.
  ' 'Twas right,' said they, 'such birds to slay,
  That bring the fog and mist.'

  "The fair breeze blew, the white foam flew,
  The furrow¹⁶ followed free;
105 We were the first that ever burst
  Into that silent sea.

  "Down dropped the breeze, the sails dropped down, ☆
  'Twas sad as sad could be;
  And we did speak only to break
110 The silence of the sea!

  "All in a hot and copper sky,
  The bloody Sun, at noon,
  Right up above the mast did stand,
  No bigger than the Moon.

115 "Day after day, day after day,
  We stuck, nor breath nor motion;
  As idle as a painted ship
  Upon a painted ocean.

  "Water, water, everywhere,
120 And all the boards did shrink;
  Water, water, everywhere,
  Nor any drop to drink.

But when the fog cleared off, they justify the same, and thus make themselves accomplices in the crime.

The fair breeze continues; the ship enters the Pacific Ocean and sails northward, even till it reaches the Line.

The ship hath been suddenly becalmed.

And the Albatross begins to be avenged.

---

15. *Uprist* means "arose."
16. The *furrow* is the ship's wake.

Listening and Speaking Practice

Share Ideas Encourage students to compare their summaries of key events in the poem. Allow each student to read a summary aloud. After several have been read, have students identify the strengths and weaknesses of each summary and create one version that captures the essential events as concisely as possible. Remind students that an effective summary should omit less important details. As students share their ideas, remind them to avoid generalizations and support their constructive criticisms with examples.

"The very deep did rot: O Christ!
That ever this should be!
125 Yea, slimy things did crawl with legs
Upon the slimy sea.

"About, about, in reel and rout[17]
The death-fires[18] danced at night;
The water, like a witch's oils,
130 Burned green and blue and white.

"And some in dreams assurèd were
Of the Spirit that plagued us so;
Nine fathom deep he had followed us
From the land of mist and snow.

135 "And every tongue, through utter drought,
Was withered at the root;
We could not speak, no more than if
We had been choked with soot.

"Ah! well a-day! what evil looks
140 Had I from old and young!
Instead of the cross, the Albatross
About my neck was hung.

PART III

"There passed a weary time. Each throat
Was parched, and glazed each eye.
145 A weary time! a weary time!
How glazed each weary eye,
When looking westward, I beheld
A something in the sky.

"At first it seemed a little speck,
150 And then it seemed a mist;
It moved and moved, and took at last
A certain shape, I wist.[19]

---

17. *In reel and rout* means "in riotous, whirling movements."
18. *Death-fires* are luminous glowings supposedly seen over dead bodies.
19. *Wist* means "knew."

Monitor Comprehension *Why would the Mariner's shipmates hang the albatross around his neck?* **2**

A Spirit had followed them; one of the invisible inhabitants of this planet, neither departed souls nor angels. . . . They are very numerous, and there is no climate or element without one or more.

The shipmates, in their sore distress, would fain throw the whole guilt on the ancient Mariner: in sign whereof they hang the dead sea bird round his neck.

The ancient Mariner beholdeth a sign in the element afar off.

SAMUEL TAYLOR COLERIDGE **769**

Teach

View the Art ★

Gustave Doré's artistic ability with woodcut prints led to the popularity of folio-size, or large-scale, illustrated books in Europe. His flair for dramatic portrayals is evident in his interpretation of the crew's demise. **Ask:** Why do you think Doré decided not to picture the Mariner in this illustration? *(He might have wanted to emphasize the crew's terrible fate without focusing on the Mariner's reaction to it.)*

Cursed ship is sent to the equator where crew perish, 1875. Gustave Doré. Engraving. ★

"A speck, a mist, a shape, I wist!
And still it neared and neared:
155   As if it dodged a water sprite,
It plunged and tacked and veered.

"With throats unslaked,[20] with black lips baked,
We could nor laugh nor wail;
Through utter drought all dumb we stood!
160   I bit my arm, I sucked the blood,
And cried, 'A sail! a sail!'

> At its nearer approach, it seemeth him to be a ship; and at a dear ransom he freeth his speech from the bonds of thirst.

"With throats unslaked, with black lips baked,
Agape[21] they heard me call:
Gramercy![22] they for joy did grin,
165   And all at once their breath drew in,
As they were drinking all.

> A flash of joy;

"See! see! (I cried) she tacks no more!
Hither to work us weal;[23]
Without a breeze, without a tide,
170   She steadies with upright keel!

> And horror follows. For can it be a ship that comes onward without wind or tide?

"The western wave was all aflame.
The day was well nigh done!
Almost upon the western wave
Rested the broad bright Sun;

---

20. *Unslaked* means "unrelieved of thirst."
21. *Agape* means "with mouths open in wonder."
22. *Gramercy* is an exclamation of surprise or sudden feeling similar to "Have mercy on us!"
23. *Work us weal* means "do us good; benefit us."

770   UNIT 4   THE TRIUMPH OF ROMANTICISM

Literary Element Practice

SPIRAL REVIEW **Personification** Remind students that personification is a figure of speech in which an animal, an object, a force of nature, or an idea is given human qualities. Have students find an example of personification in lines 199–203. *("The stars rush out"; "At one stride comes the dark"; the specter ship is heard to "whisper.")*

Ask: How does Coleridge's use of personification add to his depiction of the fantastic in this poem? *(Personification makes all elements of the world seem alive.)*

175 When that strange shape drove suddenly
Betwixt us and the Sun.

"And straight²⁴ the Sun was flecked with bars,
(Heaven's Mother send us grace!)
As if through a dungeon grate he peered
180 With broad and burning face.

"Alas! (thought I, and my heart beat loud)
How fast she nears and nears!
Are those *her* sails that glance in the Sun,
Like restless gossameres?²⁵

185 "Are those *her* ribs through which the Sun
Did peer, as through a grate?
And is that Woman all her crew?
Is that a Death? and are there two?
Is Death that woman's mate?

190 "*Her* lips were red, *her* looks were free,
Her locks were yellow as gold:
Her skin was as white as leprosy,
The Nightmare Life-in-Death was she,
Who thicks man's blood with cold.

195 "The naked hulk alongside came,
And the twain were casting dice;
'The game is done! I've won! I've won!'
Quoth she, and whistles thrice.

"The Sun's rim dips; the stars rush out:
200 At one stride comes the dark;
With far-heard whisper, o'er the sea,
Off shot the specter bark.²⁶

"We listened and looked sideways up!
Fear at my heart, as at a cup,
205 My lifeblood seemed to sip!
The stars were dim, and thick the night,
The steersman's face by his lamp gleamed white;

It seemeth him but the skeleton of a ship.

And its ribs are seen as bars on the face of the setting Sun. The Specter-Woman and her Death mate, and no other on board the skeleton ship.

Like vessel, like crew!

Death and Life-in-Death have diced for the ship's crew, and she (the latter) winneth the ancient Mariner.

No twilight within the courts of the Sun.

At the rising of the Moon,

---

24. Here, *straight* means "immediately."
25. *Gossameres* (or gossamers) are fine films of cobwebs.
26. *Specter bark* means "ghost ship."

Nature and the Imagination *How does the strange ship represent the supernatural?*

Monitor Comprehension *What happens in this stanza?*

Teach

Big Idea | 1

Nature and the Imagination
Answer: *It is a skeleton ship with sails and ribs that one can see through; the ship moves even though there is no tide or wind.*

Reading Strategy | 2

Monitor Comprehension
Answer: *Life-in-Death wins the dice game and the Mariner, who will live.*

(ENGLISH LEARNERS) For English learners, **ask:** Who is the *she* in "How fast she nears and nears"? (line 182) *(the ship)* Explain that in English, ships are commonly referred to as *she*. Ask students what *her* refers to in lines 183 and 185.

English Learners

DIFFERENTIATED INSTRUCTION

Intermediate Make sure that students recognize that Coleridge's capitalization of nouns is an artistic choice. For example, his capitalization of the word *Sun* suggests that it is a proper noun or a character's name. Similarly, *Death* is capitalized because it appears as an actual character in the poem.

Approaching Level

DIFFERENTIATED INSTRUCTION

Established Ask students to find three examples of phrases with inverted word order in lines 195–202 (*The naked hulk alongside came; Quoth she; Off shot the specter bark*). Have them restate the

sentences using conventional word order. Remind them to pay attention to the verb forms they are using.

Teach

Reading Strategy   1

Monitor Comprehension
Answer: *The Mariner's ship-mates fall down dead because Life-in-Death has won only the Mariner. The other members of the crew are Death's prize.*

Literary Element   2

Narrative Poetry   Answer:
This image recalls the Mariner's shooting of the albatross with his crossbow. It suggests that the horrible events to befall the ship result from the Mariner's arbitrary decision to shoot the seabird.

[ENGLISH LEARNERS] Explain to English learners that *onomato-poeia* means words whose spoken sounds resemble the sounds they describe. Have students read line 223 aloud, focusing on the word *whiz*. Ask why they think Coleridge chose to use this word.

Reading Strategy   3

Monitor Comprehension
Answer: *The Wedding Guest is frightened because he thinks the Mariner might be a ghost.*

Cultural History ☆

Christian Afterlife Point out that the phrase "bliss or woe" alludes to the Christian belief in the afterlife. After the dead are judged according to their deeds in this life, they enter the "bliss" of heaven or suffer the "woe" of hell.

From the sails the dew did drip—
Till clomb²⁷ above the eastern bar
210   The hornèd Moon,²⁸ with one bright star
Within the nether²⁹ tip.

"One after one, by the star-dogged Moon,³⁰
Too quick for groan or sigh,
Each turned his face with a ghastly pang,
215   And cursed me with his eye.

"Four times fifty living men,
(And I heard nor sigh nor groan)
With heavy thump, a lifeless lump,
They dropped down one by one.

220   "The souls did from their bodies fly—
They fled to bliss or woe! ☆
And every soul, it passed me by,
Like the whiz of my crossbow!"

PART IV

"I fear thee, ancient Mariner!
225   I fear thy skinny hand!
And thou art long, and lank, and brown,
As is the ribbed sea-sand.

"I fear thee and thy glittering eye,
And thy skinny hand, so brown."—
230   "Fear not, fear not, thou Wedding Guest!
This body dropped not down.
"Alone, alone, all, all alone,
Alone on a wide, wide sea!

---

27. *Clomb* means "climbed."
28. A *hornèd Moon* is a crescent moon.
29. *Nether* means "lower."
30. Sailors believed that a *star-dogged Moon* was a sign of impending evil.

1   Monitor Comprehension *What happens to the Mariner's ship-mates and why?*

2   Narrative Poetry *What image does this line recall? What does this suggest?*

3   Monitor Comprehension *Why is the Wedding Guest frightened?*

One after another,

His shipmates drop down dead.

But Life-in-Death begins her work on the ancient Mariner.

The Wedding Guest feareth that a Spirit is talking to him;

But the ancient Mariner assureth him of his bodily life, and proceedeth to relate his horrible penance.

Grammar Practice

Inverted Order Remind students that in most sentences the subject precedes the verb. Explain that poets and other writers sometimes put the verb before the subject to fit a specific meter, draw attention to a specific word, or create variety. Have students identify the inverted order in lines 209–210 *("Til clomb above the eastern bar / The horned Moon")*, and ask them to say the sentence in normal word order. *(The horned Moon clomb above the eastern bar.)* Ask students to identify other examples of inverted word order in this poem.

And never a saint took pity on
235 My soul in agony.

"The many men, so beautiful!
And they all dead did lie:
And a thousand thousand slimy things
Lived on; and so did I.

240 "I looked upon the rotting sea,
And drew my eyes away;
I looked upon the rotting deck,
And there the dead men lay.

"I looked to heaven, and tried to pray;
245 But or[31] ever a prayer had gushed,
A wicked whisper came, and made
My heart as dry as dust.

"I closed my lids, and kept them close,
And the balls like pulses beat;
250 For the sky and the sea, and the sea and the sky
Lay like a load on my weary eye,
And the dead were at my feet.

"The cold sweat melted from their limbs,
Nor rot nor reek did they:
255 The look with which they looked on me
Had never passed away.

"An orphan's curse would drag to hell
A spirit from on high;
But oh! more horrible than that
260 Is the curse in a dead man's eye!
Seven days, seven nights, I saw that curse,
And yet I could not die.

"The moving Moon went up the sky,
And nowhere did abide:
265 Softly she was going up,
And a star or two beside—

---

31. Here, *or* means "before."

Monitor Comprehension *What has the Mariner seen for the last
seven days and seven nights and what has he tried to do? Look
back at line 244.*

4

*Death and Life play dice on skeleton
ship,* 1875. Gustave Doré. Engraving.

View the Art Do you think this
engraving captures the mood and
atmosphere of the scene in the poem?
Why or why not?

He despiseth the creatures of the
calm.

And envieth that they should live,
and so many lie dead.

But the curse liveth for him in the
eye of the dead men.

In his loneliness and fixedness he
yearneth towards the journeying
Moon, and the stars that still sojourn
. . . ; and everywhere the blue sky
belongs to them, and is their
appointed rest, and their native
country and their own natural
homes, which they enter
unannounced, as lords that are
certainly expected, and yet there is a
silent joy at their arrival.

Teach

Reading Strategy | 4

Monitor Comprehension
Answer: *The Mariner has looked
at the dead bodies of the crew. He
has tried to pray but could not.*

View the Art ★

Answer: *Most students will
agree that the engraving captures
the mood of the scene. They
should point to details such as
the posture of Death, the apparent disarray of the ship's ropes
and equipment, and the facial
expressions of the two figures.
This depiction of Death and Life-
in-Death illustrates Doré's passion
for portraying grotesque figures,
a penchant that appealed to the
Romantic fascination with the
bizarre.*

SAMUEL TAYLOR COLERIDGE **773**

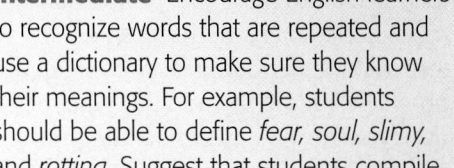

English Learners

DIFFERENTIATED INSTRUCTION

Intermediate Encourage English learners
to recognize words that are repeated and
use a dictionary to make sure they know
their meanings. For example, students
should be able to define *fear, soul, slimy,*
and *rotting.* Suggest that students compile
a glossary to help them learn unfamiliar
terms.

Approaching Level

DIFFERENTIATED INSTRUCTION

Emerging Students may need help identifying shifts in speaker. For example, Part
III ends with lines spoken by the Mariner,
but Part IV begins with lines spoken by the
Wedding Guest. Emphasize that referring to the marginal notes may help them
detect a change in speaker.

Teach

Literary Element | 1

Narrative Poetry
Answer: *He blesses the sea creatures "unaware," thereby acknowledging the beauty of all God's creatures; this is the first step in the process of the Mariner's redemption.*

[ADVANCED] Ask advanced students to reflect on what this development says about Coleridge's view of human nature. **Ask:** Would this transformed Mariner have shot the albatross? *(likely answer: no)* Why did he shoot the albatross before his enlightenment? *(possible answer: he did not recognize it as part of nature's perfection)* Do you think the Mariner symbolizes humanity? *(Answers will vary. Have students support their ideas with examples from the poem.)*

Literary Element | 2

Narrative Poetry **Answer:**
The Mariner was unable to die or to sleep. However, he now sinks into a deep and soothing sleep, sent as a blessing from the Virgin Mary.

Writer's Technique ☆

Imagery Coleridge repeats some images to create a unified world and suggest parallels between events. In lines 290–291, he describes how the Albatross finally fell from the Mariner's neck and "sank/Like lead into the sea." **Ask:** How does Coleridge repeat this image in these lines? *(Like the albatross, the ship also sinks like lead.)* Why might he have decided to repeat this image? *(The sinking of the Albatross and the skeletal ship mark different stages in the Mariner's spiritual journey from sin toward redemption.)*

"Her beams bemocked the sultry main,[32]
Like April hoarfrost[33] spread;
But where the ship's huge shadow lay,
270 The charmèd water burned alway[34]
A still and awful red.

"Beyond the shadow of the ship,
I watched the water snakes:
They moved in tracks of shining white,
275 And when they reared, the elfish light
Fell off in hoary[35] flakes.

"Within the shadow of the ship
I watched their rich attire:
Blue, glossy green, and velvet black,
280 They coiled and swam; and every track
Was a flash of golden fire.

"O happy living things! no tongue
Their beauty might declare:
A spring of love gushed from my heart,
285 And I blessed them unaware:
Sure my kind saint took pity on me,
And I blessed them unaware.

"The selfsame moment I could pray;
And from my neck so free
290 The Albatross fell off, and sank
Like lead into the sea."

PART V

"Oh sleep! it is a gentle thing,
Beloved from pole to pole!
To Mary Queen the praise be given! ☆
295 She sent the gentle sleep from Heaven
That slid into my soul.

By the light of the Moon, he beholdeth God's creatures of the great calm.

Their beauty and their happiness.

He blesseth them in his heart.

The spell begins to break.

By grace of the holy Mother, the ancient Mariner is refreshed with rain.

---

32. This line means "Her moonbeams mocked the hot sea."
33. *Hoarfrost* is frost, especially the white coating it forms on surfaces.
34. *Alway* means "all along."
35. *Hoary* means "white."

1 Narrative Poetry *How does the Mariner's action contribute unwittingly to his salvation?*

2 Narrative Poetry *How has the Mariner's situation changed?*

Research Practice

Electronic Texts Point out that many classic works are available electronically on the Internet. Encourage students to use a search engine to locate an e-text of this poem and compare and contrast the print version with the online version. Most online e-texts lack additional notes or background information, but the ability to search a text makes some questions much easier to answer using an e-text. **Ask:** Coleridge describes sleep as *gentle* in lines 292 and 295. What else does he describe as *gentle* later in the poem? (The weather in line 431)

"The silly[36] buckets on the deck,
That had so long remained,
I dreamed that they were filled with dew;
300 And when I awoke, it rained.

"My lips were wet, my throat was cold,
My garments all were dank;
Sure I had drunken in my dreams,
And still my body drank.

305 "I moved, and could not feel my limbs:
I was so light—almost
I thought that I had died in sleep,
And was a blessèd ghost.

"And soon I heard a roaring wind:
310 It did not come anear;
But with its sound it shook the sails
That were so thin and sere.[37]

"The upper air burst into life!
And a hundred fire-flags sheen,[38]
315 To and fro they were hurried about!
And to and fro, and in and out,
The wan[39] stars danced between.

"And the coming wind did roar more loud,
And the sails did sigh like sedge;[40]
320 And the rain poured down from one black cloud;
The Moon was at its edge.

"The thick black cloud was cleft,[41] and still
The Moon was at its side:
Like waters shot from some high crag,
325 The lightning fell with never a jag,
A river steep and wide.

"The loud wind never reached the ship,
Yet now the ship moved on!

He heareth sounds and seeth strange sights and commotions in the sky and the element.

The bodies of the ship's crew are inspired, and the ship moves on; [Inspired means "breathed life into" or "animated by divine or supernatural influence."]

---

36. Here, *silly* means "useless."
37. *Sere* means "worn."
38. *Fire-flags* may refer to the aurora australis, or southern lights. *Sheen* means "shone."
39. *Wan* means "faint" or "dull" (compared with the fire-flags).
40. *Sedge* is marsh grass.
41. *Cleft* means "split."

Teach

Cultural History ☆

Mary Queen Point out that Mary Queen refers to the Virgin Mary, not to a living queen. Although the exact time of the events in the poem is not given, the Mariner states that his crew was the first to enter the Pacific Ocean. Since Magellan was acknowledged as the first European to enter the Pacific in 1520, Coleridge implies that the poem's events take place before that date.

English Learners

DIFFERENTIATED INSTRUCTION

PARTNERS

Beginning Suggest that students use a dictionary or work with a partner to find synonyms for unfamiliar words in the poem. You might suggest these examples: abide (line 264)—live; attire (line 278)—clothing. Encourage students to use synonyms when summarizing or paraphrasing.

Approaching Level

DIFFERENTIATED INSTRUCTION

PARTNERS

Established Have approaching-level students work in pairs to confirm their comprehension of the stanzas on this spread. Tell each partner to write five factual questions about what takes place in these stanzas. Help students make sure they are using correct word order and verb forms in their questions. Have partners answer each other's questions.

Teach

Big Idea   1

Nature and the Imagination
Answer: *Blessed spirits inhabit the corpses of the crew members.*

Writer's Technique ☆

Theme The events in the plot of *The Rime of the Ancient Mariner* work on two levels. One involves a physical journey from a familiar environment to wild, remote regions of the globe and back. The other, a spiritual journey, takes the Mariner from innocence to the brink of damnation and then back toward a state of redemption. **Say:** The crew's bodies do not return to life but are inhabited by spirits. **Ask:** How does this detail relate to both the Mariner's physical and spiritual journeys? *(It relates to his physical journey because the crew can now sail the boat; it relates to his spiritual journey because he is now accompanied by blessed spirits.)*

Beneath the lightning and the Moon
330 The dead men gave a groan.

"They groaned, they stirred, they all uprose,
Nor spake, nor moved their eyes;
It had been strange, even in a dream,
To have seen those dead men rise.

335 "The helmsman steered, the ship moved on;
Yet never a breeze up-blew;
The mariners all 'gan work the ropes,
Where they were wont[42] to do;
They raised their limbs like lifeless tools—
340 We were a ghastly crew.

"The body of my brother's son
Stood by me, knee to knee:
The body and I pulled at one rope,
But he said nought to me."

345 "I fear thee, ancient Mariner!"
"Be calm, thou Wedding Guest!
'Twas not those souls that fled in pain,
Which to their corses[43] came again,
But a troop of spirits blessed: ☆

350 "For when it dawned—they dropped their arms,
And clustered round the mast;
Sweet sounds rose slowly through their mouths,
And from their bodies passed.

"Around, around, flew each sweet sound,
355 Then darted to the Sun;
Slowly the sounds came back again,
Now mixed, now one by one.

"Sometimes a-dropping from the sky
I heard the skylark sing;
360 Sometimes all little birds that are,
How they seemed to fill the sea and air
With their sweet jargoning![44]

But not by the souls of the men, nor by demons of earth or middle air, but by a blessed troop of angelic spirits, sent down by the invocation of the guardian saint.

---

42. *Wont* means "accustomed."
43. *Corses* are corpses.
44. *Jargoning* means "warbling."

1 **Nature and the Imagination** *What is the Mariner's explanation for the crew's revival?*

Reading Practice

SPIRAL REVIEW **Contrast** Have students improve their comprehension by finding meaningful contrasts among the events in this poem. For example, students might contrast the becalmed ship in lines 111–138 with the ship returned to motion by the spirit crew in lines 350–388. Encourage students to draw direct contrasts between the language and the imagery. *(The imagery of the becalmed ship is hot and tortured. The imagery of the ship restored to motion is sweet and musical.)* Suggest that students choose two other events from the poem to contrast, jotting down their ideas in a chart.

"And now 'twas like all instruments,
Now like a lonely flute;
365 And now it is an angel's song,
That makes the heavens be mute.

"It ceased; yet still the sails made on
A pleasant noise till noon,
A noise like of a hidden brook
370 In the leafy month of June,
That to the sleeping woods all night
Singeth a quiet tune.

"Till noon we quietly sailed on,
Yet never a breeze did breathe:
375 Slowly and smoothly went the ship,
Moved onward from beneath.

"Under the keel nine fathom deep, **2**
From the land of mist and snow,
The Spirit slid: and it was he
380 That made the ship to go.
The sails at noon left off their tune,
And the ship stood still also.

"The Sun, right up above the mast,
Had fixed her to the ocean:
385 But in a minute she 'gan stir,
With a short uneasy motion—
Backwards and forwards half her length
With a short uneasy motion.

"Then like a pawing horse let go,
390 She made a sudden bound:
It flung the blood into my head,
And I fell down in a swound.

"How long in that same fit I lay,
I have not to declare;
395 But ere my living life returned,
I heard, and in my soul discerned
Two voices in the air.

" 'Is it he?' quoth one, 'Is this the man?
By him who died on cross,
400 With his cruel bow he laid full low
The harmless Albatross.

Monitor Comprehension *Summarize what has happened so far in Part V.* **3**

The lonesome Spirit from the South Pole carries on the ship as far as the Line, in obedience to the angelic troop, but still requireth vengeance.

The Polar Spirit's fellow demons, the invisible inhabitants of the element, take part in his wrong; and two of them relate, one to the other, that penance long and heavy for the ancient Mariner hath been accorded to the Polar Spirit, who returneth southward.

Teach

Literary Element　　2

Narrative Poetry **Ask:** How does the ship seem to function as a character in this section? *(The ship, guided by the Spirit, seems to have a mind of its own. It starts, stops, and heaves unpredictably, ignoring the rules of the natural world.)*

(APPROACHING) Have approaching-level students focus on lines 373–388. Ask them to summarize the action described in each stanza.

Reading Strategy　　3

Monitor Comprehension **Answer:** *The Mariner sleeps and rain falls. The Mariner awakens but thinks he has died. Wind shakes the sails, the southern lights appear in the sky, and a storm comes. As the ship moves, the dead crew rise up and take their posts around the ship. The Mariner works near the silent body of his brother's son. The Wedding Guest interrupts to repeat his fear of the Mariner. The Mariner explains that good spirits have inhabited the bodies of the dead crew and they sing sweet and lovely songs.*

(ENGLISH LEARNERS) For English learners, **ask:** What clues let you know when the Wedding Guest is speaking? *(quotation marks, the person addressing the Mariner, the Mariner responding afterward)*

English Learners

DIFFERENTIATED INSTRUCTION

Intermediate Point out that Coleridge uses the word *blessèd* in line 308 and *blessed* in line 349. Both words have the same meaning but different pronunciations. The diacritic in *blessèd* indicates that the word should be pronounced as two syllables. He uses different versions of the word to preserve meter.

Approaching Level

DIFFERENTIATED INSTRUCTION

 PARTNERS **Emerging** Visual learners may have difficulty interpreting the rapidly changing imagery of the poem. Encourage partners to read the poem stanza by stanza, pausing after each one to visualize and describe the images presented. Suggest that students draw quick sketches to identify the positions of the characters.

Teach

Vocabulary | 1

Related Words The word *penance* shares a root with both *penitent* (expressing regret for sins or actions committed) and *penitentiary* (a prison). **Ask:** What is the relationship between penance and a penitentiary? *(Penance is an act of self-punishment because of sorrow for sin; a penitentiary is a place where criminals are punished by an authorized power, such as a government.)*

Literary Element | 2

Narrative Poetry Answer: *FIRST VOICE and SECOND VOICE are two spirits discussing the Mariner's fate. They are important to the narration because they know and disclose information the Mariner could not otherwise know.*

(APPROACHING) For approaching-level students, **ask:** Who are the voices talking about? *(the Mariner)* What kind of information are they revealing? *(They are explaining what is happening and why.)*

View the Art ★

The art world treasures Doré's illustrations of literary classics. Other works he illustrated include Dante's *Divine Comedy*, Milton's *Paradise Lost*, Cervantes' *Don Quixote* and the Bible.

778

" 'The Spirit who bideth by himself
In the land of mist and snow,
He loved the bird that loved the man
405   Who shot him with his bow.'

"The other was a softer voice,
As soft as honeydew:
Quoth he, 'The man hath penance done, **1**
And **penance** more will do.' "

PART VI

FIRST VOICE

410   " 'But tell me, tell me! speak again,
Thy soft response renewing—
What makes that ship drive on so fast?
What is the ocean doing?'

SECOND VOICE

" 'Still as a slave before his lord,
415   The ocean hath no blast;[45]
His great bright eye most silently
Up to the Moon is cast—

" 'If he may know which way to go;
For she guides him smooth or grim.
420   See, brother, see! how graciously
She looketh down on him.'

FIRST VOICE

" 'But why drives on that ship so fast,
Without or wave or wind?'

SECOND VOICE

" 'The air is cut away before,
425   And closes from behind.'

---

45. *Blast* means "wind."

2 Narrative Poetry *Who are these voices and why are they important?*

Vocabulary

penance (pen′ əns) *n.* an act of self-punishment to show repentance for a sin

778   UNIT 4   THE TRIUMPH OF ROMANTICISM

The Mariner hath been cast into a trance; for the angelic power causeth the vessel to drive northward faster than human life could endure.

The supernatural motion is retarded; the Mariner awakes, and his penance begins anew.

Angels remove the curse, 1875. Gustave Doré. Engraving. ★

Listening and Speaking Practice

PARTNERS **Perform a Dialogue** Ask partners to prepare oral readings of the dialogue between the two spirits in Part VI. Share these guidelines for presenting a dialogue:

- Use stresses and pauses to build suspense and to convey an atmosphere of tension or mystery when appropriate.
- Vary volume, pitch, and tone.
- Use facial expressions and gestures to help convey meaning.

Suggest that students first rehearse using their own paraphrases of the dialogue in order to understand the basic meaning of the scene before practicing with the poetic language of the text.

"'Fly, brother, fly! more high, more high!
Or we shall be belated:[46]
For slow and slow that ship will go,
When the Mariner's trance is abated.'

430 "I woke, and we were sailing on
As in a gentle weather:
'Twas night, calm night, the moon was high;
The dead men stood together.

"All stood together on the deck,
435 For a charnel-dungeon[47] fitter:
All fixed on me their stony eyes,
That in the Moon did glitter. **3**

"The pang, the curse, with which they died,
Had never passed away:
440 I could not draw my eyes from theirs,
Nor turn them up to pray.

"And now this spell was snapped: once more
I viewed the ocean green,
And looked far forth, yet little saw
445 Of what had else been seen—

"Like one, that on a lonesome road
Doth walk in fear and dread,
And having once turned round walks on,
And turns no more his head;
450 Because he knows, a frightful fiend
Doth close behind him tread.

"But soon there breathed a wind on me,
Nor sound nor motion made:
Its path was not upon the sea,
455 In ripple or in shade.

"It raised my hair, it fanned my cheek
Like a meadow-gale of spring—
It mingled strangely with my fears,
Yet it felt like a welcoming.

---

46. *Belated* means "made late."
47. A *charnel-dungeon* is a burial vault.

Narrative Poetry *How do these lines signal a new phase of the story?* **4**

The curse is finally expiated.
[*Expiated* means "paid for" or "made amends for."]

Teach

Big Idea   3

Nature and the Imagination
Say: Through-out the poem, the Sun and the Moon are portrayed as characters. The Sun is depicted as masculine and is associated with punishment and harsh reality; the Moon is portrayed as feminine and is associated with mercy and imagination. **Ask:** What does this contrast suggest? (*Reality and the imagination are complementary aspects of human experience*)

Literary Element   4

Narrative Poetry
Answer: *The spell is broken, and the Mariner now sees clearly.*
Ask: How does the Mariner's current view of the ocean contrast with earlier imagery? (*The ocean now is a peaceful green color; earlier it had been depicted as molten hot, tumultuous, at times dark, and always mysterious. Even when the ship was calm and motionless before, the ocean was never tranquil.*)

English Learners

DIFFERENTIATED INSTRUCTION

Intermediate Remind English learners that the Mariner is telling his story to the Wedding Guest. Within that story, he presents the exact words of these two Voices. The single quotation mark indicates that a speech is quoted within another speech. Point out that in line 430, the Mariner resumes his own words.

Guide students to read aloud lines 426–433 and adjust their voice to reflect the change in speech.

Approaching Level

DIFFERENTIATED INSTRUCTION

Established Remind students to read for complete sentences and to pause at the end of a line only if they come upon a mark of punctuation. Coleridge's sentences could be written as prose with traditional punctuation, with the exception of the capitalization of words at the beginning of each line.

Teach

Narrative Poetry   Answer:
They are angels or blessed spirits, who inhabited the bodies of the dead crew members to man the ship on its voyage home.

Cultural History ☆

Angels of the First Order

In the Christian tradition, there are nine orders, or ranks, of celestial beings. The seraphim (plural of seraph) are the highest. They stand by God's throne and reflect God's love with such intensity that they seem to burn with it. The color crimson in lines 483 and 485 may symbolically suggest seraphim.

---

460   "Swiftly, swiftly flew the ship,
     Yet she sailed softly too:
     Sweetly, sweetly blew the breeze—
     On me alone it blew.

     "Oh! dream of joy! is this indeed
465   The lighthouse top I see?
     Is this the hill? is this the kirk?
     Is this mine own countree?

     "We drifted o'er the harbor bar,[48]
     And I with sobs did pray—
470   O let me be awake, my God!
     Or let me sleep alway.

     "The harbor bay was clear as glass,
     So smoothly it was strewn!
     And on the bay the moonlight lay,
475   And the shadow of the Moon.

     "The rock shone bright, the kirk no less,
     That stands above the rock:
     The moonlight steeped in silentness
     The steady weathercock.

480   "And the bay was white with silent light,
     Till, rising from the same,
     Full many shapes, that shadows were,
     In crimson colors came. ☆

     "A little distance from the prow
485   Those crimson shadows were:
     I turned my eyes upon the deck—
     Oh, Christ! what saw I there!

     "Each corse lay flat, lifeless and flat,
     And, by the holy rood![49]
490   A man all light, a seraph[50] man,
     On every corse there stood.

     "This seraph band, each waved his hand:
     It was a heavenly sight!
     They stood as signals to the land,
495   Each one a lovely light;

And the ancient Mariner beholdeth his native country.

The angelic spirits leave the dead bodies,

And appear in their own forms of light.

---

48. A *harbor bar* is a bank of sand across the mouth of a harbor, obstructing navigation.
49. The *holy rood* is the cross symbolizing the Christian faith.
50. A *seraph* is an angel of the highest rank.

1   Narrative Poetry   *Who are these characters?*

Writing Practice

ⓣ Hypertext Links

 **SMALL GROUP**   Remind students that texts on the Internet often include hypertext links, which are highlighted or underlined words and phrases that enable readers to access related information, such as definitions, explanations, or relevant Web sites. Have teams suggest how they might create an online version of *The Rime of the Ancient Mariner*. Have them list at least twenty hypertext links they might include. For example, students might suggest highlighting the first occurrence of the word *seraph* in line 490 and linking it to a text explaining the Christian tradition of the nine orders of angels.

"This seraph band, each waved his hand,
No voice did they **impart**— 2
No voice; but oh! the silence sank
Like music on my heart.

500 "But soon I heard the dash of oars,
I heard the Pilot's[51] cheer;
My head was turned perforce[52] away,
And I saw a boat appear.

"The Pilot and the Pilot's boy,
505 I heard them coming fast:
Dear Lord in Heaven! it was a joy
The dead men could not blast.

"I saw a third—I heard his voice:
It is the Hermit good!
510 He singeth loud his godly hymns
That he makes in the wood.
He'll shrieve[53] my soul, he'll wash away
The Albatross's blood."

PART VII

"This Hermit good lives in that wood
515 Which slopes down to the sea.
How loudly his sweet voice he rears!
He loves to talk with mariners
That come from a far countree.

"He kneels at morn, and noon, and eve—
520 He hath a cushion plump:
It is the moss that wholly hides
The rotted old oak stump.

"The skiff[54] boat neared: I heard them talk,

---

51. A *pilot* is a person who steers ships in and out of a harbor.
52. *Perforce* means "of necessity."
53. To *shrieve* is to hear confession and grant forgiveness.
54. A *skiff* is a small seagoing boat, used for sailing or rowing.

3 Monitor Comprehension *What role does the Mariner think the Hermit will play?*

Vocabulary
impart (im pärt′) *v.* to give; donate

The Hermit of the wood

Hermit saves the Mariner, 1875. Gustave Doré. Engraving.

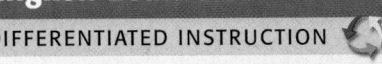 Doré's work was often admired for its fanciful, outrageous qualities. Are these qualities present in this image? Explain. ★

SAMUEL TAYLOR COLERIDGE **781**

Teach

Vocabulary 2

Multiple Meanings Point out that the verb *impart* has two common definitions: "to give" and "to communicate information." Ask students to give examples of sentences using each definition. (*For example:* The sun imparted a feeling of warmth. The messenger imparted important information.)

Reading Strategy 3

Monitor Comprehension
Answer: *The Mariner thinks the Hermit will hear the Mariner's confession and absolve him from his sin.*

APPROACHING Direct approaching-level students' attention to lines 511–512. **Ask:** Does the Mariner want the Hermit to literally wash the Albatross's blood off him? *(no)* To what is the Albatross's blood being compared in this metaphor? *(the Mariner's guilt over killing the bird)*

View the Art ★

Answer: *The posture of the mariner on the ship, the pile of skeletons at his side, the wild waves and the ominous figure of the Hermit in a boat, along with the bold, dark clouds, are all fanciful and dramatic details that fit well with the Romantic aesthetic.*

Teach

Nature and the Imagination

Answer: *The images echo the horror of the events at sea. The hermit mentions skeletons of leaves and a wolf eating its own young.*

ENGLISH LEARNERS Point out the word *owlet* in line 536. Ask English learners to divide the word into root and affix and tell you what they think it means *(probably, a kind of owl)*. Have students look up *owlet* in the dictionary and tell what they think the affix *(-let)* means *(an animal's young)*. Ask students what *piglet* means.

'Why, this is strange, I trow![55]
525　Where are those lights so many and fair,
　　That signal made but now?'

" 'Strange, by my faith!' the Hermit said—
　　'And they answered not our cheer![56]
　　The planks looked warped! and see those sails,
530　How thin they are and sere!
　　I never saw aught[57] like to them,
　　Unless perchance it were

" 'Brown skeletons of leaves that lag
　　My forest brook along;
535　When the ivy tod[58] is heavy with snow,
　　And the owlet whoops to the wolf below,
　　That eats the she-wolf's young.'

" 'Dear Lord! it hath a fiendish look—
　　(The Pilot made reply)
540　I am a-feared'—'Push on, push on!'
　　Said the Hermit cheerily.

"The boat came closer to the ship,
　　But I nor spake nor stirred;
　　The boat came close beneath the ship,
545　And straight[59] a sound was heard.

"Under the water it rumbled on,
　　Still louder and more dread:
　　It reached the ship, it split the bay;
　　The ship went down like lead. ☆

550　"Stunned by that loud and dreadful sound,
　　Which sky and ocean smote,[60]
　　Like one that hath been seven days drowned
　　My body lay afloat;
　　But swift as dreams, myself I found
555　Within the Pilot's boat.

---

55. *Trow* means "suppose" or "believe."
56. Here, *cheer* means "shout of welcome."
57. *Aught* means "anything."
58. An *ivy tod* is a bush of ivy.
59. Here, *straight* means "immediately."
60. *Smote* means "struck."

1 **Nature and the Imagination** *How are the images from nature in this stanza similar to other images you have already encountered in the poem?*

Approacheth the ship with wonder.

The ship suddenly sinketh.

The ancient Mariner is saved in the Pilot's boat.

Vocabulary Practice

Connotations Remind students that a word's connotations are implied meanings that go beyond its denotation. Ask students to look for examples of weighted language that Coleridge uses and to identify the connotations that make each word effective. One useful strategy is to consider synonyms the writer might have chosen. For example, in line 584, the Mariner refers to his "ghastly tale." Coleridge might have selected many synonyms, such as *terrible or frightening*. However, the word *ghastly* carries an additional connotation of ghostliness, suggesting a supernatural tale.

"Upon the whirl, where sank the ship,
The boat spun round and round;
And all was still, save that the hill
Was telling of the sound.

560 "I moved my lips—the Pilot shrieked
And fell down in a fit;
The holy Hermit raised his eyes,
And prayed where he did sit.

"I took the oars: the Pilot's boy,
565 Who now doth crazy go,
Laughed loud and long, and all the while
His eyes went to and fro.
'Ha! ha!' quoth he, 'full plain I see,
The Devil knows how to row.'

570 "And now, all in my own countree,
I stood on the firm land!
The Hermit stepped forth from the boat,
And scarcely he could stand.

" 'O shrieve me, shrieve me, holy man!'
575 The Hermit crossed his brow.[61]
'Say quick,' quoth he, 'I bid thee say—
What manner of man art thou?'

"Forthwith this frame of mine was wrenched
With a woeful agony,
580 Which forced me to begin my tale;
And then it left me free.

"Since then, at an uncertain hour,
That agony returns:
And till my ghastly tale is told,
585 This heart within me burns.

"I pass, like night, from land to land;
I have strange power of speech;
That moment that his face I see,
I know the man that must hear me:
590 To him my tale I teach.

---

61. *Crossed his brow* means "made the sign of the cross on his forehead."

Narrative Poetry *How do those in the boat react to the Mariner's movement? Why do you think they react this way?* **2**

Reviewing *Why must the Mariner tell his tale and why must the Wedding Guest listen?* **3**

The ancient Mariner earnestly entreateth the Hermit to shrieve him; and the penance of life falls on him.

And ever and anon throughout his future life an agony constraineth him to travel from land to land,

Teach

Literary Element 2

Narrative Poetry
Answer: *The Pilot shrieks and falls down in a fit, the Hermit prays, and the boy goes crazy. The Mariner's appearance is so frightening that these characters are horror-struck when he moves his lips.*

Reading Strategy 3

Review Answer: *From time to time, the Mariner is wracked with agony until he tells his story. He is given powers to recognize his listener and to hold him spell-bound. The Wedding Guest must learn the lesson about love that the Mariner's tale teaches.*

English Learners
DIFFERENTIATED INSTRUCTION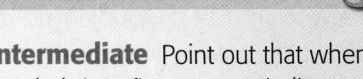

Intermediate Point out that when the word *shrieve* first appears in line 512, it is defined in the footnotes. Remind students that the word *shrieve* in line 574 means "to hear confession and grant forgiveness." Suggest that students review the footnotes to compile a glossary of religious terms.

Approaching Level
DIFFERENTIATED INSTRUCTION

Emerging Help students recognize the connection between the ship's appearance and the angelic lights. **Ask:** How does the boat change when the angelic lights vanish? *(It becomes warped and dry.)* What other ship does it resemble? *(The ship of Death and Life-in-Death)*

Teach

Big Idea | 1

Nature and the Imagination
Answer: *God created all life, large and small, and people should therefore love and respect all life.*

Point out lines 612–613, which sum up the Mariner's message. Ask students to restate "He prayeth well, who loveth well" in contemporary English. Point out that *prayeth* and *loveth* are archaic forms of *prays* and *loves*.

Literary Element | 2

Narrative Poetry
Answer: *Instead of attending the wedding feast, he goes home stunned. The next day he is sadder, but wiser.*

Cultural History ☆

Absolution Christian tradition holds that sincere confession brings about absolution, or forgiveness of sins. Absolution requires that the sinner do penance first. The Mariner's penance is to repeat his tale to others who need to hear his story and learn its lesson.

 To check students' understanding of the selection, see Unit 4 Teaching Resources Book, p. 152.

"What loud uproar bursts from that door!
The wedding guests are there:
But in the garden bower the bride
And bridemaids singing are:
595 And hark the little vesper bell,
Which biddeth me to prayer!

"O Wedding Guest! this soul hath been
Alone on a wide, wide sea:
So lonely 'twas, that God himself
600 Scarce seemèd there to be.

"O sweeter than the marriage feast,
'Tis sweeter far to me,
To walk together to the kirk
With a goodly company!—

605 "To walk together to the kirk,
And all together pray,
While each to his great Father bends,
Old men, and babes, and loving friends
And youths and maidens gay!

610 "Farewell, farewell! but this I tell ☆
To thee, thou Wedding Guest!
He prayeth well, who loveth well
Both man and bird and beast.

"He prayeth best, who loveth best
615 All things both great and small;
For the dear God who loveth us,
He made and loveth all."

The Mariner, whose eye is bright,
Whose beard with age is hoar,
620 Is gone: and now the Wedding Guest
Turned from the bridegroom's door.

He went like one that hath been stunned,
And is of sense forlorn:[62]
A sadder and a wiser man,
625 He rose the morrow morn.

---

62. *Of sense forlorn* means "stripped of his senses."

1 **Nature and the Imagination** *How does nature inform the moral of the Mariner's tale?*

2 Narrative Poetry *According to the last stanza, what does the Wedding Guest do now? How has he been changed by his experience?*

Albatross from cover binder. Sangorski and Sutcliffe, London.

And to teach, by his own example, love and reverence to all things that God made and loveth.

Literary Element Practice

SPIRAL REVIEW **Character** Point out that a dynamic character is one who changes or grows during the course of a literary work. Have students contrast two dynamic characters in this narrative: the Mariner and the Wedding Guest. Have students describe how the Mariner was changed by physical and spiritual events, while the Wedding Guest was changed by encountering the Mariner and hearing his tale. Students might write a prose scene in which the Wedding Guest explains to the bridal couple why he failed to appear at the wedding.

After You Read

Respond and Think Critically

Respond and Interpret

1. (a)What images remain in your mind from this poem? Explain. (b)What still puzzles you about this poem? Write your answer in the form of a question.

2. (a)What sin or crime does the Mariner say he has committed? (b)What happens to the ship after this deed? (c)How do the Mariner's fellow crewmen single him out for punishment?

3. (a)Who is aboard the skeleton ship in Part III and what are they doing? (b)What is the result of their activity?

4. (a)What comparison does the Mariner make between himself, the water snakes, and the dead men in lines 236–239? (b)How does his view of these water snakes change at the end of Part IV in lines 272–291?

5. (a)In Part IV what happens when the Mariner prays? (b)In lines 402–409 what does the lonesome Polar Spirit decide and why?

Analyze and Evaluate

6. (a)Do you think the Mariner is responsible for what happens to the ship? Why or why not? (b)Do you think the Mariner's punishment fits his crime? Explain.

7. Coleridge added the side notes to help the reader better follow the plot. Do you think they are helpful? Why or why not?

Connect

8. **Big Idea** **Nature and the Imagination** How does this poem exemplify Romantic ideas about nature and the imagination?

9. **Connect to the Author** Coleridge once wrote that a reader must put aside his or her understanding of reality and accept the writer's world. In what ways does this fit in with Coleridge's use of Romantic themes and devices?

Literary Element Narrative Poetry

Traditionally, there are three main types of **narrative poetry**: the epic, the romance, and the ballad. Epic poems, like *Beowulf* (page 22), are long poems written in a formal style, often tracing the story of a noble and courageous hero. Romances are similar to epics and often recount the exploits of heroic knights. *Sir Gawain and the Green Knight* (page 164) is one example. The ballad is a shorter narrative poem that is written in the form of a song.

1. Explain Coleridge's use of a frame story to present the tale of the Mariner's adventure.

2. (a)How would you characterize the Mariner? (b)Why do you think Coleridge wrote this poem in the ballad form?

3. (a)What incident sparks the conflict of the story? (b)What incident serves as the climax?

Review: Ballad Stanza

As you learned on page 200, a **literary ballad** is written in imitation of folk ballads. The writer may employ a **ballad stanza** and rhyme scheme, as well as archaic diction to achieve this effect.

Partner Activity With a classmate, talk about Coleridge's use of the elements of folk ballads in *The Rime of the Ancient Mariner*. Construct a chart and cite at least one example for each bullet.

Ballad Element	Example
• Quatrains of alternating 4 and 3 stressed syllables	
• Rhyme scheme of *abcb*	
• Iambic meter	
• Repeated lines or refrains	

SAMUEL TAYLOR COLERIDGE **785**

After You Read

Assess

1. (a) Students' responses will vary. (b) Make sure students write their answers in the form of a question.

2. (a) He kills the albatross. (b) The ship is becalmed. (c) They hang the dead bird around the Mariner's neck.

3. (a) The specters, Death and Life-in-Death, gamble for the crew. (b) Life-in-Death wins the Mariner, and Death claims the rest of the crew.

4. (a) He sees the dead men as beautiful and himself and the water snakes as repugnant. (b) He sees the water snakes as strangely beautiful and recognizes that they are God's creatures.

5. (a) The albatross falls from his neck into the sea. (b) The Polar Spirit loved the albatross and has decided that the Mariner must do more penance.

6. (a) His evil deed is the reason the spirits respond as they do. (b) Answers will vary.

7. Answers will vary.

8. It is a tale with a moral expressing the sacredness of nature.

9. Coleridge's use of dramatic, exaggerated, and emotional elements in his work creates a fictional world that often looks like the real world, but is more intense and operates differently. He is asking his readers to appreciate that world and its fantastical ways. A reader who refused to accept Death and Life-in-Death playing dice for men's souls would not be able to appreciate Coleridge's poem.

Review: Ballad Stanza

Students' answers will vary. Make sure charts are thoroughly completed.

785

Literary Element

1. The frame story provides an opportunity for the Mariner to do penance by telling his tale.

2. (a) The Mariner is brave, but frightening and tragic. (b) The Mariner is a wandering bard, which suits the ballad form.

3. (a) The Mariner's killing of the albatross (b) The Mariner's unconscious blessing of the sea creatures

Progress Check

Can students analyze narrative poetry?

If No → See Unit 4 Teaching Resources Book, p. 149.

After You Read

Assess

Reading Strategy

1. Evaluate students' summaries on their accuracy, completeness, and concision.

2. While on a voyage, the Mariner violates nature by killing an albatross. As a result, the ship is trapped in the doldrums, and the other crew members die. When the Mariner blesses God's creatures, spirits sail the ship home, and the Mariner begins his penance of roaming the world and telling his tale.

Vocabulary Practice

1. The context suggests that "sunny and bright" is the opposite of *dismal*, so *dismal* must mean "dark" or "gloomy."

2. The context suggests that *penance* means "punishment."

3. The context suggest that *imparted* means "gave."

Academic Vocabulary

Students' questions should focus on the most important elements of the poem.

 For additional assessment, see Assessment Resources, pp. 195–196.

Reading Strategy Monitor Comprehension

Summarizing the main ideas, supporting details, actions, and plot of a literary work as you review that work will aid your understanding of it.

1. Summarize each of the seven parts of *The Rime of the Ancient Mariner.*

2. Write a summary of the whole poem in two or three sentences.

Vocabulary Practice

Practice with Context Clues Identify the context clues in the following sentences that help you determine the meaning of each bold-faced vocabulary word.

1. The morning had been **dismal**, but the sky cleared and the afternoon was sunny and bright.

2. The Mariner had to do **penance** for killing the albatross by suffering on the ship.

3. My mother **imparted** her bread recipe to me, and now I make the bread myself.

Academic Vocabulary

The Mariner's killing of the albatross is **crucial** *to Coleridge's narrative.*

Crucial is an academic word. More familiar words that are similar in meaning are *critical, essential,* and *important.*

To further explore the meaning of this word, write and answer questions about the **crucial** elements of *The Rime of the Ancient Mariner.*

EXAMPLE:
Question: Why did the whole crew drop dead?
Answer: Death and Life-in-Death gambled for the crew.

For more on academic vocabulary, see pages 56 and R81.

Connect to *Art*

Assignment Choose several of the Gustave Doré engravings that accompany the poem and analyze their contribution to its events, theme, and mood. Create one or two sketches of your own to present with your analysis.

Investigate Reread *The Rime of the Ancient Mariner,* paying close attention to the engravings. Discuss your ideas with a partner. Then think about the points you want to make and how to present them—either following the chronology of the poem or in order of importance to the theme.

Create Sketch, draw, or paint a scene, or create a collage that summarizes your reaction to reading Coleridge's poem and viewing Doré's art. Use colors, textures, and subjects that reflect your emotional response.

Report Document any ideas you take from outside sources, using correct bibliographic and citation style. Refer to specific elements of the poem and engravings and incorporate your own artwork into your presentation, explaining how it supports your statements and illuminates your reaction to them.

EXAMPLE

We—and those around us—are doomed to suffer the consequences of our actions.

 Literature Online

Selection Resources For Selection Quizzes, eFlashcards, and Reading-Writing Connection activities, go to glencoe.com and enter QuickPass code GLB9817u4.

 Connect to *Art*

Students' visual representations should reveal direct connections to the poem and include analysis of the engravings appearing with the selection.

To create custom assessments using software, use ExamView Assessment Suite.

To create custom assessments online, go to Progress Reporter Online Assessment.

from
In Patagonia

Bruce Chatwin

Hawthornden Prize Winner

Learning Objectives

For pages 787–790
In studying this text, you will focus on the following objectives:

Literary Study: Making connections across literature.

Reading: Evaluating historical influences.

Set a Purpose for Reading

As you read, ask yourself, What was the historical basis for Coleridge's *Rime of the Ancient Mariner*?

Build Background

In 1591 a British fleet under the command of Thomas Cavendish sailed from Plymouth, England, on a voyage to the Pacific Ocean. The trip would end in disaster. As a result of bad weather, ill luck, and a series of miscalculations, many in the fleet's crew were lost. This disaster may have provided some of the inspiration for Samuel Taylor Coleridge's *The Rime of the Ancient Mariner*. The following selection, from Bruce Chatwin's prize-winning book *In Patagonia,* describes the circumstances surrounding the disaster.

Reading Strategy

Evaluate Historical Influences

Evaluating historical influences involves gathering and examining the background information related to the writing of a literary work. As you read, take notes on the parallels between the historical events and the events in Coleridge's poem. Use a two-column chart like the one below.

Literary Work	Historical Events
Ancient Mariner's voyage	Voyage of the <u>Desire</u>

On October 30th 1593,[1] the ship *Desire*, of 120 tons, limping home to England, dropped anchor in the river at Port Desire, this being her fourth visit since Thomas Cavendish[2] named the place in her, his flagship's, honor, seven years before.

The captain was now John Davis, a Devon man, the most skilled navigator of his generation. Behind him were three Arctic voyages in search of the North-West Passage. Before him were two books of seamanship and six fatal cuts of a Japanese pirate's sword.

Davis had sailed on Cavendish's Second Voyage "intended for the South Sea." The fleet left Plymouth on August 26th 1591, the Captain-General in the galleon *Leicester*; the other ships were the *Roebuck*, the *Desire*, the *Daintie*, and the *Black Pinnace*, the last so named for having carried the corpse of Sir Philip Sydney.[3]

---

1. Although Chatwin cites the year 1593, 1592 is more likely based on the chronology of the voyage.
2. *Thomas Cavendish* (1555–1592) was a famed explorer who led the third circumnavigation of the globe.
3. A *pinnace* is a small sailing ship. *Sir Philip Sydney* (1554–1586) was an Elizabethan poet, courtier, and soldier.

BRUCE CHATWIN **787**

Focus

Summary

In 1591, the English ship *Desire*, captained by John Davis, sailed through the Strait of Magellan and into the Atlantic after a storm. Needing food, the sailors killed twenty thousand penguins and dried, salted, and stored fourteen thousand of them in the hold. After several Indian attacks, Davis headed back to Europe. The crew and ship became infected with worms bred in the dead penguins. When the ship drifted into port in Ireland, only five men were alive and healthy enough to move. This journey is one possible source of inspiration for Coleridge's *The Rime of the Ancient Mariner*.

 For summaries in languages other than English, see Unit 4 Teaching Resources Book, pp. 154–159.

 For an audio recording of this selection, use Listening Library Audio CD-ROM.

Readability Scores

Dale-Chall: 7.0
DRP: 60
Lexile: 1050

Approaching Level

DIFFERENTIATED INSTRUCTION

Emerging Read aloud the last two sentences in the second paragraph. Explain that, in this case, *before* means "in front of" and not "earlier than." **Ask:** What is the author using *behind* and *before* to mean in these two sentences? (*Chatwin uses* behind *to mean "in his past." He uses* before *to mean "still ahead in his life."*)

Teach

Evaluate Historical Influences

Ask: When did Cavendish agree to return? *(In the spring)* And about when did he make this agreement? *(Around May 20th)*

APPROACHING Help approaching-level students understand that the seasons in the southern hemisphere are reversed from those in the northern hemisphere.

Ask: On May 20th, what is the season in the southern hemisphere? *(fall)* In the ships' location at the time, when would "the following spring" begin? *(around September)*

Nature and the Imagination

Ask: How did the sailors and captain of the *Desire* view the forces of nature? *(To them, nature was controlled by God, and God used the forces of nature to punish them.)* How does this compare to Coleridge's view? *(Coleridge also saw nature as an instrument of God, but he saw God as using nature to redeem the Mariner.)*

Context Clues

Ask: What do you think *vizzard* means? *(a mask)* What words around *vizzard* helped you figure this out? *"on their faces like dogs' faces"*

Informational Text

Cavendish was puffed up with early success, hating his officers and crew. On the coast of Brazil, he stopped to sack[4] the town of Santos. A gale scattered the ships off the Patagonian coast, but they met up, as arranged, at Port Desire.

The fleet entered the Magellan Strait[5] with the southern winter already begun. A sailor's frostbitten nose fell off when he blew it. Beyond Cape Froward, they ran into northwesterly gales and sheltered in a tight cove with the wind howling over their mastheads. Reluctantly, Cavendish agreed to revictual[6] in Brazil and return the following spring.

1 On the night of May 20th, off Port Desire, the Captain-General changed tack[7] without warning. At dawn, the *Desire* and the *Black Pinnace* were alone on the sea. Davis made for port, thinking his commander would join him as before, but Cavendish set course for Brazil and thence to St. Helena.[8] One day he lay down in his cabin and died, perhaps of apoplexy,[9] cursing Davis for desertion: "This villain that hath been the death of me."

Davis disliked the man but was no traitor. The worst of the winter over, he went south again to look for the Captain-General. Gales blew the two ships in among some undiscovered islands, now known as the Falklands.

This time, they passed the Strait and out into the Pacific. In a storm off Cape Pilar, the *Desire* lost the *Pinnace*, which went down with all hands. Davis was alone at the helm, praying for a speedy end, when the sun broke through the clouds. He took bearings, fixed his position, and so regained the calmer water of the Strait. **2**

He sailed back to Port Desire, the crew scurvied and mutinous and the lice lying in their flesh, "clusters of lice as big as peason, yea, and some as big as beanes." He repaired the ship as best he could. The men lived off eggs, gulls, baby seals, scurvy grass and the fish called *pejerrey*. On this diet they were restored to health.

Ten miles down the coast, there was an island, the original Penguin Island, where the sailors clubbed twenty thousand birds to death. They had no natural enemies and were unafraid of their murderers. John Davis ordered the penguins dried and salted and stowed fourteen thousand in the hold.

On November 11th a war-party of Tehuelche Indians[10] attacked "throwing dust in the ayre, leaping and running like brute beasts, having vizzards on their faces like dogs' faces, or else **3** their faces are dogs' faces indeed." Nine men died in the skirmish, among them the chief mutineers, Parker and Smith. Their deaths were seen as the just judgment of God.

> "The fleet entered the Magellan Strait with the southern winter already begun. A sailor's frostbitten nose fell off when he blew it."

---

4. Here, *sack* means "pillage."
5. The *Magellan Strait* connects the Atlantic and Pacific oceans near the southern tip of South America.
6. *Revictual* means to "resupply with food."
7. Here, *tack* means "course."
8. *St. Helena,* first discovered in 1502, was a British island colony and port of call off the southwestern coast of Africa.
9. *Apoplexy* is a stroke.
10. The *Tehuelche Indians* were a nomadic group that inhabited Patagonia.

Reading Practice

SPIRAL REVIEW **Tone** Throughout the selection, Chatwin describes some horrendous events and circumstances. But he does so in a simple, straightforward manner. "A sailor's frostbitten nose fell off when he blew it," is horrible, but Chatwin reports it as a simple statement of fact. The most extreme example of this may be, "One day he lay down in his cabin and died... ." Discuss with students whether this low-key style of reporting just the facts serves to downplay the horrors being described or to accentuate them.

The *Desire* sailed at nightfall on December 22nd and set course for Brazil where the Captain hoped to provision with cassava[11] flour. On January 30th he made land at the Isle of Plasencia, off Rio de Janeiro. The men foraged for fruit and vegetables in gardens belonging to the Indians.

Six days later, the coopers[12] went with a landing party to gather hoops for barrels. The day was hot and the men were bathing, unguarded, when a mob of Indians and Portuguese attacked. The Captain sent a boat crew ashore and they found the thirteen men, faces upturned to heaven, laid in a rank with a cross set by them.

4 John Davis saw pinnaces sailing out of Rio harbor. He made for open sea. He had no other choice. He had eight casks of water and they were fouled.

As they came up to the Equator, the penguins took their revenge. In them bred a "loathsome worme" about an inch long. The worms ate everything, iron only excepted—clothes, bedding, boots, hats, leather lashings, and live human flesh. The worms gnawed through the ship's side and threatened to sink her. The more worms the men killed, the more they multiplied.

☆ Around the Tropic of Cancer, the crew came down with scurvy. Their ankles swelled and their chests, and their parts swelled so horribly that "they could neither stand nor lie nor go."

The Captain could scarcely speak for sorrow. Again he prayed for a speedy end. He asked the men to be patient; to give thanks to God and accept his chastisement. But the men were rag-

Map of the Magellan Straits, from Cosmographie Universelle, 1555. Guillaume Le Testu. Watercolor on paper. Ministry of Defense, Service Historique de l'Armee de Terre, France.

ing mad and the ship howled with the groans and curses of the dying. Only Davis and a ship's boy were in health, of the seventy-six who left Plymouth. By the end there were five men who could move and work the ship.

And so, lost and wandering on the sea, with topsails and spritsails torn, the rotten hulk drifted, rather than sailed, into the harbor of Berehaven on Bantry Bay[13] on June 11th 1593. The smell disgusted the people of that quiet fishing village. . . .

---

11. *Cassava* is a tuber—the bulky, underground stem of a plant—that can be dried and milled into flour.
12. *Coopers* repair and build wooden barrels or casks.

13. *Bantry Bay* is in southwest Ireland.

BRUCE CHATWIN **789**

Teach

Reading Strategy | 4

Evaluate Historical Influences Ask: Why did Davis have no choice about sailing when he saw the ships coming out of Rio harbor? *(Based on the Cavendish's earlier sacking of Santos and the attack by the Portuguese and Indians, it's clear that the people of Brazil are enemies of the English.)*

APPROACHING For approaching-level students, ask: what happened immediately before he made this decision? *(He saw pinnaces sailing out of the harbor at Rio de Janeiro.)* What would have happened if he had stayed where he was? *(The ships would have attacked the* Desire.*)*

Cultural History ☆

Scurvy Scurvy was a disease that plagued sailors for centuries. Its symptoms included fatigue, loose teeth, joint pain, and, eventually, death. The disease, which is caused by a lack of vitamin C, ceased to be a problem when ships began stocking fruit for the sailors.

 For activities related to this selection, see Unit 4 Teaching Resources Book, pp. 154–162.

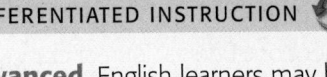
English Learners

DIFFERENTIATED INSTRUCTION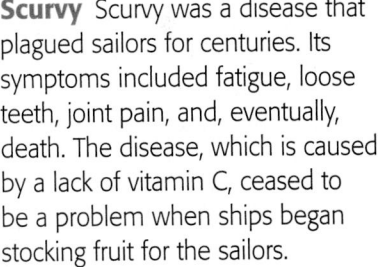

Advanced English learners may be unfamiliar with the different locations mentioned in this selection. Have them identify the different places mentioned on this page. *(Ise of Plasencia, Rio de Janeiro, Tropic of Cancer, Berehaven, Bantry Bay, and Plymouth, England)* Tell

English learners to research one of these locations, using a variety of print and online resources. After researching, have them give a brief oral presentation on general and historical information about the location of their choosing.

Assess

1. Students' summaries should outline the series of events on the *Desire.*

2. The killing of the penguins

3. (a) Cavendish accused Davis of desertion. Because the Captain-General "changed tack without warning," the *Desire* and the *Black Pinnace* were left alone, stranded from their fleet.
(b) Because Cavendish disliked his crew and officers, he was predisposed to judge them unfairly.

4. (a) They killed the penguins for food. (b) They needed a larger number in order to provide enough food for their long voyage.

5. Students' answers will vary.

6. (a) Some students will argue that Davis was only attempting to help the crew accept their fate; others will argue that he too believed they were being punished for their sins.
(b) Supernatural punishment for a crime against the natural world is at the heart of Coleridge's poem and Davis's notion of "chastisement."

7. Most students will argue that there is a clear link between the historical events and Coleridge's poem.

 For additional assessment, see Assessment Resources, pp. 197–198.

790

Informational Text

"The Southern Voyage of John Davis" appeared in Hakluyt's[14] edition of 1600. Two centuries passed and another Devon man, Samuel Taylor Coleridge, set down the 625 controversial lines of *The Ancient Mariner,* with its hammering repetitions and story of crime, wandering, and expiation.[15]

John Davis and the Mariner have these in common: a voyage to the Black South, the murder of a bird or birds, the nemesis which follows, the drift through the tropics, the rotting ship, the curses of dying men. Lines 236–9 are particularly resonant of the Elizabethan voyage:

> The many men so beautiful!
> And they all dead did lie:
> And a thousand, thousand slimy things
> Lived on and so did I.

14. *Richard Hakluyt* (1552–1616) was a British geographer and chronicler of British exploration. The second edition of his nautical record was completed and released between 1598 and 1600.

15. *Expiation* is the act of making atonement.

In *The Road to Xanadu,* the American scholar John Livingston Lowes traced the Mariner's victim to a "disconsolate Black Albitross" shot by one Hatley, the mate of Captain George Shelvocke's privateer in the eighteenth century. Wordsworth had a copy of this voyage and showed it to Coleridge when the two men tried to write the poem together. . . .

Lowes demonstrated how the voyages in Hakluyt and Purchas[16] fuelled Coleridge's imagination. "The mighty great roaring of ice" that John Davis witnessed on an earlier voyage off Greenland reappears in line 61: "It cracked and growled and roared and howled." But he did not, apparently, consider the likelihood that Davis's voyage to the Strait gave Coleridge the backbone for his poem. ☙

16. *Samuel Purchas* (1577–1626) chronicled British nautical discoveries, continuing the work of Hakluyt. His work was a favorite of Coleridge's.

Respond and Think Critically

Respond and Interpret

1. Write a brief summary of the main ideas in this excerpt before you answer the following questions. For help writing a summary, see page 435.

2. In your opinion, what aspects of this account most resemble the events in Coleridge's poem? Explain.

3. (a) As he died, what did Cavendish accuse Davis of? Describe the events that led to the accusation. (b) Why do you think Cavendish came to this conclusion?

4. (a) For what reason did the crew kill the penguins on Penguin Island? (b) Why do you think they needed so many penguins?

Analyze and Evaluate

5. On the basis of the descriptions in this passage, do you agree with Chatwin that the killing of the penguins provided Coleridge's inspiration for the killing of the albatross? Explain.

6. (a) Why do you think Davis told the crew to accept God's "chastisement"? (b) In what ways does Davis's notion of divine punishment echo the themes of Coleridge's poem?

Connect

7. Refer to the chart you made while reading. Do you believe that these events gave Coleridge "the backbone for his poem," as Chatwin claims? Support your opinion with evidence from this selection and from *The Rime of the Ancient Mariner.*

Writing Practice

Journal Entry

SPIRAL REVIEW Have students write a journal entry for Davis or one of his crewmembers. The entry should describe events of the *Desire's* journey from the point of view of the sailor. Base your assessment of students' journal entry on the accuracy of the facts retold, the reasonableness of students' conclusions and whether the facts stated support the conclusions, and correct grammar and mechanics.

Before You Read

from the Introduction to *Frankenstein*

Meet **Mary Shelley**
(1797–1851)

The daughter of two celebrated writers and social thinkers, Mary Shelley might have been destined for literary stardom even if she had never met and married the great Romantic poet Percy Bysshe Shelley. No one could have predicted, however, that at age eighteen, she would write *Frankenstein*, a novel that in its day far outstripped the popularity of her famous husband's poetry.

Mary Shelley was the daughter of the radical philosopher William Godwin and Mary Wollstonecraft Godwin, whose well-known writings included one of England's first treatises on women's rights. Nevertheless, Shelley's childhood was not a happy one. Her mother died from complications following Mary's birth; her father then married a woman with a family of her own and little time for her stepdaughter. However, Shelley did get to meet many British intellectuals of the day. Young admirers of William Godwin's writings often gathered at the philosopher's home; one of these literary lights was Percy Bysshe Shelley, the man who was to become her husband in 1816.

> "Nothing contributes so much to tranquilize the mind as a steady purpose—a point on which the soul may fix its intellectual eye."
>
> —Mary Shelley

Literary Life The Shelleys' life together was romantic but troubled. Only one of their children survived past infancy, Mary Shelley suffered a breakdown, and her husband was sometimes unfaithful. Still, the Shelleys were passionate about many of the same things, including literature and languages. They often read together, usually the classics, sharing their responses at length.

In 1816 the couple traveled to Switzerland and lived near Lord Byron—who at the time was a celebrity. It was during this time that Mary Shelley began writing the book that became one of the best-known gothic novels of all time. Published anonymously two years later, *Frankenstein; or, The Modern Prometheus* tells the story of a "mad" scientist, Victor Frankenstein, who gives life to a creature made from parts of corpses. Although Frankenstein's "monster" is sensitive and kind, his appearance arouses hatred and fear, dooming him to misery. The novel was an instant hit, and Britain was buzzing with speculations (all wrong) about its author. Mary Shelley was pleased with its success, but her happiness was short-lived: in 1822 her husband died.

New Mission Mary Shelley devoted much of the rest of her life to establishing her late husband's reputation as one of the great English poets. Her efforts were successful. A complete collection of Shelley's works, painstakingly edited by his widow, was published in 1847, and Shelley's poetry began to receive the critical acclaim that it now enjoys. Mary Shelley continued to write to support herself. Her later works, however, never matched *Frankenstein* in originality of conception or emotional power. That masterpiece remains popular with readers to this day—a testament to the overwhelming power and scope of her imagination.

LOG ON ▶ **Literature** Online

Author Search For more about Mary Shelley, go to glencoe.com and enter QuickPass code GLB9817u4.

MARY SHELLEY **791**

Before You Read

Focus

Bellringer Options

Selection Focus
Transparency 39
Daily Language Practice
Transparency 64

Or **say:** Take a few minutes to describe one of your favorite daydreams. Be sure to include a description of your role in the daydream. **Ask:** When are you most likely to daydream?

Selection Skills

Literary Elements
- Gothic Novel (SE pp. 792–798)

Reading Skills
- Activate Prior Knowledge (SE pp. 792–798)
- Preread (TE p. 792)

from **The Introduction to Frankenstein**

Vocabulary Skills
- Word Usage (SE p. 798)
- Synonyms (TE p. 792)

Listening/Speaking/Viewing Skills
- Analyze Art (SE pp. 794, 796)
- View the Movie (TE p. 796)

Writing Skills/Grammar
- Write a Story (SE p. 798)

Before You Read

Focus

Summary

While vacationing in Switzerland in 1816, the Shelleys and two friends spent many hours discussing the nature of life. The four decided to try their hands at writing ghost stories. As she lay in bed one night, Mary Shelley was kept awake by recurring thoughts of a scientist who creates life in a laboratory—with disastrous consequences. She developed the plot outline into the novel that has become a classic of horror fiction.

 For summaries in languages other than English, see Unit 4 Teaching Resources Book, pp. 163–168.

Vocabulary

Synonyms Say: When you are reading a text with new words, it is helpful to know synonyms for them. The synonym can help you figure out the meaning of a sentence. Ask students to write a sentence using each of the vocabulary words. Then have them trade papers with a partner. Students should rewrite each other's sentences, substituting synonyms for the vocabulary words.

 For additional vocabulary practice, see Unit 4 Teaching Resources Book, p. 171.

Literature and Reading Preview

Connect to the Essay

What moments of creative inspiration have you experienced? Freewrite for a few minutes about one such moment, and what might have triggered it.

Build Background

In 1831, when the novel *Frankenstein* was being prepared for a new edition, the publishers asked Mary Shelley to write an introduction that answered the question so many still asked: How could a young woman of eighteen have created a novel so far removed from her own experience? Mary Shelley's introduction offers fascinating insights into the genesis of a literary work.

Set Purposes for Reading

Big Idea Nature and the Imagination

As you read, ask yourself, What is the importance of nature and the imagination to this Romantic writer?

Literary Element Gothic Novel

Mary Shelley's *Frankenstein* is a **gothic novel**. A gothic novel has a gloomy, ominous setting and elements of mystery, horror, or the supernatural. Gothic novels sparked a fascination with not only gothic writing but gothic painting and architecture as well. As you read the introduction to *Frankenstein*, ask yourself, What elements of Gothic style does Shelley use to describe her writing experience?

Reading Strategy Activate Prior Knowledge

You derive meaning from a literary work by relating what you read to what you already know. To understand this selection, draw upon your **prior knowledge** about the act of writing, the creative process, and the story of *Frankenstein*. As you read, ask yourself, How might this relate to something I know?

....

Tip: Taking Notes In a chart like the one below, record the connections you make between your prior knowledge and the events the author describes.

Event	Prior Knowledge
Shelley struggled to find an idea for a ghost story.	I, too, sometimes have writer's block.

Learning Objectives

For pages 791–798

In studying this text, you will focus on the following objectives:

Literary Study: Analyzing a gothic novel.

Reading: Activating prior knowledge.

Writing: Writing a story.

Vocabulary

incite (in sīt´) *v.* to urge or provoke; p. 794 *The angry speaker nearly incited a riot.*

dispatch (di spach´) *v.* to send off or away with speed; p. 795 *I dispatched him to the store for extra milk.*

illustrious (i lus´ trē əs) *adj.* famous and distinguished; p. 795 *The illustrious author gave a series of lectures about her life and work.*

relinquish (ri ling´ kwish) *v.* to give up; put aside; abandon; p. 795 *Jamal's grandfather decided to relinquish his driving privileges.*

transient (tran´ shənt) *adj.* lasting only a brief time; temporary; p. 797 *Because of the cool climate, that region has only a transient growing season.*

Reading Practice

 Preread Remind students that the selection is about Shelley's inspirations for *Frankenstein*. Before they read the selection, have them preview it by reading the first paragraph and the first sentence of each paragraph that follows. Ask them to write three predictions about what they have previewed. Invite students to share one of their predictions with the class. **Ask:** What led to your prediction? *(Students should make specific references to the selection.)* As students read, have them check to see whether their predictions were accurate.

792

from The Introduction to Frankenstein

Mary Shelley

The publishers of the Standard Novels, in selecting *Frankenstein* for one of their series, expressed a wish that I should furnish them with some account of the origin of the story. I am the more willing to comply because I shall thus give a general answer to the question so very frequently asked me—how I, then a young girl, came to think of and to dilate[1] upon so very hideous an idea.

It is true that I am very averse to bringing myself forward in print, but as my account will only appear as an appendage[2] to a former production, and as it will be confined to such topics as have connection with my authorship alone, I can scarcely accuse myself of a personal intrusion.

It is not singular that, as the daughter of two persons of distinguished literary celebrity, I should very early in life have thought of writing. As a child I scribbled, and my favorite pastime during the hours given me for recreation was to "write stories." Still, I had a dearer pleasure than this, which was the formation of castles in the air—the indulging in waking dreams—the following up trains of thought, which had for their subject the formation of a succession of imaginary incidents. My dreams were at once more fantastic and agreeable than my writings. In the latter I was a close imitator—rather doing as others had done than putting down the suggestions of my own mind. What I wrote was intended at least for one other eye—my childhood's companion and friend; but my dreams were all my own. I accounted for them to nobody; they were my refuge when annoyed—my dearest pleasure when free.

I lived principally in the country as a girl and passed a considerable time in Scotland. I made occasional visits to the more picturesque parts, but my habitual residence was on the blank and dreary northern shores of the Tay, near Dundee. Blank and dreary on retrospection, I call them; they were not so to me then. They were the aerie[3] of freedom and the pleasant region where unheeded I could commune with the creatures of my fancy. I wrote then, but in a most commonplace style. It was beneath the trees of the grounds belonging to our house, or on the bleak sides of the woodless mountains near, that my

---

1. Here, *dilate* means "speak or write at length."
2. An *appendage* is an addition or accompaniment.

 1 Activate Prior Knowledge *Why might publishers ask authors to describe the origin of their stories?*

3. An *aerie* is a nest or retreat.

Teach

Reading Strategy **1**

Activate Prior Knowledge
Answer: *Publishers might believe that an author's testimony will enhance a new edition of a novel, enticing readers to purchase the book.* **Ask:** What makes you curious about an author's ideas and inspirations? *(Responses will vary.)*

[ENGLISH LEARNERS] **Write** the following questions on the board and have English learners work with a partner in answering them. What is your favorite book or story? Why? What would you like to know about its author?

 For additional practice using the reading skill or strategy, see Unit 4 Teaching Resources Book, p. 170.

Big Idea **2**

Nature and the Imagination
Ask: How does nature play a role in Mary Shelley's life as a child? *(She grew up in a rural environment and spent many hours outdoors in Scotland, writing stories and indulging in daydreams.)*

 For an audio recording of this selection, use Listening Library Audio CD-ROM.

Readability Scores
Dale-Chall: 10.5
DRP: 63
Lexile: 1210

Approaching Level

DIFFERENTIATED INSTRUCTION

SMALL GROUP **Emerging** Because this selection contains challenging vocabulary, complex sentence structures, and lengthy paragraphs, summarizing may be a useful tool for less-proficient readers. Divide students into small groups. Have them pause after reading each paragraph and identify its main ideas. Finally, have them write summaries of the paragraphs. **Model** summarizing the first paragraph: *Publishers asked Shelley to write an introduction to* Frankenstein. *They wanted her to explain how a young girl could write a horror story.*

Teach

Big Idea   1

Nature and the Imagination
Answer: *As a child, Shelley spent much time alone in nature using her imagination to create characters and stories.*

Reading Strategy   2

Activate Prior Knowledge
Answer: *Because both of Mary Shelley's parents were creative thinkers and gifted writers, her husband expected her to achieve literary success.*

Big Idea   3

Nature and the Imagination
Answer: *Nature stimulated Byron's imagination, inspiring him to write poetry about the beauty of his surroundings.*

View the Art ★

Victor Hugo (1802–1885) is better known as a writer than a painter. He is famous for writing *The Hunchback of Notre Dame* and *Les Misérables*, both of which are famous gothic works.

Answer: *The atmosphere is bleak and dreary, even menacing. The setting is similar in its mountains and shoreline.*

Castle. Victor Hugo (1802–1885). British Museum, London.

View the Art Shelley felt that her environment inspired her to write the story of *Frankenstein*. How would you describe the atmosphere in this painting? How does it compare with the setting in which Shelley found herself? ★

true compositions, the airy flights of my imagination, were born and fostered. I did not make myself the heroine of my tales. Life appeared to me too commonplace an affair as regarded myself. I could not figure to myself that romantic woes or wonderful events would ever be my lot; but I was not confined to my own identity, and I could people the hours with creations far more interesting to me at that age than my own sensations.

After this my life became busier, and reality stood in place of fiction. My husband, however, was from the first very anxious that I should prove myself worthy of my parentage and enroll myself on the page of fame. He was forever **inciting** me to obtain literary reputation, which even on my own part I cared for then, though since I have become infinitely indifferent to it. At this time he desired that I should

write, not so much with the idea that I could produce anything worthy of notice, but that he might himself judge how far I possessed the promise of better things hereafter. Still I did nothing. Traveling, and the cares of a family, occupied my time; and study, in the way of reading or improving my ideas in communication with his far more cultivated mind, was all of literary employment that engaged my attention.

In the summer of 1816, we visited Switzerland and became the neighbors of Lord Byron.[4] At first we spent our pleasant hours on the lake or wandering on its shores; and Lord Byron, who was writing the third canto[5] of *Childe Harold*,[6] was the only one among us who put his thoughts upon paper. These, as he brought them successively to us, clothed in all the light and harmony of poetry, seemed to stamp as divine the glories of heaven and earth, whose influences we partook with him.

---

1   **Nature and the Imagination** *In what ways was Shelley's childhood conducive to her future career as a novelist?*

2   **Activate Prior Knowledge** *Why did Mary Shelley's husband have such high expectations of her?*

Vocabulary

incite (in sīt´) *v.* to urge or provoke

---

4. George Gordon, *Lord Byron* (1788–1824), was an English Romantic poet.
5. A *canto* is a division of a long poem.
6. *Childe Harold's Pilgrimage* is one of Byron's best-known poems.

Nature and the Imagination *Why was nature important to Lord Byron?*   **3**

Reading Practice

Activate Prior Knowledge The premise of *Frankenstein* has gained significant cross-cultural recognition through film and television. However, characterization and plot events in some of the adaptations differ significantly from those in the novel. To ensure that students start from a similar and accurate knowledge base, ask students to share what they know about the story. Clarify for students the differences between adaptations and the text of the novel. You might suggest that students search the Internet for a plot summary.

But it proved a wet, ungenial summer, and incessant rain often confined us for days to the house. Some volumes of ghost stories translated from the German into French fell into our hands. There was the *History of the Inconstant Lover*, who, when he thought to clasp the bride to whom he had pledged his vows, found himself in the arms of the pale ghost of her whom he had deserted. There was the tale of the sinful founder of his race whose miserable doom it was to bestow the kiss of death on all the younger sons of his fated house, just when they reached the age of promise.

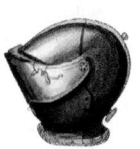

Visual Vocabulary
In a suit of armor, a *beaver* is a moveable piece on the helmet that protects the face.

His gigantic, shadowy form, clothed like the ghost in *Hamlet*, in complete armor, but with the beaver up, was seen at midnight, by the moon's fitful beams, to advance slowly along the gloomy avenue. The shape was lost beneath the shadow of the castle walls; but soon a gate swung back, a step was heard, the door of the chamber opened, and he advanced to the couch of the blooming youths, cradled in healthy sleep. Eternal sorrow sat upon his face as he bent down and kissed the forehead of the boys, who from that hour withered like flowers snapped upon the stalk. I have not seen these stories since then, but their incidents are as fresh in my mind as if I had read them yesterday.

"We will each write a ghost story," said Lord Byron, and his proposition was acceded[7] to. There were four of us.[8] The noble author[9] began a tale, a fragment of which he printed at the end of his poem of Mazeppa. Shelley, more apt to embody ideas and sentiments in the radiance of brilliant imagery and in the music of the most melodious verse that adorns our

language than to invent the machinery of a story, commenced one founded on the experiences of his early life. Poor Polidori had some terrible idea about a skull-headed lady who was so punished for peeping through a keyhole—what to see I forget: something very shocking and wrong, of course; but when she was reduced to a worse condition than the renowned Tom of Coventry,[10] he did not know what to do with her and was obliged to **dispatch** her to the tomb of the Capulets,[11] the only place for which she was fitted. The **illustrious** poets also, annoyed by the platitude[12] of prose, speedily **relinquished** their uncongenial task.

I busied myself *to think of a story*—a story to rival those which had excited us to this task. One which would speak to the mysterious fears of our nature and awaken thrilling horror—one to make the reader dread to look round, to curdle the blood, and quicken the beatings of the heart. If I did not accomplish these things, my ghost story would be unworthy of its name. I thought and pondered—vainly. I felt that blank incapability of invention which is the greatest misery of authorship, when dull Nothing replies to our anxious invocations.[13] "Have you thought of a story?" I was asked each morning, and each morning I was forced to reply with a mortifying negative.

---

10. According to legend, *Tom of Coventry* (Peeping Tom) lost his eyes as punishment for looking at Lady Godiva when she rode naked through Coventry.
11. The *tomb of the Capulets* is the setting of Romeo's and Juliet's deaths in Shakespeare's play.
12. *Platitude* means "lack of originality; dullness; triteness."
13. *Invocations* are prayers or appeals to a higher power.

Activate Prior Knowledge *What makes writer's block so frustrating?* **5**

Vocabulary

dispatch (di spach′) *v.* to send off or away with speed
illustrious (i lus′ trē əs) *adj.* famous and distinguished
relinquish (ri ling′ kwish) *v.* to give up; put aside; abandon

---

7. *Acceded* means "consented."
8. The *four of us* consisted of the Shelleys, Byron, and John Polidori, Byron's personal physician.
9. *The noble author* refers to Byron.

4 Gothic Novel *What elements in these stories are characteristic of gothic novels?*

MARY SHELLEY **795**

Teach

Literary Element | 4

Gothic Novel **Answer:**
Students might mention the spooky castle, the eerie moonlight, the ghostly knight, and the kiss of death.

APPROACHING Have approaching-level students reread the first paragraph on this page to answer the following questions. **Ask:** Who gives the kiss of death? *(a father)* What does he look like? *(He is large and wears armor.)* When does he walk? *(at night)* Who receives the kiss of death? *(his sons)*

Reading Strategy | 5

Activate Prior Knowledge
Answer: *Students may say that writer's block is so frustrating because it cuts the writer off from his or her creativity.* Invite students to share their own experiences with overcoming writer's block.

ENGLISH LEARNERS Ask English learners what it means to block a play in soccer. **Ask:** What do you think *writer's block* means? *(being stopped from writing)*

Literary History ☆

Autobiography In addition to Mary Shelley's gothic inspirations, there are parallels between *Frankenstein* and Shelley's own life. Shelley's first daughter died shortly after birth, and Shelley dreamed she brought the child back to life. She wrote the book—the action of which spans nine months—during a later pregnancy. One of the novel's important figures, Margaret Walton Saville, even shares the author's initials.

Teach

Literary Element | 1

Gothic Novel Direct students attention to the paragraph that describes Lord Byron and Shelley's conversation. **Ask:** What specific gothic elements that Lord Byron and Shelley discussed influence Shelley's novel *Frankenstein*? *(Students should mention the experiments of Dr. Darwin and a corpse being brought to life through galvanism.)*

ENGLISH LEARNERS Remind English learners to utilize the footnotes as context clues to determine the meaning of unknown words. To check their comprehension, **ask:** what does *galvanize* mean? *(to stimulate muscle tissue by using electricity)*

View the Art

Answer: *Students may note that the gloomy coloration of the engraving, the use of shadows, the mysterious cloaked figure, the man's horrified expression, and the skeleton all contribute to an overall Gothic style or mood.*

Illustration from *Frankenstein* by Mary Shelley. Theodor M. von Holst. Engraving. Private collection.

View the Art Theodor M. von Holst was known for his depictions of bold, nightmarish scenes. What aspects of the Gothic style are reflected in this engraving? ★

Everything must have a beginning, to speak in Sanchean phrase,[14] and that beginning must be linked to something that went before. The Hindus give the world an elephant to support it, but they make the elephant stand upon a tortoise. Invention, it must be humbly admitted, does not consist in creating out of void, but out of chaos; the materials must, in the first place, be afforded: it can give form to dark, shapeless substances but cannot bring into being the substance itself. In all matters of discovery and invention, even of those that appertain to the imagination, we are continually reminded of the story of Columbus and his egg.[15] Invention consists in the capacity of seizing on the capabilities of a subject and in the power of molding and fashioning ideas suggested to it.

Many and long were the conversations between Lord Byron and Shelley, to which I was a devout but nearly silent listener. During one of these, various philosophical doctrines were discussed, and among others the nature of the principle of life, and whether there was any probability of its ever being discovered and communicated. They talked of the experiments of Dr. Darwin[16] (I speak not of what the doctor really did or said that he did, but, as more to my purpose, of what was then spoken of as having been done by him), who preserved a piece of vermicelli[17] in a glass case till by some extraordinary means it began to move with voluntary motion. Not thus, after all, would life be given. Perhaps a corpse would be reanimated; galvanism[18] had given token of such things: perhaps the component parts of a creature might be manufactured, brought together, and endued with vital warmth.

Night waned upon this talk, and even the witching hour had gone by before we retired to rest. When I placed my head on my pillow, I did not sleep, nor could I be said to think. My imagination, unbidden, possessed and guided me, gifting the successive images that arose in my mind with a vividness far beyond the usual

---

14. *Sanchean phrase* refers to the character Sancho Panza in Cervantes's *Don Quixote*, who often uses proverbs to express common sense.

15. In response to claims that others could have discovered the New World before him, *Columbus* challenged guests at a banquet to make an *egg* stand on end. When nobody could do it, he tapped one end of the egg flat and stood it on the table, bolstering his claim that the others could only follow his lead.

16. Erasmus *Darwin* was a physician and scientist and the grandfather of the famous naturalist Charles Darwin.

17. *Vermicelli* (vur′mə chel′ ē) is a long, slender noodle thinner than spaghetti.

18. *Galvanism* refers to the use of electricity to stimulate muscle tissue.

Viewing Practice

SMALL GROUP **SPIRAL REVIEW** **View the Movie** Obtain a copy of the 1931 film *Frankenstein* from the library or a video store. Play the film for the class. Tell students to keep in mind their knowledge of the gothic tradition and the elements that distinguish a gothic work. Students might jot down particular points and ideas as they watch. After students have viewed the film, divide them into small groups to discuss the gothic elements of the film. Have a spokesperson from each group report the main points of their discussion to the class.

But it proved a wet, ungenial summer, and incessant rain often confined us for days to the house. Some volumes of ghost stories translated from the German into French fell into our hands. There was the *History of the Inconstant Lover*, who, when he thought to clasp the bride to whom he had pledged his vows, found himself in the arms of the pale ghost of her whom he had deserted. There was the tale of the sinful founder of his race whose miserable doom it was to bestow the kiss of death on all the younger sons of his fated house, just when they

Visual Vocabulary
In a suit of armor, a *beaver* is a moveable piece on the helmet that protects the face.

reached the age of promise. His gigantic, shadowy form, clothed like the ghost in *Hamlet*, in complete armor, but with the beaver up, was seen at midnight, by the moon's fitful beams, to advance slowly along the gloomy avenue. The shape was lost beneath the shadow of the castle walls; but soon a gate swung back, a step was heard, the door of the chamber opened, and he advanced to the couch of the blooming youths, cradled in healthy sleep. Eternal sorrow sat upon his face as he bent down and kissed the forehead of the boys, who from that hour withered like flowers snapped upon the stalk. I have not seen these stories since then, but their incidents are as fresh in my mind as if I had read them yesterday.

"We will each write a ghost story," said Lord Byron, and his proposition was acceded[7] to. There were four of us.[8] The noble author[9] began a tale, a fragment of which he printed at the end of his poem of Mazeppa. Shelley, more apt to embody ideas and sentiments in the radiance of brilliant imagery and in the music of the most melodious verse that adorns our

language than to invent the machinery of a story, commenced one founded on the experiences of his early life. Poor Polidori had some terrible idea about a skull-headed lady who was so punished for peeping through a keyhole—what to see I forget: something very shocking and wrong, of course; but when she was reduced to a worse condition than the renowned Tom of Coventry,[10] he did not know what to do with her and was obliged to **dispatch** her to the tomb of the Capulets,[11] the only place for which she was fitted. The **illustrious** poets also, annoyed by the platitude[12] of prose, speedily **relinquished** their uncongenial task.

I busied myself *to think of a story*—a story to rival those which had excited us to this task. One which would speak to the mysterious fears of our nature and awaken thrilling horror—one to make the reader dread to look ☆ round, to curdle the blood, and quicken the beatings of the heart. If I did not accomplish these things, my ghost story would be unworthy of its name. I thought and pondered—vainly. I felt that blank incapability of invention which is the greatest misery of authorship, when dull Nothing replies to our anxious invocations.[13] "Have you thought of a story?" I was asked each morning, and each morning I was forced to reply with a mortifying negative.

---

10. According to legend, *Tom of Coventry* (Peeping Tom) lost his eyes as punishment for looking at Lady Godiva when she rode naked through Coventry.
11. The *tomb of the Capulets* is the setting of Romeo's and Juliet's deaths in Shakespeare's play.
12. *Platitude* means "lack of originality; dullness; triteness."
13. *Invocations* are prayers or appeals to a higher power.

Activate Prior Knowledge *What makes writer's block so frustrating?* **5**

Vocabulary

dispatch (di spach′) *v.* to send off or away with speed
illustrious (i lus′ trē əs) *adj.* famous and distinguished
relinquish (ri ling′ kwish) *v.* to give up; put aside; abandon

---

7. *Acceded* means "consented."
8. The *four of us* consisted of the Shelleys, Byron, and John Polidori, Byron's personal physician.
9. The *noble author* refers to Byron.

4 Gothic Novel *What elements in these stories are characteristic of gothic novels?*

MARY SHELLEY **795**

Literary Element **4**

Gothic Novel Answer:
Students might mention the spooky castle, the eerie moonlight, the ghostly knight, and the kiss of death.

(APPROACHING) Have approaching-level students reread the first paragraph on this page to answer the following questions. **Ask:** Who gives the kiss of death? *(a father)* What does he look like? *(He is large and wears armor.)* When does he walk? *(at night)* Who receives the kiss of death? *(his sons)*

Reading Strategy **5**

Activate Prior Knowledge
Answer: *Students may say that writer's block is so frustrating because it cuts the writer off from his or her creativity.* Invite students to share their own experiences with overcoming writer's block.

(ENGLISH LEARNERS) Ask English learners what it means to block a play in soccer. **Ask:** What do you think *writer's block* means? *(being stopped from writing)*

Literary History ☆

Autobiography In addition to Mary Shelley's gothic inspirations, there are parallels between *Frankenstein* and Shelley's own life. Shelley's first daughter died shortly after birth, and Shelley dreamed she brought the child back to life. She wrote the book—the action of which spans nine months—during a later pregnancy. One of the novel's important figures, Margaret Walton Saville, even shares the author's initials.

English Learners

DIFFERENTIATED INSTRUCTION

Intermediate Explain to students that even though this selection is nonfiction, Mary Shelley still uses figurative language and descriptive details to create and enhance her imagery. Direct students' attention to the highlighted text at the bottom of the first column on this page. Read the entire sentence aloud to students. Then work with them to paraphrase the sentence. *(I haven't read these stories in years, but I remember them very clearly.)* When students come upon difficult words and phrases, encourage them to stop and rephrase the ideas in their own words.

Teach

Gothic Novel Direct students attention to the paragraph that describes Lord Byron and Shelley's conversation. **Ask:** What specific gothic elements that Lord Byron and Shelley discussed influence Shelley's novel *Frankenstein*? (*Students should mention the experiments of Dr. Darwin and a corpse being brought to life through galvanism.*)

ENGLISH LEARNERS Remind English learners to utilize the footnotes as context clues to determine the meaning of unknown words. To check their comprehension, **ask:** what does *galvanize* mean? (*to stimulate muscle tissue by using electricity*)

View the Art ★

Answer: *Students may note that the gloomy coloration of the engraving, the use of shadows, the mysterious cloaked figure, the man's horrified expression, and the skeleton all contribute to an overall Gothic style or mood.*

Illustration from *Frankenstein* by Mary Shelley. Theodor M. von Holst. Engraving. Private collection.

View the Art Theodor M. von Holst was known for his depictions of bold, nightmarish scenes. What aspects of the Gothic style are reflected in this engraving? ★

Everything must have a beginning, to speak in Sanchean phrase,[14] and that beginning must be linked to something that went before. The Hindus give the world an elephant to support it, but they make the elephant stand upon a tortoise. Invention, it must be humbly admitted, does not consist in creating out of void, but out of chaos; the materials must, in the first place, be afforded: it can give form to dark, shapeless substances but cannot bring into being the substance itself. In all matters of discovery and invention, even of those that appertain to the imagination, we are continually reminded of the story of Columbus and his egg.[15] Invention consists in the capacity of seizing on the capabilities of a subject and in the power of molding and fashioning ideas suggested to it.

Many and long were the conversations between Lord Byron and Shelley, to which I was a devout but nearly silent listener. During one of these, various philosophical doctrines were discussed, and among others the nature of the principle of life, and whether there was any probability of its ever being discovered and communicated. They talked of the experiments of Dr. Darwin[16] (I speak not of what the doctor really did or said that he did, but, as more to my purpose, of what was then spoken of as having been done by him), who preserved a piece of vermicelli[17] in a glass case till by some extraordinary means it began to move with voluntary motion. Not thus, after all, would life be given. Perhaps a corpse would be reanimated; galvanism[18] had given token of such things: perhaps the component parts of a creature might be manufactured, brought together, and endued with vital warmth.

Night waned upon this talk, and even the witching hour had gone by before we retired to rest. When I placed my head on my pillow, I did not sleep, nor could I be said to think. My imagination, unbidden, possessed and guided me, gifting the successive images that arose in my mind with a vividness far beyond the usual

14. *Sanchean phrase* refers to the character Sancho Panza in Cervantes's *Don Quixote*, who often uses proverbs to express common sense.

15. In response to claims that others could have discovered the New World before him, *Columbus* challenged guests at a banquet to make an *egg* stand on end. When nobody could do it, he tapped one end of the egg flat and stood it on the table, bolstering his claim that the others could only follow his lead.
16. Erasmus *Darwin* was a physician and scientist and the grandfather of the famous naturalist Charles Darwin.
17. *Vermicelli* (vur´mə chel´ē) is a long, slender noodle thinner than spaghetti.
18. *Galvanism* refers to the use of electricity to stimulate muscle tissue.

Viewing Practice

SMALL GROUP **SPIRAL REVIEW**

View the Movie Obtain a copy of the 1931 film *Frankenstein* from the library or a video store. Play the film for the class. Tell students to keep in mind their knowledge of the gothic tradition and the elements that distinguish a gothic work. Students might jot down particular points and ideas as they watch. After students have viewed the film, divide them into small groups to discuss the gothic elements of the film. Have a spokesperson from each group report the main points of their discussion to the class.

bounds of reverie. I saw—with shut eyes, but acute mental vision—I saw the pale student of unhallowed arts kneeling beside the thing he had put together. I saw the hideous phantasm[19] of a man stretched out, and then, on the working of some powerful engine, show signs of life and stir with an uneasy, half-vital motion.

Visual Vocabulary
A parquet (pär kā´) floor is made of wooden pieces, often of different colors, worked into a geometric pattern or mosaic.

Frightful must it be, for supremely frightful would be the effect of any human endeavor to mock the stupendous mechanism of the Creator of the world. His success would terrify the artist; he would rush away from his odious handiwork, horror-stricken. He would hope that, left to itself, the slight spark of life which he had communicated would fade, that this thing which had received such imperfect animation would subside into dead matter, and he might sleep in the belief that the silence of the grave would quench forever the **transient** existence of the hideous corpse which he had looked upon as the cradle of life. He sleeps; but he is awakened; he opens his eyes; behold, the horrid thing stands at his bedside, opening his curtains and looking on him with yellow, watery, but speculative eyes.

I opened mine in terror. The idea so possessed my mind that a thrill of fear ran through me, and I wished to exchange the ghastly image of my fancy for the realities around. I see them still: the very room, the dark parquet, the closed shutters with the moonlight struggling through, and the sense I had that the glassy lake and white high Alps were beyond. I could not so easily get rid of my hideous phantom; still it haunted me. I must try to think of something else. I recurred to my ghost story—my tiresome, unlucky ghost story! Oh! If I could only contrive one which would frighten my reader as I myself had been frightened that night!

Swift as light and as cheering was the idea that broke in upon me. "I have found it! What terrified me will terrify others; and I need only describe the specter which had haunted my midnight pillow." On the morrow I announced that I had *thought of a story*. I began that day with the words "It was on a dreary night of November," making only a transcript of the grim terrors of my waking dream.

At first I thought but of a few pages, of a short tale, but Shelley urged me to develop the idea at greater length. I certainly did not owe the suggestion of one incident, nor scarcely of one train of feeling, to my husband, and yet but for his incitement, it would never have taken the form in which it was presented to the world. From this declaration I must except the preface. As far as I can recollect, it was entirely written by him.

And now, once again, I bid my hideous progeny[20] go forth and prosper. I have an affection for it, for it was the offspring of happy days, when death and grief were but words,[21] which found no true echo in my heart. Its several pages speak of many a walk, many a drive, and many a conversation, when I was not alone; and my companion[22] was one who, in this world, I shall never see more. But this is for myself; my readers have nothing to do with these associations. . . . 🙠

---

19. A *phantasm* is an image or illusion.

2 Gothic Novel *Which details in this passage create an ominous mood?*

Vocabulary

transient (tran´ shənt) *adj.* lasting only a brief time; temporary

---

20. *Progeny* means "offspring"—in this case, the product of a creative effort.
21. *When death . . . words* is Shelley's reference to a time before the deaths of her husband and two of her children.
22. Shelley's *companion* was her husband, who died in a boating accident in 1822.

Activate Prior Knowledge *How did Shelley overcome her writer's block?*

MARY SHELLEY **797**

Teach

Literary Element | 2

Gothic Novel Answer: *The cold, dreary night and the strange waking dream with a hideous creature contribute to a mood of foreboding.*

ENGLISH LEARNERS For English learners, **write** the following words on the board: *unhallowed, odious, horrid, ghastly*. Have them find and reread the sentence that contains each word and use context clues to guess the word's meaning. Then, have them look up the definitions in a dictionary.

Reading Strategy | 3

Activate Prior Knowledge Answer: *Shelley overcame her writer's block by closing her eyes and surrendering herself to her imagination. She then transformed her dream into a horror story.*

Language History ☆

Frankenstein As a result of the 1931 film, *Frankenstein* entered the language in a curiously altered way. In the novel, Victor Frankenstein is the scientist who creates the creature. Shelley did not give the creature a name. In popular usage, *Frankenstein* became associated with the creature. The term is most frequently used to describe a monster, especially one that destroys its creator.

To check students' understanding of the selection, see Unit 4 Teaching Resources Book, p. 174.

Advanced Learners

DIFFERENTIATED INSTRUCTION

Read and Review the Novel Have advanced students obtain copies of the novel *Frankenstein* from the library or a bookstore. Students might even find an e-text online. Allow students time to read the novel and write a review of it. If necessary, provide examples of book reviews from the *New York Times*, the *New Yorker*, or another appropriate source. Remind students that the review should include a brief plot summary and their evaluations of and opinions about the novel supported with evidence from the text. Provide time for students to share their reviews with the rest of the class.

After You Read

Assess

1. Answers will vary.

2. (a) She complies with the publishers' request and answers the often asked question. (b) She is flexible and accommodating.

3. (a) She listened to discussions on the nature of life, Dr. Darwin's experiments, and galvanism. (b) These factors support her theory that invention involves re-arranging basic ideas or elements rather than creating something out of nothing.

4. Most students will agree that writers have creative ideas in their minds that must be drawn out.

5. Their conversations helped her conceive the plot and theme. Her husband urged her to develop the tale into a novel.

6. Shelley generates *Frankenstein* not by using her reason but by letting her imagination brood upon a conversation.

7. Answers will vary.

Reading Strategy

1. Answers will vary. Students prior knowledge of the popular "monster" image of Frankenstein may have helped most.

2. Answers will vary. Students' responses should reflect parts of the selection that they wish they had more background information on.

Progress Check

Can students identify elements of a gothic novel?

If No → See Unit 4 Teaching Resources Book, p. 169.

798

After You Read

Respond and Think Critically

Respond and Interpret

1. What insights or ideas about the writing process did this selection give you?

2. (a) Why does Shelley write this account of her story's origin even though she claims to be "averse to bringing myself forward in print"? (b) What does this contradiction tell you about her personality?

3. (a) Describe the events leading up to Shelley's idea for the plot of *Frankenstein*. (b) Do these factors support her theories about invention?

Analyze and Evaluate

4. Do you agree with Shelley's assessment of what is needed for invention? Why or why not?

5. Shelley was not alone when she conceived of and wrote *Frankenstein*. What part did other writers play in her success?

Connect

6. **Big Idea** **Nature and the Imagination** How does Shelley suggest that imagination is more important than reason?

7. **Connect to Today** Shelley sought to appeal to "the mysterious fears of our nature and awaken thrilling horror." What books or movies have you read or seen that meet this description?

Literary Element Gothic Novel

The trappings of gothic fiction include haunted castles, clanking chains, mysterious graveyards, and restless spirits. Originally the term **gothic novel** referred only to works with a medieval atmosphere or setting. Gradually, however, its meaning expanded to refer to any work that featured terror or gloom.

1. Describe the gothic elements of Shelley's waking dream that inspired *Frankenstein*.

2. In your opinion, what accounts for the popularity of gothic novels today?

 Writing

Write a Story Shelley created her novel *Frankenstein* from a single striking mental image. Brainstorm some of the key elements of gothic fiction. Write down anything particularly vivid that occurs to you. Then choose one thing you've noted and build a short story around it. Include details that reinforce the gloomy, mysterious atmosphere common to gothic novels.

 **Literature** Online

Selection Resources For Selection Quizzes, eFlashcards, and Reading-Writing Connection activities, go to glencoe.com and enter QuickPass code GLB9817u4.

Reading Strategy Activate Prior Knowledge

Review the chart you made as you read, and answer the following questions.

1. What prior knowledge helped you the most in understanding this selection?

2. Which aspects of the selection do you wish you'd known more about before reading it?

Vocabulary Practice

Practice with Usage Respond to these statements to help you explore the meanings of boldfaced vocabulary words from the selection.

1. Give an example from a movie in which a character **incited** an action.

2. How might an **illustrious** person act?

3. Identify a time when you had to **relinquish** something important to you.

4. Name an item you might **dispatch**.

5. Explain how the four seasons are **transient**.

Literary Element

1. Elements include "unhallowed arts," a phantasm, and reference to a grave.

2. The excitement and fear they provoke

For additional assessment, see Assessment Resources, pp. 199–200.

Vocabulary Practice

Students' sentences will vary.

Writing

Students' stories should incorporate gothic elements to create a mysterious atmosphere.

PART 3

The Quest for Truth and Beauty

La Belle Dame Sans Merci, 1893. John Williams Waterhouse. Oil on canvas, 44.09 x 31.89 in. Hessisches Landesmuseum, Darnstadt, Germany.

 View the Art The Romantic period, as its name suggests, changed society's view of love and other human emotions. How does Waterhouse's painting hint at the power of what Keats called "the heart's affections"?

"I am certain of nothing but the holiness of the heart's affections and the truth of imagination—what the imagination seizes as beauty must be truth—whether it existed before or not." **1**

—John Keats

799

UNIT FOUR
PART 3

Analyze and Extend

Reading Strategy **1**

Make Connections Have students read the title and the quotation. **Ask:** Where does Keats find truth? *(In the imagination's apprehension of beauty)* What do we take to be reliable sources of truth today? *(Students may have many different ideas ranging from media to intuition.)*

View the Art

Answer: *Students may say that the woman represents the power of the heart or of beauty—her dress is decorated with a heart, and she has ensnared the knight with her hair.*

John William Waterhouse (1849–1917) was known for his paintings of femmes fatales—women of great seductive charm who lead men into compromising or dangerous situations—and the painting here is one celebrated example. Waterhouse was a member of the Royal Academy.

 For additional support for English Learners, see Unit 4 Teaching Resources Book, p. 177.

Approaching Level

DIFFERENTIATED INSTRUCTION

Established Ask volunteers to read the quotation from Keats aloud. **Ask:** What does Keats imply with the phrase "whether it existed before or not"? *(Keats implies that a person with a great capacity to imagine beauty may in that act create truth.)* Would you agree with Keats that humans have the capacity to bring into being that which they imagine? How might this be so? *(Some students may point out that works of literature, art, and music come from visions that their creators form in their imaginations.)*

Before You Read

Focus

Bellringer Options

Selection Focus
   Transparency 40
Daily Language Practice
   Transparency 65

Or explain that an important element in Romanticism is an appreciation of the beauty and truth found in nature. **Say:** What emotions does the power of nature inspire in you?

Tell students to think about the power of a storm or another force of nature and to jot down adjectives that describe their reactions to this phenomenon. As they read "Apostrophe to the Ocean," have them compare their reactions with the speaker's.

Before You Read

Byron's Poetry

Meet **George Gordon, Lord Byron**
(1788–1824)

George Gordon, Lord Byron—aristocrat, poet, member of Parliament, athlete, expatriate, and freedom fighter—was perhaps the most colorful figure of his day.

Descended from two noble but flamboyant and violent families, Byron inherited his title and a large estate at the age of ten, when his great-uncle, known as the "Wicked Lord," died. Byron had been born with a clubfoot, and the physical suffering and acute embarrassment it caused him profoundly affected his temperament. "No action of Lord Byron's life—scarce a line he has written—but was influenced by his personal defect," Mary Shelley wrote. To compensate for this impairment, Byron succeeded in becoming a masterful swimmer, horseman, boxer, cricket player, and fencer.

Literary Celebrity As a student at Cambridge University, Byron was known for his lavish lifestyle and flamboyant behavior; he even kept a tame bear as a pet. After graduating from Cambridge, he embarked upon an adventurous journey, traveling on horseback across Portugal and Spain and on to distant lands that few Englishmen had visited, including Asia Minor (present-day Turkey) and mountainous Albania. While traveling, he worked his adventures into his poetry, including the first part of his long poem *Childe Harold's Pilgrimage*, which made him the toast of London society at age twenty-four. In his own words, "I awoke one morning and found myself famous." As a member of the House of Lords, he championed liberal political causes.

Soon, however, this extraordinarily handsome poet—with brown curly hair, fine features, and intensely brilliant eyes—saw his fame turn to

> "Be thou the rainbow to the
>   storms of life,
> The evening beam that smiles the
>   clouds away,
> And tints to-morrow with
>   prophetic ray!"
>
> —Lord Byron, *The Bride of Abydos*

notoriety. Personal scandals plagued him as he pursued a self-indulgent lifestyle with many love affairs.

Poet in Exile At twenty-eight, Byron exiled himself from England, never to return. He briefly lived in Switzerland, where he spent time with the Shelleys, and then settled in Italy. There, he composed *Don Juan*, a verse satire that describes the adventures of a licentious, though naive, young man. Byron died of fever shortly after his thirty-sixth birthday, having exhausted his energies training Greek troops fighting for independence from the Turks. His efforts in support of the Greek independence movement made him a national hero in Greece. Byron influenced a host of eminent writers, including Goethe in Germany, Balzac in France, Pushkin and Dostoevsky in Russia, and Hawthorne, Melville, and Poe in the United States.

 Literature Online

Author Search For more about Lord Byron, go to glencoe.com and enter QuickPass code GLB9817u4.

Selection Skills

Literary Elements
- Juxtoposition (SE pp. 801–805)

She Walks in Beauty, Apostrophe to the Ocean

Listening/Speaking/Viewing Skills
- Analyze Art (SE p. 802)
- Sounds and Emotions (TE p. 804)

Reading Skills
- Analyze Figurative Language (SE pp. 801–805)

Vocabulary Skills
- Analogies (SE pp. 801, 805)

Writing Skills/Grammar
- Write an Essay (SE p. 805)
- Pronoun Antecedent Agreement (TE p. 802)

Literature and Reading Preview

Connect to the Poems

What makes you admire something or someone? Create a list of qualities that trigger your admiration.

Build Background

In medieval times, *childe* referred to a candidate for knighthood. Byron applied that title to the hero of *Childe Harold's Pilgrimage* to suggest the character's inner nobility and his quest for meaning. Byron described Childe Harold as "the wandering outlaw of his own dark mind." "She Walks in Beauty," a lyric poem originally written for music, was inspired by the sight of the beautiful Lady Wilmot Horton, who appeared at a party dressed in a black gown covered with bits of sparkling material.

Set Purposes for Reading

Big Idea The Quest for Truth and Beauty

As you read, ask yourself, How do these poems reflect Romantic ideals of beauty?

Literary Element Juxtaposition

Juxtaposition refers to the placing of two or more distinct elements of a literary work—for example, words, phrases, images, lines, or passages—next to or close to one another. For example, in line 7 of "Apostrophe to the Ocean," Byron uses this technique to contrast the speaker's future and his past: "From all I may be, or have been before." As you read, ask yourself, What effect does this technique have on the poems?

Reading Strategy Analyze Figurative Language

When you **analyze figurative language**, you examine language that is not meant to be interpreted literally but is used for descriptive effect, often to suggest ideas. First, identify figures of speech, or specific devices of figurative language such as metaphor, simile, and personification. As you read, ask yourself, What does each device contribute to the work?

Tip: Identifying Figurative Language Use a chart to record examples of figurative language and to describe their function.

Example	Type	Function
"like a drop of rain" (line 16, "Apostrophe")	simile	suggests the insignificance of humans

GEORGE GORDON, LORD BYRON **801**

Learning Objectives

For pages 800–805

In studying these texts, you will focus on the following objectives:

Literary Study: Analyzing juxtaposition.

Reading: Analyzing figurative language.

Writing: Writing an essay.

Vocabulary Preview

spurn (spurn) *v.* to reject or drive off; p. 803 *Members of Congress spurned the unqualified nominee.*

arbiter (är′ bə tər) *n.* a judge; p. 804 *Public opinion is the final arbiter in a debate between two candidates.*

mar (mär) *v.* to spoil or damage; p. 804 *The walls of that building were marred with graffiti.*

Tip: Analogies Analogies are comparisons based on relationships between words and ideas. To complete an analogy, decide on the relationship between the first pair of words. Then apply that relationship to the second pair. Some common relationships include synonyms, antonyms, parts/wholes, and objects/characteristics.

Before You Read

Focus

Summary

In these two poems, Byron displays his mastery by matching "sound to sense." "She Walks in Beauty" describes both the physical and spiritual beauty of an admired woman. "Apostrophe to the Ocean" from *Childe Harold's Pilgrimage* examines the idea that nature is more powerful than humans.

For summaries in languages other than English, see Unit 4 Teaching Resources Book, pp. 178–183.

Vocabulary

Analogies **Write** on the board: mar:damage:: spurn:reject **Say:** To understand an analogy, find the relationship that the first pair shares with the second. *Mar* means "to damage," and *spurn* means "to reject." Have students compose their own analogies for each vocabulary word.

For additional vocabulary practice, see Unit 4 Teaching Resources Book, p. 186.

For additional context, see Glencoe Interactive Vocabulary CD-ROM.

English Learners

DIFFERENTIATED INSTRUCTION

PARTNERS **Beginning** Have students read "She Walks in Beauty" aloud to a partner. Ask them to practice any parts of the poem that cause particular difficulty.

Intermediate Say: The first line of Byron's poem "She walks in beauty, like the night" is a simile. Explain that a simile is a comparison between two unlike things. What two things is the speaker comparing? (*The speaker compares the woman's beauty to a beautiful night.*)

Teach

Reading Strategy 1

Analyze Figurative Language **Answer:** *The speaker suggests that the woman is celestial and naturally beautiful.*

[ENGLISH LEARNERS] For English learners, **ask:** *Cloudless* uses the suffix *–less* to mean that there are no clouds. What is another example of a word that uses the suffix *–less*? *(thoughtless, painless)*

 For additional practice using the reading skill or strategy, see Unit 4 Teaching Resources Book, p. 185.

View the Art ★

Answer: *Some students may say the painting is a good companion to the poem because the woman is beautiful, has both dark features (eyes) and light features (skin), and shares a hair color and hair style with the subject of the poem; others may say the woman in the poem sounds more energetic or exotic than the stationary, serene subject of the painting.*

Henry Howard (1769–1847) was an English portrait painter whose work can be seen in the National Portrait Gallery and the Tate Gallery in London. This painting of the artist's daughter was first exhibited in 1827. The title *The Florentine Girl* reflects the fact that the subject is dressed in the style of a woman from Florence, Italy.

 For an audio recording of this selection, use Listening Library Audio CD-ROM.

The Florentine Girl (The Artist's Daughter), c. 1827. Henry Howard. Oil on canvas, 965 x 610 mm. Tate Gallery, London.

View the Art The word "Florentine" in this painting's title refers to the woman's clothing, which is a style that was popular in Florence, Italy, at the time. Is this painting a good accompaniment to Byron's poem? Explain.

She Walks in Beauty

George Gordon, Lord Byron

She walks in beauty, like the night
    Of cloudless climes[1] and starry skies;
And all that's best of dark and bright
    Meet in her aspect[2] and her eyes:
5 Thus mellowed to that tender light
    Which heaven to gaudy day denies.

One shade the more, one ray the less,
    Had half impaired the nameless grace
Which waves in every raven tress,
10   Or softly lightens o'er her face;
    Where thoughts serenely sweet express
    How pure, how dear their dwelling place.

And on that cheek, and o'er that brow,
    So soft, so calm, yet eloquent,
15 The smiles that win, the tints that glow,
    But tell of days in goodness spent,
  A mind at peace with all below,
    A heart whose love is innocent!

---

1. Here, *climes* means "climates" or "atmospheres."
2. Here, *aspect* means "appearance" or "face."

 1 Analyze Figurative Language *What does the speaker suggest about the woman by using this simile?*

Grammar Practice

[SPIRAL REVIEW] **Pronoun-Antecedent Agreement Say:** An antecedent is a noun or pronoun that a pronoun refers to or replaces. A pronoun must agree with its antecedent in number (singular or plural), gender (masculine, feminine, or neuter) and person (first, second, or third). **Write** the following sentences on the board and have students identify the antecedents of the underscored pronouns:

- They both gained fame through <u>their</u> poetry. *(They)*
- Childe Harold's Pilgrimage, with <u>its</u> exotic settings, captivated readers. *(Childe Harold's Pilgrimage)*

from Childe Harold's Pilgrimage

George Gordon, Lord Byron

Apostrophe to the Ocean

There is a pleasure in the pathless woods;
There is a rapture on the lonely shore;
There is society, where none intrudes,
By the deep sea, and music in its roar.
5   I love not man the less, but nature more,
From these our interviews, in which I steal°
From all I may be, or have been before,
To mingle with the universe, and feel
What I can ne'er express, yet cannot all conceal.

10   Roll on, thou deep and dark blue ocean—roll!
Ten thousand fleets sweep over thee in vain;
Man marks the earth with ruin—his control
Stops with the shore. Upon the watery plain
The wrecks are all thy deed, nor doth remain
15   A shadow of man's ravage, save his own,
When, for a moment, like a drop of rain,
He sinks into thy depths with bubbling groan,
Without a grave, unknelled,° uncoffined, and unknown.

His steps are not upon thy paths—thy fields
20   Are not a spoil for him—thou dost arise
And shake him from thee; the vile strength he wields
For earth's destruction thou dost all despise,
Spurning him from thy bosom to the skies,
And send'st him, shivering in thy playful spray **2**
25   And howling, to his gods, where haply° lies
His petty hope in some near port or bay,
And dashest him again to earth—there let him lay.

Analyze Figurative Language *What does the personification in this passage reveal about the ocean and the speaker?* **3**

Vocabulary

spurn (spurn) *v.* to reject or drive off

6 **steal**: depart quietly.

18 **unknelled**: without the ringing of church bells.

25 **haply**: perhaps.

Teach

Literary Element **2**

Juxtaposition **Ask:** In lines 24–25, what is the effect of juxtaposing *thy playful spray* with the words *shivering* and *howling*? *(Byron contrasts the terrified human perspective to the indifferent view of the ocean.)*

ENGLISH LEARNERS For English learners, **ask:** What is Byron describing in lines 24–25? *(a shipwrecked sailor being tossed by waves)*

Reading Strategy **3**

Analyze Figurative Language **Answer:** *The speaker uses personification to convey the great power and majesty of the ocean and the intimacy of his relationship with it.*

Advanced Learners

DIFFERENTIATED INSTRUCTION

SMALL GROUP **Apostrophe** Review the literary device of apostrophe in which the speaker addresses an inanimate object, a person who is absent or dead, or an abstract concept. **Say:** Writers can use apostrophe to express many emotions, including love, fear, or contempt, but apostrophe generally conveys a tone of intimacy. Ask advanced students to lead a discussion in small groups on whether

Byron's use of apostrophe reinforces the theme of this excerpt. Then ask them individually to write a paragraph supporting their point of view on Byron's use of apostrophe.

Teach

Literary Element   1

Juxtaposition **Answer:** *The speaker suggests that impressive human weapons and massive feats of engineering are insignificant and insubstantial compared to the ocean's power.*

[APPROACHING] For approaching-level students **ask:** When Byron uses *ribs* in line 31, what does he mean? *(the structural frame of a ship's hull)*

> To check students' understanding of the selection, see Unit 4 Teaching Resources Book, p. 187.

The armaments which thunderstrike the walls
Of rock-built cities, bidding nations quake
30 And monarchs tremble in their capitals,
The oak leviathans,° whose huge ribs make
Their clay° creator the vain title take
Of lord of thee and **arbiter** of war—
These are thy toys, and as the snowy flake,
35 They melt into thy yeast° of waves, which **mar**
  Alike the Armada's pride or spoils of Trafalgar.°

Thy shores are empires, changed in all save thee—
Assyria, Greece, Rome, Carthage,° what are they?
Thy waters washed them power while they were free,
40 And many a tyrant since; their shores obey
The stranger, slave, or savage; their decay
Has dried up realms to deserts—not so thou,
Unchangeable, save to thy wild waves' play.
Time writes no wrinkle on thine azure° brow;
45   Such as creation's dawn beheld, thou rollest now.

Thou glorious mirror, where the Almighty's form
Glasses itself° in tempests; in all time,
Calm or convulsed—in breeze, or gale, or storm,
Icing the pole, or in the torrid clime°
50 Dark-heaving—boundless, endless, and sublime—
The image of eternity—the throne
Of the Invisible; even from out thy slime
The monsters of the deep are made; each zone°
  Obeys thee; thou goest forth, dread, fathomless, alone.

55 And I have loved thee, Ocean! and my joy
Of youthful sports was on thy breast to be
Borne, like thy bubbles, onward: from a boy
I wantoned° with thy breakers°—they to me
Were a delight—and if the freshening sea
60 Made them a terror, 'twas a pleasing fear,
For I was as it were a child of thee,
And trusted to thy billows far and near,
  And laid my hand upon thy mane—as I do here.

31 leviathans: large ships.
32 clay: human.

35 yeast: the foam or froth of troubled waters.
36 Armada...Trafalgar: A Spanish fleet (armada) that sailed against England in 1588 was destroyed, as were most of the French ships captured by Lord Nelson at the Spanish cape of Trafalgar in 1805.
38 Assyria, Greece, Rome, Carthage: powerful ancient empires.

44 azure: sky blue.

47 Glasses itself: reflects.

49 torrid clime: the intensely hot area near the equator.

53 zone: a climatic region of the earth.

58 wantoned: frolicked.
breakers: large waves.

---

1 **Juxtaposition** *What does the speaker suggest about the ocean's power by juxtaposing the phrases "oak leviathans" and "huge ribs" (line 31) with "thy toys" and "the snowy flake"?*

Vocabulary

arbiter (är′ bə tər) *n.* a judge
mar (mär) *v.* to spoil or damage

804   UNIT 4   THE TRIUMPH OF ROMANTICISM

Listening Practice

SPIRAL REVIEW **Sounds and Emotions** Poets and writers describe not only visual aspects of their subjects but audible aspects as well. For example, in "Apostrophe to the Ocean," Byron uses the phrase "music in its roar" to describe the ocean.

Have students listen to a recording of sounds of the ocean, a storm, or an event such as a parade or a battle. Have them note how the sounds make them feel as they listen. Then ask students to write a reflective response in which they convey the emotional impact of the sounds.

After You Read

Respond and Think Critically

Respond and Interpret

1. What new ideas about nature and beauty did these poems suggest to you?

2. (a)What qualities besides beauty does the woman in "She Walks in Beauty" have? (b)What can you infer about the speaker's feelings toward her?

3. (a)In lines 1–36 of "Apostrophe to the Ocean," how does the speaker portray the relationship between the ocean and human beings? (b)What do these lines suggest about the ability of human beings to master nature?

4. From the contrast presented in lines 37–54 of "Apostrophe to the Ocean," what can you infer about the speaker's views on humans and the ocean?

Analyze and Evaluate

5. What **images** in "She Walks in Beauty" best communicate to you the woman's beauty?

6. Byron wrote *Childe Harold's Pilgrimage* in Spenserian stanzas, a verse form named after Edmund Spenser. (a)What is the **rhyme scheme** of each stanza? (b)What effects does Byron achieve with the longer ninth line of each stanza?

Connect

7. **Big Idea** **The Quest for Truth and Beauty** In "She Walks in Beauty," what is the main idea that Byron conveys about physical beauty?

8. **Connect to the Author** Byron was a frequent traveler throughout his life. In what ways do his poems reflect this?

Literary Element Juxtaposition

By using **juxtaposition**, poets can create unexpected pairings and stunning contrasts.

1. In lines 17–18 of "She Walks in Beauty," why does the speaker juxtapose phrases about the subject's mind and heart?

2. What examples of juxtaposition in "Apostrophe to the Ocean" did you find most effective?

Writing

Write an Essay Byron's poems contain striking and descriptive figurative language. Choose one simile, metaphor, personification, or other figure of speech from "She Walks in Beauty" and one from "Apostrophe to the Ocean." Write a brief essay in which you analyze the meaning of each figure of speech and the effect it has upon the rest of the poem or passage in which it appears.

 **Literature** Online

Selection Resources For Selection Quizzes, eFlashcards, and Reading-Writing Connection activities, go to glencoe.com and enter QuickPass code GLB9817u4.

Reading Strategy Analyze Figurative Language

When you **analyze the figurative language** in a poem, you can often detect the work's tone.

1. In the last line of "Apostrophe to the Ocean," what does the word *mane* suggest about the ocean?

2. How would you contrast the tone of "Apostrophe to the Ocean" with that of "She Walks in Beauty"?

Vocabulary Practice

Practice with Analogies Choose the word that best completes each analogy.

1. spurn : snub :: obscure :
   a. conceal   **b.** upset   **c.** display

2. arbiter : judge :: error :
   a. correction   **b.** disclaimer   **c.** blunder

3. mar : repair :: insult :
   a. offend   **b.** extol   **c.** denigrate

GEORGE GORDON, LORD BYRON **805**

After You Read

Assess

1. Students' answers will vary.

2. (a) Gentleness, calmness, thoughtfulness, and innocence (b) The speaker feels admiration, love, and protectiveness.

3. (a) The ocean is powerful, and humans are weak. (b) Humans can never master nature.

4. He is disillusioned by people but believes the ocean is divine.

5. Some students may choose images that indicate the woman's physical beauty, while others may choose images that describe her personal goodness.

6. (a) *ababbcbcc* (b) The longer, ninth line (six stresses as opposed to five) stretches out the poet's concluding thought in each stanza, mimicking movement of the ocean's waves.

7. External appearance reflects the character of the soul.

8. Byron's poetry makes vivid references to various geographic formations and exotic locations that suggest a familiarity with large parts of the world.

 Writing

Students' essays should analyze the meaning of a figure of speech from each poem and the effect the literary device has on the rest of the poem.

For additional selection assessment, see Assessment Resources, pp. 201–202.

Progress Check

Can students understand juxtaposition?

If No → See Unit 4 Teaching Resources Book, p. 184.

805

Literary Element

1. They emphasize the beauty of natural innocence.

2. The use of "unknelled, uncoffined, and unknown."

Reading Strategy

1. *Mane* evokes the image of a lion and its associations of power and royalty.

2. The tone of "Apostrophe to the Ocean" is awestruck; that of "She Walks in Beauty" is tender.

Vocabulary Practice

1. a **2.** c **3.** b

Focus

Bellringer Options

Daily Language Practice Transparency 66

Or **ask**: Can you think of any present-day style setters? Who is emulated in dress, speech, writing, or activities? (*Students may mention athletes, celebrities, or political figures.*) Are there any qualities that these people share? Do they share characteristics of the Byronic hero? (*They may be iconoclasts, going against conventions.*)

The Byronic Hero

G EORGE GORDON, LORD BYRON WAS ONLY thirty-six when he died. His brief life was marked by bold adventure, lascivious scandal, and artistic accomplishment. His work and lifestyle profoundly influenced the culture of his time.

When Byron published the first two cantos of *Childe Harold's Pilgrimage* in 1812, he became famous overnight. The speaker of this long poem is an unconventional outsider, a moody, passionate, mysterious wanderer. In short, he is a Byronic hero—an antihero, alienated and rebellious. Byron himself embodied many of these traits, and the archetype that he created has become ingrained in literature and popular culture. **1**

> "Mad—bad—and dangerous to know."
>
> —Lady Caroline Lamb, on Lord Byron

Characteristics of the Byronic Hero

Literary critics have defined the Byronic hero in various ways, but most agree on the archetype's essential characteristics.

Rebellion The Byronic hero is a rebel, an individualist who questions and rejects society's laws, conventions, and morality. As the model, Byron might have looked to figures like Napoleon Bonaparte, the mysterious commoner who became emperor of France and whose genius was to transform it into a great European power.

Alienation The Byronic hero disdains society and social conventions. He rejects the assumption that people of wealth, rank, and privilege deserve advantages in life solely because of their ancestry. He is often an outcast or outlaw who supports the democratic ideals of a meritocracy.

Gloom The Byronic hero is darkly handsome, melancholy, moody, and mysterious. He can never be happy, even when good things happen. He is difficult to portray because the reader must sympathize with him, yet he must be somewhat

Manfred on the Jungfrau, 1840–1861. Ford Madox Brown. Oil on canvas. Manchester Art Gallery, England. ★

sinister. One of Byron's characters, Manfred, carries an air of melancholy that grows out of a mysterious, "half-maddening sin." Byronic heroes often have unexplained pasts that intensify their air of mystery and hint at great sorrow.

Boldness The Byronic hero is arrogant and defiant. Byron's heroes are effective, almost superhuman

806 UNIT 4 THE TRIUMPH OF ROMANTICISM

Teach

Literary Element | **1**

Poetry Forms Tell students that a canto is a major division of a long poem.

View the Art ★

Manfred was the first play Lord Byron wrote. It was highly successful and was translated into German at least 18 times during the nineteenth century.

 For an audio recording of this selection, use Listening Library Audio CD-ROM.

Reading Practice

SPIRAL REVIEW **Characterization** Remind students that two methods are used to reveal characters' personalities: direct characterization is an author's description of a character's personality; indirect characterization is a suggestion of traits by means of a character's words, actions, or appearance. Ask students to look through this selection and find examples of direct characterization and indirect characterization of the Byronic hero.

 For activities related to this selection, see Unit 4 Teaching Resources Book, pp. 189–190.

leaders who overcome obstacles and formidable, even supernatural, opponents. This confidence helps endear the Byronic hero to the reader.

Danger The Byronic hero is ultimately self-destructive and, unlike traditional heroes, unlikely to live happily ever after. That is his charm and his tragedy. Appealing as he may be to the various women who cross his path, he cannot be faithful to them. He is either incapable of such fidelity, or his wandering destiny keeps him from lasting attachments.

The Legacy of the Byronic Hero

Besides the dark, brooding characters that he created, Byron himself left a lasting impact on European culture. His style and persona mirrored the tastes of the day—his portrait in Albanian dress (see page 800) shows the era's fascination with the exotic. The famed Russian poet Alexander Pushkin, an enthusiastic admirer of Byron, had himself painted in a similarly exotic costume. As if they were making a pilgrimage, artists followed in Byron's footsteps, traveling throughout Europe, the Middle East, and North Africa and painting exotic street scenes and portraits of Arab chieftains and commoners.

Composers have immortalized several Byronic heroes as well. Hector Berlioz's *Harold in Italy* grew out of Byron's first major work, *Childe Harold's Pilgrimage*. Inspired by the Byronic hero Manfred, Robert Schumann wrote a *Manfred* Overture, and Peter Ilich Tchaikovsky wrote a *Manfred* Symphony.

Still, the most significant effect of the Byronic hero has been in literature. Many nineteenth-century novels feature brooding, mysterious characters, such as Mr. Rochester in Charlotte Brontë's *Jane Eyre* and Heathcliff in Emily Brontë's *Wuthering Heights*. In modern times, the Byronic hero has been a

regular feature of romance novels, comic books, and detective stories. He has also found his way to the big screen. In spaghetti westerns, Clint Eastwood famously portrayed nameless, roving gunslingers who embodied the archetype of the Byronic hero. Perhaps the best-known pop-culture example, though, is James Dean's lead role in *Rebel Without a Cause*.

Lord Byron Reposing in the House of a Fisherman Having Swum the Hellespont, nineteenth century. Sir William Allan. Roy Miles Fine Paintings, London.

 Literature Online

Literature and Reading For more about Byron and the Byronic hero, go to glencoe.com and enter QuickPass code GLB9817u4.

Respond and Think Critically

1. In what ways is the Byronic hero similar to and different from the traditional hero?

2. Why do you think the Byronic hero has endured in literature, movies, and art?

3. Choose a contemporary character from a comic book, movie, novel, story, or play and discuss how that character exemplifies the Byronic hero.

4. How did the Byronic hero influence the cultures of Russia and Western Europe?

LITERARY HISTORY **807**

Teach

Big Idea | **2**

The Quest for Truth and Beauty Remind students that the Romantics sought out the deepest, most intense human experiences by falling in love, writing poetry, and fighting for causes they believed in. **Ask:** How does the Byronic hero embody the spirit of the Romantics? *(He or she doesn't follow convention; rather, he or she is fiercely independent, passionate, and rebellious.)*

Assess

1. The Byronic hero's ability to act as an effective leader and his sense of chivalry are traditionally heroic traits. Byronic heroes differ from traditional heroes by being rebellious and moody and by choosing to be outsiders.

2. Students' answers will vary but may refer to the attraction many people feel to rebellious outsiders.

3. Students may mention a variety of rebellious, moody, arrogant, or self-destructive characters.

4. Byron's creation of the anti-hero or Byronic hero manifested itself in artists' work and in famous literary characters in the cultures of Russia and Western Europe.

English Learners

DIFFERENTIATED INSTRUCTION

Beginning Ask English learners whether Byronic heroes are found in their particular cultures. If so, have students share poems or stories featuring a Byronic hero with the class.

Advanced Ask students to generate two questions to help clarify their understanding of the characteristics of the Byronic hero. *(What characteristics does the Byronic hero share with a villain? How does the Byronic hero differ from a villain?)* Have students ask each other their questions until all have been answered.

Focus

Bellringer Options

Selection Focus
  Transparency 41

Daily Language Practice
  Transparency 67

Or **read** this quotation by Shelley aloud: "Poetry turns all things to loveliness … it strips the veil of familiarity from the world and lays bare the naked and sleeping beauty." **Ask:** What does the quotation mean? Do you agree that the poet's job is to reveal hidden beauty in the world? (*Answers will vary.*)

Have students, as they read, consider Shelley's Romantic view of poetry.

Before You Read

Shelley's Poetry

Meet **Percy Bysshe Shelley**
(1792–1822)

Many of our modern stereotypes of poets are derived from the life and character of Percy Shelley. He died young; he was politically radical and indifferent to the social norms of his age; he was passionate and often intemperate; and in his poems, he celebrated nature's transcendence while embracing its inherent gloom.

> *"Poets are the unacknowledged legislators of the World."*
>
> —Percy Bysshe Shelley

"Mad Shelley" Born in 1792, Shelley was the son of a country squire and an heir to a wealthy estate. He was the oldest child in a family mostly of girls. He was adored by his sisters and indulged by his father, who was unsure how to manage his unruly son. At age ten, when he attended Syon House Academy, however, he was often ridiculed. When he switched to Eton at twelve, the boys there treated him worse, calling him "Mad Shelley" and playing practical jokes on him. Shelley retreated into fantasy, writing gothic poems and melodramatic romances. He also began to gravitate toward political literature that opposed hypocrisy and injustice.

At eighteen, Shelley entered University College, Oxford, where he met his lifelong friend and biographer Thomas Hogg. The two were expelled only six months later, however, after they circulated and refused to admit authorship of the pamphlet *The Necessity of Atheism.* Shelley then traveled to London, where he met, and eventually eloped with, Harriet Westbrook. Both Shelley's family and Harriet's were opposed to the marriage. As a result, the couple had to fend for themselves with little money. After moving from place to place, they went to Dublin, Ireland.

Emerging Poet By 1813 Shelley had returned to London, where he published his first major work, *Queen Mab,* a prophetic poem that condemns war, the monarchy, and the church. That same year Harriet gave birth to their first of two children. Shelley, though, was soon to fall in love with Mary Godwin, the daughter of his mentor, radical philosopher William Godwin, and author Mary Wollstonecraft. Just before his twenty-second birthday, Shelley left for Europe with Mary. They spent the summer of 1816 on the shores of Lake Geneva, in Switzerland, where Shelley met and befriended George Gordon, Lord Byron. After two years of traveling and writing, they returned to England. Soon after their return, Harriet drowned herself. Percy and Mary were then married.

In 1818, seeking a more healthful climate, relief from his creditors, and increased proximity to Lord Byron, Shelley moved his household to Italy. In Italy, Shelley wrote some of his best poetry and essays. Yet, tragedy loomed. He and Mary lost two of their own children, and Mary suffered a severe nervous breakdown. Then, just prior to his thirtieth birthday, Shelley drowned in a boating accident. "You were all brutally mistaken about Shelley," wrote his grief-stricken friend Lord Byron. "[He was] the best and least selfish man I ever knew."

 Literature Online

Author Search For more about Percy Bysshe Shelley, go to glencoe.com and enter QuickPass code GLB9817u4.

Selection Skills

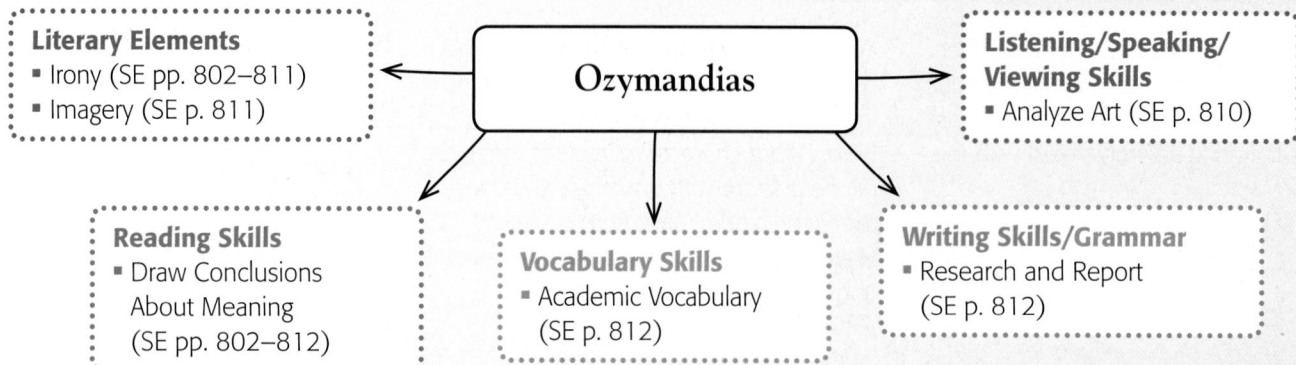

Literary Elements
- Irony (SE pp. 802–811)
- Imagery (SE p. 811)

Ozymandias

Listening/Speaking/ Viewing Skills
- Analyze Art (SE p. 810)

Reading Skills
- Draw Conclusions About Meaning (SE pp. 802–812)

Vocabulary Skills
- Academic Vocabulary (SE p. 812)

Writing Skills/Grammar
- Research and Report (SE p. 812)

Literature and Reading Preview

Connect to the Poem

What do you feel is the most enduring kind of contribution a person can make? With a small group of classmates, discuss what makes a person's legacy pass the test of time.

Build Background

"Ozymandias" is a Greek form of the name of Ramses II, the pharaoh who ruled Egypt during the thirteenth century B.C. Much of our knowledge of Ramses is derived from the large-scale monuments built to glorify his reign.

Shelley wrote "Ode to the West Wind" in 1819, in a forest beside the Arno River near Florence, Italy. "To a Skylark" celebrates the European skylark, a small bird that sings only in flight, often when it is too high to be seen.

Set Purposes for Reading

Big Idea **The Quest for Truth and Beauty**

As you read, ask yourself, How does Shelley present Romantic ideas about beauty, nature, and political radicalism?

Literary Element **Irony**

Irony takes several forms, all arising from a contrast between appearance and reality. In **verbal irony**, words that appear to mean one thing actually mean the opposite. In **situational irony**, the outcome of a situation is the opposite of what one expected. **Dramatic irony** exists when the audience or reader knows something that a character does not know. As you read "Ozymandias," ask yourself, What purpose is irony serving in the poem?

Reading Strategy **Draw Conclusions About Meaning**

A **conclusion** is a general statement based on a number of specific examples. In a work of literature, these specific examples are literary elements, rhetorical devices, and main ideas. By analyzing the specifics, a reader can draw a valid conclusion about the meaning of the literary work. As you read, ask yourself, What statement can I make about what I've read?

....

Tip: Taking Notes Note specific examples in the poem that might aid you in drawing a conclusion about its meaning. Write down each example, describe it, and then label the line in which it appears. After recording your examples, draw a conclusion about the poem's meaning.

PERCY BYSSHE SHELLEY **809**

Vocabulary Preview

dirge (durj) *n.* a song sung in grief; a mournful hymn; p. 814 *During the ceremony, a dirge was sung in honor of the missing soldiers.*

cleave (klēv) *v.* to tear or rip; to split something apart; p. 815 *It was quite easy for the axe to cleave the soft wood.*

tumult (tōō′ məlt) *n.* disorder; an uproar; p. 816 *After the show, there was a great tumult outside the theater.*

satiety (sə tī′ ə tē) *n.* a feeling of weariness or even dislike of something caused by satisfying an appetite or desire for it in excess; p. 819 *Diners suffered satiety after the enormous meal.*

Before You Read

Focus

Summary

The speaker quotes a traveler who described the ancient ruin of a monument to Ozymandias, an Egyptian pharaoh. The statue is inscribed with the king's order to behold his great works. All that remains, however, is the crumbled ruin in the desert.

 For summaries in languages other than English, see Unit 4 Teaching Resources Book, pp. 191–196.

Vocabulary

Application Discuss present-day actions or situations that apply to each word's definition. Once students are comfortable using the words, ask them what the meaning and use of these words suggests about Shelley's outlook on life.

 For additional context, see Glencoe Interactive Vocabulary CD-ROM.

 For an audio recording of this selection, use Listening Library Audio CD-ROM.

Approaching Level

DIFFERENTIATED INSTRUCTION

Emerging Approaching-level students may need additional support to understand irony and its role in "Ozymandias." Tell them that situational irony is when the outcome of a situation is the opposite of expectations. **Say:** Imagine you are on your way to the movie theater and you see a quarter lying on the ground, but you don't pick it up. When you go to pay for the movie, you find that you are one quarter short. This is situational irony.

Ask students to write their own examples of ironic situations involving a powerful person, such as a leader or famous historical figure.

Teach

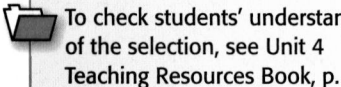

Memnonium, Thebes, from David Roberts in Egypt and Nubia, 1848. L. Haghe. Color lithograph. Institute of Civil Engineers.

View the Art Many of the Egyptian monuments sketched by Roberts have since been destroyed. Does this image capture the idea or feel of Shelley's poem? Explain.

Ozymandias

Percy Bysshe Shelley

I met a traveler from an antique land
Who said: Two vast and trunkless legs of stone
Stand in the desert . . . Near them, on the sand,
Half sunk, a shattered visage[1] lies, whose frown,
5 And wrinkled lip, and sneer of cold command, **2**
Tell that its sculptor well those passions read
Which yet survive, stamped on these lifeless things,
The hand[2] that mocked[3] them, and the heart[4] that fed:
And on the pedestal these words appear:
10 "My name is Ozymandias, king of kings:
Look on my works, ye Mighty, and despair!"
Nothing beside remains. Round the decay
Of that colossal wreck, boundless and bare
The lone and level sands stretch far away.

1. A *visage* is a face.

2. Here, *hand* refers to the hand of the sculptor.
3. *Mocked* means "imitated" or "derided."
4. *Heart* refers to the heart of Ozymandias.

1 Irony *What is ironic about the statue's inscription? What does the irony suggest about the theme of the poem?*

810 UNIT 4 THE TRIUMPH OF ROMANTICISM

After You Read

Respond and Think Critically

Respond and Interpret

1. What is your opinion of Ozymandias? Give reasons for your answer.

2. (a)At the start of the poem, what does the traveler describe? (b)What specific details help you visualize what is being described?

3. (a)What words appear on the pedestal? (b)What do these words suggest about Ozymandias's personality and character?

4. (a)How does the traveler describe the area surrounding the ruins? (b)What does this description suggest about the nature of power and fame?

Analyze and Evaluate

5. (a)In your opinion, for what purposes did Shelley write this poem? (b)How successful was he? Explain.

6. (a)Why do you think Shelley uses "a traveler from an antique land" as the storyteller within the poem? (b)What is the effect of having both a speaker and a storyteller? Explain.

Connect

7. **Big Idea** **The Quest for Truth and Beauty** How are Shelley's political radicalism and Romantic ideals evident in this poem? Explain.

8. **Connect to Today** Name a modern monument or tribute, and consider whether it will continue to be meaningful in the distant future. Explain your opinion.

Literary Element Irony

Irony can be used in many different ways in a literary work. It can be used to support the theme or main idea. It can add humor, increase suspense, or create a surprise. In "Ozymandias," there are several different examples of irony that help advance the poem's theme.

1. Find examples of irony in "Ozymandias." What type of irony is illustrated by each example? Explain.

2. How does the irony support the theme of the poem?

Review: Imagery

Imagery is the "word pictures" writers create with **sensory details**—details that appeal to sight, smell, hearing, touch, or taste. Choose an image from "Ozymandias" that strikes you as particularly vivid, and sketch your interpretation of the image on a separate sheet of paper. Share your sketch with a partner, explaining which sensory details helped you form the image in your mind.

LOG ON ▶ **Literature** Online

Selection Resources For Selection Quizzes, eFlashcards, and Reading-Writing Connection activities, go to glencoe.com and enter QuickPass code GLB9817u4.

PERCY BYSSHE SHELLEY **811**

After You Read

Assess

Literary Element

1. Possible answers: "passions ... survive"—verbal; "Look on ... despair"—dramatic

2. Irony develops the theme that all is vanity.

Review

Students should incorporate specific details from the poem in their sketches.

Progress Check

Can students identify irony?

If No ➔ See Unit 4 Teaching Resources Book, p. 197.

After You Read

Reading Strategy

1. Fame and power do not last.
2. Students' answers will vary. Some may cite images, such as, "sneer of cold command," "decay of that colossal wreck," "lone and level sands stretch far away," or the inscription "My name is Ozymandias, king of kings: look on my works, ye Mighty, and despair!"

Progress Check

Can students draw conclusions about meaning?

If No → See Unit 4 Teaching Resources Book, p. 198.

 For additional assessment, see Assessment Resources, pp. 203–204.

 To create custom assessments online, go to Progress Reporter Online Assessment.

 To create assessment using software, use ExamView Assessment Suite.

Reading Strategy Draw Conclusions About Meaning

Much of the evidence needed to draw accurate conclusions about a literary work is not explicitly stated. Therefore, it is often necessary for the reader to infer the meaning from various elements within the work.

1. What do you think is the meaning of the poem "Ozymandias"?

2. In support of your opinion, list three specific examples from the poem.

Academic Vocabulary

In the poem, Shelley **contrasts** *the image of what was once a grand statue with the decay in which it now lies.*

Contrast is an academic word. To create irony, Shelley **contrasts** reality with what a character thinks an outcome will be.

To further explore the meaning of this word, answer the following question: What kind of a room would **contrast** with the room you're in right now?

For more on academic vocabulary, see pages 56 and R81.

Research and Report

 Literary Criticism

Assignment The scholar and literary critic Donald H. Reiman has stated that Shelley "dedicated his efforts to the destruction of tyranny in all its forms." Write a short essay indicating whether you find evidence of this philosophy in "Ozymandias." Share your conclusions with the class.

Prepare Reread the poem, looking for evidence either supporting or refuting Reiman's observation. Then craft a thesis statement that expresses your main idea. Be sure to cite passages from the poem accurately, enclosing them in quotation marks and separating lines with a slash (/).

Report Present your essay to the class, using a tone of voice and gestures suited to the serious, scholarly nature of the subject. Demonstrate how the lines you quote from the poem logically support your thesis. Referring often to the text of the poem will lend your argument strength.

EXAMPLE:
The phrase "sneer of cold command" suggests
_____ and _____.

Speak slowly and clearly, frequently looking at various members of the audience. Vary the pace and volume of your voice to stress evidence that supports your thesis

Evaluate Write a paragraph evaluating the effectiveness of your report.

Academic Vocabulary

Answers will vary.

Writing

Students' essays should: argue whether or not critic Reiman's statement of Shelley's philosophy is found in the poem, include a clearly stated thesis statement, support opinions with direct quotes from the poem, and be presented to the class using appropriate tone of voice and gestures.

Literary Element Diction

Diction is an author's word choice, or the use of appropriate words to convey a particular meaning. Diction is particularly important in poetry, which uses language more economically than most prose does. As you read "Ode to the West Wind" and "To a Skylark" pay attention to Shelley's use of diction.

Reading Strategy Recognize Author's Purpose

To **recognize an author's purpose** means to recognize an author's intent. An author typically writes to accomplish one or more of the following purposes: to persuade, to instruct, to inform or explain, to entertain, to describe, or to tell a story.

Ode to the West Wind

Percy Bysshe Shelley

O wild West Wind, thou breath of Autumn's being,
Thou, from whose unseen presence the leaves dead
Are driven, like ghosts from an enchanter fleeing,

Yellow and black and pale and hectic red,°
5 Pestilence-stricken multitudes: O Thou,
Who chariotest° to their dark wintry bed

The wingèd seeds, where they lie cold and low,
Each like a corpse within its grave, until
Thine azure° sister of the Spring° shall blow

4 **hectic red:** red like the flushed cheeks of someone who has tuberculosis.
6 **chariotest:** convey in a chariot.

9 **azure:** sky blue.
sister of the Spring: the south wind.

Diction *If Shelley had used "sky blue" instead of "azure," would line 9 sound more formal or more like everyday speech?* **1**

PERCY BYSSHE SHELLEY **813**

Focus

Summary

In "Ode to the West Wind," the speaker describes the effect of the west wind on the land, sky, and sea. He expresses his envy and desire to be as free as the wind. "To a Skylark" exalts the skylark's beautiful spirit, praising its "profuse strains of unpremeditated art." The speaker asks the skylark to bestow on him its art and "gladness."

 For summaries in languages other than English, see Unit 4 Teaching Resources Book, pp. 201–206.

Teach

Literary Element | **1**

Diction Answer: *More like everyday speech*

ENGLISH LEARNERS Encourage English Learners to connect *azure* with *azul*, the Spanish word for "blue." **Ask:** What visual image does the word create for you? *(Answers will vary.)*

Selection Skills

Literary Elements
• Diction (SE pp. 813–822)
• Rhyme Scheme (SE p. 822)

Ode to the West Wind, To a Skylark

Listening/Speaking/ Viewing Skills
• Analyze Art (SE p. 817; TE pp. 815, 820)

Reading Skills
• Recognize Author's Purpose (SE pp. 813–822)

Vocabulary Skills
• Synonyms (SE p. 822)
• Academic Vocabulary (SE p. 822)

Writing Skills/Grammar
• Write a Review (SE p. 823)
• Point of View (SE p. 823)
• Use Pronouns (TE p. 820)

Teach

Diction **Answer:** *Students may say that it creates an energetic tone.*

[ENGLISH LEARNERS] Remind English learners that the purpose of imagery is to create "word pictures"—detailed language that conveys the author's feelings or ideas. Have them work with partners to locate two examples of powerful imagery on this page. Discuss what these images add to the poem.

 For additional literary element practice, see Unit 4 Teaching Resources Book, p. 207.

Literary History ☆

Odes Traditionally, odes are long lyric poems that have had serious subjects, lofty sound diction, and elaborate structure. The best early odes are credited to the Greek poet Pindar (522–443 B.C.), whose work publicly praised notable citizens such as victorious Olympic athletes. Later, the Roman poet Horace (65–8 B.C.) wrote odes on love, friendship, and the art of poetry. As the form evolved in England, the irregular ode arose with its varying rhyme scheme and stanzas. The modern Romantic ode evolved from these various forms.

---

10   Her clarion° o'er the dreaming earth and fill
      (Driving sweet buds like flocks to feed in air)
      With living hues and odors plain and hill:

      Wild Spirit, which art moving everywhere;
      Destroyer and preserver; hear, oh, hear!

2

15   Thou on whose stream, 'mid the steep sky's commotion,
      Loose clouds like Earth's decaying leaves are shed,
      Shook from the tangled boughs of Heaven and Ocean,°

      Angels° of rain and lightning: there are spread
      On the blue surface of thine aery surge,
20   Like the bright hair uplifted from the head

      Of some fierce Maenad,° even from the dim verge
      Of the horizon to the zenith's height,
      The locks of the approaching storm. Thou **dirge**

      Of the dying year, to which this closing night
25   Will be the dome of a vast sepulchre,°
      Vaulted with all thy congregated might

      Of vapors, from whose solid atmosphere
      Black rain and fire and hail will burst: oh, hear!

3 ☆

      Thou who didst waken from his summer dreams
30   The blue Mediterranean where he lay
      Lulled by the coil of his crystalline streams,

      Beside a pumice° isle in Baiae's bay,°
      And saw in sleep old palaces and towers
      Quivering within the wave's intenser day,

35   All overgrown with azure moss and flowers
      So sweet the sense faints picturing them! Thou
      For whose path the Atlantic's level powers

---

1   Diction   *What tone does this metaphor help create?*

Vocabulary

dirge (durj) *n.* a song sung in grief; a mournful hymn

10 clarion: trumpet call.

17 the tangled boughs of Heaven and Ocean: a metaphor for the way in which clouds are formed by a suspension of water **(Ocean)** in air **(Heaven)**.
18 Angels: messengers.

21 Maenad (mē´ nad): in Greek mythology, a female worshiper of Dionysus, the god of wine and wild revelry.

25 sepulchre (sep´ əl kər): tomb.

32 pumice (pum´ is): a light, porous volcanic rock.
Baiae's (bī´ ēz) **bay:** a small seaport in a volcanic area near Naples, Italy, which had been a tourist resort in ancient Roman times. Shelley had taken a boat trip there in 1818 and observed its underwater ruins.

814   UNIT 4   THE TRIUMPH OF ROMANTICISM

Reading Practice

 SMALL GROUP   SPIRAL REVIEW   **Identify Main Idea and Supporting Details**

Help students identify the main idea in section 2 of Shelley's poem *(that the West Wind transforms the sky)* and the supporting details *(the wind's driving storm clouds across the sky like leaves and spreading rain and lightning like Maenad's hair, the wind's sounding like a funeral song, and the wind's vapors vaulting the dome of night).*

Then divide students into four groups. Have each group identify the main idea and the supporting details in one of the other sections of the poem.

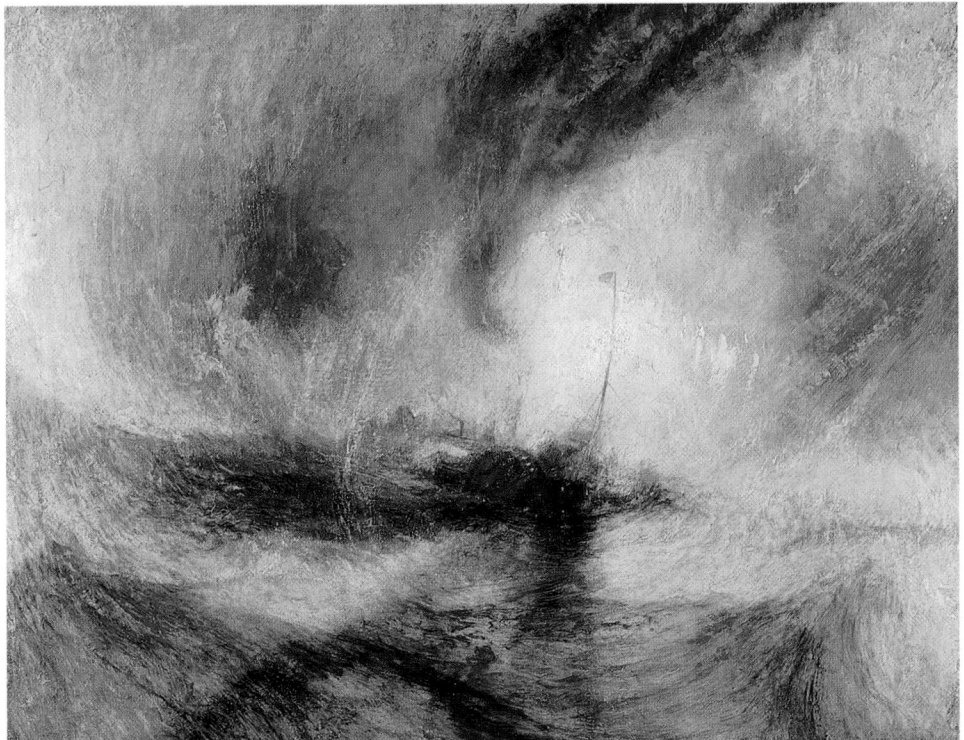

Snow Storm at Sea, 1842. Joseph Mallord William Turner. Oil on canvas, 91½ x 122 cm. Tate Gallery, London.

Cleave themselves into chasms, while far below
The sea-blooms and the oozy woods which wear
40 The sapless foliage of the ocean, know

Thy voice and suddenly grow grey with fear
And tremble and despoil themselves:° oh, hear!

39–42 The sea-blooms . . . despoil themselves: the vegetation at the bottom of the sea changes with the seasons. (Here, *despoil*, in the sense of "undress," refers to a loss of vegetation.)

Diction *Why might Shelley have chosen the word* oozy? **2**

Vocabulary

cleave (klēv) *v.* to tear or rip; to split something apart

PERCY BYSSHE SHELLEY **815**

Teach

| Literary Element | 2 |

Diction **Answer:** *The word* oozy *creates a sensory image that suggests both the texture of seaweed and its wavery appearance in the water. In addition, it echoes the vowel sound of "blooms."*

View the Art ★

Like other Romantics, J. M. W. Turner (1775–1851) was fascinated by the power of nature and the mystery of the sea. In this seascape, he captures the turbulence of the snowstorm, the upwelling waves, and the ferocious wind.

Ask: How does Turner's visual portrayal of the wind compare with Shelley's written portrayal? *(Accept all reasonable responses.)*

English Learners

DIFFERENTIATED INSTRUCTION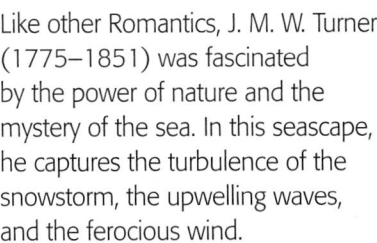

SMALL GROUP

Intermediate Point out that the West Wind is associated with the yearly cycle of decay and new growth. Many cultures have traditions that celebrate the seasonal cycle. Form cross-cultural groups and have them compare Shelley's description of the West Wind with motifs from other cultural traditions.

Advanced Learners

DIFFERENTIATED INSTRUCTION

Terza Rima Explain that terza rima is a verse form of interlocking three-line stanzas called **tercets**. The first and third lines of the first tercet rhyme; the second line provides the rhyme for the first and third lines of the next tercet, and so on. Have students research and present to the class the origins of terza rima.

Teach

Reading Strategy 　 1

Recognize Author's Purpose Answer: *They suggest that Shelley's purpose is to praise the power of the West Wind and to ask for spiritual rebirth.*

Ask: In the next stanza, what does Shelley ask of the wind? *(He asks the west wind to spread its words among people, as it spreads sparks and hot ashes from a fireplace.)*

APPROACHING If approaching-level students have difficulty understanding the author's purpose, re-read section 5 aloud and call on students to paraphrase each line. Make sure students see that Shelley compares his poetry to the leaves he has described throughout this poem.

4

If I were a dead leaf thou mightest bear;
If I were a swift cloud to fly with thee;
45　A wave to pant beneath thy power and share

The impulse° of thy strength, only less free
Than thou, O Uncontrollable! If even
I were as in my boyhood and could be

The comrade of thy wanderings over Heaven,
50　As then, when to outstrip thy skiey speed
Scarce seemed a vision, I would ne'er have striven

As thus with thee in prayer in my sore need.
Oh, lift me as a wave, a leaf, a cloud!
I fall upon the thorns of life! I bleed!

55　A heavy weight of hours has chained and bowed
One too like thee: tameless and swift and proud.

5

Make me thy lyre,° even as the forest is:
What if my leaves are falling like its own!
The **tumult** of thy mighty harmonies

60　Will take from both a deep, autumnal tone,
Sweet, though in sadness. Be thou, Spirit fierce,
My spirit! Be thou me, impetuous one!

Drive my dead thoughts over the universe
Like withered leaves to quicken a new birth!
65　And by the incantation° of this verse,

Scatter, as from an unextinguished hearth
Ashes and sparks, my words among mankind!
Be through my lips to unawakened Earth

The trumpet of a prophecy! O Wind,
70　If Winter comes, can Spring be far behind?

46 impulse: a sudden force that causes motion, such as a push.

57 lyre (līr): a harp—in this case probably an Aeolian harp, a stringed instrument that produces musical sounds when the wind passes over its strings.

65 incantation: a ritual recitation or chanting, usually of a magic charm or spell.

> **1** **Recognize Author's Purpose** *What do these lines suggest about Shelley's purpose for writing this poem?*

> **Vocabulary**
> **tumult** (tōō′ məlt) *n.* disorder; an uproar

816　UNIT 4　THE TRIUMPH OF ROMANTICISM

Reading Practice

SPIRAL REVIEW **Set a Purpose** Have students recall characteristics of Romantic poetry. Ask a volunteer to list responses on the board. Focus on the following: subjects drawn from common life, celebration of beauty in nature, expression of spontaneous feelings, and emphasis on the poet's personal responses to the subject. As they read sections 4 and 5, have students note whenever they encounter a phrase, line, or stanza that they think illustrates characteristics of Romantic poetry. Afterward, have students compare notes and elaborate on the reasons for their choices.

816

Wheatfield with Lark, 1888. Vincent van Gogh. Oil on canvas. Rijksmuseum, Amsterdam.

View the Art Van Gogh used strong, visible brushstrokes to give his paintings texture and color. What do you first notice in this image?

To a Skylark

Percy Bysshe Shelley

Hail to thee, blithe° Spirit!
    Bird thou never wert,
That from Heaven, or near it,
    Pourest thy full heart
5 In profuse° strains of unpremeditated° art.

    Higher still and higher
      From the earth thou springest
Like a cloud of fire;
    The blue deep thou wingest,
10 And singing still dost soar, and soaring ever singest.

1 **blithe:** carefree; lighthearted.

5 **profuse:** plentiful; given freely or abundantly.
unpremeditated: done without plan or forethought.

Diction *How does the diction in these lines affect their sound?*

Teach

Reading Strategy | 2

Recognize Author's Purpose Remind students that odes are songs of praise. Point out that the title *To a Skylark* is typical of odes, which are written "to" a part of nature, "to" a quality like love, or "to" an absent person.

Ask: What qualities of the skylark might Shelley admire? *(Skylarks fly high and sing lovely, spontaneous songs.)*

Literary Element | 3

Diction Answer: *The repeated 's' sound and the repetition of sing and soar create a musical effect.*

View the Art ★

Answer: *Many students will say they notice the movement of the wheat, or that they notice the bird first, because of its stark contrast with the rest of Van Gogh's sky.*

English Learners

DIFFERENTIATED INSTRUCTION

 Intermediate Have students work in pairs to find examples of *thee, thou* and *thy*. Compare these words to the Spanish words *vosotros* and *vuestro*, which are no longer used in Latin America. Then have them read aloud, substituting modern pronouns for the archaic ones.

Approaching Level

DIFFERENTIATED INSTRUCTION

AAVE For approaching-level students who use African American Vernacular English (AAVE), practice the *th* sounds in *thee, blithe*, and *thou*. Have students place their tongues at the bottom of their two front teeth and blow outward. Approaching-level students who use AAVE should try pronouncing these words using this method.

The Quest for Truth and Beauty

Answer: *The speaker knows that the skylark exists even though he cannot see it. This fits the Romantic's sense of absolute truth and elusive beauty.*

(ADVANCED) For advanced students, **ask:** In stanza 5, what is like the skylark, unseen but felt? *(Venus)* What is the author's purpose in making such a comparison? *(Although the speaker cannot always see Venus and the skylark, he feels that they are there.)*

Cultural History ☆

A Song Not Heard As he said in "Ode to the West Wind," Shelley wanted to be "the trumpet of a prophecy." Shelley saw himself as voicing ideas that would change the world, yet he did not enjoy popular success in his lifetime. By 1819, when he wrote this poem, he may have realized that he was "singing hymns unbidden" to a world that "heeded not".

In the golden lightning
    Of the sunken sun,
O'er which clouds are bright'ning,
    Thou dost float and run—
15 Like an unbodied joy whose race is just begun.

The pale purple even°
    Melts around thy flight;
Like a star of Heaven,
    In the broad daylight
20 Thou art unseen, but yet I hear thy shrill delight,

Keen° as are the arrows
    Of that silver sphere,°
Whose intense lamp narrows
    In the white dawn clear
25 Until we hardly see—we feel that it is there.

All the earth and air
    With thy voice is loud,
As, when night is bare,
    From one lonely cloud
30 The moon rains out her beams, and Heaven is overflowed.

What thou art we know not;
    What is most like thee?
From rainbow clouds there flow not
    Drops so bright to see
35 As from thy presence showers a rain of melody.

Like a poet hidden
    In the light of thought,
Singing hymns unbidden,
    Till the world is wrought
40 To sympathy with hopes and fears it heeded not: ☆

Like a high-born maiden
    In a palace tower,
Soothing her love-laden
    Soul in secret hour
45 With music sweet as love, which overflows her bower:°

16 even: evening.

21 Keen: sharp.
22 silver sphere: the planet Venus, also called the morning star because it is visible just before or at sunrise.

45 bower: a private room or bedroom.

---

1   **The Quest for Truth and Beauty** *How does Shelley's description of the skylark in this line mimic the Romantic quest for truth and beauty?*

Reading Practice

PARTNERS | SPIRAL REVIEW

Monitor Comprehension Remind students that similes are comparisons that use the words *like* or *as*. Have partners create a web like the one here. As they read, they should pause each time they encounter a simile and list the things to which the skylark is compared. Suggest they look for a common thread that unites the nouns.

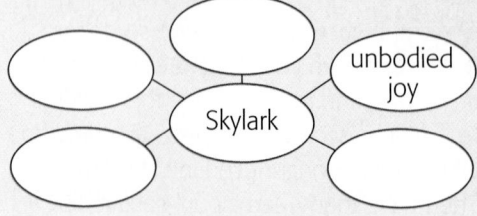

Like a glowworm golden
   In a dell° of dew,
Scattering unbeholden
   Its aerial hue
50 Among the flowers and grass, which screen it from the view!

Like a rose embowered
   In its own green leaves,
By warm winds deflowered,
   Till the scent it gives
55 Makes faint with too much sweet those heavy-wingèd thieves:

Sound of vernal° showers
   On the twinkling grass,
Rain-awakened flowers,
   All that ever was
60 Joyous and clear and fresh, thy music doth surpass:

Teach us, Sprite or Bird,
   What sweet thoughts are thine:
I have never heard
   Praise of love or wine
65 That panted forth a flood of rapture so divine.

Chorus Hymeneal,°
   Or triumphal chant,
Matched with thine would be all
   But an empty vaunt,°
70 A thing wherein we feel there is some hidden want.

What objects are the fountains°
   Of thy happy strain?°
What fields or waves or mountains?
   What shapes of sky or plain?
75 What love of thine own kind? What ignorance of pain?

With thy clear keen joyance°
   Languor° cannot be:
Shadow of annoyance
   Never came near thee:
80 Thou lovest—but ne'er knew love's sad **satiety**.

47 **dell:** a small, deep valley.

56 **vernal:** occurring in the spring.

66 **Chorus Hymeneal**
(hī′ mə nē′ əl): a wedding song—
named for Hymen, the Greek god of
marriage.
69 **vaunt:** boast.

71 **fountains:** sources.
72 **strain:** melody.

76 **joyance:** rejoicing; delight.
77 **Languor** (lang′ gər): a lack of
energy or spirit; weariness.

Diction *How does the word* panted *affect the connotation of this line?* **2**

Vocabulary

satiety (sə tī′ ə tē) *n.* a feeling of weariness or even dislike of
something caused by satisfying an appetite or desire for it in excess

---

Literary Element | **2**

Diction **Answer:** *Panted is a
charged word that can have connotations suggesting rapid breathing. Here, it is used to strengthen
the sense of "rapture so divine."*

Ask: What ideas do *panted* and
rapture suggest? *(The words
suggest the throes of passion.)*

Writer's Technique

Poetic Structure Remind students of the invocation structure
in "Ode to the West Wind." Then
ask them to identify the structural
change in line 61. *(After spending
60 lines praising the skylark, the
speaker now begins to make a
request.)* Point out that Shelley
underscores this shift in two
subtle ways. First, he breaks a
meter pattern he uses to begin
stanzas. Instead of opening with
a six-syllable line that ends in an
unstressed syllable, Shelley shaves
off that last syllable. Second, he
uses the word *sprite*, which means
"a supernatural being." This word
echoes in both sound and meaning the phrase "blithe spirit" in the
poem's first line.

Teach

Reading Strategy | 1

Recognize Author's Purpose Answer: *Shelley's beliefs that the natural world is transcendent and that nature is the best poet suggest his Romanticism. He uses the poem to praise the power of nature to inspire.*

View the Art ★

Mark Catesby (1682–1749) was an English artist and naturalist who made two extended journeys to the American colonies and the Caribbean to draw the wildlife he found there. His efforts resulted in *The Natural History of Carolina, Florida and the Bahama Islands* (1731–1747) which includes 220 hand-colored etchings.

Ask: How does the lark in this painting compare with the way Shelley describes the lark in the poem? (*Students may note that the lark in the painting is more static than the lark Shelley describes.*)

To check students' understanding of the selection, see Unit 4 Teaching Resources Book, p. 211.

> Waking or asleep,
>   Thou of death must deem°
> Things more true and deep
>   Than we mortals dream,
> 85 Or how could thy notes flow in such a crystal stream?
>
>   We look before and after,
>   And pine for what is not:
>   Our sincerest laughter
>   With some pain is fraught;
> 90 Our sweetest songs are those that tell of saddest thought.
>
>   Yet if we could scorn
>   Hate and pride and fear;
>   If we were things born
>   Not to shed a tear,
> 95 I know not how thy joy we ever should come near.
>
>   Better than all measures
>   Of delightful sound,
>   Better than all treasures
>   That in books are found,
> 100 Thy skill to poet were, thou scorner of the ground!
>
>   Teach me half the gladness
>   That thy brain must know,
>   Such harmonious madness
>   From my lips would flow
> 105 The world should listen then—as I am listening now.

82 **deem:** think, believe, or judge.

---

1 Recognize Author's Purpose *In what ways do lines 101–104 suggest both Shelley's Romanticism and his purpose for writing this poem?*

The Large Lark, 1731-1743. Mark Catesby. Academy of Natural Sciences of Philadelphia, PA. ★

Grammar Practice

SPIRAL REVIEW **Use Pronouns** Have students identify the pronouns in lines 81–85. Then ask them to name the antecedent of each pronoun. Remind them that a pronoun cannot refer to more than one antecedent. Have students rewrite these sentences to make the pronoun reference clear:

- If Shelley's Poems is on the bookshelf, you can find it.
- Shelley mastered complex rhyme schemes, and this is apparent in his poetry.

After You Read

Respond and Think Critically

Respond and Interpret

1. Which of these poems more effectively invokes the natural world? Explain.

2. (a)Sections 1–3 of "Ode to the West Wind" describe how the wind affects three aspects of nature. What are those aspects? (b)What do these descriptions reveal about the speaker's view of the West Wind?

3. (a)In lines 1–30 of "To a Skylark," what words or images help you imagine the skylark's flight and song? (b)Describe the speaker's attitude toward the skylark.

4. (a)To what people or things does the speaker compare the skylark in lines 31–60? (b)What qualities of the skylark do these comparisons suggest?

Analyze and Evaluate

5. (a)What effect does Shelley create with his use of apostrophe in "Ode to the West Wind"? (b)Do you think this technique makes the poem more powerful? Explain.

6. In "To a Skylark," what effect does the rhyme scheme create?

Connect

7. **Big Idea** **The Quest for Truth and Beauty** What ideas about truth and beauty do these poems convey?

8. **Connect to the Author** Reread the biography of Shelley on page 808. What aspects of his personality do you find reflected in "Ode to the West Wind" and "To a Skylark"? Explain, using quotations from the poems.

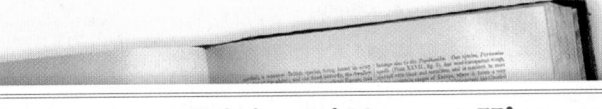

You're the Critic: Different Viewpoints

Are Shelley's Ideas Juvenile?

T. S. Eliot was one of the most important twentieth-century poets and critics. J. B. Priestley was a popular twentieth-century British novelist, dramatist, and essayist. As you read these two excerpts, try to determine your position on the issues they raise.

"Shelley's views I positively dislike. . . . When the doctrine, theory, belief, or 'view of life' presented in a poem is one which the mind of the reader can accept as coherent, mature, and founded on the facts of experience, it interposes no obstacle to the reader's enjoyment. . . . When it is one which the reader rejects as childish or feeble, it may, for a reader of well-developed mind, set up an almost complete check."

—T. S. Eliot

"[W]hen he is in full flight . . . his poetry is marvelous in its innocence and loveliness . . . as if it belonged to—and is indeed celebrating— some future Golden Age. . . . What any generous youth, preferably in rebellion against tyranny and injustice, imagines for a few minutes . . . goes soaring and glittering and singing through volume after volume of Shelley."

—J. B. Priestley

Group Activity Discuss the following questions with classmates. Refer to the excerpts and cite evidence from Shelley's poems for support.

1. (a)Why does Eliot argue that Shelley's views prevent enjoyment of the poems? (b)How might Priestley respond to Eliot's criticism?

2. With which critic do you agree more? Explain.

You're the Critic

1. (a) Eliot claims that Shelley's presentation of "childish" ideas impedes the reader's enjoyment of the earlier poet's work. (b) While Priestley might agree that the ideas are "innocent," he would insist that they sing and soar in Shelley's greatest lines.

2. Students' answers will vary. Make sure that students support their positions with evidence from the poems.

After You Read

Assess

1. Students' answers will reflect individual perceptions.

2. (a) Earth, sky, and sea (b) The west wind is a force that dominates nature as a destroyer and preserver.

3. (a) Examples should reflect an understanding of imagery and sensory details. (b) Attitudes include affection, admiration, worship, and awe.

4. (a) A rainbow, a poet, a high-born maiden, a glowworm, a rose, and spring rain (b) Beauty unites all of these images.

5. (a) The apostrophe creates a dramatic relationship between the speaker and the wind, making the poem seem prayer-like. (b) Most will agree that it increases the poem's power.

6. The *ababb* scheme creates a strong stop at the end of each stanza.

7. Natural beauty, embodied in the skylark's song, is divine.

8. Many students will say the poems highlight Shelley's tendency to think in emotional extremes and melodramatic ways. Some might note that they show his understanding of the close relationship between life, beauty, death, and gloom.

After You Read

Assess

Literary Element

1. (a) The diction is formal, elegant, and forceful. (b) The diction creates an elevated and lush mood.

2. The rhythm and rhyme reinforce the elevated diction and thus enhance the mood.

Review: Rhyme Scheme

Discussions should focus on the interlocking sequence of terza rima and on the rhyming couplet that ends each of the sonnet sections of the poem. Be sure students see that the second line of each tercet provides the rhyme for the first and third lines of the following tercet.

Reading Strategy

1. His purpose was to inform and to inspire by praising the power of art and nature.

2. The theme of both of these poems is that art and nature have the power to change the world. This theme is directly related to Shelley's purpose for writing: to impress upon his reader the power of art and nature.

Progress Check

Can students recognize the author's purpose?

If No → See Unit 4 Teaching Resources Book, p. 208.

822

Literary Element Diction

The **diction** used by a poet is closely connected to the mood that is created in the poem. For example, writers who choose plain, unadorned, straightforward language may create an unromantic, matter-of-fact mood. Writers who use florid, dense language or a great deal of figurative or connotative language will create a far different tone in their writing. In poetry, diction creates the rhymes, rhythms, and other sound devices that can contribute to the mood.

1. (a)How would you describe the diction in "Ode to the West Wind" and "To a Skylark"? (b)In your opinion, what effect does the diction have on the mood of each poem?

2. In each poem, how does Shelley's use of rhythm and rhyme affect the mood?

Review: Rhyme Scheme

As you learned on page 256, the **rhyme scheme** of a poem is the pattern that is formed in a stanza by the rhymes at the end of each line. "Ode to the West Wind" is written in the terza rima form. Shelley borrowed this poetic form from Dante and other Italian literary sources.

Partner Activity Meet with another classmate and explore the rhyme scheme of terza rima. The rhyme scheme is designated by assigning a different letter of the alphabet to each new rhyme. Make a note of any other patterns or poetic forms that you notice.

822 UNIT 4 THE TRIUMPH OF ROMANTICISM

Reading Strategy Recognize Author's Purpose

Often, a poet's purpose is directly related to the theme of a poem. To determine the theme, pay close attention to main ideas, supporting details, rhetorical strategies, and literary elements.

1. What do you think Shelley's purpose was for writing each of these poems?

2. What is the **theme**, or message about life, of each poem? How does the theme of each relate to Shelley's purpose? Explain.

Vocabulary Practice

Practice with Synonyms Match each bold-faced vocabulary word below with a synonym. Use a dictionary to check your answers. You will not use all of the answer choices.

1. dirge   **a.** commotion   **d.** lament

2. cleave   **b.** funeral   **e.** bravery

3. tumult   **c.** fullness   **f.** split

4. satiety

Academic Vocabulary

*Shelley **drafted** his first poems and romances when he was still a student.*

Draft is a word that can have several different meanings. It is important to **draft** an essay and then make revisions before handing it in.

Using context clues, determine the meaning of *drafted* in each sentence:

1. Thomas Jefferson **drafted** the Declaration of Independence; it was then modified by other committee members.

2. When he was twenty, my father was **drafted** by the military and sent to fight in Vietnam.

For more on academic vocabulary, see pages 56 and R81.

Vocabulary Practice

1. d   **2.** f   **3.** a   **4.** c

 For additional vocabulary practice, see Unit 4 Teaching Resources Book, p. 209.

Academic Vocabulary

1. wrote   **2.** called to serve

 For additional context, see Glencoe Interactive Vocabulary CD-ROM.

Respond Through Writing

Review

Learning Objectives

In this assignment, you will focus on the following objective:

Writing: Writing a review.

Writing Task Although Shelley is a highly regarded poet whose works have withstood the test of time, some readers find his writing to be overly sentimental. Write a review of Shelley's poems to be posted on a literary Web site about Shelley or poetry in general, stating whether or not you agree with this view. Support your opinion with examples from the poem, focusing specifically on the poet's diction and rhyme scheme.

Understanding the Task A **review** is a critical evaluation of a work of art, based on specific standards and supported with details from the work, expert opinions, and logical explanations.

Prewrite Reread Shelley's poems and, if possible, one or two critical essays about his work. Decide on a definition of *sentimental* and make a word web listing its components and ways they do or do not apply to Shelley's poems.

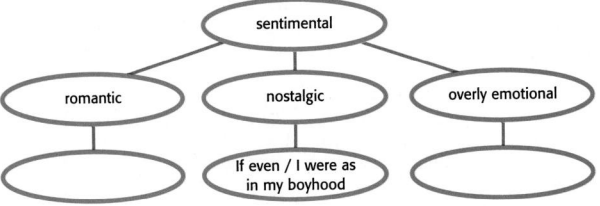

Draft Support your opinion about Shelley's sentimentality with relevant quotations from the poems. Use rhetorical and persuasive devices, such as appeals to authority or emotion, to give your argument more weight. Consider differing points of view and objections your readers might have and address them logically, explaining clearly why your perspective is correct. Use statements like the following to respond to such opposition:

Some might object that _____, but my response would be _____.

Revise Reread your review, checking to make sure your position is logically developed. Be sure you have named your sources whenever necessary. Evaluate the essay with the Writing Workshop checklists on pages 972 and 1322.

Edit and Proofread Proofread your paper, correcting any errors in spelling, grammar, and punctuation. Use the Grammar Tip in the side column to help you with point of view.

Grammar Tip

Point of View

In persuasive writing, your arguments should be clear. To avoid confusing your audience, maintain a consistent **point of view**, or perspective on your subject, by using pronouns in a consistent person.

During drafting, decide if you want the point of view used in your argument to be first (*I, me*), second (*you*), or third (*he/she, him/her*) person, and use the appropriate pronouns throughout.

I found the rhyme scheme of "Ode to the West Wind" to be annoying and intrusive. The end rhyme in every other line got ~~you~~ me into a lighthearted sing-song rhythm that contrasted with Shelley's serious message.

PERCY BYSSHE SHELLEY **823**

After You Read

Assess

Respond Through Writing

Students' reviews should: reflect whether they agree or disagree that Shelley's writing is overly sentimental, provide support for their opinions with references to the poems, focus primarily on the poet's use of diction and rhyme scheme, and use persuasive devices, such as logical and emotional appeals.

A student who meets all of these criteria should receive the equivalent of a 4-point response.

A student who fully meets two or partially meets three of these criteria should receive the equivalent of a 3-point response.

A student who fully meets one or partially meets two of these criteria should receive the equivalent of a 2-point response.

A student who partially meets one of these criteria should receive the equivalent of a 1-point response.

For additional assessment, see Assessment Resources, pp. 205–206.

Approaching Level

DIFFERENTIATED INSTRUCTION

Emerging Say: Order of importance is one of the ways you can present arguments in persuasive writing. Ask students who are struggling to create a list of their arguments to rank their arguments, with the most important coming first, and then the second most important, and so on. Encourage students to include supporting details with each argument, and tell them they may follow this hierarchy in their review.

Before You Read

Focus

Bellringer Options

Daily Language Practice Transparency 68

Or **read aloud** the displayed quotation on the student page.

Say: Keats knew from a young age what he wanted to accomplish. What do you want to accomplish in your lifetime?

Before You Read

Keats's Poetry

Meet **John Keats**

(1795–1821)

"Mortality," wrote John Keats, "weighs heavily on me like unwilling sleep." Keats wrote these words at age twenty-one, soon after launching his poetic career. Within five years, he was dead. To say he made the most of his time would be an understatement. No other poet—not even Chaucer, Shakespeare, or Milton—progressed so far by the age of twenty-five.

> "O for ten years, that I may overwhelm Myself in poesy; so I may do the deed That my own soul has to itself decreed."
>
> —John Keats, from "Sleep and Poetry"

Young Keats Keats was affected by death at an early age. When he was eight, his father died after falling from a horse; when he was fourteen, his mother died of tuberculosis. He took no special interest in literature until he was fifteen. With the encouragement of his mentor, Charles Cowden Clarke, Keats immersed himself in reading.

No sooner had Keats awakened to literature than he was pulled out of school by his practical-minded guardian and apprenticed to the pharmacist-surgeon Thomas Hammond, with whom Keats studied medicine. Keats continued to read and study with Clarke, however, and at age twenty-one Keats abandoned medicine for poetry.

The Soul's Decree Up to that time, Keats had written few poems—and certainly none of artistic importance. Then, after spending an entire night with Clarke reading from the poet George

Chapman's lively translation of Homer, Keats produced his first major poem: "On First Looking into Chapman's Homer." Leigh Hunt, a political radical, successful author, and friend of Keats's, published the poem and others by Keats in his journal, the *Examiner*. With Hunt's help, Keats found a publisher for his first book when he was only twenty-one. It sold poorly and received mixed reviews.

In the summer of 1818, Keats embarked on a walking tour of the northern British Isles. After slogging for days in pouring rain, he came down with the first symptoms of tuberculosis and returned to London. There he found that his brother Tom was gravely ill with the disease. Keats became Tom's devoted caregiver until Tom died that December. About the same time, Keats met and fell in love with Fanny Brawne. They became engaged, but their relationship was tormented by Keats's illness, poverty, and strict devotion to his work.

1819 came to be known as Keats's Great Year as a poet. Despite physical and emotional strain, Keats wrote the greatest works of his career: *The Eve of St. Agnes*, "La Belle Dame sans Merci," the great odes, and *Lamia*, among others. Within five years after he had begun writing poetry, Keats was a master. Nonetheless, time was running out. By the fall, Keats's tuberculosis made it impossible for him to sustain his creative momentum. In a desperate attempt to prolong his life, he sailed the next September for Italy. Just six months later, he died in Rome and was buried there. At his request, his marker bears no name—just this epitaph: "Here lies one whose name was writ in water."

 Literature Online

Author Search For more about John Keats, go to glencoe.com and enter QuickPass code GLB9817u4.

Selection Skills

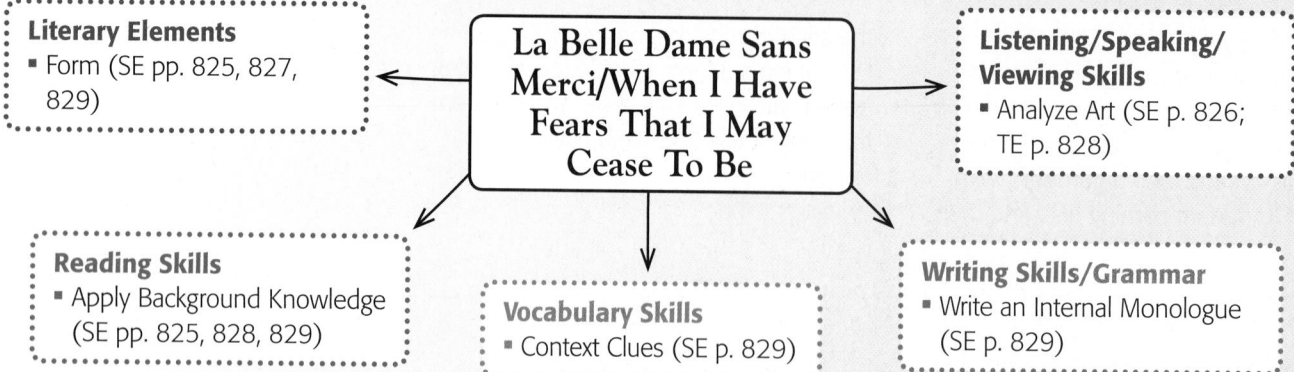

Literary Elements
- Form (SE pp. 825, 827, 829)

La Belle Dame Sans Merci/When I Have Fears That I May Cease To Be

Listening/Speaking/Viewing Skills
- Analyze Art (SE p. 826; TE p. 828)

Reading Skills
- Apply Background Knowledge (SE pp. 825, 828, 829)

Vocabulary Skills
- Context Clues (SE p. 829)

Writing Skills/Grammar
- Write an Internal Monologue (SE p. 829)

Literature and Reading Preview

Connect to the Poems

Do you ever worry that life is too short for you to fulfill all your aspirations? Freewrite for a few minutes about whether worries about time could help or hinder you in achieving your goals.

Build Background

Keats's letters reveal his evolving struggle with the problem of evil and suffering in the world and show his refusal to be comforted by religious absolutes or abstract philosophy. In a letter from 1817, he used the term "negative capability" to describe the necessity of the poet to be objective by restraining the urge to define and control his or her subject. In such instances, said Keats, "Beauty overcomes every other consideration."

Set Purposes for Reading

Big Idea **The Quest for Truth and Beauty**

As you read, ask yourself, How do the poems reflect the Romantic ideals of truth and beauty?

Literary Element **Form**

Form is the structure that governs a literary genre. "La Belle Dame sans Merci" ("The Beautiful Woman Without Pity") is a **ballad** (see page 200). "When I Have Fears That I May Cease to Be" is a **Shakespearean sonnet** (see page 243). As you read each poem, ask yourself, What clues can I find to this poem's form?

Reading Strategy **Apply Background Knowledge**

When you **apply background knowledge**, you use what you already know about an author to help you understand his or her writing. As you read, ask yourself, How does the information about Keats that I have read affect my reading?

....

Tip: Drawing Conclusions Use a graphic organizer to draw conclusions based on your background knowledge.

| Passage:
"When I have fears that I may cease to be /
Before my pen has gleaned my teeming brain" | **+** | Background:
When still young, Keats knew he didn't have long to live. His father, mother, and brother died during his lifetime. | **=** | Conclusion:
Despite his youth, it is understandable that Keats was obsessed with the subject of mortality. |

Learning Objectives

For pages 824–829

In studying these texts, you will focus on the following objectives:

Literary Study: Analyzing form.

Reading: Applying background knowledge.

Writing: Writing an interior monologue.

Vocabulary Preview

loitering (loiʹ tər ing) *adj.* standing or lingering idly about a place; p. 827 *The shop owner did not like people loitering around his entrance if they were not going to buy anything.*

glean (glēn) *v.* to collect slowly and carefully; gather crops left on a field after reaping; p. 828 *Although he sometimes thought his coursework was irrelevant, Jared had gleaned more useful knowledge than he realized.*

teeming (tēʹ ming) *adj.* full; at the point of overflowing; p. 828 *The teeming river was in danger of flooding the town.*

Before You Read

Focus

Summary

"La Belle Dame sans Merci" is a ballad about a knight who has succumbed to a beautiful woman who has no pity on him. He is enchanted by her and will not leave the eerie place even "Though the sedge is wither'd from the lake,/And no birds sing."

"When I Have Fears That I May Cease to Be" is a sonnet about the things the speaker might never live to experience.

> For summaries in languages other than English, see Unit 4 Teaching Resources, pp. 213–218.

Vocabulary

Context Have students use magazines, newspapers, and Internet sources to find sentences containing the vocabulary words. Ask them to explain for each example why the vocabulary word is appropriate in its context.

English Learners

DIFFERENTIATED INSTRUCTION

Intermediate Have students prepare a one-paragraph summary of either "La Belle Dame sans Merci" or "When I Have Fears That I May Cease to Be." Then have students exchange summaries with other students to discuss the meaning of the poems.

Advanced Say: Keats is famous for the intense emotion conveyed by his language. Have students identify three words or phrases in each poem that seem especially effective in conveying a mood.

(Answers "La Belle Dame sans Merci": "haggard," "woe-begone," and "lulled"; "When I Have Fears That I May Cease To Be": "fears," "relish," "cease," and "nothingness")

Teach

<u>View the Art</u> ★

Answer: *Some students may note that the woman seems to be about to abandon the knight or leave him behind.*

Walter Crane (1845–1915) is best known for his paintings of literary scenes, including a series of drawings depicting scenes from Tennyson's "The Lady of Shalott." **Ask:** How would you describe the woman in the painting? *(Possible response: She is beautiful and enchanting. She seems powerful and linked with nature.)* What effect does she seem to have on the knight? *(Possible response: She has somehow stripped him of his power.)*

La Belle Dame sans Merci

John Keats

La Belle Dame Sans Merci, 1865. Walter Crane. Private collection.

<u>View the Art</u> Keats's poem and this painting share a name with a fourteenth-century French poem about a rejected suitor. What in this image suggests that the beautiful lady is "sans merci"—without mercy?

Listening and Speaking Practice

Oral Performance
Divide students into pairs. One student should take the role of the person interrogating the knight, and the other student should take the role of the knight as he responds to the inquiry. Allow students time to practice their oral readings. Encourage students to use varying tone, pitch, volume, and speed to highlight emotions. Allow students time to present their oral performances to the class. As students listen, have them record comments about the reading. Remind listeners to provide constructive comments for their classmates.

O what can ail thee, knight-at-arms,
    Alone and palely **loitering**?
The sedge[1] has wither'd from the lake,
    And no birds sing.

5 O what can ail thee, knight-at-arms,
    So haggard, and so woe-begone?
The squirrel's granary[2] is full,
    And the harvest's done.

    I see a lily on thy brow,
10   With anguish moist and fever dew,
And on thy cheeks a fading rose
    Fast withereth too.

I met a lady in the meads,[3]
    Full beautiful—a fairy's child,
15 Her hair was long, her foot was light,
    And her eyes were wild.

I made a garland for her head,
    And bracelets too, and fragrant zone;[4]
She look'd at me as she did love,
20   And made sweet moan.

I set her on my pacing steed,
    And nothing else saw all day long,
For sidelong would she bend and sing
    A fairy's song.

25 She found me roots of relish sweet,
    And honey wild, and manna dew,[5]
And sure in language strange she said
    "I love thee true."

She took me to her elfin grot,[6]
30   And there she wept and sigh'd full sore,
And there I shut her wild wild eyes
    With kisses four.

And there she lulled me asleep,
    And there I dream'd—Ah! woe betide!
35 The latest[7] dream I ever dream'd
    On the cold hill side.

I saw pale kings and princes too,
    Pale warriors, death-pale were they all;
They cried, "La Belle Dame sans Merci
40   Hath thee in thrall!"[8]

I saw their starved lips in the gloam,[9]
    With horrid warning gaped wide,
And I awoke, and found me here,
    On the cold hill's side.

45 And this is why I sojourn[10] here,
    Alone and palely loitering,
Though the sedge is wither'd from the lake,
    And no birds sing.

---

1. *Sedge* refers to reedy, grasslike plants often found on wet ground or in water.
2. A *granary* is a place for storing grain.
3. *Meads* means "meadowlands."
4. *Zone* is an old-fashioned term for a belt or girdle.
5. *Manna dew* is the sweet juice from the European ash tree and certain other plants. According to Exodus 16:13–36, *manna* is also the food that God miraculously provided for the Israelites.
6. *Grot* means "cave" or "grotto."
7. *Latest* here means "last."
8. *In thrall* means "enslaved."
9. *Gloam* means "twilight."
10. A *sojourn* is a visit or temporary stay.

 Form *What makes lines 9–12 a ballad stanza? How does it deviate from the traditional ballad form?*

Vocabulary

loitering (loi´ tər ing) *adj.* standing or lingering idly about a place

The Quest for Truth and Beauty *How does the plight of the knight-at-arms reflect the Romantic quest for beauty?*

JOHN KEATS **827**

Literary Element   1

Form Answer: *The stanza is a quatrain, and only the second and fourth lines rhyme. Also, the first and third lines are iambic with four stressed syllables. The stanza deviates from the traditional form in that the second line has four stressed syllables instead of three and the fourth line is not iambic.* **Say:** Paraphrase the description given in these lines. (*I see your brow is moist and you have lost all color in your face.*)

> For additional literary element practice, see Unit 4 Teaching Resources Book, p. 219.

Big Idea   2

The Quest for Truth and Beauty Answer: *The knight "sojourns" and "loiters" by the lakeside because he has been entranced by a beautiful, elusive lady he fell in love with. His love is tragic because his quest for beauty has led to his enslavement. Keats is stressing the Romantic idea that the search for beauty, in art and in life, can be intoxicating and obsessive.*

(APPROACHING) For approaching-level students, **ask:** How does the knight learn the true nature of his situation? (*Former lovers of the lady appear to him in a dream.*)

Approaching Level

DIFFERENTIATED INSTRUCTION

Emerging Tell approaching-level students before they read that the poem is a narrative ballad. The major part of "La Belle Dame sans Merci" is told in a flashback, describing things that happened in the past as if they are happening now. One way to clarify content is to reorder the events on a timeline. Have students pause frequently to identify the main events of a stanza and place a summary of the action in the proper place on the time line. (*The main action of the flashback begins in the fourth stanza. All events following precede the action in the first three stanzas, namely the speaker asking the knight what happened.*)

Teach

Reading Strategy   1

Apply Background Knowledge **Answer:** *The speaker is afraid of dying before he has fulfilled his romantic relationship with the woman he loves. Students should point out that Keats's fatal illness and difficult relationship with Fanny Brawne might help explain this fear.*

 For additional practice using the reading skill or strategy, see Unit 4 Teaching Resources Book, p. 220.

View the Art ★

While a successful portrait painter, Welsh artist Richard Wilson (1713–1782) gained fame through his landscape paintings, which exerted a strong influence on subsequent landscape painting in England. *On Hounslow Heath* exemplifies a new type of landscape view, designed to bring a vision of a rural idyll into the city dweller's home.

On Hounslow Heath, exhibited 1770. Richard Wilson. Oil on canvas, 425 x 527 cm. Tate Gallery, London.

WHEN I HAVE FEARS THAT I MAY CEASE TO BE

John Keats

When I have fears that I may cease to be
    Before my pen has **gleaned** my **teeming** brain,
Before high-piled books, in charactery,[1]
    Hold like rich garners[2] the full-ripened grain;
5 When I behold, upon the night's starred face,
    Huge cloudy symbols of a high romance,
And think that I may never live to trace
    Their shadows, with the magic hand of chance;
And when I feel, fair creature of an hour,
10   That I shall never look upon thee more,
Never have relish in the fairy power
    Of unreflecting love—then on the shore
Of the wide world I stand alone, and think
Till love and fame to nothingness do sink.

---

1. *Charactery* means "characters" or "symbols"—in other words, letters of the alphabet.
2. *Garners* are storehouses for grain.

 Apply Background Knowledge *What is the speaker afraid of losing here? How does your background knowledge help you interpret these lines?*

Vocabulary

glean (glēn) *v.* to collect slowly and carefully; gather crops left on a field after reaping
teeming (tē´ ming) *adj.* full; at the point of overflowing

Writing Practice

SPIRAL REVIEW **Reflective Journal Entry Say:** In his poem, Keats makes it clear that his major goal in life is to achieve success as a writer. This goal causes him anxiety because he is afraid he will die before attaining it. Have students write a brief reflective journal entry about a major goal that they have for themselves. In their journals, ask them not only to define their goal and explain its significance to them, but also to consider how this goal makes them feel—apprehensive? Determined? After they have written their journals, have a discussion comparing their viewpoints to that of Keats's poem.

After You Read

Respond and Think Critically

Respond and Interpret

1. (a)Which poem did you prefer? (b)What did this poem leave you thinking or wondering?

2. (a)In "La Belle Dame sans Merci," what does the speaker ask the knight-at-arms in the first two stanzas? (b)How does the time of year reflect the knight's physical and emotional state?

3. (a)Summarize the speaker's main fears in "When I Have Fears . . ." (b)What do these fears reveal about the speaker's values and goals?

Analyze and Evaluate

4. How do you interpret the knight's dream in "La Belle Dame sans Merci"?

5. (a)What happens to the speaker's fears in "When I Have Fears . . ."? (b)What tone is established in the concluding couplet?

Connect

6. **Big Idea** **The Quest for Truth and Beauty** (a)How does "La Belle Dame sans Merci" exemplify the Romantic quest for beauty? (b)How does "When I Have Fears . . ." exemplify the Romantic quest for truth?

7. **Connect to the Author** Reread Keats's epitaph on page 824. In what ways does this demonstrate the same feelings seen in his poems? In your opinion, is the epitaph true?

Literary Element Form

The **forms** of "La Belle Dame sans Merci" and "When I Have Fears . . ." contribute to the meaning of the poems.

1. (a)How is the ballad form appropriate to the subject and theme of "La Belle Dame sans Merci"? (b)How do the first and last stanzas contribute to the poem?

2. (a)In "When I Have Fears . . .," what is the focus of each quatrain? (b)How does the final couplet resolve the issues in the three quatrains?

Writing

Write an Internal Monologue Write an internal monologue from the perspective of the speaker in "La Belle Dame sans Merci." What does he or she think about the knight-at-arms's story? Does the speaker have sympathy for the suffering knight, or find him mostly foolish? Include the speaker's reactions to other details.

 **Literature** Online

Selection Resources For Selection Quizzes, eFlashcards, and Reading-Writing Connection activities, go to glencoe.com and enter QuickPass code GLB9817u4.

Reading Strategy Apply Background Knowledge

Use your background knowledge about Keats to answer the following questions.

1. How does the sonnet "When I Have Fears . . ." illustrate Keats's principle of negative capability?

2. What aspect of Keats's life is it possible to see in "La Belle Dame sans Merci"?

Vocabulary Practice

Practice with Context Clues Look back at pages 827–828 to find context clues for the vocabulary words below. Record your findings in a chart like the one here.

loitering   glean   teeming

EXAMPLE:

Word: loitering	
Textual Clues: The knight is "sojourning" on the hill, seemingly unsure of what to do next.	
Meaning: standing or lingering idly about a place	

JOHN KEATS **829**

After You Read

Assess

1. Responses will vary.

2. (a) What ails the knight and why he is alone (b) The knight is lethargic and despondent—emotions associated with winter.

3. (a) He will die before he can fulfill his potential, experience love, and know the joy of commitment. (b) He values fame and love.

4. He appears to be under the power of the enchantress.

5. (a) They lead to the conclusion that love and fame will disappear. (b) Despair

6. (a) The knight risks enchantment by pursuing beauty. (b) The speaker arrives at truth: that the certainty of death makes all endeavors futile.

7. Keats's epitaph suggested that he felt both his life and his fame were fleeting. Students may say that his brief life and constant poverty were an illustration of this; others may say that his enduring fame after his death shows the epitaph to be false.

Literary Element

1. (a) It suits the Romantic subject. (b) The call and response effect gives the narrative closure.

2. (a) First quatrain: a lament that he will not fulfill his literary potential. Second: a lament that mortality will keep him from writing a romance. Third: regret that death will end his relationship. (b) The speaker consigns fame and love to oblivion.

Reading Strategy

1. Keats does not minimize his fears by "reaching after fact and reason."

2. Keats is the knight on a quest.

 For additional assessment, see Assessment Resources, pp. 207–208.

Vocabulary Practice

Word: glean
Textual Clues: The speaker wants to "stand alone, and think," to carefully collect knowledge for his writing.
Meaning: to collect carefully

Word: teeming
Textual Clues: The speaker fears that there is too much in the world to write down before he dies.
Meaning: full

Focus

Summary

In "Ode on a Grecian Urn," Keats contrasts the relative permanence of art with the brevity of human life.

 For summaries in languages other than English, see Unit 4 Teaching Resources Book, pp. 224–229.

Vocabulary

Word Origins Have students use a dictionary to find the etymology of the following words: **deities, desolate, sylvan, sacrifice.** For each word, ask them to find another word that shares its root. (*deities: Latin deus (god), deism; desolate: Latin solus (alone), isolate; sylvan: Latin silva (forest), Pennsylvania; sacrifice: Latin sacer (holy), sacred*)

Ode on a Grecian Urn

Connect to the Poem

How can you capture a moment in time? In a journal entry, try to capture the current moment in as much detail as possible.

Build Background

The artistic tradition of ancient Greek painted pottery can be traced to the city of Corinth in the seventh century B.C. In Athens, pottery painters began to include narrative scenes based on Greek mythology. In Keats's day, excavations in the Mediterranean region uncovered many Greek urns, sparking interest throughout Europe in all things classical. "Ode on a Grecian Urn" may have been inspired by such an urn.

Set Purposes for Reading

Big Idea **The Quest for Truth and Beauty**

As you read, ask yourself, How does Keats find the Romantic ideals of truth and beauty in the Grecian urn?

Literary Element **Ode**

An **ode** is a long, serious lyric poem that is elevated in tone and style. Some odes celebrate a person, quality, or object; others are private meditations. Nearly all feature **apostrophe**, a figure of speech in which an idea, inanimate object, or absent person is directly addressed. As you read, ask yourself, How does Keats address the Grecian urn and the figures on it?

Reading Strategy Analyze Parallelism

Parallelism is the repetition of words, phrases, or sentences that have the same grammatical form. Parallelism in a poem can help create rhythm, call attention to an idea, or balance different ideas. As you read, ask yourself, How does parallelism help Keats express the themes or images in his poem?

Tip: Taking Notes Use a chart to note instances of parallelism.

Example	Effect
Ah happy, happy boughs!" (line 21) and "more happy, happy love!" (line 25)	emphasizes the mood of the figures on the urn

---

Learning Objectives

For pages 830–834

In studying this text, you will focus on the following objectives:

Literary Study: Analyzing an ode.

Reading: Analyzing parallelism.

Research: Connecting literature to science and math.

Vocabulary Preview

deities (dē′ ə tēz) *n.* gods or goddesses; divinities; p. 831 *The streets downtown are named after ancient Greek and Roman deities.*

desolate (des′ ə lit) *adj.* destitute of inhabitants; deserted; p. 832 *After the hurricane, John returned to find his hometown desolate.*

Selection Skills

Literary Elements
- Ode (SE pp. 830–833)
- Rhetorical Devices (SE p. 833)

Vocabulary Skills
- Word Origins (SE p. 834)
- Academic Vocabulary (SE p. 834)

Ode on a Grecian Urn

Study Skills/Research/Assessment
- Internet Connection (SE p. 834)
- Research Artifacts (TE p. 832)

Reading Skills
- Analyze Parallelism (SE p. 830–834)

Ode on a Grecian Urn

John Keats

1

Thou still unravished bride of quietness,
    Thou foster child of silence and slow time,
Sylvan° historian, who canst thus express
    A flowery tale more sweetly than our rhyme:
5 What leaf-fringed legend haunts about° thy shape
    Of **deities** or mortals, or of both,
      In Tempe° or the dales of Arcady?°
What men or gods are these? What maidens loath?°
    What mad pursuit? What struggle to escape?
10   What pipes and timbrels?° What wild ecstasy?

2

Heard melodies are sweet, but those unheard
    Are sweeter; therefore, ye soft pipes, play on;
Not to the sensual° ear, but, more endeared,
    Pipe to the spirit ditties° of no tone:
15 Fair youth, beneath the trees, thou canst not leave
    Thy song, nor ever can those trees be bare;
      Bold Lover, never, never canst thou kiss,
Though winning near the goal—yet, do not grieve;
    She cannot fade, though thou hast not thy bliss,
20   Forever wilt thou love, and she be fair!

---

3 Sylvan: of the woods.

5 haunts about: surrounds.

7 Tempe: a beautiful valley in Arcadia. **Arcady:** Arcadia, a mountainous region in Greece, traditionally considered an ideal rustic landscape.
8 loath: reluctant.
10 timbrels: ancient percussion instruments similar to tambourines.

13 sensual: physical; bodily.
14 ditties: short, simple songs.

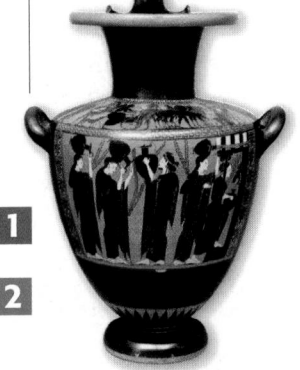

Women carrying water, 6th century B.C. Black figure Attic hydria from Vulci.

Ode *To whom does "Thou" refer? What figure of speech common to odes is Keats using in the first two lines of the poem?*   **1**

Analyze Parallelism *What lines are parallel in this part of stanza 2? What is their effect on the meaning of the stanza?*   **2**

Vocabulary

deities (dē′ ə tēz) *n.* gods or goddesses; divinities

JOHN KEATS **831**

Teach

Literary Element **1**

Ode **Answer:** *"Thou" refers to the urn. Keats uses apostrophe, a figure of speech in which the speaker directly addresses an inanimate object.*

(ADVANCED) For advanced students, **ask:** Why do you think Keats chose to address a poem to a Grecian urn? *(Answers will vary. Students may note that these urns, like poems, tell stories; also, that the urn serves as a reminder of the ancient origins of art.)*

Reading Strategy **2**

Analyze Parallelism
Answer: *Lines 11–29 contain parallelism with the repetition of the grammatical structure: adjective, noun, verb, predicate adjective. These lines emphasize imagination over reality.*

View the Art ★

The urn is identified as an Attic hydria from Vulci. The word *Attic* refers to its Grecian origin. A hydria is a type of vase that was used to carry water. Vulci was an Etruscan city located about 50 miles northwest of Rome. Notice the images of hydrias in the painting on this hydria.

Interactive Read and Write

Other options for teaching this selection can be found in

- Interactive Read and Write for EL Students, pp. 213–222
- Interactive Read and Write for Approaching-Level Students, pp. 213–222
- Interactive Read and Write for On-Level Students, pp. 213–222

Approaching Level

DIFFERENTIATED INSTRUCTION

AAVE The use of the verb *to be* after interrogatives like *who* or *what* can be an issue for approaching-level students who use African American Vernacular English (AAVE). **Write** the following questions on the board: Who are these men? What is this mad pursuit? What are these pipes? **Say:** Standard American English includes forms of *to be,* such as *is* and *are,* in questions beginning with *who* or *what.* For each of the examples, have students write three sentences following the same pattern.

831

Big Idea 1

The Quest for Truth and Beauty **Answer:** *Romantic idealists did not believe that truth or beauty could be discovered and appreciated through analysis. Instead, they believed in a grand synthesis uniting truth and beauty in an eternal, transcendental realm. For Keats and other Romantics, great art was a vehicle for reaching a transcendental state that is perfect, timeless, and immune to the disappointments and decay of the natural world.*

To check students' understanding of the selection, see Unit 4 Teaching Resources Book, p. 233.

3

Ah, happy, happy boughs! that cannot shed
    Your leaves, nor ever bid the Spring adieu;
And, happy melodist, unwearied,
    Forever piping songs forever new;
25 More happy love! more happy, happy love!
    Forever warm and still to be enjoyed,
      Forever panting, and forever young;
All breathing human passion far above,
    That leaves a heart high-sorrowful and cloyed,°
30   A burning forehead, and a parching tongue.

4

Who are these coming to the sacrifice?
    To what green altar, O mysterious priest,
Lead'st thou that heifer lowing at the skies,
    And all her silken flanks with garlands dressed?
35 What little town by river or seashore,
    Or mountain-built with peaceful citadel,°
      Is emptied of this folk, this pious morn?
And, little town, thy streets forevermore
    Will silent be; and not a soul to tell
40   Why thou art **desolate,** can e'er return.

5

O Attic° shape! Fair attitude! with brede°
    Of marble men and maidens overwrought,°
With forest branches and the trodden weed;
    Thou, silent form, dost tease us out of thought
45 As doth eternity: Cold Pastoral!°
    When old age shall this generation waste,
      Thou shalt remain, in midst of other woe
Than ours, a friend to man, to whom thou say'st,
    "Beauty is truth, truth beauty"—that is all
50   Ye know on earth, and all ye need to know.

29 cloyed: oversatisfied; burdened by excess.

36 citadel: fortress.

41 Attic: in the simple, graceful style characteristic of Attica, the region of Greece where Athens was located. **brede:** an interwoven or braided design.
42 overwrought: decorated.
45 Pastoral: a work depicting the life of shepherds, or simple rural life in general.

---

1 **The Quest for Truth and Beauty** *How does Keats's equation of truth and beauty represent a principle of Romantic idealism?*

> **Vocabulary**
>
> **desolate** (des′ ə lit) *adj.* destitute of inhabitants; deserted

832 UNIT 4 THE TRIUMPH OF ROMANTICISM

Research Practice

SPIRAL REVIEW **Research Artifacts** Explain to students that Grecian urns are cultural artifacts from ancient Greece. The artwork on the urns tells much about the lives and beliefs of the ancient Greeks. Have students conduct research on ancient Greek urns. Suggest muse-ums' Web sites or the print resources to learn more about the urns and the decorative artwork. Have students write brief essays about what they learned of ancient Greece from their research on this particular art form. Allow students to present their essays to the class.

After You Read

Respond and Think Critically

Respond and Interpret

1. What images of the Grecian urn do you find most striking? Explain.

2. (a)What metaphors does the speaker use to describe the urn in lines 1–3? (b)What do the metaphors reveal about the speaker's view of the urn?

3. Why might an "unheard" melody be sweeter than a "heard melody" (see lines 11–12)?

4. (a)What people and things does the speaker address in the second and third stanzas? (b)Why does the speaker envy them? Cite evidence from the poem.

Analyze and Evaluate

5. An oxymoron is a figure of speech in which contradictory ideas are combined for effect, as in the phrase "wise fool." Explain the oxymoron in the final stanza. What is its effect?

Connect

6. **Big Idea** **The Quest for Truth and Beauty** How have later artists and thinkers reacted to the Romantic idealism of Keats's identification of truth with beauty?

7. **Connect to the Author** Why do you think Keats found comfort and solace by contemplating the figures painted on the urn? What can you infer about Keats's views concerning the purpose of art?

Literary Element · Ode

A **Horatian ode**, named for the Roman poet Horace, has a regular pattern of stanzas and a rhyme scheme. "Ode on a Grecian Urn" is considered a Horatian ode. Keats believed that the poet should subordinate his own identity in order to enable the ode's subject to emerge fully. He called this quality "negative capability."

1. (a)What are the structure and rhyme scheme of "Ode on a Grecian Urn"? (b)How does Keats create variations on the form?

2. How does Keats achieve negative capability in "Ode on a Grecian Urn"?

Review: Rhetorical Devices

In addition to parallelism, poets often use **rhetorical devices,** such as exclamation and rhetorical questions, to enhance the meaning or emotional qualities of their poems. With a partner, complete a chart of the other rhetorical devices Keats uses in "Ode on a Grecian Urn," and their effects. You may want to use the chart below as a model.

Example	Device	Effect
"What men or gods are these?" (line 8)	rhetorical question	emphasizes the speaker's thoughts about the figures on the urn

JOHN KEATS **833**

After You Read

Assess

1. Responses will vary.

2. (a) "Unravished bride of quietness," "foster child of silence and slow time," and "Sylvan historian" (b) He admires its beauty.

3. It is perfect music in the "mind's ear," as opposed to audible music that is often imperfect.

4. (a) Fair youth, a bold lover, a melodist, pipes, and boughs (b) Time does not affect them.

5. *Pastoral* suggests a warm country scene. *Cold* means "lacking emotion." The images on the urn depict love and religion. However, the painted figures are "cold" because they are not living beings. The effect is to contrast art and human experience.

6. Realist and Naturalist writers denied that truth is always beautiful.

7. The figures belong to an imagined world beyond time and death. The purpose of art is to raise humans above transient pleasures and concentrate their attention on ideal beauty.

 For additional assessment, see Assessment Resources, pp. 209–210.

Literary Element

1. (a) The structure consists of five sections of ten lines each. The first four lines rhyme *abab*. The last six rhyme *cdecde* or a variation of that pattern. (b) The rhyme scheme of the last six lines of each stanza varies.

2. Keats explores his theme without referring to himself.

Progress Check

Can students identify an ode?

If No → See Unit 4 Teaching Resources Book, p. 230.

Review: Rhetorical Devices

Students' charts should identify rhetorical devices that Keats uses in the ode as well as the effect caused by those devices.

After You Read

Assess

Reading Strategy

1. *Forever* emphasizes the eternal state of the figures painted on the urn.
2. Students should provide correct examples of parallelism and explain why they are effective.

Vocabulary Practice

Etymology of *deities*: Latin *deus* means "god"

Etymology of *desolate*: Latin *solus* means "alone"

Sample sentences will vary.

Academic Vocabulary

The context suggests that *derived* means "originated from."

Internet Connection

Students' reports should be based on independent research. Students should have written outlines to support their reasoning and conclusion as well as an MLA style bibliography.

Reading Strategy — Parallelism

In poetry, **rhetorical devices** such as **parallelism** can enhance the lyric quality and the sound of a poem, especially when it is read aloud.

1. Explain the use of parallelism in stanza 3 and describe its effect.
2. Review the chart of examples you filled in as you read. Which examples were the most effective at expressing one of Keats's ideas, and why?

Vocabulary Practice

Practice with Word Origins Create a word map, like the one below, for each of these vocabulary words from the selection. Use a dictionary for help.

deities   desolate

EXAMPLE:

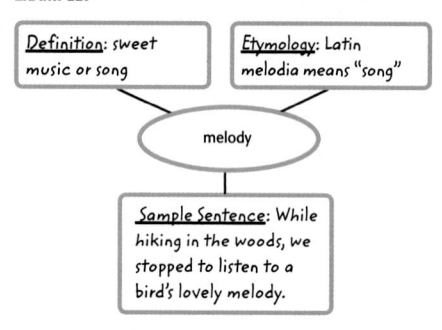

Academic Vocabulary

Keats **derived** the epigram "Beauty is truth, truth beauty" from his meditation on a Grecian urn.

Derive is an academic word. For example, a chemist might **derive** a new drug from the bark of a tree.

Using context clues, try to figure out the meaning of *derived* in the following sentence: *The modern word* poem *is* **derived** *from the ancient Greek word* poema.

For more on academic vocabulary, see pages 56 and R81.

Internet Connection

Connect to *Science* and *Math*

Assignment Keats discovered the essence of truth and beauty in an ancient Grecian urn. Scientists use more qualitative methods to examine and learn from the past. Report on the techniques archaeologists use to determine the age of artifacts such as ancient pottery.

Investigate Develop questions to guide your research and look for answers on the Internet. Check the reliability of the Web site before using the information. The site should be sponsored by a reputable organization (.edu and .gov sites are usually reliable sources). The author should be a recognized authority, and the information should have been recently updated. Bookmark each Web site you use in case you have to return to it.

Make an outline to organize the material you gather, quoting material accurately and citing the source of each fact or opinion. Look up any unfamiliar technical terms in the dictionary and include the definitions in your report.

EXAMPLE:
Methods of Dating Ancient Artifacts
I. *Potassium-argon*
II. *Radiocarbon*

Create To avoid plagiarizing, restate material in your own words and indicate the source of each fact in the body of your report. Compile a complete bibliography of your sources in appropriate MLA style at the end. Include visual aids, such as charts, computer graphics, photographs or sketches of artifacts or equipment, to give your report depth and interest. If possible, create a PowerPoint presentation or a slide show incorporating your visual aids.

Report Present your material in a logical sequence, integrating information from various sources logically and seamlessly. Include the definitions of technical terms your audience may not be familiar with. If you are using PowerPoint or another computer program, be sure that it ties in logically with what you are saying.

Reading Practice

SPIRAL REVIEW **Theme Say:** The main argument of Keats's poem depends on the idea that works of art have the same meaning to audiences in different historical periods. **Ask:** What claims does Keats make that depend on this idea? (*His interpretation of the scene; the emphasis on the eternity of the figures; "beauty is truth, truth beauty."*) Do you agree with Keats's argument? Why or why not? (*Answers will vary. Students may believe that works like the Odyssey or Greek statues have survived because they speak to successive generations. Or they may use Keats's poem itself as an example of an artwork that has changed in meaning from the time of its composition.*)

Comparing Literature
Across Time and Place

Compare Literature about Nature

The cyclical nature of the seasons inspires the three works compared here—an English Romantic poem, a series of Japanese haiku, and a memoir by a contemporary American writer. Together, they show an awareness of how a few small details in nature can lead to broader reflections on life.

COMPARE THE `Big Idea` **The Quest for Truth and Beauty**

Poets from around the world have conveyed a sense of rapture and ecstasy in exploring natural beauty. They have found transcendent power in small details, often drawing connections between humanity and the weather, the animal kingdom, and physical landscapes. As you read, ask yourself, How do the authors of these selections derive human significance from nature?

COMPARE Nature Imagery

Scenes from nature can focus on the energetic and colorful, or the bleak and unforgiving. As you read, ask yourself, How do the images, or word pictures, that describe concrete sensory details in nature also function as springboards to larger meanings in these selections by Keats, Bashō, and Dillard?

COMPARE Literary Traditions

Nature has been the theme and inspiration for works throughout history.
It provides a dramatic backdrop to evaluate the place of humans in the world. As civilization becomes more technological and urban, writers continue to explore the way nature coexists and contrasts with these developments. As you read, ask yourself, How do the authors of these selections find inspiration in nature?

Smithsonian American Art Museum, Washington, DC.

LOG ON ▶ **Literature** Online

Author Search For more about John Keats, Matsuo Bashō, and Annie Dillard, go to glencoe.com and enter QuickPass code GLB9817u4.

COMPARING LITERATURE **835**

Focus

Bellringer Options

Selection Focus Transparency 42
Daily Language Practice Transparency 69

Or **display** pictures of landscapes that reflect distinct differences between spring, summer, fall, and winter. Challenge students to think about the seasons and write down three specific details about each. The details might appeal to one or more of the five senses, or they might involve the thoughts, feelings, or moods prompted by the season.

Connect to the Reading Selections

Review some of the details most commonly provided by students in the Bellringer activity. Discuss whether and how one or more of them might lead to broader reflections on life.

Learning Objectives

For pages 835–845

In studying these texts, you will focus on the following objectives:

Literary Study: Comparing themes.

Reading: Analyzing sound devices.

Writing: Writing a poem.

Selection Skills

Literary Elements
- Imagery (SE pp. 836, 838, 839)

Comparing Literature

Listening/Speaking/ Viewing Skills
- Oral Presentation (SE p. 845)

Reading Skills
- Analyze Sound Devices (SE pp. 836, 838, 839)

Vocabulary Skills
- Word Usage (SE p. 839)
- Etymology (TE p. 836)

Writing Skills/Grammar
- Write a Poem (SE p. 839)
- Quickwrite (SE pp. 841, 844)
- Compare Imagery (SE p. 845)

Before You Read

Focus

Summary

The poem opens with images of ripening fruit and late-blooming flowers that describe early autumn before the harvest. Keats then presents several images suggesting that autumn is the season for harvesting nature's plenty. The last line of the poem evokes the approach of winter.

 For summaries in languages other than English, see Unit 4 Teaching Resources Book, pp. 237–241.

Vocabulary

Etymology Have students look up the etymology of each vocabulary word in a dictionary.

Ask: Which word has changed the most over time? *(furrow)*

Before You Read

To Autumn

Connect to the Poem

Do certain seasons inspire certain moods? Freewrite for a few minutes about the way you might feel during the first few days of spring after a long, cold winter.

Build Background

Keats wrote "To Autumn" in September 1819, after a walk on which he saw fields of stubble that looked "warm" to him.

Set Purposes for Reading

Big Idea **The Quest for Truth and Beauty**

As you read, ask yourself, How does this poem reflect the Romantic focus on the beauty of the natural world?

Literary Element **Imagery**

Writers create **imagery**, or word pictures, to evoke an emotional response in readers. As you read "To Autumn," ask yourself, What vivid images and sensory details does Keats present?

Reading Strategy **Analyze Sound Devices**

When you **analyze sound devices**, you examine devices that appeal to the ear in order to better understand a poem. **Assonance** is a sound device in which a vowel sound is repeated. **Consonance** is a repetition of consonant sounds, typically at the end of nonrhyming words. **Alliteration** is a repetition of consonant sounds at the beginnings of words. **Onomatopoeia** is the use of a word or phrase to imitate or suggest the sound of what it describes. As you read, ask yourself, What different effects does Keats employ in the poem?

Tip: Determining Patterns Organize your findings in a chart.

Sound Device	Examples
Assonance	line 7: "the hazel shells"
Consonance	
Alliteration	
Onomatopoeia	

Vocabulary Preview

conspiring (kən spī′ ring) *adj.* planning or plotting secretly; p. 837 *Maria saw her brothers whispering behind the shed, and she knew they were conspiring against her.*

furrow (fur′ ō) *n.* a long, narrow trench in the ground made by a plow; rut, groove, or wrinkle; p. 838 *When my father is in a serious mood, a deep furrow lines his forehead.*

836 UNIT 4 THE TRIUMPH OF ROMANTICISM

Reading Practice

SPIRAL REVIEW **Preread** Have students scan the three selections they will read, and note the form of each. Have them make observations about genre based on how each selection looks on the page. For example, "To Autumn" is a poem divided into three similar stanzas. Then have students compare the titles of the selections.

Ask: Are any of these titles similar? *("To Autumn" and "Haiku for Four Seasons" both have to do with seasons.)*

An Autumn Lane. Edward W. Waite. Burlington Paintings, London.

View the Art Like Keats in his ode "To Autumn," Waite incorporates color, texture, and light in his visual portrayal of autumn. What is the mood of this image? What details contribute to that mood?

To Autumn

John Keats

1

Season of mists and mellow fruitfulness,
    Close bosom-friend of the maturing sun;
Conspiring with him how to load and bless
    With fruit the vines that round the thatch-eaves run;
5 To bend with apples the mossed cottage-trees,
    And fill all fruit with ripeness to the core;
      To swell the gourd, and plump the hazel shells
    With a sweet kernel; to set budding more,
    And still more, later flowers for the bees,
10   Until they think warm days will never cease,
      For Summer has o'er-brimmed their clammy cells. **1**

> **Vocabulary**
>
> **conspiring** (kən spī′ ring) *adj.* planning or plotting secretly

English Learners

DIFFERENTIATED INSTRUCTION

Advanced The first stanza is one incomplete sentence. Its structure is "Season of mists, conspiring with [the sun] how to load and bless [vines], to bend [trees] and fill [fruit], to swell [gourd] and plump [shells], to set budding [flowers], until [bees] think [warm days will never cease], for Summer has o'er-brimmed [cells]." A similar sentence might be "Teenaged girl, friend of my sister, discussing with her

how to do their homework, to study their notes, to set out food for her pets." There is no verb here. Point out to students that changing *conspiring* to *conspires* would make a complete sentence.

Have students form a similar incomplete sentence of their own.

Teach

Reading Strategy   1

Clarify Meaning Explain to students that *o'er-brimmed* means "overfilled." **Ask:** In this line, what does *their* refer to? *(the bees)* What are the "cells"? *(the chambers in the honeycomb)* What does *clammy* mean? *(cool and damp)*

> For additional practice using the reading skill or strategy, see Unit 4 Teaching Resources Book, p. 243.

View the Art

Answer: *Most students will say that the mood is peaceful, warm, and comforting. The bright colors, combined with the two figures in the distance, the image of a home on the left, and the bright, calm sky contribute to this mood.*

Have students compare Edward Waite's *An Autumn Lane* with Keats's poem. **Ask:** In your opinion, are the artists celebrating the season or lamenting it? Do the figures in the painting represent desolation, or a oneness with nature? Have students rate autumn among all the seasons for beauty. Encourage them to provide reasons for their rankings, using Keats's claims as a gauge.

> For an audio recording of this selection, use Listening Library Audio CD-ROM.

Comparing Literature

Teach

Literary Element   1

Imagery Answer: *Keats personifies autumn as a worker, sleeping on a half-reaped row. He appeals to the senses of sight ("hook" and "the next swath with all its twinèd flowers") and smell ("fume of poppies").*

(ENGLISH LEARNERS) Have English learners read lines 15–19 one line at a time, identifying what sense or senses the imagery in each line appeals to. Clarify any words or phrases students have trouble understanding.

Reading Strategy   2

Analyze Sound Devices

Answer: *The word* oozings *is onomatopoeic, as it mimics the sound of something dripping slowly. The sound and repetition of* hours *combined with* oozings *suggests the slow, dripping action of the cider press described in the line above.*

2

Who hath not seen thee oft amid thy store?
    Sometimes whoever seeks abroad may find
Thee sitting careless on a granary[1] floor,
15   Thy hair soft-lifted by the winnowing[2] wind;
Or on a half-reaped **furrow** sound asleep,
    Drowsed with the fume of poppies, while thy hook[3]
      Spares the next swath[4] and all its twinèd flowers:
And sometimes like a gleaner[5] thou dost keep
20   Steady thy laden head across a brook;
    Or by a cider-press, with patient look,
      Thou watchest the last oozings, hours by hours.

3

Where are the songs of Spring? Ay, where are they?
    Think not of them, thou hast thy music, too—
25 While barred[6] clouds bloom the soft-dying day,
    And touch the stubble-plains with rosy hue;
Then in a wailful choir the small gnats mourn
    Among the river sallows,[7] borne aloft
      Or sinking as the light wind lives or dies;
30 And full-grown lambs loud bleat from hilly bourn;[8]
    Hedge crickets sing; and now with treble soft
    The redbreast whistles from a garden croft,[9]
      And gathering swallows twitter in the skies.

---

1. A *granary* is a storehouse for grain.
2. *Winnowing* is a process of separating wheat grain from chaff, or husks, by blowing away the chaff, which is lighter.
3. A *hook* is a curved blade used to cut grain.
4. A *swath* is a row or area of grain to be cut.
5. A *gleaner* is one who gathers grain left in the field by the reapers.
6. *Barred* means "streaked."
7. *Sallows* are low-growing willow trees.
8. *Bourn* means "region."
9. A *croft* is a small piece of enclosed land, often near a house.

1 Imagery *What image does Keats use here to describe autumn? Which senses does he appeal to?*

2 Analyze Sound Devices *How do the sound devices in these lines contribute to the poem?*

Vocabulary

furrow (fur′ō) *n.* a long, narrow trench in the ground made by a plow; rut, groove, or wrinkle

838 UNIT 4   THE TRIUMPH OF ROMANTICISM

Listening and Speaking Practice

SPIRAL REVIEW Sounds of Poetry Remind students that, unlike most prose, poetry depends on the sounds of words as well as the meanings and emotions expressed by the words. Have a student read the second stanza aloud. In addition to the sound devices mentioned in the Reading Strategy feature on page 836, have students discuss the effects of meter, word order, and rhyme on the listener.

After You Read

Respond and Think Critically

Respond and Interpret

1. Which images remain in your mind after reading the poem?

2. (a)In the first stanza, what have autumn and the sun conspired to do? (b)List examples of personification in the second stanza. (c)In what ways do these images differ from those in the first stanza?

3. (a)Cite three instances in which the spirit of autumn is personified as a farm girl. (b)What view of autumn does this personification suggest?

Analyze and Evaluate

4. (a)What are some of the descriptive details that help create a sense of abundance? (b)Why might Keats have used these images?

---

5. (a)What examples of imagery do you find in "To Autumn"? (b)What do these details contribute to your appreciation of the poem?

Connect

6. **Big Idea** **The Quest for Truth and Beauty** Keats wrote that "if poetry comes not as naturally as the leaves to a tree, it had better not come at all." In other words, human creations such as poetry should be modeled on the effortless beauty of nature. In your opinion, does "To Autumn" fulfill this Romantic ideal? Explain.

7. **Connect to the Author** Keats wrote this poem after being diagnosed with a fatal illness. Where in the poem does he seem to be addressing life? Death? Rebirth?

Literary Element Imagery

The **imagery**, or word pictures, a writer creates includes **sensory details** and **figurative language** that evoke an emotional response.

1. What types of figurative language does Keats use in "To Autumn"? Give examples from the text.

2. How does Keats's use of imagery match your expectations of a description of autumn? How is it different?

Writing

Write a Poem Keats uses sensory details and figurative language to create imagery appropriate to the season of autumn. Use these same literary devices—sensory details and imagery—to write your own poem on a different season.

> **LOG ON** **Literature** Online
>
> **Selection Resources** For Selection Quizzes, eFlashcards, and Reading-Writing Connection activities, go to glencoe.com and enter QuickPass code GLB9817u4.

Reading Strategy Analyze Sound Devices

Sound devices—such as alliteration, assonance, consonance, and onomatopoeia—are techniques used to appeal to the ear. Refer to the chart you made as you read, and answer these questions.

1. In the second stanza, which sound devices reinforce the image of autumn (as a farm girl) sleeping? Explain.

2. Line 24 responds to the question in line 23. How might the sound devices in line 24 contribute to the tone and meaning of the response?

Vocabulary Practice

Practice with Word Usage Respond to these statements to help you explore the meanings of vocabulary words from the selection.

1. Name a group of characters from literature or film who are **conspiring** to commit a crime.

2. Give an example of where you might find a **furrow**.

JOHN KEATS **839**

After You Read

Assess

1. Students' answers will vary.

2. (a) To load vines with fruit, to bend trees with apples, to ripen fruits and vegetables, and to cause late-blooming flowers to bud (b) "Sitting," "hair," "asleep," "gleaner," and "patient look." (c) They describe human acts, not nature.

3. (a) Autumn sits on the granary floor, sleeps in a furrow, and looks at the cider press. (b) An innocence or youthfulness.

4. (a) Bent apple trees, ripe fruit, budding flowers, overflowing beehives, full granaries, and cider presses. (b) To convey sights of early autumn

5. (a) ripened apples, swollen gourds, and plump hazel shells; poppies and cider press; "songs of Spring" and bleating lambs. (b) They make the description vivid.

6. The poem effortlessly conjures up images true to nature.

7. Keats addresses life, death, and rebirth in phrases such as "maturing sun," "wind lives or dies," and "soft-dying day."

Literary Element

1. Personification ("Thee sitting careless on a granary floor"), simile ("like a gleaner"), and metaphor ("barred clouds bloom")

2. Keats describes the abundance of harvest. Some of Keats's imagery—full of bursting and blooming—is often associated with spring.

Writing

Students' poems should focus on the imagery Keats used and how it appeals to the senses.

839

Reading Strategy

1. The repetition of *s* sounds (alliteration and consonance), such as "sitting careless," and "sound asleep," creates a sibilance that mimics whispering.

2. The alliteration of *th* sounds and force the line to be read slowly, reinforcing the firm tone of the command.

Vocabulary Practice

1. Students should name groups working together for an illegal result.

2. One could find a furrow in a field or someone's forehead.

> For additional assessment, see Assessment Resources, pp. 211–212.

Focus

Summary

Each of these four haiku focuses on an evocative natural detail to convey the spirit of one of the four seasons.

Literary Element	1

Imagery Have students note the verbs used in each haiku. **Ask: What is each flower doing?** *(the orchid "breathes," the hollyhock flowers are "turning")*

Build Background

Matsuo Bashō is considered the master of the haiku—a Japanese poetic form that traditionally draws a comparison between two images and consists of seventeen syllables spread out over three lines—five syllables in the first, seven in the second, and five in the third.

Haiku
for Four Seasons

Matsuo Bashō
Translated by Makoto Ueda

Spring

Ran no ka ya
Chō no tsubasa ni
Takimono su

The fragrant orchid:
Into a butterfly's wings
It breathes the incense.

Summer

Hi no michi ya
Aoi katamuku
Satsuki-ame

Toward the sun's path
Hollyhock flowers turning   **1**
In the rains of summer.

840 UNIT 4   THE TRIUMPH OF ROMANTICISM

Reading Practice

SPIRAL REVIEW **Literary Influence** Matsuo Bashō was a student of Zen Buddhism. The main tenet of this religion is that all things in the world are interconnected. Following the Zen philosophy, Bashō often took a universal truth or other large idea and compressed it into a simple image. As they read the haiku, have students look for big ideas behind the simple words.

Teach

Literary Element   2

Mood Have a volunteer read "Autumn" aloud. **Ask:** How does Bashō describe the branch the bird is sitting on? *(as bare)* What kind of bird sits on the branch? *(a crow)* What time of day is it? *(evening)* What mood does the image convey? *(A sad and desolate mood.)*
APPROACHING If approaching-level students are having difficulty, remind them that mood can often be described with a single word, such as *depressed* or *joyful*. Have them visualize the image and come up with one word to describe it.

Evening Snow at Asuka-yama, from the series *Eight Views of the Environs of Edo,* 1837–1838. Ando Hiroshige. Color woodblock print. The Cleveland Museum of Art, OH.

Autumn

Kareeda ni
Karasu no tomarikeri
Aki no kure

On a bare branch
A crow is perched—
Autumn evening.

Winter

Fuyu no hi ya
Bajō ni kōru
Kagebōshi

The winter sun—
Frozen on the horse,
My shadow.

> **Quickwrite**
>
> Study the images in one of Bashō's haiku. Then write a paragraph comparing or contrasting these images about the season. How did the poem make you rethink one of the seasons? Discuss the insights you gained from the comparison.

MATSUO BASHŌ **841**

Literary History ☆

Before Bashō's time, most haiku were based on gossip or wordplay and were meaningless to anyone who did not know their background. Bashō believed that haiku should have a universal meaning. He wrote poems that everyone could understand and enjoy.

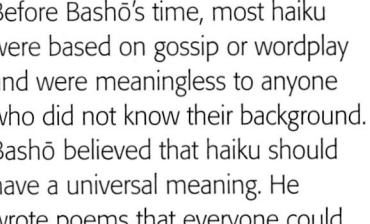 **Quickwrite**

Students' responses should address how Bashō's comparisons evoke emotions or convey insights.

English Learners
DIFFERENTIATED INSTRUCTION

Intermediate Two of the English translations contain em dashes (—). Em dashes are used to set off words, either in the middle of a sentence, like parentheses, or at the end of a sentence, to further explain an idea. Challenge students to write several sentences in which they use em dashes correctly.

Approaching Level
DIFFERENTIATED INSTRUCTION

Emerging Some students may struggle with poems that are so short and in which nothing "happens." You might want to suggest they think of a haiku as a snapshot. Each haiku presents an image frozen in time, as does a photograph.

Focus

Summary

Dillard describes a snakeskin she found in the woods. She wants to capture the moment that spring begins, but like the snakeskin, seasons have no beginning or end. She finally notes that the higher power that controls the changes of the seasons also has no beginning and no end.

Build Background

In 1971 Annie Dillard nearly died from pneumonia; this experience inspired her to appreciate life and the natural world more fully. What came of her journals from this time was the personal, reflective narrative *Pilgrim at Tinker Creek.*

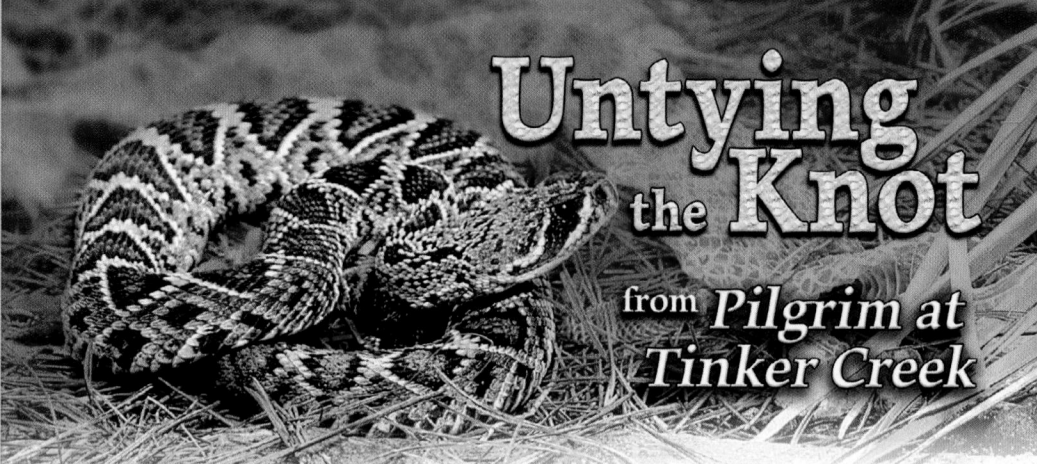

Untying the Knot

from *Pilgrim at Tinker Creek*

Annie Dillard

Yesterday I set out to catch the new season, and instead I found an old snakeskin. I was in the sunny February woods by the quarry; the snakeskin was lying in a heap of leaves right next to an aquarium someone had thrown away. I don't know why that someone hauled the aquarium deep into the woods to get rid of it; it had only one broken glass side. The snake found it handy, I imagine; snakes like to rub against something rigid to help them out of their skins, and the broken aquarium looked like the nearest likely object. Together the snakeskin and the aquarium made an interesting scene on the forest floor. It looked like an exhibit at a trial—circumstantial evidence— of a wild scene, as though a snake had burst through the broken side of the aquarium, burst through his ugly old skin, and disappeared, perhaps straight up in the air, in a rush of freedom and beauty.

The snakeskin had unkeeled scales,[1] so it belonged to a nonpoisonous snake. It was roughly five feet long by the yardstick, but I'm not sure because it was very wrinkled and dry, and every time I tried to stretch it flat it broke. I ended up with seven or eight pieces of it all over the kitchen table in a fine film of forest dust.

---

1. *Unkeeled scales* means that the snake does not have a ridge down the center of its scales. Unkeeled scales appear shiny and smooth.

Reading Practice

SPIRAL REVIEW **Preview** Have a student volunteer read the first sentence of the essay aloud. Then have students glance at the remaining text on page 842. **Ask:** What does most of the text on this page deal with? *(the snakeskin)* Discuss whether students think the entire essay will be about the snakeskin. Then have students skim over the rest of the essay. What does Dillard write about besides the snakeskin? *(the seasons, nature, and God)* Why does she even mention the snakeskin? *(She uses it as an introduction and as a segue to the larger topics she wants to discuss.)*

The point I want to make about the snake-skin is that, when I found it, it was whole and tied in a knot. Now there have been stories told, even by reputable scientists, of snakes that have deliberately tied themselves in a knot to prevent larger snakes from trying to swallow them—but I couldn't imagine any way that throwing itself into a half hitch would help a snake trying to escape its skin. Still, ever cautious, I figured that one of the neighborhood boys could possibly have tied it in a knot in the fall, for some whimsical boy-ish reason, and left it there, where it dried and gathered dust. So I carried the skin along thoughtlessly as I walked, snagging it sure enough on a low branch and ripping it in two for the first of many times. I saw that thick ice still lay on the quarry pond and that the skunk cabbage was already out in the clearings, and then I came home and looked at the skin and its knot.

The knot had no beginning. Idly I turned it around in my hand, searching for a place to untie; I came to with a start when I realized I must have turned the thing around fully ten times. Intently, then, I traced the knot's lump around with a finger; it was continuous. I couldn't untie it any more than I could untie a doughnut; it was a loop without beginning or end. These snakes *are* magic, I thought for a second, and then of course I reasoned what must have happened. The skin had been pulled inside-out like a peeled sock for several inches; then an inch or so of the inside-out part—a piece whose length was coincidentally equal to the diameter of the skin—had somehow been turned right-side out again, making a thick lump whose edges were lost in wrinkles, looking exactly like a knot.

So. I have been thinking about the change of seasons. I don't want to miss spring this year. I want to distinguish the last winter frost from the out-of-season one, the frost of spring. I want to be there on the spot the moment the grass turns green. I always miss this radical revolu-tion; I see it the next day from a window, the yard so suddenly green and lush I could envy Nebuchadnezzar[2] down on all fours eating grass. This year I want to stick a net into time and say "now," as men plant flags on the ice and snow and say, "here." But it occurred to me that I could no more catch spring by the tip of the tail than I could untie the apparent knot in the snakeskin; there are no edges to grasp. Both are continuous loops.

I wonder how long it would take you to notice the regular recurrence of the seasons if you were the first man on earth. What would it be like to live in open-ended time broken only by days and nights? You could say, "it's cold again; it was cold before," but you couldn't make the key connection and say, "it was cold this time last year," because the notion of "year" is precisely the one you lack. Assuming that you hadn't yet noticed any orderly pro-gression of heavenly bodies, how long would you have to live on earth before you could feel with any assurance that any one particular long period of cold would, in fact, end? "While the earth remaineth, seedtime and harvest, and cold and heat, and summer and winter, and day and night shall not cease": God makes this guarantee very early in Genesis to a peo-ple whose fears on this point had perhaps not been completely allayed.

It must have been fantastically important, at the real beginnings of human culture, to con-serve and relay this vital seasonal information, so that the people could anticipate dry or cold seasons, and not huddle on some November rock hoping pathetically that spring was just around the corner. We still very much stress the simple fact of four seasons to schoolchildren; even the most modern of modern new teachers, who don't seem to care if their charges can read or write or name two products of Peru, will still

2. *Nebuchadnezzar* (c. 630–561 B.C.) was the great king and military strategist of Babylonia. He was rumored to have gone mad and lived like a wild animal for seven years.

ANNIE DILLARD **843**

Comparing Literature

Teach

Vocabulary | 1

Word Origins Tell students that *vanguard* refers to either the troops at the head of an army or the leaders of a movement. It comes from the French word *avant-garde*. In French, *avant* means "before," and *garde* means "guard."

Quickwrite

Students should mention the circular shape of the snakeskin and the mystery Dillard finds in the lack of a beginning or end to its shape. Then students should explain that Dillard relates the image to the fuzzy boundaries between seasons of the year. Encourage students to incorporate their own knowledge of time and the seasons in their responses and to consider the rhetorical question Dillard poses in the selection: "I wonder how long it would take you to notice the regular recurrence of the seasons if you were the first man on earth."

Reading Practice

Analyze Archetype of Seasons
Engage students in a class discussion about the archetype of seasons. Begin by asking students what the theme is behind the archetype of the seasons. *(life, death and rebirth)* **Ask:** What types of literary devices does Keats use in order to show the theme of life and death? Cite examples. *(Students may note Keats personifies autumn as a worker in lines 17–18 or the onomatopoeia of "oozings"*

---

1 muster some seasonal chitchat and set the kids to making paper pumpkins, or tulips, for the walls. "The people," wrote Van Gogh in a letter, "are very sensitive to the changing seasons." That we are "very sensitive to the changing seasons" is, incidentally, one of the few good reasons to shun travel. If I stay at home I preserve the illusion that what is happening on Tinker Creek is the very newest thing, that I'm at the very vanguard and cutting edge of each new season. I don't want the same season twice in a row; I don't want to know I'm getting last week's weather, used weather, weather broadcast up and down the coast, old-hat weather.

But there's always unseasonable weather. What we think of the weather and behavior of life on the planet at any given season is really all a matter of statistical probabilities; at any given point, anything might happen. There is a bit of every season in each season. Green plants—deciduous green leaves—grow everywhere, all winter long, and small shoots come up pale and new in every season. Leaves die on the tree in May, turn brown, and fall into the creek. The calendar, the weather, and the behavior of wild creatures have the slimmest of connections. Everything overlaps smoothly for only a few weeks each season, and then it all tangles up again. The temperature, of course, lags far behind the calendar seasons, since the earth absorbs and releases heat slowly, like a leviathan[3] breathing. Migrating birds head south in what appears to be dire panic, leaving mild weather and fields full of insects and seeds; they reappear as if in all eagerness in January, and poke about morosely in the snow. Several years ago our October woods would have made a dismal colored photograph for a sadist's[4] calendar: a killing frost came before the leaves had even begun to brown; they drooped from every tree like crepe, blackened

---

3. *Leviathan* is an allusion to a monstrous sea creature mentioned in the Bible.
4. A *sadist* derives gratification from being cruel to others.

---

and limp. It's all a chancy, jumbled affair at best, as things seem to be below the stars.

Time is the continuous loop, the snakeskin with scales endlessly overlapping without beginning or end, or time is an ascending spiral if you will, like a child's toy Slinky. Of course we have no idea which arc on the loop is our time, let alone where the loop itself is, so to speak, or down whose lofty flight of stairs the Slinky so uncannily walks.

The power we seek, too, seems to be a continuous loop. I have always been sympathetic with the early notion of a divine power that exists in a particular place, or that travels about over the face of the earth as a man might wander—and when he is "there" he is surely not here. You can shake the hand of a man you meet in the woods; but the spirit seems to roll along like the mythical hoop snake with its tail in its mouth. There are no hands to shake or edges to untie. It rolls along the mountain ridges like a fireball, shooting off a spray of sparks at random, and will not be trapped, slowed, grasped, fetched, peeled, or aimed. "As for the wheels, it was cried unto them in my hearing, O wheel."[5] This is the hoop of flame that shoots the rapids in the creek or spins across the dizzy meadows; this is the arsonist of the sunny woods: catch it if you can. ❧

---

5. *"As for the wheels . . ."* is a passage from the Bible (Ezekiel 10:13), addressing a vision of God on Earth.

Quickwrite

Dillard uses an image of a curled-up piece of snakeskin as a springboard to discuss the continuity of life. Essay writers often identify an engaging image or anecdote from their experience and then develop it into a broader reflection on life. How does Dillard develop the metaphor of the snakeskin? Write a paragraph on this topic, citing details from the text.

---

in line 22 or "twitter" in line 33) Which images from the haikus support the archetype's theme? *(Answers will vary. Students may note flowers "breathing" in spring then the "bare branch" in autumn.)* How does the time sequence and point of view in Dillard's essay contribute? *(The chronological order and the first person point of view contribute to Dillard's final realization that "time is the continuous loop".)*

Wrap-Up: Comparing Literature

Across Time and Place

- *To Autumn* by John Keats
- *Haiku for Four Seasons* by Matsuo Bashō
- *Untying the Knot,* from *Pilgrim at Tinker Creek* by Annie Dillard

---

COMPARE THE [Big Idea] **The Quest for Truth and Beauty**

Group Activity Keats, Bashō, and Dillard express sentiments about nature that range from breathless enthusiasm to quiet, sober meditation. In a group, discuss the following questions.

1. How do you think each of these writers would define truth and beauty? Which writer's outlook is most compelling to you? Explain.

2. What do each of these writers search for through their writings on nature?

3. Compare and contrast the degrees to which each of these authors finds inspiration for his or her poetry in realm of the spiritual or the supernatural.

COMPARE Nature Imagery

Writing Write a brief essay in which you compare the imagery in two or more of the selections. Base your comparison on the sensory qualities of the images and how they contribute to the work's message about life. Refer to evidence from the selections you chose in your response.

COMPARE Literary Traditions

Speaking and Listening Research a tradition of nature writing in nonfiction or poetry. You may choose journals and reflective narratives, or poetry. Research the forces that influenced the writing and display your information in a chart. Then present your findings to the class in an oral presentation.

 **Literature** Online

Selection Resources For Selection Quizzes, eFlashcards, and Reading-Writing Connection activities, go to glencoe.com and enter QuickPass code GLB9817u4.

COMPARING LITERATURE **845**

Advanced Learners

DIFFERENTIATED INSTRUCTION

Research Have advanced students research two literary traditions and compare them in their presentation, supporting their ideas with examples from each tradition. Remind students to rehearse their presentation before delivering it to the class.

Assess

Compare the Big Idea

1. Students may discuss Keats's enthusiasm for sensory details and the effortless beauty he depicts, Bashō's light touch at describing both the loneliness and interconnectedness of life, Cullen's exuberance at the onset of spring, and Dillard's commentary about the transitions between the four seasons.

2. They seek to analyze nature and the place of humans in the natural world.

3. Students should discuss the different ways in which the selections explore nature and the seasons.

Compare Nature Imagery

Use these criteria to evaluate students' writing:

- The response describes images from different selections.
- The response shows how the image develops into a larger reflection on life.

Compare Literary Traditions

Use this criterion to evaluate students' presentations:

- The oral presentation discusses the literary and cultural patterns evident in a certain type of nature writing.
- The student gives an engaging presentation, citing evidence from the selections and independent research.

Focus

Bellringer

Bring in a powerful or moving poem and read it aloud to the students. **Ask:** Can you relate the poem to your own feelings? Does it make you reflect on something you have experienced in your own life? *Reread the poem and this time have students take a few minutes to jot down their reflections.*

Summary

In this workshop, students will write and present reflective essays about poetic themes. Students will follow the stages of the writing process, including prewriting, drafting, revising, editing, and presenting. In addition, the workshop provides two mini-lessons, one on varying sentence structure and one on using active and passive voice.

> For Writing Workshop graphic organizer and rubric, see Unit 4 Teaching Resources, pp. 247–249.

Learning Objectives

For pages 846–853

In this workshop, you will focus on the following objective:

Writing: Writing a reflective essay using the writing process.

 Writing Workshop

Reflective Essay

Literature Connection In her journal, Dorothy Wordsworth reflects on an enjoyable walk that she took through a field of daffodils and offers an insight about her observations.

> *"I never saw daffodils so beautiful. They grew among the mossy stones about and about them; some rested their heads upon these stones as on a pillow for weariness."*
>
> —Dorothy Wordsworth, from *The Journals of Dorothy Wordsworth*

In a reflective essay, a writer describes an experience or observation to better understand what it means personally and what it might teach others. A reflective essay may also describe a personal response to literature and explore the meaning of a reading experience. To write an effective essay, you will need to learn the goals of reflective writing and the strategies to achieve those goals.

Checklist

Goals	Strategies
To share your personal reflections about the meaning of a poem	☑ Draw comparisons between specific personal experiences and broader themes
	☑ Quote lines from the poem as evidence to support your ideas
	☑ Strike a balance between reflecting on the poem and reflecting on broader themes
To explain your observations and ideas in a logical order	☑ Clearly organize your ideas from beginning to end
To connect with an audience	☑ Use first-person point of view
	☑ Use fresh, natural language
	☑ Use rhetorical devices
	☑ Vary sentences
	☑ Create a tone that is consistent with your purpose, audience, and form

Writing Process

At any stage of the writing process, you may think of new ideas. Feel free to return to earlier stages as you write.

Prewrite

Draft

Revise

Focus Lesson: Sentence Structure

Edit and Proofread

Focus Lesson: Active and Passive Voice

Present

846 UNIT 4 THE TRIUMPH OF ROMANTICISM

Workshop Resources

Print Materials

- Unit 4 Teaching Resources pp. 247–249
- Writing Kit
- Success in Writing: Research and Reports
- Grammar and Language Transparencies 55, 73
- Writing Workshop Transparencies 21–25

Technology

- Literature Online: Writing Resources and Grammar Resources, www.glencoe.com
- Online Essay Grader, www.glencoe.com
- Student Presentation Builder on StudentWorks Plus CD-ROM
- Media Workshop DVD
- Online Student Edition

Assignment: Reflect on a Poem

Write a reflective essay of about 1,500 words in which you interpret the meaning of a poem, explore its personal significance, and connect that significance to a broader theme or belief. As you move through the stages of the writing process, keep your audience and purpose in mind.

Audience: teacher, classmates, and peers familiar with the chosen poem

Purpose: to explain an interpretation of a poem and support it with personal experience

Real-World Connection

Reflective writing skills are necessary for many college application essays. You may also need them for scholarship, internship, and job applications.

Analyze a Professional Model

In the essay below, poet Robin Becker reflects on the significance of her experience as an adolescent reading William Wordsworth's "Lines Composed a Few Miles Above Tintern Abbey." As you read the passage, pay close attention to the comments in the margin. They point out features to include in your own reflective essay.

From *"Wordsworth"* by Robin Becker ☆

Wordsworth is full of loss. So are adolescents. At thirteen, before I'd thought much about poetry, Miss Bickley asked us to feel the undertow of longing in the first-person voice. Reading aloud, she instructed us to listen to the unrhymed iambic pentameter, the word and phrasal repetitions, and the syntax of "Tintern Abbey." (Lousy in math and science, I thought, *I can do this.*) I learned to listen for "Once again" and "How oft," the moody signals and backward-looking words that triggered descriptions of Wordsworth's countryside and of the "lonely rooms" in which he sought consolation. With his semicolons and dashes, he built winding sentences, and though I couldn't always follow the grammar (*"Oh yeah?"* was penciled in a margin of my old *Norton* anthology), I liked the sound, the poem's steady iambic music. What I understood of "voice" I gathered from trying to leap—with Wordsworth—from concrete ("A lover of the meadows and the woods") to abstract ("soul / Of all my moral being") and to follow

First-Person Point of View

Use the pronoun *I* to "speak" directly to your reader.

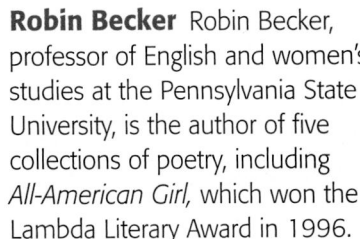

Writing and Research For prewriting, predrafting, and revising tools, go to glencoe.com and enter QuickPass code GLB9817u4.

Teach

Big Idea

Nature and the Imagination Explain that William Wordsworth and the other early English Romantics sought spiritual strength in the beauty of the natural world, the simple lives of ordinary workers, and the innocence of children. **Ask:** By writing a reflective essay, how are you echoing the pursuit of the Romantics? (*Writing a reflective essay is essentially a spiritual journey. Inspired by an external observation—of a poem, a painting, or a scene in nature—the writer explores thoughts and feelings while relating the response to personal experiences, thereby deriving strength of awareness or insight.*)

Literary History ☆

Robin Becker Robin Becker, professor of English and women's studies at the Pennsylvania State University, is the author of five collections of poetry, including *All-American Girl,* which won the Lambda Literary Award in 1996.

English Learners

DIFFERENTIATED INSTRUCTION

Intermediate Before English learners begin writing their reflective essays, have them work in small groups with proficient speakers of English who have chosen to write about the same poem.

First, have students discuss the theme. Next, have them share interpretations of key passages or images in the poem. Students should consider all opinions that can be reasonably supported. Finally, they should decide whether the new information can help them refine their own ideas. All students should take notes as they work through this activity.

Teach

Writing Skills

Interpretation Remind students that they have great freedom in interpreting their selected poems, provided that they support their views with evidence. In the words of M. H. Abrams, editor of the *Norton Anthology of Poetry,* "There is no one, right interpretation of a poem—but there is one which is more right than any of the others."

Cultural History ☆

The Wye Valley and Tintern Abbey When it became fashionable to visit wilder parts of Great Britain in the late eighteenth century, the Wye Valley became renowned for its striking natural beauty. The poet William Wordsworth and others who sought the romantic and the picturesque rediscovered Tintern Abbey, then swathed in ivy.

Literary Interpretation

Explore the personal meaning of the poem in the introduction.

Audience

Use fresh, vivid language; varied sentences; and other stylistic choices to connect with your audience. Make the experience of reading a poem come alive.

Writing Voice/Tone

Use a conversational tone to help readers sense that a real person is communicating with them.

Supporting Evidence

Cite lines from the poem to support your interpretation of the poem's meaning and themes.

Conclusion

Reveal the personal significance of the poem and connect your experience to broader themes and beliefs.

the poem's argument, which I felt, at the time, was a parable for how to grow up.

As a city kid, I knew only two rural landscapes: my beloved Camp Greylock in the Adirondacks and Wordsworth's rustic woodland. Onto his sensuous descriptions of childhood ("when like a roe / I bounded o'er the mountains") I transposed my own tomboyhood: perishable, vagabond. I identified with the poet's fall from "thoughtless youth," and I remember liking "the still, sad music of humanity" for its mournfulness. Did we discuss the sibilance? The assonance? I don't recall. But certain phrases—"the din / Of towns and cities" and "greetings where no kindness is" and "The dreary intercourse of daily life"—pleased me enormously, for they evoked my own scorn for the hypocrisy and tedium of grown-ups and gave me an ally in literature.

Another surprise: The poem turned out to have a love interest! Chaste but not austere, Wordsworth's affection for his sister, Dorothy, provided the second half of the poem with memorable metaphors:

> . . . when thy mind
> Shall be a mansion for all lovely forms,
> Thy memory be as a dwelling place
> For all sweet sounds and harmonies. . . .

Wordsworth's great fortune in having an intimate friend ("For thou art with me here upon the banks / Of this fair river; thou, my dearest Friend, / My dear, dear Friend") with whom to share his thoughts did not escape me; I, too, longed for a companionable pal. . . . At thirteen, I was consoled.

Reading-Writing Connection Think about the writing techniques that you just encountered and try them out in the reflective essay you write.

Reading Practice

Reread Before they begin to write their essay, encourage students to reread their selected poem aloud several times, noting its structure, recurring images or themes, meter, and rhyme scheme—all of the

elements that help to create its total effect.

Ask students to create a chart with the headings such as *Structure, Images,* and *Themes* and to fill it in.

Prewrite

Explore Ideas Your essay is more likely to turn out well if you choose a poem that is interesting and meaningful. Think about which poem from this unit made the deepest impression on you. Consider connections you might draw between the poem and your own experience.

Reflect on Poetic Themes Writing a reflective essay about a poetic theme involves more than describing the experience of reading a poem. As you reflect on a poem, consider the following questions:

▶ **What does the poem mean?** Become familiar with the poem's main ideas and images. Picture what the poem is saying.

▶ **Why is it significant to me?** Think about your personal responses to the poem. How does understanding the poem help you better understand yourself, your beliefs, and the human experience in general?

▶ **How does the poem connect to a broader theme?** What insight about human experience did you learn from your reflection?

Gather Details Note the images, phrases, and lines that express the theme or message you will focus on. Examine the poetic elements that also contribute to the theme, such as meter, rhyme, and other sound devices. Then explore how the poem relates to your own observations and experience and use vivid details to develop your description.

Make a Plan As you plan your essay, keep in mind that you will need to connect the poem to personal observation and experience. You may find it helpful to explore the poem's meaning by moving through it from beginning to end. Here is a chart one student used to outline a reflective essay about the poem "Ozymandias" by Percy Bysshe Shelley.

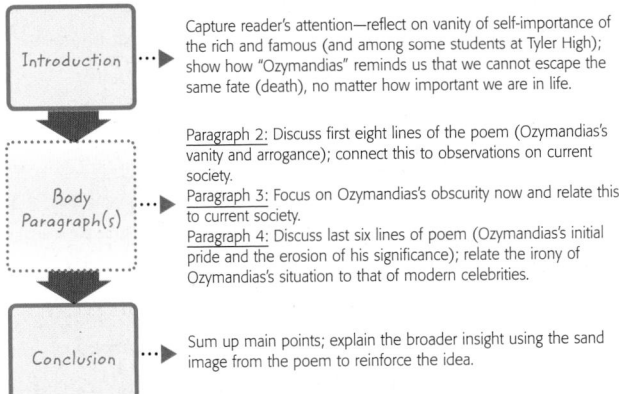

Introduction ···▶ Capture reader's attention—reflect on vanity of self-importance of the rich and famous (and among some students at Tyler High); show how "Ozymandias" reminds us that we cannot escape the same fate (death), no matter how important we are in life.

Body Paragraph(s) ▶ Paragraph 2: Discuss first eight lines of the poem (Ozymandias's vanity and arrogance); connect this to observations on current society.
Paragraph 3: Focus on Ozymandias's obscurity now and relate this to current society.
Paragraph 4: Discuss last six lines of poem (Ozymandias's initial pride and the erosion of his significance); relate the irony of Ozymandias's situation to that of modern celebrities.

Conclusion ···▶ Sum up main points; explain the broader insight using the sand image from the poem to reinforce the idea.

Freewriting

An effective prewriting strategy for stimulating the flow of ideas is freewriting. Use this method to move from what you know about a poem to associations that leap to mind during the generative act of putting pen to paper or fingers to a keyboard.

Avoid Plagiarism

This assignment does not require the use of outside sources, so do not consult them. This will help you avoid the temptation to identify someone else's words or ideas as your own. Additionally, focusing on only the poem may encourage you to read more carefully for meaning.

Teach

Writing Process

Prewrite Suggest that students jot down answers to the questions provided and that they use their notes in drafting their essays.

Also remind students to make sure that they support their views with specific evidence from the poem.

Writing Process

Make a Plan Remind students that at this stage they should jot down only notes. They can develop a plan or an outline for their essay later.

Approaching Level
DIFFERENTIATED INSTRUCTION

Emerging Poetry, particularly when written long ago, may contain unusual syntax or vocabulary. Before students begin planning their essays, tell them to be sure that they understand the language of their selected poems. Encourage students to paraphrase, or restate in their own words, especially difficult lines or phrases. Remind them to resist the temptation to skip over lines or phrases that seem unintelligible. These passages may be essential to the poem. Instead, students should consult a dictionary to define unfamiliar vocabulary.

Teach

Writing Skills

Point of View/Tone **Answer:** *The first-person point of view helps establish an informal, conversational tone that is appropriate for a reflective essay.*

Writing Skills

Literary Interpretation

Answer: *The interpretation states the personal and universal significance of the poem and provides a focus for the reflective essay.*

Writing Skills

Organization **Answer:** *The writer discusses the poem and its effects, starting with the first lines of the poem. Following the chronology of the poem in organizing the essay is logical and helps guide the reader.*

Sentence Frames

As you read the workshop model, think about the writer's use of the following frames:

- According to _____, a _____,....

- As _____ notes in <title of work>, _____.

Consider using frames like these in your own reflective essay.

Point of View/Tone

How does using first-person point of view affect the tone of this essay?

Literary Interpretation

How does interpreting the poetic theme here make the introduction more effective?

Organization

Why might the writer choose to focus on the beginning of the poem in the first body paragraph?

Draft

From Plan to Paper When you begin your first draft, use your outline as a guide to help you balance your specific reflections on the poem with more general conclusions and insights. As you write, however, be open to new observations about the poem and your personal responses.

Analyze a Workshop Model

Here is a final draft of a reflective essay. Read the essay and answer the questions in the margin. Use the answers to these questions to guide you as you write.

The Eroding Sands of Time

Some people matter and some people don't—or so many would have us believe. Nothing is easier to overestimate than the importance of one's own existence on Earth. In our culture today, that misguided assessment of one's own importance is frequently based on how much wealth or fame someone has: celebrities, in particular, often act superior to others. They also tend to confuse their current status with some kind of lasting fame or immortality. I've also seen this exaggerated sense of importance reflected in the attitudes and actions of high-profile politicians and even some students at Tyler High. These people think they are much more influential than they really are in the long run. In "Ozymandias," Percy Bysshe Shelley shows how even one of the greatest pharaohs of ancient Egypt comes to ruin and nothingness. The poem's theme is still relevant today; whether one is a pharaoh or a peasant, a president or a prom queen, we cannot escape the same fate.

Shelley devotes the first eight lines of his sonnet to describing the statue of Ozymandias, which is actually the Greek name for the Egyptian pharaoh Ramses II. The speaker in the poem, who is observing the statue, can still see the passions, power, and majesty of this great ruler reflected in the ruins of the statue. The speaker notices especially the "frown" and "sneer of cold command" carved

Writing Practice

Paragraphs To be effective, an essay must provide evidence strong enough to convince the reader of a certain position. Remind students that each middle paragraph in an essay should state a point that is credible, relevant, and well supported. Each middle paragraph should have a topic sentence, which states its main idea. The other sentences in the paragraph should include details that develop the main idea. Have students try writing a topic sentence for each middle paragraph of their essays.

on the ruler's face. This sneer represents the attitude of Ramses when he was at the height of his power. He, like the successful politician of the moment, was riding high—building, creating, transforming, and feeling invincible.

Yet the statue is broken in two parts. Only the legs of stone still stand upright, and, "Near them, on the sand, / Half sunk, a shattered visage lies." Shelley's choppy description broken by commas emphasizes the image of Ozymandias's shattered face. Despite his former power, Ozymandias now lies in pieces. His commanding sneer and "wrinkled lip" have crumbled, and the once imposing statue threatens to turn back to dust. However mighty he was at one time, Ramses' power and influence were only temporary. He is no longer important, just as today's celebrities will soon be forgotten.

The last six lines of the poem emphasize the irony of the situation. Beginning with "My name is Ozymandias," an inscription on the pedestal warns everyone about the greatness of this man. I can't help thinking this is a bit like the proclamations of famous people who walk into a restaurant and tell their name to the host, as if that gesture alone should allow them to skip the line formed by everyone else who is waiting for a table. The inscription goes on to tell others to look on the mighty works of Ozymandias and "despair," as though his works will forever dwarf those of anyone else. Similarly, rappers today often boast of their success in their songs, only to fall out of the spotlight a short time later. This poem makes it clear that the inscription and Ozymandias's fate are two different things. Thousands of years later, Ozymandias is just a broken statue. The "lone and level sands"—death and oblivion— are the fate that lies ahead for everyone. Time reduces, erodes, and obscures all human achievements, whether they are the accomplishments of a political figure, a celebrity, or an ordinary person.

If Ozymandias could have known the fate of his statue, would he have boasted? Perhaps everyone should look at Ozymandias and rethink his or her own importance. Worldly fame and importance do not last; the sands of time run out for all.

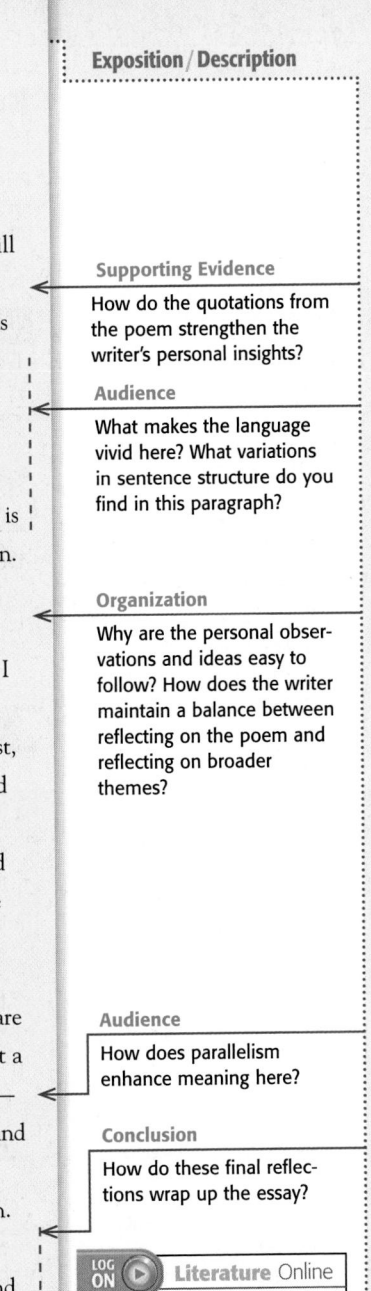

Exposition / Description

Supporting Evidence

How do the quotations from the poem strengthen the writer's personal insights?

Audience

What makes the language vivid here? What variations in sentence structure do you find in this paragraph?

Organization

Why are the personal observations and ideas easy to follow? How does the writer maintain a balance between reflecting on the poem and reflecting on broader themes?

Audience

How does parallelism enhance meaning here?

Conclusion

How do these final reflections wrap up the essay?

LOG ON ▶ **Literature** Online

Writing and Research For editing and publishing tools, go to glencoe.com and enter QuickPass code GLB9817u4.

WRITING WORKSHOP **851**

Teach

Writing Skills

Supporting Evidence
Answer: *The quotations help convince the reader that the writer's personal insights are based on a careful reading of the poem.*

Writing Skills

Audience Answer: *Phrases such as "commanding sneer" make the writing vivid. Simple, compound, and complex sentences are used.*

Writing Skills

Organization Answer: *Observations are well organized. The author presents points in order and makes connections to experiences readers can relate to, such as stars' fleeting fame, to support his observations.*

Writing Skills

Audience Answer: *The parallelism translates the poetic elements into terms that clarify the meaning.*

Writing Skills

Conclusion Answer: *Final reflections restate the main message, explain its personal significance, and connect it to universal themes. The writer leaves the reader with much to think about.*

Approaching Level

DIFFERENTIATED INSTRUCTION

Emerging Illustrating the essay may help students who process information through visual perceptions. If they are having difficulty converting the ideas on their chart into a written draft, suggest an activity like the following as a transition between the planning and drafting stages:

Have students draw pictures showing how they visualize an idea, an image, a person, or a scene. Encourage them to add as much detail as possible. Then suggest that they use the visual interpretations as a springboard to the development of written communications.

Teach

Writing Process

Revise Suggest that students take notes as they answer each of the questions in the rubric "Writing a Reflective Essay." This technique will help them recall insights that occur to them as they move through the process. If you choose to have partners read drafts aloud to each another, tell peer reviewers to jot down specific recommendations for revising. Suggest that reviewers pay close attention to issues involving clarity and the organization of ideas.

Writer's Technique ☆

Revision When writing a first draft, writers usually do not spend much time on word choice or sentence variety. The important thing is to get ideas down on paper. Do not try to perfect a rough draft as you are writing. Instead, complete the draft, set it aside for at least 24 hours, and then reread it. Now find ways to improve the variety in the sentences, choose more precise words, and add more details.

Traits of Strong Writing

Include these traits of strong writing to express your ideas effectively.

Ideas

Organization

Voice

Word Choice

Sentence Fluency

Conventions

Presentation

For more information on using the Traits of Strong Writing, see pages R28–R30.

Word Choice

Find this academic vocabulary word in the student model:

assessment (ə ses′ mənt) *n.* 1. the action of or statement of determining worth or value; 2. a determination of worth or value; an appraisal. *In our culture today, a misguided assessment of importance is frequently based on how much wealth or fame someone has.*

Using academic vocabulary may help strengthen your writing. Try to use one or two academic vocabulary words in your reflective essay. See the complete list on pages R81–R83.

Revise ☆

Peer Review E-mail the draft of your essay to one or more peer reviewers. They can provide comments in a separate document and offer suggestions for revisions. Use the checklist below to evaluate and strengthen your essay.

Checklist

☑ Do you present your personal reflections about the meaning of a poem?

☑ Do you connect with your audience through first-person point of view, fresh, natural language; and varied sentences?

☑ Do you present your observations in a logical order?

☑ Do you cite lines from the poem to support your points?

☑ Do you draw comparisons between personal experience and broader themes?

☑ Do you balance reflections on the poem with generalizations about life?

▶ Focus Lesson

Vary Sentence Structure

Vary your sentences to make your writing more lively and rhythmical. Short, simple sentences sound direct and straightforward. An interrogative sentence can create a dramatic effect.

Draft: The sentences of the paragraph have very similar structures and lengths and create a dull, predictable rhythm.

> If Ozymandias had known his statue's fate, he would not have boasted. If people looked at Ozymandias, they would rethink their own importance.

Revision: Vary length and structure to enliven the writing.

> If Ozymandias could have known the fate of his statue, would he have boasted?[1] Perhaps everyone should look at Ozymandias and rethink his or her own importance.[2]

> 1: Use a question for variation and dramatic effect.
>
> 2: Use a simple sentence to sound straightforward.

Writing Practice

The Right Word As students revise their work, tell them to avoid vague words and phrases. Also stress the importance of using precise words to express their ideas. Point out that a dictionary or a thesaurus explains different shades of meaning between synonyms.

Ask partners to help each other identify vague words and phrases in each other's writing and to suggest revisions. Tell them to underline words that are essential to the main ideas in their essays. They should consult a dictionary or a thesaurus to see whether a synonym might convey their ideas more precisely.

Edit and Proofread

Get It Right When you have completed the final draft of your essay, proofread it for errors in grammar, usage, mechanics, and spelling. Refer to the Language Handbook, pages R47–R59, as a guide.

> **Focus Lesson**

Use Active and Passive Voice

The passive voice consists of a form of the auxiliary verb *be* together with the past participle of a verb. Note these examples:

- *Ozymandias is remembered.* [present]
- *Ozymandias was remembered.* [past]

Most of the time, you should strive to use the active voice. There are times, however, when the passive voice is appropriate. For example, use it when the doer of an action is unknown or unimportant.

Ozymandias was revered.

You may also use the passive voice when it makes sense to shift the emphasis of the sentence onto the action or the object of the action.

A great statue of Ramses II was built by his followers.

(Here the emphasis falls, rightly, on the statue, rather than on the followers.)

Original: The passive voice diminishes the sentence's impact.

All human achievements are reduced, eroded, and obscured by time.

Improved: Use the active voice to make the sentence more direct and powerful.

Time reduces, erodes, and obscures all human achievements.

Present

Final Details Is your essay inviting to read? Make handwritten papers neat and legible. If you are working on a computer, follow your teacher's guidelines for formatting your final draft. Remember, appearance counts.

Peer Review Tips

A classmate may ask you to read his or her reflective essay. Take your time and jot down notes as you read so you can give constructive feedback. Use the following questions to get started:

- Are the ideas clearly organized from beginning to end?

- Has the writer used rhetorical devices and made other fresh, interesting choices in word choice and sentence structure?

Word-Processing Tips

Although word processing gives you many choices for formatting, maintain standard conventions for both horizontal and vertical space. These include one-inch margins on all sides, double spacing, no additional lines of space between paragraphs, and paragraph indents of five spaces.

Writer's Portfolio

Place a copy of your reflective essay in your portfolio to review later.

Writing Workshop

Reflective Essay

Teach

Writing Process

Edit and Proofread Encourage students to use the Proofreading Checklist on the inside back cover of this book.

Point out that some writers prefer to read their essays aloud to identify errors in grammar but that others prefer to read silently. Encourage students to try different techniques until they find the one that suits them. Students could also audiotape their essays and listen for errors as they play the recording.

Writing Process

Present Students who have written about the same poem might compile a collection of "modern literary criticism." Suggest that they choose a title for the volume and create a table of contents. They may wish to donate a copy of the work to the school or community library.

Approaching Level

DIFFERENTIATED INSTRUCTION

Established Encourage students to ask themselves the following questions as they review their writing.

Does my reflective essay

- clearly state my main idea?
- support that idea with sound analysis of evidence from the text?
- represent work I am proud of?

Have students consider their responses to these questions as they decide whether to include their essays in their portfolios.

Focus

Summary

In this workshop, students will learn techniques for planning, rehearsing, and delivering a reflective presentation.

Teach

Speaking Skills

Enliven Your Presentation

Remind students that although they may have written an inspiring reflective essay, it will not move their audience if they are stiff and unenthusiastic when delivering it. To enliven their presentations, encourage students to try to be natural and animated. Suggest that they use hand gestures and move around a little. They should never rock back and forth, however, as that action conveys nervousness.

Above all, encourage students to smile. It will make them seem more at ease and less nervous.

 For help with creating presentations, see Student Presentation Builder on StudentWorks Plus.

 For Speaking, Listening, and Viewing rubric, see Unit 4 Teaching Resources, pp. 252–253.

854

Learning Objectives

For pages 854–855

In this workshop, you will focus on the following objective:

Speaking and Listening: Delivering a reflective presentation.

Active Listening Tips

Invite your audience to follow these guidelines for effective listening:

- Prepare to listen.
- Note the topic and recall what you already know about it.
- Pay attention to the structure of the message.
- Take notes.
- Ask questions, aloud or silently.
- Listen for feelings as well as thoughts.

Speaking, Listening, and Viewing Workshop

Reflective Presentation

Literature Connection

"The idea of talking about poetry is not to get to the bottom of it, but to clarify it, to make it more a part of what you and other people know and will remember. . . . What a poem makes you feel helps you make sense of it by making the poem part of your own experience. . . . Go slow, be simple and clear, and say how it seems to you and what exact words and lines in the poem your ideas and feelings come from."

—Kenneth Koch and Kate Farrell, from *Talking about Poetry*

The poets Kenneth Koch and Kate Farrell offer some sound strategies for sharing your reflections on a poem in an oral presentation. When you reflect on a poem or other literary work, you think about what the poem means to you and explore how the literature shapes or confirms your thoughts and beliefs. As you deliver a reflective presentation on a poetic theme, you tell these ideas to others—a live audience—in order to explain what that poem has taught you and what it might teach others.

> **Assignment**   Create a reflective presentation from your reflective essay.

> Ozymandias
> I met a traveler from an antique land
> Who said: Two vast and trunkless legs
>   of stone
> Stand in the desert . . . Near them, on
>   the sand,
> Half sunk, a shattered visage lies,
>   whose frown
> And wrinkled lip, and sneer of cold
>   command,

854   UNIT 4   THE TRIUMPH OF ROMANTICISM

Speaking Practice

Voice Projection Tell students that, contrary to popular belief, projecting their voices does **not** mean shouting but raising the volume of the natural speaking voice without losing control of it (which is what shouting is). Say that projecting is like talking to someone in a restaurant rather than calling in a dog from outside.

Ask student volunteers to read random passages from their textbooks. First, have them shout a few lines; next, have them project those same lines, correcting their volume and pitch. Tell them that they should always project while giving a speech, even in a small room.

Plan Your Presentation

Adapt your reflective essay into a presentation by following these guidelines:

- Read your essay aloud to a peer. Discuss which ideas you should keep or delete. What will your audience find most interesting?
- Do not rely on your written essay to deliver your reflective presentation. Instead, jot down key words and ideas on index cards. Refer to your notes as a speaking prompt.
- Include quotations and visual images in your presentation to illustrate key ideas and to help you apply them to broad generalizations about life. If you are reflecting on a short poem, you might read the entire poem aloud at the start of your presentation.

Presenting Visual Media

Visual media, such as photographs, a collage, drawings, or a computer slide show, can not only make your presentation more interesting, but also help you maintain a balance between retelling and explaining the poem, and relating it to more general or abstract ideas. As needed, narrate or describe what your visuals show as a means of connecting them to the poem and to generalizations about life. Be sure that your visual media enhance your presentation by practicing with your props beforehand. Use the checklist below as a guide:

- ☑ Have I remembered not to block the visuals while presenting?
- ☑ Do I use color in my presentation?
- ☑ Do I face the audience and not the visuals?
- ☑ Have I used at least 24-point font for labels or captions?

Be sure to cite the source or sources for any visuals you use.

Techniques for Delivering a Reflective Presentation

Verbal Techniques	Nonverbal Techniques
☑ **Pace** Speak at a moderate speed but vary the rate and use pauses to convey your meaning.	☑ **Eye Contact** Make frequent eye contact with the audience; if you are nervous, you may look slightly above the crowd instead.
☑ **Pronunciation** Speak clearly, pronouncing all the words precisely.	☑ **Facial Expressions** Vary your facial expressions to reflect the tone and mood of what you are saying.

Speaking Frames

Consider using the following frames in your reflective presentation:

- In line ＿＿＿ of <title of poem>, the speaker says ＿＿＿. This makes me think of ＿＿＿.

- As this image of ＿＿＿ shows, ＿＿＿.

Presentation Tips

Use the following checklist to evaluate your reflective presentation.

- Did you make the specific meanings you found in the poem clear to your audience?

- Did you balance quoting from, retelling, and explaining the poem with relating it to abstract ideas or generalizations about life?

- Did your words, nonverbal techniques, and visuals work together to create a smooth and interesting presentation?

 **Literature** Online

Speaking Listening, and Viewing For project ideas, templates, and presentation ideas, go to glencoe.com and enter QuickPass code GLB9817u4.

Teach

Speaking Skills

Rehearse Encourage students to practice their presentations in front of a full-length mirror. They should keep their hands in sight and look into their own eyes. Encourage them to be as natural and confident as possible, maintaining an alert posture without looking stiff. Remind students to look up from their notes often and to look directly into their eyes whenever they do so.

Listening Skills

Respond Ask students to refer to the following criteria as they evaluate reflective presentations:

- Is the speaker well prepared?
- Does the speaker use effective pacing, gestures, volume, and eye contact?
- Does the speaker use vivid imagery and active language in his or her presentation?
- Does the speaker make effective use of any visual aids?

Approaching Level

DIFFERENTIATED INSTRUCTION

Established To reduce any stress students may feel about speaking before an audience, urge them to practice deep breathing exercises. It may strike students as odd, but impress upon them that deep breathing really does slow the heart rate, lower blood pressure, and reduce adrenaline flow. Have them practice deep breathing exercises in the classroom.

Instruct students to breathe in through the nose, holding their breath for five seconds, and then to breathe out through the mouth. Have them do this exercise several times and then describe how they felt.

Independent Reading

Focus

Summary

The purpose of Independent Reading is to encourage students to read novels from the time period that they have learned about in this unit.

Teach

Literary History ☆

Compare Novels Ask students who have read British novels written in the early nineteenth century to discuss the content of those works. **Ask:** What were the authors interested in exploring? How were the characters similar to and different from people you know?

Point out that while some authors of the period set their novels in the past or presented their characters in gothic horror, others placed their characters in realistic settings of the day. Lead students to understand that the authors were interested in exploring human behavior and its motives.

Reading Practice

Make Judgments As they read novels independently, tell students to pay attention to the opinions they form about the author's message and purpose, the characters' likability, and the credibility of the plot. Remind students that making judgments involves evaluating the work critically; encourage students to keep notes about their judgments and the reasons for them. Point out that they may revise their judgments as they continue reading.

Independent Reading

DESPITE SOME INITIAL CRITICISM, THE NOVEL BECAME WIDELY ACCEPTED during the Romantic period, inspiring a dramatic increase in fiction writing in the 1800s. Though authors used a wide range of styles, including gothic, historical, and Romantic, the basis of the novel was reality. In fact, Sir Walter Scott in 1824 defined the novel as "a fictitious narrative . . . accommodated to the ordinary train of human events."

Frankenstein

Mary Shelley

In his attempt to create a human being, Victor Frankenstein assembles body parts from corpses and ultimately gives life to a monster. This epistolary novel (or novel of letters) about the experiments of Dr. Frankenstein combines romance and science fiction to create one of the most famous gothic novels of the time. *Frankenstein*, however, transcends the gothic fascination with the supernatural to explore the nature of evil and the possible consequences of mechanization in the new industrial age. Mary Shelley, the wife of the Romantic poet Percy Bysshe Shelley, conceived the idea for the story after reading ghost stories and experiencing a terrifying nightmare.

Emma

Jane Austen

In her time, Jane Austen was nearly alone in writing the **novel of manners**, a realistic, usually satiric novel that examines the behavior and outlook of a particular social class. *Emma* is generally considered her most accomplished work, masterfully focusing on village life. The main character, Emma Woodhouse, amuses herself by making matches between her friends. With many humorous twists, this novel of manners charts Emma's journey toward greater self-awareness and, ultimately, love.

GLENCOE
LITERATURE
LIBRARY

Sense and Sensibility

Jane Austen

This classic novel tells the story of the Dashwood sisters, Elinor and Marianne, who face romantic adventures and misfortunes and try to protect each other as only sisters can.

Pride and Prejudice

Jane Austen

Austen's novel tells the story of Elizabeth Bennet and Fitzwilliam Darcy and the stubborn pride and foolish prejudice that threaten to keep them apart.

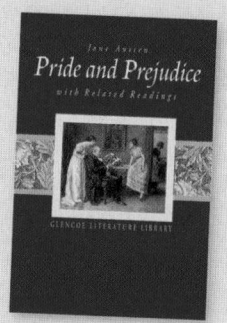

CRITICS' CORNER

"Scott's main achievement was to get people to realize that history was not just a list of political and religious dates denoting events that seemed to have happened of their own accord; instead he showed how history was the product of human decisions, human drama. Scott knew that his historical novels were nothing but educated guesses at what those human choices and human dramas really involved, but he persuaded us that the properly educated guess was the lesser lie than the flat denial of the human element."

—Nathan Uglow

Ivanhoe

Sir Walter Scott

Sir Walter Scott's novels were immensely popular during his lifetime. After completing a series of Scottish historical novels, he turned his focus to England in *Ivanhoe*, his tale of a Saxon knight who returns home from the Crusades to marry his love, Rowena. A true product of the Romantic age, Scott incorporated his fascination with the marvelous and uncommon into his work. Because of his emphasis on history, Scott is often regarded as the inventor of the historical novel. His work later influenced Charles Dickens and James Fenimore Cooper.

 Write a Reader-Response Journal

Select a book from this page to read. Keep a log of your responses to what you have read each day, and share your entries with the class.

Approaching Level

DIFFERENTIATED INSTRUCTION

Emerging To help approaching-level readers better comprehend the novels they are reading, have them write character sketches, describing each of the major characters in their books. Remind students to describe each character's appearance, personality, and role in the story. Also have students note how cultural forces from the novel's historical period, such as religion and attitudes toward social class, may have affected the characters. These sketches may help students better understand and predict characters' actions in the novels.

Teach

Reader-Response Journal

Students' logs should include daily entries that reflect their personal responses to the books.

Cultural History ☆

Literary Criticism Explain to students that Scott's critical reputation fell somewhat during the early part of the twentieth century. Recently scholars have once again embraced Scott's work. Encourage students to find representative criticism from Scott's own time period, from the early twentieth century, and from today. Ask students to compare the criticisms and discuss what may have caused Scott's reputation to rise, fall, and rise again.

Glencoe Literature Library

Glencoe Literature Library offers an extensive collection of hardcover books that can help you encourage students to read independently. Choose from among the more than 120 full-length literary works—novels, novellas, plays, and nonfiction. Each book includes related readings from a broad range of genres. Go to www.Glencoe.com for more information.

 For access to all study guides for the Glencoe Literature Library, see the Literature Library Teacher Resources CD-ROM.

Bellringer

Say: Reading comprehension makes up a significant portion of most standardized tests. What are some effective strategies to use when tackling reading passages? Have students brainstorm to compile a list of test-taking strategies they have learned so far.

Teach

Assessment Tell students that this section will reinforce their general test-taking strategies and will test the skills and vocabulary covered in the unit. Students will read a nonfiction selection and answer context-clue, comprehension, and inference questions. Then they will answer ten sentence-completion questions and ten paragraph-improvement questions and respond to a short reflective-essay question.

 To create custom assessments online, go to Progress Reporter Online Assessment.

 To create custom assessments using software, see ExamView Assessment Suite.

Assessment

English–Language Arts

Reading: Fiction

Carefully read the following passage. Use context clues to help you define any words with which you are unfamiliar. Pay close attention to the author's purpose and her use of figurative language and argument. Then, on a separate sheet of paper, answer the questions.

from *A Vindication of the Rights of Woman* by Mary Wollstonecraft

line

I once knew a weak woman of fashion, who was more than commonly proud of her delicacy and sensibility. She thought a distinguishing taste and puny appetite the height of all human perfection, and acted accordingly. I have seen this weak sophisticated being neglect all the duties of life, yet recline with self-complacency on a sofa, and boast of her want of appetite as a proof of delicacy that

5 extended to, or, perhaps, arose from, her exquisite sensibility; for it is difficult to render intelligible such ridiculous jargon. . . .

Women are everywhere in this deplorable state; for, in order to preserve their innocence, as ignorance is courteously termed, truth is hidden from them, and they are made to assume an artificial character before their faculties have acquired any strength. Taught from their infancy that beauty is

10 woman's scepter, the mind shapes itself to the body, and roaming round its gilt cage, only seeks to adore its prison. Men have various employments and pursuits which engage their attention, and give a character to the opening mind; but women, confined to one, and having their thoughts constantly directed to the most insignificant part of themselves, seldom extend their views beyond the triumph of the hour. . . .

15 This argument branches into various ramifications. Birth, riches, and every extrinsic advantage that exalt a man above his fellows, without any mental exertion, sink him in reality below them. In proportion to his weakness, he is played upon by designing men, till the bloated monster has lost all traces of humanity. . . . Educated in slavish dependence, and enervated by luxury and sloth, where shall we find men who will stand forth to assert the rights of man, or claim the privilege of moral

20 beings, who should have but one road to excellence? Slavery to monarchs and ministers, which the world will be long in freeing itself from, and whose deadly grasp stops the progress of the human mind, is not yet abolished.

Let not men then in the pride of power, use the same arguments that tyrannic kings and venal ministers have used, and fallaciously assert that woman ought to be subjected because she has

25 always been so. . . .

[I]f women be educated for dependence, that is, to act according to the will of another fallible being, and submit, right or wrong, to power, where are we to stop? Are they to be considered as vicegerents allowed to reign over a small domain, and answerable for their conduct to a higher tribunal, liable to error?

858 UNIT 4 THE TRIUMPH OF ROMANTICISM

Assessment Practice

Functional Material Explain to students that instructors often give test directions orally. Ask students to listen carefully as you read aloud the test directions at the top of this page. Ask students who clearly understand the directions to restate them. Tell students that restating or paraphrasing information is a listening strategy for checking comprehension.

30   It will not be difficult to prove that such delegates will act like men subjected by fear, and make their children and servants endure their tyrannical oppression. As they submit without reason, they will, having no fixed rules to square their conduct by, be kind, or cruel, just as the whim of the moment directs; and we ought not to wonder if sometimes, galled by their heavy yoke, they take a malignant pleasure in resting it on weaker shoulders. . . .

35   For man and woman, truth, if I understand the meaning of the word, must be the same; yet the fanciful female character, so prettily drawn by poets and novelists, demanding the sacrifice of truth and sincerity, virtue becomes a relative idea, having no other foundation than utility, and of that utility men pretend arbitrarily to judge, shaping it to their own convenience.

1. From the context, what do you conclude that the word *want* in line 4 means?
   A. need
   B. lack
   C. plan
   D. desire

2. Which of the following best describes the tone of the phrase *as ignorance is courteously termed*, in lines 7–8?
   F. sad
   G. sympathetic
   H. ironic
   J. bitter

3. Which type of figurative language is Wollstonecraft using in the phrase *beauty is woman's scepter* in lines 9–10?
   A. simile
   B. personification
   C. metaphor
   D. metaphysical conceit

4. What does Wollstonecraft claim "seeks to adore its prison" in lines 10–11?
   F. the ignorant woman's mind
   G. a beautiful woman's scepter
   H. a gilt cage
   J. an artificial character

5. According to Wollstonecraft in lines 12–14, what is the effect of women's having only one employment?
   A. They direct their thoughts to insignificant things.
   B. They open their minds and develop character.
   C. They develop insignificant character traits.
   D. They seldom extend their views past the present.

6. According to Wollstonecraft, what sinks a man below his fellows?
   F. advantage without mental exertion
   G. riches and every advantage
   H. the ramifications of argument
   J. weakness

7. From the context, what do you conclude that the word *enervated*, in line 18, means?
   A. strengthened
   B. frightened
   C. excited
   D. weakened

8. To whom does the word *delegates*, in line 30, refer?
   F. husbands
   G. women
   H. kings
   J. tyrants

1. B is the correct answer. The context makes clear that the intended meaning is "lack." [DOK 1]

2. H is the correct answer. Wollstonecraft is launching an ironic attack against the social norms that hindered a woman's education. [DOK 4]

3. C is the correct answer. In comparing unlike things indirectly, Wollstonecraft is using a metaphor. [DOK 2]

4. F is the correct answer. The subject of *seeks* in the sentence is the *mind*. [DOK 1]

5. D is the correct answer. Wollstonecraft explicitly states that women "seldom extend their views beyond the triumph of the hour." [DOK 1]

6. F is the correct answer. Wollstonecraft states explicitly that birth, riches, and every extrinsic advantage "without any mental exertion" sink the man. [DOK 1]

7. D is the correct answer. The context makes clear that the intended meaning of the word is "weakened." [DOK 1]

8. G is the correct answer. The phrase *act like men* excludes *husbands* and *kings*, so options **F** and **H** are incorrect. The sentence implies that women will become tyrannical, so option **J** is incorrect. [DOK 2]

English Learners

DIFFERENTIATED INSTRUCTION

Beginning Have students look up the following words in the dictionary: *sympathetic, bitter, adore, delegate*. Ask students to write down the meaning of each word and write a sentence using the word correctly. Check students' work. Have several volunteers share their sentences with the class. Write one sentence for each word on the board.

Assessment

Assess

9. D is the correct answer. Options **A, B,** and **C** all contradict the paragraph's message. `DOK 2`

10. F is the correct answer. It is the only option that makes sense in this context. `DOK 1`

11. C is the correct answer. Options **A, B,** and **D** all contradict either some portion or the general position of the essay. `DOK 4`

12. G is the correct answer. The overall tone is not ironic, humorous, or sarcastic; therefore, options **F, H,** and **J** are all incorrect. `DOK 4`

13. A is the correct answer. The author's purpose is clearly to persuade the reader to support equality between the sexes. `DOK 4`

14. H is the correct answer. Options **F** and **G** contradict a position taken by Wollstonecraft. Since Wollstonecraft never claims that women are more adept than men, option **J** is also incorrect. `DOK 2`

9. Which of the following is the main idea of the paragraph that begins on line 30?
   A. Men and women are naturally tyrannical.
   B. Tyranny is unavoidable in the household.
   C. Women are not capable of tyrannical behavior.
   D. The effects of tyranny are never isolated.

10. From the context, what do you conclude that the word *drawn*, in line 36, means?
    F. created
    G. closed
    H. drained
    J. confused

11. On the basis of this passage, with which of the following statements do you think Wollstonecraft would be most likely to agree?
    A. Equality between the sexes is impossible.
    B. Truth is based on utility.
    C. Arbitrary power cannot be justified.
    D. Innocence is the most desirable condition.

12. On the basis of this passage, what do you think the overall tone of this essay is?
    F. ironic
    G. authoritative
    H. humorous
    J. sarcastic

13. From your reading of this selection, what do you think the author's main purpose was?
    A. to persuade
    B. to instruct
    C. to inform
    D. to entertain

14. What is the main idea of this passage?
    F. Men and women must be treated differently.
    G. There is no such thing as truth.
    H. Inequality and tyranny are needless evils.
    J. Women are more adept than men.

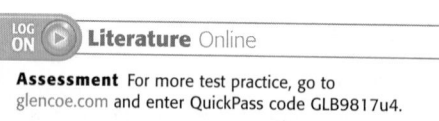

Literature Online

Assessment For more test practice, go to glencoe.com and enter QuickPass code GLB9817u4.

Reading Practice

Skim Explain that skimming involves looking over an entire selection quickly to get a general idea of what the piece is about. Skimming gives the reader a general idea of a selection's content. An effective way to practice skimming is to read, as quickly as possible, the first few sentences and the last few sentences of every paragraph. The more students practice this method, the easier it will become, as students learn to look for key verbs and nouns. Have students practice this technique, using magazine or newspaper articles.

Vocabulary Skills: Sentence Completion

For each item in the Vocabulary Skills section, choose the word or words that best complete the sentence.

1. During the Romantic period, writers chose to _____ the _____ mind embraced by the Enlightenment in favor of the imagination and intuition.
   A. relinquish . . . dismal
   B. spurn . . . rational
   C. cleave . . . bleak
   D. repose . . . congenial

2. During the 1700s, England's _____ over the Americas came to an end.
   F. dirge
   G. faculty
   H. penance
   J. dominion

3. Many of the Romantic writers at first embraced the political and cultural _____ and revolution of their day.
   A. tumult
   B. satiety
   C. teeming
   D. foresight

4. Romantic poets, including Keats and Shelley, believed in the _____ but transcendent power of the natural world.
   F. hypocritical
   G. bleak
   H. conspiring
   J. transient

5. William Blake's unconventional poetics, behavior, and religious beliefs confounded many of his _____.
   A. arbiters
   B. faculties
   C. furrows
   D. acquaintances

6. The radicalism of many of the Romantics _____ anger and indignation among _____ traditional thinkers and critics.
   F. incited . . . emphatically
   G. imparted . . . pomp
   H. loitered . . . deities
   J. relinquished . . . desolate

7. Many historians think that the American and French revolutions were the _____ outcome of royal mismanagement.
   A. uncouth
   B. inevitable
   C. illustrious
   D. kindred

8. The Romantics believed that the imagination was the most judicial and accurate _____ of the world.
   F. piety
   G. dirge
   H. arbiter
   J. indignation

9. The conditions of the Industrial Revolution forced many workers into _____ existences with little hope of improvement.
   A. secluded
   B. dismal
   C. loitering
   D. congenial

10. Mary Shelley's most famous fiction presents a disturbing and _____ view of humanity.
    F. bleak
    G. congenial
    H. transient
    J. widespread

Assessment

Assess

1. **B** is the correct answer. Options **A, C,** and **D** make no sense in this context. `DOK2`

2. **J** is the correct answer. It is the only option that makes sense in this context. `DOK1`

3. **A** is the correct answer. The word *revolution* suggests the word *tumult*. `DOK1`

4. **J** is the correct answer. Options **F, G,** and **H** have negative meanings that do not fit the context. `DOK1`

5. **D** is the correct answer. No other option makes sense in this context. `DOK1`

6. **F** is the correct answer. *Pomp* makes no sense in this context, making option **G** incorrect. *Loitered anger* and *relinquished anger* also make no sense in this context, so options **H** and **J** are also incorrect. `DOK2`

7. **B** is the correct answer. No other option makes sense in this context. `DOK1`

8. **H** is the correct answer. The word *judicial* suggests *arbiter*. `DOK1`

9. **B** is the correct answer. The phrase "little hope of improvement" suggests a dismal existence. `DOK1`

10. **F** is the correct answer. The word *disturbing* suggests no other answer but *bleak*. `DOK1`

Approaching Level
DIFFERENTIATED INSTRUCTION

Established Encourage students to read books, newspapers, and magazines for pleasure. The more students read, the more opportunities they will have to absorb new words and ideas and to expand their horizons. Suggest that students look up unfamiliar words and phrases and note them in a journal for future reference. Remind students that reading is a worthwhile activity with intangible rewards that will enrich their lives.

Teach

 Writing Skill

Active Versus Passive Voice
Remind students that an action verb is in the active voice when the subject of the sentence performs the action. Sentences in the active voice generally are clearer, more direct, and more concise than those in the passive voice. Use the passive voice only when the emphasis is intended to be on something other than the doer of the action or when the doer is unknown. On the board (or a transparency), write these two sentences:

The championship was won by the Mud Hens.

The Mud Hens won the championship.

Ask: Which of these two sentences is more effective? Why? *(The second sentence is more direct and concise.)*

Grammar and Writing: Paragraph Improvement

In the following excerpt from a student draft of a reflective essay, you will find underlined phrases and sentences. The number beneath each underlined phrase corresponds to a numbered question on the next page. Each question will prompt you to replace an underlined phrase. If you think the original should not be changed, choose "NO CHANGE."

At the end of the passage, you will also find a boxed number. This number refers to a question about a specific paragraph or to the essay as a whole.

Both the boxed number and the numbers that appear beneath underlined phrases or sentences refer to question numbers, *not* to the sequence of sentences or paragraphs.

As you read, pay close attention to the writer's use of modifiers, punctuation, and voice.

[1]
How can the world be made up of contradictions? Good and evil, light and dark, and tragedy and comedy are all at odds, and yet exist as parts of a greater whole! These contradictions are what William Blake was wrestling with as he wrote "The Tyger." This poem depicts the violence and power of a Tyger, and the awe the speaker feels for it. Enthralled by the Tyger's force, the poem is propelled by an electric and rhythmic cadence. The poet also intended the piece as a contrast and complement to the delightful and innocent Lamb, from his Songs of Innocence. The contrast of these elements—*innocence* and *experience*, as embodied by these animals—is a compelling symbol for the world in which we live.

[2]
In the first stanza, a question is posed by the speaker. This question, the backbone of the poem's theme, animates the whole purpose of both innocence and experience: "What immortal hand or eye / Could frame thy fearful symmetry?" Here Blake is asking, "What could produce such a frightening thing?" He is also asking, "How can the Tyger's nature, which contradicts that of the Lamb's, exist?" This is the "fearful symmetry" to which Blake is referring. In fact, symmetry is employed throughout the Songs of Innocence and Experience with complex echoes and counterargument. The interaction between the worlds of innocence and experience evokes many thoughts. It prompts exploration. It prompts the kinds of questions that only I ask when I see violence, or unhappiness, or when I consider natural disasters or calamities caused by human beings. I wonder how these things can exist in a world with so much potential for good.

9

862 UNIT 4 THE TRIUMPH OF ROMANTICISM

Writing Practice

Avoid Unnecessary Words Remind students that the clearest, most effective writing is simple and direct. A sentence should contain only necessary words and a paragraph only necessary sentences. Good writers make every word count.

Ask students to improve these phrases:

He is a man who . . . (He)
The reason why is that . . . (Because)
In a rapid manner . . . (Rapidly)
Owing to the fact that . . . (Since/ Because)

1. **A.** NO CHANGE
   B. *Good* and *evil*, *light* and *dark*, and *tragedy* and *comedy* are all at odds, and yet exist as parts of a greater whole!
   C. Good and evil, light and dark, and tragedy and comedy are all at odds and yet exist as parts of a greater whole.
   D. Good and evil; light and dark; tragedy and comedy; are all at odds, and yet exist as parts of a greater whole.

2. **F.** NO CHANGE
   G. Enthralled by the Tyger's force; the poem is propelled by an electric, rhythmic cadence.
   H. Enthralled by the Tyger's force. The poem is propelled by an electric, and rhythmic cadence.
   J. Enthralled by the Tyger's force, Blake made the poem seem propelled by an electric and rhythmic cadence.

3. **A.** NO CHANGE
   B. delightful and innocent Lamb from his *Songs of Innocence*.
   C. *delightful*, *innocent* Lamb, from *Songs of Innocence*.
   D. "delightful" and "innocent" Lamb—from his Songs of Innocence.

4. **F.** NO CHANGE
   G. innocence and experience as embodied by these animals. Is a *compelling* symbol for the *world* in which we live.
   H. *innocence* and *experience* as embodied by these animals—is a *compelling* symbol for the *world* in which we live.
   J. innocence and experience, as embodied by these animals—is a compelling symbol for the world in which we live.

5. **A.** NO CHANGE
   B. A question is posed in the first stanza.
   C. In the first stanza, the speaker poses a question.
   D. In the first stanza: a question is posed.

6. **F.** NO CHANGE
   G. animated the whole purpose of both innocence and experience:
   H. *animates* a purpose of innocence and experience:
   J. animates the whole purpose of both "innocence" and "experience."

7. **A.** NO CHANGE
   B. In fact, with complex echoes and counterargument, symmetry is employed throughout the *Songs of Innocence and Experience*.
   C. In fact, symmetry is employed throughout the *Songs of Innocence and Experience*.
   D. symmetry is employed throughout the *Songs of Innocence and Experience* with complex echoes and counterargument.

8. **F.** NO CHANGE
   G. Only it prompts the kinds of questions that I ask when I see violence
   H. It prompts the kinds of questions that I ask only when I see violence
   J. It prompts the questions that only I ask when I see violence

9. Which of the following would be the most logical topic for paragraph 3?
   A. Blake's poetic influences
   B. discussion of stanzas after the first stanza
   C. the relationship between "The Tyger" and "The Lamb"
   D. symbolism in "The Lamb"

Essay

Which poem from this unit affected you most? Write a reflective essay in which you discuss how the poem changed you, how it relates to your personal experience, and what the universal themes in the poem are. As you write, keep in mind that your essay will be checked for **ideas, organization, voice, word choice, sentence fluency, conventions,** and **presentation.**

Assessment

Assess

1. **C** is the correct answer. This sentence contains an unnecessary exclamation point and an incorrectly used comma between parts of a compound predicate. `DOK 1`

2. **J** is the correct answer. No other option corrects the dangling modifier. `DOK 1`

3. **B** is the correct answer. The book title should be italicized. `DOK 1`

4. **J** is the correct answer. No other option corrects the inappropriate italicization without introducing further errors. `DOK 1`

5. **C** is the correct answer. This sentence is needlessly written in the passive voice. No other option corrects this problem. `DOK 1`

6. **F** is the correct answer. This sentence contains no errors. `DOK 1`

7. **B** is the correct answer. No other option corrects the misplaced modifier without changing the content or introducing further errors. `DOK 1`

8. **H** is the correct answer. No other option corrects the misplaced modifier. `DOK 1`

9. **C** is the correct answer. In the second paragraph, the opening stanza's relevance to the thesis statement is discussed, so it would be logical to discuss the other stanzas in the next paragraph. `DOK 4`

⚡ Essay

Remind students of the key points they learned about writing a reflective essay: drawing comparisons between specific personal experiences and universal literary themes; clearly organizing their ideas from beginning to end; using first-person point of view and a thoughtful, conversational tone. Encourage students to develop their writing voice and style by keeping a journal or by writing for the school paper. `DOK 3`

Skills Scope and Sequence

Readability Scores Key: Dale-Chall/DRP/Lexile

PART 1: Optimism and the Belief in Progress

Selections and Features	Literary Elements
Unit Introduction pp. 864–878	Sensory Details **TE** p. 875
Poems *from* **In Memoriam A. H. H.,** and **Crossing the Bar,** and **Tears, Idle Tears,** by Alfred, Lord Tennyson pp. 880–889	Rhythm **SE** p. 881 Poetic Structure **TE** p. 886 Repetition (review) **SE** p. 888
Poem Ulysses, by Alfred, Lord Tennyson pp. 890–895	Assonance and Consonance **SE** p. 890 Alliteration (review) **SE** p. 894
Comparing Literature Sonnet 43, by Elizabeth Barrett Browning, **Love Is Not All: It Is Not Meat nor Drink** (poem), by Edna St. Vincent Millay, and **In My Life** (song), by John Lennon and Paul McCartney pp. 896–903	Repetition **SE** p. 898
Informational Text TIME: What Is Love? by Paul Gray 9.5/67/1070 pp. 904–907	
Poems Pied Beauty and **Spring and Fall: To a Young Child,** by Gerard Manley Hopkins pp. 908–912	Sprung Rhythm **SE** p. 909
Poem Jabberwocky, by Lewis Carroll pp. 913–916	Nonsense Verse **SE** p. 914
Literary Perspective Jabberwocky, by Wanda Coleman 7.6/68/1230 pp. 917–920	

Reading Skills and Strategies	Vocabulary	Writing Grammar	Speaking, Listening, Viewing

Use the Timeline **TE** p. 866
Analyze Graphic Information
   SE pp. 867, 869
Draw Conclusions **TE** p. 867
Make Inferences **TE** p. 868
Make Generalizations **TE** p. 869
Use Subheads to Find Main Idea
   TE p. 871
Interpret **SE** p. 873
Identify Author's Purpose **TE** p. 873
Analyze Cause and Effect **TE** p. 874,
   SE p. 875
Connect **TE** p. 876
Compare and Contrast **SE** p. 877
	Word Roots **TE** p. 876	Write a Reflective Essay
		   TE p. 878	

Analyze Mood **SE** p. 881 Compare and Contrast **TE** p. 882	Word Usage **SE** p. 889 Academic Vocabulary **SE** p. 889	Apply Rhythm **SE** p. 889	

Analyze Tone **SE** p. 890	Context Clues **SE** p. 895
	Academic Vocabulary
	   SE p. 895
		Write About Allusions
		   TE p. 892
			Oral Interpretation **SE** p. 895

Compare Theme **SE** p. 896
Compare Historical Contexts **SE** p. 896
Analyze Style **SE** p. 898
	Academic Vocabulary
	   SE p. 900
		Identify Adverbs **TE** p. 898
		Write a List **SE** p. 900
		Write an Essay **SE** p. 903
			Small Group Discussion
			   SE pp. 901, 902
			Hear the Song **TE** p. 902

Examine Connotation and Denotation **SE** p. 904	Compound Words **TE** p. 904		Hear Song Lyrics **TE** p. 906
Monitor Comprehension **SE** p. 909 Preread **TE** p. 910 Make Inferences **TE** p. 911	Word Usage **SE** p. 912	Write a Journal Entry **SE** p. 912	
Analyze Style **SE** p. 914	Identify Suffixes **TE** p. 914 Academic Vocabulary **SE** p. 916	Write a Story **SE** p. 916	
Analyze Literary Influences **SE** p. 917 Make Critical Judgments **TE** p. 918			

Readability Scores Key: Dale-Chall/DRP/Lexile

PART 2: Realism and Naturalism

Reading Skills and Strategies	Vocabulary	Writing Grammar	Speaking, Listening, Viewing
		Write About Cause and Effect **TE** p. 922	
Analyze Characterization **SE** p. 925 Recognize Author's Purpose **TE** p. 930 Discuss Antagonists and Conflict **TE** p. 930 Make Inferences **TE** p. 932	Context Clues **SE** p. 934	Draw Conclusions in an Essay **TE** p. 926	Oral Report **SE** p. 934
		Noun Clauses **SE** p. 935	
Clarify Meaning **SE** p. 937	Word Usage **SE** p. 940	Write a Letter **SE** p. 940	Read Aloud **TE** p. 938
Connect to Contemporary Issues **SE** p. 942 Identify Hyperbole **TE** p. 946	Context Clues **SE** p. 948 Academic Vocabulary **SE** p. 948	Write a Response **TE** p. 944 Write a Review **SE** p. 949 Superlative Adjectives **SE** p. 949	
	Word Origins **SE** p. 950		
Compare and Contrast Imagery **SE** p. 952 Preview **TE** p. 952	Academic Vocabulary **SE** p. 954	Write a Journal Entry **SE** p. 954	
Connect to Personal Experience **SE** p. 956 Preview **TE** p. 956	Analogies **SE** p. 958	Write an Article **SE** p. 958	
Analyze Theme **SE** p. 960 Preview **TE** p. 960	Academic Vocabulary **SE** p. 965	Apply Irony **SE** p. 965	Dramatic Monologue **TE** p. 962

Readability Scores Key: Dale-Chall/DRP/Lexile

PART 2: Realism and Naturalism *(continued)*

Selections and Features	Literary Elements
Writing Workshop pp. 966–973	
Speaking, Listening, and Viewing Workshop pp. 974–975	
Independent Reading pp. 976–977	
Assessment pp. 978–983	

Reading Skills and Strategies	Vocabulary	Writing / Grammar	Speaking, Listening, Viewing
		Respond to a Poem **SE** p. 967 Use Transitional Phrases **TE** p. 968 Prewrite **SE** p. 969 Draft **SE** p. 970 Understand Abstract Versus Concrete Nouns **TE** p. 970 Revise **SE** p. 972 Rewrite Wordy Sentences **SE** p. 972 Edit and Proofread **SE** p. 973 In-Text Quotations from Poems **SE** p. 973	Present **SE** p. 973
			Discussion Group **SE** pp. 974–975
Analyze Author's Background **TE** p. 976		Prepare an Interview **SE** p. 977	
Identify Allusion **TE** p. 978		Identify Topic Sentences **TE** p. 982 Write an Essay **SE** p. 983	

Focus

The Bayswater Omnibus, 1895. George William Joy. Oil on canvas, 47½ x 78¼ in. Museum of London.

View the Art Horse-drawn omnibuses like the one shown here were the predecessor of modern, motorized buses. What can you infer about omnibuses and their passengers from the details in this image?

Unit Introduction Skills

Literary Elements
- Sensory Details (TE p. 875)

Reading Skills
- Analyze Graphic Information (SE pp. 866–869)
- Interpret (SE pp. 872–873)
- Analyze Cause and Effect (SE pp. 874–875)
- Compare and Contrast (SE pp. 876–877)

The Victorian Age

Vocabulary Skills
- Word Roots (TE p. 876)

Listening/Speaking/Viewing Skills
- Contrast Literary Periods (SE p. 878)
- Build Visual Literacy (SE p. 878)
- Analyze Art (SE pp. 864, 873, 877)

Writing Skills/Grammar
- Take Notes (SE p. 878)

The Victorian Age

1837–1901

Looking Ahead

During the sixty-four-year reign of Queen Victoria, Britain experienced unprecedented economic and technological growth and dramatic political and social change. Britain became "the workshop of the world." About a quarter of the world's people lived within the British Empire. A growing social consciousness stirred reforms. Some Victorian writers felt an optimistic promise in the era; others saw the menace of a world driven by inhuman forces.

Keep the following questions in mind as you read:

◆ How were Britain and the British Empire changing during the Victorian age?

◆ What conditions helped stimulate Victorian optimism?

◆ How did the mood of later Victorian writers change?

865

Focus

Summary

This section briefly views the surge in power and wealth that Britain underwent from 1837 to 1901. It captures the reaction of Victorian writers to British life, including the growing concern for those left behind. The overview divides the Victorian age into distinct thematic parts: optimism and progress, realism, and disillusionment.

View the Art ★

Possible answers: *Students might infer from the passengers' clothing that omnibuses were used by the middle or upper classes. Students might note that the buses were used by both genders, and people of different ages.*

An Irish painter of the human form, George W. Joy (1844–1925) worked with narrative themes and historical allusions. For this work, point out that horse-drawn omnibuses were used in London during the 1800s. Explain that the painting, a view of modern life, is among Joy's best and according to one critic "displays his powers of observation at their keenest."

Unit Resources

Print Materials

- Unit 5 Teaching Resources, pp. 1–171
- Interactive Read and Write (On Level,/ Approaching, EL), pp. 223–256
- Novel Companion, p. 231
- Bellringer Option Transparencies: Selection Focus 43–49; Daily Language Practice 70–81

- Literary Element Transparencies 13, 24, 29, 38, 54, 61, 68, 85, 89
- Assessment Resources, Unit Assessment, pp. 33–40
- Assessment Resources, Selection Assessment, pp. 213–240

Technology

- TeacherWorks Plus CD
- StudentWorks Plus CD
- Literature Launchers: Pre-Reading Videos DVD, Unit 5
- Literature Online
- Interactive Vocabulary CD-ROM
- Listening Library CD-ROM
- ExamView CD-ROM
- Skill Level Up! CD-ROM

Teach

Reading Strategy | 1

Use the Timeline Have students examine the timeline and relate British literary milestones to major events in British and world history.

- Explain that themes of social justice in Dickens's novels reflected ideas found in the *Communist Manifesto*.

- Point out that Darwin's *On the Origin of Species* had a powerful and controversial effect on ideas of humanity's origins.

Ask: What historical event on the timeline is related to Darwin's ideas? *(Discovery of Neanderthal remains in 1856)*

Literary History ☆

"Goblin Market" Christina Rossetti's (1830–1894) fairy tale–like poem features two sisters who are tempted, threatened and attacked by goblin merchants selling fruit. Many interpretations of the poem focus on what Rossetti seems to be suggesting about the victimization of women in a male-dominated society.

Timeline 1837–1901 ❶

Charles Darwin

BRITISH LITERATURE

1835   **1865**

1841
Humorous weekly *Punch* is founded

1847
Emily Brontë publishes *Wuthering Heights*

1847
Charlotte Brontë publishes *Jane Eyre*

1850
Alfred Tennyson becomes poet laureate

1859
Charles Darwin publishes *On the Origin of Species*

1859
Edward FitzGerald publishes *Rubáiyát of Omar Khayyám*

1861
Charles Dickens publishes *Great Expectations*

1862
Christina Rossetti publishes *Goblin Market* ▼ ☆

1865
Lewis Carroll publishes *Alice's Adventures in Wonderland*

1866
Gerard Manley Hopkins becomes a Roman Catholic

1867
Matthew Arnold publishes *New Poems*

BRITISH EVENTS

1835   **1865**

1837
Victoria is crowned queen

1838
Chartists demand political reforms

1839
First real bicycle is invented in Scotland

1840
Queen Victoria marries Prince Albert

1841
Hong Kong comes under British sovereignty

1845
Irish Potato Famine begins

1851
Great Exhibition is held ▶

1854
Britain enters Crimean War

1857
Indian Mutiny breaks out

1861
Prince Albert dies

1862
John Hanning Speke identifies source of Nile

Crystal Palace

1865
Joseph Lister initiates antiseptic surgery

WORLD EVENTS

1835   **1865**

1837
John Deere invents steel plow in the United States

1848
Revolutions break out in Europe

1848
German philosophers Marx and Engels write *Communist Manifesto*

1856 ▲
Remains of Neanderthal man are discovered in Germany

1861
Alexander II emancipates Russian serfs

1865
American Civil War ends

1866
Alfred Nobel invents dynamite

1868
Meiji restoration occurs in Japan

LOG ON ▶ **Literature** Online

Literature and Reading To explore the Interactive Timeline, go to glencoe.com and enter QuickPass code GLB9817u5.

Reading Practice

SPIRAL REVIEW Ⓖ **Use Graphic Information Say:** A timeline like this one can help you to make connections between events that occured during the same time period and to draw conclusions about the connections. For instance, the 1856 discovery of Neanderthal man and the 1861 publication of *On the Origin of Species* both reflect new ideas about human origins. **Ask:** What connection can you make between John Deere's 1837 invention of the steel plow, the 1865 introduction of antiseptic surgery, and the 1898 publication of *The War of the Worlds?* *(the development of technology in the 19th century)* Have students find other ways of grouping contemporaneous events and themes that developed over time. *(Answers will vary.)*

The Mad Tea Party, John Tenniel.
The Pierpont Morgan Library,
New York.

1885

1878
Thomas Hardy publishes
The Return of the Native

1882
Robert Louis Stevenson
publishes *Treasure Island* **2**

1884
First volume of
Oxford English Dictionary
is published

1894
First issue of *The Yellow
Book* is published

1895
*The Importance of Being
Earnest* by Oscar Wilde
is produced

1896
A. E. Housman publishes
A Shropshire Lad

1897
Bram Stoker publishes
Dracula

1898
H. G. Wells publishes
The War of the Worlds ▶

1885

1866
Great Eastern lays first
successful transatlantic
cable

1869
Debtors' prisons are
abolished

1876
Queen Victoria is
proclaimed Empress of
India

1885
General Gordon is killed
at Khartoum

1897
Queen Victoria celebrates
her Diamond Jubilee ☆

1899
Boer War begins
in South Africa

1901
Commonwealth of Australia
is established ▶

1901
Queen Victoria dies;
Edward VII becomes king

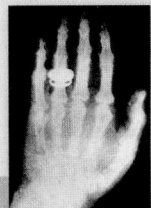

1885

1874
First Impressionist
exhibition is held in Paris

1876
Alexander Graham Bell
invents telephone in the
United States ▼

1885
Leopold II of Belgium
acquires Congo in Africa

1888
Wilhelm II becomes
emperor of Germany

1895
Italian engineer Guglielmo
Marconi invents wireless
telegraphy

1895 ▲
German physicist Wilhelm
Röntgen discovers X-rays

1901
First Nobel Prizes are
awarded

Reading Check

Analyze Graphic Information For how many
years was Queen Victoria a widow?

INTRODUCTION **867**

Teach

Reading Check

Answer: *40 years*

Reading Strategy | 2

Draw Conclusions Tell
students that the late 1800s saw
a rise in middle-class readership.
Direct them to the timeline to
find the books published in 1882,
1897, and 1898. **Ask:** On the
basis of what you know about
these stories, what conclusion
can you draw about the tastes of
middle-class readers in the late
1800s? *(Students might say these
books suggest there was a market
for adventure stories, some with
horror or science fiction themes.)*

Cultural History ☆

Victorian Ideals By the time of
Queen Victoria's Diamond Jubilee,
Victoria could see a nation that had
come to glow with achievement
during her long reign. The British
Empire now peaked as a world
power, embracing a quarter of the
world's population and area. As a
result of the new wealth, a strong
middle class had formed, and its
rigid standards and moral tone
defined the age. At the same time,
an increase in social consciousness
stirred reforms.

Teach

Reading Strategy | 1

Make Inferences Focus students' attention on the Eligible Voters chart. **Ask:** What can you infer about the kinds of voters the Reform Acts added to the polls? *(Students ought to infer from the word* reform *that more men from lower social classes gained the right to vote.)*

APPROACHING **Ask:** What does it mean to reform something? *(to improve something that is unjust or corrupt)*

Cultural History ☆

Class and Education The Victorian upper class saw no benefit to sharing education with the masses. To add to the problem, working-class families could not afford to spare a child's wages. British businesses, in turn, wanted child workers, and pauper apprentices came cheap. George Courtald, a silk-mill owner, bought children from workhouses and had them sign contracts that bound them to the mill until age 21, paying them 1.5 pounds per week.

By the Numbers

Growth in the British Electorate, 1832–1884

Through a series of reform bills, the number of male voters in Britain greatly increased during the Victorian age. Women would have to wait until the twentieth century to win the right to vote.

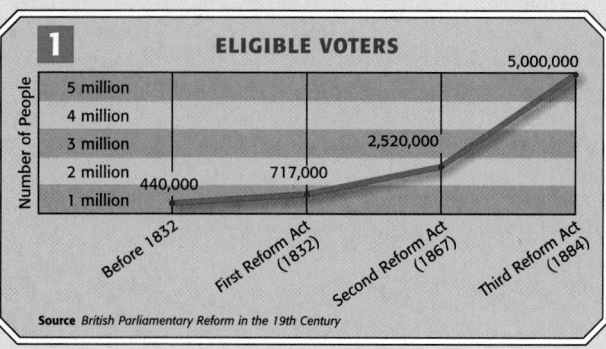

1 ELIGIBLE VOTERS

- Number of People: 1 million – 5 million
- Before 1832: 440,000
- First Reform Act (1832): 717,000
- Second Reform Act (1867): 2,520,000
- Third Reform Act (1884): 5,000,000

Source *British Parliamentary Reform in the 19th Century*

THE GREAT EXHIBITION OF 1851

Queen Victoria officially opened the "Great Exhibition of the Works of Industry of All Nations"—the first world's fair—at noon on May 1, 1851, in the mammoth Crystal Palace erected in London's Hyde Park.

- The Crystal Palace was 1,848 feet long and 408 feet wide. The central transept was 108 feet high.

- More than half of the almost 14,000 exhibitors at the Great Exhibition were from Britain and the British Empire.

- More than 6,200,000 visitors attended the exhibition—478,773 in the last week alone—before it closed on October 11, 1851.

- Among the displays were the first life-size models of creatures that scientists had named only a few years earlier: dinosaurs.

SETTLING AUSTRALIA

Between 1788 and 1868, Britain sent more than 160,000 convicts to Australia. The First Fleet consisted of 11 small ships carrying 736 criminals. Their average age was 27. The oldest male was in his sixties; the youngest was 9. The youngest female was 13; the oldest, 84.

HOME LIGHTING

Before the electric light was invented, candles and oil lamps lighted homes. One estate employed 3 or more men cutting wicks, removing wax drips, cleaning glass lamp chimneys, and filling lamps. Even a modest home could have 20 or more lamps.

CHILD MORTALITY

In 1839 nearly half the funerals in London were for children younger than 10 years old.

SERVANTS

In Victorian Britain, having at least one servant was a mark of middle-class respectability. In 1891 servants made up 16 percent of the British work force.

EDUCATION ☆

Elementary education was not compulsory in Britain until 1880. In 1871 more than 19 percent of men and 26 percent of women could not sign their names. Twenty years later, both figures had dropped to around 7 percent.

HUNTING

The Victorian upper class spent a lot of time shooting game animals on their estates. During a three-day period in 1864, hunters at one estate killed 4,045 pheasants, 3,902 rabbits, 860 hares, 59 woodcocks, and 28 creatures described as "various."

Reading Practice

SPIRAL REVIEW **Draw Conclusions** Remind students that they can skillfully draw conclusions by noting details as they read and making educated guesses about their importance to the text. Have the class look at the paragraph under "Settling Australia."

Ask: What conclusions can you draw about how the British justice system considered the age of offenders when assigning punishments? *(Since people from 9 to 84 were exiled, age was not much of a consideration.)*

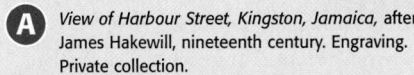
Being There

The Victorian age was a period of great expansion for the British Empire. Along with other European powers, the British engaged in a fierce competition for African colonies. The vast Indian subcontinent became "the Jewel in the Crown" of Queen Victoria, who was declared Empress of India in 1876. Britain's annexation of Australia continued throughout the Victorian age, until the entire island continent was part of the British Empire.

B *The Last of England,* Ford Madox Brown, 1852–1855. Oil on panel. Birmingham Museums and Art Gallery, United Kingdom.

A *View of Harbour Street, Kingston, Jamaica,* after James Hakewill, nineteenth century. Engraving. Private collection.

C *The British Raj Great Indian Peninsular Terminus,* unknown artist, nineteenth century. Watercolor on paper. British Library, London.

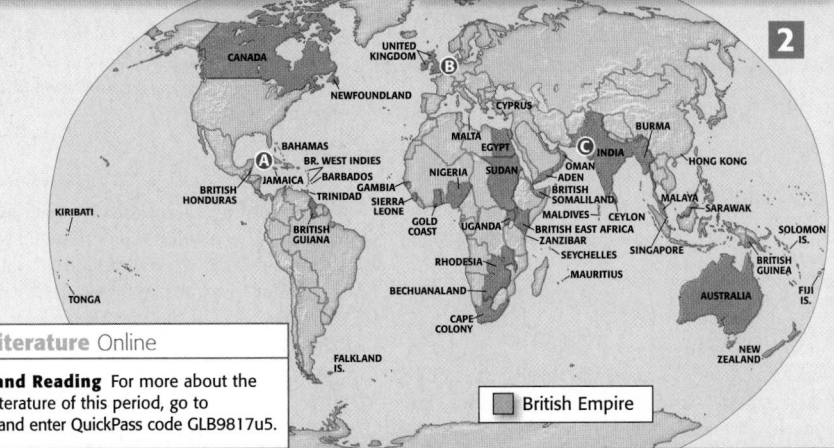

LOG ON ▶ **Literature** Online

Literature and Reading For more about the history and literature of this period, go to glencoe.com and enter QuickPass code GLB9817u5.

Reading Check

Analyze Graphic Information:

1. About how many times greater was the British electorate after 1884 than it had been before 1832?

2. Approximately how many exhibitors at the Great Exhibition were from Britain and the British Empire?

3. On what continent did the British Empire have the smallest amount of territory?

English Learners

DIFFERENTIATED INSTRUCTION

Beginning Point out the words *exhibition* and *exhibitors*. Then write on the board

| -tion | SUFFIX | "action of" |
| -or/-er | SUFFIX | "one who does" |

Have students suggest other examples of words containing these suffixes.

Intermediate **Write on the board:** jewel in the crown; The sun never sets on the British Empire. **Ask:** Figurative language was often used to describe the British Empire. What do these two expressions mean? *(the most valuable part of the empire; the empire is vast)*

Teach

Reading Check

Answers:

1. *More than 10 times greater*
2. *More than 7,000*
3. *South America*

Reading Strategy | 2

Make Generalizations Have students look at the map and pictures. **Ask:** Into what latitudes did the British Empire mostly expand in this era? *(tropical and southern latitudes.)*

View the Art

A. James Hakewill was an architect and illustrator who lived in Jamaica for two years.

B. Ford Madox Brown's painting depicts sculptor Thomas Woolner setting out on the treacherous journey to Australia. Brown wrote a poem to accompany his painting, in which the speaker states, "The last of England! O'er the seas, my dear, / Our homes to seek amid Australian fields."

C. "British Raj" refers to the area of direct British rule on the Indian subcontinent. British culture had a great impact on the countries that were under its rule.

Teach

Reading Strategy | 1

Make Generalizations Have students read the quotation on this page.

Ask: What generalization can you make from the quotation? *(Students should see that Victorian Britain saw itself as benevolent master of the world.)*

Political History ☆

Victoria, the Woman Queen Victoria had the longest reign in the history of British monarchy. In 1840, she wed her German cousin Albert, whom she adored. As Albert came to have a strong influence on the government, observers commented that he was, to all intents and purposes, the king. In 1861, Prince Albert died of typhoid fever. Grief overwhelmed the queen for her remaining forty years. While her children offered some comfort, Victoria tried to govern as Albert would have wished. But eventually she withdrew to their Scottish castle, Balmoral, becoming a remote figure.

Learning Objectives

For pages 864–878

In studying this text, you will focus on the following objectives:

Literary Study:
Analyzing a literary period. Connecting to the literature.

Reading: Evaluating historical influences.

The Victorian Age

1837–1901

Historical, Social, and Cultural Forces

☆ Queen Victoria and Her Empire

Victoria came to the British throne in 1837 as a girl of eighteen; at her death in 1901, most of her subjects had never known any other ruler. Personally, Victoria was most interested in her own family—her husband, Prince Albert, and their nine children. As "mother of the empire," however, she also played a major symbolic role in unifying Britain's widespread colonies. By Queen Victoria's sixtieth anniversary Diamond Jubilee in 1897, she ruled one-quarter of the world's population.

> **1** *"The British Empire is under Providence the greatest instrument for good that the world has seen."*
>
> —Lord Curzon, Viceroy of India

Technological Advances

Britain's imperial success was aided by technological strength. Victorian life literally sped up. For untold centuries, the fastest speeds possible—and then only for the rich—were achieved with horses and sailing ships. By the end of the century, locomotives could reach fifty miles per hour, and steamships, fifteen knots.

Many nineteenth-century inventions similarly changed the fabric and structure of daily life. Cast iron and elevators enabled people to build taller buildings; transatlantic telegraph wires and telephones meant people communicated more quickly and widely; the new aniline dyes meant people dressed more brightly. Electric light made streets safer and theatrical performances more thrilling. The discovery of vaccines and the pasteurization of milk improved health. Canned food fed soldiers and arctic explorers while bringing variety to the limitations of locally produced, seasonal diets. For the first time, photographs preserved memories. To the Victorians, speed and other technological innovations seemed to promise a better world in many respects.

Marxism and Darwinism

The stunning changes of Victorian life came at a price. The visible signs of material progress seemed to many contemporaries to underscore the lack of progress on other fronts. Governmental committees published reports on such subjects as child labor laws, conditions in mines, and sewer projects. Many of these reports, known as Blue Books because of the color of their covers, had real effects on public opinion and the laws. Despite mountains of data, however, many people felt the lack of an overarching theory to make sense of the huge changes they had witnessed. In this cultural climate, two men provided theories that continue to influence us today.

Writing Practice

 Elaborate with Facts and Statistics Point out that elaborating with facts and statistics strengthens a report. **Then write on the board:** Britain's imperial success was aided by technological strength.

Have students look at the paragraph beneath the displayed quotation. Ask them to write answers to the following questions on their paper.

1. What factual framework does the writer add to this foundation? *("Victorian life literally sped up.")*

2. What statistics are used to elaborate on the facts? *(Locomotives could reach 50 mph and steamships 15 knots.)*

The German-born philosopher Karl Marx moved to London in 1849 after being exiled from Paris for his political radicalism. In Britain, he drew on the information contained in the Blue Books to write his most famous and influential book, *Das Kapital* ("Capital"), which began to appear in English in 1886. Marx believed that class warfare was inevitable. According to him, all property and means of production should be held in common, and all means of subsistence should be shared equally: "From each according to his abilities, to each according to his needs."

Marx intended his ideas to have earth-shaking political and social consequences; the British naturalist Charles Darwin did not. He published his book *On the Origin of Species by Means of Natural Selection* in 1859, but the seeds of it had been planted more than twenty years earlier on an expedition to gather biological specimens. Darwin's long-term observations and speculations led him to view all living organisms—from pine trees and codfish to human beings—as governed by the same natural laws. For Darwin, evolution was the result of the process of natural selection

Postcard illustrating the British Empire, c. 1919. Rykoff collection. ★

acting on random mutations; there was no agent behind the changes. By the end of the century, contemporary interpreters of Darwin claimed evolution implied progress. They used biological notions of "the survival of the fittest" (not Darwin's words) to justify the power of the rich, an application known as Social Darwinism. Darwin, however, was not interested in applying his theories to human social policy.

 PREVIEW **Big Ideas** of the Victorian Age

[2]

1 Optimism and the Belief in Progress

During the Victorian era, Britain developed a huge empire. The resulting material success, coupled with technological advances and social reforms, encouraged an optimistic belief in progress that was reflected in some Victorian literature.

See pages 872–873.

2 The Emergence of Realism

In the mid-1800s, a reaction to Romanticism appeared in art and literature. This movement—Realism—aimed to explore contemporary life and ordinary experience. Many Victorian Realist writers sought to reform society.

See pages 874–875.

3 Disillusionment and Darker Visions

By the late 1800s, a movement called Naturalism had developed out of Realism. Like Realists, Naturalists presented people and their problems as accurately as possible. However, Naturalists tended toward extreme pessimism.

See pages 876–877.

Approaching Level

DIFFERENTIATED INSTRUCTION

Established Ask if students have prior knowledge about Marx or Darwin. Then point out that the work of these men still sparks controversy. **Ask:** Who might dislike the idea that a nation's wealth should be shared equally among all its people? *(The financial establishment and the wealthiest members of society)* Who might dislike the idea that natural forces shape life on Earth? *(Religious groups and*

others who believe God created all life) Invite students to use the Internet to research the rippling effects of these ideas in current news.

Teach

Reading Strategy 2

Main Idea Have students read the numbered subheads under "Big Ideas of the Victorian Age." **Ask:** How do the subheads help you understand the work you'll read? *(The subheads divide the unit into three main ideas, and the literature under each will typify that theme.)* How does reading the three subheads together establish a sense of continuity? *(It shows the rise, peak, and ultimate fall of the optimism of the time.)* **Say:** The suffix *-ical* changes the noun *technology* into the adjective *technological.* Apply the same suffix to these nouns: *biology, astrology (biological, astrological)*

View the Art ★

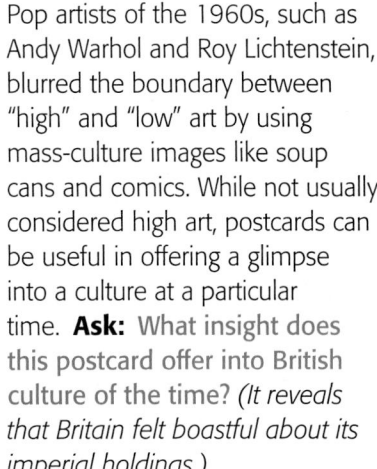

Pop artists of the 1960s, such as Andy Warhol and Roy Lichtenstein, blurred the boundary between "high" and "low" art by using mass-culture images like soup cans and comics. While not usually considered high art, postcards can be useful in offering a glimpse into a culture at a particular time. **Ask:** What insight does this postcard offer into British culture of the time? *(It reveals that Britain felt boastful about its imperial holdings.)*

Reading Strategy | 1

Make Generalizations

Ask: From the subheads, what generalizations can you make about each of these sections? *(First section: Victorian Britain valued morality. Second section: The middle class became more powerful. Third section: Britain progressed democratically. Fourth section: Britain expanded its power through colonization.)* What generalization links these sections? *Britain was progressing in many ways.)*

[APPROACHING] **Ask:** According to the section under the first subhead, what is an example of a Victorian value? *(self-improvement, earnestness, or work)*

Literary History ☆

"In Memoriam" Lord Tennyson wrote his long poem "In Memoriam A. H. H." in honor of a very close friend who died tragically young. In addition to charting the course of Tennyson's grief and his ultimate acceptance of his friend's death, the poem treats many other issues, including the inner conflict between religious beliefs and many of the new scientific theories of the time.

Big Idea 1

Optimism and the Belief in Progress

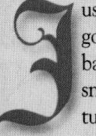 ust like styles of clothing, beliefs and ideals go out of fashion—and then often come back in again. Victorian values have been sneered at off and on for more than a century, but they show no sign of disappearing.

1 Victorian Values

Three of the most typical Victorian ideals were self-improvement, moral earnestness, and the value of work. In the bestselling *Self-Help*, published in 1859, Samuel Smiles preached a gospel of thrift, hard work, and patience: "Honorable industry travels the same road with duty; and Providence has closely linked both with happiness." Moral earnestness defined the work of Queen Victoria's favorite contemporary writer, her poet laureate, Alfred, Lord Tennyson (see page 880). After the death of her husband in 1861, the queen cherished Tennyson's long poem *In Memoriam*, which struggles to affirm the survival of love despite death and religious doubts.

> *"Not what I have, . . . but what I do is my kingdom."*
>
> —Thomas Carlyle, Sartor Resartus

The Middle-Class Public

The middle-class virtues of Victorian individualism seemed to define a new aristocracy of merit. Making something of oneself required guidance and effort. The middle class spent a lot of money on reading for self-improvement—and there was much new material for them to read. Periodicals were crammed with serialized novels, book reviews, travel writing, current events, and other educational pieces. Several Victorian novelists, including Charles Dickens (see page 941) and

William Makepeace Thackeray, edited their own journals that also published their work, ridding themselves of the burdens of patronage.

The Expansion of Democracy

Many British workers were literate and—thanks to cheaper books, municipally funded lending libraries, and Mechanics' Institutes (workingmen's colleges)—were exposed to new ideas. During this period, continental Europe experienced many violent political upheavals, coups, and revolutions, but Britain did not. One reason for this lies in the greater ability of the British to change through political means in response to pressures from below.

Although Victorian Britain was officially a representative democracy, the right to vote at the beginning of the queen's reign was very limited. Nonetheless, there was a marked trend toward increasing representation and social mobility. In 1832 the First Reform Bill brought the vote to middle-class men. In 1867 the Second Reform Bill enfranchised many workingmen, doubling the electorate. By the end of the nineteenth century, women could vote in most local elections. It was not until the end of World War I, however, that all men over twenty-one and women over thirty could vote. Many people felt that real economic, social, and political mobility was increasingly possible.

Imperialism

Britain gained its empire more through commercial expansion than through military conquest. British colonial rule did not aim at centralized control, and there could be considerable variation in local government. Colonial New Zealand, for example, in 1893 became the first country in the world to give the vote to all adults regardless of sex or race. British institutions—including the army, the civil service, and the law—offered some

Viewing Practice

[SPIRAL REVIEW] **Symbols** Have students select, organize, and produce visuals to complement and extend meaning for this spread. Tell them to use the Crystal Palace as a symbolic container for imagery of Victorian accomplishments, values, and ideals. Have students write a caption that discusses its symbolic values, for example:

- the transparency of democracy
- the ingenuity of industrialism
- the refinement of Victorian life
- the superiority of England

When the visual is complete, have students discuss the relationship of the imagery to this section's themes.

Queen Victoria Opening the 1862 Exhibition after Crystal Palace Moved to Sydenham. Joseph Nash. Private collection.

View the Art The Crystal Palace was designed to house an exhibition of recent British inventions and technological or scientific marvels. Does the building in this image seem appropriate for such an exhibition? Explain. ★

inclusion and mobility to colonials. Mohandas Gandhi, for example, was born in India and admitted to the British bar in London in 1889. His legal work to end discrimination against Indians in South Africa, another British colony, started him on his path to become the leader of the movement for Indian independence. There is no doubt that British colonial rule could be officious and insensitive. But many people in Victorian Britain truly believed they were bringing their colonial subjects the benefits of Western civilization.

One of the most influential critics of Victorian culture was the essayist and historian Thomas Carlyle.

from *Past and Present* by Thomas Carlyle

 All true Work is sacred; in all true Work, were it but true hand-labor, there is something of divineness. Labor, wide as the Earth, has its summit in Heaven. Sweat of the brow; and up from that to sweat of the brain, sweat of the heart; which includes all Kepler calculations, Newton meditations, all Sciences, all spoken Epics, all acted Heroisms, Martyrdoms,—up to that "Agony of bloody sweat," which all men have called divine! O brother, if this is not "worship," then I say, the more pity for worship; for this is the noblest thing yet discovered under God's sky. Who art thou that complainest of thy life of toil? Complain not. Look up, my wearied brother; see thy fellow Workmen there, in God's Eternity; surviving there, they alone surviving: sacred Band of the Immortals, celestial Bodyguard of the Empire of Mankind.

Reading Check

Interpret Why did Victorians such as Carlyle value work?

Reading Strategy | 2

Identify Author's Purpose Tell students that one of an author's purposes can be to persuade his or her audience. **Ask:** What is Carlyle's purpose here? *(to persuade people of the importance of work and of the importance of embracing their work)* **Ask:** How does Carlyle try to accomplish his purpose? *(He suggests there is a religious and spiritual value to work; he acknowledges different kinds of work people can do, such as work of the body and work of the mind.)*

View the Art ★

Possible answer: *Most students will say that the building is appropriate—very modern and marvelous itself, its steel framework shows intricate engineering.*

In this work Joseph Nash (1809–1878) evokes the industrial beauty and romantic elegance of the Crystal Palace. First designed by Joseph Paxton in only ten days, its iron framework towered over visitors. Its courts depicted art and architecture from ancient Egypt to the Renaissance, and the center housed a full-blown circus. The Crystal Palace burnt to the ground in 1936.

English Learners

DIFFERENTIATED INSTRUCTION

Advanced Carlyle's flowery expression and quaint phrases may be called "Victorianese." Point out this expression and others:

"O brother" *("Listen, fellow Brit")*

Have students read the excerpt and consider Carlyle's opinions with their own.

Advanced Learners

DIFFERENTIATED INSTRUCTION

Imperialism and India Have students research and analyze the history of India's relationship with Great Britain in the Victorian age. Have students share their analysis with the class.

Teach

Analyze Cause and Effect

Ask: What have you learned so far about effects of the Victorian age? *(Students should mention a sense of optimism and accomplishment, a growing middle class, and a new set of high-minded values.)* After students read "The Road to Wealth" and "Voices of Reform," write this cause-and-effect chain on the board:

Imperialism/industrial technology

↓

Greater wealth/increased population

↓

More poor people/greater suffering

As they reread the page, have students complete the chain and analyze Victorian trends.

Literary History ☆

Reactions to Utilitarianism
Although popular at the time, Utilitarianism did have its detractors. The writer William Hazlitt said that Jeremy Bentham spent a great part of his life "reducing the mind of man to a machine."

Big Idea 2
The Emergence of Realism

or the Victorians, in an age of transition where all the old values seemed in the process of being demolished, life was lived amid a babble of conflicting opinions. Whom should they trust? **1**

The Road to Wealth

At the beginning of the Industrial Revolution, the British economic theorist Adam Smith put forward the idea that a nation of individuals free to pursue their own economic self-interest without governmental interference would ultimately produce a stronger, wealthier nation. To give moral justification to such self-interest, Jeremy Bentham and John Stuart Mill came up with the theory of Utilitarianism—the view that the ethical value of an activity is measured by the extent of its usefulness. Many factory owners and businessmen, particularly in the industrial north of Britain, became strong advocates for putting free-market and Utilitarian doctrines into practice.

> "The greatest happiness of the greatest number is the foundation of morals and legislation."
>
> —Jeremy Bentham

Free-market economic policy had visible consequences. Did a forward-moving nation have a responsibility to help the poorest people among them, who produced no wealth but consumed resources? Quite a few people argued that the answer was no. Extreme Utilitarians argued that one poor person's starvation was more than offset by the full stomach of a person capable of producing something beneficial for society. Social Darwinists, erroneously believing they were

supported by Charles Darwin's writings on evolution, claimed that artificially prolonging the life of the unfit weakened a whole society.

Voices of Reform

Equally determined Victorian voices spoke out on behalf of the poor and helpless. Carlyle, for example, passionately exposed the underlying flaws in Victorian society, warning of Britain's moral, as well as literal, starvation. His writings inspired many writers and reformers, including Karl Marx and the novelist Charles Dickens.

Doctors, ministers, journalists, and private philanthropists organized many charitable organizations, including the Ladies' Society for the Education and Employment of the Female Poor, the Society for the Prevention of Cruelty to Animals, and the Young Men's Christian Association (YMCA). Reformers within Parliament used Blue Book reports to educate the well-to-do middle class about the poor. Reports on, for example, child labor in coal mines, were widely read, leading to reform laws.

The Novel and the Condition of England

In 1845 Benjamin Disraeli chose to write a novel to persuade the wealthy to unite "the two nations" of England—the rich and the poor. Many other authors wrote novels to represent, in a socially realistic way, the "Condition of England." Their characters were working-class mill-hands, clerks, seamstresses—or lower-class people, such as paupers. Plots partially depended on romance but also included riots among workers and meetings to discuss working conditions. Victorian novels proved to be powerful instruments for instructing middle-class readers. As they sat in their parlors, these readers began to imagine the humanity of those whom they might never meet.

Reading Practice

SPIRAL REVIEW **Read with Purpose** Tell students that it is important to set a purpose for reading in order to gain as much information as possible from a text. Have students describe how they would read an entertainment vs. a scholarly journal article. (They would read a journal article slowly, focusing on key concepts, while they would likely skim an entertainment article.) Ask students what the purpose of reading the Unit Introduction might be. (To learn about the history and culture of Victorian times.) Then remind students that they should read informational texts such as the this slowly and carefully to understand each big idea.

The Docks at Cardiff, 1894. Lionel Walden. Oil on canvas. Musé d'Orsay, Paris. ★

from *Hard Times* by Charles Dickens

"Now, what I want is, Facts. Teach these boys and girls nothing but Facts. Facts alone are wanted in life. Plant nothing else, and root out everything else. You can only form the minds of reasoning animals upon Facts: nothing else will ever be of any service to them. This is the principle on which I bring up my own children, and this is the principle on which I bring up these children. Stick to Facts, Sir!"

The scene was a plain, bare, monotonous vault of a school-room, and the speaker's square forefinger emphasized his observations by underscoring every sentence with a line on the schoolmaster's sleeve. The emphasis was helped by the speaker's square wall of a forehead, which had his eyebrows for its base, while his eyes found commodious cellarage in two dark caves, overshadowed by the wall. The emphasis was helped by the speaker's mouth, which was wide, thin, and hard set. The emphasis was helped by the speaker's voice, which was inflexible, dry, and dictatorial. The emphasis was helped by the speaker's hair, which bristled on the skirts of his bald **2** head, a plantation of firs to keep the wind from its shining surface, all covered with knobs, like the crust of a plum pie, as if the head had scarcely warehouse-room for the hard facts stored inside. The speaker's obstinate carriage, square coat, square legs, square shoulders,—nay, his very neck-cloth, trained to take him by the throat with an unaccommodating grasp, like a stubborn fact, as it was,—all helped the emphasis.

"In this life, we want nothing but Facts, Sir; nothing but Facts!"

The speaker, and the schoolmaster, and the third grown person present, all backed a little, and swept with their eyes the inclined plane of little vessels then and there arranged in order, ready to have imperial gallons of facts poured into them until they were full to the brim.

Reading Check

Analyze Cause and Effect Why did Victorian writers move in the direction of Realism?

Advanced Learners

DIFFERENTIATED INSTRUCTION

The Bleak Joy of Dickens Students might enjoy reading and critiquing one of the classics that have earned Dickens a place among the giants of English literature. Have them read *A Christmas Carol* and then write a literary critique of the work. Suggest that they address elements such as vivid description of everyday life in Victorian Britain, social conscience, and Dickens's gift for compelling characterization. They might also discuss the author's use of melodrama, sentimentality, and unlikely plot coincidence.

Teach

Reading Check

Answer: *They hoped to use realistic presentation of the social problems resulting from rapid industrialization and unrestrained capitalism as a means to encourage reform.*

Literary Element | 2

Sensory Details Point out that Dickens, a master of description, uses sensory details here to evoke the grimness of Victorian efficiency. **Ask:** Which sensory details does Dickens use to portray the speaker's coldness? *(He says the speaker's "square forefinger emphasized" his points; he had a "square wall of a forehead"; and his eyes sat in "two dark caves.")*

ENGLISH LEARNERS **Say:** Paraphrase in your own words Dickens's description of the speaker's hair and head. *(He has some bristly hair, but is mostly bald, with a shiny, bumpy head.)*

View the Art ★

The American artist Lionel Walden (1861–1933) studied painting in Paris. Although influenced by Impressionism, Walden moved toward Naturalism to portray contemporary themes, as in this gritty industrial cityscape.

875

Teach

Connect After students read this page, focus their attention on the first sentence of the section "Pessimism and Naturalism." **Ask:** How can you connect our world to the sentiments expressed by Thomas Carlyle? *(Students might connect Carlyle's fear of the dehumanizing effects of technology with today's concerns over computer technology alienating people from one another.)*

APPROACHING **Ask:** If someone is "mechanical in head and in heart," how does he or she act? *(without thinking, in an unfeeling way)*

Literary History ☆

Oscar Wilde If you're going to be disillusioned, be funny. Oscar Wilde (1854–1900) was both. A gifted poet and dramatist, Wilde was famous for his sharp wit and hit plays, such as *The Importance of Being Earnest.* From the golden pen of the Dublin-born writer came great observations of the era.

Big Idea 3
Disillusionment and Darker Visions

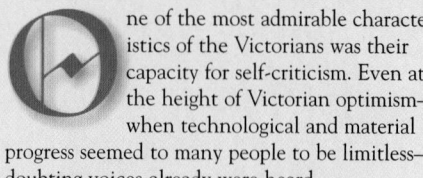

One of the most admirable characteristics of the Victorians was their capacity for self-criticism. Even at the height of Victorian optimism—when technological and material progress seemed to many people to be limitless—doubting voices already were heard.

Pessimism and Naturalism

The young Thomas Carlyle worried that, in an age that worshiped machinery, people too would grow "mechanical in head and in heart, as well as in hand." Carlyle's fellow cultural critic John Ruskin, in a series of letters addressed to British "workmen and laborers," looked around and saw a savage world: a "yelping, carnivorous crowd, mad for money and lust, tearing each other to pieces, and starving each other to death." The ugliness and brutality of the Victorian age prompted many painful questions: What could replace traditions as they disappeared? What would unify the country when religious feeling weakened? Could human nature and society improve indefinitely?

The Realist novel, which had proved itself so effective in rousing emotion, began to seem too good at raising falsely comforting feelings. A new generation of novelists were influenced in part by Darwinism to look for natural, rather than spiritual, forces guiding the course of human life. In France, for example, the novelist Émile Zola wrote novels according to a set of beliefs called Naturalism. Naturalistic novels, plays, and poems tend to present a grim, almost fatalistic view of the world, in which mostly lower-class characters are trapped by circumstances beyond their control for reasons that they cannot determine. Zola observed that he was subjecting his fictional characters to "the same analytical examination that surgeons perform on corpses." For novelists following in the path of Zola, clinical knowledge of the human condition replaced teary sympathy.

Other writers who did not identify themselves with Naturalism nonetheless shared a tendency toward a somber realization of life's randomness. The late Victorian writer Thomas Hardy (see page 959) wrote many poems as "Satires of Circumstance." We could not, he believed, even flatter ourselves that gods cared about us enough to torment us; our life here was merely a cosmic joke of happenstance.

> "How arrives it joy lies slain,
> And why unblooms the best hope
> ever sown?"
>
> —Thomas Hardy, "Hap"

Decadent Literature

As the nineteenth century drew to a close, a new mood arose in Victorian culture. Referred to as decadence (meaning "decline" or "decay"), this new cultural spirit was, like Naturalism, a reaction to the prevailing optimism of the Victorian age. Naturalist writers, however, had hoped that their literary works could influence people's opinions. By contrast, Decadent writers rejected the idea that works of art had to serve any useful purpose. Among the most notorious of the Decadents was Oscar Wilde, an Irish-born comic genius who enjoyed upending Victorian values—but always with a subversively serious intent. As Wilde wrote, "There is no such thing as a moral or an immoral book. Books are well written, or badly written. That is all." Partaking in the growing disillusionment at the end of the Victorian age, Decadent writers disdained and despised the consolations of religion and bourgeois life. They embraced life's futility through extremes of style, whether in dress, behavior, or their literary work.

Vocabulary Practice

SPIRAL REVIEW **Word Roots** Remind students that knowing word roots can help them unlock meaning. Call their attention to the first sentence on this page. **On the board, write:**

capacity ROOT *capac* "spacious" < *capere*: to take (or take in)

Ask: What is the main sense of the root *capac*? *(to be large enough to take in)* **On the board, write:**

capacious   incapacitate

Ask: What does *capacious* mean? *(big enough to contain a lot; roomy)* What does *incapacitate* mean? *(to make unable to take or do something)*

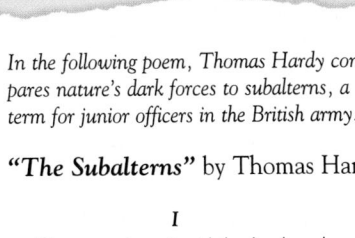

The Doubt: "Can These Drying Bones Live?", c. 1855.
Henry Alexander Bowler. Tate Gallery, London.

View the Art The title of this painting may refer
to the Christian idea of life after death. What aspects
of naturalism seem to be reflected by this image
and its title? ★

In the following poem, Thomas Hardy compares nature's dark forces to subalterns, a term for junior officers in the British army.

"The Subalterns" by Thomas Hardy

I
"Poor wanderer," said the leaden sky,
   "I fain would lighten thee,
But there be laws in force on high
   Which say it must not be."

II
—"I would not freeze thee, shorn one," cried
   The North, "knew I but how
To warm my breath, to slack my stride;
   But I am ruled as thou."

III
—"To-morrow I attack thee, wight,"
   Said Sickness. "Yet I swear
I bear thy little ark no spite,
   But am bid enter there."

IV
—"Come hither, Son," I heard Death say;
   "I did not will a grave
Should end thy pilgrimage to-day,
   But I, too, am a slave!"

V
We smiled upon each other then,
   And life to me wore less
Of that fell look it wore ere when
   They owned their passiveness.

Reading Check

Compare and Contrast How did Naturalism
differ from Realism?

English Learners

DIFFERENTIATED INSTRUCTION

Intermediate Point out that inverted
word order and old-fashioned English
account for much of the challenge of reading Hardy. Then remind students that *thee*
means "you" and *thy* means "your." Point
out that most of the words are simple and
that rereading and context can help them
unlock Hardy's meaning.

Have students work in small groups to
grasp the following words and phrases: "I
fain would lighten thee" *(I would like to
give you light)*; "shorn one" *(being without
fur)*; "knew I but how" *(if only I knew how)*;
"Come hither" *(come here)*; "ere" *(before)*.

Teach

Reading Check

Answer: *Naturalism presented
a far bleaker, more mechanistic
view of human life. Unlike Realism,
it did not offer sentiment to offset
the sadness of life.*

Reading Strategy 2

Interpret Direct students to the
last stanza of the poem. **Ask:**
How do the speaker's lines here
reflect Naturalism? *(Students
might say that the speaker seems
resigned to misfortune and to
the forces that he or she cannot
control.)*

View the Art ★

Possible answers: *The painting
and its title present a grim view of
life and death. The subject seems
to be doubting the idea of spiritual
comforts; she also seems to be
pondering the grave somewhat
calmly and coldly, without sadness.*
Henry Alexander Bowler
(1824–1903) might be thought
of as the quintessential Victorian
painter. He painted landscapes and
genre subjects in a classical manner.
He exhibited at the Royal Academy,
that bastion of British vanguard
values. His themes reflected the
culture of the day. The work shown
on this page remains his best-
known painting. Its crisp forms and
bright translucent color point to a
Pre-Raphaelite influence.

Assess

Legacy of the Period

Direct students' attention to the second and third paragraphs.
Ask: Which factors give rise to the doubts described in these paragraphs? *(class issues; social reform; evolution; technological progress vs. dehumanization)*

Cultural and Literary Links

Suggest students look for how the ideas of Victorian authors have affected the way we look at the world.

Activities

1. **Follow Up** Students should support their answers with details from this introduction and from lessons in the unit.
2. **Contrast Literary Periods** Presentations might focus on social reforms or on scientific theories such as Darwinism.
3. **Build Visual Literacy** Encourage students to share any impressions they have about the influence of cultural periods on the representations.
4. Answers will vary.

FOLDABLES®
Study Organizer

Have students make and label the Three-Tab Book. They can put note cards about each big idea under the appropriate tab.

Wrap-Up

Legacy of the Period

The fundamental problems and questions that Victorians faced, and the solutions they attempted, are still with us. Most visible are the material changes; for example, the ways in which nineteenth-century cities were organized. Like us, the Victorians were consumers with an enormous appetite for innovations and material goods—often absurd and unnecessary.

The newly complicated nineteenth-century world made more evident the need for educated and involved citizens. Social reforms and increasing democratization are two important trends of the Victorian age. We still puzzle over how large a role government should have in helping the poor. Darwinism is still hotly debated today.

Above all, we have inherited from the Victorians an uneasy faith in ourselves. We share both their hopefulness about progress and their doubts about ever achieving it.

Cultural and Literary Links

◆ The Victorian poet Gerard Manley Hopkins became an important influence on modern literature in English after an edition of his works was first published in 1918.

◆ Charlotte Brontë's *Jane Eyre* inspired Jean Rhys's novel *Wide Sargasso Sea*, which tells the story of Mr. Rochester's first wife. *Jack Maggs*, a novel by the contemporary Australian writer Peter Carey, retells Dickens's *Great Expectations*.

◆ Lewis Carroll has had a large influence on modern culture, including words he coined (such as *chortle*), and on literary works, such as the fiction of the Argentine writer Jorge Luis Borges.

 Literature Online

Unit Resources For additional skills practice, go to glencoe.com and enter QuickPass code GLB9817u5.

Activities

Choose one of the following activities to explore and develop as you read this unit.

1. **Follow Up** Go back to the Looking Ahead section on page 865 and answer the questions.

2. **Contrast Literary Periods** Work with a small group to identify ideals, traditions, or philosophies from the Victorian period that still appear, in one form or another, in modern thinking. Create a presentation for the class in which you describe how these things affect our current literature, art, or other forms of expression.

3. **Build Visual Literacy** Lewis Carroll's *Alice* books have always been popular with artists, beginning with Carroll himself, and later with Victorian cartoonist John Tenniel. Create a display of the different ways in which artists have dealt with the *Alice* books.

Discuss with other students how differences in the art and the medium might reflect differences in the culture over time.

4. **Take Notes** Use this organizer to explore your personal responses to the selections in this unit.

 FOLDABLES®
Study Organizer   **THREE-TAB BOOK**

Writing Practice

SPIRAL REVIEW **Persuasive Essay Say:** Some writers in the Victorian period took a generally optimistic view of the world and believed that society was progressing. Others had a more pessimistic perspective, feeling that life was largely marked by suffering. Have students explore, in a reflective essay, the perspective that more closely matches their own view of contemporary life. Ask them to develop their reflections with examples from their own lives, from current events, and from contemporary art or literature.

878

Part 1
Optimism and the Belief in Progress

Queen Victoria in Her Coronation Robes, 1887. Chromolithograph.
From a book celebrating the queen's Golden Jubilee.
 Queen Victoria was only eighteen at the time of her coronation.
What impression of the young queen does the painter give in this image?

> "'Tis only noble to be good.
> Kind hearts are more than coronets,
> And simple faith than Norman blood."
>
> —Alfred, Lord Tennyson, "Lady Clara Vere de Vere"

1

879

Literary Element   1

Aphorism Explain that an aphorism is a short, pointed statement expressing a wise observation about human experience. **Ask:** What observation is Tennyson making about nobility? *(He is saying that one must do good to be noble and that kindness and humble faith are nobler than crowns and royal blood.)* How is this aphorism Victorian? *(It says merit outweighs social position, inviting self-improvement.)*

View the Art

Answer: *The painting shows Victoria as young and beautiful, but very confident, regal, and determined. She is looking to the sky, and a light shines down on her face, possibly suggesting her divine right to rule.*

Emphasize that this portrait advertises wealth and royal nobility.
Ask: How does the quote literally subvert the portrait? *(The quote, which sits under the art, advocates humility and merit over crowns and royal blood.)*

 For additional support for English Learners, see Unit 5 Teaching Resources Book, p. 19

English Learners

 DIFFERENTIATED INSTRUCTION

Advanced Say: Sometimes poets leave words out of a sentence or a line in a stanza; this is called elision. **Ask:** What words has the poet omitted in the third line? *(Is more)* Why might Tennyson have omitted words in the third line? *(To keep the meter)*

Approaching Level

 DIFFERENTIATED INSTRUCTION

Established Explain to approaching-level students that Tennyson expressed a belief that had not been confronted often in British literature: what you do counts, not how rich you are or what family you were born into. Ask students to share their opinions on Tennyson's ideas.

Before You Read

Focus

Bellringer Options

Selection Focus
Transparency 43
Daily Language Practice
Transparency 71

Or tap a rhythm on the board or a table. **Ask:** What adjectives would you use to describe that rhythm? (Depending on the rhythm, answers might include slow, fast, playful, or unpredictable.) Discuss students' responses, and then ask volunteers to tap a rhythm that matches each of these adjectives: mournful, ecstatic, passionate, humorous. Point out that rhythm is one device Tennyson uses to create mood in his poetry.

Before You Read

Tennyson's Poetry

Meet **Alfred, Lord Tennyson**
(1809–1892)

Not an average child, Alfred Tennyson produced a six-thousand-line epic poem by the age of twelve. He also wrote poems in the styles of Alexander Pope, Sir Walter Scott, and John Milton before his teen years. Throughout his life, Tennyson would turn to poetry whenever he felt troubled. As he said in one of his poems, "for the unquiet heart and brain / A use in measured language lies."

Tennyson had great need of such solace. His father, a clergyman, had a long history of mental instability. When Tennyson's grandfather considered the clergyman unfit to take over the family dynasty—thereby virtually disinheriting him—Tennyson's father turned to drugs and alcohol. He often took out his bitter disappointment on the family.

> *"I suffered what seemed to me to shatter all my life so that I desired to die rather than live."*
>
> —Alfred, Lord Tennyson

Early Struggles At age eighteen, Tennyson joined his older brother at Cambridge University. Although he was painfully shy, his poetry brought him to the attention of an elite group of students known as "The Apostles." Thriving on their affection and support, Tennyson gained confidence in his abilities. His closest friend was Arthur Henry Hallam, a brilliant and popular student who later became engaged to Tennyson's sister. While at Cambridge, Tennyson published *Poems, Chiefly Lyrical*, and he accompanied Hallam and other Apostles to Spain to support the unsuccessful revolt against Ferdinand VII.

In 1831 Tennyson left Cambridge to be with his father, whose health was failing. After his father's death, Tennyson decided to pursue a career in poetry rather than return to school. His early volumes of poetry drew mixed reviews, however, and Tennyson was hurt by some stinging criticism. Then, in 1833, he learned that Arthur Hallam had died suddenly of a stroke. Tennyson fell into a deep and long depression. Nearly a decade passed before he published any poetry. However, he wrote some of his most significant poems during this period, perfecting his craft during what he later called his "ten years' silence."

Literary Renown When he was thirty-two, Tennyson brought out a new book of poems. This time, almost all of the reviews were positive. Fame came in 1850 with the publication of *In Memoriam A. H. H.*, a long cycle of poems about his grief over the loss of Hallam. That same year, Queen Victoria appointed Tennyson to succeed William Wordsworth as poet laureate. Finally confident about his future, Tennyson married Emily Sellwood, his fiancée of fourteen years.

For the rest of his life, Tennyson enjoyed remarkable prestige. His books could be found in the home of nearly every English reader. To his contemporaries, Tennyson was the great consoling voice of their age.

 Literature Online

Author Search For more about Alfred, Lord Tennyson, go to glencoe.com and enter QuickPass code GLB9817u5.

Selection Skills

Literary Elements
- Rhythm (SE pp. 881–888)
- Repetition (SE p. 888)
- Structure (TE p. 886)

Reading Skills
- Analyze Mood (SE pp. 881–889)

from In Memoriam A.H.H., Crossing the Bar, Tears, Idle Tears

Vocabulary Skills
- Word Usage (SE p. 889)
- Academic Vocabulary (SE p. 889)

Listening/Speaking/Viewing Skills
- Analyze Art (SE pp. 882, 886)

Writing Skills/Grammar
- Apply Rhythm (SE p. 889)

Literature and Reading Preview

Connect to the Poems

Why do we appreciate things more when they are gone? Freewrite for a few minutes about something you may have taken for granted—until you no longer had it.

Building Background

After Arthur Hallam's death in 1833, Tennyson wrote an **elegy**, or poem of lament, about this loss. He continued writing elegies over the next seventeen years, eventually collecting them under the title *In Memoriam A. H. H.* Tennyson wrote "Crossing the Bar" at the age of eighty-one, and asked that it be placed at the end of every edition of his work. "Tears, Idle Tears" comes from Tennyson's first long narrative poem, *The Princess*, which explores the role of women in society.

Set Purposes for Reading

Big Idea Optimism and the Belief in Progress

As you read, ask yourself, To what extent do these poems reflect the characteristic Victorian optimism?

Literary Element Rhythm

Rhythm refers to the pattern of beats created by the arrangement of stressed and unstressed syllables in lines of verse. For example, in the following line from *In Memoriam A. H. H.*, the second, fourth, sixth, and eighth syllables are stressed:

> Ă hánd thăt cán bĕ cláspĕd nŏ móre—

As you read, ask yourself, What effect does this rhythm have?

Reading Strategy Analyze Mood

To **analyze mood**, identify the elements that work together to create the emotional quality of a literary work. These elements include diction, imagery, and figurative language as well as rhythm, rhyme, repetition, and other sound devices. As you read, ask yourself, What emotion does this evoke, and why?

....

Tip: Analyzing Mood As you read, use a diagram like the one below to help you identify the elements that create mood.

Figurative Language: "like a guilty thing I creep" → Mood ← Imagery

Learning Objectives

For pages 880–889

In studying these texts, you will focus on the following objectives:

Literary Study: Analyzing rhythm.

Reading: Analyzing mood.

Writing: Applying rhythm in a poem.

Vocabulary

license (lī′ səns) *n.* freedom used irresponsibly; p. 883 *Jen often took license with her sister's belongings, "borrowing" them without asking.*

diffusive (di fū′ siv) *adj.* spread out or widely scattered; p. 885 *A diffusive energy surged through the stadium as the players ran onto the field.*

feigned (fānd) *adj.* pretended; imagined; p. 887 *Is your interest in this offer genuine or feigned?*

ALFRED, LORD TENNYSON **881**

English Learners

DIFFERENTIATED INSTRUCTION

Intermediate Tell students that sometimes we don't appreciate something until we've lost it. **Ask:** Have you ever felt this way? Is there anything specific to your native culture that you are unable to find in the United States that you miss? *(Answers will vary.)* Invite students to share their experiences with the class. Explain to students that they will read several selections that deal with Tennyson's experience of loss.

Before You Read

Focus

Summary

In the selections from *In Memoriam A. H. H.*, the speaker evolves through stages of grief—from despair to faith. In "Crossing the Bar," Tennyson uses a voyage as a metaphor to examine the universal experience of crossing the border between life and death. The speaker in "Tears, Idle Tears," grieves for the past, describing it as "Death in Life" because it now has no potential for growth or change.

 For summaries in languages other than English, see Unit 5 Teaching Resources Book, pp. 20–25.

Vocabulary

Etymology Remind students that in order to research the etymology of a vocabulary word, sometimes you have to look up a related word in the dictionary. For example, to find out about the word *catastrophic*, you might look up *catastrophe*. Tell students to use related words to find information about *diffusive* and *feigned*.

 For additional vocabulary practice, see Unit 5 Teaching Resources Book, p. 28.

 For additional context, see Glencoe Interactive Vocabulary CD-ROM.

Teach

 For an audio recording of this selection, use Listening Library Audio CD-ROM.

London Twilight from the Adelphi. Christopher Richard Wynne Nevinson (1889–1946). Oil on canvas, 44.5 x 59 cm.

View the Art Nevinson's work uses light to create a mood in his paintings. How does the mood of this image compare to the mood created by Tennyson? ★

from In Memoriam A. H. H.

Alfred, Lord Tennyson

7

Dark house, by which once more I stand
  Here in the long unlovely street,°
  Doors, where my heart was used to beat
So quickly, waiting for a hand,

5 A hand that can be clasped no more—
   Behold me, for I cannot sleep,
   And like a guilty thing I creep
At earliest morning to the door.

2 **long unlovely street:** Wimpole Street in London, where Arthur Henry Hallam lived after he left Cambridge.

Reading Practice

SPIRAL REVIEW **Compare and Contrast**
Encourage students to practice comparing and contrasting the main ideas of each section of *In Memoriam A. H. H.* Students should create a chart. Suggest that students follow these steps to construct their charts.

- State the main idea of each section.

- Describe how the main ideas are related. Are they similar? Are they opposite? (*Students might suggest that Section 7 expresses a deep grief and abysmal sorrow; Section 27 suggests that it is better to have experienced love even if it results in deep sorrow.*)

He is not here; but far away
10   The noise of life begins again,
    And ghastly through the drizzling rain
On the bald street breaks the blank day.

27

I envy not in any moods
   The captive void of noble rage,
    The linnet° born within the cage,
That never knew the summer woods;

5 I envy not the beast that takes
   His **license** in the field of time,
    Unfettered by the sense of crime,
To whom a conscience never wakes;

Nor, what may count itself as blest,
10   The heart that never plighted troth°
    But stagnates in the weeds of sloth;
Nor any want-begotten rest.°

I hold it true, whate'er befall;
   I feel it, when I sorrow most;
15 'Tis better to have loved and lost
Than never to have loved at all.

54

O, yet we trust that somehow good
   Will be the final goal of ill,
    To pangs of nature, sins of will,
Defects of doubt, and taints of blood;°

5 That nothing walks with aimless feet;
   That not one life shall be destroyed,

3 linnet: a small bird.

10 plighted troth: "pledged loyalty" or "became engaged to marry."

12 want-begotten rest: leisure that comes from a lack of commitment (as opposed to a rest that is earned through struggle).

3–4 These two lines specify four types of ills: *pangs of nature* (physical pain), *sins of will* (moral transgressions), *defects of doubt* (spiritual shortcomings), and *taints of blood* (inherited flaws).

1 Analyze Mood *What feelings does the setting evoke in the speaker?*

2 Analyze Mood *Why does the poet include this image?*

3 Optimism and the Belief in Progress *What Victorian belief do these lines reflect?*

> **Vocabulary**
> **license** (līʹsəns) *n.* freedom used irresponsibly

ALFRED, LORD TENNYSON   **883**

 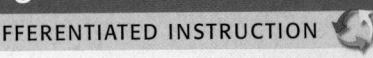
Teach

Teach

Reading Strategy | 1

Analyze Mood Answer:
The mood changes from guarded optimism to despair. The repetition of the phrase "An infant crying," and the rhyming words "night" and "light" support this mood by suggesting the sound of a wailing cry.

Literary Element | 2

Rhythm **Answer:** *The regular rhythm imitates the pealing of church bells.*

Literary History ☆

Tennyson on Writing In another section of *In Memoriam A. H. H.*, the poet describes his work as a series of "short swallow-flights of song." Reflecting on the entire poem later, he wrote "It must be remembered that this is a poem, not an actual biography. The different moods of sorrow as in a drama are dramatically given." **Ask:** Why do you think readers sometimes are tempted to view poems as "actual biography"? *(Poets may speak with a deeply personal voice that encourages readers to assume that the speaker and the poet share the same experiences.)*

Or cast as rubbish to the void,
When God hath made the pile complete;

10 That not a worm is cloven° in vain;
   That not a moth with vain desire
   Is shriveled in a fruitless fire,
Or but subserves° another's gain.

Behold, we know not anything;
   I can but trust that good shall fall
15 At last—far off—at last, to all,
And every winter change to spring.

So runs my dream; but what am I?
   An infant crying in the night;
   An infant crying for the light,
20 And with no language but a cry.

106

Ring out, wild bells, to the wild sky, ☆
   The flying cloud, the frosty light:
   The year is dying in the night;
Ring out, wild bells, and let him die.

5 Ring out the old, ring in the new,
   Ring, happy bells, across the snow:
   The year is going, let him go;
Ring out the false, ring in the true.

Ring out the grief that saps the mind,
10 For those that here we see no more;
   Ring out the feud of rich and poor,
Ring in redress to all mankind.

Ring out a slowly dying cause,
   And ancient forms of party strife;°
15 Ring in the nobler modes of life,
With sweeter manners, purer laws.

Ring out the want, the care, the sin,
   The faithless coldness of the times;

9 cloven: split.

12 subserves: "promotes" or "assists."

14 party strife: antagonism or a dispute between sides or factions.

---

1 Analyze Mood *How does the mood of this section change in the final stanza?*

2 Rhythm *What effect does the rhythm of this passage create?*

884 UNIT 5 THE VICTORIAN AGE

Research Practice

SPIRAL REVIEW **Use Print and Internet Sources** In the twentieth century, psychologists, such as psychiatrist Kubler-Ross, studied how people respond emotionally to the death of a loved one. Discuss the different stages of grief through which the speaker of *In Memoriam A. H. H.* passes. Ask students to use reliable print and internet sources to research psychologists' findings about the stages of grief. Encourage students to give a compare and contrast presentation on the stages identified by psychologists and by Tennyson.

Ring out, ring out my mournful rhymes,
20 But ring the fuller minstrel in.

Ring out false pride in place and blood,
    The civic slander and the spite;
    Ring in the love of truth and right,
Ring in the common love of good.

25 Ring out old shapes of foul disease;
    Ring out the narrowing lust of gold;
    Ring out the thousand wars of old,
Ring in the thousand years of peace.

Ring in the valiant man and free,
30   The larger heart, the kindlier hand;
    Ring out the darkness of the land,
Ring in the Christ that is to be.

130

Thy voice is on the rolling air
    I hear thee where the waters run;
    Thou standest in the rising sun,
And in the setting thou art fair.

5   What art thou then? I cannot guess;
    But though I seem in star and flower
        To feel thee some **diffusive** power,
I do not therefore love thee less.

My love involves the love before;
10   My love is vaster passion now;
    Tho' mix'd with God and Nature thou,
I seem to love thee more and more.

Far off thou art, but ever nigh;°
    I have thee still, and I rejoice;
15   I prosper, circled with thy voice;
I shall not lose thee tho' I die.

13 **nigh:** near.

Optimism and the Belief in Progress *What positive changes does the speaker hope for in the new year?* **3**

Analyze Mood *What feelings does the speaker convey in these lines?* **4**

Vocabulary

diffusive (di fū′ siv) *adj.* spread out or widely scattered

ALFRED, LORD TENNYSON **885**

Teach

Big Idea **3**

Optimism and the Belief in Progress **Answer:** *The speaker hopes that ills such as grief, class struggle, political divisiveness, poverty, sin, and lack of faith will cease and that good things will replace them.*

(APPROACHING) Make sure approaching-level students understand that the speaker's hopes for the new year are what he wants the bells to "ring in." Have students identify the lines that include the phrase "ring in" and then summarize them in their own words.

Reading Strategy **4**

Analyze Mood **Answer:** *The speaker conveys hopeful, transcendent feelings. Having found his friend in "God and Nature," the speaker believes that he will be united with him after death.*

Political History

An Influential Poem
Queen Victoria's husband, Prince Albert, greatly admired *In Memoriam A. H. H.* Sources say that his admiration played a decisive role in the queen's decision to name Tennyson poet laureate in 1850. After Prince Albert died, the widowed queen told Tennyson, "Next to the Bible, *In Memoriam* is my lasting comfort." The work had a lasting influence on the British public. The poet's son, Hallam Tennyson, noted that at his father's funeral in 1892, many of the mourners "were seen reading *In Memoriam* while waiting for the service."

Teach

Rhythm Answer: *The rhythm created by a long, slow-moving line followed by a short one suggests the ebb and flow of the tide.*

View the Art ★

Possible answers: *Some students may say that the painting creates a peaceful mood, because the waves are low and people seem to be calmly watching the boats. Others may say that the dark colors and harsh lines, along with the stormy sky, create a less peaceful impression.*

John Constable spent a fair amount of time painting shores outside of Brighton, such as Hove. These secluded beaches allowed him to concentrate on the ocean and beach itself, rather than on the tourists who frequented the more populated ones. **Ask:** How does Constable's impression of the shoreline compare with Tennyson's? *(Answers will vary.)*

Hove Beach with Fishing Boats, c.1824. John Constable. Oil on paper laid on canvas. Victoria and Albert Museum, London.

<u>View the Art</u> Note the colors and lines that stand out most in this painting. Does this scene strike you as peaceful? Explain why or why not.

Crossing the Bar Alfred, Lord Tennyson

Sunset and evening star,
   And one clear call for me!
And may there be no moaning of the bar,[1]
   When I put out to sea,

5 But such a tide as moving seems asleep,
   Too full for sound and foam,
When that which drew from out the boundless deep
   Turns again home.

Twilight and evening bell,
10   And after that the dark!
And may there be no sadness of farewell,
   When I embark;

For though from out our bourne[2] of Time and Place
   The flood[3] may bear me far,
15 I hope to see my Pilot face to face
   When I have crossed the bar.

1. A *bar,* or sandbar, is a ridge of sand formed by the action of tides or currents.
2. *Bourne* means "boundary."
3. *Flood* means "rising tide."

---

1 Rhythm *How does the rhythm reinforce the meaning of these lines?*

Literary Element Practice

SPIRAL REVIEW **Analyze Structure** Encourage students to analyze the structure of the poetic form Tennyson uses in these poems. Help students focus their investigation by pointing out that poetic structure includes rhythm, rhyme scheme, line length, and stanza divisions. **Ask:** In which poem does the poetic structure closely mirror key images in the poem? *(Students should recognize that the irregular line lengths in "Crossing the Bar" reflect the movements of the tide described in the poem.)* Is the poetic form in the poems you have read so far formal or informal? (informal)*

Tears, Idle Tears

from *The Princess*

Alfred, Lord Tennyson

Recalling the Past, 1888. Carlton Alfred Smith.
Watercolor on paper. The Stapleton Collection.

Tears, idle[1] tears, I know not what they mean,
Tears from the depth of some divine despair
Rise in the heart, and gather to the eyes,
In looking on the happy autumn fields,
5   And thinking of the days that are no more.

Fresh as the first beam glittering on a sail,
That brings our friends up from the underworld,
Sad as the last which reddens over one
That sinks with all we love below the verge;[2]
10   So sad, so fresh, the days that are no more.

Ah, sad and strange as in dark summer dawns
The earliest pipe of half-awakened birds
To dying ears, when unto dying eyes
The casement[3] slowly grows a glimmering square;
15   So sad, so strange, the days that are no more.

Dear as remembered kisses after death,
And sweet as those by hopeless fancy **feigned** 4
On lips that are for others; deep as love,
Deep as first love, and wild with all regret;
20   O Death in Life, the days that are no more.

1. Here, *idle* means "having no basis or reason."
2. *Verge* refers to the horizon.
3. A *casement* is a window that opens outward.

Analyze Mood   *How does the phrase "autumn fields" convey a feeling of loss?*   2

Analyze Mood   *What feelings does Tennyson convey by describing the past as "Death in Life"?*   3

Vocabulary

feigned (fānd) *adj.* pretended; imagined

ALFRED, LORD TENNYSON   **887**

After You Read

Assess

1. Answers will vary.

2. (a) A bird that has never been free, a beast without a conscience (b) Lost love is better than never having known love at all.

3. (a) "Remembered kisses after death," imagined kisses, "love," "first love" (b) Neither past nor imagined experiences have substance; they are like a form of death in life.

4. Serene and hopeful; "Too full for sound and foam" and "hope"

5. Some students may say that the speaker finds comfort in thoughts of past joys. The speaker of *In Memoriam* feels grief and loss when recalling the past.

6. Tears are idle because they cannot bring back the past.

7. The speaker evolves from despair to doubt to hope to faith.

8. Most students will say that Tennyson's experiences with loss and grief made him accept death as a part of life, as his tone in both "In Memoriam" and "Crossing the Bar" is somewhat sad, but not bitter.

Literary Element

1. Iambic tetrameter

2. Their steadiness helps to contain strong emotions, channeling them into meaningful measures.

After You Read

Respond and Think Critically

Respond and Interpret

1. Which lines from these poems did you find the most memorable? Why?

2. (a)In section 27 of *In Memoriam*, to what does the speaker compare those people who have never loved anyone? (b)What do these **metaphors** lead the speaker to conclude about lost love?

3. (a)In lines 16–19 of "Tears, Idle Tears," to what does the speaker compare "the days that are no more"? (b)How do these **similes** illustrate line 20?

Analyze and Evaluate

4. How would you describe the **tone** of "Crossing the Bar"? What words and phrases create this tone?

5. Sum up the speaker's attitude toward the past in "Tears, Idle Tears." Compare that attitude to the one expressed by the speaker of *In Memoriam*.

6. How does the title of "Tears, Idle Tears" relate to its **theme**, or main idea?

Connect

7. **Big Idea** Optimism and the Belief in Progress Tennyson's contemporaries found *In Memoriam* very inspirational. Explain how the speaker of this poem evolves through stages of grief, progressing to more positive emotions. Cite specific lines from the poem to support your response.

8. **Connect to the Author** Tennyson's biography on page 880 shows that he was familiar with loss and grief. From reading his poems, how would you describe his attitude toward death?

Literary Element Rhythm

Meter is a type of **rhythm** in which the alteration between stressed and unstressed syllables is predictable and regular. Note the similarities and differences between the rhythms in each of the three poems you have read.

1. What is the metrical pattern of *In Memoriam*? What effect might Tennyson have been striving for with this type of rhythm?

2. Why might poets such as Tennyson find it effective to use regular rhythms in poems that concern grief and loss?

Review: Repetition

In both poetry and prose, writers will often employ **repetition** of a word, phrase, or sound in order to emphasize a certain idea, or create a certain rhythm. With a partner, identify examples of repetition in the three poems you have just read. Then discuss what ideas they help emphasize, or how they contribute to the poem's rhythm. Record your results in a chart like the one below.

Poem	Example	Effect
"Tears, Idle Tears"	"So sad" (line 10, line 15)	emphasizes the sadness of lost time

Review: Repetition
Direct students to the conclusion that meter and rhythm help to establish an idea in the mind of the reader, which Tennyson uses to emphasize ideas about grief and loss.

Progress Check

Can students analyze rhythm?

If No → See Unit 5 Teaching Resources Book, p. 26.

Reading Strategy: Analyze Mood

Refer to the diagram you created as you read, and then answer the following questions.

1. How would you describe the mood of "Crossing the Bar"?
2. What details in the speaker's surroundings help create the mood?

Vocabulary Practice

Practice with Word Usage Respond to these statements to help you explore the meanings of vocabulary words from the selection.

1. Describe a time when someone took unfair **license** in trying to control a project or situation.
2. List some possible advantages and disadvantages of having a **diffusive** set of friends.
3. List some reasons that a person might take on a **feigned** identity.

Academic Vocabulary

"Tears, Idle Tears" demonstrates Tennyson's general **inclination** toward sorrowful, rather than joyful, subjects.

Inclination is an academic word. More familiar words that are similar in meaning are *tendency* and *leaning*.

To further explore this word, describe a situation in which you had to act against your natural **inclinations**, and explain how it made you feel.

For more on academic vocabulary, see pages 56 and R81.

Write with Style

 Apply Rhythm

Assignment Poets use the rhythm of their words to help create a mood and movement. Think of a natural or social phenomenon that has a distinct movement or pattern, such as leaves falling or traffic passing through a stoplight. Write a short poem about this phenomenon, using a rhythm that echoes that of your subject.

Get Ideas Identify the movement in the phenomenon you have chosen and gather details by journaling or making a word web. Jot down metaphors and similes that convey the rhythm of the movement and help make it concrete.

Give It Structure Develop the images you came up with in your prewriting. Make sure that the sensory details you include are relevant and advance the rhythm and message of your poem. Organize your images and details in a manner that makes sense, given the topic of your poem.

EXAMPLE:
Location: grocery store

Images:
First: Cold white aisles full of ice cream and milk
Second: Crowded butcher counter, customers shoving
Third: Slow checkout line

Look at Language Read your poem aloud, listening for the rhythm of the words. Your word choice should create specific sensory images and combine with the rhythm to contribute to a strong sense of movement.

EXAMPLE:
Moving like molasses,
Slow, slower, slowest,
The checkout line
Swallows us like quicksand.

Before You Read

Assess

Reading Strategy

1. Serious and reflective
2. The depth of the ocean, the vastness of the sky, the slow-moving tide, and twilight turning to darkness generate thoughts of separation from the human world.

Vocabulary Practice

1. License, in this situation, means having authority.
2. Diffusive means widely scattered.
3. Feigned means false.

Academic Vocabulary

Students should attempt to use *inclination* in a way that is synonymous with *tendency* or *urge*.

 Write with Style

Students should use an identifiable pattern of rhythm in their poems, utilizing imagery and sensory details.

> For additional assessment, see Assessment Resources, pp. 213–214.

English Learners

 DIFFERENTIATED INSTRUCTION

Intermediate If English learners have difficulty using figurative language in their poems, have students practice making analogies for their chosen topic. Have them create a word web with the subject of their poem in the center and things that are similar to their subject surrounding it.

When they have finished brainstorming, have students write a sentence relating their subject to the words they've written in the word web. Students should also try to include descriptive language. For example: *Autumn leaves fall gently like orange snowflakes.*

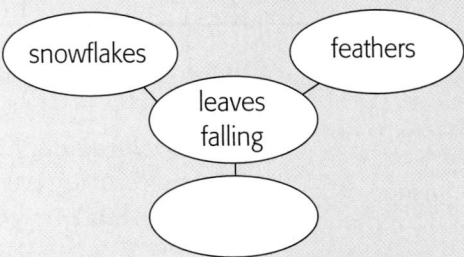

Focus

Summary

An old man, Ulysses, recognizes that he cannot be satisfied to remain an "idle king" and decides to leave the rule of Ithaca to his son, Telemachus. Ulysses determines to set forth on a final voyage with his sailors, acknowledging that although their physical strength has diminished, their spirit "to strive, to seek, to find, and not to yield" remains strong.

 For summaries in languages other than English, see Unit 5 Teaching Resources Book, pp. 31–36.

Vocabulary

Context Clues Direct students' attentions to the sentence that contains the vocabulary word *prudence* on page 892 and *abide* on page 893. **Ask:** What context clues provide meaning for each of the vocabulary words? (*Labor, slow and mild infer the meaning of* prudence; *"though much is taken" provides a contrast as a clue for* abides.)

Ulysses

Connect to the Poem

Which of your achievements do you love to relive in memory? In a small group, recount one such achievement and explain what made it important, and why you remember it so strongly.

Build Background

"Ulysses" is the Roman name of the Greek hero Odysseus, from Homer's epic poems, the *Iliad* and the *Odyssey*. Odysseus wandered for ten years after the Trojan War, facing great perils. At last, he returned home to Ithaca and was reunited with his wife, Penelope, and his son, Telemachus (tə leˊ mə kəs). "Ulysses" carries the story further, presenting an old king who longs for one last adventure.

Set Purposes for Reading

Big Idea **Optimism and the Belief in Progress**

As you read, ask yourself, What Victorian values might Ulysses and his son reflect?

Literary Element **Assonance and Consonance**

Assonance is the repetition of similar vowel sounds within non-rhyming words, as in "a l*i*on, w*i*ld, r*i*ses from sleep." **Consonance** is the repetition of consonant sounds within or at the ends of non-rhyming words, as in, "a lou*d* re*d* bir*d*." As you read, ask yourself, Where do I find these sound devices?

Reading Strategy **Analyze Tone**

When you **analyze tone**, you think critically about how the writer's attitude toward a subject is conveyed through such elements as diction, sentence structure, imagery, and figures of speech. As you read, ask yourself, What is the poet's attitude toward Ulysses?

Tip: Determining Tone Use a web like the one below to help you identify the elements that convey tone.

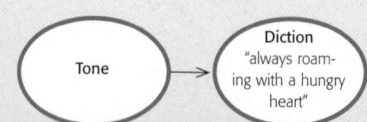

Learning Objectives

For pages 890–895

In studying this text, you will focus on the following objectives:

Literary Study: Analyzing assonance and consonance.

Reading: Analyzing tone.

Speaking and Listening: Presenting an oral interpretation.

Vocabulary

prudence (pro〓odˊ əns) *n.* sound judgment; careful management; p. 892 *Please use* prudence *in deciding how to invest the money.*

abide (ə bīdˊ) *v.* to remain; p. 893 *Though his power and wealth were lost, his family and friends* abided.

Tip: Context Clues To figure out the meaning of an unfamiliar word, look for clues in the surrounding words and sentences.

Selection Skills

Literary Elements
- Assonance and Consonance (SE pp. 890–894)
- Alliteration (SE p. 894)

Listening/Speaking/Viewing Skills
- Analyze Art (SE p. 893; TE p. 892)
- Oral Interpretation (SE p. 895)

Ulysses

Reading Skills
- Analyze Tone (SE pp. 890–895)

Vocabulary Skills
- Context Clues (SE pp. 890, 895)

Ulysses and the Sirens. Roman mosaic, 3rd century A.D. Musee National du Bardo, Tunis, Tunisia.

Ulysses
Alfred, Lord Tennyson

It little profits that an idle king,
By this still hearth, among these barren crags,°
Matched with an agèd wife, I mete and dole
Unequal laws° unto a savage race,
5   That hoard and sleep and feed, and know not me.

   I cannot rest from travel; I will drink
Life to the lees.° All times I have enjoyed
Greatly, have suffered greatly, both with those
That loved me, and alone; on shore, and when
10   Through scudding° drifts the rainy Hyades°
Vexed the dim sea. I am become a name;
For always roaming with a hungry heart
Much have I seen and known—cities of men
And manners, climates, councils, governments,
15   Myself not least, but honored of them all—

2 **barren crags:** here, the rugged landscape of Ithaca, the Greek island where Ulysses lives.
4 **Unequal laws:** rewards and punishments.

7 **lees:** sediment found at the bottom of wine and other liquids. To "drink to the lees" is to drink to the last drop.
10 **scudding:** wind-driven. **Hyades** (hī′ə dēz′): a cluster of stars. When they rose, it was believed that rain would soon follow.

Assonance and Consonance *Which words contain the short i sound? Which words contain the g sound?* **1**

Teach

Literary Element   1

Assonance and Consonance
Answer: *The words* it, little, profits, king, this, *and* still *contain the short* i *sound; the words* king *and* among *contain the* g *sound.*

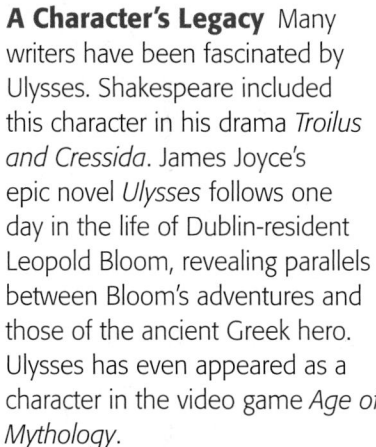 For additional literary element practice, see Unit 5 Teaching Resources Book, p. 37.

Literary History ☆
A Character's Legacy Many writers have been fascinated by Ulysses. Shakespeare included this character in his drama *Troilus and Cressida.* James Joyce's epic novel *Ulysses* follows one day in the life of Dublin-resident Leopold Bloom, revealing parallels between Bloom's adventures and those of the ancient Greek hero. Ulysses has even appeared as a character in the video game *Age of Mythology.*

 For an audio recording of this selection, use Listening Library Audio CD-ROM.

English Learners

DIFFERENTIATED INSTRUCTION

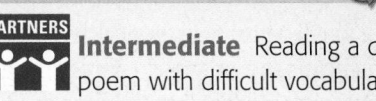 **Intermediate** Reading a dense poem with difficult vocabulary may seem like a daunting task to English learners. Have students work in pairs, reading aloud chunks of text (about 5 lines at a time) and noting any words or phrases that are unfamiliar. Have them use a dictionary and the footnotes to clarify their understanding, and then paraphrase the chunk before moving on to the next.

891

Assonance and Consonance
Answer: *The short* u *sound is heard in the words* some *and* suns, *and the* ôr *sound is heard in the words* for, store, *and* hoard.

Connotations Point out that *prudence* describes the virtue of sound judgment or careful management. However, the related noun *prude* has negative connotations, referring to someone who uses too much careful judgment and as a result is too attentive to propriety.

ENGLISH LEARNERS Have English learners identify a Spanish cognate for *prudence* (*prudencia*). Ask students to discuss whether *prudencia* has a positive or negative connotation.

View the Art ★

This print depicts Ulysses's passing through the strait of Messia, the mythological home of Scylla and Charybdis. Scylla is the sea monster eating his crew and Charybdis is a monster that sucks in water, causing the whirlpool to the left of the ship. Ulysses is placed at the front of the ship, leading it through the strait.

And drunk delight of battle with my peers,
Far on the ringing plains of windy Troy.°
I am a part of all that I have met;
Yet all experience is an arch wherethrough
20 Gleams that untraveled world, whose margin fades
Forever and forever when I move.
How dull it is to pause, to make an end,
To rust unburnished, not to shine in use!
As though to breathe were life! Life piled on life
25 Were all too little, and of one to me
Little remains; but every hour is saved
From that eternal silence, something more,
A bringer of new things; and vile it were
For some three suns to store and hoard myself,
30 And this gray spirit yearning in desire
To follow knowledge like a sinking star,
Beyond the utmost bound of human thought.
    This is my son, mine own Telemachus,
To whom I leave the scepter and the isle—
35 Well-loved of me, discerning to fulfill
This labor, by slow **prudence** to make mild **2**
A rugged people, and through soft degrees
Subdue them to the useful and the good.
Most blameless is he, centered in the sphere
40 Of common duties, decent not to fail
In offices of tenderness, and pay
Meet° adoration to my household gods,
When I am gone. He works his work, I mine.

    There lies the port; the vessel puffs her sail;
45 There gloom the dark broad seas. My mariners,
Souls that have toiled and wrought and thought with me—
That ever with a frolic welcome took
The thunder and the sunshine, and opposed
Free hearts, free foreheads—you and I are old;
50 Old age hath yet his honor and his toil;
Death closes all; but something ere the end,
Some work of noble note, may yet be done,
Not unbecoming men that strove with Gods.
The lights begin to twinkle from the rocks;
55 The long day wanes; the slow moon climbs; the deep

16–17 battle . . . Troy: the Trojan War, which the Greeks won after a ten-year siege

Print of the ship of Ulysses.

42 Meet: fitting; proper.

1 Assonance and Consonance *Which vowel sounds recur in this line?*

Vocabulary
prudence (prōōd′ əns) *n.* sound judgment; careful management

Writing Practice

 Allusion

SPIRAL REVIEW Tell students that the speaker of this poem is the great Greek mythological hero Odysseus. Tennyson legitimizes his speaker by including many references to places and people in Greek mythology that Odysseus encountered on his journey to Ithaca. Tell students that when a writer references famous works and characters, he or she is using allusion. Have students identify the allusions in this poem (*Hyades, Troy, Telemachus, Happy Isles, Achilles*) and write a brief essay discussing their significance.

Moans round with many voices. Come, my friends,
'Tis not too late to seek a newer world.
Push off, and sitting well in order smite
The sounding furrows;° for my purpose holds
60 To sail beyond the sunset, and the baths
Of all the western stars,° until I die.
It may be that the gulfs will wash us down;
It may be we shall touch the Happy Isles,°
And see the great Achilles,° whom we knew.
65 Though much is taken, much **abides**; and though
We are not now that strength which in old days
Moved earth and heaven, that which we are, we are—
One equal temper of heroic hearts,
Made weak by time and fate, but strong in will
70 To strive, to seek, to find, and not to yield.

59 sounding furrows: crashing waves.

60–61 baths . . . stars: reference to the ancient belief that the stars descended into a sea or river that encircled Earth.

63 Happy Isles: in Greek mythology, the place where mortals favored by the gods are sent to dwell after they die.

64 Achilles (ə kiꞌ lēz): the greatest warrior in the Greek assault on Troy.

Analyze Tone *Which words and phrases in these lines convey a tone of admiration?* **3**

Optimism and the Belief in Progress *What values does this line affirm?* **4**

Vocabulary

abide (ə bīdꞌ) *v.* remain

ALFRED, LORD TENNYSON **893**

Analyze Tone Answer: *"Purpose," "beyond the sunset," and "the baths of all the western stars" convey the poet's admiration for Ulysses.*

Optimism and the Belief in Progress Answer: *Self-confidence, earnest endeavor, perseverance, and progress*

(APPROACHING) Have approaching-level students recall the Victorian values discussed so far. **Ask:** Which of these values are represented in line 70? *(hard work, earnestness)*

Writer's Technique
Dramatic Monologue Tell students that a dramatic monologue is a form in which the speaker describes a crucial moment in his or her life and in the process reveals much about his or her own character. Ulysses seems to be speaking directly to the reader, revealing his most intimate thoughts.

Approaching Level

DIFFERENTIATED INSTRUCTION

Emerging Guide students in understanding Ulysses' argument as he persuades his mariners (and himself) to go back to sea. Have a volunteer read aloud lines 45–70. **Ask:** How does Ulysses describe himself and the nature of his journey? *(He is a hero, old but still able to do a noble deed. This journey could be that last heroic work.)* **Ask:** How does Ulysses try to persuade his mariners to undertake this journey? *(He points out that even though they are old, they may have time to accomplish one more great thing before they die.)*

To check students' understanding of the selection, see Unit 5 Teaching Resources Book, p. 40.

After You Read

Assess

1. Students' questions should reflect an understanding of Ulysses' character traits.

2. (a) As king, Ulysses settles petty disputes between his subjects. (b) Ulysses feels his life at home is dull and unfulfilling. His feelings are evident from details such as "idle king," "still hearth," "barren crags," and "savage race."

3. (a) Adventures, new ideas, and living life to the fullest (b) People should strive to reach their goals despite age.

4. (a) To accompany him on one last, glorious adventure (b) Some may say to create the impression that Ulysses is speaking to himself or directly to the reader; others may say that the delay builds suspense.

5. Ulysses understands how his experiences have contributed to making him who he is, while recognizing that there are experiences beyond his reach.

6. (a) Ulysses respects his son's decency as a leader. (b) Some students may find Telemachus's solidity preferable in a leader; others may prefer the vision and drive of Ulysses.

7. (a) That despite age they still have honor and usefulness and that it is not too late to seek new adventures (b) Answers will vary.

8. Ulysses is self-confident, future-oriented, and progress-minded. Telemachus displays Victorian values in his work to improve his subjects ("Subdue them to the useful and the good") and in his commitment to duty, decency, and propriety.

9. Victorian-era people placed high value on one's ability to work, an idea that is still popular today.

894

Respond and Think Critically

Respond and Interpret

1. What questions would you ask Ulysses if he were alive today?

2. (a) How does Ulysses spend his time at home? (b) How does he feel about his life at home? Use evidence from the poem to support your answer.

3. (a) What does Ulysses miss from his past? (b) Sum up Ulysses' thoughts and feelings about aging. Support your answer with evidence from the poem.

4. (a) What does Ulysses want his band of followers to do with him? (b) Why might Tennyson have chosen to wait until late in the poem before revealing whom Ulysses is addressing in his monologue?

Analyze and Evaluate

5. How do you interpret lines 18–21 of the poem?

6. (a) How does Ulysses regard his son's approach to life? (b) Which character would you rather have as a ruler—Ulysses or Telemachus? Why?

7. (a) What arguments does Ulysses present to persuade his listeners to join him? (b) Do you find his arguments persuasive? Explain why or why not.

Connect

8. **Big Idea** Optimism and the Belief in Progress Which Victorian values does Ulysses embody? Which values does his son reflect?

9. **Connect to Today** How do modern attitudes toward age and retirement compare to the attitude expressed in Tennyson's poem, or Victorian society overall?

Literary Element Assonance and Consonance

Tennyson is often praised for the musical patterns of his poetry. To help create these patterns, he sometimes uses **assonance** and **consonance**. For example, in line 5 of "Ulysses," he uses assonance, repeating long e sounds: "That hoard and sleep and feed, and know not me"; in line 17, he uses consonance, repeating the n and r sounds: "Far on the ringing plains of windy Troy."

1. Find other examples of assonance and consonance in "Ulysses."

2. How does Tennyson's use of assonance and consonance contribute to the overall effect of the poem?

LOG ON ▶ **Literature** Online

Selection Resources For Selection Quizzes, eFlashcards, and Reading-Writing Connection activitites, go to glencoe.com and enter QuickPass code GLB9817u5.

Review: Alliteration

As you learned on page 758, **alliteration** is the repetition of consonant sounds at the beginnings of words, as in the line "On the bald street breaks the blank day." Like assonance and consonance, alliteration is used to create rhythmic or musical effects.

Partner Activity Meet with a classmate to identify examples of alliteration in "Ulysses." Use a two-column chart like the one below to record your examples and describe their effects.

Example	Effect
lines 6-7 "I will drink / Life to the lees."	Creates rhythm; emphasizes the idea that Ulysses enjoys life to the fullest.

Literary Element

1. Examples: Assonance—(line 29) For some three suns to store and hoard myself; Consonance—(line 2) By this still hearth, among these barren crags.

2. These sound devices create a musical pattern and contribute to the rhythm of the poem.

Review: Alliteration

Sample answers: (line 12) hungry heart; (lines 13–14) men/And manners, climates, councils; (line 16) fades/Forever and forever; (lines 24–25) For some three suns to store; (line 49) Free hearts, free foreheads

Reading Strategy · Analyze Tone

A writer's **tone** may convey a variety of attitudes such as sympathy, irony, admiration, sadness, or bitterness. To **analyze the tone** of "Ulysses," focus on elements such as diction, imagery, and figurative language. In the following lines, for example, the image of fading light gives the speaker's words a sad, urgent tone:

> The lights begin to twinkle from the rocks;
> The long day wanes;

Review the web you filled in as you read, and then answer the following questions.

1. How would you describe the overall tone of this poem?

2. What details in the poem contribute to this tone?

Vocabulary Practice

Practice with Context Clues Identify the context clues in the following sentences that help you determine the meaning of each boldfaced vocabulary word.

1. The true hero acts not with rashness, but with **prudence**.

2. Even though heroes die, their messages **abide**, never fading away.

Academic Vocabulary

In the poem, old age is **conceived** *as a time to pursue one's goals, rather than a time to give up.*

Conceived is an academic word. It can have several different meanings. Using context clues, try to figure out the meaning of *conceived* in each sentence and explain the difference between the two meanings.

1. I first **conceived** my poem while hiking in Alaska, where the landscape inspired me.

2. I can't **conceive** of why you want to go to that concert; it seems expensive and overcrowded.

For more on academic vocabulary, see pages 56 and R81.

Speaking and Listening

 Oral Interpretation

Assignment Offer an oral interpretation of Tennyson's "Ulysses." Focus on conveying the poet's tone and revealing how it contributes to his message.

Prepare Create a script by rereading the poem several times, listening for Tennyson's tone and marking words and phrases that you should stress to help convey the poem's tone to your audience. Also note places where you can change the pace and volume of your voice to mirror the progression of Ulysses's journey and highlight the theme of the poem.

EXAMPLE:

"Death closes all;" (slow pace and pause) "but something ere the end," (increase register and volume)

"Some work of noble note," (extend arms and hands toward audience) "may yet be done...."

Rehearse your oral interpretation in front of a mirror or for friends and family. Deliver it several times, until you're comfortable looking up from your script and making eye contact often. Practice incorporating gestures and facial expressions at appropriate places.

Perform Remember that your attitude will determine your audience's receptivity, so take a deep breath, relax, and deliver your presentation with confidence. Speak loudly and clearly and use natural gestures and expressions. Understatement is often more effective than exaggeration. Be sure that your interpretation, above all, will help listeners understand the poem's meaning and theme.

Evaluate Write a critique of your performance, addressing the criteria listed on page 1163. Indicate how you would change your interpretation or delivery to improve your next presentation.

ALFRED, LORD TENNYSON **895**

Reading Strategy

1. The overall tone of this poem may be described as respectful, admiring, or celebratory. Tennyson regards Ulysses as a model of heroism for his defiance of time and relentless search for knowledge and experience.

2. Several details contribute to this tone, for example, the driving rhythm created by the infinitives in the concluding line: "To strive, to seek, to find, and not to yield."

Vocabulary Practice

1. not, rashness

2. never fading away

Academic Vocabulary

1. *Conceived* here means "thought of."

2. *Conceived* here means "understand."

 Speaking and Listening

Students' oral interpretations should emphasize the tone of adventure and excitement present in "Ulysses."

 For additional assessment, see Assessment Resources, pp. 215–216.

To create custom assessments using software, use ExamView Assessment Suite.

Focus

Comparing Literature
Across Time and Place

Bellringer Options

Selection Focus
Transparency 44

Daily Language Practice
Transparency 72

Or have students brainstorm popular songs about love. Make a short list of these songs on the board. Then, discuss what each song describes or implies about love.

Connect to the Reading Selections

Have students discuss whether it is necessary to have love in one's life. If you like, stage a brief debate with two or three students taking pro and con positions.

Compare Literature About Love

The line between love and heartache is thin and delicate, and it often defies logic. The following poems by Elizabeth Barrett Browning and Edna St. Vincent Millay and the song by John Lennon and Paul McCartney investigate the necessity of love and its power to change lives.

Sonnet 43 by Elizabeth Barrett Browning .... sonnet 897

Love Is Not All: It Is Not Meat nor Drink
by Edna St. Vincent Millay .... poem 901

In My Life by John Lennon and Paul McCartney .... song 902

COMPARE THE | Big Idea | **Optimism and the Belief in Progress**

Barrett Browning's poem describes an idealized love and reflects an optimism unburdened by certain realities of her life and times. As you read, ask yourself, How do the three selections here express idealistic views of the adventure and power of romance, while also presenting realistic hurdles between lovers?

COMPARE Theme of Passionate Love

The themes of love and desire have produced some of history's most memorable literature. As you read, ask yourself, How do the selections explore the presence and absence of love in one's life?

COMPARE Historical Contexts

The manner in which love is expressed in a poem or a song can depend upon historical context. For example, at one point it was fashionable to write religious love poems. As you read, ask yourself, How is it fashionable to express love in poetry today?

Learning Objectives

For pages 896–903

In studying these texts, you will focus on the following objectives:

Literary Study: Analyzing repetition.

Reading:
Analyzing style.
Comparing themes.
Comparing historical context.

Writing: Writing a list.

LOG ON ► Literature Online

Author Search For more about Barrett Browning, Millay, Lennon, and McCartney, go to glencoe.com and enter QuickPass code GLB9817u5.

Selection Skills

Literary Elements
- Repetition (SE pp. 898–903)

Comparing Literature

Listening/Speaking/Viewing Skills
- Discussion Starter (SE pp. 901–902)
- Oral Report (SE p. 903)

Reading Skills
- Analyze Style (SE pp. 898–903)

Vocabulary Skills
- Academic Vocabulary (SE p. 900)

Writing Skills/Grammar
- Write a List (SE p. 900)

Before You Read

Sonnet 43

Meet **Elizabeth Barrett Browning**

(1806–1861)

"I tell you hopeless grief is passionless."

—Elizabeth Barrett Browning

The eldest child of a wealthy country squire, Elizabeth Barrett spent her childhood playing in the countryside and reading. In fact, by the age of ten, she had read a stunning array of literature, from the historical works of classical Greece and Rome to the plays of Shakespeare. Reflecting on her youth, she later said, "Books and dreams were what I lived in and domestic life only seemed to buzz gently around, like bees about the grass."

Hope End Barrett grew up on a lush, opulent country estate called Hope End. Her father derived his wealth from sugar plantations in Jamaica. The business turned sour, however, while Barrett was still a youth, and the family adopted a more modest lifestyle. When she was fifteen, Barrett suffered a spinal injury, which, along with a chronic problem with her lungs, left her bedridden for much of her life. Despite her poor health, Barrett became one of the most successful and versatile poets in Victorian England. Her work was characterized by enthusiasm, directness, and a warmly felt sense of social responsibility. Still, Barrett's family life was difficult, and she struggled to cope with the tragic drowning in 1840 of her favorite brother, Edward. Additionally, her contact with the outside world was restricted by her over-protective father, who forbade any of his eleven children to marry. By the age of thirty-five, Barrett was confined to her bedroom in the family's London home because of both her health and her father's wishes.

A Great Love Story Despite her confinement, Barrett became well known for her published verses. When her poems came to the attention of the fledgling poet Robert Browning, he immediately wrote her a telegram declaring, "I love your verses with all my heart, dear Miss Barrett. I do,

as I say, love these books with all my heart—and I love you too." In contrast to Barrett's bedridden existence, Browning led an active social life. Six years her junior, Browning was determined and brash. He boldly began to visit Barrett despite her father's disapproval. The two eloped in 1846, moved quickly to Italy, and settled at Casa Guidi, an old stone house in Florence. In Italy, the couple had a child, who they nicknamed Pen, and Barrett Browning became an avid player in politics, supporting the Risorgimento movement that sought to unify the country. In 1850 Barrett Browning published *Sonnets from the Portuguese*, perhaps her most famous collection.

While her love poems still thrill readers, Barrett Browning, like other Victorian writers, also wrote literature intended to spark social reform. Her 1857 book-length poem *Aurora Leigh* was groundbreaking. The work critiques the treatment of women in Victorian society by telling the story of an independent, artistic heroine. Of the poem, Virginia Woolf wrote, "Aurora Leigh, with her passionate interest in social questions, her conflict as artist and woman, her longing for knowledge and freedom, is the true daughter of her age."

ELIZABETH BARRETT BROWNING **897**

Before You Read

Focus

Political History ☆

When the Brownings moved to Florence, Italy was not a unified country. Florence was independent and controlled much land surrounding Tuscany. Other Italian-speaking areas were either independent or controlled by foreign powers such as Spain or Austria. The Kingdom of Italy was not formed until 1861—the year of Barrett Browning's death.

English Learners

DIFFERENTIATED INSTRUCTION

Beginning Explain that Sonnet 43 repeats a certain phrase. Tell students to note the phrase as they read and pay attention to the images associated with it. When they have read

the sonnet, have them state the theme in a sentence and describe the speaker in another sentence. *(The poem is about the everlasting nature of the speaker's love. She is passionate and devoted.)*

Intermediate Ask students to think about poems, books, or stories they have read or films they have seen that have love as a major theme. Have volunteers tell how love is portrayed in these tales. Then ask each student to state which view of love he or she most closely agrees with.

Comparing Literature

Before You Read

Focus

Summary

The speaker describes her love as all encompassing and never-ending. She says that her love has reawakened emotions from her childhood. She ends by writing that, God willing, her love will live on after her death.

 For summaries in languages other than English, see Unit 5 Teaching Resources Book, pp. 43–48.

Literature and Reading Preview

Connect to the Sonnet

Is love a luxury, or a basic human need, like air and water? Debate this question with a partner.

Build Background

Elizabeth Barrett Browning wrote forty-four sonnets describing the fear, excitement, and hope she felt when, after years of ill health, she fell in love. Robert Browning, her husband, was impressed, and insisted she publish them. Not wanting to share her private feelings with the public, she published the sonnets under the title *Sonnets from the Portuguese*, hoping people would think the poems were translations rather than expressions of her own emotions.

Set Purposes for Reading

Big Idea Optimism and the Belief in Progress

As you read, ask yourself, How does Barrett Browning's poem reflect the optimism and belief in progress of her day?

Literary Element Repetition

Repetition is the recurrence of sounds, words, phrases, lines, or stanzas in a poem. As you read, ask yourself, How does this literary device call attention to particular ideas?

Reading Strategy Analyze Style

To **analyze style** is to look at the ways in which the expressive qualities of a work help reveal the author's attitude and purpose in writing. Word choice, figurative language, and imagery are key elements that help create style. Also, context matters—you might interpret a religious metaphor in a love poem differently from the same metaphor in a poem about war. As you read, ask yourself, How do these elements work together to create the writer's style?

Tip: Connecting Style and Theme As you read, identify the overall effect and the message, or theme, of the sonnet. Then, in a word web, note the stylistic elements the poet employs to help express that theme. Remember to look for examples of imagery, line and stanza patterns, figurative language, and distinctive rhythms.

Autumn, 1903. George Frederick Watts. Oil on canvas, Trustees of the Watts Gallery, Compton, Surrey, UK.

Writing Practice

SPIRAL REVIEW **Identify Adverbs** Remind students that an adverb modifies a verb, an adjective, or another adverb. Challenge students to identify adverbs in the poem. (*Most, freely, purely,* and *better*) **Write** each one on the board. **Ask:** Which word does each of these adverbs modify? (*Most modifies the adjective* quiet; *the others modify the verb* love.) Have students write a sentence using each of these adverbs correctly. Ask volunteers to write their sentences on the board and read them aloud.

Sonnet 43

Elizabeth Barrett Browning

The Painter's Honeymoon, c.1863–4. Lord Frederic Leighton. Oil on canvas, 83.8 x 77.5 cm. Museum of Fine Art, Boston.

How do I love thee? Let me count the ways.
I love thee to the depth and breadth and height
My soul can reach, when feeling out of sight
For the ends of Being and ideal Grace.
5   I love thee to the level of every day's
Most quiet need, by sun and candlelight.
I love thee freely, as men strive for Right;
I love thee purely, as they turn from Praise.
I love thee with the passion put to use
10 In my old griefs, and with my childhood's faith.
I love thee with a love I seemed to lose
With my lost saints—I love thee with the breath,
Smiles, tears, of all my life!—and, if God choose,
I shall but love thee better after death.

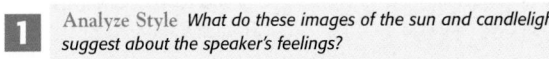

1   Analyze Style *What do these images of the sun and candlelight suggest about the speaker's feelings?*

ELIZABETH BARRETT BROWNING **899**

Approaching Level

DIFFERENTIATED INSTRUCTION

Established Some approaching-level students may wish to find out more about Elizabeth Barrett Browning and her poetry. Discuss where they might find more examples of her poetry. *(In a collection of her verse, in an anthology of Victorian poetry, or on a Web site devoted to her poetry)* Discuss with students where they might find more information about her life. *(In a book about famous poets, in an encyclopedia*

article about her, or on the Web) Then allow students to develop questions that they would like answered about her life and work. Have students use the discussed methods of research to find answers to these questions.

Teach

Reading Strategy   **1**

Analyze Style **Answer:**
The image "sun and candlelight" suggests a burning, almost spiritual devotion.

 For additional practice using the reading skill or strategy, see Unit 5 Teaching Resources Book, p. 50.

View the Art ★

Lord Frederic Leighton was an English classicist painter and sculptor. He studied extensively in Rome and Florence and, like Barrett Browning, was influenced by classical works. Tell students that his painting reflects many features of classical paintings.
Ask: How are the two people in the painting characterized? *(As a young couple, they seem to be deeply in love based on their body language (holding hands even as he paints). She is involved in or interested by his work.)*

 For an audio recording of this selection, use Listening Library Audio CD-ROM.

 To check students' understanding of the selection, see Unit 5 Teaching Resources Book, p. 51.

After You Read

Assess

1. Students' choices will vary.
2. (a) Possible paraphrase is "I love you more than you can know." (b) Her love pervades her life.
3. (a) Her love has rekindled lost innocence and allowed her to channel negative feelings in positive ways. (b) The speaker's past is disillusioning or unhappy.
4. (a) Forever (b) The final two lines
5. (a) Adoring, reverent, and idealized (b) She has intense feelings and romantic idealism.
6. Such love brings out the best in partners but may set up unrealistic expectations.
7. Lines 7–8 suggest that the speaker believes in humanity's ability to do right.
8. The expression of true love is both universal and timeless.

Literary Element

1. (a) "I love thee" occurs in lines 1, 2, 5, 7, 8, 9, 11, 12, and 14. Lines 7–8 are syntactically similar. (b) It reinforces the speaker's feelings and contributes to the rhythm.
2. The repetition introduces aspects of the speaker's love.

Progress Check

Can students analyze repetition?

If No → See Unit 5 Teaching Resources Book, p. 49.

After You Read

Respond and Think Critically

Respond and Interpret

1. The speaker of Sonnet 43 expresses her love in a variety of "ways." Which of these ways do you find most compelling? Explain.
2. (a) Paraphrase how the speaker describes her love in lines 1–8. (b) What do these lines reveal about the nature of the speaker's love?
3. (a) How does the speaker describe her love in lines 9–12? (b) What can you infer about the speaker's past from these lines?
4. (a) How long does the speaker expect her love to last? (b) What line or lines in the poem support your interpretation?

Analyze and Evaluate

5. (a) How would you describe the speaker's **tone**, or attitude toward the subject? (b) What does the speaker's tone seem to suggest about her character and personality?
6. Evaluate the advantages and disadvantages of a love as strong as the speaker's in the poem.

Connect

7. **Big Idea** Optimism and the Belief in Progress How does this poem reflect an optimistic outlook and a belief in progress? Explain.
8. **Connect to Today** Do you think this poem is too personal or that the language and imagery is too outdated to be of interest to present-day readers? Explain.

Literary Element Repetition

Repetition in a literary work often helps to highlight important concepts.

1. (a) Identify repeated words and phrases as well as syntactical repetition in Barrett Browning's poem. (b) What is the effect of this repetition?
2. How does this repetition relate to the professed purpose of the poem?

🖋 Writing

Write a List Sonnet 43 contains an idealized description of true love. Imagine that you are a marriage counselor, and write a list of the ideas or qualities that a couple should have in order to build a healthy relationship. Your list might be purely practical, or it might combine practical ideas with more romanticized examples like those in the sonnet. Share your list with a partner and discuss what makes love true, or lasting.

Reading Strategy Analyze Style

A work's style can help reveal the writer's purpose. Examine Barrett's style to answer these questions.

1. What distinguishes the style of this sonnet? Cite examples from the text.
2. How does the use of concrete imagery and abstract concepts contribute to the poem's message?

Academic Vocabulary

*Elizabeth Barrett Browning **compiled** a list of her feelings for her husband into one brief poem.*

Compiled is an academic word. In an everyday setting, a "best of" album might be advertised as a **compiled** collection of a musician's hit songs. Using context clues, try to figure out the meaning of the word in the sentence about Barrett Browning above. Check your guess in a dictionary.

For more on academic vocabulary, see pages 56 and R81.

Reading Strategy

1. The effect of the question that begins the sonnet, the variations in rhythm and the use of enjambment
2. Concrete images of light and abstract concepts that suggest religious faith underline the speaker's love.

Academic Vocabulary

Here, "compiled" means "brought together."

🖋 Writing

Students' lists should include reasonable ideas and qualities, such as respect, trust, or passion.

Build Background

To a generation of Americans who came of age during the Roaring Twenties, the poet Edna St. Vincent Millay was a symbol of the modern woman: young, independent, free-spirited, energetic, and beautiful. In fact, the line "My candle burns at both ends" from one of Millay's poems became a motto for the age.

Love Is Not All:
It Is Not Meat nor Drink

Edna St. Vincent Millay

Love is not all: it is not meat nor drink
Nor slumber nor a roof against the rain;
Nor yet a floating spar to men that sink
And rise and sink and rise and sink again;
5   Love can not fill the thickened lung with breath,
Nor clean the blood, nor set the fractured bone;
Yet many a man is making friends with death
Even as I speak, for lack of love alone.
It well may be that in a difficult hour,
10   Pinned down by pain and moaning for release,
Or nagged by want past resolution's power,
I might be driven to sell your love for peace,
Or trade the memory of this night for food.
It well may be. I do not think I would.

> **💬 Discussion Starter**
>
> Millay's poem explores both the power and the inability of love to sustain an individual. The speaker in the poem expresses both emotional and rational responses to love. Which type of response to love does the speaker most value? Discuss this question with a group of classmates, citing examples from the poem to support your views.

EDNA ST. VINCENT MILLAY **901**

Focus

Summary

The speaker says that though love cannot meet some essential needs, many people are dying from a lack of it. She admits that someday she may feel compelled to exchange love for health or peace—but probably not.

Literary Element

Repetition **Ask:** What effect does the poet achieve by repeating *not* and *nor*, and *might* and *may well*? *(She creates a contrast between the two halves of the poem, the first half focusing on what love cannot do and the second half focusing on the positive, emotional appeal of love.)*

Discussion Starter

Students' discussions should spur a debate about whether the speaker values an emotional or rational response to love more. Students should support their opinions with examples from the poem.

Approaching Level

DIFFERENTIATED INSTRUCTION

Established **Ask:** What does the title of this sonnet mean? *(It means that love alone is not enough to keep a person alive.)* What are the essential needs that love cannot provide? *(Food and drink; shelter; rescue in the open sea; respiration; filtering the blood, setting a bone)* Read lines 7 and 8 aloud. **Ask:** What is Millay saying here? *(Many people are sick or dying only because they lack love in their lives.)*

Comparing Literature

Focus

Summary

The speaker has known people, places, and moments that still live in his memory and that he still loves. But, he says, "I'll love you more."

Reading Strategy

Analyze Style Examine the songwriter's word choices. **Ask:** What types of words does Lennon and McCartney use? *(common, everyday words)* Why do you think they chose this style? *(Possible answer: The simple language makes it easy to relate to the singer's feelings.)*

Build Background

Influenced by American rock 'n' roll, the Beatles perfected the art of the pop song. As they grew as musicians, their songs became more complex and emotionally revealing. One of the first songs to demonstrate such growth was "In My Life," a song written by the guitarist and singer John Lennon for the 1965 album *Rubber Soul.* Lennon remarked, "'In My Life' was, I think, my first real, major piece of work. Up until then it had all been glib and throwaway."

In My Life

John Lennon and
Paul McCartney

There are places I'll remember all my life,
Though some have changed,
Some forever, not for better,
Some have gone and some remain.

5　All these places had their moments
With lovers and friends I still can recall.
Some are dead and some are living.
In my life I've loved them all.

But of all these friends and lovers,
10　There is no one compares with you,
And these mem'ries lose their meaning
When I think of love as something new.

Though I know I'll never lose affection
For people and things that went before,
15　I know I'll often stop and think about them,
In my life I'll love you more.

Though I know I'll never lose affection
For people and things that went before,
I know I'll often stop and think about them,
20　In my life I'll love you more.
In my life I'll love you more.

> **Discussion Starter**
>
> How is this song structured? How are songs similar to poems? What qualities associated with poetry are at work in this song? Discuss these questions with a group. If a recording of the song is available, listen to it to enrich your understanding of the lyrics.

Listening Practice

SPIRAL REVIEW **Hear the Song** If possible, bring in a recording of *In My Life* or another John Lennon song, along with copies of the song's lyrics. Have students read the lyrics and then listen to the song. Discuss how the music contributes to the mood of the lyrics. Ask students which words seemed more prominent when they read the lyrics and which were more prominent when they listened to the song. Ask students to discuss how the difference in emphasis affected their perspective on the song.

Wrap-Up: Comparing Literature

Across Time and Place

- *Sonnet 43* by Elizabeth Barrett Browning

- *Love Is Not All: It Is Not Meat nor Drink*
  by Edna St. Vincent Millay

- *In My Life* by John Lennon and Paul McCartney

COMPARE THE **Big Idea** Optimism and the Belief
in Progress

Writing What purpose does love serve in society? Does love inspire innovation and bring about a better quality of life? Does a belief in love go hand
in hand with a belief in progress? Write a brief essay comparing the arguments made by these three writers.

COMPARE Theme of Passionate Love

Group Activity With a group of classmates, discuss
the theme of love in these three selections. Then
answer the following questions.

1. How does the speaker of each work assess the
   importance of love in his or her life?

2. How is each speaker emotionally affected by the
   experience of being in love?

3. Which selection is most romantic? Which is most
   realistic? Explain.

Online Romance. Illustration. Farida Zaman.

COMPARE Historical Contexts

Speaking and Listening Writers are influenced by their
surroundings. Barrett Browning's poem is an outgrowth of her upbringing in
Victorian England. Millay's poem mirrors her frenetic lifestyle during the
Roaring Twenties. The Beatles song is influenced by sudden stardom.
Research the historical backdrop of one of these works and give a short oral
report to your class about how the context helps you better understand the
writer's portrayal of love and passion. Make a chart to use as part of your
presentation.

Selection Resources For
Selection Quizzes, eFlashcards,
and Reading-Writing Connection
activities, go to glencoe.com and
enter QuickPass code GLB9817u5.

COMPARING LITERATURE **903**

Assess

Compare the Big Idea

Students' essays should discuss
Barrett Browning's idealized version
of love, Millay's idea of love as
essential to life, and Lennon's and
McCartney's views about the importance of holding on to memories
while still living in the moment.

Compare the Theme of Passionate Love

1. Students may compare the way
Barrett Browning is liberated by her
love and the way Millay is sustained by it.

2. Encourage students to compare Millay's poem to Lennon and
McCartney's song and to examine
the power of love to consume and
to heal.

3. Answers will vary.

Compare Historical Contexts

Students' oral presentations
should:

- identify and describe the historical context

- link the context to the literature

- incorporate visual aids

Advanced Learners

DIFFERENTIATED INSTRUCTION

Compare Styles Have students compare
the style and tone of the various selections.
Ask them to think about whether they see
a progression in the styles. *(Browning's
sonnet is the most formal and stylized;
St. Millay's still uses more formal language
and form, but the sentence structure is
simpler; Lennon and McCartney's song
is simple and informal, using everyday
contemporary language.)* Ask students to

speculate on reasons for the differences in
style and tone. *(Possible answer: Society
has become less formal over time and
people have come to value simpler forms
of expression.)*

Focus

Summary

Recently scientists have begun to investigate the origins of love, which has defied scientific measurement. It has been assumed that love is a false emotion, a legacy of the French troubadours in the twelfth century. Now scientists are studying whether it is a mental construct or a biological fact.

 For summaries in languages other than English, see Unit 5 Teaching Resources Book, pp. 53–58.

 Interactive Read and Write
Other options for teaching this selection can be found in
- Interactive Read and Write for EL Students, pp. 223–234
- Interactive Read and Write for Approaching-Level Students, pp. 223–234
- Interactive Read and Write for On-Level Students, pp. 223–234

Teach

Reading Strategy   1

Examine Connotation and Denotation After students read the introduction, **ask:** What words or phrases describe love? Have students tell if they have a positive, negative, or neutral connotation. (*Wonderful, mysterious, emotional* (positive); "mushy," hard to measure, too different (negative))

Readability Scores

Dale-Chall: 9.5
DRP: 67
Lexile: 1070

Learning Objectives

For pages 904–907

In studying this text, you will focus on the following objectives:

Reading:
Analyzing informational text. Examining connotation and denotation.

Set a Purpose for Reading

You've just read three selections about the power of love. As you read this article, ask yourself, What are the results of studies on the origin of love?

Preview the Article

1. How does love influence traditions and institutions in our culture?
2. On the basis of the photographs on pages 905–907, what point do you think the writer is going to make about love?

Reading Strategy Examine Connotation and Denotation

A word's **denotation** is its literal meaning, or dictionary definition. Its **connotations** are the suggested or implied meanings associated with the word beyond its literal meaning. As you read, examine how the writer uses connotation and denotation.

904 UNIT 5

TIME

What Is LOVE?

After centuries of ignoring the subject as too vague and mushy, scientists have undergone a change of heart about the tender passion.

By PAUL GRAY

What is this thing called love? What? Is this thing called love? What is this thing called? Love.

HOWEVER PUNCTUATED, Cole Porter's simple question begs an answer. Love's symptoms are familiar enough: a drifting mooniness in thought and behavior, the mad conceit that the entire universe has rolled itself up into the person of the beloved, a conviction that no one on earth has ever felt so torrentially about a fellow creature before. Love is ecstasy and torment, freedom and slavery. Poets and songwriters would be in a fine mess without it. Plus, it makes the world go round.

Until recently, scientists wanted no part of it. The reason for this avoidance, this reluctance to study what is probably life's most intense emotion, is not difficult to track down. Love is mushy; science is hard. Anger and fear, feelings that have been considerably researched in the field and the lab, can be quantified through measurements: pulse and breathing rates, muscle contractions, a whole spider web of involuntary responses. Love does not register as definitively on the instruments; it leaves a blurred fingerprint that could be mistaken for anything from indigestion to a manic attack. Anger and fear have direct roles—fighting or running—in the survival of the species. But romantic love, and all the attendant sighing and swooning and sonnet writing, has struck many pragmatic investigators as beside the point.

So biologists and anthropologists assumed that it would be fruitless, even frivolous, to study love's origins, the way it was encoded in our genes or imprinted in our

---

Vocabulary Practice

SPIRAL REVIEW **Compound Words** Remind students that compound words are made up of two or more words. Readers can increase their understanding of compound words by examining the meaning of the separate parts. Examples of compound words in this selection include *songwriter, fingerprint,* and *playwrights.* Ask students to define these compound words.

★ **UNITED STATES**
Valentine's Day
Romantic rituals in the West have evolved into the bestowal of flowers, candy, and other sweet nothings. But the absence of such gift giving in poorer cultures does not, anthropologists are learning, mean the absence of romance.

Sandi Fellman

brains. Serious scientists simply assumed that romantic love was really all in the head, put there five or six centuries ago when civilized societies first found enough spare time to indulge in flowery prose. The task of writing the book of love was ceded to playwrights, poets, and pulp novelists.

2 But in recent years, scientists across a broad range of disciplines have had a change of heart about love. The amount of research expended on the tender passion has never been more intense. To explain this rise in interest, some point to the growing number of women scientists and suggest that they may be more willing than their male colleagues to take love seriously. Says researcher Elaine Hatfield: "When I was back at Stanford in the 1960s, they said studying love and human relationships was a quick way to ruin my career. Why not go where the

real work was being done: on how fast rats could run?" Whatever the reasons, science seems to have come around to a view that nearly everyone else has always taken for granted: Romance is real. It is not merely a conceit; it is bred into our biology.

Getting to this point logically is harder than it sounds. The love-as-cultural-delusion argument has long seemed unassailable. What actually accounts for the emotion, according to this scenario, is that people long ago made the mistake of taking fanciful literary notions seriously. Among the prime suspects are the 12th-century French troubadours who more or less invented the Art of Courtly Love, an elaborate and artificial ritual for idle aristocrats.

Ever since then, the injunction to love and to be loved has hummed nonstop through popular culture; it is a dominant theme in music, films,

novels, magazines, and nearly everything shown on TV. Love is a formidable and thoroughly proved commercial engine; people will buy and do almost anything that promises them a chance at the bliss of romance.

But does all this mean that love is merely a phony emotion that we picked up because our culture celebrates it? Psychologist Lawrence Casler, author of *Is Marriage Necessary?*, forcefully thinks so, at least at first: "I don't believe love is part of human nature, not for a minute. There are social pressures at work." Then a shadow falls over his certainty. "Even if it is a part of human nature, like crime or violence, it's not necessarily desirable."

Well, love either is or is not intrinsic to our species; having it both ways leads nowhere. And the contention that romance is an entirely acquired trait—the revenge of

WHAT IS LOVE? **905**

TIME

Teach

Big Idea	**2**

Optimism and the Belief in Progress Ask: How does this article reflect the spirit of optimism and the belief in progress? *(Answers may include that scientists are optimistic about finding the true nature of love; science is associated with progress in our understanding of our world.)*

Cultural History ☆

Valentine's Day in the United States Esther Howland (1828–1904) is considered the "Mother of the American Valentine." After receiving a fancy lace Valentine in college, she decided to start her own Valentine card business. Her business grew to $100,000 a year before she sold it in 1881. The valentines she created are now collectors' items.

English Learners

DIFFERENTIATED INSTRUCTION

PARTNERS 👥 **Intermediate** Encourage students to increase their vocabulary. Suggest that they work with English-proficient partners to select words or phrases from this spread and analyze their reactions to them. Make sure that students respond to the following: blurred fingerprint, sighing and swooning, fruitless, and all in the head. Have students classify the connotations of these words and phrases using a chart with the following headings: Positive, Negative, and Neutral. *(Answers will vary.)*

Teach

Reading Strategy | **1**

Examine Denotation and Connotation Have students point out the scientific language the author sometimes uses. **Ask:** What kind of connotation does this language create? *(The scientific language makes the tone more serious and therefore makes the author seem more credible.)*

 For activities related to this selection, see Unit 5 Teaching Resources Book, pp. 59–60.

overly imaginative love poets on those who would take them literally—has always rested on some flimsy premises.

Why, for example, has romantic love—that odd collection of tics and impulses—lasted over the centuries? Most mass hallucinations, such as the 17th-century tulip mania in Holland (when the popularity of tulips pushed the price of a single bulb sky high), flame out fairly rapidly when people realize the absurdity of what they have been doing and come to their senses. When people in love come to their senses, they tend to orbit with added energy around each other and look more helplessly loopy and self-besotted. If romance were purely a figment, unsupported by any rational or sensible evidence, then surely most folks would be immune to it by now. Look

around. It hasn't happened. Love is still in the air.

And it may be far more widespread than even romantics imagined. Those who argue that love is a cultural fantasy have tended to do so from a Eurocentric and class-driven point of view. Romance, they say, arose thanks to circumstances peculiar to the West: leisure time, a decent amount of creature comforts, a certain level of refinement in the arts and letters. Romantic love was for aristocrats, not for peasants.

But a study conducted by anthropologists William Jankowiak of the University of Nevada-Las Vegas and Edward Fischer of Tulane University found evidence of romantic love in at least 147 of the 166 cultures they studied. This discovery, if borne out, should

pretty well wipe out the idea that love is an invention of the Western mind rather than a biological fact. Says Jankowiak: "It is, instead, a universal phenomenon, a panhuman characteristic that stretches across cultures. Societies like ours have the resources to show love through candy and flowers, but that does not mean that the lack of resources in other cultures indicates the absence of love." **1**

Some scientists are not startled by this contention. One of them is anthropologist Helen Fisher, a research associate at the American Museum of Natural History. Says Fisher: "I've never not thought that love was a very primitive, basic human emotion, as basic as fear, anger, or joy. It is so evident. I guess anthropologists have just been busy doing other things."

CHINA
Courtship on Horseback
On the plains of Xinjiang, mounted Kazakh suitors play Catch the Maiden. He chases her in pursuit of a kiss. If he succeeds, she goes after him with a riding crop.

Jay Dickman

Listening Practice

SPIRAL REVIEW **Hear Song Lyrics** Have students listen to a recording of a love song. Some possible titles include "You're the One that I Want" by Olivia Newton-John or "I Wanna Hold Your Hand" by The Beatles. After playing the recording, **ask:** What words are repeated in the song? What does this reveal about love in our society?

(Repeated words generally include "love," "need," and "beautiful." Students may feel this means that finding love is highly valued in our society.)

AFRICA
Dressed Up for Display
The Woodaabe tribe recognizes two kinds of marriage: kobgal, or arranged, and teegal, made from the heart. This young male is hoping to attract a partner in teegal.

Among the things anthropologists—often knobby-kneed gents in safari shorts—tended to do in the past was ask questions about courtship and marriage rituals. This now seems a classic example, as the old song has it, of looking for love in all the wrong places. In many cultures, love and marriage do not go together. Weddings can have all the romance of corporate mergers, signed and sealed for family or territorial interests. This does not mean, Jankowiak insists, that love does not exist in such cultures; it erupts in clandestine forms, "a phenomenon to be dealt with."

But if science is going to probe and prod and then announce that we are all scientifically fated to love—and to love preprogrammed types—by our genes and chemicals, then a lot of people would just as soon not know. If there truly is a biological predisposition to love, as more and more scientists are coming to believe, then it follows that there is also an amazing diversity in the ways humans have chosen to express the feeling. The cartoon images of cavemen bopping cavewomen over the head and dragging them home by their hair? Love. Helen of Troy, subjecting her adopted city to 10 years of ruinous siege? Love. Romeo and Juliet? Ditto. Joe in Accounting making a fool of himself around the water cooler over Susan in Sales? Love. Like the universe, the more we learn about love, the more preposterous and mysterious it is likely to appear.

Respond and Think Critically

Respond

1. Write a brief summary of the main ideas in this article before you answer the following questions. For help with writing a summary, see page 435.

2. How did the article influence your preconceptions about the origin of love?

Recall and Interpret

3. (a)Why have scientists traditionally been reluctant to study the concept of love? (b)Who took on the "task of writing the book of love"?

4. (a)Paraphrase the "love-as-cultural-delusion" argument. (b)What facts tend to refute this argument?

5. (a)According to some modern anthropologists, why are courtship and marriage rituals the wrong places to look for the origins of love?

(b)Where do modern scientists look for the origin of love?

Analyze and Evaluate

6. (a)Why do you think the writer chose to use the introductory Cole Porter quotation? (b)What is the significance of the quotation?

7. (a)Why do some theorists think love is a fantasy of the West? (b)How does the study by Jankowiak and Fischer prove this theory wrong?

8. If romantic love is genetically programmed, what selective advantage does it afford the human species?

Connect

9. How do you think Victorian writers would have responded to the modern scientific view that love is biologically determined?

WHAT IS LOVE? **907**

Before You Read

Focus

Bellringer Options

Selection Focus
Transparency 45
Daily Language Practice
Transparency 73

Or have students close their eyes and imagine that they are hiking through a forest, hearing birds and a babbling brook, seeing beautiful flowers and trees. **Ask:** What are you feeling? How does nature affect you? Encourage students to share their thoughts. Then explain that the poems of Gerard Manley Hopkins reveal lessons that nature might teach them.

Before You Read

Hopkins's Poetry

Meet **Gerard Manley Hopkins**
(1844–1889)

Like many artists and writers, Gerard Manley Hopkins did not know fame during his lifetime. In fact, his poetry was not published until 1918, nearly thirty years after his death. For this reason, Hopkins was long viewed as a twentieth-century poet, although in recent decades scholars and publishers have considered his poems in their original Victorian context—all the better to understand and appreciate the extent of Hopkins's innovation and accomplishment as a poet.

From Highgate to High Church The first of nine children, Hopkins was born into a middle-class Anglican family who shared a love of literature, art, and music. He began writing as a child and won a poetry prize when he was fifteen. After a brilliant career at the Highgate School in London, Hopkins entered Oxford University in 1863. There he studied Latin and Greek and was also exposed to the newest ideas in poetry and theology. These pursuits fostered in Hopkins a dual interest in rich, imagistic verse and in rich, imagistic religion—the latter of which led him first to High Church Anglicanism and then to Roman Catholicism and the Jesuit priesthood. As a result of his conversion, Hopkins suffered a painful and enduring estrangement from his Protestant family.

> *"The world is charged with the grandeur of God.*
> *It will flame out, like shining from shook foil."*
>
> —Gerard Manley Hopkins

The Poet Priest Soon after his conversion, Hopkins burned most of his poems in a display of religious devotion. For seven years he wrote no new poetry. Then, in 1875, one of his superiors suggested that he write a poem about five nuns exiled for their faith who had drowned in the shipwreck of the *Deutschland*. "The Wreck of the Deutschland" was rejected for publication due to its unconventional style but sparked in Hopkins a renewed interest in writing poetry—which he would continue to do for the remaining fourteen years of his life.

In much of Hopkins's early poetry, the meeting of the mind and nature leads directly to a transcendent awareness of God in all things—an awareness expressed fervently and poignantly in his 1877 poem "God's Grandeur."

Late in life, however, Hopkins produced a series of "terrible sonnets" which express despair at the poet's inability to fully escape the prison of the self. This despair created for Hopkins a frustrating dilemma: isolation from the very God who made each human unique—and, therefore, isolated from one another.

Hopkins's priestly life was varied and full. His duties took him, among other places, to the slums of industrial England, where he witnessed the misery of the poor and the devastation of the natural environment. His last five years were spent teaching Greek and Latin at the Catholic University in Dublin and writing some of his most striking poetry.

Literature Online

Author Search For more about Gerard Manley Hopkins, go to glencoe.com and enter QuickPass code GLB9817u5.

Selection Skills

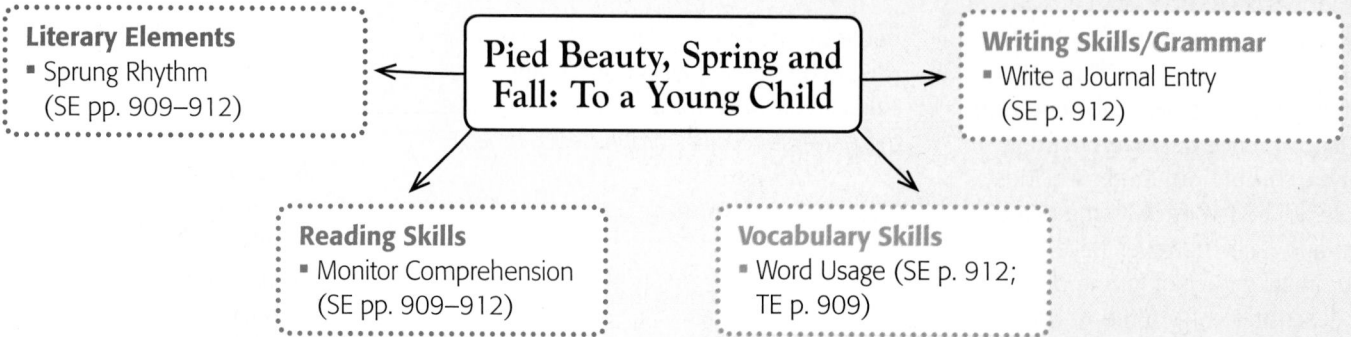

Literary Elements
- Sprung Rhythm
  (SE pp. 909–912)

Pied Beauty, Spring and Fall: To a Young Child

Writing Skills/Grammar
- Write a Journal Entry
  (SE p. 912)

Reading Skills
- Monitor Comprehension
  (SE pp. 909–912)

Vocabulary Skills
- Word Usage (SE p. 912;
  TE p. 909)

Literature and Reading Preview

Connect to the Poems

What is your impact on the natural environment? List your daily activities, and how they might affect the natural world.

Build Background

Gerard Manley Hopkins once said that "design, pattern, or what I am in the habit of calling 'inscape' is what I above all aim at in poetry." To create such an effect, Hopkins developed a style of poetry based on irregular rhythms, incomplete syntax, and repetition and alliteration. The resulting roughness, he believed, captured the complex design of the human mind.

Set Purposes for Reading

Big Idea Optimism and the Belief in Progress

Another word for progress—a central Victorian ideal—is *change*. As you read these poems, ask yourself, How can change be both beautiful and sad?

Literary Element Sprung Rhythm

Hopkins's central poetic innovation was a technique he called **sprung rhythm.** Sprung rhythm is a kind of meter in which each foot contains one stressed syllable (the first) and any number of unstressed syllables. This meter has four kinds of feet: the stressed monosyllable (´), the trochee (´ ˘), the dactyl (´ ˘ ˘), and the first paeon (´ ˘ ˘ ˘). Additional unstressed syllables are also permitted. As you read, ask yourself, How is the rhythm of these poems different from that of most poems I've read?

Reading Strategy Monitor Comprehension

To **monitor comprehension,** note whether you fully grasp the author's meaning as you read. If not, you can use strategies such as reading more slowly, rereading difficult passages, and using a graphic organizer to help. As you read, ask yourself, Am I understanding the author's meaning?

Tip: Charting Meaning Use a two-column chart to clarify the meanings of difficult phrases. Use the side notes, a dictionary, or your own prior knowledge to help you.

Difficult Phrase	Simplified Meaning
"dappled things"	"blotched or spotted things"

Vocabulary

dappled (dap´ əld) *adj.* marked with spots; p. 910 *A ray of sun warmed the fawn's dappled coat.*

fallow (fal´ ō) *n.* land plowed but left unseeded; p. 910 *Beyond the barn was a fallow, empty and waiting for next year's seeds.*

blight (blīt) *n.* a disease that makes plants wither and die; something destructive; p. 911 *A blight in the region killed thousands of saplings.*

Before You Read

Focus

Summary

"Pied Beauty" and "Spring and Fall: To a Young Child" reflect the legacy of the Romantic poets and Hopkins's feelings about God's presence in nature.

 For summaries in languages other than English, see Unit 5 Teaching Resources Book, pp. 62–67.

Vocabulary

Word Usage Ask students to write three paragraphs—one using each vocabulary word—that describe specific objects or places. The descriptions may be fiction or nonfiction, and the words may be used literally or figuratively. Challenge students to include at least five sensory details in each paragraph. Then, have volunteers read one of their paragraphs to the class.

 For additional vocabulary practice, see Unit 5 Teaching Resources Book, p. 70.

 For additional context, see Glencoe Interactive Vocabulary CD-ROM.

Approaching Level

DIFFERENTIATED INSTRUCTION

Emerging Paraphrasing may aid comprehension for students who have difficulty reading poetry. Have these students work with strong readers to paraphrase the incidents, descriptions, or feelings expressed in each poem. Model how to paraphrase the first lines of each poem. In "Pied Beauty" (page 910), the speaker praises God for things of more than one color. In "Spring and Fall: To a Young Child" (page 911), the speaker asks Márgarét if she is upset about the trees shedding their leaves in autumn.

Teach

Reading Strategy | 1

Monitor Comprehension
Answer: *Since the word* couple *means "two," skies of couple-color must mean "skies of two colors."*

[ENGLISH LEARNERS] Tell English learners that *couple* means "two." **Ask:** What two colors might you see in the sky? *(Possible response: blue and white)*

> 📁 For additional practice using the reading skill or strategy, see Unit 5 Teaching Resources Book, p. 69.

View the Art ★

Answer: *Most students will say this is a good companion image, because it presents a joyful mood and seems to portray the many, varied colors of nature. The image tends to use two or three colors for each object—the sky, for example, is made up of light and dark yellow streaks.*

Vincent van Gogh (1853–1890) was born in Zundert, Netherlands. The son of a preacher, Van Gogh studied to become a clergyman. However, his increasing obsession with religion were derided by the church, and Van Gogh was dismissed. Inspired by the work of Jean-François Millet and other artists of the period, Van Gogh began painting as a means to honor God through his creations. Though considered a master of European art, Van Gogh painted for only ten years before his death in 1890.

The Sower, 1888. Vincent van Gogh. Oil on canvas, 64 x 80.5 cm. Rijksmuseum, Netherlands.

View the Art ★ Van Gogh used strong brushstrokes and vivid colors to express the emotions his subjects evoked in him. Is this image a good companion for Hopkins's poem? Explain. ★

Pied Beauty
Gerard Manley Hopkins

Glory be to God for **dappled** things—
  For skies of couple-color as a brinded° cow;
    For rose-moles° all in stipple° upon trout that swim;
Fresh-firecoal chestnut-falls;° finches' wings;
5   Landscape plotted and pieced°—fold,° **fallow**, and plow;
      And áll trádes, their gear and tackle and trim.°

All things counter,° original, spare, strange;
  Whatever is fickle, freckled (who knows how?)
    With swift, slow; sweet, sour; adazzle, dim;
10 He fathers-forth° whose beauty is past change:
      Praise him.

2 brinded: streaked or spotted.
3 rose-moles: marks of a reddish color. **stipple:** in art, areas of small dots used to produce gradations of tone.
4 Fresh-firecoal chestnut-falls: glowing-colored fallen chestnuts newly out of their husks.
5 Landscape plotted and pieced: the patchwork pattern created by dividing land into fields. **fold:** an enclosed area for sheep
6 trim: equipment or clothing.
7 counter: contrary or opposite.
10 fathers-forth: creates.

1 Monitor Comprehension *How does your prior knowledge of the word* couple *help you understand the meaning of this unusual phrase?*

Vocabulary

dappled (dap′ əld) *adj.* marked with spots
fallow (fal′ ō) *n.* land plowed but left unseeded

910 UNIT 5 THE VICTORIAN AGE

Reading Practice

 SPIRAL REVIEW Preread Before students read, have them reflect on the poems' titles. Explain that *pied* means "having patches of different colors." Ask students to list as many associations with *pied* and *beauty* as possible. Then, have them list their associations with *spring,* *fall,* and *young child,* encouraging them to consider various definitions of those words.

Ask: What predictions can you make about each poem based on its title? *(Students may note the contrasting connotations of pied and beauty as well as the possible themes of aging and loss in "Spring and Fall.")*

910

The Wild Wood, Autumn.
Alfred Oliver (d. 1943).
Private collection.

View the Art Consider the impression of autumn that Hopkins creates in this poem. Does the painting create a similar impression of the season? Explain. ★

Spring and Fall: To a Young Child

Gerard Manley Hopkins

Márgarét, are you gríeving
Over Goldengrove unleaving?°
Leáves líke the things of man, you
With your fresh thoughts care for, can you?
5 Áh! ás the heart grows older
It will come to such sights colder
By and by, nor spare a sigh
Though worlds of wanwood° leafmeal° lie;
And yet you wíll weep and know why. **4**
10 Now no matter, child, the name:
Sórrow's spríngs áre the same.
Nor mouth had, no nor mind, expressed
What heart heard of, ghost° guessed:
It ís the **blight** man was born for,
15 It is Margaret you mourn for.

2 **Goldengrove unleaving:** a grove of trees losing its leaves in autumn.

8 **wanwood:** dim woodland. **leafmeal:** crushed, decomposing leaves on the ground.

13 **ghost:** the spirit or soul.

2 Sprung Rhythm *Which three syllables are stressed in this line? What type of foot does each stressed syllable begin?*

3 Optimism and the Belief in Progress *How do these lines express the flip side of Victorian optimism?*

Vocabulary

blight (blīt) *n.* a disease that makes plants wither and die; something destructive

GERALD MANLEY HOPKINS **911**

Teach

Literary Element | 2

Sprung Rhythm Answer: *The syllables Már and rét (in Márgarét) and gríev (in grieving) are stressed. The first begins a trochee (´ ˘), the second a dactyl (´ ˘ ˘), and the third a trochee.*

[APPROACHING] For approaching-level students, write the line on the board and divide it into feet with vertical marks.

Big Idea | 3

Optimism and the Belief in Progress Answer: *These lines link maturity not with accomplishment and progress, but with the loss of sensitivity.*

Reading Strategy | 4

Make Inferences Have students focus on line 9 in the poem. **Ask:** Why will Margaret weep as she gets older? *(Students may mention various personal disappointments and perhaps the loss or death of people she loves.)*

View the Art ★

Answer: *Some students might say that the painting, with its warm, soft colors creates a happier impression of autumn than Hopkins's poem, which speaks of fall as a sad time.*

 To check students' understanding of the selection, see Unit 5 Teaching Resources Book, p. 71.

911

After You Read

Assess

1. (a) Answers may include spotted trout, husked chestnuts, finches' wings, plots of cultivated land. (b) The speaker sees beauty in ordinary things of more than one color.

2. (a) He first notes she is grieving over the trees' loss of leaves. Later, he states she is unknowingly grieving over her own mortality. (b) Aging and death are natural stages of life, but still occasions for sadness.

3. Hopkins considers human activities as extensions of God's creation.

4. The catalog of images evokes the theme of beauty and diversity in God's creation.

5. Answers will vary.

6. It suggests human beings—and human industry—are parts of a vast creation, not masters over it.

7. Students may say that Hopkins's "imagistic" religious feeling comes out in his poetry through creative phrases like "fresh-firecoal chestnut falls" and "adazzle," or through commentary on "the things of man."

Literary Element

1. Answers will vary.

2. The jolting nature of sprung rhythm does mimic the mind's back-and-forth activity as it processes data.

Progress Check

Can students analyze sprung rhythm?

If No → See Unit 5 Teaching Resources Book, p. 68.

After You Read

Respond and Think Critically

Respond and Interpret

1. (a) In the first stanza of "Pied Beauty," for what specific things does the speaker glorify God? (b) What do the speaker's choices suggest about his concept of beauty?

2. (a) In "Spring and Fall," how does the speaker first explain Margaret's grief? How does he later explain it? (b) What can you infer from this about the speaker's philosophy of life, death, and the aging process?

Analyze and Evaluate

3. In your opinion, why does Hopkins include examples from trade ("gear and tackle and trim") in his praise of pied beauty?

Literary Element Sprung Rhythm

Hopkins chose to use **sprung rhythm** because "it is nearest to the rhythm of prose, that is, the native and natural rhythm of speech."

1. In your opinion, does sprung rhythm resemble natural, everyday speech? Support your answer, using specific examples from the poems.

2. Do you think sprung rhythm captures the movement of the mind as it perceives the world? Explain.

Writing

Write a Journal Entry Write a journal entry that Margaret, the small child in "Spring and Fall: To a Small Child," might have written after reading the poem. Consider whether she would agree with the speaker's idea of how her feelings would change. Alternately, write your entry from the perspective of a much older Margaret, looking back.

LOG ON ▶ **Literature** Online

Selection Resources For Selection Quizzes, eFlashcards, and Reading-Writing Connection activities, go to glencoe.com and enter QuickPass code GLB9817u5.

---

4. In "Pied Beauty," how does Hopkins's use of **imagery**, or word pictures, help to convey the poem's **theme**, or main idea?

5. Do you agree with the point of view expressed in lines 5–9 of "Spring and Fall"? Why or why not?

Connect

6. **Big Idea** Optimism and the Belief in Progress The Victorians felt that it was their prerogative to bend nature to their own purposes. How does "Pied Beauty" counter this idea?

7. **Connect to the Author** Consider the religious issues and convictions Hopkins confronted in his life. How are these evident in his verse?

Reading Strategy Monitor Comprehension

Remember that when you **monitor comprehension,** you pay special attention to parts of the text you don't understand.

Reread "Spring and Fall," or examine the chart you filled in. What line or phrase seemed difficult the first time you read it but is much clearer now? Explain.

Vocabulary Practice

Practice with Word Usage Respond to these statements to help you explore the meanings of vocabulary words from the selection.

blight   dappled   fallow

1. Describe how greed could be a **blight** on a person's life.

2. List some animals that have **dappled** skin or fur.

3. Explain why a farmer might leave a field **fallow** for a season.

Writing

Students' journal entries should be consistent with the characterization in the poem and be from the perspective of an older Margaret.

Reading Strategy

Some students may mention the phrase "heart heard of, ghost guessed."

Vocabulary Practice

1. Greed can cause one to lose sight of what is truly important.

2. Dalmatians, leopards.

3. Growing conditions may be poor.

📁 For additional assessment, see Assessment Resources, pp. 223–224.

Before You Read

Jabberwocky

Meet **Lewis Carroll**
(1832–1898)

Considered a dull lecturer by many of his students and a marginally important mathematician by his colleagues at Oxford University, Charles Lutwidge Dodgson might, on the surface, seem an uninteresting fellow. Yet this quiet, painfully shy man published some of the wittiest children's fiction ever written. Under the pen name Lewis Carroll, Dodgson became world famous, particularly for two books that for generations have captivated children and adults alike: *Alice's Adventures in Wonderland* and *Through the Looking Glass and What Alice Found There.*

An Inventive Youth The son of a church rector, Dodgson was the third child and oldest son in a family of eleven children. The Dodgson children

lived in an isolated country village and had few friends outside the family, but they found many ways to amuse themselves. From an early age, Dodgson entertained his younger siblings by performing magic tricks and marionette shows and by writing poetry and word games for the family's homemade magazines.

The young scholar found success at Oxford University, where he excelled in mathematics and classical studies. Graduating first in his class in mathematics, Dodgson was granted a scholarship and assumed a post as a lecturer in mathematics. As a condition of this scholarship, Dodgson

was also ordained a deacon, but a severe stammer kept him from seeking a career in preaching.

Play Makes Perfect Even though Dodgson spent twenty-six years teaching math at Oxford, he was bored by the work. In the company of children, however, Dodgson was neither bored nor shy. He was able to speak to children without stammering, and he loved to entertain young visitors—often the children of fellow faculty members—by inventing games, performing magic tricks, giving puppet shows, and telling stories. Much to Dodgson's own surprise, one of these stories eventually became *Alice in Wonderland.*

> "In a desperate attempt to strike out some new line of fairy-lore, I had sent my heroine straight down a rabbit-hole, to begin with, without the least idea what was to happen afterwards."
>
> —Lewis Carroll

Alice was not Dodgson's first publication, however. Between 1854 and 1856, several of Dodgson's comical and satirical works appeared in national publications. Then, in 1856, a poem called "Solitude" was printed under the pseudonym "Lewis Carroll." In typical word-play fashion, Dodgson had created this name by translating his given names into Latin—Carolus Ludovicus—then reversing the names and translating them back into English.

 Literature Online

Author Search For more about Lewis Carroll, go to glencoe.com and enter QuickPass code GLB9817u5.

LEWIS CARROLL **913**

Before You Read

Focus

Bellringer Options

Selection Focus
  Transparency 46
Daily Language Practice
  Transparency 74

Or **write** the following words on the board: *brillig, vorpal, outgrabe.*
Ask: Do the words seem familiar to you? Explain that these made-up words appear in a famous poem by Lewis Carroll. Have students look for other coined words as they read "Jabberwocky."

Selection Skills

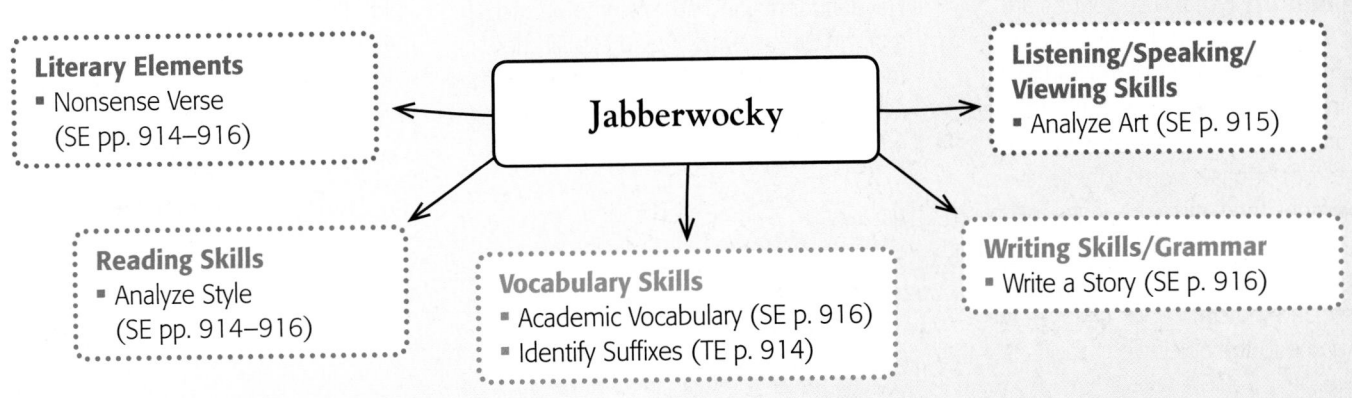

913

Before You Read

Focus

Summary

In this poem full of invented words and wonderful whimsy, a father warns his son to "beware the Jabberwock." Undaunted, the son slays the Jabberwock with his sword and then beheads it. He returns victorious to his elated father.

 For summaries in languages other than English, see Unit 5 Teaching Resources Book, pp. 73–78.

Literature and Reading Preview

Connect to the Poem

Why is the notion of inventing new things so compelling? Freewrite for a few minutes about an invention you would love to see—it does not have to exist, or even be humanly possible.

Build Background

In 1862, Dodgson told an especially amusing tale to a young girl named Alice Liddell, who begged him to write it down. In 1865 he published the story as *Alice's Adventures in Wonderland*. Six years later he published a sequel, *Through the Looking Glass and What Alice Found There*, which includes the poem "Jabberwocky."

Set Purposes for Reading

Big Idea Optimism and the Belief in Progress

Among other things, the Victorians invented the train, the toilet, the vacuum cleaner, and cola. As you read, ask yourself, How does Victorian inventiveness extend itself into this poem?

Literary Element Nonsense Verse

Nonsense verse is humorous poetry that defies logic—or, at first glance, appears to. Nonsense verse usually has a strong rhythm and contains made-up words. These words—like *galumphing* in "Jabberwocky"—are often examples of **ono-matopoeia**, the use of words whose sounds suggest their meanings. As you read, ask yourself, What clues do the sounds of these words give me about their meanings?

Reading Strategy Analyze Style

When you **analyze style**, you examine the ways in which an author makes his or her work unique. Part of Lewis Carroll's style in the poem "Jabberwocky" is the use of nonsense, or "nonce" words. To make these invented terms understandable to readers, he also uses standard **syntax**, or word order, and **diction**, or choice of words. As a result, readers have various **context clues** to help them construe the nonce words.

Tip: Analyzing Syntax When you encounter a confusing phrase or sentence, clarify the syntax by labeling the parts of speech.

> N.   ADJ. N.
> 'Twas brillig, and the slithy toves

THE SHOWER OF CARDS.

Alice and the Cards. First published in 1865.

Vocabulary Practice

SPIRAL REVIEW **Identify Suffixes** Suffixes are word parts added to the end of a root or a base word to change its meaning and sometimes its part of speech. The common suffixes *-y*, *-ish*, and *-ious* change root or base words to adjectives. For example, the suffix *-y* changes the noun *water* to the adjective *watery*; the suffix *-ish* changes the noun *child* to the adjective *childish*; and the suffix *-ious* changes the noun *grace* to the adjective *gracious*.

Have students find an example of each suffix in "Jabberwocky" and explain how the word it contains is used in the poem. (*slithy, mimsy, tulgey, frumious, beamish, uffish*)

Jabberwocky

Lewis Carroll

'Twas brillig, and the slithy toves
    Did gyre and gimble in the wabe;
All mimsy were the borogoves,
    And the mome raths outgrabe.

5 "Beware the Jabberwock, my son!
    The jaws that bite, the claws that
        catch!
Beware the Jubjub bird, and shun
    The frumious Bandersnatch!"

He took his vorpal sword in hand:
10   Long time the manxome foe he
        sought—
So rested he by the Tumtum tree,
    And stood awhile in thought.

And as in uffish thought he stood,
    The Jabberwock, with eyes of flame,
15 Came whiffling through the tulgey wood,
    And burbled as it came!

One, two! One, two! And through and
    through
    The vorpal blade went snicker-snack!
He left it dead, and with its head
20   He went galumphing back.

"And hast thou slain the Jabberwock?
    Come to my arms, my beamish boy!

O frabjous day! Callooh! Callay!"
    He chortled in his joy.

25 'Twas brillig, and the slithy toves
    Did gyre and gimble in the wabe;
All mimsy were the borogoves,
    And the mome raths outgrabe.

The Jabberwock, nineteenth century. John Tenniel. Illustration.

 View the Art Tenniel's illustrations for Lewis Carroll's books have influenced readers' views of Carroll's work ever since. Does this image capture the Jabberwock as it is described in the poem? Explain why or why not.

1 Analyze Style *Which ordinary word choices and syntax give you clues about the Jabberwock, the Jubjub bird, and the Bandersnatch?*

2 Nonsense Verse *Which of these words are onomatopoetic? What meaning does the sound of each word suggest?*

LEWIS CARROLL **915**

 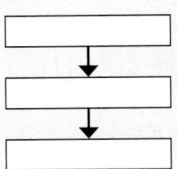

Assess

1. (a) With sword in hand, the boy searches for the foe. As the boy rests, the Jabberwock charges him. The boy slays the Jabberwock and returns home with its head. (b) The boy's courage or his desire to win his father's admiration

2. (a) Joyfully (b) He admires his son's courage and is relieved at the elimination of a threat.

3. (a) Rhythm: iambic tetrameter; rhyme scheme: *abab* (b) Possible answer: The regular meter and rhyme suggest a medieval ballad or a nursery rhyme. The effect is mock-heroic and humorous.

4. (a) Mock-terror or mock-heroic (b) The atmosphere changes to rapture in stanza 6.

5. (a) He repeats the nonsense words because the work is a mock-heroic ballad. (b) It reinforces how nonsensical he finds the vision of the heroic quest.

6. The Victorian attitudes of self-importance and conquest

7. Answers will vary.

Literary Element

1. brilliant, big;
2. flimsy;
3. rats, wrath;
4. fuming, furious;
5. puffy, iffy, elfish;
6. fabulous, gorgeous

Progress Check

Can students understand nonsense verse?

If No → See Unit 5 Teaching Resources Book, p. 79.

916

Respond and Think Critically

Respond and Interpret

1. (a) Summarize what happens in stanzas 3–5. (b) What do these events reveal about the boy's character?

2. (a) How does the father respond to his son's actions? (b) Why do you think he responds in this manner?

Analyze and Evaluate

3. (a) Describe the poem's meter (or rhythm) and rhyme scheme. (b) What effects are created by these devices?

4. (a) How would you describe the poem's atmosphere? (b) Does the atmosphere change? Explain your answer with details from the poem.

5. (a) Why do you think Carroll repeats the first stanza at the end of the poem? (b) What is the effect of this repetition?

Connect

6. **Big Idea** Optimism and the Belief in Progress What Victorian attitudes might Carroll be mocking or satirizing in this poem?

7. **Connect to Today** Can you identify any artists, writers, or musicians today who specialize in the kind of clever "nonsense" Carroll used? Explain how their work is similar to or different from "Jabberwocky."

Literary Element Nonsense Verse

Carroll provided "definitions" for many of the nonce words in "Jabberwocky." For example, he described a tove as a type of badger with short horns that "lived chiefly on cheese" and defined *slithy* as a combination of "slimy" and "lithe," meaning "smooth and active." For each word below, write one or two real words that its sound suggests.

1. brillig   2. mimsy   3. raths
4. frumious   5. uffish   6. frabjous

 Writing

Write a Story "Jabberwocky" pays tribute to the hero who slays the Jabberwock. Write a brief story from the perspective of the Jabberwock. Though you will write in prose, try to keep your story consistent with the light, nonsense tone of the poem. You may wish to borrow many of the nonsense terms that Carroll uses.

 **Literature** Online

Selection Resources For Selection Quizzes, eFlashcards, and Reading-Writing Connection activities, go to glencoe.com and enter QuickPass code GLB9817u5.

Reading Strategy Analyze Style

Remember that you can use context and syntactical clues to help you understand Carroll's style.

Partner Activity Rewrite the first stanza, substituting a real word of the same part of speech for each nonce word. Read your new stanza aloud to a partner. Discuss similarities and differences in your interpretations.

Academic Vocabulary

Although "Jabberwocky" is a nonsense poem, its structure, regular meter, and syntax create coherence.

Coherence is an academic word. In a school setting, a teacher might advise a student to improve an essay's **coherence** by including a clear thesis statement. Using context clues, try to figure out the meaning of the word in the sentence about "Jabberwocky" above. Check your guess in a dictionary.

For more on academic vocabulary, see pages 56 and R81.

Reading Strategy

Students should use words that represent the same parts of speech as the lines from "Jabberwocky."

Verbs: *gyre, gimble, outgrabe;*

Adjectives: *brillig, slithy, mimsy, mome;* Translations will vary.

 For additional assessment, see Assessment Resources, pp. 227–228.

Academic Vocabulary

The poem's structure, regular meter and rhyme, and syntax create coherence.

✍ Writing

Students' stories should use a lighthearted tone to describe the Jabberwock's slaying.

Jabberwocky

Wanda Coleman

National Book Award Winner

Set a Purpose for Reading

As you read, ask yourself, How did reading a literary classic influence a future writer?

Build Background

Wanda Coleman, a prize-winning African American poet and novelist, had a transformative experience when she read Lewis Carroll's *Alice's Adventures in Wonderland* and *Through the Looking Glass*. In particular, Carroll's poem "Jabberwocky" helped her make sense of the realities of racial discrimination. In her world, as in Alice's, nothing was ever as it seemed.

Reading Strategy

Analyze Literary Influences

Analyzing literary influences involves examining the ways that literary works affect writers. As you read, take notes about the influence of Lewis Carroll's poem on Coleman. Use a cause-and-effect diagram like the one below to help you.

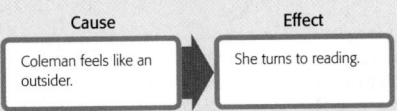

Cause		Effect
Coleman feels like an outsider.	→	She turns to reading.

Learning Objectives

For pages 917–920

In studying this text, you will focus on the following objectives:

Literary Study:
Analyzing literary influences. Making connections across literature.

The stultifying[1] intellectual loneliness of my Watts upbringing was dictated by my looks—dark skin and unconkable kinky hair. Being glowered at was a constant state of being. The eyes of adults and children alike immediately informed me that some unpleasant *ugliness* had entered their sphere and spoiled their pleasure because of its close and onerous[2] proximity. I recall one such moment very strongly: a white man was standing in front of me at such an angle that I was momentarily uncertain what he was frowning at. I turned to look behind me and saw nothing.

I have come to mark such moments—as they have recurred throughout my life—as indicative of the significance of physical likeness, beyond the issue of physical beauty: of the importance of "mirror image" (a phrase that recurs in one form or another in my poetry); in the ongoing dialogue of race, as I've struggled to grasp and respond to what others *assume* when their eyes are directed at or on me. I find the shifts in visual context as infuriating now as they were in childhood. The act of wading

---

1. *Stultifying* means "dulling."
2. *Onerous* means "burdensome."

WANDA COLEMAN **917**

Focus

Summary

In this essay, Wanda Coleman explains how "Jabberwocky" helped her deal with prejudice.

 For summaries in languages other than English, see Unit 5 Teaching Resources Book, pp. 83–88.

Teach

Reading Strategy · 1

Analyze Literary Influences
Encourage students to recall their responses to "Jabberwocky." **Ask:** How did the nonsense words and events in this poem affect you? Tell students to look for the effect the poem had on Wanda Coleman.

 For an audio recording of this selection, use Listening Library Audio CD-ROM.

Readability Scores

Dale-Chall: 7.6
DRP: 68
Lexile: 1230

 **Approaching Level**

DIFFERENTIATED INSTRUCTION

Emerging Remind students that commas are used to separate items or to set them off from the rest of a sentence. They signal places in the sentence where readers should pause briefly. Call on volunteers to read aloud the first paragraph on this page, pausing briefly after each comma.

Advanced Learners

DIFFERENTIATED INSTRUCTION

Research Draw students' attention to the authors and poets that Wanda Coleman mentions in her essay. Ask students to choose one writer and research him or her using print and Internet resources. Have students share their findings with the class.

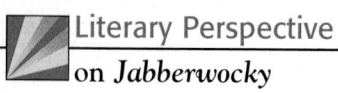
Teach

Big Idea 1

Optimism and Belief in Progress Review the Big Idea with students. **Ask:** Were optimism and the belief in progress evident in Coleman's childhood? *(Students may say that they were not evident until Coleman discovered Lewis Carroll's books about Alice.)*

APPROACHING Direct approaching-level students' attention to the second paragraph on this page (beginning *I found …*). Ask students to find and list the negative words in this paragraph *(i.e., rejection, unbearable, no, not, rejected, boring, no way, excluded).*

View the Art ★

Born in Brooklyn, New York, in 1866, Roseland became a prominent painter who focused on realism in landscapes and still lifes. A self-taught artist, he focused on the lives of post-Civil War blacks.

918

Informational Text

Budding Scholar, Henry Herman Roseland (1866–1950). Private collection. ★

through stereotypes, in order to become clearly visible in the larger society, corresponds exactly to that moment when Lewis Carroll's Alice steps through that looking glass.

Incapable of imagining my world, removed from it by gender and race as well as by time and place, Lewis Carroll had nevertheless provided me with a means (and an attitude) with which to assess, evaluate, and interpret my own journey through this bizarre actuality of late-twentieth-century America, where nothing is ever as it seems. I was a *Negro* child—yet this book, and its poem "Jabberwocky," served **1** singularly to buoy my self-esteem, constantly under assault by my Black peers, family members, and the world outside.

I found the rejection unbearable and—encouraged by my parents to read—sought an escape in books, which were usually hard to come by. In the South Central Los Angeles of the 1950s and 1960s, there were only three Black-owned bookstores, and I would not discover them until early adulthood. In my childhood there was no Harlem Renaissance, no Black arts movement; I did not encounter the poems of Paul Laurence Dunbar and James

Weldon Johnson[3] except at church socials and in the early 1960s, during Negro History "week" celebrations. There were no images of Black children *of any age* in the American literature I encountered. The sole exception was "Little Black Sambo," whom I immediately rejected upon finding the book on my desk in the first

> "If a drink
> or a slice of cake
> could transform her . . .
> Why not a transformation
> of her skin color?"

3. *Paul Laurence Dunbar* (1872–1906) was an African American poet and novelist. *James Weldon Johnson* (1871–1938) was an African American poet and a leading member of the National Association for the Advancement of Colored People.

918 UNIT 5 THE VICTORIAN AGE

Reading Practice

SPIRAL REVIEW Make Critical Judgments Discuss the ways in which an autobiographical essay, such as this one, conveys information that an encyclopedia or other reference source does not. Before students read, help them make critical judgments about the piece. **Ask:** What makes a good essay? What does an autobiographical essay convey about a subject that might not be found in other pieces of writing? After

students read, they can discuss what this essay conveys about racial discrimination and how it has affected readers.

grade—along with equally boring books featuring Dick, Jane, and Spot. There was no way in which I could "identify" with these strange images of children. I was born and raised in the white world of Southern California; it gave birth to me, but excluded me. Even the postwar Watts of the poet Arna Bontemps,[4] and the South Central Los Angeles that would riot in 1965, were predominantly working-class white neighborhoods with small Black enclaves.

Whenever my father visited public libraries, he allowed me to roam the stacks. This was my Wonderland. I was immediately enthralled with the forbidden world of adult literature, hidden away in leather-bound tomes I was neither able to reach nor allowed to touch. I hungered to enter, and my appetite had no limits. I plowed through Papa's dull issues of *National Geographic* and Mama's tepid copies of *Reader's Digest* and *Family Circle* in desperation, starved. At age ten I consumed the household copy of the complete works of Shakespeare. Although the violence was striking, and *Hamlet* engrossing (particularly Ophelia), I was too immature to appreciate the Bard until frequent rereadings in my mid-teens.

On Christmas, thereabouts, I received Johanna Spyri's[5] *Heidi* as a well-intended gift. I had exhausted our teensy library, and my father's collections of *Knight* and *Esquire*. . . . Between my raids on the adults-only stuff, there was nothing but *Heidi*, reread in desperation until I could quote chunks of the text, mentally squeezing it for what I imagined to be

---

4. *Arna Bontemps* (1902–1973) was an African American novelist, historian, and poet.

5. *Johanna Spyri* (1829–1901) was a Swiss writer.

The Children's Encyclopedia, James McDonald (b.1956). Oil on canvas. Private collection. Bourne Gallery, Reigate, Surrey, UK.

WANDA COLEMAN **919**

Literary Perspective
on *Jabberwocky*

Assess

Literary History ☆
Harlem Renaissance In the 1920s, the Harlem neighborhood of New York City experienced a creative explosion of African American literature, art, and music. Many African American writers published their works during this movement, including Zora Neale Hurston, Langston Hughes, and Countee Cullen.

For activities related to this selection, see Unit 5 Teaching Resources Book, pp. 89–90.

English Learners

DIFFERENTIATED INSTRUCTION

PARTNERS **Intermediate** Have students summarize the reading by pulling topic sentences from each paragraph. Invite students to work in pairs to brainstorm a topic sentence for each section of the essay. Then have them write supporting evidence that the author provides. Finally, have students describe how each section's topic sentence relates to the main idea.

Reading Strategy 1

Analyze Literary Influences

Ask: Why does the author see herself as Alice? *(It piqued her imagination and allowed her to feel free from racism.)*

Assess

1. Summary example: The author feels that the work of Lewis Carroll helped her to escape the widespread racism she experienced growing up in Los Angeles.

2. Students may mention details about the writer's experience of discrimination, her reading of "Jabberwocky," or her favorite authors and poems.

3. (a) These people treated her shabbily, making her feel ashamed and different.
(b) Coleman regarded literature as a means of escape from the harsh realities of racism. "Jabberwocky" tells of a young hero's triumph over a ferocious monster. The poem strengthened Coleman's resolve to slay her own monsters by triumphing over discrimination.

4. (a) Carroll's stories and poems let Coleman's imagination take flight, empowering her on magical journeys. (b) Coleman was fascinated by Alice's physical transformations. Coleman identified strongly with Alice, whom she regarded as her alter ego. She imagined Alice changing her skin color from white to black.

5. Her literary explorations and rereading of *Heidi* suggest that she was hungry to read anything and that her environment could not satisfy her intellectual curiosity.

920

Informational Text

hidden underneath. One early spring day, my adult cousin Rubyline came by the house with a nourishing belated Christmas gift: an illustrated collection of *Alice's Adventures in Wonderland* and *Through the Looking-Glass.* (She also gave me my first *Roget's*—which I still use—on my twelfth birthday in 1958.) In love with poetry since kindergarten, my "uffish" vows were startlingly renewed. I promptly retired *Heidi* and steeped myself in Alice to an iambic spazz.

In the real world I was an outsider, but in the stories and poems of Carroll I *belonged*. Why? Perhaps because when he freed Alice in the mirror, he also freed my imagination and permitted me to imagine myself living in an adventure, sans[6] the constraints of a racist society. If a drink or a slice of cake could transform her, alter her shape and size, the next leap for me was the most illogically logical of all: *Why not a transformation of her skin color?* In my frequent rereadings of Alice, I rewrote her as me.

"Jabberwocky" was and remains one of only a dozen poems I've ever loved enough to memorize. It heads the very long list of my favorite childhood poems, along with Poe's "Raven," Service's "Cremation of Sam McGee," Byron's "Prisoner of Chillon," Coleridge's "Rime of the Ancient Mariner," Henley's "Invictus," and E. A. Robinson's "Richard Cory."[7] To the astute reader, Carroll's lasting influence on my poetry is easily discerned. Many have referred to "Jabberwocky" as nonsense, but in my Los Angeles childhood, it made absolutely one hundred percent perfect sense. And within the context of Los Angeles today, that "nonsense" is dangerously and exhilaratingly profound.

---

6. *Sans* is a French word that means "without."

7. Edgar Allan *Poe* (1809–1849) was an American poet and fiction writer; Robert *Service* (1874–1958) was a Canadian poet; Lord *Byron* (1788–1824) and Samuel Taylor *Coleridge* (1772–1834) were British Romantic poets; William Ernest *Henley* (1849–1903) was a British critic and poet; and Edwin Arlington *Robinson* (1869–1935) was an American poet.

Respond and Think Critically

Respond and Interpret

1. Write a brief summary of the main ideas in this essay before you answer the following questions. For help writing a summary, see page 435.

2. Which details in this essay did you find most interesting? Why?

3. (a) How did Coleman's peers, family members, and strangers treat her as a child? (b) How did reading the poem "Jabberwocky" help buoy her self-esteem?

4. (a) Why did Coleman feel at home in Carroll's stories and poems? (b) What does the question, *"Why not a transformation of her skin color?"* reveal about Coleman's response to Alice?

Analyze and Evaluate

5. What does Coleman's exploration of magazines, the "forbidden world of adult literature," and her rereading of *Heidi* suggest about her personality and environment?

6. (a) Which words in this essay establish a comparison between reading and eating? (b) What does this comparison suggest about Coleman's regard for reading?

7. Why does Coleman maintain that "Jabberwocky" is meaningful rather than nonsensical?

Connect

8. What is the best book you have ever read? How can reading be a transformative experience?

920 UNIT 5 THE VICTORIAN AGE

---

6. (a) The words *hungered, appetite, starved, consumed,* and *nourishing* establish this comparison. (b) Reading nourishes the spirit as eating nourishes the body.

7. "Jabberwocky" is meaningful because it helped Coleman interpret her environment and build self-esteem.

8. Answers will vary. Students may say that reading can be a transformative experience by influencing one's perceptions and enhancing self-worth.

Part 2

Realism and Naturalism

On Strike, c. 1891. Sir Hubert von Herkomer.
Oil on canvas. Royal Academy of Arts, London.

 View the Art The Victorian era was marked by the prosperity of the free market, but many of the people working under that system lived lives of grinding poverty. What does this image suggest about the working poor in the Victorian era? Explain.

> *"It is a dreadful thing for the greatest and most necessary part of a very rich nation to live a hard life without dignity, knowledge, comforts, delights or hopes in the midst of plenty—which plenty they make."*
>
> —Gerard Manley Hopkins

| 1

921

Analyzing and Extending

Big Idea | 1

The Emergence of Realism
Focus students' attention on the quotation from Hopkins.
Ask: How does this comment reflect a tendency toward a philosophy of Realism in writers of the Victorian Age? (*The words boldly state that the British working class was excluded from the nation's good fortune.*)

View the Art

Answer: *The woman and children in the background suggest the suffering and misery of the working poor; the expression on the man's face suggests that they were also dignified and angry—the man's posture suggests that he is protective of his family and angry about their situation.*

Born in Germany, Hubert von Herkomer (1849–1914) first worked as a magazine illustrator in England. Unable to utilize his skills to the fullest, he set out to be a fine artist. By the 1880s, he had become wealthy as a portrait painter. Yet he continued to create works of Social Realism.

English Learners

DIFFERENTIATED INSTRUCTION

Intermediate Call students' attention to the word *dreadful* in the opening words of the quotation. Then write this on the board:

> *dread* + *-ful* = *dreadful*
> WORD   **SUFFIX**   NEW WORD

Ask: What part of speech is the word *dread*? (*either noun or verb*) What does the suffix *-ful* mean? ("*full of*" or "*characterized by*") What part of speech is

dreadful? (*adjective*) What does *dreadful* mean? ("*awful, terrible*") Have students form five other words with the *-ful* suffix.

> For additional support for English Learners, see Unit 5 Teaching Resources Book, p. 95.

Focus

Bellringer Options

Daily Language Practice Transparency 75

Or tell students that the novel reached new heights during the Victorian period. **Ask:** What are some of the subgenres of the novel? Name at least four. *(comic, sporting, romance, novel of manners, gothic, crime fiction, social-problem, regionalist)*

Teach

Literary Element 1

Novel Explain that a novel is a book-length fictional prose narrative, typically having a plot that unfolds through the actions, speech, and thoughts of characters.

Learning Objectives

For pages 922–923

In studying this text, you will focus on the following objectives:

Literary Study:
Analyzing literary periods.
Analyzing literary genres.

Reading: Evaluating historical influences.

The Age of the Novel

> *"The person, be it gentleman or lady, who has not pleasure in a good novel, must be intolerably stupid."*
>
> —Jane Austen, *Northanger Abbey*

W HILE THE NOVEL WAS BORN IN THE eighteenth century, it was not until the nineteenth century that the genre came of age. Many social **1** factors converged to propel the novel to the forefront of the literary world. First, literacy rates for England's growing middle class rose sharply, increasing readership and creating new markets for the nineteenth-century novelist. Second, the emergence of libraries in the mid-1800s allowed greater access to literature. Most of these libraries were subscription libraries that charged customers an annual usage fee. At the forefront of this emergence was businessman Charles Edward Mudie. He wielded a tremendous amount of clout in the literary world because his library purchased thousands of copies of new books to loan to its customers. During this time, novels were often published in three volumes, called "triple-decker" novels, so publishers and subscription libraries could charge readers for each volume.

Third, innovations in publishing gave rise to inexpensive literary magazines which published complete novels in a series of short monthly installments. The serial novel became a popular trend in the nineteenth century. Some authors completed their novels before publication, but others, such as Charles Dickens, used the reactions of their reads to shape the story's events. Dickens, Wilkie Collins, William Thackeray, and Thomas Hardy all published several novels in serial form.

The Artful Dodger picking a pocket to the amazement of Oliver Twist, c. 1837–1838. George Cruikshank. Book illustration. Private collection.

Finally, the novel was a new and evolving literary form; novelists from this period did not suffer from an "anxiety of influence." Thus, the novel form allowed writers to experiment with new genres, such as the comic novel or the sporting novel. Jane Austen and William Thackeray continued an eighteenth-century trend, writing romance novels and novels of manners. Wilkie Collins shaped the ☆

Literary History ☆

The Woman in White Wilkie Collins wrote *The Woman in White,* which was published first as a magazine serial beginning in 1859. It is considered to be the first mystery novel.

Writing Practice

Write About Cause and Effect Have students examine the causes and effects of the novel coming to age. Assign students to analyze the connections between the causes and effects implied and directly stated in this selection, and support their assertions with evidence from the text in a 3- to 5- paragraph essay. For example, a student may argue that evidence for the cause of the birth of the novel was rising literacy rates among England's

middle class as noted in the opening paragraph on this page. Students' essays should include an introduction, body, and conclusion.

gothic novel into the suspenseful but more realistic sensation novel or crime fiction. Two other important genres of the nineteenth century were the social-problem novel and the Regionalist novel.

Social-Problem Novels

Social-problem novels, also called "Condition of England" novels, drew attention to social ills in an attempt to spark reform. For instance, Dickens's novels *Hard Times* and *Oliver Twist* reveal the poverty and exploitation of London's lower classes, and his novel *Bleak House* focuses on the corruption in England's legal system. Elizabeth Gaskell also wrote several novels urging social reform. Her first novel, *Mary Barton,* depicts the harsh, miserable conditions of the working-class people. In the preface to the work, Gaskell wrote, "Whatever public effort can do in the way of legislation, or private effort in the way of merciful deeds . . . should be done, and that speedily." Social-problem novelists opposed blind faith in progress, and by presenting a realistic account of the negative effects of the Industrial Revolution, they raised public consciousness and triggered social reforms.

Regionalist Novels

The Regionalist novel employs a detailed setting that is often modeled on an actual, usually rural, location. Regionalist novels are examples of Realism in the sense that they emphasize accurate rather than romantic settings and explore how place influences characters and events. This type of fiction is further characterized by the use of local dialect, references to natural or physical landmarks, incorporation of the community's political or social values, and parody of local characters. For example, Thomas Hardy set all of his novels in the fictional

Philip in Church, c. 1862. Frederick Walker. Gouache on paper, 179.92 x 144.88 in. The Tate Museum, London.

county of Wessex, which was based on the county of Dorset and the town of Dorchester. Charlotte and Emily Brontë both created haunting backdrops in *Jane Eyre* and *Wuthering Heights* that echo the Yorkshire moors where they grew up.

Nineteenth-century publishing trends, such as the serial novel, may not remain popular today, but their enduring impact was the firm establishment of a public market for literature. Toward the end of the nineteenth century, free public libraries began to replace subscription libraries, ensuring that literature would remain widely available.

 Literature Online

Literature and Reading For more about the Age of the Novel, go to glencoe.com and enter QuickPass code GLB9817u5.

Respond and Think Critically

1. What changes occurred in the nineteenth-century literary market?

2. (a)What types of issues do social-problem novels address? (b)Identify some contemporary novels or films that serve a similar function.

3. Compare and contrast the way social-problem novels and Regionalist novels reflect the emerging focus on Realism in the nineteenth century.

LITERARY HISTORY **923**

Before You Read

Focus

Bellringer Options

Daily Language Practice Transparency 76

Or say: A report on child labor in Victorian England described children as "chained, belted, harnessed like dogs . . . black, saturated with wet, more than half-naked . . . dragging their heavy loads behind them."

Ask: What might a novelist or poet do to address such problems? *(Answers will vary.)*

As they read, have students consider the social and political climate of England in the 1840s.

 For summaries in languages other than English, see Unit 5 Teaching Resources Book, pp. 96–101.

 For additional vocabulary practice, see Unit 5 Teaching Resources Book, p. 104.

Before You Read

from *Jane Eyre*

Meet **Charlotte Brontë**
(1816–1855)

The daughter of an Irish-born clergyman, Charlotte Brontë grew up in the tiny village of Haworth on the edge of the bleak Yorkshire moors. Although her childhood was somewhat dismal and lonely, these experiences would later inspire her greatest stories and novels.

"It is in vain to say human beings ought to be satisfied with tranquility: they must have action; and they will make it if they cannot find it."

—Charlotte Brontë, from *Jane Eyre*

A Family Curse Born in 1816, Charlotte Brontë experienced tragedy at a young age. Her mother died in 1821. Not long afterward, her two older sisters, Maria and Elizabeth, succumbed to tuberculosis and typhus, both brought on by their stay at a poorly run girls' boarding school. This school later became the model of Charlotte's Lowood School in *Jane Eyre*. In the gloomy parsonage behind the church where their father worked, the four remaining Brontë children offset their unhappy, isolated lives by spinning tales of imaginary worlds and exotic characters. From this childhood play came a wealth of later creativity: Charlotte, Anne, and Emily all won distinction as writers; their brother Branwell became a painter. Nevertheless, their lives were tragically shortened by what seemed like a family curse, tuberculosis: Branwell died of it in September 1848; Emily, just a few months later; and Anne succumbed the following year.

Instant Literary Success Despite the specter of death that haunted her family, Charlotte was able to produce a number of poems and novels, including the novel *Jane Eyre*. Charlotte published *Jane Eyre* in 1847 under the pen name Currer Bell, but the book was an instant success that soon drew its author from anonymity. Charlotte was then free to publish other novels, including some that had been rejected before. She also became the subject of one of the Victorian era's most famous biographies, *The Life of Charlotte Brontë* by Elizabeth Gaskell, herself a well-known novelist.

An absorbing tale, *Jane Eyre* blends Realism and Romanticism in recounting, with the detail typical of Victorian fiction, the life of its title character from childhood on. Like Dickens's Oliver Twist, Jane Eyre first faces life as a penniless young orphan. The story is Brontë's most memorable work, and it leaves a lasting impression of the power of her writing. Virginia Woolf once wrote, "All her force, and it is the more tremendous for being constricted, goes into the assertion, 'I love,' 'I hate,' 'I suffer.'"

Charlotte Brontë, the only one of her siblings to reach the age of thirty, died of tuberculosis in March 1855, less than a year after she was married. She was not yet thirty-nine years old.

 Literature Online

Author Search For more about Charlotte Brontë, go to glencoe.com and enter QuickPass code GLB9817u5.

Selection Skills

Literary Elements
- Description (SE pp. 925, 927, 929, 933)
- Point of View (SE p. 933)

Reading Skills
- Analyze Characterization (SE pp. 925, 926, 928, 930, 931, 934)

from **Jane Eyre**

Vocabulary Skills
- Context Clues (SE p. 934)

Listening/Speaking/Viewing Skills
- Oral Report (SE p. 934)

Writing Skills/Grammar
- Essay (TE p. 926)

Literature and Reading Preview

Connect to the Story

How well do people know the real you? In a journal entry, write about a time when someone else misunderstood your personality or intentions. Consider reasons why someone might not see you the way you really are.

Build Background

At the beginning of the novel, Jane Eyre is a ten-year-old orphan left in the care of her aunt, Mrs. Sarah Reed. Mrs. Reed and her children, Eliza, Georgiana, and John, treat Jane with great cruelty. Jane, who is treated like a maid and ordered around by the housekeeper, Bessie, is blamed and punished whenever the Reed children misbehave. During one of these punishments, Mrs. Reed locks Jane in the red room, where Jane's uncle died. Jane is frightened and begs to be let out of the room. Mrs. Reed refuses and Jane becomes so upset she passes out. When she awakes, a physician is standing over her. He recommends that Jane be sent away to a boarding school because she is so miserable living with the Reed family. The selection you are about to read begins when Jane first meets Mr. Brocklehurst, the headmaster of the school.

Set Purposes for Reading

Big Idea Disillusionment and Darker Visions

As you read, ask yourself, What effects would conditions like Jane's have on Victorian orphans?

Literary Element Description

Description is a detailed portrayal of a person, a place, an object, or an event. Good descriptive writing appeals to the senses through imagery. As you read, ask yourself, What details give me a sense of the characters and setting in this excerpt?

Reading Strategy Analyze Characterization

Characterization is the method a writer uses to reveal the personality of a character. In **direct characterization**, the writer makes explicit statements about a character. In **indirect characterization**, the writer reveals a character through his or her words, thoughts, and actions and through what other characters think and say about that character. As you read, ask yourself, What is the writer showing me about the characters?

Tip: Taking Notes As you read, note examples of both direct and indirect characterization in the selection from *Jane Eyre*.

Learning Objectives

For pages 924–934

In studying this text, you will focus on the following objectives:

Literary Study: Analyzing description.

Reading: Analyzing characterization.

Listening and Speaking: Presenting an oral report.

Vocabulary

vacant (vā′ kənt) *adj.* empty; p. 927 *The house was vacant for months until a family moved in.*

scrutiny (skrōōt′ ən ē) *n.* close watch or examination; p. 928 *The suspect's activities were under close scrutiny by the police.*

advocate (ad′ və kāt′) *v.* to support or argue for; p. 930 *I advocate environmental protection since I firmly believe in recycling.*

retaliation (ri tal′ ē ā′ shən) *n.* getting even with; revenge; p. 931 *Ignoring them is the best retaliation again bullies.*

subside (səb sīd′) *v.* to give way or end; p. 932 *The fear about graduation eventually subsided, and I awaited the challenges ahead.*

Tip: **Context Clues** Context clues are words and sentences around an unfamiliar word that help you figure out the word's meaning. Example: *The house was vacant for months until a family moved in.* The sentence suggests that no one was living in the house, so *vacant* must mean "empty."

CHARLOTTE BRONTË **925**

Before You Read

Focus

Summary

A carriage arrives at Gateshead Hall, the home of Jane Eyre's uncaring relatives, the Reeds. Mrs. Reed introduces Jane to Mr. Brocklehurst, whom she has summoned to take Jane away to Lowood School. Reed says Jane needs discipline for being deceitful; Brocklehurst grills Jane about her character. After he leaves, Jane unleashes her fury on Mrs. Reed, accusing her of hypocrisy and cruelty. The older woman is stung by Jane's rebuke.

Vocabulary

Context Clues Divide students into five groups, and assign each group one vocabulary word. Each group should study the word and then write two related sentences, one of which uses the word. Students must incorporate enough context clues into their sentences so the class can guess the word's meaning. Have each group write their sentences on the board and, after the class has figured out the word's meaning, underline the context clues they provided.

English Learners

DIFFERENTIATED INSTRUCTION

PARTNERS **Intermediate** Help students understand the different methods of characterization by showing them how they use these methods in daily life. In direct characterization, a writer makes explicit statements about a character. **Ask:** Use direct characterization to describe a friend. *(My friend Steve is about six feet tall, with short, dark curly hair, and brown eyes. Many of Steve's teachers also taught his older brother, Jake, so some of Steve's teachers often call him Jake.)*

Ask: How might you describe your friend using indirect characterization? *(Steve says "All my friends call me Smitty, and my teachers call me Jake, but hey,*

I'm OK with that.") Tell students that what they would do to describe a friend is what authors do to describe a character. Then, put students in pairs and have them carry out the exercise, characterizing a close friend directly and indirectly.

Teach

Reading Strategy 1

Analyze Characterization

Answer: *Brontë shows Eliza's character by portraying her hoarding money and commenting that Eliza charges "usurious" interest.*

Ask: In the next paragraph, what might the first sentence suggest about Georgiana's character? *(Georgiana may be vain.)*

 For additional practice using the reading skill or strategy, see Unit 5 Teaching Resources Book, p. 103.

View the Art ★

Answer: *The pen and paper, books, and pet birds might suggest that the girl is a student who loves animals. Some students may say that because the girl seems more interested in the bird than in her writing, she is not too studious or prefers animals to books.*

 For an audio recording of this selection, use Listening Library Audio CD-ROM.

Readability Scores

Dale-Chall: 10.3
DRP: 63
Lexile: 1010

from Jane Eyre

Charlotte Brontë

A Girl Writing. Henriette Browne. Oil color on canvas, 74 cm. x 92 cm. Victoria and Albert Museum, London.

View the Art Portrait artists will often show their subjects surrounded by favorite or symbolic items, to give viewers a sense of the subject's personality. What do the objects in this painting, and the girl's pose, suggest about her?

It was the fifteenth of January, about nine o'clock in the morning. Bessie was gone down to breakfast; my cousins had not yet been summoned to their mama; Eliza was putting on her bonnet and warm garden coat to go and feed her poultry, an occupation of which she was fond, and not less so of selling the eggs to the housekeeper and hoarding up the money she thus obtained. She had a turn for traffic, and a marked propensity for saving, shown not only in the vending of eggs and chickens but also in driving hard bargains with the gardener about flower roots, seeds, and slips of plants, that functionary having orders from Mrs. Reed to buy from this young lady all the products of her parterre[1] she wished to sell; and Eliza would have sold the hair off her head if she could

have made a handsome profit thereby. As to her money, she first secreted it in odd corners, wrapped in a rag or an old curl paper; but some of these hoards having been discovered by the housemaid, Eliza, fearful of one day losing her valued treasure, consented to entrust it to her mother, at a usurious[2] rate of interest—fifty or sixty percent, which interest she exacted every quarter, keeping her accounts in a little book with anxious accuracy.

Georgiana sat on a high stool, dressing her hair at the glass, and interweaving her curls with artificial flowers and faded feathers, of which she had found a store in a drawer in the attic. I was making my bed, having received strict orders from Bessie to get it arranged before

2. *Usurious* means "excessive."

Analyze Characterization *How does Brontë reveal Eliza's character in this passage?* **1**

1. A *parterre* is a garden in which the flowerbeds are arranged to form a pattern.

Writing Practice

Draw Conclusions in an Essay

Explain that students can draw conclusions about a chracter by identifying the events a narrator stresses. **Ask:** What conclusion can you draw about the carriage's significance? *(Its arrival will affect Jane.)* What can you conclude about Jane from her reaction to the robin? *(She is engaged with the world and is kind.)* Have students write a short essay to predict what may happen to Jane at the Lowood school, based on what conclusions they have drawn from text evidence.

she returned (for Bessie now frequently employed me as a sort of under-nurserymaid,[3] to tidy the room, dust the chairs, etc.). Having spread the quilt and folded my nightdress, I went to the windowseat to put in order some picture books and doll's-house furniture scattered there; an abrupt command from Georgiana to let her playthings alone (for the tiny chairs and mirrors, the fairy plates and cups were her property) stopped my proceedings, and then, for lack of other occupation, I fell to breathing on the frostflowers with which the window was fretted, and thus clearing a space in the glass through which I might look out on the grounds, where all was still and petrified under the influence of a hard frost.

From this window were visible the porter's[4] lodge and the carriage road, and just as I had dissolved so much of the silver-white foliage veiling the panes as left room to look out, I saw the gates thrown open and a carriage roll through. I watched it ascending the drive with indifference; carriages often came to Gateshead, but none ever brought visitors in whom I was interested. It stopped in front of the house, the doorbell rang loudly, the newcomer was admitted. All this being nothing to me, my **vacant** attention soon found livelier attraction in the spectacle of a little hungry robin, which came and chirruped on the twigs of the leafless cherry tree nailed against the wall near the casement. The remains of my breakfast of bread and milk stood on the table, and having crumbled a morsel of roll, I was tugging at the sash to put out the crumb on the windowsill when Bessie came running upstairs into the nursery.

---

3. The *under-nurserymaid* helps take care of the nursery—the part of the house where children sleep, play, and study.
4. A *porter* is someone who works at the door or gate to let people inside.

 Description *How does this description help establish Jane's feelings about her surroundings?*

Vocabulary
vacant (vā′ kənt) *adj.* empty

"Miss Jane, take off your pinafore;[5] what are you doing there? Have you washed your hands and face this morning?" I gave another tug before I answered, for I wanted the bird to be secure of its bread; the sash yielded, I scattered the crumbs, some on the stone sill, some on the cherry-tree bough, then, closing the window, I replied:

"No, Bessie; I have only just finished dusting."

"Troublesome, careless child! And what are you doing now? You look quite red, as if you had been about some mischief; what were you opening the window for?"

I was spared the trouble of answering, for Bessie seemed in too great a hurry to listen to explanations; she hauled me to the washstand, inflicted a merciless but happily brief scrub on my face and hands with soap, water, and a coarse towel; disciplined my head with a bristly brush, denuded me of my pinafore, and then hurrying me to the top of the stairs, bid me go down directly, as I was wanted in the breakfast room. **3**

I would have asked who wanted me; I would have demanded if Mrs. Reed was there, but Bessie was already gone, and had closed the nursery door upon me. I slowly descended. For nearly three months, I had never been called to Mrs. Reed's presence; restricted so long to the nursery, the breakfast, dining, and drawing rooms were become for me awful regions, on which it dismayed me to intrude.

I now stood in the empty hall; before me was the breakfast-room door, and I stopped, intimidated and trembling. What a miserable little poltroon[6] had fear, engendered of unjust punishment, made of me in those days! I feared to return to the nursery, and feared to go forward to the parlor; ten minutes I stood in agitated hesitation. The vehement ringing of the breakfast-room bell decided me; I *must* enter.

"Who could want me?" I asked inwardly, as with both hands I turned the stiff door handle

---

5. A *pinafore* is a sleeveless housedress worn over a dress.
6. *Poltroon* means "a complete coward."

Description *How does this passage help to build suspense?* **4**

CHARLOTTE BRONTË **927**

English Learners

DIFFERENTIATED INSTRUCTION

Intermediate Point out that Brontë uses idioms from business and commerce. Draw students' attention to these expressions: *a turn for traffic* means "a talent for business"; *driving hard bargains* means "getting a good price"; *handsome profit* means "very good profit." Have students use these idioms in a sentence.

Approaching Level

DIFFERENTIATED INSTRUCTION

Emerging Point out the fast, forceful action unfolding as Bessie bursts into the nursery. **Ask:** What vivid action verbs does Brontë use in this passage? (*hauled, inflicted, disciplined, denuded, hurrying, bid*) Have students track the action verbs throughout the selection.

Teach

Literary Element | 2

Description **Answer:** *It creates an atmosphere that reflects Jane's loneliness.*

APPROACHING If approaching level students have difficulty, guide them in thinking about the symbolism of winter. The cold, the absence of growing things, the lack of lively movement—these details of setting reflect the life that Jane lives, snubbed by her cousins and put to work as a maid.

Big Idea | 3

Disillusionment and Darker Visions Say: As you read, note how other characters treat Jane, starting with this description of her interactions with Bessie. (*Bessie gives her strict orders to make her bed; she frequently makes Jane assist her.*) **Ask:** How do Jane's actions contrast with those of Eliza and Georgiana? (*While Eliza gets dressed to tend to her money-making chickens and Georgiana primps in the mirror, Jane works at her assigned task.*)

Literary Element | 4

Description **Answer:** *The description of Jane in the empty hall, which stands between her captivity in the nursery and her fate in the parlor, builds suspense by heightening a dramatic moment.*

Teach

Big Idea 1

Disillusionment and Darker Visions Answer: *The stranger appearing as a "black pillar" symbolizes a darker vision; his "carved mask" face suggests he will be rigid and harsh.* Be sure that students know the meanings of these words: *sable, grim.*
(ENGLISH LEARNERS) **Ask:** What does the color black often represent in literature? Guide students to recognize both the positive and negative associations of black and to focus on the negative associations as they answer the Big Idea question.

Vocabulary 2

Context Clues If students know *prolonged* means "continued," they can use it and other context clues to find the meaning of *scrutiny.* **Ask:** Where would a reader find context clues to determine the meaning of *scrutiny?* (in the previous paragraph) What was the man doing previously? (He was examining Jayne.)

Reading Strategy 3

**Analyzing Characterization
Answer:** *Brontë uses dialogue to reveal that Jane is honest and innocent and that she believes she is not a good child.*

Ask: Why do you think Jane has this opinion of herself? *(Jane sees herself as less than good because Mrs. Reed has probably told her so many times.)*

928

---

which, for a second or two, resisted my efforts. "What should I see beside Aunt Reed in the apartment? A man or a woman?" The handle turned, the door unclosed, and passing through and curtseying low, I looked up at—a black pillar!—such, at least, appeared to me, at first sight, the straight, narrow, sable-clad shape standing erect on the rug; The grim face at the top was like a carved mask, placed above the shaft by way of capital.

Mrs. Reed occupied her usual seat by the fireside; she made a signal to me to approach; I did so, and she introduced me to the stony stranger with the words: "This is the little girl respecting whom I applied to you."

He, for it was a man, turned his head slowly towards where I stood, and having examined me with the two inquisitive-looking gray eyes which twinkled under a pair of bushy brows, said solemnly, and in a bass voice: "Her size is small; what is her age?"

"Ten years."

"So much?" was the doubtful answer; and he prolonged his **scrutiny** for some minutes. Presently he addressed me:

"Your name, little girl?"

"Jane Eyre, sir."

In uttering these words, I looked up: he seemed to me a tall gentleman, but then I was very little; his features were large, and they and all the lines of his frame were equally harsh and prim.

"Well, Jane Eyre, and are you a good child?"

Impossible to reply to this in the affirmative; my little world held a contrary opinion. I was silent. Mrs. Reed answered for me by an expressive shake of the head, adding soon, "Perhaps the less said on that subject the better, Mr. Brocklehurst."

---

1 **Disillusionment and Darker Visions** *How does this description of the stranger represent a darker vision? What do you think the stranger will be like?*

Vocabulary

scrutiny (skrōōt′ ə n ē) *n.* close watch or examination

928 UNIT 5 THE VICTORIAN AGE

"Sorry indeed to hear it! She and I must have some talk," and bending from the perpendicular, he installed his person in the armchair, opposite Mrs. Reed's. "Come here," he said.

I stepped across the rug; he placed me square and straight before him. What a face he had, now that it was almost on a level with mine! what a great nose! and what a mouth! and what large prominent teeth!

"No sight so sad as that of a naughty child," he began, "especially a naughty little girl. Do you know where the wicked go after death?"

"They go to hell," was my ready and orthodox answer.

"And what is hell? Can you tell me that?"

"A pit full of fire."

"And should you like to fall into that pit, and to be burning there forever?"

"No, sir."

"What must you do to avoid it?"

I deliberated a moment; my answer, when it did come, was objectionable: "I must keep in good health, and not die."

"How can you keep in good health? Children younger than you die daily. I buried a little child of five years old only a day or two since—a good little child, whose soul is now in heaven. It is to be feared the same could not be said of you, were you to be called hence."

Not being in a condition to remove his doubts, I only cast my eyes down on the two large feet planted on the rug, and sighed, wishing myself far enough away.

"I hope that sigh is from the heart, and that you repent of ever having been the occasion of discomfort to your excellent benefactress."

"Benefactress! benefactress!" said I, inwardly. "They all call Mrs. Reed my benefactress; if so, a benefactress is a disagreeable thing."

"Do you say your prayers night and morning?" continued my interrogator.

"Yes, sir."

"Do you read your Bible?"

"Sometimes."

Analyze Characterization *How does Brontë reveal Jane's character in this passage?* **3**

Reading Practice

(SPIRAL REVIEW) **Analyze Characters** Guide students to analyze the characters of the questioner—Mr. Brocklehurst—and the questioned—Jane—in this passage, using a Question and Answer chart. Draw a simple T-chart on the board, with the left side "Questions About the Characters" and the right side "What Readers Learn from the Answers." Have students copy the chart. Then, provide opening questions: "Why doesn't Jane want to enter the room?

What forces her to do so?" Read the interview between Mr. Brocklehurst and Jane aloud, stopping to suggest or elicit questions during their dialogue. Encourage students to keep asking questions that reveal characterization as they read on.

Four Girls and a Dog on a Bridge Over the Debdon Burn.
Henry Hetherington Emmerson. Watercolor on paper. Cragside House, Northumberland, UK.

<u>View the Art</u> Examine the differences between the girl on the rocks and the girls on the bridge. Which of the girls best fits your impression of Jane? Explain.

"With pleasure? Are you fond of it?"

"I like Revelations, and the book of Daniel, and Genesis and Samuel, and a little bit of Exodus, and some parts of Kings and Chronicles, and Job and Jonah."

"And the Psalms? I hope you like them?"

"No, sir."

"No? Oh, shocking! I have a little boy, younger than you, who knows six Psalms by heart; and when you ask him which he would rather have, a gingerbread nut to eat or a verse of a Psalm to learn, he says: 'Oh! the verse of a Psalm! Angels sing Psalms'; says he, 'I wish to be a little angel here below'; he then gets two nuts in recompense for his infant piety."

"Psalms are not interesting," I remarked.

"That proves you have a wicked heart; and you must pray to God to change it, to give you a new and clean one, to take away your heart of stone and give you a heart of flesh."

I was about to propound a question, touching the manner in which that operation of changing my heart was to be performed, when Mrs. Reed interposed, telling me to sit down; she then proceeded to carry on the conversation herself.

"Mr. Brocklehurst, I believe I intimated in the letter which I wrote to you three weeks ago that this little girl has not quite the character and disposition I could wish; should you admit her into Lowood school, I should be glad if the superintendent and teachers were requested to keep a strict eye on her, and above all, to guard against her worst fault, a tendency to deceit. I mention this fact in your hearing, Jane, that you may not attempt to impose on Mr. Brocklehurst."

Well might I dread, well might I dislike Mrs. Reed, for it was her nature to wound me cruelly; never was I happy in her presence: however carefully I obeyed, however strenuously I strove to please her, my efforts were still repulsed and repaid by such sentences as the above. Now, uttered before a stranger, the accusation cut me to the heart: I dimly perceived that she was already obliterating hope from the new phase of existence which she destined me to enter; I felt, though I could not have expressed the feeling, that she was sowing aversion and unkindness along my future path; I saw myself transformed under Mr. Brocklehurst's eye into an artful, obnoxious child, and what could I do to remedy the injury?

"Nothing, indeed!" thought I, as I struggled to repress a sob, and hastily wiped away some tears, the impotent evidences of my anguish.

"Deceit is, indeed, a sad fault in a child," said Mr. Brocklehurst; "it is akin to falsehood, and all liars will have their portion in the lake

---

Description *How does Mrs. Reed's description of Jane foreshadow Jane's future treatment at Lowood?* | **4**

Teach

Literary Element | 4

Description **Answer:**
Mrs. Reed's description foreshadows that Jane will be mistreated because the staff at Lowood will think she is deceitful and deserves punishment.

APPROACHING **Ask:** In the next paragraph, how does Brontë's description reveal character and increase this sense of foreshadowing? (*Brontë's description shows that Mrs. Reed is an uncompassionate taskmaster and that Jane dislikes her.*)

Ask: What words or phrases create this foreshadowing? (*Answers may include Mrs. Reed's comments on Jane's character and disposition, her advice that Jane be watched, and her statement that Jane was deceitful.*)

<u>View the Art</u> ★

Answer: *The girls on the bridge look similar to one another—they all have blond hair and are all dressed alike. They give the impression of being related. They are carrying bunches and baskets of flowers. Most students will identify Jane with the girl in blue, since she seems sad, thoughtful, and set apart from the others.*

Tell students to observe Emmerson's placement of the figures in this painting. Have students discuss what each subject in the painting might be feeling and then compare these emotions with those expressed by characters in this selection.

English Learners

DIFFERENTIATED INSTRUCTION

Intermediate Explain that many nineteenth-century novels had a formal tone, sentence structure, and word choice. Make sure students understand difficult vocabulary words in the selection. Begin by having them focus on these words on page 923: *propound* ("put forward"), *interposed* ("offered a remark as an interruption"), *proceeded* ("began"), *intimated* ("made known"), and *disposition* ("personality"). Have students speak sentences that contain these words. As they continue to read the selection, have them write down any unfamiliar words.

Teach

Reading Strategy | 1

Analyzing Characterization

Answer: *The passage reveals Mr. Brocklehurst's character through his words, which show how he treats his students and his family. He is a hypocrite by discouraging pride as a "worldly sentiment" in the schoolgirls while fostering it in his own children.*

ENGLISH LEARNERS Help English learners understand what it means to behave hypocritically: a person claims to approve of a way of acting but does the opposite. Elicit examples of hypocritical behavior that they have witnessed. **Ask:** Do you trust Mr. Brocklehurst to be a good teacher? Why or why not? *(Answers will vary, but most students will say that they do not trust him because his actions and his words differ.)*

Reading Strategy | 2

Recognizing Author's Purpose

Point out that writers use physical description to create characterization. Describing a character as "pale and bony, with birdlike eyes" hints at something about the nature of the character.

Ask: How does the language Brontë uses to describe Mrs. Reed's face hint at her inhumanity? *(The clinical phrases "underjaw being much developed," "her brow was low," and "an eye devoid of ruth" suggest a predatory animal.)*

930

---

burning with fire and brimstone; she shall, however, be watched, Mrs. Reed; I will speak to Miss Temple and the teachers."

"I should wish her to be brought up in a manner suiting her prospects," continued my benefactress; "to be made useful, to be kept humble; as for the vacations, she will, with your permission, spend them always at Lowood."

"Your decisions are perfectly judicious, madam," returned Mr. Brocklehurst. "Humility is a Christian grace, and one peculiarly appropriate to the pupils of Lowood; I, therefore, direct that especial care shall be bestowed on its cultivation among them. I have studied how best to mortify in them the worldly sentiment of pride; and, only the other day, I had a pleasing proof of my success. My second daughter, Augusta, went with her mama to visit the school, and on her return she exclaimed: 'Oh, dear papa, how quiet and plain all the girls at Lowood look; with their hair combed behind their ears, and their long pinafores, and those little holland[7] pockets outside their frocks—they are almost like poor people's children! And,' said she, 'they looked at my dress and mama's as if they had never seen a silk gown before.'"

"This is the state of things I quite approve," returned Mrs. Reed. "Had I sought all England over, I could scarcely have found a system more exactly fitting a child like Jane Eyre. Consistency, my dear Mr. Brocklehurst; I **advocate** consistency in all things."

"Consistency, madam, is the first of Christian duties, and it has been observed in every arrangement connected with the establishment of Lowood: plain fare, simple attire, unsophisticated accommodations, hardy and

---

7. *Holland* refers to a type of linen or heavy cotton first made in Holland.

1 Analyze Characterization *How does this paragraph reveal Mr. Brocklehurst's character?*

Vocabulary

advocate (ad′ və kāt′) *v.* to support or argue for

930 UNIT 5 THE VICTORIAN AGE

---

active habits; such is the order of the day in the house and its inhabitants."

"Quite right, sir. I may then depend upon this child being received as a pupil at Lowood, and there being trained in conformity to her position and prospects?"

"Madam, you may; she shall be placed in that nursery of chosen plants—and I trust she will show herself grateful for the inestimable privilege of her election."

"I will send her, then, as soon as possible, Mr. Brocklehurst; for, I assure you, I feel anxious to be relieved of a responsibility that was becoming too irksome."

"No doubt, no doubt, madam, and now I wish you good morning. I shall return to Brocklehurst Hall in the course of a week or two; my good friend, the archdeacon,[8] will not permit me to leave him sooner. I shall send Miss Temple notice that she is to expect a new girl, so that there will be no difficulty about receiving her. Good-bye."

"Good-bye, Mr. Brocklehurst; remember me to Mrs. and Miss Brocklehurst, and to Augusta and Theodore, and Master Broughton Brocklehurst."

"I will, madam. Little girl, here is a book entitled the 'Child's Guide'; read it with prayer, especially that part containing 'an account of the awfully sudden death of Martha G—, a naughty child addicted to falsehood and deceit.'"

With these words Mr. Brocklehurst put into my hand a thin pamphlet sewed in a cover, and having rung for his carriage, he departed.

Mrs. Reed and I were left alone. Some minutes passed in silence; she was sewing, I was watching her. Mrs. Reed might be at that time some six- or seven-and-thirty; she was a woman of robust frame, square shouldered and strong limbed, not tall, and, though stout, not obese; she had a somewhat large face, the underjaw being much developed and very solid; her brow was low, her chin large and prominent, mouth and nose sufficiently regular; under her light

2

---

8. The *archdeacon,* in the Church of England, is a church official ranking just below a bishop. He assists the bishop in his duties.

Reading Practice

SPIRAL REVIEW **Antagonists and Conflict** Discuss Mr. Brocklehurst and Mrs. Reed, reminding students that each of these characters is an **antagonist**, a person who opposes the protagonist. Point out that the clash between a protagonist and antagonist is a **conflict. Ask:**

▪ What motivates Mrs. Reed in opposing Jane? *(She wants Jane out of her home.)*

▪ What may motivate Brocklehurst in condemning Jane? *(He'll make money if she attends his school.)*

▪ What does Jane want? *(She wants to be treated kindly.)*

eyebrows glimmered an eye devoid of ruth;[9] her skin was dark and opaque, her hair nearly flaxen; her constitution was sound as a bell—illness never came near her; she was an exact, clever manager; her household and tenantry[10] were thoroughly under her control; her children, only, at times defied her authority, and laughed it to scorn; she dressed well, and had a presence and port[11] calculated to set off handsome attire.

Sitting on a low stool, a few yards from her armchair, I examined her figure; I perused her features. In my hand I held the tract, containing the sudden death of the Liar, to which narrative my attention had been pointed as to an appropriate warning. What had just passed; what Mrs. Reed had said concerning me to Mr. Brocklehurst; the whole tenor of their conversation, was recent, raw, and stinging in my mind; I had felt every word as acutely as I had heard it plainly, and a passion of resentment fomented now within me.

Mrs. Reed looked up from her work; her eye settled on mine, her fingers at the same time suspended their nimble movements.

"Go out of the room; return to the nursery," was her mandate. My look or something else must have struck her as offensive, for she spoke with extreme though suppressed irritation. I got up; I went to the door; I came back again; I walked to the window, across the room, then close up to her.

Speak I must; I had been trodden on severely, and must turn, but how? What strength had I

> "People think you a good woman, but you are bad; hard-hearted. *You* are deceitful!"

to dart **retaliation** at my antagonist? I gathered my energies and launched them in this blunt sentence:

"I am not deceitful: if I were, I should say I loved *you,* but I declare I do not love you; I dislike you the worst of anybody in the world except John Reed; and this book about the liar you may give to your girl, Georgiana, for it is she who tells lies, and not I."

Mrs. Reed's hands still lay on her work inactive; her eye of ice continued to dwell freezingly on mine.

"What more have you to say?" she asked, rather in the tone in which a person might address an opponent of adult age than such as is ordinarily used to a child.

That eye of hers, that voice stirred every antipathy I had. Shaking from head to foot, thrilled with ungovernable excitement, I continued.

"I am glad you are no relation[12] of mine; I will never call you aunt again as long as I live. I will never come to see you when I am grown up; and if anyone asks me how I liked you, and how you treated me, I will say the very thought of you makes me sick and that you treated me with miserable cruelty."

"How dare you affirm that, Jane Eyre?"

"How dare I, Mrs. Reed? How dare I? Because it is the *truth.* You think I have no feelings, and that I can do without one bit of love or kindness; but I cannot live so, and you have no pity. I shall remember how you thrust me back—roughly and violently thrust me back—into the red room,[13] and locked me up

---

9. *Ruth* is compassion or pity.
10. *Tenantry* refers to tenant farmers on Mrs. Reed's estate.
11. *Port* is a way of carrying oneself.

3 Analyze Characterization *Based on the characterization in this paragraph, what kind of person do you think Mrs. Reed is?*

4 Analyze Characterization *How does this passage reveal Jane's character?*

---

12. *Relation* here means "blood relation." Mrs. Reed is Jane's aunt by marriage.
13. The *red room* is a room with red furnishings. When Jane was younger, Mrs. Reed unjustly punished her by locking her in that room, in which Jane's uncle had died.

Vocabulary

retaliation (ri tal′ ē ā′ shən) *n.* getting even with; revenge

CHARLOTTE BRONTË **931**

Teach

Disillusionment and Darker Visions Answer:
Jane's anger and passionate dislike of Mrs. Reed are aptly represented by the devouring flames of a fire.

View the Art ★

Note the title of this painting and the expression on the girl's face. Discuss characteristics that students expect the subject of this painting to have. **Ask:** Do you think Jane Eyre would be a witty girl to talk with? How do your expectations for this girl's personality compare to characteristics of Jane Eyre? *(Answers will vary but should include the fact that Jane is much wiser and smarter than her age would suggest.)*

To check students' understanding of the selection, see Unit 5 Teaching Resources Book, p. 107.

She is Witty to Talk With. Helen Jackson. Watercolor on paper, 50.8 x 43.1 cm. Private collection. The Maas Gallery, London. ★

there, to my dying day; though I was in agony, though I cried out, while suffocating with distress, 'Have mercy! Have mercy, Aunt Reed!' And that punishment you made me suffer because your wicked boy struck me—knocked me down for nothing. I will tell anybody who asks me questions this exact tale. People think you a good woman, but you are bad; hardhearted. *You* are deceitful!"

Ere I had finished this reply, my soul began to expand, to exult, with the strangest sense of freedom, of triumph, I ever felt. It seemed as if an invisible bond had burst, and that I had struggled out into unhoped-for liberty. Not without cause was this sentiment: Mrs. Reed looked frightened; her work had slipped from her knee; she was lifting up her hands, rocking herself to and fro, and even twisting her face as if she would cry.

"Jane, you are under a mistake; what is the matter with you? Why do you tremble so violently? Would you like to drink some water?"

"No, Mrs. Reed."

"Is there anything else you wish for, Jane? I assure you, I desire to be your friend."

"Not you. You told Mr. Brocklehurst I had a bad character, a deceitful disposition; and I'll let everybody at Lowood know what you are, and what you have done."

"Jane, you don't understand these things; children must be corrected for their faults."

"Deceit is not my fault!" I cried out in a savage, high voice.

"But you are passionate, Jane, that you must allow; and now return to the nursery—there's a dear—and lie down a little."

"I am not your dear. I cannot lie down; send me to school soon, Mrs. Reed, for I hate to live here."

"I will indeed send her to school soon," murmured Mrs. Reed, sotto voce;[14] and gathering up her work, she abruptly quitted the apartment.

I was left there alone—winner of the field. It was the hardest battle I had fought, and the first victory I had gained. I stood awhile on the rug, where Mr. Brocklehurst had stood, and I enjoyed my conqueror's solitude. First, I smiled to myself and felt elated; but this fierce pleasure **subsided** in me as fast as did the accelerated throb of my pulses. A child cannot quarrel with its elders, as I had done, cannot give its furious feelings uncontrolled play, as I had given mine, without experiencing afterward the pang of remorse and the chill of reaction. A ridge of lighted heath,[15] alive, glancing, devouring, would have been a meet[16] emblem of my mind when I accused and menaced Mrs. Reed; the same ridge, black and blasted after the flames are dead, would have represented as meetly my subsequent condition, when half an hour's silence and reflection had shown me the madness of my conduct, and the dreariness of my hated and hating position. ❧

---

14. *Sotto voce* means "in an undertone."
15. *Lighted heath* is moorland that has caught fire.
16. *Meet* means "suitable or appropriate."

Disillusionment and Darker Visions *Why did Brontë choose these images to describe Jane's feelings?* **1**

Vocabulary

subside (səb sīd´) *v.* to give way or end

Reading Practice

SPIRAL REVIEW **Make Inferences** Remind students that they can make inferences about characters by analyzing their dialogue and actions. Write these dialogue passages on the board:

Brocklehurst: "Your decisions are perfectly judicious, madam."

Mrs. Reed: "I advocate consistency in all things."

Ask: What inferences can you make about the characters based on their words? *(Brocklehurst is a flatterer; Reed is rigid.)* Next, have students find words and actions of the key characters from which they can infer traits.

After You Read

Respond and Think Critically

Respond and Interpret

1. Imagine you faced a situation similar to Jane Eyre's. How would you have reacted?

2. (a)With what duties is Jane often employed in the nursery? (b)What does this reveal about her role in the Reed household?

3. (a)How does Mrs. Reed describe Jane to Mr. Brocklehurst? (b)How might her comments affect the way Mr. Brocklehurst treats Jane?

4. (a)How does Jane behave after the departure of Mr. Brocklehurst? (b)What changing feelings does Jane experience after her conversation with Mrs. Reed? Why does she feel this way?

Analyze and Evaluate

5. What ironic contrasts do the details about Augusta Brocklehurst's visit to Lowood reveal about Lowood and the Brocklehursts?

6. (a)Why do you think Mrs. Reed wants to be Jane's friend at the end of the selection? (b)How does Brontë use imagery in this scene to represent opposite sides of the argument?

Connect

7. **Big Idea** Disillusionment and Darker Visions What does Jane Eyre's situation reveal about how Victorian novelists attempted to create social change?

8. **Connect to Today** How does the attitude toward children and child care in this excerpt differ from modern ideas? Are there any ways in which the attitudes are similar? Explain.

Literary Element Description

Description reveals details about people and places in a story and shapes how a reader feels about events. Writers use description to develop the **mood**, or emotional quality, of a literary work. Description also reveals the **tone**, or the attitude of the author (or narrator) toward his or her subject.

1. What qualities are revealed about Jane, Mrs. Reed, and Mr. Brocklehurst through description?

2. How does the narrator's description of her surroundings show how she feels about them?

Review: Point of View

As you learned on page 266, **point of view** is the standpoint from which a story is told. In a story with **first-person point of view**, the narrator is a character in the story and uses the words *I* and *me*, as in the selection from *Jane Eyre*. Sometimes, a narrator retells events that have already happened.

Partner Activity Work with a partner to find evidence in *Jane Eyre* that an adult narrator is retelling past events. Determine what is revealed about the adult Jane through her recollection of childhood events. Use a chart like this one to take notes.

Example Sentence	What the Reader Learns
"Well, Jane Eyre, and are you a good child?" Impossible to reply to this in the affirmative; my little world held a contrary opinion.	The adult narrator knows she was isolated in the Reed household and made to feel she was not a good girl. A child narrator might not be able to express those feelings or even recognize the situation.

Review: Point of View

Partners should alternate in identifying passages that indicate the narrator is an adult. Encourage collaboration in making inferences about the narrator through the nature and tone of her commentary. Remind students that their charts need not have lengthy inferences.

Progress Check

Can students analyze description?

If No → See Unit 5 Teaching Resources Book, p. 102.

After You Read

Assess

1. Answers will vary.

2. (a) Maid duties (b) She is treated as a servant rather than a family member.

3. (a) As a deceitful, obnoxious child (b) It will blacken her reputation at Lowood before she arrives.

4. (a)She stands up for herself. (b) Boldness; she does not really care about Jane or her future.

5. Lowood is a grim institution with substandard living conditions, while the Brocklehursts are prosperous.

6. (a) She does not really want to be Jane's friend but has a guilty conscience and is intimidated by Jane's new boldness. (b) She repeats images of fire and ice.

7. Children were not well protected in Victorian society. Novelists tried to change this by depicting likeable characters who faced difficult situations.

8. Most students will say that modern attitudes about children are different today from the ones in *Jane Eyre*. Mistreatment of children is thought to be wrong, not a way to "create humility." Children are not regarded as extra servants, or kept away from adults at most times.

Literary Element

1. Students should point out specific examples of description within the text that show that Jane is likeable and that Mr. Brocklehurst and Mrs. Reed are worthy of contempt.

2. She is intimidated and miserable. One supporting example is her initial description of Brocklehurst as a "grim . . . carved mask."

After You Read

Assess

Speaking and Listening

Students' reports should be focused on a specific research question, clearly outlined and organized, and presented with effective visual aids.

 For grammar practice, see Unit 5 Teaching Resources Book, p. 106.

Vocabulary

Word: vacant
Textual Clues: The arrival is "nothing to" Jane, so she is not paying attention.
Meaning: empty

Word: scrutiny
Textual Clues: The man is "examin[ing]" Jane "with the two inquisitive-looking gray eyes," so he is looking at her carefully.
Meaning: close watch or examination

Word: advocate
Textual Clues: Mrs. Reed says she "approves" of the "consistency" at Lowood, so she supports and condones it.
Meaning: to support or argue for

Word: retaliation
Textual Clues: Jane says she "must turn" on her "antagonist," so she wants revenge.
Meaning: getting even with; revenge

Word: subside
Textual Clues: Jane first feels "elated," but then she feels "the pang of remorse," so her elation must have faded away.
Meaning: to give way or end

 For additional assessment, see Assessment Resources, pp. 229–230.

934

Reading Strategy Analyze Characterization

Authors use **characterization** to shape the way a reader views the characters and their actions. As you read about a character, remember that by carefully selecting details, an author controls the impression the reader forms. Find examples of characterization in the selection from *Jane Eyre* that use the following techniques. Then describe what each passage reveals about the character.

1. a direct statement
2. a character's actions
3. a character's physical appearance

Vocabulary Practice

Practice with Context Clues Look back at pages 926–932 to find context clues for the boldface vocabulary words below. Record your findings in a chart like the one here.

vacant scrutiny advocate retaliation subside

EXAMPLE:

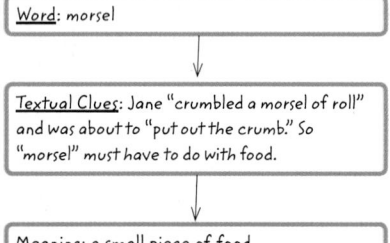

Word: morsel

Textual Clues: Jane "crumbled a morsel of roll" and was about to "put out the crumb." So "morsel" must have to do with food.

Meaning: a small piece of food

Speaking and Listening

 Oral Report

Assignment Present an oral report on orphans and orphanages in Victorian England.

Prepare Before you begin your research, decide what part of the topic you plan to make your focus. Next, develop a list of research questions on this topic. For example, if you focus on orphanages, one research question might be: "How many working orphanages were in England at the time *Jane Eyre* was written?" As you research, be sure to use a variety of reliable and authoritative sources.

Finally, organize the information you find into an outline like the one below. Use your outline as a reference while giving your report.

Victorian Orphanages

I. In London
   a. Number of orphanages
   b. Living conditions

II. In Rural England
   a.
   b.

Report Assemble three or four visual aids, such as posters, graphs, or images, relevant to your topic. These should either explain the information you are reporting or add new information. Incorporate the visual aids into your outline, so you know when to refer to each one.

Evaluate Write a paragraph in which you assess how effectively you explained each of your points, and how well you incorporated your visual aids into your presentation.

Literature Online

Selection Resources For Selection Quizzes, eFlash-cards, and Reading-Writing Connection activities, go to glencoe.com and enter QuickPass code GLB9817u5.

Reading Strategy

1. (Mrs. Reed) "Well might I dread, well might I dislike Mrs. Reed, for it was her nature to wound me cruelly." This excerpt reveals that Mrs. Reed is uncaring.

2. (Georgiana) "Georgiana sat on a high stool, dressing her hair at the glass, and interweaving her curls with artificial flowers and faded feathers." This excerpt shows that Georgiana is vain.

3. (Mr. Brocklehurst) "The grim face at the top was like a carved mask" shows that Mr. Brocklehurst is solemn and intimidating

Grammar Workshop

Noun Clauses

Literature Connection In the quotation from *Jane Eyre* below, the noun clause *who wanted me* is object of the verb phrase *would have asked,* and the noun clause *if Mrs. Reed was there* is object of the verb phrase *would have demanded.* The noun clauses answer the question *What?* of the verbs.

> *I would have asked who wanted me, I would have demanded if Mrs. Reed was there, but Bessie was already gone, and had closed the nursery door upon me.*
>
> —Charlotte Brontë, from *Jane Eyre*

Like adjective and adverb clauses, a **noun clause** is a subordinate (or dependent) clause, which cannot stand alone as a sentence. Unlike other subordinate clauses, however, it may *complete* the main clause—by serving as a subject of a verb, direct or indirect object of a verb or an infinitive, subject or object complement, object of a preposition, or appositive.

A noun clause, like other subordinate clauses, requires a connective word to link it to the rest of the sentence. Some common connectives are *whether, if, that, who, which, what, whose, when, where, why,* or *how.*

Examples

<u>Whoever Eliza wished to buy eggs from</u> was required to oblige.

The noun clause is the subject of the verb *was required.*

Bessie asked <u>whether Jane had washed her hands and face.</u>

The noun clause is the direct object of the verb *asked.*

He knew nothing about Jane except <u>what her aunt told him.</u>

The noun clause is the subject of the preposition *except.*

Proofread Identify the noun clause and its function in each sentence.

1. He directed that special care be taken to cultivate students' humility.
2. That she should keep in good health and not die was Jane's response.
3. A guardian who does not care about her charge will fail in her duty.
4. Jane's main "defect" was that she was an independent thinker.

Learning Objectives

In this workshop, you will focus on the following objectives:

Grammar:
Understanding how to use noun clauses.
Understanding how to use commas with noun clauses.

Tip

One test that may help you identify a noun clause is to read the sentence *without* the subordinate clause. If the sentence requires something else to make sense (a subject, a predicate nominative, or an object), the subordinate clause is probably a noun clause.

Punctuating Noun Clauses

Most subordinate clauses are set off with commas if they are nonrestrictive (or nonessential to the meaning of the sentence). A noun clause is always restrictive (or essential to the meaning of the sentence), so it never requires a comma.

Language Handbook

For more about noun clauses, see Language Handbook, p. R41.

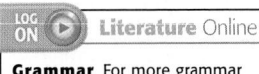 **Literature** Online

Grammar For more grammar practice, go to glencoe.com and enter QuickPass code GLB9817u5.

English Learners

DIFFERENTIATED INSTRUCTION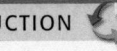

Intermediate Have students identify the common connectors and noun clauses in the following sentences: Doug wondered whether Jane would be late.

She hoped to learn if she would inherit the estate.

That I learned to drive was a miracle.
(Connectors: whether, if, that; Noun clauses: whether Jane would be late, if she would inherit the estate, that I learned to drive)

Grammar Workshop

Noun Clauses

Focus

Write on the board:

1. I should have said who came by.
2. Dave wanted to know whether you are staying for dinner.

Say: Identify the noun clauses in each sentence.

(1. who came by; 2. whether you are staying for dinner)

Teach

Noun Clauses

A noun clause functions in the same way in a sentence as a noun. Noun clauses always have markers, such as *whether, who, what,* and *where,* which cannot be left out of the sentence (except for *that,* which can be omitted occasionally).

Assess

Proofread

1. *that special care be taken to cultivate students' humility:* object of the verb *directed*
2. *that she should keep in good health and not die:* subject of the verb *was*
3. *who does not care about her charge:* appositive to the noun *guardian*
4. *that she was an independent thinker:* complement (predicate nominative) of the verb *was*

 For additional grammar practice, see Unit 5 Teaching Resources Book, p. 109.

Before You Read

Focus

Bellringer Options

Selection Focus
Transparency 47
Daily Language Practice
Transparency 77

Or write the word *jealousy* on the board. **Ask:** What do you think of when you hear the word *jealousy*? Tell students to list their first associations with the word *jealousy*. Then discuss their ideas. As they read Browning's poem, have students consider the effect of jealousy on the speaker.

Before You Read

My Last Duchess

Meet **Robert Browning**
(1812–1889)

From early in his career, English poet Robert Browning explored the darker aspects of human nature. His real self seemed completely at odds with the poet who embraced Realism and wrote about murder, madness, jealousy, deceit, and corruption. He had a pleasant demeanor, and he was a loving, devoted husband and father.

> *"It is the glory and good of Art*
> *That Art remains the one way possible*
> *Of speaking truth,—to mouths like*
> *mine, at least."*
>
> —Robert Browning

"The Poet of Men's Souls" Browning was an expert at dissecting the hearts and minds of his characters. This analytical bent was encouraged early in life by his parents. Although he attended various schools, Browning's education was gained mostly at home, where he lived with his parents until he married at age thirty-four. After spending one year at London University, Browning embarked on a writing career. Unfortunately, Browning's high expectations were quickly dashed by critics who mocked his poems and ignored his plays altogether.

Many of Browning's first poems were published in *Monthly Repository*, the most radical middle-class journal of its time. Its editor, the Unitarian W. J. Fox, espoused radical political, social, and economic reforms. Browning's close involvement with Fox and his intellectual circle exposed the poet to ideas that would not reach most of the English literati until the 1840s and 1850s.

One person who did admire Browning's work was a popular poet named Elizabeth Barrett (see page 897). After several months of correspondence, they met in person. Browning soon declared his love for Barrett, but she was reluctant to marry because of her poor health and the opposition of her overbearing father. In 1846, however, the couple eloped to Italy and settled in Florence, where they remained for the next fifteen years.

Recognition and Success The marriage between Barrett and Browning proved to be a happy one. Barrett Browning recovered her health, and in 1849 she gave birth to a son. When she died in 1861, Browning and his son moved back to England, where he finally began to receive the recognition he deserved. Another edition of his collected poems was requested in 1863, and his next book of poems, *Dramatis Personae* (1864), reached two editions. After the publication of *The Ring and the Book* (1868), a blank-verse dramatic poem based on a murder trial in Rome in 1698, Browning became a much sought-after celebrity.

Browning never remarried, even though he survived his wife by nearly thirty years. He claimed that his "heart was buried in Florence." On his last trip to Italy, he developed bronchitis. After learning of the favorable reviews of his last book of verse, Browning smiled and muttered, "How gratifying." He died a few hours later.

Literature Online
Author Search For more about Robert Browning, go to glencoe.com and enter QuickPass code GLB9817u5.

Selection Skills

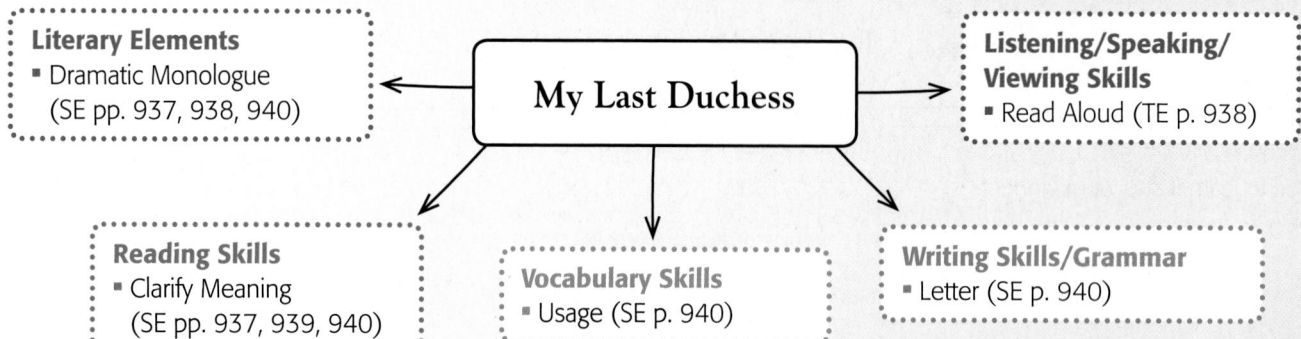

Literary Elements
- Dramatic Monologue (SE pp. 937, 938, 940)

My Last Duchess

Listening/Speaking/ Viewing Skills
- Read Aloud (TE p. 938)

Reading Skills
- Clarify Meaning (SE pp. 937, 939, 940)

Vocabulary Skills
- Usage (SE p. 940)

Writing Skills/Grammar
- Letter (SE p. 940)

Literature and Reading Preview

Connect to the Poem

How can jealousy change a person? In a journal, recall a time when you or someone you knew acted strangely out of jealousy. Describe how it affected relationships with other people.

Build Background

Browning's first work, *Pauline*, was influenced by Percy Bysshe Shelley's confessional style. One reviewer commented on the "intense self-consciousness" in the poem. Embarrassed, Browning quit using himself in his poems. He used fictional or historical speakers. "My Last Duchess" is based on the duke of Ferrara, whose wife died under mysterious circumstances.

Set Purposes for Reading

Big Idea The Emergence of Realism

As you read, ask yourself, How is Realism's focus on lives of individuals, with all their flaws, displayed in "My Last Duchess"?

Literary Element Dramatic Monologue

Dramatic monologue is a form of poetry where the speaker addresses a listener. Unlike traditional poetry in which the speaker often speaks for the poet, the speaker of the dramatic monologue is a separate character, with his or her own personality, much like a character in a story. As you read, ask yourself, How does the speaker reveal his personality through what he says?

Reading Strategy Clarify Meaning

To **clarify meaning** is to examine confusing parts of a text in order to make sense of them. When reading a poem set in the Renaissance, you may see vocabulary, imagery, and line breaks that hinder comprehension. Adjust your reading rate, reread, and paraphrase to clarify what you don't understand. As you read, ask yourself, Do I understand what I've just read?

....

Tip: Paraphrasing Important Ideas Use a chart to paraphrase important ideas in the poem.

Lines	Key Details	Paraphrase
1–4	Duchess painted, wall, as if alive	That's a painting of my former duchess on the wall. It's so lifelike.

Learning Objectives

For pages 936–940

In studying this text, you will focus on the following objectives:

Literary Study: Analyzing dramatic monologue.

Reading: Clarifying meaning.

Writing: Writing a letter.

Vocabulary

countenance (koun′ tə nəns) *n.* someone's face; the expression on someone's face; p. 938 *Bright blue eyes complemented his cheerful countenance.*

trifling (trī′ fling) *n.* treating someone or something as unimportant; showing a lack of proper respect; p. 939 *The judge lost patience with the lawyer's trifling.*

munificence (mū nif′ ə səns) *n.* great generosity; p. 939 *Through the munificence of an anonymous donor, the fundraiser was a success.*

....

Tip: Word Origins A word's origin, or **etymology**, explains its history and illustrates how the word relates to other words in English and other languages. In a dictionary, a word's origin usually appears in brackets.

Before You Read

Focus

Summary

In "My Last Duchess," a duke tells about a painting of his "last duchess." As he speaks, it becomes clear that he was jealous of the attention she paid to others and that his anger grew over time. He explains that after he objected, she stopped smiling, and finally stopped smiling altogether. As the monologue ends, readers realize that the duke is talking to an envoy who is arranging the duke's next marriage.

 For summaries in languages other than English, see Unit 5 Teaching Resources Book, pp. 110–115.

Vocabulary

Word Meanings Ask students to create a mnemonic device to help them remember the meaning of each word. (*Students may create sentences such as "I could* **count** *on his happy face every morning.*")

 For additional vocabulary practice, see Unit 5 Teaching Resources Book, p. 118.

English Learners

DIFFERENTIATED INSTRUCTION

Intermediate Preview the selection for students by explaining that much of "My Last Duchess" describes a portrait of the figure in the title. **Ask:** What parts of a person's body might a portrait include? (*face, hands, neck, hair, etc.*) Have students create a chart identifying the main body parts in one column and details to describe them in a second column. In a third column, they should write down words or phrases that the poem uses to describe each part.

Dramatic Monologue

Answer: *The speaker is a duke, since his wife was a duchess. He is wealthy enough to have hired a portrait artist. The setting seems to be the speaker's home, since his wife's picture is hung on the wall. The words "I call / That piece a wonder" seem to have a slightly haughty tone, as if the speaker appreciates the artistry more than he recalls his late wife.*

[ENGLISH LEARNERS] To help English learners, **Ask:** To whom might the duke be speaking? What is this person's reaction to the painting? Ask students to cite specific evidence from lines 1–20 in their explanation *(Students might answer that this person is an important guest who the duke wants to impress or persuade; students may point to lines 7 and 11–13, as well as, was intrigued by the portrait.)*

View the Art ★

Answer: *Students may say that the image of the duchess, like the one described, is very lifelike and that the woman's gaze is earnest and passionate. Others may read her expression as being sarcastic or witty instead.*

Sir Thomas Lawrence began his career as a child prodigy, working from his own studio at the age of 12. Because of his delicate and intricate brushwork, Lawrence eventually succeeded Reynolds as Britain's greatest portrait painter.

The Duchess of Berri, c.1825. Sir Thomas Lawrence. Oil on canvas. Musée Crozatier, Le Puy-en-Velay, France.

<u>View the Art</u> The Duchess in this image was known for supporting young artists, and also for plotting an armed rebellion in 1832. In what ways does the image reflect the speaker's description of "the depth and passion of its earnest glance"? ★

My Last Duchess

Robert Browning

That's my last Duchess painted on the wall,
Looking as if she were alive. I call
That piece a wonder, now: Frà Pandolf's[1] hands
Worked busily a day, and there she stands.
5   Will 't please you sit and look at her? I said
"Frà Pandolf" by design,[2] for never read
Strangers like you that pictured **countenance**,
The depth and passion of its earnest glance,
But to myself they turned (since none puts by[3]
10 The curtain I have drawn for you, but I)
And seemed as they would ask me, if they durst,[4]
How such a glance came there; so, not the first
Are you to turn and ask thus. Sir, 'twas not
Her husband's presence only, called that spot
15 Of joy into the Duchess' cheek: perhaps
Frà Pandolf chanced to say, "Her mantle[5] laps
Over my lady's wrist too much," or "Paint
Must never hope to reproduce the faint
Half-flush that dies along her throat." Such stuff
20 Was courtesy, she thought, and cause enough

1. *Frà* (frä), meaning "brother," is the Italian title given to members of a religious order of friars. *Frà Pandolf* is an imaginary artist and friar.
2. *By design* here means "intentionally."
3. *Puts by* means "sets aside" or "draws open."
4. *Durst* means "dared."
5. A *mantle* is a cloak.

---

1   **Dramatic Monologue** *What do you learn about the speaker and the setting of the poem from the title and the opening lines?*

Vocabulary

countenance (koun′ tə nəns) *n.* someone's face; the expression on someone's face

Listening and Speaking Practice

Read Aloud Point out to students that in this dramatic monologue the speaker's emotions shift as he reveals information about himself and his late wife. Have students read the poem silently until they gain familiarity with the language. Ask students to look for the place where the tone of the speaker's voice changes. Then ask volunteers to take turns reading the poem aloud, modulating their voices to reflect the changes in tone.

For calling up that spot of joy. She had
A heart—how shall I say?—too soon made glad,
Too easily impressed; she liked whate'er
She looked on, and her looks went everywhere.
25 Sir, 'twas all one! My favor[6] at her breast,
The dropping of the daylight in the West,
The bough of cherries some officious[7] fool
Broke in the orchard for her, the white mule
She rode with round the terrace—all and each
30 Would draw from her alike the approving speech,
Or blush, at least. She thanked men—good! but thanked
Somehow—I know not how—as if she ranked
My gift of a nine-hundred-years-old name
With anybody's gift. Who'd stoop to blame
35 This sort of **trifling**? Even had you skill
In speech—(which I have not)—to make your will
Quite clear to such an one, and say, "Just this
Or that in you disgusts me; here you miss,
Or there exceed the mark"—and if she let
40 Herself be lessoned so, nor plainly set
Her wits to yours, forsooth,[8] and made excuse,
—E'en then would be some stooping; and I choose
Never to stoop. Oh, sir, she smiled, no doubt,
Whene'er I passed her; but who passed without
45 Much the same smile? This grew; I gave commands;
Then all smiles stopped together. There she stands
As if alive. Will 't please you rise? We'll meet
The company below, then. I repeat,
The Count your master's known **munificence**
50 Is ample warrant that no just pretense
Of mine for dowry will be disallowed;[9]
Though his fair daughter's self, as I avowed
At starting, is my object. Nay, we'll go
Together down, sir! Notice Neptune,[10] though,
55 Taming a sea horse, thought a rarity,
Which Claus of Innsbruck[11] cast in bronze for me!

---

2 Clarify Meaning *In your own words, explain what the speaker is saying in this sentence (lines 25–31). What do these lines reveal about the duchess and the speaker?*

3 The Emergence of Realism *Does Browning's presentation of the speaker show Realism or Romanticism? Explain.*

ROBERT BROWNING **939**

Advanced Learners

DIFFERENTIATED INSTRUCTION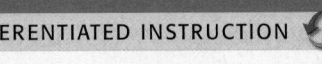

Courtship Customs This selection provides an excellent opportunity for a cross-cultural exchange of ideas about courtship customs. Discuss with students the freedom of choice at the heart of romantic love and the conventions of arranged marriages. Then have them discuss the perceived advantages and disadvantages to each system. Have students research the custom of arranged marriages and how people of different cultures set up these arrangements. Ask students to create a multimedia presentation of their findings.

Teach

Reading Strategy 2

Clarify Meaning Answer:
The duchess reacted the same to special gifts from her husband as she did to a sunset, a bouquet, or a mule. The duke resented her apparent lack of awe of his noble status.

ENGLISH LEARNERS To help English learners, point out the phrase "the dropping of the daylight in the West." **Ask:** Is something really being dropped? *(no)* To what natural event does this refer? *(sunset)* What clues help you figure that out? *(daylight, West)*

Big Idea 3

The Emergence of Realism
Answer: *The poem shows aspects of both. Romantic aspects include the setting and the speaker's obsession with his own importance. Realistic aspects include the complexity of the speaker's character.*

To check students' understanding of the selection, see Unit 5 Teaching Resources Book, p. 119.

Progress Check

Can students clarify meaning?

If No → See Unit 5 Teaching Resources Book, p. 117.

939

Footnotes (center column)

6. A *favor* here refers to a gift presented as a sign of one's love, such as a piece of jewelry or a decorative ribbon.
7. The word *officious* (ə fi´ shəs) today means "interfering" or "meddlesome." However, an archaic meaning is "kind and helpful."
8. *Forsooth* is an archaic word meaning "in truth."
9. The duke is saying here that he feels assured that the Count will approve his claim for a generous dowry.
10. *Neptune* is the god of the sea in Roman mythology. Note that the duke is referring to a sculpture of Neptune.
11. *Claus of Innsbruck* (inz´ brook) is an imaginary sculptor. Innsbruck, Austria, is the site of Emperor Maximilian's tomb, known for its bronze work.

After You Read

Assess

1. Answers will vary.
2. (a) A portrait of his late wife (b) He is implying that her tastes did not discriminate between his gift and "lesser" kindnesses.
3. (a) The duchess is "too easily impressed." (b) He felt superior, jealous, or resentful toward her.
4. (a) "Who'd stoop to blame / This sort of trifling" and "I choose / Never to stoop"
5. (a) She was murdered or sent away, as indicated by the words "I gave commands; / Then all smiles stopped together." (b) He may have wanted to add a sense of mystery to the poem.
6. He might have felt that an audience would be enticed by a poem with a sensational topic.
7. Most students will say that Browning was probably horrified by the duke. The indications in the poem are lines such as "Notice Neptune, though, / taming a sea horse…," which show how little regard the duke has for his former wife.

Literary Element

1. He is unsympathetic and conveys impatience, frustration, contempt, and prideful jealousy.
2. Students' answers will vary.

Writing

Students' letters should demonstrate an understanding of the poem and include suggestions to the duke.

> For additional assessment, see Assessment Resources, pp. 231–232.

After You Read

Respond and Think Critically

Respond and Interpret

1. If you could ask the speaker one question, what would it be and why?
2. (a) What is the speaker showing the visitor? (b) How does he account for "that spot of joy" on the duchess's cheek?
3. (a) Summarize the speaker's description of the duchess's character and behavior. (b) What can you infer about his attitude toward her?

Analyze and Evaluate

4. What words in the poem explain why the speaker didn't tell the duchess how her behavior affected him?
5. (a) What do you think happened to the duchess?

(b) Why do you think Browning doesn't explicitly state what happened to the duchess?

Connect

6. **Big Idea** The Emergence of Realism Newspaper accounts of real, scandalous, and violent events had become readily available to readers in Browning's time. How may Browning have been trying to compete for the same audience with the poem "My Last Duchess"?
7. **Connect to the Author** Browning was known for being different in his personal life from the dark, brooding poet known to the public. What might his attitude toward the duke have been? What signs of this attitude appear in this poem?

Literary Element Dramatic Monologue

The speaker of a **dramatic monologue** describes a crucial moment or situation to someone who makes no response. As we listen to this one-sided conversation, we gain insight into the speaker's character and learn his ideas about the subject.

1. Does the speaker come across as a sympathetic or unsympathetic character? Explain.
2. How do you think the listener reacted to the speaker's description of his wife? Explain.

Reading Strategy Clarify Meaning

Review the ideas you recorded in your paraphrasing chart from page 937.

1. What gift does the duke refer to in line 33? Why does he believe the duchess didn't like this gift?
2. What reference suggests the duke's new wife could have the same fate as the first duchess?

> **LOG ON** **Literature** Online
>
> **Selection Resources** For Selection Quizzes, eFlashcards, and Reading-Writing Connection activities, go to glencoe.com and enter QuickPass code GLB9817u5.

Vocabulary Practice

Practice with Usage Respond to these statements to help you explore the meanings of boldface vocabulary words from the selection.

1. Describe the **countenance** of a friend.
2. Identify a time when you felt someone was acting in a **trifling** way to you.
3. Give an example of **munificence** that you've done or seen recently.

Writing

Write a Letter Write a letter from the listener in "My Last Duchess" to his master, the count. Discuss what you have learned about the duke, and describe your reaction to the story of his late wife. Do you think the count should still allow his daughter to marry the duke? Tell the count what course of action you would advise him to take, and explain your reasoning.

Reading Strategy

1. His 900-year-old title; she made as much fuss over a bouquet of flowers from an ordinary person.
2. The statue of Neptune taming a sea horse reinforces the idea that the speaker controlled his former wife and will control his new one.

Vocabulary

Sample answers:

1. Brown hair, blue eyes, and a big smile is the countenance of my best friend.
2. I felt the basketball coach treated me in a trifling way at tryouts.
3. A recent munificence that I've done is working on a clothing drive for the homeless.

Before You Read

from *Oliver Twist*

Meet **Charles Dickens**
(1812–1870)

Charles Dickens was the most beloved British author of the Victorian age, and more than a hundred years after his death, his work is still popular, both in print and in dramatic and musical versions. The magic that millions still find in Dickens's novels can be traced, at least in part, to the eccentric and colorful array of characters that he created: villainous Fagin of *Oliver Twist*, miserly Scrooge of *A Christmas Carol*, shiftless Mr. Micawber of *David Copperfield*, and bitter Miss Havisham of *Great Expectations*. Like most Realist authors, Dickens based his characters on his own experience. In fact, many people believe that his father was the model for Micawber and that his mother inspired Mrs. Nickleby in *Nicholas Nickleby*.

Birth and Early Life Dickens was born in Portsmouth in southern England, the second of eight children. His father was a clerk who worked for the navy. During his childhood, Dickens's family repeatedly moved to escape creditors. When his father was finally sent to a debtors' prison, Dickens, then twelve, began working in a warehouse pasting labels on pots of shoe polish. After a sudden inheritance improved the family's fortunes, Dickens found work as a lawyer's clerk and then as a shorthand reporter in the law courts.

Literary Triumphs Dickens's literary career began with the success of *Sketches by Boz*, a collection of brief scenes about life in the city that he wrote for a London newspaper. *Boz* led to *The Pickwick Papers*, his first novel, which like much of his work, was published in weekly or monthly installments. Prompted by his success, Dickens married Catherine Hogarth in 1836, and they eventually had ten children. Dickens was a prolific writer. He published fifteen major novels, in addition to a plethora of stories, essays, poems, and travel notes.

> *"I don't profess to be profound; but I do lay claim to common sense."*
>
> —Charles Dickens, *David Copperfield*

Dickens and his wife separated in 1858, and about this time, he began to read his work publicly in both London and the United States. His readings were mobbed by adoring fans. Despite failing health, Dickens kept a frenetic schedule of writing, reform activities, attending theatricals, and readings. His energy, which had always seemed boundless to friends, began to wane, and his farewell reading tour exhausted him. He died in 1870, leaving an unfinished novel, *The Mystery of Edwin Drood*.

Dickens intended his novels as a means of social reform. Human welfare could not keep pace with the technological advances of his time, and Dickens did much to expose evil byproducts of industrialization: child labor, debtors' prisons, ruinous financial speculation, inhuman legal procedures, and mismanagement of schools, orphanages, prisons, and hospitals.

 Literature Online

Author Search For more about Charles Dickens, go to glencoe.com and enter QuickPass code GLB9817u5.

CHARLES DICKENS **941**

Before You Read

Focus

Bellringer Options

Daily Language Practice Transparency 78

Or have students consider the derivation of names. For example, someone with the last name of Cooper may have had an ancestor who made barrels. In Victorian England, a cooper was a barrel maker. Explain that sometimes authors give characters names that hint at what will happen to them in the story. **Ask:** What do you think Dickens was trying to tell his readers when he named the main character "Twist"?

 For summaries in languages other than English, see Unit 5 Teaching Resources Book, pp. 121–126.

Selection Skills

Literary Elements
- Exposition (SE pp. 942–945, 948)
- Satire (SE p. 948)

from **Oliver Twist**

Writing Skills/Grammar
- Review (SE p. 949)
- Superlative Adjectives (SE p. 949)

Reading Skills
- Connect to Contemporary Issues (SE pp. 942, 944, 946, 948)

Vocabulary Skills
- Context Clues (SE p. 948)
- Academic Vocabulary (SE p. 998)

Before You Read

Focus

Summary

This excerpt from *Oliver Twist* delivers a searing indictment of the workhouses established to rescue poor orphans from starvation. They are exposed as inflicting those very horrors their residents are trying to escape. The contrast between starving children and the fat gentlemen who run the workhouse is emphasized when Oliver faces dire punishment for asking for more gruel.

Vocabulary

Have students look up the Latin or Greek root of each vocabulary word, then the meaning of the prefixes *in-*, *extra-*, and *de-*. Invite students to find connections between the meanings of the root and prefix and the modern definition of each word.

 For additional vocabulary practice, see Unit 5 Teaching Resources Book, p. 129.

Literature and Reading Preview

Connect to the Story

What are some ways to call attention to social issues? In a small group, discuss possible ways of addressing today's issues, and why they would or would not be effective.

Build Background

The following selection from *Oliver Twist* introduces Oliver, an orphan who must depend on the mercies of public support. When he turns nine, Oliver becomes too old for the orphanage. He is taken to a workhouse, a place where the poor must work for their keep. When we meet him, Oliver has been given bread so he will not look hungry when he appears before the parish board of directors to be introduced to his new home.

Set Purposes for Reading

Big Idea **The Emergence of Realism**

As you read, ask yourself, How does Dickens re-create the dismal living conditions of poor orphans and highlight specific areas in need of reform?

Literary Element **Exposition**

Exposition is part of the **plot** of a fictional work. The plot begins with exposition, which introduces the story's characters and conflicts. *Oliver Twist* starts with his birth and mother's death. This selection from Chapter Two also is part of the exposition. As you read, ask yourself, What does it tell me about Oliver and his life?

Reading Strategy **Connect to Contemporary Issues**

Connecting means linking what you read to events in your own life or to world events. Associating details from literature with those from current events can help you further understand what you read. As you read, ask yourself, What details or situations do I recognize from current events?

Tip: Creating a Double-Entry Journal As you read, use a double-entry journal to ask and answer questions that link this excerpt to contemporary issues.

Questions	Answers

Vocabulary

demolition (dem´ə lish´ən) *n.* the state of being demolished or obliterated; p. 943 *All the cars were destroyed in the demolition.*

extraordinary (iks trôr´də ner´ē) *adj.* very unusual or remarkable; p. 944 *Dressing up dogs as people produces an extraordinary sight.*

philosophical (phil´ə sof´i kəl) *adj.* concerned with the deeper meaning of life; p. 944 *Jenny liked to discuss philosophical matters with her father.*

inseparable (in sep´ər ə bəl) *adj.* linked so closely that it is almost impossible to separate; p. 945 *The twin sisters were inseparable.*

Tip: Context Clues To figure out the meaning of an unfamiliar word, look for clues in the context, or the surrounding words. Consider the sentence *The demolition of the building included bulldozers and a wrecking ball.* The words *bulldozers* and *wrecking ball* help you figure out the meaning of *demolition* ("to destroy").

Reading Practice

SPIRAL REVIEW **Connect** Explain that this excerpt from *Oliver Twist* describes a institution devoted to the care of orphans and the way that it is run. Write the following questions on the board:

- Have you ever been disappointed by your expectations of something only to find out that the reality was quite different?

- What were you expectations based on? Experience? Advertisements? Someone else's opinion?

Ask students to note differences between their expectations of an orphanage and the one described in *Oliver Twist*.

View the Art Like much of Dickens's work, *Oliver Twist* was published in installments. What would you infer about the installment that had this illustration for its cover? Explain. ★

from Oliver Twist

Charles Dickens

1 Oliver had not been within the walls of the workhouse a quarter of an hour, and had scarcely completed the **demolition** of a second slice of bread, when Mr. Bumble, who had handed him over to the care of an old woman, returned; and, telling him it was a board night, informed him that the board had said he was to appear before it forthwith.

Not having a very clearly defined notion of what a live board was, Oliver was rather astounded by this intelligence, and was not quite certain whether he ought to laugh or cry.

2 Exposition *What does this passage tell you about Oliver's character?*

Vocabulary

demolition (dem′ ə lish′ ən) *n.* the state of being demolished or obliterated

He had no time to think about the matter, however; for Mr. Bumble gave him a tap on the head, with his cane, to wake him up, and another on the back to make him lively; and bidding him follow, conducted him into a large whitewashed room, where eight or ten fat gentlemen were sitting round a table. At the top of the table, seated in an armchair rather higher than the rest, was a particularly fat gentleman with a very round, red face.

"Bow to the board," said Bumble. Oliver brushed away two or three tears that were lingering in his eyes, and seeing no board but the table, fortunately bowed to that.

"What's your name, boy?" said the gentleman in the high chair.

Oliver was frightened at the sight of so many gentlemen, which made him tremble; and the

CHARLES DICKENS **943**

Approaching Level
DIFFERENTIATED INSTRUCTION

Established Have students discuss what conditions at Victorian workhouses were like. Then, have students write a journal entry that Oliver Twist might have written about his first day at the workhouse.

Big Idea 1
The Emergence of Realism
Say: How does Dickens re-create the dismal living conditions of poor orphans and highlight specific areas in need of reform? *(His description is laced with sarcasm, highlighting the need for reform.)*

Literary Element 2
Exposition Answer: *He is young, inexperienced, and sensitive; he doesn't quite know what is expected of him.*

(ENGLISH LEARNERS) Make sure English learners understand the words *defined, notion, astounded,* and *intelligence.* Have them paraphrase the first four lines of paragraph 2 by substituting simpler synonyms for these words.

View the Art ★
Answer: *Students might infer from the bright, vivid colors and the caption under Fagin's picture that this installment will be dramatic. They might infer the installment will focus on the character of Fagin and his imprisonment, since that illustration is largest and central.*

Readability Scores
Dale-Chall: 8.0
DRP: 61
Lexile: 990

Teach

Literary Element | 1

Exposition Answer: *The gentlemen treat Oliver with disdain. Oliver is merely a nuisance to the gentlemen. They have no intention of making him feel less afraid.*

Literary Element | 2

Exposition Answer: *In the past Oliver was not educated as he should have been and was treated with disdain.*

Reading Strategy | 3

Connect to Contemporary Issues Answer: *Oliver's situation is similar to that of workers in sweatshops in developing nations.*

ENGLISH LEARNERS Make sure English Learners understand a "modern global economic issue" is a problem with the way things are made, bought and sold in the world today.

Big Idea | 4

The Emergence of Realism

Answer: *As a result of the board, the poor have no alternative but to starve. Dickens's view is that the poor are being punished.*

beadle[1] gave him another tap behind, which made him cry: and these two causes made him answer in a very low and hesitating voice; whereupon a gentleman in a white waistcoat[2] said he was a fool. Which was a capital way of raising his spirits, and putting him quite at his ease.

"Boy," said the gentleman in the high chair, "listen to me. You know you're an orphan, I suppose?"

"What's that, sir?" inquired poor Oliver.

"The boy is a fool—I thought he was," said the gentleman in the white waistcoat.

"Hush!" said the gentleman who had spoken first. "You know you've got no father or mother, and that you were brought up by the parish, don't you?"

"Yes, sir," replied Oliver, weeping bitterly.

"What are you crying for?" inquired the gentleman in the white waistcoat. And to be sure it was very **extraordinary**. What *could* the boy be crying for?

"I hope you say your prayers every night," said another gentleman in a gruff voice; "and pray for the people who feed you, and take care of you—like a Christian."

"Yes, sir," stammered the boy. The gentleman who spoke last was unconsciously right. It would have been *very* like a Christian, and a marvellously good Christian, too, if Oliver had prayed for the people who fed and took care of *him.* But he hadn't, because nobody had taught him.

"Well! You have come here to be educated, and taught a useful trade," said the red-faced gentleman in the high chair.

"So you'll begin to pick oakum[3] tomorrow morning at six o'clock," added the surly one in the white waistcoat.

For the combination of both these blessings in the one simple process of picking oakum, Oliver bowed low by the direction of the beadle, and was then hurried away to a large ward, where, on a rough, hard bed, he sobbed himself to sleep. What a noble illustration of the tender laws of England! They let the paupers go to sleep!

Poor Oliver! He little thought, as he lay sleeping in happy unconsciousness of all around him, that the board had that very day arrived at a decision which would exercise the most material influence over all his future fortunes. But they had. And this was it:

The members of this board were very sage, deep, **philosophical** men; and when they came to turn their attention to the workhouse, they found out at once, what ordinary folks would never have discovered—the poor people liked it! It was a regular place of public entertainment for the poorer classes; a tavern where there was nothing to pay; a public breakfast, dinner, tea, and supper all the year round; a brick and mortar Elysium, where it was all play and no work. "Oho!" said the board, looking very knowing, "we are the fellows to set this to rights; we'll stop it all, in no time." So they established the rule, that all poor people should have the alternative (for they would compel nobody, not they), of being starved by a gradual process in the house, or by a quick one out of it. With this view, they contracted with the

---

1. A *beadle* is a minor officer of a parish, or church district.
2. A *waistcoat* (wes´ kət) is a vest.

| 1 | Exposition *How do the gentlemen treat Oliver?* |

| 2 | Exposition *What does this passage tell you about how Oliver was treated in the past?* |

Vocabulary

extraordinary (iks trôr´də ner´ ē) *adj.* very unusual or remarkable

---

3. To *pick oakum* is to tear apart old rope for the stringy fiber that was used in sealing the seams of boats.

Connect to Contemporary Issues *Oliver is forced to work at a menial job for virtually no pay. To what modern global economic issue can you connect Oliver's situation?* | 3

The Emergence of Realism *How does Dickens view the treatment of the poor?* | 4

Vocabulary

philosophical (fil´ ə sof´ i kəl) *adj.* concerned with the deeper meaning of life

---

Writing Practice

 **Extended Responses**

SPIRAL REVIEW Explain that an answer to a test question that requires an extended response is evaluated on the thoughtfulness with which the main idea of each paragraph was chosen, the clarity with which it was presented, and the relevance of details chosen to support that idea. **Ask:** Do you think that Oliver will be the most important character in the rest of the book? Write an answer in 3–4 short paragraphs. (*Students' responses might include references to Oliver as the title character and to attitudes toward the poor.*)

water-works to lay on an unlimited supply of water; and with a corn-factor to supply periodically small quantities of oatmeal; and issued three meals of thin gruel a day, with an onion twice a week, and half a roll on Sundays. They made a great many other wise and humane regulations, having reference to the ladies, which it is not necessary to repeat; kindly undertook to divorce poor married people, in consequence of the great expense of a suit in Doctors' Commons; and, instead of compelling a man to support his family, as they had theretofore done, took his family away from him, and made him a bachelor! There is no saying how many applicants for relief, under these last two heads, might have started up in all classes of society, if it had not been coupled with the workhouse; but the board were long-headed men, and had provided for this difficulty. The relief was **inseparable** from the workhouse and the gruel; and that frightened people.

For the first six months after Oliver Twist was removed, the system was in full operation. It was rather expensive at first, in consequence of the increase in the undertaker's bill, and the necessity of taking in the clothes of all the paupers, which fluttered loosely on their wasted, shrunken forms, after a week or two's gruel. But the number of workhouse inmates got thin as well as the paupers; and the board were in ecstasies.

The room in which the boys were fed, was a large stone hall, with a copper[4] at one end; out of which the master, dressed in an apron for the purpose, and assisted by one or two women, ladled the gruel at meal-times. Of this festive composition each boy had one

---

4. A *copper* is a large pot for cooking, originally made of copper.

5 The Emergence of Realism *What situation is Dickens targeting for reform?*

Vocabulary

inseparable (in sep′ ər ə bəl) *adj.* linked so closely that it is almost impossible to separate

---

porringer,[5] and no more—except on occasions of great public rejoicing, when he had two ounces and a quarter of bread besides. The bowls never wanted washing. The boys polished them with their spoons till they shone again; and when they had performed this operation (which never took very long, the spoons being nearly as large as the bowls), they would sit staring at the copper, with such eager eyes, as if they could have devoured the very bricks of which it was composed; employing themselves, meanwhile, in sucking their fingers most assiduously, with the view of catching up any stray splashes of gruel that might have been cast thereon. Boys have generally excellent appetites. Oliver Twist and his companions suffered the tortures of slow starvation for three months. At last they got so voracious and wild with hunger, that one boy, who was tall for his age, and hadn't been used to that sort of thing (for his father had kept a small cook's shop), hinted darkly to his companions, that unless he had another basin of gruel *per diem*, he was afraid he might some night happen to eat the boy who slept next him, who happened to be a weakly youth of tender age. He had a wild, hungry eye; and they implicitly believed him. A council was held; lots were cast who should walk up to the master after supper that evening and ask for more; and it fell to Oliver Twist.

The evening arrived, the boys took their places. The master, in his cook's uniform, stationed himself at the copper, his pauper assistants ranged themselves behind him; the gruel was served out; and a long grace was said over the short commons.[6] The gruel disappeared; the boys whispered to each other, and winked at Oliver; while his next neighbors nudged him. Child as he was, he was desperate with hunger, and reckless with misery. He rose from

---

5. A *porringer* is a small, shallow bowl with a handle.
6. A *common* is a ration or allowance of food.

6 Exposition *How does this passage hint at a future conflict for Oliver?*

Teach

Big Idea 5

The Emergence of Realism
Answer: *Dickens is calling attention to the exploitation of children and orphans in workhouses across England.*

Literary Element 6

Exposition Answer: *The poor conditions in the workhouse have been described. It is obvious that the board is exploiting the work of its paupers and orphans. Oliver will most likely be punished severely for asking for more food; the board will see it as an act of disrespectful rebellion.*

Cultural History

In most English workhouses, the poor were divided into groups by age and gender, and each group stayed in a separate area of the workhouse. As a result, families that entered the workhouse were immediately separated from each other. Residents of the workhouse wore uniforms made of coarse cloth, and punishments for breaking rules ranged from withholding food to solitary confinement.

Approaching Level

DIFFERENTIATED INSTRUCTION

Emerging Have students reread the scene that occurs at the workhouse when Oliver asks for more gruel. Then, after discussing the events and the lines spoken by Mr. Limbkins, Mr. Bumble, and Oliver, assign the roles to volunteers and have them read the lines aloud.

Advanced Learners

DIFFERENTIATED INSTRUCTION

Research In *Oliver Twist* Dickens sharply criticizes the abusive treatment of orphans in nineteenth-century England. Have interested students research how orphans were treated in this country in the nineteenth century and write a short comparison report on their findings.

Teach

Reading Strategy | 1

Connect to Contemporary Issues Answer: *The goal of the board members is not to have to deal with (and pay for) any troublesome boys in their care. Budget issues today often force those dependent on public services, including the mentally ill and the poor, to fend for themselves.*

ENGLISH LEARNERS Have English learners summarize the reaction of the board members when Oliver asks for more supper. **Ask:** Why are they so upset? *(They are only thinking about the cost of food.)*

View the Art ★

In the mid-nineteenth century, stories about schoolchildren became more common. As these stories grew in popularity, many famous artists were employed to illustrate them. One of these artists was Harold Copping, who illustrated a number of children's books around the turn of the century.

 To check students' understanding of the selection, see Unit 5 Teaching Resources Book, p. 132.

Progress Check

Can students analyze exposition?

If No → See Unit 5 Teaching Resources Book, p. 127.

---

the table; and advancing to the master, basin and spoon in hand, said, somewhat alarmed at his own temerity,—

"Please, sir, I want some more."

The master was a fat, healthy man; but he turned very pale. He gazed in stupefied astonishment on the small rebel for some seconds; and then clung for support to the copper. The assistants were paralyzed with wonder, the boys with fear.

"What!" said the master at length, in a faint voice.

"Please, sir," replied Oliver, "I want some more."

The master aimed a blow at Oliver's head with the ladle, pinioned him in his arms, and shrieked aloud for the beadle.

The board were sitting in solemn conclave,[7] when Mr. Bumble rushed into the room in great excitement, and addressing the gentleman in the high chair, said,—

"Mr. Limbkins, I beg your pardon, sir! Oliver Twist has asked for more!"

There was a general start. Horror was depicted on every countenance.

"For *more!*" said Mr. Limbkins. "Compose yourself, Bumble, and answer me distinctly. Do I understand that he asked for more, after he had eaten the supper allotted by the dietary?"[8]

"He did, sir," replied Bumble.

"That boy will be hung," said the gentleman in the white waistcoat. "I know that boy will be hung."

Nobody controverted the prophetic gentleman's opinion. An animated discussion took place. Oliver was ordered into instant confinement; and a bill was next morning pasted on the outside of the gate, offering a reward of five pounds to anybody who would take Oliver Twist off the hands of the parish. In other words, five

Oliver Asks for More. Harold Copping. Color lithograph. Illustration for "Character Sketches from Dickens" compiled by B. W. Matz, 1924. Private collection. ★

pounds and Oliver Twist were offered to any man or woman who wanted an apprentice[9] to any trade, business, or calling.

"I never was more convinced of anything in my life," said the gentleman in the white waistcoat, as he knocked at the gate and read the bill next morning: "I never was more convinced of anything in my life, than I am that that boy will come to be hung." ❧

---

7. A *conclave* is a private meeting.
8. A *dietary* is a daily ration or allowance of food.

1 Connect to Contemporary Issues *What does this passage tell you about the goal of the board members? Name some similar contemporary circumstances.*

9. An *apprentice* is a trainee who works in return for instruction in an art or trade.

Reading Practice

SPIRAL REVIEW **Hyperbole** Hyperbole is a figure of speech that uses exaggeration to express strong emotion, make a point, or evoke humor. Dickens uses hyperbole in describing what happens after Oliver asks for more gruel. Have students identify phrases that are examples of hyperbole and write a paraphrase of the incident without the hyperboles.

After You Read

Respond and Think Critically

Respond and Interpret

1. What was your first reaction to Oliver's plight?

2. What circumstances lead the gentlemen of the board to think Oliver a fool?

3. (a)How does the gentleman in the white waistcoat respond to Oliver's weeping? (b)What does the man's reaction reveal about him?

4. (a)How does the staff respond to Oliver's request for more food? (b)Why do they respond this way?

Analyze and Evaluate

5. How does the description of the gentlemen on the board compare to the description of the workhouse boys?

6. (a)What does Dickens suggest is the official attitude toward the poor? (b)What does the board think of its own efforts on behalf of the poor?

7. What is implied by the prediction that Oliver will be hung and by the bill posted on the gate?

8. What theme is implied by the excerpt from *Oliver Twist*? Explain.

Connect

9. **Big Idea** The Emergence of Realism
Do you think literature is an effective way to call attention to social problems? Explain.

10. **Connect to the Author** His own childhood poverty had a lasting effect on Dickens. Where in the excerpt can you see proof of this effect?

You're the Critic: Different Viewpoints

Was Dickens Too Melodramatic?

Dickens loved the theater. In fact, critics often detect a sense of melodrama in his writing. A melodrama is usually a play, but the term can apply to a work that has a strong conflict, appeals principally to the emotions, and arouses strong feelings of horror or pity. The characters are either very good or very wicked. Read the comments by critics on Dickens's use of melodrama.

> *"Some parts of [Oliver Twist] are so crude and of so clumsy a melodrama, that one is almost tempted to say that Dickens would have been greater without it. . . . It is by far the most depressing of all his books; it is in some ways the most irritating; yet its ugliness gives the last touch of honesty to all that spontaneous and splendid output."*
>
> —G. K. Chesterton

> *"The typical Dickens novel . . . always exists round a framework of melodrama. The last thing anyone ever remembers about the books is their central story. . . .*
>
> *Of course it would be absurd to say that Dickens is a vague or merely melodramatic writer. Much that he wrote is extremely factual, and in the power of evoking visual images he has probably never been equaled."*
>
> —George Orwell

Group Activity Discuss the questions with classmates. Refer to the quotations on this page and cite evidence from the *Oliver Twist* excerpt.

1. Do these critics view Dickens's melodrama as positive or negative? Explain.

2. In general, do you think the excerpt from *Oliver Twist* is melodramatic? Explain.

After You Read

Assess

1. Most students will be sympathetic to his plight.

2. Oliver weeps, from fright and the beadle's blow, when asked his name.

3. (a) The gentleman wants to know why Oliver is crying. (b) He is insensitive and blind to the suffering that the board causes.

4. (a) The master turns pale, hits Oliver, and calls for Mr. Limbkins. The assistants are shocked and paralyzed. (b) They believe that they are being helpful and that a child should be grateful.

5. The fat board members contrast with the underfed, emaciated boys.

6. (a) The poor use the workhouse for free shelter, food, and entertainment. (b) It does a good and noble job.

7. Failure to appreciate meager charity is criminal; Oliver is a social burden who is without rights or feelings.

8. That cruelty is often disguised as kindness

9. Students' responses will vary.

10. Students might find evidence of Dickens's experience in Oliver's extreme fear and embarrassment, his confused responses, his weeping and his fear of even speaking aloud to the cook.

Progress Check

Can students connect to contemporary issues?

If No → See Unit 5 Teaching Resources Book, p. 128.

You're the Critic

1. Chesterton views Dickens's melodrama as negative, but within the context of his larger work, he thinks it is illuminating. He views the melodrama as a result of overexuberant honesty, which validates the social concerns evident throughout the rest of Dickens's corpus. Orwell believes that melodrama is central to Dickens's work, but that Dickens's considerable gifts as a realist allow him to transcend such limitations.

2. In general, the scenes appeal to readers' emotions. In addition, certain characters, such as the board members, are not subtly drawn; they are totally flat characters and thus melodramatic caricatures.

After You Read

Assess

Literary Element

1. The workhouse is the setting.

2. Oliver is an orphan who has just been moved from a parish to a workhouse. As the excerpt comes to an end, he is about to be sold off as an apprentice.

3. The reader is expected to feel pity for "poor Oliver" and contempt for Mr. Bumble.

4. The major conflict occurs when Oliver asks for more food. The conflict is resolved when a sign is put up offering a reward of five pounds to anyone who will take Oliver.

Review: Satire

Have students share their organizers with partners and evaluate the effectiveness of Dickens's satiric devices.

Reading Strategy

1. Death of both parents from AIDS is a common cause of orphaned children in Africa. The casualties of war, poor nutrition, and starvation are other causes, as are poverty and neglect of children.

2. Students' answers will vary. Quality of care of orphans often depends on location.

Vocabulary

1. "By the bulldozer" and "pile of debris" suggest that demolition involves destruction.

2. "Loud applause" suggests that an extraordinary performance is an outstanding or remarkable one.

3. "Thoughtful and logical" suggests that *philosophical* relates to deep thought.

948

Literary Element Exposition

The reader learns quite a lot about Oliver and his circumstances in the **exposition** included in the excerpt.

1. What is the setting of the excerpt?

2. What is Oliver's situation?

3. What is the reader expected to feel for Oliver? For Mr. Bumble?

4. What is the major conflict of the excerpt and how is it resolved?

Review: Satire

As you learned on page 549, **satire** is writing that comments, sometimes humorously, on human flaws, ideas, social customs, or institutions. The purpose of satire may be to reform, to entertain, or both. Some satiric devices are irony, hyperbole, and understatement.

Partner Activity Meet with another classmate and discuss the satire in this excerpt from *Oliver Twist*. Then, working with your partner, create an organizer that shows the satiric devices Dickens uses. Jot down page numbers.

Satiric Devices in *Oliver Twist*		
Irony	Exaggeration	Understatement

LOG ON ▶ **Literature** Online

Selection Resources For Selection Quizzes, eFlashcards, and Reading-Writing Connection activities, go to glencoe.com and enter QuickPass code GLB9817u5.

4. "Did not like to be apart for long" suggests that inseparable means "difficult to separate."

 For additional assessment, see Assessment Resources, pp. 233–234.

 To create custom assessments online, go to Progress Reporter Online Assessment.

Reading Strategy Connect to Contemporary Issues

Review the chart you made while reading the excerpt, and answer the following questions.

1. Estimates of the number of orphans worldwide vary but are all high. What are reasons today for the high number of orphans in the world?

2. Do you think orphans are treated more humanely today than they were in Dickens's time? Explain your answer.

Vocabulary Practice

Practice with Context Clues Identify the context clues in the following sentences that help you determine the meaning of each boldfaced vocabulary word.

1. The **demolition** of the old building by the bulldozer made a large pile of debris.

2. The **extraordinary** performance of the talented pianist led to loud applause.

3. The **philosophical** debate was between two thoughtful and logical students.

4. The **inseparable** twins were very close and did not like to be apart for long.

Academic Vocabulary

*Oliver's request for more food is a **deviation** from the accepted rules of the workhouse.*

In the above sentence, *deviation* means "departure from the norm." The word *deviation* can have different meanings in different subject areas. Using context clues, try to figure out the meaning of *deviation* in each sentence.

1. The books were banned because they expressed the author's **deviation** from the government's ideals.

2. Mathematicians calculate the standard **deviation** of a set of data points in order to measure the spread between data points.

For more on academic vocabulary, see pages 56 and R81.

Academic Vocabulary

1. The context suggests that in politics, *deviation* is departure from established beliefs or ideals.

2. The context suggests that in mathematics, *standard deviation* is a measure of the spread or variability of a data set.

Respond Through Writing

Review

Convince an Audience In your opinion, is Dickens's *Oliver Twist* a book worth reading? Would you say that it is an important work of literature? Explain your position and your reasons in a book review, using evidence from the selection to support your ideas.

Understand the Task In a book review, a writer presents his or her well-supported opinions about a work of literature or nonfiction. The review may also recommend that people read the book, or suggest that they avoid it.

Prewrite First, reread the selection and determine what your controlling idea will be. Do you plan to recommend the book? Decide how you will present and organize your information. For example, you might begin with a summary of the work, and follow up with your own opinions. You may wish to organize your information with an outline. Choose an appropriate audience, such as students who might read the book for class.

Draft Create your thesis, and follow it up with the logical sequence of information you outlined during the prewriting phase. As you write, remember to support any claims you make with evidence, such as quotations from the selection. You may wish to create a chart like the one shown here to ensure that all of your points are well-supported. Use appeals to logic, emotion, or ethical beliefs whenever possible.

Evidence	Claim
Dickens uses irony to illustrate Oliver's hopeless situation and to criticize the cruelty of the authorities.	He mentions that the board "would not compel nobody, not they," when in fact the board has ensured that all poor people will be compelled to starve, one way or another.

Revise As you review, make sure you have considered the other side of the argument. Answering the possible objections will show your readers that your opinion is balanced and well-considered. Use the checklist on page 652 in Writing Workshop: Persuasive Essay to check other elements of your review, which is similar to a persuasive essay.

Edit and Proofread Proofread your paper, correcting any errors in grammar, spelling, and punctuation. Use the Grammar Tip in the side column to help you with superlative adjectives.

Learning Objectives

In this assignment, you will focus on the following objectives:

Writing: Writing a review.

Grammar: Understanding how to use superlative adjectives.

Grammar Tip

Superlative Adjectives

Many adjectives have different forms to indicate their degree of comparison. The **superlative** form compares more than two nouns or pronouns. You will usually form it by adding *-est* or *-iest*.

*Oliver is the **hungriest** of the many orphans.*

Add *most* to multisyllable adjectives that sound awkward with *-est*.

*All the children are miserable, but Oliver is the **most desperate**.*

Note that you will never add *most* to a word that already has an *-est* ending.

After You Read

Assess

Respond Through Writing

Use these criteria in evaluating student book reviews:

- It critically reviews the selection from *Oliver Twist*, supporting the opinion with evidence from the text.
- Logic and emotional appeals add weight to the argument.
- The correct forms of superlative adjectives are used to compare more than two nouns.

A student who meets all of these criteria should receive the equivalent of a 4-point response.

A student who fully meets two or partially meets three of these criteria should receive the equivalent of a 3-point response.

A student who fully meets one or partially meets two of these criteria should receive the equivalent of a 2-point response.

A student who partially meets one of these criteria should receive the equivalent of a 1-point response.

For grammar practice, see Unit 5 Teaching Resources Book, p. 131.

CHARLES DICKENS **949**

English Learners

DIFFERENTIATED INSTRUCTION

Intermediate Before writing their book reviews, students may need to develop their ideas orally. Have English learners work in pairs to answer the questions "Why should people read *Oliver Twist*?" and "What can people learn from *Oliver Twist*?"

Approaching Level

DIFFERENTIATED INSTRUCTION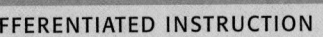

AAVE Approaching level students who are users of African American vernacular English (AAVE) may need to review how to form a possessive noun. **Write the following on the board:** Oliver's job, the cook's uniform, the board's attitude, Dickens's belief. Have them practice writing sentences about the selection.

Vocabulary Workshop

Word Origins

Focus

Say: Look up the etymology of the word *etymology* in your dictionary. What is it? *(from Greek etymon, "literal meaning," and -logy, "theory or study of")*

Teach

Prefixes and Suffixes

Remind students that prefixes and suffixes can be added to both base words and roots.

Assess

- Greek *Akadēmeia*, school where Plato taught; often refers to schools or institutions
- Late Latin *aristocratia*, "aristocracy"; member of the nobility
- Latin *meritum*, "deserving"; earned
- Latin *morārī*, "to delay"; a waiting period
- *per* + *diēs*, "for the day"; means literally "by the day"

 For additional vocabulary practice, see Glencoe Visual Vocabulary CD-ROM.

In this workshop, you will focus on the following objective:

Vocabulary: Understanding word origins.

Vocabulary Workshop

Word Origins: Politics and History

Literature Connection Whether you are reading historical or political documents, or literature like *Oliver Twist,* you are likely to encounter words that come from other languages.

> "In other words, five pounds and Oliver Twist were offered to any man or woman who wanted an apprentice to any trade, business, or calling."
>
> —Charles Dickens, from *Oliver Twist*

Much of the English language originated in Greek and Latin. For example, in the above quotation, the word *apprentice* comes from the Latin root *apprendere,* meaning "to learn."

Understanding difficult material, such as historical and political terms, will be easier if you know a word's origin, or **etymology.**

Etymology

A word's **etymology** is its history, development, and origin. By studying a word's etymology, you can learn how its use has evolved over time.

Tip

Knowing a few common Latin and Greek prefixes and suffixes will enable you to guess the meaning of many unfamiliar words you may encounter on standardized tests.

Examples

history (his′ tə rē) n. a record of events: *a history of pop music.* [Latin *historia* inquiry, history]

- What does the Latin word root mean?
- How does the word's etymology relate to its modern meaning?

political (pə li′ ti kəl) adj. of, relating to, or concerned with government: *a political campaign* [Greek *polis* city + *-al* relating to]

- What suffix is added to this root?
- What other words contain this root or suffix?

Practice Working in groups, find the etymologies of the following words in a dictionary. Record your answers in a chart like the one below.

Word	Etymology	Relevance to Modern Use
abolish	Latin, *abolēre,* "to do away with"	means to get rid of something
academy		
aristocrat		
merit		
moratorium		
per diem		

LOG ON ▶ **Literature** Online

Vocabulary For more vocabulary practice, go to glencoe.com and enter QuickPass code GLB9817u5.

Grammar Practice

Political and Historical Terms Write the following political and historical terms on the board: *diplomatic, suffragist, liberal, conservative, chronicle, annals.* **Say:** Pair up with a classmate and look these words up in your dictionary. Have students report on the etymological information they find.

Then explain that Greek and Latin roots are common in such terms. Have students work with a partner to identify the roots in these Greek or Latin words, using a dictionary: *oligarchy* (olig = "few"), *territory* (terr = "earth"), *interstate* (inter = "between"), and *antebellum.* (ante = "before" *and* bell = "war")

Before You Read

Dover Beach

Meet **Matthew Arnold**

(1822–1888)

The nineteenth century brought enormous changes to England. Yet, rapid economic and industrial progress had its price. In his poetry and prose, Matthew Arnold addressed the deep sense of loss and futility felt by many as a result of the economic and social changes that swept across Europe.

An Uninspired Student Arnold grew up as the son of the most renowned educator in early Victorian England, the headmaster of the famous Rugby School. However, to his somber father's dismay, the young Arnold neglected his studies and instead showed more interest in fanciful clothes and social repartee. Nevertheless, at eighteen, he managed to win the Rugby poetry prize as well as a scholarship to Oxford University. Oxford failed to turn Arnold into a serious student, however. But in his mid-twenties Arnold surprised his family and friends by publishing two volumes of melancholy and profoundly serious verse. Because Arnold was a perfectionist, he published the volumes anonymously; he later withdrew them from circulation because he was dissatisfied with his writing. After marrying Fanny Lucy Wightman in 1851, Arnold accepted an appointment as an inspector of schools in order to support his family. For thirty-five years he traveled over England's wretched roads and stayed at dreary inns in order to inspect the dismal schools of the period.

> *"The best poetry will be found to have a power of forming, sustaining, and delighting us, as nothing else can."*
>
> —Matthew Arnold

An Ars Poetica In 1853 Arnold published his third book of poems, *Poems: A New Edition*, which was the first to bear his name. In the preface to this book, Arnold delivered his famous dictum—poetry should not only express an author's feelings but should also "animate and ennoble" its readers. Thus, for Arnold, literature served an aesthetic and social function.

In 1857 Arnold was elected to the poetry chair at Oxford University. There he gave a series of lectures presenting his ideas on poetry, society, and education in general. As inspector of schools, Arnold studied the British and European educational systems closely. He concluded that all young children should receive a broad education in both the arts and the sciences. The goal of such an education, he felt, was "to enable a man to know himself and the world."

A Critic Is Born As Arnold wrote more prose, he wrote less poetry. In 1867 he published *New Poems*, his last major publication as a poet. From that point on, Arnold focused on social, political, and literary criticism almost exclusively. One of Arnold's best-known critical works was *Culture and Anarchy*, published in 1869. In this volume, Arnold repeated his belief that literature and culture were as necessary to society as religion. A few years later, Arnold wrote four books specifically on religion and its place in a society that was fascinated by science. Toward the end of Arnold's life, he traveled to the United States, where he lectured to enthusiastic audiences and continued to write.

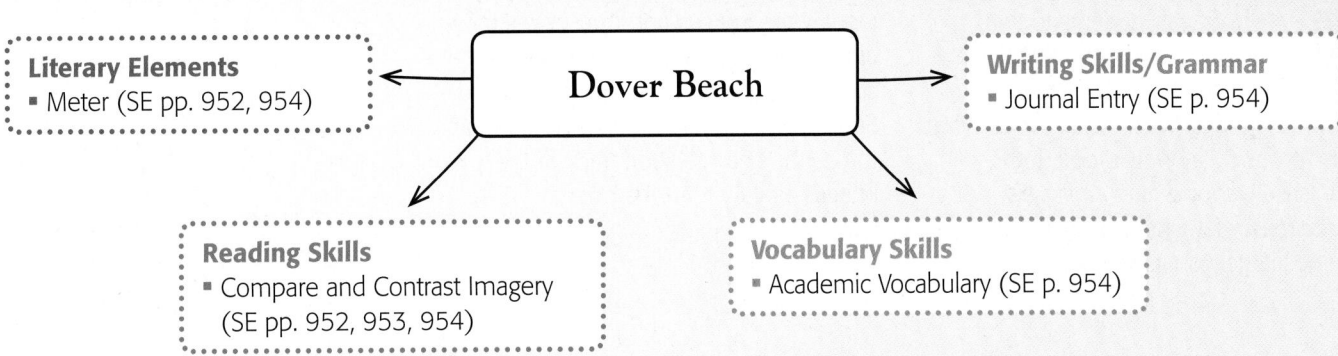

LOG ON ▶ **Literature** Online

Author Search For more about Matthew Arnold, go to glencoe.com and enter QuickPass code GLB9817u5.

Bellringer Options

Literature Launchers:
Pre-Reading Videos DVD,
Selection Launcher

Selection Focus
Transparency 48

Daily Language Practice
Transparency 79

Or ask: Do you think of yourself as an optimist or a pessimist? Why? Ask self-described optimists how they feel after reading or viewing current news about subjects such as war, famine, and environmental problems. **Ask:** Do you believe that humankind will solve its many problems or be destroyed by them? Do you believe that love can help people survive in harsh environments? Explain.

Selection Skills

Literary Elements
- Meter (SE pp. 952, 954)

Dover Beach

Writing Skills/Grammar
- Journal Entry (SE p. 954)

Reading Skills
- Compare and Contrast Imagery (SE pp. 952, 953, 954)

Vocabulary Skills
- Academic Vocabulary (SE p. 954)

Before You Read

Focus

Summary

The speaker watches the calm waters of the English Channel and compares the tides to the ebb and flow of human misery. In despair, he listens to the melancholy roar of the world's pain. He asks his sweetheart to stand with him; he is pessimistic about humanity but believes in love and fidelity between individuals. He asks his love to be true, for all they have is each other.

For summaries in languages other than English, see Unit 5 Teaching Resources Book, pp. 134–139.

> **Interactive Read and Write**
>
> Other options for teaching this selection can be found in
>
> - Interactive Read and Write for EL Students, pp. 241–248
> - Interactive Read and Write for Approaching-Level Students, pp. 241–248
> - Interactive Read and Write for On-Level Students, pp. 241–248

Literature and Reading Preview

Connect to the Poem

What comforts you when you are sad or lonely? Make a list of things, people, and actions that help you deal with hard times.

Build Background

The town of Dover, England, which is famous for its chalk-white cliffs, is about twenty miles from France. It is believed Arnold visited the town in 1851. At that time, Arnold was adjusting not only to married life but also to his position as school inspector. He also was adjusting to the transition in England from an age of faith to an age of science and technology. Arnold addressed some of these social and religious changes in "Dover Beach."

Set Purposes for Reading

Big Idea Disillusionment and Darker Visions

As you read, ask yourself, What phrases does Arnold use to show a dark vision and a sense of impermanence everywhere?

Literary Element Meter

Meter is the pattern of stressed and unstressed syllables that gives a line of poetry a fairly predictable rhythm. The basic unit of meter is known as a **foot**, which usually consists of one or two stressed syllables (marked ´) and one or more unstressed syllables (marked ˘). As you read, ask yourself, How are the syllables arranged, and what kind of rhythm do they create?

Reading Strategy Compare and Contrast Imagery

Imagery describes the word pictures that writers create to evoke a response in readers. In making effective images, writers use sensory details, or descriptions that appeal to one or more of the senses. When you **compare and contrast**, you note the similarities and differences between two or more things. As you read, ask yourself, Where can I see images of permanence and impermanence that create tension and convey a sense of loss?

....

Tip: Noting Imagery Use a chart to record imagery you find.

Images of Permanence	Images of Impermanence
the cliffs of England stand, / Glimmering and vast	on the French Coast the light / Gleams and is gone.

Learning Objectives

For pages 951–954

In studying this text, you will focus on the following objectives:

Literary Study: Analyzing meter.

Reading: Comparing and contrasting imagery.

Writing: Writing a journal entry.

A Seaside View. David Cox. Watercolor on paper. Private collection.

Reading Practice

SPIRAL REVIEW **Preview** Ask students to think about how they might perceive a body of water, such as a lake or ocean, using their five senses. **Ask:** What does the body of water look/feel/taste/smell/sound like? *(salty, sweet, wet, cold, warm)* Explain that this poem depends largely on its imagery. To help

identify the images and the senses they appeal to, have students prepare a two-column chart with headings *Image* and *Sensory perception*. Encourage students to use the chart to keep track of the images as they read the poem.

DOVER BEACH

Matthew Arnold

The sea is calm tonight.
The tide is full, the moon lies fair
Upon the straits[1]—on the French coast the light
Gleams and is gone; the cliffs of England stand,
5   Glimmering and vast, out in the tranquil bay.
Come to the window, sweet is the night air!
Only, from the long line of spray
Where the sea meets the moon-blanched land,
Listen! you hear the grating roar
10 Of pebbles which the waves draw back, and fling,
At their return, up the high strand,[2]
Begin, and cease, and then again begin,
With tremulous cadence[3] slow, and bring
The eternal note of sadness in.

15 Sophocles[4] long ago
Heard it on the Aegean,[5] and it brought
Into his mind the turbid[6] ebb and flow
Of human misery; we
Find also in the sound a thought,
20 Hearing it by this distant northern sea.

The Sea of Faith
Was once, too, at the full, and round earth's shore
Lay like the folds of a bright girdle[7] furled.
But now I only hear
25 Its melancholy, long, withdrawing roar,
Retreating, to the breath
Of the night wind, down the vast edges drear
And naked shingles[8] of the world.

Ah, love, let us be true
30 To one another! for the world, which seems
To lie before us like a land of dreams,
So various, so beautiful, so new,
Hath really neither joy, nor love, nor light,
Nor certitude, nor peace, nor help for pain;
35 And we are here as on a darkling[9] plain
Swept with confused alarms of struggle and flight,
Where ignorant armies clash by night.

1

2 Compare and Contrast Imagery *How does the description of the sea change over the course of this stanza?*

1. *Straits* refers to the Strait of Dover, a narrow channel separating England and France.
2. A *strand* is a shore.
3. *Tremulous* means "trembling." *Cadence* is a rhythmic rise and fall.
4. *Sophocles* was a Greek dramatist who lived during the fifth century B.C.
5. The *Aegean* is the arm of the Mediterranean Sea between Greece and Turkey.
6. *Turbid* means "confusing" or "in a state of turmoil."
7. A *girdle* is anything that girds, or encircles, such as a belt or sash worn around the waist.
8. *Shingles* are beaches covered with water-worn pebbles.
9. Something that is *darkling* is characterized by darkness.

MATTHEW ARNOLD **953**

Teach

Big Idea   1

Disillusionment and Darker Visions Ask: What kind of picture does Arnold paint of human life? What does he identify as the main problems? What does Arnold think can help individuals cope in this world? *(He paints a dark picture of sadness, confusion, impermanence, and war. Individuals can help each other with mutual love and fidelity.)*

APPROACHING To help approaching level students, point out that the last stanza of the poem compares the world as a "land of dreams" with way it really is. Have them identify the problems the poet lists in the final five lines.

Reading Strategy   2

Compare and Contrast Imagery Answer: *At first, the speaker describes the sea as "tranquil," but later he describes the sea's "grating roar."*

> For additional practice using the reading skill or strategy, see Unit 5 Teaching Resources Book, p. 141.

Writer's Technique ☆

Rhyme Point out to students that although the poem as a whole does not have a regular rhyme scheme, there are a surprising number of end-rhymed lines—for example, lines 1 and 3, lines 2 and 6, and lines 4, 8 and 11. Stanza 2 contains 3 rhyming pairs, and stanza 4 has the most regular rhyme scheme of all: *abbacddcc*.

After You Read

Assess

1. Answers will vary.

2. (a) The sea, the moonlight, the cliffs, and the bay (b) The roar of pebbles hitting the strand

3. (a) Sadness and misery (b) The "eternal note of sadness"

4. (a) It is still affected by sadness. (b) Answers will vary.

5. Once full but now receding.

6. Love can overcome the troubles of the world. Yes. Examples include "tranquil bay"; "sweet is the night air"; "Sea of Faith"

7. Answers will vary.

8. Some students might say that Arnold's poem is a "call to action" asking people to think harder about a changing world, or appreciate the unchanging things (being "true to one another") more strongly. Others might say that the poem's somewhat hopeless tone would not necessarily be inspiring.

Literary Element

1. (a) The iamb (b) It mirrors the poem's shift from positive stability to uncertainty.

2. The irregular meter reinforces the imagery of the ebb and flow of the sea.

Progress Check

Can students analyze meter?

If No → See Unit 5 Teaching Resources Book, p. 140.

 For additional assessment, see Assessment Resources, pp. 235–236.

954

After You Read

Respond and Think Critically

Respond and Interpret

1. What image or images made the deepest impression on you? Why?

2. (a) What does the speaker see from the window in lines 1–6? (b) What does the speaker hear in lines 7–14?

3. (a) What emotion does the speaker associate with the sound of waves? (b) According to the poem, what does Sophocles hear?

Analyze and Evaluate

4. (a) According to the speaker, how has the world not changed since Sophocles's time? (b) Do you agree or disagree with this assertion? Explain.

5. What words or images suggest that the speaker of the poem still has hope?

6. (a) What is the theme, or main idea, of the poem? (b) In your opinion, do the images of the shoreline effectively convey the theme? Explain.

Connect

7. **Big Idea** **Disillusionment and Darker Visions** How might being "true to one another" help in a world of struggle and pain?

8. **Connect to the Author** Arnold felt that poetry should "animate and enable" readers. How do you think the poem accomplishes this goal?

Literary Element Meter

Meter often gives clues to the meaning and mood of a poem.

1. (a) What is the dominant foot in the first lines of the poem? (b) How does the breakdown of this regularity contribute to the poem's meaning?

2. How does the meter in the first two stanzas support the imagery?

Reading Strategy Compare and Contrast Imagery

Look back at the chart you filled in as you read, and answer the following questions.

1. Compare and contrast the images of light and darkness that appear in the first and last stanzas.

2. Compare and contrast the imagery used to portray each body of water mentioned in the poem.

LOG ON **Literature** Online

Selection Resources For Selection Quizzes, eFlashcards, and Reading-Writing Connection activities, go to glencoe.com and enter QuickPass code GLB9817u5.

Academic Vocabulary

In "Dover Beach," Arnold **incorporates** images of the sea into a meditation on human life.

Incorporate is a word that has many different meanings. Use context clues to figure out the meaning of incorporated in each sentence and explain the difference between the meanings.

1. We were previously an informal group of consultants, but we **incorporated** last year to become a business.

2. Exercise can be **incorporated** into your daily routine: use stairs instead of elevators and walk short distances instead of driving.

For more on academic vocabulary, see pages 56 and R81.

Writing

Write a Journal Entry Imagine you are looking at the scene being described in "Dover Beach." Write a journal entry in which you describe what you see and hear through the window, including observations about how the scene affects your mood.

Reading Strategy

1. Light symbolizes faith and knowledge; the night symbolizes confusion.

2. Similar images describe the English Channel and the Aegean Sea. The description of the "Sea of Faith" is similar in that the sea makes a melancholy sound.

Academic Vocabulary

1. Here, *incorporated* means "formed into a legal corporation."

2. Here, *incorporated* means "integrated into a larger whole."

Writing

Students' writing should incorporate descriptive language to create mood.

954

Before You Read

To an Athlete Dying Young

Meet **A. E. Housman**
(1859–1936)

Solitary and brilliant, Alfred Edward Housman was known during his life for both his classical scholarship and his somber poetry. Much of Housman's poetic fame, though, came late in his life, resulting both from his own emotional upheavals and from the changes in tastes that represented the first steps in the transformation of the Victorians into Moderns.

> "With rue my heart is laden
> For golden friends I had,
> For many a rose-lipped maiden
> And many a lightfoot lad."
>
> —A. E. Housman
> from *A Shropshire Lad*

A Shropshire Lad The oldest of seven children, Housman loved learning and sharing knowledge with others, especially his younger brothers and sisters, whom he tutored throughout childhood. One anecdote in particular stands out: to demonstrate a lesson on astronomy, Housman had his siblings stand together on the front lawn. There, each took on the role of a celestial body and, under his direction, moved about according to the patterns and laws of the solar system.

At the center of this active, happy home life was Housman's mother. Her death—sadly, occurring on the young poet's twelfth birthday—was an emotional shock that affected Housman for years. Housman was a gifted student of the classics and, as a result, won a scholarship to St. John's College, Oxford. At first he did well. However, during a period of emotional struggle, and what some have

characterized as a nervous breakdown, he failed his final examinations. He had to return the following year and received a lesser "pass" degree. Housman then took a civil service job in London, working in the same office as his friend Moses Jackson, whom he had met in Oxford. On his own, Housman continued to study the Greek and Latin classics in the British Museum reading room and began to publish impressive scholarly articles. These articles eventually resulted in his being made chair of Greek and Latin at University College, London, in 1892.

Grief and Poetry That same year, Moses Jackson's brother, Adalbert, died of typhoid. After Moses's departure several years earlier for a teaching career in India, Adalbert had become Housman's closest companion. His death prompted a poetic outpouring from Housman and sparked his greatest work: *A Shropshire Lad*. This collection of sixty-three poems is tragic in tone and addresses the themes of death, aging, and loss.

In 1911 Housman became professor of Latin at Trinity College, Cambridge—a position he retained until his death. After the release of *A Shropshire Lad*, Housman's poetic output dwindled considerably. He released only one other book, *Last Poems*, during the remainder of his life. These poems are representative of Housman's understanding of the purpose of all great poetry, to "transfuse emotion" and to "entangle the reader in a net of thoughtless delight."

 Literature Online

Author Search For more about A. E. Housman, go to glencoe.com and enter QuickPass code GLB9817u5.

Before You Read

Focus

Bellringer Options

Literature Launchers:
   Pre-Reading Videos DVD
Daily Language Practice
   Transparency 80

Or hold a class discussion about the ambitions, achievements, and disappointments of young adults.

Ask: What are some important life goals most young people share? What obstacles might young people face on their path toward those goals? How would it feel to reach an important goal in life? How would it feel to fail to reach that goal?

Interactive Read and Write

Other options for teaching this selection can be found in

- Interactive Read and Write for EL Students, pp. 249–256
- Interactive Read and Write for Approaching-Level Students, pp. 249–256
- Interactive Read and Write for On-Level Students, pp. 249–256

Selection Skills

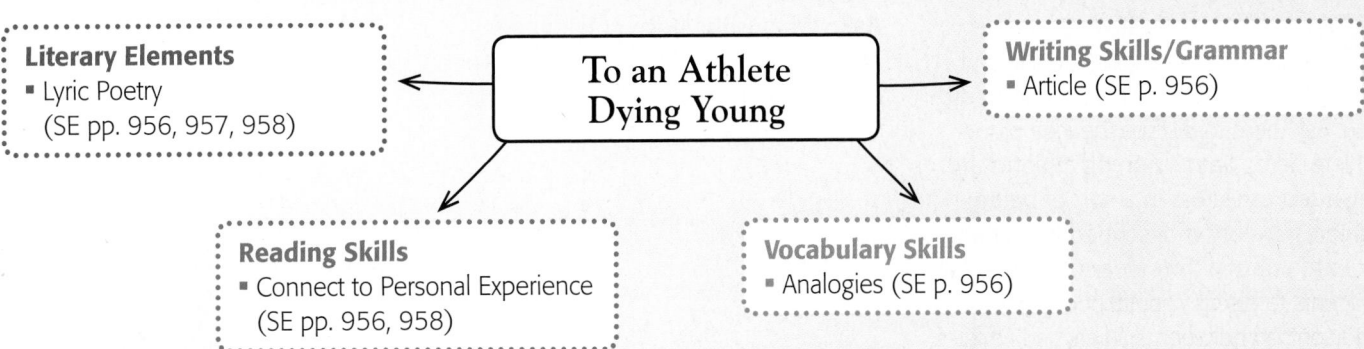

Literary Elements
- Lyric Poetry
  (SE pp. 956, 957, 958)

To an Athlete Dying Young

Writing Skills/Grammar
- Article (SE p. 956)

Reading Skills
- Connect to Personal Experience
  (SE pp. 956, 958)

Vocabulary Skills
- Analogies (SE p. 956)

Before You Read

Focus

Summary

"To an Athlete Dying Young" is a poignant elegy to an athlete who became a local hero before an early death.

 For summaries in languages other than English, see Unit 5 Teaching Resources Book, pp. 144–149.

Vocabulary

Analogy First, have students write an analogy using each word. They should omit the last word and have a classmate resolve it. Finally, instruct students to write one original sentence that uses both words.

 For additional vocabulary practice, see Unit 5 Teaching Resources Book, p. 152.

Reading Practice

SPIRAL REVIEW **Preview** Have students preview the poem by reading the title and looking at the illustration and its caption. Ask them to discuss the idea of the athlete-hero: **Say:** Winning athletes are regarded as victors in a sort of battle; athletes are often described in military or battle terms; they wear uniforms. Ask students to discuss points of comparison and contrast between soldiers and athletes.

Ask: What is the price of failure for athletes? for soldiers? (*Students may point out that soldiers risk their lives, not just their standing or their record.*)

Literature and Reading Preview

Connect to the Poem

How do you think your accomplishments will affect the way people remember you? Freewrite about what people at your school might say about you, for example, after you graduate.

Build Background

Housman was influenced by Greek and Latin lyric poetry as well as English and Scottish folk ballads. He used Shakespeare and poets William Blake and Heinrich Heine as models for poems in *A Shropshire Lad*, in which "To an Athlete Dying Young" appears. Many of Housman's favorite themes—passing youth, early death, unhappy love, the indifference of nature—derive from the disappointments and pains of his own youth.

Set Purposes for Reading

Big Idea **Disillusionment and Darker Visions**

As you read, ask yourself, How does Housman's poem adhere to the notions of Realism while expressing an inherent pessimism?

Literary Element **Lyric Poetry**

Lyric poetry expresses a speaker's thoughts and feelings and is typically short and musical. While the subject of a lyric poem might be an object, a person, or an event, the emphasis of the poem is on the experience of emotion. As you read, ask yourself, What emotion does the poet want to evoke or describe?

Reading Strategy **Connect to Personal Experience**

Connecting to personal experience means relating what you read to events in your life. Connecting personal experience to a text helps gain a greater understanding of it. As you read, ask yourself, Is this something I can relate to my own experiences?

Tip: Taking Notes Use a chart to connect your personal experience with the poem.

Text	My Experience	Significance
"And early though the laurel grows / It withers quicker than the rose."	I was a more agile athlete when I was younger. I'm not nearly as fast now.	Housman's poem seems to reflect the real world accurately.

Learning Objectives

For pages 955–958

In studying this text, you will focus on the following objectives:

Literary Study: Analyzing lyric poetry.

Reading: Connecting to personal experience.

Writing: Writing an article.

Vocabulary

threshold (thresh´hōld´) *n.* doorway; entranceway; p. 957
The groom carried the bride over the threshold of their new home.

fleet (flēt) *adj.* swift; fast; p. 957
Most of the children were fleet of foot during the race.

Tip: Analogies An **analogy** shows how the relationship between a pair of words is similar to the relationship between another pair of words. Example: in the analogy *plodding: slow :: fleet : fast*, each pair of words expresses the relationships between movement and speed.

To an Athlete Dying Young

A. E. Housman

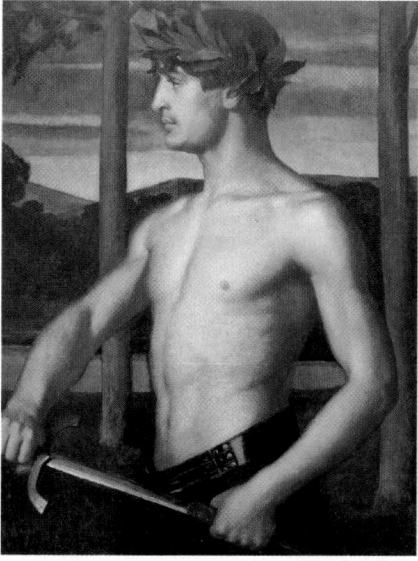

The Victor, 1898. Ottilie Wilhelmina Roederstein. Tempera on paperboard, 91 x 69.8 cm. Private collection.

The time you won your town the race
We chaired you through the market-
place;
Man and boy stood cheering by,
And home we brought you shoulder-high.

5   Today, the road all runners come,
Shoulder-high we bring you home,
And set you at your **threshold** down,
Townsman of a stiller town.

Smart lad, to slip betimes[1] away
10 From fields where glory does not stay
And early though the laurel[2] grows
It withers quicker than the rose.

Eyes the shady night has shut

Cannot see the record cut,[3]
15 And silence sounds no worse than cheers
After earth has stopped the ears:

Now you will not swell the rout[4]
Of lads that wore their honors out,
Runners whom renown outran
20 And the name died before the man.

So set, before its echoes fade,
The **fleet** foot on the sill of shade,
And hold to the low lintel[5] up
The still-defended challenge-cup.

25 And round that early-laureled head
Will flock to gaze the strengthless dead,
And find unwithered on its curls
The garland briefer than a girl's.

---

1. Here, *betimes* means "early in life."
2. *Laurel* is the symbol for victory; in ancient Greece and Rome, victorious athletes were crowned with laurel wreaths.

Lyric Poetry In what ways has Housman made these lines musical? What other element of lyric poetry do you see at work in these lines?

Vocabulary

threshold (thresh′ hōld′) *n.* doorway; entranceway

---

3. *Cut* means "broken" or "outdone."
4. In this instance, a *rout* is a particular group or class of people.
5. A *lintel* is an architectural piece spanning, and usually bearing the weight, above a door.

Vocabulary

fleet (flēt) *adj.* swift; fast

A. E. HOUSMAN   **957**

After You Read

Assess

1. Answers will vary, but students should support their positions.

2. (a) On the first occasion, the young runner is carried home in honor of a victory. On the second occasion, his dead body is carried to his grave. (b) To underscore the tragedy of the runner's early death

3. (a) Glory passes away. (b) Death is the universal equalizer, and youth and fame are short-lived.

4. (a) Iambic tetrameter; *aabb* (b) They add a lightness and musicality to the poem.

5. The poem suggests loss, despair, and resignation.

6. Answers will vary. Students should use modern examples of young, famous people to illustrate their opinions.

Progress Check

Can students connect to personal experience?

If No → See Unit 5 Teaching Resources Book, p. 151.

 For additional assessment, see Assessment Resources, pp. 237–238.

After You Read

Respond and Think Critically

Respond and Interpret

1. Do you agree with the speaker in "To an Athlete Dying Young"? Explain why or why not.

2. (a) In "To an Athlete Dying Young," compare the two occasions on which the athlete is brought home "shoulder high." What has happened to him in each case? (b) Why do you think Housman juxtaposes these two events in the poem?

3. (a) Summarize the commentary and advice the speaker gives in lines 9–28 of the poem. (b) From this, what can you infer about the speaker's attitudes toward youth, fame, and death? Explain the basis for your inference.

Analyze and Evaluate

4. (a) Briefly describe the meter and rhyme scheme in "To an Athlete Dying Young." (b) Do you think these elements are well suited to the poem's subject matter? Explain.

Connect

5. **Big Idea** **Disillusionment and Darker Visions** Briefly describe how the theme of this poem represents Naturalism's pessimistic view of the world.

6. **Connect to Today** Compare Housman's attitude toward the athlete with our current ideas about fame and glory. What do modern attitudes share with Housman's? How do they differ?

Literary Element Lyric Poetry

Poems are considered lyric if they are musical, emotional, and deemphasize narrative elements. This often means the poem will use rhyme, meter, or another musical device. In addition, lyric poetry often explores an emotionally charged subject.

1. Describe the personal thoughts and emotions expressed by the poem's speaker.

2. Why do you think Housman is considered an important lyric poet of the Victorian period? Use examples from the poem to support your views.

Reading Strategy Connect to Personal Experience

Connecting personal experience to a text can make reading more fulfilling. Based on your own experiences, does this poem seem like an accurate representation of real-life situations? Explain.

 Literature Online

Selection Resources For Selection Quizzes, eFlash-cards, and Reading-Writing Connection activities, go to glencoe.com and enter QuickPass code GLB9817u5.

Vocabulary Practice

Practice with Analogies Choose the word that best completes each analogy.

1. canal : ocean :: threshold :
   a. pedestrian   b. building   c. bolt

2. dim : bright :: fleet :
   a. slow   b. quick   c. tight

 Writing

Write an Article Write a news article covering the death and funeral of the athlete in the poem. Your article should provide details about the athlete, his friends and family's reaction to his passing, and his career. You will have to invent some details, but use the poem as a source for others.

Literary Element

1. The poem conveys mourning for the athlete.

2. The poem expresses emotion and thoughts about love and death.

 To create custom assessments online, go to Progress Reporter Online Assessment.

Reading Strategy

Students might relate to the idea of faded glory.

 To create custom assessments using software, use ExamView Assessment Suite.

Vocabulary

1. b   2. a

Writing

Students' articles should have a serious tone, use specific details from the poem, and include reactions from people who might have known him.

Before You Read

Hardy's Poetry

Meet Thomas Hardy
(1840–1928)

When Thomas Hardy was apprenticed to an architect at age sixteen, a minister denounced him for trying to rise above his class. However, the young man had even higher ambitions than the minister suspected. Each morning Hardy rose early and studied literature before going to the office. His hunger for learning eventually led to a distinguished writing career. Although it was criticized at first, Hardy's "self-taught" style gave his writing a stern, authentic voice—a voice that captured the mood of the late Victorian age without pandering to the literary fashions of the time.

> "My opinion is that a poet should express the emotion of all the ages and the thought of his own."
>
> —Thomas Hardy

Seeds of Naturalism Hardy was born and grew up in Higher Bockhampton, a small village in the county of Dorset in southwest England that would play an integral role in his literary career. The region is agricultural, and across its rugged surface stand monuments of the past: Saxon and Roman ruins, as well as the great boulders of Stonehenge. Hardy often set his writing in this bleakly beautiful landscape to emphasize nature's indifference to human suffering. This view of nature as an indifferent, implacable force is the foundation of Naturalism, which Hardy was among the first great English writers to espouse.

Having completed his apprenticeship, Hardy moved to London to work as an architect. He hoped to become a poet and spent his free time visiting museums and theaters and writing poetry. Magazines rejected his verse, however, so Hardy focused on fiction. He returned to Dorset and wrote his first novel while working as an architect. Although publishers rejected the manuscript, writer George Meredith encouraged Hardy to continue writing fiction. His third novel, *Under the Greenwood Tree*, met with success in 1874 and enabled him to devote himself to writing.

Return to Poetry At age thirty, Hardy met Emma Gifford, whom he married four years later. At first the marriage was happy, but the couple gradually drifted apart. The difficulty of sustaining love in marriage became an important theme in Hardy's work, and his later novels were often criticized for their portrayal of relationships between men and women. A particularly harsh review of *Tess of the d'Urbervilles* (1891) led Hardy to declare, "Well, if this sort of thing continues, no more novel-writing for me. A man must be a fool to deliberately stand up to be shot at." When his novel *Jude the Obscure* (1895) elicited even more outrage, Hardy decided never to write another novel, turning instead to his first passion, poetry. In the next three decades, he wrote nearly a thousand poems.

Hardy's wife died in 1912, ending decades of estrangement, but filling Hardy with regret and remorse. He expressed these feelings in "Poems of 1912–1913," often considered the peak of his achievement. Hardy wrote prolifically until the final months of his life.

 Literature Online

Author Search For more about Thomas Hardy, go to glencoe.com and enter QuickPass code GLB9817u5.

Before You Read

Focus

Bellringer Options

Selection Focus Transparency 49

Daily Language Practice Transparency 81

Or say: Think about experiences that have taught you important life lessons. What happened? What did you learn? How is it different to learn by experience rather than by being told something is true? Use these questions as a prompt for class discussion.

Selection Skills

Literary Elements
- Irony (SE pp. 960–964)
- Dramatic Monologue (SE p. 964)

Reading Skills
- Analyze Theme (SE pp. 960–963, 965)

Hardy's Poetry

Vocabulary Skills
- Academic Vocabulary (SE p. 965)

Listening/Speaking/Viewing Skills
- Dramatic Monologue (TE p. 962)

Writing Skills/Grammar
- Apply Irony (SE p. 965)

Before You Read

Focus

Summary

"The Darkling Thrush" describes a bleak winter landscape and the speaker's feelings of despair. He hears a frail bird singing joyfully and wishes that he could see a reason to hope. The speaker of "The Man He Killed" is a soldier who has killed an enemy soldier. He realizes that if the two had met under different circumstances they might have been friends. The speaker in "Ah, Are You Digging on My Grave?" is a young woman who wonders who it is she hears at her grave.

 For summaries in languages other than English, see Unit 5 Teaching Resources Book, pp. 155–160.

Literary History ☆

Hardy published this poem at the very end of the nineteenth century. Its first title was "By the Century's Deathbed." The bird in the poem is probably a missel thrush. A nature book published around the same time as this poem describes the missel thrush this way: "Midwinter is the season of the missel-thrush. . . . When there is no gleam of light anywhere, and no change in that darkness of immense ever-moving clouds . . . [this thrush] sings his loudest from a treetop."

960

Literature and Reading Preview

Connect to the Poems

How can art help society cope with death and tragedy? With a small group, discuss works of art, such as paintings and writing, that were created as a response to death. Consider how they may have been intended, and what effects they have had.

Build Background

Hardy noted the speaker in "The Man He Killed" has returned to England from the South African War, or Boer War. In Hardy's lifetime, Britain was the largest imperialist nation in the world. The South African War, in conjunction with other British conflicts around the world, provoked criticism against imperialist policies. Although Hardy claimed to be "quite outside politics," he voiced his opposition to war.

Set Purposes for Reading

Big Idea Disillusionment and Darker Visions

As you read the poems, ask yourself, Which ideas reflect Hardy's Naturalism—his focus on things such as realistic details, pessimism, and the futility of human endeavors?

Literary Element Irony

Irony is a contrast between expectation and reality. **Verbal irony** occurs when a person says one thing but means another. **Situational irony** occurs when the actual outcome of a situation is the opposite of what was expected. As you read, look for Hardy's use of verbal and situational irony. Ask yourself, Where can I find unexpected outcomes or ironic statements here?

Reading Strategy Analyze Theme

When you **analyze theme,** you examine ways a writer uses characters, imagery, and conflicts to express a larger message about life. As you read the poems, ask yourself, What elements help Hardy make his point about the idea of death?

....

Tip: Taking Notes Use a chart similar to the one below to record a detail from each poem and how it helps support the theme.

	Poem 1	Poem 2	Poem 3
Detail			
How it supports a theme			

Reading Practice

SPIRAL REVIEW **Preview** Remind students that as they read, they should look for evidence of Hardy's Naturalism. Then have students preview the poems by looking at the titles and illustrations. On the basis of the titles and illustrations alone, have students make predictions about the content of the poems (a bird, war, death), and discuss how these topics might incorporate Naturalistic themes. Students can evaluate their predictions as they read the poems.

Learning Objectives

For pages 959–965

In studying these texts, you will focus on the following objectives:

Literary Study: Analyzing irony.

Reading: Analyzing theme.

Writing: Applying irony in a narrative.

The Darkling Thrush

Thomas Hardy

Tawny Thrush. John James Audubon. 1833.

I leant upon a coppice[1] gate
    When Frost was specter-gray,
And Winter's dregs made desolate
    The weakening eye of day.
5 The tangled bine-stems[2] scored the sky
    Like strings of broken lyres,
And all mankinds that haunted nigh
    Had sought their household fires.

The land's sharp features seemed to be
10   The Century's corpse[3] outleant,[4]
His crypt the cloudy canopy,
    The wind his death-lament.
The ancient pulse of germ[5] and birth
    Was shrunken hard and dry,
15 And every spirit upon earth
    Seemed fervorless as I.

      At once a voice arose among
        The bleak twigs overhead
      In a full-hearted evensong
20   Of joy illimited;[6]
      An aged thrush, frail, gaunt, and small,
        In blast-beruffled plume,[7]
      Had chosen thus to fling his soul
        Upon the growing gloom.

25   So little cause for carolings
        Of such ecstatic sound
      Was written on terrestrial things
        Afar or nigh around,
      That I could think there trembled through
30   His happy good-night air
      Some blessed Hope, whereof he knew
        And I was unaware.

---

1. A *coppice* is a small wood or thicket.
2. *Bine-stems* are the stems of a climbing plant.
3. *The Century's corpse* refers to the passing of the nineteenth century (Hardy first published this poem on Dec. 29, 1900).
4. *Outleant* means "leaned out" or "outstretched."
5. Here, *germ* means "seed" or "bud."

6. *Illimited* means "unlimited."
7. *Blast-beruffled plume* refers to the bird's feathers, which were disturbed or made to stand on end by a gust of wind.

1 Analyze Theme *Based on the metaphor in these lines, how would you describe the speaker's attitude toward the nineteenth century?*

Irony *Reread the last four lines. What is ironic about the song of the thrush?* **2**

Teach

Teach

Reading Strategy | 1

Analyze Theme Answer:
He identifies with and feels a sense of kinship with the soldier he killed; he sees him as a fellow human being, not as an enemy.

Big Idea | 2

Disillusionment and Darker Visions Answer:
He sees himself and his "foe" as trapped in a situation beyond their control. As members of hostile armies, they are required to kill each other, although the reasons for fighting are unclear. Impersonal forces determine their fates.

(ENGLISH LEARNERS) Make sure English learners understand the use of the verb *treat* in the poem. Have them look up the word in a dictionary and decide which definition best fits the poem.

View the Art ★

Answer: *Students might infer that the soldiers are exhausted, possibly wounded, or just jaded from being at war. They are lying down in a relaxed way, but one covers his face as if he is crying or in pain. The other covers his face with a gas mask, suggesting that the scene is not as peaceful as it might appear at first. Many students will draw a parallel to the poem's speaker, since he too seems to balance between being horrified by war and being somewhat detached from it.*

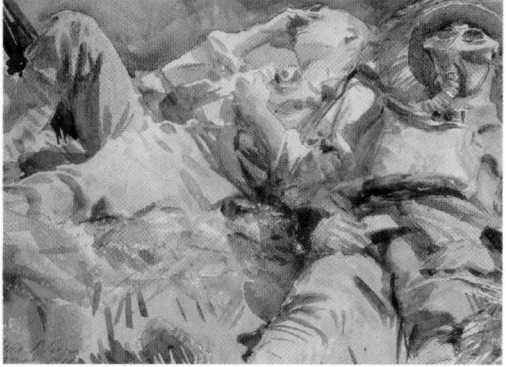

Two Soldiers at Arras, 1917. John Singer Sargent. Watercolor on paper. Christie's Images.

View the Art Sargent used his rapid brushstroke style and vivid color to capture the horrors of World War I. What impression do you have of the soldiers in this image? How does the impression compare to the speaker in Hardy's poem? ★

THE MAN HE KILLED

Thomas Hardy

"Had he and I but met
By some old ancient inn,
We should have sat us down to wet[1]
Right many a nipperkin![2]

5 "But ranged as infantry,
And staring face to face,
I shot at him as he at me,
And killed him in his place.

"I shot him dead because—
10 Because he was my foe,
Just so: my foe of course he was;
That's clear enough; although

"He thought he'd 'list,[3] perhaps,
Off-hand like—just as I—
15 Was out of work—had sold his traps[4]—
No other reason why.

"Yes; quaint and curious war is!
You shoot a fellow down
You'd treat if met where any bar is,
20 Or help to half-a-crown."[5]

1. Here, *wet* means "drink."
2. *Nipperkin* is a colloquial word for a small glass of ale.
3. Here, '*list* means "enlist in the army."
4. *Traps* are personal belongings.
5. A *half-a-crown* is a coin formerly used in Great Britain.

1 Analyze Theme *What message about soldiers and enlisted men does this line help express?*

2 Disillusionment and Darker Visions *How is the speaker's ironic attitude toward war in the final stanza an example of Naturalism?*

Listening and Speaking Practice

Dramatic Monologue Remind students that in a dramatic monologue the speaker addresses the reader directly. **Ask:** What effect does this technique have? *(The speaker seems more real and immediate; the reader can more easily identify with the speaker because he or she is addressed directly.)* Invite several volunteers to give oral readings of the poem (or stanzas from the poem). Encourage them to take on the voice and emotions of the poem's speaker and to read with expression. Discuss how hearing the readings affects students understanding.

"Ah, Are You Digging on My Grave?"

Thomas Hardy

Treasured Pets. Albert Ludovici. Anthony Mitchell Paintings, Nottingham, UK.

"Ah, are you digging on my grave
     My loved one?—planting rue?"[1]
—"No: yesterday he went to wed
One of the brightest wealth has bred.
5 'It cannot hurt her now,' he said,
     'That I should not be true.' "

"Then who is digging on my grave?
     My nearest dearest kin?"
—"Ah, no: they sit and think, 'What use!
10 What good will planting flowers produce?
No tendance[2] of her mound can loose
     Her spirit from Death's gin.' "[3]

"But some one digs upon my grave?
     My enemy?—prodding sly?"
15 —"Nay: when she heard you had passed the Gate
That shuts on all flesh soon or late,
She thought you no more worth her hate,
     And cares not where you lie."

"Then, who is digging on my grave?
20   Say—since I have not guessed!"
—"O it is I, my mistress dear,
Your little dog, who still lives near,
And much I hope my movements here
     Have not disturbed your rest?"

25 "Ah, yes! *You* dig upon my grave . . .
     Why flashed it not on me
That one true heart was left behind!
What feeling do we ever find
To equal among human kind
30   A dog's fidelity!"

"Mistress, I dug upon your grave
     To bury a bone, in case
I should be hungry near this spot
When passing on my daily trot.
35 I am sorry, but I quite forgot
     It was your resting-place."

---

1. *Rue* is a type of ornamental plant; the word can also mean "sorrow."
2. *Tendance* means "tending" or "looking after."
3. Here, *gin* means "trap."

3   Analyze Theme *Based on the first three stanzas, what generalization can you make about the speaker's relationships? What theme might Hardy be expressing through these stanzas?*

Irony *How is the dog's "apology" ironic?* **4**

THOMAS HARDY **963**

After You Read

Assess

1. Answers will vary.
2. (a) The speaker finds the bird's song to be incongruous amidst the bleak landscape. (b) The speaker knows that the thrush's song is instinctual and has nothing to do with reality.
3. (a) They might have enjoyed drinking together. (b) He shot the man because he was his "foe."
4. (a) She assumes that her dog is showing love and fidelity. (b) Indifferent to human wishes
5. Hardy locates the illusion of hope and joy in the speaker's imagination.
6. They make the bitterness of the woman's discovery darkly comical.
7. All three poems are pessimistic and depict humans as victims.
8. Many students will identify a similar theme about the absurdity of war in songs or poems from the Vietnam War era. Students should provide examples to support their opinions.

Literary Element

1. The thrush's song does not come from its "soul," but from instinct.
2. The word *quaint* carries a benign connotation, yet lines in the poem contain sinister details that belie the description *quaint*.
3. The dead woman expects her loved ones to visit her, when in fact they are not thinking about her at all. She assumes that her dog is at her grave out of fidelity, but it is merely burying a bone.

After You Read

Respond and Think Critically

Respond and Interpret

1. Which of these poems did you like best? Explain.
2. (a) Describe the speaker's emotional response to the thrush's song in "The Darkling Thrush." (b) Does the song inspire the speaker to be hopeful? Explain.
3. (a) In "The Man He Killed," what does the speaker think would have happened if he had met the man at the inn? (b) What actually happened? Why?
4. (a) In "Ah, Are You Digging on My Grave?" how does the woman react when she first learns who is digging on her grave? (b) What can you infer about nature from the digger's response? Explain.

Analyze and Evaluate

5. The attribution of human thoughts and emotions to nature or nonhuman objects or animals is called pathetic fallacy. Do you think Hardy is guilty of this fallacy in the first poem? Explain.
6. How do the dialogue and the rhyme scheme in "Ah, Are You Digging on My Grave?" enhance the poem's irony?

Connect

7. **Big Idea** **Disillusionment and Darker Visions** How do these three poems illustrate the literary movement known as Naturalism?
8. **Connect to Today** Consider songs or poems written about recent wars. How do the attitudes in modern culture compare to Hardy's attitude?

Literary Element Irony

The term **irony** derives from a character in Greek comedy called the *eiron*, meaning "dissembler" or "deceiver." The *eiron* spoke in understatement and pretended to be dimwitted to fool enemies. The current literary use of irony retains this idea of "dissembling." In **verbal irony**, what a character or speaker says is often nearly the opposite of what is meant. **Situational irony** occurs when an outcome is vastly different from what was expected.

1. Explain the verbal irony in the words "Had chosen thus to fling his soul / Upon the growing gloom" in "The Darkling Thrush."
2. In "The Man He Killed," what details suggest that the speaker employs verbal irony when he uses the word *quaint* to describe war?
3. Identify two examples of situational irony in "Ah, Are You Digging on My Grave?"

Review: Dramatic Monologue

As you learned on page 937, **dramatic monologue** is a form of poetry in which speakers address a

silent listener—and in the process reveal much about their characters. "The Man He Killed" is a dramatic monologue. The reader is the silent listener to the speaker's narrative and receives the speaker's moral lesson at the end of the monologue.

Group Activity Meet with a small group and create a chart similar to the one below to demonstrate what the reader learns about the speaker through his monologue.

Element of Dramatic Monologue	Effect on Reader
personal tone	inspires identification and compassion

1. What does the reader learn about the personality of the speaker in "The Man He Killed"?
2. What moral or lesson does the speaker convey in this poem?

Review: Dramatic Monologue

1. The speaker is a soldier who is motivated to kill out of duty but questions the logic and values of war.
2. War places human beings in unnatural and destructive relationships.

Progress Check

Can students analyze irony?

If No → See Unit 5 Teaching Resources Book, p. 161.

Reading Strategy   Analyze Theme

Examine the details you collected in your chart from page 960. What conclusions can you draw about Hardy's philosophy and ideas from his use of these details? Use these conclusions to analyze the themes in each work, as you answer the following questions.

1. What images and descriptions in "The Darkling Thrush" help Hardy express an idea about humans, and their relationship with nature?

2. How does Hardy use repetition and parallelism in "Ah, Are You Digging on My Grave?" Explain how the repetition emphasizes his message about mortality and memory.

3. Although the three poems portray different speakers and situations, each poem expresses a similar view of human life. What common theme can you trace through all three of the poems? Explain.

Write with Style

 Apply Irony

Assignment Irony can add to the excitement and humor of a piece of writing, as in Thomas Hardy's poems. Incorporate either verbal or situational irony—or both—in a short story or autobiographical narrative.

Get Ideas Consider the form and main message of your writing and the characteristics of your audience. Decide which type(s) of irony you want to incorporate and jot down ideas about how to work them in.

EXAMPLE:
I think I'll write about the time I locked the keys in the car, while it was still running. My classmates should be able to identify with that kind of situation. Using both verbal and situational irony will help emphasize my embarrassment.

Give It Structure Make a two-column chart of the ironic situations, statements, or events you came up with. List the expected events or meanings of statements in one column and the ironic ones in the other.

Look at Language Don't be afraid to exaggerate statements or situations to make sure the irony is very clear. The greater the difference between the expected and the actual, the more effective your use of irony will be.

After You Read

Assess

Reading Strategy

1. Images of "Winter's dregs made desolate" and the "Century's corpse" suggest that people interpret nature as it relates to themselves. Images of "full-hearted evensong" and "fling his soul" suggest that the bird's world is still rich and joyful. These contribute to Hardy's idea that man and nature are disconnected, and nature does not care about human suffering.

2. Hardy uses repetition and parallelism in the dialogue. It emphasizes the idea that no matter how different your relationships in life might have been, in death you are forgotten equally.

3. Possible common themes: individual people are disconnected—both from one another and from the world at large; human life is insignificant and not sacred; important-seeming events like changing centuries, death, and war are not as significant as we like to think.

For additional assessment, see Assessment Resources, pp. 239–240.

Academic Vocabulary

Possible answer: A person in a military position is expected to use force against others when necessary, whereas a civilian is not.

Write with Style

Each student's story or autobiography should exhibit either verbal or situational irony, focus on a specific event, have events arranged in logical order, and make use of exaggeration.

Writing Workshop

Literary Analysis

Focus

Bellringer

Bring in a recent review of a film, musical recording, or book. Select the paragraph in which the critic states his or her opinion of the work and read it aloud to the class.

Ask: What is the critic's opinion of the work that he or she is reviewing? Why might a reader consult such reviews? *(To decide whether to go to the film or buy the book or recording; to see how the critic's opinion compares with the reader's own)*

Summary

In this workshop, students will write literary analyses that examine the theme and meaning of a poem. Students will follow the stages of the writing process, including prewriting, drafting, revising, and editing.

 For Writing Workshop graphic organizer and rubric, see Unit 5 Teaching Resources, pp. 165-167.

Learning Objectives

For pages 966–973

In this workshop, you will focus on the following objectives:

Writing: Writing a response to literature using the writing process.

Grammar: Understanding how to punctuate in-text quotations from a poem.

Writing Process

At any stage of a writing process, you may think of new ideas. Feel free to return to earlier stages as you write.

Prewrite

Draft

Revise

Focus Lesson: Wordy Sentences

Edit and Proofread

Focus Lesson: In-Text Quotations from Poems

Present

 **Literature** Online

Writing and Research For prewriting, drafting, and revising tools, go to glencoe.com and enter QuickPass code GLB9817u5.

Writing Workshop

Literary Analysis

Literature Connection Matthew Arnold wrote not only literature but also **literary criticism**, or studies concerned with interpreting, analyzing, and evaluating other works of literature.

> *"To have the sense of creative activity is the great happiness and the great proof of being alive, and it is not denied to criticism to have it; but then criticism must be sincere, simple, flexible, ardent, ever widening its knowledge."*
>
> —Matthew Arnold, from *The Function of Criticism*

In literary analysis—a type of literary criticism—the reader studies the specific parts of a piece of literature to determine how they work together to express a theme or deeper meaning. To write a successful essay, you will need to learn the goals of literary analysis writing and the strategies for achieving those goals.

Checklist

Goals	Strategies
To analyze specific elements of the poem	☑ Show how diction, rhythm, tone, mood, sound devices, imagery, and figurative language contribute to the theme
To present and support a concise thesis statement	☑ Introduce your thesis and maintain a focus on it
	☑ Cite specific, substantial, and relevant evidence
	☑ Quote accurately and coherently; cite correctly
To organize your main points in a logical, effective order	☑ Organize your major points according to the chronological order of the poem or in order of importance
To create precision and interest	☑ Vary sentences
	☑ Use effective, precise language

Workshop Resources

Print Materials

- Unit 5 Teaching Resources pp. 165–167
- Writing Kit
- Success in Writing: Research and Reports
- Grammar and Language Transparency 87
- Writing Workshop Transparencies 26–30
- Daily Language Transparencies 13, 37, 94, 141

Technology

- Literature Online: Writing Resources and Grammar Resources, www.glencoe.com
- Online Essay Grader, www.glencoe.com
- Student Presentation Builder on StudentWorks Plus CD-ROM
- Media Workshop DVD
- Online Student Edition

Exposition

Assignment: Analyze a Poem

Write a literary analysis of at least 1,500 words that examines how particular elements of a poem express a broader theme or deeper meaning. As you work, keep your audience and purpose in mind.

Audience: teacher, classmates, and peers

Purpose: to analyze the deeper meaning or theme of a poem

Analyze a Professional Model

As you read this passage, note how David Perkins analyzes the elements of a poem to reveal a deeper theme. The comments in the margin point out features to include in your own literary analysis.

From *"Hardy and the Poetry of Isolation"* by David Perkins

Perhaps Hardy's most successful exploration of the common mental attitude which permits men to slough their questionings occurs in "The Man He Killed." Here the extreme surface simplicity, the short, almost jingling meters, the colloquial idiom, the total absence of stock poetic associations, the unwillingness to employ the glitter of poetic phrase, bespeak a rigid artistic discipline and integrity in which all has been subordinated to an interplay of character and incident. . . . The poem turns on the character of the speaker revealed in his reactions to what has taken place. The speaker begins by stating that he had no personal quarrel with the man he killed. This naturally raises the question of why he killed him, and, pondering the question, the speaker can only say that it was "Because he was my foe" (line 10). But he seems unsure and unsatisfied, and hence reiterates the explanation: "my foe of course he was; / That's clear enough" (lines 11–12). We are introduced, then, to a rather simple type of person, incapable of thinking past stock and ready-made answers ("he was my foe"), well-meaning and troubled by having killed a man toward whom he felt no rancor. At once the speaker goes on to recognize that the man was not his

Thesis

Clearly state your thesis, present an interpretation, and include the author's name and the title of the work.

Support

Support your thesis with specific, substantial, and relevant evidence.

Support

Quote accurately and cite correctly. Lead into and out of quotations to create coherence.

Real-World Connection

Publish your literary analysis by presenting your ideas during the group discussion (see pages 974–975). Alternatively, read your literary analysis aloud to other classmates who wrote about the same poem and discuss the similarities and differences in your analyses.

Teach

Big Idea

The Emergence of Realism
Remind students that in this unit they have encountered poems from the Realist movement. Whether these poems are about love, war, or everyday concerns, they often focus on the realities of contemporary life. A student's analysis of a poem might explore how the poet's language and imagery reflect time and culture.

Literary History ☆

The Two Burials of Thomas Hardy Hardy fell ill with pleurisy in December 1927 and died in January 1928, after dictating a final poem to his wife. His funeral was controversial: while his family and friends wanted him to be buried in the English village of Stinsford, his executor insisted on burying him in Poet's Corner in Westminster Abbey. A compromise was reached whereby his heart was buried at Stinsford and his ashes were interred in the abbey.

English Learners

DIFFERENTIATED INSTRUCTION

Intermediate The language and mechanics of poetry may be particularly difficult for English learners. Assist them or have other students assist them with passages they do not understand. Also, have English learners select a stanza from their selected poems and, with the help of a dictionary or thesaurus, paraphrase the stanza in simpler language.

Teach

Writing Skills

Sharing a Discovery Tell students that in a strong essay the writer shares a discovery with the reader. It may be a deeper meaning in a poem, a connection to a current event, or an unusual insight. Recite E. M. Forster's quotation: "How can I know what I think till I see what I say?" While writing the essay, students should discover their own feelings and opinions about the poem they analyze.

Writing Skills

Understatement Ask students to define *hyperbole. (a figure of speech that expresses exaggeration)* Point out that *understatement* (saying less than what is meant) is the opposite. *("It seems a bit damp here," Mark said, wading through the tub overflow.)*

Writer's Technique ☆

Point of View A writer's point of view depends on the narrator, the audience, and the style of a piece. For example, academic writing is usually written in the third person. The point of view must be used consistently throughout a piece.

Organization ☆
Arrange the essay chronologically to show the moments as they occur in the poem, or choose another logical organizational pattern.

Support
Use examples and direct quotations from the text. When citing three or more lines, use long-quotation form.

Purpose/Focus
Analyze elements of a poem (such as understatement and irony) to show how they contribute to a broader theme.

Conclusion
Close your analysis with an interesting observation or insight.

"foe" at all, but simply a man who happened, like himself, to have drifted into the army:

> "He thought he'd 'list, perhaps,
> Off-hand like—just as I—
> Was out of work—had sold his traps—
> No other reason why. (lines 13–16)

At this point, the speaker having identified himself with the man he killed, convention would seem to suggest a revulsion from the killing, and a direct attack on war and the meaningless slaughter it involves. But this would take the poem outside the limited feeling and moral awareness of the speaker. Instead the speaker merely concludes:

> "Yes; quaint and curious war is!
> You shoot a fellow down
> You'd treat if met where any bar is,
> Or help to half-a-crown." (lines 17–20)

The summing up leading to the conclusion that war is "quaint and curious" suggests that the speaker has resolved his problem and will be no more troubled by it. But in the reader the aroused sense of wrong is in no way satisfied by the words "quaint and curious." Instead, by the drastic understatement of the last stanza, Hardy forces the reader to face up to the situation more or less on his own, and exacts that "full look at the worst" which is a necessary prelude to any possible "Better." Hence it is by the limitations of the speaker that the poem makes its point. But the limitations of the speaker give an additional edge of irony to the poem. For the irony is not simply that two men who have no quarrel should fire on each other, being trapped in the blind moilings of the "Immanent Will." There is the further irony that a decent man, such as the speaker, should not be more disturbed, should be able to appease his discomfort with the words "quaint and curious."

Reading-Writing Connection Think about the writing techniques in the model, and try them out in the response to literature you write.

Writing Practice

Transitional Phrases Encourage students to use transitional phrases to create a logical flow in their writing. Ask students to find transitional words and phrases in the Perkins essay and to volunteer other examples. When students have finished, write these on the board:

after all; as a result; at any rate; at the same time; by the way; even so; for example; in addition; in fact; in other words; instead; on the contrary; on the other hand

Tell students that using transitional phrases will help them communicate and connect their ideas more clearly.

Prewrite

Choose a Poem Think about the poems in the unit that you found moving or interesting. Review your purpose and audience.

Analyze the Poem Reread the poem several times, paying attention to the form, content, and meaning.

▶ **Explore Interpretations** Review your notes about the poem. Are you still wondering about any passages, ideas, or themes? What is your interpretation? Consider how your classmates interpreted the poem differently.

▶ **Analyze Important Elements** Consider specific elements of the poem, such as speaker, imagery, structure, mood, and sound devices. How do these elements enhance the poem's meaning?

Selection	"My Last Duchess," a poem by Robert Browning
Summary	duke and a count's emissary discuss the duke's possible marriage to the count's daughter
Speaker	the duke (dramatic monologue/first-person perspective)
Figurative Language	personification of the painting ("there she stands"); metaphors of ownership ("that piece," "my gift," "my object")
Imagery	the duke's speculation on Frà Pandolf's relationship with the duchess (to make her blush)
Structure	56 lines with regular rhythm, meter, and rhyme
Tone	duke's jealous, vengeful tone
Theme/ Meaning	strategies to flaunt power ultimately undermine it

Narrow Your Thesis Summarize your topic and your main idea in one or two sentences. Include the name of the poem, the name of the author, and the meaning or theme you will discuss.

Draw Conclusions and Elaborate Be sure to support your main points with relevant evidence and precise examples from the poem. Draw conclusions, explaining how the evidence supports them.

Make a Plan In the body of your essay, organize your main points in an effective, logical order. If you are analyzing a change that occurs in the poem, use chronological order. If you organize your analysis around essential literary elements, you may wish to use order of importance.

Exposition

Literary Present Tense

Use the present tense when you write about literature. Although the poem you analyze was written long ago, the text is continuously being introduced to new readers and is being reinterpreted by those already familiar with the poem.

Avoid Plagiarism

Do not fall prey to the temptation to download a paper from the Internet. A teacher can find the paper just as easily as you did, and the consequences for such dishonesty can range from a failing grade to suspension.

English Learners

DIFFERENTIATED INSTRUCTION

Beginning An essential part of understanding poetry is knowing that many English words can have multiple meanings. For example, the word *pool* has many different meanings:

- *n.* a small body of standing liquid
- *n.* billiards
- *v.* to combine resources

Pair English learners with English speakers to discuss their poems and to look for multiple meanings that words in the poems may have.

Teach

Writing Process

Prewrite After students have chosen their poems, have them reread their poems several times, taking notes on the title, the theme, and other interesting elements. Encourage students to consider freewriting their first draft. Ask them to use the topic as the title and then to write down everything they can about the topic. The idea is to write without stopping; students can correct their grammar and mechanical mistakes during the editing-and-proofreading step.

Writing Process

Prewrite Tell students to keep this in mind: if they find something interesting in their poems, their readers probably will as well.

Writing Process

Draft Students often dread this step in the writing process because they worry about paragraphing—arranging ideas into the introductory section, the body, and the conclusion. Tell students not to spend much time on organization at this stage. Drafting is not about perfection; it is about developing ideas.

Literary Analysis

Teach

Writing Process

Audience/Purpose Answer:
The summary provides an overview for those who might otherwise not understand the poem. The summary helps other readers recall the essential parts.

Writing Process

Thesis/Point of View Answer:
The thesis presents the writer's interpretation of the effect to be analyzed and elements that contribute to that interpretation.

Writing Process

Purpose Answer: *The writer shows how a specific element contributes to the theme or meaning of the poem. Because the writer mentions figurative language in the thesis, discussing personification here helps support the thesis.*

Writing Process

Explanaton Answer: *The writer shows readers how to recognize aspects of the Duke's character in his monologue.*

Writer's Audience ☆

Writers must write with the audience—the readers—in mind. A writer trying to persuade people to engage in community service, for example, would consider the attitudes, possible objections, and values of the audience so as to construct a persuasive argument. Students should write with a larger audience in mind than just the teacher.

970

Writing Frames

As you read the workshop model, think about the writer's use of the following frames:

- Through _____, <the author> reveals _____.

- In the opening lines of the poem, _____ begins by _____.

Consider using frames like these in your own literary analysis.

☆ **Audience**

Why does the writer summarize the poem in the introduction?

Thesis

What makes this statement an effective thesis?

Purpose/Focus

How does the use of personification strengthen the analysis?

Purpose

What makes this a strong main point? How does it relate to the thesis?

970 UNIT 5

Draft

Present and Support Your Points Present your major points in a straightforward, logical way, and support them with direct evidence from the poem. As you discuss the points, be sure to explain your evidence to the reader, clarifying how it supports your thesis.

Analyze a Workshop Model

Here is a final draft of a literary analysis. Use your answers to the questions in the margin to guide you as you write.

Power and Possession in "My Last Duchess"

In his poem "My Last Duchess," Robert Browning portrays the discussion between a duke and an emissary from a count over the duke's possible marriage to the count's daughter. The duke pauses to show the emissary a painting of the former duchess. Through the duke's first-person perspective, his arrogant, jealous tone, and the figurative language in "My Last Duchess," Browning reveals how the very strategies the duke uses to attain and demonstrate his power undermine that power in the end.

In the opening lines of the poem, the duke begins by confiding in the emissary, discussing his painting and its artist as if to show off his powerful position and valuable possessions. Rather than refer to the portrait as a *painting*, the duke speaks of it as "my last Duchess painted on the wall" (line 1), personifying the image as though it actually were his wife and not just a picture of her. The personification continues as he notes, "there she stands" (line 4) having drawn back the curtain only he controls ("none puts by / The curtain . . . but I," lines 9–10). By personifying the painting, the duke appears to possess not just the painting but also, literally, the woman.

"My Last Duchess" is a dramatic monologue in which the duke controls the discussion and tells only his version of events. Yet, through his monologue, the duke reveals his jealous and tyrannical nature, probably hurting his chance for remarriage. When the duke

---

Writing Practice

Abstract Versus Concrete Nouns To provide practice in using both abstract and concrete nouns, have students replace concrete nouns with abstract nouns and abstract nouns with concrete nouns. *(Possible answers follow.)*

1. *cold* (ice)

2. *death* (skull)

3. *victory* (trophy)

4. *blood* (violence)

5. *confetti* (celebration)

6. *candle* (illumination)

describes the painting in detail, his admiration for artist Frà Pandolf's work gives way to jealousy. The duke speculates on how the artist may have made the duchess blush for the painting by complimenting her: "perhaps / Frà Pandolf chanced to say . . . 'Paint / Must never hope to reproduce the faint / Half-flush that dies along her throat'" (lines 15–19). The duke's tone and speculation reveal his jealous suspicion at the thought of someone's having any power at all over what he feels is his alone.

This desire for complete control over the duchess becomes clear as the duke explains their relationship through a series of metaphors related to possession. The duke views her "approving speech" and "blush" as gifts that should be reserved for him alone, in return for his "gift of a nine-hundred-years-old name" (line 33). Even the duchess's "thanking" others threatens the duke, as the gesture represents both a "gift" from the duchess to another man and her autonomy. As the duke confesses, he refused to discuss his jealousy with her or "let / Herself be lessoned so, nor plainly set / Her wits to yours" (lines 39–41). He then explains, "—E'en then would be some stooping; and I choose / Never to stoop" (lines 42–43). The statements reinforce that the duke sees the duchess as his property. Any reasoning with her would imply she were an equal, and that would undermine the duke's power. Echoing his statement from line 2, he finally says of the painting, "There she stands / As if alive" (lines 46–47). The repetition and the duke's satisfied tone suggest that the painting is a perfect compromise; the duchess has literally become his object.

As the duke negotiates terms for the future marriage, he affirms that, despite talk of the dowry, the "fair daughter's self, as I avowed / At starting, is my object" (lines 52–53). At this point, the duke's use of the word *object* is clearly ironic; he means it literally. By flaunting his power and rank, the duke exposes himself to the emissary as a jealous tyrant. Like Neptune, the sea god he admires, the duke must dominate, and is therefore likely to destroy, anything that compromises his power.

Exposition

Support
How does the writer create a smooth flow of related ideas while presenting quoted evidence?

Support
What makes this evidence substantial, even though the writer quotes only a word or two at a time?

Interest/Audience
How do precise language and varied sentence structure make the paper more interesting?

Organization
What is the general organization of the paper? Why is it effective for this analysis?

Conclusion
What makes this a strong conclusion?

Advanced Learners

DIFFERENTIATED INSTRUCTION

Check Out Other Poets Ask students to compare the poems they have chosen with works by other poets. To find related poems, they can search online by typing key words such as *poetry* or *poems* into a search engine along with the appropriate theme, such as mourning, death, love, war, or isolation.

 Writing Workshop

Literary Analysis

Teach

Writing Process

Support Answer: *The writer shows readers how to infer much by reading "between the lines" of the Duke's monologue.*

Writing Process

Purpose Answer: *The writer analyzes subtleties, inferring the reason for a blush and what the Duke sees as a gift to his duchess.*

Writing Process

Language Answer: *The writer draws attention to the Duke's possessiveness and the baseless suspicions revealed in the his words.*

Writing Process

Support/Elaboration Answer: *The writer points to numerous examples of relevant evidence for his thesis and interprets their significance for the reader.*

Writing Process

Organization Answer: *The writer builds up gradually to the climax: the Duke's use of terms that convey his intense need to control. The listener, at this point, cannot fail to see the danger his next wife would be in.*

Writing Process

Conclusion Answer: *Reference to the much-admired mythological god Neptune points to the Duke's view of himself as godlike, entitled to dispense life and death at will— the real premise of the poem.*

971

Teach

Writing Process

Revise Suggest that students read their completed drafts aloud to themselves. Encourage them to let their ears tell them whether the language flows smoothly and whether the points follow one another in a logical sequence.

Writing Process

Peer Review Have students in pairs read their drafts aloud to each other. The listening partner should jot down notes based on the rubric on the student page.

Writer's Technique ☆

Organization Writers pay close attention during revision to the organization of the draft. Well-organized writing flows smoothly from one idea to another so that readers can easily follow the writer's argument. A clear focus on one idea in each paragraph, appropriate transitions, and arrangement of content around a central thesis are all important parts of well-organized writing.

 A scoring rubric for this Writing Workshop can be found in the Assessment section of *Florida Treasures Standards Road Map*.

972

Traits of Strong Writing

Include these traits of strong writing to express your ideas effectively.

Ideas
Organization ☆
Voice
Word Choice
Sentence Fluency
Convention
Presentation

For more information on using the Traits of Strong Writing, see pages R28–R30.

Word Choice

This academic vocabulary word appears in the student model:

strategies (stra′ tə gēz) *n.* 1. plans or methods; 2. hidden plans for achieving a goal; 3. military methods or plans; *Browning reveals how the very strategies the duke uses to attain and demonstrate his power undermine that power in the end.*

Using academic vocabulary may help strengthen your writing. Try to use one or two academic vocabulary words in your response to literature. See the complete list on pages R81–R83.

 **Literature** Online

Writing and Research For editing and publishing tools, go to glencoe.com and enter QuickPass code GLB9817u5.

Revise

Use the checklist below to help you evaluate and strengthen your essay.

Checklist

☑ Do you show how specific elements of the poem contribute to the overall meaning or theme?

☑ Do you present a concise thesis statement?

☑ Do you organize your main points in a logical, effective order?

☑ Do you quote accurately and coherently, and do you cite correctly?

☑ Do you use specific, relevant, and substantial supporting evidence?

☑ Do you vary sentences and use precise language?

▶ Focus Lesson

Rewrite Wordy Sentences

The most effective writing is straightforward, clear, and concise. Unnecessary wordiness often creates confusion and distracts readers. This is not to say that all sentences should be short or simple but that every word, sentence, and paragraph should count. When revising, omit redundant or unnecessary words and rewrite abstract, flowery sentences in a more straightforward style.

Draft:

At this point, there is no doubt but that[1] the duke's use of the word object is clearly ironic; the reason why is that[1] the duke[2] means it literally. The duke is a man who,[1] by flaunting his power and rank, exposes himself to the emissary as a jealous tyrant and despot.[3]

Revision:

At this point, the duke's use of the word *object* is clearly ironic; he means it literally. By flaunting his power and rank, the duke exposes himself to the emissary as a jealous tyrant.

1. **Avoid needless words or phrases**
2. **Use pronouns to eliminate unnecessary repetition.**
3. **Delete redundant words and phrases.**

972 UNIT 5 THE VICTORIAN AGE

Writing Practice

Revision As they revise and edit their essays, students should consider these questions for quality control:

- Do their sentences have good rhythm and construction?
- Are their verbs primarily active ones?
- Do they ever use a rhetorical question?
- Does sentence length vary?

- Have they chosen words that convey precisely what they want to say?

Edit and Proofread

Get It Right When you have completed the final draft of your essay, proofread it for errors in grammar, usage, mechanics, and spelling. Refer to the Language Handbook, pages R47–R59, as a guide.

> **Focus Lesson**
>
> ## In-Text Quotations from Poems ☆
>
> Enclose a direct quotation from a poem in quotation marks. Cite the line(s) in parentheses after the quotation, outside the quotation marks, and before the final punctuation. To indicate a line break, separate one line from the next with a slash. If you omit words from a quotation, use ellipses (. . .) to show the omission.

Original: The quotation does not indicate the line break, and it is not punctuated or placed correctly.

Echoing his statement from line 2, he finally says of the painting, "There she stands As if alive 46–47."

Improved: The quotation is punctuated and cited correctly.

Echoing his statement from line 2, he finally says of the painting, "There she stands / As if alive" (lines 46–47).

Original: The quotation does not indicate that words have been omitted from the original lines of the poem.

The duke notes that "none puts by / The curtain but I" (lines 9–10).

Improved: Ellipses show that words have been omitted.

The duke notes that "none puts by / The curtain . . . but I" (lines 9–10).

Present

Make It Legible and Neat If you write your essay by hand, use blue or black ink and neat, legible handwriting. If you are word-processing, double-check your teacher's manuscript or format guidelines.

Long Quotations

If you are quoting more than three lines of poetry, set them off as a long quotation (indented ten letter spaces). Do not use quotation marks unless they appear in the original poem. Cite line numbers in parentheses and place the citation *after* the end punctuation.

Peer Review Tips

A classmate may ask you to read his or her literary analysis. Take your time and jot down notes as you read so you can give constructive feedback. Use the following questions to get started:

- What is the writer's thesis? How well does the evidence support it?
- Does the writer increase your understanding of the poem?
- Where does the writer quote accurately, as well as most coherently?

Writer's Portfolio

Place a clean copy of your literary analysis essay in your portfolio to review later.

Approaching Level

DIFFERENTIATED INSTRUCTION

African American Vernacular English (AAVE) As students proofread their essays, have them double-check for errors that are commonly made, including these:

- to/too/two;
- they're/their/there;
- alot/a lot;
- lose/loose;
- lay/lie;
- then/than;
- "alright"/all right.

Students who are in doubt about standard usage of any of these words should consult a dictionary.

Teach and Assess

Writing Process

Edit and Proofread Encourage students to use the Proofreading Checklist on the inside back cover. Point out that some writers find errors in grammar by reading their essays aloud but that others prefer silent reading. Encourage students to try different techniques until they find one that suits them. Suggest that students read their essays several times, each time focusing on only one type of error, such as spelling, grammar, or word choice.

Writing Process

Proofread Discuss with students the reasons for proofreading. **Ask:** What can happen when mechanical errors appear in the final copy of an essay? (*Errors may result in misreading or distract readers from the content.*)

Writer's Technique ☆

Quotations Writers incorporate quotations into their writing as support but must avoid their overuse. Quotations should be used only if the meaning in a source might be lost in a paraphrase or when a quotation makes a particular impact.

Focus

Summary

In this workshop, students will learn techniques for effectively participating in a group discussion of a literary topic.

Teach

Speaking Skills

Practice Common Courtesies

Emphasize the need to observe common courtesies in a group discussion. Some common courtesies may be established by the whole class; individual and group assessment may be conducted periodically. Review the following list of courtesies with students:

- State opinions in a respectful manner.
- Address all members of the group.
- Avoid personal comments and intrusive questions.
- Express likes and dislikes with sensitivity.
- Avoid confrontation and argument.
- Speak in a clear, calm voice.
- Avoid repeating ideas needlessly.
- Always use common courtesy in scheduled classes and outside class.

 For help with creating presentations, see Student Presentation Builder on StudentWorks Plus.

 For Speaking, Listening and Viewing rubric, see Unit 5 Teaching Resources, pp. 170–171.

974

Learning Objectives

For pages 974–975
In this workshop, you will focus on the following objective:

Speaking and Listening:
Delivering an oral response to literature.

Speaking, Listening, and Viewing Workshop

Oral Response to Literature

Literature Connection Poetry is open to many interpretations. After reading a thought-provoking poem like "The Man He Killed," readers often enjoy discussing their thoughts and reactions. A group discussion is a useful way for people to share their responses to literature and enhance their understanding of a piece of writing.

Organize a Discussion Group

Assign roles to people in your group, such as facilitator and recorder.

> **Assignment** In groups, respond to and discuss the major themes of a literary work from Unit Five.

Each group member is equally responsible for discussion.

This chart will help you understand these roles:

Role	Duties
Leader/ Facilitator	• introduces the discussion topic • invites each participant to speak • keeps the discussion focused and interactive • keeps track of the time • helps participants arrive at a consensus
Group Participants (All)	• form ideas and questions about the literature before the discussion • contribute throughout the discussion • support any opinions with detailed references to the work • avoid repeating what has been said earlier • listen carefully to other group members • evaluate opinions of others • respect the opinions of others
Recorder	• keeps track of the most important points • helps the group leader form conclusions based on the discussion • helps summarize the discussion

Speaking Practice

Useful Vocabulary Impress upon students the importance of useful vocabulary for better speaking and listening in group situations. Clarity and precision are the keys to effective word choice. Students should strive to find direct and meaningful ways of communicating their ideas. To help students develop useful vocabulary, try the following:

- Maintain classroom charts on which students may record a growing list of synonyms for certain words.
- Have students keep individual word lists to extend their speaking vocabularies.

Prepare Your Response

- Reread the work, making careful note of its major themes.
- List ways to narrate, explain, or describe how the author expressed the themes. List details about speaker, structure, characters, setting, and other aspects of the poem that reveal theme.
- Reflect on whether the theme is universal and where you have encountered it in other works.
- List other stylistic choices, such as imagery and word choice, that help express the theme. List the varying connotations or nuances and connect them with the theme(s).
- Mine the text for ambiguous details to interpret in more than one way. Reflect on how these affect your understanding of the work.

Participate

Present your responses with confidence. Be sure to look around the group as you speak. Do not read your notes, but refer to them as needed to make detailed and accurate references to the work.

As you listen to others, analyze and evaluate what you hear. Follow these guidelines.

- Direct your attention to who is speaking. Listen actively to determine where your ideas and the ideas of the speaker diverge or converge.
- Respond to comments you do not understand by asking for elaboration or clarification. If you agree, say or show it.
- If you disagree, do so respectfully. Politely state your own ideas, providing evidence for them from the text.

Techniques for Discussing Oral Responses to Literature

Verbal Techniques	Nonverbal Techniques
☑ **Pace** Allow each group member time to voice his or her opinion before moving on to the next topic.	☑ **Listen** Remain quiet until it is your turn to speak.
☑ **Discuss** Ask open-ended questions to promote discussion.	☑ **Poise** Use nonverbal communication, such as nodding and eye contact, to show you understand the speaker.
☑ **Evaluate** After discussion, take some time to evaluate how you worked together.	☑ **Gestures** Avoid movements that may distract the speaker.

Time Limits

Set time limits for your group to ensure there's enough time for each idea or topic to be discussed.

Speaking Frames

Consider using the following frames in the group discussion:

- One reason for my opinion is found in the part of the work when _____.
- That's a good point. The part of the work in which _____ also demonstrates _____.
- I'm not sure I follow. Doesn't the passage/story/character/line/speaker say _____?

Presentation Tips

Use the following checklist to evaluate your group discussion.

- Did all group members demonstrate a thorough understanding of the work, both through presenting their own ideas and by responding to the ideas of others?
- Did all group members listen and respond respectfully?
- How could the discussion be improved the next time the group meets?

 **Literature** Online

Speaking, Listening and Viewing For project ideas, templates, and presentation tips, go to glencoe.com and enter QuickPass code GLB9817u5.

English Learners

DIFFERENTIATED INSTRUCTION

Intermediate Encourage students to use transitional words and phrases in group discussions. These words and phrases signal a relationship between new information and what has already been said.

Brainstorm with students to compile a list of these transition words and phrases and to create sentences using them.

- *cause/effect:* because, since, as a result, consequently, therefore, thus

- *contrast:* but, conversely, on the other hand
- *degree of importance:* above all, least of all, primarily

Teach
Listening Skills

Lend a Good Ear Read students a brief passage or recount a personal anecdote. Then ask key questions to test their ability to listen. **Ask:** What are some ways you can become a more effective listener? Encourage students to adopt the techniques on the student page, reminding them that the better they listen, the more they will learn and be able to contribute to a discussion.

Listening Skills

Peer Assessment Ask students to evaluate their group's ability to work together according to the following criteria:

- Did each group member have enough time and opportunity to voice his or her opinion?
- Did the group leader ask questions that promoted discussion?
- Were members respectful, listening without interruption until others finished speaking?
- Did members use nonverbal communication such as nodding and making eye contact to show that they understood the speakers?

Focus

Summary

The purpose of Independent Reading is to encourage students to read other novels from the time period that they have learned about in this unit.

Teach

Literary History ☆

Compare Novels Encourage students who have read British novels from the Victorian era to discuss the style and content of those books. **Ask:** What are the author's attitudes about people and the Industrial Age? What types of characters are portrayed in the book? Students might observe that, in Victorian novels, virtue is often rewarded and evil punished. Some Victorian authors criticized social problems such as child labor and neglectful orphanages. Victorian authors wrote about people of different classes but sometimes depicted the poor in a sentimental tone.

Reading Practice

SPIRAL REVIEW Analyze Author's Background Assign students to find and read a biography of one of the authors on this spread. **Ask:** How might the major events of this person's life have influenced his or her literary works? *(Answers will vary, depending upon the chosen author.)* Point out that authors

such as Dickens often wrote about social conditions similar to those that they had experienced.

Independent Reading

Novels dominated the literary scene in Victorian times, and many became wildly popular, turning their authors into celebrated public figures. Some of these works first appeared over several months as magazine installments. This delayed gratification only served to increase the public's interest, as readers waited eagerly for each new installment to appear.

Many of these novels, though, offered more than simple entertainment; they offered serious social commentary as well as insightful portraits of Victorian lives. Unlike the previous era's Romantic fictions, these novels were intended to be realistic depictions of life in Victorian England. The novel form remains tremendously popular, with modern novels ranging from realistic to fanciful in their subjects and styles.

Charles Dickens

Great Expectations

Charles Dickens

One of Dickens's most notable achievements, *Great Expectations* was also one of his last, completed just nine years before his death. The work explores the childhood and youth of Philip Pirrip, or Pip, as he is called, and the hardships he endures, largely at the hands of others. Told from a first-person perspective, the novel is an exploration of Pip's own mind and a depiction of the inequalities and the loss of human worth in England during the Industrial Revolution.

Middlemarch: A Study of Provincial Life

George Eliot

"George Eliot" was the pen name of Mary Ann Evans, one of the most prominent Victorian novelists. *Middlemarch*, widely considered Eliot's best novel, is true to its subtitle, for it offers a detailed and riveting portrait of provincial England in the nineteenth century. The plot revolves around the frustrations of its two main characters. A Victorian woman vainly seeking intellectual fulfillment, Dorothea Brooke resorts to marrying scholarly but pompous Edward Casaubon. Meanwhile, Tertius Lydgate, an idealistic young doctor, faces ruin and disgrace brought on by his beautiful but thoughtless wife.

A Tale of Two Cities

Charles Dickens

This classic novel follows Charles Darnay during the tumultuous and bloody years leading up to the French Revolution.

The Return of the Native

Thomas Hardy

Clym Yeobright, returning to his native region of England, marries a woman bent on leaving.

Wuthering Heights

Emily Brontë

A story of revenge, love, and obsession set in the desolate Yorkshire district of England, near the end of the eighteenth century.

CRITICS' CORNER

"[Jane Eyre], indeed, is a book after our own heart. . . . The story is not only of singular interest, naturally evolved, unflagging to the last, but it fastens itself upon your attention, and will not leave you. The book closed, the enchantment continues. . . . Reality—deep, significant reality—is the great characteristic of the book. It is an autobiography,—not, perhaps, in the naked facts and circumstances, but in the actual suffering and experience. The form may be changed, and here and there some incidents invented; but the spirit remains such as it was."

—George Henry Lewes, *Fraser's Magazine,*
December 1847

Jane Eyre ☆

Charlotte Brontë

Charlotte Brontë intertwines elements of Romanticism and Realism in her first published novel, *Jane Eyre.* As she tells the romantic tale of a poor, orphaned governess and her wealthy, brooding employer, Brontë provides lyrical glimpses into English provincial life. Given the realities of her world, Jane Eyre must choose between her romantic impulses and her moral duty. As a fine Victorian woman, she chooses the latter, with very dramatic—and romantic—results.

 Prepare an Interview

Read one of the books on this list and prepare an interview with its author, consisting of 5–7 questions about the book, the author's life, or any experiences that might have inspired the author's work. Share your questions with the class.

Approaching Level

DIFFERENTIATED INSTRUCTION

Emerging To help approaching level readers better understand the novels that they are reading, have them retell the plot to a classmate at the end of each chapter. Next, encourage students to write down the gist of their retellings. These notes should help them keep track of the many plots and characters that Victorian novels have in common.

Teach

 Prepare an Interview

Students' questions should relate to the author, including the author's experience.

Cultural History ☆

Women and Literature Explain that Charlotte Brontë and her sisters, Emily and Anne, first published their books under the pseudonyms Currer, Ellis, and Acton Bell, believing that their books would be taken more seriously if people thought that men had written them. When *Jane Eyre* was published, it soon became a bestseller and received many favorable reviews. Some critics, though, thought the subject matter too "coarse," especially for a female author.

Glencoe Literature Library

Glencoe Literature Library offers an extensive collection of hardcover books that help you encourage students to read independently. Choose from among the more than 120 full-length literary works—novels, novellas, plays, and nonfiction. Each book includes related readings from a broad range of genres. Go to www.glencoe.com for more information.

 For access to all study guides for the Glencoe Literature Library, see the Literature Library Teacher Resources CD-ROM.

 To create customized reading lists from a database of more than 30,000 titles, use BookLink K–12 CD-ROM.

Say: By now, you might be suffering from examination fatigue and beginning to view testing as an unnecessary ordeal. To help you come to grips with test taking, let's discuss why you think that we have standardized tests and put so much emphasis on performing well on them.

Teach

Assessment Explain that this section is intended to reinforce students' general test-taking strategies as well as to test the skills and vocabulary covered in the unit. Students will first be asked to read a nonfiction selection and to answer comprehension, context clues, and inference questions. Then they will be asked to complete ten vocabulary items, to answer ten questions on paragraph improvement, and finally to write a short literary analysis of a poem from this unit.

 To create custom assessments online, go to Progress Reporter Online Assessment.

 To create custom assessments using software, see ExamView Assessment Suite.

Assessment

English–Language Arts

Reading: Fiction

Carefully read the following passage. Use context clues to help you define any words with which you are unfamiliar. Pay close attention to the use of figurative language, argument, and the author's purpose. Then, on a separate sheet of paper, answer the questions on pages 979–980.

from *The New Railway* from *Dombey and Son* by Charles Dickens

line

The first shock of a great earthquake had, just at that period, rent the whole neighborhood to its center. Traces of its course were visible on every side. Houses were knocked down; streets broken through and stopped; deep pits and trenches dug in the ground; enormous heaps of earth and clay thrown up; buildings that were undermined and shaking, propped by great beams of wood. . . .

5 Everywhere were bridges that led nowhere; thoroughfares that were wholly impassable; Babel towers of chimneys, wanting half their height; temporary wooden houses and enclosures, in the most unlikely situations; carcasses of ragged tenements, and fragments of unfinished walls and arches, and piles of scaffolding, and wildernesses of bricks, and giant forms of cranes, and tripods straddling above nothing. There were a hundred thousand shapes and substances of incompleteness, wildly mingled

10 out of their places, upside down, burrowing in the earth, aspiring in the air, moldering in the water, and unintelligible as any dream. . . .

 In short, the yet unfinished and unopened railroad was in progress; and from the very core of all this dire disorder, trailed smoothly away, upon its mighty course of civilization and improvement.

 But as yet, the neighborhood was shy to own the railroad. . . . Nothing was the better for it, or

15 thought of being so. If the miserable waste ground lying near it could have laughed, it would have laughed it to scorn, like many of the miserable neighbors.

 Staggs's Gardens was uncommonly incredulous. It was a little row of houses, with little squalid patches of ground before them, fenced off with old doors, barrel staves . . . and dead bushes; with bottomless tin kettles and exhausted iron fenders, thrust into the gaps. Here, the Staggs's Gardeners

20 trained scarlet beans, kept fowls and rabbits, erected rotten summer-houses (one was an old boat), dried clothes, and smoked pipes. . . . Staggs's Gardens was regarded by its population as a sacred grove not to be withered by railroads; and so confident were they generally of its long outliving any such ridiculous inventions, that the master chimney-sweeper at the corner, who was understood to take the lead in the local politics of the Gardens, had publicly declared that on the occasion of the

25 railroad opening, if ever it did open, two of his boys should ascend the flues of his dwelling, with instructions to hail the failure with derisive jeers from the chimney-pots.

* * *

 There was no such place as Staggs's Gardens. It had vanished from the earth. Where the old rotten summer-houses once had stood, palaces now reared their heads, and granite columns of

---

Reading Practice

Identify Allusion Write on the board: *He was a veritable Hercules.* **Ask:** How is this statement an example of an allusion? *(The statement is an allusion in that it refers to a well-known person, place, thing, or event—in this case, a hero from Roman mythology.)* Explain that an allusion may refer to something in literature, history, religion, or modern culture. **Ask:** Why would writers want to use allusion in their works? *(Writers may use allusions to deepen the meaning of their works.)*

gigantic girth opened a vista to the railway world beyond. . . . The old by-streets now swarmed with
30 passengers and vehicles of every kind. . . .

As to the neighborhood which had hesitated to acknowledge the railroad in its struggling days,
that had grown wise and penitent . . . and now boasted of its powerful and prosperous relation. There
were railway patterns in its drapers' shops, and railway journals in the windows of its newsmen. There
were railway hotels, coffee-houses, lodging-houses, boarding-houses; railway plans, maps, views,
35 wrappers, bottles, sandwich-boxes, and timetables. . . . There was even railway time observed in
clocks, as if the sun itself had given in. Among the vanquished was the master chimney-sweeper . . .
who now lived in a stuccoed house three stories high, and gave himself out, with golden flourishes
upon a varnished board, as contractor for the cleansing of railway chimneys by machinery.

1. From the context, what do you conclude that the word *rent*, in line 1, means?
   (A) hired
   (B) torn
   (C) paid
   (D) chartered
   (E) withheld

2. Which of the following literary elements is Dickens using in the phrase *Babel towers of chimneys*, in lines 5–6?
   (A) allusion
   (B) alliteration
   (C) simile
   (D) understatement
   (E) personification

3. Which of the following literary elements is Dickens using in *There were a hundred thousand shapes and substances of incompleteness*, in line 9?
   (A) allusion
   (B) metaphor
   (C) simile
   (D) hyperbole
   (E) personification

4. Which of the following literary elements is Dickens using in the phrase *unintelligible as any dream*, in line 11?
   (A) allusion
   (B) metaphor
   (C) simile
   (D) hyperbole
   (E) personification

5. According to the second paragraph, to what does the word *earthquake*, in line 1, refer?
   (A) the effects of the unfinished railroad
   (B) the effects of long-term neglect
   (C) the poverty in this particular urban area
   (D) the destruction of a prosperous urban area
   (E) the destruction of a civilization

6. To what does the pronoun *its* in line 13 refer?
   (A) civilization
   (B) the railway
   (C) disorder
   (D) the neighborhood
   (E) Staggs's Gardens

7. In lines 22–26, how does Dickens reveal the master chimney-sweeper's personality?
   (A) by direct characterization
   (B) by indirect characterization
   (C) in metaphors
   (D) as a symbol
   (E) by personification

Assessment

Assess

1. **B** is correct. **E** is not a definition of *rent*, and **A, C,** and **D** do not fit the context of "shock" and "earthquake." [DOK 1]

2. **A** is correct: Dickens alludes to the biblical tower of Babel. The phrase uses no alliteration **(B)**, simile **(C)**, understatement **(D)**, or personification **(E)**. [DOK 2]

3. **D** is correct. There are no allusion **(A)**, no comparison **(B** or **C)**, or no human qualities of nonhuman things **(E)**. [DOK 2]

4. **C** is correct: a comparison of unlike things using the word *as*. There are no reference to a well-known name, no exaggeration, and no personification, so **A, D,** and **E** are incorrect. The phrase contains the word *as*, so it is not a metaphor **(B)**. [DOK 2]

5. **A** is correct. Paragraph 1 describes destruction, not neglect or poverty, so **B** and **C** are incorrect. The destruction of a prosperous urban area **(D)** or of civilization **(E)** is never mentioned. [DOK 1]

6. **B** is correct. *Its* modifies *course of civilization* so the pronoun cannot refer to civilization; thus **A** is incorrect. *Disorder* **(C)** makes no sense in this context. Neither the neighborhood nor Staggs's Gardens "trailed smoothly away," so **D** and **E** are also incorrect. [DOK 1]

7. **B** is the correct answer. The master chimney-sweeper's actions show his personality indirectly. There is no direct description of the character, so **A** is incorrect. There is no metaphor **(C)**, symbolism **(D)**, or personification **(E)**. [DOK 2]

Assess

8. **E** is the correct answer. He plans to instruct boys to "hail the failure" of the railroad. **B** and **D** contradict his attitude, and the paragraph makes no mention of improving commerce or destroying the neighborhood, so **A** and **C** are incorrect. ⟨DOK 4⟩

9. **E** is correct. There are no allusion, no comparison of unlike things, and no exaggeration, so options **A, B, C,** and **D** are incorrect. ⟨DOK 2⟩

10. **D** is correct. *Angry, unsure,* and *vengeful* do not fit with boasting about the railroad, and the passage does not mention perfection, so **A, B, C,** and **E** are incorrect. ⟨DOK 1⟩

11. **E** is correct. There are no allusion, metaphor, or exaggeration, so **A, B,** and **D** are incorrect. The words *as if* could appear in a simile, but the sun is not compared to anything. Thus **C** is incorrect. ⟨DOK 2⟩

12. **C** is correct. It is ironic that a man who scoffed at the railroad now earns his living from it. The sentence betrays no uncertainty, sadness, or bitterness, so **A, B,** and **D** are incorrect. The tone is not warm enough to be sympathetic, so **E** is incorrect. ⟨DOK 4⟩

13. **C** is correct. The narrator never uses *I* or *me,* so **A** is incorrect. **B** and **E** are incorrect because they are not points of view. The narrator does not see through the eyes of a single character, so **D** is incorrect. ⟨DOK 2⟩

8. What can you infer from the master chimney-sweeper's actions in lines 22–26?
   (A) He believes that the railroad will help improve commerce in Staggs's Gardens.
   (B) He is unaware of the railroad's existence.
   (C) He is in favor of the destruction of Staggs's Gardens.
   (D) He has never seen a railroad before.
   (E) He assumes that the railroad will fail.

9. Which of the following literary elements is Dickens using in the phrase *palaces now reared their heads,* in line 28?
   (A) allusion
   (B) metaphor
   (C) simile
   (D) hyperbole
   (E) personification

10. From the context, what do you conclude that the word *penitent,* in line 32, means?
   (A) angry
   (B) perfect
   (C) unsure
   (D) repentant
   (E) vengeful

11. Which of the following literary elements is Dickens using in the phrase *as if the sun itself had given in,* in line 36?
   (A) allusion
   (B) metaphor
   (C) simile
   (D) hyperbole
   (E) personification

12. What is the tone of the last sentence in this passage?
   (A) unsure
   (B) melancholic
   (C) ironic
   (D) bitter
   (E) sympathetic

13. From what point of view is this passage written?
   (A) first person
   (B) second person
   (C) third-person omniscient
   (D) third-person limited
   (E) ironic

14. On the basis of this passage, which of the following ideas do you think Dickens would most likely agree with?
   (A) It was a terrible crime for Staggs's Gardens to have been destroyed.
   (B) The risks associated with progress far outweigh any potential benefits.
   (C) Technological progress can bring many social and economic benefits.
   (D) There is no such thing as progress.
   (E) The railroads are a destructive force and have little merit.

15. What is the overall tone of this passage?
   (A) unsure
   (B) melancholic
   (C) ironic
   (D) bitter
   (E) confrontational

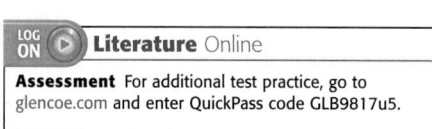

LOG ON **Literature** Online

Assessment For additional test practice, go to glencoe.com and enter QuickPass code GLB9817u5.

14. **C** is correct. The passage does not hint that destroying Staggs's Gardens was wrong, so **A** is incorrect. **B, D,** and **E** all contradict the main idea of the essay, so they are incorrect. ⟨DOK 4⟩

15. **C** is the correct answer. The writer's attitude is clearly not unsure, bitter, or confrontational, so **A, D,** and **E** are incorrect. Although the first paragraph may seem sad, the overall attitude is positive, so **B** is incorrect. ⟨DOK 4⟩

Vocabulary Skills: Sentence Completion

For each item in the Vocabulary Skills section, choose the word or words that best complete the sentence.

1. In many ways, the pessimism of the Naturalist movement was meant to _____ the Romantic view of nature.
   (A) countenance
   (B) advocate
   (C) blight
   (D) redress
   (E) dapple

2. Many in England failed to consider the _____ and widespread negative effects of the British Empire on the colonial peoples.
   (A) philosophical
   (B) extraordinary
   (C) vacant
   (D) dappled
   (E) trifling

3. The rise of literary Realism was _____ from Victorian social reform movements.
   (A) philosophical
   (B) fleet
   (C) vacant
   (D) dappled
   (E) inseparable

4. Victorian society, in general, opposed moral _____ and approved of personal restraint.
   (A) retaliation
   (B) demolition
   (C) license
   (D) threshold
   (E) countenance

5. The misery caused by the Industrial Revolution resulted in greatly increased governmental _____ and oversight.
   (A) threshold
   (B) scrutiny
   (C) munificence
   (D) demolition
   (E) countenance

6. Realism was both a reaction against the Romantic movement and a means through which to _____ social reform.
   (A) advocate
   (B) subside
   (C) license
   (D) blight
   (E) diffuse

7. Thomas Hardy's pessimism was a/an _____ conviction that arose from his experiences.
   (A) fleet
   (B) inseparable
   (C) dappled
   (D) trifling
   (E) philosophical

8. Victorians, who stood at the _____ of the modern era, expressed many modern ideas.
   (A) munificence
   (B) retaliation
   (C) threshold
   (D) countenance
   (E) demolition

9. As the Romantic movement _____, so did the portrayal of nature as divine.
   (A) subsided
   (B) retaliated
   (C) blighted
   (D) feigned
   (E) redressed

10. Some critics consider Dickens's writing melodramatic and his subjects occasionally _____ or silly.
    (A) vacant
    (B) trifling
    (C) dappled
    (D) fleet
    (E) extraordinary

Assess

1. **D** is correct. To say that pessimism was meant to "countenance" **(A)**, "advocate" **(B)**, "blight" **(C)**, or "dapple" **(E)** would make little sense. DOK 1

2. **B** is correct. *Philosophical, vacant,* and *dappled* effects make no sense in this context, so **A, C,** and **D** are all incorrect. *Widespread* suggests that it would not modify *trifling* **(E)**. DOK 1

3. **E** is correct. **A, B, C,** and **D** do not fit logically before *from* in this context. DOK 1

4. **C** is correct. The answer must contrast with *restraint,* so options **A, B, D,** and **E** are not correct. DOK 1

5. **B** is correct. Increased governmental *threshold* **(A)** or *countenance* **(E)** would make no sense. *Demolition* **(D)** might fit poor housing, not misery. *Munificence* **(C)** is not relevant to *oversight.* DOK 1

6. **A** is correct. To *subside* **(B)** or *blight* **(D)** social reform does not make grammatical sense. To *diffuse* **(E)** reform could mean to resist it, but Realism promoted social reform. To *license* **(C)** reform might mean to permit it, but *advocate* **(A)** is the better choice. DOK 1

7. **E** is correct. A conviction cannot be fleet **(A)**, dappled **(C)**, trifling **(D)** or inseparable **(B)**. DOK 1

8. **C** is correct. *Munificence* **(A)**, *retaliation* **(B)**, and *countenance* **(D)** make no sense in this context. *Demolition* **(E)** does not fit the beginning of an era. DOK 1

9. **A** is correct. Portraying nature does not fit with *retaliated* or *blighted,* so **B** and **C** are not good choices. *Feigned* and *redressed* are transitive verbs, so options **D** and **E** could not be correct. DOK 1

10. **B** is correct. *Vacant, dappled, fleet,* and *melodramatic* do not fit logically in this context, so **A, C, D,** and **E** are not correct. DOK 1

Assessment

Assess

1. C is the correct answer. A comma is missing after the long prepositional phrase. The essential appositive "Dover Beach" requires no commas, so option **A** is incorrect. Titles of short works should be enclosed in quotation marks, so option **B** is incorrect. A comma should separate coordinate adjectives, so **D** is incorrect. Because the sentence contains an error, **E** is incorrect. **DOK 2**

2. D is the correct answer. A comma is missing after the subordinate clause that begins this sentence. A comma should not separate the verb of a clause from the prepositional phrase that modifies it, so option **A** is incorrect. A semicolon can separate two independent clauses, but here dependent clauses precede *observation,* so **B** is incorrect. A comma should neither set off an introductory subordinating conjunction nor separate the subordinate clause from the word it modifies. Thus option **C** is incorrect. Because the sentence contains an error, option **E** is incorrect. **DOK 1**

3. D is correct: slash marks should show line breaks. **A** misplaces the citation, **B** italicizes a quotation, and **C** omits the citation and slashes. **E** is incorrect: there is an error. **DOK 1**

982

Grammar and Writing: Paragraph Improvement

Read carefully through the opening paragraphs from the first draft of a student's literary analysis. Pay close attention to the writer's use of **clauses, quotations,** and **punctuation.** Then, on a separate sheet of paper, answer the questions that follow.

(1) *In Matthew Arnold's brilliant, melancholy poem "Dover Beach" the speaker describes the physical sensations that he associates with the sea and the emotions that these sensations arouse.* (2) *Although the poem begins with imagery that is entirely derived from observation it expands to incorporate a broad subject.* (3) *The speaker states, "The sea is calm tonight. The tide is full, the moon lies fair Upon the straits" (lines 1–3).* (4) *These lines, however, serve only to initiate a powerful meditation on the nineteenth century's greatest intellectual struggles.*

(5) *The majority of the first stanza is fixed on one principle: simple observation of the physical world.* (6) *The final lines of this stanza, though, foreshadow the philosophical probing of the remaining stanzas.* (7) *"Begin, and cease, and then again begin, With tremulous cadence slow," writes Arnold, "and bring The eternal note of sadness in" (lines 12–14).* (8) *These lines, which describe the sounds of pebbles being washed up and down the shore, attract attention, and ensure recognition of the pebbles' symbolic importance.* (9) *The pebbles are our miseries.*

(10) *The next stanza confirms this symbol: "Into his mind the turbid ebb and flow / Of human misery (lines 17–18)."* (11) *Although this image seems to imply that the sea represents life the speaker changes course, thereby complicating the poem's theme.* (12) *The speaker claims, "The Sea of Faith / Was once, too, at the full" (lines 21–22).* (13) *The sea has become something explicitly more than simply "the sea."* (14) *It has come to represent the recession of belief and a place from which the speaker may contemplate humanity's earthly life.*

1. Which error, if any, appears in sentence 1?
   (A) The appositive "*Dover Beach*" is not set off with commas.
   (B) The title of the poem is quoted.
   (C) The long introductory phrase lacks a comma at the end.
   (D) A comma separates two adjectives.
   (E) No error appears in the sentence.

2. Which is the best way to revise sentence 2?
   (A) Insert a comma after *begins.*
   (B) Insert a semicolon after *observation.*
   (C) Insert commas after *Although* and *imagery.*
   (D) Insert a comma after *observation.*
   (E) Make no change.

3. Which is the best way to revise sentence 3?
   (A) The speaker states, "The sea is calm tonight. The tide is full, the moon lies fair Upon the straits (lines 1–3)."
   (B) The speaker states, *The sea is calm tonight. The tide is full, the moon lies fair Upon the straits* (lines 1–3).
   (C) The speaker states, "The sea is calm tonight. The tide is full, the moon lies fair Upon the straits."
   (D) The speaker states, "The sea is calm tonight. / The tide is full, the moon lies fair / Upon the straits" (lines 1–3).
   (E) Make no change.

Writing Practice

Topic Sentences Say: Define the role of the topic sentence. Help students conclude that a topic sentence is a sentence whose main idea or claim controls the rest of the paragraph. The other sentences in the paragraph explain, develop, or support the topic sentence.

On an overhead transparency or on handouts, have students identify the topic sentence of a passage. **Say:** Topic sentences help writers stay focused and keep paragraphs manageable. Topic sentences are also useful to readers as a guide through sometimes complex arguments.

4. Which error, if any, appears in sentence 7?
   (A) The citation appears outside quotation marks.
   (B) *Cease* is not capitalized.
   (C) *Cadence* is not capitalized.
   (D) Slash marks do not separate lines of poetry.
   (E) No error appears in the sentence.

5. Which is the best way to revise sentence 8?
   (A) Delete the comma after *attention*.
   (B) Change *which* to *that*.
   (C) Insert a comma after *recognition*.
   (D) Delete the comma after *lines*.
   (E) Make no change.

6. Which trait of strong writing is the student demonstrating in sentence 9?
   (A) ideas
   (B) oganization
   (C) voice
   (D) word choice
   (E) sentence fluency

7. Which error, if any, appears in sentence 10?
   (A) The colon should be a comma.
   (B) A citation appears within a quotation.
   (C) The slash mark is unnecessary.
   (D) The word *symbol* is unnecessary.
   (E) No error appears in the sentence.

8. Which error, if any, appears in sentence 11?
   (A) The subject and the verb do not agree.
   (B) No comma appears after the introductory clauses.
   (C) This is a sentence fragment.
   (D) This is a comma splice (run-on sentence).
   (E) No error appears in the sentence.

9. Which would be the most logical topic for an additional concluding paragraph?
   (A) a discussion of the stanzas following those already discussed
   (B) Arnold's poetic influences
   (C) the historical importance of Dover Beach
   (D) the literary importance of Arnold's poem "Dover Beach"
   (E) the author's feelings about "Dover Beach"

10. Which sentence would make the strongest conclusion?
   (A) Without the power of faith, as Arnold so powerfully demonstrates, there can be no hope in a world where "ignorant armies clash by night."
   (B) The miseries we experience today are the same as those experienced in Arnold's day.
   (C) In "Dover Beach," Arnold elegantly weaves together observations of the natural world with a discussion of the erosion of faith during the Victorian era.
   (D) "Dover Beach" forces readers to observe their own smallness in relation to the larger world and the way in which that world is filled with the "eternal note of sadness."
   (E) Arnold's "Dover Beach" is unsurpassed in its examination of nature's power to inspire.

Essay

Write a short literary analysis of a poem from this unit. Be sure to support your opinions with evidence from the text of the poem. As you write, keep in mind that your essay will be checked for **ideas, organization, voice, word choice, sentence fluency, conventions,** and **presentation.**

Assessment

Assess

4. **D** is correct: slash marks should show line breaks. **A** is incorrect: the citation is proper. **B** and **C** add extra capital letters. **E** fails to add slash marks. `DOK 2`

5. **A** is correct: the comma interrupts a compound predicate. A nonrestrictive clause needs *which* and commas, so **B** and **D** are incorrect. **C** separates a phrase from the word it modifies. **E** retains the comma. `DOK 1`

6. **E** is correct: the short sentence contrasts dramatically with its context. Sentence 9 does not add to ideas, organization, voice, or word choice, so **A, B, C,** and **D** are poor choices. `DOK 2`

7. **B** is correct: the citation belongs outside the quotation marks. The other punctuation is proper, so **A** and **C** are incorrect. *Symbol* avoids a vague pronoun reference, so **D** is incorrect. There is an error, so **E** is incorrect. `DOK 2`

8. **B** is correct: a comma belongs after the introductory clauses. **A** is incorrect: all verbs and subjects agree. **C** is incorrect: the main clause has a subject and a verb. **D** is incorrect: a run-on contains at least two independent clauses. There is an error, so **E** is incorrect. `DOK 2`

9. **A** is correct: the essay's order thus far follows the order of the poem. Arnold's influences and the beach itself are outside the topic, so **B** and **C** are incorrect. The essay is about the poem's meaning, so its importance **(D)** or the poet's feelings **(E)** are not relevant. `DOK 4`

10. **C** is correct: restating the thesis creates a strong conclusion. **A, B,** and **D** introduce ideas not developed in the essay. **E** fails to mention the symbolism the essay develops. `DOK 4`

Essay

Answers will vary but should be supported with evidence from the text of the poem. `DOK 3`

Skills Scope and Sequence

Readability Scores Key: Dale-Chall/DRP/Lexile

PART 1: Class Conflict, Colonialism, and the Great War

Selections and Features	Literary Elements
Unit Introduction pp. 984–998	Modernism **SE** pp. 994–995
Comparing Literature **A Cup of Tea** (short story), by Katherine Mansfield **5.7/53/650**, **Village People** (essay), by Bessie Head **6.3/54/820**, **The Parable of the Lazarus and the Rich Man** (parable) **5.8/60/990**, and *from* **The Qur'an** (sacred text) pp. 1000–1018	Motivation **SE** p. 1002
Informational Text TIME: **Down and Out in Europe,** by Aparisim Ghosh **9.9/66/1140** pp. 1019–1023	
Literary History The Modern British Short Story pp. 1024–1025	Short Story **SE** pp. 1024–1025 Realism **SE** p. 1024 Modernism **SE** p. 1025
Short Story Miss Youghal's Sais, by Rudyard Kipling **8.2/61/1100** pp. 1026–1034	Narrator **SE** p. 1027 Characterization **TE** p. 1032 Conflict (review) **SE** p. 1033
Essay Shooting an Elephant, by George Orwell **5.5/60/1060** pp. 1035–1045	Symbol **SE** p. 1036 Thesis (review) **SE** p. 1044
Grammar Workshop p. 1046	
Poem Dreamers, by Siegfried Sassoon pp. 1047–1050	Title **SE** p. 1048

Reading Skills and Strategies	Vocabulary	Writing / Grammar	Speaking, Listening, Viewing
Analyze Historical Context **SE** pp. 984–998 Analyze Graphic Information **SE** pp. 987, 989 Make Generalizations **TE** p. 988 Identify Cause and Effect **TE** p. 990 Compare and Contrast **SE** p. 998	Context Clues **TE** p. 996	Create a Graphic Organizer **TE** p. 994 Write a Biographical Narrative **TE** p. 998	Collage **TE** p. 992 Exhibit **SE** p. 998
Compare and Contrast **SE** p. 1000 Connect to Contemporary Issues **SE** p. 1002 Identify Author's Purpose **TE** p. 1002	Analogies **SE** p. 1010	Write a Character Analysis **TE** p. 1008 Write a Story **SE** p. 1010 Write a Comparison-Contrast Essay **SE** p. 1018	Analyze Art **SE** pp. 1006, 1014 Discussion **SE** pp. 1013, 1017, 1018 Visual Display **SE** p. 1018
Analyze Text Structure **SE** p. 1019 Preview **SE** p. 1019 Analyze Solutions **TE** p. 1020 Summarize **TE** p. 1024		Write a List **TE** p. 1022 Write a Summary **SE** p. 1023	
Analyze Characters **SE** p. 1027 Make Predictions **TE** p. 1028	Word Parts **SE** p. 1034 Academic Vocabulary **SE** p. 1034	Write a Character Analysis **TE** p. 1030 Write a Research Report **SE** p. 1034	
Analyze Cause-and-Effect Relationships **SE** p. 1036 Compare and Contrast **TE** p. 1036 Use Graphic Organizers **TE** p. 1038	Analogies **SE** p. 1044 Academic Vocabulary **SE** p. 1044	Write an Expository Essay **TE** p. 1040, **SE** p. 1045 Write a Literary Analysis **TE** p. 1042 Dashes **SE** p. 145	Analyze Art **SE** p. 1042
	Word Parts **TE** p. 1046	Coordinating Conjunctions **SE** p. 1046	
Compare and Contrast Imagery **SE** p. 1048 Activate Prior Knowledge **TE** p. 1048	Context Clues **SE** p. 1050	Write a Poem **SE** p. 1050	

Readability Scores Key: Dale-Chall/DRP/Lexile

PART 1: Class Conflict, Colonialism, and the Great War *(continued)*

PART 2: Modernism

Reading Skills and Strategies	Vocabulary	Writing / Grammar	Speaking, Listening, Viewing
Recognize Author's Purpose **SE** p. 1052 Make Predictions **TE** p. 1052	Synonyms **SE** p. 1054	Write a Summary **SE** p. 1054	
Synthesize Information **SE** p. 1055		Write a Summary **SE** p. 1058	

Reading Skills and Strategies	Vocabulary	Writing / Grammar	Speaking, Listening, Viewing
Draw Conclusions About Author's Meaning **SE** p. 1061 Analyze Text Structure **TE** p. 1062	Academic Vocabulary **SE** p. 1063	Write a Brochure **SE** p. 1063	
Analyze Figurative Language **SE** p. 1064	Academic Vocabulary **SE** p. 1069	Write a Poem **TE** p. 1066 Write an Expository Essay **SE** p. 1070 Transitional Expressions **SE** p. 1070	Discussion **SE** p. 1068 Oral Response to Literature **TE** p. 1070
Analyze Style **SE** p. 1072 Preview **TE** p. 1072	Word Usage **SE** p. 1076 Academic Vocabulary **SE** p. 1076	Write a Poem **SE** p. 1076	Media Presentation **TE** p. 1074
Make Inferences About Characters **SE** p. 1078 Preview **TE** p. 1078 Question **TE** p. 1082	Analogies **SE** p. 1092 Academic Vocabulary **SE** p. 1092	Write a Literary Analysis **TE** p. 1080 Write a Journal Entry **TE** p. 1086	Analyze Art **SE** p. 1086 Oral Interpretation **TE** p. 1090 Literature Group **SE** p. 1092
Make and Verify Predictions **SE** p. 1094 Preview **TE** p. 1094 Summarize **TE** p. 1096	Antonyms **SE** p. 1101 Academic Vocabulary **SE** p. 1101	Write an Autobiographical Narrative **TE** p. 1098 Evaluate Literary Criticism **SE** p. 1101	Analyze Art **SE** p. 1098
	Word Origins **SE** p. 1102		
Analyze Tone **SE** p. 1104 Preview **TE** p. 1104	Word Origins **SE** p. 1110 Academic Vocabulary **SE** p. 1110	Write a Literary Analysis **TE** p. 1106 Verb Tense **TE** p. 1108	Analyze Art **SE** p. 1107 Debate **SE** p. 1110

PART 3: World War II and Its Aftermath

Reading Skills and Strategies	Vocabulary	Writing Grammar	Speaking, Listening, Viewing
Distinguish Fact and Opinion **SE** p. 1113	Context Clues **SE** p. 1119 Academic Vocabulary **SE** p. 1119 Loaded Words **SE** p. 1120	Write an Inspirational Speech **SE** p. 1119	Analyze Art **SE** p. 1116 Analyze Speech **TE** p. 1116
Analyze Sensory Details **SE** p. 1122 Preview **TE** p. 1122	Denotation and Connotation **TE** p. 1128 Word Usage **SE** p. 1130	Create a Graphic Organizer **TE** p. 1124 Create a Timeline **TE** p. 1126 Write an Article **SE** p. 1130	Analyze Art **SE** p. 1123
Clarify Meaning **SE** p. 1132 Preview **TE** p. 1132 Analyze Free Verse **TE** p. 1134	Analogies **SE** p. 1137 Academic Vocabulary **SE** p. 1137	Write a Research Report **SE** p. 1137	Analyze Art **SE** p. 1133
Evaluate Comic Devices **SE** p. 1139	Synonyms **SE** p. 1144	Write an Internal Monologue **SE** p. 1144	Analyze Art **SE** p. 1140 Tell a Story **TE** p. 1142
		Run-on Sentences **SE** p. 1145 Coordinating Conjunctions **TE** p. 1145	
Analyze Figures of Speech **SE** p. 1147	Analogies **TE** p. 1150 Context Clues **SE** p. 1152 Academic Vocabulary **SE** p. 1152	Write an Expository Essay **SE** p. 1153 Hyphens **SE** p. 1153	Discussion **SE** p. 1151
		Write a Character Sketch **TE** p. 1156 Prewrite **SE** p. 1158 Draft **SE** p. 1158 Revise **SE** p. 1160 Use Action Verbs **SE** p. 1160 Sentence Length **TE** p. 1160 Sentence Fragments **SE** p. 1161 Write a Short Story **SE** p. 1161	
		Write a Script **TE** p. 1162	Performance of a Short Story **SE** p. 1163
		Analyze Literary Criticism **TE** p. 1164	Visual Presentation **SE** p. 1165
		Write a Comparison-Contrast Essay **SE** p. 1171	

Bellringer Options

Literature Launchers: Pre-Reading Videos DVD: Unit 6

Daily Language Practice Transparency 82

Or on the board, write: The Modern Age

Say: Think about the word *modern*. **Ask:** What are some synonyms of *modern*? *(new, up-to-date, latest, contemporary)* Draw a word web on the board with *modern* at the center. **Ask:** Do you think the word *modern* has any negative connotations? *(Students may mention the dehumanizing effects of industrialization and technology.)*

 For school-to-home activities, see Unit 6 Teaching Resources Book, pp. 5–11.

 For students who would profit from independent novel study, see Novel Companion pp. 275–330.

Interior with a Table, 1921. Vanessa Bell. Oil on canvas. 21¼ x 25¼ inches. Tate Gallery, London. ©1961 Estate of Vanessa Bell. Courtesy of Henrietta Garnett.

View the Art Vanessa Bell, the older sister of writer Virginia Woolf, was a member of a circle of Modernist writers and artists called the Bloomsbury group. From this image, what qualities or ideas can you infer Modernist painters considered important?

984

Unit Introduction Skills

Reading Skills
- Analyze Graphic Information (SE pp. 987, 989)
- Analyze Cause and Effect (SE p. 993)
- Interpret (SE p. 995)
- Compare and Contrast (SE p. 997)

The Modern Age

Listening/Speaking/Viewing Skills
- Analyze Art (SE pp. 984, 995)
- Build Visual Literacy (SE p. 998)

Study Skills/Research/Assessment
- Use Online Resources (TE p. 986)

Writing Skills/Grammar
- Author Essay (SE p. 998)

THE MODERN AGE

1901–1950

Looking Ahead

When the twentieth century began, Britain was at the height of its power. During the next half century, the British endured bitter class conflict, two world wars, global economic depression, and growing demands for independence among the colonial peoples they ruled. This period of profound change also witnessed the emergence of powerful Modernist writers, who modified and broke away from the forms and traditions of British literature.

Keep the following questions in mind as you read:

▶ How did World Wars I and II impact British literature?

▶ How was class conflict represented in British literature?

▶ How did attitudes toward the British Empire begin to change during this period?

▶ What were some major characteristics of Modernism?

985

UNIT SIX

Focus

Summary

This introduction gives an overview of British literature and world events from 1901 to 1950. It addresses the reaction of Modern writers to ideas that reinforced class boundaries, distribution of wealth, and imperialism. The Modernist saw humans as increasingly alienated and the sociopolitical order as something false and fragmenting.

View the Art ★

Possible answer: *Vivid, solid colors, bold brush strokes, and lack of specific and realistic details.*
Vanessa Bell (1879–1961) was a member of the Bloomsbury Group, which consisted of writers, artists, and economists who met in a London section called Bloomsbury. These intellectuals exerted influence on British life between 1905 and World War II and even helped bring about England's voluntary withdrawal from its colonial empire. Bell's work sprang from European art trends that emphasized personal vision and artistic license over the Impressionist ideal of raw naturalism.

Unit Resources

Print Materials

- Unit 6 Teaching Resources, pp. 1–279
- Interactive Read and Write (On Level/ Approaching, EL), pp. 257–296
- Novel Companion, pp. 275–330
- Bellringer Option Transparencies: Selection Focus 50–62; Daily Language Practice 82–99

- Literary Element Transparencies 12, 52, 86, 97
- Assessment Resources, Unit Assessment, pp. 323–324
- Assessment Resources, Selection Assessment, pp. 241–276

Technology

- TeacherWorks Plus CD
- StudentWorks Plus CD
- Literature Launchers: Pre-Reading Videos DVD, Unit 6
- Literature Online
- Visual Vocabulary CD-ROM
- Listening Library CD-ROM
- ExamView CD-ROM
- Skill Level Up! CD-ROM

Teach

Reading Strategy | 1

Use the Timeline
Have students examine the timeline and relate key events in British literary history to British and world history.

- Explain that Queen Victoria's death in 1901 marks the symbolic end of an era of convention and, to some degree, hypocrisy.
- Point out the number of entries related to women's rights (union in 1903, voting in 1918, *A Room of One's Own* in 1929)
- Explain that T. S. Eliot's poem *The Waste Land* portrayed the human condition as bleak and lonely.

Ask: What major historic event might have caused Eliot and others to view life so pessimistically? (*World War I*)

Literary History ☆

The Waste Land Point out that T. S. Eliot's poem *The Waste Land* is seen as a hallmark of Modernism. It defied poetic conventions of rhythm, rhyme, and imagery, and some saw it as "unpoetic."

TIMELINE 1901–1950 ①

BRITISH LITERATURE

1900

1901
Rudyard Kipling publishes *Kim*

1907
Rudyard Kipling wins Nobel Prize in Literature

1913
George Bernard Shaw's *Pygmalion* is first produced

1914
Modernist journal *Blast* begins publication ▼

1920

1917
William Butler Yeats publishes *The Wild Swans at Coole*

1918
Siegfried Sassoon publishes *Counter-Attack*

1920
Wilfred Owen's *Collected Poems* is published

1922
Katherine Mansfield publishes *The Garden Party*

1922
T. S. Eliot publishes *The Waste Land* ☆

1922
James Joyce publishes *Ulysses*

BRITISH EVENTS

1900

1901
Queen Victoria dies; Edward VII becomes king

1902
Boer War ends in South Africa

1903
Women's Social and Political Union is formed

1909
Old-age pension is introduced

1912
Luxury liner *Titanic* sinks

1915
Germans sink British liner *Lusitania*

1916
Easter Rebellion occurs in Dublin

1918 ▲
British women over the age of thirty gain voting rights

1920

1922
Irish Free State is established

1922
BBC begins radio broadcasts

1924
First Labour government is formed

WORLD EVENTS

1900

1903
In United States, Orville and Wilbur Wright make first successful airplane flight

1905 ▶
Einstein publishes special theory of relativity

1911
Manchu Dynasty falls in China

1914
World War I begins

1917
United States enters World War I

1918
World War I ends

1920

1922 ▶
King Tut's tomb is discovered in Egypt

LOG ON ▶ Literature Online

Literature and Reading To explore the Interactive Timeline, go to glencoe.com and enter QuickPass code GLB9817u6.

Research Practice

Use Online Resources Have students identify on the timeline an event that they would like to learn more about. Discuss appropriate resources for the information and how sources should be credited. Share this example:

"In August of 1900, Wilbur built his first glider. He then contacted the U.S. Weather Bureau for information on windy regions of the country." © 2003, The Henry Ford Museum.

Point out the two parts of the entry: the article excerpt and the copyright information. Have students write short research papers about the events they have chosen.

1925

1925 ▲
George Bernard Shaw wins
Nobel Prize in Literature

1929
Virginia Woolf publishes
A Room of One's Own

1930
W. H. Auden publishes
Poems

1931
Virginia Woolf publishes
The Waves ▼

1940

1945
George Orwell publishes
Animal Farm ▶

1945
Elizabeth Bowen publishes
The Demon Lover

1946
Dylan Thomas publishes
Deaths and Entrances

1948
T. S. Eliot wins Nobel
Prize in Literature

1949
George Orwell publishes
Nineteen Eighty-four

1925

1926
General strike begins

1928
Alexander Fleming
discovers penicillin

1936
King Edward VIII
abdicates; George VI
becomes king

1940

◀ **1940**
Winston Churchill
becomes prime minister ☆

1940
Battle of Britain begins

1945
Clement Attlee becomes
prime minister

1946
National Health Service
is established

1947
Princess Elizabeth marries
Duke of Edinburgh

1925

1927 ▲
Charles Lindbergh makes
first transatlantic solo
flight

1929
Great Depression begins

1930
Gandhi leads Salt March
in India

1940

1933
Adolf Hitler becomes
German chancellor

1936
Spanish Civil War begins

1937
Japan invades China

1939
World War II begins

1945
United States drops
atomic bombs on two
Japanese cities; World
War II ends

1945
United Nations is
established

Reading Check

Analyze Graphic Information What major British
literary works were published in 1922?

Teach

Reading Check

Answer: The Garden Party *by
Katherine Mansfield*, The Waste
Land *by T. S. Eliot*, Ulysses *by
James Joyce*

Political History ☆

Winston Churchill German
aggression led to the invasion of
Poland in 1939. Shortly thereafter,
France and Great Britain declared
war on Nazi Germany. In 1940
Winston Churchill rallied a nation
at arms. "If the British . . . last for
1,000 years, men will still say 'This
was their finest hour.'" For a year,
Britain stood alone. Defying overwhelming odds, the Royal Air Force
won the air battle against Germany,
preventing a land invasion. The
people persevered despite the
continual bombing of London and
other cities—bombings that killed
60,000 civilians. The Soviet Union
and the United States entered the
war in 1941, and the tide slowly
turned toward Allied victory.

Approaching Level

DIFFERENTIATED INSTRUCTION 🐟

Established Explain that locating
comparable events on a timeline can
provide an understanding of progress over
a period of time. **Ask:** How many years
after the Wright brothers made the first
airplane flight did Lindbergh make the
first transatlantic solo flight? *(24 years)*
Ask: What other event shows that much
effort was put into flight technology?

(United States drops atomic bombs.) How
did the flights of the Wright brothers
and Lindbergh influence events of World
War II? Invite volunteers to ask and answer
questions based on the timeline.

987

Teach

Reading Strategy | 1

Make Inferences Draw students' attention to the chart "World War I Casualties." **Ask:** What can you infer about the impact of World War I on Europe compared with its impact on the United States? *(Students should see that because of the far higher number of casualties suffered by European combatants, the war had a more devastating impact on Europe.)*

Cultural History ☆

Spanish Flu The influenza outbreak, also called the Spanish influenza epidemic, is really classified as a pandemic, meaning it affected a wide geographic area and a significant percentage of the population. It is believed that the virus originated in the United States and appeared in Europe when U.S. soldiers began arriving to fight in World War I. Over the next few years, the virus quickly spread throughout the world, facilitated by congested cities and improved transportation.

BY THE NUMBERS

World War I Casualties 1

ALLIED POWERS					
	TOTAL FORCES	TOTAL DEATHS	WOUNDED	PRISONERS AND MISSING	TOTAL CASUALTIES
Russia	12,000,000	1,700,000	4,950,000	2,500,000	9,150,000
British Empire	8,904,467	908,371	2,090,212	191,652	3,190,235
France	8,410,000	1,357,800	4,266,000	537,000	6,160,800
Italy	5,615,000	650,000	947,000	600,000	2,197,000
United States	4,355,000	116,516	204,002	4,500	323,018

CENTRAL POWERS					
	TOTAL FORCES	TOTAL DEATHS	WOUNDED	PRISONERS AND MISSING	TOTAL CASUALTIES
Germany	11,000,000	1,773,700	4,216,058	1,152,800	7,142,558
Austria-Hungary	7,800,000	1,200,000	3,620,000	2,200,000	7,020,000

Source *U.S. War Department, reprinted in Encyclopaedia Britannica*

SINKING OF THE *TITANIC*

On the night of April 14, 1912, the British luxury liner *Titanic* struck an iceberg in the North Atlantic and sank two hours and forty minutes later. Of the 2,224 passengers and crew aboard, more than 1,500 people drowned or froze to death in the icy water.

THE EVACUATION OF DUNKIRK

In late May 1940, a rapid German advance trapped a large force of British and French troops at Dunkirk on the French coast. Using a fleet of 41 large destroyers and 900 civilian boats, which ferried troops to the larger vessels, the British rescued 338,000 British and French troops.

PACKAGES FROM HOME

During World War I, British civilians sent their troops 1,742,947 scarves, 1,574,155 pairs of mittens, 6,145,673 hospital bags, 12,258,536 bandages, and 16,000,000 books.

PANDEMIC ☆

In 1918 and 1919, an influenza epidemic spread around the world with devastating results. In Britain, 228,000 people died, the highest death rate since a cholera epidemic in 1849. It has been estimated that 22 million people—or more than twice the number of people killed in World War I—died from influenza.

BOMB DAMAGE

At the end of World War II, in 1945, 700,000 London-area houses damaged by German bombs and rockets still needed repair. There were also 42,000 houses too damaged to be habitable.

VACATION TIME

During the 1920s, 1,500,000 British workers received a vacation with pay. By 1938, this figure had doubled. The Holidays with Pay Act (1938) increased the number of British workers entitled to paid vacations to 11 million in the following year.

Reading Practice

Make Generalizations Remind students that a generalization is a broad statement about a group of ideas based on a study of some of its members. **Ask:** What generalization can you make about the modern age? *(The modern age was a time of great death and destruction.)* Explain that it is important to check the validity of generalizations. Have students cite other facts that validate the generalization.

A Bomb damage in central London, October 1941. Achille Beltrame. Engraving in Italian newspaper *La Domenica del Corriere.*

BEING THERE

2 During World War I, the principal area of combat for British troops was the Western Front, where parallel systems of trenches stretched from the North Sea to the border of Switzerland.

B *The Entrance Hall, Savoy Hotel, London,* c. twentieth century. English School. Coloured lithograph.Bibliothèque des Arts Décoratifs, Paris.

C English trenches along the Western Front in WWI.

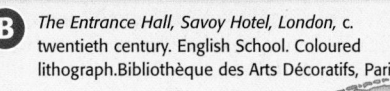

NORTH SEA

Birmingham

UNITED KINGDOM

NETHERLANDS

Bristol • London **A**
B

Portsmouth •

Strait of Dover

Brussels •
BELGIUM

GERMANY

LUXEMBOURG

English Channel

X Battle of the Somme

C

Le Havre •

Western Front, 1915

Paris •

FRANCE

Literature Online

Literature and Reading For more about the history and literature of this period, go to glencoe.com and enter QuickPass code GLB9817u6.

Reading Check

Analyze Graphic Information

1. What was the total number of British forces engaged in World War I who died of wounds, disease, or other causes?

2. Compared with workers in the 1920s, how many additional British workers received paid vacations in 1939 as a result of the Holidays with Pay Act?

3. In what country was most of the Western Front located?

Teach

Reading Check

Answers:

1. *908,371*

2. *9,500,000 additional workers*

3. *France*

Reading Strategy 2

Make Generalizations Point out that the map and illustrations show England's proximity to the World War battles in the first half of the twentieth century. **Ask:** How did the world wars affect life in England? *(The wars were fought on England's doorstep and affected the nation profoundly. In fact, England was bombed in World War II.)*

View the Art ★

A. At one point early in the war, German air raids against London went on for 57 consecutive nights.

B. The luxurious Savoy Hotel in London was the first hotel to feature private bathrooms within guests' rooms.

C. To avoid the onslaught of bullets and artillery, soldiers dug trenches into the ground for their protection. These trenches dominated the landscape of the Western Front during World War I.

English Learners

DIFFERENTIATED INSTRUCTION

Intermediate Have English learners look at the photographs on the page. Point out that the photographs show both military and civilian life. Then have students work in pairs to describe what they see in the photos. Have them discuss the different ways soldiers and civilians experience war.

Teach

Make Generalizations Have students read only the subheadings on these two pages. **Ask:** What generalization about the modern age can you make after reading the subheads on these pages? *(The period was a time of great upheaval, conflict, and change.)*

Political History ☆

Adolf Hitler In 1933, Adolf Hitler, head of the National Socialist German Labor Party (or Nazi Party), was elected chancellor of Germany on a platform of rabid nationalism and vengeance. The Treaty of Versailles, which Germany was forced to sign after World War I, required that it make expensive reparations to nations it had invaded and harmed. Hitler was against paying this economically crippling debt, and many Germans agreed. He quickly gained power and his army swept through Europe, conquering countries in just days in a *blitzkrieg,* or "lightning war." When he invaded Poland in 1939, Britain and France declared war.

Learning Objectives

For pages 984–998
In studying this text, you will focus on the following objectives:

Literary Study:
Analyzing literary periods.
Analyzing literary genres.

Reading:
Evaluating historical influences.
Connecting to the literature.

THE MODERN AGE 1901–1950

Historical, Social, and Cultural Forces

The British Empire 1

At its peak in the early twentieth century, the British Empire included about one-quarter of the world's people. Increasing nationalism in the colonies, however, challenged British rule. Ireland, Britain's first colony, became the independent Irish Free State in 1922 (with the important exception of six northern counties). India and Pakistan became independent after World War II.

World War I

In the early twentieth century, a series of political crises and a continent-wide arms race brought tensions in Europe to a head. The British viewed Germany's sudden invasion of Belgium in 1914 as a threat and declared war. Britain and its allies France and Russia were soon engaged with the Central Powers—Germany, Austria-Hungary, and Turkey—in a war fought on several continents. It was a war of mud, blood, and barbed wire, made more deadly by new tanks, machine guns, flame-throwers, and poison gas. Before the war ended in November 1918, millions of people had been killed, and the economic, social, and political order of Europe had been devastated. Monarchies in Russia, Germany, and Austria-Hungary were overthrown. As British Foreign Minister Sir Edward Grey observed at the war's outset, "The lamps are going out all over Europe; we shall not see them lit again in our lifetime."

The 1920s and the Great Depression

During the war, Britain had lost many of the markets for its industrial products to the United States and Japan. Industries such as coal, steel, and textiles declined after the war, leading to a rise in unemployment. In 1921 two million British workers were unemployed. Britain soon rebounded, however, and experienced limited prosperity from 1925 to 1929. This relatively prosperous period came to an abrupt end with the Great Depression, a major economic collapse that began when the stock market crashed in the United States in October 1929. During 1932, the worst year of the Great Depression, nearly one British worker in every four was unemployed.

> *"We shall not flag or fail. We shall go on to the end."*
>
> —Winston Churchill, speech, June 4, 1940

World War II

Europe's postwar economic and political problems encouraged the rise of dictatorships in many countries. Adolf Hitler and the Nazi Party gained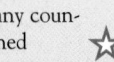

Reading Practice

Identify Cause and Effect Point out to students that they can analyze this essay on the various forces that reshaped the modern world by identifying causes and effects. Begin with the section titled "The British Empire." **Ask:** What cause-and-effect relationships can you identify in this paragraph? *(Students should see that rising nationalism in British colonies caused various peoples to challenge British rule. This in turn brought about independence.)*

Have students take notes in a cause-and-effect chart as they read the rest of the essay.

power by appeals to nationalism and ethnic hatred. Beginning in 1936, Nazi Germany began a policy of territorial expansion that would soon lead to war. On September 1, 1939, German forces attacked Poland, forcing Britain and France to declare war on Germany. World War II had begun. Germany soon overran much of Europe, including France, leaving Britain isolated and vulnerable. In May 1940 Winston Churchill became British prime minister and through his wartime speeches expressed the stubborn determination of the British people to continue the fight. In early September 1940, the German air force began subjecting Britain to the first sustained bombing of civilian targets in the history of warfare. Although thousands of people were killed or injured and enormous damage was done, British morale remained high throughout the war, until the surrenders of Germany and Japan in 1945.

Postwar Britain: New Priorities

The end of World War II left Britain with massive economic problems and bitter class conflict. In elections immediately after the war, the Labour Party, which promised far-reaching economic reforms, gained a landslide victory. In 1946 the new government passed legislation providing government aid to help the unemployed, the sick,

Battle between German and British airplanes, 1916. Bayrisches Armeemuseum, Ingolstadt, Germany. ★

and the aged. The Labour government also created a system of national health care that ensured medical services for everyone. The cost of building a welfare state that would take care of its own citizens forced Britain to reduce expenses abroad. This meant the dismantling of the British Empire. Britain was no longer able to afford the cost of being a world power.

PREVIEW **Big Ideas** of the Modern Age

2

1 **Class, Colonialism, and the Great War**

In the first half of the century, Britain's power was challenged by class conflict at home, resistance to colonialism abroad, and the outbreak of World War I. British writers responded to the profound changes in Britain's life and culture.

See pages 992–993.

2 **Modernism**

World War I decimated a generation and shattered European civilization. Responding to the war, British writers attempted to find meaning in both traditional literary forms and the innovative movement known as Modernism.

See pages 994–995.

3 **World War II and Its Aftermath**

In World War II, the British and the other Allies defeated the Axis powers, but postwar Britain dismantled its colonial empire. These years brought a deep sense of cultural anxiety and disillusionment that permeated British writing.

See pages 996–997.

INTRODUCTION **991**

Teach

Reading Strategy 2

Preview Have students read the three numbered subheadings under the heading "Big Ideas of the Modern Age." **Ask:** How can you use these headings to increase your understanding of this section and the unit in general? *(Students should recognize that these headings identify the focuses of the subsequent pages in the unit introduction pages and that they name the three major topics to which the selections in the unit will relate.)*

View the Art ★

World War I Air Battles This illustration depicts a classic dogfight between World War I airplanes. The greatest World War I flying ace, Manfred von Richthofen, had 80 confirmed kills during the war. To set himself apart, Richthofen painted his plane a blazing red. The stunt led his British rivals to nickname him the Red Baron.

Teach

Main Idea Point out that the subheads highlight the main ideas of the sections, which explain the changes propelling England into the modern age. **Ask:** What is the main idea of each of these sections? *(First section: The lower classes used politics and literature to fight for equal opportunity. Second section: Women fought for equal opportunities and won the right to vote. Third section: The views of British writers were conflicted about British colonialism. Fourth section: British troops fought in a war unlike any previous conflict.)*

Cultural History ☆

Emmeline Pankhurst During her lifetime, Emmeline Pankhurst (1858–1928) continually fought for women's suffrage. Although the motto of the WSPU was "Deeds, Not Words," Pankhurst has been credited with some fiery quotations, such as "Men make the moral code, and they expect women to accept it."

Big Idea 1

Class, Colonialism, and the Great War

People's expectations and opportunities are shaped by several factors. One of the most important is the social and economic class to which they belong. This was certainly true of Britain in the early twentieth century, when challenges to the traditional British class structure were just beginning to be heard.

Class Conflict 1

As the Victorian politician and novelist Benjamin Disraeli observed, the British upper and lower classes formed "two nations . . . as ignorant of each other's habits, thoughts, and feelings, as if they were of different planets; who are . . . fed by different food, are ordered by different manners, and are not governed by the same laws." By the early twentieth century, people of diverse groups had begun to question Britain's traditional social values. Trade unions grew, and their leaders began to agitate for a radical change to the economic system. In 1900 a new political party was formed, the Labour Party, which dedicated itself to the interests of workers. By midcentury, a group of writers known as the Angry Young Men were voicing their suspicion and resentment of the static British establishment and bitterly attacking its manners, snobbery, and hypocrisy.

> *"The argument of the broken window pane is the most valuable argument in modern politics."*
>
> —Emmeline Pankhurst

Women's Rights

Women composed another disaffected group that began to seek greater political power. The suffrage movement in Britain, which had long been work-

ing peacefully to secure votes for women, took a bold new direction after Emmeline Pankhurst founded the Women's Social and Political Union (WSPU) in 1903. Under the leadership of Pankhurst and her daughters, British suffragettes used unusual publicity stunts to call attention to their demands. They pelted government officials with eggs, chained themselves to lampposts, burned railroad cars, and smashed the windows of fashionable department stores. The British government finally relented and gave women over thirty the right to vote in 1918; ten years later, the voting age for women was lowered to twenty-one.

British Imperialism

Throughout the 1800s, Britain had continued to expand its overseas territories, in part to provide markets for British goods to replace those lost to growing commercial rivals such as Germany and the United States. Some British writers, such as Rudyard Kipling (see page 1026) defended colonialism. In a celebrated poem, he admonished, "Take up the White Man's burden— / The savage wars of peace— / Fill full the mouth of Famine / And bid the sickness cease." Other writers, such as George Orwell (see page 1035), were far more critical of British imperialism. Orwell, a colonial police officer in Burma, witnessed abuses of power that oppressed him "with an intolerable sense of guilt."

The Great War

With no historical precedent for the scale of the bloodshed and destructiveness of World War I, the British referred to it simply as the Great War. The chief battlefield for British troops, known as the Western Front, stretched for hundreds of miles across northern France. From parallel systems of defensive trenches protected with barbed wire, enemy armies faced each other across "no-man's-land," a wilderness of shell craters and rubble. The battles of the Great War were vast, prolonged

Viewing Practice

Represent Have students select, organize, and produce visuals to complement and extend this information. Ask them to focus their research on Britain in the first half of the twentieth century. Volunteers can determine and explain their purposes in choosing specific visuals. Remind students to look for images of historical events, important people, authors, cultural details (such as fashion), as well as artwork depicting the impact of war. Display students' images on a "Modern Age Images" bulletin board, and refer to it from time to time when teaching selections in Unit Six.

of the Somme, 60,000 British soldiers were killed or wounded. By the time the battle was over in mid-November, British losses amounted to more than 400,000.

The Food Queue, c. twentieth century. C. R. W. Nevinson. Pastel on brown paper. Imperial War Museum, London.

Vera Brittain wrote an autobiographical account of the years 1900 to 1925, called Testament of Youth. *Her fiancé, Roland, and her brother Edward were killed in battle. In the following passage, she writes of her feelings when the war finally ended on November 11, 1918.*

from *Testament of Youth* by Vera Brittain

I detached myself from the others and walked slowly up Whitehall, with my heart sinking in a sudden cold dismay. Already this was a different world from the one that I had known during four life-long years, a world in which people would be light-hearted and forgetful, in which themselves and their careers and their amusements would blot out political ideals and great national issues. And in that brightly lit, alien world I should have no part. All those with whom I had really been intimate were gone; not one remained to share with me the heights and the depths of my memories. As the years went by and youth departed and remembrance grew dim, a deeper and ever deeper darkness would cover the young men who were once my contemporaries.

For the time I realized, with all that full realization meant, how completely everything that had hitherto made up my life had vanished with Edward and Roland, with Victor and Geoffrey. The War was over; a new age was beginning; but the dead were dead and would never return.

2

Reading Check

Analyze Cause and Effect Why do you think the end of World War I failed to make Vera Brittain feel elated?

Teach

Reading Strategy | 1

Analyze Cause and Effect

Ask: What have you learned so far about causes of the modern age? *(Students should mention trends toward social justice, such as anticolonialism and women's rights, and the world wars.)* After students read the section "Ground-breaking Ideas," write this cause-and-effect chain on the board:

Ideas in science ⟶ New beliefs

Point out that continuing this chain will help them analyze the causes and effects of Modernism. As they finish reading this page, have them complete the chain.

Literary History ☆

Ulysses When it was first published, most readers and critics found *Ulysses* to be a literary disaster. People objected to its style, subject matter, and obscenity, along with its scorn for religion and morality. The book was banned in much of Europe and the United States until 1933. Today, many critics praise *Ulysses* as a masterpiece.

Big Idea 2
Modernism

Modernism was a literary and artistic movement that developed in the early 1900s and continued through the 1940s. Although there were forerunners to Modernism in the late nineteenth century, it did not fully emerge until the years just before, and immediately following, World War I. **1**

Groundbreaking Ideas

New scientific ideas in biology, psychology, and physics strongly influenced the development of Modernism. In the late nineteenth century, Charles Darwin's theory of evolution had already challenged traditional beliefs about the origin and nature of human beings. Around 1900, the psychological theories of Sigmund Freud, emphasizing the role of the unconscious in human personality, called into question accepted attitudes about human behavior. At about the same time, Albert Einstein's theory of relativity established new views of space, time, and energy, overturning the familiar Newtonian laws of physics, including the concept of a three-dimensional universe.

> *"Nothing can be brought to an end in the unconscious; nothing is past or forgotten."*
>
> —Sigmund Freud, *The Interpretation of Dreams*

Modern Art

During the first part of the Modernist period, artists ceased trying to create realistic depictions of the world around them. The painters Georges Braque and Pablo Picasso developed a style of art called Cubism, in which the shapes of objects or people were angular, geometric, or fragmented.

Sometimes different sides of a subject were shown simultaneously. Another artistic movement, called Surrealism, was influenced by Freud's emphasis on the subconscious and the role of dreams in human behavior. Surrealist artists such as René Magritte and Salvador Dalí created dreamlike images in their paintings.

Modernist Literature

The work of early Modernist writers was influenced by contemporary movements in the visual arts. For example, the Imagist poets, who appeared in the years before World War I, used techniques that resembled Cubism's presentation of an object from several perspectives. The horrors of the war and the alienation of modern life gave Modernist writing a dark tone of disillusionment bordering on despair. This bleak sense of spiritual emptiness is memorably conveyed in T. S. Eliot's poem *The Waste Land*. Modernist poets, such as Eliot (see page 1071), abandoned established meters to experiment with free verse.

Modernism also produced a revolution in prose fiction, such as the works of James Joyce (see page 1093) and Virginia Woolf (see page 1103). Both incorporated the new ideas of psychology into their fiction, using a literary technique known as stream of consciousness to reflect a character's free-flowing thoughts, feelings, and memories. Joyce took the stream-of-consciousness technique to its limits in *Ulysses* (1922), creating a book that is simultaneously realistic, symbolic, poetic, didactic, comic, ironic, and mythic.

The subject matter of literature changed too. With the shock of the war, technological advances, and greater social freedom, writers realized that they could and should write about anything. No subject was too dignified or undignified, too familiar or remote, to appear in a modern poem or novel.

Reading Practice

Construct a Graphic Organizer

Guide students in creating three idea webs, one for the content under each heading. In the center of the webs, have them write "Science," "Art," and "Literature." In each web, they should list the concepts that contributed to Modernist ideas in that area. Ask students to save their completed webs as critical-reading and viewing aids for later works in the unit.

Room in the second Post-Impressionist Exhibition in 1912 showing the works of Henri Matisse. Roger Fry. Oil on wood, 20.19 x 24.76 in. Louvre, Paris.

View the Art Matisse, whose paintings appear in the background of this image, was a leader of the art movement Fauvism. Fauvism relied on unstructured shapes and strong, contrasting colors. In what ways are the image itself and the paintings by Matisse similar? How do they differ?

The epic novel Ulysses, *by James Joyce, is the fictional account of the life of several Dublin citizens over the course of one day—June 16, 1904. The following passage focuses on one of the major characters, Leopold Bloom, and presents his interior monologue during a walk through the city.*

from **Ulysses** by James Joyce

Mr Bloom came to Kildare street. First I must. Library.

Straw hat in sunlight. Tan shoes. Turnedup trousers. It is. It is.

His heart quopped softly. To the right. Museum. Goddesses. He swerved to the right.

Is it? Almost certain. Won't look. Wine in my face. Why did I? Too heady. Yes, it is. The walk. Not see. Not see. Get on.

Making for the museum gate with long windy strides he lifted his eyes. Handsome building. Sir Thomas Deane designed. Not following me?

Didn't see me perhaps. Light in his eyes.

The flutter of his breath came forth in short sighs. Quick. Cold statues quiet there. Safe in a minute.

No, didn't see me. After two. Just at the gate.

My heart!

His eyes beating looked steadfastly at cream curves of stone. Sir Thomas Deane was the Greek architecture.

Look for something I.

His hasty hand went quick into a pocket, took out, read unfolded Agendath Netaim. Where did I?

Busy looking for.

He thrust back quickly Agendath.

Afternoon she said.

I am looking for that. Yes, that. Try all pockets. Handker. *Freeman.* Where did I? Ah, yes. Trousers. Purse. Potato. Where did I?

Hurry. Walk quietly. Moment more. My heart.

His hand looking for the where did I put found in his hip pocket soap lotion have to call tepid paper stuck. Ah, soap there! Yes. Gate.

Safe!

Reading Check

Interpret How does this passage reflect the influence of psychology on literature during the Modernist period?

INTRODUCTION **995**

Advanced Learners

DIFFERENTIATED INSTRUCTION

Author Study Encourage students to further explore the work of James Joyce from a Modernist perspective. Have them use the library and the Internet to find books about Joyce. Ask students to concentrate on material that places the novelist in a historical context. Students might research Joyce's reaction to World War I, his opinion of Sigmund Freud's writings, and his views on the work of Picasso, Matisse, and other Modernist artists. For extra credit, students can read a section of one of Joyce's novels and write a brief essay linking the passage to characteristic Modernist ideas.

Teach

Reading Check

Answer: *The stream-of-conscious narrative reflects the focus on the psychological workings of the mind.*

Literary Element   2

Style Remind students that style involves the expressive qualities, such as word choice and sentence structure, that distinguish an author's work. **Ask:** What qualities does Joyce's style exhibit? *(Joyce's style has a clipped and chaotic quality, with fragments, inverted word order, and word parts.)*

View the Art ★

Possible answer: *Students may say that, like the Matisse paintings, the image as a whole features unstructured shapes and flattened perspective. Unlike the Matisse paintings, the image's colors are muted and blended. The image is not very emotional.*

Roger Fry (1866–1934) gained fame in two areas: as a Postimpressionist painter and as an art critic. In 1910, Fry curated the first British show of Postimpressionist paintings. Of that exhibit, Virginia Woolf observed that "on or about December 1910, human character changed." Fry uses this painting to champion the ideals that led to Woolf's statement "Art need not show the world as it looks."

995

Teach

Make Predictions Ask students to look at the title, headings, quotation, and painting before they begin reading the text. **Ask:** What can you predict about this period in Great Britain's history? *(Students may say that this was a harsh and dark period in England's history but that the British faced it with courage and determination.)*

Cultural History ☆

World War II In 1941, German bombs destroyed large parts of London, and tens of thousands of civilians were killed. On December 7 of the same year, Japan bombed the U.S. naval base at Pearl Harbor, Hawaii. The United States, which had tried to stay out of the conflict, declared war on Japan. Prime Minister Winston Churchill joined forces with the U.S. president, Franklin Roosevelt, to find a way to end the deadly conflict. Without this personal alliance, it may have been impossible for the Allies to unify and repel the Axis powers.

Big Idea 3
World War II and Its Aftermath ▪

What is worth fighting and dying for? The disillusionment that resulted from World War I left many British people, particularly intellectuals, writers, and artists, with the opinion that traditional ideas of military heroism and national honor were worthless concepts. As the world's dictators grew more ruthless and aggressive in the 1930s, however, democratic nations such as Britain had to stand up to these totalitarian regimes or risk being taken over.

> *"Do not let us speak of darker days; let us rather speak of sterner days. These are not dark days: these are great days—the greatest days our country has ever lived."*
>
> —Winston Churchill, speech, October 1941

Wartime Britain

After the fall of France in June 1940, only the British stood between Nazi Germany and the conquest of Europe. To gain control of the skies over Britain in preparation for an invasion, the Germans began a massive bombing campaign against British cities. Under the determined leadership of their wartime prime minister, Winston Churchill (see page 1112), the British remained defiant despite nightly German air raids, which the British referred to as the Blitz. Britain's Royal Air Force fought back heroically, soon inflicting major losses on the German bombers and effectively putting an end to the planned invasion of Britain. As Churchill memorably observed of the RAF, "Never in the field of human conflict was so much owed by so many to so few." German bombing raids and later

rocket attacks took a terrible toll on British lives, however, and left large parts of some of Britain's major cities, particularly London, in ruins. Among the most vivid depictions of London during the Blitz are those contained in the fiction of Elizabeth Bowen (see page 1121).

By the end of 1941, Britain was no longer fighting alone but had been joined by the Soviet Union and the United States. Together, the Allies succeeded in defeating Germany and Japan by August 1945. However, the wartime alliance between the Soviet Union and the West collapsed when the Nazi threat had been eliminated, and the Americans and Soviets soon became rivals in a Cold War for control of the postwar world. With these superpowers in possession of atomic weapons, there was a new threat of nuclear world war. Everyone had witnessed in horror the devastating effects of the atomic bombs dropped on Japan. Fear of a nuclear holocaust was pervasive. The Cold War and its constant threat of global annihilation loomed over postwar Britain.

Postwar Britain

Britain's recovery from World War II was slow and challenging. The country was virtually bankrupt. Because of shortages, food rationing was increased. Coal rationing did not end until 1958. For a long time, Britain remained a hungry and cold nation. Two world wars also hastened the end of the British Empire. After World War II, the first in a long line of British colonies and dependencies became independent. India and Pakistan gained independence in 1947, followed a year later by Ceylon (Sri Lanka), Burma (Myanmar), and Palestine (Israel). Many British, both at home and abroad, found their country's diminished status to be a blow to national pride. For many others, however, the loss of Britain's colonies was a relief. After the hardship of two world wars, a group of reformers renounced the failed ideals of the past

Vocabulary Practice

Context Clues Remind students to use the three kinds of context clues: definition, inference, and contrast.
Write on the board:
The paper's uneven edge appeared serrated.

Anton was sagacious, but wisdom was not his only strength.

At first, few worried about the raids, but soon fear grew pervasive.

Have students define each underlined word and describe which type of context clue they used to find the word's meaning. *(Jagged: definition; wise: inference; widespread: contrast)*

Shelterers in the Tube, 1941. Henry Moore. Pencil, pen and ink, watercolour and crayon on paper, 38 1/10 x 22 in. Tate Gallery, London. ★

and saw a new opportunity to help all British citizens by alleviating economic and social injustice.

After the war, the Labour government set out to create a modern welfare state—a state in which the government takes responsibility for providing people with basic services. In 1946 the National Insurance Act and the National Health Service Act were passed to provide funds to those in need and health care for everyone. The British welfare state became the model for most western European countries after the war.

from *George Orwell's Wartime Diary*

10 September, 1940

Can't write much of the insanities of the last few days. It is not so much that the bombing is worrying in itself as that the disorganization of traffic, frequent difficulty of telephoning, shutting of shops whenever there is a raid on etc etc, combined with the necessity of getting on with one's ordinary work, wear one out and turn life into a constant scramble to catch up lost time. . . .

The delayed-action bombs are a great nuisance, but they appear to be successful in locating most of them and getting all the neighboring people out until the bomb shall have exploded. All over South London, little groups of disconsolate-looking people wandering about with suitcases and bundles, either people who have been rendered homeless or, in more cases, who have been turned out by the authorities because of an unexploded bomb. . . .

Most of last night in the public shelter, having been driven there by recurrent whistle and crash of bombs not very far away at intervals of about a quarter of an hour. Frightful discomfort owing to overcrowding, though the place was well-appointed, with electric light and fans. People, mostly elderly working class, grousing bitterly about the hardness of the seats and the longness of the night, but no defeatist talk.

Reading Check

Compare and Contrast How does the tone of the excerpt from Churchill's speech on page 1114 contrast with that of Orwell's diary?

INTRODUCTION **997**

English Learners

DIFFERENTIATED INSTRUCTION

British Phrases Some of the expressions that Orwell uses may be unfamiliar to students accustomed to American English. Be sure students understand the following phrases and can determine how the ideas they convey would be expressed in American usage: *catch up lost time; until the bomb shall have exploded; frightful discomfort; owing to overcrowding.*

Teach

Reading Check

Answer: *Orwell's expression of the stress of wartime life is a check against the optimism and pride shown in Churchill's speech.*

Literary Element | 2

Sensory Details Ask: What sensory details in Orwell's diary excerpt help you imagine what life was like during an air raid? *("Recurrent whistle and crash of bombs," "overcrowding," "electric light and fans," "grousing bitterly," "hardness of the seats")*

View the Art ★

The sculptor Henry Moore (1898–1986) achieved such blazing success that he became, in the words of the Henry Moore Foundation, a "cultural phenomenon." Unlike this work, his drawings were typically studies for sculptures, which were collected by major museums as early as the 1930s. The Moores stayed in London for much of the bombing, leaving for a remote farmhouse only when their home suffered bomb damage. In this drawing, Moore is sketching his fellow citizens during an air raid.

Assess/Close

Legacy of the Period

Ask: How did World War I change men's traditional view of war? *(War was no longer looked upon as a heroic adventure but rather as a horrific event.)* Direct students' attention to the second paragraph. **Ask:** What idea is common to the work of Modernist writers and artists? *(Both artists and writers turned away from representing the exterior world realistically.)*

Cultural and Literary Links

Suggest students consider how Modernist ideas have affected the way we view the world.

Activities

1. **Follow Up** Students should support their answers with details from this introduction and from lessons in the unit.

2. **Contrast Literary Periods** Presentations might focus on continued development of technology.

3. **Build Visual Literacy** Encourage students to share any impressions they have about the influence of cultural periods on the representations.

4. Answers will vary.

FOLDABLES
Study Organizer

Have students make and label the Three-Pocket Foldable. Then have them write words about each Big Idea on note cards to insert into the appropriate pocket of their Foldable.

WRAP-UP

Legacy of the Period

World War I was a cultural watershed for twentieth-century Britain. The war decimated a generation of young men, and many of the survivors were haunted by the horrors of the Western Front, where the traditional view of war as heroic adventure became a grimly ironic absurdity. As the poet Philip Larkin observed, "Never such innocence again."

Modernism fundamentally changed the way people looked at the world around them. Modernist visual artists transformed familiar objects into exotic new shapes or explored the content of dreams. Modernist writers, such as T. S. Eliot and James Joyce, broke away from traditional literary forms and values to create the classics of a new literature, wherein reality might be redefined not by fidelity to exterior appearances but by the patterns of myth or the flow of the subconscious mind.

Cultural and Literary Links

▶ Virginia Woolf's *A Room of One's Own* influenced and inspired the modern generation of feminists, who sympathized with Woolf's view that women, especially women artists, need privacy and financial independence.

▶ The term *newspeak*, derived from the name of the language invented by George Orwell in his novel *Nineteen Eighty-four*, has been widely used to refer to messages expressed in the media that are deliberately misleading and contradictory for the purpose of controlling public opinion. The adjective *Orwellian* is used to describe features of totalitarian governments.

▶ In a famous 1946 speech, Winston Churchill introduced the phrase "iron curtain" to refer to the political barrier isolating the nations controlled by the Soviet Union after World War II.

 Literature Online

Unit Resources For additional skills practice, go to glencoe.com and enter QuickPass code GLB9817u6.

Activities ▶

Choose one of the following activities to explore and develop as you read this unit.

1. Follow Up Go back to the Looking Ahead section on page 985 and answer the questions.

2. Contrast Literary Periods With a partner, create a two-column chart. In the first column, list the values and styles of Victorian literature. In the second column, list the values and styles of the Modernist literature you find in this unit. Which elements do the two periods have in common? Which elements of Victorian literature did Modernism reject, adapt, or develop further?

3. Build Visual Literacy Work with a small group to create an exhibit illustrating and explaining Modernism. You can include examples from literature, fine art, music, architecture, and interior design.

4. Take Notes Use this organizer to explore your personal responses to the works in this unit.

 **THREE-POCKET BOOK**

Big Idea 1 Big Idea 2 Big Idea 3

Writing Practice

Essay Have each student choose one of the writers—Virginia Woolf, George Orwell, or Winston Churchill—mentioned under "Cultural and Literary Links." **Ask:** What do you know about this person? Have students research one of the writers and write a brief essay that includes three interesting facts about the writer's life and/or work.

PART 1

Class, Colonialism, and the Great War

La Mitrailleuse, 1915. Christopher R. W. Nevinson. Tate Gallery, London.

 View the Art A *mitrailleuse* was a type of French machine gun used in the early twentieth century. In your opinion, does this image convey the same feelings about war as the quote from Wilfred Owen? Explain why or why not.

> *"What passing-bells for these who die as cattle?
> Only the monstrous anger of guns."* **1**
>
> —Wilfred Owen, "Anthem for Doomed Youth"

999

Analyze and Extend

Literary Element   1

Tone Focus attention on the quotation and ask what situation or event it refers to. *(World War I)*
Ask: What is the tone of these lines? *(sad and bitterly disillusioned)*

View the Art   ★

Answer: *Answers will vary. Some students may say that the painting gives an impression of calculated, mechanical warfare, while the quote—describing men who "die like cattle" and "monstrous anger"—describes a gritty and ugly type of war.*

C. R. W. Nevinson was a Futurist. Futurism looked to the aesthetic beauty and inevitability of machines while exploring the world's gathering speed and efficiency. Point out the painting's title. **Ask:** What do you think *La Mitrailleuse* (lah mee tray URZE) means? *(machine gun)* Why might Nevinson have used the French word for a machine gun? *(He was painting what he saw on the Western Front.)*.

English Learners

DIFFERENTIATED INSTRUCTION

Beginning Call attention to the word *colonialism* in the heading. **Ask:** What other words use the suffix *-ism*? *(Modernism and Romanticism)* This suffix often appears in nonfiction writing about history, politics, art, or literature. **Ask:** What does *-ism* mean? *("having to do with")*

Approaching Level

DIFFERENTIATED INSTRUCTION

Established Wilfred Owen meant to tell the world of the grim results of the war he witnessed. Invite students to research a war or conflict currently in the news. Ask them to investigate its toll in terms of the injuries and death. Have them share their research with the class.

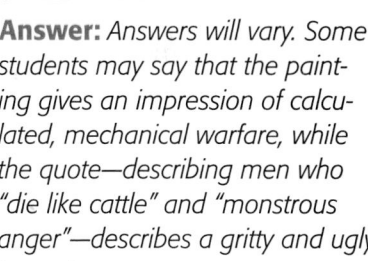 For additional support for English Learners, see Unit 6 Teaching Resources Book, p. 21.

Focus

Bellringer Options

**Selection Focus
Transparency 50**

**Daily Language Practice
Transparency 83**

Or ask volunteers to relate a time when they shared or gave up something to help another person. **Ask:** Do you think you did this to make yourself feel better or to help the other person? Do you think charity is less meaningful if you expect something in return? Have students keep their answers in mind as they read the selections.

Connect to the Reading Selections

Allow students to share their responses to the opening question. Then have students discuss what they already know about Katherine Mansfield, Bessie Head, the King James Bible, and the Qur'an.

Compare Literature About Class Conflict

What is the best way to respond to a person in need? The four selections compared here—a short story by Katherine Mansfield, an essay by Bessie Head, a parable from the Bible, and verses from the Qur'an—explore this issue and offer insights about life.

COMPARE THE Big Idea **Class, Colonialism, and the Great War**

Wealth and poverty can generate rigid classes that divide people and erode society. As you read, ask yourself, How do the writers of these selections examine the misery of poverty, the power of wealth, and the true meaning of compassion?

COMPARE Tone

Tone is a reflection of a writer's attitude toward a subject and is conveyed through such elements as word choice, punctuation, sentence structure, and figures of speech. As you read, ask yourself, How do these four selections reflect different attitudes toward poverty and the poverty-stricken?

COMPARE Past and Present

Although advances in technology have improved the quality of life for many people throughout the world today, the widening gulf between the haves and the have-nots is still a grim reality. As you read, ask yourself, How do these selections reveal the ways that different cultures of the past viewed wealth and poverty?

LOG ON ▶ **Literature** Online

Author Search For more about Katherine Mansfield and Bessie Head, go to glencoe.com and enter QuickPass code GLB9817u6.

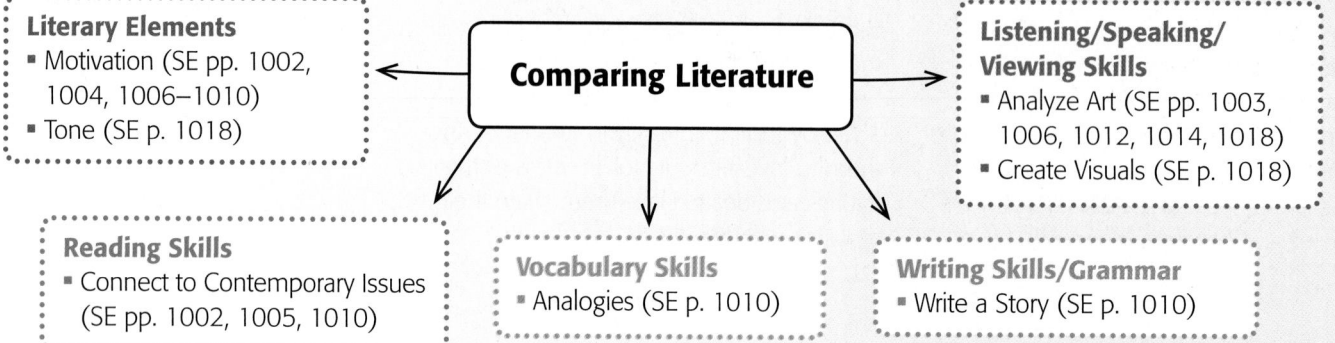

Literary Elements
- Motivation (SE pp. 1002, 1004, 1006–1010)
- Tone (SE p. 1018)

Comparing Literature

Listening/Speaking/Viewing Skills
- Analyze Art (SE pp. 1003, 1006, 1012, 1014, 1018)
- Create Visuals (SE p. 1018)

Reading Skills
- Connect to Contemporary Issues (SE pp. 1002, 1005, 1010)

Vocabulary Skills
- Analogies (SE p. 1010)

Writing Skills/Grammar
- Write a Story (SE p. 1010)

Before You Read

A Cup of Tea

Meet **Katherine Mansfield**

(1888–1923)

Katherine Mansfield lived for only thirty-four years, but in her short life she became one of the greatest short story writers and an innovator in the form. Her stories have been called delicate, beautiful, and profound. She revolutionized the concept of the short story, moving it away from the strictures of plot and external action. She was able to capture the meaning of a relationship in a series of sensations, illuminating the inner truth of a character's life.

> *"Life is, all at one and the same time, far more mysterious and far simpler than we know."*
>
> —Katherine Mansfield

Setbacks and Success Born Katherine Mansfield Beauchamp in Wellington, New Zealand, Mansfield was the daughter of a domineering father and an aloof mother. As a young child, she was nurtured primarily by her maternal grandmother. She tasted her first literary success at age nine: first prize in a school composition contest. When she was fourteen, her family sailed to London, and she enrolled in Queen's College. There, she edited the school magazine and, to her delight, discovered such authors as Oscar Wilde.

Mansfield returned briefly to New Zealand, but in 1908 she moved to England for good. Her life there got off to a rough start. She married hastily, left her husband after only a few days, suffered a miscarriage, and became increasingly disillusioned.

Then, in 1911 her life improved—Mansfield published her first book and met the man who would become her second husband, John Middleton Murry, editor of two magazines in which she published her stories. Though a member of a literary circle that included D. H. Lawrence and Virginia Woolf, Mansfield often felt alienated from it, and she criticized the intellectual snobbery she perceived in some of her artist friends.

The death of her soldier brother in 1915 affected Mansfield deeply. Dedicating herself to preserving her memories of him and their shared childhood, she wrote a series of short stories that beautifully portray her family life in New Zealand. Regarded today as masterpieces of the short-story form, these stories were published in 1920 in the collection *Bliss and Other Stories*.

Illness and Critical Acclaim Never in good health, Mansfield contracted tuberculosis in her early thirties. Despite her illness, she continued to write, producing some of her best works, including "A Cup of Tea," while desperately seeking a cure for her illness. During this period, she published the critically acclaimed collection *The Garden Party*. She completed her last story only months before her death. Two more collections of stories, *The Dove's Nest* and *Something Childish*, were published posthumously.

KATHERINE MANSFIELD **1001**

Before You Read

Focus

Political History ☆

Mapping Poverty In 1889, sociologist Charles Booth created a map showing the distribution of poverty in London. Although some parts of the city were inhabited primarily by the wealthy or by the poor, in many cases the two groups lived side by side. The map also shows that a large portion of London's population lived in severe poverty, with weekly family incomes of a pound or less.

English Learners

DIFFERENTIATED INSTRUCTION

PARTNERS **Intermediate** Pair English learners together. Ask them to discuss wealthy and poor characters from films or television shows. Have each pair make a brief oral presentation in which they describe one wealthy and one poor character.

Advanced Have students create a three-column chart with the headings *Selection, Attitude About Poverty,* and *Attitude About Wealth*. In the first column, students should list the selections' titles. As they read, have them record attitudes about poverty and wealth presented in each text.

Comparing Literature

Before You Read

Focus

Summary

A shallow woman married to a wealthy man encounters another woman begging in the street. She takes the beggar home and feeds her. She tells her she will help her and that they are to be friends. However, when her husband comments on the beggar's physical beauty, she gives the beggar a small amount of money and turns her out on the street again.

 For summaries in languages other than English, see Unit 6 Teaching Resources Book, pp. 23–28.

Vocabulary

Etymology Divide the class into two teams. Explain that for each vocabulary word, you will give the meaning of its etymological root. Some words have more than one root. Tell students to identify the vocabulary word and explain their choice. Have the teams compete to see which can make the most correct matches first. **Say:** "Hatred" (*odious*); "foreign or alien" (*exotic*); "neat or dainty" (*quaint*); "outside" (*exotic*); "twist back" (*retort*); "known" (*quaint*).

 For additional vocabulary practice, see Unit 6 Teaching Resources Book, p. 31.

 For additional context, see Glencoe Interactive Vocabulary CD-ROM.

1002

Literature and Reading Preview

Connect to the Story

Can a person ever be truly selfless? With a small group of classmates, discuss whether it is easy to do something purely for someone else's sake.

Build Background

This short story is set in England at the beginning of the twentieth century. At this time, people from different social classes did not socialize with one another, and it was considered improper for upper-class women to work outside the home. Through the use of images, dialogue, monologue, and metaphors, Mansfield showed her characters' emotional states, subtle shifts of mood, and **epiphanies**—or sudden, significant realizations.

Set Purposes for Reading

Big Idea Class, Colonialism, and the Great War

As you read, ask yourself, What does this story suggest about the upper class and class conflict in early-twentieth-century Britain?

Literary Element Motivation

A character's **motivation** is his or her reason for acting, thinking, or feeling in a certain way. This motivation may be stated in the story or implied. As you read, ask yourself, What are the motivations of the characters in this story?

Reading Strategy Connect to Contemporary Issues

One reason that great literature endures is that generations of readers recognize its relevance to their own times. When you **connect literature to contemporary issues**, you relate events and issues in a story to those in society today. As you read, ask yourself, What contemporary issues does this story address?

Tip: Identifying Connections Use a chart to record connections between Mansfield's story and contemporary issues.

Event in Story	Contemporary Issue
A stranger asks Rosemary for money.	Homeless people today sometimes ask passersby for money.

1002 UNIT 6 THE MODERN AGE

Reading Practice

SPIRAL REVIEW **Identify Author's Purpose** As they read the selection, have students note whether they think Mansfield is trying to persuade the reader of her own beliefs. (*Some students may say that Mansfield wants to persuade the reader to believe that society's attitude toward and treatment of the poor must change. Others might think she simply intends to point out some hidden truths about Rosemary and her real-life counterparts.*)

Vocabulary

quaint (kwānt) *adj.* pleasingly unusual or odd; p. 1004 *The tourists were amused to find a quaint bungalow nestled among the downtown skyscrapers.*

odious (ō´ dē əs) *adj.* causing hate, disgust, or repugnance; p. 1004 *The odious sight of the garbage dump offended us.*

exotic (ig zot´ ik) *adj.* strangely beautiful or fascinating; p. 1004 *I had never before seen that exotic flower, with its unusual leaves and petals.*

retort (ri tôrt´) *v.* to reply in a witty, quick, or sharp manner; p. 1009 *When her father refused to agree with her, the frustrated teen retorted sarcastically, "You always take my side."*

Marguerite Kelsey, 1928. Meredith Frampton. Oil on canvas, 120.8 x 141.2 cm. Tate Gallery, London.

View the Art The style of clothing in this painting reflects the popular 1920s "garçonne" style—a style that gave women's clothes a simpler, more masculine look. What details in this image are similar to the early details given about Rosemary Fell? Explain.

A Cup of Tea

Katherine Mansfield

KATHERINE MANSFIELD **1003**

View the Art

Answer: *The woman in the image is, like Rosemary, not exactly beautiful, but striking; she's very modern and fashionable for her time.*

For an audio recording of this selection, use Listening Library Audio CD-ROM.

Readability Scores

Dale-Chall: 5.7
DRP: 53
Lexile: 650

Approaching Level

DIFFERENTIATED INSTRUCTION

Established Have students read the View the Art blurb below the painting. Students may be unfamiliar with the "garçonne" style of women's clothing that was popular in the 1920s. **Ask:** Why might women who were not allowed to work outside of their homes, dress in a trend that was considered more masculine? *(Answers will vary. Students may say this presents a shift in the treatment of* women. *Others may say that the simple clothes represented the simple treatment of women.)* Have interested students investigate further by researching the political assumptions of the attitude towards and role of women in the 1920s.

Comparing Literature

Teach

Reading Strategy · 1

Analyze Character Ask: If you met Rosemary, do you think you would like her? *(Most students might say that she is fashionable, but also seems shallow.)*

 For additional practice using the reading skill or strategy, see Unit 6 Teaching Resources Book, p. 30.

Literary Element · 2

Motivation Answer: *She wants to impress others.*

Big Idea · 3

Class, Colonialism, and the Great War Answer: *Mansfield criticizes Rosemary's lavish spending and her insensitivity to the working poor, such as the shopgirl who totes her parcels.*

Literary Element · 4

Motivation Answer: *She removes her gloves out of vanity.*
(APPROACHING) Remind approaching-level students that much of the story is told from Rosemary's point of view. Have them identify words that describe her hands. *(charming, rosy, flashing)*

1004

---

1 Rosemary Fell was not exactly beautiful. No, you couldn't have called her beautiful. Pretty? Well, if you took her to pieces . . . But why be so cruel as to take anyone to pieces? She was young, brilliant, extremely modern, exquisitely well dressed, amazingly well read in the newest of the new books, and her parties were the most delicious mixture of the really important people and . . . artists—**quaint** creatures, discoveries of hers, some of them too terrifying for words, but others quite presentable and amusing.

Rosemary had been married two years. She had a duck[1] of a boy. No, not Peter—Michael. And her husband absolutely adored her. They were rich, really rich, not just comfortably well off, which is **odious** and stuffy and sounds like one's grandparents. But if Rosemary wanted to shop she would go to Paris as you and I would go to Bond Street.[2] If she wanted to buy flowers, the car pulled up at that perfect shop in Regent Street, and Rosemary inside the shop just gazed in her dazzled, rather **exotic** way, and said: "I want those and those and those. Give me four bunches of those. And that jar of roses. Yes, I'll have all the roses in the jar. No, no lilac. I hate lilac. It's got no shape." The attendant bowed and put the lilac out of sight, as though this was only too true; lilac was dreadfully shapeless. "Give me those stumpy little tulips. Those red and white

---

1. Here, *duck* probably means "darling" or "dear," although it could also mean "funny thing" or "odd but harmless person."
2. *Bond Street*—as well as *Regent Street* and *Curzon Street* mentioned later—was, and continues to be, an elegant London street lined with shops that sell expensive items.

2 Motivation *Why do you think Rosemary invites "really important people" to her parties?*

Vocabulary

quaint (kwānt) *adj.* pleasingly unusual or odd
odious (ō′ dē əs) *adj.* causing hate, disgust, or repugnance
exotic (ig zot′ ik) *adj.* strangely beautiful or fascinating

1004 UNIT 6 THE MODERN AGE

---

ones." And she was followed to the car by a thin shopgirl staggering under an immense white paper armful that looked like a baby in long clothes. . . .

One winter afternoon she had been buying something in a little antique shop in Curzon Street. It was a shop she liked. For one thing, one usually had it to oneself. And then the man who kept it was ridiculously fond of serving her. He beamed whenever she came in. He clasped his hands; he was so gratified he could scarcely speak. Flattery, of course. All the same, there was something . . .

"You see, madam," he would explain in his low respectful tones, "I love my things. I would rather not part with them than sell them to someone who does not appreciate them, who has not that fine feeling which is so rare. . . ." And, breathing deeply, he unrolled a tiny square of blue velvet and pressed it on the glass counter with his pale fingertips.

Today it was a little box. He had been keeping it for her. He had shown it to nobody as yet. An exquisite little enamel box with a glaze so fine it looked as though it had been baked in cream. On the lid a minute[3] creature stood under a flowery tree, and a more minute creature still had her arms around her neck. Her hat, really no bigger than a geranium petal, hung from a branch; it had green ribbons. And there was a pink cloud like a watchful cherub floating above their heads. Rosemary took her hands out of her long gloves. She always took off her gloves to examine such things. Yes, she liked it very much. She loved it; it was a great duck. She must have it. And, turning the creamy box, opening and shutting it, she couldn't help noticing how charming her hands were against the blue velvet.

---

3. *Minute* means "tiny."

Class, Colonialism, and the Great War *What does Mansfield criticize about Rosemary?* **3**

Motivation *Why does Rosemary remove her gloves to examine the enamel box?* **4**

Reading Practice

 SPIRAL REVIEW Make Inferences Say: "He clasped his hands; he was so gratified he could scarcely speak. Flattery, of course." **Ask:** The narrator is describing the man's behavior as flattery, but what does "of course" mean? *(The narrator expects flattery and therefore, she can easily dismiss his behavior.)* **Say:** "Flattery, of course. All the same, there was something . . ."

Ask: What is that last sentence implying? *(The narrator is implying that even if one knows that the man is not being sincere, it is pleasant to be treated that way.)*

5 The shopman, in some dim cavern of his mind, may have dared to think so too. For he took a pencil, leaned over the counter, and his pale bloodless fingers crept timidly towards those rosy, flashing ones, as he murmured gently: "If I may venture to point out to madam, the flowers on the little lady's bodice."[4]

"Charming!" Rosemary admired the flowers. But what was the price? For a moment the shopman did not seem to hear. Then a murmur reached her. "Twenty-eight guineas,[5] madame."

"Twenty-eight guineas." Rosemary gave no sign. She laid the little box down; she buttoned her gloves again. Twenty-eight guineas. Even if one is rich . . . She looked vague.[6] She stared at a plump teakettle like a plump hen above the shopman's head, and her voice was dreamy as she answered: "Well, keep it for me—will you? I'll . . ."

> *" . . . a young girl, thin, dark, shadowy— where had she come from?"*

But the shopman had already bowed as though keeping it for her was all any human being could ask. He would be willing, of course, to keep it for her forever.

The discreet door shut with a click. She was outside on the step, gazing at the winter afternoon. Rain was falling, and with the rain it seemed the dark came too, spinning down like ashes. There was a cold bitter taste in the air, and the new-lighted lamps looked sad. Sad were the lights in the houses opposite. Dimly they burned as if regretting something. And people hurried by, hidden under their hateful umbrellas. Rosemary felt a strange pang. She pressed her muff to her breast; she wished she had the little box, too, to cling to. Of course, the car was there. She'd only to cross the pavement. But still she waited. There are moments, horrible moments in life, when one emerges from shelter and looks out, and it's awful. One oughtn't to give way to them. One ought to go home and have an extra-special tea. But at the very instant of thinking that, a young girl, thin, dark, shadowy—where had she come from?—was standing at Rosemary's elbow and a voice like a sigh, almost like a sob, breathed: "Madame, may I speak to you a moment?"

"Speak to me?" Rosemary turned. She saw a little battered creature with enormous eyes, someone quite young, no older than herself, who clutched at her coat collar with reddened hands, and shivered as though she had just come out of the water.

"M-madame," stammered the voice. "Would you let me have the price of a cup of tea?"

"A cup of tea?" There was something simple, sincere in that voice; it wasn't in the least the voice of a beggar. "Then have you no money at all?" asked Rosemary.

"None, madam," came the answer.

"How extraordinary!" Rosemary peered through the dusk, and the girl gazed back at her. How more than extraordinary! And suddenly it seemed to Rosemary such an adventure. It was like something out of a novel by Dostoevsky,[7]

---

4. A *bodice* is the fitted part of a dress from the waist to the shoulder.
5. A *guinea* was a unit of money (one pound and one shilling) often used to express prices of luxury goods.
6. Here, *vague* means "uncertain."

7. Fyodor *Dostoevsky*, a Russian writer who is considered one of the world's greatest novelists, often dramatized moral and psychological issues and wrote of the poor.

Connect to Contemporary Issues   *How might a wealthy person today respond to a poor person's request for pocket change?*   **6**

KATHERINE MANSFIELD   **1005**

Comparing Literature

Teach

Vocabulary   5

Multiple-Meaning Words
Direct students to the first sentence on this page. Tell students that one meaning of *dim*, especially in Britain, is "stupid." **Ask:** Is that the meaning Mansfield is using here? (*no*) Then direct students to the use of *dimly* in the fourth full paragraph. Tell students that another meaning is "seen indistinctly or weakly." **Ask:** Is Mansfield saying Rosemary can't see the girl well in the dim light? (*no*) What is she saying? (*that Rosemary can't see the girl as a real person*)

Reading Strategy   6

Connect to Contemporary Issues **Answer:** *Some wealthy people might ignore the poor person and hurry off, pretending that he or she does not even exist. Others might stop to give the supplicant some money.*

Advanced Learners

DIFFERENTIATED INSTRUCTION

Vary Sentence Structure Say: "The new-lighted lamps looked sad. Sad were the lights in the houses opposite. Dimly they burned as if regretting something." **Ask:** Each of these sentences describes something. But how are they different? (*The first sentence has* an adjective after the subject and the verb. The other two begin with the adjective or adverb.) Why would someone write "Sad were the lights" instead of "The lights were sad"? (*Placing the adjective first emphasizes it and varies the sentence structure.*)

Comparing Literature

Teach

Literary Element   1

Motivation **Answer:**
Rosemary appears to have no knowledge of the world in which the young woman lives and views the prospect of taking her home as a thrilling adventure, like an episode in a novel. Rosemary also believes the gesture will impress her friends, who will regard her as adventurous and magnanimous.

ENGLISH LEARNERS Ask English learners if they know a Spanish word that sounds similar to *adventure. (aventura)* **Say:** Replace *adventure* with the meaning of the Spanish word. Is it a cognate? *(yes)*

View the Art ★

Answer: *The woman seems satisfied with her surroundings. Rosemary is wealthy and lives in opulence.*

Hepple is best known for his fine portraits, as well as his paintings of children. During World War II, he was an official war artist.

Firelight. Norman Hepple (1908–1994). Oil on canvas. Private collection.

View the Art Hepple was well-known for his paintings documenting World War II. How would you describe the woman's expression? Why might Rosemary have a similar expression? ★

this meeting in the dusk. Supposing she took the girl home? Supposing she did do one of those things she was always reading about or seeing on the stage, what would happen? It would be thrilling. And she heard herself saying afterwards to the amazement of her friends: "I simply took her home with me," as she stepped forward and said to that dim person beside her: "Come home to tea with me."

The girl drew back startled. She even stopped shivering for a moment. Rosemary put out a hand and touched her arm. "I mean it," she said,

---

1 Motivation *Why does Rosemary invite the young woman home?*

smiling. And she felt how simple and kind her smile was. "Why won't you? Do. Come home with me now in my car and have tea."

"You—you don't mean it, madam," said the girl, and there was pain in her voice.

"But I do," cried Rosemary. "I want you to. To please me. Come along."

The girl put her fingers to her lips and her eyes devoured Rosemary. "You're—you're not taking me to the police station?" she stammered.

"The police station!" Rosemary laughed out. "Why should I be so cruel? No, I only want to make you warm and to hear—anything you care to tell me."

Reading Practice

SPIRAL REVIEW **Understand Ellipses** Direct students' attention to Rosemary's unfinished sentence at the end of the second paragraph on page 1007. Explain that the three dots are called an ellipsis. An ellipsis is used to indicate that a sentence or thought is unfinished.
Ask: If Rosemary were to finish that sentence, what might she say?

(Students may suggest "If I'm the more fortunate, you ought to expect me to help you.") Why does Rosemary leave the sentence unfinished? *(She is interrupted by the arrival at her house as she pauses to think.)*

Hungry people are easily led. The footman held the door of the car open, and a moment later they were skimming through the dusk.

"There!" said Rosemary. She had a feeling of triumph as she slipped her hand through the velvet strap. She could have said, "Now I've got you," as she gazed at the little captive she had netted. But of course she meant it kindly. Oh, more than kindly. She was going to prove to this girl that—wonderful things did happen in life, that—fairy godmothers were real, that—rich people had hearts, and that women *were* sisters. She turned impulsively, saying: "Don't be frightened. After all, why shouldn't you come back with me? We're both women. If I'm the more fortunate, you ought to expect . . ."

But happily at that moment, for she didn't know how the sentence was going to end, the car stopped. The bell was rung, the door opened, and with a charming, protecting, almost embracing movement, Rosemary drew the other into the hall. Warmth, softness, light, a sweet scent, all those things so familiar to her she never even thought about them, she watched that other receive. It was fascinating. She was like the little rich girl in her nursery with all the cupboards to open, all the boxes to unpack.

"Come, come upstairs," said Rosemary, longing to begin to be generous. "Come up to my room." And, besides, she wanted to spare this poor little thing from being stared at by the servants; she decided as they mounted the stairs she would not even ring for Jeanne, but take off her things by herself. The great thing was to be natural!

And "There!" cried Rosemary again, as they reached her beautiful big bedroom with the curtains drawn, the fire leaping on her wonderful lacquer furniture, her gold cushions and the primrose and blue rugs.

---

2 Class, Colonialism, and the Great War *What does this passage suggest about the disparity between Rosemary's world and her guest's?*

The girl stood just inside the door; she seemed dazed. But Rosemary didn't mind that.

"Come and sit down," she cried, dragging her big chair up to the fire, "in this comfy chair. Come and get warm. You look so dreadfully cold."

"I daren't, madam," said the girl, and she edged backwards.

"Oh, please,"—Rosemary ran forward—"you mustn't be frightened, you mustn't, really. Sit down, and when I've taken off my things we shall go into the next room and have tea and be cosy. Why are you afraid?" And gently she half pushed the thin figure into its deep cradle.

But there was no answer. The girl stayed just as she had been put, with her hands by her sides and her mouth slightly open. To be quite sincere, she looked rather stupid. But Rosemary wouldn't acknowledge it. She leaned over her, saying: "Won't you take off your hat? Your pretty hair is all wet. And one is so much more comfortable without a hat, isn't one?"

There was a whisper that sounded like "Very good, madam," and the crushed hat was taken off.

"Let me help you off with your coat, too," said Rosemary.

The girl stood up. But she held on to the chair with one hand and let Rosemary pull. It was quite an effort. The other scarcely helped her at all. She seemed to stagger like a child, and the thought came and went through Rosemary's mind, that if people wanted helping they must respond a little, just a little, otherwise it became very difficult indeed. And what was she to do with the coat now? She left it on the floor, and the hat too. She was just going to take a cigarette off the mantelpiece when the girl said quickly, but so lightly and strangely: "I'm very sorry, madam, but I'm going to faint. I shall go off, madam, if I don't have something."

Class, Colonialism, and the Great War *What can you conclude about Rosemary's attitude toward her guest?* **3**

Motivation *Whose needs are uppermost in Rosemary's mind?* **4**

Comparing Literature

Teach

Big Idea **2**

Class, Colonialism, and the Great War
Answer: *Rosemary's world is one of beauty and luxury; her guest's one of squalor and need.*

ENGLISH LEARNERS Tell English learners that *the other* refers to the beggar. **Ask:** What things are "familiar" to Rosemary? *("Warmth, softness, light, a sweet scent")* Whom does she watch "receive" them? *(the beggar)*

Big Idea **3**

Class, Colonialism, and the Great War
Answer: *Rosemary, like many others of the upper class, is unable to empathize with the poor.*

Literary Element **4**

Motivation **Answer:** *Rosemary is not thinking of the young woman's needs but of her own—she needs the young woman's gratitude and adulation.*

English Learners

DIFFERENTIATED INSTRUCTION

Beginning Remind students that long dashes are called em dashes. They are used to create a break, either in the middle or at the end of a sentence. Direct students' attention to the text, "She was going to prove to this girl that—wonderful things did happen in life, that—fairly god-mothers were real—rich people had hearts, and that women were sisters." **Ask:** Why does the author use an em dash? *(to separate the reasons why Rosemary wants to help; The pause caused by the break adds a sort of fanstasy element or disbelief of what Rosemary is saying.)*

Comparing Literature

Teach

Literary Element   1

Motivation Answer: *Smith is a very common name. It is also a name that a person sometimes uses to conceal his or her real name. The young woman may have made up the name in order to avoid revealing her identity to the Fells.*

ENGLISH LEARNERS Ask English learners for examples of common surnames in their cultures.

Cultural History ☆

Low Tea Tea is, of course, a drink. But in England the term *tea* designates a light meal as well. Low tea, or afternoon tea, is usually served around four o'clock in the afternoon. It typically consists of tea or coffee, scones, sandwiches, and pastries. Many restaurants serve afternoon tea, which is often incorrectly called "high tea."

"Good heavens, how thoughtless I am!" Rosemary rushed to the bell.

"Tea! Tea at once! And some brandy immediately!"

The maid was gone again, but the girl almost cried out. "No, I don't want no brandy. I never drink brandy. It's a cup of tea I want, madam." And she burst into tears.

It was a terrible and fascinating moment. Rosemary knelt beside her chair.

"Don't cry, poor little thing," she said. "Don't cry." And she gave the other her lace handkerchief. She really was touched beyond words. She put her arm round those thin, birdlike shoulders.

Now at last the other forgot to be shy, forgot everything except that they were both women, and gasped out: "I can't go on no longer like this. I can't bear it. I shall do away with myself. I can't bear no more."

"You shan't have to. I'll look after you. Don't cry any more. Don't you see what a good thing it was that you met me? We'll have tea and you'll tell me everything. And I shall arrange something. I promise. *Do* stop crying. It's so exhausting. Please!"

☆ The other did stop just in time for Rosemary to get up before the tea came. She had the table placed between them. She plied the poor little creature with everything, all the sandwiches, all the bread and butter, and every time her cup was empty she filled it with tea, cream and sugar. People always said sugar was so nourishing. As for herself she didn't eat; she smoked and looked away tactfully so that the other should not be shy.

And really the effect of that slight meal was marvelous. When the tea table was carried away a new being, a light, frail creature with tangled hair, dark lips, deep, lighted eyes, lay back in the big chair in a kind of sweet languor,[8] looking at the blaze. Rosemary lit a fresh cigarette; it was time to begin.

"And when did you have your last meal?" she asked softly.

But at that moment the door handle turned.

"Rosemary, may I come in?" It was Philip.

"Of course."

He came in. "Oh, I'm so sorry," he said, and stopped and stared.

"It's quite all right," said Rosemary smiling. "This is my friend, Miss—"

"Smith, madam," said the languid[9] figure, who was strangely still and unafraid.

"Smith," said Rosemary. "We are going to have a little talk."

"Oh, yes," said Philip. "Quite," and his eye caught sight of the coat and hat on the floor. He came over to the fire and turned his back to it. "It's a beastly afternoon," he said curiously, still looking at that listless figure, looking at its hands and boots, and then at Rosemary again.

"Yes, isn't it?" said Rosemary enthusiastically. "Vile."

Philip smiled his charming smile. "As a matter of fact," said he, "I wanted you to come into the library for a moment. Would you? Will Miss Smith excuse us?"

> **"Her heart beat like a heavy bell. Pretty! Lovely!"**

---

8. *Languor* means "a dreamy, lazy mood or quality."
9. *Languid* means "lacking energy or vitality."

Motivation *Why does the young woman identify herself as "Smith"?*   **1**

Writing Practice

 SPIRAL REVIEW **Character Analysis** Have students analyze Mansfield's characterizations in "A Cup of Tea." **Write the following question on the board:** How does Mansfield's use of language help define her characters and convey the narrator's attitudes toward them? Ask students to reread the story, taking notes on the author's descriptions of the characters. Then, have them respond to the question with a brief essay that includes specific references to the text. *(Students may discuss the level of detail in the descriptions, interpret figurative language, or examine the sounds and connotations of specific words.)*

The big eyes were raised to him, but Rosemary answered for her. "Of course she will." And they went out of the room together.

"I say," said Philip, when they were alone. "Explain. Who is she? What does it all mean?"

Rosemary, laughing, leaned against the door and said: "I picked her up in Curzon Street. Really. She's a real pick-up. She asked me for the price of a cup of tea, and I brought her home with me."

"But what on earth are you going to do with her?" cried Philip.

"Be nice to her," said Rosemary quickly. "Be frightfully nice to her. Look after her. I don't know how. We haven't talked yet. But show her—treat her—make her feel—"

"My darling girl," said Philip, "you're quite mad, you know. It simply can't be done."

"I knew you'd say that," **retorted** Rosemary. "Why not? I want to. Isn't that a reason? And besides, one's always reading about these things. I decided—"

"But," said Philip slowly, and he cut the end of a cigar, "she's so astonishingly pretty."

"Pretty?" Rosemary was so surprised that she blushed. "Do you think so? I—I hadn't thought about it."

"Good Lord!" Philip struck a match. "She's absolutely lovely. Look again, my child. I was bowled over when I came into your room just now. However . . . I think you're making a ghastly mistake. Sorry, darling, if I'm crude and all that. But let me know if Miss Smith is going to dine with us in time for me to look up *The Milliner's Gazette*."[10]

---

10. A *milliner* is one who makes or sells women's hats. A *gazette* is a newspaper.

 Class, Colonialism, and the Great War *How would you characterize the upper-class marriage portrayed in this story?*

Vocabulary

retort (ri tôrt´) *v.* to reply in a witty, quick, or sharp manner

"You absurd creature!" said Rosemary, and she went out of the library, but not back to her bedroom. She went to her writing room and sat down at her desk. Pretty! Absolutely lovely! Bowled over! Her heart beat like a heavy bell. Pretty! Lovely! She drew her check book towards her. But no, checks would be no use, of course. She opened a drawer and took out five pound notes, looked at them, put two back, and holding the three squeezed in her hand, she went back to her bedroom.

Half an hour later Philip was still in the library, when Rosemary came in.

"I only wanted to tell you," said she, and she leaned against the door again and looked at him with her dazzled exotic gaze, "Miss Smith won't dine with us tonight."

Philip put down the paper. "Oh, what's happened? Previous engagement?"

Rosemary came over and sat down on his knee. "She insisted on going," said she, "so I gave the poor little thing a present of money. I couldn't keep her against her will, could I?" she added softly.

Rosemary had just done her hair, darkened her eyes a little, and put on her pearls. She put up her hands and touched Philip's cheeks.

"Do you like me?" said she, and her tone, sweet, husky, troubled him.

"I like you awfully," he said, and he held her tighter. "Kiss me."

There was a pause.

Then Rosemary said dreamily, "I saw a fascinating little box today. It cost twenty-eight guineas. May I have it?"

Philip jumped her on his knee. "You may, little wasteful one," said he.

But that was not really what Rosemary wanted to say.

"Philip," she whispered, and she pressed his head against her bosom, "am I *pretty*?"

Motivation *What is the real reason why Rosemary cut Miss Smith's visit short?* **3**

KATHERINE MANSFIELD **1009**

Comparing Literature

After You Read

Assess

1. (a) The owner flatters her and makes her feel respected.
(b) Rosemary is deeply insecure.

2. (a) Cold, alien, and frightening (b) It is delicate.

3. (a) Whether she is pretty (b) Despite her vanity, she needs reassurance that she is attractive to her husband.

4. Rosemary enjoys the idea of "having" Miss Smith, just as she admires the look of her hands holding the box, but Miss Smith is threatening because she comes from the "real world."

5. (a) When Philip tells Rosemary that he thinks Miss Smith is attractive (b) Besides ending Rosemary's relationship with Miss Smith, this event helps show the superficial nature of Rosemary's life.

6. Mansfield is critical of her upper-class contemporaries. She did care about the plight of London's poor, as evident in her depiction of Miss Smith.

7. Some students may feel there is no longer a class system. Other students may cite examples such as Hurricane Katrina or the health-care system to show that inequities in social classes still exist.

Literary Element

1. Rosemary believes that she is being generous and caring. Her real motive is to feel better about herself.

2. Philip is appalled to find a common street woman in his home. He likely knows that his comments about Miss Smith's beauty will prompt Rosemary to dismiss her guest.

Reading Strategy

1. Possible answer: Most people ignore or try to avoid homeless people.

2. Possible answer: Today women's lives are as freely chosen as those of men.

Vocabulary Practice

1. b   2. c   3. a   4. b

Writing

Students' writing should reflect the point of view of Philip or Miss Smith, and should retell the events and settings of the story from this character's perspective.

1010

After You Read

Respond and Think Critically

Respond and Interpret

1. (a) Why does Rosemary enjoy shopping at the antique store? (b) How would you **characterize** her from her thoughts and actions while there?

2. (a) Describe Curzon Street as it appears to Rosemary. (b) What do Rosemary's impressions of the street suggest about her emotional state?

3. (a) What does Rosemary ask her husband at the end of the story? (b) What does this reveal about their relationship? Explain your answer.

Analyze and Evaluate

4. "I picked her up in Curzon Street," Rosemary explains to Philip. In what ways is Miss Smith like the other things Rosemary picks up on Curzon Street? How is she different?

5. (a) What do you think is the **climax** in this story? (b) How does this event contribute to the story?

Connect

6. **Big Idea** **Class, Colonialism, and the Great War** What do you think is Mansfield's opinion of the upper class? Of the lower class? Support your answers with details from the story.

7. **Connect to Today** Are social and economic classes as separated today as they were in Mansfield's time? Use examples to support your opinion.

Literary Element **Motivation**

Revealing characters' **motivations** helps to make the characters believable and their actions realistic.

1. What does Rosemary believe is her reason for helping Miss Smith? What is her real motive?

2. Why does Philip discourage his wife from helping Miss Smith? Why do you think he comments on Miss Smith's beauty?

Writing

Write a Story Briefly retell the story "A Cup of Tea" from the point of view either of Philip or Miss Smith. Begin your story at the point in which that character first appears or a little before. (For example, you may want to imagine what Miss Smith was thinking before seeing Rosemary.) Record your character's impressions of events and settings from the original story.

LOG ON ▶ **Literature** Online

Selection Resources For Selection Quizzes, eFlashcards, and Reading-Writing Connection activities, go to glencoe.com and enter QuickPass code GLB9817u6.

Reading Strategy **Connect to Contemporary Issues**

Review the chart you made as you read, and then answer the following questions.

1. In your experience, how do most people behave toward the homeless today?

2. How has the role of women in society changed since the time of this story?

Vocabulary Practice

Practice with Analogies Choose the word that best completes each analogy.

1. stiff : formal :: quaint :
   a. ancient   b. unusual   c. foreign

2. unpleasant : enjoyable :: odious :
   a. repulsive   b. intense   c. attractive

3. shout : yell :: retort :
   a. reply   b. sing   c. whisper

4. cloudy : overcast :: exotic :
   a. predictable   b. unusual   c. typical

Before You Read

Focus

Summary

Head begins by explaining the desperate poverty experienced by everyone in a Botswanan village. She tells the story of an old woman who nearly passes out from hunger. Head takes her home and feeds her. Later, a relative of the woman appears to thank Head for her kindness with a bucket of water.

 For an audio recording of this selection, use Listening Library Audio CD-ROM.

Readability Scores

Dale-Chall: 6.3
DRP: 54
Lexile: 820

Build Background

Bessie Head wrote the following essay during her first years living in Serowe, Botswana, in the mid-1960s. At that time, Serowe was a village of 33,000 people who "all live in mud huts," according to Head. Botswana, a country neighboring South Africa, has a limited supply of fresh water and experiences periodic droughts.

Village People

Bessie Head

Poverty has a home in Africa—like a quiet second skin. It may be the only place on earth where it is worn with an unconscious dignity. People do not look down at your shoes which are caked with years of mud and split so that the toes stick out. They look straight and deeply into your eyes to see if you are friend or foe. That is all that matters. To some extent I think that this eye-looking, this intense human awareness, is a reflection of the earth all about. There is no end to African sky and to African land. One might say that in its vastness is a certain kind of watchfulness that strips man down to his simplest form. If that is not so, then there must be some other, unfathomable reason for the immense humanity and the extreme gentleness of the people of my village.

Poverty here has majority backing.[1] Our lives are completely adapted to it. Each day we eat a porridge of millet[2] in the morning; a thicker millet porridge with a piece of boiled meat at midday; and at evening we repeat breakfast. We use our heads to transport almost everything: water from miles and miles, bags of corn and maize, and firewood.

This adaptation to difficult conditions in a permanently drought-stricken country is full of calamity.[3] Babies die most easily of starvation and malnutrition: and yet, within this pattern of adaptation people crowd in about the mother and sit, sit in heavy silence, absorbing the pain, till, to the mother, it is only a dim, dull ache folded into the stream of life. It is not right. There is a terrible mindlessness about it. But what alternative? To step out of this mindless safety, and face the pain of life alone when the balance is heavily weighted

---

1. [Poverty . . . backing.] More people are poverty-stricken here than not.

2. *Millet* is a type of cereal grass whose grain is used for food.
3. A *calamity* is a catastrophe causing terrible loss and pain.

BESSIE HEAD **1011**

Teach

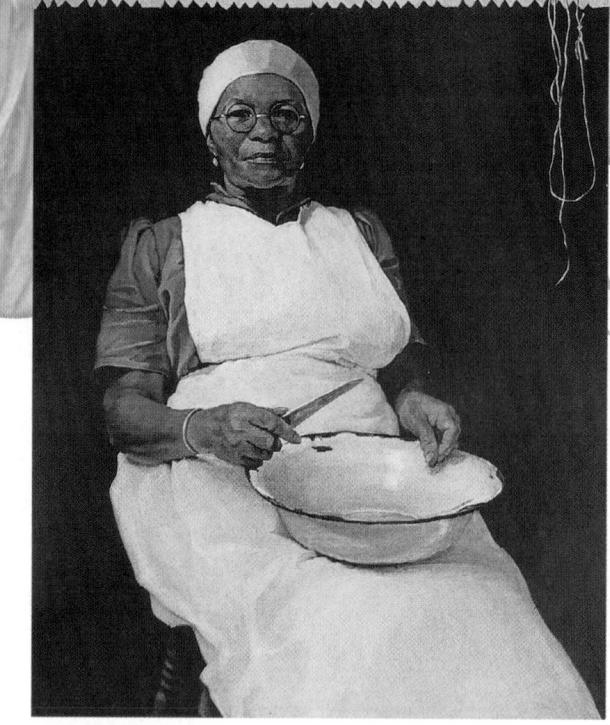

Cookie, Annie Mavata, 1956. Dorothy Kay. Oil on canvas, 69 x 57 cm.
Pretoria Art Museum, Pretoria, South Africa.

View the Art At the time this painting was done, Mavata was employed by
the artist as a cook. Black citizens in South Africa at that time were subject to
strict segregation under the apartheid system. In what ways does this image
show dignity in spite of suffering, as Head describes it?

down on one side, is for certain to face a fate
far worse. Those few who have are insane in a
strange, quiet, harmless way: walking all about
the village, freely. Only by their ceaseless muttering and half-clothed bodies are they distinguishable from others. It is not right, as it is
negative merely to strive for existence. There
must be other ingredients boiling in the pot.
Yet how? We are in the middle of nowhere.
Most communication is by ox cart or sledge.
Poverty also creates strong currents of fear and
anxiety. We are not outgoing. We tend to push
aside all new intrusions. We live and survive
by making as few demands as possible. Yet,

under the deceptive peace around us we are
more easily confused and torn apart than those
with the capacity to take in their stride the
width and the reach of new horizons.

   Do we really retain the right to develop
slowly, admitting change only in so far as it
keeps pace with our limitations, or does change
descend upon us as a calamity? I merely ask this
because, anonymous as we are, in our favor is a
great credit balance of love and warmth that
the gods somewhere should count up. It may be
that they overlook desert and semidesert places.
I should like to remind them that there are
people here too who need taking care of.

1012   UNIT 6   THE MODERN AGE

The Old Woman

2 She was so frail that her whole body swayed this way and that like a thin stalk of corn in the wind. Her arms were as flat as boards. The flesh hung loosely, and her hands which clutched the walking stick were turned outwards and knobbled with age. Under her long dress also swayed the tattered edges of several petticoats. The ends of two bony stick-legs peeped out. She had on a pair of sand-shoes. The toes were all sticking out, so that the feet flapped about in them. She wore each shoe on the wrong foot, so that it made the heart turn over with amusement.

Yet she seemed so strong that it was a shock when she suddenly bent double, retched and coughed emptily, and crumbled to the ground like a quiet sigh.

"What is it, Mmm? What is the matter?" I asked.

"Water, water," she said faintly.

"Wait a minute. I shall ask at this hut here if there is any water."

"What is the matter?" they asked.

"The old lady is ill," I said.

"No," she said curtly. "I am not ill. I am hungry."

The crowd laughed in embarrassment that she should display her need so nakedly. They turned away; but old ladies have no more shame left. They are like children. They give way to weakness and cry openly when they are hungry.

"Never mind," I said. "Hunger is a terrible thing. My hut is not far away. This small child will take you. Wait till I come back, then I shall prepare food for you."

Then, it was late afternoon. The old lady had long passed from my mind when a strange young woman, unknown to me, walked into the yard with a pail of water on her head. She set it down outside the door and squatted low.

"Good-day. How are you?" I said.

She returned the greeting, keeping her face empty and carefully averted. It is impossible to say: what do you want? Whom are you looking for? It is impossible to say this to a carefully averted face and a body that squats quietly, patiently. I looked at the sky, helplessly. I looked at the trees. I looked at the ground, but the young woman said nothing. I did not know her, inside or out. Many people I do not know who know me, inside and out, and always it is this way, this silence.

A curious neighbor looked over the hedge.

"What's the matter?" she asked.

I turned my eyes to the sky again, shrugging helplessly.

"Please ask the young woman what she wants, whom she is looking for."

The young woman turned her face to the neighbor, still keeping it averted, and said quietly:

"No, tell her she helped our relative who collapsed this morning. Tell her the relatives discussed the matter. Tell her we had nothing to give in return, only that one relative said she passes by every day on her way to the water tap. Then we decided to give a pail of water. It is all we have."

Tell them too. Tell them how natural, sensible, normal is human kindness. Tell them, those who judge my country, Africa, by gain and greed, that the gods walk about her barefoot with no ermine and gold-studded cloaks.

> 💬 **Discussion Starter**

In your opinion, is Head disillusioned by the events that take place, or are her ideals reinforced by them? Discuss this question with a small group of classmates. Use specific details from the essay to support your opinions. Then share your conclusions with the rest of the class.

BESSIE HEAD **1013**

Teach

Literary Element 2

Simile Ask: What similes does Head use to describe the old woman or parts of her body? *(Head compares the woman's body to a thin stalk of corn and her arms to boards.)*

APPROACHING Remind approaching-level students that a **simile** compares two different things using *like, as,* or another connecting word. Ask them to find the words *like* and *as* in the first paragraph on this page.

Approaching Level

DIFFERENTIATED INSTRUCTION

Established Remind students of the similes Head uses to describe the old woman. Have students choose a literary character and have them to write a short paragraph describing this character. They may describe the person's appearance, personality, or both. Encourage them to include several similes in their descriptions and challenge them to use one simile that compares their character to the character of the old woman.

Comparing Literature

Before You Read

Focus

Summary

This parable tells of a rich man and a beggar named Lazarus. Lazarus dies and goes to heaven. But after the rich man dies, he wakes up in hell. He calls up to heaven, asking Abraham to send Lazarus to help him. Abraham refuses and adds that travel between heaven and hell is impossible. The rich man asks Abraham to send Lazarus to his house to warn his brothers so that they won't end up in hell after they die. Abraham says that the brothers already have "Moses and the prophets." If the brothers ignore their warnings, they will also ignore the warnings of someone who returns from the dead.

View the Art ★

Answer: *The people at the rich man's table wear luxurious clothing, elaborate hats, and shoes. They celebrate raucously and seem oblivious to the beggar. Lazarus wears almost no clothing, his head is wrapped in a rag, and he is barefoot. He sits on the bare floor, instead of on a bench, and watches the festivities alertly.*

Build Background

A **parable** is an illustrative story answering a question or pointing to a moral or religious lesson. The most famous parables are those told by Jesus, such as the one you are about to read. In this parable, Lazarus, whose name comes from a Hebrew word meaning "God has helped," is a diseased beggar. At that time many people believed that the diseased and destitute were to blame for their afflictions, perhaps because they or an ancestor had sinned. This parable also mentions Abraham, a biblical patriarch regarded as the father of the Hebrew people.

The Parable of the Rich Man. Frans Francken the Younger. Musée Municipal, Cambrai, France.

View the Art Francken is known for his small-scale works with religious themes. How does this image show the contrast between rich and poor? Explain. ★

The Parable of Lazarus and the Rich Man

from the King James Version of the Bible

Vocabulary Practice

SPIRAL REVIEW **Word Patterns Ask:** What does the word brethren mean? If necessary, explain to students that *brethren* is a plural form of *brother*. It is an archaic word that is not generally used today. (The King James Bible was published in 1611.) When it is used, it almost always refers to the members of a specific group or profession. **Ask:** Can you think of any other words that form their plurals by adding -ren? *(child)*

There was a certain rich man, which was clothed in purple and fine linen, and fared sumptuously every day:

And there was a certain beggar named Lazarus, which was laid at his gate, full of sores,

And desiring to be fed with the crumbs which fell from the rich man's table: moreover the dogs came and licked his sores.

And it came to pass, that the beggar died, and was carried by the angels into Abraham's bosom: the rich man also died, and was buried;

And in hell he lift up his eyes, being in torments, and seeth Abraham afar off, and Lazarus in his bosom.

And he cried and said, Father Abraham, have mercy on me, and send Lazarus, that he may dip the tip of his finger in water, and cool my tongue; for I am tormented in this flame.

But Abraham said, Son, remember that thou in thy lifetime receivedst thy good things and likewise Lazarus evil things: but now he is comforted, and thou art tormented.

And beside all this, between us and you there is a great gulf fixed: so that they which would pass from hence to you cannot; neither can they pass to us, that *would come* from thence.

Then he said, I pray thee therefore, father, that thou wouldest send him to my father's house:

For I have five brethren; that he may testify unto them, lest they also come into this place of torment.

Abraham saith unto him, They have Moses and the prophets; let them hear them.

And he said, Nay, father Abraham: but if one went unto them from the dead, they will repent.

And he said unto him, If they hear not Moses and the prophets, neither will they be persuaded, though one rose from the dead. ❧

—Luke 16:19–31

Quickwrite

How do you respond to the role reversal that takes place in this parable? What does the parable imply about the lives of Lazarus and the rich man, and how does that lesson apply to all humans? Write a paragraph in which you address these questions.

COMPARING LITERATURE **1015**

Teach

Literary History ☆
Different Interpretations
Over the centuries, there has been considerable discussion about this parable. Some say its message is that we should treat people kindly in life. Others say it shows that obeying God is a person's most important responsibility, that death is the fate that awaits rich and poor alike, or that riches—or a lack of them—do not indicate a person's favor in God's eyes.

⚡ Quickwrite

Students' paragraphs should address the questions by noting that the rich man enjoys his abundance in private, ignoring the plight of the beggar at his gates, and the parable expresses the need for people to share their wealth to help the poor.

> 💿 For an audio recording of this selection, use Listening Library Audio CD-ROM.

Readability Scores
Dale-Chall: 5.8
DRP: 60
Lexile: 990

English Learners
DIFFERENTIATED INSTRUCTION

Intermediate In the parable, Abraham refers to "Moses and the prophets." Students who do not have a Judeo-Christian background may not be aware that the phrase has a specific meaning. The first five books of the Hebrew Bible—the Old Testament—are sometimes called the Pentateuch, or the Torah. They are also referred to as the Law of Moses. The rest of the Hebrew Bible is divided into two groups—the Prophets and the Writings. So when Abraham refers to "Moses and the prophets," he means the Law of Moses and the writings of the prophets. Have students identify this expression as they read.

Before You Read

Focus

Summary

The selection is a compilation of short verses from the Qur'an that deal with giving alms to the poor.

Reading Strategy   1

Draw Conclusions About Theme Direct students' attention to verse 2:273. Tell them that *importune* means "to ask persistently." **Ask:** How does the verse suggest people behave when they need money and when they give it? *(People should not beg or call attention to themselves when they give alms.)*

ADVANCED Ask advanced learners what the verse implies about the relative importance of business and religion. Have them support their answer with references to the verse. *(Religious devotion—"fighting for the cause of God"—is more important than working to earn money—"travel[ing] the land in quest of trading ventures.")* Ask students to debate whether those values are reflected in contemporary American society.

For an audio recording of this selection, use Listening Library Audio CD-ROM.

Readability Scores

Dale-Chall: 10.2
DRP: 61
Lexile: 900

Build Background

The Arabic word *Qur'an,* which means "recitation" or "reading aloud," refers to the holy book of Islam. Muslims believe that the Qur'an is the sacred word of Allah, or God, and the authoritative guide to life. According to Muslim belief, Allah directly revealed the Qur'an to Muhammad (A.D. 570–632).

The Qur'an identifies the five "pillars of Islam," or the core practices that a devout Muslim follows: acknowledging Allah as the only God, praying five times a day, fasting from dawn to dusk during the holy month of Ramadan, giving alms—donations—to the poor, and undertaking a pilgrimage to Mecca once in a lifetime, if the believer has the means.

from the Qur'an

Translated by N. J. Dawood

Attend to your prayers, render the alms levy, and kneel with those who kneel. (2:43)

Those that give their wealth for the cause of God and do not follow their almsgiving with taunts and insults shall be rewarded by their Lord; they shall have nothing to fear or to regret. (2:262)

As for those needy men who, being wholly preoccupied with fighting for the cause of God, cannot travel the land in quest of trading ventures: the ignorant take them for men of wealth on account of their modest behavior. But you can recognize them by their look—they never importune men for alms. Whatever alms you give are known to God. (2:273)

You shall never be truly righteous until you give in alms what you dearly cherish. The alms you give are known to God. (3:92)

God does not love arrogant and boastful men, who are themselves tight-fisted and enjoin others to be tight-fisted; who conceal the riches which God of His bounty has bestowed upon them (We have prepared a shameful punishment for the unbelievers) . . . (4:37)

Alms shall be only for the poor and the destitute; for those that are engaged in the management of alms and those whose hearts are sympathetic to the Faith; for the freeing of slaves and debtors; for the advancement of God's cause; and for the traveler in need. That is a duty enjoined by God. God is all-knowing and wise. (9:60)

Grammar Practice

SPIRAL REVIEW **Parse Sentences** Verses 2:273, 4:37, and 9:60 contain long sentences with atypical punctuation. Have students select one of these three verses and determine exactly how the sentences, clauses, and parenthetical elements are structured. You may want to suggest they copy the verses in their notebooks and mark them up. Have students re-write the sentences using punctuation and grammar conventions of Standard Academic English.

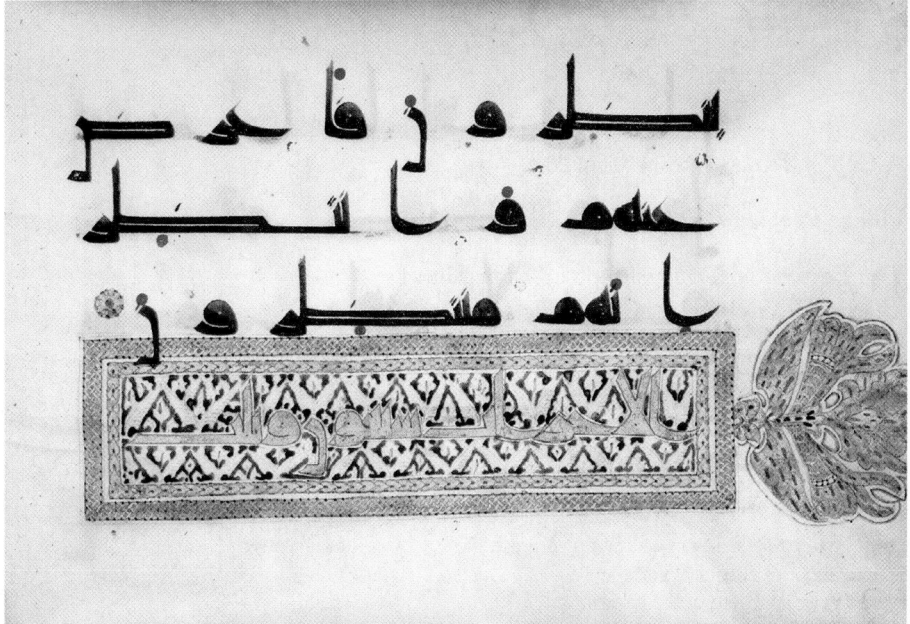

Fragment from the Qur'an. Iraq or Syria, ninth–tenth century. Ink and gold leaf on parchment, 21.5 x 32.5 cm. Museum für Islamische Kunst, Staatliche Museen zu Berlin, Germany.

The true believers, both men and women, are friends to one another. They enjoin what is just and forbid what is evil; they attend to their prayers, and render the alms levy, and obey God and His apostle. On these God will have mercy. God is mighty and wise. (9:71)

Tell My servants, those who are true believers, to be steadfast in prayer and to give alms in private and in public, before that day arrives when all trading shall cease and friendships be no more. (14:31)

Give to the near of kin their due, and also to the destitute and to the traveler in need. Do not squander your substance wastefully, for the wasteful are Satan's brothers; and Satan is ever ungrateful to his Lord. (17:27)

You are called upon to give in the cause of God. Some among you are ungenerous; yet whoever is ungenerous to this cause is ungenerous to himself. Indeed, God does not need you, but you need Him. If you pay no heed, He will replace you by others who shall bear no resemblance to yourselves. (47:38)

Have you thought of him that denies the Last Judgment? It is he who turns away the orphan and has no urge to feed the destitute. (107:1)

💬 Discussion Starter

Which verses convey the Muslim attitude toward compassion and generosity? How is the message in those verses similar to and different from the messages in the other selections in this Comparing Literature feature? Consider how the message is conveyed in each selection. Discuss these questions with a group of classmates.

COMPARING LITERATURE **1017**

Teach

Reading Strategy 2

Analyze Text Structure
Point out that the verses come from different parts of the Qur'an. **Ask:** Why do you think the giving of alms is discussed repeatedly in the Qur'an? *(Possible responses: Giving alms is one of the five pillars of Islam; people need to be reminded to take care of the poor.)*

Cultural History ☆
The Five Pillars The verses on almsgiving say that he who has an overabundance and does not share with the poor will be doomed. Explain to students that this idea is one of the five pillars of Islamic society. Students should understand that the statements of moral truths in these verses from the Qur'an are explicit, while the messages suggested by Mansfield's story, Head's essay, and the biblical parable are implicit.

English Learners

DIFFERENTIATED INSTRUCTION

Intermediate Read the first verse, 2:43, aloud. Repeat "kneel with those who kneel." **Ask:** What activity do you think the phrase refers to? *(praying)* Why would a person say that? *(Muslims—and many Christians—kneel down to pray.)*

After You Read

Teach

View the Art ★

Answer: *Similarities: The wealthier people are enjoying a meal, while the poor man has no food and watches them as they eat. They seem happy and celebratory, and pay no attention to the man outside. Differences: They do not share space, as in the Lazarus painting; he seems ashamed while Lazarus seems to look at the wealthy man accusingly.*

Assess

▣ Compare the Big Idea

Critique students' essays on the basis of these criteria:

- Does the essay compare the messages about class conflict in two or more of the selections?
- Does the essay include insights about life gained from two or more of the selections?
- Does the essay include examples and evidence to support its main points?

Compare Tone

1. Mansfield's tone conveys contempt for Rosemary's use of wealth. Head's tone conveys admiration for the poor people of her village. "The Parable…" conveys a stern warning to wealthy people who ignore other's poverty. *The Qur'an* conveys the urgent message that rich people are obligated to help the poor.

Wrap-Up: Comparing Literature

Across Time and Place

- *A Cup of Tea* by Katherine Mansfield
- *Village People* by Bessie Head
- *The Parable of Lazarus and the Rich Man*
  from the King James Version of the Bible
- from the *Qur'an*

COMPARE THE **Big Idea** **Class, Colonialism, and the Great War**

Writing Write a brief essay in which you compare the messages about class conflict and the insights about life conveyed in two or more of the selections.

COMPARE Tone

Group Activity With a small group of your classmates, discuss the tone of each selection. Then answer the following questions.

1. How does the tone of each selection convey the writer's attitude toward wealth and poverty?

2. How does each writer use language to convey his or her tone?

3. What terms would you use to describe the overall tone of each selection?

COMPARE Past and Present

Visual Display How does British culture today view wealth and poverty? Does that view differ from the one suggested by Mansfield's short story? Research the ways in which Britain currently addresses the needs of the poor. Create a visual display, such as a chart or a collage, to communicate your findings.

Thoughts of a Hungry Man. Emilio Longoni. Oil on canvas, 74.8 x 61.02 in. Museo Civico, Biella, Italy.

View the Art The contrast of social classes is a prevalent theme in many nineteenth- and twentieth-century works. How does this image's portrayal differ from the one that accompanies the parable on page 1014? In what ways is it similar? ★

LOG ON ▶ **Literature** Online

Selection Resources For Selection Quizzes, eFlashcards, and Reading-Writing Connection activities, go to glencoe.com and enter the QuickPass code GLB9817u6.

1018 UNIT 6 THE MODERN AGE

---

2. Mansfield relies heavily upon verbal and dramatic irony. Head uses rhetorical questions, detailed imagery, and dialogue. The writer of the parable uses allegory. The writer of the excerpt from *The Qur'an* uses persuasive rhetoric.

3. "A Cup of Tea" can be described as satirical, "Village People" as compassionate, "The Parable of Lazarus and the Rich Man" as didactic, and the excerpt from *The Qur'an* as moralistic.

Compare Past and Present

Students' visual displays should reflect how Britain addresses the needs of the poor in recent times. Tell students to create captions for any images in their displays.

Set a Purpose for Reading

You've read about class divisions in several cultures and eras. As you read this article about how homelessness has become a major concern in many European countries, ask yourself, What solutions have been proposed to help alleviate the problem?

Preview the Article

1. Scan the **subheads,** or smaller headlines within the article. What clues do they give you about the content of the article?

2. Examine the photograph on page 1021. Judging by this image, do you think homelessness is a serious problem in Europe? Explain.

Reading Strategy Analyze Text Structure

When you **analyze text structure,** you determine a pattern of organization within a piece of writing. Most informational texts are organized in chronological order, cause-and-effect order, or compare-and-contrast order. Identify the pattern in each subsection of the article.

1

Down and Out In Europe

The number of homeless in Western Europe is at its highest level in 50 years—and rising. What should be done?

By APARISIM GHOSH

BIG SID TELLS LIES. DURING THE COURSE OF A SINGLE three-hour conversation on a London street corner, he relates his life story four times, each version more fantastical than the last. In one, he swims to the middle of the Thames in midwinter to rescue a drowning dog. In another, he defeats a band of armed skinheads with his bare hands. Sid is a black man who says his parents came to Britain from the Caribbean. But the specific biographical details he serves up vary so dramatically he might easily be talking about three or four completely different people; the narrative of inconsistencies mounts as he works his way through a two-liter bottle of hard cider. By the halfway point, he's contradicting himself almost every other sentence, and lapsing into incoherent repetitions of his two favorite phrases: "short-term" and "long-term."

DOWN AND OUT IN EUROPE **1019**

Approaching Level

DIFFERENTIATED INSTRUCTION

Emerging Point out to students that they can anticipate the tone and content of a text by looking over the various features, such as the title, quotations, subheads, and photographs with captions. Before they begin to read, ask students to list the features in the text and to jot down information provided by each feature in their notebooks. Then have them use their notes to set a purpose for their reading.

Focus

Summary

Homelessness is a growing problem in Western Europe, where more than 3 million people have no place to live. Throwing money at the problem does not necessarily help solve it. Research shows that an accurate count of the homeless is necessary and that local governments provide a better census than centralized governments. Government must work with voluntary organizations to come up with long-term solutions.

 For summaries in languages other than English, see Unit 6 Teaching Resources Book, pp. 36–41.

Teach

Reading Strategy   **1**

Analyze Text Structure

Be sure students understand that the subsections of the article may have different patterns of organization. Invite them to think, as they complete their charts, about why a particular pattern may have been used in each case.

 For an audio recording of this selection, use Listening Library Audio CD-ROM.

Readability Scores

Dale-Chall: 9.9
DRP: 66
Lexile: 1140

Teach

Big Idea	1

Class, Colonialism, and the Great War

Ask: What do the homeless in Western Europe today have in common with the British people after the Great War? *(Possibe answer: They have suffered from a loss of family structure and have experienced disadvantages due to lack of wealth and social position.)*

Cultural History

FEANTSA FEANTSA is an international nongovernmental organization that was founded in 1989. It brings together more than 60 charitable and not-for-profit organizations that provide a wide range of vital services to homeless people.

WHERE THE HOMELESS ARE

FEANTSA, a Brussels-based umbrella body of homeless organizations, estimates that over 3 million people in Western Europe are homeless. Numbers for specific countries are hard to get. Some countries simply don't bother to count, while others have different definitions for homelessness. The numbers below are estimates based on data from government and private sources

HIGH RATES	MEDIUM RATES	LOW RATES
>3 per 1,000	1-3 per 1,000	<1 per 1,000
United Kingdom	Austria	Sweden
Germany	Finland	Greece
France	Belgium	
	Netherlands	
	Denmark	

NOTE: NO CREDIBLE DATA IS AVAILABLE FOR THE EUROPEAN COUNTRIES NOT LISTED.

> **"** That Europe's homelessness problem is roughly the same as America's **IS A SHOCK.** After all, Europe sees itself as kinder, gentler, and more socially responsible than the U.S. **"**

Depending on which version of the saga you believe, Big Sid was born in South London, or in Yorkshire—a county in England; he's a high school dropout or played football at college; he was married (and divorced) twice, or never. He may be 35, or 40. He claims to be utterly alone in the world, an orphan with no relatives at all, but asked if he will allow himself to be photographed for this article, he balks. "I have family, man," he says, his high voice abruptly dropping to an embarrassed whisper. "I don't want them to pick up your magazine and see me in this condition."

His condition is the one certain, cruel, truth about Big Sid: he is homeless. On this bitterly cold winter night, he will make a bed of flattened cardboard boxes in the recessed doorway of a music store, squeeze into a fluorescent green sleeping bag that's too small for his angular 6-foot-6-inch frame, and rest his bald head on an old mail carrier's sack that contains his every possession. He's been sleeping on the streets for much of his adult life, wandering from city to city. Once or twice a year, he will go to a shelter for homeless people, to get out of nasty weather or to have a doctor look at the sores on his feet. But these interludes rarely last more than a few days because Sid finds constant human company stressful, and is deeply suspicious of anything that smacks of officialdom. "The shelters are okay for short-term, for a bath and medical treatment," he says, "but they aren't for long-term, man, not for me."

A Huge Challenge

Finding long-term solutions for people like Big Sid is an enormous—and growing—challenge for Western Europe, where homelessness has quietly been climbing to levels not seen since the end of World War II. Hard numbers are scarce, but according to the European Federation of National Organizations Working with the Homeless (FEANTSA), a Brussels-based group of homeless organizations, at least 3 million Western Europeans are homeless. And between one-fifth and one-third of them are members of homeless families. Only a small number, less than 10%, sleep on the streets like Big Sid. Most huddle into shelters or temporary housing, live in shacks, or bed down in the homes of friends and family. Think homelessness is an American problem? Think again. As a percentage of population, it's as bad in Europe as it is in the U. S., where there are an estimated 2 million homeless, according to Dennis Culhane, a social-policy expert at the University of Pennsylvania.

That Europe's homelessness problem is roughly the same as America's—and that one of the fastest-growing segments of Europe's homeless population is families—is a shock. After all, Europe sees itself as kinder, gentler, and more socially responsible than the U.S. The continent has an extensive, expensive social safety net that's designed to help and protect its most vulnerable citizens—the kind of

Research Practice

SPIRAL REVIEW **Analyze Solutions to Poverty** Sweden and Greece have lower homeless rates than other European countries. Have students find out what programs are available in those countries. **Ask:** Do the programs account for the lower rates? If not, what seems to be working? *(Answers will vary.)* Have students share their findings with the rest of the class and discuss whether similar programs would help alleviate the problem of homelessness in the United States and in other European countries.

people who are thrown to the wolves in winner-take-all America. But that might just be the point: It's easier to be homeless in Europe, where even the down-and-out get social-welfare checks.

Activists and experts, however, don't like to make a direct cause-and-effect connection between welfare and homelessness. They point, instead, to inadequate and sometimes senseless social-welfare policies that throw money at the problem but don't do enough to move the homeless from the streets and shelters into jobs and permanent housing. "The safety net is failing some of the most vulnerable

sections of European society," says Freek Spinnewijn, FEANTSA's director. "A lot of people are falling through—people with mental-health problems, drug and alcohol problems, and people who have suffered [from] abuse." **2**

Homeless Women

Most homeless people in Europe are single or separated men, like Big Sid. But voluntary agencies say the fastest-growing segments among the homeless are like Christelle: young, female, and part of a family. The explanations range from the predictable (the scarcity of jobs) to the counterintuitive (women's

independence may be a contributor: more assertive women are more likely to dump abusive husbands and move into homeless shelters). When the numbers were small, Europe did well by homeless families and women, giving them priority in temporary and permanent government housing. But as their numbers swell, housing is being stretched thin. Spinnewijn says that single women with children make up the majority of homeless families in Europe. "One of the main reasons for the increasing number of homeless families is divorce," says Spinnewijn. "There has been a rise in the number of divorces, and often,

STREET LIFE: A homeless man beds down for the night in central London.

Phillip Hollis

DOWN AND OUT IN EUROPE **1021**

TIME

Teach

Reading Strategy | 2

Analyzing Text Structure
Tell students to stop after reading each subsection of the article to review the order the writer has used. **Ask:** How does the writer organize his information? *(He presents the problem, describes its enormity, highlights those most seriously affected, presents a view of government response, and offers a final review of what is really needed.)*

View the Photograph ★
Photographs are used to supplement the information presented in articles. Point out to students that photographs can influence how the reader feels about the subject matter. **Ask:** How do you feel about this homeless man? *(Responses will vary.)*

English Learners

DIFFERENTIATED INSTRUCTION

Intermediate Remind English learners that different conjunctions are used to express different relationships. **Write** these pairs of sentences on the board:

1. I love the movies. I didn't like *Jaws.*

2. I went to see *Jaws.* I'm afraid to swim in the ocean.

3. We went to school. Later we went to the beach.

Have them decide which type of order is used in each set of sentences, and then have them pick a conjunction to connect the two sentences. *(1. Compare-and-contrast, but; 2. Cause-and-effect, so; 3. Chronological, and)*

TIME

Teach

Reading Strategy | 1

Check Comprehension
Have students read the quotation from Susan Fallis. **Ask:** Why does she say that the homeless who stay in her hostel are often suspicious and angry? *(After living on the streets for years, the homeless are uncomfortable when they find themselves suddenly in a confined area surrounded by people.)*
APPROACHING Approaching-level students should be told that the word *hostel* means "shelter."

For activities related to this selection, see Unit 6 Teaching Resources Book, pp. 42–43.

---

divorced women with children find it very difficult to have an economically sustainable life."

Christelle, originally from northwestern France, has been living in a Paris shelter for five months. According to the French government's rules, she can only stay six months, which means she must find a new place to stay. Christelle is worried about the deadline, but is optimistic that she will have a job and an apartment soon. With no friends in Paris and what appears to be a distant relationship with her family, who live several hours away, she contacted a social-aid worker who placed her in a shelter.

Résumé in hand, she goes out each day looking for work. "I'd like a job in the hospitality industry, maybe as a receptionist," she says. But the job market is tight, and so she tries to hide her circumstances from possible employers, to duck prejudice against homeless people. "Nobody knows I don't have my own home, and I don't tell them," she says. That includes her husband from whom she is separated, and her family. When she calls her parents, she lets them believe she has a place to live.

The music of Jennifer Lopez plays on the radio in the background, and Christelle says what she'd really like to do is live in the U.S. "I dream of Los Angeles," she says. "Things just seem better there." But for the moment, it's enough to care for her daughter and keep going out every day looking for a job. "When I was young I would see people from shelters and thought it must not be easy to live like that, without a place of your own," she says with an awkward smile. "Now I know."

Heading for a Normal Life

It's hard to know what is tormenting the short, stocky man slouched on a bench in a Berlin metro station at 11 P.M. one freezing winter night. His blue eyes are bloodshot from alcohol, his brown beard mottled. Asked for his name by a worker from the Berlin City Mission—a homeless organization—he comes up with "O'Brien," although he's plainly German. He agrees to be taken to a shelter run by the Mission, which is sponsored by the Lutheran Church. There, he is required to surrender the black table lamp that he jealously guards at all times. He's then handed a bowl of hot soup, but screams out that he wants spaghetti. After some soothing words from the kitchen volunteers, he begrudgingly takes his bowl of soup to the almost-empty dining room.

A drunken tantrum is nothing more than a small nuisance for those who work with the homeless. Volunteers routinely encounter hostility, even violence, particularly from men who sleep on the streets. "Those who've been on the streets for years get very uncomfortable when they are suddenly in a confined space, surrounded by lots of people," says Susan Fallis. She is the project manager at a West London hostel, one of several run by the charity Broadway. "They are suspicious and angry, and get put off by even the simplest things." **1**

Residents at Fallis's hostel are provided hot meals, clean bedrooms, even well-being services like foot massages and aromatherapy. If any of the residents are substance abusers, they are encouraged to sign up for government programs to help them. The hostel receives around $940 a week from the British

government for each of its 30-odd residents. It also charges them a small fee, about $15 a week, for things like electricity, water, and gas. It's a small amount they can afford to pay from their welfare checks. The fee has another function: It is meant to help residents deal with simple real-world chores like paying bills. "They need to take small steps toward a normal life," Fallis says.

Money Isn't Enough

Europe's traditional response to homelessness has been to throw money at the problem, in the form of benefits. Unemployed single French citizens over the age of 25 and with no children are entitled to an allowance of around $480 a month. In Britain, people can claim $60–96 per week in unemployment benefits. In Germany, the homeless are entitled to an allowance of $11 a day. Social researchers know that "it's not a matter of giving someone [money each month] and expecting them to find a place to live and make a life," says Martin Hirsch. He is the president of Emmaus France, a voluntary organization that runs shelters and provides housing across the country. "Money isn't enough for people with problems—physical, psychological—who can't take care of themselves."

Can Europe fix its homelessness problem? Not before it acknowledges that the problem is far more serious than officials currently admit. Social researchers say an accurate count of the homeless is as crucial as an accurate national census. Central governments would be smart to pass that job on to local authorities; they're closer to the problem and better able to quantify it. This is shown by the experience of Ger-

1022 UNIT 6 THE MODERN AGE

Reading Practice

SMALL GROUP SPIRAL REVIEW

 Informational Text
Tell students that journalists seek to answer six basic questions when they write a story. The questions begin with *who, what, why, when, where,* and *how.* Have students work with a partner to write the six questions Aparisim Ghosh, the author of this article, might have been using to guide his research. Have students write the questions in

a list, leaving enough space between questions for another pair of students to write answers. *(Who are the homeless in Western Europe? What can prevent more people from becoming homeless? Why did they become homeless? When did the numbers of homeless begin growing? Where do they sleep? How do they survive?)* Have students exchange their questions with another pair and answer

each of the questions using the text. Then have the two pairs discuss the questions and answers as a small group.

many's states, which under German law are responsible for dealing with homelessness. As a result, Germany provides the most accurate picture of the problem among the major European countries. After peaking at 590,000 in 1997, the number of homeless Germans fell to 390,000 in 2000. The decline also suggests that local authorities do a better job, not just of counting the homeless but of getting them off the streets.

Other countries are coming around to the idea that workable solutions for homelessness must come from local authorities. England's Homelessness Act came into force in 2002, requiring each of its 354 local-government housing authorities to develop a homelessness plan.

So far, the response from voluntary groups has been mixed.

Alastair Jackson, director of policy for the housing organization Shelter, says the law has already "improved the quality of help" available to homeless people. But he and others worry that better coordination and cooperation among central and local governments and volunteer organizations must take place. And yes, European governments will still need to throw more money at the problem—to pay for more affordable housing, more shelters, and for the detox, rehabilitation, and therapies many homeless people need to overcome their serious personal problems.

Big Sid doesn't think that's possible. It's been two weeks since he went to a shelter, and now he's back on the streets of London after a trip to the beach resort of Brighton where he begged on the streets for

money. He's still telling tall tales, but they've taken on a much darker tone, with him playing the victim instead of the hero. The villains, inevitably, are representatives of the state, from doctors in public hospitals who don't give him the medicines he wants to police officers who beat him up for no reason. "Governments hurt people," he says, recounting years of abuse he endured—or did he?—in a state-run correctional school 20 years ago. "Government programs are all short-term, and nothing good comes of short-term." Finding long-term solutions for the Big Sids of Europe may be the hardest part of dealing with homelessness.

Respond and Think Critically

Respond and Interpret

1. Write a brief summary of the main ideas in this article before you answer the following questions. For help with writing a summary, see page 435.

2. What do you think can be done to solve the problem of homelessness in Europe and in our own society?

Recall and Interpret

3. (a)What is the estimated number of Western Europeans who are homeless? (b)Why is it "easier" to be homeless in Europe than in the United States?

4. (a)Why are women the fastest-growing segment of the homeless population? (b)Why do you think those who have suffered abuse or have mental-health issues are more likely to be homeless?

Analyze and Evaluate

5. (a)What kind of assistance is available to the homeless in Europe? (b)Why do most social researchers believe that providing money is not enough to eradicate homelessness?

6. (a)What possible solutions for homelessness does the writer suggest? (b)What evidence does the writer cite to support the viability of these suggestions?

7. (a)What kinds of text structures are used in "Down and Out in Europe"? (b)How does the structure show the short- and long-term effects of homelessness?

Connect

8. How do the profiles of homeless people in this article help you understand the class divisions in Katherine Mansfield's story "A Cup of Tea"?

DOWN AND OUT IN EUROPE **1023**

8. Possible answer: The profiles illuminate the plight of the young penniless girl and Rosemary's sympathy for her, and they demonstrate that the young girl's poverty, contrasted with the Fells' great wealth, is indicative of a huge social and economic gap between the upper and lower classes.

 For additional assessment, see Assessment Resources, pp. 243–244.

TIME

Assess

1. Students' summaries should include the main issues of poverty and the projected government aided solutions.

2. Answers will vary.

3. (a) Three million (b) European countries have extensive social "safety nets" that are designed to help their most vulnerable citizens.

4. (a) Lack of jobs, the growing independence of women, and divorce (b) They are more in need of assistance in taking care of themselves.

5. (a) Welfare checks from the government; food, shelter, and counseling at hostels for the homeless (b) Money cannot cure the psychological problems and substance abuse that plague many homeless people.

6. (a) Local authorities should keep careful records of the number of homeless people; governments should empower local authorities to build affordable housing and create social programs for the homeless. (b) German record keeping and England's Homelessness Act

7. (a) Cause and effect and compare and contrast (b) Short-term: personal portraits of homeless people like Big Sid and Christelle; long-term: analysis of statistics and legislation that has been suggested to alleviate the problem

Focus

Bellringer Options

Daily Language Practice
Transparency 84

Or invite students to name their favorite short stories. **Ask:** Who are the authors? What countries are they from? When were they written and published? Why do you think short stories originated in some countries? Lead students to discuss the elements that make the short story a distinctive literary form.

Teach

Literary Element   1

Short Story Explain that a short story is a brief fictional narrative in prose, usually focusing on a single event. Elements of the short story include plot, character, setting, point of view, and theme.

Literary History

The Modern British Short Story ▮1

> *"Short-story writers see by the light of the flash; theirs is the art of the only thing that one can be sure of— the present moment."*
>
> —Nadine Gordimer,
> from "The Flash of Fireflies"

DURING THE SECOND HALF OF THE nineteenth century, the short story gained international popularity. Pioneers of the form included Hawthorne, Poe, and Irving in the United States; Balzac, Flaubert, and Maupassant in France; and Turgenev, Tolstoy, and Chekhov in Russia. Yet in Victorian England the climate that fostered the development of the novel stifled that of the short story. Story writer and critic H. E. Bates wrote that the short story "cannot tolerate a weight of words or a weight of moral teaching, and it is highly significant that these two factors are dominant character-istics of the Victorian English novel." Around 1880, however, the British began to question the Victorian values and conventions that had unified their country (and empire) for the past fifty years. The writer Frank O'Connor suggests that the short story is typically a product of a fragmented society. Thus, as the Victorian world fell apart, writers focused on the individual and the present moment rather than on society and historical continuity. Suddenly, the concentrated form of the short story made sense.

Toward Realism

British fiction during the 1880s and 1890s reflects the transition from Victorian literary conventions to twentieth-century Realism. The short stories of Thomas Hardy, for instance, reflect a melancholy

Conversation Piece, 1912. Vanessa Bell. Oil on panel. University of Hull Art Collection, Humberside, UK. ©1961 Estate of Vanessa Bell, courtesy of Henrietta Garnett.

1024   UNIT 6   THE MODERN AGE

Reading Practice

SPIRAL REVIEW **Summarize** Remind students that a summary is a short restatement of the main ideas of a selection and the details that support them. Have students write a summary of the information about the British short story that they have read. Provide these tips:

- Identify the main ideas.
- Identify supporting details.

- Arrange the main ideas in a logical sequence.
- Summarize the main ideas in your own words.

attitude and a shift toward Realism; yet, the reality Hardy presents is undermined by the artificiality of the Victorian language he uses. Similarly, Rudyard Kipling's short stories were criticized for their focus on brief episodes and use of literary "tricks." Indeed, the short story form was widely criticized as too episodic and formulaic to contain any moral force. Joseph Conrad's short stories, on the other hand, unite the aims of Realism and Romanticism through the use of concrete, realistic details to suggest deeper symbolic and philosophical meanings. According to the critic Charles E. May, it was Conrad who, "because of the profundity of his vision and the subtlety of his use of language, effectively made the transition" and mastered the modern short story form.

Modernism

Both public literacy and the availability of reading material increased drastically during the Victorian and early modern periods. These factors broadened and fractured the reading public; writers could no longer take for granted a unified audience. The growing alienation between the artist and society during the 1890s became the dominant force of the Modernist movement. Many Modernist writers deliberately opposed popular tastes and trends.

After the turn of the century, prevailing assumptions about the individual, faith, history, materialism, and knowledge shattered. Writers no longer saw reality as a recognizable constant; rather, reality depended on each person's fragmented perception of it. "Look within," suggested Virginia Woolf. Woolf and other writers, including Katherine Mansfield, James Joyce, and D. H. Lawrence, concentrated on writing about "an ordinary mind on an ordinary day"—that is, about the mental consciousness of a character.

Sigmund Freud's psychoanalysis contributed to this focus on the internal life and spurred literary innovations, such as stream-of-consciousness writing.

Furthermore, many modern short stories are known for depicting seemingly trivial "slices of life" that depend on important moments and the manipulation of mood rather than plot to reveal meaning. For example, in his stories, Joyce established theme through realistic detail and atmosphere. He often used **epiphany**—or a moment of revelation in which something commonplace is seen in a new light—to unify and bring his stories to a close.

Mid-Twentieth-Century Style

The events of the early twentieth century, particularly the world wars and the Great Depression, irrevocably destroyed many British conventions and ideals. Like earlier Modernist writers, Elizabeth Bowen and Graham Greene wrote stories that focused on the internal psychological and moral struggles within characters. However, Bowen and Greene often linked their characters to contemporary political and social settings.

For the modern short story writer, any subject will do, and nothing needs to "happen." Yet, due to the constraints of the form, every detail must contribute to a story's meaning. As William Faulkner noted, "In a short story . . . almost every word has to be almost exactly right."

Literature Online

Literature and Reading For more about the modern British short story, go to glencoe.com and enter QuickPass code GLB9817u6.

Respond and Think Critically

1. According to H. E. Bates and Frank O'Connor, what delayed the rise of the British short story?

2. How did Conrad's short story techniques advance the modern short story in a way that Hardy's and Kipling's did not?

3. Why might the short story be a fitting form to capture "reality" as the Modernists understood it?

Before You Read

Focus

Bellringer Options

Selection Focus
Transparency 51
Daily Language Practice
Transparency 85

Or **ask:** What is your idea of romance and a good adventure? Why? Give an example from a movie you have seen or book you have read. (Responses will vary.) Tell students to explore the elements of both adventure and romance as they read Kipling's story.

Before You Read

Miss Youghal's Sais

Meet **Rudyard Kipling**

(1865–1936)

Rudyard Kipling reportedly once read in a magazine that he had died. Kipling's literary reputation has suffered a similar fate, having been buried and resurrected numerous times both in his lifetime and since his death. Readers critical of Kipling are uncomfortable with his staunch defense of British imperialism, which grew from his sincere belief that it was Britain's duty to introduce European culture to societies he believed to be less civilized. Supporters of Kipling admire the keen observations that characterize his depiction of Anglo-Indian life and find inspiration in the themes of courage, self-sacrifice, and loyalty in his works.

Childhood Influences Born to English parents living in Bombay, India, Kipling grew up speaking Hindustani better than English. His happy childhood in India made a deep impression on him and contributed to his romantic treatment of India in his fiction. When he was only five years old, Kipling was sent to live with a hired foster family in England—a common practice among British families living in India. It was an unhappy experience for Kipling, who felt deserted by his parents. At the age of twelve, he was enrolled at the United Services College, a boarding school in Devon. His experiences there instilled in him an admiration for individualism, discipline, and order—qualities that strongly influenced his thinking and writing in later years.

> "The magic of Literature lies in the words, and not in any man."
>
> —Rudyard Kipling

Literary Success At the age of sixteen, Kipling returned to India, where he worked as a journalist. He traveled widely and began to publish his first stories and poems about military life and Indian culture under British rule. In 1889 Kipling returned to England and continued his successful and prolific writing career. In 1892 Kipling married an American, Caroline Balestier, and settled in Vermont. Over the next few years, he wrote the novels *Captains Courageous* and *Kim*, as well as his beloved children's classic *The Jungle Book* and its sequel, *The Second Jungle Book*. Kipling returned to England in 1897.

A Genius of Narrative In 1907 Kipling became the first English author to be awarded the Nobel Prize in Literature. At the award ceremony, Kipling was praised as "the greatest genius in the realm of narrative that [England] has produced in our times." In later years, however, Kipling's defense of British imperialism became unfashionable among more liberal-minded thinkers in England, and his popularity declined. The British novelist George Orwell's assessment of Kipling's literary reputation echoed the debate that continues today: "I worshipped [him] at thirteen, loathed him at seventeen, enjoyed him at twenty, despised him at twenty-five, and now again rather admire him."

 Literature Online

Author Search For more about Rudyard Kipling, go to glencoe.com and enter QuickPass code GLB9817u6.

Selection Skills

Literary Elements
- Narrator (SE pp. 1027, 1029–1033)
- Conflict (SE p. 1033)

Miss Youghal's Sais

Writing Skills/Grammar
- Research Report (SE p. 1034)
- Character Analysis (TE p. 1030)

Reading Skills
- Analyze Characters (SE pp. 1027, 1029, 1030, 1032, 1034)
- Make Predictions (TE p. 1028)

Vocabulary Skills
- World Parts (SE p. 1034)
- Academic Vocabulary (SE p. 1034)

Literature and Reading Preview

Connect to the Story

What would you sacrifice for someone you care about? Make a list of things that you would give up on behalf of a good friend.

Build Background

For more than one hundred years prior to gaining independence in 1947, India was a colony of the British Empire. When India was a colony, most aspects of Indian society were dominated by the British. The story you are about to read was written early in Kipling's career, during the time he spent in India working as a journalist. It was published in his first collection of short stories, *Plain Tales from the Hills*.

Set Purposes for Reading

Big Idea Class, Colonialism, and the Great War

As you read "Miss Youghal's *Sais*," ask yourself, What details reveal Kipling's attitude toward Indian culture and the British presence in India?

Literary Element Narrator

In a literary work such as a story, a novel, or a narrative poem, the **narrator** is the person who tells the story. The narrator may be a character in the narrative or someone outside it. As you read, ask yourself, Who is the narrator, and how is he related to the protagonist (hero)?

Reading Strategy Analyze Characters

When a story contains well-written characters, their interactions will often affect the story's plot in meaningful ways. You can **analyze characters** and their effects on the plot by exploring the ways in which their words, actions, and traits contribute to different events in the story. As you read, ask yourself, How is this event dependent on or changed by the characters' actions or traits?

Tip: Taking Notes Use a chart like the one below to help you make connections between characters, their traits, and events in the story.

Character	Traits	Events Involving This Character
Miss Youghal	obedient, very proper	Leaves with her parents for Simla

Learning Objectives

For pages 1026–1034

In studying this text, you will focus on the following objectives:

Literary Study: Analyzing narrator.

Reading: Analyzing characters.

Vocabulary

unsavory (un sā′ vər ē) *adj.* sinister; morally questionable; p. 1029 *The unsavory stranger curled his lip and stared with cold, piercing eyes at the frightened children.*

perpetually (per pech′ ōō ə lē) *adv.* continually; unceasingly; p. 1029 *The kitten was perpetually ill—it came down with cold after cold, and we spent all summer at the vet's.*

compensation (kom′ pən sā′ shən) *n.* something that offsets, counterbalances, or makes up for; p. 1031 *Seeing her favorite performer in person was compensation enough for the problems Linda encountered getting to the concert.*

suppressing (sə pres′ ing) *n.* prohibiting publication or circulation; censoring; p. 1031 *Fearing a backlash from voters, the politician favored suppressing news of the tax increases he planned.*

RUDYARD KIPLING **1027**

Before You Read

Focus

Summary

Strickland, a British police officer in colonial India, is distrusted by Youghal, an officer with whose daughter he has fallen in love. When the Youghals go away to Simla, they employ Dulloo, an Indian groomsman (*sais*), who is Strickland in disguise. One day Strickland is enraged to find an English general flirting with his beloved. Learning the sais's true identity, the general helps Strickland gain favor with the Youghals.

 For summaries in languages other than English, see Unit 6 Teaching Resources Book, pp. 45–50.

Vocabulary

Word Parts Divide students into four groups, and ask each group to break up one vocabulary word into its root and affixes. Students should write each word part on a separate note card (example: un savor y). Shuffle the groups' cards; then have students reassemble the words, giving the meaning of each root and affix.

 For additional vocabulary practice, see Unit 6 Teaching Resources Book, p. 53.

English Learners

DIFFERENTIATED INSTRUCTION

Intermediate Review with students the techniques authors use to help readers get to know characters. **Ask:** How do you get to know a person you have just met? (*Talk to them, listen to them, look at how they dress and what they do, and find out what others know about them.*) Encourage students to use these questions as they analyze the characters in the story:

- What does the character say and think?
- What do other characters say and think about the character?
- How does the character dress and act?
- Does the character remind you of real people you know?

Teach

View the Art ★

Possible answers: *The solid blocks of vivid color, high contrast, and flattened perspective suggest Modernist ideas. The subject's clothing and the buildings pictured seem more traditional.*

British artist Bella Easton (1971–) is an acclaimed painter in oils as well as a master of traditional printmaking techniques. The title of her painting *Pushkar Blues* refers to the holy village of Pushkar in India, which is said to have arisen where the creator god Brahma dropped a lotus flower.

For an audio recording of this selectin, use Listening Library Audio CD-ROM.

Readability Scores

Dale-Chall: 8.2
DRP: 61
Lexile: 1100

Miss Youghal's Sais

Rudyard Kipling

View the Art Pushkar, a small town in northwestern India, is a destination for thousands of religious pilgrims every year. In what ways does this image reflect Modernist ideas? In what respects is it more traditional? ★

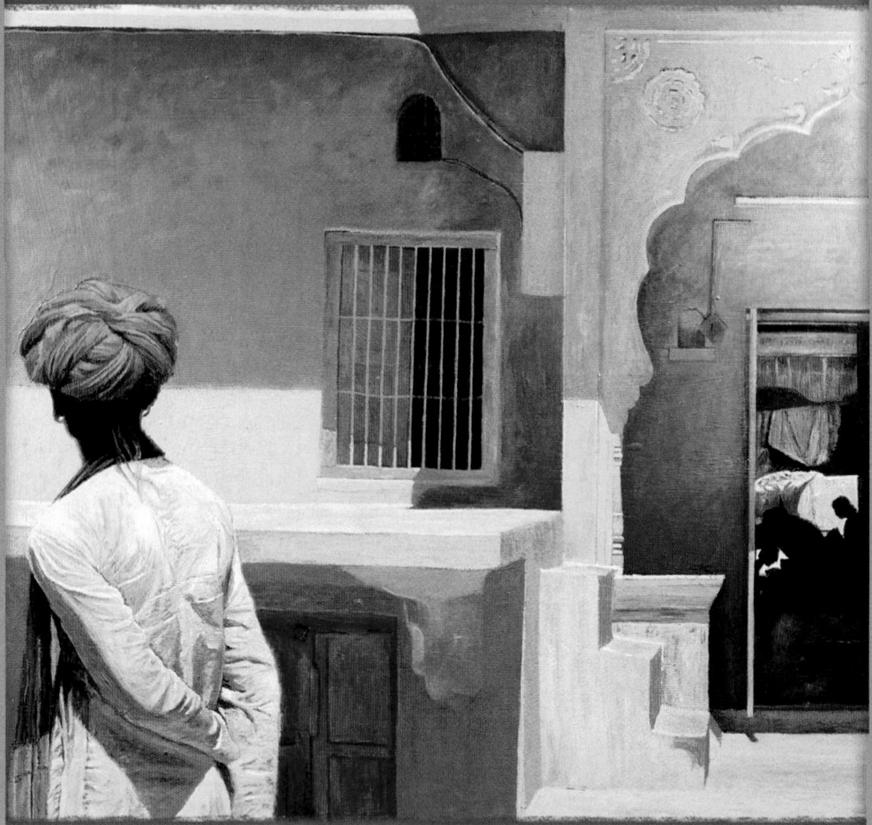

Pushkar Blues (2), c. 21st century. Bella Easton. Oil on panel, 153.6 x 137 cm. Private collection.

Reading Practice

SPIRAL REVIEW **Make Predictions** Tell students that making predictions will help them better understand and interact with the text. To make predictions, students must first gather clues from the story. From these clues, students can make educated guesses about what might happen later in the story. Finally, students should read further to verify their predictions or adjust them if necessary.

When Man and Woman are agreed, what can the Kazi[1] do?
—*Proverb.*

Some people say that there is no romance in India. Those people are wrong. Our lives hold quite as much romance as is good for us. Sometimes more.

Strickland was in the Police, and people did not understand him; so they said he was a doubtful sort of man and passed by on the other side. Strickland had himself to thank for this. He held the extraordinary theory that a Policeman in India should try to know as much about the natives as the natives themselves. Now, in the whole of Upper India there is only one man who can pass for Hindu or Mahommedan,[2] hide-dresser or priest, as he pleases. He is feared and respected by the natives from the Ghor Kathri[3] to the Jamma Musjid;[4] and he is supposed to have the gift of invisibility and executive control over many Devils. But this has done him no good in the eyes of the Indian Government.

Strickland was foolish enough to take that man for his model; and, following out his absurd theory, dabbled in **unsavory** places which no respectable man would think of exploring—all among the native riff-raff. He educated himself in this peculiar way for seven years, and people could not appreciate it. He was **perpetually** "going Fantee"[5] among natives, which, of course, no man with

any sense believes in. He was initiated into the *Sat Bhai*[6] at Allahabad[7] once, when he was on leave; he knew the Lizzard-Song of the Sansis,[8] and the *Hálli-Hukk* dance, which is a religious can-can[9] of a startling kind. When a man knows who dance the *Hálli-Hukk*, and how, and when, and where, he knows something to be proud of. He has gone deeper than the skin. But Strickland was not proud, though he had helped once, at Jagadhri,[10] at the Painting of the Death Bull, which no Englishman must even look upon; had mastered the thieves'-patter of the *chángars*; had taken a Eusufzai[11] horse-thief alone near Attock; and had stood under the sounding-board of a Border mosque and conducted service in the manner of a Sunni Mollah.[12]

His crowning achievement was spending eleven days as a *faquir* or priest in the gardens of Baba Atal at Amritsar,[13] and there picking up the threads of the great Nasiban Murder Case. But people said, justly enough, "Why on earth can't Strickland sit in his office and write up his diary, and recruit, and keep quiet, instead of showing up the incapacity of his seniors?" So the Nasiban Murder Case did him

---

1. A *kazi* (kä´ zē) is a civil judge.
2. A *Mahommedan* is a Muslim.
3. The *Ghor Kathri* (gōr kä trē´), in the city of Peshawar, Pakistan, was once a Buddhist monastery and was later a sacred Hindu temple.
4. The *Jamma Musjid* (jä´ mä mäs jid´) is the principal mosque (mosk), or Muslim place of worship, in Delhi.
5. *Going Fantee* (fän´ tē) means "mixing with the natives and conforming to their habits."

6. *Sat Bhai* (sät bī´) literally means "seven brothers."
7. *Allahabad* (al´ ə hə bad´), a city in north-central India, is a Hindu pilgrimage site.
8. The *Sansis* (sän sēz´) are a low-caste people of the Indian state of Punjab (pun jäb´). The caste system is a rigid social division characterized by hereditary status, hereditary occupation, and fixed social barriers.
9. The *can-can* is a Parisian dance characterized by exaggerated high kicking.
10. *Jagadhri* (jä gä´ drē) is a town in the Punjab.
11. The *Eusufzai* (ū soof´ zē) are a tribe of northwest Pakistan.
12. A *Sunni Mollah* (soo´ nē mə lä´) is a Muslim religious leader or teacher.
13. *Amritsar* (äm´ rit´ ser) is a city in northwestern India and the center of the Sikh (sēk) faith. Sikhs believe in one God and are disciples of the ten gurus (goo´ rooz), or teachers.

 1 Narrator *What does the narrator reveal about his attitude toward life and romance in these lines?*

 2 Analyze Characters *What does this comment reveal about Strickland's character?*

Vocabulary

unsavory (un sā´ və rē) *adj.* sinister; morally questionable

perpetually (per pech´ oo ə lē) *adv.* continually; unceasingly

 Class, Colonialism, and the Great War *What attitude toward Indian culture is expressed in this sentence?* **3**

Narrator *What is the narrator's attitude toward Strickland's accomplishments?* **4**

RUDYARD KIPLING **1029**

English Learners

DIFFERENTIATED INSTRUCTION

Intermediate English language learners may find this story confusing in places, as Kipling makes references to both English and Indian cultures. Encourage students to take notes from the very beginning.

Approaching Level

DIFFERENTIATED INSTRUCTION

AAVE For approaching-level students using African American Vernacular English (AAVE), **write** on the board: Those people wrong. Strickland in the Police. **Ask:** What part of speech is missing from each sentence? *(the verb)*

Teach

Literary Element **1**

Narrator **Answer:** *A somewhat jaded, conservative view of romance, believing that there can be more than "is good for us."*

(APPROACHING) Have approaching-level students consider what the narrator means by "romance." Encourage students to recall the romances of the Medieval period and to develop a definition that goes beyond the idea of romantic love.

Reading Strategy **2**

Analyze Character **Answer:** *Strickland is culturally aware; the word "extraordinary" suggests that he differs from most colonists in his philosophy.*

For additional practice using the reading skill or strategy, see Unit 6 Teaching Resources Book, p. 52.

Big Idea **3**

Class, Colonialism, and the Great War **Answer:** *The narrator suggests that the conventional English attitude toward Indian culture is not to become involved in it.*

Literary Element **4**

Narrator **Answer:** *He feels that it is all right for Strickland to know about another culture. He also believes, however, that Strickland should not try to become a part of that culture himself.*

Teach

Reading Strategy | 1 |

Analyze Character Answer:
The passage reveals that Miss Youghal is obedient to her parents, while Strickland is respectful and considerate. The outcome—that Strickland drops the matter and the Youghals go to Simla—would be impossible if, for example, Miss Youghal were rebellious, or Strickland were obsessive.

Literary Element | 2 |

Narrator Answer: *He is addressed as "Dear old man" by Strickland and is obviously an acquaintance of his in the government.* **Ask:** How does this information correspond with your prediction about the narrator's identity? *(Answers will vary.)*

Big Idea | 3 |

Class, Colonialism, and the Great War Answer:
She is proud because it is like the English. **Ask:** How do the Youghals personify the ideals of both classism and colonialism? *(They won't let their daughter marry Strickland because he is in a lower class. They appreciate Dulloo most for his mimicking the English.)*

no good departmentally; but, after his first feeling of wrath, he returned to his outlandish custom of prying into native life. When a man once acquires a taste for this particular amusement, it abides with him all his days. It is the most fascinating thing in the world—Love not excepted. Where other men took ten days to the Hills, Strickland took leave for what he called *shikar,*[14] put on the disguise that appealed to him at the time, stepped down into the brown crowd, and was swallowed up for a while. He was a quiet, dark young fellow—spare, black-eyed—and, when he was not thinking of something else, a very interesting companion. Strickland on Native Progress as he had seen it was worth hearing. Natives hated Strickland; but they were afraid of him. He knew too much.

When the Youghals came into the station, Strickland—very gravely, as he did everything—fell in love with Miss Youghal; and she, after a while, fell in love with him because she could not understand him. Then Strickland told the parents; but Mrs. Youghal said she was not going to throw her daughter into the worst paid department in the Empire, and old Youghal said, in so many words, that he mistrusted Strickland's ways and works, and would thank him not to speak or write to his daughter any more. "Very well," said Strickland, for he did not wish to make his lady-love's life a burden. After one long talk with Miss Youghal he dropped the business entirely.

The Youghals went up to Simla[15] in April.

In July Strickland secured three months' leave on "urgent private affairs." He locked up his house—though not a native in the Province would wittingly have touched "Estreekin

---

14. *Shikar* (shē kär´) means "hunting."
15. From 1865 to 1939, *Simla* (sĕm´ lä) was India's summer capital. It is still a popular summer resort.

| 1 | **Analyze Characters** *What does this passage reveal about the characters of Miss Youghal and Strickland? In what ways does the outcome of the situation depend on those character traits?* |

Sahib's"[16] gear for the world—and went down to see a friend of his, an old dyer, at Tarn Taran.

Here all trace of him was lost, until a *sais*[17] or groom met me on the Simla Mall with this extraordinary note:

DEAR OLD MAN,—Please give bearer a box of cheroots[18]—Supers, No. 1, for preference. They are freshest at the Club. I'll repay when I reappear; but at present I'm out of society.—Yours,
E. STRICKLAND.

I ordered two boxes, and handed them over to the sais with my love. That sais was Strickland, and he was in old Youghal's employ, attached to Miss Youghal's Arab. The poor fellow was suffering for an English smoke, and knew that, whatever happened, I should hold my tongue till the business was over.

Later on, Mrs. Youghal, who was wrapped up in her servants, began talking at houses where she called of her paragon among *saises*—the man who was never too busy to get up in the morning and pick flowers for the breakfast-table, and who *blacked*—actually blacked—the hooves of his horse like a London coachman! The turn-out[19] of Miss Youghal's Arab was a wonder and a delight. Strickland—Dulloo, I mean—found his reward in the pretty things that Miss Youghal said to him when she went out riding. Her

Visual Vocabulary
An *Arab* is an Arabian horse prized for its speed and purity of breed.

---

16. In colonial India, *Sahib* (sä hēb´) was a respectful form of address for a European man.
17. A *sais* (sä ēs´) is a servant who attends to horses and who follows on foot behind a rider or carriage.
18. *Cheroots* (shə rōōts´) are cigars.
19. *Turn-out* refers to the horse's tack, or equipment.

| **Narrator** *Who is the narrator? How do you know?* | 2 |

| **Class, Colonialism, and the Great War** *Why might Mrs. Youghal be proud that her daughter's sais blacked the horse's hooves?* | 3 |

Writing Practice

SMALL GROUP SPIRAL REVIEW Character Analysis
Point out to students that much of the plot in this story is character driven; it depends on Strickland's character. Tell students they will be writing a brief character analysis of Strickland. Ask students to consider the following questions:

- What is Strickland like as a person?
- What are his thoughts about colonialism? The natives?

- How does he behave? How do other characters respond to him?

You might lead a class discussion, using these questions. After students have finished writing their analyses, have them share their writing in small groups.

parents were pleased to find she had forgotten all her foolishness for young Strickland, and said she was a good girl.

Strickland vows that the two months of his service were the most rigid mental discipline he has ever gone through. Quite apart from the little fact that the wife of one of his fellow-*saises* fell in love with him and then tried to poison him with arsenic because he would have nothing to do with her, he had to school himself into keeping quiet when Miss Youghal went out riding with some man who tried to flirt with her, and he was forced to trot behind carrying the blanket and hearing every word! Also, he had to keep his temper when he was slanged[20] in the theater porch by a policeman—especially once when he was abused by a Naik[21] he had himself recruited from Isser Jang village—or, worse still, when a young subaltern[22] called him a pig for not making way quickly enough.

But the life had its **compensations.** He obtained great insight into the ways and thefts of *saises*—enough, he says, to have summarily convicted half the population of the Punjab if he had been on business. He became one of the leading players at knuckle-bones,[23] which all *jhampánies*[24] and many *saises* play while they are waiting outside the Government House[25] or the Gaiety Theater of nights; he learned to smoke tobacco that was three-fourths cowdung; and he heard the wisdom of the grizzled

---

20. *Slanged* means "attacked with abusive language."
21. A *Naik* (nä ēk′) is a corporal of the native infantry.
22. A *subaltern* is a junior military officer.
23. *Knuckle-bones* is a game played by tossing and catching sheep bones.
24. *Jhampánies* (jäm pän′ ēz) are bearers of a jampan, a chair that is designed to hold one person and is carried on poles by men.
25. The *Government House* is the residence of a governor or the owner or manager of an estate.

Jemadar[26] of the Government House grooms. Whose words are valuable. He saw many things which amused him; and he states, on honor, that no man can appreciate Simla properly till he has seen it from the *sais's* point of view. He also says that, if he chose to write all he saw his head would be broken in several places.

Strickland's account of the agony he endured on wet nights, hearing the music and seeing the lights in "Benmore," with his toes tingling for a waltz and his head in a horse-blanket, is rather amusing. One of these days Strickland is going to write a little book on his experiences. That book will be worth buying, and even more worth **suppressing.**

Thus he served faithfully as Jacob served for Rachel;[27] and his leave was nearly at an end when the explosion came. He had really done his best to keep his temper in the hearing of the flirtations I have mentioned; but he broke down at last. An old and very distinguished General took Miss Youghal for a ride, and began that specially offensive "you're-only-a-little-girl" sort of flirtation—most difficult for a woman to turn aside deftly, and most maddening to listen to. Miss Youghal was shaking with fear at the things he said in the hearing of her *sais.* Dulloo—Strickland—stood it as long as he could. Then he caught hold of the General's bridle, and, in most fluent English, invited him to step off and be flung over the cliff. Next minute Miss Youghal began to cry, and Strickland saw that he had hopelessly given himself away, and everything was over.

The General nearly had a fit, while Miss Youghal was sobbing out the story of the disguise

---

26. A *Jemadar* (jə mə där′) is the head of a group of servants.
27. *Jacob served for Rachel* refers to Genesis 29:15–40 in the Bible, in which Jacob served Rachel's father, Laban, for fourteen years in return for Rachel's hand in marriage.

Class, Colonialism, and the Great War *How might the thought expressed here reflect Kipling's own experiences in India?* **4**

Narrator *What does this sentence suggest about the narrator?* **5**

Big Idea **4**

Class, Colonialism, and the Great War Answer: *Kipling traveled extensively in India, immersing himself in Indian culture. It is likely that he would share Strickland's sentiments.*
Ask: What does Strickland mean by saying "his head would be broken in several places"? *(The people of India and the characteristics of the culture are so complex and profound that he could never capture the reality in writing.)*

ENGLISH LEARNERS Make sure that English learners understand that Strickland uses figurative language and that his head would not really be harmed. Tell students that Strickland uses exaggeration to explain how hard it would be to write down everything he knows. Elicit examples of exaggerated speech that students have used recently.

Literary Element **5**

Narrator Answer: *Students may say he is sophisticated and has a dry sense of humor. He sees that Strickland's experiences would be interesting to readers but embarrassing—"worth suppressing"—to some Englishmen.*

English Learners

DIFFERENTIATED INSTRUCTION

Intermediate English language learners may find this selection challenging because of the multiple cultural references included and footnoted. In order to help students comprehend the text, give them time to look over the footnotes and ask questions. Explain the religious and cultural references, and show a map of India, helping students locate the various places described in the footnotes.

After students have a basic understanding of the footnoted material, have them reread the selection with English-proficient partners if necessary.

Teach

Reading Strategy   1

Analyze Character Answer:
The General is lighthearted, with a good sense of humor. He is modest enough to know that he behaved poorly with Miss Youghal. He is fond of flirtation and seems to be a bit romantic. It makes sense for him to help the young couple, since Strickland has gone to such outrageous lengths for love.

Big Idea   2

Class, Colonialism, and the Great War Answer: *Miss Youghal's parents believe that the acceptable route to better pay and the good life of Simla is for Strickland to follow departmental routine and stop associating with Indians.*

Literary Element   3

Narrator Answer: *He recognizes that Indian society is complex and that accepted behavior shifts in subtle ways. Despite his own classism, he admits that Indian culture is interesting.*

To check students' understanding of the selection, see Unit 6 Teaching Resources Book, p. 56.

and the engagement that was not recognized by the parents. Strickland was furiously angry with himself, and more angry with the General for forcing his hand; so he said nothing, but held the horse's head and prepared to thrash the General as some sort of satisfaction. But when the General had thoroughly grasped the story, and knew who Strickland was, he began to puff and blow in the saddle, and nearly rolled off with laughing. He said Strickland deserved a V.C.,[28] if it were only for putting on a *sais*'s blanket. Then he called himself names, and vowed that he deserved a thrashing, but he was too old to take it from Strickland. Then he complimented Miss Youghal on her lover. The scandal of the business never struck him; for he was a nice old man, with a weakness for flirtations. Then he laughed again, and said that old Youghal was a fool. Strickland let go of the cob's[29] head, and suggested that the General had better help them if that was his opinion. Strickland knew Youghal's weakness for men with titles and letters after their names and high official position. "It's rather like a forty-minute farce," said the General, "but, begad, I *will* help, if it's only to escape that tremendous thrashing I deserve. Go along to your home, my *sais*-Policeman, and change into decent kit,[30] and I'll attack Mr. Youghal. Miss Youghal, may I ask you to canter home and wait?"

* * *

About seven minutes later there was a wild hurroosh[31] at the Club. A *sais*, with blanket and head-rope, was asking all the men he knew: "For Heaven's sake lend me decent clothes!" As the men did not recognize him, there were some peculiar scenes before Strickland could get a hot

---

28. A *V.C.* is a Victoria Cross, a British military decoration bestowed for conspicuous bravery in battle.
29. A *cob* is a short-legged stout variety of horse.
30. Here, *kit* means "outfit" or "uniform."
31. Here, a *hurroosh* is a commotion.

1 Analyze Characters *What kind of man is the General? Is it logical for him to want to help the young couple?*

bath, with soda in it, in one room, a shirt here, a collar there, a pair of trousers elsewhere, and so on. He galloped off, with half the Club wardrobe on his back, and an utter stranger's pony under him, to the house of old Youghal. The General, arrayed in purple and fine linen, was before him. What the General had said Strickland never knew, but Youghal received Strickland with moderate civility; and Mrs. Youghal, touched by the devotion of the transformed Dulloo, was almost kind. The General beamed and chuckled, and Miss Youghal came in, and, almost before old Youghal knew where he was, the parental consent had been wrenched out, and Strickland had departed with Miss Youghal to the telegraph office to wire for his European kit. The final embarrassment was when a stranger attacked him on the Mall and asked for the stolen pony.

In the end, Strickland and Miss Youghal were married, on the strict understanding that Strickland should drop his old ways, and stick to Departmental routine, which pays best and leads to Simla. Strickland was far too fond of his wife, just then, to break his word, but it was a sore trial to him; for the streets and the bazaars, and the sounds in them, were full of meaning to Strickland, and these called to him to come back and take up his wanderings and his discoveries. Some day I will tell you how he broke his promise to help a friend. That was long since, and he has, by this time, been nearly spoiled for what he would call *shikar*. He is forgetting the slang, and the beggar's cant,[32] and the marks, and the signs, and the drift of the undercurrents, which, if a man would master, he must always continue to learn.

But he fills in his Departmental returns beautifully. ❧

---

32. *Cant* means "jargon; specialized language."

Class, Colonialism, and the Great War *What conventional attitude toward British life in India is expressed here?* **2**

Narrator *What does this comment reveal about the narrator's attitude toward Indian culture?* **3**

Literary Element Practice

SMALL GROUP **SPIRAL REVIEW** **Characterization**
Remind students that characterization is how an author portrays a character, describing his or her actions, thoughts, feelings, and appearance, as well as the words he or she uses. The main character of a story usually displays different aspects of his or her charac-ter as the story develops. Have small groups discuss Kipling's characterization of Strickland. **Ask: Is Strickland a round character? What traits does he have?** Walk around the class to monitor students' discussions.

After You Read

Respond and Think Critically

Respond and Interpret

1. Do you think this story has a happy ending? Why or why not?

2. (a)Explain how Strickland has put into practice his theory about his job. (b)What do his past adventures reveal about his personality and character?

3. (a)What job does Strickland take on in Simla? Why? (b)What are the challenges and rewards of the job?

4. (a)How does the incident with the general lead to the final outcome of the story? (b)Do you think Strickland expected this outcome? Explain.

Analyze and Evaluate

5. (a)How is Strickland's life changed by his marriage? (b)What can you infer about his attitude toward his new life?

6. Evaluate the importance of the story's setting. How does it affect the sequence of events? Explain, using specific examples from the story.

Connect

7. **Big Idea** Class, Colonialism, and the Great War (a)What political issues of the time are reflected in this story? (b)What can you infer about Kipling's attitude toward these issues? Use evidence from the story to support your opinion.

8. **Connect to the Author** Which character in this story seems closest to a reflection of Kipling himself? What details about the character remind you of what you know about Kipling from the information on page 1026.

Literary Element Narrator

The **narrator** of a story is important for several reasons. An author's choice of narrator establishes a particular **point of view** from which the events are seen. The narrator can also dictate the **tone** of a story. Finally, a narrator can comment on the characters and events and inform the reader of ideas or **themes** the author wishes to convey. Review "Miss Youghal's *Sais*" and answer the following questions:

1. (a)Who is the narrator of this story? How do you know? (b)What seems to be his relationship to Strickland? What evidence in the story leads you to this conclusion?

2. (a)What can you infer about the narrator's personality and character from his comments and opinions? (b)How do his comments and opinions affect your perception of the other characters and the events that take place?

Review: Conflict

As you learned on page 23, a **conflict** is a struggle between opposing forces. The **protagonist**, or central character, of a story may be faced with one or more **antagonists**—people or forces that oppose the protagonist. Generally, the reader is meant to sympathize with the protagonist and to be critical or fearful of the antagonist(s).

Partner Activity With a partner, review the events of "Miss Youghal's *Sais*." Then answer these questions.

1. (a)Who is the protagonist of this story? (b)Who are the antagonists?

2. (a)What is the nature of the conflict between these opposing forces? (b)Is the conflict **external** or **internal**? Why?

3. (a)Identify the plot's **climax**. How does it serve as a turning point and lead to the resolution? (b)How is the conflict resolved?

Literary Element

1. (a) An Englishman who buys cigars for Strickland (b) His tone and description suggest he is a colleague or friend.

2. (a) He views human nature cynically but admires Strickland's adventurous spirit. (b) The reader sympathizes with Strickland and is annoyed with Miss Youghal's parents.

Review: Conflict

1. (a) Strickland (b) Miss Youghal's parents

2. (a) The Youghals refuse to allow their daughter to be with Strickland. (b) External; it exists outside.

3. (a) Strickland confronts the General, who then agrees to help him. (b) The General succeeds, leading to Strickland's marriage.

After You Read

Assess

1. Students' answers will vary.

2. (a) By posing as a native, he solved a murder. (b) Strickland has a great imagination and zest for life.

3. (a) A sais, so that he can see Miss Youghal despite her parents' disapproval (b) He is ill treated, nearly poisoned, and tormented by jealousy, but he sees Miss Youghal and learns more about India.

4. (a) It leads to the General's agreeing to intercede on Strickland's behalf. (b) He could not have predicted this outcome.

5. (a) He must abandon his old habit of associating with native Indians. (b) While he is fond of his wife, he misses the excitement of his former life.

6. It mirrors the conflict between classes that keeps Strickland and Miss Youghal apart. It also enables Strickland to carry out his plan to be near her.

7. (a) The British rule over colonial India (b) Kipling's support of Britain's presence in India is implied by the absence of any criticism of it in the story, but he also separates himself from these attitudes by expressing admiration (through the narrator) for Strickland's ability to immerse himself in Indian life.

8. Kipling likely sees himself reflected in Strickland, since Strickland is a British man living in India.

Progress Check

Can students analyze the purpose of the narrator?

If No → See Unit 6 Teaching Resources Book, p. 51.

After You Read

Assess

Reading Strategy

1. They assume he is not good enough for their daughter. Their opinion changes and both embrace him, perhaps hesitantly, when they learn of the intensity of his devotion to their daughter.

2. Strickland's dedication and determination drive the events of the story forward.

Vocabulary Practice

Possible answers:

unsavory

Prefix: *un-*, "not"

Root: *savor*, "taste"

Suffix: *-y*, "characterized by"

Sample Sentence: The unsavory stranger waited in the alley so he could attack unsuspecting people.

perpetually

Prefix: *per-*, "completely," "utterly"

Root: *pet*, "seek," "reach for"

Suffix: *-al*, "pertaining to;" *-ly*, "characterized by"

Sample Sentence: Robert was perpetually late for class, so the teacher always started without him.

compensation

Prefix: *com-*, "together," "in association"

Root: *pens*, "weigh," "consider"

Suffix: *-ion*, "condition of"

Sample Sentence: The store manager gave me a gift certificate as compensation for the rotten apple I had found in my groceries.

suppressing

Prefix: *sup-*, "under"

Root: *press*, "press"

Suffix: *-ing* (a suffix that turns a verb into a noun)

Reading Strategy · Analyze Characters

When you **analyze characters** in a story, you can develop a stronger understanding of why the story's events unfold the way they do. To help you answer the following questions, refer to the chart you created as you read.

1. What do Mr. and Mrs. Youghal assume about Strickland's character? When and why does their opinion change?

2. What is the impact of Strickland's character and personality on each of the story's main events?

Vocabulary Practice

Practice with Word Parts For each boldfaced vocabulary word in the left column, identify the related word with a shared word part in the right column. Write each word and underline the part they have in common. Look up the meaning of the new word and explain how they are related.

1. unsavory   promotion
2. perpetually   pressurize
3. compensation   unimpressive
4. suppressing   fluidly

EXAMPLE:

Absent, abduct

Abduct means "to carry away." An absent person is one who is away for some reason.

Academic Vocabulary

Strickland has to change his **conduct** *in order to marry Miss Youghal.*

Conduct is an academic word. Someone might say that a person who is courteous to others exhibits good **conduct**.

To further explore the meaning of this word, answer the following question: What would your **conduct** be like at a formal party?

For more on academic vocabulary, see pages 56 and R81.

1034 UNIT 6   THE MODERN AGE

Connect to *Social Studies*

Assignment Research and prepare a brief report about the British presence in India, addressing how this historical/cultural phenomenon influenced the assumptions and world views of the characters in Kipling's story.

Investigate Use multiple reputable Internet sources or your social studies text to collect background information on both English and Indian views of British colonialism in India during the late 1800s. Then review the cultural assumptions of various characters in Kipling's short story, indicating how the colonial attitudes you learned about might have influenced each character. To help organize your ideas, you might want to adapt the chart you made for the Reading Strategy on page 1027.

Create Synthesize your information, drawing general conclusions about colonialism in India. Then analyze each character from that perspective, supporting your analyses with examples, quotations, and logical arguments. Use a word-processing program to compile a complete bibliography of the sources you consulted.

Report Organize your report logically, grouping characters by nationality or in order of their importance to the story. Be sure to attribute all statements that are not original or common knowledge to the correct sources.

EXAMPLE:

Introduction
Background on colonialism
    British attitudes
    Indian attitudes

Effect on Kipling's characters
    Strickland
    Miss Youghal
    Miss Youghal's parents

If possible, use a computer slide-show program, such as PowerPoint, to illustrate your report.

 Literature Online

Selection Resources For Selection Quizzes, eFlashcards, and Reading-Writing Connection activities, go to glencoe.com and enter QuickPass code GLB9817u6.

Sample Sentence: The editor advocated suppressing news of the accident until more was known.

Academic Vocabulary

Possible answer: *I would exhibit more reserved conduct.*

 Connect to *Social Studies*

Students' reports should utilize a thesis statement and supporting evidence from primary and secondary sources, follow a logical order, and use a works cited page.

For addditional assessment, see Assessment Resources, pp. 245–246.

Before You Read

Shooting an Elephant

Meet **George Orwell**
(1903–1950)

Have you ever heard the expression "Big Brother is watching you"? It comes from George Orwell's *Nineteen Eighty-Four*, a novel in which government—under the guise of Big Brother, an all-powerful ruler—watches and controls every aspect of people's lives. According to Orwell, "The moral to be drawn from this dangerous nightmare situation is a simple one: *Don't let it happen. It depends on you.*" Orwell took this idea to heart, serving as the "conscience of his generation," according to the critic V. S. Pritchett.

> *"Every line of serious work that I have written since 1936 has been written, directly or indirectly, against totalitarianism."*
>
> —George Orwell,
> from "Why I Write"

Developing Social Consciousness Orwell—whose real name was Eric Blair—was born in Motihari, India, where his father worked for the British government. Orwell's parents were lower-middle-class people who scraped together enough money to send Orwell to English prep schools. When he attended private school in England, he was distinguished from the other boys by both his brilliance and his relative poverty. He found that the boys from wealthy families were treated better than he was. Being a victim of class distinctions during his school days made Orwell sympathetic to the working class and other victims of injustice, a sympathy that influenced his writing.

After graduation, Orwell applied to become a member of the Indian Imperial Police. At nineteen, he sailed to Burma (now Myanmar), where he spent the next five years working as a police officer. While on leave in England, Orwell decided, at the age of twenty-four, to resign his post in Burma and pursue a writing career. He wrote that his experiences in Burma had left him with "an immense weight of guilt. . . . I wanted to submerge myself, to get right down among the oppressed, to be one of them and on their side against their tyrants." Orwell did this by donning rags and wandering the streets of the impoverished East End of London.

Writer and Activist By his late twenties, Orwell had published only a few pieces; his book *Down and Out in Paris and London*, a fictionalized account of actual incidents in the Paris and London slums, had been rejected three times. Disheartened, he decided to take a "regular job" and accepted a teaching position at an English school for boys. But Orwell's literary fortunes soon changed. His book was published, it sold well, and his writing career began.

In 1936 Orwell was dispatched to report on the Spanish civil war, but caught up in the cause, he joined a combat unit to fight fascism. His wartime experiences and later work as a British Broadcasting Corporation radio broadcaster intensified Orwell's fear of government authority and censorship. He later wrote that a government's changing of historical fact to suit its needs "frightens me much more than bombs." His last two novels, *Animal Farm* and *Nineteen Eighty-Four*, express this fear.

 Literature Online

Author Search For more about George Orwell, go to glencoe.com and enter QuickPass code GLB9817u6.

Before You Read

Focus

Bellringer Options

Selection Focus
 Transparency 52
Daily Language Practice
 Transparency 86

Or **say:** Think about a time when you felt that you were forced to do something you didn't want to do. **Ask:** How did it make you feel? How did you react? Have students consider their experiences as they read Orwell's essay.

Skills Practice

Literary Elements
- Symbol (SE pp. 1036, 1038, 1039, 1042, 1044)
- Thesis (SE p. 1044)

Shooting an Elephant

Listening/Speaking/Viewing Skills
- Analyze Art (SE pp. 1037, 1042)

Reading Skills
- Analyze Cause and Effect Relationships (SE pp. 1036, 1037, 1040, 1041, 1044)

Vocabulary Skills
- Analogies (SE p. 1044)
- Academic Vocabulary (SE p. 1044)

Writing Skills/Grammar
- Expository Essay (SE p. 1045)
- Dashes (SE p. 1045)

Before You Read

Focus

Summary

Orwell serves as a police officer in Burma, where he is subjected to anti-European feelings. He detests the people who mock him but also detests the imperialistic system. One day Orwell is called on to stop an elephant that has killed a villager. Orwell finds the animal eating peacefully and does not want to shoot it. A huge crowd of Burmese is watching him and expects him to act.

> For summaries in languages other than English, see Unit 6 Teaching Resources Book, pp. 58–63.

Vocabulary

Analogies Have students study the vocabulary words. Then have students stand in a circle; provide a light-weight ball or bean bag for them to toss. **Say:** "Supplant— synonym," and toss the ball to a student. The student must catch the ball, give a synonym for *supplant*, and toss the ball to another student, who provides another synonym. When students run out of synonyms, ask for antonyms, traits (for example, **ask:** Who would wear garish clothes?), and other analogical relationships. Repeat for each word.

> For additional vocabulary practice, see Unit 6 Teaching Resources Book, p. 66.

1036

Literature and Reading Preview

Connect to the Essay

How does peer pressure affect your behavior? In a journal entry, write about an instance where you either gave in to or resisted peer pressure in a difficult situation.

Build Background

To understand the superior attitude prevalent among the British in Burma at the time Orwell was living there, it is helpful to know that Britain then had colonies and territories in nearly every part of the world. The empire was so vast, in fact, that the British proudly proclaimed, "The sun never sets on the British Empire," meaning that even as the sun set in one part of the empire, it was sure to be rising or still shining in another.

Set Purposes for Reading

Big Idea **Class, Colonialism, and the Great War**

As you read, ask yourself, What evidence does Orwell provide of class conflict and the effects of British colonialism in Burma?

Literary Element **Symbol**

A **symbol** is a person, animal, place, object, or event that exists on a literal level within a work but also represents something on a figurative level. As you read the essay, ask yourself, How does Orwell develop the symbolic meaning of the elephant?

Reading Strategy **Analyze Cause-and-Effect Relationships**

You can **analyze cause-and-effect relationships** in a story or essay by looking closely at why certain events happen and then determining what effects they have on other events. Often, a writer will signal that a cause-and-effect relationship exists by using specific words, such as *because*, *therefore*, or *subsequently*. As you read, ask yourself, How does Orwell indicate causes and effects in his narrative?

Tip: Taking Notes Use a chart like the one below to note cause-and-effect relationships.

Cause	Effect
The Burmese are bitter about British occupation	They insult people who work for the British

1036 UNIT 6   THE MODERN AGE

Reading Practice

SPIRAL REVIEW **Compare and Contrast Goals**

Tell students that this essay deals with a clash between cultures: the culture of the Burmese people and the culture of the European people living in and governing Burma. The people in each culture have needs and desires that sometimes overlap but more often clash.

Have students use a Venn diagram to keep track of each culture's goals as they read the essay. Students may label the left circle "What do the Burmese want?" and the right circle "What do the Europeans want?" They may label the overlap "What do people from both cultures want?" When they have finished the essay, students may use the diagram to discuss the essay's conflict.

Learning Objectives

For pages 1035–1044

In studying this text, you will focus on the following objectives:

Literary Study: Analyzing symbol.

Reading: Analyzing cause-and-effect relationships.

Vocabulary

supplant (sə plant´) v. to take the place of, often unfairly; p. 1038 *Wishing to supplant the king, the prince plotted against him.*

despotic (des pot´ ik) adj. tyrannical; oppressive; p. 1038 *The despotic ruler raised taxes for his own personal gain.*

labyrinth (lab´ ə rinth´) n. a place containing winding, interconnected passages; p. 1038 *Jessie quickly became lost in the labyrinth.*

squalid (skwol´ id) adj. dirty or broken-down from poverty or neglect; p. 1038 *The family's squalid living conditions were a direct cause of the infant's illness.*

garish (gār´ ish) adj. excessively bright; flashy; gaudy; p. 1040 *The garish party decorations were in poor taste.*

Shooting an Elephant

George Orwell

An Indian elephant and his mahout with a fortress on a hill and palm trees behind, mid-nineteenth century. Elizabeth Sophia Forbes. Woolwork panel. Dreweatt Neate Fine Art Auctioneers, Newbury, England.

 View the Art Tapestries and artwork depicting scenes from India, Burma, and other colonies were popular in Victorian England. What impression of colonial life might this tapestry be meant to convey? ★

In Moulmein, in lower Burma, I was hated by large numbers of people—the only time in my life that I have been important enough for this to happen to me. I was subdivisional police officer of the town, and in an aimless, petty[1] kind of way anti-European feeling was very bitter. No one had the guts to raise a riot, but if a European woman went through the bazaars alone somebody would probably spit betel[2] juice over her dress. As a police officer I was an obvious target and was baited whenever it seemed safe to do so. When a nimble[3] Burman tripped me up on the football field and the referee (another Burman) looked the other way, the crowd yelled with hideous laughter. This happened more than once. In the end the sneering[4] yellow faces of young men that met me everywhere, the insults hooted after me when I was at a safe distance, got badly on my nerves. The young Buddhist priests were the worst of all. There were several thousands of them in the town and none of them seemed to have anything to do except stand on street corners and jeer at Europeans.

All this was perplexing and upsetting. For at that time I had already made up my mind that imperialism[5] was an evil thing and the sooner I chucked up my job and got out of it the better. Theoretically—and secretly, of course—I was all for the Burmese and all against their oppressors, the British. As for the job I was doing, I hated it more bitterly than I can perhaps make clear. In a job like that you see the dirty work of Empire at close quarters. The wretched prisoners huddling in the stinking cages of the lockups, the gray, cowed faces of the long-term convicts, the scarred buttocks of the men who

---

1. *Petty* means "trivial" or "insignificant."
2. In Asia, the leaves and nuts of the *betel* palm, mixed with mineral lime, are chewed as a stimulant.
3. Here, *nimble* means "agile" or "quick-moving."
4. *Sneering* means "scornful."

1 Analyze Cause-and-Effect Relationships *What causes the Burmese to target Orwell, specifically?*

5. *Imperialism* is the policy of extending a nation's authority by acquisition of territory.

GEORGE ORWELL **1037**

Advanced Learners

DIFFERENTIATED INSTRUCTION

Research Have students visit the library or use the Internet to conduct research on the history of British imperialism in Burma. Invite students to form questions they would like to have answered about this history. Possible responses include the following: *How did Britain come to rule Burma? What was a job as a British police officer or official like? What was life like for the Burmese?* Have students record at least three questions and research the one that is most focused. Tell students to take notes and write a brief report on what they learned. Allow students class time to present their reports.

Teach

Reading Strategy | 1

Analyze Cause-and Effect Relationships **Answer:** *As a police officer, Orwell is a representative of the British government; while other people might be able to hide their national origins, his uniform marks him as a European and a member of the nation they despise.*

For additional practice using the reading skill or strategy, see Unit 6 Teaching Resources Book, p. 65.

View the Art ★

Possible answers: *The tapestry depicts life in colonial India as peaceful and exotic. The elephant stands quietly, the mahout looks triumphant and exotically dressed, and the background is lush.*

This tapestry depicts a common scene viewed through the colonial eyes of the British Raj in India. India came under British control in 1858 after a series of events involving the British East India Company. Not until 1885 did Burma, where Orwell's experience takes place, come under British control.

For an audio recording of this selection, use Listening Library Audio CD-ROM.

Readability Scores

Dale-Chall: 5.5
DRP: 60
Lexile: 1060

Teach

Literary Element | **1**

Symbol **Answer:** *They symbolize the oppression of British colonialism.*

Big Idea | **2**

Class, Colonialism, and the Great War **Answer:** *On the one hand, Orwell sides with the Burmese and hates the oppression of British colonialism. On the other hand, he feels bound by his duty as a British police officer.*

APPROACHING Refer approaching-level students to the Venn diagrams they are completing. Ask them to identify details that demonstrate the narrator's conflicting feelings: his sympathy for the Burmese and his duty to his own nation.

Literary Element | **3**

Symbol **Answer:** *The elephant, in its ruthless disregard for the welfare of the Burmese people, might symbolize the British Empire.* **Ask:** Where does the elephant do the most damage? *(in one of the poorest areas)* How does this fact support the interpretation of the elephant as symbolizing the British Empire? *(Some of the worst damage and destruction caused by the Empire was aimed at the poorest of the indigenous population.)*

had been flogged with bamboos—all these oppressed me with an intolerable sense of guilt. But I could get nothing into perspective. I was young and ill-educated and I had had to think out my problems in the utter silence that is imposed on every Englishman in the East. I did not even know that the British Empire is dying, still less did I know that it is a great deal better than the younger empires that are going to **supplant** it. All I knew was that I was stuck between my hatred of the empire I served and my rage against the evil-spirited little beasts who tried to make my job impossible. With one part of my mind I thought of the British Raj[6] as an unbreakable tyranny, as something clamped down, *in saecula saeculorum,*[7] upon the will of prostrate[8] peoples; with another part I thought that the greatest joy in the world would be to drive a bayonet into a Buddhist priest's guts. Feelings like these are the normal by-products of imperialism; ask any Anglo-Indian official, if you can catch him off duty.

One day something happened which in a roundabout way was enlightening. It was a tiny incident in itself, but it gave me a better glimpse than I had had before of the real nature of imperialism—the real motives for which **despotic** governments act. Early one morning the subinspector at a police station the other end of the town rang me up on the phone and said that an elephant was ravaging

---

6. *British Raj* (räj) refers to the British Empire in the East; *raj* is a Hindu word meaning "rule."
7. *In saecula saeculorum* (Latin) means "forever and ever."
8. Here, *prostrate* means "completely overcome; helpless."

1 Symbol *What do the prisoners symbolize for Orwell?*

2 Class, Colonialism, and the Great War *Summarize the conflicting feelings that Orwell identifies as "the normal by-products of imperialism."*

Vocabulary

supplant (sə plant′) *v.* to take the place of, often unfairly
despotic (des pot′ ik) *adj.* tyrannical; oppressive

---

the bazaar. Would I please come and do something about it? I did not know what I could do, but I wanted to see what was happening and I got on to a pony and started out. I took my rifle, an old .44 Winchester and much too small to kill an elephant, but I thought the noise might be useful *in terrorem.*[9] Various Burmans stopped me on the way and told me about the elephant's doings. It was not, of course, a wild elephant, but a tame one which had gone "must."[10] It had been chained up, as tame elephants always are when their attack of "must" is due, but on the previous night it had broken its chain and escaped. Its mahout,[11] the only person who could manage it when it was in that state, had set out in pursuit, but had taken the wrong direction and was now twelve hours' journey away, and in the morning the elephant had suddenly reappeared in the town. The Burmese population had no weapons and were quite helpless against it. It had already destroyed somebody's bamboo hut, killed a cow, and raided some fruit-stalls and devoured the stock; also it had met the municipal rubbish van and, when the driver jumped out and took to his heels, had turned the van over and inflicted violences upon it.

The Burmese subinspector and some Indian constables were waiting for me in the quarter where the elephant had been seen. It was a very poor quarter, a **labyrinth** of **squalid** bamboo huts, thatched with palm leaf, winding all over a steep hillside. I remember that it was a cloudy, stuffy morning at the beginning of the rains. We began questioning the people as to where the

---

9. *In terrorem* (Latin) means "to terrify."
10. Here, *must* refers to the state of frenzy a male animal periodically undergoes during mating season.
11. A *mahout* (mə hout′) is an elephant keeper.

Symbol *What might the elephant symbolize?* **3**

Vocabulary

labyrinth (lab′ ə rinth′) *n.* a place containing winding, interconnected passages
squalid (skwol′ id) *adj.* dirty or broken-down from poverty or neglect

Reading Practice

SPIRAL REVIEW **Use Graphic Organizers** Like most autobiographical writing, Orwell's essay includes personal details and opinions. Help students connect to Orwell's feelings as they analyze the telling of his experience. Write the word *target* on the board in the center of a word web. Ask students to recall times when they have felt targeted. Explain that in this selection, Orwell recalls such an experience.

Have students list the information in the outer circles of the web. *(Orwell is targeted by Buddhist priests, by a crowd watching the elephant, and by his hatred of the British imperial system, of which he is a part.)*

elephant had gone and, as usual, failed to get any definite information. That is invariably the case in the East; a story always sounds clear enough at a distance, but the nearer you get to the scene of events the vaguer it becomes. Some of the people said that the elephant had gone in one direction, some said that he had gone in another, some professed not even to have heard of any elephant. I had almost made up my mind that the whole story was a pack of lies, when we heard yells a little distance away. There was a loud, scandalized cry of "Go away, child! Go away this instant!" and an old woman with a switch in her hand came round the corner of a hut, violently shooing away a crowd of naked children. Some more women followed, clicking their tongues and exclaiming; evidently there was something that the children ought not to have seen. I rounded the hut and saw a man's dead body sprawling in the mud. He was an Indian, a black Dravidian coolie,[12] almost naked, and he could not have been dead many minutes. The people said that the elephant had come suddenly upon him round the corner of the hut, caught him with its trunk, put its foot on his back and ground him into the earth. This was the rainy season and the ground was soft, and his face had scored a trench a foot deep and a couple of yards long. He was lying on his belly with arms crucified and head sharply twisted to one side. His face was coated with mud, the eyes wide open, the teeth bared and grinning with an expression of unendurable agony. (Never tell me, by the way, that the dead look peaceful. Most of the corpses I have seen looked devilish.) The friction of the great beast's foot had stripped the

> "It had already destroyed somebody's bamboo hut, killed a cow, and raided some fruitstalls and devoured the stock . . ."

skin from his back as neatly as one skins a rabbit. As soon as I saw the dead man I sent an orderly to a friend's house nearby to borrow an elephant rifle. I had already sent back the pony, not wanting it to go mad with fright and throw me if it smelt the elephant.

The orderly came back in a few minutes with a rifle and five cartridges, and meanwhile some Burmans had arrived and told us that the elephant was in the paddy fields[13] below, only a few hundred yards away. As I started forward practically the whole population of the quarter flocked out of the houses and followed me. They had seen the rifle and were all shouting excitedly that I was going to shoot the elephant. They had not shown much interest in the elephant when he was merely ravaging their homes, but it was different now that he was going to be shot. It was a bit of fun to them, as it would be to an English crowd; besides they wanted the meat. It made me vaguely uneasy. I had no intention of shooting the elephant—I had merely sent for the rifle to defend myself if necessary—and it is always unnerving to have a crowd following you. I marched down the hill, looking and feeling a fool, with the rifle over my shoulder and an ever-growing army of people jostling at my heels. At the bottom, when you got away from the huts, there was a metaled road and beyond that a miry[14] waste of paddy fields a thousand yards across, not yet ploughed but soggy from the first rains and dotted with coarse grass. The elephant was standing eight yards from the road, his left side towards us. He took not the slightest notice of the crowd's approach. He was tearing up bunches of grass, beating them against his knees to clean them and stuffing them into his mouth.

---

12. A *Dravidian coolie* is an unskilled laborer from southern India, where Dravidian languages are spoken.

4 Symbol *What might the Dravidian coolie symbolize?*

13. *Paddy fields* are rice fields.
14. *Miry* means "swampy."

GEORGE ORWELL **1039**

Teach

Literary Element | **4**

Symbol Answer: *In his agony and "crucified" posture, he symbolizes the suffering Christ.* **Ask:** What other information supports this interpretation? *(the man's poverty, his role in society, and the oppression he suffers at the hands of the brutal Empire)*

(**ENGLISH LEARNERS**) Explain to English learners that Orwell uses the word *crucified* to bring to mind the death of Christ. The man's arms are spread out to his sides, as Christ's were at his death on the cross. Tell students that Orwell relies on this single word to bring an image to European readers' minds so that they will feel sympathy for this man.

Writer's Technique ☆

Comparisons Draw students' attention to the sentence, "It was a bit of fun to them, as it would be to an English crowd." Students might find this comparison surprising because so much time is spent describing the animosity between the two groups. Point out that Orwell uses this comparison to show that the Burmese and the English are alike in one aspect—violence is a source of entertainment for both.

English Learners

DIFFERENTIATED INSTRUCTION

Beginning Explain to students that many adverbs end in *-ly*. Adverbs are words that modify or describe verbs, adjectives, and other adverbs. **Write** on the board: The people said that the elephant had come suddenly upon him. . . . They had seen the rifle and were all shouting excitedly. Point out the underlined words and tell students they are adverbs. Ask students to identify the words the adverbs modify.

(had come; were shouting) Explain that these adverbs tell *how* an action was performed.

Teach

Reading Strategy | 1

Analyze Cause-and-Effect Relationships **Answer:** *The presence of the crowd makes Orwell rethink his decision about the elephant. They make him consider his own position in the community instead of just considering what threat the elephant poses.*

Big Idea | 2

Class, Colonialism, and the Great War **Answer:** *Orwell is saying that British rule in the East is a futile waste of effort because, paradoxically, "when the white man turns tyrant it is his own freedom that he destroys." He "shall spend his life in trying to impress the 'natives,'" and his chief motivation is to act in such a way that he will not be mocked.*

(APPROACHING) Ask approaching-level students to think of a time when they felt forced to do something they didn't want to do. **Ask:** What drove you to act against your better judgment? Do you think Orwell felt the same pressures? *(Answers will vary.)* Then return to the Big Idea question, and help students apply what they and Orwell experienced individually to what the British nation experienced as a whole.

I had halted on the road. As soon as I saw the elephant I knew with perfect certainty that I ought not to shoot him. It is a serious matter to shoot a working elephant—it is comparable to destroying a huge and costly piece of machinery—and obviously one ought not to do it if it can possibly be avoided. And at that distance, peacefully eating, the elephant looked no more dangerous than a cow. I thought then and I think now that his attack of "must" was already passing off; in which case he would merely wander harmlessly about until the mahout came back and caught him. Moreover, I did not in the least want to shoot him. I decided that I would watch him for a little while to make sure that he did not turn savage again, and then go home.

But at that moment I glanced round at the crowd that had followed me. It was an immense crowd, two thousand at the least and growing every minute. It blocked the road for a long distance on either side. I looked at the sea of yellow faces above the **garish** clothes—faces all happy and excited over this bit of fun, all certain that the elephant was going to be shot. They were watching me as they would watch a conjurer[15] about to perform a trick. They did not like me, but with the magical rifle in my hands I was momentarily worth watching. And suddenly I realized that I should have to shoot the elephant after all. The people expected it of me and I had got to do it; I could feel their two thousand wills pressing me forward, irresistibly. And it was at this moment, as I stood there with the rifle in my hands, that I first grasped the hollowness, the futility[16] of the white man's dominion in the East. Here was I, the white man with his gun, standing in front of the

unarmed native crowd—seemingly the leading actor of the piece; but in reality I was only an absurd puppet pushed to and fro by the will of those yellow faces behind. I perceived in this moment that when the white man turns tyrant it is his own freedom that he destroys. He becomes a sort of hollow, posing dummy, the conventionalized figure of a sahib.[17] For it is the condition of his rule that he shall spend his life in trying to impress the "natives," and so in every crisis he has got to do what the "natives" expect of him. He wears a mask, and his face grows to fit it. I had got to shoot the elephant. I had committed myself to doing it when I sent for the rifle. A sahib has got to act like a sahib; he has got to appear resolute, to know his own mind and do definite things. To come all that way, rifle in hand, with two thousand people marching at my heels, and then to trail feebly away, having done nothing—no, that was impossible. The crowd would laugh at me. And my whole life, every white man's life in the East, was one long struggle not to be laughed at.

---

15. A *conjurer* is a magician.
16. *Futility* means "ineffectiveness" or "uselessness."

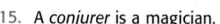 Analyze Cause-and-Effect Relationships *What effect does the crowd's attention have on Orwell?*

Vocabulary

garish (gār′ ish) *adj.* excessively bright; flashy; gaudy

---

17. *Sahib* is a title, similar to *sir*, that Indian people once used when speaking to or of a European.

Class, Colonialism, and the Great War *How does this statement epitomize Orwell's perception of the absurdity of British colonialism?*

Writing Practice

⚡ Write an Essay

SPIRAL REVIEW Have students review their webs from the Reading Practice on page 1036. First, ask students to identify the various "targets" within the text. *(Burmese people, Orwell, British Empire and its employees, the elephant, the coolie)* Then ask them to write a brief essay

about how the idea of being targeted is explored in this text. If necessary, remind students of the symbol of the elephant as the British Empire and the coolie as Christ.

But I did not want to shoot the elephant. I watched him beating his bunch of grass against his knees, with that preoccupied grandmotherly air that elephants have. It seemed to me that it would be murder to shoot him. At that age I was not squeamish about killing animals, but I had never shot an elephant and never wanted to. (Somehow it always seems worse to kill a *large* animal.) Besides, there was the beast's owner to be considered. Alive, the elephant was worth at least a hundred pounds; dead, he would only be worth the value of his tusks, five pounds, possibly. But I had got to act quickly. I turned to some experienced-looking Burmans who had been there when we arrived, and asked them how the elephant had been behaving. They all said the same thing: he took no notice of you if you left him alone, but he might charge if you went too close to him.

It was perfectly clear to me what I ought to do. I ought to walk up to within, say, twenty-five yards of the elephant and test his behavior. If he charged, I could shoot; if he took no notice of me, it would be safe to leave him until the mahout came back. But also I knew that I was going to do no such thing. I was a poor shot with a rifle and the ground was soft mud into which one would sink at every step. If the elephant charged and I missed him, I should have about as much chance as a toad under a steamroller. But even then I was not thinking particularly of my own skin, only of the watchful yellow faces behind. For at that moment, with the crowd watching me, I was not afraid in the ordinary sense, as I would have been if I had been alone. A white man mustn't be frightened in front of "natives"; and so, in general, he isn't frightened. The sole thought in my mind was that if anything went wrong those two thousand Burmans would see me pursued, caught, trampled on, and reduced to a grinning corpse like that Indian up the hill. And if that happened it was quite probable that some of them would laugh. That would never do. There was only one alternative. I shoved the cartridges into the magazine and lay down on the road to get a better aim.

 3 Analyze Cause-and-Effect Relationships *What thought finally convinces Orwell to load his gun and take aim?*

The crowd grew very still, and a deep, low, happy sigh, as of people who see the theater curtain go up at last, breathed from innumerable throats. They were going to have their bit of fun after all. The rifle was a beautiful German thing with cross-hair sights. I did not then know that in shooting an elephant one would shoot to cut an imaginary bar running from ear-hole to ear-hole. I ought, therefore, as the elephant was sideways on, to have aimed straight at his ear-hole; actually I aimed several inches in front of this, thinking the brain would be further forward.

When I pulled the trigger I did not hear the bang or feel the kick—one never does when a shot goes home—but I heard the devilish roar of glee that went up from the crowd. In that instant, in too short a time, one would have thought, even for the bullet to get there, a mysterious, terrible change had come over the elephant. He neither stirred nor fell, but every line of his body had altered. He looked suddenly stricken, shrunken, immensely old, as though the frightful impact of the bullet had paralyzed him without knocking him down. At last, after what seemed a long time—it might have been five seconds, I dare say—he sagged flabbily to his knees. His mouth slobbered. An enormous senility seemed to have settled upon him. One could have imagined him thousands of years old. I fired again into the same spot. At the second shot he did not collapse but climbed with desperate slowness to his feet and stood weakly upright, with legs sagging and head drooping. I fired a third time. That was the shot that did for him. You could see the agony of it jolt his whole body and knock the last remnant of strength from his legs. But in falling he seemed for a moment to rise, for as his hind legs collapsed beneath him he seemed to tower upward like a huge rock toppling, his trunk reaching skywards like a tree. He trumpeted, for the first and only time. And then down he came, his belly towards me, with a crash that seemed to shake the ground even where I lay.

I got up. The Burmans were already racing past me across the mud. It was obvious that the elephant would never rise again, but he was not

Reading Strategy   3

Analyze Cause-and-Effect Relationships **Answer:** *The thought that the natives will laugh at him if he is killed persuades Orwell to go ahead and shoot the elephant.*

Big Idea   4

Class, Colonialism, and the Great War **Ask:** Are you surprised by people's reaction to the imminent shooting of the elephant? Why or why not? *(Answers will vary.)* What does the crowd's reaction reveal about the society of the time? *(Violence breeds violence, and the atmosphere of the story reflects the bitter resentment that the Burmese feel toward the British. Violence is so pervasive that it is a source of perverse entertainment.)*

Approaching Level

DIFFERENTIATED INSTRUCTION

SMALL GROUP **Emerging** Some students may find advanced vocabulary in this selection challenging. To improve students' comprehension, have them work in small groups to read a portion of the text independently. Then have the groups convene and write a summary of their individual portions of the text. When students have finished reading the entire text, have them compile their summaries of smaller sections into a comprehensive summary. Have groups share their completed summaries with the rest of the class.

Teach

Symbol Answer: *The elephant might symbolize the slow, painful death of the British Empire.*

(ADVANCED) Tell advanced students to reread the selection. **Ask:** What earlier passage, or passages, might lead you to believe that the elephant symbolizes the death of the British Empire in this passage? *(Possible answers: "I did not even know the British Empire is dying. . .", or "The Burmese population had no weapons and were quite helpless against it.")* Then have them explain their choices.

Big Idea | 2

Class, Colonialism, and the Great War **Answer:** *In the eyes of the Europeans, the work done by elephants, legal justification for their actions, and saving face are more important than the rights or the lives of colonial subjects.*

View the Photograph ★

Possible answers: *Student opinions will vary.*

This photograph depicts the traditional mode of rowing of the Intha people in southern Burma. Each rower wraps his leg around the lower part of a long paddle while holding on to the top with one hand.

 To check students' understanding of the selection, see Unit 6 Teaching Resources Book, p. 69.

Leg Rowing Race, 1922. A canoe is propelled by leg power in a boat race event on a river in Burma.

View the Art Orwell lived in Burma at about the time this photograph was taken. Does the photograph portray a similar sense of life in the colonies to the image on page 1037? Explain why or why not. ★

dead. He was breathing very rhythmically with long rattling gasps, his great mound of a side painfully rising and falling. His mouth was wide open—I could see far down into caverns of pale pink throat. I waited a long time for him to die, but his breathing did not weaken. Finally I fired my two remaining shots into the spot where I thought his heart must be. The thick blood welled out of him like red velvet, but still he did not die. His body did not even jerk when the shots hit him, the tortured breathing continued without a pause. He was dying, very slowly and in great agony, but in some world remote from me where not even a bullet could damage him further. I felt that I had got to put an end to that dreadful noise. It seemed dreadful to see the great beast lying there, powerless to move and yet powerless to die, and not even to be able to finish him. I sent back for my small rifle and poured shot after shot into his heart and down his throat. They seemed to make no impression. The tortured gasps continued as steadily as the ticking of a clock.

In the end I could not stand it any longer and went away. I heard later that it took him half an hour to die. Burmans were bringing dahs[18] and baskets even before I left, and I was told they had stripped his body almost to the bones by the afternoon.

Afterwards, of course, there were endless discussions about the shooting of the elephant. The owner was furious, but he was only an Indian and could do nothing. Besides, legally I had done the right thing, for a mad elephant has to be killed, like a mad dog, if its owner fails to control it. Among the Europeans opinion was divided. The older men said I was right, the younger men said it was a damn shame to shoot an elephant for killing a coolie, because an elephant was worth more than any damn Coringhee[19] coolie. And afterwards I was very glad that the coolie had been killed; it put me legally in the right and it gave me a sufficient pretext for shooting the elephant. I often wondered whether any of the others grasped that I had done it solely to avoid looking a fool. ❧

18. *Dahs* are heavy Burmese knives.
19. *Coringhee* is a port in southeastern India.

1 Symbol *What might the elephant symbolize in this passage?*

Class, Colonialism, and the Great War *How does this paragraph reflect the distorted values of British colonialism?* **2**

Writing Practice

SPIRAL REVIEW **Theme** Remind students that the theme of a work is its main message or idea. Explain that writers use evidence to support or present their themes. Tell students that they will be doing two timed writing assignments. They will have ten minutes to answer each question. **Write on the board:** What personal theme does Orwell express in this essay? Support your answer with evidence from the text. After students finish writing, have them answer this question: What universal or political theme does Orwell present? Support your answer with evidence from the text.

1042

After You Read

Respond and Think Critically

Respond and Interpret

1. Which scene in the essay made the strongest impression on you? Explain.

2. (a)According to Orwell, what attitude did the Burmese have toward him and the other Europeans? (b)What do you think accounts for this attitude?

3. (a)How do the reactions of both older and younger Europeans to the shooting of the elephant compare with Orwell's realization at the end of the essay? (b)Looking back, what judgments does Orwell seem to be making about himself and about British imperialism?

Analyze and Evaluate

4. (a)Analyze Orwell's reasons for changing his mind about shooting the elephant. (b)Explain what his change of mind suggests about his character at the time of the incident.

5. What effects are created by Orwell's lengthy, detailed description of the elephant's fate?

6. How does Orwell's perspective on the incident differ from that of the crowd of Burmese natives?

Connect

7. **Big Idea** Class, Colonialism, and the Great War According to Orwell, what is the **paradox**, or apparent contradiction, at the heart of colonialism? How does the essay illustrate this paradox?

8. **Connect to Today** Can you think of any present-day professions that involve conflicts similar to those that Orwell faced in Burma? Use examples to support your answer.

You're the Critic: Different Viewpoints

Who Is the Greater Victim?

Read the following two excerpts of literary criticism. Notice how each critic emphasizes a different aspect of Orwell's complexity.

"The key to the moral content of 'Shooting an Elephant' lies in a chain of identifications made by the narrator, beginning with his identification of the trampled Dravidian with the victim of the crucifixion. . . . All of these identifications (Dravidian with Jesus, elephant with Dravidian, narrator with elephant) come together with an earlier image, that of the humiliated Burmese in the [i]mperial jail, the 'prostrate peoples' victimized by Empire."

—Thomas Bertonneau

"[The narrator of 'Shooting an Elephant'] is the target of physical and verbal abuse for the native population. A pivotal opposition, between individual and group, is established immediately, one that will reverberate through the narrative."

—Peter Marks

1. The two critics agree that the narrator is a victim, but each emphasizes a different aspect of the victimization. What is the difference in emphasis between the two critics?

2. (a)In your opinion, who is more victimized by the British Empire—persons such as Orwell, who must enforce the laws, or the native population, who must obey the laws?

GEORGE ORWELL **1043**

You're the Critic

1. Bertonneau emphasizes a series of personal identifications that Orwell makes between himself and the other victims—the Dravidian coolie, the elephant, and the abused prisoners. Marks emphasizes the opposition between the individual and the group—Orwell against his Burmese tormentors.

2. (a) Opinions will vary but should be supported by the text.

 For additional assessment, see Assessment Resources, pp. 247–248.

After You Read

Assess

1. Answers will vary.

2. (a) The Burmese were "very bitter." (b) The Burmese resented a foreign power making all of the decisions about their country and their lives.

3. (a) The older Europeans agree that Orwell was right in carrying out the law; the younger ones believe the elephant was more valuable than the man it killed. Orwell wonders if any of them understood that he had acted only to avoid looking foolish. (b) British rule in the East hurts both the colonizers and colonized.

4. (a) He was motivated by fear of death and of being ridiculed by the Burmese natives. (b) Orwell was young and unsure of himself, so he did what he thought was expected of him.

5. The description arouses great sympathy for the elephant.

6. Orwell views the incident as a matter of honor and keeping up appearances. The Burmese view the incident as entertainment and an opportunity to scavenge the meat of the elephant.

7. "When the white man turns tyrant it is his own freedom that he destroys." Students' responses will vary.

8. Answers will vary. Some examples might be a police officer who patrols a new neighborhood or a soldier in occupied territory.

After You Read

Assess

1. The elephant's destructiveness symbolizes the damage that British colonialism has done to the Burmese way of life.

2. (a) Orwell symbolizes the power and authority of the British Empire. (b) As a result of his position, he is seen as an exploiter and a tyrant, even though he secretly sympathizes with the Burmese.

Review: Thesis

Students may quote the following statement as the thesis of the essay: "All I knew was that I was stuck between my hatred of the empire I served and my rage against the evil-spirited little beasts who tried to make my job impossible." Make sure that the evidence students write in the outer circles of the web directly supports Orwell's thesis.

Progress Check

Can students interpret symbols?

If No → See Unit 6 Teaching Resources Book, p. 64.

Reading Strategy

1. According to Orwell, the older Europeans approve of his actions, while the younger ones think it's a shame—but only because the elephant is worth more than the Burmese man it killed. This shows that, like Orwell, many of the colonists are divided on what their role in Burma should be. It might also suggest that the attitudes of the colonists change with age.

Literary Element **Symbol**

Symbols in literature often represent abstractions. For example, in "Shooting an Elephant," the elephant might symbolize the British Empire. Both are large, powerful, fearsome things that are dying a slow death.

1. If the elephant is a symbol for the British Empire, what might the elephant's behavior suggest about the way the British rulers have treated the Burmese people?

2. (a) What do you think Orwell himself might symbolize for the people of the town? (b) How does this symbolism help explain the fact that he is "hated by large numbers of people"?

Review: Thesis

As you learned on page 696, the **thesis** is the main idea, or statement to be proved, in a work of nonfiction. A thesis may be stated or implied. The author must support the thesis with evidence in the form of reasons and examples.

Partner Activity Meet with a classmate and discuss the thesis of Orwell's essay. Create a web diagram similar to the one below. In the center circle, write the thesis. If the thesis is stated, quote it from the essay; if the thesis is implied, paraphrase it in your own words. Then, in the surrounding circles, write evidence that supports the thesis.

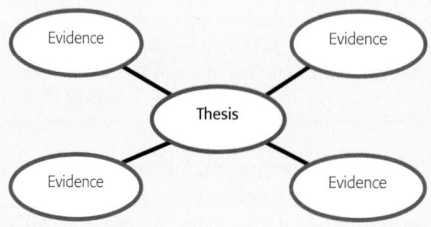

Reading Strategy Analyze Cause-and-Effect Relationships

Analyzing cause-and-effect relationships in a text can help you to better understand and interpret events in the plot and the reactions of differ-

---

ent characters. Look back at the chart you created as you read, and answer the following questions.

1. What effect does Orwell's killing of the elephant have on the European community? What does this tell you about the colonizers?

2. Orwell believes that if he does not shoot the elephant, he will have damaged the image of the European colonizers. How might killing the elephant affect the colonizers' image? Explain.

Vocabulary Practice

Practice with Analogies Choose the word that best completes each analogy below.

1. lively : somber :: garish :
   a. ugly   c. luminous
   b. bright   d. subdued

2. ill : sick :: squalid :
   a. well-maintained   c. stormy
   b. dirty   d. peaceful

3. uproot : remove :: supplant :
   a. position   c. beseech
   b. add   d. displace

4. cruel : kind :: despotic :
   a. tyrannical   c. overbearing
   b. democratic   d. kingly

5. path : lane :: labyrinth :
   a. crooked   c. maze
   b. winding   d. puzzle

Academic Vocabulary

In the story, Orwell illustrates the futility of the British **administration** *in the East.*

Administration is an academic word. In American government, the current president and cabinet are called an **administration**.

To further explore the meaning of this word, answer the following question: Which people make up the **administration** at your school?

For more on academic vocabulary, see pages 56 and R81.

---

2. Students may infer that the Burmese population will temporarily regard the Europeans with more respect, due to fear, but the anger of the elephant's owner suggests that eventually they will return to their former levels of resentment over unfair treatment.

Vocabulary Practice

1. d **2.** b **3.** d **4.** b **5.** c

Academic Vocabulary

Students might answer that the administration is made up of the principal, dean, and so forth.

Respond Through Writing

Expository Essay

Analyze Cause and Effect "Shooting an Elephant" chronicles George Orwell's experience as a British police officer in colonial Burma. Trace the cause-and-effect relationships throughout Orwell's essay and explain how they help support his theme of feeling trapped by circumstances.

Understanding the Task A **theme** is a central message of a work of literature, often expressed as a general statement about life. It can either be stated directly or be revealed indirectly through description, dialogue, and events.

Prewrite As you reread Orwell's essay, use a cause-and-effect graphic to trace the connections among the ideas and events. Keep in mind that one cause can have multiple effects and that several causes can contribute to a particular effect. Decide how these connections reflect on the essay's significant ideas, using quotations from the text to support your opinion.

Draft Organize your statements according to the information in your chart. Evaluate the evidence from the text supporting each point you make, and include the strongest examples and quotations in your essay. Consider incorporating your chart into your analysis as a visual aid. Be sure to explain clearly how each event contributes to Orwell's theme of entrapment.

In explaining causes and effects, use sentence structures like the following:

As a result of _____, the narrator _____.

Revise Ask a peer reader to review your essay, focusing specifically on the chain of causes and effects you presented. Ask for feedback both on any connections that are unclear and on those that are particularly well stated. Before making final changes, you might want to skim Orwell's essay again to ensure you've portrayed his theme correctly and haven't omitted any important points.

The narrator feels trapped between the British government, which he hates, and the Burmese people, whom he also hates. ⌃He hates the British because they abuse the Burmese people, and he hates the Burmese, who insult him for working with the British.

Edit and Proofread Proofread your paper, correcting any errors in spelling, grammar, and punctuation. Use the Grammar Tip in the side column to help you with dashes.

Grammar Tip

Dashes

The effectiveness of a cause-and-effect analysis depends on the evidence you provide to elaborate on and support your statements. Use **dashes** (—) when you want to emphasize supporting information or set off breaks in thought.

In contrast, use commas to set off closely related ideas and parentheses to set off supplementary material you don't want to emphasize.

The elephant had killed the man—not only killed, but skinned him like a rabbit—and left him to die in agony.

Literature Online

Selection Resources For Selection Quizzes, eFlashcards, and Reading-Writing Connection activities, go to glencoe.com and enter QuickPass code GLB9817u6.

After You Read

Assess

Respond Through Writing

Students' expository essays should:

- trace the cause-and-effect relationships in Orwell's essay, providing examples and quotations from the text to support statements

- relate the relationship of each event to the theme of the work and ensure it is clearly explained

- use dashes to set off supporting information that breaks a thought or provides explanation

> For grammar practice, see Unit 6 Teaching Resources Book, p. 68.

English Learners

DIFFERENTIATED INSTRUCTION

PARTNERS

Intermediate Pair English learners with English speakers to edit and proofread their papers. Have pairs trade and read each other's papers, correcting spelling and grammatical errors as they read. If English learners have difficulty with the spelling of unfamiliar words, make a dictionary available to look up words and clarify their understanding. Have students return the papers and go over them together. Encourage students to ask and answer questions about the comments on their papers.

Focus

Write on the board

and, but, or, nor, for, yet, so

Ask students to write a sentence that connects two independent clauses with one of the coordinating conjunctions on the board. *(Sentences will vary.)* Ask volunteers to share their sentence and explain why they chose the conjunction they did.

Teach

Using Commas with Coordinating Conjunctions

Tell students to use a comma before the coordinating conjunction *and, but,* or *for* when joining two independent clauses.

Assess

1. and
2. but
3. but
4. for
5. or

> For additional grammar practice, see Unit 6 Teaching Resources Book, p. 71.

Vocabulary Practice

SPIRAL REVIEW **Word Parts** To help students understand the words *coordinating* and *conjunction*, break them down into their parts.

co- means "with, together, joint"

ordinat means "arranged," from the Latin *ordinatus*

-ing is a suffix forming the present participle

con- means "with, together, thoroughly"

junct means "joining", from the Latin *junctio*

-ion is a suffix meaning "an act or process"

Give examples of other words with these parts and have student identify the parts (*cooperate, condense*).

Using Commas with Coordinating Conjunctions

Use a comma before an independent clause beginning with *but* or *and* unless the clause is very short. To avoid confusion, use a comma before a clause beginning with *for*: *She offered the book, for Sam wanted to read it.*

Tip

Before handing in a written test, make sure your coordinating conjunctions correctly show how ideas are connected.

Language Handbook

For more on coordinating conjunctions, see Language Handbook, p. R41.

LOG ON **Literature** Online

Grammar For more grammar practice, go to glencoe.com and enter QuickPass code GLB9817u6.

Grammar Workshop

Coordinating Conjunctions

Literature Connection In this quotation, George Orwell uses a coordinating conjunction to combine two thoughts and clearly show the connection between them.

> *"No one had the guts to raise a riot, but if a European woman went through the bazaars alone somebody would probably spit betel juice over her dress."*
>
> —George Orwell, from "Shooting an Elephant"

A **conjunction** is a word that joins single words or groups of words. A **coordinating conjunction** joins words or groups of words that have the same grammatical function in a sentence. Use them to link choppy sentences or join parts of a sentence. Some common coordinating conjunctions are *and, but, or, nor, for, yet,* and *so*.

Examples

Use *and* or *or* to connect similar sentence elements:

Orwell was often taunted <u>and</u> harassed by the Burmese people.

Use *but, yet,* or *nor* to connect contrasting sentence parts:

Orwell says, "I was not squeamish about killing animals, <u>but</u> I had never shot an elephant and never wanted to."

Use *for* or *so* to show cause and effect between ideas:

He was miserable, <u>for</u> he was caught between two cultures.

Revise For each sentence, select the better coordinating conjunction to join the sentence parts. Write your answers on a separate sheet of paper.

1. In his short story, Orwell uses direct language (and, so) appeals to the reader's emotions.

2. He hated the British raj (so, but) also disliked Burmese nationalism.

3. Burma was once part of the British Empire, (but, for) it gained its independence in 1948.

4. Orwell had to investigate an elephant that had killed a man, (yet, for) that was part of his job.

5. He would have to shoot the elephant, (or, yet) the natives would laugh at him.

Meet **Siegfried Sassoon**

(1886–1967)

I n January 1916, England's First Battalion dug itself into a line of trenches along the river Somme in France and waited to stage the British army's largest offensive of the Great War. Siegfried Sassoon was a transportation officer for the First Battalion, and in April of that year he proved himself a courageous soldier. He successfully rescued a number of wounded comrades while under heavy fire in no-man's-land and was awarded the Military Cross for valor. This selfless—and extremely dangerous—act of heroism and other forays into enemy territory earned him the nickname Mad Jack.

Early Life Born to a family of considerable wealth and privilege in 1886, Sassoon grew up on a country estate near Warminster, Kent, and spent his leisure time playing cricket and golf. Sassoon was educated at home by a private tutor until he reached the age of fourteen, and then he attended the New Beacon School. In 1902 he enrolled at Marlborough College, ostensibly to study law, but he became interested in writing poetry. He later went to Clare College, Cambridge, to pursue studies in history but did not complete a degree. Instead, he wrote poetry and self-published *Poems*, his first of ten collections to appear in print before he enlisted in the army and was sent to France.

The Making of a Pacifist Poet The First Battle of the Somme began on July 1 and resulted in over 57,000 British casualties on the first day. It is still considered the bloodiest single day of fighting in British military history. Five days later Sassoon captured a German trench by himself and was recommended for the Victoria Cross. Later that month he became afflicted with acute gastroenteritis and was evacuated to England, an action that saved his life. The Battle of the Somme resulted in over one million casualties, and the horrors of such bloodshed forever changed the way Sassoon viewed war.

> *"I am not protesting against the conduct of the war, but against the political errors and insincerities for which the fighting men are being sacrificed."*
>
> —Siegfried Sassoon

While Sassoon was recuperating in a military hospital, his horror and disgust at what he perceived to be the senseless slaughter of the war turned him into a pacifist. However, he felt guilty that his fellow countrymen were still fighting and dying, and he returned to the front only to be shot in the shoulder and hospitalized once again. At the encouragement of another pacifist, the philosopher Bertrand Russell, Sassoon decided to voice his opposition to the war in a letter to newspapers.

Along with other antiwar poets, such as his friend Wilfred Owen, Sassoon was able to poignantly convey the suffering and express the thoughts and feelings of the lost generation of British soldiers who succumbed to the brutal bloodbath of World War I.

 **Literature** Online

Author Search For more about Siegfried Sassoon, go to glencoe.com and enter QuickPass code GLB9817u6.

SIEGFRIED SASSOON **1047**

Bellringer Options

Daily Language Practice Transparency 88

Or **ask:** Why would the disillusionment of war best be conveyed by those most closely involved? *(Answers will vary.)*

Explain that "Dreamers" is a poem written by a genuine war hero—but one who lost faith in the reasons for which he was asked to fight. As students read the poem, ask them to look for Sassoon's attitudes about war.

Selection Skills

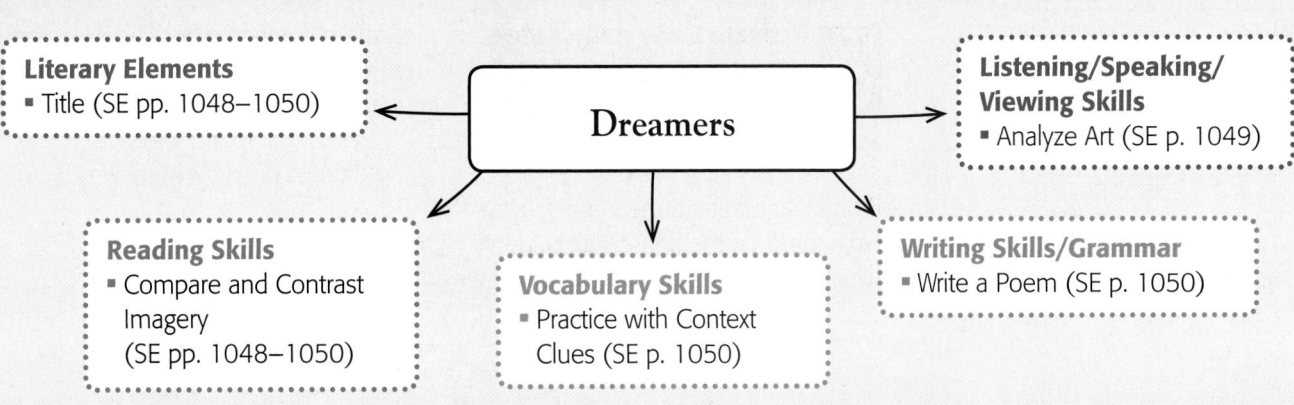

Literary Elements
- Title (SE pp. 1048–1050)

Listening/Speaking/ Viewing Skills
- Analyze Art (SE p. 1049)

Dreamers

Reading Skills
- Compare and Contrast Imagery (SE pp. 1048–1050)

Vocabulary Skills
- Practice with Context Clues (SE p. 1050)

Writing Skills/Grammar
- Write a Poem (SE p. 1050)

Before You Read

Focus

Summary

Soldiers have no future. They are required to make the ultimate sacrifice to bring about some glorious climax. Yet when soldiers are about to face death, they do not think of glory or ideals but of the ordinary, peaceful pleasures they once experienced and took for granted in civilian life.

 For summaries in languages other than English, see Unit 6 Teaching Resources Book, pp. 72–77.

Vocabulary

Connotation and Denotation Make sure students understand the difference between denotation (the literal meaning of a word) and connotation (the emotional overtones a word carries). Ask students to jot down the emotions they associate with the vocabulary words. Have them write a new sentence for each word that reflects the connotations they named.

 For additional vocabulary practice, see Unit 6 Teaching Resources Book, p. 80.

 For additional context, see Glencoe Interactive Vocabulary CD-ROM.

Literature and Reading Preview

Connect to the Poem

What circumstances might make you appreciate the mundane aspects of your daily life? With a small group, discuss how ordinary things might seem like luxuries to someone in dire straits.

Build Background

As World War I dragged on and the casualties mounted, veteran soldiers became weary and disheartened. Many felt a stark sense of separation from those at home, who could not comprehend the terror of trench warfare. Some soldiers felt so alienated from their families that they passed up opportunities to visit home on leave. Others were disgusted by patriotic tributes to heroism that glossed over the atrocities that they had endured. Much of the war poetry written during this period reflects the soldiers' feelings of abandonment and disillusionment.

Set Purposes for Reading

Big Idea Class, Colonialism, and the Great War

As you read the poem, ask yourself, How did World War I redefine notions of normalcy for both civilians and soldiers?

Literary Element Title

The **title** of a literary work is the first clue about the work's meaning. The title may help to explain the setting, provide insight into the theme, or describe the action that will take place in the work. As you read, ask yourself, How does the poem reflect ideas suggested by the title?

Reading Strategy Compare and Contrast Imagery

To **compare** two things is to focus on their similarities, while to **contrast** them is to focus on their differences. **Imagery** refers to the word pictures that a writer uses to evoke emotions in the reader through the use of vivid sensory details. As you read, ask yourself, How does Sassoon use contrasting image patterns?

Tip: Taking Notes Use a chart similar to the one below to list contrasting images of war and civilian life.

Images of Civilian Life	Images of War
"firelit homes, clean beds, and wives"	"foul dugouts, gnawed by rats"

Reading Practice

SPIRAL REVIEW **Activate Prior Knowledge** Have students read Build Background on this page and the portrait of Sassoon on the previous page. Ask them to name the key facts about World War I that are mentioned, and write them on the board. Ask students which wars they have studied, and have them contribute facts they learned about topics relevant to the poem, such as trench warfare, shell shock (now known as post-traumatic stress disorder), and the attitudes of ordinary soldiers.

Learning Objectives

For pages 1047–1050

In studying this text, you will focus on the following objectives:

Literary Study: Analyzing title.

Reading: Comparing and contrasting imagery.

Writing: Writing a poem.

Vocabulary

destiny (des´ tə nē) *n.* fate; what will necessarily happen; p. 1049 *Convinced that fame was her destiny, Wilma felt little need to practice her act.*

feud (fūd) *n.* a lengthy, bitter conflict or dispute; p. 1049 *The tribal leaders had engaged in a number of feuds that made a lasting peace nearly impossible.*

fatal (fāt´ əl) *adj.* causing death, destruction, or harm; p. 1049 *After weeks of deliberation, the jury delivered a fatal verdict.*

Wounded at the Roadside. Benjamin Strasser. Heeresgeschichtliches Museum, Vienna, Austria.

View the Art During and after World War I, many visual artists tried to show the full horror and violence of the war. What ideas or images from Sassoon's poem can you see reflected in this painting?

DREAMERS

Siegfried Sassoon

Soldiers are citizens of death's gray land,
    Drawing no dividend from time's tomorrows.
In the great hour of **destiny** they stand,
    Each with his **feuds**, and jealousies, and sorrows.
5 Soldiers are sworn to action; they must win
    Some flaming, **fatal** climax with their lives.
Soldiers are dreamers; when the guns begin
    They think of firelit homes, clean beds, and wives.

I see them in foul dugouts, gnawed by rats,
10   And in the ruined trenches, lashed with rain,
Dreaming of things they did with balls and bats,
    And mocked by hopeless longing to regain
Bank-holidays, and picture shows, and spats,
    And going to the office in the train.

Title *How do these two lines explain and expand the title of the poem?*

Vocabulary

destiny (des′ tə nē) *n.* fate; what will necessarily happen
feud (fūd) *n.* a lengthy, bitter conflict or dispute
fatal (fāt′ əl) *adj.* causing death, destruction, or harm

SIEGFRIED SASSOON **1049**

After You Read

Assess

1. Students' answers will vary.
2. (a) Ordinary men with "feuds, and jealousies, and sorrows" who are sworn to fight but who can think only about civilian life (b) He pities the soldiers and sees them as victims of war.
3. (a) The simple pleasures of civilian life (b) Their dreams contrast with the horrible realities of the trenches.
4. (a) The agony of war has made the routine tasks appear to be pleasurable. (b) Most civilians take their jobs, peace, and safety for granted.
5. (a) He calls war a mockery of the soldiers' longings and aspirations. (b) Agents of the state who have decided to sacrifice human life for victory
6. In its sorrow and hopelessness, "Dreamers" reflects the mood of most people during the Great War and its aftermath.
7. Responses will vary. Students might note that while some people consider war a big adventure, many, like Sassoon, consider it a horrifying waste.

Literary Element

1. Someone who is unrealistic or out of touch with reality
2. Sassoon implies that the war is unreal, and the soldiers' dreams of returning to civilian life constitute a longing to return to the real world.

Progress Check

Can students compare and contrast imagery?

If No → See Unit 6 Teaching Resources Book, p. 79.

1050

After You Read

Respond and Think Critically

Respond and Interpret

1. What is your reaction to the things soldiers dream about during war?
2. (a) How does the speaker describe the soldiers in the first stanza? (b) From this description, what can you infer about the speaker's attitude toward the circumstances of a soldier's life?
3. (a) According to the speaker, what do soldiers dream about? (b) How do these dreams contrast with the reality of war?

Analyze and Evaluate

4. (a) Why does the speaker include routine tasks, such as "going to the office in the train," among the civilian comforts that the soldiers long for?

(b) What moral, or lesson, might Sassoon be conveying to his readers?

5. (a) How does Sassoon convey his disillusionment with war in the poem? (b) Who or what has determined the soldiers' "destiny"?

Connect

6. **Big Idea** Class, Colonialism, and the Great War How does "Dreamers" reflect the cultural trauma experienced by the British people during and after the Great War?

7. **Connect to Today** How do current attitudes about warfare compare to the attitude expressed in Sassoon's poem? Explain.

Literary Element Title

A good **title** stimulates the reader's interest and curiosity about a literary work. The title can state or imply the subject or theme of the work, provide a clue to its meaning, or give the reader a sense of the period or setting. A title may be understated, ironic, or paradoxical.

1. What is the typical connotation of the word *dreamer*?
2. How does the poem contradict the expectations that the reader derives from the title?

Writing

Write a Poem Write your own short poem about either an unpleasant or humorous situation. Then create a title that stands in ironic contrast to the content and mood of your poem. For example, a poem about a coward might be titled "The Hero."

Selection Resources For Selection Quizzes, eFlashcards, and Reading-Writing Connection activities, go to glencoe.com and enter QuickPass code GLB9817u6.

1050 UNIT 6 THE MODERN AGE

Reading Strategy Compare and Contrast Imagery

"Dreamers" contains two contrasting image patterns—the worlds of military and civilian life.

1. Cite examples of images in the poem that represent the contrasting worlds of war and peace.
2. What generalizations can you make about these contrasting image patterns?

Vocabulary Practice

Practice with Context Clues Identify the context clues in each sentence that help you determine the meaning of the boldfaced vocabulary word.

1. He was sure that graduating was his **destiny**, so he did not study or worry about grades.
2. The warring factions' **feud** went back for several generations.
3. The doctor told the patient that his disease was **fatal** and he had only six months to live.

Reading Strategy

1. War: "death's gray land," "ruined trenches," and "foul dugouts, gnawed by rats" Civilian life: "firelit homes, clean beds, and wives" and "things they did with balls and bats"
2. The images of war reinforce the brutal conditions that soldiers face. The images of peace evoke the pleasures of civilian work and leisure.

Vocabulary Practice

1. *sure, did not worry*
2. *warring factions'*
3. *disease, only six months to live*

Writing

Students' poems should use contrasting imagery to emphasize the ironic title of their work.

Before You Read

Dulce et Decorum Est

Meet Wilfred Owen
(1893–1918)

One day in January 1917, Lieutenant Wilfred Owen and his men marched six miles over shell-pocked roads and through flooded trenches. The mud was so thick and deep in places that a number of Owen's men became stuck and had to slip out of their waders to free themselves. They continued their march with freezing and bleeding feet while suffering enemy machine-gun fire and heavy shelling. When it appeared that circumstances couldn't get worse, German soldiers fired canisters of chlorine gas at them. Through his gas mask, Owen watched one of his men choke to death in a sea-green cloud of poison. This was the incident that inspired Owen's poem "Dulce et Decorum Est."

> "My subject is War, and the pity of war. I am not concerned with Poetry. The Poetry is in the Pity."
>
> —Wilfred Owen

Soldier and Poet Owen was born to a working-class family in Oswestry, England, in 1893. He attended school at the Birkenhead Institute and graduated from the Shrewsbury Technical School. Owen gained entrance to the University of London but could not afford the tuition. To help pay for his schooling, he took a job as an assistant to the vicar of Dunsden. However, he soon became disenchanted with his position and went to France to teach English. When Britain entered World War I, Owen enlisted in the British army and left for the front to fight for his country.

One night, after falling into a fifteen-foot shell hole and badly banging his head, Owen experienced unrelenting headaches, which he believed were a result of a concussion. For two months he fought the headaches and the Germans under punishing conditions until doctors diagnosed his illness as "shell shock." Unable to lead his regiment, Owen was transported to Craiglockhart War Hospital in Edinburgh, Scotland, for treatment. When his fellow soldier and poet Siegfried Sassoon arrived at the hospital, the two became friends and exchanged poems. Sassoon helped the younger poet by introducing him to Robert Ross, a London editor. Although critics would later point out that Owen's poems exhibited greater range and technical superiority, Owen was humble about comparing himself to Sassoon. "I am not worthy to light his pipe," he wrote to his mother.

A Posthumous Legacy Owen was more sensitive and compassionate about his subject than many other war poets of the time, and he developed a direct, outspoken style that broke with the conventions of the day. Although he would become one of England's most admired war poets, he would not live long enough to see his poems in print. Tragically, he was killed in battle one week before the end of the war, and the bulk of his poems were posthumously published by Sassoon in the 1920s.

LOG ON ▶ **Literature** Online

Author Search For more about Wilfred Owen, go to glencoe.com and enter QuickPass code GLB9817u6.

Before You Read

Focus

Bellringer Options

Daily Language Practice Transparency 89

Or **ask:** What ideas about warfare have you learned from television, movies, books, or conversations with veterans? *(Answers will vary. Some may point to tales of heroic deeds, the overcoming of enemies, the horrors of battle, etc.)* Explain that this poem is a response to the author's military service in World War I.

Selection Skills

Literary Elements
- Verse Paragraph (SE pp. 1052, 1054)

Dulce et Decorum Est

Writing Skills/Grammar
- Write a Summary (SE p. 1054)

Reading Skills
- Recognize Author's Purpose (SE pp. 1052, 1054)

Vocabulary Skills
- Synonyms (SE p. 1054)
- Connotation (TE p. 1052)

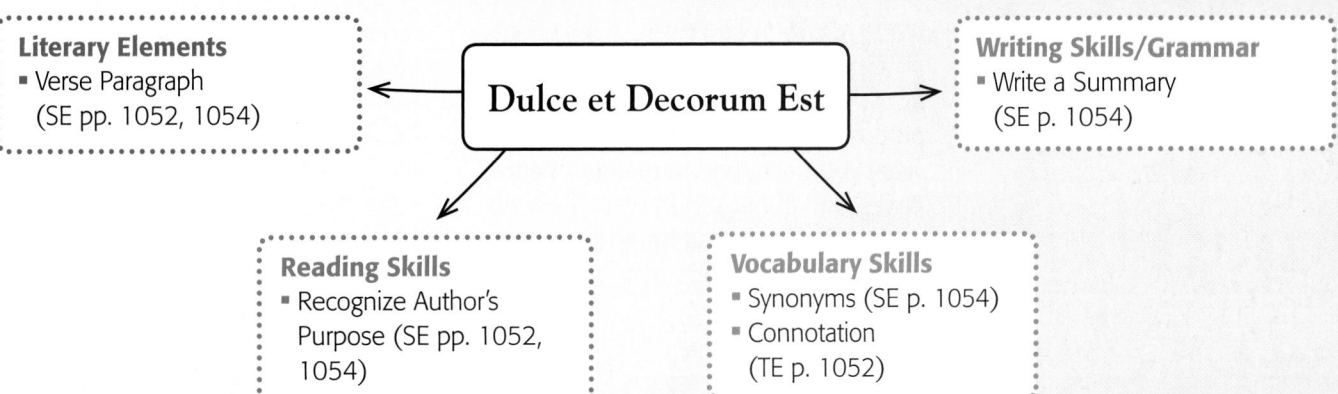

Before You Read

Focus

Summary

A group of retreating soldiers is victimized by a mustard gas attack. One soldier fails to put his gas mask on in time and dies a hideous death. The speaker addresses the reader and says that if the reader could witness this atrocity, he or she would not be so eager to inculcate children with "the old Lie" that it is sweet and honorable to die for one's country.

 For summaries in languages other than English, see Unit 6 Teaching Resources Book, pp. 83–88.

Vocabulary

Connotation Ask: Would you say the vocabulary words have a high or low intensity, or strength of meaning? *(high)* Have students brainstorm synonyms for each vocabulary word and rate the intensity of the synonyms's connotation *(e.g., walk would be a low-intensity synonym for trudge).* Ask students to write a sentence using one of the vocabulary words and then substitute a synonym of a different intensity. Ask them how the change affects the mood of the sentence.

 For additional vocabulary practice, see Unit 6 Teaching Resources Book, p. 91.

Literature and Reading Preview

Connect to the Poem

Is it always honorable and glorious to die for one's country? Freewrite for a few minutes on the less glorious aspects of war.

Build Background

During World War I, new technologies brought unprecedented dangers to soldiers and civilians alike. Machine guns and tanks killed more efficiently and caused considerably more destruction than previous weapons. Chemicals such as mustard gas, chlorine, and phosphorus poisoned and maimed troops. Mortars, which fired shells more than half a mile, decimated fighting forces and civilian centers. For the first time in the history of warfare, entire companies of soldiers could be destroyed before they could catch sight of their enemies.

Set Purposes for Reading

Big Idea Class, Colonialism, and the Great War

The strength and confidence of Britain as a military power came under scrutiny as the war progressed. As you read, ask yourself, How might the suffering and deaths of large numbers of soldiers have affected morale in the field and at home?

Literary Element Verse Paragraph

A **verse paragraph** and a prose paragraph have a similar function—to convey a main idea that is supported by details. Unlike a stanza, a verse paragraph does not have a fixed number of lines. Verse paragraphs are indicated on the page by blank spaces between groups of lines. As you read, ask yourself, What is the main idea of this section?

Reading Strategy Recognize Author's Purpose

An **author's purpose** is usually one of the following: to persuade, to inform or explain, to entertain, to describe, or to tell a story. Novelists and poets tend to imply their purposes. Examining the title, tone, theme, and figurative language in "Dulce et Decorum Est" can help you determine Owen's purpose. As you read, ask yourself, What do these words imply about Owen and his reasons for writing?

Tip: Asking Questions As you read, ask yourself questions like the following:

- Why does Owen use a Latin quotation for his title?
- How does the speaker's **tone** help fulfill Owen's purpose?

Learning Objectives

For pages 1051–1054

In studying this text, you will focus on the following objectives:

Literary Study: Analyzing verse paragraph.

Reading: Recognizing author's purpose.

Writing: Writing a summary.

Vocabulary

trudge (truj) *v.* to walk wearily or laboriously; p. 1053 *After the loss, the coach made the entire football team trudge behind the bus for a mile.*

ecstasy (ek′ stə sē) *n.* a state beyond reason or self-control; p. 1053 *The musicians moved the audience to a state of collective ecstasy.*

vile (vīl) *adj.* repulsive or disgusting; p. 1053 *When the landlord unlocked the door, he was almost knocked over by the vile odor coming from the trash can.*

Reading Practice

SPIRAL REVIEW **Make Predictions** Ask students to make predictions about the tone of the poem and about Owen's purpose in writing it. **Ask:** Based on what you have read here about Wilfred Owen and about World War I, how do you think Owen felt about the war? *(Likely answer: He was against it.)* What tone do the vocabulary words suggest to you? *(Possible answer: dramatic, intense)* With this in mind, what do you think the poem's purpose will be? *(Possible answer: to convince people that war is horrible)*

DULCE ET DECORUM EST

Wilfred Owen

Bent double, like old beggars under sacks,
Knock-kneed, coughing like hags, we cursed through sludge,
Till on the haunting flares we turned our backs
And towards our distant rest began to **trudge**.
5   Men marched asleep. Many had lost their boots
But limped on, blood-shod. All went lame; all blind;
Drunk with fatigue; deaf even to the hoots
Of tired, outstripped Five-Nines° that dropped behind.

Gas! GAS! Quick, boys!—An **ecstasy** of fumbling,
10   Fitting the clumsy helmets° just in time;
But someone still was yelling out and stumbling
And flound'ring like a man in fire or lime . . .
Dim, through the misty panes and thick green light,
As under a green sea, I saw him drowning.

15   In all my dreams, before my helpless sight,
He plunges at me, guttering, choking, drowning.

If in some smothering dreams you too could pace
Behind the wagon that we flung him in,
And watch the white eyes writhing in his face,
20   His hanging face, like a devil's sick of sin;
If you could hear, at every jolt, the blood
Come gargling from the froth-corrupted lungs,
Obscene as cancer, bitter as the cud
Of **vile**, incurable sores on innocent tongues,—
25   My friend, you would not tell with such high zest
To children ardent° for some desperate glory,
The old Lie: *Dulce et decorum est*
Pro patria mori.°

8   Five-Nines: artillery shells used during World War I.

10   clumsy helmets: a reference to gas masks.

26   ardent: eager.

27–28   Dulce . . . mori: These Latin words, meaning "It is sweet and honorable to die for one's country," are from a poem by the ancient Roman poet Horace.

Class, Colonialism, and the Great War   *How do these similes challenge the notion that war is glorious?*   **1**

Vocabulary

trudge (truj) *v.* to walk wearily or laboriously
ecstasy (ek′ stə sē) *n.* a state beyond reason or self-control
vile (vīl) *adj.* repulsive or disgusting

Big Idea   1

Class, Colonialism, and the Great War   Answer: *The similes portray the retreating soldiers as bedraggled victims worthy of pity rather than heroes worthy of adulation.*

 For an audio recording of this selection, use Listening Library Audio CD-ROM.

 To check students' understanding of the selection, see Unit 6 Teaching Resources Book, p. 92.

Approaching Level

DIFFERENTIATED INSTRUCTION

PARTNERS
Established A simile is a comparison of two essentially unlike things using the word *like* or *as*. In the opening lines of the poem, Owen uses a simile to compare soldiers to "old beggars under sacks." The word *like* should signal to students that a comparison is being made between the physical posture of the young soldiers trudging through mud and that of old beggars bent by years of poverty. Have students work in pairs with more proficient readers to identify the similes in the poem and the word or phrase that sets each off.

After You Read

Assess

1. Answers will vary.
2. (a) Children should not be told that it is honorable to die for one's country. (b) The death described is hideous and pathetic.
3. (a) "Blood-shod"; the soldiers have no boots and are "wearing blood." (b) Assonance and slant rhyme
4. (a) The speaker compares the soldier's face to that of a "devil" and his hemorrhaging lungs to "cancer." (b) Revulsion
5. (a) They have been brainwashed. (b) He views it as propaganda.
6. Answers will vary. Students should support their responses with examples.
7. Students may respond that Owen's experiences at war were too horrific to be expressed by the language and style of the Romantics.

Literary Element

1. To portray a war incident
2. The narrator explains how the incident affected him.

Progress Check

Can students analyze verse paragraphs?

If No → See Unit 6 Teaching Resources Book, p. 89.

 For additional assessment, see Assessment Resources, pp. 251–252.

After You Read

Respond and Think Critically

Respond and Interpret

1. How did you feel when the speaker addresses the reader in the final verse paragraph?
2. (a)What theme, or message, do you think the speaker wants to convey in lines 25–28? (b)What evidence does the speaker present to prove that the Latin quotation is a lie?

Analyze and Evaluate

3. (a)Explain the **metaphor** in line 6. (b)What sound effects make this metaphor particularly effective?
4. (a)What **similes** does the speaker use in the final verse paragraph? (b)What is the cumulative effect of these similes?

5. (a)Why are the children in line 26 eager for "desperate glory"? (b)Why do you think Owen describes the glory as "desperate"?

Connect

6. **Big Idea** **Class, Colonialism, and the Great War** Most of Owen's poems were published after the war. How do you think most people in Britain would have reacted to "Dulce et Decorum Est" when they first read it? Do you think the poem may have affected their opinions about the war effort? Explain.

7. **Connect to the Author** Why might Owen have adopted a more plainspoken, direct style than the poets—Keats and Shelley—he admired?

Literary Element Verse Paragraph

Whereas poems written before the twentieth century usually contain stanzas, many contemporary poems are made up of **verse paragraphs**.

1. What is the function of the first two verse paragraphs of "Dulce et Decorum Est"?
2. How do lines 15–16 function as a transitional verse paragraph?

 Writing

Write a Summary "Dulce et Decorum Est" recounts a series of events through sensory details and figurative language. Write a summary of the events of the poem in plain prose. Remember that a summary should be shorter than the original because its purpose is to highlight the main points of the original. For help with writing a summary, see page 55.

LOG ON ▶ **Literature** Online

Selection Resources For Selection Quizzes, eFlashcards, and Reading-Writing Connection activities, go to glencoe.com and enter QuickPass code GLB9817u6.

Reading Strategy Recognize Author's Purpose

Sometimes an author has more than one purpose for writing. However, he or she usually considers one purpose more important than the others.

1. What do you think was Owen's main purpose in writing "Dulce et Decorum Est"?
2. How do Owen's **tone** and **figurative language** contribute to his purpose?

Vocabulary Practice

Practice with Synonyms With a partner, match each boldfaced vocabulary word below with its synonym. Use a thesaurus or dictionary to check your answers. You will not use all of the answer choices.

1. trudge	a. offensive
2. ecstasy	b. plod
3. vile	c. pathetic
	d. disown
	e. rapture

Reading Strategy

1. Possible answer: to show the war as a tragedy
2. The tone and figurative language evoke pity for the soldiers and place blame on pro-war civilians.

Vocabulary Practice

1. b **2.** e **3.** a

Writing

Students' summaries should include the main ideas. Sample summary: A soldier breathes poison gas and chokes to death. The speaker is horrified by this event.

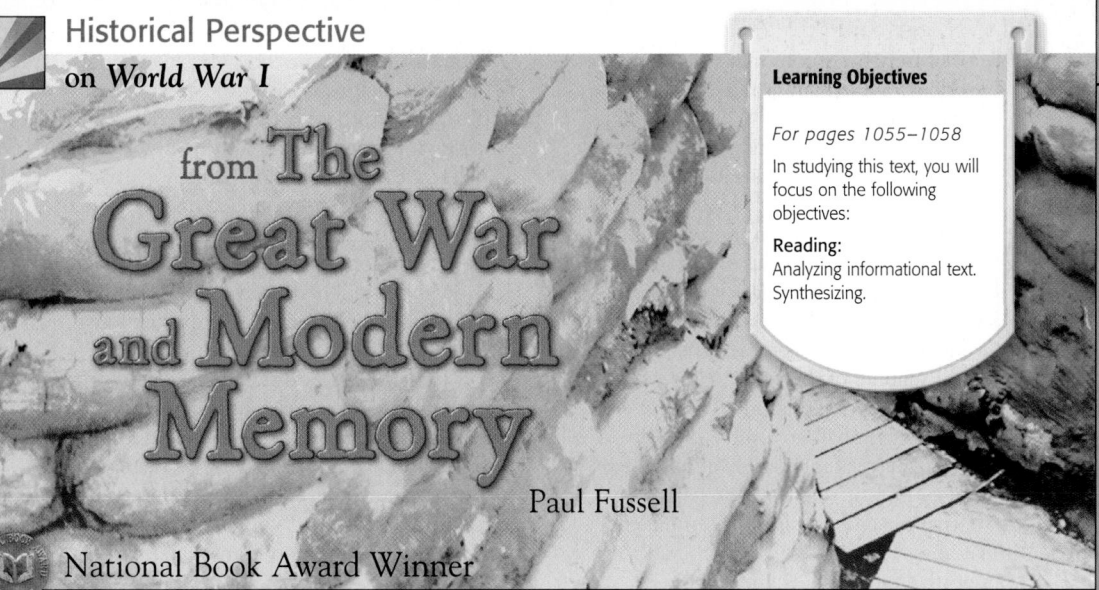

from The Great War and Modern Memory

Paul Fussell

National Book Award Winner

Learning Objectives

For pages 1055–1058

In studying this text, you will focus on the following objectives:

Reading:
Analyzing informational text. Synthesizing.

Set a Purpose for Reading

As you read, ask yourself, What am I finding out about the trenches used during World War I?

Build Background

Paul Fussell was born in California in 1924. His experiences fighting as an infantryman in World War II profoundly influenced his beliefs about the meaning of war, its causes, and its relationship to literature and the arts. In the following excerpt from *The Great War and Modern Memory*, Fussell describes the trenches that spanned the Western Front during World War I. (See map on page 989.)

Reading Strategy

Synthesize Information

To **synthesize** means to draw information from multiple sources in order to come to a conclusion. While you are reading, take notes about the lives of soldiers in the trenches. Use an evaluation chart like the one below, and include information drawn from other sources in this unit, including poetry. As you read, ask yourself, What conclusion about trench warfare can I come to on the basis of this evidence?

Information About Trench Life	Evidence	Conclusion

Henri Barbusse[1] estimates that the French front alone contained about 6250 miles of trenches. Since the French occupied a little more than half the line, the total length of the numerous trenches occupied by the British must come to about 6000 miles. We thus find over 12,000 miles of trenches on the Allied side alone. When we add the trenches of the Central Powers, we arrive at a figure of about 25,000 miles, equal to a trench sufficient to circle the earth. Theoretically it would have been possible to walk from Belgium to Switzerland entirely below ground, but although the lines were "continuous," they were not entirely seamless: occasionally mere shell holes or fortified strong-points would serve as a connecting link. Not a few survivors have performed the heady imaginative exercise of envisioning the whole line at once. Stanley Casson is one who, imagining the whole line from his position on the ground, implicitly submits the whole preposterous conception to the criterion of the "normally" rational and intelligible. As he remembers, looking back from 1935,

1. *Henri Barbusse* (1873–1935) was a French infantryman and novelist.

PAUL FUSSELL **1055**

Focus

Summary

Citing a number of primary sources, Fussell describes the trenches of World War I. The total length of all the trenches was great enough to stretch around the earth. Some soldiers imagined walking through them from Belgium to Switzerland (east–west) or from the North Sea to Switzerland (north–south)— entirely below ground. Generally there were three lines of trenches, one behind another, with connecting passages. They were six to eight feet deep and built up higher with barbed-wire divides on the side facing the enemy.

📁 For summaries in languages other than English, see Unit 6 Teaching Resources Book, pp. 94–99.

Teach

Reading Strategy **1**

Decode Expressions **Read:** "Not a few survivors have performed the heady imaginative exercise of envisioning the whole line at once." **Ask:** How many survivors imagined this sort of thing? A few? *(No, many imagined it.)* Why do you say that? *(The sentence says "Not a few," and "many" is "not a few.")* Reread the sentence, substituting "Many" for "Not a few."

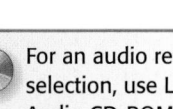
 For an audio recording of this selection, use Listening Library Audio CD-ROM.

Teach

Recognize Sources Call students' attention to the first paragraph on this page. **Ask:** Did Paul Fussell fight in World War I? *(No, he was born after it ended.)* Are these Paul Fussell's words? *(no)* Whose words are they? *(Stanley Casson's)* How can you tell? *(Fussell mentions Casson on the preceding page, introducing the quotation with, "As he remembers…")*

Cultural History ☆

Trench Warfare Although soldiers have been digging trenches since ancient times, World War I was the first (and last) war to be fought almost entirely from trenches. The invention of the machine gun and improvements in weapons made it impossible to simply charge an enemy force without protection.

Readability Scores

Dale-Chall: 9.2
DRP: 66
Lexile: 1190

 Our trenches stood on a faint slope, just overlooking German ground, with a vista of vague plainland below. Away to right and left stretched the great lines of defense as far as eye and imagination could stretch them. I used to wonder how long it would take for me to walk from the beaches of the North Sea to that curious end of all fighting against the Swiss boundary; to try to guess what each end looked like; to imagine what would happen if I passed a verbal message, in the manner of the parlor game, along to the next man on my right to be delivered to the end man of all up against the Alps. Would anything intelligible at all emerge?

Another imagination has contemplated a similar absurd transmission of sound all the way from north to south. Alexander Aitken[2] remembers the Germans opposite him celebrating some happy public event in early June, 1916, presumably either the (ambiguous) German success at the naval battle of Jutland (May 31–June 1) or the drowning of Lord Kitchener, lost on June 5 when the cruiser *Hampshire* struck a mine and sank off the Orkney Islands.[3] Aitken writes, "There had been a morning in early June when a tremendous tin-canning and beating of shell-gongs had begun in the north and run south down their lines to end, without doubt, at Belfort and Mulhausen[4] on the Swiss frontier." Impossible to believe, really, but in this mad setting, somehow plausible.

2. *Alexander Aitken* (1895–1967) was a soldier, war memoirist, and famed mathematician.
3. The *naval battle of Jutland,* which took place off the coast of Denmark, was the only major naval battle of the war. It ended without a decisive victor. *Lord Kitchener* (1850–1916) was a British field marshal and secretary of state for war. The *Orkney Islands* sit off the northeast coast of Scotland.
4. *Belfort,* the capital of the Territoire de Belfort in eastern France, was successfully defended by the Allies during World War I. *Mulhausen* is an industrial town in northeastern France.

"When all is said and done," Sassoon[5] notes, "the war was mainly a matter of holes and ditches." And in these holes and ditches extending for ninety miles, continually, even in the quietest times, some 7000 British men and officers were killed and wounded daily, just as a matter of course. "Wastage," the Staff called it.

There were normally three lines of trenches. The front-line trench was anywhere from fifty yards or so to a mile from its enemy counterpart. Several hundred yards behind it was the support trench line. And several hundred yards behind that was the reserve line. There were three kinds of trenches: firing trenches, like these; communication trenches, running roughly perpendicular to the line and connecting the three lines; and "saps," shallower ditches thrust out into No Man's Land, provid-

---

5. Siegfried *Sassoon* (see page 1047) was a poet who wrote about the war.

Soldier cleaning a trench in the Champagne region of France.

Reading Practice

SPIRAL REVIEW **Find Corroboration** Review Alexander Aitken's anecdote about a German celebration that spread through the trenches as word of the good news was relayed from one end of the front to the other. Fussell describes the story as "impossible to believe, really, but in this mad setting, somehow plausible." Challenge students to research the incident and then attempt to determine whether it happened or not. You may also want them to research another "unbelievable" incident that occurred during World War I—the Christmas Truce of 1914.

A French front line trench from WWI.

ing access to forward observation posts, listening posts, grenade-throwing posts, and machine gun positions. The end of a sap was usually not manned all the time: night was the favorite time for going out. Coming up from the rear, one reached the trenches by following a communication trench sometimes a mile or more long. It often began in a town and gradually deepened. By the time pedestrians reached the reserve line, they were well below ground level.

A firing trench was supposed to be six to eight feet deep and four or five feet wide. On the enemy side a parapet[6] of earth or sandbags rose about two or three feet above the ground. A corresponding "parados"[7] a foot or so high was often found on top of the friendly side. Into the sides of trenches were dug one- or two-man holes ("funk-holes"), and there were deeper dugouts, reached by dirt stairs, for use as command posts and officers' quarters. On the enemy side of a trench was a fire-step two feet high on which the defenders were supposed to stand, firing and throwing grenades, when repelling attack. A well-built trench did not run straight for any distance: that would have

been to invite enfilade[8] fire. Every few yards a good trench zig-zagged. It had frequent traverses designed to contain damage within a limited space. Moving along a trench thus involved a great deal of weaving and turning. The floor of a proper trench was covered with wooden duckboards, beneath which were sumps a few feet deep designed to collect water. The walls, perpetually crumbling, were supported by sandbags, corrugated iron, or bundles of sticks or rushes. Except at night and in half-light, there was of course no looking over the top except through periscopes, which could be purchased in the "Trench Requisites" section of the main London department stores. The few snipers on duty during the day observed No Man's Land through loopholes cut in sheets of armor plate.

The entanglements of barbed wire had to be positioned far enough out in front of the trench to keep the enemy from sneaking up to grenade-throwing distance. Interestingly, the two novelties that contributed most to the personal menace of the war could be said to be American inventions. Barbed wire had first appeared on the American frontier in the late nineteenth century for use in restraining animals. And the machine gun was the brainchild of Hiram Stevens Maxim (1840–1916), an American who, disillusioned with native patent law, established his Maxim Gun Company in England and began manufacturing his guns in 1889. He was finally knighted for his efforts. At first the British regard for barbed wire was on a par with Sir Douglas Haig's[9] understanding of the machine gun. In the autumn of

---

6. A *parapet* is a wall used to protect soldiers.
7. A *parados* was the side of a trench that faced away from the enemy.

8. *Enfilade* is gunfire from the flank of a battle line, directed along the line's length.
9. *Sir Douglas Haig* (1861–1928) was a British field marshal and commander in chief of British forces in France.

PAUL FUSSELL **1057**

Teach

Vocabulary | 2

Determine Meaning **Ask:**
What does the word *funk* mean? *(Most students will probably provide definitions involving music or an odor.)* Tell students that another meaning of funk is "fear." **Ask:** Why do you think the holes dug into the sides of trenches were called "funk-holes"? *(Because soldiers who were afraid would hide in them.)*

Reading Strategy | 3

Synthesize Information
World War I was called the "war to end all wars" because of the great loss of life among the nations who fought in it. **Ask:** What inventions or actions made this quote true at the time? Have students list the inventions and actions they find in the text as they read. *(Possible answers: machine guns, poison gas, barbed wire, enfilade firing)*

 For activities related to this selection, see Unit 6 Teaching Resources Book, pp. 100–101.

English Learners

DIFFERENTIATED INSTRUCTION

Advanced Challenge English learners to find all the hyphenated words on this page. *(grenade-throwing, one- or two-man, funk-holes, fire-step, well-built, zig-zagged, half-light)* **Say:** Two or more words are hyphenated when they work together to form an adjective—but only if they appear before the noun. Find

examples in the selection. *(one- or two-man, well-built, and grenade-throwing)* Find examples of two or more words hyphenated to make a compound word. *(funk-holes, fire-step, zig-zagged, and half-light)*

Assess

1. Students should summarize main events of the selection, such as Fussell's description that there were three lines of trenches with connecting passages.

2. Answers will vary. Students should support their opinions with evidence from the text.

3. (a) "Wastage" was the term for the 7,000 soldiers who were killed or wounded every day. (b) Students should understand that the staff was attempting to blunt the reality of the war's heavy toll by resorting to military jargon.

4. (a) They referred to the trenches by using the names of streets in London. (b) The soldiers were homesick and wished to remind themselves of London and their lives before the war. They also may have been using sardonic humor.

5. (a) Students' answers will vary. Many will point out that the anecdotes seem emblematic of the war's oddity. The anecdotes also give a sense of the great distances traversed by the trenches. (b) Both anecdotes give the reader a sense of the huge scale of the conflict.

A view of the German Trench Avenue on the Western Front, showing the elaborate construction erected by the Germans.

1914, the first wire Private Frank Richards saw emplaced before the British positions was a single strand of agricultural wire found in the vicinity. Only later did the manufactured article begin to arrive from England in sufficient quantity to create the thickets of mock-organic rusty brown that helped give a look of eternal autumn to the front.

The whole British line was numbered by sections, neatly, from right to left. A section, normally occupied by a company, was roughly 300 yards wide. One might be occupying front-line trench section 51; or support trench S 51, behind it; or reserve trench SS 51, behind both. But a less formal way of identifying sections of trench was by place or street names with a distinctly London flavor. *Piccadilly* was a favorite; popular also were *Regent Street* and *Strand*; junctions were *Hyde Park Corner* and *Marble Arch*. Directional and traffic control signs were everywhere in the trenches, giving the whole system the air of a parody modern city, although one literally "underground."

Respond and Think Critically

Respond and Interpret

1. Write a brief summary of the main ideas in this excerpt before answering the following questions. For help with writing a summary, see page 435.

2. In what way has this passage changed your understanding of life in the trenches? Explain.

3. (a)According to Fussell, what did the British staff refer to as "wastage"? (b)Why do you think they used this term?

4. (a)How did the British identify sections of the trench when speaking informally? (b)For what reason do you think they did this?

Analyze and Evaluate

5. (a)For what reason might Fussell describe the two instances of the "transmission of sound all the way from north to south"? (b)In your opinion, why are these anecdotes effective?

6. (a)How are the trenches like a "modern city"? (b)In your opinion, how successful is Fussell's description of the trenches? Explain.

Connect

7. In what ways does Fussell's description of trench life resemble the descriptions in the poetry of Wilfred Owen and Siegfried Sassoon? On the basis of these similarities and the evaluation chart you made as you read, what conclusions can you draw about life in the trenches?

6. (a) The trenches resemble a modern city because they are massive, complex networks in which humans live. (b) Answers will vary. Students should support their opinions with evidence from the text.

7. Students should recognize that the poems and this essay reflect the brutal, surrealistic, violent, and heroic qualities of trench life.

 For additional assessment, see Assessment Resources, pp. 253–254.

PART 2

Modernism

The Arrival, ca. 1913. Christopher R. W. Nevinson. Oil on canvas, 30 x 25 in. Tate Gallery, London.

 View the Art This image is an example of Futurist art, which focused on urban and mechanical subjects and imagery. How does this painting emphasize science and progress?

> "The most beautiful thing we can
> experience is the mysterious. It is **1**
> the source of all art and science."
>
> —Albert Einstein, "What I Believe"

1059

Reading Strategy   **1**

Evaluate Point out the quotation by Einstein. Explain that Modernism was in part a literary response to the disillusionment that followed the chaos and barbarism of World War I. **Ask:** How do Einstein's words relate to the Modernists' search for meaning? *(Einstein's words suggest a journey beyond the grim reality of events and toward the hidden meaning of things.)*

 View the Art ★

Answer: *By splitting the image into several different facets, Nevinson is able to highlight the individual mechanical parts of the ship. The approaching ship and the smoke blowing back suggest forward movement or progress.*

C. R. W. Nevinson (1889–1946) was a Futurist who looked to the aesthetic beauty of machines, the power of cities, and the speed of modernity.

For additional support for English Learners, see Unit 6 Teaching Resources Book, p. 104.

English Learners

DIFFERENTIATED INSTRUCTION

Intermediate Have students work in groups of four to "reassemble" the fragmented picture by identifying the feature of the ship in each fragment. Encourage students to think about what the text means as well. **Ask:** What kind of ship is this? *(It is an ocean liner that carries passengers and cargo from continent to continent.)*

Approaching Level

DIFFERENTIATED INSTRUCTION

Emerging Help students use their interpretations of the painting to draw conclusions about Modernism. *Modernism* is an umbrella term for a variety of movements that all had in common a desire to break with the past, to change the very structure of literature and all the arts.

Before You Read

Focus

Bellringer Options

Selection Focus
  Transparency 53
Daily Language Practice
  Transparency 90

Or have students recall a special place that lives in their imagination. **Ask:** How would you describe this place? How do you feel when you relive your memories of it? Have students consider, as they read, why Innisfree means so much to the speaker.

Before You Read

Yeats's Poetry

Meet **William Butler Yeats**
(1865–1939)

William Butler Yeats (yāts) is universally regarded as one of the greatest poets of the twentieth century. Born into an Anglo-Irish Protestant family in the Dublin suburb of Sandymount, Yeats loved to read and daydream as a child, especially during his summers at his grandparents' home in County Sligo, where he rode his pony about the scenic countryside and discovered Irish folklore and mythology.

Irish Romantic The son of a distinguished portrait painter, Yeats briefly studied painting but turned to writing poetry in his teens. His early work was influenced by the Romantics, particularly William Blake. Yeats even dressed the part of the romantic young poet, wearing a flowing tie, brown velvet jacket, and his father's old cape and wide-brimmed hat.

When Yeats was twenty-three, he published his first book of verse, and soon afterward a young woman named Maud Gonne arrived at his home to tell him that his poetry had moved her deeply. This meeting began Yeats's long obsession with Gonne, an actress and Irish patriot who inspired him to join the fight to free Ireland from British rule.

Although Gonne refused Yeats's many marriage proposals, she haunted his imagination and became a central figure in his poetry. Yeats did not end his pursuit of her until 1916, more than twenty years after they had first met. He later wrote that it was a "miserable love affair" and that he might as well have been offering his heart to a statue in a museum. Fortunately, Yeats found contentment in 1917, when he married Georgie Hyde-Lees.

Yeats combined his passions for literature and for Irish nationalism by joining the Celtic Revival, a cultural and political movement dedicated to Irish independence and to the use of Irish folklore in literature. He also presided over the Irish National Theatre Society at the Abbey Theatre in Dublin with his friend and patron, Augusta, Lady Gregory, and the playwright J. M. Synge. Yeats contributed many of his own plays to this theater, including *The Land of Heart's Desires*. He hoped to unite Catholics and Protestants in Ireland through a national literature that transcended religious differences.

> *"We should write out our own thoughts in as nearly as possible the language we thought them in, as though in a letter to an intimate friend."*
>
> —William Butler Yeats

From Romantic to Modernist In middle age, when Yeats reread the poems of his youth, he found "little but romantic convention, unconscious drama." He began to write in a less romantic style that more closely resembled natural speech. His poetry became less dreamlike and more energetic; his imagery became more economical and his tone more conversational. "Sentimentality," he declared, "is deceiving oneself; rhetoric is deceiving other people." Yeats received the Nobel Prize in Literature in 1923.

Author Search For more about William Butler Yeats, go to glencoe.com and enter QuickPass code GLB9817u6.

Selection Skills

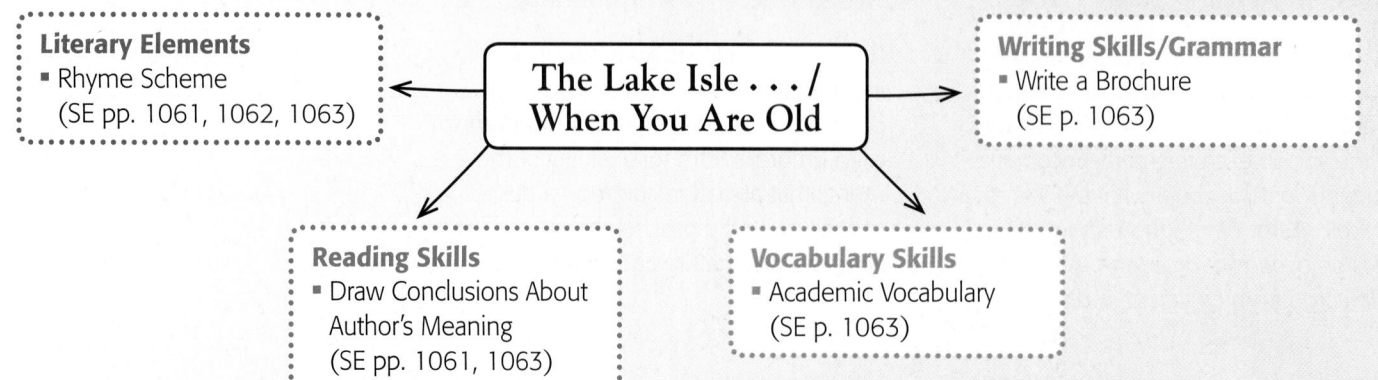

Literary Elements
- Rhyme Scheme
  (SE pp. 1061, 1062, 1063)

**The Lake Isle . . . /
When You Are Old**

Writing Skills/Grammar
- Write a Brochure
  (SE p. 1063)

Reading Skills
- Draw Conclusions About
  Author's Meaning
  (SE pp. 1061, 1063)

Vocabulary Skills
- Academic Vocabulary
  (SE p. 1063)

Literature and Reading Preview

Connect to the Poems

Where would you like to go to find peace and renewal? Write a list of details that make a place peaceful to you.

Build Background

Yeats's poems "The Lake Isle of Innisfree" and "When You Are Old" are romantic and dreamlike. "The Lake Isle of Innisfree" was influenced by Yeats's reading of *Walden* by Henry David Thoreau, who described his retreat from the city to a simple cabin by a forest pond. Yeats wrote his poem after the sight of a small fountain in a shop window in London brought the sound of Sligo's lake water lapping back into his consciousness.

Set Purposes for Reading

Big Idea Modernism

The Modernist poets were fascinated with contrast and the tension between opposites. As you read, ask yourself, How does Yeats's early poetry reflect this characteristic?

Literary Element Rhyme Scheme

The pattern that end rhymes form in a stanza or poem is known as its rhyme scheme. The **rhyme scheme** is designated by assigning a different letter of the alphabet to each new rhyme. As you read, ask yourself, What patterns of rhyme can I see here, and what is their effect?

Reading Strategy Draw Conclusions About Author's Meaning

Drawing conclusions is part of inferring, or making informed guesses about what an author suggests. Poets suggest meaning rather than state it directly, so drawing conclusions is essential when reading a poem. When you draw a conclusion, you make a statement supported by evidence. As you read, ask yourself, What details and evidence led me to Yeats's higher meaning?

Tip: Taking Notes Use a chart like the one below to record conclusions you draw from the details presented in the poems.

Details	Conclusions
Speaker plans to build a cabin and raise bees.	The speaker dreams of a simple life close to nature.

Learning Objectives

For pages 1060–1063

In studying these texts, you will focus on the following objectives:

Literary Study: Analyzing rhyme scheme.

Reading: Drawing conclusions about author's meaning.

Writing: Writing a brochure.

Juliette Drouet, 1883. Jules Bastien-Lepage. Oil on canvas, 36 x 31 cm. Musée Victor Hugo, Paris.

WILLIAM BUTLER YEATS **1061**

Before You Read

Focus

Summary

Yeats's early poems were often simple, musical, romantic, and dreamlike. In "The Lake Isle of Innisfree," the speaker dreams of a peaceful, self-sufficient life close to nature. In "When You Are Old," the speaker imagines his beloved in old age, reading and reminiscing.

Vocabulary

Adjectives Explain that Yeats uses adjectives creatively to bring his poems to life and develop their tone. Tell students to pay attention to the adjectives when as read the poems and think about how they create the poems' tone. Have students practice writing colorful adjectives by having them brainstorm words that could be used to describe the face of Juliette Drouet in the portrait. Tell them to group the adjectives according to the type of tone they develop.

Teach

Big Idea   1

Modernism **Ask:** In "The Lake Isle of Innisfree," what does the speaker want to escape? *(the aesthetic and spiritual poverty of modern life)* What is he seeking? *(a pastoral retreat to nourish his spirit)*

Literary Element   2

Rhyme Scheme **Answer:** *Lines 1 and 3 rhyme, and so do lines 2 and 4.*

Ask advanced level students to read "The Lake Isle of Innisfree" aloud several times and note the meter of the poem. **Ask:** Does the poem have a regular meter? *(no)* Why do you think the poem made that choice? *(possible answer: to reflect the poems theme of freedom from civilization)*

Literary History ☆

Yeats and Thoreau Henry David Thoreau's *Walden*, which encourages living in harmony with nature rather than pursuing material goods, influenced Yeats's "The Lake Isle of Innisfree." Yeats took Thoreau's message to heart: "I did not wish to live what was not life, living is so dear."

To check students' understanding of the selection, see Unit 6 Teaching Resources Book, p. 113.

The Lake Isle of Innisfree ☆
William Butler Yeats

I will arise and go now, and go to Innisfree,[1]
And a small cabin build there, of clay and wattles[2] made:
Nine bean-rows will I have there, a hive for the honeybee,
And live alone in the bee-loud glade.[3]

5 And I shall have some peace there, for peace comes
    dropping slow,
Dropping from the veils of the morning to where the
    cricket sings;
There midnight's all a glimmer, and noon a purple glow,
And evening full of the linnet's[4] wings.

I will arise and go now, for always night and day
10 I hear lake water lapping with low sounds by the shore;
While I stand on the roadway, or on the pavements gray, **1**
I hear it in the deep heart's core.

1. *Innisfree* is an island in County Sligo. Yeats had wanted to go to Innisfree since hearing of it as a child.
2. *Wattles* are walls made of twigs.
3. A *glade* is an open space in the forest.
4. A *linnet* is a small brown songbird.

When You Are Old
William Butler Yeats

When you[1] are old and gray and full of sleep,
And nodding by the fire, take down this book,
And slowly read, and dream of the soft look
Your eyes had once, and of their shadows deep;

5 How many loved your moments of glad grace,
And loved your beauty with love false or true,
But one man loved the pilgrim soul in you,
And loved the sorrows of your changing face;

And bending down beside the glowing bars,[2]
10 Murmur, a little sadly, how Love fled
And paced upon the mountains overhead
And hid his face amid a crowd of stars.

1. Some critics think that the *you* Yeats is addressing is Maud Gonne, the woman he loved and who rejected his proposals of marriage. However, this poem is actually a free translation of Pierre de Ronsard's sonnet to *his* love Hélène (see page 452).
2. *Glowing bars* refers to the grate in front of the fireplace.

2   Rhyme Scheme *Which lines rhyme in this stanza?*

Reading Practice

SPIRAL REVIEW **Text Structure** Point out that both "The Lake Isle of Innisfree" and "When You Are Old" consist of three stanzas. Each stanza is known as a quatrain because it contains four lines. The last line of each quatrain in "The Lake Isle of Innisfree" has fewer feet than the preceding three lines. Ask students what effect this has. *(By ending somewhat abruptly, each quatrain gives the impression that something is missing, reinforcing the speaker's lack of fulfillment.)*

After You Read

Respond and Think Critically

Respond and Interpret

1. Would you like to live on Innisfree or a place like it? Why or why not?

2. (a)List three details from "The Lake Isle of Innisfree" that describe this special place. (b)What can you infer about this place from the speaker's description of it?

3. (a)According to the speaker in "When You Are Old," how does his love differ from that of others? (b)What might you infer about the relationship between the woman and the speaker?

Analyze and Evaluate

4. In "The Lake Isle of Innisfree," what do you think Innisfree symbolizes for the speaker?

5. In "When You Are Old," what does the personification of love seem to suggest about the woman? About the speaker's love for her?

6. Evaluate the speaker's tone, or attitude toward the subject, in "When You Are Old." Does the speaker seem disillusioned? Why or why not? Use details from the poem to support your answer.

Connect

7. **Big Idea** Modernism What contrasts does the speaker suggest in these poems?

8. **Connect to the Author** From which phase in Yeats's life—his Romantically inclined youth or his more Modernist middle age—would you guess these poems are? Explain.

Literary Element Rhyme Scheme

In these poems, Yeats adopts a traditional form of lyric poems with a pattern of rhyming sounds.

1. What is the rhyme scheme of "When You Are Old"?

2. How does the rhyme help reinforce the meaning?

Reading Strategy Draw Conclusions About Author's Meaning

Look at the chart you created as you read to help you answer the following questions.

1. Will the speaker in "The Lake Isle of Innisfree" ever really go to Innisfree? Explain.

2. In "When You Are Old," what does the speaker want the woman to feel as she reads the poem? What clues support your conclusion?

 Literature Online

Selection Resources For Selection Quizzes, eFlashcards, and Reading-Writing Connection activities, go to glencoe.com and enter QuickPass code GLB9817u6.

Academic Vocabulary

Yeats's early poetry shows a liberal, romantic vision of life.

Liberal is an academic word. For instance, a person who does not always conform to traditional views could be called **liberal**. Using context clues, try to figure out the meaning of the word in the sentence about Yeats above. Check your guess in a dictionary.

For more on academic vocabulary, see pages 56 and R81.

Writing

Write a Brochure Using Yeats's poem as a reference, create a travel brochure for the island of Innisfree. If you plan to describe additional aspects of the island that Yeats does not mention in the poem, do research on Innisfree and on other islands around Ireland. In your brochure, explain why people would find an escape from their everyday world in Innisfree.

After You Read

Assess

1. Students' answers will vary.

2. (a) "midnight's all a glimmer, and noon a purple glow, / And evening full of the linnet's wings." (b) It is isolated.

3. (a) He loves the woman's inner nature. (b) She does not recognize the depth of the speaker's love.

4. Peace and sanctuary

5. The woman was cruel to the speaker. The speaker's love was lofty, idealistic, and timeless.

6. The tone seems melancholy and the speaker seems saddened.

7. In "The Lake Isle of Innisfree," he contrasts his present location and the place that beckons him. In "When You Are Old," he contrasts the woman in youth and in old age.

8. Some students may say that the simple language suggests the poems come from Yeats's older years. Others may say that the regular rhymes, structures, and use of the Ronsard poem as inspiration might mean they come from his more romantic early years.

Literary Element

1. *abba cddc effe*

2. The regularity contributes to a subdued tone.

Writing

Students' brochures should be persuasive and include specific details from the poem and from their research.

Reading Strategy

1. His idealized portrayal of Innisfree suggests that it may be only a figment of the imagination.

2. He wants the woman to feel regret.

Academic Vocabulary

liberal

Definition: giving freely

Synonyms: generous, altruistic

Antonyms: ungenerous, stingy, parsimonious

Sentence: My math teacher is liberal with her time, so I go to her office every day for help.

Before You Read

Focus

Summary

In "Sailing to Byzantium," an old man seeks spiritual joy in the timeless world of art. "The Second Coming" depicts the chaos of the modern world and the birth of a cruel order.

Vocabulary

Related Forms Tell students that knowing the noun form of a word will enable them to recognize related words. Have students use a dictionary to find related forms of *artifice* and *anarchy* (*artificial, anarchist, anarchic, anarchism*).

Interactive Read and Write

Other options for teaching this selection can be found in

- Interactive Read and Write for EL Students pp. 257–266
- Interactive Read and Write for Appoaching-Level Students, 257–266
- Interactive Read and Write for On-Level Students, 257–266

Before You Read

Sailing to Byzantium and *The Second Coming*

Connect to the Poems

Are conditions in the world getting better or worse? Discuss the question with a partner. In "Sailing to Byzantium," the speaker describes a timeless realm of the imagination; in "The Second Coming," the speaker utters a prophecy triggered by trends he observes in the modern world. As you read, think about a place you would choose to symbolize the kingdom of imagination.

Build Background

The capital of Byzantium, the eastern division of the Roman Empire, was a great center of artistic activity during the Middle Ages. Yeats regarded Byzantium as a city of the imagination, a perfect blend of the practical, spiritual, and artistic. "The Second Coming" is based on Yeats's theory that cycles of history and nature occur every two thousand years. During this time, one civilization evolves and decays, eventually replaced by another.

Set Purposes for Reading

Big Idea Modernism

Yeats exerted enormous influence on the Modernist poets, particularly in his use of symbolism. As you read, ask yourself, What makes the symbolism in these poems so rich?

Literary Element Structure

Structure is the framework of a literary work. It refers to the relationship of the parts to each other and to the whole piece. As you read, ask yourself, How is the poem constructed?

Reading Strategy Analyze Figurative Language: Metaphor

Analyzing is the process of looking at the separate parts of a literary work to understand the whole. When you **analyze metaphors**, you identify figures of speech that make comparisons without using the words *like* or *as*. As you read, ask yourself, What does Yeats achieve by using metaphors not literal words?

Tip: Identifying Metaphors As you read, record your interpretations of the metaphors in the poems.

1064 UNIT 6 THE MODERN AGE

Learning Objectives

For pages 1064–1069

In studying these texts, you will focus on the following objectives:

Literary Study: Analyzing structure.

Reading: Analyzing figurative language and metaphor.

Vocabulary

artifice (är′ tə fis) *n.* trickery; deception; p. 1065 *Her friendly attitude was a mere artifice.*

anarchy (an′ ər kē) *n.* a complete lack of political order; chaos; p. 1067 *Mobs of citizens rioted, storming the capitol and ushering in a state of anarchy.*

conviction (kən vik′ shən) *n.* a strong belief; p. 1067 *My conviction is that writing helps you think.*

vex (veks) *v.* disturb; trouble; irritate; p. 1067 *Eager to buy tickets, he was vexed by the slow line.*

Tip: Context Clues You can figure out the meanings of unfamiliar words by looking for clues in the **context**, or the surrounding words and sentences. Consider the sentence: *Eager to buy tickets, he was vexed by the slow line.* If you wanted to buy tickets to your favorite group, a line being slow would probably disturb and annoy you. Therefore, you can infer that *vexed* means "disturbed" or "irritated."

Selection Skills

Literary Elements
- Structure (SE pp. 1064, 1065, 1067, 1069)
- Meter (SE p. 1069)

Sailing to Byzantium / The Second Coming

Listening/Speaking/ Viewing Skills
- Analyze Art (SE p. 1066)

Reading Skills
- Analyze Figurative Language: Metaphor (SE pp. 1064, 1069)

Vocabulary Skills
- Context Clues (SE pp. 1064, 1069)
- Academic Vocabulary (SE p. 1069)

Writing Skills/Grammar
- Expository Essay (SE p. 1070)
- Transitional Expressions (SE p. 1070)

SAILING TO BYZANTIUM

William Butler Yeats

I

1 That is no country for old men. The young
In one another's arms, birds in the trees
—Those dying generations—at their song,
The salmon-falls,[1] the mackerel-crowded
    seas,
5 Fish, flesh, or fowl, commend all summer
    long
Whatever is begotten, born, and dies.
Caught in that sensual music all neglect
Monuments of unaging intellect.

II

An aged man is but a paltry[2] thing,
10 A tattered coat upon a stick, unless
Soul clap its hands and sing, and louder
    sing
For every tatter in its mortal dress,
Nor is there singing school but studying
Monuments of its own magnificence;
15 And therefore I have sailed the seas and
    come
To the holy city of Byzantium.

III

O sages[3] standing in God's holy fire

As in the gold mosaic of a wall,
Come from the holy fire, perne in a gyre,[4]
20 And be the singing-masters of my soul.
Consume my heart away; sick with desire
And fastened to a dying animal
It knows not what it is; and gather me
Into the **artifice** of eternity.

IV

25 Once out of nature I shall never take
My bodily form from any natural thing,
But such a form as Grecian goldsmiths
    make
Of hammered gold and gold enameling
To keep a drowsy Emperor awake;[5]
30 Or set upon a golden bough to sing
To lords and ladies of Byzantium
Of what is past, or passing, or to come.

---

4. *Perne in a gyre* means to spin around in a spiral motion. Yeats associated gyres with the spinning of fate; here, the speaker asks the images on the wall to come down and spin him into their timeless state of being.
5. *But such a form . . . awake* refers to something Yeats once read about: An emperor in Byzantium had a tree made of gold and silver upon which artificial birds sat and sang.

> **Structure** *How might the last two stanzas of this poem contrast with the first two?* **2**

Vocabulary

artifice (är′ tə fis) n. trickery; deception

---

1. *Salmon-falls* are the rapids in rivers that salmon swim up to spawn.
2. *Paltry* means "worthless."
3. *Sages* are the wise men pictured on the walls of the churches in Byzantium.

English Learners

DIFFERENTIATED INSTRUCTION

Intermediate An oral reading of "Sailing to Byzantium" will help students focus on the imagery and the contrasts in the poem. Give students the following tips:

- Read slowly and clearly.
- Continue reading until you come to punctuation or a pause.

Approaching Level

DIFFERENTIATED INSTRUCTION

Emerging Explain that metaphors compare two unlike things to help readers "see" what is being described. For example, "The sun is butter on a bright blue plate" helps readers see the sun in a blue sky. Have pairs analyze the metaphor "a tattered coat upon a stick."

Teach

Big Idea	1

Modernism Ask: What symbols can you find in these poems? *(In "Sailing to Byzantium," Yeats uses the symbol of a "tattered coat upon a stick" to stand for old age, while youth is symbolized by "birds in the trees." The act of sailing to Byzantium is a symbol of achieving a sense of timelessness through art. In "The Second Coming," spiral motion symbolizes rapid change culminating in the world whirling out of control. Meanwhile, a "rough beast" slouches toward Bethlehem to inaugurate a new order.)*

Literary Element	2

Structure Answer: *The first two stanzas illustrate the speaker's problem of living in his own country, Ireland; the last two stanzas present his solution to that problem.*

(APPROACHING) Ask approaching level students to visualize a tattered coat on a stick. **Ask:** In what ways might this image remind someone of a very old person? *(a tattered coat could be like aging skin; the stick is like a very thin person)*

 For additional literary element practice, see Unit 6 Teaching Resources Book, p. 121.

Teach

View the Art ★

Answer: *The upward rays, bold colors, and upward-reaching people in the foreground suggest progress and movement, while also evoking the idea of newness or creation. It is not clear which of the spheres is supposed to be the "new" planet, but the crowds seem to greet the creation joyfully.*

A noted Russian painter and theater designer, Konstantin Juon (1875–1958) thrived as an Impressionist painter before going on to explore Symbolism, as in the painting *New Planet,* which shows the October (or Bolshevik) Revolution of 1917. He also designed sets for theater and opera and later, until his death, worked as a strict social-realist artist, producing paintings such as *Parade in Red Square on November 7, 1941.*

The New Planet, 1921. Konstantin Fiodorvich Juon. Tempera on cardboard, 71 x 101 cm. Tretjakov Gallery, Moscow.

View the Art Russian Constructivist artists of the early 1920s celebrated the dawning of a new modern era in their works. How do the visual details of this image support its title and evoke the modern world?

The Second Coming

William Butler Yeats

Writing Practice

Poem As Yeats wrote a poem reacting to the events of his time, have students write a poem (no more than 20–25 lines) that reacts to an event in our times, such as the war in Iraq, Hurricane Katrina, or the avian (bird) flu. Encourage them to use figurative language, such as metaphor, alliteration, and personification. Have them consider Yeats's poem as a model for their own poems, in spirit if not in form. After they have finished, ask for student volunteers to read their poems aloud to the class. Use the poems as points of discussion and comparison between the events the students describe and those Yeats addresses.

Turning and turning in the widening gyre[1]
The falcon cannot hear the falconer;
Things fall apart; the center cannot hold; ☆
Mere **anarchy** is loosed upon the world,
5 The blood-dimmed tide is loosed, and everywhere
The ceremony of innocence is drowned;
The best lack all **conviction**, while the worst
Are full of passionate intensity.

Surely some revelation is at hand;
10 Surely the Second Coming is at hand.
The Second Coming! Hardly are those words out
When a vast image out of *Spiritus Mundi*[2]
Troubles my sight: somewhere in sands of the desert
A shape with lion body and the head of a man,[3]
15 A gaze blank and pitiless as the sun,
Is moving its slow thighs, while all about it
Reel shadows of the indignant desert birds.
The darkness drops again; but now I know
That twenty centuries of stony sleep[4]
20 Were **vexed** to nightmare by a rocking cradle,[5]
And what rough beast, its hour come round at last,
Slouches towards Bethlehem[6] to be born?

---

1. A *gyre* is a circular form or motion.
2. The Latin phrase *Spiritus Mundi* means "Spirit of the World." Yeats believed that all people are connected through this spirit and that it constitutes the collective, inherited body of myths and symbols common to all cultures.
3. *A shape . . . man* This figure is meant to resemble the Egyptian sphinx.
4. *That twenty . . . sleep* The speaker is referring to the two-thousand-year period before the birth of Christ.
5. *Rocking cradle* refers to the birth of the infant Jesus.
6. *Bethlehem* was the birthplace of Jesus Christ.

 1 Structure *With which image in the first part of this poem does the image of "the indignant desert birds" contrast?*

 2 Modernism *What might the "rough beast" symbolize?*

Vocabulary

anarchy (an′ ər kē) *n.* a complete lack of political order; chaos
conviction (kən vik′ shən) *n.* a strong belief
vex (veks) *v.* disturb; trouble; irritate

WILLIAM BUTLER YEATS **1067**

Teach

Literary Element | 1

Structure Answer: *The image of the hovering desert birds contrasts with that of the soaring falcon orbiting beyond the falconer's call.*

Big Idea | 2

Modernism Answer: *The "rough beast" symbolizes a new savage god coming into the world.*
(ADVANCED) Tell advanced level students that the "rough beast" in line 21 symbolizes the Antichrist. Have students read the passages in the Bible that refer to the Antichrist (1 John 2:18, 1 John 2:22, 1 John 4:3, and 2 John 1:7). and discuss how the image of the Antichrist fits in with the rest of the poem. Ask them to infer what kind of future Yeats envisioned for humankind.

Cultural History ☆

"Things Fall Apart" When Yeats wrote "The Second Coming," he believed that the Christian era was coming to an end. As evidence that this era was ending, Yeats cited recent events such as World War I, the Russian Revolution, and Ireland's violent struggle for independence from England.

After You Read

Assess

1. Students' answers will vary.
2. (a) The present-day world, where the elderly feel neglected by the young (b) To achieve immortality by entering into works of art
3. (a) Take his heart away and subsume his soul into a timeless world (b) He longs to escape time and feel a sense of worth.
4. (a) The world is on the brink of destruction, with anarchy rampant and innocence gone. (b) Bewilderment
5. He wants to transcend the sufferings of old age and death.
6. The mood is one of darkness and horror. His fear and the nightmare he envisions add to it.
7. Victorian ideals were shattered by the gruesome reality of modern warfare. The events described in the poem are nightmarish, suggesting catastrophic change.
8. In the first stanza, birds in the trees are described as "dying generations—at their song." These are literal birds that will age and die, and their music is transient. In the second stanza, an old man is but a "paltry thing" unless he produces a spiritual song. Finally, in the fourth stanza, the speaker envisions himself as a marvelous bird, singing on a golden bough (line 30). The bird and the bough symbolize the union of art and nature.
9. Students may say that Yeats's response to death and destruction after World War I might have resonated with more recent authors who were coping with their own cultural and political traumas.

1068

After You Read

Respond and Think Critically

Respond and Interpret

1. What line or lines from the poems made the strongest impression on you? Why?
2. (a) What is the country described in the first stanza of "Sailing to Byzantium" like? (b) Why does the speaker travel to Byzantium?
3. (a) In lines 17–24 of "Sailing to Byzantium," what does the speaker ask the sages to do? (b) Why do you think the speaker makes these requests?
4. (a) In "The Second Coming," how does the speaker describe the state of the world and human affairs in the first stanza? (b) What seems to be the speaker's attitude toward this situation?

Analyze and Evaluate

5. In "Sailing to Byzantium," how would you describe the speaker's attitude toward aging and death?

6. Evaluate the mood of "The Second Coming." How does the speaker's tone, or attitude toward the subject, contribute to that mood?
7. Yeats wrote "The Second Coming" shortly after the end of World War I. What relationship can you see between the devastation of war and the events described in this poem?

Connect

8. **Big Idea** Modernism Explain how Yeats uses the notions of song and singing in a symbolic way in "Sailing to Byzantium."
9. **Connect to the Author** The phrases "things fall apart" (line 3) and "slouching toward Bethlehem" (adapted from line 22) from "The Second Coming" became the titles of works by Chinua Achebe and Joan Didion. Both wrote during times of social and political unrest. Why might they have felt inspired by "The Second Coming"? Explain.

Visual Literacy

Organizing Details in Poetry

You can often use graphic organizers to record details in a literary work and your ideas about them. For example, you might organize the details in "The Second Coming" in a diagram like the one below. Copy this organizer on a separate sheet of paper and fill it in.

STANZA 1 DETAILS:
"The falcon cannot hear the falconer"

Suggests:

STANZA 2 DETAILS:
"some revelation is at hand"

Result?

Group Activity Discuss the following questions with classmates. Refer to your graphic organizer and cite evidence from "The Second Coming" for support.

1. Do the details in the first stanza lead you to conclude that the "Second Coming" is at hand? Explain.
2. Yeats does not indicate what will result after the "rough beast" is born in Bethlehem. What do you imagine will happen then?
3. How will the "rough beast" differ from Christ?

Visual Literacy

1. They suggest that violent upheaval is imminent.
2. Violence will overwhelm the world.
3. The "rough beast" is both man and animal, whereas Christ was man and God. The "rough beast" emerges from the desert and has a pitiless stare; Christ comes from heaven and is all-merciful.

Literary Element · Structure

Structure refers to the sequence of thoughts and images that work together to impart the meaning of a poem.

1. In what way is the structure of "Sailing to Byzantium" symmetrical?

2. How would you describe the structure of "The Second Coming"? Consider the subject matter of each stanza.

Review: Meter

As you learned on page 952, **meter** refers to a regular pattern of stressed and unstressed syllables that gives a line of poetry a predictable rhythm. In "Sailing to Byzantium," Yeats uses **iambic pentameter**, meaning that each line of verse usually contains five feet in which a stressed syllable follows an unstressed one.

An octave is a stanza that consists of eight lines. **Ottava rima** is a stanza written in iambic pentameter with an *abababcc* rhyme scheme.

1. Copy a stanza from "Sailing to Byzantium." Scan the meter and mark the rhyme scheme. Is the stanza written in ottava rima? Explain.

2. What effects do the meter and rhyme scheme create in "Sailing to Byzantium"? Give examples.

LOG ON ▶ **Literature** Online

Selection Resources For Selection Quizzes, eFlashcards, and Reading-Writing Connection activities, go to glencoe.com and enter QuickPass code GLB9817u6.

Reading Strategy · Analyze Figurative Language: Metaphor

When you **analyze metaphors**, you look critically at examples of this figure of speech to determine what they contribute to the poem as a whole.

1. In "Sailing to Byzantium," to what does the speaker compare "an aged man" in line 9? What does this comparison suggest?

2. Why is the metaphor of a "dying animal" in line 22 effective?

3. In "The Second Coming," what is "the ceremony of innocence" in line 6?

Vocabulary Practice

Practice with Context Clues Identify the context clues in the following sentences that help you determine the meaning of each boldfaced vocabulary word.

1. An ingenious **artifice**, her kind attitude covered her true selfishness.

2. Some frontier towns were in a state of **anarchy** until federal marshals and judges restored order.

3. You must stand up for your **convictions** when others challenge them.

4. The teacher was **vexed** when the blaring horn from a passing car interrupted his lecture.

Academic Vocabulary

The development of Yeats's poetry shows the slow **erosion** *of his romantic views about life.*

Erosion is an academic word. For example, rust might cause **erosion** of the body of a car, eventually rendering the car unusable.

Using context clues, try to figure out the meaning of *erosion* in the following sentence: *The powerful river's* **erosion** *of the cliffs caused the people who lived on top of them to fear for their safety.*

For more on academic vocabulary, see pages 56 and R81.

After You Read

Assess

Literary Element

1. The first two stanzas portray the speaker's problem and his sense of alienation; the second two stanzas portray the speaker's solution: liberating his soul in Byzantium through immersion in works of art.

2. The images in the first stanza suggest that civilization is disintegrating. The images in the second stanza describe the savage god of the future.

Review: Meter

1. Each stanza is written in ottava rima: The metrical pattern is iambic pentameter; the rhyme scheme is *abababcc*.

2. The opening is rushed and full of slant rhymes, suggesting emotional discord. The highly disciplined stanza form reflects the artistic intricacy and unity of Byzantium. The meter changes to reflect emotional shifts the speaker experiences.

Reading Strategy

1. The speaker compares "an aged man" to "a tattered coat upon a stick." The comparison suggests a scarecrow. Both an old man and a scarecrow have skeleton-like support.

2. It conveys the speaker's attitude toward his failing body.

3. The "ceremony of innocence" is baptism, a sacrament usually conferred upon infants in Christian ritual.

Vocabulary

1. The context suggests that *artifice* is something that covers or conceals the truth.

2. The context suggests that *anarchy* is the opposite of law and order.

3. According to the sentence, *convictions* are things that you must "stand up for," which suggests that *convictions* means "strong beliefs."

4. A blaring car horn in the middle of a lecture would be irritating, so *vexed* must mean "irritated."

Academic Vocabulary

Since the people fear for their safety, *erosion* seems to mean "wearing away."

After You Read

Respond Through Writing

Use these criteria in evaluating expository essays:

- It correctly identifies Yeats's use of metaphors and structural elements.
- The contribution of the stylistic elements to the poems' meaning are clearly explained and supported with quotations.
- Appropriate transitional expressions are used to compare and contrast ideas.

A student who meets all of these criteria should receive the equivalent of a 4-point response.

A student who fully meets two or partially meets three of these criteria should receive the equivalent of a 3-point response.

A student who fully meets one or partially meets two of these criteria should receive the equivalent of a 2-point response.

A student who partially meets one of these criteria should receive the equivalent of a 1-point response.

Respond Through Writing

Expository Essay

Analyze Figurative Language In his poetry, Yeats weaves imaginative figurative language into a rich tapestry that reads like everyday speech. Analyze how his use of metaphor and the structure of his poems contribute to and help convey the nuances of their meaning.

Prewrite As you review Yeats's poems, record their metaphors and structural elements in one column of a chart. In the other column, indicate how the element contributes to the poem's meaning. If you are unable to fill in the entire second column, you can come back to it later.

Stylistic element	Meaning
"twenty centuries of stony sleep"	people unawakened (to their spirituality?)
rhyme in "Byzantium"	illustrates theme of repetition/connection—"what is past, or passing, or to come"

Draft Review your chart. Then organize your ideas into a coherent pattern, either following the development of metaphors throughout the poems, or presenting images and structures in the order of their importance. Refer directly to the text when you can, paying extra attention to ambiguous or complex examples.

Use sentence structures like the following to identify the significant metaphors and structural elements in Yeats's poems:

Some examples of _____ in the poems are _____, _____, and _____.

Revise Make sure you have identified the important elements of Yeats's style and correctly interpreted their contribution to the meaning of the poems. Apply the standards in the Writing Workshop checklist on page 972 to your essay and make any necessary changes.

Edit and Proofread Proofread your paper, correcting any errors in spelling, grammar, and punctuation. Use the Grammar Tip in the side column to help you with transitional expressions.

> ### Grammar Tip
>
> **Transitional Expressions**
>
> In analyzing the rich metaphors and complex structure of Yeats's poems, you will need to compare and contrast his images and techniques.
>
> Use **transitional expressions** such as *like, unlike, compared with, in the same way, in contrast*, and *on the other hand* to make these comparisons clear.
>
> **Like** the images "aged man" and "dying animal" in "Sailing to Byzantium," the startling metaphor "the artifice of eternity" touches on the idea of impermanence.

Speaking Practice

SPIRAL REVIEW **Oral Response to Literature**
After students complete their essays, have them turn them into oral responses to literature. Encourage them to analyze the language and themes of Yeats's poetry through a combination of narration, description and exposition. Their presentations should show that they fully understand Yeats's significant ideas. Their presentations should also support the main ideas with detailed references to the poems or with quotations from the poems. Refer students to the Speaking, Listening, and Viewing Workshop on page 974 for tips on oral responses to literature.

Before You Read

Preludes

Meet **T. S. Eliot**
(1888–1965)

In 1917 customers of Lloyds Bank on London's Queen Henrietta Street might have been surprised to learn that the shy young American they knew as Mr. Eliot the banker was known in literary circles as T. S. Eliot the poet. Eliot's supervisors at the bank knew that he wrote poetry, but they dismissed his writing as a curious hobby. In reality, poetry was far more than just a hobby to Eliot, and by the time he left the bank eight years later, he was one of the leading poets and critics of his age.

> "The experience of a poem is the experience both of a moment and of a lifetime."
>
> —T. S. Eliot

Education and Groundbreaking Poems
Thomas Stearns Eliot was born in St. Louis, Missouri. An excellent student, Eliot studied philosophy and literature at Harvard University, the Sorbonne in Paris, and Oxford University in England. While in school, he began writing poetry, composing such groundbreaking poems as "Preludes." In London he met poet Ezra Pound, who immediately recognized his genius and brought Eliot's work to the attention of various publishers. Pound praised Eliot's Modernist verse and encouraged him to continue writing.

Eliot decided to stay in England. At age twenty-six, he married a British woman named Vivienne Haigh-Wood. Soon after, she became seriously ill; to pay for her mounting medical expenses, Eliot took on a number of jobs, including the position at Lloyds Bank. After work he wrote poetry and,

to supplement his income, literary essays and reviews. These articles had an impact far beyond his expectations, helping to shape literary criticism for years to come. However, his wife's illness, their financial difficulties, and his long workdays took a toll on him, and he was close to collapse. While resting for a few months in a Swiss sanatorium, he worked on *The Waste Land*, a long poem about the spiritual breakdown of the modern world. It proved to be one of the most influential poems of the twentieth century.

Spiritual Renewal and International Acclaim
At the age of thirty-six, Eliot left Lloyds to become an editor at Faber & Faber, a London publishing house. He also continued to write, composing a number of distinguished poems and plays. In his late thirties, Eliot became a British citizen. Always a deeply spiritual man, Eliot was also baptized into the Church of England. His later poems, such as "Ash Wednesday" and *Four Quartets*, show the influence of his conversion to Anglo-Catholicism. At the age of sixty, Eliot received the Nobel Prize in Literature. He died in London sixteen years later. At the time of his death, many considered Eliot the most important poet and critic writing in the English language.

 Literature Online

Author Search For more about T. S. Eliot, go to glencoe.com and enter QuickPass code GLB9817u6.

Before You Read

Focus

Bellringer Options

Literature Launchers:
 Pre-Reading Videos DVD,
 Selection Launcher
Selection Focus
 Transparency 54
Daily Language Practice
 Transparency 91

Or display several photographs of urban life, including ones that depict grim realities such as poverty, isolation, and entrapment. **Ask:** What feelings do these images evoke in you? Have students consider how Eliot describes city life.

Interactive Read and Write

Other options for teaching this selection can be found in

- Interactive Read and Write for EL Students pp. 267–274
- Interactive Read and Write for Approaching-Level Students, pp. 267–274
- Interactive Read and Write for On-Level Students, pp. 267–274

Selection Skills

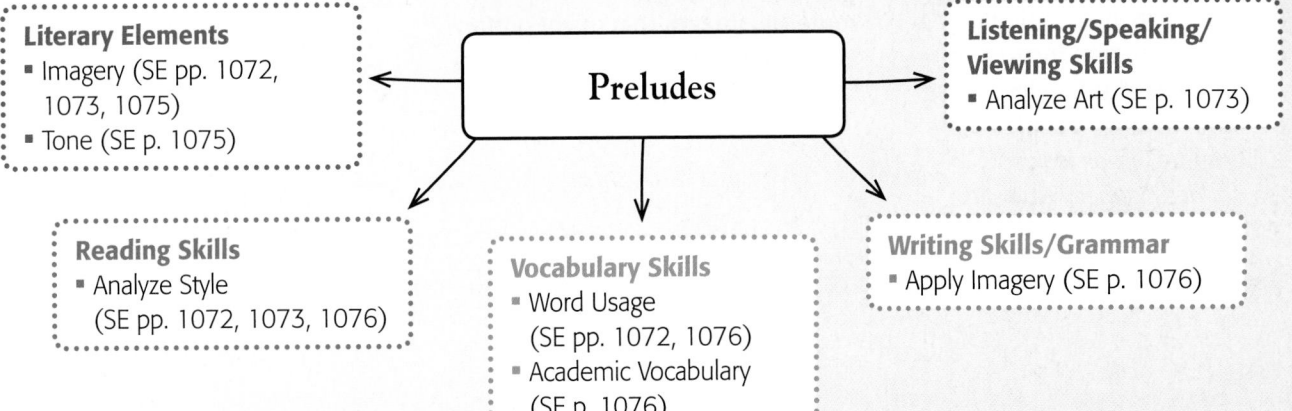

Literary Elements
- Imagery (SE pp. 1072, 1073, 1075)
- Tone (SE p. 1075)

Reading Skills
- Analyze Style (SE pp. 1072, 1073, 1076)

Preludes

Vocabulary Skills
- Word Usage (SE pp. 1072, 1076)
- Academic Vocabulary (SE p. 1076)

Listening/Speaking/ Viewing Skills
- Analyze Art (SE p. 1073)

Writing Skills/Grammar
- Apply Imagery (SE p. 1076)

Before You Read

Focus

Summary

In "Preludes," the speaker describes the dark world of the city and the futility of its inhabitants in the early twentieth century. Yet the hopeful dreams of the people trapped in this world move the speaker to identify with the oppressed. "I am moved by fancies that are curled / Around these images, and cling: / The notion of some infinitely gentle / Infinitely suffering thing."

Vocabulary

Word Usage Using new vocabulary in context helps to reinforce understanding. **Ask:** What body of government does the Senate and House of Representatives constitute together? *(Congress)* If a mathematical series continues infinitely, when does it end? *(never)* Ask students to write their own sentences using these two words.

Literature and Reading Preview

Connect to the Poem

What sights, sounds, and feelings do you experience while walking down a city street? Create a list of the sensory impressions you can recall from your last visit to a similar location.

Build Background

In music, preludes are short pieces that introduce longer, more complex compositions. The poem "Preludes" describes a city much like the St. Louis neighborhood of Eliot's childhood. To Eliot, the physical decay of a city represented a deeper moral and spiritual decay. This theme runs throughout much of his work.

Set Purposes for Reading

Big Idea Modernism

As you read, ask yourself, How does the poem illustrate a sense of alienation and despair typical of Modernist poetry?

Literary Element Imagery

Imagery consists of the word pictures that writers create to evoke a particular emotional response. In creating effective images, writers use **sensory details**, or descriptions that appeal to one or more of the five senses. As you read, ask yourself, What images does Eliot present?

Reading Strategy Analyze Style

Style consists of the expressive qualities that distinguish an author's work, including word choice, the length of sentences, and the use of figurative language and imagery. To **analyze style**, look at these qualities separately to determine the meaning of the entire work. Analyzing style can reveal an author's tone and purpose in writing. As you read, ask yourself, How does Eliot's style illustrate his attitude toward the subject?

Tip: Taking Notes As you read, look for stylistic elements that reveal Eliot's attitude toward his subject and his purpose in writing. Organize your examples in a chart like this one.

Stylistic Devices	Eliot's Attitude
Word Choice	
Figurative Language	
Imagery	

1072 UNIT 6 THE MODERN AGE

Learning Objectives

For pages 1071–1076
In studying this text, you will focus on the following objectives:

Literary Study: Analyzing imagery.

Reading: Analyzing style.

Writing: Applying imagery in a poem.

Vocabulary

constitute (kon′ stə to͞ot′) *v.* make up; form; p. 1074 *An hour for lunch constituted our only break from the all-day seminar.*

infinitely (in′ fə nit lē) *adv.* boundlessly; endlessly; p. 1074 *The unending array of obstructions made solving the puzzle infinitely complicated.*

Tip: Word Usage When you come across a new word, it might help you to answer a specific question about the word. For example, What **constitutes** a successful friendship, in your opinion?

Reading Practice

PARTNERS
Preview Say: T. S. Eliot's poem "Preludes" focuses on the dismal squalor of urban life. What might be some feelings people who live in a city share? *(fear, isolation, loneliness, sadness, anger)* What are some city images that might portray these feelings? *(dark alleys, a person looking out a window at night time)*

Preludes

T. S. Eliot

Tower Bridge, from the limited-edition portfolio *London,* published 1909. Photogravure. Alvin Langdon Coburn. Private collection.

 Photogravure was one of the earliest means of creating and reproducing photographic images. In what ways does this image show the intersection of old and modern? ★

I

   The winter evening settles down
   With smell of steaks in passageways. **1**
   Six o'clock.
   The burnt-out ends of smoky days.
5   And now a gusty shower wraps
   The grimy scraps
   Of withered leaves about your feet
   And newspapers from vacant lots;
   The showers beat
10 On broken blinds and chimney-pots,[1]
   And at the corner of the street
   A lonely cab-horse steams and stamps.

   And then the lighting of the lamps.

II

   The morning comes to consciousness
15 Of faint stale smells of beer
   From the sawdust-trampled[2] street
   With all its muddy feet that press
   To early coffee-stands.

   With the other masquerades[3]
20 That time resumes,
   One thinks of all the hands
   That are raising dingy shades
   In a thousand furnished rooms.[4]

---

2 Analyze Style *What effect does Eliot's word choice have on your impression of this scene?*

3 Imagery *To what senses do the images in lines 15–18 appeal? What emotions do these images evoke?*

1. *Chimney-pots* are pipes that protrude from chimney tops.
2. *Sawdust-trampled* refers to the sawdust that many bars and shops sprinkled on their floors to absorb dirt and spilled drinks. The sawdust has been carried into the streets on the soles of people's shoes.
3. Here, a *masquerade* is a pretense or act.
4. *Furnished rooms* are cheap, one-room apartments that come with beds and other basic pieces of furniture.

T. S. ELIOT **1073**

Teach

Big Idea **1**

Modernism Ask: What do you find fresh and original about Eliot's language in "Preludes"? *(Eliot's language is not flowery or poetic. It is shocking in its realism and descriptiveness.)*

Reading Strategy **2**

Analyze Style Answer: *Students might picture an urban setting with buildings scattered among open, empty areas and old newspapers strewn about, blown by the wind. The word vacant suggests something deserted and uninviting.*

Literary Element **3**

Imagery Answer: *They appeal to the senses of smell, sight, and touch. Students' emotional responses will vary. Many will suggest feelings of disapproval.*

APPROACHING To help approaching level students, **ask:** Why does the street smell faintly of beer? *(from the previous night's drinking)* Why is this repugnant? *(The smell is stale. Also, some students may say it is repugnant because people must have drinking a lot.)*

 ★

Answer: *The photograph shows the old majesty of the bridge contrasted with the crowds of boats and smokestacks. The image itself is made with technology that was new at the time.*

Modernism Answer: *Sordid suggests something dirty or corrupt. For many people, soul refers to a person's spiritual component. Eliot repeats a recurring theme in his poetry: the corruption of spiritual values in contemporary life.*

Cultural History ☆

World War I The terrible cost in human life and the tragic consequences of World War I caused many artists and intellectuals to question their assumptions about the world. The growth of Modernism was a response to the perceived irrelevance of former values to contemporary life. Writers sought new styles that would reflect the fragmented and meaningless nature of the modern world.

III

You tossed a blanket from the bed,
25 You lay upon your back, and waited;
You dozed, and watched the night revealing
The thousand sordid images
Of which your soul was **constituted;**
They flickered against the ceiling.
30 And when all the world came back
And the light crept up between the shutters
And you heard the sparrows in the gutters,
You had such a vision of the street
As the street hardly understands;
35 Sitting along the bed's edge, where
You curled the papers from your hair,
Or clasped the yellow soles of feet
In the palms of both soiled hands.

IV

His soul stretched tight across the skies
40 That fade behind a city block,
Or trampled by insistent feet
At four and five and six o'clock;
And short square fingers stuffing pipes,
And evening newspapers, and eyes
45 Assured of certain certainties,
The conscience of a blackened street
Impatient to assume the world.

I am moved by fancies that are curled
Around these images, and cling:
50 The notion of some **infinitely** gentle
Infinitely suffering thing.

Wipe your hand across your mouth, and laugh;
The worlds revolve like ancient women ☆
Gathering fuel in vacant lots.

---

1   Modernism *In what sense do the words* sordid *and* soul *contrast with one another? What comment is Eliot making in lines 27–28 about contemporary life?*

Vocabulary

constitute (kon′ stə tōōt′) *v.* make up; form
infinitely (in′ fə nit lē) *adv.* boundlessly; endlessly

Speaking Practice

SPIRAL REVIEW **Media Presentation** Have students incorporate sound, images, and other media into an oral presentation of the poem. Encourage them to select media that reflect the poem's mood, tone, and imagery, and to combine the media with the text in an appropriate fashion. Students should work with a partner to evaluate the effectiveness of their presentation and revise accordingly, before presenting to the class.

After You Read

Respond and Think Critically

Respond and Interpret

1. What images in "Preludes" did you find especially vivid?

2. (a)What sights, sounds, and odors are described in the first prelude? (b)What mood do these images evoke?

3. (a)What images are described in the second prelude? (b)What do these images have in common?

4. (a)In the fourth prelude, what moves the speaker? (b)What does this tell you about the speaker?

5. (a)Explain the progression of time from the first prelude to the fourth prelude. (b)How does this progression illustrate the revolving of the worlds described in lines 53–54?

Analyze and Evaluate

6. (a)To what does the speaker compare the revolving of the worlds? (b)In your own words, explain what this simile means. (c)How does it help sum up the main point of the poem?

7. (a)What parts of the preludes were most meaningful to you? (b)What parts were most challenging to understand? In each case, explain why.

Connect

8. **Big Idea** Modernism (a)Cite examples from "Preludes" that illustrate characteristics of Modernist poetry. (b)Do you like Modernist poetry, traditional forms, or both? Support your opinion with reasons.

9. **Connect to Today** Brainstorm about some recent portrayals of "life in the city"—in literature, music, or art. Are the current attitudes toward cities similar to or different from Eliot's? Explain.

Literary Element Imagery

In "Preludes," Eliot creates a series of word pictures that present a dreary view of twentieth-century urban life.

1. (a)To what sense do the images in lines 2–4 and line 15 appeal? To what other sense(s) might these images appeal? (b)Are the images pleasant? Explain.

2. (a)Cite examples of images from the poem that appeal to sight, hearing, and touch. (b)What emotions do these images evoke?

Review: Tone

A writer's **tone** is the attitude he or she expresses toward a subject. Word choice, figurative language, and imagery all contribute to the tone of a work. The tone in "Preludes" has often been described as melancholy, pessimistic, or sad. At the same time, Eliot often uses images that suggest great beauty.

Partner Activity With a partner, create a chart listing some of the different tones that appear throughout the poem, and the words, phrases, or images that help create them.

 **Literature** Online

Selection Resources For Selection Quizzes, eFlashcards, and Reading-Writing Connection activities, go to glencoe.com and enter QuickPass code GLB9817u6.

T. S. ELIOT **1075**

After You Read

Assess

1. Answers will vary.

2. (a) Sights: "withered leaves," "a lonely cab-horse," "lighting of the lamps"; sounds: showers beating "on broken blinds"; the horse stamping; odors: "steaks in passageways"; "burnt-out ends" (b) Desolation

3. (a) The smell of stale beer, a street with sawdust footprints, hands raising shades (b) They are isolated and grim.

4. (a) The fancies that cling to images of souls in solitude (b) He feels that all humans are suffering in their isolation.

5. (a) The first is set in the evening. The second in the morning. The third begins at night and ends with morning. The fourth is again set in the evening. (b) The reference to worlds seems to look to the whole universe of revolving planets and stars.

6. (a) To ancient women gathering wood for fuel in vacant lots (b) The ancient women represent individuals living lonely, perhaps purposeless lives. (c) It suggests that a loss of spiritual values has created a society of individuals who live without meaning or purpose.

7. Answers will vary.

8. (a) Examples should focus on the intellectually challenging ideas expressed, the use of images that seem disconnected, and the suggestions of irony. (b) Answers will vary.

9. Modern depictions of city life will vary. Some students may say that Eliot's cynical attitude toward urban areas persists in modern culture. Others may say that modern culture glamorizes the city more than Eliot did.

Literary Element

1. (a) The sense of smell; the smells might also suggest tastes associated with them. (b) The "smell of steaks" might be pleasant; yet, when combined with "burnt-out ends of smoky days," an unpleasant smell is implied.

2. Answers will vary.

Review: Tone

Students should cite specific lines and images from the poems in order to discuss the tone that is created.

1075

After You Read

Reading Strategy

1. Answers will vary.
2. The line is set apart, in effect isolating it. "And then" reinforces the idea of a pause or break. There is no verb, which suggests a lack of action.

Vocabulary

1. Students should mention activities they like to do on weekends.
2. Students should name something that seemed to go on forever, perhaps because it was unpleasant.

Academic Vocabulary

Students should mention actions that would benefit their community, such as volunteering at a hospital, participating in cleanup projects, and so forth.

Progress Check

Can students analyze style?

If No → See Unit 6 Teaching Resources Book, p. 133.

Reading Strategy Analyze Style

Review the Reading Strategy notes you wrote down while reading "Preludes." Note how the word choices, figurative language, and structure of the poem contribute to its theme.

1. Which words from the poem convey a dreary or pessimistic attitude?
2. Line 13 contains no emotionally charged words, yet it conveys a melancholy attitude. Explain how the placement and construction of this sentence might account for this attitude.

Vocabulary Practice

Practice with Word Usage Respond to these statements to help explore the meanings of the boldfaced vocabulary words from the selection.

1. Name some things that **constitute** a fun weekend for you.
2. Describe a task you had to do that seemed to go on **infinitely**.

Academic Vocabulary

Eliot writes about the isolation that results from the disintegration of the world **community**.

Community is an academic word. Words that are similar in meaning to *community* are *group, collective,* and *population.*

To further explore the meaning of this word, complete the following sentence: *I can serve my* **community** *by* _____.

For more on academic vocabulary, see pages 56 and R81.

Write with Style

 Apply Imagery

Assignment Images like *The burnt-out ends of smoky days* in "Preludes" paint powerful sensory pictures. Write a poem capturing the essence of a particular place. Use sensory images—sights, sounds, smells, tastes, and tactile experiences—to re-create it for your readers.

Get Ideas Make a chart or word web to gather sensory images of the location you've chosen. Find concrete words and metaphors that create the sights, sounds, smells, tastes, and tactile sensations of being there.

Give It Structure Use the chart or word web you have developed to help plan your poem. Additionally, decide on how you will structure your ideas. What form will your poem take? Will you write discrete stanzas with end-rhyme and a regular rhythmic pattern, or will the more open structure of free verse work better?

Look at Language The trick in writing poetry is to make your images both concrete and original. Avoid clichés and mixed metaphors. Choose words that suggest images which readers can easily re-create in their own minds; this will keep them interested in your poem and subject. Be careful that your words do not accidentally contradict the emotional tone you are trying to create.

EXAMPLE:

The ~~blood-red~~ *ripe-plum* sunset

~~Drowned~~ *Coated* the lake like a polished fingernail.

Write with Style

Use these criteria in evaluating student writing:

- The poem describes a specific place.
- It uses sensory details to create vivid imagery.
- The images are concrete and fresh.

Before You Read

The Rocking-Horse Winner

Meet **D. H. Lawrence**
(1885–1930)

David Herbert Lawrence helped to define modern literature with his carefully constructed, highly original, and socially conscious novels and short stories. Yet his attitudes about life and writing were often in direct contrast to the opinions held by society at the time.

Turmoil and Controversy Lawrence was born in a small mining village near Nottingham, England, to an illiterate coal miner and a retired schoolteacher mother. As a young child, Lawrence suffered a severe attack of pneumonia from which he never fully recovered. This affliction, however, enabled him to escape from a life of work in the coal mines. Instead, he attended school on a scholarship but was forced to abandon his education at sixteen to work as a clerk in a factory. After a short time, however, Lawrence again fell ill. While recuperating, he formed a close friendship with Jessie Chambers, a local farmer's daughter. Soon Lawrence became a pupil-teacher, later earning a teacher's certificate at University College, Nottingham. Encouraged by Jessie, he also started writing poetry and fiction.

Lawrence's mid-twenties were turbulent: He broke with Jessie, his mother died, his first novels were published, and he decided to give up teaching and support himself solely by writing. During this time, Lawrence fell in love and eloped with a German woman named Frieda von Richtofen. For the next two years, the couple traveled extensively throughout Europe. Frieda became the prototype for many of Lawrence's best-known heroines.

The onset of the First World War forced Lawrence and his wife to return to England, where at first they settled on the south coast. Because of Frieda's nationality and Lawrence's outspoken criticism of the war, however, many local residents suspected them of being spies. Persecuted, they were forced to live on the run, traveling throughout England until the end of the war.

During this time, Lawrence published a novel called *The Rainbow*, which was seized by the police and declared obscene. Throughout his career, Lawrence's work so scandalized the public that some of his books were banned.

> "Be still when you have nothing to say; when genuine passion moves you, say what you've got to say, and say it hot."
>
> —D. H. Lawrence

Writer in Exile Disgusted with England, Lawrence and his wife left for Italy in 1919 and spent the rest of their lives traveling in search of an ideal society—as well as a warm climate for Lawrence's frequent respiratory illnesses. The couple settled for several years in Taos, New Mexico, where Lawrence fell ill and found that he was in the late stages of tuberculosis. They returned to Italy, and Lawrence finished his last and most controversial novel, *Lady Chatterley's Lover*. From Italy, Frieda took him to France in search of a cure. During this time he wrote "The Rocking-Horse Winner," as well as many other short stories. Lawrence died at the age of forty-five with Frieda at his bedside.

 Literature Online

Author Search For more about D. H. Lawrence, go to glencoe.com and enter QuickPass code GLB9817u6.

D. H. LAWRENCE **1077**

Before You Read

Focus

Bellringer Options

Selection Focus
  Transparency 55
Daily Language Practice
  Transparency 92

Or draw a horseshoe or a four-leaf clover on the board. **Ask:** Have you ever had an object or done something that you thought would bring you luck? How did your luck turn out? Encourage students to discuss how humans sometimes associate luck with certain items or rituals. Tell students to read this story by D. H. Lawrence to find out what luck means to the main character in the story.

Selection Skills

Literary Elements
- Foreshadowing (SE pp. 1078–1091)
- Motivation (SE p. 1091)

Reading Skills
- Make Inferences About Characters (SE pp. 1078–1092)

The Rocking-Horse Winner

Vocabulary Skills
- Analogies (SE p. 1092)
- Academic Vocabulary (SE p. 1092)

Listening/Speaking/Viewing Skills
- Analyze Art (SE pp. 1079, 1086, 1087)
- Literature Groups (SE p. 1092)

Writing Skills/Grammar
- Literary Analysis (TE p. 1080)
- Journals (TE p. 1086)

Before You Read

Focus

Paul, a young boy, desperately needs to be lucky in order to gain his mother's love. He finds luck by riding his rocking horse, which gives him the power to foresee which horses will win races. When Paul shares this secret with his uncle, they create a plan whereby Paul's mother receives some of his winnings to pay off debts. His mother spends the money on new things, however, and Paul feels pressure to make even more money. The pressure leads to his death.

Vocabulary

Analogies Write on the board: emancipate: free:: vex: bother Say: This analogy makes sense because the words on each side share the same relationship. To *emancipate* is "to free," and to *vex* is "to bother." Have students construct analogies for the other vocabulary words.

Literature and Reading Preview

Connect to the Story

Do you agree with the saying "Money can't buy happiness"? In a group, discuss how money can affect your state of mind.

Build Background

"The Rocking-Horse Winner" takes place in England in the early part of the twentieth century. At that time, social classes were quite distinct, and many people who were not born wealthy lived beyond their means in an effort to attain the prestige of a higher social class. This story mentions many popular horse races held in England, including the Ascot and the St. Leger. The Turf Commission operates a bank where bettors can deposit funds for future bets.

Set Purposes for Reading

Big Idea Modernism

As you read, ask yourself, How does this story reflect Lawrence's concerns about society's emphasis on money?

Literary Element Foreshadowing

Foreshadowing is the author's use of hints or clues to prepare readers for events that will happen later in a story. Mood, atmosphere, events, physical objects, and even character traits can foreshadow later events. As you read, ask yourself, How might this detail hint at a future event?

Reading Strategy Make Inferences About Characters

Making inferences involves making educated guesses about what an author implies or suggests. Because authors often do not directly state what they want readers to know, making inferences is essential to constructing meaning. In reading Lawrence's story, you must examine details about the characters and then infer what they believe, how they feel, and why they act as they do. As you read, ask yourself, What does this tell me about the character?

Tip: Taking Notes Use a chart to record your inferences about the characters in the story.

Details	Inferences About Characters

Learning Objectives

For pages 1077–1092

In studying this text, you will focus on the following objectives:

Literary Study: Analyzing foreshadowing.

Reading: Making inferences about characters.

Speaking and Listening: Participating in a literature group.

Vocabulary

parry (par′ ē) *v.* to respond, as to a question or argument, by warding off or diverting; p. 1082 *Instead of answering directly, she parried the question by telling an amusing story.*

obstinately (ob′ stə nit lē′) *adv.* in a manner not yielding to argument, persuasion, or reason; inflexibly; p. 1085 *Obstinately remaining silent, he fixed his eyes on the floor.*

reiterate (rē it′ ə rāt′) *v.* to say or do again; to repeat; p. 1085 *I reiterated the question because he seemed not to hear it.*

emancipate (i man′ sə pāt′) *v.* to free; to liberate; p. 1089 *The governor pardoned several criminals, emancipating them from prison.*

Reading Practice

SPIRAL REVIEW **Preview Say:** The first sentence of "The Rocking-Horse Winner" is: "There was a woman who was beautiful, who started with all the advantages, yet she had no luck." What kind of story does this first sentence remind you of, if any? *(a fairy tale)* Have students discuss and list the elements that make up a fairy tale, including magic, significant animals, and a happy ending. Then, as they read the story, ask them to keep track of the aspects of the story that make it like a fairy tale and the aspects that make it unlike one.

1078

The Rocking-Horse Winner

D. H. Lawrence

Teach

View the Art ★

Ask students to predict, on the basis of this illustration and the story's title, what they think this story is about. *(Students may mention horse racing, horse training, betting, and winning or losing a fortune.)* **Ask:** What famous race-horses do you know? *(Possible answers: Man O' War, Seabiscuit, Secretariat, Affirmed, Seattle Slew)*

For an audio recording of this selection, use Listening Library Audio CD-ROM.

Readability Scores

Dale-Chall: 5.3
DRP: 49
Lexile: 690

Approaching Level

DIFFERENTIATED INSTRUCTION

Emerging Some students may have difficulty determining what is real in the story and what is imaginary. Their ideas about illusion and reality may also change as the story progresses. Have students keep charts, detailing which events in the story are real and which occur only in people's minds. Encourage students to add to and revise their entries as they read.

Real Events	Imagined Events

Teach

Reading Strategy | 1

Make Inferences About Characters **Answer:** *The mother's attitude might make the children feel insecure and desperate to win her approval.*

Big Idea | 2

Modernism **Answer:** *Lawrence criticizes the desire for status that destroys a family financially and spiritually.*

ENGLISH LEARNERS To help English learners, **ask:** What does Lawrence mean when he says that the style was always "kept up"? *(The family maintained their style of living despite financial problems.)*

Reading Strategy | 3

Make Inferences About Characters **Answer:** *The children imagine the secret whispers because they are susceptible to their parents' anxiety.*

Cultural History ☆

The Family Car This story takes place only a few years after automobiles began to be mass-produced in factories, although they had been on the market since about 1903. Therefore, wealthier families owned the majority of cars.

There was a woman who was beautiful, who started with all the advantages, yet she had no luck. She married for love, and the love turned to dust. She had bonny[1] children, yet she felt they had been thrust upon her, and she could not love them. They looked at her coldly, as if they were finding fault with her. And hurriedly she felt she must cover up some fault in herself. Yet what it was that she must cover up she never knew. Nevertheless, when her children were present, she always felt the centre of her heart go hard. This troubled her, and in her manner she was all the more gentle and anxious for her children, as if she loved them very much. Only she herself knew that at the centre of her heart was a hard little place that could not feel love, no, not for anybody. Everybody else said of her: "She is such a good mother. She adores her children."

Only she herself, and her children themselves, knew it was not so. They read it in each other's eyes.

There were a boy and two little girls. They lived in a pleasant house, with a garden, and they had discreet servants, and felt themselves superior to anyone in the neighbourhood.

Although they lived in style, they felt always an anxiety in the house. There was never enough money. The mother had a small income, and the father had a small income, but not nearly enough for the social position which they had to keep up. The father went into town to some office. But though he had good prospects, these prospects never materialised. There was always the grinding sense of the shortage of money, though the style was always kept up.

At last the mother said: "I will see if *I* can't make something." But she did not know where to begin. She racked her brains, and tried this thing and the other, but could not find anything successful. The failure made deep lines come into her face. Her children were growing up, they would have to go to school. There must be more money, there must be more money. The father, who was always very handsome and expensive in his tastes, seemed as if he never *would* be able to do anything worth doing. And the mother, who had a great belief in herself, did not succeed any better, and her tastes were just as expensive.

And so the house came to be haunted by the unspoken phrase: *There must be more money! There must be more money!* The children could hear it all the time, though nobody said it aloud. They heard it at Christmas, when the expensive and splendid toys filled the nursery. Behind the shining modern rocking-horse, behind the smart doll's house, a voice would start whispering: "There *must* be more money! There *must* be more money!" And the children would stop playing, to listen for a moment. They would look into each other's eyes, to see if they had all heard. And each one saw in the eyes of the other two that they too had heard. "There *must* be more money! There *must* be more money!"

It came whispering from the springs of the still-swaying rocking-horse, and even the horse, bending his wooden, champing head, heard it. The big doll, sitting so pink and smirking in her new pram,[2] could hear it quite plainly, and seemed to be smirking all the more self-consciously because of it. The foolish puppy, too, that took the place of the teddy bear, he was looking so extraordinarily foolish for no other reason but that he heard the secret whisper all over the house: "There *must* be more money!"

Yet nobody ever said it aloud. The whisper was everywhere, and therefore no one spoke it. Just as no one ever says: "We are breathing!" in spite of the fact that breath is coming and going all the time.

---

1. *Bonny* means "good-looking; robust."

> **1** Make Inferences About Characters **What effect might the mother's attitude have on her children?**

> **2** Modernism **What does Lawrence criticize about middle-class life?**

---

2. A *pram* (short for *perambulator*) is a baby carriage.

> Make Inferences About Characters **Do the children really hear the secret whispers? Explain.** **3**

Writing Practice

 SPIRAL REVIEW **Literary Analysis Say:** Throughout the story, Lawrence refers to the unfulfilled need to have enough money. As you read, take notes on examples from the text that illustrate this theme. Have students write a brief essay on the "The Rocking-Horse Winner." Encourage students to address how these examples contribute to plot development. Ask them to use specific details to support their analysis.

"Mother," said the boy Paul one day, "why don't we keep a car of our own? Why do we always use uncle's, or else a taxi?"

"Because we're the poor members of the family," said the mother.

"But why *are* we, mother?"

"Well—I suppose," she said slowly and bitterly, "it's because your father has no luck."

The boy was silent for some time.

"Is luck money, mother?" he asked, rather timidly.

"No, Paul. Not quite. It's what causes you to have money."

"Oh!" said Paul vaguely. "I thought when Uncle Oscar said *filthy lucker,* it meant money."

"*Filthy lucre*³ does mean money," said the mother. "But it's lucre, not luck."

"Oh!" said the boy. "Then what *is* luck, mother?"

"It's what causes you to have money. If you're lucky you have money. That's why it's better to be born lucky than rich. If you're rich, you may lose your money. But if you're lucky, you will always get more money."

"Oh! Will you? And is father not lucky?"

"Very unlucky, I should say," she said bitterly.

The boy watched her with unsure eyes.

"Why?" he asked.

"I don't know. Nobody ever knows why one person is lucky and another unlucky."

"Don't they? Nobody at all? Does *nobody* know?"

"Perhaps God. But He never tells."

"He ought to, then. And aren't you lucky either, mother?"

"I can't be, if I married an unlucky husband."

"But by yourself, aren't you?"

"I used to think I was, before I married. Now I think I am very unlucky indeed."

"Why?"

"Well—never mind! Perhaps I'm not really," she said.

The child looked at her to see if she meant it. But he saw, by the lines of her mouth, that she was only trying to hide something from him.

"Well, anyhow," he said stoutly, "I'm a lucky person."

"Why?" said his mother, with a sudden laugh.

He stared at her. He didn't even know why he had said it.

"God told me," he asserted, brazening⁴ it out.

"I hope He did, dear!" she said, again with a laugh, but rather bitter.

"He did, mother!"

"Excellent!" said the mother, using one of her husband's exclamations.

The boy saw she did not believe him; or rather, that she paid no attention to his assertion. This angered him somewhere, and made him want to compel her attention.

He went off by himself, vaguely, in a childish way, seeking for the clue to "luck." Absorbed, taking no heed of other people, he went about with a sort of stealth, seeking inwardly for luck. He wanted luck, he wanted it, he wanted it. When the two girls were playing dolls in the nursery, he would sit on his big rocking-horse, charging madly into space, with a frenzy that made the little girls peer at him uneasily. Wildly the horse careered,⁵ the waving dark hair of the boy tossed, his eyes had a strange glare in them. The little girls dared not speak to him.

When he had ridden to the end of his mad little journey, he climbed down and stood in front of his rocking-horse, staring fixedly into its lowered face. Its red mouth was slightly open, its big eye was wide and glassy-bright.

---

3. *Lucre* (lōō′ kər) is Latin for "profit." Here, it refers to money, especially that gained through greed or dishonesty.

4. Here, *brazening* means "stating confidently."
5. *Careered* means "rushed forward."

---

4 Modernism *What does Lawrence imply about the mother's values?*

5 Make Inferences About Characters *What is Paul's mother trying to hide?*

Make Inferences About Characters *How might the mother's answer influence Paul?* **6**

Foreshadowing *What might Paul's frenzied riding foreshadow?* **7**

Approaching Level

DIFFERENTIATED INSTRUCTION

AAVE Approaching level students who use African American Vernacular English (AAVE) may be accustomed to using nonstandard forms of negation in sentences. Write on the board: *Isn't father lucky? Nobody ever knows why one person is lucky and another isn't. Don't they? Does nobody know? Aren't you lucky, mother?* Have students identify the examples of negation in these sentences and explain why the negation takes the form that it does. Then ask them to write three new sets of sentences following this pattern, but using *happy, successful,* and *good* in the place of *lucky.*

Teach

Big Idea | 4

Modernism Answer: *Lawrence implies that the mother's values are shallow. Like the social class she represents, she is convinced that money is more important than anything else—even love.*

Reading Strategy | 5

Make Inferences About Characters Answer: *The mother's ideas about luck and her bitterness toward her husband might convince Paul that money is the most important thing in life. Paul might absorb his mother's confusion about luck and love.*

Reading Strategy | 6

Make Inferences About Characters Answer: *Paul's mother is trying to hide either her belief that she is unable to love him or her unhappiness with her family.* APPROACHING **Ask:** What effect does Lawrence's use of direct quotation have? *(He shows his characters' evasions without commenting on them directly.)*

Literary Element | 7

Foreshadow Answer: *Paul's frenzied riding might foreshadow that he will do something desperate in this story and maybe even harm himself.* ENGLISH LEARNERS **Ask:** What are two or three adjectives that describe Paul's behavior in this paragraph? *(intense, obsessive, disturbing)*

Teach

Reading Strategy 1

Make Inferences About Characters **Answer:** *Uncle Oscar appears unconcerned about Paul in encouraging him in his frenzied riding instead of asking him to stop it.*
Ask: What does Paul's mother's reaction to his riding reveal about her? *(Instead of being concerned for her son's well-being, she is worried that he is too old to be riding a rocking horse.)*

Reading Strategy 2

Make Inferences About Characters **Answer:** *Bassett is extremely serious about racing. His belief that it is like a religion might induce Paul, who is highly impressionable, to feel the same way.*
(APPROACHING) To help approaching level students, **ask:** Bassett says, "Master Paul comes and asks me." What does Paul ask Bassett about? *(horse racing)*

Literary History ☆

Adaptations In 1950, this story was adapted into a full-length film, with the famous British actor John Mills playing Bassett. In a short film made in 1997, Eric Stolz played the gambling uncle. Both of these films, along with an opera inspired by the story and a reading of the story by actor John Shea, are available on a single DVD.

"Now!" he would silently command the snorting steed. "Now, take me to where there is luck! Now take me!"

And he would slash the horse on the neck with the little whip he had asked Uncle Oscar for. He *knew* the horse could take him to where there was luck, if only he forced it. So he would mount again and start on his furious ride, hoping at last to get there. He knew he could get there.

"You'll break your horse, Paul!" said the nurse.

"He's always riding like that! I wish he'd leave off!" said his elder sister Joan.

But he only glared down on them in silence. Nurse gave him up. She could make nothing of him. Anyhow, he was growing beyond her.

One day his mother and his Uncle Oscar came in when he was on one of his furious rides. He did not speak to them.

"Hallo, you young jockey! Riding a winner?" said his uncle.

"Aren't you growing too big for a rocking-horse? You're not a very little boy any longer, you know," said his mother.

But Paul only gave a blue glare from his big, rather close-set eyes. He would speak to nobody when he was in full tilt. His mother watched him with an anxious expression on her face.

At last he suddenly stopped forcing his horse into the mechanical gallop and slid down.

"Well, I got there!" he announced fiercely, his blue eyes still flaring, and his sturdy long legs straddling apart.

"Where did you get to?" asked his mother.

"Where I wanted to go," he flared back at her.

"That's right, son!" said Uncle Oscar. "Don't you stop till you get there. What's the horse's name?"

"He doesn't have a name," said the boy.

> "I only know the winner," said the boy.

"Gets on without all right?" asked the uncle.

"Well, he has different names. He was called Sansovino last week."

"Sansovino, eh? Won the Ascot. How did you know this name?"

"He always talks about horse-races with ☆ Bassett," said Joan.

The uncle was delighted to find that his small nephew was posted with all the racing news. Bassett, the young gardener, who had been wounded in the left foot in the war and had got his present job through Oscar Cresswell, whose batman[6] he had been, was a perfect blade of the "turf."[7] He lived in the racing events, and the small boy lived with him.

Oscar Cresswell got it all from Bassett.

"Master Paul comes and asks me, so I can't do more than tell him, sir," said Bassett, his face terribly serious, as if he were speaking of religious matters.

"And does he ever put anything on a horse he fancies?"

"Well—I don't want to give him away—he's a young sport, a fine sport, sir. Would you mind asking him himself? He sort of takes a pleasure in it, and perhaps he'd feel I was giving him away, sir, if you don't mind."

Bassett was serious as a church.

The uncle went back to his nephew and took him off for a ride in the car.

"Say, Paul, old man, do you ever put anything on a horse?" the uncle asked.

The boy watched the handsome man closely.

"Why, do you think I oughtn't to?" he **parried**.

---

6. A *batman* is a British army orderly, or personal attendant.
7. A *blade of the "turf"* is a horse-racing fan.

Make Inferences About Characters *What does this detail suggest about Bassett?* **2**

Vocabulary

parry (par´ ē) *v.* to respond, as to a question or argument, by warding off or diverting

---

1 **Make Inferences About Characters** *What are your first impressions of Uncle Oscar?*

1082 UNIT 6 THE MODERN AGE

Reading Practice

SPIRAL REVIEW **Question** A story as ambiguous in tone and meaning as "The Rocking-Horse Winner" raises many questions. Students can organize their questions to clarify their thoughts about the story's meaning. Have students write their questions in a chart like the one shown.

Questions About Tone
Questions About Character
Questions About Plot
Questions About Meaning

"Not a bit of it! I thought perhaps you might give me a tip for the Lincoln."

The car sped on into the country, going down to Uncle Oscar's place in Hampshire.

"Honour bright?"[8] said the nephew.

"Honour bright, son!" said the uncle.

"Well, then, Daffodil."

"Daffodil! I doubt it, sonny. What about Mirza?"

"I only know the winner," said the boy. "That's Daffodil."

"Daffodil, eh?"

There was a pause. Daffodil was an obscure horse comparatively.

"Uncle!"

"Yes, son?"

"You won't let it go any further, will you? I promised Bassett."

"Bassett be damned, old man! What's he got to do with it?"

"We're partners. We've been partners from the first. Uncle, he lent me my first five shillings,[9] which I lost. I promised him, honour bright, it was only between me and him; only you gave me that ten-shilling note I started winning with, so I thought you were lucky. You won't let it go any further, will you?"

The boy gazed at his uncle from those big, hot, blue eyes, set rather close together. The uncle stirred and laughed uneasily.

"Right you are, son! I'll keep your tip private. Daffodil, eh? How much are you putting on him?"

"All except twenty pounds,"[10] said the boy. "I keep that in reserve."

The uncle thought it a good joke.

"You keep twenty pounds in reserve, do you, you young romancer? What are you betting, then?"

"I'm betting three hundred," said the boy gravely. "But it's between you and me, Uncle Oscar! Honour bright?"

The uncle burst into a roar of laughter.

"It's between you and me all right, you young Nat Gould,"[11] he said, laughing. "But where's your three hundred?"

"Bassett keeps it for me. We're partners."

"You are, are you! And what is Bassett putting on Daffodil?"

"He won't go quite as high as I do, I expect. Perhaps he'll go a hundred and fifty."

"What, pennies?" laughed the uncle.

"Pounds," said the child, with a surprised look at his uncle. "Bassett keeps a bigger reserve than I do."

Between wonder and amusement Uncle Oscar was silent. He pursued the matter no further, but he determined to take his nephew with him to the Lincoln races.

"Now, son," he said, "I'm putting twenty on Mirza, and I'll put five on for you on any horse you fancy. What's your pick?"

"Daffodil, uncle."

"No, not the fiver on Daffodil!"

"I should if it was my own fiver," said the child.

"Good! Good! Right you are! A fiver for me and a fiver for you on Daffodil."

The child had never been to a race-meeting before, and his eyes were blue fire. He pursed his mouth tight and watched. A Frenchman just in front had put his money on Lancelot. Wild with excitement, he flayed his arms up and down, yelling *Lancelot! Lancelot!* in his French accent.

Daffodil came in first, Lancelot second, Mirza third. The child, flushed and with eyes blazing, was curiously serene. His uncle brought him four five-pound notes, four to one.

"What am I to do with these?" he cried, waving them before the boy's eyes.

---

8. *Honour bright* is an expression used to declare that one is speaking the truth (as in "on your honour").

9. *Shillings* were British coins worth one twentieth of a pound.

10. *Pounds* are currency used in Britain. Twenty pounds in the mid-1920s would be worth about $1,000 today.

11. *Nat Gould* was a sports journalist who often wrote about horse racing.

3 Make Inferences About Characters *Why does Paul reveal his prediction about the race to Uncle Oscar?*

4 Make Inferences About Characters *Why does Paul feel so peaceful?*

D. H. LAWRENCE **1083**

Teach

Reading Strategy ▮ 1

Make Inferences About Characters **Answer:** *Paul might believe that his luck will change if his mother knows about the partnership or that she will put a stop to his gambling. Also, he wants to surprise her with his winnings and earn her love.*

Literary Element ▮ 2

Foreshadow **Answer:** *Bassett's remark might foreshadow the disclosure of the mysterious means that Paul uses to pick the winners.*

Cultural History ☆

Freud and the Unconscious Will D. H. Lawrence was influenced by Sigmund Freud, especially Freud's views on the unconscious mind. According to Freud, human beings repress feelings (such as aggression) and desires in their unconscious, and these feelings and desires erupt in irrational or neurotic behavior. In this story, Lawrence explores the force of the unconscious will.

Horse Race #14. Robert McIntosh.

"I suppose we'll talk to Bassett," said the boy. "I expect I have fifteen hundred now; and twenty in reserve; and this twenty."

His uncle studied him for some moments.

"Look here, son!" he said. "You're not serious about Bassett and that fifteen hundred, are you?"

"Yes, I am. But it's between you and me, uncle. Honour bright?"

"Honour bright all right, son! But I must talk to Bassett."

"If you'd like to be a partner, uncle, with Bassett and me, we could all be partners. Only, you'd have to promise, honour bright, uncle, not to let it go beyond us three. Bassett and I are lucky, and you must be lucky, because it was your ten shillings I started winning with. . . ."

Uncle Oscar took both Bassett and Paul into Richmond Park for an afternoon, and there they talked.

"It's like this, you see, sir," Bassett said. "Master Paul would get me talking about racing events, spinning yarns, you know, sir. And he was always keen on knowing if I'd made or if I'd lost. It's about a year since, now, that I put five shillings on Blush of Dawn for him: and we lost. Then the luck turned, with that ten shillings he had from you: that we put on Singhalese. And since that time, it's been pretty steady, all things considering. What do you say, Master Paul?"

"We're all right when we're sure," said Paul. "It's when we're not quite sure that we go down."

"Oh, but we're careful then," said Bassett.

"But when are you *sure?*" smiled Uncle Oscar.

"It's Master Paul, sir," said Bassett in a secret, religious voice. "It's as if he had it from heaven. Like Daffodil, now, for the Lincoln. That was as sure as eggs."

"Did you put anything on Daffodil?" asked Oscar Cresswell.

---

1 Make Inferences About Characters *Why does Paul not want Uncle Oscar to reveal the partnership?*

Foreshadowing *What event might Bassett's remark foreshadow?* **2**

Reading Practice

Author's Purpose Have students analyze why Lawrence makes racing so important in the story. **Ask:** How is the attempt to make money by gambling different from the attempt to make money at a job? *(Students may point out that, when making money at a job, one has an agreed-upon salary that can be expected, whereas when trying to make money at the races, one can never be sure of the money that may result, if at all.)* How does racing "raise the stakes" in the narrative? *(Since the outcome of a race is never certain, the reader is never sure what will happen to Paul and his family.)*

"Yes, sir. I made my bit."

"And my nephew?"

Bassett was **obstinately** silent, looking at Paul.

"I made twelve hundred, didn't I, Bassett? I told uncle I was putting three hundred on Daffodil."

"That's right," said Bassett, nodding.

"But where's the money?" asked the uncle.

"I keep it safe locked up, sir. Master Paul he can have it any minute he likes to ask for it."

"What, fifteen hundred pounds?"

"And twenty! And *forty*, that is, with the twenty he made on the course."

"It's amazing!" said the uncle.

"If Master Paul offers you to be partners, sir, I would, if I were you: if you'll excuse me," said Bassett.

Oscar Cresswell thought about it.

"I'll see the money," he said.

They drove home again, and, sure enough, Bassett came round to the garden-house with fifteen hundred pounds in notes. The twenty pounds reserve was left with Joe Glee, in the Turf Commission deposit.

"You see, it's all right, uncle, when I'm *sure!* Then we go strong, for all we're worth. Don't we, Bassett?"

"We do that, Master Paul."

"And when are you sure?" said the uncle, laughing.

"Oh, well, sometimes I'm *absolutely* sure, like about Daffodil," said the boy; "and sometimes I have an idea; and sometimes I haven't even an idea, have I, Bassett? Then we're careful, because we mostly go down."

"You do, do you! And when you're sure, like about Daffodil, what makes you sure, sonny?"

"Oh, well, I don't know," said the boy uneasily. "I'm sure, you know, uncle; that's all."

"It's as if he had it from heaven, sir," Bassett **reiterated.**

"I should say so!" said the uncle.

But he became a partner. And when the Leger was coming on Paul was "sure" about Lively Spark, which was a quite inconsiderable horse. The boy insisted on putting a thousand on the horse, Bassett went for five hundred, and Oscar Cresswell two hundred. Lively Spark came in first, and the betting had been ten to one against him. Paul had made ten thousand.

"You see," he said, "I was absolutely sure of him."

Even Oscar Cresswell had cleared two thousand.

"Look here, son," he said, "this sort of thing makes me nervous."

"It needn't, uncle! Perhaps I shan't be sure again for a long time."

"But what are you going to do with your money?" asked the uncle.

"Of course," said the boy, "I started it for mother. She said she had no luck, because father is unlucky, so I thought if I was lucky, it might stop whispering."

"What might stop whispering?"

"Our house. I *hate* our house for whispering."

"What does it whisper?"

"Why—why"—the boy fidgeted—"why, I don't know. But it's always short of money, you know, uncle."

"I know it, son, I know it."

"You know people send mother writs,[12] don't you, uncle?"

"I'm afraid I do," said the uncle.

"And then the house whispers, like people laughing at you behind your back. It's awful, that is! I thought if I was lucky——"

"You might stop it," added the uncle.

The boy watched him with big blue eyes, that had an uncanny cold fire in them, and he said never a word.

---

12. Here, *writs* are legal notices demanding payment for outstanding bills.

Make Inferences About Characters *Why is Uncle Oscar nervous?* **3**

Modernism *What does this whispering suggest about society's values?* **4**

D. H. LAWRENCE **1085**

Teach

Teach

Literary Element | 1

Foreshadow Ask: What might Uncle Oscar's concern about the birthday money foreshadow? *(Paul's mother may not handle the money well, and so it may increase her debt in the long run.)*

View the Art ★

Answer: *The mood is claustrophobic and tense, like that of the story.*

The British artist Pam (P. J.) Crook (1945–) typically paints crowd scenes in public spaces or intimate personal scenes in interiors or in dreamlike spaces. Crook's images tend to have a theatrical quality due to their composition, technique, and dramatic content. They also have an undercurrent of mystery and unease, which is fueled by her use of dark outlines, strong colors, full shadows, and surreal perspectives. The rock band King Crimson has used her art for several of their album/CD covers.

5 O'Clock Cowboy. P. J. Crook (b. 1945). Acrylic on wood, 43 x 53 cm. Private collection.

View the Art P. J. Crook often emphasizes the three-dimensional nature of her scenes and subjects. How would you describe the mood of this work? How does it compare with the mood of the story? ★

"Well, then!" said the uncle. "What are we doing?"

"I shouldn't like mother to know I was lucky," said the boy.

"Why not, son?"

"She'd stop me."

"I don't think she would."

"Oh!"—and the boy writhed in an odd way—"I *don't* want her to know, uncle."

"All right, son! We'll manage it without her knowing."

They managed it very easily. Paul, at the other's suggestion, handed over five thousand pounds to his uncle, who deposited it with the family lawyer, who was then to inform Paul's mother that a relative had put five thousand pounds into his hands, which sum was to be paid out a thousand pounds at a time, on the mother's birthday, for the next five years.

"So she'll have a birthday present of a thousand pounds for five successive years," said Uncle Oscar. "I hope it won't make it all the **1** harder for her later."

Paul's mother had her birthday in November. The house had been "whispering" worse than ever lately, and, even in spite of his luck, Paul could not bear up against it. He was very anxious to see the effect of the birthday letter, telling his mother about the thousand pounds.

When there were no visitors, Paul now took his meals with his parents, as he was beyond the nursery control. His mother went into town nearly every day. She had discovered that she had an odd knack of sketching furs and dress materials, so she worked secretly in the studio of a friend who was the chief "artist" for the leading drapers.[13] She drew the figures of ladies in furs and ladies in silk and sequins for the newspaper advertisements. This young

---

13. *Drapers* are dealers in cloth and other dry goods.

Writing Practice

 Journals

SPIRAL REVIEW One way to strengthen students' interest in a selection is to ask them to make connections between ideas in the text and their own ideas. As a way to explore the theme of this selection, have students think about what Paul and his mother say about luck, money, and families. Have students write journal entries describing their own ideas about the meaning of luck, the importance of money, and the roles of both in family life.

Horse Race #5. Robert McIntosh.

View the Art Compare this image with the one on page 1084. How does this image convey motion? Is it more or less effective than the earlier image? ★

woman artist earned several thousand pounds a year, but Paul's mother only made several hundreds, and she was again dissatisfied. She so wanted to be first in something, and she did not succeed, even in making sketches for drapery advertisements.

She was down to breakfast on the morning of her birthday. Paul watched her face as she read her letters. He knew the lawyer's letter. As his mother read it, her face hardened and became more expressionless. Then a cold, determined look came on her mouth. She hid the letter under a pile of others, and said not a word about it.

"Didn't you have anything nice in the post for your birthday, mother?" said Paul.

"Quite moderately nice," she said, her voice cold and absent.

 Make Inferences About Characters *What reaction from his mother was Paul hoping for?*

She went away to town without saying more.

But in the afternoon Uncle Oscar appeared. He said Paul's mother had had a long interview with the lawyer, asking if the whole five thousand could not be advanced at once, as she was in debt.

"What do you think, uncle?" said the boy.

"I leave it to you, son."

"Oh, let her have it, then! We can get some more with the other," said the boy.

"A bird in the hand is worth two in the bush, laddie!" said Uncle Oscar.

"But I'm sure to *know* for the Grand National; or the Lincolnshire; or else the Derby. I'm sure to know for *one* of them," said Paul.

So Uncle Oscar signed the agreement, and Paul's mother touched the whole five thousand. Then something very curious happened. The voices in the house suddenly went mad, like a ☆ chorus of frogs on a spring evening. There were

D. H. LAWRENCE **1087**

Advanced Learners

DIFFERENTIATED INSTRUCTION

Problem and Solution Paul's parents choose to ignore their financial problems. Have students discuss why facing financial issues is important. Then ask them to draft solutions to the problems Paul's family faces. Encourage them to first identify the problems, then brainstorm possible solutions, and finally choose the best solution for each problem. Have students write their solutions as a plan for the family to follow.

Teach

Literary Element   1

Foreshadow **Answer:** *This detail creates an eerie and ominous mood. This mood might foreshadow a dark ending to this story.*

Reading Strategy   2

Make Inferences About Characters Answer: *She really does, in her way, love her son and worry about him.*

(APPROACHING) To guide approaching level students, **ask:** What words or phrases in this passage tell you that she really does care about Paul? *(looking down at him anxiously, her heart curiously heavy because of him)*

Reading Strategy   3

Make Inferences About Characters Answer: *Paul's mother does not know her son's real feelings.*

(ADVANCED) **Ask:** Paul wants to stay at home until the Derby so he can bet on it. What other reasons might he have for not wanting to be sent away? *(If his mother were to send him away, it would symbolically confirm that she doesn't care for him.)*

certain new furnishings, and Paul had a tutor. He was *really* going to Eton,[14] his father's school, in the following autumn. There were flowers in the winter, and a blossoming of the luxury Paul's mother had been used to. And yet the voices in the house, behind the sprays of mimosa and almond-blossom, and from under the piles of iridescent cushions, simply trilled and screamed in a sort of ecstasy: "There *must* be more money! Oh-h-h; there *must* be more money. Oh, now, now-w! Now-w-w—there *must* be more money!—more than ever! More than ever!"

It frightened Paul terribly. He studied away at his Latin and Greek with his tutor. But his intense hours were spent with Bassett. The Grand National had gone by: he had not "known," and had lost a hundred pounds. Summer was at hand. He was in agony for the Lincoln. But even for the Lincoln he didn't "know," and he lost fifty pounds. He became wild-eyed and strange, as if something were going to explode in him.

"Let it alone, son! Don't you bother about it!" urged Uncle Oscar. But it was as if the boy couldn't really hear what his uncle was saying.

"I've got to know for the Derby! I've got to know for the Derby!" the child reiterated, his big blue eyes blazing with a sort of madness.

His mother noticed how overwrought he was.

"You'd better go to the seaside. Wouldn't you like to go now to the seaside, instead of waiting? I think you'd better," she said, looking down at him anxiously, her heart curiously heavy because of him.

But the child lifted his uncanny blue eyes.

"I couldn't possibly go before the Derby, mother!" he said. "I couldn't possibly!"

"Why not?" she said, her voice becoming heavy when she was opposed. "Why not? You can still go from the seaside to see the Derby

with your Uncle Oscar, if that's what you wish. No need for you to wait here. Besides, I think you care too much about these races. It's a bad sign. My family has been a gambling family, and you won't know till you grow up how much damage it has done. But it has done damage. I shall have to send Bassett away, and ask Uncle Oscar not to talk racing to you, unless you promise to be reasonable about it: go away to the seaside and forget it. You're all nerves!"

"I'll do what you like, mother, so long as you don't send me away till after the Derby," the boy said.

"Send you away from where? Just from this house?"

"Yes," he said, gazing at her.

"Why, you curious child, what makes you care about this house so much, suddenly? I never knew you loved it."

He gazed at her without speaking. He had a secret within a secret, something he had not divulged, even to Bassett or to his Uncle Oscar.

But his mother, after standing undecided and a little bit sullen for some moments, said:

"Very well, then! Don't go to the seaside till after the Derby, if you don't wish it. But promise me you won't let your nerves go to pieces. Promise you won't think so much about horse-racing and *events*, as you call them!"

"Oh no," said the boy casually. "I won't think much about them, mother. You needn't worry. I wouldn't worry, mother, if I were you."

"If you were me and I were you," said his mother, "I wonder what we *should* do!"

"But you know you needn't worry, mother, don't you?" the boy repeated.

"I should be awfully glad to know it," she said wearily.

"Oh, well, you *can*, you know. I mean, you *ought* to know you needn't worry," he insisted.

"Ought I? Then I'll see about it," she said.

Paul's secret of secrets was his wooden horse, that which had no name. Since he

---

14. *Eton* is a prestigious private school in England.

1 Foreshadowing *What mood does this detail create? What might this mood foreshadow?*

2 Make Inferences About Characters *What can you conclude about Paul's mother?*

Make Inferences About Characters *What does this passage reveal about the mother's insights into her son?* **3**

Reading Practice

SPIRAL REVIEW **Symbolism Ask:** What physical feature does Lawrence frequently emphasize in describing Paul? *(eyes)* What feature of the mother does he emphasize? *(mouth)* Have students find examples of Lawrence's descriptions of the boy's eyes and the mother's mouth. **Ask:** What traits do these physical features represent? *(The boy's eyes are described as blazing with cold fire, signifying his determination and desire; the mother's mouth is described as cold and shut off, symbolizing her coldness toward her child, as well as resembling the coldness of Paul's stare.)*

was **emancipated** from a nurse and a nursery-governess, he had had his rocking-horse removed to his own bedroom at the top of the house.

"Surely you're too big for a rocking-horse!" his mother had remonstrated.[15]

"Well, you see, mother, till I can have a *real* horse, I like to have *some* sort of animal about," had been his quaint answer.

"Do you feel he keeps you company?" she laughed.

"Oh yes! He's very good, he always keeps me company, when I'm there," said Paul.

So the horse, rather shabby, stood in an arrested prance in the boy's bedroom.

The Derby was drawing near, and the boy grew more and more tense. He hardly heard what was spoken to him, he was very frail, and his eyes were really uncanny. His mother had sudden strange seizures of uneasiness about him. Sometimes, for half an hour, she would feel a sudden anxiety about him that was almost anguish. She wanted to rush to him at once, and know he was safe.

Two nights before the Derby, she was at a big party in town, when one of her rushes of anxiety about her boy, her first-born, gripped her heart till she could hardly speak. She fought with the feeling, might and main, for she believed in common sense. But it was too strong. She had to leave the dance and go downstairs to telephone to the country. The children's nursery-governess was terribly surprised and startled at being rung up in the night.

"Are the children all right, Miss Wilmot?"

"Oh yes, they are quite all right."

"Master Paul? Is he all right?"

"He went to bed as right as a trivet. Shall I run up and look at him?"

---

15. *Remonstrated* means "objected."

4 Foreshadowing *What might this description foreshadow?*

Vocabulary

emancipate (i man′ sə pāt′) *v.* to free; to liberate

"No," said Paul's mother reluctantly. "No! Don't trouble. It's all right. Don't sit up. We shall be home fairly soon." She did not want her son's privacy intruded upon.

"Very good," said the governess.

It was about one o'clock when Paul's mother and father drove up to their house. All was still. Paul's mother went to her room and slipped off her white fur cloak. She had told her maid not to wait up for her. She heard her husband downstairs, mixing a whisky and soda.

And then, because of the strange anxiety at her heart, she stole upstairs to her son's room. Noiselessly she went along the upper corridor. Was there a faint noise? What was it?

She stood, with arrested muscles, outside his door, listening. There was a strange, heavy, and yet not loud noise. Her heart stood still. It was a soundless noise, yet rushing and powerful. Something huge, in violent, hushed motion. What was it? What in God's name was it? She ought to know. She felt that she knew the noise. She knew what it was.

Yet she could not place it. She couldn't say what it was. And on and on it went, like a madness.

Softly, frozen with anxiety and fear, she turned the door handle.

The room was dark. Yet in the space near the window, she heard and saw something plunging to and fro. She gazed in fear and amazement.

Then suddenly she switched on the light, and saw her son, in his green pyjamas, madly surging on the rocking-horse. The blaze of light suddenly lit him up, as he urged the wooden horse, and lit her up, as she stood, blonde, in her dress of pale green and crystal, in the doorway.

"Paul!" she cried. "Whatever are you doing?"

"It's Malabar!" he screamed in a powerful, strange voice. "It's Malabar!"

His eyes blazed at her for one strange and senseless second, as he ceased urging his wooden horse. Then he fell with a crash to the ground,

---

Foreshadowing *What feelings does this description evoke? What does it suggest might happen?* **5**

D. H. LAWRENCE **1089**

Teach

Reading Strategy 1

Make Inferences About Characters Answer: *The mother knows that Paul discusses horse races with Bassett, so she believes that he might be able to elicit some response from her feverish son.*

Big Idea 2

Modernism Answer: *This passage suggests that money means more than love in modern society.*

(ENGLISH LEARNERS) To guide English language learners, **ask:** What does Uncle Oscar mean when he calls Paul a "poor devil"? *(It is an expression of sympathy; he means that Paul was an unfortunate victim.)*

Progress Check

Can students identify foreshadowing?

If No → See Unit 6 Teaching Resources Book, p. 144.

and she, all her tormented motherhood flooding upon her, rushed to gather him up.

But he was unconscious, and unconscious he remained, with some brain-fever. He talked and tossed, and his mother sat stonily by his side.

"Malabar! It's Malabar! Bassett, Bassett, I *know*! It's Malabar!"

So the child cried, trying to get up and urge the rocking-horse that gave him his inspiration.

"What does he mean by Malabar?" asked the heart-frozen mother.

"I don't know," said the father stonily.

"What does he mean by Malabar?" she asked her brother Oscar.

"It's one of the horses running for the Derby," was the answer.

And, in spite of himself, Oscar Cresswell spoke to Bassett, and himself put a thousand on Malabar: at fourteen to one.

The third day of the illness was critical: they were waiting for a change. The boy, with his rather long, curly hair, was tossing ceaselessly on the pillow. He neither slept nor regained consciousness, and his eyes were like blue stones. His mother sat, feeling her heart had gone, turned actually into a stone.

In the evening, Oscar Cresswell did not come, but Bassett sent a message, saying could he come up for one moment, just one moment? Paul's mother was very angry at the intrusion, but on second thoughts she agreed. The boy was the same. Perhaps Bassett might bring him to consciousness.

The gardener, a shortish fellow with a little brown moustache and sharp little brown eyes,

> "It's Malabar! Bassett . . . I know!"

tiptoed into the room, touched his imaginary cap to Paul's mother, and stole to the bedside, staring with glittering, smallish eyes at the tossing, dying child.

"Master Paul!" he whispered. "Master Paul! Malabar came in first all right, a clean win. I did as you told me. You've made over seventy thousand pounds, you have; you've got over eighty thousand. Malabar came in all right, Master Paul."

"Malabar! Malabar! Did I say Malabar, mother? Did I say Malabar? Do you think I'm lucky, mother? I knew Malabar, didn't I? Over eighty thousand pounds! I call that lucky, don't you, mother? Over eighty thousand pounds! I knew, didn't I know I knew? Malabar came in all right. If I ride my horse till I'm sure, then I tell you, Bassett, you can go as high as you like. Did you go for all you were worth, Bassett?"

"I went a thousand on it, Master Paul."

"I never told you, mother, that if I can ride my horse, and *get there*, then I'm absolutely sure—oh, absolutely! Mother, did I ever tell you? I *am* lucky!"

"No, you never did," said his mother.

But the boy died in the night.

And even as he lay dead, his mother heard her brother's voice saying to her: "My God, Hester, you're eighty-odd thousand to the good, and a poor devil of a son to the bad. But, poor devil, poor devil, he's best gone out of a life where he rides his rocking-horse to find a winner." ❧

---

1 | **Make Inferences About Characters** *Why does the mother believe that Bassett might be able to help Paul?*

Modernism *What does this passage suggest about love and money in modern society?* | **2**

Listening and Speaking Practice

Oral Interpretation The passage in which Paul's mother finds him riding his rocking horse in his room is the climax of this story and offers a perfect opportunity for pairs of students to provide an oral interpretation. Encourage them to use facial expressions and gestures and to vary inflections and tone of voice to bring the piece to life.

After You Read

Respond and Think Critically

Respond and Interpret

1. What went through your mind at the end of the story?

2. (a)How does the mother feel about her children at the beginning of the story? (b)Do you think her feelings for Paul change over the course of the story? Explain.

3. (a)What does the house whisper? (b)Why might only the children hear what the house is whispering?

4. (a)How does Paul use the rocking horse to gain luck? (b)What might the rocking horse **symbolize** to Paul?

5. (a)How does Paul arrange to give his mother his winnings? (b)What does Paul's mother's reaction to the gift of money reveal about her?

Analyze and Evaluate

6. In your opinion, should anyone be held responsible for what happens to Paul? Explain.

7. This story is written almost like a fairy tale. Do you find this **style** effective? Why or why not?

8. This story has an **omniscient**, or all-knowing, narrator. How might the story change if it were told from the point of view of Paul or his mother?

Connect

9. **Big Idea** Modernism What effect does society's emphasis on money have on the characters in this story?

10. **Connect to the Author** Lawrence wrote "The Rocking-Horse Winner" late in his life, after he and his wife fled social persecution in England. How might his experiences in England have influenced this story?

Literary Element Foreshadowing

Foreshadowing often helps to build suspense or interest in a story. It makes readers predict what will happen and encourages them to keep reading to see if their predictions prove to be correct.

1. Cite several examples of foreshadowing from the story. What later events do these examples predict?

2. What events does the title of the story foreshadow?

Review: Motivation

As you learned on page 1002, **motivation** refers to a character's reason for acting, thinking, or feeling in a certain way. A character's motivation may be stated directly or only implied.

Partner Activity Meet with a partner to discuss what the following passage reveals about Paul's motivation. Then answer the questions.

"Well, anyhow," he said stoutly, "I'm a lucky person."

"Why?" said his mother, with a sudden laugh. He stared at her. He didn't even know why he had said it.

"God told me," he asserted, brazening it out.

"I hope He did, dear!" she said, again with a laugh, but rather bitter.

1. What is Paul's motivation for seeking luck?

2. What prompts Paul to claim that God told him he was lucky?

After You Read

Assess

1. Students' answers will vary.

2. (a) She does not appear to love them. (b) She loves Paul when she begins to lose him.

3. (a) "There *must* be more money." (b) Because they are attuned to their parents' worries

4. (a) To learn the names of winning horses so he can bet on them (b) A conduit to his mother's heart

5. (a) Paul has Uncle Oscar give his mother the money through a lawyer as if a relative had donated it. (b) That she will never have enough money to be satisfied

6. Some may say the adults should be held responsible for allowing Paul to feel so unloved and worried. Others may say society is at fault for placing so much emphasis on money.

7. Answers will vary.

8. From the mother's point of view, we would see more clearly that her values are twisted and that her understanding of her son is limited. From Paul's point of view, we would understand Paul's world only as he sees it.

9. It breeds anxiety in the family, damaging all the characters emotionally and, in Paul's case, physically too.

10. Students will probably say that Lawrence experienced England as being cold, exclusionary, and socially rigid—all traits that the adults in "Rocking-Horse Winner" exhibit.

Literary Element

1. Students may cite the passage in which Paul's mother finally begins to feel anxious about her son, which foreshadows Paul's sickness and death.

2. Paul's winnings at the racetrack and, ironically, his winning of his mother's love, which occurs too late to save him.

Review: Motivation

1. To win his mother's love, to make the house stop whispering, and to alleviate his mother's anxiety about money.

2. Paul is trying to convince his mother that he is lucky and therefore worthy of her love.

After You Read

Assess

Reading Strategy

1. Because the children stop playing and begin to stare at one another when they hear the whispers, one can infer that they are anxious and confused. The children do not understand why their parents are so tense and unhappy or why they need more money, especially since they seem to have more than enough.

2. Most students will say that the story's theme relates to materialism's destructive qualities. Some students may choose Uncle Oscar's remarks at the end of the story, supporting their choice by stating that in a world where money is valued over love, sensitive children may be better off dead.

Vocabulary

1. a 2. c 3. b 4. a

Academic Vocabulary

Students should write and answer questions about amounts of money in the story.

 To create custom assessments using software, use ExamView Assessment Suite.

Making inferences about the characters in a story can help you understand their actions and discover the author's theme, or message about life.

1. What can you infer about Paul and the children from their reactions to the whispering house?

2. What is the story's theme? Which character's statement from the story sums up the theme?

Vocabulary Practice

Practice with Analogies Choose the word that best completes each analogy.

1. emancipate : enslave :: admire :
   a. disdain   c. worship
   b. love   d. fear

2. parry : confront :: tow :
   a. suspend   c. push
   b. pull   d. bury

3. reiterate : repeat :: examine :
   a. negate   c. overlook
   b. inspect   d. ignore

4. obstinately : inflexibly :: courageously :
   a. valiantly   c. timidly
   b. indignantly   d. lethargically

Academic Vocabulary

In the story, Paul amasses a large **sum** *of money by winning bets on horse races.*

Sum is an academic word. For instance, you would calculate the **sum** *of a dinner bill by adding the cost of the food, drinks, and tax.*

To further explore the meaning of this word, write and answer questions about the **sums** *of characters' winnings in the story.*

EXAMPLE:
Question: What sum did Paul bet at first?
Answer: He bet five shillings, which he lost.

For more on academic vocabulary, see pages 56 and R81.

Speaking and Listening

 Literature Groups

Assignment Bassett and Uncle Oscar both support Paul's obsession with betting, even though they realize how damaging it is to the boy. In a small group, discuss the motivation of these characters, considering their thoughts, words, and actions; and the comments about them by other characters and the narrator.

Prepare Reread "The Rocking-Horse Winner," noting clues to the characters and motivations of Bassett and Uncle Oscar. Think about issues such as Bassett's description of Paul's gift and Uncle Oscar's original hesitation. Create a word web, chart, or Venn diagram to help you organize the information. Also review the oral communication skills on page 975 to guide your participation in the discussion.

Discuss When it is your turn to speak, support your points with logical arguments and specific examples from the short story. Listen to others' points of view, responding respectfully with agreement, questions, or counterarguments.

EXAMPLE:
Some might say that _____ and _____ suggest that Uncle Oscar is initially concerned about Paul, because _____.
On the other hand, actions such as _____ and _____ suggest _____.

Report Summarize the points made in the discussion, ranking the arguments in order of their persuasive logic and support.

Evaluate Write a paragraph in which you assess your peers' participation in the discussion and how well the discussion's objectives were accomplished.

LOG ON ▶ **Literature** Online

Selection Resources For Selection Quizzes, eFlashcards, and Reading-Writing Connection activities, go to glencoe.com and enter QuickPass code GLB9817u6.

Literature Groups

Use these criteria in evaluation student literature groups:

- The group discussion focuses on the motives of Bassett and Uncle Oscar in "The Rocking-Horse Winner."
- Statements are supported with relevant material from the text and presented logically.

- The group summarized the points brought out in the discussion, ranking arguments in order of strength.
- Individual group members respectfully and accurately critique each others' participation.

Before You Read

Araby

Meet **James Joyce**
(1882–1941)

Although James Joyce was born and grew up in Dublin, Ireland, and set all of his work there, he found the voice to write about the city only in exile. Leaving Dublin (the city Joyce termed "the center of paralysis") allowed him the distance to imaginatively re-create the city in his fiction.

> "*Welcome, O life! I go to encounter for the millionth time the reality of experience and to forge in the smithy of my soul the uncreated conscience of my race.*"
>
> —James Joyce

Early Exile The oldest of ten children, Joyce was born into an affluent Catholic family that sank into poverty due to his father's heavy drinking and irresponsibility. However, Joyce did have happy memories of his father, especially from the time they lived on North Richmond Street—the setting of "Araby." Joyce's father often walked the streets of Dublin with young James, telling stories about the people who lived there.

Although Joyce received most of his education in Catholic schools, he later rebelled against Catholicism and what he felt was the stifling environment of Dublin. After graduating from Dublin's University College in 1902, Joyce left Dublin for Paris to seek freedom from narrow religious and social conventions. When his mother contracted a fatal illness, he returned to Ireland and began working on the stories that would become *Dubliners*.

In 1904 he met and fell in love with Nora Barnacle, an uneducated but witty and intelligent working-class girl whom he persuaded to leave Ireland with him for good. She became his lifelong companion.

A Struggling Genius Moving throughout Europe, Joyce spent most of his time in Trieste, Paris, Zurich, and Rome, teaching languages and writing in his spare time. Although he was convinced of his own genius, Joyce's frankness and his experiments with form made it difficult for him to get his writing published. When his work did get published, it was often considered scandalous and was banned by censors. As a result, Joyce earned very little income from his writing until his later years. In addition to publishing difficulties and poverty, he suffered from severe eye diseases and endured over twenty operations—some of which left him temporarily blind.

By the end of his life, Joyce was recognized as one of the most innovative and influential writers of the twentieth century. He experimented with language, plot, and characterization, focusing on the inner reality of his characters through the literary technique known as stream of consciousness. He gained acclaim for his autobiographical novel *A Portrait of the Artist as a Young Man*, as well as for his finely crafted stories in *Dubliners*. A perfectionist who was devoted to his art, Joyce spent seven years writing his masterpiece, *Ulysses*. Joyce's fiction represents Dublin as a microcosm for all human experience.

 Literature Online

Author Search For more about James Joyce, go to glencoe.com and enter QuickPass code GLB9817u6.

JAMES JOYCE **1093**

Before You Read

Focus

Summary

A boy has recently discovered his passion for the sister of his friend Mangan. He longs to do something to prove his love for her, in the manner of the knights who quested for the Holy Grail. Instead, he promises to bring her something from the local bazaar, which is called Araby. When he arrives at the bazaar, he finds it darkened, with only money counters and a few vendors left. He overhears a conversation and realizes that his love, like his desire for the exotic atmosphere of Araby, is nothing more than a childish illusion.

Vocabulary

Word Origins Have students research the Latin root and etymology of each vocabulary word. Point out that the prefix *im-* (or *in-*) can mean many things, including "not," "toward," and "in." Have them decide which meaning the prefix has in the words *imperturbable* and *impinge*.

Literature and Reading Preview

Connect to the Story

Have you ever looked forward to an important event that turned out differently from what you expected? Write a journal entry about your expectations, the reality, and your reaction.

Build Background

Realistic and gritty, the content of *Dubliners* discouraged potential publishers. After many rejections and nearly a decade after original negotiations began, a firm finally agreed to print the book. During printing, however, parts of the manuscript were lost, and hundreds of Joyce's corrections were never made.

Set Purposes for Reading

Big Idea Modernism

As you read, ask yourself, How does Joyce gain meaning from traditional and innovative literary movements and techniques?

Literary Element Epiphany

An **epiphany** is a moment of sudden realization of the true meaning of a situation, person, or object. Joyce was an innovator in the use of the technique and suggested the glimpses offered a kind of revelation into a character. With an epiphany, a character has an intuitive moment in which a simple thing is seen in a new light that triggers a deeper insight into the world or the inner life of the character. As you read, ask yourself, Which event seems to shift the narrator's perception?

Reading Strategy Make and Verify Predictions

When you **make predictions**, you make educated guesses about what will happen later in a selection. You then **verify predictions** by looking for textual evidence that confirms their accuracy. As you read, ask yourself, What predictions can I make about later events and the outcome of "Araby"? Then verify the accuracy of your predictions.

Tip: Taking Notes Use a chart like the one below to make and verify predictions as you read.

Prediction	Evidence for Prediction	Verification

Learning Objectives

For pages 1093–1101

In studying this text, you will focus on the following objectives:

Literary Study: Analyzing epiphany.

Reading: Making and verifying predictions.

Writing: Reporting on literary criticism.

Vocabulary

imperturbable (im′ pər tur′ bə bəl) *adj.* not easily excited or disturbed; calm; p. 1095 *The guard was imperturbable despite the boys' attempts to goad him to anger.*

diverge (dī vurj′) *v.* to move in different directions from a common point; to branch out; p. 1096 *When the detective asked about the thief's identity, the witnesses' stories diverged.*

converge (kən vurj′) *v.* to come together in a common interest or conclusion; to center; p. 1096 *Revelers converge on Times Square every New Year's Eve.*

impinge (im pinj′) *v.* to strike or dash; to collide; p. 1097 *He felt the blast of the bass impinge on his eardrums.*

amiability (ā′ mē ə bil′ ə tē) *n.* kindliness; friendliness; p. 1097 *Mrs. Lorca's amiability made her popular in the neighborhood.*

Reading Practice

SPIRAL REVIEW **Prereading** Have students preview the illustrations on the pages of the story. **Ask:** Based on the illustrations, where do you think the story is set and in what time period? *(The story takes place in an urban setting in the early part of the 20th century.)* What details in the illustrations led you to your conclusions about the setting?

(The buildings look close together, like in a city. The boys' clothing looks like the type worn during the early part of the 20th century.) Then, have students list words that describe the mood of each illustration.

Araby

James Joyce

A Glasgow Close. Joan Eardley (1921–1963). Oil on canvas, 24 x 20 in.
Hunterian Art Gallery, University of Glasgow, Scotland.

View the Art This image depicts a particular segment of urban life in the early half of the twentieth century. What can you infer about these subjects and their lifestyles?

1 North Richmond Street, being blind,[1] was a quiet street except at the hour when the Christian Brothers' School set the boys free. An uninhabited house of two stories stood at the blind end, detached from its neighbors in a square ground. The other houses of the street, conscious of decent lives within them, gazed at one another with brown **imperturbable** faces. The former tenant of our house, a priest, had died in the back drawing room. Air, musty from having been long enclosed, hung in all the rooms, and the waste room behind the kitchen was littered with old useless papers. Among

these I found a few paper-covered books, the pages of which were curled and damp: *The Abbot*, by Walter Scott, *The Devout Communicant* and *The Memoirs of Vidocq*.[2] I liked the last best because its leaves were yellow. The wild garden behind the house contained a central apple tree and a few straggling bushes under one of which I found the late tenant's rusty bicycle pump. He had been a very charitable priest; in his will he had left all his money to institutions and the furniture of his house to his sister.

When the short days of winter came dusk fell before we had well eaten our dinners. When we met in the street the houses had grown somber. The space of sky above us was the color of ever-changing violet and towards it the lamps of the

---

1. Here, *blind* means "dead-end."

Vocabulary

imperturbable (im′ pər tur′ bə bəl) *adj.* not easily excited or disturbed; calm

---

2. *The Abbot* is a historical novel; *The Devout Communicant* is a religious manual; *The Memoirs of Vidocq* is the story of a French detective.

JAMES JOYCE **1095**

English Learners

DIFFERENTIATED INSTRUCTION

Intermediate English language learners may benefit from organizing the elements of this complex story into a sequence chart. As they read, students can fill in the chart, showing how one event leads to another. Most stories begin with a problem, move to a rising action followed by falling action and conclude with a resolution.

Teach

Reading Strategy   1

Make and Verify Predictions Answer: *The narrator describes Mangan's sister as "defined by the light" when she is standing in the half-opened door waiting for her brother. Given this description, most students will predict that the narrator will fall in love with her.*

Big Idea   2

Modernism Answer: *The narrator describes the ordinary sights and sounds of the marketplace as his "foes" and imagines himself on a quest to protect his romantic image of Mangan's sister from the coarse street life.*

street lifted their feeble lanterns. The cold air stung us and we played till our bodies glowed. Our shouts echoed in the silent street. The career of our play brought us through the dark muddy lanes behind the houses where we ran the gantlet[3] of the rough tribes from the cottages, to the back doors of the dark dripping gardens where odors arose from the ashpits, to the dark odorous stables where a coachman smoothed and combed the horse or shook music from the buckled harness. When we returned to the street, light from the kitchen windows had filled the areas. If my uncle was seen turning the corner we hid in the shadow until we had seen him safely housed. Or if Mangan's sister came out on the doorstep to call her brother in to his tea we watched her from our shadow peer up and down the street. We waited to see whether she would remain or go in and, if she remained, we left our shadow and walked up to Mangan's steps resignedly. She was waiting for us, her figure defined by the light from the half-opened door. Her brother always teased her before he obeyed and I stood by the railings looking at her. Her dress swung as she moved her body and the soft rope of her hair tossed from side to side.

Every morning I lay on the floor in the front parlor watching her door. The blind was pulled down to within an inch of the sash so that I could not be seen. When she came out on the doorstep my heart leaped. I ran to the hall, seized my books and followed her. I kept her brown figure always in my eye and, when we came near the point at which our ways **diverged**, I quickened my pace and passed her.

This happened morning after morning. I had never spoken to her, except for a few casual words, and yet her name was like a summons to all my foolish blood.

Her image accompanied me even in places the most hostile to romance. On Saturday evenings when my aunt went marketing I had to go to carry some of the parcels. We walked through the flaring streets, jostled by drunken men and bargaining women, amid the curses of laborers, the shrill litanies[4] of shopboys who stood on guard by the barrels of pigs' cheeks, the nasal chanting of street singers, who sang a *come-you-all* about O'Donovan Rossa,[5] or a ballad about the troubles in our native land. These noises **converged** in a single sensation of life for me: I imagined that I bore my chalice safely through a throng of foes. Her name sprang to my lips at moments in strange prayers and praises which I myself did not understand. My eyes were often full of tears (I could not tell why) and at times a flood from my heart seemed to pour itself out into my bosom. I thought little of the future. I did not know whether I would ever speak to her or not or, if I spoke to her, how I could tell her of my confused adoration. But my body was like a harp and her words and gestures were like fingers running upon the wires.

One evening I went into the back drawing room in which the priest had died. It was a dark rainy evening and there was no sound in the house. Through one of the broken panes I

---

3. *Gantlet* [or *gauntlet*] refers to an outdated punishment in which the offender was made to run between two rows of men who struck at him with switches or weapons as he passed. Here, it means "a series of challenges."

1 Make and Verify Predictions *Based on the narrator's description of Mangan's sister, what do you think his feelings for her are?*

Vocabulary

diverge (dī vurj´) v. to move in different directions from a common point; to branch out

---

4. As it is used here, *litany* is a repetitive announcement to attract customers.

5. A *come-you-all* is a ballad; *O'Donovan Rossa* was a nineteenth-century Irish nationalist.

Modernism *The chalice is a religious icon—the Holy Grail, or drinking cup of Christ for which the knights of the Round Table quested. How does Joyce make use of this traditional symbol in a modern setting?*   **2**

Vocabulary

converge (kən vurj´) v. to come together in a common interest or conclusion; to center

Reading Practice

SPIRAL REVIEW **Summarize** "Araby" focuses on a boy's sudden transition from the illusions of childhood to the insights of maturity. Some students may have trouble recognizing this change and may benefit from summarizing and charting the stages of the boy's emotional growth.

Details of Childhood	Moment of Change (Epiphany)	Details of Maturity

Have students fill in charts similar to the one shown.

heard the rain **impinge** upon the earth, the fine incessant needles of water playing in the sodden beds. Some distant lamp or lighted window gleamed below me. I was thankful that I could see so little. All my senses seemed to desire to veil themselves and, feeling that I was about to slip from them, I pressed the palms of my hands together until they trembled, murmuring: *O love! O love!* many times.

At last she spoke to me. When she addressed the first words to me I was so confused that I did not know what to answer. She asked me was I going to *Araby*.[6] I forget whether I answered yes or no. It would be a splendid bazaar, she said; she would love to go.

—And why can't you? I asked.

While she spoke she turned a silver bracelet round and round her wrist. She could not go, she said, because there would be a retreat[7] that week in her convent.[8] Her brother and two other boys were fighting for their caps and I was alone at the railings. She held one of the spikes, bowing her head towards me. The light from the lamp opposite our door caught the white curve of her neck, lit up her hair that rested there and, falling, lit up the hand upon the railing. It fell over one side of her dress and caught the white border of a petticoat, just visible as she stood at ease.

—It's well for you, she said.

—If I go, I said, I will bring you something.

What innumerable follies laid waste my waking and sleeping thoughts after that evening! I wished to annihilate the tedious intervening days. I chafed against the work of school. At night in my bedroom and by day in the classroom her image came between me and the page

---

6. *Araby* was a bazaar held in 1894 in Dublin.
7. A *retreat* is a group withdrawal for prayer and meditation.
8. Here, a *convent* is a school run by an order of Catholic nuns.

 Make and Verify Predictions *Given the narrator's attitude in the passage, what do you predict will happen concerning his "sight"?*

I strove to read. The syllables of the word *Araby* were called to me through the silence in which my soul luxuriated and cast an Eastern enchantment over me. I asked for leave to go to the bazaar on Saturday night. My aunt was surprised and hoped it was not some Freemason[9] affair. I answered few questions in class. I watched my master's face pass from **amiability** to sternness; he hoped I was not beginning to idle. I could not call my wandering thoughts together. I had hardly any patience with the serious work of life which, now that it stood between me and my desire, seemed to me child's play, ugly monotonous child's play.

On Saturday morning I reminded my uncle that I wished to go to the bazaar in the evening. He was fussing at the hall stand, looking for the hat brush, and answered me curtly:

—Yes, boy, I know.

As he was in the hall I could not go into the front parlor and lie at the window. I left the house in bad humor and walked slowly towards the school. The air was pitilessly raw and already my heart misgave me.

When I came home to dinner my uncle had not yet been home. Still it was early. I sat staring at the clock for some time and, when its ticking began to irritate me, I left the room. I mounted the staircase and gained the upper part of the house. The high cold empty gloomy rooms liberated me and I went from room to room singing. From the front window I saw my companions playing below in the street. Their cries reached me weakened and indistinct and, leaning my forehead against the cool glass, I looked over at the dark house where she lived. I may have stood there for an hour, seeing nothing but the brown-clad figure cast by my imagination, touched discreetly by the lamplight at the curved neck, at the hand upon the railings and at the border below the dress.

---

9. The *Freemasons* are part of a secret fraternity whose members are primarily Protestant.

Teach

Reading Strategy   3

Make and Verify Predictions **Answer:**
Students may predict he will have an experience that forces him to shed his blindness and to "see," or become aware of, something concealed.

Advanced Learners

DIFFERENTIATED INSTRUCTION

Religious Imagery Some students may not grasp the significance of the biblical allusions in "Araby." Have volunteers prepare oral reports that explain the religious significance of the chalice or grail, the garden with the central apple tree, the Madonna (analogues for Mangan's sister), and the moneylenders in the temple.

Teach

Make and Verify Predictions Answer: *Up to this point, the narrator has regarded the bazaar (and everything having to do with Mangan's sister) as holy and exotic. The aunt's matter-of-fact tone and ordinary language puncture the romantic aura surrounding the bazaar. Her tone reminds the boy that his quest is contingent upon his uncle's returning home early enough to give the boy the money that he needs for admission and to buy a gift for Mangan's sister. Students may predict that the reality of the bazaar will fall short of the narrator's high expectations.*

View the Art ★

Answer: *The subjects of the painting, like the narrator and his friends, meet in the streets and conduct their days as a group. The body language is somewhat confident and even rebellious, and the narrator describes his friends as being saucy and confident in their play and teasing.*

Maria Bashkirtseff was a gifted artist and diarist who was born in Russia but later settled in Paris. She spent much of her childhood traveling across Europe. She is best known for the journal she began to keep at the age of thirteen. This journal documents her struggles as a female artist. Maria dealt with poor health most of her life and died of tuberculosis when she was 25.

A Meeting, 1884. Maria Bashkirtseff. Oil on canvas, 195 x 177 cm. Musée d'Orsay, Paris.

<u>View the Art</u> Examine the clothing and posture of the children in this image. In what ways are they similar to the narrator and his friends? ★

When I came downstairs again I found Mrs. Mercer sitting at the fire. She was an old garrulous woman, a pawnbroker's widow, who collected used stamps for some pious purpose. I had to endure the gossip of the tea table. The meal was prolonged beyond an hour and still my uncle did not come. Mrs. Mercer stood up to go: she was sorry she couldn't wait any longer, but it was after eight o'clock and she did not like to be out late, as the night air was bad for her. When she had gone I began to walk up and down the room, clenching my fists. My aunt said:

—I'm afraid you may put off your bazaar for this night of Our Lord.

---

1 Make and Verify Predictions *How does the aunt's statement undermine what Araby symbolizes for the narrator? What might her casual remark foreshadow for the rest of the story?*

At nine o'clock I heard my uncle's latch-key in the hall door. I heard him talking to himself and heard the hall stand rocking when it had received the weight of his overcoat. I could interpret these signs. When he was midway through his dinner I asked him to give me the money to go to the bazaar. He had forgotten.

—The people are in bed and after their first sleep now, he said.

I did not smile. My aunt said to him energetically:

—Can't you give him the money and let him go? You've kept him late enough as it is.

My uncle said he was very sorry he had forgotten. He said he believed in the old saying: *All work and no play makes Jack a dull boy.* He asked me where I was going and, when I had told him a second time he asked me did I know *The Arab's Farewell to His Steed*.[10] When I left the kitchen he was about to recite the opening lines of the piece to my aunt.

I held a florin[11] tightly in my hand as I strode down Buckingham Street towards the station. The sight of the streets thronged with buyers and glaring with gas recalled to me the purpose of my journey. I took my seat in a third-class carriage of a deserted train. After an intolerable delay the train moved out of the station slowly. It crept onward among ruinous houses and over the twinkling river. At Westland Row Station a crowd of people pressed to the carriage doors; but the porters moved them back, saying that it was a special train for the bazaar. I remained alone in the bare carriage. In a few minutes the train drew up beside an improvised wooden platform. I passed out on to the road and saw by the lighted dial of a clock that it was ten minutes

---

10. *The . . . Steed* is a sentimental poem by Caroline Norton.
11. A *florin* was a coin worth two shillings, which, at the time, equaled about fifty cents.

Writing Practice

 **Voice**

SPIRAL REVIEW Explain to students that Joyce carefully constructs the narrator's voice by changing perspective and offering images to convey feelings. Have volunteers point out phrases that show the speaker's feelings. Next, have students freewrite on subjects that stir their emotions, endeavoring to express themselves in clear and distinctive voices.

to ten. In front of me was a large building which displayed the magical name.

I could not find any sixpenny entrance and, fearing that the bazaar would be closed, I passed in quickly through a turnstile, handing a shilling to a weary-looking man. I found myself in a big hall girdled at half its height by a gallery. Nearly all the stalls were closed and the greater part of the hall was in darkness. I recognized a silence like that which pervades a church after a service. I walked into the center of the bazaar timidly. A few people were gathered about the stalls which were still open. Before a curtain, over which the words *Café Chantant*[12] were written in colored lamps, two men were counting money on a salver.[13] I listened to the fall of the coins.

Remembering with difficulty why I had come I went over to one of the stalls and examined porcelain vases and flowered tea sets. At the door of the stall a young lady was talking and laughing with two young gentlemen. I remarked their English accents and listened vaguely to their conversation.

—O, I never said such a thing!

—O, but you did!

—O, but I didn't!

—Didn't she say that?

—Yes. I heard her.

—O, there's a . . . fib!

Observing me the young lady came over and asked me did I wish to buy anything. The tone of her voice was not encouraging; she seemed to have spoken to me out of a sense of duty. I looked humbly at the great jars that stood like eastern guards at either side of the dark entrance to the stall and murmured:

—No, thank you.

The young lady changed the position of one of the vases and went back to the two young men. They began to talk of the same subject.

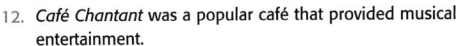

---

12. *Café Chantant* was a popular café that provided musical entertainment.
13. A *salver* is a tray commonly used to serve food and drinks.

La Gare, 1991. P. J. Crook. Acrylic on canvas and wood, 116.8 x 91.4 cm. Private collection.

View the Art Much of Crook's work depicts large crowds in various settings—both urban and rural. How would you describe the atmosphere of this work? What scene does it remind you of in the story? Why?

Once or twice the young lady glanced at me over her shoulder.

I lingered before her stall, though I knew my stay was useless, to make my interest in her wares seem the more real. Then I turned away slowly and walked down the middle of the bazaar. I allowed the two pennies to fall against the sixpence in my pocket. I heard a voice call from one end of the gallery that the light was out. The upper part of the hall was now completely dark.

Gazing up into the darkness I saw myself as a creature driven and derided by vanity; and my eyes burned with anguish and anger. ❧

Epiphany *What is the boy's epiphany in the final passage of the story? How does the conversation between the "young lady" and the "two young gentlemen" help bring about the boy's epiphany?* **2**

Teach

Literary Element | **2**

Epiphany Answer: *The boy now sees himself clearly and realizes that his romantic feelings for Mangan's sister are a delusion. The casual flirtation among the three young people reveals to the boy that his feelings for Mangan's sister and all his romantic illusions are nothing but a "fib"—a childish lie.*

> For additional literary element practice, see Unit 6 Teaching Resources Book, p. 157.

View the Art ★

Answer: *The atmosphere of the painting is ominous. The main figure, like the narrator in "Araby," observes a bustling crowd at a train station.*

P. J. Crook, a British artist, is known for her ability to capture the mysterious, disturbing side of reality. The main focus of many of Crook's paintings is a spectator observing an unsettling scene.

Approaching Level

DIFFERENTIATED INSTRUCTION

Established Point out to students that Joyce uses a first-person narrator in this story. Tell them that readers must analyze how the story is told to come to conclusions about aspects of the main character. **Ask:** How much time has passed between the events of the story and the telling of it? *(Considerable amount, since the narrator seems highly educated and there is distance between* himself as an adult telling the story and as a child experiencing it.) Is the narrator reliable? *(Answers will vary but should include that he is educated but also very passionate.)*

After You Read

Assess

1. Students' answers will vary.

2. (a) Dingy but respectable poverty
(b) Despite their poverty and shabby surroundings, the people are proud and "decent."

3. (a) In the morning and evening; he thinks of her much of the time, especially when alone. (b) He does not know her well at all; his feelings are based on his romantic fantasies.

4. (a) His uncle arrives home late, and the narrator waits until his uncle is midway through his dinner before asking him for money for the bazaar. (b) A loveless, distant one

5. It represents the romantic impulses and illusions the narrator has. It is the place where he hopes to fulfill his promise to Mangan's sister.

6. (a) He does not relish the mundane reality of his world. (b) He chooses not to become a part of the materialism of the bazaar.

7. Fantasies provide only temporary escape and inevitable disappointment.

8. Joyce uses religious symbols and images that connect the narrator's romantic quest to that of the Holy Grail.

9. Students will probably note that the narrator and his friends go to school and run errands much as present-day kids do, but may say they seem to have more freedom than modern students.

After You Read

Respond and Think Critically

Respond and Interpret

1. (a) What were your feelings toward the narrator at the end of the story? (b) Were you surprised by the outcome? Explain.

2. (a) Describe the neighborhood in the opening scene of the story. (b) What does the **personification** of the houses in the first paragraph tell you about the people who live in the neighborhood?

3. (a) At what time of day does the narrator see Mangan's sister? When does he think of her? (b) How well does the narrator know her, and upon what do his feelings seem to be based?

4. (a) What causes the narrator to be delayed in going to the bazaar? (b) Based on the uncle's words and actions, what sort of relationship does he seem to have with his nephew?

Analyze and Evaluate

5. Explain at least two reasons why you think Araby becomes so important to the narrator. What might the bazaar represent to him?

6. (a) What do the narrator's illusions and disillusions tell you about his personality? (b) Why do you think the narrator buys nothing from the stall with the porcelain vases?

7. What broader message or theme might Joyce be revealing through the story?

Connect

8. **Big Idea** Modernism How does Joyce connect traditional symbols and images to the modern world in "Araby"?

9. **Connect to Today** Consider the daily lives of the narrator and his friends. How do they compare to the lives of present-day children?

Literary Element Epiphany

Earlier writers had used and discussed the occurrence of a character's sudden revelation or recognition, referring to it as "the moment," but Joyce gave the term **epiphany** a spiritual dimension. The name derives from a Greek word denoting the manifestation of a deity. Joyce remarked that the "something" that triggers an epiphany is its "soul, its whatness [that] leaps to us from the vestment of its appearance." Note how the narrator's epiphany affords him a spiritual insight into himself and the world.

1. Where does the narrator's epiphany occur in the story and what events trigger the epiphany?

2. (a) What revelation does the epiphany offer the narrator about the world? (b) What spiritual revelation does the epiphany give the narrator about himself?

Review: Symbol

As you learned on page 715, a **symbol** is any object, person, place, or experience that exists on a literal level but also represents something beyond itself, on a figurative level.

Partner Activity Meet with a partner to discuss the meaning of the religious symbols in the passage below. Then answer the questions that follow.

"I imagined that I bore my chalice safely through a throng of foes. Her name sprang to my lips at moments in strange prayers and praises which I myself did not understand. . . . I did not know whether I would ever speak to her or not or, if I spoke to her, how I could tell her of my confused adoration."

1. In Roman Catholic dogma, the chalice is the vessel that holds the consecrated wine transformed by the priest into the blood of Christ. In this passage, what does the chalice symbolize?

2. How does Mangan's sister function as a symbol in this passage?

Literary Element

1. The epiphany occurs in the last sentence. Specifically, he is disillusioned by the men counting money, the many deserted stalls, and the conversation between the girl and the two men.

2. (a) The real world is spiritually impoverished compared with the idealized world of his imagination.

(b) His romantic fantasies are driven by vanity.

Review: Symbol

1. The narrator's romantic vision of Mangan's sister, which he bears through the teeming streets of Dublin.

2. She is depicted as a celestial figure reminiscent of the Blessed Virgin.

Reading Strategy — Make and Verify Predictions

Review the chart you made while reading the story and answer the following questions.

1. What clues throughout the story suggest that the narrator might be exaggerating the significance of his relationship with Mangan's sister?

2. How did the narrator form his initial concept of Araby as a place of mystery and delight?

3. How might the narrator's daily life have led him to create romantic fantasies about Mangan's sister and about Araby?

Vocabulary Practice

Practice with Antonyms With a partner, brainstorm three antonyms for each boldfaced vocabulary word below. Then discuss your choices with your classmates. Be prepared to explain why you chose your words.

> imperturbable   diverge   converge
> impinge   amiability

EXAMPLE: *descend*
<u>Antonyms</u>: *ascend, rise, increase*
<u>Sample explanation</u>: *If a stock was descending, its value would be going down, but if it was rising, its value would be going up.*

Academic Vocabulary

*At the end of "Araby," the speaker realizes that he has a **distorted** view of the real and the ideal.*

*Distorted is an academic word. A mirror with a wavy surface would cause objects to appear **distorted**.*

*To further explore the meaning of this word, complete the following sentence: A person who _____ might be said to have a **distorted** sense of reality.*

For more on academic vocabulary, see pages 56 and R81.

Research and Report

 Literature Criticism

Assignment Write a short essay evaluating literary criticism of Joyce's "Araby" based on your understanding of the short story. Present your assessment to the class.

Prepare Read the following quotation about Joyce's work by the critic Edmund Wilson:

"Images or words in the conscious mind take on an ominous significance . . . incidents swell with meaning."

Identify an image that appears throughout "Araby" and trace its unfolding and "swelling" as the story develops. Consider imagery such as light and darkness, religious symbolism, or exotic descriptions. Alternatively, trace imagery that remains static. Develop a thesis that explains the image's significance to the story, and gather examples from the selection for support. You may want to create a flowchart to help consolidate your thoughts.

EXAMPLE:
Light vs. darkness
Richmond Street "blind" → violet winter sky → Mangan's sister "defined by light" → "thankful I could see so little" → bazaar hall in darkness → "my eyes burned with anguish and anger"

Practice your presentation until you're comfortable with the material and your delivery.

Report Present your ideas in a logical order, to help convince the audience that your thesis is valid. Speak clearly and with confidence, altering your tone of voice and pacing and incorporating appropriate body language to support your statements.

Evaluate Assess the impact of your presentation, focusing on the criteria delineated in the chart on page 1325.

 Literature Online

Selection Resources For Selection Quizzes, eFlashcards, and Reading-Writing Connection activities, go to glencoe.com and enter QuickPass code GLB9817u6.

JAMES JOYCE **1101**

Reading Strategy

1. Students may note the exalted religious imagery and symbolism, as well as the narrator's obsession with a girl whom he scarcely knows. He does not even know her first name.

2. The narrator has no basis for his initial concept of Araby other than the sound of the word and its connotations of magic and romance.

3. The narrator's daily life appears to be dull, lonely, and regimented. It is not surprising that he would try to escape from his daily routine. Also, his familiarity with the rituals and iconography of the Catholic Church fed his longing for a transcendent, or "holy," adventure.

Academic Vocabulary

Possible answer: A person who thought that money was the most important thing in the world might be said to have a distorted sense of reality.

Research and Report

Use these criteria in evaluation student responses to literary criticism:

- The response directly addresses the criticism and is support with quotations and examples from the story.
- The presentation is clear, supported by appropriate gestures and voice modulation, and appropriate for the audience.
- The self-evaluation is fair and accurate, addressing the relevant criteria.

Vocabulary

imperturbable <u>Antonyms</u>: volatile, excitable, edgy; <u>Sample explanation</u>: An imperturbable person stays calm; a volatile person is prone to outbursts.

diverge <u>Antonyms</u>: unify, unite, meet; <u>Sample explanation</u>: If two rivers diverge, they split; if they unite, they come together.

converge <u>Antonyms</u>: disperse, divide, separate; <u>Sample explanation</u>: At the start of a meeting, people converge; at the end, they disperse.

impinge <u>Antonyms</u>: detach, disconnect, disjoin; <u>Sample explanation</u>: If a person impinges negatively upon your life, you want him or her to detach from you.

amiability <u>Antonyms</u>: rudeness, animosity, nastiness; <u>Sample explanation</u>: You want to spend time around amiable people and not animosity.

Vocabulary Workshop

Word Origins

Focus

Students can figure out the meanings of unfamiliar math and science terms by examining their roots and suffixes. Ask students to choose a math or science term and break it into its parts.

Teach

Roots and Suffixes Remind students that the main part of a word is its root. When the root is a complete word, it is sometimes called a base word. A root or base word can be thought of as the "spine" of a word. It gives the word its backbone of meaning. Suffixes are word parts added to the end of a root or a base word to change its meaning and sometimes its part of speech.

Assess

1. geometry   **2.** florescence

3. telegrapher   **4.** astronomy

5. autocrat

Vocabulary Practice

Math and Science Terms Write the following terms on the board: *biology, chemistry, geology, trigonometry, decimal, metric, algebra, calculus*. Ask students to pair up and look up the etymologies of these words in a dictionary. Have students report on the information they find.

Learning Objectives

In this workshop, you will focus on the following objective:

Vocabulary: Understanding word parts.

Etymology

Etymology is the study of word origins. You can find the origins of most words in a dictionary.

Tip

When faced with an unfamiliar word in a reading passage, break it into its parts. Then think of familiar words that include those parts.

Vocabulary Workshop

Word Origins: Math and Science

Literature Connection The word *florin*, the name of a coin, in the quotation below comes from the Latin *flor-* meaning "flower."

> "I held a florin tightly in my hand as I strode down Buckingham Street towards the station."

—James Joyce, from "Araby"

Originally made in Florence, the coin was stamped with the image of a lily. The common English words *flour, flourish,* and *Florida* also come from this Latin root.

Examples

You can discern the meaning of many math and science terms if you know some common word parts. Study the word parts and their definitions in the chart below.

Roots		Suffixes	
astr/o	star	*-crat*	ruler
auto	self	*-escence*	becoming
flor	flower	*-grapher*	writer
ge/o	earth	*-nomy*	laws/knowledge
tele	distant	*-metry*	measure

Practice Answer the following questions by combining word parts from both columns above. Consult a dictionary to check your answers.

1. What word describes a branch of mathematics?

2. What word means "blossoming"?

3. What word describes someone who sends long-distance messages?

4. What word describes the scientific study of the objects in outer space?

5. What word describes a ruler with unlimited power?

 **Literature** Online

Vocabulary For more vocabulary practice, go to glencoe.com and enter QuickPass code GLB9817u6.

 For additional vocabulary practice, see Glencoe Interactive Vocabulary CD-ROM.

Before You Read

from *A Room of One's Own*

Meet **Virginia Woolf**
(1882–1941)

As a child, Virginia Woolf was tutored by one of the most prominent intellectuals and literary critics in England—her father, Sir Leslie Stephen. Following in his footsteps, Woolf began her career as an essayist and critic. She went on, however, to write some of the most untraditional and influential novels of the early twentieth century. Her work was a deliberate attempt to break the conventions of fiction, and she challenged the way traditional novels presented the flow of time and individual experience. She saw life not as a neatly arranged series of events but as a process we live every day. To be faithful to this idea, Woolf's fiction avoids plot as we know it and instead swirls through the consciousness of characters, revealing the essence of their lives.

> *"A woman must have money and a room of her own if she is to write fiction."*
>
> —Virginia Woolf, "A Room of One's Own"

Bloomsbury Virginia Woolf, born Adeline Virginia Stephen, was the next to youngest in a family of four children. At the age of thirteen, her mother died, a loss that plunged Woolf into a deep depression. Woolf periodically suffered serious mental breakdowns for the rest of her life. After the death of her father, when she was in her early twenties, Woolf, her brother, and her two sisters moved to the Bloomsbury district of London. Soon Woolf had made her mark as an essayist and critic for the *Times Literary Supplement*. The home of Woolf and her sister Vanessa, a painter, quickly became a center of English intellectual activity and a salon that attracted eminent authors and thinkers, such as E. M. Forster, George Bernard Shaw, and economist John Maynard Keynes. This loose collection of artists and thinkers, dubbed the Bloomsbury Group, shared a passion for the arts and an intense dislike of the restrictions of Victorian England.

The Hogarth Press The outbreak of World War I caused Woolf's depression to recur, despite her progression as a writer and the publication of her first novel, *The Voyage Out* (1915). Hoping a new artistic outlet would restore her health, she and her husband, essayist and journalist Leonard Woolf, set up a printing press in the basement of Hogarth House, their home. From this humble beginning grew one of the most important publishing ventures of the day—Hogarth Press. The press became a leading force in the popularization of modern, experimental literature and philosophy, publishing the writing of such important literary figures as Katherine Mansfield and T. S. Eliot and such influential thinkers as Sigmund Freud. Hogarth Press also published Woolf's own novels, including *Mrs. Dalloway* and *To the Lighthouse*, two of her most popular, respected, and experimental works.

When Woolf was in her late fifties, she lost her last battle with mental illness. In 1941 she drowned herself in the river near her home in Sussex. Yet, her legacy lies in her innovative style as well as her passion for women's equality.

 Literature Online

Author Search For more about Virginia Woolf, go to glencoe.com and enter QuickPass code GLB9817u6.

VIRGINIA WOOLF **1103**

Before You Read

Focus

Summary

In "A Room of One's Own," Virginia Woolf looks back at women in the sixteenth century and wonders why there were no great female poets at that time. She imagines that Shakespeare had a sister and creates a fictional world where this woman is kept uneducated and unchallenged. Even if she had been able to write, Woolf argues, this woman would have been so tormented by society and by her own internal conflict that she would have endangered her health and sanity.

Vocabulary

Etymology Have students use a dictionary to trace the etymologies of the vocabulary words. Point out that each word has a different source. **Ask:** From what languages were the following words taken? *thwart (Old Norse), hinder (Anglo-Saxon), dilemma (Greek), morbid (Latin)* Explain that *guffaw* is onomatopoeic: it mimics the sound it describes.

Literature and Reading Preview

Connect to the Essay

How do you think society views the "ideal woman"? Write a list of the qualities a woman in our society is expected to possess.

Build Background

Woolf wrote the essay "A Room of One's Own" during a time in which England's woman suffrage movement had won substantial victories. In 1918 the English government extended the right to vote to all British female citizens over the age of thirty. In 1928, a year before "A Room of One's Own" was published, the voting age for women was lowered to twenty-one. Woolf was an active supporter of the suffrage movement and other women's rights movements of the time even though many of the intellectuals she associated with scorned the agitation for increased women's rights. "A Room of One's Own" is based on "Women and Fiction," a series of lectures she delivered at Newnham and Girton colleges, Cambridge. In these lectures, she discussed the educational, social, and financial disadvantages that she believed had prevented women of the past from becoming successful writers.

Set Purposes for Reading

Big Idea Modernism

Modernism represented a break with both literary and social traditions. As you read, ask yourself, How does Woolf's essay reflect these changes?

Literary Element Argument

Argument is a type of persuasive writing in which logic or reason is used to try to influence a reader's ideas or actions. As you read Woolf's essay, ask yourself, How does she construct her argument about the obstacles faced by women writers?

Reading Strategy Analyze Tone

When you **analyze tone**, you think critically about how the writer's attitude toward a subject is conveyed through such elements as diction, sentence structure, imagery, and figures of speech. As you read, ask yourself, How does Woolf show her attitude toward traditional women's roles?

....

Tip: Interpreting Tone As you read, pause from time to time to consider Woolf's attitude toward the idea that women are inherently incapable of creating great art.

Learning Objectives

For pages 1103–1110

In studying this text, you will focus on the following objectives:

Literary Study: Interpreting argument.

Reading: Analyzing tone.

Listening and Speaking: Participating in a debate.

Vocabulary

guffaw (gu fô′) *v.* to laugh loudly and boisterously; p. 1106 *He guffawed at Marvin's ridiculous suggestion.*

thwart (thwôrt) *v.* to prevent from doing or achieving something; p. 1108 *The criminal was able to thwart detectives for several years.*

hinder (hin′ dər) *v.* to make difficult the progress of; to hold back; p. 1108 *If the drought continues, it will hinder the growth of corn.*

dilemma (di lem′ ə) *n.* a situation requiring a choice between equally undesirable alternatives; p. 1108 *When I was admitted to only the colleges I least wanted to attend, I faced the dilemma of choosing which offer to accept.*

morbid (môr′ bid) *adj.* overly sensitive to death and decay; not cheerful or wholesome; p. 1108 *People who suffer from depression are usually inclined toward morbid and unhappy thoughts.*

Reading Practice

SPIRAL REVIEW **Preview** Before students read the selection, have them preview it by skimming the first and last paragraphs. Ask them to write down their initial observations about the essay's topic, tone, and other features. Lead a discussion about their impressions, and have them support their comments with references to the text. (*Students should identify the topic as women writers and* *may describe the tone as ironic, angry, or sad.*) Then, ask them to begin reading carefully and to revise their notes as they clarify their understanding of Woolf's argument.

from

A Room of One's Own

Virginia Woolf

The Music Room, 30 Strandgade, 1907. Vilhelm Hammershoi. Oil on canvas. Private collection.

View the Art Solitude is a recurring theme in Hammershoi's paintings. What details create a sense of solitude or stillness in this image? ★

Here am I asking why women did not write poetry in the Elizabethan age, and I am not sure how they were educated; whether they were taught to write; whether they had sitting-rooms to themselves; how many women had children before they were twenty-one; what, in short, they did from eight in the morning till eight at night. They had no money evidently; according to Professor Trevelyan[1] they were married whether they liked it or not before they were out of the nursery, at fifteen or sixteen very likely. It would have been extremely odd, even upon this showing, had one of them suddenly written the plays of Shakespeare, I concluded, and I thought of that old gentleman, who is dead now, but was a bishop, I think, who declared that it was impossible for any woman, past, present, or to come, to have the genius of Shakespeare. He wrote to the papers about it. He also told a lady who applied to him for information that cats do not as a matter of fact go to heaven, though they have, he added, souls of a sort. How much thinking those old gentlemen used to save one! How the borders of ignorance shrank back at their approach! Cats do not go to heaven. Women cannot write the plays of Shakespeare.

Be that as it may, I could not help thinking, as I looked at the works of Shakespeare on the

---

1. *Professor Trevelyan* was a British historian and author who often wrote about the history of England.

Analyze Tone *How would you characterize Woolf's tone in this passage?* **2**

VIRGINIA WOOLF **1105**

Teach

Literary Element 1

Argument **Answer:** *Woolf tells the story of the bishop so that she can discredit his position. His story sets up the story of Shakespeare's fictional sister. Woolf is going to use the story of Judith to examine why a woman could not "have written the plays of Shakespeare in the age of Shakespeare."*

Literary Element 2

Argument **Answer:** *Woolf is setting up a contrast between the ways creative men and women are treated by society.*

Reading Strategy 3

Analyze Tone **Answer:** *Woolf is very matter-of-fact here. She has just portrayed the beating of a creative young girl. Thus, the answer to these questions is obvious. Woolf is disdainful of the idea that women are inherently incapable of creating great art.*

shelf, that the bishop was right at least in this; it would have been impossible, completely and entirely, for any woman to have written the plays of Shakespeare in the age of Shakespeare. Let me imagine, since facts are so hard to come by, what would have happened had Shakespeare had a wonderfully gifted sister, called Judith, let us say. Shakespeare himself went, very probably—his mother was an heiress—to the grammar school, where he may have learnt Latin—Ovid, Virgil, and Horace[2]—and the elements of grammar and logic. He was, it is well known, a wild boy who poached[3] rabbits, perhaps shot a deer, and had, rather sooner than he should have done, to marry a woman in the neighborhood, who bore him a child rather quicker than was right. That escapade[4] sent him to seek his fortune in London. He had, it seemed, a taste for the theater; he began by holding horses at the stage door. Very soon he got work in the theater, became a successful actor, and lived at the hub of the universe, meeting everybody, knowing everybody, practicing his art on the boards,[5] exercising his wits[6] in the streets, and even getting access to the palace of the queen. Meanwhile his extraordinarily gifted sister, let us suppose, remained at home. She was as adventurous, as imaginative, as agog[7] to see the world as he was. But she was not sent to school. She had no chance of learning grammar and logic, let alone of reading Horace and Virgil. She picked up a book now and then, one of her brother's perhaps, and read a few pages. But then her parents came in and told her to mend the stockings or mind the stew and not moon[8] about

---

2. *Ovid, Virgil,* and *Horace* were famous poets from ancient Rome who were commonly studied by students.
3. Here, *poached* means "hunted illegally."
4. An *escapade* is an unconventional adventure.
5. Here, *on the boards* means "onstage."
6. As it is used here, *wits* means "intelligence."
7. *Agog* means "full of interest or anticipation."
8. Here, *moon* means "to wander or pass time aimlessly."

---

1 Argument *Why does Woolf tell the story of the bishop? Why does she imagine that Shakespeare had a sister?*

2 Argument *What contrast is Woolf drawing here?*

with books and papers. They would have spoken sharply but kindly, for they were substantial people who knew the conditions of life for a woman and loved their daughter—indeed, more likely than not she was the apple of her father's eye. Perhaps she scribbled some pages up in an apple loft on the sly, but was careful to hide them or set fire to them. Soon, however, before she was out of her teens, she was to be betrothed[9] to the son of a neighboring wool stapler. She cried out that marriage was hateful to her, and for that she was severely beaten by her father. Then he ceased to scold her. He begged her instead not to hurt him, not to shame him in this matter of her marriage. He would give her a chain of beads or a fine petticoat, he said; and there were tears in his eyes. How could she disobey him? How could she break his heart? The force of her own gift alone drove her to it. She made up a small parcel of her belongings, let herself down by a rope one summer's night and took the road to London. She was not seventeen. The birds that sang in the hedge were not more musical than she was. She had the quickest fancy, a gift like her brother's, for the tune of words. Like him, she had a taste for the theater. She stood at the stage door; she wanted to act, she said. Men laughed in her face. The manager—a fat, loose-lipped man—**guffawed.** He bellowed something about poodles dancing and women acting—no woman, he said, could possibly be an actress. He hinted—you can imagine what. She could get no training in her craft. Could she even seek her dinner in a tavern or roam the streets at midnight? Yet her genius was for fiction and lusted to feed abundantly upon the lives of men and women and the study of their ways. At last—for she was very young, oddly like Shakespeare the poet in her face, with the same gray eyes and rounded brows—at last

---

9. *Betrothed* means "engaged to be married."

Analyze Tone *What is the tone of these questions? How do they demonstrate Woolf's attitude toward her subject?* **3**

Vocabulary

guffaw (gu fô´) *v.* to laugh loudly and boisterously

Writing Practice

Analyze an Essay

SPIRAL REVIEW Students will better understand and appreciate an essay if they can identify the author's purpose. Writing about what they read can help them. Remind students that the main purposes for writing are to express oneself, to inform, to entertain, and to persuade. Have students write analyses of "A Room of One's Own" in which they answer the following questions: What does the author want to accomplish in this essay? Does she succeed? Instruct students to include their own opinions as well.

A Maid with a Pail in the Backyard, c. 1660–1661. Pieter de Hooch. Oil on canvas, 48.2 x 42.9 cm. Private collection.

View the Art Pieter de Hooch depicted the domestic, middle class world in which he lived. How does this scene compare to the life Woolf describes for Judith Shakespeare?

Nick Greene the actor-manager took pity on her; she found herself with child by that gentleman and so—who shall measure the heat and violence of the poet's heart when caught and tangled in a woman's body?—killed herself one winter's night and lies buried at some crossroads where the omnibuses[10] now stop outside the Elephant and Castle.

That, more or less, is how the story would run, I think, if a woman in Shakespeare's day had had Shakespeare's genius. But for my part, I agree with the deceased bishop, if such he was—it is unthinkable that any woman in Shakespeare's day should have had Shakespeare's genius. For genius like Shakespeare's is not born among laboring, uneducated, servile people. It was not born in England among the Saxons and the Britons. It is not born today among the working classes. How, then, could it have been born among women whose work began, according to Professor Trevelyan, almost before

they were out of the nursery, who were forced to it by their parents and held to it by all the power of law and custom? Yet genius of a sort must have existed among women as it must have existed among the working classes. Now and again an Emily Brontë or a Robert Burns[11] blazes out and proves its presence. But certainly it never got itself on to paper. When, however, one reads of a witch being ducked, of a woman possessed by devils, of a wise woman selling herbs, or even of a very remarkable man who had a mother, then I think we are on the track of a lost novelist, a suppressed poet, of some mute and inglorious Jane Austen,[12] some Emily Brontë who dashed her brains out on the moor

---

11. *Brontë* overcame the obstacle of being a woman, and *Burns* overcame the obstacle of being from the working class; both became famous writers.
12. *[Some . . . Austen]* alludes to a line from Thomas Gray's "Elegy Written in a Country Churchyard," which reads, "Some mute inglorious Milton here may rest."

Modernism *How does this statement represent a break with traditional beliefs?* **5**

---

10. *Omnibuses* is another term for "buses."

VIRGINIA WOOLF **1107**

Teach

Literary Element 4

Imagery Ask: How does Woolf describe the despair of the young woman? *(Woolf writes of the "heat and violence" in the poet's heart, which are "caught and tangled" in her body.)*

ENGLISH LEARNERS Tell English learners that *heat and violence* and *caught and tangled* are examples of figurative language. **Ask:** What feeling might heat and violence describe? *(anger)* What feelings do caught and tangled suggest? *(frustration, fear)*

Big Idea 5

Modernism Answer: *Woolf is challenging the traditional view that the upper classes are inherently more intelligent and creative. The lack of literature by women and members of the working class is related to a lack of time rather than a lack of genius.*

View the Art

Answer: *The woman seems preoccupied with chores. She seems isolated and unhappy.*

A Dutch painter and manservant, Pieter de Hooch (1629–1684) painted scenes with which he was quite familiar: middle-class life and domesticity. When attempting to paint scenes depicting upper-class life, de Hooch was not successful. Fading into obscurity, he died in an insane asylum in 1684.

1107

Teach

Argument Answer: *Woolf describes in great detail the plight of a woman author whose genius rivals Shakespeare's but who is denied the opportunity to write because of her gender.*

[ENGLISH LEARNERS] **Ask:** What does Woolf say would have happened to a 16th century woman with a gift for writing? Cite words from the text to support your answer. *(She would have "gone crazed," shot herself, or had been feared and labeled a witch or wizard.)*

View the Art ★

Answer: *The mood of the painting is one of quiet, stillness, order, or solitude. Student interpretations of Woolf's reaction will vary, but many will say that Woolf might see the painting as depicting the loneliness and tedium of a domestic woman's life.*

Ask: How does this scene confirm the tedium of everyday life for women in the past? *(Students' answers will vary.)*

Interior with Sewing Woman, early nineteenth century. Ascribed to Fedor Petrovich Tolstoi. Oil on canvas, 42 x 46.8 cm. Tretjakov Gallery, Moscow.

View the Art Like the image on page 1107, this painting depicts the life of a middle-class woman. What is the mood of this image? What might Woolf read into it?

or mopped and mowed about the highways crazed with the torture that her gift had put her to. Indeed, I would venture to guess that Anon,[13] who wrote so many poems without signing them, was often a woman. It was a woman Edward FitzGerald,[14] I think, suggested who made the ballads and the folk songs, crooning them to her children, beguiling her spinning with them, or the length of the winter's night.

This may be true or it may be false—who can say?—but what is true in it, so it seemed to me, reviewing the story of Shakespeare's sister as I had made it, is that any woman born with a great gift in the sixteenth century would certainly have gone crazed, shot herself, or ended her days in some lonely cottage outside the village, half witch, half wizard, feared and mocked at. For it needs little skill in psychology to be sure that a highly gifted girl who had tried to use her gift for poetry would have been so **thwarted** and **hindered** by other people, so tor-

tured and pulled asunder by her own contrary instincts, that she must have lost her health and sanity to a certainty. No girl could have walked to London and stood at a stage door and forced her way into the presence of actor-managers without doing herself a violence and suffering an anguish which may have been irrational—for chastity[15] may be a fetish invented by certain societies for unknown reasons—but were none the less inevitable. Chastity had then, it has even now, a religious importance in a woman's life, and has so wrapped itself round with nerves and instincts that to cut it free and bring it to the light of day demands courage of the rarest. To have lived a free life in London in the sixteenth century would have meant for a woman who was poet and playwright a nervous stress and **dilemma** which might well have killed her. Had she survived, whatever she had written would have been twisted and deformed, issuing from a strained and **morbid** imagination. And undoubtedly, I thought, looking at the shelf where there are no plays by women, her work would have gone unsigned. ∾

---

15. *Chastity* is the quality or state of being morally pure.

Argument *How does Woolf's argument support this statement?* **1**

Vocabulary

dilemma (di lem′ ə) *n.* a situation requiring a choice between equally undesirable alternatives
morbid (môr′ bid) *adj.* overly sensitive to death and decay; not cheerful or wholesome

---

13. *Anon* is the abbreviation for "Anonymous."
14. *Edward FitzGerald* was an English poet and translator.

Vocabulary

thwart (thwôrt) *v.* to prevent from doing or achieving something
hinder (hin′ dər) *v.* to make difficult the progress of; to hold back

1108 UNIT 6 THE MODERN AGE

Grammar Practice

SPIRAL REVIEW **Verb Tenses** Explain to students that each of the six verb tenses has a progressive form that describes a continuing action. Each progressive form is created by combining an appropriate tense of the verb *be* with the present participle of the main verb.

He *is dancing* to swing music.

We *were reading* the whole time.

Have students write five sentences about "A Room of One's Own" in which they use progressive verb forms.

Respond and Think Critically

Respond and Interpret

1. What was your response to Woolf's argument?

2. (a)How does Woolf feel about the bishop's comments about women? (b)Summarize and explain the extended **analogy** in the second paragraph that Woolf uses to support her view.

3. (a)In the third paragraph, who is "Anon"? (b)What point does Woolf make through the use of this name?

Analyze and Evaluate

4. What is the main message of Woolf's essay?

5. (a)In your opinion, was Woolf's primary purpose to inform, persuade, entertain, or disprove the views of others? Explain. (b)Do you believe Woolf effectively fulfills her purpose? Why or why not?

6. (a)How do you think a sixteenth-century Englishman might define the "ideal woman"? (b)In your opinion, are Woolf's views still relevant today? Explain.

Connect

7. **Big Idea** **Modernism** How does Woolf's essay reflect the Modernist break with tradition?

8. **Connect to Today** The bishop in Woolf's essay has concrete notions about the roles of men and women. What assumptions about gender roles do we have—or struggle with—today?

Literary Element **Argument**

An **argument** is an opinion supported by carefully chosen facts and logical reasoning.

1. (a)Summarize Professor Trevelyan's and the unnamed bishop's comments about women, as presented in the first paragraph. (b)What point might Woolf be making by including the comment about cats?

2. (a)In the fourth paragraph, what fate does Woolf believe a gifted sixteenth-century woman would have suffered? (b)What evidence does Woolf offer in support of her view?

Review: Rhetorical Devices

When an author's purpose is to persuade an audience, the author will often employ rhetorical devices, or techniques meant to create a particular effect or emotional response. Common persuasive rhetorical devices include **analogies**—comparisons that bring out the similarities between otherwise different things—and **rhetorical questions**, or questions whose answers are so obvious, they need not be stated.

This excerpt from "A Room of One's Own" contains an elaborate analogy comparing the life of Shakespeare, a creative man, with the hypothetical life of a creative woman in Shakespeare's time.

Partner Activity With a partner, fill in a chart tracking the rhetorical questions Woolf poses throughout the essay. In the right-hand column of the chart, note how Woolf expects her readers to answer each question.

Rhetorical Question	Expected Answer
"Could she even seek her dinner in a tavern or roam the streets at midnight?"	Of course not, it would not have been proper.

1. Students' answers will vary.

2. (a) Women could have genius but could not express it. (b) Shakespeare's fictional sister's genius was destroyed because she was a woman.

3. (a) "Anon" may have been female. (b) Women did not dare use their own names.

4. Women were denied opportunities.

5. (a) Woolf wanted to persuade her readers that women's genius has always existed but has been unrecognized. (b) Answers will vary.

6. (a) Women's main purpose was to marry and bear children and not be educated. (b) Answers will vary.

7. The conventions and social structure associated with literature have inhibited innovation and the participation of women.

8. Student answers will vary.

Literary Element

1. (a) Trevelyan remarks that women were married very early; the bishop believed women could never have been Shakespeare's equal. (b) Just as cats cannot go to heaven, women cannot write.

2. (a) A gifted woman would have lost her health, her sanity, or even her life through desperation. (b) Society would have tortured such a woman.

Review: Rhetorical Devices

Student's charts should use text evidence to support their answers to each question Woolf poses.

After You Read

Reading Strategy

1. Woolf's comments about the professor and the bishop and about chastity are sarcastic.

2. The overall tone is angry; Woolf's statement that a woman who wrote would have produced "twisted and deformed" work is evidence of her anger.

Vocabulary

guffaw; <u>Definition</u>: to laugh loudly and boisterously; <u>Etymology</u>: Scots *gawf* means "to laugh noisily";

thwart; <u>Definition</u>: to prevent from doing or achieving something; <u>Etymology</u>: Old Norse *tvert* means "across";

hinder; <u>Definition</u>: to make difficult the progress of; <u>Etymology</u>: Old English *hindrian* means "to keep back";

dilemma; <u>Definition</u>: a situation requiring a choice between two alternatives; <u>Etymology</u>: Greek *dilemma* means "double proposition";

morbid; <u>Definition</u>: not cheerful or wholesome; <u>Etymology</u>: Latin *morbidus* means "diseased";

Sample Sentences will vary.

Academic Vocabulary

1. Students should infer that *normal* means "healthy" or "as usual."

2. Students should infer that a *normal distribution* is a mathematical term referring to a bell curve.

Writers use a variety of literary elements to craft **tone**, including text structure and imagery.

1. At what points in the essay is Woolf sarcastic?

2. In your opinion, what is the overall tone of the essay? Support your opinion with passages and ideas from the selection.

Vocabulary Practice

Practice with Word Origins Create a word map for each of the boldface vocabulary words from the selection. Use a dictionary for help.

guffaw   thwart   hinder   dilemma   morbid

EXAMPLE:

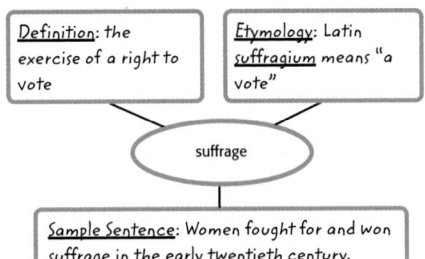

Academic Vocabulary

Woolf argues that in Shakespeare's time, it was **normal** *for women to be denied their potential.*

Normal is an academic word. Something that conforms to a standard is called **normal**. This word can have different meanings in different subject areas. Using context clues, try to figure out the meaning of *normal* in each sentence:

1. He had been home from the hospital for a week and was finally feeling **normal** again.

2. The teacher wanted a **normal** distribution of grades so they would form a bell curve.

For more on academic vocabulary, see pages 56 and R81.

Speaking and Listening

 Debate

Assignment In this selection from "A Room of One's Own," Woolf uses a highly creative analogy to support her ideas about women. Hold a debate on the validity and effectiveness of this analogy.

Prepare Clearly and simply state your thesis about Woolf's analogy. Then gather evidence and formulate logical arguments to create a persuasive case. Take notes and use a graphic organizer, such as an outline or chart, to help order your thoughts.

Debate In presenting your point of view, think about your audience's perspective and craft your arguments to address their concerns. Argue both deductively—from the general to the specific—and inductively—from the specific to the general—using emotional appeals to bolster your evidence and reasoning. Also, consider using analogies of your own to explain your reaction to Woolf's analogy.

EXAMPLE:

Woolf's analogy between Shakespeare and his hypothetical sister is like comparing _____ and _____. The effect of her argument is _____.

Evaluate Assess your own as well as your classmates' debate skills. Consider elements such as the clarity of presentation, effectiveness of support, and appropriateness of diction and tone of voice. Based on these elements, name the side with the strongest, most effective presentation the "winner" of the debate, and explain your choice.

Speaking and Listening

Use these criteria in evaluating student debates:

- The discussion stays focused on the effectiveness of Woolf's analogy.

- Statements exhibit solid reasoning, adequate support, and persuasive emotional appeals.

- Individuals accurately evaluate their own and others' participation in the debate based on appropriate criteria.

PART 3

World War II and Its Aftermath

It's a Long, Long Way, 1941. Henry Lamb. Oil on canvas. South African National Gallery, Cape Town.

<u>View the Art</u> Henry Lamb was a member of a group of artists called the Camden Town group, which took its inspiration from everyday life in British industrial towns. In what ways does this image have an "everyday" style?

"What is absurd and monstrous about war is that men who have no personal quarrel should be trained to murder one another in cold blood."

1

—Aldous Huxley, "Words and Behavior"

Analyze and Extend

Big Idea **1**

World War II and Its Aftermath Focus students' attention on the quotation. **Ask:** What attitude toward war do Huxley's words express? *(Disillusionment; opposition to war. He calls war "absurd and monstrous" and describes combat as "murder[ing] one another in cold blood.")*

<u>View the Art</u>

Answer: *Most students will say that the casual poses of the soldiers, the lack of any specific activity, and the peaceful surroundings give the painting an "everyday" feel.*

A founding member of the Camden Town Group in 1911, Henry Lamb (1883–1960) was mostly a Postimpressionist. The Camden Town Group drew inspiration from a painter who created dark paintings in a gritty, working-class section of London. In addition to serving as a medic in World War I, Lamb was an Official War Artist in both world wars. **Ask:** What do you think was the artist's purpose in creating this work? *(perhaps to capture a typical moment in the war)*

Approaching Level

DIFFERENTIATED INSTRUCTION

Established Have students look at the quotation and determine the writer's attitude toward war. Explain that the attitude apparent in a piece of writing is called tone. Point out that word choice helps create tone. **Ask:** What is the tone of the quotation? *(bitter, disillusioned)* Which words help create that tone? *(monstrous,* *murder, cold blood)* Encourage students to be alert for tone as they read the works in Part 3.

 For additional support for English Learners, see Unit 6 Teaching Resources Book, p. 178.

Before You Read

Be Ye Men of Valor

Meet **Winston Churchill**
(1874–1965)

"Blood, toil, tears, and sweat." These unforgettable words of Winston Churchill were not merely a rallying cry, but his approach to life. He is perhaps one of the most renowned prime ministers of Great Britain, inspiring a nation and leading it to victory in the face of World War II.

"You ask, what is our aim? I can answer in one word: Victory—victory at all costs, victory in spite of all terror; victory, however long and hard the road may be."

—Winston Churchill

Lasting Influences Churchill's childhood profoundly influenced his beliefs and career (in addition to his political positions, Churchill was a soldier, journalist, writer, historian, and painter). Born to Lord Randolph Churchill, a conservative member of Parliament, and the American heiress Jennie Jerome, Churchill was unable to form a bond with either of his parents, particularly his aloof father, whom he greatly admired. From an early age he was fascinated with soldiers and historic battles, and his father enrolled him in England's Royal Military College at Sandhurst. After graduation Churchill served as a junior officer in the British army and later as a war correspondent in Cuba, India, and South Africa. After his famous escape from a Pretoria prisoner-of-war camp, Churchill used the profits from his writings and lectures to pursue a career in politics. Throughout his career—even after his father's death—Churchill's political interests would mirror those of his father.

Political Career Churchill's military experience and his background as a writer gave him a unique advantage in the political realm. He served in numerous positions in Parliament, including home secretary, first lord of the Admiralty, minister of munitions, secretary of state for war and air, and secretary for the colonies. In 1940 Churchill became prime minister just as the Germans invaded Belgium—a post he held until the end of the war and the defeat of the Axis powers.

A Literary Knight At the age of seventy-one, Churchill was voted out of office as prime minister, but he was reelected six years later. In 1953 he was knighted and awarded the Nobel Prize in Literature for his work on history and politics, *The Second World War* (published in six volumes, 1948–1953), in particular. Ten years later Churchill left public office to spend his last years writing, painting, and traveling. The scope of his achievements impacted not only England but the entire world.

Literature Online

Author Search For more about Winston Churchill, go to glencoe.com and enter QuickPass code GLB9817u6.

Selection Skills

Literary Elements
 ▪ Rhetoric (SE pp. 1113, 1117, 1118)
 ▪ Structure (SE p. 1118)

Be Ye Men of Valor

Listening/Speaking/ Viewing Skills
 ▪ Analyze Art (SE pp. 1114, 1116)

Reading Skills
 ▪ Distinguish Fact and Opinion (SE pp. 1113, 1115, 1116, 1118)

Vocabulary Skills
 ▪ Context Clues (SE p. 1119)
 ▪ Academic Vocabulary (SE p. 1119)

Writing Skills/Grammar
 ▪ Speech (SE p. 1119)

Literature and Reading Preview

Connect to the Speech

Have you ever found your courage tested? Freewrite for a few minutes about the event and its effect on you.

Build Background

Delivered on May 19, 1940, "Be Ye Men of Valor" was Churchill's first radio broadcast as British prime minister. In the speech, Churchill refuses to negotiate or compromise with Adolf Hitler. Initially, Churchill believed Britain would be fighting the Nazis alone. "There is one thing that will bring Hitler down, and that is an absolutely devastating, exterminating attack by very heavy bombers from this country upon the Nazi homeland," Churchill wrote, describing the bombing plan. He was still carrying out these strategies when the United States joined the war after the attack on Pearl Harbor in 1941.

Set Purposes for Reading

Big Idea World War II and Its Aftermath

As you read, ask yourself, How does Churchill inspire confidence and courage in the British people?

Literary Element Rhetoric

Rhetoric is the art of using language to present facts and ideas in order to persuade an audience. As you read Churchill's speech, ask yourself, How does he combine logic, emotion, and artful phrases to inform the public about the German advance and to express his confidence in his troops and the Allied cause?

Reading Strategy Distinguish Fact and Opinion

A **fact** is a statement that can be proved true. An **opinion**, however, is a statement of someone's personal beliefs or feelings, and it cannot be proved. As you read, ask yourself, Is this statement provable, or is it an opinion?

....

Tip: Taking Notes Use a chart to distinguish facts from opinions in Churchill's speech.

Facts	Opinions
"our heavy bombers are striking nightly . . ."	"It would be foolish, however, to disguise the gravity of the hour."

Learning Objectives

For pages 1112–1119

In studying this text, you will focus on the following objectives:

Literary Study: Understanding rhetoric.

Reading: Distinguishing fact and opinion.

Writing: Applying parallelism in a speech.

Vocabulary

ravage (rav′ ij) *v.* to lay waste to; destroy; p. 1115 *The air raids will ravage the city, destroying churches, homes, and factories.*

grapple (grap′ əl) *v.* to attempt to deal with; struggle; p. 1116 *He grappled with the idea of conceding but realized victory was the only option.*

imperious (im pēr′ ē əs) *adj.* imperative; urgent; p. 1117 *The nation faced imperious problems and needed to utilize all of its resources to survive.*

indomitable (in dom′ ə tə bəl) *adj.* incapable of being subdued or overcome; p. 1117 *The captain's indomitable spirit carried his men through the horrible battle.*

Before You Read

Focus

Summary

In this speech, Prime Minister Churchill speaks over the radio to the people of Great Britain to tell them of the German advance into France. He attempts to instill confidence about the British and French efforts to keep the Germans at bay, but he also warns that it is possible that the German forces will be unleashed on England. Churchill expresses his determination to fight to the end and to win the war or, if the war is lost, to lose by dying gloriously in battle.

 For summaries in languages other than English, see Unit 6 Teaching Resources Book, pp. 179–184.

Vocabulary

Use the vocabulary words to preview the selection and to practice identifying and explaining rhetoric. **Ask:** If Churchill's goal is to inspire the British people, why might he have chosen these words? What effect would they have on people? *(to make the public aware of the threat or to assure victory)* Discuss with students the contexts in which each word is likely to be discussed. *(battles; the sacrifices of citizens; negotiations by politicians)*

 For additional vocabulary practice, see Unit 6 Teaching Resources Book, p. 187.

English Learners

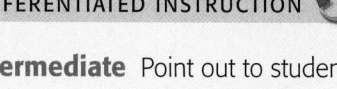

DIFFERENTIATED INSTRUCTION

Intermediate Point out to students that the use of rhetoric is not limited to Churchill but is a skill students encounter every day. Ask students to recall a speech they heard recently from a parent, coach, religious figure, or politician. **Ask:** What was this person trying to persuade you to do? What did they do to convince you? *(Answers will vary.)* Encourage students to identify specific words, tones of voice, or actions adopted by the speaker. Write these purposes and techniques on the board and discuss as a class ways people try to persuade others. Then preview the selection by reminding students that Churchill had to persuade an entire country to go to war.

Teach

View the Photograph ★

Answer: *Churchill might have wanted to show both the British and the Germans that British leadership was not afraid of bombings or invasion and would remain calm and strong in the face of destruction.*

Point out that the photographic images created during wartime not only provide information but also serve as powerful tools of propaganda.

For an audio recording of this selection, use Listening Library Audio CD-ROM.

Readability Scores

Dale-Chall: 8.2
DRP: 66
Lexile: 1280

Prime Minister Churchill inspects a bomb crater.

View the Photograph From late 1940 to early 1941, the city of London and much of its surroundings were the target of sustained bombing by German planes. Why might Churchill have wanted photographs of his visits to bomb craters? ★

Be Ye Men of Valor

Winston Churchill

Study Skills Practice

Note Taking Encourage students to research the following events in World War II:

a. Hitler annexes Austria

b. The Battle of Britain

c. Victory in Europe

d. Germany invades Poland

e. Victory over Japan

f. United States enters the war

g. France falls

Ask students to focus their research by first drawing on their knowledge to place the events in chronological order. *(a, d, g, b, f, c, e)* Students' notes should include the exact date of each event as well as a brief summary.

BBC, LONDON, 19 MAY 1940

I speak to you for the first time as Prime Minister in a solemn hour for the life of our country, of our Empire, of our Allies,[1] and, above all, of the cause of Freedom. A tremendous battle is raging in France and Flanders. The Germans, by a remarkable combination of air bombing and heavily armored tanks, have broken through the French defenses north of the Maginot Line,[2] and strong columns of their armored vehicles are **ravaging** the open country, which for the first day or two was without defenders. They have penetrated deeply and spread alarm and confusion in their track. Behind them there are now appearing infantry in lorries,[3] and behind them, again, the large masses are moving forward. The regroupment of the French armies to make head against, and also to strike at, this intruding wedge has been proceeding for several days, largely assisted by the magnificent efforts of the Royal Air Force.

We must not allow ourselves to be intimidated by the presence of these armored vehicles in unexpected places behind our lines. If

they are behind our Front, the French are also at many points fighting actively behind theirs. Both sides are therefore in an extremely dangerous position. And if the French Army, and our own Army, are well handled, as I believe they will be; if the French retain that genius for recovery and counter-attack for which they have so long been famous; and if the British Army shows the dogged endurance and solid fighting power of which there have been so many examples in the past— then a sudden transformation of the scene might spring into being.

It would be foolish, however, to disguise the gravity[4] of the hour. It would be still more foolish to lose heart and courage or to suppose that well-trained, well-equipped armies numbering three or four millions of men can be overcome in the space of a few weeks, or even months, by a scoop, or raid of mechanized vehicles, however formidable.[5] We may look with confidence to the stabilization of the Front in France, and to the general engagement of the masses, which will enable the qualities of the French and British soldiers to be matched squarely against those of their adversaries.[6] For myself, I have invincible confidence in the French Army and its leaders. Only a very small part of that splendid army has yet been heavily engaged; and only a very small part of France has yet been invaded. There is good evidence to show that practically the whole of the specialized and mechanized forces of the enemy have been already thrown into the battle; and we know that very heavy losses have been inflicted upon them. No officer or man, no brigade or division,

> "No officer or man, no brigade or division, which grapples at close quarters with the enemy, wherever encountered, can fail to make a worthy contribution to the general result."

---

1. At the date of this speech, Britain's allies were France and several smaller countries that were occupied by German troops.
2. The *Maginot Line* was a heavily fortified line of defense in France that was assembled to stave off the Germans.
3. *Lorries* are British motor trucks.

 World War II and Its Aftermath *How do Churchill's opening lines reflect the attitude of the British during World War II?*

 Distinguish Fact and Opinion *What major fact is Churchill talking about? In his opinion, how should the British deal with that fact?*

Vocabulary

ravage (rav´ ij) *v.* to lay waste to; destroy

---

4. Here, *gravity* means "seriousness" or "importance."
5. *Formidable* means "arousing fear or dread."
6. *Adversaries* are opponents.

WINSTON CHURCHILL **1115**

Teach

Teach

Reading Strategy | 1

Distinguish Fact and Opinion Answer: *That the British are shooting down enemy planes is a fact; Churchill's confidence in the Allies' ability is an opinion.*

(ADVANCED) To challenge advanced students, **ask:** How does Churchill's use of diction in this paragraph express his opinion and persuade his listeners? *(Verbs like* cutting *and* clawing *and phrases like "fighting our own battles" and "the taproot of German mechanized power" convey the valor of the British fighting forces.)*

View the Photograph ★

Answer: *The photo underscores the gravity of war and its destruction. It conveys the devastation that will occur across Great Britain.*

Ask: What is the mood of the photograph, and how does the photographer create it? *(The photographer achieves a stark, pensive mood by creating a high-contrast image. Churchill and Bracken appear as dark silhouettes against a brightly lit scene of destruction.)*

which **grapples** at close quarters with the enemy, wherever encountered, can fail to make a worthy contribution to the general result. The Armies must cast away the idea of resisting behind concrete lines or natural obstacles, and must realize that mastery can only be regained by furious and unrelenting assault. And this spirit must not only animate the High Command, but must inspire every fighting man.

In the air—often at serious odds—often at odds hitherto thought overwhelming —we have been clawing down three or four to one of our enemies; and the relative balance of the British and German Air Forces is now considerably more favorable to us than at the beginning of the battle. In cutting down the German bombers, we are fighting our own battle as well as that of France. My confidence in our ability to fight it out to the finish with the German Air Force has been strengthened by the fierce encounters which have taken place and are taking place. At the same time, our heavy bombers are striking nightly at the taproot[7] of German mechanized power, and have already inflicted serious damage upon the oil refineries on which the Nazi effort to dominate the world directly depends.

We must expect that as soon as stability is reached on the Western Front, the bulk of that

---

7. As it is used here, *taproot* means "the most important part."

1 **Distinguish Fact and Opinion** *Which elements of this paragraph are fact and which are opinion?*

Vocabulary

grapple (grap′ əl) *v.* to attempt to deal with; struggle

Prime Minister Winston Churchill and Brendan Bracken survey bomb damage to the Houses of Parliament, London.

View the Photograph Londoners during the "Blitz," as it came to be called, led their lives as normally as possible despite devastating damage, injuries, and fatalities. Does seeing this photograph of actual war damage add to your appreciation of the speech? Explain. ★

hideous apparatus of aggression which gashed Holland into ruin and slavery in a few days, will be turned upon us. I am sure I speak for all when I say we are ready to face it; to endure it; and to retaliate against it—to any extent that the unwritten laws of war permit. There will be many men, and many women, in this island who when the ordeal comes upon them, as come it will, will feel comfort, and even a pride—that they are sharing the perils of our lads at the Front—soldiers, sailors, and airmen, God bless them—and are drawing away from them a part at least of the onslaught they have

Listening and Speaking Practice

Identify Types of Persuasive Speech
Have students listen to this speech on the StudentWorks Plus CD, the Online Student Edition, or the Listening Library CD, paying special attention to the speaker's pattern of organization, use of persuasive language, reasoning, and proof. Ask students to identify which of the four basic types of persuasive speech (propositions of fact, value, problem, or policy) the selection

represents, and to identify any logical fallacies the speaker uses. Refer students to pages R60 and R62 of the Logic and Persuasion Handbook for more on persuasive techniques.

to bear. Is not this the appointed time for all to make the utmost exertions in their power? If the battle is to be won, we must provide our men with ever-increasing quantities of the weapons and ammunition they need. We must have, and have quickly, more airplanes, more tanks, more shells, more guns. There is **2** imperious need for these vital munitions. They increase our strength against the powerfully armed enemy. They replace the wastage of the obstinate[8] struggle; and the knowledge that wastage will speedily be replaced enables us to draw more readily upon our reserves and throw them in now that everything counts so much.

Our task is not only to win the battle—but to win the War. After this battle in France abates[9] its force, there will come the battle for our island—for all that Britain is, and all that Britain means. That will be the struggle. In that supreme emergency we shall not hesitate to take every step, even the most drastic, to call forth from our people the last ounce and the last inch of effort of which they are capable. The interests of property, the hours of labor, are nothing compared with the struggle for life and honor, for right and freedom, to which we have vowed ourselves.

I have received from the Chiefs of the French Republic, and in particular from its **indomitable** Prime Minister, M. Reynaud, the most sacred pledges that whatever happens they will fight to the end, be it bitter or be it glorious. Nay, if we fight to the end, it can only be glorious.

Having received His Majesty's commission, I have found an administration of men and women of every party and of almost every point of view. We have differed and quarreled in the past; but now one bond unites us all— to wage war until victory is won, and never to surrender ourselves to servitude and shame, whatever the cost and the agony may be. This is one of the most awe-striking periods in the long history of France and Britain. It is also beyond doubt the most sublime. Side by side, unaided except by their kith and kin in the great Dominions and by the wide Empires which rest beneath their shield—side by side, the British and French peoples have advanced to rescue not only Europe but mankind from the foulest and most soul-destroying tyranny which has ever darkened and stained the pages of history. Behind them—behind us—behind the armies and fleets of Britain and France— gather a group of shattered States and blud-geoned[10] races: the Czechs, the Poles, the Norwegians, the Danes, the Dutch, the Belgians—upon all of whom the long night of barbarism will descend, unbroken even by a star of hope, unless we conquer, as conquer we must; as conquer we shall.

Today is Trinity Sunday.[11] Centuries ago words were written to be a call and a spur to the faithful servants of Truth and Justice: "Arm yourselves, and be ye men of valor, and be in readiness for the conflict; for it is better for us to perish in battle than to look upon the out-rage of our nation and our altar. As the Will of God is in Heaven, even so let it be."[12]

---

8. *Obstinate* means "stubborn."
9. *Abates* means "reduces in intensity."

10. As it is used here, *bludgeoned* means "bullied or beaten."
11. *Trinity Sunday* is the first Sunday after Pentecost (the fiftieth day after Easter) in the Christian calendar.
12. In this quotation from 1 Maccabees 3:58–60, Judas Maccabeus, the leader of a Jewish rebellion during the second century B.C., urges his army before a battle against the Syrians, who then ruled Judaea.

3 Rhetoric *In what way does Churchill use rhetoric here? What is the effect?*

4 Rhetoric *Is Churchill exaggerating in this passage? What rhetorical technique does he use?*

English Learners

DIFFERENTIATED INSTRUCTION

Beginning Encourage students to collect examples of the emotional words that Churchill chooses. Have students classify the words as positive (*honor, glorious, sublime, valor*) and negative (*hideous, servitude, shame, foulest, soul-destroying, barbarism*).

Advanced Learners

DIFFERENTIATED INSTRUCTION

Audio Analysis Winston Churchill's distinctive voice was an important part of his effectiveness as a speaker. Encourage students to locate recordings of Churchill's speeches on the Internet. Ask them to characterize Churchill's speaking style.

Teach

Vocabulary　2

Multiple Meanings
Say: Many words, such as *imperious*, can have more than one meaning. Have students compare dictionary definitions to the one on the page. **Ask:** How can you tell which meaning of the word Churchill uses? (*The word describes a need, not a person, so* urgency *fits best.*)

(ENGLISH LEARNERS) Explain to English learners who speak Spanish that the Spanish form of *imperi-ous (imperioso)* has the same dual meaning. Have students write a sentence in Spanish for each definition and discuss appropriate contexts for using the term.

Literary Element　3

Rhetoric **Answer:** *His loaded words appeal to emotion, invoking patriotism and sacrifice.*

(APPROACHING) Ask approaching level students to identify specific words that demonstrate Churchill's use of rhetoric in this section. Call on students to explain the words' ideological or emotional conno-tations and to discuss why they might be persuasive.

Literary Element　4

Rhetoric **Answer:** *Many students will notice that loaded words like* foulest *and* soul-destroying *are examples of hyperbole.*

To check students' understanding of the selection, see Unit 6 Teaching Resources Book, p. 190.

After You Read

Assess

1. Perhaps awed or patriotic

2. (a) Movements of the Germans in France (b) Perhaps fear or urgency

3. (a) The French have genius for counterattack; the British, dogged endurance. (b) To keep hope alive

4. Most students will find his language effective; he evokes emotions of fear and pride.

5. (a) The oppression of German occupation (b) Students may find it effective; it inspires courage and hope. (c) Many students will agree, because the war stopped the Nazis.

6. Churchill portrays war as noble to incite a sense of patriotism.

7. Answers will vary. One example might be the speech given by George W. Bush after the terrorist attacks in New York and Washington, D.C., on September 11, 2001.

Literary Element

He appeals primarily to emotion. Emotional appeals might bolster people's courage.

Review: Structure

Students should accurately characterize the main argument and the arrangement of ideas and should plausibly evaluate the contribution of structure to the speech's persuasiveness.

Progress Check

Can students distinguish fact and opinion?

If No → See Unit 6 Teaching Resources Book, p. 186.

After You Read

Respond and Think Critically

Respond and Interpret

1. If you had been listening to the live broadcast of this speech as a British citizen, how might you have felt? Explain.

2. (a) What does Churchill describe in the first paragraph? (b) What emotions does he convey with his use of descriptive language?

3. (a) How does Churchill describe the British and French armies? (b) Why might he describe them this way?

Analyze and Evaluate

4. Is Churchill's use of **loaded words**—language that expresses strong emotion—effective? Explain.

5. Churchill ends his speech with a quote: "it is better for us to perish in battle than to look upon the outrage of our nation and our altar." (a) What outrage might he be referring to? (b) Is this an effective end to his speech? Explain. (c) Do you agree with his assertion? Why or why not?

Connect

6. **Big Idea** World War II and Its Aftermath Churchill chooses to foster the idea that war is a noble, even a sublime, effort. Why do you think he portrays war in this manner?

7. **Connect to Today** Have any recent events prompted the kind of "call to action" that you find in Churchill's speech? Explain, giving example.

Literary Element Rhetoric

Common rhetorical devices include **rhetorical questions**, or questions to which no answer is expected; **parallelism**, in which words, phrases, or sentences are balanced in structure; and **loaded words**, which appeal to emotion.

Does Churchill appeal primarily to emotions or to intellect? How might this choice have helped persuade his audience?

Review: Structure

Writers can improve the persuasive power of a speech or a work of literature by paying close attention to how they structure their arguments. An argument organized in a meaningful way will carry more weight than one with points scattered throughout, or unclear connections between ideas.

Partner Activity With a partner, outline the main argument of Churchill's speech. Then write two or three paragraphs evaluating the structure he uses. Does the arrangement of ideas make the speech more persuasive? Support your opinion.

Reading Strategy Distinguish Fact and Opinion

Distinguishing fact and opinion enables listeners and readers to evaluate the information they receive.

Does Churchill rely more heavily on facts or on opinions to persuade his audience? Explain. Why does Churchill include his opinions in his speech?

LOG ON Literature Online

Selection Resources For Selection Quizzes, eFlashcards, and Reading-Writing Connection activities, go to glencoe.com and enter QuickPass code GLB9817u6.

Reading Strategy

Churchill uses facts but relies more heavily on his opinions and emotions. Much of what he says cannot be proven. His opinions are meant to inspire his audience.

For additional assessment, see Assessment Resources, pp. 267–268.

Vocabulary Practice

Practice with Context Clues Look back at pages 1115–1117 to find context clues for the vocabulary words below. Record your findings in a chart like the one here.

ravage   grapple   imperious   indomitable

EXAMPLE:

Word: *ravage*

Textual Clues: The Germans have "spread alarm and confusion in their track," so they must be causing destruction and terror.

Meaning: to lay waste to; to destroy

Academic Vocabulary

Churchill urges the British people to rally together and support the war effort; only **thereby** *can they hope to defeat Germany.*

Thereby is an academic word that can be used to describe everyday cause-effect relationships. For example, a football player might score a touchdown, **thereby** winning the game for his team.

Using context clues, try to figure out the meaning of *thereby* in the following sentence: *My grandmother gave me money, and I paid for the guitar I wanted* **thereby**.

For more on academic vocabulary, see pages 56 and R81.

Write with Style

 Apply Parallelism

Assignment Winston Churchill was a master of rhetoric and used language like a razor-sharp sword. Using Churchill's address as a model, compose an inspirational speech to be delivered at a graduation ceremony. Include rhetorical techniques such as emotional appeals and parallelism.

Get Ideas Make an outline of the points you want to include in your speech. By each point, jot down emotional appeals or parallelism—similar phrasing of words, phrases, or sentences—you can use to strengthen your presentation.

Into the Future!

I. What we took from high school.

    a. friends ("friends who will stand with us through thick and thin"

    b. knowledge

II. What we can look forward to

    a.

    b.

Give It Structure Remember that your purpose is to inspire your audience, so take their knowledge and interests into consideration as you write. Organize your statements logically and support each with examples, facts, or statistics.

EXAMPLE:
You'll never be more hopeful, never be more primed, and never be more empowered to chart the course of your future than you are today. The world is your sandbox—so play in it, dream how to make it better, and work to build a praiseworthy life.

Look at Language Choose concrete, specific terms that express your ideas precisely. Make sure that your parallel structures are actually grammatically parallel—that is, that they repeat not only similar words, but the same parts of speech as well.

WINSTON CHURCHILL **1119**

Vocabulary

Word: *grapple*

Textual Clues: People grapple with their "enemy," and this "make[s] a worthy contribution" to the war effort, so the word must mean "fight" or "struggle."

Meaning: to attempt to deal with; to struggle

Word: *imperious*

Textual Clues: The munitions are "vital" and the troops "must have" them, so they are urgently needed.

Meaning: imperative; urgent

Word: *indomitable*

Textual Clues: The French prime minister says he will "fight to the end," so he must be strong and difficult to defeat.

Meaning: incapable of being subdued or overcome

Academic Vocabulary

Students should infer that *thereby* means "by means of that" or "with that."

Write with Style

Use these criteria in evaluating student writing:

- The speech is logically organized and inspirational.
- The message is appropriate for the specific audience.
- Parallelism and emotional appeals make it effective and memorable.

 For grammar practice, see Unit 6 Teaching Resources Book, p. 189.

 To create custom assessments online, go to Progress Reporter Online Assessment.

 To create custom assessments using software, see ExamView Assessment Suite.

Focus

Tell students that they need to be aware of loaded words in order to understand the writer's viewpoint and purpose.

Teach

Denotation and Connotation

Denotation is the literal meaning of a word. Connotation is the suggested or implied meanings associated with a word. Have students give the denotation and connotation of a word from the text.

Assess

1. Never, so much, so many, so few (*hyperbole, propaganda*)
2. survival, Christian, civilization (*hyperbole, propaganda*)
3. blood, toil, tears, sweat (*hyperbole*)
4. ruins, ashes, tamely, abjectly, enslaved (*bias, hyperbole*)

Vocabulary Practice

Loaded Words Have students reread one selection from Unit Six and keep track of any words they find emotionally charged or with strong positive or negative connotations. After reading, have them look up each word in a dictionary to find its definition, then describe how the denotation of each word compares with its connotation. Students may want to organize their notes in a three-column chart: word/denotation/connotation.

For additional vocabulary practice, see Glencoe Visual Vocabulary CD-ROM.

1120

Learning Objectives

In this workshop, you will focus on the following objective:

Vocabulary: Understanding denotation and connotation.

Loaded Words

Loaded words express strong opinions or emotions. Some reveal **bias,** or prejudice. **Hyperbole** is the use of exaggeration to make a point. **Propaganda** is language that may distort the truth to be persuasive.

Tip

When you read test passages, consider the author's purpose and point of view. Look for evidence in the text that suggests the author's position.

LOG ON **Literature** Online

Vocabulary For more vocabulary practice, go to glencoe.com and enter QuickPass code GLB9817u6.

Vocabulary Workshop

Loaded Words

Literature Connection In this excerpt from his World War II speech, Winston Churchill's language is charged with conviction. He appeals to the British people directly, using a persuasive tone and words loaded with emotion.

> *"We must expect that as soon as stability is reached on the Western Front, the bulk of that hideous apparatus of aggression which gashed Holland into ruin and slavery in a few days, will be turned upon us."*
>
> —Winston Churchill, from "Be Ye Men of Valor"

Highly charged phrases such as "hideous apparatus of aggression" and "gashed Holland into ruin and slavery" helped Churchill mobilize the British people to fight a brutal war. His **loaded words** helped inspire a country's commitment to a necessary action, but people often use such words to manipulate public opinion for personal, political, or commercial gain.

- **Bias** is language that expresses a one-sided point of view. Connotations can reveal bias. Churchill's positive bias lends his words authority.
  For myself, I have <u>invincible confidence</u> in the French Army and its leaders.

- **Hyperbole** is exaggeration used for effect.
  After this battle in France abates its force, there will come the battle for our island—for <u>all that Britain is</u>, and <u>all that Britain means</u>.

- **Propaganda** is language used to influence the public. It often includes bias and hyperbole and may distort the truth.
  Nay, if we <u>fight to the end</u>, it can only be <u>glorious</u>.

Practice For each of the following quotations from speeches by Churchill, underline the loaded words and identify the persuasive techniques being used. Write your answers on a separate piece of paper.

1. "Never in the field of human conflict was so much owed by so many to so few."
2. "Upon this battle depends the survival of Christian civilization."
3. "I have nothing to offer but blood, toil, tears and sweat."
4. "[W]e would rather see London laid in ruins and ashes than that it should be tamely and abjectly enslaved."

Before You Read

The Demon Lover

Meet **Elizabeth Bowen**
(1899–1973)

Elizabeth Bowen once said, "If you look at life one way, there is always cause for alarm." Though she may have experienced more causes for alarm than most people, Bowen maintained her sense of perspective and her composure throughout her life. In view of the many hardships she faced at an early age, this strong sense of self and her world no doubt came in very handy.

A Difficult Childhood Born into the Anglo-Irish gentry, Elizabeth Dorothea Cole Bowen spent her early childhood in Dublin and at Kildorrey. Before her eighth birthday, Bowen's father was hospitalized with a long-term illness, and she and her mother left for England to live with family. Five years later her mother died of cancer. Bowen was then taken in by her aunts on the Kentish seacoast of England and sent to a boarding school.

When World War I broke out, Bowen, still in her teens, went to work in an Irish hospital for soldiers suffering from shell shock, or what is now typically referred to as post-traumatic stress syndrome.

> "*I feel happiest, in the sense of poetic truth, in the short story. Yet if I wrote only short stories, I should feel I was shrinking.*"
>
> —Elizabeth Bowen

The Literary Life After World War I, the twenty-year-old Bowen began to write. She published her first collection of short stories, *Encounters*, in 1923 at the age of twenty-four. She also married Alan Cameron. The couple lived together for a number of years in London. By the time she was thirty, Bowen had become associated with the renowned Bloomsbury Group, which included such literary heavyweights as Virginia Woolf and E. M. Forster.

In 1930 Bowen inherited her family's home, Bowen's Court, in County Cork, Ireland. But she remained in London until 1940, when, as part of her job with the English Ministry of Information, she was posted in Dublin. Her function was to send back to England reports on the Irish people's sentiments about World War II. Bowen moved into Bowen's Court in 1952, but after a few years she moved back to London, where she would reside for the rest of her life.

Bowen's work was influenced by the grim changes World War II brought to English life. The brooding silence of London's abandoned bomb-torn neighborhoods fills many of her works, including her novel *The Heat of the Day*. Many of her short stories, such as "The Demon Lover" and "The Cat Jumps," also subtly weave in supernatural elements. Her work is filled with small but powerful details and an unfailingly accurate sense of time and place.

Bowen's most effective work deals with Britain's upper class. Her stories won her a reputation as an acute observer of both human nature and English society. Her work lives on at least in part because of her flair for description and her particular gift for revealing subtle changes of light, sound, landscape, and human emotion.

LOG ON ▶ **Literature** Online

Author Search For more about Elizabeth Bowen, go to glencoe.com and enter QuickPass code GLB9817u6.

Before You Read

Focus

Bellringer Options

Selection Focus Transparency 59

Daily Language Practice Transparency 96

Or ask: Have you ever had an experience that took you vividly back to an earlier period in your life? Why did one experience remind you of the other? Was there anything that seemed "otherworldly" about returning so vividly to the past? Use these questions to lead a class discussion.

 For summaries in languages other than English, see Unit 6 Teaching Resources Book, pp. 192–197.

Selection Skills

Literary Elements
- Flashback (SE pp. 1122, 1125, 1126, 1128, 1130)

Reading Skills
- Analyze Sensory Details (SE pp. 1122–1130)

The Demon Lover

Vocabulary Skills
- Usage (SE p. 1130)
- Denotation and Connotation (TE p. 1128)

Listening/Speaking/Viewing Skills
- Analyze Art (SE pp. 1123, 1129)

Writing Skills/Grammar
- Article (SE p. 1130)
- Identify Thematic Details (TE p. 1124)

Before You Read

Focus

Summary

"The Demon Lover" takes place in London, between bombings during World War II. The protagonist, Mrs. Drover, returns to her closed-up home for some personal belongings. She finds a letter, with that day's date, from her fiancé, long presumed dead. She flashes back to her last troubling meeting with him 25 years earlier, before he went missing while in the military during World War I. The story concludes with her riding away in a taxi, screaming.

Vocabulary

Dictionary Have students look up each vocabulary word in a dictionary and create a chart to list the etymology, alternative definitions, synonyms, and antonyms of each word.

For additional vocabulary practice, see Unit 6 Teaching Resources Book, p. 200.

For additional context, see Glencoe Visual Vocabulary CD-ROM.

Literature and Reading Preview

Connect to the Story

What makes a story scary, to you? Create a list of qualities that are common to most of the scary tales you know.

Build Background

This story, which is based loosely on a gothic ballad, takes place during World War II during the German bombing of London known as the Blitz. On fifty-seven consecutive nights, the German Luftwaffe bombed London in an effort to obliterate the city and destroy the fighting spirit of Britain's people. Many families moved to the country to get out of harm's way. Those who could not afford to move had to take shelter where they could find it. The story also contains a flashback to World War I, when the main character became engaged to a young soldier.

Set Purposes for Reading

Big Idea World War II and Its Aftermath

As you read "The Demon Lover," ask yourself, What details express the main character's dark pessimism and create an overwhelming sense of foreboding?

Literary Element Flashback

A **flashback** is an interruption in the chronological order of a narrative to show an event that happened earlier. This gives readers information that may help them to figure out the main events of a story. As you read, ask yourself, How do details from the flashback frame the rest of the story?

Reading Strategy Analyze Sensory Details

In creating effective images, writers use **sensory details**, or descriptions that appeal to one or more of the five senses: sight, hearing, touch, taste, and smell. Like diction and sentence structure, sensory details influence the tone and meaning of a literary work. As you read, ask yourself, What senses is the writer appealing to with this detail?

Tip: Using Your Senses Create a chart to keep track of the senses you use as you read "The Demon Lover."

Image or Description	Senses
"it had been a steamy, showery day"	touch

Learning Objectives

For pages 1121–1130

In studying this text, you will focus on the following objectives:

Literary Study: Analyzing flashback.

Reading: Analyzing sensory details.

Writing: Writing an article.

Vocabulary

prosaic (prō zā′ ik) *adj.* commonplace; ordinary; p. 1124 *The students' more prosaic expectations were upset by the instructor's non-traditional approach.*

intermittent (in′ tər mit′ ənt) *adj.* alternately starting and stopping; p. 1125 *During the storm, weather bulletins interrupted regular programming on an intermittent basis.*

precipitately (pri sip′ ə tət′ lē) *adv.* without deliberation; hastily; abruptly; p. 1125 *Rushing out of the store, Cal precipitately knocked the vase off the shelf.*

emanate (em′ ə nāt′) *v.* to come forth from a source; issue; p. 1128 *On Thanksgiving Day, wonderful smells emanate from the kitchen.*

impassively (im pas′ iv lē) *adv.* in an emotionless manner; p. 1128 *Surprisingly, the patient accepted the grim diagnosis impassively.*

Reading Practice

SPIRAL REVIEW **Preview** Have students look at the title, the illustrations, and the pull quote in the story. **Ask:** What do you learn about the story from the title? *(The plot may pertain to a love relationship, perhaps one that has gone bad.)* **Ask:** What do you learn about the setting and mood of the story from the illustrations and from the displayed quotation? *(It is set in London. The mood seems ominous.)*

1122

The Gallery, 1952. Leonard Campbell Taylor. Oil on canvas. Private collection.

View the Art Though Taylor was a well-respected painter, he preferred to work as a journalist—he found it more exciting. What is the mood of this painting? How does the image compare to the description of the Drover house on page 1124? ★

The Demon Lover

Elizabeth Bowen

Towards the end of her day in London Mrs. Drover went round to her shut-up house to look for several things she wanted to take away. Some belonged to herself, some to her family, who were by now used to their country life. It was late August; it had been a steamy, showery day: at the moment the trees down the pavement glittered in an escape of humid yellow afternoon sun.

Against the next batch of clouds, already piling up ink-dark, broken chimneys and parapets[1] stood out.

---

1. A *parapet* is a low, protective railing or wall along the edge of a roof or balcony.

Analyze Sensory Details *In what ways does this paragraph appeal to your senses?* **1**

ELIZABETH BOWEN **1123**

Teach

Reading Strategy   1

Analyze Sensory Details

Answer: *Students may cite the ink-dark clouds, glittering pavement, yellow sun, and broken chimneys as appealing to their sense of sight.*

Ask: Which details give information about the time and place? *(The broken chimneys and parapets reveal damage from the Blitz of London during World War II.)*

View the Art ★

Answer: *The mood is one of stillness and isolation. Like the Drovers' house, the hall in this picture is populated only by one woman, along with some untouched-looking furniture. However, the furniture is in good repair, and there are rugs on the floor—it does not look abandoned.*

A respected painter and portraitist, Leonard Campbell Taylor (1874–1969) considered the study of art to be tedious and preferred the work of a journalist in his early years. Ask students to survey the painting and note any details that affect the mood. **Ask:** How does the woman in the distance compare to the other objects in the painting? Does the relatively small space she occupies on the canvas affect your impression of her? *(Answers will vary.)*

 For an audio recording of this selection, use Listening Library Audio CD-ROM.

Readability Scores

Dale-Chall: 8.4
DRP: 58
Lexile: 990

1123

Teach

Reading Strategy | 1

Analyze Sensory Details

[ENGLISH LEARNERS] **Ask:** What do you learn here about Mrs. Drover's house? *(The windows are boarded up; the small details of the house are very familiar to her; her piano has been put into storage; some dust has seeped in; the hearth is cold.)* Point out to English learners whose first language is Spanish that *escritoire* is a cognate with *escritorio*. Both denote types of writing desks.

Big Idea | 2

World War II and Its Aftermath **Answer:** *The bombing of London has ruined much of the city, and no one is sure when the bombing will stop.*

Reading Strategy | 3

Analyzing Sensory Details

Answer: *The dark, low clouds and overgrown, weedy lawns add to the feeling of loneliness and foreboding.*

Writing Practice

Identify Thematic Details Ask students to create a graphic organizer like the one below to record details in the text that indicate the writer's beliefs about darkness and destruction during war:

Darkness	Destruction
_____	_____
_____	_____
_____	_____

Then have students use the graphic organizer to write a one-paragraph summary of the writer's beliefs about war.

In her once familiar street, as in any unused channel, an unfamiliar queerness had silted up;[2] a cat wove itself in and out of railings, but no human eye watched Mrs. Drover's return. Shifting some parcels under her arm, she slowly forced round her latchkey in an unwilling lock, then gave the door, which had warped, a push with her knee. Dead air came out to meet her as she went in.

The staircase window having been boarded up, no light came down into the hall. But one door, she could just see, stood ajar, so she went quickly through into the room and unshuttered the big window in there. Now the **prosaic** woman, looking about her, was more perplexed[3] than she knew by everything that she saw, by

Visual Vocabulary
An *escritoire* is a writing table or desk.

traces of her long former habit of life—the yellow smoke stain up the white marble mantelpiece, the ring left by a vase on the top of the escritoire; the bruise in the wall-paper where, on the door being thrown open widely, the china handle had always hit the wall. The piano, having gone away to be stored, had left what looked like claw marks on its part of the parquet.[4] Though not much dust had seeped in, each object wore a film of another kind; and, the only ventilation being the chimney, the whole drawing room smelled of the cold hearth. Mrs. Drover put down her parcels on the escritoire and left the room to proceed upstairs; the things she wanted were in a bedroom chest.

She had been anxious to see how the house was—the part-time caretaker she shared with some neighbors was away this week on his

---

2. Here, *silted* up means "built up."
3. *Perplexed* means "bewildered" or "puzzled."
4. *Parquet* is inlaid wood, often of different colors, that is worked into geometric patterns or mosaic and is used especially for flooring.

Vocabulary

prosaic (prō zā′ ik) *adj.* commonplace; ordinary

---

holiday, known to be not yet back. At the best of times he did not look in often, and she was never sure that she trusted him. There were some cracks in the structure, left by the last bombing,[5] on which she was anxious to keep an eye. Not that one could do anything—

A shaft of refracted[6] daylight now lay across the hall. She stopped dead and stared at the hall table—on this lay a letter addressed to her.

She thought first—then the caretaker must be back. All the same, who, seeing the house shuttered, would have dropped a letter in at the box? It was not a circular,[7] it was not a bill. And the post office redirected, to the address in the country, everything for her that came through the post. The caretaker (even if he were back) did not know she was due in London today—her call here had been planned to be a surprise—so his negligence in the manner of this letter, leaving it to wait in the dusk and the dust, annoyed her. Annoyed, she picked up the letter, which bore no stamp. But it cannot be important, or they would know . . . She took the letter rapidly upstairs with her, without a stop to look at the writing till she reached what had been her bedroom, where she let in light. The room looked over the garden and other gardens: the sun had gone in; as the clouds sharpened and lowered, the trees and rank[8] lawns seemed already to smoke with dark. Her reluctance to look again at the letter came from the fact that she felt intruded upon—and by someone contemptuous[9] of her ways. However, in the tenseness preceding the fall of rain she read it: it was a few lines.

---

5. *The last bombing* indicates that the story takes place during World War II.
6. *Refracted* means "coming in at an angle."
7. Here, a *circular* is a printed advertisement.
8. As it is used here, *rank* means "overgrown with weeds."
9. *Contemptuous* means "scornful."

World War II and Its Aftermath *Why is Mrs. Drover unable to do anything about her crumbling house?* **2**

Analyze Sensory Details *What does this description of the lawns and garden contribute to the story's overall mood?* **3**

Dear Kathleen: You will not have forgotten that today is our anniversary, and the day we said. The years have gone by at once slowly and fast. In view of the fact that nothing has changed, I shall rely upon you to keep your promise. I was sorry to see you leave London, but was satisfied that you would be back in time. You may expect me, therefore, at the hour arranged. Until then . . .   K.

Mrs. Drover looked for the date: it was today's. She dropped the letter on to the bedsprings, then picked it up to see the writing again—her lips, beneath the remains of lipstick, beginning to go white. She felt so much the change in her own face that she went to the mirror, polished a clear patch in it and looked at once urgently and stealthily[10] in. She was confronted by a woman of forty-four, with eyes starting out under a hat brim that had been rather carelessly pulled down. She had not put on any more powder since she left the shop where she ate her solitary tea. The pearls her husband had given her on their marriage hung loose round her now rather thinner throat, slipping in the V of the pink wool jumper her sister knitted last autumn as they sat round the fire. Mrs. Drover's most normal expression was one of controlled worry, but of assent.[11] Since the birth of the third of her little boys, attended by a quite serious illness, she had had an **intermittent** muscular flicker to the left of her mouth, but in spite of this she could always sustain a manner that was at once energetic and calm.

Turning from her own face as **precipitately** as she had gone to meet it, she went to the chest where the things were, unlocked it, threw up the lid and knelt to search. But as rain began to come crashing down she could not

keep from looking over her shoulder at the stripped bed on which the letter lay. Behind the blanket of rain the clock of the church that still stood struck six—with rapidly heightening apprehension she counted each of the slow strokes. "The hour arranged . . . My God," she said, "*what* hour? How should I . . . ? After twenty-five years . . ."

The young girl talking to the soldier in the garden had not ever completely seen his face. It was dark; they were saying good-bye under a tree. Now and then—for it felt, from not seeing him at this intense moment, as though she had never seen him at all—she verified his presence for these few moments longer by putting out a hand, which he each time pressed, without very much kindness, and painfully, on to one of the breast buttons of his uniform. That cut of the button on the palm of her hand was, principally, what she was to carry away. This was so near the end of a leave from France that she could only wish him already gone. It was August 1916.[12] Being not kissed, being drawn away from and looked at intimidated Kathleen till she imagined spectral[13] glitters in the place of his eyes. Turning away and looking back up the lawn she saw, through branches of trees, the drawing-room window alight: she caught a breath for the moment when she could go running back there into the safe arms of her mother and sister, and cry: "What shall I do, what shall I do? He has gone."

---

12. *August 1916* indicates that this flashback takes place during the First World War.
13. *Spectral* means "ghostly."

Flashback *What clues indicate that a flashback is beginning?*   **4**

Analyze Sensory Details *What does the pain Mrs. Drover experiences here suggest to you about her relationship with the young soldier?*   **5**

---

10. *Stealthily* means "secretly."
11. Here, *assent* means "resignation."

Vocabulary

intermittent (in´ tər mit´ ənt) *adj.* alternately starting and stopping
precipitately (pri sip´ ə tət´ lē) *adv.* without deliberation; hastily; abruptly

ELIZABETH BOWEN   **1125**

Approaching Level

DIFFERENTIATED INSTRUCTION

Emerging As practice in **reading fluency**, have students work in small groups to read aloud the long paragraph that details Mrs. Drover's reaction to the letter. Ask them to practice until each group member can read the paragraph fluidly, expressively, and at a normal speaking pace. Have students use context clues to identify the meanings of unfamiliar words and verify the meanings with a dictionary.

Teach

Literary Element   4

Flashback **Answer:** *The last words before the break in the text are a clue that Mrs. Drover may be thinking back to a past event. The shift of scene to a garden is also a clue. "The young girl" indicates that Mrs. Drover is thinking back to a scene from her youth. The ornament before this paragraph begins also indicates a shift.*

For additional literary element practice, see Unit 6 Teaching Resources Book, p. 198.

Reading Strategy   5

Analyzing Sensory Details
Answer: *He treated her roughly and demanded much of her emotions; he caused her pain but didn't seem to notice or care about what she was feeling.*

(ENGLISH LEARNERS) Point out to English learners that "being drawn away from" means that the soldier took a step back in order to see Kathleen, not that the soldier drew a picture of her.

Teach

| Literary Element | 1 |

Flashback *Answer: The soldier's promise suggests that he wrote the letter.*

View the Art ★

Born in Leeds, England, John Atkinson Grimshaw (1836–1893) was only twenty-four when he decided to leave his position as a clerk for the railroad and become an artist. Grimshaw's parents were strict Baptists who refused his wish to become a painter; at one time his mother destroyed his paints and forbade his work. The dark scene depicted here would have been typical of London in the late nineteenth century, with industrial pollution contributing to fog at night.

Writing Practice

Timeline Have students draw a timeline of the events in the story that they have read, including the flashback. Make sure that students understand that the flashback occurred 25 years before the rest of the narration.

St. Paul's Cathedral from Ludgate Circus, London, England. John Atkinson Grimshaw. ★

Hearing her catch her breath, her fiancé said, without feeling: "Cold?"

"You're going away such a long way."

"Not so far as you think."

"I don't understand?"

"You don't have to," he said. "You will. You know what we said."

"But that was—suppose you—I mean, suppose."

"I shall be with you," he said, "sooner or later. You won't forget that. You need do nothing but wait."

Only a little more than a minute later she was free to run up the silent lawn. Looking in through the window at her mother and sister, who did not for the moment perceive her, she already felt that unnatural promise drive down between her and the rest of all human kind. No other way of having given herself could have made her feel so apart, lost and foresworn.[14] She could not have plighted a more sinister troth.[15]

Kathleen behaved well when, some months later, her fiancé was reported missing, presumed killed. Her family not only supported her but were able to praise her courage without stint[16] because they could not regret, as a husband for her, the man they knew almost nothing about. They hoped she would, in a year or two, console herself—and had it been only a question of consolation things might have gone much

---

14. Here, *foresworn* means "abandoned."
15. *She . . . troth.* She could not have pledged herself to a more evil promise.
16. To praise without *stint* is to praise generously and without reservation.

1 **Flashback** *What does the soldier's promise suggest about the letter Kathleen receives?*

1126 UNIT 6 THE MODERN AGE

straighter ahead. But her trouble, behind just a little grief, was a complete dislocation from everything. She did not reject other lovers, for these failed to appear: for years she failed to attract men—and with the approach of her thirties she became natural enough to share her family's anxiousness on this score. She began to put herself out, to wonder; and at thirty-two she was very greatly relieved to find herself being courted by William Drover. She married him, and the two of them settled down in this quiet, arboreal[17] part of Kensington:[18] in this house the years piled up, her children were born and they all lived till they were driven out by the bombs of the next war. Her movements as Mrs. Drover were circumscribed,[19] and she dismissed any idea that they were still watched.

As things were—dead or living the letter writer sent her only a threat. Unable, for some minutes, to go on kneeling with her back exposed to the empty room, Mrs. Drover rose from the chest to sit on an upright chair whose back was firmly against the wall. The desuetude[20] of her former bedroom, her married London home's whole air of being a cracked cup from which memory, with its reassuring power, had either evaporated or leaked away, made a crisis—and at just this crisis the letter writer had, knowledgeably, struck. The

> You have no time to run from a face you do not expect.

hollowness of the house this evening canceled years on years of voices, habits, and steps. Through the shut windows she only heard rain fall on the roofs around. To rally[21] herself, she said she was in a mood—and for two or three seconds shutting her eyes, told herself that she had imagined the letter. But she opened them—there it lay on the bed.

On the supernatural side of the letter's entrance she was not permitting her mind to dwell. Who, in London, knew she meant to call at the house today? Evidently, however, this had been known. The caretaker, *had* he come back, had had no cause to expect her: he would have taken the letter in his pocket, to forward it, at his own time, through the post. There was no other sign that the caretaker had been in—but, if not? Letters dropped in at doors of deserted houses do not fly or walk to tables in halls. They do not sit on the dust of empty tables with the air of certainty that they will be found. There was needed some human hand—but nobody but the caretaker had a key. Under circumstances she did not care to consider, a house can be entered without a key. It was possible that she was not alone now. She might be being waited for, downstairs. Waited for—until when? Until "the hour arranged." At least that was not six o'clock: six has struck.

She rose from the chair and went over and locked the door.

The thing was, to get out. To fly? No, not that: she had to catch her train. As a woman whose utter dependability was the keystone of her family life she was not willing to return to

---

17. *Arboreal* indicates that there were many trees where they lived.
18. *Kensington* is a wealthy district in London.
19. *Circumscribed* means "restricted."
20. *Desuetude* (des′ wə tood′) means "state of disuse."

---

3 World War II and Its Aftermath *In what way might Mrs. Drover's home represent the whole of London?*

21. Here, *rally* means "to calm and encourage."

ELIZABETH BOWEN **1127**

2

3

Teach

Literary Element | 2

Flashback Ask: How does Bowen lead readers back to the present after Mrs. Drover's flashback to 25 years in the past? *(Bowen gives a brief, poignant summary of events that followed Mrs. Drover's last meeting with her fiancé, leading up to the present.)* APPROACHING For approaching level students, **ask:** In which sentence is the reader back in the narrative present? *("As things were---dead or living the letter writer sent her only a threat.")*

Big Idea | 3

World War II and Its Aftermath Answer: *Both the home and the city are broken; they are filled with evidence of death and destruction.* ENGLISH LEARNERS To check comprehension of English learners, **ask:** What does it mean to be broken? *(To be broken can mean to be literally or figuratively destroyed.)* **Ask:** How is London broken? *(London has buildings that are destroyed and people who have lost hope.)*

Approaching Level

DIFFERENTIATED INSTRUCTION

African American Vernacular English
Approaching level students who use African American vernacular English may have difficulty with forming the simple past tense. Have students describe the information contained in the flashback in the simple past tense, including the standard forms of irregular verbs such as *be, have,* and *do.*

Teach

Literary Element 1

Flashback Answer: *He clasped her hand so tightly it left a painful mark. He seemed to want to possess her without actually loving, or even liking, her.*

Big Idea 2

World War II and Its Aftermath Ask: In addition to the mysterious and eerie presence of the letter, what else is probably contributing to Mrs. Drover's sense of unrest and foreboding? *(She had a troubled engagement with a soldier who went missing during World War I and who was presumed dead. She had difficulty finding a suitable mate after that. She had a serious illness at the time of the birth of her third son. Her family was forced to leave their home in London because of intense bombings during World War II.)*

Reading Strategy 3

Analyze Sensory Details Say: A sensory experience leads Mrs. Drover to a moment of intense dread and fear. What does she feel, and what does she believe it means? Do you think she is perceiving the situation accurately? Why or why not? *(She feels and smells a draft of stale air; she believes that someone has opened a door or window in the basement to leave the house at that moment. Some students may believe that she is highly attuned to a real danger, but some may argue that Mrs. Drover's anxiety is causing her to imagine an intruder.)*

the country, to her husband, her little boys and her sister, without the objects she had come up to fetch. Resuming work at the chest she set about making up a number of parcels in a rapid, fumbling-decisive way. These, with her shopping parcels, would be too much to carry; these meant a taxi—at the thought of the taxi her heart went up and her normal breathing resumed. I will ring up the taxi now; the taxi cannot come too soon: I shall hear the taxi out there running its engine, till I walk calmly down to it through the hall. I'll ring up—But no: the telephone is cut off . . . She tugged at a knot she had tied wrong.

The idea of flight . . . He was never kind to me, not really. I don't remember him kind at all. Mother said he never considered me. He was set on me, that was what it was—not love. Not love, not meaning a person well. What did he do, to make me promise like that? I can't remember—But she found that she could.

She remembered with such dreadful acuteness that the twenty-five years since then dissolved like smoke and she instinctively looked for the weal[22] left by the button on the palm of her hand. She remembered not only all that he said and did but the complete suspension of *her* existence during that August week. I was not myself—they all told me so at the time. She remembered—but with one white burning blank as where acid has dropped on a photograph: *under no conditions* could she remember his face.

So, wherever he may be waiting, I shall not know him. You have no time to run from a face you do not expect.

The thing was to get to the taxi before any clock struck what could be the hour. She would slip down the street and round the side of the square to where the square gave on the main road. She would return in the taxi, safe, to her own door, and bring the solid driver into the

house with her to pick up the parcels from room to room. The idea of the taxi driver made her decisive, bold: she unlocked her door, went to the top of the staircase and listened down.

She heard nothing—but while she was hearing nothing the *passé*[23] air of the staircase was disturbed by a draft that traveled up to her face. It **emanated** from the basement: down there a door or window was being opened by someone who chose this moment to leave the house.

The rain had stopped; the pavements steamily shone as Mrs. Drover let herself out by inches from her own front door into the empty street. The unoccupied houses opposite continued to meet her look with their damaged stare. Making towards the thoroughfare and the taxi, she tried not to keep looking behind. Indeed, the silence was so intense—one of those creeks of London silence exaggerated this summer by the damage of war—that no tread could have gained on hers unheard. Where her street debouched[24] on the square where people went on living, she grew conscious of, and checked, her unnatural pace. Across the open end of the square two buses passed each other: women, a perambulator, cyclists, a man wheeling a barrow signalized, once again, the ordinary flow of life. At the square's most populous corner should be— and was—the short taxi

Visual Vocabulary
A *perambulator* is a baby carriage.

rank. This evening, only one taxi—but this, although it presented its blank rump, appeared already to be alertly waiting for her. Indeed, without looking round the driver started his

---

22. A *weal* is a bruise or mark on the skin; a welt.

23. As it is used here, *passé* means "stale."
24. *Debouched* (di boosht´) means "emerged."

Vocabulary

emanate (em´ ə nāt´) *v.* to come forth from a source; issue

impassively (im pas´ iv lē) *adv.* in an emotionless manner

1 Flashback *How is this sentiment reflected in the soldier's past behavior?*

1128 UNIT 6 THE MODERN AGE

Vocabulary Practice

Denotation and Connotation
Explain that a denotation is a dictionary meaning and that connotations are suggested or implied meanings. Have volunteers identify and share examples of each from this page. Students can work with partners as necessary. Have students hypothesize about why Bowen chooses

denotation or connotation to convey information and what effects her choices have on readers.

The Strand by Night, 1937. Christopher Richard Wynne Nevinson. Bradford Art Galleries and Museums, West Yorkshire, UK.

View the Art The Strand was London's center of theater and nightlife during the Victorian era. How does the mood of this image compare to Bowen's description of the street in which Mrs. Drover finds herself?

engine as she panted up from behind and put her hand on the door. As she did so, the clock struck seven. The taxi faced the main road: to make the trip back to her house it would have to turn— she had settled back on the seat and the taxi *had* turned before she, surprised by its knowing movement, recollected that she had not "said where." She leaned forward to scratch at the glass panel that divided the driver's head from her own.

The driver braked to what was almost a stop, turned round and slid the glass panel back: the jolt of this flung Mrs. Drover forward till her face was almost into the glass. Through the aperture[25] driver and passenger, not six inches between them, remained for an eternity eye to eye. Mrs. Drover's mouth hung open for some seconds before she could issue her first scream. After that she continued to scream freely and to beat with her gloved hands on the glass all round as the taxi, accelerating without mercy, made off with her into the hinterland[26] of deserted streets. ✍

---

25. An *aperture* (ap′ ər chər) is an opening.
26. *Hinterland* means "remote regions."

Analyze Sensory Details *What details in this passage contribute to the ominous mood?* **4**

ELIZABETH BOWEN **1129**

Teach

Reading Strategy   4

Analyze Sensory Details
Answer: *Mrs. Drover's screams, her being trapped in the taxi, the deserted streets*

APPROACHING To help approaching level students, **ask:** What details in the text hint at the identity of the driver? *(The clock strikes seven; the driver seems to know the direction to Mrs. Drover's home; Mrs. Drover screams after staring eye to eye with the driver.)*

View the Art

Answer: *The mood of this image is vibrant, populated, and bright. The streets in which Mrs. Drover finds herself are described as a "deserted," silent "hinterland." One passage mentions people and buses in the street, but they are moving slowly and without interest or vibrancy.*

During World War I, Christopher Richard Wynne Nevinson (1889–1946) served as an ambulance driver for the Red Cross. He later served in the official role of an artist for the War Propaganda Bureau. His paintings during this period depict battles and wounded soldiers in the trenches of the front lines. Later in his career, Nevinson's focus turned to painting urban scenes, like the one depicted here.

To check students' understanding of the selection, see Unit 6 Teaching Resources Book, p. 203.

1129

Assess

1. Some students may have found the story frightening or eerie.
2. (a) It makes her tense; she wonders how it got there. (b) That she is a private, pragmatic woman
3. (a) She blocked out the memory because it was frightening. (b) It adds to its eeriness.
4. Many students will expect a grim outcome.
5. (a) The wartime setting adds to the threatening mood. (b) They have made her emotionally fragile and dislocated.
6. Student answers will vary.

Literary Element

1. She was probably relieved, but her promise keeps her from moving on with her life.
2. Possible answer: The flashback intensifies the eerie atmosphere with the fiancé's frightening, faceless figure.

⚡ Writing

Students' articles should include specific details and descriptions, reveal an understanding of the story, and be written in a newspaper format.

> 📁 For grammar practice, see Unit 6 Teaching Resources Book, p. 202.

Progress Check

Can students analyze sensory details?

If No → See Unit 6 Teaching Resources Book, p. 199.

After You Read

Respond and Think Critically

Respond and Interpret

1. What was your reaction to the conclusion of this story? Explain.
2. (a)How does Mrs. Drover react to finding the letter on the hall table? (b)What does her reaction suggest about her personality and way of life?

Analyze and Evaluate

3. (a)Mrs. Drover cannot, under *any* circumstances, remember her fiancé's face. What does this suggest to you? (b)How does this detail contribute to the story's mood?

Literary Element Flashback

Reread the **flashback** sequence on pages 1125–1127. Then answer the questions about how the information from the flashback affected your understanding of the story.

1. How did Mrs. Drover's younger self really feel when her fiancé was presumed dead?
2. Do you think Bowen's use of the flashback interrupts the flow of the story, or does it intensify the suspense? Explain.

⚡ Writing

Write an Article Consider what Mrs. Drover's disappearance must have looked like from the perspective of her husband, family, and strangers. Write a news article covering her disappearance. Your article should include only information that someone other than Mrs. Drover could have known, such as where she was last seen or the known facts of her history.

> **LOG ON ▶** Literature Online
>
> **Selection Resources** For Selection Quizzes, eFlashcards, and Reading-Writing Connection activities, go to glencoe.com and enter QuickPass code GLB9817u6.

4. What do you think happens to Mrs. Drover at the end? Explain.

Connect

5. **Big Idea** World War II and Its Aftermath (a)Why do you think Bowen chose war-torn London as the setting for this story? (b)In your opinion, how might both world wars have affected Mrs. Drover's emotional health?
6. **Connect to the Author** What can you infer from details in "The Demon Lover" about the effect World War II had on Bowen? Explain.

Reading Strategy Analyze Sensory Details

Review the chart you started on page 1122 and answer the following questions.

1. (a)What sensory details does Bowen use to describe the London house? (b)How do the details contribute to the story's atmosphere?
2. (a)What sensory details describe the day on which the story takes place? (b)How do these details create suspense?

Vocabulary Practice

Practice with Usage Respond to the following statements to help you explore the meanings of these vocabulary words from the selection.

1. Describe a **prosaic** Saturday afternoon in your neighborhood.
2. If your violin practice was **intermittent**, would your playing be likely to get better?
3. What kinds of scents might **emanate** from a bakery in the morning?
4. Name someone who reacts **impassively** even when things are going wrong.
5. If someone you were talking with jumped up **precipitately**, would you be concerned?

Reading Strategy

1. (a) It is a place filled with exhausted memories, yellowing stains, chilly drafts, and old bumps and marks on the dingy walls. (b) The details are vivid, and the sensory experience heightens the reader's awareness of Mrs. Drover's dangerous surroundings.

2. (a) The pavement is wet; the air is "humid yellow" and "steamy." (b) The threatening storm that might break at any moment parallels the possible arrival of the demon lover.

Vocabulary

Students' responses will vary but should demonstrate an understanding of the words' meanings.

Before You Read

Musée des Beaux Arts and The Unknown Citizen

Meet **W. H. Auden**
(1907–1973)

For much of the middle part of the twentieth century, Wystan Hugh Auden was hailed as the greatest poet of his generation—the successor to T. S. Eliot and William Butler Yeats. His poetry was brilliant and political. Auden often used traditional formal techniques to explore modern social and spiritual concerns. His prolific output and versatile abilities helped clear the way for a new poetic style in the post–World War II period.

> *"Poetry makes nothing happen. It survives in the valley of its saying."*
>
> —W. H. Auden

The Auden Group Born in York, the son of a distinguished doctor, the young Auden had no particular literary ambitions; he had originally planned to become a mining engineer. His absorbing interest during childhood and adolescence was science, primarily biology. However, by 1922 he discovered a knack for poetry—publishing his first poem two years later, at the age of seventeen. After entering Oxford in 1925, Auden famously declared to his English tutor that he planned to become "a great poet."

While at Oxford, Auden became friends with a group of some of the brightest young poets in England, including Stephen Spender, Cecil Day-Lewis, and Louis MacNeice. Auden's influence in this illustrious group was so great that it was known as the "Auden Group," and later dubbed by journalists and critics as the Auden Generation. After college Auden began teaching in Scotland and England. A somewhat eccentric teacher, he was nonetheless liked by his students. Soon after Auden began teaching, his first book of verse was published.

By the age of twenty-five, with the publication of a second volume, Auden had made a mark on the literary landscape. At the time, his poems were characterized, in part, by his belief that poetry could act as a kind of therapy, performing a function similar to psychoanalysis.

An American Citizen Although his writing was primarily psychological, Auden, like many of his contemporaries, was active in the politics of his day. "I am not one of those who believe that poetry need or even should be directly political," he wrote, "but in a critical period such as ours, I do believe that the poet must have direct knowledge of the major political events." He went to Spain in 1937 during the Spanish Civil War, hoping to aid the Loyalists in their fight against fascism. This visit inspired the poem *Spain*, one of Auden's most famous works. In 1938, just before the start of World War II, Auden moved to the United States. "The attractiveness of America to a writer is its openness," he said. Auden became a U.S. citizen in 1946. The next year he won the Pulitzer Prize for *The Age of Anxiety*.

In the late 1940s, Auden divided his time between Europe and the United States. From 1956 to 1961, he was professor of poetry at Oxford University. Throughout the rest of his life he continued to write, creating a diverse body of work that includes not only poetry but also drama, criticism, blues music, musical librettos, and nonsense verse.

 Literature Online

Author Search For more about W. H. Auden, go to glencoe.com and enter QuickPass code GLB9817u6.

Before You Read

Focus

Bellringer Options

Selection Focus Transparency 60

Daily Language Practice Transparency 97

Or tell students that some of W. H. Auden's poems feature an everyman—a "typical" person of the time in which Auden lived. **Ask:** How would you describe an everyman of today? What are some attitudes, problems, and hopes he or she might have? Use these questions to spur a class discussion of a contemporary everyman.

> For summaries in languages other than English, see Unit 6 Teaching Resources Book, pp. 205–210.

Selection Skills

Literary Elements
- Irony (SE pp. 1132, 1133, 1135, 1136)
- Diction (SE p. 1136)

Musée des Beaux Arts / The Unknown Citizen

Listening/Speaking/ Viewing Skills
- Analyze Art (SE pp. 1133, 1134)

Reading Skills
- Clarify Meaning (SE pp. 1132, 1137)

Vocabulary Skills
- Analogies (SE pp. 1132, 1137)
- Academic Vocabulary (SE p. 1137)

Writing Skills/Grammar
- Research Report (SE p. 1137)

Before You Read

Focus

Summary

"Musée des Beaux Arts" is about a painting called *The Fall of Icarus*, by Peter Brueghel the Elder. Icarus plunges to his death in the background of a pastoral scene, in which other figures are unconcerned with his fate.

"The Unknown Citizen" describes the life and death of an everyman of his time. The man is described in ironically generic terms.

Vocabulary

Use a Dictionary Have students look up each vocabulary word and record its definition and etymology, along with related words (for example, *revere* and *reverent* are related to *reverently*). Then have them compose sentences containing the vocabulary words and related words.

For additional vocabulary practice, see Unit 6 Teaching Resources Book, p. 213.

For additional context, see Glencoe Interactive Vocabulary CD-ROM.

Literature and Reading Preview

Connect to the Poems

Are people immune to the suffering and loss of others? In a journal entry, consider a time when it seemed life just went on normally, in spite of tragedy.

Build Background

The title of the poem "Musée des Beaux Arts" refers to the Royal Museum of Fine Arts in Brussels, Belgium. This museum owns the painting *The Fall of Icarus*, to which Auden refers in his poem. This painting, by Pieter Brueghel the Elder, depicts the Greek myth of Icarus. In this myth, Icarus and his father, Daedalus, escape from prison by making artificial wings of feathers and wax. Daedalus warns Icarus not to fly too close to the sun because it could melt the wax, but Icarus ignores his father's warning and falls to his death. In Brueghel's rendition, Icarus's legs can be seen disappearing into the sea in a corner of the painting, while everything else appears normal.

Set Purposes for Reading

Big Idea World War II and Its Aftermath

As you read, ask yourself, How does Auden address human isolation, cultural anxiety, and disillusionment with society?

Literary Element Irony

Irony is a discrepancy between appearance and reality. **Verbal irony** in poetry exists when the speaker says one thing, but the poet clearly means something different; **dramatic irony** occurs when the audience or reader knows something that the speaker of the poem or one of its characters does not. As you read, ask yourself, How is irony used in this poem?

Reading Strategy Clarify Meaning

To **clarify meaning** means to focus on difficult sections of a text in order to understand them better. Often this involves rereading, summarizing, and asking questions. As you read, ask yourself, Is the meaning of this poem clear to me?

Tip: Asking Questions As you read Auden's poems, ask yourself questions like the following:

- What is the stanza basically saying?
- How could I restate these lines to improve my comprehension?
- What does this image seem to represent?

Viewing Practice

Preview Direct students' attention to the painting *The Fall of Icarus* on page 1133. Ask a volunteer to relate the story of Icarus and Daedalus, or explain this myth to students. Afterward, have students describe what they see in the painting. Have them write three ideas or questions they have about Icarus, Brueghel, or the painting itself. As students read the poem, have them evaluate how their ideas and questions compare with Auden's ideas.

Vocabulary

reverently (rev′ rənt lē) *adv.* respectfully; with deep affection or veneration; p. 1133 *The child spoke reverently about his favorite teacher.*

forsaken (fôr sāk′ ən) *adj.* deserted or lonely; p. 1133 *The windswept mountains are a forsaken place during the winter.*

sensible (sen′ sə bəl) *adj.* having good judgment or sound thinking; p. 1135 *Most commentators agreed that the jury's decision was well reasoned and very sensible.*

Tip: Analogies An **analogy** applies the relationship between one pair of words to another pair of words. For example, in the analogy *brief: long :: rational : illogical,* the word *brief* is an antonym of *long,* and the word *rational* is an antonym of *illogical.* Analogies can also be based on cause-effect relationships, part-whole relationships, and other types of relationships.

Musée des Beaux Arts

W. H. Auden

The Fall of Icarus, c. 1558–1566. Pieter Brueghel the Elder. Oil on canvas, 73.7 x 111.8 cm. Musée Royaux des Beaux-Arts de Belgique, Brussels, Belgium.

View the Art Brueghel's works are known for their intense focus on detail. In your opinion, does Auden's description of the painting seem accurate? Explain. ★

About suffering they were never wrong,
The Old Masters:[1] how well they understood
Its human position; how it takes place
While someone else is eating or opening a window or just walking dully along; **1**
5 How, when the aged are **reverently**, passionately waiting
For the miraculous birth, there always must be
Children who did not specially want it to happen, skating
On a pond at the edge of the wood:
They never forgot
10 That even the dreadful martyrdom must run its course
Anyhow in a corner, some untidy spot
Where the dogs go on with their doggy life and the torturer's horse
Scratches its innocent behind on a tree.

In Bruegel's *Icarus,* for instance: how everything turns away
15 Quite leisurely from the disaster; the ploughman may
Have heard the splash, the **forsaken** cry,
But for him it was not an important failure; the sun shone
As it had to on the white legs disappearing into the green
Water; and the expensive delicate ship that must have seen
20 Something amazing, a boy falling out of the sky,
Had somewhere to get to and sailed calmly on.

---

1. *The Old Masters* refers to great European artists of the sixteenth to eighteenth centuries.

2 Irony *What is ironic about the ship sailing "calmly on"?*

Vocabulary

reverently (rev′ rənt lē) *adv.* respectfully; with deep affection or veneration
forsaken (fôr sāk′ ən) *adj.* deserted or lonely

W. H. AUDEN **1133**

English Learners

DIFFERENTIATED INSTRUCTION

Advanced Point out to English learners that the first stanza of the poem is like a thesis statement about the Old Masters, whereas the second stanza provides evidence to support the thesis.

Have students summarize the poet's main argument as stated in the first stanza of the poem. Then have them explain the supporting details set forth in the second stanza.

Teach

Motor Manufacturing – Empire buying makes busy factories, 1928. Poster. Victoria & Albert Museum, London.

View the Art Poster art in the 1920s shared many characteristics with fine art—bold, strong shapes, bright colors, and a focus on progress and technology. What do you infer about the people shown in this image? ★ How might this relate to Auden's title?

The Unknown Citizen

W. H. Auden

Reading Practice

*(To JS/07/M/378
This Marble Monument Is Erected by the State)*[1]

He was found by the Bureau of Statistics to be
One against whom there was no official complaint,
And all the reports on his conduct agree
That, in the modern sense of an old-fashioned word, he was a saint,
5   For in everything he did he served the Greater Community.
Except for the War till the day he retired
He worked in a factory and never got fired,
But satisfied his employers, Fudge Motors Inc.
Yet he wasn't a scab[2] or odd in his views,
10   For his Union reports that he paid his dues,
(Our report on his Union shows it was sound)
And our Social Psychology workers found
That he was popular with his mates and liked a drink.
The Press are convinced that he bought a paper every day
15   And that his reactions to advertisements were normal in every way.
Policies taken out in his name prove that he was fully insured,
And his Health-card shows he was once in hospital but left it cured.
Both Producers Research and High-Grade Living declare
He was fully **sensible** to the advantages of the Installment Plan
20   And had everything necessary to the Modern Man,
A phonograph, a radio, a car, and a frigidaire.
Our researchers into Public Opinion are content
That he held the proper opinions for the time of year;
When there was peace, he was for peace; when there was war, he went.
25   He was married and added five children to the population,
Which our Eugenist[3] says was the right number for a parent of his generation,
And our teachers report that he never interfered with their education.
Was he free? Was he happy? The question is absurd:
Had anything been wrong, we should certainly have heard.

---

1. A quotation or a short inscription at the beginning of a poem is called an *epigraph*.
2. A *scab* is slang for someone who does not want to join a union.
3. A *Eugenist* is someone who studies or supports the hereditary enhancement of the human race by controlled breeding.

1 | Irony *How do you know that this passage is ironic?*

2 | World War II and Its Aftermath *Do you think Auden believes that this is all people in the modern world need? What do you think he is suggesting in these lines?*

Vocabulary

sensible (sen′ sə bəl) *adj.* having good judgment or sound thinking

W. H. AUDEN   **1135**

English Learners

DIFFERENTIATED INSTRUCTION

Beginning Inform English learners that Auden's use of capitalization is not typical. Explain that terms such as *Greater Community, War, Press,* and *Modern Man* are meant to signify abstract ideas. Have student find and read aloud other examples of atypical capitalization in the poem. (*Union, Social Psychology, Health-card, Installment Plan*)

Approaching Level

DIFFERENTIATED INSTRUCTION

Strategic Have students find the beginning and end of the poem's sentences. Discuss the poetic lines' relationship to the sentences. Pair students to read the poem aloud, indicating sentences by phrasing.

Teach

Literary Element | 1

Irony **Answer:** *This statement is hyperbolic and clarifies a common idiom that would not normally need clarification; a person is not a saint just because he or she leads a normal life. The idiom itself is ironic; the state considers the unknown citizen to be a saint because he did nothing out of the ordinary.*

APPROACHING To aid approaching level learners, encourage them to first describe what the expression "he was a saint" usually means. Then have them compare this definition with the actions of the unknown citizen.

Big Idea | 2

World War II and Its Aftermath **Answer:** *Auden does not believe that this is all people in the modern world need. He may be suggesting that consumer goods are a poor substitute for spiritual fulfillment.*

 To check students' understanding of the selection, see Unit 6 Teaching Resources Book, p. 214.

After You Read

Assess

1. Students might comment on people's being disconnected and not having good priorities.

2. (a) Its "human position"; suffering is generally ignored amidst everyday life. (b) The dogs go on with their lives; the horse scratches its behind. (c) Nature is indifferent.

3. (a) Icarus falls from the sky. (b) "Everything" turns away from the event.

4. (a) The citizen is described as a factory worker, a war veteran, and an ordinary person. (b) The epigraph suggests that the citizen is a statistic more than an actual human being.

5. (a) People ignore the suffering of others. (b) Some might disagree, since suffering is often in the news.

6. (a) Auden uses three central images of suffering: birth, martyrdom, and a scene from a myth. (b) Many will select Icarus's fall, since it is described in more detail.

7. (a) A mindless, mechanized government that views its citizens only as letters and numbers dehumanizes individuals. (b) Students' responses will vary.

8. Both suggest disillusionment with society and government.

9. Students' answers will vary.

Literary Element

1. It is ironic that children do not "specially want" the miraculous birth, that the martyrdom takes place in "some untidy spot," and that no one would investigate the crash of a flying boy. All are examples of insensitivity toward suffering.

2. Examples of verbal irony include the citizen's saintliness, the citizen's having "everything necessary to the Modern Man," and the poem's final lines. Irony is essential to the poem.

> For additional assessment, see Assessment Resources, pp. 271–272.

Review: Diction

1. Examples include "horse scratches its innocent behind" (lines 12–13) and "Had somewhere to get to" (line 21). Both provide contrast to the exotic, fantastic events of the poem.

2. It emphasizes that ignored suffering is ordinary.

After You Read

Respond and Think Critically

Respond and Interpret

1. What is your opinion of Auden's portrayal of humanity in both poems?

2. (a)According to the speaker in "Musée des Beaux Arts," what did the "Old Masters" understand about suffering? (b)What do the dogs do and how does "the torturer's horse" behave? (c)What does this suggest about nature's reaction to human suffering?

3. (a)What "disaster" occurs in the second stanza? (b)According to the speaker of the poem, how does "everything" in Brueghel's painting react to this disaster?

4. (a)In "The Unknown Citizen," how is the citizen described? (b)What effect does the epigraph have on the poem as a whole?

Analyze and Evaluate

5. (a)What is the message of "Musée des Beaux Arts"? (b)Do you agree with this message? Explain.

6. (a)How does Auden use **imagery** to convey his ideas about suffering in "Musée des Beaux Arts"? (b)Which image do you believe is most effective? Explain.

7. (a)What is the message of "The Unknown Citizen"? (b)Do you agree or disagree with this message?

Connect

8. **Big Idea** World War II and Its Aftermath In what ways do these poems suggest the disillusionment of British writers during this time?

9. **Connect to Today** In what ways are people today disconnected from the world around us? Is culture still preoccupied with statistics instead of emotion? Explain.

Literary Element Irony

Irony is an important element to identify and analyze because it can completely shade the message of a literary work. For example, if you do not grasp the irony in Auden's "The Unknown Citizen" you will miss the main message of the poem.

1. Find several examples of **dramatic irony** in "Musée des Beaux Arts" and explain how they support the poem's theme.

2. Cite several examples of **verbal irony** in "The Unknown Citizen" and explain how they help to convey the poem's message.

Review: Diction

As you learned on page 744, an author's word choice, or use of appropriate words to convey a particular meaning, is called **diction**. Good writers choose their words carefully to express their intended meaning precisely. Diction is particularly important in poetry, which uses language more economically than most prose does. In "Musée des Beaux Arts," Auden deliberately uses language that is plain, straightforward, even earthy—as when he describes a corner "where the dogs go on with their doggy life." In this example, Auden's diction creates an unromantic matter-of-fact tone.

Partner Activity Work with a partner to answer the following questions.

1. Find another example of mundane or earthy language in "Musée des Beaux Arts." What effect is created by this choice of language?

2. In your opinion, how does Auden's diction help convey the **theme**, or message about life, of "Musée des Beaux Arts"?

Reading Strategy · Clarify Meaning

The meaning of a poem can sometimes be difficult to determine. When a passage in a literary work is not clear to you, ask yourself questions and rephrase it in your own words.

1. Paraphrase lines 10–13 of "Musée des Beaux Arts." How do these lines add to the theme?

2. Examine lines 24–26 in "The Unknown Citizen." What is the tone of these lines?

Vocabulary Practice

Practice with Analogies Choose the word that best completes each analogy. To complete an analogy, decide on the relationship represented by the first pair of words. Then apply that relationship to the second set of words.

1. violently : peacefully :: reverently :
   a. disrespectfully
   b. happily
   c. swiftly

2. bold : brave :: forsaken :
   a. unhealthy
   b. desolate
   c. meaningful

3. vivid : bright :: sensible :
   a. cluttered
   b. sensational
   c. reasonable

Academic Vocabulary

In Auden's poem, **statistics** *show that nothing could have been wrong with the citizen.*

Statistics is an academic word. Someone might use **statistics** as objective data, when arguing.

Explore the meaning of this word by creating questions about **statistics** in the poem.

EXAMPLE:
Question: How many children did the citizen have?
Answer: He had five children.

For more on academic vocabulary, see pages 56 and R81.

Connect to *Art*

Assignment Research the work of the artist Brueghel the Elder, including *The Fall of Icarus* referred to in and displayed with "Musée des Beaux Arts." Write a short report on Brueghel's art, looking for consistent elements, such as subject matter, theme, and tone.

Investigate First, reread "Musée des Beaux Arts" and carefully examine *The Fall of Icarus.* If you are not familiar with the myth of Icarus, look under "Greek mythology" in an encyclopedia. Take notes on what you learn.

Then consult reliable art resources in your library and on the Internet. Include both primary sources—other paintings by Brueghel the Elder—and secondary ones—commentary about the artist by art historians and critics. Identify any unfamiliar terms and look up their definitions—you will want to include these in your report. Finally, make a chart summarizing your information.

EXAMPLE:

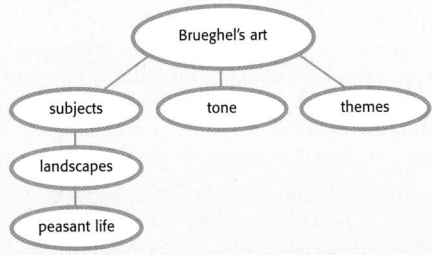

Create Make photocopies of Brueghel's paintings or display them using a slide show program on your computer. Also consider presenting your graphic organizer to summarize your material.

Report In a presentation for the class, tie in what you have learned about Brueghel's work with any inferences you had made about him from Auden's poem. Use presentation techniques such as appropriate eye contact, tone of voice, and body language.

W. H. AUDEN **1137**

After You Read

Reading Strategy

1. "When a terrible killing occurs, dogs and horses will go on with their lives." These lines state the theme of the poem: nature carries on regardless of suffering.

2. The tone is cold and clinical.

Vocabulary

1. a 2. b 3. c

Academic Vocabulary

Students should write and answer questions about objective facts presented in the poem.

Progress Check

Can students analyze irony?

If No → See Unit 6 Teaching Resources Book, p. 211.

Progress Check

Can students clarify meaning?

If No → See Unit 6 Teaching Resources Book, p. 212.

Connect to *Art*

Use these criteria in evaluating student oral reports:

- The report represents an analysis of Pieter Brueghel the Elder's art.

- Information is drawn from a number of reliable sources to address the artists' subject matter, tone, and themes.

- Visual aids and appropriate presentation techniques are incorporated into the delivery of the report.

 To create custom assessments online, go to Progress Reporter Online Assessment.

 To create custom assessments using software, use ExamView Assessment Suite.

Before You Read

A Shocking Accident

Bellringer Options

**Selection Focus
Transparency 61**

**Daily Language Practice
Transparency 98**

Or discuss how people respond to bad news. **Ask:** Do you think there are right and wrong ways to react to bad news, or is any response appropriate? *(Students might suggest that many responses are acceptable, but some, such as violence, are never appropriate.)* Is humor ever appropriate when discussing serious events? *(Answers will vary. In some cases, humor might be used as a defense mechanism to mitigate the power or impact of the event.)*

Meet **Graham Greene**
(1904–1991)

Among the finest writers of postwar Britain, Graham Greene produced a string of popular spy thrillers, which he called his "entertainments," as well as more serious works of literature. The grandnephew of Victorian writer Robert Louis Stevenson, Greene was a masterful storyteller who achieved both popular and critical success.

Headmaster's Son Greene grew up in Hertfordshire, north of London. He attended the exclusive Berkhamsted School, of which his father was headmaster, and came to detest the brutalities of boarding-school life, especially since he was often tormented for being the headmaster's son. At seventeen he suffered an emotional breakdown and ran away. Later, recalling his tortured years at the school, Greene wrote: "One met for the first time characters, adult and adolescent, who bore about them the genuine quality of evil."

As a result of running away from boarding school, Greene spent six months under the care of a London psychoanalyst, who also happened to be a writer. Later Greene would call these months the happiest time of his life. Not only did he escape the hated boarding school, but he began to write for himself with the encouragement of the sympathetic doctor. The experience also sparked Greene's lifelong interest in psychoanalysis.

Writing and Spying Greene attended Oxford University and, upon graduation in 1925, published a volume of poetry. For the next few years, he worked as a journalist, eventually finding himself on the staff of one of Britain's best newspapers, the London *Times*. After several years, he resigned to become a full-time writer. With the publication of *The Man Within* (1929), Greene established himself as a novelist. Not long afterward came two

major novels: *Brighton Rock* (1938) and *The Power and the Glory* (1940).

Along with many other English authors, Greene served in British intelligence during World War II. His experience helped him in the writing of his spy novels, many of which were turned into popular films. Greene also found there was plenty to spy on in his own society. A careful observer, he was attentive to the smallest details: "You're there, listening to every word, but part of you is observing. Everything is useful to a writer, you see—every scrap, even the longest and most boring of luncheon parties."

> *"The great advantage of being a writer is that you can spy on people."*
>
> —Graham Greene

Literary Success A convert to Roman Catholicism, Greene often treated moral and religious themes in his more serious fiction. He also was a worldwide traveler and is noted for his realistic depiction of Cold War and colonial politics in novels like *The Heart of the Matter* (1948), *The Quiet American* (1956), and *The Comedians* (1966). In addition, he produced such humorous satires as *Our Man in Havana* (1958), a parody of his own spy thrillers.

 Literature Online

Author Search For more about Graham Greene, go to glencoe.com and enter QuickPass code GLB9817u6.

Selection Skills

Literary Elements
- Character (SE pp. 1139–1144)
- Recognize Author's Purpose (TE p. 1140)

Listening/Speaking/Viewing Skills
- Analyze Art (SE p. 1140)
- Storytelling (TE p. 1142)

A Shocking Accident

Reading Skills
- Evaluate Comic Devices (SE pp. 1139–1144)

Vocabulary Skills
- Synonyms (SE p. 1144)
- Word Usage (TE p. 1139)

Writing Skills/Grammar
- Interior Monologue (SE p. 1144)

Literature and Reading Preview

Connect to the Story

Why do people sometimes find humor in shocking situations? In a small group, discuss why people might react this way.

Build Background

"A Shocking Accident" draws on Greene's early school experiences and reflects his more satirical side. In England, "public schools" are expensive private schools: the term *public* merely dates back to a time when these schools were the first schools opened outside the home. Two prestigious public schools mentioned in this story are Marlborough and Rugby.

Set Purposes for Reading

Big Idea World War II and Its Aftermath

During the years after World War II, a sense of cultural anxiety and disillusionment permeated British writing. As you read, ask yourself, What is Greene criticizing or satirizing in this story?

Literary Element Character

A **character** is a person or animal portrayed in a literary work. Less important characters, known as **minor characters**, are used by a writer to "fill out" a scene, to provide dialogue, or to further the plot in some way. As opposed to **main characters**, who are typically fully developed, minor characters display few personality traits and generally act in a consistent manner. As you read, ask yourself, How would I classify each character in this story?

Reading Strategy Evaluate Comic Devices

The humor in a work of literature can come from a number of different literary elements. Sometimes it comes from exaggerated or ironic situations. Sometimes the characters themselves have comic traits. Often, the use of language—such as **hyperbole**, or exaggeration used to express strong emotion—can give a story its comic tone. When you **evaluate comic devices**, you decide how effectively the writer has used those devices to create humor. As you read, ask yourself, Why do I find this funny?

···

Tip: Taking Notes Use a chart to record examples of comic devices in the story and their effectiveness.

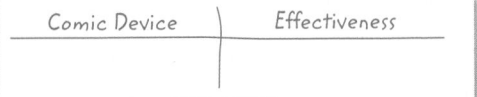

Comic Device	Effectiveness

Learning Objectives

For pages 1138–1144

In studying this text, you will focus on the following objectives:

Literary Study: Analyzing character.

Reading: Evaluating comic devices.

Writing: Writing an interior monologue.

Vocabulary

callousness (kal′ əs nəs) *n.* hardness in mind or feelings; insensitivity; p. 1141 *The reporters showed callousness in interviewing the mourners at the funeral.*

commiseration (kə miz′ ə rā′ shən) *n.* a feeling or expression of sympathy; compassion; p. 1141 *Those players who grumbled about the referee's calls received no commiseration from their coach.*

intrinsically (in trin′ zik lē) *adv.* inherently; in its very nature; p. 1142 *The head of the social services department believes that people are intrinsically good.*

brevity (brev′ ə tē) *n.* shortness in speech or writing; p. 1142 *By deleting unnecessary words, you give your writing brevity, clarity, and force.*

appease (ə pēz′) *v.* to bring to a state of peace or quiet; satisfy; p. 1143 *Sometimes, only a bottle of warm milk can appease a crying baby.*

GRAHAM GREENE **1139**

Before You Read

Focus

Summary

At preparatory school, young Jerome is informed that his father, a travel writer, has died in Naples. The cause of death, a "shocking accident," is a falling pig. The weight of the pig caused a balcony to break as Jerome's father was unluckily walking below. In the following years, Jerome rehearses ways of relating the tragedy without eliciting laughter from the listener. When he falls in love with Sally, he dreads telling her the story. To his great relief, she reacts with appropriate horror, and he knows they are meant to marry.

 For summaries in languages other than English, see Unit 6 Teaching Resources Book, pp. 216–221.

Vocabulary

Word Usage Divide students into small groups. Have each group write a short paragraph using each of the vocabulary words correctly. When all of the groups have finished, ask one member from each group to share the paragraph they have created.

 For additional vocabulary practice, see Unit 6 Teaching Resources Book, p. 224.

 For additional context, see Glencoe Interactive Vocabulary CD-ROM.

English Learners

DIFFERENTIATED INSTRUCTION

 PARTNERS **Intermediate** Have English learners work in pairs. With their partner, have them recount a time in their life when they found humor in an event not intended to be funny. For example, if someone was showing off on a skateboard and fell, they may have laughed even though accidents are not supposed to be funny. Once students have discussed their personal experiences, ask volunteers to share their stories with the class. Discuss why people sometimes have this reaction to shocking or upsetting events.

View the Art ★

Answer: *The geometric patterns give the image an orderly, rigid feel, which is disturbed by the pig and the apples he has scattered around the ground.*

Austrian-born artist Ditz lives in England, where she creates popular images that appear in galleries as well as on greeting cards, ceramics, and textiles. She often turns her artistic eye to animals, from cats and dogs to farmyard horses, pigs, and sheep.

For an audio recording of this selection, use Listening Library Audio CD-ROM.

Readability Scores

Dale-Chall: 8.9
DRP: 56
Lexile: 1030

A Shocking Accident

Graham Greene

The Apple-Tub, 1992. Ditz. Private collection.

View the Art This image relies heavily on geometric, repeating patterns. What "feel" does this give the scene? What effect does the pig's action have on the scene? ★

1

Jerome was called into his housemaster's[1] room in the break between the second and the third class on a Thursday morning. He had no fear of trouble, for he was a warden—the name that the proprietor and headmaster of a rather expensive preparatory school had chosen to give to approved, reliable boys in the lower forms[2] (from a warden one became a guardian and finally before leaving, it was hoped for Marlborough or Rugby, a crusader). The housemaster, Mr. Wordsworth, sat behind his desk with an appearance of perplexity[3] and apprehension.[4] Jerome had the odd impression when he entered that he was a cause of fear.

"Sit down, Jerome," Mr. Wordsworth said. "All going well with the trigonometry?"

"Yes, sir."

"I've had a telephone call, Jerome. From your aunt. I'm afraid I have bad news for you."

"Yes, sir?"

"Your father has had an accident."

"Oh."

Mr. Wordsworth looked at him with some surprise. "A serious accident."

"Yes, sir?"

Jerome worshipped his father: the verb is exact. As man re-creates God, so Jerome re-created his father—from a restless widowed author into a mysterious adventurer who traveled in far places—Nice, Beirut, Majorca, even the Canaries. The time had arrived about his eighth birthday when Jerome believed that his father either "ran guns"[5] or was a member of the British Secret Service. Now it occurred to him that his father might have been wounded in "a hail of machine-gun bullets."

Mr. Wordsworth played with the ruler on his desk. He seemed at a loss how to continue. He said, "You know your father was in Naples?"

"Yes, sir."

"Your aunt heard from the hospital today."

"Oh."

5. *Ran guns* means "smuggled firearms and ammunition."

Character *How does Jerome react to the news of his father's accident?* **1**

Character *Why does this thought pop into Jerome's mind?* **2**

1. A *housemaster* is a teacher who supervises a residence hall of a boys' school.
2. Here, *forms* means "grades."
3. *Perplexity* is the state of being puzzled or confused.
4. Here, *apprehension* means "dread."

1140 UNIT 6 THE MODERN AGE

Mr. Wordsworth said with desperation, "It was a street accident."

"Yes, sir?" It seemed quite likely to Jerome that they would call it a street accident. The police of course had fired first; his father would not take human life except as a last resort.

"I'm afraid your father was very seriously hurt indeed."

"Oh."

"In fact, Jerome, he died yesterday. Quite without pain."

"Did they shoot him through the heart?"

"I beg your pardon. What did you say, Jerome?"

"Did they shoot him through the heart?"

"Nobody shot him, Jerome. A pig fell on him." An inexplicable convulsion took place in the nerves of Mr. Wordsworth's face; it really looked for a moment as though he were going to laugh. He closed his eyes, composed his features and said rapidly as though it were necessary to expel the story as quickly as possible, "Your father was walking along a street in Naples when a pig fell on him. A shocking accident. Apparently in the poorer quarters of Naples they keep pigs on their balconies. This one was on the fifth floor. It had grown too fat. The balcony broke. The pig fell on your father."

Mr. Wordsworth left his desk rapidly and went to the window, turning his back on Jerome. He shook a little with emotion.

Jerome said, "What happened to the pig?"

2

This was not **callousness** on the part of Jerome, as it was interpreted by Mr. Wordsworth to his colleagues (he even discussed with them whether, perhaps, Jerome was yet fitted to be a warden). Jerome was only attempting to visualize the strange scene to get the details right. Nor was Jerome a boy who cried; he was a boy who brooded,[6] and it never

occurred to him at his preparatory school that the circumstances of his father's death were comic—they were still part of the mystery of life. It was later, in his first term at his public school, when he told the story to his best friend, that he began to realize how it affected others. Naturally after that disclosure he was known, rather unreasonably, as Pig.

Unfortunately his aunt had no sense of humor. There was an enlarged snapshot of his father on the piano; a large sad man in an unsuitable dark suit posed in Capri with an umbrella (to guard him against sunstroke), the Faraglione rocks forming the background. By the age of sixteen Jerome was well aware that the portrait looked more like the author of *Sunshine and Shade* and *Rambles in the Balearics* than an agent of the Secret Service. All the same he loved the memory of his father: he still possessed an album filled with picture-postcards (the stamps had been soaked off long ago for his other collection), and it pained him when his aunt embarked with strangers on the story of his father's death.

"A shocking accident," she would begin, and the stranger would compose his or her features into the correct shape for interest and **commiseration.** Both reactions, of course, were false, but it was terrible for Jerome to see how suddenly, midway in her rambling discourse,[7] the interest would become genuine. "I can't think how such things can be allowed in a civilized country," his aunt would say. "I suppose one has to regard Italy as civilized. One is prepared for all kinds of things abroad, of course, and my brother was a great traveler. He always carried a water filter with him. It was far less expensive, you know, than buying all those

---

6. *Brooded* means "pondered unhappily."

7. As it is used here, *discourse* means "story."

World War II and Its Aftermath *What does Greene criticize about British public schools?*

> **Vocabulary**
>
> **callousness** (kal′ əs nəs) *n.* hardness in mind or feelings; insensitivity

> **Vocabulary**
>
> **commiseration** (kə miz′ ə rā′ shən) *n.* a feeling or expression of sympathy; compassion

GRAHAM GREENE **1141**

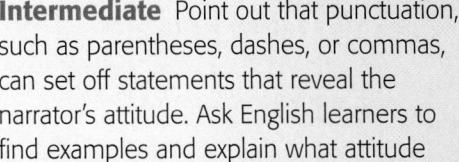

English Learners
DIFFERENTIATED INSTRUCTION

Intermediate Point out that punctuation, such as parentheses, dashes, or commas, can set off statements that reveal the narrator's attitude. Ask English learners to find examples and explain what attitude the author expresses.

Approaching Level
DIFFERENTIATED INSTRUCTION

SMALL GROUP

Emerging The scene between Jerome and his housemaster is presented with little commentary to explain the characters' feelings. Have approaching-level students work in small groups to read the dialogue and discuss how the character feels.

World War II and Its Aftermath Answer: *Greene criticizes the cruelty of public-school students who ridicule classmates and call them by demeaning nicknames.*

Teach

Evaluate Comic Devices

Answer: *Jerome's intense concern over how to explain his father's death to a biographer is ironic because nobody plans to write a biography of his father. Student evaluations of the passage's effectiveness will vary, but it does illustrate the fact that Jerome is much too worried about reactions to the pig story.*

 For additional practice using the reading skill or strategy, see Unit 6 Teaching Resources Book, p. 223.

Vocabulary | 2

Word Roots Say: Use your knowledge of word roots to predict what might be on display at a hydrographic museum. *(Students should identify roots meaning "water" (hydr) and "writing" (graph). Hydrography is the study and mapping of the earth's waters. A hydrographic museum might display maps of oceans, lakes, and rivers.)*

Cultural History ☆

Times Literary Supplement
This London weekly bills itself as "the world's most authoritative review of literature, scholarship and the visual and performing arts." It probably is the most prestigious publication in which Jerome might hope to see his father mentioned.

---

bottles of mineral water. My brother always said that his filter paid for his dinner wine. You can see from that what a careful man he was, but who could possibly have expected when he was walking along the Via Dottore Manuele Panucci on his way to the Hydrographic[8] Museum that a pig would fall on him?" That was the moment when the interest became genuine.

Jerome's father had not been a very distinguished writer, but the time always seems to come, after an author's death, when somebody thinks it worth his while to write a letter to the *Times Literary Supplement* announcing the preparation of a biography and asking to see any letters or documents or receive any anecdotes from friends of the dead man. Most of the biographies, of course, never appear—one wonders whether the whole thing may not be an obscure form of blackmail and whether many a potential writer of a biography or thesis finds the means in this way to finish his education at Kansas or Nottingham.[9] Jerome, however, as a chartered accountant, lived far from the literary world. He did not realize how small the menace[10] really was, or that the danger period for someone of his father's obscurity had long passed. Sometimes he rehearsed the method of recounting his father's death so as to reduce the comic element to its smallest dimensions—it would be of no use to refuse information, for in that case the biographer would undoubtedly visit his aunt who was living to a great old age with no sign of flagging.[11]

It seemed to Jerome that there were two possible methods—the first led gently up to the accident, so that by the time it was described the listener was so well prepared that the death came really as an anticlimax. The chief danger

---

8. *Hydrographic* means "relating to the scientific analysis of the physical conditions of water."
9. *Nottingham*, a city in central England, is home to several universities.
10. A *menace* is a threat.
11. *Flagging* means "weakening."

1 **Evaluate Comic Devices** *What is ironic about Jerome's concerns in this passage? Do the wording and tone of the passage express this irony clearly?*

---

of laughter in such a story was always surprise. When he rehearsed this method Jerome began boringly enough.

"You know Naples and those high tenement buildings? Somebody once told me that the Neapolitan[12] always feels at home in New York just as the man from Turin[13] feels at home in London because the river runs in much the same way in both cities. Where was I? Oh, yes. Naples, of course. You'd be surprised in the poorer quarters what things they keep on the balconies of those sky-scraping tenements—not washing, you know, or bedding, but things like livestock, chickens or even pigs. Of course the pigs get no exercise whatever and fatten all the quicker." He could imagine how his hearer's eyes would have glazed by this time. "I've no idea, have you, how heavy a pig can be, but these old buildings are all badly in need of repair. A balcony on the fifth floor gave way under one of those pigs. It struck the third floor balcony on its way down and sort of ricocheted into the street. My father was on the way to the Hydrographic Museum when the pig hit him. Coming from that height and that angle it broke his neck." This was really a masterly attempt to make an **intrinsically** interesting subject boring.

The other method Jerome rehearsed had the virtue of **brevity**.

"My father was killed by a pig."

"Really? In India?"

"No, in Italy."

"How interesting. I never realized there was pig-sticking in Italy. Was your father keen on polo?"

In course of time, neither too early nor too late, rather as though, in his capacity as a chartered accountant, Jerome had studied the

---

12. A *Neapolitan* is one who lives in Naples, Italy.
13. *Turin* is a city in Italy.

Vocabulary

intrinsically (in trin′ zik lē) *adv.* inherently; in its very nature
brevity (brev′ ə tē) *n.* shortness in speech or writing

Listening and Speaking Practice

Storytelling Jerome rehearses different ways to tell the story of his father's death. Encourage students to try telling versions of this story to achieve one of the following objectives:

- to encourage an audience to see the lighter side of the story
- to focus on the seriousness of it
- to present Jerome's personality

Listeners should comment on which goal they think the storyteller achieved.

statistics and taken the average, he became engaged to be married: to a pleasant fresh-faced girl of twenty-five whose father was a doctor in Pinner.[14] Her name was Sally, her favorite author was still Hugh Walpole,[15] and she had adored babies ever since she had been given a doll at the age of five which moved its eyes and made water. Their relationship was contented rather than exciting, as became the love affair of a chartered accountant; it would never have done if it had interfered with the figures.

One thought worried Jerome, however. Now that within a year he might himself become a father, his love for the dead man increased; he realized what affection had gone into the picture-postcards. He felt a longing to protect his memory, and uncertain whether this quiet love of his would survive if Sally were so insensitive as to laugh when she heard the story of his father's death. Inevitably she would hear it when Jerome brought her to dinner with his aunt. Several times he tried to tell her himself, as she was naturally anxious to know all she could that concerned him.

"You were very small when your father died?"

"Just nine."

"Poor little boy," she said.

"I was at school. They broke the news to me."

"Did you take it very hard?"

"I can't remember."

"You never told me how it happened."

"It was very sudden. A street accident."

"You'll never drive fast, will you, Jemmy?" (She had begun to call him "Jemmy.") It was too late then to try the second method—the one he thought of as the pig-sticking one.

They were going to marry quietly in a registry office and have their honeymoon at Torquay.[16] He avoided taking her to see his aunt until a week before the wedding, but then the night came, and he could not have told himself

whether his apprehension was more for his father's memory or the security of his own love.

The moment came all too soon. "Is that Jemmy's father?" Sally asked, picking up the portrait of the man with the umbrella.

"Yes, dear. How did you guess?"

"He has Jemmy's eyes and brow, hasn't he?"

"Has Jerome lent you his books?"

"No."

"I will give you a set for your wedding. He wrote so tenderly about his travels. My own favorite is *Nooks and Crannies*. He would have had a great future. It made that shocking accident all the worse."

"Yes?"

Jerome longed to leave the room and not see that loved face crinkle with irresistible amusement.

"I had so many letters from his readers after the pig fell on him." She had never been so abrupt before.

And then the miracle happened. Sally did not laugh. Sally sat with open eyes of horror while his aunt told her the story, and at the end, "How horrible," Sally said. "It makes you think, doesn't it? Happening like that. Out of a clear sky."

Jerome's heart sang with joy. It was as though she had **appeased** his fear forever. In the taxi going home he kissed her with more passion than he had ever shown and she returned it. There were babies in her pale blue pupils, babies that rolled their eyes and made water.

"A week today," Jerome said, and she squeezed his hand. "Penny for your thoughts, my darling."

"I was wondering," Sally said, "what happened to the poor pig?"

"They almost certainly had it for dinner," Jerome said happily and kissed the dear child again.

---

14. *Pinner* is a town in England.
15. *Hugh Walpole* was an English novelist.
16. *Torquay* is a town in southwestern England.

3 | Character *What conflict must Jerome resolve?*

Character *What does Sally's question reveal about her?* | **4**

Vocabulary

appease (ə pēz′) *v.* to bring to a state of peace or quiet; satisfy

GRAHAM GREENE **1143**

After You Read

Assess

1. Answers will vary.
2. (a) His father was wounded while spying; he has romanticized his father. (b) The man died when a pig fell onto him from a balcony.
3. One method is very brief, omitting the balcony; the other builds up gradually. Both versions attempt to keep listeners from laughing.
4. The father's death is the opposite of the glamour Jerome imagines.
5. (a) A given set of facts can be perceived in different ways. (b) Students' answers will vary.
6. The cruelty of schoolchildren and the artificiality of polite conversation
7. Jerome's boarding school experience is gentler than the one described by Greene. But Jerome, like Greene, experiences an insensitive headmaster and needless cruel taunting by students.

Literary Element

1. Jerome is a flat character. We see mainly his conventional personality and his feelings toward his father.
2. Jerome is mainly static, although his perspective changes slightly at the end of the story.

Progress Check

Can students analyze character?

If No → See Unit 6 Teaching Resources Book, p. 222.

After You Read

Respond and Think Critically

Respond and Interpret

1. How did you react when you learned what had happened to Jerome's father? Do you think your reaction was appropriate? Why or why not?
2. (a)When Jerome first hears about his father's accident, what does he assume has happened? Why? (b)What actually happened in the accident?

Analyze and Evaluate

3. Compare the methods Jerome devises for telling the story of the accident. In your opinion, why does he devise these two different methods?

4. Find an example of **situational irony** in the story and evaluate the effect it creates.
5. (a)What **theme**, or message about life, do you think Greene wanted to convey through this story? (b)Do you agree with this message?

Connect

6. **Big Idea** World War II and Its Aftermath Which aspects of British society does this story criticize or satirize? Support your response.
7. **Connect to the Author** Reread the biography on page 1138. What aspects of Greene's own experiences appear in "A Shocking Accident"?

Literary Element Character

In this story Jerome is the main character, and the other characters are minor. Characters that show varied and sometimes contradictory traits are called **round**; characters who reveal only a single personality trait are called **flat**.

1. Is Jerome a round or a flat character? Explain.
2. Is he static or dynamic? Give reasons for your answer.

Writing

Write an Interior Monologue Greene does not give readers much insight into the thoughts of his minor characters as he does into Jerome's thoughts, fears, and feelings. Write a brief interior monologue for the headmaster of Jerome's school, detailing his thoughts as he tries to tell Jerome the bad news. What "emotion" is he shaking with on page 1141? Try to keep your monologue consistent with what you already know about the character.

LOG ON ▶ **Literature** Online

Selection Resources For Selection Quizzes, eFlashcards, and Reading-Writing Connection activities, go to glencoe.com and enter QuickPass code GLB9817u6.

Reading Strategy Evaluate Comic Devices

Review the chart you created as you read, and then answer the following questions.

1. Look through your chart for examples of hyperbole. Why might Greene's employ hyperbole where he does? Is it effective?
2. Greene uses both situational and verbal irony throughout "A Shocking Accident." Explain which ironies in the story you found effective, and why.

Vocabulary Practice

Practice with Synonyms With a partner, match each boldfaced vocabulary word below with its synonym. Use a thesaurus or dictionary to check your answers. You will not use all of the answer choices.

1. callousness   a. satisfy
2. commiseration   b. innately
3. intrinsically   c. insensitivity
4. brevity   d. concision
5. appease   e. provoke
                        f. sympathy

1144 UNIT 6   THE MODERN AGE

Reading Strategy

1. Possible answers: Greene seems to use hyperbole most often in describing Jerome's thoughts. It is effective because it shows the reader how seriously Jerome is affected by things, despite his lack of outward reaction.
2. Answers will vary.

Vocabulary Practice

1. c 2. f 3. b 4. d 5. a

Writing

Students' interior monologues should reflect the fears and feelings of Jerome which are not expressed in the story.

Grammar Workshop

Run-On Sentences

Literature Connection In the passage below, Graham Greene presents connected ideas in a **compound sentence**—a sentence that has two or more main clauses.

> *"You can see from that what a careful man he was, but who could possibly have expected when he was walking along the Via Dottore Manuele Panucci on his way to the Hydrographic Museum that a pig would fall on him?"*
>
> —Graham Greene, from "A Shocking Accident"

The conjunction *but* separates the two main clauses, and it prevents a **run-on sentence,** or two or more complete sentences written as though they were one.

Problem The clauses of a run-on sentence have no punctuation between them or are separated only by a comma (an error called a comma splice).

Jerome's friends tease him thoughtlessly they don't understand his difficulty in dealing with his father's bizarre accident.

Jerome's friends tease him thoughtlessly, they don't understand his difficulty in dealing with people.

Solution A Divide the sentence into two sentences.

Jerome's friends tease him thoughtlessly. They don't understand his difficulty in dealing with his father's bizarre accident.

Solution B Separate the clauses with a semicolon.

Jerome's friends tease him thoughtlessly; they don't understand his difficulty in dealing with his father's bizarre accident.

Solution C Insert a comma and a coordinating conjunction between the clauses.

Jerome's friends tease him thoughtlessly, <u>for</u> they don't understand his difficulty in dealing with his father's bizarre accident.

Revise Correct each of the following run-on sentences.

1. Jerome admired his father in fact, he worshipped him.

2. Jerome did not cry, he brooded.

3. Mr. Wordsworth tried to hide a laugh, Jerome found the accident mysterious rather than funny.

4. Sally recognized the old man's photograph she had not read his books.

Learning Objectives

In this workshop, you will focus on the following objectives:

Grammar:
Understanding how to avoid run-on sentences. Understanding how to use commas and coordinating conjunctions.

Compound and Run-On Sentences

A **compound sentence** is a sentence that contains more than one main clause. In a **run-on sentence,** the clauses are written as though they expressed only one main idea.

Coordinating Conjunctions

and	or
but	so
for	yet
nor	

Tip

To avoid run-on sentences, reviewing your work and insert correct punctuation and conjunctions in sentences that present more than one complete idea.

Language Handbook

For more about sentence structure, see the Language Handbook, pp. R47–R48.

 Literature Online

Grammar For more grammar practice, go to glencoe.com and enter QuickPass code GLB9817u6.

Approaching Level

DIFFERENTIATED INSTRUCTION

 Emerging Have student pairs create run-on sentences and have the pairs exchange their sentences and correct them. **Ask:** How do the corrections make sentences more effective? *(Answers will vary.)*

Grammar Workshop

Run-On Sentences

Focus

On the board, write the following:

Mary's mother berated her constantly she had high expectations that Mary couldn't meet. **Ask:** What is wrong with this sentence? *(It is a run-on sentence.)* How can it be corrected? *(In any of three ways. Make it two sentences, insert a semicolon, or insert a comma and conjunction.)*

Teach

Coordinating Conjunctions

Use *and* or *or* to show similarity. Use *but, yet,* or *nor* to show contrast. Use *for* or *so* to show cause and effect.

Assess

Possible rewrites:

1. Jerome admired his father; in fact, he worshipped him.

2. Jerome did not cry. He brooded.

3. Mr. Wordsworth tried to hide a laugh, yet Jerome found the accident mysterious rather than funny.

4. Sally recognized the old man's photograph, but she had not read his books.

 For additional grammar practice, see Unit 6 Teaching Resources Book, p. 229.

1145

Before You Read

Fern Hill and *Do Not Go Gentle into That Good Night*

Meet **Dylan Thomas**
(1914–1953)

Dylan Thomas once wrote, "A poet is a poet for such a very tiny bit of his life; for the rest, he is a human being." Thomas certainly tried to live his life to the fullest. He loved parties; he was an entertaining conversationalist; and he enjoyed speaking and reading his poems in public.

> *"A good poem is a contribution to reality. The world is never the same once a good poem has been added to it."*
>
> —Dylan Thomas

Early Success Born in Swansea (swän′ zē), South Wales, Thomas was the son of a farmer's daughter and an English teacher. He attended the Swansea grammar school, where he gained a wide breadth of knowledge of English poetry, though he was an average student in most subjects. He displayed an early aptitude for writing poetry, submitting "decent verse" to his school newspaper when he was only eleven years old.

At age seventeen, Thomas decided not to continue his education and took a job at the local newspaper, writing book and theater reviews. When he was nineteen, he published his first poem in the *New English Weekly*, and within the year he was publishing a poem every month in various literary journals. At age twenty, he published his first book of poetry, *Eighteen Poems*, for which he received instant critical acclaim. At such a young age, he had already gained a literary reputation for the "wildness" of his imagery, for his use of sound and rhythm, and for his exploration of the inner workings of the mind.

In 1934 Thomas left Wales to live the freewheeling life of a writer in London. To support himself he worked as a journalist, actor, screenwriter, and broadcaster for the British Broadcasting Corporation. During this period he wrote several volumes of short stories and memoirs in addition to poetry. One of his most famous and popular works, "A Child's Christmas in Wales," was a memoir of his childhood in Swansea.

In 1937 Thomas married and then returned to Wales, settling in the small picturesque fishing village of Laugharne, Carmarthenshire. He and his wife, Caitlin, and their three children lived in a converted boathouse overlooking the sea—a setting that inspired many of his poems.

Poet and Performer In 1950, Thomas made his first visit to the United States to embark on a series of whirlwind poetry-reading and speaking tours at American universities. Considered one of the best performers of poetry in modern times, he was idolized by the literary establishment. In 1953, during his third tour of America, he collapsed in New York after a party celebrating his thirty-ninth birthday. He fell into a coma and died several days later of complications from alcoholism.

Shortly before his death Thomas completed *Under Milk Wood*, a radio play celebrating daily life in a small Welsh village. Thomas, who saw himself as a modern-day descendant of the English Romantics, remains best known for his radiant and resonant verse.

 Literature Online

Author Search For more about Dylan Thomas, go to glencoe.com and enter QuickPass code GLB9817u6.

1146 UNIT 6 THE MODERN AGE

Selection Skills

Literary Elements
- Assonance and Consonance (SE pp. 1147–1152)

Reading Skills
- Analyze Figures of Speech (SE pp. 1147–1152)

Fern Hill / Do Not Go Gentle into That Good Night

Vocabulary Skills
- Context Clues (SE p. 1152)
- Academic Vocabulary (SE p. 1152)

Listening/Speaking/ Viewing Skills
- Interview (TE p. 1148)
- Analyze Art (TE p. 1150)

Writing Skills/Grammar
- Expository Essay (SE p. 1153)
- Hyphens (SE p. 1153)

Literature and Reading Preview

Connect to the Poems

How do you feel about the passing of time? Freewrite for a few minutes on the ways that time's passing has affected you.

Build Background

"Fern Hill" is a fine example of Thomas's characteristic use of original images, rich symbols, and dazzling language. This poem was inspired by visits to Fernhill Farm, the home of his aunt Ann Jones. Thomas also enjoyed a particularly close relationship with his father, whom he addressed in "Do Not Go Gentle into That Good Night." The elder Thomas encouraged his son's writing, and Thomas composed many of his early poems seated at his father's desk in the study at their family home in Swansea.

Set Purposes for Reading

Big Idea World War II and Its Aftermath

After World War II, when disillusionment permeated Britain, Thomas sought to affirm the values of home and family. As you read, ask yourself, How do the poems reflect those values?

Literary Element Assonance and Consonance

The repetition of nearby vowel sounds in stressed syllables is called **assonance**, as in the phrase *my wild life*. The repetition of consonant sounds, typically within or at the end of non-rhyming words, is called **consonance**, as in the *d* sounds in this line from Yeats's "The Second Coming": "The blood-dimmed tide is loosed." As you read, ask yourself, How do these techniques affect the poem?

Reading Strategy Analyze Figures of Speech

Analyzing figures of speech involves looking critically at specific kinds of figurative language, such as metaphor, personification, simile, or symbol. Another, less common device is known as **oxymoron**, which combines two contradictory terms. As you read, ask yourself, What do figures of speech help Thomas express?

Tip: Charting Figures of Speech Use a chart to record your interpretations of figures of speech in these poems.

Figure of speech	Interpretation
Simile: "happy as the grass was green"	Joy was intrinsic to the speaker as a child.

Learning Objectives

For pages 1146–1152

In studying these texts, you will focus on the following objectives:

Literary Study: Analyzing assonance and consonance.

Reading: Analyzing figures of speech.

Vocabulary

hail (hāl) *v.* to acclaim; pay tribute to; p. 1148 *A crowd gathered to hail the championship team on its triumphant return.*

spellbound (spel′ bound) *adj.* fascinated; affected as if by enchantment; p. 1149 *Roger stared as if spellbound at the flickering colored lights on the water.*

heedless (hēd′ lis) *adj.* careless; not paying attention; p. 1149 *Ignoring the ranger's warnings, the heedless boys dragged their sleds to the top of the steep hill.*

frail (frāl) *adj.* delicate; fragile; p. 1150 *The frail old men, with their canes and walkers, sat on benches outside the nursing home.*

DYLAN THOMAS **1147**

Before You Read

Focus

Summary

In "Fern Hill," the speaker remembers an idyllic childhood with a poignant sense of nostalgia for the freedom and innocence of that time. Vivid images of a fresh, green countryside combine with repetitive sounds to create a rich portrait of childhood's simplicity and naturalness.

In "Do Not Go Gentle into That Good Night," the speaker urges men to rage against the world rather than calmly accepting their fate. The speaker offers this advice to all men, whether they be wise, good, wild, grave, or even his own father.

 For summaries in languages other than English, see Unit 6 Teaching Resources Book, pp. 230–235.

Vocabulary

Etymology Point out that the word *spellbound* is a compound word made up of *spell* and *bound*. As students look up the etymology of each vocabulary word, have them look up *spell* and *bound* separately.

 For additional vocabulary practice, see Unit 6 Teaching Resources Book, p. 238.

 For additional context, see Glencoe Interactive Vocabulary CD-ROM.

English Learners

DIFFERENTIATED INSTRUCTION

PARTNERS **Intermediate Ask:** How do we keep track of time? Have students form pairs and discuss the various ways we keep track of what day, week, and year it is. Have each pair make a list of their ideas, then share their lists with the class. (*Examples might include calendars, daylight, meal or class times, clocks, weekdays/weekends, seasonal changes, and holidays.*)

1147

Teach

Reading Strategy | 1

Analyze Figures of Speech
Answer: *That time is an authority figure who allowed the speaker to enjoy his childhood play*

[ENGLISH LEARNERS] Have English learners read "Time let me play and be golden in the mercy of his means" as a sentence, identifying its subject and verb.

Big Idea | 2

World War II and Its Aftermath **Answer:** *The images of simple childhood on the farm imply that home life can be happy and satisfying—even wondrous. The speaker's family, though not mentioned specifically, supports these happy activities and helps nurture him.*

[APPROACHING] Have approaching level students list the images in lines 10–18.

Literary Element | 3

Assonance and Consonance
Point out that this poem does not have a formal rhyme scheme, but the poet uses assonance at the ends of some lines—words which do not rhyme but have the same vowel sounds. **Ask:** Which lines end with assonant words? *(lines 4/5, 11/12, 13/14, 16/17)* Why might Thomas have chosen assonance over a traditional rhyme scheme? *(Possible answer: It allows the poet's remembrances to flow more freely and more easily.)*

 For additional literary element practice, see Unit 6 Teaching Resources Book, p. 236.

1148

FERN HILL

Dylan Thomas

Now as I was young and easy under the apple boughs
About the lilting¹ house and happy as the grass was green,
      The night above the dingle² starry,
            Time let me **hail** and climb
5   Golden in the heydays of his³ eyes, **3**
And honored among wagons I was prince of the apple towns
And once below a time I lordly had the trees and leaves
            Trail with daisies and barley
      Down the rivers of the windfall light.

10   And as I was green and carefree, famous among the barns
About the happy yard and singing as the farm was home,
      In the sun that is young once only,
            Time let me play and be
      Golden in the mercy of his means,
15   And green and golden I was huntsman and herdsman, the calves
Sang to my horn, the foxes on the hills barked clear and cold,
            And the sabbath rang slowly
      In the pebbles of the holy streams.

1. *Lilting* means "lively" or "cheerful."
2. A *dingle* is a small wooded valley.
3. A *heyday* is the prime of one's existence; *his* refers to Time.

---

1 Analyze Figures of Speech *What does this personification suggest about time?*

2 World War II and Its Aftermath *What do the images in this stanza imply about the speaker's home and family?*

Vocabulary
hail (hāl) *v.* to acclaim; pay tribute to

1148   UNIT 6   THE MODERN AGE

Listening and Speaking Practice

Interview The speaker in "Fern Hill" is nostalgic about the days of his youth. Encourage students to locate recordings of this poem on the Internet. Ask students to characterize the poet's speaking style, and evaluate whether or not this style is effective. Follow up by asking students how this activity helped them better understand the speaker's feelings.

All the sun long it was running, it was lovely, the hay
20 Fields high as the house, the tunes from the chimneys, it was air
      And playing, lovely and watery
        And fire green as grass.
      And nightly under the simple stars
As I rode to sleep the owls were bearing the farm away, ☆
25 All the moon long I heard, blessed among stables, the nightjars[4]
      Flying with the ricks,[5] and the horses
        Flashing into the dark.

And then to awake, and the farm, like a wanderer white
With the dew, come back, the cock on his shoulder: it was all
30   Shining, it was Adam and maiden,[6]
        The sky gathered again
      And the sun grew round that very day.
So it must have been after the birth of the simple light
In the first, spinning place, the **spellbound** horses walking warm
35   Out of the whinnying green stable
        On to the fields of praise.

And honored among foxes and pheasants by the gay house
Under the new made clouds and happy as the heart was long,
      In the sun born over and over,
40   I ran my **heedless** ways,
      My wishes raced through the house high hay
And nothing I cared, at my sky blue trades, that time allows
In all his tuneful turning so few and such morning songs
        Before the children green and golden
45   Follow him out of grace,[7]

Nothing I cared, in the lamb white days, that time would take me
Up to the swallow thronged loft by the shadow of my hand,
        In the moon that is always rising,
          Nor that riding to sleep
50   I should hear him fly with the high fields
And wake to the farm forever fled from the childless land.
Oh as I was young and easy in the mercy of his means,
        Time held me green and dying
      Though I sang in my chains like the sea.

---

 4 Assonance and Consonance *What examples of consonance do you see in these lines?*

 5 Analyzing Figures of Speech *What was the speaker like as a child?*

Vocabulary

spellbound (spel′ bound) *adj.* fascinated; affected as if by enchantment
heedless (hēd′ lis) *adj.* careless; not paying attention

---

4. *Nightjars* are nocturnal birds.
5. *Ricks* are haystacks.
6. *Adam and maiden* refers to the biblical Adam and Eve in the Garden of Eden.
7. *Follow . . . grace* is a reference to Adam's fall from grace and innocence.

Teach

Literary Element 4

Assonance and Consonance
Answer: *The* k *sound in* a*w*a*k*e, ba*ck*, *and* co*ck* *is an example of consonance; as is the* w *sound in* a*w*ake, *w*anderer, *w*hile *and* *w*ith. **Ask:** What is the effect of repeating the *k* sound, as opposed to another consonant sound? (*The* k *sound is a harsh and abrupt sound. Thomas might be using this hard sounds to highlight the sense of waking up to the rooster's vibrant crowing.*)

Reading Strategy 5

Analyze Figures of Speech **Answer:** *The speaker was utterly joyous, unaware of the bonds of time.*

(**ENGLISH LEARNERS**) Point out to English learners that *my chains* refer to the chains, or bondage, of time. **Ask:** Why would the speaker sing while in chains? (*He was not aware of them; they were unimportant to him.*)

Writer's Technique ☆
Imagery Writers look for new, fresh ways to express human experiences, and "Fern Hill" is full of such imagery. For example, the phrase "riding to sleep" is the poet's way of expressing what people often mean when they say "drifting off to sleep." Instead of drifting into sleep, it is as if the speaker is riding a horse into sleep.

1149

View the Art ★

The Danish painter Laurits Andersen Ring (1854–1933) apprenticed to a house painter before studying painting at the Royal Academy of Fine Arts in Copenhagen. His artwork frequently depicts the country landscapes of his youth and gives artistic importance to the lives of everyday people.

 To check students' understanding of the selection, see Unit 6 Teaching Resources Book, p. 240.

Do Not Go Gentle into That Good Night

Dylan Thomas

Old Man Walking in a Rye Field, 1905. Laurits Andersen Ring. Oil on canvas, 68 x 56 cm.

Do not go gentle into that good night,
Old age should burn and rave at close of day;
Rage, rage against the dying of the light.

Though wise men at their end know dark is right,
5 Because their words had forked no lightning they
Do not go gentle into that good night.

Good men, the last wave by, crying how bright
Their **frail** deeds might have danced in a green bay,
Rage, rage against the dying of the light.

10 Wild men who caught and sang the sun in flight,
And learn, too late, they grieved it on its way,
Do not go gentle into that good night.

Grave men, near death, who see with blinding sight
Blind eyes could blaze like meteors and be gay,
15 Rage, rage against the dying of the light.

And you, my father, there on the sad height,
Curse, bless, me now with your fierce tears, I pray.
Do not go gentle into that good night.
Rage, rage against the dying of the light.

1 Assonance and Consonance *What examples of assonance does this line contain?*

2 Analyze Figures of Speech *What kinds of words might fork lightning?*

Vocabulary

frail (frāl) *adj.* delicate; fragile

Vocabulary Practice

Complete Analogies Analogies show the relationship between pairs of words. One type of relationship between words is that they are opposites:
harsh : gentle :: rave : whisper

Other analogies use synonyms:
rage : anger :: grieved : mourned
Ask students to make their own analogies, using words from the poem.

After You Read

Respond and Think Critically

Respond and Interpret

1. With which of the two poems do you identify more? Why?

2. (a)What has the speaker lost in the last stanza of "Fern Hill"? (b)In your opinion, what are the speaker's "chains"?

3. (a)What four types of people are mentioned in "Do Not Go Gentle into That Good Night"? (b)Why does each rage against death?

Analyze and Evaluate

4. What might Fern Hill **symbolize** for the speaker?

5. In your opinion, does the speaker in "Do Not Go Gentle into That Good Night" express greater love by urging his father to rage than by wishing him a peaceful death? Explain.

6. What might dark and light **symbolize** in "Do Not Go Gentle into That Good Night"?

Connect

7. **Big Idea** **World War II and Its Aftermath** How do these poems affirm the values of home and family?

8. **Connect to the Author** Thomas considered himself a Romantic poet, like Keats or Shelley, rather than a Modernist poet like T. S. Eliot. What evidence of Romantic ideals—such as love and beauty or strong emotion—do you find in these poems?

Visual Literacy: Fine Art

Illustrating the Welsh Countryside

Sir Cedric Morris (1889–1982) spent his formative years in and around Swansea. Largely self-taught, he painted portraits, still lifes, and landscapes. In the oil painting titled *Llanmadoc* 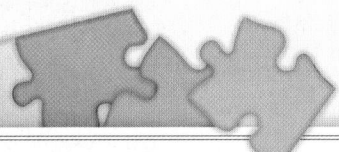 *Hill, Gower Peninsula, 1928,* he depicts a typical farm and outbuildings set among the hills that distinguish the Welsh countryside. The simplicity and clarity of Morris's style enhance his close observation of people and nature. Throughout his career, he used strong colors and bold designs drawn from his association with prominent avant-garde artists of the 1920s.

Group Activity Discuss the following questions with a small group of your classmates.

1. What is the mood of this painting? How does Morris convey this mood?

2. Which details in "Fern Hill" does the painting call to mind?

Llanmadoc Hill, Gower Penninsula, 1928. Sir Cedric Morris. Oil on canvas, 65.4 x 81.2 cm. Glynn Vivian Art Gallery, Swansea, Wales.

DYLAN THOMAS **1151**

After You Read

Assess

1. Answers will vary.

2. (a) The glorious childhood world (b) The constraints of time

3. (a) Wise men, good men, wild men, and grave men (b) Wise men because their words did not exert influence; good men for the good they might have done; wild men because their high living hastened their deaths; grave men for not having risen above their limitations

4. The innocent happiness of Eden

5. Students might say by urging his father to rage he shows passion and a spark of life.

6. Light symbolizes the world of the living; dark symbolizes death.

7. "Fern Hill" presents a loving, almost idyllic, view of home and family. "Do Not Go Gentle into That Good Night" expresses love of family in the speaker's impassioned pleas to his father.

8. Students may say that the nature imagery in Fern Hill and the strong emotions of "Do Not Go Gentle" are similar to the ideals of the Romantic poets.

Visual Literacy

1. Tranquil, even serene; soft lines and blue colors help set that mood.

2. "Apple boughs," "grass was green," "the dingle," "trees and leaves," "barns," "hills," "chimneys," "fields," and "sky blue"

After You Read

Assess

Literary Element

1. 1–2: <u>bou</u>ghs, <u>a</u>bout, h<u>ou</u>se; l10: gr<u>ee</u>n, caref<u>ree</u>; 49–50: r<u>i</u>ding, <u>I</u>, fl<u>y</u>, h<u>igh</u>

2. 5: h<u>eyday</u>s, h<u>i</u>s, <u>eye</u>s; 11: far<u>m</u>, ho<u>m</u>e; 46: la<u>m</u>b, ti<u>m</u>e

3. In "Fern Hill" the repeated g, h, and c sounds in lines 15 and 16 and the <u>f</u>arm <u>f</u>orever <u>f</u>led in line 51; in "Do Not Go Gentle," <u>d</u>eeds and <u>d</u>anced in line 8; <u>s</u>ang and <u>s</u>un in line 10; and <u>bl</u>ind and <u>bl</u>aze in line 14

4. They strengthen imagery and enhance the poems' sound.

Review: Form

1. The verb phrase do not go and the repeated verb rage, which are used as imperatives in stanzas 1 and 6, become verbs for the subjects wise men, good men, wild men, and grave men in stanzas 2, 3, 4, and 5 respectively.

2. To unify the details and drive home the poem's main point

3. To produce a dignified effect

Reading Strategy

1. Time is the child's friend at first. It makes him realize he is aging.

2. That near death people experience a flash of spiritual insight

3. A curse because his father suffers; a blessing because his father is defying death

---

Literary Element Assonance and Consonance

Both **assonance** and **consonance**, together with other sound devices such as alliteration (the repetition of initial consonant sounds), contribute to a poem's musical qualities.

1. What examples of assonance do lines 1–2, 10, and 49–50 of "Fern Hill" contain?

2. Point out examples of consonance in lines 5, 11, and 46 of "Fern Hill."

3. What instances of **alliteration** can you find in these poems?

4. What effects do these sound devices produce?

Review: Form

As you learned on page 457, **form** is the structure a literary work has. Dylan Thomas chose to use the **villanelle** form for his poem "Do Not Go Gentle into That Good Night." This intricate form contains nineteen lines divided into five tercets (three-line stanzas), each with the rhyme scheme aba, and a final quatrain (four-line stanza) with the rhyme scheme abaa. The first line is repeated as a **refrain** at the end of the second and fourth stanzas. The last line of the first stanza is repeated at the end of the third and fifth stanzas. Both lines reappear as the final two lines of the poem.

Partner Activity With another classmate, discuss Thomas's use of the villanelle form in "Do Not Go Gentle into That Good Night."

1. How does Thomas weave lines 1 and 3 into the sentence structures of stanzas 2, 3, 4, and 5?

2. What purpose do the refrains serve in this poem?

3. Why might Thomas have chosen this highly structured form for such a personal and moving subject?

LOG ON ▶ **Literature** Online

Selection Resources For Selection Quizzes, eFlashcards, and Reading-Writing Connection activities, go to glencoe.com and enter QuickPass code GLB9817u6.

Reading Strategy Analyze Figures of Speech

By **analyzing figures of speech**, such as simile, metaphor, personification, symbol, and oxymoron, you can explore the theme of a poem and the author's purpose for writing.

1. In "Fern Hill," how is time **personified**? How would you interpret the speaker's views of the passage of time?

2. In "Do Not Go Gentle into That Good Night," what does the **oxymoron** "blinding sight" (line 13) suggest?

3. How might the father's "fierce tears" (line 17) both curse and bless the speaker?

Vocabulary Practice

Practice with Context Clues Identify the context clues in the following sentences that help you determine the meaning of each bold-faced vocabulary word.

1. The candidate's supporters gathered to **hail** her victory on election night.

2. The children were **spellbound** by the new toy and did not speak until lunch.

3. The **heedless** driver accidentally ran through a red light.

4. My elderly aunt is so **frail** that we are afraid she will fall down and injure herself.

Academic Vocabulary

In "Fern Hill," Thomas adds **layers** to his theme as the poem progresses.

Layer is an academic word. For instance, someone might say that a literary work has several **layers** of meaning.

Using context clues, try to figure out the meaning of layer in the following sentence: Symbols and allusions can add **layers** to a poem's meaning.

For more on academic vocabulary, see pages 56 and R81.

Vocabulary Practice

1. A victory is something worth acknowledging and celebrating, so hail must mean "pay tribute to."

2. The children do not notice what else is going on, so spellbound must mean "fascinated."

3. The driver runs the red light accidentally, so heedless must mean "not paying attention."

4. They are worried that the aunt will fall, so frail must mean "weak and delicate."

Academic Vocabulary

Students should infer that layer means "a single thickness."

Respond Through Writing

Expository Essay

Evaluate Imagery Dylan Thomas sought to taste everything life has to offer and to express the full spectrum of those experiences in his poetry. Write a response to literature in which you discuss how effectively Thomas uses figures of speech to create the imagery of light and dark in his poems, and to add nuance to their themes.

Prewrite With several classmates, brainstorm a list of figures of speech in the poems. Discuss the images of light and dark that each invokes. Then decide whether you will discuss all the imagery in one poem, then all the imagery in the other, or discuss each image as it is represented in both poems.

Draft Be sure to state the message, or meaning, of each poem in your own words. Then return to your list of figures of speech and explain the image of light or darkness that each creates and how that image contributes to the poem's message.

In "Fern Hill," vivid sensory language creates luscious images of light. The days are marked by a personified sun "born over and over." Continuing the personification, Thomas says that the "sun grew round," in a metaphoric pregnancy awaiting "the birth of the simple light." Even the night in the poem is filled by a moon that is a metaphor for the sun—"always rising" and "flashing into the dark."

Sentence structures like the following are helpful in identifying imagery in the poems:

Thomas uses details such as _____ and _____ to create imagery of _____.

Revise Exchange papers with a classmate and respond to each others' essays. Look specifically for nuances, ambiguities, or complexities that have been omitted or misinterpreted. After reviewing your peer reader's comments, use the Writing Workshop checklist on page 972 to make sure you've met the criteria listed there. Then revise your essay accordingly.

Edit and Proofread Proofread your paper, correcting any errors in spelling, grammar, and punctuation. Use the Grammar Tip in the side column to help you with hyphens.

Learning Objectives

In this assignment, you will focus on the following objectives:

Writing: Writing an expository essay.

Literary Study: Evaluating imagery.

▶ Grammar Tip

Hyphens

Use **hyphens** in your expository essay to avoid combinations that could lead to misunderstanding, such as *re-creation* or *re-covered*, (which have different meanings when not hyphenated). Hyphens also clarify letter combinations such as *re-enter, semi-independent, micro-organism*, and *shell-like*.

The days are marked by a personified sun "born over and over." This image helps us experience life as a continuing re-creation of not only our own birth, but also that of the earth itself.

After You Read

Assess

Respond Through Writing

Students' expository essays should:

- focus on Thomas's images of light and dark and the figures of speech that create them
- interpret the poems' nuances and support interpretations with accurately cited quotations from the text
- use hyphens to avoid awkward or misleading unions of letters

A student who meets all of these criteria should receive the equivalent of a 4-point response.

A student who fully meets two or partially meets all of these criteria should receive the equivalent of a 3-point response.

A student who fully meets one or partially meets two of these criteria should receive the equivalent of a 2-point response.

A student who partially meets one of these criteria should receive the equivalent of a 1-point response.

 For grammar practice, see Unit 5 Teaching Resources Book, p. 131.

 For additional assessment, see Assessment Resources, pp. 275–276.

 To create custom assessments online, go to Progress Reporter Online Assessment.

 To create custom assessments using software, use ExamView Assessment Suite.

Approaching Level

DIFFERENTIATED INSTRUCTION

Emerging Since the poems contain a great deal of figurative language, review the different types of figurative language with students before they begin their essays. Review the characteristics of **symbol, personification, simile**, and **metaphor**, and ask students for examples of each from the poems. Discuss which examples relate to images of light and darkness.

Focus

Bellringer

Ask: What is conflict? *(an open clash between groups or individuals)* Have students suggest examples of conflict—experienced personally and globally. Then explain that conflict is the basis for drama, in any genre, and that students will be both creating and resolving it in a short story.

Summary

In this workshop, students will write short stories that create and resolve clear conflicts. They will follow the stages of the writing process, including prewriting, drafting, revising, editing, proofreading, and presenting. In addition, the workshop includes two focus lessons, on using action verbs and on correcting sentence fragments.

> For Writing Workshop graphic organizer and rubric, see Unit 6, Teaching Resources, pp. 242–244.

Learning Objectives

For pages 1154–1161

In this workshop, you will focus on the following objective:

Writing: Write a short story using the writing process.

Writing Workshop

Short Story

Literature Connection In "Miss Youghal's *Sais,*" Rudyard Kipling presents a conflict between the main character, Strickland, and Miss Youghal's parents.

> *"His leave was nearly at an end when the explosion came. He had really done his best to keep his temper in the hearing of the flirtations . . . but he broke down at last."*

Kipling then creates an interesting resolution to this situation. In a short story, your most important job is to create and resolve a conflict. To do this, you must also think about characters, setting, and other fictional elements. To write a successful short story, study the features in the chart below.

Checklist

Goals	Strategies
To tell a good story	☑ Craft an engaging plot with a clear conflict
	☑ Pace the story to show changes in time, place, and mood
	☑ Use chronological order, or create flashbacks or foreshadowing
	☑ Choose and maintain a point of view
To create interesting characters in a clearly defined setting	☑ Use dialogue, appearances, gestures, and movements as methods of characterization
	☑ Locate scenes in specific places and times
To entertain the reader from beginning to end	☑ Use fresh, natural language to create a tone
	☑ Use figurative language, sensory images, and specific details
	☑ Open with interest, close in a satisfying way, and build up the conflict in between

---

Writing Process

At any stage of the writing process, you may think of new ideas. Feel free to return to earlier stages as you write.

Prewrite

Draft

Revise

Focus Lesson:
Using Action Verbs

Edit and Proofread

Focus Lesson:
Sentence Fragments

Present

LOG ON **Literature** Online

Writing and Research For prewriting, drafting, and revising tools, go to glencoe.com and enter QuickPass code GLB9817u6.

1154 UNIT 6 THE MODERN AGE

Workshop Resources

Print Materials

- Unit 6 Teaching Resources pp. 242–244
- Writing Kit
- Success in Writing: Research and Reports
- Grammar and Language Transparency 11
- Writing Workshop Transparencies 31–35
- Daily Language Transparencies 27, 43, 79, 85, 95

Technology

- Literature Online: Writing Resources and Grammar Resources, www.glencoe.com
- Online Essay Grader, www.glencoe.com
- Student Presentation Builder on StudentWorks Plus CD-ROM
- Media Workshop DVD
- Online Student Edition

Teach

Class, Colonialism, and the Great War Have students create a two-column chart to help them compare and contrast the conflicts that existed in post-Victorian England (such as clashes between upper and lower classes, emerging resistance to colonialism abroad, and the outbreak of World War I) with the conflicts that exist in our world today. Encourage students to reflect on these larger issues, as Kipling and Orwell did, as they write their stories.

Literary History ☆

R. K. Narayan Narayan was born in Madras (now Chennai), India, in 1906. Most of his work, starting from his first novel, *Swami and Friends* (1935), is set in the fictional town of Malgudi, which has as much personality as his human characters. Bringing his heritage as well as his travels into his writing, Narayan comments on daily life, while integrating traditional Hindu lore into his stories.

Narration

Assignment: Write a Short Story   **1**

Write a short story of at least 1,500 words in which you create and resolve a clear conflict.

Audience: your peers, classmates, and teacher

Purpose: to entertain by presenting all the elements of a good short story, including setting, characters, and plot.

Analyze a Professional Model

Notice how the narrator of this story presents the conflict, intensifies it, and resolves it in an ambiguous but satisfying way. The comments in the margin point out features you might want to include in your story.

"A Snake in the Grass" by R. K. Narayan ☆

On a sunny afternoon, when the inmates of the bungalow were at their siesta, a cyclist rang his bell at the gate frantically and announced: "A big cobra has got into your compound. It crossed my wheel." He pointed to its track under the gate, and resumed his journey.

The family consisting of the mother and her four sons assembled at the gate in great agitation. The old servant, Dasa, was sleeping in the shed. They shook him out of his sleep and announced to him the arrival of the cobra. "There is no cobra," he replied and tried to dismiss the matter. They swore at him and forced him to take an interest in the cobra. "The thing is somewhere here. If it is not found before the evening, we will dismiss you. Your neglect of the garden and the lawns is responsible for all these dreadful things coming in." Some neighbors dropped in. They looked accusingly at Dasa: "You have the laziest servant on earth," they said. "He ought to keep the surroundings tidy." "I have been asking for a grass-cutter for months," Dasa said. In one voice they ordered him to manage with the available things and learn not to make demands. He persisted. They began to speculate how much it would cost to buy a grass-cutter. A neighbor declared

Conflict/Audience/Purpose

Grab your reader's interest by introducing the conflict early.

Point of View

Maintain a consistent point of view throughout the story.

Dialogue/Purpose

Add natural-sounding dialogue to reveal characters' backgrounds, personalities, and motives, or to advance the plot.

Work with your class and your teacher to collect all the students' short stories and assemble them in a booklet. You might also want to make an electronic version of your literary magazine to store on a school computer.

WRITING WORKSHOP **1155**

English Learners

DIFFERENTIATED INSTRUCTION

Intermediate English language learners learn best when they have an opportunity to speak about a topic before they begin to write. Before students begin their stories, have them form groups in which they discuss the characters, conflicts, themes, and settings they are considering.

Suggest that students from other backgrounds choose settings from their families' countries of origin.

Teach

Writing Skills

Choose a Narrative Remind students that they can write their story from the first-person point of view, "I," as if they were one of the characters; from the third-person-limited point of view, "he or she," as a detached narrator who presents one character's thoughts and observations; or from the third-person-omniscient point of view, also "he or she," as a detached narrator who presents the thoughts and observations of all of the characters.

Writing Skills

Use Dialogue Encourage students to use dialogue to make their story realistic, as well as to make their characters seem believable and identifiable to the reader. Challenge students to use dialogue in direct quotations, such as writing "Go there!" rather than in indirect quotations, such as "She told him to go there."

Fictional Elements: Character

Describe specific feelings, gestures, and actions to reveal characters.

Fictional Elements: Setting

Locate scenes in specific places. Use concrete details, sensory images, and figurative language to describe setting.

Chronological Order

Tell the events in the order they happen, or use flashbacks and foreshadowing to vary the order.

that you could not think of buying any article made of iron till after the war. He chanted banalities of wartime prices. The second son of the house asserted that he could get anything he wanted at controlled prices. The neighbor became eloquent about the black market. A heated debate followed. The rest watched in apathy. At this point the college boy of the house butted in with: "I read in an American paper that 30,000 people die of snake bite every year." Mother threw up her arms in horror and arraigned Dasa. The boy elaborated the statistics. "I have worked it out, 83 a day. That means every twenty minutes someone is dying of cobra bite. As we have been talking here, one person has lost his life somewhere." Mother nearly screamed on hearing it. The compound looked sinister. The boys brought in bamboo sticks and pressed one into the hands of the servant also. He kept desultorily poking it into the foliage with a cynical air. "The fellow is beating about the bush," someone cried aptly. They tucked up their dhoties, seized every available knife and crowbar, and began to hack the garden. Creepers, bushes, and lawns were laid low. What could not be trimmed was cut to the root. The inner walls of the house brightened with the unobstructed glare streaming in. When there was nothing more to be done Dasa asked triumphantly, "Where is the snake?"

An old beggar cried for alms at the gate. They told her not to pester when they were engaged in a snake hunt. On hearing it the old woman became happy. "You are fortunate. It is God Subramanya who has come to visit you. Don't kill the snake." Mother was in hearty agreement: "You are right. I forgot all about the promised Abhishekam. This is a reminder." She gave a coin to the beggar, who promised to send down a snake-charmer as she went. Presently an old man appeared at the gate and announced himself as a snake-charmer. They gathered around him. He spoke to them of his life and activities and his power over snakes. They asked admiringly: "How do you catch them?" "Thus," he said, pouncing upon a hypothetical snake on the ground. They pointed the direction in which the cobra had gone and asked him to go ahead. He looked helplessly

Writing Practice

Develop Characters

In order for students to develop "living, breathing," multifaceted characters, it is important that students understand their characters. Have students write mini-bios for their main characters, considering these five areas:

- **Appearance:** age, height, dress
- **Action:** what they do
- **Background:** where they are from, type of family, socioeconomic class

- **Speech:** how they talk and what they say
- **Thoughts:** goals, dreams, secrets

about and said: "If you show me the snake, I'll at once catch it. Otherwise what can I do? The moment you see it again, send for me. I live nearby." He gave his name and address and departed.

At five in the afternoon, they threw away their sticks and implements and repaired to the veranda to rest. They had turned up every stone in the garden and cut down every grass blade and shrub, so that the tiniest insect coming into the garden should have no cover. They were loudly discussing the various measures they would take to protect themselves against reptiles in the future, when Dasa appeared before them carrying a water-pot whose mouth was sealed with a slab of stone. He put the pot down and said: "I have caught him in this. I saw him peeping out of it . . . . I saw him before he could see me." He explained at length the strategy he had employed to catch and seal up the snake in the pot. They stood at a safe distance and gazed on the pot. Dasa had the glow of a champion on his face. "Don't call me an idler hereafter," he said. Mother complimented him on his sharpness and wished she had placed some milk in the pot as a sort of religious duty. Dasa picked up the pot cautiously and walked off saying that he would leave the pot with its contents with the snake-charmer living nearby. He became the hero of the day. They watched him in great admiration and decided to reward him adequately.

It was five minutes since Dasa was gone when the youngest son cried: "See there!" Out of a hole in the compound wall a cobra emerged. It glided along towards the gate, paused for a moment to look at the gathering in the veranda with its hood half open. It crawled under the gate and disappeared along a drain. When they recovered from the shock they asked, "Does it mean that there are two snakes here?" The college boy murmured: "I wish I had taken the risk and knocked the water-pot from Dasa's hand; we might have known what it contained."

Reading-Writing Connection Think about the writing techniques that you have just encountered and try them out in your short story.

Tone
Use fresh, natural language to create your tone.

Rising Action/Pacing
Present a series of events that intensifies the conflict. Pick up or slow down the pace to show shifts in time or mood.

Climax
Be sure to include a clear climax, or the most exciting or suspenseful moment in your story.

Sensory Details
Make effective use of sensory details in your descriptions.

Audience/Purpose
Create an engaging ending with satisfying, surprising, or ambiguous details.

 **Writing Workshop**

Short Story

Teach

Writing Skills

Rising Action Explain that each event in the rising action should be more intense than the one before, until the action reaches a peak in the climax. Have students think of rising action as water heating up. The molecules become more and more agitated until the water boils.

Writing Skills

Climax Explain that the climax, in the metaphor above, is the moment when the water boils. The building tension—the rising action—is resolved as the problem (human rival, nature, inner demon) is solved, often through the intelligence, creativity, courage, or other positive attribute of the protagonist.

Cultural History ☆

The Sacred Cow Dairy products hold a special place in Hindu religious practices. From about the seventh century B.C.E., people in parts of India have protected cows as sustainers of life. Eventually, killing milk-producing cows (once used for food) was forbidden. Hindu mythology associates cows with religious figures such as Shiva, Indra, and Krishna.

Advanced Learners

DIFFERENTIATED INSTRUCTION

Difference Between a Short Story and a Novel The elements of a short story are plot, characters, language, theme, voice, setting, and imagery. Tell students to list the elements of their short stories and to add notes under each heading. In small groups, have students discuss which elements of

their stories could be stronger and how they could strengthen each element.

Teach

Writing Skills

Gather Ideas Suggest that students "trawl" for story ideas in newspapers, magazines, photographs, and anecdotes that their parents, friends, or neighbors have recounted to them.

Writing Skills

Brainstorming When they have ideas for their short stories, encourage students to explore and expand the ideas by brainstorming. On a separate sheet of paper, have them create cluster diagrams in which students freewrite words and phrases around their centered main ideas and main characters. In the free flow of ideas, students will find that they can generate gems they can use in their stories.

Writer's Technique ☆

Drafting When writers complete their prewriting, they begin drafting. Creating a draft does not mean putting together a perfect copy of the paper but focusing on getting ideas down on paper. Once the ideas are written down, revision and editing can be employed to polish the draft.

Prewrite

Gather Ideas Find ideas by observing. For example, perhaps you notice a new person riding the bus you take. What makes this stranger stand out? Imagine different scenarios: Where is the person going? Why? What if . . . ? Use your imagination to develop the conflict and events.

Imagine Characters and Setting Who is your story about? Will you show conflict through two opposing characters? Consider what the characters look like; how they speak, move, and behave; and what they want. Then decide where and when the story will take place.

Add Dialogue Add natural-sounding dialogue to reveal a character's background, personality, and motives, or to present the conflict or events.

Plan the Plot The plot, or sequence of events, is what happens in a story. Keep the plot focused on the conflict. An **external conflict** occurs when a character struggles against an outside force, such as another character, society, or the environment. An **internal conflict** occurs when the character struggles with his or her feelings. Before writing, fill out a story map like the one below.

Setting	Characters
• Time: • Place:	
Problem/Conflict:	
Main Events: 1. 2. 3. Climax:	
Resolution:	

Choose the Point of View The story's narrator may be a character in the story or someone unnamed, outside the story.

Draft

Create Paragraphs Create separate paragraphs for separate events. In dialogue, start a new paragraph each time the speaker changes.

Pace the Story

Pacing involves telling story events at an effective rate. A good story usually builds slowly to a climax, then quickly comes to a resolution.

Avoid Plagiarism

One way to avoid the urge to copy a published story or a friend's work is to put a strong effort into the prewriting process. The better you've mapped out your characters and events, the easier it will be to create a satisfying story on your own.

Writing Practice

Realistic Dialogue As an aid to writing realistic dialogue, students might situate themselves in public places—the cafeteria, a park bench, the mall—and transcribe the various conversations they overhear. Encourage students to pay close attention to how people really speak: talking in fragments, repeating words, stammering, interrupting, and so on. Adding realistic dialogue will help bring their characters to "life."

Analyze a Workshop Model

Here is a final draft of a student's short story. Read it and answer the questions in the margin. Use your answers to guide you as you write.

A Prior Engagement

Every Saturday afternoon for several years, Eudora Stills invited herself to our house for tea. A busybody and remarkably bad judge of character, she held my mother captive for hours with her gossip. How my mother tolerated her none of us understood.

One Saturday, Eudora didn't call. My mother set out tea and scones just the same. Finally, she coaxed my father to walk to Eudora's house to check on her. When he returned, he said, "Well, she's not dead," then, with a sly grin, "She's engaged!" He said that Eudora had been seeing Brad Mites, a man we all distrusted, for almost a year. When he proposed to Eudora, she said yes, just like that. Worse, she was planning to move east with this cheat.

Hearing the news, my mother grew somber. "I'm surprised Eudora never told me," she said to no one in particular.

When Eudora came to discuss her move with my mother, she proudly flashed her large, ill-fitting, and possibly fake, diamond ring. After Eudora left, my mother remained seated in the living room until evening fell. My dad reminded her to make supper.

The next night I saw my mother peering into the bathroom sink drain. She lifted the stopper and pulled out Eudora's diamond ring. We both knew what trouble that spelled. How could Eudora tell her fiancé she'd lost it? He'd drop her for sure. My mother slipped the ring into her pocket. Then she stunned me by saying, "I guess that's that for Brad Mites."

When Eudora came the next Saturday, I knew my mother hadn't told her about the ring. A week later, when Eudora confessed in a panicked voice that she had lost the ring, my mother offered tea and sympathy but nothing more. A month later, when Eudora told my mother that the engagement was over, all I heard my mother say was "Scone?"

Conflict/Setting/Tone
How does the opening create interest and introduce the conflict and the setting? What is the tone and which words create it?

Characterization
How do dialogue, actions, and gestures reveal characters?

Rising Action/Audience
How do events intensify the conflict or make the story more interesting?

Point of View
Who is narrating the events of the story? Is the narrative point of view consistent? Explain.

Climax/Pacing
What is the high point of tension, or turning point, of the story? How does the pacing change?

Audience/Purpose
Is this a satisfying ending? Explain.

Approaching Level

DIFFERENTIATED INSTRUCTION

African American Vernacular English
As many students do, speakers of AAVE may write informally, the way they talk, often using a nonstandard form of *be* verbs. Have students reread their papers, circling any *be* verbs from which (for example) a present participle has been omitted. Students should correct these misuses, conforming their drafts to academic writing, not casual conversation.

Teach

Writing Skills

Conflict/Setting/Tone
Answer: *Interest is created in the apparent conflict between characters.* Busybody *and* captive *convey the humorous tone.*

Writing Skills

Characterization **Answer:**
They let characters reveal themselves, rather than be described.

Writing Skills

Rising Action/Audience
Answer: *Eudora's failure to call is out of character, her engagement is interesting, and her fiancé's being a well-known cheat creates suspense about what will happen to her.*

Writing Skills

Point of View Answer: *The child tells the whole story from the first-person point of view, using the pronouns* I *and* my. *The characters' dialogue and actions speak for themselves, even though these are reported by the child.*

Writing Skills

Climax/Pacing Answer: *The mother puts the ring in her pocket and says something to suggest that she will not return the ring.*

Writing Skills

Audience/Purpose Answer:
The ending is very satisfying. It demonstrates the character of the mother, who probably enjoys the company of this "busybody" after all. Some students may note that the mother's protective instincts are flawed by dishonesty.

1159

Writing Workshop

Short Story

Teach

Writing Process

Revise Try to arrange time to let students' drafts rest for a week. Then have students mark sections they believe are weak, according to the revising rubric. Have they addressed every question? Students should revise accordingly.

Writing Skills

Peer Review As a further check, have students exchange drafts. After they read them, encourage students to begin their comments on a positive note before offering any negative observations.

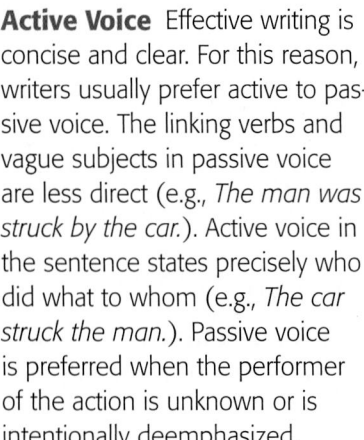

Writer's Technique ☆

Active Voice Effective writing is concise and clear. For this reason, writers usually prefer active to passive voice. The linking verbs and vague subjects in passive voice are less direct (e.g., *The man was struck by the car.*). Active voice in the sentence states precisely who did what to whom (e.g., *The car struck the man.*). Passive voice is preferred when the performer of the action is unknown or is intentionally deemphasized.

Word Choice

Find this academic vocabulary word in the student model:

period (pir′ē əd) *n.* **1.** a length of time; **2.** a mark of punctuation with which declarative and some imperative sentences close. *Every Saturday afternoon for several years, Eudora Stills invited herself to our house for tea.*

Using academic vocabulary can strengthen your writing. Try to use two academic vocabulary words in your short story. See the complete list on pages R81–R83.

LOG ON ▶ **Literature** Online

Writing and Research For editing and publishing tools, go to glencoe.com and enter QuickPass code GLB9817u6.

Revise

Use the checklist below to evaluate your writing.

Checklist
☑ Do you create an engaging plot?
☑ Do you choose and maintain a consistent point of view?
☑ Do you use dialogue, appearances, gestures, and movements to show your characters?
☑ Do you create interest through the use of sensory details and figurative language?
☑ Do you pace your story to show changes in mood?
☑ Do you present events in chronological order or use foreshadowing or flashbacks?
☑ Do you locate scenes in precise times and places?

▶ **Focus Lesson**

Use Action Verbs

An action verb tells what someone or something does. Action verbs can express either physical action (*She flashed her ring at me*) or mental action (*She stunned me*). For the most impact, use precise and vivid action verbs instead of state-of-being verbs, such as *is*.

Draft:

> Every Saturday afternoon for years Eudora Stills was over to our house for tea. A well-known busybody and a remarkably bad judge of character, she was always holding my mother captive for hours. How my mother tolerated her was understood by none of us.

Revision:

> Every Saturday afternoon for years, Eudora Stills invited herself[1] to our house for tea. A well-known busybody and a remarkably bad judge of character, she held[2] my mother captive for hours, repeating the same gossip. How my mother tolerated her none of us understood.[3]

1: Use action verbs to convey precise information.

2: Replace wordy constructions with precise verbs.

3: Use the active voice whenever possible. ☆

Writing Practice

Variation in Sentence Length Explain to students that too many sentences of the same length can produce a boring, singsong tone in a a paragraph. Have students check their stories for this problem, paragraph by paragraph. When necessary, students should vary sentence length by combining short sentences that have the same subject or by breaking long sentences into shorter ones. If this does not solve the problem, they should consider replacing sentences altogether.

Edit and Proofread

Get It Right When you have completed the final draft of your story, proofread it for errors in grammar, usage, mechanics, and spelling. Refer to the Language Handbook, pages R47–R59, as a guide.

> **Focus Lesson**

Correct Sentence Fragments

A sentence fragment results from punctuating an incomplete sentence as if it were a complete sentence. In most of your writing, and especially on tests, avoid sentence fragments. Review your work to make sure that each sentence includes a subject and a verb, and correct any subordinate clauses you punctuated as complete sentences.

Problem: The sentence uses a verb form that cannot stand alone.
My dad reminding her to make supper.

Solution 1: Add a helping verb.
My dad was reminding her to make supper.

Solution 2: Change the form of the verb.
My dad reminded her to make supper.

Problem: A sentence has no verb and does not express a complete thought.
When he proposed to Eudora, she said yes. Just like that.

Solution: Eliminate the fragment by combining it with the previous sentence.
When he proposed to Eudora, she said yes, just like that.

Present

Follow Manuscript Guidelines Remember that your handwritten work must be extremely legible; if your handwriting is difficult to read, be sure to word-process your paper instead. Carefully follow all guidelines for margins and other vertical and horizontal spacing.

Punctuating Dialogue

Use quotation marks around the speaker's exact words only, and always place a period or comma *inside* closing quotation marks:

When he returned, he said, "Well, she's not dead."

Peer Review Tips

A classmate may ask you to read his or her short story. Take your time and jot down notes as you read so you can give constructive feedback. Use the following questions to get started:

- Where is the plot especially interesting?
- Where do the sensory details, figurative language, and other details draw you into the story?

Word-Processing Tips

If your teacher requires the use of a cover sheet or title page but does not set specific requirements, be sure it includes the following in the upper right-hand corner:

- your name
- the course name
- your teacher's name
- the date

Writer's Portfolio

Place a copy of your short story in your portfolio to review later.

Teach

Writing Process

Edit and Proofread Encourage students to use the Proofreading Checklist inside the back cover of the book. Students can begin by checking any direct quotations in their short stories for incorrect punctuation marks. Next, students should check their work for grammar, usage, mechanics, and spelling errors. Some students may find it helpful to read aloud as they edit their work.

Writing Process

Present Encourage students to submit their stories to literary magazines or short story contests. Make them aware that some contests require an entry fee. Students should also make sure that they have formatted their stories to satisfy any required standards set by a magazine or contest.

English Learners

DIFFERENTIATED INSTRUCTION

Intermediate Pair an English speaker with an English learner. Have each read the other's paper. Instruct both partners to notice spelling, grammar, and sentence-construction problems as well as appropriate word choice and organization. In this way English learners can be especially alerted to English constructions or words they do not know. After reading each other's paper, the partners should confer and discuss their positive and negative observations.

Focus

Summary

In this workshop, students will learn techniques for effectively planning and delivering a performance of a short story they have read in Unit Six.

Teach

Political History ☆

Good Speaking Techniques
Show students recordings on film or DVD of a speech by a statesman or -woman known to have inspired an audience (e.g., Winston Churchill, Eleanor Roosevelt, Martin Luther King). **Ask:** How does this person engage the audience? *(e.g., tone of voice, facial expressions, gestures, air of sincerity or conviction)* Remind students to incorporate these elements into their plan and rehearsal for their presentations.

 For help with creating presentations, see Student Presentation Builder on StudentWorks Plus.

Speaking, Listening, and Viewing Workshop

Performance of a Short Story

Literature Connection

"It's Malabar!" he screamed, in a powerful, strange voice. "It's Malabar!" His eyes blazed at her for one strange and senseless second, as he ceased urging his wooden horse. Then he fell with a crash to the ground. . . .

—D. H. Lawrence, "The Rocking-Horse Winner"

Short stories do not just communicate a theme. They also present characters, a setting, and a series of events that can be as vivid and dramatic as the one above. In this workshop, you will work with group members to present a dramatic performance of a short story.

> **Assignment** Plan and deliver a performance of the short story you wrote or of a short story you read in Unit Six.

Plan Your Presentation

Follow these steps to plan and develop your performance.

Choose a story. Start by considering an original short story written by a member of your group: it may be the most practical choice because of its length. As you evaluate a story for performance, remember to look for events, scenes, and conflicts that you can clearly and dramatically recreate for an audience.

Break the story down into scenes. After you select a story, break it down into a minimum of three scenes. If the story you selected will not yield three scenes, consider selecting another story. With a work of literature, it is fine to condense the action somewhat, as long as you can still convey the theme of the story and the most important action.

Develop ideas for artistic staging. Begin with the setting. You will want to have some kind of backdrop or set for your performance. Remember that a backdrop can be concrete, or representational, and show things such as houses, trees, or a kitchen; it can also present abstract colors and symbols. Also think about props. Props are especially helpful for showing scene changes because they help locate events in particular places and times.

Speaking Practice

Prepare a Script Encourage students to prepare scripts for their own use during their presentations. Have them mark the scripts with notes and guides that will help them during their performances. They might underline the words they want to emphasize or insert marks to indicate where they plan to pause for breath and where to gesture or move around the room.

 For help with creating presentations, see Student Presentation Builder on StudentWorks Plus.

Write your script. Use all the stages of a writing process to develop a script. First, as a group, discuss ideas for what must be said or shown to present each scene and which characters must take part. Look carefully at the dialogue in the original story to see what you can use or adapt.

Get into character. Part of the process of writing your script will be reading through its various incarnations to see how well they work. As you do so, discuss the chief characteristics and personality traits of each character. Develop ideas for appearance, such as adding a cane, a wig, a hat, or another costume or make-up device. Analyze each character's speech, and develop performance ideas such as a lilt in the voice, a drawl, a hesitation or urgency about speaking, or dialect. Also develop ideas for posture, such as a straight-backed rigidity, a slouching nonchalance, or an uncertain or shy hesitation in gait or gestures. As you read through each evolving draft of your script, take parts and get into character.

Add effects. Evaluate when to use different kinds of effects, such as sound effects that might range from a knocking at the door to a crash of thunder, as well as musical effects that might range from subtle background music to dramatic rolls of a drum.

Rehearse

Rehearse the performance several times before presenting it to a small audience. As you perform, keep the speaking techniques below in mind. As you watch others present their performances, keep the listening and viewing tips in mind.

Techniques for Dramatic Performances

Speaking Techniques	Listening and Viewing Techniques
☑ **Use Audience Feedback** Study the expressions on viewers' faces for feedback.	☑ **Focus** Look directly at the actors, concentrating on what they do.
☑ **Volume** Adjust your volume to the size of your audience: no one should feel as if you're shouting, and no one should strain to hear you.	☑ **Respond** Show interest by responding to various effects as well as through upright posture.
☑ **Entertain** "Get into" the character and part you are presenting on the stage.	☑ **Evaluate** Identify the most successful aspects of the performance.

Speaking Frames

As you adapt your story into a script, you may find yourself needing to spell out relationships between characters and scenes that were only narrated or implied in the original. Consider using speaking frames like these:

- "I wonder if _____." (to imply foreshadowing or illustrate a character's thoughts)
- "Let's go _____." (to explain an action or departure)
- "I remember that _____." (to introduce a flashback)

Presentation Tips

Use the following checklist to evaluate your performance:

- ☆ Did you engage and entertain your audience from beginning to end?
- Did you accurately and effectively recreate the story?
- Did you convey the setting and scenes, and did you present interesting characters and compelling events?

Speaking, Listening and Viewing For project ideas, templates, and presentation tips, go to glencoe.com and enter QuickPass code GLB9817u6.

Teach
Speaking Skills

Use Visual Aids Have students practice their presentation with their visual aids so that they become comfortable using them. Remind students to keep things simple, using just one or two aids to clarify key points.

Listening Skills

Peer Assessment Ask students to evaluate their classmates' performances according to the following criteria:

- Did the speaker present a clear thesis and support it with evidence and examples?
- Did the speaker vary his or her volume, pace, and tone according to the needs of the material?
- Did the speaker effectively convey the meaning and theme of the story?
- Did the speaker make eye contact with the audience?
- Did the speaker use gestures and visual aids effectively to emphasize important ideas?

Approaching Level
DIFFERENTIATED INSTRUCTION

Emerging Remind students that the credibility of a speaker can be undermined by the use of the dreaded *like*, *uh*, and *you know*. If students catch themselves using these or other fillers, it usually means that they are nervous and are stalling for time to think of the next word. Encourage students to slow down, take a breath, and think about what they are saying. Students should concentrate on removing one bad habit at a time. Trying to correct everything at once may make them more nervous and self-conscious when they speak. They can start, for example, by getting rid of *like*.

Focus

Summary

The purpose of Independent Reading is to encourage students to read other novels from the time period that they have learned about in this unit.

Teach

Literary History ☆

Compare Novels Have students compare novels from the early twentieth century to British novels of the Victorian Era. **Ask:** How do the authors depict British society of the early twentieth century? Explain to students that many authors in the early twentieth century took a critical look at British society, including its empire. Help students understand that these books are much more likely to end unhappily than most Victorian novels. Discuss how novels of the early twentieth century often delve deeply into the interior life of the characters portrayed.

⚡ Analyze Literary Criticism
Assign students to read one of the novels on this spread, as well as a critical essay or article on the novel. **Ask:** What elements of this literary criticism do you find accurate? How does your own overall impression of the work compare with the critic's? (*Answers will vary depending on which novel the student*

chose to read.) Have students summarize their chosen novel and give a brief synopsis of the literary criticism for the class.

Independent Reading

THE NOVEL, which had come to prominence during the Victorian period, continued to dominate the literary scene in the early half of the twentieth century. Many novels from this period reveal and criticize the destructive influences of colonial power on society and on the individual. The emphasis on the individual as well as on character development and motivation reflected a continued interest in the theories of psychoanalysis. ☆

Heart of Darkness

Joseph Conrad

In this tale, Charles Marlow, a thoughtful sailor, tells of his physical and psychological journey up the Congo River. He is attempting to reach the Inner Station to relieve Mr. Kurtz, the agent for a company that trades in ivory. The trip takes Marlow through the African jungle, where he encounters widespread inefficiency and cruelty at various company stations. When Marlow arrives at the Inner Station, he discovers that Kurtz rules the native population with force and brutality. Marlow takes the agent aboard his steamboat, but Kurtz is ill and cannot be saved.

A Passage to India

E. M. Forster

Set in turn-of-the-century India, this three-part novel explores several themes including the relationship between the power of the earth and the imagination and the relationship between East (India) and West (Britain). In the novel, Adela Quested, a young Englishwoman eager to discover the "real" India, visits the country and befriends the respected Dr. Aziz. After a cultural misunderstanding, she accuses him of attacking her. He is imprisoned, but during the ensuing trial, she withdraws her charges. One of Aziz's British friends, Mr. Fielding, defends Aziz. However, when Mr. Fielding befriends Adela, the friendship between the two men ends. Several years later, Dr. Aziz encounters Mr. Fielding, but they cannot find common ground. Their ethnic and social differences become all too clear.

Animal Farm

George Orwell

Written as a fable, this novel presents a satire of Communist Russia and its revolution.

All Quiet on the Western Front

Erich Maria Remarque

This novel depicts the horrors of World War I from a German soldier's viewpoint.

The Time Machine *and* The War of the Worlds

H. G. Wells

The Time Machine tells of a scientist who travels into the future. *The War of the Worlds* is the story of a Martian invasion of Earth.

CRITICS' CORNER

"To the Lighthouse . . . *is a book of interrelationships among people. . . . Those who reject* To the Lighthouse *as inferior to* Mrs. Dalloway*. . . must fail to notice the richer qualities of mind and imagination and emotion which Mrs. Woolf, perhaps not wanting them, omitted from* Mrs. Dalloway*.*"

—Louis Kronenberger, *The New York Times*, May 8, 1927

To the Lighthouse ☆

Virginia Woolf

This novel, written in stream of consciousness, is driven by character and imagination, rather than a strict narrative. On Scotland's Isle of Skye, where the Ramsay family has a summer residence, Mr. and Mrs. Ramsay play out the roles traditionally expected of them. Mr. Ramsay, a once famous philosopher, smugly exhibits his rational approach to life while Mrs. Ramsay attends to her guests, her children, and her husband's ego. Woolf reveals the flaws of British society and of the Ramsays by contrasting them with Lily Briscoe, an artist who is a guest of the family.

 Create Visual Art

Read one of the books listed on these pages, and then create a piece of visual art that reflects a character, setting, or theme in the book.

Teach

Cultural History ☆

An Empire in Decline By the turn of the twentieth century, the British were questioning the morality and ideology of their empire. Conrad and Forster criticized the relationship between the British and those whom they colonize. *All Quiet on the Western Front*, on the other hand, questions the morality of World War I, dealing directly with the disenchantment experienced by soldiers in the Great War. *To the Lighthouse*, written after World War I, captures a sense of disillusionment.

Glencoe Literature Library

Glencoe Literature Library offers an extensive collection of hardcover books that help you encourage your students to read independently. Choose from among the more than 120 full-length literary works—novels, novellas, plays, and nonfiction. Each book includes related readings from a broad range of genres. Go to www.glencoe.com for more information.

 For access to all study guides for the Glencoe Literature Library, see the Literature Library Teacher Resources CD-ROM.

 To create customized reading lists from a database of more than 30,000 titles, use BookLink K–12 CD-ROM.

Approaching Level

DIFFERENTIATED INSTRUCTION

Established To help readers better understand the novel that they are reading, have them think about the author's purpose in writing this book. Was the author merely intending to entertain? Was the author interested in exploring human psychology? Alternatively, was he or she critiquing British society or a political movement? Point out that knowing the author's purpose will help students determine the novel's theme. Remind students that a theme is the main idea, or message, of a literary work. Challenge students to write their own short stories that have a similar theme.

Focus

Bellringer

Naturally, students often go into test-taking situations with a little anxiety, if not outright fear. Encourage students to take more control of the situation. **Ask: What can you do to have more confidence when you face a test?** (*Get plenty of sleep the night before; study; arrive early.*) Remind students that they are taking the test; it is not taking them.

Teach

Assessment

Explain to students that this section is intended to reinforce their general test-taking strategies, as well as to test their mastery of the skills and vocabulary covered in the unit. They will first be asked to read an essay and to answer comprehension, context-clue, and inference questions. Then they will be asked to complete ten vocabulary items, answer ten paragraph-improvement questions, and write a short essay on a poetry selection.

 To create custom assessments online, go to Progress Reporter Online Assessment.

 To create custom assessments using software, see ExamView Assessment Suite.

1166

Assessment

English–Language Arts

Reading: Essay

Carefully read the following passage. Use context clues to help you define any words with which you are unfamiliar. Pay close attention to the use of figurative language, character, the main idea, and the author's purpose. Then, on a separate sheet of paper, answer the questions that follow.

from **"Old Mrs. Grey"** by Virginia Woolf

line

There are moments even in England, now, when even the busiest, most contented suddenly let fall what they hold—it may be the week's washing. Sheets and pyjamas crumble and dissolve in their hands, because, though they do not state this in so many words, it seems silly to take the washing round to Mrs. Peel when out there over the fields over the hills, there is no washing; no pinning of
5   clothes to lines; mangling and ironing; no work at all, but boundless rest. Stainless and boundless rest; space unlimited; untrodden grass; wild birds flying; hills whose smooth uprise continue that wild flight.
    Of all this however only seven foot by four could be seen from Mrs. Grey's corner. That was the size of her front door which stood wide open, though there was a fire burning in the grate. The fire looked like a small spot of dusty light feebly trying to escape from the embarrassing pressure of the
10   pouring sunshine.
    Mrs. Grey sat on a hard chair in the corner looking—but at what? Apparently at nothing. She did not change the focus of her eyes when visitors came in. Her eyes had ceased to focus themselves; it may be that they had lost the power. They were aged eyes, blue, unspectacled. They could see, but without looking. She had never used her eyes on anything minute and difficult; merely upon faces,
15   and dishes and fields. And now at the age of ninety-two they saw nothing but a zigzag of pain wriggling across the door, pain that twisted her legs as it wriggled; jerked her body to and fro like a marionette. Her body was wrapped round the pain as a damp sheet is folded over a wire. The wire was spasmodically jerked by a cruel invisible hand. She flung out a foot, a hand. Then it stopped. She sat still for a moment.
20   In that pause she saw herself in the past at ten, at twenty, at twenty-five. She was running in and out of a cottage with eleven brothers and sisters. The line jerked. She was thrown forward in her chair.
    "All dead. All dead," she mumbled. "My brothers and sisters. And my husband gone. My daughter too. But I go on. Every morning I pray God to let me pass."
    The morning spread seven foot by four green and sunny. Like a fling of grain the birds settled on
25   the land. She was jerked again by another tweak of the tormenting hand.
    "I'm an ignorant old woman. I can't read or write, and every morning when I crawls down stairs, I say I wish it were night; and every night, when I crawls up to bed, I say, I wish it were day. I'm only an

---

Reading Practice

Identify Imagery Ask: What is the definition of *imagery*? (*figurative language that evokes mental images*) **Why does a writer need to use imagery?** (*to allow the reader to experience the action more vividly*) **Write on the board:** The snake came toward us in the grass. Ask students to add imagery to the sentence to make it more vivid. (*Answers will vary.*)

ignorant old woman. But I prays to God: O let me pass. I'm an ignorant old woman—I can't read or write."

30   So when the color went out of the doorway, she could not see the other page which is then lit up; or hear the voices that have argued, sung, talked for hundreds of years.

The jerked limbs were still again.

"The doctor comes every week. The parish doctor now. Since my daughter went, we can't afford Dr. Nicholls. But he's a good man. He says he wonders I don't go. He says my heart's nothing but

35   wind and water. Yet I don't seem able to die."

So we—humanity—insist that the body shall still cling to the wire. We put out the eyes and the ears; but we pinion it there, with a bottle of medicine, a cup of tea, a dying fire, like a rook on a barn door; but a rook that still lives, even with a nail through it.

1. According to the context, what does the word *boundless* in line 5 most nearly mean?
   - (A) unconscious
   - (B) beautiful
   - (C) finishing
   - (D) endless
   - (E) bright

2. Which of the following literary elements is Woolf using in line 6 in the phrases *untrodden grass; wild birds flying; hills whose smooth uprise continue that wild flight*?
   - (A) personification
   - (B) idiom
   - (C) foreshadowing
   - (D) imagery
   - (E) epiphany

3. Which of the following literary elements is Woolf using in lines 9–10 in the phrase *dusty light feebly trying to escape from the embarrassing pressure of the pouring sunshine*?
   - (A) metaphor
   - (B) simile
   - (C) personification
   - (D) idiom
   - (E) symbol

4. Which device is Woolf using in the phrase *Apparently at nothing* in line 11?
   - (A) sentence fragment
   - (B) rhetorical question
   - (C) parallelism
   - (D) repetition
   - (E) figurative language

5. According to the context, what does the word *minute* in line 14 most nearly mean?
   - (A) convoluted
   - (B) a short period of time
   - (C) distant
   - (D) academic
   - (E) small

6. Which of the following literary elements is Woolf using in the phrase *jerked her body to and fro like a marionette* in lines 16–17?
   - (A) metaphor
   - (B) simile
   - (C) personification
   - (D) idiom
   - (E) symbol

Assessment

Assess

1. **D** is the correct answer. No other option makes sense in this context. `DOK 1`

2. **D** is the correct answer. Each example calls images to mind. `DOK 2`

3. **C** is the correct answer. Light is described as a person trying to escape. `DOK 2`

4. **A** is the correct answer. This sentence is not complete. `DOK 2`

5. **E** is the correct answer. No other option makes sense in this context. `DOK 1`

6. **B** is the correct answer. The word *like* is used in this comparison. `DOK 2`

Approaching Level

DIFFERENTIATED INSTRUCTION

Emerging Tell students that the reading-comprehension questions on the SAT measure their ability to understand and interpret what they read. Remind them that they get points for answering questions correctly, so they should try to read each passage quickly and spend most of their time answering questions. They can return to the passage to find the specific details they need in order to answer questions.

Assessment

Assess

7. B is the correct answer. The word *like* is used in this comparison. (DOK2)

8. E is the correct answer. The letter *t* is repeated in this phrase. (DOK2)

9. C is the correct answer. The nonstandard English is dialect. (DOK2)

10. A is the correct answer. No other option makes sense in this context. (DOK1)

11. A is the correct answer. This direct comparison does not contain the word *like* or *as*. (DOK2)

12. E is the correct answer. No change in Mrs. Grey is shown during this essay. (DOK2)

13. B is the correct answer. This essay is not hopeful, humorous, witty, or boisterous. (DOK4)

14. C is the correct answer. The narrator tells the whole story. (DOK2)

15. B is the correct answer. This sentence clearly summarizes the main idea of this passage. (DOK2)

---

7. Which of the following literary elements is Woolf using in *Like a fling of grain the birds settled on the land* in lines 24–25?
   (A) metaphor
   (B) simile
   (C) personification
   (D) idiom
   (E) symbol

8. What sound device is Woolf using in the phrase *tweak of the tormenting hand* in line 25?
   (A) consonance
   (B) assonance
   (C) rhyme
   (D) onomatopoeia
   (E) alliteration

9. What is the dialogue beginning in line 26 an example of?
   (A) apostrophe
   (B) onomatopoeia
   (C) dialect
   (D) idiom
   (E) rhetoric

10. To what does the word *voices* in line 31 refer?
    (A) writers and their works
    (B) birdsong
    (C) Mrs. Grey's childhood
    (D) Mrs. Grey's siblings and husband
    (E) the world outside Mrs. Grey's home

11. Which of the following literary elements is being used in the phrase *He says my heart's nothing but wind and water* in lines 34–35?
    (A) metaphor
    (B) simile
    (C) personification
    (D) idiom
    (E) epiphany

12. Which of the following best describes Mrs. Grey's character?
    (A) dynamic
    (B) minor
    (C) round
    (D) direct
    (E) static

13. Which of the following best describes the overall mood of this passage?
    (A) hopeful
    (B) grim
    (C) humorous
    (D) witty
    (E) boisterous

14. From which point of view is this passage narrated?
    (A) first person
    (B) second person
    (C) third-person omniscient
    (D) third-person limited
    (E) ironic

15. Which of the following best summarizes this essay's main idea?
    (A) Without fail, life always brings new experiences.
    (B) Life is sometimes harsh and can feel like a prison.
    (C) Human dignity is always derived from the family.
    (D) All people have the right to a happy domestic life.
    (E) Life must always come to an end.

LOG ON ▶ **Literature** Online

Assessment For additional test practice, go to glencoe.com and enter QuickPass code GLB9817u6.

Reading Practice

Retrieve Information Exams demand that students retrieve information from their "knowledge warehouse." Retrieval, like any other skill, must be practiced. After students carefully and actively read over a passage, have them try to recover what they know about it by writing down the main points on a piece of paper. This will make them practice retrieval and will also determine the extent of their knowledge of the topic. If they cannot recall what is in the passage, they "must go back over it." This practice will show them how to pay active attention, the first time through, to what they are reading.

Vocabulary Skills: Sentence Completion

For each item in the Vocabulary Skills section, choose the word or words that best complete the sentence.

1. The bloody stalemate that emerged during World War I completely _____ Europe.
   - (A) retorted
   - (B) grappled
   - (C) appeased
   - (D) converged
   - (E) ravaged

2. The harsh restrictions imposed on Germany at the end of World War I were _____ related to the rise of Hitler.
   - (A) intrinsically
   - (B) impassively
   - (C) heedlessly
   - (D) perpetually
   - (E) reverently

3. Many in Germany held the conviction that its _____ was to _____ the British Empire.
   - (A) labyrinth . . . brevity
   - (B) feud . . . ecstasy
   - (C) destiny . . . supplant
   - (D) callousness . . . compensation
   - (E) vileness . . . amiability

4. Modernism _____ radically from the literary movements of the Victorian period.
   - (A) supplanted
   - (B) commiserated
   - (C) trudged
   - (D) hailed
   - (E) diverged

5. While the Realists were reacting to the _____ conditions of urban life, the Modernists were, in part, reacting to the horrors of mechanized war.
   - (A) squalid
   - (B) spellbound
   - (C) imperturbable
   - (D) dogged
   - (E) exotic

6. The start of the twentieth century was marred by the rise of numerous _____ European governments.
   - (A) quaint
   - (B) intermittent
   - (C) despotic
   - (D) prosaic
   - (E) sensible

7. Many of the heads of Europe were _____ of the threat posed by Nazi Germany.
   - (A) callous
   - (B) heedless
   - (C) sensible
   - (D) unsavory
   - (E) quaint

8. The _____ spirit of the British was shown during the bombing of London.
   - (A) imperious
   - (B) garish
   - (C) forsaken
   - (D) indomitable
   - (E) frail

9. Although the Nazis _____ Europe for years, the continent was eventually emancipated from Nazism.
   - (A) frail
   - (B) suppressed
   - (C) exotic
   - (D) emanated
   - (E) despotic

10. During the twentieth century, Modernism was _____ by many critics, who recognized the movement's great inventiveness.
   - (A) precipitated
   - (B) converged
   - (C) hailed
   - (D) impinged
   - (E) retorted

Assessment

Assess

1. **E** is the correct answer. No other option makes sense in this context. **DOK 1**
2. **A** is the correct answer. No other option makes sense in this context. **DOK 1**
3. **C** is the correct answer. No other option makes sense in this context. **DOK 2**
4. **E** is the correct answer. INo other option makes sense in this context. **DOK 1**
5. **A** is the correct answer. No other option makes sense in this context. **DOK 1**
6. **C** is the correct answer. No other option makes sense in this context. **DOK 1**
7. **B** is the correct answer. No other option makes sense in this context. **DOK 1**
8. **D** is the correct answer. No other option makes sense in this context. **DOK 1**
9. **B** is the correct answer. No other option makes sense in this context. **DOK 1**
10. **C** is the correct answer. No other option makes sense in this context. **DOK 1**

Approaching Level

DIFFERENTIATED INSTRUCTION

Emerging Explain that comparing and contrasting possible answers will help students determine a correct answer. Suggest that when they are struggling with a sentence-completion exercise, they should try out each choice and think about whether the word makes sense in the sentence.

Assessment

Assess

Grammar and Writing: Paragraph Improvement

Read carefully through the opening paragraphs from the first draft of a student's short story. Pay close attention to **sentence structure, punctuation,** and the writer's **use of conjunctions.** Then on a separate sheet of paper, answer the questions that follow.

(1) *There were three things that really upset Frank Mead, the first was rudeness.* (2) *He couldn't stand it when someone spoke out of turn, cut in line, or failed to adhere to proper driving etiquette, he absolutely hated cell phones.* (3) *Second, Frank hated books. "Just a lot of dead people," Frank would say.* (4) *For good measure he'd add, "yet they're boring too."* (5) *Third, and most important, Frank hated to work.* (6) *Few ever saw Frank walked up stairs or lift anything larger than a lunch pail.* (7) *However, his disdain for work was made far more complicated by the fact that the region's busiest construction firm employed him.*

(8) *As of late, the firm for which he worked—Big Briggs—was busier than ever.* (9) *Big Briggs had landed an account with a very small, but very wealthy, private college.* (10) *The dean of this college, it turns out, was a rabid hockey fan, his love for the sport had started to influence his duties as dean.* (11) *At official dinners, during lectures, and even at commencement ceremonies— this year's ceremony was notably bad—he found ways in which to introduce pucks, sticks, nets, and goalies.*

(12) *That fall, the college had received an unexpected and very generous donation, the dean immediately earmarked the money for the building of an expansive hockey rink.* (13) *This rink, it was hoped, would become the envy of even professional teams, to the dean, this meant great prestige.* (14) *Big Briggs was contracted within days of the donation, and with that contract came Frank Mead.*

1. Which is the best revision of sentence 1?
   (A) The three things that really upset Frank Mead were rudeness.
   (B) There were three things that really upset Frank Mead. The first was rudeness.
   (C) There were three things that really upset Frank Mead; The first was rudeness.
   (D) Rudeness really upset Frank Mead.
   (E) Frank Mead was really upset by rudeness.

2. Which error appears in sentence 2?
   (A) sentence fragment
   (B) lack of subject-verb agreement
   (C) lack of pronoun-antecedent agreement
   (D) run-on sentence
   (E) No error appears.

3. Which is the best revision of sentence 4?
   (A) For good measure he'd add, yet they're boring.
   (B) For good measure he would add, "yet they're boring too."
   (C) For good measure he'd add, "And they're boring too."
   (D) He'd add, "yet they're boring too."
   (E) He would add, "yet they're boring too."

4. Which error appears in sentence 6?
   (A) run-on sentence
   (B) sentence fragment
   (C) incorrect verb form
   (D) incorrect parallelism
   (E) misplaced modifier

Reading Practice

Reread Tell students that paragraph-improvement exercises are like puzzles. Students will have to read the passage more than once to figure out the most logical sequence of sentences and paragraphs. To help students become more comfortable with these exercises, provide practice models that they can work on during their free time. You might take a passage from a book that the class is reading and rearrange the sentences to give students help.

5. What are the dashes in sentence 8 used to do?
   (A) set off an appositive phrase
   (B) emphasize an idea
   (C) indicate a break in thought
   (D) complicate the sentence structure
   (E) provide unnecessary information

6. Which is the best revision of sentence 10?
   (A) A rabid hockey fan the dean of this college.
   (B) The dean of this college was, it turns out, a rabid hockey fan, yet his love for the sport was influencing his duties as dean.
   (C) The dean of this college was a rabid hockey fan; His love for the sport was influencing him.
   (D) The dean of this college was, it turns out, a rabid hockey fan, and his love for the sport was influencing his duties as dean.
   (E) The dean of this college was, it turns out, a rabid hockey fan, however his love for the sport was influencing his duties as dean.

7. What are the dashes in sentence 11 used to do?
   (A) set off an appositive phrase
   (B) emphasize an idea
   (C) indicate a break in thought
   (D) complicate the sentence structure
   (E) provide essential information

8. Which error appears in sentence 12?
   (A) run-on sentence
   (B) sentence fragment
   (C) incorrect coordinating conjunction
   (D) incorrect parallelism
   (E) improper use of dialogue

9. Which is the best revision of sentence 13?
   (A) This rink, it was hoped, would become the envy of even professional teams, but to the dean this meant great prestige.
   (B) This rink—it was hoped—would become the envy of even professional teams, to the dean this meant prestige.
   (C) This rink would become the envy of even professional teams, this meant great prestige.
   (D) This rink, it was hoped, would become the envy of even professional teams; to the dean, this meant great prestige.
   (E) To the dean this meant great prestige.

10. This passage includes which parts of a plot?
    (A) exposition and rising action
    (B) exposition, rising action, and climax
    (C) rising action, climax, and falling action
    (D) exposition, rising action, climax, falling action, and resolution
    (E) only the resolution

Essay

In "The Second Coming," William Butler Yeats wrote the following:

> Things fall apart; the center cannot hold;
> Mere anarchy is loosed upon the world,
> The blood-dimmed tide is loosed, and everywhere
> The ceremony of innocence is drowned;
> The best lack all conviction, while the worst
> Are full of passionate intensity.

Write a short essay in which you explore the continuing relevance and validity of this passage for us today. As you write, keep in mind that your essay will be checked for **ideas, organization, voice, word choice, sentence fluency, conventions,** and **presentation.**

ASSESSMENT   **1171**

Assess

5. **A** is the correct answer. The dashes set off an appositive phrase. DOK 2

6. **D** is the correct answer. This sentence contains two main clauses separated only by a comma. It is a run-on sentence or comma splice. No other option corrects this problem without introducing further errors. DOK 1

7. **C** is the correct answer. The dashes in this sentence indicate a break in thought. DOK 2

8. **A** is the correct answer. This sentence contains two main clauses separated by a comma. It is a run-on sentence or comma splice. DOK 2

9. **D** is the correct answer. This sentence contains two main clauses separated only by a comma. It is a run-on sentence or comma splice. No other option corrects this problem without changing the content or introducing further errors. DOK 1

10. **A** is the correct answer. This passage contains only exposition and rising action. DOK 4

Essay

Check to be sure that each student's essay focuses on the relevance pf the passage in today's world and that it is well organized and free of grammatical errors. DOK 4

Approaching Level

DIFFERENTIATED INSTRUCTION

Established Remind students of the key points they learned about writing a literary analysis—showing how specific elements of a poem contribute to its overall meaning or theme. They should cite evidence from the poem to support their points, organizing their main points in a logical, effective order and drawing their own conclusions.

Skills Scope and Sequence

Readability Scores Key: Dale-Chall/DRP/Lexile

PART 1: The British Isles: Making and Remaking Traditions

Selections and Features	Literary Elements
Unit Introduction pp. 1172–1186	Rhythm **TE** p. 1181 Rhyme **TE** p. 1183
Poem Not Waving but Drowning, by Stevie Smith pp. 1188–1191	Speaker **SE** p. 1189
Short Story At the Pitt-Rivers, by Penelope Lively **7.2/55/920** pp. 1192–1203	Vernacular **SE** p. 1193 Narrator (review) **SE** p. 1202
Comparing Literature **Shall We Choose Death?** (radio speech) **10.0/59/1360**, by Bertrand Russell, **The Tribe with Its Eyes on the Sky** (short story) **10.6/60/1180**, by Italo Calvino, and **Political Science** (song), by Randy Newman pp. 1204–1215	Structure **SE** p. 1206
Poem Follower, by Seamus Heaney pp. 1216–1219	Slant Rhyme **SE** p. 1217
Poem Wind, by Ted Hughes pp. 1220–1223	Personification **SE** p. 1221
Drama That's All, by Harold Pinter pp. 1224–1229	Theater of the Absurd **SE** p. 1225 Dialogue (review) **SE** p. 1228
Literary History British Drama—from the Drawing Room to the Kitchen Sink pp. 1230–1231	Drama **SE** p. 1230
Poem What We Lost, by Eavan Boland pp. 1232–1236	Voice **SE** p. 1233

Reading Skills and Strategies	Vocabulary	Writing / Grammar	Speaking, Listening, Viewing

Identify Genre **TE** p. 1174
Activate Prior Knowledge **TE** p. 1176
Analyze Text Structure **TE** p. 1178
Analyze Figurative Language
   TE p. 1180
	Prefixes **TE** p. 1182	Write a Summary **TE** p. 1176
		Write Persuasive Arguments
		   TE p. 1186
			Analyze Art **SE** p. 1172
			Discussion **TE** p. 1184

Question **SE** p. 1189 Summarize **TE** p. 1190	Academic Vocabulary **SE** p. 1191	Write a Poem **SE** p. 1191	

Synthesize **SE** p. 1193	Denotation and Connotation
	   SE p. 1202
	Academic Vocabulary
	   SE p. 1202
		Write an Essay **TE** p. 1196
		Write a Review **TE** p. 1200
		Write an Autobiographical
		   Narrative **SE** p. 1203
		Sentence Fragments
		   SE p. 1203
			Monologue **TE** p. 1198

Analyze Political Assumptions **SE** p. 1206 Preview **TE** p. 1206	Context Clues **SE** p. 1209	Write a Dialogue **SE** p. 1209 Write a Song **TE** p. 1214	Debate **TE** p. 1212

Make Generalizations **SE** p. 1217
Preview **TE** p. 1218
	Academic Vocabulary
	   SE p. 1219
		Write an Autobiography
		   SE p. 1219	

Analyze Language **SE** p. 1221 Preview **TE** p. 1222	Analogies **SE** p. 1223	Write a Journal Entry **SE** p. 1223	

Scan **TE** p. 1224
Make Inferences About Characters
   SE p. 1225
	Academic Vocabulary
	   SE p. 1229
		Write an Essay **TE** p. 1226	Performance **SE** p. 1229

	Compound Words **TE** p. 1230		
Clarify Meaning **SE** p. 1233 Build Background **TE** p. 1234	Academic Vocabulary **SE** p. 1236	Write a Letter **SE** p. 1236	

Reading Skills and Strategies	Vocabulary	Writing / Grammar	Speaking, Listening, Viewing

Analyze Conflict **SE** p. 1239
Make Predictions **TE** p. 1240
	Compound Words **TE** p. 1242
	Word Origins **SE** p. 1247
	Academic Vocabulary
	  SE p. 1247
		Write a Description
		  TE p. 1244
		Write a Persuasive Essay
		  SE p. 1248
		Apostrophes **SE** p. 1248
			Analyze Art **SE** p. 1242
			Discussion **SE** p. 1246
			Persuasive Speech
			  TE p. 1248

Visualize **SE** p. 1250
Question **TE** p. 1250
	Context Clues **SE** p. 1257
	Academic Vocabulary
	  SE p. 1257
		Write a Dialogue **TE** p. 1254
		Write a Description
		  SE p. 1257	

Analyze Characterization **SE** p. 1259
Identify Sequence **TE** p. 1262
	Compound Words
	  TE p. 1260
	Word Usage **SE** p. 1264
	Academic Vocabulary
	  SE p. 1264
		Write a Reflective Essay
		  SE p. 1265
		Nominative Absolutes
		  SE p. 1265
			Analyze Art **SE** p. 1260
			Discussion **SE** p. 1263

	Homophones **SE** p. 1266		
Connect to Contemporary Issues **SE** p. 1268 Preview **TE** p. 1268	Synonyms **SE** p. 1271	Write a Script **TE** p. 1270 Write a Poem **SE** p. 1271	

Identify Sequence **SE** p. 1273
Evaluate Sources **TE** p. 1274
	Word Origins **SE** p. 1278
	Academic Vocabulary
	  SE p. 1278
		Write a Comparison-Contrast
		  Essay **TE** p. 1276
			Literature Group **SE** p. 1278

Evaluate Sound Devices **SE** p. 1280	Synonyms **SE** p. 1282	Write a Descriptive Essay **SE** p. 1282	Analyze Art **SE** p. 1281

Draw Conclusions About Meaning
  SE p. 1284
Make Inferences **TE** p. 1288
	Analogies **SE** p. 1291
	Academic Vocabulary
	  SE p. 1291
		Contractions **TE** p. 1286
		Apply Diction **SE** p. 1291
			Interview **TE** p. 1284
			Analyze Art **SE** p. 1285

Identify Assumptions and Ambiguity **SE** p. 1292 Connect **TE** p. 1292		Write a Summary **SE** p. 1295	

Connect to Personal Experience
  SE p. 1297
Identify Cause and Effect **TE** p. 1302
	Word Usage **SE** p. 1305
	Academic Vocabulary
	  SE p. 1305
		Create an Instruction Manual
		  SE p. 1305
			Analyze Art **SE** p. 1298

Readability Scores Key: Dale-Chall/**DRP**/Lexile

PART 2: Around the World: Extending and Evaluating Traditions *(continued)*

Focus

Bellringer Options

**Literature Launcher
  Pre-Reading Video: Unit 7**

**Daily Language Practice
  Transparency 100**

Or say: Name some countries in which English is a popular, if not the primary, language.

(The United Kingdom, the United States, Canada, Australia, Jamaica, South Africa, Kenya, the Philippines, India, Ireland.) **Ask:** Why is English spoken in so many countries spread around the globe? *(Most of these countries have a historical connection to the United Kingdom)*

For students who would profit from independent novel study, see Novel Companion pp. 335–378.

For school-to-home activities, see Unit 7 Teaching Resources Book, pp. 5–11.

The Light Programme, 2002. Mark Copeland. Oil on canvas, 12.20 x 16.14 in. Private collection.

View the Art Mark Copeland is known for his ironic, surrealist images, particularly landscapes. What are some of the ironies in this image?

1172

Unit Introduction Skills

Literary Elements
- Identify Genres (TE p. 1174)
- Figurative Language (TE p. 1180)

Writing Skills/Grammar
- Write a Summary (TE p. 1176)

Study Skills/Research/Assessment
- Take Notes (SE p. 1186)

An International Literature

Vocabulary Skills
- Prefixes (TE p. 1182)

Listening/Speaking/Viewing Skills
- Panel Discussion (SE p. 1186)
- Present a Display (SE p. 1186)

Reading Skills
- Analyze Graphic Information (SE p. 1175, 1177)
- Compare and Contrast (SE p. 1181)
- Analyze Cause and Effect (SE p. 1183)
- Interpret (SE p. 1185)
- Use Text Structure (TE p. 1178)

An International Literature

1950–Present

Looking Ahead

For the British, the period after World War II was marked by declining status abroad and enormous changes at home. The British Empire was gradually dismantled, and former British colonies struggled to adjust to home rule. Britain's economy sputtered, and the traditional class system no longer seemed secure. Responding to these upheavals, writers in Britain and in its former colonies produced a great outpouring of literature.

Keep the following questions in mind as you read:

▶ What are some major characteristics of contemporary British literature?

▶ What problems resulted from the collapse of the British Empire?

▶ What factors helped make English a global language?

1173

Unit Resources

Print Materials

- Unit 7 Teaching Resources, pp. 1–262
- Interactive Read and Write (On Level, Approaching, EL), pp. 297–334
- Novel Companion, pp. 331–374. Bellringer Option Transparencies: Selection Focus 63–73; Daily Language Practice 100–116
- Assessment Resources, Selection Assessment, pp. 277–312

Technology

- TeacherWorks Plus CD
- StudentWorks Plus CD
- Literature Launchers: Pre-Reading Videos DVD, Unit 7
- Literature Online
- Interactive Vocabulary CD-ROM
- Listening Library CD-ROM
- ExamView CD-ROM
- Skill Level Up! CD-ROM

Focus

Summary

This introduction gives an overview of British literature and events and world events from 1950 to the present. It discusses the changes that took place in the period after World War II, during which literature reflected the reshaping of traditions, the development of a postcolonial perspective, and the growth of globalization.

Teach

View the Art ★

Possible answers: Some ironies in the image include the fact that the people in the painting are camping, presumably to experience nature, but instead are surrounding a giant transistor radio. Other ironies include: the lush landscape is blocked from their view by the radio; the non-natural item has become part of the landscape itself, and even dominates the landscape.

Mark Copeland (1956–) often creates surreal scenes in which an oversized object dominates a landscape. Inspired by his work as a model maker for the film *The Borrowers*, Copeland has depicted a giant cabbage floating beneath Tower Bridge in London and a mammoth teapot floating above Boston Harbor. **Ask:** What point might Copeland be making about the importance of media? *(The artist might be suggesting that media, such as radio, dominate our lives.)*

Teach

Reading Strategy   1

Use the Timeline Help students read the timeline and relate key events in British literary history to British and world history.

- Explain that the European Economic Community was established in 1958 to make member countries more competitive in world markets. The first members were Belgium, France, Italy, Luxembourg, the Netherlands, and West Germany.

- Point out that DNA transmits hereditary information and codes for proteins responsible for each cell's structure and function.

Ask: Which event on the time line is in the same field as Watson and Crick's 1953 genetic discovery? *(The first "test-tube" baby is born in 1978.)*

Timeline   1950–Present   1

BRITISH LITERATURE

1950

1952
Nadine Gordimer publishes *The Soft Voice of the Serpent*

1953
Samuel Beckett's play *Waiting for Godot* is produced

1954
William Golding publishes *Lord of the Flies*

1957
Stevie Smith publishes *Not Waving but Drowning*

1958
Chinua Achebe publishes *Things Fall Apart*

1961
Muriel Spark publishes *The Prime of Miss Jean Brodie*

1963
National Theatre Company opens

Muriel Spark

1966
Tom Stoppard's play *Rosencrantz and Guildenstern Are Dead* is produced

1970
Ted Hughes publishes *Crow*

1978
Iris Murdoch publishes *The Sea, the Sea*

1979
V. S. Naipaul publishes *A Bend in the River*

BRITISH EVENTS

1950   1960

1952
George VI dies; Elizabeth II becomes queen ▼

1953
James Watson and Francis Crick reveal the double helical structure of the DNA molecule

1954
Wartime food rationing ends

1959
First Hovercraft crosses the English Channel

1962 ▲
Beatles have their first hit single, "Love Me Do"

1969
Violence erupts in Northern Ireland

1973
Britain joins European Economic Community

1978
First "test-tube" baby is born

1979
Margaret Thatcher becomes first woman to serve as prime minister

WORLD EVENTS

1950   1960

1957 ▶
Soviet Union launches *Sputnik I*, first artificial satellite to orbit Earth 1957

1961
Soviet cosmonaut Yuri Gagarin becomes the first human in space

1963
President John F. Kennedy is assassinated ▶

1966
China's Cultural Revolution begins

1969
U.S. *Apollo XI* spacecraft lands on Moon

1975
Vietnam War ends

LOG ON ▶ **Literature** Online

Literature and Reading To explore the Interactive Timeline, go to glencoe.com and enter QuickPass code GLB9817u7.

Reading Practice

Identify Genres Encourage students to classify the works of British literature listed in the timeline according to genre. Ask students to begin by noting genres that are named in the timeline. *(Both* Waiting for Godot *and* Rosencrantz and Guildenstern Are Dead *are labeled as plays.)* Then have students name the genres of works with which they are familiar. For example, many students will know that *Lord of the Flies* is a novel. Encourage students to use Internet tools to quickly identify the genres of the remaining works cited in the timeline.

The Old Vic Theatre in London

1980

1981
Salman Rushdie publishes *Midnight's Children*

1985
Margaret Atwood publishes *The Handmaid's Tale*

1986
Wole Soyinka wins Nobel Prize in Literature

1990
Derek Walcott publishes *Omeros*

1991
Nadine Gordimer wins Nobel Prize in Literature

1992
Derek Walcott wins Nobel Prize in Literature

1995
Seamus Heaney wins Nobel Prize in Literature

1996
New Globe Theatre opens

2000

2000
Seamus Heaney publishes translation of *Beowulf*

2000
Zadie Smith publishes *White Teeth* ▶

2001
V. S. Naipaul wins Nobel Prize in Literature

2005
Harold Pinter wins Nobel Prize in Literature **2**

1980

1981
Prince Charles marries Lady Diana Spencer

1982
Britain defeats Argentina in Falklands War

1986
Andrew Lloyd Webber's musical *Phantom of the Opera* premieres

1988
Terrorists blow up airliner over Lockerbie, Scotland

1994
"Chunnel" opens—railway tunnel under English Channel, linking England with France

1997
Princess Diana is killed in car accident

British forensic officers gather evidence.

2005 ▲
Terrorist bombings in London claim more than fifty lives

1980

1981
First case of AIDS is reported

1989
Germany opens Berlin Wall ▶

1989
Chinese government suppresses Tiananmen Square protests

1991
Soviet Union is dissolved

1993
European Union is established

1994
Nelson Mandela is elected president of South Africa

2000

2001
Terrorist attacks destroy World Trade Center in New York

2004 ▲
Massive tsunami devastates Southeast Asia

Reading Check

Analyzing Graphic Information How long did food rationing continue in Britain after the end of World War II in 1945?

Teach

Reading Check

Answer: *Nine years*

Reading Strategy   **2**

Make Inferences **Ask:** Why do you think six Nobel Prizes are included in this timeline? *(The Nobel Prize in Literature is a prestigious award that reflects a writer's prominence in world literature. The different backgrounds of these six writers reflect a broadening of English literature's scope and cultural references.)*

Cultural History ☆

A Noteworthy Debut Zadie Smith published her first novel, *White Teeth*, when she was 25. Her sweeping tale depicts a multicultural world in which the histories of three families overlap. One family's roots are in Bangladesh; another has roots in Britain and Jamaica; the third family has both Jewish and Catholic roots. The surprising combinations suggest a new and rapidly changing view of traditions and cultural heritage.

Approaching Level

DIFFERENTIATED INSTRUCTION

Established Encourage students to brainstorm a list of influential people and events from this time period. Students may draw on their own experiences and cultures. Suggest that small groups work together to choose three specific items they would add to the timeline.

English Learners

DIFFERENTIATED INSTRUCTION

Intermediate Point out to students that the events on this timeline are recent enough that they may remember some of them. Have students point out events that they remember. **Ask:** Which of these events might have had the greatest effect on your life?

Teach

Activate Prior Knowledge

Direct students to the graph that shows oil production in the North Sea. **Ask:** What are some issues that could arise out of decreased oil production? (*Students may mention rising gas prices, international tensions, and new technologies that are less oil dependent.*)

Political History ☆

Partition Leading up to India's independence in August 1947, a group named the Muslim League called for the separation of India into separate Hindu and Muslim states. When India achieved its independence, two other nations were also created—West Pakistan (present-day Pakistan) and East Pakistan (present-day Bangladesh).

By the Numbers

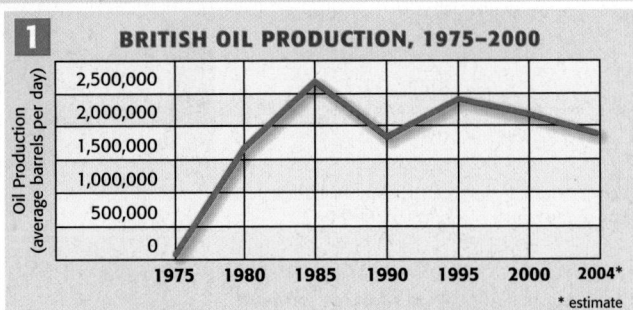

1 **BRITISH OIL PRODUCTION, 1975–2000**

Oil Production (average barrels per day)

| | 1975 | 1980 | 1985 | 1990 | 1995 | 2000 | 2004* |

* estimate
Source Energy Information Administration

In 1975 Britain began oil production in the North Sea, the arm of the Atlantic Ocean that separates the British Isles from the European mainland. Oil production boomed during the 1980s and 1990s. However, after peaking in the late 1990s, North Sea oil has declined. Some analysts predict that production will remain stagnant or continue to decrease—creating concern over the supply of oil.

End of Empire

Listed below are some of the former British colonies and dependencies that achieved home rule after World War II (former names are in parentheses).

☆ India—1947
☆ Pakistan—1947
  Sri Lanka (Ceylon)—1948
  Myanmar (Burma)—1948
  Israel (Palestine)—1948
  Ghana (Gold Coast)—1957
  Nigeria—1960
  Tanzania (Tanganyika)—1961
  Jamaica—1962
  Uganda—1962
  Kenya—1963
  Zambia (Northern Rhodesia)—1964
  Malta—1964
  Guyana (British Guiana)—1966
  Fiji and Tonga—1970
  Bahamas—1973
  Belize—1981
  Brunei—1984

IMMIGRATION

In the late twentieth century, the ethnic make-up of Britain began to change when immigrants, mostly from the West Indies, began to arrive. In 1948, 547 immigrants from Jamaica arrived; by 1955 that number had increased to 18,561. Immigrants from the Indian subcontinent and then from Asia, Africa, and the Middle East followed.

EDUCATION

One of the major changes in postwar Britain was the establishment of a system of comprehensive schools, or secondary schools that admit pupils from all ability levels. In 1971, 34 percent of British secondary school students attended comprehensive schools; by 1980, that figure had risen to 80 percent.

CONSUMER SPENDING

Between 1955 and 1960, the number of British people who owned refrigerators rose from 6 percent to 16 percent; those owning washing machines, from 25 percent to 44 percent; and those owning automobiles, from 18 percent to 32 percent. Shopping in postwar Britain became Americanized, with more than 800 supermarkets opening from 1956 to 1961.

ENGLISH SPEAKERS

Approximately 350 million people throughout the world speak English as a first language, and another 450 million use it as a second language. About one-seventh of the world's population speaks English, and that number continues to rise.

Writing Practice

 Summarize

SMALL GROUP
Point out the variety of ways in which information is presented on this page: in a graph, in a list, and in text blocks. **Ask:** Which way of presenting information helps you learn facts most quickly? Why? (*Answers will vary but should be explained.*)

Then break the class into three groups. Assign each group a segment of the information: the graph, the list, or the text blocks. **Ask:** How do you summarize information? (*Study the information till you can determine the main idea; then write that idea in your own words.*)

Tell each group to produce a summary of the assigned information in two or three sentences. Have groups write their summaries on the board and discuss their strategy for summarizing the information presented in different forms.

Being There

After World War II, the sun did set over the British Empire, which dissolved into the Commonwealth of Nations. This federation of nations voluntarily recognizes the British monarchy as a symbol of their economic alliance and collaborates on economic and social policies. Today, the Commonwealth (shown in orange on the map below) comprises fifty-three countries, including Canada, Australia, India, Pakistan, Nigeria, and South Africa.

B *Kano State, Nigeria, 2002.*

C *Hanbury Street, London, 1996.*

A ★

An elephant walks down a street amid traffic as it rains in Mumbai, 2005.

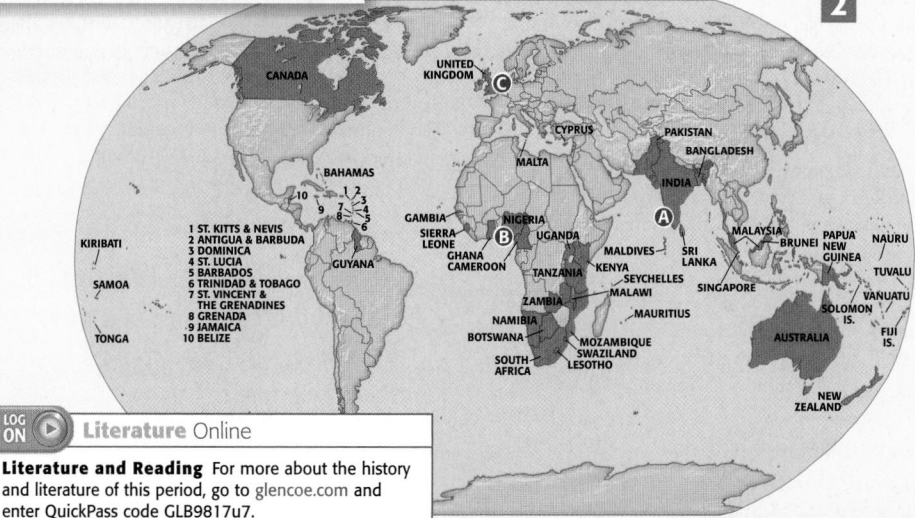

2

1 ST. KITTS & NEVIS
2 ANTIGUA & BARBUDA
3 DOMINICA
4 ST. LUCIA
5 BARBADOS
6 TRINIDAD & TOBAGO
7 ST. VINCENT & THE GRENADINES
8 GRENADA
9 JAMAICA
10 BELIZE

LOG ON ▶ **Literature** Online

Literature and Reading For more about the history and literature of this period, go to glencoe.com and enter QuickPass code GLB9817u7.

Reading Check

Analyze Graphic Information

1. About how many times greater was West Indian immigration to Britain in 1955 than it had been in 1948?

2. Approximately how many people throughout the world speak English as a first or second language?

3. Which continents have countries that belong to the British Commonwealth of Nations?

Teach

Reading Check

Answers:

1. *About 34 times greater*

2. *Approximately 800 million people*

3. *Europe, North America, South America, Africa, Asia, and Australia*

Reading Strategy   2

Analyze Maps Have students examine the locations of Commonwealth countries on the map. **Ask:** How do the locations of Commonwealth countries help explain why there are so many English speakers in the world? *(Six continents have Commonwealth countries; some densely populated areas are part of the Commonweatlth, thus increasing the number of people who speak English.)*

View the Art ★

A. This photo shows a striking clash between traditional and modern cultures in India.

B. More than 250 ethnic groups make up Nigeria's population.

C. This street is near Brick Lane, a London neighborhood famous for its Bangladeshi community.

English Learners

DIFFERENTIATED INSTRUCTION

Beginning Remind students that *-tion* is a suffix found in many abstract nouns. Have students locate this suffix in page headings (*production, immigration, education, inflation*) and name the related verbs (*produce, immigrate, educate, inflate*).

Approaching Level

DIFFERENTIATED INSTRUCTION

Emerging Some students may have difficulty interpreting statistics. Remind them to read graph labels carefully. Suggest that partners work together to paraphrase statistics in their own words. Then have students explain why each statistic is significant.

Teach

Reading Strategy | 1

Evaluate As they read "End of the Empire," encourage students to consider the troubles newly independent nations faced.

Ask: Given the troubles new nations dealt with, do you think it was a good thing that so many nations achieved home rule? Why or why not? *(Students may argue that it was a good thing, since the nations were no longer reliant on Britain and could decide for themselves how they wanted to be ruled.)*

Literary History ☆

Cry, the Beloved Country
In 1948, the novel *Cry, the Beloved Country,* by the South African writer Alan Paton, was published. The novel tells the story of a black minister who witnesses racial tensions in Johannesburg when his son is accused of murder. The novel is especially notable for bringing the issue of apartheid to the world's attention.

Learning Objectives

For pages 1172–1186
In studying this text, you will focus on the following objectives:

Literary Study:
Analyzing literary periods.
Analyzing literary genres.

Reading:
Evaluating historical influences.
Connecting to the literature.

An International Literature
1950–Present

Historical, Social, and Cultural Forces

Domestic and Foreign Problems

The end of World War II left Britain saddled with serious economic problems. After a landslide victory in 1946, the Labour Party instituted a series of programs to strengthen the economy. The government assumed responsibility for housing, pensions, unemployment, and the nation's railroads and mines. A national health program made medical care available to everyone. The British welfare state became the model for many other postwar European countries.

Another thorny problem involved relations with Britain's neighbor Ireland. In the late 1960s, violence erupted in Northern Ireland between the Protestant Unionists, who wanted to remain in the United Kingdom, and the Catholic Nationalists, who wanted to break with Britain and join the Republic of Ireland. In the 1970s and 1980s terrorists from the Irish Republican Army carried out bombings in Britain.

End of the Empire

To strengthen its economy, Britain had to reduce expenses abroad, and it gradually agreed to many colonies' demands for home rule. Colony by colony, the British Empire was dismantled. In Asia and Africa, the new nations created from former British colonies faced an array of formidable problems, including overpopulation, poverty, and ethnic and religious strife. In India, for example, despite

government efforts, the population grew at the alarming rate of more than two percent each year during the 1950s and 1960s. This growth wreaked havoc on the economy, increasing poverty in that new nation.

Newly created African nations struggled to resolve the tension between modern and traditional lifestyles. Some African leaders supported Western-style capitalism. Others, such as Julius Nyerere (ni râr´ ē) of Tanzania, believed that economic and political life should imitate that found in a traditional African community—a village inhabited by an extended family.

> *"To be free is not merely to cast off one's chains, but to live in a way that respects and enhances the freedom of others."*
>
> —Nelson Mandela, from *Long Walk to Freedom*

Though South Africa had been independent since 1910, its political system remained controlled by whites. In the late 1940s, South African whites codified the laws separating whites and blacks into a system of racial segregation known as apartheid

Reading Practice

Use Text Structure Encourage students to use the subheadings to organize notes and ideas about the unit. Suggest that students follow these steps:

- Express the spread title ("Historical, Social, and Cultural Forces") in your own words.

- Create a three-column foldable and label each column with the subheads on page 1179.

- Summarize the key ideas in each section. Be sure you have included the main idea of each.

- Add ideas of your own that are directly related to each topic.

("apartness"). Under the leadership of the African National Congress (ANC), blacks in South Africa demonstrated against legalized segregation. The government brutally repressed these demonstrations, sentencing ANC leader Nelson Mandela to life imprisonment in 1964. Under the administration of the anti-apartheid president F. W. de Klerk, Mandela was released from prison in 1990.

Joining Europe

The loss of its colonial empire brought Britain closer to its Western European allies. As the Cold War developed between the two superpowers, the United States and the Soviet Union, Britain sought security by joining the North Atlantic Treaty Organization (NATO), a defensive alliance formed in 1949. Britain also sought closer economic ties with the nations of Western Europe. In 1973 Britain joined the free-trade zone of the European Economic Community (EEC), or Common Market, despite uncertainty over the consequences of this step. Britain's political ties to the continent grew stronger when the EEC morphed into the European Union in 1993. ☆

COMPLETE INDEPENDENCE 1961

Julius Nyerere carried by supporters, 1961.

PREVIEW **Big Ideas** of An International Literature

1 Making and Remaking Traditions	**2** Colonialism and Postcolonialism	**3** Globalization
Since the end of World War II, Britain has struggled through an identity crisis. Every cultural trait and tradition, from the monarchy to the stiff upper lip, has been called into question. Contemporary British writers have created variations and innovations upon traditional forms and themes. **See pages 1180–1181.**	Beginning in 1947, with the partition of British India into the independent states of India and Pakistan, a long succession of former British colonies declared independence. Writers in these new nations broadened the scope of English literature in both subject matter and style. **See pages 1182–1183.**	One of the most important cultural legacies of the British Empire was the establishment of English as a global language. As a result, contemporary literature in English is enriched by the voices and experiences of writers from a great variety of cultures throughout the world. **See pages 1184–1185.**

INTRODUCTION **1179**

Teach

Reading Strategy   2

Question **Ask:** What was apartheid? (*Apartheid was a system of racial separation in South Africa.*) How did the system originate? (*South Africa was politically controlled by white South Africans from 1910 until the end of apartheid in 1990; they created the system to prevent black South Africans from gaining political power.*) Who was Nelson Mandela? (*Mandela was a leader of the African National Congress who was imprisoned for demonstrating against apartheid.*) [ADVANCED] Challenge students to research the etymology of the term *apartheid*. Students can use dictionaries and on-line sources to determine the word's meaning; then, have them consider how a Dutch word came into use to name a power structure in an African nation.

Political History ☆

European Union The European Union allows member nations to compete as a single market. One key feature of this union is the euro, a single currency adopted by 12 of the 25 member nations, sometimes called the "eurozone." Launched as a currency in 2002, the euro rose in value relative to many foreign currencies, strengthening both economic and political ties among these countries.

Cultural History ☆

The British Empire At its most powerful, the British Empire spread across the world, yet many British citizens had only vague notions about the colonies. **Ask:** Why didn't knowledge of the colonies become a strong part of British culture? (*Students might suggest that the colonies existed only for economic gain; few British people traveled to the colonies.*) What process led to greater multicultural awareness after 1950? (*Immigration brought cultures into direct contact.*)

Big Idea 1
Making and Remaking Traditions

Early in the twentieth century, Britain was supreme among the nations of the world. Fifty years later, with its empire lost, Britain's preeminence disappeared, and British confidence eroded. Both internally and externally, Britain found it had to achieve a new identity.

An Identity Crisis

For most of the British people, the loss of the empire produced few shock waves. To ordinary people in Britain—rather than the relatively small number of the middle and upper classes who had served as colonial administrators—the British Empire had always been a rather distant, if glorious, prospect. Even if the empire had been remote, however, its loss seemed ominous and darkly symbolic of British decline.

In addition to the dissolution of the British Empire, economic woes contributed to the alarming sense that something was very wrong. Economic recovery after World War II was painfully slow. Burdened with heavy debt and a shortage of goods, postwar Britain imposed a program of austerity on its war-weary citizens. Fresh fruit, canned goods, meat, and butter were among the rationed foods. Persistently high rates of unemployment triggered bitter labor disputes, fueling fears that joblessness might be a permanent condition in Britain. By the mid-1970s, inflation was increasing faster than at any time since the war. The economy fluctuated under the direction of prime ministers Margaret Thatcher and John Major in the 1980s and 1990s. Under Tony Blair, Britain continued to face daunting economic challenges, exacerbated by rising security costs because of terrorist threats.

Shift in Values

Meanwhile, various social changes generated widespread anxiety. The youth rebellion that affected American society in the 1960s had its counterpart in Britain. Many British, particularly older people, objected to the increasing "permissiveness" they observed in mass media, including advertising, movies, television, and popular music. The relationship among the long-established classes of English society began to break down as the power of the common people increased. Nothing in postwar Britain seemed safe and secure.

> "I thought it would last my time—The sense that, beyond the town, There would always be fields and farms . . ."
>
> —Philip Larkin, "Going, Going"

Contemporary British Literature

After decades of Modernist innovation, British poets after World War II were free to reexamine literary tradition. Ted Hughes's poetry looked beyond the Modernists to create a vision of nature that combines beauty and brutality.

Many of the greatest prose writers working today are British novelists. Indian-born author Salman Rushdie's *Midnight's Children* has been universally hailed for its innovative postmodern take on Indian history. Zadie Smith's novel *White Teeth* (2000) was a critically acclaimed postmodern narrative about immigrant communities in London. Kazuo Ishiguro's novels, including *The Remains of the Day* (1989) and *Never Let Me Go* (2005), are more straightforward narratives infused with subtle emotion. Other writers from the Commonwealth, including South African Nobel laureate J. M. Coetzee and Englishmen Ian McEwen and Julian Barnes, have been consistently lauded for their varied works in prose.

Reading Practice

Analyze Figurative Language Ask students to answer these questions to analyze the metaphors in "Thistles":

- How does the speaker compare thistles to dangerous weapons? (*He says they are "splintered weapons" thrust up from the ground.*)

- What is "the underground stain of a decayed Viking"? (*the nutrients from a dead Viking, providing sustenance for the plant*)

- What is the "plume of blood"? (*the purple color of the thistle's flower*)

- Who "grow grey, like men"? (*the thistle plants after they flower*)

- What are "their sons"? (*the new plants that grow from seed*)

My Parents, 1977. David Hockney. Tate Gallery, London.

View the Art David Hockney's works tend to show ordinary, realistic scenes rendered in a simple but highly accurate way. What mood does this scene create? What is the effect of the poses of its subjects? ★

Beginning in the mid-1950s, an extraordinary group of playwrights revolutionized the British theater. Samuel Beckett's play *Waiting for Godot* (1953) became an instant classic of absurdist drama. In plays such as *The Caretaker* (1960) and *The Homecoming* (1965), Harold Pinter (see page 1224) created characters unable to communicate and devoid of love.

"Thistles" by Ted Hughes

Against the rubber tongues of cows and the hoeing
   hands of men
Thistles spike the summer air
Or crackle open under a blue-black pressure.

Every one a revengeful burst
Of resurrection, a grasped fistful
Of splintered weapons and Icelandic frost thrust up

From the underground stain of a decayed Viking.
They are like pale hair and the gutturals of dialects.
Every one manages a plume of blood.

Then they grow grey, like men.
Mown down, it is a feud. Their sons appear,
Stiff with weapons, fighting back over the same ground. **2**

Reading Check

Compare and Contrast How would you compare Hughes's view of nature with that of traditional Romantics?

INTRODUCTION **1181**

Approaching Level

DIFFERENTIATED INSTRUCTION

Emerging Explain that personification is giving human characteristics to an animal, object, or idea. **Ask:** What is personified in "Thistles"? *(the thistles)* **Ask:** What is the poem's setting? How does the poet portray that setting? *(Farm fields are portrayed as battlefields.)* Help students identify the warring enemies: the farmers, who want to get rid of the weedy thistles, and the thistles, who want to thrive and reproduce. **Ask:** Which enemy seems to be winning the battle? How do you know? *(The thistles are winning; no matter how many the farmers hoe up, new crops grow in their place.)* Then have students consider why the poet used personification. **Ask:** Would you have less sympathy for the thistles if the poet had simply described them as plants?

Teach
Reading Check

Answer: *Hughes' view of nature seems Romantic in that he presents beautiful natural images and shows nature as untamed. However, the images of warfare suggest a brutal conflict between humans and nature, which is not a Romantic concept.*

Literary Element   2

Rhythm **Ask:** Is the rhythm of this poem regular or irregular? *(irregular; it does not follow a set metrical pattern)* How do the rhythm and form of Hughes's poem reflect his subject? *(The jagged lines and irregular rhythm reflect the spiky thistles and support Hughes' violent and aggressive depiction.)*

[APPROACHING] Write the first two lines of the poem on the board, and read them aloud, vocally emphasizing the accented syllables and marking them as you read. ("Against' the rub'ber tongues' of cows' and the hoe'ing hands' of men' . . . .") Then, have students repeat the process with the other lines.

View the Art ★

Answer: *Students may identify the mood as peaceful, quiet, or still, or cheerful. Opinions on the effects of the poses will vary; students may say that the mother's pose adds to the cheerful mood, while the father's suggests a casual, relaxed mood.*

Teach

Reading Strategy | 1

Evaluate Ask: Of these words, which do you think has greater negative connotations: *colonialism* or *imperialism*? *(Although both words name systems that are inherently unequal, imperialism has strongly negative connotations, suggesting that one country is completely dominating another and destroying its culture.)* How can the language used to describe a political system affect the way the system is interpreted or accepted? *(Governments sometimes use words with positive or neutral connotations to describe policies that will actually have negative effects; they also use neutral language to minimize negative events.)*

ENGLISH LEARNERS Write on the board: *colonialism* and *imperialism*. **Ask:** *Which Spanish words look like these words? (colonialismo, imperialismo)* Ask a student to write the words in Spanish on the board. Remind students that if they know a word in Spanish that looks similar to an English word, it might mean the same thing.

Big Idea 2
Colonialism and Postcolonialism

From the earliest days of the British Empire, many of its colonies struggled to gain independence. Though most of these early struggles failed, the American Revolution, of course, proved a notable exception.

British Colonial Rule

During the nineteenth and early twentieth centuries, Britain colonized large portions of the world. Markedly different from earlier and more limited British colonialism, especially in Africa and Asia, this "new imperialism" aimed at total control over vast territories. Although based on economic exploitation and influenced by racist attitudes toward colonial peoples, British imperialism also promoted humanitarian goals, such as building railroads, telegraphs, schools, and hospitals. In a poem written in 1899, British poet Rudyard Kipling coined the phrase "the white man's burden" to capture the odd blend of racism and humanitarianism inherent in British imperialism.

> "People go to Africa and confirm what they already have in their heads and so they fail to see what is there in front of them."
>
> —Chinua Achebe

Throughout the British Empire, however, even well-intentioned administrators and zealous missionaries often came into conflict with colonial peoples. In a series of novels that includes his masterpiece, *Things Fall Apart* (1958), the Nigerian writer Chinua Achebe (see page 1258) describes the devastating effect of colonialism and Christianity on the traditional African way of life.

Problems of Independence

As the British Empire collapsed, independence brought serious problems to former British colonies. For example, British India consisted of two countries, one Hindu (India) and the other Muslim (Pakistan). When India and Pakistan became independent in 1947, millions of people fled across the new borders, with Hindus streaming toward India and Muslims toward Pakistan. In the ensuing violence, more than a million people perished. Mohandas Gandhi, the renowned Indian nationalist leader and advocate of nonviolence, was assassinated by a Hindu militant on January 30, 1948.

During the 1950s and 1960s, many former British colonies in Africa achieved independence, but their national spirit was undermined by ethnic clashes. Civil warfare was a tragic aftermath of colonialism. In building colonial empires, Britain and other European powers had drawn up the boundaries of African nations with little regard to the inhabitants' ethnic diversity.

In South Africa, the process of achieving political independence for non-whites was complicated by apartheid, the official system of racial segregation in force since the late 1940s. After decades of resistance, apartheid was finally overturned, and in 1994 free elections brought Nelson Mandela to power as the first black president of South Africa. Among the most outspoken critics of South African racism were the writers Doris Lessing (see page 1238) and Nadine Gordimer (see page 1249).

Postcolonial Literature

Many writers from former British colonies, including Achebe, Wole Soyinka, Derek Walcott, and V. S. Naipaul, have addressed the political and social problems that continue to plague these countries even after independence. Postcolonial writers constantly grapple with the tension between native and colonial cultures while

Vocabulary Practice

Prefixes Have students compare the meanings of the words *colonialism* and *postcolonialism*. *(Postcolonialism is the period after the fall of colonialism.)* Highlight the prefix *post-* as it is used in this term. Point out that another word frequently used to describe a movement in the late twentieth century is *postmodern*. **Ask:** How is this term an oxymoron? *(Modern means "current," so* postmodern *could mean "after what is current" or something that has not yet occurred.)* Explain that the word *postmodern* usually refers to a reaction to or against the Modernist movement.

A wooden carving of a car with a European and his driver, c. twentieth century. Zaire Luba. Museum of Central Africa, Tervuren, Belgium.

addressing themes of identity, racism, and cultural dominance. Because English is so widely spoken, many postcolonial writers have felt compelled to adopt this language even if it is not their native tongue.

In the nineteenth century, the British had boasted that "the sun never set" on their worldwide empire. After World War II, as colony after colony became independent, Britain's national prestige was dealt a severe blow.

"Homage to a Government" by Philip Larkin

Next year we are to bring the soldiers home
For lack of money, and it is all right.
Places they guarded, or kept orderly,
Must guard themselves, and keep themselves orderly.
We want the money for ourselves at home
Instead of working. And this is all right.

It's hard to say who wanted it to happen,
But now it's been decided nobody minds.
The places are a long way off, not here.
Which is all right, and from what we hear

The soldiers there only made trouble happen.
Next year we shall be easier in our minds.

Next year we shall be living in a country
That brought its soldiers home for lack of money.
The statues will be standing in the same
Tree-muffled squares, and look nearly the same.
Our children will not know it's a different country.
All we can hope to leave them now is money. **2**

Reading Check
Analyze Cause and Effect According to the speaker in Larkin's poem, why did Britain give up its colonies?

Teach
Reading Check

Answer: *Britain gave up its colonies because of a lack of money. The speaker also suggests that some people "wanted it to happen" for unspecified political reasons, which the speaker associates with the British welfare state.*

Literary Element | 2

Rhyme **Ask:** How would you describe the pattern found in this poem's line endings? *(The line endings in each stanza follow the pattern abccab. However, it is not a rhyme pattern because the same words repeat, except for a homophone pair.)* What is the effect of this pattern of repetition? *(It suggests that the speaker has a limited worldview and is possibly parroting ideas of others.)*

View the Art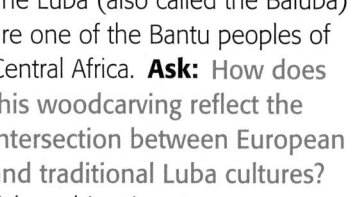
The Luba (also called the Baluba) are one of the Bantu peoples of Central Africa. **Ask:** How does this woodcarving reflect the intersection between European and traditional Luba cultures? *(The subject is a European car and rider, but the style and design look like traditional African art.)*

Approaching Level
DIFFERENTIATED INSTRUCTION

Established To improve **reading fluency**, encourage students to read the poem aloud once to gain an understanding of its rhythms. Have them identify an appropriate tone for an oral reading.

English Learners
DIFFERENTIATED INSTRUCTION

Intermediate Have students identify verbs in the poem that refer to the future. (are, shall be, will be, will not know) Remind students that verbs in the present tense can refer to future events, as in the opening line of the poem. **Ask:** What phrase clearly indicates that the event takes place in the future? *("Next year")*

Teach

Reading Strategy   1

Compare and Contrast Ask:
How is globalization different
from colonization? *(Globalization
is the development of a shared
global culture; colonization involves
one country ruling another.)*

[ADVANCED] Challenge students
to identify three ways in which
the people of a globalized nation
benefit, whereas the people of a
colonized nation do not.

Reading Strategy   2

Evaluate Ask: Does the
spread of the English language
promote colonization or globalization? *(The dominance of English
promotes globalization because
many places now share the same
language, which is an important
aspect of a shared culture.)*

[APPROACHING] **Ask:** What are the
advantages and disadvantages
of knowing more than one
language? Have students list the
pros and cons; then guide them to
return to the question and apply
their conclusions to it.

Big Idea 3
Globalization 1

What does the term *English literature*
convey to you? In the Middle Ages,
the term applied only to the writings produced on an island off the
northwest coast of Europe. Even
three hundred years ago, in the early stages of the
British Empire, the meaning of the term extended
only to the works created by British colonists in
New England and Virginia. Today, writers
throughout the world create masterpieces in
English. How did this extraordinary turn of events
come about?

Movement of Peoples

From its beginning more than three centuries ago,
the British Empire spurred the migration of people. Emigrants left Britain to settle in India,
Canada, Australia, New Zealand, South Africa,
and a host of other British colonies.

> *"I am a word in a foreign language."*
> —Margaret Atwood, "Disembarking at Quebec"

People also moved from one colony to another
within the British Empire in search of work on
plantations or in mines. The family of the writer
V. S. Naipaul (see page 1283) emigrated from
British India to Trinidad in the West Indies. In
Prologue to an Autobiography, Naipaul describes his
complex heritage: "There was a migration from
India to be considered, a migration within the
British Empire. There was my Hindu family, with
its fading memories of India; there was India itself.
And there was Trinidad, with its past of slavery,
its mixed population, its racial antagonisms, and
its changing political life."

Exporting English

During its heyday as an empire-builder, Britain
exported many goods, from cotton products and
cricket bats to policies and laws. Undoubtedly, the
most important British export was the English
language itself. It traveled widely in the three centuries during which Britain ruled much of the
world. The emergence of Britain's former colony,
the United States of America, as a superpower
after World War II also contributed to the global
dominance of English.

A Global Literature

Just as improvements and innovations in transportation and technology have enabled people from
different countries to communicate more easily,
the spread of the English language and British culture throughout the world has given rise to an
international literature in English. The Nobel
Prize in Literature serves as a yardstick to measure
the increase in the number of writers throughout
the world creating works in English. Before World
War II, only one Nobel laureate writing in
English, the Indian writer Rabindranath Tagore
(rə bin′ drə nät′ tə gôr′), was neither British,
Irish, nor American. Since World War II, Nobel
laureates writing in English include Patrick White
from Australia, Nadine Gordimer and J. M.
Coetzee from South Africa, Wole Soyinka from
Nigeria, and Derek Walcott and V. S. Naipaul
from the Caribbean.

In the twenty-first century, with all its advances in
technology, the world seems to be a smaller place.
Nevertheless, literature remains a major source of
understanding and entertainment, just as it was in
the times of Chaucer, Shakespeare, and Keats.
Throughout this worldwide community, the global
village, people continue to look to British literature for a glorious tradition that is still growing
and seeking new directions.

Speaking and Listening Practice

Discuss English Authors Have students consider whether they can identify a
writer's country of origin by reading his or
her works.

- Have each student select sample text
  from one of the authors discussed in
  this unit introduction.

- Students should read the excerpts aloud
  without identifying the authors.

- Listeners should try to guess each
  author's nation of origin.

Point out that some clues will reflect
physical or geographic details; other clues
might be subtle uses of language or style.

Britain Seen from the North, 1981. Tony Cragg. Plastic and mixed media, 173.22 x 314.96 x 3.93 in. Tate Gallery, London.

View the Art Tony Cragg's early works often consisted of items salvaged from the trash or the streets. What message might this work be trying to send about Britain? ★

Among the themes addressed by the writers of this global literature in English are the effects of colonialism, the nature of cultural identity, and the experience of crossing boundaries, either geographical or historical. Published in 1981, Salman Rushdie's novel Midnight's Children opens with this account of the narrator's birth at the exact moment when India became independent.

from *Midnight's Children* by Salman Rushdie

I was born in the city of Bombay . . . once upon a time. No, that won't do, there's no getting away from the date: I was born in Doctor Narlikar's Nursing Home on August 15th, 1947. And the time? The time matters, too. Well then: at night. No, it's important to be more . . . On the stroke of midnight, as a matter of fact. Clock-hands joined palms in respectful greeting as I came. Oh, spell it out, spell it out: at the precise instant of India's arrival at independence, I tumbled forth into the world. There were gasps. And, outside the window, fireworks and crowds. A few seconds later, my father broke his big toe; but his accident was a mere trifle when set beside what had befallen me in the benighted moment, because thanks to the occult tyrannies of those blandly saluting clocks I had been mysteriously handcuffed to history, my destinies indissolubly chained to those of my country. For the next three decades, there was to be no escape. Soothsayers had prophesied me, newspapers celebrated my arrival, politicos ratified my authenticity. I was left entirely without a say in the matter.

Reading Check

Interpret Why might some writers from former British colonies feel "handcuffed to history," as Rushdie's narrator does?

Teach

Reading Check

Answer: *These writers come from societies strongly influenced by the history and values of the British Empire; they write in English, in itself a legacy of the empire.*

Reading Strategy | 3

Questioning **Ask:** What is the symbolic importance of the date of the narrator's birth? *(The narrator was born at the very instant that India became an independent nation.)*

View the Art ★

(Possible answers: Students may say the image suggests that Britain is fragmented, cluttered with the debris of the past, or has lost direction [since North faces to the right instead of upward, as on a traditional map].)

Tony Cragg (1949–) was born in Liverpool but lives in Germany. Like many of his wall sculptures, this work is an assemblage of a variety of objects to create a larger image. The figure at the right is a self-portrait of the artist. **Ask:** What is unusual about the figure's perspective on Britain? *(Not only is north at the right instead of the traditional top, but most of the world and the former empire views Britain from the south.)*

Approaching Level

DIFFERENTIATED INSTRUCTION

Emerging Students may have difficulty following the narrative digressions of the speaker in *Midnight's Children*. Encourage students to read aloud, using punctuation marks as a guide for when to pause.

English Learners

DIFFERENTIATED INSTRUCTION

Beginning Explain that an ellipsis can suggest that a speaker is trailing off, hesitating, or confused. **Ask:** What do you think the speaker was going to say after the second ellipsis? *(Exact; precise)*

Assess

Legacy of the Period

Discuss how technology may contribute to the continued spread of English. **Ask:** How has the Internet contributed to the spread of English around the globe? *(People around the world can visit English-language sites.)*

Cultural and Literary Links

Suggest that, as they read the unit, students look for ways in which the authors have influenced other forms of media.

FOLDABLES®
Study Organizer

Have students make and label the Four-Tab Book. When they read a selection, encourage them to classify it by writing its name under the appropriate book flap. Students can also include a main idea for each selection.

Wrap-Up

Legacy of the Period

English is the main or official language in more than sixty nations and is used on every continent. The reasons for the spread of English point to the influence of the once global British Empire and the emergence of the United States as a world power. The spread of the English language has created a vast audience for traditional British literature. More important, it has provided an opportunity for writers throughout the world to create modern classics in the English language. Drawing upon their cultural traditions and life experiences, these writers have broadened and enriched British literature.

The Modernist movement had run its course when World War II ended. Postmodernism, with its emphasis on literature as a self-consciously artificial form, influenced postwar literature in Britain (Julian Barnes's novel *Flaubert's Parrot* is one notable example), but much contemporary British poetry and fiction adapted traditional literary forms. British drama is perhaps the genre richest in innovation, as the plays of Samuel Beckett, John Osborne, Harold Pinter, and Wole Soyinka attest.

Cultural and Literary Links

▶ In his recent translation of *Beowulf*, Seamus Heaney stated that he sought to evoke the traditional English that he heard as a child in Northern Ireland.

▶ In his book-length narrative poem *Omeros*, Derek Walcott invests his tale of a Caribbean fisherman's voyage to his ancestral African home with allusions to the Homeric epics.

▶ V. S. Naipaul's novel *A Bend in the River* is a postcolonial account of the African region first described by Joseph Conrad in his novel *Heart of Darkness* (1902).

 LOG ON ▶ **Literature** Online

Unit Resources For additional skills practice, go to glencoe.com and enter QuickPass code GLB9817u7.

Activities ▶

Choose one of the following activities to explore and develop as you read this unit.

1. Follow Up Go back to Looking Ahead on page 1173 and answer the questions.

2. Contrast Literary Periods Work with several other students to hold a panel discussion, contrasting one of this period's big ideas with current American culture. Use examples from literature, fine art, music, movies, and other kinds of expression to support your ideas.

3. Build Visual Literacy Held in 1951, the Festival of Britain celebrated the centennial of the Great Exhibition. Research the festival and create a

display showing some of its buildings, artifacts, and attractions.

4. Take Notes Use this study organizer to keep track of the three big ideas in the unit.

FOLDABLES®
Study Organizer   **FOUR-TAB BOOK**

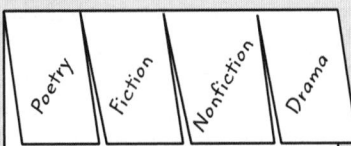

Writing Practice

Construct Persuasive Arguments
Remind students that they have just read about the global importance of the English language. **Ask:** What other languages have grown in importance globally? *(Answers may include Spanish and Chinese).* Then **ask:** Since English is spoken around the world, why should English speakers learn to speak other languages?

Divide the class in half. Assign one group the task of writing three persuasive, well-explained reasons why English speakers should learn other languages. The other group should write three reasons why English speakers do not need to speak another language. Have students write their reasons on the board.

Before the class decides which group's reasons are more persuasive, discuss the traits of solid persuasive reasons:

- the reason is based on sufficient evidence
- the reason does not manipulate readers' feelings
- the reason is written in unbiased language

Part 1

The British Isles:
Making and Remaking Traditions

Untitled, from a series of five, 1973. Tim Mara. Silkscreen print, 34.76 x 34.76 in. Wolverhampton Art Gallery, West Midlands, UK.

View the Art The Pop Art movement in Britain tended to incorporate themes of technology or mass culture into images that critiqued modern society. What comments on society might this image be making? ★

"You're hurt because everything's changed. Jimmy's hurt because everything's the same. And neither of you can face it." **1**

—Alison in John Osborne's *Look Back in Anger*

1187

Analyze and Extend

Reading Strategy   1

Analyze Direct students to read the quotation from *Look Back in Anger*. Explain that writing this 1956 drama earned John Osborne a reputation as an "angry young man," launching a British theater movement focusing on the lives of the working class. **Ask:** What conflict does this quotation suggest? *(Some people want to maintain the status quo. Others want things to improve rapidly. Because both results are unlikely to happen, people who hold on to these firm beliefs are frustrated.)*

View the Art ★

Possible answers: Responses will vary. Some students may note that while everyone is looking at something, nobody looks at each other—suggesting that people have become disconnected.

Printmaker Tim Mara (1948–1997) often created vivid interiors in electric colors. **Ask:** How do the colors and shapes of this print reflect the relationships between the figures shown? *(The colors are strident and sharp, isolating each figure in its own space. The figures are focused on newspapers, the window, or themselves, not one another.)*

1187

Before You Read

Focus

Bellringer Options

Selection Focus
  Transparency 63
Daily Language Practice
  Transparency 101

Or say: Write about a time when you felt totally overwhelmed. What caused you to feel that way? How did you handle the situation? *(Responses will vary.)*

Before You Read

Not Waving but Drowning

Meet **Stevie Smith**
(1902–1971)

Florence Margaret Smith got her nickname Stevie as a young girl when she and a friend were riding horses in a London park. Smith's horse was slow, and she rose in the saddle to urge it on. A few boys playing in the park saw her unsuccessful attempt to speed her mount and taunted, "Come on, Steve," referring to Steve Donaghue, a famous jockey of the day. Smith's companion loved the joke and began referring to Smith as Steve. Other friends soon were affectionately calling the petite, jockey-sized woman Stevie. The name stuck for the rest of her life.

Smith grew up with her mother, her aunt, and her older sister in a suburb of London. When Smith was three years old, her father deserted the family to become a sailor. As a child, Smith was a smart but unmotivated student. Her sister once noted that although Smith shirked school work, she could "get to the heart of the matter in two ticks."

> "The times will just have to enlarge themselves to make room for me, won't they?"
>
> —Stevie Smith

The World of Work Not considered academically suited for college, Smith attended secretarial school and soon got a job as secretary of the head of a publishing firm. She worked there for thirty years, supporting herself and her aunt, who lived with her for her entire life. In her spare time, Smith wrote poetry and read prodigiously, keeping a log of what she read and copying down passages that stimulated or impressed her.

Smith had her first poems published in a magazine in 1935. With this success, she approached an editor at a publishing house with a collection of her poems. The editor told Smith that before she was likely to get a book of poetry published she needed to "go away and write a novel." Smith did just that, completing her book in about six weeks. Against the advice of the editor who had encouraged Smith, the publishing house turned down Smith's novel. However, another publisher soon accepted it. *A Novel on Yellow Paper* was published in 1937 and a book of Smith's poetry was published soon afterward.

The Pendulum of Popularity Smith achieved sudden fame that launched her to the center of London's literary circles. She continued writing prose, but poetry was her real love. In fact, Smith's prose often exhibits the musicality and rhythm of poetry. One short story she wrote had such perfect meter that she later had it published as a poem, adding only line breaks and stanza divisions.

World War II interrupted Smith's writing career. She served as a volunteer fire-watcher during the nighttime air raid attacks on London. After the war, Smith's poetry didn't sell, and her publisher was reluctant to print her new work. Smith's popularity resurged in the late 1950s, however, and in the 1960s she received awards for her poems. In 1969 Queen Elizabeth honored her by giving her the Gold Medal for Poetry. A few years later, Smith died of an inoperable brain tumor.

 Literature Online

Author Search For more about Stevie Smith, go to glencoe.com and enter QuickPass code GLB9817u7.

Selection Skills

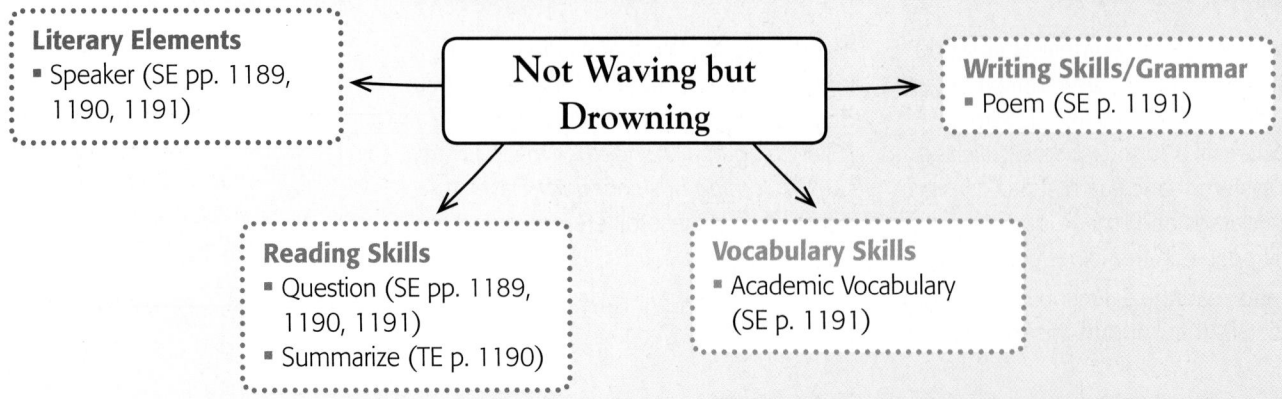

Literary Elements
- Speaker (SE pp. 1189, 1190, 1191)

Not Waving but Drowning

Writing Skills/Grammar
- Poem (SE p. 1191)

Reading Skills
- Question (SE pp. 1189, 1190, 1191)
- Summarize (TE p. 1190)

Vocabulary Skills
- Academic Vocabulary (SE p. 1191)

Literature and Reading Preview

Connect to the Poem

How do people respond when someone is in trouble? With a small group of classmates, discuss the ways in which both individuals and society as a whole respond to calls for help.

Build Background

Smith believed that "a poet should get on with his work and not be bothered by what his status is in the community." By following this principle, she developed a unique and independent style that differed greatly from that of her contemporaries. One of her most distinctive approaches was the use of humorous verse to express what were in fact profoundly serious themes. Another distinctive characteristic was her use of her own sketches to illustrate her poems.

Set Purposes for Reading

Big Idea Making and Remaking Traditions

As you read, ask yourself, How does Smith use both conventional poetic forms, including rhyme and meter, and unconventional elements in the poem?

Literary Element Speaker

In prose fiction, the narrator is the person, object, or force telling the story. In poetry, this role is taken by the **speaker**. The speaker may or may not be the poet. As you read "Not Waving but Drowning," ask yourself, Who is making this statement?

Reading Strategy Question

Questioning is a reading strategy that involves asking yourself specific questions to aid your comprehension. As you read, ask yourself, What might this mean? and Why is this important?

....

Tip: Asking Questions Make three or more copies of a diagram like the one below. As you read each stanza of "Not Waving but Drowning," fill in a copy of the diagram to ask and answer questions about the poem. If you wish, you can fill in more than one diagram per stanza.

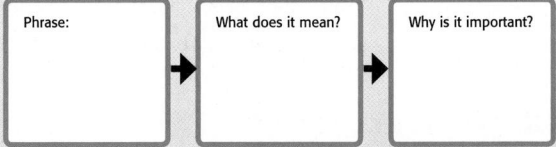

| Phrase: | → | What does it mean? | → | Why is it important? |

STEVIE SMITH **1189**

Summary

"Not Waving but Drowning" concerns a dead man misunderstood by the people who knew him.

For summaries in languages other than English, see Unit 7 Teaching Resources Book, pp. 20–25.

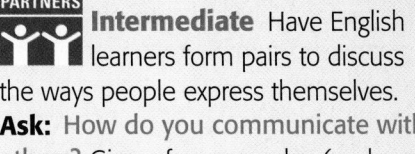

Learning Objectives

For pages 1188–1191

In studying this text, you will focus on the following objectives:

Literary Study: Analyzing speaker.

Reading: Questioning.

Writing: Writing a poem.

English Learners

DIFFERENTIATED INSTRUCTION

PARTNERS **Intermediate** Have English learners form pairs to discuss the ways people express themselves. **Ask:** How do you communicate with others? Give a few examples (such as speech, gestures, poetry), then have vol- unteers offer additional suggestions. Have students work together with their partners to generate a list of ideas, and then share them with another pair.

Teach

Big Idea   1

Making and Remaking Traditions **Ask:** Does this poem follow a particular rhyme scheme? *(Yes)* What is it? *(abcb defe gbhb)* How does this poem break from traditional verse? *(Possible response: The speaker changes within the poem.)*

Literary Element   2

Speaker **Answer:** *In line 2, an unnamed narrator is speaking; in line 3, the dead man, who is the subject of the poem, is speaking.*

Reading Strategy   3

Question **Answer:** *The word* cold *relates not only to temperature but also to a lack of emotional connection.*

[ENGLISH LEARNERS] Have English learners look up the word *cold* in the dictionary and decide which definitions apply to the way *cold* is used in the poem.

View the Art ★

Ask: What is the mood of this image? *(It is ominous, sad, or gloomy. Students may reply that it is ambiguous because you cannot tell where the waving man is standing or what his gesture means, or whether he is in or above the water.)*

Not Waving but Drowning   Stevie Smith   ★

Nobody heard him, the dead man,
But still he lay moaning:
I was much further out than you thought
And not waving but drowning.

5   Poor chap, he always loved larking[1]
And now he's dead
It must have been too cold for him his heart gave way,
They said.

Oh, no no no, it was too cold always
10   (Still the dead one lay moaning)
I was much too far out all my life
And not waving but drowning.

---

1. *Larking* means "engaging in harmless pranks."

2   Speaker *Who is speaking in these two lines?*

3   Question *What connotations does the word* cold *have here?*

Reading Practice

Summarize Tell students that one way to improve comprehension is to stop at the end of each stanza and write a brief summary. Remind students that summaries should include only the main ideas presented in the text. Ask students to determine the main idea of the first two lines. *(A dead man is moaning even though no one hears him.)* Ask them to identify the main idea of lines 3–4. *(The subject of the poem explains that he was* too far out and was calling for help, but no one realized it.) Have students work with partners to summarize the remainder of the poem.

After You Read

Respond and Think Critically

Respond and Interpret

1. Did the subject of the poem match what you predicted the poem would be about, based on its title? Why or why not?

2. (a)In the first stanza, what statement does the dead man make? (b)Do you think he tried to communicate this while he was living? Explain.

3. (a)In the second stanza, what do "they" believe caused the man's death? (b)In your opinion, who are "they"? What do you infer about their relationship with the drowned man?

Analyze and Evaluate

4. (a)Which words and phrases in the poem have double meanings? (b)What do these plays on words suggest about the dead man's ability to be understood by others?

5. Do you think this poem is tragic, comic, both, or something else? Explain.

Connect

6. **Big Idea** **Making and Remaking Traditions** (a)What poetic conventions does "Not Waving but Drowning" employ? (b)In what ways is this poem unconventional?

7. **Connect to the Author** With which speaker do you think Smith herself would have most closely identified? Explain, supporting your answer with what you know about Smith's life and attitude.

Literary Element | Speaker

On the surface, "Not Waving but Drowning" is a simple poem. There are no long, complex words, and the phrasing is conversational. But identifying the different **speakers** reveals layers of complexity.

1. Identify the different speakers in the poem. In which lines is each person speaking?

2. What clues helped you figure out who was speaking and when there was a shift in speakers?

🖋 Writing

Write a Poem In "Not Waving But Drowning," Smith's speakers reveal that the dead man has been fatally misunderstood. Write your own poem in which two speakers address each other but do not really communicate. Be sure to provide clues showing when there is a shift from one speaker to the other.

Reading Strategy | Question

To understand poetry, you need to ask **questions** both as you read a poem and as you analyze it.

1. What connotations do the words *too far out* and *drowning* have in the context of this poem? How do they add to the meaning of the poem?

2. In terms of his ability to communicate, has anything changed for the man over the course of the poem? Explain your answer.

Academic Vocabulary ▶

*The poem describes an ambiguous set of **circumstances**: a person who appears to be waving is actually drowning.*

Circumstance is an academic word. In the legal system, judges try to consider all the **circumstances** surrounding a case before sentencing.

To further explore the meaning of this word, complete the following sentence: *Under difficult **circumstances**, I usually try to _____.*

For more on academic vocabulary, see pages 56 and R81.

Reading Strategy

1. *Too far out* refers to emotional distance; *drowning* refers to being overwhelmed by fear. These words help bring out the poem's symbolism.

2. Students should support their responses.

Progress Check

Can students identify the speaker?

If No → See Unit 7 Teaching Resources Book, p. 26.

After You Read

Assess

1. Responses will vary.
2. (a) He says he was much further out than everyone thought and he was drowning. (b) He tried to communicate the thought but was misinterpreted.
3. (a) The cold water and heart failure (b) The dead man's friends and relations who misunderstood him
4. (a) An example is the word *cold*. (b) He was misunderstood.
5. Possible answer: Tragic situation but comic presentation
6. (a) Rhyme and mainly iambic pentameter (b) Irregular line lengths and everyday speech
7. Responses will vary. Students should use the information in the Building Background or Biography sections to support their answers.

Literary Element

1. An observer in lines 1–2, 5–8, and 10, and the dead man in lines 3–4, 9, and 11–12.
2. The observer refers to the dead man as *he*; the colon in line 2 indicates that the dead man will speak; the use of parentheses in line 10 gives a clue that the observer is speaking.

🖋 Writing

Students' poems should show a shift at some point to highlight the miscommunication between the speaker and listener.

Academic Vocabulary

Possible answer: When I find myself in difficult circumstances, I usually try to stay positive.

Bellringer Options

Daily Language Practice
Transparency 102

Or ask: Have you ever taken the time to watch people in a public place? Who was most striking? *(Responses will vary.)*

Say: The story you will read chronicles a young man's impressions of a couple he watches at a museum.

Meet **Penelope Lively**

(born 1933)

Have you ever wondered how your life might have changed if you had made a different decision at a critical turning point? In her autobiographical novel *Making It Up*, Penelope Lively imagines alternate life paths, exploring what might have happened if her family, fleeing Cairo, Egypt, during World War II, had headed for South Africa instead of their actual destination, Palestine. Would the ship on which they sailed have been torpedoed, as so many other ships had been? She also wonders what would have happened if she had had children at a younger age than she did, if her husband-to-be had been sent to fight in the Korean War, if she had married a different man, or if she had gone on an archaeological dig as a student. Did the choices she made cut off more rewarding paths, or did they avert disasters?

> *"It seems to me that the challenge of writing novels and short stories is to transcend and translate personal experience . . ."*
>
> —Penelope Lively

Childhood Upheaval Lively was born in Cairo and spent much of her childhood there. Her father, a bank manager, was so busy that she rarely saw him, and her mother was often occupied with social engagements. As a child Lively spent most of her time with a young English woman named Lucy, who started out as her nurse and then became her governess. Lively had no formal education until 1945, when she was sent to a boarding school in England after her parents divorced.

Already dealing with the trauma of parental neglect, Lively now had to endure permanent separation from Lucy, to whom she had become attached. She saw England as "not home at all—a mysterious, grey, wet place where it rained all the time."

Literary Pursuits After graduating from high school, Lively went on to college, earning a degree in history at Oxford. She married Jack Lively, a university professor, and they had two children. She and her husband had a long and happy marriage until his death in 1998. While raising her children, Lively began writing children's books. Her first published novel, *Astercote*, is about modern English villagers who fear the return of the medieval plague. She has written more than twenty novels for children, set mostly in rural England and concerned with the significance of memory and history.

By the mid-1970s, Lively began shifting her focus to literature for adults, although she continued to write for children well into the 1980s. "I began to feel that I was in danger of writing the same children's books over and over again," she explains. "More than that, I'd exhausted the ways in which I could explore my own preoccupations and interests within children's books." Her adult novels continue to explore the themes of the past and memory, but in the context of how such themes can affect one's philosophy or perspective on life. Lively won the Booker Prize for her novel *Moon Tiger* in 1987.

LOG ON **Literature** Online

Author Search For more about Penelope Lively, go to glencoe.com and enter QuickPass code GLB9817u7.

Selection Skills

Literary Elements
- Vernacular (SE pp. 1193, 1194, 1198, 1202)
- Narrator (SE p. 1202)

At the Pitt-Rivers

Listening/Speaking/ Viewing Skills
- Analyze Art (SE p. 1196)
- Monologue (TE p. 1198)

Reading Skills
- Synthesize (SE pp. 1193, 1195, 1197, 1198, 1200, 1202)

Vocabulary Skills
- Denotation and Connotation (SE p. 1202)
- Academic Vocabulary (SE p. 1202)

Writing Skills/Grammar
- Autobiography (SE p. 1203)
- Sentence Fragments (SE p. 1203)

Literature and Reading Preview

Connect to the Story

Why do we love to speculate about the lives of others? Freewrite for a few minutes about the ways in which our society observes people—such as tabloids—and why people are so fond of them.

Build Background

The setting of this story is the Pitt Rivers Museum of Anthropology and World Archaeology, located at Oxford University. The museum was established in 1884, when General Augustus Pitt Rivers donated his collection of artifacts (more than 18,000 objects) to the university. The museum now has more than half a million objects, most of them on display, identified with small handwritten labels. One holding is the three-floors-high totem pole mentioned in the story.

Set Purposes for Reading

Big Idea Making and Remaking Traditions

As you read, ask yourself, In what ways is this a conventional love story? In what ways is it unconventional?

Literary Element Vernacular

Vernacular is the ordinary speech of a particular country or region. It is more casual than cultivated, formal speech and includes slang and **dialect**. Another important feature of vernacular is the use of **idiom**—a term that has meaning only in a particular language. Like a metaphor, an idiom departs from literal meaning, as in the expression "catch his eye." As you read, ask yourself, What does the vernacular language in the story reveal about the narrator?

Reading Strategy Synthesize

When you **synthesize**, you combine various details or simple ideas to arrive at a more complex idea. Synthesizing information helps you reach a deeper understanding of a literary text. As you read, ask yourself, How can these ideas be combined to suggest something larger?

Tip: Taking Notes In a chart or a list, record significant details from the story, as well as relevant background information. Then synthesize your information and details to gain new insights into the story.

Learning Objectives

For pages 1192–1202

In studying this text, you will focus on the following objectives:

Literary Study: Analyzing vernacular.

Reading: Synthesizing.

Vocabulary

benign (bi nīn′) *adj.* pleasant and friendly; p. 1196 *The nurse gave her patient a benign smile.*

explicit (eks plis′ it) *adj.* plainly and clearly expressed; definite; p. 1197 *The children had explicit instructions to return to the house.*

compulsory (kəm pul′ sər ē) *adj.* obligatory; required; p. 1197 *Midterms for that course are compulsory, so don't miss that day!*

radiant (rā′ dē ənt) *adj.* beaming, as with joy, love, or energy; p. 1198 *The bride was radiant as she looked at her new husband.*

envious (en′ vē əs) *adj.* feeling jealous or discontented because of the good fortune or superior abilities of another; p. 1198 *Jeremy was envious of his brother's amazing athletic ability.*

Before You Read

Focus

Summary

A teenaged narrator visits the Pitt-Rivers Museum regularly to look at the various objects and work on his poetry. One day he sees a woman who is not traditionally attractive but is "radiant." He realizes she is in love and reflects on his own experiences with a girl. He repeatedly sees the woman with a man at the museum and admires the way they interact. His last time seeing them, he witnesses their break-up and realizes how little he knows about life.

 For summaries in languages other than English, see Unit 7 Teaching Resources Book, pp. 30–35.

Vocabulary

Etymology Have a student volunteer read aloud either an alternate definition or the etymology of a vocabulary word, and have other students try to guess the word. Repeat with a different word and another volunteer.

 For additional vocabulary practice, see Unit 7 Teaching Resources Book, p. 38.

English Learners

DIFFERENTIATED INSTRUCTION

Intermediate Have English Learners recall a time they observed a stranger in a public place, such as a grocery store or restaurant. In pairs or small groups, have them orally describe the person's appearance and actions. You may want to model this by taking the first turn: *When I was at the grocery store, I saw a woman with a baby. She was wearing a sweater and jeans. The baby was crying, and she was trying to quiet the child.*

Teach

Literary Element | 1

Vernacular **Answer:** *The dashes suggest that the narrator is quickly adding afterthoughts. The narrator uses sentence fragments. The word* umpteen *is slang.* **Ask:** What does the phrase "get up to" mean? *(It means what people are doing.)*

[ENGLISH LEARNERS] English Learners may not be familiar with the word *umpteen*. Have students note its context as well as the word part "teen." Then have them offer suggestions as to its meaning.

View the Art ★

Lincoln Seligman studied to be a lawyer before becoming a professional artist. He is known mainly for his large-scale designs, most notably suspended sculptures found in building entrances around the world. He is also a painter and muralist. **Ask:** What kind of relationship might the two people in the painting have based upon their body language? *Some students might infer that the age difference, his hunched posture versus her straight, energetic pose, and difference in styles of clothing suggest that the two are strangers; some may infer that they might be father and daughter, since they are standing close together and share an interest in the painting.*

Readability Scores

Dale-Chall: 7.2
DRP: 55
Lexile: 920

At the Pitt-Rivers

Penelope Lively

Man and Woman in an Art Gallery. Lincoln Seligman. Private collection.

They've got this museum in Oxford, called the Pitt-Rivers; I spend a lot of time there. It's a weird place, really weird, stuff from all over the world crammed into glass cases like some kind of mad junk-shop—native things from New Guinea and Mexico and Sumatra and wherever you like to think of. Spears and stone axes and masks and a thousand different kinds of fish-hook. And bead jewelry and peculiar musical instruments. And a great totem from Canada. You can learn a lot there about what people get up to: it makes you think. Mostly it's pretty depressing—umpteen different nasty ways of killing each other.

I didn't start going there to learn anything; just because it was a nice quiet place to mooch around[1] and be on my own, Saturdays, or after

---

1. *Mooch around* is British slang for "idle away time."

Vernacular *How do punctuation and diction give this paragraph an informal feel?* **1**

1194 UNIT 7 AN INTERNATIONAL LITERATURE

Research Practice

[SPIRAL REVIEW] **Use the Internet** Explain to students that they will spend much time researching information when they go to college. If they enter the workforce immediately, they will likely also need to have strong research and Internet skills. Have students use a search engine to look up the Pitt-Rivers Museum. Suggest that students use the name of the museum as a keyword. Then tell students to choose a collection to explore online. Students should take notes about what they find in the collection, what they thought was most interesting, and what they would like to learn more about.

school. It got to be a kind of habit. There aren't often people there—the odd art student, a few kids gawping at the shrunken heads, one or two serious-looking blokes wandering around. The porter's usually reading the *Sun*[2] or having a snooze; there's not a lot of custom. The Natural History Museum is a bigger draw; you have to go through that to get into the Pitt-Rivers. You'll always get an audience for a dinosaur and a few nasty-looking jellyfish in formalin.[3] Actually I'm partial to the Natural History Museum myself; that makes you think, too. All those fossils, and then in the end you and me. I had a go at reading *The Origin of Species*[4] last term, not that I got very far. There's a room upstairs in the museum where Darwin's friend—Huxley—had this great argument with that bishop[5] and the rest of them. It says so on the door. I like that, it seems kind of respectful. Putting up a plaque to an argument, instead of just JOE SOAP WAS BORN HERE or whatever. It should be done more often.

It was in the Natural History Museum—underneath the central whale—that I first saw her, and since my mind was on natural selection I thought she wasn't all that good an example of it. I remember thinking that it was funny it doesn't seem to operate with girls, so you got them getting prettier and prettier, because good-looking girls have a better deal than bad-looking ones, you've only got to observe a bit to see that. I always notice girls, to see if they're pretty or not, and she wasn't. She wasn't specially ugly; just very ordinary—

2. The *Sun* is a British tabloid newspaper.
3. *Formalin* is a liquid—a solution of formaldehyde (a disinfectant) with a small amount of methanol (an alcohol)—used to preserve biological specimens.
4. *The Origin of Species* is a book by Charles Darwin that explains his theory of evolution by natural selection.
5. In 1860 Bishop Samuel Wilberforce lost a famous debate with Thomas Henry Huxley over the issue of evolution.

2 Synthesize *What new understanding do you gain about the narrator by synthesizing his comments in this paragraph?*

you wouldn't look at her twice. She was sitting on a bench, watching the entrance.

All the girls I know—at school or round where I live—are either attractive or they're not. If they're attractive they have lots of blokes after them and if they're not they don't. It's as simple as that. If they're attractive just looking at them makes you think of all sorts of things, imagine what it would be like and so forth, and if they're not then it doesn't really occur to you, except in so far as it occurs to you a good deal of the time, actually. This girl was definitely not attractive. In the first place she was in fact quite old, not far off thirty, I should think, and in the second she hadn't got a nice figure; her legs were kind of dumpy and she didn't have pretty hair or anything like that. I gave her a look, just automatically, to check, and then didn't bother with her.

Until I came alongside, where I could see her face clearly, and then I looked again. And again. She still wasn't pretty, but she had the most beautiful expression I've ever seen in my life. She glowed; that's the only way I can put it. She sat there with her hands in her lap, watching the door, and radiating away so that in a peculiar fashion it made you feel good just to look at her, a bit like you were joining in how she felt. Stupid, I daresay, but that's how it was.

And I thought to myself: oh ho . . . I mean, I've seen films and I've read books and I know a bit about things.

As a matter of fact I've been in love myself twice. The first time was with a girl in my class at school and I suppose it was a bit of a trial run, really, I mean I'm not altogether sure how much I was feeling it but it seemed quite important when it was going on. The second time was last year, when I was fifteen. She came to stay with her married sister who lives round the corner from us and though it's months and months ago now I still feel quite faint and weak when I go past the house.

Synthesize *What new side of the narrator is revealed through his observations of the woman in the museum?* **3**

Teach

| Literary Element | 1 |

Vernacular **Ask:** What does the narrator mean when he says the man "couldn't be much"? *(He doesn't expect the man to be handsome.)*

View the Art ★

Possible answer: Some students may say that the subject of the painting appears quiet and reserved and seems to be watching someone or something outside the frame, which is similar to the narrator quietly watching the couple at the Pitt-Rivers.

Although he began his studies in England, Maxwell Ashby Armfield (1882–1972) produced some of his most notable landscape paintings during a seven-year tour of the United States. He relied primarily on tempera, a painting medium that utilizes protein-based substances such as egg yolk, instead of oil. In addition to painting, Armfield wrote many books, including poetry and a book about tempera painting. Keith Henderson, the subject of the portrait, is another tempera painter with whom Armfield studied.

Portrait of Keith Henderson in a Black Hood, 1902. Maxwell Ashby Armfield. 16.5 x 17.5 cm. Collection of Andrew McIntosh Patrick, UK.

View the Art The person in this image is a painter who studied new materials and new techniques with the artist. How does he compare with the mental image you have of the narrator? Explain. ★

Oh ho, I thought. I felt kindly—sort of **benign**—and a bit curious to see what the **1** bloke would be like. I thought he couldn't be much because of her not being pretty. I mean, in films you can always tell who's going to fall for who because they'll be the two good-lookers and while I'm not saying real life's like that there is a way people match each other, isn't there, you've only got to look round at married people. Let me hasten to say that I'm not all that good-looking myself, only about B+. Not too bad, but not all that marvelous either.

Vocabulary
benign (bi nīn′) *adj.* pleasant and friendly

But he didn't show up and I wanted to get on into the Pitt-Rivers, so I left her there, waiting. What I haven't said is that one of the things I go to the Pitt-Rivers for is to write poetry. I write quite a lot of poetry. I could do it at home—I often do—and it's not that I'm coy or anything, my parents know about it and they're quite interested, but I just like the idea of having a special place to go to. It's quiet there, and a bit odd like I've said, and nobody takes any notice of me.

Sometimes I feel I'm getting somewhere with this poetry, and other times it looks to me pretty awful. I showed a few poems to our English master and he was very helpful: he said what was good and pointed out where I'd used words badly, or not worked out what I was thinking very well,

---

Writing Practice

SPIRAL REVIEW **Compare and Contrast** Tell students that they will be writing an essay that compares and contrasts the narrator of this story with another narrator or character. For example, they might compare Holden Caufield from *The Catcher in the Rye* with the narrator of this selection given that they have several similar characteristics. Or students might compare this narrator with a dissimilar character. Tell students to use the five-paragraph structure with the first paragraph as introduction, the last paragraph as conclusion, and the three middle paragraphs as support.

so that was quite encouraging. He's a nice bloke. I like his lessons. He's very good at explaining poetry. I mean, I think poetry's amazingly difficult: sometimes you read a thing again and again and you just can't see what the hell the person's getting at. He reads all sorts of poetry to us, our English master, and you really get the hang of it after a bit—hard stuff like Hopkins[6] and The Hound of Heaven,[7] and Donne.[8] He read us some of those Donne poems about love the other day which are all very **explicit** and I must say first time round I hadn't quite got the point—'Licence my roving hands . . .' and so forth—but he wasn't embarrassed or anything, our English master, and when you realize that it's not geography he's talking about, the poet, then as a matter of fact I think that poem's lovely.[9] I got a bit fed up with the way some of my mates were sniggering about it, being all-knowing; truth to tell I doubt if they know any more than I do, it's all just show. And that's a beautiful poem: I mean, if anything makes it clear that there's nothing wrong about sex, that poem does, they ought to make it **compulsory** reading for some people.

Anyway, I went on into the Pitt-Rivers and I was up on the first floor, in a favorite corner of mine among the arrow-heads, when I saw her again, and I must say I got quite a shock. Because the man with her was an old bloke: he was older than my father, fiftyish and more, he must have been at least twenty years older than

her. So I reckoned I must have made a mistake. Not that at all.

They were talking, though I couldn't hear what they were saying because they were on the far side of the gallery. They stopped in front of a case and I could see their faces quite clearly. They stood there looking at each other, not talking anymore, and I realized I hadn't made a mistake after all. Absolutely not. They didn't touch each other, they just stood and looked; it seemed like ages. I don't imagine they knew I was there.

And that time I was shocked. Really shocked. I don't mind telling you, I thought it was disgusting. He was an ordinary-looking person—he might have been a schoolmaster or something, he wore those kind of clothes, old trousers and sweater, and he had greyish hair, a bit long. And there was she, and as I've said she wasn't pretty, not at all, but she had this marvelous look about her, and she was years and years younger.

It was because of him, I realized, that she had that look.

I didn't like it at all. I got up, from where I was sitting, with quite a clatter to make sure they heard me and I went stumping off out of the museum. I wasn't going to write any more poetry that day, I could see. I went off home and truth to tell I didn't really think much more about them, that man and the girl, mainly because of being rather disgusted, like I said.

A couple of weeks later they were there again. They were on the ground floor, at the back, by the rush matting[10] and ceremonial gear for with-it tribesmen, leaning up against a glass case that they weren't looking into, and talking. At least he was talking, quiet and serious, and she was listening, and nodding from time to time. I was busy with some thinking I wanted to do, and I tried not to take any notice of them; I mean, they were neither here nor there as far as I was concerned, none of my

---

6. *Hopkins* refers to the British poet Gerard Manley Hopkins (1844–1889).
7. "The Hound of Heaven" is a poem by British poet Francis Thompson (1859–1907).
8. *Donne* refers to John Donne (1572–1631), an Anglican cleric and poet.
9. The Donne poem referred to here is "Elegy XIX: On My Mistress Going to Bed."

2 Synthesize *What new insight about the narrator do you gain from a synthesis of the details in this passage?*

Vocabulary

explicit (eks plis′ it) *adj.* plainly and clearly expressed; definite
compulsory (kəm pul′ sər ē) *adj.* obligatory; required

---

10. *Rush* is a type of marsh plant with cylindrical, often hollow stems; it is used to make chair bottoms and mats. The term *rush matting* refers to mats made out of rush.

Reading Strategy | **2**

Synthesize **Answer:** *We learn that the narrator is trying to be a serious poet and to learn about poetry from his English master, which is one reason he resents the "sniggering" of his classmates. We also learn that, although the narrator praises erotic poetry, he is sexually inexperienced.*

(ENGLISH LEARNERS) Have English Learners listen as one paragraph at a time is read aloud. Pause so that students can paraphrase each paragraph.

English Learners

DIFFERENTIATED INSTRUCTION

Beginning Tell students that this selection gives them a perfect opportunity to practice reading aloud. Divide students into pairs. Give them several minutes to discuss what they know about the narrator and to hypothesize what the narrator's voice sounds like. Then, have students take turns reading columns of the selection in the character of the narrator. If students find

a particular passage difficult, have them reread it aloud several times until it becomes automatic. Finally, have students read an entire page aloud. Circulate around the room to monitor students' progress.

Teach

Big Idea   1

Making and Remaking Traditions Answer: *The wide disparity in the ages of the two lovers violates the narrator's traditional belief that it is unseemly or "disgusting" for people of different ages to fall in love with each other.*

Reading Strategy   2

Synthesize Answer: *At first he is repelled by the prospect of a relationship between the young girl and the older man. When he observes their behavior, however, he begins to realize that they share an emotional and intellectual relationship that endears them to him.* **Ask:** *How do his observations of the couple's relationship compare with the narrator's own experience with the neighbor's sister? (The couple at the museum seems to have a real connection that the narrator realizes is missing from his interaction on the date with the neighbor's sister.)*

business, though I still thought it was a bit creepy. I couldn't see *why*, frankly. You fancy people your own age, and that's all there is to it, is what I thought. What I'd always thought.

So I ignored them, except that I couldn't quite. I kept sneaking a look, every now and then, and the more I did the more I felt kind of friendly towards them; I liked them. Which was a bit weird considering they didn't know I even existed—they certainly weren't interested in me—so it was a pretty one-sided kind of relationship. I thought he seemed like a nice bloke, whatever you thought about him and her and all that. It was something about the way he smiled, and the way he told her things (not that I ever heard a word they said, I wasn't eavesdropping, not ever, let's be quite clear about that) that made her look interested and say things back and so on. I thought it was obvious they like talking to each other, quite apart from anything else. I thought that was nice.

I only took out that girl I mentioned—the one who came to stay with her sister—once, and as a matter of fact we couldn't find much to talk about. I was still in love with her—no doubt about that—but it was a bit sticky, I don't mind admitting. In fact I was quite glad when it was time to take her back to her sister's. In many ways the best part was just thinking about her.

Every time I looked at the girl—the Pitt-Rivers one, that is—I found myself imagining what it must be like being able to feel that you've made someone look like that. **Radiant**, like she was. Which is what that bloke must

have been able to feel. I found myself putting myself in his place, as it were, and wondering. I've done a lot of wondering about things like that—everybody does, I suppose—but mostly it's been more kind of basic. Now, I began to think I didn't really know anything. Looking at those two—watching them, if you like—was a bit like seeing something go on behind a thick glass window, so it was half removed from you. You could see but not hear, hear but not touch, or whatever. I could see, but I didn't know.

I suppose you could say I was envious, in a funny kind of way. I don't mean jealous in that I fancied the girl, or anything like that. As I've said already, she wasn't pretty, or even attractive. And I wasn't **envious** like you might be envious of someone for being happier than you are, because I'm not specially unhappy, as it happens. I think I was envious of them for being what they were—as though one fossil creature might be envious of a more evolved kind of fossil creature, which of course is a stupid idea.

When I was in the Pitt-Rivers again I looked for them, quite deliberately, but they weren't there. I was disappointed, though I pretended to myself it really didn't matter. I wondered about why they went there in the first place; I mean, people have to meet each other somewhere but why *there*? It doesn't exactly spring to mind as a romantic spot. I supposed there were reasons they didn't want to meet somewhere obvious

---

1   **Making and Remaking Traditions** *How does the couple in the story violate the narrator's traditional concept of love?*

2   **Synthesize** *Based on what you already know about the narrator, why do you think he has begun to change his negative attitude toward the couple?*

Vocabulary

radiant (rā′ dē ənt) *adj.* beaming, as with joy, love, or energy

Vernacular *What does the idiom* spring to mind *mean? Why might the writer have chosen to use an idiomatic expression here?*   **3**

Vocabulary

envious (en′ vē əs) *adj.* feeling jealous or discontented because of the good fortune or superior abilities of another

1198   UNIT 7   AN INTERNATIONAL LITERATURE

Listening and Speaking Practice

SPIRAL REVIEW   **Monologue** Have each student choose a particular scene from the story to read as a monologue in front of the class. After students have chosen their scenes, allow them time to practice reading the monologues aloud, possibly in front of a mirror. Tell students to read with emotion, capturing and presenting the narrator's feelings to their audience. Students can read from the book, but encourage them to familiarize

themselves as much as possible with the text so that they can maintain eye contact with the audience and add actions and gestures to their monologues. Allot time for students to present their monologues to the class.

The flashlights of visitors cast tracks in Pitt Rivers Museum in Oxford.

Vernacular Answer: *The idiom spring to mind means "to suddenly think of something." The idiom fits the informal tone of the passage and is meant to be humorously ironic.*

[ENGLISH LEARNERS] Have English Learners define "spring" and look at the context of the phrase "spring to mind." Have them suggest possible meanings for the phrase.

and public: maybe he was married, I thought, or maybe she was, even. I wondered if that was the only place they met, or did they have others. Once walking through the botanical gardens, I found myself looking for them in the big glasshouses there.

I know the inside of the Pitt-Rivers pretty well by now. Considering it's not anthropology or ethnology or whatever I went there for in the first place, it's quite surprising what a lot I could tell you about the things people believe and do. Primitive people, that is—what the Pitt-Rivers calls primitive people. And I think

it's all very sad, actually: sad because it's like children, not understanding how things work and getting it all wrong, and carving each other up because of it a lot of the time. It does actually make you feel things get better—wars and bombs and everything notwithstanding. Nobody wants to go on being a child all their lives.

I was thinking about this—looking at a case full of particularly loony stuff to do with witchcraft—when I saw them again. At least I saw her first, standing by the totem with her hands in her coat pockets, and I didn't have to

PENELOPE LIVELY   **1199**

Established Point out that the narrator shares his observations of the woman, the man, and their interactions and information about his life. Draw a chart like the following on the board:

Observations of Couple	Information About Narrator

Tell students to copy the chart in their notebooks. Have students work in groups to review the text and complete the chart.

Teach

Reading Strategy 1

Synthesize Answer: *The two people are not talking, the girl looks miserable, and they hold on to each other; most likely they are ending the relationship.*

Reading Strategy 2

Synthesize Answer: *The narrator comes to admire the glowing radiance that the man inspires in the young woman. He hopes that he might be able to inspire a similar reaction someday. He strongly identifies with the couple and feels their separation as a personal loss.*

 To check students' understanding of the selection, see Unit 7 Teaching Resources Book, p. 41.

look at the door to know he'd arrived: her face told you that. He came up to her and gave her a kind of hug—arm round her shoulders and then quickly off again—and they wandered away up the stairs, heads together, talking.

I didn't follow them; it had been nice to see them again, and know they were there, and that was it. I was busy on a poem I'd been writing and unpicking and rewriting for some time. It was a poem about an old man sitting on a bench in a park and getting into conversation with a boy—someone around my age—and they swap opinions and observations (it's all dialogue, this poem, like a long conversation) and it's not till the end you realize they're the same person. It sounds either corny, or pretentious, I know; and what I could never decide was whether to have it as though the old man's looking back, or the boy's kind of projecting forward—imagining himself, as it were. So I went on fiddling about with this, and didn't really think much about the man and the girl, until I saw it was latish and there was no one else in the museum except me and some feet on the wooden floor of the gallery overhead, walking round and round, round and round. Two pairs of feet. They'd been doing that for ages, I realized; I'd been hearing them without registering.

I saw them go past—just their heads, above the glass cases—and something wasn't right. They weren't talking. She had her arm through his, and she was looking straight in front of her, and when I saw her face I had a nasty kind of twinge in my stomach. Because she was miserable. Once, she looked at him, and they both managed a bleak sort of smile. And then they walked on, round the gallery again, and next time past they still weren't talking, just holding on to each other like that, like people who're

ill, or very old. And then the attendant rang the bell, and I heard them come down the stairs, and they came past me and went out into the Natural History Museum.

I went after them. I saw them stop—under the central whale, just where I first saw her—and then they did say something to each other. I couldn't see her face; she had her back to me. He went off then, on his own, out through the main entrance, quickly, and she sat down on a bench. For a moment or two she just sat staring at that wretched whale, and then she felt in her bag and got out a comb and did her hair, as though that might help. And then she dropped the comb and didn't seem to have noticed, even, because she just sat; she didn't bother to pick it up or anything. I could see her face then, and I hope I don't ever see anyone look so unhappy again. I truly hope that.

I don't know what had happened. I never will. Somehow, I don't think they were ever going to see each other again, but why . . . well, that's their concern, just like the rest of it was, except that in this peculiar way I'd come to feel it was mine too. I didn't think there was anything disgusting about them anymore, or creepy—I hadn't for a long time. I suppose you could say I'd learned something else in the Pitt-Rivers, by accident. I never did go on with that poem. I tore it up, as far as it had got; I wasn't so sure anymore about that conversation, that there could even be one, or not like I'd been imagining, anyway. ∾

Synthesize *What new understanding do you reach about the couple's relationship when you synthesize the details in this paragraph?* **1**

Synthesize *Why do you think the narrator feels personally involved in the couple's lives?* **2**

Writing Practice

Write a Review

SPIRAL REVIEW Have students create a rough draft of the review they will develop on page 1201. Reviewers should carefully read the narrative, then respond in writing with a short summary of the narrative, an outline or diagram of the plot, and a list and description of the characters in the story. Reviewers may also offer three or four questions they had

about the story—aspects of the plot they did not fully understand, or areas where they would have liked more explanation. Writers may find these questions helpful as they revise their stories.

After You Read

Respond and Think Critically

Respond and Interpret

1. What would you have liked to ask the narrator at the end of the story?

2. (a)Why does the narrator spend so much time at the Pitt-Rivers? (b)What might this suggest about his home life?

3. (a)Why is the narrator shocked and disgusted at first by the relationship between the two people? (b)What does this reveal about his attitude toward love?

Analyze and Evaluate

4. (a)Consider the scene in which the two people appear to separate permanently. Explain how the author indicates that both of them suffer greatly at this moment. (b)How does the narrator react to their separation?

5. (a)What evidence in the story suggests that the two people have an emotional and intellectual, rather than a physical, relationship? (b)What do you think is the most likely reason that the couple decided to end their relationship?

Connect

6. **Big Idea** Making and Remaking Traditions What elements of Lively's style make this story different from others you have read in this textbook? Explain.

7. **Connect to Today** Are attitudes like the narrator's original one—to be offended by an age difference within a couple—still common? Give examples of present-day couples, such as actors or politicians, who help to show society's view on the subject.

Primary Source Quotation

The Functions of Fiction

Read the two comments by Penelope Lively below. Notice how each quotation expresses Lively's attitudes toward life, memory, and the functions of fiction.

> *"I have never come to terms with life, and I wouldn't wish anyone else to do so; if fiction is to help at all in the process of living, it is by illuminating its conflicts and ambiguities."*

> *"I don't imagine that I am ever going to find the answer to the questions prompted by the workings of memory; all I can do is pose these questions in fictional form and see what happens."*

Group Activity Discuss the following questions with a group of classmates. Refer to the quotations and cite evidence from "At the Pitt-Rivers" for support.

1. (a)What does Lively believe to be the function of fiction? (b)How does "At the Pitt-Rivers" fulfill this function?

2. (a)How might the "workings of memory" have contributed to this story?

After You Read

Assess

1. Responses will vary.

2. (a) He likes the idea of going to a special place where he can write poetry without intrusion. (b) His home life does not offer privacy.

3. (a) He thinks the man is too old for the young woman. (b) He thinks only people of the same age should date each other.

4. (a) Their body language is much different from the way it was when they were happier. They keep pacing, they smile bleakly, and then they hold on to each other as if they are ill or very old. (b) The narrator shares their sense of loss.

5. (a) Their meeting in a museum and talking so much (b) Responses will vary but should be based on the text.

6. Lively's use of punctuation, tone, and sentence structure reflect a teenager's perspective. She combines a casual tone with profound themes.

7. Responses will vary. Students may use examples of Hollywood couples to show that, generally, society is more or less accepting of age differences, though they still prompt some gossip.

Primary Source Quotation

Students' discussions should touch on the following points:

1. (a) To reveal life's complexities (b) The narrator has a limited and flawed understanding of the couple's relationship. He does not receive an epiphany at the end of the story; rather, the conflicts and ambiguities behind the couple's estrangement result in a state of disillusionment that motivates him to tear up his poem.

2. (a) "At the Pitt-Rivers" may be based on a memory of an event. The fact that Lively went to Oxford and married a professor is circumstantial evidence for such a hypothesis.

After You Read

Assess

Literary Element

1. (a) Possible responses: "you wouldn't look at her twice"; her legs are "kind of dumpy"; he "gave her a look" and "then didn't bother with her" (b) It reveals his adolescent conception of beauty.
2. Responses will vary depending on chosen paragraphs and rewordings.
3. "Trial run" is an expression used to mean "to test or try." The narrator means his first relationship wasn't real, but a practice attempt or test.

Review: Narrator

Students should note that Lively's narrator is a character in the story. He observes the couple from a distance, but all the information in the story comes from his point of view. Lively does not give the reader a perspective from an observer outside the story.

Reading Strategy

1. Possible responses: He claims to have been in love, but he could not communicate with the girl. He enjoys writing poetry at the Pitt-Rivers because "It's quiet there . . . and nobody takes any notice of me." He appears to be alienated from his male classmates who laugh at his favorite Donne poem.
2. The narrator is fond of weighty reading matter in both science (Darwin) and literature, particularly the sophisticated love poetry of Donne. He longs for love and companionship, but he seeks it on an abstract, intellectual plane .

1202

The use of the **vernacular** gives an informal feel to a work of literature. For example, in "At the Pitt-Rivers," the narrator addresses the reader as if he were having a casual conversation with a friend.

1. (a)How does the narrator use the vernacular to describe his first impressions of the young woman? (b)What characteristics does the narrator's vernacular speech reveal about himself?
2. (a)Choose a paragraph from the story that has examples of vernacular language and reword it into Standard English. (b)How does the tone of the new paragraph compare to the original?
3. When the narrator is talking about the first time he was in love, he calls it a "trial run." How would you explain this idiom to someone who is just learning English?

Review: Narrator

As you learned on page 1027, a **narrator** is the voice that tells the story in a work of fiction. Sometimes, the narrator is a character in the story; at other times, the narrator is an outside observer.

Partner Activity Meet with a classmate and discuss the narrator in "At the Pitt-Rivers." Is he a character in the story, an outside observer, or a combination of both? To help in your analysis, complete a graphic organizer like the one below.

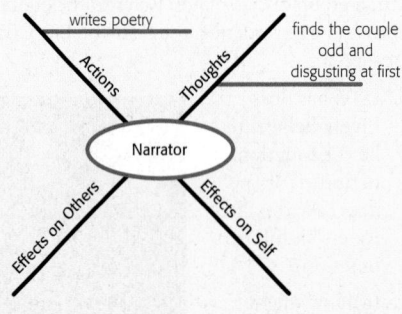

writes poetry

Actions

Thoughts

finds the couple odd and disgusting at first

Narrator

Effects on Others

Effects on Self

LOG ON ▶ **Literature** Online

Selection Resources For Selection Quizzes, eFlashcards, and Reading-Writing Connection activities, go to glencoe.com and enter QuickPass code GLB9817u7.

Synthesizing story details, footnotes, background information, information about the author, and your own prior knowledge can help you interpret a story.

1. What details can you synthesize from the story to characterize the narrator as a lonely introvert?
2. Based on the references to the narrator's reading habits, what idea can you synthesize about the way he thinks and acts, in general?

Vocabulary Practice

Practice with Denotation and Connotation Work with a partner to complete a graphic organizer like the one below for each vocabulary word. Include the vocabulary word in one box and a word that has a similar denotation in another. Then explain which word has the stronger connotation.

benign   explicit   compulsory
radiant   envious

EXAMPLE:

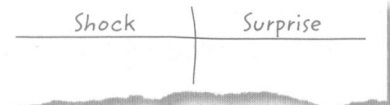

Shock | Surprise

Academic Vocabulary

Although he does not know the woman at the museum, the narrator develops a deep invest-ment in her happiness.

Investment is an academic word that appears in everyday usage. For example, a stock that creates financial returns is an **investment**.

Using context clues, try to figure out the meaning of the word *investment* in the sentence about "At the Pitt-Rivers" above. Check your guess in a dictionary.

For more on academic vocabulary, see pages 56 and R81.

Academic Vocabulary

The context suggests that *investment* means "devotion" or "emotional energy."

Vocabulary

Possible answers:

Vocabulary word: *benign*
Similar word: *benevolent*

Explanation: *Benevolent* has the stronger connotation. *Benign* implies amiability, while *benevolent* implies generosity and kindness.

Vocabulary word: *explicit*
Similar word: *absolute*

Explanation: *Absolute* has the stronger connotation. *Explicit* implies clarity, while *absolute* implies complete and total certainty.

Respond Through Writing

Autobiography

Apply Point of View Write a narrative of 1,500 words or more about a time when you were conflicted about your relationship with a friend or relative. Using Lively's "At the Pitt-Rivers" as a model, incorporate dialect and idiomatic expressions into your narrator's voice.

Understanding the Task Dialect is the speech of people from a specific time, place, and class. **Idiomatic expressions** are phrases (for example, *to fall for someone*) that have a meaning different from the literal meanings of the words. Idioms in dialogue lend authenticity to characters and settings.

Prewrite Look back through your journals or create a new entry to remind yourself of a conflict you have had with someone you were close to. Then state the controlling idea of your autobiographical incident. List the characters and main events involved and jot down any dialogue that comes to mind during this process.

Draft Be sure to set the scene for your readers by describing exact locations and their details for each point in the narrative. Relate the events clearly in the order that they happened. Tell your story in the first person, using the pronouns *I, me, my,* and *myself,* being sure to maintain a consistent point of view.

Try to capture the speech of the characters. Use realistic dialect and idiomatic expressions and show, rather than just tell, what they do and feel.

In the darkness of the theater I looked over at Tom and Maya. They weren't holding hands or looking at each other or whispering. What was up with that? I remembered Maya snapping at me before we left, saying, "We're fine, okay? We're totally happy. Let it go!" But she didn't sound happy. Then again, what did I know about all this lovey-dovey stuff?

Revise Make sure you have set the scene for your incident, including concrete sensory details that will recreate the time and place for your readers. Pay attention to the pace of your story, revising it if it doesn't fit with the mood or tone of a scene. Use the Writing Workshop checklists on pages 214 and 1160 to help you review your work.

Edit and Proofread Proofread your paper, correcting any errors in spelling, grammar, and punctuation. Use the Grammar Tip in the side column to help you with sentence fragments.

Learning Objectives

In this assignment, you will focus on the following objectives:

Writing:
Writing an autobiographical narrative.
Applying point of view.

> **Grammar Tip**

A **sentence fragment** is a "sentence" that is missing a subject, a predicate, or both.

Actual speech often includes sentence fragments, so incorporate them as needed in your dialogue to make your characters believable.

Used sparingly, sentence fragments can also create striking dramatic effects:

"No way," I screamed. "Unbelievable! Nothing short of unbelievable!"

After You Read

Assess

Respond Through Writing

Use these criteria in evaluating autobiographical incidents:

- The incident describes a conflict between the writer and a friend or relative.
- The setting is vividly described and realistic dialogue includes dialect and idiomatic expressions.
- Sentence fragments are incorporated in dialogue as part of everyday speech and, occasionally, to create dramatic effects.
- A student who meets all of these criteria should receive the equivalent of a 4-point response.
- A student who fully meets two or partially meets three of these criteria should receive the equivalent of a 3-point response.
- A student who fully meets one or partially meets two of these criteria should receive the equivalent of a 2-point response.
- A student who partially meets one of these criteria should receive the equivalent of a 1-point response.

Vocabulary word: *compulsory*

Similar word: *forced*

Explanation: *Forced* has the stronger connotation. *Compulsory* implies that something is simply required, while *forced* implies that it is being pushed on people against their will.

Vocabulary word: *radiant*

Similar word: *cheery*

Explanation: *Radiant* has the stronger connotation. *Cheery* implies positivity, while *radiant* implies glowing, beaming happiness.

Vocabulary word: *envious*

Similar word: *wishful*

Explanation: *Envious* has the stronger connotation. *Wishful* simply implies desire, while *envious* implies strong jealousy of another person.

Focus

Bellringer Options

Literature Launchers:
 Pre-Reading Videos DVD,
 Selection Launcher
Daily Language Practice
 Transparency 103

Or **say:** The possibility of nuclear war has many people concerned about the future.
Ask: What issues make you concerned about the future? Have students discuss issues that concern them. Ask students to consider consequences of these issues and solutions for them.

Compare Literature About Nuclear Weapons

Point out to students that schools during the Cold War were often designated as fallout shelters. Discuss how reminders of the possibility of nuclear war could affect everyday life.

Compare Literature About Nuclear Weapons

After the United States developed the atomic bomb during World War II and used it against the Japanese cities of Hiroshima and Nagasaki, other nations hastened to acquire nuclear weapons of their own. The threat of nuclear warfare quickly became a major source of fear among the peoples of the world. These three works by Bertrand Russell, Italo Calvino, and Randy Newman reflect that fear in very different ways.

Learning Objectives

For pages 1204–1215
In studying these texts, you will focus on the following objectives:
Literary Study: Analyzing text structure.
Reading: Analyzing political assumptions.
Writing: Writing a dialogue.

COMPARE THE Big Idea **Making and Remaking Traditions**

Events in world history frequently lead writers to extend or remake the traditions in which they work. Uncertainty about the future, economic ups and downs, and political conflicts can lead to significant changes in the ways people write and the subjects they write about. As you read, ask yourself, What twentieth-century concerns helped to shape these works?

COMPARE Political Assumptions

A writer's political assumptions—including his or her vision of an ideal world and of the means that might be used to bring such a world about—can color all the writer's work, even when the assumptions are not overtly expressed. As you read, ask yourself, What political views may lie behind this work, and how may they have affected its content?

COMPARE Genres

Persuasive speeches, short stories, and popular songs require their writers to employ quite different literary techniques and forms of expression. As you read, ask yourself, What features of these works are determined by the genres in which the writers chose to work, and what features are the writers' personal contributions?

 Literature Online

Author Search For more about Bertrand Russell, Italo Calvino, and Randy Newman, go to glencoe.com and enter QuickPass code GLB9817u7.

Selection Skills

Literary Elements
- Structure (SE pp. 1206, 1208, 1209)
- Similes (TE p. 1206)

Reading Skills
- Analyze Political Assumptions (SE pp. 1206, 1207, 1209)
- Preview (TE p. 1206)

Comparing Literature

Vocabulary Skills
- Context Clues (SE p. 1209; TE p. 1206)

Listening/Speaking/Viewing Skills
- Discussion Starter (SE p. 1214)
- Research Report (SE p. 1215)
- Logical Fallacies (TE p. 1208)
- Debate (TE p. 1212)

Writing Skills/Grammar
- Dialogue (SE p. 1209)
- Quickwrite (SE p. 1212)
- Essay/Short Story (SE p. 1215)
- Write a Song (TE p. 1214)

Before You Read

Shall We Choose Death?

Meet **Bertrand Russell**
(1872–1970)

Born into an aristocratic family, Bertrand Russell became one of the most prominent British philosophers of the twentieth century, and perhaps the most influential. He was, however, better known to the people of Britain for his controversial writings and speeches on political and ethical issues, which attracted attention throughout the world.

> "*War does not determine who is right, only who is left.*"
>
> —Bertrand Russell

Philosophical Work Russell studied mathematics and philosophy at Cambridge University, where he became acquainted with Alfred North Whitehead and other prominent British philosophers of the day. His interest in both subjects led him to explore the notion that mathematics was nothing but a form of logic, an idea that formed the basis of two works—*The Principles of Mathematics* (1903) and, with Whitehead, *Principia Mathematica* (1910–1913)— that established his reputation as one of Britain's leading philosophers. In later years, he became more interested in epistemology (the study of how humans come to have knowledge of the external world) and produced a number of works in this field; but his work in logic was what would have the most lasting impact on later philosophical thought throughout the world. In 1945 he published *A History of Western Philosophy*, which became a best-seller.

Activism Russell had always shown an interest in social and political problems, and this came to the fore during World War I, when his outspoken opposition to the war and the British draft caused him to be twice charged with crimes by the British government. As a result, he lost his teaching position at Cambridge and served a six-month sentence in prison. Thereafter, he devoted a great deal of his energy to writing and speaking out on political subjects, producing numerous books, as well as articles in newspapers and magazines, on various political topics and becoming a familiar voice on British radio broadcasts.

Tireless in his opposition to war, Russell continued to engage in antiwar activities throughout his life. After World War II, he frequently called for nuclear disarmament and participated in mass peace demonstrations, even being briefly jailed again in 1961, at the age of 89, for inciting civil disobedience. In 1950 he received the Nobel Prize in Literature for "his varied and significant writings in which he champions humanitarian ideals and freedom of thought," and in 1963 he was awarded the first Jerusalem Prize, for writers concerned with the issue of individuals' freedom in society.

BERTRAND RUSSELL **1205**

Comparing Literature

Before You Read

Focus

Summary

Russell argues that the advent of nuclear weapons ultimately requires the abolition of war. Large-scale war with hydrogen bombs could lead to the extinction of the human race. An end to war would mean adopting a new outlook on human beings as a whole, but the only other option is universal death.

 For summaries in languages other than English, see Unit 7 Teaching Resources Book, pp. 44–49.

Interactive Read and Write
Other options for teaching this selection can be found in
- Interactive Read and Write for EL Students, pp. 321–334.
- Interactive Read and Write for Approaching-Level Students, pp. 321–334.
- Interactive Read and Write for On-Level Students, pp. 321–334.

English Learners

DIFFERENTIATED INSTRUCTION

Intermediate Say: A rhetorical question is a question used by a speaker not to request information, but to make a point. For example, a speaker who says *"Isn't it time to end this problem?"* is making a statement. Russell uses rhetorical questions to structure his speech. Have students identify rhetorical questions in Russell's speech. Then ask them to paraphrase the meaning of these questions.

Advanced Learners

DIFFERENTIATED INSTRUCTION

Research Have advanced students use print or Internet resources to conduct research on atomic testing. Ask them to construct a timeline showing the dates of significant tests or of treaties regulating atomic testing.

Comparing Literature

Before You Read

Focus

Vocabulary

Context Clues Have students locate the vocabulary words *obliterate* and *abolish* in Russell's text. Then ask them to identify any context clues in the speech that can help them to understand the meaning of the words.

 For additional context, see Glencoe Interactive Vocabulary CD-ROM.

Literature and Reading Preview

Connect to the Speech

What developments in the world today cause you to feel anxiety or fear? Write a journal entry about some current events that you find troubling.

Build Background

This speech was delivered as radio broadcast on December 30, 1954. For several years, the United States and the Soviet Union had been testing atomic bombs in remote locations; but on March 1 of that year the United States had detonated a hydrogen bomb with a power vastly greater than that of any previous weapon—about 1,000 times the force of the bombs that were dropped on Hiroshima and Nagasaki at the end of World War II.

Set Purposes for Reading

Big Idea Making and Remaking Tradition

As you read this radio address, ask yourself, How might the points being made differ from the ideas in speeches delivered in other times?

Literary Element Structure

The **structure** of a persuasive speech is usually based on a logical sequence of main ideas that support the speaker's position and that are, in turn, supported by relevant details. As you read, ask yourself, Why did Russell choose to present his points in the particular order he did?

Reading Strategy Analyze Political Assumptions

To **analyze political assumptions** is to infer political attitudes and viewpoints that may have influenced a writer's statements. As you read, ask yourself, What political assumptions may be reflected in these arguments?

Tip: Taking Notes Use a chart to record significant statements and the underlying assumptions that you infer.

Statement	Assumption

Vocabulary

obliteration (ə blit′ ə rā′ shən) *n.* complete destruction or removal; p. 1207 *The general sought not just victory but the obliteration of the enemy troops.*

abolish (ə bol′ ish) *v.* to put an end to; do away with; p. 1208 *John Brown was a leader in the struggle to abolish slavery in the United States.*

Reading Practice

SPIRAL REVIEW **Preview** Ask students to fill in a graphic organizer to preview "Shall We Choose Death?" For each text feature, they should make a prediction about what they expect to read. Then, as they read, they should note whether their prediction was correct.

Text Feature	I Predict...	Was the Prediction Right?
Title		
Illustration		
First Sentence		

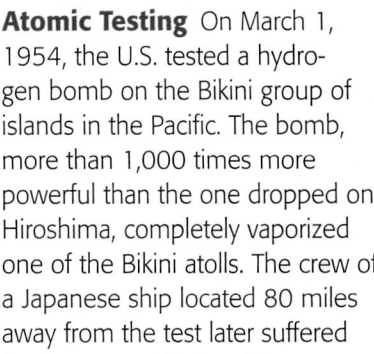

Shall We Choose Death?

Bertrand Russell

I am speaking not as a Briton, not as a European, not as a member of a western democracy, but as a human being, a member of the species Man, whose continued existence is in doubt. The world is full of conflicts: Jews and Arabs; Indians and Pakistanis; white men and Negroes in Africa; and, overshadowing all minor conflicts, the titanic struggle between communism and anti-communism.

Almost everybody who is politically conscious has strong feelings about one or more of these issues; but I want you, if you can, to set aside such feelings for the moment and consider yourself only as a member of a biological species which has had a remarkable history and whose disappearance none of us can desire. I shall try to say no single word which should appeal to one group rather than to another. All, equally, are in peril, and, if the peril is understood, there is hope that they may collectively avert it. We have to learn to think in a new way. We have to learn to ask ourselves not what steps can be taken to give military victory to whatever group we prefer, for there no longer are such steps. The question we have to ask ourselves is: What steps can be taken to prevent a military contest of which the issue must be disastrous to all sides?

The general public, and even many men in positions of authority, have not realized what would be involved in a war with hydrogen bombs. The general public still thinks in terms of the **obliteration** of cities. It is understood that the new bombs are more powerful than the old and that, while one atomic bomb could obliterate Hiroshima, one hydrogen bomb could obliterate the largest cities such as London, New York, and Moscow. No doubt in a hydrogen-bomb war great cities would be obliterated. But this is one of the minor disasters that would have to be faced. If everybody in London, New York, and Moscow were exterminated, the world might, in the course of a few centuries, recover from the blow. But we now know, especially since the Bikini test,[1] that hydrogen bombs can gradually spread destruction over a much wider area than had been supposed. It is stated on very good authority that a bomb can now be manufactured which will be 25,000 times as powerful as that which destroyed Hiroshima. Such a bomb, if exploded near the ground or under water, sends radioactive particles into the

---

1. *Bikini test* refers to an experimental explosion, by the United States, of a hydrogen bomb on Bikini Atoll in the South Pacific Ocean (March 1, 1954).

Vocabulary

obliteration (ə blit´ ə rā´ shən) *n.* complete destruction or removal

BERTRAND RUSSELL **1207**

1 Analyze Political Assumptions *What is Russell assuming about the political situation at the time?*

Comparing Literature

Teach

Literary Element | 1

Structure Answer: *This sentence is an emotional appeal to the reader to make the reader question if this could be the end.*

[ENGLISH LEARNERS] Tell English learners that the word *cosmos* in the second to last paragraph means the same in Spanish and English. A related word in Spanish is *universo*. **Ask:** What English word means the same as *universo?* (universe)

Writer's Technique

Anaphora Anaphora is the use of repetition at the beginning of successive phrases, clauses, or sentences, as in Tennyson's "To strive, to seek, to find, and not to yield." Russell uses anaphora when he asks: "Is our race so destitute of wisdom, so incapable of impartial love, so blind even to the simplest dictates of self-preservation. . .?"

upper air. They sink gradually and reach the surface of the earth in the form of a deadly dust or rain. It was this dust which infected the Japanese fishermen and their catch of fish although they were outside what American experts believed to be the danger zone. No one knows how widely such lethal radioactive particles might be diffused, but the best authorities are unanimous in saying that a war with hydrogen bombs is quite likely to put an end to the human race. It is feared that if many hydrogen bombs are used there will be universal death—sudden only for a fortunate minority, but for the majority a slow torture of disease and disintegration. . . .

Here, then, is the problem which I present to you, stark and dreadful and inescapable: Shall we put an end to the human race; or shall mankind renounce war? People will not face this alternative because it is so difficult to **abolish** war. The abolition of war will demand distasteful limitations of national sovereignty. But what perhaps impedes understanding of the situation more than anything else is that the term "mankind" feels vague and abstract. People scarcely realize in imagination that the danger is to themselves and their children and their grandchildren, and not only to a dimly apprehended humanity. And so they hope that perhaps war may be allowed to continue provided modern weapons are prohibited. I am afraid this hope is illusory. Whatever agreements not to use hydrogen bombs had been reached in time of peace, they would no longer be considered binding in time of war, and both sides would set to work to manufacture hydrogen bombs as soon as war broke out, for if one side manufactured the bombs and the other did not, the side that manufactured them would inevitably be victorious. . . .

As geological time is reckoned, Man has so far existed only for a very short period—one million years at the most. What he has achieved, especially during the last 6,000 years, is something utterly new in the history of the Cosmos, so far at least as we are acquainted with it. For countless ages the sun rose and set, the moon waxed and waned, the stars shone in the night, but it was only with the coming of Man that these things were understood. In the great world of astronomy and in the little world of the atom, Man has unveiled secrets which might have been thought undiscoverable. In art and literature and religion, some men have shown a sublimity[2] of feeling which makes the species worth preserving. Is all this to end in trivial horror because so few are able to think of Man rather than of this or that group of men? Is our race so destitute of wisdom, so incapable of impartial love, so blind even to the simplest dictates of self-preservation, that the last proof of its silly cleverness is to be the extermination of all life on our planet?—for it will be not only men who will perish, but also the animals, whom no one can accuse of communism or anti-communism.

I cannot believe that this is to be the end. I would have men forget their quarrels for a moment and reflect that, if they will allow themselves to survive, there is every reason to expect the triumphs of the future to exceed immeasurably the triumphs of the past. There lies before us, if we choose, continual progress in happiness, knowledge, and wisdom. Shall we, instead, choose death, because we cannot forget our quarrels? I appeal, as a human being to human beings: Remember your humanity, and forget the rest. If you can do so, the way lies open to a new Paradise; if you cannot, nothing lies before you but universal death. ∾

2. Sublimity means "loftiness" or "nobility."

Vocabulary

abolish (ə bol´ ish) *v.* to put an end to; do away with

Structure *What purpose does this sentence serve within the speech's structure?* | 1

Listening and Speaking Practice

[SPIRAL REVIEW] **Identify Logical Fallacies** Have students listen to this speech on Studentworks+, the Online Student Edition, or the Listening Library. Ask students to identify any logical fallacies— such as false causality, red herrings, or overgeneralizations—the speaker uses. Refer students to page R62 of the Logic and Persuasion Handbook for more on these propositions.

After You Read

Respond and Think Critically

Respond and Interpret

1. Do you find Russell's speech persuasive? Why or why not?

2. (a) In the first paragraph, what world conflict does Russell say overshadows all others? (b) What may have been his reasons for emphasizing that one?

3. (a) In the fifth paragraph, what accomplishments of humankind does Russell list? (b) How are these related to the "silly cleverness" he mentions in that paragraph's final sentence?

4. (a) In the final paragraph, what new idea does Russell introduce into the speech? (b) Does that idea add to the effectiveness of his appeal? Explain.

Analyze and Evaluate

5. Why does Russell, at the beginning of the second paragraph, ask his audience to set aside their political feelings?

6. (a) Does this speech appeal mainly to the emotions or to the intellect? (b) Why might Russell have chosen this approach?

Connect

7. **Big Idea** Making and Remaking Tradition In what ways does this address differ from Churchill's "Be Ye Men of Valor" (page 1115)?

8. **Connect to Today** Do you think subsequent world events have made Russell's message less relevant today than it was in 1954? Explain.

Literary Element Structure

A persuasive speech's **structure** usually includes a statement of the author's view, a series of supporting paragraphs, and a conclusion in which the view is restated and reinforced.

Summarize, in a single sentence, the main idea of each of the six paragraphs of this speech. What notion, present in each paragraph, serves to unite them and connect them with the conclusion?

Writing

Write a Dialogue Russell says that "even many men in positions of authority" do not realize the results of a nuclear war. Write a dialogue in which Russell advocates renouncing war and a politician opposes his arguments, advocating the stockpiling of nuclear weapons to defend his nation.

> **LOG ON**  **Literature** Online
>
> **Selection Resources** For Selection Quizzes, eFlashcards, and Reading-Writing Connection activities, go to glencoe.com and enter QuickPass code GLB9817u7.

Reading Strategy Analyze Political Assumptions

Sometimes, a writer's political assumptions are fairly obvious. For instance, Russell clearly assumes that the necessity of avoiding nuclear war outweighs all other political considerations.

Review the chart you made as you read. What more subtle assumptions did you note? How might they increase or decrease the persuasiveness of Russell's arguments?

Vocabulary Practice

Practice with Context Clues Identify the context clues that help you determine the meaning of each boldfaced vocabulary word.

1. George had expected to see evidence of the destruction of a few trees, not the **obliteration** of the entire forest.

2. How can we **abolish** hatred in the world when we allow it to grow in our own hearts?

BERTRAND RUSSELL **1209**

After You Read

Assess

1. Students should support their answers with references to the speech.

2. (a) The struggle between communism and anti-communism (b) This is a political struggle opposed to a conflict of religion or race.

3. (a) Discovering the atom and contributions to science, art, literature and religion (b) He feels the human race is clever enough that we should take measure to preserve our species instead of to destroy it.

4. (a) This is not the end (b) Yes, he appeals to human emotions

5. He wants people to recognize themselves as members of the human race rather than an individual political party.

6. (a) Students should recognize that the speech appeals mostly to emotions (b) Answers will vary.

7. Students should contrast the differences in both speeches.

8. Answers will vary. Some students may say no because he presents an emotional appeal to the human race and asks people to put their political affiliations aside.

Literary Element

Students' sentences should summarize the main ideas and connect them with the conclusion.

Progress Check

Can students analyze structure?

If No → See Unit 7 Teaching Resources Book, p. 50.

Reading Strategy

Students should note Russell's subtle political assumptions.

Vocabulary Practice

1. destruction, entire

2. can we, when we allow it

Writing

Students' dialogues should reflect opposing views of renouncing nuclear war and using nuclear weapons.

Comparing Literature

Focus

Summary

The narrator, a member of a tribe that lives by gathering coconuts, describes watching missiles pass overhead. Members of the tribe debate whether the missiles signal the fulfillment of a Great Prophecy. Meanwhile, the missiles poison the earth with their back-and-forth trajectories, and the tribe suffers under the terms of its contract with the Nicer Nut Corporation.

Teach

Literary Element   1

Structure Ask: What themes of the story are introduced in its opening line? *(the conflict between natural beauty and human warfare)*

APPROACHING For approaching-level students, **ask:** What detail seems out of place in this sentence? *(The missiles don't fit with the beautiful night or summer sky.)*

Writer's Technique ☆

Fables Italo Calvino believed that the most fundamental kind of narrative was the fable. His work has been described as "fables for adults." In "The Tribe with Its Eyes on the Sky," the clear moral point of the story reflects its character as a fable.

Readability Scores

DRP: 60
Dale-Chall: 10.6
Lexile: 1180

Build Background

In works such as *Cosmicomics, Invisible Cities,* and *If on a Winter's Night a Traveler,* the Italian author Italo Calvino (1923–1985) created his own special fusion of realism, fantasy, science fiction, and sheer literary playfulness. Of the goal of his work, he wrote, "I have tried to remove weight, sometimes from people, sometimes from heavenly bodies, sometimes from cities: above all I have tried to remove weight from the structure of stories and from language."

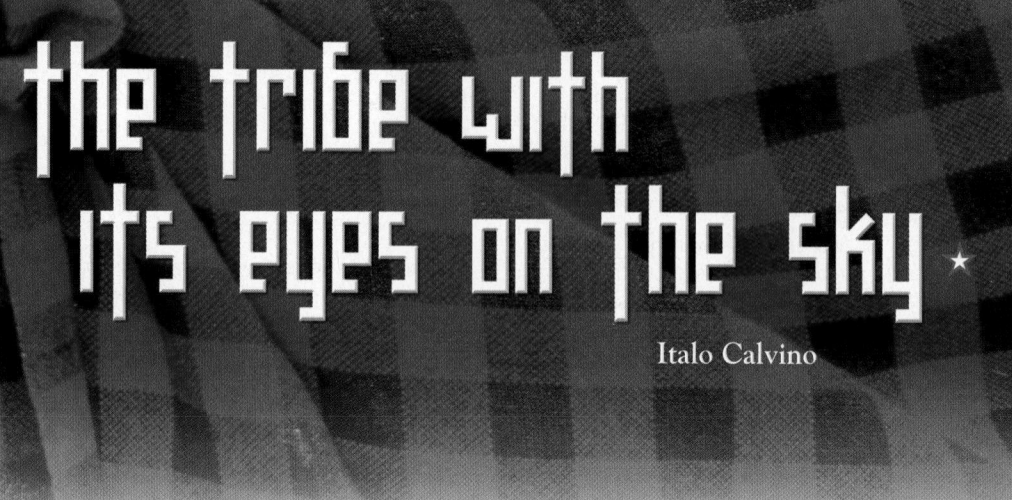

the tribe with its eyes on the sky ★

Italo Calvino

1 The nights are beautiful and missiles cross the summer sky.

Our tribe lives in huts of straw and mud. In the evening when we get back tired from gathering coconuts we sit at the entrances, some on their heels, some on a mat, the children, bellies big as footballs, playing round about, and we watch the sky. For a long time, perhaps since time began, the eyes of our tribe, these poor trachoma-inflamed eyes[1] of ours, have been gazing at the sky: but especially since new celestial bodies began to cross the starry vault above our village: jet planes with white trails, flying saucers, rockets, and now these guided missiles, so high and fast you can't see or hear them, but in the sparkle of the Southern Cross,[2] if you look very hard, you can pick up a sort of shiver, a tremor, at which the most expert of us say: "There, a missile passing at twenty thousand kilometres an hour; a little slower, if I'm not mistaken, than the one that went by last Thursday."

---

1. *Trachoma-inflamed eyes* are infected with a bacterial disease.

2. The *Southern Cross* is a group of four bright stars visible in the Southern Hemisphere.

Reading Practice

SPIRAL REVIEW **Create Similes Say:** Calvino uses a simile in the second paragraph when he says "bellies big as footballs." Have students fill in the graphic organizer to create similes describing the given objects.

Item	Comparison	Simile
missile		
night sky		
village		

Now, since this missile business has been in the air, many of us have been seized by a strange euphoria. Some of the village witch-doctors, in fact, have led us to believe, by inference, that since this shooting star originates from beyond Kilimanjaro,[3] it is the sign foreseen in the Great Prophecy, and hence the day fast approaches, as promised by the Gods, when after centuries of slavery and poverty our tribe will reign over the whole valley of the Great River, and the barren savannah will bring forth millet and maize.[4] So—these witch-doctors appear to be insinuating—it is hardly worth us racking our brains over new ways of emerging from our present situation; we should trust in the Great Prophecy, rally round its only rightful interpreters, without asking to know more.

It has to be said, however, that even though we are a poor tribe of coconut gatherers, we are well informed about everything that goes on: we know what a nuclear missile is, how it

works, how much it costs; we know that it won't only be the cities of the white sahibs[5] which will be scythed down like fields of millet, that as soon as they really start to fire them these things will leave the whole of the earth's crust as spongey and cracked as a termites' nest. No one forgets for one moment that the missile is a diabolical weapon, not even the witch-doctors; on the contrary, in line with the teaching of the Gods, they are always heaping curses on it. But that doesn't change the fact that it is convenient to consider the missile in a good light too, as the shooting star of the prophecy; not letting one's mind dwell too much on it perhaps, but just leaving a little mental window open to that possibility, partly so as to let all our other worries fly out the same way.

The problem is—and we've seen this time and again—that a little while after some devilry appears in the sky above our village coming, as the prophecy foresaw, from beyond Kilimanjaro, another, worse than the first, always appears from the opposite direction,

---

3. *Kilimanjaro,* in the country of Tanzania, is the highest mountain in Africa.
4. *Millet* and *maize* are grain crops.
5. *Sahibs* are people of rank or authority.

ITALO CALVINO **1211**

Comparing Literature

Teach

Reading Strategy | 2

Analyze Political Assumptions Ask: What attitude do the witch doctors recommend toward the threat of nuclear holocaust? *(Trust in them)* What attitude do you think Calvino has toward this recommendation? *(He seems to present it ironically.)*

ENGLISH LEARNERS For English learners, **ask:** What does it mean to call someone a rightful interpreter? *(That person has the authority to say what something means)*

Cultural History ☆

Astrology The use of the stars and planets to make predictions about events on earth is known as astrology. The rediscovery of Greek astrological manuscripts led to a revival of astrology in Europe beginning in the 1400s. Soon afterward, the rise of astronomy, the scientific study of celestial bodies, led to a sharp decline in the influence of astrology.

English Learners

DIFFERENTIATED INSTRUCTION

Intermediate Say: You can use clues from context to help you guess at the meaning of unfamiliar words. For instance, Calvino says, "The eyes of our tribe have been gazing at the sky." Since *gazing* is something you do with your eyes, you might conclude that it means looking, or looking carefully. Have students use the context given by the story to try to guess the meanings of the following words: *celestial, tremor, euphoria, barren, diabolical, trajectories.*

Then have them check their guesses with a dictionary.

Comparing Literature

Teach

Big Idea   1

Making and Remaking Tradition Ask: How has the life of the tribe remained similar to the way it was in the past? *(They still rely on prophecy based on events in the sky.)* How has it changed? *(Now there are missiles in the sky and the Nicer Nut Corporation runs the coconut trade.)*

[APPROACHING] Have approaching-level students paraphrase this sentence: "It is in the power of these shooting stars that our entire destiny lies." *(The paths of the shooting stars determine what happens to us.)*

Quickwrite

Students' paragraphs should note that the narrator observes the missiles without having the ability to control them, while the "white sahibs" actively decide to launch them. Also, the narrator recognizes the effect of the missiles on the entire world, while the missiles' launchers seem to focus solely on their own conflicts.

---

and shoots away to vanish beyond the peak of Kilimanjaro: and this is a sign of ill-omen, dashing our hopes that the Great Day is approaching. Thus, one moment in hope the next in fear, we stare up at an ever more armed and lethal sky, as once we read our destiny in the serene trajectories of the stars, the wandering comets.

The only thing people talk about in our tribe now are guided missiles, while we are still going about armed with crude axes and spears and blowpipes. Why worry? We are the last village at the edge of the jungle. Nothing is going to change here, until the Great Day of the prophets dawns.

Yet even here these are no longer the times when a white merchant would occasionally arrive in his piragua[6] to buy our coconuts, and sometimes he would cheat us on the price and sometimes it was us fooled him: now we have the Nicer Nut Corporation, who buy the whole harvest *en bloc*,[7] imposing their prices on us, and we have to gather the nuts faster than before in teams that work shifts day and night to reach the targets laid down in the contract.

Nevertheless there are those among us who say that the times promised in the Great Prophecy are nearer than ever, not because of the celestial omens, but because the miracles announced by the Gods are now just so many

---

6. A *piragua* is a kind of flat-bottomed boat.
7. The French expression *en bloc* means "as a whole."

---

technical problems that only we, and not the Nicer Nut Corporation, can solve. Easier said than done! Meantime, you try and touch the Nicer Nut Corporation! Seems their agents with their feet up on the tables of their offices in the docks on the Great River, glasses of whisky in their hands, are only concerned about whether this new missile mightn't be bigger than the last; in short, they don't talk about anything but missiles either. There is agreement, here, between what they say and what the witch-doctors say: it is in the power of these shooting stars that our entire destiny lies.

I too, sitting at the entrance to my hut, look up at the stars and at the rockets appearing and disappearing, I think of the explosions poisoning the fish in the sea, and of the courtesies those people who decide the explosions exchange with each other between one missile and the next. I'd like to understand more: certainly the will of the Gods is made manifest in these signs, certainly they foretell the ruin or the fortune of our tribe. . . . Still, there's one idea I can't get out of my head: that a tribe that relies entirely on the will of shooting stars, whatever fortune they may bring, will always be selling off its coconuts cheap. ✺

Quickwrite

What distinguishes the attitude of this story's narrator from the attitude of the "white sahibs" who "decide the explosions"? Write a paragraph or two to explain your views.

Speaking Practice

SMALL GROUP   SPIRAL REVIEW

Debate Say: Sometimes the participants in a debate do not necessarily believe the side they argue for; however, a skilled debater will put their opinions aside and make a persuasive argument.

Divide the class into two groups and assign each group the side of the tribe or the side of the "white sahibs." Have students expand upon the attitudes they wrote about in the Quickwrite exercise and hold a debate about the missiles launched.

Build Background

From the 1960s through the early 1980s, Randy Newman was known as a prolific composer and performer of pop songs—many of them satiric—including such hits as "Short People" and "I Love L.A." ("Political Science" is from his 1972 album *Sail Away*.) In the years since, he has focused mainly on composing music for films and television; a number of his scores, such as those for the films *The Natural* and *Toy Story*, have been nominated for Academy Awards. He was inducted into the Songwriters Hall of Fame in 2002.

Political Science

Randy Newman ☆

No one likes us, I don't know why.
We may not be perfect, but heaven knows we try.
But all around even our big friends put us down.
Let's drop the big one and see what happens.

5 We give them money, but are they grateful?
No, they're spiteful and they're hateful.
They don't respect us, so let's surprise 'em.
We'll drop the big one and pulverize 'em.

Asia's crowded and Europe's too old.
10 Africa is far too hot and Canada's too cold.
South America stole our name.
Let's drop the big one, there'll be no one left to blame us.

We'll save Australia.
Don't wanna hurt no kangaroo.
15 We'll build an All American amusement park there.
They got surfin' too.

1

RANDY NEWMAN **1213**

Focus

Summary

The speaker in Newman's satirical song argues for dropping the nuclear bomb to repay other countries for their poor attitudes. The song argues for sparing no place except Australia, which can be recreated as a new America. At the end of the song, the speaker looks forward to enjoying the products of now-destroyed nations such as Japan and Italy.

Teach

Literary Element	2

Structure **Ask:** How do the rhymes in "Political Science" help to reinforce the song's main idea? *(Light-sounding rhymes such as* grateful/hateful *and* kangaroo/too *emphasize the lack of seriousness with which the speaker considers nuclear war.)*

Literary History ☆

Songwriter From the beginning of his career as a songwriter and performer in the late 1960s, Randy Newman attracted critical acclaim. He also enjoyed popular success with such hits as "Short People" and "I Love LA." More recently, Newman has been known primarily as a composer of soundtracks. He won the 2002 Best Song Academy Award for the song "If I Didn't Have You" from the movie *Monsters, Inc.*

Comparing Literature

Teach

Reading Strategy | 1

Analyze Political Assumptions Ask: What attitude toward citizens of other countries does the speaker of the song display? *(Their lives are unimportant compared to the needs of Americans.)* How do you think Newman feels about the narrator's attitude? *(He is presenting it as ridiculous.)*

View the Photograph ★

Ask: What symbolic significance does the mushroom cloud have in modern culture? *(The mushroom cloud is often seen as a symbol of the paradox of technological mastery and moral horror.)*

Discussion Starter

Students may note that Newman is satirizing a tendency to view other countries as anti-American and potentially available for exploitation. Some students may point out that Newman's song was written during the Vietnam War and may reflect Newman's anger about that war.

★

Boom goes London and boom Paree.[1]
More room for you and more room for me.   **1**
And ev'ry city the whole world 'round
20 Will just be another American town.
Oh, how peaceful it'll be.
We'll set ev'rybody free.
You'll wear a Japanese kimono and there'll be Italian
   shoes for me.
They all hate us anyhow.
25 So let's drop the big one now.
Let's drop the big one now.

---

1. *Paree* is a pronunciation spelling of *Paris.*

💬 Discussion Starter

One technique often used by writers of satires is the exaggeration of particular attitudes, assumptions, and ideas until they become ridiculous. With a group of classmates, discuss what actual political assumptions Newman may have been satirizing through the exaggerated statements of this song's speaker.

1214   UNIT 7   AN INTERNATIONAL LITERATURE

Writing Practice

SPIRAL REVIEW **Write a Song** If possible, play students Newman's recording of "Political Science." **Say:** Newman's song doesn't have a chorus. Instead, he uses the repeated line "Let's drop the big one" to organize the several verses. Have students write a satirical song like "Political Science." First ask them to select a topic of current interest, either locally or nationally. Then have them compose a line that could be repeated throughout the song. Finally, have them write four or five verses of their song, using an AABB rhyme scheme like Newman's. Have students perform their songs for the class.

Wrap-Up: Comparing Literature

Across Time and Place

- *Shall We Choose Death?* by Bertrand Russell
- *The Tribe with Its Eyes on the Sky* by Italo Calvino
- *Political Science* by Randy Newman

COMPARE THE **Big Idea** Making and Remaking Traditions

Group Activity Reread Queen Elizabeth I's speech to her troops at Tilbury (page 247), James Joyce's "Araby" (page 1095), and Jonathan Swift's "A Modest Proposal" (page 550). With a group of classmates, discuss how Elizabeth's speech compares with Russell's, how Joyce's short story compares with Calvino's, and how Swift's satire compares with Newman's. Focus on the differences in style, literary devices, and concerns that separate the later writers from the earlier ones.

COMPARE Political Assumptions

Writing In different ways, the works by Russell, Calvino, and Newman all reveal an underlying assumption that the use of nuclear weapons would be irrational and unproductive under any circumstances. Can a case be made that their use might sometimes be necessary? Write a brief essay or short story in which you envision a situation to which the use of such weapons might be a reasonable response.

COMPARE Genres

Speaking and Listening In the second half of the twentieth century, reactions to the threat of nuclear war found expression in many media—from films to newsmagazines, from paintings and sculptures to comic books. Research a few such works in different media, and report to your classmates on how the conventions of a particular medium and genre helped to shape the form and content of each work.

Selection Resources For Selection Quizzes, eFlashcards, and Reading-Writing Connection activities, go to glencoe.com and enter QuickPass code GLB9817u7.

COMPARING LITERATURE **1215**

Compare the Big Idea

Students' discussions should analyze the differences in style, literary devices and concerns of earlier and later writers, specific to the assigned speeches.

Compare Political Assumptions

Students' essays or short stories should reflect a situation in which nuclear weapons might be reasonable to use. Note that some students may feel strongly that there will never be such a scenario.

Compare Genres

Students' presentations should focus on how a particular medium expressed the reaction to the threat of nuclear war. Encourage students to bring in their researched media to show the class if possible.

Advanced Learners

DIFFERENTIATED INSTRUCTION

The Nuclear Age Have advanced learners research one of the following topics related to nuclear warfare:

- mutual assured destruction
- the nuclear freeze movement
- the Strategic Defense Initiative
- present-day measures against nuclear proliferation
- another topic of the students' choice

Ask them to use library and Internet resources to gather information about the topic and understand its significance. Then have them present the results of their research to the class.

Before You Read

Follower

Bellringer Options

Show students a few images of farming or farm life. **Ask:** What do you think life as a farmer might be like? What might someone enjoy about that lifestyle? After they read, have students think about how the speaker of the poem feels about his work on a farm.

Meet **Seamus Heaney**

(born 1939)

Seamus Heaney is one of the most honored and popular poets writing today. His collections of poems have sold in the tens of thousands, and his poetry readings draw enthusiastic crowds throughout the world.

"Be true to your own solitude, true, true to your own secret knowledge"

—Seamus Heaney

Poet and Teacher Born to Roman Catholic parents, Heaney was raised in County Derry, Northern Ireland, in what he once described as "a farming household with enlightened values and a special sense of worth." The eldest of nine children, he became aware at a very early age of his homeland's violent history. His education led him away from rural life at the age of twelve when he won a scholarship to St. Columb's College, a Catholic boarding school. He described this transition as moving from "the earth of farm labor to the heaven of education."

An avid reader, he began writing poetry when he was a student at Queen's University in Belfast. After graduating, he continued developing his poetry while supporting himself by teaching secondary school. He has said that he has "a poetic, protective notion that [his] poetry should not be a meal ticket." Later he taught at Queens University and the University of California at Berkeley, the University of Oxford, and Harvard University, where he joined the faculty in 1982. In 1984 he was named Boylston Professor of Rhetoric and Oratory at Harvard, a prestigious position that allows him to spend several months of the year in Dublin, writing and enjoying time with his wife and children.

Heaney's first volume of poems, *Death of a Naturalist* (1966), contains the acclaimed poem "Follower." Though his early poems show the influence of Robert Frost, they take for their subject domestic rural life in Northern Ireland. In fact, the greatest influence on Heaney's work is his Irish heritage.

Nobel Laureate Deeply rooted in the Irish countryside, Heaney's poetry depicts the people, crafts, politics, history, and the myths of his native land, particularly the bitter conflicts between Ireland and England over the independence and unification of the divided Irish state. Heaney's fascination with archaic lore extends beyond Irish forebears to Danes, Normans, and Vikings, who battled for control of the British Isles during the Anglo-Saxon period. In 2000 his magnificent translation of the epic poem Beowulf earned critical and popular acclaim. Heaney is also an accomplished essayist on poetry and both modern and ancient Irish history.

Heaney's poetry is known for its phrasing, which is fresh and striking, and for its vivid imagery, which is often tactile, energetic, and violent. In 1995, in recognition of his many achievements as a poet, Heaney was awarded the Nobel Prize in Literature. According to critic Richard Tillinghast, Heaney's poetry serves as a "powerful tonic" against the disillusionment and alienation expressed by many contemporary writers.

 Literature Online

Author Search For more about Seamus Heaney, go to glencoe.com and enter QuickPass code GLB9817u7.

1216 UNIT 7 AN INTERNATIONAL LITERATURE

Selection Skills

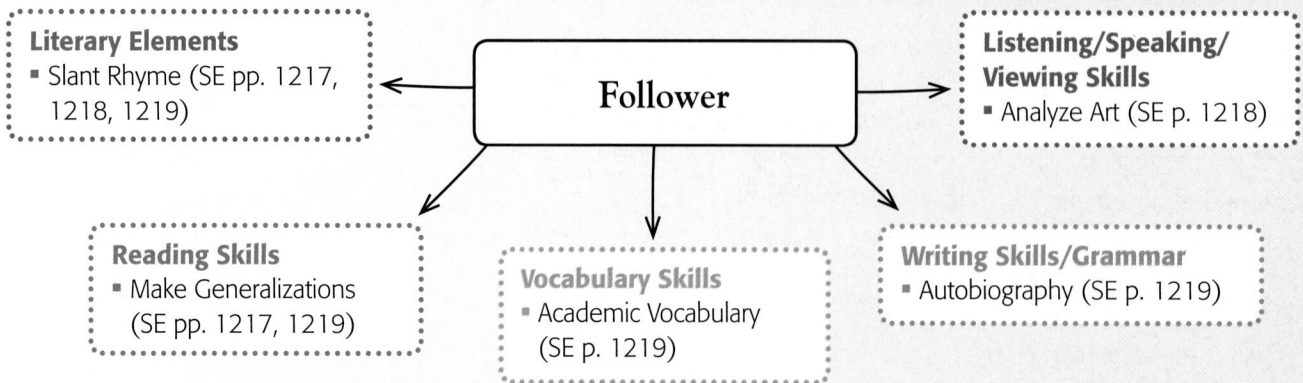

Literary Elements
- Slant Rhyme (SE pp. 1217, 1218, 1219)

Follower

Listening/Speaking/ Viewing Skills
- Analyze Art (SE p. 1218)

Reading Skills
- Make Generalizations (SE pp. 1217, 1219)

Vocabulary Skills
- Academic Vocabulary (SE p. 1219)

Writing Skills/Grammar
- Autobiography (SE p. 1219)

Literature and Reading Preview

Connect to the Poem

When you were a child, what adults did you regard as role models, and why? Discuss this question with a small group.

Build Background

Seamus Heaney has said that his poetry is a "quest for precision and definition." His poems are rich with description, which he calls "the living speech of a landscape I was born with." Unlike many other poets of his generation, Heaney often structures his poetry around traditional forms (such as stanzas with fixed rhyme schemes) and sets his poems in rural areas similar to the ones he knew as a child. His poems are often compared to those of William Wordsworth, the Romantic poet who wrote about the harmony and beauty of nature. Heaney has said that "Wordsworth was lucky and . . . I was lucky in having this kind of rich, archetypal subject matter as part of growing up."

Set Purposes for Reading

Big Idea Making and Remaking Traditions

As you read, ask yourself, What is traditional and what is original in this poem?

Literary Element Slant Rhyme

Slant rhyme is an approximate or near rhyme. For example, the repetition of the *k* consonant sound in the words *sock* and *pluck* forms a slant rhyme. As you read, ask yourself, Where do I find slant rhyme, and what effect does it have?

Reading Strategy Make Generalizations

Making generalizations involves generating statements that can apply to more than one item or group. Making generalizations is part of the process of inferring.

....

Tip: Taking Notes Use a chart to record your generalizations based on the details in Heaney's poem.

Detail	Generalization
"I was a nuisance, tripping, falling / Yapping always."	Children sometimes feel that they are in the way.

Learning Objectives

For pages 1216–1219

In studying this text, you will focus on the following objectives:

Literary Study: Analyzing slant rhyme.

Reading: Making generalizations.

Writing: Writing an autobiographical sketch.

Irish countryside in Limavady District, Northern Ireland.

Before You Read

Focus

Summary

The speaker describes himself as a child, following behind his father as he plows the fields. His father guides the horses with strength and skill, but the boy stumbles behind him on the uneven ground. In the last two lines, the speaker tells us that now his father is stumbling behind him.

 For summaries in languages other than English, see Unit 7 Teaching Resources Book, pp. 55–60.

English Learners

DIFFERENTIATED INSTRUCTION

Intermediate Students whose first language is not English may use alternative vowel sounds in their pronunciation of English words. If so, you may want to list the rhyme pairs from the poem (strung/tongue, round/ground, sod/plod, arm/farm, and today/away) on the board. You may want to note two near-rhymes: wing/breaking (the rhyming syllable is unstressed in "breaking") and plow/follow (the final vowel sound is pronounced differently). If you have any students who are from Ireland or have parents who are, ask them if any of these words would be pronounced differently there.

Teach

Big Idea

Make and Remake Traditions Discuss with students some of the aspects of traditional poetry, including the forms they have read about in this program. **Ask:** How is modern poetry different from traditional poetry? Try to keep the discussion on aspects of the poetry and not on which ones students like better.

APPROACHING Have students name the elements of poetry that they have studied so far, such as rhyme, diction, imagery, and meter. Ask them to describe traditional and modern poetry using these terms.

Literary Element | 1

Slant Rhyme Answer: *The words* plow *and* follow *form a slant rhyme.*

View the Art ★

Responses will vary. Some lines that seem closely connected to the image are lines 4 ["The horses strained…"] and 9–10 ["the sweating team turned around/and back into the land"].

Follower

Seamus Heaney

Ploughing. Nancy Smith (flourished 1940–1950). Transport poster. Stapleton Collection, UK.

View the Art Bold colors and clean lines give this poster a modern look, despite the old-fashioned subject matter. What lines in this poem do you feel are reflected by the image?

My father worked with a horse plow,
His shoulders globed like a full sail strung
Between the shafts and the furrow.[1]
The horses strained at his clicking tongue.

5　An expert. He would set the wing
And fit the bright steel-pointed sock.[2]
The sod rolled over without breaking.
At the headrig,[3] with a single pluck

Of reins, the sweating team turned round
10　And back into the land. His eye
Narrowed and angled at the ground,
Mapping the furrow exactly.

I stumbled in his hobnailed[4] wake,[5]
Fell sometimes on the polished sod;
15　Sometimes he rode me on his back
Dipping and rising to his plod.

I wanted to grow up and plow,
To close one eye, stiffen my arm.
All I ever did was follow
20　In his broad shadow round the farm.

I was a nuisance, tripping, falling,
Yapping always. But today
It is my father who keeps stumbling
Behind me, and will not go away.

---

1. A *furrow* is a trench made by a plow.
2. A *sock* is the blade of a plow.
3. A *headrig* is the mechanism on a plow that turns the blade used to cut the soil.

4. A *hobnail* is a short nail with a thick head that protects the soles of shoes.
5. A *wake* is the visible trail left by a moving body, such as the trail left by a ship as it cuts through water.

Slant Rhyme *What example of slant rhyme is found in this stanza?* | 1

1218 UNIT 7 AN INTERNATIONAL LITERATURE

Reading Practice

SPIRAL REVIEW Preview Have students preview the poem by reading the first line of each stanza. Have them predict the subject of the poem while you write their predictions on the board. As students read the poem, have them cross off predictions that prove to be incorrect.

1218

After You Read

Respond and Think Critically

Respond and Interpret

1. What are your impressions of the speaker in this poem? Explain.

2. (a)In stanzas 1–3, what task does the speaker describe? (b)How does he feel about the way his father performs this task? What words or phrases reveal the speaker's feelings toward his father?

3. (a)Who is the follower in lines 1–22? In lines 22–24? (b)Make inferences about the changes that the father and the son have undergone. How have these changes affected their relationship?

Analyze and Evaluate

4. Heaney's poetry is often praised for its vivid **imagery**. (a)Which words and phrases in this poem suggest images of the sea and sailing?

(b)Why do you think Heaney uses this image pattern?

5. In stanzas 4 and 6, how does the repetition of forms of "stumble" help reveal the changes the father and son have undergone?

6. Why might the speaker feel haunted by the memory of his father?

Connect

7. **Big Idea** Making and Remaking Traditions In what ways is "Follower" a traditional poem? In what ways does it depart from tradition? Explain.

8. **Connect to the Author** What signs of Heaney's appreciation of his heritage can you see in this poem?

Literary Element Slant Rhyme

Slant rhyme is based on **assonance**, the repetition of a vowel sound, or **consonance**, the repetition of a consonant sound at the ends of words.

1. What examples of slant rhyme can you find in "Follower"?

2. Contrast the true rhymes in the poem with the slant rhymes you identified. How might you explain the difference between the two types of rhyme?

Writing

Write an Autobiography Using the poem and the information on page 1216, write a brief autobiographical sketch by the speaker's father, focusing on either the young father's relationship with his son or their relationship when he is an old man.

> **LOG ON** ▶ **Literature** Online
>
> **Selection Resources** For Selection Quizzes, eFlashcards, and Reading-Writing Connection activities, go to glencoe.com and enter QuickPass code GLB9817u7.

Reading Strategy Make Generalizations

To **make a generalization** about a poem, ask yourself what broad statement is supported by particular details in the poem.

What general statement can you make about the lives of farmers like the speaker's father?

Academic Vocabulary

In Heaney's poem, the father and son eventually switch **roles**, *with the son becoming the leader and the father the follower.*

Role is an academic word that appears in everyday usage. For example, in a job interview, the interviewer's **role** is to ask questions.

To further explore the meaning of this word, answer the following question: What are two areas of your life in which you play different **roles?** Explain.

For more on academic vocabulary, see pages 56 and R81.

After You Read

Assess

1. Answers will vary.

2. (a) His father plowing a field (b) The speaker presents him as powerful and as an "expert" at "mapping" the ground.

3. (a) The speaker as a child; the aged father (b) The father now depends upon the son who once idealized him.

4. (a) "Like a full sail strung/ Between the shafts and the furrow," "mapping the furrow," "hobnailed wake," and "dipping and rising" (b) To suggest that farming is as skillful a craft as sailing

5. The changed roles and the cyclic nature of the change

6. Because he did not follow his father's way of life

7. Traditional in its use of stanzas and rhyme; original in its portrayal of the lack of communication and its occasional use of slant rhyme

8. Responses will vary. Students may say that the speaker's desire to follow in his father's footsteps connects to Heaney's fondness for his Irish past and roots.

Literary Element

1. Other examples include *wake/ back, wing/breaking,* and *falling/stumbling.*

2. True rhymes repeat the stressed vowel sounds and any succeeding sounds in two or more words. Slant rhymes repeat only a stressed vowel sound within words or consonant sounds at the ends of words.

Reading Strategy

1. Irish farmers lived hard lives, used simple tools, and plowed like craftsmen.

> To create custom assessments using software, use ExamView Assessment Suite.

Academic Vocabulary

Possible answer: When I babysit, I play the role of a caregiver, but at home, I play the role of a younger sister.

Writing

Students' sketches should be consistent with details in the poem and represent the idea that the father symbolizes the speaker's unbreakable tie to the past.

Meet **Ted Hughes**

(1930–1998)

In 1984 the British government took the world by surprise when it named Ted Hughes as its poet laureate. The honor usually goes to a poet who writes conservative, mainstream verse. Hughes's poetry, however, is sometimes controversial and dark. He often portrayed nature as fiercely beautiful and violent.

A Love of Nature and Wild Places Hughes grew up in the rugged landscape of Yorkshire, England. From a young age, he loved being out in nature, hiking, hunting, and fishing. He began writing poetry in high school, and after graduating and gaining admission to Cambridge University on scholarship, he deferred his enrollment for two years to serve in the Royal Air Force. He had a post as a radio mechanic at a radar station in a remote area on the east coast of England. With a lot of time on his hands, Hughes read and reread Shakespeare. By the time his term of service was up, he knew all the plays intimately.

At Cambridge, Hughes began as an English major but later changed his major to anthropology. Although he always planned to be a poet, he loved studying folklore and felt it gave him good background for his writing. After graduating in 1954, Hughes took a number of odd jobs in London, devoting his free time to writing.

> "*Maybe all poetry . . . is a revealing of something that the writer doesn't actually want to say, but desperately needs to communicate.*"
>
> —Ted Hughes

About a year after Hughes graduated, he met the American postgraduate student Sylvia Plath, who would later become a famous poet. They fell in love and were married four months later.

Life on a Roller Coaster Plath made a practice of submitting her poems to many different magazines and was often published. Soon, she was typing up Hughes's poetry and submitting it as well. Plath entered several dozen of Hughes's poems in a poetry contest sponsored by a major publisher, and a panel of distinguished U.S. poets chose Hughes as the winner among almost three hundred entrants. The prize was the publication of Hughes's first book, *Hawk in the Rain*, which received good reviews and even won another prestigious award several years later. The poem "Wind" appeared in that collection.

Literary Success The publication of *Hawk in the Rain*, when Hughes was only twenty-seven, launched his career as a poet. After Plath died in 1963, Hughes focused on teaching and raising their children, Frieda and Nicholas. His writing career continued and, over his lifetime, Hughes wrote more than two dozen books of poetry, sixteen children's books, and more than a dozen plays.

Literary Elements
- Personification
  (SE pp. 1221, 1223)

Wind

Writing Skills/Grammar
- Journal Entry (SE p. 1223)

Reading Skills
- Analyze Language
  (SE pp. 1221, 1222, 1223)
- Preview (TE p. 1222)

Vocabulary Skills
- Analogies (SE p. 1223)

Literature and Reading Preview

Connect to the Poem

What feelings and moods do you associate with the wind? Write down your associations in a list.

Build Background

"Wind" is set in Yorkshire, the wild and sometimes inhospitable region of England where Hughes grew up. Many of Hughes's poems celebrate the unbridled energy of nature, treating it as an almost magical force that can release the power of human emotion. His poems also explore the adversarial relationship between people and nature as well as people's isolation from both nature and one another.

Set Purposes for Reading

Big Idea Making and Remaking Traditions

Notice the ways in which "Wind" follows literary tradition and the ways in which it is a nontraditional poem. As you read, ask yourself, Which approach—traditional or nontraditional—is strongest here?

Literary Element Personification

Personification is a figure of speech in which a nonhuman thing is given human characteristics. For example, if you say "the trees are sighing in the wind" you are personifying the trees, because people sigh. As you read "Wind," ask yourself, How does Hughes use personification?

Reading Strategy Analyze Language

Analyzing language involves noticing the word choices and figures of speech a poet uses to determine what makes a poem especially effective. As you read, ask yourself, What language choices stand out?

....

Tip: Taking Notes Use a chart like the one below to record and analyze words, phrases, and figures of speech in the poem.

Line	Word, Phrase, or Figure of Speech	Why Effective
1	far out at sea	It's surprising to think of a house far out at sea.

TED HUGHES **1221**

Learning Objectives

For pages 1220–1223

In studying this text, you will focus on the following objectives:

Literary Study: Analyzing personification.

Reading: Analyzing language

Writing: Writing a journal entry.

Vocabulary

flounder (floun′ dər) *v.* to struggle to obtain footing; p. 1222 *I slipped in the mud and was floundering, flinging my arms in circles to try to regain my balance.*

luminous (lōō′ mə nəs) *adj.* emitting a glowing light; p. 1222 *The moon on the horizon was luminous and orange like a jack-o'-lantern.*

grimace (grim′ is) *n.* a look of pain or disgust; p. 1222 *The grimace on my teacher's face told me my answer wasn't even close.*

Before You Read

Focus

Summary

Ted Hughes developed a deep love of nature, especially in its most extreme manifestations. In "Wind," he describes the conflict between the weather and the people indoors.

 For summaries in languages other than English, see Unit 7 Teaching Resources Book, pp. 65–70.

Vocabulary

Etymology Explain to students that the spelling and pronunciation of words change over time. Have students look up the words *flounder* and *founder*, compare their definitions and roots, and then describe the etymology of *flounder*.

English Learners

DIFFERENTIATED INSTRUCTION

Intermediate On the board, list these words from the selection: *scaled, coal-house, black-back gull*. Encourage English learners to look these words up in the dictionary and the encyclopedia for meanings that may apply in the poem. Students should notice that one meaning of *scaled* is *climbed*; that a *coal-house* is a small building where a rural family's coal supply was kept; and that a *black-back gull* is a large, aggressive bird with a shrill voice. Discuss ways in which these words might contribute to the violence of the scene described.

Big Idea   1

Making and Remarking Traditions **Ask:** In the second stanza, which two lines end in a slant rhyme and which two end in a true rhyme? *(The second and third lines of the stanza, ending with* wielded *and* emerald, *have a slant rhyme; the first and fourth lines of the stanza, ending with* eye *and* sky, *have a true rhyme.)*

Reading Strategy   2

Analyze Language
Answer: *The words* crashing *and* booming *appeal to hearing. Students might imagine tree branches or trees falling due to high winds, and wind or thunder echoing off the hills.*

ENGLISH LEARNERS Have English learners close their eyes and imagine this image as you read it aloud. **Ask:** What do you see? What do you hear? *(Accept all reasonable responses).*

View the Art ★

Carel Weight was a 20th-century British painter, who was born in London in 1908. His paintings often include people going about their daily lives. **Ask:** What is the relationship between the painting and its title *(Accept all reasonable responses.)*

Wind

Ted Hughes

Bitter Wind. Carel Weight. Oil on board. Private collection. ★

This house has been far out at sea all night,
The woods crashing through darkness, the booming hills,
Winds stampeding the fields under the window
Floundering black astride and blinding wet

5   Till day rose; then under an orange sky
The hills had new places, and wind wielded
Blade-light, **luminous** black and emerald,
Flexing like the lens of a mad eye. **1**

At noon I scaled along the house-side as far as
10   The coal-house door. Once I looked up—
Through the brunt wind° that dented the balls of my eyes
The tent of the hills drummed and strained its guy rope,°

The fields quivering, the skyline a **grimace,**
At any second to bang and vanish with a flap:
15   The wind flung a magpie° away and a black-
Back gull bent like an iron bar slowly. The house

Rang like some fine green goblet in the note
That any second would shatter it.° Now deep
In chairs, in front of the great fire, we grip
20   Our hearts and cannot entertain book, thought,

Or each other. We watch the fire blazing,
And feel the roots of the house move, but sit on,
Seeing the window tremble to come in,
Hearing the stones cry out under the horizons.

11 **brunt wind:** a wind of shockingly great force.
12 **guy rope:** a cord or cable used for steadying or guiding.

15 **magpie:** a kind of bird.

17–18 **Rang like . . . shatter it:** a reference to the fact that most objects vibrate at specific frequencies. If, for example, a singer produces a note that is the natural frequency of a glass goblet, the goblet will begin to vibrate and may shatter.

2   Analyze Language   *Which two words in this line appeal to the sense of hearing? What do you imagine when you read this line?*

Vocabulary

flounder (floun′ dər) *v.* to struggle to obtain footing
luminous (loo′ mə nəs) *adj.* emitting a glowing light
grimace (grim′ is) *n.* a look of pain or disgust

1222   UNIT 3   FROM PURITANISM TO THE ENLIGHTENMENT

Reading Practice

SPIRAL REVIEW **Preview** Have students look at the painting *Bitter Wind* by Carel Weight. Ask them to describe what they see in the painting—what the people are doing, what their faces and body language express, how the wind seems to affect the people. **Ask:** Is the overall impression positive or negative? Then have students write a short paragraph about the positive and negative ways we think of wind (bitter wind vs. warm summer breeze).

After You Read

Respond and Think Critically

Respond and Interpret

1. What image or idea in this poem did you find most interesting or surprising? Explain.

2. (a)According to the speaker, where has the house been during the night? (b)How do you know that this is a figurative description?

3. What effect has the wind had on the landscape, the house, and the people who live there? Support your answers with specific evidence from the poem.

Analyze and Evaluate

4. (a)How does Hughes change or mix metaphors in this poem? (b)Does this mixing of metaphors bother you? Why or why not?

5. (a)What **symbolism** do you see in this poem? Consider the problem or conflict the poem centers on and the images used in the poem. (b)Which stylistic or literary device is most effective in illustrating the symbolism?

Connect

6. **Big Idea** Making and Remaking Traditions (a)In what ways do Hughes's word choices, sound effects, or style make this poem traditional? (b)In what ways do they make the poem nontraditional?

7. **Connect to the Author** Hughes often portrays nature as violent and frightening, but he himself had a deep love of the wilderness. What evidence of that love do you find in "Wind"?

Literary Element Personification

Not only can the use of **personification** make descriptions vivid, it can also help intensify the drama of a work of literature.

1. How is the wind personified in the first stanza? What does the wind do and what effect does this action have on the landscape?

2. How does Hughes's use of personification in describing the wind and the house intensify the mood and help bring out the poem's theme?

Writing

Write a Journal Entry In his poem "Wind," Hughes mentions a second person with him. Write a journal entry from the perspective of that second person. Find your own ways of describing a powerful wind, either through personification or careful word choice.

Reading Strategy Analyze Language

In writing this poem about the wind, Hughes has chosen many words that sound like what they describe. This use of language is called **onomatopoeia**. Refer to the chart you made as you read, then answer these questions.

1. In line 2, why might the words *crashing* and *booming* be better suited to the poem than synonyms such as *falling* and *loud*?

2. Find two more examples of onomatopoeia in this poem. Explain why you think these word choices are particularly effective.

Vocabulary Practice

Practice with Analogies Choose the word that best completes each analogy below.

1. noisy : quiet :: luminous :
   a. light   b. dim   c. unlucky

2. quiver : tremble :: flounder :
   a. favor   b. flash   c. thrash

3. laughter : humor :: grimace :
   a. triumph   b. success   c. pain

After You Read

Assess

1. Answers will vary.

2. (a) "far out at sea" (b) Because, based on line 9, the house is a normal house

3. The wind causes the fields to be "stampeded," the hills to shift position, the fields to quiver, the skyline to grimace, the house to ring with sound and people to forego normal pursuits.

4. (a) In line 1, the house is out at sea; in lines 16–17, it is a goblet; in line 22, it is a plant with roots (b) The mixing of metaphors contributes to the powerful imagery.

5. (a) The wind is a symbol of the power of nature. (b) Personification

6. (a) Occasional use of true rhyme and his use of consonance, assonance, personification, and extended metaphor (b) The slant rhyme, the mixing of metaphors, the unusual images, and the jarring line breaks

7. Students may say that Hughes's love of nature shows in his speaker's descriptions, which are admiring even if they describe a violent scene. The speaker goes out into the wind, even though it "dents the balls of [his] eyes," he and his companion are completely captivated by it and cannot focus on manmade pursuits.

Literary Element

1. As an animal that stampedes the fields; student interpretations will vary.

2. Power is attributed to the wind and frailty to the house, bringing out the theme of the stunning power of nature.

Reading Strategy

1. *Crashing* and *booming* sound more like the actions they refer to.

2. *Drummed, bang, flap, rang,* and *shatter*

Vocabulary

1. b **2.** c **3.** c

Writing

Students' journal entries should use second person to describe the wind, staying consistent with the details provided by Hughes.

Before You Read

Focus

Bellringer Options

Selection Focus
 Transparency 65

Daily Language Practice
 Transparency 105

Or ask: What kind of conversation do we call "small talk"? (*casual conversation about conventional topics*) Have students share their favorite examples. **Ask:** Why do you think it's called "small talk"? (*It's usually about nothing important.*) Explain that *That's All* is a scene of small talk between two women. Encourage students to watch for important meanings beneath the chatter

Before You Read

That's All

Meet **Harold Pinter**
(born 1930)

Harold Pinter was a twenty-seven-year-old actor when he received a phone call from a friend, a drama student at Bristol University, who had an assignment to direct a production. The friend asked Pinter to write a play. Although currently making a living by acting, Pinter had already done some writing: he'd had a few of his poems published in a literary magazine and was working on an autobiographical novel. However, Pinter had never written a play, and his friend had a tight deadline—the play had to be ready in six days. Pinter not only met the deadline; he exceeded it, finishing the one-act play in four days.

> "Firstly and finally, and all along the line, you write because there's something you want to write, have to write. For yourself."
>
> —Harold Pinter

An Actor Turns Playwright This one-act play, called *The Room*, was a success at Bristol University and another drama school associated with the university decided to put on the play, entering it into a drama competition. An influential critic gave *The Room* a favorable review. About a month later, an independent producer who had read about Pinter's play in a newspaper contacted Pinter to see if he had any other works completed. Pinter, encouraged by the praise he had received for *The Room*, had already written two more plays. The producer bought options on one of the two. Pinter's career as a playwright had begun.

When Pinter began writing plays, he drew heavily on his experience as an actor. This experience helped him pace his plays and write what he referred to as "speakable dialogue." He also drew on his experience writing poetry, which helped him craft dialogue to help convey his characters' underlying emotions.

A Distinguished Career After the modest success of *The Room*, Pinter wrote nine plays in six years. His first major success was *The Caretaker*, which was produced when Pinter was thirty-one. This full-length play, which was nominated for a Tony award, appeared on Broadway in New York. By 1964, when he wrote the short play, or sketch, *That's All*, Pinter had won three more important awards. About his short plays Pinter said, "There is no real difference between my sketches and my plays. In both I am interested primarily in people. I want to present living people to the audience, worthy of their interest basically because they are, they exist."

Since writing *That's All*, Pinter has written dozens of sketches, plays, screenplays, and radio and television dramas. He has also published his own poetry and collected the poetry of others in anthologies. In 2005 Pinter won the Nobel Prize in Literature.

 Literature Online

Author Search For more about Harold Pinter, go to glencoe.com and enter QuickPass code GLB9817u7.

Reading Practice

SPIRAL REVIEW Scan Have students preview the selection by scanning the text. **Ask:** What do you know about this selection, even without reading it? (*It is a dialogue between two women, Mrs. A and Mrs. B; it is a play.*) **Ask:** Which woman talks the most? (*Mrs. A*) Explain to students that, as they read, they will make inferences about the characters in the play. Explain that they can use a simple two-column chart to list details

from the text and inferences that they make based on those details. To begin, have them list the information they learned by scanning the text in their chart. Students can add details and inferences to the chart as they read the selection.

Literature and Reading Preview

Connect to the Play

What does your conversation style say about you? In a small group, examine the habits you have while talking with others.

Build Background

Pinter's plays are characterized by unexplained circumstances and an atmosphere of menace. His characters are often unable to communicate their needs, feelings, or motivations. They begin thoughts without finishing them, and do not listen carefully to one another. However, understatement and silent pauses reveal the inner thoughts beneath their banal remarks.

Set Purposes for Reading

Big Idea Making and Remaking Traditions

Notice the ways in which Pinter's play breaks away from traditional drama. As you read, ask yourself, What elements am I not used to finding in a play? What elements are familiar?

Literary Element Theater of the Absurd

Pinter, along with other playwrights such as Samuel Beckett and Eugène Ionesco, is often associated with the movement known as the **theater of the absurd**. These playwrights depict life as illogical and meaningless. They often ignore or parody the conventions of traditional drama, such as unified plot and coherent dialogue. As you read *That's All*, ask yourself, What meanings are hidden in this conversation?

Reading Strategy Make Inferences About Characters

Making inferences about characters involves putting together clues from their dialogue or actions to draw conclusions about the characters that are not directly stated. You might make inferences about the characters' feelings, motivations, or what the characters themselves symbolize. As you read, ask yourself, What is this character saying about him or herself?

....

Tip: Take Notes *That's All* presents two characters who talk about a third person who does not appear in the play. Use a chart to record the inferences you make about the characters.

Character	Line	Inference
Mrs. A		

Focus

Summary

The sketch opens in the middle of a conversation between Mrs. A and Mrs. B. The women's chat reveals that a neighbor of Mrs. A's has moved away. Unable to find a butcher near her new home, she returns to her former neighborhood on Thursdays, when she visits the butcher and stops in for tea with Mrs. A. The sketch concludes with Mrs. A's admission that the former neighbor does not return that often.

 For summaries in languages other than English, see Unit 7 Teaching Resources Book, pp. 76–81.

Learning Objectives

For pages 1224–1229

In studying this text, you will focus on the following objectives:

Literary Study: Understanding genre

Reading: Making inferences about characters.

Speaking and Listening: Performing a dialogue.

Selection Skills

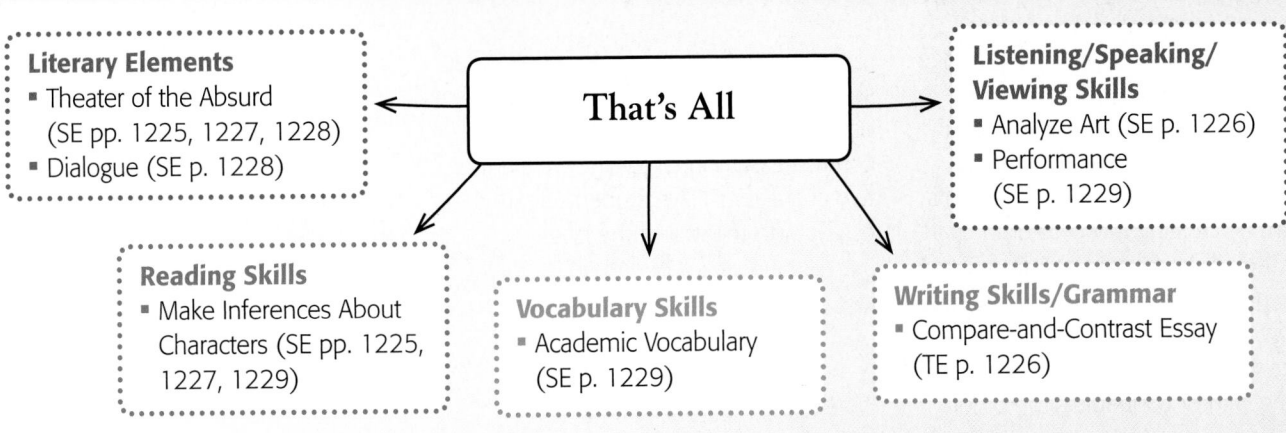

Literary Elements
- Theater of the Absurd (SE pp. 1225, 1227, 1228)
- Dialogue (SE p. 1228)

That's All

Listening/Speaking/ Viewing Skills
- Analyze Art (SE p. 1226)
- Performance (SE p. 1229)

Reading Skills
- Make Inferences About Characters (SE pp. 1225, 1227, 1229)

Vocabulary Skills
- Academic Vocabulary (SE p. 1229)

Writing Skills/Grammar
- Compare-and-Contrast Essay (TE p. 1226)

Teach

View the Photograph ★

Possible answers: *Most students will infer that the women are close friends or relatives, based on their similar body language and how close they stand to one another.*

Say: As you read the following dialogue, think about which woman in the picture is most like Mrs. A and which woman is most like Mrs. B. After students have finished the play, encourage them to return to the picture and discuss which woman should play each role and why. *(Students might say that the woman on the left would probably play Mrs. A because she seems very chatty and animated, and the woman on the right would play Mrs. B because she seems to be listening more than talking.)*

 For an audio recording of this selection, use Listening Library Audio CD-ROM.

View the Photograph Body language, such as posture and gestures, can reveal much about people's moods and relationships. What can you infer about the relationship between these two women from what you see in this image?

That's All

Harold Pinter

1226 UNIT 7 AN INTERNATIONAL LITERATURE

Writing Practice

Compare and Contrast Encourage students to compare and contrast Mrs. A and Mrs. B. **Ask:** Are Mrs. A and Mrs. B two of a kind? What do their similarities or differences mean? Have students brainstorm by creating a two-column chart in which they distinguish Mrs. A from Mrs. B. For each character, ask students to think about how she speaks, what she contributes to the conversation, whether she goes along with or contradicts the other character, and what opinions or attitudes she seems to express. Then have students use these details to write compare-and-contrast essays in which they relate the two characters. Have students share their essays with the rest of the class.

1226

MRS. A. I always put the kettle on about that time.

MRS. B. Yes. [*Pause.*]

MRS. A. Then she comes round.

MRS. B. Yes. [*Pause.*]

MRS. A. Only on Thursdays.

MRS. B. Yes. [*Pause.*]

MRS. A. On Wednesdays I used to put it on. When she used to come round. Then she changed it to Thursdays.

MRS. B. Oh yes.

MRS. A. After she moved. When she used to live round the corner, then she always came in on Wednesdays, but then when she moved she used to come down to the butcher's on Thursdays. She couldn't find a butcher up there.

MRS. B. No.

MRS. A. Anyway, she decided she'd stick to her own butcher. Well, I thought, if she can't find a butcher, that's the best thing.

MRS. B. Yes. [*Pause.*]

MRS. A. So she started to come down on Thursdays. I didn't know she was coming down on Thursdays until one day I met her in the butcher.

MRS. B. Oh yes.

MRS. A. It wasn't my day for the butcher. I don't go to the butcher on Thursday.

MRS. B. No, I know. [*Pause.*]

MRS. A. I go on Friday.

MRS. B. Yes. [*Pause.*]

MRS. A. That's where I see you.

MRS. B. Yes. [*Pause.*]

MRS. A. You're always in there on Fridays.

MRS. B. Oh yes. [*Pause.*]

MRS. A. But I happened to go in for a bit of meat, it turned out to be a Thursday. I wasn't going in for my usual weekly on Friday. I just slipped in, the day before.

MRS. B. Yes.

MRS. A. That was the first time I found out she couldn't find a butcher up there, so she decided to come back here, once a week, to her own butcher.

MRS. B. Yes.

MRS. A. She came on Thursday so she'd be able to get meat for the weekend. Lasted her till Monday, then from Monday to Thursday they'd have fish. She can always buy cold meat, if they want a change.

MRS. B. Oh yes. [*Pause.*]

MRS. A. So I told her to come in when she came down after she'd been to the butcher's and I'd put a kettle on. So she did. [*Pause.*]

MRS. B. Yes. [*Pause.*]

MRS. A. It was funny because she always used to come in Wednesdays. [*Pause.*] Still, it made a break. [*Long pause.*]

MRS. B. She doesn't come in no more, does she? [*Pause.*]

MRS. A. She comes in. She doesn't come in so much, but she comes in. [*Pause.*]

MRS. B. I thought she didn't come in. [*Pause.*]

MRS. A. She comes in. [*Pause.*] She just doesn't come in so much. That's all.

Make Inferences About Characters *Based on this information, what can you infer about the friendship between Mrs. A and the unnamed woman?*

Theater of the Absurd *What elements of the theater of the absurd can you detect in this dialogue?* **3**

1 Making and Remaking Traditions *What do you think Pinter's use of pauses here is intended to indicate about the conversation between Mrs. A and Mrs. B?*

English Learners

DIFFERENTIATED INSTRUCTION

Intermediate English learners may be unacquainted with the nuances of meaning in casual conversation and not realize that strategic silences can change otherwise innocent statements. Demonstrate by engaging a volunteer in an ordinary exchange of small talk—first as it is expected to be and then with pauses interjected. Discuss ways in which a sense of strangeness occurs and what it might mean. To help students recognize the effects of Pinter's pauses, have volunteers perform the scene, first preparing carefully so that their timing matches that of the script.

Teach

Big Idea   1

Making and Remaking Traditions Answer: *Most conversations have some pauses, but this dialogue contains so many of them that the conversation has a surreal air.*

(APPROACHING) Ask: Which woman do you think is responsible for most of the pauses? *(Students may suggest Mrs. B.)*

Reading Strategy   2

Make Inferences About Characters Answer: *Since the unnamed woman didn't let Mrs. A know that she was coming to the neighborhood, the unnamed woman didn't consider her friendship with Mrs. A important.*

For additional practice using the reading skill or strategy, see Unit 7 Teaching Resources Book, p. 83.

Literary Element   3

Theater of the Absurd Answer: *Mrs. B challenges Mrs. A for the first time. Mrs. A's final admission that "She just doesn't come in so much" is a poignant confession that her friendship with the visitor has come to an end.*

(ENGLISH LEARNERS) English learners may find the repetition in this section confusing. Have students read aloud Mrs. B's lines in a challenging tone of voice and Mrs. A's lines in a hesitant or defensive tone.

 To check students' understanding of the selection, see Unit 7 Teaching Resources Book, p. 85.

1227

After You Read

Assess

1. Answers will vary.
2. (a) To confirm that the unnamed woman no longer comes in to visit; Mrs. A admits that the unnamed woman does not come in as often as she did. (b) Anger, sadness, or loneliness are behind her response.
3. (a) To emphasize their insignificance or universality (b) Answers will vary.
4. (a) It suggests that the women have nothing more important to talk about. (b) They suggest that life consists of nothing more than superficial encounters.
5. (a) Some students may see subtle humor in the repetitiveness and banality of the conversation. (b) Mrs. A's pretense of friendship with the unnamed woman is a pathetic attempt to avert the tragedy of alienation.
6. In much traditional drama, the "speeches" are artificial in their coherence. But Pinter's dialogue makes audiences aware that conversations in real life are often repetitive, trivial, and full of hesitations.
7. Responses will vary, but students should cite shows, plays, or films that use realistic dialogue, repetition, and convey messages about human life or relationships without stating them explicitly.

Progress Check

Can students identify theater of the absurd?

If No → See Unit 7 Teaching Resources Book, p. 82.

1228

After You Read

Respond and Think Critically

Respond and Interpret

1. What did you think of the dialogue in the play? In what ways does it resemble conversations you have had or overheard?
2. (a) What does Mrs. B ask Mrs. A toward the end of the play? How does Mrs. A respond? (b) What attitudes or feelings can you infer from Mrs. A's response?

Analyze and Evaluate

3. (a) Why do you think Pinter named these characters as he did? (b) Do you think the names strengthen the message of the play? Explain.
4. (a) Why do you think Pinter chose the title *That's All* for this sketch? (b) Why do you think he ended the sketch with these words?

5. (a) In your opinion, is this short play a comedy? Explain. (b) Can you detect a tragic undercurrent in the play? Explain.

Connect

6. **Big Idea** Making and Remaking Traditions In what way might the dialogue in *That's All* be more realistic than the dialogue in much traditional drama?
7. **Connect to Today** Where do you see elements of theater of the absurd today? In TV? Movies? Stage plays? Provide examples and explain how they illustrate theater of the absurd.

Literary Element Theater of the Absurd

To portray what they see as the fundamental absurdity of life, playwrights of this school often write fragmented dialogue interrupted by long silences between lonely characters desperately seeking meaning or identity.

1. What is Mrs. A desperately searching for in this play? How does she try to deceive herself that she has found what she is looking for?
2. What does Mrs. B force Mrs. A to admit at the end of the play? What motive might Mrs. B have for shattering Mrs. A's illusions?

Review: Dialogue

Because plays, sketches, and screenplays often lack a narrator, **dialogue**—the speech between characters—becomes the primary way for an author to convey details about characters, create a tone, and express ideas. With a partner, determine the tone of each speaker in Pinter's *That's All*. Then list the words, phrases, lines, and speech patterns that help create that character's tone.

Literature Online

Selection Resources For Selection Quizzes, eFlashcards, and Reading-Writing Connection activities, go to glencoe.com and enter QuickPass code GLB9817u7.

Literary Element

1. Friendship; she tells herself that she has found a friend in the unnamed woman whom she invites to her home.
2. That her "friend" is avoiding her; Mrs. B wants Mrs. A to be as lonely as she is.

Review: Dialogue

Some students may find the tone of the selection as bleak and alienated; others may find comedy in the simple absurdity of Pinter's language. Students should support their opinions with examples from the text.

Reading Strategy — Make Inferences About Characters

To understand the theme of the play, you must make inferences about the characters and their lives. Look at the chart you made as you read, and then answer the following questions.

1. (a) What are the two women in this play talking about? (b) Based on their conversation, what can you infer about Mrs. A's life?

2. What can you infer about the relationship between Mrs. A and Mrs. B?

3. What point do you think Pinter is making about the majority of human relationships?

Academic Vocabulary

Mrs. A prefers to keep her daily routine **constant**, *so she is distressed by the unnamed woman's changing behavior.*

Constant is an academic word that is used in many different disciplines. For example, scientists will often mention the importance of keeping **constant** all but one variable in an experiment.

Using context clues, try to figure out the meaning of the word *constant* in the sentence about *That's All* above. Check your guess in a dictionary.

For more on academic vocabulary, see pages 56 and R81.

Speaking and Listening

 Performance

Assignment Write and perform a dialogue that takes place in the school hallway between classes. Model your dialogue on "That's All," incorporating elements of theater of the absurd.

Prepare Review the elements of the theater of the absurd. Then think of a situation involving two characters and write the dialogue that they exchange. In the tradition of theater of the absurd, the conversation shouldn't make much sense or involve any real communication.

Decide in advance what postures and tones of voice your characters should use for each line. Indicate these as stage directions in parentheses.

EXAMPLE:

Marius: "I forgot to bring my gym shoes and it was supposed to rain today, but it probably won't."

Avi (nods): "Uh huh."

Marius: "And the locusts. . . ." (Voice drifts off, he looks away)

Avi (interrupts, quickly): "What about the locusts?"

Marius: I don't know, what about them?"

Avi: I certainly don't know. I didn't bring them up."

Marius (waves a hand dismissing Avi): "You must've. I've never even seen one."

Perform Rehearse your lines with a classmate. Choose tones of voice, postures (maybe facing away from each other), and pacing (leaving long pauses or interrupting each other) that emphasize the absurdity of the conversation.

Make sure, though, that you keep your audience in mind. Speak loudly enough for them to hear the dialogue and remain within their line of sight.

Evaluate Use the criteria on page 1163 to assess the performance of your classmates' dialogues. In addition to meeting these general guidelines, consider how well the dialogues reflect the elements of theater of the absurd.

HAROLD PINTER **1229**

After You Read

Assess

Reading Strategy

1. (a) They are describing a friend who moved away but still comes back once a week to visit the butcher. (b) Mrs. A's life is uneventful.

2. They are cordial and polite but do not truly confide in each other.

3. Most people are alienated from each other.

Speaking and Listening

Use these criteria in evaluating student performances:

- The performance uses appropriate postures and tones.
- The performance uses appropriate pacing.
- The performance follows the dialogue conventions for theater of the absurd.

 For grammar practice, see Unit 7 Teaching Resources Book, p. 84.

Academic Vocabulary

The fact that Mrs. A is distressed by the woman's "changing behavior" suggests that *constant* means "unchanging."

 For additional assessment, see Assessment Resources, pp. 287–288.

Approaching Level

DIFFERENTIATED INSTRUCTION

Established Have students work together to plan a performance of their dialogues for an audience (such as another class). The performance should include several dialogues written by members of the class, and may also include Pinter's work. To prepare, have students rehearse the dialogues and organize other aspects of the performance, such as props, music and sound effects, and transitions between dialogues.

It might be helpful for students who are not performing to write a short introduction to theater of the absurd, so that audience members can more easily understand the performance.

Focus

Bellringer Options

Daily Language Practice
Transparency 106

Or tell students that in the 1950s, the subject matter of British drama changed from formulaic plays with upper-class characters to plays with working-class, angry, realistic characters. The transition to these "kitchen-sink dramas" was fueled by frustrations with postwar society. As they read, students should consider which aspects of society contributed to the "anger" in drama.

Teach

Literary Element   1

Drama Explain that a drama is a story intended to be performed by actors in front of an audience.

Ask: Have you ever performed in a drama? *(Answers will vary based on student experiences.)* Have students select a scene or soliloquy from a play in their textbooks, rehearse it, and perform it in front of the class.

 For activities related to this selection, see Unit 7 Teaching Resources Book, pp. 87–88.

Learning Objectives

For pages 1230–1231

In studying this text, you will focus on the following objectives:

Literary Study: Analyzing literary genres.

Reading: Evaluating historical influences.

British Drama—from the Drawing Room to the Kitchen Sink

1   The late twentieth century was a period of extraordinary richness for British drama, when exciting young playwrights forged bold new paths for theater in England. The devastation of World War II had a major impact on these developments. Despite social reforms enacted by the Labour Party in the aftermath of the war, widespread bitterness and frustration remained in British society. Wartime rationing of clothing, gasoline, and food continued into the 1950s. College educations failed to lead to meaningful jobs. An anger born of desire for social change and intensified by Britain's slow postwar recovery was reflected in many British novels and plays of the early 1950s. John Osborne was the playwright who first dramatized this bitterness. When his play *Look Back in Anger* opened on May 8, 1956, it challenged audiences with a working-class hero, his brutal language, and the rage he expressed toward the traditional British class system.   **2**

> *"What do I know of man's destiny? I could tell you more about radishes."*
> —Samuel Beckett, from "Enough"

Kitchen-Sink Drama

The successful British playwrights of the 1930s and 1940s, such as Noel Coward and W. Somerset Maugham, crafted witty, formulaic plays often described as "drawing-room comedies" since the action frequently took place in a living, or drawing, room. Their upper class characters spoke in refined accents and employed servants. To the audiences of such plays, *Look Back in Anger* came as a distinct shock.

Osborne's working-class hero in the play, Jimmy Porter, marries above his social status. University educated, he still sells candy in a street market because he can't find a job equal to his schooling or his ego. Frustrated, he verbally attacks his wife, her

Scene from *Waiting for Godot,* 1994.

Vocabulary Practice

Compound Words Remind students that a compound word is made up of two or more words put together. Readers can increase their understanding of both familiar and unfamiliar words by examining the meaning of the separate parts. **Write**

on the board: playwrights, widespread, screenplay, highlight. Explain that these are examples of compound words in this feature. Ask students to define them.

upper-middle-class background, and, by extension, the entire British class system. Porter's furious, self-pitying rants stunned audiences and gave rise to the term "Angry Young Men," which soon categorized a group of young writers who attacked British society in their plays and novels.

Absurdists and Contemporaries

Another important work of postwar British drama is the Irish-born playwright Samuel Beckett's *Waiting for Godot* (1952). Beckett's tragicomic play presents characters who are clown-like vagrants repeating senseless phrases in an unending round of pointless activity. Drama critic Martin Esslin used the term "theater of the absurd" to describe postwar plays that express "bewilderment, anxiety, and wonder in the face of an inexplicable universe." Reflecting postwar pessimism, Beckett's plays—including *Endgame* and *Happy Days*—emphasize inaction and futility. Among the British playwrights influenced by Beckett, who won the Nobel Prize in Literature in 1969, are Tom Stoppard and Harold Pinter.

The Czech-born playwright Tom Stoppard became famous with *Rosencrantz and Guildenstern Are Dead*, a play based on two minor characters in *Hamlet*. His other important works include *The Real Inspector Hound* (a parody of the conventions of stage thrillers) and *Jumpers* (a satire of academics). Stoppard displays a strong theatrical sense as well as an understanding of modern science and modern ethics. Using puns and other kinds of word play, he creates dramas that provoke and amuse.

Harold Pinter is a prolific writer who explores the mysteries and underlying meanings in everyday dialogue. His first full-length play, *The Birthday Party*, was followed by *The Caretaker, The*

Rosencrantz and Guildenstern Are Dead, 1995.

Homecoming, Betrayal, and numerous screenplays. Unlike Beckett, Pinter writes plays that have the appearance of Realism.

What links Pinter to Beckett is his use of dialogue, which employs a variety of strategies—from the banalities of small talk to extended silences—to highlight the difficulties of communication. In 2005 Pinter won the Nobel Prize in Literature. In his Nobel lecture he noted, "Truth in drama is forever elusive. You never quite find it but the search for it is compulsive. The search is clearly what drives the endeavor."

Contemporary British drama continues to investigate political and social issues. Caryl Churchill has written political plays that express socialist and feminist themes. *Top Girls*, one of Churchill's best-known plays, introduces famous women from legend and history, such as the medieval figure Pope Joan and the Victorian traveler Isabella Bird, into an analysis of contemporary feminism. Today, British playwrights continue to push the boundaries of theme, form, and production.

LOG ON ▶ **Literature** Online

Literature and Reading For more about British drama, go to glencoe.com and enter QuickPass code GLB9817u7.

Respond and Think Critically

1. How do you think you would have responded if you had been in the audience when *Look Back in Anger* was first produced?

2. What do you think marked the major change between prewar and postwar British drama?

3. What are some of the essential features of late twentieth-century British drama?

4. What does the popularity of and critical acclaim for playwrights like Pinter and Beckett suggest about the modern audience?

LITERARY HISTORY **1231**

 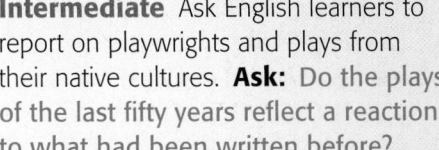

What We Lost

Meet **Eavan Boland**
(born 1944)

E avan Boland's early life was marked by the disruptions of moving from place to place and the struggles associated with learning where one belongs. In 1950, at the age of five, she left her native Ireland when her father became ambassador to the Court of St. James in London. She vividly remembers the anti-Irish hostility she faced from Londoners at the time as well as the feelings of isolation and humiliation that such cruelty prompted in her.

Cultural Isolation In 1956 her father was named Irish ambassador to the United Nations, and again Boland found herself uprooted in a move that took her family clear across the Atlantic to New York City. Boland enrolled in the Convent of the Sacred Heart School, and she thought New York was a "beautiful, bizarre city." However, her new surroundings did little to diminish her feeling that she was an outsider. It was at this time that she found hints of an emerging aesthetic that would shape her work as a writer: the deepening "feeling that your reality is an inner rather than an outer" experience.

In 1959 Boland returned to Ireland to go to boarding school at Holy Child Convent in Killiney, County Dublin, where she stayed until 1962. Again she felt chillingly distant from her own culture because of her long absence. She did not speak Gaelic and her upbringing in London and New York set her apart. Nevertheless, it was an important time for her as she became reacquainted with Ireland, and she found that her loneliness was conducive to writing.

Family Influences Boland was not exactly alone when it came to seriously exploring her artistic side, though. Her mother, Frances Kelly Boland, was an accomplished painter who had studied

with the postexpressionists in Paris in the 1930s. While Boland insists that both her parents "were profoundly influential" on her work, her mother promoted the kind of confidence that would help Boland challenge the male-dominated literary traditions of Ireland.

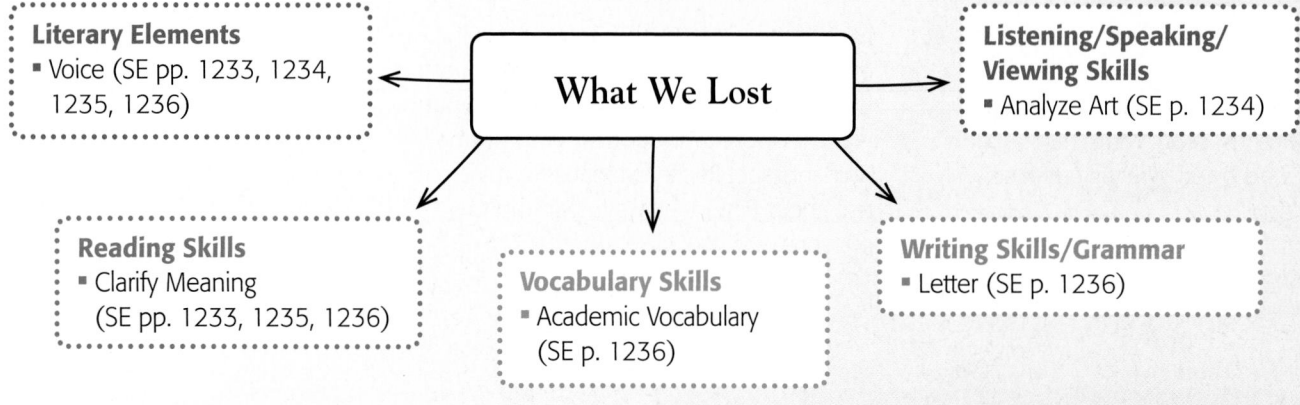

> *"The idea of a poetry which can fathom silences, follow the outsider's trail—that draws me in."*
>
> —Eavan Boland

Teacher and Writer After graduating from Holy Child, Boland worked as a hotel housekeeper and used her wages to publish a chapbook entitled *23 Poems* (1962). She went on to study English at Trinity College, Dublin, during the next four years, earning a first-class honors degree. Boland taught for a while at Trinity but felt she "was completely unsuited to being an academic." However, she has lectured at the School of Irish Studies in Dublin since the late 1960s and writes reviews and articles for the *Irish Times*. Since 1996 she has taught graduate level workshops in poetry in the Stanford Creative Writing Program in California.

LOG ON ▶ **Literature** Online

Author Search For more about Eavan Boland, go to glencoe.com and enter QuickPass code GLB9817u7.

Bellringer Options

Daily Language Practice Transparency 107

Or ask: Have you ever been in a setting where you felt completely out of place? What was it like? As students provide examples, elicit the idea that an unfamiliar setting often gives rise to feelings of estrangement, discomfort, and alienation. Explain that writer Eavan Boland had similar feelings when she moved to America. As students read, have them consider how "What We Lost" reflects these feelings.

 For an audio recording of this selection, use Listening Library Audio CD-ROM.

Selection Skills

Literary Elements
- Voice (SE pp. 1233, 1234, 1235, 1236)

What We Lost

Listening/Speaking/ Viewing Skills
- Analyze Art (SE p. 1234)

Reading Skills
- Clarify Meaning (SE pp. 1233, 1235, 1236)

Vocabulary Skills
- Academic Vocabulary (SE p. 1236)

Writing Skills/Grammar
- Letter (SE p. 1236)

Literature and Reading Preview

Connect to the Poem

Why is it important to hold on to stories of the past? In a journal entry, write about something you have learned from your family's history, or something you would want your children and grandchildren to learn from you.

Build Background

In her 1995 book of prose *Object Lessons*, Boland writes about the life of her grandmother, a woman she knows almost nothing about. In the book, Boland constructs a story that intimately ties her own life together with that of her grandmother while revealing the parallel construction of Boland's own persona as poet, wife, and mother in the traditional, male-dominated literary world.

Set Purposes for Reading

Big Idea Making and Remaking Traditions

As you read, ask yourself, Which traditional poetic conventions are missing here?

Literary Element Voice

The author's distinctive use of language to convey the speaker's personality to the reader is referred to as **voice**. Various elements of style can determine a writer's voice. These elements may include sentence structure, word choice, sound devices, pace, and tone. As you read the poem, ask yourself, Can I "hear" a distinctive voice emerging from the piece?

Reading Strategy Clarify Meaning

Rereading passages in a literary work can help to clarify the meaning of the text. The sequence or cause of events, challenging language, or even puzzling ideas may become clearer when you slowly reread the material. As you read, ask yourself, Where does the meaning of the poem become vague?

Tip: Taking Notes As you read Boland's poem, make a chart like the one below to help you clarify meaning.

Difficult Line or Phrase	Possible Meaning	Meaning After Rereading
The distance is a crystal earshot	The surroundings are frozen and glistening.	Crystal suggests something hard and clear.

Learning Objectives

For pages 1232–1236

In studying this text, you will focus on the following objectives:

Literary Study: Analyzing voice.

Reading: Clarifying meaning.

Writing: Writing a letter.

Rack Picture for William Malcolm Bunn, 1882. John Frederick Peto. Oil on canvas, 24 x 20 in. Smithsonian American Art Museum, Washington, DC.

EAVAN BOLAND **1233**

Before You Read

Focus

Summary

In "What We Lost," the poem's speaker describes a time that her mother spent with her grandmother one winter afternoon. The grandmother related an important story, but her young daughter soon forgot it.

 For summaries in languages other than English, see Unit 3 Teaching Resources Book, pp. 89–94.

Teach

Literary Element | 1

Voice **Answer:** *The sentences are direct and exact. Students may conclude that the voice is confident and matter-of-fact.*

 For additional literary element practice, see Unit 7 Teaching Resources Book, p. 95.

Vocabulary | 2

Word Meanings Students may need clarification of some words. Explain that *sprigged* (line 6) is a verbal form of *sprig*, a small shoot or twig. *Lavender* (line 7) is an aromatic herb that is bundled into sachets to impart fragrance to linens or clothes. *Tobacco silk* (line 12) is colorful swatches of silk once enclosed as premiums in packages of smoking tobacco; women collected these and sewed them into quilts or, as here, used them to trim garments. *Flax* (line 14) is a pale-colored, fibrous herb that was hand-processed into cordage and mats.

View the Art ★

Possible answer: *The left half has soft colors, indistinct lines, and little detail or shadow. The images—a dog and a coffee cup— suggest home, relaxation, and leisure. The right half has intense colors and harder lines. The items—sepia pictures, a spinning wheel, an old woman—suggest the past, darkness, and hard work. The halves might represent youth and age or present and past.*

1234

What We Lost

Eavan Boland

Marion McLean. Ian Fleming. Oil on canvas. The Fleming-Wyfold Art Foundation.

View the Art ★ Ian Fleming was a painter of the Glasgow school who is better known for traditional portraits and etchings than for images like this one. Compare and contrast the two halves of this painting. What might they represent?

It is a winter afternoon.
The hills are frozen. Light is failing.
The distance is a crystal earshot.
A woman is mending linen in her kitchen.

5   She is a countrywoman.
Behind her cupboard doors she hangs sprigged,
stove-dried lavender in muslin.°
Her letters and mementos and memories

7 **muslin:** a strong, often sheer cotton fabric.

1 Voice *What do these short opening sentences contribute to the speaker's voice?*

Reading Practice

Build Background Much of "What We Lost" deals with the various fabrics that were important to the household of the speaker's grandmother: *linen, muslin, satin, gabardine, worsted, cambric, tobacco silk,* and *flax.* To familiarize students with these textiles, have them consult an encyclopedia or the Internet to identify their appearance and function.

Have volunteers present their findings to the class, showing actual samples of the fabrics if possible.

are packeted in satin at the back with
10   gaberdine and worsted and
the cambric° she has made into bodices;°
the good tobacco silk for Sunday Mass.

She is sewing in the kitchen.
The sugar-feel of flax is in her hands.
15   Dusk. And the candles brought in then.
One by one. And the quiet sweat of wax.

There is a child at her side.
The tea is poured, the stitching put down.
The child grows still, sensing something of importance.
20   The woman settles and begins her story.

Believe it, what we lost is here in this room
on this veiled evening.
The woman finishes. The story ends.
The child, who is my mother, gets up, moves away.

25   In the winter air, unheard, unshared,
the moment happens, hangs fire, leads nowhere.
The light will fail and the room darken,
the child fall asleep and the story be forgotten.

The fields are dark already.
30   The frail connections have been made and are broken.
The dumb-show° of legend has become language,
is becoming silence and who will know that once

words were possibilities and disappointments,
were scented closets filled with love letters
35   and memories and lavender hemmed into muslin,
stored in sachets,° aired in bed linen;

and traveled silks and the tones of cotton
tautened into bodices, subtly shaped by breathing;
were the rooms of childhood with their griefless peace,
40   their hands and whispers, their candles weeping brightly?

10–11 gaberdine and worsted and the cambric: kinds of cloth. **bodices:** the upper parts of women's dresses.

31 dumb-show: a play or scene presented in gestures, without words.

36 sachets: small perfumed bags placed in drawers to scent clothing during storage.

Clarify Meaning   *Reread the context surrounding this line after you've finished the poem. What was lost?*   **3**

Voice   *How has sentence length changed from the opening lines of the poem? How does that change affect the voice?*   **4**

EAVAN BOLAND   **1235**

Approaching Level

DIFFERENTIATED INSTRUCTION

Established Have students widen their perspective on rural life in early 20th-century Ireland by finding pictures and descriptions of everyday activities such as home spinning. Women like the speaker's grandmother made many of their fabrics by hand, and illustrations of their spinning wheels,

bobbins, and other paraphernalia should be easy to find. Students may present their items to the class in a show-and-tell demonstration.

Teach

Reading Strategy   3

Clarify Meaning   **Answer:** *The story the mother told to her daughter.*

(APPROACHING) Students may think that lines 21 and 22 are the story that the woman told. Explain that these lines simply replace the story but are still from the speaker's point of view. Have students paraphrase this sentence. *(Example: The forgotten past is coming back to the speaker.).*

Literary Element   4

Voice   **Answer:** *The sentences become longer and more detailed, and the speaker's voice more earnest, more generalized, and less specific as she drifts into memory..*

 To check students' understanding of the selection, see Unit 7 Teaching Resources Book, p. 97.

Language History   ☆

The literal meaning of the term *hang fire* is "to misfire." The expression originated with the 17th-century flintlock musket, in which the priming powder would often ignite but fail to explode the main charge. Here it expresses the moment when the child, disappointed in the "unheard, unshared" connection with her mother, moves away and forgets the story. This moment of possible intimacy "leads nowhere."

After You Read

Assess

1. (a) The speaker's grandmother (b) Perhaps the speaker knows little about her.

2. (a) Muslin, satin, gabardine, worsted, cambric, tobacco silk (b) Physical things are remembered, but the words are not.

3. (a) To her daughter, who forgets the story (b) It would have provided additional family history.

4. (a) The physical details transport the reader to a specific time and place. (b) Responses will vary.

5. The question begins with "Who will know that once." Possible rephrasing: "Who will know that words once captured the dreams and losses of the past, its familiar things, and the sweet world of childhood?"

6. The poem does not rhyme, and its rhythm is irregular. It does have consistent four-line stanzas, however.

7. Possible answer: Boland's childhood, during which she always felt like an outsider, may have prompted her to feel strongly about being connected to a family or group.

Progress Check

Can students clarify meaning?

If No → See Unit 7 Teaching Resources Book, p. 96.

Literary Element

1. Responses will vary.
2. Students may say that the voice is earnest, sincere, somber, serious, wistful, or thoughtful.

 For additional assessment, see Assessment Resources, pp. 289–290.

1236

After You Read

Respond and Think Critically

Respond and Interpret

1. (a)Who is "the woman" in the poem? (b)Why doesn't the speaker describe her more fully?

2. (a)List three of the fabrics mentioned in the early stanzas of the poem. (b)How do these concrete things contrast with what was lost?

3. (a)To whom is the woman's story told, and with what results? (b)Is the story important? Explain.

Analyze and Evaluate

4. (a)What effect is created by the vivid and immediate descriptions of scenes before the speaker's birth? (b)Is the poem effective at drawing you into the visual aspects of the past?

5. The last line ends with a question mark. Reread the end of the poem to determine where the question begins. Rephrase the question in your own words. What is being asked?

Connect

6. **Big Idea** Making and Remaking Traditions In this poem, how does Boland depart from traditional poetic techniques? Consider rhyme, sound effects, and rhythm.

7. **Connect to the Author** Why do you think Boland would have such strong feelings about family stories being shared? Consider what you know from the biography on page 1232.

Literary Element Voice

A piece of writing can be magical when a reader can hear an original **voice** coming from the page. Even when the words are read silently, their placement and rhythms can create a distinctive sound.

1. Choose a stanza from "What We Lost" and explain specifically how word choice, pace, or other elements contribute to the voice in that stanza.

2. Characterize the overall voice you hear in the poem and provide examples to support your opinion.

 Writing

Write a Letter "What We Lost" describes how important things can be lost or forgotten if they are not appreciated at the time. Write a letter to an old friend or a relative, recounting a favorite story or an anecdote about your lives together. In your letter, explain why the story is an important one, and why you feel it's unforgettable.

LOG ON ▶ **Literature** Online

Selection Resources For Selection Quizzes, eFlashcards, and Reading-Writing Connection activities, go to glencoe.com and enter QuickPass code GLB9817u7.

1236 UNIT 7 AN INTERNATIONAL LITERATURE

Reading Strategy Clarify Meaning

Rereading a passage that appears difficult at first can often unlock its meaning. However, it helps to identify parts of the text that seem clear, and use them to shed light on difficult sections.

Using the chart you made as you read, choose a passage that was unclear at first and re-examine it in relation to parts of the poem that seem absolutely clear to you. What is your interpretation of the difficult passage now? Explain.

Academic Vocabulary ▶

In "What We Lost," the woman's packets of letters **denote** her attachment to her past.

Denote is an academic word that appears in everyday usage. For example, we say that a word's denotation is its concrete meaning.

Use context clues to figure out the meaning of the word denoted in the following sentence: Though the infant could not yet speak, his smile **denoted** happiness.

For more on academic vocabulary, see pages 56 and R81.

Reading Strategy

Students should cite a passage such as the sixth stanza, which at first may seem part of the woman's story. Their interpretations will vary but should be plausible.

▶ To create custom assessments online, go to Progress Reporter Online Assessment.

 Writing

Students' letters should use descriptive sensory details to recount an anecdote between family or friends.

Academic Vocabulary

The words "could not speak," implying a comparison with speech, indicate that denoted means "signified."

Part 2

Around the World: Extending and Evaluating Traditions

Man's Natural World, c. twentieth century. Sir Peter Scott. Oil on canvas. Private collection.

 View the Art Sir Peter Markham Scott was a British conservationist as well as an artist. What can you infer about his attitudes toward man's relationship with the world from this image?

"The English language is nobody's special property. It is the property of the imagination: it is the property of the language itself."

1

—Derek Walcott

1237

Analyze and Extend

Reading Strategy   1

Analyze Argument Direct students to read the quotation from Walcott. **Ask:** What argument does the quotation counter? *(the idea that the English language belongs to Great Britain)* What evidence might you give to support or oppose Walcott's argument? *(Students supporting Walcott's argument might provide evidence demonstrating that English is now spoken in many countries. Students who oppose this argument might suggest that the language will always contain elements that reflect its origins.)*

View the Art

Answer: *The image is ambiguous. Some students will reply that Scott considers modern society essentially destructive. Others may infer that he sees modern society as balancing the destruction by preserving wildlife. Sir Peter Scott (1909–1989) combined many interests as an ornithologist, a conservationist, and a painter.*

 For additional support for English Learners, see Unit 7 Teaching Resources Book, p. 100.

English Learners

DIFFERENTIATED INSTRUCTION

Beginning Remind students that English is spoken in more than 60 nations. These nations often have very different cultures. Therefore, two people who speak English do not necessarily share anything more than the same language. Have students name countries in which English is the native language. *(U.S., Australia, New Zealand, United Kingdom, Ireland, Jamaica, etc.)*

Approaching Level

DIFFERENTIATED INSTRUCTION

Emerging Read Walcott's quotation aloud to students. **Ask:** How can language be "the property of the imagination"? *(Language shapes how we think and create.)*

Bellringer Options

Selection Focus
Transparency 66
Daily Language Practice
Transparency 108

Or **ask:** What advantages are there in learning by first hand experience rather than getting information second hand? Have you ever had to take someone's word for the truth in an important situation? Was the information you got reliable? Explain your answers. Use these questions to lead a class discussion.

Before You Read

A Mild Attack of Locusts

Meet **Doris Lessing**
(born 1919)

After visiting South Africa in 1956, Doris Lessing was escorted to the airport by two police officers and told never to return. She was banned for twenty-five years from entering South Africa and Southern Rhodesia (now Zimbabwe) because of her political views and her opposition to apartheid, South Africa's former official policy of racial segregation. Throughout her life, Lessing has caused a stir with her novels and her clearly articulated political views.

An Uncomfortable Childhood Lessing was born to English parents in Persia (now Iran), where her father had been a captain in the British Army. In 1924 Lessing's parents moved to the British colony in the African country of Southern Rhodesia, where Lessing would spend the next twenty-five years of her life.

Lessing has described her childhood as a mixture of some pleasure and more pain. Only excursions into the natural world provided Lessing with some relief from the strict governance of her mother, who was determined to raise a "proper" daughter. As a young adolescent, Lessing was sent to an all-girls' school in the nation's capital, Salisbury. Miserable, she dropped out at the age of thirteen, ending her formal education.

> "I wasn't thinking about being a writer then—I was just thinking about how to escape."
>
> —Doris Lessing

An Unbounded Career Soon after dropping out of school, Lessing left home and began working—

first as a nursemaid, then later as a typist. By her early twenties, Lessing had been married twice, and at age thirty she left her second husband to live in England with her son.

Lessing took with her to England the manuscript of her first novel, *The Grass Is Singing*, and with its publication, she began a successful career as a novelist. Much of Lessing's work is autobiographical, based upon her experiences in Africa and as a mother and wife bound by social expectations. Her stories set in Africa chronicle the struggle between native black Africans and the white colonials who claimed their land.

Critics have tried to label Lessing both a feminist and a writer about race relations, but Lessing dislikes such labels. Unlike some of her contemporaries, who enjoy the fame that accompanies a writing career, Lessing claims she prefers not to give book tours and interviews. She once said to an interviewer, "I told my publishers it would be far more useful for everyone if I stayed at home, writing another book."

In addition to her numerous novels (which include a five-volume science fiction series), Lessing has also published several collections of short stories, as well as poetry, essays, travel writings, and two autobiographical works. In 1995 Lessing visited South Africa for the first time since being forcibly removed in 1956. Recognized at last as a significant and revolutionary writer, Lessing was, on this occasion, welcomed with open arms. In 2007, Lessing was awarded the Nobel Prize for Literature. When told of this honor, she replied, "I can't say I'm overwhelmed with surprise."

Literature Online

Author Search For more about Doris Lessing, go to glencoe.com and enter QuickPass code GLB9817u7.

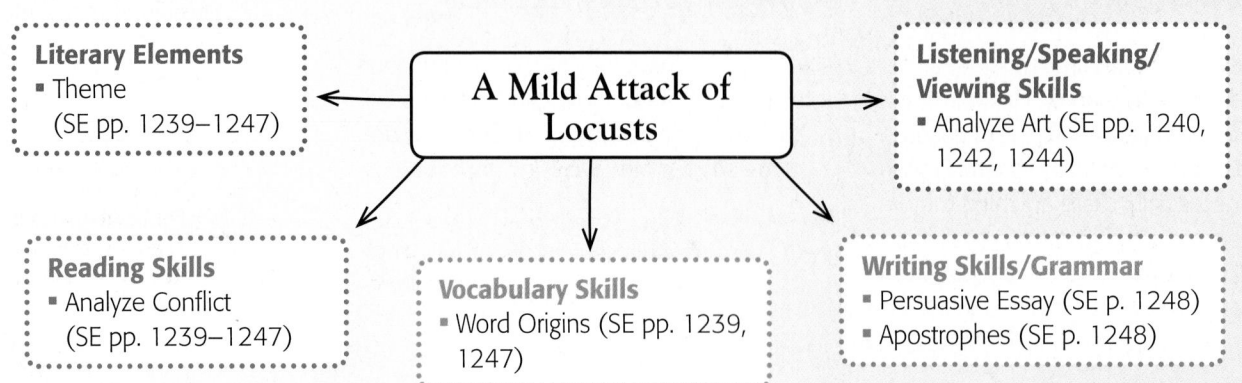

Literary Elements
- Theme (SE pp. 1239–1247)

A Mild Attack of Locusts

Listening/Speaking/ Viewing Skills
- Analyze Art (SE pp. 1240, 1242, 1244)

Reading Skills
- Analyze Conflict (SE pp. 1239–1247)

Vocabulary Skills
- Word Origins (SE pp. 1239, 1247)

Writing Skills/Grammar
- Persuasive Essay (SE p. 1248)
- Apostrophes (SE p. 1248)

Literature and Reading Preview

Connect to the Story

How does your family or school prepare for natural hazards? With a small group, discuss effective ways of being prepared.

Build Background

Lessing was five when her father moved the family to a farm in Southern Rhodesia. One of the many hazards of farming in this region was frequent locust swarms. The name *locust* refers to a number of jumping insects, including the periodical cicada (sə kā′ də)—which appears every seven, thirteen, or seventeen years—and the true locust, a migratory grasshopper. Locusts severely damage crops wherever they swarm.

Set Purposes for Reading

Big Idea Colonialism and Postcolonialism

Southern Rhodesia (now Zimbabwe) declared independence from Britain in 1923. As you read, ask yourself, What signs of British influence are still visible in this story?

Literary Element Theme

Theme refers to a central idea about life that is expressed in a work of literature. These themes may be universal—widely held across human cultures. A theme is different from a topic. A topic is a broad category, such as "hardship," whereas a theme conveys a complete idea *about* a topic; for example, "Hardship is best met with a sense of humor." As you read, ask yourself, What messages can I find in this story?

Reading Strategy Analyze Conflict

Conflict is the central struggle in a story or drama. This struggle might be between two or more people, between people and nature, or between people and their own feelings. To analyze conflict, as you read, ask yourself, Is the character struggling against something on the outside, something on the inside, or both? Then watch to see how each conflict is resolved.

....

Tip: Identifying Conflict As you read, use a graphic organizer like the one below to identify conflicts in the story.

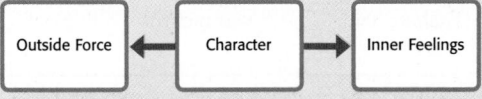

Vocabulary

acrid (ak′ rid) *adj.* burning, biting, or irritating to the taste or smell; p. 1241 *Where is that acrid stench coming from?*

irremediable (ir i mē′ dē ə bəl) *adj.* not subject to remedy or cure; p. 1243 *The tornado left irremediable damage in its wake.*

imminent (im′ ə nənt) *adj.* about to happen; impending; p. 1245 *A clap of thunder told us that a rainstorm was imminent.*

Tip: Word Origins Many words in English derive from, or come from, words in other languages. For example, the word *locust* derives from the Latin word *locusta*, meaning "grasshopper." Knowing a word's origin, or **etymology**, can help you better understand its meaning.

DORIS LESSING **1239**

English Learners

DIFFERENTIATED INSTRUCTION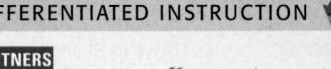

 PARTNERS

Intermediate Discuss with English learners some types of natural disasters. **Write** their answers on the board. Then have students divide into pairs. Have pairs discuss ways in which people can prepare for each type of natural disaster on the list. Encourage pairs to share their ideas with the class.

Before You Read

Focus

Summary

Margaret has been living on her husband's farm in southern Africa for just three years. Her adjustment to farm life is interrupted by a dramatic invasion of locusts, which devastate the land. Through this experience, Margaret begins to understand the hardships of a farmer's life and work.

 For summaries in languages other than English, see Unit 7 Teaching Resources Book, pp. 101–106.

Vocabulary

Affixes Have students note that the vocabulary word *irremediable* is related to the word *remedy*. Have them look up *remedy* in a dictionary and compare its definition to *irremediable*. Ask students to draw conclusions as to the meaning of the prefix *ir-* and the suffix *-able*.

For additional vocabulary practice, see Unit 7 Teaching Resources Book, p. 109.

Cultural History ☆

Locust Plagues Locust swarms have devastated countless crops in Africa and Asia over thousands of years. In one day, a ton of locusts (a small part of a swarm) eats enough food for 2,500 people. Scientists still don't know just what causes locust swarms or how to prevent or control them.

Teach

Literary Element   1

Theme Answer: *The paragraph says that experience is required to truly understand anything.*

Ask: Do you agree with this message? Why or why not? *(Most students will probably agree that firsthand experience is the best way to truly understand something.)*

[ENGLISH LEARNERS] English learners may have trouble with the phrase "even to know about what seems a simple thing" due to its unusual syntax. Point out that "to know about" means "to understand." Then have students paraphrase the sentence.

 For additional literary element practice, see Unit 6 Teaching Resources Book, p. 107.

View the Photograph ★

Answer: *Responses will vary. Students may say that the barren land in the photograph evokes a somber, lonely mood.*

 For an audio recording of this selection, use Listening Library Audio CD-ROM.

Readability Scores

Dale-Chall: 6.4
DRP: 56
Lexile: 870

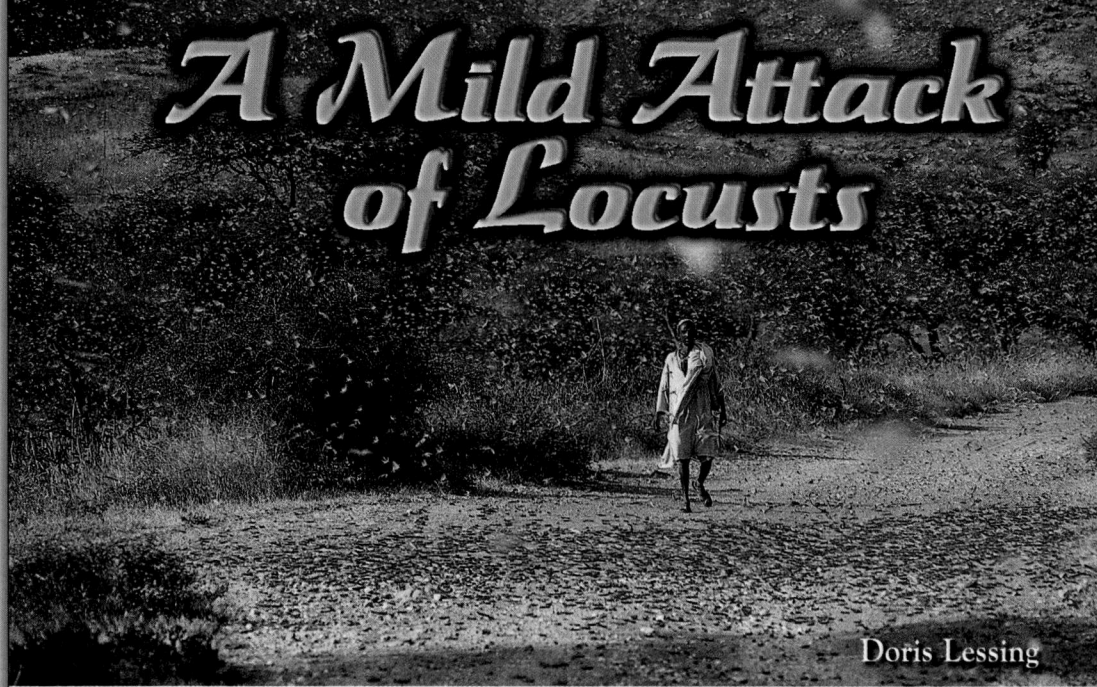

A Mild Attack of Locusts

Doris Lessing

Swarm of desert locusts.

View the Photograph Swarms of locusts tend to form when their habitat changes rapidly. What emotional response, or mood, does this photograph evoke for you?

The rains that year were good; they were coming nicely just as the crops needed them—or so Margaret gathered[1] when the men said they were not too bad. She never had an opinion of her own on matters like the weather, because even to know about what seems a simple thing like the weather needs experience. Which Margaret had not got.

The men were Richard her husband, and old Stephen, Richard's father, a farmer from way back; and these two might argue for hours whether the rains were ruinous or just ordinarily exasperating. Margaret had been on the farm three years. She still did not understand how they did not go bankrupt altogether, when the men never had a good word for the weather, or

the soil, or the government. But she was getting to learn the language. Farmers' language. And they neither went bankrupt nor got very rich. They jogged along doing comfortably.

Their crop was maize. Their farm was three thousand acres on the ridges that rise up toward the Zambesi escarpment[2]—high, dry wind-swept country, cold and dusty in winter, but now, in the wet season, steamy with the heat rising in wet soft waves off miles of green foliage. Beautiful it was, with the sky blue and brilliant halls of air, and the bright green folds and hollows of country beneath, and the mountains lying sharp and bare twenty miles off across the rivers. The sky made her eyes ache; she was not used to it. One does not look so much at the sky in the city she came from. So that evening when Richard said: "The government is sending out

---

1. As it is used here, *gathered* means "concluded."

 Theme *What idea about life is expressed in the opening paragraph?*

---

2. The *Zambesi escarpment* is a series of steep cliffs along the Zambesi River in southern Africa.

Reading Practice

 SPIRAL REVIEW Make Predictions Point out that the author has introduced the main characters and the setting on the first page of the story and has alluded to what will happen. Explain that making predictions is a good way to focus on the story's main elements. Have students reread this page and make predictions about the story's plot. *(Students might guess that the crops will be destroyed by a locust plague.)* Have students explain

their responses by identifying story details that led them to make these predictions. Invite them to continue reading to see whether their predictions are correct.

warnings that locusts are expected, coming down from the breeding grounds up North," her instinct was to look about her at the trees. Insects—swarms of them—horrible! But Richard and the old man had raised their eyes and were looking up over the mountain. "We haven't had locusts in seven years," they said. "They go in cycles, locusts do." And then: "There goes our crop for this season!"

But they went on with the work of the farm just as usual until one day they were coming up the road to the homestead for the midday break, when old Stephen stopped, raised his finger and pointed: "Look, look, there they are!"

Out ran Margaret to join them, looking at the hills. Out came the servants from the kitchen. They all stood and gazed. Over the rocky levels of the mountain was a streak of rust-colored air. Locusts. There they came.

At once Richard shouted at the cookboy. Old Stephen yelled at the houseboy. The cook-boy ran to beat the old ploughshare[3] hanging from a tree branch, which was used to summon the laborers at moments of crisis. The house-boy ran off to the store to collect tin cans, any old bit of metal. The farm was ringing with the clamor of the gong; and they could see the laborers come pouring out of the compound, pointing at the hills and shouting excitedly. Soon they had all come up to the house, and Richard and old Stephen were giving them orders—Hurry, hurry, hurry.

And off they ran again, the two white men with them, and in a few minutes Margaret could see the smoke of fires rising from all around the farmlands. Piles of wood and grass had been pre-pared there. There were seven patches of bared soil, yellow and oxblood color and pink, where

the new mealies[4] were just showing, making a film of bright green; and around each drifted up thick clouds of smoke. They were throwing wet leaves on to the fires now, to make it **acrid** and black. Margaret was watching the hills. Now there was a long, low cloud advancing, rust-color still, swelling forward and out as she looked. The telephone was ringing. Neighbors—quick, quick, there come the locusts. Old Smith had had his crop eaten to the ground. Quick, get your fires started. For of course, while every farmer hoped the locusts would overlook his farm and go on to the next, it was only fair to warn each other; one must play fair. Everywhere, fifty miles over the countryside, the smoke was rising from myriads[5] of fires. Margaret answered the tele-phone calls, and between calls she stood watching the locusts. The air was darkening. A strange darkness, for the sun was blazing—it was like the darkness of a veldt[6] fire, when the air gets thick with smoke. The sunlight comes down distorted,[7] a thick, hot orange. Oppressive it was, too, with the heaviness of a storm. The locusts were coming fast. Now half the sky was darkened. Behind the reddish veils in front, which were the advance guards of the swarm, the main swarm showed in dense black cloud, reaching almost to the sun itself.

Margaret was wondering what she could do to help. She did not know. Then up came old Stephen from the lands. "We're finished, Margaret, finished! Those beggars can eat every leaf and blade off the farm in half an hour! And it is only early afternoon—if we can make enough smoke, make enough noise till the

---

3. A *ploughshare* is the cutting blade of a plow.

Analyze Conflict What external conflict does everyone on the farm face? What additional internal conflict does Margaret face?

Colonialism and Postcolonialism What does the locust crisis reveal about the relationship between the landowners and the laborers?

---

4. A *mealie* is an ear of corn.
5. *Myriads* means "a great or countless number."
6. The *veldt* (velt, felt) is a rolling grassland region in southern Africa that has scattered bushes and trees.
7. Here, *distorted* means "unnatural in appearance."

Analyze Conflict What competing feelings or desires is Margaret struggling with? [4]

Vocabulary

acrid (ak′ rid) *adj.* burning, biting, or irritating to the taste or smell

---

Teach

Reading Strategy | 2

Analyze Conflict Answer:
They all face external conflict with the locusts. Margaret also faces the internal conflict of her fear.

Big Idea | 3

Colonialism and Postcolonialism Answer:
All the men—both owners and laborers—work together side by side.

ADVANCED To challenge advanced students, **ask:** What economic reality made it necessary for landowners and laborers to cooperate during the crisis? *(If the crop were lost, both laborers and landowners would suffer.)*

Reading Strategy | 4

Analyze Conflict Answer:
Her desire to help and her feeling of ignorance.

English Learners

DIFFERENTIATED INSTRUCTION

Intermediate As they read the story, help English learners comprehend challenging vocabulary. Tell them to use context to determine meaning and to look up unfamiliar words. Remind students that Lessing chooses words carefully to evoke a specific time and place.

Advanced Learners

DIFFERENTIATED INSTRUCTION

Research Challenge advanced students to use the Internet to learn more about locust plagues. Students may begin their research on the United Nations Web site: www.fao.org/ag/locusts. Allow students to present their findings creatively in televi-sion news reports that offer "on the scene" accounts of a locust plague in Africa.

Teach

Analyze Conflict **Answer:**
She overcomes her fear and ignorance by doing what the others are doing.

(ENGLISH LEARNERS) English learners may find it difficult to understand the phrase "set her teeth." Explain that this phrase means something like "clenched her teeth together" and is an indication that a person is determined. Have students visualize Margaret clenching her teeth as she runs outside.

View the Photograph ★

Answer: *Most students will reply that the image shares certain details with Lessing's description, such as "the air was thick, locusts everywhere," and "like looking into the driving rain." It does not include the close-up descriptions of the insects, or show their effects on human structures, as Lessing does.*

Brown locusts are found mainly in South Africa and are known for being particularly destructive. Over the years, research has been done to determine how to minimize the damage done by locust swarms. After a swarm, the focus is on eliminating the eggs laid by the locusts. During a swarm, a hopperdozer may be used. A hopperdozer is a wheeled contraption consisting of a screen and a box of water mixed with kerosene. The screen and box are wheeled into the field, and the locusts fly into the screen, are stunned, and drop into the box, where they die.

Brown Locust Swarm, South Africa

View the Photograph When a locust swarm has already begun, there is almost nothing that can stop it. How does the swarm in this image compare to the description in this excerpt? Do you think Lessing's choice of the word "attack" is accurate? ★

sun goes down, they'll settle somewhere else perhaps. . . ." And then: "Get the kettle going. It's thirsty work, this."

So Margaret went to the kitchen, and stoked up the fire, and boiled the water. Now, on the tin roof of the kitchen she could hear the thuds and bangs of falling locusts, or a scratching slither as one skidded down. Here were the first of them. From down on the lands came the beating and banging and clanging of a hundred gasoline cans and bits of metal. Stephen impatiently waited while one gasoline can was filled with tea, hot, sweet and orange-colored, and the other with water. In the meantime, he told Margaret about how twenty years back he was eaten out, made bankrupt, by the locust armies. And then, still talking, he hoisted up the gasoline cans, one in each hand, by the wood pieces set cornerwise across each, and jogged off down to the road to the thirsty laborers. By now the locusts were falling like hail on to the roof of the kitchen. It sounded like a heavy storm. Margaret looked out and saw the air dark with a crisscross of the insects,

and she set her teeth and ran out into it—what the men could do, she could. Overhead the air was thick, locusts everywhere. The locusts were flopping against her, and she brushed them off, heavy red-brown creatures, looking at her with their beady old-men's eyes while they clung with hard, serrated[8] legs. She held her breath with disgust and ran through into the house. There it was even more like being in a heavy storm. The iron roof was reverberating,[9] and the clamor of iron from the lands was like thunder. Looking out, all the trees were queer and still, clotted with insects, their boughs weighed to the ground. The earth seemed to be moving, locusts crawling everywhere, she could not see the lands at all, so thick was the swarm. Toward the mountains it was like looking into driving rain—even as she watched, the sun was blotted out with a fresh onrush of them. It was a half-night, a perverted blackness. Then came a sharp crack from the bush—a branch had snapped off. Then another. A tree down the slope leaned over and settled heavily to the ground. Through the hail of insects a man came running. More tea, more water was needed. She supplied them. She kept the fires stoked and filled cans with liquid, and then it was four in the afternoon, and the locusts had been pouring across overhead for a couple of hours. Up came old Stephen again, crunching locusts underfoot with every step, locusts clinging all over him; he was cursing and swearing, banging with his old hat at the air. At the doorway he stopped briefly, hastily pulling at the clinging insects and throwing them off, then he plunged into the locust-free living room.

---

1 Analyze Conflict *How does Margaret handle her ignorance and fear?*

---

8. *Serrated* means "jagged" or "saw-toothed."
9. *Reverberating* means "echoing."

Vocabulary Practice

SPIRAL REVIEW **Compound Words** Explain that a compound word is made up of two or more shorter words; the shorter words may offer clues to the compound word's meaning. **Write** these compound words from the story on the board: *cornerwise, crisscross, onrush, underfoot.* **Ask:** What does each of these words mean? How can you use the meanings of the shorter words to guess the meaning of the compound word? Have students find two more common compound words on this page. *(everywhere, afternoon)* Invite volunteers to explain the meanings of these words.

"All the crops finished. Nothing left," he said.

But the gongs were still beating, the men still shouting, and Margaret asked: "Why do you go on with it, then?"

"The main swarm isn't settling. They are heavy with eggs. They are looking for a place to settle and lay. If we can stop the main body settling on our farm, that's everything. If they get a chance to lay their eggs, we are going to have everything eaten flat with hoppers[10] later on." He picked a stray locust off his shirt and split it down with his thumbnail—it was clotted inside with eggs. "Imagine that multiplied by millions. You ever seen a hopper swarm on the march? Well, you're lucky."

Margaret thought an adult swarm was bad enough. Outside now the light on the earth was a pale, thin yellow, clotted with moving shadows; the clouds of moving insects thickened and lightened like driving rain. Old Stephen said, "They've got the wind behind them, that's something."

"Is it very bad?" asked Margaret fearfully, and the old man said emphatically: "We're finished. This swarm may pass over, but once they've started, they'll be coming down from the North now one after another. And then there are the hoppers—it might go on for two or three years."

Margaret sat down helplessly, and thought: Well, if it's the end, it's the end. What now? We'll all three have to go back to town. . . . But at this, she took a quick look at Stephen, the old man who had farmed forty years in this country, been bankrupt twice, and she knew nothing would make him go and become a clerk in the city. Yet her heart ached for him, he looked so tired, the worry lines deep from nose to mouth. Poor old man. . . . He had lifted up a locust that had got itself somehow into his pocket, holding it in the air by one leg. "You've got the strength of a steel-spring in those legs of yours," he was telling the locust, good-humoredly. Then, although he had been fighting locusts, squashing locusts, yelling at locusts, sweeping them in great mounds into the fires to burn for the last three

hours, nevertheless he took this one to the door and carefully threw it out to join its fellows, as if he would rather not harm a hair of its head. This comforted Margaret; all at once she felt irrationally cheered. She remembered it was not the first time in the last three years the man had announced their final and **irremediable** ruin.

"Get me a drink, lass," he then said, and she set the bottle of whisky by him.

In the meantime, out in the pelting storm of insects, her husband was banging the gong, feeding the fires with leaves, the insects clinging to him all over—she shuddered. "How can you bear to let them touch you?" she asked. He looked at her, disapproving. She felt suitably humble—just as she had when he had first taken a good look at her city self, hair waved and golden, nails red and pointed. Now she was a proper farmer's wife, in sensible shoes and a solid skirt. She might even get to letting locusts settle on her—in time.

Having tossed back a whisky or two, old Stephen went back into the battle, wading now through glistening brown waves of locusts.

Five o'clock. The sun would set in an hour. Then the swarm would settle. It was as thick overhead as ever. The trees were ragged mounds of glistening brown.

Margaret began to cry. It was all so hopeless— if it wasn't a bad season, it was locusts; if it wasn't locusts, it was army-worm[11] or veldt fires. Always something. The rustling of the locust armies was like a big forest in the storm; their settling on the roof was like the beating of the rain; the ground was invisible in a sleek, brown, surging tide—it was like being drowned in locusts, submerged by the loathsome brown flood. It seemed as if the roof might sink in under the weight of them, as if

---

11. An *army-worm* is any of various insect larvae that travel in groups and destroy vegetation.

Analyze Conflict *What new insight do we gain about old Stephen's struggle against the locusts?* **2**

Vocabulary

irremediable (ir i mē′ dē ə bəl) *adj.* not subject to remedy or cure

---

10. *Hoppers* are baby locusts.

DORIS LESSING **1243**

Approaching Level

DIFFERENTIATED INSTRUCTION

PARTNERS **Established** Have students work in pairs to practice *reading fluency* by reading the dialogue between Stephen and Margaret on this page. Ask them to take turns reading paragraphs 1–5 on this page. They should practice until each partner can read both passages fluidly, expressively, and at a normal

speaking pace, smoothly incorporating the dialogue and the exposition in the story. Challenge students to "perform" the reading, using expression to convey the characters' emotions.

Teach

Under the Acacia Tree, 1991. Tilly Willis. Oil on board, 25 x 35 cm. Private collection.

View the Art Acacia trees are native to hot, dry environments like those found in Africa and Australia. What sense of the story's setting do you get from this painting? ★

the door might give in under their pressure and these rooms fill with them—and it was getting so dark . . . she looked up. The air was thinner; gaps of blue showed in the dark, moving clouds. The blue spaces were cold and thin—the sun must be setting. Through the fog of insects she saw figures approaching. First old Stephen, marching bravely along, then her husband, drawn and haggard with weariness. Behind them the servants. All were crawling all over with insects. The sound of the gongs had stopped. She could hear nothing but the ceaseless rustle of a myriad wings.

The two men slapped off the insects and came in.

"Well," said Richard, kissing her on the cheek, "the main swarm has gone over."

☆ "For the Lord's sake," said Margaret angrily, still half-crying, "what's here is bad enough, isn't it?" For although the evening air was no longer black and thick, but a clear blue, with a pattern of insects whizzing this way and that across it, everything else—trees, buildings, bushes, earth, was gone under the moving brown masses.

---

1   Theme *How does Richard's attitude differ from Margaret's?*

"If it doesn't rain in the night and keep them here—if it doesn't rain and weight them down with water, they'll be off in the morning at sunrise."

"We're bound to have some hoppers. But not the main swarm—that's something."

Margaret roused herself, wiped her eyes, pretended she had not been crying, and fetched them some supper, for the servants were too exhausted to move. She sent them down to the compound to rest.

She served the supper and sat listening. There is not one maize plant left, she heard. Not one. The men would get the planters out the moment the locusts had gone. They must start all over again.

But what's the use of that, Margaret wondered, if the whole farm was going to be crawling with hoppers? But she listened while they discussed the new government pamphlet that said how to defeat the hoppers. You must have men out all the time, moving over the farm to watch for movement in the grass. When you find a patch of hoppers, small lively black things, like crickets, then you dig trenches around the patch or spray them with poison from pumps supplied by the government. The government wanted them to cooperate in a world plan for eliminating this plague forever. You should attack locusts at the source. Hoppers, in short. The men were talking as if they were planning a war, and Margaret listened, amazed.

In the night it was quiet; no sign of the settled armies outside, except sometimes a branch snapped, or a tree could be heard crashing down.

Margaret slept badly in the bed beside Richard, who was sleeping like the dead, exhausted with the afternoon's fight. In the morning she woke to yellow sunshine lying across the bed—clear sunshine, with an occasional blotch of shadow moving over it. She went to the window. Old Stephen was ahead of her. There he stood outside, gazing down over the bush. And she gazed, astounded—and entranced, much against her will. For it looked as if every tree, every bush, all the earth, were lit with pale flames. The locusts were fanning their wings to free them of the night dews. There was a shimmer of red-tinged gold light everywhere.

She went out to join the old man, stepping carefully among the insects. They stood and watched. Overhead the sky was blue, blue and clear.

"Pretty," said old Stephen, with satisfaction.

Well, thought Margaret, we may be ruined, we may be bankrupt, but not everyone has seen an army of locusts fanning their wings at dawn.

Over the slopes, in the distance, a faint red smear showed in the sky, thickened and spread. "There they go," said old Stephen. "There goes the main army, off south."

And now from the trees, from the earth all round them, the locusts were taking wing. They were like small aircraft, maneuvering for the take-off, trying their wings to see if they were dry enough. Off they went. A reddish brown steam was rising off the miles of bush, off the lands, the earth. Again the sunlight darkened.

And as the clotted branches lifted, the weight on them lightening, there was nothing but the black spines of branches, trees. No green left, nothing. All morning they watched, the three of them, as the brown crust thinned and broke and dissolved, flying up to mass with the main army, now a brownish-red smear in the southern sky. The lands which had been filmed with green, the new tender mealie plants, were stark and bare. All the trees stripped. A devastated landscape. No green, no green anywhere.

By midday the reddish cloud had gone. Only an occasional locust flopped down. On the ground were the corpses and the wounded. The African laborers were sweeping these up with branches and collecting them in tins.

"Ever eaten sun-dried locust?" asked old Stephen. "That time twenty years ago, when I went broke, I lived on mealie meal and dried locusts for three months. They aren't bad at all—rather like smoked fish, if you come to think of it."

But Margaret preferred not even to think of it.

After the midday meal the men went off to the lands. Everything was to be replanted. With a bit of luck another swarm would not come traveling down just this way. But they hoped it would rain very soon, to spring some new grass, because the cattle would die otherwise—there was not a blade of grass left on the farm. As for Margaret, she was trying to get used to the idea of three or four years of locusts. Locusts were going to be like bad weather, from now on, always **imminent.** She felt like a survivor after war—if this devastated and mangled countryside was not ruin, well, what then was ruin?

But the men ate their supper with good appetites.

"It could have been worse," was what they said. "It could be much worse."

---

2 Analyze Conflict *Why do you think the men go about resolving their conflict with the locusts in this manner?*

3 Theme *How has Margaret's view of the locusts changed?*

Colonialism and Postcolonialism *What message about history itself might Lessing want to convey?* **4**

Vocabulary

imminent (im′ ə nənt) *adj.* about to happen; impending

Teach

Reading Strategy   2

Analyze Conflict **Answer:** *Through experience, they have learned that locusts (and other natural challenges) are part of their lives as farmers.*

Literary Element   3

Theme **Answer:** *She has learned to see the locusts as a part of nature, not as a personal enemy.*

Big Idea   4

Colonialism and Postcolonialism **Answer:** *Lessing suggests that human beings can survive and recover from devastation.*

(APPROACHING) To help approaching-level students answer the question, have them explain what the people in the story do after the locusts have moved on.

> To check students' understanding of the selection, see Unit 7 Teaching Resources Book, p. 111.

English Learners

DIFFERENTIATED INSTRUCTION

Beginning Point out examples of Margaret's internal monologue from this page. *(Well, thought Margaret, we may be ruined. . . .)* Explain that these words of Margaret's are unspoken, so they are not punctuated as spoken dialogue would be. Have English learners describe what Margaret is thinking based on her internal monologue.

Approaching Level

DIFFERENTIATED INSTRUCTION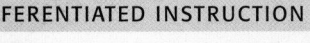

PARTNERS Emerging Distribute index cards and have approaching-level students work in pairs to write a two-to-three-sentence summary of each page of the story. Partners can mix up their summary cards and trade with another pair; students should be able to put each others' summaries into proper sequence.

After You Read

Assess

1. Students may suggest feeling dread or even despair.

2. (a) She does not understand the ways of farming in general, and she knows that the farms often see little or no profit. (b) "Farmer's language" may employ understatement because the effect of the locust attack is anything but "mild."

3. (a) Because the farm's situation seems hopeless (b) The locusts' destruction would probably unnerve anyone who had not witnessed it before. The farmers had survived locust attacks before, so they knew what to expect and how to recover.

4. City dwellers do not have as much exposure to nature; their lives tend to revolve around business and industry, not agriculture.

5. (a) "Lit with pale flames" and "shimmer of red-tinged gold light" (b) The images add to the story's realism and help show the locusts as creatures of nature.

6. The descriptions of the setting and the fact that the farmers are at the mercy of the insects with whom they share the land

7. Lessing grew up on an African maize farm. She probably would have been familiar with "farmer's language," farm work, and the threat of locusts.

After You Read

Respond and Think Critically

Respond and Interpret

1. How might you have felt if you had seen these locusts approaching your home?

2. (a) Why doesn't Margaret understand how the farm does not go bankrupt? (b) What can you infer about the nature of "farmer's language"? Why?

3. (a) Why does Margaret cry at the end of the first day? (b) Why is Margaret so disturbed by the locusts? Why aren't the farmers as upset as she is?

Analyze and Evaluate

4. Why might people who live in the city have a different attitude toward nature than those who live in the country?

5. (a) What words and phrases best help you to picture the locusts fanning their wings in the morning? (b) In your opinion, what do these images add to the story?

Connect

6. **Big Idea** Colonialism and Postcolonialism Lessing writes that "I believe that the chief gift from Africa to writers . . . is the continent itself. . . . Africa gives you the knowledge that man is a small creature, among other creatures, in a large landscape." How does Lessing communicate this feeling of smallness in "A Mild Attack of Locusts"?

7. **Connect to the Author** Lessing's fiction has been called "deeply autobiographical." Reread the biographical information on page 1238. What elements of her life might Lessing have used in this story?

Primary Visual Artifact

Locust Swarms

The species of locust featured in Lessing's story is known as the desert locust. Desert locusts are short-horned grasshoppers (family *Acrididae*)  that are known to change their behavior and form swarms of adults or bands of hoppers. Swarms typically fly with the wind at a speed of about 16–19 kilometers an hour and can travel up to 130 kilometers a day. Locust swarms can vary from less than one square kilometer to several hundred square kilometers. There can be at least 40 million and sometimes as many as 80 million locust adults in each square kilometer of swarm. A very small part of an average swarm eats the same amount of food in one day as about ten elephants, twenty-five camels, or 2,500 people.

Group Activity Discuss the following questions with your classmates.

1. Find a short passage in "A Mild Attack of Locusts" that this photo might be used to illustrate.

2. How does the photo help you understand Margaret's feelings of hopelessness and despair?

Primary Visual Artifact

1. The photo could be used to illustrate the passage "Looking out, all the trees were queer and still, clotted with insects, their boughs weighed to the ground."

2. It shows how pervasive, overwhelming, and intimidating a swarm of locusts can be.

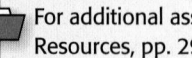 For additional assessment, see Assessment Resources, pp. 291–292.

Literary Element   Theme

A story's **theme**, or central message about life, is sometimes stated, or expressed directly. More often, though, the theme is **implied**, or revealed gradually through events, dialogue, description, or a character's actions. Remember, though, that works of literature can have more than one theme. Because of this, a story might directly express one theme and then imply a range of others.

One way to identify a story's theme is to ask yourself what the main character learns during the course of the story. What does the character think or believe at the story's outset? How, at the end of the story, has this perspective changed? Usually, the lesson learned by the main character has a strong connection to the message the author hopes to send the reader.

1. What stated theme appears in the first paragraph of the story?

2. What lesson about farming does Margaret learn from her experiences in the story?

3. What more general lesson about life—what implied theme—can you extrapolate from the lesson Margaret learns?

Review: Title

As you learned on page 1048, the **title** of a literary work may serve a number of purposes. It may identify the setting, provide insight into the theme, or describe the story's main action. The title "A Mild Attack of Locusts" serves several purposes. First, it describes what will appear in the story—a swarm of locusts. Second, it describes the farmers' reaction to the attack, which they say was not as bad as it might have been.

1. In what way is the title an understatement? What idea does Lessing wish to emphasize?

2. Come up with another title for this story. Why do you think your alternate title is appropriate?

 **Literature** Online

Selection Resources For Selection Quizzes, eFlashcards, and Reading-Writing Connection activities, go to glencoe.com and enter QuickPass code GLB9817u7.

Reading Strategy   Analyze Conflict

When conflict is **external**, a struggle occurs between a character and some outside force. When conflict is **internal**, a character struggles with two or more competing feelings or desires. Review the chart you made as you read.

1. With what internal feelings does Margaret struggle?

2. Which of these do you consider more central to the story? Why?

Vocabulary Practice

Practice with Word Origins Create a word map, like the one below, for each of these vocabulary words from the selection. Use a dictionary for help.

acrid   irremediable   imminent

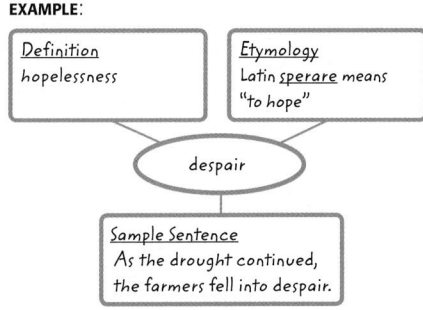

Academic Vocabulary

The initial energetic response of the men in the story contradicts their **overall** *attitude of calm resignation toward the locusts.*

Overall is an academic word that also appears in everyday usage. A runner in a marathon, for example, might be said to have finished first in his age category and fourth **overall**.

To further explore the meaning of this word, answer the following question: What is your **overall** impression of the story's characters?

For more on academic vocabulary, see pages 56 and R81.

DORIS LESSING   **1247**

After You Read

Assess

Literary Element

1. To have an opinion requires experience.

2. Calamities are a part of farm life, and they can be faced and overcome.

3. Suggested theme: humans have the ability to survive disaster.

Review: Title

1. The locust attack was actually quite severe, stripping all vegetation from the farm. Lessing wants to emphasize the fact that farmers can overcome most disasters.

2. Answers may relate to Margaret's character or to a theme.

Reading Strategy

1. Her fear of the locusts and feelings of ignorance.

2. Answers will vary. Some may say Margaret's internal conflicts because Margaret learns that her attitude toward locusts—and toward any outside threat—can be altered.

Progress Check

Can students analyze conflict?

If No → See Unit 7 Teaching Resources Book, p. 108.

Vocabulary Practice

acrid

Definition: burning, biting, or irritating to the taste or smell

Etymology: Latin *acer* means "sharp" or "sour"

Sample Sentence: I accidentally melted the plastic handle of the spatula, filling the kitchen with an *acrid* smell.

irremediable

Definition: not subject to remedy or cure

Etymology: Latin *remedium* means "to heal"

Sample Sentence: The doctors tried their best, but my grandfather's illness was *irremediable*.

imminent

Definition: about to happen; impending

Etymology: Latin *imminere* means "to overhang"

Sample Sentence: Having forgotten to study for the test, I sensed that failure was *imminent*.

Academic Vocabulary

Possible answer: My overall impression is that their lives are difficult and unpredictable.

After You Read

Assess

 ## Respond Through Writing

Students' persuasive essays should:

- take a clear position on what will happen to Margaret
- be supported with examples and quotations from the text, logical explanations, and persuasive techniques
- use apostrophes correctly to show possession in subjects with both regular and irregular plurals

> For grammar practice, see Unit 7 Teaching Resources Book, p. 110.

 # Respond Through Writing

Persuasive Essay

Argue a Position Do you think that Margaret will successfully adapt to life as a farmer? Explain and defend your opinion in a persuasive essay. Support your argument using evidence from the selection as well as from your own experiences and knowledge of human nature.

Prewrite Reread the selection, using a two-column chart to take notes on statements and actions that reveal aspects of Margaret's character and can help you predict how she will change. In one column, record quotations and examples that suggest she will adjust to farm life and in the other, evidence that suggests she will not.

Will adjust	Won't adjust
was learning farmers' language	didn't know how to help
"felt like a survivor after war"	"was trying to get used to the idea of three or four years of locusts"

Then evaluate the entries in your chart, weighing the support for each column to determine which point of view you support.

Draft State your opinion clearly and succinctly. Next, present your evidence, explaining logically how each fact, example, or quotation supports your claim. Use persuasive techniques, such as emotional appeals and choice of words with appropriate connotations, to strengthen your arguments.

Also consider opposing arguments and refute them with solid evidence and reasoning. Sentence structures like the following can help you support your own claims and critique those of others' objections.

Their assertion that _____ is contradicted by _____.

Revise Ask a peer reader to review your draft, focusing on its logical structure and the support for your arguments. Rework your writing as necessary, being sure to note sources for your information. Then use the Writing Workshop checklist on page 652 to determine where your essay may need further revision.

Edit and Proofread Proofread your paper, correcting any errors in spelling, grammar, and punctuation. Use the Grammar Tip in the side column to help you with apostrophes.

1248 UNIT 7 AN INTERNATIONAL LITERATURE

> **Grammar Tip**
>
> **Apostrophes**
>
> Use **apostrophes** in your argument to show possession and clearly attribute ideas and opinions.
>
> Use **'s** to show possession for irregular plural subjects—those that don't end in *s* (e.g., *people's, men's*) as well as all singular subjects (e.g., *Margaret's, lass's*).
>
> *I suspect that most **people's** predictions would be that Margaret would adjust well to her life.*
>
> Add an apostrophe alone for regular plural subjects that end in *s* (e.g., *farmers'*).
>
> *I think that the **locusts'** invasion was just the beginning of Margaret's challenges*

Listening and Speaking Practice

 **Persuasive Speech** Have students use their persuasive essay to prepare a speech or presentation. Using their essay as a starting point, have students adapt the language as necessary and rehearse their speech with a partner to practice intonation, expression, and eye contact. You may want to have students with opposing viewpoints prepare a debate or forum-style presentation.

Meet **Nadine Gordimer**
(born 1923)

Nadine Gordimer grew up in a South Africa that was divided along racial lines. Born in a mining town near the capital, Johannesburg, Gordimer was the daughter of wealthy parents of European descent. As a member of the white minority—and in the care of an overprotective mother—Gordimer was sheltered from the harsher effects of apartheid, South Africa's official policy of racial segregation (which was abolished in the early 1990s). During frequent trips to the library, the young Gordimer began reading about the injustices suffered by her black compatriots, and as her awareness of their problems grew, so did her desire to help.

> "I did not, at the beginning, expect to earn a living by being read. I wrote as a child out of the joy of apprehending life through my senses—the look and scent and feel of things."
>
> —Nadine Gordimer

In Black and White Gordimer began writing by the age of nine, and her first story was published in a Johannesburg magazine when she was only fifteen. Gordimer has referred to herself as a "natural writer"—one who never made a conscious decision to write.

As Gordimer matured, her writing became more consciously concerned with the dehumanizing effects of racial prejudice. Throughout the 1950s and 1960s, Gordimer published novels and collections of short stories that explored issues related to apartheid: the narrow-mindedness of small-town life, the psychology of the master/servant relationship, the paranoia resulting from colonialism, and the superficial liberalism of her privileged peers.

Writing and Politics Gordimer is often praised for her skillful handling of sensitive political and social themes. Her writing is distinguished by a dispassionate tone that is free from sentimentality or bias. To achieve objectivity, Gordimer often presents several different, opposing perspectives on an event or situation in her stories. Gordimer claims that an author can transcend his or her own politics but still remain engaged in the political realities of the time.

Although several of her books were banned in South Africa before the demise of apartheid, Gordimer, unlike many of her contemporaries, refused to go into exile. Gordimer has periodically left South Africa for lecture tours and teaching assignments in the United States, but she has remained a citizen of her native country to this day. She is a long-time member of the African National Congress, the nation's governing political party since 1994, and is a founding member of the Congress of South African Writers. Gordimer has received many awards for her work, including the Nobel Prize in Literature in 1991.

LOG ON ▶ **Literature** Online

Author Search For more about Nadine Gordimer, go to glencoe.com and enter QuickPass code GLB9817u7.

Bellringer Options

Selection Focus
Transparency 67

Daily Language Practice
Transparency 109

Or have students think about a time they had to bargain or haggle for something. **Ask:** What reasons might a person have for bargaining, or haggling, for something? Do you think most people haggle to get a fair deal, or do you think they are trying to take advantage of a buyer or seller? (Students' responses will vary, but they should justify their responses.)

Selection Skills

Literary Elements
- Setting (SE pp. 1250–1256)
- Symbol (SE p. 1256)

The Train from Rhodesia

Listening/Speaking/ Viewing Skills
- Analyze Art (SE pp. 1251, 1253)

Reading Skills
- Visualize (SE pp. 1250–1257)

Vocabulary Skills
- Context Clues (SE p. 1250, 1257)

Writing Skills/Grammar
- Apply Figurative Language (SE p. 1257)
- Use Repetition (TE p. 1254)

Before You Read

Focus

Summary

While an African train is standing in the station, local artisans offer their wares to the passengers. Among the passengers are a young husband and wife on holiday. The wife is interested in buying a carving of a lion but decides that the price is too high. Without her knowledge, her husband buys it for a bargained price. When he presents it to her, she feels furious and empty when she thinks of how little the artisan was paid.

 For summaries in languages other than English, see Unit 7 Teaching Resources Book, pp. 113–118.

Vocabulary

Context Clues Remind students that a word's context is the text that surrounds it: the sentence in which it appears and the sentences around it. **Ask:** What kinds of clues to a word's meaning might you find in its context? (*synonyms, antonyms, definitions, explanations*) Then, have students, working in four groups, provide context clues for the vocabulary words.

 For additional vocabulary practice, see Unit 7 Teaching Resources Book, p. 121.

1250

Literature and Reading Preview

Connect to the Story

Have you ever traveled someplace where you felt a distinct divide between tourists and local people? Freewrite for a few minutes about what it means to be a good traveler in another culture.

Build Background

"The Train from Rhodesia" takes place during the early or mid-1900s at an African train station, where black merchants are selling their wares to white passengers. Under apartheid, blacks in South Africa could not vote in elections, own property, or live in certain areas. Denied basic rights, many blacks lived in poverty, eking out a living by selling goods to white tourists.

Set Purposes for Reading

Big Idea Colonialism and Postcolonialism

In "The Train from Rhodesia," the physical separation of characters symbolizes a broader social barrier between groups of people. As you read, ask yourself, What signs of separation can I find here?

Literary Element Setting

Setting refers to the time and place in which the events of a story occur. The setting of a story can include not only physical surroundings, but also the ideas, customs, values, and beliefs of the people who live there. As you read this story, ask yourself, How do the characters interact with their surroundings?

Reading Strategy Visualize

When you **visualize**, you form mental pictures of what is happening in the story based on the details provided by the narrator. Picturing the story's setting or events in your mind's eye can help you determine when the point of view, or perspective, is shifting from one character to another. As you read, ask yourself, What picture does this description call to mind?

Tip: Taking Notes As you read, note how certain objects or events appear—and who is viewing them.

Appearance or Effect	Observer
"The train came out of the red horizon ..."	the stationmaster

Learning Objectives

For pages 1249–1257

In studying this text, you will focus on the following objectives:

Literary Study: Analyzing setting.

Reading: Visualizing.

Writing: Applying figurative language in a description.

Vocabulary

vendor (ven′ dər) *n.* one who sells goods; p. 1251 *The vendor offered a selection of sandwiches and drinks.*

career (kə rēr′) *v.* to move or run with a swift headlong motion; to rush or dash along; p. 1253 *The children careered toward the playground with squeals of delight.*

wryly (rī′ lē) *adv.* in a twisted or distorted manner; p. 1255 *Her face twisted wryly with displeasure.*

sinew (sin′ ū) *n.* a tendon; p. 1255 *The sculpture represented every muscle and sinew in the athlete's body.*

Tip: Context Clues You can often figure out the meaning of an unfamiliar word by looking for clues in the surrounding words or sentences. Consider the sentence *The vendor sold a wide variety of fresh fruits and vegetables.* Since the vendor sells fruits and vegetables, you can infer that a *vendor* is someone who sells something.

Reading Practice

 **Develop Questions** Tell students that they can frame questions about a story before they begin to read. Then, as they read, they will look for answers to their questions. Have students work in pairs to generate two questions about an element of the story. Model the activity. **Say:** I wonder what will happen in the story when the tourists interact with local people?

Remind students that they can draw questions from the Before You Read pages as well, such as "I wonder what Postcolonialism has to do with the story?" Then, after they read, revisit the questions to see what answers students found in the story.

The Refreshment Car. Poster, 1928. Victoria and Albert Museum, London.

<u>View the Art</u> In the early part of the twentieth century, railroad travel was considered an elegant way to travel, and wealthy travelers could expect any possible luxury. What details in this image suggest this view of railways? How does the image compare to railway cars you have seen recently?

The Train from Rhodesia

Nadine Gordimer

☆ The train came out of the red horizon and bore down toward them over the single straight track. The stationmaster came out of his little brick station with its pointed chalet roof, feeling the creases in his serge[1] uniform in his legs as well. A stir of preparedness rippled through

the squatting native <u>vendors</u> waiting in the dust; the face of a carved wooden animal, eternally surprised, stuck out of a sack. The stationmaster's barefoot children wandered over. From the gray mud huts with the untidy heads that stood within a decorated mud wall, chick-

---

1. *Serge* is a twilled cloth.

1 Setting *In what physical surroundings is this story set?*

Vocabulary

vendor (ven′ dər) n. one who sells goods

NADINE GORDIMER **1251**

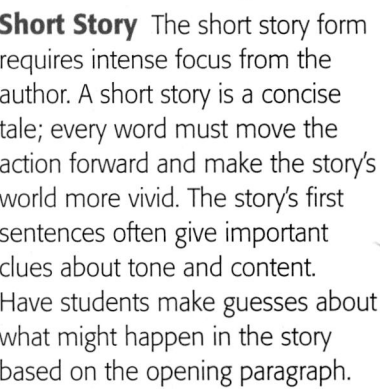

Teach

For additional literary element practice, see Unit 7 Teaching Resources Book, p. 119.

Big Idea | 1

Colonialism and Postcolonialism **Say:** This page begins with many details about the stationmaster's family. On the basis of these details, is the stationmaster a powerful person or a member of the servant class in this society? *(He is a member of the servant class.)*

ENGLISH LEARNERS Help English learners understand the figurative language used in this passage. Tell students that the "faces . . . drinking beer" stands for the people in the dining car. **Ask:** What barrier keeps the man from seeing and knowing the people in the dining car? *(the glass windows)*

Reading Strategy | 2

Visualize **Answer:** *The woman is in the train, looking down on the old man on the ground. This arrangement symbolizes the fact that in colonial Africa white Europeans perceived themselves as superior to black natives.*

Literary Element | 3

Setting **Answer:** *The interior world of the train represents the insulated, wealthy white world of the Europeans; the exterior world of the station platform represents the impoverished world of native Africans.*

---

1 ens, and dogs with their skin stretched like parchment over their bones, followed the piccanins[2] down to the track. The flushed and perspiring west cast a reflection, faint, without heat, upon the station, upon the tin shed marked "Goods," upon the walled kraal,[3] upon the gray tin house of the stationmaster and upon the sand, that lapped all around, from sky to sky, cast little rhythmical cups of shadow, so that the sand became the sea, and closed over the children's black feet softly and without imprint.

The stationmaster's wife sat behind the mesh of her verandah. Above her head the hunk of a sheep's carcass moved slightly, dangling in a current of air.

They waited.

The train called out, along the sky; but there was no answer; and the cry hung on: I'm coming . . . I'm coming . . .

The engine flared out now, big, whisking a dwindling body behind it; the track flared out to let it in.

Creaking, jerking, jostling, gasping, the train filled the station.

Here, let me see that one—the young woman curved her body further out of the corridor window. Missus? smiled the old boy, looking at the creatures he held in his hand. From a piece of string on his gray finger hung a tiny woven basket; he lifted it, questioning. No, no, she urged, leaning down toward him, across the height of the train, toward the man in the piece of old rug; that one, that one, her hand commanded. It was a lion, carved out of soft dry wood that looked like spongecake; heraldic,[4] black and white, with impressionistic detail burnt in. The old man held

---

2. *Piccanins* is a name some people used for black children in Africa.
3. A *kraal* is an enclosure for livestock.
4. The lion is *heraldic* because it resembles the rearing lions often found on coats of arms (or family crests). Heraldry is the craft of describing and representing coats of arms.

2 Visualize *Visualize the arrangement in space of the woman and the old man. What does it tell you about their relationship?*

1252 UNIT 7   AN INTERNATIONAL LITERATURE

---

it up to her still smiling, not from the heart, but at the customer. Between its Vandyke teeth, in the mouth opened in an endless roar too terrible to be heard, it had a black tongue. Look, said the young husband, if you don't mind! And round the neck of the thing, a piece of fur (rat? rabbit? meerkat?); a real mane, majestic, telling you somehow that the artist had delight in the lion.

Visual Vocabulary
Vandyke means "V-shaped," as in a Vandyke beard.

All up and down the length of the train in the dust the artists sprang, walking bent, like performing animals, the better to exhibit the fantasy held toward the faces on the train. Buck, startled and stiff, staring with round black and white eyes. More lions, standing erect, grappling[5] with strange, thin, elongated warriors who clutched spears and showed no fear in their slits of eyes. How much, they asked from the train, how much?

Give me penny, said the little ones with nothing to sell. The dogs went and sat, quite still, under the dining car, where the train breathed out the smell of meat cooking with onion.

A man passed beneath the arch of reaching arms meeting gray-black and white in the exchange of money for the staring wooden eyes, the stiff wooden legs sticking up in the air; went along under the voices and the bargaining, interrogating the wheels. Past the dogs; glancing up at the dining car where he could stare at the faces, behind glass, drinking beer, two by two, on either side of a uniform railway vase with its pale dead flower. Right to the end, to the guard's van, where the stationmaster's children had just collected their mother's two loaves of bread; to the engine itself, where the stationmaster and

---

5. *Grappling* means "wrestling."

Setting *What two worlds, or settings, are divided by the window? What do these two worlds represent?* **3**

Literary Element Practice

SPIRAL REVIEW **Figurative Language** Gordimer uses metaphors, similes, and personification to describe vividly. In the first paragraph, "the sand became the sea, and closed over the children's black feet . . ." In the fourth paragraph, the train "called out . . . I'm coming . . . I'm coming . . ." **Ask:** Are these descriptions meant literally or figuratively? How do these descriptions help readers to form a mental image of what happens in the story? Is each an example of metaphor, simile, or personification? Challenge students to find and discuss other examples of figurative language on this page.

Compartment C, Car 293, 1938. Edward Hopper. Oil on canvas.

 View the Art Like Gordimer, Hopper often focused on themes of isolation or alienation. How does this image compare with your mental picture of the young woman in the story? ★

the driver stood talking against the steaming complaint of the resting beast.

The man called out to them, something loud and joking. They turned to laugh, in a twirl of steam. The two children **careered** over the sand, clutching the bread, and burst through the iron gate and up the path through the garden in which nothing grew.

5 Passengers drew themselves in at the corridor windows and turned into compartments to fetch money, to call someone to look. Those sitting inside looked up: suddenly different, caged faces, boxed in, cut off, after the contact of outside. There was an orange a piccanin

4 Colonialism and Postcolonialism *How does this sentence portray European colonists in Africa?*

Vocabulary

career (kə rēr′) *v.* to move or run with a swift head-long motion; to rush or dash along

would like. . . . What about that chocolate? It wasn't very nice. . . .

A young girl had collected a handful of the hard kind, that no one liked, out of the chocolate box, and was throwing them to the dogs, over at the dining car. But the hens darted in, and swallowed the chocolates, incredibly quick and accurate, before they had even dropped in the dust, and the dogs, a little bewildered, looked up with their brown eyes, not expecting anything. **5**

—No, leave it, said the girl, don't take it. . . .

Too expensive, too much, she shook her head and raised her voice to the old boy, giving up the lion. He held it up where she had handed it to him. No, she said, shaking her head. Three-and-six?[6] insisted her husband,

6. *Three-and-six* is three shillings and sixpence, the equivalent today of somewhere between five and twenty American dollars, depending on the exact time the story takes place.

NADINE GORDIMER **1253**

English Learners

DIFFERENTIATED INSTRUCTION

Intermediate As they read the story, support English learners' comprehension of long sentences. Model breaking long sentences into smaller parts, or "chunks." Have students determine the meaning of each sentence part. Then model how to synthesize the meanings.

Approaching Level

DIFFERENTIATED INSTRUCTION

Emerging Explain to approaching-level students that Gordimer often moves her focus from one place or character to another, similar to a movie camera. Ask them to reread this page and identify how Gordimer switches her focus.

Big Idea | **4**

Colonialism and Postcolonialism **Answer:**
The sentence implies that the European colonists are intruders in Africa, alienated by wealth, power, and comfort from the land and its people.

(APPROACHING) To guide approaching-level students, **write** these words and phrases on the board: *caged, boxed in, cut off.* **Ask:** What do these phrases often describe? *(animals in zoos, prisoners in cells, people trying to get somewhere but held back by obstacles)*

Literary Element | **5**

Setting **Say:** The stationmaster's children are shown clutching bread and bursting into a garden where nothing grows. The girl on the train throws chocolates to the animals below. **Ask:** What does this indicate about how these people live? *(Some people struggle to meet their basic needs, while others have luxuries.)*

View the Art ★

Answer: *The young woman in the image, like the one in Gordimer's story, seems well-off, a bit isolated, and sits alone in a compartment like the one described. Unlike the woman in the story, she is calm and collected.*

Originally trained as a commercial illustrator, Edward Hopper (1882–1967) gradually focused his creative energy on painting realistic urban settings. Critics often comment on the feeling of loneliness conveyed by many of Hopper's paintings, which sometimes feature solitary figures.

Teach

Setting **Answer:** *She realizes that the artifacts the old man is selling derive their beauty from their native setting and that when they are removed from Africa, they may look out of place and lose their beauty and significance.*

ENGLISH LEARNERS Have English learners reread the sentence that precedes the woman's questions that she asks herself beginning with "But the wooden buck…"

Ask: What do the words *they* and *them* refer to in the woman's questions? *(the wooden artifacts–the buck, hippos, and elephants–that the woman has already collected during her trip to Africa)*

Colonialism and Postcolonialism **Answer:** *After reboarding the train, the Europeans feel "safe" within their cocoon of wealth and luxury. The implication is that native Africans and the world they live in are dangerous, inferior, or contaminated. The Europeans "could not see beyond" these prejudices because they are insulated from reality behind the symbolic glass barrier of the train window.*

loudly. Yes baas! laughed the boy. *Three-and-six?*—the young man was incredulous. Oh leave it—she said. The young man stopped. Don't you want it? he said, keeping his face closed to the boy. No, never mind, she said, leave it. The old native kept his head on one side, looking at them sideways, holding the lion. Three-and-six, he murmured, as old people repeat things to themselves.

The young woman drew her head in. She went into the coupé[7] and sat down. Out of the window, on the other side, there was nothing; sand and bush; a thorn tree. Back through the open doorway, past the figure of her husband in the corridor, there was the station, the voices, wooden animals waving, running feet. Her eye followed the funny little valance of scrolled wood that outlined the chalet roof of the station; she thought of the lion and smiled. That bit of fur round the neck. But the wooden buck, the hippos, the elephants, the baskets that already bulked out of their brown paper under the seat and on the luggage rack! How will they look at home? Where will you put them? What will they mean away from the

---

7. On British trains, a *coupé* is a half-compartment at the end of a passenger car with only one row of seats.

1 Setting *What realization about an artifact and its setting does the woman have?*

places you found them? Away from the unreality of the last few weeks? The man outside. But he is not part of the unreality; he is for good now. Odd . . . somewhere there was an idea that he, that living with him, was part of the holiday, the strange places.

Outside, a bell rang. The stationmaster was leaning against the end of the train, green flag rolled in readiness. A few men who had got down to stretch their legs sprang on to the train, clinging to the observation platforms, or perhaps merely standing on the iron step, holding the rail; but on the train, safe from the one dusty platform, the one tin house, the empty sand.

There was a grunt. The train jerked. Through the glass the beer drinkers looked out, as if they could not see beyond it. Behind the fly-screen, the stationmaster's wife sat facing back at them beneath the darkening hunk of meat.

There was a shout. The flag drooped out. Joints not yet coordinated, the segmented body of the train heaved and bumped back against itself. It began to move; slowly the scrolled chalet moved past it, the yells of the natives, running alongside, jetted up into the air, fell back at different levels. Staring wooden faces waved drunkenly, there, then gone, questioning for the last time at the windows. Here, one-and-six baas!—As one automatically opens a hand to catch a thrown ball, a man fumbled wildly down his pocket, brought up the shilling and sixpence and threw them out; the old native, gasping, his skinny toes splaying the sand, flung the lion.

The piccanins were waving, the dogs stood, tails uncertain, watching the train go: past the mud huts, where a woman turned to look, up from the smoke of the fire, her hand pausing on her hip.

The stationmaster went slowly in under the chalet.

The old native stood, breath blowing out the skin between his ribs, feet tense, balanced

---

Colonialism and Postcolonialism *What is implied in this passage about the European colonialists' attitude toward, and understanding of, native black Africans?* **2**

Writing Practice

PARTNERS SPIRAL REVIEW **Use Repetition** Have students practice the technique of repetition in their own writing to assess the technique's effectiveness. Have students pair up and **say:** Imagine that a seven-year-old child has spotted a small toy while shopping with a parent. The child has set his or her heart on the toy, but the parent does not intend to buy it. Write a dialogue in which both characters use repetition to win the argument—but do not tell who wins. When students have finished their dialogues, have them read their lines dramatically. For each dialogue, **ask:** What words and phrases were repeated effectively? Which character will win the dispute?

in the sand, smiling and shaking his head. In his opened palm, held in the attitude of receiving, was the retrieved shilling and sixpence.

The blind end of the train was being pulled helplessly out of the station.

The young man swung in from the corridor, breathless. He was shaking his head with laughter and triumph. Here! he said. And waggled the lion at her. One-and-six!

What? she said.

He laughed. I was arguing with him for fun, bargaining—when the train had pulled out already, he came tearing after. . . . One-and-six Baas! So there's your lion.

She was holding it away from her, the head with the open jaws, the pointed teeth, the black tongue, the wonderful ruff of fur facing her. She was looking at it with an expression of not seeing, of seeing something different. Her face was drawn up, **wryly,** like the face of a discomforted child. Her mouth lifted nervously at the corner. Very slowly, cautious, she lifted her finger and touched the mane, where it was joined to the wood.

But how could you, she said. He was shocked by the dismay of her face.

Good Lord, he said, what's the matter?

If you wanted the thing, she said, her voice rising and breaking with the shrill impotence of anger, why didn't you buy it in the first place? If you wanted it, why didn't you pay for it? Why didn't you take it decently, when he offered it? Why did you have to wait for him to run after the train with it, and give him one-and-six? One-and-six!

She was pushing it at him, trying to force him to take it. He stood astonished, his hands hanging at his sides.

But you wanted it! You liked it so much?

—It's a beautiful piece of work, she said fiercely, as if to protect it from him.

You liked it so much! You said yourself it was too expensive—

Oh *you*—she said, hopeless and furious. *You.* . . . She threw the lion on to the seat.

He stood looking at her.

She sat down again in the corner and, her face slumped in her hand, stared out of the window. Everything was turning round inside her. One-and-six. One-and-six. One-and-six for the wood and the carving and the **sinews** of the legs and the switch of the tail. The mouth open like that and the teeth. The black tongue, rolling, like a wave. The mane round the neck. To give one-and-six for that. The heat of shame mounted through her legs and body and sounded in her ears like the sound of sand pouring. Pouring, pouring. She sat there, sick. A weariness, a tastelessness, the discovery of a void made her hands slacken their grip, atrophy[8] emptily, as if the hour was not worth their grasp. She was feeling like this again. She had thought it was something to do with singleness, with being alone and belonging too much to oneself.

She sat there not wanting to move or speak, or to look at anything, even; so that the mood should be associated with nothing, no object, word or sight that might recur and so recall the feeling again. . . . Smuts blew in grittily, settled on her hands. Her back remained at exactly the same angle, turned against the young man sitting with his hands drooping between his sprawled legs, and the lion, fallen on its side in the corner.

The train had cast the station like a skin. It called out to the sky, I'm coming, I'm coming; and again, there was no answer.

---

8. Here, *atrophy* means "go slack; weaken."

Colonialism and Postcolonialism What **epiphany,** or sudden realization, does the woman experience in this passage? **3**

Visualize What does the body language of each character symbolize? **4**

NADINE GORDIMER **1255**

Teach

Big Idea   3

Colonialism and Postcolonialism Answer:
She recognizes the demeaning nature of the relationship between European colonialists and native Africans. She is ashamed that by haggling over the price of the artifact, her husband has devalued the old man's craftsmanship and ignored his need to earn a livelihood. She feels that all of her values have been shattered.

ENGLISH LEARNERS Have English learners use a dictionary to learn the meaning of *wryly* and *sinews.* Then, have them demonstrate their understanding by having them smile wryly. Finally, have them apply both words' meanings in original sentences.

Reading Strategy   4

Visualize **Answer:** *The woman's posture symbolizes rejection of the man's values. Her husband's posture symbolizes helplessness and bewilderment. Both disregard the carved lion, which symbolizes their estrangement.*

Writer's Technique

Repetition The author repeats the phrase "one-and-six" many times to underscore the woman's shame and incredulity that her husband has paid so little to the artist who made the lion figure.

 To check students' understanding of the selection, see Unit 7 Teaching Resources Book, p. 124.

After You Read

Assess

1. Answers will vary.
2. (a) A carving of a roaring lion painted black-and-white and adorned with a fur collar (b) A well-crafted work of art that the old man takes pride in—not a mere souvenir
3. (a) The price is too much. (b) She has had a sudden insight into the exploitation of native Africans by Europeans.
4. The carving is a work of art and worth more than her husband paid.
5. It may force the reader to concentrate more on what the characters are saying.
6. The buying and selling of goods is skewed in favor of the Europeans.
7. Most students will say that yes, the narrator seems to have some sympathy for the young woman, especially when she has had her epiphany. Gordimer may have wanted to give the impression that she felt both sides suffered under the social codes, although the colonists suffered less, and should have done things differently.

Literary Element

1. Leaving the time and place unspecified gives the story a universal feeling, suggesting that the effects of colonialism are far-reaching in both time and space.
2. The woman and, to a greater extent, her husband become cheapened as their desire for souvenirs—and the "fun" of haggling—are exposed as exploitation.

After You Read

Respond and Think Critically

Respond and Interpret

1. Were you surprised by the woman's reaction to her husband's purchase of the carving? Explain.
2. (a) Describe the artifact the old man wants to sell to the woman. (b) What does the description of the artifact imply about its value?
3. (a) Why does the woman decide against buying the carved lion? (b) What does her reaction to her husband's "bargain" suggest about her new perspective?

Analyze and Evaluate

4. The man is confused by the woman's reaction to the purchase. How would you explain to him what she is feeling?

5. Gordimer does not use quotation marks to set off the dialogue in this story. How does this aspect of her style affect your reading of the story?

Connect

6. **Big Idea** Colonialism and Postcolonialism How might the economics at work in this story be viewed as a microcosm, or small-scale representation, of colonial economics?

7. **Connect to the Author** Do you think the narrator is sympathetic to the young woman in the story? Why might Gordimer want to give—or not give—that impression?

Literary Element | Setting

In a sense, "The Train from Rhodesia" is a story about setting itself—and about what happens when two very different settings collide. Occupying the world *inside* the train—the European world of tourism and travel—are the woman who admires the merchant's carved lion and the husband who haggles over it "for fun." Occupying the world *outside* the train is the vendor himself, whose livelihood depends upon haggling effectively. As the woman interacts with this foreign setting and its inhabitants, she comes to realize that she lives in a fantasy world and that the real world exists outside. By juxtaposing these two settings, Gordimer also invites the reader to expand or revise his or her view of Africa—to consider how it has been altered, and in some ways infected, by its colonial history.

1. Why do you think Gordimer does not specify the exact time and place of the story?
2. One result of the contact between the two worlds is that the lion carving becomes cheapened. What else—or who else—becomes cheapened in the transaction? Explain.

Review: Symbol

As you learned on page 715, a **symbol** is any object, person, place, or experience that exists on a literal level but also represents something beyond itself. Stories are not limited to a single symbol, however. Often, objects and events that occur around the central symbol extend or deepen the symbolic power of the story as a whole.

Group Activity Read each quotation from the story in the three examples below. Then discuss possible symbolic meanings of the boldfaced words.

1. "From a piece of string on his gray finger hung a tiny woven basket; he lifted it, questioning. No, no, she urged, **leaning down toward him**, across the height of the train . . . that one, that one, her hand commanded. It was a **lion**, carved out of soft dry wood . . . "
2. "All up and down the length of the train in the dust **the artists** sprang, walking bent, like performing animals, the better to exhibit the fantasy held toward the **faces on the train**."
3. "The **train** had cast the **station** like a skin."

Review: Symbol

1. The woman's leaning may symbolize condescending European colonial attitudes toward native Africans; the carved lion may symbolize the goods extracted by European colonialists.
2. The artists may symbolize native Africans who demean themselves by entertaining Europeans; the faces on the train may symbolize Europeans who take advantage of Africans by passing through their land without contributing to it.
3. The train may symbolize British colonial presence in Africa; the station may symbolize Africa, which the colonialists leave behind as a snake sloughs off its skin.

Reading Strategy — Visualize

In the same way that an artist arranges people and objects on a canvas, an author arranges people and objects in the space of a story's setting. **Visualizing** these spatial arrangements can help you understand the relationships and conflicts between characters.

Read each passage from the story below. Then identify the perspective or the relationship suggested by the description.

1. "Creaking, jerking, jostling, gasping, the train filled the station." (page 1252)

2. "Back through the open doorway, past the figure of her husband in the corridor, there was the station, the voices, wooden animals waving, running feet." (page 1254)

Vocabulary Practice

Practice with Context Clues Identify the context clues in each of the following sentences that help you determine the meaning of the boldfaced vocabulary word.

1. The **vendor** searched through his bag of wares to find the item the shopper requested.

2. The roller coaster began to **career** toward the ground with thrilling speed.

3. She smiled **wryly** upon seeing the mess.

4. The muscles and **sinews** in the cheetah's hind legs flexed as the large cat prepared to leap.

Academic Vocabulary

*The man in the story buys the carving on his wife's **behalf**, but his action ends up angering her.*

Behalf is an academic word that is used in everyday settings. For example, a person might accept an award on **behalf** of an entire group.

To further explore the meaning of this word, describe a time when someone interceded or acted on your **behalf**.

For more on academic vocabulary, see pages 56 and R81.

Write with Style

 Apply Figurative Language

Assignment By using striking figurative language—including personification of the train—in her short story, Nadine Gordimer helps you experience the Rhodesia of her youth first-hand. Use personification and other figurative language to help create a vivid description of an ordinary place.

Get Ideas Journal about the details that make a particular place memorable for you. If possible, revisit the place you're describing. Then create a two-column chart, listing features of the place in one column and human traits or figures of speech describing them in the other.

Give It Structure Flesh out the details you recorded in your chart, using personification to create vivid comparisons. Focus on the descriptive purpose of your writing and the people who will read it.

Look at Language Make sure that the images of figurative language support, rather than compete with, each other. For example, you might want to personify the place as a whole and extend that image as you describe the parts.

EXAMPLE:

As you enter my grandfather's garage, you're sucked into the mouth of a killer whale. Precarious piles of boxes line the walls like flesh-rending teeth, and a tangled intestinal maze of waste swallows you in fetid darkness.

Look over your choice of words to make sure your descriptions are original, not clichéd. The description should sound like your own voice, too—not too stilted or formal.

 Literature Online

Selection Resources For Selection Quizzes, eFlashcards, and Reading-Writing Connection activities, go to glencoe.com and enter QuickPass code GLB9817u7.

NADINE GORDIMER **1257**

Write with Style

Use these criteria in evaluating students' writing:

- It focuses on a specific place.
- The word choice and sentence structure contribute to an original, personal style.
- Personification effectively contributes to a vivid impression of the setting.

 For grammar practice, see Unit 7 Teaching Resources Book, p. 123.

 For additional assessment, see Assessment Resources, pp. 293–294.

After You Read

Assess

Reading Strategy

1. The perspective is that of the stationmaster or one of the vendors at the station. The relationship between the train and those in the station seems to be one of invasion and uproar.

2. The perspective is that of the woman. She has mentally left her husband behind and entered the reality of the train station and its workers and vendors.

Progress Check

Can students visualize?

If No → See Unit 7 Teaching Resources Book, p. 120.

Vocabulary Practice

1. The vendor has "wares" that he is giving to a "shopper," so he must be a person who sells goods.

2. The roller coaster moves with "thrilling speed," so *careered* must mean "moved forward swiftly."

3. The baby "screw[s] up his face," so *wryly* must mean "in a twisted manner."

4. The sinews "flex" along with the cheetah's muscles, indicating that *sinews* means "ligaments" or "tendons."

Academic Vocabulary

Students should describe a time when someone did something to help them.

Bellringer Options

Selection Focus
Transparency 68
Daily Language Practice
Transparency 110

Or show students a map of Africa and have them locate Nigeria. Explain that like many other African nations, Nigeria was once a colony of a European nation, in this case Britain. Tell students that although Nigeria is an oil-rich country with modern cities, many of its people still live in traditional ways. Common occupations include fishing, farming, and herding. Have students look for the two faces of Nigeria in this selection.

Meet **Chinua Achebe**

(born 1930)

Nigerian author Chinua Achebe (chē noo′ ə ə chä′ bä) is considered one of Africa's finest fiction writers. A "strange, early tribute" helped inspire him to pursue a writing career. When he was a university student in Nigeria, a retired English ambassador visited the school and read aloud an amusing limerick Achebe had written. At the time, Achebe had not thought about becoming a writer, but he said, "when I heard my name and nonsense poem recited . . . you could have knocked me over with a feather."

A member of the Ibo (ē′ bō) tribe, Achebe grew up in the village of Ogidi, where his father taught at the local missionary school. His parents, who were devout Protestants, gave him the name Albert. While studying at the University College at Ibadan (which was also the alma mater of prominent Nigerian writer Wole Soyinka), Achebe rejected his European name and adopted the African name Chinualumogu, meaning "My spirit come fight for me." He majored in English literature and decided he wanted to become a writer.

> "At the University I read some appalling European novels about Africa . . . and realized that our story could not be told for us by anyone else."
>
> —Chinua Achebe

Crusader for Biafra From 1954 to 1963, Achebe worked as a producer for the Nigerian Broadcasting Company (NBC) in Lagos, the Nigerian capital. While holding this position, he began his career as a writer with the publication of *Things Fall Apart*

(1958), an immediate triumph. In this novel, Achebe explores the traumatic effects of African contact with Western ways. The protagonist of the novel is a proud village leader who refuses to adopt Western culture.

After Nigeria gained independence from England in 1960, Achebe was one of many who grew disillusioned with the new government, a military dictatorship, and attempted to establish a separate nation in eastern Nigeria called Biafra. As chairman of the Biafra National Guidance Committee, Achebe traveled abroad with other writers, seeking support for the Biafran cause. In the ensuing civil war, approximately one million Ibo died fighting for independence, many from disease and starvation. The collapse of Biafra and its reunification with Nigeria in 1970 prompted Achebe to retire from political life and live abroad, devoting himself to writing and teaching.

Acclaimed Novelist In the late 1970s, when Nigeria once again became a republic, Achebe returned to his native country. A car accident near Lagos in 1990 left him paralyzed below the waist and confined to a wheelchair. He then accepted a teaching position at Bard College in New York.

Achebe's fiction, remarkable for its psychological depth and social insight, is popular throughout the world. In addition to *Things Fall Apart*, his novels include *No Longer at Ease* (1960), *Arrow of God* (1964), *A Man of the People* (1966), and *Anthills of the Savannah* (1987). In 2007, Achebe won the Man Booker International Prize for his work.

Literature Online

Author Search For more about Chinua Achebe, go to glencoe.com and enter QuickPass code GLB9817u7.

Selection Skills

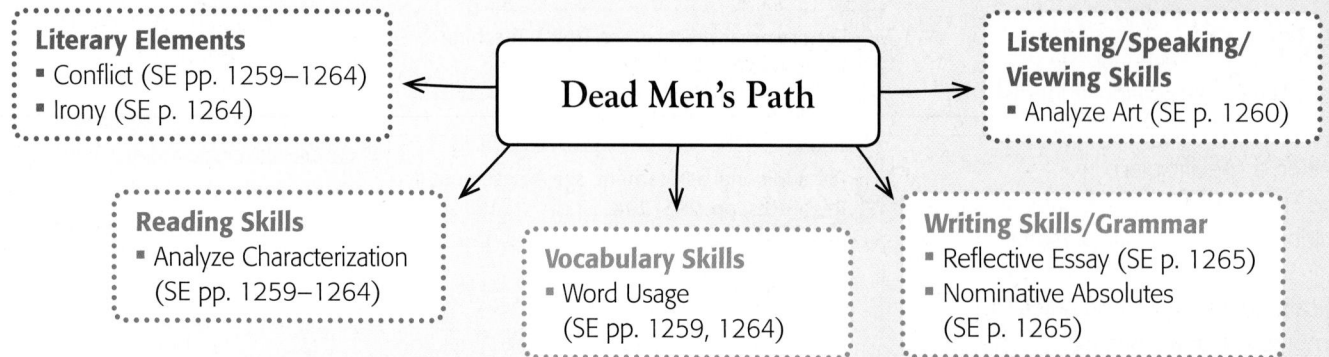

Literary Elements
- Conflict (SE pp. 1259–1264)
- Irony (SE p. 1264)

Dead Men's Path

Listening/Speaking/Viewing Skills
- Analyze Art (SE p. 1260)

Reading Skills
- Analyze Characterization (SE pp. 1259–1264)

Vocabulary Skills
- Word Usage (SE pp. 1259, 1264)

Writing Skills/Grammar
- Reflective Essay (SE p. 1265)
- Nominative Absolutes (SE p. 1265)

Literature and Reading Preview

Connect to the Story

Is progress always a good thing? With a partner, discuss or debate the positives and negatives of modernization.

Build Background

This story is set in a mission school near a small village in Nigeria in 1949. At that time, Nigeria was still a British colony. Mission schools sought to give students a solid academic education and to instruct them in Christian beliefs and traditions. Many of Achebe's stories depict the effects of Western cultures on African traditions. He wrote: "We have been subjected—and have subjected ourselves too—to this period during which we have accepted everything alien as good and practically everything local or native as inferior."

Set Purposes for Reading

Big Idea Colonialism and Postcolonialism

As you read "Dead Men's Path," ask yourself, What is the result of the clash between old African ways and new Western ideas?

Literary Element Conflict

A **conflict**, or struggle between two opposing forces, is central to all plots. In an **external conflict**, the main character struggles against an outside force. This force may be another character, society, nature, or fate. As you read, ask yourself, What external element or obstacle do the characters struggle with?.

Reading Strategy Analyze Characterization

When you **analyze characterization**, you identify and examine the methods that authors use to reveal characters. These methods include describing a character's appearance, actions, speech, and thoughts. As you read, ask yourself, What do I know about this character, and how do I know it?

Tip: Mapping Character Use a web to map Michael Obi's character. Also create webs for Obi's wife and the village priest.

CHINUA ACHEBE **1259**

Learning Objectives

For pages 1258–1265

In studying this text, you will focus on the following objectives:

Literary Study: Identifying conflict.

Reading: Analyzing characterization.

Vocabulary

pivotal (piv′ ət əl) *adj.* of central or vital importance; p. 1260 *Maria's experiences in the army were pivotal in developing her character.*

denigration (den′ i grā′ shən) *n.* defamation of one's character or reputation; slander; p. 1261 *The leader suffered ongoing denigration from his enemies and a hostile press.*

superannuated (sōō pər an′ ū ā tid) *adj.* out of date; p. 1261 *The teenager considered her mother old-fashioned and her taste in clothes superannuated.*

Tip: Word Usage Answering specific questions can help you explore the meaning of a new word. For example, Have you ever participated in the **denigration** of another person and then regretted it?

Before You Read

Focus

Summary

Michael Obi becomes headmaster of a mission school in a village. He and his wife set out to improve the school. When Obi discovers villagers are crossing the school compound, he closes the path. The village priest explains that the path is needed by souls entering and leaving the world. When a young villager dies in childbirth, a diviner calls for a sacrifice to appease the ancestors. Overnight, the school gardens are destroyed, and Obi gets a bad report from his supervisor.

 For summaries in languages other than English, see Unit 7 Teaching Resources Book, pp. 126–131.

Vocabulary

Word Usage Ask: What is more likely to be *pivotal*, a battle or a suitcase? *(battle)* If you received *denigration*, would you be happy or angry? *(angry)*

For additional vocabulary practice, see Unit 7 Teaching Resources Book, p. 134.

Teach

Reading Strategy   1

Analyze Characterization
Answer: *His strength is his desire to help students learn; his pride and intolerance are weaknesses.*

[ENGLISH LEARNERS] For English learners, **say:** Give an antonym for each of the following words: *enthusiasm, condemnation, narrow, older. (indifference, praise, broad, younger)*

View the Art ★

Answer: *Some students will note that the large object at left resembles a bug. The bands on the right side may remind students of snake scales, zebra stripes, wings, or flowers.*

An art form practiced by the Igbo people of Nigeria, *Uli*, began as the practice of women painting each other's bodies. According to legend, the women were copying the designs the earth goddess painted on animals. The practice eventually expanded to painting wall murals. There is no set style, and it can be abstract or representative, but common features include asymmetrical design, the use of concentric patterns, and a reliance on four primary colors—black, reddish-brown, yellow, and white.

For an audio recording of this selection, use Listening Library Audio CD-ROM.

Readability Scores
Dale-Chall: 7.3
DRP: 58
Lexile: 900

DEAD MEN'S PATH
Chinua Achebe

An Igbo mural painting, c. 1980.

View the Art Many recent Nigerian artists continue to use traditional patterns and images, which are said to be based in nature. What patterns or images in this mural remind you of things found in nature?

Michael Obi's hopes were fulfilled much earlier than he had expected. He was appointed headmaster of Ndume Central School in January 1949. It had always been an unprogressive school, so the Mission authorities decided to send a young and energetic man to run it. Obi accepted this responsibility with enthusiasm. He had many wonderful ideas and this was an opportunity to put them into practice. He had had sound secondary school education which designated him a "**pivotal**" teacher in the official records and set him apart from the other headmasters in the mission field. He was outspoken in his condemnation[1] of the narrow views of these older and often less-educated ones.

---

1. *Condemnation* means "the act of severely disapproving of something."

Analyze Characterization *What strengths and weaknesses does Obi bring to his job?*   **1**

Vocabulary

pivotal (piv′ ət əl) *adj.* of central or vital importance

Vocabulary Practice

[SPIRAL REVIEW] **Compound Words** Review with students that a compound word is made up of two or more words put together. In some cases, the words are linked by a hyphen. Readers can sometimes decipher the meanings of these words by examining the meanings of their separate parts. Some examples in this selection are *headmaster, downcast, stoop-shouldered, deep-set, schoolroom,* and *footpath.*

Give students practice by asking them to define these compound words: *wheelchair, chairman, highway, thoroughfare, moonlight, bobsled,* and *countryside.*

"We shall make a good job of it, shan't we?" he asked his young wife when they first heard the joyful news of his promotion.

"We shall do our best," she replied. "We shall have such beautiful gardens and everything will be just *modern* and delightful . . ." In their two years of married life she had become completely infected by his passion for "modern methods" and his **denigration** of "these old and **superannuated** people in the teaching field who would be better employed as traders in the Onitsha² market." She began to see herself already as the admired wife of the young headmaster, the queen of the school.

The wives of the other teachers would envy her position. She would set the fashion in everything . . . Then, suddenly, it occurred to her that there might not be other wives. Wavering between hope and fear, she asked her husband, looking anxiously at him.

"All our colleagues are young and unmarried," he said with enthusiasm which for once she did not share. "Which is a good thing," he continued.

"Why?"

"Why? They will give all their time and energy to the school."

Nancy was downcast. For a few minutes she became skeptical about the new school; but it was only for a few minutes. Her little personal misfortune could not blind her to her husband's happy prospects. She looked at him as he sat folded up in a chair. He was stoop-shouldered and looked frail. But he sometimes surprised people with sudden bursts of physical energy. In his present posture, however, all his bodily strength seemed to have retired behind his deep-set eyes, giving them an extraordinary power of penetration. He was only twenty-six,

but looked thirty or more. On the whole, he was not unhandsome.

"A penny for your thoughts, Mike," said Nancy after a while, imitating the woman's magazine she read.

"I was thinking what a grand opportunity we've got at last to show these people how a school should be run."

Ndume School was backward in every sense of the word. Mr. Obi put his whole life into the work, and his wife hers too. He had two aims. A high standard of teaching was insisted upon, and the school compound³ was to be turned into a place of beauty. Nancy's dream-gardens came to life with the coming of the rains, and blossomed. Beautiful hibiscus and allamanda hedges in brilliant red and yellow marked out the carefully tended school compound from the rank neighborhood bushes.

One evening as Obi was admiring his work he was scandalized to see an old woman from the village hobble right across the compound, through a marigold flower bed and the hedges. On going up there he found faint signs of an almost disused path from the village across the school compound to the bush on the other side.

"It amazes me," said Obi to one of his teachers who had been three years in the school, "that you people allowed the villagers to make use of this footpath. It is simply incredible." He shook his head.

"The path," said the teacher apologetically, "appears to be very important to them. Although it is hardly used, it connects the village shrine with their place of burial."

"And what has that got to do with the school?" asked the headmaster.

"Well, I don't know," replied the other with a shrug of the shoulders. "But I remember there was a big row⁴ some time ago when we attempted to close it."

---

2. *Onitsha* is a commercial city in Nigeria.

 Colonialism and Postcolonialism *How has modernization affected young Nigerians like Obi's wife?*

Vocabulary

denigration (den′ i grā′ shən) *n.* defamation of one's character or reputation; slander

superannuated (soo̅′ pər an′ u̅ ā′ tid) *adj.* out of date

---

3. A *compound* is a group of buildings.
4. As it is used here, a *row* (rou) is a noisy disturbance or quarrel.

Analyze Characterization *What does this detail reveal about Obi?*

Teach

Literary Element | 1

Conflict Answer: *Obi's assertion sets the conflict between his school and the villagers in motion. The villagers sometimes use the path that traverses the school's grounds.*

 For additional literary element practice, see Unit 7 Teaching Resources Book, p. 132.

Reading Strategy | 2

**Analyze Characterization
Answer:** *Tradition*

Literary Element | 3

Conflict Answer: *The Supervisor appreciates the seriousness of exacerbating tension between the school and the village.*

ENGLISH LEARNERS Ask English learners: How could you paraphrase the quotation from the Supervisor? *(the conflict between the school and village that the headmaster brought on through mistaken enthusiasm)*

 To check students' understanding of the selection, see Unit 7 Teaching Resources Book, p. 136.

"That was some time ago. But it will not be used now," said Obi as he walked away. "What will the Government Education Officer think of this when he comes to inspect the school next week? The villagers might, for all I know, decide to use the schoolroom for a pagan[5] ritual during the inspection."

Heavy sticks were planted closely across the path at the two places where it entered and left the school premises. These were further strengthened with barbed wire.

Three days later the village priest of *Ani* called on the headmaster. He was an old man and walked with a slight stoop. He carried a stout walking stick which he usually tapped on the floor, by way of emphasis, each time he made a new point in his argument.

"I have heard," he said after the usual exchange of cordialities, "that our ancestral footpath has recently been closed . . . "

"Yes," replied Mr. Obi. "We cannot allow people to make a highway of our school compound."

"Look here, my son," said the priest bringing down his walking stick, "this path was here before you were born and before your father was born. The whole life of this village depends on it. Our dead relatives depart by it and our ancestors visit us by it. But most important, it is the path of children coming in to be born . . . "

Mr. Obi listened with a satisfied smile on his face.

"The whole purpose of our school," he said finally, "is to eradicate just such beliefs as that. Dead men do not require footpaths. The whole idea is just fantastic. Our duty is to teach your children to laugh at such ideas."

"What you say may be true," replied the priest, "but we follow the practices of our fathers. If you reopen the path we shall have nothing to quarrel about. What I always say is: let the hawk perch and let the eagle perch." He rose to go.

"I am sorry," said the young headmaster. "But the school compound cannot be a thoroughfare. It is against our regulations. I would suggest your constructing another path, skirting our premises. We can even get our boys to help in building it. I don't suppose the ancestors will find the little detour too burdensome."

"I have no more words to say," said the priest, already outside.

Two days later a young woman in the village died in childbed. A diviner[6] was immediately consulted and he prescribed heavy sacrifices to propitiate[7] ancestors insulted by the fence.

Obi woke up next morning among the ruins of his work. The beautiful hedges were torn up not just near the path but right round the school, the flowers trampled to death and one of the school buildings pulled down . . . That day, the white Supervisor came to inspect the school and wrote a nasty report on the state of the premises but more seriously about the "tribal-war situation developing between the school and the village, arising in part from the misguided zeal[8] of the new headmaster." ❧

---

5. *Pagan* means "relating to a religion that involves many gods."

1 Conflict *What conflict does Obi's assertion set in motion?*

2 Analyze Characterization *What does the village priest value?*

---

6. A *diviner* is a fortune teller.
7. To *propitiate* is to appease.
8. *Zeal* is earnest enthusiasm.

Conflict *How does the Supervisor's assessment of the conflict differ from Obi's?* **3**

Reading Practice

SPIRAL REVIEW **Sequence Events** Have students pay close attention to the order in which events occur. **Draw** a story line on the board and provide the first and last events. *(First event: Obi is appointed headmaster of Ndume School; last event: Obi receives a bad report from the Supervisor.)* **Ask** students to place the following events in order on the story line.

- Obi first learns that the footpath has special meaning to the villagers.

- The village priest visits Obi.
- Obi has the footpath fenced off with barbed wire.
- The garden is destroyed.

After You Read

Respond and Think Critically

Respond and Interpret

1. Were you surprised by the end of the story? Why or why not?

2. (a)What do the Obis hope to accomplish when they take charge of the school? (b)How might the path stand in the way of what Mr. Obi has set out to accomplish?

3. (a)Why is the path important to the villagers? (b)What can you infer about the villagers' attitudes toward their ancestors and their heritage? Support your inference with evidence from the story.

4. (a)What **proverb**, or short saying, does the village priest tell Mr. Obi he always says? (b)What message is the village priest trying to convey to Mr. Obi through this proverb?

Analyze and Evaluate

5. (a)What qualities do you think are important in a headmaster? (b)Which of these qualities do you think Mr. Obi possesses?

6. With his training and attitudes, do you think Mr. Obi could have reacted any differently to the problems he encountered? Explain.

Connect

7. **Big Idea** Colonialism and Postcolonialism What does this story suggest about the way people should treat another culture's traditional beliefs?

8. **Connect to Today** What recent events can you think of that represent a clash between old and new ideas? Explain, giving examples.

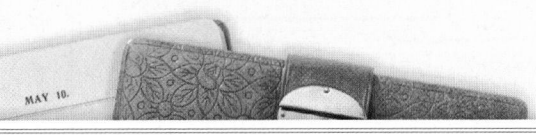

Daily Life & Culture

Life in a Nigerian Village

Achebe does not specify the exact location of his story. However, the habits of the local villagers—and Achebe's own background—suggest that it is set in eastern Nigeria, near a traditional Ibo village. The villages can range in population from several hundred to several thousand.

Though most Nigerians are Muslims or Christians, ancient tribal beliefs still persist. The Ibo, for example, traditionally believed in a god so powerful that he had to be approached through lesser deities, each affiliated with a different Ibo village. The Ibo view death

as the transition between the human and the spirit world. After a sojourn in the spirit world, the soul is believed to be reborn into a new life.

Each village is served by a priest or priestess who advises in spiritual matters and presides over religious rituals and ceremonies. Additionally, people known as diviners seek to discern and report the will of the gods. The diviner's message from the gods guides decision-making.

Group Activity Discuss the following questions with your classmates.

1. Which aspects of traditional Ibo life are reflected in "Dead Men's Path"?

2. What evidence does the story provide of the importance of the diviner in village life?

Igbo mask with knobbed headgear.

CHINUA ACHEBE **1263**

Daily Life & Culture

1. Ibo religious beliefs are reflected in the villagers' veneration of the path and their reaction to the death of the young woman in childbirth.

2. It is the diviner who prescribes "heavy sacrifices" to appease the ancestors who are insulted by the fence Obi has erected. The vandalism of the school compound suggests that the villagers immediately responded to the diviner's directives.

After You Read

Assess

1. Students may not be surprised that someone reopened the path but may be surprised by the vandalism.

2. (a) To raise the standard of teaching and to beautify the school compound (b) The path symbolizes the "fantasies" occupying the villagers' minds. Mr. Obi wants his students to think in more modern ways and to scorn such traditional views.

3. (a) The villagers believe the path is needed by souls being born or dying and by souls returning to visit the village. (b) They have a deep respect for their ancestors and their heritage.

4. (a) "Let the hawk perch and let the eagle perch." (b) The priest (representing tradition) and Obi (representing modern ways) should respect each other rather than try to change each other.

5. (a) Possible answers: A logical mind, the courage to try new ideas, the ability to appreciate other people's positions, a willingness to compromise (b) Obi possesses only the first two qualities.

6. Obi could have been inspired by his training to modernize the school without alienating the villagers, but his intolerant attitude left him unable to react differently.

7. The story suggests that people should respect another culture's traditional beliefs.

8. Responses will vary, but should show a distinction between two schools of thought or opinions, one of which is traditional and one of which is new.

After You Read

Assess

Literary Element

1. Obi struggles against the villagers and against tradition. Obi's opponent wins, both physically and philosophically.

2. The villagers would not have ruined the school grounds, and the white Supervisor might have commended Obi.

Review: Irony

Obi zealously tries to do a good job, but his zeal leads to failure. He closes the path in part to avoid problems but causes even greater ones.

Reading Strategy

1. Self-important, opinionated, zealously efficient, insensitive

2. Possible response: Obi erects barbed-wire fences to close the villagers' path across the school compound. This action leads to a visit from the village priest, which intensifies the conflict between the two parties.

3. Optimistic, loyal, materialistic, shallow, and easily influenced

4. The priest because his use of the proverb "Let the hawk perch and let the eagle perch" reflects his willingness to tolerate the school's presence despite the new ideas it teaches.

Progress Check

Can students analyze characterization?

If No → See Unit 7 Teaching Resources Book, p. 133.

Literary Element Conflict

In an **external conflict**, the main character is not always a "good" character, nor is the outside force with which he or she struggles always "bad."

1. What is the outside force with which Obi struggles? How is this external conflict resolved?

2. How might the story have ended if Obi had followed the village priest's advice?

Review: Irony

As you learned on page 1132, **irony** is a contrast or discrepancy between expectation and reality. **Situational irony** occurs when the outcome of a situation is the opposite of what someone expected.

Partner Activity With a partner, identify and explain the ironies in this story. Use a diagram like the following to record your information.

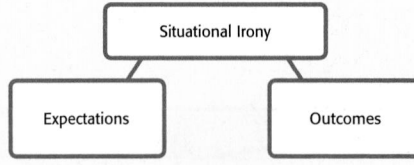

Igbo mask, Leja village

Literature Online

Selection Resources For Selection Quizzes, eFlashcards, and Reading-Writing Connection activities, go to glencoe.com and enter QuickPass code GLB9817u7.

Reading Strategy Analyze Characterization

As you **analyze characterization**, remember that by carefully selecting details, an author controls the reader's impression of a character. Review the character webs you made as you read, and then answer the following questions.

1. What are Michael Obi's chief personality traits?

2. Choose one of Obi's actions listed in your web. How does that action help drive the plot forward?

3. What are Obi's wife's main qualities?

4. Who is more tolerant, Obi or the village priest? Explain.

Vocabulary Practice

Practice with Word Usage Respond to these statements to help you explore the meanings of vocabulary words from the selection.

1. Describe a **pivotal** experience from your childhood.

2. Describe a situation you have experienced or heard about in which someone suffered unfair public **denigration**.

3. List any policies in your school or community that you consider to be **superannuated**.

Academic Vocabulary

*To control the villagers' activities, Obi institutes the **regulation** that they may not use the path.*

Regulation is an academic word that appears in everyday usage. In sports, the word is often used to refer to the standard length of a game, as in the sentence *They scored three points in the last seconds of **regulation**.*

Using context clues, try to figure out the meaning of the word *regulation* in the sentence about "Dead Men's Path" above. Check your guess in a dictionary.

For more on academic vocabulary, see pages 56 and R81.

Vocabulary Practice

1. Students should name an experience that was integral to their development.

2. Students might name an instance in which a peer was singled out and unfairly teased.

3. Students should name policies that they believe are outdated or old-fashioned.

Academic Vocabulary

The context indicates that a *regulation* is a rule or policy instituted to control the activities of others.

Respond Through Writing

Reflective Essay

Explore Conflict Achebe's story focuses on the conflicts that arose in the clash of traditional African culture under European colonialism. In a reflective essay, consider a time in your life when you experienced a conflict between old and new ways. Use description and dialogue to characterize the people involved and help your readers understand the conflict.

Understanding the Task A **reflective essay** is a commentary on something you have experienced, read, discussed, written, or learned. **Characterization** refers to the techniques a writer uses to reveal a character's personality. These methods can be direct—through statements about the character by the narrator or other characters—or indirect—through the character's own thoughts, actions, and words.

Prewrite Write a statement briefly describing the conflict you will discuss. Then create a timeline to record the main events. For each event, note the setting, the people involved, and any actions or dialogue.

Conflict: Spoiled only child realizes he's nothing special when he goes to camp.

1st time away from home (me at age 11/horse camp/ interior monologue: "I'm free!")	1st time rooming with someone (Ellis and me/ bunkhouse/ arguing about everything)	"If you think you're the only person in the world, think again!"	

Draft Fill in the details of your story, using dialogue and description to explain the conflict and the significance of events. You may also want to use rhetorical devices, such as anecdotes or analogies, to help readers understand the situation and your reactions to it. Compare the events and emotions in your experience with the situation described in Achebe's story. What larger idea might both of these incidents express about conflict?

Revise Exchange your draft with a partner, making sure each essay has not just related a series of events, but also explained how they illustrate the essay's main conflict and its resolution (if it was resolved at all).

Edit and Proofread Proofread your paper, correcting any errors in spelling, grammar, and punctuation. Use the Grammar Tip in the side column to help you with nominative absolutes.

CHINUA ACHEBE **1265**

Learning Objectives

In this assignment, you will focus on the following objectives:

Writing: Writing a reflective essay.

Literary Study: Exploring conflict.

Grammar Tip

Nominative Absolutes

The **nominative absolute** is a free-standing part of a sentence that often consists of a noun modified by a participial phrase.

Nominative absolute:

His voice rising alarmingly, Ellis announced, _"You have ten seconds!"_

One way to identify a nominative absolute is to add a verb to it.

Complete sentence:

His voice **was** rising alarmingly.

After You Read

Assess

Respond Through Writing

Students' reflective essays should:

- describe a conflict the writer experienced between the old and the new
- present settings, characters, and dialogue vividly and explain their significance
- use nominative absolutes to indicate intent or obligation

> For grammar practice, see Unit 7 Teaching Resources Book, p. 135.

> For additional assessment, see Assessment Resources, pp. 295–296.

English Learners

DIFFERENTIATED INSTRUCTION

PARTNERS **Intermediate** **Say:** Achebe shows his readers a great deal about his characters through dialogue. Have English learners in pairs act out Obi's conversations with his wife, the teacher, and the village priest. Ask them to think about matching their tone of voice to the words that they are speaking. After reading the dialogues aloud, discuss what students have discovered about the characters. **Ask:** How does Obi behave in these conversations? _(He does not really listen to those he talks with, but only presses his own views.)_

Focus

Write this sentence group on the board: *The prisoner paced in the tiny <u>cell</u>. Every <u>cell</u> is surrounded by a membrane. I have to <u>sell</u> magazine subscriptions to raise money for the band.* Read the sentences aloud. Point out the underlined words and **ask:** Are these words pronounced the same or differently? *(the same)* What does the underlined word in each sentence mean? *(a place for confining prisoners; a building block of a living organism; to offer for purchase).* **Say:** These three words are *homophones*, words that sound exactly the same but have different meanings. As you can see, sometimes homophones have the same spelling and sometimes they do not.

Teach

Homophones

Remind students that homophones sound alike but have different spellings and meanings.

Assess

1. new
2. hear
3. sight
4. tale

 For additional vocabulary practice, see Glencoe Interactive Vocabulary CD-ROM.

Homophones

Homophones are words that are pronounced the same way yet have completely different meanings and different spellings.

Tip

To determine the meaning of a homophone, look for context clues. These clues will help you tell what meaning is intended.

LOG ON **Literature** Online

Vocabulary For more vocabulary practice, go to glencoe.com and enter QuickPass code GLB9817u7.

Vocabulary Workshop

Homophones

Literature Connection In this passage from "Dead Men's Path," Chinua Achebe uses the homophone *week*.

> " 'What will the Government Education Officer think of this when he comes to inspect the school next week?' "
>
> —Chinua Achebe, from "Dead Men's Path"

Homophones are words that have different meanings and spellings but share the same pronunciation. *Week and weak* are homophones. *Week* means "a series of seven days," and *weak* means "frail."

Here is a brief list of homophones.

Word	Meaning	Example
bear	an animal; to cope	The brown *bear* came dangerously close to camp.
bare	lacking clothing	The doctor examined his *bare* shoulder.
break	to crack, split, or smash	Enslaved people endeavored to *break* their bonds.
brake	to stop a movement	The negligent driver failed to *brake* for the pedestrian.
piece	a part of something	I completed the last *piece* of the puzzle.
peace	tranquility	During war, people long for *peace*.
stairs	a series of steps	Take the *stairs* because it's quicker than the elevator.
stares	fixed gazes	The new student was intimidated by the *stares* of the class.

When you are unsure about the meanings of homophones, use context clues to help you determine the meaning or consult a dictionary. Remember, a computer's spell-check feature cannot identify incorrect homophones, because a computer cannot discern the meaning you intend. Carefully proofreading your work will help you eliminate any mistakes with homophones.

Practice Choose the correct homophone in each sentence.

1. Michael Obi was enthralled with <u>knew / new</u> ways of doing things.
2. Obi did not want to <u>hear / here</u> what the tribal priest had to say.
3. Michael and his wife, Nancy, lost <u>sight / site</u> of the sacred values of African culture.
4. I found "Dead Men's Path" to be a thoughtful <u>tail / tale</u>.

Vocabulary Practice

SPIRAL REVIEW **Use Homophones Correctly** Ask students to use each of the above pairs or groups of homophones in the same sentence. Ask volunteers to share their sentences with the class.

If students experience difficulty with homophones, encourage them to keep a log of homophones they encounter and to look up the different meanings of the similar-sounding words.

Before You Read

Telephone Conversation

Meet **Wole Soyinka**
(born 1934)

Wole Soyinka (wä´ lā shä ying´ ka) has earned an international reputation as one of the most distinguished and powerful voices for social change and human rights. His plays, poetry, novels, and essays have not only helped to introduce the world to the traditions and folklore of Africa, but they have also exposed Nigeria's struggles with colonial rule, oppression and injustice, dictatorship, modernization, and civil war. As Soyinka has said, "Books and all forms of writing have always been objects of terror to those who seek to suppress the truth."

> *"I have one abiding religion—human liberty . . . my writing grows more and more preoccupied with the theme of the oppressive boot, the irrelevance of the color of the foot that wears it and the struggle for individuality."*
>
> —Wole Soyinka

Cultural Conflicts Soyinka was born in Nigeria when it was still under British rule. His parents were educators and were able to provide him with a strong English education. Soyinka's grandfather taught him about African tradition and the Yoruba gods and folklore, which influenced his later writing. Thus, from an early age, Soyinka was keenly aware of the cultural conflicts between African tradition and British modernization. Soyinka's lifelong political activism was inspired during his childhood by the independence movement in Nigeria and a revolt against a tax on women led by his mother. Soyinka graduated from college in England in 1958 and returned to Nigeria in 1960, shortly after the country gained its independence.

A Voice of Truth
In 1966 a military coup overthrew the freely elected Nigerian government. The next year, a section of the country seceded, forming the Republic of Biafra, and the Nigerian civil war began. In the same year, Soyinka was falsely accused of helping the Biafrans buy jet fighters and was imprisoned for more than two years. The military government kept him in solitary confinement in a four-by-eight-foot cell. To save his sanity and communicate with his supporters, Soyinka manufactured his own ink and began a diary using anything he could find to write on—toilet paper, cigarette packages, and book pages. These notes were later published in *The Man Died: Prison Notes of Wole Soyinka*. Although Soyinka was released in 1969, it would not be the last time he found himself in legal trouble. More than two decades later, he was charged with treason for criticizing the government and sentenced to death, forcing Soyinka into self-imposed exile for four years.

In 1986 Soyinka became the first African to receive the Nobel Prize in Literature, which was a mixed blessing for him. He remarked, "It has such a prestige and such a hold on people's imagination in all corners and on all levels that you become the property of the world."

LOG ON ▶ **Literature** Online

Author Search For more about Wole Soyinka, go to glencoe.com and enter QuickPass code GLB9817u7.

WOLE SOYINKA **1267**

Before You Read

Focus

Selection Skills

Literary Elements
- Free Verse (1268–1271)

Telephone Conversation

Listening/Speaking/Viewing Skills
- Analyze Art (TE p. 1269)

Reading Skills
- Connect to Contemporary Issues (SE pp. 1268–1271)

Vocabulary Skills
- Synonyms (SE pp. 1268, 1271)

Writing Skills/Grammar
- Write a Poem (SE p. 1271)
- Multimedia Presentations (TE p. 1270)

Before You Read

Focus

Summary

In this poem, a caller hoping to rent an apartment admits that he is African. The conversation then focuses on the potential tenant's race.

 For summaries in languages other than English, see Unit 7 Teaching Resources Book, pp. 138–143.

Vocabulary

Word Webs Have students use a dictionary to look up the vocabulary words. Have them make a word web that includes the definition, root, synonyms, and antonyms of each word.

 For additional vocabulary practice, see Unit 7 Teaching Resources Book, p. 146.

 For additional context, see Glencoe Interactivve Vocabulary CD-ROM.

Reading Practice

SPIRAL REVIEW **Preread** Have students preview the poem by looking at the title and scanning the text. **Ask:** Based on the title, what do you think this poem is going to be about? (*a telephone conversation*) **Ask:** Is there anything unusual about the text of the poem? (*There are several lines written in all caps.*) Have students speculate as to why these lines are in all caps.

1268

Literature and Reading Preview

Connect to the Poem

Have you ever faced discrimination—for example, due to your age, race, or background? In a journal entry, write about your reaction to incidents of discrimination, either against you or others.

Build Background

African tradition was an important part of Soyinka's childhood and has played an essential and recurring role in his work. "Telephone Conversation" reflects his ability to create dramatic dialogue that uses irony and humor to satirize racial prejudice.

Set Purposes for Reading

Big Idea Colonialism and Postcolonialism

As you read, ask yourself, How do the imagery and dialogue contribute to the portrayal of racial prejudice?

Literary Element Free Verse

Poetry that has no fixed pattern of meter, rhyme, line length, or stanza arrangement is called **free verse**. Notice how he uses techniques such as repetition and alliteration to create lyrical patterns; also note his use of irony and imagery to emphasize meaning and capture the formlessness that he perceives in modern life. As you read, ask yourself, What effect does the free verse form have on the sound and meaning of the poem?

Reading Strategy Connect to Contemporary Issues

Connecting means linking what you read to events in your own life, to world events, or to other selections you have read. To **connect to contemporary issues**, compare how issues in a text have been treated over time and how they are treated today. As you read, ask yourself, How would this be different—or the same—today?

Tip: Comparing and Contrasting Use a Venn diagram to compare today's issues of racism and prejudice with those in "Telephone Conversation."

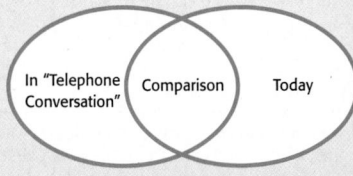

In "Telephone Conversation" — Comparison — Today

Learning Objectives

For pages 1267–1271

In studying this text, you will focus on the following objectives:

Literary Study: Analyzing free verse.

Reading: Connecting to contemporary issues.

Writing: Writing a poem.

Vocabulary

rancid (ran′ sid) *adj.* having an offensive or foul odor or taste; p. 1270 *The rancid food smelled like garbage.*

revelation (rev′ ə lā′ shən) *n.* the act of making something known; something that is revealed; p. 1270 *Her revelation brought attention to the way society discriminated against women.*

assent (ə sent′) *v.* to agree to something after consideration; concur; p. 1270 *He would assent only after he carefully analyzed all of his options.*

friction (frik′ shən) *n.* the clashing between two people or groups of opposed views; p. 1270 *After their argument, the friction between the couple was evident to us all.*

Tip: Synonyms A **synonym** is a word that has the same or nearly the same meaning as another word. For example, *mislead* and *deceive* are synonyms.

Telephone Conversation

Wole Soyinka

Teach

View the Photograph

As they read the selection, ask students to think about what is being communicated in this poem. Direct students' attention to the photograph on this page. **Ask:** What might this phone booth represent to the author? *(Students may say that for someone like Soyinka, the phone booth might represent both "home" and the oppression of colonies, or communication between two cultures.)*

For an audio recording of this selection, use Listening Library Audio CD-ROM.

English Learners

DIFFERENTIATED INSTRUCTION

PARTNERS **Intermediate** Help English learners prepare for some of the vocabulary in the poem by identifying the relationships among words with common origins. Pair students with strong English speakers to write sentences using these related words:

confess: confessor, confession
adjust: adjustment, readjust, adjustor
shame: shameful, ashamed, shameless

Approaching Level

DIFFERENTIATED INSTRUCTION

Established Discuss with approaching-level students how someone might find an apartment to rent. Point out that most people check want ads in newspapers or on the Internet. Have students analyze want ads to locate specific kinds of apartments.

Teach

Literary Element 1

Free Verse Answer: *It has no fixed pattern of rhyme or meter; it sounds like natural speech.*

[APPROACHING] If approaching-level students are having difficulty recognizing the natural speech rhythms in the poem, have them try reading it aloud, ignoring the line breaks.

 For additional literary element practice, see Unit 7 Teaching Resources Book, p. 144.

Big Idea 2

Colonialism and Postcolonialism Answer:

As his passport indicates, the speaker of this poem is African. The landlady cannot see past his race. She can see only race, not the speaker as a human being. This is an attitude that colonialism and racism breed.

 To check students' understanding of the selection, see Unit 7 Teaching Resources Book, p. 148.

The price seemed reasonable, location
Indifferent. The landlady swore she lived
Off premises. Nothing remained
But self-confession. "Madam," I warned,
5 "I hate a wasted journey—I am—African."
Silence. Silenced transmission of
Pressurized good breeding. Voice, when it came,
Lipstick-coated, long gold-rolled
Cigarette-holder pipped. Caught I was, foully.
10 "HOW DARK?" . . . I had not misheard . . . "ARE YOU LIGHT
OR VERY DARK?" Button B. Button A. Stench
Of **rancid** breath of public hide-and-speak.
Red booth. Red pillar-box.[1] Red double-tiered
Omnibus[2] squelching tar. It was real! Shamed
15 By ill-mannered silence, surrender
Pushed dumbfoundment to beg simplification.
Considerate she was, varying the emphasis—
"ARE YOU DARK? OR VERY LIGHT?" **Revelation** came.
"You mean—like plain or milk chocolate?"
20 Her **assent** was clinical, crushing in its light
Impersonality. Rapidly, wavelength adjusted,
I chose, "West African sepia"[3]—and as an afterthought,
"Down in my passport." Silence for spectroscopic
Flight of fancy,[4] till truthfulness clanged her accent
25 Hard on the mouthpiece. "WHAT'S THAT?" conceding[5]
"DON'T KNOW WHAT THAT IS." "Like brunette."
"THAT'S DARK, ISN'T IT?" "Not altogether.
Facially, I am brunette, but madam, you should see
The rest of me. Palm of my hand, soles of my feet
30 Are a peroxide blond. **Friction**, caused—
Foolishly madam—by sitting down, has turned
My bottom raven black—One moment madam!"—sensing
Her receiver rearing on the thunderclap
About my ears—"Madam," I pleaded, "Wouldn't you rather
35 See for yourself?"

---

1 Free Verse *How does the beginning of this selection defy traditional poetic conventions?*

2 Colonialism and Postcolonialism *How does this passage represent the cultural conflict created by colonialism and racism?*

Vocabulary

rancid (ran′ sid) *adj.* having an offensive or foul odor or taste
revelation (rev′ ə lā′ shən) *n.* the act of making something known; something that is revealed
assent (ə sent′) *v.* to agree to something after consideration; concur
friction (frik′ shən) *n.* the clashing between two people or groups of opposed views

1270 UNIT 7 AN INTERNATIONAL LITERATURE

---

1. A *pillar-box* is a mailbox.
2. A *double-tiered omnibus* is a bus that has two levels.
3. *Sepia* is a brownish gray to dark olive brown color.
4. A spectroscope is an instrument scientists use to examine the spectrum, or range, of colors in white light. The phrase "spectroscopic flight of fancy" indicates that the woman has paused to consider the range of colors she knows.
5. Here, *conceding* means "admitting."

Writing Practice

 Multimedia Presentations Have students write a script for a multimedia presentation that reflects current day issues of discrimination similar to the poem, where the potential tenant is being judged by the landlord based on race. Tell students to incorporate images and other media that reflect the poem's mood, tone, and imagery. Students should work with a partner to evaluate the effectiveness of their presentation and revise accordingly, before handing in their scripts.

After You Read

Respond and Think Critically

Respond and Interpret

1. (a) What is the "self-confession" the speaker makes to the landlady? (b) What does his confession imply about his past experience? Explain.

2. **Verbal irony** occurs when the meaning of a statement is the reverse of what is meant. How is the word "considerate" in line 17 an example of verbal irony?

3. (a) How does the telephone conversation end? (b) What does the speaker's final plea suggest about his attitude toward the landlady?

Analyze and Evaluate

4. Humor is often used to point out human failings. How effective is Soyinka's use of humor in presenting the gravity of racism? Explain.

5. How does Soyinka's style help address the sensitive issue of racism? Consider his use of humor, irony, and imagery.

Connect

6. **Big Idea** **Colonialism and Postcolonialism** Soyinka became the first African writer to win a Nobel Prize. How might poems such as "Telephone Conversation" broaden the scope of English literature?

7. **Connect to the Author** What inferences do you make about Soyinka himself, based on the choices he's made in writing "Telephone Conversation"?

Literary Element **Free Verse**

Many twentieth-century poets, striving to emphasize the relationship between form and meaning in a poem, have written in **free verse** to capture the formlessness that they perceive in modern life.

1. Why might Soyinka have wanted this poem to follow natural speech patterns? Explain.

2. From what past tradition might Soyinka be trying to break? Explain.

📝 Writing

Write a Poem Think of a time when you had to endure an unfair or discriminatory situation. Write a short free-verse poem about this situation. You may want to incorporate bits of dialogue, or parts of your surroundings that you remember most clearly. Use imagery that conveys your attitude—then and now—about the situation and the people involved in it.

 **Literature** Online

Selection Resources For Selection Quizzes, eFlashcards, and Reading-Writing Connection activities, go to glencoe.com and enter QuickPass code GLB9817u7.

Reading Strategy **Connect to Contemporary Issues**

Artists continue to respond to racism and prejudice today. Refer to the Venn diagram you made as you read to answer the following questions.

1. How have other contemporary artists, such as writers and musicians, addressed these issues?

2. How do their views and ideas compare with Soyinka's work?

Academic Vocabulary

Practice with Synonyms With a partner, brainstorm three synonyms for each boldfaced vocabulary word below. Then discuss your choices with your classmates.

> rancid   revelation   assent   friction

EXAMPLE: *affection*
<u>Synonyms</u>: *love, liking, attachment*

<u>Sample explanation</u>: <u>Affection</u> and <u>love</u> both denote "fondness," though the word <u>love</u> usually has stronger connotations than the word <u>affection</u>.

WOLE SOYINKA   **1271**

After You Read

Assess

1. (a) He is African.
(b) That the speaker has faced racial prejudice before

2. The landlady is actually inconsiderate

3. (a) The speaker pleads to state his case in person. (b) He seems willing to try to change her mind to get the apartment.

4. Humor characterizes the speaker and allows readers to be more receptive to the message about racism.

5. Soyinka uses an everyday event (finding an apartment to rent) in order to show the effects of racism on ordinary encounters.

6. Soyinka's work brought attention to the struggles of Africans not only in Africa but everywhere.

7. Responses will vary. Students may infer that Soyinka has had personal experience with racism, that he has a sense of humor, that he is proud of his ethnicity, that he has a modern approach to poetry.

📝 Writing

Students' poems should be free verse, refer to a specific situation, and reveal how attitudes toward the situation have changed over time.

Literary Element

1. To re-create a telephone conversation

2. From traditional poetic structure

Vocabulary Practice

rancid
<u>Synonyms</u>: *rotten, decomposing, putrid*
<u>Sample explanation</u>: Spoiled food could be described as either *rotten* or *rancid*.

revelation
<u>Synonyms</u>: *disclosure, insight*
<u>Sample explanation</u>: These words mean to expose something hidden.

assent
<u>Synonyms</u>: *agree, concur, comply*
<u>Sample explanation</u>: These words suggest going along with an idea.

friction
<u>Synonyms</u>: *tension, hostility, antagonism*
<u>Sample explanation</u>: These words suggest disagreement.

Reading Strategy

1. Answers will vary.

2. Students may say that contemporary views are similar to those of Soyinka.

1271

Before You Read

Focus

Before You Read

Two Sheep

Meet **Janet Frame**
(1924–2004)

In 1947 Janet Frame voluntarily checked into a mental institution. Mistakenly diagnosed as schizophrenic, she spent the next eight years in and out of hospitals. In her autobiography, she describes this dark, bleak existence: "I inhabited a territory of loneliness which I think resembles that place where the dying spend their time before death, and from where those who do return living to the world bring inevitably a unique point of view that is a nightmare, a treasure, and a lifelong possession." In fact, Frame's lifelong love of creative writing provided her with an emotional outlet; while hospitalized, she published her first collection of short stories, *The Lagoon*. Horrifyingly, Frame was scheduled to receive a frontal lobotomy, an operation in which doctors cut nerve fibers in the brain, potentially leaving the patient in a permanently vegetative state. Just before the procedure, however, Frame's doctors informed her that *The Lagoon* had won a prestigious literary award. They cancelled the surgery, and Frame was discharged from the hospital.

> "It is little wonder that I value writing as a way of life when it actually saved my life."
>
> —Janet Frame, from *An Autobiography*

Family Misfortunes Janet Frame was born in Dunedin, a city bordering the Pacific Ocean on the southeastern coast of New Zealand. Her father was a railroad worker, and her mother wrote poetry, which she sold to neighbors. After several moves, the family settled in the small town of Oamaru. A shy child, Frame spent her time reading and writing. She became acquainted with illness and tragedy at an early age; her brother had epilepsy, and two of her sisters drowned during childhood. As a young adult, Frame trained to become a teacher. But on the morning she was to receive her final evaluation for certification, she panicked. Greeted by the headmaster and inspector at the start of class, she asked to be excused for a moment, and, as she reported in her autobiography, "I walked out of the room and out of the school, knowing I would never return."

No "Mad Genius" Frame's subsequent breakdown, which led to her numerous stays in psychiatric wards, proved to be a turning point in her life. Following the critical success of *The Lagoon*, she went on to pursue a productive writing career. Readers and critics who knew of Frame's hospitalizations dubbed her a "mad genius," believing that her creative powers sprang from mental instability, but Frame (and a team of London doctors) proved them wrong. During the late 1950s, while living in London, Frame sought an explanation for the loneliness and depression that plagued her at times. After submitting to several interviews and a psychiatric evaluation, she was told that she was not schizophrenic and was not mentally ill.

In her prolific career, Frame published not only short stories but also novels, poetry, and a three-volume autobiography. New Zealand film director Jane Campion adapted Frame's autobiography into the film *An Angel at My Table*. As her fame increased, Frame traveled internationally to promote her work, and lived for brief periods of time in both England and the United States. She returned permanently to her birthplace, Dunedin, in 1997.

 Literature Online

Author Search For more about Janet Frame, go to glencoe.com and enter QuickPass code GLB9817u7.

Selection Skills

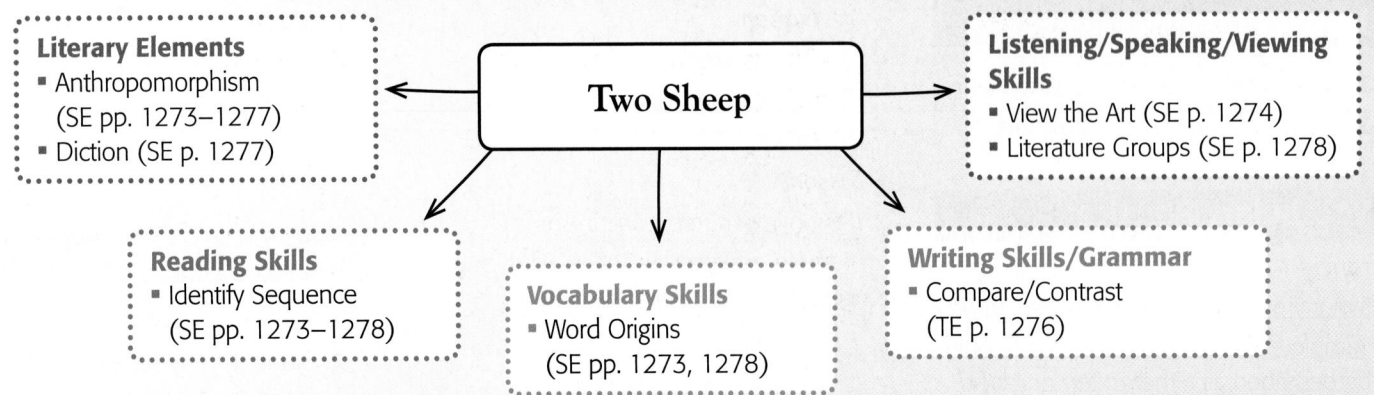

Literary Elements
- Anthropomorphism (SE pp. 1273–1277)
- Diction (SE p. 1277)

Two Sheep

Listening/Speaking/Viewing Skills
- View the Art (SE p. 1274)
- Literature Groups (SE p. 1278)

Reading Skills
- Identify Sequence (SE pp. 1273–1278)

Vocabulary Skills
- Word Origins (SE pp. 1273, 1278)

Writing Skills/Grammar
- Compare/Contrast (TE p. 1276)

Literature and Reading Preview

Connect to the Fable

Do you think that "ignorance is bliss"? Discuss the question with a partner, making sure to cover all possible sides of the issue.

Build Background

In 1963, Frame turned her attention to allegory. The fable "Two Sheep" was first published in *You Are Now Entering the Human Heart* (1983). A **fable** is a short, often simple story intended to teach a lesson about human behavior. The moral or lesson is usually implied by the plot of the story and then stated explicitly at the end. "Two Sheep" is an example of a beast fable, in which animals represent human types. Unlike most fables, the moral or lesson here must be inferred.

Set Purposes for Reading

Big Idea Globalization

As you read, ask yourself, In what ways does this story illustrate the rich diversity of contemporary English literature?

Literary Element Anthropomorphism

Anthropomorphism is the practice of ascribing human form or characteristics to nonhuman objects or animals. This element is often found in fables, where the main characters are commonly animals that have the ability to speak and think. As you read "Two Sheep," ask yourself, In what ways do the animals behave like humans?

Reading Strategy Identify Sequence

To **identify sequence** is to recognize the pattern of organization that a writer uses to present information. In narrative writing, writers often use chronological, or time, order to present a sequence of events in the order in which they happen. As you read, ask yourself, In what order do these events appear?

....

Tip: Making a Sequence Chart As you read, identify and record the sequence of events. When you finish, study the sequence to determine the moral or lesson of the story.

> Sequence of Events in "Two Sheep"
> 1. Two sheep are traveling to the saleyards.
> 2. _____

JANET FRAME **1273**

Learning Objectives

For pages 1272–1278

In studying this text, you will focus on the following objectives:

Literary Study: Analyzing anthropomorphism.

Reading: Identifying sequence.

Speaking and Listening: Participating in a literature group.

Vocabulary

pall (pôl) *n.* an atmosphere of dark and gloom; p. 1275 *The rain clouds overhead cast a pall on our picnic.*

barren (bar′ ən) *adj.* having little or no vegetation; bare; p. 1276 *The barren landscape was devoid of all plant life.*

unperturbed (un pər turbd′) *adj.* undisturbed; not troubled; p. 1276 *Dressed in a warm, furry parka, Tom was unperturbed by the subzero temperature.*

Tip: Word Origins A word's origin, or **etymology**, explains its history and illustrates how the word relates to other words in English and other languages. In a dictionary, a word's etymology usually appears in brackets.

Before You Read

Focus

Summary

As a flock of sheep is being driven to slaughter, a sheep who knows their fate comments on the beauties of the day. Another sheep belittles the idea that they may die. Then the second sheep realizes the truth and also expresses appreciation for the beautiful day. The first sheep is mistaken for dead at the freezing works, is discarded, and gets away. He slips into another flock and realizes the course of his future: to escape slaughter and join a new flock, again and again, always wondering about the dual nature of reality.

 For summaries in languages other than English, see Unit 7 Teaching Resources Book, pp. 150–155.

Vocabulary

Suffixes Say: The noun *pall* from the vocabulary list means "dark" and "gloomy;" however, when the suffixes *–or* and *–id* are added to the word *pall,* the meaning changes. Look up the meaning of *pallor* and *pallid* in the dictionary and then use each word in a sentence.

 For additional vocabulary practice, see Unit 7 Teaching Resources Book, p. 158.

 For additonal context, see Glencoe Interactive Vocabulary CD-ROM.

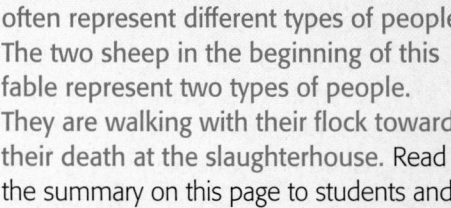

English Learners

DIFFERENTIATED INSTRUCTION

Intermediate Say: In a fable, animals often represent different types of people. The two sheep in the beginning of this fable represent two types of people. They are walking with their flock towards their death at the slaughterhouse. Read the summary on this page to students and have them describe the type of character represented by each sheep. *(The first sheep is positive and aware of his fate,* while the second sheep is negative and naïve.) **Ask:** Why would the sheep who knows where they are going be more positive about nature than the one who does not know? *(The first sheep appreciates things in nature that he will not see again.)*

| Literary Element | 1 |

Anthropomorphism
Answer: *The words* knew *and* know *in the first paragraph imply that the sheep can think. The sheep can also talk and reason.*

 For additional literary element practice, see Unit 7 Teaching Resources Book, p. 156.

| Reading Strategy | 2 |

Identify Sequence Answer: *Here, and in the second paragraph of the story, the first sheep seems pleased and perhaps moved by the beauty and calm of his surroundings. The second sheep has the opposite reaction. It seems odd that the sheep who knows that he is headed for the slaughterhouse would be in a happy and peaceful mood and that the sheep who does not know his fate would be irritable.*

View the Photograph ★

Answer: *Some students might feel the direct gaze of the sheep seems a little bit human; some will say there's nothing or very little anthropomorphic about the image.*

 For an audio recording of this selection, use Listening Library Audio CD-ROM.

Readability Scores

Dale-Chall: 5.9
DRP: 57
Lexile: 1130

Two Sheep
Janet Frame

View the Photograph Sheep are often used as a metaphor for people who obey or follow the crowd without thinking. Do the sheep in this image seem human in any way? Explain. ★

Two sheep were traveling to the saleyards. The first sheep knew that after they had been sold their destination was the slaughterhouse at the freezing works. The second sheep did not know of their fate. They were being driven with the rest of the flock along a hot dusty valley road where the surrounding hills leaned in a sun-scorched wilderness of rock, tussock,[1] and old rabbit warrens.[2] They moved slowly, for the drover[3] in his trap was in no hurry, and had even taken one of the dogs to sit beside him while the other scrambled from side to side of the flock, guiding them.

"I think," said the first sheep who was aware of their approaching death, "that the sun has never shone so warm on my fleece, nor, from what I see with my small sheep's eye, has the sky seemed so flawless, without seams or tucks or cracks or blemishes."

"You are crazy," said the second sheep who did not know of their approaching death. "The sun is warm, yes, but how hot and dusty and heavy my wool feels! It is a burden to go trotting along this oven shelf. It seems our journey will never end."

"How fresh and juicy the grass appears on the hill!" the first sheep exclaimed. "And not a hawk in the sky!"

---

1. A *tussock* is a clump or tuft of grass.
2. *Warrens* are places where rabbits are kept and bred.
3. A *drover* is one who drives sheep.

Anthropomorphism *What human characteristics are attributed to the sheep?* **1**

Identify Sequence *What attitude does each sheep express toward his surroundings? What seems odd or ironic about their respective attitudes?* **2**

Research Practice

 SPIRAL REVIEW **Evaluate Internet Sources**
Point out that to do online research effectively, students need to evaluate the reliability of the Web sites. Have students use these guidelines in researching the author:

- Identify the Web site's source. Is it authoritative? For example, is it sponsored by a well-established institution, such as a library or museum?

- Check for current information. Has the Web site been recently updated?

- Does the site contain typographical errors or mistakes in grammar and spelling? Such mistakes are often clues to less-than-reliable sources.

"I think," replied the second sheep, "that something has blinded you. Just look up in the sky and see those three hawks waiting to swoop and attack us!"

They trotted on further through the valley road. Now and again the second sheep stumbled.

"I feel so tired," he said. "I wonder how much longer we must walk on and on through this hot dusty valley?"

But the first sheep walked nimbly and his wool felt light upon him as if he had just been shorn. He could have gamboled like a lamb in August.

"I still think," he said, "that today is the most wonderful day I have known. I do not feel that the road is hot and dusty. I do not notice the stones and grit that you complain of. To me the hills have never seemed so green and enticing, the sun has never seemed so warm and comforting. I believe that I could walk through this valley forever, and never feel tired or hungry or thirsty."

"Whatever has come over you?" the second sheep asked crossly. "Here we are, trotting along hour after hour, and soon we shall stand in our pens in the saleyards while the sun leans over us with its branding irons and our overcoats are such a burden that they drag us to the floor of our pen where we are almost trampled to death by the so dainty feet of our fellow sheep. A fine life that is. It would not surprise me if after we are sold we are taken in trucks to the freezing works and killed in cold blood. But," he added, comforting himself, "that is not likely to happen. Oh no, that could never happen! I have it on authority that even when they are trampled by their fellows, sheep do not die. The tales we hear from time to time are but malicious rumors, and those vivid dreams which strike us in the night as we sleep on the sheltered hills, they are but illusions. Do you not agree?" he asked the first sheep.

They were turning now from the valley road, and the saleyards were in sight, while drawn up in the siding on the rusty railway lines, the red

trucks stood waiting, spattered inside with sheep and cattle dirt and with white chalk marks, in cipher,[4] on the outside. And still the first sheep did not reveal to his companion that they were being driven to certain death.

When they were jostled inside their pen the first sheep gave an exclamation of delight.

"What a pleasant little house they have let to us! I have never seen such smart red-painted bars, and such four-square corners. And look at the elegant stairway which we will climb to enter those red caravans for our seaside holiday!"

"You make me tired," the second sheep said. "We are standing inside a dirty pen, nothing more, and I cannot move my feet in their nicely polished black shoes but I tread upon the dirt left by sheep which have been imprisoned here before us. In fact I have never been so badly treated in all my life!" And the second sheep began to cry. Just then a kind elderly sheep jostled through the flock and began to comfort him.

"You have been frightening your companions, I suppose," she said angrily to the first sheep. "You have been telling horrible tales of our fate. Some sheep never know when to keep things to themselves. There was no need to tell your companion the truth, that we are being led to certain death!"

But the first sheep did not answer. He was thinking that the sun had never blessed him with so much warmth, that no crowded pen had ever seemed so comfortable and luxurious. Then suddenly he was taken by surprise and hustled out a little gate and up the ramp into the waiting truck, and suddenly too the sun shone in its true colors, battering him about the head with gigantic burning bars, while the hawks congregated above, sizzling the sky with their wings, and a **pall** of dust clung to the

---

4. Here, *in cipher* means "in code."

> Identify Sequence *In what way does the arrival of the third sheep advance the plot of the story?* **4**

Vocabulary

pall (pôl) *n.* an atmosphere of dark and gloom

---

3 Anthropomorphism *What human failing is revealed by the second sheep's denials?*

Teach

Literary Element | **3**

Anthropomorphism
Answer: *The second sheep admits to having heard malicious rumors but dismisses them as illusions, revealing the human tendency to deny or ignore unpleasant realities.*

ENGLISH LEARNERS Be sure that English learners understand the meaning of *illusions*. Have them use a dictionary to look up the meaning of this word.

Reading Strategy | **4**

Identify Sequence Answer: *The third sheep reveals the truth that the first sheep had kept to himself, forcing the second sheep to confront his fate.*

Literary History ☆

Fables The Greek story-teller Aesop in the sixth century B.C. is credited with the first fables in Western culture. Other notable fables were written in the 1600s by the French writer La Fontaine. Fables from other ancient sources such as the *Panchatantra* of India also found their way into Western literature.

Approaching Level

DIFFERENTIATED INSTRUCTION

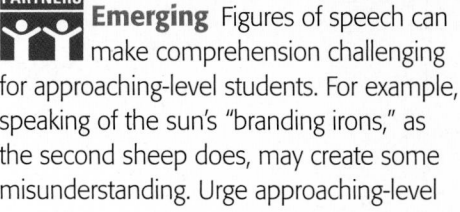

PARTNERS

Emerging Figures of speech can make comprehension challenging for approaching-level students. For example, speaking of the sun's "branding irons," as the second sheep does, may create some misunderstanding. Urge approaching-level students to take the time to make sense of such language. Have students work with stronger readers to make charts in which they list figures of speech from the fable as well as explanations and interpretations.

Teach

Literary Element   1

Anthropomorphism
Answer: *He has gained insight and understanding.*

[APPROACHING] To help approaching-level students, **ask:** Which words describe the actions of the first sheep when he learns that he will die? *(He began to struggle and cry out)*

Reading Strategy   2

Identify Sequence **Answer:** *The first sheep decides to keep what he knows to himself. He will live the rest of his life in timidity, uncertainty, and silence. His experiences—repeatedly escaping death by mere chance—have broken his spirit and, as a result, destroyed his ability to face the ups and downs of life with a positive attitude.*

To check students' understanding of the selection, see Unit 7 Teaching Resources Book, p. 160.

barren used-up hills, and everywhere was commotion, pushing, struggling, bleating, trampling.

"This must be death," he thought, and he began to struggle and cry out.

The second sheep, having at last learned that he would meet his fate at the freezing works, stood **unperturbed** now in the truck with his nose against the wall and his eyes looking through the slits.

"You are right," he said to the first sheep. "The hill has never seemed so green, the sun has never been warmer, and this truck with its neat red walls is a mansion where I would happily spend the rest of my days."

But the first sheep did not answer. He had seen the approach of death. He could hide from it no longer. He had given up the struggle and was lying exhausted in a corner of the truck. And when the truck arrived at its destination, the freezing works, the man whose duty it was to unload the sheep noticed the first lying so still in the corner that he believed it was dead.

"We can't have dead sheep," he said. "How can you kill a dead sheep?"

So he heaved the first sheep out of the door of the truck onto the rusty railway line.

"I'll move it away later," he said to himself. "Meanwhile here goes with this lot."

And while he was so busy moving the flock, the first sheep, recovering, sprang up and trotted away along the line, out the gate of the freezing works, up the road, along another road, until he saw a flock being driven before him.

"I will join the flock," he said. "No one will notice, and I shall be safe."

While the drover was not looking, the first sheep hurried in among the flock and was soon trotting along with them until they came to a hot dusty road through a valley where the hills

leaned in a sun-scorched wilderness of rock, tussock, and old rabbit warrens.

By now he was feeling very tired. He spoke for the first time to his new companions.

"What a hot dusty road," he said. "How uncomfortable the heat is, and the sun seems to be striking me for its own burning purposes."

The sheep walking beside him looked surprised.

"It is a wonderful day," he exclaimed. "The sun is warmer than I have ever known it, the hills glow green with luscious grass, and there is not a hawk in the sky to threaten us!"

"You mean," the first sheep replied slyly, "that you are on your way to the saleyards, and then to the freezing works to be killed."

The other sheep gave a bleat of surprise.

"How did you guess?" he asked.

"Oh," said the first sheep wisely, "I know the code. And because I know the code I shall go around in circles all my life, not knowing whether to think that the hills are bare or whether they are green, whether the hawks are scarce or plentiful, whether the sun is friend or foe. For the rest of my life I shall not speak another word. I shall trot along the hot dusty valleys where the hills are both barren and lush with spring grass.

"What shall I do but keep silent?"

And so it happened, and over and over again the first sheep escaped death, and rejoined the flock of sheep who were traveling to the freezing works. He is still alive today. If you notice him in a flock, being driven along a hot dusty road, you will be able to distinguish him by his timidity, his uncertainty, the frenzied expression in his eyes when he tries, in his condemned silence, to discover whether the sky is at last free from hawks, or whether they circle in twos and threes above him, waiting to kill him. ❧

Anthropomorphism *Considering the first sheep's response here, what has he gained from his experiences?*   **1**

Identify Sequence *As a result of all the things that have happened to him in the story, what does the first sheep resolve to do? Why do you think he reaches this conclusion?*   **2**

Vocabulary

barren (bar′ ən) *adj.* having little or no vegetation; bare

unperturbed (un pər turbd′) *adj.* undisturbed; not troubled

Writing Practice

[SPIRAL REVIEW] **Compare/Contrast Say:** This fable deals with both similarities and differences. Have students list the similarities and differences that they notice in the fable. **Ask:** What two different views of life does the fable present? *(a positive view that life is* wonderful and a negative view that life is awful) Have students write one or two paragraphs in which they use examples from the story to illustrate each view about life.

After You Read

Respond and Think Critically

Respond and Interpret

1. What aspects of this fable did you enjoy most? Why?

2. (a)At the beginning of the story, what does the first sheep know that the second sheep does not? (b)How does the first sheep's knowledge at the beginning affect his perception of his surroundings?

3. (a)How does the first sheep perceive the sun and the hawks after he's been taken by surprise and hustled into the truck? (b)What accounts for the first sheep's change in perception as he stands in the truck?

4. (a)How does the first sheep escape "certain death" at the freezing works? (a)In what way does he not really escape?

5. (a)At the end of the story, what does the first sheep say his life will be like? (b)How will observers be able to distinguish him from the other sheep traveling to the freezing works? (c)What do these admissions reveal about his attitude toward what he has learned?

Analyze and Evaluate

6. (a)What does the first sheep literally mean when he says, "I know the code"? (b)What might knowing the code mean symbolically? (c)In what ways might one's life be affected by knowing the code?

7. (a)What is the moral of this fable? (b)In your opinion, how effectively does the author convey this moral? Explain.

Connect

8. **Big Idea** Globalization Why might Frame's fable appeal to a variety of worldwide cultures?

9. **Connect to Today** Think of a current situation to which people respond both optimistically and pessimistically. What themes or ideas from the story can you apply to that situation?

Literary Element Anthropomorphism

Assigning human traits to animal characters in a fable allows writers to teach valuable lessons about life in an engaging, entertaining, and inoffensive way. Review the behavior of the sheep in the fable you have just read.

1. What general human traits or characteristics do the sheep possess?

2. What specific attitudes, emotions, and opinions do they express? Support your answer with examples from the fable.

3. The second sheep convinces himself that being killed at the freezing works "is not likely to happen." Does this seem like a typical human reaction to the concept of approaching death? Explain.

Review: Diction

As you learned on page 813, **diction**, an author's choice of words, is an important component of an author's voice or style. (Other components include sentence structure, choice of sensory details, and use of figures of speech.) In "Two Sheep," Janet Frame uses simple words and dialogue to tell her story.

Partner Activity With a partner, answer these questions:

1. (a)Why is simple language appropriate for a children's fable? (b)In what other ways besides diction does "Two Sheep" resemble a children's fable?

2. (a)In what significant way is "Two Sheep" more like an adult fable than a children's fable? (b)Would using more difficult or sophisticated language increase or decrease the effectiveness of "Two Sheep"? Explain.

After You Read

Assess

1. Students' opinions will vary.

2. (a) That they are going to the slaughterhouse (b) It makes him more appreciative of his surroundings.

3. (a) He sees the sun as punishing him and the hawks as threatening him. (b) The knowledge that death is very near

4. (a) A worker mistakes him for dead and tosses him out of the truck. (b) He joins another herd of sheep only to repeat the cycle.

5. (a) He will escape death and join flocks again and again. (b) By his timidity, uncertainty, and silence (c) He feels defeated.

6. (a) He is aware that he (the first sheep) is inevitably headed for the slaughterhouse. (b) Confronting rather than avoiding mortality (c) Confronting one's mortality might influence how one copes with the ups and downs of daily life.

7. (a) That people can view life as wonderful, or horrible, or both simultaneously, and their happiness will depend on how they adapt to their view of life (b) Students' responses will vary.

8. Frame's theme is universal; in the end we all share the same fate. In addition, her story speaks to a world where our individuality is increasingly at risk and certainty is increasingly undermined.

9. Answers and examples will vary; one current situation might be the global warming debate, since the people with knowledge of the risks and dangers have more to worry about than those who lack that knowledge.

Literary Element

1. They think, talk, express emotions, and have opinions.

2. Appreciation for their surroundings, fear of death, and resignation to the uncertainties of life

3. Students may suggest that people often try to deny unpleasant facts.

Review: Diction

1. (a) Simple language allows children to understand the ideas in a story easily. (b) It contains talking animals, and the narrative develops a simple conflict.

2. (a) The ideas are complex and mature. (b) If the language were more difficult, it would be that much harder to absorb and evaluate the ideas in the story. The story gains meaning by working on multiple levels.

After You Read

Assess

Reading Strategy

1. The third sheep tells the uninformed one the truth, confronting his fate; the first sheep escapes, giving him a reprieve from fate; the first sheep talks to a sheep in the new flock he has joined, giving insight into life that he has acquired.

2. (a) Possible responses: people deny or ignore what is unpleasant; confronting death makes one appreciate life more; life is filled with uncertainties. (b) Possible responses: Your happiness will depend on your attitude towards life.

Progress Check

Can students identify sequence?

If No → See Unit 7 Teaching Resources Book, p. 157.

Vocabulary Practice

pall

Definition: an atmosphere of dark and gloom Etymology: Latin *pallium* means "cloak" Sample Sentence: Her foul mood cast a *pall* on my birthday party.

barren

Definition: having little or no vegetation; bare Etymology: Middle Welsh *brynar* means "fallow land" Sample Sentence: The plain lay barren after the long drought.

unperturbed

Definition: undisturbed; not troubled Etymology: Latin *perturbare* means "to throw into disorder" Sample Sentence: He seemed surprisingly unperturbed by the car accident.

1278

Reading Strategy Identify Sequence

Review the sequence of events that you recorded in your sequence chart as you read. Then answer the following questions.

1. Identify the three events in the story that trigger significant changes in the development or direction of the plot. Explain the significance of each of these events.

2. (a)What observations about life are expressed or implied as the story progresses? (b)What morals or lessons do they teach?

Vocabulary Practice

Practice with Word Origins Create a word map for each of these vocabulary words from the selection. Use a dictionary for help.

| pall | barren | unperturbed |

EXAMPLE:

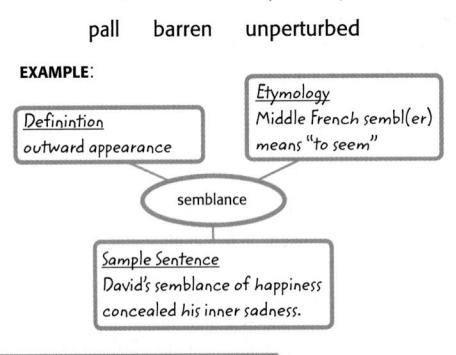

Academic Vocabulary

*The slaughterhouse is their **final** destination.*

Final is an academic word that appears in everyday usage. If someone gives his or her "**final** answer," it is a definitive conclusion.

To study this word further, fill out the graphic organizer below.

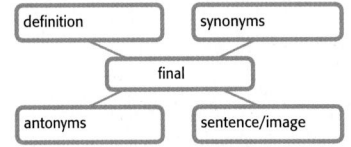

For more on academic vocabulary, see pages 56 and R81.

1278 UNIT 7   AN INTERNATIONAL LITERATURE

Speaking and Listening

 Literature Groups

Assignment Writers often anthropomorphize animals or inanimate objects to communicate an idea or message about humans. In a small group, discuss whether the anthropomorphism in "Two Sheep" effectively supports the author's message or acts more as a distraction. Continue the discussion until you reach a consensus.

Prepare Reread the short story, focusing on the effect of the anthropomorphism. Organize your ideas in an outline or a chart.

With the members of your group, decide what will constitute consensus. Will you work for unanimity, or will a majority be acceptable?

Discuss Hold your discussion, exercising good speaking and listening skills. State your point of view clearly and succinctly, supporting your statements with sound arguments and examples from the story. Respond to others' statements respectfully and logically, rather than emotionally.

Report Write a summary of the consensus reached in your discussion, focusing on the strongest arguments. Have a group member present the results orally, using diction, tone of voice, and gestures to engage the audience.

EXAMPLE:

The human characteristics demonstrated by each sheep—over-thinking, or unquestioning obedience—characterize two extreme human types. Seeing them portrayed in nonhuman creatures creates distance and humor, which helps clarify the author's message.

Evaluate Write a paragraph assessing your participation in the group. Bear in mind how well the group reached consensus or settled on a majority.

LOG ON ▶ **Literature** Online

Selection Resources For Selection Quizzes, eFlashcards, and Reading-Writing Connection activities, go to glencoe.com and enter QuickPass code GLB9817u7.

Academic Vocabulary

Possible answer:

final

Definition: at the end; ultimate
Synonyms: *last, concluding*
Antonyms: *beginning, first, initial*
Sentence/Image: The final exam is a culmination of all the material from the course.

Speaking and Listening

Students' literature groups should:

- address the effectiveness of anthropomorphism in conveying the message
- deliver statements logically and respectfully
- report the group's results appropriately and clearly
- provide a self-evaluation that is accurate and based on relevant criteria

Meet **Derek Walcott**

(born 1930)

Inspired by their schoolteacher mother, Derek Walcott and his twin brother, Roderick, enjoyed reading literature and improvising plays at an early age. Both boys grew up to be writers, following in the footsteps of their father, an amateur poet and artist who died when the boys were only a year old.

> "The fate of poetry is to fall in love with the world."
>
> —Derek Walcott

A Young Poet Derek Walcott grew up in a middle-class family on the Caribbean island of Saint Lucia. His father worked for the government and his mother was an elementary school teacher. The arts were valued highly in the Walcott home, and in this enriched environment, Walcott quickly developed a lasting love of art and language. By the time he was eight years old, he had decided to become a poet. In his youth he began a practice of writing a poem a day in the notebooks his mother gave him for this purpose. She also guided him by giving him famous poems to copy and imitate. In this way, Walcott began to internalize different forms of poetry and gain an appreciation of sound devices, rhythm, and cadence.

As a teenager, Walcott had several of his poems published in a local newspaper. When he was eighteen, he borrowed two hundred dollars from his mother and used it to publish his first book of poetry, which he then sold on the streets of Castries, his hometown and the capital of Saint Lucia. The book, *25 Poems*, received good reviews, and Walcott was soon able to pay his mother back for the loan.

Caribbean Theater Although he continued writing poetry, Walcott soon became involved in theater. In 1950 he helped found the Saint Lucia Arts Guild, for which he wrote several plays. He received a fellowship to study theater in New York City in 1958. He continued his involvement with Caribbean theater when he moved to Trinidad in 1959, founding with his brother the Trinidad Theatre Workshop. Walcott's plays often incorporate Caribbean folktales or local history. About writing these plays, Walcott has said, "The great challenge for me was to write as powerfully as I could without writing down to the audience, so that the large emotions could be taken in by a fisherman or a guy on the street, even if he didn't understand every line."

Walcott has written more than thirty plays; *Ti-Jean and His Brothers* (1958) and *Dream on Monkey Mountain* (1967) are two of the most famous. In addition, he wrote an epic poem, *Omeros* (1990), which is based on Homer's *Odyssey*. Walcott received the Nobel Prize in Literature in 1992. In addition to writing poetry and plays, Walcott paints and teaches, dividing his time between the Caribbean and the United States.

 **Literature** Online

Author Search For more about Derek Walcott, go to glencoe.com and enter QuickPass code GLB9817u7.

DEREK WALCOTT **1279**

Bellringer Options

Selection Focus Transparency 71

Daily Language Practice Transparency 113

Or **display** a photograph or painting of a Caribbean Island. **Ask:** Have you ever tried to describe the natural beauty of an island? What words or phrases would you use to describe this picture? Encourage students to discuss how poets use descriptive words to create vivid images in their poems. Tell students to read Walcott's poem to find examples of such imagery.

Selection Skills

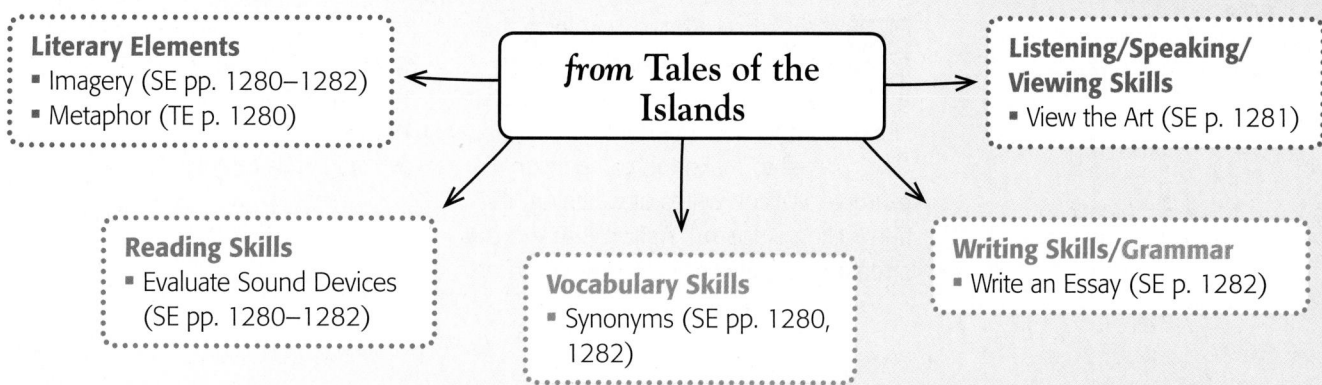

Literary Elements
- Imagery (SE pp. 1280–1282)
- Metaphor (TE p. 1280)

from Tales of the Islands

Listening/Speaking/ Viewing Skills
- View the Art (SE p. 1281)

Reading Skills
- Evaluate Sound Devices (SE pp. 1280–1282)

Vocabulary Skills
- Synonyms (SE pp. 1280, 1282)

Writing Skills/Grammar
- Write an Essay (SE p. 1282)

Before You Read

Focus

Summary

This poem by Derek Walcott describes the speaker's sadness as he watches from an airplane a beautiful island that he loves and arrives in a city where it had rained.

 For summaries in languages other than English, see Unit 7 Teaching Resources Book, pp. 162–167.

Vocabulary

Etymology Have students look up the Latin root of each vocabulary word. Ask them to compare the meaning of the root with the definition of the vocabulary word. **Ask:** Which word is most similar to its Latin root's meaning? *(fidelity)*

 For additonal vocabulary practice, see Unit 7 Teaching Resources Book, p. 170.

 For additional context, see Glencoe Interactive Vocabulary CD-ROM.

 For an audio recording of this selection, use Listening Library Audio CD-ROM.

1280

Literature and Reading Preview

Connect to the Poem

What feelings do you have when you leave a place that you love? In a journal entry, write about the thoughts, feelings, and wishes you've had in departing from somewhere special.

Build Background

Saint Lucia is a small island in the eastern Caribbean. It was settled by the French in 1635 and was taken over by the British in 1814. In the 1700s and early 1800s, enslaved Africans were brought to work on the large sugar plantations run by Europeans. The island gained independence in 1979.

Set Purposes for Reading

Big Idea Colonialism and Postcolonialism

As you read, ask yourself, What references to French Creole customs and English literary tradition appear in this poem?

Literary Element Imagery

The word pictures in a work of literature are called **imagery**. Such images appeal to one or more of the five senses and evoke an emotional response in the reader. As you read, ask yourself, Which sense does Walcott's imagery appeal to most?

Reading Strategy Evaluate Sound Devices

Sound devices include a variety of techniques that writers use to appeal to the ear and to add a musical quality to their writing. Some common sound devices include repetition, rhyme, alliteration, assonance, and caesura. Use the Literary Terms Handbook to review the definition of each of these devices. As you read, ask yourself, What device creates this "sound," and is it effective?

Tip: **Taking Notes** Use a chart like the one below to record examples of the different sound devices in this poem.

Device	Line	Example
Assonance	Epigraph	The "u" sounds in "Adieu" and "foulard"
Alliteration		
Caesura		
Repetition		

1280 UNIT 7 AN INTERNATIONAL LITERATURE

Literary Element Practice

SPIRAL REVIEW **Metaphor** Remind students that a metaphor is a figure of speech that compares two unlike things. Unlike a simile, a metaphor does not use "like" or "as" to make the comparison. For example, Walcott writes of watching "the fine writing of foam." **Ask:** What did the speaker actually see? *(He saw foam at* the edge of the cliffs.) Why would he compare this foam to writing? *(The word "writing" conveys the image of a narrow line or that the foam is "writing" the speaker's farewell.)*

Vocabulary

precipice (pres′ ə pis) *n.* a very steep or overhanging mass of rock as on a cliff; p. 1281 *The precipice plunged into the sea, without even a beach at its base.*

fidelity (fi del′ ə tē) *n.* the quality or state of being faithful; p. 1281 *The fidelity of a true friend is priceless.*

Tip: **Synonyms** Synonyms are words that have the same or nearly the same meaning. For example, *divide* and *separate* are synonyms.

from
Tales of the Islands

Derek Walcott

Chapter X

"Adieu foulard . . ."[1]

I watched the island narrowing the fine
Writing of foam around the **precipices** then
The roads as small and casual as twine
Thrown on its mountains; I watched till the plane **1**
5   Turned to the final north and turned above
The open channel with the gray sea between
The fishermen's islets[2] until all that I love
Folded in cloud; I watched the shallow green
That broke in places where there would be reef,
10   The silver glinting on the fuselage,[3] each mile
Dividing us and all **fidelity** strained
Till space would snap it. Then, after a while
I thought of nothing; nothing, I prayed, would change;
When we set down at Seawell[4] it had rained.

---

2   Imagery *From this image, determine where the speaker is in relation to the roads and mountains.*

Vocabulary

precipice (pres′ ə pis) *n.* a very steep or overhanging mass of rock as on a cliff
fidelity (fi del′ ə tē) *n.* the quality or state of being faithful

View the Photograph

The island of Saint Lucia is only 27 miles long. What lines or phrases of the poem does this image most closely reflect?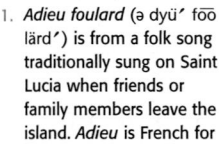

1.   *Adieu foulard* (ə dyü′ fo͞o lärd′) is from a folk song traditionally sung on Saint Lucia when friends or family members leave the island. *Adieu* is French for "good-bye," and a *foulard* is a neckerchief worn by the people of Saint Lucia.
2.   *Islets* are little islands.
3.   A *fuselage* is the central body of the aircraft.
4   *Seawell* is a city in Barbados.

Teach

Reading Strategy | 1

Evaluate Sound Devices
Explain that a caesura is a pause in the middle of a line of poetry. **Ask:** Where does a caesura occur in this poem? *(After the semicolon between* mountains *and* I watched *in line 4)* Can you find other examples of caesuras? *(After the semicolons in lines 8 and 13; after the period between "it" and "Then" in line 12)*

Literary Element | 2

Imagery **Answer:** *The speaker is above them in an airplane.*

 For additional practice using the reading skill or strategy, see Unit 7 Teaching Resources Book, p. 169.

View the Photograph

Answer: *"the shallow green/ That broke in places," "fishermen's islets," "roads as small and casual as twine"*

This photograph of Saint Lucia shows an aerial view of part of an island, mirroring the speaker's vantage point in this poem.

To check students' understanding of the selection, see Unit 7 Teaching Resources Book, p. 171.

English Learners

DIFFERENTIATED INSTRUCTION

SMALL GROUP

Beginning Give English learners several photographs of beautiful places in the world. Have them divide into small groups and give each group a few of the photos. Have students in each group take turns describing one of the photographs. **Ask:** Would you like to live there? Why or why not? Have them think of a place they have lived, or would like to live and orally describe these places.

After You Read

Assess

1. (a) A Caribbean island (b) He is sad and perhaps fearful about leaving St. Lucia. In line 7, the speaker says that all he loves is below, on the island.
2. (a) That nothing will change (b) He loves the island.
3. (a) Fourteen lines; *ababcdcdefgfgg;* the b's and the g's are slant rhymes; sonnet (b) The number of lines and the rhyme scheme fit the form; the lack of one rhyming pair in the third quatrain and the use of caesura depart from the form.
4. (a) The tone ceases to be laudatory and becomes sad. (b) It makes the poem universal.
5. (a) The epigraph is from a traditional song. (b) The sonnet is a classic English form.
6. Students should note that Walcott's biography mentions numerous relocations. He may have become very nostalgic about home, and is most familiar with leaving it.

Literary Element

1. A comparison between the roads on the mountainsides and a looping piece of twine; the comparison suggests an aerial view of the roads.
2. Fidelity is likened to a piece of elastic that will snap under great strain. The metaphor appeals to the senses of hearing, sight, and touch and suggests the speaker's tension.

Progress Check

Can students evaluate imagery?

If No → See Unit 7 Teaching Resources Book, p. 168.

After You Read

Respond and Think Critically

Respond and Interpret

1. (a)What is the setting of this poem? (b)What is the speaker's attitude toward the subject? What clues helped you figure out the speaker's attitude?
2. (a)What does the speaker pray for in line 13? (b)What does this prayer imply about his feelings as he leaves the island?

Analyze and Evaluate

3. (a)Count the number of lines and analyze the rhyme scheme of this poem. Use this information to identify the form of the poem. (b)In what ways does this poem fit this traditional form? How does it depart from the form?
4. (a)Near the end of the poem, how does the tone change? (b)Do you think this change adds meaning to the poem? Explain.

Connect

5. **Big Idea** Colonialism and Postcolonialism Although English is the official language of Saint Lucia, many people there also speak French Creole. (a)How does the poem pay homage to Saint Lucia's alternate language? (b)How does the poem fit into the tradition of English classics?
6. **Connect to the Author** Reread the biography on page 1279. What aspects of Walcott's life might have led him to write about leaving Saint Lucia, instead of about the island itself?

Literary Element Imagery

Images can appeal to any of the five senses. They can be simple references to color, odor, taste, sound, or texture. They can also be more complex, incorporating similes or metaphors.

1. Evaluate Walcott's use of simile in lines 3–4. What comparison is being made? Does this simile help you better envision the scene? Explain.
2. Evaluate the metaphor in lines 11–12. Which senses are being appealed to, and what is being compared? Does this metaphor help you understand the speaker's feelings? Explain.

Writing

Write an Essay Write a brief essay describing a trip you have taken, either by car, bus, train, or airplane. Focus on the act of traveling itself. Use figurative language, such as simile and metaphor, to express the sensory details you recall.

LOG ON Literature Online

Selection Resources For Selection Quizzes, eFlashcards, and Reading-Writing Connection activities, go to glencoe.com and enter QuickPass code GLB9817u7.

Reading Strategy Evaluate Sound Devices

Refer to the chart you made on page 1280 for examples of assonance and alliteration from the poem. Then answer these questions.

1. How does the use of assonance affect the pace of the poem?
2. Why do you think Walcott uses alliteration at specific points in this poem? Do you think these lines convey dramatic tension or serve some other purpose? Explain.

Vocabulary Practice

Practice with Synonyms With a partner, match each boldfaced vocabulary word below with its synonym. Use a dictionary or thesaurus to check your answers. You will not use all of the answer choices.

1. **precipice**	a. faithfulness
2. **fidelity**	b. valley
	c. malfeasance
	d. cliff

Reading Strategy

1. The use of assonance in lines 2–3 and 11–12 slows the pace.
2. Walcott uses alliteration mainly in lines 11–12, with the repetition of the s sound at the beginning of *strained*, *space*, and *snap*, to create dramatic tension related to the speaker's leaving his home.

Vocabulary

1. d 2. a

Writing

Students' essays should use figurative language to describe the details and experience of a specific trip.

Meet **V. S. Naipaul**
(born 1932)

V. S. (Vidiadhar Surajprasad) Naipaul chose to become a writer at age eleven because he thought of writing as a noble occupation. However, writing did not come easily for Naipaul. "I do not believe in natural genius. I do not believe in the spontaneous outpouring of the soul. Style is essentially a matter of hard thinking," Naipaul once told writer and poet Derek Walcott in an interview.

Early Years and Education Naipaul was born on the Caribbean island of Trinidad. His grandparents on both sides of his family had come to the West Indies from India as indentured servants. Within a few decades, Naipaul's mother's family had achieved wealth; his father's family had not. However, education was important to his father's family, and Naipaul's father completed school and got a job writing for a Trinidad newspaper. Naipaul received a good education and graduated from Trinidad's most prestigious school. In 1950 he won a scholarship to attend Oxford University, and he graduated in 1953 with a degree in English.

A Literary Life in London After graduating, Naipaul moved to London. There he got a part-time job with the British Broadcasting Company (BBC) editing and presenting a weekly radio program about literature that was designed for a Caribbean audience. When Naipaul wasn't working on his radio program, he worked toward his goal of becoming a writer. Naipaul's first literary works were based on memories of his years in Trinidad. The novels *The Mystic Masseur* (1957) and *The Suffrage of Elvira* (1958) and the short story collection *Miguel Street* (which contains the story "B. Wordsworth") were well-received by critics and readers. But Naipaul's status as a great author was secured with the publication of *A House for Mr. Biswas* (1961). The novel's title character is based on Naipaul's father and the work presents a fictionalized account of Naipaul's childhood in Trinidad.

> "A book should speak to you directly. You should be able to pick up things in your own experience and if you can't pick things up, then for you, the book has failed, I think."
>
> —V. S. Naipaul

A Cosmopolitan Writer In 1960 the government of Trinidad gave Naipaul a grant to return to the Caribbean. Based on his travels, he wrote a nonfiction book, *The Middle Passage*, detailing his views of the region. This book was the first of many nonfiction books Naipaul wrote documenting his travels through India, the Middle East, Africa, and the Caribbean. Many of his novels, too, are set in developing nations struggling to form new national identities after the end of colonialism.

Naipaul has won numerous prizes, including the Nobel Prize in Literature in 2001. Knighted in 1990, he is now entitled to be called Sir V. S. Naipaul.

LOG ON **Literature** Online

Author Search For more about V. S. Naipaul, go to glencoe.com and enter QuickPass code GLB9817u7.

Bellringer Options

Selection Focus Transparency 72

Daily Language Practice Transparency 114

Or **ask:** What do you think poets are like? *(Students responses might include that they are sensitive, observant, unusual, or eccentric.)* What skills do you think a poet needs to have? *(Student responses may include a lively imagination, good language skills, and keen observational skills.)* Have students consider what a poet is as they read Naipaul's short story.

Selection Skills

Literary Elements
- Dialect (SE pp. 1284–1290)
- Foreshadowing (SE p. 1290)

B. Wordsworth

Listening/Speaking/Viewing Skills
- Analyze Art (SE pp. 1285, 1288)
- Interview (TE p. 1284)

Reading Skills
- Draw Conclusions About Meaning (SE pp. 1284–1291)

Vocabulary Skills
- Analogies (SE p. 1291)
- Academic Vocabulary (SE p. 1291)

Writing Skills/Grammar
- Apply Diction (SE p. 1291)

Before You Read

Focus

Summary

An unusual man comes to a young boy's house, asking to watch bees there. A friendship blooms between the two, and the man who calls himself "Black Wordsworth" tells the boy that they are both poets. He also shares details about his life. One day, when the boy visits the man, he sees that he is dying. B. Wordsworth says that the stories he has told the boy about writing poetry and about his past are not true. Afterward, the boy mourns his friend.

 For summaries in languages other than English, see Unit 7 Teaching Resources Book, pp. 173–178.

Vocabulary

Word Roots Have students look up the etymologies of the vocabulary words to find their Latin roots, or tell students the roots (*hospit* = guest; *stell* = star; *patron* = protector; *still* = drop). Ask them to think of other words that contain the roots. (*hospitality, stellar, patron, instill*)

 For additional vocabulary practice, see Unit 7 Teaching Resources Book, p. 181.

Literature and Reading Preview

Connect to the Story

What are the qualities of a poet? Create a list of traits, habits, or skills that make a person a poet—literally or figuratively.

Build Background

"B. Wordsworth" is set in the city of Port-of-Spain, which is the capital city of the Caribbean island of Trinidad, now part of the Republic of Trinidad and Tobago. People of many different backgrounds live in Port-of-Spain, including people of African descent, people of European descent, people of mixed heritage, and people from the subcontinent of India whose families moved to Trinidad in the 1800s. Formerly a British colony, Trinidad and Tobago became an independent republic in 1962.

Set Purposes for Reading

Big Idea Globalization

As you read, ask yourself, What makes this story specific to a particular place, and what makes it universal?

Literary Element Dialect

Dialect is a variation of a language that is spoken in a particular region or by a particular group of people. Dialects may differ from the standard form of a language in vocabulary, pronunciation, or grammar. As you read, ask yourself, How does the dialect used by the characters differ from Standard English?

Reading Strategy Draw Conclusions About Meaning

Drawing conclusions about meaning means making a generalization about the main idea, or theme, of a story from clues supplied by the author. These clues can be found in the characters' dialogue, in the narrator's commentary, and in the specific details used to describe setting. As you read, ask yourself, What might the author want to express with these details?

Tip: Taking Notes Use a chart similar to the one below to write down clues that you think may help you draw conclusions about the meaning of this story.

Detail	Meaning

Learning Objectives

For pages 1283–1291

In studying this text, you will focus on the following objectives:

Literary Study: Analyzing dialect.

Reading: Drawing conclusions about meaning.

Writing: Applying diction in a story or dialogue.

Vocabulary

hospitable (hos´ pi´ tə bəl) *adj.* offering generous and cordial welcome to guests; p. 1285 *A hospitable person is gracious when people come to visit.*

constellation (kon´ stə lā´ shən) *n.* any of eighty-eight groups of stars, many of which traditionally represent characters and objects in ancient mythology; p. 1287 *We could identify several constellations when we studied the patterns of stars in the night sky.*

patronize (pā´ trə nīz´) *v.* to be a customer of; p. 1288 *They preferred to patronize locally owned stores rather than large chain stores.*

distill (dis til´) *v.* to extract the essence of; p. 1288 *Distilling information means expressing it in as few words as possible.*

Listening and Speaking Practice

 Conduct an Interview Have students think about what type of person becomes a poet. **Ask:** What skills would such a person have? What would his or her personality be like? *(Answers will vary.)* Brainstorm a list of skills and personality traits with students and write them on the board.

Divide students into pairs and have them write an interview between a reporter and a poet. The reporter wants to know why the poet chose poetry as a career and what it takes to be a real poet. Students may use words from the board in their questions and answers. Give students a chance to practice their interview before they role-play it in front of the class.

Landscape, Trinidad, c. 1921. James Wilson Morrice. Oil on canvas, 74 x 92.2 cm. Art Gallery of Toronto.

 View the Art In the late nineteenth and early twentieth centuries, artists like Morrice and Paul Gauguin traveled to tropical locations like Trinidad and Tahiti to paint. What elements of this image by Morrice might illustrate the appeal of such locations to an artist? ★

B. Wordsworth

V. S. Naipaul

1 Three beggars called punctually every day at the **hospitable** houses in Miguel Street. At about ten an Indian came in his dhoti[1] and white jacket, and we poured a tin of rice into the sack he carried on his back. At twelve an old woman smoking a clay pipe came and she got a cent. At two a blind man led by a boy called for his penny. Sometimes we had a

rogue.[2] One day a man called and said he was hungry. We gave him a meal. He asked for a cigarette and wouldn't go until we had lit it for him. That man never came again.

The strangest caller came one afternoon at about four o'clock. I had come back from school and was in my home-clothes. The man said to me, "Sonny, may I come inside your yard?"

He was a small man and he was tidily dressed. He wore a hat, a white shirt, and black trousers.

---

1. A *dhoti* is a loincloth worn by Hindu men in India.

Vocabulary

hospitable (hos´ pi´ tə bəl) *adj.* offering generous and cordial welcome to guests

---

2. One might be described as a *rogue* if one is somehow different or set apart from a group. *Rogue* can also mean a beggar.

V. S. NAIPAUL **1285**

Teach

Literary Element　1

Dialect Answer: *Two specific differences are* it have *rather than* there is *and* He say he want *rather than* He says he wants.

📁 For additional literary element practice, see Unit 7 Teaching Resources Book, p. 179.

Big Idea　2

Globalization Answer: *It indicates that B. Wordsworth, in Trinidad, has learned to love English literature and considers it a part of his heritage. He feels a kinship with the English poet William Wordsworth through a common language and a love of poetry.*

Reading Strategy　3

Draw Conclusions About Meaning Answer: *Some students may say that he finds B. Wordsworth an interesting character, that he is flattered that B. Wordsworth considers him a poet, and that he finds B. Wordsworth to be a gentle, educated person.*

I asked, "What do you want?"

He said, "I want to watch your bees."

We had four small gru-gru palm trees and they were full of uninvited bees.

I ran up the steps and shouted, "Ma, it have a man outside here. He say he want to watch the bees."

My mother came out, looked at the man, and asked in an unfriendly way, "What you want?"

The man said, "I want to watch your bees."

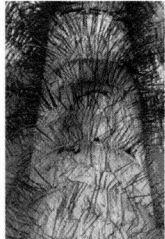

Visual Vocabulary
Gru-gru palm trees are spiny-trunked palms that grow in the West Indies.

His English was so good, it didn't sound natural, and I could see my mother was worried.

She said to me, "Stay here and watch him while he watch the bees."

The man said, "Thank you, Madam. You have done a good deed today."

He spoke very slowly and very correctly as though every word was costing him money.

We watched the bees, this man and I, for about an hour, squatting near the palm trees.

The man said, "I like watching bees. Sonny, do you like watching bees?"

I said, "I ain't have the time."

He shook his head sadly. He said, "That's what I do, I just watch. I can watch ants for days. Have you ever watched ants? And scorpions, and centipedes, and *congorees*[3]—have you watched those?"

I shook my head.

I said, "What you does do, mister?"

He got up and said, "I am a poet."

I said, "A good poet?"

He said, "The greatest in the world."

"What's your name, mister?"

"B. Wordsworth."

"B for Bill?"

---

3. *Congorees* is a West Indian term for millipedes (long, many-legged arthropods).

1 Dialect *How does the boy's dialect differ from Standard English? List two specific differences.*

"Black. Black Wordsworth. White Wordsworth[4] was my brother. We share one heart. I can watch a small flower like the morning glory and cry."

I said, "Why you does cry?"

"Why, boy? Why? You will know when you grow up. You're a poet, too, you know. And when you're a poet you can cry for everything."

I couldn't laugh.

He said, "You like your mother?"

"When she not beating me."

He pulled out a printed sheet from his hip-pocket and said, "On this paper is the greatest poem about mothers and I'm going to sell it to you at a bargain price. For four cents."

I went inside and I said, "Ma, you want to buy a poetry for four cents?"

My mother said, "Tell that blasted man to haul his tail away from my yard, you hear."

I said to B. Wordsworth, "My mother say she ain't have four cents."

B. Wordsworth said, "It is the poet's tragedy."

And he put the paper back in his pocket. He didn't seem to mind.

I said, "Is a funny way to go round selling poetry like that. Only calypsonians[5] do that sort of thing. A lot of people does buy?"

He said, "No one has yet bought a single copy."

"But why you does keep on going round, then?"

He said, "In this way I watch many things, and I always hope to meet poets."

I said, "You really think I is a poet?"

"You're as good as me," he said.

And when B. Wordsworth left, I prayed I would see him again.

---

4. *White Wordsworth* is a reference to the English poet William Wordsworth (1770–1850).

5. *Calypsonians* are folk musicians who sing calypso music— satirical street ballads native to Trinidad and Tobago that are often improvised.

2 Globalization *What does this statement tell you about the globalization of English?*

3 Draw Conclusions About Meaning *Why do you think the boy wants to see B. Wordsworth again?*

1286　UNIT 7　AN INTERNATIONAL LITERATURE

Writing Practice

SPIRAL REVIEW 🌀 **Contractions Say:** A contraction is a word in which two words are joined but one or more letters are left out. An apostrophe replaces the missing letter or letters, as in the word *aren't*, a contraction of *are not*. Point out that Naipaul uses contractions to convey informal speech. Note that both characters use contractions, though

B. Wordsworth speaks Standard English, whereas the boy speaks a type of English dialect. Have students make contraction charts that include the contractions and the words that the contractions stand for.

1286

About a week later, coming back from school one afternoon, I met him at the corner of Miguel Street.

He said, "I have been waiting for you for a long time."

I said, "You sell any poetry yet?"

He shook his head.

He said, "In my yard I have the best mango tree in Port of Spain. And now the mangoes are ripe and red and very sweet and juicy. I have waited here for you to tell you this and to invite you to come and eat some of my mangoes."

He lived in Alberto Street in a one-roomed hut placed right in the center of the lot. The yard seemed all green. There was the big mango tree. There was a coconut tree and there was a plum tree. The place looked wild, as though it wasn't in the city at all. You couldn't see all the big concrete houses in the street.

He was right. The mangoes were sweet and juicy. I ate about six, and the yellow mango juice ran down my arms to my elbows and down my mouth to my chin and my shirt was stained.

My mother said when I got home, "Where you was? You think you is a man now and could go all over the place? Go cut a whip for me."

She beat me rather badly, and I ran out of the house swearing that I would never come back. I went to B. Wordsworth's house. I was so angry, my nose was bleeding.

B. Wordsworth said, "Stop crying, and we will go for a walk."

I stopped crying, but I was breathing short. We went for a walk. We walked down St. Clair Avenue to the Savannah[6] and we walked to the racecourse.

B. Wordsworth said, "Now, let us lie on the grass and look up at the sky, and I want you to think how far those stars are from us."

I did as he told me, and I saw what he meant. I felt like nothing, and at the same time I had

never felt so big and great in all my life. I forgot all my anger and all my tears and all the blows.

When I said I was better, he began telling me the names of the stars, and I particularly remembered the **constellation** of Orion the Hunter, though I don't really know why. I can spot Orion even today, but I have forgotten the rest.

Then a light was flashed into our faces, and we saw a policeman. We got up from the grass.

The policeman said, "What you doing here?"

B. Wordsworth said, "I have been asking myself the same question for forty years."

Visual Vocabulary
Orion the Hunter is the constellation named for a mythological giant hunter.

We became friends, B. Wordsworth and I. He told me, "You must never tell anybody about me and about the mango tree and the coconut tree and the plum tree. You must keep that a secret. If you tell anybody, I will know, because I am a poet."

I gave him my word and I kept it.

I liked his little room. It had no more furniture than George's[7] front room, but it looked cleaner and healthier. But it also looked lonely.

One day I asked him, "Mister Wordsworth, why you does keep all this bush in your yard? Ain't it does make the place damp?"

He said, "Listen, and I will tell you a story. Once upon a time a boy and girl met each other and they fell in love. They loved each other so much they got married. They were both poets. He loved words. She loved grass and flowers and trees. They lived happily in a single room, and then one

---

7. *George* is a character in Naipaul's book of short stories *Miguel Street.*

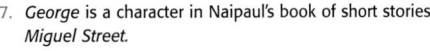
Dialect *What difference do you detect between the speech of the policeman and that of B. Wordsworth?* **5**

Vocabulary

constellation (kon´ stə lā´ shən) *n.* any of eighty-eight groups of stars, many of which traditionally represent characters and objects in ancient mythology

---

6. *Savannah* is a two-hundred-acre park in Port-of-Spain, Trinidad, that includes a racecourse.

 4
Draw Conclusions About Meaning *What does the boy learn from B. Wordsworth in this passage?*

V. S. NAIPAUL **1287**

Teach

Reading Strategy   4

Draw Conclusions About Meaning   Answer:
B. Wordsworth teaches the boy about humans' relationship to the vast cosmos, which makes the boy forget about his personal problems.

(APPROACHING) To help approaching level students, **ask:** Why did the narrator feel like "nothing" when he looked at the stars? *(He was thinking about how big the sky is in comparison to himself.)*

Literary Element   5

Dialect   Answer: *The policeman speaks in dialect, whereas B. Wordsworth speaks Standard English.*

Approaching Level

DIFFERENTIATED INSTRUCTION

Established To give approaching-level students practice with short-answer test questions, have them write three to five sentences in response to the following question. **Say:** When a policeman asks B. Wordsworth what he is doing there, B. Wordsworth tells him that he has been asking himself that same question for forty years. **Ask:** What does he mean?

(Students might write that he is making a joke about his purposeless life. Alternatively, students may write that he is saying something literally true—he has wondered what he is and should be doing on earth.)

Teach

Reading Strategy   1

Draw Conclusions About Meaning **Answer:** *He believes that ordinary life is very special, almost sacred. He believes in treating each event in his life as a fresh experience to be cherished in the present moment.*

Reading Strategy   2

Draw Conclusions About Meaning **Answer:** *Considering that B. Wordsworth is an old man, his plan of finishing a great poem in 22 years by writing one line per month is preposterous. The reader begins to suspect that B. Wordsworth enjoys beguiling the boy by concocting fanciful stories about his life.*

ENGLISH LEARNERS For English learners, **ask:** What does *present* mean in the phrase "at the present rate"? Does it mean the same as *gift*? *(no)* Have students look up *present* in the dictionary and choose the correct meaning for this context. *(current)* If students' first language is Spanish, note that the Spanish noun *presente* means "the present time" or "the present tense."

View the Art ★

Answer: *Most students will identify the image with the narrator, because of the person's age; some may say the person's watchfulness reminds them of B. Wordsworth.*

day, the girl poet said to the boy poet, 'We are going to have another poet in the family.' But this poet was never born, because the girl died, and the young poet died with her, inside her. And the girl's husband was very sad, and he said he would never touch a thing in the girl's garden. And so the garden remained, and grew high and wild."

I looked at B. Wordsworth, and as he told me this lovely story, he seemed to grow older. I understood his story.

We went for long walks together. We went to the Botanical Gardens and the Rock Gardens. We climbed Chancellor Hill in the late afternoon and watched the darkness fall on Port of Spain, and watched the lights go on in the city and on the ships in the harbor.

He did everything as though he were doing it for the first time in his life. He did everything as though he were doing some church rite.

He would say to me, "Now, how about having some ice cream?"

And when I said yes, he would grow very serious and say, "Now, which café shall we **patronize**?" As though it were a very important thing. He would think for some time about it, and finally say, "I think I will go and negotiate the purchase with that shop."

The world became a most exciting place.

One day, when I was in his yard, he said to me, "I have a great secret which I am now going to tell you."

I said, "It really secret?"

"At the moment, yes."

I looked at him, and he looked at me. He said, "This is just between you and me, remember. I am writing a poem."

"Oh." I was disappointed.

He said, "But this is a different sort of poem. This is the greatest poem in the world."

I whistled.

---

1 Draw Conclusions About Meaning *What does this statement indicate about B. Wordsworth's philosophy of life?*

Vocabulary

patronize (pā′ trə nīz′) *v.* to be a customer of
distill (dis til′) *v.* to extract the essence of

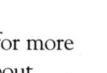

Watching, 1995. Betye Saar. Mixed media on metal, 13½ x 9½ in. Courtesy of Michael Rosenfeld Gallery, New York.

View the Art This image gets its coloring from the metal that is beneath the paint. What character would you most identify with this image? ★

He said, "I have been working on it for more than five years now. I will finish it in about twenty-two years from now, that is, if I keep on writing at the present rate."

"You does write a lot, then?"

He said, "Not any more. I just write one line a month. But I make sure it is a good line."

I asked, "What was last month's good line?"

He looked up at the sky, and said, *"The past is deep."*

I said, "It is a beautiful line."

B. Wordsworth said, "I hope to **distill** the experiences of a whole month into that single line of poetry. So, in twenty-two years, I shall have written a poem that will sing to all humanity."

Draw Conclusions About Meaning *What does the reader begin to suspect about B. Wordsworth in this passage?* **2**

1288 UNIT 7   AN INTERNATIONAL LITERATURE

Reading Practice

SPIRAL REVIEW **Make Inferences** Remind students that making inferences involves using one's own knowledge of people and the clues in the text to better comprehend the story. **Ask:** Why does B. Wordsworth tell the narrator about his "greatest poem in the world"? *(He wants to impress or entertain the boy. He is so involved in his writing that he wants to share his work with someone.)* **Say:** Make an inference about the reason B. Wordsworth stops talking about the poem. *(B. Wordsworth regrets that he lied to the boy or that his writing is not going well, so he would rather not talk about it.)*

I was filled with wonder.

Our walks continued. We walked along the seawall at Docksite one day, and I said, "Mr. Wordsworth, if I drop this pin in the water, you think it will float?"

He said, "This is a strange world. Drop your pin, and let us see what will happen."

The pin sank.

I said, "How is the poem this month?"

But he never told me any other line. He merely said, "Oh, it comes, you know. It comes."

Or we would sit on the seawall and watch the liners come into the harbor.

But of the greatest poem in the world I heard no more.

I felt he was growing older.

"How you does live, Mr. Wordsworth?" I asked him one day.

He said, "You mean how I get money?"

When I nodded, he laughed in a crooked way.

 He said, "I sing calypsos in the calypso season."

"And that last you the rest of the year?"

"It is enough."

"But you will be the richest man in the world when you write the greatest poem?"

He didn't reply.

One day when I went to see him in his little house, I found him lying on his little bed. He looked so old and so weak, that I found myself wanting to cry.

He said, "The poem is not going well."

He wasn't looking at me. He was looking through the window at the coconut tree, and he was speaking as though I wasn't there. He said, "When I was twenty I felt the power within myself." Then, almost in front of my eyes, I could see his face growing older and more tired. He said, "But that—that was a long time ago."

And then—I felt it so keenly, it was as though I had been slapped by my mother. I could see it clearly on his face. It was there for everyone to see. Death on the shrinking face.

He looked at me, and saw my tears and sat up. He said, "Come." I went and sat on his knees.

He looked into my eyes, and he said, "Oh, you can see it, too. I always knew you had the poet's eye."

He didn't even look sad, and that made me burst out crying loudly.

He pulled me to his thin chest, and said, "Do you want me to tell you a funny story?" and he smiled encouragingly at me.

But I couldn't reply.

He said, "When I have finished this story, I want you to promise that you will go away and never come back to see me. Do you promise?"

I nodded.

He said, "Good. Well, listen. That story I told you about the boy poet and the girl poet, do you remember that? That wasn't true. It was something I just made up. All this talk about poetry and the greatest poem in the world, that wasn't true, either. Isn't that the funniest thing you have heard?"

But his voice broke.

I left the house, and ran home crying, like a poet, for everything I saw.

I walked along Alberto Street a year later, but I could find no sign of the poet's house. It hadn't vanished, just like that. It had been pulled down, and a big, two-storied building had taken its place. The mango tree and the plum tree and the coconut tree had all been cut down, and there was brick and concrete everywhere.

It was just as though B. Wordsworth had never existed.

Draw Conclusions About Meaning *In your opinion, what is B. Wordsworth's motivation for extracting this promise from the boy?* **3**

Draw Conclusions About Meaning *What lesson has B. Wordsworth taught the boy by denying the truth of his stories? Why does the boy run home crying?* **4**

V. S. NAIPAUL **1289**

Teach

Reading Strategy | 3

Draw Conclusions About Meaning **Answer:** *B. Wordsworth made the boy promise to go away for good to spare the boy from witnessing his death.*

Reading Strategy | 4

Draw Conclusions About Meaning **Answer:** *He has taught the boy that for a creative writer, the literal truth of a story is unimportant. What is important is the symbolic, or universal, truths and emotions that the poet reveals. The boy cries because B. Wordsworth has inspired him to be a poet who can "cry for everything" when he grows up (page 1286).*

Cultural History ☆

Calypso Point out to students that calypso music has been popular in Trinidad for well over a hundred years. Explain that calypso has its roots in African, French, and British music styles and that calypso singers used to pass on the news of the day in their songs. Tell students that the best-known calypso song in the United States is "The Banana Boat Song" as recorded by Harry Belafonte. Encourage students to find recordings of calypso music to play for the class.

To check students' understanding of the selection, see Unit 7 Teaching Resources Book, p. 184.

After You Read

Assess

1. Answers will vary.
2. (a) He asks for permission to watch the bees. (b) The request shows his love for nature. He believes that natural beauty can sustain the spirit.
3. (a) The poet William Wordsworth; they "share one heart." (b) They both appreciate the beauty of nature and can "cry for everything."
4. (a) They walk about town together, watch the stars, talk, visit gardens, and sometimes eat together. (b) Nature's power to move the heart and imagination
5. (a) That his story about the poet whose wife and baby died was a lie, as was the story about "the greatest poem in the world" The narrator runs home in tears. (b) He cries for everything he sees.
6. A change in setting would not alter the story of friendship and the power of the imagination.
7. Poetry allows him to experience life to its fullest.
8. Trinidad has a diverse population, yet everyone in the story speaks English.
9. Possible reflections of Naipaul's experience include the location and the development of a love of writing.

Literary Element

1. When characters use dialect, their verbs do not agree with their subjects in person and number. Sometimes verbs are omitted entirely, and sometimes the word *it* is omitted at the beginning of a sentence. The phrase *it have* is used in place of *there is*; the slang contraction *ain't* is used.

1290

After You Read

Respond and Think Critically

Respond and Interpret

1. What was the main emotion you felt at the end of the story? Explain.
2. (a) How does B. Wordsworth's request differ from the requests of the others who visit "the hospitable houses of Miguel Street"? (b) What does this request suggest about him? How does it set him apart from the others?
3. (a) Who does B. Wordsworth say is his brother? What do they have in common, according to B. Wordsworth? (b) In what ways does the thing B. Wordsworth and his "brother" share make them both poets?
4. (a) What are some of the things B. Wordsworth and the narrator do together? (b) What does B. Wordsworth teach the narrator to value?
5. (a) What does B. Wordsworth tell the narrator on his deathbed? How does the narrator respond to B. Wordsworth's revelation? (b) How has the narrator become "like a poet"?

Analyze and Evaluate

6. Is this story unique to Trinidad, or does it contain universal qualities? How might a different setting change the story?
7. How would you describe B. Wordsworth's perspective on poetry?

Connect

8. **Big Idea** Globalization How does this story demonstrate that twentieth-century English is a global language?
9. **Connect to the Author** Naipaul has said that a reader should see elements of his or her own experience in a story. What elements of his own experience might Naipaul see in "B. Wordsworth"?

Literary Element Dialect

Authors incorporate **dialect** into their writing for various reasons. They might include dialect to help convey a sense of place or the social context of the character. Review the story, looking for examples of dialect, and then answer the following questions.

1. In terms of grammar and vocabulary, how does the dialect spoken by some characters in this story differ from Standard English?
2. Which characters in the story use dialect and which use Standard English? What does this speech difference tell you about the characters?
3. What difference do you notice between the boy's speech when he is narrating the story and when he is engaged in dialogue with the other characters? What might account for this difference?

Review: Foreshadowing

As you learned on page 1078, **foreshadowing** is an author's use of clues to prepare readers for events that will happen later in a story.

Partner Activity Meet with a classmate and find two or more examples of foreshadowing in this story. What do you think each example foreshadows? Working with your partner, create a chart similar to the one below in which you list the examples of foreshadowing you have found.

Examples of Foreshadowing	What the Example Foreshadows
"You will know when you grow up . . . And when you're a poet you can cry for everything."	After his last meeting with B. Wordsworth, the boy "ran home crying, like a poet, for everything I saw."

---

2. Only B. Wordsworth uses Standard English. B. Wordsworth was educated in British schools or comes from a higher social class than the other characters.
3. In dialogue, the boy speaks in dialect; as narrator, he uses Standard English. This difference probably indicates that the narrator is an educated adult who tells a story about his youth.

Review: Foreshadowing

Other examples of foreshadowing: (1) The mother's words "You think you is a man now and could go all over the place?" foreshadow the boy's step toward maturity at the end of the story. (2) B. Wordsworth's extraction of a promise from the boy not to talk about him foreshadows the end of his existence, except in the boy's memory.

Reading Strategy Draw Conclusions About Meaning

Review the chart you made while reading the selection, and then answer the following questions.

1. What conclusions can you draw about B. Wordsworth's influence on the story's narrator?

2. Why do you think B. Wordsworth confesses to the narrator at their final meeting that his stories about himself are false?

Vocabulary Practice

Practice with Analogies Choose the word that best completes each analogy.

1. stars : constellation :: ships :
   a. fleet **b.** port **c.** galley

2. kind : good-hearted :: hospitable :
   a. healing **b.** hostile **c.** generous

3. instill : remove :: distill :
   a. extract **b.** dilute **c.** inject

4. patronize : favor :: despise :
   a. humiliate **b.** hate **c.** acclaim

Academic Vocabulary

In the end, the narrator finds out the events in Wordsworth's stories never actually **occurred**.

Occur is an academic word that has different meanings. For example, if you summarized "B. Wordsworth," you would need to relate all the important events that **occur** in the story.

Using context clues, try to figure out the meaning of *occur* in each sentence and explain the difference between the two meanings.

1. Chess Club meetings will **occur** every Wednesday at 4:00 P.M.

2. When I learned I was getting an allowance increase, it **occurred** to me that I might be able to afford a new bike after all.

For more on academic vocabulary, see pages 56 and R81.

Write with Style

 Apply Diction

Assignment There is hardly anything more interesting than conversations between people—with all their vibrant accents, dialects, and slang. Write a brief story or dialogue in which one or more characters speak in a strong dialect or use vivid slang, like the narrator or his mother in "B. Wordsworth."

Get Ideas With other students, brainstorm about conversations you have had or heard that involve dialect or slang. Then think about places where you may have seen that dialect written out phonetically, or heard it recorded. If possible, consult these sources. As you examine the chosen dialect or slang, list as many of its details as accurately as you can.

Give It Structure Record dialogue exactly as it occurred. If the conversation wasn't coherent or didn't develop logically, you may want to eliminate repetition and irrelevant comments and reorganize statements slightly, so that they have a more logical progression.

Look at Language: Use phonetic spelling to re-create the sound of people's diction. You can check the effectiveness of your spellings by going back and sounding out the words. Do they re-create the dialect's sound correctly? Choose strong, specific verbs to describe each person's manner of speaking. Keep your style consistent throughout.

EXAMPLE:

"We-ell, dahlin,' ah nevah did heer of any sich thing," she drawled.

"Mebbe hit's because you ain't nevah been list'nin," he snapped back.

 Literature Online

Selection Resources For Selection Quizzes, eFlashcards, and Reading-Writing Connection activities, go to glencoe.com and enter QuickPass code GLB9817u7.

V. S. NAIPAUL **1291**

Write with Style

Use these criteria in evaluating student writing:

- The dialogue is realistic and believable, including dialect or slang.
- The conversation is coherent and well-organized.
- Diction is recorded by means of easily understandable phonetic spellings.

 For grammar practice, see Unit 7 Teaching Resources Book, p. 183.

 To create custom assessments online, go to Progress Reporter Online Assessment.

After You Read

Assess

Reading Strategy

1. B. Wordsworth expands the narrator's mind by introducing him to the creative process of storytelling, by encouraging him to be a poet, and by teaching him to observe the wonders of the universe and to savor the present moment.

2. B. Wordsworth is teaching the boy that the literal truth is unimportant to the creative artist. What is important is the emotional power and symbolic truth that a story conveys to the reader.

Progress Check

Can students draw conclusions about meaning?

If No → See Unit 7 Teaching Resources Book, p. 180.

Vocabulary Practice

1. a **2.** c **3.** b **4.** b

Academic Vocabulary

1. The context suggests that *occur* means "happen" or "take place."

2. The context suggests that *occur* means "come to mind" or "become apparent."

 For additional assessment, see Assessment Resources, pp. 303–304.

Focus

Summary

Rushdie describes a visit to the house in Bombay where he grew up. He remembers it mostly from an old black-and-white photograph and is surprised to see that it is colorful. He writes of how expatriate authors sometimes feel they belong to two cultures, and sometimes to none. Rushdie then focuses on Anglo-Indian writers, who, he says, can write with a double perspective, offering readers a "stereoscopic vision."

 For summaries in languages other than English, see Unit 7 Teaching Resources Book, pp. 186–191.

Teach

Political History ☆

Fatwa Against Rushdie

Rushdie's 1988 novel *The Satanic Verses* offended many Muslims. The leader of Iran, the Ayatollah Khomeni, issued a *fatwa* against Rushdie, declaring that any Muslim who saw Rushdie must kill him. Rushdie went into hiding, but he continued to write. The fatwa was lifted in 1998, and Rushdie has written more novels since then.

 For an audio recording of this selection, use Listening Library Audio CD-ROM.

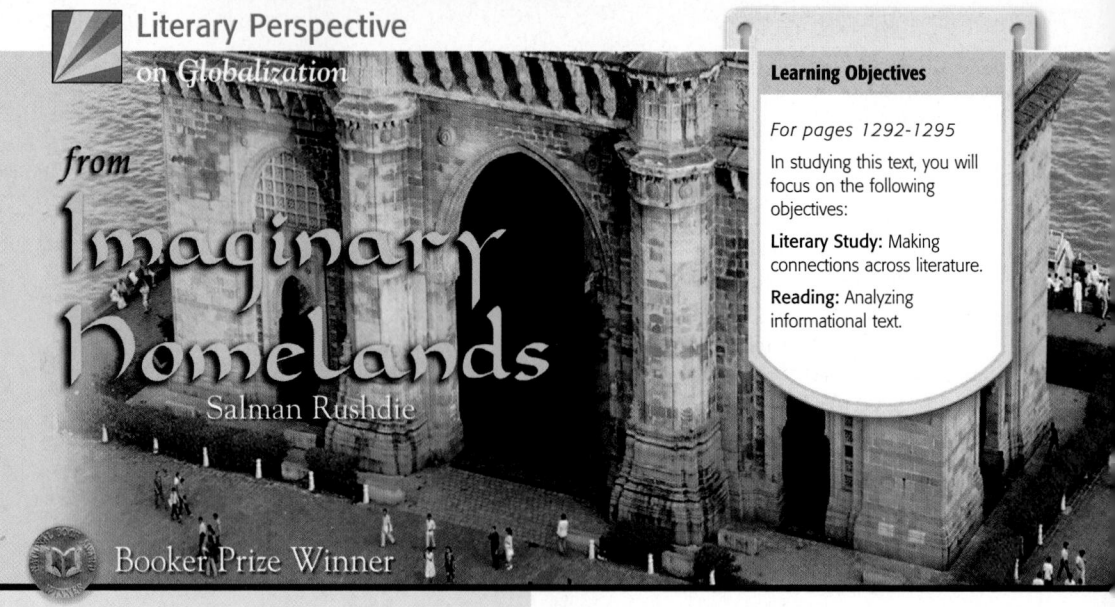

Literary Perspective
on *Globalization*

from
Imaginary Homelands
Salman Rushdie

Booker Prize Winner

Set a Purpose for Reading

Read to understand a novelist's perspective on writing in this new global age.

Build Background

Indian-born author Salman Rushdie has written some of the most well-regarded works of the past twenty-five years. His novel *Midnight's Children* was awarded the prestigious Booker Prize for Fiction in 1981. The following excerpt is from *Imaginary Homelands,* a book of criticism and essays.

Reading Strategy

Identify Assumptions and Ambiguity

An **assumption** is an idea or a belief that a person takes for granted without any actual proof. **Ambiguity** is the state of having more than one meaning. Use a two-column chart, like the one below, to help you to identify assumptions and ambiguities as you read the essay.

Assumptions	Ambiguities

An old photograph in a cheap frame hangs on a wall of the room where I work. It's a picture dating from 1946 of a house into which, at the time of its taking, I had not yet been born. The house is rather peculiar—a three-storeyed gable affair with tiled roofs and round towers in two corners, each wearing a pointy tiled hat. "The past is a foreign country," goes the famous opening sentence of L. P. Hartley's[1] novel *The Go-Between*, "they do things differently there." But the photograph tells me to invert this idea; it reminds me that it's my present that is foreign, and that the past is home, albeit a lost home in a lost city in the mists of lost time.

A few years ago I revisited Bombay, which is my lost city, after an absence of something like half my life. Shortly after arriving, acting on an impulse, I opened the telephone directory and looked for my father's name. And, amazingly, there it was; his name, our old address, the unchanged telephone number, as if we had never gone away to the unmentionable country across the border. It was an eerie discovery. I felt as if I were being claimed, or informed that the

---

1. *L. P. Hartley* (1895–1972) was an English critic, novelist, and short story writer.

Reading Practice

SPIRAL REVIEW **Connect** Explain to students that when they recall information and experiences that are uniquely their own and combine them with the words on a page, they can gain a deeper understanding of what they read. **Ask:** What experience is Rushdie writing about in the first paragraph? Have you had a similar experience? What effect did it have on your life?

Invite volunteers to share with the class the experience of moving away from one city to another or from one country to another and the effect the move had on them.

facts of my faraway life were illusions, and that this continuity was the reality. Then I went to visit the house in the photograph and stood outside it, neither daring nor wishing to announce myself to its new owners. (I didn't want to see how they'd ruined the interior.) I was overwhelmed. The photograph had naturally been taken in black and white; and my memory, feeding on such images as this, had begun to see my childhood in the same way, monochromatically. The colors of my history had seeped out of my mind's eye; now my other two eyes were assaulted by colors, by the vividness of the red tiles, the yellow-edged green of cactus-leaves, the brilliance of bougainvillea creeper.[2] It is probably not too romantic to say that that was when my novel *Midnight's Children* was really born; when I realized how much I wanted to restore the past to myself, not in the faded grays of old family-album snapshots, but whole, in CinemaScope and glorious Technicolor.

Bombay is a city built by foreigners upon reclaimed land; I, who had been away so long that I almost qualified for the title, was gripped by the conviction that I, too, had a city and a history to reclaim.

It may be that writers in my position, exiles or emigrants or expatriates, are haunted by some sense of loss, some urge to reclaim, to look back, even at the risk of being mutated into pillars of salt. But if we do look back, we must also do so in the knowledge—which gives rise to profound uncertainties—that our physical alienation from India almost inevitably means that we will not be capable of reclaiming precisely the thing that was lost; that we will, in short, create fictions, not actual cities or villages, but invisible ones, imaginary homelands, Indias of the mind.

Writing my book in North London, looking out through my window on to a city scene totally unlike the ones I was imagining on to paper, I was constantly plagued by this problem, until I felt obliged to face it in the text, to make clear that (in spite of my original . . . ambition to unlock the gates of lost time so

that the past reappeared as it actually had been, unaffected by the distortions of memory) what I was actually doing was a novel of memory and about memory, so that my India was just that: "my" India, a version and no more than one version of all the hundreds of millions of possible versions. I tried to make it as imaginatively true as I could, but imaginative truth is simultaneously honorable and suspect, and I knew that my India may only have been one to which I (who am no longer what I was, and who by quitting Bombay never became what perhaps I was meant to be) was, let us say, willing to admit I belonged. . . .

So literature can, and perhaps must, give the lie to official facts. But is this a proper function of those of us who write from outside India? Or are we just dilettantes[3] in such affairs, because we are not involved in their day-to-day unfolding, because by speaking out we take no risks, because our personal safety is not threatened? What right do we have to speak at all?

My answer is very simple. Literature is self-validating. That is to say, a book is not justified by its author's worthiness to write it, but by the quality of what has been written. There are terrible books that arise directly out of experience, and extraordinary imaginative feats dealing with themes which the author has been obliged to approach from the outside.

Literature is not in the business of copyrighting certain themes for certain groups. And as for risk: the real risks of any artist are taken in the work, in pushing the work to the limits of what is possible, in the attempt to increase the sum of what it is possible to think. Books become good when they go to this edge and risk falling over it—when they endanger the artist by reason of what he has, or has not *artistically* dared.

So if I am to speak for Indian writers in England I would say this, paraphrasing G. V. Desani's[4] H. Hatterr: The migrations of the fif-

---

2. *Bougainvillea creeper* is a tropical ornamental plant.

3. Here, *dilettantes* means "amateurs" or "those with a superficial understanding."
4. *G. V. Desani* (1909–2000) was an Indian novelist and journalist. His best-known work is the novel *All About H. Hatterr.*

SALMAN RUSHDIE **1293**

English Learners

DIFFERENTIATED INSTRUCTION

Intermediate Read aloud: *It may be that . . . exiles or emigrants or expatriates are haunted by some sense of loss.* Tell English learners that the three words *exiles, emigrants,* and *expatriates* have similar meanings. Challenge English learners to find definitions of all three words. Then discuss the similarities and differences among the words. *(All three words refer*

to people living in a country other than where they were born. In fact, that is what an expatriate is. Emigrants have moved to a new country permanently. Exiles are not allowed to return to their native country.)

Literary Perspective
on *Globalization*

Teach

Vocabulary	1

Context Clues Direct students' attention to the phrase "who by quitting Bombay" towards the end of the first paragraph in the second column. **Ask:** What does *quitting* mean here? *("leaving")* Tell students that *quit* has several other meanings as well. It can mean "to stop or cease" (*Quit bothering me*), "to give up or resign" (*He quit his job*), or "to set free or release" (*They quit themselves of their belongings*).

Literary History ☆

"Pillars of Salt" In the Hebrew Bible, God decides to destroy the cities of Sodom and Gomorrah because the people who live there are evil. However, he sends two angels to warn a man in Sodom named Lot. The angels tell Lot to take his family and leave the city before it is destroyed. They also warn him not to look back as the cities are being destroyed. Lot and his family escape to a nearby village, but Lot's wife does look back. As a result, she is changed into a pillar of salt.

For activities related to this selection, see Unit 7 Teaching Resources Book, pp. 192–193.

Teach

Globalization Have a volunteer read this paragraph and the following two paragraphs aloud. **Ask:** How does this relate to the big idea? *(Rushdie is saying that as more South Asian writers come to live in Britain, more South Asian literature will be written in English.)*

Political History ☆

"Indians"—a Diverse Community Pakistan borders India on the northwest. It was originally part of India, but when India gained independence from Britain in 1947, Pakistan was recognized as a separate country. In 1971, the eastern part of Pakistan gained independence and became Bangladesh. South Africa has a large Indian minority. Mohandas Gandhi started his career as a lawyer and his efforts as an activist while he was living in South Africa.

Reading Practice

Metaphor Read this sentence aloud: *Sometimes we feel that we straddle two cultures; at other times, that we fall between two stools.* **Ask:** What does Rushdie mean when he says that emigrant Indian writers feel that they "straddle two cultures"? *(They feel they belong to both their native culture and their adopted one.)*

---

ties and sixties happened. "We are. We are here." And we are not willing to be excluded from any part of our heritage; which heritage includes . . . the right of any member of this post-diaspora⁵ community to draw on its roots for its art, just as all the world's community of displaced writers has always done.

Let me override at once the faintly defensive note that has crept into these last few remarks. The Indian writer, looking back at India, does so through guilt-tinted spectacles. (I am of course, once more, talking about myself.) I am speaking now of those of us who emigrated . . . and I suspect that there are times when the move seems wrong to us all. . . . Sometimes we feel that we straddle two cultures; at other times, that we fall between two stools. But however ambiguous and shifting this ground may be, it is not an infertile territory for a writer to occupy. If literature is in part the business of finding new angles at which to enter reality, then once again our distance, our long geographical perspective, may provide us with such angles. Or it may be that that is simply what we must think in order to do our work. . . .

☆ England's Indian writers are by no means all the same type of animal. Some of us, for instance, are Pakistani. Others Bangladeshi. Others West, or East, or even South African. And V. S. Naipaul, by now, is something else entirely. This word "Indian" is getting to be a pretty scattered concept. Indian writers in England include political exiles, first-generation migrants, affluent expatriates whose residence here is frequently temporary, naturalized Britons, and people born here who may never have laid eyes on the subcontinent. Clearly, nothing that I say can apply across all these categories. But one of the interesting things about this diverse community is that, as far as Indo-British fiction is concerned, its existence changes the ball game, because that fiction is in future going to come as much from addresses in London, Birmingham and Yorkshire as from Delhi or Bombay.

One of the changes has to do with attitudes towards the use of English. Many have referred to the argument about the appropriateness of this language to Indian themes. And I hope all of us share the view that we can't simply use the language in the way the British did; that it needs remaking for our own purposes. Those of us who do use English do so in spite of our ambiguity towards it, or perhaps because of that, perhaps because we can find in that linguistic struggle a reflection of other struggles taking place in the real world, struggles between the cultures within ourselves and the influences at work upon our societies. To conquer English may be to complete the process of making ourselves free.

But the British Indian writer simply does not have the option of rejecting English, anyway. His children, her children, will grow up speaking it, probably as a first language; and in the forging of a British Indian identity the English language is of central importance. It must, in spite of everything, be embraced. (The word "translation" comes, etymologically, from the Latin for "bearing across." Having been borne across the world, we are translated men. It is normally supposed that something always gets lost in translation; I cling, obstinately, to the notion that something can also be gained.)

To be an Indian writer in this society is to face, every day, problems of definition. What does it mean to be "Indian" outside India? How can culture be preserved without becoming ossified?⁶ How should we discuss the need for change within ourselves and our community without seeming to play into the hands of our racial enemies? What are the consequences, both spiritual and practical, of refusing to make any concessions to Western ideas and practices? What are the consequences of embracing those ideas and practices and turning away from the ones that came here with us? These questions are all a single, existential question. How are we to live in the world?

---

5. *Diaspora* means "the scattering of a people from their homeland."

6. Here, *ossified* means "rigidly conventional."

1294 UNIT 7 AN INTERNATIONAL LITERATURE

What does he mean when he says that they "fall between two stools"? *(They belong to neither their native culture nor their adopted one.)*

I do not propose to offer, prescriptively, any answers to these questions; only to state that these are some of the issues with which each of us will have to come to terms.

To turn my eyes outwards now, and to say a little about the relationship between the Indian writer and the majority white culture in whose midst he lives, and with which his work will sooner or later have to deal:

In common with many Bombay-raised middle-class children of my generation, I grew up with an intimate knowledge of, and even sense of friendship with, a certain kind of England: a dream-England. . . . I wanted to come to England. I couldn't wait. And to be fair, England has done all right by me; but I find it a little difficult to be properly grateful. I can't escape the view that my relatively easy ride is not the result of the dream-England's famous sense of tolerance and fair play, but of my social class, my freak fair skin and my "English" English accent. Take away any of these, and the story would have been very different. Because of course the dream-England is no more than a dream. . . .

As Richard Wright[7] found long ago in America, black and white descriptions of society are no longer compatible. Fantasy, or the mingling of fantasy and naturalism, is one way of dealing with these problems. It offers a way of echoing in the form of our work the issues faced by all of us: how to build a new, "modern" world out of an old, legend-haunted civilization, an old culture which we have brought into the heart of a newer one. But whatever technical solutions we may find, Indian writers in these islands, like others who have migrated into the north from the south, are capable of writing from a kind of double perspective: because they, we, are at one and the same time insiders and outsiders in this society. This stereoscopic vision[8] is perhaps what we can offer in place of "whole sight."

---

7. *Richard Wright* (1908–1960) was an African American novelist.
8. *Stereoscopic vision* refers to the combining of two images—often photographs of the same thing taken at slightly different angles—into a single three-dimensional image, with the aid of a stereoscope.

Respond and Think Critically

Respond and Interpret

1. Write a brief summary of the main ideas in this essay before you answer the following questions. For help writing a summary, see page 435.

2. In what ways has this essay changed your understanding of the effects of globalization on literature?

3. (a)When Rushdie revisited his childhood home in Bombay, what realization did he have? (b)What metaphor does Rushdie use to examine his feelings? Explain.

4. (a)According to Rushdie, what "can, and perhaps must," literature do? (b)In his opinion, what have displaced writers always done?

5. How does Rushdie describe England and his life there?

Analyze and Evaluate

6. (a)Rushdie claims that Indian writers cannot use English "in the way the British did" and "that it needs remaking." Why does Rushdie say this? (b)Do you agree with this claim? Why or why not?

7. (a)Briefly state the main ideas of this essay. (b)With which ideas do you agree? With which do you disagree? Explain your reasoning.

Connect

8. How is the "stereoscopic vision" described by Rushdie at the end of this essay demonstrated by other writers in this unit?

SALMAN RUSHDIE **1295**

Assess

1. Students' summaries will vary but should include the main ideas of the essay.
2. Students' answers will vary.
3. (a) Rushdie realized that he wanted to recapture or reclaim his past and his cultural traditions. He claims to have been overwhelmed by the color of the house. (b) He uses the monochromatic photograph as a metaphor. He views his past in black and white, but he desires to see it in color.
4. (a) Create what is imaginatively true (b) Drawn upon their traditional roots to create art.
5. Rushdie says that living in England has had its advantages. However, England's reputation for tolerance and fair play is an illusion. He says that the "dream-England is no more than a dream."
6. (a) Rushdie means that English is a colonial language and thus has negative implications for many Indians. In Rushdie's view, Anglo-Indians must appropriate the English language and remodel it for their own uses. (b) Students' answers will vary.

---

7. (a) Emigrants are faced with a great loss that can be translated into fertile artistic territory; great literature transcends boundaries; an author has the right to tackle any subject that he or she desires; good literature justifies itself; what it means to be an Indian writer is constantly shifting because of globalization. (b) Students' answers will vary.

8. Students might refer to V. S. Naipaul's "B. Wordsworth," in which the characters are clearly bound to multiple cultures.

> For additional assessment, see Assessment Resources, pp. 305–306.

Before You Read

Games at Twilight

Meet **Anita Desai**

(born 1937)

Many of Anita Desai's novels brilliantly portray life in India, its past and present, and the struggles that many Indians, especially women and children, face. Her novels and short stories are often full of vivid imagery and ornate detail. As Nobel Prize–winning novelist J. M. Coetzee has stated, "Desai's strength as a writer has always been her eye for detail . . . her gift for telling metaphor, and above all her feel for the sun and sky, heat and dust, for the elemental reality of central India."

A Distinct Genius Desai was born Anita Mazumdar in Mussoorie, India, north of Delhi, to a German mother and an Indian father. Hers was a family of bookworms, and she treasured the amount of time and privacy she had as a child to read and dream. "I grew up in a home where three languages were spoken together—Hindi, English, and German—but English was my literary language—the one I read and wrote in. I am grateful for that because it opened to me the literature of the world and I made myself at home in it and was not restricted to any one region." Desai came to appreciate each language for "its own distinct genius." She found English the most flexible of languages, however, and the one in which she could best work "to convey the rhythms, accents, tones, and pace of Indian life."

Desai began to write in English at the age of seven, publishing her first story at age nine. After graduating with a B.A. in English literature from Delhi University in 1957, she married Ashvin Desai, a businessman; they later had four children.

In 1963, when she was twenty-six, Desai published her first novel, *Cry, the Peacock*, which deals with the oppression of Indian women. *Where Shall We Go This Summer?* also explores the theme of despairing women. Many of her novels, such as *Bye-Bye Blackbird* and *Fire on the Mountain*, focus on the profound cultural changes that India has experienced since the dissolution of the British Empire.

> *"I believe literature and art really contain the essence of life and the world, uncover its innermost secrets and present those truths that one might ordinarily miss or ignore, and so [are] closer to the truth than life itself."*
>
> —Anita Desai

An International Teacher In addition to several collections of short stories, Desai has published some books for children, acquiring a strong international reputation as a children's writer. In 1987 she came to the United States to teach creative writing at Smith College in Massachusetts. Since that time she has alternated between living and teaching in the United States and in India. She is also a Fellow of England's Royal Society of Literature.

 Literature Online

Author Search For more about Anita Desai, go to glencoe.com and enter QuickPass code GLB9817u7.

Selection Skills

Literary Elements
- Point of View (SE pp. 1297–1304)
- Mood (SE p. 1304)

Games at Twilight

Listening/Speaking/Viewing Skills
- Analyze Art (SE pp. 1298, 1301; TE p. 1303)

Reading Skills
- Connect to Personal Experience (SE pp. 1297–1305)

Vocabulary Skills
- Word Usage (SE p. 1305)
- Academic Vocabulary (SE p. 1305)

Writing Skills/Grammar
- Create a Brochure (SE p. 1305)

Literature and Reading Preview

Connect to the Story

What were some of your favorite games as a child? When you played, how important was winning? Freewrite for a few minutes about your most vivid memories of childhood games.

Build Background

A counting-out game is a game, played by an indeterminate number of participants, usually for the purpose of choosing a person to be "it" in the playing of another, different game. Many countries have their own versions of counting-out games. Some of the most common of these games are rock, paper, scissors; odd or even; coin flipping; drawing straws; and rhymes such as "Eeny, Meeny, Miny, Mo" or (in England) "Tinker, Tailor, Soldier, Sailor." The game played near the start of "Games at Twilight" is an example of a counting-out game.

Set Purposes for Reading

Big Idea Globalization

As you read, ask yourself, How does the Indian culture in the story reflect British influences?

Literary Element Point of View

Point of view is the standpoint from which a story is told. In a first-person story, the narrator is a character in the story. In a third-person story, the narrator stands outside the story and describes the actions. As you read, ask yourself, How does the narrator's relationship to the story affect its telling?

Reading Strategy Connect to Personal Experience

You can bring your own **personal experiences** and world knowledge to bear on any reading situation to help you understand and assess what is happening. This is especially useful when you read literature in which cultural comparisons are explicit or implicit. As you read, ask yourself, In what ways can I personally relate to this?

Tip: Taking Notes Use a chart to list similarities and differences between your experiences and those of characters in the story.

Similarities	Differences

ANITA DESAI **1297**

Vocabulary

stridently (strīd′ ənt lē) *adv.* in a harsh, grating manner; p. 1298 *Len's classmates stridently denounced his opinion.*

defunct (di fungkt′) *adj.* no longer existing or active; dead; p. 1300 *The little mom-and-pop grocery store that used to be on our corner is now defunct.*

temerity (tə mer′ ə tē) *n.* excessive or reckless boldness; rashness; p. 1300 *We were amazed at Linda's temerity as she faced down the bullies.*

fray (frā) *n.* a heated dispute or contest; p. 1301 *The game of dodgeball had already degenerated into a free-for-all before George entered the fray.*

lugubrious (loo goo′ brē əs) *adj.* excessively mournful or sorrowful; p. 1303 *The little girl's expression as she held her broken doll was so lugubrious that I couldn't help but sympathize.*

Before You Read

Focus

Summary

Children play hide-and-seek on a hot day in India. The oldest boy, Raghu, is chosen as "It" and soon catches the little ones. But Ravi slips into an abandoned shed. In his boldness, he feels a surge of pride and stays till after dark. Long after the game ends, Ravi comes out and declares himself winner. When he does so, he discovers that the others have forgotten about him and gone on to play other games.

 For summaries in languages other than English, see Unit 7 Teaching Resources Book, pp. 195–200.

Vocabulary

Word Usage Explain to students that the more often they use a new word, the better they will understand its meaning. Have students work in pairs to ask and answer at least two questions that incorporate each vocabulary word.

 For additional vocabulary practice, see Unit 7 Teaching Resources Book, p. 203.

 For additional context, see Glencoe Interactive Vocabulary CD-ROM.

Approaching Level

DIFFERENTIATED INSTRUCTION

 Established Remind approaching-level students that **skimming** involves reading a story quickly to find the main idea or general theme, whereas **scanning** is doing a quick review of the story to pick out certain pieces of information. Tell students that both techniques are good ways of previewing a story before they read.

Have students work in heterogeneous groups. Ask them to scan the story to identify the main characters, and then skim to get the general theme. Have group members compare their findings.

Teach

Reading Strategy   1

Connect to Personal Experience Have students read the dialogue on this page. Then have them read the text that follows, in which Desai describes the mother's giving in to the children's demands. **Ask:** From your experience, what do you think of the children's promises? *(They probably would say anything to get outside.)*

  For additional practice using the reading skill or strategy, see Unit 7 Teaching Resources Book, p. 202.

View the Art ★

Answer: *The light in this image creates the vivid blue shadows of tree branches that dominate the painting.*

  For an audio recording of this selection, use Listening Library Audio CD-ROM.

Readability Scores

Dale-Chall: 7.2
DRP: 60
Lexile: 1220

Games at Twilight

Anita Desai

Girl on a Swing, India, 2000. Andrew Macara. Oil on canvas, 63.5 x 76.2 cm. Private collection.

View the Art Macara says that much of his work is inspired by the different effects of light on the exotic locations he paints. What effect does light have on this image? ★

It was still too hot to play outdoors. They had had their tea, they had been washed and had their hair brushed, and after the long day of confinement in the house that was not cool but at least a protection from the sun, the children strained to get out. Their faces were red and bloated with the effort, but their mother would not open the door, everything was still curtained and shuttered in a way that stifled the children, made them feel that their lungs were stuffed with cotton wool and their noses with dust and if they didn't burst out into the light and see the sun and feel the air, they would choke.

"Please, ma, please," they begged. "We'll play in the veranda and porch—we won't go a step out of the porch."

"You will, I know you will, and then—"

"No—we won't, we won't," they wailed so horrendously that she actually let down the bolt of the front door so that they burst out like seeds from a crackling, overripe pod into the veranda, with such wild, maniacal[1] yells that she retreated to her bath and the shower of talcum powder and the fresh sari[2] that were to help her face the summer evening.

They faced the afternoon. It was too hot. Too bright. The white walls of the veranda glared **stridently** in the sun. The bougainvillea[3] hung about it, purple and magenta, in livid balloons. The garden outside was like a tray made of beaten brass, flattened out on the red gravel and the stony soil in all shades of metal—aluminum, tin, copper, and brass. No life stirred at this arid time of day—the birds still drooped, like dead fruit, in the papery tents of the trees; some squirrels lay limp on the wet earth under the garden tap. The outdoor dog lay stretched as if dead on the veranda mat, his paws and ears and tail all reaching out like dying travelers in search of water. He rolled his eyes at the children—two white marbles rolling in the purple sockets, begging for sympathy—and attempted to lift his tail ☆

---

2. A *sari* is an outer garment worn mainly by Hindu women.
3. *Bougainvillea* is a woody, tropical vine with flowers.

Vocabulary

stridently (strīd′ ənt lē) *adv.* in a harsh, grating manner

---

1. *Maniacal* means "marked by excessive enthusiasm."

1298 UNIT 7   AN INTERNATIONAL LITERATURE

Reading Practice

SPIRAL REVIEW **Figurative Language** Remind students that Desai's figurative language helps readers sense the scene: a stiflingly hot day in India. **Write** this sentence on the board: *The bougainvillea hung about it, purple and magenta, in livid balloons.* **Ask:** How does Desai's verb phrase "hung about" add to the sense of punishing heat? *(It suggests the lazy exhaustion of heat.)* Call students' attention to the word *livid,* which means "discolored by a bruise; black-and-blue." **Ask:** How does this word affect the imagery? *(It makes the plant seem bruised and suffering.)*

Little Indian Girl with a Leaf, 1998. Penelope Anstice. Oil on canvas. Private collection.

in a wag but could not. It only twitched and lay still.

Then, perhaps roused by the shrieks of the children, a band of parrots suddenly fell out of the eucalyptus tree, tumbled frantically in the still, sizzling air, then sorted themselves out into battle formation and streaked away across the white sky.

The children, too, felt released. They too began tumbling, shoving, pushing against each other, frantic to start. Start what? Start their business. The business of the children's day which is—play.

"Let's play hide-and-seek."

"Who'll be It?"

"You be It."

"Why should I? You be—"

"You're the eldest—"

2
Connect to Personal Experience *Based on your memories of childhood, do the children's pent-up energy and eagerness to play seem believable? Explain.*

"That doesn't mean—"

The shoves became harder. Some kicked out. The motherly Mira intervened. She pulled the boys roughly apart. There was a tearing sound of cloth but it was lost in the heavy panting and angry grumbling and no one paid attention to the small sleeve hanging loosely off a shoulder.

"Make a circle, make a circle!" she shouted, firmly pulling and pushing till a kind of vague circle was formed. "Now clap!" she roared and, clapping, they all chanted in melancholy unison: "Dip, dip, dip—my blue ship—" and every now and then one or the other saw he was safe by the way his hands fell at the crucial moment—palm on palm, or back of hand on palm—and dropped out of the circle with a yell and a jump of relief and jubilation.

Raghu was It. He started to protest, to cry "You cheated—Mira cheated—Anu cheated—" but it was too late, the others had all already streaked away. There was no one to hear when he called out, "Only in the veranda—the porch—Ma said—Ma *said* to stay in the porch!" No one had stopped to listen, all he saw were their brown legs flashing through the dusty shrubs, scrambling up brick walls, leaping over compost heaps and hedges, and then the porch stood empty in the purple shade of the bougainvillea and the garden was as empty as before; even the limp squirrels had whisked away, leaving everything gleaming, brassy and bare.

Only small Manu suddenly reappeared, as if he had dropped out of an invisible cloud or from a bird's claws, and stood for a moment in the center of the yellow lawn, chewing his finger and near to tears as he heard Raghu shouting, with his head pressed against the veranda wall, "Eighty-three, eighty-five, eighty-nine, ninety..." and then made off in a panic, half of him wanting to fly north, the other half counseling south. Raghu turned just in time to see the flash of his white shorts and the uncertain skittering of his red sandals, and charged after him with such a blood-curdling yell that Manu stumbled over the hosepipe, fell into its rubber coils, and lay there weeping, "I won't be It—you have to find them all—all—All!"

ANITA DESAI **1299**

Reading Strategy | 2

Connect to Personal Experience **Answer:** *Most students will probably remember having similar feelings when they were children.*

(APPROACHING) To help approaching level students, **say:** Think of a time when you were a child and had to wait to do something you wanted. **Ask:** How did you feel while you were waiting? *(impatient, frustrated)* How did you feel when you finally got to do what you wanted? *(happy, excited, energetic)*

Writer's Technique ☆

Sensory Images Desai uses sensory images to capture the children's high energy and to make the hot day palpable. In a simile, Desai has the children "burst out like seeds from a crackling, over-ripe pod." The garden is "like a tray made of beaten brass." The eyes of the dog become "two white marbles rolling in the purple sockets, begging for sympathy."

DIFFERENTIATED INSTRUCTION

Emerging Have approaching-level students track the story's sounds. Begin with the dialogue in the first column of page 1299. Now read the next two paragraphs. **Ask:** How are the children speaking? *(quickly, loudly)* What words does the writer use to suggest sounds? *("tearing sound," "heavy panting," "angry grumbling")* How would you describe the sounds? *(loud, excited, fast, rough)* After discussion, have students read the scene and imagine the sounds.

Teach

Literary Element | 1

Point of View Answer: *The point of view has shifted from third-person omniscient to third-person limited, and the fact that the reader now knows Ravi's thoughts and feelings suggests that he is the character that the story will focus on.*

Big Idea | 2

Globalization Answer: *Raghu is larger, stronger, and more mature than Ravi. In addition, he plays soccer in school—a fairly aggressive game that demands athletic prowess and that separates him from the children who enjoy simple, childhood games such as hide-and-seek.*

"I know I have to, idiot," Raghu said, superciliously kicking him with his toe. "You're dead," he said with satisfaction, licking the beads of perspiration off his upper lip, and then stalked off in search of worthier prey, whistling spiritedly so that the hiders should hear and tremble.

Ravi heard the whistling and picked his nose in a panic, trying to find comfort by burrowing the finger deep-deep into that soft tunnel. He felt himself too exposed, sitting on an upturned flowerpot behind the garage. Where could he burrow? He could run around the garage if he heard Raghu come—around and around and around—but he hadn't much faith in his short legs when matched against Raghu's long, hefty, hairy footballer legs. Ravi had a frightening glimpse of them as Raghu combed the hedge of crotons and hibiscus,[4] trampling delicate ferns underfoot as he did so. Ravi looked about him desperately, swallowing a small ball of snot in his fear.

The garage was locked with a great heavy lock to which the driver had the key in his room, hanging from a nail on the wall under his work shirt. Ravi had peeped in and seen him still sprawling on his string-cot in his vest and striped underpants, the hair on his chest and the hair in his nose shaking with the vibrations of his phlegm-obstructed snores. Ravi had wished he were tall enough, big enough to reach the key on the nail, but it was impossible, beyond his reach for years to come. He had sidled away and sat dejectedly on the flowerpot. That at least was cut to his own size.

But next to the garage was another shed with a big green door. Also locked. No one even knew who had the key to the lock. That shed wasn't opened more than once a year when Ma turned out all the old broken bits of furniture and rolls of matting and leaking buckets, and the white anthills were broken and swept away and Flit sprayed into the spiderwebs and rat holes so that the whole operation was like the looting of a poor, ruined, and conquered city. The green leaves of the door sagged. They were nearly off their rusty hinges. The hinges were large and made a small gap between the door and the walls—only just large enough for rats, dogs, and, possibly, Ravi to slip through.

Ravi had never cared to enter such a dark and depressing mortuary[5] of **defunct** household goods seething with such unspeakable and alarming animal life but, as Raghu's whistling grew angrier and sharper and his crashing and storming in the hedge wilder, Ravi suddenly slipped off the flowerpot and through the crack and was gone. He chuckled aloud with astonishment at his own **temerity** so that Raghu came out of the hedge, stood silent with his hands on his hips, listening, and finally shouted "I heard you! I'm coming! Got you—" and came charging round the garage only to find the upturned flowerpot, the yellow dust, the crawling of white ants in a mud hill against the closed shed door—nothing. Snarling, he bent to pick up a stick and went off, whacking it against the garage and shed walls as if to beat out his prey.

Ravi shook, then shivered with delight, with self-congratulation. Also with fear. It was dark, spooky in the shed. It had a muffled smell, as of graves. Ravi had once got locked into the linen cupboard and sat there weeping for half an hour

---

4. *Crotons* and *hibiscus* are tropical plants.

1 **Point of View** *Note the shift in point of view. What about this new point of view suggests that Ravi has become the main character?*

2 **Globalization** *Football, known as soccer in the United States, is a part of British culture that caught on in the colonies. Explain why this detail about Raghu might be significant.*

5. A *mortuary* is a place where dead bodies are kept before burial.

Vocabulary

defunct (di fungkt´) *adj.* no longer existing or active; dead

temerity (tə mer´ ə tē) *n.* excessive or reckless boldness; rashness

Reading Practice

SPIRAL REVIEW **Motif** Over the next few pages, readers are cut off, in a sense, from the sunlight and playful children. Explain that because of the third-person limited point of view, we sit in the dark with Ravi and his thoughts. **Ask:** What does the phrase "in the dark" mean? *(unaware, not knowing)* In this case, how is being in the dark more illuminating than being in the sunlight with the other children? *(In the quiet darkness, we discover Ravi's thoughts and learn more about him than if he were running around the yard.)* Point out that Desai uses motifs of light and darkness in the story.

Abstract Day, 2005. Lou Wall. Private collection.

 View the Art Abstract art relies on color and form to convey emotion, since no actual objects appear. What passage in the story seems to reflect the mood and emotions conveyed in this image?

before he was rescued. But at least that had been a familiar place, and even smelled pleasantly of starch, laundry, and, reassuringly, of his mother. But the shed smelled of rats, anthills, dust, and spiderwebs. Also of less definable, less recognizable horrors. And it was dark. Except for the white-hot cracks along the door, there was no light. The roof was very low. Although Ravi was small, he felt as if he could reach up and touch it with his fingertips. But he didn't stretch. He hunched himself into a ball so as not to bump into anything, touch or feel anything. What might there not be to touch him and feel him as he stood there, trying to see in the dark? Something cold, or slimy—like a snake. Snakes! He leaped up as Raghu whacked the wall with his stick—then, quickly realizing what it was, felt

almost relieved to hear Raghu, hear his stick. It made him feel protected.

But Raghu soon moved away. There wasn't a sound once his footsteps had gone around the garage and disappeared. Ravi stood frozen inside the shed. Then he shivered all over. Something had tickled the back of his neck. It took him a while to pick up the courage to lift his hand and explore. It was an insect—perhaps a spider—exploring him. He squashed it and wondered how many more creatures were watching him, waiting to reach out and touch him, the stranger.

There was nothing now. After standing in that position—his hand still on his neck, feeling the wet splodge of the squashed spider gradually dry—for minutes, hours, his legs began to tremble with the effort, the inaction. By now he could see enough in the dark to make out the large solid shapes of old wardrobes, broken buckets, and bedsteads piled on top of each other around him. He recognized an old bathtub—patches of enamel glimmered at him and at last he lowered himself onto its edge.

He contemplated slipping out of the shed and into the **fray.** He wondered if it would not be better to be captured by Raghu and be returned to the milling crowd as long as he could be in the sun, the light, the free spaces of the garden, and the familiarity of his brothers, sisters, and cousins. It would be evening soon. Their games would become legitimate. The parents would sit out on the lawn on cane basket chairs and watch them as they tore around the garden or gathered in knots to share a loot of mulberries or black, teeth-splitting *jamun*[6]

---

6. *Jamun* is a tropical fruit.

Connect to Personal Experience *How might these "legitimate" games be different from the game the children have been playing?* | 4 |

Vocabulary

fray (frā) n. a heated dispute or contest

| 3 | Point of View *What have you found out about Ravi in this section so far that you could not learn if the story were told from a different point of view?* |

ANITA DESAI **1301**

Teach

Literary Element | 3 |

Point of View Answer: *We learn of a number of emotions that Ravi experiences in quick succession, emotions that he does not necessarily show through actions or facial expressions.*

Reading Strategy | 4 |

Connect to Personal Experience Answer: *Because the parents watch the children play, the games become safe, acceptable, and therefore "legitimate."*

View the Art ★

Answer: *Students might say that it reflects Ravi's situation in his hiding place. He is in a dark place, with only cracks of light, and the painting is of a dark landscape with light seeping in. Also, the ill-defined, abstract shapes could reflect Ravi's eyes' adjusting to the dark.*

English Learners

DIFFERENTIATED INSTRUCTION

Intermediate Explain to English learners that although *shed* can be a verb meaning "to cast off or lose," here it is a noun that means "a small building, usually used for storage." Students might also explore multiple meanings of these words: *leaves, hedge, bore, sound.*

Advanced Learners

DIFFERENTIATED INSTRUCTION

Mood Have advanced students analyze the mood of "Games at Twilight" by exploring how any three of the following elements affect the story's mood: setting, description, diction, motif, plot. Have students write three to five paragraphs, citing the text to support their analysis.

Teach

Reading Strategy | 1

Connect to Personal Experience Answer: *Most students will probably feel that Ravi's situation is believable and will have experienced a comparable situation.*

[ENGLISH LEARNERS] For English learners, **ask:** Who is describing Ravi's experience, Ravi himself or the narrator? *(the narrator)* From what point of view is the story told? *(third person)*

Writer's Technique ☆

Textured Images In a review of *Diamond Dust,* a collection of Desai's stories published in 2000, the *New York Times* described the author's work as "nicely textured." In the passage on this page, Desai laces the prose with moody descriptive images of light and color. Point out the way she depicts the late afternoon light as fading to "crumbling yellow pollen."

Ask: Can you imagine and describe what this light looks like? *(Accept all reasonable responses.)* Discuss with students the effect of other color images in the passage, including "blue fur," "green scent," and "purple shadows."

---

from the garden trees. The gardener would fix the hosepipe to the water tap and water would fall lavishly through the air to the ground, soaking the dry yellow grass and the red gravel and arousing the sweet, the intoxicating scent of water on dry earth—that loveliest scent in the world. Ravi sniffed for a whiff of it. He half rose from the bathtub, then heard the despairing scream of one of the girls as Raghu bore down upon her. There was the sound of a crash, and of rolling about in the bushes, the shrubs, then screams and accusing sobs of, "I touched the den—" "You did not—" "I did—" "You liar, you did *not*" and then a fading away and silence again.

Ravi sat back on the harsh edge of the tub, deciding to hold out a bit longer. What fun if they were all found and caught—he alone left unconquered! He had never known that sensation. Nothing more wonderful had ever happened to him than being taken out by an uncle and bought a whole slab of chocolate all to himself, or being flung into the soda man's pony cart and driven up to the gate by the friendly driver with the red beard and pointed ears. To defeat Raghu—that hirsute,[7] hoarse-voiced football champion—and to be the winner in a circle of older, bigger, luckier children—that would be thrilling beyond imagination. He hugged his knees together and smiled to himself almost shyly at the thought of so much victory, such laurels.[8]

There he sat smiling, knocking his heels against the bathtub, now and then getting up and going to the door to put his ear to the broad crack and listening for sounds of the game, the pursuer and the pursued, and then returning to his seat with the dogged determination of the true winner, a breaker of records, a champion.

☆ It grew darker in the shed as the light at the door grew softer, fuzzier, turned to a kind of crumbling yellow pollen that turned to yellow fur, blue fur, gray fur. Evening. Twilight. The sound of water gushing, falling. The scent of earth receiving water, slaking its thirst in great gulps and releasing that green scent of freshness, coolness. Through the crack Ravi saw the long purple shadows of the shed and the garage lying still across the yard. Beyond that, the white walls of the house. The bougainvillea had lost its lividity, hung in dark bundles that quaked and twittered and seethed with masses of homing sparrows. The lawn was shut off from his view. Could he hear the children's voices? It seemed to him that he could. It seemed to him that he could hear them chanting, singing, laughing. But what about the game? What had happened? Could it be over? How could it when he was still not found?

It then occurred to him that he could have slipped out long ago, dashed across the yard to the veranda, and touched the "den." It was necessary to do that to win. He had forgotten. He had only remembered the part of hiding and trying to elude[9] the seeker. He had done that so successfully, his success had occupied him so wholly that he had quite forgotten that success had to be clinched by that final dash to victory and the ringing cry of "Den!"

With a whimper he burst through the crack, fell on his knees, got up and stumbled on stiff, benumbed legs across the shadowy yard, crying heartily by the time he reached the veranda so that when he flung himself at the white pillar and bawled, "Den! Den! Den!" his voice broke with rage and pity at the disgrace of it all and he felt himself flooded with tears and misery.

Out on the lawn, the children stopped chanting. They all turned to stare at him in amazement. Their faces were pale and triangular in the dusk. The trees and bushes around them stood inky and sepulchral, spilling long shadows across them. They stared, wondering at his reappearance, his passion, his wild animal howling. Their mother rose from her basket chair and came towards him, worried, annoyed, saying, "Stop it, stop it, Ravi. Don't be a baby. Have you hurt yourself?" Seeing him attended to, the children

---

9. To *elude* is to escape from.

Connect to Personal Experience *Do you think Ravi's predicament in this passage is believable? Explain.* | **1**

---

7. *Hirsute* means "covered with hair."
8. *Laurels* means "glory and honor."

Reading Practice

SPIRAL REVIEW **Identify Cause and Effect** Point out that Ravi's changing feelings inform the story's thematic message. Explain that students can track and analyze the causes of these changes in a chart like the one shown. Remind them to first identify and list effects in the chart.

Effects	Causes
When Ravi reaches the "den," he feels rage and pity.	His expectations of victory are not met.

Children's Play (detail), 1987. Shanti Panchal.
Watercolor on paper, 130 x 100 cm. Private collection.

went back to clasping their hands and chanting "The grass is green, the rose is red . . . ."

But Ravi would not let them. He tore himself out of his mother's grasp and pounded across the lawn into their midst, charging at them with his head lowered so that they scattered in surprise. "I won, I won, I won," he bawled, shaking his head so that the big tears flew. "Raghu didn't find me. I won, I won—"

It took them a minute to grasp what he was saying, even who he was. They had quite forgotten him. Raghu had found all the others long ago. There had been a fight about who was to be It next. It had been so fierce that their mother had emerged from her bath and made them change to another game. Then they had played another and another. Broken mulberries from the tree and eaten them. Helped the driver wash the car when their father returned from work. Helped the gardener water the beds till he roared at them and swore he would complain to their parents. The parents had come out, taken up their positions on the cane chairs. They had begun to play

again, sing and chant. All this time no one had remembered Ravi. Having disappeared from the scene, he had disappeared from their minds. Clean.

"Don't be a fool," Raghu said roughly, pushing him aside, and even Mira said, "Stop howling, Ravi. If you want to play, you can stand at the end of the line," and she put him there very firmly.

The game proceeded. Two pairs of arms reached up and met in an arc. The children trooped under it again and again in a **lugubrious** circle, ducking their heads and intoning[10]

"The grass is green,
The rose is red;
Remember me
When I am dead, dead, dead,
dead . . . "

And the arc of thin arms trembled in the twilight, and the heads were bowed so sadly, and their feet tramped to that melancholy refrain so mournfully, so helplessly, that Ravi could not bear it. He would not follow them, he would not be included in this funereal game. He had wanted victory and triumph—not a funeral. But he had been forgotten, left out, and he would not join them now. The ignominy[11] of being forgotten—how could he face it? He felt his heart go heavy and ache inside him unbearably. He lay down full length on the damp grass, crushing his face into it, no longer crying, silenced by a terrible sense of his insignificance. ∿

---

10. *Intoning* is chanting.
11. *Ignominy* means "humiliation and dishonor."

Connect to Personal Experience *Have you ever experienced this feeling of being "out of sight, out of mind"? Does it seem realistic here? Explain.* **2**

Point of View *In what ways does the point of view affect the story's climax?* **3**

Vocabulary

lugubrious (loo gōō′ brē əs) *adj.* excessively mournful or sorrowful

ANITA DESAI **1303**

Teach

Reading Strategy   2

Connect to Personal Experience **Possible answer:** *Yes; children, especially, forget about things and even people when they are not constantly in sight.*

ENGLISH LEARNERS Point out to English learners the one-word sentence "Clean" in this passage. Explain the idiom "I clean forgot." **Ask:** What does the word "clean" mean in this context? *(completely)* Have students discuss why the author chose to break the rules of grammar and express herself in this way.

Literary Element   3

Point of View **Answer:** *Because the point of view is third-person limited, the narrator focuses on Ravi's thoughts and feelings exclusively, allowing the climax to occur mostly inside Ravi's mind.*

View the Art ★

Although Shanti Panchal left India in 1978 to move to Britain, his native country remained a significant influence on his artistic creations. Beyond the autobiographical nature of his paintings, his use of color reflects the earthen colors of his Indian homeland. He believes that much of his artistic vision stems from his Hindu spirituality.

To check students' understanding of the selection, see Unit 7 Teaching Resources Book, p. 206.

After You Read

Assess

1. Responses will vary.

2. (a) Playing a game of hide-and-seek (b) They immediately disobey the mother by leaving the porch. They treat each other rudely. Only Mira seems to have any control over them.

3. (a) In a shed; because he is small enough to squeeze through a crack (b) He begins to think that he might become "a breaker of records."

4. (a) He must go back to the veranda and touch "the den." (b) The narrator connects Ravi's tears with feelings of "rage and pity at the disgrace of it all."

5. (a) They treat him as the baby of the family; he does seem to be the youngest—except, perhaps, for Manu. (b) Near the ending, the dialogue is sharp, condescending, and abrasive when aimed at Ravi.

6. (a) When he realizes they have forgotten him, he is devastated and lies face-down in the grass. (b) His sense of being forgotten hurts him.

7. Apart from certain details, such as the bougainvillea and the Indian sun, this story might take place in any number of places around the world. This might show that British influence pervaded India. The only specifically Indian reference is the mother's sari.

8. Answers will vary.

Progress Check

Can students analyze point of view?

If No → See Unit 7 Teaching Resources Book, p. 201.

1304

After You Read

Respond and Think Critically

Respond and Interpret

1. What is your overall impression of the children and their games throughout the story? Explain.

2. (a)What are the children doing at the beginning of the story? (b)What does the children's behavior at the beginning tell you about the relationships among them?

3. (a)Where does Ravi hide? Why does he choose that place? (b)What idea builds in Ravi's mind as he hides?

4. (a)What does Ravi suddenly realize he must do to win the game? (b)In your opinion, why is Ravi crying as he leaves his hiding place and heads for the "den"?

Analyze and Evaluate

5. (a)How do the other children tend to treat Ravi throughout the story? Why do you think this is so? (b)How does the dialogue help to convey these relationships?

6. (a)How does Ravi react to the other children's behavior toward him at the end? (b)What seems to affect him more deeply, not winning or having been forgotten? Explain.

Connect

7. **Big Idea** Globalization Cite elements in this story that demonstrate the effects of globalization. Does any element maintain a uniquely Indian flavor? Explain.

8. **Connect to Today** What elements of the story have parallels in your own childhood? In the lives of children today?

Literary Element Point of View

In a story written from the **third-person limited** point of view, the narrator stands outside the story and reveals the thoughts, feelings, and observations of only one, or a limited number, of characters. In a story written from the **third-person omniscient**, or all knowing, point of view, the narrator knows everything about the characters and events and may reveal details that the characters themselves could not reveal.

1. From which point of view is "Games at Twilight" written, third-person limited or omniscient? How can you tell?

2. How does the point of view affect this story? What might have been different if the story had been told from a different point of view?

Review: Mood

As you learned on page 78, **mood** is the emotional quality of a literary work. Choice of language, subject matter, setting, and tone, as well as such sound devices as rhyme and rhythm, contribute to the mood of a work.

Partner Activity Meet with another classmate and discuss how the mood changes during the course of this story. Construct a graphic organizer like the one below, in order to trace the sequence of moods in the story and to note which events and literary elements create these moods.

MOODS IN "GAMES AT TWILIGHT"

Boisterous
"The children, too, felt released. They too began tumbling, shoving, pushing against each other, frantic to start."

↓

↓

Literary Element

1. Most of the story is told from the third-person limited point of view. The narrator does not reveal the thoughts and feelings of all of the characters; only Ravi's are presented to the reader.

2. Without the third-person limited point of view, the reader would not know Ravi's thoughts—he is in no position to act them out or to tell them to someone else—and would not understand how deeply he is affected by his experience.

Review: Mood

Partners should work together to identify changes in mood and find supporting passages in the text. Remind them to consider such literary elements as diction, description, and point of view when identifying shifts in mood.

Reading Strategy — Connect to Personal Experience

You can use your personal experiences and knowledge of the world to help you understand what you read. Think about your own childhood experiences as you answer the following questions.

1. Do you think Desai effectively captures the emotions of a child in this situation? Explain.

2. If you were Ravi's sibling, what might you have said to him when he reappeared in the yard?

Vocabulary Practice

Practice with Word Usage Respond to these statements to help you explore the meanings of boldface vocabulary words from the selection.

1. Describe a regulation that, if instituted at your school, would cause you to protest **stridently**.

2. List some factors that might cause an organization to become **defunct**.

3. Give an example from a book or movie in which a character showed **temerity**.

4. Explain how a minor disagreement might escalate into a **fray**.

5. Name a song whose lyrics are **lugubrious**.

Academic Vocabulary

*Ravi hides in a an abandoned shed, thinking that this is an **area** of the property where the others will not look.*

In the above sentence, *area* means "a part of a space." The word *area* can have different meanings. Using context clues, try to figure out the meaning of *area* in each sentence.

1. The greater Chicago **area** is home to a large number of natural attractions, including forest preserves and beaches.

2. The total **area** of a rectangle, or the amount of space it takes up, is calculated by multiplying its length by its height.

For more on academic vocabulary, see pages 56 and R81.

Research and Report

Internet Connection

Assignment Use the Internet to investigate childhood games played around the world. Prepare a manual explaining the objectives, rules, and scoring methods of the game you select.

Get Ideas Choose a country and research the games that are played there. Alternately, you may choose a game and research the countries in which it is commonly played. Create a list of questions to guide your research. Consider using primary sources, such as interviews and oral histories, in addition to the Internet.

Research Evaluate the reliability of your information, assessing its authority, accuracy, objectivity, and timeliness. Record information that pertains to your research, making sure to quote and cite sources precisely. If you find conflicting statements, look for corroboration in other sources and accept and report the most widely accepted and reliable information.

Report Create your manual in the form of a brochure, using publishing technology and other digital tools to produce a professional-looking product.

EXAMPLE

The Rules of Boules	
Also known as pétanque, this game is extremely popular in France.	
Players: Two teams of two or three players	Playing field: One-to-two-foot circle drawn in the dirt
Equipment: Three steel balls (boules) and a small wooden ball (cochonnet)	Object: To get close to or hit the cochonnet with your boules, driving it away from your opponent's boules

 Literature Online

Selection Resources For Selection Quizzes, eFlashcards, and Reading-Writing Connection activities, go to glencoe.com and enter QuickPass code GLB9817u7.

After You Read

Assess

Reading Strategy

1. Students may think that Ravi responds emotionally to the circumstances, as might many children with something to prove.

2. Students may say that they would have expressed concern over Ravi's whereabouts.

Research and Report

Use these criteria in evaluating students' Internet searches and brochures:

- A variety of sources are consulted for information about the game.
- Sources are evaluated for reliability, and information is properly quoted and attributed.
- The rules of the game are presented in an attractive, easy-to-read brochure created with suitable technology and visual aids.

 For grammar practice, see Unit 7 Teaching Resources Book, p. 205.

For additional assessment, see Assessment Resources, pp. 307–308.

Vocabulary

1. Students should explain why they would object so strongly to the measure they have named.

2. Students might mention a lack of cooperation between members or a lack of funding.

3. Students should give an example in which a person showed rashness or boldness.

4. Students might say that a minor disagreement could escalate into a fray if people started using violence or if many bystanders became involved.

5. Students should explain their choices of a mournful song or movie.

Academic Vocabulary

1. The context suggests that *area* means "geographical region."

2. The context suggests that *area* means "the space occupied by a two-dimensional geometrical figure."

Before You Read

Focus

Bellringer Options

Daily Language Practice Transparency 116

Or display images of various extinct and endangered species. **Say:** According to a 1998 survey of 400 biologists by the American Museum of Natural History, nearly 70 percent believe we are in the early stages of a human-caused mass extinction. **Ask:** To what emotions should writers appeal in trying to help stop our insensitive use of the Earth? *(Accept all reasonable responses.)*

Before You Read

Elegy for the Giant Tortoises

Meet **Margaret Atwood**
(born 1939)

"I began as a profoundly apolitical writer," Canadian poet and novelist Margaret Atwood once told *Ms.* magazine, "but then I began to do what all novelists and some poets do: I began to describe the world around me." Over the course of her more than forty years as an author, Atwood's unblinking description of the world as she sees it has won her legions of fans all over the globe.

A Split Personality Atwood was born in Ottawa, Ontario, the daughter of an entomologist. She spent the better part of her first seven years in the forested bush of northwestern Quebec, where her father was doing research on insects. The family lived far from civilization for much of each year, which meant Atwood grew up without many playmates, movies, or even a consistently working radio. As a result she learned to read at an early age, and she has been a voracious reader ever since.

During the coldest months of the year, the family packed up and moved to various cities. This moving between forest solitude and the bustle of the city, Atwood would later claim, endowed her with the split personality necessary to become a poet. Even as a very young child she wrote stories, comic books, and plays. When she was seven years old, Atwood and her family relocated to Toronto, Ontario, where she spent her adolescence. It was during this time that, without warning, she transformed into a poet. As she describes it, she was walking home from school when, "a large invisible thumb descended from the sky and pressed down on the top of my head. A poem formed. . . . It was a gift, this poem—a gift from an anonymous donor."

Atwood studied at the University of Toronto and went on to get her master's degree from Radcliffe College in Massachusetts. She was only in her mid-twenties when her poetry collection *The Circle*

Game won the prestigious Governor General's Literary Award for Poetry. Perhaps as a result of her early years in the bush, many of Atwood's poems, including those in *The Circle Game*, explore themes of humankind's precarious relationship with the natural world. She published a number of volumes of poetry in the years that followed. It has been as a novelist, however, that Atwood has made her greatest mark upon the literary world.

> *"I hope that people will finally come to realize that there is only one 'race'— the human race—and that we are all members of it."*
>
> —Margaret Atwood

Atwood's Women Margaret Atwood's novels are peopled with strong women who have complicated, and often troubled, emotional lives. Much of her work dissects modern life through a frankly feminist lens. Atwood's probing insights into human behavior have made her one of the most popular and critically acclaimed writers of her time.

 Literature Online

Author Search For more about Margaret Atwood, go to glencoe.com and enter QuickPass code GLB9817u7.

Selection Skills

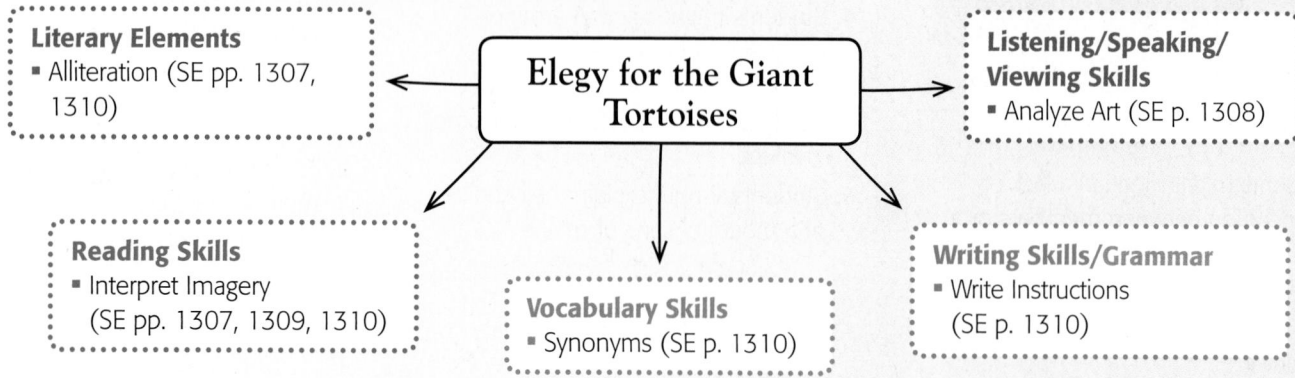

Literary Elements
- Alliteration (SE pp. 1307, 1310)

Reading Skills
- Interpret Imagery (SE pp. 1307, 1309, 1310)

Elegy for the Giant Tortoises

Vocabulary Skills
- Synonyms (SE p. 1310)

Listening/Speaking/ Viewing Skills
- Analyze Art (SE p. 1308)

Writing Skills/Grammar
- Write Instructions (SE p. 1310)

Literature and Reading Preview

Connect to the Poem

What is our responsibility to the environment? In a group, discuss goals humanity should strive for in caring for our planet.

Build Background

Her early experiences in the Canadian wilderness focused Atwood's attention on nature. "Later on I studied chemistry and botany and zoology," she recalls, "and if I hadn't been a writer I'd have gone on with that." Atwood believes that the struggle to survive in nature is a theme that runs throughout Canadian literature. She sees herself as a strongly nationalistic Canadian writer and views Canadian literature as distinct from its American and British counterparts. She believes that a single unifying and defining symbol or theme identifies each country or culture. For the United States, it is the frontier, and for England, it is the island. For Canada, Atwood believes, this defining theme is survival.

Set Purposes for Reading

Big Idea Globalization

Atwood's work reflects a global perspective, an acknowledgment of the many nations and cultures that make up the modern world. As you read "Elegy for the Giant Tortoises," ask yourself, What serious global issues are at the poem's core?

Literary Element Alliteration

Alliteration is the repetition of consonant sounds at the beginnings of words. It can be used to reinforce meaning or create a musical effect. As you read "Elegy for the Giant Tortoises," listen for the sounds of repeated consonants. Ask yourself, What might Atwood's intention be in using them?

Reading Strategy Interpret Imagery

Imagery refers to the word pictures that writers create to evoke an emotional response. In creating effective images, writers use **sensory details**, or descriptions that appeal to one or more of the five senses. As you read, ask yourself, to which senses does this appeal, and what mental picture does it create?

....

Tip: Focusing on Images As you read, note the images in the poem and what they might mean.

Learning Objectives

For pages 1306–1310

In studying this text, you will focus on the following objectives:

Literary Study: Analyzing alliteration.

Reading: Interpreting imagery.

Writing: Writing a set of instructions.

Vocabulary

withering (with′ ər ing) *adj.* becoming dry; shriveling from lack of moisture; p. 1308 *The bunch of grapes I left on the picnic table were withering from the heat.*

periphery (pə rif′ ər ē) *n.* the outward or farthest boundary; p. 1309 *The girls were dancing together in the middle of the room while the boys hung back on the periphery.*

plodding (plod′ ding) *adj.* walking heavily and/or slowly; p. 1309 *The tired mule was plodding through the yard dragging the broken plow behind him.*

lumbering (lum′ bər ing) *adj.* moving heavily and clumsily; p. 1309 *The old dog came lumbering up the steps.*

obsolete (ob′ sə lēt′) *adj.* no longer in use; out-dated; p. 1309 *The new, faster computers made the old ones obsolete.*

MARGARET ATWOOD **1307**

Before You Read

Focus

Summary

The speaker sets out to meditate on, or grieve over, the possible extinction of giant tortoises. In describing her efforts, she sees an image of the endangered tortoises plodding along a road, without water. Finally they walk up the steps of a typically neoclassical natural history museum and into their glass display cases, "brittle gods" we "have destroyed."

For summaries in languages other than English, see Unit 7 Teaching Resources Book, pp. 208–213.

Vocabulary

Etymology Have students research the etymology of each vocabulary word. Remind students to look up the most basic form of the word—for example, *wither* for *withering*, *lumber* for *lumbering*, and *plod* for *plodding*.

For additional vocabulary practice, see Unit 7 Teaching Resources Book, p. 216.

For additional context, see Glencoe Visual Vocabulary CD-ROM.

English Learners

DIFFERENTIATED INSTRUCTION

Intermediate Preview the words *specialize* (line 3), *materialize* (line 13), and *paralyzed* (line 19). Explain that the suffix *-ize* (*-yze* for words whose penultimate syllable ends in *y*, such as *paralysis*) turns an adjective or a noun into a verb. **Write** the suffix *-ize* on the board and include the following definitions: (1) "to become" (2) "to cause to become" (3) "to engage or act in." Have English learners brainstorm a list of other words that contain the suffix *-ize*. Then point out that Atwood uses the three *-ize* words at the end of lines, which creates a distant-rhyme effect.

Teach

Big Idea   1

Globalization Answer: *They are either extinct (passenger pigeon and dodo) or endangered (whooping crane) species of animals or ethnic groups whose traditional ways of life are endangered (Eskimo or Inuit).*

Literary Element   2

Imagery Point out the image in line 6: "[tortoises] withering finally on a remote island." **Ask:** What effect does the word *withering* have? (*The word* withering *makes the image sad and painful.*) How do the words *finally* and *remote* add sadness to the speaker's vision? (*Finally* deepens the sadness by suggesting that death is at hand; remote *suggests that the tortoises are dying alone, unseen.*)

[ENGLISH LEARNERS] If English learners encounter unfamiliar vocabulary (such as *withering, finally,* or *remote*), have them consult a dictionary for definitions.

View the Art ★

Possible answer: *Like Atwood's tortoises, this turtle seems "remote," stranded between the other objects in the painting.*

Fantaise, 1975. Peter Kinsley. Private collection.

View the Art In this image, thick brushstrokes and simple, limited colors create a resemblance to a child's drawing. How does the turtle in this image compare to Atwood's description of the giant tortoises?

Elegy for the Giant Tortoises
Margaret Atwood

Let others pray for the passenger pigeon,
the dodo,[1] the whooping crane, the eskimo:
everyone must specialize

I will confine myself to a meditation
5 upon the giant tortoises
withering finally on a remote island. **2**

---

1. A *dodo* was a heavy flightless bird, now extinct.

1 **Globalization** *What might the passenger pigeon, dodo, whooping crane, and Eskimo (Inuit) have in common?*

Vocabulary

withering (wi<u>th</u>′ ər ing) *adj.* becoming dry; shriveling from lack of moisture

Reading Practice

SPIRAL REVIEW Preview Have students preview the poem by looking at its form. **Ask:** Is there a pattern of rhyming words at the end of the lines? *(no)* **Ask:** How is the poem organized? *(into stanzas of three lines)* Tell students that some writers may break a poem into lines and stanzas to follow a specific form or rhyme scheme, whereas others use stanzas and line breaks to control the pace of the poem. As they read, have students notice how line and stanza breaks affect the pace of this poem.

I concentrate in subway stations,
in parks, I can't quite see them,
they move to the **peripheries** of my eyes

10 but on the last day they will be there;
already the event
like a wave travelling shapes vision:

on the road where I stand they will materialize,
plodding past me in a straggling line
15 awkward without water

their small heads pondering
from side to side, their useless armor
sadder than tanks and history,

in their closed gaze ocean and sunlight paralyzed,
20 **lumbering** up the steps, under the archways
toward the square glass altars

where the brittle gods are kept,
the relics of what we have destroyed,
our holy and **obsolete** symbols.

---

3 | Interpret Imagery *What does the speaker mean by the statement that the ocean and sunlight are "paralyzed" in the tortoise's closed gaze?*

Vocabulary

periphery (pə rif′ ər ē) *n.* the outward or farthest boundary
plodding (plod′ ding) *adj.* walking heavily and/or slowly
lumbering (lum′ bər ing) *adj.* moving heavily and clumsily
obsolete (ob′ sə lēt′) *adj.* no longer in use; outdated

MARGARET ATWOOD **1309**

Approaching Level

DIFFERENTIATED INSTRUCTION

Established To build **reading fluency** have approaching-level students read the poem aloud. Doing so shines a light on sound devices like rhythm, alliteration, and assonance (repetition of vowel sounds). To teach the latter elements, **write** line 15 on the board: *awkward without water*
Have a volunteer read the line aloud.
Then ask the following questions:

- Which consonant sound does Atwood repeat? *(the w sound)*
- How does Atwood use assonance to infuse the line with music and mood? *(by repeating the ô sound)*

Teach

Reading Strategy | **3**

Interpret Imagery **Answer:**
That the images of ocean and sun have frozen like photographs in the tortoises' eyes, since they can no longer enjoy them

(APPROACHING) Have approaching-level students who are having difficulty break the line into two parts: "in their closed gaze" and "ocean and sunlight paralyzed." Then have them paraphrase each part.

Progress Check

Can students interpret imagery?

If No → See Unit 7 Teaching Resources Book, p. 215.

Cultural History
Natural History Museums
In the nineteenth century, natural history museums began to open in Europe and the United States. These imposing buildings were replete with the neoclassical "archways" Atwood refers to in line 20. Many of the men who ran these institutions had trained as taxonomists. They stuffed animals and placed them in vitrines, or "square glass altars," as Atwood says in line 21.

 To check students' understanding of the selection, see Unit 7 Teaching Resources Book, p. 218.

1309

After You Read

Assess

1. Students' answers will vary.
2. (a) To subway stations and parks (b) These locations are as close as the speaker can get to the tortoises' natural environment.
3. (a) To useless armor and tanks (b) War is often a useless act, which, like the tortoise's shell, does little to prevent harm.
4. To a museum, because that is where we go to look at extinct species from past times
5. Feelings of sadness and loss, as well as anger
6. (a) To a church, by using words such as *gods, relics, holy,* and *altars* (b) The tortoises will be displayed in museums as the relics of saints are displayed in churches.
7. The poem is a reminder and a warning about our planet's fragility.
8. This poem exhibits Atwood's poetic ability as well as her knowledge of the natural world.

 For additional assessment, see Assessment Resources, pp. 309–310.

Progress Check

Can students analyze alliteration?

If No → See Unit 7 Teaching Resources Book, p. 214.

Literary Element

1. The staccato sounds of the two words beginning with *s* create a feeling of the hustle and bustle of the city.
2. They create a slow rhythm in keeping with the waddling tortoises.

After You Read

Respond and Think Critically

Respond and Interpret

1. What was your emotional response to the poem's ending? Why?
2. (a) Where does the speaker go to concentrate on the tortoises? (b) Are these appropriate places to go? Explain.
3. (a) To what does the speaker compare the tortoises' shells? (b) What point does the speaker seem to be making with this comparison?
4. Where does the speaker imply we will have to go to see tortoises in the future? Why?

Analyze and Evaluate

5. What emotions do you think Atwood wanted to evoke in readers with this poem?
6. (a) To what does the poet compare the museum in the final two stanzas? (b) Why do you think Atwood uses this particular comparison?

Connect

7. **Big Idea** Globalization How might the theme of this poem be said to reflect global concerns?
8. **Connect to the Author** How does Atwood's "split personality" show in this elegy? Explain.

Literary Element Alliteration

Alliteration is the repetition of consonants or consonant sounds at the beginnings of words in close proximity to one another. In "Elegy for the Giant Tortoises," Atwood uses alliteration to reinforce rhythm and musicality and to emphasize particular points.

1. Listen to the way the phrase "subway station" sounds in line 7. What does this sound reinforce given the context of the stanza?
2. What sort of rhythm do the phrases "plodding past" (line 14) and "side to side" (line 17) create?

Writing

Write a Set of Instructions Atwood's poem offers suggestions on how humans should approach nature. Use her poem "Elegy for the Giant Tortoises" as a model for a set of general instructions entitled "How to Show Respect for Another Species." Number or letter your steps to guide readers through the process. For help in writing a set of instructions, see page R27.

 **Literature** Online

Selection Resources For Selection Quizzes, eFlashcards, and Reading-Writing Connection activities, go to glencoe.com and enter QuickPass code GLB9817u7.

Reading Strategy Interpret Imagery

By **interpreting** the **imagery** in the poem, you may note that the speaker suggests a person should not pray for all species; it is necessary to specialize.

1. Why do you think Atwood uses the images of prayer and church to make her point?
2. (a) Identify three images in the poem that relate to war. (b) How do you interpret the significance of these images?

Vocabulary Practice

Practice with Synonyms With a partner, brainstorm three synonyms for each boldfaced vocabulary word below. Then discuss your choices with your classmates. Be prepared to explain why you chose your words.

withering   periphery   plodding
lumbering   obsolete

EXAMPLE
zenith

Synonyms: summit, pinnacle, apex
Sample explanation: Both zenith and summit mean "top," although zenith has slightly stronger connotations.

Reading Strategy

Possible answers:

1. The poem points out that we should worship nature, not after it is destroyed but while we can still do something to protect it.
2. (a) "useless armor," "sadder than tanks and history," "battle gods" (b) The giant tortoises, like soldiers, are in a losing battle for the survival of the species.

Vocabulary

Answers will vary.

Writing

Check that each step in students' instructions are relevant to the topic and that the steps are logically ordered.

Set a Purpose for Reading

As you read, ask yourself, How can music establish cultural identity and serve as a universal language spread by globalization?

Preview the Article

1. Examine the title. What might "global" mean in this context?

2. Read the *deck,* or the sentence in large type that appears underneath the headline. What connection might the writer make between music and traditions?

Reading Strategy Activate Prior Knowledge

When you recall information and personal experiences that are uniquely your own, you are **activating prior knowledge.**

As you read, ask yourself, How does the article relate to my prior knowledge and experiences?

TIME

Music Goes Global

From Kingston to Cape Town, from New Delhi to New York, musicians are rocking old traditions. Your world will never be the same.

By CHRISTOPHER JOHN FARLEY

IT'S EARLY EVENING IN KINGSTON. THE SLUMBERING HILLS that surround the capital of Jamaica are covered in warm blankets of shadows. It has been a season of heat—the sugarcane crop is shriveling for lack of rain and the streets are dusty and dry. The heat makes tensions rise.

Independence Day is coming, the anniversary of Jamaica's emergence from the control of Britain. Outside club Asylum, one of the city's most popular night spots, young Jamaicans have begun to gather. Inside, things are slow as the drone of foreign acts—Britney Spears, Whitney Houston, 'N Sync—echoes across the empty dance floor. But out on the streets, kids are making their own scene, to their own sounds. Ragga (a rap-influenced form of reggae) booms out of parked cars. Young Jamaican men with white scarves tied around their heads vibrate to the music—some of which are songs of protest.

It is a scene like those that nowadays are taking place in cities all over the planet—in Tokyo, in Cape Town, in Reykjavik. In such ways, in such places, a fresh sound in global music is being born. It's the beating heart of a new world.

Bob Marley, the great Jamaican reggae star, once posed the question "Won't you help me sing these songs of freedom?" Music can be a tool: for relaxation, for stimulation, for communication—and for social change. In fact, it is often a rhythm of resistance:

MUSIC GOES GLOBAL **1311**

TIME

Focus

Summary

Music around the world has changed dramatically in the last fifty years. Radio was the medium that brought music from the outside world to Africa in the 1940s and 1950s. In the 1970s, the audiocassette tape made it possible for third world musicians to spread their music. In the 21st century, the Internet has been instrumental in opening up the entire world of music.

Teach

Reading Strategy | 1

Activate Prior Knowledge
Point out that each person brings his or her unique knowledge and memories to encounters with music. What we have heard, played, or sung before affects how we react to new music. **Say:** The word *global* means "relating to the whole world, without borders or boundaries." Music referred to as *crossover* combines two types of music into one.

(ENGLISH LEARNERS) For English learners, **ask:** What are the two types of music in the following crossovers: ragga, rockabilly, and folk rock? *(Ragga combines rap and reggae. Rockabilly combines rock and country. Folk rock combines folk and rock.)*

Readability Scores
Dale-Chall: 6.4
DRP: 67
Lexile: 1040

TIME

Teach

Big Idea   1

Globalization **Ask:** In what ways, besides music, are our everyday lives affected by globalization? *(Answers might include that many products are no longer manufactured in the United States; some service industries have been moved overseas, so when we call for help on a product, the person answering the phone may be in India or another country; the same businesses are found around the world.)*

For activities related to this selection, see Unit 7 Teaching Resources Book, pp. 220–227.

For an audio recording of this selection, use Listening Library Audio CD-ROM.

---

against war, against social injustice, against government corruption.

The U.S., in this one-superpower age, has perhaps never been so dominant—economically, militarily, culturally. That strength attracts immigrants, who bring with them new forms of music. That strength also inspires competition. Musicians and performers in other countries, mindful of American influence, assert their national identities and culture and create new musical genres they can call their own: garage in Britain, kwaito in South Africa, ever evolving forms of reggae in Jamaica. America may be the world's policeman, but citizens of the world—and the New Americans who have come here—have turned up their **1** car stereos and are dancing like never before.

The quest for change has often been a family affair: many top global-music performers, including Nigeria's Femi Kuti (son of Fela), Jamaica's Ziggy Marley (son of Bob) and Brazil's Max de Castro (son of Wilson Simonal), are the children of musical pioneers. In recent years around the world, old traditions have been revived, remolded, and returned to prominence by a new generation and new technology. In Tijuana, Mexico, young DJs have crossed traditional norteno (a polka-like music) with not-at-all-traditional techno to create a fresh genre, Nortec. In Bogota, Colombia, the rock duo Aterciopelados mixed old-time accordion-driven vallenato with clubland drum-'n'-bass beats. In Rio de Janeiro, Brazil, the great chanteuse Marisa Monte smoothly blended samba and art-pop.

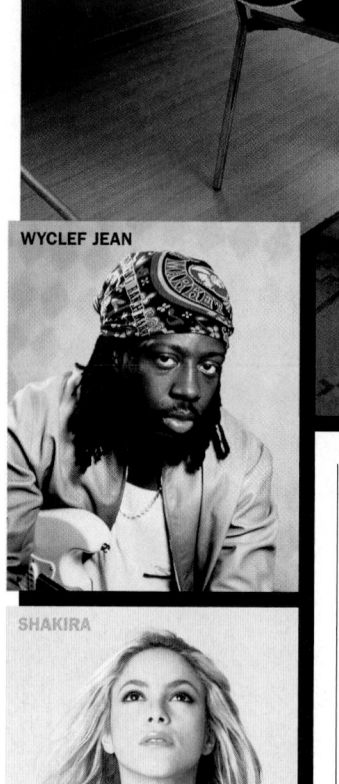

WYCLEF JEAN

DE CASTRO

SHAKIRA

Centuries of customs have changed in just decades. In the 1940s and '50s, radio brought the music of the outside world to much of Africa for the first time. In the 1970s, audiocassette tapes made it possible for Third World musicians to spread their own music quickly, cheaply, and profitably. Acts like the Congo's Papa Wemba became continent-wide superstars.

In the 21st century, the Internet has opened up the world to itself. In the distant past—say, a decade ago—global-music fans had to wait for a record label to decide whether to distribute a foreign artist in their country. A few years later, Internet file-sharing services were allowing users to listen to whatever they

---

Vocabulary Practice

Adjectives Say: A varied and specific use of adjectives in writing gives the reader a more complete sensory experience: sight, sound, touch, smell, and taste. **Write** on the board: *large, green, quiet* Ask the class for more specific adjectives for each of the words. Review the suggestions made with the class, and ask students how each word could affect a reader's reaction.

Write on the board: *slumbering, warm blankets, dusty, dry* **Ask:** How do these adjectives in the first paragraph make you feel? *(Answers will vary.)*

HIKARU

MIKE D

Phil Knott/Camerapress/Retna

SHIRLEY MANSON

Niels Van Iperenn/Retna

Michael Halsband/TIME

MARC ANTHONY

Michael Lavine/CORBIS

wanted, anywhere they chose, anytime they pleased. Today, online music stores tend to have wider and more diverse inventories than their bricks-and-mortar counterparts.

The we-are-the-world maxim is this: music is the universal language. For the mainstream record industry in the U.S., however, music in languages other than English often wasn't considered universal; it was controversial.

Richie Valens hit it big with "La Bamba" in 1959. The music industry didn't wholeheartedly embrace another Latin rocker until Santana's late-in-life success in 1999. After that, tongues became untied. Wyclef Jean's platinum hip-hop CDs, *The Carnival* and *The Ecleftic*, mixed English and Haitian Creole. Christina Aguilera, who launched her career singing English-language teen pop,

recorded a CD entirely in Spanish. Increasingly, world-beaters are collaborating and connecting with one another. Colombian rocker Shakira had a CD executive-produced by Cuban-American Emilio Estefan Jr. that drew from Argentine tango.

The new global music doesn't exclude America. After all, one of America's biggest rock stars of the past few years was Dave Matthews, a white African; the Japanese pop star Utada Hikaru hailed from Manhattan. The old-school term *world music* is a joke, a wedge, a way of separating English-language performers from the rest of the planet. But there has always been crossover. In 1958 Dean Martin scored a hit with the Italian tune "Volare"; in 1967 Frank Sinatra recorded an album of songs by Brazilian composer Antonio Carlos

2

MUSIC GOES GLOBAL **1313**

TIME

Teach

| Big Idea | 2 |

Globalization Ask: Will globalization erase the differences between cultures? Will all societies end up the same, one barely distinguishable from another? Ask students to write paragraphs expressing their opinions on these questions. Ask volunteers to share their paragraphs with the class. APPROACHING Have approaching-level students think about how music can strengthen the connection between people in different countries. **Ask:** What limitations in connecting people might the globalization of music face? What obstacles—both political and personal—might not be easy to overcome? *(Possible barriers: language, opposition because of strict observance of moral codes or concern that new music may evoke a spirit of rebellion.)*

English Learners

DIFFERENTIATED INSTRUCTION

Intermediate Tell English learners that rereading an article like "Music Goes Global" will help them identify the article's main ideas and supporting details, the author's tone and purpose for writing, and unfamiliar words. **Write** the following note headings on the board, and have students copy them onto a piece of paper to guide their note taking as they reread:

Main Ideas and Supporting Details
Tone
Author's Purpose
Unfamiliar Words

TIME

Teach

FASSIE

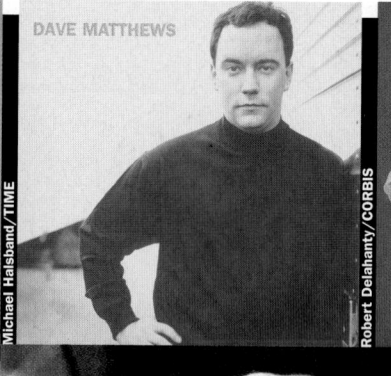
DAVE MATTHEWS

ATERCIOPELADOS

ZIGGY MARLEY

Reading Strategy 1

Activate Prior Knowledge
Ask: What does the author mean by "There's a sense that geography doesn't have to equal destiny"? *(Answers will vary. Students should note that where you are from is not necessarily where you will be in the future.)* Encourage students to explore this concept of location determining destiny. Have students combine images, videos, interviews, and sound clips of their favorite musician or music group in a brief presentation. Students should tailor their choice of materials to the focus of their presentation. Remind them to edit sound clips and videos both for length and for appropriateness. Have the class prepare evaluations for each presentation and offer constructive feedback to the speaker, with suggestions for revision.

(Tom) Jobim. Elvis Presley's "Can't Help Falling in Love" is based on the 18th century French ballad "Plaisir d'amour."

Pop music and global music aren't mutually exclusive categories. In the 1980s Paul Simon, David Byrne, and Peter Gabriel blended world beats. Later, Sting scored a hit with Algerian rai star Cheb Mami, Lauryn Hill covered Bob Marley on MTV Unplugged, and Britney Spears made a habit of working with Swedish songwriter Max Martin. Over the years, Madonna's sound—and style—has been inspired by many cultures.

Musicians performing in different languages often strike similar chords. Listen to the intense, undulant wail of Assane Ndiaye on the song "Nguisstal," a track on *Streets of Dakar: Generation Boul Fale*, a compilation of young Senegalese acts. *Boul fale* is a Wolof phrase that means, loosely, "Never mind." The American punk group Nirvana's great album of teen angst was also titled *Nevermind*. Alienation, it seems, is a nation without borders.

Lyrics are important, but they don't have to matter. Even when Bob Dylan, arguably America's finest lyricist, mumbles through a number, the poetry of his words comes out in the phrasing. "How does it feel?" Dylan famously asked on "Like a Rolling Stone." We may not have known exactly what he meant, but we knew how it felt. Today's musicians have taken that lesson to heart. Thom Yorke of the British band Radiohead wrote some songs for his classic album *Kid A* by cutting up lyric sheets and pulling lines out of a top hat. The Icelandic band Sigur Ros sang some songs in a made-up tongue it called Hopelandic.

Many of today's global musicians move back and forth from their native tongues to English, on the same album, sometimes on the same song. There's a sense that geography doesn't have 1 to equal destiny. The Tokyo-based rock trio the Brilliant Green produced a CD almost entirely in Japanese. It was recorded in Tokyo. The CD's title? *Los Angeles*.

Cultural History ☆

Bob Dylan In the early 1960s, an American folk artist named Bob Dylan emerged onto the popular music scene. His songs were embraced by the antiwar and civil rights movements of the time. After over 40 years of playing music, Dylan has run the gamut of folk, country/blues, rock 'n' roll, and jazz.

Writing Practice

Write a Letter The author of the article, Christopher John Farley, states, "Lyrics are important, but they don't have to matter." Ask students whether they agree or disagree with this statement. **Ask:** What examples does Farley give to support this statement? *(Radiohead pulling lyrics out of a hat; Sigur Rose making up its own language)* After the discussion, have them write a letter to Farley, explaining whether they think that music lyrics matter.

Have students use specific examples from familiar music to support their position. *(Students might discuss tone and mood of music as being more powerful than the lyrics; classical music which tells a story with no lyrics; the significance of the specific lyrics of a song to them)*

Listening to music in an unfamiliar tongue can be more thrilling than listening to a song whose lyrics are instantly understandable. That's because if you can connect with another person beyond lyrics, beyond language, then you have engaged in a kind of telepathy. You have managed to escape the everyday realm of ordinary communication and entered a place where souls communicate directly. It's cooler than instant messaging. Cherif Mbaw is a Senegalese singer-guitarist living in Paris; the songs on his brilliant CD *Kham Kham* are in his native Wolof. But when Mbaw, with his beatific tenor, soars into a passage of staccato vocals and jittery guitar work on "Saay

Saay," you know exactly what he means even if you don't know what he's saying. His intent is in his inflection; his eloquence is in his emotion. Boundaries fall away.

Is a sense of cultural uniqueness lost in the global-pop blender? If they are grooving to America's latest pop star in Kingston, is there anywhere to hide? The first years of the 21st century have been haunted by the specter of globalization. Our star-spangled world with its parade of powerful letters—the U.N., the WTO, the IMF—hammers the diversity of the planet into homogenized goop. But the Colombian duo Aterciopelados insists on recording its CDs in its hometown of Bogotá. And Max de Castro projects

blown-up images of old Brazilian LPs at some of his concerts to remind audiences of his country's heritage. Many new global artists have the curiosity to wander the earth with their music and the integrity to stay connected to their homelands. This is the help Marley asked for. These are freedom songs.

It's getting hot in club Asylum, but the dancers just keep on going. At this club and ones like it around the world—in Sao Paulo, in Dakar, in Havana, in New York City— Independence Day is every night.

Respond and Think Critically

Respond and Interpret

1. Write a brief summary of the main ideas in this article before you answer the following questions. For help on writing a summary, see page 435.

2. What was your reaction to the music described in the article? How is it different from or similar to the music you listen to?

3. (a)How did technology inspire a global music revolution? (b)How has technology continued to make access to music easier?

Analyze and Evaluate

4. (a)What similarities does the writer point out between American and world music? (b)What effect does this point have on his argument?

5. (a)How did your prior experiences and personal interests relate to the article? (b)Explain whether the writer assumes readers have a prior knowledge of music. Cite specific examples from the text.

Connect

6. How does this article connect global music to some themes of contemporary British literature?

TIME

Assess

1. Summaries will vary but should mention issues such as varied traditions and cultures, changing attitudes, rebellion, government opposition, morality, progress, and bridges to international understanding.

2. Some students may be unfamiliar with the music described in the text, while others may be more familiar with it. Ask them to discuss their thoughts on listening to music in another language.

3. (a) Cassette tapes made access to music cheaper for consumers and more profitable for musicians. (b) Online music stores and file-sharing services on the Internet allow quick, easy access to music from all over the world.

4. (a) He uses examples such as Nirvana's "Nevermind" and Bob Dylan's "Like a Rolling Stone" to show how global music represents feelings rather than language. (b) This supports his argument that music represents emotion rather than language.

 For additional assessment, see Assessment Resources, pp. 311–312.

5. (a) Students' responses will vary. (b) He assumes readers are familiar because he provides examples of many popular American musicians, such as Bob Dylan and Nirvana, to support his argument.

6. Students should mention the connection made between global music and the freedom of former British colonies, such as Jamaica, and the dispersion of culture throughout the countries of the world. These developments are relevant to the selections in Unit Seven, Part 2.

Focus

Bellringer

Ask students about a film that most are likely to have seen.

Ask: How would you describe this film? What did you like or dislike about it and why? After they give their answers, tell students that they have just presented a critical review.

Summary

In this workshop, students will write critical reviews in which they analyze the literary merits of a short story. They will follow the stages of the writing process, including prewriting, drafting, revising, editing, proofreading, and presenting. In addition, the workshop includes two focus lessons, one on adding evidence to support a viewpoint and one on correcting verb tense.

> For Writing Workshop graphic organizer and rubric, see Unit 7 Teaching Resources, pp. 229–231.

Learning Objectives

For pages 1316–1323

In this workshop, you will focus on the following objective:

Writing: Writing a critical review using the writing process.

▶ Writing Process

At any stage of the writing process, you may think of new ideas to include. Feel free to return to earlier stages as you write.

Prewrite

Draft

Revise

Focus Lesson:
Support a Viewpoint

Edit and Proofread

Focus Lesson:
Verb Tense

Present

LOG ON ▶ **Literature** Online

Writing and Research For prewriting, drafting, and revising tools, go to glencoe.com and enter QuickPass code GLB9817u7.

 **Writing Workshop**

Critical Review

Literature Connection In *Imaginary Homelands,* Salman Rushdie discusses what, in his opinion, an artist must successfully attempt in order to create great literature.

> *"The real risks of any artist are taken in the work, in pushing the work to the limits of what is possible. . . . Books become good when they go to this edge and risk falling over it."*

More narrowly, in a critical review you examine what an artist has attempted to achieve in a particular work and evaluate his or her relative success, citing specific strengths and weaknesses to support your opinion. To write a successful critical review, learn the goals of critical writing and the strategies for achieving those goals.

Checklist

Goals	Strategies
To state a position or claim about a story's literary merits	☑ Develop an insightful thesis to express your overall critical judgment
To support your claim with evidence	☑ Analyze and assess important literary elements to show that your thesis is valid
	☑ Include direct evidence and examples from the work, and use reasoning to support your evaluation
To present a logically organized critical review of the story	☑ Summarize briefly and state your thesis in the introduction
	☑ State your reasons and supporting evidence in your body paragraphs
	☑ End persuasively
To persuade the reader to accept your evaluation of the story	☑ Use third-person point of view to establish objectivity, but establish your own tone.
	☑ In the conclusion, consider readers' expectations and address opposing viewpoints
	☑ Use persuasive techniques

1316 UNIT 7 AN INTERNATIONAL LITERATURE

Workshop Resources

Print Materials

- Unit 7 Teaching Resources pp. 229–231
- Writing Kit
- Success in Writing: Research and Reports
- Grammar and Language Transparencies 62, 80
- Writing Workshop Transparencies 26–30
- Daily Language Transparencies 61, 97, 99, 102

Technology

- Literature Online: Writing Resources and Grammar Resources, www.glencoe.com
- Online Essay Grader, www.glencoe.com
- Student Presentation Builder on Student-Works Plus CD-ROM
- Media Workshop DVD
- Online Student Edition

Assignment: Evaluate a Literary Work

Write a critical review of at least 1,500 words in which you analyze the literary merits of a work and make a critical evaluation of the work. As you write, keep your audience and purpose in mind.

Audience: peers and others who may be interested in the work

Purpose: to evaluate a work and convince an audience of the validity of your evaluation

Analyze a Professional Model

In this critical review, the *New York Times* writer Selden Rodman reviews V. S. Naipaul's collection of short stories *Miguel Street,* praising the story "B. Wordsworth" in particular. As you read the review, notice how Rodman makes a critical evaluation and supports it with examples and evidence from the text. Pay close attention to the comments in the margin. They point out features that you may want to include in your own critical review.

from *"Catfish Row, Trinidad"* by Selden Rodman ☆

The mystifying thing about Trinidad writers—most recently Samuel Selvon, Geoffrey Holder, and the present author—is why they ever leave the island. Existence in this corner of the British West Indies may not be paradise, but compared with the slums of London or New York, this is life among those who know how to live it. Certainly it has never a dull moment. V. S. Naipaul, born in Trinidad of Hindu parents and educated at Oxford, proved he knew the region in his novel, "The Mystic Masseur." He proves it again with these short, delightful sketches of Miguel Street, the Catfish Row of Port of Spain. . . .

The finest of this really fine collection of portraits is the one entitled "B. Wordsworth." B stands for Black, and it is about a poet who wanders in one day just to "watch the bees" and who answers a policeman who asks what he's doing lying on his back in a public place, "I have been asking myself the same question for forty years." The young narrator takes this character to meet his mother:

Persuasion / Exposition

Real-World Connection

You will use the ability to analyze, state your opinion, and support your opinion in a host of workplace documents that range from creating new business plants to advocating for new materials and methods in tasks ranging from building bridges to setting up exhibits.

Point of View

Use the third-person point of view, but establish your own tone.

Introduction/Audience/ Purpose

In your introduction, include the author and the title of the work you are to review, as well as your thesis, or overall critical judgment of the work.

Summary/Audience

Give a brief summary so that readers unfamiliar with the work will understand your review.

Teach

Big Idea

Globalization As technology continues to make our world smaller, we are exposed to more art and culture from other countries. Challenge students to be especially curious and open-minded as they approach their selected works from foreign writers. Have them search the stories for elements that are specific to the writer's background as well as elements that are universal.

Literary History ☆

Selden Rodman Selden Rodman (1909–2002) was an acclaimed poet, author, and critic of modern culture. Born into a wealthy family in New York, he grew into a rebellious young man and ended up as a famous champion of the Western Hemisphere's folk arts, particularly Haitian paintings, which he called a "crystallization of joy." He rocked the modern art establishment by branding Abstract Expressionism "the cerebral put-ons of the avant-garde."

English Learners

DIFFERENTIATED INSTRUCTION

Intermediate Writing an effective critical review requires a clear understanding of the basic literary elements in a work of literature. Make sure that students understand the nature of these elements. Discuss character, plot, setting, theme, and conflict before the reviews are begun.

Approaching Level

DIFFERENTIATED INSTRUCTION

Emerging Remind approaching level readers to refer to the notes next to Rodman's critical review on pages 1317–1318. Explain that his review, like any good composition, contains a clear thesis, a plot summary of the analyzed work, support from the story, and a conclusion. **Ask:** From which point of view is Rodman's review written? *(third-person)*

Critical Review

Teach

Writing Skills

Support To illustrate V. S. Naipaul's gift of characterization, Rodman includes several direct quotations from "B. Wordsworth." **Ask:** Why do you think Rodman chooses to use direct quotations where he does? (*Possible answer: The use of Naipaul's own words may be a more effective way of showing the author's vivid and often humorous depiction of a character than retelling or summarizing the writing would be.*)

Writing Skills

Conclusion An effective conclusion returns to the thesis stated in the opening paragraph. Have students note how Rodman introduces his conclusion in the line before the last paragraph: "a fact which brings us back to the original question." Then, in his conclusion, Rodman sums up his review by hinting that he would like to see the story expanded into a novel. Challenge students to write a conclusion that sums up the review but also leaves the reader with something to think about.

Support

Support your evaluation with critical evidence, including examples and direct quotations.

Opposing Viewpoints/ Audience

Answer possible objections to your evaluation to persuade your reader that your opinion is balanced.

Purpose/Persuasive Techniques

Use persuasive techniques such as word choice, repetition, and rhetorical questions to help achieve your writing purpose.

"He pulled out a printed sheet from his hip-pocket and said, 'On this paper is the greatest poem about mothers and I'm going to sell it to you at a bargain price. For four cents.'

"I went inside and I said, 'Ma, you want to buy a poetry for four cents?'

"My mother said, 'Tell that blasted man to haul his tail away from my yard, you hear?'

"I said to B. Wordsworth, 'My mother say she ain't have four cents.'

"B. Wordsworth said, 'It is the poet's tragedy.'"

He put the paper back in his pocket. He didn't seem to mind. The ending of this little classic is a sad one. But the prevailing mood of the stories is comic, and most of the characters fulfill themselves through their idiosyncrasies—a fact which brings us back to the original question.

In the final chapter the narrator is about to join his fellow story-tellers abroad ("The Americans gave me a visa after making me swear I wouldn't overthrow their government by armed force"). In the airport lounge, filled with haughty tourists in sun-glasses looking "too rich, too comfortable," he wishes he had never got a scholarship. Wouldn't it be interesting now to have a novel about one of these children of nature in our frigid cities—and then, the native's return?

Reading-Writing Connection Think about the writing techniques that you have just encountered and try them out in the critical review you write.

Writing Practice

Practice Aloud Students may find that an effective prewriting strategy is to explain the plan of a review aloud to a partner. Pair up students and have partners present their theses to each other before they put their ideas on paper. Encourage the listening partner to ask probing questions. Remind students that it is especially important to ask where in the text the writer finds evidence that supports his or her interpretation of the story.

Prewrite

Choose a Work Choose a work from Unit Seven that left you with a strong positive or negative impression.

Examine and Evaluate the Work Reread the work several times. Determine the author's purpose and the literary elements used to achieve it. Ask yourself:

▶ What is the author trying to achieve? Did he or she succeed? How?

▶ What is the theme of the work and how is it conveyed?

▶ If there is a plot, is it believable? Is it engaging or suspenseful? Why?

▶ If the work is a poem, what is unique or compelling about the language, the imagery, the speaker, the sound devices, or the form?

▶ If there are characters, how are they developed? Are they believable?

▶ In your opinion, what element is most important to the overall success or failure of the work?

Develop a Thesis What is your overall opinion of the work? Distill that opinion into a clear thesis statement that presents your critical judgment.

Identify Critical Evidence Remember that a critical review involves more than just stating your opinion; you need to give logical reasons why your opinion is valid and deserves your audience's consideration.

Outline Your Review Create an outline to organize your ideas. Follow the structure of an essay and include needed background information.

Discuss Your Ideas Once you finish organizing, share your thesis and outline with a partner. Help your partner clarify his or her thesis, organize reasons, and identify additional supporting evidence.

Introduction	Give the story's title and author. Summarize the plot briefly. State your overall critical judgment in your thesis.	"The Train from Rhodesia" by Nadine Gordimer Thesis: Through realistic description and full characterization, Gordimer shows how the complex and pervasive force of racism damages the victim, the oppressor, and those caught in between.
Body Paragraphs	Focus on the major elements that contribute to the story's success or failure. State your opinions, support them with reasons.	Gordimer uses vivid descriptions and a detached voice to suggest the existence of racism, using rich characterization to powerfully show how it affects the characters.
Conclusion	Restate your evaluation and make a recommendation to the reader.	Although Gordimer's subtlety and complex characters may be frustrating at first, most readers will find her story powerful and almost haunting.

Persuasion / Exposition

Review the Reviews

Sharpen your critical sense by reading book and film reviews published in current newspapers and magazines. Notice the voice and tone of the reviews, the evaluations presented, and how those evaluations are supported.

Avoid Plagiarism

Always attribute your sources. Attribute the literature, your primary source in a critical review, by quoting it accurately and by using quotation marks or indenting it as a long quotation of four or more lines. Attribute outside sources by citing them in parenthetical references (see page R34).

Teach

Writing Process

Prewrite Suggest that students freewrite an introduction, a body, and a conclusion. They may find that a plan has already formed in their minds or that their main idea needs to be reworked before they begin. There is no need for them to edit as they go; the key is to write straight through and include as many ideas as possible. The revising and editing will come later.

Writing Skills

Introduction Explain to students that the introductory paragraph is the most critical part of the essay. A stellar opening may be able to carry a shoddy essay, but a second-rate introduction will cripple an otherwise capable paper. Challenge students to engage their audience at the outset. Encourage them to write a "zinger" of a first sentence to capture the audience's attention and then to present a clearly stated thesis.

English Learners

DIFFERENTIATED INSTRUCTION

Intermediate Have small groups identify the elements of specific stories. Encourage students to focus on key details and on the ways the author uses the literary elements. **Ask:** How do the theme, plot, setting, and characters contribute to the development of the story?

Approaching Level

DIFFERENTIATED INSTRUCTION

Established As a class, analyze a short story together. Ask students to pinpoint various literary elements (imagery, setting, plot, character) and to examine the effects of these elements on the story. Then have students work together to develop a thesis.

Writer's Technique ☆

Contextualization Rodman provides information valuable to rirst-time readers of Naipaul's work: notes about Naipaul's biography and that of writers who resemble him, and details related to the cultural background of his writing.

Teach

Writing Skills

Introduction/Point of View

Answer: *The introduction supplies information to help orient the reader: the story title and the author's name and nationality. The point of view is third person omniscient.*

Writing Skills

Summary/Audience **Possible**

answer: *The summary provides enough information to familiarize a reader with the basic story without revealing many details.*

Writing Skills

Thesis **Answer:** *The thesis is a judgment of the story based on evaluation of the description, characterization, and literary merits.*

Writing Skills

Tone/Repetition/Purpose

Answer: *Phrases such as "get caught up in" and "we are there" and the second-person pronouns lend a natural, conversational tone to the review. Repetition and parallelism reinforce the premise.*

Writing Skills

Support **Answer:** *Summaries and explanations are clearer and more concise than quotations.*

Writing Frames

As you read the model, think about the writer's use of these frames:

- Through _____, <title of work> shows how _____.

- Perhaps the most compelling aspect of the work is _____.

Consider using frames like these in your own critical review.

Introduction/Point of View

What makes this a strong introduction? What is the point of view?

Summary/Audience

Does this plot summary provide enough information for the reader? Explain.

Thesis

What details make this an appropriate thesis for a critical review?

Tone/Repetition/Purpose

How would you describe the tone of the review? Which words help create the tone? How do repetition and parallelism make the writing more persuasive?

Support

Why might the writer include this example but not quote the passage directly here?

Draft

Stay Flexible As you draft your review, use your outline as a guide but be flexible as your evaluation evolves. You may change your opinion about the work as you explore it.

Analyze a Workshop Model

Here is a final draft of a critical review. Read it and answer the questions in the margin. Use your answers to guide you as you write your review.

"The Train from Rhodesia": A Subtle Message

"The Train from Rhodesia" by South African writer Nadine Gordimer is a haunting story that explores the damaging effects of racism in a subtle but powerful way. Gordimer begins the story with a rich description of an African train station just as a train pulls in. The story revolves around a seemingly trivial event: a woman is interested in buying a carved lion from a native artist but decides it is too expensive. Without her knowledge, her husband bargains with the artist and buys the carving at a much cheaper price. Through realistic description and full characterization, the story shows how the complex and pervasive forces of colonialism and racism damage the victim, the oppressor, and those caught in between.

It is easy to get caught up in Gordimer's vivid images. From the very first line, readers are *there*, feeling the train bearing down on the station, seeing and hearing it "creaking, jerking, jostling, gasping." Through the precise descriptions, readers are seeing and hearing the evidence of blatant racial tension at the station and on the train, without any mention of it directly. At the station, the native vendors are "squatting" and "waiting in the dust." The stationmaster's "barefoot" children approach the train, where they are enclosed in shadows. On the train, we hear needier native children begging the travelers for a penny, an orange, or a chocolate; a moment later we see a young girl throwing a handful of unwanted chocolates to the dogs instead. No words are exchanged between the girl and the chil-

---

Writing Practice

 **Precise Language** Writers should strive for precise language to represent the selection and to explain their interpretations. They should change vague words to more exact ones or add specific details. **Write:** *She went there for lunch.*

Ask students to use more precise language to make the sentence more telling. (*Possible answer: Maria drove to the café to meet Sarah for a bagel.*)

In peer review groups, have students exchange drafts of their critical essays and make specific suggestions about how to use more precise language.

dren, and the narrator does not explain or comment on the action. This type of subtlety and detachment throughout the story makes the events and interactions especially disturbing.

Perhaps the most compelling aspect of Gordimer's story, though, is her sharp characterization of people, both black and white, who encounter the complex issue of racism in one way or another. As a contrast to the girl with the candy, Gordimer paints the wife as sympathetic and self-aware. The wife sees the lion's mouth "opened in an endless roar too terrible to be heard" and its fur mane, "a real mane, majestic, telling you somehow that the artist had delight in the lion." Here, again, Gordimer's realistic details suggest much more than they actually describe.

At the same time, however, Gordimer weaves contrasting details into the narrative, exposing contradictions in the characters. From the limited third-person perspective, the reader learns the wife's intimate thoughts—her sympathy toward the artist, for example, but also her more automatic, conventional attitudes. Whatever respect the wife has for the artist, she always speaks gruffly to him in person, in a commanding, almost annoyed tone. And even though the artist, unlike the wife, has no choice in the matter, doesn't he, too, conform to racist social conventions? He calls the wife "Missus" and the husband "Baas" (boss) more out of the need to make a sale than out of respect. When the husband pays him after bargaining for a cheaper price, the artist, "smiling and shaking his head," appears more happy than humiliated, at least for the moment.

Gordimer's detached tone and complex characters may leave some readers frustrated. The ending of the story asks more questions than it answers, yet one theme becomes clear: the lingering effects of colonialism and racism are damaging to all those involved, no matter which side of the color line they're on. Read "The Train from Rhodesia" and you'll find that Gordimer's vivid images and powerful characters stay with you long after you finish the story.

Persuasion / Exposition

Support/Purpose
How does this information strengthen the writer's review?

Organization
How are the first two body paragraphs organized? Why is this an effective way of organizing the review?

Word Choice/Purpose
Which word choices are especially persuasive? Why?

Persuasive Techniques/ Purpose
How does this rhetorical question support an effective argument?

Opposing Viewpoints/ Audience
How does telling readers that they might be "frustrated" with the story help support the writer's evaluation? Explain.

Conclusion
What makes this a strong conclusion?

Teach

Writing Skills

Support/Purpose Answer: *By connecting the evidence to the thesis, the writer helps the reader recognize the validity of the thesis.*

Writing Skills

Organization Answer: *The paragraphs (first description and then characterization) follow the organization of the thesis.*

Writing Skills

Word Choice/Purpose
Possible answer: Contrasting *and* contradictions *point up the wife's conflicting emotions.* Conventional *and* condescending *demonstrate how naturally racism was accepted at the time.*

Writing Skills

Persuasive Techniques/ Purpose Answer: *The question highlights the wife's own questioning of the status quo.*

Writer's Technique ☆
Transitional Devices The author of this composition effectively uses transitional elements to signal the logic of the essay's argument. Words and phrases such as *though*, *as a contrast*, and *however* make the point of various details clear.

Intermediate Students' critical writing will be more effective if they can recognize word connotations. Encourage students to consult a dictionary or a thesaurus as they write. Then pair them with fluent English speakers, who can help them understand connotations of key words.

Emerging Some students may benefit from creating essay outlines based on the workshop model. Have students work with partners to create the outlines, filling them in with key sentences and ideas from the model. Then ask students to identify the organizational pattern the writer used.

Critical Review

Teach

Writing Process

Revise Before they revise their drafts, have students reread the essay on "The Train from Rhodesia." Ask them to pay close attention to the elements that make the piece flow and succeed. When students shift their focus to their own essays, challenge them to adopt those winning elements, as well as to consider carefully the questions in the checklist on page 1322.

Writing Skills

Peer Review Remind students that even the most accomplished writers are judged by their peers. Encourage students not to accept or reject comments immediately but to consider them at some point during the revision process. Advise students, however, to pay particular attention to comments concerning clarity of expression.

Traits of Strong Writing

Include these traits of strong writing to express your ideas effectively.

Ideas
Organization
Voice
Word Choice
Sentence Fluency
Conventions
Presentation

For more information on using the Traits of Strong Writing, see pages R28–R30.

Word Choice

This academic vocabulary word appears in the student model:

contrast (kon´ trast) *n.* something that shows a striking dissimilarity; 2. the act of contrasting or showing differences. *As a contrast to the girl with the candy, Gordimer paints the wife as sympathetic and self-aware.*

Using academic vocabulary may help strengthen your writing. Try to use one or two academic vocabulary words in your critical review. See the complete list on pages R81–R83.

 **Literature** Online

Writing and Research For editing and publishing tools, go to glencoe.com and enter QuickPass code GLB9817u7.

Revise

Use the checklist below to help you evaluate and strengthen your review.

Checklist:

☑ Do you state a clear, insightful position or claim?

☑ Do you use the third-person point of view?

☑ Do you support ideas with reasons, examples, and direct quotations?

☑ Do you organize ideas logically and for greatest effect?

☑ Do you use persuasive techniques such as repetition, effective word choice, and parallelism?

☑ Do you anticipate and address audience concerns?

▶ **Focus Lesson**

Add Evidence to Support a Viewpoint

Check to be sure that you fully support your viewpoint with reasons and that you back up the reasons with examples and quotations.

Draft:

> Perhaps the most compelling aspect of Gordimer's story, though, is her sharp characterization of people, both black and white, who encounter the complex but familiar issue of racism in one way or another.

Revision:

> Perhaps the most compelling aspect of Gordimer's story, though, is her sharp characterization of people, both black and white, who encounter the complex but familiar issue of racism in one way or another. <u>As a contrast to the girl with the candy, Gordimer paints the wife as sympathetic and self-aware.</u>[1] <u>The wife sees the lion's mouth "opened in an endless roar too terrible to be heard" and its fur mane, "a real mane, majestic, telling you somehow that the artist had delight in the lion."</u>[2] <u>Here, again, Gordimer's realistic details suggest much more than they actually describe.</u>[3]

1: <u>Add example from the text.</u>   **2:** <u>Add direct quotations.</u>
3: <u>Show how your evidence supports your thesis.</u>

Writing Practice

End Strongly Explain that an effective conclusion must anchor the thesis in readers' minds, not just restate the main idea. Refer students to the final paragraph of the review of "The Train from Rhodesia," on page 1321.

- End with a broad comment about the text or the writer (e.g., "Gordimer's vivid images and powerful characters stay with the reader long after the final paragraph has been read."). Restate the thesis powerfully (e.g., "One theme becomes clear: the lingering effects of colonialism and racism are damaging to all those involved.").

Edit and Proofread

Get It Right When you have completed the final draft of your review, proofread it for errors in grammar, usage, mechanics, and spelling. Refer to the Language Handbook, pages R40–R59, as a guide.

> ### ▶ Focus Lesson
>
> ### Correct Verb Tense
>
> When you write about events in—or the writing of—a literary work, use the **literary present tense**.
>
> **Original:** The statement describing the writing is in the past tense.
>
> *As a contrast to the girl with the candy, Gordimer painted the wife as sympathetic and self-aware.*
>
> **Improved:** Even though the action you describe technically happened in the past, use the literary present tense.
>
> *As a contrast to the girl with the candy, Gordimer paints the wife as sympathetic and self-aware.*
>
> **Original:** The description of story events, like the quotation, is in the past tense.
>
> *One of the first images occurred at the station, where the stationmaster's barefoot children watched the train and wandered over as shadows "closed over the children's black feet softly and without imprint."*
>
> **Improved:** Do not change the tense in the quoted material, but describe the events in the present tense.
>
> *One of the first images occurs at the station, where the stationmaster's barefoot children watch the train and wander over as shadows "closed over the children's black feet softly and without imprint."*

Present

Take One Last Look Before you turn in your critical review, take a last look to make sure that you have followed your teacher's guidelines.

Persuasion / Exposition

Peer Review Tips

A classmate may ask you to read his or her critical review. Take your time and jot down notes as you read so you can give constructive feedback. Use the following questions to get started:

- Does the writer increase your understanding or appreciation of the work through an insightful thesis and substantial, relevant, and accurate support?

- Does the writer persuade you, in part, through the effective use of persuasive techniques including effective word choice?

Word-Processing Tips

To achieve a professional-looking, unblemished presentation, make sure your word-processed paper appears entirely uniform, with standard indents, one-inch margins, and no additional lines of space in the body of your paper. Do not enclose the title of your paper in quotations or add excess formatting; similarly, do not add extra formatting or flourishes to your own name or the page numbers.

Writer's Portfolio

Place a clean copy of your critical review in your portfolio to review later.

English Learners

DIFFERENTIATED INSTRUCTION

Beginning English learners and others may find the formal tone and specific language of critical writing confusing. Read aloud sections of the models on pages 1317–1318 and 1320–1321. Then discuss the tone and word choices. Ask students to reflect these choices in their own writing.

Approaching Level

DIFFERENTIATED INSTRUCTION

Emerging Some students may benefit from talking with partners or small groups about writing their critical reviews. Have students discuss particularly challenging or easy parts of the process. Encourage sharing of strategies or tips that proved helpful.

⚡ Writing Workshop

Critical Review

Teach

Writing Process

Edit and Proofread Encourage students to use the Proofreading Checklist inside the back cover of the textbook. Point out that run-on sentences are a frequent mistake in writing but one that is usually easy to correct.

Writing Process

Present Students who decide to submit their work to literary magazines should be aware of the guidelines that those magazines have established and should realize that their work may not be accepted for publication. They may also want to explore the possibility of publishing their work on the Internet. Alternatively, students may wish to publish their own literary journal to share with readers in the school library.

Writer's Technique ☆

Tone Achieving an appropriate tone in a piece of literary criticism requires attention to word choice and sentence structure. Both the reviewer, Rodman, and the author of the essay, Gordimer, succeed in maintaining a balanced, analytical tone as well as reader interest.

Focus

Summary

In this workshop, students will learn techniques for effectively planning and delivering an oral critique of a literary work in the style of a television or radio broadcast.

Teach

Speaking Skills

Ensure That You Are Understood Explain to students that there are many deceptively simple steps they can take to ensure that their oral communication is the best it can be. They include the following:

- Keep the message clear.
- Keep the message simple.
- Keep the message concise.
- Be prepared.
- Be natural.
- Make your delivery expressive.

 For Speaking, Listening, and Viewing rubric, see Unit 7 Teaching Resources, pp. 234–235.

 For help with creating presentations, see Student Presentation Builder on StudentWorks Plus.

Use a Model

Watch an evening newscast for examples of critical reviews. These may be reviews of movies, sporting events, or public policy. Pay attention to tone, pacing, and gestures. What do you find effective about the journalists' presentation? What do you think could be improved? Make a note of these findings for your own presentation.

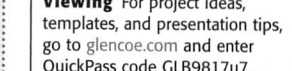 **Literature** Online

Speaking, Listening and Viewing For project ideas, templates, and presentation tips, go to glencoe.com and enter QuickPass code GLB9817u7.

Speaking, Listening, and Viewing Workshop

Oral Critical Review

Literature Connection A critical review is a way to share your impressions about a work of literature. When you deliver a critical review, you evaluate what a writer attempted to achieve and whether you feel he or she succeeded. You encounter different kinds of critical reviews nearly every day, sometimes without even realizing it. A critical review can take the form of a newspaper editorial, a book review in a magazine, or a commentary on a radio or news broadcast.

> **Assignment** In groups, plan and deliver a critical review in the style of a television or radio broadcast.

Plan Your Presentation

There are a variety of ways you can arrange to record the audio and visual elements of your review. For example, you can use a home video camera to create a talk show–style newscast or a hand-held tape recorder to develop a radio broadcast. However, your radio or television broadcast does not have to be complicated. You might simply pretend to have an "on-air" set and present your review to an audience of your classmates.

Prepare to Present

- Decide which parts of your critical review you want to share with your audience. In a radio or television format, you may not have enough time to cover everything. Therefore, limit your presentation to your most important points.
- Before presenting, read your critical review several times to become familiar with the key ideas in the order they appear. If you are presenting a television broadcast, don't try to memorize the words verbatim; on the other hand, avoid simply reading the review aloud.
- If you are presenting a television broadcast, experiment with gestures, facial expressions, and postures to show excitement, dismay, and other emotions. Try practicing in front of a mirror before you record your presentation.
- Consider playing background music as part of your presentation.

Speaking Practice

Rehearse Encourage students to practice their presentations by speaking into a recording device. After recording, they should listen and time their presentations. By listening to themselves, students will discover what to delete and what to elaborate upon.

A good way to plan a short presentation is to allow one minute for the opening, one minute for each of the three points they want to make, and one minute for the conclusion.

Rehearse and Present

Transform your written critical review into an effective oral presentation by using your voice as a persuasive instrument. As you rehearse, experiment with volume, pitch, pace, and emphasis. Strive to develop a tone that is both engaging and authoritative. If you are presenting a radio broadcast, remember that your voice is all you have for reinforcing your message.

If you are presenting a television broadcast, develop visual aids, such as posters illustrating key ideas in the work. As you rehearse, establish seamless ways of introducing these aids. Experiment with verbal techniques until you achieve the right emphasis, tone, and pacing.

As you rehearse, keep the following evaluation criteria in mind. Also use them when you evaluate others' presentations.

Techniques for Listening to and Evaluating a Critical Review

☑ **Listen Purposefully** Be sure to identify the thesis or claim. If you need to, jot it down. Then listen for the reasons and evidence that support the writer's thesis or claim. Note the best uses of persuasive techniques.

☑ **Listen Responsively** Show interest through focus, including eye contact, as well as through posture. Sit up straight and do not prop your head on your hand.

☑ **Evaluate the Message** Think about whether you have been persuaded, or whether your understanding or appreciation for the work has been deepened.

☑ **Evaluate the Delivery** Decide how well the performer used his or her voice as a persuasive instrument by considering volume, pitch, tone, pace, and emphasis. Also evaluate the use of nonverbal techniques, including eye contact, gestures, movements, and, if applicable, visual aids.

Technology Skills

If you decide to record your presentation, there are many resources available to provide technology assistance. Both the Internet and the library are valuable resources for technology help. Additionally, your school may have an audio-visual department that can provide assistance.

Speaking Frames

Consider using the following frames in your critical review:

- One aspect of the (story's/ poem's/ essay's) power is _____.

- Perhaps the part of the work that shows this best is _____.

- How could any (word/ phrase/bit of characterization/detail) be more apt than _____?

Presentation Tips

Use the following checklist to evaluate your critical review.

- Did you present a clear, insightful thesis and strong, well-supported arguments?

- Did you use appropriate tone and other effective verbal techniques?

- Did you capture and hold your audience's attention from beginning to end?

English Learners

DIFFERENTIATED INSTRUCTION

Intermediate Encourage English learners to listen actively to authentic speech. Have them note in particular the little words and expressions that are used to link ideas, start sentences, give opinions, and change the subject. Challenge students to repeat phrases or whole sentences and to attempt to imitate the pronunciation, the intonation, and the speed of the original. If possible, have students record themselves, using a tape recorder or an interactive CD-ROM so that they can compare recordings and rerecord if necessary.

Teach

Speaking Skills

Variety Encourage students to speak with vocal *variety*. They should slow down for dramatic points and speed up to show excitement. They also need to pause occasionally for effect. Challenge students not just to stand in one position behind the podium or desk but to move a step away, from time to time, to make a point.

Speaking Skills

Use Visual Aids Encourage students to introduce their visuals effectively rather than simply "throw" them at their audience. Students should keep talking as they show the visual(s) and continue to look at the audience the whole time. Remind students that *they* are still the main event and that their visual is only an aid.

Listening Skills

Peer Assessment Ask students to evaluate their classmates' performance by reviewing each of the criteria in the Techniques rubric on page 1325.

Focus

Summary

In this workshop, students will take part in discussions to analyze the strategies deployed in several media examples, including a campaign poster, a news transcript, a public service announcement, and a news photograph. The workshop also contains a focus lesson on persuasive techniques.

 For video presentations related to this workshop, see Media Workshop DVD.

Workshop Resources

Print Materials

- Unit 7 Teaching Resources, p. 236
- Writing Kit
- Success in Writing: Research and Reports

Technology

- Literature Online: Writing Resources and Grammar Resources, www.glencoe.com
- Online Essay Grader, www.glencoe.com
- Student Presentation Builder on Student-Works Plus CD-ROM
- Media Workshop DVD
- Online Student Edition

1326

Media Workshop

Analyze Media Messages

Literature Connection In the short story "The Train from Rhodesia," Nadine Gordimer addresses South Africa's policy of apartheid—a system of racial segregation and economic discrimination. The poverty, racism, and injustice of life under apartheid affected millions of Africans—both black and white. As citizens and governments around the world put political, economic, and media pressure on the government of South Africa, apartheid began to crumble in the early 1990s. Other human-rights and humanitarian organizations have also come to rely on media campaigns to help raise awareness—and funds—for their causes.

Forms of Media

You encounter media messages, in both print and electronic forms, many times throughout the day. **Print media**—such as newspapers, magazines, books, and billboards—feature printed words or images. **Electronic media** include radio, television, CDs, DVDs, movies, video-tapes, documentary films, and the Internet.

Each type of medium helps determine the way messages are presented and the way they will affect you as reader, listener, or viewer. Consider the difference between watching a two-minute TV news report on a natural disaster and reading a lengthy newspaper article about the same event. Which medium covers the story more completely? Which one is more informative? Each medium has distinctive characteristics, strengths, and weaknesses and affects the audience differently.

Media Strategies

All media messages contain information intended to shape the audience's attitudes. That information, however, reflects the viewpoints, beliefs, or even biases of the people who create the message. The creators use a broad range of techniques to make their message as powerful and effective as possible. How can you make informed opinions as you read, listen, or view media messages in your everyday life? Refer to the checklist to help you analyze, or deconstruct, media strategies.

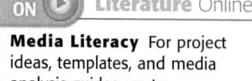

Media Literacy For project ideas, templates, and media analysis guides, go to glencoe.com and enter QuickPass code GLB9817u7.

Strategy		Questions to ask yourself
source	☑	Who created the message? How do the creators' viewpoints or biases affect the message?
purpose	☑	Why was the message created? To persuade? To inform? To entertain?
word choice	☑	What kind of language is used to express the message? Is figurative language used to make the message seem more meaningful? Is technical language used to make it seem more informative?
cultural elements	☑	Does the message transmit, or communicate, culture—values that reflect a particular group or nation?
symbols	☑	Does the message represent ideas, principles, or people through symbols? How might using symbols have an impact on the audience?
target audience	☑	Is the messaged tailored to a specific intended audience? Do the creators of the message use stereotypes of people—for example, children or teenagers—to connect with the audience?
design elements and/ or film techniques	☑	How is the message visually composed? Do design elements such as color, line, and texture enhance the message? Are film techniques or special effects used to manipulate the audience's reaction?

> **Focus Lesson**

Persuasive Techniques: Logical Fallacies

Media messages that urge an audience to agree with a viewpoint or to take a specific action use a variety of persuasive techniques—both logical and illogical. Errors in reasoning, or logical fallacies, undermine sound arguments. Such faulty reasoning may appear in propaganda (the use of ideas, information, or rumors to spread information or beliefs). Try to spot these types of logical fallacies in media:

- **false cause**—inaccurately drawing a cause-and-effect relationship between two events that follow one after another

- **overgeneralization**—making a sweeping statement that does not provide any reasonable supporting evidence as proof

- **bandwagon**—urging the audience to do something because everyone else is doing it

- *ad hominem*—personally attacking someone in order to shift attention away from his or her views

- **either-or fallacy**—presenting only two possible sides or solutions to an issue when there are more possibilities

- **red herring**—changing the subject in order to avoid the issue

> **Activity**
>
> **Create a Chart**
>
> Use the media-strategies chart on this page as a guide to examine a print or an online advertisement. Make a chart with a third column in which you respond to the questions in the second column.

Big Idea

Globalization Point out that many American brands have a worldwide media presence. **Ask:** What differences might an American advertiser have to consider when producing ads for markets in other countries? *(Possible answers: linguistic, cultural, and religious differences)*

Cultural History

False Cause One famous historical example of the fallacy of false cause is belief in spontaneous generation. Before the discovery of microorganisms, many people believed that nonliving matter, such as meat or bread, could produce living things such as flies or mice, because these creatures were observed after the meat or bread was left alone for extended periods.

English Learners

DIFFERENTIATED INSTRUCTION

Intermediate Ask: What is the base word in the term *overgeneralization?* *(general)* What words are combined to form *bandwagon?* *(band, wagon)*

Approaching Level

DIFFERENTIATED INSTRUCTION

Emerging Write on the board: Everybody cheats—why shouldn't I? If I don't become a doctor, I'll never be happy. Have students identify these fallacies. *(bandwagon, either-or)*

Teach
Speaking and Listening

1. Answers will vary. Many students may say that the picture of Mandela projects an image of experience, trustworthiness, and maturity.

2. The campaign slogan, by suggesting that all people can make their own decisions, may influence more voters to participate in the election.

3. Answers will vary.

Political History ☆

Nelson Mandela Nelson Mandela was imprisoned from 1962 to 1990 for his opposition to South Africa's system of apartheid. After his release, he worked with then-President F. W. de Klerk to end the apartheid system. The two shared the Nobel Peace Prize in 1993.

Reading Practice

Rhetorical Analysis Say: Logical fallacies, such as bandwagon appeals or false causes, can also be found in written documents. Have students work in small groups to download a speech or policy statement from the website of a current political candidate. Ask students to identify a fallacious argument—such as bandwagon appeal, appeal ad hominem, or false cause—that appears in the chosen document. Then have students write two or three sentences each identifying the logical fallacy and explaining the problems with its reasoning.

Media Impact: **Campaign Poster**

Activity

Listening and Speaking

Meet in a small group to discuss the following questions:

1. Why do you think the African National Congress, the organization that created this poster, chose this photo of Nelson Mandela? Explain.

2. How might the campaign slogan "The People's Choice!" influence voters' attitudes about participating in a democratic election?

3. What Internet or TV political campaign ads have you viewed that had a strong impact on you as a future voter? Describe the ads and identify the media strategies. (Refer to the chart on page 1327.)

Media Image

The close-up picture of Nelson Mandela's face shows a smiling, friendly older man. In the time between his release from prison in 1990 and the 1994 election, most South Africans saw news images of Mandela portrayed as the wise survivor.

Logical Fallacy

The poster's bandwagon appeal urges viewers to vote like all other citizens—"the people."

Build Background In 1994, South Africa held its first democratic national election. The African National Congress (ANC), a political party that had been banned from 1960 until 1990, won a landslide victory. ANC's long-imprisoned leader, Nelson Mandela, was elected president. ☆ In his inaugural address, Mandela expressed his hopes for unity: "We shall build a society in which all South Africans, both black and white, will be able to walk tall, without any fear in their hearts, assured of their inalienable right to human dignity."

Symbol

The colors in the poster's border correspond to the symbolic colors of the African National Congress flag.

black = the South African people
green = the land
yellow = mineral wealth

Media Impact: **News Transcript**

Build Background In August 2007, a nine-foot-tall statue of Nelson Mandela, cast in bronze, was officially presented to the public in London. Ian Walters, the sculptor of the statue, shows Mandela delivering a speech and gesturing with open arms and hands. This statue stands near statues of Abraham Lincoln and Winston Churchill—two other champions of freedom and democracy.

Mandela Statue Unveiled in London
by Raphael G. Satter, Associated Press Writer

Nelson Mandela paid tribute to the anti-apartheid struggle Wednesday as Britain unveiled a towering statue in his honor outside the Houses of Parliament, saying it symbolized the sacrifices made by all who fight oppression.

Speaking to thousands of supporters as African hymns echoed from the walls of Westminster Abbey, the 89-year-old Nobel Peace Prize winner recalled the many brave men and women who joined the campaign to end apartheid in South Africa.

"The history of the struggle in South Africa is rich with the stories of heroes and heroines, some of them leaders, some of them followers. All of them deserve to be remembered," Mandela declared after Prime Minister Gordon Brown pulled away a rainbow-striped cloth covering the statue.

"Though this statue is of one man, it should in actual fact symbolize all those who have resisted oppression, especially in my country."

Activity

Listening and Speaking

Meet in a small group to discuss the following questions:

1. How does Nelson Mandela interpret the cultural value and symbolic meaning of his statue?

2. Besides sculptures, what other visual artworks have you seen that were created to honor political leaders? Give descriptive details.

3. How would you use media to create a visual image of a leader you admire?

Cultural Elements

The photo of the statue shows a striking visual representation and creates a grand image of a revered leader—Nelson Mandela.

Lead

The opening paragraph—the lead—captures the reader's attention and summarizes the main point of the news story.

Word choice

The reporter's vivid language helps readers imagine the sights and sounds of the scene.

Symbol

The rainbow-striped cloth covering the statue might represent cultural diversity and unity.

Media Workshop

Analyze Media Messages

Teach
Speaking and Listening

1. Mandela says that the statue should symbolize all people who resist oppression, especially those from South Africa.
2. Answers will vary.
3. Answers will vary.

Cultural History ☆

Westminster Abbey Westminster Abbey is a church in London often used for official British ceremonies, such as the coronation of kings and queens. It contains the famous Poet's Quarter, where writers such as Geoffrey Chaucer and Robert Browning are buried.

English Learners

DIFFERENTIATED INSTRUCTION

Intermediate Say: Newspaper articles, such as this one reporting the unveiling of Mandela's statue. are structured around the five questions *who, what, where, when,* and *why*. In an effective article, the answers to these questions can be found in the first paragraph. Have students identify the answers to these questions from the article. *(Who: Mandela; what: had a statue unveiled; where: outside Parliament; when: Wednesday; why: to symbolize the anti-apartheid movement)*

Teach
Speaking and Listening

1. Possible answers: (first image) The woman's raised foot represents the slogan *"Stamp out racism."* (second image) The hand holding an eraser represents the slogan *"Erase Racism."* (third image) The silhouette of a figure in a wheelchair shows quick movement to represent the slogan *"Outpace racism."*

2. Possible answers: Silhouettes avoid focusing viewers' attention on details in the images, allowing them to focus on the slogans.

3. Possible answer: The impact is simple, unambiguous, and forceful.

4. Answers will vary.

Cultural History ☆

University of Toronto The University of Toronto, founded in 1827, is one of Canada's oldest universities. It is also, with more than 70,000 students, Canada's largest. Famous Toronto alumni include the filmmaker David Cronenberg and the writer Margaret Atwood.

Media Impact:
Public Service Announcement

PSAs

Public service announcements (PSAs) persuade an audience to take action on a cultural, social, or political issue.

Build Background In 2005, the Anti-Racism and Cultural Diversity Office at Canada's University of Toronto launched a hard-hitting awareness campaign to spread a compelling message—that everyone on campus had a role to play in wiping out prejudice. The colorful poster below was designed to mimic the power of electronic media, such as big-screen video ads and computerized billboards. ☆

Word Choice

The strong action verbs over each of the three panels are forceful and direct. The rhyming of *erase* with *outpace* creates a musical effect.

Design Elements

The artist chose vibrant colors and silhouettes for each panel.

Activity

Listening and Speaking

Meet with a partner to discuss the following questions:

1. Describe the image represented in each silhouette on a colored panel. What do you think was the artist's purpose?

2. Why might the artist have chosen to use silhouettes rather than photographs or more traditional depictions of people?

3. How do the text and the images persuade the viewer?

4. Do you find this public service announcement effective? Why or why not?

www.antiracism.utoronto.ca

University of Toronto Anti-Racism and Cultural Diversity Office

Word Choice

The repetition of the word *racism* three times reinforces the key issue of the PSA.

Writing Practice

Multimedia Presentation Have students work in small groups to develop multimedia presentations evaluating public service announcements on topics that frequently inspire public service messages (such as smoking, drug abuse, or voting). Ask each group to find three to five examples of public service announcements related to their topic in a variety of media (including print advertising, billboards, and television). Have them prepare a presentation evaluating the effectiveness of each example, employing a variety of media (including text, images, and video) in their presentation.

Media Impact: **News Photograph**

Build Background Peaceful protests broke out in Myanmar, a former British colony, in August 2007, when the military government dramatically hiked fuel prices. As a result, the cost of food also soared. The military government began using force to stop the pro-democracy demonstrations, which included thousands of Buddhist monks. The photograph captures one of the monks' marches through the capital city of Rangoon.

Photojournalism

Unlike portrait photography, photojournalism attempts to capture a real life event as it happens and to tell a story with the image. News photographers not only present factual information but also convey their views of events.

Symbol

To the people of Myanmar, the monks' familiar red robes symbolize Buddhism (the country's main religion), peace, and unity.

Design Elements

Notice the strong lines in the photo: the vertical lines of the pillars and the angled lines of the marchers, trucks, and cars.

Composition

The photographer places the subject—the monks—in the center of the frame, slanting across nearly the entire photo.

Activity

Listening and Speaking

Meet with a small group of classmates to discuss the following questions:

1. What seems unusual about this news photo?

2. How do you think the people in the photo regard the marching monks? Explain.

3. What story do you think the photographer is trying to tell with this photo?

Teach
Speaking and Listening

1. The center throng of marchers are all bals and dressed in red.

2. Possible answer: They seem respectful. In fact, some have joined hands to hold back traffic or others who might intrude.

3. Possible answer: He or she may wish to show that the protest is supported by a majority.

Political History ☆

Aung San Suu Kyi Aung San Suu Kyi is the most prominent opponent of the military regime in Myanmar (formerly Burma). The daughter of a Burmese prime minister who was assassinated, she won the Nobel Peace Prize in 1991 for her prodemocracy activities. Since 2003 she has been under house arrest by Myanmar authorities.

Advanced Learners

DIFFERENTIATED INSTRUCTION

Photojournalism Say: The photograph on this page uses framing and perspective effectively to convey the significance of the march. Have students, in pairs or small groups, document a local event with photographs, using the photo on this page as a model. Then have students present their photographs to the class. Lead a discussion of how the visual aspects of the photographs communicate the meaning of the event to viewers who were not present.

Focus

Summary

The purpose of Independent Reading is to encourage students to read novels from the time period that they have learned about in this unit.

Teach

Cultural History ☆

Plays of the Age Explain to students that, by the mid-twentieth century, British playwrights such as Samuel Beckett and Harold Pinter were exploring (often with wit) the issues of menace and survival versus oblivion. **Ask:** How might historical events of the twentieth century have influenced their writing? Explain that these authors lived through World War II, experiencing its devastation, and the Cold War that followed. With the British Empire collapsing, the British public was reevaluating long-held beliefs and values. After the violence and loss, the issue of whether, and how, to go on became a literary theme.

Independent Reading

ENGLISH LITERATURE IN THE LATTER HALF OF THE TWENTIETH CENTURY BECAME INCREASINGLY global and far more inclusive. Women and minority writers—groups that had been largely excluded from critical examination—produced acclaimed works of fiction, poetry, and drama. Through literature, colonized peoples began to find a means by which to explore issues related to colonialism, such as race and cultural identity. Also, writing became increasingly experimental and innovative, as genres, traditions, and national boundaries blurred or were abandoned altogether.

Waiting for Godot

Samuel Beckett ☆

This play, which is Beckett's most well known, is one of the leading works of the twentieth-century dramatic movement known as the theater of the absurd. Structured in two acts, *Waiting for Godot* is stripped bare of theatrical pretense; the stage is empty during much of the play except for four characters and a leafless tree. The main characters, Vladimir and Estragon, are unsure of their purpose but are convinced that they are waiting for an unseen, possibly nonexistent character named Godot.

Possession: A Romance

A. S. Byatt

Brilliantly weaving together multiple story-lines and genres, Byatt's novel explores the relationships between the past and the present, writers and their readers, and women and men. *Possession*, which won the Booker Prize in 1990, focuses on two young literary scholars, Roland Michell and Maud Bailey, who uncover a secret romance that existed between two poets from the Victorian age. Through letters and manuscripts, Michell and Bailey piece together this hidden history, which forces them to reevaluate the meaning of their own lives and scholarship.

Reading Practice

SPIRAL REVIEW **Analyze Author's Influences**
Assign students to read one of the plays or novels on this spread. Have students search for recent book reviews or articles about Beckett, Byatt, Achebe, Markandaya, Naipual, or Rushdie. **Ask:** According to the book review, what political, ethical, or social influences may have shaped the author's writing? What influences can you infer? How has this author responded to globalization and global events through his or her work? Prompt students to discuss connections between any of the author's more recent works and the ones students have already read.

GLENCOE LITERATURE LIBRARY

Things Fall Apart
Chinua Achebe

As Britain's imperial ambitions extend into Africa, a centuries-old way of life vanishes and Okonkwo, a figure of heroic proportions, meets his moving, tragic end.

Nectar in a Sieve
Kamala Markandaya

Nectar in a Sieve explores painful and disturbing aspects of poverty and a village's transformation from agriculture to industry.

A House for Mr. Biswas
V. S. Naipaul

Set in Trinidad, this novel draws largely from the author's own childhood experiences as a Hindu Indian living in what was then a British colony.

CRITICS' CORNER

"The literary map of India is about to be redrawn. . . . Serious English-language novelists from India (often called Indo-Anglians), or those from abroad who use Indian material, have steered a steady course between . . . two vast, mutually obliterating realities. . . . What this fiction has been missing is a different kind of ambition, something just a little coarse, a hunger to swallow India whole and spit it out. . . . Now, in Midnight's Children, Salman Rushdie has realized that ambition. . . . This is a book to accept on its own terms, and an author to welcome into world company."

—Clark Blaise, *The New York Times*, April 19, 1981

Midnight's Children ☆
Salman Rushdie

Midnight's Children begins in 1947, on the first night of India's independence. This controversial novel combines elements of magical realism, myth, family, and the modern history of India in the postcolonial period.

 Prepare an Interview

Read one of the books on this page and prepare and interview with the author, asking about the influences of global culture on his or her work.

INDEPENDENT READING **1333**

Literary History ☆

Magical Realism After World War II some authors embraced magical realism, a genre that mixes realistic and fantastical story elements.

Ask students to read a section from *Midnight's Children* and to compare it to a work of nineteenth-century naturalism they have read.

Glencoe Literature Library

Glencoe Literature Library offers an extensive collection of hardcover books that can help you encourage your students to read independently. Choose from among the more than 120 full-length literary works—novels, novellas, plays, and works of nonfiction. Each book includes related readings from a broad range of genres. Go to www.glencoe.com for more information.

Prepare an Interview

Students' interviews should include questions that pertain to the influence of global culture on the author's work.

> For access to all study guides for the Glencoe Literature Library, see the Literature Library Teacher Resources CD-ROM.

> To create customized reading lists from a database of more than 30,000 titles, use BookLink K–12 CD-ROM.

Approaching Level

DIFFERENTIATED INSTRUCTION

Emerging To help approaching level readers better comprehend what they are reading, have them pay special attention to the writer's use of irony, common in post–World War II British literature. For example, in *Things Fall Apart*, we read an entire book about an African man, yet by the end of the novel we learn that his tragic story will be reduced to a paragraph in a report.

Encourage students to note examples of irony. Point out that there may be disagreement about what is considered irony. Ask groups to discuss examples and the author's purpose in including irony in the text.

Have students think of past exams in which they did not perform as well as they had hoped. **Ask: What did you learn from these exams? What can you do differently to perform better on the next one?** *(Possible answers: Study well in advance versus cramming; read directions thoroughly; stay calm; review work).* Considering the time spent in mastering other skills, a few minutes devoted to test-taking skills seems a small price to pay for reaping great potential rewards.

Teach

Assessment

Explain that students will first be asked to read a poem and to answer comprehension, context, and inference questions. Then they will be asked to complete ten vocabulary items, answer ten paragraph-improvement questions, and finally write a critical review of a selection from Unit 7.

 To create custom assessments online, go to Progress Reporter Online Assessment.

 To create custom assessments using software, see ExamView Assessment Suite.

Assessment

English–Language Arts

Reading: Poetry

Carefully read the following poem. Use context clues to help you define any words with which you are unfamiliar. Pay close attention to the poem's form, use of figurative language, and sound devices. Then, on a separate sheet of paper, answer the questions that follow.

"Winding Up" by Derek Walcott

line

I live on the water,
alone. Without wife and children,
I have circled every possibility
to come to this:

5 a low house by grey water,
with windows always open
to the stale sea. We do not choose such things,

but we are what we have made.
We suffer, the years pass,
10 we shed freight but not our need

for encumbrances. Love is a stone
that settled on the sea-bed
under grey water. Now, I require nothing

from poetry but true feeling,
15 no pity, no fame, no healing. Silent wife,
we can sit watching grey water,

and in a life awash
with mediocrity and trash
live rock-like.

20 I shall unlearn feeling,
unlearn my gift. That is greater
and harder than what passes there for life.

Literary Element Practice

Simile, Metaphor, and Personification Remind students that figurative language allows a poet to speak of one thing in terms of another.

1. A **simile** is a stated comparison of two seemingly dissimilar things.

2. A **metaphor** is an indirect comparison without connective words such as *like*.

3. **Personification** is the attribution of human characteristics to inanimate objects or to animals.

Have students suggest examples for each type of figurative language.

1. From which point of view is this poem written?
   (A) first person
   (B) second person
   (C) third-person limited
   (D) third-person omniscient
   (E) third-person expansive

2. Which of the following literary elements is Walcott using in lines 5 and 6?
   (A) personification
   (B) idiom
   (C) foreshadowing
   (D) imagery
   (E) epiphany

3. What sound device are the words *stale sea*, in line 7, an example of?
   (A) consonance
   (B) assonance
   (C) rhyme
   (D) onomatopoeia
   (E) alliteration

4. The pronoun *we*, in lines 7–10, refers to the speaker and what or whom else?
   (A) the sea
   (B) all humanity
   (C) poetry
   (D) the speaker's wife and children
   (E) the speaker's home

5. From the context, what do you conclude that the word *encumbrances*, in line 11, most nearly means?
   (A) movements
   (B) changes
   (C) burdens
   (D) graces
   (E) exchanges

6. Which of the following literary elements is Walcott using in the clause *Love is a stone*, in line 11?
   (A) metaphor
   (B) simile
   (C) personification
   (D) flashback
   (E) paradox

7. Which of the following two sound devices appear in line 12?
   (A) consonance and onomatopoeia
   (B) consonance and personification
   (C) alliteration and consonance
   (D) assonance and meter
   (E) meter and rhyme

8. What does the phrase *silent wife*, in line 15, refer to?
   (A) the speaker
   (B) the sea
   (C) freight
   (D) poetry
   (E) mediocrity

9. The end words in lines 17 and 18 are an example of which of the following sound devices?
   (A) alliteration
   (B) onomatopoeia
   (C) meter
   (D) rhythm
   (E) slant rhyme

10. What does the phrase *my gift*, in line 21, refer to?
    (A) feeling
    (B) mediocrity
    (C) poetry
    (D) life
    (E) loneliness

Assessment

Assess

1. **A** is the correct answer. The speaker uses first-person pronouns throughout. `DOK 2`

2. **D** is the correct answer. Walcott is using sensory details to create imagery. `DOK 2`

3. **E** is the correct answer. Walcott repeats consonant sounds at the beginning of the adjacent words, creating alliteration. `DOK 2`

4. **B** is the correct answer. In these lines, the speaker is making general statements about humanity. `DOK 1`

5. **C** is the correct answer. In the context, clearly the intended meaning of the word *encumbrances* is "burdens." `DOK 1`

6. **A** is the correct answer. Walcott is comparing two unlike things without using the word *like* or *as*. `DOK 2`

7. **C** is the correct answer. Walcott repeats consonant sounds at the beginnings and ends of words. `DOK 2`

8. **D** is the correct answer. *Silent wife* clearly does not refer to the speaker, the sea, freight, or mediocrity. `DOK 1`

9. **E** is the correct answer. *Awash* and *trash* both end in *ash* but are pronounced differently. `DOK 2`

10. **C** is the correct answer. In line 14, the speaker declares feelings to be a component of poetry. Feeling is also said to be greater than life. Options **B** and **E** make no sense in this context. `DOK 1`

English Learners

DIFFERENTIATED INSTRUCTION

Intermediate Ask: What prefix appears in the word *unlearn*? *(un-)* What is another example of a word with this prefix? *(undo, unnerve, unsettle, etc.)*

Approaching Level

DIFFERENTIATED INSTRUCTION

African American Vernacular English (AAVE) Write on the board: I live on the water. I require nothing. Have students rewrite these sentences, substituting the third-person pronoun (*he* for *I*) and the necessary changes in the verb forms. *(He lives on the water. He requires nothing.)*

Assessment

Assess

11. D is the correct answer. The poem meets none of the formal requirements of a sonnet, blank verse terza rima, or a villanelle. It has no regular meter, no set rhyme scheme, and no stanzaic pattern. (**DOK 2**)

12. B is the correct answer. All but one of the stanzas in the poem are three lines long and therefore tercets. (**DOK 2**)

13. A is the correct answer. The speaker refers to no conflict with an outside element. (**DOK 4**)

14. B is the correct answer. This poem suggests resignation; no humor, hope, or desperation is evident, and the poem is not ironic. (**DOK 4**)

15. D is the correct answer. The poem never states that it is best to avoid commitment or that peace of mind is available only to those without any hope, and the statements that life is awash in mediocrity and that fame may not be worth pursuing are made only in passing. (**DOK 2**)

---

11. Which of the following best describes the form of this poem?
    (A) sonnet
    (B) blank verse
    (C) terza rima
    (D) free verse
    (E) villanelle

12. Which of the following describes the majority of this poem's stanzas?
    (A) couplets
    (B) tercets
    (C) quatrains
    (D) octaves
    (E) sestets

13. Which of the following best describes the conflict that appears in this poem?
    (A) internal
    (B) external
    (C) man versus nature
    (D) man versus fate
    (E) man versus man

14. Which of the following best describes the overall mood of this poem?
    (A) hopeful
    (B) resigned
    (C) desperate
    (D) comic
    (E) ironic

15. Which of the following statements best describes the theme of this poem?
    (A) It is best to avoid committing oneself emotionally to other people.
    (B) Peace of mind is available only to those who have no hope.
    (C) Life is awash in mediocrity.
    (D) Sometimes it is best to resign oneself to life and accept it as it is.
    (E) Fame is not worth pursuing.

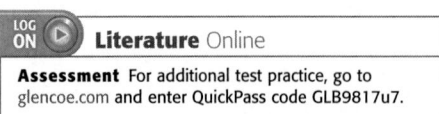

Literature Online

Assessment For additional test practice, go to glencoe.com and enter QuickPass code GLB9817u7.

Reading Practice

Reading Tests Remember that reading comprehension involves a wide range of skills.

- Determining main idea
- Understanding author's purpose
- Comparing and contrasting
- Making inferences
- Defining vocabulary within context
- Identifying pertinent details
- Identifying setting and plot
- Generalizing through analogies
- Interpreting figures of speech
- Drawing conclusions

Make a classroom poster of all of these skills and refer to them throughout the school year as you teach each skill.

Vocabulary Skills: Sentence Completion

For each item in the Vocabulary Skills section, choose the word or words that best complete the sentence.

1. As English became a global language, groups that had been on the _____ of the British Empire began to create influential works.
   (A) temerity
   (B) periphery
   (C) friction
   (D) sinew
   (E) denigration

2. After the war, many young people _____ opposed Britain's cultural traditions, which they felt were both _____ and out of touch.
   (A) hospitably . . . envious
   (B) wryly . . . explicit
   (C) stridently . . . luminous
   (D) hospitably . . . radiant
   (E) stridently . . . superannuated

3. The collapse of the British Empire was a/an _____ event in postwar English literature.
   (A) acrid
   (B) unperturbed
   (C) pivotal
   (D) defunct
   (E) barren

4. It became clear that the faults of the empire were _____, and its collapse was likely.
   (A) rancid
   (B) withering
   (C) envious
   (D) plodding
   (E) irremediable

5. Although many effects of the British Empire's collapse were _____, there were also some negative consequences, such as the rise of apartheid in South Africa.
   (A) benign
   (B) imminent
   (C) compulsory
   (D) lugubrious
   (E) plodding

6. When England's economic woes threatened to cause the country to _____, the government established a welfare state.
   (A) distill
   (B) patronize
   (C) career
   (D) lumber
   (E) flounder

7. Although many postwar writers rejected the past, some demonstrated a great _____ to traditional forms, topics, and techniques.
   (A) fray
   (B) vendor
   (C) precipice
   (D) fidelity
   (E) revelation

8. Economic and social problems caused a deep _____ to be cast across postwar Britain.
   (A) friction
   (B) assent
   (C) temerity
   (D) pall
   (E) fray

9. As the threat of nuclear disaster seemed _____, the United States and Western European nations formed NATO.
   (A) imminent
   (B) radiant
   (C) luminous
   (D) withering
   (E) lugubrious

10. To many critics, the postcolonial body of English literature came as a _____.
    (A) temerity
    (B) revelation
    (C) vendor
    (D) sinew
    (E) denigration

1. **B** is the correct answer. No other option makes sense in this context. **DOK 1**
2. **E** is the correct answer. In this sentence, the phrase *out of touch* suggests no other word but *superannuated*. **DOK 2**
3. **C** is the correct answer. No other option makes sense in this context. **DOK 1**
4. **E** is the correct answer. No other option makes sense in this context. **DOK 1**
5. **A** is the correct answer. The structure of this sentence implies that the answer will be an antonym of *negative*. **DOK 1**
6. **E** is the correct answer. *Distill, patronize, career,* and *lumber* make no sense in this context. **DOK 1**
7. **D** is the correct answer. In this sentence, the preposition *to* implies no other word but *fidelity*. **DOK 1**
8. **D** is the correct answer. In this sentence, the phrase *to be cast* suggests no other word but *pall*. **DOK 1**
9. **A** is the correct answer. No other option makes sense in this context. **DOK 1**
10. **B** is the correct answer. No other option makes sense in this context. **DOK 1**

Approaching Level

DIFFERENTIATED INSTRUCTION

Emerging Remind students that when they are asked to choose a definition for a word in a passage, the word will usually be italicized. Encourage them to scan the passage to find the word. Reading the line before, the line containing the word, and the line following the word will usually provide enough information to answer the question correctly. Provide students with several opportunities to develop their ability to "scan" written material in a variety of activities and lessons.

Assessment

Assess

1. D is the correct answer. The nonessential clause *who spent much of her young life on a farm in Africa* must be set off with commas. No other option corrects this error without changing the content or introducing further errors. **DOK 1**

2. A is the correct answer. This sentence contains an incorrect verb tense. The verb *were* should be *are*. No other option corrects this error without changing the content or introducing further errors. **DOK 1**

3. B is the correct answer. This sentence contains an incorrect verb tense. The verb *had* should be *have*. No other option corrects this error without changing the content or introducing further errors. **DOK 1**

Grammar and Writing: Paragraph Improvement

Carefully read the opening paragraphs from the first draft of a student's critical review. Pay close attention to **verb tense, punctuation,** and **organization.** Then, on a separate sheet of paper, answer the questions that follow.

(1) *Doris Lessing's "A Mild Attack of Locusts" is a smartly constructed fable that explores the ability of some people to survive in the face of nature's unforgiving and often destructive power.* (2) *Lessing who spent much of her young life on a farm in Africa begins by describing the story's three principal characters, the farm on which they live, and their struggles against bankruptcy.* (3) *This struggle is thrown into high relief by a government announcement that swarms of locusts were expected.* (4) *With strong character development, compelling dialogue, and vivid sensory details, Lessing illustrates how personal histories affect individual perceptions of nature's threat.*

(5) *The story's three main characters—Margaret; her husband, Richard; and Richard's father, old Stephen—all had different perceptions.* (6) *Each character bases their perceptions on their own experiences.* (7) *For example, Margaret, who is not from a farming background, is horrified by the swarming locusts.* (8) *On seeing her husband covered in locusts, she asks, "How can you bear to let them touch you?"* (9) *Later Margaret is shown crying, thinking that "it was all so hopeless—if it wasn't a bad season, it was locusts."* (10) *This was not the response, though, of either her husband or old Stephen.* (11) *Throughout A Mild Attack of Locusts, Richard and old Stephen waver between statements of total despair and actions that suggest hope.* (12) *While this might create the impression that these characters are inconsistent, their behavior is actually the result of something altogether different.* (13) *In particular, old Stephen who has been bankrupted twice in the past acts hopeful but sounds despairing.*

1. Which is the best way to revise sentence 2?
   (A) Insert commas after *life* and after *Africa*.
   (B) Delete both commas in the sentence.
   (C) Delete *who spent much of her young life on a farm*.
   (D) Insert commas before *who* and after *Africa*.
   (E) Insert a comma after *begins*.

2. Which is the best way to revise sentence 3?
   (A) Change *were* to *are*.
   (B) Change *is* to *was*.
   (C) Delete *that swarms of locusts were expected*.
   (D) Insert *to come* after *expected*.
   (E) Make no change.

3. Which is the best revision of sentence 5?
   (A) All three main characters—Margaret, her husband Richard, and Richard's father, old Stephen—had different perceptions.
   (B) The story's three main characters—Margaret; her husband, Richard; and Richard's father, old Stephen—all have different perceptions.
   (C) The story's three main characters: Margaret; her husband, Richard; and Richard's father, old Stephen, all had different perceptions.
   (D) Margaret, her husband Richard, and Richard's father, old Stephen, had different perceptions.
   (E) Make no change.

Reading Practice

TEST PREPARATION: Skip Questions

First remind students that the questions for each section of the SAT and other standardized tests are arranged in ascending order of difficulty. The easier questions are at the beginning of each section, and the more difficult ones are at the end of the section. **Say:** If you find yourself working too long on a single question, make a mark next to it in the test booklet and continue with the next question. After you have answered the remaining questions, return to the ones you skipped.

4. Which is the best revision of sentence 6?
   (A) Each character bases their perceptions on personal experience.
   (B) Each character bases their perceptions on his or her experience.
   (C) Each character's perceptions are based on their experience.
   (D) Each character bases his or her perceptions on personal experience.
   (E) All characters base their perceptions on his or her experience.

5. Which persuasive technique appears in sentences 8 and 9?
   (A) rhetorical question
   (B) thesis statement
   (C) evidence from the text
   (D) addressing opposing viewpoints
   (E) plot summary

6. Which is the best revision of sentence 10?
   (A) This is not the response, though, of either her husband or old Stephen.
   (B) This was not the response though of either her husband or old Stephen.
   (C) This was not the response—though—of either her husband or old Stephen.
   (D) Old Stephen, though, did not respond this way.
   (E) Though this was not the response of either her husband or old Stephen.

7. Which error appears in sentence 11?
   (A) *A Mild Attack of Locusts* does not have quotation marks around it.
   (B) This is a run-on (comma splice) sentence.
   (C) The subject and verb disagree.
   (D) This is a sentence fragment.
   (E) No error appears.

8. Which persuasive technique appears in sentence 12?
   (A) rhetorical question
   (B) thesis statement
   (C) evidence from the text
   (D) addressing opposing viewpoints
   (E) plot summary

9. Which is the best revision of sentence 13?
   (A) In particular, old Stephen who has been bankrupted twice in the past acted hopeful but sounded despairing.
   (B) In particular; old Stephen who has been bankrupted twice in the past acts hopeful but sounds despairing.
   (C) In particular, old Stephen who has been bankrupted twice in the past.
   (D) In particular, old Stephen: who has been bankrupted twice in the past acts hopeful but sounds despairing.
   (E) In particular, old Stephen, who has been bankrupted twice in the past, acts hopeful but sounds despairing.

10. Which of the following should the author present next in this essay?
    (A) examples of how dialogue illustrates each character's perception of nature
    (B) details from Lessing's time spent on an African farm
    (C) a comparison between the setting in this story and those in similar works
    (D) an analysis of the rhetorical devices used in this story
    (E) an evaluation of Lessing's use of sound devices in this story

Essay

Write a critical review of one selection from this unit. Analyze how imagery, rhetorical devices, and figurative language function in the work and what ideas these devices help convey. As you write, keep in mind that your essay will be checked for **ideas, organization, voice, word choice, sentence fluency, conventions,** and **presentation.**

Assess

4. **D** is the correct answer. Neither pronoun in this sentence agrees in number with the singular antecedent, *each*. No other option corrects this error without changing the content or introducing further errors. `DOK 1`

5. **C** is the correct answer. The author quotes directly from the text, providing evidence to support an argument. `DOK 2`

6. **A** is the correct answer. This sentence contains an incorrect verb tense. The verb *was* should be *is*. No other option corrects this error without changing the content or introducing further errors. `DOK 1`

7. **A** is the correct answer. This sentence incorrectly puts in italics the title of a short story. No other option corrects this error without changing the content or introducing further errors. `DOK 2`

8. **D** is the correct answer. The author is anticipating and responding to possible counterarguments. `DOK 2`

9. **E** is the correct answer. No commas appear around the nonessential phrase *who . . . past*. No other option corrects this error without changing the content or introducing further errors. `DOK 1`

10. **A** is the correct answer. The thesis statement of this review suggests that the author will discuss character development, dialogue, and sensory details. The second paragraph discusses character development. `DOK 4`

 **Essay**

Students' reviews must deal with a selection from unit seven. Reviews should include a thesis statement with an overall critical judgment of the selection. Students should provide supporting evidence, including direct quotations and examples. Students should show an understanding of the terms *imagery, rhetorical device,* and *figurative language.* Students also should demonstrate what ideas these devices convey. Consider paying special attention to the unity of the reviews.

Reference Section

Literary Terms Handbook

A

Act A major unit of a drama, or play. Modern dramas generally have one, two, or three acts. Older dramas, including Shakespeare's, often have five acts. Acts may be divided into one or more scenes.

See also *DRAMA, SCENE.*

Allegory A literary work in which all or most of the characters, settings, and events stand for ideas, qualities, or figures beyond themselves. The overall purpose of an allegory is to teach a moral lesson.

See page 525.

See also *SYMBOL.*

Alliteration The repetition of consonant sounds, generally at the beginnings of words. Alliteration can be used to emphasize words, reinforce meaning, or create a musical effect. Note the repeated *s* and *d* sounds in the following line from Hopkins's "Pied Beauty":

> With <u>s</u>wift, <u>s</u>low; <u>s</u>weet, <u>s</u>our; a<u>d</u>azzle, <u>d</u>im;

See pages 758, 1307.

See also *SOUND DEVICES.*

Allusion A reference to a well-known character, place, or situation from history, music, art, or another work of literature. Discovering the meaning of an allusion can often be essential to the understanding of a work.

See page 512.

Ambiguity The state of having more than one meaning. The richness of literary language lies in its ability to evoke multiple layers of meaning.

See also *CONNOTATION.*

Analogy A comparison that shows similarities between two things that are otherwise dissimilar. A writer may use an analogy to explain something unfamiliar by comparing it to something familiar. Shakespeare pokes fun at analogies in "Sonnet 130," claiming, "My mistress' eyes are nothing like the sun."

See also *METAPHOR, SIMILE.*

Anapest A metrical foot of three syllables in which two unstressed syllables are followed by a stressed one (˘˘´). In the following line from Dylan Thomas's "Fern Hill" the feet are divided by slashes:

> ˘ ˘ ´ ˘ ˘ ´ ˘ ˘ ´
> Though I sang / in my chains / like the sea.

See also *FOOT, METER, SCANSION.*

Anecdote A brief account of an interesting happening. Essayists often use anecdotes to support their opinions, clarify their ideas, get the reader's attention, or entertain. Biographers often include anecdotes to illustrate points about their subjects. Boswell's *The Life of Samuel Johnson* contains an anecdote about the first time Boswell was introduced to Johnson by Thomas Davies.

Antagonist A person or a force that opposes the protagonist, or central character, in a story or drama. The reader is generally meant not to sympathize with the antagonist. In *Beowulf,* Grendel is an antagonist.

See also *CONFLICT, PROTAGONIST.*

Anthropomorphism The assignment of human characteristics to gods, animals, or inanimate objects. It is a key element in fables, where the main characters are often animals. The sheep in Janet Frame's "Two Sheep" have human characteristics.

See page 1273.

See also *FABLE.*

Aphorism A short, pointed statement that expresses a wise or clever observation about human experience, such as Pope's saying from *An Essay on Criticism:*

> We think our fathers fools, so wise we grow;
> Our wiser sons, no doubt, will think us so.

See also *EPIGRAM.*

Apostrophe A figure of speech in which a speaker addresses an inanimate object, an idea, or an absent person. In Percy Bysshe Shelley's "Ode to the West Wind," the speaker addresses the wind.

See page 262.

See also *PERSONIFICATION.*

Archetype A symbol, a character, an image, or a story pattern that recurs frequently in literature and evokes strong responses, often based on unconscious memory. The story of a hero who embarks on a dangerous quest is a recurring story in literature and film.

See page 164.

See also *SYMBOL*.

Argument A type of persuasive writing in which logic or reason is used to try to influence a reader's ideas or actions. In *A Vindication of the Rights of Woman,* Mary Wollstonecraft presents a powerful argument for the education of women. *Argument* can also refer to a prose summary or synopsis of what is in a story or play.

See pages 417, 1104.

See also *PERSUASION*.

Aside In a play, a character's comment that is directed to the audience or another character but is not heard by any other characters on the stage. Asides, which are rare in modern drama, reveal what a character is thinking or feeling. An example occurs in Act 1, scene 4, of Shakespeare's *Macbeth.*

> King.   My worthy Cawdor!
>
> Macbeth. [*Aside.*] The Prince of Cumberland!
>
>   That is a step
>
> On which I must fall down, or else o'erleap.

See also *SOLILOQUY*.

Assonance The repetition of the same or similar vowel sounds in stressed syllables that end with different consonant sounds. For example, the long *i* sound is repeated in the opening line from Ben Jonson's "On My First Son":

> Farewell, thou child of my right hand, and joy; . . .

See pages 890, 1147.

See also SOUND DEVICES.

Atmosphere The dominant emotional feeling of a literary work that contributes to the mood. Orwell's description of the natives' dislike of him in "Shooting an Elephant" builds an atmosphere of suspense and foreboding.

See page 306.

See also *MOOD*.

Author's purpose An author's intent in writing a literary work. Authors typically write for one or more of the following purposes: to persuade, to inform, to explain, to entertain, or to describe.

See page 270.

See also *DICTION, STYLE, THEME*.

Autobiography The story of a person's life written by that person. Autobiographies can give insights into the author's view of himself or herself and of the society in which he or she lived. *The Book of Margery Kempe* is the autobiography of a medieval woman.

See page 156.

See also *BIOGRAPHY, DIARY, MEMOIR, NONFICTION*.

B

Ballad A narrative song or poem. Folk ballads, which usually recount an exciting or dramatic episode, were passed down by word of mouth for generations before being written down. Literary ballads are written in imitation of folk ballads but have a known author. Coleridge's *The Rime of the Ancient Mariner* is a literary ballad. "Bonny Barbara Allan" is a folk ballad.

See page 200.

See also *FOLKLORE, NARRATIVE POETRY, ORAL TRADITION*.

Ballad stanza A quatrain, or four-line stanza, in which the first and third lines have four stressed syllables, and the second and fourth lines have three stressed syllables. Only the second and fourth lines rhyme. Although the basic foot in this stanza is the iamb (˘´), there tend to be many irregularities, as in this stanza from "Get Up and Bar the Door."

> It fell about the Martinmas time,
>
> And a gay time it was then,
>
> When our goodwife got puddings to make,
>
> And she's boiled them in the pan.

See page 202.

See also *QUATRAIN, SCANSION*.

Bias An inclination toward a certain opinion or position on a topic, possibly stemming from prejudice.

See also *NONFICTION*.

Biography An account of a person's life written by someone other than the subject. Biographies have been written of many of the writers in this book. Boswell's *The Life of Samuel Johnson* is a famous example.

See page 633.

See also *AUTOBIOGRAPHY, DIARY, JOURNAL, MEMOIR.*

Blank verse Poetry or lines of dramatic verse written in unrhymed iambic pentameter. Each line has five feet, with each foot made up of an unstressed syllable followed by a stressed syllable. Because blank verse may attempt to imitate spoken English, every line need not be perfectly regular. Most of Shakespeare's characters speak in blank verse—as Macbeth does, for example, when he addresses the floating dagger in Act 2, scene 1:

⏑ ´ ⏑ ´ ⏑ ´ ⏑ ´ ⏑ ´
And on thy blade and dudgeon gouts of blood,

See also *FOOT, IAMBIC PENTAMETER, SCANSION.*

Byronic hero See *HERO.*

C

Cadence The rhythmic rise and fall of language when it is spoken or read aloud.

See also *FREE VERSE, METER.*

Caesura A pause in a line of poetry, usually near the middle of a line, with two stressed syllables before and two after, creating a strong rhythm. A caesura is used to produce variations in meter and to draw attention to certain words. Some pauses are indicated by punctuation, others by phrasing or meaning. In the lines below, from Tennyson's *In Memoriam A. H. H.*, the caesuras are marked by double vertical lines.

Ring out the old, || ring in the new,
Ring, happy bells, || across the snow;

See also *RHYTHM.*

Carpe diem A Latin phrase meaning "seize the day"; in other words, "make the most of each moment." In *carpe diem* poems, the speaker emphasizes the shortness of life—usually to persuade a young woman to yield to love while she still has her youth and beauty.

See page 448.

Cavalier poetry The work of a group of English poets in the 1600s who were loyal to the monarchy. Cavalier poetry is generally intended to entertain rather than to instruct. It is characterized by regular rhythmic patterns, carefully structured stanzas, and simple but eloquent language. Love is a popular theme. Herrick, Suckling, and Lovelace were Cavalier poets.

Character A person portrayed in a literary work. A **main character** is central to the story and is typically fully developed. A **minor character** displays few personality traits and is used to help develop the story. Characters who show varied and sometimes contradictory traits are called **round.** Characters who reveal only one personality trait are called **flat.** A **stereotype,** or stock character, is typically flat. A **dynamic character** grows and changes during the story. A **static character** remains basically the same throughout a story. Things happen to the character, but he or she does not change.

See page 1139.

See also *CHARACTERIZATION, STEREOTYPE.*

Characterization The methods a writer uses to reveal the personality of a character. In **direct characterization,** the writer makes explicit statements about a character. In **indirect characterization,** the writer reveals a character through his or her words, thoughts, and actions and through what other characters think and say about that character.

See page 101.

See also *CHARACTER.*

Cliché A word or phrase that is so overused that it is virtually meaningless. "Dead as a doornail," "piece of cake," and "last but not least" are all clichés.

Climax See *PLOT.*

Colloquialism Informal language used in everyday conversation but not in formal writing or speech. In Mansfield's "A Cup of Tea," Miss Smith is speaking colloquially when she says, "I can't go on no longer . . . I can't bear no more."

See also *DIALECT, VERNACULAR.*

Comedy A type of drama that is humorous and often has a happy ending. A **heroic comedy** focuses on the exploits of a larger-than-life hero.

See also *DRAMA, FARCE, HUMOR, PARODY, SATIRE, WIT.*

Comic relief A humorous scene, event, or speech in a serious drama. It provides relief from emotional intensity while at the same time highlighting the seriousness of the story.

Conceit An elaborate figure of speech that makes a comparison between two significantly different things. The conceit draws an analogy between some object from nature or everyday life and the subject or theme of a poem. A **metaphysical conceit** is an intellectual comparison—rather than one based on nature—that can develop a wide range of ideas and capture a broad range of emotions.

See page 430.

See also *ANALOGY, EXTENDED METAPHOR, METAPHYSICAL POETRY, SIMILE.*

Conflict The central struggle between two opposing forces in a story or drama. An **external conflict** exists when a character struggles against some outside force, such as another person, nature, society, or fate. An **internal conflict** is a struggle that takes place within the mind of a character who is torn between opposing feelings, desires, or goals.

See pages 23, 1259.

See also *ANTAGONIST, PLOT, PROTAGONIST.*

Connotation The suggested or implied meanings associated with a word beyond its dictionary definition, or denotation. A word can have a positive, negative, or neutral connotation.

See also *AMBIGUITY, DENOTATION, FIGURATIVE LANGUAGE.*

Consonance The repetition of consonant sounds, typically at the end of nonrhyming words and preceded by different vowel sounds, as in this succession of echoing *d* sounds in William Butler Yeats's "The Second Coming":

> The bloo*d*-dimme*d* ti*d*e is loose*d*, . . .

See pages 890, 1147.

See also *SOUND DEVICES.*

Couplet Two consecutive, rhymed lines of poetry that follow the same rhythmic pattern. The last two lines of Shakespeare's "Sonnet 29" are a couplet:

> For thy sweet love rememb'red such wealth brings
> That then I scorn to change my state with kings.

See also *HEROIC COUPLET, RHYME, SONNET.*

Crisis See *PLOT.*

D

Dactyl A three-syllable metrical foot, in which the first syllable is stressed and the following two are unstressed. The following line from Tennyson's "Tears, Idle Tears" has a basic dactylic rhythm:

> / ˘ ˘ / ˘ ˘ / ˘ ˘ /
> Tears, idle/ tears, I know/ not what they/ mean,

See also *FOOT, METER, SCANSION.*

Denotation The literal, or dictionary, meaning of a word.

See also *CONNOTATION.*

Dénouement See *PLOT.*

Description A detailed portrayal of a person, a place, an object, or an event. Good descriptive writing appeals to the senses through imagery.

See page 925.

See also *FIGURATIVE LANGUAGE, IMAGERY.*

Dialect A variation of a language spoken by a particular region or class. Dialects may differ from the standard form of a language in vocabulary, pronunciation, or grammatical form. In Naipaul's story "B. Wordsworth," the narrator and his mother speak a dialect of English.

> I ran up the steps and shouted, "Ma, it have a man outside here. He say he want to watch the bees."

See pages 690, 1284.

See also *VERNACULAR.*

Dialogue Conversation between characters in a literary work. Dialogue can contribute to characterization, create mood, advance the plot, and develop theme.

See page 727.

Diary An individual's daily record of impressions, events, or thoughts, written for personal use rather than for publication. Samuel Pepys's diary, written between 1660 and 1669, is a famous example.

See page 538.

See also *JOURNAL.*

Diction A writer's choice of words; an important element in the writer's "voice" or style. Skilled writers choose their words carefully to convey a particular meaning or feeling.

See pages 744, 813.

See also *AUTHOR'S PURPOSE, CONNOTATION, STYLE, TONE, VOICE.*

Dimeter A line of verse consisting of two feet.

See also *FOOT, METER, SCANSION.*

Drama A story intended to be performed by actors before an audience. The script of a dramatic work, or **play,** often includes the author's instructions to the actors and director, known as stage directions. A drama may be divided into acts, which may also be broken up into scenes, indicating changes in location or the passage of time.

See also *ACT, COMEDY, PROPS, SCENE, STAGE DIRECTIONS, TRAGEDY.*

Dramatic irony See *IRONY.*

Dramatic monologue A form of dramatic poetry in which a speaker addresses a silent listener. The speaker may be a fictional or historical figure and is clearly distinct from the poet. Robert Browning's poem "My Last Duchess" is a dramatic monologue.

See page 937.

See also *DRAMATIC POETRY, MONOLOGUE.*

Dramatic poetry Poetry in which characters are revealed through dialogue and monologue, as well as through description. Hardy's "Ah, Are You Digging on My Grave?" is an example of dramatic poetry.

See also *DIALOGUE, DRAMATIC MONOLOGUE.*

Dramatic structure The structure of a serious play. Common elements are exposition, rising action, climax, falling action, and resolution.

See also *PLOT.*

Dynamic character See *CHARACTER.*

E

Elegy A poem mourning a death or another great loss. Tennyson's *In Memoriam A. H. H.* is an elegy.

See pages 438.

End rhyme The rhyming of words at the ends of lines, as in Housman's "To an Athlete Dying Young."

End-stopped line A line of poetry that contains a complete thought, thus requiring a semicolon or period at the end, as in Blake's "A Poison Tree":

> I was angry with my friend;
> I told my wrath, my wrath did end.

See also *ENJAMBMENT.*

Enjambment The continuation of a sentence from one line of a poem to another, without a pause, as in the following lines from Shakespeare's "Sonnet 116":

> Let me not to the marriage of true minds
> Admit impediments; love is not love
> Which alters when it alteration finds . . .

Enjambment enables poets to create a conversational tone, breaking lines at points where people would normally pause in conversation yet still maintaining the unity of thought.

See page 739.

See also *RHYTHM.*

Epic A long narrative poem that recounts the adventures of a larger-than-life hero. This **epic hero** is usually a man of high social status who embodies the ideals of his people. He is often of great historical or legendary importance. Epic plots typically involve supernatural events, long time periods, distant journeys, and life-and-death struggles between good and evil. Works such as *Beowulf* are called **folk epics** because they have no certain authorship and arise, usually through storytelling, from the collective experiences of a people. **Literary epics,** such as John Milton's *Paradise Lost,* are written by known authors.

See page 20.

See also *LEGEND, MYTH, ORAL TRADITION.*

Epigram A short, witty verse or saying. Samuel Taylor Coleridge defined *epigram* with an epigram of his own:

> What is an Epigram? A dwarfish whole,
> Its body brevity, and wit its soul.

See also *APHORISM.*

Epigraph A quotation from another work or source that suggests the theme or main idea of the work at hand. It is often up to the reader to determine how the quoted work relates to the literature it introduces. An epigraph generally serves as an introductory passage at the beginning of a literary work. Kipling's "Miss Youghal's *Sais*" begins with an epigraph.

Epilogue A concluding statement or section added to a work of literature.

Epiphany A moment of sudden understanding of the true meaning of a situation, a person, or an object. In Katherine Mansfield's "A Cup of Tea," Rosemary Fell's realization that her husband finds Miss Smith pretty is an epiphany.

See pages 1025, 1094.

Epistle Any letter, such as Lady Mary Wortley Montagu's "Letter to Her Daughter." Often the term is applied to a more literary work than the informal communication written by most people. Pope called the four poems that make up *An Essay on Man* "verse epistles."

Epitaph A brief statement commemorating a dead person, often inscribed on a gravestone. Thomas Gray's "Elegy Written in a Country Churchyard" ends with an epitaph, as does Malory's *Le Morte d'Arthur.*

See page 681.
See also *ELEGY.*

Epithet A word or brief phrase used to characterize a person, place, or thing. Royal epithets are common: Good Queen Bess, Richard the Lionheart, Edward the Black Prince, Charles the Bold, and Philip the Good, for example.

Essay A short piece of nonfiction writing on any topic. The purpose of the essay is to communicate an idea or opinion. A **formal essay** is serious and impersonal, often with the purpose of instructing or persuading. Typically, the author strikes a serious tone and develops a main idea, or thesis, in a logical, highly organized way. An **informal** or **personal essay** entertains while it informs, usually in light, conversational style.

See also *NONFICTION, THESIS.*

Exaggeration See *HYPERBOLE.*

Exemplum A brief story used as an example to illustrate a moral point. Chaucer's "The Pardoner's Tale" is an exemplum.

See also *ANECDOTE, FABLE.*

Exposition See *PLOT.*

Extended metaphor A metaphor that compares two unlike things in various ways throughout a paragraph, a stanza, or an entire selection.

See page 585.
See also *METAPHOR.*

F

Fable A short, often humorous tale intended to teach a lesson about human behavior or to give advice about how to behave. Many fables end by stating the moral, or lesson to be learned, while others leave it up to the reader to infer the moral. In a **beast fable,** animals talk and act like humans.

See also *LEGEND, MORAL, PARABLE, THEME.*

Fairy tale A type of folktale that features supernatural elements, such as spirits, talking animals, and magic.

See also *FOLKTALE.*

Falling action See *PLOT.*

Fantasy A literary work that is set in an unreal world and that often concerns incredible characters and events. There are elements of fantasy in Swift's *Gulliver's Travels.*

See also *SCIENCE FICTION.*

Farce A type of comedy with ridiculous situations, characters, or events.

See also *COMEDY, HUMOR, PARODY, SATIRE.*

Fiction A narrative in which situations and characters are invented by the writer. Some aspects of a fictional work may be based on fact or experience. Fictional works include short stories, novels, and plays.

See also *DRAMA, NONFICTION, NOVEL, SHORT STORY.*

Figurative language Language used for descriptive effect in order to convey ideas or emotions. Figurative expressions are not literally true but express some truth beyond the literal level. Figurative language is especially common in poetry.

See page 251.

See also *FIGURE OF SPEECH.*

Figure of speech A specific kind of figurative language such as metaphor, personification, or simile.

See also *CONNOTATION, FIGURATIVE LANGUAGE, METAPHOR, OXYMORON, PERSONIFICATION, SIMILE, SYMBOL.*

Flashback An interruption in the chronological order of a narrative to describe an event that happened earlier. A flashback gives readers information that may help explain the main events of a story.

See page 1122.
See also *FORESHADOWING.*

Flash-forward An interruption in the chronological sequence of a narrative to leap forward in time.

See also *FLASHBACK.*

Flat character See *CHARACTER.*

Foil A character whose attitudes, beliefs, or behavior differ significantly from those of another character. Often a foil is a minor character who serves, through contrast, to emphasize the distinctive characteristics of the main character.

See also *ANTAGONIST, CHARACTER, CHARACTERIZATION, PROTAGONIST.*

Folklore Beliefs, customs, stories, songs, and dances of a culture. Folklore is passed down through oral tradition and is based on the concerns of ordinary people.

See also *BALLAD, EPIC, FOLKTALE, LEGEND, MYTH, ORAL TRADITION.*

Folktale A traditional story passed down orally long before being written down. Folktales include animal stories, trickster stories, fairy tales, myths, legends, and tall tales.

See also *FOLKLORE.*

Foot The basic unit in the measurement of a line of metrical poetry. A foot usually contains one stressed syllable (´) and one or more unstressed syllables (˘). The basic metrical feet are the **anapest** (˘ ˘ ´), **dactyl** (´ ˘ ˘), **iamb** (˘ ´), **spondee** (´ ´), and **trochee** (´ ˘).

See also *METER, RHYTHM, SCANSION, STANZA.*

Foreshadowing An author's use of clues to prepare readers for events that will happen later in a story. D. H. Lawrence prepares the reader for future happenings by stating at the beginning of "The Rocking-Horse Winner" that there was "always an anxiety in the house. There was never enough money."

See page 1078.

See also *FLASHBACK, PLOT, SUSPENSE.*

Form The structure of a poem. Many modern writers use loosely structured poetic forms instead of following traditional or formal patterns. These poets vary the lengths of lines and stanzas, relying on emphasis, rhythm, pattern, or the placement of words and phrases to convey meaning.

See pages 457, 825

See also *FREE VERSE, RHYTHM, STANZA, STRUCTURE.*

Formal essay See *ESSAY.*

Frame story A story that surrounds another story or that serves to link several stories together. The frame is the outer story, which usually precedes and follows the inner, more important story. Chaucer's *The Canterbury Tales* is a frame story. The pilgrimage is the outer story, or frame, unifying the tales or inner stories told by the pilgrims.

See also *STRUCTURE.*

Free verse Poetry that has no fixed pattern of meter, rhyme, line length, or stanza arrangement. T. S. Eliot's "Preludes" is an example of free verse. Although poets who write free verse ignore traditional rules, they use techniques such as repetition and alliteration to create musical patterns in their poems.

See page 1268.

See also *FORM, METER, RHYME, RHYTHM, STANZA.*

Genre A category or type of literature. Examples of genres are poetry, drama, fiction, and nonfiction.

Gothic novel A novel that has a gloomy, foreboding setting and contains strong elements of horror, mystery, and the supernatural. English writer Horace Walpole is credited with writing the first gothic novel, *The Castle of Otranto*, in 1765. *Gothic* originally referred to a style of architecture in western Europe during the Middle Ages. Since the setting of Walpole's novel is a medieval castle, the term was applied to this type of writing.

See page 792.
See also *NOVEL.*

Haiku An ancient Japanese form of poetry that has three lines and seventeen syllables. The first and third lines have five syllables each; the middle line has seven syllables. Usually about nature, a traditional haiku uses striking imagery to evoke an insight or capture a mood.

See also *IMAGERY.*

Heptameter A metrical line of seven feet.

See also *FOOT, METER, SCANSION.*

Hero The chief character in a literary work, typically one whose admirable qualities or noble deeds arouse admiration. Although the word *hero* is applied only to males in traditional usage—*heroine* being the term used for females—modern usage applies the term to either gender. A **Byronic hero** is the unconventional, brooding, romantic character popularized by Lord Byron in some of his verse.

See pages 20, 806.

See also *EPIC, LEGEND, MYTH, PROTAGONIST, TRAGEDY.*

Heroic couplet A pair of rhymed lines in iambic pentameter that work together to express an idea or make a point. A heroic couplet is based on the poetic form used by ancient Greek and Roman poets in their heroic epics. The following lines from Pope's *An Essay on Man* form a heroic couplet:

> And, spite of pride, in erring reason's spite,
> One truth is clear, Whatever is, is right.

See page 572.
See also *IAMBIC PENTAMETER, METER, RHYTHM.*

Heroic stanza A group of four poetic lines (a quatrain) in iambic pentameter having a rhyme scheme of *abab*, also known as the **elegiac stanza**. Gray's "Elegy Written in a Country Churchyard" features heroic, or elegiac, stanzas.

See also *IAMBIC PENTAMETER, QUATRAIN, RHYME SCHEME.*

Hexameter Line of verse consisting of six feet.

See also *FOOT, METER, SCANSION.*

Historical fiction Fiction that sets characters against the backdrop of a period other than the author's own. Some works of historical fiction include actual historical people along with fictitious characters.

See page 603.

See also *FICTION, NOVEL.*

Historical narrative A work of nonfiction that tells the story of important historical events or developments. Bede's *The Ecclesiastical History of the English People* tells of the influence of the Christian church on English civilization.

See page 87.

See also *HISTORY, NONFICTION.*

History A factual account of real events that occurred in the past. Typically, a history is arranged chronologically and seeks to provide an objective description of what happened.

See also *HISTORICAL FICTION, NONFICTION.*

Hubris Extreme pride or arrogance. Hubris often results in the downfall of a protagonist who violates a human, natural, or divine law. In his sonnet "Ozymandias," Percy Bysshe Shelley provides a concise portrait of hubris in the doomed king whose empire lies in ruins around him.

See also *TRAGEDY.*

Humor The quality of a literary work that makes the characters and their situations seem funny, amusing, or silly. Humor often points out human failings and the irony found in many situations. Humorous language includes sarcasm, exaggeration, and verbal irony.

See page 133.

See also *COMEDY, FARCE, PARODY, PUN, SATIRE, WIT.*

Hymn A lyric poem or song addressed to a divine being or expressing religious sentiments.

See also *LYRIC.*

Hyperbole A figure of speech that uses exaggeration to express strong emotion, to make a point, or to evoke humor. The following passage from Andrew Marvell's "To His Coy Mistress" contains hyperbole:

> An hundred years should go to praise
> Thine eyes, and on thy forehead gaze; . . .

See page 465.

See also *FIGURATIVE LANGUAGE, UNDERSTATEMENT.*

I

Iamb A two-syllable metrical foot consisting of one unstressed syllable and one stressed syllable, as in the word *divide.*

Iambic pentameter A poetic meter in which each line is composed of five feet (**pentameter**); each foot—known as an **iamb**—consists of one unstressed syllable (ˇ) followed by one stressed syllable (´). In order to imitate the natural flow of spoken English, poets using iambic pentameter often vary its rhythm. The following line from Spenser's "Sonnet 75" is a perfect example of this metrical form:

> But came / the tide, / and made / my pains /
>
> his prey.

See also *BLANK VERSE, FOOT, HEROIC COUPLET, METER, RHYTHM, SCANSION.*

Idiom An expression whose meaning is different from the literal meaning of the words that make it up. Phrases such as "catch his eye," "turn the tables," "over the hill," and "keep tabs on" are idiomatic expressions understood by native speakers but often puzzling to nonnative speakers. Idioms can add realism to dialogue in a story and contribute to characterization.

See also *DIALECT.*

Imagery The "word pictures" that writers create to evoke an emotional response. In creating effective images, writers use **sensory details,** or descriptions that appeal to one or more of the five senses: sight, hearing, touch, taste, and smell. Note Yeats's use of imagery in "The Lake Isle of Innisfree."

See pages 836, 1072, 1280.

See also *FIGURATIVE LANGUAGE.*

Informal essay See *ESSAY.*

Interior monologue A technique that records a character's emotions, memories, and opinions. Interior monologue contributes to the stream-of-consciousness effect. Joyce's "Araby" contains interior monologue.

See also *STREAM OF CONSCIOUSNESS.*

Internal conflict See *CONFLICT.*

Internal rhyme Rhyme that occurs within a single line of poetry. Poets use internal rhyme to convey meaning, to evoke mood, or simply to create a musical effect.

See also *RHYME.*

Inversion Reversal of the usual word order for emphasis or variety. Writers use inversion to maintain rhyme scheme or meter, or to emphasize certain words. In the first line that follows from Gray's "Elegy Written in a Country Churchyard," the verb (*fades*) comes before the subject (*landscape*), a reversal of the usual order. In the second line, the object (*stillness*) comes before the verb (*holds*).

> Now fades the glimmering landscape on the
>   sight,
> And all the air a solemn stillness holds, . . .

See page 534.

See also *STYLE.*

Irony A contrast or discrepancy between appearance and reality. **Situational irony** exists when the outcome of a situation is the opposite of expectations, as in Hardy's poem "Ah, Are You Digging on My Grave?" **Verbal irony** occurs when the meaning of a statement is the reverse of what is meant, as in Swift's *A Modest Proposal.* **Dramatic irony** occurs when readers or viewers know something that the characters do not.

See pages 125, 809, 960, 1132.

J–L

Journal A daily record of events kept by a participant in those events or a witness to them. A journal is usually less intimate than a diary, emphasizing events rather than emotions. Dorothy Wordsworth's journal, kept from 1800 to 1803, provides a glimpse into English country life.

See page 754.

See also *DIARY, NONFICTION.*

Juxtaposition The placing of two or more distinct things side by side in order to contrast or compare them. It is commonly used to evoke an emotional response in the reader.

See page 801.

Kenning A descriptive figure of speech that takes the place of a common noun, especially in Anglo-Saxon and Norse poetry. In *Beowulf*, for example, the sea is described as the "whale road."

See also *FIGURATIVE LANGUAGE.*

Legend A traditional story handed down from the past, based on actual people and events, and tending to become more exaggerated and fantastical over time. Often legends celebrate the heroic qualities of a national or cultural leader. Legends about King Arthur and his knights of the Round Table have evolved from a real warrior who led the British in battle in the eighth century A.D.

See page 189.

See also *FOLKLORE, FOLKTALE, HERO, ORAL TRADITION.*

Literary criticism A type of writing in which the writer analyzes and evaluates a literary work.

Lyric poetry Poetry that expresses a speaker's personal thoughts and feelings. A lyric poem is usually short and creates a single, unified impression.

See pages 441, 956.

See also *POETRY.*

M

Maxim A short saying that contains a general truth or gives practical advice, particularly about morality and behavior. Also known as an adage or aphorism.

See also *APHORISM.*

Melodrama A melodrama is usually a play, but it can be any work that has a strong conflict and appeals primarily to the emotions. In a melodrama, the characters are either extremely good or extremely wicked.

See also *DRAMA.*

Memoir A type of narrative nonfiction that presents the story of a period in the writer's life. It is usually written from the first-person point of view and emphasizes the narrator's own experience of this period. It may also reveal the impact of significant historical events on his or her life.

See also *AUTOBIOGRAPHY, BIOGRAPHY.*

Metaphor A figure of speech that compares or equates two seemingly unlike things to help readers perceive the first thing more vividly. In contrast to a simile, a metaphor implies the comparison instead of stating it directly; hence there is no use of connectives such as *like* or *as*. The lines below from Sir Philip Sidney's "Sonnet 39" contain metaphors:

> **Come sleep! O sleep, the certain knot of peace,**
> **The baiting place of wit, the balm of woe, . . .**

See page 284.

See also *EXTENDED METAPHOR, FIGURATIVE LANGUAGE, SIMILE.*

Metaphysical poetry The work of a group of seventeenth-century English poets led by John Donne. Metaphysical poetry is written in a conversational style, emphasizes complex meanings, contains unusual imagery, and extends the range of metaphors into areas of science, religion, and learning.

See also *CONCEIT, METAPHOR.*

Meter A regular pattern of stressed (´) and unstressed (˘) syllables that gives a line of poetry a more or less predictable rhythm. The basic unit of meter is the foot, consisting of one or two stressed syllables and/or one or two unstressed syllables. The iamb, for example, consists of two syllables: one unstressed followed by one stressed. The length of a metrical line can be expressed in terms of the number of feet it contains:

> dimeter, two feet
> trimeter, three feet
> tetrameter, four feet
> pentameter, five feet
> hexameter, six feet
> heptameter, seven feet

The following lines from Marlowe's "The Passionate Shepherd to His Love" are in iambic tetrameter:

˘ ´ ˘ ´ ˘ ´ ˘ ´
Come live / with me, / and be / my love,

˘ ´ ˘ ´ ˘ ´ ˘ ´
And we / will all / the plea / sures prove.

See pages 423, 952.

See also *FOOT, IAMBIC PENTAMETER, RHYTHM, SCANSION.*

Metonymy A figure of speech in which a word or phrase is substituted for another that is related. For example, the executive branch of the British government is often referred to as Downing Street, where the prime minister lives in London.

See also *FIGURATIVE LANGUAGE.*

Miracle play A medieval religious drama presenting a story from the Bible or the lives of the saints; also called a **mystery play.**

See also *MORALITY PLAY.*

Mock-epic An imitation epic, or long narrative poem, that makes fun of the trivial values of a society by using elevated language to describe a mundane event. Pope's "The Rape of the Lock" is a mock-epic.

See page 576.

See also *EPIC.*

Modernism A term applied to a variety of twentieth-century artistic movements that shared a desire to break with the past. In addition to technical experimentation, Modernist playwrights, writers, and artists in the first half of the twentieth century were interested in the irrational or inexplicable, as well as in the workings of the unconscious mind. The poetry of T. S. Eliot, with its new subject matter, diction, and metrical patterns, came to define Modernism. Other Modernist writers include Virginia Woolf and James Joyce.

See also *STREAM OF CONSCIOUSNESS.*

Monologue A long speech by a character in a literary work, spoken either to others or as if alone.

See also *DRAMATIC MONOLOGUE, SOLILOQUY.*

Mood The emotional quality of a literary work. A writer's choice of language, subject matter, setting, and tone, as well as sound devices such as rhyme and rhythm, contribute to creating mood. *Mood* is a broader term than *tone,* which refers to the attitude of a writer toward the subject matter or the audience. It also differs from *atmosphere,* which is concerned mainly with the physical qualities that contribute to a mood, such as time, place, and weather.

See page 78.

See also *ATMOSPHERE, SETTING, TONE.*

Moral A practical lesson about right and wrong conduct taught in a fable or parable.

See also *FABLE, PARABLE.*

Morality play A medieval religious play popular in the 1400s and 1500s. The plays centered on the moral struggles of everyday people and were designed to teach lessons about salvation and the struggle between virtue and vice. Characters were personifications of abstract qualities such as vice, virtue, mercy, ignorance, and poverty. *The Creation of Adam and Eve* is a morality play.

See also *MIRACLE PLAY.*

Motif A significant word, phrase, image, description, idea, or other element repeated throughout a literary work and related to the theme. Luck is a motif in D. H. Lawrence's "The Rocking-Horse Winner."

See page 327.

See also *THEME.*

Motivation The stated or implied reason for a character's actions. Motivation may be an external circumstance or an internal moral or emotional impulse.

See page 1002.

Myth A traditional story that deals with goddesses, gods, heroes, and supernatural forces. A myth may explain a belief, a custom, or a force of nature. Milton's *Paradise Lost* has mythic elements.

See also *EPIC, FOLKLORE, LEGEND, ORAL TRADITION.*

N

Narrative Writing or speech that tells a story. Narratives may be fiction or nonfiction, prose or poetry.

See also *NARRATIVE POETRY, NARRATOR.*

Narrative poetry Verse that tells a story. **Ballads, epics,** and **romances** are all types of narrative poetry. "The Rime of the Ancient Mariner" by Samuel Taylor Coleridge is a narrative poem.

See page 762.

See also *BALLAD, DRAMATIC MONOLOGUE, EPIC, NARRATIVE.*

Narrator The person who tells a story. The narrator may be a character in the story, as in James Joyce's "Araby," or outside the story, as in Doris Lessing's "A Mild Attack of Locusts."

See page 1027.

See also *NARRATIVE, PERSONA, POINT OF VIEW, SPEAKER.*

Naturalism A literary movement characterized by a belief that people are part of the natural world and have little control over their own lives. Writers such as Hardy and Lawrence focused on the powerful economic, social, and environmental forces that shape the lives of individuals.

See also *REALISM.*

Neoclassicism A term often applied to English literature of the Neoclassical period, from 1660 to the end of the eighteenth century. This period, which is also known as the Age of Reason, corresponds to Unit Three in the text. Neoclassical writers valued order, reason, balance, and clarity over emotion. The work of Alexander Pope is an example of Neoclassicism.

See also *RESTORATION AGE.*

Nonfiction Literature that deals with real people, places, and events. Among the categories of nonfiction are biographies, autobiographies, and essays.

See also *AUTOBIOGRAPHY, BIOGRAPHY, ESSAY, FICTION, HISTORY, MEMOIR.*

Nonsense verse Humorous poetry that defies logic. It usually has a strong rhythm and contains made-up words known as **nonce words.** Lewis Carroll's "Jabberwocky" is nonsense verse.

See page 914.

Novel A book-length fictional prose narrative having a plot, characters, setting, and a theme. A short novel is often called a **novella.**

See also *FICTION, PLOT, SHORT STORY.*

Novel of manners A realistic work that deals with the conventions and values of a particular society or social class, such as those depicted in Jane Austen's novels of nineteenth-century English country life.

O

Octave The first eight lines of a **Petrarchan,** or **Italian,** sonnet. The octave usually presents a situation, an idea, or a question.

See also *SONNET.*

Octet A group of eight lines in a poem.

Ode A serious lyric poem, dignified and sincere in tone and style. Some odes celebrate a person, an event, or even a power; others are more private meditations. A **Horatian ode,** named for the Roman poet Horace, has a regular stanza pattern and rhyme scheme. An **irregular ode** has no set rhyme scheme or stanza pattern.

See page 830.

See also *LYRIC POETRY.*

Onomatopoeia The use of a word or phrase that imitates or suggests the sound of what it describes. The words *mew, crack, swish, hiss, caw,* and *buzz* are onomatopoeic words.

See also *SOUND DEVICES.*

Oral tradition The passing of literature by word of mouth from one generation to the next. Oral literature is a way of recording the past, glorifying leaders, and teaching morals and traditions to young people.

See also *BALLAD, EPIC, FOLKLORE, FOLKTALE, LEGEND, MYTH.*

Ottava rima A stanza of eight lines written in iambic pentameter with the rhyme scheme *ababababcc.* Yeats's

"Sailing to Byzantium" is written in ottava rima.

See also *IAMBIC PENTAMETER, RHYME SCHEME, STANZA.*

Oxymoron A figure of speech in which opposite ideas are combined. Examples are "bright darkness," "wise fool," and "hateful love."

See also *FIGURATIVE LANGUAGE, PARADOX.*

P–Q

Parable A simple story pointing to a moral or religious lesson. It differs from a fable in that the characters are people instead of animals.

See also *FABLE, MORAL.*

Paradox A situation or statement that seems to be impossible or contradictory but is nevertheless true, literally or figuratively. The fifth line of Elizabeth I's poem "On Monsieur's Departure" contains two paradoxes:

> I am and not, I freeze and yet am burned,

See page 461.

See also *OXYMORON.*

Parallelism The use of a series of words, phrases, or sentences that have similar grammatical form. Parallelism shows the relationship between ideas and helps emphasize thoughts. Winston Churchill's speech "Be Ye Men of Valor" contains parallelism:

> <u>The interests of property, the hours of labor,</u> are nothing compared with the struggle <u>for life and honor, for right and freedom,</u> to which we have vowed ourselves.

See page 274.

See also *REPETITION.*

Parody A humorous imitation of a literary work that aims to point out the work's shortcomings. A parody may imitate the plot, characters, or style of another work, usually through exaggeration. Shakespeare's "Sonnet 130" is a parody of Renaissance love poetry.

See page 559.

See also *COMEDY, FARCE, HUMOR, SATIRE.*

Pastoral Poetry that idealizes the simple lives of shepherds in a rural setting. Pastoral poems often exaggerate the rural pleasures and the innocence of country people living in harmony with nature.

Pathetic fallacy The attribution of human thoughts and emotions to nature or to nonhuman objects or animals. In "The Tyger," William Blake speaks of the stars as if they were capable of human feeling:

> When the stars threw down their spears
> And watered heaven with their tears

The pathetic fallacy is a type of personification but refers specifically to feelings, not to all human qualities.

See also *PERSONIFICATION.*

Pentameter A metrical line of five feet.

See also *BLANK VERSE, FOOT, METER.*

Persona The person created by the author to tell a story. Whether the story is told by an omniscient narrator or by one of the characters, the author of the work often adopts a persona—a personality different from his or her real one. The attitudes and beliefs of the persona may not be the same as those of the author. Jonathan Swift is the author of *Gulliver's Travels*; however, the first-person narrator, Lemuel Gulliver, is the voice through which Swift chose to tell his story.

See also *NARRATOR, POINT OF VIEW.*

Personification A figure of speech in which an animal, an object, a force of nature, or an idea is given human characteristics. Yeats personifies love in these lines from "When You Are Old":

> Murmur, a little sadly, how Love fled
> And paced upon the mountains overhead
> And hid his face amid a crowd of stars.

See pages 509, 1221.

See also *APOSTROPHE, FIGURATIVE LANGUAGE, PATHETIC FALLACY.*

Persuasion Writing, usually nonfiction, that attempts to convince readers to think or act in a particular way.

Persuasion Writing, usually nonfiction, that attempts to convince readers to think or act in a particular way. Writers of persuasive works use appeals to logic or emotion and other techniques to sway their readers. Mary Wollstonecraft's *A Vindication of the Rights of Woman* is an excellent example of persuasive writing.
See also *ARGUMENT*.

Petrarchan sonnet See *SONNET*.

Play See *DRAMA*.

Plot The sequence of events in a short story, novel, or drama. Most plots deal with a problem and develop around a **conflict,** a struggle between opposing forces. The plot begins with **exposition,** which introduces the story's characters, setting, and situation. The **rising action** adds complications to the conflicts, or problems, leading to the **climax,** or **crisis,** the point of highest emotional pitch. The climax gives way rapidly to its logical result in the **falling action** and finally to the **resolution** (sometimes called the **dénouement**), in which the final outcome is revealed.
See pages 360, 942.
See also *CONFLICT*.

Poetry A form of literary expression that differs from prose in emphasizing the line, rather than the sentence, as the unit of composition. Many other traditional characteristics of poetry apply to some poems but not to others. Some of these characteristics are emotional, imaginative language; use of metaphor, simile, and other figures of speech; division into stanzas; and the use of rhyme and regular patterns of meter.
See also *FIGURATIVE LANGUAGE, FREE VERSE, METER, PROSE, RHYME, STANZA*.

Point of view The standpoint from which a story is told. In a story with **first-person** point of view, the narrator is a character in the story and uses the words *I* and *me*. In a story told from **third-person** point of view, the narrator is someone who stands outside the story and describes the characters and action. **Third-person omniscient,** or all-knowing point of view, means that the narrator knows everything about the characters and events and may reveal details that the characters themselves could not reveal. If the narrator describes events as only one character perceives them, as in Elizabeth Bowen's "The Demon Lover," the point of view is called **third-person limited.** An objec-
tive point of view is that of a narrator who presents a story in a completely impersonal way, describing only external aspects of characters and events and never directly referring to thoughts or emotions.
See pages 266, 1297.
See also *NARRATOR, SPEAKER*.

Postmodernism A broad contemporary movement in art, music, film, literature, and other cultural areas that is viewed as growing out of or replacing Modernism. Many of the characteristic features of postmodernist literature extend or exaggerate tendencies of Modernism. For example, Modernist writers turned away from the apparent objectivity of Realism; postmodernists go further, introducing a frankly artificial, self-conscious playfulness into their works.
See also *MODERNISM*.

Prologue An introductory section of a play, a speech, or another literary work. Chaucer's *The Canterbury Tales* contains a long prologue.
See also *EPILOGUE*.

Propaganda Written or spoken material designed to bring about a change or to damage a cause through use of emotionally charged words, name-calling, or other techniques.

Props A theater term (a shortened form of *properties*) for articles used in a stage play or movie or television set.
See also *DRAMA*.

Prose Written language that is not versified. Novels, short stories, and essays are usually written in prose.
See also *POETRY*.

Protagonist The central character in a literary work, around whom the main conflict revolves. Generally, the audience is meant to sympathize with the protagonist.
See also *ANTAGONIST, CONFLICT, HERO, PLOT*.

Proverb A saying that expresses some truth about life or contains some bit of popular wisdom such as "faint heart never won fair lady," "marry in haste, repent at leisure," or "out of sight, out of mind."
See also *APHORISM, EPIGRAM*.

Psalm A song of praise most commonly found in the biblical book of Psalms. David, king of Israel around 1000 B.C., wrote many of these psalms. Occasionally a modern poet will title his or her poem a psalm.

Pun A humorous use of words that are similar in sound (*merry* and *marry*) or of a word with several meanings. In Shakespeare's *Romeo and Juliet*, when Mercutio is fatally wounded, he says, "Ask for me tomorrow, and you shall find me a <u>grave</u> man," meaning both "serious" and "dead."

Puritan writing The work of early seventeenth-century writers who supported the Puritan cause. John Milton and John Bunyan were two major Puritan writers.

Quatrain A stanza of four lines.
See also *BALLAD STANZA, COUPLET, HEROIC STANZA, SESTET, STANZA.*

R

Rationalism A philosophy that values reason over feeling or imagination. It was most influential during the Neoclassical period.
See also *NEOCLASSICISM, ROMANTICISM.*

Realism A literary movement first prominent in the late nineteenth and early twentieth centuries. Realism seeks to portray life as it is really lived. Realistic fiction often focuses on middle- or working-class conditions and characters, often with reformist intent. Charles Dickens was a Realist writer.
See also *NATURALISM.*

Refrain A line or lines repeated regularly, usually in a poem or song. In Dylan Thomas's "Do Not Go Gentle into That Good Night," the line "Rage, rage against the dying of the light" serves as a refrain.
See also *REPETITION.*

Regionalism An emphasis on themes, characters, customs, and settings of a particular geographical region.
See also *DIALECT, VERNACULAR.*

Repetition The recurrence of sounds, words, phrases, lines, or stanzas in a speech or literary work. Repetition increases the sense of unity in a work and can draw attention to particular ideas.
See page 898.
See also *PARALLELISM, REFRAIN.*

Renaissance A word meaning "rebirth." The Renaissance in Europe marked a transition from the medieval period to the modern world. The height of the English Renaissance occurred in the late sixteenth and early seventeenth centuries, when William Shakespeare was active.

Resolution See *PLOT.*

Restoration Age The short period immediately following the restoration of the Stuarts to the throne in 1660. The age is marked by the return of drama to the English stage.

Rhetoric The art of using language—often in public speaking—to present facts and ideas in order to persuade. **Rhetorical devices** are techniques writers use to manipulate language for effect or to evoke an emotional response in the reader. These may include repetition, parallelism, analogy, logic, and the skillful use of connotation and anecdote. Effective rhetoric often appeals to logic, emotion, morality, or authority. A **rhetorical question** is a question to which no answer is expected or the answer is obvious.
See page 1113.
See also *ANALOGY, ANECDOTE, ARGUMENT, CONNOTATION, PARALLELISM, REPETITION.*

Rhyme The repetition of the same stressed vowel sounds and any succeeding sounds in two or more words. **End rhyme** occurs at the ends of lines of poetry. **Internal rhyme** occurs within a single line.
See also *RHYME SCHEME, SLANT RHYME.*

Rhyme scheme The pattern that end rhymes form in a stanza or a poem. Rhyme scheme is designated by the assignment of a different letter of the alphabet to each new rhyme. The rhyme scheme of the following lines from Thomas Hardy's "The Man He Killed" is *abab*:

"Had he and I but met	a
By some old ancient inn,	b
We should have sat us down to wet	a
Right many a nipperkin!	b

See pages 256, 1061.

See also *RHYME*.

Rhythm The pattern of beats created by the arrangement of stressed and unstressed syllables, especially in poetry. Rhythm gives poetry a musical quality, can add emphasis to certain words, and may help convey the poem's meaning. Rhythm can be regular, with a predictable pattern or meter, or irregular. Note the regular rhythm in the following lines from A. E. Housman's "To an Athlete Dying Young":

The time you won your town the race

We chaired you through the market-place;

See page 881.

See also *IAMBIC PENTAMETER, METER, SCANSION, SPRUNG RHYTHM*.

Rising action See *PLOT*.

Romance Historically, a term used to describe long narrative works about the exploits and love affairs of chivalric heroes such as King Arthur and Sir Lancelot. The term *romance* can also be applied to any story that involves noble heroes, idealized love, or fantastic events that seem remote from everyday life.

See also *LEGEND*.

Romanticism An artistic movement that began in Europe and valued imagination and feeling over intellect and reason. The works of William Wordsworth, Coleridge, Byron, and Keats represent the height of Romantic poetry.

S

Sarcasm The use of bitter or caustic language to point out shortcomings or flaws.

See also *IRONY, SATIRE*.

Satire Writing that exposes to ridicule the vices or follies of people or societies through devices such as hyperbole, understatement, and irony. The purpose of satire may be to reform or to entertain.

See page 549.

See also *COMEDY, HYPERBOLE, IRONY, PARODY, UNDERSTATEMENT, WIT*.

Scansion The analysis of the meter of a line of verse. To scan a line of poetry means to note the stressed and unstressed syllables and to divide the line into its feet, or rhythmic units. Stressed syllables are marked (´) and unstressed syllables (˘). Note the scansion of these lines from Byron's "She Walks in Beauty":

She walks / in beau / ty, like / the night

Of cloud / less climes / and star / ry skies; . . .

Since each line has four feet and the rhythm is iambic, the lines can be described as iambic tetrameter.

See also *FOOT, METER, RHYTHM*.

Scene A subdivision of an act in a play. A scene is shorter than an act.

See also *ACT, DRAMA*.

Science fiction Fiction that deals with the impact of science and technology—real or imagined—on society and on individuals. Sometimes occurring in the future, science fiction commonly portrays space travel, exploration of other planets, and possible future societies.

Sensory details See *IMAGERY*.

Sestet A six-line stanza.

See also *SONNET*.

Setting The time and place in which the events of a literary work occur. Setting includes not only the physical surroundings but also the ideas, customs, values, and beliefs of a particular time and place. Setting often helps create an atmosphere or a mood. Setting plays an important part in Lessing's "A Mild Attack of Locusts."

See page 1250.

Shakespearean songs Shakespeare used songs in his plays to heighten the drama, making what is merry merrier or what is sad sadder. His plays include love songs, nonsense songs, and **dirges**, songs that mourn a death.

Shakespearean sonnet See *SONNET.*

Short story A brief fictional narrative that generally includes the following major elements: setting, characters, plot, point of view, and theme.

See page 1024.

See also *FICTION, NOVEL, PLOT.*

Simile A figure of speech that uses *like* or *as* to compare seemingly unlike things. In the following example from Andrew Marvell's "To His Coy Mistress," the poet compares his love's complexion to dew:

> Now, therefore, while the youthful hue
> Sits on thy skin like morning dew,

See pages 284, 288.

See also *ANALOGY, FIGURATIVE LANGUAGE, METAPHOR.*

Slant rhyme An approximate rhyme occurring when words include sounds that are similar but not identical (*jackal* and *buckle*). Slant rhyme typically involves some variation of **consonance** (the repetition of similar consonant sounds) or **assonance** (the repetition of similar vowel sounds). In "Follower," Seamus Heaney features slant rhyme in word pairs such as *sock/pluck* and *plow/furrow.*

See page 1217.

See also *RHYME.*

Soliloquy In drama, a long speech by a character who is alone on stage. A soliloquy reveals the private thoughts and emotions of that character. In Act 3, scene 1 of Shakespeare's *Macbeth*, Macbeth delivers a soliloquy that begins

> To be thus is nothing, but to be safely thus—
> Our fears in Banquo stick deep, . . .

See also *ASIDE, DRAMATIC MONOLOGUE, MONOLOGUE.*

Sonnet A lyric poem of fourteen lines, typically written in iambic pentameter and usually following strict

patterns of stanza divisions and rhymes. The **Shakespearean,** or **English,** sonnet consists of three **quatrains,** or four-line stanzas, followed by a **couplet,** or pair of rhyming lines. The rhyme scheme is typically *abab, cdcd, efef, gg.* The couplet often presents a conclusion to the issues or questions presented in the three quatrains. Like a Shakespearean sonnet, the **Spenserian sonnet** has three quatrains and a couplet, but it follows the rhyme scheme *abab bcbc cdcd ee.* This interlocking rhyme scheme pushes the sonnet toward the final couplet, which makes a key point or comment. In the **Petrarchan,** or **Italian,** sonnet, fourteen lines are divided into two stanzas, the eight-line **octave** and the six-line **sestet.** The sestet usually responds to a question or situation posed by the octave. The rhyme scheme for the octave is typically *abbaabba*; for the sestet, the rhyme scheme is typically *cdecde.*

See page 242.

See also *COUPLET, LYRIC POETRY, RHYME SCHEME, STANZA.*

Sonnet sequence A series of sonnets focused on a particular theme. Elizabeth Barrett Browning's *Sonnets from the Portuguese* is a sonnet sequence.

See also *SONNET.*

Sound devices Techniques used, especially in poetry, to appeal to the ear. Writers use sound devices to enhance the sense of rhythm, to emphasize particular sounds, or to add a musical quality to their work.

See also *ALLITERATION, ASSONANCE, CONSONANCE, ONOMATOPOEIA, RHYME.*

Speaker The person who is speaking in a poem, similar to a narrator in a work of prose. Sometimes the speaker's voice is that of the poet, sometimes that of a fictional person or even a thing. The speaker's words communicate a particular tone, or attitude, toward the subject of the poem. One should never assume that the speaker and the writer are identical, however.

See page 1189.

See also *DRAMATIC MONOLOGUE, NARRATOR, TONE.*

Spondee A metrical foot of two stressed syllables.
See also *FOOT, METER.*

Sprung rhythm A kind of irregular rhythm in which each foot has one stressed syllable, usually the first, and a varied number of unstressed syllables. Gerard Manley Hopkins, who invented the term and the technique, believed this to be the rhythm of natural speech.

See page 909.

See also *METER, RHYTHM.*

Stage directions Instructions written by a playwright to describe the appearance and actions of characters, as well as the sets, costumes, and lighting.

See also *DRAMA.*

Stanza A group of lines forming a unit in a poem or song. A stanza in a poem is similar to a paragraph in prose. Typically, stanzas in a poem are separated by a line of space.

See page 720.

See also *BALLAD STANZA, COUPLET, HEROIC STANZA, QUATRAIN, SONNET, SPENSERIAN STANZA.*

Stereotype A character who is not developed as an individual but instead represents a collection of traits and mannerisms supposedly shared by all members of a group.

See also *CHARACTER.*

Stream of consciousness The literary representation of a character's free-flowing thoughts, feelings, and memories. Stream-of-consciousness writing does not always employ conventional sentence structure or other rules of grammar and usage.

Structure The particular order or pattern a writer uses to present ideas. Narratives commonly follow a chronological order, while the structure of persuasive or expository writing may vary. Listing detailed information, using cause and effect, or describing a problem and then offering a solution are some other ways a writer can present a topic.

See pages 1064, 1206.

See also *FORM.*

Style The expressive qualities that distinguish an author's work, including word choice and the length and arrangement of sentences, as well as the use of figurative language and imagery. Style can reveal an author's attitude and purpose in writing.

See pages 407, 595.

See also *AUTHOR'S PURPOSE, DICTION, FIGURATIVE LANGUAGE, IMAGERY, TONE.*

Subject The topic of a literary work.

Suspense A feeling of curiosity, uncertainty, or even dread about what is going to happen next in a story. Writers increase the level of suspense by creating a threat to the central character and raising questions in a reader's mind about the outcome of a conflict.

Symbol Any object, person, place, or experience that exists on a literal level but also represents something else, usually something abstract.

See pages 715, 1036.

See also *ALLEGORY, FIGURATIVE LANGUAGE.*

Synecdoche A figure of speech in which a part is used for the whole or a whole is used for a part. In this line from the book of Revelation in the Bible, "All nations, and kindreds, and people, and tongues," *tongues* (a part) is used for the whole (languages).

See also *METONYMY.*

T

Terza rima A verse form consisting of a sequence of interlocking three-line stanzas, or tercets. The first and third lines of the first stanza rhyme, and the second line provides the rhyme for the first and third lines of the next stanza, forming the rhyme scheme *aba, bcb, cdc,* and so on.

Tetrameter A metrical line of four feet.

See also *FOOT, METER.*

Theater of the absurd Drama, primarily of the 1950s and 1960s, that presents a series of scenes in which the characters—often confused and anxious—exist in a meaningless world. Harold Pinter is a leading English dramatist of absurdist and other plays.

See page 1225.

See also *DRAMA.*

Theme The message of a story, poem, novel, or play. A literary work may have more than one theme. Some themes are universal, meaning that they are widely held ideas about life. Themes and **subjects** are different. The subject of a work might be love; the theme would be what the writer says about love—for example, love is cruel; love is wonderful; love is fleeting.

See pages 292, 1239.

See also *AUTHOR'S PURPOSE, MORAL.*

Thesis The main idea of a work of nonfiction. The thesis may be stated directly or implied. The thesis of Francis Bacon's "Of Studies" is that books have multiple uses and readers have multiple needs and capabilities.

See page 696.

See also *NONFICTION.*

Title The name given to a literary work. The title can help explain the setting, provide insight into the theme, or describe the action that will take place in the work.

See page 1048.

Tone An author's attitude toward his or her subject matter or the audience. Tone is conveyed through elements such as word choice, punctuation, sentence structure, and figures of speech. A writer's tone might convey a variety of attitudes such as sympathy, amusement, or superiority.

See page 245.

See also *AUTHOR'S PURPOSE, NARRATOR, SPEAKER, STYLE, VOICE.*

Tragedy A play in which a main character suffers a downfall. That character, the **tragic hero,** is typically a person of dignified or heroic stature. The downfall may result from outside forces or from a weakness within the character, which is known as a **tragic flaw.**

See page 380.

See also DRAMA, HERO, HUBRIS.

Trochee A metrical foot made up of one stressed and one unstressed syllable. The line below, from Shakespeare's *Macbeth*, has four trochees and can be described as trochaic tetrameter.

    ´ ˘   ´ ˘   ´ ˘   ´ ˘

   Double, / double, / toil and / trouble;

See also *FOOT, METER.*

U–W

Understatement Language that makes something seem less important than it really is. Understatement may be used to add humor or to focus the reader's

attention on something the author wants to emphasize.

See also *HYPERBOLE.*

Vernacular Ordinary speech of a particular country or region. Vernacular is more casual than cultivated, formal speech. Slang, dialect, and idiom are commonly included as part of the vernacular. Writers often employ vernacular to enhance the realism of their narrative or dialogue. See page 1193.

See also *DIALECT, IDIOM, REGIONALISM.*

Verse paragraph A group of lines in a poem that form a unit. Unlike a stanza, a verse paragraph does not have a fixed number of lines. While poems written before the twentieth century usually contain stanzas, many contemporary poems are made up of verse paragraphs. Verse paragraphs help to organize a poem into thoughts, as paragraphs help to organize prose.

See page 1052.

See also *STANZA.*

Villanelle A nineteen-line poem divided into five tercets, or stanzas of three lines, each with the rhyme scheme *aba,* and a final quatrain with the rhyme scheme *abaa.* The first line is repeated as a refrain at the end of the second and fourth stanzas. The last line of the first stanza is repeated at the end of the third and fifth stanzas. Both lines reappear as the final two lines of the poem. This six-stanza form was originally used in French pastoral poetry.

See also *QUATRAIN, REFRAIN, STANZA.*

Voice The distinctive use of language that conveys the author's or narrator's personality to the reader. Voice is determined by elements of style such as word choice and tone.

See pages 295, 624, 1233.

See also *AUTHOR'S PURPOSE, DICTION, NARRATOR, STYLE, TONE.*

Wit An exhibition of cleverness and humor. Jonathan Swift, Alexander Pope, and Lewis Carroll are authors famous for their wit.

See also *COMEDY, HUMOR, SATIRE.*

 **Reading and Thinking with Foldables®**

by Dinah Zike, M.Ed., Creator of Foldables®

Using Foldables® Makes Learning Easy and Enjoyable

Anyone who has paper, scissors, and maybe a stapler or some glue can use Foldables in the classroom. Just follow the illustrated step-by-step directions. Check out the following sample:

 **Reading Objective:** to understand how one character's actions affect other characters in a short story

Use this Foldable to keep track of what the main character does and how his or her actions affect the other characters.

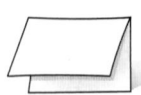 **Step ❶** Place a sheet of paper in front of you so that the short side is at the top. Fold the paper in half from top to bottom.

 **Step ❷** Fold in half again, from side to side, to divide the paper into two columns. Unfold the paper so that the two columns show.

 **Step ❸** Draw a line along the column crease. Then, through the top layer of paper, cut along the line you drew, forming two tabs.

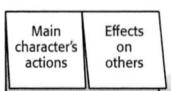 **Step ❹** Label the tabs *Main character's actions* and *Effects on others.*

Step ❺ As you read, record the main character's actions under the first tab. Record how each of those actions affects other characters under the second tab.

 **Short Story**

Reading Objective: to analyze a short story on the basis of its literary elements

As you read, use the following Foldable to keep track of five literary elements in the short story.

 Step ❶ Stack three sheets of paper with their top edges about a half-inch apart. Be sure to keep the side edges straight.

 **Step ❷** Fold up the bottom edges of the paper to form six tabs, five of which will be the same size.

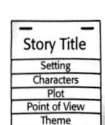 **Step ❸** Crease the paper to hold the tabs in place and staple the sheets together along the crease.

Step ❹ Turn the sheets so that the stapled side is at the top. Write the title of the story on the top tab. Label the five remaining tabs *Setting, Characters, Plot, Point of View,* and *Theme.*

Step ❺ Use your Foldable as you read the short story. Under each labeled tab, jot down notes about the story in terms of that element.

You may adapt this simple Foldable in several ways.

• Use it with dramas, longer works of fiction, and some narrative poems—wherever five literary elements are present in the story.

• Change the labels to focus on something different. For example, if a story or a play has several settings, characters, acts, or scenes, you could devote a tab to each one.

 Drama

Reading Objective: to understand conflict and plot in a drama

As you read the drama, use the following Foldable to keep track of conflicts that arise and ways that those conflicts are resolved.

 **Step ❶** Place a sheet of paper in front of you so that the short side is at the top. Fold the paper in half from side to side.

 **Step ❷** Fold the paper again, one inch from the top as shown here.

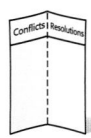 **Step ❸** Unfold the paper and draw lines along all of the folds. This will be your chart.

Step ❹ At the top, label the left column *Conflicts* and the right column *Resolutions.*

Step ❺ As you read, record in the left column the various conflicts that arise in the drama. In the right column, explain how each conflict is resolved by the end of the drama.

You may adapt this simple Foldable in several ways.

- Use it with short stories, longer works of fiction, and many poems—wherever conflicts and their resolutions are important.
- Change the labels to focus on something different. For example, you could record the actions of two characters, or you could record the thoughts and feelings of a character before and after the story's climax.

 Lyric Poem

Reading Objective: to interpret the poet's message by understanding the speaker's thoughts and feelings

As you read the poem, use the following Foldable to help you distinguish between what the speaker *says* and what the poet *means.*

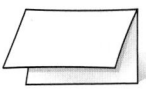 **Step ❶** Place a sheet of paper in front of you so that the short side is at the top. Fold the paper in half from top to bottom.

 **Step ❷** Fold the paper in half again from left to right.

 **Step ❸** Unfold and cut through the top layer of paper along the fold line. This will make two tabs.

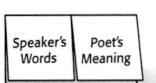 **Step ❹** Label the left tab *Speaker's Words.* Label the right tab *Poet's Meaning.*

Step ❺ Use your Foldable to jot down notes on as you read the poem. Under the left tab, write down key things the speaker says. Under the right tab, write down what you think the poet means by having the speaker say those things.

You may adapt this simple Foldable in several ways.

- Use it to help you visualize the images in a poem. Just replace *Speaker's Words* with *Imagery* and replace *Poet's Meaning* with *What I See.*
- Replace the label *Speaker's Words* with *Speaker's Tone* and under the tab write adjectives that describe the tone of the speaker's words.
- If the poem you are reading has two stanzas, you might devote each tab to notes about one stanza.

Functional Documents

Functional documents are specialized forms of expository writing that serve specifc purposes. Functional documents are an every day part of business, school, and even home life. They must be clear, concise, accurate, and correct in style and usage.

Letter of Application

A letter of application is a form of business writing. It can be used when applying for a job, an internship, or a scholarship. In most cases, the letter is intended to accompany a résumé or an application. Because detailed information is usually included in the accompanying form, a letter of application should provide a general overview of your qualifications and the reasons you are submitting an application. A letter of application should be concise. You should clearly state which position you are applying for and then explain why you are interested and what makes you qualified. The accompanying material should speak for itself.

> 32 South Street
> Austin, Texas 78746
> May 6, 2009
>
> Melissa Reyes
> City Life magazine
> 2301 Davis Avenue
> Austin, Texas 78764
>
> ❶ Re: Internship
> ❷ Dear Ms. Reyes:
> I am a junior at City High School and editor of the City High Herald. I am
> ❸ writing to apply for your summer internship at City Life magazine. As a journalism student and a longtime fan of your magazine, I feel that an internship with your magazine would provide me with valuable experience in the field of journalism. I believe that my role with the City High Herald has
> ❹ given me the skills necessary to be a useful contributor to your magazine this summer. In addition, my enclosed application shows that I am also a
> ❺ diligent worker.
>
> I thank you for considering my application for your summer internship, and I hope to be working with you in the coming months.
>
> Sincerely,
> *Anne Moris*
> Anne Moris

❶ The optional subject line indicates the topic of the letter.

❷ In a business letter, the greeting is followed by a colon.

❸ The writer states her purpose directly and immediately.

❹ The writer comments briefly on her qualifications.

❺ The writer makes reference to the accompanying material.

Activity

Choose a local business where you might like to work. Write a letter of application for an internship at that business. Assume that you will be submitting this letter along with a résumé or an internship application that details your experience and qualifications.

Résumé

The purpose of a résumé is to provide the employer with a comprehensive record of your background information, related experience, and qualifications. Although a résumé is intended to provide a great deal of information, the format is designed to provide this information in the most efficient way possible.

❶ Jane Wiley
909 West Main Street, Apt. #1
Urbana, Illinois 61802
(217) 555-0489 • jane@internet.edu

Goal
Seeking position in television news production

❷ Education
Junior standing in the College of Communications at the University of Illinois, Urbana-Champaign
2005 Graduate of City High School

Honors
Member of National Honor Society

Activities
❸ Member, Asian American Association: 2005–Present
Environmental Committee Chairperson, Asian American Association: August 2006–May 2007

Work Experience
❹ Radio Reporter, WPGU, 107.1 FM, Champaign, Illinois: May 2007–Present
❺ • Rewrote and read stories for afternoon newscasts
• Served as field reporter for general assignments

Cashier, Del's Restaurant, Champaign, Illinois: May 2006–August 2006
• Responsible for taking phone orders
• Cashier for pickup orders

Assistant Secretary, Office of Dr. George Wright, Woodstock, Illinois: May 2005–August 2005
• Answered phones
• Made appointments

❶ Header includes all important contact information.

❷ All important education background is included.

❸ Related dates are included for all listed activities.

❹ Job title is included along with the place of employment.

❺ Job responsibilities are briefly listed, with a parallel structure used in each bulleted item.

Activity
Create an outline that lists the information that you would want to include in a résumé. Use a word processor to help format your outline.

Job Application

When applying for a job, you usually need to fill out a job application. When you fill out the application, read the instructions carefully. Examine the entire form before beginning to fill it out. If you fill out the form by hand, make sure that your handwriting is neat and legible. Fill out the form completely, providing all information directly and honestly. If a question does not apply to you, indicate that by writing *n/a*, short for "not applicable." Keep in mind that you will have the opportunity to provide additional information in your résumé, in your letter of application, or during the interview process.

❶ Please type or print neatly in blue or black ink.

❷ Name: _____ Today's date: _____

Address: _____

Phone #: _____ Birth date: _____ Sex: __ Soc. Sec. #: ___

****

❸ Job History (List each job held, starting with the most recent job.)

1. Employer: _____ Phone #: _____

Dates of employment: _____

Position held: _____

❹ Duties: _____

2. Employer: _____ Phone #: _____

Dates of employment: _____

Position held: _____

Duties: _____

****

Education (List the most recent level of education completed.)

_____

****

Personal References:

1. Name: _____ Phone #: _____

Relationship: _____

2. Name: _____ Phone #: _____

Relationship: _____

❶ The application provides specific instructions.

❷ All of the information requested should be provided in its entirety.

❸ The information should be provided legibly and succinctly.

❹ Experience should be stated accurately and without embellishment.

Activity

Pick up a job application from a local business or use the sample application shown. Complete the application thoroughly. Fill out the application as if you were actually applying for the job. Be sure to pay close attention to the guidelines mentioned above.

Memos

A memorandum (memo) conveys precise information to another person or a group of people. A memo begins with a leading block. It is followed by the text of the message. A memo does not have a formal closing.

TO: All Employees
FROM: Jordan Tyne, Human Resources Manager
❶ SUBJECT: New Human Resources Assistant Director
DATE: November 3, 2009

❷ Please join me in congratulating Daphne Rudy on her appointment as assistant director in the Human Resources Department. Daphne comes to our company with five years of experience in the field. Daphne begins **❸** work on Monday, November 10. All future general human resource inquiries should be directed to Daphne.

Please welcome Daphne when she arrives next week.

❶ The topic of the memo is stated clearly in the subject line.

❷ The announcement is made in the first sentence.

❸ All of the important information is included briefly in the memo.

Business E-mail

E-mail is quickly becoming the most common form of business communication. While e-mail may be the least formal and most conversational method of business writing, it shouldn't be written carelessly or too casually. The conventions of business writing—clarity, attention to your audience, proper grammar, and the inclusion of relevant information—apply to e-mail.

An accurate subject line should state your purpose briefly and directly. Use concise language and avoid rambling sentences.

To: LiamS@internet.com
From: LisaB@internet.com
CC: EricC@internet.com
Date: January 7, 8:13 a.m.
❶ Subject: New Product Conference Call

Liam,

❷ I just wanted to make sure that arrangements have been made for next week's conference call to discuss our new product. The East Coast sales team has already scheduled three sales meetings at the end of the month with potential buyers, so it's important that our sales team is prepared to talk about the product. Please schedule the call when the manufacturing director **❸** is available, since he will have important information for the sales team.

Lisa

❶ Subject line clearly states the topic.

❷ The purpose is stated immediately and in a conversational tone.

❸ Important details are included in a brief, direct fashion.

Activity

Write an e-mail to your coworkers. Inform them of a change in company procedure that will affect them.

Travel Directions

When planning an event or a social occasion, it is often necessary to provide people with detailed directions to the location. These directions must be clear enough that anyone who is unfamiliar with the surrounding area can easily find their way. Creating a map that shows the route with clearly labeled streets can also be a great help.

Directions to Darien High School's Graduation Ceremony

From I-95 North, take Exit 11. **❶**

Turn Left onto Post Road (Route 1).

At the first light, turn Left onto Samuel Avenue. Travel 2.5 miles. **❷**

Turn Right onto Cherry Hill Road.

Turn Left onto High School Lane. **❸**

Follow signs to Visitor Parking.

❶ Begins at a point from which most people will be coming

❷ Offers travel distances to help travelers locate streets

❸ Gives the name of each street along the route

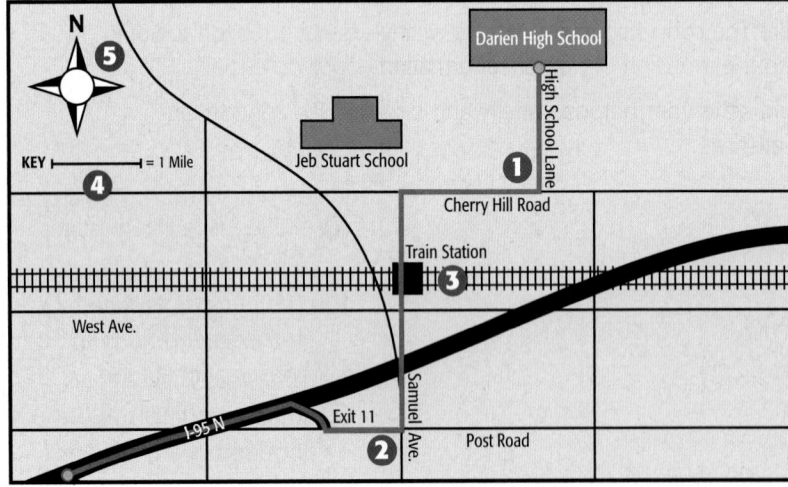

❶ Clearly labels all streets to be traveled

❷ Labels major cross streets so the traveler can keep better track of his or her progress

❸ Includes landmarks to help identify the area

❹ Includes legend to show scale

❺ Includes compass rose to help orientate the traveler

Activity

Write directions and draw an accompanying map to a location in your town. Be sure to include enough details and give enough clear directions so that even someone who is unfamiliar with the area could find the destination.

Technical Writing

Technical writing involves the use of very specific vocabulary and a special attention to detail. The purpose of technical writing is to describe a process clearly enough so that the reader can perform the steps and reach the intended goal, such as installing software, connecting a piece of equipment, or programming a device.

Instructions for Connecting DVD Player to HDTV

1 Your DVD player can be connected to an HDTV using RCA cables or, for best picture quality, an HDMI cable.

Connecting with RCA Cables:

2 **Step 1:** Insert the ends of the red, white, and yellow cables into the jacks labeled "AUDIO/VIDEO OUT." Be sure to match the colors of the cable with the color of the jack.

Step 2: Insert the other ends of the RCA cables into the jacks labeled "AUDIO/VIDEO IN" on your HDTV. These are usually located on the side or the back of the television. Again, be sure to match the colors of the cables with the colors of the jacks.

Connecting with HDMI Cable:

Step 1: Insert one end of the HDMI cable into the HDMI port located on the back of the DVD player.

Step 2: Insert the other end of the HDMI cable into the HDMI port on your HDTV.

3 **Note:** Your HDTV may have more than one HDMI port. If so, be sure that you set your HDTV to the correct input when viewing.

1 Uses specific language to clearly describe the process

2 Lists each step individually

3 Directs attention to possible variations the reader may encounter

Activity

Choose a device that you own or have access to, such as an mp3 player or a cell phone. Write brief step-by-step directions on how to perform a specific function on the device, so that someone else can follow your instructions and perform the function successfully.

Writing Handbook

Using the Traits of Strong Writing

What are some basic terms you can use to discuss your writing with your teacher or classmates? What should you focus on as you revise and edit your compositions? Check out the following terms, or traits, that describe the qualities of strong writing. Learn the meaning of each trait and find out how using the traits can improve your writing.

Ideas

The message or the theme and the details that develop it

Writing is clear when readers can grasp the meaning of your ideas right away. Check to see whether you're getting your message across.

- ☑ Does the title suggest the theme of the composition?

- ☑ Does the composition focus on a single narrow topic?

- ☑ Is the thesis—the main point or central idea—clearly stated?

- ☑ Do well-chosen details elaborate your main point?

Organization

The arrangement of main ideas and supporting details

An effective plan of organization points your readers in the right direction and guides them easily through your composition from start to finish. Find a structure, or order, that best suits your topic and writing purpose. Check to see whether you've ordered your key ideas and details in a way that keeps your readers on track.

- ☑ Are the beginning, middle, and end clearly linked?

- ☑ Is the internal order of ideas easy to follow?

- ☑ Does the introduction capture your readers' attention?

- ☑ Do sentences and paragraphs flow from one to the next in a way that makes sense?

- ☑ Does the conclusion wrap up the composition?

Voice

A writer's unique way of using tone and style

Your writing voice comes through when your readers sense that a real person is communicating with them. Readers will respond to the **tone** (or attitude) that you express toward a topic and to the **style** (the way that you use language and shape your sentences). Read your work aloud to see whether your writing voice comes through.

☑ Does your writing sound interesting?

☑ Does your writing reveal your attitude toward your topic?

☑ Does your writing sound like you—or does it sound like you're imitating someone else?

Word Choice

The vocabulary a writer uses to convey meaning

Words work hard. They carry the weight of your meaning, so make sure you choose them carefully. Check to see whether the words you choose are doing their jobs well.

☑ Do you use lively verbs to show action?

☑ Do you use vivid words to create word pictures in your readers' minds?

☑ Do you use precise words to explain your ideas simply and clearly?

Sentence Fluency

The smooth rhythm and flow of sentences that vary in length and style

The best writing is made up of sentences that flow smoothly from one sentence to the next. Writing that is graceful also sounds musical—rhythmical rather than choppy. Check for sentence fluency by reading your writing aloud.

☑ Do your sentences vary in length and structure?

☑ Do transition words and phrases show connections between ideas and sentences?

☑ Does parallelism help balance and unify related ideas?

Conventions

Correct spelling, grammar, usage, and mechanics

A composition free of errors makes a good impression on your readers. Mistakes can be distracting, and they can blur your message. Try working with a partner to spot errors and correct them. Use this checklist to help you.

☑ Are all words spelled correctly?

☑ Are all proper nouns—as well as the first word of every sentence—capitalized?

☑ Is your composition free of sentence fragments?

☑ Is your composition free of run-on sentences?

☑ Are punctuation marks—such as apostrophes, commas, and end marks—inserted in the right places?

Presenting and Publishing

The formatting of writing for various purposes

For many writers, the writing process is not complete until they present their work to an audience. This can mean submitting your writing for publication in a school paper or a national magazine, or it can simply mean preparing your writing in a neat and presentable format. For readers to fully appreciate your writing, it is very important that you present it neatly, effectively, and according to professional standards.

Format

- The standard typeface setting for most writing submissions is Courier 12 point.
- Double-space your work so that it is easy to read.
- Leave one-inch margins on all sides of every page.
- Italicize titles or when using terms from other languages. You may also italicize words to add emphasis, but do this only when it is necessary to make your point clear. (If you are submitting your writing to a professional publication, underline words that should appear in italics.)
- Most word processing programs make it easy to set the page number to appear in the upper right-hand corner of each page. Include your last name before each page number after the first page.
- If you are including charts, graphs, maps, or other visual aids, consider setting them on their own page. This will allow you to show the graphic at a full size that is easy to read.

Organization

- On a separate sheet of paper, center your name under the title of your work. If you are submitting your writing for publication, include the total number of words in the upper right-hand corner, and your name and address in the upper left-hand corner.
- The body of your work follows immediately.
- End your presentation with you list of works cited.

Research Paper Writing

More than any other type of paper, research papers are the product of a search—a search for data, for facts, for informed opinions, for insights, and for new information.

Selecting a topic

- If a specific topic is not assigned, choose a topic. Begin with the assigned subject or a subject that interests you. Read general sources of information about that subject and narrow your focus to some aspect of it that interests you. Good places to start are encyclopedia articles and the tables of contents of books on the subject. A computerized library catalog will also display many subheads related to general topics. Find out if sufficient information about your topic is available.

- As you read about the topic, develop your paper's central idea, which is the purpose of your research. Even though this idea might change as you do more research, it can begin to guide your efforts. For example, if you were assigned the subject of the Civil War, you might find that you're interested in women's roles during that war. As you read, you might narrow your topic down to women who went to war, women who served as nurses for the Union, or women who took over farms and plantations in the South.

Conducting a broad search for information

- Generate a series of researchable questions about your chosen topic. Then research to find answers to your questions.

- Among the many sources you might use are the card catalog, the computer catalog, the *Reader's Guide to Periodical Literature* (or an electronic equivalent), newspaper indexes, and specialized references such as biographical encyclopedias.

- If possible, use primary sources as well as secondary sources. A **primary source** is a firsthand account of an event—for example, the diary of a woman who served in the army in the Civil War is a primary source. **Secondary sources** are sources written by people who did not experience or influence the event. Locate specific information efficiently by using the table of contents, indexes, chapter headings, and graphic aids.

Developing a working bibliography

If a work seems useful, write a **bibliography card** for it. On an index card, write down the author, title, city of publication, publisher, date of publication, and any other information you will need to identify the source. Number your cards in the upper right-hand corner so you can keep them in order.

Following are model bibliography, or source, cards.

Book

❶ Settle, Mary Lee   ❷ 6
❸ <u>All the Brave Promises.</u>
❹ Columbia: University of
     South Carolina
❺ Press, 1995.

❻ Evanston Public Library   D810.W754

❶ Author   ❺ Date of publication
❷ Source number   ❻ Location of source
❸ Title   ❼ Library call number
❹ City of publication/
     Publisher

Periodicals

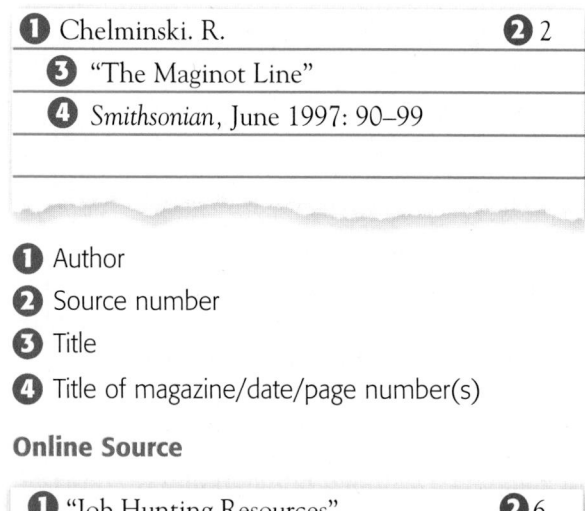

1 Author

2 Source number

3 Title

4 Title of magazine/date/page number(s)

Online Source

1 Title   **4** Sponsoring organization

2 Source number   **5** Date of access

3 Title of database   **6** URL

Evaluating your sources

Your sources should be authoritative, reliable, timely, and suitable **(arts)**.

- The source should be **authoritative.** The author should be well-known in the field. An author who has written several books or articles about a subject or who is frequently quoted may be considered an authority. You might also consult *Book Review Index* and *Book Review Digest* to find out how other experts in the field have evaluated a book or an article.

- The source should be **reliable.** If possible, avoid material from popular magazines in favor of that from more scholarly journals. Be especially careful to evaluate material from online sources. For example, the Web site of a well-known university is more reliable than that of an individual. (You might also consult a librarian or your instructor for guidance in selecting reliable online sources.)

- The source should be **timely.** Use the most recent material available, particularly for subjects of current importance. Check the publication date of books as well as the month and year of periodicals.

- The source should be **suitable,** or **appropriate.** Consider only material that is relevant to the purpose of your paper. Do not waste time on books or articles that have little bearing on your topic. If you are writing on a controversial topic, you should include material that represents more than one point of view.

Compiling and organizing note cards

Careful notes will help you to organize the material for your paper.

- As you reread and study sources, write useful information on index cards. Be sure that each note card identifies the source (use the number of the bibliography card that corresponds to each source).

- In the lower right-hand corner of the card, write the page number on which you found the information. If one card contains several notes, write the page number in parentheses after the relevant material.

- Three helpful ways to take notes are paraphrasing, summarizing, and quoting directly.

  1. **Paraphrase** important details that you want to remember; that is, use your own words to restate specific information.
  2. **Summarize** main ideas that an author presents. When you summarize several pages, be sure to note the page on which the material begins and the page on which it ends—for example, 213–221.
  3. **Quote** the exact words of an author only when the actual wording is important. Be careful about placing the author's words in quotation marks.

- Identify the subject of each note card with a short phrase written in the upper left.

See the sample note card below, which includes information about careers and goals from three pages.

> Careers and goals   12
> Many people "crave work that will
> spark . . . excitement and energy." (5)
> Sher recognizes that a career does
> not necessarily satisfy a person's aim
> in life. (24) She also offers ads on how
> to overcome obstacles that people
> experience in defining their goals. (101)

- Organize your note cards to develop a **working outline.** Begin by sorting them into piles of related cards. Try putting the piles together in different ways that suggest an organizational pattern. (If, at this point, you discover that you do not have enough information, go back and do further research.) Many methods of organization are possible. You might also combine methods of organization.

Developing a thesis statement

A thesis statement tells what your topic is and what you intend to say about it—for example, "World War II changed the lives of African Americans and contributed to the rise of the civil rights movement."

- Start by examining your central idea.
- Refine it to reflect the information that you gathered in your research.
- Next, consider your approach to the topic. What is the purpose of your research? Are you proving or disproving something? illustrating a cause-and-effect relationship? offering a solution to a problem? examining one aspect of the topic thoroughly? predicting an outcome?
- Revise your central idea to reflect your approach.
- Be prepared to revise your thesis statement if necessary.

Drafting your paper

Consult your working outline and your notes as you start to draft your paper.

- Concentrate on getting your ideas down in a complete and logical order.
- Write an introduction and a conclusion. An effective introduction creates interest, perhaps by beginning with a question or a controversial quotation; it should also contain your thesis statement. An effective conclusion will summarize main points, restate your thesis, explain how the research points to important new questions to explore, and bring closure to the paper.

Avoiding Plagiarism

Plagiarism is the act of presenting an author's words or ideas as if they were your own. This is not only illegal, it is also unethical. You must credit the source not only for material directly quoted but also for any facts or ideas obtained from the source.

Consider this example:

From the original SparkNotes study guide by Melissa and Stephanie Martin

> Throughout the novel, Twain depicts the society that surrounds Huck as little more than a collection of degraded rules and precepts that defy logic. This faulty logic appears early in the novel, when the new judge in town allows Pap to keep custody of Huck.

Plagiarized usage

> Twain's depiction of society is as a collection of illogical rules and principles. A good example of this is when Pap is awarded custody of Huck.

Simply rewording the original passage is not enough. In order to legally and ethically use the words or ideas of another writer you must credit the writer of the original or rework the original into your own new idea.

Using Material Without Plagiarizing

1. **Quote the original directly and credit the author.**

   As Melissa and Stephanie Martin note in their SparkNotes study guide, Huck lives in a society that is "little more than a collection of degraded rules and precepts that defy logic." They offer the example of Pap being awarded custody of Huck.

2. **Paraphrase the original and credit the author.**

   In their SparkNotes study guide, Melissa and Stephanie Martin note that Twain's depiction of society is as a collection of illogical rules and principles. A good example of this is when Pap is awarded custody of Huck.

3. **Use the information in the original to create your own idea.**

   It is hard to blame Huck for wanting to escape from a world where he is forced to follow arbitrary rules, and where he is forced to live with an abusive father.

Crediting your source is not only fair to the writer of the original source, it is also the law. Plagiarism is a serious offence and can result in failing grades, expulsion, and even legal action.

- In addition to citing books and periodicals from which you take information, cite song lyrics, letters, and excerpts from literature.

- Also credit original ideas that are expressed graphically in tables, charts, and diagrams, as well as the sources of any visual aids you may include, such as photographs.

- You do not need to cite the source of any information that is common knowledge, such as "John F. Kennedy was assassinated in 1963 in Dallas, Texas."

In-text citations The most common method of crediting sources is with parenthetical documentation within the text. Generally a reference to the source and page number is included in parentheses at the end of each quotation, paraphrase, or summary of information borrowed from a source. An in-text citation points readers to a corresponding entry in your **works-cited list**—a list of all your sources, complete with publication information, that will appear as the final page of your paper. The Modern Language Association (MLA) recommends the following guidelines for crediting sources in text. You may wish to refer to the *MLA Handbook for Writers of Research Papers* by Joseph Gibaldi for more information and examples.

- Put in parentheses the author's last name and the page number where you found the information. An art historian has noted, "In Wood's idyllic farmscapes, man lives in complete harmony with Nature; he is the earth's caretaker" (Corn 90).

- If the author's name is mentioned in the sentence, put only the page number in parentheses. Art historian Wanda Corn has noted, "In Wood's idyllic farmscapes, man lives in complete harmony with Nature; he is the earth's caretaker" (90).

- If no author is listed, put the title or a shortened version of the title in parentheses. Include a page number if you have one. Some critics believe that Grant Wood's famous painting *American Gothic* pokes fun at small-town life and traditional American values ("Gothic").

Compiling a list of works cited

At the end of your text, provide an alphabetized list of published works or other sources cited.

- Include complete publishing information for each source.

- For magazine and newspaper articles, include the page numbers. If an article is continued on a different page, use + after the first page number.

- For online sources, include the date accessed.

- Cite only those sources from which you actually use information.

- Arrange entries in alphabetical order according to the author's last name. Write the last name first. If no author is given, alphabetize by title.

- For long entries, indent five spaces every line after the first.

How to cite sources

On the next three pages, you'll find sample style sheets that can help you prepare your list of sources—the final page of the research paper. Use the one your teacher prefers.

MLA Style

MLA style is most often used in English and social studies classes. Center the title *Works Cited* at the top of your list.

Source	Style
Book with one author	Isaacson, Walter. *Einstein: His Life and Universe.* New York: Simon & Schuster, 2007.
Book with two or three authors	Mortenson, Greg and Relin, David Oliver. *Three Cups of Tea: One Man's Mission to Promote Peace…One School at a Time.* New York: Penguin Books, 2006. [If a book has more than three authors, name only the first author and then write "et al." (Latin abbreviation for "and others")]
Book with editor(s)	Lehman, David and McHugh, Heather, eds. The Best American Poetry 2007. New York: Scribner, 2007.
Book with an organization or a group as author or editor	Adobe Creative Team. *Adobe Photoshop CS3 Classroom in a Book.* Berkeley: Adobe Press, 2007.
Work from an anthology	Kilmer, Joyce. "Trees." *The Poetry Anthology, 1912–2002.* Ed. Joseph Parisi. Chicago: Ivan R. Dee, 2004. 7
Introduction in a published book	Jackson, Peter. Introduction. *The Making of* Star Wars*: The Definitive Story Behind the Original Film.* By. J.W. Rinzler. New York: Del Rey, 2007. iii.
Encyclopedia article	"Jazz." *Encyclopedia Britannica.* 15th ed. 2007.
Weekly magazine article	Sacks, Oliver. "A Bolt from the Blue." *The New Yorker.* 23 July 2007: 38–42.
Monthly magazine article	Plotnikoff, David. "Hungry Man." *Saveur.* July 2007: 35–36.
Newspaper article	Long, Ray and Meitrodt, Jeffrey. "Some Budget Progress Made." *Chicago Tribune.* 26 July 2007: B3. [If no author is named, begin the entry with the title of the article.]
Internet	"Americans Embracing 'Green' Cleaning." *ABC News.* 30 January 2006. ABC News Internet Ventures. 1 August 2007 <http://abcnews.go.com/Technology/Business/story?id=1544322>.
Online magazine article	Parks, Bob. "Robot Buses Pull In to San Diego's Fastest Lane." *Wired Magazine.* 15.08 (July 2007). 25. Oct. 2007 <http://www.wired.com/cars/futuretransport/magazine/15-08/st_robot>.
Radio or TV program	"Jungles." *Planet Earth.* Animal Planet. Discovery Channel. 25 July. 2007.
Videotape or DVD	Guggenheim, David, dir. *An Inconvenient Truth.* DVD. Paramount, 2006. [For a videotape (VHS) version, replace "DVD" with "Videocassette."]
Interview	Campeche, Tanya. E-mail interview. 25 Feb. 2004. [If an interview takes place in person, replace "E-mail" with "Personal"; if it takes place on the telephone, use "Telephone."]

CMS Style

CMS style was created by the University of Chicago Press to meet its publishing needs. This style, which is detailed in *The Chicago Manual of Style* (CMS), is used in a number of subject areas. Center the title *Bibliography* at the top of your list.

Source	Style
Book with one author	Isaacson, Walter. *Einstein: His Life and Universe.* New York: Simon & Schuster, 2007.
Book with two or three authors	Mortenson, Greg and Relin, David Oliver. *Three Cups of Tea: One Man's Mission to Promote Peace…One School at a Time.* New York: Penguin Books, 2006. [If a book has more than ten authors, name only the first seven and then write "et al." (Latin abbreviation for "and others")].
Book with editor(s)	Lehman, David and McHugh, Heather, eds. *The Best American Poetry 2007.* New York: Scribner, 2007.
Book with an organization or a group as author or editor	Adobe Creative Team. *Adobe Photoshop CS3 Classroom in a Book.* Berkeley: Adobe Press, 2007.
Work from an anthology	Kilmer, Joyce. "Trees." *The Poetry Anthology, 1912–2002.* Ed. Joseph Parisi, 7. Chicago: Ivan R. Dee, 2004.
Introduction in a published book	Rinzler, J.W. *The Making of* Star Wars: *The Definitive Story Behind the Original Film.* Introduction by Peter Jackson. New York: Del Rey, 2007.
Encyclopedia article	[Credit for encyclopedia articles goes in your text, not in your bibliography.]
Weekly magazine article	Sacks, Oliver. "A Bolt from the Blue." *The New Yorker,* July 23, 2007, 38–42.
Monthly magazine article	Plotnikoff, David. "Hungry Man." *Saveur.* July 2007, 35–36.
Newspaper article	Long, Ray and Meitrodt, Jeffrey. "Some Budget Progress Made." *Chicago Tribune.* July 26, 2007, B3. [Credit for unsigned newspaper articles goes in your text, not in your bibliography.]
Internet	ABC News Internet Ventures. "Americans Embracing 'Green' Cleaning." *ABC News.* http://abcnews.go.com/Technology/Business/story?id=1544322.
Online magazine article	Parks, Bob. "Robot Buses Pull In to San Diego's Fastest Lane." *Wired Magazine.* 15.08 (July 2007). http://www.wired.com/cars/futuretransport/magazine/15-08/st_robot.
Radio or TV program	[Credit for radio and TV programs goes in your text, not in your bibliography.]
Videotape or DVD	Guggenheim, David, dir. *An Inconvenient Truth.* Paramount, 2006. DVD. [For a videotape (VHS) version, replace "DVD" with "Videocassette."]
Interview	[Credit for interviews goes in your text, not in your bibliography.]

APA Style

The American Psychological Association (APA) style is commonly used in the sciences. Center the title References at the top of your list.

Source	Style
Book with one author	Isaacson, Walter. (2007). *Einstein: His life and universe.* New York: Simon & Schuster.
Book with two or three authors	Mortenson, Greg and Relin, David Oliver. *Three cups of tea: One man's mission to promote peace…One school at a time.* New York: Penguin Books, 2006. [If a book has more than ten authors, name only the first seven and then write "et al." (Latin abbreviation for "and others")].
Book with editor(s)	Lehman, David and McHugh, Heather. (Eds.). (2007). The best American poetry 2007. New York: Scribner.
Book with an organization or a group as author or editor	Adobe Creative Team. (2007). *Adobe Photoshop CS3 Classroom in a Book.* Berkeley: Adobe Press.
Work from an anthology	Kilmer, Joyce. "Trees." *The Poetry Anthology, 1912–2002.* Ed. Joseph Parisi, 7. Chicago: Ivan R. Dee, 2004.
Introduction in a published book	[Credit for introductions goes in your text, not in your references.]
Encyclopedia article	Jazz. (2007). In *Encyclopedia Britannica.* (Vol. 6, pp. 519). Chicago: Encyclopedia Britannica.
Weekly magazine article	Sacks, Oliver. (2007, July 23).A bolt from the blue. *The New Yorker,* 38–42.
Monthly magazine article	Plotnikoff, David. (2007, July). Hungry man. *Saveur,* 103, 35–36.
Newspaper article	Long, Ray and Meitrodt, Jeffrey. (2007, July 26). Some budget progress made. *Chicago Tribune,* p. B3. [If no author is named, begin the entry with the title of the article.]
Internet	ABC News Internet Ventures. (2006, January 30). *ABC News.* "Americans Embracing 'Green' Cleaning." Retrieved August 1, 2007, from http://abcnews. go.com/Technology/Business/story?id=1544322.
Online magazine article	Parks, Bob. (2007, July). Robot buses pull in to San Diego's fastest lane." *Wired Magazine.*15.08.Retreived July 25, 2007, from http://www.wired.com/cars/ futuretransport/magazine/15-08/st_robot.
Radio or TV program	Jungles. (2007, July 25). *Planet Earth* [Television series episode]. Animal Planet. Silver Spring, MD: Discovery Channel.
Videotape or DVD	Guggenheim, David (Director). (2006). *An inconvenient truth.* DVD. Paramount, 2006. [For a videotape (VHS) version, replace "DVD" with "Videocassette."]
Interview	[Credit for interviews goes in your text, not in your bibliography.]

Reading Handbook

Reading Handbook

Being an active reader is a crucial part of being a lifelong learner. It is also an ongoing task. Good reading skills are recursive; that is, they build on each other, providing the tools you'll need to understand text, to interpret ideas and themes, and to read critically.

Understanding Text Structure

To follow the logic and message of a selection and to remember it, analyze the **text structure,** or organization of ideas, within a writer's work. Recognizing the pattern of organization can help you discover the writer's purpose and will focus your attention on important ideas in the selection. **Look for signal words** to point you to the structure.

- **Spatial sequence** uses words or phrases such as *nearby, to the left, above,* and *behind* to show the physical arrangement of people and objects in an area.

- **Order of importance** will use words such as *most important* and *least necessary* to compare the importance of things or ideas.

- **Chronological order** often uses such words as *first, then, after, later,* and *finally* to show a sequence of events in time.

- **Cause-and-effect order** discusses chains of events using words or phrases such as *therefore, because, subsequently,* or *as a result.*

- **Comparison-contrast order** may use words or phrases such as *similarly, in contrast, likewise,* or *on the other hand.*

- **Problem-solution order** presents a problem and then offers one or more solutions. A problem-solution structure may incorporate other structures such as order of importance, chronological order, or comparison-contrast order.

Comprehension Strategies

Because understanding is the most critical reading task, lifelong learners use a wide variety of reading strategies before, during, and after reading to ensure their comprehension.

Determining the Main Idea

The **main idea** of a selection is the writer's purpose in writing the selection. As you read, it will be helpful to determine the main idea not only of the entire piece, but also of each paragraph. After identifying the important details in each paragraph, pause and ask yourself

- What is the main point of this selection?

- What do these details add up to?

- What is the writer trying to communicate?

Summarizing

A summary is a short restatement of the main ideas and important details of a selection. Summarizing what you have read is an excellent tool for understanding and remembering a passage. To summarize a selection:

- Identify the **main ideas.**

- Determine the essential **supporting details.**

- Relate all the main ideas and essential details in a **logical sequence.**

- **Paraphrase**—that is, restate the selection in your own words.

- Answer **who, what, where, when,** and **why** questions.

The best summaries can easily be understood by someone who has not read the selection. If you're not sure whether an idea is a main idea or a supporting detail, try taking it out of your summary. Does your summary still sound complete?

Distinguishing between fact and opinion

It is always important to be able to tell whether the ideas in a selection are facts or the writer's opinions.

- **Facts** can be proven or measured; you can verify them in reference materials. Sometimes you can observe or test them yourself.

  Example: Chicago is about 800 miles from New York City.

- **Opinions** are often open to interpretation and contain phrases such as "I believe" or "from my point of view."

  Example: Chicago to New York is too far to drive.

As you read a selection, evaluate any facts as well as any opinions you find. Ask yourself:

- Are the facts relevant? Are they actually true?
- Are the opinions well informed and based on verifiable facts? Are they persuasive?

Drawing inferences and supporting them

An **inference** involves using your reason and experience to come up with an idea based on what a writer implies or suggests but does not directly state.

- **Drawing a conclusion** is making a general statement you can explain with reason or with supporting details from the text.
- **Making a generalization** is generating a statement that can apply to more than one item or group.

What is most important when inferring is to be sure that you have accurately based your thoughts on supporting details from the text as well as on your own knowledge.

Making a prediction

A **prediction** is an educated guess about what a text will be about based on initial clues a writer provides. You can also make predictions about what will happen next in a story as you read.

- Take breaks during your reading and **ask yourself questions** about what will happen next, such as, "How will this character react to this news?"
- **Answer these questions for yourself,** supporting your answers with evidence from the text. For example, "Sam will be jealous when he hears the news, because he is in love with Antonia."
- As you continue reading, **verify** your predictions.

Reading silently for sustained periods

When you read for long periods of time, your task is to avoid distractions. Check your comprehension regularly by summarizing what you've read so far. Using study guides or graphic organizers can help you get through difficult passages. Take regular breaks when you need them and vary your reading rate with the demands of the task.

Keep in mind:

Whichever strategies you choose to use while reading, it will always be helpful to:

- Read slowly and carefully.
- Reread difficult passages.
- Take careful notes.

Also, when reading more difficult material, consider these steps to modify or change your reading strategies when you don't understand what you've read.

- Reread the passage.
- Consult other sources, including text resources, teachers, and other students.
- Write comments or questions on another piece of paper for later review or discussion.

Language Handbook

Grammar Glossary

This glossary will help you quickly locate information on parts of speech and sentence structure.

A

Absolute phrase. *See* Phrase.

Abstract noun. *See* Noun chart.

Action verb. *See* Verb.

Active voice. *See* Voice.

Adjective A word that modifies a noun or pronoun by limiting its meaning. Adjectives appear in various positions in a sentence. (**The** *gray* **cat purred. The cat is** *gray*.)

Many adjectives have different forms to indicate degree of comparison. (**short, shorter, shortest**)

The positive degree is the simple form of the adjective. (**easy, interesting, good**)

The comparative degree compares two persons, places, things, or ideas. (**easier, more interesting, better**)

The superlative degree compares more than two persons, places, things, or ideas. (**easiest, most interesting, best**)

A predicate adjective follows a linking verb and further identifies or describes the subject. (**The child is happy.**)

A proper adjective is formed from a proper noun and begins with a capital letter. Many proper adjectives are created by adding these suffixes: -*an, -ian, -n, -ese,* and *-ish.* (**Chinese, African**)

Adjective clause. *See* Clause chart.

Adverb A word that modifies a verb, an adjective, or another adverb by making its meaning more specific. When modifying a verb, an adverb may appear in various positions in a sentence. (**Cats** *generally* **eat less than dogs.** *Generally,* **cats eat less than dogs.**) When modifying an adjective or another adverb, an adverb appears directly before the modified word. (**I was** *quite* **pleased that they got along so well.**) The word *not* and the contraction

-n't are adverbs. (**Mike** *wasn't* **ready for the test today.**) Certain adverbs of time, place, and degree also have a negative meaning. (**He's** *never* **ready.**)

Some adverbs have different forms to indicate degree of comparison. (**soon, sooner, soonest**)

The comparative degree compares two actions. (**better, more quickly**)

The superlative degree compares three or more actions. (**fastest, most patiently, least rapidly**)

Adverb clause. *See* Clause chart.

Antecedent. *See* Pronoun.

Appositive A noun or a pronoun that further identifies another noun or pronoun. (**My friend** *Julie* **lives next door.**)

Appositive phrase. *See* Phrase.

Article The adjective *a, an,* or *the.*

Indefinite articles (*a* **and** *an*) refer to one of a general group of persons, places, or things. (**I eat** *an* **apple** *a* **day.**)

The definite article (**the**) indicates that the noun is a specific person, place, or thing. (*The* **alarm woke me up.**)

Auxiliary verb. *See* Verb.

B

Base form. *See* Verb tense.

C

Clause A group of words that has a subject and a predicate and that is used as part of a sentence. Clauses fall into two categories: *main clauses,* which are also called *independent clauses,* and *subordinate clauses,* which are also called *dependent clauses.*

A main clause can stand alone as a sentence.

Types of Subordinate Clauses			
Clause	**Function**	**Example**	**Begins with . . .**
Adjective clause	Modifies a noun or a pronoun	Songs *that have a strong beat* make me want to dance.	A relative pronoun such as *which, who, whom, whose,* or *that*
Adverb clause	Modifies a verb, an adjective, or an adverb	*Whenever Al calls me,* he asks to borrow my bike.	A subordinating conjuction such as *after, although, because, if, since, when,* or *where*
Noun clause	Serves as a subject, an object, or a predicate nominative	*What Philip did* surprised us.	Words such as *how, that, what, whatever, when, where, which, who, whom, whoever, whose,* or *why*

There must be at least one main clause in every sentence. (*The rooster crowed,* and *the dog barked.*)

A subordinate clause cannot stand alone as a sentence. A subordinate clause needs a main clause to complete its meaning. Many subordinate clauses begin with subordinating conjunctions or relative pronouns. (**When Geri sang her solo,** the audience became quiet.) The chart on the next page shows the main types of subordinate clauses.

Collective noun. *See* Noun chart.

Common noun. *See* Noun chart.

Comparative degree. *See* Adjective; Adverb.

Complement A word or phrase that completes the meaning of a verb. The four basic kinds of complements are *direct objects, indirect objects, object complements,* and *subject complements.*

A direct object answers the question *What?* or *Whom?* after an action verb. (**Kari found a dollar. Larry saw Denise.**)

An indirect object answers the question *To whom? For whom? To what?* or *For what?* after an action verb. (**Do me a favor. She gave the child a toy.**)

An object complement answers the question *What?* after a direct object. An object complement is a noun, a pronoun, or an adjective that completes the meaning of a direct object by identifying or describing it. (**The director made me the understudy for the role. The little girl called the puppy hers.**)

A subject complement follows a subject and a linking verb. It identifies or describes a subject. The two kinds of subject complements are *predicate nominatives* and *predicate adjectives.*

A predicate nominative is a noun or pronoun that follows a linking verb and tells more about the subject. (**The author of "The Raven" is Poe.**)

A predicate adjective is an adjective that follows a linking verb and gives more information about the subject. (**Ian became angry at the bully.**)

Complex sentence. *See* Sentence.

Compound preposition. *See* Preposition.

Compound sentence. *See* Sentence.

Compound-complex sentence. *See* Sentence.

Conjunction A word that joins single words or groups of words.

A coordinating conjunction *(and, but, or, nor, for, yet, so)* joins words or groups of words that are equal in grammatical importance. (**David and Ruth are twins. I was bored, so I left.**)

Correlative conjunctions *(both . . . and, just as . . . so, not only . . . but also, either . . . or, neither . . . nor, whether . . . or)* work in pairs to join words and groups of words of equal importance.

(Choose *either* the muffin *or* the bagel.)

A subordinating conjunction *(after, although, as if, because, before, if, since, so that, than, though, until, when, while)* joins a dependent idea or clause to a main clause. (Beth acted *as if* she felt ill.)

Conjunctive adverb An adverb used to clarify the relationship between clauses of equal weight in a sentence. Conjunctive adverbs are used to replace *and (also, besides, furthermore, moreover)*; to replace *but (however, nevertheless, still)*; to state a result *(consequently, therefore, so, thus)*; or to state equality *(equally, likewise, similarly).* (Ana was determined to get an A; *therefore,* she studied often.)

Coordinating conjunction. *See* Conjunction.

Correlative conjunction. *See* Conjunction.

D

Declarative sentence. *See* Sentence.

Definite article. *See* Article.

Demonstrative pronoun. *See* Pronoun.

Direct object. *See* Complement.

E

Emphatic form. *See* Verb tense.

F

Future tense. *See* Verb tense.

G

Gerund A verb form that ends in *-ing* and is used as a noun. A gerund may function as a subject, the object of a verb, or the object of a preposition. (*Smiling* uses fewer muscles than *frowning.* Marie enjoys *walking.*)

Gerund phrase. *See* Phrase.

I

Imperative mood. *See* Mood of verb.

Imperative sentence. *See* Sentence chart.

Indicative mood. *See* Mood of verb.

Indirect object. *See* Complement.

Infinitive A verb form that begins with the word *to* and functions as a noun, an adjective, or an adverb. (No one wanted *to answer.*) Note: When *to* precedes a verb, it is not a preposition but instead signals an infinitive.

Infinitive phrase. *See* Phrase.

Intensive pronoun. *See* Pronoun.

Interjection A word or phrase that expresses emotion or exclamation. An interjection has no grammatical connection to other words. Commas follow mild ones; exclamation points follow stronger ones. (*Well,* have a good day. *Wow!*)

Interrogative pronoun. *See* Pronoun.

Intransitive verb. *See* Verb.

Inverted order In a sentence written in *inverted order,* the predicate comes before the subject. Some sentences are written in inverted order for variety or special emphasis. (Up the beanstalk *scampered Jack.*) The subject also generally follows the predicate in a sentence that begins with *here* or *there.* (*Here* was the solution to his problem.) Questions, or interrogative sentences, are generally written in inverted order. In many questions, an auxiliary verb precedes the subject, and the main verb follows it. (*Has* anyone *seen* Susan?) Questions that begin with *who* or *what* follow normal word order.

Irregular verb. *See* Verb tense.

L

Linking verb. *See* Verb.

M

Main clause. *See* Clause.

Mood of verb A verb expresses one of three moods: indicative, imperative, or subjunctive.

The indicative mood is the most common. It makes a statement or asks a question. (We *are* out of bread. *Will* you *buy* it?)

The imperative mood expresses a command or makes a request. (*Stop* acting like a child! Please *return* my sweater.)

Types of Nouns		
Noun	Function	Examples
Abstract noun	Names an idea, a quality, or a characteristic	capitalism, terror
Collective noun	Names a group of things or persons	herd, troop
Common noun	Names a general type of person, place, thing, or idea	city, building
Compound noun	Is made up of two or more words	checkerboard, globe-trotter
Noun of direct addrress	Identifies the person or persons being spoken to	*Maria,* please stand.
Possessive noun	Shows possession, ownership, or the relationship between two nouns	my *sister's* room
Proper noun	Names a particular person, place, thing, or idea	Cleopatra, Italy, Christianity

The subjunctive mood is used to express, indirectly, a demand, suggestion, or statement of necessity (**I demand that he** *stop* **acting like a child. It's necessary that she** *buy* **more bread.**) The subjunctive is also used to state a condition or wish that is contrary to fact. This use of the subjunctive requires the past tense. (**If you** *were* **a nice person, you** *would return* **my sweater.**)

N

Nominative pronoun. *See* Pronoun.

Noun A word that names a person, a place, a thing, or an idea. The chart on this page shows the main types of nouns.

Noun clause. *See* Clause chart.

Noun of direct address. *See* Noun chart.

Number A noun, pronoun, or verb is *singular* in number if it refers to one; *plural* if it refers to more than one.

O

Object. *See* Complement.

P

Participle A verb form that can function as an adjective. Present participles always end in *-ing.* (**The**
woman comforted the *crying* child.) Many past participles end in *-ed.* (**We bought the beautifully** *painted* **chair.**) However, irregular verbs form their past participles in some other way. (**Cato was Caesar's** *sworn* **enemy.**)

Passive voice. *See* Voice.

Past tense. *See* Verb tense.

Perfect tense. *See* Verb tense.

Personal pronoun. *See* Pronoun, Pronoun chart.

Phrase A group of words that acts in a sentence as a single part of speech.

An absolute phrase consists of a noun or pronoun that is modified by a participle or participial phrase but has no grammatical relation to the complete subject or predicate. (***The vegetables being done,* we finally sat down to eat dinner.**)

An appositive phrase is an appositive along with any modifiers. If not essential to the meaning of the sentence, an appositive phrase is set off by commas. (**Jack plans to go to the jazz concert,** *an important musical event.*)

A gerund phrase includes a gerund plus its complements and modifiers. (***Playing the flute* is her hobby.**)

An infinitive phrase contains the infinitive plus its complements and modifiers. (**It is time *to leave for school.***)

A participial phrase contains a participle and any modifiers necessary to complete its meaning. (**The woman** *sitting over there* **is my grandmother.**)

A prepositional phrase consists of a preposition, its object, and any modifiers of the object. A prepositional phrase can function as an adjective, modifying a noun or a pronoun. (**The dog** *in the yard* **is very gentle.**) A prepositional phrase may also function as an adverb when it modifies a verb, an adverb, or an adjective. (**The baby slept** *on my lap.*)

A verb phrase consists of one or more auxiliary verbs followed by a main verb. (**The job** *will have been completed* **by noon tomorrow.**)

Positive degree. *See* Adjective.

Possessive noun. *See* Noun chart.

Predicate The verb or verb phrase and any objects, complements, or modifiers that express the essential thought about the subject of a sentence.

A simple predicate is a verb or verb phrase that tells something about the subject. (**We** *ran.*)

A complete predicate includes the simple predicate and any words that modify or complete it. (**We** *solved the problem in a short time.*)

A compound predicate has two or more verbs or verb phrases that are joined by a conjunction and share the same subject. (**We** *ran to the park and began to play baseball.*)

Predicate adjective. *See* Adjective; Complement.

Predicate nominative. *See* Complement.

Preposition A word that shows the relationship of a noun or pronoun to some other word in the sentence. Prepositions include *about, above, across, among, as, behind, below, beyond, but, by, down, during, except, for, from, into, like, near, of, on, outside, over, since, through, to, under, until, with.* (**I usually eat breakfast** *before* **school.**)

A compound preposition is made up of more than one word. (**according to, ahead of, as to, because of, by means of, in addition to, in spite of, on account of**) (**We played the game** *in spite of* **the snow.**)

Prepositional phrase. *See* Phrase.

Present tense. *See* Verb tense.

Progressive form. *See* Verb tense.

Pronoun A word that takes the place of a noun, a group of words acting as a noun, or another pronoun. The word or group of words that a pronoun refers to is called its antecedent. (**In the following sentence,** *Mari* **is the antecedent of** *she. Mari likes Mexican food, but she doesn't like Italian food.*)

A demonstrative pronoun points out specific persons, places, things, or ideas. (*this, that, these, those*)

An indefinite pronoun refers to persons, places, or things in a more general way than a noun does. (*all, another, any, both, each, either, enough, everything, few, many, most, much, neither, nobody, none, one, other, others, plenty, several, some*)

An intensive pronoun adds emphasis to another noun or pronoun. If an intensive pronoun is omitted, the meaning of the sentence will be the same. (**Rebecca** *herself* **decided to look for a part-time job.**)

An interrogative pronoun is used to form questions. (*who? whom? whose? what? which?*)

A personal pronoun refers to a specific person or thing. Personal pronouns have three cases: nominative, possessive, and objective. The case depends upon the function of the pronoun in a sentence. The first chart on this page shows the case forms of personal pronouns.

A reflexive pronoun reflects back to a noun or pronoun used earlier in the sentence, indicating that the same person or thing is involved. (**We told** *ourselves* **to be patient.**)

A relative pronoun is used to begin a subordinate clause. (*who, whose, that, what, whom, whoever, whomever, whichever, whatever*)

Proper adjective. *See* Adjective.

Proper noun. *See* Noun chart.

R

Reflexive pronoun. *See* Pronoun.

Relative pronoun. *See* Pronoun.

S

Sentence A group of words expressing a complete thought. Every sentence has a subject and a predicate. Sentences can be classified by function or by structure. The second chart on this page shows the categories by function; the following subentries describe the categories by structure. *See also* Subject; Predicate; Clause.

A simple sentence has only one main clause and no subordinate clauses. *(Alan found an old violin.)* A simple sentence may contain a compound subject or a compound predicate or both. *(Alan and Teri found an old violin. Alan found an old violin and tried to play it. Alan and Teri found an old violin and tried to play it.)* The subject and the predicate can be expanded with adjectives, adverbs, prepositional phrases, appositives, and verbal phrases. As long as the sentence has only one main clause, however, it remains a simple sentence. *(Alan, rummaging in the attic, found an old violin.)*

A compound sentence has two or more main clauses. Each main clause has its own subject and predicate, and these main clauses are usually joined by a comma and a coordinating conjunc-tion. *(Cats meow, and dogs bark, but ducks quack.)* Semicolons may also be used to join the main clauses in a compound sentence. *(The helicopter landed; the pilot had saved four passengers.)*

A complex sentence has one main clause and one or more subordinate clauses. *(Since the movie starts at eight, we should leave here by seven-thirty.)*

A compound-complex sentence has two or more main clauses and at least one subordinate clause. *(If we leave any later, we may miss the previews, and I want to see them.)*

Simple predicate. *See* Predicate.

Simple subject. *See* Subject.

Subject The part of a sentence that tells what the sentence is about.

A simple subject is the main noun or pronoun in the subject. *(Babies crawl.)*

A complete subject includes the simple subject and any words that modify it. *(The man from New Jersey won the race.)* In some sentences, the simple subject and the complete subject are the same. *(Birds fly.)*

Personal Pronouns			
Clause	Singular Pronouns	Plural Pronouns	Function in Sentence
Nominative	I, you, she, he, it	we, you, they	subject or predicate nominative
Objective	me, you, her, him, it	us, you, them	direct object, indirect object, or object of a preposition

Types of Sentences			
Sentence Type	Function	Ends with . . .	Examples
Declarative sentence	Makes a statement	A period	I did not enjoy the movie.
Exclamatory sentence	Expresses strong emotion	An exclamation point	What a good writer Consuela is!
Imperative sentence	Makes a request or gives a command	A period or an exclamation point	Please come to the party. Stop!
Interrogative sentence	Asks a question	A question mark	Is the composition due?

A compound subject has two or more simple subjects joined by a conjunction. The subjects share the same verb. (*Firefighters* and *police officers* protect the community.)

Subjunctive mood. *See* Mood of verb.

Subordinate clause. *See* Clause.

Subordinating conjunction. *See* Conjunction.

Superlative degree. *See* Adjective; Adverb.

T

Tense. *See* Verb tense.

Transitive verb. *See* Verb.

V

Verb A word that expresses action or a state of being. *(cooks, seem, laughed)*

An action verb tells what someone or something does. Action verbs can express either physical or mental action. (**Crystal** *decided* to *change* **the tire herself.**)

A transitive verb is an action verb that is followed by a word or words that answer the question *What?* or *Whom?* (**I** *held* **the baby.**)

An intransitive verb is an action verb that is not followed by a word that answers the question *What?* or *Whom?* (**The baby** *laughed.*)

A linking verb expresses a state of being by linking the subject of a sentence with a word or an expression that identifies or describes the subject. (**The lemonade** *tastes* **sweet. He** *is* **our new principal.**) The most commonly used linking verb is be in all its forms *(am, is, are, was, were, will be, been, being).* Other linking verbs include *appear, become, feel, grow, look, remain, seem, sound, smell, stay, taste.*

An auxiliary verb, or helping verb, is a verb that accompanies the main verb to form a verb phrase. (**I** *have been* **swimming.**) The forms of *be* and *have* are the most common auxiliary verbs: *(am, is, are, was, were, being, been; has, have, had, having).* Other auxiliaries include *can, could, do, does, did, may, might, must, shall, should, will, would.*

Verbal A verb form that functions in a sentence as a noun, an adjective, or an adverb. The three kinds of verbals are gerunds, infinitives, and participles. *See* Gerund; Infinitive; Participle.

Verb tense The tense of a verb indicates when the action or state of being occurs. All the verb tenses are formed from the four principal parts of a verb: a base form *(talk)*, a present participle *(talking)*, a simple past form *(talked)*, and a past participle *(talked)*. A regular verb forms its simple past and past participle by adding *-ed* to the base form. *(climb, climbed)* An irregular verb forms its past and past participle in some other way. *(get, got, gotten)*

In addition to present, past, and future tenses, there are three perfect tenses.

The present perfect tense expresses an action or a condition that occurred at some indefinite time in the past. This tense also shows an action or a condition that began in the past and continues into the present. (**She** *has played* **the piano for four years.**)

The past perfect tense indicates that one past action or condition began *and* ended before another past action started. (**Andy** *had finished* **his homework before I even began mine.**)

The future perfect tense indicates that one future action or condition will begin *and* end before another future event starts. Use *will have* or *shall have* with the past participle of a verb. (**By tomorrow, I** *will have finished* **my homework, too.**)

The progressive form of a verb expresses a continuing action with any of the six tenses. To make the progressive forms, use the appropriate tense of the verb *be* with the present participle of the main verb. (**She** *is swimming.* **She** *has been swimming.*)

The emphatic form adds special force, or emphasis, to the present and past tense of a verb. For the emphatic form, use *do, does,* or *did* with the base form. (**Toshi** *did want* **that camera.**)

Voice The voice of a verb shows whether the subject performs the action or receives the action of the verb.

A verb is in the active voice if the subject of the sentence performs the action. (**The referee** *blew* **the whistle.**)

A verb is in the passive voice if the subject of the sentence receives the action of the verb. (**The whistle** *was blown* **by the referee.**)

Troubleshooter

The Troubleshooter will help you recognize and correct errors that you might make in your writing.

Sentence Fragment

Problem: A fragment that lacks a subject
The grass is wet. Can't be mowed now.

Solution: Add a subject to the fragment to make it a complete sentence.
The grass is wet. It can't be mowed now.

Problem: A fragment that lacks a complete verb
We enjoyed our dinner. Beans, rice, and salad.
The storm was fierce. The wind blowing hard.

Solution A: Add either a complete verb or a helping verb to make the sentence complete.
We enjoyed our dinner. Beans, rice, and salad make a good meal.
The storm was fierce. The wind was blowing hard.

Solution B: Combine the fragment with another sentence.
We enjoyed our dinner of beans, rice, and salad.
The storm was fierce with the wind blowing hard.

Problem: A fragment that is a subordinate clause
We went to the park. Where we had often gone before.
Jan won the swimming medal. Which she gave to her parents.

Solution A: Combine the fragment with another sentence.
We went to the park, where we had often gone before.
Jan won the swimming medal, which she gave to her parents.

Solution B: Rewrite the fragment as a complete sentence, eliminating the subordinating conjunction or the relative pronoun and adding a subject or other words necessary to make a complete thought.
We went to the park. We had often gone there before.
Jan won the swimming medal. She gave it to her parents.

Problem: A fragment that lacks both a subject and a verb
The birds woke us with their songs. At six in the morning.

Solution: Combine the fragment with another sentence.
The birds woke us with their songs at six in the morning.

Rule of Thumb: Sentence fragments can make your writing hard to understand. Make sure every sentence has a subject and a verb.

Note: In almost all of the writing you do, especially for school, you should avoid sentence fragments. However, sentence fragments can be used to create special effects, such as adding emphasis or conveying realistic dialogue.
"Not again!" she cried.
The pizza was gone. All of it.

Run-On Sentence

Problem: Comma splice—two main clauses separated only by a comma
The sky is pitch black, there is no moon.

Solution A: Replace the comma with an end mark of punctuation, such as a period or a question mark, and begin the new sentence with a capital letter.
The sky is pitch black. There is no moon.

Solution B: Place a semicolon between the two main clauses.
The sky is pitch black; there is no moon.

Solution C: Add a coordinating conjunction after the comma.
The sky is pitch black, and there is no moon.

Problem: Two main clauses with no punctuation between them.
We picked the apples then we made pies.

Solution A: Separate the main clauses with an end mark of punctuation, such as a period or question mark, and begin the second sentence with a capital letter.
We picked the apples. Then we made pies.

Solution B: Separate the main clauses with a semicolon.
We picked the apples; then we made pies.

Solution C: Add a comma and a coordinating conjunction between the main clauses.
We picked the apples, and then we made pies.

Problem: The main clauses with no comma before the coordinating conjunction
Elephants still live in the wild but they are endangered.

Solution: Add a comma before the coordinating conjunction to separate the two main clauses.
Elephants still live in the wild, but they are endangered.

Rule of Thumb: It often helps to have someone else read your longer sentences to see if they are clear. Since you know what the sentences are supposed to mean, you might miss the need for punctuation.

Lack of Subject-Verb Agreement

Problem: A subject that is separated from the verb by an intervening prepositional phrase
Ten pieces of the puzzle is on the floor.
The shoe department in each of our stores are closing.

Solution: Make the verb agree with the subject, which is never the object of a preposition.
Ten pieces of the puzzle are on the floor.
The shoe department in each of our stores is closing.

Problem: A predicate nominative that differs in number from the subject
Hamburgers is tonight's dinner.
Tonight's dinner are hamburgers.

Solution: Ignore the predicate nominative, and make the verb agree with the subject of the sentence.
Hamburgers are tonight's dinner.
Tonight's dinner is hamburgers.

Problem: A subject that follows the verb
On my desk is two letters from my dad.
Here is my answers to them both.

Solution: In an inverted sentence look for the subject after the verb. Then make sure the verb agrees with the subject.
On my desk are two letters from my dad.
Here are my answers to them both.

Rule of Thumb: Reversing the order of an inverted sentence may help you decide on the verb form to use: "My answers to them both are here."

Problem: A collective noun as the subject
The cross country team are in first place.
The team gathers at the captain's house after each meet.

Solution A: If the collective noun refers to a group as a whole, use a singular verb.
The cross country team is in first place.

Solution B: If the collective noun refers to each member of a group individually, use a plural verb.
The team gather at the captain's house after each meet.

Problem: A noun of amount as the subject
Five bushels are a great many tomatoes.
Three marbles is in my pocket.

Solution: Determine whether the noun of amount refers to one unit and is therefore singular or whether it refers to a number of individual unites and is therefore plural.
Five bushels is a great many tomatoes.
Three marbles are in my pocket.

Problem: A compound subject that is joined by *and*
The hill and the lake makes a lovely setting for a picnic.
Spaghetti and meatballs are her favorite dinner.

Solution A: If the parts of the compound subject do not belong to one unit or if they refer to different people of things, use a plural verb.
The hill and the lake make a lovely setting for a picnic.

Solution B: If the parts of the compound subject belong to one unit or if both parts refer to the same person or thing, use a singular verb.
Spaghetti and meatballs is her favorite dinner.

Problem: A compound subject that is joined by *or* or *nor*
Neither those trees nor that shrub are healthy.

Solution: Make the verb agree with the subject that is closer to it.
Neither those trees nor that shrub is healthy.

Problem: A compound subject that is preceded *by many a, every,* or *each*
Many a dog and cat ends up in an animal shelter or a pound.

Solution: When *many a, every,* or *each* precedes a compound subject, the subject is considered singular. Use a singular verb.
Many a dog and cat ends up in an animal shelter or a pound.

Problem: A subject that is separated from the verb by an intervening expression
That issue, as well as several others, are bothering me.

Solution: Certain expressions, such as these beginning with *as well as, in addition to,* and *together with,* do not change the number of the subject. Ignore an intervening expression between a subject and its verb, and make the verb agree with the subject.
That issue, along with several others, is bothering me.

Problem: An indefinite pronoun as the subject
Neither of the boys are on time.

Solution: Determine whether the indefinite pronoun is singular or plural, and make the verb agree. Some indefinite pronouns are singular—*another, anyone, everyone, one, each, either, neither, anything, everything, something,* and *somebody.* Some are plural—*both, many, few, several,* and *others.* Some can be singular or plural—*some, all, any, more, most,* and *none.* In these cases, find the noun to which the pronoun refers to determine which verb form to use.
Neither of the boys is on time.

Lack of Pronoun-Antecedent Agreement

Problem: A singular antecedent that can be either male or female.
A climber must check his equipment carefully.

Solution A: Traditionally, a masculine pronoun has been used to refer to an antecedent that may be either male or female. This usage ignores or excludes females. Reword the sentence to use *he or she, him or her,* and so on.
A climber must check his or her equipment carefully.

Solution B: Reword the sentence so that both the antecedent and the pronoun are plural.
Climbers must check their equipment carefully.

Solution C: Reword the sentence to eliminate the pronoun.
A climber must check the equipment carefully.

Rule of Thumb: Although you may see the masculine forms used exclusively in older literature, they are not acceptable in contemporary writing.

Problem: A second-person pronoun that refers to a third-person antecedent
Juan likes sitcoms that make you think as well as laugh.

Solution A: Use the appropriate third-person pronoun.
Juan likes sitcoms that make him think as well as laugh.

Solution B: Use an appropriate noun instead of a pronoun.
Juan likes sitcoms that make people think as well as laugh.

Problem: A singular indefinite pronoun as an antecedent
Each of the volumes has their own index.

Solution: *Each, every, either, neither,* and *one* are singular and therefore require singular personal pronouns even when followed by a prepositional phrase that contains a plural noun.
Each of the volumes has its own index.

Rule of Thumb: To help you remember that *each, either,* and *neither* are singular, think *each one, either one,* and *neither one.*

Lack of Clear Pronoun Reference [Unclear Antecedent]

Problem: A pronoun reference that is weak or vague
We spent several weeks at the farm this summer, and it was exciting.
The label says to shake it before pouring a serving.

Solution A: Rewrite the sentence, adding a clear antecedent for the pronoun.
We spent our vacation at the farm this summer, and it was exciting.

Solution B: Rewrite the sentence, substituting a noun for the pronoun.

The label says to shake the bottle of salad dressing before pouring a serving.

Problem: A pronoun that could refer to more than one antecedent

Lauren and Abby wrote six songs, and she recorded them all.

Don't buy a car from that dealership: it will let you down.

Solution A: Rewrite the sentence, substituting a noun for the pronoun.

Lauren and Abby wrote six songs, and Abby recorded them all.

Solution B: Rewrite the sentence, making the antecedent of the pronoun clear.

A car from that dealership will let you down; don't buy one there.

Problem: The indefinite use of *you* or *they*

You just have to laugh at that scene in the movie.
They say the weather will be clear tomorrow.

Solution A: Rewrite the sentence, substituting a noun for the pronoun.

The audience just has to laugh at that scene in the movie.

Solution B: Rewrite the sentence, eliminating the pronoun entirely.

According to the forecast, the weather will be clear tomorrow.

Shift in Pronoun

Problem: An incorrect shift in person between two pronouns

Lynn likes the front seat, where you are most comfortable.

The Chins planted a maple on the south side of the house, where you need shade the most.

Solution A: Replace the incorrect pronoun with a pronoun that agrees with its a antecedent.

Lynn likes the front seat, where she is most comfortable.

Solution B: Replace the incorrect pronoun with an appropriate noun.

The Chins plants a maple on the south side of the house, where the house needs shade the most.

Shift in Verb Tense

Problem: An unnecessary shift in tense.

The children will give their mother flowers, and they kiss her.
After the party ended, we go home.

Solution: When two or more events occur at the same time, be sure to use the same verb tense to describe each event.

The children will give their mother flowers, and they will kiss her.
After the party ended, we went home.

Problem: A lack of correct shift in tenses to show that one event precedes or follows another

By the time the concert ended, we sat for four hours.

Solution: When two past events being described have occurred at different times, shift from the past tense to the past perfect tense to indicate that one action began and ended before another past action began. Use the past perfect tense for the earlier of the two actions.

By the time the concert ended, we had sat for four hours.

Rule of Thumb: When you need to use several verb tenses in your writing, it may help to first jot down the sequence of events you're writing about. Be clear in your mind what happened first, next, last.

Incorrect Verb Tense or Form

Problem: An incorrect or missing verb ending

When I began taking lessons, I learn about quarter, half, and whole notes.
I had start the lessons two months ago.

Solution: Add −ed to a regular verb to form the past tense and the past participle.

When I began taking lessons, I learned about quarter, half, and whole notes.
I had started the lessons two months ago.

Problem: An improperly formed irregular verb

James brung the book back to the library.
Catherine has writed six pages on that topic.

Solution: Irregular verbs form their past and past participles in some way other than by adding −ed. Memorize these forms, or look them up.

James brought the book back to the library.
Catherine has written six pages on that topic.

Problem: Confusion between the past form and the past participle
We have ate too many apples.
She had swam the Chesapeake last July.

Solution: Use the past participle form of an irregular verb, not the past form, when you use the auxiliary verb *have.*
We have eaten too many apples.
She had swum the Chesapeake last July.

Problem: Improper use of the past participle
The catcher thrown several runners out.
The DiCaprios done a fine job rearing those children.

Solution A: The past participle of an irregular verb cannot stand alone as a verb. Add a form of the auxiliary verb *have* to the past participle to form a complete verb.
The catcher had thrown several runners out.
The DiCaprios have done a fine job rearing those children.

Solution B: Replace the past participle with the past form of the verb.
The catcher threw several runners out.
The DiCaprios did a fine job rearing those children.

Misplaced or Dangling Modifier

Problem: A misplaced modifier
The children were swimming in the photograph.
Swooping down on a fish, I spotted the gull.
I saw a man at the movies eating popcorn.

Solution: Modifiers that modify the wrong word or seem to modify more than own word in a sentence are called misplaced modifiers. Move the misplaced phrase as close as possible to the word or words it modifies.
The children in the photograph were swimming.
I spotted the gull swooping down on a fish.
I saw a man eating popcorn at the movies.

Problem: Incorrect placement of the adverb *only*
Tricia only has enough money to buy a pencil.

Solution: Place the adverb only immediately before the word or group of words it modifies.
Only Tricia has enough money to buy a pencil.
Tricia has enough money to buy only a pencil.
Tricia has only enough money to buy a pencil.

Rule of Thumb: Note that each time *only* is moved,

the meaning of the sentence changes. Check to be sure your sentence says what you mean.

Problem: A dangling modifier
Croaking loudly, I listened to the sounds of the frogs in the bog.
Stealing home, the game was won for the Pirates.

Solution: Dangling modifiers do not seem to logically modify any word in the sentence. Rewrite the sentence, adding a noun to which the dangling phrase clearly refers. Often you will have to add other words too.
I listened to the sounds of the frogs croaking loudly in the bog.
Stealing home, Layla won the game for the Pirates.

Missing or Misplaced Possessive Apostrophe

Problem: Singular nouns
The womans child loved the circus trapeze artists.

Solution: Use an apostrophe and –s to form the possessive of a singular noun, even one that ends in *s.*
The woman's child loved the circus's trapeze artist.

Problem: Plural nouns ending in – s
The hikers cars were parked at the base of the trail.

Solution: Use an apostrophe alone to form the possessive of a plural noun that ends in –s.
The hikers' cars were parked at the base of the trail.

Problem: Plural nouns not ending in –s
Did Brian join the mens group?

Solution: Use an apostrophe and –s to form the possessive of a plural noun that does not end in –s.
Did Brian join the men's group?

Problem: Pronouns
Everyones contribution helps.
These pencils are your's, and those pencils are their's.

Solution A: Use an apostrophe and –s to form the possessive of a singular indefinite pronoun.
Everyone's contribution helps.

Solution B: Do not use an apostrophe with any of the possessive personal pronouns.
These pencils are yours, and those pencils are theirs.

Problem: Confusion between *its* and *it's*
Will you tell me when its ten o'clock?
The cat licked it's fur.

Solution: Do not use an apostrophe to form the possessive of *it*. Use an apostrophe to form the contraction of *it is*.
Will you tell me when it's ten o'clock?
The cat licked its fur.

Missing Commas with Nonessential Element

Problem: Missing commas with nonessential participles, infinitives, and their phrases
Pounding hard on the roof the rain awakened me.
The whole set of cups chipped from many years of use was discarded.
To answer you question this software package is worth the price.

Solution: Determine whether the participle, infinitive, or phrase is essential to the meaning of the sentence. If it is not essential, set off the phrase with commas.
Pounding hard on the roof, the rain awakened me.
The whole set of cups, chipped from many years of use, was discarded.
To answer your question, this software package is worth the price.

Problem: Missing commas with nonessential adjective clauses
My mother who is a very generous woman gave us investment tips.

Solution: Determine whether the clause is essential to the meaning of the sentence. If it is not essential, set off the clause with commas.
My mother, who is a very generous woman, gave us investment tips.

Problem: Missing comas with nonessential appositives
John the lead-off batter singles on a line drive

Solution: Determine whether the appositive is essential to the meaning of the sentence. If it is not essential, set off the appositive with commas.
John, the lead-off batter, singled on a line drive.

Rule of Thumb: To determine whether a word or phrase is essential, try reading the sentence without it.

Problem: Missing commas with interjections and parenthetical expressions
Wow what a great cat that is
On Saturdays as a rule we sleep late.

Solution: Set off the interjection or parenthetical expression with commas.
Wow, what a great cat that is!
On Saturdays, as a rule, we sleep late.

Missing Commas in a Series

Problem: Missing commas in a series of words, phrases, or clauses
Alicia Nirupam and Matt made the honor roll.
Mark made the dough kneaded it and left it to rise
The firefighter carries the child out of the apartment down the stairs and into the arms of her mother.
Joe pitched the tent Meg gathered firewood and Bud unloaded the truck.

Solution: When there are three or more elements in a series, use a comma after each element that precedes the conjunction
Alicia, Nirupam, and Matt made the honor roll.
Mark made the dough, kneaded it, and left it to rise.
The firefighter carries the child out of the apartment, down the stairs, and into the arms of her mother.
Joe pitched the tent, Meg gathered firewood, and Bud unloaded the truck.

Rule of Thumb: When you're having difficulty with a rule of usage, try rewriting the rule in your own words. Then check with your teacher to be sure you have grasped the concept.

Mechanics

This section will help you use correct capitalization, punctuation, and abbreviations in your writing.

Capitalization

This section will help you recognize and use correct capitalization in sentences.

Rule: Capitalize the first word in any sentence, including direct quotations and sentences in parentheses unless they are included in another sentence.

Example: *She said, "Come back soon."*

Example: *Emily Dickinson became famous only after her death. (She published only six poems during her lifetime.)*

Rule: Always capitalize the pronoun *I* no matter where it appears in the sentence.

Example: *Some of my relatives think that I should become a doctor.*

Rule: Capitalize proper nouns, including
a. names of individuals and titles used in direct address preceding a name or describing a relationship.
Example: *George Washington; Dr. Morgan; Aunt Margaret*

b. names of ethnic groups, national groups, political parties and their members, and languages.
Example: *Italian Americans; Aztec; the Republican Party; a Democrat; Spanish*

c. names of organizations, institutions, firms, monuments, bridges, buildings, and other structures.
Example: *Red Cross; Stanford University; General Electric; Lincoln Memorial; Tappan Zee Bridge; Chrysler Building; Museum of Natural History*

d. trade names and names of documents, awards, and laws.
Example: *Microsoft; Declaration of Independence; Pulitzer Prize; Sixteenth Amendment*

e. geographical terms and regions or localities.
Example: *Hudson River; Pennsylvania Avenue; Grand Canyon; Texas; the Midwest*

f. names of planets and other heavenly bodies.
Example: *Venus; Earth; the Milky Way*

g. names of ships, planes, trains, and spacecraft.
Example: *USS Constitution; Spirit of St. Louis; Apollo 11*

h. names of most historical events, eras, calendar items, and religious names and items.
Example: *World War II; Age of Enlightenment; June; Christianity; Buddhists; Bible; Easter; God*

i. titles of literary works, works of art, and musical compositions.
Example: *"Why I Live at the P.O."; The Starry Night; Rhapsody in Blue*

j. names of specific school courses.
Example: *Advanced Physics; American History*

Rule: Capitalize proper adjectives (adjectives formed from proper nouns).

Example: *Christmas tree; Hanukkah candles; Freudian psychology; American flag*

Punctuation

This section will help you use these elements of punctuation correctly.

Rule: Use a period at the end of a declarative sentence or a polite command.

Example: *I'm thirsty.*
Example: *Please bring me a glass of water.*

Rule: Use an exclamation point to show strong feeling or after a forceful command.

Example: *I can't believe my eyes!*
Example: *Watch your step!*

Rule: Use a question mark to indicate a direct question.

Example: *Who is in charge here?*

Rule: Use a colon
a. to introduce a list (especially after words such as these, the following, or as follows) and to introduce material that explains, restates, or illustrates previous material.

Example: *The following states voted for the amendment: Texas, California, Georgia, and Florida.*
Example: *The sunset was colorful: purple, orange, and red lit up the sky.*

b. to introduce a long or formal quotation.
Example: *It was Mark Twain who stated the following proverb: "Man is the only animal that blushes. Or needs to."*

c. in precise time measurements, biblical chapter and verse references, and business letter salutations.
Example:
3:35 P.M.   *7:50 A.M.*
Gen. 1:10–11   *Matt. 2:23*
Dear Ms. Samuels: *Dear Sir:*

Rule: Use a semicolon
a. to separate main clauses that are not joined by a coordinating conjunction.
Example: *There were two speakers at Gettysburg that day; only Lincoln's speech is remembered.*

b. to separate main clauses joined by a conjunctive adverb or by *for example* or *that is.*
Example: *Because of the ice storm, most students could not get to school; consequently, the principal canceled all classes for the day.*

c. to separate the items in a series when these items contain commas.
Example: *The students at the rally came from Senn High School, in Chicago, Illinois; Niles Township High School, in Skokie, Illinois; and Evanston Township High School, in Evanston, Illinois.*

d. to separate two main clauses joined by a coordinating conjunction when such clauses already contain several commas.
Example: *The designer combined the blue silk, brown linen, and beige cotton into a suit; but she decided to use the yellow chiffon, yellow silk, and white lace for an evening gown.*

Rule: Use a comma
a. between the main clauses of a compound sentence.
Example: *Ryan was late getting to study hall, and his footsteps echoed in the empty corridor.*

b. to separate three or more words, phrases, or clauses in a series.
Example: *Mel bought carrots, beans, pears, and onions.*

c. between coordinate modifiers.

Example: *That is a lyrical, moving poem.*

d. to set off parenthetical expressions, interjections, and conjunctive adverbs.
Example: *Well, we missed the bus again.*
Example: *The weather is beautiful today; however, it is supposed to rain this weekend.*

e. to set off nonessential words, clauses, and phrases, such as:
   —adverbial clauses
Example: *Since Ellen is so tall, the coach assumed she would be a good basketball player.*
   —adjective clauses
Example: *Scott, who had been sleeping, finally woke up.*
   —participles and participial phrases
Example: *Having found what he was looking for, he left.*
   —prepositional phrases
Example: *On Saturdays during the fall, I rake leaves.*
   —infinitive phrases
Example: *To be honest, I'd like to stay awhile longer.*
   —appositives and appositive phrases
Example: *Ms. Kwan, a soft-spoken woman, ran into the street to hail a cab.*

f. to set off direct quotations.
Example: *"My concert," Molly replied, "is tonight."*

g. to set off an antithetical phrase.
Example: *Unlike Tom, Rob enjoys skiing.*

h. to set off a title after a person's name.
Example: *Margaret Thomas, Ph.D., was the guest speaker.*

i. to separate the various parts of an address, a geographical term, or a date.
Example: *My new address is 324 Indian School Road, Albuquerque, New Mexico 85350.*
   I moved on March 13, 1998.

j. after the salutation of an informal letter and after the closing of all letters.
Example: *Dear Helen,   Sincerely,*

k. to set off parts of a reference that direct the reader to the exact source.
Example: *You can find the article in the* Washington Post, *April 4, 1997, pages 33–34.*

l. to set off words or names used in direct address and in tag questions.

Example: *Yuri, will you bring me my calculator?*
  Lottie became a lawyer, didn't she?

Rule: Use a dash to signal a change in thought or to emphasize parenthetical material.

Example: *During the play, Maureen—and she'd be the first to admit it—forgot her lines.*

Example: *There are only two juniors attending—Mike Ramos and Ron Kim.*

Rule: Use parentheses to set off supplemental material. Punctuate within the parentheses only if the punctuation is part of the parenthetical expression.

Example: *If you like jazz (and I assume you do), you will like this CD. (The soloist is Miles Davis.)*
Example: *The upper Midwest (which states does that include?) was hit by terrible floods last year.*

Rule: Use brackets to enclose information that you insert into a quotation for clarity or to enclose a parenthetical phrase that already appears within parentheses.

Example: *"He serves his [political] party best who serves the country best."—Rutherford B. Hayes*
Example: *The staircase (which was designed by a famous architect [Frank Lloyd Wright]) was inlaid with ceramic tile.*

Rule: Use ellipsis points to indicate the omission of material from a quotation.

Example: *". . . Neither an individual nor a nation can commit the least act of injustice against the obscurest individual. . . ." —Henry David Thoreau*

Rule: Use quotation marks
a. to enclose a direct quotation, as follows:
Example: *"Hurry up!" shouted Lisa.*

When a quotation is interrupted, use two sets of quotation marks.

Example: *"A cynic," wrote Oscar Wilde, "is someone who knows the price of everything and the value of nothing."*

Use single quotation marks for a quotation within a quotation.

Example: *"Did you say 'turn left' or 'turn right'?" asked Leon.*

In writing dialogue, begin a new paragraph and use a new set of quotation marks every time the speaker changes.

Example: *"Do you really think the spaceship can take off?" asked the first officer.*
"Our engineer assures me that we have enough power," the captain replied.

b. o enclose titles of short works, such as stories, poems, essays, articles, chapters, and songs.
Example: *"The Lottery" [short story]*
  "Provide, Provide" [poem]
  "Civil Disobedience" [essay]

c. to enclose unfamiliar slang terms and unusual expressions.
Example: *The man called his grandson a "rapscallion."*

d. to enclose a definition that is stated directly.
Example: *Gauche is a French word meaning "left."*

Rule: Use italics
a. for titles of books, lengthy poems, plays, films, television series, paintings and sculptures, long musical compositions, court cases, names of newspapers and magazines, ships, trains, airplanes, and spacecraft. Italicize and capitalize articles (a, an, the) at the beginning of a title only when they are part of the title.
Example: E.T. *[film];* The Piano Lesson *[play]*
  The Starry Night *[painting]*
  the New Yorker *[magazine]*
  Challenger *[spacecraft]*
  The Great Gatsby *[book]*
  the Chicago Tribune *[newspaper]*

b. for foreign words and expressions that are not used frequently in English.
Example: *Luciano waved good-bye, saying, "Arrivederci."*

c. for words, letters, and numerals used to represent themselves.
Example: *There is no Q on the telephone keypad.*
Example: *Number your paper from 1 through 10.*

Rule: Use an apostrophe

a. for a possessive form, as follows:

Add an apostrophe and *s* to all singular nouns, plural nouns not ending in *s,* singular indefinite pronouns, and compound nouns. Add only an apostrophe to a plural noun that ends in *s.*

Example: *the tree's leaves*
the man's belt
the bus's tires
the children's pets
everyone's favorite
my mother-in-law's job
the attorney general's decision
the baseball player's error
the cats' bowls

If two or more persons possess something jointly, use the possessive form for the last person named. If they possess it individually, use the possessive form for each one's name.

Example: *Ted and Harriet's family*
Ted's and Harriet's bosses
Lewis and Clark's expedition
Lewis's and Clark's clothes

b. to express amounts of money or time that modify a noun.
Example: *two cents' worth*
Example: *three days' drive (You can use a hyphenated adjective instead: a three-day drive.)*

c. in place of omitted letters or numerals.
Example: *haven't [have not]   the winter of '95*

d. to form the plural of letters, numerals, symbols, and words used to represent themselves. Use an apostrophe and *s.*
Example: *You wrote two 5's instead of one.*
Example: *How many s's are there in Mississippi?*
Example: *Why did he use three !'s at the end of the sentence?*

Rule: Use a hyphen

a. after any prefix joined to a proper noun or proper adjective.
Example: *all-American   pre-Columbian*

b. after the prefixes *all-, ex-,* and *self-* joined to any noun or adjective, after the prefix *anti-* when it joins a word beginning with *i,* after the prefix *vice-* (except in some instances such as *vice president*), and to avoid confusion between words that begin with *re-* and look like another word.

Example: *ex-president*
self-important
anti-inflammatory
vice-principal
re-creation of the event
recreation time
re-pair the socks
repair the computer

c. in a compound adjective that precedes a noun.
Example: *a bitter-tasting liquid*

d. in any spelled-out cardinal or ordinal numbers up to *ninety-nine* or *ninety-ninth,* and with a fraction used as an adjective.
Example: *twenty-three   eighty-fifth*
one-half cup

e. to divide a word at the end of a line between syllables.
Example: *air-port   scis-sors*
fill-ing   fin-est

Abbreviations

Abbreviations are shortened forms of words.

Rule: Use only one period if an abbreviation occurs at the end of a sentence. If the sentence ends with a question mark or an exclamation point, use the period and the second mark of punctuation.

Example: *We didn't get home until 3:30 A.M.*
Example: *Did you get home before 4:00 A.M.?*
Example: *I can't believe you didn't get home until 3:30 A.M.!*

Rule: Capitalize abbreviations of proper nouns and abbreviations related to historical dates.

Example: *John Kennedy Jr.   P.O. Box 333*
800 B.C.   A.D. 456   1066 C.E.

Use all capital letters and no periods for most abbreviations of organizations and government agencies.
Example: *CBS   CIA   PIN*
CPA   IBM   NFL
MADD   GE   FBI

Spelling

The following basic rules, examples, and exceptions will help you master the spellings of many words.

Forming plurals

English words form plurals in many ways. Most nouns simply add *s*. The following chart shows other ways of forming plural nouns and some common exceptions to the pattern.

General Rules for Forming Plurals		
if the word ends in	**Rule**	**Example**
ch, s, sh, x, z	add *es*	glass, glasses
a consonant + *y*	change *y* to *i* and add *es*	caddy, caddies
a vowel + *y* or *o*	add only *s*	cameo, cameos monkey, monkeys
a consonant + *o* common exceptions	generally add *es* but sometimes add only *s*	potato, potatoes cello, cellos
f or *ff* common exceptions	add *s* change *f* to *v* and add *es*	cliff, cliffs hoof, hooves
lf	change *f* to *v* and add *es*	half, halves

A few plurals are exceptions to the rules in the previous chart, but they are easy to remember. The following chart lists these plurals and some examples.

Special Rules for Forming Plurals	
Rule	**Example**
To form the plural of most proper names and one-word compound nouns, follow the general rules for plurals.	Cruz, Cruzes Mancuso, Mancusos crossroad, crossroads
To form the plural of hyphenated compound nouns or compound nouns of more than one word, make the most important word plural.	sister-in-law, sisters-in-law motion picture, motion pictures
Some nouns have unusual plural forms.	goose, geese child, children
Some nouns have the same singular and plural forms.	moose scissors pants

Adding prefixes

When adding a prefix to a word, keep the original spelling of the word. Use a hyphen only when the original word is capitalized or with prefixes such as *all-*, *ex-*, and *self-* joined to a noun or adjective.

co + operative = cooperative
inter + change = interchange
pro + African = pro-African
ex + partner = ex-partner

Suffixes and the silent *e*

Many English words end in a silent letter *e*. Sometimes the *e* is dropped when a suffix is added. When adding a suffix that begins with a consonant to a word that ends in silent *e*, keep the *e*.

like + ness = likeness   sure + ly = surely
COMMON EXCEPTIONS awe + ful = awful;
judge + ment = judgment

When adding a suffix that begins with a vowel to a word that ends in silent *e*, usually drop the *e*.

believe + able = believable
expense + ive = expensive
COMMON EXCEPTION mile + age = mileage

When adding a suffix that begins with *a* or *o* to a word that ends in *ce* or *ge*, keep the *e* so the word will retain the soft *c* or *g* sound.

notice + able = noticeable
courage + ous = courageous

When adding a suffix that begins with a vowel to a word that ends in *ee* or *oe*, keep the final *e*.

see + ing = seeing   toe + ing = toeing

Drop the final silent *e* after the letters *u* or *w*.

argue + ment = argument
owe + ing = owing

Keep the final silent *e* before the suffix *-ing* when necessary to avoid ambiguity.

singe + ing = singeing

Suffixes and the final *y*

When adding a suffix to a word that ends in a consonant + *y*, change the *y* to *i* unless the suffix begins with *i*. Keep the *y* in a word that ends in a vowel + *y*.

try + ed = tried   fry + ed = fried
stay + ing = staying   display + ed = displayed
copy + ing = copying joy + ous = joyous

Adding *ly* and *ness*

When adding *ly* to a word that ends in a single *l*, keep the *l*, but when the word ends in a double *l*, drop one *l*. When the word ends in a consonant + *le*, drop the *le*. When adding *-ness* to a word that ends in *n*, keep the *n*.

casual + ly = casually
practical + ly = practically
dull + ly = dully
probable + ly = probably
open + ness = openness
mean + ness = meanness

Doubling the final consonant

Double the final consonant in words that end in a consonant preceded by a single vowel if the word is one syllable, if it has an accent on the last syllable that remains there even after the suffix is added, or if it is a word made up of a prefix and a one-syllable word.

stop + ing = stopping
admit + ed = admitted
replan + ed = replanned

Do not double the final consonant if the accent is not on the last syllable, or if the accent shifts when the suffix is added. Also do not double the final consonant if the final consonant is *x* or *w*. If the word ends in a consonant and the suffix begins with a consonant, do not double the final consonant.

benefit + ed = benefited
similar + ly = similarly
raw + er = rawer
box + like = boxlike
friend + less = friendless
rest + ful = restful

Forming Compound Words

When joining a word that ends in a consonant to a word that begins with a consonant, keep both consonants.

out + line = outline
after + noon = afternoon
post + card = postcard
pepper + mint = peppermint

ie and *ei*

Learning this rhyme can save you many misspellings: "Write *i* before *e* except after *c,* or when sounded like *a* as in *neighbor* and *weigh.*" There are many exceptions to this rule, including *seize, seizure, leisure, weird, height, either, neither, forfeit.*

-cede, -ceed, and *-sede*

Because of the relatively few words with *sēd* sounds, these words are worth memorizing.

These words use *-cede:* **accede, precede, secede.**
One word uses *-sede:* **supersede.**
Three words use *-ceed:* **exceed, proceed, succeed.**

Logic and Persuasion Handbook

Persuasion

Propositions

One of the main reasons people write and talk is to persuade each other. Persuasive writing and speaking attempts to convince someone of the truth of a **proposition,** that is, a statement or claim. There are four basic types of proposition:

- A proposition of **fact** is a claim that certain information is correct.
  Candidate Wilkins comes from Illinois.

- A proposition of **value** is a statement that a feeling or judgment is valid.
  Candidate Wilkins is a friendly woman.

- A proposition about a **problem** combines fact and judgment.
  Candidate Wilkins is not qualified to run.

- A proposition of **policy** is a claim that someone should do something.
  Everyone should vote for candidate Wilkins.

A proposition may be **true** or **false.** In evaluating persuasive speaking and writing, you need to know which type of proposition is being made so that you can decide whether it is true or false.

Evidence and Arguments

Persuasive writing and speaking usually includes **evidence,** that is, reasons why someone should accept a proposition. Together, a proposition and a reason for accepting it make up an **argument.**

Everyone should vote for candidate Wilkins, because she is the most qualified.

An argument may be **valid** or **invalid,** that is, reasonable or unreasonable.

Appeals

Arguments are meant to appeal to certain beliefs, values, or feelings belonging to the reader or listener. Most reasons given in support of a proposition make at least one of four types of **appeal:**

- An **appeal to logic** is a claim based on fact and reason.
  Wilkins is unqualified, because she does not meet the age requirement.

- An **appeal to ethics or values** is a claim based on shared values or judgments.
  Wilkins is best, because she is the most honest and caring.

- An **appeal to authority** is a claim based on sources believed to be reliable.
  Wilkins is best, because the Metropolitan Bar Association supports her.

- An **appeal to emotion** is a claim based on shared feelings.
  Wilkins is best, because she has overcome hardship.

In evaluating arguments, you need to know which type of appeal is being made so that you can decide whether it is valid or invalid. Note that an argument may involve more than one type of appeal.

Exercise: Analyzing an Argument

Read the following statements. For each statement, identify the type of proposition made and the type of appeal used to support it..

1. If we want clean beaches, then we need to provide trash cans and arrange for garbage removal in the summer.

2. It is our responsibility as human beings to keep ocean ecosystems healthy by polluting them as little as possible or not at all.

3. According to eminent marine biologists, we have a lot to learn about the animals that live in the ocean depths.

4. Restricting owners of beachfront property from building wherever they want to on their property is highly unfair.

Statement	Proposition	Appeal
1	about a problem	
2		
3		
4		to ethics or values

Logic

Inductive Reasoning

Inductive reasoning involves putting facts together to come up with a generalized statement as a conclusion.

Specific facts:

> **Fact 1.** *Star Wars* is the second-biggest money maker of all time.

> **Fact 2.** The number one movie at the box office in 2004 was *Shrek 2*.

> **Fact 3.** *Spider-man* broke many box office records in 2002.

Generalization: Science fiction and fantasy films do very well at the box office.

Errors In Inductive Reasoning

To avoid errors in inductive reasoning, be sure you use a large enough sample of specific facts, and of course, make sure your facts are accurate. Assuming you have a large enough sample of accurate facts, make sure that your generalization is logical.

For example, it would be illogical to conclude from the facts above that movies whose titles begin with the letter *S* do well at the box office.

Deductive Reasoning

Deductive reasoning is essentially the opposite of inductive reasoning. With deductive reasoning you start with a generalization to come to a conclusion about a specific case.

Generalization: Paul can only eat vegetarian food.

Specific fact: The Glory Diner offers vegetarian food.

Conclusion: Paul can eat at the Glory Diner.

Syllogisms

A syllogism is a formal statement of a deductive argument. It consists of a **major premise,** or general statement; a **minor premise,** or related fact; and a **conclusion** based on the two.

Major premise: People who travel between countries need a passport.

Minor premise: Jody is flying from the United States to Spain.

Conclusion: Jody needs a passport.

Errors In Deductive Reasoning

Errors in deductive reasoning result from faulty construction of the argument. Make sure the major premise is a universal statement, that both premises are true, and that the conclusion follows logically from the premises.

Note: A syllogism is *valid* if it follows the rules of deductive reasoning. A syllogism is *true* if the statements are factually accurate. Therefore, a perfectly valid syllogism can be untrue. For example:

Major premise: All voters are good citizens. [There is more to good citizenship than voting.]

Minor premise: My parents are voters.

Conclusion: Therefore, my parents are good citizens.

This conclusion is valid according to the premises; however, it isn't necessarily true because the major premise is flawed.

Exercise: Analyzing Logical Reasoning

For each argument below, identify whether inductive or deductive reasoning is used. Evaluate whether the conclusion is valid or invalid and explain your evaluation.

1. An epic poem is a serious, long narrative poem centered on the life of a cultural or national hero or heroine. *El Cid* is an epic poem. In more than 30,000 lines, it celebrates the life and accomplishments of a Spanish military and political leader who lived in the eleventh century.

2. If a computer can play compact discs, the computer must have been built after 1985. This computer can play CDs. This computer must have been built after 1985.

3. Many humorists use puns. Mark Twain used puns in his writing and his speeches. Ogden Nash used puns in his poems. Woody Allen uses puns in his movies.

Exercise: Using Logical Reasoning

Write a short essay arguing a proposition. In your argument, use at least two examples each of valid inductive and deductive reasoning.

Logical Fallacies

A **logical fallacy** is a particular type of faulty reasoning. Fallacies often seem reasonable at face value, so they are often used, both intentionally and unintentionally. Some fallacies are so common that they have names.

To identify fallacies in the writing and speaking of others and to avoid it in your own persuasive communication, you need to be able to identify fallacies and to understand why they are illogical.

- **Ad Hominem**
  Don't listen to what Smyth says about the election; he spent time in prison.
  An ad hominem argument (literally, an argument "against the person") implies that a defect in a person's character or behavior is evidence that what he says is unreliable. Note that the ad hominem fallacy contains a hidden premise: *People who have spent time in prison cannot have valid opinions.* Because this premise is untrue, the argument about Smyth is untrue also.

- **Non Sequitur or False Causality**
  This shirt is unlucky: every time I wear it, something bad happens.
  Non sequitur literally means "it doesn't follow." Just because two events occur together, it doesn't follow logically that one caused the other.

- **Glittering Generalities**
  If you love freedom, vote for Jack.
  Glittering generalities are words with overwhelmingly positive connotations, used to make it seem impossible to disagree with an idea. How can you argue against the idea of freedom? A listener's initial reaction to this statement might be, "Freedom is a good thing, so I must vote for Jack."

- **Overgeneralization and Stereotype**
  Tall people make excellent basketball players.
  An overgeneralization is any conclusion that may be accurate about a small group, but is inaccurate when applied to a much larger group. An overgeneralization about a group of people is called a stereotype.

- **Argument from Authority and Celebrity Endorsement**
  Four out of five doctors recommend Pumpidox for most heart conditions.
  Argument from authority is the quoting of an alleged expert on a certain topic. As a logical fallacy, arguments from authority rely solely on the mention of the word "expert," and give no clear facts from the expert. Companies often hire celebrities to appear in commercials for their products in the hope that audiences will respond to the likability of the famous person, even if that person has no real expert knowledge about the product.

- **The Bandwagon Effect**
  Choose America's favorite toothpaste!
  The term "jumping on the bandwagon" means doing or thinking something because everyone else is doing it or thinking it. This type of reasoning provides no evidence to support a decision or viewpoint.

- **Card Stacking**
  Senator Porter voted against childcare laws and recycling programs. It's time for new leadership!
  Card stacking involves piling on evidence that supports one side of an argument while ignoring or suppressing valid evidence supporting the other side. Saying that a politician voted against positive-sounding programs does not mean that he or she didn't have good reason to, or that the opposition has a better record.

Ethical Reasoning and Propaganda

Propaganda

Propaganda is the process of persuading by deliberately misleading or confusing an audience. Through the use of combinations of logical fallacies, propaganda can appeal to ethics or values, authority, or emotion, but they do so in a way that is unsupported or inappropriate.

Political propaganda

A vote for Marmelard is a vote for the enemy!

America: You're with us or against us!

Advertising

Be the best parent you can be: Serve your kids Super Goody cereal.

The most successful people shop at Blorland's Department Store.

Ethical Reasoning

Reasoning that persuades by helping its intended audience make informed decisions is called **ethical reasoning.** As a writer or speaker, you have the responsibility to use ethical reasoning and avoid propaganda. This means that you must gather complete information about a topic, check your facts for accuracy, and make sure that your reasoning includes no errors in logic or false conclusions. You should address opposing evidence with clear and accurate argumentation. Using ethical reasoning in your persuasive writing or speeches will strengthen your positions as your audience sees that you have logically addressed all sides of an idea.

Identifying Unethical Persuasive Techniques

The following essay contains several examples of faulty reasoning. Read through the entire text once, then go back and look for logical fallacies, invalid arguments, and manipulative appeals. For each example you find, make an entry in a chart like the one shown. Then write a paragraph evaluating the essay's argument.

Passage	Type(s) of Appeals	Why Invalid
"Principal Spaly"	Appeal to logic	Card stacking

Don't Take Away Our Freedom

The school board recently announced plans to remove all vending machines from our schools' cafeterias. They say that candy, snacks, and cola are bad for students. But is starvation good for students? Is taking away freedom to choose good for students?

Every expert on nutrition agrees that it is not healthy for kids to go for hours between meals without some sort of snack in between to tide them over. If the school board has its way, students will be passing out at their desks from hunger and dehydration. Principal Spaly claims that students are more likely to pass out from a "sugar crash." This is the same Principal Spaly who recently showed what he thought of students when he denied sophomores the right to park at the high school.

We are taught in these very schools that America is a land of democracy, freedom, and liberty. It is clear that the school board has forgotten this. Any student who loves his or her school will write to the school board and let them know how we feel.

Glossary/Glosario

This glossary lists the vocabulary words found in the selections in this book. The definition given is for the word as it is used in the selection; you may wish to consult a dictionary for other meanings of these words. The key below is a guide to the pronunciation symbols used in each entry.

Pronounciation Key					
a	**a**t	ō	h**o**pe	ng	si**ng**
ā	**a**pe	ô	f**o**rk, **a**ll	th	**th**in
ä	f**a**ther	oo	w**oo**d, p**u**t	<u>th</u>	**th**is
e	**e**nd	o͞o	f**oo**l	zh	trea**s**ure
ē	m**e**	oi	**oi**l	ə	**a**go, tak**e**n, penc**i**l,
i	**i**t	ou	**ou**t		lem**o**n, circ**u**s
ī	**i**ce	u	**u**p	′	indicates primary stress
o	h**o**t	ū	**u**se	′	indicates secondary

English

A

abide (ə bīd′) *v.* remain; **p. 893**

abolish (ə bol′ ish) *v.* to put an end to; do away with; **p. 1208**

abundantly (ə bun′ dənt lē) *adv.* plentifully; **p. 409**

acquaintance (ə kwānt′ əns) *n.* the state of being familiar with; **p. 730**

acrid (ak′ rid) *adj.* burning, biting, or irritating to the taste or smell; **p. 1241**

admonish (ad mon′ ish) *v.* to warn; to reprimand; **p. 80**

adversary (ad′ vər ser′ ē) *n.* opponent; enemy; **p. 126**

advocate (ad′ və kāt′) *v.* to support or argue for; **p. 930**

aggregated (ag′ rə gā′ təd) *adj.* collected; gathered into a whole; **p. 626**

alteration (ôl′ tə rā′ shən) *n.* change; modification; **p. 285**

Español

A

abide/permanecer *v.* subsistir; **p. 893**

abolish/abolir *v.* poner fin a; eliminar; **p. 1208**

abundantly/abundantemente *adv.* en gran cantidad; cuantiosamente; **p. 409**

acquaintance/conocido(a) *s.* persona con quien se tiene trato o relación, sin ser amistad; **p. 730**

acrid/acre *adj.* irritante, amargo o desagradable al gusto y al olfato; **p. 1241**

admonish/amonestar *v.* advertir; reprender; **p. 80**

adversary/adversario *s.* oponente; enemigo; **p. 126**

advocate/abogar *v.* defender o hablar a favor de alguien; **p. 930**

aggregated/agregado *adj.* sumado; unido a un todo; **p. 626**

alteration/alteración *s.* cambio; modificación; **p. 285**

amends (ə mendz′) *n.* something done or given to make up for injury, loss, etc.; **p. 356**

amiability (ā′ mē ə bil′ ə tē) *n.* kindliness; friendliness; **p. 1097**

anarchy (an′ ər kē) *n.* a complete lack of political order; chaos; **p. 1067**

antidote (an′ ti dōt′) *n.* a medicine used to counteract the effects of a poison; any counteracting remedy; **p. 386**

appall (ə pôl′) *v.* to fill with horror and shock; **p. 353**

appease (ə pēz′) *v.* to bring to a state of peace or quiet; to satisfy; **p. 1143**

arbiter (är′ bə tər) *n.* a judge; **p. 804**

arrogance (ar′ ə gəns) *n.* overbearing pride or self-importance; **p. 144**

artifice (är′ tə fis) *n.* trickery; deception; **p. 1065**

aspire (əs pīr′) *v.* to strive for; **p. 91**

assent (ə sent′) *v.* to agree to something after consideration; concur; **p. 1270**

avarice (av′ ər is) *n.* greed; **p. 373**

awry (ə rī′) *adj.* wrong; in a faulty way; **p. 297**

amends/reparación *s.* desagravio, compensación o satisfacción por una ofensa, daño o injuria; **p. 356**

amiability/afabilidad *s.* amabilidad, cordialidad; **p. 1097**

anarchy/anarquía *s.* desconcierto o desorganización por ausencia de una autoridad; **p. 1067**

antidote/antídoto *s.* medicina usada para contrarrestar los efectos de una substancia venenosa; contraveneno; **p. 386**

appall/consternar *v.* horrorizar, conmocionar; **p. 353**

appease/apaciguar *v.* aquietar; tranquilizar o calmar; **p. 1143**

arbiter/árbitro(a) *s.* persona que actúa como un juez en un conflicto; **p. 804**

arrogance/arrogancia *s.* altanería, demasiado orgullo o soberbia; **p. 144**

artifice/artificio *s.* habilidad; arte o ingenio con lo que algo está hecho; **p. 1065**

aspire/aspirar *v.* anhelar; **p. 91**

assent/acordar *v.* determinar o deliberar individualmente; estar de acuerdo; **p. 1270**

avarice/avaricia *s.* codicia; **p. 373**

awry/mal *adj.* contrariamente a lo previsto o a lo deseado; **p. 297**

B

barren (bar′ ən) *adj.* having little or no vegetation; bare; **p. 1276**

beguile (bi gīl′) *v.* to mislead by trickery; to deceive; **p. 412**

benign (bi nīn′) *adj.* pleasant and friendly; **p. 1196**

blanch (blanch) *v.* to turn white or become pale; **p. 82**

bleak (blēk) *adj.* cold; harsh; raw; **p. 692**

blight (blīt) *n.* a disease caused by parasites that makes plants and trees wither and die; **p. 911**

blithe (blīth) *adj.* carefree; lighthearted; **p. 179**

brandish (bran′ dish) *v.* to shake or swing threateningly, as a weapon; **p. 195**

brevity (brev′ ə tē) *n.* shortness in speech or writing; **p. 1142**

B

barren/yermo *adj.* que tiene poca o ninguna vegetación; pelado; **p. 1276**

beguile/embaucar *v.* despistar mediante trampas; engañar; **p. 412**

benign/benigno(a) *adj.* afable, benévolo, piadoso; **p. 1196**

blanch/blanqueado(a) *adj.* decoloración; **p. 82**

bleak/helado(a) *adj.* crudo; brutal; riguroso; **p. 692**

blight/roya *s.* hongo parásito que ataca plantas y árboles; **p. 911**

blithe/alegre *adj.* despreocupado; tranquilo **p. 179**

brandish/blandir *v.* levantar o mover de modo amenazante, como un arma; **p. 195**

brevity/brevedad *s.* corta extensión o duración de un discurso o escrito; **p. 1142**

C

calamity (kə lam′ ə tē) *n.* disaster; extreme misfortune; **p. 297**

callousness (kal′ əs nəs) *n.* hardness in mind or feelings; insensitivity; **p. 1141**

career (kə rēr′) *v.* to move or run with a swift headlong motion; to rush or dash along; **p. 1253**

cavalcade (kav′ əl kād′) *n.* a ceremonial procession; **p. 540**

censure (sen′ shər) *n.* strong disapproval; condemnation as wrong; **p. 292**

cleave (klēv) *v.* to tear or rip; to split something apart; **p. 815**

commend (kə mend′) *v.* to praise; to express approval of; **p. 574**

commiseration (kə miz′ ə rā′ shən) *n.* a feeling or expression of sympathy; compassion; **p. 1141**

compensation (kom′ pən sā′ shən) *n.* something that offsets, counterbalances, or makes up for; **p. 1031**

complaisance (kəm plā′ səns) *n.* a willingness to please, be gracious, or be courteous; **p. 598**

composure (kəm pō′ zhər) *n.* a calm or tranquil state of mind; **p. 159**

compulsory (kəm pul′ sər ē) *adj.* obligatory; required; **p. 1197**

concede (kən sēd′) *v.* to admit as true; acknowledge; **p. 137**

concord (kon′ kôrd) *n.* an agreement of interests or feelings; **p. 247**

condescend (kon′ di send′) *v.* to lower oneself; **p. 701**

confining (kən′ fīn ing) *adj.* restricting; limiting; **p. 605**

confound (kən found′) *v.* to confuse; to defeat or overthrow; to bewilder; **p. 580**

congeal (kən jēl′) *v.* harden; thicken; **p. 267**

congenial (kən jēn′ ē əl) *adj.* compatible; agreeable; **p. 700**

congregation (kong′ grə gā′ shən) *n.* a group of people who gather for religious worship; **p. 431**

C

calamity/calamidad *s.* desgracia; infortunio; **p. 297**

callousness/insensibilidad *s.* dureza al pensar o actuar; crueldad; **p. 1141**

career/apresurarse *v.* moverse o correr de prisa; avanzar con rapidez; **p. 1253**

cavalcade/cabalgata *s.* desfile ceremonial; **p. 540**

censure/censura *s.* reprobación; crítica o juicio negativos; **p. 292**

cleave/partir *v.* rajar o hender; dividir algo en dos o más partes; **p. 815**

commend/elogiar *v.* ensalzar; alabar; **p. 574**

commiseration/conmiseración *s.* sentimiento o expresión de compasión; lástima; **p. 1141**

compensation/compensación *s.* algo que se da para compensar, remunerar o retribuir algo; **p. 1031**

complaisance/afabilidad *s.* amabilidad; deseo de complacer o ser cortés; **p. 598**

composure/compostura *s.* estado mental de tranquilidad o calma; **p. 159**

compulsory/obligatorio(a) *adj.* que tiene que ser hecho, cumplido u obedecido; **p. 1197**

concede/conceder *v.* admitir; reconocer, convenir; **p. 137**

concord/pacto *s.* acuerdo, convenio, lo que se decide entre dos partes; **p. 247**

condescend/condescender *v.* dignarse; acceder; **p. 701**

confining/restrictivo *adj.* que restringe; **p. 605**

confound/confundir *v.* turbar; desconcertar; **p. 580**

congeal/congelar(se) *v.* solidificar(se); cuajar(se); espesar(se); **p. 267**

congenial/compatible *adj.* afín; que concuerda; **p. 700**

congregation/congregación *s.* grupo de personas que se reúne para orar; **p. 431**

conjecture (kən jek′ chər) *v.* to infer from inconclusive evidence; to guess; **p. 559**

conspiring (kən spīr′ ing) *adj.* planning or plotting secretly; **p. 837**

constitute (kon′ stə to͞ot′) *v.* make up; form; **p. 1074**

contemplation (kon′ təm plā′ shən) *n.* careful thought or consideration; meditation; **p. 432**

converge (kən vurj′) *v.* to come together in a common interest or conclusion; to center; **p. 1096**

conviction (kən vik′ shən) *n.* a strong belief; **p. 1067**

copiously (kō′ pē əs lē) *adv.* plentifully; **p. 167**

countenance (koun′ tə nəns) *n.* someone's face; the expression on someone's face; **p. 938**

covetousness (kuv′ it əs nəs) *n.* great desire for something belonging to another; **p. 432**

D

dappled (dap′ əld) *adj.* marked with spots; **p. 910**

dauntless (dônt′ lis) *adj.* daring; not easily discouraged; **p. 178**

deem (dēm) *v.* regard as; consider; **p. 263**

deference (def′ ər əns) *n.* courteous respect; **p. 553**

deftly (deft′ lē) *adv.* skillfully; nimbly; **p. 131**

defunct (di fungkt′) *adj.* no longer existing or active; dead; **p. 1300**

defy (di fī′) *v.* to resist; to refuse to cooperate with; **p. 606**

deities (dē′ ə tēz) *n.* gods or goddesses; divinities; **p. 831**

deluge (del′ ūj) *n.* anything that overwhelms as if by a flood; **p. 515**

demolition (dem′ ə lish′ ən) *n.* the state of being demolished or obliterated; **p. 943**

denigration (den′ i grā′ shən) *n.* defamation of one's character or reputation; slander; **p. 1261**

conjecture/conjeturar *v.* inferir sin evidencias suficientes o claras; suponer; **p. 559**

conspiring/conspirar *v.* unirse o aliarse para preparar una acción contra algo; **p. 837**

constitute/constituió *v.* formó; compuso; **p. 1074**

contemplation/contemplación *s.* consideración o reflexión cuidadosa; meditación; **p. 432**

converge/converger *v.* llegar a una conclusión o interés común; dirigirse a un mismo punto; **p. 1096**

conviction/convicción *s.* ideas en las que se cree firmemente; **p. 1067**

copiously/copiosamente *adv.* de modo abundante; **p. 167**

countenance/semblante *s.* cara; expresión del rostro; **p. 938**

covetousness/codicia *s.* deseo intenso de obtener algo que pertenece a otro; **p. 432**

D

dappled/moteado(a) *adj.* adornado con manchas o lunares; **p. 910**

dauntless/intrépido *adj.* sin miedo; atrevido; **p. 178**

deem/considerar *v.* estimar; juzgar; **p. 263**

deference/deferencia *s.* tratamiento cortés o respetuoso; **p. 553**

deftly/diestramente *adv.* hábilmente; ágilmente; **p. 131**

defunct/difunto *adj.* que ya no existe; muerto; **p. 1300**

defying/desafiante *adj.* que se niega a cooperar; **p. 606**

deities/deidades *s.* dioses o diosas; divinidades; **p. 831**

deluge/diluvio *s.* torrente; algo que abruma o cae como un diluvio; **p. 515**

demolition/demolición *s.* derribo o destrucción; **p. 943**

denigration/denigración *s.* acción de ofender o desacreditar a alguien; calumnia; **p. 1261**

desolate (des′ ə lit) *adj.* destitute of inhabitants; deserted; **p. 832**

despotic (des pot′ ik) *adj.* tyrannical; oppressive; **p. 1038**

destiny (des′ tə nē) *n.* fate; what will necessarily happen; **p. 1049**

diffusive (di fū′ siv) *adj.* spread out or widely scattered; **p. 885**

digress (dī′ gres) *v.* to stray from the main subject; **p. 554**

dilemma (di lem′ ə) *n.* a situation requiring a choice between equally undesirable alternatives; **p. 1108**

diligently (dil′ ə jənt lē) *adv.* persistently; **p. 90**

direful (dīr′ fəl) *adj.* terrible; dreadful; **p. 310**

dirge (durj) *n.* a song sung in grief; a mournful hymn; **p. 814**

discern (di surn′) *v.* to perceive; to detect; **p. 515**

discord (dis′ kôrd) *n.* a lack of agreement or harmony; **p. 574**

discourse (dis′ kôrs′) *n.* verbal communication in speech or writing; **p. 275**

discreet (dis krēt′) *adj.* having or showing careful judgment in speech and action; prudent; **p. 111**

discretion (dis kresh′ ən) *n.* good judgment; **p. 418**

disdainful (dis dān′ fəl) *adj.* feeling or showing contempt; scornful; **p. 115**

dismal (diz′ məl) *adj.* dark and gloomy; **p. 766**

disperse (dis purs′) *v.* to scatter about; distribute widely; **p. 141**

diverge (dī vurj′) *v.* to move in different directions from a common point; to branch out; **p. 1096**

diverse (di vurs′) *adj.* markedly different; **p. 527**

diversion (di vur′ zhən) *n.* an amusement; an entertainment; **p. 587**

divulge (di vulj′) *v.* to make known; disclose; **p. 158**

doleful (dōl′ fəl) *adj.* sad; **p. 192**

dominion (də min′ yən) *n.* control or the exercise of control; **p. 691**

doom (do͞om) *n.* that which cannot be escaped; death, ruin, or destruction; **p. 285**

desolate/desolado(a) *adj.* falto de habitantes; desierto; **p. 832**

despotic/déspota *adj.* tiránico; opresivo; **p. 1038**

destiny/destino *n.* fortuna; encadenamiento de sucesos necesario e inevitable; **p. 1049**

diffusive/difuso(a) *adj.* difundido o esparcido; **p. 885**

digress/divagar *v.* desviarse del tema principal; **p. 554**

dilemma/dilema *s.* situación de duda en la que hay que elegir; **p. 1108**

diligently/diligentemente *adv.* de modo persistente; **p. 90**

direful/espantoso(a) *adj.* terrible; atroz; **p. 310**

dirge/endecha *s.* canción triste o de lamento; himno fúnebre; **p. 814**

discern/discernir *v.* percibir; detectar; **p. 515**

discord/discordia *s.* sin acuerdo en las opiniones; sin armonía; **p. 574**

discourse/discurso *s.* comunicación oral o escrita; **p. 275**

discreet/discreto *adj.* cuidadoso al hablar o actuar; prudente; **p. 111**

discretion/discreción *s.* tacto, sensatez; **p. 418**

disdainful/desdeñoso *adj.* que siente o muestra desprecio; **p. 115**

dismal/sombrío(a) *adj.* con poca luz y melancólico; **p. 766**

disperse/dispersar(se) *v.* separado; extendido o repartido; **p. 141**

diverge/divergir *v.* moverse en diferentes direcciones desde un punto común; desviarse; **p. 1096**

diverse/diverso *adj.* patentemente diferente; **p. 527**

diversion/diversión *s.* entretenimiento; distracción; **p. 587**

divulge/divulgar *v.* dar a conocer; revelar; **p. 158**

doleful/afligido *adj.* triste; **p. 192**

dominion/dominio *s.* poder o control sobre algo; **p. 691**

doom/sino *s.* fuerza desconocida que actúa sobre las cosas y determina sucesos; fatalidad; **p. 285**

dwell (dwel) *v.* to live as a resident; **p. 203**

dull (dul) *adj.* slow in thinking or responding; **p. 458**

E

ecstasy (ek′ stə sē) *n.* a state beyond reason or self-control; **p. 1053**

edifice (ed′ ə fis) *n.* a building, especially a large one; **p. 586**

elate (i lāt′) *v.* to make happy; **p. 589**

emanate (em′ ə nāt′) *v.* to come forth from a source; to issue; **p. 1128**

emancipate (i man′ sə pāt′) *v.* to free; to liberate; **p. 1089**

emphatic (em fat′ ik) *adj.* with strong emphasis; **p. 731**

endure (en door′) *v.* bear; tolerate; put up with; **p. 418**

enmity (en′ mə tē) *n.* ill will; hostility; **p. 412**

envious (en′ vē əs) *adj.* feeling jealous or discontented because of the good fortune or superior abilities of another; **p. 1198**

estimable (es′ tə mə bəl) *adj.* deserving of esteem; admirable; **p. 110**

execute (ek′ sə kūt′) *v.* to carry out; to put into effect; **p. 275**

exotic (ig zot′ ik) *adj.* strangely beautiful or fascinating; **p. 1004**

explicit (eks plis′ it) *adj.* plainly and clearly expressed; definite; **p. 1197**

exploit (eks′ ploit) *n.* bold deed; **p. 367**

expound (iks pound′) *v.* to set forth in detail; explain; **p. 89**

extraordinary (iks trôr′ də ner′ ē) *adj.* very unusual or remarkable; **p. 944**

F

faculty (fak′ əl tē) *n.* capacity of the mind; ability; aptitude; **p. 700**

fallow (fal′ ō) *n.* land plowed but left unseeded; **p. 910**

dwell/residir *v.* habitar, morar; **p. 203**

dull/tonto *adj.* lento en pensar o responder; **p. 458**

E

ecstasy/éxtasis *s.* arrobamiento; un estado más alla de razón o dominio de sí mismo; **p. 1053**

edifice/edificio *s.* construcción alta; se refiere particularmente a un edificio alto y de aspecto imponente; **p. 586**

elate/regocijar *v.* hacer feliz; **p. 589**

emanate/emanar *v.* salir de una fuente; expedir; **p. 1128**

emancipate/emancipar *v.* liberar; poner en libertad; **p. 1089**

emphatic/enfático(a) *adj.* que se expresa con énfasis; **p. 731**

endure/soportar *v.* resistir; tolerar; aguantar; **p. 418**

enmity/enemistad *s.* hostilidad; **p. 412**

envious/envidioso(a) *adj.* que siente dolor o pesar del bien de otros; que desea lo que no posee; **p. 1198**

estimable/estimable *adj.* que merece aprecio; admirable; **p. 110**

execute/ejecutar *v.* llevar a cabo; realizar; **p. 275**

exotic/exótico(a) *adj.* extrañamente hermoso o fascinante; **p. 1004**

explicit/explícito(a) *adj.* que expresa claramente y determinadamente; **p. 1097**

exploit/hazaña *s.* proeza; **p. 367**

expound/exponer *v.* presentar en detalle; explicar; **p. 89**

extraordinary/extraordinario(a) *adj.* que excede lo normal o lo ordinario; **p. 944**

F

faculty/facultad *s.* capacidad mental; habilidad; aptitud; **p. 700**

fallow/barbecho *s.* tierra arada y sin sembrar para dejarla descansar; **p. 910**

fatal (fāt′ əl) *adj.* causing death, destruction, or harm; **p. 1049**

feigned (fānd) *adj.* pretended; imagined; **p. 887**

feud (fūd) *n.* lengthy, bitter conflict or dispute; **p. 1049**

fidelity (fi del′ ə tē) *n.* the quality or state of being faithful; **p. 1281**

fleet (flēt) *adj.* swift; fast; **p. 957**

flounder (floun′ dər) *v.* struggle to obtain footing; **p. 1222**

flourish (flur′ ish) *v.* to exist at the peak of development or achievement; to thrive; **p. 81**

folly (fol′ ē) *n.* foolishness; an irrational and useless undertaking; **p. 293**

foremost (fôr′ mōst′) *adj.* ahead of all others or in the first position; **p. 206**

foresight (fôr′ sīt′) *n.* preparation or concern for the future; **p. 692**

forged (fôrjd) *adj.* formed or shaped, often with blows or pressure after heating; **p. 25**

forsaken (fôr sāk′ ən) *adj.* deserted or lonely; **p. 1133**

frail (frāl) *adj.* delicate; fragile; **p. 1150**

fray (frā) *n.* a heated dispute or contest; **p. 1301**

friction (frik′ shən) *n.* the clashing between two people or groups of opposed views; **p. 1270**

frivolous (friv′ ə ləs) *adj.* not serious; silly; **p. 91**

furrow (fur′ ō) *n.* a long, narrow trench in the ground made by a plow; a rut, groove, or wrinkle; **p. 838**

G

garish (gār′ ish) *adj.* excessively bright; flashy; gaudy; **p. 1040**

genial (jē′ nē əl) *adj.* giving warmth and comfort; pleasant or cheerful; **p. 684**

glean (glēn) *v.* to collect slowly and carefully; to gather crops left on a field after reaping; **p. 828**

grapple (grap′ əl) *v.* to attempt to deal with; to struggle; **p. 1116**

fatal/crucial *adj.* que es decisivo o muy importante porque condiciona el desarrollo de algo; **p. 1049**

feigned/fingido(a) *adj.* simulado; imaginado; **p. 887**

feud/contiendas. *adj.* lidia, pelea; disputa o discusión; **p. 1049**

fidelity/fidelidad *s.* lealtad y constancia que se debe a las ideas, afectos, obligaciones; **p. 1281**

fleet/ligero(a) *adj.* apresurado; rápido; **p. 957**

flounder/tambaleando *v.* moviéndose como si fuese a caer; **p. 1222**

flourish/florecer *v.* alcanzar el máximo desarrollo o progreso; prosperar; **p. 81**

folly/locura *s.* disparate; hecho o dicho imprudentes o insensatos; **p. 293**

foremost/primer(o-a) *adj.* antes de todo, destacado o en primer lugar; **p. 206**

foresight/previsión *s.* preparación o preocupación para atender contingencias o evitar males futuros; **p. 692**

forged/forjado *adj.* formado o moldeado, a menudo mediante golpes o presión después de calentarse; **p. 25**

forsaken/desolado(a) *adj.* despoblado, desierto; **p. 1133**

frail/frágil *adj.* delicado; débil; **p. 1150**

fray/riña *s.* disputa o contienda ardiente; **p. 1301**

friction/fricción *n.* enfrentamientos o desacuerdos entre personas o colectividades; **p. 1270**

frivolous/frívolo *adj.* que no es serio; tonto; **p. 91**

furrow/surco *s.* hendidura hecha en la tierra con el arado; ranura; arruga en la cara; **p. 838**

G

garish/chillón *adj.* excesivamente brillante; llamativo; **p. 1040**

genial/cordial *adj.* afectuoso y amable; agradable y amistoso; **p. 684**

glean/cosechar *v.* conseguir o lograr resultados luego de trabajar por ellos; recoger cultivos cuando están maduros; **p. 828**

grapple/forcejear *v.* tratar de resolver; luchar; **p. 1116**

gratify (grat′ ə fī′) *v.* to satisfy; indulge; **p. 130**

grimace (grim′ is) *n.* a look of pain or disgust; **p. 1222**

guffaw (gu fô′) *v.* to laugh loudly and boisterously; **p. 1106**

H

hail (hāl) *v.* acclaim; pay tribute to; **p. 1148**

heedless (hēd′ lis) *adj.* careless; not paying attention; **p. 1149**

hinder (hin′ dər) *v.* to make difficult the progress of; to hold back; **p. 1108**

hue (hū′) *n.* color, shade, or tint; **p. 467**

hypocritical (hip′ ə krit′ i kəl) *adj.* pretending to believe one thing but doing the opposite; **p. 730**

I

illustrious (i lus′ trē əs) *adj.* famous and distinguished; **p. 795**

imminent (im′ ə nənt) *adj.* about to happen; impending; **p. 1245**

immutably (i mū′ tə blē) *adv.* unchangeably; permanently; **p. 626**

impart (im pärt′) *v.* to give; donate; **p. 781**

impassively (im pas′ iv lē) *adv.* in an emotionless manner; **p. 1128**

impediment (im ped′ ə mənt) *n.* an obstruction; an obstacle; **p. 276**

imperious (im pēr′ ē əs) *adj.* imperative; urgent; **p. 1117**

imperturbable (im′ pər tur′ bə bəl) *adj.* not easily excited or disturbed; calm; **p. 1095**

impetuous (im pech′ o͞o əs) *adj.* characterized by rushing headlong into things; impulsive; **p. 637**

impinge (im pinj′) *v.* to strike or dash; to collide; **p. 1097**

incense (in sens′) *v.* to make enraged; filled with anger; **p. 346**

incite (in sīt′) *v.* to urge or provoke; **p. 794**

indictment (in dīt′ mənt) *n.* a formal accusation; **p. 528**

gratify/gratificar *v.* satisfacer; complacer; **p. 130**

grimace/mueca *s.* mirada de dolor o disgusto; **p. 1222**

guffaw/carcajear *v.* reír a carcajadas o vulgarmente; **p. 1106**

H

hail/vitorear *v.* ovacionar; aclamar; **p. 1148**

heedless/indiferente *adj.* despreocupado; sin prestar atención; **p. 1149**

hinder/estorbar *v.* impedir el progreso; obstaculizar; **p. 1108**

hue/matiz(ces) *s.* color, grado o tono; **p. 467**

hypocritical/hipócrita *adj.* persona que finge ideas, sentimientos o cualidades diferentes de los que tiene en realidad; **p. 730**

I

illustrious/ilustre *adj.* famoso y distinguido; **p. 795**

imminent/inminente *adj.* que está por ocurrir; próximo; **p. 1245**

immutably/inmutablemente *adv.* de un modo que no cambia; permanentemente; **p. 626**

impart/impartir *v.* dar; repartir; **p. 781**

impassively/impasiblemente *adv.* sin mostrar emoción; **p. 1128**

impediment/impedimento *s.* obstáculo; tropiezo; **p. 276**

imperious/imperioso *adj.* imperativo; urgente; **p. 1117**

imperturbable/imperturbable *adj.* que no se emociona o molesta fácilmente; calmado; **p. 1095**

impetuous/impetuoso *adj.* apresurado; impulsivo; **p. 637**

impinge/tropezar *v.* golpear; chocar; **p. 1097**

incense/indignado(a) *adj.* enfadado; irritado; **p. 346**

incite/incitar *v.* urgir o provocar; **p. 794**

indictment/acusación *s.* denuncia formal; **p. 528**

indignation (in′ dig nā′ shən) *n.* anger aroused by something unjust or mean; **p. 697**

indissoluble (in′ di sol′ yə bəl) *adj.* incapable of being broken; permanent; **p. 343**

indomitable (in dom′ ə tə bəl) *adj.* incapable of being subdued or overcome; **p. 1117**

inevitable (i nev′ ə tə bəl) *adj.* incapable of being avoided or prevented; certain; **p. 683**

infamous (in′ fə məs) *adj.* having a bad reputation; notorious; **p. 31**

infinitely (in′ fə nit lē) *adv.* boundlessly; endlessly; **p. 1074**

infirmity (in fur′ mə tē) *n.* weakness; state of being feeble or unable; **p. 300**

ingenuity (in′ jə nōō′ ə tē) *n.* cleverness; inventiveness; **p. 639**

inseparable (in sep′ ər ə bəl) *adj.* linked so closely that it is almost impossible to separate; **p. 945**

instigation (in′ stə gā′ shən) *n.* the act of inciting or urging on; **p. 158**

intermittent (in′ tər mit′ ənt) *adj.* alternately starting and stopping; **p. 1125**

intrepid (in trep′ id) *adj.* fearless; courageous; **p. 169**

intrinsically (in trin′ zik lē) *adv.* inherently; in its very nature; **p. 1142**

intuitive (in tōō′ ə tiv) *adj.* known or perceived without deliberate thought; **p. 626**

inveterate (in vet′ ə rit) *adj.* firmly established; deep-rooted; **p. 588**

irrational (i rash′ ən əl) *adj.* lacking reason; ill-advised; **p. 599**

irremediable (ir i mē′ dē ə bəl) *adj.* not subject to remedy or cure; **p. 1243**

J

jeopardy (jep′ ər dē) *n.* danger; **p. 195**

jest (jest) *n.* an utterance or act offered humorously or mockingly; **p. 424**

indignation/indignación *s.* ira provocada por algo injusto o malo; **p. 697**

indissoluble/indisoluble *adj.* que no se puede desunir o separar; **p. 343**

indomitable/indomable *adj.* incapaz de ser gobernado o sometido; rebelde; **p. 1117**

inevitable/inevitable *adj.* que no se puede evitar o prevenir; **p. 683**

infamous/infame *adj.* desacreditado; de mala reputación; **p. 31**

infinitely/infinitamente *adv.* ilimitadamente; sin termino; **p. 1074**

infirmity/enfermedad *s.* padecimiento; dolencia o alteración de la salud; **p. 300**

ingenuity/ingenio *s.* talento; inventiva; **p. 639**

inseparable/inseparable *adj.* persona estrechamente unida a otra por vínculos de amor o amistad; imposible de separar; **p. 945**

instigation/instigación *s.* acto de incitar o impulsar; **p. 158**

intermittent/intermitente *adj.* que se inicia y se detiene alternativamente; **p. 1125**

intrepid/intrépido *adj.* temerario; valiente; **p. 169**

intrinsically/intrínsecamente *adv.* de modo inherente o esencial; dentro de su misma naturaleza; **p. 1142**

intuitive/intuitivo *adj.* que se piensa o percibe de inmediato sin necesidad de razonar; **p. 626**

inveterate/arraigado *adj.* firmemente establecido; crónico; empedernido; **p. 588**

irrational/irracional *adj.* absurdo; incoherente; **p. 599**

irremediable/irremediable *adj.* que no se puede evitar o remediar; **p. 1243**

J

jeopardy/riesgo *s.* peligro; **p. 195**

jest/broma *s.* lo que se hace o se dice para que alguien se ría sin mala intención; **p. 424**

jovial (jō′ vē al) *adj.* full of good humor; genial and playful; **p. 348**

jovial/jovial *adj.* de buen humor; alegre y festivo; **p. 348**

K

keen (kēn) *adj.* having a sharp edge or point; **p. 293**

kindred (kin′ drid) *adj.* like; allied; similar; **p. 685**

K

keen/agudo(a) *adj.* que tiene un punto o filo afilado; **p. 293**

kindred/semejante *adj.* casi igual; análogo; similar; **p. 685**

L

labyrinth (lab′ ə rinth′) *n.* a place containing winding, interconnected passages; **p. 1038**

lament (lə ment′) *n.* expression of sorrow; song or literary composition that mourns a loss or death; **p. 25**

languished (lang′ gwisht) *adj.* dispirited; lacking vitality; **p. 263**

license (lī′ səns) *n.* freedom used irresponsibly; **p. 883**

loath (lōth) *adj.* reluctant; unwilling; **p. 542**

loitering (loi′ tər ing) *adj.* standing or lingering idly about a place; **p. 827**

lugubrious (loo goo′ brē əs) *adj.* excessively mournful or sorrowful; **p. 1303**

lumbering (lum′ bər ing) *v.* moving heavily and clumsily; **p. 1309**

luminous (loo′ mə nəs) *adj.* emitting a glowing light; **p. 1222**

L

labyrinth/laberinto *s.* lugar que tiene pasajes o recovecos interconectados; **p. 1038**

lament/lamento *s.* expresión de pesar; canción o composición literaria que expresa dolor por una pérdida o muerte; **p. 25**

languished/lánguido(a) *adj.* falto de ánimo; sin fuerzas; **p. 263**

license/libertinaje *s.* abuso de la libertad sin tener en cuenta a los demás; **p. 883**

loath/reacio *adj.* que se opone a hacer algo; remiso; **p. 542**

loitering/vagando *v.* andar libre y sin rumbo; holgazaneando; **p. 827**

lugubrious/lúgubre *adj.* afligido, sombrío o tétrico; **p. 1303**

lumbering/moverse pesadamente *frase verbal.* moviéndose trabajosa y torpemente; **p. 1309**

luminous/luminoso(a) *adj.* que despide luz; **p. 1222**

M

magnitude (mag′ nə tood′) *n.* greatness of size or extent; **p. 565**

malicious (mə lish′ əs) *adj.* deliberately harmful; **p. 544**

mar (mär) *v.* to spoil or damage; **p. 804**

morbid (môr′ bid) *adj.* overly sensitive to death and decay; not cheerful or wholesome; **p. 1108**

mortal (môrt′ əl) *adj.* destined to die; **p. 268**

M

magnitude/magnitud *s.* de gran tamaño o extensión; **p. 565**

malicious/malicioso *adj.* que provoca daño deliberadamente; **p. 544**

mar/estropear *v.* maltratar o deteriorar; **p. 804**

morbid/mórbido *adj.* muy sensible a la muerte o descomposición; que no es saludable ni alegre; **p. 1108**

mortal/mortal *adj.* que ha de morir; **p. 268**

mourn (môrn) *v.* to show or feel sadness; grieve; **p. 535**

munificence (mū nif′ ə səns) *n.* great generosity; **p. 939**

mute (mūt) *adj.* unable to speak; refraining from producing vocal sounds; **p. 246**

myriad (mir′ ē əd) *n.* a great or countless number; **p. 516**

N

negligence (neg′ li jəns) *n.* an air of careless ease or casualness; **p. 598**

O

obliteration (ə blit′ e rā′ shən) *n.* complete destruction or removal; **p. 1207**

oblivion (ə bliv′ ē ən) *n.* a state of forgetting; **p. 299**

obsolete (ob′ sə lēt′) *adj.* no longer in use; outdated; **p. 1309**

obstinately (ob′ stə nit lē′) *adv.* in a manner not yielding to argument, persuasion, or reason; inflexibly; **p. 1085**

odious (ō′ dē əs) *adj.* causing hate, disgust, or repugnance; **p. 1008**

oppressed (ə prest′) *adj.* burdened; weighed down; **p. 606**

P

pageant (paj′ ənt) *n.* an elaborately staged drama or spectacular exhibition; **p. 300**

pall (pôl) *n.* an atmosphere of dark and gloom; **p. 1275**

parry (par′ ē) *v.* to respond, as to a question or argument, by warding off or diverting; **p. 1082**

passion (pash′ ən) *n.* powerful emotion; love; **p. 535**

peerless (pēr′ lis) *adj.* unrivaled; without equal; **p. 319**

mourn/acongojar *v.* mostrar tristeza o dolor por la muerte de alguien; lamentar una pérdida; **p. 535**

munificence/munificencia *s.* gran generosidad; **p. 939**

mute/mudo(a) *adj.* incapacidad que impide el habla; sin palabras, sin voz o sin sonidos; **p. 246**

myriad/miríada *s.* multitud o infinidad de personas, cosas o asuntos; **p. 516**

N

negligence/neglicencia *s.* actitud de descuido o indiferencia; **p. 598**

O

obliteration/obliteración *n.* destrucción o eliminación completa; **p. 1207**

oblivion/inconsciencia *s.* estado en que la persona no se da cuenta de las cosas; **p. 299**

obsolete/obsoleto(a) *adj.* desusado, inadecuado; anticuado, caduco; **p. 1309**

obstinately/obstinadamente *adv.* de modo que no cede a ningún razonamiento o persuasión; inflexiblemente; **p. 1085**

odious/odioso(a) *adj.* que causa odio, disgusto, o repugnancia; **p. 1008**

oppressed/oprimido *adj.* agobiado; abatido; **p. 606**

P

pageant/espectáculo *s.* función o diversión públicas; **p. 300**

pall/palio *s.* manto; atmósfera obscura y sombría; **p. 1275**

parry/esquivar *v.* desviar la conversación cuando no se quiere tratar un tema; **p. 1082**

passion/pasión *s.* sentimiento intenso; afección; **p. 535**

peerless/incomparable *adj.* sin par; sin igual; **p. 319**

penance (pen′ əns) *n.* an act of self-punishment to show repentance for a sin; **p. 778**

peril (per′ əl) *n.* risk of injury, loss, or destruction; **p. 193**

periphery (pə rif′ ər ē) *n.* the outward or farthest boundary; **p. 1309**

pernicious (pər nish′ əs) *adj.* destructive; deadly; **p. 366**

perpetually (pər pech′ o͞o əl) *adv.* constantly occurring; **p. 1029**

pertain (pər tān′) *v.* to be connected to or have relevance to; **p. 377**

philosophical (phil′ ə sof′ i kəl) *adj.* concerned with the deeper meaning of life; **p. 944**

piety (pī′ ə tē) *n.* devoutness; reverence; **p. 741**

pivotal (piv′ ət əl) *adj.* of central or vital importance; **p. 1260**

plenteous (plen′ tē əs) *adj.* abundant; fruitful; **p. 318**

plodding (plod′ ing) *v.* walking heavily and/or slowly; **p. 1309**

pomp (pomp) *n.* splendid or dignified display; **p. 683**

precept (prē′ sept) *n.* a rule intended as a guide for conduct or action; **p. 638**

precipice (pres′ ə pis) *n.* a very steep or overhanging mass of rock as on a cliff; **p. 1281**

precipitately (pri sip′ ə tət′ lē) *adv.* without deliberation; hastily; abruptly; **p. 1029**

predominance (pri dom′ ə nəns) *n.* the state of being most important, common, or noticeable; **p. 339**

prevail (pri vāl′) *v.* be in general use; succeed; **p. 458**

prevarication (pri var′ ə kā shən) *n.* the act of evading the truth; lying; **p. 120**

penance/penitencia *s.* acto realizado para mostrar arrepentimiento por los pecados; **p. 778**

peril/peligro *s.* riesgo de herida, pérdida o destrucción; **p. 193**

periphery/periferia *s.* espacio que rodea un núcleo cualquiera; **p. 1309**

pernicious/pernicioso(a) *adj.* perjudicial; gravemente dañoso; **p. 366**

perpetually/perpetuo(a) *adj.* que dura y permanece; **p. 1029**

pertain/relacionar *v.* que está conectado o asociado a algo; **p. 377**

philosophical/filosófico(a) *adj.* relacionado a los aspectos esenciales de la vida; **p. 944**

piety/piedad *s.* devoción; reverencia; **p. 741**

pivotal/central *adj.* de enorme importancia; **p. 1260**

plenteous/abundante *adj.* en gran cantidad; copioso; **p. 318**

plodding/caminar trabajosamente *frase verbal;* moviéndose lenta y pesadamente, con trabajo; **p. 1309**

pomp/pompa *s.* acompañamiento suntuoso y solemne; **p. 683**

precept/precepto *s.* regla o pauta de comportamiento o acción; **p. 638**

precipice/precipicio *s.* despeño o caída violenta y profunda, casi vertical; **p. 1281**

precipitately/precipitadamente *adv.* sin pensarlo; apresuradamente; abruptamente; **p. 1029**

predominance/predominancia *s.* condición de ser lo más importante, común o notorio; **p. 339**

prevail/prevalecer *v.* perdurar, subsistir; sobresalir; tener superioridad; **p. 458**

prevarication/engaño *s.* acto de evadir la verdad; mentira; **p. 120**

prodigious (prə dij' əs) *adj.* great in size, number, or degree; enormous; **p. 607**

prophetic (prə fet' ik) *adj.* having the quality of foretelling future events; **p. 314**

prosaic (prō zā' ik) *adj.* commonplace; ordinary; **p. 1124**

provoke (prə vōk') *v.* to call forth; to stir to action or feeling; **p. 334**

prowess (prou' is) *n.* superior ability; skill; **p. 393**

prudence (prōōd' əns) *n.* sound judgment; careful management; **p. 892**

prudent (prōōd' ənt) *adj.* cautious; careful; **p. 129**

purge (purj) *n.* the process of getting rid of impurities or undesirable elements; **p. 385**

Q

quaint (kwānt) *adj.* pleasingly unusual or odd; **p. 1004**

quench (kwench) *v.* to put out; to extinguish; **p. 542**

R

radiant (rā' dē ənt) *adj.* beaming, as with joy, love, or energy; **p. 1198**

rancid (ran' sid) *adj.* having an offensive or foul odor or taste; **p. 1270**

rancor (rang' kər) *n.* bitter malice or resentment; **p. 81**

rational (rash' ən əl) *adj.* able to reason; sensible; **p. 697**

ravage (rav ij') *v.* to lay waste to; to destroy; **p. 1115**

reconciled (rek' ən sīld) *adj.* brought to acceptance of; **p. 529**

redress (ri dres') *v.* to set right; to remedy; **p. 371**

refined (ri fīnd') *adj.* freed from imperfections; improved; **p. 426**

reiterate (rē it' ə rāt') *v.* to say or do again; to repeat; **p. 1085**

prodigious/descomunal *adj.* extraordinario en tamaño, número o grado; enorme; **p. 607**

prophetic/profético *adj.* que tiene la cualidad de anticipar futuros sucesos; **p. 314**

prosaic/prosaico *adj.* común; ordinario o vulgar; **p. 1124**

provoke/provocar *v.* mover o incitar; inducir a alguien a que haga algo; **p. 334**

prowess/destreza *s.* habilidad para hacer algo bien hecho; arte o primor; **p. 393**

prudence/prudencia *s.* buen juicio; sensatez; **p. 892**

prudent/prudente *adj.* cuidadoso; cauto; **p. 129**

purge/purga *s.* eliminación de impurezas o elementos inconvenientes; **p. 385**

Q

quaint/pintoresco(a) *adj.* agradablemente raro o peculiar; **p. 1004**

quench/extinguir *v.* apagar; aplacar; **p. 542**

R

radiant/radiante *adj.* brillante, como con alegría, amor, o energía; **p. 1198**

rancid/rancio(a) *adj.* que ha adquirido olor o sabor más fuertes, mejorándose o echándose a perder; **p. 1270**

rancor/rencor *s.* fuerte resentimiento u odio; **p. 81**

rational/racional *adj.* que es capaz de razonar; sensible; **p. 697**

ravage/asolar *v.* arruinar; destruir; **p. 1115**

reconciled/reconciliado *adj.* que ha aceptado o perdonado; **p. 529**

redress/reparar *v.* arreglar; remediar o corregir; **p. 371**

refined/refinar *v.* eliminar impurezas; hacer más fino o más puro; **p. 426**

reiterate/reiterar *v.* decir o hacer de nuevo; repetir; **p. 1085**

relinquish (ri ling′ kwish) *v.* to give up; put aside; to abandon; **p. 795**

repentance (ri pent′ əns) *n.* feeling of sorrow for wrongdoing; remorse; **p. 317**

replenish (ri plen′ ish) *v.* to refill or make complete again; to add a new supply to; **p. 409**

repose (ri pōz′) *v.* lie at rest; rest from work or toil; **p. 744**

reprove (ri proōv′) *v.* to scold or correct, usually gently or out of kindness; **p. 135**

restrain (ri strān′) *v.* to hold back; restrict; **p. 159**

retaliation (ri tal′ ē ā′ shən) *n.* getting even with; revenge; **p. 931**

retort (ri tôrt′) *v.* to reply in a witty, quick, or sharp manner; **p. 1009**

revelation (rev′ ə lā′ shən) *n.* the act of making something known; something that is revealed; **p. 1270**

reverently (rev′ rənt lē) *adv.* respectfully; with deep affection or veneration; **p. 1133**

S

satiety (sə tī′ ə tē) *n.* a feeling of weariness or even dislike of something caused by satisfying an appetite or desire for it in excess; **p. 819**

scorn (skôrn) *v.* to reject as contemptible or unworthy; **p. 263**

scruple (skroō′ pəl) *n.* a moral or ethical principle that restrains action; **p. 337**

scrutiny (skroōt′ ən ē) *n.* close watch or examination; **p. 928**

secluded (si kloō did) *adj.* shut off from others; undisturbed; **P. 744**

sensible (sen′ sə bəl) *adj.* having good judgment or sound thinking; **p. 1135**

shroud (shroud) *n.* burial cloth; **p. 30**

siege (sēj) *n.* blockade; the surrounding of a fortified place by an opposing army intending to invade it; **p. 388**

relinquish/renunciar *v.* ceder; rendirse; abandonar; **p. 795**

repentance/arrepentimiento *s.* pena o pesar de haber hecho algo; remordimiento; **p. 317**

replenish/reabastecer *v.* llenar o completar de nuevo; agregar o volver a surtir; **p. 409**

repose/reposar *v.* permanecer en quietud; descansar en medio de un trabajo o fatiga; **p. 744**

reprove/reprender *v.* corregir, regañar o amonestar a alguien desaprobando su conducta; **p. 135**

restrain/refrenar *v.* aguantar; reprimir; **p. 159**

retaliation/represalia *s.* revancha por una agresión; venganza; **p. 931**

retort/replicar *v.* responder en una manera ingeniosa, rápida, o aguda; **p. 1009**

revelation/revelación *s.* descubrimiento de algo secreto u oculto; manifestación de algo oculto; **p. 1270**

reverently/reverentemente *adv.* con respeto; que muestra veneración; **p. 1133**

S

satiety/hartazgo *s.* sensación de molestia o cansancio que puede darse por la satisfacción completa o excesiva, esp. de comida o bebida; **p. 819**

scorn/despreciar *v.* desairar, desdeñar; no apreciar el valor de algo; **p. 263**

scruple/escrúpulo *s.* principio moral o ético que limita una acción; **p. 337**

scrutiny/escrutinio *s.* examen y averiguación exacta de algo; **p. 928**

secluded/apartado(a) *adj.* retirado, separado, remoto; **p. 744**

sensible/sensato(a) *adj.* prudente, de buen juicio, que piensa antes de actuar; **p. 1135**

shroud/mortaja *s.* tela o paño para el entierro; **p. 30**

siege/sitio *s.* asedio; cerco puesto a una plaza o fortaleza para combatirla o apoderarse de ella; **p. 388**

sinew (sin′ ū) *n.* a tendon; **p. 1255**

slander (slan′ dər) *v.* to utter false or malicious statements about; **p. 158**

sloth (slôth) *n.* laziness; **p. 275**

solicitous (sə lis′ ə təs) *adj.* full of concern; **p. 106**

sordid (sôr′ did) *adj.* filthy; selfish; greedy; mean; **p. 740**

spellbound (spel′ bound) *adj.* fascinated; affected as if by enchantment; **p. 1149**

spurn (spurn) *v.* to reject or drive off; **p. 803**

squalid (skwol′ id) *adj.* dirty or broken down due to poverty or neglect; **p. 1038**

stealthy (stel′ thē) *adj.* secret; sly; **p. 329**

stratagem (strat′ ə jəm) *n.* a deception; a military tactic designed to surprise an enemy; **p. 578**

stridently (strīd′ ənt lē) *adv.* in a harsh, grating manner; **p. 1298**

strife (strīf) *n.* unrest or violent conflict; **p. 467**

subdue (səb do̅o̅′) *v.* conquer; overcome; quiet; **p. 535**

subside (səb sīd′) *v.* to give way or end; **p. 932**

subterranean (səb′ tə rā′ nē ən) *adj.* below the earth's surface; underground; **p. 520**

suffice (sə fīs′) *v.* to be enough for; **p. 148**

superannuated (so̅o̅′ pər an′ ū ā′ tid) *adj.* out of date; **p. 1261**

supplant (sə plant′) *v.* to take the place of, often unfairly; **p. 1038**

suppressed (sə presd′) *adj.* subdued; held back; **p. 246**

suppressing (sə pres′ ing) *n.* prohibiting publication or circulation; censoring; **p. 1031**

surfeited (sur′ fit əd) *adj.* overfed; **p. 330**

sustenance (sus′ tə nəns) *n.* food or other items that support life; **p. 550**

sinew/tendón *s.* tejido fibroso; **p. 1255**

slander/calumniar *v.* desacreditar; difamar; **p. 158**

sloth/flojera *s.* pereza; **p. 275**

solicitous/solícito *adj.* preocupado o interesado; deseoso de servir; **p. 106**

sordid/sórdido(a) *adj.* sucio; mísero; avariento; mezquino; **p. 740**

spellbound/embelesado(a) *adj.* fascinado; que arroba y cautiva los sentidos; **p. 1149**

spurn/rechazar *v.* despreciar; ahuyentar; **p. 803**

squalid/mísero *adj.* sucio o deteriorado debido a la pobreza y el descuido; **p. 1038**

stealthy/furtivo(a) *adj.* hecho a escondidas; sigiloso; **p. 329**

stratagem/estratagema *s.* engaño o fingimiento; ardid de guerra para conseguir un objetivo; **p. 578**

stridently/estridentemente *adv.* de modo áspero y chirriante; **p. 1298**

strife/conflicto *n.* combate, contienda, disputa; **p. 467**

subdue/someter *v.* conquistar; subyugar; pacificar; **p. 535**

subside/decaer *v.* calmar(se), pasar(se); **p. 932**

subterranean/subterráneo *adj.* que opera o existe bajo la superficie; debajo de la tierra; **p. 520**

suffice/bastar *v.* ser suficiente; **p. 148**

superannuated/anticuado *adj.* pasado de moda o fuera de uso; **p. 1261**

supplant/suplantar *v.* tomar el lugar de; **p. 1038**

suppressed/contenido(a) *adj.* reprimir; refrenar; **p. 246**

suppressing/supresión *s.* prohibición de la publicación o circulación; censura; **p. 1031**

surfeited/saciado(a) *adj.* harto; que ha satisfecho el apetito con comida y bebida; **p. 330**

sustenance/sustento *s.* alimento y otros medios que conservan la vida; **p. 550**

T

teeming (tēm' ing) *adj.* full; at the point of overflowing; **p. 828**

temerity (tə mer' ə tē) *n.* excessive or reckless boldness; rashness; **p. 1300**

tempest (tem' pist) *n.* a violent storm; a violent outburst or disturbance; **p. 285**

threshold (thresh' hōld') *n.* doorway; entranceway; **p. 957**

thwart (thwôrt) *v.* to prevent from doing or achieving something; **p. 1108**

transgress (trans gres') *v.* to break or violate a law; to go beyond a limit; **p. 514**

transient (tran' shənt) *adj.* lasting only a brief time; temporary; **p. 797**

treachery (treach' ər ē) *n.* willful betrayal of trust; treason; **p. 247**

tread (tred) *v.* to walk or step upon; **p. 286**

trifling (trī' fling) *n.* treating someone or something as unimportant; showing a lack of proper respect; **p. 939**

trudge (truj) *v.* to walk wearily or laboriously; **p. 1053**

tumult (tōō' məlt) *n.* disorder; an uproar; **p. 816**

tyrant (tī' rənt) *n.* a cruel, oppressive ruler; a ruler with unlimited power; **p. 292**

U

uncouth (un kōōth') *adj.* crude; lacking polish, culture, or refinement; **p. 685**

unperturbed (un pər turbd') *adj.* undisturbed; not troubled; **p. 1276**

unsavory (un sā' vər ē) *adj.* sinister; morally questionable; **p. 1029**

usurper (ū surp' ər) *n.* one who seizes the power, position, or rights of another by force; **p. 393**

T

teeming/rebosante *adj.* muy lleno; lleno en grado extremo; **p. 828**

temerity/temeridad *s.* excesivo atrevimiento o imprudencia; audacia; **p. 1300**

tempest/tempestad *s.* tormenta fuerte y violenta; agitación de los ánimos; **p. 285**

threshold/umbral *s.* entrada; parte inferior o escalón; **p. 957**

thwart/obstruir *v.* impedir que se haga o logre algo; **p. 1108**

transgress/transgredir *v.* violar una ley; sobrepasar un límite; **p. 514**

transient/transitorio *adj.* que tan sólo dura un tiempo breve; temporal; **p. 797**

treachery/traición *s.* acción que rompe la confianza o fidelidad; deslealtad; **p. 247**

tread/pisar *v.* caminar o poner el pie encima; **p. 286**

trifling/jugando (con) *v.* tratar algo o a alguien sin la consideración o el respeto que merece; no respetar o burlarse de alguien; **p. 939**

trudge/caminar (con dificultad) *frase verbal* marchar penosamente y con mucho trabajo; **p. 1053**

tumult/tumulto *s.* confusión; alboroto; **p. 816**

tyrant/tirano(a) *s.* gobernante que abusa de su poder y autoridad de manera injusta; quien tiene el poder absoluto; **p. 292**

U

uncouth/tosco(a) *adj.* burdo, grosero; sin delicadeza, cultura o educación; **p. 685**

unperturbed/imperturbable *adj.* sereno; tranquilo; **p. 1276**

unsavory/ultrajante *adj.* ofensivo; deshonroso; **p. 1029**

usurper/usurpador *s.* quien toma el poder, la posición o los derechos de otro mediante la fuerza; **p. 393**

V

vacant (vā′ kənt) *adj.* empty; **p. 927**

vain (vān) *adj.* conceited; excessively pleased with oneself; **p. 268**

valor (val′ ər) *n.* courage and boldness, as in battle; bravery; **p. 247**

vendor (ven′ dər) *n.* one who sells goods; **p. 1251**

veneration (ven′ ə rā′ shən) *n.* deep respect or reverence; **p. 634**

vex (veks) *v.* disturb; trouble; irritate; **p. 1067**

vigilance (vij′ ə ləns) *n.* careful watchfulness; **p. 626**

vile (vīl) *adj.* repulsive or disgusting; **p. 1053**

W

wan (won) *adj.* pale; **p. 263**

withering (with′ ər ing) *v.* becoming dry; shriveling from lack of moisture; **p. 1308**

writhing (rīth′ ing) *adj.* twisting, as in pain; **p. 32**

wryly (rī′ lē) *adv.* in a twisted or distorted manner; **p. 1255**

Z

zealous (zel′ əs) *adj.* filled with intense, enthusiastic devotion; **p. 637**

V

vacant/desocupado(a) *adj.* vacío; **p. 927**

vain/vanidoso(a) *adj.* presuntuoso; deseo excesivo de mostrar las cualidades y de que se le reconozcan y alaben; **p. 268**

valor/valentía *s.* hecho heroico con arrojo y coraje; bravura; **p. 247**

vendor/vendedor *s.* el que vende algo; **p. 1251**

veneration/veneración *s.* profundo respeto o adoración; **p. 634**

vex/enfadar *v.* disgustar; enojar; irritar; **p. 1067**

vigilance/vigilancia *s.* atención cuidadosa; **p. 626**

vile/repugnante *adj.* asqueroso o desagradable; **p. 1053**

W

wan/pálido(a) *adj.* decolorado; **p. 263**

withering/marchitando *v.* ponerse mustio; resecarse y perder frescura; **p. 1308**

writhing/retorcido *adj.* que flexiona el cuerpo, como cuando se siente dolor; **p. 32**

wryly/tergiversadamente *adv.* de modo distorsionado o enredado; **p. 1255**

Z

zealous/fervoroso *adj.* lleno de entusiasmo y devoción; **p. 637**

Academic Word List

To succeed academically in high school and prepare for college, it is important to know academic vocabulary–special terms used in classroom discussion, assignments, and tests. These words are also used in the workplace and among friends to share information, exchange ideas, make decisions, and build relationships. Research has shown that the words listed below, compiled by Averil Coxhead in 2000, are the ones most commonly used in these ways. You will encounter many of them in the Glencoe Language Arts program. You will also focus on specific terms in connection with particular reading selections.

Note: The lists are ordered by frequency of use from most frequent to least frequent.

List One

analysis
approach
area
assessment
assume
authority
available
benefit
concept
consistent
constitutional
context
contract
create
data
definition
derived
distribution
economic
environment
established
estimate
evidence
export
factors
financial
formula
function
identified
income
indicate
individual
interpretation
involved
issues
labor
legal
legislation
major
method
occur
percent
period
policy
principle
procedure
process
required
research
response
role
section
sector
significant
similar
source
specific
structure
theory
variables

List Two

achieve
acquisition
administration
affect
appropriate
aspects
assistance
categories
chapter
commission
community
complex
computer
conclusion
conduct
consequences
construction
consumer
credit
cultural
design
distinction
elements
equation
evaluation
features
final
focus
impact
injury
institute
investment
items
journal
maintenance
normal
obtained
participation
perceived
positive
potential
previous
primary
purchase
range
region
regulations
relevant
resident
resources
restricted
security
select
site
sought
strategies
survey
text
traditional
transfer

List Three

alternative
circumstances
comments
compensation
components
consent
considerable
constant
constraints
contribution
convention
coordination
core
corporate
corresponding
criteria
deduction
demonstrate
document
dominant
emphasis
ensure
excluded
framework
funds
illustrated
immigration
implies
initial

instance
interaction
justification
layer
link
location
maximum
minorities
negative
outcomes
partnership
philosophy
physical
proportion
published
reaction
registered
reliance
removed
scheme
sequence
sex
shift
specified
sufficient
task
technical
techniques
technology
validity
volume

List Four

access
adequate
annual
apparent
approximated
attitudes
attributed
civil
code
commitment
communication

concentration
conference
contrast
cycle
debate
despite
dimensions
domestic
emerged
error
ethnic
goals
granted
hence
hypothesis
implementation
implications
imposed
integration
internal
investigation
job
label
mechanism
obvious
occupational
option
output
overall
parallel
parameters
phase
predicted
principal
prior
professional
project
promote
regime
resolution
retained
series
statistics
status

stress
subsequent
sum
summary
undertaken

List Five

academic
adjustment
alter
amendment
aware
capacity
challenge
clause
compounds
conflict
consultation
contact
decline
discretion
draft
enable
energy
enforcement
entities
equivalent
evolution
expansion
exposure
external
facilitate
fundamental
generated
generation
image
liberal
license
logic
marginal
medical
mental
modified
monitoring

network
notion
objective
orientation
perspective
precise
prime
psychology
pursue
ratio
rejected
revenue
stability
styles
substitution
sustainable
symbolic
target
transition
trend
version
welfare
whereas

List Six

abstract
accurate
acknowledged
aggregate
allocation
assigned
attached
author
bond
brief
capable
cited
cooperative
discrimination
display
diversity
domain
edition
enhanced

estate
exceed
expert
explicit
federal
fees
flexibility
furthermore
gender
ignored
incentive
incidence
incorporated
index
inhibition
initiatives
input
instructions
intelligence
interval
lecture
migration
minimum
ministry
motivation
neutral
nevertheless
overseas
preceding
presumption
rational
recovery
revealed
scope
subsidiary
tapes
trace
transformation
transport
underlying
utility

List Seven

adaptation
adults
advocate
aid
channel
chemical
classical
comprehensive
comprise
confirmed
contrary
converted
couple
decades
definite
deny
differentiation
disposal
dynamic
eliminate
empirical
equipment
extract
file
finite
foundation
global
grade
guarantee
hierarchical
identical
ideology
inferred
innovation
insert
intervention
isolated
media
mode
paradigm
phenomenon
priority
prohibited
publication
quotation
release
reverse
simulation
solely
somewhat
submitted
successive
survive
thesis
topic
transmission
ultimately
unique
visible
voluntary

List Eight

abandon
accompanied
accumulation
ambiguous
appendix
appreciation
arbitrary
automatically
bias
chart
clarity
conformity
commodity
complement
contemporary
contradiction
crucial
currency
denote
detected
deviation
displacement
dramatic
eventually
exhibit
exploitation
fluctuations
guidelines
highlighted
implicit
induced
inevitably
infrastructure
inspection
intensity
manipulation
minimized
nuclear
offset
paragraph
plus
practitioners
predominantly
prospect
radical
random
reinforced
restore
revision
schedule
tension
termination
theme
thereby
uniform
vehicle
via
virtually
visual
widespread

List Nine

accommodation
analogous
anticipated
assurance
attained
behalf
bulk
ceases
coherence
coincide
commenced
concurrent
confined
controversy
conversely
device
devoted
diminished
distorted
duration
erosion
ethical
format
founded
incompatible
inherent
insights
integral
intermediate
manual
mature
mediation
medium
military
minimal
mutual
norms
overlap
passive
portion
preliminary
protocol
qualitative
refine
relaxed
restraints
revolution
rigid
route
scenario
sphere
subordinate
supplementary
suspended
team
temporary
trigger
unified
violation
vision

List Ten

adjacent
albeit
assembly
collapse
colleagues
compiled
conceived
convinced
depression
encountered
enormous
forthcoming
inclination
integrity
intrinsic
invoked
levy
likewise
nonetheless
notwithstanding
odd
ongoing
panel
persistent
posed
reluctant
so-called
straightforward
undergo
whereby

Index of Skills

References beginning with **R** refer to handbook pages.

Literary Concepts

Allegory 525, 530
Alliteration 266, 268, 758, 761, 836, 839, 894, 1307, 1310
Allusion 522, 582, 703
Ambiguity 1292
Analogy 93, 279, 1109
Antagonist 183, 1033
Anthropomorphism 1273, 1277
Apostrophe 262, 264
Archetype 164, 183, 197
Argument 417, 419, 421, 585, 696, 703, 704, 894, 1104, 1109
Assonance 836, 839, 890, 894, 1147, 1152, 1219
Assumptions 1292
Atmosphere 306, 326
Author's beliefs 417, 419, 538, 546
Author's purpose 270, 272, 278, 557, 813, 822, 1052, 1054
Autobiography 156, 160
Ballad
    folk 200, 201
    hero 201
    literary 200
Ballad stanza 202, 207, 785
Bias 1120
Biography 633
Carpe diem 445, 446, 448, 450, 468
Character 1139, 1144
    antagonist 183, 1033
    dynamic 207
    flat 1144
    main 1139
    minor 1139
    protagonist 183, 1033
    round 1144
    static 207
Characterization 101, 124, 150, 160, 530, 727, 736, 925, 1259, 1264
    direct 124, 530, 727, 925
    indirect 124, 530, 727, 925
Comic devices 1139, 1144

Conceit 421, 445
    metaphysical 430, 434
Conflict 23, 183, 522, 1033, 1239, 1259
    external 23, 54, 83, 183, 522, 1247, 1259, 1264
    internal 23, 54, 83, 94, 248, 522, 1247
Connotation 262, 264, 591, 641, 703, 904, 1202
Consonance 836, 839, 890, 894, 1147, 1152, 1219
Couplet 720
    heroic 572, 575
Cultural context 58, 72, 446, 455, 601, 617, 1018
    daily life and culture 149, 395, 702, 723
Denotation 262, 591, 641, 703, 904, 1202
Description 925, 933
Dialect 690, 694, 1193, 1203, 1284, 1290
Dialogue 727, 735, 1228
Diary 538, 545
Diction 744, 751, 752, 813, 822, 1136, 1277
Drama
    British 1230–1231
    religious 15
Dramatic monologue 937, 940, 964
Dynamic character 207
Elegy 438, 440, 681, 687
Emotional appeals/language 419, 624
Enjambment 739, 743
Epic 20–21
Epic hero 21, 54
Epiphany 1025, 1094, 1100
Epitaph 681, 687
Essay 274, 592–593
    formal 592–593
    informal 593
Exaggeration 557
Exposition 942, 948
Fable 1273
Fiction, historical 603, 608
Figurative language. *See* Figures of speech.
Figures of speech 251, 253, 302, 423, 429, 801, 805, 1064, 1070, 1147

    apostrophe 262, 264
    hyperbole 465, 468, 948
    metaphor 253, 284, 287, 302, 423, 429, 585, 590, 1064, 1147, 1221, 1223
    oxymoron 1147
    personification 264, 284, 287, 302, 423, 429, 509, 511, 1147
    simile 253, 284, 287, 288, 290, 302, 423, 429, 1147
    symbol 53, 284, 287, 715, 719, 1036, 1044, 1100, 1147, 1256, 1328, 1329, 1331
First-person point of view 266, 823, 933, 1297
Flashback 1122, 1130
Foil 342, 359
Foreshadowing 1078, 1091, 1290
Form 133, 150, 445, 457, 459, 575, 825, 829, 1152
Frame story 101
Free verse 1268, 1271
Genre 739, 743
Gothic novel 792, 798
Hero 20, 58, 72
    Byronic 806–807
    epic 21, 54
    tragic 396
Heroic couplet 572, 575
Historical context 185, 720, 724, 896, 903
Historical fiction 603, 608
Historical influences 787
Historical journal 754, 756
Historical narrative 87, 94
Horatian ode 833
Humor 133, 150, 468
Hyperbole 465, 468, 948, 1120, 1139
Iambic pentameter 242, 572, 1069
Idiom/Idiomatic expression 1193, 1203
Imagery 523, 576, 583, 681, 688, 811, 835, 836, 845, 952, 1048, 1050, 1072, 1075, 1153, 1271, 1280, 1282, 1307, 1310
Inversion 534, 536
Irony 125, 132, 396, 569, 809, 811, 948, 960, 964, 1132, 1136, 1264

Reading and Critical Thinking

Writing

Interdisciplinary Activities

Index of Authors and Titles

Acknowledgments

Unit 1

"The Battle of Maldon" from *An Anthology of Old English Poetry,* edited by Charles W. Kennedy, translated by Charles W. Kennedy, copyright © 1960 by Oxford University Press, Inc. Used by permission of Oxford University Press, Inc.

From "The Creation of Adam and Eve" from *Everyman and Medieval Miracle Plays,* edited by A. C. Cawley. Reprinted by permission of Everyman's Library, Northburgh House, 10 Northburgh Street, London EC1V 0AT.

From *Beowulf,* translated by Burton Raffel, copyright © 1963 renewed © 1991 by Burton Raffel. Used by permission of Dutton Signet, a division of Penguin Group (USA) Inc.

Excerpt from *Gilgamesh: A Verse Narrative* by Herbert Mason. Copyright © 1970 by Herbert Mason. Reprinted by permission of Houghton Mifflin Company. All rights reserved.

Excerpt from "The Battle of the Pelennor Fields" from *The Lord of the Rings* by J. R. R. Tolkien, edited by Christopher Tolkien. Copyright © 1954, 1955, 1965, 1966 by J. R. R. Tolkien. Copyright © renewed 1982, 1983 by Christopher R. Tolkien, Michael H. R. Tolkien, John F. R. Tolkien and Priscilla M. A. R. Tolkien. Copyright © renewed 1993, 1994 by Christopher R. Tolkien, John F. R. Tolkien and Priscilla M. A. R. Tolkien. Reprinted by permission of Houghton Mifflin Company. All rights reserved.

"The Seafarer" from *Poems and Prose from the Old English,* translated by Burton Raffel. Edited by Alexandra H. Olsen and Burton Raffel. Copyright © 1998 by Yale University. Reprinted by permission of Yale University Press.

From *The Canterbury Tales* by Geoffrey Chaucer, translated by Neville Coghill. Reproduced with permission of Curtis Brown Group Ltd, London on behalf of the Estate of Neville Coghill. Copyright © Neville Coghill 1952.

From *The Book of Margery Kempe,* translated by Tony D. Triggs. Reprinted by permission of the Continuum International Publishing Group.

From *The Complete Works of the Gawain Poet* by John Gardner. Copyright © 1965 by The University of Chicago. Reprinted by permission of The University of Chicago Press.

Excerpt from *Sir Gawain and the Green Knight,* translated with an introduction by Brian Stone (Penguin Classics, 1959). Copyright © Brian Stone, 1959, 1964, 1974. Reprinted by permission of Penguin Group (UK).

From *A Distant Mirror* by Barbara W. Tuchman, copyright © 1978 by Barbara W. Tuchman. Used by permission of Alfred A. Knopf, a division of Random House, Inc.

Reprinted with the permission of Scribner, an imprint of Simon & Schuster Adult Publishing Group, from *Le Morte d'Arthur* by Sir Thomas Malory, edited by R. M. Lumiansky. Copyright © 1982 by R. M. Lumiansky.

From *A House Unlocked* by Penelope Lively, copyright © 2001 by Penelope Lively. Used by permission of Grove/ Atlantic, Inc.

Unit 2

From *Shakespeare on Screen,* reproduced by permission of Curtis Brown Group Ltd, London on behalf of Daniel Rosenthal. Copyright © Daniel Rosenthal 1957.

From *Rubáiyát of Omar Khayyám* translated by Edward FitzGerald, copyright © 1983 by St. Martin's Press, LLC, and reprinted with permission.

Unit 3

Excerpt from *The History of the Peloponnesian War* by Thucydides, translated by Rex Warner, with an introduction and notes by M. I. Finley (Penguin Classics 1954, Revised edition 1972). Translation copyright © Rex Warner, 1954. Introduction and Appendices copyright © M. I. Finley, 1972. Reprinted by permission of Penguin Group (UK) and The Random House Group Ltd.

From *The Plague* by Albert Camus, translated by Stuart Gilbert, copyright 1948 by Stuart Gilbert. Used by permission of Alfred A. Knopf, a division of Random House, Inc.

Excerpt from *Samuel Johnson* by Walter Jackson Bate. Copyright © 1975, 1977 by Walter Jackson Bate. Reprinted by permission of William B. Goodman.

Unit 4

Abridged from *In Patagonia* by Bruce Chatwin. Copyright © 1977 by Bruce Chatwin. Used by permission of Simon & Schuster Adult Publishing Group.

"To John Keats Poet at Springtime" from *On These I Stand* by Countee Cullen. Copyrights held by Amistad Research Center, Tulane University, administered by Thompson and Thompson, Brooklyn, NY.

Unit 5

Unit 6

"Fern Hill" by Dylan Thomas, from *The Poems of Dylan Thomas,* copyright © 1945 by The Trustees for the Copyrights of Dylan Thomas. Reprinted by permission of New Directions Publishing Corp.

"Do Not Go Gentle into That Good Night" by Dylan Thomas, from *The Poems of Dylan Thomas,* copyright © 1952 by Dylan Thomas. Reprinted by permission of New Directions Publishing Corp.

"A Snake in the Grass" by R. K. Narayan, from *Under the Banyan Tree* by R. K. Narayan, copyright © 1985 by R. K. Narayan. Used by permission of Viking Penguin, a division of Penguin Group (USA) Inc.

"Old Mrs. Grey" from *The Death of the Moth and Other Essays* by Virginia Woolf, copyright 1942 by Harcourt, Inc. and renewed 1970 by Marjorie T. Parsons, Executrix, reprinted by permission of the publisher.

Unit 7

"Thistles" from *Wodwo* by Ted Hughes. Copyright © 1961 by Ted Hughes. Reprinted by permission of HarperCollins Publishers.

Excerpts from *Midnight's Children,* © 1980 by Salman Rushdie, by permission of The Wylie Agency.

"Not Waving, But Drowning" by Stevie Smith, from *Collected Poems of Stevie Smith,* copyright © 1972 by Stevie Smith. Reprinted by permission of New Directions Publishing Corp.

"At the Pitt–Rivers" from *A Pack of Cards and Other Stories* by Penelope Lively. Copyright © 1978, 1980, 1981, 1982, 1984, 1985, 1986 by Penelope Lively. Used by permission of Grove/Atlantic, Inc.

"Shall We Choose Death" by Bertrand Russell. Copyright The Bertrand Russell Peace Foundation Ltd. Reprinted by permission.

"The Tribe with Its Eyes on the Sky" translated by Timothy Parks, from *Numbers in the Dark* by Italo Calvino, translated by Timothy Parks, English translation copyright © 1995 by Timothy Parks. Used by permission of Pantheon Books, a division of Random House, Inc.

"Follower" from *Poems 1965–1975* by Seamus Heaney. Copyright © 1980 by Seamus Heaney. Reprinted by permission of Farrar, Straus & Giroux, Inc.

"Mnemonic" by Li–Young Lee. Reprinted by permission of BOA Editions and The Permissions Company.

"Photograph" "Photo of Parents" from *Running in the Family* by Michael Ondaatje. Copyright © 1982 by Michael Ondaatje. Used by permission of W. W. Norton & Company, Inc.

"Wind" from *Selected Poems 1957–1967* by Ted Hughes. Copyright © 1956 by Ted Hughes. Reprinted by permission of HarperCollins Publishers.

"That's All" from *Complete Plays: Three* by Harold Pinter. Copyright © 1978 by H. Pinter Ltd. Used by permission of Grove/Atlantic, Inc.

"What We Lost" from *Outside History: Selected Poems 1980–1990* by Eavan Boland. Copyright © 1990 by Eavan Boland. Used by permission of W. W. Norton & Company, Inc.

"A Mild Attack of Locusts" from *The Habit of Loving* by Doris Lessing. Copyright © 1957 by Doris Lessing. Reprinted by permission of HarperCollins Publishers.

"The Train from Rhodesia" by Nadine Gordimer, reprinted by the permission of Russell & Volkening, as agents for the author. Copyright © 1950 by Nadine Gordimer, renewed 1978 by Nadine Gordimer.

"Dead Men's Path," copyright © 1972, 1973 by Chinua Achebe, from *Girls at War and Other Stories* by Chinua Achebe. Used by permission of Doubleday, a division of Random House, Inc.

"Telephone Conversation" copyright © 1962 by Wole Soyinka. Reprinted with permission by Melanie Jackson Agency, LLC.

Janet Frame, "Two Sheep" from *Snowman, Snowman: Fables and Fantasies* (New York: George Braziller, Inc., 1962).

Chapter X, "Adieu foulard . . . " from "Tales of the Islands" from *Collected Poems 1948–1984* by Derek Walcott. Copyright © 1986 by Derek Walcott. Reprinted by permission of Farrar, Straus & Giroux Inc.

"B. Wordsworth" from *Miguel Street* by V. S. Naipaul, copyright © 1959 by V. S. Naipaul. Used by permission of Alfred A. Knopf, a division of Random House, Inc.

Excerpts from *Imaginary Homelands,* © 1991 by Salman Rushdie, by permission of The Wylie Agency.

"Games at Twilight" from by Anita Desai. Copyright © 1978 by Anita Desai. Reproduced by permission of the author c/o Rogers, Coleridge & White, Ltd., 20 Powis Mews, London W11 1JN.

Reference Section

Maps

Photography

Cambridge, UK/Bridgeman Art Library; **682** Johnny van Haeften Gallery, London/Bridgeman Art Library; **689** Mary Evans Picture Library; **691** Bridgeman Art Library, London/SuperStock; **693** Mary Evans Picture Library; **695** Tate Gallery, London/Art Resource, NY; **698** Private Collection/Bridgeman Art Library; **702** (c l)Getty Images; **703** Neue Pinakothek/akg- Images; **707** Barry Iverson; **708** Ayman Mroueh; **709** Etienne Boyer/SIPA; **710–711** Barry Iverson; **714** National Portrait Gallery, London/SuperStock; **715** The Art Archive; **716** Fitzwilliam Museum, University of Cambridge/Bridgeman Art Library; **717 718** The Huntington Library, Art Collections and Botanical Gardens, San Marino, CA/SuperStock; **721** Yale Center for British Art, Paul Mellon Collection, USA/ Bridgeman Art Library; **722** Fitzwilliam Museum, University of Cambridge, UK/Bridgeman Art Library; **723** (c l)Getty Images; **724** City of Westminster Archive Centre, London/Bridgeman Art Library; **726** Ozias Humphrey/Private Collection/Bridgeman Art Library; **728** Courtesy of Thomas Brod and Patrick Pilkington/Bridgeman Art Library; **730** Bonhams, London/Bridgeman Art Library; **733** Gavin Graham Gallery, London/Bridgeman Art Library; **737** Paul Mellon Collection/Bridgeman Art Library; **738** National Portrait Gallery, London, UK, Giraudon/ Bridgeman Art Library; **740** Victoria & Albert Museum, London/Art Resource, NY; **742** Private Collection, Christie's Images/Bridgeman Art Library; **745** Private Collection, Agnew's, London/Bridgeman Art Library; **748** Tate Gallery, London/Bridgeman Art Library; **750** The McGraw-Hill Companies; **751** The Art Archive/ Culver Pictures; **753** Abbot Hall Art Gallery, Kendal, Cumbria, UK/Bridgeman Art Library; **754** Bryan Reinhart/Masterfile; **757** National Portrait Gallery of London; **758** British Museum, London/Bridgeman Art Library; **759 760** Bibliotheque Nationale, Paris/ akg-images; **763** Christie's Images; **765 768 770 773 778 781** E.T. Archive; **786** Bridgeman Art Library; **789** Min. Defense, Service Historique de l'Armee de Terre, France, Giraudon/Bridgeman Art Library; **791** National Portrait Gallery, London/ Superstock; **794** British Museum/E.T. Archive; **795** (l)The Stapleton Collection/Bridgeman Art Library; **796** Private Collection/Bridgeman Art Library; **797** Yelagin Island Palace, St. Petersburg, Russia/ Bridgeman Art Library; **799** Hessisches Landesmuseum, Darmstadt, Germany/Bridgeman Art Library; **800** National Portrait Gallery/Superstock; **802** Tate Gallery, London/Art Resource, NY; **806** Manchester Art Gallery, UK/Bridgeman Art Library; **807** Roy Miles Fine Paintings/Bridgeman Art Library; **808** Bettmann/Corbis; **810** Mary Evans Picture Library/INS. OF CIVIL ENGINEERS; **812** Erich Lessing/Art Resource, NY; **815** Tate Gallery, London/SuperStock; **817** Rijksmuseum Vincent Van Gogh, Amsterdam, The Netherlands/Bridgeman Art Library; **820** Academy of Natural Sciences of Philadelphia/CORBIS; **821** Getty Images; **822** National Portrait Gallery/akg-images; **824** Lincolnshire County Council, Usher Gallery, Lincoln, UK/Bridgeman Art Library; **826** Walter Crane/Bridgeman Art Library; **828** Tate Gallery, London/Art Resource, NY; **831** Nimatallah/Art Resource, NY; **835** Smithsonian American Art Museum, Washington, DC/Art Resource, NY; **837** Fine Art Photographic Library, London/Art Resource, NY; **840** Rudi Von Briel/ CORBIS; **841** Christie's Images/CORBIS; **842** Joe McDonald/CORBIS; **845** Smithsonian American Art Museum, Washington, DC/Art Resource, NY; **854** McGraw-Hill Companies; **856** (br)Aaron Haupt, (l)Everett Collection, (r)Getty Images; **864** Museum of London/Bridgeman Art Library; **866** (b)Bildarchiv Preussischer Kulturbesitz/Art Resource, NY, (bc)CORBIS, (t)Mary Evans Picture Library, (tc)The Art Archive/British Museum/Eileen Tweedy; **867** (b)Bridgeman-Giraudon/Art Resource, NY, (bc)Getty Images, (c)Mary Evans Picture Library, (t)The Pierpont Morgan Library/Art Resource, NY, (tr)Bettmann/CORBIS; **869** (bl)Private Collection, Christie's Images/Bridgeman Art Library, (br)British Library, London/Bridgeman Art Library, (t)Birmingham Museums and Art Gallery/Bridgeman Art Library; **871** Rykoff Collection/CORBIS; **873** Private Collection/ Bonhams, London/Bridgeman Art Library; **875** Réunion des Musées Nationaux/Art Resource, NY; **877** Tate Gallery, London/Art Resource, NY; **879** The Art Archive/Dagli Orti; **880** National Portrait Gallery of London; **882** Tate, London 2007/Christie's Images; **886** Victoria & Albert Museum, London/Art Resource, NY; **887** The Stapleton Collection/Bridgeman Art Library; **891** Erich Lessing/Art Resource, NY; **892** Underwood & Underwood/CORBIS; **893** Erich Lessing/Art Resource, NY; **896** Victoria & Albert Museum, London/Art Resource - NY; **897** Private Collection/Bridgeman Art Library; **899** Museum of Fine Arts, Boston, Charles H. Bayley Picture and Painting Fund; **903** Images.com/CORBIS; **905** Sandi Fellman; **906** Jay Dickman; **907** Carol Beckwith/ Millennium Tribal Wisdom of the Modern World; **908** Getty Images; **910** Erich Lessing/Art Resource, NY; **911** Fine Art Photographic Library, London/Art Resource, NY; **913** Christ Church College, Oxford by N. Herkomer/E.T. Archive; **914** Mary Evans Picture Library/The Image Works; **915** Mary Evans Picture Library; **918** Private Collection/Christie's Images/ Bridgeman Art Library; **919** Private Collection, Bourne Gallery, Reigate, Surrey/Bridgeman Art Library; **921** Royal Academy of Arts, London/Bridgeman Art Library; **922** Image Select/Art Resource, NY; **923** Erich Lessing/Art Resource, NY; **924** Getty Images; **926** Victoria & Albert Museum, London/Art Resource, NY; **929** Cragside House, Northumberland, UK/ National Trust Photographic Library/Derrick E. Witty/ Bridgeman Art Library; **932** Private Collection, The Maas Gallery, London/Bridgeman Art Library; **936**

National Portrait Gallery, London/Superstock; **938** Musée Crozatier, Le Puy-en-Velay, France/Bridgeman Art Library; **941** Hulton Archive/Getty Images; **943** Private Collection, Barbara Singer/Bridgeman Art Library; **946** Private Collection/Bridgeman Art Library; **947 951** Getty Images; **952** Charles Plante Fine Arts English/Bridgeman Art Library; **955** Hulton-Deutsch Collection/CORBIS; **957** akg Images; **959** Towner Art Gallery, Eastbourne, East Sussex,UK/Bridgeman Art Library; **961** Geoffrey Clements/CORBIS; **962** Christie's Images/Bridgeman Art Library; **963** Fine Art Photographic Library, London/Art Resource, NY; **976** (l)Hulton Archive/Getty Images, (r)Aaron Haupt; **984–985** Tate Gallery, London/Art Resource, NY; **986** (b)The Art Archive/Culver Pictures, (bc)Scala/Art Resource, NY, (t)Percy Wyndham Lewis/Stapleton Collection, UK/Bridgeman Art Library, (tc)Snark/Art Resource, NY; **987** (b)The Art Archive/Culver Pictures, (bc)Getty Images, (tc)Vanessa Bell/Private Collection, The Stapleton Collection/Bridgeman Art Library, (tl)Sava Botzaris/Private Collection, Bonhams, London/Bridgeman Art Library, (tr)Halas & Batchelor Collection Ltd./Bridgeman Art Library; **989** (b)Snark/Art Resource, NY, (tl)The Art Archive/Domenica del Corriere/Dagli Orti, (tr)Bibliotheque des Arts Decoratifs, Paris, Archives Charmet/Bridgeman Art Library; **991** Erich Lessing/Art Resource, NY; **993** The Art Archive/Imperial War Museum; **995** Réunion des Musées Nationaux/Art Resource, NY; **997 999** Tate Gallery, London/Art Resource, NY; **1000** Indianapolis Museum of Art, Gift of Mr. and Mrs. Harrison Eiteljorg/Bridgeman Art Library; **1001** Topical Press Agency/Getty Images; **1003** Tate, London/Art Resource, NY; **1006** Private Collection/Bridgeman Art Library; **1012** Pretoria Art Museum, Pretoria, South Africa; **1014** Bridgeman-Giraudon/Art Resource, NY; **1017** Bildarchiv Preussischer Kulturbesitz/Art Resource, NY; **1018** Alinari/Art Resource, NY; **1021** Phillip Hollas/TIME; **1024** Vanessa Bell/University of Hull Art Collection, Humberside, UK/Bridgeman Art Library; **1026** John Collier/Bateman's, East Sussex, UK/National Trust Photographic Library/John Hammond/Bridgeman Art Library; **1028** Private Collection/Bridgeman Art Library; **1030** Tom Brakefield/Photodisc; **1035** AKG Photo/London; **1037** Dreweatt Neate Fine Art Auctioneers, Newbury/Bridgeman Art Library; **1040** Joe McDonald/Animals, Animals; **1042** Hulton-Deutsch Collection/CORBIS; **1043** Getty Images; **1047** George C. Beresford/Beresford/Getty Images; **1049** Erich Lessing/Art Resource, NY; **1051** Getty Images; **1055** Colin Woodbridge/Alamy Images; **1056** Archives Larousse, Paris, Giraudon/Bridgeman Art Library; **1057** POPPERFOTO/Alamy Images; **1058** Bettman/CORBIS; **1059** Tate Gallery, London/Art Resource, NY; **1060** Getty Images; **1061** Musée Victor Hugo/akg-images; **1065** Erich Lessing/Art Resource, NY; **1066** Tretjakov Gallery/akg-images;

1071 Alfred Eisenstaedt/Time Life Pictures/Getty Images; **1073** Private Collection/The Stapleton Collection Bridgeman Art Library; **1077** Hulton Getty Picture Collection **1079** Images.com/CORBIS; **1082** Kevin Summers/Getty Images; **1084** CORBIS; **1086** Private Collection/Bridgeman Art Library; **1087** CORBIS; **1090 1091** Kevin Summers/Getty Images; **1093** Hulton Archive/Getty Images; **1095** Hunterian Art Gallery, University of Glasgow; **1098** Erich Lessing/Art Resource, NY; **1099** Private Collection/Bridgeman Art Library; **1103** George C. Beresford/Getty Images; **1105** Christie's Images, Ltd.; **1107 1108** akg-images; **1111** South African National Gallery, Cape Town, South Africa/Bridgeman Art Library; **1112** Art Resource, NY; **1114** Archive Photos; **1116** Getty Images; **1121** Mary Evans Picture Library/Robin Adler; **1123** Private Collection/Bridgeman Art Library; **1124** William Morris Gallery, Walthamstow, UK/Bridgeman Art Library; **1126** Fine Art Photographic Library/CORBIS; **1128** Hulton-Deutsch Collection/Corbis; **1129** Bradford Art Galleries and Museums, West Yorkshire, UK/Bridgeman Art Library; **1131** Jerry Cooke/Time & Life Pictures/Getty Images; **1133** Musee Royaux des Beaux-Arts de Belgique, Brussels /Bridgeman Art Library; **1134** Victoria & Albert Museum, London/Art Resource, NY; **1138** Bettmann/CORBIS; **1140** Private Collection/Bridgeman Art Library; **1146** G.D. Hackett/Getty Images; **1148** Horace Bristol/Corbis; **1150** Christie's Images/SuperStock; **1151** Sir Cedric Morris/Glynn Vivian Art Gallery, Swansea, Wales/Bridgeman Art Library; **1164** (bl)Hulton-Deutsch Collection/Corbis, (t)Bettmann/CORBIS; **1165** (cr)Mary Evans Picture Library; **1172** Mark Copelad/Private Collection, Portal Gallery Ltd/Bridgeman Art Library; **1174** (b)Bettmann/CORBIS, (cl)Government of Northern Ireland, Stormont, N., Ireland/Bridgeman Art Library, (cr)Getty Images, (t)Alexander Moffat/Scottish National Portrait Gallery, Edinburgh,/Bridgeman Art Library, (tl)Rykoff Collection/CORBIS; **1175** (b)Wolfgang Kaehler/CORBIS, (cl)Sion Touhig/CORBIS, (cr)Benjamin Lowy/CORBIS, (tl)London, Boltin Picture Library/Bridgeman Art Library, (tr)MC PHERSON COLIN/CORBIS SYGMA; **1177** (bl)DESMOND BOYLAN/Reuters/Corbis, (br)Kim Sayer/CORBIS, (t)Getty Images; **1179** Bettmann/CORBIS; **1181** Tate Gallery, London/Art Resource, NY; **1183** Werner Forman/Art Resource, NY; **1185** Tate Gallery, London/Art Resource, NY; **1187** Wolverhampton Art Gallery, West Midlands, UK/Bridgeman Art Library; **1188** Hulton Archive/Getty Images; **1190** Arthur Tress/Photonica/Getty Images; **1192** Getty Images; **1194** Private Collection/Bridgeman Art Library; **1196** Collection of Andrew McIntosh Patrick, UK/Bridgeman Art Library; **1199–2000** Robert Judges/Alamy; **1201** Getty Images; **1204 1205** CORBIS; **1207** Getty Images; **1210** Brand X Pictures/PunchStock; **1211** J. Stephen